The Ice Pages IV

Minor Professional Hockey Guide

1999-2000

TS Hockey Publications
Chandler, Arizona

Cover Photo of Houston's Mark Freer courtesy of IHL

The Ice Pages/Meet the Minors
Minor Professional Hockey Guide 1999-2000

Compiled by Thomas Schettino Jr.

Published by: Athletic Guide Publishing, P.O. Box 1050, Flagler Beach, FL 32136 • (800) 255-1050

First Printing 1996
Second Printing 1997, completely revised
Third Printing 1998, completely revised
Fourth Printing 1999, completely revised

ISBN-1-880941-41-4

Acknowledgments:

It is hard to believe that this is my fourth time doing the Ice Pages. It seems not so long ago that I finished the first book. I'd like to start by saying that this book is Y2K compliant. If there aren't any catastrophes and nothing bad happens you should get hours of reading enjoyment from the Ice Pages. However, should the power go out; this hefty journal will burn and give you light and heat for a long while.

As always the first kudos goes out to the people who purchase the Ice Pages. Obviously this project wouldn't be worth doing if you folks weren't picking up a copy, or more in some cases. Secondly I would like to thank the folks who contribute to the project either by submitting features or photos. A big thanks goes out to Sean Krabach and the IHL for arranging for the cover shot for this season's book.

As usual this was an enjoyable season to watch. The sport of hockey at all levels, but especially at the minor-pro stage, continues to enjoy tremendous growth. It is also enjoyable to me to watch folks like Don Waddell, Barry Trotz, Bobby Francis, John Torchetti, Rob Valicevic, Steve Ludzik and all of the other coaches and players who worked their way up from the minor leagues get a shot in the NHL. There are thousands of players and coaches at the minor-pro level with NHL dreams, and I know that they cheer on the guys who do make it to the top.

Another fond memory from this season was Mike Modano's rise to champion. To me Modano is a player who persevered despite some scathing criticism throughout his career. Not only did the Michigan-native win the Stanley Cup, he shook off injury and assisted on the Stars last five goals to do so. It goes to show what persistence and the willingness to work with others can do for a person.

Naturally I include on this list of thanks the various league and team Media Directors who are always of help with this project. It is the rare case indeed where it takes two phone calls to get the desired information. Special thanks go out to Howe Sports Data, Ron Matejko, Phil Komarny, Joe Levandovsky, Steve Cherwonak, Sammy Wallace, Tom Keegan and the many other folks who help with this publication.

Table Of Contents

Welcome to the Fourth Annual ***Ice Pages*** Minor Hockey League Guide produced in conjecture with the In the Crease's Meet the Minors Webpages

WWW.inthecrease.com

I did it again. What seemed to be just an innocent idea at the time expanded into a major endeavor. Many of the coaches who purchased this book mentioned that it would be "great" if I had some European stats included. Now that I am all done with the project, it was indeed a pretty good idea. But at the time it was, and still is, a bit of a challenge. First off is the fact that there is no one like a Howe Sports Data over there. There are some leagues that take care of the business with their statistics. But for each country that kept decent statistics, there were two who apparently couldn't care less. There was one memorable situation where a well-known netminder appeared in all of his team's games, but the only record of his play was an assist and a few penalty minutes.

Finding the information wasn't always easy either due to that pesky language barrier. I soon learned how to say "statistics" and "roster" in many different languages. But not without one significant event. Once in a crazy blaze of confidence I called some of my co-workers around to observe my new-found language skills. While I was explaining which words I had learned in a particular language, I announced, "this link here will get me the information I want." Sadly, my language skills weren't as solid as I had hoped, and with my mixed gender audience watching on, two folks popped onto my computer screen. Let's just say they weren't playing hockey....

All of that aside, I have gathered quite a bit of information dealing with European hockey. There are some holes, but I will continue to work on patching them. This season's book also includes some of the trades made over the years. I followed the transaction wire during the season and if a trade was officially announced it is included in this book.

The result of all the added information is a few more added pages in the book. Back from last season are the feature columns and we have some good ones indeed from some of the top columnists in minor-pro hockey. Enjoy this year's hockey season and thanks again for picking up a copy of the Ice Pages.

My bottom line with this guide is accuracy. If you believe that I have omitted something or have made an error please help me out. I will appreciate any comment or correction that you can make. Please send those comments or corrections to:

TS Hockey Publications
949 East Manor Drive
Chandler, AZ 85525

In order for me to make final resolution of the issue in question, please include your source showing your correction along too.

Thank you very much.

Abbreviations and Terms

Player Abbreviations
League: The league that the player appeared in
GP: Games played
G: Goals
A: Assists
PTS: Points
PIM: Penalties in minutes (AKA: penalty minutes)

Goaltender Abbreviations
League: The league the player appeared in.
GP: Games played
W: Wins
L: Losses
T: Ties (known as (OTL) overtime losses in every league except the American League and the NHL.
MP: Minutes played
SO: shutouts
GAVG: Goals against average. Value is determined by dividing MP (minutes played) by 60 and the number of goals against.

League Abbreviations:
NHL: National Hockey League World's premier hockey league.

AHL: American Hockey League The top developmental league in the world. Each NHL team is stocked with AHL-alumni. The league welcomes two new teams this season, including one in Quebec that is the Montreal Canadiens top farm club.

IHL: International Hockey League Flux describes the IHL this season. They did lose a few franchises over the summer, but leaner is meaner. The IHL reloaded with NHL affiliations and will have one of their two conferences loaded with affiliated clubs. The league hasn't seen the end of the franchise-shuffling and is taking a bit of a PR hit around the hockey world, but soon you will begin hearing of the league's "revival".

ECHL: East Coast Hockey League This league just keeps growing and growing in many ways. They are adding teams while watching their licensing and marketing grow. They continue to be the top AA-league in the world. One expansion city even chose an ECHL franchise over a NHL-backed AHL franchise.

CeHL: Central Hockey League The addition of the Indianapolis franchise helps this league. While the teams in the West receive much of the press and attention the last two champions (Columbus and Huntsville) are from the East. All AA-minor league fans are looking forward to the CHL-WCHL All-Star game later this year.

UHL: United Hockey League No league has grown as much as the UHL has this offseason. The league shuffled some clubs around while picking up the Fort Wayne franchise from the IHL and the Adirondack club from the AHL. The challenge will be to keep the hockey at a high-level with all the moving about.

WCHL: West Coast Hockey League Bakersfield is the team to watch in this league. They had a huge jump in attendance due to their new arena and head coach Kevin MacDonald is currently building a solid team with an entire summer to plan. This league is quickly gaining a reputation with the players as "the place to be" due to the fact that the teams mainly, if not exclusively, travel by air rather than bus.

WPHL: Western Professional Hockey League It is hard to believe this league is just four years old. In just that period of time the league has become very competitive on and off the ice. This league truly believes in marketing and giving fans a "door-to-door" good time. The league gets rave reviews from players and coaches alike.

Some other leagues you will see on the stats listings;

BSL: British Superleague
MJHL: Manitoba Junior Hockey League
SJHL: Saskatchewan Junior Hockey League
AFHL: American Frontier Hockey League
SEHL: Southern Elite Hockey League

Terms:
Entry Draft: Annual Draft held each summer to allocate 18 year old (+) players to NHL organizations.

Re-Entry: Player did not sign with team that drafted him and re-entered Entry Draft.

Supplemental Draft: Draft of players graduating unsigned from college hockey. The Supplemental draft was put in place to avoid high-priced free agencies by graduating unsigned players. It has since been discontinued.

Traded: Sent to another team for a player or cash.

Sold: "Traded for cash".

Released: Team who holds players contracted rights decides to release player from all obligations.

Signed as free agent: Player with no obligations to another club signed to a contract.

Meet The Minors

The Meet the Minors section of the In The Crease website (www.inthecrease.com) is a great place to keep up-dated on all of the players in this book. Each and every league has a column that is updated at least once a week and also features interviews with players and coaches. We also held a logo contest which wound up attracting over 90,000 votes. This season we hope to do something quite different and exciting for a contest.

The playoffs are our crowning jewel. We had an update from each and every playoff game from the first game of the post season until the final game in the final league was completed.

We are always looking for contributors, so drop on by the site and see how you can get your own words into "cyperspace"

Congratulations

We would like to congratulate the current league champions. It takes a lot of hard work to win in these highly competitive leagues and you can bet that everyone will be gunning at these teams in the upcoming season. For the first time in recent memory no team repeated as champion in any of the leagues.

NHL: Dallas Stars
AHL: Providence Bruins
IHL: Houston Aeros
ECHL: Mississippi SeaWolves
CHL: Huntsville Channel Cats
UHL: Muskegon Fury
WCHL: Tacoma Sabrecats
WPHL: Shreveport Mudbugs

Tero Aaltonen — Defenseman

Regular Season / Playoffs

Season	Team	League	GP	G	A	PTS	PIM	GP	G	A	PTS	PIM
96-97	Neuwied	German 1	55	16	20	36	NA	NA	NA	NA	NA	NA
97-98	Kalix	Sweden 1	10	1	7	8	NA	NA	NA	NA	NA	NA
97-98	Duisberg	German 1	24	11	17	28	NA	NA	NA	NA	NA	NA
98-99	Fresno	WCHL	58	1	14	15	141	2	0	1	1	6

Born: 11/6/71, Helsinki, Finland. 5-11, 197.

Jason Abel — Forward

Regular Season / Playoffs

Season	Team	League	GP	G	A	PTS	PIM	GP	G	A	PTS	PIM
98-99	San Angelo	WPHL	63	4	14	18	92	12	0	1	1	8

Born: 4/27/77, Kinuson, Alberta. 5-8, 175

Sheldon Abell — Forward

Regular Season / Playoffs

Season	Team	League	GP	G	A	PTS	PIM	GP	G	A	PTS	PIM
98-99	El Paso	WPHL	6	1	0	1	2	—	—	—	—	—

Born: 2/4/77, Taber, Alberta. 6-1, 235.

Tobias Ablad — Defenseman

Regular Season / Playoffs

Season	Team	League	GP	G	A	PTS	PIM	GP	G	A	PTS	PIM
96-97	Jacksonville	ECHL	70	11	26	37	86	—	—	—	—	—
97-98	Louisiana	ECHL	12	0	6	6	8	—	—	—	—	—
97-98	Louisville	ECHL	27	1	9	10	30	—	—	—	—	—
97-98	Tallahassee	ECHL	8	1	2	3	4	—	—	—	—	—
98-99	London	BSL	7	0	0	0	8	—	—	—	—	—
98-99	Grefrather	German 1	2	0	0	0	2	—	—	—	—	—
	ECHL	Totals	117	13	43	56	128	—	—	—	—	—

Born: 04/02/71, Stockholm, Sweden. 5-11, 207. Traded to Louisville by Louisiana for Gary Roach (12/97).

Brett Abrahamson — Defenseman

Regular Season / Playoffs

Season	Team	League	GP	G	A	PTS	PIM	GP	G	A	PTS	PIM
98-99	Baton Rouge	ECHL	70	5	8	13	35	6	0	2	2	0

Born: 11/16/74, Oakdale, Minnesota. 6-0, 180. Last amateur club; Minnesota (WCHA).

Elias Abrahamsson — Defenseman

Regular Season / Playoffs

Season	Team	League	GP	G	A	PTS	PIM	GP	G	A	PTS	PIM
97-98	Providence	AHL	29	0	1	1	47	—	—	—	—	—
98-99	Providence	AHL	75	2	9	11	184	4	0	0	0	7
	AHL	Totals	104	2	10	12	231	4	0	0	0	7

Born: 06/15/77, Uppsala, Sweden. 6-3, 227. Drafted by Boston Bruins (6th choice, 132nd overall) in 1996 Entry Draft. Member of 1998-99 AHL Champion Providence Bruins. Last amateur club; Halifax (QMJHL).

Chad Ackerman — Defenseman

Regular Season / Playoffs

Season	Team	League	GP	G	A	PTS	PIM	GP	G	A	PTS	PIM
96-97	Portland	AHL	2	1	0	1	0	—	—	—	—	—
96-97	Hampton Roads	ECHL	65	9	11	20	50	5	2	1	3	8
97-98	Portland	AHL	1	0	0	0	0	—	—	—	—	—
97-98	Syracuse	AHL	9	0	0	0	4	—	—	—	—	—
97-98	Hampton Roads	ECHL	56	14	19	33	35	20	2	13	15	12
98-99	Hampton Roads	ECHL	69	10	26	36	49	4	1	2	3	0
	AHL	Totals	12	1	0	1	4	—	—	—	—	—
	ECHL	Totals	190	33	56	89	134	29	5	16	21	20

Born: 06/15/73, Rochester, Michigan. 5-8, 190. Member of 1997-98 ECHL Champion Hampton Roads Admirals. Last amateur club: Bowling Green State

Akil Adams — Defenseman

Regular Season / Playoffs

Season	Team	League	GP	G	A	PTS	PIM	GP	G	A	PTS	PIM
95-96	Carolina	AHL	61	8	17	25	42	—	—	—	—	—
96-97	Port Huron	CoHL	6	1	1	2	6	—	—	—	—	—
97-98	Port Huron	UHL	45	4	21	25	26	—	—	—	—	—
97-98	Muskegon	UHL	2	0	1	1	0	11	1	3	4	6
98-99	Michigan	IHL	8	0	0	0	6	—	—	—	—	—
98-99	Arkansas	WPHL	16	3	12	15	26	3	1	2	3	4
	UHL	Totals	53	5	23	28	32	11	1	3	4	6

Born: 8/13/74, Detroit, Michigan. 5-10, 200. Selected by Mohawk Valley in 1998 UHL Expansion Draft. Traded to Muskegon by Port Huron for Ryan Caley (3/98). Last amateur club: Ottawa 67's (OHL).

Andy Adams — Goaltender

Regular Season / Playoffs

Season	Team	League	GP	W	L	T	MIN	SO	AVG	GP	W	L	MIN	SO	AVG
95-96	Guelph	OHL	31	21	8	1	1809	1	2.82	—	—	—	—	—	—
95-96	S.S. Marie	OHL	16	9	4	1	895	0	3.55	3	0	3	180	0	3.67
95-96	Detroit	CoHL	—	—	—	—	—	—	—	1	0	1	59	0	5.07
96-97	Regina	WHL	50	28	14	3	2774	2	3.29	5	1	4	301	0	4.19
96-97	South Carolina	ECHL	—	—	—	—	—	—	—	2	0	1	88	0	5.48
97-98	Columbus	ECHL	4	1	1	1	159	0	3.78	—	—	—	—	—	—
97-98	Wichita	CHL	3	1	2	0	178	0	5.06	—	—	—	—	—	—
97-98	Fayetteville	CHL	9	1	7	0	473	0	6.22	—	—	—	—	—	—
98-99	Topeka	CHL	9	1	8	0	524	0	4.35	—	—	—	—	—	—
	CHL	Totals	21	3	17	0	1175	0	5.21	—	—	—	—	—	—
	ECHL	Totals	4	1	1	1	159	0	3.78	2	0	1	88	0	5.48

Born; 2/10/76, Thornhill, Ontario. 6-1, 205. Last amateur club; Regina (WHL).

Gerad Adams — Defenseman

Regular Season / Playoffs

Season	Team	League	GP	G	A	PTS	PIM	GP	G	A	PTS	PIM
98-99	Regina	WHL	42	16	20	36	136	—	—	—	—	—
98-99	Kelowna	WHL	15	6	10	16	28	6	1	1	2	6
98-99	Portland	AHL	3	0	0	0	4	—	—	—	—	—

Born: 3/5/78, Regina, Saskatchewan. 6-0, 195. Last amateur club; Kelowna

Jamie Adams — Left Wing

Regular Season / Playoffs

Season	Team	League	GP	G	A	PTS	PIM	GP	G	A	PTS	PIM
92-93	Knoxville	ECHL	60	29	25	54	14	—	—	—	—	—
93-94	Johnstown	ECHL	43	16	21	37	16	—	—	—	—	—
93-94	Nashville	ECHL	17	8	11	19	6	2	0	0	0	2
94-95	Dallas	CeHL	65	17	30	47	24	—	—	—	—	—
95-96	Reno	WCHL	56	20	40	60	38	3	1	2	3	0
96-97	Reno	WCHL	60	21	32	53	66	—	—	—	—	—
97-98	Reno	WCHL	60	29	22	51	44	3	1	0	1	24
98-99	Alexandria	WPHL	4	0	0	0	0	—	—	—	—	—
98-99	Bakersfield	WCHL	59	17	24	41	36	2	0	0	0	2
	WCHL	Totals	235	87	118	205	184	8	2	2	4	26
	ECHL	Totals	120	53	57	110	36	2	0	0	0	2

Born: 11/24/71, Pittsburgh, Pennsylvania. 6-1, 175. Selected by Tucson in 1998 WCHL Dispersal Draft. Last amateur club; Colby College (ECAC).

Kevyn Adams — Center

Regular Season / Playoffs

Season	Team	League	GP	G	A	PTS	PIM	GP	G	A	PTS	PIM
96-97	Grand Rapids	IHL	82	22	25	47	47	5	1	1	2	4
97-98	Toronto	NHL	5	0	0	0	7	—	—	—	—	—
97-98	St. John's	AHL	59	17	20	37	99	4	0	0	0	4
98-99	Toronto	NHL	1	0	0	0	0	7	0	2	2	14
98-99	St. John's	AHL	80	15	35	50	85	5	2	0	2	4
	NHL	Totals	6	0	0	0	7	7	0	2	2	14
	AHL	Totals	139	32	55	87	184	9	2	0	2	8

Born; 10/8/74, Washington, District of Columbia, 6-1, 182. First choice, 25th overall by Boston Bruins in 1993 Entry Draft. Signed as a free agent by Grand Rapids Griffins. Signed as a free agent by Toronto Maple Leafs (8/7/97). Last amateur club; Miami of Ohio (CCHA).

Steve Adams — Defenseman

Regular Season / Playoffs

Season	Team	League	GP	G	A	PTS	PIM	GP	G	A	PTS	PIM
96-97	Austin	WPHL	5	0	0	0	0	—	—	—	—	—
96-97	Mississippi	ECHL	2	0	0	0	0	—	—	—	—	—
96-97	Nashville	CeHL	28	1	1	2	158	—	—	—	—	—
97-98	Phoenix	WCHL	6	0	0	0	13	—	—	—	—	—
97-98	Mississippi	ECHL	20	0	1	1	65	—	—	—	—	—
97-98	Louisville	ECHL	3	0	0	0	17	—	—	—	—	—
97-98	Jacksonville	ECHL	1	0	0	0	0	—	—	—	—	—
97-98	Mobile	ECHL	3	0	0	0	0	—	—	—	—	—
98-99	Topeka	CHL	3	0	0	0	10	—	—	—	—	—
98-99	Mohawk Valley	UHL	2	0	0	0	29	—	—	—	—	—
98-99	Saginaw	UHL	3	0	0	0	14	—	—	—	—	—
98-99	Waco	WPHL	8	0	0	0	39	—	—	—	—	—
	CHL	Totals	31	1	1	2	168	—	—	—	—	—
	ECHL	Totals	29	0	1	1	82	—	—	—	—	—
	WPHL	Totals	13	0	0	0	39	—	—	—	—	—
	UHL	Totals	5	0	0	0	43	—	—	—	—	—

Born: 4/11/75, Edmonton, Alberta. 6-1, 215.

Jayme Adduono — Left Wing

Regular Season / Playoffs

Season	Team	League	GP	G	A	PTS	PIM	GP	G	A	PTS	PIM
98-99	Mohawk Valley	UHL	2	0	0	0	2	—	—	—	—	—
98-99	Fort Worth	CHL	7	1	3	4	8	—	—	—	—	—
98-99	Tupelo	WPHL	13	3	1	4	40	—	—	—	—	—

Born; 6/3/77, Thunder Bay, Ontario. 6-1, 190.

Jeremy Adduono — Right Wing

Regular Season / Playoffs

Season	Team	League	GP	G	A	PTS	PIM	GP	G	A	PTS	PIM
98-99	Canada	National	44	10	18	28	10	—	—	—	—	—

Born: 8/4/78, Thunder Bay, Ontario. 6-0, 182. Drafted by Buffalo Sabres (8th choice, 184th overall) in 1997 Entry Draft. Last amateur club; Sudbury (OHL).

David Aebischer — Goaltender

Regular Season / Playoffs

Season	Team	League	GP	W	L	T	MIN	SO	AVG	GP	W	L	MIN	SO	AVG
96-97	Fribourg	Switz.	10	—	—	—	577	—	3.53	3	—	—	184	—	4.24
97-98	Hershey	AHL	2	0	0	1	80	0	3.76	—	—	—	—	—	—
97-98	Chesapeake	ECHL	17	5	7	2	931	0	3.35	—	—	—	—	—	—
97-98	Wheeling	ECHL	10	5	3	1	564	1	3.19	—	—	—	—	—	—
97-98	Fribourg	Switz.	1	—	—	—	60	—	1.00	4	—	—	240	—	4.25
98-99	Hershey	AHL	38	17	10	5	1932	2	2.45	3	1	2	152	0	2.37
	AHL	Totals	40	17	10	6	2012	2	2.51	3	1	2	152	0	2.37
	ECHL	Totals	27	10	10	3	1495	1	3.29	—	—	—	—	—	—

Born; 2/7/78, Fribourg, Switzerland. Drafted by Colorado Avalanche (7th choice, 161st overall) in 1997 Entry Draft.

Denis Afinogev — Left Wing

Regular Season / Playoffs

Season	Team	League	GP	G	A	PTS	PIM	GP	G	A	PTS	PIM
98-99	Torpedo Yaroslavl	Russia	14	3	2	5	0	—	—	—	—	—
98-99	Muskegon	UHL	30	15	13	28	12	17	7	6	13	10

Born: 3/15/74, Ufa, Russia. 6-0, 200. Member of 1998-99 UHL Champion Muskegon Fury.

Ryan Aikia — Defenseman

Regular Season / Playoffs

Season	Team	League	GP	G	A	PTS	PIM	GP	G	A	PTS	PIM
97-98	Madison	UHL	69	2	24	26	94	7	0	5	5	15
98-99	Madison	UHL	64	5	43	48	141	—	—	—	—	—
98-99	Milwaukee	IHL	2	0	0	0	0	—	—	—	—	—
	UHL	Totals	133	7	67	74	235	7	0	5	5	15

Born; 3/24/74, Sudbury, Ontairo. 6-3, 200. Last amateur club; University of Wisconsin-Stevens Point (NCHA).

Johnathan Aitken — Defenseman

Regular Season / Playoffs

Season	Team	League	GP	G	A	PTS	PIM	GP	G	A	PTS	PIM
98-99	Providence	AHL	65	2	9	11	92	13	0	0	0	17

Born: 5/24/78, Edmonton, Alberta. 6-4, 215. Drafted by Boston Bruins (1st choice, 8th overall) in 1996 Entry Draft. Member of 1998-99 AHL Champion Providence Bruins. Last amateur club; Brandon (WHL).

Micah Aivazoff — Center

Regular Season / Playoffs

Season	Team	League	GP	G	A	PTS	PIM	GP	G	A	PTS	PIM
89-90	New Haven	AHL	77	20	39	59	71	—	—	—	—	—
90-91	New Haven	AHL	79	11	29	40	84	—	—	—	—	—
91-92	Adirondack	AHL	61	9	20	29	50	19	2	8	10	25
92-93	Adirondack	AHL	79	32	53	85	100	11	8	6	14	10
93-94	Detroit	NHL	59	4	4	8	38	—	—	—	—	—
94-95	Edmonton	NHL	21	0	1	1	2	—	—	—	—	—
95-96	Islanders	NHL	12	0	1	1	6	—	—	—	—	—
95-96	Utah	IHL	59	14	21	35	58	22	3	5	8	33
96-97	Binghamton	AHL	75	12	36	48	70	4	1	1	2	0
97-98	San Antonio	IHL	54	13	33	46	33	—	—	—	—	—
98-99	Utah	IHL	79	25	22	47	67	—	—	—	—	—
	NHL	Totals	92	4	6	10	46	—	—	—	—	—
	AHL	Totals	371	84	177	261	375	34	11	15	26	35
	IHL	Totals	192	52	76	128	158	22	3	5	8	33

Born: 5/4/69, Powell River, British Columbia. 6-0, 195. Last amateur club: Victoria, (WHL). Signed as a free agent by Detroit Red Wings (3/18/93). Claimed by Pittsburgh Penguins from Detroit in NHL Waiver Draft (1/18/95). Claimed by Edmonton Oilers from Pittsburgh (1/18/95). Signed as a free agent by New York Islanders (8/10/95). Signed as a free agent by New York Rangers (8/23/96). Member of 1991-92 AHL champion Adirondack Red Wings. Member of 1995-96 IHL champion Utah Grizzlies.

Simon Alary — Left Wing

Regular Season / Playoffs

Season	Team	League	GP	G	A	PTS	PIM	GP	G	A	PTS	PIM
98-99	Winston-Salem	UHL	37	2	1	3	96	—	—	—	—	—
98-99	Jacksonville	ECHL	3	0	0	0	0	—	—	—	—	—

Born: 1/3/77, Hearst, Ontario. 6-2, 212. Last amateur club; Rayside (OCAA).

Jim Alauria — Defenseman

Regular Season / Playoffs

Season	Team	League	GP	G	A	PTS	PIM	GP	G	A	PTS	PIM
98-99	Alabama-Hunstville	NCHA	19	7	11	18	65	—	—	—	—	—
98-99	Greenville	ECHL	16	1	1	2	17	—	—	—	—	—

Born: Phoenix, Arizona. 6-2, 220. Last amateur club; Alabama-Huntsville

Chad Alban — Goaltender

Regular Season / Playoffs

Season	Team	League	GP	W	L	T	MIN	SO	AVG	GP	W	L	MIN	SO	AVG
98-99	Houston	IHL	5	1	3	1	284	0	2.95	—	—	—	—	—	—
98-99	Mobile	ECHL	34	16	14	3	1960	1	3.40	2	0	2	119	0	4.53

Born; 4/27/76, Kalamazoo, Michigan. 5-9, 165. Last amateur club; Michigan State (CCHA).

Chris Albert — Right Wing

Regular Season / Playoffs

Season	Team	League	GP	G	A	PTS	PIM	GP	G	A	PTS	PIM
95-96	San Antonio	CeHL	37	8	12	20	54	13	3	1	4	35
96-97	San Antonio	CeHL	55	19	29	48	48	—	—	—	—	—
97-98	Detroit	IHL	2	0	0	0	2	—	—	—	—	—
97-98	Fort Worth	WPHL	68	21	29	50	205	13	7	5	12	20
98-99	Michigan	IHL	23	3	3	6	44	—	—	—	—	—
98-99	Cincinnati	AHL	17	4	3	7	109	—	—	—	—	—
98-99	Philadelphia	AHL	22	1	3	4	88	15	5	5	10	22
	AHL	Totals	39	5	6	11	197	15	5	5	10	22
	IHL	Totals	25	3	3	6	46	—	—	—	—	—
	CeHL	Totals	92	27	41	68	102	13	3	1	4	35

Born; 10/12/72, Ottawa, Ontario. 5-11, 197. Signed as a free agent by Philadelphia Flyers (7/14/99). Last amateur club; Union (ECAC)

Francois Albert — Center

Regular Season / Playoffs

Season	Team	League	GP	G	A	PTS	PIM	GP	G	A	PTS	PIM
97-98	Fredonia	SUNY	28	25	25	50	NA	—	—	—	—	—
97-98	Fort Worth	CHL	3	1	0	1	2	—	—	—	—	—
98-99	Fort Worth	CHL	2	0	1	1	0	—	—	—	—	—
98-99	San Angelo	WPHL	8	0	1	1	2	—	—	—	—	—
98-99	Fort Worth	WPHL	41	12	22	34	18	12	1	1	2	0
	WPHL	Totals	49	12	23	35	20	12	1	1	2	0
	CHL	Totals	5	1	1	2	2	—	—	—	—	—

Born; 12/3/75, Edmundston, New Brunswick. 5-9, 175. Last amateur club; State Univeristy of New York-Fredonia (SUNY).

Rod Aldoff — Defenseman

Regular Season / Playoffs

Season	Team	League	GP	G	A	PTS	PIM	GP	G	A	PTS	PIM
95-96	Tallahassee	ECHL	70	13	44	57	74	12	1	4	5	10
96-97	Utah	IHL	24	1	4	5	10	—	—	—	—	—
96-97	Ambri-Priotta	Switz.	13	3	7	10	20	—	—	—	—	—
97-98	Pee Dee	ECHL	70	12	20	32	118	8	3	4	7	10
98-99	Pee Dee	ECHL	70	12	32	44	55	13	1	4	5	10
	ECHL	Totals	210	37	96	133	247	33	5	12	17	30

Born: 1/30/71, Lethbridge, Alberta. 5-10, 190. Last amateur club; University of Minnesota-Duluth (WCHA).

Chris Aldous — Defenseman

Regular Season / Playoffs

Season	Team	League	GP	G	A	PTS	PIM	GP	G	A	PTS	PIM
98-99	Fredericton	AHL	3	0	0	0	2	—	—	—	—	—
98-99	Baton Rouge	ECHL	55	3	20	23	22	—	—	—	—	—

Born: 11/19/75, Massena, New York. 6-3, 181. Drafted by Montreal Canadiens (12th choice, 252nd overall) in 1994 Entry Draft. Last amateur club; RPI

Keith Aldridge — Defenseman

Regular Season / Playoffs

Season	Team	League	GP	G	A	PTS	PIM	GP	G	A	PTS	PIM
95-96	Lake Superior State	CCHA	38	14	36	50	88	—	—	—	—	—
95-96	Baltimore	AHL	7	0	2	2	2	—	—	—	—	—
96-97	Baltimore	AHL	51	4	9	13	92	3	0	0	0	4
97-98	Detroit	IHL	79	13	21	34	89	23	1	9	10	67
98-99	Detroit	IHL	66	15	28	43	130	11	2	7	9	49
	IHL	Totals	145	28	49	77	219	34	3	16	19	116
	AHL	Totals	58	4	11	15	94	3	0	0	0	4

Born: 7/20/73, Detroit, Michigan. 5-11, 185. Last amateur club; Lake Superior State (CCHA).

Alexandre Alepin — Defenseman

Regular Season / Playoffs

Season	Team	League	GP	G	A	PTS	PIM	GP	G	A	PTS	PIM
96-97	Pensacola	ECHL	3	0	0	0	14	—	—	—	—	—
96-97	Huntington	ECHL	43	1	5	6	94	—	—	—	—	—
97-98	Jacksonville	ECHL	8	1	2	3	4	—	—	—	—	—
97-98	Mississippi	ECHL	10	0	1	1	26	—	—	—	—	—
97-98	Pee Dee	ECHL	31	1	8	9	50	6	0	1	1	8
98-99	Bakersfield	WCHL	15	2	6	8	28	—	—	—	—	—
98-99	Idaho	WCHL	31	2	3	5	49	—	—	—	—	—
98-99	Phoenix	WCHL	13	2	4	6	18	3	0	0	0	6
	ECHL	Totals	95	3	16	19	188	6	0	1	1	8
	WCHL	Totals	59	6	13	19	95	3	0	0	0	6

Born: 9/18/75, Montreal, Quebec. 5-11, 205. Traded to Phoenix with Mario Therrien for Stu Kulak and Jason Rose (2/26/99).

Alexander Alexeev — Defenseman

Regular Season / Playoffs

Season	Team	League	GP	G	A	PTS	PIM	GP	G	A	PTS	PIM
94-95	Tacoma	WHL	54	14	32	46	55	4	0	3	3	4
94-95	Portland	AHL	2	0	2	2	4	—	—	—	—	—
95-96	Portland	AHL	34	3	10	13	30	1	0	0	0	0
96-97	Portland	AHL	8	0	0	0	8	—	—	—	—	—
96-97	Hampton Roads	ECHL	63	6	26	32	124	9	1	6	7	18
97-98	Hampton Roads	ECHL	57	6	36	42	115	20	4	12	16	36
98-99	Las Vegas	IHL	10	0	3	3	4	—	—	—	—	—
98-99	Tacoma	WCHL	26	2	11	13	28	10	1	12	13	22
	AHL	Totals	44	3	12	15	42	1	0	0	0	0
	ECHL	Totals	120	12	62	74	239	29	5	18	23	54

Born: 3/21/74, Kiev, Russia. 6-0, 216. Drafted by Winnipeg Jets (5th choice, 132nd overall) in 1992 Entry Draft. Signed as a free agent by Washington Capitals (4/8/95). Member of 1997-98 ECHL Champion Hampton Roads Admirals. Member of 1998-99 WCHL Champion Tacoma Sabrecats. Last amateur club;

Chad Allan — Defenseman

Regular Season / Playoffs

Season	Team	League	GP	G	A	PTS	PIM	GP	G	A	PTS	PIM
96-97	Syracuse	AHL	73	3	10	13	83	3	0	1	1	0
97-98	Syracuse	AHL	73	2	10	12	121	5	0	0	0	4
98-99	Syracuse	AHL	60	2	8	10	98	—	—	—	—	—
	AHL	Totals	206	7	28	35	302	8	0	1	1	4

Born: 7/12/76, Saskatoon, Saskatchewan. 6-1, 192. Selected by Vancouver Canucks, (4th choice, 65th overall) in 1994 Entry Draft. Last amateur club Saska-

Jamie Allan — Right Wing

Regular Season / Playoffs

Season	Team	League	GP	G	A	PTS	PIM	GP	G	A	PTS	PIM
91-92	St. Thomas	CoHL	58	8	18	26	124	9	4	1	5	59
92-93	St. Thomas	CoHL	46	15	35	50	108	13	2	9	11	28
93-94	St. Thomas	CoHL	18	10	12	22	87	—	—	—	—	—
93-94	Chatham	CoHL	48	26	45	71	206	15	3	7	10	*95
94-95	Detroit	CoHL	65	24	41	65	239	7	2	0	2	20
95-96	Utica	CoHL	18	4	6	10	45	—	—	—	—	—
95-96	Winston-Salem	SHL	46	20	35	55	233	9	3	2	5	30
96-97	Wichita	CeHL	9	4	2	6	36	—	—	—	—	—
96-97	New Mexico	WPHL	28	10	17	27	110	—	—	—	—	—
97-98	Reno	WCHL	16	3	5	8	55	—	—	—	—	—
97-98	Phoenix	WCHL	47	9	25	34	254	9	2	3	5	64
98-99	Phoenix	WCHL	43	11	12	23	281	3	0	2	2	18
	CoHL	Totals	253	87	157	244	809	44	11	17	28	202
	WCHL	Totals	106	23	42	65	590	12	2	5	7	82

Born: 3/18/70, Ottawa, Ontario. 6-0, 195. Last amateur club; Ottawa (OHL).

Sandy Allan — Goaltender

Regular Season / Playoffs

Season	Team	League	GP	W	L	T	MIN	SO	AVG	GP	W	L	MIN	SO	AVG
95-96	Springfield	AHL	1	0	0	0	31	0	0.00	—	—	—	—	—	—
95-96	Richmond	ECHL	30	18	4	7	1682	0	3.25	—	—	—	—	—	—
96-97	Saint John	AHL	2	0	2	0	119	0	7.04	—	—	—	—	—	—
96-97	Richmond	ECHL	3	2	0	0	140	1	2.57	—	—	—	—	—	—
96-97	Louisville	ECHL	37	19	13	4	2104	1	3.48	—	—	—	—	—	—
97-98	Pee Dee	ECHL	46	21	15	8	2612	0	2.73	8	3	5	423	1	3.97
98-99	Pee Dee	ECHL	35	21	11	2	1958	1	2.48	11	7	4	627	0	2.68
	AHL	Totals	3	0	2	0	150	0	5.60	—	—	—	—	—	—
	ECHL	Totals	151	81	43	21	8496	3	2.96	19	10	9	1050	1	3.20

Born: 1/22/74, Nassau, Bahamas. 5-11, 180. Drafted by Los Angeles Kings (2nd choice, 63rd overall) in 1992 Entry Draft. Last amateur club; Prince Albert

Chris Allen — Defenseman

Regular Season / Playoffs

Season	Team	League	GP	G	A	PTS	PIM	GP	G	A	PTS	PIM
96-97	Kingston	OHL	61	14	29	43	81	5	1	2	3	4
96-97	Carolina	AHL	9	0	0	0	2	—	—	—	—	—
97-98	Kingston	OHL	66	38	57	95	91	10	4	2	6	6
97-98	Florida	NHL	1	0	0	0	2	—	—	—	—	—
98-99	New Haven	AHL	58	8	27	35	43	—	—	—	—	—
	AHL	Totals	67	8	27	35	45	—	—	—	—	—

Born: 5/8/78, Chatham, Ontario. 6-2, 193. Drafted by Florida Panthers (2nd choice, 60th overall) in 1996 Entry Draft. Last amateur club; Kingston (OHL).

Peter Allen — Defenseman

Regular Season / Playoffs

Season	Team	League	GP	G	A	PTS	PIM	GP	G	A	PTS	PIM
93-94	Prince Edward Island	AHL	6	0	1	1	6	—	—	—	—	—
93-94	Richmond	ECHL	52	2	16	18	62	—	—	—	—	—
94-95	Canadian	National	52	5	15	20	36	—	—	—	—	—
95-96	Pittsburgh	NHL	8	0	0	0	8	—	—	—	—	—
95-96	Cleveland	IHL	65	3	45	48	55	3	0	0	0	2
96-97	Cleveland	IHL	81	14	31	45	75	14	0	6	6	24
97-98	Kentucky	AHL	72	0	18	18	73	3	0	1	1	4
98-99	Kentucky	AHL	72	3	17	20	48	12	1	1	2	8
	AHL	Totals	150	3	36	39	127	15	1	2	3	12

Born: 3/6/70, Calgary, Alberta. 6-2, 185. Drafted by Boston Bruins (1st choice, 24th overall) in 1991 Supplemental Draft. Signed as a free agent by Pittsburgh Penguins (8/10/95). Signed as a free agent by San Jose Sharks (8/15/97). Last amateur club; Yale (ECAC).

Blair Allison — Goaltender

Regular Season / Playoffs

Season	Team	League	GP	W	L	T	MIN	SO	AVG	GP	W	L	MIN	SO	AVG
96-97	Canada	National	33	22	5	2	1827	—	2.61	—	—	—	—	—	—
96-97	Orlando	IHL	1	0	1	0	41	0	7.38	—	—	—	—	—	—
97-98	Tallahassee	ECHL	21	7	9	0	1026	0	3.80	—	—	—	—	—	—
97-98	Jacksonville	ECHL	9	3	2	3	469	0	2.17	—	—	—	—	—	—
98-99	Tacoma	WCHL	48	33	5	5	2592	2	*2.66	*11	*9	2	*672	*2	*2.05
	ECHL	Totals	30	10	11	3	1495	0	3.29	—	—	—	—	—	—

Born: 6/26/72, Golden, Alberta. 5-11, 200. 1998-99 WCHL Outstanding Goaltender. 1998-99 WCHL First Team All-Star. 1998-99 WCHL Playoff MVP. Member of 1998-99 WCHL Champion Tacoma Sabrecats. Last amateur club; University of Maine (Hockey East).

Jamie Allison — Defenseman

Regular Season / Playoffs

Season	Team	League	GP	G	A	PTS	PIM	GP	G	A	PTS	PIM
94-95	Detroit	OHL	50	1	14	15	119	18	2	7	9	35
94-95	Calgary	NHL	1	0	0	0	0	—	—	—	—	—
95-96	Saint John	AHL	71	3	16	19	223	14	0	2	2	16
96-97	Calgary	NHL	20	0	0	0	35	—	—	—	—	—
96-97	Saint John	AHL	46	3	6	9	139	5	0	1	1	4
97-98	Calgary	NHL	43	3	8	11	104	—	—	—	—	—
97-98	Saint John	AHL	16	0	5	5	49	—	—	—	—	—
98-99	Saint John	AHL	5	0	0	0	23	—	—	—	—	—
98-99	Indianapolis	IHL	3	1	0	1	10	—	—	—	—	—
98-99	Chicago	NHL	38	2	2	4	62	—	—	—	—	—
	NHL	Totals	102	5	10	15	201	—	—	—	—	—
	AHL	Totals	138	6	27	33	434	19	0	3	3	20

Born: 5/13/75, Lindsay, Ontario. 6-1, 190. Drafted by Calgary Flames (2nd choice, 44th overall) in 1993 Entry Draft. Traded to Chicago Blackhawks by Calgary with Erik Andersson and Marty McInnis for Jeff Shantz and Steve Dubinsky (10/27/98). Last amateur club: Detroit (OHL).

Scott Allison — Center

Regular Season / Playoffs

Season	Team	League	GP	G	A	PTS	PIM	GP	G	A	PTS	PIM
92-93	Cape Breton	AHL	49	3	5	8	34	—	—	—	—	—
92-93	Wheeling	ECHL	6	3	3	6	8	—	—	—	—	—
93-94	Cape Breton	AHL	75	19	14	33	202	3	0	1	1	2
94-95	Cape Breton	AHL	58	6	14	20	104	—	—	—	—	—
95-96	Prince Edward Island	AHL	63	11	16	27	133	4	1	0	1	15
96-97	Manitoba	IHL	42	4	12	16	140	—	—	—	—	—
96-97	Grand Rapids	IHL	12	2	1	3	41	4	0	0	0	21
96-97	Pensacola	ECHL	12	4	5	9	104	—	—	—	—	—
97-98	Sheffield	BSL	52	27	26	53	191	8	6	6	12	53
98-99	Sheffield	BSL	49	18	24	42	113	6	3	1	4	12
	AHL	Totals	245	39	49	88	473	7	1	0	1	17
	IHL	Totals	54	6	13	19	181	4	0	0	0	21
	ECHL	Totals	18	7	8	15	112	—	—	—	—	—
	BSL	Totals	101	45	50	95	304	14	9	7	16	65

Born: 4/22/72, St. Boniface, Manitoba. 6-4, 195. Drafted by Edmonton Oilers (1st choice, 17th overall) in 1990 Entry Draft. Last amateur club; Moose Jaw (WHL).

Doug Altschul — Defenseman

Regular Season / Playoffs

Season	Team	League	GP	G	A	PTS	PIM	GP	G	A	PTS	PIM
98-99	Madison	UHL	4	0	1	1	9	—	—	—	—	—

Born:

Mike Alunno

Regular Season / Playoffs

Season	Team	League	GP	G	A	PTS	PIM	GP	G	A	PTS	PIM
98-99	Saginaw	UHL	3	0	0	0	0	—	—	—	—	—

Born:

Matt Alvey — Forward

Regular Season / Playoffs

Season	Team	League	GP	G	A	PTS	PIM	GP	G	A	PTS	PIM
96-97	Lake Superior State	CCHA	18	10	8	18	49	—	—	—	—	—
96-97	Pensacola	ECHL	7	1	2	3	0	3	0	0	0	4
97-98	Charlotte	ECHL	38	17	15	32	37	7	3	1	4	6
98-99	Greenville	ECHL	65	15	16	31	26	—	—	—	—	—

Born, 5/15/75, Troy, New York. 6-5, 208. Drafted by Boston Bruins (2nd choice, 51st overall) in 1993 Entry Draft. Last amateur club: Lake Superior State

Peter Ambroziak — Left Wing

Regular Season / Playoffs

Season	Team	League	GP	G	A	PTS	PIM	GP	G	A	PTS	PIM
91-92	Ottawa	OHL	49	32	49	81	50	11	3	7	10	33
91-92	Rochester	AHL	2	0	1	1	0	—	—	—	—	—
92-93	Rochester	AHL	50	8	10	18	37	12	4	3	7	16
93-94	Rochester	AHL	22	3	4	7	53	—	—	—	—	—
94-95	Buffalo	NHL	12	0	1	1	0	—	—	—	—	—
94-95	Rochester	AHL	46	14	11	25	35	4	0	0	0	6
95-96	Albany	AHL	8	2	1	3	25	—	—	—	—	—
95-96	Cornwall	AHL	50	9	15	24	42	8	1	1	2	4
96-97	Fort Wayne	IHL	57	15	5	20	28	—	—	—	—	—
97-98	Hershey	AHL	63	7	11	18	61	5	0	1	1	6
98-99	Flint	UHL	40	19	27	46	90	5	0	2	2	12
98-99	Detroit	IHL	33	5	8	13	30	2	0	0	0	0
	AHL	Totals	241	43	53	96	253	29	5	5	10	32
	IHL	Totals	90	20	13	33	58	2	0	0	0	0

Born: 9/15/71, Toronto, Ontario. 6-0, 200. Drafted by Buffalo Sabres (4th choice, 72nd overall) in 1991 Entry Draft. Last amateur club; Ottawa (OHL).

Bujar Amidovski — Goaltender

Regular Season / Playoffs

Season	Team	League	GP	W	L	T	MIN	SO	AVG	GP	W	L	MIN	SO	AVG
96-97	Kingston	OHL	36	11	14	4	1797	0	3.87	5	1	3	280	0	5.14
96-97	Dayton	ECHL	3	1	1	0	91	0	3.31	2	0	2	118	0	4.56
97-98	Toronto	OHL	48	12	25	7	2697	0	3.40	—	—	—	—	—	—
98-99	Louisiana	ECHL	27	17	5	3	1525	3	2.32	—	—	—	—	—	—
98-99	Philadelphia	AHL	2	2	0	0	120	0	2.50	—	—	—	—	—	—
98-99	Saint John	AHL	6	2	2	0	243	0	4.69	—	—	—	—	—	—
	AHL	Totals	8	4	2	0	363	0	3.97	2	0	2	118	0	4.56
	ECHL	Totals	30	18	6	3	1616	3	2.38	—	—	—	—	—	—

Born; 2/19/77, Toronto, Ontario. 5-11, 173. Last amateur club: Toronto (OHL).

Mike Anastasio — Right Wing

Regular Season / Playoffs

Season	Team	League	GP	G	A	PTS	PIM	GP	G	A	PTS	PIM
97-98	Odessa	WPHL	4	0	0	0	7	—	—	—	—	—
97-98	Tulsa	CHL	2	0	0	0	6	—	—	—	—	—
97-98	Macon	CHL	29	14	3	17	23	3	0	0	0	6
98-99	Macon	CHL	52	16	12	28	45	—	—	—	—	—
	CHL	Totals	83	30	15	45	74	3	0	0	0	6

Born: 11/29/75, Cromwell, Connecticut. 5-10, 185. Traded to Macon by Tulsa with Francois Leroux for Craig Coxe and Dave Wiletjo (12/97). Claimed by Macon in 1999 CHL Dispersal Draft. Last amateur club; Middlebury (ECAC).

Mike Ancuta — Defenseman

Regular Season / Playoffs

Season	Team	League	GP	G	A	PTS	PIM	GP	G	A	PTS	PIM
98-99	Mississauga	OHL	35	1	0	1	64	—	—	—	—	—
98-99	Abilene	WPHL	1	0	0	0	7	—	—	—	—	—

Born: 5/12/79, Beaverton, Ontario. 6-1, 190. Last amateur club; Mississauga

Bo Andersen — Forward

Regular Season / Playoffs

Season	Team	League	GP	G	A	PTS	PIM	GP	G	A	PTS	PIM
98-99	Odessa	WPHL	27	5	6	11	35	—	—	—	—	—

Born: 3/22/79, Aalborg, Denmark. 5-10, 181.

Eric Andersen — Defenseman

Regular Season / Playoffs

Season	Team	League	GP	G	A	PTS	PIM	GP	G	A	PTS	PIM
98-99	Louisiana	ECHL	2	0	0	0	14	—	—	—	—	—
98-99	Birmingham	ECHL	2	0	0	0	0	—	—	—	—	—
98-99	Alexandria	WPHL	10	0	0	0	8	—	—	—	—	—
98-99	Arkansas	WPHL	23	1	6	7	16	—	—	—	—	—
98-99	Amarillo	WPHL	14	0	1	1	12	—	—	—	—	—
	WPHL	Totals	47	1	7	8	36	—	—	—	—	—
	ECHL	Totals	4	0	0	0	14	—	—	—	—	—

Born: 10/25/76, Swan River, British Columbia. 6-1, 203. Last amateur club; Bemidji State (NCHA).

Darcy Anderson — Right Wing

Regular Season / Playoffs

Season	Team	League	GP	G	A	PTS	PIM	GP	G	A	PTS	PIM
95-96	Basingstoke	BHL	8	2	0	2	6	—	—	—	—	—
95-96	Saginaw	UHL	10	0	0	0	5	—	—	—	—	—
96-97												
97-98	Memphis	CHL	2	0	0	0	2	—	—	—	—	—
98-99	Greenville	ECHL	14	3	2	5	0	—	—	—	—	—

Born: 7/25/74, Thunder Bay, Ontario. 6-0, 195.

Ryan Anderson — Right Wing

Regular Season / Playoffs

Season	Team	League	GP	G	A	PTS	PIM	GP	G	A	PTS	PIM
96-97	Austin	WPHL	59	2	7	9	222	6	0	1	1	30
97-98	Austin	WPHL	69	1	7	8	309	5	1	1	2	16
98-99	Austin	WPHL	63	0	4	4	235	—	—	—	—	—
	WPHL	Totals	191	3	18	21	766	11	1	2	3	46

Born; 2/27/75, Dowsman, Alberta. 6-2, 190. Last amateur club; Neepawa

Shawn Anderson — Defenseman

Regular Season / Playoffs

Season	Team	League	GP	G	A	PTS	PIM	GP	G	A	PTS	PIM
86-87	Buffalo	NHL	41	2	11	13	23	—	—	—	—	—
86-87	Rochester	AHL	15	2	5	7	11	—	—	—	—	—
87-88	Buffalo	NHL	23	1	2	3	17	—	—	—	—	—
87-88	Rochester	AHL	22	5	16	21	19	6	0	0	0	0
88-89	Buffalo	NHL	33	2	10	12	18	5	0	1	1	4
88-89	Rochester	AHL	31	5	14	19	24	—	—	—	—	—
89-90	Buffalo	NHL	16	1	3	4	8	—	—	—	—	—
89-90	Rochester	AHL	39	2	16	18	41	9	1	0	1	4
90-91	Quebec	NHL	31	3	10	13	21	—	—	—	—	—
90-91	Halifax	AHL	4	0	1	1	2	—	—	—	—	—
91-92	Weisswasser	Germany	38	7	15	22	83	—	—	—	—	—
92-93	Washington	NHL	60	2	6	8	18	6	0	0	0	0
92-93	Baltimore	AHL	10	1	5	6	8	—	—	—	—	—
93-94	Washington	NHL	50	0	9	9	12	8	1	0	1	12
94-95	Philadelphia	NHL	1	0	0	0	0	—	—	—	—	—
94-95	Hershey	AHL	31	9	21	30	18	6	2	3	5	19
95-96	Milwaukee	IHL	79	22	39	61	68	5	0	7	7	0
96-97	Wedemark	German-2	8	1	0	1	4	—	—	—	—	—
96-97	Utah	IHL	31	2	12	14	21	—	—	—	—	—
96-97	Manitoba	IHL	17	2	7	9	5	—	—	—	—	—
97-98	Revier Lowen	Germany	32	5	14	19	45	—	—	—	—	—
98-99	Klagenfurter	Austria										
	NHL	Totals	255	11	51	62	117	19	1	1	2	16
	AHL	Totals	172	24	78	102	123	21	3	4	7	23
	IHL	Totals	127	26	58	84	94	5	0	7	7	0

Born; 2/7/68, Monteral, Quebec. 6-1, 200. Drafted by Buffalo Sabres (1st choice, 5th overall) in 1986 Entry Draft. Traded to Washington Capitals by Buffalo for Bill Houlder (9/30/90). Claimed by Quebec Nordiques from Washington in NHL Waiver Draft (10/1/90). Traded to Winnipeg Jets by Quebec for Sergei Kharin (10/22/91). Traded to Washington by Winnipeg for future considerations (10/23/91). Signed as a free agent by Philadelphia Flyers (8/16/94). Last amateur

Trevor Anderson — Goaltender

Regular Season / Playoffs

Season	Team	League	GP	W	L	T	MIN	SO	AVG	GP	W	L	MIN	SO	AVG
97-98	Charlotte	ECHL	7	2	2	2	379	0	3.48	—	—	—	—	—	—
97-98	San Angelo	WPHL	29	8	13	5	1535	0	4.92	1	0	0	20	0	6.00
98-99	Atlantis	German-2	49												

Born: Medicine Hat, Alberta. 6-1, 180. Last amateur club; Moose Jaw (WHL).

Erik Andersson — Right Wing

Regular Season / Playoffs

Season	Team	League	GP	G	A	PTS	PIM	GP	G	A	PTS	PIM
97-98	Calgary	NHL	12	2	1	3	8	—	—	—	—	—
97-98	Saint John	AHL	29	5	9	14	29	—	—	—	—	—
98-99	Saint John	AHL	5	0	0	0	4	—	—	—	—	—
98-99	Indianapolis	IHL	48	5	7	12	24	4	0	0	0	12
	AHL	Totals	34	5	9	14	33	—	—	—	—	—

Born: 8/19/71, Stockholm, Sweden. 6-3, 210. Drafted by Los Angeles Kings (5th choice, 112th overall) in 1990 Entry Draft. Re-entered Entry Draft, Calgary's (6th choice, 70th overall) in 1997 Entry Draft. Traded to Chicago Blackhawks by Calgary with Jamie Allison and Marty McInnis for Steve Dubinsky and Jeff Shantz (10/27/98). Last amateur club; University of Denver (WCHA).

Jens Andersson — Defenseman

Regular Season / Playoffs

Season	Team	League	GP	G	A	PTS	PIM	GP	G	A	PTS	PIM
98-99	Waco	WPHL	50	3	7	10	53	3	0	0	0	2

Born: 6/29/77, Umea, Sweden. 6-0, 200. Last overseas club; Bjorkloven

Niklas Andersson — Left Wing
Regular Season — Playoffs

Season	Team	League	GP	G	A	PTS	PIM	GP	G	A	PTS	PIM
91-92	Halifax	AHL	57	8	26	34	41	—	—	—	—	—
92-93	Quebec	NHL	3	0	1	1	2	—	—	—	—	—
92-93	Halifax	AHL	76	32	50	82	42	—	—	—	—	—
93-94	Cornwall	AHL	42	18	34	52	8	—	—	—	—	—
94-95	Denver	IHL	66	22	39	61	28	15	8	13	21	10
95-96	Islanders	NHL	47	14	12	26	12	—	—	—	—	—
95-96	Utah	IHL	30	13	22	35	25	—	—	—	—	—
96-97	Islanders	NHL	74	12	31	43	57	—	—	—	—	—
97-98	San Jose	NHL	5	0	0	0	2	—	—	—	—	—
97-98	Kentucky	AHL	37	10	28	38	54	—	—	—	—	—
97-98	Utah	IHL	21	6	20	26	24	4	3	1	4	4
98-99	Chicago	IHL	65	17	47	64	49	10	2	2	4	10
	NHL	Totals	129	26	44	70	73	—	—	—	—	—
	AHL	Totals	212	68	138	206	145	—	—	—	—	—
	IHL	Totals	182	58	128	176	126	29	13	16	29	24

Born: 5/20/71, Kungaly, Sweden. 5-9, 175. Drafted by Quebec Nordiques (5th choice, 68th overall) in 1989 Entry Draft. Signed as a free agent by New York Islanders (7/15/94). Signed as a free agent by San Jose (9/10/97). Signed as a free agent by Toronto Maple Leafs (9/4/98). Last overseas club; Frolumda (Sweden).

Vitali Andreev — Forward
Regular Season — Playoffs

Season	Team	League	GP	G	A	PTS	PIM	GP	G	A	PTS	PIM
98-99	Alexandria	WPHL	53	11	8	19	44	—	—	—	—	—

Born: 3/17/74, Tallin, Estonia. 5-9, 175. Last amateur club; Miami (CCHA).

Greg Andrusak — Defenseman
Regular Season — Playoffs

Season	Team	League	GP	G	A	PTS	PIM	GP	G	A	PTS	PIM
92-93	Cleveland	IHL	55	3	22	25	78	2	0	0	0	2
92-93	Muskegon	CoHL	2	0	3	3	7	—	—	—	—	—
93-94	Pittsburgh	NHL	3	0	0	0	2	—	—	—	—	—
93-94	Cleveland	IHL	69	13	26	39	109	—	—	—	—	—
94-95	Detroit	IHL	37	5	26	31	50	—	—	—	—	—
94-95	Pittsburgh	NHL	7	0	4	4	6	—	—	—	—	—
94-95	Cleveland	IHL	8	0	8	8	14	—	—	—	—	—
95-96	Pittsburgh	NHL	2	0	0	0	0	—	—	—	—	—
95-96	Detroit	IHL	58	6	30	36	128	—	—	—	—	—
95-96	Minnesota	IHL	5	0	4	4	8	—	—	—	—	—
96-97	Eisbaren	Germany	45	5	17	22	170	8	1	1	2	20
97-98	Eisbaren	Germany	34	3	7	10	65	9	0	1	1	8
98-99	Eisbaron	Germany	19	2	5	7	12	—	—	—	—	—
98-99	Houston	IHL	3	0	1	1	2	6	1	4	5	16
98-99	Pittsburgh	NHL	7	0	1	1	4	7	0	1	1	4
	NHL	Totals	19	0	5	5	12	7	0	1	1	4
	IHL	Totals	235	27	117	144	389	8	1	4	5	18

Born; 11/14/69, Cranbrook, British Columbia. 6-1, 190. Drafted by Pittsburgh Penguins (5th choice, 88th overall) in 1988 Entry Draft. Signed as a free agent by Pittsburgh Penguins (3/19/99). Signed as a free agent by Toronto Maple Leafs (7/9/99). Member of 1998-99 IHL Champion Houston Aeros. Last amateur club; Minnesota (WCHA).

Mel Angelstad — Left Wing
Regular Season — Playoffs

Season	Team	League	GP	G	A	PTS	PIM	GP	G	A	PTS	PIM
92-93	Nashville	ECHL	1	0	0	0	14	—	—	—	—	—
92-93	Thunder Bay	CoHL	45	2	5	7	256	5	0	0	0	10
93-94	Prince Edward Island	AHL	1	0	0	0	5	—	—	—	—	—
93-94	Thunder Bay	CoHL	58	1	20	21	374	9	1	2	3	65
94-95	Prince Edward Island	AHL	3	0	0	0	16	—	—	—	—	—
94-95	Thunder Bay	CoHL	46	0	8	8	317	7	0	3	3	62
95-96	Phoenix	IHL	5	0	0	0	43	—	—	—	—	—
95-96	Thunder Bay	CoHL	51	3	3	6	335	16	0	6	6	94
96-97	Thunder Bay	CoHL	66	10	21	31	422	7	0	1	1	21
97-98	Las Vegas	IHL	3	0	0	0	5	—	—	—	—	—
97-98	Orlando	IHL	63	1	3	4	321	8	0	0	0	29
97-98	Fort Worth	WPHL	19	1	6	7	102	—	—	—	—	—
98-99	Michigan	IHL	78	3	5	8	*421	5	1	0	1	16
	IHL	Totals	149	4	8	12	790	13	1	0	1	45
	AHL	Totals	4	0	0	0	21	—	—	—	—	—
	CoHL	Totals	266	16	57	73	1704	44	1	12	13	252

Born; 10/31/71, Saskatoon, Saskatchewan. 6-2, 210. Signed as a free agent by Dallas Stars (7/27/98). Member of 1993-94 CoHL champion Thunder Bay Senators. Member of 1994-95 CoHL champion Thunder Bay Senators.

Dorian Anneck — Right Wing
Regular Season — Playoffs

Season	Team	League	GP	G	A	PTS	PIM	GP	G	A	PTS	PIM
97-98	Monroe	WPHL	50	17	15	32	16	—	—	—	—	—
98-99	Monroe	WPHL	69	44	41	85	14	6	3	4	7	2
	WPHL	Totals	119	61	56	117	30	6	3	4	7	2

Born; 4/24/76, Winnipeg, Manitoba. 6-2, 210. Drafted by Winnipeg Jets (2nd choice, 56th overall) in 1994 Entry Draft. Last amateur club; Brandon (WHL).

Chad Antonishyn — Defenseman
Regular Season — Playoffs

Season	Team	League	GP	G	A	PTS	PIM	GP	G	A	PTS	PIM
96-97	Central Texas	WPHL	33	0	1	1	46	—	—	—	—	—
96-97	Waco	WPHL	15	1	0	1	30	—	—	—	—	—
97-98	Waco	WPHL	5	0	0	0	16	—	—	—	—	—
97-98	Fort Worth	CHL	55	2	7	9	134	—	—	—	—	—
98-99	Topeka	CHL	47	0	3	3	89	—	—	—	—	—
	CHL	Totals	102	2	10	12	223	—	—	—	—	—
	WPHL	Totals	53	1	1	2	92	—	—	—	—	—

Born; 5/25/74, Regina, Saskatchewan. 6-2, 210. Selected by Topeka in 1998 CHL Expansion Draft.

Jeff Antonovich — Center
Regular Season — Playoffs

Season	Team	League	GP	G	A	PTS	PIM	GP	G	A	PTS	PIM
95-96	Minnesota	IHL	1	0	0	0	2	—	—	—	—	—
95-96	Quad City	CoHL	66	20	34	54	32	4	1	1	2	0
96-97	Bakersfield	WCHL	44	22	31	53	35	—	—	—	—	—
96-97	Reno	WCHL	6	1	2	3	6	—	—	—	—	—
97-98	Nashville	CHL	66	25	38	63	36	9	3	4	7	2
98-99	Tulsa	CHL	70	40	60	100	66	—	—	—	—	—
	CHL	Totals	136	65	98	163	102	9	3	4	7	2
	WCHL	Totals	50	23	33	56	41	—	—	—	—	—

Born; 2/5/74, Greenway, Minnesota. 5-8, 170. Last amateur club; Kamloops

Anthony Aquino — Right Wing
Regular Season — Playoffs

Season	Team	League	GP	G	A	PTS	PIM	GP	G	A	PTS	PIM
98-99	Peoria	ECHL	10	1	0	1	19	—	—	—	—	—

Born: Selected by Arkansas in ECHL Expansion Draft.

Francois Archambeault — Forward

Regular Season / Playoffs

Season	Team	League	GP	G	A	PTS	PIM	GP	G	A	PTS	PIM
97-98	New Orleans	ECHL	16	2	4	6	34	—	—	—	—	—
97-98	Johnstown	ECHL	49	14	14	28	51	—	—	—	—	—
98-99	Abilene	WPHL	61	26	26	52	139	3	0	0	0	4
	ECHL	Totals	65	16	18	34	85	—	—	—	—	—

Born; 4/1/76, Chateauguay, Quebec. 6-0, 195. Last amateur club; Val D'Or (QMJHL).

Dave Archibald — Left Wing

Regular Season / Playoffs

Season	Team	League	GP	G	A	PTS	PIM	GP	G	A	PTS	PIM
87-88	Minnesota	NHL	78	13	20	33	26	—	—	—	—	—
88-89	Minnesota	NHL	72	14	19	33	14	5	0	1	1	0
89-90	Minnesota	NHL	12	1	5	6	6	—	—	—	—	—
89-90	Rangers	NHL	19	2	3	5	6	—	—	—	—	—
89-90	Flint	IHL	41	14	38	52	16	4	3	2	5	0
90-91	Canada	National	29	19	12	31	20	—	—	—	—	—
91-92	Canada	National	58	20	43	63	64	—	—	—	—	—
91-92	Canada	Olympic	8	7	1	8	18	—	—	—	—	—
91-92	Bolzano	Italy	5	4	3	7	16	7	8	5	13	7
92-93	Binghamton	AHL	8	6	3	9	10	—	—	—	—	—
92-93	Ottawa	NHL	44	9	6	15	32	—	—	—	—	—
93-94	Ottawa	NHL	33	10	8	18	14	—	—	—	—	—
94-95	Ottawa	NHL	14	2	2	4	19	—	—	—	—	—
95-96	Ottawa	NHL	44	6	4	10	18	—	—	—	—	—
95-96	Utah	IHL	19	1	4	5	10	—	—	—	—	—
96-97	Islanders	NHL	7	0	0	0	4	—	—	—	—	—
96-97	Frankfurt	Germany	34	10	19	29	48	9	4	2	6	15
97-98	San Antonio	IHL	55	11	21	32	10	—	—	—	—	—
98-99	Utah	IHL	76	23	25	48	32	—	—	—	—	—
	NHL	Totals	323	57	67	124	139	5	0	1	1	0
	IHL	Totals	191	49	88	137	68	4	3	2	5	0

Born; 4/14/69, Chilliwack, British Columbia. 6-1, 210. Drafted by Minnesota North Stars (1st choice, 6th overall) in 1987 Entry Draft. Traded to New York Rangers by Minnesota for Jayson More (11/1/89). Traded to Ottawa by Rangers for Ottawa's fifth round choice (later traded to Los Angeles—Los Angeles selected Frederic Beaubien) in 1993 Entry Draft (11/5/92) Signed as a free agent by New York Islanders (10/10/96). Last amateur club; Portland (WHL).

Bill C. Armstrong — Defenseman

Regular Season / Playoffs

Season	Team	League	GP	G	A	PTS	PIM	GP	G	A	PTS	PIM
90-91	Hershey	AHL	56	1	9	10	115	—	—	—	—	—
91-92	Hershey	AHL	80	2	14	16	159	3	0	0	0	2
92-93	Hershey	AHL	80	2	10	12	205	—	—	—	—	—
93-94	Providence	AHL	66	0	7	7	200	—	—	—	—	—
94-95	Providence	AHL	75	3	10	13	244	13	0	2	2	8
95-96	Cleveland	IHL	63	1	3	4	183	3	0	0	0	2
96-97	Cleveland	IHL	41	0	6	6	91	—	—	—	—	—
96-97	Providence	AHL	13	1	1	2	71	10	0	1	1	26
97-98	Providence	AHL	63	0	4	4	141	—	—	—	—	—
98-99	Providence	AHL	6	0	0	0	32	—	—	—	—	—
	AHL	Totals	439	9	55	64	1169	26	0	3	3	36
	IHL	Totals	104	1	9	10	274	3	0	0	0	2

Born; 5/18/70, Richmond Hill, Ontario. 6-5, 220. Drafted by Philadelphia Flyers (6th choice, 46th overall) in 1990 Entry Draft. Signed as a free agent by Boston Bruins (7/22/93). Acquired from Cleveland Lumberjacks for Mark Cornforth, 1997. Last amateur club; Oshawa (OHL).

Chris Armstrong — Defenseman

Regular Season / Playoffs

Season	Team	League	GP	G	A	PTS	PIM	GP	G	A	PTS	PIM
93-94	Moose Jaw	WHL	64	13	55	68	54	—	—	—	—	—
93-94	Cincinnati	IHL	1	0	0	0	0	10	1	3	4	2
94-95	Moose Jaw	WHL	66	17	54	71	61	10	2	12	14	22
94-95	Cincinnati	IHL	—	—	—	—	—	9	1	3	4	10
95-96	Carolina	AHL	78	9	33	42	65	—	—	—	—	—
96-97	Carolina	AHL	66	9	23	32	38	—	—	—	—	—
97-98	Fort Wayne	IHL	79	8	36	44	66	4	0	2	2	4
98-99	Milwaukee	IHL	5	0	3	3	4	—	—	—	—	—
98-99	Hershey	AHL	65	12	32	44	30	5	0	1	1	0
	AHL	Totals	209	30	88	118	133	5	0	1	1	0
	IHL	Totals	85	8	39	47	70	19	1	6	8	12

Born; 6/26/75, Regina, Saskatechewan. 6-0, 198. Drafted by Florida Panthers (3rd choice, 57th overall) in 1993 Entry Draft. Selected by Nashville Predators in 1998 Expansion Draft. Last amateur club; Moose Jaw Warriors (WHL).

Derek Armstrong — Center

Regular Season / Playoffs

Season	Team	League	GP	G	A	PTS	PIM	GP	G	A	PTS	PIM
93-94	Islanders	NHL	1	0	0	0	0	—	—	—	—	—
93-94	Salt Lake City	IHL	76	23	35	58	61	—	—	—	—	—
94-95	Denver	IHL	59	13	18	31	65	6	0	2	2	0
95-96	Islanders	NHL	19	1	3	4	14	—	—	—	—	—
95-96	Worcester	AHL	51	11	15	26	33	—	—	—	—	—
96-97	Islanders	NHL	50	6	7	13	33	—	—	—	—	—
96-97	Utah	IHL	17	4	8	12	10	6	0	4	4	4
97-98	Hartford	AHL	54	16	30	46	40	15	2	6	8	22
97-98	Detroit	IHL	10	0	1	1	2	—	—	—	—	—
98-99	Rangers	NHL	3	0	0	0	0	—	—	—	—	—
98-99	Hartford	AHL	59	29	51	80	73	7	5	4	9	10
	NHL	Totals	73	7	10	17	47	—	—	—	—	—
	AHL	Totals	164	56	96	152	146	22	7	10	17	32
	IHL	Totals	162	40	62	102	138	12	0	6	6	4

Born; 4/23/73, Ottawa, Ontario. 5-11, 188. Drafted by New York Islanders (5th choice, 128th overall) in 1992 Entry Draft. Signed as a free agent by Ottawa Senators (7/28/97). Signed as a free agent by New York Rangers (7/20/98). Member of 1994-95 IHL champion Denver Grizzlies. Last amateur club; Sudbury

Scott Arniel — Left Wing

Regular Season / Playoffs

Season	Team	League	GP	G	A	PTS	PIM	GP	G	A	PTS	PIM
81-82	Winnipeg	NHL	17	1	8	9	14	3	0	0	0	0
82-83	Winnipeg	NHL	75	13	5	18	46	2	0	0	0	0
83-84	Winnipeg	NHL	80	21	35	56	68	2	0	0	0	5
84-85	Winnipeg	NHL	79	22	22	44	81	8	1	2	3	9
85-86	Winnipeg	NHL	80	18	25	43	40	3	0	0	0	12
86-87	Buffalo	NHL	63	11	14	25	59	—	—	—	—	—
87-88	Buffalo	NHL	73	17	23	40	61	6	0	1	1	5
88-89	Buffalo	NHL	80	18	23	41	46	5	1	0	1	4
89-90	Buffalo	NHL	79	18	14	32	77	5	1	0	1	4
90-91	Winnipeg	NHL	75	5	17	22	87	—	—	—	—	—
91-92	Boston	NHL	29	5	3	8	20	—	—	—	—	—
91-92	New Haven	AHL	11	3	3	6	10	—	—	—	—	—
91-92	Maine	AHL	14	4	4	8	8	—	—	—	—	—
92-93	San Diego	IHL	79	35	48	83	116	14	6	5	11	16
93-94	San Diego	IHL	79	34	43	77	121	7	6	3	9	24
94-95	Houston	IHL	72	37	40	77	102	4	1	0	1	10
95-96	Houston	IHL	64	18	28	46	94	—	—	—	—	—
95-96	Utah	IHL	14	3	3	6	29	22	10	7	17	28
96-97	Manitoba	IHL	73	23	27	50	16	—	—	—	—	—
97-98	Manitoba	IHL	79	28	42	70	84	3	1	0	1	10
98-99	Manitoba	IHL	70	16	35	51	82	5	1	2	3	0
	NHL	Totals	730	149	189	338	599	34	3	3	6	39
	IHL	Totals	530	159	266	425	644	55	25	17	42	88
	AHL	Totals	25	7	7	14	18	—	—	—	—	—

Born; 9/17/62, Kingston, Ontario. 6-1, 190. Last amateur club; Cornwall Royals (OHL). Drafted by Winnipeg Jets (2nd choice, 22nd overall) in 1981 Entry Draft. Traded to Buffalo Sabres by Winnipeg for Gilles Hamel (6/21/86). Traded to Winnipeg by Buffalo with Phil Housley, Jeff Parker and first round choice (Keith Tkachuk) in 1990 Entry Draft for Dale Hawerchuk, first round choice (Brad May) in 1990 Entry Draft and future considerations (6/16/90). Greg Paslawski sent to Buffalo to complete deal (2/5/91). Traded to Boston Bruins by Winnipeg for future considerations (11/22/91). Signed as a free agent by San Diego Gulls (10/7/92). Member of 1995-96 IHL champion Utah Grizzlies.

Dave Arsenault — Goaltender

Regular Season / Playoffs

Season	Team	League	GP	W	L	T	MIN	SO	AVG	GP	W	L	MIN	SO	AVG
97-98	Adirondack	AHL	10	3	5	0	563	0	4.37	—	—	—	—	—	—
97-98	Toledo	ECHL	22	13	4	3	1261	0	2.85	—	—	—	—	—	—
98-99	Adirondack	AHL	5	0	4	0	250	0	4.80	—	—	—	—	—	—
98-99	Toledo	ECHL	21	10	8	1	1171	0	3.69	—	—	—	—	—	—
	AHL	Totals	15	3	9	0	813	0	4.50	—	—	—	—	—	—
	ECHL	Totals	43	23	12	4	2432	0	3.26	—	—	—	—	—	—

Born; 3/21/77, Frankfurt, Germany. 6-2, 165. Drafted by Detroit Red Wings (6th choice, 126th overall) in 1995 Entry Draft. Last amateur club; Oshawa (OHL).

Peter Arvanitis — Forward

Regular Season / Playoffs

Season	Team	League	GP	G	A	PTS	PIM	GP	G	A	PTS	PIM
96-97	Nashville	CeHL	36	5	10	15	50	—	—	—	—	—
97-98	Oklahoma City	CHL	68	17	16	33	*403	11	1	2	3	45
98-99	Oklahoma City	CHL	58	13	20	33	280	10	1	3	4	26
	CHL	Totals	162	35	46	81	733	21	2	5	7	71

Born; 4/29/74, Montreal, Quebec. 5-10, 185. Last amateur club; Dawson College (MCHL).

Arron Asham — Right Wing

Regular Season / Playoffs

Season	Team	League	GP	G	A	PTS	PIM	GP	G	A	PTS	PIM
97-98	Red Deer	WHL	67	43	49	92	153	5	0	2	2	8
97-98	Fredericton	AHL	2	1	1	2	0	2	0	1	1	0
98-99	Montreal	NHL	7	0	0	0	0	—	—	—	—	—
98-99	Fredericton	AHL	60	16	18	34	118	13	8	6	14	11
	AHL	Totals	62	17	19	36	118	15	8	7	15	11

Born; 4/13/78, Portage La Prairie, Manitoba. 5-10, 170. Drafted by Montreal Canadiens (3rd choice, 71st overall) in 1996 Entry Draft. Last amateur club; Red Deer (WHL).

Thomas Ashe — Defenseman

Regular Season / Playoffs

Season	Team	League	GP	G	A	PTS	PIM	GP	G	A	PTS	PIM
96-97	Baton Rouge	ECHL	30	2	10	12	26	—	—	—	—	—
97-98	Grand Rapids	IHL	53	5	8	13	38	3	1	0	1	6
98-99	Grand Rapids	IHL	76	1	7	8	84	—	—	—	—	—
	IHL	Totals	129	6	15	21	122	3	1	0	1	6

Born; Springfield, Massachusetts. 5-9, 184. Last amateur club; Boston College. Signed as a free agent by Grand Rapids Griffins (7/27/98).

Tom Askey — Goaltender

Regular Season / Playoffs

Season	Team	League	GP	W	L	T	MIN	SO	AVG	GP	W	L	MIN	SO	AVG
96-97	Baltimore	AHL	40	17	18	2	2239	1	3.75	3	0	3	138	0	4.79
97-98	Anaheim	NHL	7	0	1	2	273	0	2.64	—	—	—	—	—	—
97-98	Cincinnati	AHL	32	10	16	4	1753	3	3.56	—	—	—	—	—	—
98-99	Anaheim	NHL	—	—	—	—	—	—	—	1	0	1	30	0	4.00
98-99	Cincinnati	AHL	53	21	22	3	2893	3	2.72	3	0	3	178	0	4.39
	NHL	Totals	7	0	1	2	273	0	2.64	1	0	1	30	0	4.00
	AHL	Totals	125	48	56	9	6885	7	3.27	6	0	6	316	0	4.55

Born: 10/4/74, Kenmore, New York. 6-2, 185. Drafted by Anaheim Mighty Ducks (8th choice, 186th overall) in 1993 Entry Draft. Last amateur club; Ohio State (CCHA).

Carlos Assayag — Right Wing

Regular Season / Playoffs

Season	Team	League	GP	G	A	PTS	PIM	GP	G	A	PTS	PIM
96-97	El Paso	WPHL	2	1	0	1	0	—	—	—	—	—
96-97	Fort Worth	CeHL	13	7	5	12	10	—	—	—	—	—
96-97	San Antonio	CeHL	21	7	7	14	14	—	—	—	—	—
97-98	Fort Worth	CHL	13	5	3	8	32	—	—	—	—	—
97-98	Tulsa	CHL	40	9	14	23	64	4	0	1	1	12
98-99	Tulsa	CHL	63	21	18	39	99	—	—	—	—	—
	CHL	Totals	150	49	47	96	219	4	0	1	1	12

Born; 2/11/72, Ste. Foy, Quebec. 5-10, 205. Last amateur club; St. Thomas University (AUAA).

Doug Ast — Center

Regular Season / Playoffs

Season	Team	League	GP	G	A	PTS	PIM	GP	G	A	PTS	PIM
96-97	Syracuse	AHL	61	6	14	20	19	—	—	—	—	—
96-97	Wheeling	ECHL	4	1	2	3	2	—	—	—	—	—
97-98	Long Beach	IHL	82	22	41	63	75	17	2	4	6	14
98-99	Long Beach	IHL	50	16	22	38	54	8	4	2	6	6
	IHL	Totals	132	38	63	101	129	25	6	6	12	20

Born; 4/17/73, Chilliwack, British Columbia. 5-11, 177. 1997-98 IHL Ironman Trophy winner. Last amateur club; British Columbia (CWUAA).

Kaspars Astashenko — Defenseman

Regular Season / Playoffs

Season	Team	League	GP	G	A	PTS	PIM	GP	G	A	PTS	PIM
98-99	Cincinnati	IHL	74	3	11	14	166	3	0	2	2	6
98-99	Dayton	ECHL	2	0	1	1	4	—	—	—	—	—

Born; 2/7/75, Riga, Latvia. 6-2. 183. Drafted by Tampa Bay Lightning (5th choice, 127th overall) in 1999 Entry Draft. Last overseas club; Moscow CKSA

Mark Astley — Defenseman

Regular Season / Playoffs

Season	Team	League	GP	G	A	PTS	PIM	GP	G	A	PTS	PIM
92-93	Lugano	Switz.	30	10	12	22	57	—	—	—	—	—
92-93	Canada	National	22	4	14	18	14	—	—	—	—	—
93-94	Buffalo	NHL	1	0	0	0	0	—	—	—	—	—
93-94	Canada	National	13	4	8	12	6	—	—	—	—	—
93-94	Canada	Olympic	8	0	1	1	4	—	—	—	—	—
94-95	Rochester	AHL	46	5	24	29	49	3	0	2	2	2
94-95	Buffalo	NHL	14	2	1	3	12	2	0	0	0	0
95-96	Buffalo	NHL	60	2	18	20	80	—	—	—	—	—
96-97	Phoenix	IHL	52	6	11	17	43	—	—	—	—	—
97-98	Lugano	Switz.	19	1	5	6	19	4	0	1	1	0
98-99	Lugano	Swtiz.	41	3	2	5	30	16	0	1	1	33
	NHL	Totals	75	4	19	23	92	2	0	0	0	0

Born; 3/30/69, Calgary, Alberta. Drafted by Buffalo Sabres (9th choice, 194th overall) in 1989 Entry Draft. Last amateur club; Lake Superior State (CCHA).

J.F. Aube — Right Wing

Regular Season / Playoffs

Season	Team	League	GP	G	A	PTS	PIM	GP	G	A	PTS	PIM
95-96	Charlotte	ECHL	50	18	41	59	12	—	—	—	—	—
96-97	Charlotte	ECHL	66	34	49	83	24	1	0	0	0	0
97-98	Pensacola	ECHL	53	23	43	66	51	17	11	6	17	8
98-99	Charlotte	ECHL	70	32	50	82	32	—	—	—	—	—
	ECHL	Totals	239	107	183	290	119	18	11	6	17	8

Born; 4/5/73, Montreal, Quebec.6-0, 182. Last amateur club; Northeastern University.

Jean-Sebastien Aubin — Goaltender

Regular Season / Playoffs

Season	Team	League	GP	W	L	T	MIN	SO	AVG	GP	W	L	MIN	SO	AVG
97-98	Syracuse	AHL	8	2	4	1	380	0	4.10	—	—	—	—	—	—
97-98	Dayton	ECHL	21	15	2	2	1178	1	3.01	3	1	1	142	0	1.69
98-99	Pittsburgh	NHL	17	4	3	6	756	2	2.22	—	—	—	—	—	—
98-99	Kansas City	IHL	13	5	7	1	751	0	3.27	—	—	—	—	—	—

Born; 7/19/77, Montreal, Quebec. 5-11, 179. Drafted by Pittsburgh Penguins (2nd choice, 76th overall) in 1995 Entry Draft. Last amateur club; Sherbrooke

Serge Aubin — Center

Regular Season / Playoffs

Season	Team	League	GP	G	A	PTS	PIM	GP	G	A	PTS	PIM
95-96	Cleveland	IHL	2	0	0	0	0	2	0	0	0	0
95-96	Hampton Roads	ECHL	62	24	62	86	74	3	1	4	5	10
96-97	Cleveland	IHL	57	9	16	25	38	2	0	0	0	0
97-98	Syracuse	AHL	55	6	14	20	57	—	—	—	—	—
97-98	Hershey	AHL	5	2	1	3	0	7	1	3	4	6
98-99	Colorado	NHL	1	0	0	0	0	—	—	—	—	—
98-99	Hershey	AHL	64	30	39	69	58	3	0	1	1	2
	AHL	Totals	124	38	54	92	115	10	1	4	5	8
	IHL	Totals	59	9	16	25	38	4	0	0	0	0

Born; 2/15/75, Val D'Or, Quebec. 6-0, 189. Drafted by Pittsburgh Penguins (9th choice, 161st overall) in 1994 Entry Draft. Signed as a free agent by Colorado Avalanche (12/23/98). Last amateur club; Granby (QMJHL).

Ron Aubrey — Left Wing

Regular Season / Playoffs

Season	Team	League	GP	G	A	PTS	PIM	GP	G	A	PTS	PIM
87-88	Maine	AHL	1	0	0	0	0	—	—	—	—	—
88-89	Erie	ECHL	28	3	4	7	182	—	—	—	—	—
88-89	Knoxville	ECHL	6	1	0	1	48	—	—	—	—	—
89-90	Nashville	ECHL	6	1	0	1	7	—	—	—	—	—
89-90	Winston-Salem	ECHL	5	0	0	0	74	—	—	—	—	—
89-90	Moncton	AHL	1	0	0	0	0	—	—	—	—	—
90-91	Roanoke Valley	ECHL	13	1	1	2	157	—	—	—	—	—
90-91	Winston-Salem	ECHL	7	4	0	4	33	—	—	—	—	—
90-91	Louisville	ECHL	3	1	0	1	47	—	—	—	—	—
90-91	Newmarket	AHL	8	0	0	0	55	—	—	—	—	—
90-91	New Haven	AHL	2	0	0	0	9	—	—	—	—	—
90-91	Adirondack	AHL	8	0	1	1	69	—	—	—	—	—
91-92	Louisville	ECHL	10	0	0	0	36	—	—	—	—	—
91-92	Toledo	ECHL	32	5	12	17	293	3	0	1	1	57
92-93	Fort Worth	CHL	32	2	6	8	237	—	—	—	—	—
92-93	Knoxville	ECHL	11	1	2	3	85	—	—	—	—	—
93-94	Fort Worth	CHL	23	2	6	8	96	—	—	—	—	—
93-94	Toledo	ECHL	1	0	0	0	2	—	—	—	—	—
93-94	Cornwall	AHL	4	0	0	0	19	—	—	—	—	—
94-95	Oklahoma City	CHL	16	4	3	7	155	—	—	—	—	—
94-95	San Antonio	CHL	24	3	2	5	163	6	0	1	1	43
95-96	Toledo	ECHL	6	0	1	1	52	—	—	—	—	—
95-96	Alaska	WCHL	4	0	1	1	24	—	—	—	—	—
95-96	San Diego	WCHL	5	1	3	4	21	—	—	—	—	—
96-97	Nashville	CHL	7	3	2	5	110	—	—	—	—	—
96-97	San Antonio	CHL	7	0	2	2	65	—	—	—	—	—
96-97	Reno	WCHL	3	0	0	0	18	—	—	—	—	—
96-97	Waco	WPHL	1	0	0	0	2	—	—	—	—	—
97-98	Oklahoma City	CHL	8	0	0	0	47	—	—	—	—	—
98-99	Wichita	CHL	6	3	1	4	33	—	—	—	—	—
	AHL	Totals	24	0	1	1	152	—	—	—	—	—
	ECHL	Totals	128	17	20	37	1016	3	0	1	1	57
	CHL	Totals	123	17	22	39	906	6	0	1	1	43
	WCHL	Totals	12	1	4	5	63	—	—	—	—	—

Born; 9/27/67, Portland, Maine. 6-4, 230.

Philippe Audet — Left Wing

Regular Season / Playoffs

Season	Team	League	GP	G	A	PTS	PIM	GP	G	A	PTS	PIM
96-97	Granby	QMJHL	67	52	56	108	138	4	4	1	5	35
96-97	Adirondack	AHL	3	1	1	2	0	1	1	0	1	0
97-98	Adirondack	AHL	50	7	8	15	43	1	0	0	0	0
98-99	Detroit	NHL	4	0	0	0	0	—	—	—	—	—
98-99	Adirondack	AHL	70	20	20	40	77	2	1	0	1	4
	AHL	Totals	123	28	29	57	120	4	2	0	2	4

Born: 6/4/77, Ottawa, Ontario. 6-2, 175. Drafted by Detroit Red Wings (2nd choice, 52nd overall) in 1995 Entry Draft. Last amateur club; Granby (QMJHL).

Keith Audy — Forward

Regular Season / Playoffs

Season	Team	League	GP	G	A	PTS	PIM	GP	G	A	PTS	PIM
98-99	Tupelo	WPHL	4	0	0	0	2	—	—	—	—	—

Born: 6/24/73.

Patrick Augusta — Left Wing

Regular Season / Playoffs

Season	Team	League	GP	G	A	PTS	PIM	GP	G	A	PTS	PIM
93-94	Toronto	NHL	2	0	0	0	0	—	—	—	—	—
93-94	St. John's	AHL	77	*53	43	96	105	11	4	8	12	4
94-95	St. John's	AHL	71	37	32	69	98	4	2	0	2	7
95-96	Los Angeles	IHL	79	34	51	85	83	—	—	—	—	—
96-97	Long Beach	IHL	82	45	42	87	96	18	4	4	8	33
97-98	Long Beach	IHL	82	41	40	81	84	17	11	7	18	20
98-99	Washington	NHL	2	0	0	0	0	—	—	—	—	—
98-99	Long Beach	IHL	68	24	35	59	125	8	4	6	10	4
	NHL	Totals	4	0	0	0	0	—	—	—	—	—
	IHL	Totals	311	144	168	312	388	43	19	17	36	57
	AHL	Totals	223	122	120	242	277	23	9	11	20	34

Born; 7/3/73, Jihlava, Czechoslovakia. 5-10, 169. Drafted by Toronto Maple Leafs (8th choice, 149th overall) in 1992 Entry Draft. Signed as a free agent by Washington Capitals (12/11/98). 1993-94 AHL Second Team All-Star. 1996-97 IHL Second Team All-Star. Last overseas club; Dukla Jihlava (Czech)

Darcy Austin — Goaltender

Regular Season / Playoffs

Season	Team	League	GP	W	L	T	MIN	SO	AVG	GP	W	L	MIN	SO	AVG
93-94	Flint	CoHL	21	7	10	2	1126	0	5.06	2	2	0	112	0	3.21
93-94	Brantford	CoHL	6	0	2	1	246	0	7.31	—	—	—	—	—	—
94-95															
95-96															
96-97															
97-98	Tucson	WCHL	5	2	3	0	300	0	6.20	—	—	—	—	—	—
98-99	Tucson	WCHL	7	1	4	1	355	0	4.91	—	—	—	—	—	—
98-99	Abilene	WPHL	11	5	4	2	610	0	3.54	—	—	—	—	—	—
	CoHL	Totals	27	7	12	3	1372	0	5.47	2	2	0	112	0	3.21
	WCHL	Totals	12	3	7	1	655	0	5.49	—	—	—	—	—	—

Born; 4/17/72, Red Deer, Alberta. 5-11, 190. Selected by Lubbock in 1999 WPHL Expansion Draft. Last amateur club; Lethbridge (CWUAA).

Jesse Austin — Defenseman

Regular Season / Playoffs

Season	Team	League	GP	G	A	PTS	PIM	GP	G	A	PTS	PIM
95-96	Muskegon	CoHL	13	0	0	0	26	—	—	—	—	—
95-96	Brantford	CoHL	8	0	0	0	26	—	—	—	—	—
96-97	Brantford	CoHL	21	0	1	1	171	—	—	—	—	—
96-97	Dayton	CoHL	22	0	3	3	120	—	—	—	—	—
97-98	San Angelo	WPHL	10	0	0	0	53	—	—	—	—	—
97-98	Fresno	WCHL	12	0	0	0	63	—	—	—	—	—
98-99	Fresno	WCHL	21	0	0	0	141	—	—	—	—	—
98-99	Idaho	WCHL	10	2	0	2	86	1	0	0	0	7
	CoHL	Totals	64	0	4	4	343	—	—	—	—	—
	WCHL	Totals	43	2	0	2	290	1	0	0	0	7

Born; 1/12/75, Hamilton, Ontario. 6-3, 220. Traded to Idaho with John Batten by Fresno for Stu Kulak (2/26/99).

George Avery — Right Wing

Regular Season / Playoffs

Season	Team	League	GP	G	A	PTS	PIM	GP	G	A	PTS	PIM
98-99	Space Coast	SEHL	17	12	10	22	142	—	—	—	—	—
98-99	Idaho	WCHL	3	0	0	0	0	—	—	—	—	—

Born: Denver, Colorado. 6-1, 180. Last amateur club; Space Coast

George Awada — Right Wing

Regular Season / Playoffs

Season	Team	League	GP	G	A	PTS	PIM	GP	G	A	PTS	PIM
98-99	St. Cloud	WCHA	39	14	16	30	38	—	—	—	—	—
98-99	Albany	AHL	10	1	1	2	8	1	0	0	0	0

Born: 6/2/75, Mendota Heights, Minnesota. 6-2, 205. Signed as a free agent by New Jersey Devils (5/13/99). Last amateur club; St. Cloud State (WCHA).

Jeffrey Azar Left Wing
Regular Season Playoffs

Season	Team	League	GP	G	A	PTS	PIM	GP	G	A	PTS	PIM
96-97	Adirondack	AHL	2	0	0	0	0	—	—	—	—	—
96-97	Utica	CoHL	70	28	36	64	53	3	0	0	0	0
97-98	Fayetteville	CHL	68	39	36	75	41	—	—	—	—	—
98-99	Winston-Salem	UHL	71	38	45	83	45	5	1	2	3	21
	UHL	Totals	141	66	81	147	98	8	1	2	3	21

Born; 9/7/73, Quincy, Massachusetts. 5-10, 175. Member of 1996-97 CoHL Rookie Team. Last amateur club; SUNY-Plattsburgh (NCAA 3).

Travis Scott was named the ECHL Playoff MVP after leading Mississippi to the Kelly Cup
Photo Bill Vaughan

Tom Perry responded to extra ice time in his sophomore season with 84 points
Photo by Kelly Virtanen

Bill Baaki — Right Wing

Season	Team	League	GP	G	A	PTS	PIM	GP	G	A	PTS	PIM
			Regular Season					Playoffs				
98-99	Huntington	ECHL	57	5	4	9	54	—	—	—	—	—

Born; 11/26/75, Detroit, Michigan. 5-11, 190. Last amateur club; Colgate

Yuri Babenko — Center

Season	Team	League	GP	G	A	PTS	PIM	GP	G	A	PTS	PIM
			Regular Season					Playoffs				
98-99	Hershey	AHL	74	11	15	26	47	2	0	1	1	0

Born; 1/2/78, Penza, USSR. 6-0, 185. Drafted by Colorado Avalanche (2nd choice, 51st overall in 1996 Entry Draft. Last amateur club; Plymouth (OHL).

Ryan Bach — Goaltender

Season	Team	League	GP	W	L	T	MIN	SO	AVG	GP	W	L	MIN	SO	AVG
			Regular Season							Playoffs					
96-97	Adirondack	AHL	13	2	3	1	451	0	3.86	1	0	0	46	0	3.92
96-97	Toledo	ECHL	20	5	11	3	1169	0	3.80	—	—	—	—	—	—
96-97	Utica	CoHL	2	0	1	1	119	0	4.03	—	—	—	—	—	—
97-98	Houston	IHL	43	26	9	6	2453	5	2.32	—	—	—	—	—	—
98-99	Los Angeles	NHL	3	0	3	0	108	0	4.44	—	—	—	—	—	—
98-99	Utah	IHL	4	2	1	0	197	0	2.74	—	—	—	—	—	—
98-99	Long Beach	IHL	27	10	9	5	1491	1	2.98	3	0	2	152	0	2.77
	IHL	Totals	31	12	10	5	1688	1	2.95	3	0	2	152	0	2.77

Born; 10/21/73, Sherwood Park, Alberta. 6-1, 180. Drafted by Detroit Red Wings (11th choice, 262nd overall) in 1992 Entry Draft. Traded to Los Angeles Kings by Detroit for a conditional 2000 draft pick (10/22/98). Signed as a free agent by Florida Panthers (7/21/99). Last amateur club; Colorado (WCHA).

Don Back — Defenseman

Season	Team	League	GP	G	A	PTS	PIM	GP	G	A	PTS	PIM
			Regular Season					Playoffs				
97-98	Mississippi	ECHL	42	0	3	3	41	—	—	—	—	—
97-98	Richmond	ECHL	12	1	1	2	15	—	—	—	—	—
98-99	Richmond	ECHL	11	0	0	0	10	—	—	—	—	—
98-99	Greenville	ECHL	38	1	8	9	38	—	—	—	—	—
	ECHL	Totals	103	2	12	14	107	—	—	—	—	—

Born; 9/9/76, Hamilton, Ontario. 6-2, 200. Last amateur club; Brock University (OUAA).

John Badduke — Right Wing

Season	Team	League	GP	G	A	PTS	PIM	GP	G	A	PTS	PIM
			Regular Season					Playoffs				
93-94	Hamilton	AHL	55	6	8	14	*356	4	0	1	1	18
93-94	Columbus	ECHL	7	0	3	3	60	—	—	—	—	—
93-94	Brantford	CoHL	1	1	0	1	7	—	—	—	—	—
94-95	Syracuse	AHL	44	6	0	6	334	—	—	—	—	—
95-96	Syracuse	AHL	46	2	2	4	245	—	—	—	—	—
95-96	Wheeling	ECHL	4	1	2	3	15	—	—	—	—	—
96-97	Syracuse	AHL	24	0	0	0	70	—	—	—	—	—
96-97	Wheeling	ECHL	12	2	1	3	51	—	—	—	—	—
97-98	Tallahassee	ECHL	26	0	5	5	178	—	—	—	—	—
98-99	Miami	ECHL	53	3	5	8	255	—	—	—	—	—
	AHL	Totals	169	14	10	24	1005	4	0	1	1	18
	ECHL	Totals	102	6	16	22	559	—	—	—	—	—

Born; 6/21/72, Calgary, Alberta. 6-2, 217. Signed as a free agent by Vancouver Canucks (2/2/94). Last amateur club; Portland (WHL).

Brad Bagu — Defenseman

Season	Team	League	GP	G	A	PTS	PIM	GP	G	A	PTS	PIM
			Regular Season					Playoffs				
97-98	Brantford	UHL	1	0	0	0	2	8	1	0	1	5
98-99	El Paso	WPHL	50	1	11	12	36	3	0	0	0	0

Born; 2/18/73, Fernie, British Columbia. 6-0, 195.

Greg Bailey — Defenseman

Season	Team	League	GP	G	A	PTS	PIM	GP	G	A	PTS	PIM
			Regular Season					Playoffs				
93-94	Huntington	ECHL	52	0	3	3	257	—	—	—	—	—
94-95	Birmingham	ECHL	18	0	2	2	149	—	—	—	—	—
94-95	Brantford	CoHL	2	1	0	1	2	—	—	—	—	—
94-95	Flint	CoHL	15	0	1	1	20	—	—	—	—	—
95-96	Utica	CoHL	2	0	0	0	8	—	—	—	—	—
95-96	Detroit	CoHL	2	0	0	0	2	—	—	—	—	—
95-96	Wichita	CeHL	8	0	0	0	38	—	—	—	—	—
95-96	San Antonio	CeHL	9	0	2	2	45	—	—	—	—	—
95-96	Tulsa	CeHL	5	0	1	1	48	—	—	—	—	—
96-97	Roanoke	ECHL	3	0	0	0	0	—	—	—	—	—
96-97	Nashville	CeHL	11	0	3	3	71	—	—	—	—	—
96-97	San Antonio	CeHL	10	2	2	4	45	—	—	—	—	—
96-97	Brantford	CoHL	16	0	2	2	15	—	—	—	—	—
96-97	Madison	CoHL	7	0	0	0	7	5	0	0	0	20
97-98	Wheeling	ECHL	1	0	0	0	7	—	—	—	—	—
97-98	Odessa	WPHL	23	0	6	6	168	—	—	—	—	—
97-98	Lake Charles	WPHL	26	0	1	1	98	4	1	0	1	34
98-99	Alexandria	WPHL	24	0	2	2	99	—	—	—	—	—
98-99	Mohawk Valley	UHL	44	0	8	8	123	—	—	—	—	—
	UHL	Totals	88	1	11	12	177	5	0	0	0	20
	ECHL	Totals	74	0	5	5	413	—	—	—	—	—
	WPHL	Totals	73	0	9	9	365	4	1	0	1	34
	CeHL	Totals	43	2	8	10	247	—	—	—	—	—

Born; 10/3/73, St. Thomas, Ontario. 6-4, 227. Traded to Lake Charles by Odessa for David Shute and Ryan Connelly (1/98). Selected by Alexandria in 1998 WPHL Entry Draft. Last amateur club; Newmarket (OHL).

Scott Bailey — Goaltender

Season	Team	League	GP	W	L	T	MIN	SO	AVG	GP	W	L	MIN	SO	AVG
			Regular Season							Playoffs					
92-93	Johnstown	ECHL	36	13	15	3	1750	1	3.84	—	—	—	—	—	—
93-94	Providence	AHL	7	2	2	2	377	0	3.82	—	—	—	—	—	—
93-94	Charlotte	ECHL	36	22	11	3	2180	1	3.58	3	1	2	187	0	3.83
94-95	Providence	AHL	52	25	16	9	2936	2	3.00	9	4	4	504	*2	3.69
95-96	Boston	NHL	11	5	1	2	571	0	3.26	—	—	—	—	—	—
95-96	Providence	AHL	37	15	19	3	2209	1	3.26	2	1	1	119	0	3.03
96-97	Boston	NHL	8	1	5	0	394	0	3.65	—	—	—	—	—	—
96-97	Providence	AHL	31	11	17	2	1735	0	3.87	7	3	4	453	0	3.05
97-98	San Antonio	IHL	37	11	17	3	1898	1	3.73	—	—	—	—	—	—
98-99	Orlando	IHL	17	5	7	0	749	0	2.88	—	—	—	—	—	—
98-99	Birmingham	ECHL	27	16	8	2	1557	1	3.47	5	2	3	299	0	4.21
	NHL	Totals	19	6	6	2	965	0	3.42	—	—	—	—	—	—
	AHL	Totals	127	53	54	16	7257	3	3.32	18	8	9	1076	2	3.34
	IHL	Totals	54	16	24	3	2647	1	3.49	—	—	—	—	—	—
	ECHL	Totals	99	51	34	8	5487	3	3.63	8	3	5	486	0	4.07

Born; 5/2/72, Calgary, Alberta. 6-0, 195. Drafted by Boston Bruins (3rd choice, 112th overall) in 1992 Entry Draft. Last amateur club; Spokane (WHL).

Paul Bailley — Left Wing

Season	Team	League	GP	G	A	PTS	PIM	GP	G	A	PTS	PIM
			Regular Season					Playoffs				
97-98	Saskatoon	WHL	1	0	0	0	0	—	—	—	—	—
97-98	Richmond	ECHL	6	0	1	1	16	—	—	—	—	—
98-99	Greenville	ECHL	29	0	7	7	22	—	—	—	—	—
	ECHL	Totals	35	0	8	8	38	—	—	—	—	—

Born; 8/7/76, Winnipeg, Manitoba. 6-2, 220. Selected by Arkansas in 1999 ECHL Expansion Draft. Last amateur club; Saskatoon (WHL).

Mike Bajurny — Left Wing

Regular Season / Playoffs

Season	Team	League	GP	G	A	PTS	PIM	GP	G	A	PTS	PIM
94-95	Wheeling	ECHL	1	0	0	0	0	—	—	—	—	—
95-96	Brantford	CoHL	48	0	2	2	176	—	—	—	—	—
95-96	Utica	CoHL	18	0	2	2	63	—	—	—	—	—
96-97	Brantford	CoHL	30	2	4	6	95	—	—	—	—	—
96-97	Dayton	CoHL	42	3	4	7	167	—	—	—	—	—
97-98	Tulsa	CHL	61	5	4	9	224	4	0	0	0	4
98-99	Winston-Salem	UHL	6	0	1	1	7	—	—	—	—	—
98-99	Columbus	CHL	10	1	2	3	29	—	—	—	—	—
98-99	San Angelo	WPHL	26	5	1	6	71	—	—	—	—	—
98-99	Odessa	WPHL	14	2	2	4	36	2	0	2	2	4
	UHL	Totals	144	5	13	18	508	—	—	—	—	—
	CHL	Totals	71	6	6	12	253	4	0	0	0	4
	WPHL	Totals	40	7	3	10	107	2	0	2	2	4

Born; 9/28/74, Walkerton, Ontario. 6-2, 212. Selected by Topeka in 1998 CHL Expansion Draft. Traded to Odessa by San Angelo for future considerations

Jeremy Baker — Right Wing

Regular Season / Playoffs

Season	Team	League	GP	G	A	PTS	PIM	GP	G	A	PTS	PIM
96-97	Columbus	CHL	8	1	0	1	2	—	—	—	—	—
96-97	Waco	WPHL	6	2	1	3	5	—	—	—	—	—
97-98	Binghamton	UHL	59	16	25	41	14	5	1	2	3	2
98-99	Mohawk Valley	UHL	22	5	4	9	10	—	—	—	—	—
	UHL	Totals	81	21	29	50	24	5	1	2	3	2

Born; 1/27/72, Dover, Minnesota. 6-0, 185. Last amateur club; Elmira College (NCAA 3).

Mike Bales — Goaltender

Regular Season / Playoffs

Season	Team	League	GP	W	L	T	MIN	SO	AVG	GP	W	L	MIN	SO	AVG
92-93	Boston	NHL	1	0	0	0	25	0	2.40	—	—	—	—	—	—
92-93	Providence	AHL	44	22	17	0	2363	1	4.21	2	0	2	118	0	4.07
93-94	Providence	AHL	33	9	15	4	1757	0	4.44	—	—	—	—	—	—
94-95	Ottawa	NHL	1	0	0	0	3	0	0.00	—	—	—	—	—	—
94-95	PEI	AHL	45	25	16	3	2649	2	3.62	9	6	3	530	*2	2.72
95-96	Ottawa	NHL	20	2	14	1	1040	0	4.15	—	—	—	—	—	—
95-96	PEI	AHL	2	0	2	0	118	0	5.58	—	—	—	—	—	—
96-97	Ottawa	NHL	1	0	1	0	52	0	4.62	—	—	—	—	—	—
96-97	Baltimore	AHL	46	13	21	8	2544	3	3.07	—	—	—	—	—	—
97-98	Rochester	AHL	39	13	19	5	2230	0	3.42	—	—	—	—	—	—
98-99	Michigan	IHL	32	11	17	3	1773	1	3.25	—	—	—	—	—	—
	NHL	Totals	23	2	15	1	1120	0	4.12	—	—	—	—	—	—
	AHL	Totals	209	82	90	20	11661	6	3.73	11	6	5	648	2	2.96

Born; 8/6/71, Prince Albert, Saskatchewan. 6-1, 180. Drafted by Boston Bruins (4th choice, 105th overall) in 1990 Entry Draft. Signed as a free agent by Ottawa Senators, 7/4/94. Loaned to Baltimore by Ottawa, 1996. Signed as a free agent by Buffalo Sabres (8/14/97). Signed as a free agent by Dallas Stars (7/9/98). (Note: PEI=Prince Edward Island) Last amateur club; Ohio State (CCHA).

Steve Bancroft — Defenseman

Regular Season / Playoffs

Season	Team	League	GP	G	A	PTS	PIM	GP	G	A	PTS	PIM
90-91	Newmarket	AHL	9	0	3	3	22	—	—	—	—	—
90-91	Maine	AHL	53	2	12	14	46	2	0	0	0	2
91-92	Maine	AHL	26	1	3	4	45	—	—	—	—	—
91-92	Indianapolis	IHL	36	8	23	31	49	—	—	—	—	—
92-93	Chicago	NHL	1	0	0	0	0	—	—	—	—	—
92-93	Indianapolis	IHL	53	10	35	45	138	—	—	—	—	—
92-93	Moncton	AHL	21	3	13	16	16	5	0	0	0	16
93-94	Cleveland	IHL	33	2	12	14	58	—	—	—	—	—
94-95	Detroit	IHL	6	1	3	4	0	—	—	—	—	—
94-95	Ft. Wayne	IHL	50	7	17	24	100	—	—	—	—	—
94-95	St. John's	AHL	4	2	0	2	2	5	0	3	3	8
95-96	Los Angeles	IHL	15	3	10	13	22	—	—	—	—	—
95-96	Chicago	IHL	64	9	41	50	91	9	1	7	8	22
96-97	Chicago	IHL	39	6	10	16	66	—	—	—	—	—
96-97	Las Vegas	IHL	36	9	28	37	64	3	0	0	0	2
97-98	Las Vegas	IHL	70	15	44	59	148	—	—	—	—	—
97-98	Saint John	AHL	9	0	4	4	12	19	2	11	13	30
98-99	Saint John	AHL	8	1	4	5	22	—	—	—	—	—
98-99	Providence	AHL	62	7	34	41	78	15	0	6	6	28
	IHL	Totals	402	70	223	293	736	12	1	7	8	24
	AHL	Totals	192	16	73	89	243	46	2	20	22	84

Born; 10/6/70, Toronto, Ontario. 6-1, 214. Drafted by Toronto Maple Leafs (3rd choice, 21st overall) in 1989 Entry Draft. Traded to Boston Bruins by Toronto for Rob Cimetta (11/9/90). Traded to Chicago Blackhawks by Boston with Boston's 11th round choice (later traded to Winnipeg, Winnipeg selected Russell Hewson) in 1993 Entry Draft for Chicago's eleventh round choice (Eugene Pavlov) in 1993 Entry Draft. (1/9/92). Traded to Winnipeg Jets by Chicago with future considerations for Troy Murray (2/21/93). Claimed by Florida Panthers from Winnipeg in Expansion Draft (6/24/93). Signed as a free agent by Pittsburgh Penguins (8/2/93). Traded to Saint John by Las Vegas with Justin Kurtz for Sami Helenius, Keith McCambridge and Paxton Schulte (3/98). Signed as a free agent by Carolina Hurricanes (8/4/99). Member of 1998-99 AHL Champion Providence Bruins. Last amateur team; Belleville (OHL).

Frank Banham — Right Wing

Regular Season / Playoffs

Season	Team	League	GP	G	A	PTS	PIM	GP	G	A	PTS	PIM
95-96	Saskatoon	WHL	72	*83	69	152	116	4	6	0	6	2
95-96	Baltimore	AHL	9	1	4	5	0	7	1	1	2	2
96-97	Anaheim	NHL	3	0	0	0	0	—	—	—	—	—
96-97	Baltimore	AHL	21	11	13	24	4	—	—	—	—	—
97-98	Anaheim	NHL	21	9	2	11	12	—	—	—	—	—
97-98	Cincinnati	AHL	35	7	8	15	39	—	—	—	—	—
98-99	Cincinnati	AHL	66	22	27	49	20	3	0	1	1	0
	NHL	Totals	24	9	2	11	12	—	—	—	—	—
	AHL	Totals	131	41	52	93	63	10	1	2	3	2

Born; 4/14/75, Calahoo, Alberta. 6-0, 185. Drafted by Washington Capitals (4th choice, 147th overall) in 1993 Entry Draft. Signed as a free agent by Anaheim (1/27/96). Last amateur club; Saskatoon (WHL).

Cory Banika — Right Wing

Regular Season / Playoffs

Season	Team	League	GP	G	A	PTS	PIM	GP	G	A	PTS	PIM
90-91	Hampton Roads	ECHL	15	4	2	6	56	—	—	—	—	—
91-92	St. John's	AHL	2	1	0	1	2	—	—	—	—	—
91-92	Brantford	CoHL	53	10	22	32	247	6	0	1	1	27
92-93	Brantford	CoHL	56	24	26	50	318	15	4	5	9	79
93-94	Hershey	AHL	2	0	0	0	2	—	—	—	—	—
93-94	Rochester	AHL	7	1	0	1	12	3	0	0	0	0
93-94	Johnstown	ECHL	48	16	14	30	262	—	—	—	—	—
93-94	Brantford	CoHL	8	7	9	16	30	7	0	3	3	63
94-95	Cornwall	AHL	56	3	11	14	225	7	1	0	1	47
95-96	Cornwall	AHL	5	1	0	1	15	—	—	—	—	—
95-96	Muskegon	CoHL	2	0	0	0	10	5	4	1	5	14
96-97	Hershey	AHL	43	7	5	12	232	23	5	3	8	47
97-98	Hershey	AHL	55	5	9	14	266	7	1	3	4	4
98-99	Muskegon	UHL	50	11	17	28	184	15	3	5	8	58
98-99	Chicago	IHL	1	0	0	0	6	—	—	—	—	—
	AHL	Totals	170	18	25	43	754	40	7	6	13	98
	UHL	Totals	169	52	74	126	789	48	11	15	26	241
	ECHL	Totals	63	20	16	36	318	—	—	—	—	—

Born; 4/9/70, Oshawa, Ontario. 5-10, 190. Member of 1992-93 Colonial League Champion Brantford Smoke. Member of 1996-97 AHL Champion Hershey Bears. Member of 1998-99 UHL Champion Muskegon Fury. Last amateur team; Cornwall (OHL).

Darren Banks — Left Wing

Regular Season / Playoffs

Season	Team	League	GP	G	A	PTS	PIM	GP	G	A	PTS	PIM
89-90	Salt Lake City	IHL	6	0	0	0	11	1	0	0	0	10
89-90	Fort Wayne	IHL	2	0	1	1	0	—	—	—	—	—
89-90	Knoxville	ECHL	52	25	22	47	258	—	—	—	—	—
90-91	Salt Lake City	IHL	56	9	7	16	286	3	0	1	1	6
91-92	Salt Lake City	IHL	55	5	5	10	303	—	—	—	—	—
92-93	Boston	NHL	16	2	1	3	64	—	—	—	—	—
92-93	Providence	IHL	43	9	5	14	199	1	0	0	0	0
93-94	Boston	NHL	4	0	1	1	9	—	—	—	—	—
93-94	Providence	AHL	41	6	3	9	189	—	—	—	—	—
94-95	Detroit	CoHL	22	9	10	19	51	12	3	5	8	59
94-95	Adirondack	AHL	20	3	2	5	65	—	—	—	—	—
94-95	Portland	AHL	12	1	2	3	38	—	—	—	—	—
94-95	Las Vegas	IHL	2	0	0	0	19	—	—	—	—	—
95-96	Las Vegas	IHL	5	0	2	2	10	10	0	0	0	54
95-96	Detroit	CoHL	38	11	17	28	290	—	—	—	—	—
95-96	Utica	CoHL	6	1	2	3	22	—	—	—	—	—
96-97	Detoit	IHL	64	10	13	23	306	20	4	5	9	40
97-98	San Antonio	IHL	7	0	0	0	6	—	—	—	—	—
97-98	Quebec	IHL	4	0	1	1	9	—	—	—	—	—
97-98	Detroit	IHL	59	16	14	30	175	21	2	3	5	*97
98-99	Detroit	IHL	58	6	12	18	296	3	0	0	0	35
	NHL	Totals	20	2	2	4	73	—	—	—	—	—
	IHL	Totals	248	46	55	101	1421	58	6	9	15	242
	AHL	Totals	116	19	12	31	491	1	0	0	0	0
	CoHL	Totals	66	21	29	50	363	12	3	5	8	59

Born; 3/18/66, Toronto, Ontario. 6-2, 228. Signed as a free agent by Calgary Flames (12/12/90). Signed as a free agent by Boston Bruins (7/16/92). Member of 1996-97 IHL Champion Detroit Vipers. Last amateur club; Brock University

Drew Bannister — Defenseman

Regular Season / Playoffs

Season	Team	League	GP	G	A	PTS	PIM	GP	G	A	PTS	PIM
94-95	Atlanta	IHL	72	5	7	12	74	5	0	2	2	22
95-96	Tampa Bay	NHL	13	0	1	1	4	—	—	—	—	—
95-96	Atlanta	IHL	61	3	13	16	105	3	0	0	0	4
96-97	Tampa Bay	NHL	64	4	13	17	44	—	—	—	—	—
96-97	Edmonton	NHL	1	0	1	1	0	12	0	0	0	30
97-98	Edmonton	NHL	34	0	2	2	42	—	—	—	—	—
97-98	Anaheim	NHL	27	0	6	6	47	—	—	—	—	—
98-99	Las Vegas	IHL	16	2	1	3	73	—	—	—	—	—
98-99	Tampa Bay	NHL	21	1	2	3	24	—	—	—	—	—
	NHL	Totals	160	5	25	30	161	12	0	0	0	30
	IHL	Totals	149	10	21	31	252	8	0	2	2	22

Born; 9/4/74, Belleville, Ontario. 6-2, 200. Drafted by Tampa Bay Lightning (2nd choice, 26th overall) in 1992 Entry Draft. Traded to Edmonton Oilers by Tampa Bay with Tampa Bay's sixth round choice (Peter Sarno) in 1997 Entry Draft for Jeff Norton (3/18/97). Traded to Anaheim Mighty Ducks by Edmonton for Bobby Dollas (1/9/98). Traded to Tampa Bay by Anaheim for Tampa Bay's fifth choice in 2000 Entry Draft (12/10/98). Last amateur club; Sault Ste. Marie (OHL)

Ralph Barahona — Center

Regular Season / Playoffs

Season	Team	League	GP	G	A	PTS	PIM	GP	G	A	PTS	PIM
90-91	Maine	AHL	72	24	33	57	14	2	1	1	2	0
90-91	Boston	NHL	3	2	1	3	0	—	—	—	—	—
91-92	Maine	AHL	26	1	3	4	45	—	—	—	—	—
91-92	Boston	NHL	3	0	1	1	0	—	—	—	—	—
92-93	Cincinnati	IHL	30	8	6	14	4	—	—	—	—	—
92-93	Fort Wayne	IHL	7	0	2	2	2	—	—	—	—	—
92-93	Utica	AHL	2	0	0	0	0	—	—	—	—	—
93-94	Raleigh	ECHL	36	14	21	35	12	—	—	—	—	—
93-94	Hampton Roads	ECHL	27	13	20	33	12	7	3	5	8	4
94-95												
95-96	San Diego	WCHL	56	31	56	87	36	9	2	7	9	6
96-97												
97-98												
98-99	Phoenix	WCHL	8	2	2	4	0	3	0	2	2	0
	NHL	Totals	6	2	2	4	0	—	—	—	—	—
	AHL	Totals	98	25	36	61	59	2	1	1	2	0
	IHL	Totals	37	8	8	16	6	—	—	—	—	—
	WCHL	Totals	64	33	58	91	36	12	2	9	11	6
	ECHL	Totals	63	27	41	68	24	7	3	5	8	4

Born; 11/16/65, Lakewood, California. Signed as a free agent by Boston Bruins (9/90). Member of 1995-96 WCHL Champion San Diego Gulls. Last amateur club; Wiconsin-Stevens Point (NCAA 2).

Scott Barber — Goaltender

Regular Season / Playoffs

Season	Team	League	GP	W	L	T	MIN	SO	AVG	GP	W	L	MIN	SO	AVG
95-96	Lakeland	SHL	31	20	7	3	1783	0	3.60	3	0	3	174	0	4.14
96-97	Columbus	CeHL	23	9	9	3	1261	0	4.10	—	—	—	—	—	—
97-98	DNP														
98-99	Corpus Christi	WPHL	25	9	11	2	1392	1	3.23	—	—	—	—	—	—

Born; 6/29/72, Troy, New York. 5-10, 175. Last amateur club; Mercyhurst (NCAA 2).

Matt Barnes — Goaltender

Regular Season / Playoffs

Season	Team	League	GP	W	L	T	MIN	SO	AVG	GP	W	L	MIN	SO	AVG
98-99	Dayton	ECHL	2	0	0	0	63	0	1.90	—	—	—	—	—	—

Born; 7/25/74, Brantford, Ontario. 5-4, 145. Last amateur club; Western Michigan (CCHA).

Steve Barnes — Defenseman

Regular Season / Playoffs

Season	Team	League	GP	G	A	PTS	PIM	GP	G	A	PTS	PIM
94-95	Huntington	ECHL	29	1	9	10	36	—	—	—	—	—
94-95	Toledo	ECHL	31	3	10	13	18	4	0	0	0	0
95-96	Manchester	BHL	51	15	61	76	63	—	—	—	—	—
96-97	Nottingham	BHL	18	0	3	3	2	—	—	—	—	—
97-98												
98-99	Huntington	ECHL	4	0	1	1	4	—	—	—	—	—
	ECHL	Totals	64	4	20	24	58	4	0	0	0	0

Born; 7/19/70, Grovenhurst, Ontario. 5-11, 190. Last amateur club; Lake Superior State (CCHA).

Scott Barney — Right Wing

Regular Season / Playoffs

Season	Team	League	GP	G	A	PTS	PIM	GP	G	A	PTS	PIM
98-99	Peterborough	OHL	44	41	26	67	80	5	4	1	5	4
98-99	Springfield	AHL	5	0	0	0	2	1	0	0	0	2

Born; 3/27/79, Oshawa, Ontario. 6-4, 198. Drafted by Los Angeles Kings (3rd choice, 29th overall) in 1998 Entry Draft. Last amateur club; Peterborough

David Barozzino — Defenseman

Regular Season / Playoffs

Season	Team	League	GP	G	A	PTS	PIM	GP	G	A	PTS	PIM
96-97	Quebec	IHL	11	0	4	4	8	—	—	—	—	—
96-97	Pensacola	ECHL	57	16	27	43	121	12	2	4	6	24
		Italy										
97-98	Lake Charles	WPHL	40	16	29	45	75	—	—	—	—	—
98-99	Lake Charles	WPHL	59	11	29	40	82	11	1	8	9	22
	WPHL	Totals	99	27	58	85	157	11	1	8	9	22

Born; 1/4/73, Toronto, Ontario. 6-2, 203. Traded to San Antonio Dragons (8/97). Last amateur club; Lowell University (Hockey East).

Kevin Barrett — Defenseman

Regular Season / Playoffs

Season	Team	League	GP	G	A	PTS	PIM	GP	G	A	PTS	PIM
93-94	Muskegon	CoHL	61	11	14	25	307	3	0	1	1	8
94-95	Flint	COHL	71	16	14	30	254	6	0	0	0	27
95-96	Oklahoma City	CeHL	58	8	18	26	286	13	2	1	3	42
96-97	Bakersfield	WCHL	61	5	25	30	271	3	0	0	0	32
97-98	Shreveport	WPHL	60	7	19	26	296	8	0	4	4	51
98-99	Bakersfield	WCHL	57	0	12	12	187	2	0	0	0	15
	CoHL	Totals	132	27	28	55	561	9	0	1	1	35
	WCHL	Totals	118	5	37	42	458	5	0	0	0	47

Born; 11/3/70, Winnipeg, Manitoba. 6-3, 220. Member of 1995-96 CeHL champion Oklahoma City Blazers. Selected by Corpus Christi in 1998 WPHL Expan-

Len Barrie — Center

Regular Season / Playoffs

Season	Team	League	GP	G	A	PTS	PIM	GP	G	A	PTS	PIM
89-90	Kamloops	WHL	70	*85	*100	*185	108	17	*14	23	*37	24
89-90	Philadelphia	NHL	1	0	0	0	0	—	—	—	—	—
90-91	Hershey	AHL	63	26	32	58	60	7	4	0	4	12
91-92	Hershey	AHL	75	42	43	85	78	3	0	2	2	32
92-93	Philadelphia	NHL	8	2	2	4	9	—	—	—	—	—
92-93	Hershey	AHL	61	31	45	76	162	—	—	—	—	—
93-94	Florida	NHL	2	0	0	0	0	—	—	—	—	—
93-94	Cincinnati	IHL	77	45	71	116	246	11	8	13	21	60
94-95	Pittsburgh	NHL	48	3	11	14	66	4	1	0	1	8
94-95	Cleveland	IHL	28	13	30	45	137	—	—	—	—	—
95-96	Pittsburgh	NHL	5	0	0	0	18	—	—	—	—	—
95-96	Cleveland	IHL	55	29	43	72	178	3	3	2	5	6
96-97	San Antonio	IHL	57	26	40	66	196	9	5	5	10	20
97-98	Frankfurt	Germany	25	11	19	30	32	6	2	3	5	35
97-98	San Antonio	IHL	32	7	13	20	90	—	—	—	—	—
98-99	Frankfurt	Germany	41	24	35	59	105	8	2	4	6	43
	NHL	Totals	64	5	13	18	93	4	1	0	1	8
	IHL	Totals	249	120	197	317	847	27	17	18	35	94
	AHL	Totals	199	99	120	219	300	10	4	2	6	44

Born; 6/4/69, Kimberly, British Columbia. 6-0, 200. Drafted by Edmonton Oilers (7th choice, 124th overall) in 1988 Entry Draft. Signed as a free agent by Philadelphia Flyers (2/28/90). Signed as a free agent by Florida Panthers 7/20/93). Signed as a free agent by Pittsburgh Penguins (8/15/94). Signed as a free agent by Los Angeles Kings (7/21/99). 1993-94 IHL Second Team All-Star. Last amateur club: Last amateur club; Kamloops (WHL).

Mike Barrie — Center

Regular Season / Playoffs

Season	Team	League	GP	G	A	PTS	PIM	GP	G	A	PTS	PIM
93-94	Red Deer	WHL	19	11	14	25	53	—	—	—	—	—
93-94	Seattle	WHL	48	24	28	52	119	9	5	3	8	14
93-94	Rochester	AHL	—	—	—	—	—	3	0	1	1	0
94-95	Rochester	AHL	16	1	3	4	40	—	—	—	—	—
94-95	South Carolina	ECHL	39	8	14	22	122	—	—	—	—	—
95-96	South Carolina	ECHL	41	13	6	19	72	—	—	—	—	—
95-96	Hampton Roads	ECHL	12	2	6	8	42	—	—	—	—	—
96-97	Peoria	ECHL	51	17	34	51	70	—	—	—	—	—
96-97	Birmingham	ECHL	15	10	4	14	45	8	2	3	5	31
97-98	Birmingham	ECHL	69	41	37	78	250	4	3	2	5	6
98-99	Birmingham	ECHL	23	13	15	28	85	—	—	—	—	—
98-99	Frankfurt	Germany	22	2	5	7	69	7	0	1	1	27
	AHL	Totals	16	1	3	4	40	3	0	1	1	0
	ECHL	Totals	250	104	116	220	686	12	5	5	10	37

Born; 3/16/74, Kelowna, British Columbia. 6-1, 170. Drafted by Buffalo Sabres (6th choice, 194th overall) in 1993 Entry Draft. Traded to Birmingham by Peoria for Max Williams and Brendan Creagh, 1997. Last amateur club; Seattle (WHL).

Karol Bartanus — Right Wing

Regular Season / Playoffs

Season	Team	League	GP	G	A	PTS	PIM	GP	G	A	PTS	PIM
98-99	Springfield	AHL	1	0	1	1	0	—	—	—	—	—
98-99	Mississippi	ECHL	50	19	21	40	50	—	—	—	—	—
98-99	Wheeling	ECHL	13	6	5	11	8	—	—	—	—	—
	ECHL	Totals	63	25	26	51	58	—	—	—	—	—

Born; 4/9/78, Liptovsky Mikulas, Slovakia. 6-2, 185. Drafted by Boston Bruins (6th choice, 81st overall) in 1997 Entry Draft. Last amateur club; Val d'Or

Lubos Bartecko — Left Wing

Regular Season / Playoffs

Season	Team	League	GP	G	A	PTS	PIM	GP	G	A	PTS	PIM
97-98	Worcester	AHL	34	10	12	22	24	10	4	2	6	2
98-99	St. Louis	NHL	32	5	11	16	6	5	0	0	0	2
98-99	SKP Poprad	Slovakia	1	1	0	1	0	—	—	—	—	—
98-99	Worcester	AHL	49	14	24	38	22	—	—	—	—	—
	AHL	Totals	83	24	36	60	46	10	4	2	6	1

Born; 7/14/76, Kezmarok, Slovakia. 6-1, 200. Signed as a free agent by St. Louis Blues (10/3/97). Last amateur club; Drummondville (QMJHL).

Brad Barton — Defenseman

Regular Season / Playoffs

Season	Team	League	GP	G	A	PTS	PIM	GP	G	A	PTS	PIM
93-94	Chatham	CoHL	38	1	10	11	125	15	0	4	4	41
94-95	Brantford	CoHL	65	5	15	20	122	—	—	—	—	—
95-96	Brantford	CoHL	5	0	1	1	20	—	—	—	—	—
95-96	Quad City	CoHL	61	2	18	20	116	2	0	0	0	0
96-97	Chicago	IHL	3	0	0	0	0	—	—	—	—	—
96-97	Quad City	CoHL	70	5	26	31	139	15	3	4	7	27
97-98	Chicago	IHL	3	0	0	0	0	—	—	—	—	—
97-98	Quad City	UHL	58	2	12	14	143	14	2	1	3	44
98-99	Fayetteville	CHL	19	1	5	6	24	—	—	—	—	—
	IHL	Totals	6	0	0	0	0	—	—	—	—	—
	UHL	Totals	297	15	82	97	665	46	5	9	14	112

Born; 5/15/72, Uxbridge, Ontario. 6-2, 215. Drafted by Vancouver Canucks (9th choice, 205th overall) in 1991 Entry Draft. Member of 1996-97 Colonial League champion Quad City Mallards. Member of 1997-98 United League Champion Quad City Mallards. Last amateur club; Kingston (OHL).

Pat Barton — Right Wing

Regular Season / Playoffs

Season	Team	League	GP	G	A	PTS	PIM	GP	G	A	PTS	PIM
94-95	Cape Breton	AHL	2	0	0	0	0	—	—	—	—	—
94-95	Wheeling	ECHL	27	3	7	10	49	—	—	—	—	—
95-96	Wheeling	ECHL	28	6	10	16	25	—	—	—	—	—
96-97	Dayton	CoHL	7	1	0	1	11	—	—	—	—	—
97-98	Odessa	WPHL	17	6	2	8	19	—	—	—	—	—
98-99	Tupelo	WPHL	10	1	1	2	0	—	—	—	—	—
98-99	Winston-Salem	UHL	24	1	1	2	42	3	0	1	1	2
	ECHL	Totals	55	9	17	26	74	—	—	—	—	—
	UHL	Totals	31	2	1	3	53	3	0	1	1	2
	WPHL	Totals	27	7	3	10	19	—	—	—	—	—

Born; 5/4/74, Montreal, Quebec. 5-11, 205. Last amateur club; Detroit (OHL).

Shannon Basaraba — Forward

Regular Season / Playoffs

Season	Team	League	GP	G	A	PTS	PIM	GP	G	A	PTS	PIM
98-99	Charlotte	ECHL	58	10	21	31	34	—	—	—	—	—

Born; 5/27/75, International Falls, Minnesota. 5-10, 191. Last amateur club; Lowell (Hockey East)

Dave Baseggio — Defenseman

Regular Season / Playoffs

Season	Team	League	GP	G	A	PTS	PIM	GP	G	A	PTS	PIM
89-90	Indianapolis	IHL	10	1	7	8	2	10	2	4	6	6
89-90	Rochester	AHL	41	3	15	18	41	—	—	—	—	—
90-91	Rochester	AHL	35	3	13	16	32	1	0	0	0	0
91-92	Rochester	AHL	29	5	11	16	14	—	—	—	—	—
91-92	New Haven	AHL	31	3	19	22	8	3	0	0	0	2
92-93												
93-94	Bolzano	Italy	29	12	18	30	44	—	—	—	—	—
94-95	Detroit	IHL	1	0	0	0	0	—	—	—	—	—
94-95	Worcester	AHL	72	10	28	38	38	—	—	—	—	—
95-96	Cleveland	IHL	76	8	33	41	100	3	0	2	2	6
96-97	Cleveland	IHL	4	0	0	0	6	—	—	—	—	—
96-97	Houston	IHL	76	13	33	46	44	13	3	7	10	8
97-98	Cleveland	IHL	62	11	27	38	70	10	1	6	7	6
98-99	Cleveland	IHL	55	12	30	42	72	—	—	—	—	—
	IHL	Totals	284	45	130	175	288	36	6	19	25	26
	AHL	Totals	208	24	86	110	133	4	0	0	0	2

Born; 10/28/67, Niagara Falls, Ontario. 6-0, 195. Drafted by Buffalo Sabres (5th choice, 68th overall) in 1986. Member of 1989-90 IHL champion Indianapolis Ice. Last amateur club; Yale University (ECAC).

Andrei Bashkirov — Left Wing

Regular Season / Playoffs

Season	Team	League	GP	G	A	PTS	PIM	GP	G	A	PTS	PIM
93-94	Providence	AHL	1	0	0	0	2	—	—	—	—	—
93-94	Charlotte	ECHL	62	28	42	70	25	3	1	0	1	0
94-95	Charlotte	ECHL	61	19	27	46	20	3	0	0	0	0
95-96	Huntington	ECHL	55	19	39	58	35	—	—	—	—	—
96-97	Detroit	IHL	2	0	0	0	0	—	—	—	—	—
96-97	Las Vegas	IHL	27	10	12	22	0	2	0	0	0	0
96-97	Huntington	ECHL	47	29	41	70	12	—	—	—	—	—
97-98	Las Vegas	IHL	15	2	3	5	5	—	—	—	—	—
97-98	Fort Wayne	IHL	65	28	48	76	16	4	2	2	4	2
97-98	Port Huron	UHL	3	1	3	4	0	—	—	—	—	—
98-99	Montreal	NHL	10	0	0	0	0	—	—	—	—	—
98-99	Fredericton	AHL	13	7	5	12	4	—	—	—	—	—
98-99	Fort Wayne	IHL	34	11	25	36	10	—	—	—	—	—
	IHL	Totals	143	51	88	139	31	6	2	2	4	2
	AHL	Totals	14	7	5	12	6	—	—	—	—	—
	ECHL	Totals	225	95	149	244	92	6	1	0	1	0

Born; 6/22/70, Omsk, CIS. Signed as a free agent by Las Vegas Thunder, 1997. Traded to Fort Wayne by Las Vegas for Trent McCleary (2/1/97). Drafted by Montreal Canadiens (4rth choice, 132nd overall) in 1998 Entry Draft. Last overseas club; Yermak Angarsk (CIS-3).

Ryan Bast — Defenseman

Regular Season / Playoffs

Season	Team	League	GP	G	A	PTS	PIM	GP	G	A	PTS	PIM
96-97	Saint John	AHL	12	0	0	0	21	5	0	0	0	4
96-97	Las Vegas	IHL	49	2	3	5	266	—	—	—	—	—
96-97	Toledo	ECHL	12	2	2	4	75	—	—	—	—	—
97-98	Saint John	AHL	77	3	8	11	187	21	0	1	1	55
98-99	Philadelphia	NHL	2	0	1	1	0	—	—	—	—	—
98-99	Saint John	AHL	2	0	0	0	5	—	—	—	—	—
98-99	Philadelphia	AHL	69	0	11	11	160	16	0	0	0	30
	AHL	Totals	160	3	19	22	368	42	0	1	1	89

Born; 8/27/75, Regina, Saskatchewan. 6-3, 193. 1997-98 AHL Second Team All-Star. Signed as a free agent by Philadelphia Flyers (5/18/98). Traded to Philadelphia by Calgary Flames with eight round choice in 1999 (David Nystrom) for Philadelphia's third round choice (later traded to New York Rangers-Rangers selected Patrick Aufiero) in 1999 Entry Draft (10/13/98). . Last amateur club; Swift Current (WHL).

Shawn Bates — Center

Regular Season / Playoffs

Season	Team	League	GP	G	A	PTS	PIM	GP	G	A	PTS	PIM
97-98	Boston	NHL	13	2	0	2	2	—	—	—	—	—
97-98	Providence	AHL	50	15	19	34	22	—	—	—	—	—
98-99	Providence	AHL	37	25	21	46	39	—	—	—	—	—
98-99	Boston	NHL	33	5	4	9	2	12	0	0	0	4
	NHL	Totals	46	7	4	11	4	12	0	0	0	4
	AHL	Totals	87	40	40	80	61	—	—	—	—	—

Born; 4/3/75, Melrose, Massachusetts. 5-11, 205. Drafted by Boston Bruins (4th choice, 103rd overall) in 1993 Entry Draft. Last amateur club; Boston University (Hockey East).

Norm Batherson — Center

Regular Season / Playoffs

Season	Team	League	GP	G	A	PTS	PIM	GP	G	A	PTS	PIM
93-94	Prince Edward Island	AHL	67	14	23	37	85	—	—	—	—	—
93-94	Thunder Bay	CoHL	3	1	2	3	2	—	—	—	—	—
94-95	Portland	AHL	77	27	34	61	64	7	3	4	7	4
95-96	Portland	AHL	45	6	21	27	72	24	11	8	19	16
96-97	Portland	AHL	53	15	28	43	43	5	2	1	3	0
97-98	Portland	AHL	17	3	5	8	4	—	—	—	—	—
97-98	Fort Wayne	IHL	54	8	18	26	46	—	—	—	—	—
98-99	Revier Kowen	Germany	50	18	12	30	57	—	—	—	—	—
	AHL	Totals	259	65	111	176	268	36	16	13	29	20

Born; 3/27/69, Sydney, Nova Scotia. 6-1, 195. Signed as a free agent by Washington Capitals (8/95). Last amateur club; Acadia University (AUAA).

Doug Battaglia — Forward

Regular Season / Playoffs

Season	Team	League	GP	G	A	PTS	PIM	GP	G	A	PTS	PIM
98-99	Charlotte	ECHL	23	5	5	10	6	—	—	—	—	—
98-99	Wheeling	ECHL	39	4	4	8	26	—	—	—	—	—
	ECHL	Totals	62	9	9	18	32	—	—	—	—	—

Born; 10/26/75, Newmarket, Ontario. 6-1, 195. Drafted by Detroit Red Wings (5th choice, 127th overall) in 1994 Entry Draft. Last amateur club; R.I.P.

John Batten — Defenseman/Left Wing

Regular Season / Playoffs

Season	Team	League	GP	G	A	PTS	PIM	GP	G	A	PTS	PIM
91-92	Erie	ECHL	15	4	2	6	49	—	—	—	—	—
92-93	Memphis	CeHL	29	11	15	26	210	—	—	—	—	—
93-94	Brantford	CoHL	29	11	20	31	155	—	—	—	—	—
93-94	St. Thomas	CoHL	28	16	18	34	133	3	1	2	3	10
94-95	London	CoHL	9	7	10	17	46	—	—	—	—	—
94-95	Utica	CoHL	1	0	0	0	2	—	—	—	—	—
95-96	Houston	IHL	1	0	0	0	0	—	—	—	—	—
95-96	Flint	CoHL	44	15	31	46	165	10	2	7	9	41
95-96	Jacksonville	SHL	8	3	9	12	54	—	—	—	—	—
96-97	Quad City	CoHL	52	29	39	68	191	10	3	5	8	52
97-98	Quad City	UHL	8	3	4	7	29	—	—	—	—	—
97-98	Winston-Salem	UHL	27	10	22	32	52	—	—	—	—	—
97-98	Flint	UHL	28	10	23	33	43	17	4	17	21	50
98-99	Fresno	WCHL	42	12	24	36	176	—	—	—	—	—
98-99	Idaho	WCHL	8	4	9	13	25	2	0	0	0	18
	UHL	Totals	226	101	167	268	816	40	10	31	40	153
	WCHL	Totals	50	16	33	49	201	2	0	0	0	18

Born; 2/1/70, Toronto, Ontario. 6-3, 225. Member of 1995-96 Colonial Cup Champion Flint Generals. Member of 1996-97 Colonial League champion Quad City Mallards. 1996-97 Second Team CoHL All-Star. Traded to Winston-Salem by Quad City for Wayne Muir (John Vecchiarelli sent from Winston-Salem to Flint in three-way deal), 11/97. Traded to Flint by Winston-Salem with Brent Daugherty and Paul Vincent for Dmitri Rodine (1/98). Traded to Idaho with Jesse Austin by Fresno for Stu Kulak (2/99).

Ruslan Batyrshin — Defenseman

Regular Season / Playoffs

Season	Team	League	GP	G	A	PTS	PIM	GP	G	A	PTS	PIM
95-96	Los Angeles	NHL	2	0	0	0	6	—	—	—	—	—
95-96	Phoenix	IHL	71	1	9	10	144	2	0	0	0	2
96-97	Phoenix	IHL	59	3	4	7	123	—	—	—	—	—
97-98	Springfield	AHL	47	0	6	6	130	—	—	—	—	—
97-98	Grand Rapids	IHL	22	0	2	2	54	—	—	—	—	—
98-99	Dynamo Moscow	Russia	29	0	4	4	42	15	0	1	1	16
	IHL	Totals	152	4	15	19	321	2	0	0	0	2

Born; 2/19/75, Moscow, Russia. 6-1, 180. Drafted by Winnipeg Jets (4th round, 79th overall) in 1993 Entry Draft. Rights traded to Los Angeles Kings by Winnipeg with Winnipeg's second round choice (Marian Cisar) in 1996 Entry Draft for Brent Thompson and future considerations (8/8/94).

Kent Baumbach — Goaltender

Regular Season / Playoffs

Season	Team	League	GP	W	L	T	MIN	SO	AVG	GP	W	L	MIN	SO	AVG
98-99	Anchorage	WCHL	16	5	6	1	669	0	4.93	—	—	—	—	—	—

Born; 5/25/75, Red Deer, Alberta. 6-0, 170.

Nolan Baumgartner — Defenseman

Regular Season / Playoffs

Season	Team	League	GP	G	A	PTS	PIM	GP	G	A	PTS	PIM
95-96	Kamloops	WHL	28	13	15	28	45	16	1	9	10	26
95-96	Washington	NHL	1	0	0	0	0	1	0	0	0	10
96-97	Portland	AHL	8	2	2	4	4	—	—	—	—	—
97-98	Washington	NHL	4	0	1	1	0	—	—	—	—	—
97-98	Portland	AHL	70	2	24	26	70	10	1	4	5	10
98-99	Portland	AHL	38	5	14	19	62	—	—	—	—	—
98-99	Washington	NHL	5	0	0	0	0	—	—	—	—	—
	NHL	Totals	10	0	1	1	0	1	0	0	0	10
	AHL	Totals	116	9	40	49	136	10	1	4	5	10

Born; 3/23/76, Calgary, Alberta. 6-1, 200. Drafted by Washington Capitals (1st choice, 10th overall) in 1994 Entry Draft. Last amateur club; Kamloops (WHL).

Robin Bawa — Right Wing

Regular Season / Playoffs

Season	Team	League	GP	G	A	PTS	PIM	GP	G	A	PTS	PIM
87-88	Fort Wayne	IHL	55	12	27	39	239	6	1	3	4	24
88-89	Baltimore	AHL	75	23	24	47	205	—	—	—	—	—
89-90	Washington	NHL	5	1	0	1	6	—	—	—	—	—
89-90	Baltimore	AHL	61	7	18	25	189	11	1	2	3	49
90-91	Fort Wayne	IHL	72	21	26	47	381	18	4	4	8	87
91-92	Vancouver	NHL	2	0	0	0	0	1	0	0	0	0
91-92	Milwaukee	IHL	70	27	14	41	238	5	2	2	4	8
92-93	San Jose	NHL	42	5	0	5	47	—	—	—	—	—
92-93	Hamilton	AHL	23	3	4	7	58	—	—	—	—	—
92-93	Kansas City	IHL	5	2	0	2	20	—	—	—	—	—
93-94	Anaheim	NHL	12	0	1	1	7	—	—	—	—	—
93-94	San Diego	IHL	25	6	15	21	54	6	0	0	0	52
94-95	Kalamazoo	IHL	71	22	12	34	184	—	—	—	—	—
94-95	Milwaukee	IHL	4	1	1	2	19	15	1	5	6	48
95-96	San Fransisco	IHL	77	23	25	48	234	4	0	2	2	4
96-97	Fort Wayne	IHL	54	10	23	33	181	—	—	—	—	—
97-98	Fort Wayne	IHL	58	12	15	27	125	—	—	—	—	—
98-99	Fort Wayne	IHL	74	11	17	28	194	—	—	—	—	—
	NHL	Totals	61	6	1	7	60	1	0	0	0	0
	IHL	Totals	565	147	175	322	1869	54	8	16	24	223
	AHL	Totals	159	33	46	79	452	11	1	2	3	49

Born; 3/26/66, Duncan, British Columbia. 6-2, 210. Signed as a free agent by Washington Capitals (5/22/87). Traded to Vancouver Canucks by Washington for cash (7/31/91). Traded to San Jose Sharks by Vancouver for Rick Lessard (12/5/82). Claimed by Anaheim Mighty Ducks from San Jose in Expansion Draft (6/24/93). Signed as a free agent by Dallas Stars (7/22/94). Last amateur club; Kamloops (WHL).

Steve Beadle — Defenseman

Regular Season / Playoffs

Season	Team	League	GP	G	A	PTS	PIM	GP	G	A	PTS	PIM
90-91	Hershey	AHL	24	1	12	13	8	—	—	—	—	—
91-92	Hershey	AHL	6	0	2	2	0	—	—	—	—	—
91-92	Johnstown	ECHL	4	1	1	2	4	—	—	—	—	—
91-92	Michigan	CoHL	41	12	27	39	14	5	1	5	6	8
92-93	Capital District	AHL	4	0	1	1	0	—	—	—	—	—
92-93	Detroit	CoHL	57	16	36	52	48	6	4	4	8	4
93-94	Huntsville	ECHL	42	7	18	25	67	—	—	—	—	—
93-94	Detroit	CoHL	15	7	12	19	8	3	1	2	3	0
94-95	Detroit	IHL	4	0	0	0	2	—	—	—	—	—
94-95	Detroit	CoHL	75	5	40	45	61	12	1	7	8	4
95-96	Flint	CoHL	74	8	27	35	62	15	1	7	8	10
96-97	Flint	CoHL	64	9	24	33	42	14	1	1	2	20
97-98	Flint	UHL	47	4	17	21	8	10	0	3	3	2
98-99	Flint	UHL	6	1	1	2	0	—	—	—	—	—
	AHL	Totals	34	2	15	17	8	—	—	—	—	—
	UHL	Totals	379	62	184	246	243	65	9	29	38	48
	ECHL	Totals	46	8	19	27	71	—	—	—	—	—

Born; 5/30/68, Lansing, Michigan. 5-11, 195. Member of 1995-96 Colonial Cup Champion Flint Generals. Last amateur club; Michigan State University (CCHA).

Mike Beale — Goaltender

Regular Season / Playoffs

Season	Team	League	GP	W	L	T	MIN	SO	AVG	GP	W	L	MIN	SO	AVG
98-99	Johnstown	ECHL	1	0	0	0	8	0	0.00	—	—	—	—	—	—
98-99	Toledo	ECHL	1	0	0	0	15	0	2.53	—	—	—	—	—	—
98-99	Peoria	ECHL	1	0	0	0	30	0	7.95	—	—	—	—	—	—
	ECHL	Totals	3	0	0	0	54	0	5.57	—	—	—	—	—	—

Born; Spencerport, New York. 6-3, 195. Last amateur club; Nichols (NCAA-3).

Colin Beardsmore — Center

Regular Season / Playoffs

Season	Team	League	GP	G	A	PTS	PIM	GP	G	A	PTS	PIM
98-99	Adirondack	AHL	17	0	1	1	2	—	—	—	—	—
98-99	Toledo	ECHL	52	22	35	57	33	7	4	2	6	2

Born; 2/17/78, Peterborough, Ontario. 5-9, 183. Drafted by Detroit Red Wings (7th choice, 189th overall) in 1996 Entry Draft. Last amateur club; Owen Sound

Vern Beardy — Defenseman

Regular Season / Playoffs

Season	Team	League	GP	G	A	PTS	PIM	GP	G	A	PTS	PIM
97-98	Wichita	CHL	15	0	3	3	9	—	—	—	—	—
98-99	Wichita	CHL	25	1	2	3	13	—	—	—	—	—
	CHL	Totals	40	1	5	6	22	—	—	—	—	—

Born; 2/21/76, Thompson, Manitoba. 6-2, 230. Last amateur club; Lebret (SJHL).

Frederic Beaubien — Goaltender

Regular Season / Playoffs

Season	Team	League	GP	W	L	T	MIN	SO	AVG	GP	W	L	MIN	SO	AVG
95-96	Phoenix	IHL	36	13	9	7	1831	1	3.28	2	0	2	119	0	4.52
96-97	Mississippi	ECHL	40	13	19	4	2217	2	3.52	3	0	3	189	0	4.45
97-98	Central Texas	WPHL	4	2	1	0	131	0	6.87	—	—	—	—	—	—
97-98	New Mexico	WPHL	16	11	2	1	865	2	2.29	—	—	—	—	—	—
97-98	Idaho	WCHL	23	10	9	4	1344	0	3.71	4	1	3	239	0	3.26
98-99	Utah	IHL	7	3	2	1	371	0	2.91	—	—	—	—	—	—
98-99	Idaho	WCHL	45	22	18	3	2532	0	3.72	2	0	2	87	0	5.52
	WCHL	Totals	68	32	27	7	3876	0	3.72	6	1	5	316	0	3.98
	WPHL	Totals	20	13	3	1	996	2	2.89	—	—	—	—	—	—

Born; 4/1/75, Lauzon, Quebec. 6-1, 205. Drafted by Los Angeles Kings (4th choice, 105th overall) in 1993 Entry Draft. Last amateur club; St. Hyacinthe

Marc Beaucage — Center

Regular Season / Playoffs

Season	Team	League	GP	G	A	PTS	PIM	GP	G	A	PTS	PIM
97-98	Courmaosta	Italy	51	45	60	105	NA	—	—	—	—	—
98-99	Fredericton	AHL	79	25	26	51	64	9	2	3	5	12

Born; 2/14/73, Trois, Rivieres, Quebec. 6-0, 180. Signed as a free agent by Montreal Canadiens (5/28/96). Last amateur club; Quebec-Trois Rivieres (OUAA).

Nic Beaudoin — Left Wing

Regular Season / Playoffs

Season	Team	League	GP	G	A	PTS	PIM	GP	G	A	PTS	PIM
96-97	Hershey	AHL	34	4	3	7	51	—	—	—	—	—
97-98	Canada	National	49	10	16	26	107	—	—	—	—	—
98-99	Roanoke	ECHL	22	6	7	13	38	—	—	—	—	—
98-99	Lowell	AHL	49	9	9	18	18	3	1	0	1	7
	AHL	Totals	83	13	12	25	69	3	1	0	1	7

Born; 12/25/76, Ottawa, Ontario. 6-3, 205. Drafted by Colorado Avalanche (2nd choice, 51st overall) in 1995 Entry Draft. Acquired by New York Islanders from Colorado for cash (9/10/98). Last amateur club; Detroit (OHL).

Paul Beaudoin — Left Wing

Regular Season / Playoffs

Season	Team	League	GP	G	A	PTS	PIM	GP	G	A	PTS	PIM
98-99	Corpus Christi	WPHL	8	0	0	0	4	—	—	—	—	—

Born; 9/5/71.

Etienne Beaudry — Right Wing

Regular Season / Playoffs

Season	Team	League	GP	G	A	PTS	PIM	GP	G	A	PTS	PIM
97-98	Pensacola	ECHL	57	12	22	34	27	—	—	—	—	—
97-98	Richmond	ECHL	13	6	6	12	10	—	—	—	—	—
98-99	Pensacola	ECHL	37	4	4	8	34	—	—	—	—	—
	ECHL	Totals	107	22	32	54	71	—	—	—	—	—

Born; 10/16/75, Montreal, Quebec. 5-11, 188. Traded to Richmond by Pensacola with Brandon Gray for Keith O'Connell (3/98).

Joey Beaudry — Right Wing

Regular Season / Playoffs

Season	Team	League	GP	G	A	PTS	PIM	GP	G	A	PTS	PIM
97-98	Memphis	CHL	2	1	0	1	27	—	—	—	—	—
97-98	Oklahoma City	CHL	16	7	5	12	32	—	—	—	—	—
97-98	Tucson	WCHL	11	2	7	9	33	—	—	—	—	—
97-98	Bakersfield	WCHL	15	0	1	1	55	—	—	—	—	—
98-99	Austin	WPHL	22	2	2	4	55	—	—	—	—	—
98-99	Topeka	CHL	38	3	4	7	115	3	0	0	0	14
	CHL	Totals	56	11	9	20	174	3	0	0	0	14
	WCHL	Totals	26	2	8	10	88	—	—	—	—	—

Born; 6/8/76, Prince Albert, Saskatchewan. 6-2, 200.

Mark Beaufait — Center

Regular Season / Playoffs

Season	Team	League	GP	G	A	PTS	PIM	GP	G	A	PTS	PIM
92-93	San Jose	NHL	5	1	0	1	0	—	—	—	—	—
92-93	Kansas City	IHL	66	19	40	59	22	9	1	1	2	8
93-94	Kansas City	IHL	21	12	9	21	18	—	—	—	—	—
93-94	United States	National	51	22	29	51	36	—	—	—	—	—
93-94	United States	Olympic	8	1	4	5	2	—	—	—	—	—
94-95	San Diego	IHL	68	24	39	63	22	5	2	2	4	2
95-96	Orlando	IHL	77	30	79	109	87	22	9	19	28	22
96-97	Orlando	IHL	80	26	65	91	63	10	5	8	13	18
97-98	Orlando	IHL	76	24	61	85	56	17	6	16	22	10
98-99	Orlando	IHL	71	28	43	71	38	15	2	12	14	14
	IHL	Totals	459	163	336	499	306	78	25	58	83	74

Born; 5/13/70, Hamilton, Ontario. 5-7, 155. Drafted by San Jose Sharks (2nd choice, 7th overall) in 1991 Supplemental Draft. 1996-97 IHL Second Team All-Star. Last amateur club; Northern Michigan University (CCHA).

David Beauregard — Left Wing

Regular Season / Playoffs

Season	Team	League	GP	G	A	PTS	PIM	GP	G	A	PTS	PIM
96-97	Hull	QMJHL	17	14	6	20	8	—	—	—	—	—
96-97	Shawinigan	QMJHL	21	13	22	35	24	7	3	4	7	12
96-97	Kentucky	AHL	5	0	3	3	0	—	—	—	—	—
97-98	Kansas City	IHL	15	2	2	4	6	—	—	—	—	—
97-98	Wichita	CHL	57	42	29	71	86	13	3	5	8	31
98-99	Muskegon	UHL	51	34	21	55	30	—	—	—	—	—
98-99	Flint	UHL	18	18	8	26	10	12	5	3	8	12
	UHL	Totals	69	52	29	81	40	12	5	3	8	12

Born; 1/28/76, Montreal, Quebec. 6-0, 190. Drafted by San Jose Sharks (12th choice, 271st overall) in 1994 Entry Draft. Traded to Flint by Muskegon with Jan Klimes and Mark Vilneff for Mike Bondy and Chad Grills. 1997-98 CHL Rookie of the Year. Last amateur club; Shawinigan (QMJHL).

Stephane Beauregard — Goaltender

Regular Season / Playoffs

Season	Team	League	GP	W	L	T	MIN	SO	AVG	GP	W	L	MIN	SO	AVG
88-89	Moncton	AHL	15	4	8	2	824	0	4.51	—	—	—	—	—	—
88-89	Fort Wayne	IHL	16	9	5	0	830	0	3.10	9	4	4	484	*1	*2.60
89-90	Winnipeg	NHL	19	7	8	3	1079	0	3.28	4	1	3	238	0	3.03
89-90	Fort Wayne	IHL	33	20	8	3	1949	0	3.54	—	—	—	—	—	—
90-91	Winnipeg	NHL	16	3	10	1	836	0	3.95	—	—	—	—	—	—
90-91	Moncton	AHL	9	3	4	1	504	1	2.38	1	1	0	60	0	1.00
90-91	Fort Wayne	IHL	32	14	14	2	1761	0	3.71	*19	*10	9	*1158	0	2.95
91-92	Winnipeg	NHL	26	6	8	6	1267	2	2.89	—	—	—	—	—	—
92-93	Philadelphia	NHL	16	3	9	0	802	0	4.41	—	—	—	—	—	—
92-93	Hershey	AHL	13	5	5	3	794	0	3.63	—	—	—	—	—	—
93-94	Winnipeg	NHL	13	0	4	1	418	0	4.48	—	—	—	—	—	—
93-94	Moncton	AHL	37	18	11	6	2082	1	3.49	*21	*12	9	*1305	*2	2.62
94-95	Springfield	AHL	24	10	11	3	1381	2	3.17	—	—	—	—	—	—
95-96	San Francisco	IHL	*69	*36	24	8	*4022	1	3.09	4	1	3	241	0	2.49
96-97	Quebec	IHL	67	35	20	11	3946	4	2.65	9	5	3	498	0	2.29
97-98	Chicago	IHL	18	10	6	0	918	1	3.20	14	10	4	820	1	2.63
98-99	Davos	Switz.	45							6					
	NHL	Totals	90	19	39	11	4402	2	3.65	4	1	3	238	0	3.03
	IHL	Totals	168	89	56	13	13425	2	3.12	55	30	23	3201	2	2.68
	AHL	Totals	98	40	39	15	5585	4	3.48	22	13	9	1365	2	2.55

Born; 1/10/68, Cowansville, Quebec. 5-11, 190. Drafted by Winnipeg Jets (3rd choice, 52nd overall) in 1988 Entry Draft. Traded to Buffalo Sabres by Winnipeg for Christian Ruuttu and future considerations (6/15/92). Traded to Chicago Blackhawks by Buffalo with Buffalo's fourth round draft choice (Eric Daze) in 1993 Entry Draft for Dominik Hasek (8/7/92). Traded to Winnipeg by Chicago for Christian Ruuttu (8/10/92). Traded to Philadelphia Flyers by Winnipeg for future considerations (10/1/92). Traded to Winnipeg by Philadelphia for future considerations (6/11/93). Acquired by Quebec Rafales after San Francisco disbanded (1996). 1995-96 IHL MVP. 1995-96 IHL First All-Star Team. Member of 1997-98 IHL Champion Chicago Wolves. Last amateur club; St. Jean (QMJHL).

Luc Beausoleil — Right Wing

Regular Season / Playoffs

Season	Team	League	GP	G	A	PTS	PIM	GP	G	A	PTS	PIM
88-89	Murryfield	BHL	33	79	77	156	38	—	—	—	—	—
89-90		France										
90-91		France										
91-92		France										
92-93	Tulsa	CeHL	16	7	9	16	6	11	5	8	13	12
93-94	Tulsa	CeHL	60	64	50	114	110	7	4	4	8	20
94-95	Tulsa	CeHL	41	27	26	53	26	7	3	2	5	2
95-96	Reno	WCHL	15	14	8	22	40	—	—	—	—	—
96-97	Tulsa	CeHL	62	60	35	95	57	5	6	7	13	6
97-98	San Antonio	IHL	2	0	0	0	0	—	—	—	—	—
97-98	Tulsa	CHL	68	*74	53	*127	86	4	4	2	6	2
98-99	Tulsa	CHL	48	29	39	68	30	—	—	—	—	—
	CHL	Totals	295	261	212	473	315	34	22	23	45	42

Born; 10/8/67, Montreal, Quebec. 5-8, 165. Played in goal for 13:48 for Tulsa during 1998-99 season and allowed one goal on sixteen shots for a GAA of 4.35. Member of 1993 CeHL Champion Tulsa Oilers. 1996-97 CeHL Second Team All-Star. Last amateur club; Laval (QMJHL).

Jerome Bechard — Left Wing

Regular Season / Playoffs

Season	Team	League	GP	G	A	PTS	PIM	GP	G	A	PTS	PIM
90-91	New Haven	AHL	59	8	11	19	131	—	—	—	—	—
90-91	Phoenix	IHL	15	0	0	0	11	—	—	—	—	—
91-92	New Haven	AHL	62	8	11	19	129	5	0	3	3	7
92-93	Cincinnati	IHL	1	0	0	0	2	—	—	—	—	—
92-93	Birmingham	ECHL	64	24	41	65	216	—	—	—	—	—
93-94	Birmingham	ECHL	68	26	32	58	345	9	4	4	8	54
94-95	Birmingham	ECHL	67	22	26	48	427	7	1	3	4	14
95-96	Birmingham	ECHL	67	9	22	31	373	—	—	—	—	—
96-97	Columbus	CeHL	59	20	43	63	297	2	1	0	1	23
97-98	Columbus	CHL	51	11	22	33	247	13	4	5	9	36
98-99	Columbus	CHL	70	21	20	41	298	10	2	1	3	43
	AHL	Totals	121	16	22	38	260	5	0	3	3	7
	IHL	Totals	16	0	0	0	13	—	—	—	—	—
	ECHL	Totals	266	81	121	202	1361	16	5	7	12	68
	CHL	Totals	180	52	85	137	842	25	7	6	13	102

Born; 3/30/69, Regina, Saskatchewan. 5-11, 190. Drafted by Hartford Whalers (5th choice, 115th overall) in 1989 Entry Draft. Member of 1997-98 CHL Champion Columbus Cottonmouths. Last amateur club; Moose Jaw (WHL).

Louis Bedard — Right Wing

Regular Season / Playoffs

Season	Team	League	GP	G	A	PTS	PIM	GP	G	A	PTS	PIM
96-97	Tallahassee	ECHL	58	7	10	17	358	3	1	0	1	11
97-98	Tallahassee	ECHL	61	4	16	20	320	—	—	—	—	—
98-99	Tallahassee	ECHL	32	2	9	11	117	—	—	—	—	—
98-99	Hampton Roads	ECHL	32	3	6	9	208	4	0	0	0	24
	ECHL	Totals	183	16	41	57	1003	7	1	0	1	35

Born; 10/14/75, Montreal, Quebec. 5-10, 210. Last amateur club; Sherbrooke (QMJHL).

Clayton Beddoes — Center

Regular Season / Playoffs

Season	Team	League	GP	G	A	PTS	PIM	GP	G	A	PTS	PIM
94-95	Providence	AHL	65	16	20	36	39	13	3	1	4	18
95-96	Boston	NHL	39	1	6	7	44	—	—	—	—	—
95-96	Providence	AHL	32	10	15	25	24	4	2	3	5	0
96-97	Boston	NHL	21	1	2	3	13	—	—	—	—	—
96-97	Providence	AHL	36	11	23	34	60	7	2	0	2	4
97-98	Detroit	IHL	65	22	24	46	63	22	5	10	15	16
98-99	Berlin	Germany	52	17	26	43	12	—	—	—	—	—
	NHL	Totals	60	2	8	10	57	—	—	—	—	—
	AHL	Totals	133	37	58	95	123	24	7	4	11	22

Born; 11/10/70, Bentley, Alberta. 5-11, 190. Signed as a free agent by Boston Bruins (6/2/94). Signed as a free agent by Ottawa Senators (7/28/97). Last amateur club; Lake Superior State (CCHA).

Jared Bednar — Defenseman

Regular Season / Playoffs

Season	Team	League	GP	G	A	PTS	PIM	GP	G	A	PTS	PIM
93-94	Huntington	ECHL	66	8	11	19	115	—	—	—	—	—
94-95	Huntington	ECHL	64	9	36	45	211	2	0	2	2	4
95-96	Huntington	ECHL	25	4	10	14	90	—	—	—	—	—
95-96	South Carolina	ECHL	39	2	22	24	126	8	0	0	0	26
96-97	St. John's	AHL	55	1	2	3	151	—	—	—	—	—
96-97	South Carolina	ECHL	15	1	2	3	28	15	1	4	5	59
97-98	Rochester	AHL	19	0	2	2	49	—	—	—	—	—
97-98	South Carolina	ECHL	36	4	4	8	126	5	1	2	3	17
98-99	Grand Rapids	IHL	74	3	18	21	220	—	—	—	—	—
	AHL	Totals	74	1	4	5	200	—	—	—	—	—
	ECHL	Totals	245	28	85	113	696	30	2	8	10	106

Born; 2/28/72, Yorktown, Saskatchewan. 6-3, 200. Member of 1997 ECHL Champion South Carolina Stingrays. Last amateur club; Prince Albert (WHL).

Bob Beers — Defenseman

Regular Season / Playoffs

Season	Team	League	GP	G	A	PTS	PIM	GP	G	A	PTS	PIM
89-90	Boston	NHL	3	0	1	1	6	14	1	1	2	18
89-90	Maine	AHL	74	7	36	43	63	—	—	—	—	—
90-91	Boston	NHL	16	0	1	1	10	6	0	0	0	4
90-91	Maine	AHL	36	2	16	18	21	—	—	—	—	—
91-92	Boston	NHL	31	0	5	5	29	1	0	0	0	0
91-92	Maine	AHL	33	6	23	29	24	—	—	—	—	—
92-93	Providence	AHL	6	1	2	3	10	—	—	—	—	—
92-93	Tampa Bay	NHL	64	12	24	36	70	—	—	—	—	—
92-93	Atlanta	IHL	1	0	0	0	0	—	—	—	—	—
93-94	Tampa Bay	NHL	16	1	5	6	12	—	—	—	—	—
93-94	Edmonton	NHL	66	10	27	37	74	—	—	—	—	—
94-95	Islanders	NHL	22	2	7	9	6	—	—	—	—	—
95-96	Islanders	NHL	13	0	5	5	10	—	—	—	—	—
95-96	Utah	IHL	65	6	36	42	54	22	1	12	13	16
96-97	Boston	NHL	27	3	4	7	8	—	—	—	—	—
96-97	Providence	AHL	45	10	12	22	18	—	—	—	—	—
97-98	DNP											
98-99	Providence	AHL	10	1	2	3	4	5	0	1	1	2
	NHL	Totals	258	28	79	107	225	21	1	1	2	22
	AHL	Totals	204	27	91	118	140	5	0	1	1	2
	IHL	Totals	66	6	36	42	54	22	1	12	13	16

Born; 5/20/67, Pittsburgh, Pennsylvania. 6-2, 200. Drafted by Boston Bruins (10th choice, 210th overall) in 1985 Entry Draft. Traded to Tampa Bay Lightning by Boston for Stephane Richer (10/28/92). Traded to Edmonton Oilers by Tampa Bay for Chris Joseph (11/11/93). Signed as a free agent by New York Islanders (8/29/94). Signed as a free agent by Boston (8/5/96). Member of 1995-96 IHL Champion Utah Grizzlies. Last amateur club; Maine (Hockey East).

Steve Begin — Center

Regular Season / Playoffs

Season	Team	League	GP	G	A	PTS	PIM	GP	G	A	PTS	PIM
96-97	Val d'Or	QMJHL	58	13	33	46	229	10	0	3	3	8
96-97	Saint John	AHL	—	—	—	—	—	4	0	2	2	6
97-98	Val d'Or	QMJHL	35	18	17	35	73	15	2	12	14	34
97-98	Calgary	NHL	5	0	0	0	23	—	—	—	—	—
98-99	Saint John	AHL	73	11	9	20	156	7	2	0	2	18
	AHL	Totals	73	11	9	20	156	11	2	2	4	24

Born; 6/14/78, Trois-Rivieres, Quebec. 5-11, 180. Drafted by Calgary Flames (3rd choice, 40th overall) in 1996 Entry Draft. Last amateur club; Val d'Or

Derek Bekar — Left Wing

Regular Season / Playoffs

Season	Team	League	GP	G	A	PTS	PIM	GP	G	A	PTS	PIM
98-99	Worcester	AHL	51	16	20	36	6	4	0	0	0	0

Born; 9/15/75, Burnaby, British Columbia. 6-3, 185. Drafted by St. Louis Blues (7th choice, 205th overall) in 1995 Entry Draft. Last amateur club; New Hampshire (Hockey East).

Graham Belak
Defenseman

Regular Season / Playoffs

Season	Team	League	GP	G	A	PTS	PIM	GP	G	A	PTS	PIM
97-98	Edmonton	WHL	47	5	5	10	168	—	—	—	—	—
97-98	Hershey	AHL	1	0	0	0	15	—	—	—	—	—
98-99	Kootenay	WHL	45	3	1	4	201	7	0	0	0	38

Born; 8/1/79, Battleford, Saskatchewan. 6-4, 210. Drafted by Colorado Avalanche (2nd choice, 53rd overall) in 1997 Entry Draft. Last amateur club;

Wade Belak
Defensman

Regular Season / Playoffs

Season	Team	League	GP	G	A	PTS	PIM	GP	G	A	PTS	PIM
94-95	Saskatoon	WHL	72	4	14	18	290	9	0	0	0	36
94-95	Cornwall	AHL	—	—	—	—	—	11	1	2	3	40
95-96	Saskatoon	WHL	63	3	15	18	207	4	0	0	0	9
95-96	Cornwall	AHL	5	0	0	0	18	2	0	0	0	2
96-97	Colorado	NHL	5	0	0	0	11	—	—	—	—	—
96-97	Hershey	AHL	65	1	7	8	320	16	0	1	1	61
97-98	Colorado	NHL	8	1	1	2	27	—	—	—	—	—
97-98	Hershey	AHL	11	0	0	0	30	—	—	—	—	—
98-99	Colorado	NHL	22	0	0	0	71	—	—	—	—	—
98-99	Calgary	NHL	9	0	1	1	23	—	—	—	—	—
98-99	Hershey	AHL	17	0	1	1	49	—	—	—	—	—
98-99	Saint John	AHL	12	0	2	2	43	6	0	1	1	23
	NHL	Totals	44	1	2	3	132	—	—	—	—	—
	AHL	Totals	110	1	10	11	460	35	1	4	5	126

Born; 3/7/75, Saskatoon, Saskatchewan. 6-4, 203. Drafted by Quebec Nordiques (1st choice, 12th overall) in 1994 Entry Draft. Traded to Calgary Flames by Colorado Avalanche with Rene Corbet, Robyn Regehr and a conditional draft choice for Chris Dingman and Theo Fleury (2/28/99). Member of 1996-97 AHL Champion Hershey Bears. Last amateur club; Saskatoon (WHL).

Chris Belanger
Defenseman

Regular Season / Playoffs

Season	Team	League	GP	G	A	PTS	PIM	GP	G	A	PTS	PIM
93-94	Huntsville	ECHL	31	11	20	31	47	—	—	—	—	—
93-94	Toledo	ECHL	23	6	18	24	36	3	0	3	3	26
94-95	Saginaw	CoHL	22	3	13	16	67	—	—	—	—	—
95-96	EC Graz	Austria	32	10	14	24	75	—	—	—	—	—
96-97		Austria										
97-98	Villach	Austria	39	9	19	28	67	—	—	—	—	—
98-99	Vipitano	Italy	23	9	21	30	37	3	1	2	3	2
98-99	Topeka	CHL	10	3	6	9	27	—	—	—	—	—
	ECHL	Totals	54	17	38	55	83	3	0	3	3	26

Born; 4/4/72, Welland, Ontario. 6-1, 190. Last amateur club; Western Michigan (CCHA).

Eric Belanger
Center

Regular Season / Playoffs

Season	Team	League	GP	G	A	PTS	PIM	GP	G	A	PTS	PIM
97-98	Fredericton	AHL	56	17	34	51	28	4	2	1	3	2
98-99	Springfield	AHL	33	8	18	26	10	3	0	1	1	2
98-99	Long Beach	IHL	1	0	0	0	0	—	—	—	—	—
	AHL	Totals	89	25	52	77	38	7	2	2	4	4

Born; 12/16/77, Sherbrooke, Quebec. 5-11, 170. Drafted by Los Angeles Kings (5th choice, 96th overall) in 1996 Entry Draft. Last amateur club; Rimouski

Francis Belanger
Left Wing

Regular Season / Playoffs

Season	Team	League	GP	G	A	PTS	PIM	GP	G	A	PTS	PIM
98-99	Philadelphia	AHL	58	13	13	26	242	16	4	3	7	16

Born; 1/15/78, Bellefeuille, Quebec. 6-2, 216. Drafted by Philadelphia Flyers (5th choice, 124th overall) in 1998 Entry Draft. Last amateur club; Rimouski

Hugo Belanger
Center

Regular Season / Playoffs

Season	Team	League	GP	G	A	PTS	PIM	GP	G	A	PTS	PIM
95-96	Laval	QMJHL	64	27	44	71	71	—	—	—	—	—
95-96	Birmingham	ECHL	6	3	5	8	0	—	—	—	—	—
96-97	Birmingham	ECHL	70	23	54	77	34	8	2	7	9	4
97-98	Birmingham	ECHL	65	21	39	60	83	4	0	5	5	0
98-99	Birmingham	ECHL	70	34	40	74	20	5	2	0	2	2
	ECHL	Totals	211	81	138	219	137	17	4	10	14	6

Born; 3/27/75, Mascouche, Quebec. 6-0, 172. Last amateur club; Laval

Hugo P. Belanger
Left Wing

Regular Season / Playoffs

Season	Team	League	GP	G	A	PTS	PIM	GP	G	A	PTS	PIM
93-94	Indianapolis	IHL	75	23	15	38	8	—	—	—	—	—
94-95	Indianapolis	IHL	66	20	25	45	8	—	—	—	—	—
95-96	Atlanta	IHL	4	0	0	0	4	—	—	—	—	—
95-96	Nashville	ECHL	67	54	*90	*144	49	5	3	4	7	2
96-97	Phoenix	IHL	3	0	0	0	0	—	—	—	—	—
96-97	Pensacola	ECHL	53	22	40	62	14	12	6	9	15	0
97-98	Phoenix	WCHL	63	40	79	119	22	9	6	8	14	2
98-99	Fort Wayne	IHL	6	0	2	2	0	—	—	—	—	—
98-99	Phoenix	WCHL	61	51	61	112	22	3	2	1	3	0
	IHL	Totals	154	43	42	85	20	—	—	—	—	—
	WCHL	Totals	124	91	140	231	44	12	8	9	17	2
	ECHL	Totals	120	76	130	206	63	17	9	13	22	2

Born; 5/28/70, St. Hubert, Quebec. 6-1, 190. Drafted by Chicago Blackhawks (6th choice, 163rd overall) in 1990 Entry Draft. 1995-96 ECHL MVP. 1995-96 ECHL First Team All-Star. 1997-98 WCHL Second Team All-Star. 1998-99 WCHL MVP. 1998-99 WCHL First Team All-Star. Last amateur club; Clarkson

Jesse Belanger
Center

Regular Season / Playoffs

Season	Team	League	GP	G	A	PTS	PIM	GP	G	A	PTS	PIM
90-91	Fredericton	AHL	75	40	58	98	30	6	2	4	6	0
91-92	Montreal	NHL	4	0	0	0	0	—	—	—	—	—
91-92	Fredericton	AHL	65	30	41	71	26	7	3	3	6	2
92-93	Montreal	NHL	19	4	2	6	4	9	0	1	1	0
92-93	Fredericton	AHL	39	19	32	51	24	—	—	—	—	—
93-94	Florida	NHL	70	17	33	50	16	—	—	—	—	—
94-95	Florida	NHL	47	15	14	29	18	—	—	—	—	—
95-96	Florida	NHL	63	17	21	38	10	—	—	—	—	—
95-96	Vancouver	NHL	9	3	0	3	4	3	0	2	2	2
96-97	Edmonton	NHL	6	0	0	0	0	—	—	—	—	—
96-97	Hamilton	AHL	6	4	3	7	0	—	—	—	—	—
96-97	Quebec	IHL	47	34	28	62	18	9	3	5	8	13
97-98	SC Herisau	Switz.	5	4	3	7	4	—	—	—	—	—
97-98	Las Vegas	IHL	54	32	36	68	20	4	0	1	1	0
98-99	Cleveland	IHL	22	9	13	22	10	—	—	—	—	—
	NHL	Totals	218	56	70	126	52	12	0	3	3	2
	AHL	Totals	185	93	134	227	80	13	5	7	12	2
	IHL	Totals	123	75	77	152	48	13	3	6	9	13

Born; 6/15/69, St. Georges de Beauce, Quebec. 6-1, 190. Last amateur club; Granby (QMJHL). Signed as a free agent by Montreal Canadiens, 10/3/90. Claimed by Florida Panthers from Montreal in Expansion Draft, 6/24/93. Traded to Vancouver Canucks by Florida for Vancouver's third round choice (Oleg Kvasha) in 1996 Entry Draft and future considerations, 3/30/96. Signed as a free agent by Edmonton, 8/28/96. Signed as a free agent by Tampa Bay Lightning (8/1/98). Signed as a free agent by Montreal Canadiens (7/9/99). Member of 1992-93 Stanley Cup Champion Montreal Canadiens. Last amateur club; Granby

Martin Belanger
Defenseman

Regular Season / Playoffs

Season	Team	League	GP	G	A	PTS	PIM	GP	G	A	PTS	PIM
96-97	Macon	CeHL	57	5	24	29	43	5	0	0	0	6
97-98	Macon	CHL	44	3	5	8	37	3	0	0	0	0
98-99	Macon	CHL	55	2	17	19	22	—	—	—	—	—
	CHL	Totals	156	10	46	56	102	8	0	0	0	6

Born; 2/3/76, LaSalle, Quebec. 6-0, 205. Drafted by Montreal Canadiens (5th choice, 74th overall) in 1994 Entry Draft. Last amateur club; St-Hyacinthe

Brent Belecki — Goaltender

Regular Season / Playoffs

Season	Team	League	GP	W	L	T	MIN	SO	AVG	GP	W	L	MIN	SO	AVG
98-99	Miami	ECHL	54	21	24	5	2938	0	3.53	—	—	—	—	—	—

Born; 12/22/77, 5-10, 180. Selected by Greensboro in 1999 ECHL Dispersal Draft. Last amateur club; Portland (WHL).

Bob Bell — Goaltender

Regular Season / Playoffs

Season	Team	League	GP	W	L	T	MIN	SO	AVG	GP	W	L	MIN	SO	AVG
95-96	Adirondack	AHL	1	0	0	0	29	0	2.03	—	—	—	—	—	—
95-96	Tallahassee	ECHL	13	5	5	0	666	0	4.05	—	—	—	—	—	—
95-96	Toledo	ECHL	3	1	0	2	161	0	4.10	1	0	0	17	0	3.42
96-97	Thunder Bay	CoHL	41	22	11	4	2340	0	3.49	2	0	2	63	0	7.62
97-98	Binghamton	UHL	7	3	0	2	303	0	3.57	4	1	3	248	0	6.78
97-98	Monroe	WPHL	18	7	10	0	934	0	3.40	—	—	—	—	—	—
97-98	Shreveport	WPHL	3	0	1	0	90	0	6.67	—	—	—	—	—	—
97-98	Waco	WPHL	9	2	6	0	498	0	3.86	—	—	—	—	—	—
98-99	Augusta	ECHL	2	0	1	0	24	0	7.53	—	—	—	—	—	—
98-99	Tupelo	WPHL	29	10	16	3	1642	1	4.31	—	—	—	—	—	—
	WPHL	Totals	59	19	33	3	3164	1	4.03	—	—	—	—	—	—
	UHL	Totals	48	25	11	6	2643	0	3.50	6	1	5	311	0	6.95
	ECHL	Totals	18	6	6	2	851	0	4.16	1	0	0	17	0	3.42

Born; 5/28/71, New Westminster, British Columbia, 5-10, 185. Monroe traded Brady Blain and Cory Keenan to Shreverport for Bob Bell (1/98). Last amateur club; Providence (Hockey East).

David Bell — Defenseman

Regular Season / Playoffs

Season	Team	League	GP	G	A	PTS	PIM	GP	G	A	PTS	PIM
97-98	Ottawa	OHL	34	8	14	22	59	13	4	2	6	21
97-98	Louisville	ECHL	10	1	5	6	57	—	—	—	—	—
98-99	Miami	ECHL	68	7	15	22	213	—	—	—	—	—
	ECHL	Totals	78	8	20	28	270	—	—	—	—	—

Born; 3/24/77, Hepworth, Ontario. 5-11, 198. Selected by Greenville in 1999 ECHL Dispersal Draft. Last amateur club; Ottawa (OHL).

Scot Bell — Right Wing

Regular Season / Playoffs

Season	Team	League	GP	G	A	PTS	PIM	GP	G	A	PTS	PIM
96-97	Birmingham	ECHL	14	2	1	3	4	—	—	—	—	—
96-97	Dayton	ECHL	13	2	2	4	0	—	—	—	—	—
96-97	Raleigh	ECHL	5	0	3	3	0	—	—	—	—	—
97-98	Memphis	CHL	68	16	52	68	46	4	2	2	4	4
98-99	Memphis	CHL	66	15	54	69	83	4	3	4	7	12
	CHL	Totals	134	31	106	137	129	8	5	6	11	16
	ECHL	Totals	32	4	6	10	4	—	—	—	—	—

Born; 4/18/72, Winchester, Ontario. 6-0, 205. Last amateur club; Ferris State (CCHA).

Brad Belland — Center

Regular Season / Playoffs

Season	Team	League	GP	G	A	PTS	PIM	GP	G	A	PTS	PIM
91-92	Michigan	CoHL	23	7	13	20	21	5	2	4	6	26
92-93	Birmingham	ECHL	27	10	14	24	31	—	—	—	—	—
93-94												
94-95												
95-96	San Diego	WCHL	51	30	*72	102	117	9	5	*13	*18	10
96-97	Utah	IHL	1	0	0	0	0	—	—	—	—	—
96-97	San Diego	WCHL	54	22	68	90	132	8	5	*12	*17	18
97-98	San Diego	WCHL	58	21	35	56	161	13	5	*19	*24	30
98-99	San Diego	WCHL	44	15	23	38	94	—	—	—	—	—
	WCHL	Totals	207	88	198	286	504	30	15	44	59	58

Born; 1/4/67, Belle River, Ontario. 6-1, 180. Drafted by Chicago Blackhawks (5th choice, 95th overall) in 1985 Entry Draft. Member of 1995-96 WCHL champion San Diego Gulls. Member of 1996-97 WCHL champion San Diego Gulls. 1995-96 First Team WCHL All-Star. Member of 1997-98 WCHL Champion San Diego Gulls. Last amateur club; Cornwall (OHL).

Shane Belter — Defenseman

Regular Season / Playoffs

Season	Team	League	GP	G	A	PTS	PIM	GP	G	A	PTS	PIM
98-99	Providence	AHL	5	0	0	0	0	—	—	—	—	—
98-99	Greenville	ECHL	54	5	17	22	59	—	—	—	—	—

Born; 10/5/77, Swift Current, Saskatchewan. 6-1, 205. Signed as a free agent by Boston Bruins (4/20/98). Last amateur club; Kamloops (WHL).

Carl Benazic — Defenseman

Regular Season / Playoffs

Season	Team	League	GP	G	A	PTS	PIM	GP	G	A	PTS	PIM
94-95	Medicine Hat	WHL	71	9	23	32	166	5	0	1	1	19
94-95	Rochester	AHL	2	0	0	0	0	—	—	—	—	—
95-96	Medicine Hat	WHL	57	7	35	42	159	5	0	0	0	20
96-97												
97-98	Amburg	Germany	47	11	19	30	213	—	—	—	—	—
98-99	Lake Charles	WPHL	67	10	27	37	160	11	1	4	5	22

Born; 9/29/75, MacKenzie, British Columbia. 6-3, 195. Drafted by Buffalo Sabres (5th choice, 147th overall) in 1994 Entry Draft. Last amateur club; Medicine Hat (WHL).

Rick Bennett — Left Wing

Regular Season / Playoffs

Season	Team	League	GP	G	A	PTS	PIM	GP	G	A	PTS	PIM
89-90	Providence	H.E.	31	12	24	36	74	—	—	—	—	—
89-90	Rangers	NHL	6	1	0	1	5	—	—	—	—	—
90-91	Binghamton	AHL	71	27	32	59	206	10	2	1	3	27
90-91	Rangers	NHL	6	0	0	0	6	—	—	—	—	—
91-92	Binghamton	AHL	69	19	23	42	112	11	0	1	1	23
91-92	Rangers	NHL	3	0	1	1	2	—	—	—	—	—
92-93	Binghamton	AHL	76	15	22	37	114	10	0	0	0	30
93-94	Springfield	AHL	67	9	19	28	82	6	1	0	1	31
94-95	Springfield	AHL	34	3	5	8	74	—	—	—	—	—
94-95	Hershey	AHL	30	3	4	7	40	3	2	1	3	14
95-96	Cincinnati	IHL	4	0	1	1	0	1	0	0	0	2
95-96	Jacksonville	ECHL	67	28	34	62	182	18	5	10	15	30
96-97	Albany	AHL	4	0	0	0	0	—	—	—	—	—
96-97	Jacksonville	ECHL	64	23	33	56	120	—	—	—	—	—
97-98	Pee Dee	ECHL	68	12	30	42	137	8	3	2	5	14
98-99	Pee Dee	ECHL	66	21	18	39	103	11	3	1	4	33
	NHL	Totals	15	1	1	2	13	—	—	—	—	—
	AHL	Totals	351	76	105	181	628	40	5	3	8	125
	ECHL	Totals	265	84	115	199	542	37	11	13	24	77

Born; 7/24/67, Springfield, Massachusetts. 6-4, 215. Drafted by Minnesota North Stars (4th choice, 54th overall) in 1986 Entry Draft. Rights traded by Minnesota with Brian Lawton and Igor Liba to New York Rangers for Mark Tinordi, Paul Jerrard, Mike Sullivan, Brett Barnett and Los Angeles Kings third round pick (Murray Garbutt) in 1989 draft. Signed as a free agent by Hartford Whalers (8/93). Last amateur club; Providence College (H.E.).

Sean Berens — Center

Regular Season / Playoffs

Season	Team	League	GP	G	A	PTS	PIM	GP	G	A	PTS	PIM
98-99	Las Vegas	IHL	61	24	18	42	62	—	—	—	—	—
98-99	Saint John	AHL	11	2	0	2	6	2	0	0	0	0
98-99	Tacoma	WCHL	5	1	3	4	4	—	—	—	—	—

Born; 4/6/76, Chicago, Illinois. 5-10, 185. Last amateur club; Michigan State (CCHA).

Bill Berg — Left Wing

Season	Team	League	GP	G	A	PTS	PIM	GP	G	A	PTS	PIM
			Regular Season					Playoffs				
85-86	Toronto	OHL	64	3	35	38	143	4	0	0	0	19
85-86	Springfield	AHL	4	1	1	2	4	—	—	—	—	—
86-87	Toronto	OHL	57	3	15	18	138	—	—	—	—	—
87-88	Springfield	AHL	76	6	26	32	148	—	—	—	—	—
87-88	Peoria	IHL	5	0	1	1	8	7	0	3	3	31
88-89	Islanders	NHL	7	1	2	3	10	—	—	—	—	—
88-89	Springfield	AHL	69	17	32	49	122	—	—	—	—	—
89-90	Springfield	AHL	74	12	42	54	74	15	5	12	17	35
90-91	Islanders	NHL	78	9	14	23	67	—	—	—	—	—
91-92	Islanders	NHL	47	5	9	14	28	—	—	—	—	—
91-92	Capital District	AHL	3	0	2	2	16	—	—	—	—	—
92-93	Islanders	NHL	22	6	3	9	49	—	—	—	—	—
92-93	Toronto	NHL	58	7	8	15	54	21	1	1	2	18
93-94	Toronto	NHL	83	8	11	19	93	18	1	2	3	10
94-95	Toronto	NHL	32	5	1	6	26	7	0	1	1	4
95-96	Toronto	NHL	23	1	1	2	33	—	—	—	—	—
95-96	Rangers	NHL	18	2	1	3	8	10	1	0	1	0
96-97	Rangers	NHL	67	8	6	14	37	3	0	0	0	2
97-98	Rangers	NHL	67	1	9	10	55	—	—	—	—	—
98-99	Hartford	AHL	16	4	7	11	23	—	—	—	—	—
98-99	Ottawa	NHL	44	2	2	4	28	2	0	0	0	0
	NHL	Totals	546	55	67	122	488	61	3	4	7	34
	AHL	Totals	272	40	108	148	387	15	5	12	17	35

Born; 10/21/67, St. Catharines, Ontario. 6-1, 205. Drafted by New York Islanders (3rd choice, 59th overall) in 1986 Entry Draft. Claimed on waivers by Toronto Maple Leafs from Islanders (12/3/92). Traded to New York Rangers by Toronto for Nick Kypreos (2/29/96). Traded to Ottawa Senators by Rangers with a second round draft choice (later traded to Anaheim-Anaheim selected Jordan Leopold) in 1999 Entry Draft for Stan Neckar (11/27/99). Member of 1989-90 AHL Champion Springfield Indians. Last amateur club; Toronto (OHL).

Bob Berg — Left Wing

Season	Team	League	GP	G	A	PTS	PIM	GP	G	A	PTS	PIM
			Regular Season					Playoffs				
90-91	Niagara Falls	OHL	21	8	4	12	11	—	—	—	—	—
90-91	Sudbury	OHL	23	12	15	27	34	5	2	1	3	6
90-91	New Haven	AHL	19	0	1	1	8	—	—	—	—	—
91-92	Phoenix	IHL	24	2	8	10	18	—	—	—	—	—
91-92	Richmond	ECHL	37	19	14	33	65	6	2	1	3	0
92-93	Phoenix	IHL	1	0	0	0	0	—	—	—	—	—
92-93	Muskegon	CoHL	49	19	24	43	87	6	1	1	2	5
93-94	Wichita	CeHL	64	43	58	101	141	10	9	8	17	17
94-95	Wichita	CeHL	66	55	46	101	122	11	6	17	23	21
95-96	Houston	IHL	2	0	0	0	0	—	—	—	—	—
95-96	Louisiana	ECHL	68	59	50	109	127	5	3	5	8	6
96-97	Wichita	CeHL	56	36	49	85	105	9	5	5	10	29
97-98	Muskegon	UHL	73	43	65	108	39	10	9	5	14	0
98-99	Augusta	ECHL	69	28	39	67	104	2	0	1	1	0
	IHL	Totals	27	2	8	10	18	—	—	—	—	—
	CeHL	Totals	186	134	153	287	368	30	20	30	50	67
	ECHL	Totals	174	106	103	209	296	13	5	7	12	6
	UHL	Totals	122	62	89	151	126	16	10	6	16	5

Born; 7/2/70, Beamsville, Ontario. 6-2, 190. Drafted by Los Angeles Kings (3rd choice, 49th overall) in 1990 Entry Draft. Selected by Greensboro in 1999 ECHL Expansion Draft. 1993-94 CeHL Second Team All-Star. 1994-95 CeHL First Team All-Star. 1995-96 ECHL Second Team All-Star. 1996-97 CeHL Second Team All-Star. Member of 1993-94 CeHL champion Wichita Thunder. Member of 1994-95 CeHL champion Wichita Thunder. Last amateur club; Sudbury

Mike Berger — Defenseman

Season	Team	League	GP	G	A	PTS	PIM	GP	G	A	PTS	PIM
			Regular Season					Playoffs				
86-87	Spokane	WHL	65	26	49	75	80	2	0	0	0	2
86-87	Indianapolis	IHL	4	0	3	3	4	6	0	1	1	13
87-88	Minnesota	NHL	29	3	1	4	65	—	—	—	—	—
87-88	Kalamazoo	IHL	36	5	10	15	94	6	2	0	2	8
88-89	Minnesota	NHL	1	0	0	0	2	—	—	—	—	—
88-89	Kalamazoo	IHL	67	9	16	25	96	6	0	2	2	8
89-90	Binghamton	AHL	10	0	4	4	10	—	—	—	—	—
89-90	Phoenix	IHL	51	5	12	17	75	—	—	—	—	—
90-91	Kansas City	IHL	46	7	14	21	43	—	—	—	—	—
90-91	Knoxville	ECHL	7	1	7	8	31	—	—	—	—	—
91-92	Thunder Bay	CoHL	54	17	27	44	127	10	6	7	13	16
92-93	Thunder Bay	CoHL	8	3	5	8	20	—	—	—	—	—
92-93	Tulsa	CeHL	47	16	26	42	116	7	2	3	5	4
93-94	Tulsa	CeHL	58	15	19	34	134	11	7	4	11	22
94-95	Tulsa	CeHL	46	10	20	30	64	6	2	3	5	54
95-96	Tulsa	CeHL	45	9	18	27	110	6	0	1	1	22
96-97	Tulsa	CeHL	64	9	33	42	68	5	0	3	3	10
97-98	Tulsa	CHL	63	11	28	39	121	3	2	1	3	2
98-99	Tulsa	CHL	69	25	35	60	93	—	—	—	—	—
	NHL	Totals	30	3	1	4	67	—	—	—	—	—
	IHL	Totals	204	26	55	81	312	18	2	3	5	29
	CHL	Totals	392	95	179	274	706	37	13	15	28	114
	CoHL	Totals	62	20	32	52	147	10	6	7	13	16

Born; 6/2/67, Edmonton, Alberta. 6-0, 230.Drafted by Minnesota North Stars (2nd choice, 69th overall) in 1985 Entry Draft. Traded to Hartford Whalers by Minnesota for Kevin Sullivan (10/7/89). 1992-93 CeHL Second Team All-Star. 1998-99 CHL Community Service Award. Member of 1991-92 CoHL champion Thunder Bay Senators. Member of 1992-93 CeHL champion Tulsa Oilers. Last amateur club; Spokane (WHL).

Chris Bergeron — Center

Season	Team	League	GP	G	A	PTS	PIM	GP	G	A	PTS	PIM
			Regular Season					Playoffs				
93-94	Adirondack	AHL	41	6	5	11	37	1	0	0	0	0
93-94	Toledo	ECHL	18	10	10	20	26	5	7	3	10	2
94-95	Cincinnati	IHL	14	1	3	4	2	2	0	0	0	0
94-95	Birmingham	ECHL	53	27	55	82	128	7	4	8	12	2
95-96	Cincinnati	IHL	25	3	2	5	8	1	0	0	0	0
95-96	Carolina	AHL	2	0	1	1	2	—	—	—	—	—
95-96	Birmingham	ECHL	33	21	38	59	85	—	—	—	—	—
95-96	Toledo	ECHL	6	3	2	5	2	10	3	8	11	4
96-97	Las Vegas	IHL	3	0	1	1	2	—	—	—	—	—
96-97	Cincinnati	IHL	62	7	18	25	68	1	0	1	1	0
96-97	Toledo	ECHL	9	6	9	15	8	—	—	—	—	—
97-98	Cincinnati	IHL	6	1	0	1	2	—	—	—	—	—
97-98	Columbus	CHL	65	65	54	119	97	12	6	5	11	14
98-99	Cincinnati	IHL	1	0	1	1	2	3	0	0	0	0
98-99	Port Huron	UHL	53	26	43	69	18	7	3	1	4	4
	IHL	Totals	111	12	25	37	84	7	0	1	1	0
	AHL	Totals	43	6	6	12	39	1	0	0	0	0
	ECHL	Totals	119	67	114	181	249	22	14	19	33	8

Born; 11/28/70, Wallaceburg, Ontario. 5-11, 190. Member of 1993-94 ECHL champion Toledo Storm. Member of 1997-98 CHL champion Columbus Cottonmouths. Last amateur club; Miami of Ohio (CCHA).

Tony Bergin — Defenseman

Season	Team	League	GP	G	A	PTS	PIM	GP	G	A	PTS	PIM
			Regular Season					Playoffs				
97-98	Raleigh	ECHL	63	7	17	24	35	—	—	—	—	—
98-99	Shreveport	WPHL	64	10	21	31	33	12	3	1	4	12

Born; 4/24/74, Fredericton, New Brunswick. 6-3, 225. Member of 1998-99 WPHL Champion Shreveport Mudbugs. Last amateur club; Cornell (ECAC).

Stefan Bergkvist — Defenseman

Regular Season / Playoffs

Season	Team	League	GP	G	A	PTS	PIM	GP	G	A	PTS	PIM
95-96	Pittsburgh	NHL	2	0	0	0	2	4	0	0	0	2
95-96	Cleveland	IHL	61	2	8	10	58	3	0	0	0	14
96-97	Pittsburgh	NHL	5	0	0	0	7	—	—	—	—	—
96-97	Cleveland	IHL	33	0	1	1	54	4	0	0	0	0
97-98	Cleveland	IHL	71	3	6	9	129	10	0	2	2	24
98-99	Leksands IF	Sweden	42	0	2	2	167	3	0	0	0	4
	NHL	Totals	5	0	0	0	9	4	0	0	0	2
	IHL	Totals	165	5	15	20	241	14	0	2	2	24

Born; 3/10/75, Leksand, Sweden. 6-2, 224. Drafted by Pittsburgh Penguins (1st choice, 26th overall) in 1993 Entry Draft. Last amateur club; London (OHL).

Tim Bergland — Right Wing

Regular Season / Playoffs

Season	Team	League	GP	G	A	PTS	PIM	GP	G	A	PTS	PIM
87-88	Fort Wayne	IHL	13	2	1	3	9	—	—	—	—	—
87-88	Binghamton	AHL	63	21	26	47	31	4	0	0	0	0
88-89	Baltimore	AHL	78	24	29	53	39	—	—	—	—	—
89-90	Washington	NHL	32	2	5	7	31	15	1	1	2	10
89-90	Baltimore	AHL	47	12	19	31	55	—	—	—	—	—
90-91	Washington	NHL	47	5	9	14	21	11	1	1	2	12
90-91	Baltimore	AHL	15	8	9	17	16	—	—	—	—	—
91-92	Washington	NHL	22	1	4	5	2	—	—	—	—	—
91-92	Baltimore	AHL	11	6	10	16	5	—	—	—	—	—
92-93	Tampa Bay	NHL	27	3	3	6	11	—	—	—	—	—
92-93	Atlanta	IHL	49	18	21	39	26	9	3	3	6	10
93-94	Tampa Bay	NHL	51	6	5	11	6	—	—	—	—	—
93-94	Washington	NHL	3	0	0	0	4	—	—	—	—	—
93-94	Atlanta	IHL	19	6	7	13	6	—	—	—	—	—
94-95	Chicago	IHL	81	12	21	33	70	3	1	2	3	4
95-96	Chicago	IHL	81	9	19	28	45	9	0	1	1	4
96-97	Chicago	IHL	82	20	22	42	26	4	1	1	2	0
97-98	HIFK Helsinki	Finland	7	2	1	3	39	—	—	—	—	—
97-98	Chicago	IHL	49	8	10	18	18	10	2	0	2	16
98-99	Chicago	IHL	68	4	9	13	20	—	—	—	—	—
	NHL	Totals	182	17	26	43	75	26	2	2	4	22
	IHL	Totals	442	79	110	189	220	35	7	7	14	34
	AHL	Totals	214	71	93	164	146	4	0	0	0	0

Born; 1/11/65, Crookston, Minnesota. 6-3, 194. Drafted by Washington Capitals (1st choice, 75th overall) in 1983 Entry Draft. Claimed by Tampa Bay Lightning from Washington in Expansion Draft (6/18/92). Claimed on waivers by Washington Capitals from Tampa Bay (3/19/94). Member of 1997-98 IHL Champion Chicago Wolves. Last amateur club; University of Minnesota (WCHA).

Jason Bermingham — Left Wing

Regular Season / Playoffs

Season	Team	League	GP	G	A	PTS	PIM	GP	G	A	PTS	PIM
97-98	Quebec	QMJHL	25	7	14	21	33	14	4	10	14	18
97-98	Huntington	ECHL	34	4	7	11	40	—	—	—	—	—
98-99	Huntington	ECHL	69	22	19	41	62	—	—	—	—	—
	ECHL	Totals	103	26	26	52	102	—	—	—	—	—

Born; 1/17/77, Montreal, Quebec. 6-0, 193. Last amateur club; Quebec

Jim Bermingham — Center

Regular Season / Playoffs

Season	Team	League	GP	G	A	PTS	PIM	GP	G	A	PTS	PIM
92-93	Adirondack	AHL	21	0	2	2	8	—	—	—	—	—
92-93	Toledo	ECHL	18	8	9	17	21	—	—	—	—	—
93-94	Wheeling	ECHL	66	33	28	61	54	6	1	2	3	4
94-95	Worcester	AHL	10	3	4	7	4	—	—	—	—	—
94-95	Huntington	ECHL	43	29	36	65	96	4	3	1	4	4
95-96	Worcester	AHL	4	0	0	0	2	—	—	—	—	—
95-96	Huntington	ECHL	60	35	50	85	115	—	—	—	—	—
96-97	Huntington	ECHL	52	28	38	66	63	—	—	—	—	—
96-97	Fredericton	AHL	27	4	2	6	40	—	—	—	—	—
97-98	Michigan	IHL	—	—	—	—	—	4	0	0	0	2
97-98	Huntington	ECHL	67	41	59	100	116	4	0	1	1	2
98-99	Huntington	ECHL	64	16	63	79	85	—	—	—	—	—
98-99	Providence	AHL	2	1	0	1	4	—	—	—	—	—
98-99	Lowell	AHL	5	1	0	1	0	—	—	—	—	—
98-99	Hamburg	German 1	5	0	0	0	2	—	—	—	—	—
	AHL	Totals	69	9	8	17	58	—	—	—	—	—
	ECHL	Totals	370	190	283	473	550	14	4	4	8	10

Born; 12/11/71, Montreal, Quebec. 6-4, 220. Drafted by Detroit Red Wings (7th choice, 186th overall) in 1991 Entry Draft. Last amatuer club; Laval (QMJHL).

Chris Bernard — Goaltender

Regular Season / Playoffs

Season	Team	League	GP	W	L	T	MIN	SO	AVG	GP	W	L	MIN	SO	AVG
98-99	Fayetteville	CHL	13	6	5	0	620	0	4.16	—	—	—	—	—	—
98-99	Mohawk Valley	UHL	6	0	2	0	232	0	6.99	—	—	—	—	—	—

Born; 5/2/76, Brashear Falls, New York, 6-3, 190. Last amateur club; Clarkson (ECAC).

Louis Bernard — Defenseman

Regular Season / Playoffs

Season	Team	League	GP	G	A	PTS	PIM	GP	G	A	PTS	PIM
94-95	Fredericton	AHL	31	2	1	3	34	1	0	0	0	0
94-95	Wheeling	ECHL	20	1	5	6	26	—	—	—	—	—
95-96	Fredericton	AHL	28	1	2	3	60	—	—	—	—	—
95-96	Wheeling	ECHL	29	4	5	9	30	3	0	1	1	2
96-97	Raleigh	ECHL	41	3	12	15	28	—	—	—	—	—
96-97	Toledo	ECHL	27	5	9	14	20	5	0	3	3	0
97-98	Adirondack	AHL	4	0	1	1	0	—	—	—	—	—
97-98	Detroit	IHL	1	0	0	0	0	—	—	—	—	—
97-98	Toledo	ECHL	64	7	39	46	62	7	1	7	8	4
98-99	Toledo	ECHL	11	0	9	9	4	—	—	—	—	—
98-99	Charlotte	ECHL	55	7	17	24	62	—	—	—	—	—
	AHL	Totals	63	3	4	7	94	1	0	0	0	0
	ECHL	Totals	247	27	96	123	232	15	1	11	15	6

Born; 7/10/74, Victoriaville, Quebec. 6-2, 205. Drafted by Montreal Canadiens (5th choice, 82nd overall) in 1992 Entry Draft. Last amateur club; Sherbrooke

Mark Bernard — Goaltender

Regular Season / Playoffs

Season	Team	League	GP	W	L	T	MIN	SO	AVG	GP	W	L	MIN	SO	AVG
89-90	Johnstown	ECHL	9	1	3	0	385	0	7.32	—	—	—	—	—	—
90-91	Hampton Roads	ECHL	23	12	6	2	1172	0	4.45	1	0	0	20	0	0.00
91-92	Hampton Roads	ECHL	40	24	12	2	2327	3	3.35	*14	*12	2	*871	*1	*2.62
92-93	Rochester	AHL	1	0	0	0	20	0	3.00	—	—	—	—	—	—
92-93	Baltimore	AHL	2	0	1	0	64	0	6.56	—	—	—	—	—	—
92-93	Hampton Roads	ECHL	21	10	7	3	1150	0	4.02	1	0	1	61	0	4.92
93-94	Erie	ECHL	48	19	25	3	2788	0	5.06	—	—	—	—	—	—
94-95	London	CoHL	14	4	10	0	775	0	6.04	—	—	—	—	—	—
94-95	San Antonio	CeHL	29	16	8	3	1500	*3	3.72	13	5	6	636	0	4.43
95-96	Hampton Roads	ECHL	42	16	13	5	2024	*2	3.47	1	0	0	28	0	4.33
96-97	Bracknell	BSL	49	NA	NA	NA	2916	0	4.29	—	—	—	—	—	—
97-98	Bracknell	BSL	41	NA	NA	NA	2436	NA	3.65	5	NA	NA	227	NA	5.29
98-99	Bracknell	BSL	8	NA	NA	NA	490	NA	3.66	—	—	—	—	—	—
98-99	Fayetteville	CHL	15	6	5	2	821	0	5.41	—	—	—	—	—	—
	AHL	Totals	3	0	1	0	84	0	5.71	—	—	—	—	—	—
	ECHL	Totals	183	82	66	15	9846	5	4.22	17	12	3	980	1	2.76

Born; 2/1/69, Hamilton, Ontario. 5-7, 188. 1991-92 ECHL Playoff MVP. Member of 1990-91 ECHL Champion Hampton Roads Admirals. Member of 1991-92 ECHL Champion Hampton Roads Admirals.

Paul Berrington — Right Wing

Regular Season / Playoffs

Season	Team	League	GP	G	A	PTS	PIM	GP	G	A	PTS	PIM
96-97	Huntsville	CeHL	3	1	0	1	7	—	—	—	—	—
97-98	Columbus	ECHL	5	0	1	1	9	—	—	—	—	—
97-98	Odessa	WPHL	32	15	21	36	42	—	—	—	—	—
98-99	Macon	CHL	22	4	12	16	13	—	—	—	—	—
98-99	Tupelo	WPHL	20	2	2	4	12	—	—	—	—	—
	WPHL	Totals	52	17	23	40	54	—	—	—	—	—
	CHL	Totals	25	5	12	17	20	—	—	—	—	—

Born; 1/24/75, Kitchener, Ontario. 5-10, 175.

Brad Berry — Defenseman

Regular Season / Playoffs

Season	Team	League	GP	G	A	PTS	PIM	GP	G	A	PTS	PIM
85-86	North Dakota	WCHA	40	6	29	35	26	—	—	—	—	—
85-86	Winnipeg	NHL	13	1	0	1	10	3	0	0	0	0
86-87	Winnipeg	NHL	52	2	8	10	60	7	0	1	1	14
87-88	Winnipeg	NHL	48	0	6	6	75	—	—	—	—	—
87-88	Moncton	AHL	10	1	3	4	14	—	—	—	—	—
88-89	Winnipeg	NHL	38	0	9	9	45	—	—	—	—	—
88-89	Moncton	AHL	38	3	16	19	39	—	—	—	—	—
89-90	Winnipeg	NHL	12	1	2	3	6	1	0	0	0	0
89-90	Moncton	AHL	38	1	9	10	58	—	—	—	—	—
90-91	Brynas	Sweden	38	3	1	4	38	—	—	—	—	—
90-91	Canada	National	4	0	1	1	0	—	—	—	—	—
91-92	Minnestoa	NHL	7	0	0	0	6	2	0	0	0	2
91-92	Kalamazoo	IHL	65	5	18	23	90	5	2	0	2	6
92-93	Minnesota	NHL	63	0	3	3	109	—	—	—	—	—
93-94	Dallas	NHL	8	0	0	0	12	—	—	—	—	—
94-95	Kalamazoo	IHL	65	4	11	15	146	1	0	0	0	0
95-96	Michigan	IHL	80	4	13	17	73	10	0	5	5	12
96-97	Michigan	IHL	77	4	7	11	68	4	0	0	0	4
97-98	Michigan	IHL	67	3	8	11	60	—	—	—	—	—
98-99	Michigan	IHL	5	0	1	1	10	—	—	—	—	—
	NHL	Totals	241	4	28	32	323	13	0	1	1	16
	IHL	Totals	359	20	58	78	447	20	2	5	7	22
	AHL	Totals	86	5	28	33	111	—	—	—	—	—

Born; 1/1/65, Bashaw, Alberta. 6-2, 190. Drafted by Winnipeg Jets (3rd choice, 29th overall) in 1983 Entry Draft. Signed as a free agent by Minnesota North Stars (10/4/91). Last amateur club; University of North Dakota (WCHA).

Rick Berry — Defenseman

Regular Season / Playoffs

Season	Team	League	GP	G	A	PTS	PIM	GP	G	A	PTS	PIM
98-99	Hershey	AHL	62	2	6	8	153	—	—	—	—	—

Born; 11/4/78, Brandon, Manitoba. 6-1, 192. Drafted by Colorado Avalanche (3rd choice, 55th overall) in 1997 Entry Draft. Last amateur club; Spokane (WHL).

Daniel Berthiaume — Goaltender

Regular Season / Playoffs

Season	Team	League	GP	W	L	T	MIN	SO	AVG	GP	W	L	MIN	SO	AVG
85-86	Chicoutimi	QMJHL	*66	34	29	3	*3718	1	4.62	9	4	5	580	0	3.72
85-86	Winnipeg	NHL	—	—	—	—	—	—	—	1	0	1	68	0	3.53
86-87	Winnipeg	NHL	31	18	7	3	1758	1	3.17	8	4	4	439	0	2.87
86-87	Sherbrooke	AHL	7	4	3	0	420	0	3.29	—	—	—	—	—	—
87-88	Winnipeg	NHL	56	22	19	7	3010	2	3.51	5	1	4	300	0	5.00
88-89	Winnipeg	NHL	9	0	8	0	443	0	5.96	—	—	—	—	—	—
88-89	Moncton	AHL	21	6	9	2	1083	0	4.21	3	1	2	180	0	3.67
89-90	Winnipeg	NHL	24	10	11	3	1387	1	3.72	—	—	—	—	—	—
89-90	Minnesota	NHL	5	1	3	0	240	0	3.50	—	—	—	—	—	—
90-91	Los Angeles	NHL	37	20	11	4	2119	1	3.31	—	—	—	—	—	—
91-92	Los Angeles	NHL	19	7	10	1	979	0	4.04	—	—	—	—	—	—
91-92	Boston	NHL	8	1	4	2	399	0	3.16	—	—	—	—	—	—
92-93	Graz	ALP	28	—	—	—	—	0	4.07	—	—	—	—	—	—
92-93	Ottawa	NHL	25	2	17	1	1326	0	4.30	—	—	—	—	—	—
93-94	Ottawa	NHL	1	0	0	0	1	0	120.00	—	—	—	—	—	—
93-94	PEI	AHL	30	8	16	3	1640	0	4.76	—	—	—	—	—	—
93-94	Adirondack	AHL	11	7	2	0	552	0	3.80	11	6	4	632	0	2.85
94-95	Providence	AHL	2	0	1	1	126	0	3.32	—	—	—	—	—	—
94-95	Wheeling	ECHL	10	6	1	1	599	0	4.10	—	—	—	—	—	—
94-95	Roanoke	ECHL	21	15	4	2	1196	0	2.36	8	4	4	464	1	2.97
94-95	Detroit	IHL	—	—	—	—	—	—	—	5	2	3	331	0	2.53
95-96	Detroit	IHL	7	4	3	0	401	2	2.84	—	—	—	—	—	—
95-96	Roanoke	ECHL	39	22	13	3	2109	*2	3.19	2	0	2	116	0	3.09
96-97	Cen. Texas	WPHL	*54	30	20	0	*3033	*2	*3.38	*11	5	*6	*678	*1	3.80
97-98	Roanoke	ECHL	30	17	8	3	1712	2	*2.59	2	2	0	120	0	2.00
98-99	Roanoke	ECHL	35	18	12	5	2105	2	2.77	10	6	4	608	1	1.87
	NHL	Totals	215	81	90	21	11662	5	3.67	14	5	9	807	0	3.72
	AHL	Totals	71	25	31	6	3821	0	4.26	14	7	6	812	0	3.03
	IHL	Totals	7	4	3	0	401	2	2.84	5	2	3	331	0	2.53

Born; 1/26/66, Longueuil, Quebec. 5-9, 155. Drafted by Winnipeg Jets (3rd choice, 60th overall) in 1985 Entry Draft. Traded to Minnesota North Stars by Winnipeg for future considerations (1/22/90). Traded to Los Angeles Kings by Minnesota for Craig Duncanson (9/6/90). Traded to Boston Bruins by Los Angeles for future considerations (1/18/92). Traded to Winnipeg by Boston for Doug Evans (6/10/92). Signed as a free agent by Ottawa Senators (12/15/92). Traded to Detroit Red Wings by Ottawa for Steve Konroyd (3/21/94). 1996-97 WPHL Goaltender of the Year. Last amateur club; Chicoutimi (QMJHL). Note:

Jurgis Bertins — Center

Regular Season / Playoffs

Season	Team	League	GP	G	A	PTS	PIM	GP	G	A	PTS	PIM
98-99	Tacoma	WCHL	50	3	11	14	29	—	—	—	—	—

Born; 6/26/74, Riga, Latvia. 6-0, 185.

Eric Bertrand — Left Wing

Regular Season / Playoffs

Season	Team	League	GP	G	A	PTS	PIM	GP	G	A	PTS	PIM
95-96	Albany	AHL	70	16	13	29	199	4	0	0	0	6
96-97	Albany	AHL	77	16	27	43	204	8	3	3	6	15
97-98	Albany	AHL	76	20	29	49	256	13	5	5	10	4
98-99	Albany	AHL	78	34	31	65	160	5	4	2	6	0
	AHL	Totals	301	86	100	186	819	30	12	10	22	25

Born; 4/16/75, St. Ephrem, Quebec. 6-1, 195. Drafted by New Jersey Devils (9th choice, 207th overall) in 1994 Entry Draft. Last amateur club; Granby (QMJHL).

Hugo Bertrand — Defenseman

Regular Season / Playoffs

Season	Team	League	GP	G	A	PTS	PIM	GP	G	A	PTS	PIM
97-98	New Mexico	WPHL	40	5	7	12	51	—	—	—	—	—
98-99	New Mexico	WPHL	42	6	3	9	117	—	—	—	—	—
	WPHL	Totals	82	11	10	21	168	—	—	—	—	—

Born; 10/4/76, Mirabill, Quebec. 5-11, 210. Last amateur club; Shawinigan (QMJHL).

Ron Bertrand

Goaltender

Regular Season / Playoffs

Season	Team	League	GP	W	L	T	MIN	SO	AVG	GP	W	L	MIN	SO	AVG
92-93	Chatham	CoHL	18	8	7	0	861	0	4.46	—	—	—	—	—	—
93-94	St. Thomas	CoHL	53	16	23	5	2537	0	5.09	3	0	3	159	0	6.77
94-95	Columbus	ECHL	1	1	0	0	65	0	4.62	—	—	—	—	—	—
94-95	Utica	CoHL	11	5	5	0	636	0	4.53	—	—	—	—	—	—
95-96	Utica	CoHL	41	16	17	3	2169	1	4.09	—	—	—	—	—	—
95-96	Quad City	CoHL	—	—	—	—	—	—	—	1	0	1	60	0	4.01
96-97	Port Huron	CoHL	2	0	1	0	72	0	2.49	—	—	—	—	—	—
96-97	Utica	CoHL	31	9	21	0	1619	1	5.23	—	—	—	—	—	—
96-97	Madison	CoHL	10	6	2	1	525	0	3.20	1	0	0	20	0	3.00
97-98	Binghamton	UHL	37	5	*25	3	1966	1	5.19	1	0	1	59	0	4.05
98-99	Waco	WPHL	2	1	1	0	118	0	3.06	—	—	—	—	—	—
98-99	Austin	WPHL	16	4	5	1	696	0	4.31	—	—	—	—	—	—
	UHL	Totals	203	65	101	12	10385	2	4.72	6	0	5	298	0	5.43
	WPHL	Totals	18	5	6	1	814	0	4.13	—	—	—	—	—	—

Born; 1/13/72, Ottawa, Ontario. 5-11, 185. Last amateur club; North Bay (OHL).

Yves Bertrand

Forward

Regular Season / Playoffs

Season	Team	League	GP	G	A	PTS	PIM	GP	G	A	PTS	PIM
98-99	Point Rouge	QSHL	33	28	32	60	NA	—	—	—	—	—
98-99	Birmingham	ECHL	4	1	0	1	0	—	—	—	—	—

Born;

Jeff Bes

Center

Regular Season / Playoffs

Season	Team	League	GP	G	A	PTS	PIM	GP	G	A	PTS	PIM
92-93	Guelph	OHL	59	48	67	115	128	5	3	5	8	4
92-93	Kalamazoo	IHL	3	1	3	4	6	—	—	—	—	—
93-94	Kalamazoo	IHL	30	2	12	14	30	—	—	—	—	—
93-94	Dayton	ECHL	2	2	0	2	12	—	—	—	—	—
94-95	Kalamazoo	IHL	52	8	17	25	47	—	—	—	—	—
95-96	Springfield	AHL	57	20	23	43	77	9	3	4	7	13
96-97	SaiPa Lappeenranta	Finland	40	10	12	22	146	—	—	—	—	—
97-98	Chicago	IHL	24	3	5	8	20	—	—	—	—	—
97-98	Orlando	IHL	15	1	2	3	8	—	—	—	—	—
98-99	Kassel	Germany	6	0	0	0	6	—	—	—	—	—
	IHL	Totals	124	15	39	54	111	—	—	—	—	—

Born; 7/31/73, Tillsonburg, Ontario. 6-0, 190. Drafted by Minnesota North Stars (2nd choice, 58th overall) in 1992 Entry Draft. Claimed on waivers by Hartford Whalers from Dallas (7/29/95). Last amateur club; Guelph (OHL).

Mark Best

Forward

Regular Season / Playoffs

Season	Team	League	GP	G	A	PTS	PIM	GP	G	A	PTS	PIM
98-99	Quad City	UHL	1	0	0	0	0	—	—	—	—	—

Born; 1/4/74, Calgary, Alberta. 1998-99 Assistant coach for Quad City Mallards.

Randy Best

Defenseman

Regular Season / Playoffs

Season	Team	League	GP	G	A	PTS	PIM	GP	G	A	PTS	PIM
97-98	Fayetteville	CHL	43	2	9	11	95	—	—	—	—	—
97-98	Raleigh	ECHL	16	2	4	6	30	—	—	—	—	—
97-98	Louisville	ECHL	7	0	0	0	4	—	—	—	—	—
98-99	Greenville	ECHL	23	2	3	5	27	—	—	—	—	—
98-99	Birmingham	ECHL	4	0	0	0	0	—	—	—	—	—
98-99	Saginaw	UHL	28	2	7	9	12	—	—	—	—	—
	ECHL	Totals	50	4	7	11	61	—	—	—	—	—

Born; 3/5/74, Woodsbury, Minnesota. 6-2, 200. Last amateur club; St. Cloud State (WCHA).

Karel Betik

Defenseman

Regular Season / Playoffs

Season	Team	League	GP	G	A	PTS	PIM	GP	G	A	PTS	PIM
98-99	Tampa Bay	NHL	3	0	2	2	2	—	—	—	—	—
98-99	Cleveland	IHL	74	5	11	16	97	—	—	—	—	—

Born; 10/28/78, Karvina, Czechoslovakia. 6-2, 208. Drafted by Tampa Bay Lightning (6th choice, 112th overall) in 1997 Entry Draft. Last amateur club; Kelowna (WHL).

Derek Beuselink

Defenseman

Regular Season / Playoffs

Season	Team	League	GP	G	A	PTS	PIM	GP	G	A	PTS	PIM
98-99	Madison	UHL	74	3	9	12	129	—	—	—	—	—

Born; 12/17/73, Deloraine, Manitoba. 5-10, 185. Last amateur club; Ohio State (CCHA).

Andy Bezeau

Left Wing

Regular Season / Playoffs

Season	Team	League	GP	G	A	PTS	PIM	GP	G	A	PTS	PIM
91-92	Richmond	ECHL	12	1	1	2	71	—	—	—	—	—
91-92	Johnstown	ECHL	28	11	10	21	142	—	—	—	—	—
92-93	Brantford	CoHL	38	18	13	31	278	14	2	4	6	*132
92-93	Moncton	AHL	2	0	0	0	4	—	—	—	—	—
93-94	Brantford	CoHL	22	18	16	34	240	—	—	—	—	—
93-94	St. Thomas	CoHL	1	2	0	2	12	—	—	—	—	—
93-94	South Carolina	ECHL	36	10	10	20	352	2	0	0	0	23
94-95	Phoenix	IHL	6	0	0	0	23	—	—	—	—	—
94-95	Fort Wayne	IHL	3	0	1	1	26	—	—	—	—	—
94-95	Brantford	CoHL	17	8	10	18	185	—	—	—	—	—
94-95	Muskegon	CoHL	46	14	17	31	357	17	9	7	16	88
95-96	Fort Wayne	IHL	74	10	11	21	590	5	0	2	2	28
96-97	Fort Wayne	IHL	45	4	5	9	320	—	—	—	—	—
97-98	Michigan	IHL	1	0	1	1	4	—	—	—	—	—
97-98	Detroit	IHL	54	9	10	19	309	19	2	1	3	95
97-98	Muskegon	UHL	17	7	9	16	100	—	—	—	—	—
98-99	Detroit	IHL	44	2	7	9	308	8	2	1	3	31
	IHL	Totals	227	25	35	60	1580	32	4	4	8	154
	CoHL	Totals	141	67	65	132	1172	31	11	11	22	220
	ECHL	Totals	76	22	21	43	565	2	0	0	0	23

Born; 3/30/70, St. John, New Brunswick. 5-9, 185. Drafted by Boston Bruins (10th choice, 231st overall) in 1990 Entry Draft. Last amateur club; Niagara Falls

Frank Bialowas

Left Wing

Regular Season / Playoffs

Season	Team	League	GP	G	A	PTS	PIM	GP	G	A	PTS	PIM
91-92	Roanoke	ECHL	23	4	2	6	150	3	0	0	0	4
92-93	St. John's	AHL	7	1	0	1	28	1	0	0	0	0
92-93	Richmond	ECHL	60	3	18	21	261	1	0	0	0	2
93-94	Toronto	NHL	3	0	0	0	12	—	—	—	—	—
93-94	St. John's	AHL	69	2	8	10	352	7	0	3	3	25
94-95	St. John's	AHL	51	2	3	5	277	4	0	0	0	12
95-96	Portland	AHL	65	4	3	7	211	7	0	0	0	42
96-97	Philadelphia	AHL	67	7	6	13	254	6	0	2	2	41
97-98	Philadelphia	AHL	65	5	7	12	259	19	0	0	0	26
98-99	Philadelphia	AHL	24	0	3	3	42	—	—	—	—	—
98-99	Portland	AHL	6	0	0	0	10	—	—	—	—	—
98-99	Indianapolis	IHL	16	1	0	1	27	2	0	0	0	6
	AHL	Totals	354	21	30	51	1433	44	0	5	5	150
	ECHL	Totals	83	7	20	27	411	4	0	0	0	6

Born; 9/25/70, Winnipeg, Manitoba. 6-0, 235. Signed as a free agent by Toronto Maple Leafs (3/20/94). Signed as a free agent by Washington Capitals (8/10/95). Traded to Philadelphia Flyers by Washington for future considerations (7/18/96). Traded to Chicago Blackhawks by Philadelphia for Dennis Bonvie (1/8/99). Member of 1997-98 AHL Champion Philadelphia Phantoms.

Joe Bianchi

Center

Regular Season / Playoffs

Season	Team	League	GP	G	A	PTS	PIM	GP	G	A	PTS	PIM
98-99	Bad Tolz	Germany	5	1	3	4	0	—	—	—	—	—
98-99	Richmond	ECHL	53	26	26	52	68	18	7	5	12	22

Born; 8/17/75, Bloomington, Minnesota. 5-9, 185. Last amateur club; Wisconsin (WCHA).

Radim Bicanek — Defenseman

Regular Season / Playoffs

Season	Team	League	GP	G	A	PTS	PIM	GP	G	A	PTS	PIM
94-95	Belleville	OHL	49	13	26	39	61	16	6	5	11	30
94-95	Ottawa	NHL	6	0	0	0	0	—	—	—	—	—
94-95	Prince Edward Island	AHL	—	—	—	—	—	3	0	1	1	0
95-96	Prince Edward Island	AHL	74	7	19	26	87	5	0	2	2	6
96-97	Ottawa	NHL	21	0	1	1	8	7	0	0	0	8
96-97	Worcester	AHL	44	1	15	16	22	—	—	—	—	—
97-98	Ottawa	NHL	1	0	0	0	0	—	—	—	—	—
97-98	Detroit	IHL	9	1	3	4	16	—	—	—	—	—
97-98	Manitoba	IHL	42	1	7	8	52	—	—	—	—	—
98-99	Ottawa	NHL	7	0	0	0	4	—	—	—	—	—
98-99	Chicago	NHL	7	0	0	0	6	—	—	—	—	—
98-99	Grand Rapids	IHL	46	8	17	25	48	—	—	—	—	—
	NHL	Totals	42	0	1	1	32	7	0	0	0	8
	AHL	Totals	118	8	34	42	109	8	0	3	3	6
	IHL	Totals	97	10	27	37	116	—	—	—	—	—

Born; 1/18/75, Uherske Hradiste, Czechoslovakia. 6-1, 195. Drafted by Ottawa Senators (2nd choice, 27th overall) in 1993 Entry Draft. Traded to Chicago Blackhawks by Ottawa for Ottawa's sixth round choice (later traded to Dallas-Dallas selected Justin Cox) in 1999 Entry Draft. Last amateur club; Belleville

Jiri Bicek — Left Wing

Regular Season / Playoffs

Season	Team	League	GP	G	A	PTS	PIM	GP	G	A	PTS	PIM
97-98	Albany	AHL	50	10	10	20	22	13	1	6	7	4
98-99	Albany	AHL	79	15	45	60	102	5	2	2	4	2
	AHL	Totals	129	25	55	80	124	18	3	8	11	6

Born; 12/3/78, Kosice, Czechoslovakia. 5-11, 183. Drafted by New Jersey Devils (4th choice, 131st overall) in 1997 Entry Draft. Last overseas club; Kosice (Slovakia).

Daniel Bienvenue — Left Wing

Regular Season / Playoffs

Season	Team	League	GP	G	A	PTS	PIM	GP	G	A	PTS	PIM
97-98	Rochester	AHL	10	0	0	0	17	—	—	—	—	—
97-98	South Carolina	ECHL	50	10	11	21	4	—	—	—	—	—
98-99	Jacksonville	ECHL	2	0	0	0	2	—	—	—	—	—
98-99	Baton Rouge	ECHL	37	3	3	6	19	—	—	—	—	—
	ECHL	Totals	89	13	14	27	25	—	—	—	—	—

Born; 6/10/77, Val D'Or, Quebec. 6-0, 196. Drafted by Buffalo Sabres (8th choice, 123rd overall) in 1995 Entry Draft. Last amateur club; Val D'Or

Zac Bierk — Goaltender

Regular Season / Playoffs

Season	Team	League	GP	W	L	T	MIN	SO	AVG	GP	W	L	MIN	SO	AVG
97-98	Tampa Bay	NHL	13	1	4	1	433	0	4.16	—	—	—	—	—	—
97-98	Adirondack	AHL	12	1	6	1	558	0	3.87	—	—	—	—	—	—
98-99	Cleveland	IHL	27	11	12	4	1556	0	3.05	—	—	—	—	—	—
98-99	Tampa Bay	NHL	1	0	1	0	59	0	2.03	—	—	—	—	—	—
	NHL	Totals	14	1	5	1	492	0	3.90	—	—	—	—	—	—

Born; 9/17/76, Peterborough, Ontario. 6-4, 186. Drafted by Tampa Bay Lightning (8th choice, 212th overall) in 1995 Entry Draft. Last amateur club; Peterborough (OHL).

Mark Biesenthal — Right Wing

Regular Season / Playoffs

Season	Team	League	GP	G	A	PTS	PIM	GP	G	A	PTS	PIM
98-99	Elmira	NCAA-3	25	20	15	35	NA	—	—	—	—	—
98-99	Augusta	ECHL	8	0	2	2	6	2	0	0	0	0

Born; 5/9, 150. Last amateur club; Elmira (NCAA-3).

Don Biggs — Center

Regular Season / Playoffs

Season	Team	League	GP	G	A	PTS	PIM	GP	G	A	PTS	PIM
84-85	Oshawa	OHL	60	48	69	117	105	5	3	4	7	6
84-85	Minnesota	NHL	1	0	0	0	0	—	—	—	—	—
84-85	Springfield	AHL	6	0	3	3	0	2	1	0	1	0
85-86	Springfield	AHL	28	15	16	31	46	—	—	—	—	—
85-86	Nova Scotia	AHL	47	6	23	29	36	—	—	—	—	—
86-87	Nova Scotia	AHL	80	22	25	47	165	5	1	2	3	4
87-88	Hershey	AHL	77	38	41	79	151	12	5	*11	*16	22
88-89	Hershey	AHL	76	36	67	103	158	11	5	9	14	30
89-90	Philadelphia	NHL	11	2	0	2	8	—	—	—	—	—
89-90	Hershey	AHL	66	39	53	92	125	—	—	—	—	—
90-91	Otten	Switz.										
90-91	Rochester	AHL	65	31	57	88	115	15	9	*14	*23	14
91-92	Binghamton	AHL	74	32	50	82	122	11	2	7	10	8
92-93	Binghamton	AHL	78	54	*84	138	112	14	3	9	12	32
93-94	Cincinnati	IHL	80	30	59	89	128	11	8	9	17	29
94-95	Cincinnati	IHL	77	27	49	76	152	10	1	9	10	29
95-96	Cincinnati	IHL	82	27	57	84	160	17	9	19	19	24
96-97	Cincinnati	IHL	82	25	41	66	128	3	1	2	3	19
97-98	Cincinnati	IHL	82	25	52	77	88	9	5	4	9	27
98-99	Cincinnati	IHL	23	3	17	20	33	—	—	—	—	—
98-99	Utah	IHL	60	19	36	55	73	—	—	—	—	—
	NHL	Totals	12	2	0	2	8	—	—	—	—	—
	AHL	Totals	597	273	419	692	1030	70	26	52	78	110
	IHL	Totals	486	156	311	447	762	70	24	43	67	128

Born; 4/7/65, Mississauga, Ontario. 5-8, 180. Drafted by Minnesota North Stars (9th choice, 156th overall) in 1983 Entry Draft. Traded to Edmonton Oilers by Minnesota with Gord Sherven for Marc Habscheid, Don Barber and Emanuel Viveiros (12/20/85). Signed as a free agent by Philadelphia Flyers (7/17/87). Traded to New York Rangers by Philadelphia Flyers for future considerations (8/8/91). 1992-93 AHL MVP. 1992-93 AHL First Team All-Star. Member of 1987-88 AHL champion Hershey Bears. Last amateur club; Oshawa (OHL).

Beau Bilek — Defenseman

Regular Season / Playoffs

Season	Team	League	GP	G	A	PTS	PIM	GP	G	A	PTS	PIM
95-96	Indianapolis	IHL	5	0	0	0	4	—	—	—	—	—
95-96	Columbus	ECHL	64	6	25	31	78	3	0	0	0	6
96-97	Indianapolis	IHL	2	0	1	1	0	—	—	—	—	—
96-97	Columbus	ECHL	68	10	35	45	83	8	1	1	2	4
97-98	Indianapolis	IHL	4	0	0	0	0	—	—	—	—	—
97-98	Columbus	ECHL	66	4	24	28	51	—	—	—	—	—
98-99	Columbus	ECHL	68	9	37	46	94	4	0	0	0	8
98-99	Kentucky	AHL	1	0	0	0	0	—	—	—	—	—
98-99	Cincinnati	AHL	2	1	0	1	2	—	—	—	—	—
98-99	Cleveland	IHL	3	0	0	0	2	—	—	—	—	—
	IHL	Totals	10	0	1	1	6	—	—	—	—	—
	AHL	Totals	3	1	0	1	2	—	—	—	—	—
	ECHL	Totals	200	25	97	122	255	15	1	1	2	12

Born; 5/3/73, Des Moines, Iowa. 6-1, 200. Selected by Greensboro in 1999 ECHL Dispersal Draft. Last amateur club; US Air Force Academy.

Laurie Billeck — Defenseman

Regular Season / Playoffs

Season	Team	League	GP	G	A	PTS	PIM	GP	G	A	PTS	PIM
98-99	Tacoma	WCHL	5	0	2	2	6					

Born;

Cedric Billequey — Goaltender

Regular Season / Playoffs

Season	Team	League	GP	W	L	T	MIN	SO	AVG	GP	W	L	MIN	SO	AVG
98-99	Al. Huntsville	NCAA	18	13	4	1	1092	2	2.64	—	—	—	—	—	—
98-99	Huntsville	CHL	2	2	0	0	120	0	2.00	—	—	—	—	—	—

Born; Montreal, Quebec. 6-0, 175. Last amateur club; Huntsville (NCAA-1).

Brent Bilodeau — Defenseman

Season	Team	League	GP	G	A	PTS	PIM	GP	G	A	PTS	PIM
	Regular Season							Playoffs				
93-94	Fredericton	AHL	72	2	5	7	89	—	—	—	—	—
94-95	Fredericton	AHL	50	4	8	12	146	12	3	3	6	28
95-96	San Fransisco	IHL	65	3	14	17	123	4	1	0	1	2
96-97	Saint John	NHL	24	2	1	3	29	—	—	—	—	—
96-97	San Antonio	IHL	48	4	7	11	178	—	—	—	—	—
96-97	Las Vegas	IHL	3	0	0	0	0	—	—	—	—	—
97-98	Las Vegas	IHL	15	0	1	1	39	—	—	—	—	—
97-98	Kansas City	IHL	48	3	12	15	114	5	0	0	0	4
97-98	Tacoma	WCHL	2	0	1	1	2	—	—	—	—	—
98-99	Kansas City	IHL	35	0	4	4	66	—	—	—	—	—
	IHL	Totals	214	10	38	48	520	9	1	0	1	6
	AHL	Totals	146	8	14	22	264	12	3	3	6	28

Born; 3/27/73, Dallas, Texas. 6-3, 217. Drafted by Montreal Canadiens (1st choice, 17th overall) in 1991 Entry Draft. Last amateur club; Swift Current

Craig Binns — Defenseman

Season	Team	League	GP	G	A	PTS	PIM	GP	G	A	PTS	PIM
	Regular Season							Playoffs				
94-95	Columbus	ECHL	48	7	10	17	110	3	0	1	1	4
95-96	Columbus	ECHL	3	0	1	1	2	—	—	—	—	—
95-96	Mobile	ECHL	41	1	18	19	99	—	—	—	—	—
96-97	Mobile	ECHL	65	1	10	11	217	—	—	—	—	—
97-98	Chicago	IHL	37	1	3	4	56	—	—	—	—	—
97-98	Mobile	ECHL	3	0	0	0	2	—	—	—	—	—
98-99	Mobile	ECHL	53	0	8	8	94	2	0	0	0	2
	ECHL	Totals	210	9	47	56	522	5	0	1	1	6

Born; 7/18/74, Ottawa, Ontario. 6-4, 225. Last amateur club; Owen Sound

Jamie Bird — Defenseman

Season	Team	League	GP	G	A	PTS	PIM	GP	G	A	PTS	PIM
	Regular Season							Playoffs				
95-96	San Antonio	CeHL	25	3	12	15	22	—	—	—	—	—
95-96	Fort Worth	CeHL	35	5	12	17	30	—	—	—	—	—
96-97	Knoxville	ECHL	44	3	10	13	26	—	—	—	—	—
97-98	Springfield	AHL	3	0	0	0	0	—	—	—	—	—
97-98	Binghamton	UHL	72	3	54	57	32	5	0	4	4	2
98-99	Binghamton	UHL	71	6	45	51	45	5	0	2	2	2
98-99	Syracuse	AHL	1	0	0	0	0	—	—	—	—	—
	AHL	Totals	4	0	0	0	0	—	—	—	—	—
	UHL	Totals	143	9	99	108	77	10	0	6	6	4
	CeHL	Totals	60	8	24	32	52	—	—	—	—	—

Born; 3/7/74, Rochester, New York. 5-11, 189. Last amateur club; Hull

Martin Biron — Goaltender

Season	Team	League	GP	W	L	T	MIN	SO	AVG	GP	W	L	MIN	SO	AVG
	Regular Season									Playoffs					
95-96	Beauport	QMJHL	55	29	17	7	3201	1	2.85	*19	*12	7	1134	0	3.39
95-96	Buffalo	NHL	3	0	2	0	119	0	5.04	—	—	—	—	—	—
96-97	Beauport	QMJHL	18	6	9	1	928	1	3.94	—	—	—	—	—	—
96-97	Hull	QMJHL	16	11	4	1	974	2	2.65	6	3	1	325	0	3.51
97-98	Rochester	AHL	41	14	18	6	2312	*5	2.93	4	1	3	239	0	4.01
97-98	South Carolina	ECHL	2	0	1	1	86	0	2.09	—	—	—	—	—	—
98-99	Rochester	AHL	52	36	13	3	3129	*6	*2.07	*20	12	*8	1166	1	*2.16
98-99	Buffalo	NHL	6	1	2	1	281	0	2.14	—	—	—	—	—	—
	NHL	Totals	9	1	4	1	400	0	3.00	—	—	—	—	—	—
	AHL	Totals	95	50	31	9	5441	11	2.44	24	13	11	1405	1	2.48

Born; 8/15/77, Lac St. Charles, Quebec. 6-1, 154. Drafted by Buffalo Sabres (2nd choice, 16th overall) in 1995 Entry Draft. Shared 1998-99 AHL fewest goals against with Tom Draper. 1998-99 AHL Goaltender of the Year. 1998-99 AHL First Team All-Star. Last amateur club; Hull (QMJHL).

Anders Bjork — Center

Season	Team	League	GP	G	A	PTS	PIM	GP	G	A	PTS	PIM
	Regular Season							Playoffs				
97-98	Denver	WCHA	29	17	18	35	30	—	—	—	—	—
97-98	Orlando	IHL	7	2	2	4	9	17	3	4	7	16
98-99	Grand Rapids	IHL	35	8	6	14	17	—	—	—	—	—
98-99	Cincinnati	AHL	36	5	8	13	22	2	0	0	0	0
	IHL	Totals	42	10	8	18	26	17	3	4	7	16

Born; 10/17/73, Stockholm, Sweden. 6-2, 188. Last amateur club; University of Denver (WCHA).

Clint Black — Center

Season	Team	League	GP	G	A	PTS	PIM	GP	G	A	PTS	PIM
	Regular Season							Playoffs				
95-96	Wichita	CeHL	64	33	35	68	51	—	—	—	—	—
96-97	Wichita	CeHL	54	16	25	41	70	9	2	2	4	18
97-98	Wichita	CHL	34	8	11	19	33	—	—	—	—	—
97-98	Tulsa	CHL	35	18	22	40	55	1	0	0	0	0
98-99	Tulsa	CHL	70	8	33	41	127	—	—	—	—	—
	CHL	Totals	257	83	126	209	336	10	2	2	4	18

Born; 9/17/72, Duncan, British Columbia. 5-9, 175.

James Black — Center

Season	Team	League	GP	G	A	PTS	PIM	GP	G	A	PTS	PIM
	Regular Season							Playoffs				
89-90	Hartford	NHL	1	0	0	0	0	—	—	—	—	—
89-90	Binghamton	AHL	80	37	35	72	34	—	—	—	—	—
90-91	Hartford	NHL	1	0	0	0	0	—	—	—	—	—
90-91	Springfield	AHL	79	35	61	96	34	18	9	9	18	6
91-92	Hartford	NHL	30	4	6	10	10	—	—	—	—	—
91-92	Springfield	AHL	47	15	25	40	33	10	3	2	5	18
92-93	Minnesota	NHL	10	2	1	3	4	—	—	—	—	—
92-93	Kalamazoo	IHL	63	25	45	70	40	—	—	—	—	—
93-94	Dallas	NHL	13	2	3	5	2	—	—	—	—	—
93-94	Buffalo	NHL	2	0	0	0	0	—	—	—	—	—
93-94	Rochester	AHL	45	19	32	51	28	4	2	3	5	0
94-95	Las Vegas	IHL	78	29	44	73	54	10	1	6	7	4
95-96	Chicago	NHL	13	3	3	6	16	8	1	0	1	2
95-96	Indianapolis	IHL	67	32	50	82	56	—	—	—	—	—
96-97	Chicago	NHL	64	12	11	23	20	5	1	1	2	2
97-98	Chicago	NHL	52	10	5	15	8	—	—	—	—	—
98-99	Chicago	IHL	5	6	0	6	0					
98-99	Washington	NHL	75	16	14	30	14	—	—	—	—	—
	NHL	Totals	261	49	43	92	74	13	2	1	3	4
	AHL	Totals	251	106	153	259	129	32	14	14	28	24
	IHL	Totals	213	92	139	231	150	10	1	6	7	4

Born; 8/15/69, Regina, Saskatchewan. 6-0, 202. Drafted by Hartford Whalers (4th choice, 94th overall) in 1989 Entry Draft. Traded to Minnesota North Stars for Mark Janssens (9/3/92). Traded to Buffalo Sabres by Dallas Stars with Dallas' 7th round choice (Steve Webb) in 1994 Entry Draft. for Gord Donnelly (12/15/93). Signed as a free agent by Chicago Blackhawks (9/18/95). Traded to Washington Capitals by Chicago for fourth round choice (later traded to Florida-Florida selected Morgan McCormick) in 1999 Entry Draft. (10/15/99). Member of 1990-91 AHL Champion Springfield Indians. Last amateur club; Portland

Jamie Black — Center

Season	Team	League	GP	G	A	PTS	PIM	GP	G	A	PTS	PIM
	Regular Season							Playoffs				
93-94	Cleveland	IHL	71	12	16	28	36	—	—	—	—	—
94-95	Muskgeon	CoHL	56	18	28	46	35	12	3	12	15	6
94-95	Cleveland	IHL	20	5	10	15	20	—	—	—	—	—
95-96	Bakersfield	WCHL	6	5	2	7	0	—	—	—	—	—
95-96	EV Zeltwig	Austria	33	10	13	23	26	—	—	—	—	—
96-97	Basingstoke	BHL	42	7	13	20	50	—	—	—	—	—
97-98	Basingstoke	BSL	54	17	31	48	54	6	0	3	3	8
98-99	Newcastle	BSL	50	13	18	31	18	6	0	0	0	2
	IHL	Totals	91	17	26	43	56	—	—	—	—	—

Born; 8/3/69, Regina, Saskatchewan. 6-1, 185.

Ryan Black — Center
Regular Season — Playoffs

Season	Team	League	GP	G	A	PTS	PIM	GP	G	A	PTS	PIM
95-96	St. Thomas	AUAA	22	15	22	37	14	—	—	—	—	—
95-96	Hampton Roads	ECHL	5	1	1	2	0	3	1	2	3	0
96-97	Fort Worth	CeHL	52	27	20	47	44	17	5	6	11	10
97-98	Cincinnati	AHL	12	2	1	3	2	—	—	—	—	—
97-98	Port Huron	UHL	54	23	31	54	38	—	—	—	—	—
97-98	Quad City	UHL	6	4	5	9	0	19	6	7	13	14
98-99	Fort Worth	WPHL	68	22	45	67	65	12	7	5	12	12
	UHL	Totals	60	27	36	63	38	19	6	7	13	14

Born; 10/25/73, Elmira, Ontario. 6-1, 195. Drafted by New Jersey Devils (6th choice, 114th overall) in 1992 Entry Draft. Member of 1996-97 CeHL Champion Fort Worth Fire. Member of 1997-98 UHL Champion Quad City Mallards. Scored overtime Colonial Cup-winning goal in Game 7 of 97-98 season. Traded to Quad City by Port Huron for Steve Sangermano (3/98). Last amateur club; St. Thomas (AUAA).

Brant Blackned — Left Wing
Regular Season — Playoffs

Season	Team	League	GP	G	A	PTS	PIM	GP	G	A	PTS	PIM
95-96	Erie	ECHL	15	1	4	5	34	—	—	—	—	—
95-96	Thunder Bay	CoHL	15	4	10	14	17	5	0	0	0	0
96-97	Thunder Bay	CoHL	70	49	51	100	79	11	3	6	9	12
97-98	Thunder Bay	UHL	73	*63	70	133	78	5	1	5	6	2
98-99	Thunder Bay	UHL	70	41	55	96	60	13	5	8	13	12
	CoHL	Totals	228	157	186	343	234	34	9	19	28	26

Born; 4/4/74, Weminji, Quebec. 6-0, 200. 1997-98 UHL First All-Star Team. Last amateur club; Halifax (QMJHL).

Brady Blain — Forward
Regular Season — Playoffs

Season	Team	League	GP	G	A	PTS	PIM	GP	G	A	PTS	PIM
97-98	Pee Dee	ECHL	3	0	0	0	0	—	—	—	—	—
97-98	Shreveport	WPHL	12	4	4	8	4	—	—	—	—	—
98-99	Bakersfield	WCHL	60	4	20	24	14	2	0	0	0	0

Born; 7/1/74, Chatham, Ontario. 6-0, 192. Last amateur club; University of Western Ontario (OUAA).

Jason Blake — Center
Regular Season — Playoffs

Season	Team	League	GP	G	A	PTS	PIM	GP	G	A	PTS	PIM
98-99	North Dakota	WCHA	38	28	41	69	49	—	—	—	—	—
98-99	Los Angeles	NHL	1	1	0	1	0	—	—	—	—	—
98-99	Orlando	IHL	5	3	5	8	6	13	3	4	7	20

Born; 9/23/73, Moorhead, Minnesota. 5-10, 180. Signed as a free agent by Los Angeles Kings (4/20/99). Last amateur club; North Dakata (WCHA).

Sean Blanchard — Defenseman
Regular Season — Playoffs

Season	Team	League	GP	G	A	PTS	PIM	GP	G	A	PTS	PIM
98-99	Springfield	AHL	10	0	1	1	4	—	—	—	—	—
98-99	Mississippi	ECHL	58	5	24	29	30	17	0	8	8	4

Born; 3/29/78, Sudbury, Ontario. 5-11, 198. Drafted by Los Angeles Kings (5th choice, 99th overall) in 1997 Entry Draft. Member of 1998-99 ECHL Champion Mississippi SeaWolves. Last amateur club; Ottawa (OHL).

Keith Bland — Defenseman
Regular Season — Playoffs

Season	Team	League	GP	G	A	PTS	PIM	GP	G	A	PTS	PIM
97-98	Amarillo	WPHL	55	0	6	6	251	—	—	—	—	—
98-99	Amarillo	WPHL	10	0	2	2	59	—	—	—	—	—
98-99	Central Texas	WPHL	47	2	5	7	274	2	0	0	0	16
	WPHL	Totals	112	2	13	15	584	2	0	0	0	16

Born; 2/19/75, Paramus, New Jersey. 6-0, 198. Last amateur club; Alaska-Anchorage (WCHA).

Andrej Blasko — Defenseman
Regular Season — Playoffs

Season	Team	League	GP	G	A	PTS	PIM	GP	G	A	PTS	PIM
98-99	Austin	WPHL	1	0	0	0	0	—	—	—	—	—
98-99	Flint	UHL	5	0	0	0	2	—	—	—	—	—

Born; 11/11/78, Bratislavia, Slovakia. 6-0, 200.

Joe Blaznek — Forward
Regular Season — Playoffs

Season	Team	League	GP	G	A	PTS	PIM	GP	G	A	PTS	PIM
97-98	Lake Superior	CCHA	36	13	10	23	48	—	—	—	—	—
97-98	Long Beach	IHL	5	1	1	2	4	1	0	1	1	0
98-99	Richmond	ECHL	59	38	23	61	37	18	10	5	15	8
98-99	Kentucky	AHL	15	1	7	8	4	—	—	—	—	—

Born; 9/8/75, Allen Park, Michigan. 6-0, 193. Last amateur club; Lake Superior State (CCHA).

John Blessman — Defenseman
Regular Season — Playoffs

Season	Team	League	GP	G	A	PTS	PIM	GP	G	A	PTS	PIM
87-88	Utica	AHL	24	0	2	2	50	—	—	—	—	—
88-89	Utica	AHL	26	2	3	5	46	—	—	—	—	—
88-89	Indianapolis	IHL	31	2	5	7	60	—	—	—	—	—
89-90	Hershey	AHL	1	0	0	0	0	—	—	—	—	—
89-90	Winston-Salem	ECHL	17	1	6	7	108	—	—	—	—	—
89-90	Greensboro	ECHL	19	0	7	7	81	11	3	6	9	50
90-91	Greensboro	ECHL	29	7	14	21	131	13	1	9	10	36
91-92	Kansas City	IHL	25	0	2	2	24	—	—	—	—	—
91-92	Cape Breton	AHL	27	2	8	10	16	5	0	1	1	2
92-93	Baltimore	AHL	6	0	0	0	4	—	—	—	—	—
92-93	Greensboro	ECHL	5	3	1	4	16	—	—	—	—	—
92-93	West Palm Beach	SUN	22	5	12	17	60	—	—	—	—	—
94-95	Toledo	ECHL	16	1	2	3	33	—	—	—	—	—
94-95	Raleigh	ECHL	31	4	14	18	109	—	—	—	—	—
94-95	San Antonio	CeHL	16	2	10	12	13	13	4	*17	21	12
95-96	Syracuse	AHL	1	0	1	1	0	—	—	—	—	—
95-96	Wheeling	ECHL	67	8	18	26	176	7	1	3	4	2
96-97	Syracuse	AHL	23	4	4	8	9	—	—	—	—	—
96-97	Wheeling	ECHL	31	14	9	23	64	3	2	0	2	8
97-98	New Orleans	ECHL	7	0	1	1	33	—	—	—	—	—
97-98	South Carolina	ECHL	53	13	13	26	34	5	0	0	0	12
98-99	Greenville	ECHL	19	1	0	1	19	—	—	—	—	—
	AHL	Totals	108	8	18	26	125	5	0	1	1	2
	IHL	Totals	56	2	7	9	84	—	—	—	—	—
	ECHL	Totals	289	52	85	137	804	39	7	18	25	108

Born; 4/27/67, Agincourt, Ontario. 6-3, 220. Drafted by New Jersey Devils (8th choice, 170th overall) in 1987 Entry Draft. Traded to South Carolina by New Orleans for Wayne Strachan (11/97). Selected by Greenville in 1998 ECHL Expansion Draft. Member of 1989-90 ECHL champion Greensboro Monarchs. Last amateur club; Toronto (OHL).

Joakim Blink — Right Wing
Regular Season — Playoffs

Season	Team	League	GP	G	A	PTS	PIM	GP	G	A	PTS	PIM
97-98	Odessa	WPHL	7	3	2	5	2	—	—	—	—	—
98-99	Odessa	WPHL	15	3	3	6	0	—	—	—	—	—
	WPHL	Totals	22	6	5	11	2	—	—	—	—	—

Born; 2/16/76, Upplands Vasby, Sweden. 6-1, 185.

Dieter Bloem — Defenseman
Regular Season — Playoffs

Season	Team	League	GP	G	A	PTS	PIM	GP	G	A	PTS	PIM
92-93												
93-94												
94-95												
95-96	Landshut	Germany	39	5	4	9	111	—	—	—	—	—
96-97	Schwenninger	Germany	3	0	1	1	0	—	—	—	—	—
96-97	Ratinger	Germany	38	3	3	6	59	—	—	—	—	—
97-98												
98-99	Hamburg	Germany	4	3	1	4	2	—	—	—	—	—
98-99	Waco	WPHL	32	1	8	9	47	4	0	1	1	0

Born; 3/31/71, Saratoga Springs, New York. 6-3, 205.

Jeff Bloemberg — Defenseman

Regular Season — Playoffs

Season	Team	League	GP	G	A	PTS	PIM	GP	G	A	PTS	PIM
87-88	North Bay	OHL	46	9	26	35	60	4	1	4	5	2
87-88	Colorado	IHL	5	0	0	0	0	11	1	0	1	8
88-89	Rangers	NHL	9	0	0	0	0	—	—	—	—	—
88-89	Denver	IHL	64	7	22	29	55	1	0	0	0	0
89-90	Rangers	NHL	28	3	3	6	25	7	0	3	3	5
89-90	Flint	IHL	41	7	14	21	24	—	—	—	—	—
90-91	Rangers	NHL	3	0	2	2	0	—	—	—	—	—
90-91	Binghamton	AHL	77	16	46	62	28	10	0	6	6	10
91-92	Rangers	NHL	3	0	1	1	0	—	—	—	—	—
91-92	Binghamton	AHL	66	6	41	47	22	11	1	10	11	10
92-93	Cape Breton	AHL	76	6	45	51	34	16	5	10	15	10
93-94	Springfield	AHL	78	8	28	36	36	6	0	3	3	8
94-95	Adirondack	AHL	44	5	19	24	10	4	0	0	0	0
95-96	Adirondack	AHL	72	10	28	38	32	3	0	1	1	4
96-97	Adirondack	AHL	69	5	31	36	24	4	0	3	3	2
97-98	Berlin	Germany	27	3	7	10	16	—	—	—	—	—
98-99	Revier Lowen	Germany	52	3	17	20	54	—	—	—	—	—
	NHL	Totals	43	3	6	9	25	7	0	3	3	5
	AHL	Totals	482	56	238	294	186	54	6	33	39	44
	IHL	Totals	110	14	36	50	79	12	1	0	1	8

Born; 1/31/68, Listowel, Ontario. 6-2, 205. Drafted by New York Rangers (5th choice, 93rd overall) in 1986 Entry Draft. Claimed by Tampa Bay Lightning from Rangers in Expansion Draft (6/18/92). Traded to Edmonton Oilers by Tampa Bay for future considerations (9/25/92). Signed as a free agent by Hartford Whalers (8/9/93). Signed as a free agent by Detroit Red Wings (5/9/95). 1990-91 AHL Second Team All-Star. Member of 1992-93 AHL Champion Cape Breton Oilers. Last amateur club; North Bay (OHL).

Jean Blouin — Right Wing

Regular Season — Playoffs

Season	Team	League	GP	G	A	PTS	PIM	GP	G	A	PTS	PIM
91-92	Muskegon	IHL	19	4	5	9	12	—	—	—	—	—
92-93	Louisville	ECHL	2	3	1	4	0	—	—	—	—	—
92-93	Atlanta	IHL	61	11	11	22	69	—	—	—	—	—
93-94	Prince Edward Island	AHL	8	2	0	2	7	—	—	—	—	—
93-94	Thunder Bay	CoHL	23	22	12	34	31	7	0	4	4	11
94-95	Prince Edward Island	AHL	1	0	0	0	0	—	—	—	—	—
94-95	Thunder Bay	CoHL	66	70	39	109	60	11	*16	11	27	38
95-96	Thunder Bay	CoHL	13	8	7	15	27	19	*23	8	31	20
96-97	Carolina	AHL	1	0	1	1	0	—	—	—	—	—
96-97	Grand Rapids	IHL	1	0	0	0	0	—	—	—	—	—
96-97	Port Huron	CoHL	39	32	22	54	23	5	2	6	8	2
97-98	Port Huron	UHL	2	0	0	0	0	—	—	—	—	—
97-98	San Angelo	WPHL	48	63	44	107	19	3	0	1	1	2
98-99	San Angelo	WPHL	57	47	44	91	98	17	*13	9	22	23
	IHL	Totals	81	15	16	31	81	—	—	—	—	—
	AHL	Totals	10	2	1	3	7	—	—	—	—	—
	UHL	Totals	143	132	80	212	141	42	41	29	70	71
	WPHL	Totals	105	110	88	198	117	20	13	10	23	25

Born; 2/26/71, Beauport, Quebec. 6-1, 205. 1994-95 CoHL First Team All-Star. Member of 1993-94 CoHL champion Thunder Bay Senators. Member of 1994-95 CoHL champion Thunder Bay Senators. Last amateur club; Laval (QMJHL).

Sylvain Blouin — Left Wing

Regular Season — Playoffs

Season	Team	League	GP	G	A	PTS	PIM	GP	G	A	PTS	PIM
94-95	Binghamton	AHL	10	1	0	1	46	2	0	0	0	24
94-95	Chicago	IHL	1	0	0	0	2	—	—	—	—	—
94-95	Charlotte	ECHL	50	5	7	12	280	3	0	0	0	6
95-96	Binghamton	AHL	71	5	8	13	352	4	0	3	3	4
96-97	Rangers	NHL	6	0	0	0	18	—	—	—	—	—
96-97	Binghamton	AHL	62	13	17	30	301	4	2	1	3	16
97-98	Rangers	NHL	1	0	0	0	5	—	—	—	—	—
97-98	Hartford	AHL	53	8	9	17	286	9	0	1	1	63
98-99	Montreal	NHL	5	0	0	0	19	—	—	—	—	—
98-99	Fredericton	AHL	67	6	10	16	333	15	2	0	2	*87
	NHL	Totals	12	0	0	0	42	—	—	—	—	—
	AHL	Totals	263	33	44	77	1318	34	4	5	9	194

Born; 5/21/74, Montreal, Quebec. 6-2, 216. Drafted by New York Rangers (5th choice, 104th overall) in 1994 Entry Draft. Traded to Montreal Canadiens by Rangers with Rangers 6th round choice (later traded to Phoenix-Phoenix selected Erik Leverstrom) in 1999 Entry Draft for Peter Popovic (6/30/98). Last amateur club; Laval (QMJHL).

Jeff Blum — Defenseman

Regular Season — Playoffs

Season	Team	League	GP	G	A	PTS	PIM	GP	G	A	PTS	PIM
95-96	Detroit	CoHL	71	6	30	36	137	10	2	5	7	14
96-97	Port Huron	CoHL	71	11	22	33	111	5	0	0	0	4
97-98	Milwaukee	IHL	5	0	1	1	7	—	—	—	—	—
97-98	Port Huron	UHL	62	10	17	27	56	4	1	3	4	8
98-99	Port Huron	UHL	71	6	18	24	79	7	0	1	1	16
98-99	Milwaukee	IHL	2	0	0	0	5	—	—	—	—	—
	IHL	Totals	7	0	1	1	12	—	—	—	—	—
	UHL	Totals	204	27	69	96	304	19	3	8	11	26

Born; 4/24/72, Detroit, Michigan. 6-1, 195. Selected by Fort Wayne in 1999 UHL Expansion Draft. Last amateur club; Illinois-Chicago (CCHA).

Ken Blum — Left Wing

Regular Season — Playoffs

Season	Team	League	GP	G	A	PTS	PIM	GP	G	A	PTS	PIM
91-92	Toledo	ECHL	8	0	2	2	2	—	—	—	—	—
91-92	Winston-Salem	ECHL	8	0	1	1	14	—	—	—	—	—
91-92	Roanoke	ECHL	30	3	2	5	64	7	0	1	1	19
92-93	Roanoke	ECHL	63	16	21	37	132	—	—	—	—	—
93-94	Richmond	ECHL	61	11	25	36	215	—	—	—	—	—
94-95	Flint	CoHL	54	6	23	29	164	5	1	0	1	10
95-96	Carolina	AHL	1	0	0	0	0	—	—	—	—	—
95-96	Detroit	CoHL	59	22	13	35	154	10	4	1	5	26
96-97	Saginaw	CoHL	59	24	33	57	165	—	—	—	—	—
97-98	Saginaw	UHL	37	11	16	27	42	—	—	—	—	—
97-98	Madison	UHL	16	5	3	8	10	—	—	—	—	—
98-99	Mohawk Valley	UHL	11	2	0	2	6	—	—	—	—	—
98-99	Tupelo	WPHL	15	2	7	9	10	—	—	—	—	—
	UHL	Totals	236	70	88	158	541	15	5	1	6	36
	ECHL	Totals	170	30	51	81	427	7	0	1	1	19

Born; 6/8/71, Hackensack, New Jersey. Drafted by Minnesota North Stars (10th choice, 175th overall) in 1989 Entry Draft. Traded to Madison by Saginaw with Dave Ivaska for Jason Smith (1/98). Selected by Mohawk Valley in 1998 UHL Expansion Draft. Last amateur club; Lake Superior State (CCHA).

Stewart Bodtker — Forward

Regular Season — Playoffs

Season	Team	League	GP	G	A	PTS	PIM	GP	G	A	PTS	PIM
98-99	Syracuse	AHL	31	5	5	10	12	—	—	—	—	—
98-99	Augusta	ECHL	47	17	15	32	58	—	—	—	—	—

Born; 9/15/76, Vancouver, British Columbia. 6-1, 190. Drafted by Vancouver Canucks (7th choice, 170th overall) in 1995 Entry Draft. Last amateur club; Colorado (WCHA).

Jeff Boettger — Defenseman

Regular Season / Playoffs

Season	Team	League	GP	G	A	PTS	PIM	GP	G	A	PTS	PIM
97-98	Chesapeake	ECHL	48	2	5	7	37	3	0	0	0	0
98-99	Chesapeake	ECHL	56	1	5	6	59	—	—	—	—	—
98-99	Baton Rouge	ECHL	16	0	0	0	8	6	0	0	0	0
	ECHL	Totals	120	3	10	13	104	9	0	0	0	0

Born; 3/8/72, McLennan, Alberta. 6-2, 205. Last amateur club; Bethel College (NCAA 3).

Eric Boguniecki — Center

Regular Season / Playoffs

Season	Team	League	GP	G	A	PTS	PIM	GP	G	A	PTS	PIM
97-98	Fort Wayne	IHL	35	4	8	12	29	4	1	2	3	10
97-98	Dayton	ECHL	26	19	18	37	36	—	—	—	—	—
98-99	Fort Wayne	IHL	72	32	34	66	100	2	0	1	1	2
	IHL	Totals	107	36	42	78	129	6	1	3	4	12

Born; 5/6/75, New Haven, Connecticut. 5-8, 192. Drafted by St. Louis Blues (6th choice, 193rd overall) in 1993 Entry Draft. Signed as a free agent by Florida Panthers (7/20/99). Last amateur club; New Hampshire University (Hockey East).

Aaron Boh — Defenseman

Regular Season / Playoffs

Season	Team	League	GP	G	A	PTS	PIM	GP	G	A	PTS	PIM
93-94	Medicine Hat	WHL	28	4	15	19	99	—	—	—	—	—
93-94	Tri-City	WHL	27	3	7	10	97	—	—	—	—	—
93-94	Columbus	ECHL	10	1	9	10	31	—	—	—	—	—
94-95	Atlanta	IHL	20	2	6	8	15	—	—	—	—	—
94-95	Columbus	ECHL	58	5	25	30	186	—	—	—	—	—
95-96	Rochester	AHL	12	0	4	4	10	—	—	—	—	—
95-96	Minnesota	IHL	3	0	0	0	2	—	—	—	—	—
95-96	Columbus	ECHL	37	17	31	48	136	—	—	—	—	—
95-96	Louisiana	ECHL	17	5	8	13	58	5	1	7	8	10
96-97	Houston	IHL	3	0	0	0	2	—	—	—	—	—
96-97	Louisiana	ECHL	52	11	54	65	193	17	4	17	21	93
97-98	Fort Wayne	IHL	6	0	1	1	8	—	—	—	—	—
97-98	Fayetteville	CHL	56	15	43	58	230	—	—	—	—	—
98-99	Toledo	ECHL	65	11	28	39	226	7	3	6	9	28
	IHL	Totals	26	2	6	8	19	—	—	—	—	—
	ECHL	Totals	239	50	155	205	830	29	8	30	38	131

Born; 4/4/74, Lethbridge, Alberta. 6-2, 185. Drafted by Vancouver Canucks (12th choice, 261st overall) in 1992 Entry Draft. 1995-96 ECHL Second Team All-Star. Last amateur club; Tri-City (WHL).

Lonny Bohonos — Right Wing

Regular Season / Playoffs

Season	Team	League	GP	G	A	PTS	PIM	GP	G	A	PTS	PIM
94-95	Syracuse	AHL	67	30	45	75	71	—	—	—	—	—
95-96	Vancouver	NHL	3	0	1	1	0	—	—	—	—	—
95-96	Syracuse	AHL	74	40	39	79	82	16	14	8	22	16
96-97	Vancouver	NHL	33	11	11	22	10	—	—	—	—	—
96-97	Syracuse	AHL	41	22	30	52	28	3	2	2	4	4
97-98	Vancouver	NHL	31	2	1	3	4	—	—	—	—	—
97-98	Toronto	NHL	6	3	3	6	4	—	—	—	—	—
97-98	Syracuse	AHL	17	12	12	24	8	—	—	—	—	—
97-98	St. John's	AHL	11	7	9	16	10	2	1	1	2	2
98-99	Toronto	NHL	7	3	0	3	4	9	3	6	9	2
98-99	St. John's	AHL	70	34	48	82	40	5	2	4	6	2
	NHL	Totals	80	19	16	35	22	9	3	6	9	2
	AHL	Totals	280	145	183	328	239	26	19	15	34	24

Born; 3/26/70, Winnipeg, Manitoba. 5-11, 190. Signed as a free agent by Vancouver Canucks (5/31/94). Traded to Toronto Maple Leafs for Brandon Convery (3/7/98). Last amateur club; Portland (WHL).

Alexandre Boikov — Defenseman

Regular Season / Playoffs

Season	Team	League	GP	G	A	PTS	PIM	GP	G	A	PTS	PIM
96-97	Kentucky	AHL	61	1	19	20	182	4	0	1	1	4
97-98	Kentucky	AHL	69	5	14	19	153	3	0	1	1	8
98-99	Kentucky	AHL	55	5	13	18	116	—	—	—	—	—
98-99	Rochester	AHL	13	0	1	1	15	17	1	3	4	24
	AHL	Totals	198	11	47	58	466	24	1	5	6	36

Born; 2/7/75, Chelyabinsk, USSR. 6-0, 180. Signed as a free agent by San Jose Sharks (4/22/96). Signed as a free agent by Nashville Predators (7/26/99). Last amateur club; Tri-City (WHL).

Patrick Boileau — Defenseman

Regular Season / Playoffs

Season	Team	League	GP	G	A	PTS	PIM	GP	G	A	PTS	PIM
95-96	Portland	AHL	78	10	28	38	41	19	1	3	4	12
96-97	Washington	NHL	1	0	0	0	0	—	—	—	—	—
96-97	Portland	AHL	67	16	28	44	63	5	1	1	2	4
97-98	Portland	AHL	47	6	21	27	53	10	0	1	1	8
98-99	Washington	NHL	4	0	1	1	2	—	—	—	—	—
98-99	Portland	AHL	52	6	18	24	52	—	—	—	—	—
98-99	Indianapolis	IHL	29	8	13	21	27	4	0	1	1	2
	NHL	Totals	5	0	1	1	2	—	—	—	—	—
	AHL	Totals	244	38	95	133	209	34	2	5	7	24

Born; 2/22/75, Montreal, Quebec. 6-0, 190. Drafted by Washington Capitals (3rd choice, 69th overall) in 1993 Entry Draft. Last amateur club; Laval (QMJHL).

Martin Boisvenue — Center

Regular Season / Playoffs

Season	Team	League	GP	G	A	PTS	PIM	GP	G	A	PTS	PIM
98-99	Philadelphia	AHL	5	0	1	1	2	1	0	0	0	0

Born; 4/24/77, Cornwall, Ontario. 6-0, 192. Signed as a free agent by Philadelphia Flyers (10/2/96). Last amateur club; Baie-Comeau (QMJHL).

Claude Boivin — Left Wing

Regular Season / Playoffs

Season	Team	League	GP	G	A	PTS	PIM	GP	G	A	PTS	PIM
90-91	Hershey	AHL	65	13	32	45	159	7	1	5	6	28
91-92	Hershey	AHL	20	4	5	9	96	—	—	—	—	—
91-92	Philadelphia	NHL	58	5	13	18	187	—	—	—	—	—
92-93	Philadelphia	NHL	30	5	4	9	76	—	—	—	—	—
93-94	Hershey	AHL	4	1	6	7	6	—	—	—	—	—
93-94	Philadelphia	NHL	26	1	1	2	57	—	—	—	—	—
93-94	Ottawa	NHL	15	1	0	1	38	—	—	—	—	—
94-95	Prince Edward Island	AHL	22	10	9	19	89	9	1	2	3	32
94-95	Ottawa	NHL	3	0	1	1	6	—	—	—	—	—
95-96												
96-97												
97-98	Quebec	IHL	13	2	3	5	46	—	—	—	—	—
97-98	Grand Rapids	IHL	31	12	5	17	69	3	0	0	0	8
97-98	Pensacola	ECHL	10	0	1	1	45	—	—	—	—	—
98-99	Vipiteno	Italy	41	13	29	42	195	5	3	2	5	51
	NHL	Totals	132	12	19	31	364	—	—	—	—	—
	AHL	Totals	111	28	52	80	350	16	2	7	9	60
	IHL	Totals	44	14	8	22	115	3	0	0	0	8

Born; 3/1/70, St. Foy, Quebec. 6-2, 200. Drafted by Philadelphia Flyers (1st choice, 14th overall) in 1988 Entry Draft. Traded to Ottawa Senators with Kirk Daubenspeck by Flyers for Mark Lamb (3/5/94). Last amateur club; Laval

Dave Bolduc — Defenseman

Regular Season / Playoffs

Season	Team	League	GP	G	A	PTS	PIM	GP	G	A	PTS	PIM
98-99	Quad City	UHL	8	1	0	1	13	—	—	—	—	—

Born; 2/9/77, Thretford Mines, Quebec. 6-2, 220.

Rob Boleski — Defenseman

Regular Season — Playoffs

Season	Team	League	GP	G	A	PTS	PIM	GP	G	A	PTS	PIM
97-98	Saskatoon	WHL	18	0	0	0	58	—	—	—	—	—
97-98	Hampton Roads	ECHL	7	0	0	0	7	—	—	—	—	—
98-99	Hampton Roads	ECHL	9	0	1	1	18	—	—	—	—	—
98-99	Huntington	ECHL	9	0	2	2	45	—	—	—	—	—
98-99	Quad City	UHL	6	0	0	0	23	—	—	—	—	—
	ECHL	Totals	25	0	3	3	70	—	—	—	—	—

Born; 1/4/77, North Vancouver, British Columbia. 6-2, 220. Last amateur club; Saskatoon (WHL).

Kevin Bolibruck — Defenseman

Regular Season — Playoffs

Season	Team	League	GP	G	A	PTS	PIM	GP	G	A	PTS	PIM
97-98	Canada	National	49	2	5	7	65	—	—	—	—	—
98-99	Hamilton	AHL	64	1	6	7	42	11	0	1	1	4

Born; 2/8/77, Peterborough, Ontario. 6-1, 200. Drafted by Ottawa Senators (4th choice, 89th overall) in 1995 Entry Draft. Rights traded to Chicago Blackhawks by Ottawa with Densi Chasse and Ottawa's 6th round choice in 1998 Entry Draft (returned to Ottawa, Ottawa selected Christopher Neil) for Mike Prokopec (3/18/97). Re-entered draft and selected by Edmonton Oilers (7th choice, 176th overall) in 1997 Entry Draft. Last amateur club; Peterborough (OHL).

Leonardo Bonanno — Right Wing

Regular Season — Playoffs

Season	Team	League	GP	G	A	PTS	PIM	GP	G	A	PTS	PIM
98-99	Memphis	CHL	67	26	53	79	220	4	2	3	5	28

Born; 4/2/74, Montreal, Quebec. 5-9, 170.

Igor Bonderev — Defenseman

Regular Season — Playoffs

Season	Team	League	GP	G	A	PTS	PIM	GP	G	A	PTS	PIM
94-95	Birmingham	ECHL	3	0	1	1	0	—	—	—	—	—
94-95	Dallas	CeHL	9	1	9	10	12	—	—	—	—	—
94-95	Fort Worth	CeHL	41	5	19	24	32	—	—	—	—	—
95-96	Huntsville	SHL	54	16	28	44	32	10	3	8	11	2
96-97	Huntsville	CeHL	60	38	53	91	26	9	1	12	13	0
97-98	Huntsville	CHL	68	23	61	84	63	3	2	1	3	2
98-99	Las Vegas	IHL	3	0	0	0	0	—	—	—	—	—
98-99	Huntsville	CHL	64	26	78	104	86	15	5	11	16	12
	CHL	Totals	242	93	220	313	219	27	8	24	32	14

Born; 2/9/74, Riga, Latvia. 6-0, 195. 1996-97 CeHL First Team All-Star. 1998-99 CHL Defenseman on the Year. Member of 1995-96 SHL Champion Huntsville Channel Cats. Member of 1998-99 CHL Champion Huntsville Channel Cats.

Mike Bondy — Defenseman

Regular Season — Playoffs

Season	Team	League	GP	G	A	PTS	PIM	GP	G	A	PTS	PIM
97-98	Huntsville	CHL	61	20	19	39	56	3	0	0	0	2
98-99	Detroit	IHL	14	3	1	4	2	—	—	—	—	—
98-99	Flint	UHL	46	6	22	28	68	—	—	—	—	—
98-99	Port Huron	UHL	8	2	6	8	12	7	2	0	2	6
	UHL	Totals	54	8	28	36	80	7	2	0	2	6

Born; 5/9/72, Horrow, Ontario. 6-0, 185. Selected by Topeka in 1998 CHL Expansion Draft. Traded to Muskegon by Flint with Chad Grills for Jan Klimes, Mark Vilneff and David Beauregard (2/99). Traded to Port Huron by Muskegon for Kevin Boyd and Chris Neil (3/99). Last amateur club; St. Thomas Univeristy

Josh Boni — Center

Regular Season — Playoffs

Season	Team	League	GP	G	A	PTS	PIM	GP	G	A	PTS	PIM
94-95	Fife	BHL	10	3	9	12	16	—	—	—	—	—
94-95	Durham	BHL	21	17	15	32	96	—	—	—	—	—
95-96	Milton Keynes	BHL	38	18	32	50	99	—	—	—	—	—
96-97	Telford	BNL	51	35	88	123	210	—	—	—	—	—
97-98	Central Texas	WPHL	34	15	27	42	94	4	1	1	2	6
98-99	Central Texas	WPHL	35	24	30	54	94	—	—	—	—	—
98-99	Monroe	WPHL	30	14	38	52	74	6	2	5	7	18
	WPHL	Totals	99	53	93	146	260	10	3	6	9	24

Born; 8/26/74, Toronto, Ontario. 6-2, 220. Traded to Monroe by Central Texas for Darren Dougan (1/99).

Brian Bonin — Center

Regular Season — Playoffs

Season	Team	League	GP	G	A	PTS	PIM	GP	G	A	PTS	PIM
96-97	Cleveland	IHL	60	13	26	39	18	1	1	0	1	0
97-98	Syracuse	AHL	67	31	38	69	46	5	1	3	4	6
98-99	Kansas City	IHL	19	2	5	7	10	—	—	—	—	—
98-99	Adirondack	AHL	54	19	16	35	31	2	0	0	0	0
	AHL	Totals	121	50	54	104	77	7	1	3	4	6
	IHL	Totals	79	15	31	46	28	1	1	0	1	0

Born; 11/28/73, White Bear Lake, Minnesota. 5-10, 185. Drafted by Pittsburgh Penguins (9th choice, 211th overall) in 1992 Entry Draft. Last amateur club; University of Minnesota (WCHA).

Rob Bonneau — Left Wing

Regular Season — Playoffs

Season	Team	League	GP	G	A	PTS	PIM	GP	G	A	PTS	PIM
96-97	Massachusetts	H.E.	34	16	31	47	58	—	—	—	—	—
96-97	Portland	AHL	1	1	1	2	0	—	—	—	—	—
97-98	Portland	AHL	20	4	6	10	8	—	—	—	—	—
97-98	Hampton Roads	ECHL	43	19	31	50	43	20	8	5	13	22
98-99	Orlando	IHL	45	7	13	20	34	—	—	—	—	—
98-99	Utah	IHL	20	6	13	19	8	—	—	—	—	—
	IHL	Totals	65	13	26	39	42	—	—	—	—	—
	AHL	Totals	21	5	7	12	8	20	8	5	13	22

Born; 11/2/73, Springfield, Massachusetts. 6-0, 175. Member of 1997-98 ECHL Champion Hampton Roads Admirals. Last amateur club; University of Massachusetts (Hockey East).

Doug Bonner — Goaltender

Regular Season — Playoffs

Season	Team	League	GP	W	L	T	MIN	SO	AVG	GP	W	L	MIN	SO	AVG
96-97	St. John's	AHL	11	0	4	1	366	0	4.27	—	—	—	—	—	—
96-97	Peoria	ECHL	23	13	8	1	1315	1	2.87	10	6	3	541	0	3.10
97-98	St. John's	AHL	2	2	0	0	120	1	1.50	—	—	—	—	—	—
97-98	Louisiana	ECHL	54	*36	11	6	3165	1	3.03	12	8	4	772	1	3.65
98-99	St. John's	AHL	4	0	3	1	175	0	4.47	—	—	—	—	—	—
98-99	Louisiana	ECHL	45	28	13	3	2593	1	3.03	5	2	3	299	0	2.61
	AHL	Totals	17	2	7	1	661	1	3.81	—	—	—	—	—	—
	ECHL	Totals	122	77	32	10	7073	3	3.00	27	16	10	1612	1	3.28

Born; 10/15/76, Tacoma, Washington. 5-10, 175. Drafted by Toronto Maple Leafs (3rd choice, 139th overall) in 1995 Entry Draft. Last amateur club; Seattle

Gene Bono — Goaltender

Regular Season — Playoffs

Season	Team	League	GP	W	L	T	MIN	SO	AVG	GP	W	L	MIN	SO	AVG
97-98	Lake Charles	WPHL	1	0	1	0	60	0	6.00	—	—	—	—	—	—
98-99	Phoenix	WCHL	13	4	6	0	630	0	4.38	—	—	—	—	—	—

Born; 10/15/74, Boston, Massachusetts. 6-1, 190. Last amateur club; Massachusetts-Boston (NCAA 3).

Jason Bonsignore — Center
Regular Season / Playoffs

Season	Team	League	GP	G	A	PTS	PIM	GP	G	A	PTS	PIM
94-95	Niagara Falls	OHL	26	12	21	33	51	—	—	—	—	—
94-95	Sudbury	OHL	23	15	14	29	45	17	13	10	23	12
94-95	Edmonton	NHL	1	1	0	1	0	—	—	—	—	—
95-96	Sudbury	OHL	18	10	16	26	37	—	—	—	—	—
95-96	Edmonton	NHL	20	0	2	2	4	—	—	—	—	—
95-96	Cape Breton	AHL	12	1	4	5	12	—	—	—	—	—
96-97	Hamilton	AHL	78	21	33	54	78	7	0	0	0	4
97-98	Tampa Bay	NHL	35	2	8	10	22	—	—	—	—	—
97-98	Hamilton	AHL	8	0	2	2	14	—	—	—	—	—
97-98	San Antonio	IHL	22	3	8	11	34	—	—	—	—	—
97-98	Cleveland	IHL	6	4	0	4	32	8	1	1	2	20
98-99	Cleveland	IHL	48	14	19	33	68	—	—	—	—	—
98-99	Tampa Bay	NHL	23	0	3	3	8	—	—	—	—	—
	NHL	Totals	79	3	13	16	34	—	—	—	—	—
	AHL	Totals	98	22	39	61	104	7	0	0	0	4
	IHL	Totals	76	21	27	48	134	8	1	1	2	20

Born; 4/15/76, Rochester, New York. 6-4, 208. Drafted by Edmonton Oilers (1st choice, 4rth overall) in 1994 Entry Draft. Traded to Tampa Bay Lightning by Edmonton with Bryan Marchment and Steve Kelly for Roman Hamrlik and Paul Comrie (12/30/97). Signed as a free agent by Toronto Maple Leafs (7/15/99). Last amateur club; Sudbury (OHL).

Dennis Bonvie — Right Wing
Regular Season / Playoffs

Season	Team	League	GP	G	A	PTS	PIM	GP	G	A	PTS	PIM
93-94	Cape Breton	AHL	63	1	10	11	278	4	0	0	0	11
94-95	Edmonton	NHL	2	0	0	0	0	—	—	—	—	—
94-95	Cape Breton	AHL	74	5	15	20	422	—	—	—	—	—
95-96	Edmonton	NHL	8	0	0	0	47	—	—	—	—	—
95-96	Cape Breton	AHL	38	13	14	27	269	—	—	—	—	—
96-97	Hamilton	AHL	73	9	20	29	*522	22	3	11	14	*91
97-98	Edmonton	NHL	4	0	0	0	27	—	—	—	—	—
97-98	Hamilton	AHL	57	11	19	30	295	9	0	5	5	18
98-99	Chicago	NHL	11	0	0	0	44	—	—	—	—	—
98-99	Portland	AHL	3	1	0	1	16	—	—	—	—	—
98-99	Philadelphia	AHL	37	4	10	14	158	14	3	3	6	26
	NHL	Totals	25	0	0	0	118	—	—	—	—	—
	AHL	Totals	345	43	88	131	1960	49	6	19	25	146

Born; 7/23/73, Antigosh, Nova Scotia. 5-11, 210. Signed as a free agent by Edmonton Oilers (8/25/94). Selected by Chicago Blackhawks from Edmonton in NHL Waiver Draft (10/5/98).Traded to Philadelphia Flyers by Chicago for Frank Bialowas (1/8/99). Last amateur club; North Bay (OHL).

Derek Booth — Defenseman
Regular Season / Playoffs

Season	Team	League	GP	G	A	PTS	PIM	GP	G	A	PTS	PIM
91-92	Phoenix	IHL	35	2	11	13	58	—	—	—	—	—
91-92	Toledo	ECHL	20	3	17	20	46	—	—	—	—	—
92-93	Adirondack	AHL	8	0	1	1	25	—	—	—	—	—
92-93	Toledo	ECHL	57	18	46	64	198	16	7	14	21	65
93-94	Rochester	AHL	45	2	8	10	82	—	—	—	—	—
93-94	South Carolina	ECHL	3	0	1	1	15	—	—	—	—	—
94-95	South Carolina	ECHL	66	3	30	36	158	9	3	4	7	28
95-96	Vienna	Austria	33	9	19	28	81	—	—	—	—	—
96-97		Austria										
97-98	Klagenfurter	Austria	44	4	10	14	56	—	—	—	—	—
98-99	Abilene	WPHL	68	6	37	43	110	3	0	0	0	4
	AHL	Totals	53	2	9	11	107	—	—	—	—	—
	ECHL	Totals	146	24	94	118	417	25	10	18	28	93

Born; 7/19/70, Niagara Falls (OHL). 6-1, 195. 1992-93 ECHL Defenseman of the Year. 1992-93 ECHL First Team All-Star. Member of 1992-93 ECHL Champion Toledo Storm. Last amateur club; Niagara Falls (OHL).

Ken Boone — Left Wing
Regular Season / Playoffs

Season	Team	League	GP	G	A	PTS	PIM	GP	G	A	PTS	PIM
98-99	Peoria	ECHL	61	3	4	7	318	4	1	0	1	13

Born; 4/21/76, Hamilton, Ontario. 6-3, 210. Last amateur club; Cambria (CIAU).

Nick Bootland — Left Wing
Regular Season / Playoffs

Season	Team	League	GP	G	A	PTS	PIM	GP	G	A	PTS	PIM
98-99	Hershey	AHL	62	3	6	9	122	—	—	—	—	—

Born; 7/31/78, Shelbourne, Ontario. 6-0, 210. Drafted by Dallas Stars (8th choice, 220th overall) in 1996 Entry Draft. Signed as a free agent by Colorado Avalanche (8/6/98). Last amateur club; Guelph (OHL).

Andy Borggaard — Left Wing
Regular Season / Playoffs

Season	Team	League	GP	G	A	PTS	PIM	GP	G	A	PTS	PIM
93-94	Nashville	ECHL	18	5	1	6	45	—	—	—	—	—
93-94	Charlotte	ECHL	2	1	0	1	5	—	—	—	—	—
93-94	Huntington	ECHL	13	2	2	4	2	—	—	—	—	—
94-95	Raleigh	ECHL	4	0	0	0	0	—	—	—	—	—
94-95	West Palm Beach	SUN	3	1	0	1	0	—	—	—	—	—
94-95	Lakeland	SUN	3	0	2	2	9	1	0	0	0	4
94-95	Tulsa	CHL	4	2	1	3	0	—	—	—	—	—
94-95	Dallas	CHL	6	1	0	1	6	—	—	—	—	—
95-96	Detroit	CoHL	4	1	3	4	19	—	—	—	—	—
96-97	Knoxville	ECHL	1	0	0	0	2	—	—	—	—	—
97-98												
98-99	Augusta	ECHL	1	0	0	0	0	—	—	—	—	—
98-99	Baton Rouge	ECHL	5	1	0	1	24	—	—	—	—	—
98-99	Charlotte	ECHL	2	0	0	0	0	—	—	—	—	—
98-99	Jacksonville	ECHL	8	3	1	4	2	—	—	—	—	—
98-99	Tallahassee	ECHL	2	0	0	0	4	—	—	—	—	—
	ECHL	Totals	56	12	4	16	84	—	—	—	—	—
	CHL	Totals	10	3	1	4	6	—	—	—	—	—
	SUN	Totals	6	1	2	3	9	1	0	0	0	4

Born; 11/17/71, Worcester, Massachusetts. 6-1, 201.

George Bosak — Goaltender
Regular Season / Playoffs

Season	Team	League	GP	W	L	T	MIN	SO	AVG	GP	W	L	MIN	SO	AVG
95-96	Winston-Salem	SHL	21	5	6	1	872	0	4.89	1	0	0	18	0	3.25
97-98	Binghamton	UHL	6	0	2	0	184	0	7.50	—	—	—	—	—	—
98-99	Waco	WPHL	19	3	7	3	785	1	4.74	—	—	—	—	—	—

Born; 8/22/72, Philadelphia, Pennsylvania. 6-0, 185.

Joel Boschman — Defenseman
Regular Season / Playoffs

Season	Team	League	GP	G	A	PTS	PIM	GP	G	A	PTS	PIM
97-98	Spokane	WHL	9	0	0	0	16	—	—	—	—	—
97-98	Red Deer	WHL	27	0	6	6	61	—	—	—	—	—
97-98	Prince Albert	WHL	29	1	7	8	69	—	—	—	—	—
97-98	Wichita	WCHL	8	0	4	4	9	15	0	0	0	25
98-99	Lake Charles	WPHL	64	3	12	15	138	9	0	1	1	28

Born; 8/17/77, Saskatoon, Saskatchewan. 6-2, 210. Last amateur club; Prince Albert (WHL).

Scott Boston — Defenseman

Regular Season / Playoffs

Season	Team	League	GP	G	A	PTS	PIM	GP	G	A	PTS	PIM
92-93	Atlanta	IHL	76	2	17	19	75	2	0	0	0	0
93-94	Atlanta	IHL	7	0	0	0	2	—	—	—	—	—
93-94	Knoxville	ECHL	64	9	30	39	213	—	—	—	—	—
94-95	Rochester	AHL	16	1	1	2	6	—	—	—	—	—
94-95	South Carolina	ECHL	48	18	33	51	137	9	2	8	10	33
95-96	South Carolina	ECHL	67	12	46	58	163	8	3	10	13	18
96-97	St. John's	AHL	6	0	1	1	0	—	—	—	—	—
96-97	South Carolina	ECHL	42	12	30	42	85	—	—	—	—	—
96-97	Louisville	ECHL	18	2	6	8	28	—	—	—	—	—
97-98	Tacoma	WCHL	63	17	50	67	104	12	1	9	10	14
98-99	Tacoma	WCHL	64	11	49	60	102	11	5	10	15	20
	IHL	Totals	83	2	17	19	77	2	0	0	0	0
	AHL	Totals	22	1	2	3	6	—	—	—	—	—
	ECHL	Totals	239	53	145	198	806	17	5	18	23	51
	WCHL	Totals	127	28	99	127	206	23	6	19	25	34

Born; 7/13/71, Ottawa, Ontario. 6-2, 180. Signed as a free agent by Tampa Bay Lightning (8/13/92). Traded to Louisville RiverFrogs with Kyle Ferguson by South Carolina for Chris Rowland (1997). 1994-95 ECHL Second Team All-Star. 1998-99 WCHL Second Team All-Star. Member of 1998-99 WCHL Champion Tacoma Sabrecats. Last amateur club: Belleville (OHL).

Jason Botterill — Left Wing

Regular Season / Playoffs

Season	Team	League	GP	G	A	PTS	PIM	GP	G	A	PTS	PIM
97-98	Dallas	NHL	4	0	0	0	19	—	—	—	—	—
97-98	Michigan	IHL	50	11	11	22	82	4	0	0	0	5
98-99	Dallas	NHL	17	0	0	0	23	—	—	—	—	—
98-99	Michigan	IHL	56	13	25	38	106	5	2	1	3	4
	NHL	Totals	21	0	0	0	42	—	—	—	—	—
	IHL	Totals	106	24	36	60	188	9	2	1	3	9

Born; 5/19/76, Edmonton, Alberta. 6-3, 205. Drafted by Dallas Stars (1st choice, 20th overall) in 1994 Entry Draft. Traded to Atlanta Thrashers by Dallas for Jamie Pushor (7/15/99). Last amateur club; University of Michigan (CCHA).

Frederic Bouchard — Defenseman

Regular Season / Playoffs

Season	Team	League	GP	G	A	PTS	PIM	GP	G	A	PTS	PIM
97-98	Michigan	IHL	53	2	12	14	46	—	—	—	—	—
97-98	Dayton	ECHL	3	1	2	3	0	5	1	5	6	2
98-99	Michigan	IHL	3	0	1	1	17	—	—	—	—	—
98-99	Dayton	ECHL	50	3	18	21	75	—	—	—	—	—
	IHL	Totals	56	2	13	15	63					
	ECHL	Totals	53	4	20	24	75	5	1	5	6	2

Born; 7/30/76, Beauport, Quebec. 6-0, 181. Signed as a free agent by Dallas Stars (8/14/97). Last amateur club; Chicoutimi (QMJHL).

J-F Bouchard — Right Wing

Regular Season / Playoffs

Season	Team	League	GP	G	A	PTS	PIM	GP	G	A	PTS	PIM
96-97	Macon		61	15	43	58	63	—	—	—	—	—
97-98												
98-99	Tulsa	CHL	2	0	1	1	0	—	—	—	—	—
	CHL	Totals	63	15	44	59	63	—	—	—	—	—

Born; 2/24/75, St. Jean, Quebec. 6-0, 192.

Robin Bouchard — Right Wing

Regular Season / Playoffs

Season	Team	League	GP	G	A	PTS	PIM	GP	G	A	PTS	PIM
94-95	Columbus	ECHL	46	30	33	63	188	3	0	3	3	38
94-95	Roanoke	ECHL	10	1	0	1	25	—	—	—	—	—
95-96	Flint	CoHL	73	56	51	107	247	15	8	9	17	52
96-97	Fort Wayne	IHL	2	1	0	1	2	—	—	—	—	—
96-97	Flint	CoHL	16	6	12	18	60	—	—	—	—	—
96-97	Muskegon	CoHL	52	34	23	57	220	3	2	1	3	6
97-98	Muskegon	UHL	72	55	48	103	126	11	4	5	9	34
98-99	Muskegon	UHL	70	48	34	82	148	18	*13	9	22	34
	UHL	Totals	283	199	168	367	801	47	27	24	51	126
	ECHL	Totals	56	31	33	64	213	3	0	3	3	38

Born; 10/22/73, Jomquiere, Quebec. 5-11, 185. Traded to Muskegon Fury for CoHL rights to Steve Walker by Flint (1996). Member of 1995-96 Colonial Cup Champion Flint Generals. Member of 1998-99 UHL Champion Muskegon Fury. Last amateur club; Shawinagan (QMJHL).

Brian Boucher — Goaltender

Regular Season / Playoffs

Season	Team	League	GP	W	L	T	MIN	SO	AVG	GP	W	L	MIN	SO	AVG
97-98	Philadelphia	AHL	34	16	12	3	1901	0	3.19	2	0	0	31	0	1.95
98-99	Philadelphia	AHL	36	20	8	5	2061	2	2.59	16	9	7	947	0	2.85
	AHL	Totals	70	36	20	8	3962	2	2.88	18	9	7	978	0	2.82

Born; 1/2/77, Woonsocket, Rhode Island. 6-1, 190. Drafted by Philadelphia Flyers (1st choice, 22nd overall) in 1995 Entry Draft. Member of 1997-98 AHL Champion Philadelphia Phantoms. Last amateur club; Tri-City (WHL).

Tyler Boucher — Center

Regular Season / Playoffs

Season	Team	League	GP	G	A	PTS	PIM	GP	G	A	PTS	PIM
96-97	Utah	IHL	5	0	0	0	17	—	—	—	—	—
96-97	New Mexico	WPHL	48	9	17	26	263	6	1	1	2	12
97-98	New Mexico	WPHL	55	12	20	32	185	10	2	3	5	38
98-99	Corpus Christi	WPHL	44	9	9	18	115	3	0	0	0	12
	WPHL	Totals	147	30	46	76	563	19	3	4	7	62

Born; 4/27/72, The Pas, Manitoba. 5-8, 165. Last amateur club; Brandon University (CWUAA).

Carl Boudreau — Center

Regular Season / Playoffs

Season	Team	League	GP	G	A	PTS	PIM	GP	G	A	PTS	PIM
92-93	Oklahoma City	CeHL	48	27	44	71	109	11	8	5	13	20
93-94	Oklahoma City	CeHL	64	40	67	107	93	7	5	4	9	14
94-95		France										
95-96	Oklahoma City	CeHL	59	22	49	71	98	12	5	7	12	16
96-97	Reno	WCHL	55	32	53	85	57	—	—	—	—	—
97-98	San Angelo	WPHL	68	35	*92	*127	60	3	1	0	1	16
98-99	San Angelo	WPHL	68	33	*85	*118	88	17	7	*18	*25	25
	CeHL	Totals	171	89	160	249	300	30	18	16	34	50
	WPHL	Totals	136	68	177	245	148	20	8	18	26	41

Born; 8/31/71, Victoriaville, Quebec. 5-11, 180. 1992-93 CeHL First Team All-Star. Member of 1995-96 CeHL champion Oklahoma City Blazers. Last amateur club; Trois Rivieres (QMJHL).

Francois Bouillon — Defenseman

Regular Season / Playoffs

Season	Team	League	GP	G	A	PTS	PIM	GP	G	A	PTS	PIM
96-97	Wheeling	ECHL	69	10	32	42	77	3	0	2	2	10
97-98	Quebec	IHL	71	8	27	35	76	—	—	—	—	—
98-99	Fredericton	AHL	79	19	36	55	174	5	2	1	3	0

Born; 10/17/75, New York, New York. 5-9, 160. Signed as a free agent by Montreal Canadiens (8/18/98). Last amateur club; Granby (QMJHL).

Jesse Boulerice — Right Wing

Regular Season / Playoffs

Season	Team	League	GP	G	A	PTS	PIM	GP	G	A	PTS	PIM
98-99	Philadelphia	AHL	24	1	2	3	82	—	—	—	—	—
98-99	New Orleans	ECHL	12	0	1	1	38	—	—	—	—	—

Born; 8/10/78, Plattsburgh, New York. 6-1, 214. Drafted by Philadelphia Flyers (4th choice, 133rd overall) in 1996 Entry Draft. Last amateur club; Plymouth

Eric Boulton — Left Wing
Regular Season / Playoffs

Season	Team	League	GP	G	A	PTS	PIM	GP	G	A	PTS	PIM
96-97	Binghamton	AHL	23	2	3	5	67	3	0	0	0	4
96-97	Charlotte	ECHL	44	14	11	25	325	3	0	1	1	6
97-98	Fort Wayne	IHL	8	0	2	2	42	—	—	—	—	—
97-98	Charlotte	ECHL	53	11	16	27	202	4	1	0	1	0
98-99	Florida	ECHL	26	9	13	22	143	—	—	—	—	—
98-99	Houston	IHL	7	1	0	1	41	—	—	—	—	—
98-99	Kentucky	AHL	34	3	3	6	154	10	0	1	1	36
	AHL	Totals	57	5	6	11	221	13	0	1	1	40
	IHL	Totals	15	1	2	3	83	—	—	—	—	—
	ECHL	Totals	97	25	27	52	527	7	1	1	2	6

Born; 8/17/76, Halifax, Nova Scotia. Drafted by New York Rangers (12th choice, 234th overall) in 1994 Entry Draft. Traded by Charlotte to Florida for future considerations (9/98). Last amateur club; Sarnia (OHL).

Francois Bourbeau — Goaltender
Regular Season / Playoffs

Season	Team	League	GP	W	L	T	MIN	SO	AVG	GP	W	L	MIN	SO	AVG
98-99	El Paso	WPHL	22	11	4	3	1147	0	3.35	—	—	—	—	—	—

Born; 8/13/75, Boucherville, Quebec. 5-11, 170. Last amateur club; Middlebury (NCAA 3).

Francois Bourdeau — Defenseman
Regular Season / Playoffs

Season	Team	League	GP	G	A	PTS	PIM	GP	G	A	PTS	PIM
93-94	Johnstown	ECHL	63	6	17	23	61	3	0	1	1	0
94-95	Fort Worth	CeHL	60	7	21	28	119	—	—	—	—	—
95-96												
96-97		France	20	5	11	16	NA	—	—	—	—	—
97-98	Dragon Roven	France	34	6	24	30	NA	—	—	—	—	—
98-99	Idaho	WCHL	43	3	10	13	50	—	—	—	—	—
98-99	Hampton Roads	ECHL	23	1	8	9	34	4	0	1	1	2
	ECHL	Totals	86	7	25	32	95	7	0	2	2	2

Born; 8/28/72, LaSalle, Quebec. 6-0, 195. Last amateur club; Hull (QMJHL).

Brad Bourhis — Right Wing
Regular Season / Playoffs

Season	Team	League	GP	G	A	PTS	PIM	GP	G	A	PTS	PIM
98-99	Wichita	CHL	1	0	0	0	0	—	—	—	—	—

Born; 9/20/75, Saskatoon, Saskatchewan. 5-11, 205.

David Bouskill — Left Wing
Regular Season / Playoffs

Season	Team	League	GP	G	A	PTS	PIM	GP	G	A	PTS	PIM
98-99	Fort Worth	CHL	1	0	0	0	2	—	—	—	—	—
98-99	Muskegon	UHL	40	2	2	4	28	2	0	0	0	0

Born; 11/9/76, Georgetown, Ontario. 6-4, 218. Member of 1998-99 UHL Champion Muskegon Fury. Last amateur club; Georgetown (OHA).

Dany Bousquet — Center
Regular Season / Playoffs

Season	Team	League	GP	G	A	PTS	PIM	GP	G	A	PTS	PIM
95-96	Canada	National	42	15	16	31	34	—	—	—	—	—
95-96	Hamton Roads	ECHL	5	2	0	2	12	3	3	1	4	0
96-97	Birmingham	ECHL	68	54	53	107	39	8	6	7	13	12
97-98	Cincinnati	IHL	1	0	0	0	0	—	—	—	—	—
97-98	Birmingham	ECHL	70	50	49	99	84	4	3	1	4	0
98-99	Pee Dee	ECHL	62	36	54	90	63	13	7	12	19	20
98-99	Cincinnati	AHL	8	0	2	2	4	—	—	—	—	—
	ECHL	Totals	205	142	156	298	114	28	19	21	40	32

Born; 4/3/73, Montreal, Quebec. 5-11, 165. Drafted by Washington Capitals (10th choice, 277th overall) in 1993 Entry Draft. 1996-97 ECHL Rookie of the Year. 1996-97 ECHL Second Team All-Star.

J.F. Boutin — Left Wing
Regular Season / Playoffs

Season	Team	League	GP	G	A	PTS	PIM	GP	G	A	PTS	PIM
97-98	Wheeling	ECHL	64	23	30	53	134	15	4	6	10	49
98-99	Worcester	AHL	2	1	0	1	2	—	—	—	—	—
98-99	Orlando	IHL	2	0	0	0	4	—	—	—	—	—
98-99	Peoria	ECHL	61	28	34	62	114	4	1	2	3	4
	ECHL	Totals	125	51	64	115	248	19	5	8	13	53

Born; 11/17/76, Fleurimont, Quebec. 5-11, 193. Traded to Peoria by Wheeling with Alex Matvichuk for Rob Giffin (8/98). Last amateur club; Chicoutimi

Chris Bowen — Left Wing
Regular Season / Playoffs

Season	Team	League	GP	G	A	PTS	PIM	GP	G	A	PTS	PIM
97-98	Oklahoma City	CHL	19	2	4	6	21	—	—	—	—	—
97-98	Louisiana	ECHL	2	0	0	0	15	—	—	—	—	—
97-98	New Orleans	ECHL	2	0	0	0	0	—	—	—	—	—
97-98	Johnstown	ECHL	2	0	0	0	0	—	—	—	—	—
98-99	Topeka	CHL	47	3	2	5	96	3	0	0	0	0
	CHL	Totals	66	5	6	11	117	3	0	0	0	0
	ECHL	Totals	6	0	0	0	15	—	—	—	—	—

Born; 3/7/76, Barrie, Ontario. 6-1 195.

Curtis Bowen — Left Wing
Regular Season / Playoffs

Season	Team	League	GP	G	A	PTS	PIM	GP	G	A	PTS	PIM
94-95	Adirondack	AHL	64	6	11	17	71	4	0	2	2	4
95-96	Adirondack	AHL	3	0	0	0	0	—	—	—	—	—
95-96	Canada	National	31	8	8	16	48	—	—	—	—	—
96-97	Adirondack	AHL	78	11	11	22	110	4	0	0	0	2
97-98	Canada	National	46	8	22	30	73	—	—	—	—	—
98-99	Manitoba	IHL	45	10	12	22	54	—	—	—	—	—
	AHL	Totals	145	17	22	39	181	8	0	2	2	6

Born; 3/24/74, Kenora, Ontario. 6-1, 195. Drafted by Detroit Red Wings (1st choice, 22nd overall) 1992 Entry Draft. Last amateur club; Ottawa (OHL).

Jason Bowen — Left Wing
Regular Season / Playoffs

Season	Team	League	GP	G	A	PTS	PIM	GP	G	A	PTS	PIM
92-93	Tri-City	WHL	62	10	12	22	219	3	1	1	2	18
92-93	Philadelphia	NHL	7	1	0	1	2	—	—	—	—	—
93-94	Philadelphia	NHL	56	1	5	6	87	—	—	—	—	—
94-95	Philadelphia	NHL	4	0	0	0	0	—	—	—	—	—
94-95	Hershey	AHL	55	5	5	10	116	6	0	0	0	46
95-96	Philadelphia	NHL	2	0	0	0	2	—	—	—	—	—
95-96	Hershey	AHL	72	6	7	13	128	4	2	0	2	13
96-97	Philadelphia	NHL	4	0	1	1	8	—	—	—	—	—
96-97	Philadelphia	AHL	61	10	12	22	160	6	0	1	1	10
97-98	Edmonton	NHL	4	0	0	0	10	—	—	—	—	—
97-98	Philadelphia	AHL	3	0	0	0	19	—	—	—	—	—
97-98	Hamilton	AHL	51	5	14	19	108	7	1	1	2	22
98-99	Hamilton	AHL	58	3	3	6	178	11	0	1	1	16
	NHL	Totals	77	2	6	8	109	—	—	—	—	—
	AHL	Totals	300	29	41	70	709	34	3	3	6	107

Born; 11/9/73, Port Alice, British Columbia. 6-4, 208. Drafted by Philadelphia Flyers (2nd choice, 15th overall) in 1992 Entry Draft. Traded to Edmonton Oilers by Philadelphia for Brantt Myhres (10/15/97). Last amateur club; Tri-City

Rodney Bowers — Left Wing
Regular Season / Playoffs

Season	Team	League	GP	G	A	PTS	PIM	GP	G	A	PTS	PIM
97-98	Pensacola	ECHL	32	5	4	9	18	—	—	—	—	—
97-98	Peoria	ECHL	3	1	0	1	0	—	—	—	—	—
97-98	Tucson	WCHL	19	4	13	17	10	—	—	—	—	—
98-99	Red Deer College	CIAU										
	ECHL	Totals	35	6	4	10	18	—	—	—	—	—

Born; 3/10/76, Red Deer, Alberta. 6-0, 180.

Bill Bowler — Center

Regular Season / Playoffs

Season	Team	League	GP	G	A	PTS	PIM	GP	G	A	PTS	PIM
94-95	Windsor	OHL	61	22	102	135	63	10	7	15	22	13
94-95	Las Vegas	IHL	—	—	—	—	—	1	0	0	0	0
95-96	Las Vegas	IHL	75	31	55	86	26	14	3	5	8	22
96-97	Houston	IHL	78	22	43	65	79	13	2	5	7	6
97-98	Hamilton	AHL	46	7	24	31	22	—	—	—	—	—
97-98	Manitoba	IHL	30	9	25	34	30	3	0	2	2	4
98-99	Manitoba	IHL	82	26	67	93	59	5	6	5	11	6
	IHL	Totals	265	88	190	278	194	33	11	15	26	34

Born; 9/25/74, Toronto, Ontario. 5-9, 180. Traded to Houston Aeros by Las Vegas Thunder to complete earlier trade (7/96). 1998-99 IHL Second Team All-Star. Last amateur club; Windsor (OHL).

Cody Bowtell — Left Wing

Regular Season / Playoffs

Season	Team	League	GP	G	A	PTS	PIM	GP	G	A	PTS	PIM
97-98	Dayton	ECHL	39	6	3	9	35	—	—	—	—	—
97-98	Pee Dee	ECHL	2	0	1	1	10	—	—	—	—	—
97-98	Mississippi	ECHL	14	7	11	18	6	—	—	—	—	—
98-99	Mississippi	ECHL	49	18	24	42	25	18	3	4	7	4
	ECHL	Totals	104	31	39	70	76	18	3	4	7	4

Born; 4/25/74, Wainswright, Alberta. 5-11, 188. Traded to Mississippi by Pee Deewith Vaclav Nedomansky for Forbes MacPherson (3/98). Member of 1998-99 ECHL Champion Mississippi SeaWolves. Last amateur club; Alaska-Fairbanks (CCHA).

Marc Boxer — Left Wing

Regular Season / Playoffs

Season	Team	League	GP	G	A	PTS	PIM	GP	G	A	PTS	PIM
95-96	Louisville	ECHL	62	7	27	34	66	3	0	1	1	2
96-97	Memphis	CeHL	64	20	33	53	120	14	4	7	11	18
97-98	Memphis	CHL	62	13	40	53	154	4	0	2	2	14
98-99	Bayreuth	German 1	22	8	13	21	34	—	—	—	—	—
98-99	Tucson	WCHL	21	4	13	17	66	—	—	—	—	—
98-99	Bakersfield	WCHL	15	3	4	7	20	2	0	0	0	0
	CHL	Totals	126	33	73	106	274	18	4	9	13	32
	WCHL	Totals	36	7	17	24	86	2	0	0	0	0

Born; 1/27/71, Fort Worth, Texas. 5-10, 185. Selected by San Antonio in 1998 CHL Expansion Draft. Selected by Bakersfield in 1998 WCHL Dispersal Draft. Last amateur club; Miami of Ohio (CCHA).

Ian Boyce — Left Wing

Regular Season / Playoffs

Season	Team	League	GP	G	A	PTS	PIM	GP	G	A	PTS	PIM
90-91	Fort Wayne	IHL	39	10	12	22	11	19	5	4	9	0
90-91	Rochester	AHL	12	1	2	3	2	—	—	—	—	—
91-92	Fort Wayne	IHL	38	12	15	27	29	—	—	—	—	—
91-92	Rochester	AHL	20	5	8	13	4	16	3	1	4	0
92-93	Fort Wayne	IHL	69	19	34	53	63	12	3	1	4	6
93-94	Fort Wayne	IHL	55	12	16	28	26	18	3	6	9	2
94-95	Fort Wayne	IHL	76	26	22	48	20	4	2	1	3	4
95-96	San Francisco	IHL	77	25	22	47	60	4	0	1	1	10
96-97	Kansas City	IHL	68	16	26	42	43	3	1	0	1	0
97-98	Fort Wayne	IHL	66	15	13	28	14	2	0	0	0	0
98-99	Fort Wayne	IHL	75	20	24	44	80	2	0	0	0	0
	IHL	Totals	563	155	184	339	346	64	14	13	27	22
	AHL	Totals	32	6	10	16	6	16	3	1	4	0

Born; 1/24/68, St. Laurent, Quebec. 5-9, 177. Member of 1992-93 IHL champion Ft. Wayne Komets. Last amateur club; Vermont (ECAC).

Kevin Boyd — Left Wing

Regular Season / Playoffs

Season	Team	League	GP	G	A	PTS	PIM	GP	G	A	PTS	PIM
97-98	Detroit	IHL	2	0	0	0	2	—	—	—	—	—
97-98	Raleigh	ECHL	33	2	5	7	79	—	—	—	—	—
97-98	Dayton	ECHL	25	4	1	5	77	4	0	1	1	5
98-99	Port Huron	UHL	49	10	15	25	67	—	—	—	—	—
98-99	Muskegon	UHL	7	1	3	4	17	9	1	0	1	29
	ECHL	Totals	58	6	6	12	156	4	0	1	1	5
	UHL	Totals	56	11	18	29	84	9	1	0	1	29

Born; 5/19/77, Fredericton, New Brunswick. 6-4, 220. Drafted by Ottawa Senators (5th choice, 103rd overall) in 1995 Entry Draft. Traded to Dayton by Raleigh for cash and future considerations (1/98). Traded to Muskegon by Port Huron with Chris Neil for Mike Bondy (3/99). Member of 1998-99 UHL Champion Muskegon Fury. Last amateur club; London (OHL).

Rick Boyd — Right Wing

Regular Season / Playoffs

Season	Team	League	GP	G	A	PTS	PIM	GP	G	A	PTS	PIM
88-89	Indianapolis	IHL	27	2	1	3	113	—	—	—	—	—
88-89	Flint	IHL	27	4	0	4	73	—	—	—	—	—
89-90	Binghamton	AHL	3	0	0	0	7	—	—	—	—	—
89-90	Maine	AHL	11	0	2	2	29	—	—	—	—	—
89-90	Johnstown	ECHL	45	5	12	17	284	—	—	—	—	—
90-91	Johnstown	ECHL	26	5	10	15	128	—	—	—	—	—
90-91	Knoxville	ECHL	1	0	0	0	0	—	—	—	—	—
90-91	Hampton Roads	ECHL	23	0	12	12	108	13	3	2	5	63
91-92												
92-93												
93-94												
94-95												
95-96	Johnstown	ECHL	50	3	15	18	253	—	—	—	—	—
96-97	Johnstown	ECHL	23	3	4	7	141	—	—	—	—	—
97-98												
98-99	Roanoke	ECHL	4	0	0	0	8	—	—	—	—	—
	IHL	Totals	54	6	1	7	186	—	—	—	—	—
	AHL	Totals	14	0	2	2	36	—	—	—	—	—
	ECHL	Totals	172	16	53	69	922	13	3	2	5	63

Born; 12/30/64, Fort St. John, British Columbia. 6-2, 210. Member of 1990-91 ECHL Champion Hampton Roads Admirals.

Zac Boyer — Right Wing

Regular Season / Playoffs

Season	Team	League	GP	G	A	PTS	PIM	GP	G	A	PTS	PIM
92-93	Indianapolis	IHL	59	7	14	21	26	—	—	—	—	—
93-94	Indianapolis	IHL	54	13	12	25	67	—	—	—	—	—
94-95	Dallas	NHL	1	0	0	0	0	2	0	0	0	0
94-95	Kalamazoo	IHL	22	9	7	16	22	15	3	9	12	8
95-96	Dallas	NHL	2	0	0	0	0	—	—	—	—	—
95-96	Michigan	IHL	67	24	27	51	27	10	4	8	12	2
96-97	Orlando	IHL	80	25	49	74	63	3	0	1	1	2
97-98	Heraklith	Austria	6	3	5	8	4	—	—	—	—	—
97-98	SC Herisau	Swiss	19	7	16	23	77	—	—	—	—	—
97-98	Dusseldorfer	German	15	2	0	2	8	2	0	0	0	0
98-99	Houston	IHL	61	16	23	39	40	1	0	0	0	0
	NHL	Totals	3	0	0	0	0	2	0	0	0	0
	IHL	Totals	343	94	132	226	245	29	7	18	25	12

Born; 10/25/71, Inuvik, Northwest Territories. 6-2, 200. Drafted by Chicago Blackhawks (4th choice, 88th overall) in 1991 Entry Draft. Signed as a free agent by Dallas Stars (7/25/94). Signed as a free agent by Houston Aeros (7/27/98). Member of 1998-99 IHL Champion Houston Aeros. Last amateur club; Kam-

Dan Boyle — Defenseman

Regular Season / Playoffs

Season	Team	League	GP	G	A	PTS	PIM	GP	G	A	PTS	PIM
97-98	Miami-Ohio	CCHA	37	14	26	40	58	—	—	—	—	—
97-98	Cincinnati	IHL	8	0	3	3	20	5	0	1	1	4
98-99	Florida	NHL	22	3	5	8	6	—	—	—	—	—
98-99	Kentucky	AHL	53	8	34	42	87	12	3	5	8	16

Born; 7/12/76, Ottawa, Ontario. 5-11, 190. Signed as a free agent by Florida Panthers (3/30/98). 1998-99 AHL All-Rookie Team. Last amateur club; University of Miami-Ohio (CCHA).

Martin Bradette
Regular Season — Goaltender — Playoffs

Season	Team	League	GP	W	L	T	MIN	SO	AVG	GP	W	L	MIN	SO	AVG
97-98	Chesapeake	ECHL	26	9	9	3	1095	0	3.73	—	—	—	—	—	—
98-99	Cleveland	IHL	4	1	2	0	206	0	4.95	—	—	—	—	—	—
98-99	Chesapeake	ECHL	1	0	0	0	13	0	9.33	—	—	—	—	—	—
98-99	Birmingham	ECHL	3	1	1	0	100	0	6.59	—	—	—	—	—	—
98-99	Winston-Salem	UHL	17	5	8	1	864	0	4.52	—	—	—	—	—	—
	ECHL	Totals	30	10	10	3	1208	0	4.02	—	—	—	—	—	—

Born; 1/20/77, Laval, Quebec. 5-11, 165. Last amateur club; Drummondville (QMJHL).

E.J. Bradley
Regular Season — Center — Playoffs

Season	Team	League	GP	G	A	PTS	PIM	GP	G	A	PTS	PIM
98-99	Johnstown	ECHL	66	13	22	35	36	—	—	—	—	—

Born; 1/1/75, New Hyde Park, New York. 5-11, 185. Last amateur club; Wisconsin (WCHA).

Matt Bradley
Regular Season — Right Wing — Playoffs

Season	Team	League	GP	G	A	PTS	PIM	GP	G	A	PTS	PIM
98-99	Kentucky	AHL	79	23	20	43	57	10	1	4	5	4

Born; 6/13/78, Stittsville, Ontario. 6-2, 195. Drafted by San Jose Sharks (4th choice, 102nd overall) in 1996 Entry Draft. Last amateur club; Kingston (OHL).

Neil Brady
Regular Season — Center — Playoffs

Season	Team	League	GP	G	A	PTS	PIM	GP	G	A	PTS	PIM
88-89	Utica	AHL	75	16	21	37	56	4	0	3	3	0
89-90	New Jersey	NHL	19	1	4	5	13	—	—	—	—	—
89-90	Utica	AHL	38	10	13	23	21	5	0	1	1	10
90-91	New Jersey	NHL	3	0	0	0	0	—	—	—	—	—
90-91	Utica	AHL	77	33	63	96	91	—	—	—	—	—
91-92	New Jersey	NHL	7	1	0	1	4	—	—	—	—	—
91-92	Utica	AHL	33	12	30	42	28	—	—	—	—	—
92-93	Ottawa	NHL	55	7	17	24	57	—	—	—	—	—
92-93	New Haven	AHL	8	6	3	9	2	—	—	—	—	—
93-94	Dallas	NHL	5	0	1	1	21	—	—	—	—	—
93-94	Kalamazoo	IHL	43	10	16	26	188	5	1	1	2	10
94-95	Kalamazoo	IHL	70	13	45	58	140	15	5	14	19	22
95-96	Michigan	IHL	61	14	20	34	127	10	1	4	5	8
96-97	Michigan	IHL	76	13	20	33	62	4	1	0	1	0
97-98	Houston	IHL	65	9	26	35	56	4	2	0	2	34
98-99	Manitoba	IHL	13	1	5	6	8	—	—	—	—	—
	NHL	Totals	89	9	22	31	95	—	—	—	—	—
	IHL	Totals	328	60	132	192	581	38	10	19	29	74
	AHL	Totals	231	77	130	207	198	9	0	4	4	10

Born; 4/12/68, Montreal, Quebec. 6-3, 205. Drafted by New Jersey Devils (1st choice, 3rd overall) in 1986 Entry Draft. Traded to Ottawa Senators by New Jersey for future considerations (9/3/92). Signed as a free agent by Dallas Stars (12/3/93). Last amateur club; Medicine Hat (WHL).

Sean Brady
Regular Season — Center — Playoffs

Season	Team	League	GP	G	A	PTS	PIM	GP	G	A	PTS	PIM
96-97	Waco	WPHL	62	20	37	57	31	—	—	—	—	—
97-98	Waco	WPHL	69	18	28	46	42	—	—	—	—	—
98-99	Fort Worth	WPHL	45	19	18	37	33	12	1	9	10	16
	WPHL	Totals	176	57	83	140	106	12	1	9	10	16

Born; 6/14/73, Napanee, Ontario. 6-1, 190. Last amateur club; Hamilton (ECAC-

Rod Branch
Regular Season — Goaltender — Playoffs

Season	Team	League	GP	W	L	T	MIN	SO	AVG	GP	W	L	MIN	SO	AVG
96-97	New Mexico	WPHL	10	7	3	0	517	0	3.94	—	—	—	—	—	—
96-97	Tulsa	CeHL	18	10	7	1	1054	0	3.76	5	2	3	291	0	3.51
97-98	Tulsa	CHL	54	24	23	4	3106	1	3.84	2	0	2	103	0	4.64
98-99	Tulsa	CHL	11	2	5	2	636	0	4.53	—	—	—	—	—	—
98-99	Topeka	CHL	37	20	16	0	2181	3	2.78	3	0	3	179	0	4.70
	CHL	Totals	120	56	51	7	6976	4	3.56	10	2	8	573	0	4.08

Born; 4/14/75, Fort St. John, British Columbia. 5-8, 160. 1997-98 CHL Community Service Award winner. Last amateur club; Prince Albert (WHL).

Aaron Brand
Regular Season — Center — Playoffs

Season	Team	League	GP	G	A	PTS	PIM	GP	G	A	PTS	PIM
95-96	Sarnia	OHL	66	46	*73	*119	110	10	7	11	18	18
95-96	St. John's	AHL	1	0	1	1	0	4	0	0	0	4
96-97	St. John's	AHL	75	15	25	40	80	11	3	2	5	2
97-98	St. John's	AHL	79	10	20	30	107	4	2	2	4	6
98-99	St. John's	AHL	80	7	26	33	88	5	1	2	3	8
	AHL	Totals	235	32	72	104	275	24	6	6	12	20

Born; 6/14/75, Toronto, Ontario. 6-0, 190. Signed as a free agent by Toronto Maple Leafs (3/21/97). Last amateur club; Sarnia (OHL).

Bob Brandon
Regular Season — Left Wing — Playoffs

Season	Team	League	GP	G	A	PTS	PIM	GP	G	A	PTS	PIM
96-97	New England	NCAA 3	24	10	13	23	NA	—	—	—	—	-
96-97	Peoria	ECHL	3	0	0	0	7	—	—	—	—	—
97-98	Fayetteville	CHL	53	13	13	26	141	—	—	—	—	—
98-99	Mississippi	ECHL	4	0	2	2	0	—	—	—	—	—
98-99	Muskegon	UHL	7	0	1	1	17	—	—	—	—	—
98-99	Asheville	UHL	15	4	8	12	25	—	—	—	—	—
98-99	Winston-Salem	UHL	39	7	5	12	72	5	0	2	2	2
	UHL	Totals	61	11	14	25	114	5	0	2	2	2
	ECHL	Totals	7	0	2	2	7	—	—	—	—	—

Born; 1/2/74, Burlington, Ontario. 6-0, 200. Traded to Asheville by Muskegon with Lubos Krajcovic for Joakim Wassberger (12/98). Traded to Winston-Salem by Asheville for Chris Torkoff (1/99). Selected by Madison in 1999 UHL Expansion Draft. Last amateur club; New England College (ECAC).

Stefan Brannare
Regular Season — Left Wing — Playoffs

Season	Team	League	GP	G	A	PTS	PIM	GP	G	A	PTS	PIM
97-98	Wheeling	ECHL	67	9	9	18	213	14	0	1	1	12
98-99	Wheeling	ECHL	60	7	12	19	149	—	—	—	—	—
	ECHL	Totals	127	16	21	37	362	14	0	1	1	12

Born; 10/17/72, Pitea, Sweden. 5-9, 192. Last amateur club; Providence College (Hockey East).

Dampy Brar
Regular Season — Right Wing — Playoffs

Season	Team	League	GP	G	A	PTS	PIM	GP	G	A	PTS	PIM
96-97	Toledo	ECHL	8	0	2	2	8	—	—	—	—	—
96-97	Nashville	CeHL	7	4	3	7	6	—	—	—	—	—
96-97	San Antonio	CeHL	40	21	19	40	48	—	—	—	—	—
97-98	Tacoma	WCHL	55	20	38	58	50	12	7	11	18	6
98-99	Las Vegas	IHL	8	1	0	1	0	—	—	—	—	—
98-99	Tacoma	WCHL	58	33	32	65	49	11	5	4	9	10
	WCHL	Totals	113	53	70	123	99	23	12	15	27	16
	CeHL	Totals	47	25	22	47	54	—	—	—	—	—

Born; 5/22/76, Sparwood, British Columbia. 6-3, 205. Selected by Wichita in San Antonio dispersal draft (6/10/97). Member of 1998-99 WCHL Champion Tacoma Sabrecats.

Chris Brassard — Right Wing

Regular Season / Playoffs

Season	Team	League	GP	G	A	PTS	PIM	GP	G	A	PTS	PIM
98-99	Fayetteville	CHL	11	1	7	8	11	—	—	—	—	—
98-99	Macon	CHL	24	6	13	19	64	3	0	1	1	11
	CHL	Totals	35	7	20	27	75	3	0	1	1	11

Born; 8/9/75, Toronto, Ontario. 6-0, 205.

Johnny Brdarovic — Left Wing

Regular Season / Playoffs

Season	Team	League	GP	G	A	PTS	PIM	GP	G	A	PTS	PIM
98-99	Utah	IHL	2	0	0	0	0	—	—	—	—	—
98-99	Fort Wayne	IHL	2	0	3	3	0	—	—	—	—	—
98-99	San Antonio	CHL	68	56	59	115	38	8	4	8	12	6
	IHL	Totals	4	0	3	3	0	—	—	—	—	—

Born; 3/21/75, Scarboro, Ontario. 5-11, 205. 1998-99 CHL Roookie of the Year. Last amateur club; York (OUAA).

Pete Brearley — Right Wing

Regular Season / Playoffs

Season	Team	League	GP	G	A	PTS	PIM	GP	G	A	PTS	PIM
97-98	Roanoke	ECHL	70	24	30	54	20	9	2	3	5	10
98-99	Roanoke	ECHL	8	2	0	2	6	—	—	—	—	—
98-99	Charlotte	ECHL	8	3	3	6	7	—	—	—	—	—
98-99	Huntington	ECHL	39	10	8	18	11	—	—	—	—	—
	ECHL	Totals	125	39	41	80	44	9	2	3	5	10

Born; 6/27/75, Bothwell, Ontario. 6-3, 215. Last amateur club; University of Waterloo (OUAA).

Trevor Bremner — Left Wing

Regular Season / Playoffs

Season	Team	League	GP	G	A	PTS	PIM	GP	G	A	PTS	PIM
98-99	Saginaw	UHL	10	0	1	1	32	—	—	—	—	—
98-99	Madison	UHL	18	0	2	2	48	—	—	—	—	—
98-99	Flint	UHL	29	0	4	4	80	—	—	—	—	—
	UHL	Totals	57	0	7	7	160	—	—	—	—	—

Born; 7/19/76, Oshawa, Ontario. 5-10, 180.

Richard Brennan — Defenseman

Regular Season / Playoffs

Season	Team	League	GP	G	A	PTS	PIM	GP	G	A	PTS	PIM
95-96	Cornwall	AHL	36	4	8	12	61	7	0	0	0	6
95-96	Brantford	CoHL	5	1	2	3	2	—	—	—	—	—
96-97	Colorado	NHL	2	0	0	0	0	—	—	—	—	—
96-97	Hershey	AHL	74	11	45	56	88	23	2	*16	18	22
97-98	San Jose	NHL	11	1	2	3	2	—	—	—	—	—
97-98	Kentucky	AHL	42	11	17	28	71	—	—	—	—	—
97-98	Hartford	AHL	9	2	4	6	12	15	4	5	9	14
98-99	Rangers	NHL	24	1	3	4	23	—	—	—	—	—
98-99	Hartford	AHL	47	4	24	28	42	—	—	—	—	—
	NHL	Totals	37	2	5	7	25	—	—	—	—	—
	AHL	Totals	208	32	98	130	274	45	6	21	27	42

Born; 11/26/72, Schenectady, New York. 6-2, 200. Drafted by Quebec Nordiques (3rd choice, 46th overall) in 1991 Entry Draft. Signed as a free agent by San Jose Sharks (7/9/97). Traded to New York Rangers by San Jose for Jason Muzzatti (3/24/98). Member of 1996-97 AHL Champion Hershey Bears. Last amateur club; Boston University (Hockey East).

Matt Brenner — Defenseman

Regular Season / Playoffs

Season	Team	League	GP	G	A	PTS	PIM	GP	G	A	PTS	PIM
96-97	Central Texas	WPHL	64	3	14	17	39	11	2	4	6	25
97-98	Central Texas	WPHL	60	1	16	17	30	3	0	0	0	2
98-99	Central Texas	WPHL	11	0	2	2	11	—	—	—	—	—
98-99	Amarillo	WPHL	37	1	10	11	30	—	—	—	—	—
	WPHL	Totals	172	5	42	47	110	14	2	4	6	27

Born; 6/22/72, Helena, Montana. 5-10, 200. Last amateur club; Illinois-Chicago (CCHA).

Dan Brenzavich — Goaltender

Regular Season / Playoffs

Season	Team	League	GP	W	L	T	MIN	SO	AVG	GP	W	L	MIN	SO	AVG
98-99	Thunder Bay	UHL	23	12	5	1	1160	1	3.00	—	—	—	—	—	—

Born; 5/27/75, Thunder Bay, Ontario. 5-9, 170. Selected by Madison in 1999 UHL Expansion Draft. Last amateur club; Colgate (ECAC).

Tim Breslin — Left Wing

Regular Season / Playoffs

Season	Team	League	GP	G	A	PTS	PIM	GP	G	A	PTS	PIM
91-92	Phoenix	IHL	45	8	21	29	12	—	—	—	—	—
92-93	Phoenix	IHL	79	14	30	44	55	—	—	—	—	—
93-94	South Carolina	ECHL	9	3	3	6	4	—	—	—	—	—
93-94	Phoenix	IHL	50	9	18	27	29	—	—	—	—	—
94-95	Chicago	IHL	71	7	21	28	62	3	1	1	2	0
95-96	Chicago	IHL	62	11	11	22	56	9	2	2	4	12
96-97	Chicago	IHL	44	2	10	12	18	4	0	2	2	4
97-98	Chicago	IHL	81	10	26	36	90	21	1	3	4	22
98-99	Chicago	IHL	72	7	14	21	72	4	0	0	0	4
	IHL	Totals	504	68	151	219	394	41	4	8	12	42

Born; 12/8/67, Downers Grove, Illinois. 6-0, 180. Member of 1997-98 IHL Champion Chicago Wolves. Last amateur club; Lake Superior State (CCHA).

Chad Breszynskie — Forward

Regular Season / Playoffs

Season	Team	League	GP	G	A	PTS	PIM	GP	G	A	PTS	PIM
98-99	Central Texas	WPHL	3	0	1	1	2	2	0	0	0	4

Born; 11/28/74. Last amateur club; Wilfrid Laurier (OUAA).

Reggie Brezeault — Center

Regular Season / Playoffs

Season	Team	League	GP	G	A	PTS	PIM	GP	G	A	PTS	PIM
93-94	Fort Worth	CeHL	3	1	0	1	0	—	—	—	—	—
93-94	Roanoke	ECHL	26	4	4	8	75	—	—	—	—	—
94-95	Roanoke	ECHL	8	0	1	1	20	—	—	—	—	—
94-95	West Palm Beach	SUN	23	13	15	28	116	—	—	—	—	—
94-95	Charlotte	ECHL	8	1	0	1	48	3	0	0	0	4
95-96	Louisville	ECHL	19	2	7	9	81	—	—	—	—	—
95-96	Birmingham	ECHL	15	0	0	0	36	—	—	—	—	—
96-97	Port Huron	UHL	11	1	3	4	10	—	—	—	—	—
96-97	Macon	CeHL	3	0	0	0	9	—	—	—	—	—
97-98												
98-99	Charlotte	ECHL	24	3	3	6	63	—	—	—	—	—
	ECHL	Totals	100	10	15	25	323	3	0	0	0	4

Born; 4/27/72, Montreal, Quebec. 6-0, 210.

Corey Bricknell — Defenseman

Regular Season / Playoffs

Season	Team	League	GP	G	A	PTS	PIM	GP	G	A	PTS	PIM
94-95	Niagara Falls	OHL	38	2	14	16	124	—	—	—	—	—
94-95	Huntington	ECHL	34	0	8	8	136	—	—	—	—	—
95-96	Huntington	ECHL	2	0	0	0	2	—	—	—	—	—
95-96	Columbus	ECHL	17	0	5	5	76	—	—	—	—	—
96-97	Columbus	ECHL	62	3	15	18	331	8	0	2	2	43
97-98	Brantford	UHL	51	1	10	11	178	—	—	—	—	—
97-98	Binghamton	UHL	10	1	1	2	42	5	1	0	1	29
98-99	Shreveport	WPHL	31	1	3	4	163	—	—	—	—	—
98-99	Fort Worth	WPHL	23	0	3	3	65	12	0	1	1	27
	ECHL	Totals	115	3	28	31	545	8	0	2	2	43
	UHL	Totals	61	2	11	13	220	5	1	0	1	29
	WPHL	Totals	54	1	6	7	228	12	0	1	1	27

Born; 10/16/75, Port Perry, Ontario. 6-2, 185. Traded to Binghamton by Brantford with Greg Pajor and Chris Grenville for Rob MacInnis (3/98). Last amateur club; Niagara Falls (OHL).

Daniel Briere
Center

Regular Season / Playoffs

Season	Team	League	GP	G	A	PTS	PIM	GP	G	A	PTS	PIM
97-98	Phoenix	NHL	5	1	0	1	2	—	—	—	—	—
97-98	Springfield	AHL	68	36	56	92	42	4	1	2	3	4
98-99	Las Vegas	IHL	1	1	1	2	0	—	—	—	—	—
98-99	Phoenix	NHL	64	8	14	22	30	—	—	—	—	—
98-99	Springfield	AHL	13	2	6	8	20	3	0	1	1	2
	NHL	Totals	69	9	14	23	32	—	—	—	—	—
	AHL	Totals	81	38	62	100	62	7	1	3	4	6

Born; 10/6/77, Gatineau, Quebec. 5-9, 160. Drafted by Phoenix Coyotes (2nd choice, 24th overall) in 1996 Entry Draft. 1997-98 AHL Rookie of the Year. 1997-98 AHL First Team All-Star. 1997-98 AHL All-Rookie Team. Last amateur club; Drummondville (QMJHL).

Travis Brigley
Left Wing

Regular Season / Playoffs

Season	Team	League	GP	G	A	PTS	PIM	GP	G	A	PTS	PIM
97-98	Calgary	NHL	2	0	0	0	2	—	—	—	—	—
97-98	Saint John	AHL	79	17	15	32	28	8	0	0	0	0
98-99	Saint John	AHL	74	15	35	50	48	7	3	1	4	2
	AHL	Totals	153	32	50	82	76	15	3	1	4	2

Born; 6/16/77, Coronation, Alberta. 6-1, 190. Drafted by Calgary Flames (2nd choice, 39th overall) in 1996 Entry Draft. Last amateur club; Lethbridge (WHL).

Aris Brimanis
Defenseman

Regular Season / Playoffs

Season	Team	League	GP	G	A	PTS	PIM	GP	G	A	PTS	PIM
93-94	Philadelphia	NHL	1	0	0	0	0	—	—	—	—	—
93-94	Hershey	AHL	75	8	15	23	65	11	2	3	5	12
94-95	Hershey	AHL	76	8	17	25	68	6	1	1	2	14
95-96	Philadelphia	NHL	17	0	2	2	12	—	—	—	—	—
95-96	Hershey	AHL	54	9	22	31	64	5	1	2	3	4
96-97	Philadelphia	NHL	3	0	1	1	0	—	—	—	—	—
96-97	Philadelphia	AHL	65	14	18	32	69	10	2	2	4	13
97-98	Philadephia	AHL	30	1	11	12	26	—	—	—	—	—
97-98	Michigan	IHL	35	3	9	12	24	4	1	0	1	4
98-99	Grand Rapids	IHL	66	16	21	37	70	—	—	—	—	—
98-99	Fredericton	AHL	8	2	4	6	6	15	3	10	13	18
	NHL	Totals	21	0	3	3	12	—	—	—	—	—
	AHL	Totals	308	42	87	129	298	47	9	18	27	61
	IHL	Totals	101	19	30	49	94	4	1	0	1	4

Born; 3/14/72, Cleveland, Ohio. 6-3, 210. Drafted by Philadelphia Flyers (4th choice, 86th overall) in 1991 Entry Draft. Last amateur club; Bowling Green (CCHA).

Ryan Brindley
Defenseman

Regular Season / Playoffs

Season	Team	League	GP	G	A	PTS	PIM	GP	G	A	PTS	PIM
98-99	Miami-Ohio	CCHA	34	4	11	15	62	—	—	—	—	—
98-99	Cincinnati	AHL	8	0	0	0	16	3	0	0	0	2
98-99	Dayton	ECHL	4	1	2	3	16	—	—	—	—	—

Born; 7/9/76, Thunder Bay Ontario. 6-0, 204. Last amateur club; Miami-Ohio (CCHA).

Byron Briske
Defenseman

Regular Season / Playoffs

Season	Team	League	GP	G	A	PTS	PIM	GP	G	A	PTS	PIM
96-97	Baltimore	AHL	69	0	6	6	131	1	0	0	0	0
97-98	Cincinnati	AHL	59	0	9	9	95	—	—	—	—	—
98-99	Cincinnati	AHL	55	0	6	6	130	3	0	0	0	2
	AHL	Totals	183	0	21	21	356	4	0	0	0	2

Born; 1/23/76, Humboldt, Saskatchewan. 6-2, 194. Drafted by Anaheim Mighty Ducks (4th choice, 80th overall) in 1994 Entry Draft. Last amateur club; Tri-City (WHL).

Martin Brochu
Goaltender

Regular Season / Playoffs

Season	Team	League	GP	W	L	T	MIN	SO	AVG	GP	W	L	MIN	SO	AVG
93-94	Fredericton	AHL	32	10	11	3	1505	2	3.03	—	—	—	—	—	—
94-95	Fredericton	AHL	44	18	18	4	2475	0	3.51	—	—	—	—	—	—
95-96	Fredericton	AHL	17	6	8	2	986	0	4.26	—	—	—	—	—	—
95-96	Portland	AHL	5	2	2	1	287	0	3.14	12	7	4	700	2	2.40
95-96	Wheeling	ECHL	19	10	6	2	1060	1	2.89	—	—	—	—	—	—
96-97	Portland	AHL	55	23	17	7	2962	2	3.04	5	2	3	324	0	2.41
97-98	Portland	AHL	37	16	14	1	1926	2	2.99	6	3	2	297	0	3.24
98-99	Washington	NHL	2	0	2	0	120	0	3.00	—	—	—	—	—	—
98-99	Portland	AHL	20	6	10	3	1164	2	2.94	—	—	—	—	—	—
98-99	Utah	IHL	5	1	3	1	298	0	2.62	—	—	—	—	—	—
	AHL	Totals	210	81	80	21	11305	6	3.23	23	12	9	1321	2	2.59

Born; 3/10/73, Anjou, Quebec. 5-10, 200. Signed as a free agent by Montreal Canadiens (10/22/92). Traded to Washington Capitals by Montreal for future considerations (3/15/96). Last amateur club; Hull (QMJHL).

Stephan Brochu
Defenseman

Regular Season / Playoffs

Season	Team	League	GP	G	A	PTS	PIM	GP	G	A	PTS	PIM
87-88	Colorado	IHL	52	4	10	14	70	12	3	3	6	13
88-89	Rangers	NHL	1	0	0	0	0	—	—	—	—	—
88-89	Denver	IHL	67	5	14	19	109	3	0	0	0	0
89-90	Flint	IHL	5	0	0	0	2	—	—	—	—	—
89-90	Fort Wayne	IHL	63	9	19	28	98	5	0	2	2	6
90-91	Fort Wayne	IHL	73	14	29	43	49	14	1	3	4	31
91-92	Kansas City	IHL	3	0	0	0	2	—	—	—	—	—
91-92	Flint	CoHL	52	13	27	40	80	—	—	—	—	—
92-93	Flint	CoHL	44	6	28	34	77	6	4	8	12	22
93-94	Flint	CoHL	54	8	32	40	116	10	1	4	5	2
94-95	Flint	CoHL	60	12	37	49	39	6	0	9	9	8
95-96	Flint	CoHL	68	4	41	45	68	15	5	12	17	18
96-97	Adirondack	AHL	18	0	8	8	12	—	—	—	—	—
96-97	Detroit	IHL	1	0	0	0	2	—	—	—	—	—
96-97	Flint	CoHL	42	8	45	53	32	14	5	*20	*25	14
97-98	Detroit	IHL	3	0	0	0	2	—	—	—	—	—
97-98	Fort Wayne	IHL	2	1	0	1	0	—	—	—	—	—
97-98	Chicago	IHL	1	0	0	0	0	—	—	—	—	—
97-98	Flint	UHL	54	10	62	72	52	17	2	18	20	12
98-99	Flint	UHL	58	12	55	67	39	8	1	3	4	8
	IHL	Totals	269	33	72	105	334	34	4	8	12	50
	UHL	Totals	432	73	327	400	503	76	18	74	92	84

Born; 8/15/67, Sherbrooke, Quebec. 6-2, 195. Drafted by New York Rangers (9th round, 175th overall) 6/15/85. 1997-98 UHL Second All-Star Team. 1998-99 UHL Top Defenseman. 1998-99 UHL First Team All-Star. Member of 1995-96 Colonial League Champion Flint Generals. Last amateur club; St. Jean (QMJHL).

Ritchie Bronilla
Defenseman

Regular Season / Playoffs

Season	Team	League	GP	G	A	PTS	PIM	GP	G	A	PTS	PIM
95-96	Hampton Roads	ECHL	29	2	0	2	36	—	—	—	—	—
96-97	Huntington	ECHL	67	6	21	27	40	—	—	—	—	—
97-98	Fort Wayne	IHL	3	0	0	0	0	—	—	—	—	—
97-98	Huntington	ECHL	68	7	37	44	72	4	0	3	3	2
98-99	Lowell	AHL	2	0	0	0	0	—	—	—	—	—
98-99	Huntington	ECHL	62	6	26	32	30	—	—	—	—	—
	ECHL	Totals	226	21	84	105	178	4	0	3	3	2

Born; 7/15/75, Toronto, Ontario. 6-1, 215. Last amateur club; Ottawa (OHL).

Christian Bronsard
Goaltender

Regular Season / Playoffs

Season	Team	League	GP	W	L	T	MIN	SO	AVG	GP	W	L	MIN	SO	AVG
97-98	Canada	National	26	14	4	7	1469	NA	2.53	—	—	—	—	—	—

Born; 12/25/77, Orleans, Ontario. 5-8, 165. Last amateur club; Hull (QMJHL).

Wade Brookbank — Defenseman

Regular Season / Playoffs

Season	Team	League	GP	G	A	PTS	PIM	GP	G	A	PTS	PIM
97-98	Anchorage	WCHL	7	0	0	0	46	4	0	0	0	20
98-99	Anchorage	WCHL	56	0	4	4	337	5	0	0	0	47
	WCHL	Totals	63	0	4	4	383	9	0	0	0	67

Born; 9/29/77, Lahigan, Saskatchewan. 6-4, 225. Traded to San Diego by Anchorage with Kevin Epp for Kyles Reeves (6/99).

Brendan Brooks — Center

Regular Season / Playoffs

Season	Team	League	GP	G	A	PTS	PIM	GP	G	A	PTS	PIM
97-98	Owen Sound	OHL	25	3	10	13	6	—	—	—	—	—
97-98	North Bay	OHL	32	7	5	12	26	—	—	—	—	—
97-98	Mississippi	ECHL	1	0	1	1	0	—	—	—	—	—
98-99	Quad City	UHL	61	18	17	35	67	15	3	1	4	8

Born; 11/26/78, St. Catharines, Ontario. 5-9, 185. Last amateur club; North Bay (OHL).

Chris Brooks — Center

Regular Season / Playoffs

Season	Team	League	GP	G	A	PTS	PIM	GP	G	A	PTS	PIM
96-97	Amarillo	WPHL	64	45	*65	*110	34	—	—	—	—	—
97-98	Springfield	AHL	2	2	2	4	0	2	0	1	1	0
97-98	Mobile	ECHL	70	30	52	82	54	3	3	0	3	4
98-99	Amarillo	WPHL	61	*48	57	105	44	—	—	—	—	—
	WPHL	Totals	125	93	122	215	78	—	—	—	—	—

Born; 9/19/72, Stratford, Ontario. 5-8, 170. 1996-97 WPHL Most Valuable Player. Last amateur club; Western Michigan (CCHA).

David Brosseau — Right Wing

Regular Season / Playoffs

Season	Team	League	GP	G	A	PTS	PIM	GP	G	A	PTS	PIM
96-97	Binghamton	AHL	2	0	0	0	0	1	0	0	0	0
96-97	Charlotte	ECHL	68	37	18	55	65	3	1	3	4	12
97-98	Hartford	AHL	4	0	0	0	2	—	—	—	—	—
97-98	Charlotte	ECHL	67	40	21	61	64	6	3	0	3	4
98-99	Charlotte	ECHL	70	33	28	61	66	—	—	—	—	—
	AHL	Totals	6	0	0	0	2	1	0	0	0	0
	ECHL	Totals	205	110	67	177	195	9	4	3	7	16

Born; 1/16/76, Montreal, Quebec. 6-2, 189. Drafted by New York Rangers (8th choice, 156th overall) in 1994 Entry Draft. Last amateur club; Granby (QMJHL).

Paul Broten — Right Wing

Regular Season / Playoffs

Season	Team	League	GP	G	A	PTS	PIM	GP	G	A	PTS	PIM
88-89	Denver	IHL	77	28	31	59	133	4	0	2	2	6
89-90	Rangers	NHL	32	5	3	8	26	6	1	1	2	2
89-90	Flint	IHL	28	17	9	26	55	—	—	—	—	—
90-91	Rangers	AHL	28	4	6	10	18	5	0	0	0	2
90-91	Binghamton	AHL	8	2	2	4	4	—	—	—	—	—
91-92	Rangers	NHL	74	13	15	28	102	13	1	2	3	10
92-93	Rangers	NHL	60	5	9	14	48	—	—	—	—	—
93-94	Dallas	NHL	64	12	12	24	30	9	1	1	2	2
94-95	Dallas	NHL	47	7	9	16	36	5	1	2	3	2
95-96	St. Louis	NHL	17	0	1	1	4	—	—	—	—	—
95-96	Worcester	AHL	50	22	21	43	42	3	0	0	0	0
96-97	Fort Wayne	IHL	59	19	28	47	82	—	—	—	—	—
97-98	Cincinnati	IHL	81	9	12	21	80	9	3	1	4	8
98-99	Berlin	Germany	50	8	15	23	100	—	—	—	—	—
	NHL	Totals	322	46	55	101	264	38	4	6	10	18
	IHL	Totals	245	47	51	98	221	9	3	1	4	8
	AHL	Totals	58	24	23	47	46	3	0	0	0	0

Born; 10/27/65, Roseau, Minnesota. 5-11, 190. Drafted by New York Rangers (3rd choice, 77th overall) in 1984 Entry Draft. Claimed by Dallas Stars from Rangers in NHL Waiver Draft (10/3/93). Traded to St. Louis Blues by Dallas for Guy Carbonneau (10/2/95). Last amateur club; University of Minnesota

Paul Brousseau — Right Wing

Regular Season / Playoffs

Season	Team	League	GP	G	A	PTS	PIM	GP	G	A	PTS	PIM
93-94	Cornwall	AHL	69	18	26	44	35	1	0	0	0	0
94-95	Cornwall	AHL	57	19	17	36	29	7	2	1	3	10
95-96	Colorado	NHL	8	1	1	2	2	—	—	—	—	—
95-96	Cornwall	AHL	63	21	22	43	60	8	4	0	4	2
96-97	Tampa Bay	NHL	6	0	0	0	0	—	—	—	—	—
96-97	Adirondack	AHL	66	35	31	66	25	4	1	2	3	0
97-98	Tampa Bay	NHL	11	0	2	2	27	—	—	—	—	—
97-98	Adirondack	AHL	67	*45	20	65	18	3	1	1	2	0
98-99	Milwaukee	IHL	5	1	1	2	2	—	—	—	—	—
98-99	Hershey	AHL	39	11	21	32	15	5	1	1	2	0
	NHL	Totals	25	1	3	4	29	—	—	—	—	—
	AHL	Totals	361	149	137	286	182	28	9	5	14	12

Born; 9/18/73, Pierrefonds, Quebec. 6-2, 212. Drafted by Quebec Nordiques (2nd choice, 28th overall) in 1992 Entry Draft. Signed as a free agent by Tampa Bay Lightning (9/10/96). Selected by Nashville Predators in 1998 NHL Expansion Draft. 1997-98 AHL Second Team All-Star. Last amateur club; Hull (QMJHL).

Bobby Brown — Center

Regular Season / Playoffs

Season	Team	League	GP	G	A	PTS	PIM	GP	G	A	PTS	PIM
96-97	Roanoke	ECHL	39	9	14	23	61	—	—	—	—	—
96-97	Baton Rouge	ECHL	24	7	8	15	26	—	—	—	—	—
97-98	Saint John	AHL	2	0	0	0	0	—	—	—	—	—
97-98	Dayton	ECHL	65	25	28	53	117	5	3	2	5	6
98-99	Manitoba	IHL	2	0	0	0	0	—	—	—	—	—
98-99	Cincinnati	IHL	2	0	0	0	0	—	—	—	—	—
98-99	Dayton	ECHL	66	30	30	60	125	4	2	1	3	2
	IHL	Totals	4	0	0	0	0	—	—	—	—	—
	ECHL	Totals	194	71	80	151	329	9	5	3	8	8

Born; 9/26/75, 6-0, 200. Signed as a free agent by Calgary Flames (8/6/96). Last amateur club; Brandon (WHL).

Cam Brown — Left Wing

Regular Season / Playoffs

Season	Team	League	GP	G	A	PTS	PIM	GP	G	A	PTS	PIM
90-91	Vancouver	NHL	1	0	0	0	7	—	—	—	—	—
90-91	Milwaukee	IHL	74	11	13	24	218	3	0	0	0	0
91-92	Milwaukee	IHL	51	6	8	14	179	1	0	0	0	0
91-92	Columbus	ECHL	10	11	6	17	64	—	—	—	—	—
92-93	Rochester	AHL	4	0	0	0	26	—	—	—	—	—
92-93	Hamilton	AHL	1	0	0	0	2	—	—	—	—	—
92-93	Columbus	ECHL	36	13	18	31	218	—	—	—	—	—
92-93	Erie	ECHL	15	4	3	7	50	5	0	1	1	62
93-94												
94-95	Adirondack	AHL	10	0	1	1	30	4	0	0	0	24
94-95	Erie	ECHL	60	14	28	42	341	—	—	—	—	—
95-96	Erie	ECHL	64	18	26	44	307	—	—	—	—	—
96-97	Baton Rouge	ECHL	57	10	13	23	220	—	—	—	—	—
97-98	Baton Rouge	ECHL	62	18	19	37	205	—	—	—	—	—
98-99	Baton Rouge	ECHL	68	17	23	40	213	6	6	1	7	42
	IHL	Totals	125	17	21	38	397	4	0	0	0	0
	AHL	Totals	15	0	1	1	78	4	0	0	0	24
	ECHL	Totals	372	105	136	241	1618	11	6	2	8	104

Born; 5/15/69, Saskatchewan, Saskatoon. 6-1, 210. Signed as a free agent by Vancouver Canucks (4/6/90). Last amateur club; Brandon (WHL).

Craig Brown — Goaltender

Regular Season / Playoffs

Season	Team	League	GP	W	L	T	MIN	SO	AVG	GP	W	L	MIN	SO	AVG
94-95	Nashville	ECHL	52	24	20	3	2848	2	3.48	13	8	4	731	0	3.04
95-96	Atlanta	IHL	2	1	1	0	119	0	3.03	—	—	—	—	—	—
95-96	Nashville	ECHL	*53	*32	14	4	*2934	0	4.05	5	2	3	251	0	5.26
96-97	Pensacola	ECHL	21	11	7	2	1217	0	4.09	—	—	—	—	—	—
97-98	Pensacola	ECHL	17	7	7	3	976	0	3.32	2	0	0	45	0	2.67
98-99	Pensacola	ECHL	16	5	10	0	910	0	3.76	—	—	—	—	—	—
	ECHL	Totals	159	79	58	12	8885	2	3.76	20	10	7	1027	0	3.56

Born; 2/29/72, Scarborough, Ontario. 5-11, 175. Last amateur club; Western Michigan (CCHA).

Dan Brown — Defenseman

Regular Season / Playoffs

Season	Team	League	GP	G	A	PTS	PIM	GP	G	A	PTS	PIM
94-95	Prince Edward Island	AHL	1	0	1	1	0	—	—	—	—	—
94-95	Memphis	CeHL	62	10	24	34	112	—	—	—	—	—
95-96	Memphis	CeHL	59	13	46	59	223	6	1	3	4	50
96-97	Memphis	CeHL	54	12	47	59	144	16	3	6	9	84
97-98	Memphis	CHL	51	15	18	33	158	—	—	—	—	—
97-98	Macon	CHL	12	1	11	12	12	3	1	1	2	8
98-99	Columbus	CHL	52	5	39	44	93	—	—	—	—	—
98-99	Wichita	CHL	8	1	7	8	40	4	0	3	3	2
	CHL	Totals	298	57	192	249	782	29	5	13	18	144

Born; 9/13/70, Milton, Ontario. 5-11, 195. Traded to Macon by Memphis for Matt McElwee, Sebastien Parent and Marcel Chagnon (3/98). 1995-96 CeHL First Team All-Star. 1995-96 CeHL Defenseman of the Year. 1996-97 CeHL Second Team All-Star. Last amateur club; Queen's College (OUAA).

Eric Brown — Defenseman

Regular Season / Playoffs

Season	Team	League	GP	G	A	PTS	PIM	GP	G	A	PTS	PIM
98-99	Baton Rouge	ECHL	4	0	0	0	2	—	—	—	—	—

Born; 3/23/75, Sault Ste. Marie, Ontario. 5-9, 186. Last amateur club; Wisconsin-Stevens Point (NCAA 3).

Jeff Brown — Defenseman

Regular Season / Playoffs

Season	Team	League	GP	G	A	PTS	PIM	GP	G	A	PTS	PIM
98-99	Hartford	AHL	9	0	2	2	21	—	—	—	—	—
98-99	Charlotte	ECHL	12	1	2	3	20	—	—	—	—	—
98-99	Canada	National	13	0	2	2	8	—	—	—	—	—

Born; 4/24/78, Mississauga, Toronto. 6-1, 217. Drafted by New York Rangers (1st choice 21st overall) in 1996 Entry Draft. Last amateur club; London (OHL).

Jeremy Brown — Right Wing

Regular Season / Playoffs

Season	Team	League	GP	G	A	PTS	PIM	GP	G	A	PTS	PIM
97-98	Providence	AHL	1	1	0	1	0	—	—	—	—	—
97-98	Cincinnati	AHL	9	0	1	1	2	—	—	—	—	—
97-98	Wheeling	ECHL	66	28	34	62	54	9	1	4	5	6
98-99	Springfield	AHL	2	0	0	0	0	—	—	—	—	—
98-99	Providence	AHL	47	12	12	24	20	19	6	7	13	4
98-99	Wheeling	ECHL	22	9	9	18	24	—	—	—	—	—
	AHL	Totals	59	13	13	26	22	19	6	7	13	4
	ECHL	Totals	88	37	43	80	78	9	1	4	5	6

Born; 6/23/74, Barrie, Ontario. 5-10, 195. Member of 1998-99 AHL Champion Providence Bruins. Last amateur club; Western Michigan (CCHA).

Jim Brown — Center

Regular Season / Playoffs

Season	Team	League	GP	G	A	PTS	PIM	GP	G	A	PTS	PIM
93-94	Owen Sound	OHL	22	18	17	35	24	—	—	—	—	—
93-94	Newmarket	OHL	40	26	28	54	48	—	—	—	—	—
93-94	Hampton Roads	ECHL	1	2	0	2	0	7	6	7	13	4
94-95	Hampton Roads	ECHL	49	24	21	45	50	—	—	—	—	—
94-95	Knoxville	ECHL	15	7	5	12	42	4	3	2	4	8
95-96	Knoxville	ECHL	69	50	70	120	80	8	4	7	11	4
96-97	Knoxville	ECHL	64	44	48	92	66	—	—	—	—	—
97-98	Quad City	UHL	71	41	49	90	100	20	*13	12	25	22
98-99	Springfield	AHL	7	2	0	2	6	—	—	—	—	—
98-99	Pee Dee	ECHL	60	23	42	65	44	8	1	2	3	4
	ECHL	Totals	258	150	186	336	282	27	14	18	32	20

Born; 6/17/73, Scarborough, Ontario. 5-11, 185. 1995-96 ECHL First Team All-Star. 1997-98 UHL Playoff MVP. Member of 1997-98 UHL Champion Quad City Mallards. Last amateur club; Newmarket (OHL).

Kevin Brown — Right Wing

Regular Season / Playoffs

Season	Team	League	GP	G	A	PTS	PIM	GP	G	A	PTS	PIM
94-95	Dayton	ECHL	66	29	42	71	34	8	5	4	9	2
95-96	Peoria	IHL	3	2	1	3	0	—	—	—	—	—
95-96	Cornwall	AHL	2	0	0	0	0	—	—	—	—	—
95-96	Dayton	ECHL	55	26	35	61	30	3	1	1	2	6
96-97	Dayton	ECHL	31	9	12	21	8	—	—	—	—	—
96-97	Toledo	ECHL	16	7	12	19	6	5	1	3	4	2
97-98	Toledo	ECHL	68	26	35	61	18	7	4	4	8	2
98-99	Port Huron	UHL	45	23	20	43	36	1	0	0	0	0
	ECHL	Totals	236	97	136	233	96	23	11	12	23	12

Born; 4/1/70, Scarborough, Ontario. 5-11, 180. Traded to Toledo Storm by Dayton Bombers for Norm Dezainde (1997). Last amateur club; Belleville (OHL).

Kevin Brown — Right Wing

Regular Season / Playoffs

Season	Team	League	GP	G	A	PTS	PIM	GP	G	A	PTS	PIM
94-95	Los Angeles	NHL	23	2	3	5	18	—	—	—	—	—
94-95	Phoenix	IHL	48	19	31	50	64	—	—	—	—	—
95-96	Los Angeles	NHL	7	1	0	1	4	—	—	—	—	—
95-96	Phoenix	IHL	45	10	16	26	39	—	—	—	—	—
95-96	Prince Edward Island	AHL	8	3	6	9	2	3	1	3	4	0
96-97	Hartford	NHL	11	0	4	4	6	—	—	—	—	—
96-97	Springfield	AHL	48	32	16	48	45	15	*11	6	17	24
97-98	Carolina	NHL	4	0	0	0	0	—	—	—	—	—
97-98	New Haven	AHL	67	28	44	72	65	3	0	2	2	0
98-99	Edmonton	NHL	12	4	2	6	0	—	—	—	—	—
98-99	Hamilton	AHL	32	9	14	23	47	—	—	—	—	—
98-99	Hartford	AHL	9	3	2	5	14	5	1	3	4	4
	NHL	Totals	57	7	9	16	28	—	—	—	—	—
	AHL	Totals	164	75	82	157	173	26	13	14	27	28
	IHL	Totals	93	29	47	76	103	—	—	—	—	—

Born; 5/11/74, Birmingham, England. 6-1, 212. Drafted by Los Angeles Kings (3rd choice, 87th overall) in 1992 Entry Draft. Traded to Ottawa Senators by Los Angeles for Jaroslav Modry and Ottawa's 8th round pick (Kai Nurminen) in 1996 Entry Draft. Traded to Anaheim Mighty Ducks by Ottawa for Mike Maneluk (7/1/96). Traded to Hartford Whalers by Anaheim for the rights to Espen Knutsen (10/1/96). Signed as a free agent by Edmonton Oilers (7/22/98). Traded to New York Rangers by Edmonton for Vladimir Vorobiev (3/23/99). Last amateur club;

Ryan Brown — Defenseman

Regular Season / Playoffs

Season	Team	League	GP	G	A	PTS	PIM	GP	G	A	PTS	PIM
95-96	Atlanta	IHL	16	0	0	0	66	—	—	—	—	—
95-96	Nashville	ECHL	18	1	0	1	64	4	1	1	2	9
96-97	Adirondack	AHL	6	0	0	0	39	—	—	—	—	—
96-97	Raleigh	ECHL	43	7	3	10	122	—	—	—	—	—
97-98	Adirondack	AHL	23	1	2	3	31	1	0	0	0	6
97-98	Chesapeake	ECHL	16	3	2	5	21	2	0	1	1	4
98-99	Cleveland	IHL	4	0	0	0	5	—	—	—	—	—
98-99	Hershey	AHL	4	0	0	0	9	—	—	—	—	—
98-99	Chesapeake	ECHL	37	5	9	14	102	8	1	2	3	18
	AHL	Totals	33	1	2	3	79	1	0	0	0	6
	IHL	Totals	20	0	0	0	75	—	—	—	—	—
	ECHL	Totals	114	16	14	30	309	14	2	4	6	31

Born; 9/19/74, Boyle, Alberta. 6-4, 220. Drafted by Tampa Bay Lightning (5th choice, 107th overall) in 1993 Entry Draft. Last amateur club; Tri-City (WHL).

Tom Brown — Defenseman

Regular Season / Playoffs

Season	Team	League	GP	G	A	PTS	PIM	GP	G	A	PTS	PIM
97-98	Charlotte	ECHL	56	2	5	7	49	2	0	0	0	2
98-99	Charlotte	ECHL	48	1	8	9	57	—	—	—	—	—
98-99	Wheeling	ECHL	18	1	0	1	29	—	—	—	—	—
	ECHL	Totals	122	4	13	17	135	2	0	0	0	2

Born; 11/11/77, Hamilton, Ontario. 6-4, 200. Drafted by Boston Bruins (8th choice, 182nd overall) in 1996 Entry Draft. Traded to Wheeling by Charlotte for futures (3/99). Last amateur club; Sudbury (OHL).

Pat Brownlee — Defenseman

Regular Season / Playoffs

Season	Team	League	GP	G	A	PTS	PIM	GP	G	A	PTS	PIM
98-99	Charlotte	ECHL	22	1	6	7	28	—	—	—	—	—
98-99	Richmond	ECHL	22	2	10	12	22	—	—	—	—	—
	ECHL	Totals	44	3	16	19	50	—	—	—	—	—

Born; 3/10/75, Minneapolis, Minnesota. 6-0, 205. Last amateur club; R.P.I. (ECAC).

David Bruce — Left Wing

Regular Season / Playoffs

Season	Team	League	GP	G	A	PTS	PIM	GP	G	A	PTS	PIM
84-85	Fredericton	AHL	56	14	11	25	104	5	0	0	0	37
85-86	Vancouver	NHL	12	0	1	1	14	1	0	0	0	0
85-86	Fredericton	AHL	66	25	16	41	151	2	0	1	1	12
86-87	Vancouver	NHL	50	9	7	16	109	—	—	—	—	—
86-87	Fredericton	AHL	17	7	6	13	73	—	—	—	—	—
87-88	Vancouver	NHL	28	7	3	10	57	—	—	—	—	—
87-88	Fredericton	AHL	30	27	18	45	115	—	—	—	—	—
88-89	Vancouver	NHL	53	7	7	14	65	—	—	—	—	—
89-90	Milwaukee	IHL	68	40	35	75	148	6	5	3	8	0
90-91	St. Louis	NHL	12	1	2	3	14	2	0	0	0	2
90-91	Peoria	IHL	60	*64	52	116	78	18	*18	11	*29	40
91-92	San Jose	NHL	60	22	16	38	46	—	—	—	—	—
91-92	Kansas City	IHL	7	5	5	10	6	—	—	—	—	—
92-93	San Jose	NHL	17	2	3	5	33	—	—	—	—	—
93-94	San Jose	NHL	2	0	0	0	0	—	—	—	—	—
93-94	Kansas City	IHL	72	40	24	64	115	—	—	—	—	—
94-95	Kansas City	IHL	63	33	25	58	80	—	—	—	—	—
95-96	Kansas City	IHL	62	27	26	53	84	1	0	0	0	8
96-97	Kansas City	IHL	79	45	24	69	90	3	0	0	0	2
97-98	Kansas City	IHL	54	20	12	32	58	11	3	2	5	21
98-99	Landshut	Germany	43	4	9	13	20	2	0	0	0	2
	NHL	Totals	234	48	39	87	338	3	0	0	0	2
	IHL	Totals	465	274	203	477	659	39	26	16	42	71
	AHL	Totals	169	73	51	124	443	7	0	1	1	49

Born; 10/7/64, Thunder Bay, Ontario. 5-11, 190. Drafted by Vancouver Canucks (2nd choice, 30th overall) in 1983 Entry Draft. Signed as a free agent by St. Louis (7/6/90). Claimed by San Jose Sharks from St. Louis in Expansion Draft (5/30/91). 1989-90 IHL First Team All-Star. 1990-91 IHL First Team All-Star. 1990-91 IHL MVP. Member of 1990-91 IHL champion Peoria Rivermen. Last amateur club; Kitchener (OHL).

Lars Bruggermann — Defenseman

Regular Season / Playoffs

Season	Team	League	GP	G	A	PTS	PIM	GP	G	A	PTS	PIM
97-98	Jacksonville	ECHL	49	1	6	7	91	—	—	—	—	—
98-99	Krefeld	Germany	38	5	1	6	98	3	0	0	0	4

Born; 3/2/76, Hemer, Germany. 6-3, 220. Selected by Greenville in 1998 ECHL Expansion Draft.

Brett Bruininks — Right Wing

Regular Season / Playoffs

Season	Team	League	GP	G	A	PTS	PIM	GP	G	A	PTS	PIM
96-97	Philadelphia	AHL	45	3	2	5	54	4	1	1	2	2
97-98	Philadelphia	AHL	6	0	1	1	13	—	—	—	—	—
97-98	Indianapolis	IHL	43	5	6	11	79	2	0	0	0	4
97-98	Johnstown	ECHL	8	3	2	5	35	—	—	—	—	—
98-99	Florida	ECHL	42	3	5	8	26	—	—	—	—	—
	AHL	Totals	51	3	3	6	67	4	1	1	2	2
	ECHL	Totals	50	6	7	13	61	—	—	—	—	—

Born; 3/10/72, Minneapolis, Minnesota. 6-4, 230. Last amateur club; Notre Dame (CCHA).

Eric Brule — Defenseman

Regular Season / Playoffs

Season	Team	League	GP	G	A	PTS	PIM	GP	G	A	PTS	PIM
91-92	Muskegon	IHL	70	4	14	18	48	5	0	4	4	2
92-93	Fredericton	AHL	17	1	5	6	16	—	—	—	—	—
92-93	Wheeling	ECHL	4	0	0	0	2	—	—	—	—	—
92-93	Fort Worth	CeHL	36	7	33	40	66	—	—	—	—	—
93-94	Fort Worth	CeHL	37	9	17	26	98	—	—	—	—	—
93-94	South Carolina	ECHL	18	7	11	18	14	3	1	1	2	8
94-95	N/A											
95-96	Erie	ECHL	65	15	27	42	117	—	—	—	—	—
96-97	N/A											
97-98	Milwaukee	IHL	3	0	0	0	2	—	—	—	—	—
97-98	New Orleans	ECHL	69	19	36	55	105	4	0	0	0	4
98-99	Michigan	IHL	9	0	3	3	2	—	—	—	—	—
98-99	Long Beach	IHL	2	0	0	0	0	—	—	—	—	—
98-99	Abilene	WPHL	57	14	42	56	65	3	0	0	0	4
	IHL	Totals	84	4	17	21	52	5	0	4	4	2
	ECHL	Totals	156	41	74	115	238	7	1	1	2	12
	CeHL	Totals	73	16	50	66	164	—	—	—	—	—

Born; 1/17/70, Victoriaville, Quebec. 5-10, 188. 1998-99 WPHL Defenseman of the Year. Last amateur club; Chicoutimi (QMJHL).

Steve Brule — Center

Regular Season / Playoffs

Season	Team	League	GP	G	A	PTS	PIM	GP	G	A	PTS	PIM
94-95	St. Jean	QMJHL	69	44	64	108	42	7	3	4	7	8
94-95	Albany	AHL	3	1	4	5	0	14	9	5	14	4
95-96	Albany	AHL	80	30	21	51	37	4	0	0	0	17
96-97	Albany	AHL	79	28	48	76	27	15	7	7	14	12
97-98	Albany	AHL	80	34	43	77	34	13	8	3	11	4
98-99	Albany	AHL	78	32	52	84	35	5	3	1	4	4
	AHL	Totals	320	125	168	293	133	51	27	16	43	41

Born; 1/15/75, Montreal, Quebec. 5-11, 185. Drafted by New Jersey Devils (6th choice, 143rd overall) in 1993 Entry Draft. Member of 1994-95 Calder Cup champion Albany RiverRats. Last amateur club; St. Jean (QMJHL).

David Brumby — Goaltender

Regular Season / Playoffs

Season	Team	League	GP	W	L	T	MIN	SO	AVG	GP	W	L	MIN	SO	AVG
96-97	Baltimore	AHL	2	0	1	0	60	0	7.00	—	—	—	—	—	—
96-97	Columbus	ECHL	18	9	5	2	997	0	4.09	1	0	0	10	0	0.00
97-98	Cleveland	IHL	2	0	1	0	99	0	2.42	—	—	—	—	—	—
97-98	Columbus	ECHL	18	8	8	1	1015	2	2.72	—	—	—	—	—	—
97-98	Wheeling	ECHL	23	15	4	4	1349	2	2.85	15	8	7	963	*2	2.24
98-99	Providence	AHL	2	1	1	0	119	0	3.02	—	—	—	—	—	—
98-99	Wheeling	ECHL	31	11	14	4	1741	0	3.07	—	—	—	—	—	—
98-99	Charlotte	ECHL	6	3	1	0	299	0	3.61	—	—	—	—	—	—
	AHL	Totals	4	1	2	0	179	0	4.36	—	—	—	—	—	—
	ECHL	Totals	96	46	32	11	5401	4	3.17	16	8	7	973	2	2.22

Born; 5/21/75, Victoria, British Columbia. 6-1, 190. Drafted by Toronto Maple Leafs (6th choice, 201st overall) in 1993 Entry Draft. Traded to Wheeling by Columbus with Jason Sisher for Scott Kirton (1/98). Last amateur club; Lethbridge (WHL).

Jayson Brunette — Left Wing

Regular Season / Playoffs

Season	Team	League	GP	G	A	PTS	PIM	GP	G	A	PTS	PIM
98-99	Abilene	WPHL	68	14	11	25	93	3	0	0	0	0

Born; 1/9/76, Fargo, North Dakota. 5-10, 202. Last amateur club; Minnesota-Crookston (NAIA).

Matt Brush — Forward

Regular Season / Playoffs

Season	Team	League	GP	G	A	PTS	PIM	GP	G	A	PTS	PIM
98-99	Florida	ECHL	63	6	14	20	14	6	0	2	2	2

Born; 9/13/74, Birmingham, Michigan. 5-10, 175. Last amateur club; Princeton (ECAC).

Jeff Buchanan — Defenseman
Regular Season / Playoffs

Season	Team	League	GP	G	A	PTS	PIM	GP	G	A	PTS	PIM
92-93	Atlanta	IHL	68	4	18	22	282	9	0	0	0	26
93-94	Atlanta	IHL	76	5	24	29	253	14	0	1	1	20
94-95	Atlanta	IHL	4	0	1	1	9	—	—	—	—	—
94-95	Indianapolis	IHL	25	3	9	12	63	—	—	—	—	—
95-96	Indianapolis	IHL	77	4	14	18	277	5	0	1	1	9
96-97	Orlando	IHL	81	11	27	38	246	—	—	—	—	—
97-98	Orlando	IHL	61	5	20	25	131	—	—	—	—	—
97-98	Kansas City	IHL	7	2	3	5	6	11	0	2	2	40
98-99	Colorado	NHL	6	0	0	0	6	—	—	—	—	—
98-99	Hershey	AHL	38	4	6	10	102	5	0	1	1	4
	IHL	Totals	399	34	116	150	1267	39	0	4	4	95

Born; 5/23/71, Swift Current, Saskatchewan. 5-10, 165. Signed as a free agent by Tampa Bay Lightning (7/13/92). Traded to Chicago Blackhawks by Tampa Bay with Jim Cummins and Tom Tilley for Paul Ysebaert and Rich Sutter (2/22/95). Traded to Kansas City by Orlando with Bill H. Armstrong for Reggie Savage and Jason Herter (3/98). Signed as a free agent by Colorado Avalanche (8/18/98). Member of 1993-94 IHL champion Atlanta Knights. Last amateur club; Saska-

Trevor Buchanan — Left Wing
Regular Season / Playoffs

Season	Team	League	GP	G	A	PTS	PIM	GP	G	A	PTS	PIM
91-92	Louisville	ECHL	62	38	28	66	259	13	3	4	7	77
92-93	Louisville	ECHL	64	23	38	61	270	—	—	—	—	—
93-94	Louisville	ECHL	65	26	26	52	422	6	3	3	6	52
94-95	Houston	IHL	9	1	0	1	18	—	—	—	—	—
94-95	San Antonio	CeHL	48	30	27	57	268	2	0	1	1	19
95-96	San Antonio	CeHL	63	34	27	61	336	13	6	4	10	*83
96-97	Louisville	ECHL	23	4	5	9	96	—	—	—	—	—
96-97	Pensacola	ECHL	34	4	7	11	64	—	—	—	—	—
97-98	Shreveport	WPHL	69	31	32	63	282	8	3	2	5	33
98-99	Shreveport	WPHL	68	32	45	77	161	12	5	11	16	26
	ECHL	Totals	248	95	104	199	1111	19	6	7	13	148
	CeHL	Totals	111	64	54	118	604	15	6	5	11	102
	WPHL	Totals	137	63	77	140	443	20	8	13	21	59

Born; 6/7/69, Thompson, Manitoba. 6-1, 190. Drafted by Hartford Whalers (9th choice, 199th overall) in 1989 Entry Draft. Member of 1998-99 WPHL Champion Shreveport Mudbugs. Last amateur club; Victoria (WHL).

Ashley Buckberger — Right Wing
Regular Season / Playoffs

Season	Team	League	GP	G	A	PTS	PIM	GP	G	A	PTS	PIM
95-96	Carolina	AHL	67	8	9	17	25	—	—	—	—	—
96-97	Carolina	AHL	69	8	10	18	24	—	—	—	—	—
97-98	New Haven	AHL	66	6	11	17	9	2	0	0	0	0
98-99	Canada	National	35	6	5	11	18	—	—	—	—	—
98-99	Grand Rapids	IHL	11	1	2	3	0	—	—	—	—	—
98-99	Las Vegas	IHL	24	3	5	8	6	—	—	—	—	—
	AHL	Totals	202	22	30	52	58	2	0	0	0	0
	IHL	Totals	35	4	7	11	6	—	—	—	—	—

Born; 2/19/75, Esterhazy, Saskatchewan. 6-2, 206. Drafted by Quebec Nordiques (3rd choice, 49th overall) in 1993 Entry Draft. Signed as a free agent by Florida Panthers (8/3/95). Last amateur club; Kamloops (WHL).

Tom Buckley — Center
Regular Season / Playoffs

Season	Team	League	GP	G	A	PTS	PIM	GP	G	A	PTS	PIM
96-97	Springfield	AHL	62	7	12	19	39	2	0	0	0	4
96-97	Richmond	ECHL	3	0	0	0	14	—	—	—	—	—
97-98	New Haven	AHL	14	1	0	1	4	—	—	—	—	—
97-98	Richmond	ECHL	58	23	32	55	102	—	—	—	—	—
98-99	New Haven	AHL	73	8	16	24	48	—	—	—	—	—
	AHL	Totals	149	16	28	44	91	2	0	0	0	4
	ECHL	Totals	61	23	32	55	116	—	—	—	—	—

Born; 5/26/76, Buffalo, New York. 6-1, 204. Drafted by Hartford Whalers (4th choice, 187th overall) in 1994 Entry Draft. Last amateur club; Detroit (OHL).

Jan Bulis — Center
Regular Season / Playoffs

Season	Team	League	GP	G	A	PTS	PIM	GP	G	A	PTS	PIM
97-98	Washington	NHL	48	5	11	16	18	—	—	—	—	—
97-98	Portland	AHL	3	1	4	5	12	—	—	—	—	—
98-99	Washington	NHL	38	7	16	23	6	—	—	—	—	—
98-99	Cincinnati	IHL	10	2	2	4	14	—	—	—	—	—
	NHL	Totals	86	12	27	39	24	—	—	—	—	—

Born; 3/18/78, Pardubice, Czechoslovakia. 6-0, 194. Drafted by Washington Capitals (3rd choice, 43rd overall) in 1996 Entry Draft. Last amateur club; Barrie

Greg Bullock — Center
Regular Season / Playoffs

Season	Team	League	GP	G	A	PTS	PIM	GP	G	A	PTS	PIM
95-96	San Francisco	IHL	79	15	32	47	62	3	0	0	0	2
96-97	St. John's	AHL	75	21	52	73	65	11	2	6	8	17
97-98	St. John's	AHL	34	3	17	20	56	—	—	—	—	—
97-98	Grand Rapids	IHL	35	9	19	28	58	3	0	1	1	4
98-99	Augsburger	Germany	48	10	10	20	22	4	0	0	0	12
	IHL	Totals	114	24	51	75	120	6	0	1	1	6
	AHL	Totals	109	24	69	93	121	11	2	6	8	17

Born; 2/10/73, Cambridge, Ontario. 5-11, 180. Signed as a free agent by Toronto Maple Leafs (8/16/96). Sold to Grand Rapids by Saint John (1/98). Last amateur club; Lowell (Hockey East).

Mark Bultje — Center
Regular Season / Playoffs

Season	Team	League	GP	G	A	PTS	PIM	GP	G	A	PTS	PIM
93-94	Huntsville	ECHL	12	4	3	7	10	—	—	—	—	—
93-94	Erie	ECHL	15	1	5	6	19	—	—	—	—	—
94-95												
95-96	Jacksonville	SHL	50	30	40	70	90	—	—	—	—	—
96-97	Jacksonville	ECHL	16	4	3	7	36	—	—	—	—	—
97-98												
98-99	Mohawk Valley	UHL	39	17	25	42	47	—	—	—	—	—
98-99	Winston-Salem	UHL	18	6	11	17	14	5	2	0	2	6
	UHL	Totals	57	23	36	59	61	5	2	0	2	6
	ECHL	Totals	43	9	11	20	35	—	—	—	—	—

Born; 6/8/73, Etibicoke, Ontario. 5-10, 187. Traded to Saginaw by Mohawk Valley with Mike Hiebert for Dominic Chiasson and Eric Kelly (2/99). Traded to Winston-Salem by Sagina for Chris Palmer (2/99).

Geoff Bumstead — Right Wing
Regular Season / Playoffs

Season	Team	League	GP	G	A	PTS	PIM	GP	G	A	PTS	PIM
94-95	Neusser	Germany	42	51	73	124	181	—	—	—	—	—
95-96	Alaska	WCHL	58	31	36	67	170	5	0	0	0	*34
96-97	New Mexico	WPHL	5	2	0	2	62	3	0	2	2	28
97-98	Utah	IHL	1	0	0	0	0	—	—	—	—	—
97-98	Reno	WCHL	51	14	15	29	214	3	0	0	0	17
98-99	Corpus Christi	WPHL	66	32	38	70	274	4	2	2	4	4
	WCHL	Totals	109	45	51	96	384	8	0	0	0	51
	WPHL	Totals	71	34	38	72	336	7	0	2	2	45

Born; 6/8/72, Winnipeg, Manitoba. 5-10, 205. Selected by Phoenix in 1998 WCHL Dispersal Draft. Last amateur club; Cornell (ECAC).

Scott Burfoot — Center

Regular Season / Playoffs

Season	Team	League	GP	G	A	PTS	PIM	GP	G	A	PTS	PIM
91-92	Erie	ECHL	1	2	1	3	0	—	—	—	—	—
92-93	Roanoke	ECHL	48	28	32	60	22	—	—	—	—	—
93-94	Peoria	IHL	4	0	0	0	0	—	—	—	—	—
93-94	Huntsville	ECHL	62	31	65	96	80	3	4	5	9	4
94-95	Fort Wayne	IHL	10	4	2	6	6	—	—	—	—	—
94-95	Erie	ECHL	56	29	*68	*97	66	—	—	—	—	—
95-96	Flint	CoHL	52	21	54	75	30	14	12	19	31	8
96-97	Richmond	ECHL	62	32	62	94	37	8	5	10	15	8
97-98	Richmond	ECHL	69	26	51	77	75	—	—	—	—	—
98-99	Quad City	UHL	58	18	61	79	40	16	4	11	15	18
	IHL	Totals	14	4	2	6	6	—	—	—	—	—
	ECHL	Totals	298	148	279	427	280	11	9	15	24	12
	UHL	Totals	110	39	115	154	70	30	16	30	46	26

Born; 9/23/67, Winnipeg, Manitoba. 5-9, 170. 1994-95 Second Team ECHL All-Star. 1995-96 CoHL Most Sportsmanlike Player and Playoff MVP. Member of 1995-96 Colonial Cup Champion Flint Generals. Selected by Fort Wayne in 1999 UHL Expansion Draft. Last amateur club; Mercy hurst (NCAA-3).

Dru Burgess — Center

Regular Season / Playoffs

Season	Team	League	GP	G	A	PTS	PIM	GP	G	A	PTS	PIM
98-99	Roanoke	ECHL	64	21	23	44	20	12	1	2	3	4

Born; 12/7/74, Hamilton, Ontario 5-11, 195. Last amateur club; Colgate (ECAC).

Van Burgess — Center

Regular Season / Playoffs

Season	Team	League	GP	G	A	PTS	PIM	GP	G	A	PTS	PIM
95-96	Huntington	ECHL	69	20	35	55	108	—	—	—	—	—
96-97	Huntington	ECHL	70	47	47	94	50	—	—	—	—	—
97-98												
98-99	Hamburg	Germany	46	29	30	59	65	—	—	—	—	—
	ECHL	Totals	139	67	82	149	158	—	—	—	—	—

Born; 7/5/73, Lahr, Germany. 5-11, 190.

Dennis Burke — Center

Regular Season / Playoffs

Season	Team	League	GP	G	A	PTS	PIM	GP	G	A	PTS	PIM
97-98	Bracknell	BSL	57	12	10	22	20	6	3	0	3	0
98-99	Bracknell	BSL	25	5	5	10	18	—	—	—	—	—
98-99	Greenville	ECHL	4	2	0	2	0	—	—	—	—	—
98-99	Columbus	ECHL	5	0	0	0	0	—	—	—	—	—
	ECHL	Totals	9	2	0	2	0	—	—	—	—	—

Born; 12/7/74, Newton, Massachusetts. 6-1, 180.

Toby Burkitt — Center

Regular Season / Playoffs

Season	Team	League	GP	G	A	PTS	PIM	GP	G	A	PTS	PIM
97-98	Shreveport	WPHL	69	30	35	65	49	8	3	7	10	6
98-99	Shreveport	WPHL	68	29	50	79	48	12	4	11	15	2
	WPHL	Totals	137	59	85	144	97	20	7	18	25	8

Born; 2/4/72, Oshawa, Ontario. 6-0, 190. Member of 1998-99 WPHL Champion Shreveport Mudbugs. Last amateur club; University of New Brunswick (AUAA).

Garrett Burnett — Defenseman

Regular Season / Playoffs

Season	Team	League	GP	G	A	PTS	PIM	GP	G	A	PTS	PIM
95-96	Utica	CoHL	15	0	1	1	78	—	—	—	—	—
95-96	Oklahoma City	CeHL	3	0	0	0	20	—	—	—	—	—
95-96	Tulsa	CeHL	6	1	0	1	94	—	—	—	—	—
95-96	Nashville	ECHL	3	0	0	0	22	—	—	—	—	—
95-96	Jacksonville	ECHL	8	0	1	1	38	1	0	0	0	0
96-97	Knoxville	ECHL	50	5	11	16	321	—	—	—	—	—
97-98	Philadelphia	AHL	14	1	2	3	129	—	—	—	—	—
97-98	Johnstown	ECHL	34	1	1	2	331	—	—	—	—	—
98-99	Kentucky	AHL	31	1	0	1	186	—	—	—	—	—
	AHL	Totals	45	2	2	4	315	—	—	—	—	—
	ECHL	Totals	95	6	13	19	712	1	0	0	0	0
	CeHL	Totals	9	1	0	1	114	—	—	—	—	—

Born; 9/23/75, Coquitlim, British Columbia. 6-3, 220. Signed as a free agent by San Jose Sharks (7/22/98). Last amateur club; Kitchener (OHL).

Shawn Burr — Left Wing

Regular Season / Playoffs

Season	Team	League	GP	G	A	PTS	PIM	GP	G	A	PTS	PIM
84-85	Kitchener	OHL	48	24	42	66	50	4	3	3	6	2
84-85	Detroit	NHL	9	0	0	0	2	—	—	—	—	—
84-85	Adirondack	AHL	4	0	0	0	2	—	—	—	—	—
85-86	Kitchener	OHL	59	60	67	127	104	5	2	3	5	8
85-86	Detroit	NHL	5	1	0	1	4	—	—	—	—	—
85-86	Adirondack	AHL	3	2	2	4	2	17	5	7	12	32
86-87	Detroit	NHL	80	22	25	47	107	16	7	2	9	20
87-88	Detroit	NHL	78	17	23	40	97	9	3	1	4	14
88-89	Detroit	NHL	79	19	27	46	78	6	1	2	3	6
89-90	Detroit	NHL	76	24	32	56	82	—	—	—	—	—
89-90	Adirondack	AHL	3	4	2	6	2	—	—	—	—	—
90-91	Detroit	NHL	80	20	30	50	112	7	0	4	4	15
91-92	Detroit	NHL	79	19	32	51	118	11	1	5	6	10
92-93	Detroit	NHL	80	10	25	35	74	7	2	1	3	2
93-94	Detroit	NHL	51	10	12	22	31	7	2	0	2	6
94-95	Detroit	NHL	42	6	8	14	60	16	0	2	2	6
95-96	Tampa Bay	NHL	81	13	15	28	119	6	0	2	2	8
96-97	Tampa Bay	NHL	74	14	21	35	106	—	—	—	—	—
97-98	San Jose	NHL	42	6	6	12	50	6	0	0	0	8
98-99	San Jose	NHL	18	0	1	1	29	—	—	—	—	—
98-99	Kentucky	AHL	26	10	14	24	29	12	4	9	13	10
	NHL	Totals	874	181	257	438	1069	91	16	19	35	95
	AHL	Totals	36	16	18	34	35	29	9	16	25	42

Born; 7/1/66, Sarnia, Ontario. 6-1, 205. Drafted by Detroit Red Wings (1st choice, 7th overall) in 1984 Entry Draft. Traded to Tampa Bay Lightning by Detroit with Detroit's third round choice (later traded to Bostonb-Boston selected Jason Doyle) in 1996 Entry Draft for Marc Bergevin and Ben Hankinson (8/17/95). Traded to San Jose Sharks by Tampa Bay for San Jose's fifth round selection (Mark Thompson) in 1997 Entry Draft (6/21/97). Traded to Tampa Bay Lightning by San Jose with Andrei Zyuzin, Bill Houlder and Steve Guolla for Niklas Sundstrom and a third round draft choice in 2000 (8/4/99). Member of 1985-86 AHL Champion Adirondack Red Wings. Last amateur club; Kitchener

Randy Burridge — Left Wing

Regular Season / Playoffs

Season	Team	League	GP	G	A	PTS	PIM	GP	G	A	PTS	PIM
85-86	Peterborough	OHL	17	15	11	26	23	3	1	3	4	2
85-86	Boston	NHL	52	17	25	42	28	3	0	4	4	12
85-86	Moncton	AHL	—	—	—	—	—	3	0	2	2	2
86-87	Boston	NHL	23	1	4	5	16	2	1	0	1	2
86-87	Moncton	AHL	47	26	41	67	139	3	1	2	3	30
87-88	Boston	NHL	79	27	28	55	105	23	3	10	12	16
88-89	Boston	NHL	80	31	30	61	39	10	5	2	7	6
89-90	Boston	NHL	63	17	15	32	47	21	4	11	15	14
90-91	Boston	NHL	62	15	13	28	40	19	0	3	3	39
91-92	Washington	NHL	66	23	44	67	50	2	0	1	1	0
92-93	Washington	NHL	4	0	0	0	0	4	1	0	1	0
92-93	Baltimore	AHL	2	0	1	1	2	—	—	—	—	—
93-94	Washington	NHL	78	25	17	42	73	11	0	2	2	12
94-95	Washington	NHL	2	0	0	0	2	—	—	—	—	—
94-95	Los Angeles	NHL	38	4	15	19	8	—	—	—	—	—
95-96	Buffalo	NHL	74	25	33	58	30	—	—	—	—	—
96-97	Buffalo	NHL	55	10	21	31	20	12	5	1	6	2
97-98	Buffalo	NHL	30	4	6	10	0	—	—	—	—	—
97-98	Rochester	AHL	6	0	1	1	19	1	0	1	1	0
98-99	Las Vegas	IHL	25	7	12	19	8	—	—	—	—	—
98-99	Hannover	Germany	14	7	6	13	65	—	—	—	—	—
	NHL	Totals	696	199	251	450	478	107	18	34	52	103
	AHL	Totals	55	26	43	69	160	7	1	5	6	32

Born; 1/7/66, Fort Erie, Ontario. 5-9, 188. Drafted by Boston Bruins (7th choice, 157th overall) in 1985 Entry Draft. Traded to Washington Capitals by Boston for Stephen Leach (6/21/91). Traded to Los Angles Kings by Washington for Warren Rychel (2/10/95). Signed as a free agent by Buffalo Sabres (10/5/95). Last amateur club; Peterborough (OHL).

Scott Burt — Left Wing

Regular Season / Playoffs

Season	Team	League	GP	G	A	PTS	PIM	GP	G	A	PTS	PIM
97-98	Red Deer	WHL	15	6	4	10	22	—	—	—	—	—
97-98	Edmonton	WHL	53	35	32	67	77	—	—	—	—	—
97-98	Toledo	ECHL	6	1	2	3	0	5	1	0	1	4
98-99	Toledo	ECHL	58	18	19	37	111	7	1	5	6	6
	ECHL	Totals	64	19	21	40	111	12	2	5	7	10

Born; 2/7/77, Grand Forks, British Columbia. 6-0, 180. Last amateur club; Edmonton (WHL).

Joe Burton — Center

Regular Season / Playoffs

Season	Team	League	GP	G	A	PTS	PIM	GP	G	A	PTS	PIM
92-93	Oklahoma City	CeHL	55	35	26	61	25	11	8	7	15	4
93-94	Oklahoma City	CeHL	54	32	24	56	28	7	4	3	7	4
94-95	Oklahoma City	CeHL	66	*59	38	97	20	5	3	4	7	4
95-96	Oklahoma City	CeHL	64	66	32	98	53	13	6	3	9	2
96-97	Oklahoma City	CeHL	66	53	41	94	39	4	2	5	7	14
97-98	Oklahoma City	CHL	69	*74	50	124	43	11	9	9	18	12
98-99	Oklahoma City	CHL	69	*73	37	110	41	11	6	7	13	2
	CHL	Totals	443	392	248	640	249	62	38	38	76	42

Born; 4/23/67, Garden City, Michigan. 5-9, 170. 1994-95 CeHL First Team All-Star. 1995-96 CeHL Second Team All-Star. 1996-97 CeHL First Team All-Star. 1997-98 CHL MVP. Member of 1995-96 CeHL champion Oklahoma City Blazers. Last amateur club; University of Michigan-Dearborn (NCAA).

Sven Butenschon — Defenseman

Regular Season / Playoffs

Season	Team	League	GP	G	A	PTS	PIM	GP	G	A	PTS	PIM
96-97	Cleveland	IHL	75	3	12	15	68	10	0	1	1	4
97-98	Pittsburgh	NHL	8	0	0	0	6	—	—	—	—	—
97-98	Syracuse	AHL	65	14	23	37	66	5	1	2	3	0
98-99	Pittsburgh	NHL	17	0	0	0	6	—	—	—	—	—
98-99	Houston	IHL	57	1	4	5	81	—	—	—	—	—
	NHL	Totals	25	0	0	0	12	—	—	—	—	—
	IHL	Totals	132	4	16	20	149	10	0	1	1	4

Born; 3/22/76, Itzehoe, West Germany. 6-5, 201. Drafted by Pittsburgh Penguins (3rd choice, 57th overall) in 1994 Entry Draft. Last amateur club; Brandon

David Butler — Forward

Regular Season / Playoffs

Season	Team	League	GP	G	A	PTS	PIM	GP	G	A	PTS	PIM
98-99	Corpus Christi	WPHL	4	0	0	0	0	—	—	—	—	—

Born; Selected by Lubbock in 1999 WPHL Expansion Draft. Last amateur club; McGill (OUAA).

Rod Butler — Right Wing/Defenseman

Regular Season / Playoffs

Season	Team	League	GP	G	A	PTS	PIM	GP	G	A	PTS	PIM
95-96	Mobile	ECHL	42	5	4	9	46	—	—	—	—	—
96-97	Macon	CeHL	2	0	0	0	17	—	—	—	—	—
96-97	Nashville	CeHL	22	9	13	22	26	—	—	—	—	—
97-98	Tallahasee	ECHL	6	1	0	1	0	—	—	—	—	—
97-98	Nashville	CHL	39	6	10	16	60	9	3	1	4	32
98-99	Fayetteville	CHL	40	4	12	16	76	—	—	—	—	—
98-99	Oklahoma City	CHL	25	7	9	16	40	12	2	1	3	33
	CHL	Totals	128	26	44	70	219	21	5	2	7	69

Born; 2/27/75, Los Angeles, California. 6-3, 200. Selected by San Antonio in 1998 CHL Expansion Draft. Traded to Oklahoma City by Fayetteville for Jasen Rintala (1/99). Last amateur club; Tacoma (WHL).

Viacheslav Butseyev — Center

Regular Season / Playoffs

Season	Team	League	GP	G	A	PTS	PIM	GP	G	A	PTS	PIM
92-93	Philadelphia	NHL	52	2	14	16	61	—	—	—	—	—
92-93	Hershey	AHL	24	8	10	18	51	—	—	—	—	—
93-94	Philadelphia	NHL	47	12	9	21	58	—	—	—	—	—
93-94	San Jose	NHL	12	0	2	2	10	—	—	—	—	—
94-95	Togliatti	Russia	9	2	6	8	6	—	—	—	—	—
94-95	San Jose	NHL	6	2	0	2	0	—	—	—	—	—
94-95	Kansas City	IHL	13	3	4	7	12	3	0	0	0	2
95-96	Anaheim	NHL	7	1	0	1	0	—	—	—	—	—
95-96	Baltimore	AHL	62	23	42	65	70	12	4	8	12	28
96-97	Farjestad	Sweden	40	6	7	13	108	8	3	4	7	41
97-98	Fort Wayne	IHL	76	36	51	87	128	4	2	2	4	4
98-99	Florida	NHL	1	0	0	0	2	—	—	—	—	—
98-99	Ottawa	NHL	2	0	1	1	2	—	—	—	—	—
98-99	Fort Wayne	IHL	71	28	44	72	123	2	1	0	1	4
	NHL	Totals	127	17	26	43	133	—	—	—	—	—
	IHL	Totals	160	67	99	166	263	9	3	2	5	10
	AHL	Totals	86	31	52	83	121	12	4	8	12	28

Born; 6/13/70, Togliatti, USSR. 6-2, 200. Drafted by Philadelphia Flyers (10th choice, 109th overall) in 1990 Entry Draft. Traded to San Jose Sharks by Philadelphia for Rob Zettler (2/1/94). Signed as a free agent by Anaheim Mighty Ducks (10/19/95). Signed as a free agent by Florida Panthers (8/12/98). Traded to Ottawa Senators by Florida for sixth round choice (later traded to Dallas-Dallas selected Justin Cox) in 1999 Entry Draft. . 1997-98 IHL Second Team All-Star.

Jamie Butt — Left Wing

Regular Season / Playoffs

Season	Team	League	GP	G	A	PTS	PIM	GP	G	A	PTS	PIM
97-98	Tacoma	WCHL	50	13	11	24	105	12	2	4	6	38
98-99	Tacoma	WCHL	25	3	2	5	57	1	0	0	0	0
	WCHL	Totals	75	16	13	29	162	13	2	4	6	38

Born; 4/4/76, Richmond, Alberta. 6-0, 190. Drafted by New York Rangers (14th choice, 267th overall) in 1994 Entry Draft. Member of 1998-99 WCHL Champion Tacoma Sabrecats.

Kevin Butt — Goaltender

Regular Season										Playoffs					
Season	Team	League	GP	W	L	T	MIN	SO	AVG	GP	W	L	MIN	SO	AVG
90-91	Detroit	OHL	30	—	—	—	1592	0	4.57	—	—	—	—	—	—
90-91	Greensboro	ECHL	1	0	0	0	18	0	6.66	—	—	—	—	—	—
91-92	St. Thomas	CoHL	30	13	10	3	1606	1	4.22	12	7	5	744	0	4.11
92-93	St. Thomas	CoHL	41	17	16	3	2199	0	4.94	14	8	6	854	1	3.44
93-94	Knoxville	ECHL	1	1	0	0	60	0	4.00	—	—	—	—	—	—
93-94	Chatham	CoHL	43	28	11	2	2376	0	4.37	15	8	6	888	0	4.05
94-95	Saginaw	CoHL	45	21	15	4	2412	1	3.95	10	5	3	542	0	4.31
95-96	Quad City	CoHL	37	15	8	2	2075	0	4.16	—	—	—	—	—	—
95-96	Detroit	CoHL	7	4	2	1	406	0	5.17	5	1	3	233	0	4.90
96-97	Port Huron	CoHL	46	25	15	3	2451	0	3.72	3	1	1	136	0	3.96
97-98	Port Huron	UHL	1	0	0	1	60	0	2.00	—	—	—	—	—	—
97-98	Saginaw	UHL	41	12	20	5	2195	0	4.46	—	—	—	—	—	—
98-99	Saginaw	UHL	1	0	1	0	60	0	5.00	—	—	—	—	—	—
	UHL	Totals	292	135	98	24	15840	2	4.27	59	30	24	3397	1	4.01
	ECHL	Totals	2	1	0	0	78	0	4.62	—	—	—	—	—	—

Born; 6/16/70, Oshawa, Ontario. 5-8, 181. Last amateur club; Detroit (OHL).

Mike Buzak — Goaltender

Regular Season										Playoffs					
Season	Team	League	GP	W	L	T	MIN	SO	AVG	GP	W	L	MIN	SO	AVG
95-96	Worcester	AHL	30	9	10	5	1671	0	3.05	—	—	—	—	—	—
96-97	Worcester	AHL	19	9	4	3	973	1	2.53	1	0	1	59	0	3.06
96-97	Baton Rouge	ECHL	3	0	2	0	109	0	3.87	—	—	—	—	—	—
97-98	Long Beach	IHL	31	18	6	5	1763	*6	*1.97	5	0	3	216	0	3.06
97-98	Tucson	WCHL	2	0	2	0	107	0	3.37	—	—	—	—	—	—
97-98	Phoenix	WCHL	6	3	3	0	358	0	4.53	—	—	—	—	—	—
98-99	Albany	AHL	48	22	13	3	2382	0	2.57	5	2	1	272	0	2.65
	AHL	Totals	97	40	27	11	5026	1	2.72	6	2	2	331	0	2.72
	WCHL	Totals	8	3	5	0	465	0	4.26	—	—	—	—	—	—

Born; 2/10/73, Edson, Alberta. 6-3, 183. Drafted by St. Louis Blues (5th choice, 167th overall) in 1993 Entry Draft. Signed as a free agent by Los Angeles Kings (1998). Signed as a free agent by New Jersey Devils (7/16/98). 1997-98 Shared IHL's Norris Trophy (fewest goals against) with Kay Whitmore. Last amateur club; Michigan State (CCHA).

Petr Buzek — Defenseman

Regular Season							Playoffs				
Season	Team	League	GP	G	A	PTS	PIM	GP	G	A	PTS	PIM
96-97	Michigan	IHL	67	4	6	10	48	—	—	—	—	—
97-98	Dallas	NHL	2	0	0	0	2	—	—	—	—	—
97-98	Michigan	IHL	60	10	15	25	58	2	0	1	1	17
98-99	Dallas	NHL	2	0	0	0	2	—	—	—	—	—
98-99	Michigan	IHL	74	5	14	19	68	5	0	0	0	10
	NHL	Totals	4	0	0	0	4	—	—	—	—	—
	IHL	Totals	201	19	35	54	174	7	0	1	1	27

Born; 4/26/77, Jihlava, Czechoslovakia. 6-0, 205. Drafted by Dallas Stars (3rd choice, 63rd overall) in 1995 Entry Draft. Selected by Atlanta Thrashers in 1999 NHL Expansion Draft (6/25/99).

John Byce — Right Wing

Regular Season							Playoffs				
Season	Team	League	GP	G	A	PTS	PIM	GP	G	A	PTS	PIM
89-90	Wisconsin	WCHA	46	27	44	71	20	—	—	—	—	—
89-90	Boston	NHL	—	—	—	—	—	8	2	0	2	2
90-91	Maine	AHL	53	19	29	48	20	—	—	—	—	—
90-91	Boston	NHL	18	1	3	4	6	—	—	—	—	—
91-92	Maine	AHL	55	29	21	50	41	—	—	—	—	—
91-92	Baltimore	AHL	20	9	5	14	4	—	—	—	—	—
91-92	Boston	NHL	3	1	0	1	0	—	—	—	—	—
92-93	Baltimore	AHL	62	35	44	79	26	7	4	5	9	4
93-94	Milwaukee	IHL	28	7	4	11	10	3	2	1	3	0
94-95	Portland	AHL	6	1	1	2	2	—	—	—	—	—
94-95	San Diego	IHL	5	2	3	5	2	—	—	—	—	—
94-95	Milwaukee	IHL	30	9	11	20	10	15	4	5	9	4
95-96	Los Angeles	IHL	82	39	46	85	40	—	—	—	—	—
96-97	Long Beach	IHL	80	29	29	58	14	18	6	7	13	4
97-98	Long Beach	IHL	17	9	8	17	10	12	4	1	5	4
98-99	Long Beach	IHL	37	8	11	19	8	—	—	—	—	—
98-99	Utah	IHL	35	11	20	31	18	—	—	—	—	—
	NHL	Totals	21	2	3	5	6	8	2	0	2	2
	IHL	Totals	304	114	132	246	112	48	16	14	30	12
	AHL	Totals	196	93	100	193	93	7	4	5	9	4

Born; 8/9/67, Madison, Wisconsin. 6-1, 180. Drafted by Boston Bruins (11th choice, 220th overall) in 1985 Entry Draft. Traded to Washington Capitals by Boston Bruins with Dennis Smith for Brent Hughes and future considerations (2/24/92). Last amateur club; University of Wisconsin (WCHA).

Dan Bylsma — Right Wing

Regular Season							Playoffs				
Season	Team	League	GP	G	A	PTS	PIM	GP	G	A	PTS	PIM
92-93	Greensboro	ECHL	60	25	35	60	66	1	0	1	1	10
92-93	Rochester	AHL	2	0	1	1	0	—	—	—	—	—
93-94	Greensboro	ECHL	25	14	16	30	52	—	—	—	—	—
93-94	Albany	AHL	3	0	1	1	2	—	—	—	—	—
93-94	Moncton	AHL	50	12	16	28	25	21	3	4	7	31
94-95	Phoenix	IHL	81	19	23	42	41	9	4	4	8	4
95-96	Los Angeles	NHL	4	0	0	0	0	—	—	—	—	—
95-96	Phoenix	IHL	78	22	20	42	48	4	1	0	1	2
96-97	Los Angeles	NHL	79	3	6	9	32	—	—	—	—	—
97-98	Los Angeles	NHL	65	3	9	12	33	2	0	0	0	0
97-98	Long Beach	IHL	8	2	3	5	0	—	—	—	—	—
98-99	Los Angeles	NHL	8	0	0	0	2	—	—	—	—	—
98-99	Long Beach	IHL	58	10	8	18	53	4	0	0	0	8
98-99	Springfield	AHL	2	0	2	2	2	—	—	—	—	—
	NHL	Totals	156	6	15	21	67	2	0	0	0	0
	IHL	Totals	225	53	54	107	142	17	5	4	9	14
	AHL	Totals	57	12	19	31	29	21	3	4	7	31
	ECHL	Totals	85	39	51	90	118	1	0	1	1	10

Born; 9/19/70, Grand Haven, Michigan. 6-2, 215. Drafted by Winnipeg Jets (7th choice, 109th overall) in 1989 Entry Draft. Signed as a free agent by Los Angeles Kings (7/7/94). Last amateur club; Bowling Green (CCHA).

Jason Byrnes — Left Wing

Regular Season							Playoffs				
Season	Team	League	GP	G	A	PTS	PIM	GP	G	A	PTS	PIM
98-99	Baton Rouge	ECHL	27	1	2	3	42	—	—	—	—	—

Born; 5/9/77, Brockville, Ontario. 5-11, 198. Last amateur club; Kitchener

Chad Cabana
Regular Season — Left Wing — Playoffs

Season	Team	League	GP	G	A	PTS	PIM	GP	G	A	PTS	PIM
95-96	Carolina	AHL	59	4	9	13	159	—	—	—	—	—
96-97	Carolina	AHL	55	8	5	13	221	—	—	—	—	—
96-97	Port Huron	CoHL	14	7	9	16	49	—	—	—	—	—
97-98	New Haven	AHL	34	5	5	10	163	2	0	0	0	7
97-98	Fort Wayne	IHL	6	0	0	0	22	—	—	—	—	—
98-99	New Haven	AHL	66	6	5	11	251	—	—	—	—	—
	AHL	Totals	214	23	24	47	794	2	0	0	0	7

Born; 10/1/74, Bonnyville, Alberta. 6-1, 200. Drafted by Florida Panthers (11th choice, 213th overall) in 1993 Entry Draft. Last amateur club; Tri-City (WHL).

Clint Cabana
Regular Season — Defenseman — Playoffs

Season	Team	League	GP	G	A	PTS	PIM	GP	G	A	PTS	PIM
96-97	Medicine Hat	WHL	4	0	1	1	10	—	—	—	—	—
96-97	Edmonton	WHL	67	3	12	15	302	—	—	—	—	—
96-97	Syracuse	AHL	2	0	0	0	2	—	—	—	—	—
97-98	Edmonton	WHL	17	1	5	6	60	—	—	—	—	—
97-98	Regina	WHL	34	1	1	2	140	8	1	0	1	16
98-99	Syracuse	AHL	19	0	1	1	86	—	—	—	—	—
98-99	Augusta	ECHL	6	0	0	0	37	2	0	0	0	2
	AHL	Totals	21	0	1	1	88	—	—	—	—	—

Born; 4/28/78, Bonnyville, ALberta. 6-2, 195. Drafted by Vancouver Canucks (6th choice, 175th overall) in 1996 Entry Draft. Last amateur club; Regina

Cory Cadden
Regular Season — Goaltender — Playoffs

Season	Team	League	GP	W	L	T	MIN	SO	AVG	GP	W	L	MIN	SO	AVG
92-93	Knoxville	ECHL	42	15	23	3	2413	0	4.70	—	—	—	—	—	—
93-94	Knoxville	ECHL	40	26	8	4	2349	*2	3.09	3	1	2	179	0	4.68
94-95	Knoxville	ECHL	46	19	20	5	2688	0	3.44	4	1	3	247	0	3.89
95-96	Knoxville	ECHL	17	6	9	1	915	0	4.39	—	—	—	—	—	—
95-96	Dayton	ECHL	14	7	6	0	765	0	3.61	3	0	2	160	0	3.74
96-97	Peoria	ECHL	5	2	2	1	278	0	3.89	—	—	—	—	—	—
96-97	South Carolina	ECHL	18	8	4	2	921	0	3.91	—	—	—	—	—	—
97-98	Saint John	AHL	3	0	1	1	145	0	4.55	—	—	—	—	—	—
97-98	South Carolina	ECHL	45	30	11	1	2566	0	2.85	5	2	3	304	1	2.57
98-99	South Carolina	ECHL	45	22	13	6	2449	3	3.09	—	—	—	—	—	—
	ECHL	Totals	272	135	96	23	15344	5	3.53	15	4	10	790	1	4.02

Born; 2/21/69, Edmonton, Alberta. 6-2, 195. 1993-94 ECHL Top Goaltender. 1993-94 ECHL First Team All-Star. Last amateur club; North Dakota (WCHA).

Mark Cadotte
Regular Season — Left Wing — Playoffs

Season	Team	League	GP	G	A	PTS	PIM	GP	G	A	PTS	PIM
98-99	Pee Dee	ECHL	18	1	8	9	29	—	—	—	—	—
98-99	Roanoke	ECHL	44	10	10	20	77	—	—	—	—	—
	ECHL	Totals	62	11	18	29	106	—	—	—	—	—

Born; Last amateur club; London (OHL).

Darcy Cahill
Regular Season — Center — Playoffs

Season	Team	League	GP	G	A	PTS	PIM	GP	G	A	PTS	PIM
91-92	St. Thomas	CoHL	54	22	48	70	44	7	2	5	7	14
92-93	St. Thomas	CoHL	54	25	44	69	53	5	2	1	3	0
93-94	Lee Valley	BHL	44	79	157	236	82	—	—	—	—	—
94-95	Humberside	BHL	44	50	76	126	32	—	—	—	—	—
95-96	Humberside	BHL	35	24	47	71	128	—	—	—	—	—
95-96	Chelmsford	BHL	14	15	25	40	88	—	—	—	—	—
96-97	San Antonio	CeHL	3	0	1	1	4	—	—	—	—	—
96-97	Nashville	CeHL	8	3	7	10	14	—	—	—	—	—
97-98	Columbus	ECHL	20	0	5	5	27	—	—	—	—	—
98-99	Swindon											
98-99	Waco	WPHL	5	1	4	5	7	—	—	—	—	—
98-99	Austin	WPHL	5	2	1	3	0	—	—	—	—	—
	CoHL	Totals	108	47	92	139	97	12	4	6	10	14
	WPHL	Totals	10	3	5	8	7	—	—	—	—	—
	CeHL	Totals	11	3	8	11	18	—	—	—	—	—

Born; 8/19/70, Kingston, Ontario. 6-0, 188. Last amateur club; Hamilton (OHL).

Aaron Cain
Regular Season — Left Wing — Playoffs

Season	Team	League	GP	G	A	PTS	PIM	GP	G	A	PTS	PIM
96-97	Northern Michigan	CCHA	38	6	3	9	69	—	—	—	—	—
96-97	Richmond	ECHL	5	0	0	0	23	—	—	—	—	—
97-98	Fayetteville	CHL	70	19	20	39	211	—	—	—	—	—
98-99	Johnstown	ECHL	68	14	12	26	100	—	—	—	—	—
	ECHL	Totals	73	14	12	26	123	—	—	—	—	—

Born; 2/16/73, Regina, Saskatchewan. 6-3, 215. Last amateur club; Northern Michigan (WCHA).

Eric Cairns
Regular Season — Defenseman — Playoffs

Season	Team	League	GP	G	A	PTS	PIM	GP	G	A	PTS	PIM
94-95	Birmingham	ECHL	11	1	3	4	49	—	—	—	—	—
94-95	Binghamton	AHL	27	0	3	3	134	9	1	1	2	28
95-96	Binghamton	AHL	46	1	13	14	192	4	0	0	0	37
95-96	Charlotte	ECHL	6	0	1	1	34	—	—	—	—	—
96-97	Rangers	NHL	40	0	1	1	147	3	0	0	0	0
96-97	Binghamton	AHL	10	1	1	2	96	—	—	—	—	—
97-98	Rangers	NHL	39	0	3	3	92	—	—	—	—	—
97-98	Hartford	AHL	7	1	2	3	43	—	—	—	—	—
98-99	Islanders	NHL	9	0	3	3	23	—	—	—	—	—
98-99	Hartford	AHL	11	0	2	2	49	—	—	—	—	—
98-99	Lowell	AHL	24	0	0	0	91	3	1	0	1	32
	NHL	Totals	88	0	7	7	262	3	0	0	0	0
	AHL	Totals	125	3	21	24	605	16	2	1	3	97
	ECHL	Totals	17	1	4	5	83	—	—	—	—	—

Born; 6/27/74, Oakville, Ontario. 6-5, 230. Drafted by New York Rangers (3rd choice, 72nd overall) in 1992 Entry Draft. Claimed on waivers by New York Islanders from Rangers (12/23/98). Last amateur club; Detroit (OHL).

Shane Calder
Regular Season — Right Wing — Playoffs

Season	Team	League	GP	G	A	PTS	PIM	GP	G	A	PTS	PIM
95-96	Columbus	ECHL	28	5	5	10	124	—	—	—	—	—
95-96	Nashville	ECHL	26	7	7	14	115	5	0	4	4	12
96-97	Pensacola	ECHL	64	18	19	37	221	10	1	1	2	77
97-98	Pensacola	ECHL	64	20	17	37	170	19	8	3	11	39
98-99	Pensacola	ECHL	70	17	39	56	213	—	—	—	—	—
	ECHL	Totals	252	67	87	154	643	34	9	8	17	128

Born; 8/28/74, Portage la Praire, Quebec. 5-11, 180. Last amateur club; Saskatoon (WHL).

Everett Cardwell
Regular Season — Right Wing — Playoffs

Season	Team	League	GP	G	A	PTS	PIM	GP	G	A	PTS	PIM
91-92	Dayton	ECHL	1	0	0	0	0	—	—	—	—	—
92-93	Birmingham	ECHL	11	0	0	0	0	—	—	—	—	—
93-94	Fort Worth	CHL	3	0	0	0	0	—	—	—	—	—
94-95												
95-96												
96-97												
97-98												
98-99	Birmingham	ECHL	12	0	0	0	6	—	—	—	—	—
	ECHL	Totals	24	0	0	0	6	—	—	—	—	—

Born; 6/23/63, Chesley, Ontario. 5-11, 200.

Ryan Caley
Regular Season — Goaltender — Playoffs

Season	Team	League	GP	W	L	T	MIN	SO	AVG	GP	W	L	MIN	SO	AVG
96-97	Muskegon	CoHL	23	10	8	2	1284	0	3.55	2	0	2	119	0	*2.53
97-98	Muskegon	UHL	28	14	9	4	1611	2	3.13	—	—	—	—	—	—
97-98	Port Huron	UHL	6	2	4	0	358	0	3.52	1	0	1	60	0	6.00
98-99	Port Huron	UHL	4	3	1	0	240	0	2.00	—	—	—	—	—	—
98-99	Mohawk Valley	UHL	19	7	8	3	1046	0	3.32	—	—	—	—	—	—
98-99	Winston-Salem	UHL	14	4	5	1	688	0	3.58	1	0	1	60	0	5.00

Born; 12/12/75, Owen Sound, Ontario. 6-2, 205. Traded to Port Huron by Muskegon for Akil Adams (3/98). Traded to Mohawk Valley by Port Huron with Mike Hiebert for Wayne Muir (11/98). Traded to Winston-Salem by Mohawk Valley for Josh Tymchak and Doug Reynolds (2/99).

Troy Caley — Center

Season	Team	League	GP	G	A	PTS	PIM	GP	G	A	PTS	PIM
			Regular Season					Playoffs				
96-97	Utica	CoHL	2	0	0	0	0	—	—	—	—	—
96-97	Muskegon	CoHL	2	0	0	0	0	—	—	—	—	—
96-97	Saginaw	CoHL	7	0	0	0	2	—	—	—	—	—
97-98	Tulsa	CHL	61	22	27	49	57	4	3	1	4	6
98-99	Tulsa	CHL	65	41	29	70	68	—	—	—	—	—
	CHL	Totals	126	63	56	119	125	4	3	1	4	6
	CoHL	Totals	11	0	0	0	2	—	—	—	—	—

Born; 1/14/74, Owen Sound, Ontario. 5-10, 180.

Jan Caloun — Right Wing

Season	Team	League	GP	G	A	PTS	PIM	GP	G	A	PTS	PIM
			Regular Season					Playoffs				
94-95	Kansas City	IHL	76	34	39	73	50	21	13	10	23	18
95-96	San Jose	NHL	11	8	3	11	0	—	—	—	—	—
95-96	Kansas City	IHL	61	38	30	68	58	5	0	1	1	6
96-97	San Jose	NHL	2	0	0	0	2	—	—	—	—	—
96-97	Kentucky	AHL	66	43	43	86	68	4	0	1	1	4
97-98	HIFK	Finland	41	22	26	48	8	9	6	11	17	6
98-99	HIFK	Finland	51	24	57	81	95	8	8	6	14	31
	NHL	Totals	13	8	3	11	2	—	—	—	—	—
	IHL	Totals	137	72	69	141	108	26	13	11	24	24

Born; 12/20/72, Usti-ned-laben, Czechoslovakia. 5-10, 175. Drafted by San Jose Sharks (4th choice, 75th overall) in 1992 Entry Draft. 1996-97 AHL Second Team All-Star.

Brian Callahan — Left Wing

Season	Team	League	GP	G	A	PTS	PIM	GP	G	A	PTS	PIM
			Regular Season					Playoffs				
97-98	Hampton Roads	ECHL	7	0	1	1	0	—	—	—	—	—
97-98	Johnstown	ECHL	49	8	13	21	91	—	—	—	—	—
98-99	Chesapeake	ECHL	70	20	14	34	132	8	0	1	1	12
	ECHL	Totals	126	28	28	56	223	8	0	1	1	12

Born; 7/13/74, Melrose, Massachusetts. 6-1, 190. Drafted by Pittsburgh Penguins (10th choice, 235th overall) in 1992 Entry Draft. Sold to Johnstown by Hampton Roads (11/97). Last amateur club; Boston College (Hockey East).

Greg Callahan — Defenseman

Season	Team	League	GP	G	A	PTS	PIM	GP	G	A	PTS	PIM
			Regular Season					Playoffs				
96-97	Wheeling	ECHL	11	0	1	1	11	—	—	—	—	—
96-97	Johnstown	ECHL	47	2	10	12	156	—	—	—	—	—
97-98	Syracuse	AHL	3	0	0	0	0	—	—	—	—	—
97-98	Johnstown	ECHL	63	4	16	20	214	—	—	—	—	—
98-99	Hershey	AHL	5	0	0	0	29	—	—	—	—	—
98-99	Mobile	ECHL	38	5	9	14	138	—	—	—	—	—
98-99	Tallahassee	ECHL	21	1	5	6	42	—	—	—	—	—
	AHL	Totals	8	0	0	0	29	—	—	—	—	—
	ECHL	Totals	180	12	41	53	561	—	—	—	—	—

Born; 4/25/73, Chestnut Hill, Massachusetts. 6-1, 210. Traded to Tallahassee by Mobile for Mitch Vig and Ken Ruddick (2/99). Last amateur club; Boston College (Hockey East).

Jock Callander — Center

Season	Team	League	GP	G	A	PTS	PIM	GP	G	A	PTS	PIM
			Regular Season					Playoffs				
82-83	Salt Lake City	IHL	68	20	27	47	26	6	0	1	1	9
83-84	Montana	CHL	72	27	32	59	69	—	—	—	—	—
83-84	Toledo	IHL	2	0	0	0	0	—	—	—	—	—
84-85	Muskegon	IHL	82	39	68	107	86	17	8	13	21	33
85-86	Muskegon	IHL	82	39	72	111	121	14	*12	11	*23	12
86-87	Muskegon	IHL	82	54	82	*136	110	15	13	7	20	23
87-88	Pittsburgh	NHL	41	11	16	27	45	—	—	—	—	—
87-88	Muskegon	IHL	31	20	36	56	49	6	2	3	5	25
88-89	Pittsburgh	NHL	30	6	5	11	20	10	2	5	7	10
88-89	Muskegon	IHL	48	25	39	64	40	7	5	5	10	30
89-90	Pittsburgh	NHL	30	4	7	11	49	—	—	—	—	—
89-90	Muskegon	IHL	46	29	49	78	118	15	6	*14	20	54
90-91	Muskegon	IHL	30	14	20	34	102	—	—	—	—	—
91-92	Pittsburgh	NHL	—	—	—	—	—	12	1	3	4	2
91-92	Muskegon	IHL	81	42	70	112	160	10	4	10	14	13
92-93	Tampa Bay	NHL	8	1	1	2	2	—	—	—	—	—
92-93	Atlanta	IHL	69	34	50	84	172	9	*7	5	12	25
93-94	Cleveland	IHL	81	31	70	101	126	—	—	—	—	—
94-95	Cleveland	IHL	61	24	36	60	90	4	2	2	4	6
95-96	Cleveland	IHL	81	42	53	95	150	3	1	0	1	8
96-97	Cleveland	IHL	61	20	34	54	56	14	7	6	13	10
97-98	Cleveland	IHL	72	20	33	53	105	10	5	6	11	6
98-99	Cleveland	IHL	81	28	26	54	121	—	—	—	—	—
	NHL	Totals	109	22	29	51	116	22	3	8	11	12
	IHL	Totals	1058	481	732	1213	1732	130	72	83	155	254

Born; 4/23/61, Regina, Saskatchewan. 6-1, 188. Signed as a free agent by St. Louis Blues (9/28/81). Signed as a free agent by Pittsburgh Penguins (7/31/87). Signed as a free agent by Tampa Bay Lightning (7/29/92). Signed by Cleveland Lumberjacks as a free agent (8/12/93). 1985-86 IHL Playoff MVP. 1986-87 Shared IHL MVP Award with Jeff Pyle. 1986-87 IHL First Team All-Star. 1991-92 IHL First Team All-Star. Member of 1990-91 Stanley Cup champion Pittsburgh Penguins. Member of 1985-86 IHL champion Muskegon Lumberjacks. Member of 1988-89 IHL champion Muskegon Lumberjacks. Last amateur club;

Dean Campanale — Left Wing

Season	Team	League	GP	G	A	PTS	PIM	GP	G	A	PTS	PIM
			Regular Season					Playoffs				
97-98	Massachusetts	H.E.	29	9	4	13	12	—	—	—	—	—
97-98	Johnstown	ECHL	9	0	2	2	2	—	—	—	—	—
98-99	Jacksonville	ECHL	25	9	8	17	16	—	—	—	—	—
98-99	Hampton Roads	ECHL	34	9	5	14	12	4	0	1	1	0
	ECHL	Totals	68	18	15	33	30	4	0	1	1	0

Born; 11/22/74, Quincy, Massachusetts. 5-11,190. Last amateur club; University of Massachusetts (Hockey East).

Brian Campbell — Defenseman

Season	Team	League	GP	G	A	PTS	PIM	GP	G	A	PTS	PIM
			Regular Season					Playoffs				
98-99	Ottawa	OHL	62	12	75	87	27	9	2	10	12	6
98-99	Rochester	AHL	—	—	—	—	—	2	0	0	0	0

Born; 5/23/79, Strathroy, Ontario. 5-11, 185. Drafted by Buffalo Sabres (7th choice, 156th overall) in 1997 Entry Draft. Last amateur club; Ottawa (OHL).

Ed Campbell — Defenseman

Season	Team	League	GP	G	A	PTS	PIM	GP	G	A	PTS	PIM
			Regular Season					Playoffs				
96-97	Binghamton	AHL	74	5	17	22	108	4	0	0	0	2
97-98	Hartford	AHL	9	0	1	1	9	14	0	2	2	33
97-98	Fort Wayne	IHL	50	10	5	15	147	—	—	—	—	—
98-99	Fort Wayne	IHL	46	1	16	17	137	—	—	—	—	—
98-99	Hartford	AHL	18	0	3	3	24	7	0	3	3	14
	AHL	Totals	101	5	21	26	141	25	0	5	5	49
	IHL	Totals	96	11	21	32	284	—	—	—	—	—

Born; 11/26/74, Westboro, Massachusetts. 6-2, 202. Drafted by New York Rangers (9th choice, 190th overall) in 1993 Entry Draft. Last amateur club; Lowell University (Hockey East).

Scott Campbell — Center

Season	Team	League	GP	G	A	PTS	PIM	GP	G	A	PTS	PIM
			Regular Season					Playoffs				
98-99	Roanoke	ECHL	46	11	15	26	24	12	0	1	1	8

Born; 8/6/74, Plattsburgh, New York. 5-11, 185. Last amateur club; Northeastern (Hockey East).

Scott Campbell — Defenseman

Season	Team	League	GP	G	A	PTS	PIM	GP	G	A	PTS	PIM
			Regular Season					Playoffs				
92-93	Niagara Falls	OHL	31	4	26	30	65	4	0	1	1	4
92-93	Cape Breton	AHL	10	0	0	0	8	—	—	—	—	—
93-94	Muskegon	CoHL	34	2	15	17	40	3	2	2	4	14
94-95	Rochester	AHL	3	0	0	0	13	—	—	—	—	—
94-95	Muskegon	CoHL	51	7	28	35	79	16	2	8	10	58
95-96	Newcastle	BHL	14	4	7	11	104	—	—	—	—	—
95-96	South Carolina	ECHL	3	0	1	1	27	—	—	—	—	—
95-96	Brantford	CoHL	29	1	10	11	91	9	0	0	0	22
96-97	Sheffield	BHL	39	1	10	11	99	—	—	—	—	—
97-98	Bracknell	BSL	45	2	8	9	64	4	1	0	1	48
98-99	Courmostra	Italy										
	CoHL	Totals	114	10	53	63	210	28	4	10	14	94
	ECHL	Totals	49	11	16	27	51	12	0	1	1	8

Born; 1/22/72, Glasgow, Scotland. 6-1, 190.

Christian Campeau — Right Wing

Season	Team	League	GP	G	A	PTS	PIM	GP	G	A	PTS	PIM
			Regular Season					Playoffs				
92-93	Atlanta	IHL	66	3	5	8	40	3	0	0	0	2
93-94	Atlanta	IHL	65	8	9	17	74	14	1	0	1	2
94-95	Atlanta	IHL	76	10	13	23	96	5	1	0	1	11
95-96	Atlanta	IHL	75	3	19	22	95	3	1	0	1	4
96-97	Quebec	IHL	81	14	13	27	71	9	0	1	1	2
97-98	Quebec	IHL	47	3	4	7	69	—	—	—	—	—
97-98	Cleveland	IHL	12	1	0	1	8	4	1	1	2	4
98-99	Merano	Italy										
	IHL	Totals	423	42	63	105	453	38	4	2	6	25

Born; 6/2/71, Verdun, Quebec. 5-10, 180. Signed as a free agent by Tampa Bay Lightning (7/10/92). Member of 1993-94 IHL champion Atlanta Knights.

Bob Cancelli — Center

Season	Team	League	GP	G	A	PTS	PIM	GP	G	A	PTS	PIM
			Regular Season					Playoffs				
98-99	Memphis	CHL	7	1	1	2	8	—	—	—	—	—

Born; 8/11/75, Mississauga, Ontario. 6-0, 180. Last amateur club; Dartmouth (ECAC).

Jason Cannon — Defenseman

Season	Team	League	GP	G	A	PTS	PIM	GP	G	A	PTS	PIM
			Regular Season					Playoffs				
98-99	Toronto	OHL	61	8	26	34	52	—	—	—	—	—
98-99	Toledo	ECHL	8	1	1	2	27	7	1	1	2	12

Born; 2/22/78, Toledo, Ohio. 5-11, 170. Last amateur club; Toronto (OHL).

Kris Cantu — Left Wing

Season	Team	League	GP	G	A	PTS	PIM	GP	G	A	PTS	PIM
			Regular Season					Playoffs				
97-98	Saint John	AHL	4	0	0	0	0	—	—	—	—	—
97-98	Rochester	AHL	4	0	0	0	0	—	—	—	—	—
97-98	Roanoke	ECHL	52	30	20	50	78	—	—	—	—	—
98-99	Roanoke	ECHL	59	27	26	53	104	6	0	1	1	6
	AHL	Totals	8	0	0	0	0	—	—	—	—	—
	ECHL	Totals	111	57	46	103	182	6	0	1	1	6

Born; 1/12/76, Warren, Michigan. 6-0, 175. Last amateur club; Seattle (WHL).

Curtis Capjack — Left Wing

Season	Team	League	GP	G	A	PTS	PIM	GP	G	A	PTS	PIM
			Regular Season					Playoffs				
98-99	Austin	WPHL	2	0	1	1	2	—	—	—	—	—

Born; 8/5/77, Edmonton, Alberta. 6-0, 177. Last amateur club; Tri-City (WHL).

Anthony Cappelletti — Defenseman

Season	Team	League	GP	G	A	PTS	PIM	GP	G	A	PTS	PIM
			Regular Season					Playoffs				
98-99	Massachusetts	H.E.	36	13	19	32	56	—	—	—	—	—
98-99	Portland	AHL	5	1	1	2	4	—	—	—	—	—

Born; 2/1/76, Sudbury, Ontario. 5-11, 189. Last amateur club; Massachusetts

Frank Caprice — Goaltender

Season	Team	League	GP	W	L	T	MIN	SO	AVG	GP	W	L	MIN	SO	AVG
			Regular Season							Playoffs					
81-82	London	OHL	45	24	17	2	2614	0	4.50	4	1	3	240	0	4.50
81-82	Dallas	CHL	3	0	3	0	178	0	6.40	—	—	—	—	—	—
82-83	Vancouver	NHL	1	0	0	0	20	0	9.00	—	—	—	—	—	—
82-83	Fredericton	AHL	14	5	8	1	819	0	3.67	—	—	—	—	—	—
83-84	Vancouver	NHL	19	8	2	2	1099	1	3.38	—	—	—	—	—	—
83-84	Fredericton	AHL	18	11	5	2	1089	2	2.70	—	—	—	—	—	—
84-85	Vancouver	NHL	28	8	14	3	1523	0	4.81	—	—	—	—	—	—
85-86	Fredericton	AHL	26	12	11	2	1526	0	4.29	6	2	4	333	0	3.96
85-86	Vancouver	NHL	7	0	3	2	308	0	5.45	—	—	—	—	—	—
86-87	Fredericton	AHL	12	5	5	0	686	0	4.11	—	—	—	—	—	—
86-87	Vancouver	NHL	25	8	11	2	1390	0	3.84	—	—	—	—	—	—
87-88	Vancouver	NHL	22	7	10	2	1250	0	4.18	—	—	—	—	—	—
88-89	Milwaukee	IHL	39	24	12	0	2204	2	3.89	—	—	—	—	—	—
89-90	Maine	AHL	10	2	6	1	550	0	5.02	—	—	—	—	—	—
89-90	Milwaukee	IHL	20	—	—	—	1098	0	4.32	3	—	—	142	0	4.23
90-91															
91-92															
92-93															
93-94															
94-95															
95-96															
96-97	Cardiff	BSL	10	—	—	—	1195	0	2.75	—	—	—	—	—	—
97-98	Cardiff	BSL	29	—	—	—	1722	0	2.68	2	—	—	120	0	2.00
98-99	Ayr	BSL	7	—	—	—	391	—	3.68	4	—	—	210	—	3.14
98-99	Corpus Christi	WPHL	15	9	5	1	847	0	3.40	—	—	—	—	—	—
	NHL	Totals	102	31	40	11	5589	1	4.20	—	—	—	—	—	—
	AHL	Totals	82	35	35	6	4670	2	3.87	6	2	4	333	0	3.96
	IHL	Totals	59	24	12	0	3302	2	4.03	3	—	—	142	0	4.23

Born; 5/2/62, Hamilton, Ontario. 5-9, 160. Drafted by Vancouver Canucks (8th choice, 178th overall) in 1981 Entry Draft. Traded to Boston Bruins by Vancouver for a twelfth round choice (Jan Bergman) in 1989 Entry Draft. Last amateur club; London (OHL).

Luciano Caravaggio — Goaltender

Season	Team	League	GP	W	L	T	MIN	SO	AVG	GP	W	L	MIN	SO	AVG
			Regular Season							Playoffs					
97-98	Pee Dee	ECHL	25	11	8	2	1329	1	3.03	2	0	0	62	0	1.94
98-99	Wheeling	ECHL	43	16	22	2	2289	3	3.64	—	—	—	—	—	—
	ECHL	Totals	68	27	30	4	3618	4	3.42	2	0	0	62	0	1.94

Born; 10/3/73, Etobicoke, Ontario. 5-11, 175. Drafted by New Jersey Devils (7th choice, 155th overall) in 1994 Entry Draft. Last amateur club; Michigan Tech (WCHA).

Joe Carderelli — Left Wing

Season	Team	League	GP	G	A	PTS	PIM	GP	G	A	PTS	PIM
			Regular Season					Playoffs				
97-98	Adirondack	AHL	30	0	3	3	2	—	—	—	—	—
97-98	Chesapeake	ECHL	8	2	4	6	4	—	—	—	—	—
98-99	Cleveland	IHL	50	7	7	14	8	—	—	—	—	—
98-99	Chesapeake	ECHL	17	2	6	8	8	—	—	—	—	—
	ECHL	Totals	25	4	10	14	12	—	—	—	—	—

Born; 6/13/77, Vancouver, British Columbia. 6-0, 203. Drafted by Tampa Bay Lightning (7th choice, 186th overall) in 1995 Entry Draft. Last amateur club; Spokane (WHL).

Reg Cardinal — Left Wing

Season	Team	League	GP	G	A	PTS	PIM	GP	G	A	PTS	PIM
			Regular Season					Playoffs				
97-98	Johnstown	ECHL	49	13	12	25	55	—	—	—	—	—
98-99	Tallahassee	ECHL	50	13	21	34	34	—	—	—	—	—
	ECHL	Totals	99	26	33	59	89	—	—	—	—	—

Born; 7/7/71, Edmonton, Alberta. 5-10, 175. Last amateur club; University of Maine (Hockey East).

Robert Cardinal — Defenseman

Regular Season / Playoffs

Season	Team	League	GP	G	A	PTS	PIM	GP	G	A	PTS	PIM
98-99	Winston-Salem	UHL	6	0	0	0	0	—	—	—	—	—

Born; 11/4/78, Edmonton, Alberta. 5-10, 190.

Justin Cardwell — Center

Regular Season / Playoffs

Season	Team	League	GP	G	A	PTS	PIM	GP	G	A	PTS	PIM
97-98	Pee Dee	ECHL	4	0	1	1	4	—	—	—	—	—
97-98	Chesapeake	ECHL	61	40	14	54	54	3	3	0	3	2
98-99	Canada	National	45	20	24	44	60	—	—	—	—	—
98-99	Indianapolis	IHL	4	2	0	2	0	7	0	2	2	6
	ECHL	Totals	65	40	15	55	58	3	3	0	3	2

Born; 11/26/73, Whitby, Ontario. 6-0, 205. Traded to Chesapeake by Pee Dee for cash and future considerations (10/97). Last amateur club; Western Michigan (CCHA).

Jason Carey — Goaltender

Regular Season / Playoffs

Season	Team	League	GP	W	L	T	MIN	SO	AVG	GP	W	L	MIN	SO	AVG
96-97	Saginaw	CoHL	36	9	16	1	1585	0	5.34	—	—	—	—	—	—
97-98	El Paso	WPHL	31	19	5	3	1684	0	3.31	3	1	1	133	0	4.98
98-99	Central Texas	WPHL	45	22	12	8	2421	*4	3.20	2	0	2	120	0	4.50
	WPHL	Totals	76	41	17	11	4105	4	3.24	5	1	3	253	0	4.74

Born; 3/31/73, Winnipeg, Manitoba. 5-10, 190. Member of 1997-98 WPHL Champion El Paso Buzzards. Last amateur club; University of Manitoba

Jim Carey — Goaltender

Regular Season / Playoffs

Season	Team	League	GP	W	L	T	MIN	SO	AVG	GP	W	L	MIN	SO	AVG
94-95	Portland	AHL	55	30	14	11	3281	*6	2.76	—	—	—	—	—	—
94-95	Washington	NHL	28	18	6	3	1604	4	2.13	7	2	4	358	0	4.19
95-96	Washington	NHL	71	35	24	9	4069	*9	2.26	3	0	1	97	0	6.19
96-97	Washington	NHL	40	17	18	3	2293	1	2.75	—	—	—	—	—	—
96-97	Boston	NHL	19	5	13	0	1004	0	3.82	—	—	—	—	—	—
97-98	Boston	NHL	10	3	2	1	496	2	2.90	—	—	—	—	—	—
97-98	Providence	AHL	10	2	7	1	605	0	3.97	—	—	—	—	—	—
98-99	St. Louis	NHL	4	1	2	0	202	0	3.86	—	—	—	—	—	—
98-99	Providence	AHL	30	17	8	3	1750	3	2.33	—	—	—	—	—	—
98-99	Cincinnati	IHL	2	1	0	1	120	0	1.00	—	—	—	—	—	—
	NHL	Totals	172	79	65	16	9668	16	2.58	10	2	5	455	0	4.62

Born; 5/31/74, Dorchester, Massachusetts. 6-2, 205. Drafted by Washington Capitals (2nd choice, 32nd overall) in 1992 Entry Draft. 1994-95 AHL First All-Star Team. 1994-95 AHL Top Netminder. 1994-95 NHL All-Rookie Team. 1995-96 NHL First All-Star Team. 1995-96 Vezina Trophy winner. Traded to Boston by Washington with Anson Carter, Jason Allison, Washington's third round choice (Lee Goren) in 1997 Entry Draft and a conditional chioce in 1998 Entry Draft for Bill Ranford, Adam Oates and Rick Tocchet (3/1/97). Signed as a free agent by St. Louis Blues (3/1/99). Last amateur club; University of Wisconsin

Matt Carey — Defenseman

Regular Season / Playoffs

Season	Team	League	GP	G	A	PTS	PIM	GP	G	A	PTS	PIM
97-98	Quad City	UHL	24	2	2	4	6	12	3	4	7	2
98-99	Quad City	UHL	41	5	9	14	27	—	—	—	—	—
	UHL	Totals	65	7	11	18	33	12	3	4	7	2

Born; 5/19/73, Neenah, Wisconsin. 5-11, 215. Member of 1997-98 UHL champion Quad City Mallards. Last amateur club; University of Wisconsin-Stevens Point (NCAA 3).

C.J. Carlson — Center

Regular Season / Playoffs

Season	Team	League	GP	G	A	PTS	PIM	GP	G	A	PTS	PIM
98-99	Space Coast	SEHL	38	62	68	130	41	NA	NA	NA	NA	NA
98-99	Jacksonville	ECHL	18	1	1	2	4	—	—	—	—	—

Born; 4/22/78, Marquette, Michigan. 5-10, 175. Last amateur club; Space Coast (SEHL).

Kenneth Carlsson — Defenseman

Regular Season / Playoffs

Season	Team	League	GP	G	A	PTS	PIM	GP	G	A	PTS	PIM
98-99	Waco	WPHL	37	0	2	2	80	—	—	—	—	—

Born; 4/13/76, Sweden. 6-1, 216.

Matt Carmichael — Goaltender

Regular Season / Playoffs

Season	Team	League	GP	W	L	T	MIN	SO	AVG	GP	W	L	MIN	SO	AVG
96-97	North Bay	OHL	16	4	7	4	940	1	3.77	—	—	—	—	—	—
96-97	Roanoke	ECHL	4	1	1	0	144	0	4.18	2	0	1	59	0	4.05
97-98	North Bay	OHL	59	15	34	5	3335	2	4.05	—	—	—	—	—	—
97-98	Louisville	ECHL	2	1	0	0	41	0	2.93	—	—	—	—	—	—
98-99	Port Huron	UHL	11	2	5	1	536	1	4.59	—	—	—	—	—	—
	ECHL	Totals	6	2	1	0	185	0	3.90	2	0	1	59	0	4.05

Born; 7/26/77, Shawville, Quebec. 5-9, 160. Last amateur club; North Bay

Dana Carnegie — Goaltender

Regular Season / Playoffs

Season	Team	League	GP	W	L	T	MIN	SO	AVG	GP	W	L	MIN	SO	AVG
97-98	Madison	UHL	1	0	1	0	60	0	3.02	—	—	—	—	—	—
98-99	Memphis	CHL	2	0	2	0	99	0	7.29	—	—	—	—	—	—

Born; 1/15/73, Toronto, Ontario. 6-3, 225.

Dan Carney — Forward

Regular Season / Playoffs

Season	Team	League	GP	G	A	PTS	PIM	GP	G	A	PTS	PIM
94-95	Nashville	ECHL	58	7	17	24	36	13	2	3	5	8
95-96	Nashville	ECHL	33	5	12	17	30	—	—	—	—	—
95-96	Erie	ECHL	15	1	3	4	8	—	—	—	—	—
96-97	Amarillo	WPHL	15	2	1	3	16	—	—	—	—	—
96-97	Jacksonville	ECHL	50	5	12	17	36	—	—	—	—	—
97-98	Hampton Roads	ECHL	62	2	12	14	43	19	1	1	2	2
98-99	Macon	CHL	17	2	5	7	14	—	—	—	—	—
98-99	Peoria	ECHL	35	5	3	8	26	4	0	1	1	6
	ECHL	Totals	253	25	59	84	179	36	3	5	8	16

Born; 12/23/71, Brooklyn, New York. 5-10, 170. Member of 1997-98 ECHL champion Hampton Roads Admirals. Last amateur club; University of Wisconsin-River Falls (NCAA 3).

Pat Caron — Left Wing

Regular Season / Playoffs

Season	Team	League	GP	G	A	PTS	PIM	GP	G	A	PTS	PIM
91-92	Raleigh	ECHL	3	0	2	2	31	—	—	—	—	—
92-93												
93-94												
95-96	West Palm Beach	SHL	11	10	5	15	56	—	—	—	—	—
95-96	Fort Worth	CeHL	36	9	14	23	87	—	—	—	—	—
96-97												
97-98	Adendorfer	Germany	43	23	41	64	60	—	—	—	—	—
98-99	San Antonio	CHL	33	17	10	27	95	—	—	—	—	—
	CHL	Totals	69	26	24	50	182	—	—	—	—	—

Born; 3/28/70, Campbellton, New Brunswick. 6-0, 196. Last amateur club; St. Jean (QMJHL).

Steve Carpenter — Defenseman

Regular Season / Playoffs

Season	Team	League	GP	G	A	PTS	PIM	GP	G	A	PTS	PIM
95-96	Richmond	ECHL	43	9	29	38	100	—	—	—	—	—
96-97	Solihull	BNL	45	27	41	68	178	—	—	—	—	—
96-97	Fresno	WCHL	6	2	4	6	10	5	1	1	2	30
97-98	Nottingham	BSL	51	6	15	21	75	6	2	0	2	2
98-99	Nottingham	BSL	42	4	24	28	38	8	0	3	3	2
	BSL	Totals	93	10	39	49	113	14	2	3	5	4

Born; 3/31/71, Prince George, British Columbia. 5-11, 181.

Benjamin Carpentier — Defenseman

Regular Season / Playoffs

Season	Team	League	GP	G	A	PTS	PIM	GP	G	A	PTS	PIM
98-99	Hartford	AHL	21	0	1	1	31	—	—	—	—	—
98-99	Charlotte	ECHL	23	4	6	10	68	—	—	—	—	—

Born; 6/13/78, Grand-Mere, Quebec. 6-2, 195. Signed as a free agent by New York Rangers (10/3/96). Last amateur club; Laval (QMJHL).

Brandon Carper — Defenseman

Regular Season / Playoffs

Season	Team	League	GP	G	A	PTS	PIM	GP	G	A	PTS	PIM
95-96	Toledo	ECHL	58	10	24	34	44	11	1	4	5	22
96-97	Fresno	WCHL	56	10	27	37	46	—	—	—	—	—
96-97	Reno	WCHL	7	1	2	3	0	—	—	—	—	—
97-98	Mobile	ECHL	43	2	5	7	14	3	0	3	3	4
98-99	Mobile	ECHL	69	7	29	36	57	2	0	0	0	4
	ECHL	Totals	170	19	58	77	115	16	1	7	8	30
	WCHL	Totals	63	11	29	40	46	—	—	—	—	—

Born; 4/2/72, Highland Park, Illinois. 6-2, 200. Drafted by Calgary Flames (10th choice, 198th overall) in 1992 Entry Draft. Last amateur club; Bowling Green State (CCHA).

Jason Carriere — Left Wing/Defenseman

Regular Season / Playoffs

Season	Team	League	GP	G	A	PTS	PIM	GP	G	A	PTS	PIM
95-96	Alaska	WCHL	2	0	0	0	0	—	—	—	—	—
95-96	Jacksonville	SHL	10	0	4	4	44	—	—	—	—	—
95-96	Huntsville	SHL	5	3	0	3	8	—	—	—	—	—
97-98	Reno	WCHL	13	2	2	4	44	—	—	—	—	—
97-98	Tucson	WCHL	5	1	0	1	7	—	—	—	—	—
97-98	Macon	CHL	5	2	0	2	9	—	—	—	—	—
97-98	Fort Worth	CHL	27	3	13	16	73	—	—	—	—	—
98-99	Fort Worth	CHL	38	12	11	23	80	—	—	—	—	—
98-99	South Carolina	ECHL	11	1	1	2	22	—	—	—	—	—
98-99	Augusta	ECHL	5	0	1	1	16	—	—	—	—	—
98-99	Miami	ECHL	3	0	0	0	5	—	—	—	—	—
	CHL	Totals	70	17	24	41	162	—	—	—	—	—
	WCHL	Totals	20	3	2	5	51	—	—	—	—	—
	ECHL	Totals	19	1	2	3	43	—	—	—	—	—
	SHL	Totals	15	3	4	7	52	—	—	—	—	—

Born; 4/22/74, Calgary, Alberta. 6-3, 240. Traded to Fort Worth by Macon with Claude Fillion for Richie Walcott (1/98). Selected by Arkansas in 1999 ECHL Dispersal Draft.

Anson Carter — Center

Regular Season / Playoffs

Season	Team	League	GP	G	A	PTS	PIM	GP	G	A	PTS	PIM
96-97	Washington	NHL	19	3	2	5	7	—	—	—	—	—
96-97	Portland	AHL	27	19	19	38	11	—	—	—	—	—
97-98	Boston	NHL	78	16	27	43	31	6	1	1	2	0
98-99	Utah	IHL	6	1	1	2	0	—	—	—	—	—
98-99	Boston	NHL	55	24	16	40	22	12	4	3	7	0
	NHL	Totals	171	51	50	101	62	18	5	4	9	0

Born; 6/6/74, Toronto, Ontario. 6-1, 185. Drafted by Quebec Nordiques (11th chocie, 220th overall) in 1992 Entry Draft. Traded to Washington Capitals by Colorado for Washington's fourth round choice (Ben Storey) in 1996 Entry Draft (4/3/96). Traded to Boston Bruins by Washington with Jim Carey, Jason Allison and Washington's third round choice (Lee Goren) in 1997 Entry Draft for Bill Ranford, Adam Oates and Rick Tocchet (3/1/97). Last amateur club; Michigan

Shawn Carter — Left Wing

Regular Season / Playoffs

Season	Team	League	GP	G	A	PTS	PIM	GP	G	A	PTS	PIM
96-97	Orlando	IHL	53	22	25	47	40	—	—	—	—	—
96-97	St. John's	AHL	18	5	6	11	15	7	1	2	3	6
97-98	St. John's	AHL	80	14	16	30	117	4	1	0	1	4
98-99	Orlando	IHL	79	13	26	39	103	17	1	4	5	10
	IHL	Totals	132	35	51	86	143	17	1	4	5	10
	AHL	Totals	98	19	22	41	132	11	2	2	4	10

Born; 4/16/73, Eagle River, Wisconsin. 6-2, 210. Signed as a free agent by Toronto Maple Leafs (2/14/97). Last amateur club; University of Wisconsin

Steve Carter — Defenseman

Regular Season / Playoffs

Season	Team	League	GP	G	A	PTS	PIM	GP	G	A	PTS	PIM
96-97	Fort Worth	CeHL	64	5	18	23	95	17	0	5	5	18
97-98	Fort Worth	WPHL	64	5	18	23	98	12	0	3	3	19
98-99	Fort Worth	WPHL	45	6	7	13	111	—	—	—	—	—
	WPHL	Totals	109	11	25	36	209	12	0	3	3	19

Born; 3/8/75, Kingston, Ontario. 6-1, 201. Member of 1996-97 CeHL Champion Fort Worth Fire. Last amateur club; Belleville (OHL).

Chuck Carvey — Defenseman

Regular Season / Playoffs

Season	Team	League	GP	G	A	PTS	PIM	GP	G	A	PTS	PIM
98-99	Flint	UHL	2	0	0	0	0	—	—	—	—	—

Born; 6/14/69, Farmington, Michigan.

Todd Cary — Center

Regular Season / Playoffs

Season	Team	League	GP	G	A	PTS	PIM	GP	G	A	PTS	PIM
98-99	Richmond	ECHL	3	0	1	1	0	—	—	—	—	—

Born; 12/17/72, Indianapolis, Indiana. 5-7, 150.

Brian Casey — Defenseman

Regular Season / Playoffs

Season	Team	League	GP	G	A	PTS	PIM	GP	G	A	PTS	PIM
98-99	Canada	National	46	5	9	14	10	—	—	—	—	—

Born; 1/10/73, Grand-Falls Windsor, Newfoundland. 6-0, 195. Last amateur club; Acadia (AUAA).

Mike Casselman — Left Wing

Regular Season / Playoffs

Season	Team	League	GP	G	A	PTS	PIM	GP	G	A	PTS	PIM
91-92	Adirondack	AHL	1	0	0	0	0	—	—	—	—	—
91-92	Toledo	ECHL	61	39	60	99	83	5	0	1	1	6
92-93	Adirondack	AHL	60	12	19	31	27	8	3	3	6	0
92-93	Toledo	ECHL	3	0	1	1	2	—	—	—	—	—
93-94	Adirondack	AHL	77	17	38	55	34	12	2	4	6	10
94-95	Adirondack	AHL	60	17	43	60	42	4	0	0	0	2
95-96	Florida	NHL	3	0	0	0	0	—	—	—	—	—
95-96	Carolina	AHL	70	34	68	102	46	—	—	—	—	—
96-97	Cincinnati	IHL	68	30	34	64	54	3	1	0	1	2
97-98	Cincinnati	IHL	55	19	28	47	44	—	—	—	—	—
97-98	Rochester	AHL	25	8	7	15	14	4	1	1	2	2
98-99	Landshut	Germany	49	20	29	49	64	3	0	1	1	0
	AHL	Totals	293	88	175	263	163	28	6	8	14	14
	IHL	Totals	123	49	62	111	98	—	—	—	—	—
	ECHL	Totals	64	39	61	100	85	5	0	1	1	6

Born; 8/23/68, Morrisburg, Ontaio. 5-11, 185. Drafted by Detroit Red Wings (1st choice, 3rd overall) in 1990 Supplemental Draft. Traded to Rochester by Cincinnati (IHL) with Steven King for Martin Menard and Brent Fedyk (2/98). 1992 ECHL Second Team All-Star. Last amateur club; Clarkson (ECAC).

Frederic Cassivi — Goaltender

Regular Season / Playoffs

Season	Team	League	GP	W	L	T	MIN	SO	AVG	GP	W	L	MIN	SO	AVG
95-96	PEI	AHL	41	20	14	3	2346	1	3.27	5	2	3	317	0	4.54
95-96	Thunder Bay	CoHL	12	6	4	2	715	0	4.28	—	—	—	—	—	—
96-97	Syracuse	AHL	55	23	22	8	3069	2	3.21	1	0	1	60	0	3.01
97-98	Worcester	AHL	45	20	22	2	2594	1	3.24	6	3	3	326	0	3.31

Born; 6/12/75, Sorel, Quebec. 6-4, 205. Drafted by Ottawa Senators (7th choice, 210th overall) in 1994 Entry Draft. Last amateur club; St. Jean (QMJHL). Note: PEI=Prince Edward Island.

Chris Catellier — Defenseman
Regular Season / Playoffs

Season	Team	League	GP	G	A	PTS	PIM	GP	G	A	PTS	PIM
97-98	Monroe	WPHL	68	3	15	18	95	—	—	—	—	—
98-99	Monroe	WPHL	2	0	0	0	2	—	—	—	—	—
	WPHL	Totals	70	3	15	18	97	—	—	—	—	—

Born; 8/18/72, Winnipeg, Manitoba. 6-0, 200. Last amateur club; University of Manitoba (CWUAA).

Peter Cava — Center
Regular Season / Playoffs

Season	Team	League	GP	G	A	PTS	PIM	GP	G	A	PTS	PIM
97-98	Sault Ste. Marie	OHL	64	30	60	90	86	—	—	—	—	—
97-98	St. John's	AHL	2	0	0	0	0	—	—	—	—	—
97-98	Thunder Bay	UHL	—	—	—	—	—	5	2	4	6	4
98-99	Sarnia	OHL	62	33	48	81	63	5	1	5	6	8

Born; 2/14/78, Thunder Bay, Ontario. 5-11, 175. Drafted by Toronto Maple Leafs (7th choice, 110th overall) in 1996 Entry Draft. Last amateur club; S.S. Marie (OHL).

Mark Cavallin — Goaltender
Regular Season / Playoffs

Season	Team	League	GP	W	L	T	MIN	SO	AVG	GP	W	L	MIN	SO	AVG
93-94	Chatham	CoHL	4	1	1	1	192	0	4.05	2	0	1	53	0	6.74
94-95	Tulsa	CeHL	26	11	10	3	1463	0	4.10	—	—	—	—	—	—
95-96															
96-97															
97-98	Lake Charles	WPHL	*57	30	20	5	3177	2	3.78	—	—	—	—	—	—
98-99	London	BSL	44	—	—	—	2496	—	4.11	—	—	—	—	—	—

Born; 10/20/71, Missisauga, Ontario. 5-9, 170. Last amateur club; Mt. Allison (AUAA).

Chad Cavanaugh — Forward
Regular Season / Playoffs

Season	Team	League	GP	G	A	PTS	PIM	GP	G	A	PTS	PIM
98-99	Sault Ste. Marie	OHL	68	40	39	79	77	5	5	4	9	4
98-99	Birmingham	ECHL	2	0	0	0	0	5	1	0	1	0

Born; 2/13/78, Peterborough, Ontario. 5-11, 166. Drafted by Washington Capitals (12th choice, 232nd overall) in 1996 Entry Draft. Last amateur club; Sault Ste. Marie (OHL).

Colum Cavilla — Goaltender
Regular Season / Playoffs

Season	Team	League	GP	W	L	T	MIN	SO	AVG	GP	W	L	MIN	SO	AVG
96-97	Ayr	BNL	24	—	—	—	1304	0	3.25	—	—	—	—	—	—
97-98	Ayr	BSL	21	—	—	—	1250	2	2.50	—	—	—	—	—	—
98-99	Manchester	BSL	4	—	—	—	240	—	1.75	—	—	—	—	—	—

Born; 11/7/73, Lethbridge, Alberta. 5-11, 185. Last amateur club; Lethbridge (CWUAA).

Mattias Cederlund — Right Wing
Regular Season / Playoffs

Season	Team	League	GP	G	A	PTS	PIM	GP	G	A	PTS	PIM
97-98	Fort Worth	CHL	2	0	0	0	4	—	—	—	—	—
97-98	Binghamton	UHL	57	6	6	12	64	—	—	—	—	—
98-99	San Angelo	WPHL	5	1	1	2	4	—	—	—	—	—
98-99	Mississippi	ECHL	2	0	1	1	2	—	—	—	—	—

Born; 5/13/75, Sundsvall, Sweden. 6-0, 190. Selected by Mohawk Valley in 1998 UHL Expansion Draft.

Dan Ceman — Center
Regular Season / Playoffs

Season	Team	League	GP	G	A	PTS	PIM	GP	G	A	PTS	PIM
96-97	Windsor	OUAA	26	25	40	65	NA	—	—	—	—	—
96-97	Kentucky	AHL	11	1	4	5	23	—	—	—	—	—
97-98	Portland	AHL	4	0	1	1	2	—	—	—	—	—
97-98	Hampton Roads	ECHL	58	15	21	36	47	20	11	5	16	33
98-99	Providence	AHL	3	1	0	1	0	2	0	0	0	0
98-99	Hampton Roads	ECHL	70	38	39	77	66	4	1	4	5	2
	AHL	Totals	18	2	5	7	25	2	0	0	0	0
	ECHL	Totals	128	53	60	113	113	24	12	9	21	35

Born; 7/25/73, Windsor, Ontario. 6-1, 195. Member of 1997-98 ECHL Champion Hampton Roads Admirals. Member of 1998-99 AHL Champion Providence Bruins. Last amateur club; University of Windsor (OUAA).

Joey Centrella — Forward
Regular Season / Playoffs

Season	Team	League	GP	G	A	PTS	PIM	GP	G	A	PTS	PIM
97-98	Fayetteville	CHL	3	0	1	1	0	—	—	—	—	—
98-99	Asheville	UHL	2	0	1	1	6	—	—	—	—	—

Born; 7/30/73, Tewksbury, Massachusetts. 5-8, 175. Last amateur club; Fitchburg State (NCAA 3).

Miloslav Cermak — Right Wing
Regular Season / Playoffs

Season	Team	League	GP	G	A	PTS	PIM	GP	G	A	PTS	PIM
97-98	Tucson	WCHL	63	14	34	48	31	—	—	—	—	—
98-99	Central Texas	WPHL	5	0	0	0	0	—	—	—	—	—
98-99	Shreveport	WPHL	1	0	0	0	0	—	—	—	—	—
	WPHL	Totals	6	0	0	0	0	—	—	—	—	—

Born; 12/5/75, Beroun, Czech Republic. 6-1, 216.

Peter Cermak — Left Wing
Regular Season / Playoffs

Season	Team	League	GP	G	A	PTS	PIM	GP	G	A	PTS	PIM
96-97	Jacksonville	ECHL	2	0	0	0	0	—	—	—	—	—
96-97	Johnstown	ECHL	3	0	0	0	0	—	—	—	—	—
96-97	Madison	CoHL	28	8	7	15	14	—	—	—	—	—
97-98	Madison	UHL	10	2	0	2	6	—	—	—	—	—
97-98	Saginaw	UHL	55	10	12	22	16	—	—	—	—	—
98-99	Binghamton	UHL	67	16	15	31	20	5	1	1	2	15
	UHL	Totals	160	36	34	70	56	5	1	1	2	15
	ECHL	Totals	5	0	0	0	0	—	—	—	—	—

Born; 4/16/76, Bratislava, Czechoslovakia. 6-0, 180. Selected by Fort Wayne in 1999 UHL Expansion Draft.

Kord Cernich — Defenseman
Regular Season / Playoffs

Season	Team	League	GP	G	A	PTS	PIM	GP	G	A	PTS	PIM
90-91	Binghamton	AHL	52	5	10	15	36	—	—	—	—	—
91-92	San Diego	IHL	64	5	18	23	53	3	1	0	1	0
91-92	Binghamton	AHL	5	1	3	4	6	—	—	—	—	—
92-93	Capital District	AHL	6	0	0	0	4	—	—	—	—	—
92-93	Rochester	AHL	4	0	0	0	2	—	—	—	—	—
92-93	Flint	CoHL	31	5	12	17	18	6	3	3	6	4
92-93	San Diego	IHL	17	1	5	6	4	3	0	0	0	2
93-94	Nottingham	BHL	33	6	12	18	58	—	—	—	—	—
93-94	Fort Wayne	IHL	3	0	0	0	4	—	—	—	—	—
93-94	Dayton	ECHL	21	4	13	17	14	3	1	2	3	4
94-95												
95-96	Anchorage	WCHL	57	4	24	28	57	—	—	—	—	—
96-97	Anchorage	WCHL	54	8	12	20	24	9	1	2	3	2
97-98	Anchorage	WCHL	64	4	19	23	64	8	0	2	2	12
98-99	Anchorage	WCHL	71	7	47	54	42	1	0	0	0	0
	IHL	Totals	84	6	23	29	61	6	1	0	1	2
	AHL	Totals	67	6	13	19	48	—	—	—	—	—
	WCHL	Totals	246	23	102	125	187	18	1	4	5	14

Born; 10/20/66, Ketchikan, Alaska. 5-11, 194. Last amateur club; Lake Superior State (CCHA).

Martin Cerven — Center

Regular Season / Playoffs

Season	Team	League	GP	G	A	PTS	PIM	GP	G	A	PTS	PIM
97-98	Philadelphia	AHL	50	7	11	18	27	8	1	2	3	2
98-99	Philadelphia	AHL	46	6	4	10	20	1	0	1	1	0
98-99	Mohawk Valley	UHL	16	4	8	12	20	—	—	—	—	—
	AHL	Totals	96	13	15	28	47	9	1	3	4	2

Born; 3/7/77, Trencin, Czechoslovakia. 6-4, 200. Drafted by Edmonton Oilers (6th choice, 161st overall) in 1995 Entry Draft. Traded to Philadelphia Flyers by Edmonton for Philadelphia's seventh round choice (Chad Hinz) in 1997 Entry Draft (6/18/97). Member of 1997-98 AHL Champion Philadelphia Phantoms. Selected by Missouri in 1999 UHL Expansion Draft. Last amateur club; Seattle

Frederic Chabot — Goaltender

Regular Season / Playoffs

Season	Team	League	GP	W	L	T	MIN	SO	AVG	GP	W	L	MIN	SO	AVG
89-90	Fort Wayne	IHL	23	6	13	3	1208	1	4.32	—	—	—	—	—	—
89-90	Sherbrooke	AHL	2	1	1	0	119	0	4.03	—	—	—	—	—	—
90-91	Montreal	NHL	3	0	0	1	108	0	3.33	—	—	—	—	—	—
90-91	Fredericton	AHL	35	9	15	5	1800	0	4.07	—	—	—	—	—	—
91-92	Fredericton	AHL	30	17	9	4	1761	2	*2.69	7	3	4	457	0	2.63
91-92	Winston-Salem	ECHL	24	15	7	2	1449	0	*2.94	—	—	—	—	—	—
92-93	Montreal	NHL	1	0	0	0	40	0	1.50	—	—	—	—	—	—
92-93	Fredericton	AHL	45	22	17	4	2544	0	3.33	4	1	3	261	0	3.68
93-94	Montreal	NHL	1	0	1	0	60	0	5.00	—	—	—	—	—	—
93-94	Philadelphia	NHL	4	0	1	1	70	0	4.29	—	—	—	—	—	—
93-94	Fredericton	AHL	3	0	1	1	143	0	5.03	—	—	—	—	—	—
93-94	Hershey	AHL	28	13	5	6	1464	2	*2.58	11	7	4	665	0	2.89
93-94	Las Vegas	IHL	2	1	1	0	110	0	2.72	—	—	—	—	—	—
94-95	Cincinnati	IHL	48	25	12	7	2622	1	2.93	5	3	2	326	0	2.94
95-96	Cincinnati	IHL	38	23	9	4	2147	3	2.46	14	9	5	853	1	2.60
96-97	Houston	IHL	*72	*39	26	7	*4265	*7	2.53	13	8	5	777	*1	2.63
97-98	Los Angeles	NHL	12	3	3	2	554	0	3.14	—	—	—	—	—	—
97-98	Houston	IHL	22	12	7	2	1237	1	2.23	4	1	3	239	0	3.06
98-99	Montreal	NHL	11	1	3	0	430	0	2.23	—	—	—	—	—	—
98-99	Houston	IHL	21	16	4	1	1258	3	2.34	—	—	—	—	—	—
	NHL	Totals	32	4	8	4	1262	0	2.95	—	—	—	—	—	—
	IHL	Totals	226	122	72	24	12847	16	2.72	36	21	15	219	2	2.68

Born; 2/12/68, Herbertville, Quebec. 5-11, 177. Drafted by New Jersey Devils (10th choice, 192nd overall) in 1986 Entry Draft. Signed as a free agent by Montreal Canadiens (1/16/90). Claimed by Tampa Bay Lightning from Montreal in Expansion Draft (6/18/92). Traded to Montreal by Tampa Bay for J.C. Bergeron (6/19/92). Traded to Philadelphia Flyers by Montreal for cash (2/21/94). Signed as a free agent by Florida Panthers (8/11/94). Signed as a free agent by Houston Aeros (1996). Signed as a free agent by Los Angeles Kings (9/4/97). Selected by Nashville Predators in 1998 NHL Expansion Draft. Claimed on waivers by Los Angeles from Nashville (7/21/98). Won Baz Bastien Award (best goaltender as selected by AHL coaches) 1993-94. 1995-96 IHL Second Team All-Star. 1996-97 IHL First Team All-Star. 1996-97 IHL Most Valuable Player. Last amateur club; Prince Albert (WHL).

Nicholas Chabot — Goaltender

Regular Season / Playoffs

Season	Team	League	GP	W	L	T	MIN	SO	AVG	GP	W	L	MIN	SO	AVG
98-99	Baie-Comeau	QMJHL	30	6	16	5	1666	0	4.36	—	—	—	—	—	—
98-99	Colorado	WCHL	7	4	3	0	324	0	4.07	—	—	—	—	—	—
98-99	Idaho	WCHL	5	1	3	0	280	0	4.71	1	0	0	33	0	1.81
	WCHL	Totals	10	5	6	0	604	0	4.37	1	0	0	33	0	1.81

Born; 2/8/78, Montreal, Quebec. 5-10, 190. Last amateur club; Baie-Comeau (QMJHL).

Rene Chapdelaine — Right Wing

Regular Season / Playoffs

Season	Team	League	GP	G	A	PTS	PIM	GP	G	A	PTS	PIM
89-90	New Haven	AHL	41	0	1	1	35	—	—	—	—	—
90-91	Los Angeles	NHL	3	0	1	1	10	—	—	—	—	—
90-91	Phoenix	IHL	17	0	2	2	10	11	0	0	0	8
90-91	New Haven	AHL	65	3	11	14	49	—	—	—	—	—
91-92	Los Angeles	NHL	16	0	1	1	10	—	—	—	—	—
91-92	Phoenix	IHL	62	4	22	26	87	—	—	—	—	—
91-92	New Haven	AHL	—	—	—	—	—	4	0	2	2	0
92-93	Los Angeles	NHL	13	0	0	0	12	—	—	—	—	—
92-93	Phoenix	IHL	44	1	17	18	54	—	—	—	—	—
92-93	San Diego	IHL	9	1	1	2	8	14	0	1	1	27
93-94	Peoria	IHL	80	8	9	17	100	6	1	3	4	10
94-95	Peoria	IHL	45	3	2	5	62	9	0	2	2	12
95-96	Peoria	IHL	70	2	10	12	135	12	1	0	1	8
96-97	San Antonio	IHL	69	7	11	18	125	9	2	3	5	10
97-98	San Antonio	IHL	73	2	11	13	128	—	—	—	—	—
98-99	Utah	IHL	19	2	2	4	16	—	—	—	—	—
98-99	Long Beach	IHL	29	1	1	2	28	8	0	2	2	18
	NHL	Totals	32	0	2	2	32	—	—	—	—	—
	IHL	Totals	517	31	88	119	753	69	4	11	15	93
	AHL	Totals	106	3	12	15	84	4	0	2	2	0

Born; 9/27/66, Weyburn, Saskatchewan. 6-1, 195. Drafted by Los Angeles Kings (7th choice, 149th overall) in 1986 Entry Draft. Last amateur club; Lake Superior State (CCHA).

Brian Chapman — Defense

Regular Season / Playoffs

Season	Team	League	GP	G	A	PTS	PIM	GP	G	A	PTS	PIM
86-87	Belleville	OHL	54	4	32	36	142	6	1	1	2	10
86-87	Binghamton	AHL	—	—	—	—	—	1	0	0	0	0
87-88	Belleville	OHL	63	11	57	68	180	6	1	4	5	13
88-89	Binghamton	AHL	71	5	25	30	216	—	—	—	—	—
89-90	Binghamton	AHL	68	2	15	17	180	—	—	—	—	—
90-91	Binghamton	NHL	3	0	0	0	29	—	—	—	—	—
90-91	Springfield	AHL	60	4	23	27	200	18	1	4	5	62
91-92	Springfield	AHL	73	3	26	29	245	10	2	2	4	25
92-93	Springfield	AHL	72	17	34	51	212	15	2	5	7	43
93-94	Phoenix	IHL	78	6	35	41	280	—	—	—	—	—
94-95	Phoenix	IHL	60	2	23	25	181	9	1	5	6	31
95-96	Phoenix	IHL	66	8	11	19	187	4	0	1	1	14
96-97	Phoenix	IHL	69	9	16	25	109	—	—	—	—	—
96-97	Long Beach	IHL	14	1	7	8	67	17	0	3	3	38
97-98	Long Beach	IHL	6	0	1	1	15	—	—	—	—	—
97-98	Manitoba	IHL	77	3	25	28	159	3	0	0	0	10
98-99	Manitoba	IHL	76	3	15	18	127	5	0	0	0	12
	IHL	Totals	446	32	133	165	1125	38	1	9	10	105
	AHL	Totals	344	31	123	154	1053	44	5	11	16	130

Born; 2/10/68, Brockville, Ontario. 6-0, 195. Drafted by Hartford Whalers (3rd choice, 74th overall) in 1986 Entry Draft. Signed as a free agent by Phoenix Roadrunners (7/16/93). Traded to Long Beach Ice Dogs by Phoenix to complete trade for Todd Gillingham. Traded to Manitoba by Long Beach for Russ Romaniuk (10/97). Member of 1990-91 AHL champion Springfield Indians. Last amateur club; Belleville (OHL).

Craig Chapman — Center

Regular Season / Playoffs

Season	Team	League	GP	G	A	PTS	PIM	GP	G	A	PTS	PIM
95-96	Fresno	WCHL	57	21	38	59	49	7	1	4	5	6
96-97	Fresno	WCHL	57	21	30	51	100	5	2	2	4	14
97-98	Fresno	WCHL	42	20	16	36	43	5	0	4	4	6
98-99	Sheffield	BSL	52	4	13	17	44	6	0	1	1	10
	WCHL	Totals	156	62	84	146	192	17	3	10	13	26

Born; 2/12/71, Williams Lake, British Columbia. 5-10, 190.

Daniel Chaput — Defenseman

Regular Season / Playoffs

Season	Team	League	GP	G	A	PTS	PIM	GP	G	A	PTS	PIM
92-93	Ferris State	CCHA	39	3	22	25	79	—	—	—	—	—
92-93	Hampton Roads	ECHL	—	—	—	—	—	1	0	1	1	2
93-94	Hampton Roads	ECHL	68	10	36	46	95	7	2	8	10	15
94-95	Richmond	ECHL	39	8	13	21	122	—	—	—	—	—
95-96												
96-97	Knoxville	ECHL	45	2	18	20	85	—	—	—	—	—
96-97	Richmond	ECHL	22	2	10	12	55	8	1	4	5	14
97-98	San Angelo	WPHL	41	2	15	17	77	3	0	1	1	8
98-99	San Angelo	WPHL	66	7	26	33	86	17	1	4	5	23
	ECHL	Totals	174	22	77	99	357	16	3	13	16	31
	WPHL	Totals	107	9	41	50	163	20	1	5	6	31

Born; 1/2/71, St. Anne, Manitoba. 6-1, 195. Last amateur club; Ferris State

Zdeno Chara — Defenseman

Regular Season / Playoffs

Season	Team	League	GP	G	A	PTS	PIM	GP	G	A	PTS	PIM
97-98	Islanders	NHL	25	0	1	1	50	—	—	—	—	—
97-98	Kentucky	AHL	48	4	9	13	125	1	0	0	0	4
98-99	Islanders	NHL	59	2	6	8	83	—	—	—	—	—
98-99	Lowell	AHL	23	2	2	4	47	—	—	—	—	—
	NHL	Totals	84	2	7	9	133	—	—	—	—	—
	AHL	Totals	71	6	11	17	172	1	0	0	0	4

Born; 3/18/77, Trencin, Czechoslovakia. Drafted by New York Islanders (3rd choice, 56th overall) in 1996 Entry Draft. 1997-98 AHL All-Rookie Team. Last amateur club; Prince George (WHL).

L.P. Charbonneau — Right Wing

Regular Season / Playoffs

Season	Team	League	GP	G	A	PTS	PIM	GP	G	A	PTS	PIM
95-96	Cornwall	AHL	1	0	0	0	0	—	—	—	—	—
95-96	Roanoke	ECHL	22	6	1	7	94	—	—	—	—	—
95-96	Erie	ECHL	25	2	3	5	187	—	—	—	—	—
96-97	Syracuse	AHL	2	0	0	0	2	—	—	—	—	—
96-97	Jacksonville	ECHL	27	3	6	9	241	—	—	—	—	—
96-97	Wheeling	ECHL	23	4	3	7	159	1	0	0	0	0
97-98	Chesapeake	ECHL	53	16	10	26	201	3	0	0	0	9
98-99	Chesapeake	ECHL	46	9	7	16	*271	—	—	—	—	—
98-99	Greenville	ECHL	19	4	3	7	*95	—	—	—	—	—
	AHL	Totals	3	0	0	0	2	—	—	—	—	—
	ECHL	Totals	215	44	33	77	1248	4	0	0	0	9

Born; 10/27/74, Montreal, Quebec. 6-1, 204. Traded to Greenville by Chesapeake for Kam White (3/99). Last amateur club; Hull (QMJHL).

Patrice Charbonneau — Defenseman

Regular Season / Playoffs

Season	Team	League	GP	G	A	PTS	PIM	GP	G	A	PTS	PIM
97-98	Macon	CHL	69	3	11	14	75	3	0	0	0	10
98-99	Macon	CHL	66	3	14	17	78	1	0	0	0	0
	CHL	Totals	135	6	25	31	153	4	0	0	0	10

Born; 3/28/75, Sherbrooke, Quebec. 6-0, 210. Selected by Indianapolis in 1999 CHL Expansion Draft.

Patrick Charbonneau — Defenseman

Regular Season / Playoffs

Season	Team	League	GP	G	A	PTS	PIM	GP	G	A	PTS	PIM
96-97	Birmingham	ECHL	34	0	2	2	42	1	0	0	0	0
97-98	Wheeling	ECHL	43	0	7	7	50	—	—	—	—	—
97-98	Roanoke	ECHL	20	3	2	5	17	3	0	0	0	0
98-99	Saginaw	UHL	72	10	17	27	92	—	—	—	—	—
	ECHL	Totals	97	3	11	14	109	4	0	0	0	0

Born; 6/5/75, Napierville, Quebec. 5-10, 183. Last amateur club; Drummondville (QMJHL).

Patrick Charbonneau — Goaltender

Regular Season / Playoffs

Season	Team	League	GP	W	L	T	MIN	SO	AVG	GP	W	L	MIN	SO	AVG
93-94	Victoriaville	QMJHL	56	11	34	2	2948	0	5.31	5	1	4	212	0	6.79
93-94	PEI	AHL	3	2	1	0	180	0	3.67	—	—	—	—	—	—
94-95	Victoriaville	QMJHL	47	15	27	1	2339	0	5.16	4	0	3	142	0	8.45
94-95	PEI	AHL	2	2	0	0	120	0	2.00	3	0	2	137	0	5.24
95-96	PEI	AHL	17	5	8	0	864	0	4.79	—	—	—	—	—	—
95-96	Thunder Bay	CoHL	29	16	7	3	1587	1	3.25	19	10	8	942	0	4.01
96-97	Syracuse	AHL	2	1	0	0	80	1	2.25	—	—	—	—	—	—
96-97	Raleigh	ECHL	40	18	14	4	2105	0	4.13	—	—	—	—	—	—
97-98	Cincinnati	IHL	1	1	0	0	60	0	1.00	—	—	—	—	—	—
97-98	New Orleans	ECHL	6	2	3	1	327	0	3.85	—	—	—	—	—	—
97-98	Birmingham	ECHL	28	13	9	2	1489	0	3.67	—	—	—	—	—	—
98-99	Syracuse	AHL	1	1	0	0	36	0	0.00	—	—	—	—	—	—
98-99	Mohawk Valley	UHL	54	19	26	5	2881	2	3.60	—	—	—	—	—	—
	AHL	Totals	24	10	9	0	1244	1	4.20	3	0	2	137	0	5.24
	UHL	Totals	83	35	33	8	4468	3		19	10	8	942	0	4.01
	ECHL	Totals	74	33	26	7	3921	0	3.93	—	—	—	—	—	—

Born; 7/22/75, St. Jean, Quebec. 5-11, 217. Drafted by Ottawa Senators (3rd choice, 53rd overall) in 1993 Entry Draft. Sold to Birmingham b y New Orleans (11/97). Last amateur club; Victoriaville (QMJHL).

Sebastien Charpentier — Goaltender

Regular Season / Playoffs

Season	Team	League	GP	W	L	T	MIN	SO	AVG	GP	W	L	MIN	SO	AVG
97-98	Portland	AHL	4	1	3	0	230	0	2.61	—	—	—	—	—	—
97-98	Hampton Roads	ECHL	43	20	16	6	2389	0	2.86	18	*14	4	*1183	1	1.93
98-99	Portland	AHL	3	0	3	0	179	0	3.34	—	—	—	—	—	—
98-99	Quad City	UHL	6	0	0	0	4	0	0.00	—	—	—	—	—	—
	AHL	Totals	7	1	6	0	409	0	2.93	—	—	—	—	—	—

Born; 4/18/77, Drummondville, Quebec. 5-9, 161. Drafted by Washington Capitals (4th choice, 93rd overall) in 1995 Entry Draft. 1997-98 ECHL Playoff MVP. Member of 1997-98 ECHL Champion Hampton Roads Admirals. Last amateur club; Shawinigan (QMJHL).

Craig Charron — Center

Regular Season / Playoffs

Season	Team	League	GP	G	A	PTS	PIM	GP	G	A	PTS	PIM
90-91	Albany	IHL	5	0	2	2	0	—	—	—	—	—
90-91	Winston-Salem	ECHL	30	11	16	27	10	—	—	—	—	—
91-92	Cincinnati	ECHL	64	41	55	96	97	9	5	5	10	10
92-93	Cleveland	IHL	27	6	8	14	8	—	—	—	—	—
92-93	Birmingham	ECHL	23	9	17	26	18	—	—	—	—	—
93-94												
94-95	Cornwall	AHL	6	5	0	5	0	2	0	0	0	0
94-95	Fort Wayne	IHL	2	1	0	1	4	—	—	—	—	—
94-95	Kalamazoo	IHL	2	0	0	0	0	—	—	—	—	—
94-95	Dayton	ECHL	48	35	47	82	82	9	9	13	22	10
95-96	Rochester	AHL	72	43	52	95	79	19	7	10	17	12
96-97	Rochester	AHL	72	24	41	65	42	10	2	7	9	4
97-98	Rochester	AHL	75	25	53	78	51	4	1	1	2	0
98-99	Lowell	AHL	71	22	39	61	41	3	1	2	3	8
	AHL	Totals	225	97	146	243	172	35	10	18	28	16
	IHL	Totals	36	7	10	17	12	—	—	—	—	—
	ECHL	Totals	165	96	135	231	207	18	14	18	32	20

Born; 11/15/67, North Easton, Massachusetts. 5-10, 183. 1997-98 AHL Fred T. Hunt Trophy (dedication and sportsmanship). Member of 1995-96 AHL champion Rochester Americans. Signed as a free agent by New York Islanders (9/9/98). Last amateur club; University of Lowell (H.E.).

Eric Charron
Defenseman

Season	Team	League	GP	G	A	PTS	PIM	GP	G	A	PTS	PIM
			Regular Season					Playoffs				
88-89	Trois-Rivieres	QMJHL	38	2	16	18	111	—	—	—	—	—
88-89	Verdun	QMJHL	28	2	15	17	66	—	—	—	—	—
88-89	Sherbrooke	AHL	1	0	0	0	0	—	—	—	—	—
89-90	St-Hyacinthe	QMJHL	68	13	38	51	152	11	3	4	7	67
89-90	Sherbrooke	AHL	—	—	—	—	—	2	0	0	0	0
90-91	Fredericton	AHL	71	1	11	12	108	2	1	0	1	29
91-92	Fredericton	AHL	59	2	11	13	98	6	1	0	1	4
92-93	Montreal	NHL	3	0	0	0	2	—	—	—	—	—
92-93	Fredericton	AHL	54	3	13	16	93	—	—	—	—	—
92-93	Atlanta	IHL	11	0	2	2	12	3	0	1	1	6
93-94	Tampa Bay	NHL	4	0	0	0	2	—	—	—	—	—
93-94	Atlanta	IHL	66	5	18	23	144	14	1	4	5	28
94-95	Tampa Bay	NHL	45	1	4	5	26	—	—	—	—	—
95-96	Tampa Bay	NHL	14	0	0	0	18	—	—	—	—	—
95-96	Washington	NHL	4	0	1	1	4	6	0	0	0	8
95-96	Portland	AHL	45	0	8	8	88	20	1	1	2	33
96-97	Washington	NHL	25	1	1	2	20	—	—	—	—	—
96-97	Portland	AHL	29	6	8	14	55	5	0	3	3	0
97-98	Calgary	NHL	2	0	0	0	4	—	—	—	—	—
97-98	Saint John	AHL	56	8	20	28	136	20	1	7	8	55
98-99	Calgary	NHL	12	0	1	1	14	—	—	—	—	—
98-99	Saint John	AHL	50	10	12	22	148	3	1	0	1	22
	NHL	Totals	115	2	7	9	90	6	0	0	0	8
	AHL	Totals	365	30	83	113	726	58	5	11	16	143
	IHL	Totals	77	5	20	25	156	17	1	5	6	34

Born; 1/14/70, Verdun, Quebec. 6-3, 192. Drafted by Montreal Canadiens (1st choice, 20th overall) in 1988 Entry Draft. Traded to Tampa Bay Lightning by Montreal with Alain Cote and future considerations for Rob Ramage (3/20/93). Traded to Washington Capitals by Tampa Bay for conditional pick in 1997 Entry Draft (11/16/97). Traded to Calgary Flames by Washington for future considerations (9/4/97). Member of 1993-94 IHL champion Atlanta Knights. Last amateur club; St. Hyacinthe (QMJHL).

Scott Chartier
Defenseman

Season	Team	League	GP	G	A	PTS	PIM	GP	G	A	PTS	PIM
			Regular Season					Playoffs				
93-94	San Diego	IHL	49	2	6	8	84	4	0	0	0	6
94-95	San Diego	IHL	8	0	0	0	0	—	—	—	—	—
94-95	Greensboro	ECHL	30	6	14	20	82	18	2	3	5	41
95-96	Baltimore	AHL	3	0	0	0	2	—	—	—	—	—
95-96	Jacksonville	ECHL	52	16	19	35	121	18	2	8	10	37
96-97	Jacksonville	ECHL	10	1	7	8	26	—	—	—	—	—
97-98	Amarillo	WPHL	60	3	27	30	89	—	—	—	—	—
98-99	Tallahassee	ECHL	41	12	18	30	107	—	—	—	—	—
	IHL	Totals	57	2	6	8	84	4	0	0	0	6
	ECHL	Totals	133	35	58	93	336	36	4	11	15	78

Born; 1/9/72, Birlte, Manitoba. 6-1, 200. Signed as a free agent by Anaheim Mighty Ducks (7/30/93). Last amateur club; Western Michigan University

Brad Chartrand
Right Wing

Season	Team	League	GP	G	A	PTS	PIM	GP	G	A	PTS	PIM
			Regular Season					Playoffs				
96-97	Canada	National	54	10	14	24	42	—	—	—	—	—
97-98	Canada	National	60	24	30	54	47	—	—	—	—	—
98-99	St. John's	AHL	64	16	14	30	48	5	0	2	2	2

Born; 12/14/74, Winnipeg, Manitoba. 5-11, 180. Signed as a free agent by Los Angeles Kings (7/21). Last amateur club; Cornell (ECAC).

Don Chase
Right Wing

Season	Team	League	GP	G	A	PTS	PIM	GP	G	A	PTS	PIM
			Regular Season					Playoffs				
96-97	Fredericton	AHL	12	0	0	0	2	—	—	—	—	—
96-97	Wheeling	ECHL	53	23	25	48	26	3	2	4	6	0
97-98	Mississippi	ECHL	56	20	18	38	82	—	—	—	—	—
97-98	Pee Dee	ECHL	12	4	5	9	8	8	1	0	1	4
98-99	Pensacola	ECHL	67	21	24	45	55	—	—	—	—	—
	ECHL	Totals	188	68	72	140	171	11	3	4	7	4

Born; 3/17/74, Springfield, Massachusetts. 5-11, 190. Drafted by Montreal Canadiens (7th choice, 116th overall) in 1992 Entry Draft. Last amateur club; Boston College (Hockey East).

Tim Chase
Defenseman

Season	Team	League	GP	G	A	PTS	PIM	GP	G	A	PTS	PIM
			Regular Season					Playoffs				
92-93	Brown	ECAC	13	3	4	7	12	—	—	—	—	—
92-93	Fredericton	AHL	25	4	8	12	16	3	0	0	0	0
93-94	Fredericton	AHL	8	0	4	4	0	—	—	—	—	—
93-94	Atlanta	IHL	1	1	0	1	0	—	—	—	—	—
93-94	Knoxville	ECHL	37	2	15	17	65	—	—	—	—	—
94-95												
95-96	Jacksonville	ECHL	54	13	18	31	134	16	5	8	13	6
96-97	Jacksonville	ECHL	9	0	2	2	10	—	—	—	—	—
96-97	Louisville	ECHL	25	6	15	21	20	—	—	—	—	—
96-97	Tallahassee	ECHL	11	1	3	4	18	—	—	—	—	—
97-98												
98-99	Tallahassee	ECHL	65	10	22	32	46	—	—	—	—	—
	AHL	Totals	33	4	12	16	16	3	0	0	0	0
	ECHL	Totals	136	22	53	75	247	16	5	8	13	6

Born; 3/23/70, Gaithersburg, Maryland. 6-2, 180. Drafted by Montreal Canadiens (8th choice, 146th overall) in 1992 Entry Draft. Selected by Arkansas in 1999 ECHL Expansion Draft. Last amateur club; Brown (ECAC).

Denis Chasse
Right Wing

Season	Team	League	GP	G	A	PTS	PIM	GP	G	A	PTS	PIM
			Regular Season					Playoffs				
91-92	Halifax	AHL	73	26	35	61	254	—	—	—	—	—
92-93	Halifax	AHL	75	35	41	76	242	—	—	—	—	—
93-94	St. Louis	NHL	3	0	1	1	15	—	—	—	—	—
93-94	Cornwall	AHL	48	27	39	66	194	—	—	—	—	—
94-95	St. Louis	NHL	47	7	9	16	133	7	1	7	8	23
95-96	St. Louis	NHL	42	3	0	3	108	—	—	—	—	—
95-96	Washington	NHL	3	0	0	0	5	—	—	—	—	—
95-96	Winnipeg	NHL	15	0	0	0	12	—	—	—	—	—
95-96	Worcester	AHL	3	0	0	0	6	—	—	—	—	—
96-97	Ottawa	NHL	22	1	4	5	19	—	—	—	—	—
96-97	Detroit	IHL	9	2	1	3	33	—	—	—	—	—
96-97	Indianapolis	IHL	3	0	0	0	10	4	1	1	2	23
97-98	Augsburg	German	29	6	6	12	97	—	—	—	—	—
97-98	Mannheim	German	15	2	5	7	72	—	—	—	—	—
98-99	Bracknell	BSL	33	13	22	35	108	1	0	1	1	8
	NHL	Totals	132	11	14	25	292	—	—	—	—	—
	AHL	Totals	199	88	115	203	696	7	1	7	8	23
	IHL	Totals	12	2	1	3	43	4	1	1	2	23

Born; 2/7/70, Montreal, Quebec. 6-2, 200. Signed as a free agent by Quebec Nordiques (5/14/91). Traded to St. Louis Blues with Steve Duchesne by Quebec for Ron Sutter, Bob Bassen and Garth Butcher (1/23/94). Traded to Washington Capitals by Blues for Rob Pearson (1/29/ 96). Traded to Winnipeg Jets by Washington for Stewart Malgunas (2/15/96). Traded to Chicago Blackhawks by Ottawa with the rights to Kevin Bolibruck and Ottawa's sixth round draft choice in 1998 Entry Draft (traded back to Ottawa-Ottawa selected Chris Neil) for Mike Prokopec (3/18/97). Last amateur club; Drummondville (QMJHL).

Brooke Chateau
Defenseman

Season	Team	League	GP	G	A	PTS	PIM	GP	G	A	PTS	PIM
			Regular Season					Playoffs				
98-99	Charlotte	ECHL	66	8	7	15	107	—	—	—	—	—

Born; Utica, Michigan. 6-0, 215. Last amateur club; Miami (CCHA).

Colin Chaulk
Left Wing

Season	Team	League	GP	G	A	PTS	PIM	GP	G	A	PTS	PIM
			Regular Season					Playoffs				
98-99	Adirondack	AHL	4	0	0	0	4	—	—	—	—	—
98-99	Utah	IHL	6	1	1	2	2	—	—	—	—	—
98-99	Tallahassee	ECHL	7	0	5	5	14	—	—	—	—	—
98-99	Jacksonville	ECHL	24	8	22	30	49	2	2	1	3	6
98-99	Austin	WPHL	23	7	16	23	28	—	—	—	—	—
	ECHL	Totals	31	8	27	35	63	2	2	1	3	6

Born; 1/7/77, Toronto, Ontario. 6-0, 199. Last amateur club; Kingston (OHL).

Vladimir Chebaturkin — Defenseman

Regular Season / Playoffs

Season	Team	League	GP	G	A	PTS	PIM	GP	G	A	PTS	PIM
96-97	Utah	IHL	68	0	4	4	34	—	—	—	—	—
97-98	Islanders	NHL	2	0	2	2	0	—	—	—	—	—
97-98	Kentucky	AHL	54	6	8	14	52	2	0	0	0	4
98-99	Islanders	NHL	8	0	0	0	12	—	—	—	—	—
98-99	Lowell	AHL	69	2	12	14	85	3	0	0	0	0
	NHL	Totals	10	0	2	2	12	—	—	—	—	—
	AHL	Totals	123	8	20	28	137	5	0	0	0	4

Born; 4/23/75, Tyumen, Russia. 6-2, 189. Drafted by New York Islanders (3rd choice, 66th overall) in 1993 Entry Draft. Last overseas club; Kristall (CIS).

Nick Checco — Left Wing

Regular Season / Playoffs

Season	Team	League	GP	G	A	PTS	PIM	GP	G	A	PTS	PIM
97-98	Cincinnati	AHL	12	0	0	0	2	—	—	—	—	—
97-98	Columbus	ECHL	58	19	20	39	36	—	—	—	—	—
98-99	Florida	ECHL	61	11	14	25	31	6	2	2	4	2
	ECHL	Totals	119	30	34	64	67	6	2	2	4	2

Born; 11/18/74, Bloomington, Minnesota. 5-11, 195. Last amateur club; University of Minnesota (WCHA).

Steve Chelios — Defenseman

Regular Season / Playoffs

Season	Team	League	GP	G	A	PTS	PIM	GP	G	A	PTS	PIM
89-90	Virginia	ECHL	5	1	2	3	4	—	—	—	—	—
90-91	Roanoke	ECHL	7	1	3	4	28	—	—	—	—	—
90-91	Richmond	ECHL	5	0	2	2	4	—	—	—	—	—
90-91	Johnstown	ECHL	7	0	3	3	8	—	—	—	—	—
90-91	Louisville	ECHL	3	0	1	1	4	—	—	—	—	—
91-92	Roanoke	ECHL	18	2	4	6	44	—	—	—	—	—
91-92	Nashville	ECHL	24	5	11	16	47	—	—	—	—	—
92-93	Dallas	CeHL	30	3	19	22	60	—	—	—	—	—
92-93	Wichita	CeHL	12	4	12	16	32	—	—	—	—	—
93-94	Wichita	CeHL	61	8	51	59	153	9	0	11	11	18
94-95	Daytona	SUN	26	6	31	37	101	—	—	—	—	—
95-96	Birmingham	ECHL	10	1	1	2	4	—	—	—	—	—
95-96	Madison	CoHL	2	1	0	1	0	—	—	—	—	—
95-96	Daytona	SHL	29	5	42	47	152	—	—	—	—	—
96-97	Quad City	CoHL	14	2	8	10	13	14	2	13	15	18
97-98	Quad City	UHL	16	0	8	8	27	—	—	—	—	—
97-98	Huntsville	CHL	3	1	2	3	2	3	1	1	2	16
98-99	Bakersfield	WCHL	31	1	11	12	45	—	—	—	—	—
	CHL	Totals	106	16	84	100	247	12	1	12	13	34
	ECHL	Totals	79	10	27	37	143	—	—	—	—	—
	SHL	Totals	55	11	73	84	253	—	—	—	—	—
	UHL	Totals	32	3	16	19	40	14	2	13	15	18

Born; 8/24/68, San Diego, California. 5-9, 180. Member of 1993-94 CeHL champion Wichita Thunder. Member of 1996-97 CoHL champion Quad City Mallards.

Steve Cheredaryk — Defenseman

Regular Season / Playoffs

Season	Team	League	GP	G	A	PTS	PIM	GP	G	A	PTS	PIM
94-95	Medicine Hat	WHL	72	3	35	38	151	3	0	1	1	9
94-95	Springfield	AHL	3	0	1	1	0	—	—	—	—	—
95-96	Springfield	AHL	32	0	1	1	36	—	—	—	—	—
95-96	Knoxville	ECHL	13	0	10	10	72	6	2	4	6	12
96-97	Springfield	AHL	46	1	2	3	69	—	—	—	—	—
96-97	Fredericton	AHL	14	0	1	1	24	—	—	—	—	—
96-97	Mississippi	ECHL	9	0	1	1	33	—	—	—	—	—
97-98	Fredericton	AHL	4	0	0	0	8	—	—	—	—	—
97-98	New Orleans	ECHL	59	4	16	20	214	2	0	0	0	16
98-99	New Orleans	ECHL	58	8	15	23	135	11	3	4	7	26
	AHL	Totals	99	1	5	6	137	—	—	—	—	—
	ECHL	Totals	139	12	42	54	454	19	5	8	13	54

Born; 11/20/75, Calgary, Alberta. 6-2, 197. Drafted by Winnipeg Jets (4th choice, 82nd overall) in 1994 Entry Draft. Traded to Montreal Canadiens by Phoenix Coyotes for Pat Jablonski. (3/18/97). Last amateur club; Medicine Hat (WHL).

Greg Cherne — Right Wing

Regular Season / Playoffs

Season	Team	League	GP	G	A	PTS	PIM	GP	G	A	PTS	PIM
98-99	Colorado	WCHL	3	0	0	0	2	—	—	—	—	—
98-99	Idaho	WCHL	8	1	2	3	2	—	—	—	—	—
98-99	Fort Worth	CHL	21	6	2	8	12	—	—	—	—	—
98-99	Memphis	CHL	7	0	1	1	0	—	—	—	—	—
	CHL	Totals	28	6	3	9	12	—	—	—	—	—
	WCHL	Totals	11	1	2	3	4	—	—	—	—	—

Born; 11/26/74, Euclid, Ohio. 5-11, 210.

Stefan Cherneski — Right Wing

Regular Season / Playoffs

Season	Team	League	GP	G	A	PTS	PIM	GP	G	A	PTS	PIM
98-99	Hartford	AHL	11	1	2	3	41	—	—	—	—	—

Born; 9/19/78, Winnipeg, Manitoba. 6-0, 195. Drafted by New York Rangers (1st choice, 19th overall) in 1997 Entry Draft. Last amateur club; Brandon (WHL).

Mikhail Chernov — Defenseman

Regular Season / Playoffs

Season	Team	League	GP	G	A	PTS	PIM	GP	G	A	PTS	PIM
98-99	Philadelphia	AHL	56	4	3	7	98	14	1	0	1	8

Born; 11/11/78, Prokopjevsk, USSR. 6-2, 196. Drafted by Philadelphia Flyers (4th choice, 103rd overall) in 1997 Entry Draft. Last amateur club; Yaroslav

John Cherubini — Defenseman

Regular Season / Playoffs

Season	Team	League	GP	G	A	PTS	PIM	GP	G	A	PTS	PIM
97-98	Bakersfield	WCHL	4	0	1	1	0	—	—	—	—	—
97-98	Memphis	CHL	3	0	0	0	2	—	—	—	—	—
97-98	Fort Worth	CHL	2	0	0	0	2	—	—	—	—	—
98-99	Mohawk Valley	UHL	2	0	0	0	0	—	—	—	—	—
	CHL	Totals	5	0	0	0	4	—	—	—	—	—

Born; 1/31/73, Clinton, Massacusetts. 6-2, 190. Last amateur club; Fitchburg State (NCAA 3).

Denis Chervyakov — Defenseman

Regular Season / Playoffs

Season	Team	League	GP	G	A	PTS	PIM	GP	G	A	PTS	PIM
92-93	Boston	NHL	2	0	0	0	2	—	—	—	—	—
92-93	Providence	AHL	48	4	12	16	99	—	—	—	—	—
92-93	Atlanta	IHL	1	0	0	0	0	—	—	—	—	—
93-94	Providence	AHL	58	2	16	18	128	—	—	—	—	—
94-95	Providence	AHL	65	1	18	19	130	10	0	2	2	14
95-96	Providence	AHL	64	3	7	10	58	4	1	0	1	21
96-97	Kentucky	AHL	52	2	11	13	78	—	—	—	—	—
97-98	Assat Pori	Finland	2	0	0	0	2	—	—	—	—	—
97-98	Lukko Rauma	Finland	24	0	0	0	14	—	—	—	—	—
97-98	Tappara Tampere	Finland	14	0	2	2	14	4	0	0	0	0
98-99	Portland	AHL	13	0	0	0	15	—	—	—	—	—
98-99	Baton Rouge	ECHL	4	1	3	4	16	—	—	—	—	—
98-99	Cincinnati	IHL	32	3	3	6	62	—	—	—	—	—
98-99	Orlando	IHL	12	0	2	2	39	9	0	0	0	16
	AHL	Totals	248	10	53	63	415	14	1	2	3	35
	IHL	Totals	45	3	5	8	101	9	0	0	0	16

Born; 4/20/70, St. Petersburg, Russia. 6-0, 190. Drafted by Boston Bruins (9th choice, 256th overall) in 1992 Entry Draft. Signed as a free agent by New York Islanders (9/12/96).

Dominic Chiasson — Left Wing

Regular Season / Playoffs

Season	Team	League	GP	G	A	PTS	PIM	GP	G	A	PTS	PIM
97-98	Val d'Or	QMJHL	49	25	35	60	27	18	14	15	29	11
97-98	Quebec	IHL	12	1	1	2	4	—	—	—	—	—
98-99	Saginaw	UHL	49	15	26	41	8	—	—	—	—	—
98-99	Mohawk Valley	UHL	23	15	8	23	6	—	—	—	—	—
	UHL	Totals	72	30	34	64	14	—	—	—	—	—

Born; 1/18/77, Valleyfield, Quebec. 5-10, 170. Traded to Mohawk Valley by Saginaw with Eric Kelly for Mark Bultje and Mike Hiebert (2/99). Member of 1998-99 UHL All-Rookie Team. Last amateur club; Val D'Or (QMJHL).

Jason Chimera
Center
Regular Season / Playoffs

Season	Team	League	GP	G	A	PTS	PIM	GP	G	A	PTS	PIM
97-98	Medicine Hat	WHL	72	34	32	66	93	—	—	—	—	—
97-98	Hamilton	AHL	4	0	0	0	8	—	—	—	—	—
98-99	Medicine Hat	WHL	37	18	22	40	84	—	—	—	—	—
98-99	Brandon	WHL	21	14	12	26	32	5	2	1	3	9

Born; 5/2/79, Edmonton, Alberta. 6-0, 160. Drafted by Edmonton Oilers (5th choice, 121st overall) in 1997 Entry Draft. Last amateur club; Brandon (WHL).

Todd Chinnick
Defenseman
Regular Season / Playoffs

Season	Team	League	GP	G	A	PTS	PIM	GP	G	A	PTS	PIM
98-99	Mobile	ECHL	2	0	0	0	5	—	—	—	—	—
98-99	Saginaw	UHL	4	0	0	0	0	—	—	—	—	—

Born; 2/6/77, Chatham, Ontario.

Andrew Chlebas
Forward
Regular Season / Playoffs

Season	Team	League	GP	G	A	PTS	PIM	GP	G	A	PTS	PIM
97-98	Mississippi	ECHL	3	0	1	1	0	—	—	—	—	—
98-99	Columbus	ECHL	16	0	0	0	0	—	—	—	—	—
	ECHL	Totals	19	0	1	1	0	—	—	—	—	—

Born; 2/4/72, Beaconsfield, Quebec. 6-1, 190. Sold to Columbus by Mississippi (2/99). Last amateur club; Concordia (OUAA).

Eric Chouinard
Center
Regular Season / Playoffs

Season	Team	League	GP	G	A	PTS	PIM	GP	G	A	PTS	PIM
98-99	Quebec	QMJHL	62	50	59	109	56	13	8	10	18	8
98-99	Fredericton	AHL	—	—	—	—	—	6	3	2	5	0

Born; 7/8/80, Atlanta, Georgia. 6-2, 195. Drafted by Montreal Canadiens (1st choice, 16th overall) in 1998 Entry Draft. Last amateur club; Quebec (QMJHL).

Marc Chouinard
Center
Regular Season / Playoffs

Season	Team	League	GP	G	A	PTS	PIM	GP	G	A	PTS	PIM
97-98	Cincinnati	AHL	8	1	2	3	4	—	—	—	—	—
98-99	Cincinnati	AHL	69	7	8	15	20	3	0	0	0	4
	AHL	Totals	77	8	10	18	24	3	0	0	0	4

Born; 5/5/77, Charlesbourg, Ontario. 6-5, 187. Drafted by Winnipeg Jets (2nd choice, 32nd overall) in 1995 Entry Draft. Traded to Anaheim Mighty Ducks by Winnipeg with Teemu Selanne and Winnipeg's fourth round choice (later traded to Totronto-later traded to Montreal-Montreal selected Kim Staal) in 1996 Entry Draft for Chad Kilger, Oleg Tverdovsky and Anaheim's third round choice (Per-Anton Ludstrom) in 1996 Entry Draft. Suffered torn achilles tendon (10-31-97). Last amateur club; Halifax QMJHL).

Martin Chouinard
Center
Regular Season / Playoffs

Season	Team	League	GP	G	A	PTS	PIM	GP	G	A	PTS	PIM
97-98	Quebec	IHL	24	2	6	8	8	—	—	—	—	—
97-98	Pensacola	ECHL	25	7	18	25	36	19	3	8	11	16
98-99	New Orleans	ECHL	9	1	0	1	4	—	—	—	—	—
	ECHL	Totals	34	8	18	26	40	19	3	8	11	16

Born; 5/6/77, Quebec City, Quebec. 6-4, 200. Selected by Arkansas in 1999 ECHL Expansion Draft. Last amateur club; Granby (QMJHL).

Troy Christensen
Defenseman
Regular Season / Playoffs

Season	Team	League	GP	G	A	PTS	PIM	GP	G	A	PTS	PIM
95-96	Nashville	ECHL	3	1	0	1	4	—	—	—	—	—
96-97	Dayton	ECHL	46	3	8	11	30	2	0	0	0	0
97-98	Dayton	ECHL	23	0	4	4	19	—	—	—	—	—
98-99	Asheville	UHL	4	0	0	0	4	—	—	—	—	—
98-99	Chesapeake	ECHL	1	0	0	0	0	—	—	—	—	—
98-99	Dayton	ECHL	16	0	2	2	11	—	—	—	—	—
	ECHL	Totals	89	4	14	18	64	2	0	0	0	0

Born; 4/6/75, Winnipeg, Manitoba. 5-9, 185.

Jeff Christian
Left Wing
Regular Season / Playoffs

Season	Team	League	GP	G	A	PTS	PIM	GP	G	A	PTS	PIM
90-91	Utica	AHL	80	24	42	66	165	—	—	—	—	—
91-92	New Jersey	NHL	2	0	0	0	2	—	—	—	—	—
91-92	Utica	AHL	76	27	24	51	198	4	0	0	0	16
92-93	Utica	AHL	22	4	6	10	39	—	—	—	—	—
92-93	Hamilton	AHL	11	2	5	7	35	—	—	—	—	—
92-93	Cincinnati	IHL	36	5	12	17	113	—	—	—	—	—
93-94	Albany	AHL	76	34	43	77	227	5	1	2	3	19
94-95	Pittsburgh	NHL	1	0	0	0	0	—	—	—	—	—
94-95	Cleveland	IHL	56	13	24	37	126	2	0	1	1	8
95-96	Pittsburgh	NHL	3	0	0	0	2	—	—	—	—	—
95-96	Cleveland	IHL	66	23	32	55	131	3	0	1	1	8
96-97	Pittsburgh	NHL	11	2	2	4	13	—	—	—	—	—
96-97	Cleveland	IHL	69	40	40	80	262	12	6	8	14	44
97-98	Phoenix	NHL	1	0	0	0	0	—	—	—	—	—
97-98	Las Vegas	IHL	30	12	15	27	90	4	2	2	4	20
98-99	Houston	IHL	80	45	41	86	252	18	4	12	16	32
	NHL	Totals	18	2	2	4	17	—	—	—	—	—
	IHL	Totals	337	138	164	302	974	39	12	24	36	112
	AHL	Totals	265	91	120	211	664	9	1	2	3	35

Born; 7/30/70, Burlington, Ontario. 6-2, 210. Drafted by New Jersey Devils (2nd choice, 23rd overall) in 1988 Entry Draft. Signed as a free agent by Pittsbugh Penguins (8/2/94). Signed as a free agent by Phoenix Coyotes (8/28/97). Member of 1998-99 IHL Champion Houston Aeros. 1998-99 IHL Comeback Player of the Year. Last amateur club; Owen Sound (OHL).

Tim Christian
Right Wing
Regular Season / Playoffs

Season	Team	League	GP	G	A	PTS	PIM	GP	G	A	PTS	PIM
95-96	Roanoke	ECHL	66	24	26	50	33	3	0	1	1	2
96-97	Roanoke	ECHL	68	25	28	53	35	2	1	0	1	0
97-98	Roanoke	ECHL	65	24	18	42	20	8	1	3	4	4
98-99	Roanoke	ECHL	70	22	30	52	29	12	4	2	6	6
	ECHL	Totals	269	95	102	197	117	25	6	6	12	12

Born; 5/11/71, Grand Rapids, Michigan. 6-0, 180. Last amateur club; Ferris State (CCHA).

Jason Christie
Right Wing
Regular Season / Playoffs

Season	Team	League	GP	G	A	PTS	PIM	GP	G	A	PTS	PIM
91-92	Columbus	ECHL	61	28	56	84	218	—	—	—	—	—
92-93	Hamilton	AHL	11	3	2	5	8	—	—	—	—	—
92-93	Columbus	ECHL	63	20	41	61	190	—	—	—	—	—
93-94	Hamilton	AHL	28	6	9	15	36	—	—	—	—	—
93-94	Charlotte	ECHL	27	10	14	24	55	3	1	1	2	2
94-95	Portland	AHL	71	20	40	60	130	3	1	0	1	0
95-96	Portland	AHL	65	7	21	28	86	23	6	10	16	49
96-97	Manitoba	IHL	34	4	12	16	29	—	—	—	—	—
96-97	Portland	AHL	33	4	14	18	42	5	1	3	4	4
97-98	Manitoba	IHL	54	12	15	27	47	2	0	0	0	0
97-98	Portland	AHL	8	2	1	3	12	—	—	—	—	—
98-99	Columbus	ECHL	35	9	28	37	70	4	1	1	2	4
	AHL	Totals	216	42	87	129	314	31	8	13	21	53
	IHL	Totals	88	16	27	43	76	2	0	0	0	0
	ECHL	Totals	186	67	139	206	533	7	2	2	4	6

Born; 4/25/69, Gibbons, Alberta. 5-8, 180.

Ryan Christie
Left Wing
Regular Season / Playoffs

Season	Team	League	GP	G	A	PTS	PIM	GP	G	A	PTS	PIM
98-99	Michigan	IHL	48	4	5	9	74	3	1	1	2	2

Born; 7/3/78, Beamsville, Ontario. 6-2, 175. Drafted by Dallas Stars (4th choice, 112th overall) in 1996 entry Draft. Last amateur club; Owen Sound (OHL).

Dave Chudomel
Defenseman
Regular Season / Playoffs

Season	Team	League	GP	G	A	PTS	PIM	GP	G	A	PTS	PIM
98-99	Port Huron	UHL	4	0	0	0	7	—	—	—	—	—

Born; 2/25/76, Prague, Czech. Republic. 6-3, 210.

Alexsander Chunchukov — Right Wing

Regular Season / Playoffs

Season	Team	League	GP	G	A	PTS	PIM	GP	G	A	PTS	PIM
94-95	Raleigh	ECHL	32	7	18	25	30	—	—	—	—	—
94-95	Nashville	ECHL	29	11	25	36	32	11	4	11	15	4
95-96	Nashville	ECHL	55	20	31	51	51	—	—	—	—	—
96-97	Johnstown	ECHL	70	34	58	92	75	—	—	—	—	—
97-98	Nashville	CHL	69	33	69	102	45	9	3	8	11	8
98-99	Fayetteville	CHL	45	24	36	60	36	—	—	—	—	—
	ECHL	Totals	186	72	132	204	188	11	4	11	15	4
	CHL	Totals	114	57	105	162	81	9	3	8	11	8

Born; 4/3/71, Riga, Latvia. 6-1, 195. Selected by Fort Worth in 1998 CHL Dispersal Draft.

Brad Church — Left Wing

Regular Season / Playoffs

Season	Team	League	GP	G	A	PTS	PIM	GP	G	A	PTS	PIM
96-97	Portland	AHL	50	4	8	12	92	1	0	0	0	0
97-98	Washington	NHL	2	0	0	0	0	—	—	—	—	—
97-98	Portland	AHL	59	6	5	11	98	9	2	4	6	14
98-99	Portland	AHL	10	1	3	4	18	—	—	—	—	—
98-99	Hamilton	AHL	9	0	2	2	4	—	—	—	—	—
98-99	Hampton Roads	ECHL	24	10	9	19	129	—	—	—	—	—
98-99	New Orleans	ECHL	5	3	4	7	4	11	1	1	2	22
	AHL	Totals	128	11	18	29	212	10	2	4	6	14
	ECHL	Totals	29	13	13	26	133	11	1	1	2	22

Born; 11/14/76, Dauphin, Manitoba. 6-1, 210. Drafted by Washington Capitals (1st choice, 17th overall) in 1995 Entry Draft. Traded to Edmonton Oilers by Washington for the rights to Barrie Moore (2/3/99). Last amateur club; Prince

Dave Chyzowski — Left Wing

Regular Season / Playoffs

Season	Team	League	GP	G	A	PTS	PIM	GP	G	A	PTS	PIM
89-90	Kamloops	WHL	4	5	2	7	17	17	11	6	17	46
89-90	Islanders	NHL	34	8	6	14	45	—	—	—	—	—
89-90	Springfield	AHL	4	0	0	0	7	—	—	—	—	—
90-91	Islanders	NHL	56	5	9	14	61	—	—	—	—	—
90-91	Capital District	AHL	7	3	6	9	22	—	—	—	—	—
91-92	Islanders	NHL	12	1	1	2	17	—	—	—	—	—
91-92	Capital District	AHL	55	15	18	33	121	6	1	1	2	23
92-93	Capital District	AHL	66	15	21	36	177	3	2	0	2	0
93-94	Islanders	NHL	3	1	0	1	4	2	0	0	0	0
93-94	Salt Lake City	IHL	66	27	13	40	151	—	—	—	—	—
94-95	Islanders	NHL	13	0	0	0	11	—	—	—	—	—
94-95	Kalamazoo	IHL	4	0	4	4	8	16	9	5	14	27
95-96	Adirondack	AHL	80	44	39	83	160	3	0	0	0	6
96-97	Chicago	NHL	8	0	0	0	6	—	—	—	—	—
96-97	Indianapolis	IHL	76	34	40	74	261	4	0	2	2	38
97-98	Orlando	IHL	17	9	7	16	32	—	—	—	—	—
97-98	San Antonio	IHL	10	1	5	6	39	—	—	—	—	—
97-98	Kansas City	IHL	38	19	14	33	88	11	5	4	9	11
98-99	Kansas City	IHL	67	24	15	39	147	—	—	—	—	—
	NHL	Totals	126	15	16	31	144	2	0	0	0	0
	IHL	Totals	278	114	98	212	726	31	14	11	25	76
	AHL	Totals	212	77	84	161	487	12	3	1	4	29

Born; 7/11/71, Edmonton, Alberta. 6-1, 193. Drafted by New York Islanders (1st choice, 2nd overall) 1989 Entry Draft. Signed as a free agent by Detroit Red Wings (8/29/95). Signed as a free agent by Chicago Blackhawks (9/26/96). Signed as a free agent by Orlando Solar Bears (8/97). Traded to San Antonio by Orlando with Dave Smith and Chris LiPuma for Scott Hollis, Grigori Panteleyev and Dave MacIntyre (11/97). Traded to Kansas City by San Antonio for Brent Cullaton (1/98). Last amateur club; Kamloops (WHL).

Peter Ciavaglia — Center

Regular Season / Playoffs

Season	Team	League	GP	G	A	PTS	PIM	GP	G	A	PTS	PIM
91-92	Buffalo	NHL	2	0	0	0	0	—	—	—	—	—
91-92	Rochester	AHL	77	37	61	98	16	6	2	5	7	6
92-93	Buffalo	NHL	3	0	0	0	0	—	—	—	—	—
92-93	Rochester	AHL	64	35	67	102	32	17	9	16	25	12
93-94	United States	National	18	2	9	11	6	—	—	—	—	—
93-94	United States	Olympic	8	2	4	6	0	—	—	—	—	—
93-94	Leksand	Sweden	39	14	18	32	34	4	1	2	3	0
94-95	Detroit	IHL	73	22	59	81	83	5	1	1	2	6
95-96	Detroit	IHL	75	22	56	78	38	12	6	11	17	12
96-97	Detroit	IHL	72	21	51	72	54	21	*14	19	*33	32
97-98	Detroit	IHL	35	11	30	41	10	23	8	11	19	12
98-99	Detroit	IHL	59	27	31	58	33	11	1	8	9	10
	NHL	Totals	5	0	0	0	0	—	—	—	—	—
	IHL	Totals	314	103	227	330	218	51	16	31	47	40
	AHL	Totals	141	72	128	200	48	23	11	21	32	18

Born; 7/15/69, Albany, New York. 5-10, 180. Drafted by Calgary Flames (8th choice, 145th overall) in 1987 Entry Draft. Signed as a free agent by Buffalo Sabres (8/30/91). 1996-97 IHL Playoff MVP. Member of 1996-97 IHL Champion Detroit Vipers. Last amateur club; Harvard (ECAC).

Enrico Ciccone — Defenseman

Regular Season / Playoffs

Season	Team	League	GP	G	A	PTS	PIM	GP	G	A	PTS	PIM
90-91	Kalamazoo	IHL	57	4	9	13	384	4	0	1	1	58
91-92	Minnesota	NHL	11	0	0	0	48	—	—	—	—	—
91-92	Kalamazoo	IHL	53	4	16	20	406	10	0	1	1	58
92-93	Minnesota	NHL	31	0	1	1	115	—	—	—	—	—
92-93	Kalamazoo	IHL	13	1	3	4	50	—	—	—	—	—
92-93	Hamilton	AHL	6	1	3	4	44	—	—	—	—	—
93-94	Washington	NHL	46	1	1	2	174	—	—	—	—	—
93-94	Portland	AHL	6	0	0	0	27	—	—	—	—	—
93-94	Tampa Bay	NHL	11	0	1	1	52	—	—	—	—	—
94-95	Tampa Bay	NHL	41	2	4	6	*225	—	—	—	—	—
95-96	Tampa Bay	NHL	55	2	3	5	258	—	—	—	—	—
95-96	Chicago	NHL	11	0	1	1	48	9	1	0	1	30
96-97	Chicago	NHL	67	2	2	4	233	4	0	0	0	18
97-98	Carolina	NHL	14	0	3	3	83	—	—	—	—	—
97-98	Vancouver	NHL	13	0	1	1	47	—	—	—	—	—
97-98	Tampa Bay	NHL	12	0	0	0	45	—	—	—	—	—
98-99	Tampa Bay	NHL	16	1	1	2	24	—	—	—	—	—
98-99	Washington	NHL	43	2	0	2	103	—	—	—	—	—
98-99	Cleveland	IHL	6	0	0	0	23	—	—	—	—	—
	NHL	Totals	371	10	18	28	1455	13	1	0	1	48
	IHL	Totals	129	9	28	37	840	14	0	2	2	90
	AHL	Totals	12	1	3	4	71	—	—	—	—	—

Born; 4/10/70, Montreal, Quebec. 6-5, 220. Drafted by Minnesota North Stars (5th choice, 92nd overall) in 1990 Entry Draft. Traded to Washington Capitals by Dallas Stars to complete transaction that sent Paul Cavallini to Dallas (6/20/93)-6/25/93. Traded to Tampa Bay Lightning by Washington with Washington's third round choice (later traded to Anaheim-Anaheim selected Craig Reichert) in 1994 Entry Draft and the return of future draft choices transferred in the Pat Elynuik trade for Joe Reekie, 3/21/94. Traded to Chicago Blackhawks by Tampa Bay with Tampa Bay's 2nd round choice (Jeff Paul) in 1996 Entry Draft for Patrick Poulin, Igor Ulanov and Chicago's second round choice (later traded to New Jersey-New Jersey selected Pierre Dagenais) in 1996 Entry Draft, 3/20/96. Traded to Carolina Hurricanes by Chicago for Ryan Risidore and Carolina's fifth round choice (later traded to Toronto-Toronto selected Morgan Warren) in 1998 Entry Draft, 7/25/97. Traded to Vancouver Canucks by Carolina with Sean Burke and Geoff Sanderson for Kirk McLean and Martin Gelinas, 1/3/98. Traded to Tampa Bay by Vancouver for Jamie Huscroft, 3/14/98. Sold to Washington by Tampa Bay (12/28/98). Last amateur club; Trois-Rivieres (QMJHL).

Ivan Ciernik — Left Wing

Regular Season / Playoffs

Season	Team	League	GP	G	A	PTS	PIM	GP	G	A	PTS	PIM
97-98	Ottawa	NHL	2	0	0	0	0	—	—	—	—	—
97-98	Worcester	AHL	53	9	12	21	38	1	0	0	0	2
98-99	Adirondack	AHL	21	1	4	5	4	—	—	—	—	—
98-99	Cincinnati	AHL	32	10	3	13	10	2	0	0	0	2
	AHL	Totals	106	20	19	39	52	3	0	0	0	4

Born; 10/30/77, Levice, Czechoslovakia. 6-1, 198. Drafted by Ottawa Senators (6th choice, 216th overall) in 1996 Entry Draft.

Jozef Cierny
Left Wing
Regular Season / Playoffs

Season	Team	League	GP	G	A	PTS	PIM	GP	G	A	PTS	PIM
92-93	Rochester	AHL	54	27	27	54	36	—	—	—	—	—
93-94	Edmonton	NHL	1	0	0	0	0	—	—	—	—	—
93-94	Cape Breton	AHL	73	30	27	57	88	4	1	1	2	4
94-95	Cape Breton	AHL	73	28	24	52	58	—	—	—	—	—
95-96	Detroit	IHL	20	2	5	7	16	—	—	—	—	—
95-96	Los Angeles	IHL	43	23	16	39	36	—	—	—	—	—
96-97	Long Beach	IHL	68	27	27	54	106	16	8	5	13	7
97-98	Nurnberg	Germany	45	20	22	42	61	—	—	—	—	—
98-99	Nurnberg	Germany	47	22	21	43	65	13	3	2	5	37
	AHL	Totals	200	85	78	163	182	4	1	1	2	4
	IHL	Totals	131	52	48	100	158	16	8	5	13	7

Born; 5/13/74, Zvolen, Czechoslovakia. 6-2, 185. Drafted by Buffalo Sabres (2nd choice, 35th overall) in 1992 Entry Draft. Traded to Edmonton Oilers by Buffalo with Buffalo's fourth round choice (Jussi Tarvainen) in 1994 Entry Draft for Craig Simpson, 9/1/93.

Tony Cimellaro
Center
Regular Season / Playoffs

Season	Team	League	GP	G	A	PTS	PIM	GP	G	A	PTS	PIM
92-93	New Haven	AHL	76	18	16	34	73	—	—	—	—	—
92-93	Ottawa	NHL	2	0	0	0	0	—	—	—	—	—
93-94	Asiago	Italy	16	16	11	27	13	—	—	—	—	—
93-94	Prince Edward Island	AHL	19	1	0	1	30	—	—	—	—	—
94-95	Durham	BHL	4	2	5	7	10	—	—	—	—	—
94-95	Blackburn	BNL	24	40	33	73	76	—	—	—	—	—
95-96												
96-97	Ratinger	Germany	46	4	13	17	42	—	—	—	—	—
97-98	Adendorfer	Germany	50	25	39	64	131	—	—	—	—	—
98-99	Waco	WPHL	61	28	53	81	110	4	2	1	3	4
	AHL	Totals	95	19	16	35	103	—	—	—	—	—

Born; 6/14/71, Kingston, Ontario. 5-11, 179. Signed as a free agent by Ottawa Senators (7/30/92). Last amateur club; Belleville (OHL).

Jason Cipolla
Center
Regular Season / Playoffs

Season	Team	League	GP	G	A	PTS	PIM	GP	G	A	PTS	PIM
94-95	Yale	ECAC	28	15	19	34	38	—	—	—	—	—
94-95	St. John's	AHL	4	0	0	0	0	—	—	—	—	—
95-96	St. John's	AHL	38	8	9	17	42	4	0	1	1	2
95-96	South Carolina	ECHL	39	21	32	53	73	—	—	—	—	—
96-97	St. John's	AHL	45	7	13	20	74	—	—	—	—	—
96-97	South Carolina	ECHL	9	7	4	11	20	18	11	13	24	20
97-98	South Carolina	ECHL	23	11	21	32	26	—	—	—	—	—
97-98	Milwaukee	IHL	50	12	32	44	79	10	1	9	10	20
98-99	Milwaukee	IHL	79	21	46	67	122	2	0	2	2	6
	IHL	Totals	129	33	78	111	201	12	1	11	12	26
	AHL	Totals	87	15	22	37	116	4	0	1	1	2
	ECHL	Totals	71	39	57	96	119	18	11	13	24	20

Born; 12/30/72, Toronto, Ontario. 5-9, 170. Member of 1996-97 ECHL Champion South Carolina Stingrays. Last amateur club; Yale (ECAC).

Aigars Cipruss
Center
Regular Season / Playoffs

Season	Team	League	GP	G	A	PTS	PIM	GP	G	A	PTS	PIM
94-95	Atlanta	IHL	11	3	7	10	2	—	—	—	—	—
94-95	Nashville	ECHL	57	25	32	57	96	12	5	10	15	20
95-96	Atlanta	IHL	2	0	2	2	0	—	—	—	—	—
95-96	Providence	AHL	15	3	3	6	6	—	—	—	—	—
95-96	Nashville	ECHL	49	26	50	76	57	—	—	—	—	—
96-97	Grand Rapids	IHL	1	0	1	1	0	—	—	—	—	—
96-97	Quebec	IHL	41	7	24	31	2	—	—	—	—	—
96-97	Muskegon	CoHL	23	13	19	32	13	—	—	—	—	—
97-98	Lukko Rauma	Finland	48	12	23	35	18	—	—	—	—	—
98-99	Lukko Rauma	Finland	54	9	26	35	28	—	—	—	—	—
	IHL	Totals	55	10	34	44	4	—	—	—	—	—
	ECHL	Totals	106	51	82	133	153	12	5	10	15	20

Born; 1/12/72, Riga, Latvia. 5-10, 175.

Ryan Cirillo
Left Wing
Regular Season / Playoffs

Season	Team	League	GP	G	A	PTS	PIM	GP	G	A	PTS	PIM
98-99	Jacksonville	ECHL	38	5	5	10	49	—	—	—	—	—

Born; Last amateur club; Oshawa (OHL).

John Cirjak
Center
Regular Season / Playoffs

Season	Team	League	GP	G	A	PTS	PIM	GP	G	A	PTS	PIM
98-99	Chesapeake	ECHL	5	1	0	1	0	—	—	—	—	—

Born; 2/10/77, Vancouver, Washington. 6-2, 180. Drafted by Colorado Avalanche (6th choice, 155th overall) in 1995 Entry Draft. Last amateur club;

Jason Cirone
Center
Regular Season / Playoffs

Season	Team	League	GP	G	A	PTS	PIM	GP	G	A	PTS	PIM
91-92	Winnipeg	NHL	3	0	0	0	2	—	—	—	—	—
91-92	Moncton	AHL	64	32	27	59	124	10	1	1	2	8
92-93	Asiago	Alpen.	25	24	14	38	36	—	—	—	—	—
92-93	Asiago	Italy	16	6	5	11	18	2	1	5	6	18
93-94	Cincinnati	IHL	26	4	2	6	61	—	—	—	—	—
93-94	Birmingham	ECHL	11	3	3	6	45	10	8	8	16	*67
94-95	Cincinnati	IHL	74	22	15	37	170	9	1	1	2	14
95-96	Rochester	AHL	24	4	5	9	34	—	—	—	—	—
95-96	Los Angeles	IHL	26	8	10	18	47	—	—	—	—	—
95-96	San Diego	WCHL	3	2	1	3	20	—	—	—	—	—
96-97	Long Beach	IHL	11	4	3	7	14	—	—	—	—	—
96-97	Kansas City	IHL	70	18	38	56	88	3	0	3	3	2
97-98	Kansas City	IHL	82	22	30	52	166	11	3	3	6	20
98-99	Kansas City	IHL	82	42	26	68	151	3	1	0	1	8
	IHL	Totals	371	120	124	244	697	26	5	7	12	44
	AHL	Totals	88	36	32	68	158	10	1	1	2	8

Born; 2/21/71, Toronto, Ontario. 5-9, 184. Drafted by Winnipeg Jets (3rd choice, 46th overall) in 1989 Entry Draft. Traded to Florida Panthers by Winnipeg for Dave Tomlinson (8/3/93). Signed as a free agent by Kansas City Blades (7/9/989). Last amateur club; Windsor (OHL).

Marian Cisar
Right Wing
Regular Season / Playoffs

Season	Team	League	GP	G	A	PTS	PIM	GP	G	A	PTS	PIM
98-99	Milwaukee	IHL	51	11	17	28	31	2	0	0	0	12

Born; 2/25/78, Bratislavia, Czechoslovakia. 6-0, 176. Drafted by Los Angeles Kings (2nd choice, 37th overall) in 1996 Entry Draft. Traded to Nashville Predators by Los Angeles for future considerations, 5/29/98. Last amateur club;

Derek Clancey
Center
Regular Season / Playoffs

Season	Team	League	GP	G	A	PTS	PIM	GP	G	A	PTS	PIM
91-92	Erie	ECHL	16	7	6	13	24	—	—	—	—	—
91-92	Toledo	ECHL	5	2	5	7	0	—	—	—	—	—
91-92	Winston-Salem	ECHL	9	4	3	7	2	—	—	—	—	—
92-93	Detroit	CoHL	11	4	13	17	6	1	0	0	0	2
93-94	Columbus	ECHL	45	16	42	58	34	6	1	5	6	4
94-95	Columbus	ECHL	63	21	66	87	20	3	3	2	5	6
95-96	Columbus	ECHL	67	32	77	109	40	3	0	2	2	0
96-97	Waco	WPHL	9	3	10	13	2	—	—	—	—	—
96-97	Columbus	ECHL	46	26	33	59	32	8	1	2	3	8
97-98	Chesapeake	ECHL	70	28	77	105	20	3	0	1	1	2
98-99	Chesapeake	ECHL	70	21	58	79	48	8	1	8	9	12
	ECHL	Totals	391	157	367	525	220	32	6	20	26	34

Born; 4/16/69, St. John's, Newfoundland. 5-10, 180. Named coach of Jackson (ECHL) beginning with 1999-2000 season.

Chris Clancy
Left Wing

Regular Season — Playoffs

Season	Team	League	GP	G	A	PTS	PIM	GP	G	A	PTS	PIM
96-97	Guelph	OUAA										
96-97	Syracuse	AHL	3	0	1	1	0	2	0	0	0	0
97-98	Fresno	WCHL	62	12	13	25	96	5	3	0	3	4
98-99	Madison	UHL	1	0	0	0	0	—	—	—	—	—

Born; 11/28/72, Kitchener, Ontario. 6-3, 195. Drafted by Buffalo Sabres (12th choice, 251st overall) in 1992 Entry Draft. Last amateur club; University of Guelph (OUAA).

Greg Clancy
Center

Regular Season — Playoffs

Season	Team	League	GP	G	A	PTS	PIM	GP	G	A	PTS	PIM
97-98	Grand Rapids	IHL	49	9	3	12	26	—	—	—	—	—
97-98	Muskegon	UHL	13	2	3	5	4	11	5	5	10	10
98-99	Miami	ECHL	59	28	25	53	40	—	—	—	—	—

Born; 11/15/72, Kingston, Ontario. 6-1, 196. Selected by Tallahassee in 1999 ECHL Dispersal Draft. Last amateur club; Acadia (AUAA).

Marty Clapton
Right Wing

Regular Season — Playoffs

Season	Team	League	GP	G	A	PTS	PIM	GP	G	A	PTS	PIM
97-98	Portland	AHL	2	0	0	0	0	—	—	—	—	—
97-98	Hampton Roads	ECHL	47	11	8	19	29	12	2	3	5	22
98-99	Hampton Roads	ECHL	70	18	36	54	79	4	1	0	1	15
	ECHL	Totals	117	29	44	73	108	16	3	3	6	37

Born; 7/1/74, Newton, Masachussets. 6-3, 220. Member of 1997-98 ECHL Champion Hampton Roads Admirals. Last amateur club; Brown University

Brett Clark
Defenseman

Regular Season — Playoffs

Season	Team	League	GP	G	A	PTS	PIM	GP	G	A	PTS	PIM
96-97	Canada	National	57	6	21	27	52	—	—	—	—	—
97-98	Montreal	NHL	41	1	0	1	20	—	—	—	—	—
97-98	Fredericton	AHL	20	0	6	6	6	4	0	1	1	17
98-99	Montreal	NHL	61	2	2	4	16	—	—	—	—	—
98-99	Fredericton	AHL	3	1	0	1	0	—	—	—	—	—
	NHL	Totals	102	3	2	5	36	—	—	—	—	—
	AHL	Totals	23	1	6	7	20	4	0	1	1	17

Born; 12/23/76, Moosomin, Saskatchewan. 6-0, 175. Drafted by Montreal Canadiens (7th choice, 154th overall) in 1996 Entry Draft. Selected by Atlanta Thrashers in 1999 NHL Expansion Draft (6/25/99). Last amateur club; Maine (Hockey

Brian Clark
Forward

Regular Season — Playoffs

Season	Team	League	GP	G	A	PTS	PIM	GP	G	A	PTS	PIM
98-99	Winston-Salem	UHL	1	0	0	0	0	—	—	—	—	—

Born;

Chris Clark
Right Wing

Regular Season — Playoffs

Season	Team	League	GP	G	A	PTS	PIM	GP	G	A	PTS	PIM
98-99	Saint John	AHL	73	13	27	40	123	7	2	4	6	15

Born; 3/8/76, Manchester, Connecticut. 6-0, 190. Drafted by Calgary Flames (3rd choice, 77th overall) in 1994 Entry Draft. Last amateur club; Clarkson (ECAC).

Jason Clark
Left Wing

Regular Season — Playoffs

Season	Team	League	GP	G	A	PTS	PIM	GP	G	A	PTS	PIM
96-97	Syracuse	AHL	11	3	3	6	2	—	—	—	—	—
96-97	Wheeling	ECHL	38	10	14	24	14	—	—	—	—	—
96-97	Jacksonville	ECHL	28	10	24	34	8	—	—	—	—	—
97-98	Jacksonville	ECHL	65	18	36	54	55	—	—	—	—	—
98-99	Revier Lowen	Germany	52	11	26	37	55	—	—	—	—	—
98-99	San Angelo	WPHL	3	0	6	6	0	17	4	12	16	8
	ECHL	Totals	131	38	74	112	77	—	—	—	—	—

Born; 5/6/72, Belmont, Ontario. 6-1, 185. Drafted by Vancouver Canucks (8th choice, 141st overall) in 1992 Entry Draft. Last amateur club; Bowling Green State (CCHA).

Cosmo Clarke
Left Wing

Regular Season — Playoffs

Season	Team	League	GP	G	A	PTS	PIM	GP	G	A	PTS	PIM
94-95	Brantford	CoHL	5	0	0	0	2	—	—	—	—	—
95-96	Flint	CoHL	4	0	0	0	2	—	—	—	—	—
95-96	Huntsville	SHL	52	21	27	48	83	9	0	0	0	9
96-97	Dayton	CoHL	69	27	21	48	77	—	—	—	—	—
97-98	Fort Worth	CHL	54	24	22	46	22	—	—	—	—	—
98-99	Fort Worth	CHL	61	21	19	40	24	—	—	—	—	—
	CHL	Totals	115	45	41	86	46	—	—	—	—	—
	CoHL	Totals	78	27	21	48	81	—	—	—	—	—

Born; 5/1/70, Kanata, Ontario. 6-3, 238. Selected by Memphis in 1999 CHL Dispersal Draft. Member of 1995-96 SHL champion Huntsville Channel Cats.

Jason Clarke
Right Wing

Regular Season — Playoffs

Season	Team	League	GP	G	A	PTS	PIM	GP	G	A	PTS	PIM
93-94	Erie	ECHL	3	1	0	1	57	—	—	—	—	—
93-94	Charlotte	ECHL	11	2	2	4	100	—	—	—	—	—
93-94	Brantford	CoHL	24	8	13	21	264	1	0	0	0	0
94-95	Roanoke	ECHL	63	11	18	29	*467	8	1	4	5	64
95-96	Roanoke	ECHL	59	20	18	38	491	3	0	1	1	20
96-97	Brimingham	ECHL	8	1	2	3	90	—	—	—	—	—
96-97	Central Texas	WPHL	31	7	13	20	226	9	1	4	5	63
97-98	San Angelo	WPHL	22	7	10	17	195	—	—	—	—	—
97-98	Anchorage	WCHL	3	0	2	2	27	—	—	—	—	—
98-99	Tallahassee	ECHL	48	12	5	17	287	—	—	—	—	—
98-99	Pensacola	ECHL	2	0	1	1	27	—	—	—	—	—
	ECHL	Totals	194	47	46	93	1519	11	1	5	6	84
	WPHL	Totals	53	14	23	37	421	9	1	4	5	63

Born; 2/28/73, Cobourg, Ontario. 6-1, 232. Last amateur club; Niagara Falls

Ray Clarke
Left Wing

Regular Season — Playoffs

Season	Team	League	GP	G	A	PTS	PIM	GP	G	A	PTS	PIM
98-99	Las Vegas	IHL	1	0	0	0	0	—	—	—	—	—

Born;

Travis Clayton
Left Wing

Regular Season — Playoffs

Season	Team	League	GP	G	A	PTS	PIM	GP	G	A	PTS	PIM
97-98	Wichita	CHL	70	27	35	62	84	15	5	2	7	12
98-99	Wichita	CHL	69	25	57	82	95	4	1	0	1	8
	CHL	Totals	139	52	92	144	179	19	6	2	8	20

Born; 9/3/76, Paradise Hill, Saskatchewan. 5-8, 180. Last amateur club; North Battleford (SJHL).

Daniel Cleary
Left Wing

Regular Season — Playoffs

Season	Team	League	GP	G	A	PTS	PIM	GP	G	A	PTS	PIM
97-98	Belleville	OHL	30	16	31	47	14	10	6	*17	*23	10
97-98	Chicago	NHL	6	0	0	0	0	—	—	—	—	—
97-98	Indianapolis	IHL	4	2	1	3	6	—	—	—	—	—
98-99	Chicago	NHL	35	4	5	9	24	—	—	—	—	—
98-99	Portland	AHL	30	9	17	26	74	—	—	—	—	—
98-99	Hamilton	AHL	9	0	1	1	7	3	0	0	0	0
	NHL	Totals	41	4	5	9	24	—	—	—	—	—
	AHL	Totals	39	9	18	27	81	3	0	0	0	0

Born; 12/18/78, Carbonear, Newfoundland. 6-0, 203. Drafted by Chicago Blackhawks (1st choice, 11th overall) in 1997 Entry Draft. Traded to Edmonton Oilers with Chad Kilger, Ethan Moreau, Christian Laflamme and Chicago's second round choice (Alexei Semenov) in 1999 Entry Draft for Boris Mironov, Dean McAmmond, Jonas Elofsson and Edmonton's second round choice (Dmitri Levinski) in 1999 Entry Draft. Last amateur club; Belleville (OHL).

Levi Clegg
Right Wing

Regular Season — Playoffs

Season	Team	League	GP	G	A	PTS	PIM	GP	G	A	PTS	PIM
98-99	San Antonio	CHL	1	0	1	1	0	—	—	—	—	—

Born; 6-2, 195.

Bobby Clouston — Center

Regular Season / Playoffs

Season	Team	League	GP	G	A	PTS	PIM	GP	G	A	PTS	PIM
93-94	Miami-Ohio	CCHA	10	1	4	5	2	—	—	—	—	—
93-94	Huntington	ECHL	7	1	1	2	6	—	—	—	—	—
94-95	Flint	CoHL	33	3	9	12	29	—	—	—	—	—
94-95	Utica	CoHL	27	5	5	10	22	—	—	—	—	—
95-96	Quad City	CoHL	2	0	0	0	0	—	—	—	—	—
95-96	Huntsville	SHL	46	19	45	64	124	10	3	14	17	22
96-97	Dayton	CoHL	60	9	50	59	64	—	—	—	—	—
97-98	Port Huron	UHL	3	0	2	2	0	—	—	—	—	—
97-98	San Angelo	WPHL	49	7	22	29	204	3	2	0	2	7
98-99	Fort Worth	CHL	16	3	10	13	73	—	—	—	—	—
	UHL	Totals	65	8	16	24	51	—	—	—	—	—

Born; 8/14/73, Detroit, Michigan. 5-8, 175. Member of 1995-96 SHL champion Huntsville Channel Cats. Last amateur club; Miami-Ohio (CCHA).

Eric Cloutier — Left Wing

Regular Season / Playoffs

Season	Team	League	GP	G	A	PTS	PIM	GP	G	A	PTS	PIM
95-96	Providence	AHL	6	0	0	0	31	—	—	—	—	—
95-96	Charlotte	ECHL	14	2	5	7	133	—	—	—	—	—
95-96	Louisiana	ECHL	15	5	3	8	104	4	0	2	2	8
96-97	Houston	IHL	3	0	0	0	6	—	—	—	—	—
96-97	Jacksonville	ECHL	47	13	11	24	334	—	—	—	—	—
97-98	Louisiana	ECHL	50	10	6	16	398	9	1	3	4	74
98-99	Louisiana	ECHL	33	6	6	12	284	—	—	—	—	—
	ECHL	Totals	159	36	31	67	1253	13	1	5	6	82

Born; 3/7/75, Mont-Laurier, Quebec. 6-0, 185. Last amateur club; Laval

Sylvain Cloutier — Center

Regular Season / Playoffs

Season	Team	League	GP	G	A	PTS	PIM	GP	G	A	PTS	PIM
93-94	Guelph	OHL	66	45	71	116	127	9	7	9	16	32
93-94	Adirondack	AHL	2	0	2	2	2	—	—	—	—	—
94-95	Adirondack	AHL	71	7	26	33	144	—	—	—	—	—
95-96	Adirondack	AHL	65	11	17	28	118	3	0	0	0	4
95-96	Toledo	ECHL	6	4	2	6	4	—	—	—	—	—
96-97	Adirondack	AHL	77	13	36	49	190	4	0	2	2	4
97-98	Adirondack	AHL	72	14	22	36	155	—	—	—	—	—
97-98	Detroit	IHL	8	0	1	1	18	21	7	5	12	31
98-99	Chicago	NHL	7	0	0	0	0	—	—	—	—	—
98-99	Indianapolis	IHL	73	21	33	54	128	7	3	2	5	12
	AHL	Totals	215	31	81	112	454	7	0	2	2	8
	IHL	Totals	81	21	34	55	146	28	10	7	17	43

Born; 2/13/74, Mont-Laurier, Quebec. 6-0, 195. Drafted by Detroit Red Wings (3rd choice, 70th overall) 1992 Entry Draft. Signed as a free agent by Chicago Blackhawks (8/17/98). Last amateur club; Guelph (OHL).

Brodie Coffin — Right Wing

Regular Season / Playoffs

Season	Team	League	GP	G	A	PTS	PIM	GP	G	A	PTS	PIM
96-97	Huntington	ECHL	63	12	13	25	147	—	—	—	—	—
97-98	Huntington	ECHL	63	13	18	31	169	4	0	0	0	0
98-99	Huntington	ECHL	63	16	18	34	151	—	—	—	—	—
	ECHL	Totals	189	41	49	90	467	4	0	0	0	0

Born; 4/9/74, Charlottetown, Prince Edward Island. 6-1, 195. Last amateur club; St. Mary's (OUAA).

Dan Colacito — Right Wing

Regular Season / Playoffs

Season	Team	League	GP	G	A	PTS	PIM	GP	G	A	PTS	PIM
96-97	Anchorage	WCHL	2	0	0	0	0	—	—	—	—	—
97-98	Winston-Salem	UHL	3	0	0	0	0	—	—	—	—	—
98-99	Mohawk Valley	UHL	1	0	0	0	0	—	—	—	—	—
	UHL	Totals	4	0	0	0	0	—	—	—	—	—

Born; 7/19/73, Toronto, Ontario. 6-0, 205.

Brett Colbourne — Defenseman

Regular Season / Playoffs

Season	Team	League	GP	G	A	PTS	PIM	GP	G	A	PTS	PIM
98-99	Asiago	Italy										
98-99	Fayetteville	CHL	23	10	11	21	21	—	—	—	—	—

Born; 4/2/73, Clearwater, British Columbia. 5-9, 185. Last amateur club; Ferris State (CCHA).

Cam Colbourne — Forward

Regular Season / Playoffs

Season	Team	League	GP	G	A	PTS	PIM	GP	G	A	PTS	PIM
98-99	Winston-Salem	UHL	1	0	0	0	2	—	—	—	—	—

Born;

Darren Colbourne — Right Wing

Regular Season / Playoffs

Season	Team	League	GP	G	A	PTS	PIM	GP	G	A	PTS	PIM
91-92	Kalamazoo	IHL	1	0	1	1	0	—	—	—	—	—
91-92	Dayton	ECHL	64	*69	50	119	70	3	1	0	1	14
92-93	Peoria	IHL	6	1	1	2	2	—	—	—	—	—
92-93	Dayton	ECHL	32	19	11	30	41	—	—	—	—	—
92-93	Richmond	ECHL	29	26	23	49	12	1	0	1	1	0
93-94	St. John's	AHL	1	0	0	0	0	—	—	—	—	—
93-94	Richmond	ECHL	68	69	35	104	100	—	—	—	—	—
95-96	Raleigh	ECHL	36	27	14	41	16	4	0	0	0	0
96-97	Raleigh	ECHL	69	53	48	101	32	—	—	—	—	—
97-98	Raleigh	ECHL	52	30	26	56	49	—	—	—	—	—
97-98	Ayr	BSL	23	9	8	17	12	—	—	—	—	—
98-99	Augusta	ECHL	70	30	37	67	54	2	1	0	1	0
	IHL	Totals	7	1	2	3	2	—	—	—	—	—
	ECHL	Totals	420	323	244	567	374	6	2	1	3	2

Born; 1/5/68, Corner Brook, Newfoundland. 6-0, 195. Drafted by Detroit Red Wings (10th choice, 227th overall) in 1988 Entry Draft. 1991-92 ECHL Rookie of the Year. 1991-92 ECHL First Team All-Star. 1993-94 ECHL Second Team

Danton Cole — Right Wing

Regular Season / Playoffs

Season	Team	League	GP	G	A	PTS	PIM	GP	G	A	PTS	PIM
89-90	Winnipeg	NHL	2	1	1	2	0	—	—	—	—	—
89-90	Moncton	AHL	80	31	42	73	18	—	—	—	—	—
90-91	Winnipeg	NHL	66	13	11	24	24	—	—	—	—	—
90-91	Moncton	AHL	3	1	1	2	0	—	—	—	—	—
91-92	Winnipeg	NHL	52	7	5	12	32	—	—	—	—	—
92-93	Tampa Bay	NHL	67	12	15	27	23	—	—	—	—	—
92-93	Atlanta	IHL	1	1	0	1	2	—	—	—	—	—
93-94	Tampa Bay	NHL	81	20	23	43	32	—	—	—	—	—
94-95	Tampa Bay	NHL	26	3	3	6	6	—	—	—	—	—
94-95	New Jersey	NHL	12	1	2	3	8	1	0	0	0	0
95-96	Islanders	NHL	10	1	0	1	0	—	—	—	—	—
95-96	Chicago	NHL	2	0	0	0	0	—	—	—	—	—
95-96	Utah	IHL	34	28	15	43	22	—	—	—	—	—
95-96	Indianapolis	IHL	32	9	12	21	20	5	1	5	6	8
96-97	Grand Rapids	IHL	35	8	18	26	24	5	3	1	4	2
97-98	Grand Rapids	IHL	81	13	13	26	36	3	1	1	2	0
98-99	Grand Rapids	IHL	72	14	11	25	50	—	—	—	—	—
	NHL	Totals	318	58	60	118	125	1	0	0	0	0
	IHL	Totals	255	73	69	142	154	13	5	7	12	10
	AHL	Totals	83	32	43	75	18	—	—	—	—	—

Born; 1/10/67, Pontiac, Michigan. 5-11, 185.Drafted by Winnipeg Jets (6th choice, 123rd overall) in 1985 Entry Draft. Traded to Tampa Bay Lightning by Winnipeg for future considerations (6/19/92). Traded to New Jersey Devils by Tampa Bay with Shawn Chambers for Alexander Semak and Ben Hankinson (3/14/95). Signed as a free agent by New York Islanders (8/26/95). Traded to Chicago Blackhawks by Islanders for Bob Halkidis (2/2/96). Last amateur club;

Lee Cole — Defenseman

Regular Season / Playoffs

Season	Team	League	GP	G	A	PTS	PIM	GP	G	A	PTS	PIM
96-97	North Bay	OHL	42	3	18	21	231	—	—	—	—	—
96-97	Toledo	ECHL	8	0	1	1	18	1	0	0	0	2
97-98	Toledo	ECHL	59	3	9	12	244	—	—	—	—	—
98-99	Port Huron	UHL	68	4	18	22	246	7	0	1	1	12
	ECHL	Totals	67	3	10	13	262	1	0	0	0	2

Born; 7/13/76, Timmons, Ontario. 6-2, 220. Last amateur club; North Bay (OHL).

Jon Coleman — Defenseman

Regular Season / Playoffs

Season	Team	League	GP	G	A	PTS	PIM	GP	G	A	PTS	PIM
97-98	Detroit	IHL	1	0	0	0	0	—	—	—	—	—
97-98	Adirondack	AHL	54	2	29	31	23	2	0	0	0	0
98-99	Adirondack	AHL	72	12	26	38	32	3	0	0	0	0
	AHL	Totals	126	14	55	69	55	5	0	0	0	0

Born; 3/9/75, Boston, Massachusetts. 6-1, 190. Drafted by Detroit Red Wings (2nd choice, 48th overall) in 1993 Entry Draft. Last amateur club; Boston University (Hockey East).

Bruce Coles — Right Wing

Regular Season / Playoffs

Season	Team	League	GP	G	A	PTS	PIM	GP	G	A	PTS	PIM
91-92	Winston-Salem	ECHL	16	2	6	8	37	—	—	—	—	—
91-92	Johnstown	ECHL	43	32	45	77	113	6	3	1	4	12
92-93	Canadian	National	27	9	22	31	20	—	—	—	—	—
92-93	Johnstown	ECHL	28	28	26	54	61	5	1	3	4	29
93-94	Johnstown	ECHL	24	23	20	43	56	3	0	1	1	10
94-95	Hershey	AHL	51	16	25	41	73	6	1	5	6	14
94-95	Johnstown	ECHL	29	20	25	45	56	—	—	—	—	—
95-96	Hershey	AHL	68	23	29	52	75	5	2	2	4	6
96-97	Philadelphia	AHL	79	31	49	80	152	10	2	5	7	28
97-98	Philadelphia	AHL	39	19	23	42	55	17	4	3	7	12
98-99	Springfield	AHL	9	3	4	7	12	—	—	—	—	—
98-99	Grand Rapids	IHL	15	1	7	8	10	—	—	—	—	—
98-99	Manitoba	IHL	11	1	3	4	6	2	0	1	1	0
98-99	Baton Rouge	ECHL	23	8	16	24	43	—	—	—	—	—
	AHL	Totals	246	92	130	222	367	38	9	15	24	60
	IHL	Totals	26	2	10	12	16	2	0	1	1	0
	ECHL	Totals	163	113	138	251	366	14	4	5	9	51

Born; 12/6/68, Montreal, Quebec. 5-9, 185. Drafted by Montreal Canadiens (1st choice, 23rd overall) in 1990 Supplemental Draft. Signed as a free agent by Philadelphia Flyers (5/31/95). Traded to Grand Rapids Griffins by Philadelphia for Mark Greig (7/21/98). Member of 1997-98 AHL Champion Philadelphia Phantoms. Last amateur club; RPI (ECAC).

Geoff Collard — Defenseman

Regular Season / Playoffs

Season	Team	League	GP	G	A	PTS	PIM	GP	G	A	PTS	PIM
98-99	Western Michigan	CCHA	34	2	5	7	69	—	—	—	—	—
98-99	Orlando	IHL	1	0	0	0	4	—	—	—	—	—

Born; Flint, Michigan. 6-0, 205.

Mark Collicutt — Defenseman

Regular Season / Playoffs

Season	Team	League	GP	G	A	PTS	PIM	GP	G	A	PTS	PIM
97-98	Huntsville	CHL	55	2	6	8	210	2	0	0	0	2
98-99	Flint	UHL	33	0	4	4	141	—	—	—	—	—

Born; 2/5/76, Peterborough, Ontario. 6-4, 205.

Clint Collins — Right Wing

Regular Season / Playoffs

Season	Team	League	GP	G	A	PTS	PIM	GP	G	A	PTS	PIM
95-96	Fort Worth	CeHL	2	1	0	1	39	—	—	—	—	—
95-96	Tulsa	CeHL	2	1	0	1	4	—	—	—	—	—
96-97	New Mexico	WPHL	7	1	1	2	82	—	—	—	—	—
96-97	Wichita	CeHL	4	0	0	0	57	—	—	—	—	—
96-97	Columbus	CeHL	5	1	2	3	63	3	1	0	1	14
97-98	Fresno	WCHL	27	9	8	17	219	—	—	—	—	—
97-98	Wheeling	ECHL	11	0	2	2	156	—	—	—	—	—
97-98	Cincinnati	AHL	16	0	0	0	97	—	—	—	—	—
98-99	Huntsville	CHL	25	6	5	11	212	—	—	—	—	—
98-99	Corpus Christi	WPHL	3	0	1	1	19	—	—	—	—	—
	CHL	Totals	38	9	7	16	375	3	1	0	1	14
	WPHL	Totals	10	1	2	3	101	—	—	—	—	—

Born; 8/5/74, Vancouver, British Columbia. 6-0, 192. Selected by Florida in 1998 ECHL Expansion Draft.

Paul Comrie

Regular Season / Playoffs

Season	Team	League	GP	G	A	PTS	PIM	GP	G	A	PTS	PIM
98-99	Denver	WCHA	40	18	31	49	84	—	—	—	—	—
98-99	Hamilton	AHL	7	0	1	1	0	8	1	3	4	2

Born; Last amateur club; Denver (WCHA).

Brendan Concannon — Right Wing

Regular Season / Playoffs

Season	Team	League	GP	G	A	PTS	PIM	GP	G	A	PTS	PIM
96-97	Pensacola	ECHL	68	15	31	46	41	12	3	4	7	9
97-98	Pensacola	ECHL	70	40	43	83	36	19	7	18	25	2
98-99	Pensacola	ECHL	21	4	7	11	4	—	—	—	—	—
98-99	Louisiana	ECHL	4	0	0	0	6	—	—	—	—	—
98-99	South Carolina	ECHL	22	7	12	19	6	3	1	1	2	0
	ECHL	Totals	185	66	93	159	93	34	11	23	34	11

Born; 9/8/72, Boston, Massachusetts. 5-10, 185. Traded to South Carolina by Tallahassee for Jeff McLean (2/99). Last amateur team; Salem State (NCAA 3).

Rob Concannon — Left Wing

Regular Season / Playoffs

Season	Team	League	GP	G	A	PTS	PIM	GP	G	A	PTS	PIM
95-96	St. John's	AHL	20	1	2	3	4	—	—	—	—	—
95-96	South Carolina	ECHL	45	18	28	46	28	4	0	3	3	10
96-97	South Carolina	ECHL	69	24	46	70	163	18	3	5	8	39
97-98	South Carolina	ECHL	65	25	20	45	152	5	1	0	1	12
98-99	South Carolina	ECHL	69	21	16	37	258	3	1	1	2	20
	ECHL	Totals	248	88	110	198	601	30	5	9	14	81

Born; 12/2/70, Dorchester, Massachusetts. 6-0, 175. Member of 1996-97 ECHL Champion South Carolina Stingrays.

Craig Conley — Right Wing

Regular Season / Playoffs

Season	Team	League	GP	G	A	PTS	PIM	GP	G	A	PTS	PIM
95-96	Detroit	CoHL	20	7	13	20	12	—	—	—	—	—
95-96	Lakeland	SHL	7	4	7	11	2	—	—	—	—	—
95-96	Winston-Salem	SHL	15	3	7	10	2	9	2	5	7	8
96-97	Saginaw	CoHL	16	4	13	17	14	—	—	—	—	—
96-97	Dayton	CoHL	28	6	12	18	18	—	—	—	—	—
96-97	Flint	CoHL	15	0	4	4	8	—	—	—	—	—
97-98	Lake Charles	WPHL	5	2	4	6	4	—	—	—	—	—
97-98	Fort Worth	CHL	47	17	34	51	101	—	—	—	—	—
98-99	Fort Worth	CHL	70	25	52	77	92	—	—	—	—	—
	CHL	Totals	117	42	86	128	193	—	—	—	—	—
	CoHL	Totals	79	17	42	59	52	—	—	—	—	—
	SHL	Totals	22	7	14	21	4	9	2	5	7	8

Born; 10/25/70, St. Clair Shores, Michigan. 5-11, 170. Selected by Topeka in 1999 CHL Expansion Draft.

Ryan Connolly — Defenseman

Regular Season / Playoffs

Season	Team	League	GP	G	A	PTS	PIM	GP	G	A	PTS	PIM
97-98	Lake Charles	WPHL	27	1	6	7	59	—	—	—	—	—
97-98	Odessa	WPHL	23	1	4	5	27	—	—	—	—	—
98-99	San Angelo	WPHL	10	1	0	1	8	—	—	—	—	—
98-99	Tulsa	CHL	5	0	0	0	8	—	—	—	—	—
98-99	Fort Worth	CHL	9	2	1	3	39	—	—	—	—	—
98-99	Mohawk Valley	UHL	3	0	0	0	7	—	—	—	—	—
	WPHL	Totals	60	3	10	13	94	—	—	—	—	—
	CHL	Totals	14	2	1	3	47	—	—	—	—	—

Born; 2/16/76, Pickering, Ontario. 6-4, 225. Traded to Odessa with David Shute to Lake Charles for Greg Bailey (1/98). Selected by Fayetteville in 1999 CHL Dispersal Draft. Last amateur club; Wilfrid Laurier University (CIUA).

Paul Constantin — Left Wing

Regular Season / Playoffs

Season	Team	League	GP	G	A	PTS	PIM	GP	G	A	PTS	PIM
92-93	Green Bay	AHA	12	3	14	17	4	—	—	—	—	—
92-93	Muskegon	CoHL	9	1	3	4	4	—	—	—	—	—
92-93	Flint	CoHL	11	3	2	5	4	—	—	—	—	—
92-93	Jacksonville	SUN	24	11	13	24	11	—	—	—	—	—
93-94	Bracknell	BNL	39	52	45	97	70	—	—	—	—	—
94-95	Bracknell	BNL	14	15	14	29	8	—	—	—	—	—
94-95	Lee Valley	BNL	28	42	36	78	106	—	—	—	—	—
95-96	Chelmsford	BNL	9	10	9	19	6	—	—	—	—	—
96-97	Medway	BNL	51	58	57	115	119	—	—	—	—	—
97-98	Peterborough	BNL	31	34	41	75	55	8	10	11	21	4
97-98	Winston-Salem	UHL	6	0	1	1	0	—	—	—	—	—
98-99	Mohawk Valley	UHL	18	4	5	9	0	—	—	—	—	—
98-99	New Mexico	WPHL	8	2	3	5	6	—	—	—	—	—
	UHL	Totals	44	8	11	19	8	—	—	—	—	—

Born; 5/16/68, Burlington, Ontario. 6-1, 190. Last amateur club; Lake Superior (CCHA).

Peter Constantine — Defenseman

Regular Season / Playoffs

Season	Team	League	GP	G	A	PTS	PIM	GP	G	A	PTS	PIM
98-99	Rochester Inst.	NCAA										
98-99	Augusta	ECHL	5	0	2	2	2	2	0	0	0	0

Born; Toronto, Ontario. 6-4, 215. Last amateur club; Rochester Institute of Technologay (NCAA 3).

D.J. Conte — Defenseman

Regular Season / Playoffs

Season	Team	League	GP	G	A	PTS	PIM	GP	G	A	PTS	PIM
96-97	Fresno	WCHL	2	0	0	0	0	—	—	—	—	—
97-98	Saginaw	UHL	62	0	6	6	209	—	—	—	—	—
98-99	Saginaw	UHL	35	0	2	2	103	—	—	—	—	—
	UHL	Totals	97	0	8	8	312	—	—	—	—	—

Born; 5/22/73, Lawrence, Massachusetts. 6-1, 200. Last amateur club; Fitchburg State

Trevor Converse — Right Wing

Regular Season / Playoffs

Season	Team	League	GP	G	A	PTS	PIM	GP	G	A	PTS	PIM
91-92	Thunder Bay	CoHL	22	8	12	20	84	13	4	7	11	18
91-92	Richmond	ECHL	13	4	7	11	75	—	—	—	—	—
92-93	Thunder Bay	CoHL	7	0	5	5	23	—	—	—	—	—
92-93	Richmond	ECHL	2	0	0	0	4	—	—	—	—	—
95-96	Fort Worth	CeHL	62	14	21	35	195	—	—	—	—	—
96-97	Baltimore	AHL	2	0	1	1	12	—	—	—	—	—
96-97	Hershey	AHL	2	0	0	0	5	—	—	—	—	—
96-97	Johnstown	ECHL	42	6	8	14	160	—	—	—	—	—
96-97	Mobile	ECHL	10	2	2	4	53	3	2	1	3	2
97-98	Phoenix	WCHL	34	9	11	20	105	—	—	—	—	—
97-98	Fort Worth	WPHL	8	0	0	0	6	13	3	2	5	43
98-99	Long Beach	IHL	3	0	0	0	7	—	—	—	—	—
98-99	San Antonio	CHL	3	0	0	0	28	—	—	—	—	—
98-99	Colorado	WCHL	25	2	6	8	135	—	—	—	—	—
98-99	Fresno	WCHL	13	1	4	5	19	—	—	—	—	—
98-99	San Diego	WCHL	2	0	0	0	20	1	0	1	1	0
	AHL	Totals	4	0	1	1	17	—	—	—	—	—
	WCHL	Totals	74	12	21	33	279	1	0	1	1	0
	ECHL	Totals	67	12	17	29	292	3	2	1	3	2
	CHL	Totals	65	14	21	35	223	—	—	—	—	—
	CoHL	Totals	29	8	17	25	107	13	4	7	11	18

Born; 2/4/70, North Battleford, Saskatchewan. 6-1, 210. Member of 1991-92 CoHL champion Thunder Bay Senators.

Brandon Convery — Center

Regular Season / Playoffs

Season	Team	League	GP	G	A	PTS	PIM	GP	G	A	PTS	PIM
92-93	Sudbury	OHL	7	7	9	16	6	—	—	—	—	—
92-93	Niagara Falls	OHL	51	38	39	77	24	4	1	3	4	4
92-93	St. John's	AHL	3	0	0	0	0	5	0	1	1	0
93-94	Niagara Falls	OHL	29	24	29	53	30	—	—	—	—	—
93-94	Belleville	OHL	23	16	19	35	22	12	4	10	14	13
93-94	St. John's	AHL	—	—	—	—	—	1	0	0	0	0
94-95	St. John's	AHL	76	34	37	71	43	5	2	2	4	4
95-96	Toronto	NHL	11	5	2	7	4	5	0	0	0	2
95-96	St. John's	AHL	57	22	23	45	28	—	—	—	—	—
96-97	Toronto	NHL	39	2	8	10	20	—	—	—	—	—
96-97	St. John's	AHL	25	14	14	28	15	—	—	—	—	—
97-98	Vancouver	NHL	7	0	2	2	0	—	—	—	—	—
97-98	St. John's	AHL	49	27	36	63	35	—	—	—	—	—
97-98	Syracuse	AHL	2	1	2	3	5	—	—	—	—	—
98-99	Vancouver	NHL	12	2	7	9	8	—	—	—	—	—
98-99	Los Angeles	NHL	3	0	0	0	4	—	—	—	—	—
98-99	Long Beach	IHL	14	4	3	7	10	—	—	—	—	—
98-99	Springfield	AHL	31	9	14	23	45	—	—	—	—	—
	NHL	Totals	72	9	19	28	36	5	0	0	0	2
	AHL	Totals	243	107	126	233	171	11	2	3	5	4

Born; 2/4/74, Kingston, Ontario. 6-0, 180. Drafted by Toronto Maple Leafs (1st choice, 8th overall) in 1992 Entry Draft. Traded to Vancouver Canucks by Toronto for Lonny Bohonos (3/7/98). Claimed by Los Angeles Kings on waivers from Vancouver (11/26/98). Last amateur club; Belleville (OHL).

Brad Cook — Defenseman

Regular Season / Playoffs

Season	Team	League	GP	G	A	PTS	PIM	GP	G	A	PTS	PIM
94-95	Detroit	OHL	1	0	0	0	0	—	—	—	—	—
94-95	Erie	ECHL	7	0	0	0	2	—	—	—	—	—
95-96												
96-97	Dayton	CoHL	61	4	19	23	53	—	—	—	—	—
97-98	San Angelo	WPHL	55	3	28	31	76	3	0	1	1	0
98-99	San Angelo	WPHL	69	11	26	37	90	17	0	9	9	34
	WPHL	Totals	124	14	54	68	166	20	0	10	10	34

Born; 2/26/75, Southgate, Michigan. 5-10, 195. Last amateur club; Detroit

Jamie Cooke — Right Wing

Season	Team	League	GP	G	A	PTS	PIM	GP	G	A	PTS	PIM
			Regular Season					Playoffs				
91-92	Hershey	AHL	66	15	26	41	49	—	—	—	—	—
92-93	Hershey	AHL	36	11	7	18	12	—	—	—	—	—
93-94	Birmingham	ECHL	52	24	23	47	55	10	1	4	5	8
94-95	Memphis	CeHL	35	23	22	45	11	—	—	—	—	—
95-96	Memphis	CeHL	63	28	43	71	37	6	3	2	5	11
96-97	Memphis	CeHL	59	25	31	56	57	18	8	13	21	22
97-98	Idaho	WCHL	62	30	40	70	100	4	1	1	2	6
98-99	Bakersfield	WCHL	50	24	26	50	63	2	1	0	1	5
	AHL	Totals	102	26	33	59	61	—	—	—	—	—
	CeHL	Totals	157	76	96	172	155	24	11	15	26	33
	WCHL	Totals	112	54	66	120	163	6	2	1	3	11

Born; 5/11/68, Toronto, Ontario. 6-1, 200. Drafted by Philadelphia Flyers (8th choice, 140th overall) in 1988 Entry Draft. Last amateur club; Colgate (ECAC).

Matt Cooke — Center

Season	Team	League	GP	G	A	PTS	PIM	GP	G	A	PTS	PIM
			Regular Season					Playoffs				
98-99	Vancouver	NHL	30	0	2	2	27	—	—	—	—	—
98-99	Syracuse	AHL	37	15	18	33	119	—	—	—	—	—

Born; 9/7/78, Belleville, Ontario. 5-11, 200. Drafted by Vancouver Canucks (8th choice, 144th overall) in 1997 Entry Draft. Last amateur club; Kingston (OHL).

Joe Coombs — Left Wing

Season	Team	League	GP	G	A	PTS	PIM	GP	G	A	PTS	PIM
			Regular Season					Playoffs				
96-97	Columbus	ECHL	66	28	31	59	127	8	3	4	7	10
97-98	Brantford	UHL	41	16	19	35	14	—	—	—	—	—
97-98	Saginaw	UHL	9	4	3	7	4	—	—	—	—	—
98-99	Topeka	CHL	47	19	19	38	63	3	0	0	0	6
	UHL	Totals	50	20	22	42	18	—	—	—	—	—

Born; 1/6/75, Brantford, Ontario. 5-10, 195. Last amateur club; Belleville (OHL).

Matt Cooney — Left Wing

Season	Team	League	GP	G	A	PTS	PIM	GP	G	A	PTS	PIM
			Regular Season					Playoffs				
97-98	Jacksonville	ECHL	64	12	24	36	125	—	—	—	—	—
98-99	Indianapolis	IHL	29	2	9	11	52	—	—	—	—	—
98-99	Columbus	ECHL	25	5	16	21	72	3	0	1	1	11
	ECHL	Totals	89	17	40	57	197	3	0	1	1	11

Born; 8/3/74, Wilcox, Saskatchewan. 6-1, 188. Last amateur club; Cornell

David Cooper — Defenseman

Season	Team	League	GP	G	A	PTS	PIM	GP	G	A	PTS	PIM
			Regular Season					Playoffs				
92-93	Medicine Hat	WHL	63	15	50	65	88	10	2	2	4	32
92-93	Rochester	AHL	—	—	—	—	—	2	0	0	0	2
93-94	Rochester	AHL	68	10	25	35	82	4	1	1	2	2
94-95	Rochester	AHL	21	2	4	6	48	—	—	—	—	—
94-95	South Carolina	ECHL	39	9	19	28	90	9	3	8	11	24
95-96	Rochester	AHL	67	9	18	27	79	8	0	1	1	12
96-97	Toronto	NHL	19	3	3	6	16	—	—	—	—	—
96-97	St. John's	AHL	44	16	19	35	65	—	—	—	—	—
97-98	Toronto	NHL	9	0	4	4	8	—	—	—	—	—
97-98	St. John's	AHL	60	19	23	42	117	4	0	1	1	6
98-99	Saint John	AHL	65	18	24	42	121	7	1	4	5	10
	NHL	Totals	28	3	7	10	24	—	—	—	—	—
	AHL	Totals	325	74	113	187	512	25	2	7	9	32

Born; 11/2/73, Williamsville, New York. 6-2, 204. Drafted by Buffalo Sabres (1st choice, 11th overall) in 1992 Entry Draft. Signed as a free agent by Toronto Maple Leafs (9/26/96). Traded to Calgary Flames by Toronto for Ladislav Kohn (7/2/98). 1997-98 AHL Second Team All-Star. Member of 1995-96 AHL champion Rochester Americans. Last amateur club; Medicine Hat (WHL).

Kory Cooper — Goaltender

Season	Team	League	GP	W	L	T	MIN	SO	AVG	GP	W	L	MIN	SO	AVG
			Regular Season							Playoffs					
96-97	Belleville	OHL	61	20	31	5	3317	2	3.02	6	2	4	360	0	4.33
96-97	Portland	AHL	3	1	0	0	51	0	5.89	—	—	—	—	—	—
97-98	Sudbury	OHL	21	9	10	1	1159	0	3.78	10	4	5	511	0	3.64
97-98	Indianapolis	IHL	6	2	3	0	254	0	4.49	—	—	—	—	—	—
97-98	Jacksonville	ECHL	21	9	11	0	1124	0	3.52	—	—	—	—	—	—
98-99	Waco	WPHL	59	36	14	4	3232	*4	2.77	4	1	3	251	0	3.58

Born; 2/21/77, Winsloe, Prince Edward Island. 5-10, 170. 1998-99 WPHL Goaltender of the Year. 1998-99 WPHL Rookie of the Year. Last amateur club; Belleville (OHL).

Adam Copeland — Right Wing

Season	Team	League	GP	G	A	PTS	PIM	GP	G	A	PTS	PIM
			Regular Season					Playoffs				
98-99	Hamilton	AHL	30	3	6	9	6	—	—	—	—	—
98-99	New Orleans	ECHL	23	9	9	18	15	11	3	1	4	6

Born; 6/5/76, St. Catherines, Ontario. 6-1, 215. Drafted by Edmonton Oilers (6th choice, 79th overall) in 1994 Entry Draft. Last amateur club; Miami-Ohio

Olivier Coqueux — Center

Season	Team	League	GP	G	A	PTS	PIM	GP	G	A	PTS	PIM
			Regular Season					Playoffs				
98-99	Edinburgh	BNL	21	10	8	18	14	—	—	—	—	—
98-99	Tucson	WCHL	13	2	2	4	21	—	—	—	—	—

Born;

Jeff Corbett — Left Wing

Season	Team	League	GP	G	A	PTS	PIM	GP	G	A	PTS	PIM
			Regular Season					Playoffs				
97-98	Phoenix	WCHL	7	1	0	1	31	—	—	—	—	—
97-98	Hampton Roads	ECHL	38	2	2	4	155	14	0	0	0	26
98-99	Hampton Roads	ECHL	30	0	0	0	145	—	—	—	—	—
	ECHL	Totals	68	2	2	4	300	14	0	0	0	26

Born; 1/22/75, Langley, British Columbia. 6-1, 200. Selected by Trenton in 1999 ECHL Expansion Draft. Member of 1997-98 ECHL Champion Hampton Roads Admirals.

Yvan Corbin — Left Wing

Season	Team	League	GP	G	A	PTS	PIM	GP	G	A	PTS	PIM
			Regular Season					Playoffs				
92-93	Chatham	CoHL	16	16	7	23	0	—	—	—	—	—
93-94	Fredericton	AHL	6	0	0	0	2	—	—	—	—	—
93-94	Knoxville	ECHL	9	4	1	5	4	—	—	—	—	—
93-94	Columbus	ECHL	10	2	2	4	17	—	—	—	—	—
94-95	Daytona Beach	SuHL	22	27	21	48	25	—	—	—	—	—
94-95	South Carolina	ECHL	35	15	20	35	10	7	1	4	5	0
95-96	Fort Wayne	IHL	1	0	0	0	0	—	—	—	—	—
95-96	Louisiana	ECHL	5	2	1	3	4	—	—	—	—	—
95-96	Johnstown	ECHL	9	5	6	11	4	—	—	—	—	—
95-96	Erie	ECHL	2	0	1	1	0	—	—	—	—	—
95-96	Winston-Salem	SHL	47	52	43	95	72	9	*14	*16	*30	22
96-97	Mississippi	ECHL	6	1	5	6	2	—	—	—	—	—
97-98		France										
98-99	Anchorage	WCHL	71	*60	63	123	47	6	6	1	7	2
	ECHL	Totals	76	29	36	65	41	7	1	4	5	0

Born; 10/4/72, Kapuskasing, Ontario. 6-0, 185. 1998-99 WCHL Second Team All-Star. Last amateur club; Kitchener (OHL).

Mario Cormier — Defenseman

Season	Team	League	GP	G	A	PTS	PIM	GP	G	A	PTS	PIM
			Regular Season					Playoffs				
96-97	Moncton	QMJHL	70	2	15	17	144	—	—	—	—	—
96-97	South Carolina	ECHL	4	0	0	0	4	2	0	1	1	2
97-98	South Carolina	ECHL	18	1	2	3	18	—	—	—	—	—
98-99	Abilene	WPHL	66	1	12	13	50	3	0	0	0	2
	ECHL	Totals	22	1	2	3	22	2	0	1	1	2

Born; 2/24/76, Moncton, New Brunswick. 5-11, 192. Last amateur club; Moncton (QMJHL).

Mark Cornforth — Defenseman

Regular Season — Playoffs

Season	Team	League	GP	G	A	PTS	PIM	GP	G	A	PTS	PIM
94-95	Merrimack	H.E.	30	8	20	28	93	—	—	—	—	—
94-95	Syracuse	AHL	2	0	1	1	2	—	—	—	—	—
95-96	Boston	NHL	6	0	0	0	4	—	—	—	—	—
95-96	Providence	AHL	65	5	10	15	117	4	0	0	0	4
96-97	Providence	AHL	61	8	12	20	47	—	—	—	—	—
96-97	Cleveland	IHL	13	1	4	5	25	14	1	3	4	29
97-98	Cleveland	AHL	68	5	15	20	146	—	—	—	—	—
97-98	Grand Rapids	IHL	8	1	2	3	20	3	0	0	0	17
98-99	Providence	AHL	15	1	1	2	16	—	—	—	—	—
98-99	Springfield	AHL	5	0	0	0	2	—	—	—	—	—
	AHL	Totals	148	14	24	38	184	4	0	0	0	4
	IHL	Totals	89	7	21	28	191	17	1	3	4	46

Born; 11/13/72, Montreal, Quebec. 6-1, 193. Signed as a free agent by Boston Bruins (10/6/95). Last amateur club; Merrimack (Hockey East).

Keli Corpse — Center

Regular Season — Playoffs

Season	Team	League	GP	G	A	PTS	PIM	GP	G	A	PTS	PIM
95-96	Fredericton	AHL	5	0	1	1	0	—	—	—	—	—
95-96	Wheeling	ECHL	63	32	62	94	40	6	0	4	4	4
96-97	Baltimore	AHL	2	0	1	1	2	—	—	—	—	—
96-97	Grand Rapids	IHL	19	3	4	7	2	—	—	—	—	—
96-97	Fort Wayne	IHL	33	4	15	19	26	—	—	—	—	—
96-97	Wheeling	ECHL	24	12	17	29	10	—	—	—	—	—
97-98	Straubing	Germany	16	13	18	31	62	—	—	—	—	—
97-98	Merano	Italy	26	17	19	36	44	—	—	—	—	—
98-99	Pensacola	ECHL	43	8	29	37	14	—	—	—	—	—
98-99	Wheeling	ECHL	30	7	23	30	18	—	—	—	—	—
	IHL	Totals	52	7	19	26	28	—	—	—	—	—
	AHL	Totals	7	0	2	2	2	—	—	—	—	—
	ECHL	Totals	160	59	131	190	82	6	0	4	4	4

Born; 5/14/74, London, Ontario. 5-11, 175. Drafted by Montreal Canadiens (3rd choice, 44th overall) in 1992 Entry Draft. Traded to Wheeling by Pensacola for future considerations (1/99). 1995-96 ECHL Rookie of the Year. 1995-96 ECHL Second Team All-Star. Last amateur club; Kingston (OHL).

Daniel Corso — Center

Regular Season — Playoffs

Season	Team	League	GP	G	A	PTS	PIM	GP	G	A	PTS	PIM
98-99	Worcester	AHL	63	14	14	28	26	—	—	—	—	—

Born; 4/3/78, Montreal, Quebec. 5-9, 155. Drafted by St. Louis Blues (6th choice, 169th overall) in 1996 Entry Draft. Last amateur club; Victoriaville (QMJHL).

Joe Corvo — Defenseman

Regular Season — Playoffs

Season	Team	League	GP	G	A	PTS	PIM	GP	G	A	PTS	PIM
98-99	Springfield	AHL	50	5	15	20	32	—	—	—	—	—
98-99	Hampton Roads	ECHL	5	0	0	0	15	4	0	1	1	0

Born; 6/20/77, Oak Park, Illinois. 6-0, 205. Drafted by Los Angeles Kings (4th choice, 83rd overall) in 1997 Entry Draft. Last amateur club; Western Michigan (CCHA).

Bryan Cossette — Defenseman

Regular Season — Playoffs

Season	Team	League	GP	G	A	PTS	PIM	GP	G	A	PTS	PIM
96-97	Rochester Institute	NCAA 3	29	12	15	27	NA	—	—	—	—	—
96-97	Roanoke	ECHL	3	0	1	1	2	2	0	0	0	0
97-98	Memphis	CHL	70	15	24	39	99	4	0	0	0	12
98-99	Memphis	CHL	40	2	8	10	50	—	—	—	—	—
98-99	Austin	WPHL	3	0	1	1	2	—	—	—	—	—
	CHL	Totals	110	17	32	49	149	4	0	0	0	12

Born; 5/29/73, Estevan, Saskatchewan. 6-0, 200. Last amateur club; Rochester Institue of Technology (NCAA 3).

Mark Costea — Defenseman

Regular Season — Playoffs

Season	Team	League	GP	G	A	PTS	PIM	GP	G	A	PTS	PIM
96-97	Fresno	WCHL	1	0	0	0	0	—	—	—	—	—
96-97	Alaska	WCHL	30	3	16	19	34	—	—	—	—	—
97-98	Phoenix	WCHL	33	9	10	19	16	—	—	—	—	—
97-98	El Paso	WPHL	7	0	3	3	25	—	—	—	—	—
98-99	El Paso	WPHL	47	10	17	27	28	3	0	2	2	0
	WCHL	Totals	64	12	26	38	50	—	—	—	—	—
	WPHL	Totals	54	10	20	30	53	3	0	2	2	0

Born; 1/26/74, Welland, Ontario. 5-8, 190.

Alain Cote — Left Wing

Regular Season — Playoffs

Season	Team	League	GP	G	A	PTS	PIM	GP	G	A	PTS	PIM
94-95	Thunder Bay	CoHL	74	13	11	24	20	11	1	4	5	4
95-96	Winston-Salem	SHL	60	19	25	44	35	9	0	2	2	0
96-97	Macon	CeHL	65	23	33	56	76	5	2	1	3	2
97-98	Macon	CHL	69	13	25	38	41	3	0	0	0	2
98-99	Monroe	WPHL	69	6	19	25	24	6	1	0	1	2
	CHL	Totals	134	36	58	94	117	8	2	1	3	4

Born; 8/13/73, Beauport, Quebec. 5-11, 200. Member of 1994-95 Colonial League champion Thunder Bay Senators. Last amateur club; Laval (QMJHL).

Gary Coupal — Right Wing

Regular Season — Playoffs

Season	Team	League	GP	G	A	PTS	PIM	GP	G	A	PTS	PIM
94-95	Sudbury	OHL	17	1	5	6	61	—	—	—	—	—
94-95	Muskegon	CoHL	18	4	4	8	100	12	0	0	0	95
95-96	Columbus	ECHL	54	12	12	24	408	2	0	1	1	24
96-97	Columbus	ECHL	10	0	0	0	67	—	—	—	—	—
97-98	Muskegon	UHL	26	7	5	12	101	—	—	—	—	—
97-98	Central Texas	WPHL	20	3	6	9	79	4	0	0	0	11
98-99	Central Texas	WPHL	52	12	10	22	251	—	—	—	—	—
	WPHL	Totals	72	15	16	31	330	4	0	0	0	11
	ECHL	Totals	64	12	12	24	475	2	0	1	1	24
	UHL	Totals	44	11	9	20	201	12	0	0	0	95

Born; 9/16/74, Sudbury, Ontario. 6-1, 195. Traded to Tupelo by Central texas to complete earlier trade (5/99). Last amateur club; Sudbury (OHL).

Jason Courtemanche — Defenseman

Regular Season — Playoffs

Season	Team	League	GP	G	A	PTS	PIM	GP	G	A	PTS	PIM
93-94	Nashville	ECHL	46	6	6	12	140	2	0	0	0	10
94-95	Nashville	ECHL	45	1	8	9	223	—	—	—	—	—
95-96	Johnstown	ECHL	60	5	15	20	363	—	—	—	—	—
95-96	San Diego	WCHL	5	0	1	1	2	9	0	1	1	13
96-97	Houston	IHL	1	0	0	0	5	—	—	—	—	—
96-97	Utah	IHL	2	0	0	0	0	—	—	—	—	—
96-97	Long Beach	IHL	12	0	0	0	25	2	0	0	0	5
96-97	San Diego	WCHL	45	13	16	29	285	6	1	2	3	50
97-98	San Diego	WCHL	42	7	11	18	291	12	0	1	1	50
98-99	San Diego	WCHL	61	5	12	17	276	10	0	2	2	23
	IHL	Totals	15	0	0	0	30	2	0	0	0	5
	WCHL	Totals	153	25	40	65	854	37	1	6	7	136
	ECHL	Totals	151	12	29	41	726	2	0	0	0	10

Born; 7/31/70, Hartford, Connecticut. 6-1, 215. Member of 1995-96 WCHL champion San Diego Gulls. Member of 1996-97 WCHL Champion San Diego Gulls. Member of 1997-98 WCHL Champion San Diego Gulls. Last amateur club; Elmira (NCAA 3).

Ed Courtenay
Right Wing

Regular Season / Playoffs

Season	Team	League	GP	G	A	PTS	PIM	GP	G	A	PTS	PIM
88-89	Granby	QMJHL	68	59	55	114	68	4	1	1	2	22
88-89	Kalamazoo	IHL	1	0	0	0	0	1	0	0	0	2
89-90	Kalamazoo	IHL	57	25	28	53	16	3	0	0	0	0
90-91	Kalamazoo	IHL	76	35	36	71	37	8	2	3	5	12
91-92	San Jose	NHL	5	0	0	0	0	—	—	—	—	—
91-92	Kansas City	IHL	36	14	12	26	46	15	8	9	17	15
92-93	San Jose	NHL	39	7	13	20	10	—	—	—	—	—
92-93	Kansas City	IHL	32	15	11	26	25	—	—	—	—	—
93-94	Kansas City	IHL	62	27	21	48	60	—	—	—	—	—
94-95	Chicago	IHL	47	14	16	30	20	—	—	—	—	—
94-95	Peoria	IHL	9	5	0	5	4	9	5	3	8	2
95-96	San Fransisco	IHL	20	6	3	9	8	—	—	—	—	—
95-96	Jacksonville	ECHL	3	0	2	2	4	18	5	12	17	23
95-96	Reno	WCHL	7	3	7	10	8	—	—	—	—	—
96-97	South Carolina	ECHL	68	54	56	*110	70	—	—	—	—	—
97-98	Sheffield	BSL	40	27	21	48	16	8	4	4	8	14
98-99	Sheffield	BSL	53	33	29	62	37	6	5	3	8	0
	NHL	Totals	44	7	13	20	10	—	—	—	—	—
	IHL	Totals	340	141	127	268	216	36	15	15	30	31
	ECHL	Totals	71	54	58	112	74	18	5	12	17	23
	BSL	Totals	93	60	50	110	53	14	9	7	16	14

Born; 2/2/68, Verdun, Quebec. 6-4, 200. Signed as a free agent by Minnesota North Stars (10/1/89). Selected by San Jose Sharks in NHL dispersal draft (5/30/91). 1996-97 ECHL First Team All-Star. Last amateur club; Granby

Larry Courville
Left Wing

Regular Season / Playoffs

Season	Team	League	GP	G	A	PTS	PIM	GP	G	A	PTS	PIM
93-94	Newmarket	OHL	39	20	19	39	134	—	—	—	—	—
93-94	Moncton	AHL	8	2	0	2	37	10	2	2	4	27
94-95	Sarnia	OHL	16	9	9	18	58	—	—	—	—	—
94-95	Oshawa	OHL	28	25	30	55	72	7	4	10	14	10
95-96	Vancouver	NHL	3	1	0	1	0	—	—	—	—	—
95-96	Syracuse	AHL	71	17	32	49	127	14	5	3	8	10
96-97	Vancouver	NHL	19	0	2	2	11	—	—	—	—	—
96-97	Syracuse	AHL	54	20	24	44	103	3	0	1	1	20
97-98	Vancouver	NHL	11	0	0	0	5	—	—	—	—	—
97-98	Syracuse	AHL	29	6	12	18	84	—	—	—	—	—
98-99	Syracuse	AHL	71	13	28	41	155	—	—	—	—	—
	NHL	Totals	33	1	2	3	16	—	—	—	—	—
	AHL	Totals	233	58	96	154	506	27	7	6	13	57

Born; 4/2/74, Timmins, Ontario. 6-1, 180. Drafted by Winnipeg Jets (6th choice, 119th overall) in 1993 Entry Draft. Re-entered Entry Draft, selected by Vancouver Canucks (2nd choice, 61st overall) in 1995 Entry Draft. Last amateur club; Oshawa (OHL).

Dan Cousineau
Defenseman

Regular Season / Playoffs

Season	Team	League	GP	G	A	PTS	PIM	GP	G	A	PTS	PIM
98-99	Ohio State	CCHA	32	6	4	10	38	—	—	—	—	—
98-99	Columbus	ECHL	3	1	0	1	2	2	0	1	1	0

Born; 5/22/75, Waterloo, Ontario. 6-0, 200. Last amateur club; Ohio State

Marcel Cousineau
Goaltender

Regular Season / Playoffs

Season	Team	League	GP	W	L	T	MIN	SO	AVG	GP	W	L	MIN	SO	AVG
93-94	St. John's	AHL	37	13	11	9	2015	0	3.51	—	—	—	—	—	—
94-95	St. John's	AHL	58	22	27	6	3342	4	3.07	3	0	3	179	0	3.01
95-96	St. John's	AHL	62	21	26	13	3629	1	3.17	4	1	3	257	0	2.56
96-97	Toronto	NHL	13	3	5	1	566	1	3.29	—	—	—	—	—	—
96-97	St. John's	AHL	19	7	8	3	1053	0	3.30	11	6	5	658	0	2.55
97-98	Toronto	NHL	2	0	0	0	17	0	0.00	—	—	—	—	—	—
97-98	St. John's	AHL	57	17	25	13	3306	1	3.03	4	1	3	254	0	2.36
98-99	Islanders	NHL	6	0	4	0	293	0	2.87	—	—	—	—	—	—
98-99	Lowell	AHL	53	26	17	7	3034	3	2.75	3	0	3	186	0	4.20
	NHL	Totals	21	3	9	1	876	1	3.08	—	—	—	—	—	—
	AHL	Totals	286	106	114	51	16379	9	3.10	25	8	17	1534	0	2.78

Born; 4/30/73, Delson, Quebec. 5-9, 180. Drafted by Boston Bruins (3rd choice, 62nd overall) in 1991 Entry Draft. Signed as a free agent by Toronto Maple Leafs (11/13/93). Signed as a free agent by New York Islanders (7/14/98). Traded to Los Angeles Kings by Islanders with Zigmund Palffy, Bryan Smolinski and New Jersey's fourth round choice (Daniel Johansson) in 1999 Entry Draft for Olli Jokinen, Josh Green, Mathieu Biron and Los Angeles' first round choice (Taylor Pyatt) in 1999 Entry Draft (6/20/99). Shared a shutout with Felix Potvin (12/3/96) versus St. Louis. Shared a shutout with Glenn Healy (11/4/97) versus San Jose. Last amateur club; Drummondville (QMJHL).

Alexandre Couture
Defenseman

Regular Season / Playoffs

Season	Team	League	GP	G	A	PTS	PIM	GP	G	A	PTS	PIM
98-99	Peoria	ECHL	58	7	20	27	78	4	0	2	2	4

Born; 12/18/77, Hamnord, Quebec. 6-4, 197. Drafted by Florida Panthers (7th choice, 183rd overall) in 1996 Entry Draft. Last amateur club; Halifax (QMJHL).

Patrick Couture
Goaltender

Regular Season / Playoffs

Season	Team	League	GP	W	L	T	MIN	SO	AVG	GP	W	L	MIN	SO	AVG
98-99	Rouyn-Noranda	QMJHL	1	0	1	0	40	0	6.00	—	—	—	—	—	—

Born; 5/28/78, Quebec City, Quebec. 5-11, 180. Last amateur club; Rouyn-Noranda (QMJHL).

Sylvain Couturier
Left Wing

Regular Season / Playoffs

Season	Team	League	GP	G	A	PTS	PIM	GP	G	A	PTS	PIM
88-89	Los Angeles	NHL	16	1	3	4	2	—	—	—	—	—
88-89	New Haven	AHL	44	18	20	38	33	10	2	2	4	11
89-90	New Haven	AHL	50	9	8	17	47	—	—	—	—	—
90-91	Los Angeles	NHL	3	0	1	1	0	—	—	—	—	—
90-91	Phoenix	IHL	66	50	37	87	49	10	8	2	10	10
91-92	Los Angeles	NHL	14	3	1	4	2	—	—	—	—	—
91-92	Phoenix	IHL	39	19	20	39	68	—	—	—	—	—
92-93	Phoenix	IHL	38	23	16	39	63	—	—	—	—	—
92-93	Fort Wayne	IHL	—	—	—	—	—	4	2	3	5	2
92-93	Adirondack	AHL	29	17	17	34	12	11	3	5	8	10
93-94	Milwaukee	IHL	80	41	51	92	123	4	1	2	3	2
94-95	Milwaukee	IHL	77	31	41	72	77	15	1	4	5	10
95-96	Milwaukee	IHL	82	33	52	85	60	5	1	0	1	2
96-97	Milwaukee	IHL	79	26	24	50	42	3	0	1	1	2
97-98	Revier Lowen	Germany	42	12	13	25	56	—	—	—	—	—
98-99	Berlin	Germany	50	19	12	31	62	—	—	—	—	—
	NHL	Totals	33	4	5	9	4	—	—	—	—	—
	IHL	Totals	461	223	241	464	482	36	12	12	24	26
	AHL	Totals	123	44	45	89	92	21	5	7	12	21

Born; 4/23/68, Greenfield Park, Quebec. 6-2, 205. Drafted by Los Angeles Kings (3rd choice, 65th overall) in 1986 Entry Draft. Traded to Detroit Red Wings with Paul Coffey and Jim Hiller for Jimmy Carson, Marc Potvin and Gary Shuchuk (1/29/93). Member of 1992-93 IHL Champion Fort Wayne Komets. Last amateur club; Laval (QMJHL).

Michel Couvrette — Center

Regular Season / Playoffs

Season	Team	League	GP	G	A	PTS	PIM	GP	G	A	PTS	PIM
89-90	Virginia	ECHL	11	12	11	23	10	—	—	—	—	—
90-91	Albany	IHL	8	5	4	9	0	—	—	—	—	—
91-92												
92-93	Lee Valley	BHL	15	30	25	55	26	—	—	—	—	—
92-93	Green Bay	AHA	14	10	19	29	29	—	—	—	—	—
93-94	Detroit	CoHL	6	1	1	2	0	—	—	—	—	—
93-94	Utica	CoHL	1	0	0	0	0	—	—	—	—	—
93-94	Jacksonville	SUN	11	5	6	11	4	—	—	—	—	—
94-95	Tulsa	CeHL	40	22	19	41	27	—	—	—	—	—
94-95	Memphis	CeHL	3	0	1	1	0	—	—	—	—	—
94-95	Oklahoma City	CeHL	10	1	3	4	4	5	3	1	4	14
95-96	San Diego	WCHL	52	22	36	58	73	9	1	1	2	8
96-97	San Antonio	CeHL	7	4	1	5	6	—	—	—	—	—
96-97	San Diego	WCHL	7	2	4	6	6	—	—	—	—	—
96-97	Bakersfield	WCHL	11	8	8	16	10	—	—	—	—	—
97-98	Phoenix	WCHL	8	0	2	2	4	—	—	—	—	—
97-98	El Paso	WPHL	5	0	5	5	2	—	—	—	—	—
98-99	Phoenix	WCHL	36	9	12	21	43	—	—	—	—	—
	WCHL	Totals	114	41	62	103	136	9	1	1	2	8
	CeHL	Totals	60	27	24	51	37	5	3	1	4	14
	CoHL	Totals	7	1	1	2	0	—	—	—	—	—

Born; 11/11/65, Verdun, France. 5-10, 193. Member of 1995-96 WCHL Champion San Diego Gulls.

Chris Coveny — Defenseman

Regular Season / Playoffs

Season	Team	League	GP	G	A	PTS	PIM	GP	G	A	PTS	PIM
98-99	Peoria	ECHL	58	4	19	23	138	4	0	1	1	4

Born; 6/15/74. 6-1, 205. Last amateur club; Ottawa (OUAA).

Jeff Cowan — Left Wing

Regular Season / Playoffs

Season	Team	League	GP	G	A	PTS	PIM	GP	G	A	PTS	PIM
96-97	Saint John	AHL	22	5	5	10	8	—	—	—	—	—
96-97	Roanoke	ECHL	47	21	13	34	42	—	—	—	—	—
97-98	Saint John	AHL	69	15	13	28	23	13	4	1	5	14
98-99	Saint John	AHL	71	7	12	19	117	4	0	1	1	10
	AHL	Totals	162	27	30	57	148	17	4	2	6	24

Born; 9/27/76, Scarborough, Ontario. 6-2, 185. Signed as a free agent by Calgary Flames (10/2/95). Last amateur club; Barrie (OHL).

Craig Coxe — Center

Regular Season / Playoffs

Season	Team	League	GP	G	A	PTS	PIM	GP	G	A	PTS	PIM
84-85	Vancouver	NHL	9	0	0	0	49	—	—	—	—	—
84-85	Fredericton	AHL	62	8	7	15	242	4	2	1	3	16
85-86	Vancouver	NHL	57	3	5	8	176	3	0	0	0	2
86-87	Vancouver	NHL	15	1	0	1	31	—	—	—	—	—
86-87	Fredericton	AHL	46	1	12	13	168	—	—	—	—	—
87-88	Vancouver	NHL	64	5	12	17	186	—	—	—	—	—
87-88	Calgary	NHL	7	2	3	5	32	2	1	0	1	16
88-89	St. Louis	NHL	41	0	7	7	127	—	—	—	—	—
88-89	Peoria	IHL	8	2	7	9	38	—	—	—	—	—
89-90	Vancouver	NHL	25	1	4	5	66	—	—	—	—	—
89-90	Milwaukee	IHL	5	0	5	5	4	—	—	—	—	—
90-91	Vancouver	NHL	7	0	0	0	27	—	—	—	—	—
90-91	Milwaukee	IHL	36	9	21	30	116	6	3	2	5	22
91-92	San Jose	NHL	10	2	0	2	19	—	—	—	—	—
91-92	Kansas City	IHL	51	17	21	38	106	—	—	—	—	—
91-92	Kalamazoo	IHL	6	4	5	9	13	10	2	4	6	37
92-93	Kalamazoo	IHL	12	1	1	2	8	—	—	—	—	—
92-93	Cincinnati	IHL	20	5	3	8	34	—	—	—	—	—
93-94	Tulsa	CeHL	64	26	57	83	236	11	4	9	13	38
94-95	Tulsa	CeHL	12	7	7	14	28	7	0	1	1	30
95-96	Huntsville	SHL	20	7	13	20	56	10	8	13	21	33
96-97	Tulsa	CeHL	64	29	59	88	95	5	2	2	4	8
97-98	Tulsa	CHL	25	11	22	33	34	—	—	—	—	—
97-98	Wichita	CHL	31	9	29	38	75	15	1	10	11	62
98-99	Corpus Christi	WPHL	53	10	30	40	44	4	1	1	2	6
	NHL	Totals	235	14	31	45	713	5	1	0	1	18
	IHL	Totals	138	38	63	101	319	16	5	6	11	59
	AHL	Totals	108	9	19	28	410	4	2	1	3	16
	CeHL	Totals	196	82	174	256	468	38	7	22	29	138

Born; 1/21/64, Chula Vista, California. 6-4, 220. Drafted by Detroit Red Wings (4th choice, 66th overall) in 1982 Entry Draft. Traded by Vancouver Canucks to Calgary Flames for Brian Bradley, Peter Bakovic and future considerations (Kevan Guy) (3/88). Traded to St. Louis Blues by Calgary with Mike Bullard and Tim Corkey for Doug Gilmour, Mark Hunter, Steve Bozek and Michael Dark (9/5/88). Sold to Chicago Blackhawks by St. Louis to complete future considerations of Rik Wilson trade made on September 27 (9/28/89). Claimed by Canucks in NHL waiver draft (10/2/89). Selected by San Jose Sharks in 1991 NHL expansion draft (5/30/91). Traded to Macon with Dave Wiletjo for Francois Leroux and Mike Anastasio (12/97). Traded to Wichita by Macon for Jude Boulianne (1/98). Member of 1995-96 SHL champion Huntsville Channel Cats. Last amateur club;

David Craievich — Defenseman

Regular Season / Playoffs

Season	Team	League	GP	G	A	PTS	PIM	GP	G	A	PTS	PIM
91-92	Utica	AHL	9	0	0	0	4	1	0	0	0	4
91-92	Cincinnati	ECHL	50	11	29	40	166	8	1	8	9	15
92-93	Cincinnati	IHL	21	0	3	3	33	—	—	—	—	—
92-93	Birmingham	ECHL	56	10	35	45	139	—	—	—	—	—
93-94	Cincinnati	IHL	3	0	0	0	0	—	—	—	—	—
93-94	Birmingham	ECHL	61	18	58	76	218	10	5	10	15	14
94-95	Minnesota	IHL	2	0	0	0	0	—	—	—	—	—
94-95	Birmingham	ECHL	59	20	46	66	140	7	4	4	8	10
95-96	Mobile	ECHL	65	23	51	74	157	—	—	—	—	—
96-97	Hershey	AHL	2	0	0	0	2	—	—	—	—	—
96-97	Mobile	ECHL	65	13	25	38	125	3	0	1	1	0
97-98	Mobile	ECHL	70	17	48	65	116	3	0	1	1	8
97-98	Chicago	IHL	3	0	0	0	2	17	0	1	1	6
98-99	Chicago	IHL	1	0	0	0	0	—	—	—	—	—
98-99	Mobile	ECHL	60	10	38	48	90	—	—	—	—	—
	IHL	Totals	30	0	3	3	35	17	0	1	1	6
	AHL	Totals	11	0	0	0	6	1	0	0	0	4
	ECHL	Totals	486	122	330	452	1151	31	10	24	34	47

Born; 5/3/71, Chatham, Ontario. 6-2, 208. Drafted by New Jersey Devils (7th choice, 143rd overall) in 1991 Entry Draft. 1993-94 ECHL Second Team All-Star. 1995-96 ECHL Second Team All-Star. 1997-98 ECHL Second Team All-Star. Member of 1997-98 IHL Champion Chicago Wolves. Last amateur club;

Mike Craig — Right Wing

Regular Season / Playoffs

Season	Team	League	GP	G	A	PTS	PIM	GP	G	A	PTS	PIM
90-91	Minnesota	NHL	39	8	4	12	32	10	1	1	2	20
91-92	Minnesota	NHL	67	15	16	31	155	4	1	0	1	7
92-93	Minnesota	NHL	70	15	23	38	106	—	—	—	—	—
93-94	Dallas	NHL	72	13	24	37	139	4	0	0	0	2
94-95	Toronto	NHL	37	5	5	10	12	2	0	1	1	2
95-96	Toronto	NHL	70	8	12	20	42	6	0	0	0	18
96-97	Toronto	NHL	65	7	13	20	62	—	—	—	—	—
97-98	San Antonio	IHL	12	4	1	5	18	—	—	—	—	—
97-98	Kansas City	IHL	59	14	33	47	68	11	5	5	10	28
98-99	San Jose	NHL	1	0	0	0	0	—	—	—	—	—
98-99	Kentucky	AHL	52	27	17	44	72	12	5	4	9	18
	NHL	Totals	421	71	97	168	548	26	2	2	4	49
	IHL	Totals	123	45	51	96	158	11	5	5	10	28

Born; 6/6/71, St. Mary's, Ontario. 6-1, 180. Drafted by Minnesota North Stars (2nd choice, 28th overall) in 1989 Entry Draft. Signed as a free agent by Toronto Maple Leafs (7/29/94). Traded to Kansas City by San Antonio with Reggie Savage for Darrin Kimble and John Purves (11/97). Signed as a free agent by San Jose Sharks (7/14/98). Last amateur club; Oshawa (OHL).

Joe Craigen — Center

Regular Season / Playoffs

Season	Team	League	GP	G	A	PTS	PIM	GP	G	A	PTS	PIM
97-98	Peoria	ECHL	69	18	26	44	30	3	0	0	0	0
98-99	Peoria	ECHL	50	10	14	24	20	—	—	—	—	—
98-99	Huntington	ECHL	13	4	1	5	2	—	—	—	—	—
	ECHL	Totals	132	32	41	73	52	3	0	0	0	0

Born; 2/15/75, Kitchener, Ontario. 5-11, 190. Traded to Huntington by Peoria for Kevin Paden (2/99). Selected by Greenville in 1999 ECHL Expansion Draft. Last amateur club; Harvard (ECAC).

John Craighead — Right Wing

Regular Season / Playoffs

Season	Team	League	GP	G	A	PTS	PIM	GP	G	A	PTS	PIM
91-92	West Palm Beach	SUN	39	12	17	29	160	—	—	—	—	—
92-93	West Palm Beach	SUN	36	12	9	21	158	—	—	—	—	—
92-93	Louisville	ECHL	5	1	0	1	33	—	—	—	—	—
93-94	Huntington	ECHL	9	4	2	6	44	—	—	—	—	—
93-94	Richmond	ECHL	28	18	12	30	89	—	—	—	—	—
94-95	Detroit	IHL	44	5	7	12	285	3	0	1	1	4
95-96	Detroit	IHL	63	7	9	16	368	10	2	3	5	28
96-97	Toronto	NHL	5	0	0	0	10	—	—	—	—	—
96-97	St. John's	AHL	53	9	10	19	318	7	1	1	2	22
97-98	Cleveland	IHL	49	9	7	16	233	—	—	—	—	—
97-98	Quebec	IHL	13	2	2	4	73	—	—	—	—	—
98-99	Nurnberg	Germany	34	4	6	10	144	13	1	4	5	60
	IHL	Totals	169	23	25	48	959	13	2	4	6	32
	SUN	Totals	75	24	26	50	318	—	—	—	—	—
	ECHL	Totals	42	23	14	37	166	—	—	—	—	—

Born; 11/23/71, Vancouver, British Columbia. 6-1, 200. Signed as a free agent by Toronto Maple Leafs (7/22/96). Traded to Quebec by Cleveland with Ryan Mougenel, Rick Hayward, Eric Perrin, Burke Murphy's rights and Pat Jablonski for Rick Girard, Dale DeGray, Darcy Simon, Tom Draper and Jason Ruff (3/98). Last amateur club; British Columbia (BCJHL).

Dale Craigwell — Center

Regular Season / Playoffs

Season	Team	League	GP	G	A	PTS	PIM	GP	G	A	PTS	PIM
91-92	San Jose	NHL	32	5	11	16	8	—	—	—	—	—
91-92	Kansas City	IHL	48	6	19	25	29	12	4	7	11	4
92-93	San Jose	NHL	8	3	1	4	4	—	—	—	—	—
92-93	Kansas City	IHL	60	15	38	53	24	12	*7	5	12	2
93-94	San Jose	NHL	58	3	6	9	16	—	—	—	—	—
93-94	Kansas City	IHL	5	3	1	4	0	—	—	—	—	—
94-95	Injured	DNP										
95-96	San Fransico	IHL	75	11	49	60	38	4	2	0	2	2
96-97	Kansas City	IHL	82	17	51	68	34	3	1	0	1	0
97-98	Kansas City	IHL	81	13	42	55	12	11	2	9	11	2
98-99	Augsberger	Germany										
98-99	Kansas City	IHL	61	11	28	39	14	3	0	2	2	2
	NHL	Totals	98	11	18	29	28	—	—	—	—	—
	IHL	Totals	412	76	228	304	151	45	16	23	39	12

Born; 4/24/71, Toronto, Ontario. 5-10, 178. Drafted by San Jose Sharks (11th choice, 199th overall) in 1991 Entry Draft. Member of 1991-92 IHL Champion Kansas City Blades. Last amateur club; Oshawa (OHL).

Jason Crane — Right Wing

Regular Season / Playoffs

Season	Team	League	GP	G	A	PTS	PIM	GP	G	A	PTS	PIM
95-96	Lakeland	SHL	48	12	22	34	24	4	0	2	2	2
96-97	Columbus	CeHL	43	11	14	25	16	2	1	0	1	2
97-98	Tucson	WCHL	63	7	11	18	82	—	—	—	—	—
98-99	Tucson	WCHL	21	2	7	9	20	—	—	—	—	—
	WCHL	Totals	84	9	18	27	102	—	—	—	—	—

Born; 1/13/72, Toronto, Ontario. 5-9, 180. Last amateur club; Miami of Ohio (CCHA).

Derek Crawford — Left Wing

Regular Season / Playoffs

Season	Team	League	GP	G	A	PTS	PIM	GP	G	A	PTS	PIM
90-91	Greensboro	ECHL	8	2	5	7	73	—	—	—	—	—
91-92	Dayton	ECHL	61	37	37	74	231	3	0	0	0	14
92-93	Green Bay	AHA	5	2	4	6	27	—	—	—	—	—
92-93	Dayton	ECHL	21	4	9	13	91	—	—	—	—	—
92-93	Dallas	CeHL	22	19	11	30	37	7	5	2	7	27
93-94	Dallas	CeHL	61	26	50	76	171	7	1	4	5	27
94-95	Dallas	CeHL	27	6	4	10	111	—	—	—	—	—
95-96	Reno	WCHL	57	19	21	40	139	2	0	1	1	2
96-97	New Mexico	WPHL	53	15	25	40	206	6	1	3	4	18
97-98	New Mexico	WPHL	53	19	26	45	159	10	3	2	5	35
98-99	New Mexico	WPHL	62	13	24	37	168	—	—	—	—	—
	WPHL	Totals	168	47	75	122	533	16	4	5	9	53
	CeHL	Totals	110	51	65	116	319	14	6	6	12	54
	ECHL	Totals	90	43	51	94	395	3	0	0	0	14

Born; 4/14/69, Hamilton, Ontario. 6-3, 220.

Matt Cressman — Left Wing

Regular Season / Playoffs

Season	Team	League	GP	G	A	PTS	PIM	GP	G	A	PTS	PIM
97-98	Monroe	WPHL	69	16	27	43	54	—	—	—	—	—
98-99	Jacksonville	ECHL	69	16	23	39	55	2	0	0	0	2

Born; 6/19/75, Cambridge, Ontario. 6-0, 175. Last amateur club; Western Michigan (CCHA).

Derek Crimin — Center

Regular Season / Playoffs

Season	Team	League	GP	G	A	PTS	PIM	GP	G	A	PTS	PIM
95-96	Ferris State	CCHA	37	16	12	28	42	—	—	—	—	—
95-96	Nashville	ECHL	4	1	5	6	0	2	1	0	1	0
96-97	Pensacola	ECHL	16	5	10	15	4	—	—	—	—	—
96-97	Wheeling	ECHL	29	8	8	16	8	—	—	—	—	—
96-97	Charlotte	ECHL	16	2	8	10	8	3	2	1	3	8
97-98	Charlotte	ECHL	59	7	17	24	16	6	0	0	0	8
98-99	Columbus	CHL	64	23	28	51	52	9	2	0	2	12
	ECHL	Totals	124	23	48	71	36	11	3	1	4	16

Born; 4/3/73, Sault Ste. Marie, Michigan. 6-0, 185. Last amateur club; Ferris State (CCHA).

Earl Cronan — Left Wing

Regular Season / Playoffs

Season	Team	League	GP	G	A	PTS	PIM	GP	G	A	PTS	PIM
96-97	Fredericton	AHL	50	5	3	8	33	—	—	—	—	—
97-98	Fredericton	AHL	28	3	6	9	33	2	0	0	0	8
97-98	New Orleans	ECHL	4	0	1	1	6	—	—	—	—	—
98-99	Cincinnati	IHL	4	0	1	1	0	—	—	—	—	—
98-99	Chesapeake	ECHL	50	19	16	35	95	8	2	1	3	15
	AHL	Totals	78	8	9	17	66	2	0	0	0	8
	ECHL	Totals	54	19	17	36	101	8	2	1	3	15

Born; 1/2/73, Warwick, Rhode Island. 6-1, 195. Drafted by Montreal Canadiens (11th choice, 212th overall) in 1992 Entry Draft. Last amateur club; Colgate (ECAC).

Paul Croteau — Defenseman

Regular Season / Playoffs

Season	Team	League	GP	G	A	PTS	PIM	GP	G	A	PTS	PIM
95-96	Roanoke	ECHL	23	2	2	4	2	—	—	—	—	—
95-96	Raleigh	ECHL	4	0	0	0	0	—	—	—	—	—
95-96	Erie	ECHL	28	1	9	10	4	—	—	—	—	—
96-97	Baton Rouge	ECHL	61	5	29	34	24	—	—	—	—	—
97-98	Baton Rouge	ECHL	44	4	4	8	6	—	—	—	—	—
98-99	Baton Rouge	ECHL	68	8	23	31	14	6	1	0	1	4
	ECHL	Totals	228	20	67	87	50	6	1	0	1	4

Born; 5/21/72, Lewiston, Maine. 6-0, 200. Last amateur club; Bowdoin College (NCAA 3).

Troy Crowder — Right Wing

Regular Season / Playoffs

Season	Team	League	GP	G	A	PTS	PIM	GP	G	A	PTS	PIM
87-88	North Bay	OHL	9	1	2	3	44	—	—	—	—	—
87-88	Belleville	OHL	46	12	27	39	103	6	2	3	5	24
87-88	Utica	AHL	3	0	0	0	36	—	—	—	—	—
87-88	New Jersey	NHL	—	—	—	—	—	1	0	0	0	12
88-89	Utica	AHL	62	6	4	10	152	2	0	0	0	25
89-90	New Jersey	NHL	10	0	0	0	23	2	0	0	0	10
89-90	Nashville	ECHL	3	0	0	0	15	—	—	—	—	—
90-91	New Jersey	NHL	59	6	3	9	182	—	—	—	—	—
91-92	Detroit	NHL	7	0	0	0	35	1	0	0	0	0
92-93	DNP	Injured										
93-94	DNP	Injured										
94-95	Los Angeles	NHL	29	1	2	3	99	—	—	—	—	—
95-96	Los Angeles	NHL	15	1	0	1	42	—	—	—	—	—
96-97	Vancouver	NHL	30	1	2	3	52	—	—	—	—	—
96-97	Syracuse	AHL	2	0	0	0	0	—	—	—	—	—
97-98	Hannover	Germany	19	1	0	1	34	2	0	1	1	33
98-99	Hershey	AHL	25	0	1	1	44	—	—	—	—	—
	NHL	Totals	150	9	7	16	433	4	0	0	0	22
	AHL	Totals	92	6	5	11	232	2	0	0	0	25

Born; 5/3/68, Sudbury, Ontario. 6-4, 220. Drafted by New Jersey Devils (6th choice, 108th overall) in 1986 Entry Draft. Signed as a free agent by Detroit Red Wings (8/27/91). Signed as a free agent by Los Angeles Kings (8/31/94). Signed as a free agent by Vancouver Canucks (10/4/96). Last amateur club. Belleville

Calvin Crowe — Left Wing

Regular Season / Playoffs

Season	Team	League	GP	G	A	PTS	PIM	GP	G	A	PTS	PIM
97-98	Manitoba	IHL	1	0	0	0	17	—	—	—	—	—
97-98	Dayton	ECHL	66	5	15	20	*400	1	0	0	0	7
98-99	Dayton	ECHL	14	2	3	5	70	—	—	—	—	—
98-99	Pensacola	ECHL	12	1	0	1	39	—	—	—	—	—
	ECHL	Totals	92	8	18	26	509	1	0	0	0	7

Born; 3/1/76, Tehran, Iran. 6-3, 210.

Phil Crowe — Left Wing

Regular Season / Playoffs

Season	Team	League	GP	G	A	PTS	PIM	GP	G	A	PTS	PIM
91-92	Adirondack	AHL	6	1	0	1	29	—	—	—	—	—
91-92	Columbus	ECHL	32	4	7	11	145	—	—	—	—	—
91-92	Toledo	ECHL	2	0	0	0	0	5	0	0	0	58
92-93	Phoenix	IHL	53	3	3	6	190	—	—	—	—	—
93-94	Fort Wayne	IHL	5	0	1	1	26	—	—	—	—	—
93-94	Phoenix	IHL	2	0	0	0	0	—	—	—	—	—
93-94	Los Angeles	NHL	31	0	2	2	77	—	—	—	—	—
94-95	Hershey	AHL	46	11	6	17	132	6	0	1	1	19
95-96	Philadelphia	NHL	16	1	1	2	28	—	—	—	—	—
95-96	Hershey	AHL	39	6	8	14	105	5	1	2	3	19
96-97	Ottawa	NHL	26	0	1	1	30	3	0	0	0	16
96-97	Detroit	IHL	41	7	7	14	83	—	—	—	—	—
97-98	Ottawa	NHL	9	3	0	3	24	—	—	—	—	—
97-98	Detroit	IHL	55	6	13	19	160	11	2	9	11	2
98-99	Ottawa	NHL	8	0	1	1	4	—	—	—	—	—
98-99	Detroit	IHL	2	0	0	0	9	—	—	—	—	—
98-99	Cincinnati	IHL	39	2	6	8	62	—	—	—	—	—
98-99	Las Vegas	IHL	14	1	3	4	18	—	—	—	—	—
	NHL	Totals	90	4	5	9	163	3	0	0	0	16
	IHL	Totals	211	19	33	52	548	11	2	9	11	2
	AHL	Totals	91	18	14	32	266	11	1	3	4	37
	ECHL	Totals	34	4	7	11	145	5	0	0	0	58

Born; 4/14/70, Nanton, Alberta. 6-2, 220. Signed as a free agent by Los Angeles Kings (11/8/93). Signed as a free agent by Philadelphia Flyers (7/19/94). Signed as a free agent by Ottawa Senators (7/29/96). Selected in NHL Expansion Draft by Atlanta Thrashers (6/25/99). Traded to Nashville Predators by Atlanta for future considerations (6/26/99).

Mike Crowley — Defenseman

Regular Season / Playoffs

Season	Team	League	GP	G	A	PTS	PIM	GP	G	A	PTS	PIM
97-98	Anaheim	NHL	8	2	2	4	8	—	—	—	—	—
97-98	Cincinnati	AHL	76	12	26	38	91	—	—	—	—	—
98-99	Anaheim	NHL	20	2	3	5	16	—	—	—	—	—
98-99	Cincinnati	AHL	44	5	23	28	42	3	0	3	3	2
	NHL	Totals	28	4	5	9	24	—	—	—	—	—
	AHL	Totals	120	17	49	66	133	3	0	3	3	2

Born; 7/4/75, Bloomington, Minnesota. 5-11, 175. Drafted by Philadelphia Flyers (5th choice, 140th overall) in 1993 Entry Draft. Traded to Anaheim Mighty Ducks by Philadelphia with Anatoli Semenov for Brian Wesenberg (3/19/96). Last amateur club; University of Minnesota. (WCHA).

Ted Crowley — Defenseman

Regular Season / Playoffs

Season	Team	League	GP	G	A	PTS	PIM	GP	G	A	PTS	PIM
91-92	United States	National	42	6	7	13	65	—	—	—	—	—
91-92	St. John's	AHL	29	5	4	9	33	10	3	1	4	11
92-93	St. John's	AHL	79	19	38	57	41	9	2	2	4	4
93-94	United States	National	48	9	13	22	80	—	—	—	—	—
93-94	United States	Olympic	8	0	2	2	8	—	—	—	—	—
93-94	Hartford	NHL	21	1	2	3	10	—	—	—	—	—
94-95	Chicago	IHL	53	8	23	31	68	—	—	—	—	—
94-95	Houston	IHL	23	4	9	13	35	3	0	1	1	0
95-96	Providence	AHL	72	12	30	42	47	4	1	2	3	2
96-97	Cincinnati	IHL	39	9	9	18	24	—	—	—	—	—
96-97	Phoenix	IHL	30	5	8	13	21	—	—	—	—	—
97-98	Springfield	AHL	78	14	35	49	55	4	1	1	2	2
98-99	Colorado	NHL	7	0	1	1	2	—	—	—	—	—
98-99	Islanders	NHL	6	1	1	2	0	—	—	—	—	—
98-99	Hershey	AHL	18	1	5	6	27	—	—	—	—	—
98-99	Lowell	AHL	41	3	22	25	51	3	0	0	0	6
	NHL	Totals	34	2	4	6	12	—	—	—	—	—
	AHL	Totals	317	54	134	188	254	30	7	6	13	25
	IHL	Totals	145	26	49	75	148	3	0	1	1	0

Born; 5/3/70, Boxborough, Massachusetts. 6-2, 188. Drafted by Toronto Maple Leafs (4th choice, 69th overall) in 1988 Entry Draft. Traded to Hartford Whalers by Toronto for Mark Greig and Hartford's sixth round choice (later traded to New York Rangers, Rangers selected Yuri Litvinov) in 1994 Entry Draft (1/25/94). Signed as a free agent by Boston Bruins (8/9/95). Signed as a free agent by Phoenix Coyotes (6/27/97). Signed as a free agent by Colorado Avalanche (8/14/98). Traded to New York Islanders by Colorado for Michael Gaul (12/15/98). Last amateur club; Boston College (Hockey East).

Trent Cull
Defenseman
Regular Season / Playoffs

Season	Team	League	GP	G	A	PTS	PIM	GP	G	A	PTS	PIM
94-95	Brantford	CoHL	4	0	0	0	14	—	—	—	—	—
94-95	St. John's	AHL	43	0	1	1	53	—	—	—	—	—
95-96	St. John's	AHL	46	2	1	3	118	4	0	0	0	6
96-97	St. John's	AHL	75	4	5	9	219	8	0	1	1	18
97-98	Houston	IHL	72	4	8	12	201	4	0	0	0	4
98-99	Houston	IHL	72	2	14	16	232	19	0	2	2	34
	AHL	Totals	164	6	7	13	390	12	0	1	1	24
	IHL	Totals	144	6	22	28	433	23	0	2	2	38

Born; 9/27/73, Georgetown, Ontario. 6-3, 210. Signed as a free agent by Toronto Maple Leafs (6/4/94). Member of 1998-99 IHL Champion Houston Aeros. Last amateur club; Kingston (OHL).

Brent Cullaton
Right Wing
Regular Season / Playoffs

Season	Team	League	GP	G	A	PTS	PIM	GP	G	A	PTS	PIM
96-97	Kansas City	IHL	67	19	14	33	32	3	0	1	1	0
96-97	Mobile	ECHL	4	1	4	5	16	—	—	—	—	—
97-98	Kansas City	IHL	30	5	9	14	10	—	—	—	—	—
97-98	San Antonio	IHL	23	2	8	10	24	—	—	—	—	—
97-98	Peoria	ECHL	7	8	8	16	19	3	1	2	3	2
98-99	Orlando	IHL	6	1	2	3	7	—	—	—	—	—
98-99	Tallahassee	ECHL	59	23	38	61	72	—	—	—	—	—
	IHL	Totals	126	27	33	60	73	3	0	1	1	0
	ECHL	Totals	70	32	50	82	107	3	1	2	3	2

Born; 11/12/74, Cambridge, Ontario. 6-0, 210. Traded to San Antonio by Kansas City for Dave Chyzowski (1/98). Last amateur club; Miami of Ohio (CCHA).

John Cullen
Center
Regular Season / Playoffs

Season	Team	League	GP	G	A	PTS	PIM	GP	G	A	PTS	PIM
87-88	Flint	IHL	81	48	*109	*157	113	16	11	*15	26	16
88-89	Pittsburgh	NHL	79	12	37	49	112	11	3	6	9	28
89-90	Pittsburgh	NHL	72	32	60	92	138	—	—	—	—	—
90-91	Pittsburgh	NHL	65	31	63	94	83	—	—	—	—	—
90-91	Hartford	NHL	13	8	8	16	18	6	2	7	9	10
91-92	Hartford	NHL	77	26	51	77	141	7	2	1	3	12
92-93	Hartford	NHL	19	5	4	9	58	—	—	—	—	—
92-93	Toronto	NHL	47	13	28	41	53	12	2	3	5	0
93-94	Toronto	NHL	53	13	17	30	67	3	0	0	0	0
94-95	Pittsburgh	NHL	46	13	24	37	66	9	0	2	2	8
95-96	Tampa Bay	NHL	76	16	34	50	65	5	3	3	6	0
96-97	Tampa Bay	NHL	70	18	37	55	95	—	—	—	—	—
97-98	Tampa Bay	NHL	DNP									
98-99	Tampa Bay	NHL	4	0	0	0	2	—	—	—	—	—
98-99	Cleveland	IHL	6	2	7	9	0	—	—	—	—	—
	NHL	Totals	621	187	363	550	898	53	12	22	34	58
	IHL	Totals	87	50	116	166	113	16	11	15	26	16

Born; 8/2/64, Fort Erie, Ontario. 5-10, 182. Signed as a free agent by Pittsburgh Penguins (6/21/88). Traded to Hartford Whalers by Pittsburgh with Jeff Parker and Zarley Zalapski for Ron Francis, Grant Jennings and Ulf Samuelsson (3/4/91). Traded to Toronto Maple Leafs by Hartford for future considerations (11/24/92). Signed as a free agent by Pittsburgh (8/3/94). Signed as a free agent by Tampa Bay Lightning (9/11/95). 1987-88 IHL First All-Star Team. 1987-88 IHL MVP. 1987-88 Shared IHL Rookie of the Year with Ed Belfour. 1998-99 NHL Masterton Trophy Winner (perserverance, sportsmanship and dedication). Missed entire 1997-98 season recovering from treatment and surgery for non-Hodgkins Lymphoma. Last amateur club; Boston University (Hockey East).

Matt Cullen
Center
Regular Season / Playoffs

Season	Team	League	GP	G	A	PTS	PIM	GP	G	A	PTS	PIM
96-97	St. Cloud State	WCHA	36	15	30	45	70	—	—	—	—	—
96-97	Baltimore	AHL	6	3	3	6	7	3	0	2	2	0
97-98	Anaheim	NHL	61	6	21	27	23	—	—	—	—	—
97-98	Cincinnati	AHL	18	15	12	27	2	—	—	—	—	—
98-99	Anaheim	NHL	75	11	14	25	47	4	0	0	0	0
98-99	Cincinnati	AHL	3	1	2	3	8	—	—	—	—	—
	NHL	Totals	136	17	35	52	70	4	0	0	0	0
	AHL	Totals	27	19	17	36	17	3	0	2	2	0

Born; 11/2/76, Virginia, Minnesota. 6-1, 182. Drafted by Anaheim Mighty Ducks (2nd choice, 35th overall) in 1996 Entry Draft. Last amateur club; St. Cloud (WCHA).

Thom Cullen
Defenseman
Regular Season / Playoffs

Season	Team	League	GP	G	A	PTS	PIM	GP	G	A	PTS	PIM
97-98	Tacoma	WCHL	29	6	13	19	54	11	6	5	11	22
97-98	Las Vegas	IHL	27	0	4	4	20	—	—	—	—	—
98-99	Miami	ECHL	64	4	12	16	60	—	—	—	—	—

Born; St. Lambert, Quebec. 6-1, 220. Drafted by New Jersey Devils (8th choice, 195th overall) in 1993 Entry Draft. Last amateur club; St. Lawrence University (ECAC).

Barry Cummins
Defenseman
Regular Season / Playoffs

Season	Team	League	GP	G	A	PTS	PIM	GP	G	A	PTS	PIM
97-98	Phoenix	WCHL	22	4	3	7	23	—	—	—	—	—
97-98	Fort Worth	WPHL	4	0	0	0	0	—	—	—	—	—
98-99	Fort Worth	WPHL	44	5	11	16	22	10	3	3	6	4
	WPHL	Totals	48	5	11	16	22	10	3	3	6	4

Born; 4/12/70, Saskatoon, Saskatchewan. 5-11, 195.

Randy Cunneyworth
Left Wing
Regular Season / Playoffs

Season	Team	League	GP	G	A	PTS	PIM	GP	G	A	PTS	PIM
80-81	Ottawa	OHA	67	54	74	128	240	15	5	8	13	35
80-81	Buffalo	NHL	1	0	0	0	2	—	—	—	—	—
80-81	Rochester	AHL	1	0	1	1	2	—	—	—	—	—
81-82	Buffalo	NHL	20	2	4	6	47	—	—	—	—	—
81-82	Rochester	AHL	57	12	15	27	86	9	4	0	4	30
82-83	Rochester	AHL	78	23	33	56	111	16	4	4	8	35
83-84	Rochester	AHL	54	18	17	35	85	17	5	5	10	55
84-85	Rochester	AHL	72	30	38	68	148	5	2	1	3	16
85-86	Pittsburgh	NHL	75	15	30	45	74	—	—	—	—	—
86-87	Pittsburgh	NHL	79	26	27	53	142	—	—	—	—	—
87-88	Pittsburgh	NHL	71	35	39	74	141	—	—	—	—	—
88-89	Pittsburgh	NHL	70	25	19	44	156	11	3	5	8	26
89-90	Winnipeg	NHL	28	5	6	11	34	—	—	—	—	—
89-90	Hartford	NHL	43	9	9	18	41	4	0	0	0	2
90-91	Hartford	NHL	32	9	5	14	49	1	0	0	0	0
90-91	Springfield	AHL	2	0	0	0	5	—	—	—	—	—
91-92	Hartford	NHL	39	7	10	17	71	7	3	0	3	39
92-93	Hartford	NHL	39	5	4	9	63	—	—	—	—	—
93-94	Hartford	NHL	63	9	8	17	87	—	—	—	—	—
93-94	Chicago	NHL	16	4	3	7	13	6	0	0	0	8
94-95	Ottawa	NHL	48	5	5	10	68	—	—	—	—	—
95-96	Ottawa	NHL	81	17	19	36	130	—	—	—	—	—
96-97	Ottawa	NHL	76	12	24	36	99	7	1	1	2	10
97-98	Ottawa	NHL	71	2	11	13	63	6	0	1	1	6
98-99	Buffalo	NHL	14	2	2	4	0	3	0	0	0	0
98-99	Rochester	AHL	52	10	18	28	55	20	3	*14	17	58
	NHL	Totals	866	189	225	414	1280	45	7	7	14	61
	AHL	Totals	316	93	122	215	492	67	18	24	42	194

Born; 5/10/61, Etobicoke, Ontario. 6-0, 198. Drafted by Buffalo Sabres (9th choice, 167th overall) in 1980 Entry Draft. Traded to Pittsburgh Penguins by Buffalo with Mike Moller for Pat Hughes (10/4/85). Traded to Winnipeg Jets by Pittsburgh with Rick Tabaracci and Dave McLlwain for Jim Kyte, Andrew McBain and Randy Gilhen (6/17/89) Traded to Hartford Whalers by Winnipeg for Paul MacDermid (12/13/89). Traded to Chicago Blackhawks by Hartford with Gary Suter and Hartford's third round chioce (later traded to Vancouver-Vancouver selected Larry Courville) in 1995 Entry Draft for Frantisek Kucera and Jocelyn Lemieux (3/11/94). Signed as a free agent by Ottawa Senators (7/15/94). Signed as a free agent by Buffalo (8/27/98). Member of 1982-83 AHL Champion Rochester Americans. Last amateur club; Ottawa (OHA).

David Cunniff
Center
Regular Season / Playoffs

Season	Team	League	GP	G	A	PTS	PIM	GP	G	A	PTS	PIM
96-97	Jacksonville	ECHL	16	4	5	9	75	—	—	—	—	—
96-97	Raleigh	ECHL	46	14	6	20	67	—	—	—	—	—
97-98	Albany	AHL	4	0	0	0	13	—	—	—	—	—
97-98	Raleigh	ECHL	62	12	12	24	168	—	—	—	—	—
98-99	Albany	AHL	48	2	9	11	118	5	0	1	1	4
	AHL	Totals	52	2	9	11	131	5	0	1	1	4
	ECHL	Totals	124	30	23	53	310	—	—	—	—	—

Born; 10/9/73, South Boston, Massachusetts. 5-10, 185. Signed as a free agent by New Jersey Devils (10/1/97). Last amateur club; Salem State (NCAA 3).

Bob Cunningham — Left Wing

Regular Season / Playoffs

Season	Team	League	GP	G	A	PTS	PIM	GP	G	A	PTS	PIM
95-96	Mobile	ECHL	25	5	9	14	16	—	—	—	—	—
96-97	Fort Worth	CeHL	10	4	7	11	15	—	—	—	—	—
96-97	Memphis	CeHL	56	33	38	71	79	17	4	7	11	22
97-98	Tucson	WCHL	16	8	13	21	40	—	—	—	—	—
97-98	Anchorage	WCHL	36	20	20	40	63	4	2	1	3	2
98-99	Anchorage	WCHL	59	29	28	57	74	6	1	1	2	2
	WCHL	Totals	111	57	61	118	177	10	3	2	5	4
	CeHL	Totals	66	37	45	82	94	17	4	7	11	22

Born; 8/13/75, Delson, Quebec. 6-3, 205.

Mark Cupolo — Left Wing

Regular Season / Playoffs

Season	Team	League	GP	G	A	PTS	PIM	GP	G	A	PTS	PIM
85-86	Peoria	IHL	60	9	14	23	87	3	0	0	0	2
86-87												
87-88		Italy										
87-88	Peoria	IHL	37	4	7	11	22	—	—	—	—	—
87-88	Nova Scotia	AHL	5	0	1	1	0	—	—	—	—	—
88-89	Asiago	Italy										
89-90	Asiago	Italy										
90-91	Asiago	Italy										
91-92	Asiago	Italy										
92-93												
94-94												
94-95												
95-96	Reno	WCHL	16	8	8	16	6	—	—	—	—	—
96-97	Ayr	BHL	48	9	12	21	60	7	0	0	0	0
97-98	Odessa	WPHL	3	2	2	4	10	—	—	—	—	—
97-98	Murrayfield	BNL	7	4	3	7	32	—	—	—	—	—
98-99	Thunder Bay	UHL	7	0	2	2	2	—	—	—	—	—
	IHL	Totals	97	13	21	34	109	3	0	0	0	2

Born; 11/17/65, Niagra Falls, Ontario. 6-0, 185. Drafted by St. Louis Blues (14th choice, 217th overall) in 1984 Entry Draft. Last amateur club; Peterborough

Joe Curran — Center

Regular Season / Playoffs

Season	Team	League	GP	G	A	PTS	PIM	GP	G	A	PTS	PIM
98-99	Winston-Salem	UHL	1	0	0	0	0	—	—	—	—	—

Born;

Dan Currie — Left Wing

Regular Season / Playoffs

Season	Team	League	GP	G	A	PTS	PIM	GP	G	A	PTS	PIM
87-88	Sault Ste. Marie	OHL	57	50	59	109	53	6	3	9	12	4
87-88	Nova Scotia	AHL	3	4	2	6	0	5	4	3	7	0
88-89	Cape Breton	AHL	77	29	36	65	29	—	—	—	—	—
89-90	Cape Breton	AHL	77	36	40	76	28	6	4	4	8	0
90-91	Edmonton	NHL	5	0	0	0	0	—	—	—	—	—
90-91	Cape Breton	AHL	71	47	45	92	51	4	3	1	4	8
91-92	Edmonton	NHL	7	1	0	1	0	—	—	—	—	—
91-92	Cape Breton	AHL	66	*50	42	92	39	5	4	5	9	4
92-93	Edmonton	NHL	5	0	0	0	4	—	—	—	—	—
92-93	Cape Breton	AHL	75	57	41	98	73	16	7	4	11	29
93-94	Los Angeles	NHL	5	1	1	2	0	—	—	—	—	—
93-94	Phoenix	IHL	74	37	49	86	96	—	—	—	—	—
94-95	Phoenix	IHL	16	2	6	8	8	—	—	—	—	—
94-95	Minnesota	IHL	54	18	35	53	34	3	0	0	0	2
95-96	Chicago	IHL	79	39	34	73	53	9	5	4	9	12
96-97	Chicago	IHL	55	18	10	28	18	—	—	—	—	—
96-97	Fort Wayne	IHL	24	10	12	22	6	—	—	—	—	—
97-98	Fort Wayne	IHL	77	29	22	51	17	4	0	2	2	2
98-99	Hannover	Germany	44	6	12	18	50	—	—	—	—	—
	NHL	Totals	22	2	1	3	4	—	—	—	—	—
	IHL	Totals	379	153	168	321	236	16	5	6	11	14
	AHL	Totals	369	223	206	429	220	36	22	17	39	41

Born; 3/15/68, Burlington, Ontario. 6-2, 195. Drafted by Edmonton Oilers (4th choice, 84th overall) in 1986 Entry Draft. Signed as a free agent by Los Angeles Kings (7/16/93). 1991-92 AHL Second Team All-Star. 1992-93 AHL First Team All-Star. Member of 1992-93 AHL champion Cape Breton Oilers. Last amateur club; Sault Ste. Marie (OHL).

Jason Currie — Right Wing

Regular Season / Playoffs

Season	Team	League	GP	G	A	PTS	PIM	GP	G	A	PTS	PIM
98-99	Winston-Salem	UHL	14	1	3	4	23	—	—	—	—	—

Born; 6/14/74, Fort Quapell, Saskatchewan. 6-4, 240.

Luke Curtin — Left Wing

Regular Season / Playoffs

Season	Team	League	GP	G	A	PTS	PIM	GP	G	A	PTS	PIM
97-98	Kelowna	WHL	51	29	48	77	42	7	4	7	11	4
97-98	Hershey	AHL	2	0	0	0	2	—	—	—	—	—
98-99	Portland	AHL	4	0	1	1	4	—	—	—	—	—
98-99	Grand Rapids	IHL	4	0	0	0	2	—	—	—	—	—
98-99	Baton Rouge	ECHL	56	28	29	57	32	6	3	4	7	4
	AHL	Totals	6	0	1	1	6	—	—	—	—	—

Born; 9/23/77, St. Paul, Minnesota. 6-2, 190. Drafted by Colorado Avalanche (6th choice, 134th overall) in 1996 Entry Draft. Last amateur club; Kelowna

Marcin Cwikla — Left Wing

Regular Season / Playoffs

Season	Team	League	GP	G	A	PTS	PIM	GP	G	A	PTS	PIM
98-99	Chesapeake	ECHL	5	0	0	0	7	—	—	—	—	—

Born;

Cory Cyrenne — Left Wing

Regular Season / Playoffs

Season	Team	League	GP	G	A	PTS	PIM	GP	G	A	PTS	PIM
98-99	Manitoba	IHL	46	4	14	18	18	5	1	0	1	2
98-99	Louisiana	ECHL	21	6	9	15	6	—	—	—	—	—

Born; 8/25/77, Winnipeg, Manitoba. 5-9, 170. Drafted by San Jose Sharks (7th choice, 191st overall) in 1996 Entry Draft. Last amateur club; Brandon (WHL).

Jeff Christian - IHL Comeback Player of the Year Photo by Joe Costa

Jamie Dabonovich — Defenseman
Regular Season / Playoffs

Season	Team	League	GP	G	A	PTS	PIM	GP	G	A	PTS	PIM
91-92	Flint	CoHL	3	1	0	1	14	—	—	—	—	—
91-92	Knoxville	ECHL	36	4	9	13	23	—	—	—	—	—
92-93	Knoxville	ECHL	12	1	1	2	37	—	—	—	—	—
92-93	West Palm Beach	SUN	44	9	40	49	43	—	—	—	—	—
92-93	Chatham	CoHL	35	7	15	22	9	15	1	3	4	4
94-95	Detroit	CoHL	43	7	11	18	18	5	0	0	0	2
96-97	Port Huron	CoHL	60	9	18	27	60	5	0	2	2	0
97-98	Saginaw	UHL	52	5	24	29	42	—	—	—	—	—
97-98	Madison	UHL	15	1	11	12	17	7	2	1	3	6
98-99	Madison	UHL	74	10	37	47	48	—	—	—	—	—
	UHL	Totals	282	40	116	156	208	32	3	6	9	12
	ECHL	Totals	48	5	10	15	60	—	—	—	—	—

Born; 8/8/68, Sarnia, Ontario. 6-0, 210.

Jeff DaCosta — Defenseman
Regular Season / Playoffs

Season	Team	League	GP	G	A	PTS	PIM	GP	G	A	PTS	PIM
96-97	New Mexico	WPHL	55	7	39	46	63	—	—	—	—	—
96-97	El Paso	WPHL	2	1	0	1	2	10	1	5	6	10
97-98	Chesapeake	ECHL	34	7	15	22	26	—	—	—	—	—
97-98	Tallahassee	ECHL	4	0	1	1	4	—	—	—	—	—
97-98	Columbus	ECHL	27	6	15	21	40	—	—	—	—	—
98-99	Nottingham	BSL	46	3	17	20	24	8	1	1	2	4
	ECHL	Totals	65	13	31	44	70	—	—	—	—	—
	WPHL	Totals	57	8	39	47	65	10	1	5	6	10

Born; 5/16/76, Toronto, Ontario. 5-10, 201. Sold to Columbus by Tallahassee (10/97). Member of 1996-97 WPHL Champion El Paso Buzzards. Last amateur club; Kingston (OHL).

Pierre Dagenais — Left Wing
Regular Season / Playoffs

Season	Team	League	GP	G	A	PTS	PIM	GP	G	A	PTS	PIM
98-99	Albany	AHL	69	17	13	30	37	4	0	0	0	0

Born; 3/4/78, Blainville, Quebec. 6-4, 200. Drafted by New Jersey Devils (4th choice, 47th overall) in 1996 Entry Draft. Re-entered NHL Draft; drafted by New Jersey Devils (6th choice, 105th overall) in 1998 Entry Draft. Last amateur club; Rouyn-Noranda (QMJHL).

Kevin Dahl — Defenseman
Regular Season / Playoffs

Season	Team	League	GP	G	A	PTS	PIM	GP	G	A	PTS	PIM
90-91	Fredericton	AHL	32	1	15	16	45	9	0	1	1	11
90-91	Winston-Salem	ECHL	36	7	17	24	58	—	—	—	—	—
91-92	Salt Lake City	IHL	13	0	2	2	12	5	0	0	0	13
92-93	Calgary	NHL	61	2	9	11	56	6	0	2	2	8
93-94	Calgary	NHL	33	0	3	3	23	6	0	0	0	4
93-94	Saint John	AHL	2	0	0	0	0	—	—	—	—	—
94-95	Calgary	NHL	34	4	8	12	38	3	0	0	0	0
95-96	Calgary	NHL	32	1	1	2	26	1	0	0	0	0
95-96	Saint John	AHL	23	4	11	15	37	—	—	—	—	—
96-97	Phoenix	NHL	2	0	0	0	0	—	—	—	—	—
96-97	Las Vegas	IHL	73	10	21	31	101	3	0	0	0	2
97-98	Calgary	NHL	19	0	1	1	6	—	—	—	—	—
97-98	Chicago	IHL	45	8	9	17	61	20	1	8	9	32
98-99	Toronto	NHL	3	0	0	0	2	—	—	—	—	—
98-99	Chicago	IHL	34	3	6	9	61	10	2	3	5	8
	NHL	Totals	184	7	22	29	151	16	0	2	2	12
	IHL	Totals	165	21	38	59	235	38	3	11	14	55
	AHL	Totals	57	5	26	31	82	9	0	1	1	11

Born; 12/30/68, Regina, Saskatchewan. 5-11, 190. Drafted by Montreal Canadiens (12th choice, 230th overall) in 1987 Entry Draft. Signed as a free agent by Calgary Flames (7/27/91). Signed as a free agent by Phoenix Coyotes (9/4/96). Signed as a free agent by Calgary Flames (9/8/97). Signed as a free agent by St. Louis Blues (9/4/98). Selected by Toronto Maple Leafs from St. Louis in 1998 Waiver Draft (10/5/98). Member of 1997-98 IHL Champion Chicago Wolves. Last amateur club; Bowling Green (CCHA).

Phil Daigle — Center
Regular Season / Playoffs

Season	Team	League	GP	G	A	PTS	PIM	GP	G	A	PTS	PIM
95-96	Huntington	ECHL	2	0	0	0	0	—	—	—	—	—
95-96	Utica	CoHL	8	2	1	3	10	—	—	—	—	—
95-96	Jacksonville	SUN	9	3	4	7	57	—	—	—	—	—
95-96	Huntsville	SHL	8	4	3	7	36	10	1	5	6	45
96-97	Huntsville	CeHL	55	18	23	41	217	9	6	4	10	16
97-98	Huntsville	CHL	61	17	19	36	333	—	—	—	—	—
97-98	Wichita	CHL	6	1	5	6	2	14	1	1	2	64
98-99	Huntsville	CHL	70	19	23	42	264	15	2	4	6	31
	CHL	Totals	192	55	70	125	816	38	9	9	18	111
	SHL	Totals	17	7	7	14	93	10	1	5	6	45

Born; 12/21/69, Fredericton, Manitoba. 5-7, 180. Traded to Wichita by Huntsville for Eddy Marchant and Hugo Hamelin (3/98). Member of 1995-96 SHL champion Huntsville Channel Cats. Member of 1998-99 CHL Champion Huntsville Channel Cats.

Sylvain Daigle — Goaltender
Regular Season / Playoffs

Season	Team	League	GP	W	L	T	MIN	SO	AVG	GP	W	L	MIN	SO	AVG
96-97	Springfield	AHL	13	8	3	0	691	1	2.00	6	1	4	312	0	3.47
96-97	Las Vegas	IHL	1	0	0	0	42	0	7.17	—	—	—	—	—	—
96-97	Mississippi	ECHL	34	20	8	5	1951	2	3.08	—	—	—	—	—	—
97-98	Springfield	AHL	21	7	9	2	1094	0	3.73	2	0	0	23	0	0.00
98-99	Springfield	AHL	27	8	12	2	1393	1	2.89	—	—	—	—	—	—
	AHL	Totals	61	23	24	4	3178	2	2.98	8	1	4	325	0	3.32

Born; 10/20/76, St. Hyacinthe, Quebec. 5-8, 185. Drafted by Winnipeg Jets (7th choice, 136th overall) in 1995 Entry Draft. Last amateur club; Shawinigan (QMJHL).

Jason Dailey — Defenseman
Regular Season / Playoffs

Season	Team	League	GP	G	A	PTS	PIM	GP	G	A	PTS	PIM
98-99	Roanoke	ECHL	63	5	15	20	41	—	—	—	—	—

Born; 2/15/76, Pittsford, New York. 5-10, 193. Last amateur club; Cornell

Mike Dairon — Left Wing
Regular Season / Playoffs

Season	Team	League	GP	G	A	PTS	PIM	GP	G	A	PTS	PIM
98-99	Central	WPHL	69	29	36	65	66	2	0	0	0	2

Born; 8/25/75, Vancouver, British Columbia. 6-1, 185. Last amateur club; Denver (WCHA).

Andrew Dale — Center
Regular Season / Playoffs

Season	Team	League	GP	G	A	PTS	PIM	GP	G	A	PTS	PIM
96-97	Phoenix	IHL	32	7	6	13	19	—	—	—	—	—
96-97	Mississippi	ECHL	19	6	9	15	16	2	0	1	1	0
97-98	Springfield	AHL	40	3	6	9	32	—	—	—	—	—
97-98	Mississippi	ECHL	3	1	2	3	2	—	—	—	—	—
98-99	London	BSL	28	4	11	15	20	—	—	—	—	—
98-99	Mississippi	ECHL	21	6	2	8	15	12	5	3	8	10
	ECHL	Totals	43	13	13	26	33	14	5	4	9	10

Born; 2/16/76, Sudbury, Ontario. 6-1, 196. Drafted by Los Angeles Kings (6th choice, 189th overall) in 1994 Entry Draft. Member of 1998-99 ECHL Champion Mississippi SeaWolves. Last amateur club; Kitchener (OHL).

Gerry Daley — Right Wing
Regular Season / Playoffs

Season	Team	League	GP	G	A	PTS	PIM	GP	G	A	PTS	PIM
93-94	Roanoke	ECHL	13	6	3	9	10	—	—	—	—	—
93-94	Louisville	ECHL	14	2	6	8	34	—	—	—	—	—
93-94	Nashville	ECHL	30	12	13	25	20	2	0	0	0	0
94-95												
95-96	Johnstown	ECHL	4	1	0	1	2	—	—	—	—	—
95-96	Charlotte	ECHL	19	4	6	10	0	—	—	—	—	—
96-97	Charlotte	ECHL	4	1	2	3	0	—	—	—	—	—
97-98												
98-99	Charlotte	ECHL	3	0	0	0	2	—	—	—	—	—
	ECHL	Totals	87	26	30	56	68	2	0	0	0	0

Born; 9/16/69, Gloucester, Massachusetts. 5-10, 190. Last amateur club; Lowell (H.E.)

Darcy Dallas — Defenseman
Regular Season / Playoffs

Season	Team	League	GP	G	A	PTS	PIM	GP	G	A	PTS	PIM
97-98	Orlando	IHL	2	0	0	0	0	—	—	—	—	—
97-98	Pee Dee	ECHL	69	7	8	15	126	8	0	1	1	24
98-99	Pee Dee	ECHL	70	15	24	39	123	13	0	3	3	42
	ECHL	Totals	139	22	32	54	249	21	0	4	4	66

Born; 2/10/72, Calgary, Alberta. 6-0, 190. Last amateur club; Northern Michigan (CCHA).

Marty Dallman — Center
Regular Season / Playoffs

Season	Team	League	GP	G	A	PTS	PIM	GP	G	A	PTS	PIM
84-85	New Haven	AHL	78	18	39	57	26	—	—	—	—	—
85-86	New Haven	AHL	69	23	33	56	92	5	0	4	4	4
86-87	Baltimore	AHL	6	0	1	1	0	—	—	—	—	—
86-87	Newmarket	AHL	42	24	24	48	44	—	—	—	—	—
87-88	Newmarket	AHL	76	50	39	89	52	—	—	—	—	—
87-88	Toronto	NHL	2	0	1	1	0	—	—	—	—	—
88-89	Toronto	NHL	4	0	0	0	0	—	—	—	—	—
88-89	Newmarket	AHL	37	26	20	46	24	—	—	—	—	—
89-90	Vienna	Austria	35	42	31	73	NA	—	—	—	—	—
90-91	Vienna	Austria	41	39	28	67	NA	—	—	—	—	—
91-92	Vienna	Austria	40	35	41	76	NA	—	—	—	—	—
92-93	Zell Am See	Austria	46	37	41	78	NA	—	—	—	—	—
93-94	Graz	Austria	48	52	37	89	NA	—	—	—	—	—
94-95	Fribourg	Germany	4	2	2	4	0	—	—	—	—	—
94-95	South Carolina	ECHL	22	11	16	27	22	6	5	9	14	4
95-96	Vienna	Austria	33	22	29	51	67	—	—	—	—	—
96-97	Nottingham	BHL	40	24	32	56	28	—	—	—	—	—
97-98	Nottingham	BSL	45	22	28	50	22	6	3	2	5	0
98-99	Abilene	WPHL	59	30	37	67	48	3	2	2	4	0
	NHL	Totals	6	0	1	1	0	—	—	—	—	—
	AHL	Totals	308	141	156	297	238	5	0	4	4	4

Born; 2/15/63, Niagara Falls, Ontario. 5-10, 188. Drafted by Los Angeles Kings (3rd choice, 81st overall) in 1981 Entry Draft. 1987-88 AHL Second Team All-Star. Last amateur club; R.P.I. (ECAC). Named coach of the Abilene Aviators (WPHL) to begin with the 1999-2000 season.

Duncan Dalmao — Defenseman
Regular Season / Playoffs

Season	Team	League	GP	G	A	PTS	PIM	GP	G	A	PTS	PIM
98-99	Jacksonville	ECHL	68	1	7	8	78	2	0	0	0	0

Born; Last amateur club; Peterborough (OHL).

Chad Dameworth — Defenseman
Regular Season / Playoffs

Season	Team	League	GP	G	A	PTS	PIM	GP	G	A	PTS	PIM
94-95	Northern Michigan	WCHA	39	0	4	4	46	—	—	—	—	—
94-95	Cape Breton	AHL	1	0	0	0	0	—	—	—	—	—
95-96	Cape Breton	AHL	24	2	2	4	31	—	—	—	—	—
95-96	Wheeling	ECHL	35	2	9	11	10	—	—	—	—	—
96-97	Worcester	AHL	36	1	6	7	101	4	0	0	0	4
96-97	Wheeling	ECHL	20	1	3	4	25	—	—	—	—	—
96-97	Johnstown	ECHL	4	2	0	2	4	—	—	—	—	—
97-98	Orlando	IHL	29	0	4	4	36	—	—	—	—	—
97-98	Springfield	AHL	3	0	2	2	0	—	—	—	—	—
97-98	Mississippi	ECHL	35	1	5	6	44	—	—	—	—	—
98-99	Fort Wayne	IHL	36	0	6	6	33	2	0	0	0	0
98-99	Detroit	IHL	2	0	0	0	0	—	—	—	—	—
98-99	Port Huron	UHL	32	6	7	13	31	1	0	0	0	0
	IHL	Totals	67	0	10	10	69	2	0	0	0	0
	AHL	Totals	64	3	10	13	132	4	0	0	0	4
	ECHL	Totals	94	6	17	23	83	—	—	—	—	—

Born; 7/6/72, Marquette, Michigan. 6-2, 215. Drafted by Edmonton Oilers (1st choice, 6th overall) in 1994 Supplemental Draft. Last amateur club; Northern Michigan (CCHA).

Jean-Francois Damphousse — Goaltender
Regular Season / Playoffs

Season	Team	League	GP	W	L	T	MIN	SO	AVG	GP	W	L	MIN	SO	AVG
98-99	Moncton	QMJHL	40	19	17	2	2163	1	3.36	4	0	4	200	0	3.60
98-99	Albany	AHL	1	0	1	0	59	0	3.06	—	—	—	—	—	—

Born; 7/21/79, St. Alexis-des-Monts, Quebec. 6-0, 175. Drafted by New Jersey Devils (1st choice, 24th overall) in 1997 Entry Draft. Last amateur club;

Eric Dandenault — Defenseman
Regular Season / Playoffs

Season	Team	League	GP	G	A	PTS	PIM	GP	G	A	PTS	PIM
91-92	Hershey	AHL	69	6	13	19	149	3	0	0	0	4
92-93	Hershey	AHL	72	20	19	39	118	—	—	—	—	—
93-94	Johnstown	ECHL	2	1	1	2	6	—	—	—	—	—
93-94	Hershey	AHL	14	2	1	3	49	—	—	—	—	—
95-96	Cincinnati	IHL	16	1	2	3	45	17	1	6	7	30
95-96	Saginaw	CoHL	61	5	30	35	160	—	—	—	—	—
96-97	Cincinnati	IHL	77	5	14	19	240	3	0	0	0	7
97-98	Cincinnati	IHL	81	2	11	13	230	9	0	2	2	18
98-99	Cincinnati	IHL	63	4	13	17	180	3	0	0	0	2
	IHL	Totals	237	12	40	52	695	32	1	8	9	57
	AHL	Totals	155	28	33	61	316	3	0	0	0	4

Born; 3/10/70, Sherbrooke, Quebec. 6-0, 193. Signed as a free agent by Philadelphia Flyers (10/4/91). Last amateur club; Drummondville (QMJHL).

Jeff Daniels — Left Wing

Season	Team	League	GP	G	A	PTS	PIM	GP	G	A	PTS	PIM
			Regular Season					Playoffs				
88-89	Muskegon	IHL	58	21	21	42	58	11	3	5	8	11
89-90	Muskegon	IHL	80	30	47	77	39	6	1	1	2	7
90-91	Pittsburgh	NHL	11	0	2	2	2	—	—	—	—	—
90-91	Muskegon	IHL	62	23	29	52	18	5	1	3	4	2
91-92	Pittsburgh	NHL	2	0	0	0	0	—	—	—	—	—
91-92	Muskegon	IHL	44	19	16	35	38	10	5	4	9	9
92-93	Pittsburgh	NHL	58	5	4	9	14	12	3	2	5	0
92-93	Cleveland	IHL	3	2	1	3	0	—	—	—	—	—
93-94	Pittsburgh	NHL	63	3	5	8	20	—	—	—	—	—
93-94	Florida	NHL	7	0	0	0	0	—	—	—	—	—
94-95	Florida	NHL	3	0	0	0	0	—	—	—	—	—
94-95	Detroit	IHL	25	8	12	20	6	5	1	0	1	0
95-96	Springfield	AHL	72	22	20	42	32	10	3	0	3	2
96-97	Hartford	NHL	10	0	2	2	0	—	—	—	—	—
96-97	Springfield	AHL	38	18	14	32	19	16	7	3	10	4
97-98	Carolina	NHL	2	0	0	0	0	—	—	—	—	—
97-98	New Haven	AHL	71	24	27	51	34	3	0	1	1	0
98-99	Nashville	NHL	9	1	3	4	2	—	—	—	—	—
98-99	Milwaukee	IHL	62	12	31	43	19	2	1	1	2	0
	NHL	Totals	165	9	16	25	38	12	3	2	5	0
	IHL	Totals	405	139	184	323	212	39	12	14	26	29
	AHL	Totals	110	40	34	74	51	29	10	4	14	6

Born; 6/24/68, Oshawa, Ontario. 6-1, 200. Drafted by Pittsburgh Penguins (6th choice, 109th overall) in 1986 Entry Draft. Traded to Florida Panthers by Pittsburgh for Greg Hawgood (3/19/94). Signed as a free agent by Hartford Whalers (7/18/95). Selected by Nashville Predators in 1998 NHL Expansion Draft. Last amateur club; Oshawa (OHL).

Kimbi Daniels — Center

Season	Team	League	GP	G	A	PTS	PIM	GP	G	A	PTS	PIM
			Regular Season					Playoffs				
90-91	Swift Current	WHL	69	54	64	118	68	3	4	2	6	6
90-91	Philadelphia	NHL	2	0	1	1	0	—	—	—	—	—
91-92	Seattle	WHL	19	7	14	21	133	15	5	10	15	27
91-92	Philadelphia	NHL	25	1	1	2	4	—	—	—	—	—
92-93	Tri-City	WHL	9	9	12	21	12	3	0	1	1	8
93-94	Salt Lake City	IHL	25	6	9	15	8	—	—	—	—	—
93-94	Detroit	CoHL	23	11	28	39	42	—	—	—	—	—
94-95	Minnesota	IHL	10	1	4	5	2	—	—	—	—	—
95-96	Baltimore	AHL	7	2	1	3	2	—	—	—	—	—
95-96	Jacksonville	ECHL	26	12	22	34	129	—	—	—	—	—
95-96	Charlotte	ECHL	18	16	14	30	6	16	8	6	14	24
96-97	Rochester	AHL	6	1	3	4	2	—	—	—	—	—
96-97	Hamilton	AHL	3	0	0	0	0	16	5	8	13	4
96-97	Charlotte	ECHL	32	12	24	36	116	—	—	—	—	—
96-97	Wheeling	ECHL	17	5	24	29	10	3	1	4	5	6
97-98	Providence	AHL	32	2	5	7	30	—	—	—	—	—
97-98	San Antonio	IHL	13	2	12	14	20	—	—	—	—	—
97-98	Quebec	IHL	28	7	9	16	69	—	—	—	—	—
98-99	Laibach	Austria										
98-99	New Orleans	ECHL	29	11	28	39	61	—	—	—	—	—
	NHL	Totals	27	1	2	3	4	—	—	—	—	—
	IHL	Totals	76	16	34	50	99	—	—	—	—	—
	AHL	Totals	48	5	9	14	34	16	5	8	13	4
	ECHL	Totals	122	56	112	168	322	19	9	10	19	30

Born; 1/19/72, Brandon, Manitoba. 5-10, 175. Drafted by Philadelphia Flyers (5th choice, 44th overall) in 1990 Entry Draft. Member of 1995-96 ECHL champion Charlotte Checkers. Last amateur club; Seattle (WHL).

Scott Daniels — Left Wing

Season	Team	League	GP	G	A	PTS	PIM	GP	G	A	PTS	PIM
			Regular Season					Playoffs				
90-91	Springfield	AHL	40	2	6	8	121	—	—	—	—	—
90-91	Louisville	ECHL	9	5	3	8	34	1	0	2	2	0
91-92	Springfield	AHL	54	7	15	22	213	10	0	0	0	32
92-93	Hartford	NHL	1	0	0	0	19	—	—	—	—	—
92-93	Springfield	AHL	60	11	12	23	181	12	2	7	9	12
93-94	Springfield	AHL	52	9	11	20	185	6	0	1	1	53
94-95	Hartford	NHL	12	0	2	2	55	—	—	—	—	—
94-95	Springfield	AHL	48	9	5	14	277	—	—	—	—	—
95-96	Hartford	NHL	53	3	4	7	254	—	—	—	—	—
95-96	Springfield	AHL	6	4	1	5	17	—	—	—	—	—
96-97	Philadelphia	NHL	56	5	3	8	237	—	—	—	—	—
97-98	New Jersey	NHL	26	0	3	3	102	1	0	0	0	0
98-99	New Jersey	NHL	1	0	0	0	0	—	—	—	—	—
98-99	Albany	AHL	13	1	5	6	97	—	—	—	—	—
	NHL	Totals	149	8	12	20	667	1	0	0	0	0
	AHL	Totals	273	43	55	98	1091	28	2	8	10	97

Born; 9/19/69, Prince Albert, Saskatchewan. 6-3, 215. Drafted by Hartford Whalers (6th choice, 136th overall) in 1989 Entry Draft. Signed as a free agent by Philadelphia Flyers (6/27/96). Claimed by New Jersey Devils from Philadelphia in NHL Waiver Draft (9/28/97). Last amateur club; Regina (WHL).

Cam Danyluk — Forward

Season	Team	League	GP	G	A	PTS	PIM	GP	G	A	PTS	PIM
			Regular Season					Playoffs				
93-94	Hamilton	AHL	60	11	12	23	159	2	1	0	1	0
94-95	South Carolina	ECHL	50	26	27	53	188	9	5	4	9	76
94-95	Syracuse	AHL	12	1	3	4	19	—	—	—	—	—
95-96												
96-97	Alberta	CWUAA	37	13	16	29	113	—	—	—	—	—
97-98	Alberta	CWUAA	43	25	29	54	86	—	—	—	—	—
98-99	Alberta	CWUAA										
98-99	South Carolina	ECHL	3	0	2	2	8	3	0	0	0	4
	AHL	Totals	72	12	15	27	178	2	1	0	1	0
	ECHL	Totals	53	26	29	55	196	12	5	4	9	80

Born; 9/6/72, Andrew, Alberta. 6-4, 215. Last amateur club; University of Alberta (CWUAA).

Craig Darby — Center

Season	Team	League	GP	G	A	PTS	PIM	GP	G	A	PTS	PIM
			Regular Season					Playoffs				
93-94	Fredericton	AHL	66	23	33	56	51	—	—	—	—	—
94-95	Montreal	NHL	10	0	2	2	0	—	—	—	—	—
94-95	Islanders	NHL	3	0	0	0	0	—	—	—	—	—
94-95	Fredericton	AHL	64	21	47	68	82	—	—	—	—	—
95-96	Islanders	NHL	10	0	2	2	0	—	—	—	—	—
95-96	Worcester	AHL	68	22	28	50	47	4	1	1	2	2
96-97	Philadelphia	NHL	9	1	4	5	2	—	—	—	—	—
96-97	Philadelphia	AHL	59	26	33	59	24	10	3	6	9	0
97-98	Philadelphia	NHL	3	1	0	1	0	—	—	—	—	—
97-98	Philadelphia	AHL	77	42	45	87	34	20	5	9	14	4
98-99	Milwaukee	IHL	81	32	22	54	33	2	3	0	3	0
	NHL	Totals	35	2	8	10	2	—	—	—	—	—
	AHL	Totals	334	134	186	320	238	34	9	16	25	6

Born; 9/25/67, Oneida, New York. 6-1, 195. Drafted by Montreal Canadiens (3rd choice, 43rd overall) in 1991 Entry Draft. Traded to New York Islanders by Montreal with Kirk Muller and Mathieu Schneider for Pierre Turgeon and Vladimir Malakhov (4/5/95). Claimed on waivers by Philadelphia Flyers from Islanders (6/4/96). Selected by Nashville Predators in 1998 NHL Expansion Draft. 1997-98 AHL First All-Star Team. Member of 1997-98 AHL Champion Philadelphia Phantoms. Last amateur club; Providence (Hockey East).

Michael Dark — Defenseman

Regular Season / Playoffs

Season	Team	League	GP	G	A	PTS	PIM	GP	G	A	PTS	PIM
86-87	St. Louis	NHL	13	2	0	2	2	—	—	—	—	—
86-87	Peoria	IHL	42	4	11	15	93	—	—	—	—	—
87-88	St. Louis	NHL	30	3	6	9	12	—	—	—	—	—
87-88	Peoria	IHL	37	21	12	33	97	2	0	0	0	4
88-89	Salt Lake City	IHL	36	3	12	15	57	—	—	—	—	—
88-89	New Haven	AHL	7	0	4	4	4	—	—	—	—	—
89-90												
90-91												
91-92	Flint	CoHL	1	0	0	0	15	—	—	—	—	—
91-92	St. Thomas	CoHL	2	0	0	0	0	—	—	—	—	—
92-93												
93-94												
94-95												
95-96	Brantford	CoHL	11	3	12	15	33	3	1	0	1	2
96-97	Port Huron	CoHL	17	0	2	2	10	5	1	3	4	0
97-98	Port Huron	UHL	12	1	6	7	6	4	0	0	0	4
98-99	Port Huron	UHL	2	0	0	0	0	—	—	—	—	—
	NHL	Totals	43	5	6	11	14	—	—	—	—	—
	IHL	Totals	115	28	35	63	247	2	0	0	0	4
	UHL	Totals	45	4	20	24	64	12	2	3	5	6

Born; 9/17/63, Sarnia, Ontario. 6-3, 210. Drafted by Montreal Canadiens (10th choice, 124th overall) in 1982 Entry Draft. NHL Rights traded to St. Louis Blues with Mark Hunter and future considerations for St. Louis' first round choice (Jose Charbonneau) and a switch of other choices (6/85). Last amateur club; RPI

Dion Darling — Defenseman

Regular Season / Playoffs

Season	Team	League	GP	G	A	PTS	PIM	GP	G	A	PTS	PIM
93-94	Spokane	WHL	45	1	8	9	190	—	—	—	—	—
93-94	Moose Jaw	WHL	23	4	6	10	96	—	—	—	—	—
93-94	Wheeling	ECHL	3	0	1	1	7	9	0	1	1	14
94-95	Fredericton	AHL	51	0	2	2	153	—	—	—	—	—
94-95	Wheeling	ECHL	4	0	0	0	24	—	—	—	—	—
95-96	Fredericton	AHL	74	3	2	5	215	6	0	0	0	5
96-97	Fredericton	AHL	58	2	6	8	150	—	—	—	—	—
97-98	Fredericton	AHL	64	1	7	8	188	2	0	0	0	10
98-99	Fort Wayne	IHL	71	4	18	22	267	2	0	0	0	4
	AHL	Totals	247	6	17	23	706	8	0	0	0	15
	ECHL	Totals	7	0	1	1	31	9	0	1	1	14

Born; 10/22/74, Edmonton, Alberta. 6-3, 210. Drafted by Montreal Canadiens (7th choice, 125th overall) in 1993 Entry Draft. Last amateur club; Moose Jaw

David Dartsch — Forward

Regular Season / Playoffs

Season	Team	League	GP	G	A	PTS	PIM	GP	G	A	PTS	PIM
96-97	Richmond	ECHL	65	4	20	24	214	8	1	1	2	51
97-98	Cleveland	IHL	2	0	0	0	6	—	—	—	—	—
97-98	Richmond	ECHL	54	17	23	40	246	—	—	—	—	—
97-98	Tallahassee	ECHL	12	3	3	6	35	—	—	—	—	—
98-99	Tallahassee	ECHL	61	12	21	33	169	—	—	—	—	—
	ECHL	Totals	192	36	67	103	664	8	1	1	2	51

Born; 2/17/74, Pointe-Claire, Quebec. 5-10, 187. Traded to Tallahassee by Richmond for rights to Shawn Reid (3/98). Last amateur club; Lowell (Hockey East).

Chris Dashney — Defenseman

Regular Season / Playoffs

Season	Team	League	GP	G	A	PTS	PIM	GP	G	A	PTS	PIM
96-97	Tulsa	CeHL	66	1	15	16	56	5	0	0	0	14
97-98	Tulsa	CHL	35	6	20	26	30	—	—	—	—	—
97-98	Wichita	CHL	34	1	15	16	45	15	1	13	14	17
98-99	Wichita	CHL	61	5	28	33	94	4	1	2	3	0
	CHL	Totals	196	13	78	91	225	24	2	15	17	31

Born; 10/16/72, Ottawa, Ontario. 6-1, 195. Last amateur club; St. Lawrence University (ECAC).

Kirk Daubenspeck — Goaltender

Regular Season / Playoffs

Season	Team	League	GP	W	L	T	MIN	SO	AVG	GP	W	L	MIN	SO	AVG
97-98	Indianapolis	IHL	18	6	9	0	953	0	3.65	—	—	—	—	—	—
97-98	Jacksonville	ECHL	32	20	9	2	1866	1	2.96	—	—	—	—	—	—
98-99	Indianapolis	IHL	12	2	8	1	650	0	3.97	—	—	—	—	—	—
98-99	Jacksonville	ECHL	8	5	3	0	424	0	2.55	—	—	—	—	—	—
98-99	Chesapeake	ECHL	13	7	2	4	774	2	2.40	7	3	4	424	1	1.70
	IHL	Totals	30	8	17	1	1603	0	3.78	—	—	—	—	—	—
	ECHL	Totals	53	32	14	6	3064	3	2.77	7	3	4	424	1	1.70

Born; 7/16/74, Madison, Wisconsin. 6-0, 190. Drafted by Philadelphia Flyers (7th chioce, 151st overall) in 1992 Entry Draft. Traded to Ottawa Senators by Philadelphia with Claude Boivin for Mark Lamb (3/5/94). Last amateur club; University of Wisconsin (WCHA).

Bill Davidson — Defenseman

Regular Season / Playoffs

Season	Team	League	GP	G	A	PTS	PIM	GP	G	A	PTS	PIM
90-91	Louisville	ECHL	5	0	2	2	19	—	—	—	—	—
90-91	Knoxville	ECHL	14	1	5	6	45	—	—	—	—	—
91-92												
92-93												
93-94	West Palm Beach	SUN	44	3	12	15	62	5	0	4	4	6
94-95	Fresno	SUN	2	0	0	0	0	—	—	—	—	—
94-95	Memphis	CeHL	11	1	1	2	17	—	—	—	—	—
95-96												
96-97	New Mexico	WPHL	28	1	3	4	120	—	—	—	—	—
97-98												
98-99	Corpus Christi	WPHL	1	0	0	0	0	—	—	—	—	—
	SUN	Totals	46	3	12	15	62	5	0	4	4	6
	WPHL	Totals	29	1	3	4	120	—	—	—	—	—
	ECHL	Totals	19	1	7	8	64	—	—	—	—	—

Born; 4/16/67, Edmonton, Alberta. 6-0, 195. Member of 1993-94 Sunshine League Champion West Palm Beach Blaze.

Lee Davidson — Center

Regular Season / Playoffs

Season	Team	League	GP	G	A	PTS	PIM	GP	G	A	PTS	PIM
90-91	Moncton	AHL	69	15	17	32	24	—	—	—	—	—
91-92	Moncton	AHL	43	3	12	15	32	—	—	—	—	—
91-92	Fort Wayne	IHL	22	4	10	14	30	7	2	5	7	8
92-93	Fort Wayne	IHL	60	22	20	42	58	12	2	0	2	21
93-94	Fort Wayne	IHL	74	25	42	67	32	17	4	12	16	10
94-95	Chicago	IHL	76	28	37	65	36	3	2	0	2	2
95-96	Chicago	IHL	18	6	14	20	18	—	—	—	—	—
95-96	Atlanta	IHL	55	25	36	61	34	3	3	1	4	0
96-97	Fort Wayne	IHL	73	24	51	75	60	—	—	—	—	—
97-98	Fort Wayne	IHL	76	14	48	62	54	4	1	1	2	8
98-99	Hannover	Germany	51	10	18	28	40	—	—	—	—	—
	IHL	Totals	454	148	258	406	322	46	14	19	33	49
	AHL	Totals	112	18	29	47	56	—	—	—	—	—

Born; 6/30/68, Winnipeg, Manitoba. 5-11, 180. Drafted by Washington Capitals (9th choice, 166th overall) in 1986 Entry Draft. Signed as a free agent by Winnipeg Jets (9/4/90). Member of 1992-93 IHL champion Fort Wayne Komets. Last amateur club; University of North Dakota (WCHA).

Matt Davidson — Right Wing

Regular Season / Playoffs

Season	Team	League	GP	G	A	PTS	PIM	GP	G	A	PTS	PIM
97-98	Rochester	AHL	72	15	12	27	12	3	1	0	1	2
98-99	Rochester	AHL	80	26	15	41	42	18	2	1	3	6
	AHL	Totals	152	41	27	68	54	21	3	1	4	8

Born; 8/9/77, Flin Flon, Manitoba. 6-2, 190. Drafted by Buffalo Sabres (5th choice, 94th overall) in 1995 Entry Draft. Last amateur club; Portland (WHL).

Robert Davidson — Defenseman

Regular Season / Playoffs

Season	Team	League	GP	G	A	PTS	PIM	GP	G	A	PTS	PIM
98-99	Alexandria	WPHL	47	1	5	6	49	—	—	—	—	—

Born; 11/9/77, Brantford, Ontario. 6-4, 220.

Johan Davidsson — Center
Regular Season — Playoffs

Season	Team	League	GP	G	A	PTS	PIM	GP	G	A	PTS	PIM
98-99	Anaheim	NHL	64	3	5	8	14	1	0	0	0	0
98-99	Cincinnati	AHL	9	1	6	7	2	—	—	—	—	—

Born; 1/6/76, Jonkoping, Sweden. 6-1, 190. Drafted by Anaheim Mighty Ducks (2nd choice, 28th overall) in 1994 Entry Draft. Last overseas club; HV 71

Dan Davies — Right Wing
Regular Season — Playoffs

Season	Team	League	GP	G	A	PTS	PIM	GP	G	A	PTS	PIM
98-99	Asheville	UHL	63	11	7	18	95	2	0	0	0	4

Born; 3/14/73, Vancouver, British Columbia. 5-10, 195.

Scott Davis — Defenseman
Regular Season — Playoffs

Season	Team	League	GP	G	A	PTS	PIM	GP	G	A	PTS	PIM
96-97	New Mexico	WPHL	10	0	5	5	18	5	0	0	0	9
97-98	Bakersfield	WCHL	8	0	0	0	21	—	—	—	—	—
97-98	Idaho	WCHL	54	5	22	27	125	4	0	0	0	6
98-99	Idaho	WCHL	46	1	12	13	58	1	0	0	0	2
	WCHL	Totals	108	6	34	40	204	5	0	0	0	8

Born; 5/25/71, Winnipeg, Manitoba. 6-0, 188. Drafted by Quebec Nordiques (8th choice, 190th overall) in 1990 Entry Draft. Traded to Idaho by Bakersfield for Don Lester and Kelly Hrycun (11/97). Last amateur club; Manitoba (CWUAA).

Jeff Daw — Center
Regular Season — Playoffs

Season	Team	League	GP	G	A	PTS	PIM	GP	G	A	PTS	PIM
96-97	Hamilton	AHL	56	11	8	19	39	19	4	5	9	0
96-97	Wheeling	ECHL	13	3	8	11	26	—	—	—	—	—
97-98	Hamilton	AHL	79	28	35	63	20	9	6	3	9	0
98-99	Hamilton	AHL	66	18	29	47	10	11	0	3	3	4
	AHL	Totals	201	57	72	129	69	39	10	11	21	4

Born; 2/28/72, Carlisle, Ontario. 6-3, 200. Signed as a free agent by Edmonton Oilers (8/1/96). Last amateur club; Lowell University (Hockey East).

Jake Deadmarsh — Defenseman
Regular Season — Playoffs

Season	Team	League	GP	G	A	PTS	PIM	GP	G	A	PTS	PIM
96-97	Kamloops	WHL	12	1	1	2	13	—	—	—	—	—
96-97	Charlotte	ECHL	9	0	0	0	15	—	—	—	—	—
96-97	Huntington	ECHL	16	0	3	3	6	—	—	—	—	—
97-98	Huntington	ECHL	50	2	8	10	82	—	—	—	—	—
98-99	Huntington	ECHL	5	0	0	0	8	—	—	—	—	—
98-99	Shreveport	WPHL	26	2	6	8	20	10	1	0	1	2
	ECHL	Totals	80	2	11	13	103	—	—	—	—	—

Born; 1/30/77, Fruitvale, British Columbia. 6-0, 195. Drafted by San Jose Sharks (6th choice, 164th overall) in 1996 Entry Draft. Member of 1998-99 WPHL Champion Shreveport Mudbugs. Last amateur club; Kamloops (WHL).

Mike DeAngelis — Defenseman
Regular Season — Playoffs

Season	Team	League	GP	G	A	PTS	PIM	GP	G	A	PTS	PIM
87-88	Minnesota	CCHA	41	13	32	45	26	—	—	—	—	—
87-88	Kalamazoo	IHL	8	1	5	6	2	7	1	4	5	6
88-89												
89-90												
90-91												
91-92												
92-93												
93-94	Milan	Italy										
94-95												
95-96	Lugano	Italy										
96-97												
97-98	Nottingham	BSL	18	2	4	6	10	6	0	1	1	6
97-98	Reno	WCHL	20	3	16	19	4	—	—	—	—	—
98-99	Mannheim	Germany	11	0	1	1	8	12	1	0	1	12
98-99	Tacoma	WCHL	14	1	8	9	8	—	—	—	—	—
	WCHL	Totals	34	4	24	28	12	—	—	—	—	—

Born; 5-10, 185. Minneapolis, Minnesota. Last amateur club; University of Minnesota-Duluth (WCHA).

Mark Deazeley — Left Wing
Regular Season — Playoffs

Season	Team	League	GP	G	A	PTS	PIM	GP	G	A	PTS	PIM
92-93	Toledo	ECHL	63	27	18	45	263	15	8	6	14	66
93-94	Toledo	ECHL	57	41	36	77	231	14	*16	10	*26	37
93-94	Fort Wayne	IHL	1	0	0	0	2	—	—	—	—	—
94-95	Springfield	AHL	26	2	0	2	141	—	—	—	—	—
94-95	Toledo	ECHL	14	5	1	6	136	—	—	—	—	—
95-96	Tallahassee	ECHL	67	29	36	65	141	12	7	6	13	17
96-97	Austin	WPHL	20	5	8	13	28	—	—	—	—	—
96-97	Tallahassee	ECHL	43	17	10	27	89	3	0	0	0	14
97-98	Toledo	ECHL	41	11	7	18	123	7	1	0	1	28
98-99	Toledo	ECHL	36	9	7	16	96	7	2	0	2	5
	ECHL	Totals	321	139	115	254	1079	58	34	22	56	167

Born; 4/8/72, Toronto, Ontario. 6-4, 237. Signed as a free agent by Winnipeg Jets (6/17/94). 1993-94 ECHL Playoff MVP. Member of 1992-93 ECHL champion Toledo Storm. Member of 1993-94 ECHL champion Toledo Storm. Last amateur club; Oshawa (OHL).

Louie DeBrusk — Left Wing
Regular Season — Playoffs

Season	Team	League	GP	G	A	PTS	PIM	GP	G	A	PTS	PIM
90-91	London	OHL	61	31	33	64	223	7	2	2	4	14
90-91	Binghamton	AHL	2	0	0	0	7	2	0	0	0	9
91-92	Edmonton	NHL	25	2	1	3	124	—	—	—	—	—
91-92	Cape Breton	AHL	28	2	2	4	73	—	—	—	—	—
92-93	Edmonton	NHL	51	8	2	10	205	—	—	—	—	—
93-94	Edmonton	NHL	48	4	6	10	185	—	—	—	—	—
93-94	Cape Breton	AHL	5	3	1	4	58	—	—	—	—	—
94-95	Edmonton	NHL	34	2	0	2	93	—	—	—	—	—
95-96	Edmonton	NHL	38	1	3	4	96	—	—	—	—	—
96-97	Edmonton	NHL	32	2	0	2	94	6	0	0	0	4
97-98	Tampa Bay	NHL	54	1	2	3	166	—	—	—	—	—
97-98	San Antonio	IHL	17	7	4	11	130	—	—	—	—	—
98-99	Phoenix	NHL	15	0	0	0	34	6	2	0	2	6
98-99	Las Vegas	IHL	26	3	6	9	160	—	—	—	—	—
98-99	Long Beach	IHL	24	5	5	10	134	—	—	—	—	—
98-99	Springfield	AHL	3	1	0	1	0	—	—	—	—	—
	NHL	Totals	297	20	14	34	997	12	2	0	2	10
	IHL	Totals	67	15	15	30	424	—	—	—	—	—
	AHL	Totals	38	6	3	9	138	2	0	0	0	9

Born; 3/19/71, Cambridge, Ontario. 6-2, 215. Drafted by New York Rangers (4th choice, 49th overall) in 1989 Entry Draft. Traded to Edmonton Oilers by Rangers with Bernie Nicholls and Steven Rice for Mark Messier and future considerations (10/4/91). Signed as a free agent by Tampa Bay Lightning (9/23/97). Traded to Phoenix Coyotes by Tampa Bay with Tampa's fifth round choice (Jay Leach) in 1998 Entry Draft for Craig Janney (6/11/98). Last amateur club; London (OHL).

Steve Debus — Goaltender
Regular Season — Playoffs

Season	Team	League	GP	W	L	T	MIN	SO	AVG	GP	W	L	MIN	SO	AVG
97-98	Minnesota	WCHA	34	14	20	0	1893	3	3.14	—	—	—	—	—	—
97-98	Houston	IHL	1	0	0	0	28	0	2.16	—	—	—	—	—	—
98-99	Mobile	ECHL	39	15	17	5	2215	0	3.58	—	—	—	—	—	—

Born; 11/8/72, Rochester, Minnesota. 5-9, 177. Last amateur club; University of Minnesota (WCHA).

Rob DeCiantis — Right Wing
Regular Season — Playoffs

Season	Team	League	GP	G	A	PTS	PIM	GP	G	A	PTS	PIM
97-98	Birmingham	ECHL	66	24	28	52	108	4	1	2	3	6
98-99	Birmingham	ECHL	39	24	19	43	24	—	—	—	—	—
98-99	New Orleans	ECHL	31	23	22	45	32	11	11	11	*22	8
	ECHL	Totals	136	71	69	140	164	15	12	13	25	14

Born; 6/11/77, Toronto, Ontario. 6-0, 198. Drafted by Winnipeg Jets (11th choice, 214th overall) in 1995 Entry Draft. 1998-99 ECHL Second Team All-Star. Last amateur club; Kitchener (OHL).

Alexei Deev — Center

Regular Season — Playoffs

Season	Team	League	GP	G	A	PTS	PIM	GP	G	A	PTS	PIM
93-94	Charlotte	ECHL	10	3	3	6	0	—	—	—	—	—
93-94	Huntington	ECHL	12	3	6	9	2	—	—	—	—	—
94-95	Charlotte	ECHL	6	0	0	0	0	—	—	—	—	—
95-96	Winston-Salem	SHL	59	37	51	88	78	9	5	8	13	8
96-97	Macon	CeHL	66	38	54	92	28	4	2	2	4	6
97-98	Macon	CHL	67	25	40	65	35	3	0	0	0	0
98-99	Winston-Salem	UHL	74	35	49	84	14	5	2	2	4	2
	CHL	Totals	133	63	94	157	63	7	2	2	4	6
	ECHL	Totals	28	6	9	15	2	—	—	—	—	—

Born; 12/29/73, Siberia, Russia. 5-11, 172. Selected by Topeka in 1998 CHL Expansion Draft.

David Defrancesco — Defenseman

Regular Season — Playoffs

Season	Team	League	GP	G	A	PTS	PIM	GP	G	A	PTS	PIM
97-98	Huntsville	CHL	43	1	6	7	102	—	—	—	—	—
98-99	Huntsville	CHL	5	1	1	2	5	—	—	—	—	—
	CHL	Totals	48	2	7	9	107	—	—	—	—	—

Born; 2/19/78, Toronto, Ontario. 6-4, 232.

Frank DeFrenza — Defenseman

Regular Season — Playoffs

Season	Team	League	GP	G	A	PTS	PIM	GP	G	A	PTS	PIM
95-96	South Carolina	ECHL	1	0	0	0	2	—	—	—	—	—
96-97												
97-98	Reno	WCHL	37	9	17	26	92	—	—	—	—	—
98-99	Sterving	Austria										
98-99	Asheville	UHL	36	19	16	35	30	—	—	—	—	—

Born; 9/26/74, Burnaby, British Columbia. 6-3, 210.

Dale DeGray — Defenseman

Regular Season — Playoffs

Season	Team	League	GP	G	A	PTS	PIM	GP	G	A	PTS	PIM
83-84	Colorado	CHL	67	16	14	30	67	6	1	1	2	2
84-85	Moncton	AHL	77	24	37	61	63	—	—	—	—	—
85-86	Calgary	NHL	1	0	0	0	0	—	—	—	—	—
85-86	Moncton	AHL	76	10	31	41	128	6	0	1	1	0
86-87	Calgary	NHL	27	6	7	13	29	—	—	—	—	—
86-87	Moncton	AHL	45	10	22	32	57	5	2	1	3	19
87-88	Toronto	NHL	56	6	18	24	63	5	0	1	1	16
87-88	New Haven	AHL	8	2	10	12	38	—	—	—	—	—
88-89	Los Angeles	NHL	63	6	22	28	97	8	1	2	3	12
89-90	Buffalo	NHL	6	0	0	0	6	—	—	—	—	—
89-90	New Haven	AHL	16	2	10	12	38	—	—	—	—	—
89-90	Rochester	AHL	50	6	25	31	118	17	5	6	11	59
90-91	Rochester	AHL	64	9	25	34	121	15	3	4	7	*76
91-92	Italy											
92-93	San Diego	IHL	79	18	64	82	181	14	3	11	14	77
93-94	San Diego	IHL	80	20	50	70	163	9	2	1	3	8
94-95	Detroit	IHL	14	1	8	9	18	—	—	—	—	—
94-95	Cleveland	IHL	64	19	49	68	134	4	0	4	4	10
95-96	Cincinnati	IHL	79	13	46	59	96	16	1	6	7	35
96-97	Cincinnati	IHL	30	5	16	21	55	—	—	—	—	—
96-97	Manitoba	IHL	44	9	15	24	42	—	—	—	—	—
97-98	Manitoba	IHL	15	0	7	7	16	—	—	—	—	—
97-98	Quebec	IHL	31	4	9	13	27	—	—	—	—	—
97-98	Cleveland	IHL	11	1	9	10	4	9	3	7	10	8
98-99	Indianapolis	IHL	27	3	11	14	18	—	—	—	—	—
	NHL	Totals	153	18	47	65	195	13	1	3	4	28
	IHL	Totals	474	93	331	424	754	52	9	29	38	138
	AHL	Totals	336	63	160	223	533	43	10	12	22	154

Born; 9/3/63, Oshawa, Ontario. 6-0, 206. Drafted by Calgary Flames (7th choice, 162nd overall) in 1981 Entry Draft. Traded to Toronto Maple Leafs by Calgary for future considerations (9/87). Selected by Los Angeles Kings in 1988 Waiver Draft (10/3/88). Traded to Buffalo Sabres by Los Angeles for Bob Halkidis (11/24/89). Signed as a free agent by San Diego Gulls (8/27/92). Signed as a free agent by Detroit Vipers (1994). Traded by Detroit to Cleveland Lumberjacks to complete earlier trade (11/16/94). Traded to Quebec by Manitoba with Rick Girard for Craig Martin, Jeff Parrott and Michel Mongeau (12/97). Traded to Cleveland by Quebec with Rick Girard, Darcy Simon, Tom Draper and Jason Ruff for Ryan Mougenal, Rick Hayward, John Craighead, Eric Perrin, Pat Jablonski and the rights to Burke Murphy (3/98). 1984-85 AHL Second All-Star Team. 1992-93 IHL Second Team All-Star. 1994-95 IHL Second Team All-Star. Last

Mike DeGurse — Left Wing

Regular Season — Playoffs

Season	Team	League	GP	G	A	PTS	PIM	GP	G	A	PTS	PIM
95-96	Winston-Salem	SHL	56	18	20	38	302	9	1	0	1	40
96-97	Huntsville	CeHL	62	31	15	46	282	8	3	6	9	46
97-98	Huntsville	CHL	56	38	27	65	335	3	2	1	3	11
98-99	Hunstville	CHL	44	23	18	41	212	14	*8	0	8	32
	CHL	Totals	162	92	60	152	829	25	13	7	20	89

Born; 10/4/74, Sarnia Reserve, Ontario. 6-2, 220. Member of 1998-99 CHL Champion Huntsville Channel Cats.

Raymond Delarosbil — Defenseman

Regular Season — Playoffs

Season	Team	League	GP	G	A	PTS	PIM	GP	G	A	PTS	PIM
96-97	Macon	CeHL	4	0	2	2	5	5	0	2	2	2
97-98	Macon	CHL	55	3	14	17	94	3	1	1	2	4
98-99	Macon	CHL	69	8	18	26	69	3	0	0	0	0
	CHL	Totals	218	11	34	45	168	11	1	3	4	6

Born; 1/14/73, Drummondville, Quebec. 5-10, 210. Last amateur club; University of Moncton (AUAA).

Jason Deleurme — Right Wing

Regular Season — Playoffs

Season	Team	League	GP	G	A	PTS	PIM	GP	G	A	PTS	PIM
98-99	Hampton Roads	ECHL	26	9	6	15	74	—	—	—	—	—

Born; 2/1/77, Kelowna, British Columbia. 5-8, 185. Last amateur club; Kelowna (WHL).

Matt DelGuidice — Goaltender

Regular Season — Playoffs

Season	Team	League	GP	W	L	T	MIN	SO	AVG	GP	W	L	MIN	SO	AVG
90-91	Boston	NHL	1	0	0	0	10	0	0.00	—	—	—	—	—	—
90-91	Maine	AHL	52	23	18	9	2893	2	3.32	2	1	1	82	0	3.66
91-92	Boston	NHL	10	2	5	1	424	0	3.96	—	—	—	—	—	—
91-92	Maine	AHL	25	5	15	0	1369	0	4.43	—	—	—	—	—	—
92-93	Providence	AHL	9	0	7	1	478	0	7.28	—	—	—	—	—	—
92-93	San Diego	IHL	1	0	0	0	20	0	6.00	—	—	—	—	—	—
93-94	Albany	AHL	5	1	2	2	310	0	3.68	—	—	—	—	—	—
93-94	Springfield	AHL	1	0	0	1	65	0	2.77	—	—	—	—	—	—
93-94	Raleigh	ECHL	31	18	9	4	1878	1	2.94	12	6	4	707	0	3.14
94-95	Atlanta	IHL	1	0	0	0	53	0	5.70	—	—	—	—	—	—
94-95	Charlotte	ECHL	5	2	2	1	303	0	2.97	—	—	—	—	—	—
94-95	Nashville	ECHL	18	7	8	2	1009	0	4.82	2	0	1	74	0	4.84
95-96	Albany	AHL	1	0	0	0	0	0	0.00	—	—	—	—	—	—
95-96	Raleigh	ECHL	35	13	10	3	1738	0	3.56	2	0	1	60	0	2.98
96-97	Amarillo	WPHL	49	13	*26	7	2620	0	4.42	—	—	—	—	—	—
97-98	Amarillo	WPHL	31	7	17	4	1599	0	4.65	—	—	—	—	—	—
97-98	Monroe	WPHL	16	9	7	0	923	2	3.12	—	—	—	—	—	—
98-99	Monroe	WPHL	8	5	3	0	477	0	4.52	—	—	—	—	—	—
98-99	Corpus Christi	WPHL	4	1	2	1	199	0	3.31	—	—	—	—	—	—
	NHL	Totals	11	2	5	1	434	0	3.87	—	—	—	—	—	—
	AHL	Totals	93	29	42	13	5115	2	4.00	2	1	1	82	0	3.66
	IHL	Totals	2	0	0	0	73	0	5.74	—	—	—	—	—	—
	WPHL	Totals	108	35	55	12	5818	2	4.25	—	—	—	—	—	—
	ECHL	Totals	84	40	29	10	4928	1	3.54	16	6	6	841	0	3.28

Born; 3/15/67, West Haven, Connecticut. 5-10, 170. Drafted by Boston Bruins (4th choice, 77th overall) in 1987 Entry Draft. Traded to Monroe by Amarillo for Ryan MacDonald. Last amateur club; University of Maine (Hockey East).

Dan Delisle — Defenseman

Regular Season — Playoffs

Season	Team	League	GP	G	A	PTS	PIM	GP	G	A	PTS	PIM
97-98	Kansas City	IHL	4	0	0	0	9	—	—	—	—	—
97-98	Wichita	CHL	60	5	16	21	108	15	2	2	4	33
98-99	Austin	WPHL	48	4	13	17	60	—	—	—	—	—

Born; 11/28/76, Montreal, Quebec. 6-3, 215.

Jonathan Delisle — Right Wing

Regular Season — Playoffs

Season	Team	League	GP	G	A	PTS	PIM	GP	G	A	PTS	PIM
97-98	Fredericton	AHL	78	15	21	36	138	4	0	1	1	7
98-99	Montreal	NHL	1	0	0	0	0	—	—	—	—	—
98-99	Fredericton	AHL	78	7	29	36	118	15	3	6	9	39
	AHL	Totals	156	22	50	72	256	19	3	7	10	46

Born; 11/28/76, Montreal, Quebec. 6-3, 215. Drafted by Montreal Canadiens (4th chioce, 86th overall) in 1995 Entry Draft. Last amateur club; Hull (QMJHL).

Xavier Delisle — Center

Regular Season — Playoffs

Season	Team	League	GP	G	A	PTS	PIM	GP	G	A	PTS	PIM
97-98	Adirondack	AHL	76	10	19	29	47	3	0	0	0	0
98-99	Tampa Bay	NHL	2	0	0	0	0	—	—	—	—	—
98-99	Cleveland	IHL	77	15	29	44	36	—	—	—	—	—

Born; 5/24/77, Quebec City, Quebec. 5-11, 182. Drafted by Tampa Bay Lightning (5th choice, 157th overall) in 1996 Entry Draft. Last amateur club; Granby (QMJHL).

Dion Delmonte — Center

Regular Season — Playoffs

Season	Team	League	GP	G	A	PTS	PIM	GP	G	A	PTS	PIM
95-96		Italy										
96-97	Nurnberg	Germany	41	6	13	19	26	9	3	5	8	14
97-98	Sheffield	BSL	56	11	35	46	70	9	1	2	3	10
98-99	Madison	UHL	72	40	53	93	86	—	—	—	—	—

Born; 1028/72, Toronto, Ontario. 5-10, 175. Last amateur club; Dartmouth

Andy Delmore — Defenseman

Regular Season — Playoffs

Season	Team	League	GP	G	A	PTS	PIM	GP	G	A	PTS	PIM
96-97	Sarnia	OHL	64	18	60	78	39	12	2	10	12	10
96-97	Fredericton	AHL	4	0	1	1	0	—	—	—	—	—
97-98	Philadelphia	AHL	73	9	30	39	46	18	4	4	8	21
98-99	Philadelphia	NHL	2	0	1	1	0	—	—	—	—	—
98-99	Philadelphia	AHL	70	5	18	23	51	15	1	4	5	6
	AHL	Totals	147	14	49	63	97	33	5	8	13	27

Born; 12/26/76, LaSalle, Ontario. 6-1, 192. Signed as a free agent by Philadelphia Flyers (6/9/97). Member of 1997-98 AHL Champion Philadelphia Phantoms. Last amateur club; Sarnia (OHL).

Leon Delorme — Right Wing

Regular Season — Playoffs

Season	Team	League	GP	G	A	PTS	PIM	GP	G	A	PTS	PIM
98-99	Wheeling	ECHL	32	1	1	2	208	—	—	—	—	—

Born; 2/9/77, Flying Dust, Saskatchewan. 5-11, 210.

Marc Delorme — Goaltender

Regular Season — Playoffs

Season	Team	League	GP	W	L	T	MIN	SO	AVG	GP	W	L	MIN	SO	AVG
94-95	Brantford	CoHL	25	12	8	2	1339	1	3.85	—	—	—	—	—	—
95-96	Brantford	CoHL	*55	*35	13	3	*3020	1	3.40	12	7	4	688	1	3.31
96-97	Detroit	IHL	1	0	0	1	38	0	0.00	—	—	—	—	—	—
96-97	Louisiana	ECHL	56	*36	14	3	3115	2	3.06	14	7	*6	753	0	4.54
97-98	Reno	WCHL	14	6	8	0	785	0	4.36	—	—	—	—	—	—
97-98	Birmingham	ECHL	23	18	3	2	1339	0	3.18	4	1	3	245	0	3.91
98-99	Saginaw	UHL	33	10	*19	4	1946	1	3.88	—	—	—	—	—	—
98-99	Winston-Salem	UHL	27	12	*13	1	1465	1	4.01	4	1	3	247	0	4.86
	UHL	Totals	140	69	53	10	7770	4	3.71	16	8	7	935	1	3.72

Born; 6/19/70, Montreal, Quebec. 5-11, 170. 1995-96 CoHL Second Team All-Star. 1996-97 ECHL Goaltender of the Year. 1996-97 ECHL First Team All-Star. Traded to Birmingham by Louisiana for Ryan Shanahan, Mario Dumoulin and cash (1/98). Traded to Winston-Salem by Saginaw for John Nelson, Kevin Tucker and Brian Kreft (1/99).

Nate DeMars — Center

Regular Season — Playoffs

Season	Team	League	GP	G	A	PTS	PIM	GP	G	A	PTS	PIM
98-99	Chesapeake	ECHL	6	1	0	1	9	—	—	—	—	—

Born; Mahtomedi, Minnesota. 6-0, 190. Last amateur club; St. Mary's (NCAA 3).

Matt Demarski — Forward

Regular Season — Playoffs

Season	Team	League	GP	G	A	PTS	PIM	GP	G	A	PTS	PIM
98-99	Florida	ECHL	65	31	28	59	36	3	2	1	3	2

Born; 1/11/77, Winnipeg, Manitoba. 6-0, 192. Last amateur club; Seattle (WHL).

Trevor Demmans — Defenseman

Regular Season — Playoffs

Season	Team	League	GP	G	A	PTS	PIM	GP	G	A	PTS	PIM
97-98	Baton Rouge	ECHL	38	7	8	15	53	—	—	—	—	—
97-98	Wheeling	ECHL	25	8	17	25	29	15	0	2	2	19
98-99	Wheeling	ECHL	42	5	15	20	83	—	—	—	—	—
98-99	Pee Dee	ECHL	14	1	7	8	8	13	1	6	7	12
	ECHL	Totals	119	21	47	68	173	28	1	8	9	31

Born; 10/3/74, Nipawin, Saskatchewan. 6-0, 198. Last amateur club; Lake Superior State (CCHA).

Nathan Dempsey — Defenseman

Regular Season / Playoffs

Season	Team	League	GP	G	A	PTS	PIM	GP	G	A	PTS	PIM
92-93	Regina	WHL	72	12	29	41	95	13	3	8	11	14
92-93	St. John's	AHL	—	—	—	—	—	2	0	0	0	0
93-94	Regina	WHL	56	14	36	50	100	4	0	0	0	4
94-95	St. John's	AHL	74	7	30	37	91	5	1	0	1	11
95-96	St. John's	AHL	73	5	15	20	103	4	1	0	1	9
96-97	Toronto	NHL	14	1	1	2	2	—	—	—	—	—
96-97	St. John's	AHL	52	8	18	26	108	6	1	0	1	4
97-98	St. John's	AHL	68	12	16	28	85	4	0	0	0	0
98-99	St. John's	AHL	67	2	29	31	70	5	0	1	1	2
	AHL	Totals	334	34	108	142	457	26	3	1	4	26

Born; 7/14/74, Spruce Grove, Alberta. 6-0, 170. Drafted by Toronto Maple Leafs (11th choice, 148th overall) in 1992 Entry Draft. Last amateur club; Regina

Marc Denis — Goaltender

Regular Season / Playoffs

Season	Team	League	GP	W	L	T	MIN	SO	AVG	GP	W	L	MIN	SO	AVG
96-97	Chicoutimi	QMJHL	41	22	15	2	2323	4	*2.69	*21	*11	10	*1229	*1	3.42
96-97	Colorado	NHL	1	0	1	0	60	0	3.00	—	—	—	—	—	—
96-97	Hershey	AHL	—	—	—	—	—	—	—	4	1	0	56	0	*1.08
97-98	Hershey	AHL	47	17	23	4	2589	1	2.90	6	3	3	347	0	2.59
98-99	Colorado	NHL	4	1	1	1	217	0	2.49	—	—	—	—	—	—
98-9	Hershey	AHL	52	20	23	5	2908	4	2.83	3	1	1	143	0	2.93
	NHL	Totals	5	1	2	1	277	0	2.60	—	—	—	—	—	—
	AHL	Totals	99	37	46	9	5497	5	2.86	13	5	4	546	0	2.53

Born; 8/1/77, Montreal, Quebec. 6-0, 188. Drafted by Colorado Avalanche (1st choice, 25th overall) in 1995 Entry Draft. Member of 1996-97 AHL Champion Hershey Bears. Last amateur club; Chicoutimi (QMJHL).

Dan Dennis — Goaltender

Regular Season / Playoffs

Season	Team	League	GP	W	L	T	MIN	SO	AVG	GP	W	L	MIN	SO	AVG
97-98	Johnstown	ECHL	36	12	17	2	1765	0	4.15	—	—	—	—	—	—
98-99	Peterborough	BNL													
98-99	Fayetteville	CHL	16	8	5	2	920	0	3.46	—	—	—	—	—	—

Born; 9/30/72, Prince Albert, Saskatchewan. 5-10, 190. Last amateur club; Providence (Hockey East).

Mike Dennis — Defenseman

Regular Season / Playoffs

Season	Team	League	GP	G	A	PTS	PIM	GP	G	A	PTS	PIM
94-95	Dayton	ECHL	3	0	1	1	15	—	—	—	—	—
94-95	Johnstown	ECHL	59	5	18	23	86	5	0	1	1	28
95-96	Raleigh	ECHL	19	2	2	4	35	—	—	—	—	—
95-96	Mobile	ECHL	45	5	18	23	104	—	—	—	—	—
96-97	Mobile	ECHL	59	6	21	27	155	3	0	0	0	6
97-98												
98-99	Mobile	ECHL	1	0	0	0	0	—	—	—	—	—
	ECHL	Totals	182	18	60	78	395	8	0	1	1	34

Born; 5/18/71, Kansas City, Kansas. 5-10, 185. Last amateur club; Illinois-Chicago (CCHA).

John DePourcq — Center

Regular Season / Playoffs

Season	Team	League	GP	G	A	PTS	PIM	GP	G	A	PTS	PIM
93-94	Erie	ECHL	28	14	29	43	4	—	—	—	—	—
94-95	Wichita	CeHL	59	28	53	81	10	6	2	6	8	2
95-96	Louisiana	ECHL	55	22	53	75	20	3	2	1	3	0
96-97	Louisiana	ECHL	68	28	63	91	14	13	2	8	10	6
97-98												
98-99	Louisiana	ECHL	3	0	1	1	4	—	—	—	—	—
	ECHL	Totals	154	64	146	210	42	16	4	9	13	6

Born; 2/6/68, Summerside, British Columbia. 5-8, 171. Member of 1994-95 CeHL Champion Wichita Thunder.

Geoff Derouin — Goaltender

Regular Season / Playoffs

Season	Team	League	GP	W	L	T	MIN	SO	AVG	GP	W	L	MIN	SO	AVG
98-99	Wichita	CHL	6	2	3	0	339	0	4.60	—	—	—	—	—	—
98-99	Fayetteville	CHL	5	0	3	1	213	0	3.10	—	—	—	—	—	—
	CHL	Totals	11	2	6	1	552	0	4.02	—	—	—	—	—	—

Born; 11/22/77, Fort St. John, British Columbia. 5-10, 170.

Phillipe DeRouville — Goaltender

Regular Season / Playoffs

Season	Team	League	GP	W	L	T	MIN	SO	AVG	GP	W	L	MIN	SO	AVG
94-95	Pittsburgh	NHL	1	1	0	0	60	0	3.00	—	—	—	—	—	—
94-95	Cleveland	IHL	41	24	10	5	2369	1	3.32	4	1	3	263	0	4.09
95-96	Cleveland	IHL	38	19	11	3	2007	1	3.86	—	—	—	—	—	—
96-97	Pittsburgh	NHL	2	0	2	0	111	0	3.24	—	—	—	—	—	—
96-97	Kansas City	IHL	26	11	11	4	1470	2	2.82	2	0	1	33	0	7.35
97-98	Utah	IHL	30	18	9	1	1525	3	2.56	2	1	1	129	0	3.25
97-98	Hartford	AHL	3	0	2	1	184	0	3.26	—	—	—	—	—	—
97-98	Louisville	ECHL	8	5	2	1	480	0	3.38	—	—	—	—	—	—
98-99	Fredericton	AHL	19	6	6	2	921	0	3.00	—	—	—	—	—	—
98-99	Utah	IHL	5	0	2	0	142	0	5.07	—	—	—	—	—	—
98-99	San Antonio	CHL	5	3	2	0	181	0	4.32	—	—	—	—	—	—
	NHL	Totals	3	1	2	0	171	0	3.16	—	—	—	—	—	—
	IHL	Totals	140	72	43	13	7513	7	3.24	8	2	5	425	0	4.10
	AHL	Totals	22	6	8	3	1105	0	3.04	—	—	—	—	—	—

Born; 8/7/74, Victoriaville, Quebec. 6-1, 183. Drafted by Pittsburgh Penguins (5th choice, 115th overall) in 1992 Entry Draft. Last amateur club; Verdun (QMJHL).

Dmitry Deryabin — Defenseman

Regular Season / Playoffs

Season	Team	League	GP	G	A	PTS	PIM	GP	G	A	PTS	PIM
98-99	Binghamton	UHL	12	0	1	1	10	—	—	—	—	—

Born; 1/21/78, Riga, Latvia. 6-2, 203.

Mark Desantis — Defenseman

Regular Season / Playoffs

Season	Team	League	GP	G	A	PTS	PIM	GP	G	A	PTS	PIM
93-94	San Diego	IHL	54	5	10	15	95	—	—	—	—	—
94-95	San Diego	IHL	8	0	0	0	23	—	—	—	—	—
94-95	Greensboro	ECHL	57	10	34	44	196	15	0	4	4	71
95-96	Baltimore	AHL	8	0	0	0	21	—	—	—	—	—
95-96	Jacksonville	ECHL	51	12	32	44	243	18	6	15	21	56
96-97	San Antonio	IHL	61	7	15	22	184	2	0	1	1	2
97-98	San Antonio	IHL	61	5	12	17	108	—	—	—	—	—
98-99	Grand Rapids	IHL	7	0	0	0	9	—	—	—	—	—
98-99	Louisiana	ECHL	27	4	10	14	85	—	—	—	—	—
98-99	Augusta	ECHL	25	1	13	14	46	2	0	0	0	2
	IHL	Totals	191	17	37	54	419	2	0	1	1	2
	ECHL	Totals	160	27	89	116	570	35	6	19	25	129

Born; 1/12/72, Brampton, Ontario. 6-0, 205. Signed as a free agent by Anaheim Mighty Ducks (8/2/93). Traded to Augusta by Tallahassee for Alex LaPorte and Garry Gruber (1/99). Last amateur club; Newmarket (OHL).

Frederic Deschenes — Goaltender

Regular Season / Playoffs

Season	Team	League	GP	W	L	T	MIN	SO	AVG	GP	W	L	MIN	SO	AVG
96-97	Rochester	AHL	38	15	13	3	1898	2	2.85	10	6	4	628	0	2.68
96-97	Flint	CoHL	3	3	0	0	180	0	1.67	—	—	—	—	—	—
97-98	Quebec	IHL	38	9	23	3	2115	0	3.57	—	—	—	—	—	—
98-99	Portland	AHL	3	0	2	1	165	0	5.09	—	—	—	—	—	—
98-99	Orlando	IHL	12	2	7	2	638	1	3.58	—	—	—	—	—	—
98-99	Birmingham	ECHL	39	20	16	2	2224	2	3.45	—	—	—	—	—	—
	IHL	Totals	50	11	30	5	2753	1	3.57	—	—	—	—	—	—
	AHL	Totals	41	15	15	4	2063	2	3.03	10	6	4	628	0	2.68

Born; 1/12/76, Quebec, Quebec. 5-9, 164. Drafted by Detroit Red Wings (4th choice, 114th overall) in 1994 Entry Draft. Last amateur club; Granby (QMJHL).

Matthieu Descoteaux — Defenseman

Regular Season / Playoffs

Season	Team	League	GP	G	A	PTS	PIM	GP	G	A	PTS	PIM
97-98	Hamilton	AHL	67	2	8	10	70	2	0	0	0	0
98-99	Hamilton	AHL	74	6	12	18	49	4	0	0	0	0
	AHL	Totals	141	8	20	28	119	6	0	0	0	0

Born; 9/23/77, Pierreville, Quebec. 6-3, 220. Drafted by Edmonton Oilers (2nd choice, 19th overall) in 1996 Entry Draft. Last amateur club; Hull (QMJHL).

Sergei Deshevy — Defenseman

Regular Season / Playoffs

Season	Team	League	GP	G	A	PTS	PIM	GP	G	A	PTS	PIM
98-99	Austin	WPHL	2	1	0	1	0	—	—	—	—	—

Born; 6/25/77, Kiev, Ukraine.

Jason Desjardins — Goaltender

Regular Season / Playoffs

Season	Team	League	GP	W	L	T	MIN	SO	AVG	GP	W	L	MIN	SO	AVG
98-99	Fort Worth	CHL	8	3	2	1	363	0	5.29	—	—	—	—	—	—
98-99	Tulsa	CHL	5	1	3	0	296	0	9.33	—	—	—	—	—	—
98-99	San Antonio	CHL	1	0	1	0	36	0	10.00	—	—	—	—	—	—
	CHL	Totals	14	4	6	1	695	0	7.25	—	—	—	—	—	—

Born; 3/10/77, Sudbury, Ontario. 5-9, 170.

Stephane Desjardins — Defenseman

Regular Season / Playoffs

Season	Team	League	GP	G	A	PTS	PIM	GP	G	A	PTS	PIM
93-94	Fort Worth	CeHL	37	7	16	23	58	—	—	—	—	—
93-94	Dayton Beach	SUN	12	1	5	6	94	—	—	—	—	—
94-95	Roanoke	ECHL	58	2	5	7	64	7	0	0	0	9
95-96	Nashville	ECHL	39	3	13	16	55	—	—	—	—	—
95-96	Columbus	ECHL	20	1	3	4	6	3	0	0	0	0
96-97	Austin	WPHL	37	2	8	10	84	—	—	—	—	—
96-97	Central Texas	WPHL	8	2	3	5	24	—	—	—	—	—
96-97	Waco	WPHL	16	4	3	7	18	—	—	—	—	—
97-98	Waco	WPHL	10	1	0	1	25	—	—	—	—	—
97-98	Lake Charles	WPHL	39	7	8	15	95	4	0	1	1	6
97-98	Reno	WCHL	5	0	1	1	23	—	—	—	—	—
98-99	Lake Charles	WPHL	5	0	1	1	4	—	—	—	—	—
98-99	Topeka	CHL	60	5	20	25	123	3	0	0	0	4
	ECHL	Totals	117	6	21	27	125	10	0	0	0	9
	WPHL	Totals	115	16	23	39	250	4	0	1	1	6
	CHL	Totals	97	12	36	48	181	3	0	0	0	4

Born; 6/23/72, Anjou, Quebec. 5-11, 195. Last amateur club; Laval (QMJHL).

Jason Desloover — Defenseman

Regular Season / Playoffs

Season	Team	League	GP	G	A	PTS	PIM	GP	G	A	PTS	PIM
98-99	Jacksonville	ECHL	4	0	1	1	2	—	—	—	—	—
98-99	Winston-Salem	UHL	41	2	8	10	59	—	—	—	—	—
98-99	Flint	UHL	24	1	2	3	19	9	0	2	2	2
	UHL	Totals	65	3	10	13	78	9	0	2	2	2

Born; 1/30/74, Saginaw, Michigan. 6-1, 185. Traded to Flint by Winston-Salem for Tom Moulton (2/99). Last amateur club; Plattsburgh (NCAA 3).

Ray DeSouza — Defenseman

Regular Season / Playoffs

Season	Team	League	GP	G	A	PTS	PIM	GP	G	A	PTS	PIM
91-92	Thunder Bay	CoHL	7	0	1	1	17	—	—	—	—	—
91-92	Dayton	ECHL	4	0	0	0	2	—	—	—	—	—
92-93	Nashville	ECHL	26	0	6	6	115	—	—	—	—	—
92-93	Birmingham	ECHL	29	1	7	8	86	—	—	—	—	—
93-94	Huntsville	ECHL	7	1	1	2	31	—	—	—	—	—
93-94	Fort Worth	CeHL	29	0	8	8	102	—	—	—	—	—
93-94	Memphis	CeHL	6	0	4	4	6	—	—	—	—	—
94-95	Dallas	CeHL	35	4	13	17	97	—	—	—	—	—
95-96												
96-97												
97-98	Fort Worth	CHL	49	7	11	18	131	—	—	—	—	—
97-98	Wichita	CHL	4	0	0	0	18	15	0	0	0	36
98-99	Fort Worth	CHL	39	3	7	10	76	—	—	—	—	—
98-99	Memphis	CHL	12	2	9	11	28	4	0	1	1	10
	CHL	Totals	174	16	52	68	458	19	0	1	1	46
	ECHL	Totals	66	2	14	16	234	—	—	—	—	—

Born; 3/26/67, Dublin, Ireland. 6-4, 220.

Jarrett Deuling — Left Wing

Regular Season / Playoffs

Season	Team	League	GP	G	A	PTS	PIM	GP	G	A	PTS	PIM
94-95	Worcester	AHL	63	11	8	19	37	—	—	—	—	—
95-96	Islanders	NHL	14	0	1	1	11	—	—	—	—	—
95-96	Worcester	AHL	57	16	7	23	57	4	1	2	3	2
96-97	Islanders	NHL	1	0	0	0	0	—	—	—	—	—
96-97	Kentucky	AHL	58	15	31	46	57	4	3	0	3	8
97-98	Milwaukee	IHL	64	18	18	36	84	10	4	3	7	36
98-99	Kentucky	AHL	60	22	31	53	68	12	3	6	9	8
	NHL	Totals	15	0	1	1	11	—	—	—	—	—
	AHL	Totals	238	64	77	141	219	20	7	8	15	18

Born; 3/4/74, Vernon, British Columbia. 5-11, 195. Drafted by New York Islanders (2nd choice, 56th overall) in 1992 Entry Draft. Signed as a free agent by San Jose Sharks (8/27/98). Last amateur club; Kamloops (WHL).

Boyd Devereaux — Center

Regular Season / Playoffs

Season	Team	League	GP	G	A	PTS	PIM	GP	G	A	PTS	PIM
96-97	Kitchener	OHL	54	28	41	69	37	13	4	11	15	8
96-97	Hamilton	AHL	—	—	—	—	—	1	0	1	1	0
97-98	Edmonton	NHL	38	1	4	5	6	—	—	—	—	—
97-98	Hamilton	AHL	14	5	6	11	6	9	1	1	2	8
98-99	Edmonton	NHL	61	6	8	14	23	1	0	0	0	0
98-99	Hamilton	AHL	7	4	6	10	2	8	0	3	3	4
	NHL	Totals	99	7	12	19	29	1	0	0	0	0
	AHL	Totals	21	9	12	21	8	18	1	5	6	12

Born; 4/16/78, Seaforth, Ontario. Drafted by Edmonton Oilers (1st choice, 6th overall) in 1996 Entry Draft. Last amateur club; Kitchener (OHL).

Kirk Dewaele — Defenseman

Regular Season / Playoffs

Season	Team	League	GP	G	A	PTS	PIM	GP	G	A	PTS	PIM
97-98	Tallahassee	ECHL	68	1	5	6	117	—	—	—	—	—
98-99	Tallahassee	ECHL	21	0	3	3	36	—	—	—	—	—
98-99	Pensacola	ECHL	47	3	3	6	63	—	—	—	—	—
	ECHL	Totals	136	4	11	15	216	—	—	—	—	—

Born; 3/24/76, Calgary, Alberta. 6-1, 202. Last amateur club; Spokane (WHL).

Joshua DeWolf — Defenseman

Regular Season / Playoffs

Season	Team	League	GP	G	A	PTS	PIM	GP	G	A	PTS	PIM
97-98	St. Cloud State	WCHA	37	9	9	18	78	—	—	—	—	—
97-98	Albany	AHL	2	0	0	0	0	—	—	—	—	—
98-99	Albany	AHL	75	1	17	18	111	5	0	0	0	2
	AHL	Totals	77	1	17	18	111	5	0	0	0	2

Born; 7/25/77, Bloomington, Minnesota. 6-2, 190. Drafted by New Jersey Devils (3rd choice, 41st overall) in 1996 Entry Draft. Last amateur club; St. Cloud (WCHA).

Brad Dexter — Defenseman

Season	Team	League	GP	G	A	PTS	PIM	GP	G	A	PTS	PIM
			Regular Season					Playoffs				
96-97	Raleigh	ECHL	52	8	32	40	20	—	—	—	—	—
96-97	South Carolina	ECHL	16	0	17	17	12	18	3	*23	26	8
97-98	South Carolina	ECHL	70	11	38	49	54	5	2	4	6	0
98-99	South Carolina	ECHL	70	19	36	55	46	3	1	1	2	2
	ECHL	Totals	208	38	123	161	132	26	6	28	34	10

Born; 3/29/72, Kingston, Ontario. 6-3, 180. Member of 1996-97 ECHL Champion South Carolina Stingrays. 1998-99 ECHL Second Team All-Star. Last amateur club; Colgate (ECAC).

Jason Dexter — Center

Season	Team	League	GP	G	A	PTS	PIM	GP	G	A	PTS	PIM
			Regular Season					Playoffs				
94-95	Birmingham	ECHL	19	5	10	15	0	7	3	4	7	2
95-96	Birmingham	ECHL	63	18	18	36	20	—	—	—	—	—
96-97	Columbus	CeHL	66	29	44	73	27	3	1	1	2	0
97-98	Nashville	CHL	36	10	9	19	18	9	2	2	4	2
98-99	Madison	UHL	37	13	24	37	4	—	—	—	—	—
98-99	Asheville	UHL	26	12	11	23	12	—	—	—	—	—
98-99	Mohawk Valley	UHL	12	7	7	14	2	—	—	—	—	—
	CHL	Totals	102	39	53	92	45	12	3	3	6	2
	ECHL	Totals	82	23	28	51	20	7	3	4	7	2
	UHL	Totals	75	32	42	74	18	—	—	—	—	—

Born; 3/12/71, Kingston, Ontario. 6-1, 210. Selected by Macon in 1998 CHL Dispersal Draft. Traded to Asheville by Madison with Jeff Foster for Chris Newans and Jeff Smith (1/99). Last amateur club; New Hampshire (Hockey

Mark Deyell — Center

Season	Team	League	GP	G	A	PTS	PIM	GP	G	A	PTS	PIM
			Regular Season					Playoffs				
96-97	St. John's	AHL	58	15	27	42	30	10	1	5	6	6
97-98	St. John's	AHL	72	20	43	63	75	4	1	1	2	4
98-99	St. John's	AHL	44	20	27	47	39	3	0	3	3	0
	AHL	Totals	174	55	97	152	144	17	2	9	11	10

Born; 3/26/76, Regina, Saskatchewan. 5-11, 170. Drafted by Toronto Maple Leafs (4th choice, 126th overall) in 1994 Entry Draft. Last amateur club; Saskatoon (WHL).

Tony Deynzer

Season	Team	League	GP	G	A	PTS	PIM	GP	G	A	PTS	PIM
			Regular Season					Playoffs				
98-99	San Antonio	CHL	1	0	0	0	0	—	—	—	—	—

Born;

Norm Dezainde — Left Wing

Season	Team	League	GP	G	A	PTS	PIM	GP	G	A	PTS	PIM
			Regular Season					Playoffs				
93-94	Kitchener	OHL	62	30	42	72	104	5	6	3	9	20
93-94	Toledo	ECHL	—	—	—	—	—	6	0	1	1	6
94-95	Syracuse	AHL	6	0	1	1	17	—	—	—	—	—
94-95	Toledo	ECHL	20	6	15	21	47	—	—	—	—	—
94-95	South Carolina	ECHL	9	0	0	0	6	—	—	—	—	—
95-96	Toledo	ECHL	66	21	19	40	238	5	0	1	1	8
96-97	Adirondack	AHL	2	1	0	1	4	—	—	—	—	—
96-97	Toledo	ECHL	49	7	16	23	197	—	—	—	—	—
96-97	Dayton	ECHL	15	3	4	7	78	4	3	0	3	10
97-98	Michigan	IHL	2	0	0	0	5	—	—	—	—	—
97-98	Cincinnati	IHL	8	0	1	1	10	—	—	—	—	—
97-98	Dayton	ECHL	46	15	19	34	248	5	0	1	1	27
98-99	Cincinnati	IHL	2	1	0	1	0	—	—	—	—	—
98-99	Dayton	ECHL	30	14	17	31	123	4	2	2	4	18
98-99	Bracknell	BSL	32	8	16	24	80	—	—	—	—	—
	IHL	Totals	10	0	1	1	15	—	—	—	—	—
	AHL	Totals	8	1	1	2	21	—	—	—	—	—
	ECHL	Totals	205	52	73	125	814	20	3	3	6	51

Born; 1/29/73, Jarvis, Ontario. 5-10, 180. Member of 1993-94 ECHL champion Toledo Storm. Last amateur club; Kitchener (OHL).

Kevin Diachina — Defenseman

Season	Team	League	GP	G	A	PTS	PIM	GP	G	A	PTS	PIM
			Regular Season					Playoffs				
98-99	Windsor	OUAA	24	1	17	18	32	—	—	—	—	—
98-99	Toledo	ECHL	3	0	0	0	4	5	0	0	0	11

Born; Last amateur club; Windsor (OUAA).

Marty Diamond — Right Wing

Season	Team	League	GP	G	A	PTS	PIM	GP	G	A	PTS	PIM
			Regular Season					Playoffs				
94-95	Lakeland	SUN	27	18	22	40	98	—	—	—	—	—
95-96	Lakeland	SUN	60	31	58	89	137	5	3	1	4	19
96-97												
97-98	Columbus	CHL	19	4	6	10	26	—	—	—	—	—
97-98	San Angelo	WPHL	30	17	16	33	68	3	0	3	3	9
98-99	San Angelo	WPHL	66	26	35	61	113	12	5	4	9	*63
	WPHL	Totals	96	43	51	94	181	15	5	7	12	72
	SUN	Totals	87	49	80	129	235	5	3	1	4	19

Born; 12/19/71, Holly, Michigan. 6-2, 220. Selected by Arkansas in 1998 WPHL Expansion Draft. Traded to Austin by Arkansas with Rusty McKie for Tim Findlay (8/98). Traded to San Angelo by Austin for Eric Preston and future considerations (9/98). Last amateur club; SUNY-Fredonia (NCAA 3).

Mike Dick — Center

Season	Team	League	GP	G	A	PTS	PIM	GP	G	A	PTS	PIM
			Regular Season					Playoffs				
97-98	Central Texas	WPHL	45	12	10	22	31	—	—	—	—	—
98-99	Central Texas	WPHL	11	0	2	2	4	—	—	—	—	—
98-99	Corpus Christi	WPHL	13	2	2	4	12	—	—	—	—	—
98-99	Fort Worth	CHL	28	13	13	26	14	—	—	—	—	—
	WPHL	Totals	69	14	14	28	47	—	—	—	—	—

Born; 3/22/75, Altona, Alberta. 6-0, 180. Selected by Wichita in 1999 CHL Dispersal Draft. Selected by Indianapolis in 1999 CHL Expansion Draft. Last amateur club; Bemidji State (NCHA).

Scott Dickson — Center

Season	Team	League	GP	G	A	PTS	PIM	GP	G	A	PTS	PIM
			Regular Season					Playoffs				
97-98	Wheeling	ECHL	2	0	0	0	2	—	—	—	—	—
98-99	Wichita	CHL	6	0	0	0	28	—	—	—	—	—
98-99	Topeka	CHL	30	2	3	5	48	—	—	—	—	—
	CHL	Totals	36	2	3	5	76	—	—	—	—	—

Born; 12/5/76, Brandon, Manitoba. 6-1, 215.

Derek Diener — Defenseman

Season	Team	League	GP	G	A	PTS	PIM	GP	G	A	PTS	PIM
			Regular Season					Playoffs				
97-98	Worcester	AHL	32	2	5	7	88	—	—	—	—	—
97-98	Peoria	ECHL	4	2	2	4	4	—	—	—	—	—
98-99	Worcester	AHL	39	1	5	6	39	—	—	—	—	—
	AHL	Totals	71	3	10	13	127	—	—	—	—	—

Born; 7/13/76, Burnaby, British Columbia. 6-3, 185. Drafted by Philadelphia Flyers (6th choice, 192nd overall) in 1994 Entry Draft. Signed as a free agent by St. Louis Blues (3/19/97). Last amateur club; Kelowna (WHL).

Sam Dietelbaum — Goaltender

Season	Team	League	GP	W	L	T	MIN	SO	AVG	GP	W	L	MIN	SO	AVG
			Regular Season							Playoffs					
98-99	Pensacola	ECHL	2	0	0	0	73	0	3.28	—	—	—	—	—	—

Born;

Travis Dillabough — Center

Season	Team	League	GP	G	A	PTS	PIM	GP	G	A	PTS	PIM
			Regular Season					Playoffs				
97-98	Huntington	ECHL	59	9	14	23	44	3	0	0	0	6
98-99	Dayton	ECHL	54	7	18	25	91	4	0	2	2	8
	ECHL	Totals	113	16	32	48	135	7	0	2	2	14

Born; 6/20/75, Peterborough, Ontario. 6-0, 195. Last amateur club; Providence (Hockey East).

Joe Dimaline — Goaltender

Regular Season / Playoffs

Season	Team	League	GP	W	L	T	MIN	SO	AVG	GP	W	L	MIN	SO	AVG
97-98	Muskegon	UHL	43	26	11	4	2434	2	2.88	11	6	*5	684	0	3.68
98-99	Muskegon	UHL	44	29	9	4	2412	*4	*2.36	*16	*11	5	*920	*2	2.74
	UHL	Totals	87	55	20	8	4846	6	2.62	27	17	10	1604	2	3.14

Born; 9/7/72, North York, Ontario. 5-9, 171. 1998-99 UHL Goaltender of the Year. 1998-99 UHL First Team All-Star. Member of 1998-99 UHL Champion Muskegon Fury. Last amateur club; York (OUAA).

Gord Dineen — Defenseman

Regular Season / Playoffs

Season	Team	League	GP	G	A	PTS	PIM	GP	G	A	PTS	PIM
82-83	Islanders	NHL	2	0	0	0	4	—	—	—	—	—
82-83	Indianapolis	CHL	73	10	47	57	78	13	2	10	12	29
83-84	Islanders	NHL	43	1	11	12	32	9	1	1	2	28
83-84	Indianapolis	CHL	26	4	13	17	63	—	—	—	—	—
84-85	Islanders	NHL	48	1	12	13	89	10	0	0	0	26
84-85	Springfield	AHL	25	1	8	9	46	—	—	—	—	—
85-86	Islanders	NHL	57	1	8	9	81	3	0	0	0	2
85-86	Springfield	AHL	11	2	3	5	20	—	—	—	—	—
86-87	Islanders	NHL	71	4	10	14	110	7	0	4	4	4
87-88	Islanders	NHL	57	4	12	16	62	—	—	—	—	—
87-88	Minnesota	NHL	13	1	1	2	21	—	—	—	—	—
88-89	Minnesota	NHL	2	0	1	1	2	—	—	—	—	—
88-89	Pittsburgh	NHL	38	1	2	3	42	11	0	2	2	8
88-89	Kalamazoo	IHL	25	2	6	8	49	—	—	—	—	—
89-90	Pittsburgh	NHL	69	1	8	9	125	—	—	—	—	—
90-91	Pittsburgh	NHL	9	0	0	0	4	—	—	—	—	—
90-91	Muskegon	IHL	40	1	14	15	57	5	0	2	2	0
91-92	Pittsburgh	NHL	1	0	0	0	0	—	—	—	—	—
91-92	Muskegon	IHL	79	8	37	45	83	14	2	4	6	33
92-93	Ottawa	NHL	32	2	4	6	30	—	—	—	—	—
92-93	San Diego	IHL	41	6	23	29	36	—	—	—	—	—
93-94	Ottawa	NHL	77	0	21	21	89	—	—	—	—	—
93-94	San Diego	IHL	3	0	0	0	2	—	—	—	—	—
94-95	Islanders	NHL	9	0	0	0	2	—	—	—	—	—
94-95	Denver	IHL	68	5	27	32	75	17	1	6	7	8
95-96	Utah	IHL	82	1	17	18	89	22	0	3	3	14
96-97	Utah	IHL	81	5	29	34	62	7	0	3	3	4
97-98	Utah	IHL	82	3	34	37	63	4	0	2	2	2
98-99	Utah	IHL	77	5	22	27	78	—	—	—	—	—
	NHL	Totals	528	16	90	106	693	40	1	7	8	68
	IHL	Totals	578	36	209	245	594	69	3	20	23	61
	CHL	Totals	99	14	60	74	141	13	2	10	12	29
	AHL	Totals	36	3	11	14	66	—	—	—	—	—

Born; 9/21/62, Quebec City, Quebec. 6-0, 195. Drafted by New York Islanders (2nd choice, 42nd overall) in 1981 Entry Draft. Traded to Minnesota North Stars by Islanders for Chris Pryor and future considerations (3/8/88). Traded to Pittsburgh Penguins by Minnesota with Scott Bjustad for Ville Siren and Steve Gotaas (12/17/88). Signed as a free agent by Ottawa Senators (8/31/92). Signed as a free agent by Islanders (7/26/94). 1982-83 CHL First All-Star Team. 1982-83 Won Bob Gassoff Trophy (CHL's Most Improved Defenseman). 1982-83 Won Bobby Orr Trophy (CHL's Top Defenseman). 1991-92 IHL First Team All-Star. 1997-98 IHL Second Team All-Star. Member of 1982-83 CHL champion Indianapolis Checkers. Member of 1994-95 IHL champion Denver Grizzlies. Member of 1995-96 IHL champion Utah Grizzlies. Last amateur club; Sault Ste. Marie (OHL).

Chris Dingman — Left Wing

Regular Season / Playoffs

Season	Team	League	GP	G	A	PTS	PIM	GP	G	A	PTS	PIM
95-96	Brandon	WHL	40	16	29	45	109	19	12	11	23	60
95-96	Saint John	AHL	—	—	—	—	—	1	0	0	0	0
96-97	Saint John	AHL	71	5	6	11	195	—	—	—	—	—
97-98	Calgary	NHL	70	3	3	6	149	—	—	—	—	—
98-99	Calgary	NHL	2	0	0	0	17	—	—	—	—	—
98-99	Colorado	NHL	1	0	0	0	7	—	—	—	—	—
98-99	Saint John	AHL	50	5	7	12	140	—	—	—	—	—
98-99	Hershey	AHL	17	1	3	4	102	5	0	2	2	6
	NHL	Totals	73	3	3	6	173	—	—	—	—	—
	AHL	Totals	138	11	16	27	437	6	0	2	2	6

Born; 7/6/76, Edmonton, Alberta. 6-4, 245. Drafted by Calgary Flames (1st choice, 19th overall) in 1994 Entry Draft. Traded to Colorado Avalanche by Calgary with Theo Fleury for Rene Corbet, Wade Belak, Robyn Regehr and a conditional draft pick (2/28/99). Last amateur club; Brandon (WHL).

Jim Dinneen — Goaltender

Regular Season / Playoffs

Season	Team	League	GP	W	L	T	MIN	SO	AVG	GP	W	L	MIN	SO	AVG
98-99	Fort Worth	WPHL	11	2	5	2	547	0	4.06	—	—	—	—	—	—
98-99	Binghamton	UHL	2	0	1	0	63	0	4.75	—	—	—	—	—	—

Born; 8/27/75, Hanover, Massachusetts. 5-9, 170. Last amateur club; Elmira (NCAA 3).

Gilbert Dionne — Left Wing

Regular Season / Playoffs

Season	Team	League	GP	G	A	PTS	PIM	GP	G	A	PTS	PIM
90-91	Montreal	NHL	2	0	0	0	0	—	—	—	—	—
90-91	Fredericton	AHL	77	40	47	87	62	9	6	5	11	8
91-92	Montreal	NHL	39	21	13	34	10	11	3	4	7	10
91-92	Fredericton	AHL	29	19	27	46	20	—	—	—	—	—
92-93	Montreal	NHL	75	20	28	48	63	20	6	6	12	20
92-93	Fredericton	AHL	3	4	3	7	0	—	—	—	—	—
93-94	Montreal	NHL	74	19	26	45	31	5	1	2	3	0
94-95	Montreal	NHL	6	0	3	3	2	—	—	—	—	—
94-95	Philadelphia	NHL	20	0	6	6	2	3	0	0	0	4
95-96	Philadelphia	NHL	2	0	1	1	0	—	—	—	—	—
95-96	Florida	NHL	5	1	2	3	0	—	—	—	—	—
95-96	Carolina	AHL	55	43	58	101	29	—	—	—	—	—
96-97	Carolina	AHL	72	41	47	88	69	—	—	—	—	—
97-98	Cincinnati	IHL	76	42	57	99	54	9	3	4	7	28
98-99	Cincinnati	IHL	76	35	53	88	123	3	0	2	2	6
	NHL	Totals	223	61	79	140	108	39	10	12	22	34
	AHL	Totals	164	106	135	241	111	9	6	5	11	8
	IHL	Totals	152	77	110	187	177	12	3	6	9	34

Born; 9/19/70, Drummondville, Quebec. 6-0, 194. Drafted by Montreal Canadiens (5th choice, 81st overall) in 1990 Entry Draft. Traded to Philadelphia Flyers by Montreal with Eric Desjardins and John LeClair for Mark Recchi and Philadelphia's third round choice (Martin Hohenberger) in 1995 Entry Draft (2/9/95). Signed as a free agent by Florida Panthers (1/29/96). Member of 1992-93 Stanley Cup champion Montreal Canadiens. 1995-96 AHL Second Team All-Star. 1997-98 IHL First Team All-Star. Last amateur club; Kitchener (OHL).

Paul DiPietro — Center

Regular Season / Playoffs

Season	Team	League	GP	G	A	PTS	PIM	GP	G	A	PTS	PIM
90-91	Fredericton	AHL	78	39	31	70	38	9	5	6	11	2
91-92	Montreal	NHL	33	4	6	10	25	—	—	—	—	—
91-92	Fredericton	AHL	43	26	31	57	52	7	3	4	7	8
92-93	Montreal	NHL	29	4	13	17	14	17	8	5	13	8
92-93	Fredericton	AHL	26	8	16	24	16	—	—	—	—	—
93-94	Montreal	NHL	70	13	20	33	37	7	2	4	6	2
94-95	Montreal	NHL	22	4	5	9	4	—	—	—	—	—
94-95	Toronto	NHL	12	1	1	2	6	7	1	1	2	0
95-96	Toronto	NHL	20	4	4	8	4	—	—	—	—	—
95-96	St. John's	AHL	2	2	2	4	0	—	—	—	—	—
95-96	Houston	IHL	36	18	23	41	44	—	—	—	—	—
95-96	Las Vegas	IHL	13	5	6	11	10	13	4	8	12	16
96-97	Los Angeles	NHL	6	1	0	1	6	—	—	—	—	—
96-97	Phoenix	IHL	33	9	20	29	32	—	—	—	—	—
96-97	Cincinnati	IHL	32	15	14	29	28	3	1	1	2	2
97-98	Kassel	Germany	48	20	32	52	16	—	—	—	—	—
98-99	Ambri-Piotta	Switz.	45	38	44	82	22	15	6	12	18	22
	NHL	Totals	192	31	49	80	96	31	11	10	21	10
	AHL	Totals	149	75	80	155	110	16	8	10	18	10
	IHL	Totals	114	47	63	110	114	16	5	9	14	18

Born; 9/18/70, Sault Ste. Marie, Ontario. 5-9, 181. Drafted by Montreal Canadiens (6th choice, 102nd overall) in 1990 Entry Draft. Traded to Toronto Maple Leafs by Montreal for a conditional fourth round choice (Phoenix's 1996 choice-previously acquired by Toronto-Montreal selected Kim Staal) (4/6/95). Signed as a free agent by Los Angeles Kings (7/23/96). Member of 1992-93 Stanley Cup Champion Montreal Canadiens. Last amateur club; Sudbury (OHL).

Jason Disher — Defenseman

Regular Season / Playoffs

Season	Team	League	GP	G	A	PTS	PIM	GP	G	A	PTS	PIM
95-96	Prince Edward Island	AHL	10	0	1	1	13	—	—	—	—	—
95-96	Thunder Bay	CoHL	40	0	15	15	167	18	1	4	5	73
96-97	Thunder Bay	CoHL	60	9	13	22	240	11	6	3	9	56
97-98	Columbus	ECHL	21	1	5	6	122	—	—	—	—	—
97-98	Wheeling	ECHL	32	3	6	9	111	15	1	3	4	33
98-99	Michigan	IHL	1	0	0	0	0	—	—	—	—	—
98-99	Milwaukee	IHL	2	0	0	0	0	—	—	—	—	—
98-99	Madison	UHL	51	6	9	15	158	—	—	—	—	—
98-99	Thunder Bay	UHL	7	0	2	2	21	13	0	4	4	14
	IHL	Totals	3	0	0	0	0	—	—	—	—	—
	UHL	Totals	158	15	39	54	586	42	7	11	18	143
	ECHL	Totals	53	4	11	15	233	15	1	3	4	33

Born; 5/28/75, Windsor, Ontario. 6-2, 208. Drafted by Ottawa Senators (7th choice, 183rd overall) in 1993 Entry Draft. Traded to Wheeling by Columbus with David Brumby for Scott Kirton (1/98). Traded to Thunder Bay by Madison for Chris Torkoff and Dan Myre (3/99). Last amateur club; Kingston (OHL).

Brian Dobbin — Right Wing

Regular Season / Playoffs

Season	Team	League	GP	G	A	PTS	PIM	GP	G	A	PTS	PIM
85-86	London	OHL	59	38	55	93	113	5	2	1	3	9
85-86	Hershey	AHL	2	1	0	1	0	18	5	5	10	21
86-87	Philadelphia	NHL	12	2	1	3	14	—	—	—	—	—
86-87	Hershey	AHL	52	26	35	61	66	5	4	2	6	15
87-88	Philadelphia	NHL	21	3	5	8	6	—	—	—	—	—
87-88	Hershey	AHL	54	36	47	83	58	12	7	8	15	15
88-89	Philadelphia	NHL	14	0	1	1	8	2	0	0	0	17
88-89	Hershey	AHL	59	43	48	91	61	11	7	6	13	12
89-90	Philadelphia	NHL	9	1	1	2	11	—	—	—	—	—
89-90	Hershey	AHL	68	38	47	85	58	—	—	—	—	—
90-91	Hershey	AHL	80	33	43	76	82	7	1	2	3	7
91-92	Boston	NHL	7	1	0	12	22	—	—	—	—	—
91-92	New Haven	AHL	33	16	21	37	20	—	—	—	—	—
91-92	Maine	AHL	33	21	15	36	14	—	—	—	—	—
92-93	Milwaukee	IHL	80	39	45	84	50	6	4	3	7	6
93-94	Milwaukee	IHL	81	48	53	101	73	4	1	0	1	4
94-95	Milwaukee	IHL	76	21	40	61	62	9	0	4	4	2
95-96	Cincinnati	IHL	82	28	37	65	97	17	2	2	4	14
96-97	Grand Rapids	IHL	29	4	5	9	39	—	—	—	—	—
96-97	Muskegon	CoHL	2	0	0	0	2	—	—	—	—	—
96-97	Austin	WPHL	23	14	18	32	25	6	2	5	7	11
97-98	Port Huron	UHL	71	38	46	84	54	4	2	1	3	2
98-99	Port Huron	UHL	21	10	13	23	16	7	0	0	0	0
	NHL	Totals	63	7	8	15	61	2	0	0	0	17
	IHL	Totals	348	140	180	320	321	36	7	9	16	26
	AHL	Totals	331	214	256	470	240	53	24	23	47	70
	UHL	Totals	94	48	59	107	72	11	2	1	3	2

Born; 8/18/66, Petrolia, Ontario. 6-1, 205. Drafted by Philadelphia Flyers (6th choice, 100th overall) in 1984 Entry Draft (6/9/84). Traded to Boston Bruins by Philadelphia with Gord Murphy and third round pick in 1992 Draft (Sergei Zholtok) for Garry Galley, Wes Walz and future considerations (1/2/92). 1988-89 AHL First Team All-Star. 1989-90 AHL Second Team All-Star. 1993-94 IHL Second Team All-Star. Last amateur club; London (OHL).

Josh Dobbyn — Forward

Regular Season / Playoffs

Season	Team	League	GP	G	A	PTS	PIM	GP	G	A	PTS	PIM
98-99	Columbus	CHL	2	0	0	0	5	—	—	—	—	—

Born; Last amateur club; Regina (WHL).

Curtis Doell — Defenseman

Regular Season / Playoffs

Season	Team	League	GP	G	A	PTS	PIM	GP	G	A	PTS	PIM
98-99	Kentucky	AHL	53	2	8	10	166	—	—	—	—	—

Born; 10/3/76, Saskatoon, Saskatchewan. 6-1, 220. Signed as a free agent by Florida Panthers (6/5/98). Last amateur club; Minnesota-Duluth (WCHA).

Paul Doherty — Defenseman

Regular Season / Playoffs

Season	Team	League	GP	G	A	PTS	PIM	GP	G	A	PTS	PIM
98-99	Miami	ECHL	27	5	8	13	34	—	—	—	—	—

Born; 5/28/73, Sudbury, Ontario. 5-11, 200. Selected by Greenville in 1999 ECHL Dispersal Draft. Last amateur club; Acadia (AUAA).

Jason Doig — Defenseman

Regular Season / Playoffs

Season	Team	League	GP	G	A	PTS	PIM	GP	G	A	PTS	PIM
95-96	Laval	QMJHL	5	3	6	9	20	—	—	—	—	—
95-96	Granby	QMJHL	24	4	30	34	91	20	10	22	32	*110
95-96	Winnipeg	NHL	15	1	1	2	28	—	—	—	—	—
95-96	Springfield	AHL	5	0	0	0	28	—	—	—	—	—
96-97	Granby	QMJHL	39	14	33	47	211	5	0	4	4	27
96-97	Las Vegas	IHL	6	0	1	1	19	—	—	—	—	—
96-97	Springfield	AHL	5	0	3	3	2	17	1	4	5	37
97-98	Phoenix	NHL	4	0	1	1	12	—	—	—	—	—
97-98	Springfield	AHL	46	2	25	27	153	3	0	0	0	2
98-99	Phoenix	NHL	9	0	1	1	10	—	—	—	—	—
98-99	Springfield	AHL	32	3	5	8	67	—	—	—	—	—
98-99	Hartford	AHL	8	1	4	5	40	7	1	1	2	39
	NHL	Totals	28	1	3	4	50	—	—	—	—	—
	AHL	Totals	96	6	37	43	290	27	2	5	7	78

Born; 1/29/77, Montreal, Quebec. 6-3, 216. Drafted by Winnipeg Jets (3rd choice, 34th overall) in 1995 Entry Draft. Traded to New York Rangers by Phoenix Coyotes with a sixth round pick (Jay Dardis) in 1999 Entry Draft for Stan Neckar (3/23/99). Last amateur club; Granby (QMJHL).

Andy Doktorchik — Center

Regular Season / Playoffs

Season	Team	League	GP	G	A	PTS	PIM	GP	G	A	PTS	PIM
98-99	Bonnyville	SJHL	61	55	61	116	136	—	—	—	—	—
98-99	Hampton Roads	ECHL	10	1	1	2	4	4	1	0	1	6

Born; Last amateur club; Bonnyville (SJHL).

Robert Dome — Right Wing

Regular Season / Playoffs

Season	Team	League	GP	G	A	PTS	PIM	GP	G	A	PTS	PIM
95-96	Utah	IHL	56	10	9	19	28	—	—	—	—	—
96-97	Long Beach	IHL	13	4	6	10	14	—	—	—	—	—
96-97	Las Vegas	IHL	43	10	7	17	22	—	—	—	—	—
97-98	Pittsburgh	NHL	30	5	2	7	12	—	—	—	—	—
97-98	Syracuse	AHL	36	21	25	46	77	—	—	—	—	—
98-99	Syracuse	AHL	48	18	17	35	70	—	—	—	—	—
98-99	Houston	IHL	20	2	4	6	24	—	—	—	—	—
	IHL	Totals	132	26	26	52	88	—	—	—	—	—
	AHL	Totals	84	39	42	81	147	—	—	—	—	—

Born; 1/29/79, Skalica, Czechoslovakia. 6-2, 205. Drafted by Pittsburgh Penguins (1st choice, 17th overall) in 1997 Entry Draft.

Hnat Domenichelli — Center

Regular Season / Playoffs

Season	Team	League	GP	G	A	PTS	PIM	GP	G	A	PTS	PIM
96-97	Hartford	NHL	13	2	1	3	7	—	—	—	—	—
96-97	Calgary	NHL	10	1	2	3	2	—	—	—	—	—
96-97	Springfield	AHL	39	24	24	48	12	—	—	—	—	—
96-97	Saint John	AHL	1	1	1	2	0	5	5	0	5	2
97-98	Calgary	NHL	31	9	7	16	6	—	—	—	—	—
97-98	Saint John	AHL	48	33	13	46	24	19	7	8	15	14
98-99	Calgary	NHL	23	5	5	10	11	—	—	—	—	—
98-99	Saint John	AHL	51	25	21	46	26	7	4	4	8	2
	NHL	Totals	77	17	15	32	26	—	—	—	—	—
	AHL	Totals	139	83	59	142	62	31	16	12	28	18

Born; 2/17/76, Edmonton, Alberta. 6-0, 175. Drafted by Hartford Whalers (2nd choice, 83rd overall) in 1994 Entry Draft. Traded to Calgary Flames by Hartford with Glen Featherstone, Second round pick (originally acquired from New Jersey—Flames selected Dimitri Kokorev), and third round pick in 1998 Entry Draft for Steve Chiasson and third round pick (originally acquired from Colorado and New York Islanders—Hurricanes selected Francis Lessard), March 5, 1997. Last amateur club; Kamloops (WHL).

Brad Domonsky — Right Wing

Regular Season / Playoffs

Season	Team	League	GP	G	A	PTS	PIM	GP	G	A	PTS	PIM
96-97	Sudbury	OHL	58	10	14	24	301	—	—	—	—	—
96-97	Dayton	ECHL	6	0	0	0	40	—	—	—	—	—
97-98	Chesapeake	ECHL	59	7	6	13	244	3	0	0	0	2
98-99	Waco	WPHL	56	5	15	20	314	4	0	0	0	17
	ECHL	Totals	65	7	6	13	304	3	0	0	0	2

Born; 9/2/77, Sudbury, Ontario. 6-0, 190. Last amateur club; Sudbury (OHL).

Mike Donaghue — Defenseman

Regular Season / Playoffs

Season	Team	League	GP	G	A	PTS	PIM	GP	G	A	PTS	PIM
98-99	Wichita	CHL	25	1	6	7	10	4	0	1	1	2

Born; 9/4/73, Bemidji, Minnesota. 5-11, 175. Last amateur club; Bemidji State (NCAA 2).

Neil Donovan — Left Wing

Regular Season / Playoffs

Season	Team	League	GP	G	A	PTS	PIM	GP	G	A	PTS	PIM
97-98	Houston	IHL	3	0	0	0	0	—	—	—	—	—
97-98	Quebec	IHL	9	0	1	1	12	—	—	—	—	—
97-98	Mobile	ECHL	59	8	6	14	59	—	—	—	—	—
98-99	Paisley	BNL	26	7	12	19	69	—	—	—	—	—
	IHL	Totals	12	0	1	1	12	—	—	—	—	—

Born; 2/1/73, Boston, Massachusetts. 6-2, 195. Last amateur club; Lowell (Hockey East).

Rob Dopson — Goaltender

Regular Season / Playoffs

Season	Team	League	GP	W	L	T	MIN	SO	AVG	GP	W	L	MIN	SO	AVG
90-91	Muskegon	IHL	24	10	10	0	1243	0	4.34	—	—	—	—	—	—
90-91	Louisville	ECHL	3	3	0	0	180	0	4.00	5	3	1	270	0	3.55
91-92	Muskegon	IHL	28	13	12	2	1655	4	3.26	12	8	4	697	0	3.44
92-93	Cleveland	IHL	50	26	15	3	2825	1	3.55	4	0	4	203	0	5.91
93-94	Pittsburgh	NHL	2	0	0	0	45	0	4.00	—	—	—	—	—	—
93-94	Cleveland	IHL	32	9	10	8	1681	0	3.89	—	—	—	—	—	—
94-95	Houston	IHL	41	17	16	2	2102	0	3.40	1	0	0	40	0	9.00
95-96	Louisiana	ECHL	2	1	0	1	120	0	2.00	—	—	—	—	—	—
95-96	Houston	IHL	38	10	13	3	1700	0	3.74	—	—	—	—	—	—
96-97	Houston	IHL	12	5	4	1	637	0	3.39	—	—	—	—	—	—
97-98	Ayr	BSL	40	—	—	—	2394	4	2.48	9	—	—	567	1	2.01
98-99	Ayr	BSL													
98-99	Lake Charles	WPHL	—	—	—	—	—	—	—	9	4	5	541	1	3.21
	IHL	Totals	225	90	80	19	11843	5	3.58	17	8	8	940	0	4.21

Born; 8/21/67, Smith Falls, Ontario. 6-0, 205. Signed as a free agent by Pittsburgh Penguins (7/15/91). Signed as a free agent by Houston (7/6/91). Last amateur club; Wilfrid Laurier (OUAA).

Cory Dosdall — Center

Regular Season / Playoffs

Season	Team	League	GP	G	A	PTS	PIM	GP	G	A	PTS	PIM
96-97	Wichita	CeHL	62	36	36	72	272	9	2	3	5	23
97-98	Wichita	CHL	65	33	39	72	261	14	5	1	6	79
98-99	Wichita	CHL	1	2	0	2	0	—	—	—	—	—
	CHL	Totals	128	71	75	146	533	23	7	4	11	102

Born; 2/1/73, Regina, Saskatchewan. 5-10, 185. 1996-97 CeHL Rookie of the Year. Selected by Topeka in 1998 CHL Expansion Draft. Last amateur club; University of Regina (CWUAA).

Dave Doucette — Defenseman

Regular Season / Playoffs

Season	Team	League	GP	G	A	PTS	PIM	GP	G	A	PTS	PIM
89-90	Erie	ECHL	37	6	31	37	17	—	—	—	—	—
89-90	Winston-Salem	ECHL	21	3	23	26	22	10	0	8	8	4
90-91	Erie	ECHL	40	0	24	24	25	5	0	0	0	2
91-92	Raleigh	ECHL	46	3	14	17	12	2	0	1	1	2
92-93	Dallas	CeHL	50	10	46	56	66	7	0	10	10	10
93-94	Dallas	CeHL	52	9	53	62	93	—	—	—	—	—
93-94	Tulsa	CeHL	10	1	10	11	8	11	2	11	13	6
94-95	Wichita	CeHL	64	20	70	90	81	11	2	12	14	6
95-96	Wichita	CeHL	39	9	28	37	132	—	—	—	—	—
96-97	New Mexico	WPHL	51	5	35	40	45	6	2	5	7	2
97-98	Shreveport	WPHL	68	10	45	55	24	5	4	3	7	0
98-99	Fort Wayne	IHL	1	0	0	0	0	—	—	—	—	—
98-99	San Antonio	CHL	58	11	59	70	110	—	—	—	—	—
	CHL	Totals	273	60	266	326	490	29	4	33	37	22
	ECHL	Totals	144	12	92	104	76	17	0	9	9	8
	WPHL	Totals	119	15	80	95	71	11	6	8	14	2

Born; 9/22/65, Toronto, Ontario. 5-11, 190. 1989-90 ECHL First Team All-Star. 1992-93 CeHL Defenseman of the Year. 1992-93 CeHL First Team All-Star. 1993-94 CeHL First Team All-Star. 1994-95 CeHL First Team All-Star. Member of 1994-95 CeHL champion Wichita Thunder. Last amateur club; Plattsburgh

Darren Dougan — Center

Regular Season / Playoffs

Season	Team	League	GP	G	A	PTS	PIM	GP	G	A	PTS	PIM
97-98	Utah	IHL	1	0	0	0	0	—	—	—	—	—
97-98	Monroe	WPHL	62	29	51	80	46	—	—	—	—	—
98-99	Monroe	WPHL	38	9	32	41	18	—	—	—	—	—
98-99	Central Texas	WPHL	31	19	34	53	14	2	0	0	0	2
	WPHL	Totals	131	57	117	174	78	2	0	0	0	2

Born; 2/21/72, Azilda, Ontario. 5-11, 195. Traded to Central Texas Stampede by Monroe for Josh Boni (1/99). Last amateur club; Laurentian University (OUAA).

Todd Dougherty — Defenseman

Regular Season / Playoffs

Season	Team	League	GP	G	A	PTS	PIM	GP	G	A	PTS	PIM
94-95	Richmond	ECHL	3	0	0	0	15	—	—	—	—	—
94-95	Utica	CoHL	21	0	7	7	92	—	—	—	—	—
94-95	Lakeland	SUN	5	2	1	3	19	—	—	—	—	—
95-96	Huntsville	SHL	37	3	15	18	164	6	0	1	1	29
96-97	Huntsville	CeHL	44	3	12	15	201	6	0	0	0	28
97-98	Idaho	WCHL	22	1	3	4	54	—	—	—	—	—
98-99	Huntsville	CHL	61	4	12	16	96	2	0	0	0	0
	CHL	Totals	105	7	24	31	297	8	0	0	0	28
	SHL	Totals	42	5	16	21	183	6	0	1	1	29

Born; 2/17/71, Alburg, Vermont. 6-0, 215. Member of 1995-96 SHL champion Huntsville Channel Cats. Member of 1998-99 CHL Champion Huntsville Channel Cats. Last amateur club; Rochester Institute of Technology (NCAA 3).

Steve Douglas — Defenseman

Regular Season / Playoffs

Season	Team	League	GP	G	A	PTS	PIM	GP	G	A	PTS	PIM
97-98	Cape Breton	QMJHL	32	2	2	4	145	—	—	—	—	—
97-98	Wheeling	ECHL	10	0	2	2	44	—	—	—	—	—
98-99	Amarillo	WPHL	66	3	13	16	202	—	—	—	—	—

Born; 7/25/77, Scarborough, Ontario. 6-6, 222. Last amateur club; Cape Breton (QMJHL).

Doug Doull — Left Wing

Regular Season / Playoffs

Season	Team	League	GP	G	A	PTS	PIM	GP	G	A	PTS	PIM
98-99	Michigan	IHL	55	4	11	15	227	3	1	1	2	4

Born; 5/31/74, Green Bay, Nova Scotia. 6-2, 216.

Peter Douris — Right Wing

Regular Season / Playoffs

Season	Team	League	GP	G	A	PTS	PIM	GP	G	A	PTS	PIM
85-86	Winnipeg	NHL	11	0	0	0	0	—	—	—	—	—
85-86	Canadian	Olympic	33	16	7	23	18	—	—	—	—	—
86-87	Winnipeg	NHL	6	0	0	0	0	—	—	—	—	—
86-87	Sherbrooke	AHL	62	14	28	42	24	17	7	*15	*22	16
87-88	Winnipeg	NHL	4	0	2	2	0	1	0	0	0	0
87-88	Moncton	AHL	73	42	37	79	53	—	—	—	—	—
88-89	Peoria	IHL	81	28	41	69	32	4	1	2	3	0
89-90	Boston	NHL	36	5	6	11	15	8	0	1	1	8
89-90	Maine	AHL	38	17	20	37	14	—	—	—	—	—
90-91	Boston	NHL	39	2	5	7	9	7	0	1	1	6
90-91	Maine	AHL	35	16	15	31	9	2	3	0	3	2
91-92	Boston	NHL	54	10	13	23	10	7	2	3	5	0
91-92	Maine	AHL	12	4	3	7	2	—	—	—	—	—
92-93	Boston	NHL	19	4	4	8	4	4	1	0	1	0
92-93	Providence	AHL	50	29	26	55	12	—	—	—	—	—
93-94	Anaheim	NHL	74	12	22	34	21	—	—	—	—	—
94-95	Anaheim	NHL	46	10	11	21	12	—	—	—	—	—
95-96	Anaheim	NHL	31	8	7	15	9	—	—	—	—	—
96-97	Milwaukee	IHL	80	36	36	72	14	3	2	2	4	2
97-98	Dallas	NHL	1	0	0	0	0	—	—	—	—	—
97-98	Michigan	IHL	78	26	31	57	29	4	0	5	5	2
98-99	Landshut	Germany	51	17	26	43	59	3	1	0	1	0
	NHL	Totals	321	54	67	121	80	27	3	5	8	14
	AHL	Totals	270	122	129	251	114	19	10	15	25	18
	IHL	Totals	239	90	108	198	75	11	3	9	12	4

Born; 2/19/66, Toronto, Ontario. 6-1, 195. Drafted by Winnipeg Jets (1st choice, 30th overall) in 1984 Entry Draft. Traded to St. Louis Blues by Winnipeg for Kent Carlson and St. Louis' twelfth round selection (Sergei Kharin) in 1989 Entry Draft and St. Louis' fourth round choice (Scott Levins) in 1990 Entry Draft, 9/29/88. Signed as a free agent by Boston Bruins (6/27/89). Signed as a free agent by Anaheim Mighty Ducks (7/22/93). Signed as a free agent by Dallas Stars (7/16/97). Last amateur club; University of New Hampshire (Hockey East).

Pat Dovigi — Goaltender

Regular Season / Playoffs

Season	Team	League	GP	W	L	T	MIN	SO	AVG	GP	W	L	MIN	SO	AVG
97-98	Erie	OHL	41	17	17	2	2174	0	4.44	—	—	—	—	—	—
97-98	New Orleans	ECHL	2	1	1	0	120	0	6.50	—	—	—	—	—	—
98-99	Erie	OHL	12	6	5	0	655	1	4.58	—	—	—	—	—	—
98-99	Toronto	OHL	39	13	21	1	2004	0	4.28	—	—	—	—	—	—

Born; 7/2/79, Sault Ste. Marie, Ontario. 6-0, 180. Drafted by Edmonton Oilers (2nd choice, 46th overall) in 1997 Entry Draft. Last amateur club; Erie (OHL).

Dave Dow — Goaltender

Regular Season / Playoffs

Season	Team	League	GP	W	L	T	MIN	SO	AVG	GP	W	L	MIN	SO	AVG
98-99	San Antonio	CHL	1	0	0	0	20	0	6.00	—	—	—	—	—	—

Born;

Shane Dow — Defenseman

Regular Season / Playoffs

Season	Team	League	GP	G	A	PTS	PIM	GP	G	A	PTS	PIM
97-98	Winston-Salem	UHL	45	1	9	10	23	—	—	—	—	—
97-98	Fort Worth	CHL	1	0	0	0	2	—	—	—	—	—
98-99	Binghamton	UHL	12	0	0	0	6	—	—	—	—	—
	UHL	Totals	57	1	9	10	29	—	—	—	—	—

Born; 10/01/76, Peterborough, Ontario. 6-1, 205.

Jim Dowd — Center

Regular Season / Playoffs

Season	Team	League	GP	G	A	PTS	PIM	GP	G	A	PTS	PIM
91-92	New Jersey	NHL	1	0	0	0	0	—	—	—	—	—
91-92	Utica	AHL	78	17	42	59	47	4	2	2	4	4
92-93	New Jersey	NHL	1	0	0	0	0	—	—	—	—	—
92-93	Utica	AHL	78	27	45	72	62	5	1	7	8	10
93-94	New Jersey	NHL	15	5	10	15	0	19	2	6	8	8
93-94	Albany	AHL	58	26	37	63	76	—	—	—	—	—
94-95	New Jersey	NHL	10	1	4	5	0	11	2	1	3	8
95-96	New Jersey	NHL	28	4	9	13	17	—	—	—	—	—
95-96	Vancouver	NHL	38	1	6	7	6	1	0	0	0	0
96-97	Islanders	NHL	3	0	0	0	0	—	—	—	—	—
96-97	Utah	IHL	48	10	21	31	27	—	—	—	—	—
96-97	Saint John	AHL	24	5	11	16	18	5	1	2	3	0
97-98	Calgary	NHL	48	6	8	14	12	—	—	—	—	—
97-98	Saint John	AHL	35	8	30	38	20	19	3	13	16	10
98-99	Edmonton	NHL	1	0	0	0	0	—	—	—	—	—
98-99	Hamilton	AHL	51	15	29	44	82	11	3	6	9	8
	NHL	Totals	145	17	37	54	35	31	4	7	11	16
	AHL	Totals	324	98	194	292	223	25	7	17	24	22

Born; 12/25/68, Brick, New Jersey. 6-1, 190. Drafted by New Jersey Devils (7th choice, 149th overall) in 1987 Entry Draft. Traded to Hartford Whalers by New Jersey with New Jersey second round choice in 1997 Entry Draft (Dmitri Kokorev) for Jocelyn Lemieux and Hartford's second round choice in 1998 Entry Draft, (12/19/95). Traded to Vancouver Canucks by Hartford with Frantisek Kucera and Hartford's second round choice (Ryan Bonni) in 1997 Entry Draft for Jeff Brown and Vancouver's third round choice in 1998 Entry Draft, (12/19/95). Claimed by Islanders from Vancouver in NHL Waiver Draft (9/30/96). Signed as a free agent by Calgary (8/10/97). Traded to Nashville Predators by Calgary for future considerations (6/26/98). Member of 1994-95 Stanley Cup champion New Jersey Devils. Last amateur club; Lake Superior (CCHA).

John Dowd — Forward

Regular Season / Playoffs

Season	Team	League	GP	G	A	PTS	PIM	GP	G	A	PTS	PIM
98-99	Odessa	WPHL	5	0	0	0	0	—	—	—	—	—

Born; 7/3/73.

Steve Dowhy — Center

Regular Season / Playoffs

Season	Team	League	GP	G	A	PTS	PIM	GP	G	A	PTS	PIM
95-96	Bakersfield	WCHL	58	36	53	89	58	—	—	—	—	—
96-97	Bakersfield	WCHL	63	51	73	124	84	4	2	3	5	12
97-98	Bakersfield	WCHL	63	37	60	97	96	4	0	3	3	5
98-99	Bakersfield	WCHL	67	33	55	88	101	2	1	1	2	2
	WCHL	Totals	251	157	241	398	339	10	3	7	10	19

Born; 7/18/74, Winnipeg, Manitoba. 6-0, 190. 1996-97 WCHL First Team All-Star. Last amateur club; Prince George (WHL).

Aaron Downey — Right Wing

Regular Season / Playoffs

Season	Team	League	GP	G	A	PTS	PIM	GP	G	A	PTS	PIM
95-96	Hampton Roads	ECHL	65	12	11	23	354	—	—	—	—	—
96-97	Manitoba	IHL	2	0	0	0	17	—	—	—	—	—
96-97	Portland	AHL	3	0	0	0	19	—	—	—	—	—
96-97	Hampton Roads	ECHL	64	8	8	16	338	9	0	3	3	26
97-98	Providence	AHL	78	5	10	15	*407	—	—	—	—	—
98-99	Providence	AHL	75	10	12	22	*401	19	1	1	2	46
	AHL	Totals	156	15	22	37	827	19	1	1	2	46
	ECHL	Totals	129	20	19	39	692	9	0	3	3	26

Born; 8/27/74, Shelbourne, Ontario. 6-0, 205. Signed as free agent by Providence (9/30/97). Member of 1998-99 AHL Champion Providence Bruins. Last amateur club; Coral Harbor (Tier II).

Brian Downey — Left Wing

Season	Team	League	GP	G	A	PTS	PIM	GP	G	A	PTS	PIM
			Regular Season					Playoffs				
92-93	New Haven	AHL	6	0	2	2	0	—	—	—	—	—
92-93	Thunder Bay	CoHL	43	17	31	48	14	11	4	5	9	14
93-94	Thunder Bay	CoHL	61	30	51	81	17	9	3	11	14	2
94-95	Thunder Bay	CoHL	25	13	18	31	23	11	5	7	12	2
95-96	Madison	CoHL	74	30	50	80	62	6	1	6	7	2
96-97	Milwaukee	IHL	1	0	0	0	0	—	—	—	—	—
96-97	Madison	CoHL	63	25	49	74	26	5	0	3	3	2
97-98	Madison	UHL	73	20	86	106	48	7	3	6	9	6
98-99	Milwaukee	IHL	5	0	1	1	0	—	—	—	—	—
98-99	Madison	UHL	63	23	49	72	41	—	—	—	—	—
	IHL	Totals	6	0	1	1	0	—	—	—	—	—
	UHL	Totals	402	158	334	492	231	49	16	38	54	28

Born; 6/30/68, Ottawa, Ontario. 6-1, 190. Selected by Missouri in 1999 UHL Expansion Draft. 1995-96 CoHL Best Defensive Forward. 1996-97 CoHL Best Defensive Forward. 1997-98 UHL First Team All-Star. Member of 1993-94 CoHL Champion Thunder Bay Senators. Member of 1994-95 Colonial Cup Champion Thunder Bay Senators. Last amateur club; University of Maine

Jason Downey — Defenseman

Season	Team	League	GP	G	A	PTS	PIM	GP	G	A	PTS	PIM
			Regular Season					Playoffs				
93-94	Fredericton	AHL	15	0	1	1	35	—	—	—	—	—
93-94	Dayton	ECHL	35	2	22	24	176	3	0	0	0	12
94-95	Cornwall	AHL	—	—	—	—	—	7	0	0	0	28
94-95	Kalamazoo	IHL	3	0	0	0	2	—	—	—	—	—
94-95	Peoria	IHL	4	0	0	0	14	—	—	—	—	—
94-95	Dayton	ECHL	62	7	23	30	282	9	2	15	17	57
95-96	Dayton	ECHL	58	8	22	30	354	3	0	0	0	32
96-97	Dayton	ECHL	50	3	7	10	166	4	1	2	3	16
97-98	New Orleans	ECHL	67	0	17	17	295	4	0	2	2	15
98-99	New Orleans	ECHL	51	1	8	9	213	11	0	2	2	37
	AHL	Totals	15	0	1	1	35	7	0	0	0	28
	IHL	Totals	7	0	0	0	16	—	—	—	—	—
	ECHL	Totals	323	21	99	120	1486	34	3	21	24	169

Born; 7/22/72, Sault Ste. Marie, Ontario. 5-8, 198. Last amateur club; Sherbrooke (QMJHL).

Shane Doyle — Defenseman

Season	Team	League	GP	G	A	PTS	PIM	GP	G	A	PTS	PIM
			Regular Season					Playoffs				
87-88	Oshawa	OHL	21	3	18	21	66	—	—	—	—	—
87-88	Utica	AHL	14	0	1	1	38	—	—	—	—	—
87-88	Flint	IHL	13	1	1	2	81	—	—	—	—	—
88-89	Indianapolis	IHL	62	4	36	40	224	—	—	—	—	—
89-90	Winston-Salem	ECHL	7	1	4	5	44	—	—	—	—	—
90-91												
91-92												
92-93												
93-94												
94-95												
95-96	Detroit	CoHL	13	0	2	2	62	—	—	—	—	—
95-96	Saginaw	CoHL	15	1	3	4	68	—	—	—	—	—
95-96	Toledo	ECHL	2	0	0	0	23	—	—	—	—	—
95-96	Daytona Beach	SHL	8	4	7	11	48	4	0	0	0	50
96-97	Alaska	WCHL	22	3	13	16	106	—	—	—	—	—
96-97	Jacksonville	ECHL	14	0	4	4	83	—	—	—	—	—
97-98												
98-99	Arkansas	WPHL	41	2	12	14	166	—	—	—	—	—
	IHL	Totals	75	5	37	42	305	—	—	—	—	—
	CoHL	Totals	28	1	5	6	130	—	—	—	—	—
	ECHL	Totals	23	1	8	9	150	—	—	—	—	—

Born; 4/26/67, Lindsay, Ontario. 6-3, 222. Drafted by Vancouver Canucks (3rd choice, 85th overall) in 1985 Entry Draft. Last amateur club; Oshawa (OHL).

Trevor Doyle — Defenseman

Season	Team	League	GP	G	A	PTS	PIM	GP	G	A	PTS	PIM
			Regular Season					Playoffs				
94-95	Cincinnati	IHL	52	0	3	3	139	6	0	0	0	13
95-96	Carolina	AHL	48	1	2	3	117	—	—	—	—	—
96-97	Carolina	AHL	47	3	10	13	288	—	—	—	—	—
97-98	Fort Wayne	IHL	36	1	1	2	201	4	0	0	0	23
98-99	Berlin	Germany	15	1	5	6	8	—	—	—	—	—
98-99	Saint John	AHL	2	0	0	0	5	—	—	—	—	—
98-99	Michigan	IHL	4	0	0	0	2	—	—	—	—	—
	AHL	Totals	97	4	12	16	410	—	—	—	—	—
	IHL	Totals	92	1	4	5	342	10	0	0	0	36

Born; 1/1/74, Ottawa, Ontario. 6-3, 212. Drafted by Florida Panthers (9th choice, 161st overall) in 1993 Entry Draft. Last amateur club; Kingston (OHL).

Etienne Drapeau — Center

Season	Team	League	GP	G	A	PTS	PIM	GP	G	A	PTS	PIM
			Regular Season					Playoffs				
98-99	Victoriaville	QMJHL	4	1	3	4	7	—	—	—	—	—
98-99	Johnstown	ECHL	14	2	4	6	4	—	—	—	—	—

Born; 1/10/78, Quebec City, Quebec. 6-1, 181. Drafted by Montreal Canadiens (5th choice, 99th overall) in 1996 Entry Draft. Last amateur club; Victoriaville (QMJHL).

Tom Draper — Goaltender

Season	Team	League	GP	W	L	T	MIN	SO	AVG	GP	W	L	MIN	SO	AVG
			Regular Season							Playoffs					
87-88	Tappara	Finland	28	16	3	9	1619	0	3.22	—	—	—	—	—	—
88-89	Winnipeg	NHL	2	1	1	0	120	0	6.00	—	—	—	—	—	—
88-89	Moncton	AHL	*54	27	17	5	*2962	2	3.46	7	5	2	419	0	3.44
89-90	Winnipeg	NHL	6	2	4	0	359	0	4.35	—	—	—	—	—	—
89-90	Moncton	AHL	51	20	24	3	2844	1	3.52	—	—	—	—	—	—
90-91	Moncton	AHL	30	15	13	2	1779	1	3.20	—	—	—	—	—	—
90-91	Fort Wayne	IHL	10	5	3	1	564	0	3.40	—	—	—	—	—	—
90-91	Peoria	IHL	10	6	3	1	584	0	3.70	4	2	1	214	0	2.80
91-92	Buffalo	NHL	26	10	9	5	1403	1	3.21	7	3	4	433	1	2.63
91-92	Rochester	AHL	9	4	3	2	531	0	3.16	—	—	—	—	—	—
92-93	Buffalo	NHL	11	5	6	0	664	0	3.70	—	—	—	—	—	—
92-93	Rochester	AHL	5	3	2	0	303	0	4.36	—	—	—	—	—	—
93-94	Islanders	NHL	7	1	3	0	227	0	4.23	—	—	—	—	—	—
93-94	Salt Lake City	IHL	35	7	23	3	1933	0	4.34	—	—	—	—	—	—
94-95	Minnesota	IHL	59	25	20	6	3063	1	3.66	2	0	2	118	0	5.07
95-96	Winnipeg	NHL	1	0	0	0	34	0	5.29	—	—	—	—	—	—
95-96	Milwaukee	IHL	31	14	12	3	1793	1	3.38	—	—	—	—	—	—
96-97	Long Beach	IHL	39	28	7	3	2267	2	2.39	*18	*13	5	*1097	*2	2.24
97-98	Quebec	IHL	43	15	*22	4	2419	2	3.25	—	—	—	—	—	—
97-98	Cleveland	IHL	9	4	*2	2	497	0	2.41	10	5	5	582	0	3.30
98-99	Rochester	AHL	26	14	9	3	1568	0	2.30	2	0	0	86	0	2.79
	NHL	Totals	53	19	23	5	2807	1	3.70	7	3	4	433	1	2.63
	IHL	Totals	236	104	92	23	13120	4	3.36	34	20	13	2011	2	2.77
	AHL	Totals	175	83	68	15	9987	4	3.26	9	5	2	505	0	3.33

Born; 11/20/66, Outremont, Quebec. 5-11, 180. Drafted by Winnipeg Jets (8th choice, 165th overall) in 1985 Entry Draft. Traded to St. Louis Blues by Winnipeg for future considerations (Jim Vesey, 5/24/91) (2/28/91). Traded to Winnipeg by St. Louis for future considerations (5/24/91). Traded to Buffalo Sabres by Winnipeg for Buffalo's seventh round choice (Artur Oktyabrev) in 1992 Entry Draft (6/22/91). Traded to New York Islanders by Buffalo for Islanders' seventh round choice (Steve Plouffe) in 1994 Entry Draft (9/30/93). Signed as a free agent by Winnipeg Jets (12/14/95). Traded to Cleveland by Quebec with Rick Girard, Dale DeGray, Darcy Simon and Jason Ruff for Ryan Mougenal, Rick Hayward, John Craighead, Eric Perrin, Pat Jablonski and rights to Burke Murphy (3/98). Signed as a free agent by Buffalo (10/29/98). 1988-89 AHL Second Team All-Star. 1998-99 Shared Lowest GAA with Martin Biron (Rochester). Member of 1990-91 IHL champion Peoria Rivermen. Last amateur club; Vermont (ECAC).

Barry Dreger — Defenseman

Regular Season / Playoffs

Season	Team	League	GP	G	A	PTS	PIM	GP	G	A	PTS	PIM
91-92	Columbus	ECHL	57	4	24	28	362	—	—	—	—	—
92-93	Columbus	ECHL	37	4	12	16	301	—	—	—	—	—
92-93	Hamilton	AHL	13	0	3	3	50	—	—	—	—	—
93-94	San Diego	IHL	57	2	6	8	166	1	0	0	0	2
94-95	San Diego	IHL	60	5	6	11	217	—	—	—	—	—
95-96	Orlando	IHL	70	4	5	9	314	23	2	1	3	51
96-97	Orlando	IHL	81	10	14	24	387	10	0	0	0	57
97-98	Orlando	IHL	73	3	10	13	385	15	2	1	3	34
98-99	Adirondack	AHL	65	2	2	4	259	—	—	—	—	—
98-99	Orlando	IHL	8	0	0	0	57	13	1	3	4	38
	IHL	Totals	349	24	41	65	1526	62	5	5	10	182
	AHL	Totals	78	2	5	7	309	—	—	—	—	—
	ECHL	Totals	94	8	36	44	663	—	—	—	—	—

Born; 11/28/69, Winnipeg, Manitoba. 6-0, 190. Signed by Detroit Red Wings as a free agent (8/25/98).

Greg Dreveny — Goaltender

Regular Season / Playoffs

Season	Team	League	GP	W	L	T	MIN	SO	AVG	GP	W	L	MIN	SO	AVG
96-97	Birmingham	ECHL	35	21	10	1	1816	0	3.77	8	5	3	511	0	3.87
97-98	Huntington	ECHL	2	0	2	0	120	0	6.00	—	—	—	—	—	—
97-98	Birmingham	ECHL	10	1	7	1	533	0	4.95	—	—	—	—	—	—
97-98	Memphis	CHL	2	1	1	0	120	0	4.50	—	—	—	—	—	—
98-99	Birmingham	ECHL	8	0	4	0	312	0	5.78	—	—	—	—	—	—
	ECHL	Totals	55	22	23	2	2781	0	4.31	8	5	3	511	0	3.87

Born; 6/23/72, Dresden, Ontario. 6-0, 204. Last amateur club; Dalhousie

Scott Drevitch — Defenseman

Regular Season / Playoffs

Season	Team	League	GP	G	A	PTS	PIM	GP	G	A	PTS	PIM
88-89	Maine	AHL	75	10	21	31	51	—	—	—	—	—
89-90	Maine	AHL	13	0	1	1	10	—	—	—	—	—
89-90	Virginia	ECHL	40	14	31	45	46	4	3	3	6	10
90-91	New Haven	AHL	14	1	6	7	4	—	—	—	—	—
90-91	Albany	IHL	20	2	9	11	13	—	—	—	—	—
90-91	Phoenix	IHL	3	0	1	1	4	—	—	—	—	—
91-92	Richmond	ECHL	49	7	42	49	26	7	0	5	5	4
91-92	San Diego	IHL	7	0	0	0	13	—	—	—	—	—
92-93	Richmond	ECHL	34	8	18	26	16	—	—	—	—	—
92-93	Dayton	ECHL	27	9	21	30	20	3	2	4	6	2
95-96	Jacksonville	ECHL	23	5	11	16	83	—	—	—	—	—
95-96	Huntington	ECHL	45	8	22	30	52	—	—	—	—	—
97-98	Grand Rapids	IHL	3	0	0	0	0	—	—	—	—	—
97-98	Las Vegas	IHL	8	0	1	1	2	—	—	—	—	—
97-98	Tacoma	WCHL	57	11	64	75	85	10	2	7	9	18
98-99	Las Vegas	IHL	1	0	0	0	0	—	—	—	—	—
98-99	Tacoma	WCHL	70	11	64	75	79	11	4	11	15	12
	AHL	Totals	102	11	27	38	65	—	—	—	—	—
	IHL	Totals	42	2	11	13	32	—	—	—	—	—
	ECHL	Totals	218	51	145	196	243	14	5	12	17	16
	WCHL	Totals	127	22	128	150	164	21	6	18	24	30

Born; 9/9/65, Brookline, Massachusetts. 5-10, 180. Signed as a free agent by Maine (10/88). 1989-90 ECHL Second Team All-Star. 1997-98 WCHL Second Team All-Star. 1998-99 WCHL Defenseman of the Year. 1998-99 WCHL First Team All-Star. Member of 1998-99 WCHL Champion Tacoma Sabrecats. Last amateur club; Lowell (Hockey East).

Chris Droeske — Defenseman

Regular Season / Playoffs

Season	Team	League	GP	G	A	PTS	PIM	GP	G	A	PTS	PIM
98-99	Bakersfield	WCHL	18	0	0	0	153	—	—	—	—	—

Born; 4/18/68, Ottawa, Ontario. 6-4, 225.

Jimmy Drolet — Defenseman

Regular Season / Playoffs

Season	Team	League	GP	G	A	PTS	PIM	GP	G	A	PTS	PIM
96-97	Fredericton	AHL	57	3	2	5	43	—	—	—	—	—
97-98	Fredericton	AHL	28	1	3	4	38	—	—	—	—	—
97-98	New Orleans	ECHL	10	1	3	4	2	4	1	4	5	0
98-99	Fredericton	AHL	57	3	10	13	61	6	1	2	3	0
	AHL	Totals	142	7	15	22	142	6	1	2	3	0

Born; 2/19/76, Vanier, Quebec. 6-1, 180. Drafted by Montreal Canadiens (7th choice, 122nd overall) in 1994 Entry Draft. Last amateur club; Granby (QMJHL).

P.C. Drouin — Left Wing

Regular Season / Playoffs

Season	Team	League	GP	G	A	PTS	PIM	GP	G	A	PTS	PIM
96-97	Boston	NHL	3	0	0	0	0	—	—	—	—	—
96-97	Providence	AHL	42	12	11	23	10	—	—	—	—	—
97-98	Providence	AHL	7	0	2	2	4	—	—	—	—	—
97-98	Charlotte	ECHL	62	21	46	67	57	7	2	4	6	4
98-99	Bracknell	BSL	52	18	27	45	26	7	4	1	5	0
	AHL	Totals	49	12	13	25	14	—	—	—	—	—

Born; 4/22/76, St. Lambert, Quebec. 6-2, 205. Signed as a free agent by Boston Bruins (10/14/96). Last amateur club; Cornell (ECAC).

John Druce — Right Wing

Regular Season / Playoffs

Season	Team	League	GP	G	A	PTS	PIM	GP	G	A	PTS	PIM
86-87	Binghamton	AHL	77	13	9	22	131	12	0	3	3	28
87-88	Binghamton	AHL	68	32	29	61	82	1	0	0	0	0
88-89	Washington	NHL	48	8	7	15	62	1	0	0	0	0
88-89	Baltimore	AHL	16	2	11	13	10	—	—	—	—	—
89-90	Washington	NHL	45	8	3	11	52	15	14	3	17	23
89-90	Baltimore	AHL	26	15	16	31	38	—	—	—	—	—
90-91	Washington	NHL	80	22	36	58	46	11	1	1	2	7
91-92	Washington	NHL	67	19	18	37	39	7	1	0	1	2
92-93	Winnipeg	NHL	50	6	14	20	37	2	0	0	0	0
93-94	Los Angeles	NHL	55	14	17	31	50	—	—	—	—	—
93-94	Phoenix	IHL	8	5	6	11	9	—	—	—	—	—
94-95	Los Angeles	NHL	43	15	5	20	20	—	—	—	—	—
95-96	Los Angeles	NHL	64	9	12	21	14	—	—	—	—	—
95-96	Philadelphia	NHL	13	4	4	8	13	2	0	2	2	2
96-97	Philadelphia	NHL	43	7	8	15	12	13	1	0	1	2
97-98	Philadelphia	NHL	23	1	2	3	2	2	0	0	0	2
97-98	Philadelphia	AHL	39	21	28	49	45	—	—	—	—	—
98-99	Hannover	Germany	36	15	7	22	34	—	—	—	—	—
	NHL	Totals	531	113	126	239	347	53	17	6	23	38
	AHL	Totals	226	83	93	176	306	13	0	3	3	28

Born; 2/23/66, Peterborough, Ontario. 6-2, 195. Drafted by Washington Capitals (2nd choice, 40th overall) in 1985 Entry Draft. Traded to Winnipeg Jets by Washington with Toronto's fourth round choice (previously acquired by Washington-later traded to Detroit Red Wings-Detroit selected John Jakopin) in 1993 Entry Draft. for Pat Elynuik (10/1/92). Signed as a free agent by Los Angeles Kings (8/2/93). Traded to Philadelphia Flyers by Los Angeles with Los Angeles' seventh round draft chioce (Todd Fedoruk) in 1997 Entry Draft for Los Angeles' fourth round choice (previously acquired by Philadelphia-Los Angeles selected Mikael Simons) in 1996 Entry Draft. Last amateur club; Peterborough (OHL).

Stan Drulia — Right Wing

Regular Season / Playoffs

Season	Team	League	GP	G	A	PTS	PIM	GP	G	A	PTS	PIM
88-89	Niagara Falls	OHL	47	52	93	145	59	17	11	*26	37	18
88-89	Maine	AHL	3	1	1	2	0	—	—	—	—	—
89-90	Cape Breton	AHL	31	5	7	12	2	—	—	—	—	—
89-90	Phoenix	IHL	16	6	3	9	2	—	—	—	—	—
90-91	Knoxville	ECHL	64	*63	77	*140	39	3	3	2	5	4
91-92	New Haven	AHL	77	49	53	102	46	5	2	4	6	4
92-93	Tampa Bay	NHL	24	2	1	3	10	—	—	—	—	—
92-93	Atlanta	IHL	47	28	26	54	38	3	2	3	5	4
93-94	Atlanta	IHL	79	54	60	114	70	14	13	12	25	8
94-95	Atlanta	IHL	66	41	49	90	60	5	1	5	6	2
95-96	Atlanta	IHL	75	38	56	94	80	3	0	2	2	18
96-97	Detroit	IHL	73	33	38	71	42	21	5	*21	26	14
97-98	Detroit	IHL	58	25	35	60	50	15	2	4	6	16
98-99	Detroit	IHL	82	23	52	75	64	11	5	4	9	10
	IHL'	Totals	496	248	319	567	406	72	28	51	79	72
	AHL	Totals	111	55	61	116	48	5	2	4	6	4

Born; 1/5/68, Elmira, New York. 5-10, 180. Drafted by Pittsburgh Penguins (11th choice, 214th overall) in 1986 Entry Draft. Signed as a free agent by Edmonton Oilers (5/89). Signed as a free agent by Tampa Bay Lightning (9/1/92). 1990-91 First Team ECHL All-Star. 1990-91 ECHL MVP. 1991-92 AHL Second Team All-Star. 1993-94 IHL First Team All-Star. 1994-95 IHL First Team All-Star. 1998-99 IHL Ironman of the Year. Member of 1993-94 IHL champion Atlanta Knights. Member of 1996-97 IHL Champion Detroit Vipers. Last amateur club;

Christian Dube — Right Wing

Regular Season / Playoffs

Season	Team	League	GP	G	A	PTS	PIM	GP	G	A	PTS	PIM
96-97	Hull	QMJHL	19	15	22	37	37	14	7	16	23	14
96-97	Rangers	NHL	27	1	1	2	4	3	0	0	0	0
97-98	Hartford	AHL	79	11	46	57	46	9	0	4	4	6
98-99	Rangers	NHL	6	0	0	0	0	—	—	—	—	—
98-99	Hartford	AHL	58	21	30	51	20	6	0	3	3	4
	NHL	Totals	33	1	1	2	4	3	0	0	0	0
	AHL	Totals	137	32	76	108	66	15	0	7	7	10

Born; 4/25/77, Sherbrooke, Quebec. 5-11, 170. Drafted by New York Rangers (1st choice, 39th overall) in 1995 Entry Draft. Last amateur club; Hull (QMJHL).

Jean-Yves Dube — Goaltender

Regular Season / Playoffs

Season	Team	League	GP	W	L	T	MIN	SO	AVG	GP	W	L	MIN	SO	AVG
98-99	Flint	UHL	12	0	2	0	260	0	5.77	—	—	—	—	—	—
98-99	Saginaw	UHL	2	0	1	0	108	0	8.29	—	—	—	—	—	—
	UHL	Totals	14	0	3	0	369	0	6.51	—	—	—	—	—	—

Born; 1/23/75, Sept-Iles, Quebec. 6-4, 225.

Eric Dubois — Defenseman

Regular Season / Playoffs

Season	Team	League	GP	G	A	PTS	PIM	GP	G	A	PTS	PIM
91-92	Halifax	AHL	14	0	0	0	8	—	—	—	—	—
91-92	New Haven	AHL	1	0	0	0	2	—	—	—	—	—
91-92	Greensboro	ECHL	36	7	17	24	62	11	4	4	8	40
92-93	Oklahoma City	CeHL	25	5	20	25	70	—	—	—	—	—
92-93	Atlanta	IHL	43	3	9	12	44	9	0	0	0	10
93-94	Atlanta	IHL	80	13	26	39	174	14	0	7	7	48
94-95	Atlanta	IHL	56	3	25	28	56	5	0	3	3	24
95-96	Atlanta	IHL	20	1	5	6	40	—	—	—	—	—
95-96	Chicago	IHL	45	2	8	10	39	—	—	—	—	—
96-97	Manitoba	IHL	80	8	17	25	60	—	—	—	—	—
97-98	Revier Lowen	Germany	46	2	8	10	110	—	—	—	—	—
98-99	Nottingham	BSL	49	1	16	17	34	8	0	4	4	0
	IHL	Totals	324	30	90	120	413	28	0	10	10	82
	AHL	Totals	15	0	0	0	10	—	—	—	—	—

Born; 5/9/70, Montreal, Quebec. 6-0, 195. Drafted by Quebec Nordiques (6th choice, 76th overall) in 1989 Entry Draft. Signed as a free agent by Tampa Bay Lightning (6/2/93). Member of 1993-94 IHL Champion Atlanta Knights. Last amateur club; Laval (QMJHL).

Jonathan DuBois — Center

Regular Season / Playoffs

Season	Team	League	GP	G	A	PTS	PIM	GP	G	A	PTS	PIM
95-96	Huntsville	SHL	59	28	55	83	230	10	5	6	11	37
95-96	Flint	CoHL	1	0	0	0	0	8	1	1	2	14
96-97	Huntsville	CeHL	62	15	49	64	307	9	2	13	15	17
97-98	Huntsville	CHL	70	37	87	124	220	3	0	5	5	4
98-99	Manitoba	IHL	2	1	0	1	0	—	—	—	—	—
98-99	Huntsville	CHL	58	28	71	99	140	15	3	*16	*19	19
	CHL	Totals	190	80	207	287	667	27	5	34	39	40

Born; 3/8/74, Drummondville, Quebec. 5-9, 180. Member of 1995-96 SHL Champion Huntsville Channel Cats. Member of 1995-96 CoHL Champion Flint Generals. Member of 1998-99 CHL Champion Huntsville Channel Cats.

Robert DuBois — Left Wing

Regular Season / Playoffs

Season	Team	League	GP	G	A	PTS	PIM	GP	G	A	PTS	PIM
96-97	Dayton	CoHL	12	3	4	7	8	—	—	—	—	—
96-97	Thunder Bay	CoHL	21	6	7	13	6	—	—	—	—	—
96-97	Brantford	CoHL	18	7	5	12	22	—	—	—	—	—
96-97	Madison	CoHL	6	2	4	6	4	3	0	0	0	0
97-98												
98-99	Monroe	WPHL	13	2	2	4	2	—	—	—	—	—
	CoHL	Totals	57	18	20	38	40	3	0	0	0	0

Born; 3/19/76, Sudbury, Ontario. 6-0, 220. Last amateur club; Barrie (OHL).

Bryan Duce — Right Wing

Regular Season / Playoffs

Season	Team	League	GP	G	A	PTS	PIM	GP	G	A	PTS	PIM
98-99	Albany	AHL	2	0	0	0	2	—	—	—	—	—
98-99	Augusta	ECHL	68	17	27	44	33	2	0	0	0	0

Born; 1/15/78, Thunder Bay, Ontario. 6-0, 190. Signed as a free agent by New Jersey Devils (8/12/97). Last amateur club; Sault Ste. Marie (OHL).

Landon Duchon — Center

Regular Season / Playoffs

Season	Team	League	GP	G	A	PTS	PIM	GP	G	A	PTS	PIM
97-98	Straubing	Germany	25	9	20	29	18	—	—	—	—	—
98-99	Central Texas	WPHL	15	6	7	13	6	—	—	—	—	—
98-99	Ingolstadt	Germany	8	0	0	0	2	—	—	—	—	—

Born; 4/6/73, Winnipeg, Manitoba. 5-10, 180.

Jason Duda — Left Wing

Regular Season / Playoffs

Season	Team	League	GP	G	A	PTS	PIM	GP	G	A	PTS	PIM
96-97	Oklahoma City	CeHL	15	2	6	8	11	—	—	—	—	—
96-97	Wichita	CeHL	39	15	15	30	34	9	2	7	9	19
97-98	Wichita	CHL	60	32	33	65	62	15	9	12	21	10
98-99	Wichita	CHL	34	13	24	37	20	4	1	0	1	2
	CHL	Totals	148	62	78	140	127	28	12	19	31	31

Born; 5/5/75, Sexsmith, Alberta. 5-10, 185. Traded to Wichita Thunder by Oklahoma City Blazers for David Shute (1997).

Rhett Dudley — Defenseman

Regular Season / Playoffs

Season	Team	League	GP	G	A	PTS	PIM	GP	G	A	PTS	PIM
95-96	Wheeling	ECHL	1	0	0	0	0	—	—	—	—	—
95-96	Knoxville	ECHL	3	0	0	0	14	—	—	—	—	—
96-97	Tulsa	CeHL	65	8	12	20	114	5	0	2	2	10
97-98	Tulsa	CHL	67	13	28	41	126	4	0	1	1	4
98-99	Wichita	CHL	53	8	26	34	149	4	0	3	3	6
	CHL	Totals	185	29	66	95	389	13	0	6	6	20
	ECHL	Totals	4	0	0	0	14	—	—	—	—	—

Born; 11/9/74, Wetaskiwia, Alberta. 6-1, 185.

David Duerden — Left Wing

Regular Season / Playoffs

Season	Team	League	GP	G	A	PTS	PIM	GP	G	A	PTS	PIM
97-98	Fort Wayne	IHL	7	0	1	1	0	—	—	—	—	—
97-98	New Haven	AHL	36	6	7	13	10	—	—	—	—	—
97-98	Port Huron	UHL	7	0	4	4	10	—	—	—	—	—
98-99	Kentucky	AHL	36	8	9	17	9	6	0	2	2	0
98-99	Miami	ECHL	13	10	7	17	0	—	—	—	—	—
	AHL	Totals	72	14	16	30	19	6	0	2	2	0

Born; 4/11/77, Oshawa, Onatrio. 6-2, 201. Drafted by Florida Panthers (4th chioce, 80th overall) in 1995 Entry Draft. Last amateur club; Peterborough

Parris Duffus — Goaltender

Regular Season / Playoffs

Season	Team	League	GP	W	L	T	MIN	SO	AVG	GP	W	L	MIN	SO	AVG
92-93	H. Roads	ECHL	4	3	1	0	245	0	3.18	—	—	—	—	—	—
92-93	Peoria	IHL	37	16	15	4	2149	0	3.96	1	0	1	59	0	5.08
93-94	Peoria	IHL	36	19	10	3	1845	0	4.58	2	0	1	92	0	3.88
94-95	Peoria	IHL	29	17	7	3	1581	*3	2.69	7	4	2	409	0	2.49
95-96	Minnesota	IHL	35	10	17	2	1812	1	3.31	—	—	—	—	—	—
96-97	Phoenix	NHL	1	0	0	0	29	0	2.07	—	—	—	—	—	—
96-97	Las Vegas	IHL	58	28	19	6	3266	3	3.23	3	0	3	175	0	2.73
97-98	Hameenlinna	Finland	31	11	13	0	1436	0	3.30	—	—	—	—	—	—
98-99	Berlin	Germany	38	—	—	—	2256	1	3.35	—	—	—	—	—	—
98-99	Jokerit	Finland	15	7	8	0	894	5	2.28	3	0	3	167	0	4.67
	IHL	Totals	195	90	68	18	10654	7	3.55	13	4	7	560	0	2.93

Born; 1/27/70, Denver, Colorado. 6-2, 192. Drafted by St. Louis Blues (6th choice, 180th overall) in 1990 Entry Draft. Signed as a free agent by Winnipeg Jets (8/4/95). Last amateur club; Cornell (ECAC).

Pierre Dufour — Defenseman

Regular Season / Playoffs

Season	Team	League	GP	G	A	PTS	PIM	GP	G	A	PTS	PIM
97-98	Nashville	ECHL	63	12	37	49	33	9	1	12	13	14
98-99	Tucson	WCHL	9	2	5	7	10	—	—	—	—	—
98-99	Fresno	WCHL	31	5	15	20	11	—	—	—	—	—
98-99	Bakersfield	WCHL	15	3	10	13	6	—	—	—	—	—
	WCHL	Totals	55	10	30	40	27	—	—	—	—	—

Born; 8/3/73, Montreal, Quebec. 5-10, 180. Selected by Tulsa in 1998 CHL Dispersal Draft. Last amateur club; Ohio State (CCHA).

Ron Duguay — Center

Regular Season / Playoffs

Season	Team	League	GP	G	A	PTS	PIM	GP	G	A	PTS	PIM
77-78	Rangers	NHL	71	20	20	40	43	3	1	1	2	2
78-79	Rangers	NHL	79	27	36	63	35	18	5	4	9	11
79-80	Rangers	NHL	73	28	22	50	37	9	5	2	7	11
80-81	Rangers	NHL	50	17	21	38	83	14	8	9	17	16
81-82	Rangers	NHL	72	40	36	76	82	10	5	1	6	31
82-83	Rangers	NHL	72	19	25	44	58	9	2	2	4	28
83-84	Detroit	NHL	80	33	47	80	34	4	2	3	5	2
84-85	Detroit	NHL	80	38	51	89	51	3	1	0	1	7
85-86	Detroit	NHL	67	19	29	48	26	—	—	—	—	—
85-86	Pittsburgh	NHL	13	6	7	13	6	—	—	—	—	—
86-87	Pittsburgh	NHL	40	5	13	18	30	—	—	—	—	—
86-87	Rangers	NHL	34	9	12	21	9	6	2	0	2	4
87-88	Rangers	NHL	48	4	4	8	23	—	—	—	—	—
87-88	Colorado	IHL	2	0	0	0	0	—	—	—	—	—
87-88	Los Angeles	NHL	15	2	6	8	17	2	0	0	0	0
88-89	Los Angeles	NHL	70	7	17	24	48	11	0	0	0	6
89-90												
90-91	San Diego	IHL	51	15	24	39	87	—	—	—	—	—
91-92	San Diego	IHL	60	18	18	36	32	4	0	1	1	0
92-93												
93-94												
94-95												
95-96	San Diego	WCHL	12	8	9	17	10	7	0	2	2	2
96-97	San Diego	WCHL	2	1	1	2	0	—	—	—	—	—
97-98	San Diego	WCHL	3	0	3	3	2	—	—	—	—	—
98-99	Jacksonville	ECHL	1	0	0	0	0	—	—	—	—	—
	NHL	Totals	864	274	346	620	582	89	31	22	53	118
	IHL	Totals	113	33	42	75	119	4	0	1	1	0
	WCHL	Totals	17	9	13	22	12	7	0	2	2	2

Born; 7/6/57, Sudbury, Ontario. 6-2, 210. Drafted by New York Rangers (2nd choice, 13th overall) in 1977 Amateur Draft. Traded to Detroit Red Wings by Rangers with Eddie Mio and Eddie Johnstone for Willie Huber, Mark Osborne and Mike Blaisdell (6/13/83). Traded to Pittsburgh Penguins by Detroit for Doug Shedden (3/11/86). Traded to Rangers by Pittsburgh for Chris Kontos (1/21/87). Traded to Los Angeles Kings by Rangers for Mark Hardy (2/23/88). Member of 1995-96 WCHL Champion San Diego Gulls. Last amateur club; Sudbury (OHL).

Jim Duhart — Right Wing

Regular Season / Playoffs

Season	Team	League	GP	G	A	PTS	PIM	GP	G	A	PTS	PIM
02-93	West Palm Beach	SUN	44	32	27	59	86	—	—	—	—	—
93-94	Flint	CoHL	62	18	24	42	211	9	1	4	5	70
94-95	Raleigh	ECHL	20	8	8	16	112	—	—	—	—	—
94-95	Flint	CoHL	30	10	7	17	110	—	—	—	—	—
95-96	Flint	CoHL	57	8	25	33	285	5	0	0	0	20
96-97	Saginaw	CoHL	27	11	10	21	79	—	—	—	—	—
96-97	Madison	CoHL	41	26	16	42	108	5	3	4	7	8
97-98	Madison	UHL	73	50	53	103	200	7	5	3	8	12
98-99	Madison	UHL	72	40	28	68	218	—	—	—	—	—
	UHL	Totals	358	161	164	325	1211	26	9	11	20	110

Born; 7/24/71, Ottawa, Ontario. 5-10, 202. Member of 1995-96 Colonial Cup Champion Flint Generals.

Steve Duke — Defenseman

Regular Season / Playoffs

Season	Team	League	GP	G	A	PTS	PIM	GP	G	A	PTS	PIM
98-99	Saint John	AHL	2	0	0	0	0	—	—	—	—	—
98-99	Johnstown	ECHL	54	4	23	27	58	—	—	—	—	—

Born; 8/31/75, Georgetown, Ontario. 5-11, 195. Last amateur club; Western Michigan (CCHA).

Rob Dumas
Regular Season

Defenseman
Playoffs

Season	Team	League	GP	G	A	PTS	PIM	GP	G	A	PTS	PIM
88-89	Peoria	IHL	10	0	0	0	51	4	0	0	0	23
89-90												
90-91	Greensboro	ECHL	64	4	29	33	201	13	2	0	2	32
91-92	Nashville	ECHL	63	9	37	46	215	—	—	—	—	—
92-93	Milwaukee	IHL	1	0	0	0	0	—	—	—	—	—
92-93	Nashville	ECHL	63	13	45	58	191	9	2	0	2	37
93-94	Milwaukee	IHL	8	0	0	0	16	—	—	—	—	—
93-94	Nashville	ECHL	52	11	36	47	203	2	1	0	1	2
94-95	Nashville	ECHL	22	3	8	11	47	—	—	—	—	—
94-95	Tallahassee	ECHL	35	8	27	35	68	13	4	3	7	40
95-96	Milton Keynes	BHL	38	21	38	59	127	—	—	—	—	—
95-96	Billingham	BHL	7	4	5	9	55	—	—	—	—	—
96-97	Tallahassee	ECHL	63	17	33	50	118	3	0	1	1	5
97-98	Cleveland	IHL	2	0	1	1	2	—	—	—	—	—
97-98	Idaho	WCHL	62	10	38	48	93	4	0	1	1	6
98-99	Idaho	WCHL	64	19	38	57	137	2	0	1	1	0
	IHL	Totals	21	0	1	1	69	4	0	0	0	23
	ECHL	Totals	362	65	215	280	1043	40	9	4	13	116
	WCHL	Totals	216	29	76	105	230	6	0	2	2	6

Born; 5/19/69, Spirit River, Alberta. 6-0, 200. Drafted by St. Louis Blues (9th choice, 180th overall) in 1987 Entry Draft. Last amateur club; Seattle (WHL).

Steve Dumonski
Regular Season

Right Wing
Playoffs

Season	Team	League	GP	G	A	PTS	PIM	GP	G	A	PTS	PIM
97-98	Toronto	OHL	27	6	8	14	70	—	—	—	—	—
97-98	Richmond	ECHL	8	2	2	4	17	—	—	—	—	—
98-99	Richmond	ECHL	64	7	12	19	199	17	7	1	8	38
	ECHL	Totals	72	9	14	23	216	17	7	1	8	38

Born; 2/15/77, Dorion, Ontario. 6-1, 210. Last amateur club; Toronto (OHL).

Jean-Pierre Dumont
Regular Season

Right Wing
Playoffs

Season	Team	League	GP	G	A	PTS	PIM	GP	G	A	PTS	PIM
98-99	Chicago	NHL	25	9	6	15	10	—	—	—	—	—
98-99	Portland	AHL	50	32	14	46	39	—	—	—	—	—
98-99	Indianapolis	IHL	—	—	—	—	—	10	4	1	5	6

Born; 4/1/78, Montreal, Quebec. 6-1, 187. Drafted by New York Islanders (1st choice, 3rd overall) in 1996 Entry Draft. Rights traded to Chicago Blackhawks by Islanders for Dmitri Nabokov (5/30/98). 1998-99 AHL All-Rookie Team. Last amateur club; Val d'Or (QMJHL).

Louis Dumont
Regular Season

Center
Playoffs

Season	Team	League	GP	G	A	PTS	PIM	GP	G	A	PTS	PIM
94-95	Tallahassee	ECHL	5	1	0	1	4	—	—	—	—	—
94-95	Wheeling	ECHL	62	25	33	58	81	3	1	1	2	4
95-96	Wheeling	ECHL	66	24	39	63	57	6	0	3	3	6
96-97	Louisiana	ECHL	64	42	45	87	106	17	6	11	17	8
97-98	Manitoba	IHL	5	0	2	2	0	—	—	—	—	—
97-98	Louisiana	ECHL	66	31	48	79	71	12	6	5	11	17
98-99	Louisiana	ECHL	55	30	44	74	66	5	1	1	2	10
	ECHL	Totals	308	153	209	363	385	43	14	21	35	45

Born; 1/30/73, Calgary, Alberta. 5-10, 180. Last amateur club; Kamloops (WHL).

Mario Dumoulin
Regular Season

Defenseman
Playoffs

Season	Team	League	GP	G	A	PTS	PIM	GP	G	A	PTS	PIM
94-95	Halifax	QMJHL	72	23	51	74	240	7	0	5	5	27
94-95	Greensboro	ECHL	—	—	—	—	—	3	0	0	0	4
95-96	Brantford	CoHL	63	3	15	18	102	—	—	—	—	—
95-96	Detroit	CoHL	7	2	1	3	20	7	0	1	1	6
96-97	Birmingham	ECHL	61	3	12	15	328	8	1	6	7	28
97-98	Birmingham	ECHL	5	0	1	1	2	—	—	—	—	—
97-98	Louisiana	ECHL	31	4	8	12	100	—	—	—	—	—
98-99	Abilene	WPHL	33	2	15	17	173	—	—	—	—	—
98-99	Odessa	WPHL	13	3	7	10	34	3	0	0	0	26
	ECHL	Totals	97	7	21	28	430	11	1	6	7	32
	CoHL	Totals	70	5	16	21	122	7	0	1	1	6
	WPHL	Totals	46	5	22	27	207	3	0	0	0	26

Born; 1/11/74, Drummondville, Quebec. 6-1, 193. Traded to Louisiana by Birmingham with Ryan Shanahan and cash for Marc Delorme (1/98). Traded to Odessa by Abilene for Don Lavergne (1/99). Last amateur club; Halifax

Darren Duncalfe
Regular Season

Defenseman
Playoffs

Season	Team	League	GP	G	A	PTS	PIM	GP	G	A	PTS	PIM
97-98	Central Texas	WPHL	28	2	9	11	45	—	—	—	—	—
97-98	San Angelo	WPHL	16	0	4	4	37	—	—	—	—	—
98-99	Central Texas	WPHL	49	2	10	12	93	1	0	0	0	0
	WPHL	Totals	93	4	23	27	175	1	0	0	0	0

Born; 4/21/72, Brandon, Manitoba. 5-11, 190. Last amateur club; Brandon University (CWUAA).

Brett Duncan
Regular Season

Defenseman
Playoffs

Season	Team	League	GP	G	A	PTS	PIM	GP	G	A	PTS	PIM
94-95	Raleigh	ECHL	63	4	4	8	216	—	—	—	—	—
95-96	Saint John	AHL	19	0	0	0	109	—	—	—	—	—
95-96	Los Angeles	IHL	7	0	0	0	32	—	—	—	—	—
96-97	Birmingham	ECHL	27	2	1	3	99	8	0	1	1	8
97-98	Tacoma	WCHL	34	2	5	7	78	9	1	1	2	31
98-99	Tacoma	WCHL	47	0	4	4	81	11	0	1	1	12
	ECHL	Totals	90	6	5	11	315	8	0	1	1	8
	WCHL	Totals	81	2	9	11	159	20	1	2	3	43

Born; 2/15/73, Kitchener, Ontario. 6-0, 220. Drafted by Tampa Bay Lightning (10th choice, 237th overall) in 1993 Entry Draft. Member of 1998-99 WCHL Champion Tacoma Sabrecats. Last amateur club; Seattle (WHL).

Chris Duncan
Regular Season

Defenseman
Playoffs

Season	Team	League	GP	G	A	PTS	PIM	GP	G	A	PTS	PIM
98-99	Fayetteville	CHL	2	0	0	0	6	—	—	—	—	—
98-99	Oklahoma City	CHL	26	1	11	12	40	—	—	—	—	—
	CHL	Totals	28	1	11	12	46	—	—	—	—	—

Born; 3/18/77, Kanata, Ontario. 6-1, 180.

Jon Dunmar
Regular Season

Defenseman
Playoffs

Season	Team	League	GP	G	A	PTS	PIM	GP	G	A	PTS	PIM
97-98	Pensacola	ECHL	28	1	4	5	34	4	0	0	0	4
98-99	Tucson	WCHL	9	0	0	0	15	—	—	—	—	—
98-99	Phoenix	WCHL	7	0	0	0	9	—	—	—	—	—
	WCHL	Totals	16	0	0	0	24	—	—	—	—	—

Born; Westport, Connecticut. 6-1, 200. Selected by Greenville in 1998 ECHL Expansion Draft. Last amateur club; University of Connecticut (NCAA 3).

Jamie Dunn
Regular Season

Right Wing
Playoffs

Season	Team	League	GP	G	A	PTS	PIM	GP	G	A	PTS	PIM
96-97	Waco	WPHL	55	27	24	51	85	—	—	—	—	—
97-98	Waco	WPHL	64	20	25	45	100	—	—	—	—	—
97-98	Reno	WCHL	4	0	3	3	11	—	—	—	—	—
98-99	Odessa	WPHL	58	15	19	34	46	1	0	0	0	0
	WPHL	Totals	177	62	68	130	231	1	0	0	0	0

Born; 11/28/72, Calgary, Alberta. 6-2, 200. Traded to Lake Charles to complete trade for Don Riendeau (5/99).

Dennis Dunphy — Left Wing
Regular Season / Playoffs

Season	Team	League	GP	G	A	PTS	PIM	GP	G	A	PTS	PIM
98-99	Colorado	WCHL	2	0	0	0	32	—	—	—	—	—
98-99	Mohawk Valley	UHL	2	0	0	0	2	—	—	—	—	—

Born; 1/30/76, Boston, Massachusetts. 6-1, 212.

Cosmo DuPaul — Center
Regular Season / Playoffs

Season	Team	League	GP	G	A	PTS	PIM	GP	G	A	PTS	PIM
94-95	Victoriaville	QMJHL	66	26	46	72	32	5	2	2	4	6
94-95	Prince Edward Island	AHL	3	0	1	1	2	1	0	0	0	0
95-96	Thunder Bay	CoHL	63	25	32	57	20	19	5	11	16	4
95-96	Prince Edward Island	AHL	8	1	1	2	2	—	—	—	—	—
96-97	Raleigh	ECHL	14	4	6	10	6	—	—	—	—	—
97-98	Fort Worth	WPHL	68	40	59	99	32	13	5	10	15	6
98-99	Fort Worth	WPHL	67	34	37	71	40	12	7	11	18	2
	AHL	Totals	11	1	2	3	4	1	0	0	0	0
	WPHL	Totals	135	74	96	170	72	25	12	21	33	8

Born; 4/11/75, Pointe-Claire, Quebec. 6-0, 186. Drafted by Ottawa Senators (4th choice, 91st overall) in 1993 Entry Draft. Last amateur club; Victoriaville

George Dupont — Center
Regular Season / Playoffs

Season	Team	League	GP	G	A	PTS	PIM	GP	G	A	PTS	PIM
93-94	Oklahoma City	CeHL	4	4	0	4	27	7	4	4	8	48
94-95	Oklahoma City	CeHL	65	27	78	105	250	5	2	4	6	31
95-96	Oklahoma City	CeHL	61	28	83	111	274	13	2	12	14	64
96-97	Oklahoma City	CeHL	63	31	60	91	328	4	0	6	6	13
97-98	New Mexico	WPHL	69	30	79	109	208	10	4	9	13	37
98-99	New Mexico	WPHL	63	16	55	71	172	—	—	—	—	—
	CeHL	Totals	193	90	221	311	879	29	8	26	34	156
	WPHL	Totals	132	46	134	180	380	10	4	9	13	37

Born; 3/12/67, Nepean, Ontario. 5-10, 200. 1994-95 CeHL Second Team All-Star. Member of 1995-96 CeHL champion Oklahoma City Blazers. Named head coach of the Tupelo T-Rex (WPHL) to begin with 1999-2000 season. Last amateur club; Acadia (AUAA).

Guy Dupuis — Defenseman
Regular Season / Playoffs

Season	Team	League	GP	G	A	PTS	PIM	GP	G	A	PTS	PIM
90-91	Adirondack	AHL	57	4	10	14	73	—	—	—	—	—
91-92	Adirondack	AHL	49	3	6	9	59	3	0	0	0	4
91-92	Fort Wayne	IHL	10	2	7	9	0	—	—	—	—	—
92-93	Fort Wayne	IHL	53	4	11	15	57	4	0	1	1	6
92-93	Adirondack	AHL	1	0	0	0	0	—	—	—	—	—
93-94	Fort Wayne	IHL	73	9	26	35	70	17	1	7	8	28
94-95	Fort Wayne	IHL	77	9	26	35	125	4	0	0	0	6
95-96	Fort Wayne	IHL	81	5	29	34	118	5	0	0	0	2
96-97	Fort Wayne	IHL	80	6	23	29	84	—	—	—	—	—
97-98	Fort Wayne	IHL	77	10	19	29	108	4	0	0	0	4
98-99	Fort Wayne	IHL	58	3	15	18	52	2	1	0	1	0
	IHL	Totals	509	48	156	204	614	36	2	8	10	46
	AHL	Totals	107	7	16	23	132	3	0	0	0	4

Born; 5/10/70, Moncton, New Brunswick. 6-2, 200. Drafted by Detroit Red Wings (3rd choice, 47th overall) in 1988 Entry Draft. Member of 1992-93 IHL champion Fort Wayne Komets. Last amateur club; Hull (QMJHL).

Marc Dupuis — Defenseman
Regular Season / Playoffs

Season	Team	League	GP	G	A	PTS	PIM	GP	G	A	PTS	PIM
96-97	Indianapolis	IHL	32	0	3	3	14	1	0	0	0	0
96-97	Columbus	ECHL	23	2	13	15	8	8	0	3	3	4
97-98	Orlando	IHL	44	6	13	19	10	—	—	—	—	—
97-98	Fort Wayne	IHL	20	0	4	4	22	1	0	1	1	0
98-99	Indianapolis	IHL	55	4	17	21	56	—	—	—	—	—
98-99	Rochester	AHL	11	0	2	2	2	16	0	0	0	4
98-99	Columbus	ECHL	4	0	1	1	2	—	—	—	—	—
	IHL	Totals	151	10	37	47	92	2	0	1	1	0
	ECHL	Totals	27	2	14	16	10	8	0	3	3	4

Born; 4/22/76, Cornwall, Ontario. 6-0, 200. Drafted by Chicago Blackhawks (4th chioce, 118th overall) in 1994 Entry Draft. Last amateur club; Belleville (OHL).

Mark Dutiaume — Left Wing
Regular Season / Playoffs

Season	Team	League	GP	G	A	PTS	PIM	GP	G	A	PTS	PIM
96-97	Brandon	WHL	48	12	11	23	73	6	2	2	4	13
96-97	Rochester	AHL	6	1	1	2	0	—	—	—	—	—
97-98	Rochester	AHL	11	1	0	1	4	—	—	—	—	—
97-98	South Carolina	ECHL	28	3	4	7	24	2	0	0	0	2
98-99	Rochester	AHL	3	0	0	0	0	—	—	—	—	—
98-99	Binghamton	UHL	67	27	35	62	43	1	1	0	1	0
	AHL	Totals	20	2	1	3	4	—	—	—	—	—

Born; 1/31/77, Winnipeg, Manitoba. 6-0, 200. Drafted by Buffalo Sabres (3rd choice, 42nd overall) in 1995 Entry Draft. Last amateur club; Brandon (WHL).

Ales Dvorak — Defenseman
Regular Season / Playoffs

Season	Team	League	GP	G	A	PTS	PIM	GP	G	A	PTS	PIM
98-99	Binghamton	UHL	58	1	5	6	34	5	0	0	0	2

Born; 2/16/78, Czech Budweis, Czech Republic. 6-2, 212. Last amateur club; Bow Valley (Jr. A).

Michal Dvorak — Left Wing
Regular Season / Playoffs

Season	Team	League	GP	G	A	PTS	PIM	GP	G	A	PTS	PIM
98-99	Kitchener	OHL	50	23	23	46	41	1	0	0	0	0
98-99	Peoria	ECHL	4	0	2	2	0	3	0	1	1	2

Born; Last amateur club; Kitchener (OHL)

Gordie Dwyer — Left Wing
Regular Season / Playoffs

Season	Team	League	GP	G	A	PTS	PIM	GP	G	A	PTS	PIM
98-99	Fredericton	AHL	14	0	0	0	46	—	—	—	—	—
98-99	New Orleans	ECHL	36	1	3	4	163	11	0	0	0	27

Born; 1/25/78, Dalhousie, New Brunswick. 6-2, 190. Drafted by St. Louis Blues (2nd choice, 67th overall) in 1996 Entry Draft. Re-entered NHL draft; selected by Monteral Canadiens (5th choice, 152nd overall) in 1998 Entry Draft. Last amateur club; Quebec (QMJHL).

Paul Dyck — Defenseman
Regular Season / Playoffs

Season	Team	League	GP	G	A	PTS	PIM	GP	G	A	PTS	PIM
91-92	Muskegon	IHL	73	6	21	27	40	14	1	3	4	4
92-93	Cleveland	IHL	69	6	21	27	69	1	0	0	0	0
93-94	Cleveland	IHL	60	1	10	11	57	—	—	—	—	—
94-95	Cleveland	IHL	79	5	12	17	59	4	1	3	4	4
95-96	Kansas City	IHL	51	2	5	7	76	—	—	—	—	—
95-96	Detroit	IHL	5	1	1	2	8	7	0	0	0	12
96-97	Kansas City	IHL	49	2	8	10	39	—	—	—	—	—
96-97	Houston	IHL	30	1	4	5	32	13	0	1	1	12
97-98	Houston	IHL	81	6	13	19	82	4	0	0	0	10
98-99	Houston	IHL	76	4	18	22	62	19	2	3	5	18
	IHL	Totals	573	34	113	147	524	62	4	10	14	60

Born; 4/15/71, Winnipeg, Manitoba. 6-1, 200. Drafted by Pittsburgh Penguins (11th pick, 236th overall) in 1991 Entry Draft. Member of 1998-99 IHL Champion Houston Aeros. Last amateur club; Moose Jaw (WHL).

Joe Dziedzic — Left Wing
Regular Season / Playoffs

Season	Team	League	GP	G	A	PTS	PIM	GP	G	A	PTS	PIM
94-95	Cleveland	IHL	68	15	15	30	74	4	1	0	1	10
95-96	Pittsburgh	NHL	69	5	5	10	68	16	1	2	3	19
96-97	Pittsburgh	NHL	59	9	9	18	63	5	0	1	1	4
97-98	Cleveland	IHL	65	21	20	41	176	10	3	4	7	28
98-99	Springfield	AHL	61	18	27	45	128	3	1	1	2	20
	NHL	Totals	128	14	14	28	131	21	1	3	4	23
	IHL	Totals	133	36	35	71	250	14	2	3	5	38

Born; 12/18/71, Minneapolis, Minnesota. 6-3, 227. Drafted by PIttsburgh Penguins (2nd choice, 61st overall) in 1990 Entry Draft. Signed as a free agent by Phoenix Coyotes (8/27/99). Last amateur club; University of Minnesota

Joe Eagan — Defenseman
Regular Season / Playoffs

Season	Team	League	GP	G	A	PTS	PIM	GP	G	A	PTS	PIM
92-93	Northeastern	H.E.	2	0	0	0	0	—	—	—	—	—
92-93	Dallas	CeHL	16	1	2	3	12	4	0	1	1	2
93-94	Louisville	ECHL	21	0	2	2	49	—	—	—	—	—
94-95	Birmingham	ECHL	12	1	0	1	18	—	—	—	—	—
94-95	Johnstown	ECHL	3	0	0	0	2	—	—	—	—	—
95-96	Bakersfield	WCHL	22	0	9	9	73	—	—	—	—	—
96-97	Nashville	CeHL	31	5	14	19	112	—	—	—	—	—
96-97	Tulsa	CeHL	25	1	2	3	24	5	0	1	1	4
97-98	Tulsa	CHL	57	2	12	14	123	3	0	0	0	0
98-99	Jacksonville	ECHL	14	0	0	0	24	—	—	—	—	—
98-99	Baton Rouge	ECHL	46	0	5	5	79	6	0	0	0	6
	CeHL	Totals	129	9	30	39	271	12	0	2	2	6
	ECHL	Totals	96	1	7	8	172	6	0	0	0	6

Born; 4/30/70, Darien, Connecticut. 5-11, 190. Selected by San Antonio in 1998 CHL Expansion Draft. Last amateur club; Northeastern (Hockey East).

Dallas Eakins — Defenseman
Regular Season / Playoffs

Season	Team	League	GP	G	A	PTS	PIM	GP	G	A	PTS	PIM
88-89	Baltimore	AHL	62	0	10	10	139	—	—	—	—	—
89-90	Moncton	AHL	75	2	11	13	189	—	—	—	—	—
90-91	Moncton	AHL	75	1	12	13	132	9	0	1	1	44
91-92	Moncton	AHL	67	3	13	16	136	11	2	1	3	16
92-93	Winnipeg	NHL	14	0	2	2	38	—	—	—	—	—
92-93	Moncton	AHL	55	4	6	10	132	—	—	—	—	—
93-94	Florida	NHL	1	0	0	0	0	—	—	—	—	—
93-94	Cincinnati	IHL	80	1	18	19	143	8	0	1	1	41
94-95	Florida	NHL	17	0	1	1	35	—	—	—	—	—
94-95	Cincinnati	IHL	59	6	12	18	69	—	—	—	—	—
95-96	St. Louis	NHL	16	0	1	1	34	—	—	—	—	—
95-96	Winnipeg	NHL	2	0	0	0	0	—	—	—	—	—
95-96	Worcester	AHL	4	0	0	0	12	—	—	—	—	—
96-97	Phoenix	NHL	4	0	0	0	10	—	—	—	—	—
96-97	Rangers	NHL	3	0	0	0	6	4	0	0	0	4
96-97	Springfield	AHL	38	6	7	13	63	—	—	—	—	—
96-97	Binghamton	AHL	19	1	7	8	15	—	—	—	—	—
97-98	Florida	NHL	23	0	1	1	44	—	—	—	—	—
97-98	New Haven	AHL	4	0	1	1	7	—	—	—	—	—
98-99	Toronto	NHL	18	0	2	2	24	1	0	0	0	0
98-99	Chicago	IHL	2	0	0	0	0	—	—	—	—	—
98-99	St. John's	AHL	20	3	7	10	16	5	0	1	1	6
	NHL	Totals	98	0	7	7	191	5	0	0	0	4
	AHL	Totals	419	20	74	94	841	25	2	3	5	66
	IHL	Totals	141	7	30	37	212	8	0	1	1	41

Born; 2/27/67, Dade City, Florida. 6-2, 195. Drafted by Washington Capitals (11th choice, 208th overall) in 1985 Entry Draft. Signed as a free agent by Winnipeg Jets (10/17/89). Signed as a free agent by Florida Panthers (7/8/93). Traded to St. Louis Blues by Florida for St. Louis' fourth round choice in 1997 Entry Draft (Ivan Novoseltsev), 9/28/95. Claimed on waivers by Winnipeg from St. Louis (3/20/96). Traded to New York Rangers with Mike Eastwood by Phoenix Coyotes for Jayson More (2/6/97). Signed as a free agent by Florida (7/30/97). Signed as a free agent by Toronto Maple Leafs (7/28/89). Last amateur club;

James D. Eaton — Right Wing
Regular Season / Playoffs

Season	Team	League	GP	G	A	PTS	PIM	GP	G	A	PTS	PIM
95-96	Utica	CoHL	58	5	9	14	184	—	—	—	—	—
96-97	Saginaw	CoHL	64	22	34	56	301	—	—	—	—	—
97-98	Saginaw	UHL	26	10	8	18	74	—	—	—	—	—
97-98	Port Huron	UHL	47	9	12	21	107	4	0	0	0	2
98-99	Fort Worth	CHL	67	15	32	47	251	—	—	—	—	—
	UHL	Totals	195	46	63	109	666	4	0	0	0	2

Born; 5/28/73, Sudbury, Ontario. 5-11, 205. Traded to Port Huron by Saginaw with Joel Gardner and David Geris for Jason Renard, Dale Greenwood and Bobby Ferraris. Selected by Huntsville in 1999 CHL Dispersal Draft. Last amateur club; Laurentian (OUAA).

Mark Eaton — Defenseman
Regular Season / Playoffs

Season	Team	League	GP	G	A	PTS	PIM	GP	G	A	PTS	PIM
98-99	Philadelphia	AHL	74	9	27	36	38	16	4	8	12	0

Born; 5/6/77, Wilmington, Delaware. 6-3, 195. Signed as a free agent by Philadelphia Flyers (7/28/98). Last amateur club; Notre Dame (CCHA).

Derek Eberle — Defenseman
Regular Season / Playoffs

Season	Team	League	GP	G	A	PTS	PIM	GP	G	A	PTS	PIM
93-94	Providence	AHL	17	0	3	3	20	—	—	—	—	—
93-94	Charlotte	ECHL	46	8	21	29	97	3	0	3	3	4
94-95	Atlanta	IHL	13	2	1	3	4	2	0	0	0	0
94-95	Nashville	ECHL	57	25	32	57	96	12	5	10	15	20
95-96	Nashville	IHL	2	0	0	0	0	—	—	—	—	—
95-96	Nashville	ECHL	50	15	43	58	20	5	2	6	8	10
96-97	Carolina	AHL	7	0	3	3	0	—	—	—	—	—
96-97	Manitoba	IHL	3	0	0	0	0	—	—	—	—	—
96-97	Port Huron	CoHL	63	11	40	51	62	—	—	—	—	—
97-98	Fort Wayne	IHL	44	0	9	9	52	4	0	1	1	2
97-98	Dayton	ECHL	21	2	19	21	22	—	—	—	—	—
98-99	Jacksonville	ECHL	70	19	34	53	82	2	0	2	2	0
	IHL	Totals	62	2	10	12	56	6	0	1	1	2
	AHL	Totals	24	0	6	6	20	—	—	—	—	—
	ECHL	Totals	244	69	149	218	317	22	7	21	28	34

Born; 7/18/72, Regina, Saskatchewan. 5-10, 205. Last amateur club; Regina

Ken Eddy — Defenseman
Regular Season / Playoffs

Season	Team	League	GP	G	A	PTS	PIM	GP	G	A	PTS	PIM
92-93	Fargo-Moorhead	AHA	1	0	0	0	0	—	—	—	—	—
93-94												
94-95												
95-96	Daytona Beach	SHL	35	3	6	9	48	4	0	0	0	2
95-96	Quad City	CoHL	8	1	0	1	0	—	—	—	—	—
96-97												
97-98												
98-99	Quad City	UHL	13	0	2	2	10	—	—	—	—	—
98-99	Topeka	CHL	3	0	0	0	0	—	—	—	—	—
	UHL	Totals	21	1	2	3	10	—	—	—	—	—

Born; 4/8/69, Rochester, Minnesota. 5-10, 170. Last amateur club; Kent State (CCHA).

Mark Edmundson — Forward
Regular Season / Playoffs

Season	Team	League	GP	G	A	PTS	PIM	GP	G	A	PTS	PIM
98-99	Saint Thomas	AUAA	23	20	18	38	NA	—	—	—	—	—
98-99	Louisiana	ECHL	13	1	1	2	2	—	—	—	—	—

Born; Last amateur club; Saint Thomas (AUAA).

Jeff Edwards — Left Wing
Regular Season / Playoffs

Season	Team	League	GP	G	A	PTS	PIM	GP	G	A	PTS	PIM
98-99	South Carolina	ECHL	67	6	9	15	75	1	0	0	0	2

Born; 3/25/74, Fort Frances, Ontario. 6-1, 217. Last amateur club; Alaska-Anchorage (WCHA).

Troy Edwards — Defenseman
Regular Season / Playoffs

Season	Team	League	GP	G	A	PTS	PIM	GP	G	A	PTS	PIM
97-98	Idaho	WCHL	62	7	12	19	136	4	0	0	0	10
98-99	Idaho	WCHL	55	3	10	13	88	2	0	0	0	15
	WCHL	Totals	117	10	22	32	224	6	0	0	0	25

Born; 2/2/72, Broadview, Saskatchewan. 6-0, 225. Last amateur club; Bemidji State (NCHA).

Allan Egelund — Center

Regular Season — Playoffs

Season	Team	League	GP	G	A	PTS	PIM	GP	G	A	PTS	PIM
94-95	Atlanta	IHL	60	8	16	24	112	5	0	1	1	16
95-96	Tampa Bay	NHL	5	0	0	0	2	—	—	—	—	—
95-96	Atlanta	IHL	68	22	22	44	182	3	0	1	1	0
96-97	Tampa Bay	NHL	4	0	0	0	5	—	—	—	—	—
96-97	Adirondack	AHL	52	18	32	50	184	2	0	1	1	4
97-98	Tampa Bay	NHL	8	0	0	0	9	—	—	—	—	—
97-98	Adirondack	AHL	35	11	22	33	78	3	0	2	2	10
98-99	Orlando	IHL	62	7	23	30	182	—	—	—	—	—
98-99	Saint John	AHL	14	5	5	10	49	7	1	4	5	21
	NHL	Totals	17	0	0	0	16	—	—	—	—	—
	IHL	Totals	190	37	61	98	476	8	0	1	1	16
	AHL	Totals	101	34	59	93	311	12	1	7	8	35

Born; 1/31/73, Lethbridge, Alberta. 6-0, 184. Drafted by Tampa Bay Lightning (3rd choice, 55th overall) in 1993 Entry Draft. Traded to Saint John by Orlando with Arttu Kayhko for Tyler Moss and Eric Healey (3/22). Last amateur club; Tacoma (WHL).

Tracy Egeland — Right Wing

Regular Season — Playoffs

Season	Team	League	GP	G	A	PTS	PIM	GP	G	A	PTS	PIM
90-91	Indianapolis	IHL	79	17	22	39	205	7	2	1	3	21
91-92	Indianapolis	IHL	66	20	11	31	214	—	—	—	—	—
92-93	Indianapolis	IHL	43	11	14	25	122	—	—	—	—	—
93-94	Hershey	AHL	57	7	11	18	266	4	0	0	0	2
94-95	Hershey	AHL	37	5	5	10	83	—	—	—	—	—
95-96	Los Angeles	IHL	54	5	1	6	182	—	—	—	—	—
96-97	Huntington	ECHL	43	36	27	63	156	—	—	—	—	—
97-98	Orlando	IHL	1	0	1	1	5	—	—	—	—	—
97-98	Huntington	ECHL	45	15	28	43	107	4	3	1	4	10
98-99	Fort Wayne	IHL	26	10	5	15	24	2	0	1	1	0
98-99	Huntington	ECHL	47	38	18	56	113	—	—	—	—	—
	IHL	Totals	269	63	54	117	752	9	2	2	4	21
	AHL	Totals	94	12	16	28	349	4	0	0	0	2
	ECHL	Totals	135	89	73	162	376	4	3	1	4	10

Born; 8/20/70, Lethbridge, Alberta. 6-2, 180. Drafted by Chicago Blackhawks (5th choice, 132nd overall) in 1989 Entry Draft. Signed as a free agent by Philadelphia Flyers (8/4/93). Last amateur club; Prince Albert (WHL).

Trent Eigner — Defenseman

Regular Season — Playoffs

Season	Team	League	GP	G	A	PTS	PIM	GP	G	A	PTS	PIM
94-95	Raleigh	ECHL	7	1	2	3	10	—	—	—	—	—
94-95	Huntington	ECHL	59	8	25	33	164	4	0	1	1	12
95-96	Huntington	ECHL	70	6	34	40	209	—	—	—	—	—
96-97	Huntington	ECHL	8	0	1	1	8	—	—	—	—	—
96-97	El Paso	WPHL	50	14	43	57	89	11	1	8	9	29
97-98	El Paso	WPHL	65	11	47	58	105	15	1	10	11	24
98-99	El Paso	WPHL	67	3	16	19	127	3	2	0	2	2
	WPHL	Totals	182	28	106	134	321	29	4	18	22	55
	ECHL	Totals	144	15	62	77	391	4	0	1	1	12

Born; 7/6/70, Oshkosh, Wisconsin. 6-0, 195. Member of 1996-97 WPHL Champion El Paso Buzzards. Member of 1997-98 WPHL Champion El Paso Buzzards. Last amateur club; Miami of Ohio (CCHA).

Neil Eisenhut — Center

Regular Season — Playoffs

Season	Team	League	GP	G	A	PTS	PIM	GP	G	A	PTS	PIM
91-92	Milwaukee	IHL	76	13	23	36	26	2	1	2	3	0
92-93	Hamilton	AHL	72	22	40	62	41	—	—	—	—	—
93-94	Vancouver	NHL	13	1	3	4	21	—	—	—	—	—
93-94	Hamilton	AHL	60	17	36	53	30	4	1	4	5	0
94-95	Calgary	NHL	3	0	0	0	0	—	—	—	—	—
94-95	Saint John	AHL	75	16	39	55	30	5	1	1	2	6
95-96	Orlando	IHL	59	10	18	28	30	—	—	—	—	—
95-96	Binghamton	AHL	10	3	3	6	2	4	3	2	5	0
96-97	Binghamton	AHL	55	25	26	51	16	4	1	2	3	0
96-97	Flint	CoHL	21	10	33	43	20	5	1	4	5	8
97-98	Krefeld	Germany	42	9	13	22	16	3	1	2	3	2
98-99	Krefeld	Germany	46	18	25	43	69	4	1	1	2	8
	NHL	Totals	16	1	3	4	21	—	—	—	—	—
	AHL	Totals	272	83	144	227	119	17	6	9	15	6
	IHL	Totals	135	23	41	64	56	2	1	2	3	0

Born; 6/9/67, Osoyoos, British Columbia. 6-1, 195. Drafted by Vancouver Canucks (11th choice, 238th overall) in 1987 Entry Draft. Signed as a free agent by Calgary Flames (6/16/94). Last amateur club; North Dakota (WCHA).

Matt Eisler — Goaltender

Regular Season — Playoffs

Season	Team	League	GP	W	L	T	MIN	SO	AVG	GP	W	L	MIN	SO	AVG
98-99	Saint John	AHL	15	4	8	1	760	0	4.18	—	—	—	—	—	—
98-99	Johnstown	ECHL	43	14	20	7	2457	2	3.54	—	—	—	—	—	—

Born; 9/19/75, West Milford, New Jersey. 6-1, 185. Last amateur club; Notre Dame (CCHA).

Per Eklund — Center

Regular Season — Playoffs

Season	Team	League	GP	G	A	PTS	PIM	GP	G	A	PTS	PIM
97-98	Adirondack	AHL	73	21	29	50	12	3	0	0	0	0
98-99	Djurgardens	Sweden	48	14	9	23	49	4	0	0	0	6

Born; 7/9/70, Sollentuna, Sweden. 5-11, 196. Drafted by Detroit Red Wings (8th choice, 182nd overall) in 1995 Entry Draft.

Brian Elder — Goaltender

Regular Season — Playoffs

Season	Team	League	GP	W	L	T	MIN	SO	AVG	GP	W	L	MIN	SO	AVG
97-98	Manitoba	IHL	2	0	2	0	85	0	2.12	—	—	—	—	—	—
97-98	Oklahoma City	CHL	40	28	8	1	2258	2	*2.82	*11	6	*5	*669	1	2.87
98-99	Austin	WPHL	14	6	4	2	656	0	3.38	—	—	—	—	—	—
98-99	Oklahoma City	CHL	6	5	0	0	317	0	3.03	1	0	1	60	0	2.01
	CHL	Totals	46	33	8	1	2575	2	2.84	12	6	6	729	1	2.80

Born; 6/8/76, Oak Lake, Manitoba. 6-0, 175. 1997-98 CHL Goaltender of the Year. Last amateur club; Brandon (WHL).

Jason Elders — Left Wing

Regular Season — Playoffs

Season	Team	League	GP	G	A	PTS	PIM	GP	G	A	PTS	PIM
95-96	Mobile	ECHL	70	38	31	69	28	—	—	—	—	—
96-97	Kansas City	IHL	2	1	0	1	0	—	—	—	—	—
96-97	Mobile	ECHL	68	42	43	85	22	3	1	1	2	0
97-98	Cortina	Italy	26	22	8	30	6	—	—	—	—	—
97-98	Mobile	ECHL	27	23	17	40	4	3	3	3	6	4
98-99	Mobile	ECHL	68	29	46	75	24	2	0	1	1	0
	ECHL	Totals	233	132	137	269	78	8	4	5	9	4

Born; 12/28/70, Winnipeg, Manitoba. 5-10, 195. 1996-97 ECHL Second Team All-Star. Last amateur club; University of Denver (WCHA).

Matt Eldred
Defenseman

Regular Season / Playoffs

Season	Team	League	GP	G	A	PTS	PIM	GP	G	A	PTS	PIM
97-98	Michigan	IHL	4	0	0	0	2	—	—	—	—	—
97-98	Indianapolis	IHL	1	0	0	0	0	—	—	—	—	—
97-98	Jacksonville	ECHL	55	7	7	14	126	—	—	—	—	—
98-99	Milwaukee	IHL	15	0	0	0	31	—	—	—	—	—
98-99	Jacksonville	ECHL	38	5	6	11	108	—	—	—	—	—
98-99	Johnstown	ECHL	22	1	4	5	68	—	—	—	—	—
	IHL	Totals	20	0	0	0	33	—	—	—	—	—
	ECHL	Totals	115	13	17	30	302	—	—	—	—	—

Born; 3/17/74, Rocky River, Ohio. 6-0, 195. Traded to Johnstown by Jacksonville for Lukas Smital (2/99). Last amateur club; Bowling Green (CCHA).

Charlie Elezi
Defenseman

Regular Season / Playoffs

Season	Team	League	GP	G	A	PTS	PIM	GP	G	A	PTS	PIM
98-99	Oklahoma City	CHL	41	4	7	11	188	—	—	—	—	—

Born; 1/24/77, Warren, Michigan. 6-4, 220.

Calvin Elfring
Defenseman

Regular Season / Playoffs

Season	Team	League	GP	G	A	PTS	PIM	GP	G	A	PTS	PIM
98-99	Hershey	AHL	7	1	1	2	0	—	—	—	—	—
98-99	Cincinnati	AHL	4	0	0	0	0	—	—	—	—	—
98-99	Pee Dee	ECHL	10	1	2	3	14	—	—	—	—	—
98-99	Roanoke	ECHL	40	8	16	24	41	11	3	5	8	10
	AHL	Totals	11	1	1	2	0	—	—	—	—	—
	ECHL	Totals	50	9	18	27	55	11	3	5	8	10

Born; 4/23/76, Lethbridge, Alberta. 6-0, 170. Drafted by Quebec Nordiques (9th choice, 165th overall) in 1994 Entry Draft. Last amateur club; Colorado

Mickey Elick
Defenseman

Regular Season / Playoffs

Season	Team	League	GP	G	A	PTS	PIM	GP	G	A	PTS	PIM
96-97	Binghamton	AHL	1	0	1	1	2	—	—	—	—	—
96-97	Charlotte	ECHL	70	25	36	61	79	3	1	0	1	14
97-98	Canadian	National	61	20	28	48	60	—	—	—	—	—
98-99	Saint John	AHL	62	2	11	13	50	—	—	—	—	—
98-99	Grand Rapids	IHL	17	3	6	9	8	—	—	—	—	—
	AHL	Totals	63	2	12	14	52	—	—	—	—	—

Born; 3/17/74, Calgary, Alberta. 6-1, 180. Drafted by New York Rangers (8th choice, 192nd overall) in 1992 Entry Draft. Signed as a free agent by Calgary Flames (7/10/98). Traded to Grand Rapids by Saint John for Gaetan Royer (3/99). Last amateur club; University of Wisconsin (WCHA).

Jason Elliot
Goaltender

Regular Season / Playoffs

Season	Team	League	GP	W	L	T	MIN	SO	AVG	GP	W	L	MIN	SO	AVG
98-99	Adirondack	AHL	51	14	*27	5	2710	2	3.23	1	0	1	59	0	2.04

Born; 11/10/75, Inuvik, Nortwest Territories. 6-2, 183. Drafted by Detroit Red Wings (7th choice, 205th overall) in 1994 Entry Draft. Last amateur club; Cornell (ECAC).

Mikka Elomo
Left Wing

Regular Season / Playoffs

Season	Team	League	GP	G	A	PTS	PIM	GP	G	A	PTS	PIM
96-97	Portland	AHL	52	8	9	17	37	—	—	—	—	—
97-98	Portland	AHL	33	1	1	2	54	—	—	—	—	—
98-99	TPS Turku	Finland	36	5	10	15	76	10	3	5	8	6
	AHL	Totals	85	9	10	19	91	—	—	—	—	—

Born; 4/21/77, Turku, Finland. 6-0, 180. Drafted by Washington Capitals (2nd choice, 23rd overall) in 1995 Entry Draft.

Daniel Elsener
Defenseman

Regular Season / Playoffs

Season	Team	League	GP	G	A	PTS	PIM	GP	G	A	PTS	PIM
91-92	Cincinnati	ECHL	11	0	6	6	17	—	—	—	—	—
92-93	Muskegon	CoHL	4	0	3	3	10	—	—	—	—	—
92-93	Memphis	CeHL	26	2	8	10	54	—	—	—	—	—
92-93	Wichita	CeHL	8	0	4	4	15	—	—	—	—	—
92-93	St. Petersburg	SUN	7	1	3	4	2	—	—	—	—	—
92-93	Lakeland	SUN	14	0	5	5	20	—	—	—	—	—
93-94	Flint	CoHL	47	6	9	15	49	—	—	—	—	—
94-95												
95-96												
96-97	Chaux-de-Fonds	Switz.	41	1	4	5	112	—	—	—	—	—
96-97	San Diego	WCHL	8	0	8	8	4	3	0	2	2	4
97-98	Herisau	Switz.	34	1	1	2	32	—	—	—	—	—
98-99	San Diego	WCHL	23	0	5	5	12	—	—	—	—	—
	CoHL	Totals	51	6	12	18	59	—	—	—	—	—
	CeHL	Totals	34	2	12	14	69	—	—	—	—	—
	WCHL	Totals	31	0	13	13	16	3	0	2	2	4
	SUN	Totals	21	1	8	9	22	—	—	—	—	—

Born; 7/6/66, Kloten, Switzerland. 5-11, 195. Member of 1996-97 WCHL Champion San Diego Gulls.

Dmitri Emilyantsev
Right Wing

Regular Season / Playoffs

Season	Team	League	GP	G	A	PTS	PIM	GP	G	A	PTS	PIM
98-99	Muskegon	UHL	5	0	0	0	2	—	—	—	—	—
98-99	Mohawk Valley	UHL	9	3	2	5	2	—	—	—	—	—
	UHL	Totals	14	3	2	5	4	—	—	—	—	—

Born; 3/19/77, Moscow, Russia. 5-10, 195.

Rick Emmett
Defenseman

Regular Season / Playoffs

Season	Team	League	GP	G	A	PTS	PIM	GP	G	A	PTS	PIM
95-96	Brantford	CoHL	1	1	0	1	0	—	—	—	—	—
95-96	South Carolina	ECHL	7	0	2	2	4	—	—	—	—	—
95-96	Columbus	ECHL	7	1	4	5	0	—	—	—	—	—
95-96	Johnstown	ECHL	24	2	15	17	12	—	—	—	—	—
96-97	Quad City	CoHL	46	11	26	37	32	15	5	8	13	24
97-98	Chicago	IHL	1	0	0	0	0	—	—	—	—	—
97-98	Quad City	UHL	63	10	38	48	63	19	5	9	14	22
98-99	Quad City	UHL	55	12	34	46	72	13	2	5	7	16
	UHL	Totals	165	34	98	132	167	47	12	22	34	62
	ECHL	Totals	38	3	21	24	16	—	—	—	—	—

Born; 2/12/75, Etobicoke, Ontario. 5-10, 195. Selected by Mohawk Valley in 1998 UHL Expansion Draft. Member of 1996-97 CoHL Champion Quad City Mallards. 1997-98 UHL Champion Quad City Mallards. Last amateur club;

John Emmons
Center

Regular Season / Playoffs

Season	Team	League	GP	G	A	PTS	PIM	GP	G	A	PTS	PIM
96-97	Fort Wayne	IHL	1	0	0	0	0	—	—	—	—	—
96-97	Dayton	ECHL	69	20	37	57	62	4	0	1	1	2
97-98	Michigan	IHL	81	9	25	34	85	4	1	1	2	10
98-99	Detroit	IHL	75	13	22	35	172	11	4	5	9	22
	IHL	Totals	157	22	47	69	257	15	5	6	11	32

Born; 8/17/74, San Jose, California. 6-2, 205. Drafted by Calgary Flames (7th choice, 122nd overall) in 1993 Entry Draft. Signed as a free agent by Ottawa Senators (7/28/98). Last amateur club; Yale (ECAC).

Marco Emond
Goaltender

Regular Season / Playoffs

Season	Team	League	GP	W	L	T	MIN	SO	AVG	GP	W	L	MIN	SO	AVG
98-99	Topeka	CHL	5	0	2	1	219	0	4.66	—	—	—	—	—	—
98-99	Chesapeake	ECHL	2	0	1	0	43	0	2.82	—	—	—	—	—	—

Born; 11/20/77, Valleyfield, Quebec. 5-10, 180.

Larry Empey — Defenseman
Regular Season / Playoffs

Season	Team	League	GP	G	A	PTS	PIM	GP	G	A	PTS	PIM
94-95	Syracuse	AHL	1	0	0	0	0	—	—	—	—	—
94-95	Erie	ECHL	23	0	1	1	52	—	—	—	—	—
94-95	Utica	CoHL	27	0	5	5	29	6	0	1	1	6
95-96	Utica	CoHL	72	4	8	12	106	—	—	—	—	—
96-97	Utica	CoHL	73	1	10	11	83	3	0	1	1	6
97-98	Winston-Salem	UHL	71	2	10	12	74	—	—	—	—	—
98-99	Winston-Salem	UHL	74	0	8	8	120	5	0	0	0	4
	CoHL	Totals	317	7	41	48	412	14	0	2	2	16

Born; 7/25/73, Swift Current, Saskatchewan. 6-3, 220.

R.J. Enga — Left Wing
Regular Season / Playoffs

Season	Team	League	GP	G	A	PTS	PIM	GP	G	A	PTS	PIM
95-96	Atlanta	IHL	6	1	0	1	2	—	—	—	—	—
95-96	Nashville	ECHL	68	36	58	94	47	5	1	4	5	0
96-97	Erding	Germany	72	46	75	121	50	—	—	—	—	—
97-98	Tallahassee	ECHL	70	27	41	68	45	—	—	—	—	—
98-99	Colorado	WCHL	71	38	64	102	83	3	5	3	8	2
	ECHL	Totals	138	63	99	162	92	5	1	4	5	0

Born; 2/15/72, Bittburg, Germany. 6-0, 190. Last amateur club; Colorado College (WCHA).

Brad Englehart — Center
Regular Season / Playoffs

Season	Team	League	GP	G	A	PTS	PIM	GP	G	A	PTS	PIM
97-98	Wisconsin	WCHA	33	11	9	20	62	—	—	—	—	—
97-98	Cincinnati	AHL	7	1	1	2	2	—	—	—	—	—
98-99	Johnstown	ECHL	50	15	13	28	63	—	—	—	—	—

Born; 9/16/75, Woodstock, New Brunswick. 5-11, 80. Drafted by Anaheim Mighty Ducks (8th choice, 184th overall) in 1994 Entry Draft. Last amateur club; University of Wisconsin (WCHA).

Martin Engren — Goaltender
Regular Season / Playoffs

Season	Team	League	GP	W	L	T	MIN	SO	AVG	GP	W	L	MIN	SO	AVG
98-99	Monroe	WPHL	11	6	2	1	602	0	3.59	—	—	—	—	—	—

Born; 8/13/77, Stockholm, Sweden. 5-9, 180.

Vadim Epanchintsev — Center
Regular Season / Playoffs

Season	Team	League	GP	G	A	PTS	PIM	GP	G	A	PTS	PIM
97-98	Cleveland	IHL	34	3	6	9	18	—	—	—	—	—
97-98	Hampton Roads	ECHL	25	5	10	15	44	11	2	3	5	0
98-99	Novokuznetsk	Russia	38	9	19	28	12	6	0	0	0	10

Born; 3/16/76, Orsk, USSR. 5-10, 175. Drafted by Tampa Bay Lightning (3rd choice, 55th overall) in 1994 Entry Draft. Member of 1997-98 ECHL Champion Hampton Roads Admirals.

Kevin Epp — Defenseman
Regular Season / Playoffs

Season	Team	League	GP	G	A	PTS	PIM	GP	G	A	PTS	PIM
98-99	Anchorage	WCHL	67	4	16	20	72	5	1	1	2	2

Born; 8/27/74, Cranbrook, British Columbia. 6-0, 190. Traded to San Diego Gulls by Anchorage with Wade Brookbank for Kyle Reeves (6/99). Last amateur club; Alaska-Fairbanks (CCHA).

Ryan Equale — Forward
Regular Season / Playoffs

Season	Team	League	GP	G	A	PTS	PIM	GP	G	A	PTS	PIM
96-97	Roanoke	ECHL	39	4	10	14	47	4	0	0	0	2
97-98	Chesapeake	ECHL	17	3	3	6	19	—	—	—	—	—
97-98	Odessa	WPHL	32	14	17	31	41	—	—	—	—	—
98-99	Odessa	WPHL	49	20	14	34	87	—	—	—	—	—
98-99	Lake Charles	WPHL	17	10	13	23	4	11	5	3	8	10
	WPHL	Totals	98	44	44	88	132	11	5	3	8	10
	ECHL	Totals	56	7	13	20	66	4	0	0	0	2

Born; 2/22/73, Wilton, Connecticut. 6-0, 195. Traded to Lake Charles by Odessa for Paul Vincent (2/99). Last amateur club; University of Connecticut (ECAC 2).

Josh Erdman — Forward
Regular Season / Playoffs

Season	Team	League	GP	G	A	PTS	PIM	GP	G	A	PTS	PIM
98-99	Huntsville	CHL	67	8	18	26	107	7	1	1	2	4

Born; 1/14/74, Prince Albert, Saskatchewan. 6-1, 215. Member of 1998-99 CHL Champion Huntsville Channel Cats. Last amateur club; South Alberta Institute of Technology.

Chad Erickson — Goaltender
Regular Season / Playoffs

Season	Team	League	GP	W	L	T	MIN	SO	AVG	GP	W	L	MIN	SO	AVG
91-92	New Jersey	NHL	2	1	1	0	120	0	4.50	—	—	—	—	—	—
91-92	Utica	AHL	44	18	19	3	2341	2	3.77	2	0	2	127	0	5.20
92-93	Cincinnati	IHL	10	2	6	1	516	0	4.88	—	—	—	—	—	—
92-93	Birmingham	ECHL	14	6	6	2	856	0	3.79	—	—	—	—	—	—
92-93	Albany	AHL	9	1	7	1	505	0	5.58	—	—	—	—	—	—
93-94	Albany	AHL	4	2	1	0	184	0	4.25	—	—	—	—	—	—
93-94	Raleigh	ECHL	32	19	9	3	1884	0	3.22	6	3	1	287	0	4.40
94-95	Albany	AHL	1	1	0	0	60	0	2.00	—	—	—	—	—	—
94-95	Providence	AHL	7	1	6	0	351	0	5.63	—	—	—	—	—	—
94-95	Springfield	AHL	1	0	0	0	23	0	7.78	—	—	—	—	—	—
94-95	Raleigh	ECHL	11	1	8	1	587	0	4.60	—	—	—	—	—	—
95-96	Birmingham	ECHL	44	16	20	4	2410	0	5.00	—	—	—	—	—	—
96-97	Austin	WPHL	32	18	11	2	1875	0	3.90	5	2	2	281	0	4.06
97-98	Austin	WPHL	52	26	14	10	3048	0	3.50	—	—	—	—	—	—
98-99	San Angelo	WPHL	49	31	14	3	2841	0	3.29	17	*9	*7	*1033	0	3.37
	AHL	Totals	66	23	33	4	3464	2	4.24	2	0	2	127	0	5.20
	WPHL	Totals	133	75	39	15	7764	0	3.52	22	11	9	1314	0	3.52
	ECHL	Totals	101	42	43	10	5737	0	3.63	6	3	1	287	0	4.40

Born; 8/21/70, Minneapolis, Minnesota. 5-9, 175. Drafted by New Jersey Devils (8th choice, 138th overall) in 1988 Entry Draft. Last amatuer club; University of Minnesota (WCHA).

Valeri Ermolov — Center
Regular Season / Playoffs

Season	Team	League	GP	G	A	PTS	PIM	GP	G	A	PTS	PIM
96-97	Huntington	ECHL	40	5	29	34	18	—	—	—	—	—
97-98	Huntington	ECHL	33	3	4	7	4	—	—	—	—	—
98-99	Lake Charles	WPHL	3	2	1	3	0	—	—	—	—	—
98-99	Odessa	WPHL	26	5	16	21	4	—	—	—	—	—
98-99	Alexandria	WPHL	12	1	9	10	2	—	—	—	—	—
	ECHL	Totals	73	8	33	41	22	—	—	—	—	—
	WPHL	Totals	41	8	26	34	6	—	—	—	—	—

Born; 8/22/75, Minsk, Belarus. 6-2, 200. Traded to Alexandria by Odessa for future considerations (2/99).

Derek Ernest — Defenseman
Regular Season / Playoffs

Season	Team	League	GP	G	A	PTS	PIM	GP	G	A	PTS	PIM
98-99	Hampton Roads	ECHL	60	1	4	5	234	1	0	0	0	2

Born; 6/23/77, Moose Jaw, Saskatchewan. 6-2, 220.

Bob Errey — Left Wing

Regular Season / Playoffs

Season	Team	League	GP	G	A	PTS	PIM	GP	G	A	PTS	PIM
83-84	Pittsburgh	NHL	65	9	13	22	29	—	—	—	—	—
84-85	Pittsburgh	NHL	16	0	2	2	7	—	—	—	—	—
84-85	Baltimore	AHL	59	17	24	41	14	8	3	4	7	11
85-86	Pittsburgh	NHL	37	11	6	17	8	—	—	—	—	—
85-86	Baltimore	AHL	18	8	7	15	28	—	—	—	—	—
86-87	Pittsburgh	NHL	72	16	18	34	46	—	—	—	—	—
87-88	Pittsburgh	NHL	17	3	6	9	18	—	—	—	—	—
88-89	Pittsburgh	NHL	76	26	32	58	124	11	1	2	3	12
89-90	Pittsburgh	NHL	78	20	19	39	109	—	—	—	—	—
90-91	Pittsburgh	NHL	79	20	22	42	115	24	5	2	7	29
91-92	Pittsburgh	NHL	78	19	16	35	119	14	3	0	3	10
92-93	Pittsburgh	NHL	54	8	6	14	76	—	—	—	—	—
92-93	Buffalo	NHL	8	1	3	4	4	4	0	1	1	10
93-94	San Jose	NHL	64	12	18	30	216	14	3	2	5	10
94-95	San Jose	NHL	13	2	2	4	27	—	—	—	—	—
94-95	Detroit	NHL	30	6	11	17	31	18	1	5	6	30
95-96	Detroit	NHL	71	11	21	32	66	14	0	4	4	8
96-97	Detroit	NHL	36	1	2	3	27	—	—	—	—	—
96-97	San Jose	NHL	30	3	6	9	20	—	—	—	—	—
97-98	Dallas	NHL	59	2	9	11	46	—	—	—	—	—
97-98	Rangers	NHL	12	0	0	0	7	—	—	—	—	—
98-99	Hartford	AHL	69	18	27	45	59	7	0	3	3	8
	NHL	Totals	895	170	212	382	1005	99	13	16	29	109
	AHL	Totals	146	43	58	101	101	15	3	7	10	19

Born; 9/21/64, Monteral, Quebec. 5-10, 185. Drafted by Pittsbugh Penguins (1st choice, 15th overall) in 1983 Entry Draft. Traded to Buffalo Sabres by Pittsburgh for Mike Ramsey (3/22/93). Signed as a free agent by San Jose Sharks (8/17/93). Traded to Detroit Red Wings by San Jose for Detroit's fifth round choice (Michael Bros) in 1995 Entry Draft, (2/27/95). Claimed on waivers by San Jose from Detroit (2/8/97). Signed as a free agent by Dallas Stars (7/28/97). Traded to New York Rangers by Dallas with Todd Harvey and Dallas' 4th round choice (Boyd Kane) in 1998 Entry Draft for Brian Skrudland, Mike Keane and Rangers 6th round choice (Pavel Patera) in 1998 Entry Draft, (3/24/98). Member of 1990-91 Stanley Cup Champion Pittsburgh Penguins. Member of 1991-92 Stanley Cup Champion Pittsburgh Penguins. Last amateur club; Peterborough (OHL).

Robert Esche — Goaltender

Regular Season / Playoffs

Season	Team	League	GP	W	L	T	MIN	SO	AVG	GP	W	L	MIN	SO	AVG
98-99	Phoenix	NHL	3	0	1	0	130	0	3.23	—	—	—	—	—	—
98-99	Springfield	AHL	55	24	20	6	2957	1	2.80	1	0	1	60	0	4.02

Born; 1/22/78, Utica, New York. 6-0, 188. Drafted by Phoenix Coyotes (5th choice, 139th overall) in 1996 Entry Draft. 1998-99 AHL All-Rookie Team. Last amateur club; Plymouth (OHL).

Ryan Esselmont — Defenseman

Regular Season / Playoffs

Season	Team	League	GP	G	A	PTS	PIM	GP	G	A	PTS	PIM
98-99	Huntsville	CHL	5	0	0	0	0	—	—	—	—	—
98-99	Memphis	CHL	48	7	30	37	42	3	0	0	0	2
	CHL	Totals	53	7	30	37	42	3	0	0	0	2

Born; 4/20/74, 6-1, 195.

Brad Essex — Center

Regular Season / Playoffs

Season	Team	League	GP	G	A	PTS	PIM	GP	G	A	PTS	PIM
96-97	Peoria	ECHL	53	6	9	15	181	10	0	4	4	34
97-98	Peoria	ECHL	28	3	5	8	144	—	—	—	—	—
98-99	Mississippi	ECHL	59	15	14	29	190	14	2	4	6	25
	ECHL	Totals	140	24	28	52	515	24	2	8	10	59

Born; 7/15/75, Squamish, British Columbia, 6-0, 190. Member of 1998-99 ECHL Champion Mississippi SeaWolves.

John Evangelista — Forward

Regular Season / Playoffs

Season	Team	League	GP	G	A	PTS	PIM	GP	G	A	PTS	PIM
98-99	Saginaw	UHL	67	17	21	38	32	—	—	—	—	—

Born; 7/15/75, St. Catherines, Ontario. 5-10, 187. Last amateur club; Mercyhurst (NCAA 2).

David Evans — Center

Regular Season / Playoffs

Season	Team	League	GP	G	A	PTS	PIM	GP	G	A	PTS	PIM
97-98	Baton Rouge	ECHL	45	15	22	37	39	—	—	—	—	—
98-99	Mohawk Valley	UHL	72	19	25	44	72	—	—	—	—	—

Born; 5/19/72, St. John's New Brunswick. 5-8, 170.

Doug Evans — Left Wing

Regular Season / Playoffs

Season	Team	League	GP	G	A	PTS	PIM	GP	G	A	PTS	PIM
84-85	Peoria	IHL	81	36	61	97	189	20	18	14	32	*88
85-86	St. Louis	NHL	13	1	0	1	2	—	—	—	—	—
85-86	Peoria	IHL	69	46	51	97	179	10	4	6	10	32
86-87	St. Louis	NHL	53	3	13	16	91	5	0	0	0	10
86-87	Peoria	IHL	18	10	15	25	39	—	—	—	—	—
87-88	St. Louis	NHL	41	5	7	12	49	2	0	0	0	0
87-88	Peoria	IHL	11	4	16	20	64	—	—	—	—	—
88-89	St. Louis	NHL	53	7	12	19	81	7	1	2	3	16
89-90	St. Louis	NHL	3	0	0	0	0	—	—	—	—	—
89-90	Winnipeg	NHL	27	10	8	18	33	7	2	2	4	10
89-90	Peoria	IHL	42	19	28	47	128	—	—	—	—	—
90-91	Winnipeg	NHL	70	7	27	34	108	—	—	—	—	—
91-92	Winnipeg	NHL	30	7	7	14	68	1	0	0	0	2
91-92	Peoria	IHL	16	5	14	19	38	—	—	—	—	—
91-92	Moncton	AHL	10	7	8	15	10	—	—	—	—	—
92-93	Philadelphia	NHL	65	8	13	21	70	—	—	—	—	—
93-94	Peoria	IHL	76	27	63	90	108	6	2	6	8	10
94-95	Peoria	IHL	74	13	39	52	103	9	2	9	11	10
95-96	Peoria	IHL	74	19	48	67	81	1	0	0	0	0
96-97	Peoria	ECHL	67	23	59	82	128	10	10	12	22	20
97-98	Peoria	ECHL	52	27	37	64	98	3	0	1	1	4
98-99	Peoria	ECHL	57	14	46	60	112	4	0	5	5	10
	NHL	Totals	355	48	87	135	502	22	3	4	7	38
	IHL	Totals	461	179	335	514	929	46	26	35	61	140
	ECHL	Totals	176	64	142	206	338	17	10	18	28	34

Born; 6/2/63, Peterborough, Ontario. 5-9, 185. Signed as a free agent by St. Louis Blues (6/10/85). Traded to Winnipeg Jets by St. Louis for Ron Wilson (1/22/90). Loaned to Peoria Rivermen (11/9/91, returned 12/15/91). Traded to Boston Bruins by Winnipeg for Daniel Berthiaume (6/10/92). Selected by Philadelphia Flyers in NHL waiver draft (10/4/92). Signed as a free agent by Peoria (8/2/93). 1985-86 IHL First Team All-Star. Member of 1984-85 IHL champion Peoria Rivermen. Last amateur club; Peterborough (OHL).

Josh Evans — Goaltender

Regular Season / Playoffs

Season	Team	League	GP	W	L	T	MIN	SO	AVG	GP	W	L	MIN	SO	AVG
98-99	Mississauga	OHL	41	1	35	2	2212	0	6.37	—	—	—	—	—	—
98-99	Jacksonville	ECHL	3	0	1	0	53	0	4.50	—	—	—	—	—	—

Born; 4/9/79, Whitby, Ontario. 6-1, 175. Last amateur club; Mississauga (OHL).

Shawn Evans — Defenseman

Regular Season / Playoffs

Season	Team	League	GP	G	A	PTS	PIM	GP	G	A	PTS	PIM
85-86	Peoria	IHL	55	8	26	34	36	—	—	—	—	—
85-86	St. Louis	NHL	7	0	0	0	2	—	—	—	—	—
86-87	Nova Scotia	AHL	55	7	28	35	29	5	0	4	4	6
87-88	Nova Scotia	AHL	79	8	62	70	109	5	1	1	2	40
88-89	Springfield	AHL	68	9	50	59	125	—	—	—	—	—
89-90	Islanders	NHL	2	1	0	1	0	—	—	—	—	—
89-90	Springfield	AHL	63	6	35	41	102	18	6	11	17	35
90-91		Switz.										
90-91	Maine	AHL	51	9	37	46	44	2	0	1	1	0
91-92	Springfield	AHL	80	11	67	78	81	11	0	8	8	16
92-93	Milwaukee	IHL	79	13	65	78	83	6	0	3	3	6
93-94	Milan	Italy	21	2	12	14	26	—	—	—	—	—
94-95	Milwaukee	IHL	58	6	34	40	20	—	—	—	—	—
94-95	Fort Wayne	IHL	11	2	8	10	6	4	1	3	4	2
95-96	Fort Wayne	IHL	81	5	61	66	78	5	3	3	6	2
96-97	Fort Wayne	IHL	41	7	13	20	34	—	—	—	—	—
96-97	Manitoba	IHL	17	2	3	5	4	—	—	—	—	—
96-97	Cincinnati	IHL	21	3	9	12	24	3	0	0	0	19
97-98	Cincinnati	IHL	3	0	0	0	2	—	—	—	—	—
97-98	Baton Rouge	ECHL	49	5	17	22	40	—	—	—	—	—
98-99	Mohawk Valley	UHL	11	0	5	5	20	—	—	—	—	—
	NHL	Totals	9	1	0	1	2	—	—	—	—	—
	AHL	Totals	396	50	279	329	490	41	7	25	32	97
	IHL	Totals	366	46	219	265	287	18	4	9	13	29

Born; 9/7/65, Kingston, Ontario. 6-3, 190. Drafted by New Jersey Devils (2nd choice, 24th overall) in 1983 Entry Draft. Traded to St. Louis Blues by New Jersey with fifth round pick (Mike Wolak) in 1986 for Mark Johnson (9/19/85). Traded to Edmonton Oilers by St. Louis for Todd Ewen (10/15/86). Signed as a free agent by New York Islanders (6/20/88). Signed as a free agent by Hartford Whalers (8/14/91). 1991-92 AHL First Team All-Star. 1992-93 AHL First Team All-Star. Member of 1989-90 AHL champion Springfield Indians. Last amateur club; Peterborough (OHL).

Pavel Evstigneev — Right Wing

Regular Season / Playoffs

Season	Team	League	GP	G	A	PTS	PIM	GP	G	A	PTS	PIM
98-99	Las Vegas	IHL	10	2	0	2	0	—	—	—	—	—
98-99	Corpus Christi	WPHL	43	22	15	37	12	3	0	0	0	0

Born; 7/5/73, Moscow, Russia. 6-1, 190.

Dean Ewen — Left Wing

Regular Season / Playoffs

Season	Team	League	GP	G	A	PTS	PIM	GP	G	A	PTS	PIM
89-90	Springfield	AHL	34	0	7	7	194	—	—	—	—	—
90-91												
91-92	Capital District	AHL	41	5	8	13	106	—	—	—	—	—
93-94	San Diego	IHL	19	0	3	3	45	3	1	0	1	8
94-95	San Diego	IHL	36	4	3	7	187	4	0	0	0	10
95-96	Kansas City	IHL	50	1	6	7	203	5	0	1	1	11
96-97	Kansas City	IHL	36	7	2	9	132	2	0	0	0	0
97-98	Kansas City	IHL	47	2	2	4	178	2	0	0	0	0
98-99	Las Vegas	IHL	66	3	5	8	251	—	—	—	—	—
	IHL	Totals	254	17	21	38	996	16	1	1	2	29
	AHL	Totals	75	5	15	20	300	—	—	—	—	—

Born; 2/28/69, St. Albert, Alberta. 6-1, 225. Drafted by New York Islanders (3rd choice, 55th overall) in 1987 Entry Draft. Signed as a free agent by Anaheim Mighty Ducks (1/21/94). Signed as a free agent by Kansas City Blades (7/19/95). Last amateur club; Seattle (WHL).

Detroit's Stan Drulia tips the puck behind Kansas City's Patick Lalime while Steven Low (22) looks on

Photo by John Gacioch

Dominic Fafard — Defenseman
Regular Season / Playoffs

Season	Team	League	GP	G	A	PTS	PIM	GP	G	A	PTS	PIM
94-95	Wheeling	ECHL	39	2	8	10	44	—	—	—	—	—
94-95	South Carolina	ECHL	7	0	1	1	4	8	1	0	1	6
95-96	Wheeling	ECHL	2	0	0	0	0	—	—	—	—	—
95-96	Raleigh	ECHL	4	0	1	1	2	—	—	—	—	—
95-96	Oklahoma City	CeHL	56	6	26	32	77	13	0	3	3	10
96-97	Oklahoma City	CeHL	66	2	20	22	111	4	1	0	1	4
97-98	Oklahoma City	CHL	11	1	5	6	20	11	1	1	2	10
98-99	Oklahoma City	CHL	67	3	26	29	86	13	0	0	0	10
	CHL	Totals	200	12	77	89	294	41	2	4	6	34
	ECHL	Totals	52	2	10	12	50	8	1	0	1	6

Born; 7/13/74, Longeuil, Quebec. 6-5, 230. Signed as a free agent by Edmonton Oilers (9/30/94). Member of 1995-96 CeHL champion Oklahoma City Blazers. Last amateur club; Victoriaville (QMJHL).

Andrew Fagan — Left Wing
Regular Season / Playoffs

Season	Team	League	GP	G	A	PTS	PIM	GP	G	A	PTS	PIM
96-97	Quad City	CoHL	5	0	2	2	20	—	—	—	—	—
97-98	Richmond	ECHL	8	0	0	0	53	—	—	—	—	—
97-98	Columbus	ECHL	53	2	5	7	199	—	—	—	—	—
98-99	Columbus	ECHL	63	7	7	14	257	4	0	0	0	16
	ECHL	Totals	124	9	12	21	509	4	0	0	0	16

Born; 5/2/77, Orillia, Ontario. 6-1, 205. Selected by Huntington in 1999 ECHL Dispersal Draft. Last amateur club; London (OHL).

Quinn Fair — Defenseman
Regular Season / Playoffs

Season	Team	League	GP	G	A	PTS	PIM	GP	G	A	PTS	PIM
96-97	Grand Rapids	IHL	2	0	0	0	0	—	—	—	—	—
96-97	Baltimore	AHL	9	0	0	0	2	—	—	—	—	—
96-97	Mississippi	ECHL	58	12	22	34	54	3	0	1	1	0
97-98	Springfield	AHL	14	1	3	4	10	—	—	—	—	—
97-98	Mississippi	ECHL	56	8	14	22	100	—	—	—	—	—
98-99	Mississippi	ECHL	69	11	18	29	38	18	3	10	13	22
	AHL	Totals	23	1	3	4	12	—	—	—	—	—
	ECHL	Totals	183	31	54	85	192	21	3	11	14	22

Born; 5/23/73, Campbell River, British Columbia. 6-1, 210. Drafted by Los Angeles Kings (1st choice, 7th overall) in 1994 Supplemental Draft. Member of 1998-99 ECHL Champion Mississippi SeaWolves. Last amateur club; Bowling Green University (CCHA).

Kelly Fairchild — Center
Regular Season / Playoffs

Season	Team	League	GP	G	A	PTS	PIM	GP	G	A	PTS	PIM
94-95	St. John's	AHL	53	27	23	50	51	4	0	2	2	4
95-96	Toronto	NHL	1	0	1	1	2	—	—	—	—	—
95-96	St. John's	AHL	78	29	47	78	85	2	0	1	1	4
96-97	Toronto	NHL	22	0	2	2	2	—	—	—	—	—
96-97	St. John's	AHL	29	9	22	31	36	—	—	—	—	—
96-97	Orlando	IHL	25	9	6	15	20	9	6	5	11	16
97-98	St. John's	AHL	17	5	2	7	24	—	—	—	—	—
97-98	Orlando	IHL	22	2	6	8	20	—	—	—	—	—
97-98	Milwaukee	IHL	40	20	24	44	32	10	5	2	7	4
98-99	Michigan	IHL	74	17	33	50	88	5	2	2	4	16
	NHL	Totals	23	0	3	3	4	—	—	—	—	—
	AHL	Totals	177	70	94	164	196	6	0	3	3	8
	IHL	Totals	161	48	69	117	160	24	13	9	22	36

Born; 4/9/73, Hibbing, Minnesota. 5-11, 180. Drafted by Los Angeles Kings (7th choice, 152nd overall) in 1991 Entry Draft. Traded to Toronto Maple Leafs by Los Angeles with Dixon Ward, Guy Leveque and Shayne Toporowski for Eric Lacroix, Chris Snell and Toronto's fourth round choice (Eric Belanger) in 1996 Entry Draft. Traded to Milwaukee by Orlando with Dave MacIntyre for Sean McCann and Dave Mackey (1/98). Signed as a free agent by Dallas Stars (7/2/98). Last amateur club; University of Wisconsin (WCHA).

Chris Farion — Goaltender
Regular Season / Playoffs

Season	Team	League	GP	W	L	T	MIN	SO	AVG	GP	W	L	MIN	SO	AVG
98-99	Dayton	ECHL	2	0	1	0	28	0	8.70	—	—	—	—	—	—
98-99	Mobile	ECHL	1	0	0	0	13	0	4.63	—	—	—	—	—	—
	ECHL	Totals	3	0	1	0	41	0	7.40	—	—	—	—	—	—

Born; Beaconsfield, Quebec. 5-9, 165. Last amateur club; Middlebury (NCAA 3).

Brian Farrell — Left Wing
Regular Season / Playoffs

Season	Team	League	GP	G	A	PTS	PIM	GP	G	A	PTS	PIM
94-95	Cleveland	IHL	46	7	11	18	28	—	—	—	—	—
95-96	Utah	IHL	1	0	0	0	6	—	—	—	—	—
95-96	Jacksonville	ECHL	41	14	22	36	128	—	—	—	—	—
95-96	Toledo	ECHL	20	6	7	13	41	11	3	4	7	10
96-97	Fort Wayne	IHL	45	8	7	15	36	—	—	—	—	—
96-97	Chicago	IHL	22	5	5	10	16	4	2	0	2	4
97-98	Springfield	AHL	11	2	0	2	4	—	—	—	—	—
97-98	Mississippi	ECHL	59	20	26	46	54	—	—	—	—	—
98-99	Tallahassee	ECHL	53	20	13	33	71	—	—	—	—	—
	IHL	Totals	47	7	11	18	34	—	—	—	—	—
	ECHL	Totals	173	60	68	128	294	11	3	4	7	10

Born; 4/16/72, Hartford, Connecticut. 5-11, 170. Drafted by Pittsburgh Penguins (4th choice, 89th overall) in 1990 Entry Draft. Last amateur club; Harvard

Andy Faulkner — Center
Regular Season / Playoffs

Season	Team	League	GP	G	A	PTS	PIM	GP	G	A	PTS	PIM
96-97	Quad City	CoHL	69	20	25	45	18	14	1	4	5	6
97-98	Quad City	UHL	66	12	26	38	16	20	2	5	7	4
98-99	Madison	UHL	74	23	24	47	30	—	—	—	—	—
	UHL	Totals	209	55	75	130	64	34	3	9	21	10

Born; 1/8/71, Enderby, British Columbia. 5-11, 195. Traded to Madison by Quad City for cash and future considerations (9/98). Member of 1996-97 Colonial League Champion Quad City Mallards. Member of 1997-98 UHL Champion Quad City Mallards.

Randy Favaro — Forward
Regular Season / Playoffs

Season	Team	League	GP	G	A	PTS	PIM	GP	G	A	PTS	PIM
97-98	Raleigh	ECHL	20	1	2	3	20	—	—	—	—	—
97-98	Lake Charles	WPHL	28	2	6	8	55	4	0	1	1	4
98-99	Lake Charles	WPHL	64	19	20	39	94	11	5	4	9	12
	WPHL	Totals	92	21	26	47	149	15	5	5	10	16

Born; 2/12/78, North Delta, British Columbia. 6-0, 200. Last amateur club; Portland (WHL).

Chris Fawcett — Right Wing
Regular Season / Playoffs

Season	Team	League	GP	G	A	PTS	PIM	GP	G	A	PTS	PIM
97-98	Massachusetts	H.E.	31	3	8	11	12	—	—	—	—	—
97-98	Johnstown	ECHL	7	3	0	3	0	—	—	—	—	—
98-99	Dayton	ECHL	2	0	0	0	0	—	—	—	—	—
98-99	Central Texas	WPHL	54	21	20	41	14	2	0	0	0	0
	ECHL	Totals	9	3	0	3	0	—	—	—	—	—

Born; 4/15/75, Gloucester, Ontario. 6-0, 185. Last amateur club; Massachusetts (H.E.).

Kent Fearns — Defenseman

Regular Season — Playoffs

Season	Team	League	GP	G	A	PTS	PIM	GP	G	A	PTS	PIM
95-96	Cape Breton	AHL	6	0	0	0	4	—	—	—	—	—
95-96	Flint	CoHL	24	5	6	11	23	—	—	—	—	—
95-96	Knoxville	ECHL	21	1	8	9	24	8	1	5	6	6
96-97	Las Vegas	IHL	21	3	8	11	6	—	—	—	—	—
96-97	Manitoba	IHL	10	1	4	5	6	—	—	—	—	—
96-97	Knoxville	ECHL	37	11	21	32	37	—	—	—	—	—
97-98	Manitoba	IHL	65	10	23	33	32	3	0	0	0	2
98-99	Manitoba	IHL	66	14	27	41	66	5	1	5	6	8
	IHL	Totals	162	28	62	90	110	8	1	5	6	10
	ECHL	Totals	58	12	29	41	61	8	1	5	6	6

Born; 9/13/72, Langley, British Columbia. 6-0, 190. Last amateur club; Colorado College (WCHA).

Mike Feasby — Right Wing

Regular Season — Playoffs

Season	Team	League	GP	G	A	PTS	PIM	GP	G	A	PTS	PIM
96-97	York	OUAA	10	1	1	2	28	—	—	—	—	—
96-97	Muskegon	CoHL	5	1	0	1	5	3	0	0	0	12
97-98	Muskegon	UHL	68	3	4	7	169	6	0	0	0	2
98-99	Muskegon	UHL	49	0	8	8	80	2	0	0	0	4
	UHL	Totals	122	4	12	16	249	11	0	0	0	22

Born; 4/19/73, Port Perry, Ontario. 6-2, 205. Member of 1998-99 UHL Champion Muskegon Fury. Last amateur club; York University (OUAA).

Scott Feasby — Defenseman

Regular Season — Playoffs

Season	Team	League	GP	G	A	PTS	PIM	GP	G	A	PTS	PIM
90-91	Ottawa	OHL	29	2	10	12	67	17	3	8	11	22
90-91	Roanoke	ECHL	24	3	5	8	57	—	—	—	—	—
91-92	Raleigh	ECHL	20	0	5	5	47	—	—	—	—	—
91-92	Brantford	CoHL	36	2	11	13	40	6	2	1	3	4
92-93												
93-94	Muskegon	CoHL	62	7	17	24	156	3	0	1	1	5
94-95	Detroit	IHL	1	0	0	0	2	—	—	—	—	—
94-95	Kalamazoo	IHL	2	0	1	1	0	—	—	—	—	—
94-95	Phoenix	IHL	6	0	0	0	4	—	—	—	—	—
94-95	Muskegon	CoHL	63	4	15	19	75	17	0	4	4	10
95-96	Detroit	IHL	4	0	2	2	0	—	—	—	—	—
95-96	Los Angeles	IHL	22	0	1	1	34	—	—	—	—	—
95-96	Rochester	AHL	12	0	2	2	6	1	0	0	0	0
95-96	Muskegon	CoHL	44	4	8	12	107	—	—	—	—	—
96-97	Detroit	IHL	5	0	1	1	2	—	—	—	—	—
96-97	Rochester	AHL	1	0	0	0	2	—	—	—	—	—
96-97	Muskegon	CoHL	69	5	31	36	122	3	0	0	0	4
97-98	Grand Rapids	IHL	4	0	1	1	0	—	—	—	—	—
97-98	Muskegon	UHL	71	5	30	35	84	11	1	3	4	20
98-99	Muskegon	UHL	60	3	16	19	117	17	3	4	7	38
	IHL	Totals	44	0	6	6	42	—	—	—	—	—
	AHL	Totals	13	0	2	2	8	1	0	0	0	0
	UHL	Totals	405	30	128	158	701	57	6	13	19	81
	ECHL	Totals	44	3	10	13	104	—	—	—	—	—

Born; 11/20/70, Oxbridge, Ontario. 6-2, 200. Member of 1995-96 AHL champion Rochester Americans. Member of 1998-99 UHL Champion Muskegon Fury. Last amateur club; Ottawa (OHL).

Glen Featherstone — Defenseman

Regular Season — Playoffs

Season	Team	League	GP	G	A	PTS	PIM	GP	G	A	PTS	PIM
88-89	St. Louis	NHL	18	0	2	2	22	6	0	0	0	25
88-89	Peoria	IHL	37	5	19	24	97	—	—	—	—	—
89-90	St. Louis	NHL	58	0	12	12	145	12	0	2	2	47
89-90	Peoria	IHL	15	1	4	5	43	—	—	—	—	—
90-91	St. Louis	NHL	68	5	15	20	204	9	0	0	0	31
91-92	Boston	NHL	7	1	0	1	20	—	—	—	—	—
92-93	Boston	NHL	34	5	5	10	102	—	—	—	—	—
92-93	Providence	AHL	8	3	4	7	60	—	—	—	—	—
93-94	Boston	NHL	58	1	8	9	152	1	0	0	0	0
94-95	Rangers	NHL	6	1	0	1	18	—	—	—	—	—
94-95	Hartford	NHL	13	1	1	2	32	—	—	—	—	—
95-96	Hartford	NHL	68	2	10	12	138	—	—	—	—	—
96-97	Hartford	NHL	41	2	5	7	87	—	—	—	—	—
96-97	Calgary	NHL	13	1	3	4	19	—	—	—	—	—
97-98	Indianapolis	IHL	73	10	28	38	187	5	0	3	3	16
98-99	Chicago	IHL	62	5	21	26	191	10	0	3	3	26
	NHL	Totals	384	19	61	80	939	28	0	2	2	103
	IHL	Totals	187	21	72	93	518	15	0	6	6	42

Born; 7/8/68, Toronto, Ontario. 6-4, 209. Drafted by St. Louis Blues (4th choice, 73rd overall) in 1986 Entry Draft. Signed as a free agent by Boston Bruins (7/25/91). Traded to New York Rangers by Boston for Daniel Lacroix (8/19/94). Traded to Hartford Whalers by Rangers with Michael Stewart. New York Rangers' first round choice (Jean-Sebastien Giguere) in 1995 Entry Draft and fourth round choice (Steve Wasylko) in 1996 Entry Draft for Pat Verbeek (3/23/95). Traded to Calgary Flames by Hartford with Hnat Domenichelli, New Jersey's second round choice (previously acquired by Hartford-Calgary selected Dimitri Kokerev) in 1997 Entry Draft and Vancouver's third round choice (previously acquired by Hartford) in 1998 Entry Draft for Steve Chiasson and Colorado's third round choice (previously acquired by Calgary-Carolina selected Francis Lessard) in 1997 Entry Draft, (3/5/97). Last amateur club; Windsor

Brad Federenko — Forward

Regular Season — Playoffs

Season	Team	League	GP	G	A	PTS	PIM	GP	G	A	PTS	PIM
97-98	Jacksonville	ECHL	67	20	24	44	6	—	—	—	—	—
98-99	Jacksonville	ECHL	69	27	39	66	34	2	1	0	1	2
	ECHL	Totals	136	47	63	110	40	2	1	0	1	2

Born; 4/13/72, Prince Albert, Saskatchewan. 6-0, 203. Last amateur club; Minnesota-Duluth (WCHA).

Anton Fedorov — Center

Regular Season — Playoffs

Season	Team	League	GP	G	A	PTS	PIM	GP	G	A	PTS	PIM
94-95	Detroit	CoHL	4	0	0	0	0	—	—	—	—	—
94-95	Raleigh	ECHL	21	2	6	8	6	—	—	—	—	—
94-95	Johnstown	ECHL	13	5	6	11	2	5	1	1	2	0
95-96	Wichita	CeHL	64	26	38	64	62	—	—	—	—	—
96-97	Kansas City	IHL	2	0	0	0	0	—	—	—	—	—
96-97	Wichita	CeHL	66	24	41	65	79	9	0	3	3	5
97-98	Mobile	ECHL	18	4	5	9	10	—	—	—	—	—
97-98	Baton Rouge	ECHL	42	9	19	28	28	—	—	—	—	—
98-99	Colorado	WCHL	62	24	31	55	91	3	1	2	3	0
	CeHL	Totals	130	50	79	129	141	9	0	3	3	5
	ECHL	Totals	94	20	36	56	46	5	1	1	2	0

Born; 6/29/72, St. Petersbug, Russia. 5-11, 198. Traded to Baton Rouge by Mobile for Jamie Ling (12/97). Last amateur club; University of Michigan (CCHA).

Fedor Fedorov — Center

Regular Season — Playoffs

Season	Team	League	GP	G	A	PTS	PIM	GP	G	A	PTS	PIM
98-99	Port Huron	UHL	42	2	5	7	20	—	—	—	—	—

Born; 6/11/81, Moscow, Russia. 6-3, 180. Drafted by Tampa Bay Lightning (7th choice, 182nd overall) in 1999 Entry Draft.

Sergei Fedotov — Defenseman

Regular Season / Playoffs

Season	Team	League	GP	G	A	PTS	PIM	GP	G	A	PTS	PIM
96-97	Detroit	OHL	52	10	27	37	60	5	0	2	2	9
96-97	Springfield	AHL	2	0	0	0	2	—	—	—	—	—
97-98	Plymouth	OHL	38	5	11	16	33	15	3	2	5	10
97-98	New Haven	AHL	5	0	0	0	0	—	—	—	—	—
97-98	Richmond	ECHL	5	1	1	2	4	—	—	—	—	—
98-99	New Haven	AHL	3	0	0	0	2	—	—	—	—	—
98-99	Florida	ECHL	47	9	15	24	28	3	1	0	1	2
	AHL	Totals	10	0	0	0	4	—	—	—	—	—
	ECHL	Totals	52	10	16	26	32	3	1	0	1	2

Born; 1/24/77, Moscow, Russia. 6-1, 185. Drafted by Hartford Whalers (2nd choice, 35th overall) in 1995 Entry Draft. Last amateur club; Plymouth (OHL).

Drew Felder — Defenseman

Regular Season / Playoffs

Season	Team	League	GP	G	A	PTS	PIM	GP	G	A	PTS	PIM
98-99	Mississauga	OHL	36	1	7	8	68	—	—	—	—	—
98-99	Roanoke	ECHL	6	0	0	0	12	3	0	0	0	5

Born; 4/12/79, Rodney, Ontario. 6-1, 195. Selected by Greensboro in 1999 ECHL Expansion Draft. Last amateur club; Mississauga (OHL).

Chris Felix — Defenseman

Regular Season / Playoffs

Season	Team	League	GP	G	A	PTS	PIM	GP	G	A	PTS	PIM
87-88	Canada	National	68	7	27	34	68	—	—	—	—	—
87-88	Fort Wayne	IHL	19	5	17	22	24	6	4	4	8	0
88-89	Baltimore	AHL	50	8	29	37	44	—	—	—	—	—
88-89	Washington	NHL	21	0	8	8	8	1	0	1	1	0
89-90	Baltimore	AHL	73	19	42	61	115	12	0	11	11	18
89-90	Washington	NHL	6	1	0	1	2	—	—	—	—	—
90-91	Washington	NHL	8	0	4	4	0	—	—	—	—	—
90-91	Baltimore	AHL	27	4	24	28	26	6	1	4	5	6
91-92		Austria										
92-93		Austria										
93-94		Austria										
94-95		Austria										
95-96		Switz.										
96-97	Ilves Tampere	Finland	49	2	12	14	50	8	0	1	1	22
97-98	Adler Mannheim	Germany	25	0	1	1	6	3	1	0	1	4
98-99	South Carolina	ECHL	70	5	15	20	70	3	0	2	2	8
	NHL	Totals	35	1	12	13	10	1	0	1	1	0
	AHL	Totals	150	31	95	126	185	18	1	15	16	24

Born; 5/27/64, Bramalea, Ontario. 5-11, 193.Signed as a free agent by Washington Capitals (3/87). Last amateur club; Sault Ste. Marie (OHL).

Brian Felsner — Left Wing

Regular Season / Playoffs

Season	Team	League	GP	G	A	PTS	PIM	GP	G	A	PTS	PIM
96-97	Orlando	IHL	75	29	41	70	38	7	2	3	5	6
97-98	Chicago	NHL	12	1	3	4	12	—	—	—	—	—
97-98	Indianapolis	IHL	53	17	36	53	36	—	—	—	—	—
97-98	Milwaukee	IHL	15	7	8	15	20	10	3	9	12	12
98-99	Detroit	IHL	72	20	35	55	49	11	4	6	10	12
	IHL	Totals	215	73	120	193	143	28	9	18	27	30

Born; 11/7/72, Mt. Clemens, Michigan. 6-0, 190. Signed as a free agent by Chicago Blackhawks (8/27/97). Traded to Ottawa Senators by Chicago for Justin Hocking (8/21/98). 1996-97 IHL American Born Rookie of the Year. Last amateur club; Lake Superior State (CCHA).

Denny Felsner — Right Wing

Regular Season / Playoffs

Season	Team	League	GP	G	A	PTS	PIM	GP	G	A	PTS	PIM
91-92	Michigan	CCHA	44	42	52	94	46	—	—	—	—	—
91-92	St. Louis	NHL	3	0	1	1	0	1	0	0	0	0
92-93	St. Louis	NHL	6	0	3	3	2	9	2	3	5	2
92-93	Peoria	IHL	29	14	21	35	8	—	—	—	—	—
93-94	St. Louis	NHL	6	1	0	1	2	—	—	—	—	—
93-94	Peoria	IHL	6	8	3	11	14	—	—	—	—	—
94-95	St. Louis	NHL	3	0	0	0	2	—	—	—	—	—
94-95	Peoria	IHL	25	10	12	22	14	8	2	3	5	0
95-96	Syracuse	AHL	66	23	34	57	22	14	5	12	17	0
96-97	Chicago	IHL	39	10	12	22	4	—	—	—	—	—
96-97	Milwaukee	IHL	14	1	3	4	2	—	—	—	—	—
97-98	Detroit	IHL	3	0	0	0	0	—	—	—	—	—
97-98	Chesapeake	ECHL	50	30	37	67	6	—	—	—	—	—
98-99	Chesapeake	ECHL	50	29	45	74	32	8	4	1	5	2
	NHL	Totals	18	1	4	5	6	10	2	3	5	2
	IHL	Totals	116	43	51	94	42	8	2	3	5	0
	ECHL	Totals	100	59	82	141	38	8	4	1	5	2

Born; 4/29/70, Warren, Michigan. 6-0, 195. Drafted by St. Louis Blues (3rd choice, 55th overall) in 1989 Entry Draft. 1998-99 ECHL First All-Star Team. Last amateur club; University of Michigan (CCHA).

Wade Fennig — Center

Regular Season / Playoffs

Season	Team	League	GP	G	A	PTS	PIM	GP	G	A	PTS	PIM
97-98	Tallahassee	ECHL	48	11	16	27	22	—	—	—	—	—
98-99	Colorado	WCHL	65	11	20	31	58	3	0	0	0	0

Born; 9/13/73, Edmonton, Alberta. 6-1, 190. Last amateur club; Northern Alberta (CWUAA).

Eric Fenton — Right Wing

Regular Season / Playoffs

Season	Team	League	GP	G	A	PTS	PIM	GP	G	A	PTS	PIM
93-94	Hampton Roads	ECHL	24	12	16	28	39	—	—	—	—	—
93-94	Portland	AHL	25	2	5	7	104	—	—	—	—	—
94-95	Charlotte	ECHL	58	11	26	37	269	2	0	0	0	4
94-95	Peoria	IHL	8	1	1	2	20	2	0	0	0	8
95-96	Peoria	IHL	33	2	7	9	102	12	3	1	4	38
95-96	Charlotte	ECHL	4	2	1	3	36	4	1	0	1	33
96-97	Milwaukee	IHL	43	3	5	8	169	3	1	0	1	6
96-97	Charlotte	ECHL	29	15	9	24	163	—	—	—	—	—
97-98	Milwaukee	IHL	78	21	19	40	331	10	0	3	3	41
98-99	Milwaukee	IHL	5	1	2	3	24	—	—	—	—	—
	IHL	Totals	167	28	34	62	646	27	4	4	8	93
	ECHL	Totals	115	40	52	92	507	6	1	0	1	37

Born; 7/17/69, Troy, New York. 6-2, 190. Member of 1995-96 ECHL Champion Charlotte Checkers. Last amateur club; University of Maine (Hockey East).

Andrew Ference — Defenseman

Regular Season / Playoffs

Season	Team	League	GP	G	A	PTS	PIM	GP	G	A	PTS	PIM
98-99	Portland	WHL	40	11	21	32	104	4	1	4	5	10
98-99	Kansas City	IHL	5	1	2	3	4	3	0	0	0	9

Born; 3/17/79, Edmonton, Alberta. 5-10, 187. Drafted by Pittsburgh Penguins (8th choice, 208th overall) in 1997 Entry Draft. Last amateur club; Portland

Craig Ferguson — Center
Regular Season / Playoffs

Season	Team	League	GP	G	A	PTS	PIM	GP	G	A	PTS	PIM
92-93	Fredericton	AHL	55	15	13	28	20	5	0	1	1	2
92-93	Wheeling	ECHL	9	6	5	11	24	—	—	—	—	—
93-94	Montreal	NHL	2	0	1	1	0	—	—	—	—	—
93-94	Fredericton	AHL	57	29	32	61	60	—	—	—	—	—
94-95	Montreal	NHL	1	0	0	0	0	—	—	—	—	—
94-95	Fredericton	AHL	80	27	35	62	62	17	6	2	8	6
95-96	Montreal	NHL	10	1	0	1	2	—	—	—	—	—
95-96	Calgary	NHL	8	0	0	0	4	—	—	—	—	—
95-96	Saint John	AHL	18	5	13	18	8	—	—	—	—	—
95-96	Phoenix	IHL	31	6	9	15	25	4	0	2	2	6
96-97	Florida	NHL	3	0	0	0	0	—	—	—	—	—
96-97	Carolina	AHL	74	29	41	70	57	—	—	—	—	—
97-98	New Haven	AHL	64	24	28	52	41	3	2	1	3	2
98-99	New Haven	AHL	61	18	27	45	76	—	—	—	—	—
	NHL	Totals	24	1	1	2	6	—	—	—	—	—
	AHL	Totals	409	147	189	336	324	25	8	4	12	10

Born; 8/4/70, Castro Valley, California. 6-0, 185. Drafted by Montreal Canadiens (7th choice, 146th overall) in 1989 Entry Draft. Traded to Calgary Flames by Montreal with Yves Sarault for Calgary's eighth round choice (Peter Kubos) in 1997 Entry Draft (11/26/95). Traded to Los Angeles Kings by Calgary for Pat Conacher (2/10/96). Signed as a free agent by Florida Panthers (8/24/96). Last amateur club; Yale University (ECAC).

Dallas Ferguson — Defenseman
Regular Season / Playoffs

Season	Team	League	GP	G	A	PTS	PIM	GP	G	A	PTS	PIM
96-97	Alaska	WCHL	15	1	13	14	12	—	—	—	—	—
96-97	Richmond	ECHL	18	1	2	3	6	—	—	—	—	—
97-98	Anchorage	WCHL	62	2	23	25	12	8	0	5	5	4
98-99	Anchorage	WCHL	63	2	19	21	35	6	0	0	0	4
	WCHL	Totals	140	5	55	60	59	14	0	5	5	8

Born; 11/24/72, Wainwright, Alberta. 5-10, 200. Last amateur club; Alaska-Fairbanks (WCHA).

Jeff Ferguson — Goaltender
Regular Season / Playoffs

Season	Team	League	GP	W	L	T	MIN	SO	AVG	GP	W	L	MIN	SO	AVG
94-95	Fresno	SUN	8	3	4	0	367	0	5.06	—	—	—	—	—	—
95-96	Fresno	WCHL	47	22	17	7	2719	1	3.75	1	1	0	60	0	4.00
96-97	Fresno	WCHL	51	26	18	6	2895	0	3.92	5	3	2	286	0	4.62
97-98	Fresno	WCHL	*54	28	24	2	*3168	1	3.81	5	2	3	300	0	3.99
98-99	Fresno	WCHL	*59	31	24	3	3336	1	4.06	7	3	*4	418	0	3.88
	WCHL	Totals	211	107	93	18	12118	3	3.89	18	9	9	1064	0	4.12

Born; 7/23/69, Calgary, Alberta. 5-8, 175. 1996-97 WCHL Second Team All-

Scott Ferguson — Defenseman
Regular Season / Playoffs

Season	Team	League	GP	G	A	PTS	PIM	GP	G	A	PTS	PIM
94-95	Cape Breton	AHL	58	4	6	10	103	—	—	—	—	—
94-95	Wheeling	ECHL	5	1	5	6	16	—	—	—	—	—
95-96	Cape Breton	AHL	80	5	16	21	196	—	—	—	—	—
96-97	Hamilton	AHL	74	6	14	20	115	21	5	7	12	59
97-98	Edmonton	NHL	1	0	0	0	0	—	—	—	—	—
97-98	Hamilton	AHL	77	7	17	24	150	9	0	3	3	16
98-99	Anaheim	NHL	2	0	1	1	0	—	—	—	—	—
98-99	Cincinnati	AHL	78	4	31	35	144	3	0	0	0	4
	NHL	Totals	3	0	1	1	0	—	—	—	—	—
	AHL	Totals	367	26	84	110	708	33	5	10	15	79

Born; 1/6/73, Camrose, Alberta. 6-1, 191. Signed as a free agent by Edmonton Oilers (6/2/94). Traded to Ottawa by Edmonton for Frank Musil (3/9/98). Signed as a free agent by Anaheim Mighty Ducks (7/22/98). Last amateur club; Kam-

Tim Ferguson — Left Wing
Regular Season / Playoffs

Season	Team	League	GP	G	A	PTS	PIM	GP	G	A	PTS	PIM
86-87	Salt Lake City	IHL	80	28	39	67	44	17	3	0	3	6
87-88	Peoria	IHL	55	3	16	19	37	—	—	—	—	—
87-88	Springfield	AHL	3	0	0	0	2	—	—	—	—	—
88-89												
89-90												
90-91												
91-92												
92-93												
93-94												
94-95	Augsberg	Germany	43	8	11	19	52	3	7	1	8	12
95-96	Augsberg	Germany	50	11	19	30	30	—	—	—	—	—
96-97	Augsberg	Germany	48	6	10	16	48	4	1	0	1	0
97-98	Indianapolis	IHL	3	1	1	2	0	—	—	—	—	—
97-98	Nashville	CHL	53	26	30	56	28	9	5	2	7	8
98-99	Florida	ECHL	67	33	36	69	53	6	2	1	3	2
	IHL	Totals	138	32	56	88	81	17	3	0	3	6

Born; 9/9/66, Kingston, Ontario. 5-10, 192. Member of 1986-87 IHL Champion Salt Lake City. Selected by San Antonio in 1998 CHL Expansion Draft.

Robert Ferm — Defenseman
Regular Season / Playoffs

Season	Team	League	GP	G	A	PTS	PIM	GP	G	A	PTS	PIM
98-99	Asheville	UHL	1	0	1	1	0	—	—	—	—	—

Born; 10/9/73, Goteberg, Sweden.

Manny Fernandez — Goaltender
Regular Season / Playoffs

Season	Team	League	GP	W	L	T	MIN	SO	AVG	GP	W	L	MIN	SO	AVG
94-95	Dallas	NHL	1	0	1	0	59	0	3.05	—	—	—	—	—	—
94-95	Kalamazoo	IHL	46	21	10	9	2470	2	2.79	14	10	2	753	1	2.71
95-96	Dallas	NHL	5	0	1	1	249	0	4.58	—	—	—	—	—	—
95-96	Michigan	IHL	47	22	15	9	2663	4	3.00	6	5	1	372	0	2.26
96-97	Michigan	IHL	48	20	24	2	2721	2	3.13	4	1	3	277	0	3.25
97-98	Dallas	NHL	2	1	0	0	69	0	1.74	1	0	0	2	0	0.00
97-98	Michigan	IHL	55	27	17	5	3023	5	2.76	2	0	2	89	0	4.73
98-99	Dallas	NHL	1	0	1	0	60	0	2.00	—	—	—	—	—	—
98-99	Houston	IHL	50	34	6	9	2949	2	2.36	*19	*11	*8	*1126	1	2.61
	NHL	Totals	9	1	3	1	437	0	3.57	1	0	0	2	0	0.00
	IHL	Totals	246	124	72	34	13814	15	2.80	45	27	16	2617	2	2.73

Born; 8/27/74, Etobicoke, Ontario. 6-0, 185. Drafted by Quebec Nordiques (4th choice, 52nd overall) in 1992 Entry Draft. Rights traded to Dallas Stars by Quebec for Tommy Sjodin and Dallas' third round choice (Chris Drury) in 1994 Entry Draft (2/13/94). Member of 1998-99 IHL Champion Houston Aeros. Last amateur club; Laval (QMJHL).

Mark Ferner — Defenseman

Regular Season / Playoffs

Season	Team	League	GP	G	A	PTS	PIM	GP	G	A	PTS	PIM
85-86	Rochester	AHL	63	3	14	17	87	—	—	—	—	—
86-87	Buffalo	NHL	13	0	3	3	9	—	—	—	—	—
86-87	Rochester	AHL	54	0	12	12	157	—	—	—	—	—
87-88	Rochester	AHL	69	1	25	26	165	7	1	4	5	31
88-89	Buffalo	NHL	2	0	0	0	2	—	—	—	—	—
88-89	Rochester	AHL	55	0	18	18	97	—	—	—	—	—
89-90	Washington	NHL	2	0	0	0	0	—	—	—	—	—
89-90	Baltimore	AHL	74	7	28	35	76	11	1	2	3	21
90-91	Washington	NHL	7	0	1	1	4	—	—	—	—	—
90-91	Baltimore	AHL	61	14	40	54	38	6	1	4	5	24
91-92	Baltimore	AHL	57	7	38	45	67	—	—	—	—	—
91-92	St. John's	AHL	15	1	8	9	6	14	2	14	16	38
92-93	New Haven	AHL	34	5	7	12	69	—	—	—	—	—
92-93	San Diego	IHL	26	0	15	15	34	11	1	2	3	8
93-94	Anaheim	NHL	50	3	5	8	30	—	—	—	—	—
94-95	Anaheim	NHL	14	0	1	1	6	—	—	—	—	—
94-95	Detroit	NHL	3	0	0	0	0	—	—	—	—	—
94-95	San Diego	IHL	46	3	12	15	51	—	—	—	—	—
94-95	Adirondack	AHL	3	0	0	0	2	1	0	0	0	0
95-96	Orlando	IHL	43	4	18	22	37	23	4	10	14	8
96-97	Orlando	IHL	61	12	18	30	55	—	—	—	—	—
96-97	Long Beach	IHL	17	2	6	8	31	18	3	4	7	6
97-98	Long Beach	IHL	65	1	30	31	66	16	2	11	13	10
98-99	Long Beach	IHL	59	2	24	26	78	8	1	3	4	14
	NHL	Totals	91	3	10	13	51	—	—	—	—	—
	AHL	Totals	485	38	198	236	764	39	5	24	29	114
	IHL	Totals	317	24	123	147	342	76	11	30	41	46

Born; 9/5/65, Regina, Saskatchewan. 6-0, 195. Drafted by Buffalo Sabres (12th choice, 194th overall) in 1983 Entry Draft. Traded to Washington Capitals by Buffalo for Scott McCrory (6/1/89). Traded to Toronto Maple Leafs by Washington for future considerations (2/27/92). Signed as a free agent by Ottawa Senators (8/6/92). Claimed by Anaheim Might Ducks from Ottawa in Expansion Draft (6/24/93). Traded to Detroit Red Wings by Anaheim with Stu Grimson and Anaheim's sixth pick (Magnus Nilsson) for Mike Sillinger and Jason York (4/4/95). 1990-91 AHL Second Team All-Star. Last amateur club; Kamloops (WHL).

Paul Ferone — Left Wing

Regular Season / Playoffs

Season	Team	League	GP	G	A	PTS	PIM	GP	G	A	PTS	PIM
97-98	Syracuse	AHL	20	1	3	4	85	—	—	—	—	—
97-98	Raleigh	ECHL	30	7	5	12	68	—	—	—	—	—
98-99	Syracuse	AHL	28	0	2	2	109	—	—	—	—	—
	AHL	Totals	48	1	5	6	194	—	—	—	—	—

Born; 4/12/76, Vancouver, British Columbia. 5-11, 185. Signed as a free agent by Vancouver Canucks (9/19/97). Last amateur club; Seattle (WHL).

Steve Ferranti — Center

Regular Season / Playoffs

Season	Team	League	GP	G	A	PTS	PIM	GP	G	A	PTS	PIM
97-98	Peoria	ECHL	10	0	2	2	4	—	—	—	—	—
97-98	Louisville	ECHL	43	10	14	24	36	—	—	—	—	—
98-99	Amarillo	WPHL	47	27	31	58	17	—	—	—	—	—
98-99	Arkansas	WPHL	10	0	4	4	2	3	0	2	2	0
	WPHL	Totals	57	27	35	62	19	3	0	2	2	0
	ECHL	Totals	53	10	16	26	40	—	—	—	—	—

Born; 1/12/74, Windsor, Ontario. 5-10, 182. Selected by Greenville in 1998 ECHL Expansion Draft. Traded to Arkansas by Amarillo for Eric Andersen and future considerations (2/99). Last amateur club; Michigan State (CCHA).

Robert Ferraris — Defenseman

Regular Season / Playoffs

Season	Team	League	GP	G	A	PTS	PIM	GP	G	A	PTS	PIM
97-98	Saginaw	UHL	26	2	4	6	12	—	—	—	—	—
97-98	Port Huron	UHL	45	2	1	3	41	4	0	0	0	6
98-99	Mohawk Valley	UHL	74	3	19	22	139	—	—	—	—	—
	UHL	Totals	145	7	24	31	192	4	0	0	0	6

Born; 9/6/74, Weymouth, Massachusetts. 6-2, 205. Traded to Port Huron from Saginaw with Dale Greenwood and Jason Renard for James D. Eaton, Joel Gardner and David Geris (12/97). Last amateur club; St. Anselm (ECAC 2).

Chris Ferraro — Center

Regular Season / Playoffs

Season	Team	League	GP	G	A	PTS	PIM	GP	G	A	PTS	PIM
93-94	United States	National	48	8	34	4	58	—	—	—	—	—
94-95	Atlanta	IHL	54	13	14	27	72	—	—	—	—	—
94-95	Binghamton	AHL	13	6	4	10	38	10	2	3	5	16
95-96	Rangers	NHL	2	1	0	1	0	—	—	—	—	—
95-96	Binghamton	AHL	77	32	67	99	208	4	4	2	6	13
96-97	Rangers	NHL	12	1	1	2	6	—	—	—	—	—
96-97	Binghamton	AHL	53	29	34	63	94	—	—	—	—	—
97-98	Pittsburgh	NHL	46	3	4	7	43	—	—	—	—	—
98-99	Edmonton	NHL	2	1	0	1	0	—	—	—	—	—
98-99	Hamilton	AHL	72	35	41	76	104	11	8	5	13	20
	NHL	Totals	62	6	5	11	49	—	—	—	—	—
	AHL	Totals	215	102	146	248	444	25	14	10	24	49

Born; 1/24/73, Port Jefferson, New York. 5-10, 185. Drafted by New York Rangers (4th choice, 85th overall) in 1992 Entry Draft. Claimed on waivers by Pittsburgh Penguins from Rangers (10/1/97). Signed as a free agent by Edmonton Oilers (8/13/98). Signed as a free agent by New York Islanders (7/7/99). Last amateur club; Maine (Hockey East).

Peter Ferraro — Right Wing

Regular Season / Playoffs

Season	Team	League	GP	G	A	PTS	PIM	GP	G	A	PTS	PIM
94-95	Atlanta	IHL	61	15	24	39	118	—	—	—	—	—
94-95	Binghamton	AHL	12	2	6	8	67	11	4	3	7	51
95-96	Rangers	NHL	5	0	1	1	0	—	—	—	—	—
95-96	Binghamton	AHL	68	48	53	101	157	4	1	6	7	22
96-97	Rangers	NHL	2	0	0	0	0	2	0	0	0	0
96-97	Binghamton	AHL	75	38	39	77	171	4	3	1	4	18
97-98	Pittsburgh	NHL	29	3	4	7	12	—	—	—	—	—
97-98	Rangers	NHL	1	0	0	0	2	—	—	—	—	—
97-98	Hartford	AHL	36	17	23	40	54	15	8	6	14	59
98-99	Boston	NHL	46	6	8	14	44	—	—	—	—	—
98-99	Providence	AHL	16	15	10	25	14	19	9	12	*21	38
	NHL	Totals	37	3	5	8	14	2	0	0	0	0
	AHL	Totals	191	105	121	226	449	53	25	28	53	188

Born; 1/24/73, Long Island, New York. 5-10, 190. Drafted by New York Rangers (1st choice, 24th overall) in 1992 Entry Draft. Claimed in 1998 Waiver Draft by Pittsburgh Penguins. Claimed on waivers by Rangers. Signed as a free agent by Boston Bruins (7/21/98). Selected by Atlanta Thrashers in 1999 NHL Expansion Draft (6/25/99). Traded to Boston by Atlanta for Randy Robitaille (6/25/99). 1995-96 AHL First Team All-Star. 1998-99 AHL Playoff MVP. Member of 1998-99 IHL Champion Providence Bruins. Last amateur club; University of

Joe Ferras (Ferraccioli) — Center

Regular Season / Playoffs

Season	Team	League	GP	G	A	PTS	PIM	GP	G	A	PTS	PIM
88-89	Adirondack	AHL	35	7	8	15	8	—	—	—	—	—
89-90	Halifax	AHL	6	1	2	3	2	—	—	—	—	—
89-90	Winston-Salem	ECHL	49	45	63	108	56	10	3	*13	16	30
90-91	Winston-Salem	ECHL	20	17	23	40	8	—	—	—	—	—
90-91	Richmond	ECHL	26	15	35	50	17	4	0	5	5	6
91-92												
92-93												
93-94	Streatham	BHL	5	7	6	13	4	—	—	—	—	—
93-94	Milan	Italy										
93-94	Fassa	Italy	22	12	33	45	14	—	—	—	—	—
94-95	Milan	Italy										
95-96	Milan	Italy										
96-97	Bracknell	BHL	23	5	7	12	16	—	—	—	—	—
97-98	Bracknell	BSL	57	15	49	64	36	6	3	3	6	0
98-99	Bracknell	BSL	49	13	39	52	30	7	2	5	7	14
	AHL	Totals	41	8	10	18	10	—	—	—	—	—
	ECHL	Totals	95	77	121	198	81	14	3	18	21	36

Born; 5/1/66. 5-9, 180. 1989-90 ECHL Second Team All-Star. Last amateur club; Plattsburgh (SUNY-NCAA 3).

Pat Ferschweiler — Center

Regular Season / Playoffs

Season	Team	League	GP	G	A	PTS	PIM	GP	G	A	PTS	PIM
93-94	Roanoke	ECHL	68	27	58	85	79	2	0	1	1	2
94-95	Roanoke	ECHL	22	8	22	30	44	—	—	—	—	—
94-95	Minnesota	IHL	1	0	0	0	0	—	—	—	—	—
94-95	Kansas City	IHL	49	11	18	29	28	20	2	4	6	22
95-96	Kansas City	IHL	16	0	3	3	8	—	—	—	—	—
95-96	San Francisco	IHL	42	3	7	10	42	4	0	0	0	0
96-97	Kansas City	IHL	49	4	6	10	42	2	0	1	1	2
97-98	Kansas City	IHL	79	16	27	43	73	10	2	2	4	8
98-99	Kansas City	IHL	80	7	38	45	66	3	0	1	1	2
	IHL	Totals	306	41	99	140	259	39	4	8	12	34
	ECHL	Totals	90	35	80	115	113	2	0	1	1	2

Born; 2/20/70, Rochester, Minnesota. 6-1, 205. Last amateur club; Western Michigan (CCHA).

David Ficenec — Defenseman

Regular Season / Playoffs

Season	Team	League	GP	G	A	PTS	PIM	GP	G	A	PTS	PIM
98-99	Johnstown	ECHL	21	0	1	1	2	—	—	—	—	—

Born; 5/16/78, Rhadec Kralove, Czech Republic. 6-1, 185.

Jakub Ficenec — Defenseman

Regular Season / Playoffs

Season	Team	League	GP	G	A	PTS	PIM	GP	G	A	PTS	PIM
98-99	Portland	AHL	5	3	2	5	4	—	—	—	—	—
98-99	Johnstown	ECHL	59	18	23	41	54	—	—	—	—	—

Born; 2/11/77, Rhadec Kralove, Czech Republic. 5-11, 198. Last amateur club; Surrey (BCJHL).

Eric Fichaud — Goaltender

Regular Season / Playoffs

Season	Team	League	GP	W	L	T	MIN	SO	AVG	GP	W	L	MIN	SO	AVG
95-96	Islanders	NHL	24	7	12	2	1234	1	3.31	—	—	—	—	—	—
95-96	Worcester	AHL	34	13	15	6	1989	1	2.93	2	1	1	127	0	3.30
96-97	Islanders	NHL	34	9	14	4	1759	0	3.10	—	—	—	—	—	—
97-98	Islanders	NHL	17	3	8	3	807	0	2.97	—	—	—	—	—	—
97-98	Utah	IHL	1	0	0	0	40	0	4.45	—	—	—	—	—	—
98-99	Nashville	NHL	9	0	6	0	447	0	3.22	—	—	—	—	—	—
98-99	Milwaukee	IHL	8	5	2	1	480	0	3.13	—	—	—	—	—	—
	NHL	Totals	84	19	40	9	4247	1	3.15	—	—	—	—	—	—
	IHL	Totals	9	5	2	1	520	0	3.23	—	—	—	—	—	—

Born; 11/4/75, Anjou, Quebec. 5-11, 171. Drafted by Toronto Maple Leafs (1st chioce, 13th overall) in 1994 Entry Draft. Traded to New York Islanders by Toronto for Benoit Hogue, Islanders third choice (Ryan Pepperall) in 1995 Entry Draft and fifth round choice (Brandon Sugden) in 1996 Entry Draft (4/6/95) Traded to Edmonton Oilers for Mike Watt (6/18/98). Traded to Nashville Predators by Edmonton with Drake Berehowsky and Greg DeVries for Mikhail Shtalenkov and Jim Dowd (10/1/98). Traded to Carolina Hurricanes by Nashville for Carolina's fourth round choice (Yevgeny Pavlov) in 1999 Entry Draft (6/26/99). Last amateur club; Chicoutimi (QMJHL).

Jed Fiebelkorn — Right Wing

Regular Season / Playoffs

Season	Team	League	GP	G	A	PTS	PIM	GP	G	A	PTS	PIM
95-96	Worcester	AHL	13	0	1	1	5	—	—	—	—	—
95-96	Jacksonville	ECHL	29	3	8	11	57	—	—	—	—	—
95-96	Tallahassee	ECHL	21	6	6	12	18	12	1	2	3	10
96-97	Tallahassee	ECHL	66	21	18	39	101	3	0	0	0	4
97-98	Michigan	IHL	46	7	6	13	64	3	0	0	0	2
98-99	Grand Rapids	IHL	5	0	2	2	5	—	—	—	—	—
98-99	Fort Wayne	IHL	10	0	5	5	6	—	—	—	—	—
98-99	Miami	ECHL	46	18	17	35	103	—	—	—	—	—
	IHL	Totals	61	7	13	20	75	3	0	0	0	2
	ECHL	Totals	162	48	49	97	279	15	1	2	3	14

Born; 9/1/72, Minneapolis, Minnesota. 6-3, 220. Drafted by St. Louis Blues (9th choice, 197th overall) in 1991 Entry Draft. Last amateur club; University of Minnesota (WCHA).

Tom Field — Right Wing

Regular Season / Playoffs

Season	Team	League	GP	G	A	PTS	PIM	GP	G	A	PTS	PIM
98-99	Pee Dee	ECHL	39	4	9	13	30	13	3	1	4	0

Born; Braintree, Massachusetts. 5-9, 175. Last amateur club; Salem State (NCAA 3).

Sam Fields — Defenseman

Regular Season / Playoffs

Season	Team	League	GP	G	A	PTS	PIM	GP	G	A	PTS	PIM
96-97	Nashville	CeHL	23	2	6	8	88	—	—	—	—	—
96-97	Wichita	CeHL	2	0	0	0	16	—	—	—	—	—
96-97	Huntsville	CeHL	6	0	0	0	25	—	—	—	—	—
97-98	Tucson	WCHL	21	0	2	2	110	—	—	—	—	—
97-98	Idaho	WCHL	21	0	3	3	38	2	0	0	0	15
98-99	Las Vegas	IHL	1	0	0	0	10	—	—	—	—	—
98-99	Memphis	CHL	21	1	3	4	95	—	—	—	—	—
98-99	Dayton	ECHL	4	0	0	0	7	—	—	—	—	—
98-99	Bakersfield	WCHL	22	1	3	4	83	—	—	—	—	—
	WCHL	Totals	64	1	8	9	231	2	0	0	0	15
	CHL	Totals	52	3	9	12	224	—	—	—	—	—

Born; 8/31/76, Chicago, Illinois. 6-3, 200.

Mike Figliomeni — Left Wing

Regular Season / Playoffs

Season	Team	League	GP	G	A	PTS	PIM	GP	G	A	PTS	PIM
95-96	Michigan Tech.	WCHA	42	7	23	30	38	—	—	—	—	—
95-96	South Carolina	ECHL	5	2	2	4	2	—	—	—	—	—
96-97	Waco	WPHL	14	4	4	8	6	—	—	—	—	—
96-97	Thunder Bay	CoHL	53	22	35	57	21	11	2	5	7	4
97-98	Thunder Bay	UHL	69	52	75	127	38	5	3	5	8	2
98-99	Fassa	Italy	16	10	8	18	16	—	—	—	—	—
	UHL	Totals	122	74	110	184	59	16	5	10	16	6

Born; 5/3/72, Thunder Bay, Ontario. 5-5, 155. Last amateur club; Michigan Technical University (WCHA).

Jean-ian Filiatrault — Goaltender

Regular Season / Playoffs

Season	Team	League	GP	W	L	T	MIN	SO	AVG	GP	W	L	MIN	SO	AVG
95-96	Oklahoma City	CeHL	42	*30	7	2	2350	1	3.57	12	8	4	722	0	2.74
96-97	Oklahoma City	CeHL	41	26	9	4	2186	1	*2.80	—	—	—	—	—	—
97-98	Macon	CHL	9	5	1	2	498	0	3.37	1	0	1	59	0	2.04
97-98	Dayton	ECHL	10	4	4	0	475	0	3.79	—	—	—	—	—	—
97-98	Jacksonville	ECHL	2	0	1	0	96	0	6.88	—	—	—	—	—	—
98-99	Oklahoma City	CHL	43	30	12	1	2532	*6	*2.54	12	9	3	733	*1	2.45
	CHL	Totals	135	91	29	9	7566	8	2.99	25	17	8	1514	1	2.58
	ECHL	Totals	12	4	5	0	571	0	4.31	—	—	—	—	—	—

Born; 3/5/74, Laval West, Quebec. 5-11, 165. Traded to Jacksonville by Dayton for Scott Thompson (12/97). 1995-96 CeHL Goaltender of the Year. 1995-96 CeHL Second Team All-Star. 1995-96 President Trophy (CeHL Playoff MVP) winner. Member of 1995-96 CeHL Champion Oklahoma City Blazers. 1996-97 CeHL Second Team All-Star. 1998-99 CHL Goaltender of the Year.

Ron Filion — Right Wing

Regular Season / Playoffs

Season	Team	League	GP	G	A	PTS	PIM	GP	G	A	PTS	PIM
98-99	Tucson	WCHL	17	1	4	5	10	—	—	—	—	—

Born; 9/2/65, Montreal, Quebec. 5-9, 185.

Claude Fillion — Defenseman

Regular Season / Playoffs

Season	Team	League	GP	G	A	PTS	PIM	GP	G	A	PTS	PIM
94-95	Halifax	QMJHL	28	1	9	10	133	—	—	—	—	—
94-95	St. Jean	QMJHL	23	0	6	6	87	7	1	0	1	31
94-95	Providence	AHL	1	0	0	0	0	—	—	—	—	—
95-96	Hampton Roads	ECHL	39	2	14	16	144	3	0	2	2	8
96-97	Macon	CeHL	62	15	30	45	246	5	1	2	3	36
97-98	Macon	CHL	35	5	14	19	178	—	—	—	—	—
97-98	Columbus	CHL	30	5	8	13	111	2	1	0	1	4
98-99	Columbus	CHL	30	2	15	17	75	8	1	5	6	38
	CHL	Totals	157	27	67	94	610	15	3	7	10	78

Born; 7/9/74, Baie-St. Paul, Quebec. 6-3, 207. Traded to Memphis from Columbus with cash for Dan Brown (6/99). Member of 1997-98 CHL Champion Columbus Cottonmouths. Last amateur club; St. Jean (QMJHL).

Martin Fillion — Goaltender

Regular Season / Playoffs

Season	Team	League	GP	W	L	T	MIN	SO	AVG	GP	W	L	MIN	SO	AVG
97-98	Lowell	H.E.	26	12	10	1	1378	1	3.27	—	—	—	—	—	—
97-98	Wheeling	ECHL	—	—	—	—	—	—	—	1	0	0	20	0	3.00
98-99	Quad City	UHL	38	21	8	3	2028	1	3.37	3	1	1	164	0	2.57

Born; 6/12/73, Winnipeg, Manitoba. 5-9, 185. Selected by Fort Wayne in 1999 UHL Expansion Draft. Last amateur club; Lowell University (Hockey East).

Rick Findlay — Defenseman

Regular Season / Playoffs

Season	Team	League	GP	G	A	PTS	PIM	GP	G	A	PTS	PIM
98-99	Fort Worth	CHL	15	1	2	3	19	—	—	—	—	—
98-99	South Carolina	ECHL	4	0	0	0	0	—	—	—	—	—

Born; 9/22/75, Halifax, Nova Scotia. 6-2, 205.

Tim Findlay — Right Wing

Regular Season / Playoffs

Season	Team	League	GP	G	A	PTS	PIM	GP	G	A	PTS	PIM
96-97	Windsor	OHL	59	39	43	82	22	5	5	5	10	10
96-97	Syracuse	AHL	2	0	0	0	0	—	—	—	—	—
97-98	Houston	IHL	2	0	0	0	0	—	—	—	—	—
97-98	Austin	WPHL	50	42	32	74	8	5	4	1	5	0
98-99	Arkansas	WPHL	69	45	64	109	80	3	2	2	4	0
	WPHL	Totals	119	87	96	183	88	8	6	3	9	0

Born; 9/20/76, Windsor, Ontario. 6-0, 190. Traded to Arkansas by Austin for Marty Diamond and Rusty McKie (8/98). Last amateur club; Windsor (OHL).

Tim Fingerhut — Left Wing

Regular Season / Playoffs

Season	Team	League	GP	G	A	PTS	PIM	GP	G	A	PTS	PIM
92-93	Chatham	CoHL	5	1	2	3	0	—	—	—	—	—
92-93	Muskegon	CoHL	44	13	7	20	9	—	—	—	—	—
93-94	Utica	CoHL	58	24	34	58	53	—	—	—	—	—
94-95	Utica	CoHL	56	28	30	58	79	6	1	4	5	4
95-96	Utica	CoHL	58	25	23	58	95	—	—	—	—	—
95-96	Detroit	CoHL	13	3	7	10	25	10	4	2	6	12
96-97	Port Huron	CoHL	35	7	11	18	45	—	—	—	—	—
96-97	Utica	CoHL	39	9	23	32	42	3	1	0	1	9
97-98	Fort Wayne	IHL	2	0	0	0	0	—	—	—	—	—
97-98	Cincinnati	AHL	4	0	1	1	2	—	—	—	—	—
97-98	Columbus	ECHL	64	29	30	59	167	—	—	—	—	—
98-99	Cleveland	IHL	1	0	0	0	0	—	—	—	—	—
98-99	Columbus	ECHL	62	24	29	53	148	4	1	3	4	4
	IHL	Totals	3	0	0	0	0	—	—	—	—	—
	CoHL	Totals	308	110	137	247	348	19	6	6	12	25
	ECHL	Totals	126	53	59	112	315	4	1	3	4	4

Born; 5/20/71, Pennsauken, New Jersey. 6-0, 195. Drafted by Pittsburgh Penguins (12th choice, 194th overall) in 1990 Entry Draft. Selected by Wheeling in 1999 Dispersal Draft. Last amateur club; University of Vermont (ECAC).

Jeff Finley — Defenseman

Regular Season / Playoffs

Season	Team	League	GP	G	A	PTS	PIM	GP	G	A	PTS	PIM
87-88	Islanders	NHL	10	0	5	5	15	1	0	0	0	2
87-88	Springfield	AHL	52	5	18	23	50	—	—	—	—	—
88-89	Islanders	NHL	4	0	0	0	6	—	—	—	—	—
88-89	Springfield	AHL	65	3	16	19	55	—	—	—	—	—
89-90	Islanders	NHL	11	0	1	1	0	5	0	2	2	2
89-90	Springfield	AHL	57	1	15	16	41	13	1	4	5	23
90-91	Islanders	NHL	11	0	0	0	4	—	—	—	—	—
90-91	Capital District	AHL	67	10	34	44	34	—	—	—	—	—
91-92	Islanders	NHL	51	1	10	11	26	—	—	—	—	—
91-92	Capital District	AHL	20	1	9	10	6	—	—	—	—	—
92-93	Capital District	AHL	61	6	29	35	34	4	0	1	1	0
93-94	Philadelphia	NHL	55	1	8	9	24	—	—	—	—	—
94-95	Hershey	AHL	36	2	9	11	33	6	0	1	1	8
95-96	Winnipeg	NHL	65	1	5	6	81	6	0	0	0	4
95-96	Springfield	AHL	14	3	12	15	22	—	—	—	—	—
96-97	Phoenix	NHL	65	3	7	10	40	1	0	0	0	2
97-98	Rangers	NHL	63	1	6	7	55	—	—	—	—	—
98-99	Rangers	NHL	2	0	0	0	0	—	—	—	—	—
98-99	St. Louis	NHL	30	1	2	3	20	13	1	2	3	8
98-99	Hartford	AHL	42	2	10	12	28	—	—	—	—	—
	NHL	Totals	367	8	44	52	271	26	1	4	5	18
	AHL	Totals	413	33	152	185	303	23	1	6	7	31

Born; 4/14/67, Edmonton, Alberta. 6-2, 205. Drafted by New York Islanders (4th choice, 55th overall) in 1985 Entry Draft. Traded to Ottawa Senators by Islanders for Chris Luongo (6/30/93). Signed as a free agent by Philadelphia Flyers (7/30/93). Traded to Winnipeg Jets by Philadelphia for Russ Romaniuk (6/27/95). Signed as a free agent by New York Rangers (8/18/97). Traded to St. Louis Blues by Rangers with Geoff Smith and cash for Chris Kenady (2/13/99). Last amateur club; Portland (WHL).

Shannon Finn — Defenseman

Regular Season / Playoffs

Season	Team	League	GP	G	A	PTS	PIM	GP	G	A	PTS	PIM
94-95	Illinois-Chicago	CCHA	37	9	23	32	40	—	—	—	—	—
94-95	Canada	National	9	0	2	2	2	—	—	—	—	—
94-95	Minnesota	IHL	3	0	2	2	6	—	—	—	—	—
95-96	Peoria	IHL	67	4	22	26	75	12	1	1	2	10
96-97	Fort Wayne	IHL	1	0	1	1	0	—	—	—	—	—
96-97	Utah	IHL	2	0	2	2	0	—	—	—	—	—
96-97	Milwaukee	IHL	70	7	8	15	83	3	1	1	2	2
97-98	Milwaukee	IHL	74	5	28	33	108	10	4	5	9	10
98-99	Milwaukee	IHL	35	6	11	17	22	2	0	0	0	6
98-99	Hershey	AHL	42	4	15	19	57	—	—	—	—	—
	IHL	Totals	252	22	74	96	294	29	6	7	13	28

Born; 1/25/72, Toronto, Ontario. 6-2, 195. Drafted by Philadelphia Flyers (1st choice, 10th overall) in 1993 Supplemental Draft. Signed as a free agent by Nashville Predators (8/26/98). Last amateur club; University of Illinois-Chicago (CCHA).

Jon Finstrom — Left Wing

Regular Season / Playoffs

Season	Team	League	GP	G	A	PTS	PIM	GP	G	A	PTS	PIM
92-93	Daytona Beach	SUN	37	6	16	22	44	—	—	—	—	—
92-93	Minnesota	AHA	3	1	1	2	6	—	—	—	—	—
93-94	Huntsville	ECHL	5	0	1	1	0	—	—	—	—	—
93-94	Daytona Beach	SUN	54	8	18	26	107	2	0	1	1	2
94-95	Daytona Beach	SUN	4	0	1	1	17	—	—	—	—	—
95-96	Detroit	CoHL	68	15	23	38	211	10	0	1	1	33
96-97	Port Huron	CoHL	49	4	12	16	64	5	2	5	7	8
97-98	Port Huron	UHL	63	5	29	34	78	3	0	1	1	4
98-99	Mohawk Valley	UHL	3	0	0	0	2	—	—	—	—	—
98-99	Saginaw	UHL	20	1	2	3	21	—	—	—	—	—
98-99	Miami	ECHL	8	0	2	2	6	—	—	—	—	—
	UHL	Totals	203	25	66	91	376	18	2	7	9	45
	SUN	Totals	95	14	35	49	168	2	0	1	1	2
	ECHL	Totals	13	0	3	3	6	—	—	—	—	—

Born; 9/2/71, Los Angeles, California. 5-10, 180.

Paul Fiorini
Left Wing

Season	Team	League	GP	G	A	PTS	PIM	GP	G	A	PTS	PIM
			Regular Season					Playoffs				
97-98	Lake Charles	WPHL	15	4	0	4	*86	—	—	—	—	—
97-98	Odessa	WPHL	43	8	15	23	*239	—	—	—	—	—
98-99	Odessa	WPHL	26	3	9	12	111	—	—	—	—	—
98-99	Lake Charles	WPHL	33	2	8	10	84	8	1	0	1	16
	WPHL	Totals	117	17	32	49	520	8	1	0	1	16

Born; 8/7/76, Calgary, Alberta. 6-2, 215. Traded to Odessa by Lake Charles for Mike Henderson and Jeff Smith (11/97).

Jason Firth
Center

Season	Team	League	GP	G	A	PTS	PIM	GP	G	A	PTS	PIM
			Regular Season					Playoffs				
92-93	New Haven	AHL	4	0	1	1	4	—	—	—	—	—
92-93	Thunder Bay	CoHL	49	36	64	100	10	11	8	9	17	2
93-94	Prince Edward Island	AHL	61	15	46	61	66	—	—	—	—	—
93-94	Thunder Bay	CoHL	13	10	16	26	2	—	—	—	—	—
94-95	Prince Edward Island	AHL	4	1	0	1	2	—	—	—	—	—
94-95	Syracuse	AHL	20	4	13	17	4	—	—	—	—	—
94-95	Thunder Bay	CoHL	59	29	65	94	37	11	6	*22	28	8
95-96	Thunder Bay	CoHL	74	39	94	133	50	19	10	*23	*33	24
96-97	Thunder Bay	CoHL	56	37	83	120	22	11	7	14	21	8
97-98	Thunder Bay	UHL	69	*63	99	162	46	3	2	1	3	0
98-99	Thunder Bay	UHL	73	50	*91	*141	32	13	6	13	19	0
	AHL	Totals	89	20	60	80	76	—	—	—	—	—

Born; 3/29/71, Dartmouth, Nova Scotia. 5-11, 186. Drafted by Detroit Red Wings (8th choice, 208th overall) in 1991 Entry Draft. 1992-93 CoHL Rookie of the Year. 1992-93 CoHL MVP. 1992-93 CoHL Second Team All-Star. 1995-96 CoHL Second Team All-Star. Member of 1994-95 CoHL champion Thunder Bay Senators. 1996-97 Second Team CoHL All-Star. 1997-98 UHL MVP. 1997-98 UHL First Team All-Star. 1998-99 UHL MVP. 1998-99 UHL First All-Star Team. Last amateur club; North Bay (OHL).

Craig Fisher
Center

Season	Team	League	GP	G	A	PTS	PIM	GP	G	A	PTS	PIM
			Regular Season					Playoffs				
89-90	Miami-Ohio	CCHA	39	37	29	66	38	—	—	—	—	—
89-90	Philadelphia	NHL	2	0	0	0	0	—	—	—	—	—
90-91	Philadelphia	NHL	2	0	0	0	0	—	—	—	—	—
90-91	Hershey	AHL	77	43	36	79	46	7	5	3	8	2
91-92	Cape Breton	AHL	60	20	25	45	28	1	0	0	0	0
92-93	Cape Breton	AHL	75	32	29	61	74	1	0	0	0	0
93-94	Winnipeg	NHL	4	0	0	0	2	—	—	—	—	—
93-94	Cape Breton	AHL	16	5	5	10	11	—	—	—	—	—
93-94	Moncton	AHL	46	26	35	61	36	21	11	11	22	28
94-95	Indianapolis	IHL	77	53	40	93	65	—	—	—	—	—
95-96	Orlando	IHL	82	*74	56	130	81	14	10	7	17	6
96-97	Florida	NHL	4	0	0	0	0	—	—	—	—	—
96-97	Utah	IHL	15	6	7	13	4	—	—	—	—	—
96-97	Carolina	AHL	42	33	29	62	16	—	—	—	—	—
97-98	Kolner Haie	German	34	9	8	17	34	—	—	—	—	—
98-99	Rochester	AHL	70	29	52	81	28	20	9	11	20	10
	NHL	Totals	12	0	0	0	2	—	—	—	—	—
	AHL	Totals	386	188	211	399	239	50	25	25	50	40
	IHL	Totals	174	133	103	236	150	14	10	7	17	6

Born; 6/30/70, Oshawa, Ontario. 6-3, 180. Drafted by Philadelphia Flyers (3rd choice, 56th overall) in 1988 Entry Draft. Traded to Edmonton Oilers by Philadelphia with Scott Mellanby and Craig Berube for Dave Brown, Corey Foster and Jari Kurri (5/30/91). Traded to Winnipeg Jets by Edmonton for cash (12/9/93). Signed as a free agent by Chicago (6/9/94). Signed as a free agent by New York Islanders (8/96). Traded to Florida Panthers by Islanders for cash (12/7/96). Signed as a free agent by Buffalo Sabres (7/30/98). 1995-96 IHL First Team All-Star. Member of 1992-93 AHL champion Cape Breton Oilers. Last amateur club; Miami-Ohio (CCHA).

Darrin Fisher
Right Wing

Season	Team	League	GP	G	A	PTS	PIM	GP	G	A	PTS	PIM
			Regular Season					Playoffs				
98-99	Port Huron	UHL	1	0	0	0	0	—	—	—	—	—

Born; 5/13/77, Southgate, Michigan.

Rob Fitzgerald
Forward

Season	Team	League	GP	G	A	PTS	PIM	GP	G	A	PTS	PIM
			Regular Season					Playoffs				
97-98	Fort Worth	WPHL	7	1	1	2	2	—	—	—	—	—
98-99	Flint	UHL	14	2	2	4	6	—	—	—	—	—
98-99	Port Huron	UHL	13	3	2	5	6	—	—	—	—	—
	UHL	Totals	27	5	4	9	12	—	—	—	—	—

Born; 5/17/77, Peterborough, Ontario. 5-9, 175. Last amateur club; Belleville (OHL).

Rusty Fitzgerald
Center

Season	Team	League	GP	G	A	PTS	PIM	GP	G	A	PTS	PIM
			Regular Season					Playoffs				
94-95	Minnesota-Duluth	WCHA	34	16	22	38	50	—	—	—	—	—
94-95	Cleveland	IHL	2	0	1	1	0	3	3	0	3	6
94-95	Pittsburgh	NHL	4	1	0	1	0	5	0	0	0	4
95-96	Pittsburgh	NHL	21	1	2	3	12	—	—	—	—	—
95-96	Cleveland	IHL	46	17	19	36	90	1	0	0	0	2
96-97	DNP	Injured										
97-98	Cleveland	IHL	34	3	5	8	36	1	0	0	0	0
98-99	Quad City	UHL	53	29	25	54	40	12	4	4	8	9
	NHL	Totals	25	2	2	4	12	5	0	0	0	4
	IHL	Totals	82	20	25	45	126	5	3	0	3	8

Born; 10/4/72, Minneapolis, Minnesota. 6-1, 210. Drafted by Pittsburgh Penguins (2nd choice, 38th overall) in 1991 Entry Draft. Last amateur club; Minnesota-Duluth (WCHA).

Blaine Fitzpatrick
Right Wing

Season	Team	League	GP	G	A	PTS	PIM	GP	G	A	PTS	PIM
			Regular Season					Playoffs				
97-98	Peterborough	OHL	56	32	18	50	176	4	0	0	0	10
97-98	South Carolina	ECHL	4	0	0	0	0	4	0	0	0	23
98-99	Peoria	ECHL	50	14	13	27	159	3	0	2	2	17
	ECHL	Totals	54	14	13	27	159	7	0	2	2	40

Born; Selected by Mohawk Valley in 1998 UHL Expansion Draft. Last amateur club; Peterborough (OHL).

Rory Fitzpatrick
Defenseman

Season	Team	League	GP	G	A	PTS	PIM	GP	G	A	PTS	PIM
			Regular Season					Playoffs				
94-95	Sudbury	Ontario	56	12	36	48	72	18	3	15	18	21
94-95	Fredericton	AHL	—	—	—	—	—	10	1	2	3	5
95-96	Montreal	NHL	42	0	2	2	18	6	1	1	2	0
95-96	Fredericton	AHL	18	4	6	10	36	—	—	—	—	—
96-97	Montreal	NHL	6	0	1	1	6	—	—	—	—	—
96-97	St. Louis	NHL	2	0	0	0	2	—	—	—	—	—
96-97	Worcester	AHL	49	4	13	17	78	5	1	2	3	0
97-98	Worcester	AHL	62	8	22	30	111	11	0	3	3	26
98-99	St. Louis	NHL	1	0	0	0	2	—	—	—	—	—
98-99	Worcester	AHL	53	5	16	21	82	4	0	1	1	17
	NHL	Totals	51	0	3	3	28	6	1	1	2	0
	AHL	Totals	182	21	57	78	307	30	2	8	10	48

Born; 1/11/75, Rochester, New York. 6-1, 195. Drafted by Montreal Canadiens (2nd choice, 47th overall) in 1993 Entry Draft. Traded to St. Louis Blues with Pierre Turgeon and Craig Conroy by Montreal for Murray Baron, Shayne Corson and fifth round pick in 1997 Entry Draft (Gennady Razin) 10/29/96. Claimed by Boston Bruins from St. Louis in 1999 NHL Waiver Draft (10/5/98). Claimed on waivers from Boston by St. Louis (10/7/98). Last amateur club; Sudbury (OHL).

Wade Flaherty — Goaltender

Regular Season / Playoffs

Season	Team	League	GP	W	L	T	MIN	SO	AVG	GP	W	L	MIN	SO	AVG
89-90	Greensboro	ECHL	27	12	10	0	1308	0	4.40	—	—	—	—	—	—
90-91	Kansas City	IHL	*56	16	31	4	2990	0	4.49	—	—	—	—	—	—
91-92	San Jose	NHL	3	0	3	0	178	0	4.38	—	—	—	—	—	—
91-92	Kansas City	IHL	43	26	14	3	2603	1	3.23	1	0	0	1	0	0.00
92-93	San Jose	NHL	1	0	1	0	60	0	5.00	—	—	—	—	—	—
92-93	Kansas City	IHL	*61	*34	19	7	*3642	2	3.21	*12	6	6	733	*1	2.78
93-94	Kansas City	IHL	*60	32	19	9	*3564	0	3.40	—	—	—	—	—	—
94-95	San Jose	NHL	18	5	6	1	852	1	3.10	7	2	3	377	0	4.93
95-96	San Jose	NHL	24	3	12	1	1137	0	4.85	—	—	—	—	—	—
96-97	San Jose	NHL	7	2	4	0	359	0	5.18	—	—	—	—	—	—
96-97	Kentucky	AHL	19	8	6	2	1032	1	3.14	3	1	2	200	0	3.30
97-98	Islanders	NHL	16	4	4	3	694	3	1.99	—	—	—	—	—	—
97-98	Utah	IHL	24	16	5	3	1341	3	1.79	—	—	—	—	—	—
98-99	Islanders	NHL	20	5	11	2	1048	0	3.03	—	—	—	—	—	—
98-99	Lowell	AHL	5	1	3	1	305	0	3.15	—	—	—	—	—	—
	NHL	Totals	89	19	41	7	4328	4	3.62	7	2	3	377	0	4.93
	IHL	Totals	244	124	88	26	14140	6	3.40	13	6	6	734	1	2.78
	AHL	Totals	24	9	9	3	1337	1	3.14	3	1	2	200	0	3.30

Born; 1/11/68, Terrace, British Columbia. 6-0, 170. Drafted by Buffalo Sabres (10th choice, 181st overall) 1988 Entry Draft. Signed as a free agent by San Jose (9/3/91). Signed as a free agent by New York Islanders (7/22/97). Won James Norris Trophy (fewest goals against-IHL) with Arturs Irbe (1991-92). 1992-93 IHL Second All-Star Team. 1993-94 IHL Second All-Star Team. Member of 1991-92 IHL Champion Kansas City Blades. Last amateur club; Victoria (WHL).

Sheldon Flaman — Defensemann

Regular Season / Playoffs

Season	Team	League	GP	G	A	PTS	PIM	GP	G	A	PTS	PIM
98-99	Oklahoma City	CHL	56	2	12	14	91	—	—	—	—	—
98-99	Fort Worth	CHL	7	2	3	5	10	—	—	—	—	—
	CHL	Totals	63	4	15	19	101	—	—	—	—	—

Born; 3/28/77, Moosomin, Saskatchewan. 6-1, 188. Selected by Columbus in 1999 CHL Dispersal Draft.

David Fletcher — Goaltender

Regular Season / Playoffs

Season	Team	League	GP	W	L	T	MIN	SO	AVG	GP	W	L	MIN	SO	AVG
96-97	Quad City	CoHL	19	9	5	1	941	0	4.02	1	0	0	33	0	0.00
97-98	Madison	UHL	14	4	5	3	759	0	3.72	—	—	—	—	—	—
98-99	Madison	UHL	36	13	16	3	2001	2	3.54	—	—	—	—	—	—
	UHL	Totals	69	26	26	7	3701	2	3.70	1	0	0	33	0	0.00

Born; 5/27/71, Livonia, Michigan. 5-9, 171. Member of 1996-97 Colonial League Champion Quad City Mallards. Last amateur club; University of Wisconsin-Stevens Point (NCHA).

Carl Fleury — Center

Regular Season / Playoffs

Season	Team	League	GP	G	A	PTS	PIM	GP	G	A	PTS	PIM
94-95	Roanoke	ECHL	16	1	1	2	35	—	—	—	—	—
94-95	Erie	ECHL	43	13	15	28	79	—	—	—	—	—
95-96	Erie	ECHL	63	8	32	40	139	—	—	—	—	—
96-97	Johnstown	ECHL	68	30	37	67	102	—	—	—	—	—
97-98	Johnstown	ECHL	46	21	30	51	89	—	—	—	—	—
98-99	Johnstown	ECHL	22	7	7	14	31	—	—	—	—	—
	ECHL	Totals	258	80	122	202	475	—	—	—	—	—

Born; 10/22/73, St. Claire, Quebec. 6-1, 198. Last amateur club; Sherbrooke (QMJHL).

Marty Flichel — Right Wing

Regular Season / Playoffs

Season	Team	League	GP	G	A	PTS	PIM	GP	G	A	PTS	PIM
96-97	Michigan	IHL	19	2	3	5	10	—	—	—	—	—
96-97	Dayton	ECHL	28	17	16	33	24	2	0	1	1	4
97-98	Michigan	IHL	74	18	16	34	56	4	0	0	0	23
98-99	Michigan	IHL	70	15	28	43	57	1	0	0	0	0
	IHL	Totals	163	35	47	82	123	5	0	0	0	23

Born; 3/6/76, Hodgeville, Saskatchewan. 5-11, 175. Drafted by Dallas Stars (6th choice, 228th overall) in 1994 Entry Draft. Last amateur club; Kelowna (WHL).

Eric Flinton — Left Wing

Regular Season / Playoffs

Season	Team	League	GP	G	A	PTS	PIM	GP	G	A	PTS	PIM
95-96	Charlotte	ECHL	69	20	26	46	29	16	5	8	13	4
96-97	Binghamton	AHL	68	6	18	24	22	4	0	0	0	2
97-98	Charlotte	ECHL	21	6	5	11	12	—	—	—	—	—
98-99	Manchester	BSL	24	6	12	18	8	9	5	1	6	0
98-99	London	BSL	51	20	21	41	40	6	5	3	8	4
	ECHL	Totals	90	26	31	57	41	16	5	8	13	4
	BSL	Totals	75	26	33	59	48	15	10	4	14	4

Born; 2/2/72, William Lake, British Columbia. 6-2, 200. Drafted by Ottawa Senators in 1993 Supplemental Draft. Signed as a free agent by New York Rangers (9/12/95). Member of 1995-96 ECHL champion Charlotte Checkers. Last amateur club; New Hampshire (Hockey East).

Rocky Florio — Forward

Regular Season / Playoffs

Season	Team	League	GP	G	A	PTS	PIM	GP	G	A	PTS	PIM
98-99	Monroe	WPHL	1	0	0	0	0	—	—	—	—	—

Born; 8/27/77, Toronto, Ontario. 6-2, 210.

Brendan Flynn — Center

Regular Season / Playoffs

Season	Team	League	GP	G	A	PTS	PIM	GP	G	A	PTS	PIM
91-92	Richmond	ECHL	64	12	34	46	63	7	3	5	8	0
92-93	Richmond	ECHL	60	23	52	75	38	1	0	0	0	0
93-94	Salt Lake City	IHL	4	0	0	0	0	—	—	—	—	—
93-94	Richmond	ECHL	63	20	69	89	76	—	—	—	—	—
94-95												
95-96	Providence	AHL	24	2	3	5	6	—	—	—	—	—
95-96	Richmond	ECHL	31	13	36	49	67	7	4	10	14	4
96-97	Ayr	BSL	39	11	15	26	30	7	1	4	5	4
97-98	Richmond	ECHL	25	2	20	22	28	—	—	—	—	—
98-99	Pee Dee	ECHL	67	14	44	58	30	10	1	4	5	18
	ECHL	Totals	310	84	255	339	302	25	8	19	27	22

Born; 3/13/68, Boston, Massachusetts. 6-0, 175. Claimed by Greensboro in 1999 ECHL Expansion Draft. Last amateur club; Lowell (Hockey East).

Michael Flynn — Center

Regular Season / Playoffs

Season	Team	League	GP	G	A	PTS	PIM	GP	G	A	PTS	PIM
97-98	Louisville	ECHL	70	30	37	67	35	—	—	—	—	—
98-99	Miami	ECHL	70	20	50	70	30	—	—	—	—	—
	ECHL	Totals	140	50	87	137	65	—	—	—	—	—

Born; 7/15/73, West Roxbury, Massachusetts. 5-10, 185. Selected by Charlotte in 1999 Dispersal Draft. Last amateur club; Brown (ECAC).

Sean Flynn — Forward

Regular Season / Playoffs

Season	Team	League	GP	G	A	PTS	PIM	GP	G	A	PTS	PIM
98-99	Quad City	UHL	3	0	0	0	0	—	—	—	—	—

Born; 8/2/77, Chicago, Illinois. 5-10, 165.

Terry Flynn — Center

Regular Season / Playoffs

Season	Team	League	GP	G	A	PTS	PIM	GP	G	A	PTS	PIM
98-99	Odessa	WPHL	68	12	18	30	11	3	1	0	1	2

Born; 12/20/74, Braintree, Massachusetts. 6-0, 190. Last amateur club; Colby College (NCAA 3).

Dan Focht — Defenseman

Regular Season / Playoffs

Season	Team	League	GP	G	A	PTS	PIM	GP	G	A	PTS	PIM
96-97	Tri-City	WHL	28	0	5	5	92	—	—	—	—	—
96-97	Regina	WHL	22	2	2	4	59	5	0	2	2	8
96-97	Springfield	AHL	1	0	0	0	2	—	—	—	—	—
97-98	Springfield	AHL	61	2	5	7	125	3	0	0	0	4
98-99	Mississippi	ECHL	2	0	0	0	6	—	—	—	—	—
98-99	Springfield	AHL	30	0	2	2	58	3	1	0	1	10
	AHL	Totals	92	2	7	9	185	6	1	0	1	14

Born; 12/31/77, Regina, Saskatchewan. 6-6, 226. Drafted by Phoenix Coyotes (1st choice, 11th overall) in 1996 Entry Draft. Last amateur club; Regina (WHL).

Bryan Fogarty — Defenseman

Regular Season / Playoffs

Season	Team	League	GP	G	A	PTS	PIM	GP	G	A	PTS	PIM
89-90	Quebec	NHL	45	4	10	14	31	—	—	—	—	—
89-90	Halifax	AHL	22	5	14	19	6	6	2	4	6	0
90-91	Quebec	NHL	45	9	22	31	24	—	—	—	—	—
90-91	Halifax	AHL	5	0	2	2	0	—	—	—	—	—
91-92	Quebec	NHL	20	3	12	15	16	—	—	—	—	—
91-92	Halifax	AHL	2	0	0	0	2	—	—	—	—	—
91-92	New Haven	AHL	4	0	1	1	6	—	—	—	—	—
91-92	Muskegon	IHL	8	2	4	6	30	—	—	—	—	—
92-93	Pittsburgh	NHL	12	0	4	4	4	—	—	—	—	—
92-93	Cleveland	IHL	15	2	5	7	8	3	0	1	1	17
93-94	Montreal	NHL	13	1	2	3	10	—	—	—	—	—
93-94	Atlanta	IHL	8	1	5	6	4	—	—	—	—	—
93-94	Las Vegas	IHL	33	3	16	19	38	—	—	—	—	—
93-94	Kansas City	IHL	3	2	1	3	2	—	—	—	—	—
94-95	Montreal	NHL	21	5	2	7	34	—	—	—	—	—
95-96	Minnesota	IHL	17	3	12	15	24	—	—	—	—	—
95-96	Detroit	IHL	18	1	5	6	11	—	—	—	—	—
95-96	Davos	Switz.	—	—	—	—	—	3	1	1	2	0
96-97	Kansas City	IHL	22	3	9	12	10	—	—	—	—	—
96-97	Milano	Italy	16	8	20	28	30	—	—	—	—	—
96-97	Milano	Alpen.	7	3	7	10	10	—	—	—	—	—
97-98	Hannover	Germany	39	8	17	25	75	4	1	0	1	2
98-99	Indianapolis	IHL	36	7	15	22	28	—	—	—	—	—
98-99	Baton Rouge	ECHL	5	4	3	7	24	4	1	3	4	8
	NHL	Totals	156	22	52	74	119	—	—	—	—	—
	IHL	Totals	160	24	72	106	155	3	0	1	1	17
	AHL	Totals	33	5	17	22	14	6	2	4	6	0

Born; 6/11/69, Brantford, Ontario. 6-2, 198. Drafted by Quebec Nordiques (1st choice, 9th overall) in 1987 Entry Draft. Traded to Pittsburgh Penguins by Quebec for Scott Young (3/10/92). Signed as a free agent by Tampa Bay Lightning (9/28/93). Signed as a free agent by Montreal Canadiens (2/25/94). Signed as a free agent by Buffalo Sabres (9/8/95). Signed as a free agent by Chicago Blackhawks (9/2/98). Last amateur club; Niagara Falls (OHL).

Nick Foley — Goaltender

Regular Season / Playoffs

Season	Team	League	GP	W	L	T	MIN	SO	AVG	GP	W	L	MIN	SO	AVG
98-99	Mississauga	OHL	37	3	26	1	1890	0	5.90	—	—	—	—	—	—
98-99	Flint	UHL	1	0	1	0	60	0	4.00	—	—	—	—	—	—

Born; 3/22/79, Belleville, Ontario. 5-10, 170. Last amateur club; Mississauga (OHL).

Trevor Folk — Defenseman

Regular Season / Playoffs

Season	Team	League	GP	G	A	PTS	PIM	GP	G	A	PTS	PIM
98-99	Wichita	CHL	64	7	21	28	186	1	0	0	0	2

Born; 3/2/77, Pilot Butte, Saskatchewan. 6-1, 200. Last amateur club; Weyburn (SJHL).

Nick Forbes — Left Wing

Regular Season / Playoffs

Season	Team	League	GP	G	A	PTS	PIM	GP	G	A	PTS	PIM
95-96	Utica	CoHL	53	10	12	22	154	—	—	—	—	—
95-96	Flint	CoHL	7	1	3	4	32	13	2	0	2	14
96-97	Detroit	IHL	1	0	0	0	0	—	—	—	—	—
96-97	Michigan	IHL	1	0	0	0	0	—	—	—	—	—
96-97	Flint	CoHL	68	23	24	47	222	14	2	4	6	18
97-98	Flint	UHL	55	22	26	48	175	17	4	4	8	17
98-99	Flint	UHL	61	20	26	46	173	10	2	3	5	4
	IHL	Totals	2	0	0	0	0	—	—	—	—	—
	UHL	Totals	244	76	91	167	756	54	10	11	21	53

Born; 4/27/72, Montreal, Quebec. 6-1, 205. Member of 1995-96 Colonial Cup Champion Flint Generals. Last amateur club; Plattsburgh (NCAA 3).

Chad Ford — Goaltender

Regular Season / Playoffs

Season	Team	League	GP	W	L	T	MIN	SO	AVG	GP	W	L	MIN	SO	AVG
98-99	Quad City	UHL	25	18	6	1	1316	1	3.42	—	—	—	—	—	—
98-99	Mohawk Valley	UHL	4	1	2	0	168	0	4.29	—	—	—	—	—	—
	UHL	Totals	29	19	8	1	1484	1	3.52	—	—	—	—	—	—

Born; 2/28/74, Belleville, Ontario. 6-1, 200. Last amateur club; Cambrian College (OCAA).

Chris Ford — Right Wing

Regular Season / Playoffs

Season	Team	League	GP	G	A	PTS	PIM	GP	G	A	PTS	PIM
97-98	Nashville	CHL	64	23	17	40	150	9	1	5	6	9
98-99	Fayetteville	CHL	67	17	26	43	108	—	—	—	—	—
	CHL	Totals	131	40	43	83	258	9	1	5	6	9

Born; 1/7/73, Rochester, New York. 6-1, 185. Last amateur club; Union (ECAC).

Bryan Forslund — Left Wing

Regular Season / Playoffs

Season	Team	League	GP	G	A	PTS	PIM	GP	G	A	PTS	PIM
95-96	Tulsa	CeHL	59	18	15	33	78	6	0	0	0	25
96-97	Tulsa	CeHL	55	19	20	39	64	5	0	1	1	0
97-98	Raleigh	ECHL	66	31	27	58	110	—	—	—	—	—
98-99	Augusta	ECHL	8	1	2	3	20	—	—	—	—	—
98-99	Jacksonville	ECHL	65	23	46	69	46	2	0	2	2	8
	ECHL	Totals	139	55	75	130	176	2	0	2	2	8
	CeHL	Totals	114	37	35	72	142	11	0	1	1	25

Born; 6/8/74, Sherwood Park, Alberta 6-0, 190.

Francois Fortier — Left Wing

Regular Season / Playoffs

Season	Team	League	GP	G	A	PTS	PIM	GP	G	A	PTS	PIM
98-99	Sherbrooke	QMJHL	48	36	40	76	8	13	6	9	15	4
98-99	Hartford	AHL	1	0	0	0	0	—	—	—	—	—

Born; 6/13/79, Beauport, Quebec. 5-9, 161. Signed as a free agent by New York Rangers (10/8/98). Last amateur club; Sherbrooke (QMJHL).

Jason Fortier — Left Wing

Regular Season / Playoffs

Season	Team	League	GP	G	A	PTS	PIM	GP	G	A	PTS	PIM
98-99	Wichita	CHL	6	0	1	1	21	—	—	—	—	—

Born; 10/13/74, Sault Ste. Marie, Ontario. 5-9, 185.

Sebastien Fortier — Left Wing

Regular Season / Playoffs

Season	Team	League	GP	G	A	PTS	PIM	GP	G	A	PTS	PIM
93-94	Fredericton	AHL	4	0	3	3	11	—	—	—	—	—
93-94	Wheeling	ECHL	62	6	22	28	36	—	—	—	—	—
94-95	Brantford	CoHL	25	5	10	15	21	—	—	—	—	—
94-95	Utica	CoHL	33	5	14	19	86	—	—	—	—	—
95-96	Utica	CoHL	19	1	7	8	15	—	—	—	—	—
95-96	Thunder Bay	CoHL	43	3	10	13	105	17	1	2	3	96
96-97	Birmingham	ECHL	48	7	8	15	150	—	—	—	—	—
96-97	Richmond	ECHL	15	7	10	17	28	7	3	4	7	10
97-98	Phoenix	WCHL	56	14	19	33	145	9	0	1	1	41
98-99	Phoenix	WCHL	59	3	9	12	106	2	0	0	0	20
	ECHL	Totals	125	20	40	60	214	7	3	4	7	10
	CoHL	Totals	120	14	41	55	227	17	1	2	3	96
	WCHL	Totals	115	17	28	45	251	11	0	1	1	61

Born; 10/12/73, Greenfield Park, Quebec. 6-0, 198. Last amateur club; Sherbrooke (QMJHL).

Jeff Foster — Defenseman

Regular Season / Playoffs

Season	Team	League	GP	G	A	PTS	PIM	GP	G	A	PTS	PIM
97-98	Madison	UHL	72	3	13	16	50	7	0	0	0	2
98-99	Madison	UHL	25	3	5	8	24	—	—	—	—	—
98-99	Asheville	UHL	33	2	8	10	22	4	0	0	0	6
	UHL	Totals	130	8	26	34	96	11	0	0	0	8

Born; 9/4/74, Napanee, Ontario. 6-2, 195. Traded to Asheville by Madison with Jason Dexter for Chris Newans and Jeff Smith (1/99).

Ryan Foster — Left Wing

Regular Season / Playoffs

Season	Team	League	GP	G	A	PTS	PIM	GP	G	A	PTS	PIM
98-99	Canada	National	31	8	15	23	70	—	—	—	—	—

Born; 11/2/74, Brampton, Ontario. 6-0, 195. Last amateur club; Guelph (OUAA).

Mike Fountain — Goaltender

Regular Season / Playoffs

Season	Team	League	GP	W	L	T	MIN	SO	AVG	GP	W	L	MIN	SO	AVG
92-93	Canada	National	13	7	5	1	745	1	2.89	—	—	—	—	—	—
92-93	Hamilton	AHL	12	2	8	0	618	0	4.47	—	—	—	—	—	—
93-94	Hamilton	AHL	*70	*34	28	6	*4005	*4	3.61	3	0	2	146	0	4.92
94-95	Syracuse	AHL	61	25	29	7	3618	2	3.73	—	—	—	—	—	—
95-96	Syracuse	AHL	54	21	27	3	3060	1	3.61	15	8	7	915	2	3.74
96-97	Vancouver	NHL	6	2	2	0	245	1	3.43	—	—	—	—	—	—
96-97	Syracuse	AHL	25	8	14	2	1462	1	3.20	2	0	2	120	0	6.02
97-98	Carolina	NHL	3	0	3	0	163	0	3.68	—	—	—	—	—	—
97-98	New Haven	AHL	50	25	19	5	2923	3	2.85	—	—	—	—	—	—
98-99	New Haven	AHL	51	23	24	3	2989	2	3.01	—	—	—	—	—	—
	NHL	Totals	9	2	5	0	408	1	3.53	—	—	—	—	—	—
	AHL	Totals	323	138	149	26	18675	13	3.42	20	8	11	1181	2	4.12

Born; 1/26/72, North York, Ontario. 6-1, 176. Drafted by Vancouver Canucks (4th choice, 69th overall) in 1992 Entry Draft. 1993-94 AHL Second Team All-Star. Signed as a free agent by Carolina Hurricanes (8/14/97). Last amateur club; Oshawa (OHL).

Dan Fournel — Right Wing

Regular Season / Playoffs

Season	Team	League	GP	G	A	PTS	PIM	GP	G	A	PTS	PIM
93-94	Birmingham	ECHL	49	10	11	21	197	—	—	—	—	—
94-95	Huntington	ECHL	55	11	20	31	176	3	1	1	2	16
95-96	St. John's	AHL	2	0	0	0	5	—	—	—	—	—
95-96	Huntington	ECHL	23	9	10	19	132	—	—	—	—	—
95-96	South Carolina	ECHL	33	5	5	10	120	8	2	2	4	31
96-97	South Carolina	ECHL	4	1	0	1	31	—	—	—	—	—
97-98	South Carolina	ECHL	21	1	2	3	65	—	—	—	—	—
97-98	Richmond	ECHL	19	3	5	8	139	—	—	—	—	—
98-99	Richmond	ECHL	26	2	5	7	87	—	—	—	—	—
98-99	Oklahoma City	CHL	30	8	4	12	176	9	2	0	2	28
	ECHL	Totals	230	42	58	100	927	11	3	3	6	47

Born; 2/15/72, Geraldton, Ontario. 6-3, 215. Traded to Richmond by South Carolina with Kevin Knopp, Mario Cormier and Jay Moser for Mike Taylor and Jason Wright (12/97).

Luc Fournier — Forward

Regular Season / Playoffs

Season	Team	League	GP	G	A	PTS	PIM	GP	G	A	PTS	PIM
98-99	El Paso	WPHL	10	2	5	7	10	3	0	1	1	0

Born; 6/12/73, Quebec City, Quebec. 5-10, 185. Last amateur club; McGill (OUAA).

Chris Fox — Defenseman

Regular Season / Playoffs

Season	Team	League	GP	G	A	PTS	PIM	GP	G	A	PTS	PIM
98-99	New Orleans	ECHL	23	3	5	8	22	—	—	—	—	—

Born; 8/29/76, Detroit, Michigan. 6-1, 185. Last amateur club; Michigan

Mark Fox — Defenseman

Regular Season / Playoffs

Season	Team	League	GP	G	A	PTS	PIM	GP	G	A	PTS	PIM
98-99	Colorado	WCHL	63	2	4	6	47	2	0	0	0	2

Born; 10/6/77, Cambridge, Ontario. 6-2, 210.

Petr Franek — Goaltender

Regular Season / Playoffs

Season	Team	League	GP	W	L	T	MIN	SO	AVG	GP	W	L	MIN	SO	AVG
96-97	Quebec	IHL	6	3	3	0	358	0	3.02	1	0	1	40	0	6.00
96-97	Hershey	AHL	15	4	1	0	457	3	3.02	—	—	—	—	—	—
96-97	Brantford	CoHL	6	4	1	0	322	0	2.61	—	—	—	—	—	—
97-98	Hershey	AHL	43	19	14	2	2169	2	2.71	1	0	1	60	0	4.00
98-99	Utah	IHL	8	1	6	1	446	0	3.50	—	—	—	—	—	—
98-99	Las Vegas	IHL	37	17	13	2	1879	0	3.42	—	—	—	—	—	—
	AHL	Totals	58	23	15	2	2626	5	2.76	1	0	1	60	0	4.00
	IHL	Totals	51	21	22	3	2683	0	3.38	1	0	1	40	0	6.00

Born; 4/6/75, Most, Czechoslovakia. 5-11, 187. Drafted by Quebec Nordiques (10th choice, 205th overall) in 1993 Entry Draft. Last overseas club; Litvinov (Czech Republic).

Robert Francz — Left Wing

Regular Season / Playoffs

Season	Team	League	GP	G	A	PTS	PIM	GP	G	A	PTS	PIM
98-99	Peterborough	OHL	65	25	32	57	171	5	0	2	2	12
98-99	Springfield	AHL	2	1	0	1	4	1	0	0	0	0

Born; 3/30/78, Bad Muskau, Esat Germany. 6-1, 194. Drafted by Phoenix Coyotes (4th choice, 151st overall) in 1997 Entry Draft. Last amateur club; Peterborough (OHL).

Mark Franks — Right Wing

Regular Season / Playoffs

Season	Team	League	GP	G	A	PTS	PIM	GP	G	A	PTS	PIM
93-94	Erie	ECHL	14	5	6	11	22	—	—	—	—	—
93-94	Huntington	ECHL	16	12	5	17	14	—	—	—	—	—
94-95	Huntington	ECHL	55	21	16	37	34	4	3	2	5	2
95-96	Muskegon	CoHL	28	11	12	23	51	—	—	—	—	—
95-96	Quad City	CoHL	26	15	16	31	10	4	1	1	2	0
96-97		Germany	27	83	54	137	58	—	—	—	—	—
97-98		Germany	8	1	9	10	4	—	—	—	—	—
98-99	Alexandria	WPHL	6	2	2	4	2	—	—	—	—	—
98-99	Fresno	WCHL	22	14	5	19	6	5	3	1	4	2
	ECHL	Totals	85	38	27	65	70	4	3	2	5	2
	CoHL	Totals	54	26	28	54	61	4	1	1	2	0

Born; 10/12/72, Calgary, Alberta. 6-1, 198. Last amateur club; Moose Jaw

Lance Franz — Goaltender

Regular Season / Playoffs

Season	Team	League	GP	W	L	T	MIN	SO	AVG	GP	W	L	MIN	SO	AVG
98-99	Louisiana	ECHL	1	1	0	0	60	0	1.00	—	—	—	—	—	—

Born;

Shawn Frappier — Defenseman

Regular Season — Playoffs

Season	Team	League	GP	G	A	PTS	PIM	GP	G	A	PTS	PIM
96-97	Grand Rapids	IHL	3	0	0	0	0	—	—	—	—	—
96-97	Mississippi	ECHL	48	4	15	19	70	—	—	—	—	—
97-98	Orlando	IHL	8	0	1	1	2	—	—	—	—	—
97-98	Mississippi	ECHL	59	4	19	23	70	—	—	—	—	—
98-99	Mississippi	ECHL	10	1	0	1	21	—	—	—	—	—
98-99	Johnstown	ECHL	58	4	21	25	48	—	—	—	—	—
	IHL	Totals	11	0	1	1	2	—	—	—	—	—
	ECHL	Totals	175	13	55	68	209	—	—	—	—	—

Born; 7/2/75, Sudbury, Ontario. 6-0, 195. Last amateur club; Barrie (OHL).

Scott Fraser — Center

Regular Season — Playoffs

Season	Team	League	GP	G	A	PTS	PIM	GP	G	A	PTS	PIM
94-95	Fredericton	AHL	65	23	25	48	36	16	3	5	8	14
94-95	Wheeling	ECHL	8	4	2	6	8	—	—	—	—	—
95-96	Montreal	NHL	14	2	0	2	4	—	—	—	—	—
95-96	Fredericton	AHL	58	37	37	74	43	10	9	7	16	2
96-97	Fredericton	AHL	7	3	8	11	0	—	—	—	—	—
96-97	Saint John	AHL	37	22	10	32	24	—	—	—	—	—
96-97	Carolina	AHL	18	9	19	28	12	—	—	—	—	—
96-97	San Antonio	IHL	8	0	1	1	2	—	—	—	—	—
97-98	Edmonton	NHL	29	12	11	23	6	11	1	1	2	0
97-98	Hamilton	AHL	50	29	32	61	26	—	—	—	—	—
98-99	Rangers	NHL	28	2	4	6	14	—	—	—	—	—
98-99	Hartford	AHL	36	13	24	37	20	6	4	3	7	4
	NHL	Totals	71	16	15	31	24	11	1	1	2	0
	AHL	Totals	271	136	155	291	161	32	16	15	31	20

Born; 5/3/72, Moncton, New Brunswick. 6-1, 200. Drafted by Montreal Canadiens (12th choice, 193rd overall) in 1991 Entry Draft. Traded to Calgary Flames by Montreal for David Ling and Calgary's 6th round pick (Gordie Dwyer) in the 1998 Entry Draft, (10/24/96). Signed as a free agent by Edmonton Oilers (7/23/97). Signed as a free agent by New York Rangers (7/2/98). Last amateur

Trevor Fraser — Left Wing

Regular Season — Playoffs

Season	Team	League	GP	G	A	PTS	PIM	GP	G	A	PTS	PIM
98-99	Hampton Roads	ECHL	65	4	7	11	122	2	0	1	1	6

Born; 9/19/73, Leduc, Alberta. 6-0, 205. Last amateur club; Acadia (AUAA).

Kyle Freadrich — Left Wing

Regular Season — Playoffs

Season	Team	League	GP	G	A	PTS	PIM	GP	G	A	PTS	PIM
98-99	Regina	WHL	52	2	2	4	215	—	—	—	—	—
98-99	Syracuse	AHL	5	0	0	0	20	—	—	—	—	—
98-99	Louisiana	ECHL	5	0	0	0	17	4	0	0	0	2

Born; 12/28/78, Edmonton, Alberta. 6-6, 225. Drafted by Vancouver Canucks (4th choice, 64th overall) in 1997 Entry Draft. Signed as a free agent by Tampa Bay Lightning (7/17/99). Last amateur club; Regina (WHL).

Joe Frederick — Right Wing

Regular Season — Playoffs

Season	Team	League	GP	G	A	PTS	PIM	GP	G	A	PTS	PIM
92-93	Northern Michigan	WCHA	29	28	20	48	100	—	—	—	—	—
92-93	Adirondack	AHL	5	0	1	1	2	8	0	0	0	6
93-94	Adirondack	AHL	68	28	30	58	130	12	11	4	15	22
94-95	Adirondack	AHL	71	27	28	55	124	4	0	0	0	10
95-96	Orlando	IHL	63	22	14	36	194	23	6	2	8	36
96-97	Orlando	IHL	48	16	9	25	82	—	—	—	—	—
96-97	Phoenix	IHL	9	2	3	5	10	—	—	—	—	—
96-97	Chicago	IHL	8	1	1	2	14	1	1	0	1	0
97-98	Milwaukee	IHL	25	14	9	23	53	—	—	—	—	—
97-98	Manitoba	IHL	45	20	13	33	55	2	0	0	0	0
98-99	Grand Rapids	IHL	45	23	18	41	98	—	—	—	—	—
	IHL	Totals	243	98	67	165	506	26	7	2	9	36
	AHL	Totals	144	55	59	114	256	24	11	4	15	38

Born; 6/18/69, Madison, Wisconsin. 6-1, 190. Drafted by Detroit Red Wings (13th choice, 242nd overall) in 1989 Entry Draft. Last amateur club; Northern Michigan University (WCHA).

Troy Frederick — Left Wing

Regular Season — Playoffs

Season	Team	League	GP	G	A	PTS	PIM	GP	G	A	PTS	PIM
90-91	Knoxville	ECHL	4	0	3	3	41	—	—	—	—	—
90-91	Kansas City	IHL	39	2	3	5	79	—	—	—	—	—
91-92	Kansas City	IHL	13	0	3	3	29	—	—	—	—	—
92-93	Kansas City	IHL	16	0	1	1	27	—	—	—	—	—
92-93	Johnstown	ECHL	8	0	1	1	0	—	—	—	—	—
93-94	Kansas City	IHL	21	0	3	3	55	—	—	—	—	—
93-94	Fort Worth	CeHL	10	3	7	10	2	—	—	—	—	—
94-95	Fort Worth	CeHL	66	38	37	75	99	—	—	—	—	—
95-96	Foth Worth	CeHL	64	28	38	66	87	—	—	—	—	—
96-97	Central Texas	WPHL	64	35	25	60	92	11	4	5	9	10
97-98	Phoenix	WCHL	15	4	1	5	12	—	—	—	—	—
97-98	Monroe	WPHL	47	11	16	27	51	—	—	—	—	—
98-99	Topeka	CHL	64	19	17	36	87	3	1	0	1	0
	IHL	Totals	89	2	10	12	190	—	—	—	—	—
	CHL	Totals	204	88	99	187	275	3	1	0	1	0
	WPHL	Totals	111	46	41	87	143	11	4	5	9	10
	ECHL	Totals	12	0	4	4	41					

Born; 4/4/69, Virden, Manitoba. 6-5, 235. Traded to Monroe by Central Texas for Tommi Tarvainen (12/97). Last amateur club; Brandon (WHL).

Sean Freeman — Forward

Regular Season — Playoffs

Season	Team	League	GP	G	A	PTS	PIM	GP	G	A	PTS	PIM
98-99	Jacksonville	ECHL	2	0	0	0	12	—	—	—	—	—
98-99	Madison	UHL	11	1	0	1	8	—	—	—	—	—
98-99	Mohawk Valley	UHL	11	1	2	3	4	—	—	—	—	—
	UHL	Totals	22	2	2	4	12	—	—	—	—	—

Born; 11/11/75, Glencoe, Illinois. 5-11, 200. Last amateur club; Lake Forest (NCAA 3).

Mark Freer — Center

Regular Season — Playoffs

Season	Team	League	GP	G	A	PTS	PIM	GP	G	A	PTS	PIM
86-87	Peterborough	OHL	65	39	43	82	44	12	2	6	8	5
86-87	Philadelphia	NHL	1	0	1	1	0	—	—	—	—	—
87-88	Peterborough	OHL	63	38	70	108	63	12	5	12	17	4
87-88	Philadelphia	NHL	1	0	0	0	0	—	—	—	—	—
88-89	Philadelphia	NHL	5	0	1	1	0	—	—	—	—	—
88-89	Hershey	AHL	75	30	49	79	77	12	4	6	10	2
89-90	Philadelphia	NHL	2	0	0	0	0	—	—	—	—	—
89-90	Hershey	AHL	65	28	36	64	31	—	—	—	—	—
90-91	Hershey	AHL	77	18	44	62	45	7	1	3	4	17
91-92	Philadelphia	NHL	50	6	7	13	18	—	—	—	—	—
91-92	Hershey	AHL	31	13	11	24	38	6	0	3	3	2
92-93	Ottawa	NHL	63	10	14	24	39	—	—	—	—	—
93-94	Calgary	NHL	2	0	0	0	4	—	—	—	—	—
93-94	Saint John	AHL	77	33	53	86	45	7	2	4	6	16
94-95	Houston	IHL	80	38	42	80	54	4	0	1	1	4
95-96	Houston	IHL	80	22	31	53	67	—	—	—	—	—
96-97	Houston	IHL	81	21	36	57	43	12	2	3	5	4
97-98	Houston	IHL	74	14	38	52	41	4	2	2	4	4
98-99	Houston	IHL	79	17	28	45	66	19	*11	11	*22	12
	NHL	Totals	124	16	23	39	61	—	—	—	—	—
	IHL	Totals	394	112	175	287	271	39	15	17	32	24
	AHL	Totals	325	122	193	315	236	32	7	16	23	37

Born; 7/14/68, Toronto, Ontario. 5-10, 180. Signed as a free agent by Philadelphia Flyers (10/7/86). Claimed by Ottawa Senators from Philadelphia in Expansion Draft (6/18/92). Signed as a free agent by Calgary Flames (8/10/93). 1998-99 IHL Playoff MVP. Member of 1998-99 IHL Champion Houston Aeros. Last amateur club; Peterborough (OHL).

Tony Frenette — Right Wing

Regular Season / Playoffs

Season	Team	League	GP	G	A	PTS	PIM	GP	G	A	PTS	PIM
96-97	Pensacola	ECHL	9	3	3	6	8	—	—	—	—	—
96-97	Huntsville	CeHL	47	41	31	72	50	9	1	2	3	10
97-98	Huntsville	CHL	29	11	12	23	37	—	—	—	—	—
97-98	Memphis	CHL	5	3	3	6	0	4	1	2	3	4
98-99	Mohawk Valley	UHL	3	0	0	0	0	—	—	—	—	—
98-99	Point-Rouge	QSPHL	34	28	28	56	NA	—	—	—	—	—
	CHL	Totals	81	55	46	101	87	13	2	4	6	14

Born; 1/20/73, Edmonton, Alberta. 5-10, 180. Traded to Memphis for Kevin Oakenfold (3/98). Last amateur club; Maine (Hockey East).

Christian Friberg — Defenseman

Regular Season / Playoffs

Season	Team	League	GP	G	A	PTS	PIM	GP	G	A	PTS	PIM
98-99	Idaho	WCHL	60	6	7	13	52	—	—	—	—	—

Born; 4/14/76, Danderyz, Sweden. 6-4, 210. Last overseas club; Hammarby (Sweden).

Kevin Fricke — Defenseman

Regular Season / Playoffs

Season	Team	League	GP	G	A	PTS	PIM	GP	G	A	PTS	PIM
98-99	Madison	UHL	1	0	0	0	0	—	—	—	—	—

Born; 4/18/74, Edina, Minnesota. 5-9, 175. Last amateur club; Wisconsin Stevens-Point (NCAA 3).

Rob Frid — Right Wing

Regular Season / Playoffs

Season	Team	League	GP	G	A	PTS	PIM	GP	G	A	PTS	PIM
97-98	Louisville	ECHL	56	11	9	20	181	—	—	—	—	—
98-99	Quad City	UHL	38	1	1!	12	201	—	—	—	—	—

Born; 2/4/75, Burlington, Ontario. 6-2, 215. Last amateur club; St. Thomas University (AUAA).

Doug Friedman — Left Wing

Regular Season / Playoffs

Season	Team	League	GP	G	A	PTS	PIM	GP	G	A	PTS	PIM
94-95	Cornwall	AHL	55	6	9	15	56	3	0	0	0	0
95-96	Cornwall	AHL	80	12	22	34	178	8	1	1	2	17
96-97	Hershey	AHL	61	12	21	33	245	23	6	9	15	49
97-98	Edmonton	NHL	16	0	0	0	20	—	—	—	—	—
97-98	Hamilton	AHL	55	19	27	46	235	9	4	4	8	40
98-99	Nashville	NHL	2	0	1	1	14	—	—	—	—	—
98-99	Milwaukee	IHL	69	26	25	51	251	2	1	2	3	8
	NHL	Totals	18	0	1	1	34	—	—	—	—	—
	AHL	Totals	251	49	79	128	714	43	11	14	25	106

Born; 9/1/71, Cape Elizabeth, Maine. 6-1, 189. Drafted by Quebec Nordiques (11th choice, 222nd overall) in 1991 Entry Draft. Signed as a free agent by Edmonton Oilers (7/14/97). Selected by Nashville Predators in 1998 NHL Expansion Draft. Member of 1996-97 AHL Champion Hershey Bears. Last amateur club; Boston University (Hockey East).

Rob Friesen — Center

Regular Season / Playoffs

Season	Team	League	GP	G	A	PTS	PIM	GP	G	A	PTS	PIM
94-95	Guildford	BHL	37	74	69	143	26	—	—	—	—	—
95-96	Guilford	BHL	44	42	67	109	32	—	—	—	—	—
95-96	Bakersfield	WCHL	3	1	0	1	4	—	—	—	—	—
95-96	Erie	ECHL	1	0	0	0	2	—	—	—	—	—
97-98	Monroe	WPHL	57	13	25	38	21	—	—	—	—	—
98-99	Monroe	WPHL	66	12	27	39	32	5	2	3	5	2
	WPHL	Totals	123	25	52	77	53	5	2	3	5	2

Born; 5/6/68, Winnipeg, Manitoba. 5-9, 175.

Rob Friesen — Goaltender

Regular Season / Playoffs

Season	Team	League	GP	W	L	T	MIN	SO	AVG	GP	W	L	MIN	SO	AVG
97-98	Wichita	CHL	41	17	19	3	2254	1	4.31	—	—	—	—	—	—
98-99	Memphis	CHL	48	23	18	4	2692	0	4.26	—	—	—	—	—	—
	CHL	Totals	89	40	37	7	4946	1	4.28	—	—	—	—	—	—

Born; Last amateur club; Kelowna (WHL).

Terry Friesen — Goaltender

Regular Season / Playoffs

Season	Team	League	GP	W	L	T	MIN	SO	AVG	GP	W	L	MIN	SO	AVG
98-99	Kentucky	AHL	1	0	0	0	26	0	4.66	—	—	—	—	—	—
98-99	Richmond	ECHL	24	9	13	0	1277	1	3.57	1	1	0	20	0	0.00

Born; 10/29/77, Winkler, Manitoba. 5-11, 190. Drafted by San Jose Sharks (3rd choice, 55th overall) in 1996 Entry Draft. Last amateur club; Swift Current

Sam Ftorek — Forward

Regular Season / Playoffs

Season	Team	League	GP	G	A	PTS	PIM	GP	G	A	PTS	PIM
98-99	Augusta	ECHL	62	11	18	29	128	2	0	0	0	4

Born; Essex Falls, New Jersey. 6-2, 175. Last amateur club; Saint Anselm (NCAA 2).

Greg Fullerton — Defenseman

Regular Season / Playoffs

Season	Team	League	GP	G	A	PTS	PIM	GP	G	A	PTS	PIM
98-99	Thunder Bay	UHL	4	0	0	0	10	4	0	0	0	2

Born; 4/22/75. 6-4, 220. Last amateur club; Waterloo (OUAA).

Ryan Furness — Left Wing

Regular Season / Playoffs

Season	Team	League	GP	G	A	PTS	PIM	GP	G	A	PTS	PIM
97-98	Massachusetts	H.E.	32	0	3	3	37	—	—	—	—	—
97-98	Dayton	ECHL	8	0	2	2	12	5	0	0	0	15
98-99	Dayton	ECHL	55	7	10	17	106	—	—	—	—	—
98-99	Wheeling	ECHL	16	3	3	6	43	—	—	—	—	—
	ECHL	Totals	79	10	15	25	161	5	0	0	0	15

Born; 3/16/74, Salt Lake City, Utah. 6-3, 215. Last amateur club; University of Massachusetts (Hockey East).

Bryan Fuss — Right Wing

Regular Season / Playoffs

Season	Team	League	GP	G	A	PTS	PIM	GP	G	A	PTS	PIM
97-98	Lake Superior	CCHA	25	3	5	8	132	—	—	—	—	—
97-98	Nashville	CHL	6	2	1	3	2	7	1	3	4	20
98-99	Columbus	ECHL	10	1	0	1	21	—	—	—	—	—

Born; 3/4/74, Madison, Wisconsin. 5-9, 180. Selected by Fayetteville in 1998 CHL Expansion Draft. Last amateur club; Lake Superior State (CCHA).

Link Gaetz — Defenseman

Regular Season / Playoffs

Season	Team	League	GP	G	A	PTS	PIM	GP	G	A	PTS	PIM
88-89	Minnesota	NHL	12	0	2	2	53	—	—	—	—	—
88-89	Kalamazoo	IHL	37	3	4	7	192	5	0	0	0	56
89-90	Minnesota	NHL	5	0	0	0	33	—	—	—	—	—
89-90	Kalamazoo	IHL	61	5	16	21	318	9	2	2	4	59
90-91	Kalamazoo	IHL	9	0	1	1	44	—	—	—	—	—
90-91	Kansas City	IHL	18	1	10	11	178	—	—	—	—	—
91-92	San Jose	NHL	48	6	6	12	326	—	—	—	—	—
92-93	Nashville	ECHL	3	1	0	1	10	—	—	—	—	—
92-93	Kansas City	IHL	2	0	0	0	14	—	—	—	—	—
93-94	Nashville	ECHL	24	1	1	2	261	—	—	—	—	—
93-94	Cape Breton	AHL	21	0	1	1	140	—	—	—	—	—
93-94	West Palm Beach	SUN	6	0	3	3	15	3	0	1	1	8
94-95	San Antonio	CeHL	13	0	3	3	156	—	—	—	—	—
95-96	San Francisco	IHL	3	0	0	0	37	—	—	—	—	—
96-97	Madison	CoHL	26	2	4	6	178	—	—	—	—	—
97-98	Anchorage	WCHL	11	0	1	1	130	—	—	—	—	—
98-99	Toledo	ECHL	1	0	0	0	2	—	—	—	—	—
	NHL	Totals	65	6	8	14	412	—	—	—	—	—
	IHL	Totals	130	9	31	40	783	14	2	2	4	115
	ECHL	Totals	28	2	1	3	273	—	—	—	—	—

Born; 10/2/68, Vancouver, British Columbia. 6-4, 230. Drafted by Minnesota North Stars (2nd choice, 40th overall) in 19988 Entry Draft. Selected by San Jose Sharks in NHL dispersal draft (5/30/91). Traded to Edmonton Oilers by San Jose for conditional 10th round pick in 1994 Entry Draft, (9/10/93). Member of 1993-94 Sunshine League champion West Palm Beach Blaze. Last amateur club;

Mike Gaffney — Defenseman

Regular Season / Playoffs

Season	Team	League	GP	G	A	PTS	PIM	GP	G	A	PTS	PIM
98-99	Quad City	UHL	19	5	7	12	10	10	2	10	12	12
98-99	Detroit	IHL	38	2	4	6	33	—	—	—	—	—
98-99	Las Vegas	IHL	10	0	1	1	8	—	—	—	—	—
	IHL	Totals	48	2	5	7	41	—	—	—	—	—

Born; 5/18/76, Worcester, Massachusetts. 6-1, 210. Selected by Knoxville in 1999 UHL Expansion Draft. Last amateur club; Massachusetts (Hockey East).

Joaquin Gage — Goaltender

Regular Season / Playoffs

Season	Team	League	GP	W	L	T	MIN	SO	AVG	GP	W	L	MIN	SO	AVG
94-95	Edmonton	NHL	2	0	2	0	99	0	4.24	—	—	—	—	—	—
94-95	Cape Breton	AHL	54	17	28	5	3010	0	4.13	—	—	—	—	—	—
95-96	Edmonton	NHL	16	2	8	1	717	0	3.77	—	—	—	—	—	—
95-96	Cape Breton	AHL	21	8	11	0	1162	0	4.13	—	—	—	—	—	—
96-97	Hamilton	AHL	29	7	14	4	1558	0	3.50	—	—	—	—	—	—
96-97	Wheeling	ECHL	3	1	0	0	120	0	4.00	—	—	—	—	—	—
97-98	Syracuse	AHL	2	1	1	0	120	0	3.50	—	—	—	—	—	—
97-98	Raleigh	ECHL	39	19	14	3	2174	1	3.20	—	—	—	—	—	—
98-99	Portland	AHL	26	8	11	3	1429	2	2.90	—	—	—	—	—	—
98-99	Providence	AHL	3	0	2	0	130	0	4.16	—	—	—	—	—	—
98-99	Syracuse	AHL	12	2	8	2	706	0	3.91	—	—	—	—	—	—
98-99	Augusta	ECHL	5	5	0	0	300	0	3.20	—	—	—	—	—	—
	NHL	Totals	18	2	10	1	816	0	3.82	—	—	—	—	—	—
	AHL	Totals	147	43	75	11	8114	2	3.76	—	—	—	—	—	—
	ECHL	Totals	47	25	14	3	2594	1	3.24	—	—	—	—	—	—

Born; 10/19/73, Vancouver, British Columbia. 6-0, 206. Drafted by Edmonton Oilers (6th choice, 109th overall) in 1992 Entry Draft. Last amateur club; Prince Albert (WHL).

Jason Gaggi — Goaltender

Regular Season / Playoffs

Season	Team	League	GP	W	L	T	MIN	SO	AVG	GP	W	L	MIN	SO	AVG
98-99	Jacksonville	ECHL	1	0	1	0	20	0	12.00	—	—	—	—	—	—

Born; 3/2/78, Woodbridge, Ontario. 5-9, 181. Last amateur club; Sudbury (OHL).

Luc Gagne — Forward

Regular Season / Playoffs

Season	Team	League	GP	G	A	PTS	PIM	GP	G	A	PTS	PIM
98-99	Waco	WPHL	61	17	25	42	74	4	1	1	2	0

Born; 5/4/76, Sudbury, Ontario. 6-1, 200. Last amateur club; Laurentian (OUAA).

Ben Gagnon — Defenseman

Regular Season / Playoffs

Season	Team	League	GP	G	A	PTS	PIM	GP	G	A	PTS	PIM
98-99	Macon	CHL	13	1	1	2	24	—	—	—	—	—

Born;

Dave Gagnon — Goaltender

Regular Season / Playoffs

Season	Team	League	GP	W	L	T	MIN	SO	AVG	GP	W	L	MIN	SO	AVG
90-91	Detroit	NHL	2	0	1	0	35	0	10.29	—	—	—	—	—	—
90-91	Adirondack	AHL	24	7	8	5	1356	0	4.16	—	—	—	—	—	—
90-91	H. Roads	ECHL	10	7	1	2	606	2	2.57	11	*10	1	*696	0	*2.33
91-92	Toledo	ECHL	7	4	2	0	354	0	3.05	—	—	—	—	—	—
91-92	Fort Wayne	IHL	2	2	0	0	125	0	3.36	—	—	—	—	—	—
92-93	Fort Wayne	IHL	31	15	11	0	1771	0	3.93	1	0	0	6	0	0.00
92-93	Adirondack	AHL	1	0	1	0	60	0	5.00	—	—	—	—	—	—
93-94	Toledo	ECHL	20	13	5	0	1122	1	3.48	*14	*12	2	*910	0	*2.70
93-94	Fort Wayne	IHL	19	7	6	3	1026	0	3.39	—	—	—	—	—	—
94-95	Minnesota	IHL	16	5	4	2	767	0	4.30	1	0	1	60	0	9.00
94-95	Roanoke	ECHL	29	17	7	5	1738	1	2.83	—	—	—	—	—	—
95-96	Minnesota	IHL	52	18	25	4	2721	0	4.14	—	—	—	—	—	—
96-97	Roanoke	ECHL	60	34	18	6	3387	3	3.21	3	1	2	220	0	2.73
97-98	Roanoke	ECHL	43	25	13	4	2466	2	2.89	7	3	4	442	1	2.04
98-99	Roanoke	ECHL	34	20	9	5	2033	2	2.57	3	0	2	139	0	2.59
	IHL	Totals	120	37	46	9	6410	0	3.97	2	0	1	66	0	8.18
	AHL	Totals	25	7	9	5	1416	0	4.19	—	—	—	—	—	—
	ECHL	Totals	203	120	55	20	11706	11	2.96	38	26	11	2407	1	2.47

Born; 10/31/67, Windsor, Ontario. 6-0, 195. Signed as a free agent by Detroit Red Wings (6/11/90). 1990-91 ECHL Playoff MVP. 1994-95 ECHL Second Team All-Star. Member of 1990-91 ECHL champion Hampton Roads Admirals. Member of 1992-93 IHL champion Fort Wayne Komets. Member of 1993-94 ECHL champion Toledo Storm. Last amateur club; Colgate (ECAC).

Pierre Gagnon — Goaltender

Regular Season / Playoffs

Season	Team	League	GP	W	L	T	MIN	SO	AVG	GP	W	L	MIN	SO	AVG
92-93	Thunder Bay	CoHL	2	1	1	0	124	0	4.35	—	—	—	—	—	—
93-94															
94-95															
95-96															
96-97	Macon	CeHL	*57	33	18	2	*3155	1	3.27	5	2	3	308	0	2.73
97-98	Tucson	WCHL	28	8	16	3	1630	0	4.97	—	—	—	—	—	—
97-98	Shreveport	WPHL	12	4	2	4	598	0	3.41	4	1	3	202	0	3.56
98-99	Macon	CHL	50	25	16	4	2735	0	3.27	3	0	3	205	0	3.51
	CHL	Totals	107	58	34	6	5890	1	3.27	8	2	6	513	0	3.04

Born; 2/21/71, LaFontaine, Quebec. 5-8, 170. Selected by Tupelo in 1998 WPHL Expansion Draft. Last amateur club; Moncton (AUAA).

Sean Gagnon — Defenseman

Regular Season / Playoffs

Season	Team	League	GP	G	A	PTS	PIM	GP	G	A	PTS	PIM
94-95	Dayton	ECHL	68	9	23	32	339	8	0	3	3	69
95-96	Dayton	ECHL	68	7	22	29	326	3	0	1	1	33
96-97	Fort Wayne	IHL	72	7	7	14	*457	—	—	—	—	—
97-98	Phoenix	NHL	5	0	1	1	14	—	—	—	—	—
97-98	Springfield	AHL	54	4	13	17	330	2	0	1	1	17
98-99	Phoenix	NHL	2	0	0	0	7	—	—	—	—	—
98-99	Springfield	AHL	68	8	14	22	331	3	0	0	0	14
	NHL	Totals	7	0	1	1	21	—	—	—	—	—
	AHL	Totals	122	12	27	39	661	5	0	1	1	31
	ECHL	Totals	136	16	45	61	665	11	0	4	4	102

Born; 9/11/73, Sault Ste. Marie, Ontario. 6-2, 210. Signed as a free agent by Phoenix Coyotes (5/14/97). Last amateur club; Sault Ste. Marie (OHL).

Ernie Gallagher — Defenseman

Regular Season / Playoffs

Season	Team	League	GP	G	A	PTS	PIM	GP	G	A	PTS	PIM
96-97	Amarillo	WPHL	14	1	6	7	17	—	—	—	—	—
97-98	Amarillo	WPHL	55	3	4	7	41	—	—	—	—	—
98-99	Tucson	WCHL	6	0	0	0	2	—	—	—	—	—
98-99	Fort Worth	WPHL	4	0	0	0	6	—	—	—	—	—
	WPHL	Totals	73	4	10	14	64	—	—	—	—	—

Born; 6/9/74, Soldotna, Alaska. 6-0, 205.

Trevor Gallant
Forward

Regular Season — Playoffs

Season	Team	League	GP	G	A	PTS	PIM	GP	G	A	PTS	PIM
95-96	North Bay	OHL	63	47	58	105	36	—	—	—	—	—
95-96	South Carolina	ECHL	5	2	6	8	0	8	4	4	8	4
96-97	Tappara Tampere	Finland	31	4	7	11	36	3	0	1	1	2
96-97	Hermes	Finland	16	7	17	24	0	—	—	—	—	—
97-98	Canada	National	63	17	31	48	14	—	—	—	—	—
98-99	Asiago	Italy										
98-99	Canada	National	2	0	1	1	2	—	—	—	—	—

Born; Last amateur club; North Bay (OHL).

Scott Galt
Goaltender

Regular Season — Playoffs

Season	Team	League	GP	W	L	T	MIN	SO	AVG	GP	W	L	MIN	SO	AVG
95-96	Jacksonville	ECHL	11	4	5	1	619	0	4.26	—	—	—	—	—	—
96-97	Central Texas	WPHL	11	4	5	0	496	0	4.11	—	—	—	—	—	—
97-98	Lake Charles	WPHL	15	5	5	1	772	0	4.12	—	—	—	—	—	—
98-99	Lake Charles	WPHL	20	3	6	1	743	1	3.63	2	2	0	116	1	*0.52
	WPHL	Totals	46	12	16	2	2011	1	3.94	2	2	0	116	1	0.52

Born; 1/18/74, Penetanguistene, Ontario. 5-10, 175.

Mike Gamble
Center

Regular Season — Playoffs

Season	Team	League	GP	G	A	PTS	PIM	GP	G	A	PTS	PIM
95-96	Huntsville	SHL	54	31	33	64	93	—	—	—	—	—
96-97	Brantford	CoHL	36	12	13	25	55	—	—	—	—	—
96-97	Dayton	CoHL	7	2	1	3	6	—	—	—	—	—
96-97	Huntsville	CeHL	11	10	11	21	18	4	2	1	3	30
97-98	Fort Worth	CHL	6	2	2	4	33	—	—	—	—	—
97-98	Fayetteville	CHL	24	7	10	17	51	—	—	—	—	—
98-99	Huntsville	CHL	55	22	22	44	117	—	—	—	—	—
	CHL	Totals	96	41	45	86	219	4	2	1	3	30
	CoHL	Totals	43	14	14	28	24	—	—	—	—	—

Born; 8/17/75, Brantford, Ontario. 5-9, 175.

Jason Garatti
Defenseman

Regular Season — Playoffs

Season	Team	League	GP	G	A	PTS	PIM	GP	G	A	PTS	PIM
98-99	Thunder Bay	UHL	10	2	2	4	2	—	—	—	—	—

Born; 1/12/73, Thunder Bay, Ontario. 6-1, 200.

Dan Gardner
Center

Regular Season — Playoffs

Season	Team	League	GP	G	A	PTS	PIM	GP	G	A	PTS	PIM
94-95	Detroit	CoHL	2	1	0	1	0	—	—	—	—	—
95-96												
96-97												
97-98												
98-99	Madison	UHL	1	0	0	0	0	—	—	—	—	—
	UHL	Totals	3	1	0	1	0	—	—	—	—	—

Born; 5/9/71, Sarnia, Ontario. Last amateur club; Colgate (ECAC).

Joel Gardner
Center

Regular Season — Playoffs

Season	Team	League	GP	G	A	PTS	PIM	GP	G	A	PTS	PIM
90-91	Muskegon	IHL	49	9	13	22	30	2	0	1	1	0
91-92	Muskegon	IHL	5	1	2	3	2	—	—	—	—	—
91-92	Knoxville	ECHL	36	20	34	54	30	—	—	—	—	—
91-92	Michigan	CoHL	3	1	2	3	0	—	—	—	—	—
92-93	Chatham	CoHL	14	8	14	22	2	—	—	—	—	—
92-93	Raleigh	ECHL	45	22	51	73	30	—	—	—	—	—
93-94	Chatham	CoHL	42	30	54	84	50	15	8	12	20	19
94-95	Detroit	CoHL	2	1	2	3	0	12	3	0	3	8
94-95	ERC Serb											
97-98	Port Huron	UHL	20	5	10	15	2	—	—	—	—	—
97-98	Saginaw	UHL	47	20	36	56	20	—	—	—	—	—
98-99	Saginaw	UHL	3	0	3	3	2	—	—	—	—	—
98-99	Muskegon	UHL	7	0	10	10	0	—	—	—	—	—
98-99	Madison	UHL	4	0	2	2	0	—	—	—	—	—
98-99	Mohawk Valley	UHL	44	15	35	50	16	—	—	—	—	—
	IHL	Totals	54	10	15	25	32	2	0	1	1	0
	UHL	Totals	186	80	168	248	92	27	11	12	23	27
	ECHL	Totals	81	42	85	127	60	—	—	—	—	—

Born; 9/26/67, Petrolia, Ontario. 6-0, 190. Drafted by Boston Bruins (10th choice, 244th overall) in 1986 Entry Draft. Traded to Saginaw by Port Huron with J.D. Eaton and David Geris for Jason Renard, Dale Greenwood and Bobby Ferraris (12/97). Last amateur club; Colgate (ECAC).

Mathieu Garon
Goaltender

Regular Season — Playoffs

Season	Team	League	GP	W	L	T	MIN	SO	AVG	GP	W	L	MIN	SO	AVG
98-99	Fredericton	AHL	40	14	22	2	2222	3	3.08	6	1	1	208	0	3.47

Born; 1/9/78, Chandler, Quebec. 6-1, 187. Drafted by Montreal Canadiens (2nd choice, 44th overall) in 1996 Entry Draft. Last amateur club; Victoriaville (QMJHL).

Matthew Garver
Forward

Regular Season — Playoffs

Season	Team	League	GP	G	A	PTS	PIM	GP	G	A	PTS	PIM
98-99	South Carolina	ECHL	5	0	0	0	0	—	—	—	—	—

Born; 4/1/76, Pittsford, Massachusetts. 5-10, 160. Last amateur club; R.P.I.

Liam Garvey
Defenseman

Regular Season — Playoffs

Season	Team	League	GP	G	A	PTS	PIM	GP	G	A	PTS	PIM
95-96	San Antonio	CeHL	50	11	39	50	118	4	0	1	1	12
96-97	Fort Wayne	IHL	55	5	10	15	92	—	—	—	—	—
96-97	Peoria	ECHL	19	4	15	19	61	—	—	—	—	—
97-98	Quebec	IHL	69	9	21	30	75	—	—	—	—	—
98-99	Nurnburg	Germany	50	10	29	39	190	12	2	5	7	20
	IHL	Totals	124	14	31	45	167	—	—	—	—	—

Born; 1/2/73, Chicago Heights, Illinois. 5-11, 190. 1995-96 CeHL First Team All-Star. Last amateur club; Michigan Tech (WCHA).

Matt Garzone
Defenseman

Regular Season — Playoffs

Season	Team	League	GP	G	A	PTS	PIM	GP	G	A	PTS	PIM
96-97	Richmond	ECHL	39	4	13	17	38	—	—	—	—	—
96-97	Knoxville	ECHL	23	1	7	8	16	—	—	—	—	—
97-98	Louisiana	ECHL	2	1	0	1	15	—	—	—	—	—
97-98	Wheeling	ECHL	63	10	41	51	78	15	1	11	12	5
98-99	Wheeling	ECHL	20	4	10	14	14	—	—	—	—	—
98-99	South Carolina	ECHL	50	4	19	23	23	3	0	0	0	2
	ECHL	Totals	197	24	90	114	184	18	1	11	12	7

Born; 10/6/72, Sherborn, Massachusetts. 6-0, 205. Traded to Pee Dee by Louisiana for Steve Adams and Kent Fearns (10/97). Traded to Wheeling by Pee Dee with Joe Harney for Eric Royal (10/97). Last amateur club; Colgate (ECAC).

Jon Gaskins
Forward

Regular Season — Playoffs

Season	Team	League	GP	G	A	PTS	PIM	GP	G	A	PTS	PIM
98-99	Tupelo	WPHL	43	8	20	28	65	—	—	—	—	—

Born; 1/11/76, Dallas, Texas. 6-3, 205. Drafted by Edmonton Oilers (8th choice, 110th overall) in 1994 Entry Draft. Last amateur club; Michigan State (CCHA).

Pascal Gasse — Goaltender

Regular Season / Playoffs

Season	Team	League	GP	W	L	T	MIN	SO	AVG	GP	W	L	MIN	SO	AVG
98-99	Tulsa	CHL	19	8	8	1	864	0	4.65	—	—	—	—	—	—
98-99	Wichita	CHL	8	2	2	2	324	0	3.70	2	0	1	82	0	5.11
	CHL	Totals	27	10	10	3	1189	0	4.39	2	0	1	82	0	5.11

Born; 5/25/77. 6-1, 175.

Sandy Gasseau — Right Wing/Defense

Regular Season / Playoffs

Season	Team	League	GP	G	A	PTS	PIM	GP	G	A	PTS	PIM
95-96	San Diego	WCHL	14	9	11	20	20	—	—	—	—	—
96-97	San Diego	WCHL	42	26	22	48	35	6	3	3	6	14
97-98	San Diego	WCHL	56	21	15	36	82	13	3	5	8	20
98-99	San Diego	WCHL	51	14	34	48	59	—	—	—	—	—
98-99	Tacoma	WCHL	2	0	1	1	14	—	—	—	—	—
	WCHL	Totals	165	70	83	153	210	19	6	8	14	34

Born; 9/15/70, Ste. Foy, Quebec. 6-2, 195. Member of 1996-97 WCHL Champion San Diego Gulls. Member of 1997-98 WCHL Champion San Diego Gulls. Traded to Bakersfield by San Diego for Stephane St. Amour (2/99). Traded to Tacoma by Bakersfield for Brad Mehalko and Alex Mukhanov (3/99). Last amateur club; St. Cloud (WCHA).

Jim Gattolliat — Defenseman

Regular Season / Playoffs

Season	Team	League	GP	G	A	PTS	PIM	GP	G	A	PTS	PIM
96-97	Dayton	ECHL	3	0	1	1	7	4	1	2	3	7
97-98	Tacoma	WCHL	46	4	4	8	145	5	0	0	0	6
98-99	Tacoma	WCHL	64	4	11	15	121	—	—	—	—	—
98-99	Bakersfield	WCHL	4	0	1	1	6	2	0	0	0	0
	WCHL	Totals	114	8	16	24	272	7	0	0	0	6

Born; 12/18/76, Edmonton, Alberta. 5-11, 192. Traded to Bakersfield by Tacoma to complete earlier trade (3/99).

Michael Gaul — Defenseman

Regular Season / Playoffs

Season	Team	League	GP	G	A	PTS	PIM	GP	G	A	PTS	PIM
94-95	Knoxville	ECHL	68	13	41	54	51	4	2	1	3	2
94-95	Phoenix	IHL	4	0	1	1	2	—	—	—	—	—
95-96	Knoxville	ECHL	54	13	48	61	44	—	—	—	—	—
96-97	Timmendorf	Gemany-2	51	40	52	92	100	—	—	—	—	—
97-98	Hershey	AHL	60	12	47	59	69	7	0	7	7	6
97-98	Mobile	ECHL	5	0	7	7	0	—	—	—	—	—
98-99	Colorado	NHL	1	0	0	0	0	—	—	—	—	—
98-99	Lowell	AHL	18	3	5	8	14	—	—	—	—	—
98-99	Hershey	AHL	43	9	31	40	22	5	1	1	2	6
	AHL	Totals	121	24	83	107	105	12	1	8	9	12
	ECHL	Totals	127	26	96	122	95	4	2	1	3	2

Born; 4/28/73, Lachine, Quebec. 6-1, 197. Drafted by Los Angeles Kings (10th choice, 262nd overall) in 1991 Entry Draft. Signed as a free agent by New York Islanders (7/16/98). Traded to Colorado Avalanche by Islanders for Ted Crowley (12/15/98). 1997-98 AHL All-Rookie Team. Last amateur club; Laval (QMJHL).

Denis Gauthier — Defenseman

Regular Season / Playoffs

Season	Team	League	GP	G	A	PTS	PIM	GP	G	A	PTS	PIM
95-96	Saint John	AHL	5	2	0	2	8	16	1	6	7	20
96-97	Saint John	AHL	73	3	28	31	74	5	0	0	0	6
97-98	Calgary	NHL	10	0	0	0	16	—	—	—	—	—
97-98	Saint John	AHL	68	4	20	24	154	21	0	4	4	83
98-99	Calgary	NHL	55	3	4	7	68	—	—	—	—	—
98-99	Saint John	AHL	16	0	3	3	31	—	—	—	—	—
	NHL	Totals	65	3	4	7	84	—	—	—	—	—
	AHL	Totals	162	9	51	60	267	42	1	10	11	109

Born; 10/1/76, Montreal, Quebec. 6-2, 195. Drafted by Calgary Flames (1st choice, 20th overall) in 1995 Entry Draft. Last amateur club; Drummondville

Derek Gauthier — Right Wing

Regular Season / Playoffs

Season	Team	League	GP	G	A	PTS	PIM	GP	G	A	PTS	PIM
93-94	Charlotte	ECHL	52	12	15	27	118	—	—	—	—	—
94-95	Brantford	CoHL	60	16	26	42	101	—	—	—	—	—
95-96	Louisville	ECHL	65	25	32	57	177	3	1	0	1	4
96-97	Columbus	ECHL	60	33	40	73	164	8	3	4	7	18
97-98	Anchorage	WCHL	56	26	27	53	100	8	0	4	4	15
98-99	Anchorage	WCHL	61	21	24	45	168	6	0	1	1	32
	ECHL	Totals	177	70	87	157	459	11	4	4	8	22
	WCHL	Totals	117	47	51	98	268	14	0	5	5	47

Born; 4/3/73, Sudbury, Ontario. 6-0, 195. Last amateur club; Kitchener (OHL).

Sean Gauthier — Goaltender

Regular Season / Playoffs

Season	Team	League	GP	W	L	T	MIN	SO	AVG	GP	W	L	MIN	SO	AVG
91-92	Fort Wayne	IHL	18	10	4	2	978	1	3.62	2	0	0	48	0	8.75
91-92	Moncton	AHL	25	8	10	5	1415	1	3.73	2	0	0	26	0	4.62
92-93	Moncton	AHL	38	10	16	9	2196	0	3.96	2	0	1	75	0	4.80
93-94	Moncton	AHL	13	3	5	1	617	0	3.99	—	—	—	—	—	—
93-94	Fort Wayne	IHL	22	9	9	3	1139	0	3.48	—	—	—	—	—	—
94-95	Fort Wayne	IHL	5	0	2	1	218	0	4.13	—	—	—	—	—	—
94-95	Canada	Nat.	24	16	6	0	1326	0	2.40	—	—	—	—	—	—
95-96	St. John's	AHL	5	1	1	0	173	0	3.12	—	—	—	—	—	—
95-96	S. Carolina	ECHL	49	31	11	7	2891	0	3.09	8	5	3	478	0	3.01
96-97	Pensacola	ECHL	46	23	21	1	2693	1	3.74	12	8	4	750	*1	3.52
97-98	Pensacola	ECHL	54	29	17	7	*3214	0	3.62	*19	12	*7	1180	1	2.95
98-99	San Jose	NHL	1	0	0	0	3	0	0.00	—	—	—	—	—	—
98-99	Kentucky	AHL	40	18	15	6	2376	1	2.50	4	0	1	130	0	3.68
	AHL	Totals	121	40	47	21	6777	2	3.30	8	0	2	231	0	4.16
	IHL	Totals	45	19	15	6	2335	1	3.60	2	0	0	48	0	8.75
	ECHL	Totals	149	83	49	15	8798	1	3.48	39	25	14	2408	2	3.14

Born; 3/28/71, Sudbury, Ontario. 5-11, 202. Drafted by Winnipeg Jets (7th choice, 181st overall) in 1991 Entry Draft. Signed as a free agent by San Jose Sharks (7/22/98). 1995-96 ECHL Second Team All-Star. 1997-98 ECHL Second Team All-Star. Last amateur club; Kingston (OHL).

Aaron Gavey — Center

Regular Season / Playoffs

Season	Team	League	GP	G	A	PTS	PIM	GP	G	A	PTS	PIM
94-95	Atlanta	IHL	66	18	17	35	85	5	0	1	1	9
95-96	Tampa Bay	NHL	73	8	4	12	56	6	0	0	0	4
96-97	Tampa Bay	NHL	16	1	2	3	12	—	—	—	—	—
96-97	Calgary	NHL	41	7	9	16	34	—	—	—	—	—
97-98	Calgary	NHL	26	2	3	5	24	—	—	—	—	—
97-98	Saint John	AHL	8	4	3	7	28	—	—	—	—	—
98-99	Dallas	NHL	7	0	0	0	10	—	—	—	—	—
98-99	Michigan	IHL	67	24	33	57	128	5	2	3	5	4
	NHL	Totals	163	18	18	36	136	6	0	0	0	4
	IHL	Totals	133	42	50	92	213	10	2	4	6	13

Born; 2/22/74, Sudbury, Ontario 6-1, 169. Drafted by Tampa Bay Lightning (4th choice, 74th overall) in 1992 Entry Draft. Traded to Calgary Flames by Tampa Bay for Rick Tabaracci (11/19/96). Traded to Dallas Stars by Calgary for Bob Bassen (7/14/98). Last amateur club; Sault Ste. Marie (OHL).

Ryan Gelinas — Goaltender

Regular Season / Playoffs

Season	Team	League	GP	W	L	T	MIN	SO	AVG	GP	W	L	MIN	SO	AVG
97-98	Brantford	UHL	4	2	2	0	224	0	4.82	—	—	—	—	—	—
97-98	Quad City	UHL	28	14	8	1	1422	1	4.05	—	—	—	—	—	—
98-99	Windsor	OUAA	25	—	—	—	1476	—	2.48	—	—	—	—	—	—
	UHL	Totals	32	16	10	1	1646	1	4.15	—	—	—	—	—	—

Born; 10/31/77, Windsor, Ontario. 5-11, 185. Last amateur club; Windsor (OHL).

Martin Gendron — Right Wing
Regular Season / Playoffs

Season	Team	League	GP	G	A	PTS	PIM	GP	G	A	PTS	PIM
92-93	St-Hyacinthe	QMJHL	63	73	61	134	44	—	—	—	—	—
92-93	Baltimore	AHL	10	1	2	3	2	3	0	0	0	0
93-94	Hull	QMJHL	37	39	36	75	18	20	*21	17	38	8
93-94	Canada	National	19	4	5	9	2	—	—	—	—	—
94-95	Washington	NHL	8	2	1	3	2	—	—	—	—	—
94-95	Portland	AHL	72	36	32	68	54	4	5	1	6	2
95-96	Washington	NHL	20	2	1	3	8	—	—	—	—	—
95-96	Portland	AHL	48	38	29	67	39	22	*15	18	33	8
96-97	Las Vegas	IHL	81	51	39	90	20	3	2	1	3	0
97-98	Chicago	NHL	2	0	0	0	0	—	—	—	—	—
97-98	Indianapolis	IHL	17	8	6	14	16	—	—	—	—	—
97-98	Milwaukee	IHL	40	20	19	39	14	—	—	—	—	—
97-98	Fredericton	AHL	10	5	10	15	4	2	0	0	0	4
98-99	Fredericton	AHL	65	33	34	67	26	15	*12	5	17	2
	NHL	Totals	30	4	2	6	10	—	—	—	—	—
	AHL	Totals	205	113	107	220	125	46	32	24	56	16
	IHL	Totals	138	79	64	143	50	3	2	1	3	0

Born; 2/15/74, Valleyfield, Quebec. 5-8, 180. Drafted by Washington Capitals (4th choice, 71st overall) in 1992 Entry Draft. Traded to Chicago Blackhawks by Washington with a draft pick for cash (10/10/98). Traded to Milwaukee by Indianapolis with Marc Hussey for Len Esau and Kent Paynter (12/97). Traded to Montreal Canadiens by Chicago for David Ling (3/14/98). Signed as a free agent by Vancouver Canucks (8/4/99). Last amateur club; Hull (QMJHL).

Pierre Gendron — Center
Regular Season / Playoffs

Season	Team	League	GP	G	A	PTS	PIM	GP	G	A	PTS	PIM
97-98	Hamilton	AHL	3	0	0	0	2	—	—	—	—	—
97-98	New Orleans	ECHL	42	9	10	19	61	—	—	—	—	—
97-98	Charlotte	ECHL	27	10	10	20	41	7	4	6	10	10
98-99	Tallahassee	ECHL	21	11	15	26	41	—	—	—	—	—
98-99	Pensacola	ECHL	47	23	27	50	51	—	—	—	—	—
	ECHL	Totals	137	53	62	115	194	7	4	6	10	10

Born; 1/21/74, Montreal, Quebec. 5-10, 185. Traded to Charlotte by New Orleans with Mikhail Nemirovsky for Dean Moore and Stephane Soulliere (2/98). Last amateur club; McGill (OUAA).

Marc Genest — Center
Regular Season / Playoffs

Season	Team	League	GP	G	A	PTS	PIM	GP	G	A	PTS	PIM
94-95	EA Kempton	Germany	40	92	76	168	65	—	—	—	—	—
95-96	EA Kempton	Germany	25	48	39	87	38	—	—	—	—	—
96-97	South Carolina	ECHL	35	3	13	16	41	—	—	—	—	—
96-97	Raleigh	ECHL	11	1	2	3	4	—	—	—	—	—
97-98	Macon	CHL	67	24	30	54	95	3	1	3	4	2
98-99	Idaho	WCHL	65	26	48	74	72	2	0	0	0	0
	ECHL	Totals	46	4	15	19	45	—	—	—	—	—

Born; 2/19/73, Orleans, Ontario. 5-11, 188. Last amateur club; Illinois-Chicago (CCHA).

Jason Genik — Goaltender
Regular Season / Playoffs

Season	Team	League	GP	W	L	T	MIN	SO	AVG	GP	W	L	MIN	SO	AVG
98-99	Corpus Christi	WPHL	29	21	5	2	1683	*4	*2.10	4	1	3	239	0	5.26

Born; 5/9/74, Winnipeg, Manitoba. 6-1, 180. Last amateur club; Manitoba (CWUAA).

Wes Gentles — Forward
Regular Season / Playoffs

Season	Team	League	GP	G	A	PTS	PIM	GP	G	A	PTS	PIM
94-95	Fresno	SUN	11	5	5	10	11	—	—	—	—	—
95-96												
96-97												
97-98												
98-99	Fresno	WCHL	1	1	0	1	0	—	—	—	—	—

Born; 6-0, 195.

Chris George — Right Wing
Regular Season / Playoffs

Season	Team	League	GP	G	A	PTS	PIM	GP	G	A	PTS	PIM
94-95	Tallahassee	ECHL	8	1	1	2	4	—	—	—	—	—
95-96	Tallahassee	ECHL	1	0	0	0	0	—	—	—	—	—
95-96	Daytona Beach	SHL	60	45	38	83	28	4	1	3	4	4
96-97	Columbus	CeHL	3	0	1	1	6	—	—	—	—	—
96-97	Huntsville	CeHL	54	27	15	42	21	9	2	2	4	6
97-98	Huntsville	CHL	70	52	57	109	47	3	2	3	5	2
98-99	Huntsville	CHL	70	59	48	107	28	15	6	6	12	6
	CHL	Totals	197	138	121	259	102	27	10	11	21	14
	ECHL	Totals	9	1	1	2	4	—	—	—	—	—

Born; 12/3/71, Kitchener, Ontario. 5-10, 192. Member of 1998-99 CHL Champion Huntsville Channel Cats.

Darcy George — Left Wing
Regular Season / Playoffs

Season	Team	League	GP	G	A	PTS	PIM	GP	G	A	PTS	PIM
97-98	Lake Superior	CCHA	25	3	4	7	14	—	—	—	—	—
97-98	Amarillo	WPHL	13	3	3	6	4	—	—	—	—	—
98-99	Toledo	ECHL	58	8	15	23	51	6	0	1	1	4

Born; 7/23/74, Vernon, British Columbia. 6-4, 212. Last amateur club; Lake Superior State (CCHA).

Ken Gernander — Right Wing
Regular Season / Playoffs

Season	Team	League	GP	G	A	PTS	PIM	GP	G	A	PTS	PIM
91-92	Fort Wayne	IHL	13	7	6	13	2	—	—	—	—	—
91-92	Moncton	AHL	43	8	18	26	9	8	1	1	2	2
92-93	Moncton	AHL	71	18	29	47	20	5	1	4	5	0
93-94	Moncton	AHL	71	22	25	47	12	19	6	1	7	0
94-95	Binghamton	AHL	80	28	25	53	24	11	2	2	4	6
95-96	Rangers	NHL	10	2	3	5	4	6	0	0	0	0
95-96	Binghamton	AHL	63	44	29	73	38	—	—	—	—	—
96-97	Rangers	NHL	—	—	—	—	—	9	0	0	0	0
96-97	Binghamton	AHL	46	13	18	31	30	2	0	1	1	0
97-98	Hartford	AHL	80	35	28	63	26	12	5	6	11	4
98-99	Hartford	AHL	70	23	26	49	32	7	1	2	3	2
	NHL	Totals	10	2	3	5	4	15	0	0	0	0
	AHL	Totals	524	191	198	389	195	70	16	17	33	14

Born; 6/30/69, Coleraine, Minnesota. 5-10, 175. Drafted by Winnipeg Jets (4th choice, 96th overall) in 1987 Entry Draft. Signed as a free agent by New York Rangers (7/4/94). 1995-96 AHL Fred Hunt Memorial Trophy (Sportsmanship). Last amateur club; University of Minnesota (WCHA).

Peter Geronazzo — Right Wing
Regular Season / Playoffs

Season	Team	League	GP	G	A	PTS	PIM	GP	G	A	PTS	PIM
97-98	Orlando	IHL	3	0	0	0	0	—	—	—	—	—
97-98	Pee Dee	ECHL	70	25	37	62	63	8	1	3	4	17
98-99	Pee Dee	ECHL	57	27	25	52	93	13	2	5	7	20
	ECHL	Totals	127	52	62	114	156	21	3	8	11	37

Born; 2/27/71, Trail, British Columbia. 5-11, 195. Last amateur club; Colorado College (WCHA).

Hugues Gervais — Left Wing
Regular Season / Playoffs

Season	Team	League	GP	G	A	PTS	PIM	GP	G	A	PTS	PIM
96-97	Hershey	AHL	3	0	0	0	14	9	1	1	2	19
96-97	Mobile	ECHL	57	12	5	17	198	3	1	1	2	10
97-98	Hershey	AHL	44	3	8	11	146	2	0	0	0	0
97-98	Mobile	ECHL	11	2	1	3	35	—	—	—	—	—
98-99	Mobile	ECHL	66	31	20	51	167	2	0	0	0	19
	AHL	Totals	47	3	8	11	160	11	1	1	2	19
	ECHL	Totals	134	45	26	71	400	5	1	1	2	29

Born; 1/10/75, Fortierville, Quebec. 6-1, 206. Member of 1996-97 AHL Champion Hershey Bears. Last amateur club; Victoriaville (QMJHL).

Victor Gervais — Center

Regular Season / Playoffs

Season	Team	League	GP	G	A	PTS	PIM	GP	G	A	PTS	PIM
90-91	Baltimore	AHL	28	2	13	15	28	—	—	—	—	—
90-91	Hampton Roads	ECHL	8	5	14	19	15	—	—	—	—	—
91-92	Baltimore	AHL	21	1	5	6	37	—	—	—	—	—
91-92	Hampton Roads	ECHL	44	30	43	73	79	14	6	8	14	20
92-93	Baltimore	AHL	10	2	4	6	2	—	—	—	—	—
92-93	Hampton Roads	ECHL	59	38	*80	118	137	4	0	3	3	10
93-94	Portland	AHL	3	0	1	1	0	—	—	—	—	—
93-94	Cleveland	IHL	37	16	16	32	18	—	—	—	—	—
93-94	Hampton Roads	ECHL	31	22	53	75	82	—	—	—	—	—
94-95	Cleveland	IHL	52	20	32	52	55	4	1	3	4	4
95-96	Cleveland	IHL	56	10	28	38	58	3	0	1	1	2
95-96	Hampton Roads	ECHL	3	3	0	3	16	—	—	—	—	—
96-97	Grand Rapids	IHL	14	2	4	6	16	—	—	—	—	—
96-97	Hampton Roads	ECHL	52	28	60	88	170	7	2	12	14	12
97-98	Portland	AHL	9	1	6	7	8	—	—	—	—	—
97-98	Hampton Roads	ECHL	42	25	32	57	112	19	7	11	18	30
98-99	Frankfurt	Germany	49	19	24	43	89	6	0	1	1	8
	IHL	Totals	159	48	80	128	147	7	1	4	5	6
	AHL	Totals	71	6	29	35	75	—	—	—	—	—
	ECHL	Totals	239	151	282	433	611	44	15	34	49	72

Born; 3/13/69, Prince George, British Columbia. 5-9, 170. Drafted by Washington Capitals (8th choice, 187th overall) in 1989 Entry Draft. Member of 1991-92 ECHL Champion Hampton Roads Admirals. Member of 1997-98 ECHL Champion Hampton Roads Admirals. Last amateur club; Seattle (WHL).

Grant Gessell — Defenseman

Regular Season / Playoffs

Season	Team	League	GP	G	A	PTS	PIM	GP	G	A	PTS	PIM
98-99	Thunder Bay	UHL	17	0	1	1	15	—	—	—	—	—
98-99	Asheville	UHL	9	0	0	0	9	—	—	—	—	—
	UHL	Totals	26	0	1	1	24	—	—	—	—	—

Born; 10/28/76, Winnipeg, Manitoba. 6-4, 230.

Mark Giannetti — Left Wing

Regular Season / Playoffs

Season	Team	League	GP	G	A	PTS	PIM	GP	G	A	PTS	PIM
97-98	Flint	UHL	63	11	23	34	15	—	—	—	—	—
97-98	Saginaw	UHL	10	3	3	6	5	—	—	—	—	—
98-99	Las Vegas	IHL	2	0	0	0	0	—	—	—	—	—
98-99	Saginaw	UHL	56	22	25	47	24	—	—	—	—	—
98-99	Winston-Salem	UHL	10	3	7	10	12	5	2	1	3	27
	UHL	Totals	139	39	58	97	56	5	2	1	3	27

Born; 6/9/76, Metamora, Michigan. 5-11, 205.

Jason Gibson — Defenseman

Regular Season / Playoffs

Season	Team	League	GP	G	A	PTS	PIM	GP	G	A	PTS	PIM
97-98	Anchorage	WCHL	51	2	5	7	270	8	1	1	2	*87
98-99	Anchorage	WCHL	26	0	3	3	83	3	0	1	1	0
	WCHL	Totals	77	2	8	10	353	11	1	2	3	87

Born; 8/15/73, Red Deer, Manitoba. 6-1, 205. Last amateur club; Red Deer Col-

John Gibson — Defenseman

Regular Season / Playoffs

Season	Team	League	GP	G	A	PTS	PIM	GP	G	A	PTS	PIM
95-96	Huntsville	SHL	60	11	16	27	108	10	4	2	6	10
96-97	Huntsville	CeHL	66	15	50	65	111	9	5	9	14	0
97-98	Huntsville	CHL	67	6	44	50	80	3	0	2	2	4
98-99	Huntsville	CHL	70	10	35	45	120	15	2	5	7	33
	CHL	Totals	203	31	129	160	311	27	7	16	23	37

Born; 9/30/70, Kingston, Ontario. 6-2, 205. Member of 1995-96 SHL champion Huntsville Channel Cats. Member of 1998-99 CHL Champion Hunstville Channel Cats. Last amateur club; Western Ontario (OUAA).

Steve Gibson — Left Wing

Regular Season / Playoffs

Season	Team	League	GP	G	A	PTS	PIM	GP	G	A	PTS	PIM
92-93	Windsor	OHL	60	48	52	100	44	—	—	—	—	—
92-93	Johnstown	ECHL	—	—	—	—	—	3	0	1	1	2
93-94	Cape Breton	AHL	3	0	0	0	2	—	—	—	—	—
93-94	Wheeling	ECHL	55	29	30	59	47	9	1	3	4	23
94-95	Portland	AHL	12	1	3	4	2	—	—	—	—	—
94-95	Cornwall	AHL	2	0	0	0	0	—	—	—	—	—
94-95	Wheeling	ECHL	50	37	29	56	61	3	0	3	3	6
95-96	Wheeling	ECHL	70	42	53	95	54	7	5	5	10	6
96-97	Hamilton	AHL	2	0	2	2	0	2	1	0	1	2
96-97	Wheeling	ECHL	16	18	14	32	7	3	5	0	5	6
97-98	San Antonio	IHL	11	1	1	2	5	—	—	—	—	—
97-98	Quad City	UHL	58	34	47	81	80	14	8	10	18	28
98-99	Quad City	UHL	33	14	29	43	44	14	8	6	14	12
	AHL	Totals	17	1	3	4	4	—	—	—	—	—
	ECHL	Totals	191	126	126	252	169	25	11	12	23	43
	UHL	Totals	91	48	76	124	124	28	16	16	32	40

Born; 10/10/72, Listowal, Ontario. 6-0, 200. Drafted by Edmonton Oilers (7th choice, 157th overall) in 1992 Entry Draft. Member of 1997-98 UHL Champion Quad City Mallards. Last amateur club; Windsor (OHL).

Wade Gibson — Defenseman

Regular Season / Playoffs

Season	Team	League	GP	G	A	PTS	PIM	GP	G	A	PTS	PIM
94-95	Tallahassee	ECHL	41	3	7	10	129	—	—	—	—	—
94-95	Erie	ECHL	2	0	0	0	0	—	—	—	—	—
95-96	Erie	ECHL	34	4	7	11	40	—	—	—	—	—
95-96	Roanoke	ECHL	27	2	4	6	28	2	0	0	0	20
96-97	New Mexico	WPHL	58	7	15	22	141	5	0	1	1	6
97-98	Lake Charles	WPHL	41	10	22	32	50	—	—	—	—	—
98-99	Huntsville	CHL	57	10	14	24	142	15	1	6	7	32
	ECHL	Totals	104	9	18	27	197	2	0	0	0	20
	WPHL	Totals	99	17	37	54	191	5	0	1	1	6

Born; 9/13/73, Kingston, Ontario. 6-2, 205. Selected by Lake Charles in WPHL Expansion Draft (6/2/97). Member of 1998-99 CHL Champion Huntsville Channel Cats. Last amateur club; Sault Ste. Marie (OHL).

Lee Giffin — Right Wing

Regular Season / Playoffs

Season	Team	League	GP	G	A	PTS	PIM	GP	G	A	PTS	PIM
86-87	Oshawa	OHL	48	31	69	100	46	23	17	19	36	14
86-87	Pittsburgh	NHL	8	1	1	2	0	—	—	—	—	—
87-88	Pittsburgh	NHL	19	0	2	2	9	—	—	—	—	—
87-88	Muskegon	IHL	48	26	37	63	61	6	1	3	4	2
88-89	Muskegon	IHL	63	30	44	74	93	12	5	7	12	8
89-90	Flint	IHL	73	30	44	74	68	4	1	2	3	0
90-91	Kansas City	IHL	60	25	43	68	48	—	—	—	—	—
91-92	Capital District	AHL	77	19	26	45	58	7	3	3	6	18
92-93	Chatham	CoHL	29	14	26	40	65	5	6	3	9	0
93-94												
94-95	Saginaw	CoHL	13	5	7	12	13	10	2	13	15	24
95-96	Saginaw	CoHL	58	20	47	67	94	5	1	2	3	8
96-97	Kansas City	IHL	2	0	0	0	0	—	—	—	—	—
96-97	Mobile	ECHL	20	7	9	16	4	3	1	0	1	0
97-98	Mobile	ECHL	45	16	29	54	46	3	2	0	2	0
98-99	Mobile	ECHL	54	16	21	37	44	2	0	1	1	24
	NHL	Totals	27	1	3	4	9	—	—	—	—	—
	IHL	Totals	246	111	168	279	270	22	7	12	19	10
	ECHL	Totals	119	39	59	98	94	8	3	1	4	24
	CoHL	Totals	100	39	80	119	172	20	9	18	27	32

Born; 4/1/67, Chatham, Ontario. 5-11, 200. Drafted by Pittsburgh Penguins (2nd choice, 23rd overall) in 1985 Entry Draft. Signed as a free agent by New York Rangers (9/89). Member of 1989-90 IHL champion Muskegon Lumberjacks. Last amateur club; Oshawa (OHL).

Rob Giffin — Right Wing
Regular Season / Playoffs

Season	Team	League	GP	G	A	PTS	PIM	GP	G	A	PTS	PIM
97-98	Peoria	ECHL	28	6	11	17	18	2	0	0	0	0
98-99	Wheeling	ECHL	67	20	27	47	85	—	—	—	—	—
	ECHL	Totals	95	26	38	64	103	2	0	0	0	0

Born; 6/8/76, Peterborough, Ontario. 5-9, 185. Traded to Wheeling by Peoria for Alex Matvichuk and J.F. Boutin (8/98). Last amateur club; Peterborough (OHL).

Chris Gignac — Center
Regular Season / Playoffs

Season	Team	League	GP	G	A	PTS	PIM	GP	G	A	PTS	PIM
96-97	Dayton	CoHL	1	0	0	0	0	—	—	—	—	—
97-98	Windsor	OUAA	26	27	29	56	NA	—	—	—	—	—
98-99	Windsor	OUAA	22	12	27	39	NA	—	—	—	—	—
98-99	Toledo	ECHL	3	3	3	6	2	4	1	2	3	2

Born; Windsor, Ontario. Last amateur club; Windsor (OUAA).

Dale Gignac — Center
Regular Season / Playoffs

Season	Team	League	GP	G	A	PTS	PIM	GP	G	A	PTS	PIM
98-99	Muskegon	UHL	1	0	0	0	0	—	—	—	—	—

Born; 2/2/76, Penetanguishene, Ontario. 5-10, 184.

Jean-Sebastien Giguere — Goaltender
Regular Season / Playoffs

Season	Team	League	GP	W	L	T	MIN	SO	AVG	GP	W	L	MIN	SO	AVG
96-97	Halifax	QMJHL	50	28	19	3	3014	2	3.38	16	9	7	954	0	3.65
96-97	Hartford	NHL	8	1	4	0	394	0	3.65	—	—	—	—	—	—
97-98	Saint John	AHL	31	16	10	3	1758	2	2.46	10	5	3	537	0	3.02
98-99	Calgary	NHL	15	6	7	1	860	0	3.21	—	—	—	—	—	—
98-99	Saint John	AHL	39	18	16	3	2145	3	3.44	7	3	2	304	0	4.14
	NHL	Totals	23	7	11	1	1254	0	3.35	—	—	—	—	—	—
	AHL	Totals	70	34	26	6	3903	5	3.00	17	8	5	841	0	3.42

Born; 5/16/77, Montreal, Quebec. 6-0, 175. Drafted by Hartford Whalers (1st choice, 13th overall) in 1995 Entry Draft. Traded to Calgary by Carolina Hurricanes with Andrew Cassels for Gary Roberts and Trevor Kidd (8/25/97). 1997-98 AHL All-Rookie Team. 1997-98 AHL Harry "Hap" Holmes Trophy (lowest GAA) with Tyler Moss. Last amateur club; Halifax (QMJHL).

Sean Gillam — Defenseman
Regular Season / Playoffs

Season	Team	League	GP	G	A	PTS	PIM	GP	G	A	PTS	PIM
96-97	Adirondack	AHL	64	1	7	8	50	—	—	—	—	—
97-98	Adirondack	AHL	73	1	9	10	60	3	1	0	1	0
98-99	Adirondack	AHL	68	1	10	11	75	3	1	0	1	6
	AHL	Totals	205	3	26	29	185	6	2	0	2	6

Born; 5/7/76, Lethbridge, Alberta. 6-2, 187. Drafted by Detroit Red Wings (3rd choice, 75th overall) in 1994 Entry Draft. Last amateur club; Spokane (WHL).

Todd Gillingham — Left Wing
Regular Season / Playoffs

Season	Team	League	GP	G	A	PTS	PIM	GP	G	A	PTS	PIM
91-92	St. John's	AHL	66	12	35	47	306	16	4	7	11	80
91-92	Salt Lake City	IHL	1	0	0	0	2	—	—	—	—	—
92-93	Salt Lake City	IHL	75	12	21	33	267	—	—	—	—	—
93-94	St. John's	AHL	59	20	25	45	260	10	0	2	2	12
94-95	Chicago	IHL	54	8	11	19	208	—	—	—	—	—
94-95	San Diego	IHL	16	1	1	2	60	5	2	3	5	10
95-96	Los Angeles	IHL	69	26	24	50	376	—	—	—	—	—
96-97	Long Beach	IHL	37	9	15	24	129	—	—	—	—	—
96-97	Phoenix	IHL	34	9	10	19	106	—	—	—	—	—
97-98	Hartford	AHL	10	2	1	3	47	—	—	—	—	—
97-98	St. John's	AHL	50	15	13	28	157	4	1	0	1	12
98-99	St. John's	AHL	61	4	16	20	128	5	0	0	0	2
	IHL	Totals	286	65	82	147	1148	5	2	3	5	10
	AHL	Totals	246	53	86	139	898	35	5	9	14	106

Born; 1/31/70. Labrador City, Labrador. 6-2, 205. Signed as a free agent by Calgary Flames (5/1/91). Traded to Toronto Maple Leafs for cash by Calgary (1/15/92). Traded to Calgary by Toronto for cash (6/2/92). Last amateur club; Trois-Rivieres (QMJHL).

Ryan Gillis — Defenseman
Regular Season / Playoffs

Season	Team	League	GP	G	A	PTS	PIM	GP	G	A	PTS	PIM
96-97	Michigan	IHL	11	0	2	2	12	4	0	0	0	12
96-97	Saint John	AHL	4	0	0	0	0	—	—	—	—	—
96-97	Baltimore	AHL	9	1	1	2	15	—	—	—	—	—
96-97	Dayton	ECHL	35	11	12	23	44	—	—	—	—	—
97-98	Michigan	IHL	81	7	14	21	77	4	0	0	0	6
98-99	Hampton Roads	ECHL	13	2	4	6	27	4	0	1	1	8
98-99	Portland	AHL	8	0	3	3	4	—	—	—	—	—
98-99	Michigan	IHL	21	2	3	5	13	—	—	—	—	—
98-99	Cincinnati	IHL	15	2	2	4	14	—	—	—	—	—
	IHL	Totals	128	11	21	32	116	8	0	0	0	18
	AHL	Totals	21	1	4	5	19	—	—	—	—	—
	ECHL	Totals	48	13	16	29	71	4	0	1	1	8

Born; 12/31/76, Salisbury, New Brunswick. 6-1, 195. Drafted by Calgary Flames (6th choice, 176th overall) in 1995 Entry Draft. Last amateur club; North Bay (OHL).

Davc Gilmore — Left Wing
Regular Season / Playoffs

Season	Team	League	GP	G	A	PTS	PIM	GP	G	A	PTS	PIM
98-99	St. Thomas	AUAA	26	18	44	62	NA	—	—	—	—	—
98-99	St. John's	AHL	3	1	1	2	0	—	—	—	—	—

Born; 2/11/74, 5-11, 170. Last amateur club; St. Thomas (AUAA).

Darryl Gilmour — Goaltender
Regular Season / Playoffs

Season	Team	League	GP	W	L	T	MIN	SO	AVG	GP	W	L	MIN	SO	AVG
87-88	Hershey	AHL	25	14	7	0	1273	1	3.68	—	—	—	—	—	—
88-89	Hershey	AHL	38	16	14	5	2093	0	4.13	—	—	—	—	—	—
89-90	New Haven	AHL	23	10	11	2	1356	0	3.76	—	—	—	—	—	—
89-90	Nashville	ECHL	10	6	3	0	529	0	4.88	—	—	—	—	—	—
90-91	New Haven	AHL	26	5	14	3	1375	1	3.93	—	—	—	—	—	—
90-91	Phoenix	IHL	4	2	0	0	180	0	4.33	—	—	—	—	—	—
91-92	Phoenix	IHL	30	10	15	3	1774	0	4.06	—	—	—	—	—	—
92-93	Phoenix	IHL	41	7	*28	0	2281	0	4.42	—	—	—	—	—	—
93-94	Fort Wayne	IHL	28	15	7	2	1439	0	3.54	3	0	0	70	0	4.24
93-94	Muskegon	CoHL	14	8	2	0	665	0	4.51	—	—	—	—	—	—
94-95	Kalamazoo	IHL	5	3	0	0	233	0	2.06	—	—	—	—	—	—
94-95	Muskegon	CoHL	44	25	16	2	2567	1	3.88	—	—	—	—	—	—
95-96	Minnesota	IHL	9	2	3	1	348	0	4.65	—	—	—	—	—	—
95-96	Fort Wayne	IHL	1	0	0	0	1	0	0.00	—	—	—	—	—	—
95-96	Quad City	CoHL	29	9	15	3	1615	0	4.20	—	—	—	—	—	—
96-97															
97-98	Madison	UHL	53	31	15	6	3117	*4	3.33	7	3	4	424	0	3.11
98-99	Madison	UHL	43	16	24	2	2424	1	4.06	—	—	—	—	—	—
98-99	Milwaukee	IHL	5	2	1	1	155	0	4.25	—	—	—	—	—	—
	IHL	Totals	123	41	54	7	6411	0	4.04	3	0	0	70	0	4.24
	AHL	Totals	113	45	46	11	6097	2	3.89	—	—	—	—	—	—
	UHL	Totals	183	89	72	13	10388	6	3.85	7	3	4	424	0	3.11

Born; 2/13/67, Winnipeg, Manitoba. 6-0, 180. Drafted by Philadelphia Flyers (3rd choice, 48th overall) in 1985 Entry Draft. Signed as a free agent by Los Angeles Kings (12/15/89). 1997-98 UHL Goaltender of the Year. 1997-98 UHL First Team All-Star. Last amateur club; Portland (WHL).

Gaston Gingras | Defenseman
Regular Season | Playoffs

Season	Team	League	GP	G	A	PTS	PIM	GP	G	A	PTS	PIM
78-79	Birmingham	WHA	60	13	21	34	35	—	—	—	—	—
79-80	Montreal	NHL	34	2	7	10	18	10	1	6	7	8
79-80	Nova Scotia	AHL	30	11	27	38	17	—	—	—	—	—
80-81	Montreal	NHL	55	5	16	21	22	1	1	0	1	0
81-82	Montreal	NHL	34	6	18	24	28	5	0	1	1	0
82-83	Montreal	NHL	22	1	8	9	8	—	—	—	—	—
82-83	Toronto	NHL	45	10	18	28	10	3	1	2	3	2
83-84	Toronto	NHL	59	7	20	27	16	—	—	—	—	—
84-85	Toronto	NHL	5	0	2	2	0	—	—	—	—	—
84-85	St. Catherines	AHL	36	7	12	19	13	—	—	—	—	—
84-85	Sherbrooke	AHL	21	3	14	17	6	17	2	3	5	4
85-86	Montreal	NHL	34	8	18	26	12	11	2	3	5	4
85-86	Sherbrooke	AHL	42	11	20	31	14	—	—	—	—	—
86-87	Montreal	NHL	66	11	34	45	21	5	0	2	2	0
87-88	Montreal	NHL	2	0	1	1	2	—	—	—	—	—
87-88	St. Louis	NHL	68	7	22	29	18	10	1	3	4	4
88-89	St. Louis	NHL	52	3	10	13	6	7	0	1	1	2
89-90	Biel	Switz	36	17	20	37	—	6	3	3	6	—
90-91	Biel	Switz	13	1	7	8	—	—	—	—	—	—
91-92	Lugano	Switz	34	10	19	29	24	—	—	—	—	—
92-93	Val Gardena	Italy	18	3	24	27	16	—	—	—	—	—
93-94	Val Gardena	Italy	21	3	14	17	14	—	—	—	—	—
94-95	Fredericton	AHL	19	3	6	9	4	17	2	12	14	8
95-96	Fredericton	AHL	39	2	21	23	18	—	—	—	—	—
96-97												
97-98												
98-99	Chesapeake	ECHL	5	0	4	4	6	—	—	—	—	—
	NHL	Totals	476	61	174	235	161	52	6	18	24	20
	AHL	Totals	187	37	100	137	72	34	7	16	23	12

Born; 2/13/59, Temiscamgue, Quebec. 6-1, 200. Signed as an underage junior by Birmingham Bulls (1978). Drafted by Montreal Canadiens (1st choice, 27th overall) in 1979 Entry Draft. Traded to Toronto Maple Leafs by Montreal for Toronto's second round pick (Benoit Brunet) in 1985 Entry Draft. Traded to Montreal from Toronto for Larry Landon (2/14/85). Traded to St. Louis Blues by Montreal for Larry Trader and future considerations (10/13/87). Signed as a free agent by Montreal (8/10/95). Member of 1985-86 Stanley Cup champion Montreal Canadiens. Member of 1984-85 AHL champion Sherbrooke Canadiens. Last amateur club; Hamilton (OHA).

Maxime Gingras | Goaltender
Regular Season | Playoffs

Season	Team	League	GP	W	L	T	MIN	SO	AVG	GP	W	L	MIN	SO	AVG
98-99	Orlando	IHL	1	0	0	0	18	0	9.78	—	—	—	—	—	—
98-99	Richmond	ECHL	50	30	13	3	2808	*7	*2.26	*18	12	*5	1117	*5	2.31

Born; 4/22/78, Lorretteville, Quebec. 5-8, 160. 1998-99 ECHL Goaltender of the Year. 1998-99 ECHL Rookie of the Year. 1998-99 ECHL First Team All-Star. Last amateur club;

Patrick Gingras | Left Wing
Regular Season | Playoffs

Season	Team	League	GP	G	A	PTS	PIM	GP	G	A	PTS	PIM
98-99	Jacksonville	ECHL	61	9	20	29	132	2	0	0	0	10

Born; Last amateur club; Chicoutimi (QMJHL).

Rick Girard | Center
Regular Season | Playoffs

Season	Team	League	GP	G	A	PTS	PIM	GP	G	A	PTS	PIM
93-94	Swift Current	WHL	58	40	49	89	43	7	1	8	9	6
93-94	Hamilton	AHL	1	1	1	2	0	—	—	—	—	—
94-95	Syracuse	AHL	26	10	13	23	22	—	—	—	—	—
95-96	Syracuse	AHL	67	15	21	36	32	16	9	8	17	16
96-97	Syracuse	AHL	66	19	28	47	20	1	1	1	2	2
97-98	Manitoba	IHL	18	4	2	6	2	—	—	—	—	—
97-98	Quebec	IHL	35	7	10	17	15	—	—	—	—	—
97-98	Cleveland	IHL	5	1	2	3	10	3	0	0	0	0
98-99	Augsburger	Germany	49	18	23	41	22	5	1	3	4	2
	AHL	Totals	160	45	63	108	74	17	10	9	19	18
	IHL	Totals	58	12	14	26	27	3	0	0	0	0

Born; 5/1/74, Edmonton, Alberta. 5-11, 180. Drafted by Vancouver Canucks (2nd choice, 46th overall) in 1993 Entry Draft. Traded to Quebec by Manitoba with Dale DeGray for Craig Martin, Jeff Parrott and Michel Mongeau (12/97). Traded to Cleveland by Quebec with Dale DeGray, Darcy Simon, Tom Draper and Jason Ruff for Ryan Mougenel, Rick Hayward, John Craighead, Eric Perrin, Pat Jablonski and Burke Murphy (3/98). (Last amateur club; Swift Current (WHL).

Rick Girhiny | Defenseman
Regular Season | Playoffs

Season	Team	League	GP	G	A	PTS	PIM	GP	G	A	PTS	PIM
93-94	Birmingham	ECHL	15	2	1	3	10	—	—	—	—	—
93-94	Dayton	ECHL	5	2	0	2	0	—	—	—	—	—
95-96	Muskegon	CoHL	72	2	8	10	57	5	0	0	0	0
96-97	Austin	WPHL	64	10	9	19	55	6	0	1	1	16
97-98	Odessa	WPHL	68	7	26	33	44	—	—	—	—	—
98-99	Odessa	WPHL	68	9	23	32	29	3	0	0	0	0
	WPHL	Totals	200	26	58	84	218	9	0	1	1	16
	ECHL	Totals	20	4	1	5	10	—	—	—	—	—

Born; 7/11/73, Niagra Falls, Ontario. 5-9, 175.

Ray Giroux | Defenseman
Regular Season | Playoffs

Season	Team	League	GP	G	A	PTS	PIM	GP	G	A	PTS	PIM
98-99	Lowell	AHL	59	13	19	32	92	3	1	1	2	0

Born; 7/20/76, North Bay, Ontario. 6-0, 180. Drafted by Philadelphia Flyers (7th choice, 202nd overall) in 1994 Entry Draft. Rights traded to New York Islanders by Philadelphia for Islanders 6th round choice in 2000 Entry Draft. (8/25/98). Last amateur club; Yale (ECAC).

Sandis Girvitch | Defenseman
Regular Season | Playoffs

Season	Team	League	GP	G	A	PTS	PIM	GP	G	A	PTS	PIM
97-98	San Angelo	WPHL	55	2	6	8	51	1	0	0	0	0
98-99	San Angelo	WPHL	68	4	15	19	73	17	2	2	4	24
	WPHL	Totals	123	6	21	27	124	18	2	2	4	24

Born; 1/5/76, Riga, Latvia. 6-3, 190.

Jason Gladney | Defenseman
Regular Season | Playoffs

Season	Team	League	GP	G	A	PTS	PIM	GP	G	A	PTS	PIM
93-94	Kitchener	OHL	61	18	74	92	96	5	1	8	9	10
93-94	Portland	AHL	2	0	0	0	0	2	0	0	0	0
94-95	Adirondack	AHL	44	3	13	16	65	—	—	—	—	—
94-95	Toledo	ECHL	3	1	1	2	10	4	1	1	2	4
95-96	Cincinnati	IHL	9	0	2	2	8	—	—	—	—	—
95-96	Toledo	ECHL	60	16	39	55	96	11	1	8	9	17
96-97	Toledo	ECHL	63	20	46	66	120	5	1	1	2	2
97-98	Adirondack	AHL	2	0	0	0	2	—	—	—	—	—
97-98	Toledo	ECHL	45	8	24	32	61	7	2	5	7	6
98-99	Toledo	ECHL	70	5	43	48	109	—	—	—	—	—
	AHL	Totals	48	3	13	16	67	2	0	0	0	0
	ECHL	Totals	241	50	153	203	396	27	5	15	20	29

Born; 1/26/74, Toronto, Ontario. 5-11, 200. Drafted by Washington Capitals (8th choice, 225th overall) in 1993 Entry Draft. Member of 1993-94 AHL Champion Portland Pirates. Last amateur club; Kitchener (AHL).

Trent Gleason — Defenseman

Regular Season / Playoffs

Season	Team	League	GP	G	A	PTS	PIM	GP	G	A	PTS	PIM
95-96	South Carolina	ECHL	2	0	1	1	6	—	—	—	—	—
95-96	Memphis	CeHL	61	5	15	20	111	4	1	1	2	2
96-97	Memphis	CeHL	24	1	6	7	41	—	—	—	—	—
96-97	San Antonio	CeHL	25	3	9	12	25	—	—	—	—	—
97-98	Memphis	CHL	66	1	14	15	76	4	0	0	0	0
98-99	Memphis	CHL	17	0	5	5	12	—	—	—	—	—
	CHL	Totals	193	10	49	59	265	8	1	1	2	2

Born; 4/29/71, Montreal, Quebec. 6-1, 190. Last amateur club; Dalhousie

Jason Glover — Right Wing

Regular Season / Playoffs

Season	Team	League	GP	G	A	PTS	PIM	GP	G	A	PTS	PIM
95-96	Brantford	CoHL	3	0	1	1	0	—	—	—	—	—
96-97	Flint	CoHL	59	13	24	37	45	13	5	1	6	20
97-98	Detroit	IHL	1	0	0	0	0	—	—	—	—	—
97-98	Michigan	IHL	2	0	0	0	2	—	—	—	—	—
97-98	Flint	UHL	71	40	44	84	115	17	8	11	19	34
98-99	Indianapolis	IHL	1	0	2	2	0	—	—	—	—	—
98-99	Flint	UHL	66	48	48	96	91	11	1	8	9	38
	IHL	Totals	4	0	2	2	2	—	—	—	—	—
	UHL	Totals	199	101	117	218	251	41	14	20	34	92

Born; 3/29/72, London, Ontario. 6-0, 185.

Troy Glover — Left Wing

Regular Season / Playoffs

Season	Team	League	GP	G	A	PTS	PIM	GP	G	A	PTS	PIM
98-99	Flint	UHL	3	0	0	0	2	—	—	—	—	—

Born; 4/5/76, Dorchester, Ontario.

Sasha Goc — Defenseman

Regular Season / Playoffs

Season	Team	League	GP	G	A	PTS	PIM	GP	G	A	PTS	PIM
98-99	Albany	AHL	55	1	12	13	24	2	0	0	0	0

Born; 4/17/79, Calw, Germany. 6-2, 196. Drafted by New Jersey Devils (5th choice), in 1997 Entry Draft. Last overseas club; Schwenningen (Germany).

Paul Godfrey — Right Wing

Regular Season / Playoffs

Season	Team	League	GP	G	A	PTS	PIM	GP	G	A	PTS	PIM
98-99	Flint	UHL	3	0	1	1	0	—	—	—	—	—
98-99	Topeka	CHL	10	2	5	7	6	—	—	—	—	—

Born; 10/20/76, Sault Ste. Marie, Ontario. 6-0, 180.

Alexandre Godynyuk — Defenseman

Regular Season / Playoffs

Season	Team	League	GP	G	A	PTS	PIM	GP	G	A	PTS	PIM
90-91	Sokol Kiev	Russia	19	3	1	4	20	—	—	—	—	—
90-91	Toronto	NHL	18	0	3	3	16	—	—	—	—	—
90-91	Newmarket	AHL	11	0	1	1	29	—	—	—	—	—
91-92	Toronto	NHL	31	3	6	9	59	—	—	—	—	—
91-92	Calgary	NHL	6	0	1	1	4	—	—	—	—	—
91-92	Salt Lake City	IHL	17	2	1	3	24	—	—	—	—	—
92-93	Calgary	NHL	27	3	4	7	19	—	—	—	—	—
93-94	Florida	NHL	26	0	10	10	35	—	—	—	—	—
93-94	Hartford	NHL	43	3	9	12	40	—	—	—	—	—
94-95	Hartford	NHL	14	0	0	0	8	—	—	—	—	—
95-96	Hartford	NHL	3	0	0	0	2	—	—	—	—	—
95-96	Springfield	AHL	14	1	3	4	19	—	—	—	—	—
95-96	Detroit	IHL	7	0	3	3	12	—	—	—	—	—
95-96	Minnesota	IHL	45	9	17	26	81	—	—	—	—	—
96-97	Hartford	NHL	55	1	6	7	41	—	—	—	—	—
97-98	Chicago	IHL	50	5	11	16	85	1	0	0	0	0
98-99	SC Bern	Switz.	43	9	16	25	20	5	1	0	1	2
	NHL	Totals	223	10	39	49	224	—	—	—	—	—
	IHL	Totals	119	16	32	48	202	1	0	0	0	0
	AHL	Totals	25	1	4	5	48	—	—	—	—	—

Born; 1/27/70, Kiev, Ukraine. 6-0, 207. Drafted by Toronto Maple Leafs (5th choice, 115th overall) in 1990 Entry Draft. Traded to Calgary Flames by Toronto with Craig Berube, Gary Leemna, Michel Petit and Jeff Reese for Doug Gilmour, Jamie Macoun, Ric Nattress, Rick Wamsley and Kent Manderville (1/2/92). Claimed by Florida Panthers from Calgary in NHL Expansion Draft (6/24/93). Traded to Hartford Whalers by Florida for Jim McKenzie (12/16/93). Traded to St. Louis Blues by Carolina Hurricanes with Carolina's 6th round choice (Brad Vott) in 1998 Entry Draft for Stephen Leach (6/27/97). Members of 1997-98 IHL Champion Chicago Wolves.

Bob Gohde — Defenseman

Regular Season / Playoffs

Season	Team	League	GP	G	A	PTS	PIM	GP	G	A	PTS	PIM
94-95	Chicago-Illinois	CCHA	37	4	9	13	34	—	—	—	—	—
94-95	Nashville	ECHL	2	0	0	0	0	—	—	—	—	—
95-96	Jacksonville	ECHL	3	0	0	0	4	—	—	—	—	—
95-96	Huntington	ECHL	53	2	5	7	64	—	—	—	—	—
96-97	Dayton	CoHL	29	0	4	4	35	—	—	—	—	—
96-97	Brantford	CoHL	37	2	7	9	25	10	0	1	1	6
97-98	Wheeling	ECHL	3	0	0	0	2	—	—	—	—	—
97-98	Louisville	ECHL	60	3	12	15	37	—	—	—	—	—
98-99	Amarillo	WPHL	64	5	14	19	61	—	—	—	—	—
	ECHL	Totals	121	5	17	22	107	—	—	—	—	—
	CoHL	Totals	66	2	11	13	60	10	0	1	1	6

Born; 6/9/71, Rolling Meadows, Illinois. 6-1, 205. Last amateur club; University of Chicago-Illinois.

Gary Golczewski — Left Wing

Regular Season / Playoffs

Season	Team	League	GP	G	A	PTS	PIM	GP	G	A	PTS	PIM
95-96	Winston-Salem	SHL	7	2	3	5	4	—	—	—	—	—
96-97												
97-98	San Angelo	WPHL	13	0	2	2	15	3	0	0	0	0
97-98	Macon	CHL	12	2	1	3	29	—	—	—	—	—
98-99	Fort Worth	CHL	6	1	0	1	20	—	—	—	—	—
	CHL	Totals	18	3	1	4	49	—	—	—	—	—

Born; 2/16/73, Paterson, New Jersey. 6-0, 205. Drafted by Boston Bruins (6th choice, 150th overall) in 1991 NHL Entry Draft.

Matt Golden — Defenseman

Regular Season / Playoffs

Season	Team	League	GP	G	A	PTS	PIM	GP	G	A	PTS	PIM
98-99	Columbus	ECHL	61	10	19	29	98	4	0	0	0	6

Born; 4/19/77, Rolling Meadows, Illinois. Selected by Arkansas in 1999 ECHL Dispersal Draft. Last amateur club; Ferris State (CCHA).

Jeff Goldie — Left Wing

Regular Season / Playoffs

Season	Team	League	GP	G	A	PTS	PIM	GP	G	A	PTS	PIM
98-99	New Mexico	WPHL	69	27	23	50	46	—	—	—	—	—

Born; 5/27/74, Leith, Ontario. 6-3, 215. Last amateur club; Waterloo (OUAA).

Erich Goldmann — Defenseman

Regular Season / Playoffs

Season	Team	League	GP	G	A	PTS	PIM	GP	G	A	PTS	PIM
97-98	Worcester	AHL	31	0	2	2	40	—	—	—	—	—
97-98	Detroit	IHL	3	0	0	0	2	—	—	—	—	—
97-98	Dayton	ECHL	3	0	2	2	5	5	0	0	0	8
98-99	Cincinnati	IHL	5	0	1	1	7	—	—	—	—	—
98-99	Hershey	AHL	21	1	1	2	23	—	—	—	—	—
98-99	Cincinnati	AHL	32	0	2	2	18	3	0	0	0	2
	AHL	Totals	84	1	5	6	81	3	0	0	0	2
	IHL	Totals	8	0	1	1	9	—	—	—	—	—

Born; 4/7/76, Dingolfing, West Germany. 6-3, 196. Drafted by Ottawa Senators (5th choice, 212th overall) in 1996 Entry Draft. Last overseas club; Laufbeuren (Germany).

Fred Goltz — Left Wing

Regular Season / Playoffs

Season	Team	League	GP	G	A	PTS	PIM	GP	G	A	PTS	PIM
94-95	San Antonio	CeHL	61	25	19	44	150	13	2	1	3	45
95-96	Louisiana	ECHL	38	16	14	30	104	—	—	—	—	—
96-97	San Antonio	CeHL	26	13	10	23	15	—	—	—	—	—
96-97	Columbus	CeHL	14	4	9	13	16	3	0	0	0	24
97-98	Reno	WCHL	16	4	3	7	16	—	—	—	—	—
98-99	San Antonio	CHL	22	7	8	15	31	—	—	—	—	—
	CeHL	Totals	123	49	46	95	212	16	2	1	3	69

Born; 6/4/71, Kingston, Ontario. 6-0, 200.

Yan Golubovsky — Defenseman

Regular Season / Playoffs

Season	Team	League	GP	G	A	PTS	PIM	GP	G	A	PTS	PIM
94-95	Adirondack	AHL	57	4	2	6	39	—	—	—	—	—
95-96	Adirondack	AHL	71	5	16	21	97	3	0	0	0	2
96-97	Adirondack	AHL	62	2	11	13	67	4	0	0	0	0
97-98	Detroit	NHL	12	0	2	2	6	—	—	—	—	—
97-98	Adirondack	AHL	52	1	15	16	57	3	0	0	0	2
98-99	Detroit	NHL	17	0	1	1	16	—	—	—	—	—
98-99	Adirondack	AHL	43	2	2	4	32	2	0	0	0	4
	NHL	Totals	29	0	3	3	20	—	—	—	—	—
	AHL	Totals	285	14	46	60	292	12	0	0	0	8

Born; 3/9/76, Novosibirisk, Russia. 6-3, 183. Drafted by Detroit Red Wings (1st choice, 23rd overall) 1994 Entry Draft.

Tom Gomes — Right Wing

Regular Season / Playoffs

Season	Team	League	GP	G	A	PTS	PIM	GP	G	A	PTS	PIM
94-95	Oklahoma City	CeHL	57	20	22	42	52	5	4	0	4	0
95-96	Nashville	ECHL	1	0	0	0	2	—	—	—	—	—
95-96	Oklahoma City	CeHL	64	28	30	58	90	13	4	5	9	15
96-97	Oklahoma City	CeHL	66	25	25	50	155	4	1	0	1	18
97-98	Bracknell	BSL	56	20	30	50	73	6	1	2	3	4
98-99	Oklahoma City	CHL	70	18	31	49	112	13	2	6	8	34
	CHL	Totals	257	91	108	199	409	35	11	11	22	67

Born; 4/29/72, Harrow, Ontario. 5-10, 200. Member of 1995-96 CeHL champion Oklahoma City Blazers.

Daniel Goneau — Left Wing

Regular Season / Playoffs

Season	Team	League	GP	G	A	PTS	PIM	GP	G	A	PTS	PIM
96-97	Rangers	NHL	41	10	3	13	10	—	—	—	—	—
96-97	Binghamton	AHL	39	15	15	30	10	—	—	—	—	—
97-98	Rangers	NHL	11	2	0	2	4	—	—	—	—	—
97-98	Hartford	AHL	66	21	26	47	44	13	1	4	5	18
98-99	Hartford	AHL	72	20	19	39	56	2	1	0	1	0
	NHL	Totals	52	12	3	15	14	—	—	—	—	—
	AHL	Totals	177	56	60	116	110	15	2	4	6	18

Born; 1/16/76, Montreal, Quebec. 6-1, 196. Drafted by Boston Bruins (2nd choice, 47th overall) in 1994 Entry Draft. Re-entered NHL Entry Draft; selected by New York Rangers (2nd choice, 48th overall) in 1996 Entry Draft. Last amateur club; Granby (QMJHL).

Shane Googins — Left Wing

Regular Season / Playoffs

Season	Team	League	GP	G	A	PTS	PIM	GP	G	A	PTS	PIM
98-99	Madison	UHL	4	0	0	0	0	—	—	—	—	—

Born; 6/2/74, Madison, Wisconsin. 6-4, 215.

Chris Gordon — Goaltender

Regular Season / Playoffs

Season	Team	League	GP	W	L	T	MIN	SO	AVG	GP	W	L	MIN	SO	AVG
94-95	Worcester	AHL	17	7	10	0	993	0	4.05	—	—	—	—	—	—
94-95	Huntington	ECHL	30	17	6	2	1484	2	2.55	—	—	—	—	—	—
95-96	Detroit	IHL	1	0	1	0	42	0	7.11	—	—	—	—	—	—
95-96	Flint	CoHL	36	22	9	3	2042	2	2.85	9	7	2	503	0	3.22
96-97	El Paso	WPHL	50	26	18	5	2762	0	4.06	*11	*8	3	652	0	3.68
97-98	El Paso	WPHL	44	24	15	3	2449	1	3.63	*13	*10	3	*778	*1	3.47
98-99	El Paso	WPHL	45	23	18	3	2561	*4	3.07	3	1	2	179	0	4.02
	WPHL	Totals	139	73	51	11	7772	5	3.60	27	19	8	1609	1	3.62

Born; 2/16/70, Grand Rapids, Michigan. 5-11, 155. 1994-95 ECHL Goaltender of the Year. 1994-95 First Team ECHL All-Star. Member of 1995-96 Colonial Cup Champion Flint Generals. Member of 1996-97 WPHL Champion El Paso Buzzards. Member of 1997-98 WPHL Champion El Paso Buzzards. Last amateur club; Michigan (CCHA).

Ian Gordon — Goaltender

Regular Season / Playoffs

Season	Team	League	GP	W	L	T	MIN	SO	AVG	GP	W	L	MIN	SO	AVG
95-96	Saint John	AHL	19	2	12	0	768	0	4.37	—	—	—	—	—	—
96-97	Saint John	AHL	21	5	9	1	989	0	3.03	—	—	—	—	—	—
96-97	Grand Rapids	IHL	5	2	2	0	257	0	3.50	1	0	0	1	0	0.00
97-98	Grand Rapids	IHL	49	23	16	4	2573	1	2.68	2	0	2	119	0	3.54
98-99	Grand Rapids	IHL	41	16	19	3	2149	2	3.43	—	—	—	—	—	—
	IHL	Totals	95	41	37	7	4979	3	3.05	3	0	2	120	0	3.50
	AHL	Totals	40	7	21	1	1757	0	3.62	—	—	—	—	—	—

Born; 5/15/75, North Battleford, Saskatchewan. 5-10, 170. Signed as a free agent by Calgary Flames (10/6/95). Last amateur club; Saskatoon (WHL).

Rhett Gordon — Right Wing

Regular Season / Playoffs

Season	Team	League	GP	G	A	PTS	PIM	GP	G	A	PTS	PIM
95-96	Regina	WHL	66	53	50	103	68	11	9	4	13	10
95-96	Springfield	AHL	2	0	0	0	2	1	0	0	0	0
96-97	Springfield	AHL	54	11	11	22	54	8	1	2	3	6
97-98	Springfield	AHL	75	17	11	28	54	4	1	1	2	0
98-99	Manitoba	IHL	76	14	23	37	61	5	0	0	0	0
	AHL	Totals	131	28	22	50	100	13	2	3	5	6

Born; 8/26/76, Regina, Saskatchewan. 5-11, 175. Signed as a free agent by Winnipeg Jets (9/29/94). Last amateur club; Regina (WHL).

Robb Gordon — Center

Regular Season / Playoffs

Season	Team	League	GP	G	A	PTS	PIM	GP	G	A	PTS	PIM
96-97	Syracuse	AHL	63	11	14	25	18	3	0	0	0	7
97-98	Syracuse	AHL	40	4	6	10	35	—	—	—	—	—
97-98	Raleigh	ECHL	7	3	10	13	28	—	—	—	—	—
98-99	Vancouver	NHL	4	0	0	0	2	—	—	—	—	—
98-99	Syracuse	AHL	68	16	22	38	98	—	—	—	—	—
	AHL	Totals	103	15	20	35	53	3	0	0	0	7

Born; 1/13/76, Murrayville, British Columbia. 5-11, 170. Drafted by Vancouver Canucks (2nd choice, 39th overall) in 1994 Entry Draft. Last amateur club; Kelowna (WHL).

Cotton Gore — Forward

Regular Season / Playoffs

Season	Team	League	GP	G	A	PTS	PIM	GP	G	A	PTS	PIM
97-98	Waco	WPHL	17	0	2	2	9	—	—	—	—	—
98-99	Waco	WPHL	62	19	34	53	25	4	1	2	3	0
	WPHL	Totals	79	19	36	55	34	4	1	2	3	0

Born; 4/9/71, Palmer, Alaska. 6-0, 185. Selected by Lubbock in 1999 WPHL Expansion Draft. Last amateur club; Alaska-Anchorage (WCHA).

Forrest Gore — Left Wing

Regular Season / Playoffs

Season	Team	League	GP	G	A	PTS	PIM	GP	G	A	PTS	PIM
98-99	Kentucky	AHL	1	0	0	0	7	—	—	—	—	—
98-99	Richmond	ECHL	69	24	24	48	173	10	0	4	4	6

Born; 8/17/74, Palmer, Alaska. 6-0, 195. Last amateur club; Wisconsin Stevens-Point (NCAA 3).

Taner Gorica — Right Wing

Regular Season / Playoffs

Season	Team	League	GP	G	A	PTS	PIM	GP	G	A	PTS	PIM
97-98	Flint	UHL	2	0	0	0	17	—	—	—	—	—
97-98	Winston-Salem	UHL	47	6	5	11	133	—	—	—	—	—
98-99	Chesapeake	ECHL	2	0	0	0	0	—	—	—	—	—
	UHL	Totals	49	6	5	11	150	—	—	—	—	—

Born; 9/5/76, Windsor, Ontario. 5-10, 184.

Jeff Gorman — Forward

Regular Season / Playoffs

Season	Team	League	GP	G	A	PTS	PIM	GP	G	A	PTS	PIM
96-97	Bakersfield	WCHL	14	12	9	21	4	4	3	2	5	4
97-98	Bakersfield	WCHL	62	19	38	57	76	4	1	2	3	0
98-99	Amberg	Germany	NA	27	42	69	NA	—	—	—	—	—
	WCHL	Totals	76	31	47	78	80	8	4	4	8	4

Born; 1/6/73, Winnipeg, Manitoba. 5-11, 190. Last amateur club; Manitoba (CWUAA).

Robert Gorman — Goaltender

Regular Season / Playoffs

Season	Team	League	GP	W	L	T	MIN	SO	AVG	GP	W	L	MIN	SO	AVG
98-99	Louisiana	ECHL	1	0	0	0	9	0	25.99	—	—	—	—	—	—

Born; Rexdale, Ontario. 6-2, 190. Last amateur club; Wisconsin Stevens-Point (NCAA 3).

Sheldon Gorski — Right Wing

Regular Season / Playoffs

Season	Team	League	GP	G	A	PTS	PIM	GP	G	A	PTS	PIM
90-91	Indianapolis	IHL	3	1	0	1	0	—	—	—	—	—
90-91	Louisville	ECHL	62	51	53	104	106	7	5	4	9	20
91-92	Louisville	ECHL	55	56	54	100	94	13	14	8	22	15
92-93	Louisville	ECHL	63	51	47	98	103	—	—	—	—	—
93-94	Louisville	ECHL	41	22	28	50	85	6	1	7	8	4
94-95	San Antonio	CEHL	57	45	26	71	96	13	*15	12	27	12
95-96	Louisville	ECHL	48	21	18	39	47	3	1	1	2	8
96-97	Louisville	ECHL	66	38	35	73	96	—	—	—	—	—
97-98	Louisville	ECHL	68	46	29	75	114	—	—	—	—	—
98-99	Miami	ECHL	36	15	11	26	46	—	—	—	—	—
98-99	Pensacola	ECHL	32	16	17	33	24	—	—	—	—	—
	ECHL	Totals	471	301	281	582	715	29	21	20	41	47

Born; 10/16/65, Greenfell, Saskatchewan. 5-10, 185. 1990-91 ECHL Second Team All-Star. 1992-93 ECHL First Team All-Star. Last amateur club; Illinois-Chicago (CCHA).

Ben Gorwich — Forward

Regular Season / Playoffs

Season	Team	League	GP	G	A	PTS	PIM	GP	G	A	PTS	PIM
98-99	Madison	UHL	13	1	5	6	2	—	—	—	—	—

Born; 1/23/75, Thornhill, Ontario. 5-10, 185. Selected by Missouri in 1999 UHL Expansion Draft. Last amateur club; Wisconsin Stevens-Point (NCAA 3).

Christian Gosselin — Defenseman

Regular Season / Playoffs

Season	Team	League	GP	G	A	PTS	PIM	GP	G	A	PTS	PIM
96-97	Macon	CeHL	63	8	10	18	229	5	0	0	0	29
97-98	Fredericton	AHL	6	0	0	0	17	—	—	—	—	—
97-98	Pensacola	ECHL	42	6	5	11	181	19	0	1	1	54
98-99	Kentucky	AHL	31	1	1	2	107	—	—	—	—	—
	AHL	Totals	37	1	1	2	124	—	—	—	—	—

Born; 8/21/76, Montreal, Quebec. 6-5, 225. Signed as a free agent by San Jose Sharks (7/15/98). Last amateur club; Laval (QMJHL).

David Gosselin — Left Wing

Regular Season / Playoffs

Season	Team	League	GP	G	A	PTS	PIM	GP	G	A	PTS	PIM
98-99	Milwaukee	IHL	74	17	11	28	78	2	0	2	2	2

Born; 6/22/77, Levis, Quebec. 6-0, 175. Drafted by New Jersey Devils (4th choice, 78th overall) in 1995 Entry Draft. Signed as a free agent by Nashville Predators (7/1/98). Last amateur club; Chicoutimi (QMJHL).

Steve Gosselin — Defenseman

Regular Season / Playoffs

Season	Team	League	GP	G	A	PTS	PIM	GP	G	A	PTS	PIM
94-95	Houston	IHL	28	5	5	10	36	—	—	—	—	—
94-95	Chicago	IHL	19	2	2	4	43	1	0	0	0	2
95-96	Chicago	IHL	72	5	17	22	156	3	0	1	1	6
96-97	Chicago	IHL	48	3	16	19	56	—	—	—	—	—
96-97	Detroit	IHL	17	1	6	7	34	11	0	1	1	20
97-98	Lausanne	Switz.	25	3	22	25	85	—	—	—	—	—
98-99	Chicago	IHL	65	2	18	20	107	2	0	0	0	4
	IHL	Totals	249	18	64	82	432	17	0	2	2	30

Born; 3/27/73, St. Octave, Quebec. 5-9, 195. Member of 1996-97 IHL Champion Detroit Vipers. Last amateur club; Chicoutimi (QMJHL).

Jeff Greenlaw — Right Wing
Regular Season — Playoffs

Season	Team	League	GP	G	A	PTS	PIM	GP	G	A	PTS	PIM
85-86	Canada	National	57	3	16	19	81	—	—	—	—	—
86-87	Washington	NHL	22	0	3	3	44	—	—	—	—	—
86-87	Binghamton	AHL	4	0	2	2	0	—	—	—	—	—
87-88	Washington	NHL	—	—	—	—	—	1	0	0	0	19
87-88	Binghamton	AHL	56	8	7	15	142	1	0	0	0	2
88-89	Baltimore	AHL	55	12	15	27	115	—	—	—	—	—
89-90	Baltimore	AHL	10	3	2	5	26	7	1	0	1	13
90-91	Washington	NHL	10	2	0	2	10	1	0	0	0	2
90-91	Baltimore	AHL	50	17	17	34	93	3	1	1	2	2
91-92	Washington	NHL	5	0	1	1	34	—	—	—	—	—
91-92	Baltimore	AHL	37	6	8	14	57	—	—	—	—	—
92-93	Washington	NHL	16	1	1	2	18	—	—	—	—	—
92-93	Baltimore	AHL	49	12	14	26	66	7	3	1	4	0
93-94	Florida	NHL	4	0	1	1	2	—	—	—	—	—
93-94	Cincinnati	IHL	55	14	15	29	85	11	2	2	4	28
94-95	Cincinnati	IHL	67	10	21	31	117	10	2	0	2	22
95-96	Cincinnati	IHL	64	17	15	32	112	17	2	4	6	36
96-97	Cincinnati	IHL	27	6	6	12	70	1	0	1	1	2
97-98	Cincinnati	IHL	70	6	9	15	130	9	0	2	2	36
98-99	Austin	WPHL	52	25	15	40	183	—	—	—	—	—
	NHL	Totals	57	3	6	9	108	2	0	0	0	21
	IHL	Totals	283	53	66	119	514	48	6	9	15	124
	AHL	Totals	261	58	65	123	499	18	5	2	7	17

Born; 2/28/68, Toronto, Ontario. 6-0, 230. Drafted by Washington Capitals (1st choice, 19th overall) in 1986 Entry Draft. Signed as a free agent by Florida Panthers (7/14/93). Last amateur club; St. Catherines Jr. B. (Ontario).

Dale Greenwood — Center
Regular Season — Playoffs

Season	Team	League	GP	G	A	PTS	PIM	GP	G	A	PTS	PIM
96-97	Saginaw	CoHL	50	10	26	36	30	—	—	—	—	—
97-98	Saginaw	UHL	27	8	17	25	67	—	—	—	—	—
97-98	Port Huron	UHL	35	4	16	20	10	3	1	1	2	2
98-99	Asheville	UHL	9	6	6	12	15	—	—	—	—	—
	UHL	Totals	121	28	65	93	122	3	1	1	2	2

Born; 2/13/75, Mississauga, Ontario. 5-11, 185. Traded to Port Huron by Saginaw with Jason Renard and Bobby Ferraris for J.D. Eaton, Joel Gardner and David Geris (12/97).

J.F. Gregoire — Left Wing
Regular Season — Playoffs

Season	Team	League	GP	G	A	PTS	PIM	GP	G	A	PTS	PIM
96-97	Fredericton	AHL	15	1	3	4	0	—	—	—	—	—
97-98	Windsor	QSPHL										
98-99	Abilene	WPHL	67	37	45	82	42	3	0	0	0	0

Born; 12/13/72, Sherbrooke, Quebec. 6-0, 198. Last amateur club; St. Hyacinthe (QMJHL).

Dave Gregory — Defenseman
Regular Season — Playoffs

Season	Team	League	GP	G	A	PTS	PIM	GP	G	A	PTS	PIM
94-95	London	CoHL	20	0	2	2	17	—	—	—	—	—
94-95	Toledo	ECHL	9	0	1	1	9	—	—	—	—	—
95-96	Guildford	BHL	31	6	23	29	81	—	—	—	—	—
96-97	Central Texas	WPHL	16	0	4	4	22	—	—	—	—	—
96-97	Bakersfield	WCHL	6	0	1	1	0	2	0	0	0	4
97-98	Thunder Bay	UHL	65	1	8	9	76	3	1	0	1	2
98-99	Topeka	CHL	23	2	4	6	39	—	—	—	—	—
98-99	Madison	UHL	1	0	0	0	0	—	—	—	—	—
98-99	Saginaw	UHL	9	0	1	1	8	—	—	—	—	—
	UHL	Totals	95	1	101	12	101	3	1	0	1	2

Born; 5/1/67, Woodstock, Ontario. 6-1, 195.

Jack Greig — Left Wing
Regular Season — Playoffs

Season	Team	League	GP	G	A	PTS	PIM	GP	G	A	PTS	PIM
95-96	Huntsville	SHL	47	9	15	24	205	1	0	0	0	0
96-97	Dayton	CoHL	69	0	10	10	213	—	—	—	—	—
97-98	Nashville	CHL	16	1	3	4	75	—	—	—	—	—
97-98	Fort Worth	CHL	8	1	1	2	39	—	—	—	—	—
97-98	San Angelo	WPHL	40	1	2	3	154	—	—	—	—	—
98-99	Jacksonville	ECHL	4	0	0	0	5	—	—	—	—	—
98-99	Saginaw	UHL	26	1	1	2	146	—	—	—	—	—
98-99	Binghamton	UHL	15	0	2	2	51	4	0	0	0	0
	UHL	Totals	41	1	3	4	197	4	0	0	0	0
	CHL	Totals	24	2	4	6	114	—	—	—	—	—

Born; 1/11/73, Long Island, New York. 6-0, 200. Traded to Binghamton by Saginaw for Eric Kelly (2/99). Selected by Madison in 1999 UHL Expansion Draft. Member of 1995-96 SHL champion Huntsville Channel Cats.

Mark Greig — Right Wing
Regular Season — Playoffs

Season	Team	League	GP	G	A	PTS	PIM	GP	G	A	PTS	PIM
90-91	Hartford	NHL	4	0	0	0	0	—	—	—	—	—
90-91	Springfield	AHL	73	32	55	87	73	17	2	6	8	22
91-92	Hartford	NHL	17	0	5	5	6	—	—	—	—	—
91-92	Springfield	AHL	50	20	27	47	38	9	1	1	2	20
92-93	Hartford	NHL	22	1	7	8	27	—	—	—	—	—
92-93	Springfield	AHL	55	20	38	58	86	—	—	—	—	—
93-94	Hartford	NHL	31	4	5	9	31	—	—	—	—	—
93-94	Toronto	NHL	13	2	2	4	10	—	—	—	—	—
93-94	Springfield	AHL	4	0	4	4	21	—	—	—	—	—
93-94	St. John's	AHL	9	4	6	10	0	11	4	2	6	26
94-95	Calgary	NHL	8	1	1	2	2	—	—	—	—	—
94-95	Saint John	AHL	67	31	50	81	82	2	0	1	1	0
95-96	Atlanta	IHL	71	25	48	73	104	3	2	1	3	4
96-97	Quebec	IHL	5	1	2	3	0	—	—	—	—	—
96-97	Houston	IHL	59	12	30	42	59	13	5	8	13	2
97-98	Grand Rapids	IHL	69	26	36	62	103	3	0	4	4	4
98-99	Philadelphia	NHL	7	1	3	4	2	2	0	1	1	0
98-99	Philadelphia	AHL	67	23	46	69	102	7	1	5	6	14
	NHL	Totals	102	9	23	32	78	2	0	1	1	0
	AHL	Totals	325	130	226	356	402	46	8	15	23	82
	IHL	Totals	204	64	116	180	266	19	7	13	20	10

Born; 1/25/70, High River, Alberta. 5-11, 190. Drafted by Hartford Whalers (1st choice, 15th overall) in 1990 Entry Draft. Traded to Toronto Maple Leafs by Hartford with 6th round choice (later traded to New York Rangers-Rangers selected Yuri Litvinov) in 1994 Entry Draft for Ted Crowley (1/25/94). Signed as a free agent by Calgary (8/9/94). Signed as a free agent by Philadelphia Flyers (8/4/98). Member of 1990-91 AHL champion Springfield Indians. Last amateur

Roland Grelle — Defenseman
Regular Season — Playoffs

Season	Team	League	GP	G	A	PTS	PIM	GP	G	A	PTS	PIM
98-99	Dayton	ECHL	6	0	1	1	6	—	—	—	—	—

Born; 2/1/76, Cranston, Rhode Island. 6-1, 190. Last amateur club; Merrimack (Hockey East).

Jessy Grenier — Forward
Regular Season — Playoffs

Season	Team	League	GP	G	A	PTS	PIM	GP	G	A	PTS	PIM
97-98	Waco	WPHL	13	1	0	1	40	—	—	—	—	—
98-99	Saginaw	UHL	3	0	0	0	41	—	—	—	—	—
98-99	Phoenix	WCHL	10	0	1	1	59	—	—	—	—	—
98-99	South Carolina	ECHL	6	0	0	0	52	—	—	—	—	—
98-99	Pee Dee	ECHL	1	0	0	0	7	—	—	—	—	—
	ECHL	Totals	7	0	0	0	59	—	—	—	—	—

Born; Pabos Mills, Quebec.

Shawn Grenier — Goaltender
Regular Season — Playoffs

Season	Team	League	GP	W	L	T	MIN	SO	AVG	GP	W	L	MIN	SO	AVG
98-99	Saginaw	UHL	1	1	0	0	60	0	3.00	—	—	—	—	—	—

Born; 11/3/72, Fort Dix, New Jersey. 5-8, 182.

Chris Grenville — Right Wing

Regular Season / Playoffs

Season	Team	League	GP	G	A	PTS	PIM	GP	G	A	PTS	PIM
95-96	Birmingham	ECHL	40	9	7	16	40	—	—	—	—	—
96-97	Columbus	CeHL	36	13	7	20	34	—	—	—	—	—
96-97	Saginaw	CoHL	27	10	12	22	12	—	—	—	—	—
97-98	Madison	UHL	29	13	7	20	27	—	—	—	—	—
97-98	Saginaw	UHL	8	0	0	0	4	—	—	—	—	—
97-98	Binghamton	UHL	10	3	4	7	0	5	0	4	4	7
98-99	Springfield	AHL	2	0	1	1	0	—	—	—	—	—
98-99	Binghamton	UHL	74	37	34	71	105	5	2	3	5	4
	UHL	Totals	148	63	57	120	148	10	2	7	9	11

Born; 2/24/74, St. Catharines, Ontario. 6-1, 205. Traded to Binghamton by Brantford with Greg Pajor and Cory Bricknell for Rob MacInnis (3/98).

Brent Gretzky — Center

Regular Season / Playoffs

Season	Team	League	GP	G	A	PTS	PIM	GP	G	A	PTS	PIM
92-93	Atlanta	IHL	77	20	34	54	84	9	3	2	5	8
93-94	Tampa Bay	NHL	10	1	2	3	2	—	—	—	—	—
93-94	Atlanta	IHL	54	17	23	40	30	14	1	1	2	2
94-95	Tampa Bay	IHL	3	0	1	1	0	—	—	—	—	—
94-95	Atlanta	IHL	67	19	32	51	42	5	4	1	5	4
95-96	St. John's	AHL	68	13	28	41	40	4	0	6	6	0
96-97	Las Vegas	IHL	40	5	12	17	8	—	—	—	—	—
96-97	Quebec	IHL	1	0	0	0	0	—	—	—	—	—
96-97	Pensacola	ECHL	22	9	15	24	4	12	5	8	13	4
97-98	EV Graz	Austria	37	19	43	62	36	—	—	—	—	—
98-99	Asheville	UHL	32	28	42	70	29	—	—	—	—	—
98-99	Hershey	AHL	6	2	2	4	2	—	—	—	—	—
98-99	Chicago	IHL	39	9	19	28	15	3	0	1	1	0
	NHL	Totals	13	1	3	4	2	—	—	—	—	—
	IHL	Totals	239	61	101	162	164	31	8	5	13	14
	AHL	Totals	74	15	30	45	42	4	0	6	6	0

Born; 2/20/72, Brantford, Ontario. 5-10, 160. Drafted by Tampa Bay Lightning (3rd choice, 49th overall) in 1992 Entry Draft. Signed as a free agent by Toronto Maple Leafs (9/8/95). Member of 1993-94 IHL champion Atlanta Knights. Last amateur club; Belleville (OHL).

Craig Griese — Right Wing

Regular Season / Playoffs

Season	Team	League	GP	G	A	PTS	PIM	GP	G	A	PTS	PIM
98-99	Saginaw	UHL	3	0	0	0	0	—	—	—	—	—

Born; 11/21/75, Saginaw, Michigan.

Chad Grills — Center

Regular Season / Playoffs

Season	Team	League	GP	G	A	PTS	PIM	GP	G	A	PTS	PIM
94-95	Sault Ste. Marie	OHL	53	19	46	65	97	—	—	—	—	—
94-95	Flint	CoHL	3	0	1	1	8	—	—	—	—	—
95-96	Brantford	CoHL	1	0	0	0	0	—	—	—	—	—
95-96	Flint	CoHL	58	8	18	26	170	15	2	5	7	73
96-97	Detroit	IHL	1	0	0	0	0	—	—	—	—	—
96-97	Flint	CoHL	51	15	29	44	168	14	2	7	9	34
97-98	Flint	UHL	62	21	29	50	123	17	8	9	17	36
98-99	Flint	UHL	42	10	26	36	105	—	—	—	—	—
98-99	Muskegon	UHL	23	12	8	20	68	18	5	11	16	48
	UHL	Totals	240	66	111	177	642	64	17	32	49	191

Born; 12/2/74, Peterborough, Ontario. 6-1, 185. Traded to Muskegon with Mike Bondy for Jan Klimes, Mark Vilneff and David Beauregard (2/99). Member of 1995-96 Colonial Cup Champion Flint Generals. Member of 1998-99 UHL Champion Muskegon Fury. Last amateur club; Sault Ste. Marie (OHL).

Gregg Gripentrog — Right Wing

Regular Season / Playoffs

Season	Team	League	GP	G	A	PTS	PIM	GP	G	A	PTS	PIM
98-99	Pee Dee	ECHL	16	0	1	1	10	—	—	—	—	—

Born;

Nathan Grobins — Goaltender

Regular Season / Playoffs

Season	Team	League	GP	W	L	T	MIN	SO	AVG	GP	W	L	MIN	SO	AVG
93-94	Jacksonville	SuHL	24	11	10	1	1323	0	4.44	1	0	0	2	0	0.00
94-95	Daytona Beach	SuHL	23	9	10	1	1276	0	4.80	1	0	1	60	0	6.00
95-96	Daytona Beach	SHL	17	8	7	0	933	1	4.12	—	—	—	—	—	—
95-96	South Carolina	ECHL	5	1	2	1	268	0	5.36	—	—	—	—	—	—
96-97	Macon	CeHL	2	1	0	0	21	0	2.83	—	—	—	—	—	—
96-97	Waco	WPHL	9	3	3	0	381	1	3.15	—	—	—	—	—	—
97-98	Macon	CHL	1	1	0	0	60	0	3.00	—	—	—	—	—	—
97-98	Fort Worth	CHL	43	9	27	3	2349	0	5.01	—	—	—	—	—	—
98-99	Fort Worth	CHL	*60	18	*37	4	*3504	1	4.38	—	—	—	—	—	—
	CHL	Totals	106	29	64	7	5934	1	4.61	—	—	—	—	—	—
	SHL	Totals	64	28	27	2	3532	1	4.48	2	0	1	62	0	5.81

Born; 6/6/72, Houston, British Columbia. 5-11, 180. Selected by Tulsa in 1999 CHL Dispersal Draft.

Francois Groleau — Defenseman

Regular Season / Playoffs

Season	Team	League	GP	G	A	PTS	PIM	GP	G	A	PTS	PIM
93-94	Saint John	AHL	73	8	14	22	49	7	0	1	1	2
94-95	Saint John	AHL	65	6	34	40	28	—	—	—	—	—
94-95	Cornwall	AHL	8	1	2	3	7	14	2	7	9	16
95-96	Montreal	NHL	2	0	1	1	2	—	—	—	—	—
95-96	Fredericton	AHL	12	3	5	8	10	10	1	6	7	14
95-96	San Francisco	IHL	63	6	26	32	60	—	—	—	—	—
96-97	Montreal	NHL	5	0	0	0	4	—	—	—	—	—
96-97	Fredericton	AHL	47	8	24	32	43	—	—	—	—	—
97-98	Montreal	NHL	1	0	0	0	0	—	—	—	—	—
97-98	Fredericton	AHL	63	14	26	40	70	4	0	2	2	4
98-99	Augsburger	Germany	52	9	21	30	67	5	0	4	4	4
	NHL	Totals	8	0	1	1	6	—	—	—	—	—
	AHL	Totals	268	40	105	145	207	35	3	16	19	36

Born; 1/23/73. Longueuil, Quebec. 6-0, 200. Drafted by Calgary Flames (2nd choice, 41st overall) in 1991 Entry Draft. Traded to Quebec Nordiques by Calgary for Ed Ward (3/23/95). Signed as a free agent by Montreal Canadiens (6/17/95). Last amateur club; St-Jean (QMJHL).

Stanislav Gron — Left Wing

Regular Season / Playoffs

Season	Team	League	GP	G	A	PTS	PIM	GP	G	A	PTS	PIM
98-99	Kootenay	WHL	49	28	18	46	18	7	3	8	11	12
98-99	Utah	IHL	4	0	3	3	0	—	—	—	—	—

Born; 10/28/78, Bratislava, Czechoslovakia. 6-1, 190. Drafted by New Jersey Devils (2nd choice, 38th overall) in 1997 Entry Draft. Last amateur club; Koote-

Tuomas Gronman — Defenseman

Regular Season / Playoffs

Season	Team	League	GP	G	A	PTS	PIM	GP	G	A	PTS	PIM
96-97	Chicago	NHL	16	0	1	1	13	—	—	—	—	—
96-97	Indianapolis	IHL	51	5	16	21	89	4	1	1	2	6
97-98	Pittsburgh	NHL	22	1	2	3	25	1	0	0	0	0
97-98	Indianapolis	IHL	6	0	3	3	6	—	—	—	—	—
97-98	Syracuse	AHL	33	6	14	20	45	—	—	—	—	—
98-99	Kansas City	IHL	4	0	0	0	0	—	—	—	—	—
	NHL	Totals	38	1	3	4	38	1	0	0	0	0
	IHL	Totals	61	5	19	24	95	4	1	1	2	6

Born; 3/22/74. Viitasaari, Finland. 6-3, 198. Drafted by Quebec Nordiques (3rd choice, 29th overall) in 1992 Entry Draft. Rights traded to Chicago Blackhawks by Colorado for Chicago's second round choice (Phillipe Sauve) in 1998 Entry Draft (7/10/96). Traded to Pittsburgh Penguins by Chicago for Greg Johnson (10/27/98). Last amateur club; Tacoma (WHL).

Roby Gropp — Goaltender

Regular Season / Playoffs

Season	Team	League	GP	W	L	T	MIN	SO	AVG	GP	W	L	MIN	SO	AVG
98-99	Johnstown	ECHL	7	2	2	0	303	0	4.15	—	—	—	—	—	—
98-99	New Mexico	WPHL	19	7	9	0	989	1	4.00	—	—	—	—	—	—
98-99	Fort Worth	WPHL	1	0	1	0	59	0	3.03	—	—	—	—	—	—
	WPHL	Totals	20	7	10	0	1048	1	3.95	—	—	—	—	—	—

Born; 5/22/73, Kamloops, British Columbia. 6-1, 180. Last amateur club; St. Norbert (NCAA 3).

Garry Gruber — Defenseman
Regular Season / Playoffs

Season	Team	League	GP	G	A	PTS	PIM	GP	G	A	PTS	PIM
96-97	Tallahassee	ECHL	37	2	10	12	26	—	—	—	—	—
96-97	Louisville	ECHL	22	0	7	7	4	—	—	—	—	—
97-98	Huntington	ECHL	9	1	1	2	6	—	—	—	—	—
97-98	Peoria	ECHL	52	8	23	31	22	—	—	—	—	—
98-99	Augusta	ECHL	42	5	11	16	45	—	—	—	—	—
98-99	Tallahassee	ECHL	9	1	1	2	2	—	—	—	—	—
98-99	Charlotte	ECHL	21	1	2	3	17	—	—	—	—	—
	ECHL	Totals	192	18	55	73	122	—	—	—	—	—

Born; 5/9/74, Madison, Wisconsin. 6-0, 190. Traded by Augusta to Tallahassee with Alexandre LaPorte for Mark DeSantis (1/99). Last amateur club; Notre Dame (CCHA).

John Gruden — Defenseman
Regular Season / Playoffs

Season	Team	League	GP	G	A	PTS	PIM	GP	G	A	PTS	PIM
93-94	Ferris State	CCHA	38	11	25	36	52	—	—	—	—	—
93-94	Boston	NHL	7	0	1	1	2	—	—	—	—	—
94-95	Boston	NHL	38	0	6	6	22	—	—	—	—	—
94-95	Providence	AHL	1	0	1	1	0	—	—	—	—	—
95-96	Boston	NHL	14	0	0	0	4	3	0	1	1	0
95-96	Providence	AHL	39	5	19	24	29	—	—	—	—	—
96-97	Providence	AHL	78	18	27	45	52	10	3	6	9	4
97-98	Detroit	IHL	76	13	42	55	74	23	1	8	9	16
98-99	Ottawa	NHL	13	0	1	1	8	—	—	—	—	—
98-99	Detroit	IHL	59	10	28	38	52	10	0	1	1	6
	NHL	Totals	72	0	8	8	36	3	0	1	1	0
	IHL	Totals	135	23	70	93	126	33	1	9	10	22
	AHL	Totals	118	23	47	70	81	10	3	6	9	4

Born; 4/6/70, Hastings, Minnesota. 6-0, 180. Drafted by Boston Bruins (7th choice, 168th overall) in 1990 Entry Draft. Signed as a free agent by Ottawa Senators (7/22/98). 1997-98 IHL Second Team All-Star. Last amateur club; Ferris State (CCHA).

Jason Gudmunson — Right Wing
Regular Season / Playoffs

Season	Team	League	GP	G	A	PTS	PIM	GP	G	A	PTS	PIM
98-99	Amarillo	WPHL	6	4	2	6	0	—	—	—	—	—

Born; 4/9/74, Arborg, Manitoba. 5-9, 170. Last amateur club; Colorado College (WCHA).

Darren Guidlinger — Defenseman
Regular Season / Playoffs

Season	Team	League	GP	G	A	PTS	PIM	GP	G	A	PTS	PIM
98-99	Asheville	UHL	5	0	0	0	2	—	—	—	—	—

Born; 3/28/73, Estonia, Saskatchewan. 6-2, 200.

Garry Gulash — Defenseman
Regular Season / Playoffs

Season	Team	League	GP	G	A	PTS	PIM	GP	G	A	PTS	PIM
93-94	West Palm Beach	SUN	8	5	4	9	71	—	—	—	—	—
93-94	Detroit	CoHL	31	7	15	22	146	1	0	2	2	0
93-94	Johnstown	ECHL	3	0	0	0	60	—	—	—	—	—
94-95	Detroit	IHL	3	0	0	0	0	—	—	—	—	—
94-95	Detroit	CoHL	53	10	29	39	239	7	1	3	4	56
95-96	Milwaukee	IHL	4	0	0	0	11	1	0	0	0	0
95-96	Detroit	CoHL	6	1	2	3	44	—	—	—	—	—
95-96	Richmond	ECHL	37	3	9	12	260	7	0	4	4	10
96-97	Richmond	ECHL	29	1	4	5	225	—	—	—	—	—
96-97	Birmingham	ECHL	17	0	3	3	138	8	0	6	6	39
97-98	Birmingham	ECHL	60	4	19	23	387	4	0	0	0	16
97-98	Springfield	AHL	—	—	—	—	—	2	0	0	0	9
98-99	Portland	AHL	2	0	0	0	11	—	—	—	—	—
98-99	Quad City	UHL	56	10	35	45	342	16	3	4	7	53
	IHL	Totals	7	0	0	0	11	1	0	0	0	0
	AHL	Totals	2	0	0	0	11	2	0	0	0	9
	ECHL	Totals	146	8	35	43	1070	19	0	10	10	65
	UHL	Totals	146	28	81	109	771	24	4	9	13	109

Born; 9/22/72, Calgary, Alberta. 6-0, 215.

Glen Gulutzan — Center
Regular Season / Playoffs

Season	Team	League	GP	G	A	PTS	PIM	GP	G	A	PTS	PIM
95-96	Vita Hasten	Sweden	26	12	18	30	NA	—	—	—	—	—
96-97	Utah	IHL	3	0	0	0	2	—	—	—	—	—
96-97	Las Vegas	IHL	1	0	0	0	0	—	—	—	—	—
96-97	Fresno	WCHL	60	30	*80	110	52	5	0	9	9	8
97-98	Vassa	Finland	33	5	21	26	NA	—	—	—	—	—
98-99												
98-99	Fresno	WCHL	50	32	34	66	50	7	4	3	7	4
	IHL	Totals	4	0	0	0	2	—	—	—	—	—
	WCHL	Totals	110	62	114	176	102	12	4	12	16	12

Born; 8/12/71, The Pas, Manitoba. 5-10, 175. Last amateur club; University of Saskatchewan (CWUAA).

Steve Guolla — Center
Regular Season / Playoffs

Season	Team	League	GP	G	A	PTS	PIM	GP	G	A	PTS	PIM
95-96	Prince Edward Island	AHL	72	32	48	80	28	3	0	0	0	0
96-97	San Jose	NHL	43	13	8	21	14	—	—	—	—	—
96-97	Kentucky	AHL	34	22	22	44	10	4	2	1	3	0
97-98	San Jose	NHL	7	1	1	2	0	—	—	—	—	—
97-98	Kentucky	AHL	69	37	63	100	45	3	0	0	0	0
98-99	San Jose	NHL	14	2	2	4	6	—	—	—	—	—
98-99	Kentucky	AHL	53	29	47	76	33	—	—	—	—	—
	NHL	Totals	64	16	11	27	20	—	—	—	—	—
	AHL	Totals	228	120	180	300	116	10	2	1	3	0

Born; 3/15/73, Scarborough, Ontario. 6-0, 180. Drafted by Ottawa Senators (1st choice, 3rd overall) in 1994 Supplemental Draft. Signed as a free agent by San Jose Sharks (8/22/96). Traded to Tampa Bay Lightning by San Jose with Shawn Burr, Bill Houlder and Andrei Zyuzin for Niklas Sundstrom and a third round choice in the 2000 Entry Draft (8/4/99). 1997-98 AHL MVP. 1997-98 AHL Second Team All-Star. 1998-99 AHL Second Team All-Star. Last amateur club; Michigan State (CCHA).

Miloslav Guren — Defenseman
Regular Season / Playoffs

Season	Team	League	GP	G	A	PTS	PIM	GP	G	A	PTS	PIM
96-97	Fredericton	AHL	79	6	26	32	26	—	—	—	—	—
97-98	Fredericton	AHL	78	15	36	51	36	4	1	2	3	0
98-99	Monteral	NHL	12	0	1	1	4	—	—	—	—	—
98-99	Fredericton	AHL	63	5	16	21	24	15	4	7	11	10
	AHL	Totals	157	21	62	83	62	19	5	9	14	10

Born; 9/24/76, Hradiste, Czechoslovakia. 6-2, 215. Drafted by Montreal Canadiens (2nd choice, 60th overall) in 1995 Entry Draft. Last overseas club; ZPS Zlin (Czech Republic).

John Gurskis — Center
Regular Season / Playoffs

Season	Team	League	GP	G	A	PTS	PIM	GP	G	A	PTS	PIM
98-99	Columbus	ECHL	23	5	2	7	6	—	—	—	—	—
98-99	Charlotte	ECHL	32	6	6	12	12	—	—	—	—	—
	ECHL	Totals	55	11	8	19	18	—	—	—	—	—

Born; Selected by Trenton in 1999 ECHL Expansion Draft.

Sergey Gusev — Defenseman
Regular Season / Playoffs

Season	Team	League	GP	G	A	PTS	PIM	GP	G	A	PTS	PIM
95-96	Michigan	IHL	73	11	17	28	76	—	—	—	—	—
96-97	Michigan	IHL	51	7	8	15	44	4	0	4	4	6
97-98	Dallas	NHL	9	0	0	0	2	—	—	—	—	—
97-98	Michigan	IHL	36	3	6	9	36	4	0	2	2	6
98-99	Dallas	NHL	22	1	4	5	6	—	—	—	—	—
98-99	Tampa Bay	NHL	14	0	3	3	10	—	—	—	—	—
98-99	Michigan	IHL	12	0	6	6	14	—	—	—	—	—
	NHL	Totals	45	1	7	8	18	—	—	—	—	—
	IHL	Totals	172	21	37	58	170	8	0	6	6	12

Born; 7/31/75, Nizhny Tagil, Russia. 6-1, 195. Drafted by Dallas Stars (4th choice, 69th overall) in 1995 Entry Draft. Traded to Tampa Bay Lightning by Dallas for Benoit Hogue and a conditional 2001 draft pick (3/21/99). Last overseas club; Samara (CIS).

Marcus Gustafsson — Left Wing

Regular Season — Playoffs

Season	Team	League	GP	G	A	PTS	PIM	GP	G	A	PTS	PIM
98-99	Maine	H.E.	41	13	15	28	16	—	—	—	—	—
98-99	Syracuse	AHL	3	4	0	4	0	—	—	—	—	—

Born; 7/24/74, Knivsta, Sweden. 6-0, 187. Last amateur club; Maine (Hockey

Brad Guzda — Goaltender

Regular Season — Playoffs

Season	Team	League	GP	W	L	T	MIN	SO	AVG	GP	W	L	MIN	SO	AVG
94-95	Muskegon	CoHL	—	—	—	—	—	—	—	1	0	1	46	0	6.51
95-96	Muskegon	CoHL	2	0	0	0	12	0	24.46	—	—	—	—	—	—
95-96	Knoxville	ECHL	19	16	1	0	1083	0	3.82	7	3	4	433	0	3.33
96-97	Knoxville	ECHL	35	12	18	2	1853	1	5.38	—	—	—	—	—	—
96-97	Phoenix	IHL	5	0	1	2	165	0	4.37	—	—	—	—	—	—
97-98	Mississippi	ECHL	42	15	15	6	2290	0	3.17	—	—	—	—	—	—
98-99	Las Vegas	IHL	3	1	2	0	138	0	4.34	—	—	—	—	—	—
98-99	Bakersfield	WCHL	45	11	*28	4	2497	1	4.49	2	0	2	120	0	7.00
	IHL	Totals	8	1	3	2	303	0	4.36	—	—	—	—	—	—
	ECHL	Totals	96	43	34	8	5226	1	4.09	7	3	4	433	0	3.33

Born; 4/28/73, Banff, Alberta. 6-2, 175. Signed as a free agent by Los Angeles Kings (5/28/96).

Russell Guzior — Center

Regular Season — Playoffs

Season	Team	League	GP	G	A	PTS	PIM	GP	G	A	PTS	PIM
97-98	Fredericton	AHL	10	1	1	2	4	—	—	—	—	—
97-98	New Orleans	ECHL	54	11	11	22	50	4	3	1	4	9
98-99	New Orleans	ECHL	37	10	14	24	22	—	—	—	—	—
98-99	Mobile	ECHL	20	16	12	28	46	2	2	0	2	0
	ECHL	Totals	111	37	37	74	118	6	5	1	6	9

Born; 1/12/74, Chicago, Illinois. 5-10, 165. Drafted by Montreal Canadiens (13th choice, 281st overall) in 1993 Entry Draft. Traded to Mobile to New Orleans for Ken Ruddick (2/99). Last amateur club; Providence (Hockey East).

Ryan Guzior — Defenseman

Regular Season — Playoffs

Season	Team	League	GP	G	A	PTS	PIM	GP	G	A	PTS	PIM
98-99	Fayetteville	CHL	40	2	12	14	42	—	—	—	—	—

Born; 5/8/75, Thunder Bay, Ontario. 5-11, 225. Last amateur club; Merrimack (Hockey East).

Dwayne Gylywoychuk — Defenseman

Regular Season — Playoffs

Season	Team	League	GP	G	A	PTS	PIM	GP	G	A	PTS	PIM
94-95	Greensboro	ECHL	27	1	9	10	42	—	—	—	—	—
95-96	Jacksonville	ECHL	48	1	5	6	105	—	—	—	—	—
95-96	Dayton	ECHL	5	0	0	0	20	—	—	—	—	—
96-97	Central Texas	WPHL	40	1	5	6	45	8	0	1	1	10
97-98	Central Texas	WPHL	21	0	2	2	29	—	—	—	—	—
97-98	Shreveport	WPHL	30	1	4	5	32	8	0	2	2	14
98-99	Central Texas	WPHL	57	2	4	6	80	2	0	0	0	4
	WPHL	Totals	148	4	15	19	186	18	0	3	3	28
	ECHL	Totals	80	2	14	16	167	—	—	—	—	—

Born; 7/27/73, Brandon, Alberta. 6-3, 200. Drafted by Lake Charles Ice Pirates in WPHL Expansion draft. Returned by Lake Charles to Central Texas Stampede for rights to Daniel Berthiaume (6/2/97). Traded to Shreveport by Central Texas for Brandy Semchuk (1/98). Traded to Central Texas by Shreveport for Don MacPherson and future considerations (9/98). Last amateur club; Brandon

Petri Gynther — Defenseman

Regular Season — Playoffs

Season	Team	League	GP	G	A	PTS	PIM	GP	G	A	PTS	PIM
97-98	Syracuse	AHL	1	0	0	0	0	—	—	—	—	—
97-98	Chesapeake	ECHL	18	1	7	8	7	—	—	—	—	—
97-98	Raleigh	ECHL	41	4	8	12	16	—	—	—	—	—
98-99	KalPa Kuopio	Finland	43	1	3	4	12	—	—	—	—	—
	ECHL	Totals	59	5	15	20	23	—	—	—	—	—

Born; 8/20/73, Mikkeli, Finland. 6-0, 200. Traded to Raleigh by Chesapeake for Jon Larson (12/97). Selected by Florida in 1998 ECHL Expansion Draft. Last amateur club; Denver University (WCHA).

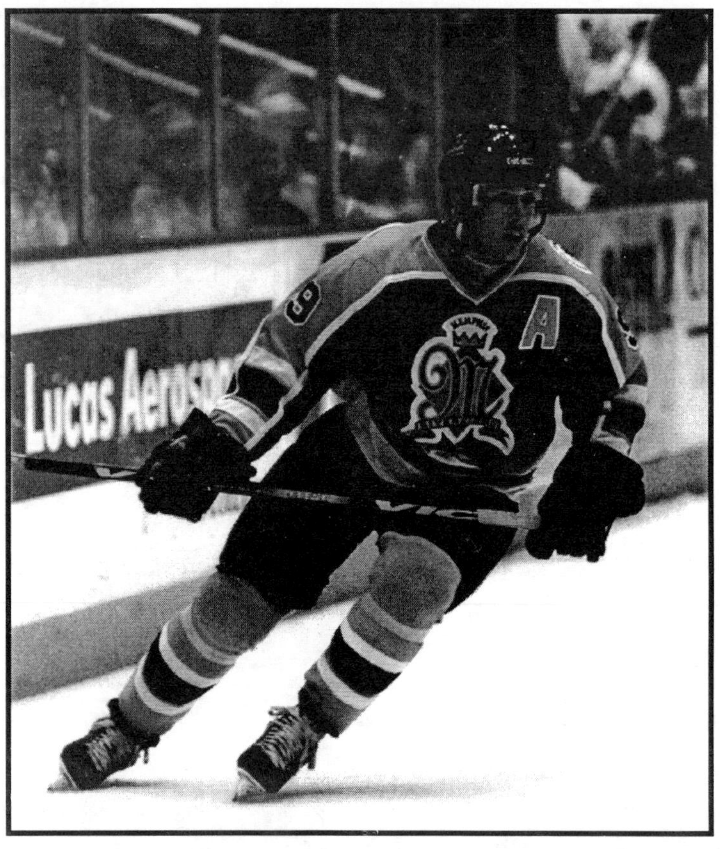

Derek Grant led the CHL in scoring with 123 points

Photo by Lindy Frank

Len Hachborn — Center
Regular Season / Playoffs

Season	Team	League	GP	G	A	PTS	PIM	GP	G	A	PTS	PIM
82-83	Maine	AHL	75	28	55	83	32	17	2	7	9	2
83-84	Springfield	AHL	28	18	42	60	15	—	—	—	—	—
83-84	Philadelphia	NHL	38	11	21	32	4	3	0	0	0	7
84-85	Philadelphia	NHL	40	5	17	22	23	4	0	3	3	0
84-85	Hershey	AHL	14	6	7	13	14	—	—	—	—	—
85-86	Hershey	AHL	23	12	22	34	34	—	—	—	—	—
85-86	Los Angeles	NHL	24	4	1	5	2	—	—	—	—	—
85-86	New Haven	AHL	12	5	8	13	21	3	0	1	1	26
86-87	Hershey	AHL	17	4	10	14	2	—	—	—	—	—
87-88	Maine	AHL	29	16	17	33	16	10	5	7	12	21
89-90	New Haven	AHL	32	13	27	40	15	—	—	—	—	—
90-91	Binghamton	AHL	50	9	27	36	8	4	0	1	1	6
91-92	San Diego	IHL	70	34	*73	107	124	4	0	2	2	17
92-93	Ayr	BHL	8	16	20	36	28	—	—	—	—	—
92-93	San Diego	IHL	59	23	36	59	49	10	2	2	4	2
94-95	Houston	IHL	53	12	30	42	10	—	—	—	—	—
94-95	Springfield	AHL	5	2	4	6	2	—	—	—	—	—
94-95	Detroit	IHL	—	—	—	—	—	1	0	1	1	0
95-96	Heilbronner	Germany	28	15	40	55	57	—	—	—	—	—
96-97	Grand Rapids	IHL	19	2	2	4	6	—	—	—	—	—
97-98	San Diego	WCHL	45	27	63	90	62	12	7	7	14	10
98-99	San Diego	WCHL	49	23	64	87	36	12	4	12	16	4
	NHL	Totals	102	20	39	59	29	7	0	3	3	7
	AHL	Totals	285	111	219	330	159	34	7	16	23	55
	IHL	Totals	201	71	141	212	189	15	2	5	7	19
	WCHL	Totals	94	50	127	177	98	24	11	19	30	14

Born; 9/4/61, Brantford, Ontario. 5-10, 180. Drafted by Philadelphia Flyers (9th choice, 184th overall) in 1981 Entry Draft. Rights sold to Los Angeles Kings by Philadelphia (12/6/85). 1991-92 IHL Second Team All Star. 1998-99 WCHL Second Team All-Star. Member of 1997-98 WCHL Champion San Diego Gulls. Last amateur club; Brantford (OHA).

Robert Haddock — Defenseman
Regular Season / Playoffs

Season	Team	League	GP	G	A	PTS	PIM	GP	G	A	PTS	PIM
93-94	Utica	CoHL	21	1	7	8	48	—	—	—	—	—
93-94	Erie	ECHL	8	0	2	2	16	—	—	—	—	—
93-94	Huntington	ECHL	2	0	0	0	17	—	—	—	—	—
94-95	Tallahassee	ECHL	43	5	14	19	55	13	1	6	7	24
95-96	Bakersfield	WCHL	39	2	17	19	81	—	—	—	—	—
96-97	El Paso	WPHL	55	8	22	30	97	6	0	2	2	14
97-98	El Paso	WPHL	69	7	17	24	62	15	4	7	11	28
98-99	El Paso	WPHL	68	10	35	45	91	3	0	1	1	0
	WPHL	Totals	192	25	74	99	250	24	4	10	14	42
	ECHL	Totals	53	5	16	21	88	13	1	6	7	24

Born; 4/7/70, Montreal, Quebec. 5-11, 195. Member of 1996-97 WPHL Champion El Paso Buzzards. Member of 1997-98 WPHL Champion El Paso Buzzards. Last amateur club; Colgate (ECAC).

Brad Haelzle — Right Wing
Regular Season / Playoffs

Season	Team	League	GP	G	A	PTS	PIM	GP	G	A	PTS	PIM
94-95	Toledo	ECHL	—	—	—	—	—	3	0	1	1	4
95-96	Fresno	WCHL	53	22	20	42	45	7	2	4	6	0
96-97	Fresno	WCHL	49	16	25	41	120	3	0	0	0	24
97-98	Fresno	WCHL	40	4	17	21	76	—	—	—	—	—
97-98	Tacoma	WCHL	13	5	6	11	37	—	—	—	—	—
97-98	Reno	WCHL	—	—	—	—	—	3	0	0	0	4
98-99	Amarillo	WPHL	67	23	24	47	73	—	—	—	—	—
	WCHL	Totals	155	47	68	115	278	13	2	4	6	28

Born; 1/5/70, Waterloo, Ontario. 6-0, 180. Selected by Bakersfield in 1998 WCHL Dispersal Draft. Last amateur club; Guelph (OUAA).

Sean Haggerty — Left Wing
Regular Season / Playoffs

Season	Team	League	GP	G	A	PTS	PIM	GP	G	A	PTS	PIM
95-96	Detroit	OHL	66	*60	51	111	78	17	15	9	24	30
95-96	Toronto	NHL	1	0	0	0	0	—	—	—	—	—
95-96	Worcester	AHL	—	—	—	—	—	1	0	0	0	2
96-97	Kentucky	AHL	77	13	22	35	60	4	1	0	1	4
97-98	Islanders	NHL	5	0	0	0	0	—	—	—	—	—
97-98	Kentucky	AHL	63	33	20	53	64	3	0	2	2	4
98-99	Lowell	AHL	77	19	27	46	40	3	0	1	1	0
	NHL	Totals	6	0	0	0	0	—	—	—	—	—
	AHL	Totals	217	65	69	134	164	11	1	3	4	10

Born; 2/11/76, Rye, New York. 6-1, 186. Drafted by Toronto Maple Leafs (2nd choice, 48th overall) in 1994 Entry Draft. Traded to New York Islanders by Toronto with Darby Hendrickson, Kenny Jonsson and Toronto's first round choice (Roberto Luongo) in 1997 Entry Draft for Wendel Clark, Mathieu Schneider and D. J. Smith (3/13/96). 1997-98 AHL Second Team All-Star. Last amateur

Johan Hagman — Forward
Regular Season / Playoffs

Season	Team	League	GP	G	A	PTS	PIM	GP	G	A	PTS	PIM
98-99	Odessa	WPHL	52	17	40	57	10	3	0	1	1	0

Born; 5/9/74, Huddinge, Sweden. 5-11, 184.

Chris Hajt — Defense
Regular Season / Playoffs

Season	Team	League	GP	G	A	PTS	PIM	GP	G	A	PTS	PIM
98-99	Hamilton	AHL	64	0	4	4	36	—	—	—	—	—

Born; 7/5/78, Saskatoon, Saskatchewan. 6-3, 206. Drafted by Edmonton Oilers (3rd choice, 32nd overall) in 1996 Entry Draft. Last amateur club; Guelph (OHL).

Ashlin Halfnight — Defense
Regular Season / Playoffs

Season	Team	League	GP	G	A	PTS	PIM	GP	G	A	PTS	PIM
97-98	New Haven	AHL	64	3	11	14	26	3	0	1	1	2
98-99	New Haven	AHL	71	2	9	11	45	—	—	—	—	—
	AHL	Totals	135	5	20	25	71	3	0	1	1	2

Born; 3/14/75, Toronto, Ontario. 6-0, 180. Drafted by Hartford Whalers (5th choice, 213th overall) in 1994 Entry Draft. Last amateur club; Harvard (ECAC).

Bob Halkidis — Defenseman

Season	Team	League	GP	G	A	PTS	PIM	GP	G	A	PTS	PIM
			Regular Season					Playoffs				
84-85	Buffalo	AHL	—	—	--	—	—	4	0	0	0	19
85-86	Buffalo	NHL	37	1	9	10	115	—	—	—	—	—
86-87	Buffalo	NHL	6	1	1	2	19	—	—	—	—	—
86-87	Rochester	AHL	59	1	8	9	144	8	0	0	0	43
87-88	Buffalo	NHL	30	0	3	3	115	4	0	0	0	22
87-88	Rochester	AHL	15	2	5	7	50	—	—	—	—	—
88-89	Buffalo	NHL	16	0	1	1	66	—	—	—	—	—
88-89	Rochester	AHL	16	0	6	6	64	—	—	—	—	—
89-90	Los Angeles	NHL	20	0	4	4	56	8	0	1	1	8
89-90	Rochester	AHL	18	1	13	14	70	—	—	—	—	—
89-90	New Haven	AHL	30	3	17	20	67	—	—	—	—	—
90-91	Los Angeles	NHL	34	1	3	4	133	3	0	0	0	0
90-91	New Haven	AHL	7	1	3	4	10	—	—	—	—	—
90-91	Phoenix	IHL	4	1	5	6	6	—	—	—	—	—
91-92	Toronto	NHL	46	3	3	6	145	—	—	—	—	—
92-93	St. John's	AHL	29	2	13	15	61	—	—	—	—	—
92-93	Milwaukee	IHL	26	0	9	9	79	5	0	1	1	27
93-94	Detroit	NHL	28	1	4	5	93	1	0	0	0	2
93-94	Adirondack	AHL	15	0	6	6	46	—	—	—	—	—
94-95	Detroit	NHL	4	0	1	1	6	—	—	—	—	—
94-95	Tampa Bay	NHL	27	1	3	4	40	—	—	—	—	—
95-96	Tampa Bay	NHL	3	0	0	0	7	—	—	—	—	—
95-96	Islanders	NHL	5	0	0	0	30	—	—	—	—	—
95-96	Atlanta	IHL	21	1	7	8	62	—	—	—	—	—
95-96	Indianapolis	IHL	3	0	2	2	8	—	—	—	—	—
95-96	Utah	IHL	27	0	7	7	72	12	1	1	2	36
96-97	Carolina	AHL	41	5	13	18	47	—	—	—	—	—
97-98	Winston-Salem	UHL	3	0	1	1	15	—	—	—	—	—
98-99	Kolner Haie	Germany	48	7	14	21	103	5	0	0	0	4
	NHL	Totals	256	8	32	40	825	20	0	1	1	51
	AHL	Totals	230	15	84	99	559	8	0	0	0	43
	IHL	Totals	81	2	30	32	227	17	1	2	3	63

Born; 3/5/66, Toronto, Ontario. 5-11, 205. Drafted by Buffalo Sabres (4th choice, 81st overall) in 1984 Entry Draft. Traded to Los Angeles Kings by Buffalo with future considerations for Dale DeGray and future considerations (11/24/89). Signed as a free agent by Toronto Maple Leafs (7/24/91). Signed as a free agent by Detroit Red Wings (9/2/93). Claimed on waivers by Tampa Bay Lightning from Detroit (2/10/95). Traded to New York Islanders by Chicago Balckhawks for Danton Cole (2/2/96). Signed as a free agent by Florida Panthers (7/25/96). Member of 1986-87 AHL champion Rochester Americans. Member of 1995-96 IHL champion Utah Grizzlies. Last amateur club; London (OHL).

Steven Halko — Defenseman

Season	Team	League	GP	G	A	PTS	PIM	GP	G	A	PTS	PIM
			Regular Season					Playoffs				
96-97	Springfield	AHL	70	1	5	6	37	11	0	2	2	8
97-98	Carolina	NHL	18	0	2	2	10	—	—	—	—	—
97-98	New Haven	AHL	65	1	19	20	44	1	0	0	0	0
98-99	Carolina	NHL	20	0	3	3	24	4	0	0	0	2
98-99	New Haven	AHL	42	2	7	9	58	—	—	—	—	—
	NHL	Totals	38	0	5	5	34	4	0	0	0	2
	AHL	Totals	177	4	31	35	139	12	0	2	2	8

Born; 3/8/74, Etobicoke, Ontario. 6-1, 183. Drafted by Hartford Whalers (10th choice, 225th overall) in 1992 Entry Draft. Last amateur club; University of Michigan (CCHA).

Maurice Hall — Forward

Season	Team	League	GP	G	A	PTS	PIM	GP	G	A	PTS	PIM
			Regular Season					Playoffs				
96-97	Bakersfield	WCHL	2	0	0	0	0	—	—	—	—	—
97-98												
98-99	Fayetteville	CHL	1	0	0	0	2	—	—	—	—	—
98-99	Memphis	CHL	5	0	1	1	0	—	—	—	—	—
98-99	Tupelo	WPHL	1	0	0	0	0	—	—	—	—	—
	CHL	Totals	6	0	1	1	2	—	—	—	—	—

Born; 2/24/74, Anchorage, Alaska. 5-7, 175.

Mike Hall — Center

Season	Team	League	GP	G	A	PTS	PIM	GP	G	A	PTS	PIM
			Regular Season					Playoffs				
96-97	Baltimore	AHL	2	0	1	1	2	—	—	—	—	—
96-97	Baton Rouge	ECHL	16	4	5	9	8	—	—	—	—	—
96-97	Raleigh	ECHL	22	3	8	11	26	—	—	—	—	—
96-97	Jacksonville	ECHL	19	8	8	16	8	—	—	—	—	—
97-98	Jacksonville	ECHL	57	20	44	64	20	—	—	—	—	—
98-99	Indianapolis	IHL	73	12	25	37	10	7	1	1	2	0
	ECHL	Totals	114	35	65	100	62	—	—	—	—	—

Born; 2/13/73, Ottawa, Ontario. 6-2, 180. Last amateur club; Bowling Green State (CCHA).

Tobias Hall — Right Wing

Season	Team	League	GP	G	A	PTS	PIM	GP	G	A	PTS	PIM
			Regular Season					Playoffs				
98-99	New Mexico	WPHL	9	0	0	0	16	—	—	—	—	—
98-99	Paisley	BNL	21	9	7	16	34	—	—	—	—	—

Born; 3/25/76, Lunde, Sweden. 6-2, 210.

Todd Hall — Left Wing

Season	Team	League	GP	G	A	PTS	PIM	GP	G	A	PTS	PIM
			Regular Season					Playoffs				
96-97	Binghamton	AHL	40	3	7	10	12	4	0	1	1	0
96-97	Charlotte	ECHL	13	0	2	2	8	—	—	—	—	—
97-98	Hartford	AHL	73	7	18	25	26	8	0	1	1	8
98-99	Hartford	AHL	72	14	15	29	12	1	0	0	0	0
	AHL	Totals	185	24	40	64	50	13	0	2	2	8

Born; 1/22/73, Hamden, Connecticut. 6-1, 212. Drafted by Hartford Whalers (3rd choice, 53rd overall) in 1991 Entry Draft. Signed as a free agent by New York Rangers (6/12/97). Last amateur club; University of New Hampshire (Hockey

Eric Hallman — Defenseman

Season	Team	League	GP	G	A	PTS	PIM	GP	G	A	PTS	PIM
			Regular Season					Playoffs				
97-98	Syracuse	AHL	9	0	0	0	6	—	—	—	—	—
97-98	Hershey	AHL	15	0	1	1	4	—	—	—	—	—
97-98	Johnstown	ECHL	24	0	9	9	23	—	—	—	—	—
97-98	Roanoke	ECHL	18	0	2	2	12	7	0	0	0	0
98-99	Kentucky	AHL	3	0	0	0	12	—	—	—	—	—
98-99	Cincinnati	AHL	5	0	0	0	0	—	—	—	—	—
98-99	Mohawk Valley	UHL	15	2	2	4	25	—	—	—	—	—
	AHL	Totals	32	0	1	1	22	—	—	—	—	—
	ECHL	Toals	42	0	11	11	35	7	0	0	0	0

Born; 5/21/73, Eden Prairie, Minnesota. 6-2, 220. Traded to Roanoke by Johnstown for Dave Tremblay (2/98). Last amateur club; University of Vermont

Jeff Halpern — Center

Season	Team	League	GP	G	A	PTS	PIM	GP	G	A	PTS	PIM
			Regular Season					Playoffs				
98-99	Princeton	ECAC	33	22	22	44	32	—	—	—	—	—
98-99	Portland	AHL	6	2	1	3	4	—	—	—	—	—

Born; 5/3/76, Washington, District of Columbia. 6-0, 195. Signed as a free agent by Washington Capitals (4/1/99). Last amateur club; Princeton (ECAC).

Trevor Halverson — Left Wing

Regular Season / Playoffs

Season	Team	League	GP	G	A	PTS	PIM	GP	G	A	PTS	PIM
91-92	Baltimore	AHL	74	10	11	21	181	—	—	—	—	—
92-93	Baltimore	AHL	67	19	21	40	170	2	1	0	1	0
92-93	Hampton Roads	ECHL	9	7	5	12	6	—	—	—	—	—
93-94	San Diego	IHL	58	4	9	13	115	—	—	—	—	—
93-94	Milwaukee	IHL	4	1	0	1	8	2	0	0	0	17
94-95	Portland	AHL	5	0	1	1	9	—	—	—	—	—
94-95	Hampton Roads	ECHL	42	14	26	40	194	4	1	1	2	2
95-96	Portland	AHL	3	0	1	1	0	—	—	—	—	—
95-96	Las Vegas	IHL	22	6	9	15	86	—	—	—	—	—
95-96	Utah	IHL	1	0	1	1	0	—	—	—	—	—
95-96	Indianapolis	IHL	12	0	1	1	18	5	0	0	0	4
95-96	Hampton Roads	ECHL	38	34	27	61	152	—	—	—	—	—
96-97	Portland	AHL	50	9	8	17	157	3	1	1	2	4
97-98	Portland	AHL	43	14	13	27	181	10	2	4	6	20
97-98	Fort Wayne	IHL	14	1	4	5	34	—	—	—	—	—
97-98	Manitoba	IHL	7	1	0	1	20	—	—	—	—	—
98-99	Washington	NHL	17	0	4	4	28	—	—	—	—	—
98-99	Portland	AHL	57	24	25	49	153	—	—	—	—	—
	AHL	Totals	299	76	80	156	851	15	4	5	9	24
	IHL	Totals	118	13	24	37	281	7	0	0	0	21
	ECHL	Totals	89	55	58	113	352	4	1	1	2	2

Born; 4/6/71, White River, Ontario. 6-1, 200. Drafted by Washington Capitals (2nd choice, 21st overall) in 1991 Entry Draft. Claimed by Anaheim Mighty Ducks in Expansion Draft (6/24/93). Signed as a free agent by Washington Capitals. Last amateur club; North Bay (OHL).

Denis Hamel — Left Wing

Regular Season / Playoffs

Season	Team	League	GP	G	A	PTS	PIM	GP	G	A	PTS	PIM
97-98	Rochester	AHL	74	10	15	25	98	4	1	2	3	0
98-99	Rochester	AHL	74	16	17	33	121	20	3	4	7	10
	AHL	Totals	148	26	32	58	219	24	4	6	10	10

Born; 5/10/77, Lachute, Quebec. 6-2, 200. Drafted by St. Louis Blues (5th choice, 153rd overall) in 1995 Entry Draft. Traded to Buffalo Sabres by St. Louis for Charlie Huddy and Buffalo's seventh round choice (Daniel Corso) in 1996 Entry Draft (3/19/96). Last amateur club; Chicoutimi (QMJHL).

Craig Hamelin — Center

Regular Season / Playoffs

Season	Team	League	GP	G	A	PTS	PIM	GP	G	A	PTS	PIM
95-96	Louisville	ECHL	2	0	2	2	4	—	—	—	—	—
95-96	Jacksonville	ECHL	2	0	1	1	2	—	—	—	—	—
95-96	Tulsa	CeHL	49	22	36	58	38	6	1	4	5	14
96-97		Finland	40	34	27	61	NA	—	—	—	—	—
96-97	New Mexico	WPHL	3	3	1	4	0	4	1	0	1	0
97-98	New Mexico	WPHL	53	24	55	79	43	10	9	4	13	16
98-99	New Mexico	WPHL	40	11	25	36	70	—	—	—	—	—
	WPHL	Totals	96	38	81	119	113	14	10	4	14	16
	ECHL	Totals	4	0	3	3	6	—	—	—	—	—

Born; 11/5/71, Renfrew, Ontario. 5-9, 175. Last amateur club; Rensselaer Polytechnic Institute (ECAC).

Hugo Hamelin — Goaltender

Regular Season / Playoffs

Season	Team	League	GP	W	L	T	MIN	SO	AVG	GP	W	L	MIN	SO	AVG
95-96	Memphis	CeHL	16	7	7	2	904	1	4.25	—	—	—	—	—	—
95-96	Huntsville	SHL	26	11	13	2	1522	0	4.93	—	—	—	—	—	—
96-97	Kansas City	IHL	1	0	0	0	2	0	0.00	—	—	—	—	—	—
96-97	Memphis	CeHL	35	16	14	2	1918	0	3.75	—	—	—	—	—	—
96-97	Wichita	CeHL	5	2	2	1	298	0	3.83	9	4	5	537	0	3.80
97-98	Kansas City	IHL	2	0	0	1	79	0	4.55	—	—	—	—	—	—
97-98	Wichita	CHL	30	15	10	1	1608	*1	3.99	—	—	—	—	—	—
97-98	Huntsville	CHL	2	1	1	0	120	*1	3.00	2	0	2	114	0	5.80
98-99	Shreveport	WPHL	39	26	9	3	2184	2	3.30	4	4	0	2400	0	1.75
	IHL	Totals	3	0	0	1	81	0	4.44	—	—	—	—	—	—
	CeHL	Totals	88	41	34	6	4848	3	3.91	11	4	7	651	0	4.15

Born; 5/5/74, Granby, Quebec. 6-0, 175. Traded to Hunstville with Eddy Marchant for Phil Daigle (3/98). Member of 1998-99 WPHL Champion Shreveport Mudbugs. Last amateur club; Val-D'Or (QMJHL).

Brian Hamilton — Goaltender

Regular Season / Playoffs

Season	Team	League	GP	W	L	T	MIN	SO	AVG	GP	W	L	MIN	SO	AVG
96-97	Peoria	ECHL	2	1	0	0	67	0	1.78	—	—	—	—	—	—
97-98	Peoria	ECHL	1	0	0	1	40	0	0.00	—	—	—	—	—	—
98-99	Peoria	ECHL	1	0	1	0	53	0	4.50	—	—	—	—	—	—
	ECHL	Totals	4	1	1	1	160	0	2.25	—	—	—	—	—	—

Born; 11/3/72, Chicago, Illinois. 5-8, 155.

Hugh Hamilton — Defenseman

Regular Season / Playoffs

Season	Team	League	GP	G	A	PTS	PIM	GP	G	A	PTS	PIM
97-98	New Haven	AHL	51	3	3	6	17	3	0	0	0	2
98-99	New Haven	AHL	1	0	0	0	0	—	—	—	—	—
98-99	Florida	ECHL	65	8	25	33	57	6	0	4	4	6
	AHL	Totals	52	3	3	6	17	3	0	0	0	2

Born; 2/11/77, Saskatoon, Saskatchewan. 6-1, 175. Drafted by Hartford Whalers (5th choice, 113th overall) in 1995 Entry Draft. Last amateur club; Spokane

Jason Hamilton — Defenseman

Regular Season / Playoffs

Season	Team	League	GP	G	A	PTS	PIM	GP	G	A	PTS	PIM
98-99	Portland	AHL	4	0	0	0	0	—	—	—	—	—
98-99	Greenville	ECHL	45	2	6	8	206	—	—	—	—	—

Born; 1/25/77, Montreal, Quebec. 6-2, 218. Signed as a free agent by Chicago Blackhawks (7/7/98). Last amateur club; Shawinigan (QMJHL).

Lee Hamilton — Defenseman

Regular Season / Playoffs

Season	Team	League	GP	G	A	PTS	PIM	GP	G	A	PTS	PIM
97-98	Birmingham	ECHL	5	0	0	0	7	—	—	—	—	—
97-98	Oklahoma City	CHL	46	7	13	20	141	10	0	2	2	18
98-99	Columbus	ECHL	22	0	2	2	82	—	—	—	—	—
98-99	Baton Rouge	ECHL	41	2	6	8	110	6	0	1	1	14
	ECHL	Totals	68	2	8	10	199	6	0	1	1	14

Born; 8/22/77, Saskatoon, Saskatchewan. 6-1, 210. Last amateur club; Kelowna (WHL).

Eric Hamlet — Right Wing

Regular Season / Playoffs

Season	Team	League	GP	G	A	PTS	PIM	GP	G	A	PTS	PIM
98-99	Johnstown	ECHL	1	0	0	0	2	—	—	—	—	—
98-99	El Paso	WPHL	2	0	0	0	0	—	—	—	—	—

Born; 5/7/73, Fairbanks, Alaska. 5-10, 180.

Ladislav Hampeis — Defenseman

Regular Season / Playoffs

Season	Team	League	GP	G	A	PTS	PIM	GP	G	A	PTS	PIM
98-99	Wheeling	ECHL	51	0	11	11	130	—	—	—	—	—

Born; 2/2/76, Pribram, Czech Republic. 6-1, 210.

Trevor Hanas — Right Wing

Regular Season / Playoffs

Season	Team	League	GP	G	A	PTS	PIM	GP	G	A	PTS	PIM
96-97	Peoria	ECHL	62	20	32	52	167	8	5	9	14	34
97-98	Peoria	ECHL	61	12	25	37	136	2	0	0	0	6
98-99	Topeka	CHL	29	3	11	14	60	—	—	—	—	—
	ECHL	Totals	123	32	57	89	303	10	5	9	14	40

Born; 1/20/75, Regina, Saskatchewan. 6-0, 190. Last amateur club; Lethbridge (WHL).

Ron Handy — Center
Regular Season / Playoffs

Season	Team	League	GP	G	A	PTS	PIM	GP	G	A	PTS	PIM
82-83	Kingston	OHL	67	52	96	148	64	—	—	—	—	—
82-83	Indianapolis	CHL	9	2	7	9	0	10	3	8	11	18
83-84	Indianapolis	CHL	66	29	46	75	40	10	2	5	7	0
84-85	Islanders	NHL	10	0	2	2	0	—	—	—	—	—
84-85	Springfield	AHL	69	29	35	64	38	3	2	2	4	0
85-86	Springfield	AHL	79	13	30	61	66	—	—	—	—	—
86-87	Indianapolis	IHL	82	*55	80	135	57	6	4	3	7	2
87-88	St. Louis	NHL	4	0	1	1	0	—	—	—	—	—
87-88	Peoria	IHL	78	53	63	116	61	7	2	3	5	4
88-89	Indianapolis	IHL	81	43	57	100	52	—	—	—	—	—
89-90	Fort Wayne	IHL	82	36	39	75	52	5	3	1	4	0
90-91	Kansas City	IHL	64	42	39	81	41	—	—	—	—	—
91-92	Kansas City	IHL	38	16	19	35	30	15	13	8	21	8
92-93	Kansas City	IHL	6	1	1	2	2	—	—	—	—	—
92-93	Peoria	IHL	18	0	7	7	16	—	—	—	—	—
92-93	Wichita	CeHL	11	6	12	18	20	—	—	—	—	—
93-94	Wichita	CeHL	57	29	80	109	98	11	12	10	22	12
94-95	Denver	IHL	1	0	0	0	0	—	—	—	—	—
94-95	Wichita	CeHL	46	24	45	69	72	11	15	16	31	4
95-96	Huntsville	SHL	3	3	1	4	0	—	—	—	—	—
95-96	Louisiana	ECHL	58	20	65	85	34	5	2	4	6	2
96-97	Louisiana	ECHL	66	33	*67	100	58	17	5	17	22	0
97-98	Huntsville	CHL	46	27	33	60	50	2	0	1	1	0
98-99	Lake Charles	WPHL	15	5	10	15	21	—	—	—	—	—
	NHL	Totals	14	0	3	3	0	—	—	—	—	—
	IHL	Totals	450	246	266	512	311	33	22	15	37	14
	AHL	Totals	148	42	65	107	104	3	2	2	4	0
	CHL (old)	Totals	75	31	53	84	40	20	5	13	18	18
	CHL (new)	Totals	160	86	170	256	240	24	27	27	54	16
	ECHL	Totals	124	53	132	185	92	22	7	21	28	2

Born; 1/5/63, Toronto, Ontario. 5-11, 175. Drafted by New York Islanders (3rd choice, 57th overall) in 1981 Entry Draft. Signed as a free agent by St. Louis Blues (9/87). Named player/coach of Indianapolis Ice (2/89). Released by St. Louis Blues (5/89). Signed as a free agent by Ft. Wayne Komets (9/89). Signed as a free agent by Kansas City Blades (8/90). Member of 1982-93 Central League champion Indianapolis Checkers. 1983-84 Central League Second Team All-Star. 1986-87 IHL Second Team All-Star. 1987-88 IHL First Team All-Star. 1991-92 IHL Playoff MVP. Member of 1991-92 IHL champion Kansas City Blades. 1993-94 CeHL Second Team All-Star. 1993-94 CeHL Playoff MVP. Member of 1993-94 CeHL champion Wichita Thunder. 1994-95 CeHL Playoff MVP. Member of 1994-95 CeHL champion Wichita Thunder. Last amateur club; Kingston (OHL).

Quinn Hancock — Right Wing
Regular Season / Playoffs

Season	Team	League	GP	G	A	PTS	PIM	GP	G	A	PTS	PIM
98-99	Worcester	AHL	13	1	2	3	4	—	—	—	—	—
98-99	Peoria	ECHL	28	8	13	21	6	—	—	—	—	—

Born; 5/18/77, Rock Creek, British Columbia. 6-1, 175. Last amateur club; Prince George (WHL).

Casey Hankinson — Left Wing
Regular Season / Playoffs

Season	Team	League	GP	G	A	PTS	PIM	GP	G	A	PTS	PIM
98-99	Portland	AHL	72	10	13	23	106	—	—	—	—	—

Born; 5/8/76, Edina, Minnesota. 6-1, 187. Drafted by Chicago Blackhawks (9th choice, 201st overall) in 1995 Entry Draft. Last amateur club; Minnesota

Randy Hankinson — Defenseman
Regular Season / Playoffs

Season	Team	League	GP	G	A	PTS	PIM	GP	G	A	PTS	PIM
98-99	Flint	UHL	36	0	6	6	35	—	—	—	—	—
98-99	Tulsa	CHL	16	1	1	2	6	—	—	—	—	—

Born; 3/4/72, West Branch, Michigan. 5-10, 185.

Scott Hannan — Defenseman
Regular Season / Playoffs

Season	Team	League	GP	G	A	PTS	PIM	GP	G	A	PTS	PIM
98-99	Kelowna	WHL	47	15	30	45	92	6	1	2	3	14
98-99	San Jose	NHL	5	0	2	2	6	—	—	—	—	—
98-99	Kentucky	AHL	2	0	0	0	2	12	0	2	2	10

Born; 1/23/79, Richmond, British Columbia. 6-2, 210. Drafted by San Jose Sharks (2nd choice, 23rd overall) in 1997 Entry Draft. Last amateur club;

Tavis Hansen — Right Wing
Regular Season / Playoffs

Season	Team	League	GP	G	A	PTS	PIM	GP	G	A	PTS	PIM
94-95	Tacoma	WHL	71	32	41	73	142	4	1	1	2	8
94-95	Winnipeg	NHL	1	0	0	0	0	—	—	—	—	—
95-96	Springfield	AHL	67	6	16	22	85	5	1	2	3	2
96-97	Springfield	AHL	12	3	1	4	23	—	—	—	—	—
96-97	Phoenix	NHL	1	0	0	0	0	—	—	—	—	—
97-98	Springfield	AHL	73	20	14	34	70	4	1	2	3	18
98-99	Phoenix	NHL	20	2	1	3	12	2	0	0	0	0
98-99	Springfield	AHL	63	23	11	34	85	3	0	1	1	5
	NHL	Totals	22	2	1	3	12	2	0	0	0	0
	AHL	Totals	215	52	42	94	263	12	2	5	7	25

Born; 6/17/75, Prince Albert, Saskatchewan. 6-1, 180. Drafted by Winnipeg Jets (3rd choice, 58th overall) in 1984 Entry Draft. Last amateur club; Tacoma

Devon Hanson — Goaltender
Regular Season / Playoffs

Season	Team	League	GP	W	L	T	MIN	SO	AVG	GP	W	L	MIN	SO	AVG
98-99	San Angelo	WPHL	2	1	1	0	119	0	3.01	—	—	—	—	—	—

Born; 10/1/75, Yorktown, Saskatchewan. 6-3, 230.

Michael Hanson — Forward
Regular Season / Playoffs

Season	Team	League	GP	G	A	PTS	PIM	GP	G	A	PTS	PIM
98-99	Windsor	OHL	58	28	30	58	216	5	4	2	6	27
98-99	Quad City	UHL	—	—	—	—	—	8	0	0	0	21

Born; 5/26/78, Oakville, Ontario. 5-11, 199. Last amateur club; Windsor (OHL).

John Hanson — Right Wing
Regular Season / Playoffs

Season	Team	League	GP	G	A	PTS	PIM	GP	G	A	PTS	PIM
95-96	San Diego	WCHL	7	2	4	6	2	—	—	—	—	—
96-97												
97-98	Lake Charles	WPHL	69	36	23	59	64	4	1	3	4	4
98-99	Lake Charles	WPHL	68	37	33	70	122	11	5	6	11	21
	WPHL	Totals	137	73	56	129	186	15	6	9	15	25

Born; 4/8/68, Eagan, Minnesota. 5-9, 180.

Michael Harder — Center
Regular Season / Playoffs

Season	Team	League	GP	G	A	PTS	PIM	GP	G	A	PTS	PIM
96-97	Colgate	ECAC	33	22	33	55	20	—	—	—	—	—
96-97	Hamilton	AHL	2	0	1	1	0	—	—	—	—	—
96-97	Milwaukee	IHL	7	1	3	4	6	2	0	1	1	0
97-98	Springfield	AHL	3	2	0	2	2	—	—	—	—	—
97-98	Rochester	AHL	8	4	2	6	0	4	3	2	5	8
97-98	Milwaukee	IHL	64	20	17	37	32	—	—	—	—	—
98-99	Rochester	AHL	79	31	48	79	39	20	2	9	11	23
	AHL	Totals	92	37	51	88	41	24	5	11	16	31
	IHL	Totals	71	21	20	41	38	2	0	1	1	0

Born; 2/8/73, Winnipeg, Manitoba. 6-0, 180. Last amateur club; Colgate (ECAC).

D.J. Harding — Defenseman
Regular Season / Playoffs

Season	Team	League	GP	G	A	PTS	PIM	GP	G	A	PTS	PIM
98-99	Huntington	ECHL	70	0	7	7	39	—	—	—	—	—

Born; 7/2/75, Salem, New Hampshire. 6-1, 185. Last amateur club; Brown

Brett Harkins — Center

Regular Season — Playoffs

Season	Team	League	GP	G	A	PTS	PIM	GP	G	A	PTS	PIM
93-94	Adirondack	AHL	80	22	47	69	23	10	1	5	6	4
94-95	Boston	NHL	1	0	1	1	0	—	—	—	—	—
94-95	Providemce	AHL	80	23	*69	92	32	13	8	14	22	4
95-96	Florida	NHL	8	0	3	3	6	—	—	—	—	—
95-96	Carolina	AHL	55	23	*71	94	172	—	—	—	—	—
96-97	Boston	NHL	44	4	14	18	8	—	—	—	—	—
96-97	Providence	AHL	28	9	31	40	32	10	2	10	12	0
97-98	Cleveland	IHL	80	32	62	94	82	10	4	13	17	14
98-99	Cleveland	IHL	74	20	67	87	84	—	—	—	—	—
	NHL	Totals	53	4	18	22	14	—	—	—	—	—
	AHL	Totals	243	77	218	295	259	33	11	29	40	8
	IHL	Totals	154	52	129	181	166	10	4	13	17	14

Born; 7/2/70, North Ridgeville, Ohio. 6-1, 185. Drafted by New York Islanders (9th choice, 133rd overall) in 1989 Entry Draft. Signed as a free agent by Boston Bruins (7/1/94). Signed as a free agent by Florida Panthers (7/24/95). Signed as a free agent by Boston (9/4/96). Last amateur club; Bowling Green (CCHA).

Todd Harkins — Center

Regular Season — Playoffs

Season	Team	League	GP	G	A	PTS	PIM	GP	G	A	PTS	PIM
90-91	Salt Lake City	IHL	79	15	27	42	113	3	0	0	0	0
91-92	Calgary	NHL	5	0	0	0	7	—	—	—	—	—
91-92	Salt Lake City	IHL	72	32	30	62	67	5	1	1	2	0
92-93	Calgary	NHL	15	2	3	5	22	—	—	—	—	—
92-93	Salt Lake City	IHL	53	13	21	34	90	—	—	—	—	—
93-94	Hartford	NHL	28	1	0	1	49	—	—	—	—	—
93-94	Saint John	AHL	38	13	9	22	64	—	—	—	—	—
93-94	Springfield	AHL	1	0	3	3	2	9	0	0	0	6
94-95	Chicago	IHL	52	18	25	43	136	—	—	—	—	—
94-95	Houston	IHL	25	9	10	19	77	4	1	1	2	28
95-96	Carolina	AHL	69	27	28	55	172	—	—	—	—	—
96-97	Fort Worth	IHL	60	12	13	25	131	—	—	—	—	—
96-97	Phoenix	IHL	16	4	3	7	24	—	—	—	—	—
97-98	Dusseldorfer	Germany	48	13	22	35	117	3	2	0	2	12
98-99	Schwenningen	Germany	51	25	9	34	137	—	—	—	—	—
	NHL	Totals	48	3	3	6	78	—	—	—	—	—
	IHL	Totals	357	103	129	232	638	12	2	2	4	28
	AHL	Totals	108	40	40	80	238	9	0	0	0	6

Born; 10/8/68, Cleveland, Ohio. 6-3, 210. Drafted by Calgary Flames (2nd choice, 42nd overall) in 1988 Entry Draft. Traded to Hartford Whalers by Calgary for Scott Morrow (1/24/94). Last amateur club; Miami (CCHA).

Tyler Harlton — Defenseman

Reg-ular Season — Playoffs

Season	Team	League	GP	G	A	PTS	PIM	GP	G	A	PTS	PIM
98-99	Worcester	AHL	58	2	5	7	94	—	—	—	—	—
98-99	Peoria	ECHL	6	0	2	2	40	—	—	—	—	—

Born; 1/11/76, Pense, Saskatchewan. 6-3, 201. Drafted by St. Louis Blues (2nd choice, 94th overall) in 1994 Entry Draft. Last amateur club; Michigan State (CCHA).

Duane Harmer — Defenseman

Regular Season — Playoffs

Season	Team	League	GP	G	A	PTS	PIM	GP	G	A	PTS	PIM
95-96	Roanoke	ECHL	69	5	13	18	120	3	0	0	0	4
96-97	Roanoke	ECHL	70	4	28	32	122	4	0	4	4	2
97-98	Roanoke	ECHL	66	10	40	50	94	9	1	2	3	16
98-99	Lowell	AHL	14	0	2	2	16	—	—	—	—	—
98-99	Providence	AHL	9	0	4	4	4	—	—	—	—	—
98-99	Roanoke	ECHL	41	6	18	24	56	12	2	5	7	0
	AHL	Totals	23	0	6	6	20	—	—	—	—	—
	ECHL	Totals	246	25	99	124	392	28	3	11	14	22

Born; 6/3/74, Fullarton, Ontario. 6-0, 190. Last amateur club; Detroit (OHL).

Joe Harney — Defenseman

Regular Season — Playoffs

Season	Team	League	GP	G	A	PTS	PIM	GP	G	A	PTS	PIM
97-98	Pee Dee	ECHL	4	0	1	1	6	—	—	—	—	—
97-98	Wheeling	ECHL	65	9	24	33	76	15	1	7	8	22
98-99	Providence	AHL	13	1	4	5	14	—	—	—	—	—
98-99	Wheeling	ECHL	15	2	4	6	24	—	—	—	—	—
98-99	Pensacola	ECHL	21	2	10	12	45	—	—	—	—	—
	ECHL	Totals	105	13	39	52	151	15	1	7	8	22

Born; 1/13/73, Hopkington, Massachusetts. 5-9, 187. Traded to Wheeling by Pee Dee with Matt Garzone for Eric Royal (10/97). Last amateur club; Boston College (Hockey East).

Derrek Harper — Defenseman

Regular Season — Playoffs

Season	Team	League	GP	G	A	PTS	PIM	GP	G	A	PTS	PIM
95-96	Tulsa	CeHL	4	0	0	0	12	—	—	—	—	—
95-96	Memphis	CeHL	3	0	0	0	0	—	—	—	—	—
95-96	Jacksonville	SHL	46	4	18	22	53	—	—	—	—	—
96-97	Memphis	CeHL	45	1	7	8	169	18	1	0	1	26
97-98	Memphis	CHL	45	3	7	10	181	3	0	0	0	10
98-99	Memphis	CHL	54	0	14	14	198	1	0	0	0	28
	CeHL	Totals	151	4	28	32	560	22	1	0	1	64

Born; 1/5/73, Princeton, British Columbia. 6-3, 210. Selected by San Antonio in 1998 CHL Expansion Draft.

Kelly Harper — Left Wing

Regular Season — Playoffs

Season	Team	League	GP	G	A	PTS	PIM	GP	G	A	PTS	PIM
94-95	Huntington	ECHL	60	12	14	26	100	4	2	1	3	2
95-96	Detroit	CoHL	7	1	1	2	7	—	—	—	—	—
95-96	Huntington	ECHL	57	13	32	45	95	—	—	—	—	—
96-97	Huntington	ECHL	58	14	49	63	52	—	—	—	—	—
97-98	Huntington	ECHL	53	31	47	78	37	4	0	2	2	2
98-99	Cincinnati	IHL	1	0	0	0	0	—	—	—	—	—
98-99	Adirondack	AHL	4	1	1	2	0	—	—	—	—	—
98-99	Lowell	AHL	7	0	1	1	0	—	—	—	—	—
98-99	Huntington	ECHL	57	23	42	65	43	—	—	—	—	—
	AHL	Totals	11	1	2	3	0	—	—	—	—	—
	ECHL	Totals	285	93	184	277	327	8	2	3	5	4

Born; 5/9/72, Sudbury, Ontario. 6-3, 190. Drafted by Calgary Flames (8th choice, 151st overall) in 1991 Entry Draft. Last amateur club; Michigan State (CCHA).

Regan Harper — Defenseman

Regular Season — Playoffs

Season	Team	League	GP	G	A	PTS	PIM	GP	G	A	PTS	PIM
96-97	Oklahoma City	CeHL	58	4	17	21	59	4	1	0	1	14
97-98	New Mexico	WPHL	64	8	28	36	56	10	0	3	3	27
98-99	Corpus Christi	WPHL	69	8	18	26	40	4	0	2	2	4
	WPHL	Totals	133	16	46	62	96	14	0	5	5	31

Born; 11/23/71, Birch Hills, Saskatchewan. 6-2, 190. Traded to Corpus Christi by New Mexico for future considerations (8/98). Last amateur club; Lethbridge (CWUAA).

Darcy Harris — Right Wing

Regular Season — Playoffs

Season	Team	League	GP	G	A	PTS	PIM	GP	G	A	PTS	PIM
98-99	Fredericton	AHL	31	3	3	6	97	3	0	0	0	0

Born; 12/22/78, O'Leary, Prince Edward Island. 6-1, 194. Drafted by Montreal Canadiens (10th choice, 247th overall) in 1998 Entry Draft. Last amateur club; Kitchener (OHL).

Ross Harris — Left Wing
Regular Season — Playoffs

Season	Team	League	GP	G	A	PTS	PIM	GP	G	A	PTS	PIM
94-95	Dallas	CeHL	40	14	21	35	15	—	—	—	—	—
94-95	San Antonio	CeHL	13	2	2	4	16	—	—	—	—	—
95-96	Bakersfield	WCHL	58	35	48	83	77	—	—	—	—	—
96-97	Oklahoma City	CeHL	15	3	4	7	4	—	—	—	—	—
96-97	Bakersfield	WCHL	22	8	7	15	42	—	—	—	—	—
96-97	Reno	WCHL	35	20	23	43	24	—	—	—	—	—
97-98	San Angelo	WPHL	57	40	61	101	52	3	1	1	2	0
98-99	San Angelo	WPHL	69	41	56	97	32	17	6	11	17	24
	WPHL	Totals	126	81	117	198	84	20	7	12	19	24
	WCHL	Totals	115	63	78	141	143	—	—	—	—	—
	CeHL	Totals	68	19	27	46	31	—	—	—	—	—

Born; 12/14/73, Victoria, British Columbia. 6-0, 185. 1995-96 WCHL Second Team All-Star. Last amateur club; Victoria (WHL).

Shawn Harris — Right Wing
Regular Season — Playoffs

Season	Team	League	GP	G	A	PTS	PIM	GP	G	A	PTS	PIM
96-97	Port Huron	CoHL	3	1	0	1	17	—	—	—	—	—
96-97	Madison	CoHL	25	4	4	8	63	3	0	0	0	0
97-98	Saginaw	UHL	3	0	0	0	14	—	—	—	—	—
98-99	Colorado	WCHL	33	3	3	6	217	1	0	0	0	35
	UHL	Totals	31	5	4	9	94	3	0	0	0	0

Born; 8/4/75, Sarnia, Ontario. 5-10, 190.

Tim Harris — Right Wing
Regular Season — Playoffs

Season	Team	League	GP	G	A	PTS	PIM	GP	G	A	PTS	PIM
93-94	South Carolina	ECHL	60	13	35	48	137	2	0	1	1	2
94-95	Utica	CoHL	60	15	28	43	92	6	2	2	4	16
95-96	Detroit	CoHL	59	22	23	45	148	10	1	3	4	14
96-97	Port Huron	CoHL	47	6	14	20	65	—	—	—	—	—
96-97	Utica	CoHL	20	10	10	20	23	3	1	1	2	0
97-98	Winston-Salem	UHL	68	11	19	30	89	—	—	—	—	—
98-99	Springfield	AHL	1	1	0	1	0	—	—	—	—	—
98-99	Mohawk Valley	UHL	71	18	27	45	60	—	—	—	—	—
	UHL	Totals	325	82	121	203	477	19	4	6	10	30

Born; 10/16/67, Uxbridge, Ontario. 6-2, 190. Drafted by Calgary Flames (5th choice, 70th overall) in 1987 Entry Draft. Selected by Mohawk Valley in 1998 UHL Expansion Draft. Last amateur club; Lake Superior State (CCHA).

Toby Harris — Forward
Regular Season — Playoffs

Season	Team	League	GP	G	A	PTS	PIM	GP	G	A	PTS	PIM
97-98	Klostersee	Germany	62	59	66	125	82	—	—	—	—	—
98-99	Salzgitter	Germany	12	10	12	22	32	—	—	—	—	—
98-99	El Paso	WPHL	44	22	39	61	29	3	2	0	2	0

Born; 1/27/73, Kingston, Massachusetts. 6-0, 198. Last amateur club; Boston College (Hockey East).

Dan Harrison — Defenseman
Regular Season — Playoffs

Season	Team	League	GP	G	A	PTS	PIM	GP	G	A	PTS	PIM
96-97	Hampton Roads	ECHL	5	1	3	4	0	—	—	—	—	—
96-97	Johnstown	ECHL	26	3	20	23	91	—	—	—	—	—
97-98	Johnstown	ECHL	66	7	23	30	153	—	—	—	—	—
98-99	Kansas City	IHL	10	1	8	9	4	—	—	—	—	—
98-99	Shreveport	WPHL	15	0	4	4	12	—	—	—	—	—
98-99	Arkansas	WPHL	41	2	14	16	107	3	0	2	2	6
	ECHL	Totals	97	11	46	57	244	—	—	—	—	—
	WPHL	Totals	56	2	18	20	119	3	0	2	2	6

Born; 4/22/75, Newmarket, Ontario. 5-11, 180. Last amateur club; Ohio State (CCHA).

Josh Harrold — Defenseman
Regular Season — Playoffs

Season	Team	League	GP	G	A	PTS	PIM	GP	G	A	PTS	PIM
98-99	Miami-Ohio	CCHA	36	3	10	13	42	—	—	—	—	—
98-99	Dayton	ECHL	7	1	4	5	8	4	0	0	0	2

Born; 6/25/76, Kirtkand Hills, Ontario. 6-1, 205. Last amateur club; Miami-Ohio (CCHA).

Ty Hartigan — Right Wing
Regular Season — Playoffs

Season	Team	League	GP	G	A	PTS	PIM	GP	G	A	PTS	PIM
97-98	Monroe	WPHL	63	13	11	24	15	—	—	—	—	—
98-99	Monroe	WPHL	13	4	0	4	4	6	1	1	2	6
	WPHL	Totals	76	17	11	28	19	6	1	1	2	6

Born; 9/18/74, St. Louis, Missouri. 6-2, 180. Selected by Alexandria in 1998 WPHL Expansion Draft. Last amateur club; University of Alabama-Huntsville

Mike Hartman — Left Wing
Regular Season — Playoffs

Season	Team	League	GP	G	A	PTS	PIM	GP	G	A	PTS	PIM
86-87	Buffalo	NHL	17	3	3	6	69	—	—	—	—	—
87-88	Buffalo	NHL	18	3	1	4	90	6	0	0	0	35
87-88	Rochester	AHL	57	13	14	27	283	4	1	0	1	22
88-89	Buffalo	NHL	70	8	9	17	316	5	0	0	0	34
89-90	Buffalo	NHL	60	11	10	21	211	6	0	0	0	18
90-91	Buffalo	NHL	60	9	3	12	204	2	0	0	0	17
91-92	Winnipeg	NHL	75	4	4	8	264	2	0	0	0	2
92-93	Tampa Bay	NHL	58	4	4	8	154	—	—	—	—	—
92-93	Rangers	NHL	3	0	0	0	6	—	—	—	—	—
93-94	Rangers	NYR	35	1	1	2	70	—	—	—	—	—
94-95	Rangers	NHL	1	0	0	0	4	—	—	—	—	—
94-95	Detroit	IHL	6	1	0	1	52	1	0	0	0	0
95-96	Orlando	IHL	77	14	10	24	243	21	2	2	4	31
96-97	Hershey	AHL	42	5	8	13	116	1	0	0	0	0
97-98	Charlotte	ECHL	53	30	18	48	79	7	4	0	4	11
98-99	Kolner Haie	Germany	43	6	3	9	156	—	—	—	—	—
	NHL	Totals	397	43	35	78	1388	21	0	0	0	106
	AHL	Totals	99	18	22	40	399	5	1	0	1	22
	IHL	Totals	83	15	10	23	295	22	2	2	4	31

Born; 2/7/67, Detroit, Michigan. 6-0, 190. Drafted by Buffalo Sabres (8th choice, 131st overall) in 1986 Entry Draft. Traded to Winnipeg Jets by Buffalo with Darrin Shannon and Dean Kennedy for Dave McLlwain, Gord Donnelly, Winnipeg's fifth round choice (Yuri Khmylev) in 1992 Entry Draft and future considerations (10/11/91). Claimed by Tampa Bay Lightning from Winnipeg in Expansion Draft (6/18/92). Traded to New York Rangers by Tampa Bay for Randy Gilhen (3/22/93). Signed as a free agent by Colorado Avalanche (9/26/96). Member of 1996-97 AHL Champion Hershey Bears. Last amateur club; North Bay

Rob Hartnell — Center
Regular Season — Playoffs

Season	Team	League	GP	G	A	PTS	PIM	GP	G	A	PTS	PIM
93-94	Richmond	ECHL	29	4	11	15	87	—	—	—	—	—
93-94	Dayton	ECHL	37	9	15	24	133	3	0	0	0	20
94-95	Dayton	ECHL	62	21	26	47	211	7	1	1	2	15
95-96	Huntington	ECHL	35	8	16	24	132	—	—	—	—	—
96-97	El Paso	WPHL	47	23	37	60	76	—	—	—	—	—
96-97	Waco	WPHL	20	8	18	26	18	—	—	—	—	—
97-98	Austin	WPHL	60	27	12	39	203	—	—	—	—	—
97-98	Amarillo	WPHL	7	6	5	11	14	—	—	—	—	—
98-99	Monroe	WPHL	45	25	32	57	96	6	2	4	6	12
	WPHL	Totals	179	89	104	193	407	6	2	4	6	12
	ECHL	Totals	163	42	68	110	563	10	1	1	2	15

Born; 11/18/72, Rocky Mountain House, Alberta. 5-9, 170. Traded to Austin by Waco for Jay Hutton and Steve Jones (10/97). Last amateur club; Tri-City

Greg Harvey — Defenseman
Regular Season — Playoffs

Season	Team	League	GP	G	A	PTS	PIM	GP	G	A	PTS	PIM
98-99	Wichita	CHL	6	0	0	0	6	—	—	—	—	—

Born; 4/8/76, Saskatoon, Saskatchewan. 6-0, 215.

Chris Haskett — Center
Regular Season / Playoffs

Season	Team	League	GP	G	A	PTS	PIM	GP	G	A	PTS	PIM
97-98	Erie	OHL	5	1	2	3	4	—	—	—	—	—
97-98	Austin	WPHL	58	4	5	9	69	—	—	—	—	—
97-98	Waco	WPHL	7	1	0	1	4	—	—	—	—	—
98-99	Macon	CHL	3	1	0	1	2	—	—	—	—	—
	WPHL	Totals	65	5	5	10	73	—	—	—	—	—

Born; 3/18/77, Lucan, Ontario. 6-1, 220. Traded to Waco by Austin with Derek Riley and Jason Rose for Rob Schriner (3/98). Last amateur club; Erie (OHL).

Brett Hauer — Defenseman
Regular Season / Playoffs

Season	Team	League	GP	G	A	PTS	PIM	GP	G	A	PTS	PIM
93-94	United States	National	57	6	14	20	88	—	—	—	—	—
93-94	United States	Olympic	8	0	0	0	10	—	—	—	—	—
93-94	Las Vegas	IHL	21	0	7	7	8	1	0	0	0	0
94-95	AJK	Sweden	37	1	3	4	38	—	—	—	—	—
95-96	Edmonton	NHL	29	4	2	6	30	—	—	—	—	—
95-96	Cape Breton	AHL	17	3	5	8	29	—	—	—	—	—
96-97	Chicago	IHL	81	10	30	40	50	4	2	0	2	4
97-98	Manitoba	IHL	82	13	48	61	58	3	0	0	0	2
98-99	Manitoba	IHL	81	15	56	71	66	5	0	5	5	4
	IHL	Totals	265	38	141	179	182	13	2	5	7	10

Born; 7/11/71, Edina, Minnesota. 6-2, 205. Drafted by Vancouver Canucks (3rd choice, 71st overall) in 1989 Entry Draft. Traded to Edmonton Oilers by Vancouver for Edmonton's seventh round pick (Larry Shapley) in 1997 Entry Draft, (8/24/95). 1998-99 IHL First Team All-Star. Last amateur club; Minnesota-

Radim Haupt — Left Wing
Regular Season / Playoffs

Season	Team	League	GP	G	A	PTS	PIM	GP	G	A	PTS	PIM
98-99	Mohawk Valley	UHL	6	1	0	1	15	—	—	—	—	—

Born; 6/24/71, Pardubice, Czech Republic. 5-11, 200.

Kyle Haviland — Defenseman
Regular Season / Playoffs

Season	Team	League	GP	G	A	PTS	PIM	GP	G	A	PTS	PIM
92-93	West Palm Beach	SUN	41	1	17	18	75	—	—	—	—	—
92-93	Roanoke	ECHL	3	0	0	0	32	—	—	—	—	—
93-94	Memphis	CeHL	59	2	11	13	151	—	—	—	—	—
94-95	Memphis	CeHL	61	7	19	26	215	—	—	—	—	—
95-96	Muskegon	CoHL	68	2	10	12	180	5	0	1	1	21
96-97	Austin	WPHL	40	1	4	5	130	6	0	1	1	40
97-98	Austin	WPHL	60	2	9	11	170	5	0	0	0	6
98-99	Topeka	CHL	63	5	3	8	147	3	0	0	0	30
	CHL	Totals	183	14	33	47	513	3	0	0	0	30
	WPHL	Totals	100	3	13	16	300	11	0	1	1	46

Born; 8/10/71, Windsor, Ontario. 6-0, 215.

Greg Hawgood — Defenseman
Regular Season / Playoffs

Season	Team	League	GP	G	A	PTS	PIM	GP	G	A	PTS	PIM
87-88	Boston	NHL	1	0	0	0	0	3	1	0	1	0
88-89	Boston	NHL	56	16	24	40	84	10	0	2	2	2
88-89	Maine	AHL	21	2	9	11	41	—	—	—	—	—
89-90	Boston	NHL	77	11	27	38	76	15	1	3	4	12
90-91	Asiago	Italy	2	3	0	3	9	—	—	—	—	—
90-91	Edmonton	NHL	6	0	1	1	6	—	—	—	—	—
90-91	Maine	AHL	5	0	1	1	13	—	—	—	—	—
90-91	Cape Breton	AHL	55	10	32	42	73	4	0	3	3	23
91-92	Edmonton	NHL	20	2	11	13	22	13	0	3	3	23
91-92	Cape Breton	AHL	56	20	55	75	26	3	2	2	4	0
92-93	Edmonton	NHL	29	5	13	18	35	—	—	—	—	—
92-93	Philadelphia	NHL	40	6	22	28	39	—	—	—	—	—
93-94	Philadelphia	NHL	19	3	12	15	19	—	—	—	—	—
93-94	Florida	NHL	33	2	14	16	9	—	—	—	—	—
93-94	Pittsburgh	NHL	12	1	2	3	8	1	0	0	0	0
94-95	Pittsburgh	NHL	21	1	4	5	25	—	—	—	—	—
94-95	Cleveland	IHL	—	—	—	—	—	3	1	0	1	4
95-96	Las Vegas	IHL	78	20	65	85	101	15	5	11	16	24
96-97	San Jose	NHL	63	6	12	18	69	—	—	—	—	—
97-98	Kolner Haie	Germany	4	0	1	1	16	—	—	—	—	—
97-98	Kolner Haie	EHL	1	0	0	0	2	—	—	—	—	—
97-98	Houston	IHL	81	19	52	71	75	4	0	4	4	0
98-99	Houston	IHL	76	17	57	74	90	19	4	8	12	24
	NHL	Totals	377	53	142	195	392	42	2	8	10	37
	IHL	Totals	235	56	117	174	266	41	10	23	33	52
	AHL	Totals	137	32	97	129	153	7	2	5	7	23

Born; 8/10/68, Edmonton, Alberta. 5-10, 190. Drafted by Boston Bruins (9th choice, 202nd overall) in 1986 Entry Draft. Traded to Edmonton Oilers by Boston for Vladimir Ruzicka (10/22/90). Traded to Philadelphia Flyers by Edmonton with Josef Beranek for Brian Benning (1/16/93). Traded to Florida Panthers by Philadelphia for cash (10/30/93). Traded to Pittsburgh Penguins by Florida for Jeff Daniels (3/19/94). Signed as a free agent by San Jose Sharks (9/25/96). 1991-92 AHL First All-Star Team. 1991-92 AHL Eddie Shore Plaque (Top Defenseman). 1995-96 IHL First All-Star Team. 1995-96 IHL Governors' Trophy (Top Defenseman). 1997-98 IHL First All-Star Team. 1998-99 IHL Governors' Trophy (Top Defenseman). 1998-99 IHL First All-Star Team. Member of 1998-99 IHL Champion Houston Aeros. Scored Turner Cup-winning goal for Aeros. Last

Todd Hawkins — Left Wing
Regular Season / Playoffs

Season	Team	League	GP	G	A	PTS	PIM	GP	G	A	PTS	PIM
87-88	Flint	IHL	50	13	13	26	337	16	3	5	8	*174
87-88	Fredericton	AHL	2	0	4	4	11	—	—	—	—	—
88-89	Vancouver	NHL	4	0	0	0	9	—	—	—	—	—
88-89	Milwaukee	IHL	63	12	14	26	307	9	1	0	1	33
89-90	Vancouver	NHL	4	0	0	0	6	—	—	—	—	—
89-90	Milwaukee	IHL	61	23	17	40	273	5	4	1	5	19
90-91	New Haven	AHL	22	2	5	7	66	—	—	—	—	—
90-91	Milwaukee	IHL	39	9	11	20	134	—	—	—	—	—
91-92	Toronto	NHL	2	0	0	0	0	—	—	—	—	—
91-92	St. John's	AHL	66	30	27	57	139	7	1	0	1	10
92-93	St. John's	AHL	72	21	41	62	103	9	1	3	4	10
93-94	Cleveland	IHL	76	19	14	33	115	—	—	—	—	—
94-95	Cleveland	IHL	4	2	0	2	29	—	—	—	—	—
94-95	Minnesota	IHL	47	10	8	18	95	3	0	1	1	12
95-96	Cincinnati	IHL	73	16	12	28	65	17	7	4	11	32
96-97	Cincinnati	IHL	81	13	13	26	162	3	0	1	1	2
97-98	Cincinnati	IHL	71	13	23	36	168	9	0	3	3	36
98-99	Cincinnati	IHL	82	20	32	52	171	3	2	1	3	8
	NHL	Totals	10	0	0	0	15	—	—	—	—	—
	IHL	Totals	647	150	157	307	1856	65	17	16	33	316
	AHL	Totals	162	53	77	130	319	16	2	3	5	20

Born; 8/2/66, Kingston, Ontario. 6-1, 195. Drafted by Vancouver Canucks (10th choice, 217th overall) in 1986 Entry Draft. Traded to Toronto Maple Leafs by Vancouver for Brian Blad (1/22/91). Signed as a free agent by Pittsburgh Penguins (8/20/93). Last amateur club; Belleville (OHL).

Dwayne Hay — Left Wing

Regular Season / Playoffs

Season	Team	League	GP	G	A	PTS	PIM	GP	G	A	PTS	PIM
97-98	Washington	NHL	2	0	0	0	2	—	—	—	—	—
97-98	Portland	AHL	58	6	7	13	35	—	—	—	—	—
97-98	New Haven	AHL	10	3	2	5	4	2	0	0	0	0
98-99	Florida	NHL	9	0	0	0	0	—	—	—	—	—
98-99	New Haven	AHL	46	18	17	35	22	—	—	—	—	—
	NHL	Totals	11	0	0	0	2	—	—	—	—	—
	AHL	Totals	114	27	26	53	61	2	0	0	0	0

Born; 2/11/77, London, Ontario. 6-1, 183. Drafted by Washington Capitals (3rd choice, 43rd overall) in 1995 Entry Draft. Traded to Florida Panthers with future considerations for Esa Tikkanen (3/9/98). Last amateur club; Guelph (OHL).

Craig Hayden — Defenseman

Regular Season / Playoffs

Season	Team	League	GP	G	A	PTS	PIM	GP	G	A	PTS	PIM
96-97	Amarillo	WPHL	31	0	3	3	22	—	—	—	—	—
97-98	Fort Worth	WPHL	52	3	12	15	44	13	0	2	2	23
98-99	Fort Worth	WPHL	50	1	5	6	61	—	—	—	—	—
98-99	Waco	WPHL	15	0	2	2	14	1	0	0	0	0
	WPHL	Totals	148	4	22	26	141	14	0	2	2	23

Born; 2/18/75, Saskatoon, Saskatchewan. 6-0, 210.

Jamie Hayden — Defenseman

Regular Season / Playoffs

Season	Team	League	GP	G	A	PTS	PIM	GP	G	A	PTS	PIM
92-93	Thunder Bay	CoHL	59	0	11	11	24	11	4	5	9	2
93-94	Thunder Bay	CoHL	43	2	13	15	22	—	—	—	—	—
93-94	Utica	CoHL	7	0	0	0	0	—	—	—	—	—
94-95	Thunder Bay	CoHL	32	1	5	6	21	—	—	—	—	—
94-95	Utica	CoHL	25	1	6	7	12	6	0	1	1	6
95-96	Thunder Bay	CoHL	42	2	6	8	26	—	—	—	—	—
95-96	Utica	CoHL	12	0	3	3	10	—	—	—	—	—
95-96	Brantford	CoHL	12	2	5	7	10	11	0	0	0	10
96-97	Brantford	CoHL	31	3	9	12	37	—	—	—	—	—
96-97	Utica	CoHL	35	1	9	10	24	3	0	0	0	2
97-98	Saginaw	UHL	74	1	14	15	48	—	—	—	—	—
98-99	Saginaw	UHL	74	3	14	17	33	—	—	—	—	—
	CoHL	Totals	446	16	95	111	265	31	4	6	10	20

Born; 4/19/72, Saskatoon, Saskatchewan. 6-0, 195. Last amateur club; Regina (WHL).

Harlin Hayes — Goaltender

Regular Season / Playoffs

Season	Team	League	GP	W	L	T	MIN	SO	AVG	GP	W	L	MIN	SO	AVG
98-99	Portland	AHL	1	0	0	0	20	0	0.00	—	—	—	—	—	—
98-99	Columbus	ECHL	18	7	7	1	934	1	3.40	2	0	1	107	0	*1.12

Born; 2/18/77, Stellarton, Nova Scotia. 6-0, 190. Selected by Johnstown in 1999 ECHL Dispersal Draft.

Rick Hayward — Defenseman

Regular Season / Playoffs

Season	Team	League	GP	G	A	PTS	PIM	GP	G	A	PTS	PIM
86-87	Sherbrook	AHL	43	2	3	5	153	3	0	1	1	15
87-88	Sherbrook	AHL	22	1	5	6	91	—	—	—	—	—
87-88	Saginaw	IHL	24	3	4	7	129	—	—	—	—	—
87-88	Salt Lake City	IHL	17	1	3	4	124	13	0	1	1	120
88-89	Salt Lake City	IHL	72	4	20	24	313	10	4	3	7	42
89-90	Salt Lake City	IHL	58	5	13	18	*419	—	—	—	—	—
90-91	Los Angeles	NHL	4	0	0	0	5	—	—	—	—	—
90-91	Phoenix	IHL	60	9	13	22	369	7	1	2	3	44
91-92	Capital District	AHL	27	3	8	11	139	7	0	0	0	58
92-93	Moncton	AHL	47	1	3	4	231	4	1	1	2	27
92-93	Capital District	AHL	19	0	1	1	80	—	—	—	—	—
93-94	Cincinnati	IHL	61	2	6	8	302	8	0	1	1	*99
94-95	Cleveland	IHL	56	1	3	4	269	3	0	0	0	13
95-96	Cleveland	IHL	53	0	6	6	244	3	0	0	0	6
96-97	Cleveland	IHL	73	2	10	12	244	13	0	0	0	36
97-98	Cleveland	IHL	41	1	3	4	191	—	—	—	—	—
97-98	Quebec	IHL	13	0	3	3	108	—	—	—	—	—
98-99	Frankfurt	Germany	22	0	0	0	113	1	0	0	0	27
	IHL	Totals	528	28	84	112	2712	57	5	7	12	360
	AHL	Totals	158	7	20	27	694	14	1	2	3	100

Born; 2/25/66, Toledo, Ohio. 6-2, 200. Drafted by Montreal Canadiens (9th choice, 162nd overall) in 1986 Entry Draft. Traded to Calgary Flames by Montreal for Martin Nicoletti (2/20/88). Signed as a free agent by Los Angeles Kings (8/90). Signed as a free agent by New York Islanders (7/25/91). Signed as a free agent by Winnipeg Jets (7/30/92). Traded to Islanders by Winnipeg for future considerations (2/22/93). Signed as a free agent by Florida Panthers (9/7/93). Signed as a free agent by Cleveland Lumberjacks (6/24/94). Traded to Quebec by Cleveland with Ryan Mougenal, John Craighead, Eric Perrin, Pat Jablonski and Burke Murphy for Rick Girard, Dale DeGray, Darcy Simon, Tom Draper and Jason Ruff (3/98). Member of 1987-88 IHL champion Salt Lake City Golden

Eric Healey — Left Wing

Regular Season / Playoffs

Season	Team	League	GP	G	A	PTS	PIM	GP	G	A	PTS	PIM
98-99	Saint John	AHL	64	14	24	38	77	—	—	—	—	—
98-99	Orlando	IHL	13	5	4	9	13	8	1	0	1	12

Born; 1/20/75, Hull, Massachusetts. 6-0, 195. Signed as a free agent by Calgary Flames. Traded to Orlando Solar Bears by Saint John Flames with Tyler Moss for Allan Egeland and Arttu Kayhko (3/99). Signed as a free agent by Phoenix Coyotes (7/26/99). Last amateur club; RPI (ECAC).

Paul Healey — Right Wing

Regular Season / Playoffs

Season	Team	League	GP	G	A	PTS	PIM	GP	G	A	PTS	PIM
95-96	Hershey	AHL	60	7	15	22	35	—	—	—	—	—
96-97	Philadelphia	NHL	2	0	0	0	0	—	—	—	—	—
96-97	Philadelphia	AHL	64	21	19	40	56	10	1	4	5	10
97-98	Philadelphia	NHL	4	0	0	0	12	—	—	—	—	—
97-98	Philadelphia	AHL	71	34	18	52	48	20	6	2	8	4
98-99	Philadelphia	AHL	72	26	20	46	39	15	4	6	10	11
	NHL	Totals	6	0	0	0	12	—	—	—	—	—
	AHL	Totals	267	88	72	160	178	45	11	12	23	25

Born; 3/20/75, Edmonton, Alberta. 6-2, 185. Drafted by Philadelphia Flyers (7th choice, 192nd overall) in 1993 Entry Draft. Last amateur club; Prince Albert

Glenn Healy — Goaltender

Regular Season / Playoffs

Season	Team	League	GP	W	L	T	MIN	SO	AVG	GP	W	L	MIN	SO	AVG
85-86	Los Angeles	NHL	1	0	0	0	51	0	7.06	—	—	—	—	—	—
85-86	New Haven	AHL	43	21	15	4	2410	0	3.98	2	0	2	49	0	5.55
86-87	New Haven	AHL	47	21	15	0	2828	1	3.67	7	3	4	427	0	2.67
87-88	Los Angeles	NHL	34	12	18	1	1869	1	4.33	4	1	3	240	0	5.00
88-89	Los Angeles	NHL	48	25	19	2	2699	0	4.27	3	0	1	97	0	3.71
89-90	Islanders	NHL	39	12	19	6	2197	2	3.50	4	1	2	166	0	3.25
90-91	Islanders	NHL	53	18	24	9	2999	0	3.32	—	—	—	—	—	—
91-92	Islanders	NHL	37	14	16	4	1960	1	3.80	—	—	—	—	—	—
92-93	Islanders	NHL	47	22	20	2	2655	1	3.30	18	9	8	1109	0	3.19
93-94	Rangers	NHL	29	10	12	2	1368	2	3.03	2	0	0	68	0	0.88
94-95	Rangers	NHL	17	8	6	1	888	1	2.36	5	2	1	230	0	3.39
95-96	Rangers	NHL	44	17	14	11	2564	2	2.90	—	—	—	—	—	—
96-97	Rangers	NHL	23	5	12	4	1357	1	2.61	—	—	—	—	—	—
97-98	Toronto	NHL	21	4	10	2	1068	0	2.98	—	—	—	—	—	—
98-99	Toronto	NHL	9	6	3	0	546	0	2.97	1	0	0	20	0	0.00
98-99	Chicago	IHL	10	6	3	1	597	0	3.32	—	—	—	—	—	—
	NHL	Totals	402	153	173	44	22221	11	3.41	37	13	15	1930	0	3.36
	AHL	Totals	90	42	30	4	5238	1	3.81	9	3	6	476	0	3.78

Born; 8/23/62, Pickering, Ontario. 5-10, 185. Signed as a free agent by Los Angeles Kings (6/13/85). Signed as a free agent by New York Islanders (8/16/89). Claimed by Anaheim Mighty Ducks from Islanders in Expansion Draft (6/24/93). Claimed by Tampa Bay Lightning from Anaheim in Phase II of Expansion Draft (6/25/93). Traded to New York Rangers by Tampa Bay for Tampa Bay's third round choice, (previously acquired, Tampa Bay selected Allan Egelund) in 1993 Entry Draft (6/25/93). Signed as a free agent by Toronto Maple Leafs (8/8/97). Member of 1993-94 Stanley Cup Champion New York Rangers. Last amateur club; Western Michigan (CCHA).

Don Hearn — Right Wing

Regular Season / Playoffs

Season	Team	League	GP	G	A	PTS	PIM	GP	G	A	PTS	PIM
97-98	Monroe	WPHL	58	18	19	37	210	—	—	—	—	—
98-99	Monroe	WPHL	66	37	23	60	102	6	2	3	5	4
	WPHL	Totals	124	55	42	97	312	6	2	3	5	4

Born; 4/11/73, Calgary, Alberta. 5-9, 215. Last amateur club; St. Norbert (NCAA

Jamie Hearn — Defenseman

Regular Season / Playoffs

Season	Team	League	GP	G	A	PTS	PIM	GP	G	A	PTS	PIM
92-93	Oklahoma City	CeHL	59	10	28	38	161	11	2	5	7	40
93-94	Wichita	CeHL	54	4	16	20	120	—	—	—	—	—
93-94	Memphis	CeHL	10	4	5	9	8	—	—	—	—	—
94-95	Memphis	CeHL	57	6	28	34	154	—	—	—	—	—
95-96	Muskegon	CoHL	48	5	22	27	139	—	—	—	—	—
95-96	Flint	CoHL	13	0	4	4	20	15	4	3	7	50
96-97	Phoenix	IHL	2	0	1	1	0	—	—	—	—	—
96-97	Waco	WPHL	62	14	39	53	166	—	—	—	—	—
97-98	Waco	WPHL	58	9	31	40	86	—	—	—	—	—
97-98	Central Texas	WPHL	10	3	8	11	21	4	1	6	7	6
98-99	Central Texas	WPHL	67	14	46	60	161	2	0	0	0	2
	WPHL	Totals	197	40	124	164	434	6	1	6	7	8
	CeHL	Totals	180	24	77	101	443	11	2	5	7	40

Born; 2/23/71, Quesnel, British Columbia. 6-1, 210. Traded to Austin by Waco for Eric Preston (9/98). Traded to Central Texas by Austin for Jeff Melnechuk and Peter Zurba (9/98). Member of 1995-96 Colonial Cup Champion Flint Gener-

Jay Hebert — Left Wing

Regular Season / Playoffs

Season	Team	League	GP	G	A	PTS	PIM	GP	G	A	PTS	PIM
98-99	Quad City	UHL	16	4	3	7	13	—	—	—	—	—
98-99	Mississippi	ECHL	3	0	1	1	0	—	—	—	—	—
98-99	Pensacola	ECHL	10	1	0	1	4	—	—	—	—	—
	ECHL	Totals	13	1	1	2	4	—	—	—	—	—

Born; 3/22/75, Troy, New York. 6-1, 210. Last amateur club; SUNY-Oswego (NCAA 3).

Jochen Hecht — Center

Regular Season / Playoffs

Season	Team	League	GP	G	A	PTS	PIM	GP	G	A	PTS	PIM
98-99	St. Louis	NHL	3	0	0	0	0	5	2	0	2	0
98-99	Worcester	AHL	74	21	35	56	48	4	1	1	2	2

Born; 6/21/77, Mannheim, Germany. 6-1, 180. Drafted by St. Louis Blues (1st choice, 49th overall) in 1995 Entry Draft. Last overseas club; Mannheim

Johan Hedberg — Goaltender

Regular Season / Playoffs

Season	Team	League	GP	W	L	T	MIN	SO	AVG	GP	W	L	MIN	SO	AVG
97-98	Baton Rouge	ECHL	2	1	1	0	100	0	4.20	—	—	—	—	—	—
97-98	Detroit	IHL	16	7	2	2	726	1	2.64	—	—	—	—	—	—
97-98	Manitoba	IHL	14	8	4	1	745	1	2.58	2	0	2	105	0	3.40
98-99	Leksand	Sweden	48	—	—	—	2940	0	2.86	4	—	—	255	0	3.53
	IHL	Totals	30	15	6	3	1471	2	2.61	2	0	2	105	0	3.40

Born; 5/5/73, Leksand, Sweden. 5-11, 180. Drafted by Philadelphia Flyers (8th choice, 218th overall) in 1994 Entry Draft. Traded to San Jose Sharks by Philadelphia for San Jose's seventh round choice (Pavel Kasparik) in 1999 Entry Draft (8/6/98).

Eric Heffler — Goaltender

Regular Season / Playoffs

Season	Team	League	GP	W	L	T	MIN	SO	AVG	GP	W	L	MIN	SO	AVG
98-99	St. Lawrence	ECAC	37	22	12	3	2206	3	2.39	—	—	—	—	—	—
98-99	Hamilton	AHL	2	1	1	0	119	0	2.52	—	—	—	—	—	—

Born; 2/29/76, Geneva, New York. 6-3, 190. Signed as a free agent by Edmonton Oilers (4/8/99). Last amateur club; St. Lawrence (ECAC).

Jason Hehr — Defenseman

Regular Season / Playoffs

Season	Team	League	GP	G	A	PTS	PIM	GP	G	A	PTS	PIM
95-96	Kansas City	IHL	7	0	1	1	11	—	—	—	—	—
95-96	Raleigh	ECHL	43	5	11	16	36	4	0	1	1	0
96-97	South Carolina	ECHL	22	6	5	11	38	17	2	7	9	27
96-97	Solihull	BHL	41	24	35	59	95	—	—	—	—	—
97-98	Chicago	IHL	3	1	0	1	0	—	—	—	—	—
97-98	South Carolina	ECHL	52	6	19	25	84	5	1	4	5	2
98-99	South Carolina	ECHL	5	0	0	0	0	—	—	—	—	—
	IHL	Totals	10	1	1	2	11	—	—	—	—	—
	ECHL	Totals	122	17	35	52	158	26	3	12	15	29

Born; 2/8/71, Medicine Hat, Alberta. 6-1, 193. Drafted by New Jersey Devils (11th choice, 253rd overall) in 1991 Entry Draft. Selected by Greensboro in 1999 ECHL Expansion Draft. Member of 1996-97 ECHL Champion South Carolina Stingrays. Last amateur club; Northern Michigan (WCHA).

Jeff Heil — Goaltender

Regular Season / Playoffs

Season	Team	League	GP	W	L	T	MIN	SO	AVG	GP	W	L	MIN	SO	AVG
97-98	Hartford	AHL	1	0	0	1	35	0	0.00	—	—	—	—	—	—
97-98	Charlotte	ECHL	22	12	5	4	1241	2	3.34	—	—	—	—	—	—
98-99	Hartford	AHL	11	2	3	0	366	0	3.60	—	—	—	—	—	—
98-99	Charlotte	ECHL	22	7	11	3	1236	0	3.74	—	—	—	—	—	—
	AHL	Totals	12	2	3	1	401	0	3.29	—	—	—	—	—	—
	ECHL	Totals	44	19	16	7	2477	2	3.54	—	—	—	—	—	—

Born; 9/17/75, Bloomington, Minnesota. 6-1, 190. Drafted by New York Rangers (7th choice, 169th overall) in 1995 Entry Draft. Last amateur club; Wisconsin-River Falls (NCHA).

Shawn Heins
Defenseman

Regular Season / Playoffs

Season	Team	League	GP	G	A	PTS	PIM	GP	G	A	PTS	PIM
95-96	Cape Breton	AHL	1	0	0	0	0	—	—	—	—	—
95-96	Mobile	ECHL	62	7	20	27	152	—	—	—	—	—
96-97	Kansas City	IHL	6	0	0	0	9	—	—	—	—	—
96-97	Mobile	ECHL	56	6	17	23	253	3	0	2	2	2
97-98	Kansas City	IHL	82	22	28	50	303	11	1	0	1	49
98-99	San Jose	NHL	5	0	0	0	13	—	—	—	—	—
98-99	Kentucky	AHL	18	2	2	4	108	12	2	7	9	10
98-99	Canada	National	36	5	16	21	66	—	—	—	—	—
	IHL	Totals	88	22	28	50	312	11	1	0	1	49
	AHL	Totals	19	2	2	4	108	12	2	7	9	10
	ECHL	Totals	118	13	37	50	405	3	0	2	2	2

Born; 12/24/73, Eganville, Ontario. 6-3, 215. Signed as a free agent by San Jose (1998).

Sami Helenius
Defenseman

Regular Season / Playoffs

Season	Team	League	GP	G	A	PTS	PIM	GP	G	A	PTS	PIM
94-95	Saint John	AHL	69	2	5	7	217	—	—	—	—	—
95-96	Saint John	AHL	68	0	3	3	231	10	0	0	0	9
96-97	Calgary	NHL	3	0	1	1	0	—	—	—	—	—
96-97	Saint John	AHL	72	5	10	15	218	2	0	0	0	0
97-98	Saint John	AHL	63	1	2	3	185	—	—	—	—	—
97-98	Las Vegas	IHL	10	0	1	1	19	4	0	0	0	25
98-99	Calgary	NHL	4	0	0	0	8	—	—	—	—	—
98-99	Tampa Bay	NHL	4	1	0	1	15	—	—	—	—	—
98-99	Chicago	IHL	4	0	0	0	11	—	—	—	—	—
98-99	Las Vegas	IHL	42	2	3	5	193	—	—	—	—	—
98-99	Hershey	AHL	8	0	0	0	29	5	0	0	0	16
	NHL	Totals	11	1	1	2	23	—	—	—	—	—
	AHL	Totals	280	8	20	28	880	17	0	0	0	25
	IHL	Totals	56	2	4	6	223	4	0	0	0	25

Born; 1/22/74, Helsinki, Finland. 6-5, 225. Drafted by Calgary Flames (5th choice, 102nd overall) in 1992 Entry Draft. Traded to Las Vegas by Saint John with Keith McCambridge and Paxton Schulte for Steve Bancroft and Justin Kurtz (3/98). Traded to Tampa Bay Lightning by Calgary for future considerations and a conditional draft pick in 1999 (1/29/99). Traded to Colorado Avalanche by Tampa Bay for a conditional draft pick in 1999 (3/23/99). Last overseas club; Reipas Lahti (Finland).

Bryan Helmer
Defenseman

Regular Season / Playoffs

Season	Team	League	GP	G	A	PTS	PIM	GP	G	A	PTS	PIM
93-94	Albany	AHL	65	4	19	23	79	5	0	0	0	9
94-95	Albany	AHL	77	7	36	43	101	7	1	0	1	0
95-96	Albany	AHL	80	14	30	44	107	4	2	0	2	6
96-97	Albany	AHL	77	12	27	39	113	16	1	7	8	10
97-98	Albany	AHL	80	14	49	63	101	13	4	9	13	18
98-99	Phoenix	NHL	11	0	0	0	23	—	—	—	—	—
98-99	St. Louis	NHL	29	0	4	4	19	—	—	—	—	—
98-99	Las Vegas	IHL	8	1	3	4	28	—	—	—	—	—
98-99	Worcester	AHL	16	7	8	15	18	4	0	0	0	12
	NHL	Totals	40	0	4	4	42	—	—	—	—	—
	AHL	Totals	395	58	169	227	519	49	8	16	24	55

Born; 7/15/72, Sault Ste. Marie, Ontario. 6-1, 190. Signed as a free agent by New Jersey Devils (7/10/94). Signed as a free agent by Phoenix Coyotes (7/22/98). Claimed on waivers by St. Louis Blues from Phoenix (12/23/97). 1997-98 AHL First Team All-Star. Member of 1994-95 Calder Cup Champion Albany River-Rats. Last amateur club; Wellington (Jr. A).

Jeff Helperl
Defenseman

Regular Season / Playoffs

Season	Team	League	GP	G	A	PTS	PIM	GP	G	A	PTS	PIM
98-99	Saskatchewan	CWUAA	37	5	31	36	55	—	—	—	—	—
98-99	Tacoma	WCHL	—	—	—	—	—	9	0	3	3	27

Born; St. Walburg, Saskatchewan. 6-2, 205. Last amateur club; Saskatchewan (CWUAA).

Ken Hemenway
Defenseman

Regular Season / Playoffs

Season	Team	League	GP	G	A	PTS	PIM	GP	G	A	PTS	PIM
98-99	Tupelo	WPHL	66	8	19	27	53	—	—	—	—	—

Born; 8/1/75, Brighton, Massachusetts. 6-2, 205. Last amateur club; Boston College (Hockey East).

Burt Henderson
Defenseman

Regular Season / Playoffs

Season	Team	League	GP	G	A	PTS	PIM	GP	G	A	PTS	PIM
96-97	Birmingham	ECHL	68	10	42	52	38	8	0	3	3	6
97-98	Cincinnati	IHL	82	5	14	19	52	9	1	0	1	6
98-99	Cincinnati	IHL	80	9	24	33	84	3	0	0	0	4
	IHL	Totals	162	14	38	52	136	12	1	0	1	10

Born; 11/5/75, Burnaby, British Columbia. 6-0, 200. Last amateur club; Kelowna (WHL).

Jay Henderson
Left Wing

Regular Season / Playoffs

Season	Team	League	GP	G	A	PTS	PIM	GP	G	A	PTS	PIM
97-98	Edmonton	WHL	72	49	45	94	130	—	—	—	—	—
97-98	Providence	AHL	11	3	1	4	11	—	—	—	—	—
98-99	Boston	NHL	4	0	0	0	2	—	—	—	—	—
98-99	Providence	AHL	55	7	9	16	172	2	0	0	0	2
	AHL	Totals	66	10	10	20	183	2	0	0	0	2

Born; 9/17/78, Edmonton, Alberta. 5-11, 190. Drafted by Boston Bruins (12th choice, 246th overall) in 1997 Entry Draft. Member of 1998-99 AHL Champion Providence Bruins. Last amateur club; Edmonton (WHL).

Matt Henderson
Left Wing

Regular Season / Playoffs

Season	Team	League	GP	G	A	PTS	PIM	GP	G	A	PTS	PIM
98-99	Nashville	NHL	2	0	0	0	2	—	—	—	—	—
98-99	Milwaukee	IHL	77	19	19	38	117	2	0	0	0	0

Born; 6/22/74, White Bear Lake, Minnesota. 6-1, 200. Signed as a free agent by Nashville Predators (7/13/98). Last amateur club; North Dakota (WCHA).

Mike Henderson
Left Wing

Regular Season / Playoffs

Season	Team	League	GP	G	A	PTS	PIM	GP	G	A	PTS	PIM
96-97	Fresno	WCHL	14	7	3	10	95	—	—	—	—	—
96-97	Amarillo	WPHL	34	7	12	19	215	—	—	—	—	—
97-98	Odessa	WPHL	9	3	3	6	52	—	—	—	—	—
97-98	Lake Charles	WPHL	52	11	11	22	187	3	0	0	0	43
98-99	Thunder Bay	UHL	57	24	30	54	287	12	1	6	7	*65
	WPHL	Totals	95	21	26	47	454	3	0	0	0	43

Born; 3/24/74, Brampton, Ontario. 6-1, 210. Traded to Lake Charles by Odessa with Jeff Smith for Paul Fiorini (11/97).

Dan Hendrickson
Center

Regular Season / Playoffs

Season	Team	League	GP	G	A	PTS	PIM	GP	G	A	PTS	PIM
97-98	Michigan	IHL	19	2	2	4	30	—	—	—	—	—
97-98	Dayton	ECHL	39	4	9	13	35	5	1	1	2	16
98-99	Dayton	ECHL	70	14	26	40	96	4	1	0	1	6
	ECHL	Totals	109	18	35	53	131	9	2	1	3	22

Born; 12/26/74, Minneapolis, Minnesota. 5-10, 185. Last amateur club; Minnesota-Twin Cities (ACHA).

Niklas Henrikkson
Defenseman

Regular Season / Playoffs

Season	Team	League	GP	G	A	PTS	PIM	GP	G	A	PTS	PIM
98-99	Tallahassee	ECHL	5	0	0	0	4	—	—	—	—	—
98-99	Birmingham	ECHL	4	0	1	1	2	—	—	—	—	—
98-99	Peoria	ECHL	8	0	3	3	8	—	—	—	—	—
	ECHL	Totals	17	0	4	4	14	—	—	—	—	—

Born;

Dale Henry — Left Wing

Regular Season / Playoffs

Season	Team	League	GP	G	A	PTS	PIM	GP	G	A	PTS	PIM
84-85	Islanders	NHL	16	2	1	3	19	—	—	—	—	—
84-85	Springfield	AHL	67	11	20	31	133	4	0	0	0	13
85-86	Islanders	NHL	7	1	3	4	15	—	—	—	—	—
85-86	Springfield	AHL	64	14	26	40	162	—	—	—	—	—
86-87	Islanders	NHL	19	3	3	6	46	8	0	0	0	2
86-87	Springfield	AHL	23	9	14	23	49	—	—	—	—	—
87-88	Islanders	NHL	48	5	15	20	115	6	1	0	1	17
87-88	Springfield	AHL	24	9	12	21	103	—	—	—	—	—
88-89	Islanders	NHL	22	2	2	4	66	—	—	—	—	—
88-89	Springfield	AHL	50	13	21	34	83	—	—	—	—	—
90-91	Albany	IHL	55	16	22	38	87	—	—	—	—	—
90-91	Springfield	AHL	20	5	9	14	31	18	2	7	9	24
91-92	Muskegon	IHL	39	5	17	22	28	14	1	4	5	36
92-93												
93-94	Milwaukee	IHL	49	5	11	16	104	—	—	—	—	—
94-95	San Antonio	CeHL	55	28	36	64	120	13	6	8	14	25
95-96	San Antonio	CeHL	62	27	40	67	177	11	3	8	11	14
96-97	San Antonio	CeHL	23	12	19	31	48	—	—	—	—	—
97-98	Shreveport	WPHL	66	34	46	80	91	8	3	5	8	29
98-99	Shreveport	WPHL	64	36	33	69	90	12	7	7	14	16
	NHL	Totals	132	13	26	39	263	14	1	0	1	19
	AHL	Totals	248	61	102	163	561	22	2	7	9	37
	IHL	Totals	143	26	50	76	219	14	1	4	5	36
	CeHL	Totals	140	67	95	162	345	24	9	16	25	39
	WPHL	Totals	130	70	79	149	181	20	10	12	22	45

Born; 9/25/64, Prince Albert, Saskatchewan. 6-0, 200. Drafted by New York Islanders (10th choice, 157th overall) in 1983 Entry Draft. Signed as a free agent by Albany Choppers (9/90). Signed as a free agent by Springfield Indians (2/16/91). Named head coach of the San Antonio Iguanas (7/9/96). 1995-96 CeHL Second Team All-Star. Member of 1990-91 AHL champion Springfield Indians. Member of 1998-99 WPHL Champion Shreveport Mudbugs. Last amateur club; Saskatoon (WHL).

Frederic Henry — Goaltender

Regular Season / Playoffs

Season	Team	League	GP	W	L	T	MIN	SO	AVG	GP	W	L	MIN	SO	AVG
96-97	Granby	QMJHL	57	33	16	6	3330	4	2.92	5	1	4	251	0	4.06
96-97	Albany	AHL	1	1	0	0	60	0	3.00	—	—	—	—	—	—
97-98	Albany	AHL	4	2	0	1	199	0	2.41	—	—	—	—	—	—
97-98	Raleigh	ECHL	34	13	17	2	1890	2	3.78	—	—	—	—	—	—
98-99	Albany	AHL	35	17	10	3	1690	1	2.98	—	—	—	—	—	—
	AHL	Totals	40	20	10	4	1949	1	2.92	—	—	—	—	—	—

Born; 8/9/77, Cap-Rouge, Quebec. 5-11, 155. Drafted by New Jersey Devils (10th choice, 200th overall) in 1995 Entry Draft. Last amateur club; Granby

Shane Henry — Center

Regular Season / Playoffs

Season	Team	League	GP	G	A	PTS	PIM	GP	G	A	PTS	PIM
94-95	Cleveland	IHL	2	0	1	1	2	—	—	—	—	—
94-95	Richmond	ECHL	57	22	47	69	34	17	3	12	15	6
95-96	Tallahassee	ECHL	45	15	38	53	22	12	2	8	10	2
96-97	Waco	WPHL	12	3	2	5	2	—	—	—	—	—
97-98	Pee Dee	ECHL	16	0	4	4	4	—	—	—	—	—
98-99	Sheffield	BSL	2	0	2	2	0	—	—	—	—	—
	ECHL	Totals	118	37	89	126	60	29	5	20	25	8

Born; 3/15/70, Vancouver, British Columbia. 5-11, 185. Member of 1994-95 ECHL Champion Richmond Renegades. Last amateur club; Lowell (HE).

Corey Heon — Center

Regular Season / Playoffs

Season	Team	League	GP	G	A	PTS	PIM	GP	G	A	PTS	PIM
97-98	El Paso	WPHL	65	29	22	51	105	10	2	2	4	28
98-99	El Paso	WPHL	41	6	16	22	102	—	—	—	—	—
	WPHL	Totals	106	35	38	73	207	10	2	2	4	28

Born; 3/8/74, Calgary, Alberta. 5-9, 180. Member of 1997-98 WPHL Champion El Paso Buzzards. Last amateur club; Southern Alberta Institute of Technology (CIAU).

Ian Herbers — Defenseman

Regular Season / Playoffs

Season	Team	League	GP	G	A	PTS	PIM	GP	G	A	PTS	PIM
92-93	Cape Breton	AHL	77	7	15	22	129	10	0	1	1	16
93-94	Edmonton	NHL	22	0	2	2	32	—	—	—	—	—
93-94	Cape Breton	AHL	53	7	16	23	122	5	0	3	3	12
94-95	Cape Breton	AHL	36	1	11	12	104	—	—	—	—	—
94-95	Detroit	IHL	37	1	5	6	46	5	1	1	2	6
95-96	Detroit	IHL	73	3	11	14	140	12	3	5	8	29
96-97	Detroit	IHL	67	3	16	19	129	21	0	4	4	34
97-98	Detroit	IHL	70	6	6	12	100	23	0	3	3	54
98-99	Detroit	IHL	82	8	16	24	142	11	1	3	4	18
	IHL	Totals	329	21	54	75	557	72	5	16	21	141
	AHL	Totals	166	15	42	57	355	15	0	4	4	28

Born; 7/18/67, Jasper, Alberta. 6-4, 225. Drafted by Buffalo Sabres (11th choice, 190th overall) in 1987 Entry Draft. Signed as a free agent by Edmonton Oilers (9/9/92). Member of 1992-93 AHL champion Cape Breton Oilers. Member of 1996-97 IHL Champion Detroit Vipers. Last amateur club; University of Alberta (CWUAA).

Alex Herbison — Defenseman

Regular Season / Playoffs

Season	Team	League	GP	G	A	PTS	PIM	GP	G	A	PTS	PIM
97-98	Brantford	UHL	59	3	12	15	24	—	—	—	—	—
97-98	Saginaw	UHL	9	1	3	4	4	—	—	—	—	—
98-99	El Paso	WPHL	18	2	3	5	4	—	—	—	—	—
98-99	Austin	WPHL	44	3	9	12	12	—	—	—	—	—
	UHL	Totals	68	4	15	19	28	—	—	—	—	—
	WPHL	Totals	62	5	12	17	16	—	—	—	—	—

Born; 7/9/73, Brantford, Ontario. 6-1, 200. Selected by Mohawk Valley in 1998 UHL Expansion Draft. Last amateur club; Saint Mary's University (AUAA).

Derek Herlofsky — Goaltender

Regular Season / Playoffs

Season	Team	League	GP	W	L	T	MIN	SO	AVG	GP	W	L	MIN	SO	AVG
95-96	Dayton	ECHL	42	19	15	4	2166	2	3.02	1	0	1	36	0	5.06
96-97	Providence	AHL	7	6	1	0	423	2	1.56	3	1	2	178	0	2.69
96-97	Michigan	IHL	9	2	4	1	442	0	3.12	—	—	—	—	—	—
96-97	Dayton	ECHL	26	17	4	4	1549	1	2.87	—	—	—	—	—	—
97-98	Cardiff	BSL	29	—	—	—	1744	3	2.68	7	—	—	448	1	2.01
98-99	Cardiff	BSL	40	—	—	—	2414	—	2.39	1	—	—	70	0	2.57
	ECHL	Totals	68	36	19	8	3715	3	2.96	1	0	1	36	0	5.06

Born; 10/1/71, Minneapolis, Minnesota. 5-10, 175. Drafted by Minnesota North Stars (7th choice, 184th overall) in 1991 Entry Draft. Last amateur club; Boston University (Hockey East).

Jay Hern — Left Wing

Regular Season / Playoffs

Season	Team	League	GP	G	A	PTS	PIM	GP	G	A	PTS	PIM
97-98	Tucson	WCHL	8	0	1	1	0	—	—	—	—	—
97-98	Odessa	WPHL	48	16	11	27	56	—	—	—	—	—
98-99	Odessa	WPHL	3	0	2	2	4	—	—	—	—	—
98-99	Shreveport	WPHL	23	3	8	11	39	—	—	—	—	—
98-99	Amarillo	WPHL	26	1	7	8	57	—	—	—	—	—
	WPHL	Totals	100	20	28	48	156	—	—	—	—	—

Born; 12/6/76, Medicine Hat, Alberta. 6-1, 195.

Steve Herniman — Defenseman

Regular Season / Playoffs

Season	Team	League	GP	G	A	PTS	PIM	GP	G	A	PTS	PIM
89-90	Virginia	ECHL	31	2	4	6	238	3	0	0	0	29
89-90	Milwaukee	IHL	15	0	0	0	102	—	—	—	—	—
90-91	Richmond	ECHL	2	0	1	1	0	4	1	1	2	9
90-91	Milwaukee	IHL	38	0	0	0	86	—	—	—	—	—
90-91	Albany	IHL	7	0	1	1	36	—	—	—	—	—
91-92	Kalamazoo	IHL	64	4	6	10	271	1	0	0	0	0
92-93	Fort Wayne	IHL	8	0	1	1	23	—	—	—	—	—
92-93	Muskegon	CoHL	49	9	22	31	173	7	1	1	2	39
93-94	Muskegon	CoHL	4	0	0	0	24	—	—	—	—	—
94-95	Muskegon	CoHL	16	0	2	2	28	—	—	—	—	—
95-96	Muskegon	CoHL	71	1	3	4	158	5	0	0	0	18
96-97	Utica	CoHL	55	0	3	3	72	3	0	0	0	2
97-98	Monroe	WPHL	69	0	6	6	134	—	—	—	—	—
98-99	Monroe	WPHL	25	0	1	1	24	—	—	—	—	—
98-99	Tupelo	WPHL	38	0	3	3	64	—	—	—	—	—
	IHL	Totals	132	4	8	12	518	1	0	0	0	0
	CoHL	Totals	195	10	30	40	455	15	1	1	2	59
	WPHL	Totals	132	0	10	10	222	—	—	—	—	—
	ECHL	Totals	33	2	5	7	238	7	1	1	2	38

Born; 6/9/68, Windsor, Ontario. 6-4, 215. Drafted by Vancouver Canucks (5th choice, 112th overall) in 1986 Entry Draft. Traded to Tupelo by Monroe for Pirre Persson (12/98), Persson dealt to Monroe (5/99). Last amateur club; Kitchener (OHL).

Chris Herperger — Left Wing

Regular Season / Playoffs

Season	Team	League	GP	G	A	PTS	PIM	GP	G	A	PTS	PIM
94-95	Seattle	WHL	59	49	52	101	106	4	4	0	4	6
94-95	Hershey	AHL	4	0	0	0	0	—	—	—	—	—
95-96	Hershey	AHL	46	8	12	20	36	—	—	—	—	—
95-96	Baltimore	AHL	21	2	3	5	17	9	2	3	5	6
96-97	Baltimore	AHL	67	19	22	41	88	3	0	0	0	0
97-98	Canada	National	63	20	30	50	102	—	—	—	—	—
98-99	Indianapolis	IHL	79	19	29	48	81	7	0	4	4	4
	AHL	Totals	138	29	37	66	141	12	2	3	5	6

Born; 2/24/74, Esterhazy, Saskatchewan. 6-0, 190. Drafted by Philadelphia Flyers (10th choice, 223rd overall) in 1992 Entry Draft. Traded by Philadelphia with Phoenix's 7th round pick (Tony Mohagen) in 1997 Entry Draft to Anaheim Mighty Ducks for Bob Corkum (2/6/96). Signed as a free agent by Chicago Blackhawks (9/2/98). Last amateur club; Seattle (WHL).

Matt Herr — Center

Regular Season / Playoffs

Season	Team	League	GP	G	A	PTS	PIM	GP	G	A	PTS	PIM
98-99	Washington	NHL	30	2	2	4	8	—	—	—	—	—
98-99	Portland	AHL	46	15	14	29	29	—	—	—	—	—

Born; 5/26/76, Hackensack, New Jersey. 6-1, 180. Drafted by Washington Capitals (4th choice, 93rd overall) in 1994 Entry Draft. Last amateur club; Michigan (CCHA).

John Herrick — Goaltender

Regular Season / Playoffs

Season	Team	League	GP	W	L	T	MIN	SO	AVG	GP	W	L	MIN	SO	AVG
97-98	Saginaw	UHL	29	5	17	0	1318	0	5.10	—	—	—	—	—	—
98-99	Mohawk Valley	UHL	2	0	1	0	65	0	4.60	—	—	—	—	—	—
98-99	Fort Worth	CHL	6	1	3	0	246	0	5.37	—	—	—	—	—	—
	UHL	Totals	31	5	18	0	1383	0	5.08	—	—	—	—	—	—

Born; 11/20/75, Concord, New Hampshire. 5-10, 180. Selected by Fayetteville in 1999 CHL Dispersal Draft. Last amateur club; St. Anselm College (ECAC 2).

Harold Hersh — Center

Regular Season / Playoffs

Season	Team	League	GP	G	A	PTS	PIM	GP	G	A	PTS	PIM
95-96	Fredericton	AHL	63	5	17	22	30	—	—	—	—	—
96-97	Fredericton	AHL	67	11	11	22	32	—	—	—	—	—
97-98	Kentucky	AHL	5	0	0	0	4	—	—	—	—	—
97-98	Detroit	IHL	22	1	1	2	14	—	—	—	—	—
97-98	Johnstown	ECHL	49	20	23	43	55	—	—	—	—	—
98-99	Kentucky	AHL	63	7	7	14	30	—	—	—	—	—
	AHL	Totals	197	23	35	58	96	—	—	—	—	—

Born; 4/18/74, Montreal, Quebec. 6-1, 188. Last amateur club; Hull (QMJHL).

Jason Herter — Defenseman

Regular Season / Playoffs

Season	Team	League	GP	G	A	PTS	PIM	GP	G	A	PTS	PIM
91-92	Milwaukee	IHL	56	7	18	25	34	1	0	0	0	2
92-93	Hamilton	AHL	70	7	16	23	68	—	—	—	—	—
93-94	Kalamazoo	IHL	68	14	28	42	92	5	3	0	3	14
94-95	Kalamazoo	IHL	60	12	20	32	70	16	2	8	10	10
95-96	Islanders	NHL	1	0	1	1	0	—	—	—	—	—
95-96	Utah	IHL	74	14	31	45	58	20	4	10	14	8
96-97	Kansas City	IHL	71	9	26	35	62	3	0	1	1	0
97-98	Kansas City	IHL	57	6	19	25	55	—	—	—	—	—
97-98	Orlando	IHL	8	1	3	4	8	17	5	7	12	20
98-99	Landshut	Germany	46	14	16	30	66	3	1	1	2	29
	IHL	Totals	394	63	145	208	379	62	14	26	40	54

Born; 10/2/70, Hafford, Saskatchewan. 6-1, 202. Drafted by Vancouver Canucks (1st choice, 8th overall) in 1989 Entry Draft. Signed as a free agent by Dallas Stars (8/6/93). Traded to New York Islanders by Dallas for cash (9/21/95). Traded to Orlando by Kansas City with Reggie Savage for Bill H. Armstrong and Jeff Buchanan (3/98). Member of 1995-96 IHL champion Utah Grizzlies. Last amateur club; University of North Dakota (WCHA).

Fred Hettle — Defenseman

Regular Season / Playoffs

Season	Team	League	GP	G	A	PTS	PIM	GP	G	A	PTS	PIM
96-97	Fresno	WCHL	44	3	13	16	51	7	2	4	6	6
96-97												
98-99	Fresno	WCHL	54	2	11	13	58	—	—	—	—	—
	WCHL	Totals	98	5	24	29	109	7	2	4	6	6

Born; 3/19/72. 6-2, 200.

Jason Heywood — Center

Regular Season / Playoffs

Season	Team	League	GP	G	A	PTS	PIM	GP	G	A	PTS	PIM
97-98	Tallahassee	ECHL	30	6	6	12	12	—	—	—	—	—
97-98	Jacksonville	ECHL	25	4	5	9	20	—	—	—	—	—
98-99	Paisley	BNL	21	20	9	29	42	—	—	—	—	—
98-99	Sheffield	BSL	32	4	8	12	26	6	1	2	3	2
	ECHL	Totals	55	10	11	21	32	—	—	—	—	—

Born; 5/11/74, St. Thomas, Ontario. 6-3, 200. Last amateur club; University of Western Ontario (OUAA).

Jamie Hicks — Center

Regular Season / Playoffs

Season	Team	League	GP	G	A	PTS	PIM	GP	G	A	PTS	PIM
91-92	Ayr	BHL	20	39	32	71	10	—	—	—	—	—
92-93	Brantford	CoHL	59	22	41	63	52	15	8	5	13	32
93-94	Rochester	AHL	2	0	0	0	4	—	—	—	—	—
93-94	Brantford	CoHL	62	37	44	81	64	7	5	5	10	2
94-95	Fort Wayne	IHL	1	0	0	0	2	—	—	—	—	—
94-95	Saginaw	CoHL	71	42	60	102	113	11	8	8	16	16
95-96	Utah	IHL	3	0	0	0	6	—	—	—	—	—
95-96	Saginaw	CoHL	73	38	78	116	64	5	2	4	6	6
96-97	Birmingham	ECHL	70	32	59	91	87	8	6	8	14	12
97-98	Houston	IHL	2	1	0	1	4	—	—	—	—	—
97-98	Birmingham	ECHL	70	44	75	119	70	4	2	3	5	0
98-99	Birmingham	ECHL	65	16	75	91	60	5	4	4	8	4
	IHL	Totals	6	1	0	1	12	—	—	—	—	—
	CoHL	Totals	265	139	223	362	293	38	23	22	45	56
	ECHL	Totals	205	92	209	301	217	17	12	15	27	16

Born; 8/23/69, Timmins, Ontario. 5-10, 175. 1993-94 CoHL Best Defensive Forward. 1997-98 ECHL MVP. 1997-98 ECHL First Team All-Star. 1998-99 ECHL Second Team All-Star. Member of 1992-93 CoHL Champion Brantford

Mike Hiebert — Defenseman

Regular Season / Playoffs

Season	Team	League	GP	G	A	PTS	PIM	GP	G	A	PTS	PIM
96-97	Reno	WCHL	3	0	0	0	15	—	—	—	—	—
96-97	Tulsa	CeHL	15	2	3	5	66	—	—	—	—	—
96-97	San Antonio	CeHL	20	2	6	8	62	—	—	—	—	—
97-98	Oklahoma City	CHL	10	0	1	1	73	—	—	—	—	—
97-98	Fayetteville	CHL	8	0	0	0	60	—	—	—	—	—
97-98	Wichita	CHL	4	0	0	0	11	—	—	—	—	—
97-98	Fort Worth	CHL	13	1	1	2	167	—	—	—	—	—
98-99	Port Huron	UHL	5	0	1	1	23	—	—	—	—	—
98-99	Mohawk Valley	UHL	33	2	5	7	114	—	—	—	—	—
98-99	Saginaw	UHL	16	2	5	7	64	—	—	—	—	—
	CHL	Totals	70	5	11	16	439	—	—	—	—	—
	UHL	Totals	54	4	11	15	201	—	—	—	—	—

Born; 4/16/75, Winnipeg, Manitoba. 6-0, 188. Traded to Mohawk Valley by Port Huron with Ryan Caley for Wayne Muir (11/98). Traded to Saginaw by Mohawk Valley with Mark Bultje for Dominic Chiasson and Eric Kelly (2/99).

Henry Higdon — Center

Regular Season / Playoffs

Season	Team	League	GP	G	A	PTS	PIM	GP	G	A	PTS	PIM
98-99	Hampton Roads	ECHL	23	2	3	5	32	2	0	0	0	0

Born; 11/17/76, Greenwich, Connecticut. 6-0, 195. Last amateur club; Harvard (ECAC).

Matt Higgins — Left Wing

Regular Season / Playoffs

Season	Team	League	GP	G	A	PTS	PIM	GP	G	A	PTS	PIM
97-98	Montreal	NHL	1	0	0	0	0	—	—	—	—	—
97-98	Fredericton	AHL	50	5	22	27	12	4	1	2	3	2
98-99	Montreal	NHL	25	1	0	1	0	—	—	—	—	—
98-99	Fredericton	AHL	11	3	4	7	6	5	0	2	2	0
	NHL	Totals	26	1	0	1	0	—	—	—	—	—
	AHL	Totals	61	8	26	34	18	9	1	4	5	2

Born; 10/29/77, Calgary, Alberta. 6-2, 170. Drafted by Montreal Canadiens (1st choice, 18th overall) in 1996 Entry Draft. Last amateur club; Moose Jaw (WHL).

Brian Hill — Center

Regular Season / Playoffs

Season	Team	League	GP	G	A	PTS	PIM	GP	G	A	PTS	PIM
98-99	Madison	UHL	15	0	5	5	10	—	—	—	—	—

Born; 2/9/72, Dubuque, Iowa. 5-9, 180. Last amateur club; Wisconsin Stevens-Point (NCAA 3).

Kevin Hill — Right Wing

Regular Season / Playoffs

Season	Team	League	GP	G	A	PTS	PIM	GP	G	A	PTS	PIM
96-97	Muskegon	UHL	2	0	0	0	0	—	—	—	—	—
97-98												
98-99	Johnstown	ECHL	1	0	0	0	0	—	—	—	—	—
98-99	Saginaw	UHL	1	0	0	0	0	—	—	—	—	—
	UHL	Totals	3	0	0	0	0	—	—	—	—	—

Born; 8/31/71, Carbondale, Illinois. 6-4, 210.

Kiley Hill — Forward

Regular Season / Playoffs

Season	Team	League	GP	G	A	PTS	PIM	GP	G	A	PTS	PIM
98-99	Dayton	ECHL	59	20	10	30	227	4	0	1	1	12
98-99	Cincinnati	IHL	1	0	1	1	0	—	—	—	—	—

Born; 1/12/75, Val Caron, Ontario. 6-3, 215. Last amateur club; Laurentian

Tim Hill — Right Wing

Regular Season / Playoffs

Season	Team	League	GP	G	A	PTS	PIM	GP	G	A	PTS	PIM
98-99	Fayetteville	CHL	47	9	15	24	102	—	—	—	—	—

Born; 3/14/74, North Bay, Ontario. 6-2, 212. Last amateur club; Dalhousie

Jon Hillebrandt — Goaltender

Regular Season / Playoffs

Season	Team	League	GP	W	L	T	MIN	SO	AVG	GP	W	L	MIN	SO	AVG
93-94	United States	National	2	1	1	0	120	0	5.00	—	—	—	—	—	—
93-94	Binghamton	AHL	7	1	3	0	294	0	3.67	—	—	—	—	—	—
93-94	Erie	ECHL	3	2	0	1	189	1	2.53	—	—	—	—	—	—
94-95	San Diego	IHL	1	0	1	0	40	0	9.00	—	—	—	—	—	—
94-95	Binghamton	AHL	—	—	—	—	—	—	—	1	0	0	5	0	12.00
94-95	Charlotte	ECHL	32	14	11	5	1790	0	4.05	3	0	2	179	0	4.01
95-96	Binghamton	AHL	36	15	14	2	1845	0	4.42	2	1	1	47	0	10.13
96-97	San Antonio	IHL	1	0	0	0	33	0	3.60	—	—	—	—	—	—
96-97	Chicago	IHL	2	0	1	0	54	0	4.46	—	—	—	—	—	—
96-97	Peoria	ECHL	26	18	4	3	1487	2	*2.82	2	1	0	80	0	3.00
97-98	Rochester	AHL	3	2	0	0	102	0	2.95	—	—	—	—	—	—
97-98	Binghamton	UHL	36	17	12	4	1891	2	3.24	—	—	—	—	—	—
98-99	Binghamton	UHL	17	8	7	0	902	*1	3.53	—	—	—	—	—	—
98-99	Port Huron	UHL	17	10	5	1	967	*3	2.30	7	3	4	438	1	2.19
	AHL	Totals	46	18	17	2	2241	0	4.26	3	1	1	52	0	10.38
	IHL	Totals	4	0	2	0	127	0	5.53	—	—	—	—	—	—
	UHL	Totals	70	35	24	5	3760	6	3.06	7	3	4	438	1	2.19
	ECHL	Totals	61	34	15	9	3466	1	3.44	5	1	2	259	0	3.70

Born; 12/18/71, Cottage Grove, Wisconsin. 5-10, 160. Drafted by New York Rangers (12th choice, 202nd overall) in 1990 Entry Draft. Traded to Port Huron by Binghamton for Mike O'Grady and Olie Sundstrom (2/99). Last amateur club; Illinois-Chicago (CCHA).

Craig Hillier — Goaltender

Regular Season / Playoffs

Season	Team	League	GP	W	L	T	MIN	SO	AVG	GP	W	L	MIN	SO	AVG
98-99	Syracuse	AHL	36	9	18	6	1919	1	3.94	—	—	—	—	—	—

Born; 2/28/78, Cole Harbour, Nova Scotia. 6-1, 176. Drafted by Pittsburgh Penguins (1st choice, 23rd overall) in 1996 Entry Draft. Last amateur club; Ottawa

Scott Hillman — Defenseman

Regular Season / Playoffs

Season	Team	League	GP	G	A	PTS	PIM	GP	G	A	PTS	PIM
98-99	Windsor	OUAA										
98-99	Toledo	ECHL	3	1	2	3	0	7	0	7	7	6

Born; Last amateur club; Windsor (OUAA).

Kevin Hilton — Center
Regular Season / Playoffs

Season	Team	League	GP	G	A	PTS	PIM	GP	G	A	PTS	PIM
96-97	Worcester	AHL	27	3	7	10	23	4	0	2	2	0
96-97	Quebec	IHL	11	1	0	1	2	—	—	—	—	—
96-97	Mississippi	ECHL	28	8	13	21	9	—	—	—	—	—
97-98	Orlando	IHL	1	0	0	0	0	—	—	—	—	—
97-98	Mobile	ECHL	69	29	53	82	50	3	0	2	2	2
98-99	Springfield	AHL	2	1	1	2	0	—	—	—	—	—
98-99	Alexandria	WPHL	16	6	17	23	17	—	—	—	—	—
98-99	Mississippi	ECHL	48	16	29	45	22	18	7	8	15	14
	AHL	Totals	29	4	8	12	23	4	0	2	2	0
	IHL	Totals	12	1	0	1	2	—	—	—	—	—
	ECHL	Totals	145	53	95	148	81	21	7	10	17	16

Born; 1/5/75, Trenton, Michigan. 5-11, 170. Drafted by Detroit Red Wings (3rd choice, 74th overall) in 1993 Entry Draft. Member of 1998-99 ECHL Champion Mississippi SeaWolves. Scored Kelly Cup-winning goal in double overtime of Game Seven for SeaWolves. Last amateur club; University of Michigan (CCHA).

Jordan Hines — Center
Regular Season / Playoffs

Season	Team	League	GP	G	A	PTS	PIM	GP	G	A	PTS	PIM
98-99	Fort Worth	WPHL	16	1	1	2	31	—	—	—	—	—
98-99	Fort Worth	CHL	3	0	0	0	0	—	—	—	—	—

Born; 6/19/76, Cleveland, Ohio. 6-3, 200.

Dan Hinote — Center
Regular Season / Playoffs

Season	Team	League	GP	G	A	PTS	PIM	GP	G	A	PTS	PIM
97-98	Oshawa	OHL	35	12	15	27	39	5	2	2	4	7
97-98	Hershey	AHL	24	1	4	5	25	—	—	—	—	—
98-99	Hershey	AHL	65	4	16	20	95	5	3	1	4	6
	AHL	Totals	89	5	20	25	120	5	3	1	4	6

Born; 1/30/77, Leesburg, Florida. 6-0, 187. Drafted by Colorado Avalanche (9th choice, 197th overall) in 1995 Entry Draft. Last amateur club; Oshawa (OHL).

Chad Hinz — Right Wing
Regular Season / Playoffs

Season	Team	League	GP	G	A	PTS	PIM	GP	G	A	PTS	PIM
98-99	Moose Jaw	WHL	71	42	75	117	40	11	4	12	16	12
98-99	Hamilton	AHL	3	0	0	0	2	—	—	—	—	—

Born; 3/21/79, Saskatoon, Saskatchewan. 5-10, 185. Drafted by Edmonton Oilers (8th choice, 187th overall) in 1997 Entry Draft. Last amateur club; Moose Jaw (WHL).

Corey Hirsch — Goaltender
Regular Season / Playoffs

Season	Team	League	GP	W	L	T	MIN	SO	AVG	GP	W	L	MIN	SO	AVG
92-93	Rangers	NHL	4	1	2	1	224	0	3.75	—	—	—	—	—	—
92-93	Binghamton	AHL	46	*35	4	5	2692	1	*2.79	14	7	7	831	0	3.32
93-94	Canadian	National	45	24	17	3	2653	0	2.80	—	—	—	—	—	—
93-94	Canadian	Olympic	8	5	2	1	495	0	2.06	—	—	—	—	—	—
93-94	Binghamton	AHL	10	5	4	1	610	0	3.73	—	—	—	—	—	—
94-95	Binghamton	AHL	57	31	20	5	3371	0	3.11	—	—	—	—	—	—
95-96	Vancouver	NHL	41	17	14	6	2338	1	2.93	6	2	3	338	0	3.73
96-97	Vancouver	NHL	39	12	20	4	2127	2	3.27	—	—	—	—	—	—
97-98	Vancouver	NHL	1	0	0	0	50	0	6.00	—	—	—	—	—	—
97-98	Syracuse	AHL	60	30	22	6	3513	1	3.19	5	2	3	297	1	2.02
98-99	Vancouver	NHL	20	3	8	3	919	1	3.13	—	—	—	—	—	—
98-99	Syracuse	AHL	5	2	3	0	300	0	2.80	—	—	—	—	—	—
	NHL	Totals	105	33	44	14	5658	4	3.15	6	2	3	338	0	3.73
	AHL	Totals	178	103	53	17	10486	2	3.08	19	9	10	1128	1	2.98

Born; 7/1/72, Medicine Hat, Alberta. 5-10, 160. Drafted by New York Rangers (8th choice, 169th overall) in 1991 Entry Draft. Traded to Vancouver Canucks by Rangers for Nathan Lafayette (4/7/95). 1992-93 AHL Rookie of the Year. 1992-93 AHL Harry "Hap" Holmes Trophy (fewest goals against) shared with Boris Rousson. 1992-93 AHL First Team All-Star. 1992-93 AHL Baz Bastien Trophy (Top Goaltender). 1995-96 NHL All-Rookie Team. Last amateur club; Kamloops

Allan Hitchen — Goaltender
Regular Season / Playoffs

Season	Team	League	GP	W	L	T	MIN	SO	AVG	GP	W	L	MIN	SO	AVG
98-99	Baton Rouge	ECHL	7	2	1	1	277	0	3.03	—	—	—	—	—	—
98-99	Charlotte	ECHL	4	0	1	1	81	0	5.92	—	—	—	—	—	—
98-99	Wheeling	ECHL	4	0	1	0	148	0	4.45	—	—	—	—	—	—
	ECHL	Totals	15	2	3	2	506	0	3.44	—	—	—	—	—	—

Born; 3/6/78, North York, Ontario. 6-1, 195. Signed as a free agent by Vancouver Canucks (10/3/96). Last amateur club; North Bay (OHL).

Martin Hlinka — Forward
Regular Season / Playoffs

Season	Team	League	GP	G	A	PTS	PIM	GP	G	A	PTS	PIM
98-99	Quad City	UHL	2	1	1	2	0	1	0	0	0	0

Born; Bratislavia, Slovakia. 6-0, 185.

Todd Hlushko — Center
Regular Season / Playoffs

Season	Team	League	GP	G	A	PTS	PIM	GP	G	A	PTS	PIM
90-91	Baltimore	AHL	66	9	14	23	55	—	—	—	—	—
91-92	Baltimore	AHL	74	16	35	51	113	—	—	—	—	—
92-93	Canadian	National	58	22	26	48	10	—	—	—	—	—
93-94	Canadian	National	55	22	6	28	61	—	—	—	—	—
93-94	Canadian	Olympic	8	5	0	5	6	—	—	—	—	—
93-94	Philadelphia	NHL	2	1	0	1	0	—	—	—	—	—
93-94	Hershey	AHL	9	6	0	6	4	6	2	1	3	4
94-95	Saint John	AHL	46	22	10	32	36	4	2	2	4	22
94-95	Calgary	NHL	2	0	1	1	2	1	0	0	0	2
95-96	Calgary	NHL	4	0	0	0	6	—	—	—	—	—
95-96	Saint John	AHL	35	14	13	27	70	16	8	1	9	26
96-97	Calgary	NHL	58	7	11	18	49	—	—	—	—	—
97-98	Calgary	NHL	13	0	1	1	27	—	—	—	—	—
97-98	Saint John	AHL	33	10	14	24	48	21	13	4	17	61
98-99	Grand Rapids	IHL	82	24	26	50	78	—	—	—	—	—
98-99	Pittsburgh	NHL	—	—	—	—	—	2	0	0	0	0
	NHL	Totals	79	8	13	21	84	3	0	0	0	2
	AHL	Totals	263	77	86	163	326	47	25	8	33	113

Born; 2/7/70, Toronto, Ontario. 5-11, 185. Drafted by Washington Capitals (14th choice, 240th overall) in 1989 Entry Draft. Signed as a free agent by Philadelphia Flyers (3/7/94). Signed as a free agent by Calgary Flames (6/17/94). Traded to Pittsburgh Penguins with German Titov for Ken Wregget and Dave Roche (6/17/98). Last amateur club; London (OHL).

Shane Hnidy — Defenseman
Regular Season / Playoffs

Season	Team	League	GP	G	A	PTS	PIM	GP	G	A	PTS	PIM
96-97	Saint John	AHL	44	2	12	14	112	—	—	—	—	—
96-97	Baton Rouge	ECHL	21	3	10	13	50	—	—	—	—	—
97-98	Grand Rapids	IHL	77	6	12	18	210	3	0	2	2	23
98-99	Adirondack	AHL	68	9	20	29	121	3	0	1	1	0
	AHL	Totals	112	11	32	43	233	3	0	1	1	0

Born; 8/11/75, Neepawa, Manitoba. 6-1, 200. Drafted by Buffalo Sabres (7th choice, 173rd overall) in 1994 Entry Draft. Signed as a free agent by Detroit Red Wings (8/6/98). Last amateur club; Prince Albert (WHL).

Justin Hocking — Defenseman
Regular Season / Playoffs

Season	Team	League	GP	G	A	PTS	PIM	GP	G	A	PTS	PIM
93-94	Medicine Hat	WHL	68	7	26	33	236	3	0	0	0	6
93-94	Los Angeles	NHL	1	0	0	0	0	—	—	—	—	—
93-94	Phoenix	IHL	3	0	0	0	15	—	—	—	—	—
94-95	Syracuse	AHL	7	0	0	0	24	—	—	—	—	—
94-95	Portland	AHL	9	0	1	1	34	—	—	—	—	—
94-95	Knoxville	ECHL	20	0	6	6	70	4	0	0	0	26
94-95	Phoenix	IHL	20	1	1	2	50	1	0	0	0	0
95-96	Prince Edward Island	AHL	74	4	8	12	251	4	0	2	2	5
96-97	Worcester	AHL	68	1	10	11	198	5	0	3	3	2
97-98	Worcester	AHL	79	5	12	17	198	11	1	2	3	19
98-99	St. John's	AHL	44	4	6	10	99	5	0	0	0	2
98-99	Indianapolis	IHL	34	2	4	6	111	—	—	—	—	—
	AHL	Totals	281	14	37	51	804	25	1	7	8	28
	IHL	Totals	57	3	5	8	176	1	0	0	0	0

Born; 1/9/74, Stettler, Alberta. 6-4, 205. Drafted by Los Angeles Kings (1st choice, 39th overall) in 1992 Entry Draft. Claimed by Ottawa Senators from Los Angeles in NHL Waiver Draft (10/2/95). Traded to Chicago Blackhawks by Ottawa for Brian Felsner (8/21/98). Signed as a free agent by Toronto Maple Leafs (7/23/99). Last amateur club; Medicine Hat (WHL).

Daniel Hodge — Defenseman
Regular Season / Playoffs

Season	Team	League	GP	G	A	PTS	PIM	GP	G	A	PTS	PIM
95-96	Providence	AHL	23	1	7	8	12	—	—	—	—	—
96-97	Peoria	ECHL	68	12	34	46	63	10	4	6	10	7
97-98	Indianapolis	IHL	22	5	6	11	12	—	—	—	—	—
97-98	Kansas City	IHL	2	0	0	0	2	—	—	—	—	—
97-98	Peoria	ECHL	33	14	19	33	22	3	0	0	0	0
98-99	Indianapolis	IHL	1	0	0	0	2	—	—	—	—	—
98-99	Peoria	ECHL	68	12	35	47	58	4	1	0	1	2
	IHL	Totals	25	5	6	11	16	—	—	—	—	—
	ECHL	Totals	169	38	88	126	143	17	5	6	11	9

Born; 9/18/71, Melrose, Massachusetts. 6-3, 205. Drafted by Boston Bruins (8th choice, 194th overall) in 1991 Entry Draft. Last amateur club; Merrimack (HE).

Kevin Hodson — Goaltender
Regular Season / Playoffs

Season	Team	League	GP	W	L	T	MIN	SO	AVG	GP	W	L	MIN	SO	AVG
92-93	Sault Ste. Marie	OHL	26	18	5	2	1470	1	*3.10	14	11	2	755	0	2.70
92-93	Indianapolis	IHL	14	5	9	0	777	0	4.09	—	—	—	—	—	—
93-94	Adirondack	AHL	37	20	10	5	2082	2	2.94	3	0	2	89	0	6.77
94-95	Adirondack	AHL	51	19	22	8	2731	1	3.54	4	0	4	237	0	3.53
95-96	Detroit	NHL	4	2	0	0	163	1	1.10	—	—	—	—	—	—
95-96	Adirondack	AHL	32	13	13	2	1654	0	3.16	3	0	2	149	0	3.21
96-97	Detroit	NHL	6	2	2	1	294	1	1.63	—	—	—	—	—	—
96-97	Quebec	IHL	2	1	1	0	118	0	3.54	—	—	—	—	—	—
97-98	Detroit	NHL	21	9	3	3	988	2	2.67	1	0	0	0	0	0.00
98-99	Detroit	NHL	4	0	2	0	175	0	3.09	—	—	—	—	—	—
98-99	Tampa Bay	NHL	5	2	1	1	238	0	2.77	—	—	—	—	—	—
98-99	Adirondack	AHL	6	1	3	2	349	0	3.27	—	—	—	—	—	—
	NHL	Totals	40	15	8	5	1858	4	2.42	1	0	0	0	0	0.00
	AHL	Totals	126	53	48	17	6816	3	3.25	10	0	8	475	0	4.04

Born; 3/27/72, Winnipeg, Manitoba. 6-0, 182. Signed as a free agent by Chicago Blackhawks (8/17/92). Signed as a free agent by Detroit Red Wings (6/16/93). Traded to Tampa Bay Lightning by Detroit with a 1999 second round choice (previously acquired from San Jose-Tampa Bay selected Sheldon Keefe) for Wendel Clark (3/23/99). Played 16 seconds in playoff game against Chicago (3/17/98). Shared a shutout with Corey Schwab vs. Boston (4/8/99). Member of 1997-98 Stanley Cup Champion Detroit Red Wings. Last amateur club; Sault Ste.

Matt Hoffman — Center
Regular Season / Playoffs

Season	Team	League	GP	G	A	PTS	PIM	GP	G	A	PTS	PIM
91-92	Oshawa	OHL	50	25	41	66	93	7	6	9	15	10
91-92	Salt Lake City	IHL	4	0	1	1	6	—	—	—	—	—
92-93	St. Thomas	CoHL	21	6	12	18	19	13	7	3	10	44
93-94	Johnstown	ECHL	58	33	40	73	85	3	0	1	1	0
94-95	Johnstown	ECHL	55	25	36	61	113	5	2	4	6	10
95-96	Mobile	ECHL	60	23	40	63	170	—	—	—	—	—
96-97	Ayr	BSL	42	13	16	29	66	—	—	—	—	—
97-98	Ayr	BSL	52	17	14	31	103	9	1	4	5	8
98-99	Ayr	BSL	41	11	13	24	69	—	—	—	—	—
98-99	Saginaw	UHL	2	0	1	1	7	—	—	—	—	—
	ECHL	Totals	173	81	116	197	368	8	2	5	7	10
	UHL	Totals	23	6	13	19	26	13	7	3	10	44
	BSL	Totals	135	41	43	84	238	9	1	4	5	8

Born; 7/6/71, Saginaw, Michigan. 6-1, 200. Drafted by Calgary Flames (8th choice, 140th overall) in 1991 Entry Draft. Last amateur club; Oshawa (OHL).

Peter Hogan — Defenseman
Regular Season / Playoffs

Season	Team	League	GP	G	A	PTS	PIM	GP	G	A	PTS	PIM
98-99	Springfield	AHL	71	1	14	15	41	2	0	0	0	0

Born; 1/10/78, Oshawa, Ontario. 6-3, 183. Drafted by Los Angeles Kings (7th choice, 123rd overall) in 1996 Entry Draft. Last amateur club; Oshawa (OHL).

Murray Hogg — Defenseman
Regular Season / Playoffs

Season	Team	League	GP	G	A	PTS	PIM	GP	G	A	PTS	PIM
96-97	Fort Worth	CeHL	66	4	13	17	197	12	1	2	3	40
97-98	Fort Worth	WPHL	69	1	7	8	153	13	1	1	2	39
98-99	Fort Worth	WPHL	68	6	10	16	158	12	0	6	6	36
	WPHL	Totals	137	7	17	24	311	25	1	7	8	75

Born; 3/15/76, Millbrook, Ontario. 6-0, 210. Member of 1996-97 CeHL Champion Fort Worth Fire. Last amateur club; Belleville (OHL).

Martin Hohenberger — Left Wing
Regular Season / Playoffs

Season	Team	League	GP	G	A	PTS	PIM	GP	G	A	PTS	PIM
97-98	Austria	Olympics	4	0	0	0	2	—	—	—	—	—
97-98	Fredericton	AHL	9	0	1	1	2	—	—	—	—	—
97-98	New Orleans	ECHL	9	1	2	3	15	3	0	0	0	0
98-99	New Orleans	ECHL	57	10	9	19	38	3	0	0	0	2
	ECHL	Totals	66	11	11	22	53	6	0	0	0	2

Born; 1/29/77, Villach, Austria. 6-1, 205. Drafted by Montreal Canadiens (3rd choice, 74th overall) in 1995 Entry Draft. Last amateur club; Lethbridge (WHL).

Brent Hoiness — Right Wing
Regular Season / Playoffs

Season	Team	League	GP	G	A	PTS	PIM	GP	G	A	PTS	PIM
98-99	Corpus Christi	WPHL	9	2	2	4	2	4	0	1	1	2
98-99	Tulsa	CHL	16	4	5	9	5	—	—	—	—	—

Born; 6/5/73, Saskatchewan, Saskatoon. 6-0, 195. Last amateur club; Brown (ECAC).

Josh Holden — Center
Regular Season / Playoffs

Season	Team	League	GP	G	A	PTS	PIM	GP	G	A	PTS	PIM
98-99	Vancouver	NHL	30	2	4	6	10	—	—	—	—	—
98-99	Syracuse	AHL	38	14	15	29	48	—	—	—	—	—

Born; 1/18/78, Calgary, Alberta. 6-0, 190. Drafted by Vancouver Canucks (1st choice, 12th overall) in 1996 Entry Draft. Last amateur club; Regina (WHL).

Juri Holik — Left Wing
Regular Season / Playoffs

Season	Team	League	GP	G	A	PTS	PIM	GP	G	A	PTS	PIM
98-99	Phoenix	WCHL	8	0	3	3	2	—	—	—	—	—

Born;

Cory Holland
Right Wing
Regular Season / Playoffs

Season	Team	League	GP	G	A	PTS	PIM	GP	G	A	PTS	PIM
97-98	Flint	UHL	8	0	2	2	17	—	—	—	—	—
97-98	Madison	UHL	50	2	3	5	177	5	0	0	0	5
98-99	Tucson	WCHL	15	1	0	1	54	—	—	—	—	—
98-99	Madison	UHL	48	1	1	2	143	—	—	—	—	—
	UHL	Totals	106	3	6	9	337	5	0	0	0	5

Born; 4/25/76, Havelock, Ontario. 5-10, 196.

Jason Holland
Defenseman
Regular Season / Playoffs

Season	Team	League	GP	G	A	PTS	PIM	GP	G	A	PTS	PIM
96-97	Islanders	NHL	4	1	0	1	0	—	—	—	—	—
96-97	Kentucky	AHL	72	14	25	39	46	4	0	2	2	0
97-98	Islanders	NHL	8	0	0	0	4	—	—	—	—	—
97-98	Kentucky	AHL	50	10	16	26	29	—	—	—	—	—
97-98	Rochester	AHL	9	0	4	4	10	4	0	3	3	4
98-99	Buffalo	NHL	3	0	0	0	8	—	—	—	—	—
98-99	Rochester	AHL	74	4	25	29	36	20	2	5	7	8
	NHL	Totals	15	1	0	1	12	—	—	—	—	—
	AHL	Totals	205	28	70	98	121	28	2	10	12	12

Born; 4/30/76, Morinville, Alberta. 6-2, 193. Drafted by New York Islanders (2nd choice, 38th overall) in 1994 Entry Draft. Member of 1996-97 AHL All-Rookie Team. Traded to Buffalo Sabres by Islanders with Paul Kruse for Jason Dawe (3/24/98). Last amateur club; Kamloops (WHL).

Kevin Holliday
Defenseman
Regular Season / Playoffs

Season	Team	League	GP	G	A	PTS	PIM	GP	G	A	PTS	PIM
96-97	Thunder Bay	CoHL	69	1	5	6	403	3	1	1	2	28
97-98	Thunder Bay	UHL	35	2	3	5	251	2	0	1	1	2
98-99	Baton Rouge	ECHL	7	0	0	0	54	—	—	—	—	—
98-99	Thunder Bay	UHL	41	2	5	7	352	12	0	0	0	42
	UHL	Totals	145	5	13	18	1006	17	1	2	3	72

Born; 5/6/75, Red Lake, Ontario. 6-2, 225.

Terry Hollinger
Defenseman
Regular Season / Playoffs

Season	Team	League	GP	G	A	PTS	PIM	GP	G	A	PTS	PIM
91-92	Lethbridge	WHL	65	23	62	85	155	5	1	2	3	13
91-92	Peoria	IHL	1	0	2	2	0	5	0	1	1	0
92-93	Peoria	IHL	72	2	28	30	67	4	1	1	2	0
93-94	St. Louis	NHL	2	0	0	0	0	—	—	—	—	—
93-94	Peoria	IHL	78	12	31	43	96	6	0	3	3	31
94-95	St. Louis	NHL	5	0	0	0	2	—	—	—	—	—
94-95	Peoria	IHL	69	7	25	32	137	4	2	4	6	8
95-96	Rochester	AHL	62	5	50	55	71	19	3	11	14	12
96-97	Rochester	AHL	73	12	51	63	54	10	2	7	9	27
97-98	Worcester	AHL	55	8	24	32	34	—	—	—	—	—
97-98	Houston	IHL	8	1	1	2	6	4	1	2	3	11
98-99	Utah	IHL	58	4	19	23	40	—	—	—	—	—
98-99	Orlando	IHL	21	9	9	18	18	17	3	5	8	14
	NHL	Totals	7	0	0	0	2	—	—	—	—	—
	IHL	Totals	307	35	115	150	364	40	7	16	23	64
	AHL	Totals	190	25	125	150	159	29	5	18	23	39

Born; 2/24/71, Regina, Saskatchewan. 6-2, 215. Drafted by St. Louis Blues (7th choice, 153rd overall) in 1991 Entry Draft. Signed as a free agent by Buffalo Sabres (8/19/95). Signed as a free agent by St. Louis Blues (7/16/97). Member of 1995-96 AHL champion Rochester Americans. 1995-96 AHL Second Team All-Star. 1996-97 AHL First Team All-Star. Last amateur club; Lethbridge (WHL).

Scott Hollis
Right Wing
Regular Season / Playoffs

Season	Team	League	GP	G	A	PTS	PIM	GP	G	A	PTS	PIM
93-94	Las Vegas	IHL	23	3	1	4	65	—	—	—	—	—
93-94	Knoxville	ECHL	28	20	16	36	99	3	3	1	4	8
94-95	Adirondack	AHL	48	12	15	27	118	—	—	—	—	—
95-96	Adirondack	AHL	55	18	19	37	111	3	0	1	1	4
95-96	Toledo	ECHL	7	7	11	18	5	—	—	—	—	—
96-97	San Antonio	IHL	73	17	17	34	187	9	1	1	2	6
97-98	San Antonio	IHL	19	15	6	21	21	—	—	—	—	—
97-98	Orlando	IHL	48	16	23	39	68	17	5	4	9	30
98-99	Orlando	IHL	3	1	1	2	6	—	—	—	—	—
98-99	Long Beach	IHL	13	2	5	7	21	—	—	—	—	—
98-99	Las Vegas	IHL	53	20	25	45	67	—	—	—	—	—
	IHL	Totals	232	74	78	152	435	26	6	5	11	36
	AHL	Totals	103	30	34	64	229	3	0	1	1	4
	ECHL	Totals	35	27	27	54	104	3	3	1	4	8

Born; 9/18/72, Kingston, Ontario. 5-11, 183. Drafted by Vancouver Canucks (9th choice, 165th overall) 1992 Entry Draft. Traded to Orlando by San Antonio with Grigori Pantaleyev and Dave MacIntyre for Chris Lipuma, Dave Smith and Dave Chyzowski (11/97). Traded to Las Vegas by Long Beach with Shawn Wansborough for Keith McCambridge and a player to be named later (Patrice Lefebvre) (12/98). Last amateur club Oshawa (OHL).

Chad Holloway
Defenseman
Regular Season / Playoffs

Season	Team	League	GP	G	A	PTS	PIM	GP	G	A	PTS	PIM
94-95	Saginaw	CoHL	60	1	2	3	97	11	0	0	0	43
95-96	Saginaw	CoHL	68	5	6	11	162	5	1	0	1	5
96-97	Brantford	CoHL	34	2	9	11	37	—	—	—	—	—
96-97	Dayton	CoHL	31	0	8	8	70	—	—	—	—	—
96-97	Utica	CoHL	6	0	1	1	7	3	0	2	2	0
97-98	KalPa Kuopio	Finland	25	1	1	2	50	—	—	—	—	—
97-98	Huntington	ECHL	5	0	0	0	6	—	—	—	—	—
98-99	Winston-Salem	UHL	61	1	14	15	47	—	—	—	—	—
98-99	Saginaw	UHL	8	0	2	2	4	—	—	—	—	—
	UHL	Totals	268	9	42	51	424	169	1	2	3	48

Born; 2/29/72, Burlington, Ontario. 6-1, 195. Selected by Fort Wayne in 1999 UHL Expansion Draft.

Tobias Holm
Left Wing
Regular Season / Playoffs

Season	Team	League	GP	G	A	PTS	PIM	GP	G	A	PTS	PIM
98-99	Wheeling	ECHL	60	9	17	26	108	—	—	—	—	—

Born; 12/5/78, Kulma, Sweden. 6-1, 200.

Randy Holmes
Center
Regular Season / Playoffs

Season	Team	League	GP	G	A	PTS	PIM	GP	G	A	PTS	PIM
96-97	Madison	CoHL	74	26	45	71	47	5	1	2	3	2
97-98	Madison	UHL	74	45	47	92	34	5	1	1	2	6
98-99	Waco	WPHL	69	33	50	83	103	4	2	1	3	6
	UHL	Totals	148	71	92	163	81	10	2	3	5	8

Born; 8/30/72, Kingston, Ontario. 5-9, 180. 1996-97 Member of CoHL All-Rookie Team. Last amateur club; Ohio State (CCHA).

Todd Holt
Right Wing
Regular Season / Playoffs

Season	Team	League	GP	G	A	PTS	PIM	GP	G	A	PTS	PIM
94-95	Roanoke	ECHL	2	0	2	2	0	—	—	—	—	—
94-95	Kansas City	IHL	28	4	4	8	12	—	—	—	—	—
95-96	Fresno	WCHL	25	14	14	28	20	—	—	—	—	—
95-96	Birmingham	ECHL	21	11	10	21	18	—	—	—	—	—
96-97	Birmingham	ECHL	63	36	31	67	45	8	6	3	9	10
97-98	Birmingham	ECHL	65	21	21	42	49	4	1	0	1	2
98-99	Heilbronner	Germany	55	38	24	62	39	—	—	—	—	—
	ECHL	Totals	151	68	64	132	112	12	7	3	10	12

Born; 1/20/73, Estevan, Saskatchewan. 5-6, 162. Drafted by San Jose Sharks (10th choice, 184th overall) in 1993 Entry Draft. Last amateur club; Swift Current

Brad Holzinger — Center

Regular Season / Playoffs

Season	Team	League	GP	G	A	PTS	PIM	GP	G	A	PTS	PIM
98-99	Jacksonville	ECHL	5	0	2	2	4	—	—	—	—	—
98-99	Chesapeake	ECHL	60	12	31	43	47	8	1	2	3	6
	ECHL	Totals	63	12	33	45	51	8	1	2	3	6

Born; 11/26/73, Parma, Ohio. 6-0, 195. Last amateur club; Bowling Green

Ryan Hoople — Goaltender

Regular Season / Playoffs

Season	Team	League	GP	W	L	T	MIN	SO	AVG	GP	W	L	MIN	SO	AVG
98-99	Kanas City	IHL	3	0	2	1	131	0	4.57	—	—	—	—	—	—
98-99	Arkansas	WPHL	44	26	14	4	2537	3	3.24	—	—	—	—	—	—

Born; 3/19/77, Edmonton, Alberta. 6-1, 188. Last amateur club; Regina (WHL).

Chris Hopf — Right Wing

Regular Season / Playoffs

Season	Team	League	GP	G	A	PTS	PIM	GP	G	A	PTS	PIM
98-99	Fort Worth	WPHL	3	0	0	0	0	—	—	—	—	—

Born; 3/5/75, Towaco, New Jersey. 5-11, 185.

Jan Horacek — Defenseman

Regular Season / Playoffs

Season	Team	League	GP	G	A	PTS	PIM	GP	G	A	PTS	PIM
98-99	Worcester	AHL	53	1	13	14	119	4	0	0	0	6

Born; 5/22/79, Benesov, Czechoslovakia. 6-3, 198. Drafted by St. Louis Blues (3rd choice, 98th overall) in 1997 Entry Draft. Last amateur club; Moncton

Brian Hosler — Goaltender

Regular Season / Playoffs

Season	Team	League	GP	W	L	T	MIN	SO	AVG	GP	W	L	MIN	SO	AVG
98-99	El Paso	WPHL	1	0	1	0	60	0	6.00	—	—	—	—	—	—

Born; 6/4/74, Calgary, Alberta. 6-1, 180.

Doug Houda — Defenseman

Regular Season / Playoffs

Season	Team	League	GP	G	A	PTS	PIM	GP	G	A	PTS	PIM
84-85	Calgary	WHL	65	20	54	74	182	8	3	4	7	29
84-85	Kalamazoo	IHL	—	—	—	—	—	7	0	2	2	10
85-86	Calgary	WHL	16	4	10	14	60	—	—	—	—	—
85-86	Medicine Hat	WHL	35	9	23	32	80	25	4	19	23	64
85-86	Detroit	NHL	6	0	0	0	4	—	—	—	—	—
86-87	Adirondack	AHL	77	6	23	29	142	11	1	8	9	50
87-88	Detroit	NHL	11	1	1	2	10	—	—	—	—	—
87-88	Adirondack	AHL	71	10	32	42	169	11	0	3	3	44
88-89	Detroit	NHL	57	2	11	13	67	6	0	1	1	0
88-89	Adirondack	AHL	7	0	3	3	8	—	—	—	—	—
89-90	Detroit	NHL	73	2	9	11	127	—	—	—	—	—
90-91	Detroit	NHL	22	0	4	4	43	—	—	—	—	—
90-91	Hartford	NHL	19	1	2	3	41	6	0	0	0	8
90-91	Adirondack	AHL	38	9	17	26	67	—	—	—	—	—
91-92	Hartford	NHL	56	3	6	9	125	6	0	2	2	13
92-93	Hartford	NHL	60	2	6	8	167	—	—	—	—	—
93-94	Hartford	NHL	7	0	0	0	23	—	—	—	—	—
93-94	Los Angeles	NHL	54	2	6	8	165	—	—	—	—	—
94-95	Buffalo	NHL	28	1	2	3	68	—	—	—	—	—
95-96	Buffalo	NHL	38	1	3	4	52	—	—	—	—	—
95-96	Rochester	AHL	21	1	6	7	41	19	3	5	8	30
96-97	Islanders	NHL	70	2	8	10	99	—	—	—	—	—
96-97	Utah	IHL	3	0	0	0	7	—	—	—	—	—
97-98	Islanders	NHL	31	1	2	3	47	—	—	—	—	—
97-98	Anaheim	NHL	24	1	2	3	52	—	—	—	—	—
98-99	Detroit	NHL	3	0	1	1	0	—	—	—	—	—
98-99	Adirondack	AHL	73	7	21	28	122	3	0	1	1	4
	NHL	Totals	559	19	63	82	1090	18	0	3	3	21
	AHL	Totals	287	33	102	135	549	44	4	17	21	128
	IHL	Totals	3	0	0	0	7	7	0	2	2	10

Born; 6/3/66, Blairmore, Alberta. 6-2, 190. Drafted by Detroit Red Wings (2nd choice, 28th overall) in 1984 Entry Draft. Traded to Hartford Whalers by Detroit for Doug Crossman (2/20/91). Traded to Los Angeles Kings by Hartford for Marc Potvin (11/3/93). Traded to Buffalo Sabres by Los Angeles for Sean O'Donnell (7/26/94). Signed as a free agent by New York Islanders (10/26/96). Traded to Anaheim Mighty Ducks by Islanders with Travis Green and Tony Tuzzolino for Joe Sacco, J.J. Daigneault and Mark Janssens (2/6/98). Traded to Detroit by Anaheim for cash and a conditional ninth round choicein 1999 (10/8/98). Signed as a free agent by Buffalo (7/13/99). 1987-88 AHL First Team All-Star. Member of 1995-96 AHL champion Rochester Americans. Last amateur club; Medicine

Eric Houde — Center

Regular Season / Playoffs

Season	Team	League	GP	G	A	PTS	PIM	GP	G	A	PTS	PIM
96-97	Montreal	NHL	13	0	2	2	2	—	—	—	—	—
96-97	Fredericton	AHL	66	30	36	66	20	—	—	—	—	—
97-98	Montreal	NHL	9	1	0	1	0	—	—	—	—	—
97-98	Fredericton	AHL	71	28	42	70	24	4	5	2	7	4
98-99	Montreal	NHL	8	1	1	2	2	—	—	—	—	—
98-99	Fredericton	AHL	69	27	37	64	32	14	2	7	9	4
	NHL	Totals	30	2	3	5	4	—	—	—	—	—
	AHL	Totals	206	85	115	190	76	18	7	9	16	8

Born; 12/19/76, Montreal, Quebec. 5-11, 191. Drafted by Montreal Canadiens (9th choice, 216th overall) in 1995 Entry Draft. Signed as a free agent by Edmonton Oilers (7/20/99). 1996-97 Member of 1996-97 AHL All-Rookie Team. Last amateur club; Halifax (QMJHL).

Mike Hough — Right Wing

Regular Season / Playoffs

Season	Team	League	GP	G	A	PTS	PIM	GP	G	A	PTS	PIM
83-84	Fredericton	AHL	69	11	16	27	142	1	0	0	0	7
84-85	Fredericton	AHL	76	21	27	48	49	6	1	1	2	2
85-86	Fredericton	AHL	74	21	33	54	68	6	0	3	3	8
86-87	Quebec	NHL	56	6	8	14	79	9	0	3	3	26
86-87	Fredericton	AHL	10	1	3	4	20	—	—	—	—	—
87-88	Quebec	NHL	17	3	2	5	2	—	—	—	—	—
87-88	Fredericton	AHL	46	16	25	41	133	15	4	8	12	55
88-89	Quebec	NHL	46	9	10	19	39	—	—	—	—	—
88-89	Halifax	AHL	22	11	10	21	87	—	—	—	—	—
89-90	Quebec	NHL	43	13	13	26	84	—	—	—	—	—
90-91	Quebec	NHL	63	13	20	33	111	—	—	—	—	—
91-92	Quebec	NHL	61	16	22	38	77	—	—	—	—	—
92-93	Quebec	NHL	77	8	22	30	69	6	0	1	1	2
93-94	Florida	NHL	78	6	23	29	62	—	—	—	—	—
94-95	Florida	NHL	48	6	7	13	38	—	—	—	—	—
95-96	Florida	NHL	64	7	16	23	37	22	4	1	5	8
96-97	Florida	NHL	69	8	6	14	48	5	1	0	1	2
97-98	Islanders	NHL	74	5	7	12	27	—	—	—	—	—
98-99	Islanders	NHL	11	0	0	0	2	—	—	—	—	—
98-99	Lowell	AHL	11	0	3	3	21	—	—	—	—	—
98-99	Utah	IHL	26	5	7	12	8	—	—	—	—	—
	NHL	Totals	707	100	156	256	675	42	5	5	10	38
	AHL	Totals	308	70	117	187	520	28	5	12	17	72

Born; 2/6/63, Montreal, Quebec. 6-1, 197. Drafted by Quebec Nordiques (7th choice, 181st overall) in 1982 Entry Draft. Traded to Washington Capitals by Quebce for Reggie Savage and Paul MacDermid (6/20/93). Claimed by Florida Panthers in Expansion Draft (6/24/93). Signed as a free agent by New York Islanders (7/21/97). Last amateur club; Kitchener (OHL).

Jean-Francois Houle — Left Wing

Regular Season / Playoffs

Season	Team	League	GP	G	A	PTS	PIM	GP	G	A	PTS	PIM
97-98	Fredericton	AHL	7	1	0	1	8	—	—	—	—	—
97-98	New Orleans	ECHL	53	25	37	62	119	4	1	1	2	16
98-99	Fredericton	AHL	62	7	22	29	101	12	1	7	8	10
	AHL	Totals	69	8	22	30	109	16	2	8	10	26

Born; 1/14/75, Charlesbourg, Quebec. 5-9, 175. Drafted by Montreal Canadiens (5th choice, 99th overall) in 1993 Entry Draft. Last amateur club; Clarkson

Bobby House — Right Wing

Regular Season / Playoffs

Season	Team	League	GP	G	A	PTS	PIM	GP	G	A	PTS	PIM
93-94	Indianapolis	IHL	42	10	8	18	51	—	—	—	—	—
93-94	Flint	CoHL	4	3	3	6	0	—	—	—	—	—
94-95	Indianapolis	IHL	26	2	3	5	26	—	—	—	—	—
94-95	Albany	AHL	26	4	7	11	12	8	1	1	2	0
94-95	Columbus	ECHL	9	11	6	17	2	—	—	—	—	—
95-96	Albany	AHL	77	37	49	86	57	4	0	0	0	4
96-97	Albany	AHL	68	18	16	34	65	16	3	2	5	23
97-98	Quebec	IHL	24	5	7	12	12	—	—	—	—	—
97-98	Albany	AHL	19	10	10	20	10	—	—	—	—	—
97-98	Hershey	AHL	20	2	6	8	8	—	—	—	—	—
97-98	Syracuse	AHL	9	5	6	11	6	5	2	0	2	4
98-99	Albany	AHL	1	0	0	0	0	—	—	—	—	—
98-99	Springfield	AHL	56	11	18	29	27	3	1	0	1	2
98-99	Augusta	ECHL	5	1	0	1	15	—	—	—	—	—
	AHL	Totals	276	87	112	199	185	36	7	3	10	33
	IHL	Totals	92	17	18	35	89	—	—	—	—	—
	ECHL	Totals	14	12	6	18	17	—	—	—	—	—

Born; 1/7/73, Whitehorse, Yukon Territories. 6-1, 200. Drafted by Chicago Blackhawks (4th choice, 66th overall) in 1991 Entry Draft. Traded to New Jersey Devils by Chicago for cash (5/21/96). Signed as a free agent by Toronto Maple Leafs (7/23/99). Member of 1994-95 Calder Cup champion Albany RiverRats. Last amateur club; Brandon (WHL).

Len Hovland — Defenseman

Regular Season / Playoffs

Season	Team	League	GP	G	A	PTS	PIM	GP	G	A	PTS	PIM
98-99	Fayetteville	CHL	70	9	22	31	113	—	—	—	—	—

Born; 12/18/73, Duluth, Minnesota. 6-3, 220. Last amateur club; Wisconsin-Superior (NCAA 3).

Todd Howarth — Center

Regular Season / Playoffs

Season	Team	League	GP	G	A	PTS	PIM	GP	G	A	PTS	PIM
91-92	Thunder Bay	CoHL	16	5	10	15	20	13	3	7	10	18
92-93	Thunder Bay	CoHL	60	37	42	79	96	11	2	13	15	12
93-94	Thunder Bay	CoHL	49	23	41	64	80	9	7	8	15	19
94-95	Thunder Bay	CoHL	67	27	47	74	168	11	8	8	16	45
95-96	Thunder Bay	CoHL	55	33	45	78	185	19	9	20	29	51
96-97	Fort Worth	CeHL	27	15	19	34	100	17	5	9	14	49
97-98	Madison	UHL	14	5	8	13	30	7	1	6	7	2
98-99	Wichita	CHL	48	23	20	43	86	—	—	—	—	—
	UHL	Totals	261	130	193	343	579	70	30	62	92	147
	CHL	Totals	75	38	39	77	186	17	5	9	14	49

Born; 6/16/70, Dryden, Ontario. 5-9, 170. 1992-93 CoHL Best Defensive Forward. Member of 1991-92 CoHL champion Thunder Bay Thunder Hawks. Member of 1993-94 CoHL champion Thunder Bay Senators. Member of 1994-95 CoHL champion Thunder Bay Senators. Member of 1996-97 CeHL Champion Fort Worth Fire. Last amateur club; Bemidji (NCAA).

Mike Howell — Defenseman

Regular Season / Playoffs

Season	Team	League	GP	G	A	PTS	PIM	GP	G	A	PTS	PIM
98-99	Asheville	UHL	2	0	0	0	0	—	—	—	—	—

Born; 12/29/74, St. Paul, Minnesota.

Nick Hriczov — Defenseman

Regular Season / Playoffs

Season	Team	League	GP	G	A	PTS	PIM	GP	G	A	PTS	PIM
96-97	Amarillo	WPHL	58	1	13	14	161	—	—	—	—	—
97-98	New Mexico	WPHL	47	1	10	11	123	—	—	—	—	—
97-98	San Angelo	WPHL	12	0	2	2	19	3	1	0	1	2
98-99	Bakersfield	WCHL	52	3	5	8	182	1	0	0	0	17
	WPHL	Totals	117	2	25	27	303	3	1	0	1	2

Born; 9/24/72, Clifton, New Jersey. 6-4, 235. Last amateur club; Oswego

Jim Hrivnak — Goaltender

Season	Team	League	GP	W	L	T	MIN	SO	AVG	GP	W	L	MIN	SO	AVG
			Regular Season							Playoffs					
88-89	Merrimack	NCAA 2	22	—	—	—	1295	4	2.41	—	—	—	—	—	—
88-89	Baltimore	AHL	10	1	8	0	502	0	6.57	—	—	—	—	—	—
89-90	Washington	NHL	11	5	5	0	609	0	3.55	—	—	—	—	—	—
89-90	Baltimore	AHL	47	24	19	2	2722	*4	3.06	6	4	2	360	0	3.17
90-91	Washington	NHL	9	4	2	1	432	0	3.61	—	—	—	—	—	—
90-91	Baltimore	AHL	42	20	16	6	2481	1	3.24	6	2	3	324	0	3.89
91-92	Washington	NHL	12	6	3	0	605	0	3.47	—	—	—	—	—	—
91-92	Baltimore	AHL	22	10	8	3	1303	0	3.36	—	—	—	—	—	—
92-93	Washington	NHL	27	13	9	2	1421	0	3.550	—	—	—	—	—	—
92-93	Winnipeg	NHL	3	2	1	0	180	0	4.33	—	—	—	—	—	—
93-94	St. Louis	NHL	23	4	10	0	970	0	4.27	—	—	—	—	—	—
94-95	Milwaukee	IHL	28	17	10	1	1634	0	3.89	—	—	—	—	—	—
94-95	Kansas City	IHL	10	3	5	2	550	0	3.81	2	0	2	118	0	3.55
95-96	Carolina	AHL	11	1	4	1	458	0	3.54	—	—	—	—	—	—
95-96	Las Vegas	IHL	13	10	1	1	712	0	2.86	—	—	—	—	—	—
95-96	Kansas City	IHL	4	1	1	0	154	0	4.29	—	—	—	—	—	—
96-97	Kolner Haie	Germany	21	—	—	—	1144	1	2.78	2	—	—	121	0	3.47
97-98	Manchester	BSL	32	—	—	—	1967	6	2.47	—	—	—	—	—	—
98-99	Hamburg	Germany	33												
	NHL	Totals	85	34	30	3	4217	0	3.73	—	—	—	—	—	—
	AHL	Totals	132	56	55	10	7466	5	3.43	12	6	5	684	0	3.51
	IHL	Totals	55	31	17	4	3050	0	3.86	2	0	2	118	0	3.55

Born; 5/28/68, Montreal, Quebec. Drafted by Washington Capitals (4th choice, 61st overall) in 1986 Entry Draft. Traded to Winnipeg Jets by Washington with Washington's second round choice (Alexei Budayev) in 1993 Entry Draft for Rick Tabaracci (3/22/93). Traded to St. Louis Blues by Winnipeg for St. Louis' seventh round choice (later traded to Florida-later traded to Edmonton-later traded to Winnipeg-Winnipeg selected Chris Kibermanis) in 1994 Entry Draft (7/29/93). Last amateur club; Merrimack (NCAA 2).

Kelly Hrycun — Right Wing

Season	Team	League	GP	G	A	PTS	PIM	GP	G	A	PTS	PIM
			Regular Season					Playoffs				
94-95	Fresno	SUN	2	0	0	0	2	—	—	—	—	—
95-96	Alaska	WCHL	34	10	20	30	6	5	4	3	7	0
96-97	Alaska	WCHL	63	38	34	72	44	—	—	—	—	—
97-98	Idaho	WCHL	4	0	1	1	2	—	—	—	—	—
97-98	Bakersfield	WCHL	55	21	32	53	18	4	1	0	1	0
98-99	Bakersfield	WCHL	68	24	20	44	40	1	0	0	0	0
	WCHL	Totals	224	93	107	200	108	10	5	3	8	0

Born; 4/21/73, Edmonton, Alberta. 5-10, 180. Selected by Tucson in 1997 WCHL Dispersal Draft. Traded to Bakersfield by Idaho with Don Lester for Scott Davis (11/97). Last amateur club; University of Denver (WCHA).

Dalen Hrooshkin — Center

Season	Team	League	GP	G	A	PTS	PIM	GP	G	A	PTS	PIM
			Regular Season					Playoffs				
98-99	New Orleans	ECHL	9	4	1	5	2	—	—	—	—	—
98-99	Mobile	ECHL	56	6	15	21	6	2	1	1	2	0
	ECHL	Totals	65	10	16	26	8	2	1	1	2	0

Born; Traded to Mobile by New Orleans for Russ Monteith (7/23/99).

Bill Huard — Left Wing

Season	Team	League	GP	G	A	PTS	PIM	GP	G	A	PTS	PIM
			Regular Season					Playoffs				
88-89	Carolina	ECHL	40	27	21	48	177	10	7	2	9	70
89-90	Utica	AHL	27	1	7	8	67	5	0	1	1	33
89-90	Nashville	ECHL	34	24	27	51	212	—	—	—	—	—
90-91	Utica	AHL	72	11	16	27	359	—	—	—	—	—
91-92	Utica	AHL	62	9	11	20	233	4	1	1	2	4
92-93	Boston	NHL	2	0	0	0	0	—	—	—	—	—
92-93	Providence	AHL	72	18	19	37	302	6	3	0	3	9
93-94	Ottawa	NHL	63	2	2	4	162	—	—	—	—	—
94-95	Ottawa	NHL	26	1	1	2	64	—	—	—	—	—
94-95	Quebec	NHL	7	2	2	4	13	1	0	0	0	0
95-96	Dallas	NHL	51	6	6	12	176	—	—	—	—	—
95-96	Michigan	IHL	12	1	1	2	74	—	—	—	—	—
96-97	Dallas	NHL	40	5	6	11	105	—	—	—	—	—
97-98	Edmonton	NHL	30	0	1	1	72	4	0	0	0	2
98-99	Edmonton	NHL	3	0	0	0	0	—	—	—	—	—
98-99	Houston	IHL	38	9	5	14	201	10	0	0	0	8
	NHL	Totals	222	16	18	34	592	5	0	0	0	2
	AHL	Totals	233	39	53	92	961	15	4	2	6	46
	IHL	Totals	50	10	6	16	275	10	0	0	0	8
	ECHL	Totals	74	51	48	99	389	10	7	2	9	70

Born; 6/24/67, Welland, Ontario. 6-1, 215. Signed as a free agent by New Jersey Devils (10/1/89). Signed as a free agent by Boston Bruins (12/4/92). Signed as a free agent by Ottawa Senators (6/30/93). Traded to Quebec Nordiques by Ottawa for Mike Stromberg and Quebec's fourth round choice (Kevin Boyd) in 1995 Entry Draft. Claimed by Dallas Stars from Colorado Avalanche in NHL Waiver Draft (10/2/95). Signed as a free agent by Edmonton Oilers (7/22/97). Signed as a free agent by Los Angeles Kings (7/21/99). Member of 1988-89 ECHL Champion Carolina Thunderbirds. Member of 1998-99 IHL Champion Houston Aeros. Last amateur club; Peterborough (OHL).

Mike Hudson — Center

Season	Team	League	GP	G	A	PTS	PIM	GP	G	A	PTS	PIM
			Regular Season					Playoffs				
87-88	Saginaw	IHL	75	18	30	48	44	10	2	3	5	20
88-89	Chicago	NHL	41	7	16	23	20	10	1	2	3	18
88-89	Saginaw	IHL	30	15	17	32	10	—	—	—	—	—
89-90	Chicago	NHL	49	9	12	21	56	4	0	0	0	2
90-91	Chicago	NHL	55	7	9	16	62	6	0	2	2	8
90-91	Indianapolis	IHL	3	1	2	3	0	—	—	—	—	—
91-92	Chicago	NHL	76	14	15	29	92	16	3	5	8	26
92-93	Chicago	NHL	36	1	6	7	44	—	—	—	—	—
92-93	Edmonton	NHL	5	0	1	1	2	—	—	—	—	—
93-94	Rangers	NHL	48	4	7	11	47	—	—	—	—	—
94-95	Pittsburgh	NHL	40	2	9	11	34	11	0	0	0	6
95-96	Toronto	NHL	27	2	0	2	29	—	—	—	—	—
95-96	St. Louis	NHL	32	3	12	15	26	2	0	1	1	4
96-97	Phoenix	NHL	7	0	0	0	2	—	—	—	—	—
96-97	Phoenix	IHL	33	6	9	15	10	—	—	—	—	—
97-98	Augsburg	Germany	15	1	5	6	16	—	—	—	—	—
97-98	Adler Mannheim	Germany	14	4	3	7	2	10	2	5	7	12
98-99	Adler Mannheim	Germany	45	6	18	24	44	12	0	3	3	14
	NHL	Totals	416	49	87	136	414	49	4	10	14	64
	IHL	Totals	141	40	58	98	64	10	2	3	5	20

Born; 2/6/67, Guelph, Ontario. 6-1, 205. Drafted by Chicago Blackhawks (6th choice, 140th overall) in 1986 Entry Draft. Traded to Edmonton Oilers by Chicago for Criag Muni (3/22/93). Claimed by New York Rangers from Edmonton in NHL Waiver Draft (10/3/93). Claimed by Pittsburgh Penguins from Rangers in NHL Waiver Draft (1/18/95). Signed as a free agent by Toronto Maple Leafs (9/22/95). Claimed on waivers by St. Louis Blues from Toronto (1/4/96). Signed as a free agent by Phoenix Coyotes (11/12/96). Last amateur

Kerry Huffman — Defenseman

Regular Season / Playoffs

Season	Team	League	GP	G	A	PTS	PIM	GP	G	A	PTS	PIM
86-87	Guelph	OHL	44	4	31	35	20	5	0	2	2	8
86-87	Philadelphia	NHL	9	0	0	0	2	—	—	—	—	—
86-87	Hershey	AHL	3	0	1	1	0	4	0	0	0	0
87-88	Philadelphia	NHL	52	6	17	23	34	2	0	0	0	0
88-89	Philadelphia	NHL	29	0	11	11	31	—	—	—	—	—
88-89	Hershey	AHL	29	2	13	15	16	—	—	—	—	—
89-90	Philadelphia	NHL	43	1	12	13	34	—	—	—	—	—
90-91	Philadelphia	NHL	10	1	2	3	10	—	—	—	—	—
90-91	Hershey	AHL	45	5	29	34	20	7	1	2	3	0
91-92	Philadelphia	NHL	60	14	18	32	41	—	—	—	—	—
92-93	Quebec	NHL	52	4	18	22	54	3	0	0	0	0
93-94	Quebec	NHL	28	0	6	6	28	—	—	—	—	—
93-94	Ottawa	NHL	34	4	8	12	12	—	—	—	—	—
94-95	Ottawa	NHL	37	2	4	6	46	—	—	—	—	—
95-96	Ottawa	NHL	43	4	11	15	63	—	—	—	—	—
95-96	Philadelphia	NHL	4	1	1	3	6	6	0	0	0	0
96-97	Las Vegas	IHL	44	5	19	24	38	3	0	0	0	2
97-98	Grand Rapids	IHL	73	4	23	27	60	3	0	0	0	2
98-99	Grand Rapids	IHL	4	0	1	1	6	—	—	—	—	—
	NHL	Totals	401	37	108	145	361	11	0	0	0	2
	AHL	Totals	77	7	43	50	36	11	1	2	3	0

Born; 1/3/68, Peterborough, Ontario. 6-2, 200. Drafted by Philadelphia Flyers (1st choice, 20th overall) in 1986 Entry Draft. Traded to Quebec Nordiques by Philadelphia with Peter Forsberg, Steve Duchesne, Mike Ricci, Ron Hextall, Chris Simon, Philadelphia's first round choice in the 1993 (Jocelyn Thibault) and 1994 (later traded to Toronto-later traded to Washington-Washington selected Nolan Baumgartner)-Entry Drafts and cash for Eric Lindros (6/30/92). Claimed on waivers by Ottawa Senators from Quebec, (1/15/94). Traded to Flyers by Senators for future considerations (3/19/96). Last amateur club; Guelph (OHL).

Brent Hughes — Right Wing

Regular Season / Playoffs

Season	Team	League	GP	G	A	PTS	PIM	GP	G	A	PTS	PIM
87-88	Moncton	AHL	73	13	19	32	206	—	—	—	—	—
88-89	Winnipeg	NHL	28	3	2	5	82	—	—	—	—	—
88-89	Moncton	AHL	54	34	34	68	286	10	9	4	13	40
89-90	Winnipeg	NHL	11	1	2	3	33	—	—	—	—	—
89-90	Moncton	AHL	65	31	29	60	277	—	—	—	—	—
90-91	Moncton	AHL	63	21	22	43	144	3	0	0	0	7
91-92	Baltimore	AHL	55	25	29	54	190	—	—	—	—	—
91-92	Boston	NHL	8	1	1	2	38	10	2	0	2	20
91-92	Maine	AHL	12	6	4	10	34	—	—	—	—	—
92-93	Boston	NHL	62	5	4	9	191	1	0	0	0	2
93-94	Boston	NHL	77	13	11	24	143	13	2	1	3	27
93-94	Providence	AHL	6	2	5	7	4	—	—	—	—	—
94-95	Boston	NHL	44	6	6	12	139	5	0	0	0	4
95-96	Buffalo	NHL	76	5	10	15	148	—	—	—	—	—
96-97	Islanders	NHL	51	7	3	10	57	—	—	—	—	—
96-97	Utah	IHL	5	2	2	4	11	—	—	—	—	—
97-98	Houston	IHL	79	19	12	31	128	4	0	3	3	20
98-99	Houston	IHL	29	4	2	6	87	—	—	—	—	—
98-99	Utah	IHL	51	13	11	24	80	—	—	—	—	—
	NHL	Totals	357	41	39	80	831	29	4	1	5	53
	AHL	Totals	328	132	142	274	1141	13	9	4	13	47
	IHL	Totals	164	38	27	65	306	4	0	3	3	20

Born; 4/5/66, New Westminster, British Columbia. 5-11, 195. Signed as a free agent by Winnipeg Jets (6/13/88). Traded to Washington Capitals by Winnipeg with Craig Duncanson and Simon Wheeldon for Bob Joyce, Tyler Larter and Kent Paynter, (5/21/91). Traded to Boston Bruins by Washington with future considerations for John Byce and Dennis Smith, (2/24/92). Claimed by Buffalo Sabres from Boston in NHL Waiver Draft (10/2/95). Signed as a free agent by New York Islanders (8/9/96). Named coach of the Austin IceBats (WPHL) beginning with the 1999-2000 season. Last amateur club; Victoria (WHL).

Jason Hughes — Defenseman

Regular Season / Playoffs

Season	Team	League	GP	G	A	PTS	PIM	GP	G	A	PTS	PIM
98-99	South Carolina	ECHL	9	1	1	2	10	2	0	0	0	17

Born; 1/16/74. 6-3, 220.

Joe Hulbig — Left Wing

Regular Season / Playoffs

Season	Team	League	GP	G	A	PTS	PIM	GP	G	A	PTS	PIM
96-97	Edmonton	NHL	6	0	0	0	0	6	0	1	1	2
96-97	Hamilton	AHL	73	18	28	46	59	16	6	10	16	6
97-98	Edmonton	NHL	17	2	2	4	2	—	—	—	—	—
97-98	Hamilton	AHL	46	15	16	31	52	3	0	1	1	2
98-99	Edmonton	NHL	1	0	0	0	2	—	—	—	—	—
98-99	Hamilton	AHL	76	22	24	46	68	11	4	2	6	18
	NHL	Totals	24	2	2	4	4	6	0	1	1	2
	AHL	Totals	195	55	68	123	179	30	10	13	23	26

Born; 9/29/73, Norwood, Massachusetts. 6-3, 215. Drafted by Edmonton Oilers (1st choice, 13th overall) in 1992 Entry Draft. Signed as a free agent by Boston Bruins (7/19/99). Last amateur club; Providence (Hockey East).

Bart Hull — Forward

Regular Season / Playoffs

Season	Team	League	GP	G	A	PTS	PIM	GP	G	A	PTS	PIM
97-98	Idaho	WCHL	1	0	0	0	0	—	—	—	—	—
98-99	Idaho	WCHL	4	0	0	0	4	—	—	—	—	—
	WCHL	Totals	5	0	0	0	4	—	—	—	—	—

Born; 2/13/69, Chicago, Illinois. 5-11, 215.

Kent Hulst — Center

Regular Season / Playoffs

Season	Team	League	GP	G	A	PTS	PIM	GP	G	A	PTS	PIM
88-89	Belleville	OHL	45	21	41	62	43	—	—	—	—	—
88-89	Flint	IHL	7	0	1	1	4	—	—	—	—	—
88-89	Newmarket	AHL	—	—	—	—	—	2	1	1	2	2
89-90	Newmarket	AHL	80	26	34	60	29	—	—	—	—	—
90-91	Newmarket	AHL	79	28	37	65	57	—	—	—	—	—
91-92	New Haven	AHL	80	21	39	60	59	5	2	2	4	0
92-93												
93-94	Portland	AHL	72	34	33	67	68	17	4	6	10	14
94-95	Portland	AHL	29	10	17	27	80	7	3	1	4	2
95-96	Portland	AHL	75	25	47	72	122	24	11	16	27	30
96-97	Portland	AHL	48	19	31	50	60	5	1	2	3	4
97-98	Portland	AHL	77	24	23	47	74	10	3	4	7	6
98-99	Portland	AHL	72	16	23	39	52	—	—	—	—	—
	AHL	Totals	540	187	261	448	549	70	25	32	57	58

Born; 4/8/68, St. Thomas, Ontario. 6-1, 195. Drafted by Toronto Maple Leafs (4th choice, 69th overall) in 1986 Entry Draft. Signed as a free agent by Quebec Nordiques (9/20/91). Signed as a free agent by Portland Pirates (1993). Member of 1993-94 AHL Champion Portland Pirates. Last amateur club; Belleville

John Hultberg — Goaltender

Regular Season / Playoffs

Season	Team	League	GP	W	L	T	MIN	SO	AVG	GP	W	L	MIN	SO	AVG
97-98	Barrie	OHL	35	15	9	4	1843	2	3.35	2	1	1	101	0	4.75
97-98	New Orleans	ECHL	1	0	0	0	1	0	0.00	—	—	—	—	—	—
98-99	New Orleans	ECHL	1	0	0	0	11	0	5.40	—	—	—	—	—	—
98-99	San Antonio	CHL	22	9	7	3	1112	0	4.26	—	—	—	—	—	—
	ECHL	Totals	2	0	0	0	12	0	5.00	—	—	—	—	—	—

Born; 4/25/77, Skokie, Illinois. 5-11, 211. Drafted by Edmonton Oilers (10th choice, 221st overall) in 1996 Entry Draft. Last amateur club; Barrie (OHL).

Kelly Hultgren — Defenseman

Regular Season / Playoffs

Season	Team	League	GP	G	A	PTS	PIM	GP	G	A	PTS	PIM
95-96	Los Angeles	IHL	40	1	7	8	54	—	—	—	—	—
95-96	Louisiana	ECHL	18	1	12	13	31	—	—	—	—	—
95-96	San Diego	WCHL	4	2	3	5	8	—	—	—	—	—
96-97	Long Beach	IHL	2	0	0	0	0	—	—	—	—	—
96-97	Pensacola	ECHL	15	6	4	10	0	10	4	5	9	6
96-97	Fresno	WCHL	44	9	28	37	45	—	—	—	—	—
97-98	Pensacola	ECHL	42	15	38	53	41	—	—	—	—	—
98-99	Pensacola	ECHL	28	4	7	11	12	—	—	—	—	—
98-99	Quad City	UHL	23	5	9	14	14	15	3	3	6	4
	IHL	Totals	42	1	7	8	54	—	—	—	—	—
	ECHL	Totals	103	26	61	87	84	10	4	5	9	6
	WCHL	Totals	48	11	31	42	53	—	—	—	—	—

Born; 4/11/71, St. Paul, Minnesota. 6-0, 190. Last amateur club; St. Cloud

Scott Humeniuk — Defenseman
Regular Season / Playoffs

Season	Team	League	GP	G	A	PTS	PIM	GP	G	A	PTS	PIM
89-90	Moose Jaw	WHL	71	23	47	70	141	—	—	—	—	—
89-90	Binghamton	AHL	4	0	1	1	11	—	—	—	—	—
90-91	Springfield	AHL	57	6	17	23	69	14	2	2	4	18
91-92	Springfield	AHL	28	2	3	5	27	—	—	—	—	—
91-92	Louisville	ECHL	26	7	21	28	93	13	1	11	12	33
92-93	Springfield	AHL	16	0	3	3	28	14	1	3	4	8
93-94	Springfield	AHL	71	15	42	57	91	6	0	3	3	8
94-95	Minnesota	IHL	47	10	15	25	55	—	—	—	—	—
94-95	Portland	AHL	8	3	1	4	30	7	3	3	6	2
95-96	Portland	AHL	29	4	10	14	50	—	—	—	—	—
95-96	Rochester	AHL	12	0	2	2	19	—	—	—	—	—
95-96	Providence	AHL	18	3	7	10	15	4	2	1	3	4
96-97	Lukko Rauma	Finland	42	6	11	17	108	—	—	—	—	—
97-98	Augsburg	Germany	42	10	12	22	104	—	—	—	—	—
98-99	Baton Rouge	ECHL	53	9	27	36	88	—	—	—	—	—
	AHL	Totals	243	33	86	119	340	45	8	12	20	34
	ECHL	Totals	79	16	48	64	181	13	1	11	12	33

Born; 9/10/69, Saskatoon, Saskatchewan. 6-0, 195. Signed as a free agent by Hartford Whalers (3/22/90). Member of 1990-91 AHL champion Springfield Indians. Last amateur club; Moose Jaw (WHL).

Casey Hungle — Right Wing
Regular Season / Playoffs

Season	Team	League	GP	G	A	PTS	PIM	GP	G	A	PTS	PIM
93-94	Erie	ECHL	64	28	17	45	51	—	—	—	—	—
94-95	Erie	ECHL	45	9	8	17	49	—	—	—	—	—
95-96	Tallahassee	ECHL	28	6	3	9	18	—	—	—	—	—
96-97	Columbus	CeHL	60	26	31	57	71	—	—	—	—	—
96-97	Wichita	CeHL	8	3	3	6	10	9	1	2	3	19
97-98	Fayetteville	CHL	47	16	16	32	56	—	—	—	—	—
98-99	Fatetteville	CHL	10	1	3	4	12	—	—	—	—	—
98-99	Tucson	WCHL	7	4	7	11	8	—	—	—	—	—
98-99	Tacoma	WCHL	50	17	16	33	40	11	3	2	5	8
	ECHL	Totals	137	43	28	71	118	—	—	—	—	—
	CHL	Totals	125	46	53	99	149	9	1	2	3	19
	WCHL	Totals	57	21	23	44	48	11	3	2	5	8

Born; 5/27/72, Shawnigan Lake, British Columbia. 5-11, 180. Member of 1998-99 WCHL Champion Tacoma Sabrecats.

Kelly Hurd — Right Wing
Regular Season / Playoffs

Season	Team	League	GP	G	A	PTS	PIM	GP	G	A	PTS	PIM
91-92	Adirondack	AHL	35	9	7	16	16	8	1	4	5	2
91-92	Fort Wayne	IHL	30	13	9	22	12	3	3	0	3	9
92-93	Fort Wayne	IHL	71	23	31	54	81	10	4	5	9	12
93-94	Fort Wayne	IHL	75	35	49	84	52	17	6	4	10	10
94-95	Fort Wayne	IHL	59	16	33	49	36	4	3	0	3	4
95-96	San Francisco	IHL	26	5	3	8	20	—	—	—	—	—
95-96	Houston	IHL	44	14	16	30	23	—	—	—	—	—
96-97	Grand Rapids	IHL	4	0	1	1	4	—	—	—	—	—
96-97	Utah	IHL	2	0	0	0	0	—	—	—	—	—
96-97	Mississippi	ECHL	57	25	33	58	72	3	1	3	4	2
97-98	Mississippi	ECHL	68	21	45	66	92	—	—	—	—	—
98-99	Mississippi	ECHL	54	20	33	53	40	18	9	11	20	4
	IHL	Totals	311	106	142	248	228	34	16	9	25	35
	ECHL	Totals	179	66	111	177	204	3	1	3	4	2

Born; 5/13/68, Castlegar, British Columbia. Drafted by Detroit Red Wings (6th choice, 143rd overall) in 1988 Entry Draft. Member of 1991-92 AHL champion Adirondack Red Wings. Member of 1992-93 IHL champion Fort Wayne Komets. Member of 1998-99 ECHL Champion Mississippi SeaWolves. Last amateur club; Michigan Tech (WCHA).

Mike Hurlbut — Defenseman
Regular Season / Playoffs

Season	Team	League	GP	G	A	PTS	PIM	GP	G	A	PTS	PIM
88-89	St. Lawrence	ECAC	36	8	25	33	30	—	—	—	—	—
88-89	Denver	IHL	8	0	2	2	13	4	1	2	3	2
89-90	Flint	IHL	74	3	34	37	38	3	0	1	1	2
90-91	San Diego	IHL	2	1	0	1	0	—	—	—	—	—
90-91	Binghamton	AHL	33	2	11	13	27	3	0	1	1	0
91-92	Binghamton	AHL	79	16	39	55	64	11	2	7	9	8
92-93	Rangers	NHL	23	1	8	9	16	—	—	—	—	—
92-93	Binghamton	AHL	45	11	25	36	46	14	2	5	7	12
93-94	Quebec	NHL	1	0	0	0	0	—	—	—	—	—
93-94	Cornwall	AHL	77	13	33	46	100	13	3	7	10	12
94-95	Cornwall	AHL	74	11	49	60	69	3	1	0	1	15
95-96	Minnesota	IHL	22	1	4	5	22	—	—	—	—	—
95-96	Houston	IHL	38	3	12	15	33	—	—	—	—	—
96-97	Houston	IHL	70	11	24	35	62	13	5	8	13	12
97-98	Buffalo	NHL	3	0	0	0	2	—	—	—	—	—
97-98	Rochester	AHL	45	10	20	30	48	4	1	1	2	2
98-99	Buffalo	NHL	1	0	0	0	0	—	—	—	—	—
98-99	Rochester	AHL	72	15	39	54	46	20	4	5	9	12
	NHL	Totals	25	1	8	9	16	—	—	—	—	—
	AHL	Totals	380	78	216	294	400	68	13	26	39	61
	IHL	Totals	214	19	76	95	168	20	6	11	17	16

Born; 10/7/66, Massensa, New York. 6-2, 200. Drafted by New York Rangers (1st choice, 5th overall) in 1988 Supplemental Draft. Traded to Quebec Nordiques by Rangers for Alexander Karpovtsev (9/7/93). 1994-95 AHL Second Team All-Star. Signed as a free agent by Buffalo Sabres (8/11/97). Last amateur club; St. Lawrence (ECAC).

Mike Hurley — Right Wing
Regular Season / Playoffs

Season	Team	League	GP	G	A	PTS	PIM	GP	G	A	PTS	PIM
98-99	Baton Rouge	ECHL	6	0	0	0	6	—	—	—	—	—

Born; 11/17/77, Charlottetown, Prince Edward Island. 5-11, 173. Drafted by Dallas Stars (3rd choice, 90th overall) in 1996 Entry Draft. Last amateur club; Portland (WHL).

Jani Hurme — Goaltender
Regular Season / Playoffs

Season	Team	League	GP	W	L	T	MIN	SO	AVG	GP	W	L	MIN	SO	AVG
97-98	Detroit	IHL	6	2	2	2	291	0	4.13	—	—	—	—	—	—
97-98	Indianapolis	IHL	29	11	11	3	1507	1	3.30	3	1	0	130	0	4.62
98-99	Detroit	IHL	12	7	3	1	643	1	2.43	—	—	—	—	—	—
98-99	Cincinnati	IHL	26	14	9	2	1428	0	3.40	—	—	—	—	—	—
	IHL	Totals	73	34	22	7	3868	2	3.26	3	1	0	130	0	4.62

Born; 1/7/75, Turku, Finland. 6-0, 187. Drafted by Ottawa Senators (2nd choice, 58th overall) in 1997 Entry Draft.

Phil Husak — Left Wing
Regular Season / Playoffs

Season	Team	League	GP	G	A	PTS	PIM	GP	G	A	PTS	PIM
97-98	Winston-Salem	UHL	48	4	7	11	47	—	—	—	—	—
98-99	Winston-Salem	UHL	6	0	0	0	2	—	—	—	—	—
98-99	Saginaw	UHL	30	2	4	6	25	—	—	—	—	—
	UHL	Totals	84	6	11	17	74	—	—	—	—	—

Born; 8/24/74, Stonewall, Manitoba. 6-0, 195.

Ryan Huska — Center
Regular Season / Playoffs

Season	Team	League	GP	G	A	PTS	PIM	GP	G	A	PTS	PIM
95-96	Indianapolis	IHL	28	2	3	5	15	5	1	1	2	27
96-97	Indianapolis	IHL	80	18	12	30	100	4	0	0	0	4
97-98	Chicago	NHL	1	0	0	0	0	—	—	—	—	—
97-98	Indianapolis	IHL	80	19	16	35	115	5	0	3	3	10
98-99	Lowell	AHL	60	5	13	18	70	2	0	0	0	0
	IHL	Totals	188	39	31	70	230	14	1	4	5	41

Born; 7/2/75, Cranbrook, British Columbia. 6-2, 194. Drafted by Chicago Blackhawks (4th choice, 76th overall) in 1993 Entry Draft. Signed as a free agent by New York Islanders (9/9/98). Last amateur club; Kamloops (WHL).

Marc Hussey — Defenseman

Regular Season / Playoffs

Season	Team	League	GP	G	A	PTS	PIM	GP	G	A	PTS	PIM
94-95	Canada	National	36	2	7	9	26	—	—	—	—	—
94-95	St. John's	AHL	11	0	1	1	20	—	—	—	—	—
95-96	Saint John	AHL	68	10	21	31	120	5	0	0	0	8
96-97	Saint John	AHL	46	6	18	24	62	—	—	—	—	—
96-97	Utah	IHL	8	0	1	1	6	—	—	—	—	—
96-97	Indianapolis	IHL	14	0	2	2	17	4	0	1	1	10
97-98	Indianapolis	IHL	23	2	5	7	14	—	—	—	—	—
97-98	Milwaukee	IHL	50	3	15	18	81	10	2	3	5	14
98-99	Fredericton	AHL	51	3	5	8	105	—	—	—	—	—
98-99	Grand Rapids	IHL	13	0	6	6	14	—	—	—	—	—
	AHL	Totals	176	19	45	64	307	5	0	0	0	8
	IHL	Totals	108	5	29	34	132	14	2	4	6	24

Born; 1/22/74, Chatham, New Brunswick. 6-4, 182. Drafted by Pittsburgh Penguins (2nd choice, 43rd overall) in 1992 Entry Draft. Traded to Chicago Blackhawks by Calgary Flames for Ravil Gusmanov (3/18/97). Traded to Milwaukee by Indiamapolis with Martin Gendron for Len Esau and Kent Paynter (12/97). Last amateur club; Medicine Hat (WHL).

Rob Hutson — Right Wing

Regular Season / Playoffs

Season	Team	League	GP	G	A	PTS	PIM	GP	G	A	PTS	PIM
95-96	Illinois-Chicago	CCHA	17	9	8	17	8	—	—	—	—	—
95-96	Toledo	ECHL	2	0	2	2	0	—	—	—	—	—
96-97	Saginaw	CoHL	5	2	2	4	4	—	—	—	—	—
96-97	Amarillo	WPHL	45	21	25	46	117	—	—	—	—	—
97-98	Amarillo	WPHL	67	31	24	55	140	—	—	—	—	—
98-99	Amarillo	WPHL	16	10	7	17	38	—	—	—	—	—
98-99	Austin	WPHL	33	9	10	19	44	—	—	—	—	—

Born; 4/9/72, Bowsman, Manitoba. 5-11, 190. Last amateur club; Illinois-Chicago (CCHA).

Geordie Hyland — Defenseman

Regular Season / Playoffs

Season	Team	League	GP	G	A	PTS	PIM	GP	G	A	PTS	PIM
98-99	Baton Rouge	ECHL	2	0	0	0	6	—	—	—	—	—
98-99	Flint	UHL	26	1	1	2	44	—	—	—	—	—
98-99	Abilene	WPHL	18	3	2	5	10	3	0	0	0	4

Born; 1/2/76, Toronto, Ontario. 6-2, 210. Last amateur club; Harvard (ECAC).

Dave Hymovitz — Left Wing

Regular Season / Playoffs

Season	Team	League	GP	G	A	PTS	PIM	GP	G	A	PTS	PIM
96-97	Indianapolis	IHL	6	0	1	1	0	1	0	0	0	0
96-97	Columbus	ECHL	58	39	32	71	29	5	4	1	5	2
97-98	Indianapolis	IHL	63	11	15	26	20	5	1	1	2	6
98-99	Indianapolis	IHL	78	46	30	76	42	5	2	3	5	2
	IHL	Totals	147	57	46	103	62	11	3	4	7	8

Born; 5/30/74, Boston, Massachusetts. 5-11, 170. Drafted by Chicago Blackhawks (9th choice, 209th overall) in 1992 Entry Draft. 1998-99 IHL Second Team All-Star. Signed as a free agent by Los Angeles Kings (6/99). Last amateur club; Boston College (Hockey East).

Chris Hynnes — Defenseman

Regular Season / Playoffs

Season	Team	League	GP	G	A	PTS	PIM	GP	G	A	PTS	PIM
93-94	Thunder Bay	CoHL	59	13	40	53	45	9	2	6	8	6
94-95	Minnesota	IHL	25	3	4	7	22	—	—	—	—	—
94-95	Prince Edward Island	AHL	14	0	1	1	4	—	—	—	—	—
94-95	Thunder Bay	CoHL	16	6	9	15	10	8	1	5	6	10
95-96	Thunder Bay	CoHL	73	26	47	73	96	19	4	17	21	32
96-97	South Carolina	ECHL	68	22	33	55	86	18	11	16	*27	44
97-98	South Carolina	ECHL	70	19	39	58	48	5	4	0	4	10
98-99	Rochester	AHL	1	0	0	0	0	—	—	—	—	—
98-99	South Carolina	ECHL	70	19	29	48	77	3	0	2	2	2
	AHL	Totals	15	0	1	1	4	—	—	—	—	—
	ECHL	Totals	208	60	101	161	211	26	15	18	33	56
	CoHL	Totals	148	45	96	141	151	36	7	28	35	48

Born; 8/12/70, Thunder Bay, Ontario. 6-0, 205. 1995-96 CoHL Best Defender. 1995-96 CoHL First Team All-Star. 1996-97 Second Team ECHL All-Star. 1997-98 ECHL First Team All-Star. Member of 1993-94 CoHL champion Thunder Bay Senators. Member of 1994-95 CoHL champion Thunder Bay Senators. Member of 1996-97 ECHL Champion South Carolina Stingrays. Last amateur club; Colorado College (WCHA).

Aldo Iaquinta — Defenseman

Regular Season / Playoffs

Season	Team	League	GP	G	A	PTS	PIM	GP	G	A	PTS	PIM
90-91	Merano	Italy										
91-92	Merano	Italy										
92-93	Tulsa	CeHL	35	2	15	17	26	12	1	0	1	12
93-94	Milan	Italy										
94-95	Milan	Italy										
95-96	Milan	Italy										
96-97	Milan	Italy										
97-98	New Mexico	WPHL	69	8	26	34	96	10	0	5	5	8
98-99	New Mexico	WPHL	40	4	20	24	60	—	—	—	—	—
98-99	Austin	WPHL	28	3	12	15	40	—	—	—	—	—
	WPHL	Totals	137	15	58	73	196	10	0	5	5	8

Born; 9/23/68, Kimberley, British Columbia. 6-4, 215. Traded to Austin by New Mexico for Daryl Lavoie (1/99). Member of 1992-93 CHL Champion Tulsa Oilers. Last amateur club; Moose Jaw (WHL).

Brian Idalski — Defenseman

Regular Season / Playoffs

Season	Team	League	GP	G	A	PTS	PIM	GP	G	A	PTS	PIM
95-96	Madison	CoHL	65	1	8	9	78	6	1	0	1	4
96-97	Madison	CoHL	58	2	15	17	83	—	—	—	—	—
97-98	Columbus	CHL	48	0	11	11	84	13	0	5	5	28
98-99	Columbus	CHL	62	2	6	8	116	6	0	3	3	10
	CoHL	Totals	123	3	23	26	161	6	1	0	1	4
	CHL	Totals	110	2	17	19	200	19	0	8	8	38

Born; 1/23/71, Warren, Michigan. 6-2, 195. Member of 1997-98 CHL Champion Columbus Cottonmouths. Last amateur club; University of Wisconsin-Stevens Point (NCHA).

Corey Ignas — Center

Regular Season / Playoffs

Season	Team	League	GP	G	A	PTS	PIM	GP	G	A	PTS	PIM
98-99	Flint	UHL	54	12	17	29	38	12	3	3	6	8

Born; 9/19/77, Trenton, Ontario. 5-11, 180. Selected by Knoxville in 1999 UHL Expansion Draft. Last amateur club; Trenton (Jr. A).

Karl Infanger — Defenseman

Regular Season / Playoffs

Season	Team	League	GP	G	A	PTS	PIM	GP	G	A	PTS	PIM
97-98	Wheeling	ECHL	70	6	22	28	102	15	1	3	4	8
98-99	Orlando	IHL	1	0	0	0	0	—	—	—	—	—
98-99	Wheeling	ECHL	54	7	20	27	67	—	—	—	—	—
98-99	Mississippi	ECHL	11	1	3	4	4	18	1	7	8	14
	ECHL	Totals	135	14	45	59	173	33	2	10	12	22

Born; 5/17/75, Lowell, Massachusetts. 6-3, 213. Member of 1998-99 ECHL Champion Mississippi SeaWolves. Last amateur club; Merrimack University (Hockey East).

Cal Ingraham — Right Wing
Regular Season / Playoffs

Season	Team	League	GP	G	A	PTS	PIM	GP	G	A	PTS	PIM
95-96	Tallahassee	ECHL	69	32	39	71	57	12	8	8	16	10
96-97	Tallahassee	ECHL	70	34	58	92	54	3	1	0	1	2
97-98	Tallahassee	ECHL	70	40	53	93	38	—	—	—	—	—
98-99	Idaho	WCHL	71	50	60	110	47	2	0	1	1	0
	ECHL	Totals	209	106	150	256	149	15	9	8	17	12

Born; 6/4/70, Haverhill, Massachusetts. 5-5, 160. 1997-98 ECHL Sportsmanship Award. Last amateur club; University of Maine (Hockey East).

Derek Innanen — Left Wing
Regular Season / Playoffs

Season	Team	League	GP	G	A	PTS	PIM	GP	G	A	PTS	PIM
96-97	Mississippi	ECHL	58	9	6	15	131	3	0	0	0	2
97-98	Amarillo	WPHL	63	18	25	43	93	—	—	—	—	—
98-99	Amarillo	WPHL	32	11	18	29	83	—	—	—	—	—
	WPHL	Totals	95	29	43	72	176	—	—	—	—	—

Born; 5/17/72, Castlegar, British Columbia. 5-11, 190. Last amateur club; Western Michigan (CCHA).

Leo Insam — Defenseman
Regular Season / Playoffs

Season	Team	League	GP	G	A	PTS	PIM	GP	G	A	PTS	PIM
93-94	Gardena	Italy										
94-95												
95-96												
96-97												
97-98	Dusseldorfer	Germany	48	2	10	12	32	3	0	0	0	2
98-99	Tucson	WCHL	4	1	1	2	6	—	—	—	—	—

Born;

Ralph Intranuovo — Left Wing
Regular Season / Playoffs

Season	Team	League	GP	G	A	PTS	PIM	GP	G	A	PTS	PIM
93-94	Cape Breton	AHL	66	21	31	52	39	4	1	2	3	2
94-95	Edmonton	NHL	1	0	1	1	0	—	—	—	—	—
94-95	Cape Breton	AHL	70	46	47	93	62	—	—	—	—	—
95-96	Edmonton	NHL	13	1	2	3	4	—	—	—	—	—
95-96	Cape Breton	AHL	52	34	29	73	84	—	—	—	—	—
96-97	Edmonton	NHL	8	1	1	2	0	—	—	—	—	—
96-97	Hamilton	AHL	68	36	40	76	88	22	8	4	12	30
97-98	Manitoba	IHL	81	26	35	61	68	3	2	0	2	4
98-99	Manitoba	IHL	71	29	31	60	70	5	2	1	3	4
	NHL	Totals	22	2	4	6	4	—	—	—	—	—
	AHL	Totals	256	137	147	284	185	26	9	6	15	32
	IHL	Totals	152	55	66	121	138	8	4	1	5	8

Born; 12/11/73, East York, Ontario. 5-8, 180. Drafted by Edmonton Oilers (5th choice, 96th overall) in 1992 Entry Draft. Calimed by Toronto Maple Leafs from Edmonton in NHL Waiver Draft (9/30/96). Claimed on waivers by Edmonton from Toronto (10/25/96). 1995 AHL Second Team All-Star. 1996-97 AHL Second Team All-Star. Last amateur club; Sault Ste. Marie (OHL).

Joel Irving — Right Wing
Regular Season / Playoffs

Season	Team	League	GP	G	A	PTS	PIM	GP	G	A	PTS	PIM
98-99	Saint John	AHL	5	0	0	0	2	—	—	—	—	—
98-99	Johnstown	ECHL	65	26	20	46	112	—	—	—	—	—

Born; 1/2/76, Lumsden, Saskatchewan. 6-3, 210. Drafted by Montreal Canadiens (8th choice, 148th overall) in 1994 Entry Draft. Signed as a free agent by Calgary Flames (7/28/98). Last amateur club; Western Michigan (CCHA).

Joel Irwin — Right Wing
Regular Season / Playoffs

Season	Team	League	GP	G	A	PTS	PIM	GP	G	A	PTS	PIM
98-99	Ferris State	CCHA	36	10	13	23	50	—	—	—	—	—
98-99	Richmond	ECHL	2	0	0	0	0	—	—	—	—	—

Born; 12/1/74, Kamloops, British Columbia. 5-10, 185. Last amateur club; Ferris State (CCHA).

Richard Irwin — Left Wing
Regular Season / Playoffs

Season	Team	League	GP	G	A	PTS	PIM	GP	G	A	PTS	PIM
97-98	Syracuse	AHL	5	0	0	0	2	—	—	—	—	—
97-98	Raleigh	ECHL	54	5	4	9	225	—	—	—	—	—
98-99	Augusta	ECHL	41	3	2	5	65	—	—	—	—	—
	ECHL	Totals	95	8	6	14	290	—	—	—	—	—

Born; 8/31/77, Toronto, Ontario. 6-3, 215. Last amateur club; Guelph (OHL).

Barry Isaac — Goaltender
Regular Season / Playoffs

Season	Team	League	GP	W	L	T	MIN	SO	AVG	GP	W	L	MIN	SO	AVG
98-99	Colorado	WCHL	1	0	0	0	8	0	14.12	—	—	—	—	—	—

Born; 1/20/71, Colorado Springs, Colorado. 5-11, 180.

Brad Isbister — Right Wing
Regular Season / Playoffs

Season	Team	League	GP	G	A	PTS	PIM	GP	G	A	PTS	PIM
96-97	Portland	WHL	24	15	18	33	45	6	2	1	3	16
96-97	Springfield	AHL	7	3	1	4	14	9	1	2	3	10
97-98	Phoenix	NHL	66	9	8	17	102	5	0	0	0	2
97-98	Springfield	AHL	9	8	2	10	36	—	—	—	—	—
98-99	Phoenix	NHL	32	4	4	8	46	—	—	—	—	—
98-99	Springfield	AHL	4	1	1	2	12	—	—	—	—	—
98-99	Las Vegas	IHL	2	0	0	0	9	—	—	—	—	—
	NHL	Totals	98	13	12	25	148	5	0	0	0	2
	AHL	Totals	20	12	4	16	62	9	1	2	3	10

Born; 5/7/77, Edmonton, Alberta. 6-2, 198. Drafted by Winnipeg Jets (4th choice, 67th overall) in 1995 Entry Draft. Traded to New York Islanders by Phoenix Coyotes with Phoenix's third round pick (Brian Collins) for Robert Reichel, Islanders' third round choice (Jason Jaspers) and Ottawa's fourth round choice (previously acquired-Phoenix selected Preston Mizzi) (3/20/99). Last amateur club; Portland (WHL).

Corey Isen — Right Wing
Regular Season / Playoffs

Season	Team	League	GP	G	A	PTS	PIM	GP	G	A	PTS	PIM
95-96	Huntington	ECHL	17	1	1	2	21	—	—	—	—	—
96-97	Utica	CoHL	22	2	7	9	60	—	—	—	—	—
96-97	Brantford	CoHL	27	10	5	15	52	10	2	1	3	10
97-98	Brantford	UHL	33	9	16	25	48	—	—	—	—	—
97-98	Saginaw	UHL	25	2	4	6	23	—	—	—	—	—
98-99	Macon	CHL	52	15	19	34	121	3	2	0	2	8
	UHL	Totals	107	23	32	55	183	10	2	1	3	10

Born; 5/26/75, London, Ontario. 5-9, 190.

Marek Ivan — Center
Regular Season / Playoffs

Season	Team	League	GP	G	A	PTS	PIM	GP	G	A	PTS	PIM
98-99	Worcester	AHL	7	0	2	2	4	—	—	—	—	—
98-99	Peoria	ECHL	61	27	25	52	206	4	2	1	3	20

Born; 11/17/78, Uhreske Hradiste, Czechoslovakia. 6-1, 182. Drafted by St. Louis Blues (9th choice, 244th overall) in 1997 Entry Draft. Last amateur club; Moose Jaw (WHL).

Raitis Ivanans — Defenseman
Regular Season / Playoffs

Season	Team	League	GP	G	A	PTS	PIM	GP	G	A	PTS	PIM
97-98	Flint	UHL	18	0	1	1	20	—	—	—	—	—
98-99	Macon	CHL	16	1	1	2	20	—	—	—	—	—
98-99	Tulsa	CHL	32	2	7	9	39	—	—	—	—	—
	CHL	Totals	48	3	8	11	59	—	—	—	—	—

Born; 1/1/79, Latvia, Russia. 6-3, 220.

Dave Ivaska — Right Wing

Season	Team	League	Regular Season GP	G	A	PTS	PIM	Playoffs GP	G	A	PTS	PIM
95-96	Detroit	CoHL	59	4	11	15	94	4	1	0	1	4
96-97	Port Huron	CoHL	61	10	9	19	102	5	1	1	2	12
97-98	Saginaw	UHL	29	1	5	6	16	—	—	—	—	—
97-98	Muskegon	UHL	45	5	12	17	67	4	0	0	0	2
98-99	Pensacola	ECHL	61	3	7	10	80	—	—	—	—	—
	UHL	Totals	194	20	37	57	279	13	2	1	3	18

Born; 4/11/73, Boston, Massachusetts. 5-10, 185. Last amateur club; Salem State (NCAA 3).

Dave Doucette's final season included a trip to the CHL All-Star Game
Photo by Angie Riemersman

Based upon his play it was not surprising to see Kevin Weekes float!
Photo by John Gachioch

Pat Jablonski — Goaltender

Regular Season / Playoffs

Season	Team	League	GP	W	L	T	MIN	SO	AVG	GP	W	L	MIN	SO	AVG
87-88	Peoria	IHL	5	2	2	1	285	0	3.58	—	—	—	—	—	—
88-89	Peoria	IHL	35	11	20	0	2051	1	4.77	3	0	2	130	0	6.00
89-90	St. Louis	NHL	4	0	3	0	208	0	4.90	—	—	—	—	—	—
89-90	Peoria	IHL	36	14	17	4	2023	0	4.89	4	1	3	223	0	5.11
90-91	St. Louis	NHL	8	2	3	3	492	0	3.05	3	0	0	90	0	3.33
90-91	Peoria	IHL	29	23	3	2	1738	0	3.00	10	7	2	532	0	2.59
91-92	St. Louis	NHL	10	3	6	0	468	0	4.87	—	—	—	—	—	—
91-92	Peoria	IHL	8	6	1	1	493	1	3.53	—	—	—	—	—	—
92-93	Tampa Bay	NHL	43	8	24	4	2268	1	3.97	—	—	—	—	—	—
93-94	Tampa Bay	NHL	15	5	6	3	834	0	3.88	—	—	—	—	—	—
93-94	St. John's	AHL	16	12	3	1	962	1	3.05	11	6	5	676	0	3.19
94-95	Chicago	IHL	4	0	4	0	216	0	4.71	—	—	—	—	—	—
94-95	Houston	IHL	3	1	1	1	179	0	3.01	—	—	—	—	—	—
95-96	St. Louis	NHL	1	0	0	0	8	0	7.50	—	—	—	—	—	—
95-96	Montreal	NHL	23	5	9	6	1264	0	2.94	1	0	0	49	0	1.22
96-97	Montreal	NHL	17	4	6	2	754	0	3.98	—	—	—	—	—	—
96-97	Phoenix	NHL	2	0	1	0	59	0	2.03	—	—	—	—	—	—
97-98	Carolina	NHL	5	1	4	0	279	0	3.01	—	—	—	—	—	—
97-98	Cleveland	IHL	34	13	13	6	1951	0	3.01	—	—	—	—	—	—
97-98	Quebec	IHL	7	3	3	0	368	0	3.42	—	—	—	—	—	—
98-99	Chicago	IHL	36	22	7	7	2119	1	3.00	3	2	1	185	0	3.57
	NHL	Totals	128	28	62	18	6634	1	3.74	4	0	0	139	0	2.59
	IHL	Totals	197	89	61	22	11423	3	3.74	20	10	8	873	0	4.54

Born; 6/20/67, Toledo, Ohio. 6-0, 180. Drafted by St. Louis Blues (6th choice, 138th overall) in 1985 Entry Draft. Traded to Tampa Bay Lightning by St. Louis with Steve Tuttle and Darin Kimble for future considerations (6/19/92). Traded to Toronto Maple Leafs by Tampa Bay for cash (2/21/94). Claimed by St. Louis Blues from Toronto in NHL Waiver Draft (10/2/95). Traded to Montreal Canadiens by St. Louis for J.J. Daigneault (11/7/95). Traded to Phoenix Coyotes by Montreal for Steve Cheredaryk (3/18/97). Signed as a free agent by Carolina Hurricanes (8/12/97). Traded to Quebec by Cleveland with Ryan Mougenel, Rick Hayward, John Craighead, Eric Perrin and Burke Murphy for Rick Girard, Dale DeGray, Darcy Simon, Tom Draper and Jason Ruff (3/98). Shared 1990-91 IHL James Norris Trophy (fewest goals allowed) with Guy Hebert. Member of 1990-91 IHL Champion Peoria Rivermen. Last amateur club; Windsor (OHL).

Richard Jackman — Defenseman

Regular Season / Playoffs

Season	Team	League	GP	G	A	PTS	PIM	GP	G	A	PTS	PIM
97-98	Sault Ste. Marie	OHL	60	33	40	73	111	—	—	—	—	—
97-98	Michigan	IHL	14	1	5	6	10	4	0	0	0	10
98-99	Michigan	IHL	71	13	17	30	106	5	0	4	4	6

Born; 6/28/78, Toronto, Ontario. 6-2, 180. Drafted by Dallas Stars (1st choice, 5th overall) in 1996 Entry Draft. Last amateur club; Sault Ste. Marie (OHL).

Dane Jackson — Right Wing

Regular Season / Playoffs

Season	Team	League	GP	G	A	PTS	PIM	GP	G	A	PTS	PIM
92-93	Hamilton	AHL	68	23	20	43	59	—	—	—	—	—
93-94	Vancouver	NHL	12	5	1	6	9	—	—	—	—	—
93-94	Hamilton	AHL	60	25	35	60	73	4	2	2	4	16
94-95	Vancouver	NHL	3	1	0	1	4	6	0	0	0	10
94-95	Syracuse	AHL	78	30	28	58	162	—	—	—	—	—
95-96	Buffalo	NHL	22	5	4	9	41	—	—	—	—	—
95-96	Rochester	AHL	50	27	19	46	132	19	3	6	10	53
96-97	Rochester	AHL	78	24	34	58	111	10	7	4	11	14
97-98	Islanders	NHL	8	1	1	2	4	—	—	—	—	—
97-98	Rochester	AHL	28	10	13	23	55	3	2	2	4	4
98-99	Lowell	AHL	80	16	27	43	103	3	0	1	1	16
	NHL	Totals	45	12	6	18	58	6	0	0	0	10
	AHL	Totals	442	155	176	331	695	39	14	15	29	103

Born; 5/17/70, Castlegar, British Columbia. 6-1, 196. Drafted by Vancouver Canucks (3rd choice, 44th overall) in 1988 Entry Draft. Signed as a free agent by Buffalo Sabres (8/16/95). Signed as a free agent by New York Islanders (7/21/97). Member of 1995-96 AHL champion Rochester Americans. Last amateur club; University of North Dakota (WCHA).

Mike Jackson — Right Wing

Regular Season / Playoffs

Season	Team	League	GP	G	A	PTS	PIM	GP	G	A	PTS	PIM
90-91	Newmarket	AHL	48	5	9	14	126	—	—	—	—	—
91-92	St. John's	AHL	1	0	0	0	0	—	—	—	—	—
91-92	Brantford	CoHL	49	7	27	34	115	6	2	5	7	8
92-93	Memphis	CeHL	57	24	28	52	182	6	1	4	5	15
93-94	Memphis	CeHL	64	26	37	63	90	—	—	—	—	—
94-95	Memphis	CeHL	52	13	22	35	67	—	—	—	—	—
95-96	Memphis	CeHL	51	12	29	41	155	3	0	0	0	7
96-97	Austin	WPHL	52	11	11	22	192	6	1	2	3	48
97-98	Austin	WPHL	40	7	17	24	186	5	1	4	5	15
98-99	Austin	WPHL	52	12	11	23	127	—	—	—	—	—
	AHL	Totals	49	5	9	14	126	—	—	—	—	—
	CeHL	Totals	224	75	116	191	494	9	1	4	5	22
	WPHL	Totals	144	30	39	69	505	11	2	6	8	63

Born; 2/4/69, Mississauga, Ontario. 6-0, 200. Drafted by Toronto Maple Leafs (12th choice, 213rd overall) in 1989 Entry Draft. Last amateur club; Cornwall

Paul Jackson — Center

Regular Season / Playoffs

Season	Team	League	GP	G	A	PTS	PIM	GP	G	A	PTS	PIM
93-94	Wichita	CeHL	59	*71	64	*135	215	11	11	*12	23	20
94-95	Sheffield	BHL	2	2	2	4	0	—	—	—	—	—
94-95	San Antonio	CeHL	53	51	49	100	251	11	7	6	13	52
95-96	Utah	IHL	1	0	0	0	0	—	—	—	—	—
95-96	San Antonio	CeHL	62	50	65	115	184	13	9	8	17	65
96-97	Las Vegas	IHL	1	0	0	0	0	—	—	—	—	—
96-97	San Antonio	CeHL	61	44	46	90	391	—	—	—	—	—
97-98	Shreveport	WPHL	68	55	60	115	249	8	3	3	6	22
98-99	San Antonio	CHL	62	14	62	103	239	8	1	10	11	67
	IHL	Totals	2	0	0	0	0	—	—	—	—	—
	CHL	Totals	297	230	286	543	1280	43	28	36	64	204

Born; 2/7/66, Toronto, Ontario. 5-10, 175. 1993-94 CeHL First Team All-Star. 1994-95 CeHL MVP. 1994-95 CeHL First Team All-Star. 1995-96 CeHL Second Team All-Star. Member of 1993-94 CeHL champion Wichita Thunder.

Ricky Jacob — Left Wing

Regular Season / Playoffs

Season	Team	League	GP	G	A	PTS	PIM	GP	G	A	PTS	PIM
97-98	Central Texas	WPHL	64	17	34	51	28	4	1	1	2	2
98-99	San Antonio	CHL	66	27	30	57	47	8	5	1	6	10

Born; 8/14/72, Cap-Tele, New Brunswick. 5-10, 180. Last amateur club; University of Moncton (CIAU).

Chris Jacobson — Center

Regular Season / Playoffs

Season	Team	League	GP	G	A	PTS	PIM	GP	G	A	PTS	PIM
98-99	South Carolina	ECHL	19	0	4	4	59	—	—	—	—	—
98-99	Wheeling	ECHL	46	4	12	16	176	—	—	—	—	—
	ECHL	Totals	65	4	16	20	235	—	—	—	—	—

Born; 2/8/77, Regina, Saskatchewan. 6-0, 188. Selected by Arkansas in 1999 ECHL Expansion Draft. Last amateur club; Portland (WHL).

Alexandre Jacques — Right Wing

Regular Season / Playoffs

Season	Team	League	GP	G	A	PTS	PIM	GP	G	A	PTS	PIM
97-98	Rimouski	QMJHL	24	17	23	40	47	10	12	10	22	6
97-98	Adirondack	AHL	16	1	1	2	0	—	—	—	—	—
97-98	Toledo	ECHL	9	6	4	10	6	—	—	—	—	—
98-99	Adirondack	AHL	68	9	13	22	25	3	0	0	0	0
	AHL	Totals	84	10	14	24	25	3	0	0	0	0

Born; 9/27/77, Laval, Quebec. 5-11, 165. Drafted by Detroit Red Wings (6th choice, 162nd overall) in 1996 Entry Draft. Last amateur club; Shawinigan

John Jakopin
Defenseman

Regular Season / Playoffs

Season	Team	League	GP	G	A	PTS	PIM	GP	G	A	PTS	PIM
96-97	Merrimack	H.E.	31	4	12	16	68	—	—	—	—	—
96-97	Adirondack	AHL	3	0	0	0	9	—	—	—	—	—
97-98	Florida	NHL	2	0	0	0	4	—	—	—	—	—
97-98	New Haven	AHL	60	2	18	20	151	3	0	0	0	0
98-99	Florida	NHL	3	0	0	0	0	—	—	—	—	—
98-99	New Haven	AHL	60	2	7	9	154	—	—	—	—	—
	NHL	Totals	5	0	0	0	4	—	—	—	—	—
	AHL	Totals	123	4	25	29	314	3	0	0	0	0

Born; 5/16/75, Toronto, Ontario. 6-5, 220. Drafted by Detroit Red Wings (4th choice, 97th overall) in 1993 Entry Draft. Signed as a free agent by Florida Panthers (5/14/97). 1997-98 AHL Man of the Year. Last amateur club; Merrimack

Trevor Janicki
Defenseman

Regular Season / Playoffs

Season	Team	League	GP	G	A	PTS	PIM	GP	G	A	PTS	PIM
97-98	Amarillo	WPHL	66	7	33	40	74	—	—	—	—	—
98-99	Amarillo	WPHL	67	4	29	33	86	—	—	—	—	—
	WPHL	Totals	133	11	62	73	160	—	—	—	—	—

Born; 7/25/73, Sudbury, Ontario. 6-1, 207. Last amateur club; Northern Michigan (CCHA).

Hakan Jansson
Defenseman

Regular Season / Playoffs

Season	Team	League	GP	G	A	PTS	PIM	GP	G	A	PTS	PIM
98-99	Las Vegas	IHL	1	0	0	0	2	—	—	—	—	—
98-99	Tucson	WCHL	17	2	4	6	44	—	—	—	—	—
98-99	Colorado	WCHL	17	0	0	0	46	—	—	—	—	—
98-99	San Diego	WCHL	30	2	4	6	83	10	0	0	0	2
	WCHL	Totals	64	4	8	12	173	10	0	0	0	2

Born; 3/23/75, Uppsala, Sweden. 6-2, 200.

Peter Jaros
Goaltender

Regular Season / Playoffs

Season	Team	League	GP	W	L	T	MIN	SO	AVG	GP	W	L	MIN	SO	AVG
98-99	Long Beach	IHL	1	0	1	0	60	0	5.00	—	—	—	—	—	—

Born; 10/20/76, Jihlava, Czech Republic. 5-8, 180.

Jan Jas
Forward

Regular Season / Playoffs

Season	Team	League	GP	G	A	PTS	PIM	GP	G	A	PTS	PIM
98-99	Miami	ECHL	6	0	3	3	0	—	—	—	—	—
98-99	Lake Charles	WPHL	8	0	0	0	5	—	—	—	—	—
98-99	Odessa	WPHL	39	15	15	30	10	3	1	2	3	0
	WPHL	Totals	47	15	15	30	15	3	1	2	3	0

Born; 6/6/78. 5-11, 180.

Peter Jas
Left Wing

Regular Season / Playoffs

Season	Team	League	GP	G	A	PTS	PIM	GP	G	A	PTS	PIM
97-98	Central Texas	WPHL	61	6	20	26	52	3	1	0	1	0
98-99	Central Texas	WPHL	15	1	6	7	8	—	—	—	—	—
98-99	Amarillo	WPHL	46	19	16	35	14	—	—	—	—	—
	WPHL	Totals	122	26	42	68	74	3	1	0	1	0

Born; 4/11/74, Presov, Czech Republic. 6-0, 185. Last amateur club; Brandon University (CIAU).

Bobby Jay
Defenseman

Regular Season / Playoffs

Season	Team	League	GP	G	A	PTS	PIM	GP	G	A	PTS	PIM
90-91	Fort Wayne	IHL	40	1	8	9	24	14	0	3	3	16
91-92	Fort Wayne	IHL	76	1	19	20	119	7	0	2	2	4
92-93	Fort Wayne	IHL	78	5	21	26	100	8	0	2	2	14
93-94	Los Angeles	NHL	3	0	1	1	0	—	—	—	—	—
93-94	Phoenix	IHL	65	7	15	22	54	—	—	—	—	—
94-95	Detroit	IHL	57	3	8	11	51	5	0	0	0	10
95-96	Detroit	IHL	17	2	2	4	22	6	0	1	1	16
96-97	Detroit	IHL	71	3	11	14	44	21	1	1	2	21
97-98	Detroit	IHL	66	5	12	17	88	8	1	3	4	8
98-99	Detroit	IHL	44	1	3	4	51	—	—	—	—	—
	IHL	Totals	514	28	99	127	553	69	2	12	14	89

Born; 11/18/65, Burlington, Massachusetts. 5-11,185. Signed as a free agent by Los Angeles Kings (7/16/93). Member of 1992-93 IHL champion Fort Wayne Komets. Member of IHL Champion Detroit Vipers 1996-97.

Yanick Jean
Defenseman

Regular Season / Playoffs

Season	Team	League	GP	G	A	PTS	PIM	GP	G	A	PTS	PIM
96-97	Mississippi	ECHL	52	2	9	11	65	3	0	3	3	8
97-98	Mobile	ECHL	69	3	5	8	196	3	0	0	0	2
98-99	Mobile	ECHL	68	2	18	20	126	2	0	1	1	4
	ECHL	Totals	189	7	32	39	387	8	0	4	4	14

Born; 11/26/75, Alma, Quebec. 6-1, 205. Drafted by Washington Capitals (5th choice, 119th overall) in 1994 Entry Draft. Traded to New Orleans by Mobile for Mark Turner (6/19/99). Last amateur club; Chicoutimi (QMJHL).

Jason Jennings
Forward

Regular Season / Playoffs

Season	Team	League	GP	G	A	PTS	PIM	GP	G	A	PTS	PIM
93-94	Raleigh	ECHL	2	0	0	0	4	—	—	—	—	—
93-94	Johnstown	ECHL	44	19	26	45	38	3	0	1	1	0
94-95	Johnstown	ECHL	67	23	31	54	57	5	0	3	3	2
95-96	Milton-Keynes	BHL	38	44	40	84	36	—	—	—	—	—
96-97	Nottingham	BHL	24	7	11	18	8	—	—	—	—	—
96-97	Straubing	Germany	7	2	3	5	14	—	—	—	—	—
97-98												
98-99	Corpus Christi	WPHL	3	0	1	1	0	—	—	—	—	—
	ECHL	Totals	113	42	57	99	99	8	0	4	4	2

Born; 3/16/71, Vancouver, British Columbia. 5-11, 195. Last amateur club; Western Michigan (CCHA).

Jim Jensen
Center

Regular Season / Playoffs

Season	Team	League	GP	G	A	PTS	PIM	GP	G	A	PTS	PIM
95-96	Mobile	ECHL	66	11	13	24	101	—	—	—	—	—
96-97	Mobile	ECHL	54	9	12	21	64	3	0	1	1	4
97-98	Mobile	ECHL	62	6	6	12	38	3	0	1	1	2
98-99	Oklahoma City	CHL	66	23	25	48	147	13	5	8	13	24
	ECHL	Totals	182	26	31	57	203	6	0	2	2	6

Born; 5/16/73, Grand Rapids, Michigan. 5-8, 185. Last amateur club; College of Holy Cross (NCAA 2).

Dave Jesiolowski
Right Wing

Regular Season / Playoffs

Season	Team	League	GP	G	A	PTS	PIM	GP	G	A	PTS	PIM
96-97	Baton Rouge	ECHL	15	2	4	6	70	—	—	—	—	—
96-97	Knoxville	ECHL	8	1	1	2	27	—	—	—	—	—
97-98	Pee Dee	ECHL	6	0	1	1	18	—	—	—	—	—
97-98	Richmond	ECHL	42	5	3	8	48	—	—	—	—	—
98-99	Alexandria	WPHL	59	13	32	45	329	—	—	—	—	—
	ECHL	Totals	71	8	9	17	163	—	—	—	—	—

Born; 1/1/74, Edmonton, Alberta. 6-0, 185. Last amateur club; University of Cape Breton (CIUA).

Mike Jickling — Center

Regular Season / Playoffs

Season	Team	League	GP	G	A	PTS	PIM	GP	G	A	PTS	PIM
98-99	Long Beach	IHL	9	1	1	2	4	—	—	—	—	—
98-99	San Diego	WCHL	1	0	2	2	0	—	—	—	—	—
98-99	New Mexico	WPHL	12	5	5	10	2	—	—	—	—	—
98-99	Florida	ECHL	47	13	32	45	35	6	1	4	5	2

Born; 1/5/73, Edmonton, Alberta. 5-10, 185. Last amateur club; Alberta

Lee Jinman — Center

Regular Season / Playoffs

Season	Team	League	GP	G	A	PTS	PIM	GP	G	A	PTS	PIM
96-97	Michigan	IHL	81	17	40	57	65	4	1	1	2	2
97-98	Michigan	IHL	61	6	19	25	54	—	—	—	—	—
97-98	Dayton	ECHL	4	1	3	4	23	—	—	—	—	—
98-99	Cincinnati	AHL	9	2	2	4	20	—	—	—	—	—
98-99	Fredericton	AHL	4	0	0	0	2	—	—	—	—	—
98-99	Michigan	IHL	3	0	0	0	0	—	—	—	—	—
98-99	Las Vegas	IHL	52	11	23	34	36	—	—	—	—	—
	IHL	Totals	197	34	82	116	155	4	1	1	2	2
	AHL	Totals	13	2	2	4	22	—	—	—	—	—

Born; 1/10/76, Toronto, Ontario. 5-10, 160. Drafted by Dallas Stars (2nd choice, 46th overall) in 1994 Entry Draft. Last amateur club; Detroit (OHL).

Trevor Jobe — Left Wing

Regular Season / Playoffs

Season	Team	League	GP	G	A	PTS	PIM	GP	G	A	PTS	PIM
88-89	Newmarket	AHL	75	23	24	47	90	5	0	1	1	12
89-90	Newmarket	AHL	1	0	1	1	2	—	—	—	—	—
89-90	Hampton Roads	ECHL	51	48	23	71	143	5	5	5	10	30
90-91	Newmarket	AHL	2	0	1	1	0	—	—	—	—	—
90-91	Nashville	ECHL	59	49	60	109	229	—	—	—	—	—
91-92	Richmond	ECHL	34	36	30	66	74	—	—	—	—	—
91-92	Nashville	ECHL	28	18	19	37	81	—	—	—	—	—
92-93	Prince Edward Island	AHL	3	1	2	3	0	—	—	—	—	—
92-93	Nashville	ECHL	61	*85	76	*161	222	9	7	7	14	38
93-94												
94-95	Nashville	ECHL	18	16	13	29	40	—	—	—	—	—
94-95	Raleigh	ECHL	23	18	22	40	42	—	—	—	—	—
95-96	Johnstown	ECHL	36	33	37	70	72	—	—	—	—	—
95-96	Tallahassee	ECHL	20	10	18	28	26	12	7	1	8	10
96-97	Wichita	CeHL	57	*56	69	*125	139	—	—	—	—	—
96-97	Columbus	CeHL	4	*5	4	*9	8	3	1	2	3	14
97-98	Columbus	CHL	12	15	18	33	16	—	—	—	—	—
97-98	Tucson	WCHL	23	15	14	29	35	—	—	—	—	—
97-98	Flint	UHL	22	24	15	39	10	17	11	17	*28	29
98-99	Baton Rouge	ECHL	22	11	12	23	26	—	—	—	—	—
98-99	Amarillo	WPHL	3	0	2	2	0	—	—	—	—	—
98-99	Alexandria	WPHL	13	3	9	12	22	—	—	—	—	—
	AHL	Totals	81	24	28	52	92	5	0	1	1	12
	ECHL	Totals	352	324	310	634	955	26	19	13	32	78
	CHL	Totals	73	76	91	167	163	3	1	2	3	14
	WPHL	Totals	16	3	11	14	22	—	—	—	—	—

Born; 5/14/67, Brandon, Manitoba. 6-1, 210. Drafted by Toronto Maple Leafs (7th choice, 133rd overall) in 1987 Entry Draft. Traded to Alexandria by Amarillo for Brent Scott (2/99). 1992-93 ECHL MVP. 1992-93 ECHL First All-Star Team. 1996-97 CeHL Second Team All-Star. 1996-97 CeHL MVP. Last amateur club; Prince Albert (WHL).

Frederick Jobin — Defenseman

Regular Season / Playoffs

Season	Team	League	GP	G	A	PTS	PIM	GP	G	A	PTS	PIM
98-99	Long Beach	IHL	35	4	4	8	88	—	—	—	—	—
98-99	San Diego	WCHL	42	6	20	26	181	11	1	7	8	47

Born; 1/28/77, Montreal, Quebec. 6-1, 204. Last amateur club; Victoriaville (QMJHL).

Bernie John — Defenseman

Regular Season / Playoffs

Season	Team	League	GP	G	A	PTS	PIM	GP	G	A	PTS	PIM
93-94	St. Thomas	CoHL	60	7	33	40	6	3	0	1	1	0
94-95	London	CoHL	46	10	22	32	10	5	1	1	2	2
95-96	Brantford	CoHL	59	6	30	36	32	12	0	18	18	23
96-97	Utah	IHL	1	0	1	1	0	—	—	—	—	—
96-97	Brantford	CoHL	69	16	54	70	25	8	4	5	9	0
97-98	Brantford	UHL	60	15	42	57	6	9	2	5	7	0
98-99	Port Huron	UHL	70	7	29	36	12	7	0	0	0	0
	UHL	Totals	364	61	210	271	91	44	7	30	37	25

Born; 6/4/72, Sudbury, Ontario. 5-11, 208. Traded to Port Huron by Asheville (Brantford) with Paul Polillo and Darryl Paquette for J.D. Eaton, Dale Greenwood, Gairin Smith and Chris Scourletis (7/99). 1996-97 CoHL Second Team All-Star. Last amateur club; Sudbury (OHL).

Andy Johnson — Defenseman

Regular Season / Playoffs

Season	Team	League	GP	G	A	PTS	PIM	GP	G	A	PTS	PIM
98-99	Asheville	UHL	1	1	1	2	0	—	—	—	—	—
98-99	Greenville	ECHL	42	2	5	7	30	—	—	—	—	—

Born; 3/6/78, Fredericton, New Brunswick. 6-3, 188. Drafted by Chicago Blackhawks (4th choice, 130th overall) in 1996 Entry Draft. Last amateur club; Peterborough (OHL).

Brent Johnson — Goaltender

Regular Season / Playoffs

Season	Team	League	GP	W	L	T	MIN	SO	AVG	GP	W	L	MIN	SO	AVG
97-98	Worcester	AHL	42	14	15	7	2241	0	3.19	6	3	2	332	0	3.43
98-99	St. Louis	NHL	6	3	2	0	286	0	2.10	—	—	—	—	—	—
98-99	Worcester	AHL	49	22	22	4	2925	2	2.99	4	1	3	238	0	3.02
	AHL	Totals	91	36	37	11	5166	2	3.08	10	4	5	570	0	3.26

Born; 3/12/77, Farmington, Michigan. Drafted by Colorado Avalanche (5th choice, 129th overall) in 1995 Entry Draft. Traded to St. Louis Blues by Colorado for San Jose's third round choice (previously acquired by St. Louis-Colorado selected Rick Berry) in 1997 Entry Draft and conditional choice in 2000 Entry Draft (5/30/97). Last amateur club; Owen Sound (OHL).

Cory Johnson — Left Wing

Regular Season / Playoffs

Season	Team	League	GP	G	A	PTS	PIM	GP	G	A	PTS	PIM
94-95	Saginaw	CoHL	57	13	29	42	22	—	—	—	—	—
94-95	Muskegon	CoHL	7	1	2	3	2	17	4	1	5	19
95-96	Muskegon	CoHL	73	17	32	49	51	5	1	1	2	7
96-97	Grand Rapids	IHL	12	1	2	3	4	—	—	—	—	—
96-97	Muskegon	CoHL	65	20	25	45	26	1	1	0	1	2
97-98	Grand Rapids	IHL	8	0	0	0	4	—	—	—	—	—
97-98	Michigan	IHL	2	0	0	0	2	—	—	—	—	—
97-98	Muskegon	UHL	1	0	0	0	0	—	—	—	—	—
97-98	Monroe	WPHL	60	26	38	64	30	—	—	—	—	—
98-99	Monroe	WPHL	69	27	25	52	20	6	0	3	3	0
	IHL	Totals	10	0	0	0	6	—	—	—	—	—
	UHL	Totals	203	51	88	139	75	23	6	2	8	28
	WPHL	Totals	129	53	63	116	50	6	0	3	3	0

Born; 9/15/73, Antigonish, Nova Scotia. 6-2, 203. Selected by Lubbock in 1999 WPHL Expansion Draft. Last amateur club; Windsor (OHL).

Craig Johnson — Right Wing

			Regular Season					Playoffs				
Season	Team	League	GP	G	A	PTS	PIM	GP	G	A	PTS	PIM
92-93	Oklahoma City	CeHL	50	8	11	19	219	11	0	2	2	67
93-94	Oklahoma City	CeHL	48	5	5	10	230	4	0	0	0	2
94-95	Birmingham	ECHL	37	3	0	3	150	—	—	—	—	—
94-95	Wichita	CeHL	14	1	0	1	99	7	2	5	7	14
95-96	Saginaw	CoHL	31	3	1	4	139	2	0	0	0	0
96-97	Michigan	IHL	2	0	0	0	2	—	—	—	—	—
96-97	Manitoba	IHL	16	2	2	4	38	—	—	—	—	—
96-97	Mobile	ECHL	4	0	0	0	74	—	—	—	—	—
96-97	Oklahoma City	CeHL	36	6	11	17	134	—	—	—	—	—
97-98	Manitoba	IHL	19	1	0	1	57	—	—	—	—	—
97-98	Oklahoma City	CHL	40	7	7	14	142	10	0	1	1	80
98-99	Houston	IHL	1	0	0	0	0	—	—	—	—	—
98-99	Austin	WPHL	43	16	9	25	164	—	—	—	—	—
98-99	Oklahoma City	CHL	9	3	7	10	63	10	2	1	3	*73
	IHL	Totals	38	3	2	5	97	—	—	—	—	—
	CHL	Totals	197	30	41	71	887	42	4	9	13	236
	ECHL	Totals	41	3	0	3	224	—	—	—	—	—

Born; 11/16/71, Montreal, Quebec. 6-5, 230. Member of 1994-95 CeHL champion Wichita Thunder.

Doug Johnson — Defenseman

			Regular Season					Playoffs				
Season	Team	League	GP	G	A	PTS	PIM	GP	G	A	PTS	PIM
97-98	Fresno	WCHL	58	0	8	8	120	3	0	0	0	2
98-99	Binghamton	UHL	69	1	6	7	114	5	1	0	1	4

Born; 2/21/76, Climax, Saskatchewan. 6-2, 195. Johnson appeared in goal for one game for the Fresno Fighting Falcons during the 1997-98 season. He faced ten shots in 17:05 of play and stopped nine of them. His goals against average was

Jay Johnson — Right Wing

			Regular Season					Playoffs				
Season	Team	League	GP	G	A	PTS	PIM	GP	G	A	PTS	PIM
94-95	Fresno	SUN	9	2	5	7	26	—	—	—	—	—
95-96	Fresno	WCHL	23	4	8	12	104	—	—	—	—	—
96-97	New Mexico	WPHL	6	1	0	1	2	—	—	—	—	—
96-97	Fresno	WCHL	1	0	1	1	2	—	—	—	—	—
97-98	Fresno	WCHL	16	3	3	6	73	—	—	—	—	—
98-99	Fresno	WCHL	3	0	1	1	13	—	—	—	—	—
	WCHL	Totals	43	7	13	20	192	—	—	—	—	—

Born; 1/18/67, Omaha, Nebraska. 5-11, 220.

Karl Johnson — Defenseman

			Regular Season					Playoffs				
Season	Team	League	GP	G	A	PTS	PIM	GP	G	A	PTS	PIM
91-92	Erie	ECHL	3	0	1	1	0	—	—	—	—	—
91-92	Springfield	AHL	34	1	11	12	17	—	—	—	—	—
92-93	Springfield	AHL	24	3	4	7	12	—	—	—	—	—
92-93	Louisville	ECHL	28	5	20	25	29	—	—	—	—	—
93-94	Raleigh	ECHL	48	14	23	37	84	12	2	3	5	4
94-95												
95-96	Knoxville	ECHL	52	2	14	16	22	7	0	0	0	6
96-97	Amarillo	WPHL	5	0	0	0	9	—	—	—	—	—
96-97	Knoxville	ECHL	3	0	0	0	4					
97-98												
98-99	Wichita	CHL	3	0	0	0	2	—	—	—	—	—
	AHL	Totals	58	4	15	19	29	—	—	—	—	—
	ECHL	Totals	134	21	58	79	139	19	2	3	5	4

Born; 8/11/67, Windsor, Ontario. 6-1, 190. Last amateur club; Lake Superior State (CCHA)

Perry Johnson — Defenseman

			Regular Season					Playoffs				
Season	Team	League	GP	G	A	PTS	PIM	GP	G	A	PTS	PIM
98-99	Canada	National	47	0	7	7	32	—	—	—	—	—

Born; 3/23/77, Vancouver, British Columbia. 5-11, 195. Last amateur club; Spokane (WHL).

Ryan Johnson — Center

			Regular Season					Playoffs				
Season	Team	League	GP	G	A	PTS	PIM	GP	G	A	PTS	PIM
96-97	Carolina	AHL	79	18	24	42	28	—	—	—	—	—
97-98	Florida	NHL	10	0	2	2	0	—	—	—	—	—
97-98	New Haven	AHL	64	19	48	67	12	3	0	1	1	0
98-99	Florida	NHL	1	1	0	1	0	—	—	—	—	—
98-99	New Haven	AHL	37	8	19	27	18	—	—	—	—	—
	NHL	Totals	11	1	2	3	0	—	—	—	—	—
	AHL	Totals	180	45	91	136	58	3	0	1	1	0

Born; 6/14/76, Thunder Bay, Ontario. 6-2, 185. Drafted by Florida Panthers (4th choice, 36th overall) in 1994 Entry Draft. Last amateur club; North Dakota (WCHA).

Trevor Johnson — Defenseman

			Regular Season					Playoffs				
Season	Team	League	GP	G	A	PTS	PIM	GP	G	A	PTS	PIM
98-99	Hampton Roads	ECHL	65	3	9	12	135	3	0	0	0	16

Born; 9/6/77, Davidson, Saskatchewan. 6-2, 190. Last amateur club; Moose Jaw (WHL).

B.J. Johnston — Right Wing

			Regular Season					Playoffs				
Season	Team	League	GP	G	A	PTS	PIM	GP	G	A	PTS	PIM
96-97	Baton Rouge	ECHL	61	17	32	49	52	—	—	—	—	—
97-98	Worcester	AHL	3	0	0	0	0	—	—	—	—	—
97-98	Baton Rouge	ECHL	65	19	26	45	78	—	—	—	—	—
98-99	Baton Rouge	ECHL	68	28	34	62	68	6	0	2	2	4
	ECHL	Totals	194	64	92	156	198	6	0	2	2	4

Born; 10/13/75, Blenheim, Ontario. 6-2, 200. Last amateur club; Ottawa (OHL).

Chris Johnston — Left Wing

			Regular Season					Playoffs				
Season	Team	League	GP	G	A	PTS	PIM	GP	G	A	PTS	PIM
95-96	Erie	ECHL	49	12	14	26	59	—	—	—	—	—
95-96	Dayton	ECHL	15	1	9	10	21	3	2	1	3	0
96-97	Dayton	ECHL	24	6	6	12	27	—	—	—	—	—
96-97	Oklahoma City	CeHL	18	8	4	12	24	4	1	0	1	35
97-98	Oklahoma City	CHL	51	27	40	67	156	11	2	2	4	52
98-99	Houston	IHL	1	0	0	0	0	—	—	—	—	—
98-99	Austin	WPHL	44	22	32	54	228	—	—	—	—	—
98-99	Oklahoma City	CHL	15	9	10	19	20	13	6	5	11	49
	ECHL	Totals	88	19	29	48	80	3	2	1	3	0
	CHL	Totals	84	44	54	98	2000	28	9	7	16	136

Born; 12/25/74, Brandon, Manitoba. 5-10, 180. Selected by Topeka in 1998 CHL Expansion Draft. Selected by Indianapolis in 1999 ECHL Expansion Draft. Last amateur club; Regina (WHL).

Kurt Johnston — Forward

			Regular Season					Playoffs				
Season	Team	League	GP	G	A	PTS	PIM	GP	G	A	PTS	PIM
98-99	Memphis	CHL	57	17	12	29	140	4	1	0	1	28

Born; 2/10/77, Peterborough, Ontario. 6-0, 215. Last amateur club; Quebec (QMJHL).

Tyler Johnston — Left Wing

			Regular Season					Playoffs				
Season	Team	League	GP	G	A	PTS	PIM	GP	G	A	PTS	PIM
97-98	Richmond	ECHL	11	0	2	2	16	—	—	—	—	—
97-98	Birmingham	ECHL	32	1	4	5	4	—	—	—	—	—
98-99	Birmingham	ECHL	66	5	21	26	67	5	0	1	1	6
	ECHL	Totals	109	6	27	33	87	5	0	1	1	6

Born; 7/14/72, Imes, Iowa. 6-2, 212. Last amateur club; Wisconsin-Stevens Point (NCHA).

Olli Jokinen — Center

Regular Season — Playoffs

Season	Team	League	GP	G	A	PTS	PIM	GP	G	A	PTS	PIM
97-98	Los Angeles	NHL	8	0	0	0	6	—	—	—	—	—
97-98	Helsinki	Finland	30	11	28	39	8	9	*7	2	9	2
98-99	Los Angeles	NHL	66	9	12	21	44	—	—	—	—	—
98-99	Springfield	AHL	9	3	6	9	6	—	—	—	—	—
	NHL	Totals	74	9	12	21	50	—	—	—	—	—

Born; 12/5/78, Kuopio, Finland. 6-3, 208. Drafted by Los Angeles Kings (1st choice, 3rd overall) in 1997 Entry Draft. Traded to New York Islanders by Los Angeles with Josh Green, Mathieu Biron and Los Angeles' first round choice (Taylor Pyatt) in 1999 Entry draft for Zigmund Palffy, Marcel Cousineau, Bryan Smolinski and fourth round choice (Daniel Johansson) in 1999 Entry Draft (6/20/99). Last amateur club; KalPa Jr. (Finland)

Jean-Francois Jomphe — Right Wing

Regular Season — Playoffs

Season	Team	League	GP	G	A	PTS	PIM	GP	G	A	PTS	PIM
93-94	San Diego	IHL	29	2	3	5	12	—	—	—	—	—
93-94	Greensboro	ECHL	25	9	9	18	41	1	1	0	1	0
94-95	Canadian	National	52	33	25	58	85	—	—	—	—	—
95-96	Anaheim	NHL	31	2	12	14	39	—	—	—	—	—
95-96	Baltimore	AHL	47	21	34	55	75	—	—	—	—	—
96-97	Anaheim	NHL	64	7	14	21	53	—	—	—	—	—
97-98	Anaheim	NHL	9	1	3	4	8	—	—	—	—	—
97-98	Cincinnati	AHL	38	9	19	28	32	—	—	—	—	—
97-98	Quebec	IHL	17	6	4	10	24	—	—	—	—	—
98-99	Phoenix	NHL	1	0	0	0	2	—	—	—	—	—
98-99	Monteral	NHL	6	0	0	0	0	—	—	—	—	—
98-99	Springfield	AHL	29	10	18	28	36	—	—	—	—	—
98-99	Fredericton	AHL	3	1	3	4	6	15	5	11	16	49
98-99	Las Vegas	IHL	32	6	14	20	63	—	—	—	—	—
	NHL	Totals	111	10	29	39	102	—	—	—	—	—
	AHL	Totals	117	41	74	115	149	15	5	11	16	49
	IHL	Totals	78	14	21	35	99	—	—	—	—	—

Born; 12/28/72, Havre' St. Pierre, Quebec. 6-1, 195. Signed as a free agent by Anaheim Mighty Ducks (9/7/93). Traded to Phoenix Coyotes by Anaheim for Jim McKenzie (6/18/98). Sold to Montreal Canadiens by Phoenix (3/23/99). Last amateur club; Sherbrooke (QMJHL).

Chris Joseph — Defenseman

Regular Season — Playoffs

Season	Team	League	GP	G	A	PTS	PIM	GP	G	A	PTS	PIM
87-88	Seattle	WHL	23	5	14	19	49	—	—	—	—	—
87-88	Pittsburgh	NHL	17	0	4	4	12	—	—	—	—	—
87-88	Edmonton	NHL	7	0	4	4	6	—	—	—	—	—
87-88	Nova Scotia	AHL	8	0	2	2	8	4	0	0	0	9
88-89	Edmonton	NHL	44	4	5	9	54	—	—	—	—	—
88-89	Cape Breton	AHL	5	1	1	2	18	—	—	—	—	—
89-90	Edmonton	NHL	4	0	2	2	2	—	—	—	—	—
89-90	Cape Breton	AHL	61	10	20	30	69	6	2	1	3	4
90-91	Edmonton	NHL	49	5	17	22	59	—	—	—	—	—
91-92	Edmonton	NHL	7	0	0	0	8	5	1	3	4	2
91-92	Cape Breton	AHL	63	14	29	43	72	5	0	2	2	8
92-93	Edmonton	NHL	33	2	10	12	48	—	—	—	—	—
93-94	Edmonton	NHL	10	1	1	2	28	—	—	—	—	—
93-94	Tampa Bay	NHL	66	10	19	29	108	—	—	—	—	—
94-95	Pittsburgh	NHL	33	5	10	15	46	10	1	1	2	12
95-96	Pittsburgh	NHL	70	5	14	19	71	15	1	0	1	8
96-97	Vancouver	NHL	63	3	13	16	62	—	—	—	—	—
97-98	Philadelphia	NHL	15	1	0	1	19	1	0	0	0	2
97-98	Philadelphia	AHL	6	2	3	5	2	—	—	—	—	—
98-99	Philadelphia	NHL	2	0	0	0	2	—	—	—	—	—
98-99	Philadelphia	AHL	51	9	29	38	26	16	3	10	13	8
98-99	Cincinnati	IHL	27	11	19	30	38	—	—	—	—	—
	NHL	Totals	420	36	99	135	525	31	3	4	7	24
	AHL	Totals	194	36	84	120	195	31	5	13	18	29

Born; 9/10/69, Burnaby, British Columbia. 6-2, 202. Drafted by Pittsburgh Penguins (1st choice, 5th overall) in 1987 Entry Draft. Traded to Edmonton Oilers by Pittsburgh with Criag Simpson, Dave Hannan and Moe Mantha for Paul Coffey, Dave Hunter and Wayne Van Dorp (11/24/87). Traded to Tampa Bay Lightning by Edmonton for Bob Beers (11/11/93). Claimed by Pittsburgh from Tampa Bay in NHL Waiver Draft (1/18/95). Claimed by Vancouver Canucks from Pittsburgh in NHL Waiver Draft (9/30/96). Signed as a free agent by Philadelphia Flyers (9/11/97). Last amateur club; Seattle (WHL).

Mike Josephson — Left Wing

Regular Season — Playoffs

Season	Team	League	GP	G	A	PTS	PIM	GP	G	A	PTS	PIM
97-98	Long Beach	IHL	22	2	3	5	43	—	—	—	—	—
97-98	San Diego	WCHL	20	6	6	12	43	—	—	—	—	—
98-99	Baton Rouge	ECHL	29	3	7	10	29	—	—	—	—	—

Born; 4/6/76, Vancouver, British Columbia. 6-0, 200. Last amateur club; Lethbridge (WHL).

Jacques Joubert — Center

Regular Season — Playoffs

Season	Team	League	GP	G	A	PTS	PIM	GP	G	A	PTS	PIM
95-96	Peoria	IHL	73	17	25	42	45	12	2	5	7	2
96-97	Milwaukee	IHL	42	7	9	16	22	—	—	—	—	—
96-97	Rochester	AHL	20	5	3	8	10	—	—	—	—	—
97-98	Tallahassee	ECHL	22	5	7	12	26	—	—	—	—	—
97-98	EC Graz	Switz.	16	6	4	10	10	—	—	—	—	—
98-99	Heilbronner	Germany	54	21	28	49	56	—	—	—	—	—
	IHL	Totals	115	24	34	58	67	12	2	5	7	2

Born; 3/23/71, South Bend, Indiana. 6-2, 201. Drafted by Dallas Stars in NHL supplemental draft (6/25/93). Last amateur club; Boston University (H.E.).

Bob Joyce — Left Wing

Regular Season — Playoffs

Season	Team	League	GP	G	A	PTS	PIM	GP	G	A	PTS	PIM
87-88	Canadian	National	46	12	10	22	28	—	—	—	—	—
87-88	Canadian	Olympic	4	1	0	1	0	—	—	—	—	—
87-88	Boston	NHL	15	7	5	12	10	23	8	6	14	18
88-89	Boston	NHL	77	18	31	49	46	9	5	2	7	2
89-90	Boston	NHL	23	1	2	3	22	—	—	—	—	—
89-90	Washington	NHL	24	5	8	13	4	14	2	1	3	9
90-91	Washington	NHL	17	3	3	6	8	—	—	—	—	—
90-91	Baltimore	AHL	36	10	8	18	14	6	1	0	1	4
91-92	Winnipeg	NHL	1	0	0	0	0	—	—	—	—	—
91-92	Moncton	AHL	66	19	29	48	51	10	0	5	5	9
92-93	Winnipeg	NHL	1	0	0	0	0	—	—	—	—	—
92-93	Moncton	AHL	75	25	32	57	52	5	0	0	0	2
93-94	Las Vegas	IHL	63	15	18	33	45	5	2	1	3	8
94-95	Las Vegas	IHL	60	15	12	27	52	10	4	3	7	26
95-96	Orlando	IHL	55	7	11	18	81	18	2	1	3	12
96-97	Orlando	IHL	76	15	33	48	98	5	0	0	0	2
97-98	Dusseldorfer	Germany	39	6	7	13	26	3	0	1	1	6
98-99	Landshut	Germany	51	4	11	15	26	3	0	0	0	0
	NHL	Totals	158	34	49	83	90	46	15	9	24	29
	IHL	Totals	254	52	74	126	276	38	8	5	13	48
	AHL	Totals	177	54	69	123	117	21	1	5	6	15

Born; 7/11/76, St. John's New Brunswick. 6-0, 195. Selected by Boston Bruins (4th choice, 82nd overall) in 1984 Entry Draft. Traded to Washington Capitals by Boston for Dave Christian (12/13/89). Traded to Winnipeg Jets by Washington with Kent Paynter and Tyler Larter for Brent Hughes, Craig Duncanson and Simon Wheeldon (5/21/91). Signed as a free agent by Las Vegas Thunder (7/8/93). Last amateur club; North Dakota (WCHA).

Jeff Jubenville — Right Wing

Regular Season — Playoffs

Season	Team	League	GP	G	A	PTS	PIM	GP	G	A	PTS	PIM
95-96	Bakersfield	WCHL	52	31	27	58	51	—	—	—	—	—
96-97	Bakersfield	WCHL	50	30	34	64	47	4	1	2	3	4
97-98	Bakersfield	WCHL	12	5	7	12	18	—	—	—	—	—
98-99	Tupelo	WPHL	18	2	2	4	8	—	—	—	—	—
98-99	Asheville	UHL	34	12	9	21	26	4	0	2	2	0
	WCHL	Totals	114	66	68	154	116	4	1	2	3	4

Born; 2/5/74, Duncan, British Columbia. 6-2, 210.

Dan Juden — Forward

Regular Season — Playoffs

Season	Team	League	GP	G	A	PTS	PIM	GP	G	A	PTS	PIM
98-99	Tupelo	WPHL	62	24	21	45	16	—	—	—	—	—

Born; 4/17/76, Beverly, Massachusetts. 6-3, 190. Drafted by Tampa Bay Lightning (5th choice, 137th overall) in 1994 Entry Draft. Last amateur club; Massachusetts (Hockey East)

Rick Judson — Left Wing

Season	Team	League	Regular Season GP	G	A	PTS	PIM	Playoffs GP	G	A	PTS	PIM
91-92	Illinois-Chicago	CCHA	35	17	19	36	26	—	—	—	—	—
91-92	Toledo	ECHL	2	1	0	1	2	—	—	—	—	—
92-93	Adirondack	AHL	7	3	0	3	0	—	—	—	—	—
92-93	Toledo	ECHL	56	23	28	51	39	16	7	16	23	10
93-94	Adirondack	AHL	2	1	0	1	0	—	—	—	—	—
93-94	Toledo	ECHL	61	39	49	88	16	14	5	13	18	6
94-95	Las Vegas	IHL	2	0	1	1	0	—	—	—	—	—
94-95	Toledo	ECHL	54	27	41	68	29	4	2	4	6	0
95-96	Utah	IHL	1	0	0	0	0	—	—	—	—	—
95-96	Michigan	IHL	2	0	1	1	0	—	—	—	—	—
95-96	Minnesota	IHL	5	0	1	1	0	—	—	—	—	—
95-96	Toledo	ECHL	59	43	38	81	38	11	9	9	18	2
96-97	Las Vegas	IHL	17	5	2	7	0	2	0	0	0	0
96-97	Toledo	ECHL	54	30	43	73	22	5	3	2	5	0
97-98	Toledo	ECHL	32	7	17	24	14	7	0	2	2	4
97-98	Manchester	BSL	20	5	6	11	0	—	—	—	—	—
98-99	Greenville	ECHL	70	16	32	48	22	—	—	—	—	—
	IHL	Totals	27	5	5	10	0	2	0	0	0	0
	AHL	Totals	9	4	0	4	0	—	—	—	—	—
	ECHL	Totals	388	186	248	434	182	57	26	46	72	22

Born; 8/13/69, Toledo, Ohio. 5-10, 200. Drafted by Detroit Red Wings (11th choice, 204th overall) in 1989 Entry Draft. 1992-93 ECHL Playoff MVP. 1993-94 ECHL Second Team All-Star. Member of 1992-93 ECHL champion Toledo Storm. Member of 1993-94 ECHL champion Toledo Storm. Last amateur club; Illinois-Chicago (CCHA).

Claude Jutras — Right Wing

Season	Team	League	Regular Season GP	G	A	PTS	PIM	Playoffs GP	G	A	PTS	PIM
94-95	Cape Breton	AHL	25	6	5	11	95	—	—	—	—	—
94-95	Wheeling	ECHL	19	7	7	14	172	3	2	1	3	20
95-96	Cape Breton	AHL	4	0	0	0	11	—	—	—	—	—
95-96	Cornwall	AHL	40	4	4	8	148	5	0	0	0	7
95-96	Brantford	CoHL	1	0	0	0	2	—	—	—	—	—
96-97	Pensacola	ECHL	13	6	5	11	132	—	—	—	—	—
96-97	Tallahassee	ECHL	20	4	8	12	126	—	—	—	—	—
96-97	Knoxville	ECHL	19	1	10	11	141	—	—	—	—	—
97-98	Long Beach	IHL	44	8	7	15	261	13	5	1	6	50
97-98	San Diego	WCHL	24	16	5	21	139	—	—	—	—	—
98-99	Long Beach	IHL	74	13	19	32	408	1	0	0	0	2
	IHL	Totals	118	21	26	47	669	14	5	1	6	52
	AHL	Totals	69	10	9	19	254	5	0	0	0	7
	ECHL	Totals	71	18	30	48	471	3	2	1	3	20

Born; 9/18/73, Hampstead, Quebec. 6-1, 200. Drafted by Philadelphia Flyers (7th choice, 175th overall) in 1992 Entry Draft. Signed as a free agent by the Cape Breton Oilers (9/30/94). Last amateur club; Hull (QMJHL).

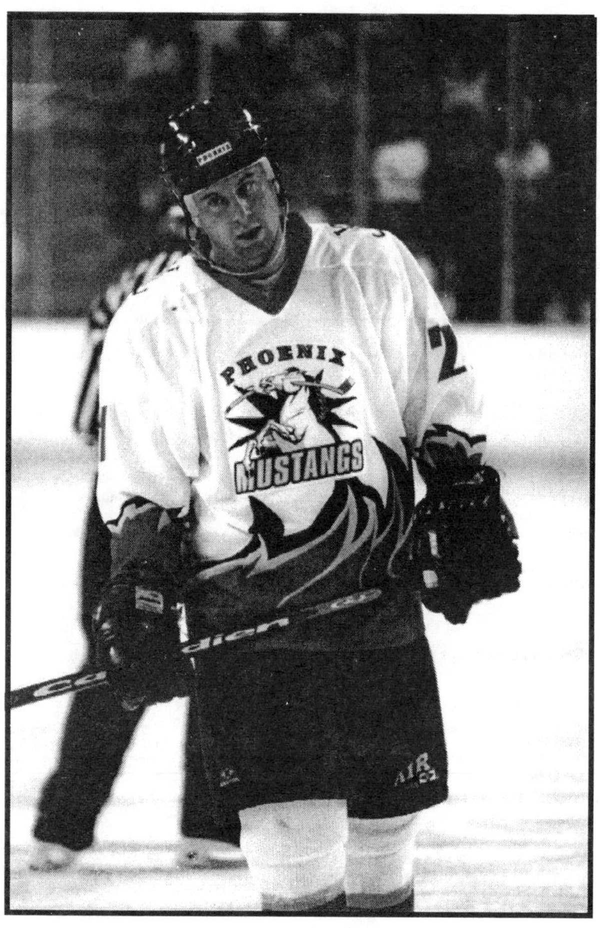

Tom Menicci is one of the up-and-coming defenseman at the AA level
Photo by Kelly Virtanen

Kevin Kerr scored his 500th goal as a professional last season
Photo by Joe Costa

John Kachur — Center

Regular Season / Playoffs

Season	Team	League	GP	G	A	PTS	PIM	GP	G	A	PTS	PIM
98-99	Wichita	CHL	65	32	25	57	60	4	1	1	2	10

Born; 2/15/77, Yorktown, Saskatchewan. 5-8, 175. Last amateur club; Red Deer (WHL).

Butch Kaebel — Left Wing

Regular Season / Playoffs

Season	Team	League	GP	G	A	PTS	PIM	GP	G	A	PTS	PIM
90-91	Knoxville	ECHL	54	17	26	43	49	1	0	0	0	0
91-92	Peoria	IHL	30	3	11	14	6	3	0	0	0	0
91-92	Dayton	ECHL	30	4	18	22	13	—	—	—	—	—
91-92	Michigan	CoHL	18	5	7	12	4	—	—	—	—	—
92-93	Birmingham	ECHL	56	17	25	42	61	—	—	—	—	—
93-94	Peoria	IHL	59	16	9	25	31	6	1	0	1	0
93-94	Dayton	ECHL	14	7	7	14	23	—	—	—	—	—
94-95	Peoria	IHL	43	7	2	9	61	3	0	0	0	2
95-96	Peoria	IHL	1	0	1	1	0	—	—	—	—	—
95-96	Quad City	CoHL	51	13	34	47	72	4	2	2	4	8
96-97	Peoria	ECHL	57	27	37	64	41	10	4	2	6	2
97-98	Peoria	ECHL	52	9	15	24	10	—	—	—	—	—
98-99	Huntington	ECHL	70	14	26	40	42	—	—	—	—	—
	IHL	Totals	133	26	23	49	98	12	1	0	1	2
	ECHL	Totals	333	95	154	249	239	11	4	2	6	2
	CoHL	Totals	69	18	41	59	76	4	2	2	4	8

Born; 11/15/66, Pekin, Illinois. 5-11, 195.

Karson Kaebel — Center

Regular Season / Playoffs

Season	Team	League	GP	G	A	PTS	PIM	GP	G	A	PTS	PIM
94-95	Cornwall	AHL	25	3	7	10	17	—	—	—	—	—
94-95	Dayton	ECHL	33	14	33	47	68	9	0	4	4	28
95-96	Jacksonville	ECHL	1	0	0	0	0	—	—	—	—	—
95-96	Quad City	CoHL	57	14	52	66	88	4	1	2	3	0
96-97	Peoria	ECHL	69	23	45	68	68	10	3	4	7	16
97-98	Fayetteville	CHL	13	5	9	14	10	—	—	—	—	—
98-99	Huntington	ECHL	63	21	32	53	60	—	—	—	—	—
	ECHL	Totals	166	58	110	168	196	19	3	8	11	44

Born; 12/5/72, Pekin, Illinois. 5-10, 204. Last amateur club; Northern Michigan (WCHA).

Dmitri Kalinen — Defenseman

Regular Season / Playoffs

Season	Team	League	GP	G	A	PTS	PIM	GP	G	A	PTS	PIM
98-99	Moncton	QMJHL	39	7	18	25	44	4	1	1	2	0
98-99	Rochester	AHL	3	0	1	1	14	7	0	0	0	6

Born; 7/22/80, Chelyabinsk, USSR. 6-2, 198. Drafted by Buffalo Sabres (1st choice, 18th overall) in 1998 Entry Draft. Last amateur club; Moncton (QMJHL).

Konstantin Kalmikov — Center

Regular Season / Playoffs

Season	Team	League	GP	G	A	PTS	PIM	GP	G	A	PTS	PIM
95-96	Flint	CoHL	38	4	12	16	16	—	—	—	—	—
95-96	Detroit	CoHL	5	0	1	1	0	—	—	—	—	—
96-97	St. John's	AHL	2	0	0	0	0	—	—	—	—	—
96-97	Sudbury	OHL	66	22	34	56	25	—	—	—	—	—
97-98	Sudbury	OHL	66	32	32	64	21	10	7	2	9	2
98-99	St. John's	AHL	52	3	4	7	4	—	—	—	—	—
	AHL	Totals	54	3	4	7	4	—	—	—	—	—
	CoHL	Totals	43	4	13	17	16	—	—	—	—	—

Born; 6/14/78, Kharkov, USSR. 6-4, 205. Drafted by Toronto Maple Leafs (4th choice, 68th overall) in 1996 Entry Draft. Last amtaeur club; Sudbury (OHL).

Erik Kaminski — Right Wing

Regular Season / Playoffs

Season	Team	League	GP	G	A	PTS	PIM	GP	G	A	PTS	PIM
97-98	Winston-Salem	UHL	3	0	0	0	0	—	—	—	—	—
97-98	Brantford	UHL	21	3	3	6	11	6	1	0	1	2
98-99	Chesapeake	ECHL	5	0	0	0	0	—	—	—	—	—
	UHL	Totals	24	3	3	6	11	6	1	0	1	2

Born; 3/23/76, Cleveland, Ohio. 6-2, 215. Drafted by Ottawa Senators (9th choice, 231st overall) in 1995 Entry Draft. Last amateur club; Northeastern

Kevin Kaminski — Center

Regular Season / Playoffs

Season	Team	League	GP	G	A	PTS	PIM	GP	G	A	PTS	PIM
88-89	Saskatoon	WHL	52	25	43	68	199	8	4	9	13	25
88-89	Minnesota	NHL	1	0	0	0	0	—	—	—	—	—
89-90	Quebec	NHL	1	0	0	0	0	—	—	—	—	—
89-90	Halifax	AHL	19	3	4	7	128	2	0	0	0	5
90-91	Halifax	AHL	7	1	0	1	44	—	—	—	—	—
90-91	Fort Wayne	IHL	56	9	15	24	*455	19	4	2	6	*169
91-92	Quebec	NHL	5	0	0	0	45	—	—	—	—	—
91-92	Halifax	AHL	63	18	27	45	329	—	—	—	—	—
92-93	Halifax	AHL	79	27	37	64	*345	—	—	—	—	—
93-94	Washington	NHL	13	0	5	5	87	—	—	—	—	—
93-94	Portland	AHL	39	10	22	32	263	16	4	5	9	*91
94-95	Portland	AHL	34	15	20	35	292	—	—	—	—	—
94-95	Washington	NHL	27	1	1	2	102	5	0	0	0	36
95-96	Washington	NHL	54	1	2	3	164	3	0	0	0	16
96-97	Washington	NHL	38	1	2	3	130	—	—	—	—	—
97-98	Portland	AHL	40	8	12	20	242	8	2	1	3	69
98-99	Las Vegas	IHL	39	7	10	17	217	—	—	—	—	—
	NHL	Totals	139	3	10	13	528	8	0	0	0	52
	AHL	Totals	281	82	122	204	1643	26	6	6	12	165
	IHL	Totals	95	16	25	41	672	19	4	2	6	169

Born; 3/13/69, Churchbridge, Saskatchewan. 5-10, 190. Drafted by Minnesota North Stars (3rd choice, 48th overall) in 1987 Entry Draft. Traded to Quebec Nordiques by Minnesota for Gaetan Duchesne (6/19/89). Traded to Washington Capitals by Quebec for Mark Matier (6/15/93). Member of 1993-94 AHL Champion Portland Pirates. Last amateur club; Saskatoon (WHL).

Yan Kaminsky — Left Wing

Regular Season / Playoffs

Season	Team	League	GP	G	A	PTS	PIM	GP	G	A	PTS	PIM
93-94	Winnipeg	NHL	1	0	0	0	0	—	—	—	—	—
93-94	Moncton	AHL	33	9	13	22	6	—	—	—	—	—
94-95	Islanders	NHL	2	1	1	2	0	—	—	—	—	—
94-95	Denver	IHL	38	17	16	33	14	15	6	6	12	0
95-96	Utah	IHL	16	3	3	6	8	21	3	5	8	4
96-97	Utah	IHL	77	28	27	55	18	7	1	4	5	0
97-98	Lukko Rauma	Finland	38	5	8	13	33	—	—	—	—	—
98-99	Utah	IHL	56	11	17	28	12	—	—	—	—	—
98-99	Grand Rapids	IHL	7	0	2	2	0	—	—	—	—	—
	NHL	Totals	3	1	1	2	0	—	—	—	—	—
	IHL	Totals	194	59	65	124	52	43	10	15	25	4

Born; 7/28/71, Penza, Russia. 6-1, 176. Drafted by Winnipeg Jets (4th choice, 99th overall) in 1991 Entry Draft. Traded to New York Islanders by Winnipeg for Wayne McBean (2/1/94). Traded to Grand Rapids by Utah for Darren Rumble (3/99). Member of 1994-95 IHL champion Denver Grizzlies. Member of 1995-96 IHL champion Utah Grizzlies.

Boyd Kane — Left Wing

Regular Season / Playoffs

Season	Team	League	GP	G	A	PTS	PIM	GP	G	A	PTS	PIM
98-99	Hartford	AHL	56	3	5	8	23	—	—	—	—	—
98-99	Charlotte	ECHL	12	5	6	11	14	—	—	—	—	—

Born; 4/18/78, Swift Current, Saskatchewan. 6-1, 207. Drafted by Pittsburgh Penguins (3rd choice, 72nd overall) in 1996 Entry Draft. Re-entered NHL draft and selected by New York Rangers (4th choice, 114th overall) in 1998. Last amatuer club; Regina (WHL). Last amateur club; Regina (WHL).

Petro Kantzavelos — Defenseman
Regular Season — Playoffs

Season	Team	League	GP	G	A	PTS	PIM	GP	G	A	PTS	PIM
98-99	Phoenix	WCHL	1	0	0	0	0	—	—	—	—	—
98-99	South Carolina	ECHL	1	0	0	0	0	—	—	—	—	—

Born; 7/9/74, Toronto, Ontario. 6-4, 220.

Kory Karlander — Left Wing
Regular Season — Playoffs

Season	Team	League	GP	G	A	PTS	PIM	GP	G	A	PTS	PIM
95-96	Columbus	ECHL	17	1	6	7	28	2	0	0	0	4
96-97	Louisville	ECHL	19	3	8	11	6	—	—	—	—	—
96-97	Raleigh	ECHL	36	8	20	28	36	—	—	—	—	—
97-98	Milwaukee	IHL	6	1	0	1	2	—	—	—	—	—
97-98	Raleigh	ECHL	60	32	48	80	71	—	—	—	—	—
98-99	Detroit	IHL	22	4	1	5	8	—	—	—	—	—
98-99	Grand Rapids	IHL	44	9	19	28	58	—	—	—	—	—
98-99	Peoria	ECHL	8	6	3	9	6	—	—	—	—	—
	IHL	Totals	72	14	20	34	68	—	—	—	—	—
	ECHL	Totals	140	50	85	135	147	2	0	0	0	4

Born; 3/21/72, Melita, Manitoba. 6-1, 190. 1997-98 ECHL Second Team All-Star. Last amateur club; Northern Michigan (WCHA).

Mark Karpen — Center
Regular Season — Playoffs

Season	Team	League	GP	G	A	PTS	PIM	GP	G	A	PTS	PIM
92-93	St. Thomas	CoHL	29	9	21	30	16	—	—	—	—	—
92-93	Johnstown	ECHL	38	17	25	42	22	5	1	4	5	4
93-94	Cleveland	IHL	17	6	5	11	0	—	—	—	—	—
93-94	Muskegon	CoHL	45	29	46	75	20	3	1	1	2	0
94-95	Wichita	CeHL	49	32	40	72	45	—	—	—	—	—
95-96	Muskegon	CoHL	9	2	4	6	8	—	—	—	—	—
95-96	Reno	WCHL	55	28	37	65	49	3	0	2	2	0
96-97	Amarillo	WPHL	57	32	36	68	38	—	—	—	—	—
97-98	Amarillo	WPHL	58	24	50	74	20	—	—	—	—	—
97-98	Reno	WCHL	7	1	5	6	2	3	0	0	0	0
98-99	Wichita	CHL	69	35	46	81	44	4	3	1	4	2
	CHL	Totals	118	67	86	153	89	4	3	1	4	2
	WPHL	Totals	115	56	86	142	58	—	—	—	—	—
	CoHL	Totals	83	40	71	111	44	3	1	1	2	0
	WCHL	Totals	62	29	42	71	51	6	0	2	2	0

Born; 5/13/69, Eveleth, Minnesota. 5-11, 170. Selected by Idaho in 1998 WCHL Dispersal Draft. 1995-96 WCHL Second Team All-Star.

Igor Karpenko — Goaltender
Regular Season — Playoffs

Season	Team	League	GP	W	L	T	MIN	SO	AVG	GP	W	L	MIN	SO	AVG
96-97	Port Huron	CoHL	23	9	9	1	1149	0	3.50	3	1	2	179	0	5.36
96-97	Las Vegas	IHL	3	0	2	0	134	0	5.38	—	—	—	—	—	—
97-98	Saint John	AHL	4	2	1	1	225	2	0.80	—	—	—	—	—	—
97-98	Port Huron	UHL	56	27	23	6	3187	0	3.77	3	0	3	180	0	4.67
98-99	Saint John	AHL	23	5	10	3	1206	0	3.43	2	0	1	63	0	4.79
98-99	Johnstown	ECHL	7	4	3	0	369	0	3.25	—	—	—	—	—	—
	AHL	Totals	27	7	11	4	1431	2	3.02	—	—	—	—	—	—
	UHL	Totals	79	36	32	7	4336	0	3.69	6	1	5	359	0	5.02

Born; 7/23/76, Kiev, Russia. Drafted by Anaheim Mighty Ducks (7th choice, 185th overall) in 1995 Entry Draft. Signed as a free agent by Calgary Flames

Avi Karunaker — Goaltender
Regular Season — Playoffs

Season	Team	League	GP	W	L	T	MIN	SO	AVG	GP	W	L	MIN	SO	AVG
98-99	Richmond	ECHL	2	0	1	0	60	0	5.00	—	—	—	—	—	—
98-99	Saginaw	UHL	28	7	17	3	1516	1	4.59	—	—	—	—	—	—

Born; 7/29/73, Kuwait. 5-11, 180. Last amateur club; Mercyhurst (ECAC 3).

Sam Katsuras
Regular Season — Playoffs

Season	Team	League	GP	G	A	PTS	PIM	GP	G	A	PTS	PIM
98-99	Belleville	OHL	6	0	2	2	4	—	—	—	—	—
98-99	Fort Worth	CHL	9	3	5	8	2	—	—	—	—	—

Born; Selected by Tulsa Oilers in 1999 CHL Dispersal Draft. Last amateur club; Belleville (OHL).

Chris Kavanagh — Defenseman
Regular Season — Playoffs

Season	Team	League	GP	G	A	PTS	PIM	GP	G	A	PTS	PIM
97-98	Elmira	NCAA	20	1	3	4	n/a	—	—	—	—	—
97-98	Binghamton	UHL	2	0	0	0	0	—	—	—	—	—
98-99	Binghamton	UHL	34	1	0	1	34	—	—	—	—	—
98-99	Mohawk Valley	UHL	12	0	2	2	21	—	—	—	—	—
	UHL	Totals	48	1	2	3	55	—	—	—	—	—

Born; 12/25/74, Framingham, Massachusetts. 6-0, 194. Last amateur club; Elmira (NCAA 3).

Arttu Kayhko — Defenseman
Regular Season — Playoffs

Season	Team	League	GP	G	A	PTS	PIM	GP	G	A	PTS	PIM
98-99	Orlando	IHL	23	0	5	5	18	—	—	—	—	—
98-99	Saint John	AHL	14	1	3	4	14	4	0	1	1	2
98-99	Mississippi	ECHL	38	5	8	13	51	—	—	—	—	—

Born; 1/5/73, Joensuu, Finland. 6-5, 230. Traded to Saint John by Orlando with Allan Egelund for Tyler Moss and Eric Healey (3/99).

Mario Kazda — Left Wing
Regular Season — Playoffs

Season	Team	League	GP	G	A	PTS	PIM	GP	G	A	PTS	PIM
98-99	Quad City	UHL	8	2	0	2	8	—	—	—	—	—

Born; 4/7/76, Dubnica, Slovakia. 6-1, 190.

Jeff Kealty — Defenseman
Regular Season — Playoffs

Season	Team	League	GP	G	A	PTS	PIM	GP	G	A	PTS	PIM
98-99	Milwaukee	IHL	70	8	14	22	134	2	0	1	1	4

Born; 4/9/76, Boston, Massachusetts. 6-4, 175. Drafted by Quebec Nordiques (2nd choice, 22nd overall) in 1994 Entry Draft. Last amateur club; Boston University (Hockey East).

Justin Kearns — Right Wing
Regular Season — Playoffs

Season	Team	League	GP	G	A	PTS	PIM	GP	G	A	PTS	PIM
98-99	Binghamton	UHL	65	16	13	29	57	5	0	1	1	6

Born; 10/02/76, Cleveland, Ohio. 6-1, 210. Selected by Fort Wayne in 1999 UHL Expansion Draft. Last amateur club; Northeastern (H.E.)

Dan Keczmer — Defensman

Regular Season / Playoffs

Season	Team	League	GP	G	A	PTS	PIM	GP	G	A	PTS	PIM
90-91	Minnesota	NHL	9	0	1	1	6	—	—	—	—	—
90-91	Kalamazoo	IHL	60	4	20	24	60	9	1	2	3	10
91-92	United States	National	51	3	11	14	56	—	—	—	—	—
91-92	Hartford	NHL	1	0	0	0	0	—	—	—	—	—
91-92	Springfield	AHL	18	3	4	7	10	4	0	0	0	6
92-93	Hartford	NHL	23	4	4	8	28	—	—	—	—	—
92-93	Springfield	AHL	37	1	13	14	38	12	0	4	4	14
93-94	Hartford	NHL	12	0	1	1	12	—	—	—	—	—
93-94	Calgary	NHL	57	1	20	21	48	3	0	0	0	4
93-94	Springfield	AHL	7	0	1	1	4	—	—	—	—	—
94-95	Calgary	NHL	28	2	3	5	10	7	0	1	1	2
95-96	Calgary	NHL	13	0	0	0	14	—	—	—	—	—
95-96	Saint John	AHL	22	3	11	14	14	—	—	—	—	—
95-96	Albany	AHL	17	0	4	4	4	1	0	0	0	0
96-97	Dallas	NHL	13	0	1	1	6	—	—	—	—	—
96-97	Michigan	IHL	42	3	17	20	24	—	—	—	—	—
97-98	Dallas	NHL	17	1	2	3	26	2	0	0	0	2
97-98	Michigan	IHL	44	1	11	12	29	—	—	—	—	—
98-99	Dallas	NHL	22	0	1	1	22	—	—	—	—	—
98-99	Nashville	NHL	16	0	0	0	12	—	—	—	—	—
98-99	Michigan	IHL	5	0	1	1	2	—	—	—	—	—
	NHL	Totals	211	8	33	41	184	12	0	1	1	8
	IHL	Totals	151	8	49	57	115	9	1	2	3	10
	AHL	Totals	101	7	33	40	70	17	0	4	4	20

Born; 5/25/68, Mt. Clemens, Michigan. 6-1, 190. Drafted by Minnesota North Stars (11th choice, 201st overall) in 1986 Entry Draft. Claimed by San Jose Sharks from Minnesota in Dispersal Draft (5/30/91). Traded to Hartford Whalers by San Jose for Dean Evason (10/2/91). Traded to Calgary Flames by Hartford for Jeff Reese (11/19/93). Traded to New Jersey Devils by Calgary Flames with Phil Housley for Tommy Albelin, Cal Hulse and Jocelyn Lemieux. Signed as a free agent by Dallas Stars (8/19/96). Claimed on waivers by Nashville Predators from Dallas (3/18/99). Last amateur club; Lake Superior State (CCHA).

Chris Kelleher — Defenseman

Regular Season / Playoffs

Season	Team	League	GP	G	A	PTS	PIM	GP	G	A	PTS	PIM
98-99	Syracuse	AHL	45	1	4	5	43	—	—	—	—	—

Born; 3/23/75, Cambridge, Massachusetts. 6-1, 215. Drafted by Pittsburgh Penguins (5th choice, 130th overall) in 1993 Entry Draft. Last amateur club; Boston University (Hockey East).

Eric Kelly — Defensman

Regular Season / Playoffs

Season	Team	League	GP	G	A	PTS	PIM	GP	G	A	PTS	PIM
97-98	Binghamton	UHL	54	5	10	15	61	4	0	0	0	2
98-99	Pee Dee	ECHL	2	0	0	0	0	—	—	—	—	—
98-99	Jacksonville	ECHL	1	0	0	0	2	—	—	—	—	—
98-99	Binghamton	UHL	28	2	2	4	36	—	—	—	—	—
98-99	Mohawk Valley	UHL	8	0	3	3	8	—	—	—	—	—
98-99	Asheville	UHL	8	1	1	2	27	3	0	0	0	2
	UHL	Totals	98	8	16	24	132	7	0	0	0	4
	ECHL	Totals	3	0	0	0	2	—	—	—	—	—

Born; 3/4/77, Binghamton, New York. 6-2, 210. Traded to Saginaw by Binghamton for Jack Greig (2/99). Traded to Mohawk Valley by Saginaw with Dominic Chiasson for Mark Bultje and Mike Hiebert (2/99). Selected by Madison in 1999 UHL Expansion Draft.

Jason Kelly — Defensman

Regular Season / Playoffs

Season	Team	League	GP	G	A	PTS	PIM	GP	G	A	PTS	PIM
95-96	Charlotte	ECHL	42	2	15	17	95	14	1	3	4	14
96-97	Baton Rouge	ECHL	60	3	14	17	81	—	—	—	—	—
97-98	Charlotte	ECHL	68	4	27	31	117	7	0	2	2	6
98-99	Kansas City	IHL	3	0	0	0	0	—	—	—	—	—
	ECHL	Totals	170	9	56	65	293	21	1	5	6	20

Born; 5/30/72, Thunder Bay,Ontario. 6-2, 208. Member of 1995-96 ECHL champion Charlotte Checkers. Last amateur club; Northeastern (Hockey East).

Steve Kelly — Center

Regular Season / Playoffs

Season	Team	League	GP	G	A	PTS	PIM	GP	G	A	PTS	PIM
96-97	Edmonton	NHL	8	1	0	1	6	6	0	0	0	2
96-97	Hamilton	AHL	48	9	29	38	111	11	3	3	6	24
97-98	Edmonton	NHL	19	0	2	2	8	—	—	—	—	—
97-98	Tampa Bay	NHL	24	2	1	3	15	—	—	—	—	—
97-98	Hamilton	AHL	11	2	8	10	18	—	—	—	—	—
97-98	Milwaukee	IHL	5	0	1	1	19	—	—	—	—	—
97-98	Cleveland	IHL	5	1	1	2	29	1	0	1	1	0
98-99	Tampa Bay	NHL	34	1	3	4	27	—	—	—	—	—
98-99	Cleveland	IHL	18	6	7	13	36	—	—	—	—	—
	NHL	Totals	75	4	6	10	56	6	0	0	0	2
	AHL	Totals	59	11	37	48	129	11	3	3	6	24
	IHL	Totals	28	7	9	16	84	1	0	1	1	0

Born; 10/26/76, Vancouver, British Columbia. 6-1, 190. Drafted by Edmonton Oilers (1st choice, 6th overall) in 1995 Entry Draft. Traded to Tampa Bay Lightning with Bryan Marchment and Jason Bonsignore to Tampa Bay for Roman Hamrlik and Paul Comrie (12/30/97). Last amateur club; Prince Albert (WHL).

Mick Kempffer — Defenseman

Regular Season / Playoffs

Season	Team	League	GP	G	A	PTS	PIM	GP	G	A	PTS	PIM
94-95	Chicago	IHL	35	2	5	7	26	—	—	—	—	—
94-95	Charlotte	ECHL	12	1	6	7	16	—	—	—	—	—
95-96	Charlotte	ECHL	65	1	21	22	82	16	0	3	3	33
96-97	Charlotte	ECHL	43	4	18	22	27	—	—	—	—	—
96-97	Jacksonville	ECHL	23	2	6	8	24	—	—	—	—	—
97-98	Columbus	CHL	61	12	53	65	99	13	2	*21	23	10
98-99	Columbus	CHL	69	19	57	76	135	10	3	13	16	30
	ECHL	Totals	143	8	51	59	149	16	0	3	3	33
	CHL	Totals	130	31	110	141	234	23	5	34	39	40

Born; 4/17/70, Duluth, Minnesota. 6-0, 184. Member of 1995-96 ECHL champion Charlotte Checkers. Member of 1997-98 CHL Champion Columbus Cottonmouths. Last amateur club; Wisconsin Stevens-Point (NCAA 3).

Chris Kenady — Right Wing

Regular Season / Playoffs

Season	Team	League	GP	G	A	PTS	PIM	GP	G	A	PTS	PIM
95-96	Worcester	AHL	43	9	10	19	58	2	0	0	0	0
96-97	Worcester	AHL	73	23	26	49	131	5	0	1	1	2
97-98	St. Louis	NHL	5	0	2	2	0	—	—	—	—	—
97-98	Worcester	AHL	63	23	22	45	84	11	1	5	6	26
98-99	Hartford	AHL	22	2	6	8	52	2	0	1	1	6
98-99	Utah	IHL	35	7	6	13	68	—	—	—	—	—
98-99	Long Beach	IHL	19	1	6	7	47	—	—	—	—	—
	AHL	Totals	201	57	64	121	241	20	1	7	8	34
	IHL	Totals	54	8	12	20	115	—	—	—	—	—

Born; 4/10/73, Mound, Minnesota. 6-2, 195. Drafted by St. Louis Blues (8th choice, 175th overall) in 1991 Entry Draft. Traded to New York Rangers by St. Louis to complete earlier trade for Jeff Finley, Geoff Smith and cash (2/22/99). (Last amateur club; Denver (WCHA).

Bryan Kennedy — Forward

Regular Season / Playoffs

Season	Team	League	GP	G	A	PTS	PIM	GP	G	A	PTS	PIM
98-99	Massachusetts	H.E.	33	3	5	8	8	—	—	—	—	—
98-99	Dayton	ECHL	5	0	1	1	2	—	—	—	—	—

Born; Toronto, Ontario. 6-1, 210. Last amateur club; Massachusetts (Hockey

Dave Kennedy — Goaltender

Regular Season / Playoffs

Season	Team	League	GP	W	L	T	MIN	SO	AVG	GP	W	L	MIN	SO	AVG
98-99	Pensacola	ECHL	1	0	0	0	20	0	3.00	—	—	—	—	—	—

Born;3/6/75. Toronto, Ohio. 5-11, 183.

Mike Kennedy — Center
Regular Season — Playoffs

Season	Team	League	GP	G	A	PTS	PIM	GP	G	A	PTS	PIM
92-93	Kalamazoo	IHL	77	21	30	51	39	—	—	—	—	—
93-94	Kalamazoo	IHL	63	20	18	38	42	3	1	2	3	2
94-95	Kalamazoo	IHL	42	20	28	48	29	—	—	—	—	—
94-95	Dallas	NHL	44	6	12	18	33	5	0	0	0	9
95-96	Dallas	NHL	61	9	17	26	48	—	—	—	—	—
96-97	Dallas	NHL	24	1	6	7	13	—	—	—	—	—
96-97	Michigan	IHL	2	0	1	1	2	—	—	—	—	—
97-98	Toronto	NHL	13	0	1	1	14	—	—	—	—	—
97-98	Dallas	NHL	2	0	0	0	2	—	—	—	—	—
97-98	St. John's	AHL	49	11	17	28	86	—	—	—	—	—
98-99	Islanders	NHL	1	0	0	0	2	—	—	—	—	—
98-99	Lowell	AHL	62	14	26	40	52	3	1	0	1	2
	NHL	Totals	145	16	36	52	112	5	0	0	0	9
	IHL	Totals	184	61	77	138	112	8	1	2	3	11
	AHL	Totals	111	25	43	68	138	3	1	0	1	2

Born; 4/13/72, Vancouver, British Columbia. 6-1, 195. Drafted by Minnesota North Stars (5th choice, 97th overall) in 1991 Entry Draft. Signed as a free agent by Toronto Maple Leafs (7/2/97). Traded to Dallas Stars by Toronto for Dallas 8th round choice (Mihail Travnicek) in 1998 Entry Draft (3/24/98). Signed as a free agent by New York Islanders (9/9/98). Last amateur club; Seattle (WHL).

Sheldon Kennedy — Right Wing
Regular Season — Playoffs

Season	Team	League	GP	G	A	PTS	PIM	GP	G	A	PTS	PIM
89-90	Detroit	NHL	20	2	7	9	10	—	—	—	—	—
89-90	Adirondack	AHL	26	11	15	26	35	—	—	—	—	—
90-91	Detroit	NHL	7	1	0	1	12	—	—	—	—	—
90-91	Adirondack	AHL	11	1	3	4	8	—	—	—	—	—
91-92	Detroit	NHL	27	3	8	11	24	—	—	—	—	—
91-92	Adirondack	AHL	46	25	24	49	56	16	5	9	14	12
92-93	Detroit	NHL	68	19	11	30	46	7	1	1	2	2
93-94	Detroit	NHL	61	6	7	13	30	7	1	2	3	0
94-95	Calgary	NHL	30	7	8	15	45	7	3	1	4	16
95-96	Calgary	NHL	41	3	7	10	36	3	1	0	1	2
95-96	Saint John	AHL	3	4	0	4	8	—	—	—	—	—
96-97	Boston	NHL	56	8	10	18	30	—	—	—	—	—
96-97	Providence	AHL	3	0	1	1	2	—	—	—	—	—
97-98	Injured	DNP										
98-99	Manitoba	IHL	24	7	7	14	14	—	—	—	—	—
98-99	Landshut	Germany	13	0	3	3	0	3	0	0	0	4
	NHL	Totals	310	49	58	107	233	24	6	4	10	20
	AHL	Totals	89	41	43	84	109	16	5	9	14	12

Born; 6/15/69, Elkhorn, Manitoba. 5-10, 180. Drafted by Detroit Red Wings (5th choice, 80th overall) in 1988 Entry Draft. Traded to Winnipeg Jets by Detroit for Winnipeg's third round choice (Darryl Laplante) in 1995 Entry Draft (5/25/94). Claimed by Calgary Flames from Winnipeg in NHL Waiver Draft (1/18/95). Signed as a free agent by Boston Bruins (8/7/96). Missed entire 1997-98 season with an off-ice leg injury. Member of 1991-92 AHL Champion Adirondack Red Wings. Last amateur club; Swift Current (WHL).

Troy Kennedy — Right Wing
Regular Season — Playoffs

Season	Team	League	GP	G	A	PTS	PIM	GP	G	A	PTS	PIM
91-92	Milton-Keynes	BHL	23	33	53	86	28	—	—	—	—	—
91-92	Telford	BHL	13	31	23	54	0	—	—	—	—	—
92-93	Telford	BHL	30	44	57	101	55	—	—	—	—	—
93-94	Telford	BHL	50	86	129	215	79	—	—	—	—	—
94-95	Trafford	BHL	10	9	10	19	8	—	—	—	—	—
94-95	Blackburn	BHL	20	20	44	64	16	—	—	—	—	—
95-96	Guildford	BHL	50	48	97	145	52	—	—	—	—	—
96-97	Central Texas	WPHL	64	16	50	66	47	11	3	9	12	12
97-98	Thunder Bay	UHL	20	6	4	10	10	—	—	—	—	—
97-98	Tacoma	WCHL	50	14	27	41	42	12	1	9	10	20
98-99	Lake Charles	WPHL	59	15	30	45	42	11	5	4	9	10
	WPHL	Totals	123	31	80	111	89	22	8	13	21	22

Born; 3/12/68, Brandon, Manitoba. Drafted by Calgary Flames (8th choice, 168th overall) in 1988 Entry Draft.

Jay Kenney — Defenseman
Regular Season — Playoffs

Season	Team	League	GP	G	A	PTS	PIM	GP	G	A	PTS	PIM
96-97	Charlotte	ECHL	62	2	14	16	61	3	0	1	1	4
97-98	Charlotte	ECHL	33	1	5	6	12	7	0	0	0	4
98-99	Peoria	ECHL	39	0	9	9	8	3	0	0	0	0
	ECHL	Totals	134	3	28	31	81	13	0	1	1	4

Born; 9/21/73, New York, New York. 6-2, 190. Drafted by Ottawa Senators (8th choice, 169th overall) in 1992 Entry Draft. Last amateur club; Providence (H.E.).

Brendan Kenny — Defenseman
Regular Season — Playoffs

Season	Team	League	GP	G	A	PTS	PIM	GP	G	A	PTS	PIM
97-98	Monroe	WPHL	69	3	4	7	117	—	—	—	—	—
98-99	Amarillo	WPHL	69	5	10	15	127	—	—	—	—	—
	WPHL	Totals	138	8	14	22	244	—	—	—	—	—

Born; 7/5/73, Edmonton, Alberta. 6-0, 210. Traded to New Mexico by Amarillo for Mitch Shawara (6/99). Traded to Monroe by New Mexico for Travis Van Tighem (7/99). Last amateur club; Western Michigan (CCHA).

Rob Kenny — Left Wing
Regular Season — Playoffs

Season	Team	League	GP	G	A	PTS	PIM	GP	G	A	PTS	PIM
92-93	Binghamton	AHL	66	12	11	23	56	8	2	4	6	8
93-94	Binghamton	AHL	63	27	14	41	90	—	—	—	—	—
94-95	Binghamton	AHL	17	2	9	11	32	—	—	—	—	—
95-96	Los Angeles	IHL	74	15	19	34	124	—	—	—	—	—
96-97	Long Beach	IHL	76	18	15	33	127	18	4	2	6	44
97-98	Long Beach	IHL	59	7	10	17	72	14	0	3	3	14
98-99	Miami	ECHL	58	22	20	42	62	—	—	—	—	—
98-99	Orlando	IHL	20	9	5	14	10	9	0	1	1	16
	IHL	Totals	229	49	49	98	333	41	4	6	10	74
	AHL	Totals	146	41	34	75	178	8	2	4	6	8

Born; 10/19/68, Bronx, New York. 6-1, 205. Selected by Johnstown in 1999 ECHL Dispersal Draft. Last amateur club; Northeastern (Hockey East).

Shane Kenny — Defenseman
Regular Season — Playoffs

Season	Team	League	GP	G	A	PTS	PIM	GP	G	A	PTS	PIM
97-98	Sarnia	OHL	45	11	21	32	91	5	0	1	1	21
97-98	Rochester	AHL	1	0	0	0	0	—	—	—	—	—
98-99	Rochester	AHL	23	2	1	3	25	1	0	0	0	10
98-99	Binghamton	UHL	7	1	1	2	4	—	—	—	—	—
	AHL	Totals	24	2	1	3	25	1	0	0	0	10

Born; 3/1/77, Oromocto, British Columbia. 6-3, 228. Selected by Mohawk Valley in 1998 UHL Expansion Draft. Selected by Fort Wayne in 1999 Expansion Draft. Last amateur club; Sarnia (OHL).

Kevin Kerr — Right Wing
Regular Season / Playoffs

Season	Team	League	GP	G	A	PTS	PIM	GP	G	A	PTS	PIM
87-88	Rochester	AHL	72	18	11	29	352	5	1	3	4	42
88-89	Rochester	AHL	66	20	18	38	306	—	—	—	—	—
89-90	Rochester	AHL	8	0	1	1	22	—	—	—	—	—
89-90	Fort Wayne	IHL	43	11	16	27	219	5	0	1	1	33
89-90	Phoenix	IHL	6	0	0	0	25	—	—	—	—	—
90-91	Fort Wayne	IHL	13	1	6	7	32	—	—	—	—	—
90-91	Cincinnati	ECHL	36	25	34	59	228	4	0	6	6	23
91-92	Utica	AHL	19	3	3	6	25	—	—	—	—	—
91-92	Cincinnati	ECHL	37	27	18	45	203	9	4	9	13	64
92-93	Cincinnati	IHL	39	18	23	41	93	—	—	—	—	—
92-93	Birmingham	ECHL	39	30	34	64	217	—	—	—	—	—
93-94	Portland	AHL	4	2	0	2	2	8	0	3	3	21
93-94	Phoenix	IHL	12	2	4	6	9	—	—	—	—	—
93-94	Flint	CoHL	45	57	55	112	299	10	6	7	13	79
94-95	Flint	CoHL	62	63	56	119	284	4	6	1	7	2
95-96	Flint	CoHL	66	53	47	100	204	15	11	15	26	24
96-97	Flint	CoHL	68	72	53	125	200	13	10	6	16	35
97-98	Flint	UHL	67	*63	48	111	208	16	9	12	21	62
98-99	Mobile	ECHL	12	6	8	14	57	—	—	—	—	—
98-99	Quad City	UHL	49	32	36	68	108	16	5	6	11	29
	AHL	Totals	169	43	33	76	707	13	1	6	7	63
	IHL	Totals	113	32	49	81	378	5	0	1	1	33
	UHL	Totals	357	340	295	635	1303	74	47	47	94	231
	ECHL	Totals	124	88	94	182	705	13	4	15	19	87

Born; 9/18/67, North Bay, Ontario. 5-10, 190. Drafted by Buffalo Sabres (4th choice, 56th overall) 6/21/86. 1993-94 CoHL First Team All-Star, 1994-95 CoHL Second Team All-Star, 1995-96 CoHL First Team All-Star. 1996-97 CoHL First Team All-Star. 1997-98 UHL First Team All-Star. Member of 1993-94 Calder Cup Champion Portland Pirates. Member of 1995-96 Colonial Cup Champion Flint Generals. Last amateur club; Windsor (OHL).

Dustin Kersey — Forward
Regular Season / Playoffs

Season	Team	League	GP	G	A	PTS	PIM	GP	G	A	PTS	PIM
98-99	Quad City	UHL	1	0	0	0	0	—	—	—	—	—

Born;

Dan Kesa — Right Wing
Regular Season / Playoffs

Season	Team	League	GP	G	A	PTS	PIM	GP	G	A	PTS	PIM
92-93	Hamilton	AHL	62	16	24	40	76	—	—	—	—	—
93-94	Vancouver	NHL	5	0	0	0	2	—	—	—	—	—
93-94	Hamilton	AHL	53	37	33	70	33	4	1	4	5	4
94-95	Syracuse	AHL	70	34	44	78	81	—	—	—	—	—
95-96	Dallas	NHL	3	0	0	0	0	—	—	—	—	—
95-96	Springfield	AHL	22	10	5	15	13	—	—	—	—	—
95-96	Michigan	IHL	15	4	11	15	33	—	—	—	—	—
95-96	Detroit	IHL	27	9	6	15	22	12	6	4	10	4
96-97	Detroit	IHL	60	22	21	43	19	20	7	5	12	20
97-98	Detroit	IHL	76	40	37	77	40	20	*13	5	18	14
98-99	Pittsburgh	NHL	67	2	8	10	27	13	1	0	1	0
98-99	Detroit	IHL	8	3	5	8	12	—	—	—	—	—
	NHL	Totals	75	2	8	10	29	13	1	0	1	0
	AHL	Totals	207	97	106	203	203	4	1	4	5	4
	IHL	Totals	186	78	80	158	1126	52	26	14	40	38

Born; 11/23/71, Vancouver, British Columbia. 6-0, 208. Drafted by Vancouver Canucks (5th choice, 95th overall) in 1991 Entry Draft. Traded to Dallas Stars by Vancouver with Greg Adams and Vancouver's fifth round choice (later traded to Los Angeles-Los Angeles selected Jason Morgan) in 1995 Entry Draft for Russ Courtnall (4/7/95) and conditional pick in 1997 Entry Draft to Hartford for Robert Petrovicky (11/29/95). Member of 1996-97 IHL Champion Detroit Vipers. Signed as a free agent by Pittsburgh Penguins (8/20/98). Last amateur club; Prince Albert

Casey Kesselring — Center
Regular Season / Playoffs

Season	Team	League	GP	G	A	PTS	PIM	GP	G	A	PTS	PIM
98-99	Johnstown	ECHL	46	18	25	43	21	—	—	—	—	—

Born; 2/5/74, Cambridge, Ontario. 6-0, 185. Last amateur club; Merrimack

Richard Keyes — Center
Regular Season / Playoffs

Season	Team	League	GP	G	A	PTS	PIM	GP	G	A	PTS	PIM
97-98	Indianapolis	IHL	2	0	0	0	0	—	—	—	—	—
97-98	Columbus	ECHL	56	23	17	40	68	—	—	—	—	—
98-99	Indianapolis	IHL	2	0	0	0	0	—	—	—	—	—
98-99	Columbus	ECHL	65	38	32	70	91	4	2	1	3	0
	IHL	Totals	4	0	0	0	0	—	—	—	—	—
	ECHL	Totals	121	61	49	110	159	4	2	1	3	0

Born; 7/7/75, Kalamazoo, Michigan. 5-10, 185. Selected by Arkansas in 1999 ECHL Dispersal Draft. Last amateur club; Michigan State (CCHA).

Tim Keyes — Goaltender
Regular Season / Playoffs

Season	Team	League	GP	W	L	T	MIN	SO	AVG	GP	W	L	MIN	SO	AVG
97-98	Syracuse	AHL	15	2	7	4	831	0	4.26	—	—	—	—	—	—
97-98	Raleigh	ECHL	1	0	1	0	60	0	4.00	—	—	—	—	—	—
97-98	Dayton	ECHL	9	1	6	2	535	0	3.70	—	—	—	—	—	—
98-99	Syracuse	AHL	11	2	7	0	582	0	4.43	—	—	—	—	—	—
98-99	Augusta	ECHL	8	4	3	0	411	0	3.65	—	—	—	—	—	—
98-99	Charlotte	ECHL	2	1	0	0	86	0	4.17	—	—	—	—	—	—
	AHL	Totals	26	4	14	4	1413	0	4.33	—	—	—	—	—	—
	ECHL	Totals	20	6	10	2	1092	0	3.74	—	—	—	—	—	—

Born; 5/28/76, Ganonoque, Ontario. 5-11, 170. Signed as a free agent by Vancouver Canucks (9/8/97). Last amateur club; Ottawa (OHL).

Ross Keys — Defenseman
Regular Season / Playoffs

Season	Team	League	GP	G	A	PTS	PIM	GP	G	A	PTS	PIM
98-99	Idaho	WCHL	2	0	1	1	4	—	—	—	—	—

Born; 10/4/74, Burnsville, Minnesota. 6-1, 225.

Sergei Kharin — Left Wing
Regular Season / Playoffs

Season	Team	League	GP	G	A	PTS	PIM	GP	G	A	PTS	PIM
90-91	Winnipeg	NHL	7	2	3	5	2	—	—	—	—	—
90-91	Moncton	AHL	66	22	18	40	38	5	1	0	1	2
91-92	Halifax	AHL	40	10	12	22	15	—	—	—	—	—
92-93	Cincinnati	IHL	60	13	18	31	25	—	—	—	—	—
92-93	Birmingham	ECHL	2	0	3	3	0	—	—	—	—	—
93-94	Dayton	ECHL	59	30	59	89	56	3	2	0	2	4
94-95	Cincinnati	IHL	56	14	29	43	24	1	0	0	0	0
95-96	Worcester	AHL	28	7	12	19	10	3	1	1	2	2
95-96	Dayton	ECHL	25	7	9	16	25	—	—	—	—	—
96-97	Port Huron	CoHL	49	20	24	44	20	—	—	—	—	—
96-97	Muskegon	CoHL	19	12	16	28	12	3	0	2	2	0
97-98	Muskegon	UHL	74	36	86	122	38	11	4	15	19	0
98-99	Muskegon	UHL	70	37	63	100	77	18	7	*17	24	10
	AHL	Totals	134	39	42	81	63	8	2	1	3	4
	IHL	Totals	116	27	47	74	49	1	0	0	0	0
	UHL	Totals	212	105	189	294	147	32	11	34	45	10
	ECHL	Totals	86	37	71	108	81	3	2	0	2	4

Born; 2/20/63, Odintsovo, Russia. 6-0, 190. Drafted by Winnipeg Jets (15th choice, 240th overall) in 1989 Entry Draft. Traded to Quebec Nordiques by Jets for Shawn Anderson (10/22/91). 1997-98 UHL Second Team All-Star. 1998-99 UHL Second All-Star Team. 1998-99 UHL Playoff MVP. Member of 1998-99 UHL Champion Muskegon Fury.

Alexander Kharlamov — Left Wing
Regular Season / Playoffs

Season	Team	League	GP	G	A	PTS	PIM	GP	G	A	PTS	PIM
95-96	Portland	AHL	65	14	18	32	35	14	2	3	5	8
96-97	Portland	AHL	56	9	15	24	28	—	—	—	—	—
97-98	Hampton Roads	ECHL	70	22	41	63	77	20	2	13	15	16
98-99	Novokuznetsk	Russia	4	0	0	0	2	—	—	—	—	—
98-99	Hampton Roads	ECHL	32	4	14	18	25	—	—	—	—	—
	AHL	Totals	121	23	33	56	63	14	2	3	5	8
	ECHL	Totals	102	26	55	81	102	20	2	13	15	16

Born; 9/23/75, Moscow, Russia. 5-11, 183. Drafted by Washington Capitals (2nd choice, 15th overall) in 1994 Entry Draft. Member of 1997-98 ECHL Champion Hampton Roads Admirals.

Denis Khlopotnov — Goaltender

Regular Season / Playoffs

Season	Team	League	GP	W	L	T	MIN	SO	AVG	GP	W	L	MIN	SO	AVG
98-99	Muskegon	UHL	37	21	8	2	1950	1	3.02	4	1	1	166	0	3.26

Born; 1/27/78, Moscow, USSR. 6-4, 198. Drafted by Florida Panthers (8th choice, 209th overall) in 1996 Entry Draft. Selected by Missouri in 1999 UHL Expansion Draft. 1998-99 UHL All-Rookie Team. Member of 1998-99 UHL Champion Muskegon Fury. Last amateur club; CSKA Moscow Jr.

Yuri Khmylev — Left Wing

Regular Season / Playoffs

Season	Team	League	GP	G	A	PTS	PIM	GP	G	A	PTS	PIM
92-93	Buffalo	NHL	68	20	19	39	28	8	4	3	7	4
93-94	Buffalo	NHL	72	27	31	58	49	7	3	1	4	8
94-95	Buffalo	NHL	48	8	17	25	14	5	0	1	1	8
95-96	Buffalo	NHL	66	8	20	28	40	—	—	—	—	—
95-96	St. Louis	NHL	7	0	1	1	0	6	1	1	2	4
96-97	St. Louis	NHL	2	1	0	1	2	—	—	—	—	—
96-97	Quebec	IHL	15	1	7	8	4	—	—	—	—	—
96-97	Hamilton	AHL	52	5	19	24	43	22	6	7	13	12
97-98	Fribourg	Switz.	17	5	6	11	2	2	1	0	1	0
98-99	St. John's	AHL	48	12	21	33	19	5	2	1	3	4
	NHL	Totals	263	64	88	152	133	26	8	6	14	24
	AHL	Totals	100	17	40	57	62	27	8	8	16	16

Born; 8/9/64, Moscow, Russia. 6-1, 189. Drafted by Buffalo Sabres (7th choice, 108th overall) in 1992 Entry Draft. Traded to St. Louis Blues by Buffalo with Buffalo's eighth round choice (Andrei Podkonicky) in 1996 Entry Draft for Jean-Luc Grand Pierre, Ottawa's second round choice (previously acquired by St. Louis—Buffalo selected Cory Sarich) in 1996 Entry Draft and St. Louis' third round selection (Maxim Afinogenov) in 1997 Entry Draft (3/20/96).

Alex Kholomeyev — Right Wing

Regular Season / Playoffs

Season	Team	League	GP	G	A	PTS	PIM	GP	G	A	PTS	PIM
92-93	Fort Worth	CeHL	42	23	22	45	124	—	—	—	—	—
93-94	Fort Worth	CeHL	53	21	21	42	76	—	—	—	—	—
94-95	Fort Worth	CeHL	63	31	29	60	91	—	—	—	—	—
95-96	Huntsville	SHL	47	36	35	71	68	10	5	5	10	23
96-97	Waco	WPHL	4	1	3	4	10	—	—	—	—	—
96-97	Huntsville	CeHL	57	37	58	95	90	9	13	1	14	24
97-98	Fort Worth	WPHL	67	34	39	73	83	5	0	1	1	0
98-99	Fort Worth	CHL	45	22	33	55	73	—	—	—	—	—
98-99	Huntsville	CHL	11	6	6	12	20	15	6	4	10	30
	CHL	Totals	271	140	169	309	474	24	19	5	24	54
	WPHL	Totals	71	35	42	77	93	5	0	1	1	0

Born; 3/29/69, St. Petersburg, Russia. 6-2, 200. Drafted by San Jose Sharks (10th choice, 219th overall) in 1992 Entry Draft. Member of 1995-96 SHL champion Huntsville Channel Cats. Member of 1998-99 CHL Champion Huntsville Channel Cats.

Justin Kieffer — Forward

Regular Season / Playoffs

Season	Team	League	GP	G	A	PTS	PIM	GP	G	A	PTS	PIM
98-99	Air Force	NCAA	34	14	23	37	NA	—	—	—	—	—
98-99	Colorado	WCHL	1	0	1	1	2	—	—	—	—	—

Born; 8/12/76, Brainerd, Minnesota. 5-11, 185. Last amateur club; Air Force (NCAA).

Joel Kimball — Goaltender

Regular Season / Playoffs

Season	Team	League	GP	W	L	T	MIN	SO	AVG	GP	W	L	MIN	SO	AVG
98-99	Anchorage	WCHL	1	0	0	0	34	0	1.74	—	—	—	—	—	—

Born;

Darin Kimble — Center

Regular Season / Playoffs

Season	Team	League	GP	G	A	PTS	PIM	GP	G	A	PTS	PIM
88-89	Quebec	NHL	26	3	1	4	149	—	—	—	—	—
88-89	Halifax	AHL	39	8	6	14	188	—	—	—	—	—
89-90	Quebec	NHL	44	5	5	10	185	—	—	—	—	—
89-90	Halifax	AHL	18	6	6	12	37	6	1	1	2	61
90-91	Quebec	NHL	35	2	5	7	114	—	—	—	—	—
90-91	St. Louis	NHL	26	1	1	2	128	13	0	0	0	38
90-91	Halifax	AHL	7	1	4	5	20	—	—	—	—	—
91-92	St. Louis	NHL	46	1	3	4	166	5	0	0	0	7
92-93	Boston	NHL	55	7	3	10	177	4	0	0	0	2
92-93	Providence	AHL	12	1	4	5	34	—	—	—	—	—
93-94	Chicago	NHL	65	4	2	6	133	1	0	0	0	5
94-95	Chicago	NHL	14	0	0	0	30	—	—	—	—	—
95-96	Indianapolis	IHL	9	1	0	1	15	—	—	—	—	—
95-96	Albany	AHL	60	4	15	19	144	3	0	0	0	2
96-97	Manitoba	IHL	39	3	4	7	115	—	—	—	—	—
96-97	Kansas City	IHL	33	9	9	18	106	2	0	0	0	0
97-98	Kansas City	IHL	16	1	3	4	60	—	—	—	—	—
97-98	San Antonio	IHL	56	6	14	20	143	—	—	—	—	—
98-99	Shreveport	WPHL	9	1	2	3	13	—	—	—	—	—
98-99	Arkansas	WPHL	51	9	17	26	133	3	0	0	0	8
	NHL	Totals	311	23	20	42	1082	23	0	0	0	52
	IHL	Totals	153	20	30	50	439	2	0	0	0	0
	AHL	Totals	136	20	35	55	423	9	1	1	2	63
	WPHL	Totals	60	10	19	29	146	3	0	0	0	8

Born; 11/22/68, Lucky Lake, Saskatchewan. 6-2, 210. Drafted by Quebec Nordiques (5th choice, 66th overall) in 1988 Entry Draft. Traded to St. Louis Blues by Quebec for Herb Raglan, Tony Twist and Andy Rymsha (2/4/91). Traded to Tampa Bay Lightning by St. Louis with Pat Jablonski and Steve Tuttle for future considerations (6/19/92). Traded to Boston Bruins by Tampa Bay with future considerations for Ken Hodge and Matt Hervey (9/4/92). Signed as a free agent by Florida Panthers (7/9/93). Traded to Chicago Blackhawks by Florida for Keith Brown (9/30/93). Traded to New Jersey Devils by Chicago for Michael Vukonich and Bill Armstrong (11/1/96). Signed as a free agent by Phoenix Coyotes (7/28/97). Traded to San Antonio by Kansas City with John Purves for Mike Craig and Reggie Savage (11/97). Last amateur club; Prince Albert (WHL).

Chris King — Goaltender

Regular Season / Playoffs

Season	Team	League	GP	W	L	T	MIN	SO	AVG	GP	W	L	MIN	SO	AVG
98-99	Topeka	CHL	1	0	1	0	40	0	4.50	—	—	—	—	—	—
98-99	Mohawk Valley	UHL	2	0	0	0	31	0	5.81	—	—	—	—	—	—
98-99	Asheville	UHL	2	0	2	0	68	0	7.02	—	—	—	—	—	—
	UHL	Totals	4	0	2	0	99	0	6.71	—	—	—	—	—	—

Born;

Scott King — Center

Regular Season / Playoffs

Season	Team	League	GP	G	A	PTS	PIM	GP	G	A	PTS	PIM
97-98	Fredericton	AHL	3	0	0	0	4	—	—	—	—	—
97-98	New Orleans	ECHL	56	26	46	72	34	4	0	6	6	6
98-99	Fredericton	AHL	70	14	29	43	42	6	2	3	5	2
	AHL	Totals	73	14	29	43	46	6	2	3	5	2

Born; 1/21/77, Saskatoon, Saskatchewan. Signed as a free agent by Montreal Canadiens (7/27/97). Last amateur club; Kelowna (WHL).

Steven King — Right Wing

Regular Season / Playoffs

Season	Team	League	GP	G	A	PTS	PIM	GP	G	A	PTS	PIM
91-92	Binghamton	AHL	66	27	15	42	56	10	2	0	2	14
92-93	Rangers	NHL	24	7	5	12	16	—	—	—	—	—
92-93	Binghamton	AHL	53	35	33	68	100	14	7	9	16	26
93-94	Anaheim	NHL	36	8	3	11	44	—	—	—	—	—
94-95	DNP	Injured										
95-96	Anaheim	NHL	7	2	0	2	15	—	—	—	—	—
95-96	Baltimore	AHL	68	40	21	62	95	12	7	5	12	20
96-97	Philadelphia	AHL	39	17	10	27	47	—	—	—	—	—
96-97	Michigan	IHL	39	15	11	26	39	4	1	2	3	12
97-98	Cincinnati	IHL	41	17	9	26	22	—	—	—	—	—
97-98	Rochester	AHL	28	15	15	30	28	4	1	1	2	4
98-99	Providence	AHL	3	1	0	1	0	13	7	4	11	12
	NHL	Totals	67	17	8	25	75	—	—	—	—	—
	AHL	Totals	257	135	94	229	326	40	17	15	32	64
	IHL	Totals	80	32	20	52	61	4	1	2	3	12

Born; 7/22/69, Greenwich, Rhode Island. 6-0, 195. Drafted by New York Rangers (1st choice. 21st overall) in 1991 Supplemental Draft. Claimed by Anaheim Mighty Ducks in Expansion Draft (6/24/93). Signed as a free agent by Philadelphia Flyers (7/31/96). Traded to Rochester by Cincinnati with Mike Casselman for Martin Menard and Brent Fedyk (2/98). Signed as a free agent by Boston Bruins (8/20/98). Signed as a free agent by Phoenix Coyotes (7/16/99).Member of 1998-99 AHL Champion Providence Bruins. Last amateur club; Brown (ECAC).

Geordie Kinnear — Defenseman

Regular Season / Playoffs

Season	Team	League	GP	G	A	PTS	PIM	GP	G	A	PTS	PIM
93-94	Albany	AHL	59	3	12	15	197	5	0	0	0	21
94-95	Albany	AHL	68	5	11	16	136	9	1	1	2	7
95-96	Albany	AHL	73	4	7	11	170	4	0	1	1	2
96-97	Albany	AHL	59	2	9	11	175	10	0	1	1	15
97-98	Albany	AHL	78	1	15	16	206	13	1	1	2	68
98-99	Albany	AHL	55	1	13	14	162	5	0	1	1	0
	AHL	Totals	392	16	67	83	1046	46	2	5	7	113

Born; 7/9/73, Simcoe, Ontario. 6-1, 200. Drafted by New Jersey Devils (7th choice, 162nd overall) in 1992 Entry Draft. Member of 1994-95 Calder Cup champion Albany RiverRats. Last amateur club; Peterborough (OHL).

Keith Kinvig — Right Wing

Regular Season / Playoffs

Season	Team	League	GP	G	A	PTS	PIM	GP	G	A	PTS	PIM
98-99	Fort Worth	CHL	12	3	1	4	21	—	—	—	—	—
98-99	Austin	WPHL	4	1	1	2	0	—	—	—	—	—

Born; 5/21/75, Medicine Hat, Alberta. 6-1, 215.

Scott Kirton — Right Wing

Regular Season / Playoffs

Season	Team	League	GP	G	A	PTS	PIM	GP	G	A	PTS	PIM
95-96	Providence	AHL	2	0	1	1	0	—	—	—	—	—
95-96	Charlotte	ECHL	56	17	19	36	176	16	4	6	10	50
96-97	Charlotte	ECHL	62	16	35	51	170	3	0	1	1	2
97-98	Fort Wayne	IHL	7	0	0	0	2	—	—	—	—	—
97-98	Wheeling	ECHL	37	18	23	41	77	—	—	—	—	—
97-98	Columbus	ECHL	33	10	18	28	74	—	—	—	—	—
98-99	London	BSL	43	9	16	25	44	6	1	3	4	12
	ECHL	Totals	188	61	95	156	487	19	4	7	11	52

Born; 10/4/71, Penetanguishene, Ontario. 6-4, 215. Drafted by Chicago Blackhawks (10th choice, 154th overall) in 1991 Entry Draft. Signed as a free agent by Boston Bruins (8/28/95). Traded to Columbus by Wheeling for David Brumby and Jason Disher (1/98). Member of 1995-96 ECHL Champion Charlotte Checkers. Last amateur club; North Dakota (WCHA).

Olaf Kjenstad — Left Wing

Regular Season / Playoffs

Season	Team	League	GP	G	A	PTS	PIM	GP	G	A	PTS	PIM
93-94	Seattle	WHL	54	30	36	66	102	9	4	9	13	16
93-94	St. John's	AHL	7	1	0	1	2	—	—	—	—	—
94-95	Birmingham	ECHL	62	29	30	59	107	7	4	2	6	8
95-96	Cape Breton	AHL	1	0	1	1	0	—	—	—	—	—
95-96	Birmingham	ECHL	67	30	36	66	128	—	—	—	—	—
96-97	Knoxville	ECHL	44	19	31	50	92	—	—	—	—	—
96-97	Tallahassee	ECHL	18	4	11	15	14	2	1	0	1	4
97-98	Columbus	CHL	69	55	70	125	183	13	12	12	24	28
98-99	Portland	AHL	5	0	0	0	4	—	—	—	—	—
98-99	Cincinnati	IHL	22	2	5	7	43	—	—	—	—	—
98-99	Columbus	CHL	3	5	1	6	2	9	4	1	5	23
98-99	Dayton	ECHL	2	1	0	1	32	—	—	—	—	—
	AHL	Totals	13	1	1	2	6	—	—	—	—	—
	ECHL	Totals	193	83	108	191	373	9	5	2	7	12
	CHL	Totals	72	60	71	131	185	22	16	13	29	51

Born; 6/15/73, Kamloops, British Columbia. 6-0, 185. Selected by San Antonio in 1998 CHL Expansion Draft. Last amateur club; Seattle (WHL).

Petr Klima — Right Wing

Regular Season / Playoffs

Season	Team	League	GP	G	A	PTS	PIM	GP	G	A	PTS	PIM
85-86	Detroit	NHL	74	32	24	56	16	—	—	—	—	—
86-87	Detroit	NHL	77	30	23	53	42	13	1	2	3	4
87-88	Detroit	NHL	78	37	25	62	46	12	10	8	18	10
88-89	Detroit	NHL	51	25	16	41	44	6	2	4	6	19
88-89	Adirondack	AHL	5	5	1	6	4	—	—	—	—	—
89-90	Detroit	NHL	13	5	5	10	6	—	—	—	—	—
89-90	Edmonton	NHL	63	25	28	53	66	21	5	0	5	8
90-91	Edmonton	NHL	70	40	28	68	113	18	7	6	13	16
91-92	Edmonton	NHL	57	21	13	34	52	15	1	4	5	8
92-93	Edmonton	NHL	68	32	16	48	100	—	—	—	—	—
93-94	Tampa Bay	NHL	75	28	27	55	76	—	—	—	—	—
94-95	Wolfsburg	Germany 2	12	27	11	38	28	—	—	—	—	—
94-95	ZPS Zlin	Czech.	1	1	0	1	0	—	—	—	—	—
94-95	Tampa Bay	NHL	47	13	13	26	26	—	—	—	—	—
95-96	Tampa Bay	NHL	67	22	30	52	68	4	2	0	2	14
96-97	Los Angeles	NHL	8	0	4	4	2	—	—	—	—	—
96-97	Pittsburgh	NHL	9	1	3	4	4	—	—	—	—	—
96-97	Cleveland	IHL	19	7	14	21	6	—	—	—	—	—
96-97	Edmonton	NHL	16	1	5	6	6	6	0	0	0	4
97-98	Krefeld	Germany	38	7	12	19	18	—	—	—	—	—
98-99	Adirondack	AHL	15	2	6	8	8	—	—	—	—	—
98-99	Detroit	NHL	13	1	0	1	4	—	—	—	—	—
	NHL	Totals	786	313	260	573	671	95	28	24	52	83
	AHL	Totals	20	7	7	14	12	—	—	—	—	—

Born; 12/23/64, Chomutov, Czech. 6-0, 190. Drafted by Detroit Red Wings (5th choice, 88th overall) in 1983 Entry Draft. Traded to Edmonton Oilers by Detroit with Joe Murphy, Adam Graves, and Jeff Sharples for Jimmy Carson, Kevin McClelland and Edmonton's fifth round choice (later traded to Montreal—Montreal selected Brad Layzell) in 1991 Entry Draft (11/2/89). Traded to Tampa Bay Lightning by Edmonton for Tampa Bay's third round choice (Brad Symes) in 1994 Entry Draft (8/16/93). Traded to Los Angeles Kings by Tampa Bay for Los Angeles' fifth round choice (Jan Sulc) in 1997 Entry Draft (8/22/96). Traded to Pittsburgh Penguins by Los Angeles for future considerations (10/25/96). Signed as a free agent by Edmonton (2/26/97). Signed as a free agent by Detroit (1/11/99). Member of 1989-90 Stanley Cup Champion Edmonton Oilers.

Sergei Klimentiev — Defenseman

Regular Season / Playoffs

Season	Team	League	GP	G	A	PTS	PIM	GP	G	A	PTS	PIM
94-95	Rochester	AHL	7	0	0	0	8	1	0	0	0	0
95-96	Rochester	AHL	70	7	29	36	74	19	2	8	10	16
96-97	Rochester	AHL	77	14	28	42	114	10	1	4	5	28
97-98	Rochester	AHL	57	4	22	26	94	—	—	—	—	—
98-99	Philadelphia	AHL	43	5	12	17	99	—	—	—	—	—
98-99	Milwaukee	IHL	35	4	11	15	59	2	0	0	0	6
	AHL	Totals	197	26	69	95	295	30	3	12	15	44

Born; 4/5/75, Kiev, Ukraine. 5-11, 200. Drafted by Buffalo Sabres (4th choice, 121st overall) in 1992 Entry Draft. Signed as a free agent by Philadelphia Flyers (7/10/98). Sold to Nashville Predators by Philadelphia (1/26/99). Member of 1995-96 AHL Champion Rochester Americans. Last amateur club; Medicine Hat

Jan Klimes — Right Wing

Regular Season / Playoffs

Season	Team	League	GP	G	A	PTS	PIM	GP	G	A	PTS	PIM
98-99	Tulsa	CHL	5	1	1	2	0	—	—	—	—	—
98-99	Muskegon	UHL	39	8	10	18	8	—	—	—	—	—
98-99	Flint	UHL	19	9	9	18	16	11	2	1	3	0
	UHL	Totals	58	17	19	36	24	11	2	1	3	0

Born; 8/12/77, Chomukov, Czech. Rebuplic. 6-1, 190. Traded to Flint by Muskegon with Mark Vilneff and David Beauregard for Mike Bondy and Chad Grills (2/99). Selected by Missouri in 1999 UHL Expansion Draft. Last amateur club; Summerside (MJHL).

Sergei Klimovich — Center

Regular Season / Playoffs

Season	Team	League	GP	G	A	PTS	PIM	GP	G	A	PTS	PIM
94-95	Indianapolis	IHL	71	14	30	44	20	—	—	—	—	—
95-96	Indianapolis	IHL	68	17	21	38	28	5	1	1	2	6
96-97	Chicago	NHL	1	0	0	0	2	—	—	—	—	—
96-97	Indianapolis	IHL	75	20	37	57	98	3	1	2	3	0
97-98	Las Vegas	IHL	25	2	8	10	6	—	—	—	—	—
97-98	Quebec	IHL	21	1	7	8	48	—	—	—	—	—
97-98	Idaho	WCHL	13	5	9	14	18	1	0	0	0	0
98-99	Augsburger	Germany	31	7	8	15	30	5	2	0	2	6
	IHL	Totals	260	54	103	157	200	8	2	3	5	6

Born; 3/8/74, Novosibrisk, Russia. 6-3, 189. Drafted by Chicago Blackhawks (3rd choice, 41st overall) in 1992 Entry Draft.

Brad Klyn — Defenseman

Regular Season / Playoffs

Season	Team	League	GP	G	A	PTS	PIM	GP	G	A	PTS	PIM
98-99	Topeka	CHL	3	0	0	0	4	—	—	—	—	—

Born; Surrey, British Columbia. 5-10, 180.

Lorne Knauft — Defenseman

Regular Season / Playoffs

Season	Team	League	GP	G	A	PTS	PIM	GP	G	A	PTS	PIM
92-93	New Haven	AHL	59	4	6	10	107	—	—	—	—	—
92-93	Thunder Bay	CoHL	3	0	0	0	2	1	0	1	1	2
93-94	Flint	CoHL	51	20	36	56	180	6	0	5	5	47
93-94	Portland	AHL	7	3	1	4	16	7	2	2	4	14
94-95	Muskegon	CoHL	16	2	7	9	48	—	—	—	—	—
94-95	Brantford	CoHL	29	12	19	31	80	—	—	—	—	—
94-95	Rochester	AHL	5	0	2	2	8	—	—	—	—	—
94-95	Adirondack	AHL	2	0	1	1	6	—	—	—	—	—
95-96	Anchorage	WCHL	41	12	27	39	180	—	—	—	—	—
96-97	Houston	IHL	7	1	0	1	2	—	—	—	—	—
96-97	Flint	CoHL	67	19	40	59	144	14	2	7	9	37
97-98	Flint	UHL	60	13	33	46	80	11	2	6	8	20
98-99	Flint	UHL	54	9	25	34	143	10	1	2	3	50
	AHL	Totals	73	7	10	17	137	7	2	2	4	14
	UHL	Totals	280	75	160	235	677	42	5	21	26	156

Born; 7/7/68, Hanna, Alberta. 6-2, 200. Member of 1993-94 AHL champion Portland Pirates. Last amateur club; Alaska-Anchorage (WCHA).

Fred Knipscheer — Center

Regular Season / Playoffs

Season	Team	League	GP	G	A	PTS	PIM	GP	G	A	PTS	PIM
93-94	Boston	NHL	11	3	2	5	14	12	2	1	3	6
93-94	Providence	AHL	62	26	13	39	50	—	—	—	—	—
94-95	Boston	NHL	16	3	1	4	2	4	0	0	0	0
94-95	Providence	AHL	71	29	34	63	81	—	—	—	—	—
95-96	St. Louis	NHL	1	0	0	0	0	—	—	—	—	—
95-96	Worcester	AHL	68	36	37	73	93	3	0	0	0	2
96-97	Phoenix	IHL	24	5	11	16	19	—	—	—	—	—
96-97	Indianapolis	IHL	41	10	9	19	46	4	0	2	2	10
97-98	Utah	IHL	58	21	32	53	69	2	0	0	0	4
97-98	Kentucky	AHL	17	0	7	7	8	3	0	1	1	7
98-99	Utah	IHL	21	4	9	13	20	—	—	—	—	—
98-99	Cincinnati	IHL	43	14	15	29	44	3	2	1	3	4
	NHL	Totals	28	6	3	9	16	16	2	1	3	6
	AHL	Totals	188	91	91	182	232	6	0	1	1	9
	IHL	Totals	187	54	76	130	198	9	2	3	5	18

Born; 9/3/69, Fort Wayne, Indiana. 5-11, 190. Signed as a free agent by Boston Bruins (4/30/93). Traded to St. Louis by Boston for Rick Zombo (10/2/95). Signed as a free agent by Chicago Blackhawks (8/16/96). Last amateur club; St. Cloud (WCHA).

Kris Knoblauch — Center

Regular Season / Playoffs

Season	Team	League	GP	G	A	PTS	PIM	GP	G	A	PTS	PIM
98-99	Kootenay	WHL	21	7	3	10	36	—	—	—	—	—
98-99	Lethbridge	WHL	52	20	22	42	102	4	1	3	4	6
98-99	Asheville	UHL	—	—	—	—	—	4	0	0	0	5

Born; 9/24/78, Imperial, Saskatchewan. 6-4, 205. Last amateur club; Lethbridge (WHL).

Kevin Knopp — Defenseman

Regular Season / Playoffs

Season	Team	League	GP	G	A	PTS	PIM	GP	G	A	PTS	PIM
95-96	Dayton	ECHL	5	0	1	1	4	—	—	—	—	—
95-96	South Carolina	ECHL	54	11	13	24	81	8	1	5	6	26
96-97	Baltimore	AHL	2	0	0	0	0	—	—	—	—	—
96-97	South Carolina	ECHL	65	10	41	51	108	18	4	2	6	43
97-98	South Carolina	ECHL	21	1	7	8	23	—	—	—	—	—
97-98	Richmond	ECHL	30	10	13	23	79	—	—	—	—	—
98-99	Richmond	ECHL	63	6	17	23	70	15	2	10	12	39
	ECHL	Totals	238	38	92	130	365	41	7	17	24	108

Born; 10/24/69, Edmonton, Alberta. 6-2, 200. Traded to Richmond by South Carolina with Dan Fournell, Mario Cormier and Jay Moser for Mike Taylor and Jason Wright (12/97). Member of 1996-97 ECHL Champion South Carolina Stingrays. Last amateur club; Acadia (AUAA).

Derek Knorr — Left Wing

Regular Season / Playoffs

Season	Team	League	GP	G	A	PTS	PIM	GP	G	A	PTS	PIM
95-96	Flint	CoHL	62	5	15	20	82	6	1	1	2	2
96-97	Muskegon	CoHL	72	26	35	61	127	3	0	3	3	8
97-98	Muskegon	UHL	72	21	40	61	104	10	2	2	4	24
98-99	Binghamton	UHL	63	31	33	64	142	5	2	2	4	8
	UHL	Totals	269	83	123	206	455	24	5	8	13	42

Born; 11/13/72, Kerrobert, Saskatchewan. 5-9, 190. Member of 1995-96 Colonial Cup Champion Flint Generals. Last amateur club; Illinois-Chicago (CCHA).

Cameron Knox — Forward

Regular Season / Playoffs

Season	Team	League	GP	G	A	PTS	PIM	GP	G	A	PTS	PIM
97-98	St. Norbert	NCHA	32	7	9	16	n/a	—	—	—	—	—
97-98	Dayton	ECHL	1	0	0	0	0	—	—	—	—	—
98-99	Central Texas	WPHL	12	0	3	3	11	—	—	—	—	—

Born; 5/2/74, Edmonton, Alberta. 6-0, 195. Last amateur club; St. Norbert College (NCHA).

Jason Knox — Defenseman
Regular Season — Playoffs

Season	Team	League	GP	G	A	PTS	PIM	GP	G	A	PTS	PIM
96-97	Fresno	WCHL	58	9	14	23	106	5	1	1	2	13
97-98	Long Beach	IHL	6	0	0	0	6	—	—	—	—	—
97-98	Fresno	WCHL	24	4	4	8	26	5	0	2	2	4
98-99	Fresno	WCHL	49	5	14	19	71	7	0	1	1	4
	WCHL	Totals	131	18	32	50	203	17	1	4	5	21

Born; 4/10/71, Williams Lake, British Columbia. 6-2, 205. Last amateur club; Mount Royal (ACAC).

Espen Knutsen — Center
Regular Season — Playoffs

Season	Team	League	GP	G	A	PTS	PIM	GP	G	A	PTS	PIM
97-98	Anaheim	NHL	19	3	0	3	6	—	—	—	—	—
97-98	Cincinnati	AHL	41	4	13	17	18	—	—	—	—	—
98-99	Djurgardens	Sweden	39	18	24	42	32	4	0	1	1	2

Born; 1/12/72, Oslo, Norway. 5-11, 180. Drafted by Hartford Whalers (9th choice, 204th overall) in 1990 Entry Draft. Rights traded to Anaheim Mighty Ducks by Hartford for Kevin Brown (10/1/96).

Jan Kobezda — Defenseman
Regular Season — Playoffs

Season	Team	League	GP	G	A	PTS	PIM	GP	G	A	PTS	PIM
98-99	Fort Wayne	IHL	4	0	0	0	4	—	—	—	—	—
98-99	Tallahassee	ECHL	60	6	14	20	56	—	—	—	—	—

Born; 7/31/75, Liava, Slovakia. 6-3, 220.

Paul Koch — Defenseman
Regular Season — Playoffs

Season	Team	League	GP	G	A	PTS	PIM	GP	G	A	PTS	PIM
95-96	Atlanta	IHL	4	0	0	0	2	—	—	—	—	—
95-96	Adirondack	AHL	3	0	1	1	0	—	—	—	—	—
95-96	Toledo	ECHL	67	6	19	25	142	8	1	6	7	10
96-97	Fort Wayne	IHL	2	0	0	0	0	—	—	—	—	—
96-97	Chicago	IHL	39	4	8	12	34	4	0	2	2	10
96-97	Toledo	ECHL	34	6	11	17	68	—	—	—	—	—
97-98	Chicago	IHL	70	1	7	8	99	—	—	—	—	—
98-99	Chicago	IHL	53	0	12	12	85	3	0	0	0	2
	IHL	Totals	168	5	27	32	220	7	0	2	2	12
	ECHL	Totals	101	10	27	37	210	8	1	6	7	10

Born; 6/30/71, St. Paul, Minnesota. 6-3, 220. Drafted by Quebec Nordiques (12th choice, 200th overall) in 1991 Entry Draft. Last amateur club; Denver (WCHA).

Dieter Kochan — Goaltender
Regular Season — Playoffs

Season	Team	League	GP	W	L	T	MIN	SO	AVG	GP	W	L	MIN	SO	AVG
97-98	Louisville	ECHL	18	7	9	2	981	1	3.73	—	—	—	—	—	—
98-99	Binghamton	UHL	40	18	16	5	2321	2	2.97	4	1	2	208	0	2.60

Born; 5/11/74, Saskatoon, Saskatchewan. 6-1, 184. Scored a goal for Binghamton during 1998-99 season. Last amateur club; Northern Michigan (CCHA).

Greg Koehler — Center
Regular Season — Playoffs

Season	Team	League	GP	G	A	PTS	PIM	GP	G	A	PTS	PIM
97-98	Lowell	H.E.	33	20	17	37	62	—	—	—	—	—
97-98	New Haven	AHL	3	0	0	0	2	—	—	—	—	—
98-99	New Haven	AHL	26	4	0	4	29	—	—	—	—	—
98-99	Florida	ECHL	29	13	14	27	62	6	2	3	5	12
	AHL	Totals	29	4	0	4	31	—	—	—	—	—

Born; 2/27/75, Scarborough, Ontario. 6-2, 195. Signed as a free agent by Carolina Hurricanes (3/31/98). Last amateur club; Lowell (Hockey East).

Trevor Koenig — Goaltender
Regular Season — Playoffs

Season	Team	League	GP	W	L	T	MIN	SO	AVG	GP	W	L	MIN	SO	AVG
98-99	Philadelphia	AHL	1	0	0	0	29	0	4.14						
98-99	Long Beach	IHL	11	5	5	0	635	0	2.74						
98-99	Detroit	IHL	6	5	0	0	300	1	2.20	—	—	—	—	—	—
98-99	Dayton	ECHL	15	9	5	0	888	0	3.04	4	1	2	203	1	1.78
	IHL	Totals	17	10	5	0	935	1	2.57	—	—	—	—	—	—

Born; 12/10/74, Edmonton, Alberta. 5-10, 170. Last amateur club; Union

Ladislav Kohn — Right Wing
Regular Season — Playoffs

Season	Team	League	GP	G	A	PTS	PIM	GP	G	A	PTS	PIM
94-95	Swift Current	WHL	65	32	60	92	122	6	2	6	8	14
94-95	Saint John	AHL	1	0	0	0	0	—	—	—	—	—
95-96	Calgary	NHL	5	1	0	1	2	—	—	—	—	—
95-96	Saint John	AHL	73	28	45	73	97	16	6	5	11	12
96-97	Saint John	AHL	76	28	29	57	81	5	0	0	0	0
97-98	Calgary	NHL	4	0	1	1	0	—	—	—	—	—
97-98	Saint John	AHL	65	25	31	56	90	21	*14	6	20	20
98-99	Toronto	NHL	16	1	3	4	4	2	0	0	0	5
98-99	St. John's	AHL	61	27	42	69	90	—	—	—	—	—
	NHL	Totals	25	2	4	6	6	2	0	0	0	5
	AHL	Totals	276	108	147	255	358	42	20	11	31	32

Born; 3/4/75, Uherske Hradiste, Czechoslovakia. 5-10, 175. Drafted by Calgary Flames (9th choice, 175th overall) in 1994 Entry Draft. Traded to Toronto Maple Leafs by Calgary for David Cooper (7/2/98). Last amateur club; Swift Current (WHL).

Mike Kolenda — Defenseman
Regular Season — Playoffs

Season	Team	League	GP	G	A	PTS	PIM	GP	G	A	PTS	PIM
95-96	Toledo	ECHL	48	0	10	10	93	7	0	0	0	47
96-97	Fort Wayne	IHL	6	1	0	1	0	—	—	—	—	—
96-97	Toledo	ECHL	52	4	15	19	73	3	0	0	0	0
97-98	Michigan	IHL	1	0	0	0	0	—	—	—	—	—
97-98	Toledo	ECHL	62	3	12	15	87	7	0	1	1	6
98-99	Greenville	ECHL	56	4	19	23	81	—	—	—	—	—
	IHL	Totals	7	1	0	1	0	—	—	—	—	—
	ECHL	Totals	218	11	56	67	334	17	0	1	1	53

Born; 3/6/72, Grand Rapids, Michigan. 6-0, 197. Selected by Greenville in 1998 ECHL Expansion Draft. Last amateur club; Ferris State (CCHA).

Mark Kolesar — Center
Regular Season — Playoffs

Season	Team	League	GP	G	A	PTS	PIM	GP	G	A	PTS	PIM
94-95	St. John's	AHL	65	12	18	30	62	5	1	0	1	2
95-96	Toronto	NHL	21	2	2	4	14	3	1	0	1	2
95-96	St. John's	AHL	52	22	13	35	47	—	—	—	—	—
96-97	Toronto	NHL	7	0	0	0	0	—	—	—	—	—
96-97	St. John's	AHL	62	22	28	50	64	10	1	3	4	6
97-98	Manitoba	IHL	30	1	9	10	29	—	—	—	—	—
97-98	St. John's	AHL	2	0	0	0	2	—	—	—	—	—
97-98	Hamilton	AHL	27	2	12	14	47	6	1	1	2	0
98-99	Nottingham	BSL	53	20	33	53	58	10	5	7	12	0
	NHL	Totals	28	2	2	4	14	3	1	0	1	2
	AHL	Totals	208	58	71	129	222	21	3	4	7	8

Born; 1/23/73, Nepawa, Manitoba. 6-1, 188. Signed as a free agent by Toronto Maple Leafs (5/24/94). Last amateur club; Brandon (WHL).

Martin Kolesar — Defenseman
Regular Season — Playoffs

Season	Team	League	GP	G	A	PTS	PIM	GP	G	A	PTS	PIM
98-99	Memphis	CHL	8	0	3	3	18	—	—	—	—	—

Born; 10/30/77, Czech Republic. 5-10, 170.

Alexei Kolkunov — Center
Regular Season — Playoffs

Season	Team	League	GP	G	A	PTS	PIM	GP	G	A	PTS	PIM
98-99	Syracuse	AHL	55	5	13	18	20	—	—	—	—	—

Born; 2/3/77, Belgorod, USSR. 6-2, 185. Drafted by Pittsburgh Penguins (5th choice, 154th overall) in 1995 Entry Draft.

Markus Kolomainen — Center

Regular Season / Playoffs

Season	Team	League	GP	G	A	PTS	PIM	GP	G	A	PTS	PIM
98-99	Bakersfield	WCHL	12	1	1	2	11	—	—	—	—	—

Born; 10/1/76, Tamperi, Finland. 6-0, 187.

Zenith Komarniski — Defenseman

Regular Season / Playoffs

Season	Team	League	GP	G	A	PTS	PIM	GP	G	A	PTS	PIM
98-99	Syracuse	AHL	58	9	19	28	89	—	—	—	—	—

Born; 8/13/78, Edmonton, Alberta. 6-0, 200. Drafted by Vancouver Canucks (2nd choice, 75th overall) in 1996 Entry Draft. Last amateur club; Spokane (WHL).

Dan Kopec — Defenseman

Regular Season / Playoffs

Season	Team	League	GP	G	A	PTS	PIM	GP	G	A	PTS	PIM
96-97	Wichita	CeHL	46	6	10	16	365	9	0	2	2	70
97-98	Raleigh	ECHL	63	0	11	11	308	—	—	—	—	—
98-99	Augusta	ECHL	65	2	6	8	313	2	0	0	0	8
	ECHL	Totals	218	2	17	19	621	2	0	0	0	8

Born; 3/3/73, Weyburn, Saskatchewan. 6-4, 225. Traded to Nashville Ice Flyers by Wichita Thunder for first pick in Dispersal Draft (6/10/97).

Dan Kordic — Left Wing

Regular Season / Playoffs

Season	Team	League	GP	G	A	PTS	PIM	GP	G	A	PTS	PIM
91-92	Philadelphia	NHL	46	1	3	4	126	—	—	—	—	—
92-93	Hershey	AHL	14	0	2	2	17	—	—	—	—	—
93-94	Philadelphia	NHL	4	0	0	0	5	—	—	—	—	—
93-94	Hershey	AHL	64	0	4	4	164	11	0	3	3	26
94-95	Hershey	AHL	37	0	2	2	121	6	0	1	1	21
95-96	Philadelphia	NHL	9	1	0	1	31	—	—	—	—	—
95-96	Hershey	AHL	52	2	6	8	101	—	—	—	—	—
96-97	Philadelphia	NHL	75	1	4	5	210	12	1	0	1	22
97-98	Philadelphia	NHL	61	1	1	2	210	—	—	—	—	—
98-99	Philadelphia	NHL	2	0	0	0	2	—	—	—	—	—
98-99	Philadelphia	AHL	9	1	1	2	43	1	0	0	0	0
98-99	Grand Rapids	IHL	3	0	0	0	0	—	—	—	—	—
	NHL	Totals	197	4	8	12	584	12	1	0	1	22
	AHL	Totals	176	3	15	18	446	18	0	4	4	47

Born; 4/18/71, Edmonton, Alberta. 6-5, 234. Drafted by Philadelphia Flyers (9th choice, 88th overall) in 1994 Entry Draft. Last amateur club, Medicine Hat

Evgeny Korolev — Defenseman

Regular Season / Playoffs

Season	Team	League	GP	G	A	PTS	PIM	GP	G	A	PTS	PIM
98-99	Lowell	AHL	54	2	6	8	48	2	0	1	1	0
98-99	Roanoke	ECHL	2	0	1	1	0	—	—	—	—	—

Born; 7/24/78, Moscow, USSR. 6-1, 186. Drafted by New York Islanders (9th choice, 192nd overall) in 1996 Entry Draft. Last amateur club; London (OHL).

Alexander Korolyuk — Right Wing

Regular Season / Playoffs

Season	Team	League	GP	G	A	PTS	PIM	GP	G	A	PTS	PIM
96-97	Soviet Wings	Russia	17	8	5	13	46	—	—	—	—	—
96-97	Manitoba	IHL	42	20	16	36	71	—	—	—	—	—
97-98	San Jose	NHL	19	2	3	5	6	—	—	—	—	—
97-98	Kentucky	AHL	44	16	23	39	96	3	0	0	0	0
98-99	San Jose	NHL	55	12	18	30	26	6	1	3	4	2
98-99	Kentucky	AHL	23	9	13	22	16	—	—	—	—	—
	NHL	Totals	74	14	21	35	32	6	1	3	4	2
	AHL	Totals	67	25	36	61	112	3	0	0	0	0

Born; 1/15/76, Moscow, Russia. 5-9, 190. Drafted by San Jose Sharks (6th choice, 141st overall) in 1994 Entry Draft.

Terho Koskela — Defenseman

Regular Season / Playoffs

Season	Team	League	GP	G	A	PTS	PIM	GP	G	A	PTS	PIM
96-97	Newcastle	BHL	42	13	13	26	20	—	—	—	—	—
97-98												
98-99	Abilene	WPHL	68	15	25	40	32	3	0	1	1	0

Born; 12/23/64, Gothenburg, Sweden. 6-0, 195.

John Kosobud — Left Wing

Regular Season / Playoffs

Season	Team	League	GP	G	A	PTS	PIM	GP	G	A	PTS	PIM
96-97	Mississippi	ECHL	52	9	12	21	40	2	0	0	0	0
97-98	Mississippi	ECHL	69	23	23	46	79	—	—	—	—	—
98-99	Springfield	AHL	2	2	0	2	4	—	—	—	—	—
98-99	Mississippi	ECHL	66	18	21	39	38	18	3	6	9	25
	ECHL	Totals	187	50	56	106	157	20	3	6	9	25

Born; 8/26/72, Fargo, North Dakota. 6-0, 205. Member of 1998-99 ECHL Champion Mississippi SeaWolves. Last amateur club; Concordia (MIAC).

Jeff Kostuch — Center

Regular Season / Playoffs

Season	Team	League	GP	G	A	PTS	PIM	GP	G	A	PTS	PIM
95-96	Hampton Roads	ECHL	67	18	23	41	60	3	0	2	2	4
96-97	Louisville	ECHL	67	19	23	42	87	—	—	—	—	—
97-98	Louisville	ECHL	61	16	31	47	37	—	—	—	—	—
98-99	Miami	ECHL	37	8	10	18	32	—	—	—	—	—
	ECHL	Totals	232	61	87	148	216	3	0	2	2	4

Born; 2/18/74, Brockville, Ontario. 6-1, 205. Last amateur club; Owen Sound (OHL).

Mark Kotary — Center

Regular Season / Playoffs

Season	Team	League	GP	G	A	PTS	PIM	GP	G	A	PTS	PIM
97-98	Richmond	ECHL	66	16	19	35	61	—	—	—	—	—
98-99	Mohawk Valley	UHL	37	10	6	16	21	—	—	—	—	—
98-99	Port Huron	UHL	17	5	7	12	12	5	0	0	0	0
	UHL	Totals	54	15	13	28	33	5	0	0	0	0

Born; 12/3/73, New Hartford, New York. 6-0, 180. Last amateur club; Oswego (SUNY).

Evgeny Kourilin — Center

Regular Season / Playoffs

Season	Team	League	GP	G	A	PTS	PIM	GP	G	A	PTS	PIM
96-97	Nashville	CeHL	6	0	0	0	0	—	—	—	—	—
97-98												
98-99	Anchorage	WCHL	42	10	9	19	18	—	—	—	—	—

Born; 1/13/79, Minsk, Belarus. Drafted by Carolina Hurricanes (9th choice, 259th overall) in 1999 NHL Entry Draft.

Jack Kowal — Right Wing

Regular Season / Playoffs

Season	Team	League	GP	G	A	PTS	PIM	GP	G	A	PTS	PIM
95-96	Alaska-Anchorage	WCHA	37	11	12	23	54	—	—	—	—	—
95-96	Anchorage	WCHL	5	2	3	5	4	—	—	—	—	—
96-97	Kentucky	AHL	40	5	8	13	37	—	—	—	—	—
96-97	Louisville	ECHL	33	11	16	27	18	—	—	—	—	—
97-98	Louisville	ECHL	70	15	28	43	56	—	—	—	—	—
98-99	Miami	ECHL	65	14	32	46	44	—	—	—	—	—
	ECHL	Totals	103	26	44	70	74	—	—	—	—	—

Born; 2/14/73, Anchorage, Alaska. 6-1, 195. Selected by Charlotte in 1999 ECHL Dispersal Draft. Last amateur club; Alaska-Anchorage (WCHA).

Rick Kowalsky — Right Wing

Regular Season								Playoffs				
Season	Team	League	GP	G	A	PTS	PIM	GP	G	A	PTS	PIM
93-94	Cornwall	AHL	65	9	8	17	86	—	—	—	—	—
94-95	Cornwall	AHL	9	2	1	3	38	—	—	—	—	—
94-95	Hampton Roads	ECHL	49	29	24	53	114	4	0	4	4	4
95-96	Hampton Roads	ECHL	52	21	29	50	121	—	—	—	—	—
96-97	Portland	AHL	22	7	8	15	10	—	—	—	—	—
96-97	Hampton Roads	ECHL	52	14	26	40	94	9	5	4	9	16
97-98	Portland	AHL	39	11	25	36	78	10	5	2	7	8
97-98	Hampton Roads	ECHL	24	11	16	27	72	—	—	—	—	—
98-99	Portland	AHL	47	6	15	21	85	—	—	—	—	—
	AHL	Totals	182	35	57	92	297	10	5	2	7	8
	ECHL	Totals	177	75	95	170	401	13	5	8	13	20

Born; 3/20/72, Simcoe, Ontario. 6-1, 195. Drafted by Buffalo Sabres (11th choice, 227th overall) in 1992 Entry Draft. Last amateur club; Sault Ste. Marie

Andrei Kozyrev — Defenseman

Regular Season								Playoffs				
Season	Team	League	GP	G	A	PTS	PIM	GP	G	A	PTS	PIM
97-98	Indianapolis	IHL	13	0	1	1	28	—	—	—	—	—
98-99	Indianapolis	IHL	61	1	2	3	81	5	0	0	0	2
98-99	Columbus	ECHL	3	0	1	1	11	—	—	—	—	—
	IHL	Totals	74	1	3	4	109	5	0	0	0	2

Born; 6/17/73, Tomsk, USSR. 6-1, 200. Drafted by Chicago Blackhawks (7th choice, 236th overall) in 1996 Entry Draft.

Ryan Kraft — Center

Regular Season								Playoffs				
Season	Team	League	GP	G	A	PTS	PIM	GP	G	A	PTS	PIM
98-99	Richmond	ECHL	63	28	36	64	35	18	10	10	20	4

Born; 11/7/75, Bottineau, North Dakota. 5-9, 181. Drafted by San Jose Sharks (11th choice, 194th overall) in 1995 Entry Draft. Last amateur club; Minnesota

Lubos Krajcovic — Right Wing

Regular Season								Playoffs				
Season	Team	League	GP	G	A	PTS	PIM	GP	G	A	PTS	PIM
98-99	Muskegon	UHL	16	2	3	5	10	—	—	—	—	—
98-99	Asheville	UHL	54	6	11	17	24	2	0	2	2	0
	UHL	Totals	70	8	14	22	34	2	0	2	2	0

Born; 10/28/76, Krupins, Slovakia. 6-3, 210. Traded to Asheville with Bob Brandon for Joakim Wassberger (12/98). Selected by Fort Wayne in 1999 UHL Expansion Draft. Last amateur club; Michigan Tech (WCHA).

Paul Krake — Goaltender

Regular Season										Playoffs					
Season	Team	League	GP	W	L	T	MIN	SO	AVG	GP	W	L	MIN	SO	AVG
92-93	Halifax	AHL	17	8	6	1	916	1	3.73	—	—	—	—	—	—
92-93	Oklahoma City	CeHL	17	13	4	0	1029	0	3.50	—	—	—	—	—	—
93-94	Cornwall	AHL	28	8	13	4	1383	0	4.17	—	—	—	—	—	—
94-95	Cornwall	AHL	7	2	4	0	359	0	4.01	—	—	—	—	—	—
94-95	Erie	ECHL	10	1	8	1	597	0	6.13	—	—	—	—	—	—
94-95	Memphis	CeHL	5	4	1	0	260	0	4.38	—	—	—	—	—	—
95-96	Charlotte	ECHL	10	3	3	0	417	0	3.59	—	—	—	—	—	—
95-96	Wichita	CeHL	22	7	9	0	1010	0	6.00	—	—	—	—	—	—
96-97	Cleveland	IHL	2	0	1	0	76	0	6.28	—	—	—	—	—	—
96-97	Brantford	CoHL	52	29	16	4	2996	*3	3.40	10	4	*6	0	596	4.43
97-98	San Angelo	WPHL	25	9	13	1	1324	0	4.35	—	—	—	—	—	—
98-99	Idaho	WCHL	15	4	8	1	809	0	4.52	—	—	—	—	—	—
	AHL	Totals	52	18	23	5	2658	1	4.00	—	—	—	—	—	—
	CeHL	Totals	44	24	14	0	2299	0	4.70	—	—	—	—	—	—
	ECHL	Totals	20	4	11	1	1014	0	5.09	—	—	—	—	—	—

Born; 3/25/69, Lloydminster, Alberta. 5-11, 180. Drafted by Quebec Nordiques (10th pick, 148th overall) in 1989 Entry Draft. Last amateur club; Alaska-Anchorage (WCHA).

Justin Krall — Defenseman

Regular Season								Playoffs				
Season	Team	League	GP	G	A	PTS	PIM	GP	G	A	PTS	PIM
96-97	Peoria	ECHL	69	10	27	37	57	10	3	5	8	8
97-98	Rochester	AHL	1	0	0	0	0	—	—	—	—	—
97-98	Peoria	ECHL	67	8	15	23	61	3	0	0	0	2
98-99	Cincinnati	IHL	1	0	0	0	0	—	—	—	—	—
98-99	Dayton	ECHL	68	16	24	40	56	4	1	2	3	2
	ECHL	Totals	204	34	66	100	174	17	4	7	11	12

Born; 2/20/74, Toledo, Ohio. 6-2, 170. Drafted by Detroit Red Wings (8th choice, 183rd overall) in 1992 Entry Draft. Last amateur club; Miami of Ohio (CCHA).

Mikhail Kravets — Right Wing

Regular Season								Playoffs				
Season	Team	League	GP	G	A	PTS	PIM	GP	G	A	PTS	PIM
91-92	Kansas City	IHL	74	10	32	42	172	15	6	8	14	12
91-92	San Jose	NHL	1	0	0	0	0	—	—	—	—	—
92-93	San Jose	NHL	1	0	0	0	0	—	—	—	—	—
92-93	Kansas City	IHL	71	19	49	68	153	10	2	5	7	55
93-94	Kansas City	IHL	63	14	44	58	171	—	—	—	—	—
94-95	Detroit	IHL	7	0	0	0	4	—	—	—	—	—
94-95	Minnesota	IHL	37	7	15	22	21	—	—	—	—	—
94-95	Syracuse	AHL	7	2	2	4	8	—	—	—	—	—
95-96	Milwaukee	IHL	7	0	1	1	4	—	—	—	—	—
95-96	Wichita	CeHL	37	14	57	71	89	—	—	—	—	—
96-97	Louisiana	ECHL	57	22	45	67	93	17	4	9	13	18
97-98	Louisiana	ECHL	28	8	18	26	41	—	—	—	—	—
97-98	Baton Rouge	ECHL	11	2	9	11	37	—	—	—	—	—
97-98	New Orleans	ECHL	4	1	0	1	2	—	—	—	—	—
97-98	Mississippi	ECHL	10	4	10	14	25	—	—	—	—	—
98-99	Mississippi	ECHL	59	17	42	59	136	18	5	8	13	10
	NHL	Totals	2	0	0	0	0	—	—	—	—	—
	IHL	Totals	259	50	141	191	525	25	8	13	21	67
	ECHL	Totals	169	54	124	178	334	35	9	17	26	28

Born; 11/12/63, Leningrad, Russia. 5-10, 182. Drafted by San Jose Sharks (13th choice, 243rd overall) in 1991 Entry Draft. Sold to New Orleans by Birminghan (2/98). Member of 1991-92 Turner Cup champion Kansas City Blades. Member of 1998-99 ECHL Champion Mississippi SeaWolves.

Brian Kreft — Goaltender

Regular Season										Playoffs					
Season	Team	League	GP	W	L	T	MIN	SO	AVG	GP	W	L	MIN	SO	AVG
97-98	Madison	UHL	9	4	3	2	499	0	3.61	—	—	—	—	—	—
97-98	Winston-Salem	UHL	10	2	5	1	519	0	4.17	—	—	—	—	—	—
98-99	Winston-Salem	UHL	23	9	12	0	1240	1	4.07	—	—	—	—	—	—
98-99	Saginaw	UHL	13	2	8	1	739	0	4.47	—	—	—	—	—	—
	UHL	Totals	55	17	28	4	2996	1	4.11	—	—	—	—	—	—

Born; Madison, Wisconsin. 6-1, 190. Traded to Saginaw by Winston-Salem with Kevin Tucker and John Nelson for Marc Delorme (1/98). Last amateur club; Wisconsin Eau-Claire (NCHA).

Kevin Kreutzer — Goaltender

Regular Season										Playoffs					
Season	Team	League	GP	W	L	T	MIN	SO	AVG	GP	W	L	MIN	SO	AVG
96-97	Canisius	MAAC	20	—	—	—	—	—	3.35	—	—	—	—	—	—
96-97	Jacksonville	ECHL	5	0	4	1	298	0	3.62	—	—	—	—	—	—
97-98	Fort Worth	CHL	2	0	2	0	119	0	5.04	—	—	—	—	—	—
97-98	Tucson	WCHL	22	5	14	1	1192	0	5.18	—	—	—	—	—	—
98-99	Charlotte	ECHL	9	4	3	1	481	0	3.62	—	—	—	—	—	—
98-99	Huntington	ECHL	13	3	7	0	651	0	3.76	—	—	—	—	—	—
98-99	Dayton	ECHL	7	3	3	1	394	0	3.50	—	—	—	—	—	—
	ECHL	Totals	34	10	17	3	1824	0	3.68						

Born; 2/16/74, Buffalo, New York. 6-3, 210. Last amateur club; Canisius College (MAAC).

Aaron Kriss

Defenseman

Regular Season / Playoffs

Season	Team	League	GP	G	A	PTS	PIM	GP	G	A	PTS	PIM
95-96	Utah	IHL	4	0	0	0	0	—	—	—	—	—
95-96	Tallahassee	ECHL	60	4	12	16	124	12	0	3	3	4
96-97	Dayton	ECHL	7	0	4	4	4	—	—	—	—	—
97-98	Michigan	IHL	4	0	0	0	7	—	—	—	—	—
97-98	Cincinnati	IHL	1	0	0	0	4	—	—	—	—	—
97-98	Dayton	ECHL	64	4	14	18	230	2	0	1	1	4
98-99	Detroit	IHL	3	0	0	0	16	—	—	—	—	—
98-99	Cincinnati	IHL	4	1	0	1	6	—	—	—	—	—
98-99	Dayton	ECHL	62	7	22	29	106	1	0	0	0	4
	IHL	Totals	16	1	0	1	33	—	—	—	—	—
	ECHL	Totals	193	15	52	67	464	15	0	4	4	12

Born; 9/17/72, Parma, Ohio. 6-2, 200. Drafted by San Jose Sharks (12th choice, 221st overall) in 1991 Entry Draft. Last amateur club; Lowell (Hockey East).

Vlastimil Kroupa

Defenseman

Regular Season / Playoffs

Season	Team	League	GP	G	A	PTS	PIM	GP	G	A	PTS	PIM
93-94	San Jose	NHL	27	1	3	4	20	14	1	2	3	21
93-94	Kansas City	IHL	39	3	12	15	12	—	—	—	—	—
94-95	Kansas City	IHL	51	4	8	12	49	12	2	4	6	22
94-95	San Jose	NHL	14	0	2	2	16	6	0	0	0	4
95-96	San Jose	NHL	27	1	7	8	18	—	—	—	—	—
95-96	Kansas City	IHL	39	5	22	27	44	5	0	1	1	6
96-97	San Jose	NHL	35	2	6	8	12	—	—	—	—	—
96-97	Kentucky	AHL	5	0	3	3	0	—	—	—	—	—
97-98	New Jersey	NHL	2	0	1	1	0	—	—	—	—	—
97-98	Albany	AHL	71	5	29	34	48	12	0	3	3	6
98-99	Kansas City	IHL	77	6	32	38	52	3	0	1	1	0
98-99	Albany	AHL	2	0	1	1	4	—	—	—	—	—
	NHL	Totals	105	4	19	23	66	20	1	2	3	25
	IHL	Totals	206	18	74	92	157	20	2	6	8	28
	AHL	Totals	78	5	33	38	52	12	0	3	3	6

Born; 4/27/75, Most, Czechoslavakia. 6-3, 205. Drafted by San Jose Sharks (3rd choice, 45th overall) in 1993 Entry Draft. Traded to New Jersey Devils by San Jose for New Jersey's third round choice (later traded to Nashville Predators-Nashville selected Geoff Koch) in 1998 Entry Draft (8/22/97).

Alexei Krovopuskov

Forward

Regular Season / Playoffs

Season	Team	League	GP	G	A	PTS	PIM	GP	G	A	PTS	PIM
98-99	Tallahassee	ECHL	23	6	9	15	73	—	—	—	—	—

Born;

Jason Kreuckl

Right Wing

Regular Season / Playoffs

Season	Team	League	GP	G	A	PTS	PIM	GP	G	A	PTS	PIM
97-98	San Angelo	WPHL	69	24	29	53	56	3	0	1	1	2
98-99	Atlantis	Germany	56	31	55	86	66	—	—	—	—	—

Born; 12/6/71, Calgary, Alberta. 6-0, 180.

Gord Krupkke

Defenseman

Regular Season / Playoffs

Season	Team	League	GP	G	A	PTS	PIM	GP	G	A	PTS	PIM
89-90	Adirondack	AHL	59	2	12	14	103	—	—	—	—	—
90-91	Detroit	NHL	4	0	0	0	0	—	—	—	—	—
90-91	Adirondack	AHL	45	1	8	9	153	—	—	—	—	—
91-92	Adirondack	AHL	65	3	9	12	208	16	0	1	1	52
92-93	Detroit	NHL	10	0	0	0	20	—	—	—	—	—
92-93	Adirondack	AHL	41	2	12	14	197	9	1	2	3	20
93-94	Detroit	NHL	9	0	0	0	12	—	—	—	—	—
93-94	Adirondack	AHL	54	2	9	11	210	12	1	3	4	32
94-95	Adirondack	AHL	48	2	9	11	157	—	—	—	—	—
94-95	St. John's	AHL	3	0	1	1	6	—	—	—	—	—
95-96	Houston	IHL	50	0	4	4	119	—	—	—	—	—
96-97	Houston	IHL	43	0	5	5	91	9	0	1	1	14
97-98	Houston	IHL	71	2	6	8	171	4	0	0	0	27
98-99	Houston	IHL	19	0	2	2	58	—	—	—	—	—
98-99	Grand Rapids	IHL	42	0	5	5	93	—	—	—	—	—
	NHL	Totals	23	0	0	0	32	—	—	—	—	—
	AHL	Totals	315	12	60	72	1034	37	2	6	8	104
	IHL	Totals	225	2	22	24	532	13	0	1	1	41

Born; 4/2/69, Slave Lake, Alberta. 6-1, 200. Drafted by Detroit Red Wings (2nd choice, 32nd overall) in 1987 Entry Draft. Traded to Toronto Maple Leafs by Detroit for other considerations (4/7/95). Member of 1991-92 AHL champion Adirondack Red Wings. Last amateur club; Prince Albert (WHL).

Todd Krygier

Left Wing

Regular Season / Playoffs

Season	Team	League	GP	G	A	PTS	PIM	GP	G	A	PTS	PIM
87-88	Connecticut	NCAA	27	32	39	71	28	—	—	—	—	—
87-88	New Haven	AHL	13	1	5	6	34	—	—	—	—	—
88-89	Binghamton	AHL	76	26	42	68	77	—	—	—	—	—
89-90	Hartford	NHL	58	18	12	30	52	7	2	1	3	4
89-90	Binghamton	AHL	12	1	9	10	16	—	—	—	—	—
90-91	Hartford	NHL	72	13	17	30	95	6	0	2	2	0
91-92	Washington	NHL	67	13	17	30	107	5	2	1	3	4
92-93	Washington	NHL	77	11	12	23	60	6	1	1	2	4
93-94	Washington	NHL	66	12	18	30	60	5	2	0	2	10
94-95	Anaheim	NHL	35	11	11	22	10	—	—	—	—	—
95-96	Anaheim	NHL	60	9	28	37	70	—	—	—	—	—
95-96	Washington	NHL	16	6	5	11	12	6	2	0	2	12
96-97	Washington	NHL	47	5	11	16	37	—	—	—	—	—
97-98	Washington	NHL	45	2	12	14	30	13	1	2	3	6
97-98	Portland	AHL	6	3	4	7	6	—	—	—	—	—
98-99	Orlando	IHL	65	19	40	59	82	17	9	10	19	16
	NHL	Totals	543	100	143	243	533	48	10	7	17	40
	AHL	Totals	95	30	51	81	117	—	—	—	—	—

Born; 10/12/65, Chicago Heights, Illinois. 6-0, 185. Selected by Hartford Whalers (1st choice, 16th overall) in 1988 Supplemental Draft. Traded to Washington Capitals by Hartford for futuer considerations (Washington's fourth round choice-later traded to Calgary-Calgary selected Jason Smith in 1993 Entry Draft) (10/3/91). Traded to Anaheim Mighty Ducks by Washington for Anaheim's fourth round choice (later traded to Dallas-Dallas selected Mike Hurley) in 1996 Entry Draft (2/2/95). Traded to Washington by Anaheim for Mike Torchia (3/8/96). Last amateur club; Connecticut (NCAA).

Mark Krys

Defenseman

Regular Season / Playoffs

Season	Team	League	GP	G	A	PTS	PIM	GP	G	A	PTS	PIM
91-92	Maine	AHL	28	1	2	3	18	—	—	—	—	—
91-92	Johnstown	ECHL	43	8	12	20	73	—	—	—	—	—
92-93	Providence	AHL	34	1	10	11	36	6	0	0	0	2
92-93	Johnstown	ECHL	25	4	14	18	18	—	—	—	—	—
92-93	Cincinnati	IHL	3	0	1	1	2	—	—	—	—	—
93-94	Providence	AHL	23	1	2	3	32	—	—	—	—	—
93-94	Rochester	AHL	58	2	13	15	77	4	0	1	1	6
94-95	Rochester	AHL	70	3	16	19	113	3	0	0	0	0
95-96	Los Angeles	IHL	78	6	11	17	96	—	—	—	—	—
96-97	Syracuse	AHL	69	10	15	25	61	—	—	—	—	—
97-98	Rosenheim	Germany	43	5	5	10	12	—	—	—	—	—
98-99	Landshut	Germany	48	1	3	4	38	3	0	0	0	2
	AHL	Totals	282	18	58	76	337	13	0	1	1	8
	ECHL	Totals	68	12	26	38	91	—	—	—	—	—

Born; 5/29/69, Timmins, Ontario. 6-0, 193. Drafted by Boston Bruins (6th choice, 165th overall) in 1988 Entry Draft. Last amateur club; Boston University

Slawomir Krzak — Right Wing

Regular Season / Playoffs

Season	Team	League	GP	G	A	PTS	PIM	GP	G	A	PTS	PIM
98-99	Central Texas	WPHL	3	1	0	1	5	—	—	—	—	—

Born; 11/4/77, Krynica, Poland. 6-1, 195.

Filip Kuba — Defenseman

Regular Season / Playoffs

Season	Team	League	GP	G	A	PTS	PIM	GP	G	A	PTS	PIM
96-97	Carolina	AHL	51	0	12	12	38	—	—	—	—	—
97-98	New Haven	AHL	77	4	13	17	58	3	1	1	2	0
98-99	Florida	NHL	5	0	1	1	0	—	—	—	—	—
98-99	Kentucky	AHL	45	2	8	10	33	10	0	1	1	4
	AHL	Totals	173	6	33	39	129	13	1	2	3	4

Born; 12/29/76, Ostrava, Czechoslovakia. 6-3, 202. Drafted by Florida Panthers (8th choice, 192nd overall) in 1995 Entry Draft. Last amateur club; Vitkovice Jr.

Pavel Kubina — Defenseman

Regular Season / Playoffs

Season	Team	League	GP	G	A	PTS	PIM	GP	G	A	PTS	PIM
97-98	Tampa Bay	NHL	10	1	2	3	22	—	—	—	—	—
97-98	Adirondack	AHL	55	4	8	12	86	1	1	0	1	14
98-99	Tampa Bay	NHL	68	9	12	21	80	—	—	—	—	—
98-99	Cleveland	IHL	6	2	2	4	16	—	—	—	—	—
	NHL	Totals	78	10	14	24	102	—	—	—	—	—

Born; 4/15/77, Celadna, Czechoslovakia. 6-3, 213. Drafted by Tampa Bay Lightning (6th choice, 179th overall) in 1996 Entry draft. Last amateur club; Moose Jaw (WHL).

Mike Kucsulain — Left Wing

Regular Season / Playoffs

Season	Team	League	GP	G	A	PTS	PIM	GP	G	A	PTS	PIM
98-99	Lake Superior	CCHA	20	4	4	8	75	—	—	—	—	—
98-99	Kentucky	AHL	4	0	1	1	14	—	—	—	—	—
98-99	Florida	ECHL	6	1	2	3	12	—	—	—	—	—

Born; 12/24/74, Flint, Michigan. 6-0, 211. Last amateur club; Lake Superior (CCHA).

Geoff Kufta — Left Wing

Regular Season / Playoffs

Season	Team	League	GP	G	A	PTS	PIM	GP	G	A	PTS	PIM
98-99	Mohawk Valley	UHL	2	0	0	0	0	—	—	—	—	—

Born; 3/15/76, Pittsbford, New York. 5-11, 197. Last amateur club; Yale

Stu Kulak — Right Wing

Regular Season / Playoffs

Season	Team	League	GP	G	A	PTS	PIM	GP	G	A	PTS	PIM
82-83	Vancouver	NHL	4	1	1	2	0	—	—	—	—	—
82-83	Victoria	WHL	50	29	33	62	130	10	10	9	19	29
83-84	Fredericton	AHL	52	12	16	28	55	5	0	0	0	59
84-85	DNP	Injured										
85-86	Fredericton	AHL	3	1	0	1	0	6	2	1	3	0
85-86	Kalamazoo	IHL	30	14	8	22	38	2	2	0	2	0
86-87	Vancouver	NHL	28	1	1	2	37	—	—	—	—	—
86-97	Edmonton	NHL	23	3	1	4	41	—	—	—	—	—
86-87	Rangers	NHL	3	0	0	0	0	—	—	—	—	—
87-88	Quebec	NHL	14	1	1	2	28	—	—	—	—	—
87-88	Moncton	AHL	37	9	12	21	58	—	—	—	—	—
88-89	Winnipeg	NHL	18	2	0	2	24	—	—	—	—	—
88-89	Moncton	AHL	51	30	29	59	98	10	5	6	11	16
89-90	Moncton	AHL	56	14	23	37	72	—	—	—	—	—
90-91	Kansas City	IHL	47	13	28	41	20	—	—	—	—	—
91-92	N/A											
92-93	Erie	ECHL	21	13	8	21	23	—	—	—	—	—
93-94	Tulsa	CeHL	59	17	29	46	101	8	0	0	0	28
94-95	San Antonio	CeHL	65	30	38	68	97	13	3	3	6	26
95-96	Reno	WCHL	43	16	25	41	60	3	1	1	2	0
96-97	Reno	WCHL	36	12	18	30	60	—	—	—	—	—
96-97	New Mexico	WPHL	5	0	0	0	0	6	1	1	2	8
97-98	Reno	WCHL	63	16	25	41	54	3	3	2	5	4
98-99	Tucson	WCHL	21	8	15	23	16	—	—	—	—	—
98-99	Phoenix	WCHL	20	3	15	18	18	—	—	—	—	—
98-99	Fresno	WCHL	9	5	6	11	8	7	2	2	4	6
	NHL	Totals	90	8	4	12	130	—	—	—	—	—
	AHL	Totals	199	66	80	146	283	21	7	7	14	75
	IHL	Totals	77	27	36	63	58	2	2	0	2	0
	WCHL	Totals	151	49	74	123	182	13	6	5	11	10
	CeHL	Totals	124	47	67	114	198	21	3	3	6	54

Born; 3/10/63, Stony Plain, Alberta. 5-10, 185. Drafted by Vancouver Canucks (5th choice, 115th overall) in 1981 Entry Draft. Acquired by Edmonton Oilers on waivers from Vancouver Canucks (12/86). Sent to New York Rangers by Edmonton as compensation for Reijo Ruotsalainen signing with Edmonton. The Rangers also sent a 12th round pick (Jesper Duus) in 1987 to the Oilers as part of the deal. Traded to Winnipeg Jets by Quebec Nordiques for Bobby Dollas. (12/87). Signed by Kansas City Blades as a free agent (9/6/90). Selected by Colorado in 1998 WCHL Dispersal Draft. Traded to Phoenix by Colorado with Marc Salsman for Don Lester and a player to be named later (9/98). Traded to Tucson by Phoenix for a player to be named later (Bobby Rapoza) (9/98). Claimed by Phoenix in 1998 Tucson Dispersal Draft. Traded to Idaho by Phoenix iwth Jason Rose for Mario Therrien and Alexandre Alepin (2/99). Traded to Fresno by Idaho for John Batten and Jesse Austin. (2/99). Last amateur club; Victoria (WHL).

Jeff Kungle — Defenseman

Regular Season / Playoffs

Season	Team	League	GP	G	A	PTS	PIM	GP	G	A	PTS	PIM
95-96	St. Lawrence	ECAC	35	10	15	25	34	—	—	—	—	—
95-96	Milwaukee	IHL	1	0	0	0	0	—	—	—	—	—
96-97	Milwaukee	IHL	3	0	0	0	0	—	—	—	—	—
96-97	Peoria	ECHL	65	6	23	29	68	10	2	4	6	11
97-98	Houston	IHL	7	0	0	0	0	—	—	—	—	—
97-98	Austin	WPHL	62	5	31	36	27	5	0	0	0	6
98-99	Duisburg	Germany	35	10	15	52		9	0	4	4	10
	IHL	Totals	11	0	0	0	0	—	—	—	—	—

Born; 10/26/72, Waka, Saskatchewan. 6-0, 205. Last amateur club; St. Lawrence (ECAC).

Arturs Kupaks — Defenseman

Regular Season / Playoffs

Season	Team	League	GP	G	A	PTS	PIM	GP	G	A	PTS	PIM
94-95	Greensboro	ECHL	63	14	30	44	89	18	5	10	15	24
95-96	Las Vegas	IHL	3	0	0	0	2	—	—	—	—	—
95-96	Detroit	CoHL	67	18	39	57	94	8	0	5	5	20
96-97	Las Vegas	IHL	6	0	0	0	10	—	—	—	—	—
96-97	Toledo	ECHL	52	13	30	43	112	—	—	—	—	—
97-98	Springfield	AHL	7	0	1	1	12	—	—	—	—	—
97-98	Chesapeake	ECHL	51	17	36	53	72	3	1	3	4	6
98-99	Chesapeake	ECHL	48	16	32	48	61	8	2	2	4	15
	IHL	Totals	9	0	0	0	12	—	—	—	—	—
	ECHL	Totals	214	60	128	188	334	29	8	15	23	45

Born; 7/14/73, Riga, Latvia. 6-0, 190. 1998-99 ECHL First Team All-Star.

Mikko Kuparinen — Defenseman

Regular Season / Playoffs

Season	Team	League	GP	G	A	PTS	PIM	GP	G	A	PTS	PIM
98-99	Grand Rapids	IHL	19	0	2	2	35	—	—	—	—	—

Born; 3/29/77. Drafted by Tampa Bay Lightning (10th choice, 244th overall) in 1999 Entry Draft.

Marcel Kuris — Goaltender

Regular Season / Playoffs

Season	Team	League	GP	W	L	T	MIN	SO	AVG	GP	W	L	MIN	SO	AVG
97-98	Peoria	ECHL	27	16	7	3	1566	1	2.87	—	—	—	—	—	—
98-99	Columbus	ECHL	3	2	1	0	179	0	4.35	—	—	—	—	—	—
98-99	Bakersfield	WCHL	20	5	7	3	942	0	3.69	—	—	—	—	—	—
	ECHL	Totals	30	18	8	3	1745	1	3.03	—	—	—	—	—	—

Born; 3/7/77, Kosice, Slovenia. 5-11, 180.

Justin Kurtz — Defenseman

Regular Season / Playoffs

Season	Team	League	GP	G	A	PTS	PIM	GP	G	A	PTS	PIM
97-98	Las Vegas	IHL	63	11	11	22	62	—	—	—	—	—
97-98	Saint John	AHL	4	0	0	0	6	6	0	0	0	0
98-99	Manitoba	IHL	38	4	6	10	40	5	0	0	0	4
98-99	Louisiana	ECHL	6	1	4	5	6	—	—	—	—	—
	IHL	Totals	101	15	17	32	102	5	0	0	0	4

Born; 1/14/77, Winnipeg, Manitoba. 6-0, 200. Drafted by Winnipeg Jets (5th choice, 84th overall) in 1995 Entry Draft. Traded to Las Vegas by Saint John with Steve Bancroft for Sami Helenius, Keith McCambridge and Paxton Schulte (3/98). Last amateur club; Brandon (WHL).

Henry Kuster — Forward

Regular Season / Playoffs

Season	Team	League	GP	G	A	PTS	PIM	GP	G	A	PTS	PIM
98-99	Augusta	ECHL	20	5	5	10	4	—	—	—	—	—

Born; 11/11/77, Edmonton, Alberta. 6-0, 195. Drafted by Boston Bruins (2nd choice, 45th overall) in 1996 Entry Draft. Last amateur club; Red Deer (WHL).

Maxim Kuznetzov — Defenseman

Regular Season / Playoffs

Season	Team	League	GP	G	A	PTS	PIM	GP	G	A	PTS	PIM
96-97	Moscow Dynamo	Russia	23	0	2	2	16	—	—	—	—	—
96-97	Adirondack	AHL	2	0	1	1	6	2	0	0	0	0
97-98	Adirondack	AHL	51	5	5	10	43	3	0	1	1	4
98-99	Adirondack	AHL	60	0	4	4	30	3	0	0	0	0
	AHL	Totals	113	5	10	15	79	8	0	1	1	4

Born; 3/24/77, Pavlodar, Russia. 6-5, 198. Drafted by Detroit Red Wings (1st choice, 26th overall) in 1995 Entry Draft.

Greg Kuznik — Defenseman

Regular Season / Playoffs

Season	Team	League	GP	G	A	PTS	PIM	GP	G	A	PTS	PIM
98-99	New Haven	AHL	27	1	0	1	33	—	—	—	—	—
98-99	Florida	ECHL	50	6	8	14	110	5	1	0	1	0

Born; 6/12/78, Prince George, British Columbia. 6-0, 182. Drafted by Hartford Whalers (7th choice, 171st overall) in 1996 Entry Draft. Last amateur club; Seattle (WHL).

Joel Kwiatkowski — Defenseman

Regular Season / Playoffs

Season	Team	League	GP	G	A	PTS	PIM	GP	G	A	PTS	PIM
98-99	Cincinnati	AHL	80	12	21	33	48	3	2	0	2	0

Born; 3/22/77, Maymont, Saskatchewan. 6-2, 200. Drafted by Dallas Stars (7th choice, 194th overall) in 1996 Entry Draft. Signed as a free agent by Anaheim Mighty Ducks (6/18/98). Last amateur club; Prince George (WHL).

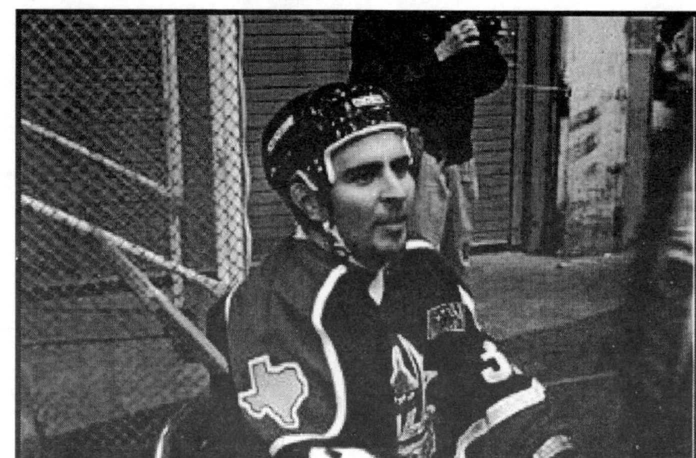

Josh Boni played for Team Texas in the WPHL All-Star Game..just days after being traded to Monroe, Louisiana

Photo by Larry Furnace

Annti Laaksonen — Left Wing

Regular Season — Playoffs

Season	Team	League	GP	G	A	PTS	PIM	GP	G	A	PTS	PIM
97-98	Providence	AHL	38	3	2	5	14	—	—	—	—	—
97-98	Charlotte	ECHL	15	4	3	7	12	6	0	3	3	0
98-99	Boston	NHL	11	1	2	3	2	—	—	—	—	—
98-99	Providence	AHL	66	25	33	58	52	19	7	2	9	28
	AHL	Totals	104	28	35	63	66	25	7	5	12	28

Born; 10/3/73, Tammela, Finland. 6-0, 180. Drafted by Boston Bruins (10th choice, 191st overall) in 1997 Entry Draft. Last amateur club; Denver (WCHA).

Jean-Francois Labbe — Goaltender

Regular Season — Playoffs

Season	Team	League	GP	W	L	T	MIN	SO	AVG	GP	W	L	MIN	SO	AVG
93-94	Thunder Bay	CoHL	52	*35	11	4	*2900	*2	*3.10	8	7	1	493	*2	*2.19
93-94	PEI	AHL	7	4	3	0	389	0	3.39	—	—	—	—	—	—
94-95	PEI	AHL	32	13	14	3	1817	2	3.10	—	—	—	—	—	—
95-96	Cornwall	AHL	55	25	21	5	2971	3	2.91	8	3	5	470	1	2.68
96-97	Hershey	AHL	66	*34	22	9	3811	*6	*2.52	*23	*14	8	*1364	1	2.60
97-98	Hamilton	AHL	52	24	17	11	3139	2	2.85	7	3	4	414	0	2.90
98-99	Hartford	AHL	*59	28	26	3	*3392	2	3.22	7	3	4	447	0	2.95
	AHL	Totals	271	128	103	31	15519	15	2.90	45	23	21	2695	2	2.72

Born; 6/15/72, Sherbrooke, Quebec. 5-9, 165. Signed as a free agent by Ottawa Senators (5/12/94). Traded to Colorado Avalanche by Ottawa for a conditional draft pick (9/20/95). Signed as a free agent by Edmonton Oilers (8/8/97). Singed as a free agent by New York Rangers (7/16/98). 1994 CoHL First Team All-Star. 1994 CoHL Rookie of the Year. 1994 CoHL Outstanding Goaltender. 1996-97 AHL Outstanding Netminder. 1996-97 AHL MVP. 1996-97 AHL First Team All-Star. Member of 1996-97 AHL Champion Hershey Bears. Last amateur club; Hull (QMJHL). Note: PEI=Prince Edward Island.

Marc LaBelle — Left Wing

Regular Season — Playoffs

Season	Team	League	GP	G	A	PTS	PIM	GP	G	A	PTS	PIM
90-91	Fredericton	AHL	24	1	4	5	95	4	0	2	2	25
90-91	Richmond	ECHL	5	1	1	2	37	—	—	—	—	—
91-92	Fredericton	AHL	62	7	10	17	238	3	0	0	0	6
92-93	New Haven	AHL	31	5	4	9	124	—	—	—	—	—
92-93	San Diego	IHL	5	0	2	2	5	—	—	—	—	—
92-93	Thunder Bay	CoHL	9	0	5	5	17	7	0	1	1	11
93-94	Cincinnati	IHL	37	2	1	3	133	4	0	1	1	6
94-95	Cincinnati	IHL	54	3	4	7	173	8	0	0	0	7
95-96	Cincinnati	IHL	57	6	11	17	218	—	—	—	—	—
95-96	Milwaukee	IHL	20	5	3	8	50	5	1	1	2	4
96-97	Milwaukee	IHL	14	1	1	2	33	—	—	—	—	—
96-97	Michigan	IHL	46	4	7	11	148	3	0	0	0	6
97-98	Cincinnati	IHL	60	2	1	3	160	9	0	1	1	38
98-99	El Paso	WPHL	47	11	25	36	182	3	1	0	1	0
	IHL	Totals	293	23	30	53	920	29	1	3	4	61
	AHL	Totals	117	13	18	31	457	7	0	2	2	31

Born; 12/20/69, Maniwaki, Quebec. 6-2, 205. Signed as a free agent by Montreal Canadiens (1/21/91). Signed as a free agent by Ottawa Senators (8/6/92). Selected by Florida Panthers in Expansion Draft (6/24/93). Signed as a free agent by Dallas Stars (4/15/96). Signed as a free agent by Ottawa (7/14/97). Last amateur club; Victoriaville (QMJHL).

Greg Labenski — Defenseman

Regular Season — Playoffs

Season	Team	League	GP	G	A	PTS	PIM	GP	G	A	PTS	PIM
98-99	North Bay	OHL	68	16	40	56	73	4	0	2	2	2
98-99	Flint	UHL	—	—	—	—	—	12	0	4	4	2

Born; 4/4/78, Welland, Ontario. 6-0, 192. Last amateur club; North Bay (OHL).

Christian LaBonte — Center

Regular Season — Playoffs

Season	Team	League	GP	G	A	PTS	PIM	GP	G	A	PTS	PIM
96-97	Utica	CoHL	2	0	0	0	0	—	—	—	—	—
96-97	Memphis	CeHL	8	4	1	5	21	—	—	—	—	—
96-97	Waco	WPHL	5	0	0	0	2	—	—	—	—	—
97-98	Tucson	WCHL	18	1	4	5	46	—	—	—	—	—
98-99	Amburg	Germany		25	28	53		—	—	—	—	—

Born; 2/4/75, Asbestos, Quebec. 5-11, 202. Last amateur club; Chicoutimi (QMJHL).

Jan Labraaten — Right Wing

Regular Season — Playoffs

Season	Team	League	GP	G	A	PTS	PIM	GP	G	A	PTS	PIM
97-98	Raleigh	ECHL	41	5	12	17	26	—	—	—	—	—
98-99	Jacksonville	ECHL	1	0	0	0	0	—	—	—	—	—
98-99	Monroe	WPHL	54	11	21	32	39	6	0	0	0	0
	ECHL	Totals	42	5	12	17	26	—	—	—	—	—

Born; 2/17/77, Karlstad, Sweden. 6-2, 198. Drafted by Calgary Flames (4th choice, 98th overall) in 1995 Entry Draft.

Emmanuel Labranche — Defenseman

Regular Season — Playoffs

Season	Team	League	GP	G	A	PTS	PIM	GP	G	A	PTS	PIM
97-98	Michigan	IHL	2	0	0	0	4	—	—	—	—	—
97-98	Brantford	UHL	60	6	8	14	138	—	—	—	—	—
97-98	Flint	UHL	9	1	2	3	51	17	1	2	3	30
98-99	Detroit	IHL	2	0	0	0	2	—	—	—	—	—
98-99	Hershey	AHL	5	0	1	1	28	—	—	—	—	—
98-99	Birmingham	ECHL	56	6	3	9	216	5	1	1	2	8
	IHL	Totals	4	0	0	0	6	—	—	—	—	—
	UHL	Totals	69	7	10	17	189	17	1	2	3	30

Born; 8/5/76, Montreal, Quebec. 6-3, 220. Last amateur club; Victoriaville (QMJHL).

Bob Lachance — Left Wing

Regular Season — Playoffs

Season	Team	League	GP	G	A	PTS	PIM	GP	G	A	PTS	PIM
95-96	Boston University	H.E.	39	15	37	52	67	—	—	—	—	—
95-96	Worcester	AHL	7	1	0	1	6	—	—	—	—	—
96-97	Worcester	AHL	74	21	35	56	66	5	0	2	2	4
97-98	Worcester	AHL	70	15	33	48	56	11	6	10	16	12
98-99	Indianapolis	IHL	70	17	46	63	59	7	1	5	6	16
	AHL	Totals	151	37	68	105	128	16	6	12	18	16

Born; 2/1/74, Northhampton, Massachusetts. 5-11, 180. Drafted by St. Louis Blues (5th choice, 134th overall) in 1991 Entry Draft. Signed as a free agent by Atlanta Thrashers (7/13/99). Last amateur club; Boston University (Hockey East).

Dan LaCouture — Left Wing

Regular Season — Playoffs

Season	Team	League	GP	G	A	PTS	PIM	GP	G	A	PTS	PIM
97-98	Hamilton	AHL	77	15	10	25	31	5	1	0	1	0
98-99	Edmonton	NHL	3	0	0	0	0	—	—	—	—	—
98-99	Hamilton	AHL	72	17	14	31	73	9	2	1	3	2
	AHL	Totals	149	32	24	56	104	14	3	1	4	2

Born; 4/18/77, Hyannis, Massachusetts. 6-2, 201. Drafted by New York Islanders (2nd choice, 29th overall) in 1996 Entry Draft. Traded to Edmonton Oilers by Islanders for Mariusz Czerkawski (8/25/97). Last amateur club; Boston University (Hockey East).

Daniel Lacroix — Center

Season	Team	League	GP	G	A	PTS	PIM	GP	G	A	PTS	PIM
			Regular Season					Playoffs				
88-89	Granby	QMJHL	70	45	49	94	320	4	1	1	2	57
88-89	Denver	IHL	2	0	1	1	0	2	0	1	1	0
89-90	Flint	IHL	61	12	16	28	128	4	2	0	2	24
90-91	Binghamton	AHL	54	7	12	19	237	5	1	0	1	24
91-92	Binghamton	AHL	52	12	20	32	149	11	2	4	6	28
92-93	Binghamton	AHL	73	21	22	43	255	—	—	—	—	—
93-94	Rangers	NHL	4	0	0	0	0	—	—	—	—	—
93-94	Binghamton	AHL	59	20	23	43	278	—	—	—	—	—
94-95	Boston	NHL	23	1	0	1	38	—	—	—	—	—
94-95	Rangers	AHL	1	0	0	0	0	—	—	—	—	—
94-95	Providence	AHL	40	15	11	26	266	—	—	—	—	—
95-96	Rangers	NHL	25	2	2	4	30	—	—	—	—	—
95-96	Binghamton	AHL	26	12	15	27	155	—	—	—	—	—
96-97	Philadelphia	NHL	74	7	1	8	163	12	0	1	1	22
97-98	Philadelphia	NHL	56	1	4	5	135	4	0	0	0	4
98-99	Edmonton	NHL	4	0	0	0	13	—	—	—	—	—
98-99	Hamilton	AHL	46	13	9	22	260	11	3	1	4	65
	NHL	Totals	187	11	7	18	379	16	0	1	1	26
	AHL	Totals	351	100	112	212	1600	27	6	5	11	117
	IHL	Totals	63	12	17	29	128	6	2	1	3	24

Born; 3/11/69, Montreal, Quebec. 6-2, 205. Drafted by New York Rangers (2nd choice, 31st overall) in 1987 Entry Draft. Traded to Boston Bruins by Rangers for Glen Featherstone (8/19/94). Claimed on waivers by Rangers from Boston (4/10/95). Signed as a free agent by Philadelphia (7/18/96). Traded to Edmonton Oilers by Philadelphia for Valeri Zelupukin (10/5/99). Last amateur cluh; Granby (QMJHL).

Nathan Lafayette — Center

Season	Team	League	GP	G	A	PTS	PIM	GP	G	A	PTS	PIM
			Regular Season					Playoffs				
93-94	St. Louis	NHL	38	2	3	5	14	—	—	—	—	—
93-94	Vancouver	NHL	11	1	1	2	4	20	2	7	9	4
93-94	Peoria	IHL	27	13	11	24	20	—	—	—	—	—
94-95	Vancouver	NHL	27	4	4	8	2	—	—	—	—	—
94-95	Rangers	NHL	12	0	0	0	0	8	0	0	0	2
94-95	Syracuse	AHL	27	9	9	18	10	—	—	—	—	—
95-96	Binghamton	AHL	57	21	27	48	32	—	—	—	—	—
95-96	Rangers	NHL	5	0	0	0	2	—	—	—	—	—
95-96	Los Angeles	NHL	12	2	4	6	6	—	—	—	—	—
96-97	Los Angeles	NHL	15	1	3	4	8	—	—	—	—	—
96-97	Phoenix	IHL	31	2	5	7	16	—	—	—	—	—
96-97	Syracuse	AHL	26	14	11	25	18	3	1	0	1	2
97-98	Los Angeles	NHL	34	5	3	8	32	4	0	0	0	2
97-98	Fredericton	AHL	28	7	8	15	36	—	—	—	—	—
98-99	Los Angeles	NHL	33	2	2	4	35	—	—	—	—	—
98-99	Long Beach	IHL	41	9	13	22	24	7	1	0	1	8
	NHL	Totals	187	17	20	37	103	32	2	7	9	8
	AHL	Totals	138	51	55	106	96	3	1	0	1	2
	IHL	Totals	99	24	29	53	60	7	1	0	1	8

Born; 2/17/73, New Westminster, British Columbia. 6-1, 195. Drafted by St. Louis Blues (3rd choice, 65th overall) in 1991 Entry Draft. Traded to Vancouver Canucks by St. Louis Blues with Jeff Brown and Bret Hedican for Craig Janney (3/21/94). Traded to New York Rangers by Vancouver for Corey Hirsch (4/7/95). Traded to Los Angeles Kings by Rangers with Ray Ferraro, Mattias Norstrom, Ian Laperriere, and Rangers fourth round choice (Sean Blanchard) in 1997 Entry Draft for Marty McSorley, Jari Kurri and Shane Churla, (3/14/96). Last amateur club; Newmarket (OHL).

Christian Laflamme — Defenseman

Season	Team	League	GP	G	A	PTS	PIM	GP	G	A	PTS	PIM
			Regular Season					Playoffs				
96-97	Chicago	NHL	4	0	1	1	2	—	—	—	—	—
96-97	Indianapolis	IHL	62	5	15	20	60	4	1	1	2	16
97-98	Chicago	NHL	72	0	11	11	59	—	—	—	—	—
98-99	Chicago	NHL	62	2	11	13	70	—	—	—	—	—
98-99	Edmonton	NHL	11	0	1	1	0	4	0	1	1	2
98-99	Portland	AHL	2	0	1	1	2	—	—	—	—	—
	NHL	Totals	149	2	24	26	131	4	0	1	1	2

Born; 11/24/76, St. Charles, Quebec. 6-1, 202. Drafted by Chicago Blackhawks (2nd choice, 45th overall) in 1995 Entry Draft. Traded to Edmonton Oilers by Chicago with Chad Kilger, Dan Cleary, Ethan Moreau for Boris Mironov, Dean McCammond, Jonas Elofson and a swap of second round choices in 1999 Enry Draft (3/20/99). Last amateur club; Beauport (QMJHL).

Brian LaFleur — Defenseman

Season	Team	League	GP	G	A	PTS	PIM	GP	G	A	PTS	PIM
			Regular Season					Playoffs				
97-98	Quebec	IHL	4	0	0	0	4	—	—	—	—	—
97-98	Pensacola	ECHL	64	11	38	49	44	19	6	10	16	19
98-99	Portland	AHL	1	0	0	0	2	—	—	—	—	—
98-99	Grand Rapids	IHL	4	0	0	0	2	—	—	—	—	—
98-99	Quad City	UHL	61	28	41	69	20	14	1	3	4	4
	IHL	Totals	8	0	0	0	6	—	—	—	—	—

Born; 3/11/75, Bloomington, Minnesota. 5-11, 197. 1998-99 UHL First Team All-Star. Last amateur club; Minnesota-Twin Cities (ACHA).

Steve Lafleur — Defenseman

Season	Team	League	GP	G	A	PTS	PIM	GP	G	A	PTS	PIM
			Regular Season					Playoffs				
98-99	Owen Sound	OHL	30	1	10	11	45	—	—	—	—	—
98-99	Kingston	OHL	35	1	10	11	47	5	0	1	1	12
98-99	Pensacola	ECHL	3	0	0	0	7	—	—	—	—	—

Born; 11/8/78, Ottawa, Ontario. 6-4, 205. Drafted by Colorado Avalanche (10th choice, 245th overall) in 1997 Entry Draft. Last amateur club; Kingston (OHL).

Marc LaForge — Defenseman

Season	Team	League	GP	G	A	PTS	PIM	GP	G	A	PTS	PIM
			Regular Season					Playoffs				
86-87	Kingston	OHL	53	2	10	12	224	12	1	0	1	79
86-87	Binghamton	AHL	—	—	—	—	—	4	0	0	0	7
88-89	Binghamton	AHL	38	2	2	4	179	—	—	—	—	—
88-89	Indianapolis	IHL	14	0	2	2	138	—	—	—	—	—
89-90	Hartford	NHL	9	0	0	0	43	—	—	—	—	—
89-90	Binghamton	AHL	25	2	6	8	111	—	—	—	—	—
89-90	Cape Breton	AHL	3	0	1	1	24	3	0	0	0	27
90-91	Cape Breton	AHL	49	1	7	8	217	—	—	—	—	—
91-92	Cape Breton	AHL	59	0	14	14	341	4	0	0	0	24
92-93	Cape Breton	AHL	77	1	12	13	208	15	1	2	3	*78
93-94	Edmonton	NHL	5	0	0	0	21	—	—	—	—	—
93-94	Cape Breton	AHL	14	0	0	0	91	—	—	—	—	—
93-94	Salt Lake City	IHL	43	0	2	2	242	—	—	—	—	—
94-95	Cape Breton	AHL	18	0	1	1	80	—	—	—	—	—
94-95	Syracuse	AHL	39	1	5	6	202	—	—	—	—	—
95-96	Minnesota	IHL	20	0	2	2	102	—	—	—	—	—
96-97	San Antonio	IHL	67	1	7	8	311	7	0	0	0	26
97-98	Manitoba	IHL	7	0	0	0	43	—	—	—	—	—
97-98	Anchorage	WCHL	27	1	10	11	124	8	0	2	2	23
98-99	San Antonio	CHL	58	0	8	8	302	7	0	0	0	43
	NHL	Totals	14	0	0	0	64	—	—	—	—	—
	AHL	Totals	322	7	48	55	1453	26	1	2	3	136
	IHL	Totals	151	1	13	14	836	7	0	0	0	26

Born; 1/3/68, Sudbury, Ontario. 6-2, 210. Drafted by Hartford Whalers (2nd choice, 32nd overall) in 1986 Entry Draft. Traded to Edmonton Oilers by Hartford for the rights to Cam Brauer (3/16/90). Traded to New York Islanders by Edmonton for Brent Grieve (12/15/93). Member of 1992-93 AHL champion Cape Breton Oilers. Last amateur club; Sudbury (OHL).

Darryl LaFrance — Right Wing

Season	Team	League	GP	G	A	PTS	PIM	GP	G	A	PTS	PIM
			Regular Season					Playoffs				
95-96	Chicago	IHL	42	5	5	10	20	5	0	0	0	2
95-96	Flint	CoHL	6	5	3	8	2	—	—	—	—	—
96-97	Chicago	IHL	47	12	14	26	18	3	1	1	2	0
96-97	Peoria	ECHL	7	4	4	8	4	—	—	—	—	—
97-98	Hamilton	AHL	7	0	2	2	0	—	—	—	—	—
97-98	New Orleans	ECHL	42	24	25	49	32	1	0	1	1	0
98-99	Hamilton	AHL	1	0	0	0	0	—	—	—	—	—
98-99	New Orleans	ECHL	55	39	39	78	41	11	6	11	17	12
	IHL	Totals	89	17	19	36	38	8	1	1	2	2
	AHL	Totals	8	0	2	2	0	—	—	—	—	—
	ECHL	Totals	104	67	68	135	77	12	6	12	18	12

Born; 3/20/74, Sudbury, Ontario. 6-0, 195. Drafted by Calgary Flames (6th choice, 121st overall) in 1993 Entry Draft. Last amateur club; Oshawa (OHL).

Scott LaGrand — Goaltender

Regular Season / Playoffs

Season	Team	League	GP	W	L	T	MIN	SO	AVG	GP	W	L	MIN	SO	AVG
92-93	Hershey	AHL	32	8	17	4	1854	0	4.69	—	—	—	—	—	—
93-94	Hershey	AHL	40	16	13	3	2032	2	3.45	—	—	—	—	—	—
94-95	Hershey	AHL	21	7	9	3	1104	1	3.86	—	—	—	—	—	—
94-95	Atlanta	IHL	21	7	7	3	993	0	4.04	3	0	2	101	0	5.91
95-96	Orlando	IHL	33	17	7	3	1618	1	3.82	3	0	0	51	0	1.17
96-97	Orlando	IHL	35	16	10	2	1747	2	2.92	4	0	2	153	0	1.96
97-98	Orlando	IHL	23	8	9	3	1265	0	3.23	—	—	—	—	—	—
97-98	Utah	IHL	7	1	1	2	361	0	3.00	—	—	—	—	—	—
97-98	Fort Wayne	IHL	11	3	5	0	488	0	3.44	2	0	1	94	0	4.47
98-99	Utah	IHL	8	4	3	1	474	1	2.53	—	—	—	—	—	—
98-99	Chicago	IHL	2	1	0	0	78	0	2.31	—	—	—	—	—	—
98-99	Tallahassee	ECHL	39	15	18	4	2159	0	3.36	—	—	—	—	—	—
	IHL	Totals	140	57	42	9	7023	4	3.35	12	0	5	399	0	3.46
	AHL	Totals	93	31	39	10	4990	3	4.00	—	—	—	—	—	—

Born; 2/11/70, Potsdam, New York. 6-0, 165. Drafted by Philadelphia Flyers (5th choice, 77th overall) in 1988 Entry Draft. Traded to Tampa Bay Lightning by Philadelphia for Mike Greenlay (2/2/95). Last amateur club; Boston College (Hockey East).

Matt Lahey — Left Wing

Regular Season / Playoffs

Season	Team	League	GP	G	A	PTS	PIM	GP	G	A	PTS	PIM
98-99	Columbus	ECHL	25	7	5	12	73	—	—	—	—	—

Born; 10/12/77, Nepean, Ontario. 6-2, 232. Drafted by Washington Capitals (8th choice, 126th overall) in 1996 Entry Draft. Selected by Pensacola in 1999 ECHL Dispersal Draft. Last amateur club; Guelph (OHL).

Jouni Lahtinen — Center

Regular Season / Playoffs

Season	Team	League	GP	G	A	PTS	PIM	GP	G	A	PTS	PIM
98-99	Kal Pa Kuopio	Finland	18	0	2	2	6	—	—	—	—	—
98-99	Fresno	WCHL	39	6	19	25	25	—	—	—	—	—

Born; 2/4/75, Kangasala, Finland. 6-2, 210.

William Laird — Left Wing

Regular Season / Playoffs

Season	Team	League	GP	G	A	PTS	PIM	GP	G	A	PTS	PIM
98-99	Asheville	UHL	11	2	0	2	24	—	—	—	—	—

Born; 11/10/77, Lar, Germany. 6-0, 200.

Sami Laine — Right Wing

Regular Season / Playoffs

Season	Team	League	GP	G	A	PTS	PIM	GP	G	A	PTS	PIM
97-98	Odessa	WPHL	64	56	28	84	59	—	—	—	—	—
98-99	Odessa	WPHL	44	31	23	54	79	3	2	1	3	2
	WPHL	Totals	108	87	51	138	138	3	2	1	3	2

Born; 12/11/70, Helsinki, Finland. 5-10, 186. 1997-98 WPHL Rookie of the Year.

Martin Laitre — Left Wing

Regular Season / Playoffs

Season	Team	League	GP	G	A	PTS	PIM	GP	G	A	PTS	PIM
94-95	Denver	IHL	1	0	0	0	18	—	—	—	—	—
94-95	Brantford	CoHL	28	2	5	7	161	—	—	—	—	—
94-95	Hampton Roads	ECHL	5	0	0	0	4	—	—	—	—	—
94-95	West Palm Beach	SUN	17	4	2	6	153	—	—	—	—	—
95-96	Cornwall	AHL	34	0	2	2	231	—	—	—	—	—
95-96	Brantford	CoHL	6	1	2	3	4	1	0	0	0	0
96-97	Hamilton	AHL	42	1	3	4	297	3	0	0	0	0
97-98	Detroit	IHL	12	0	1	1	51	—	—	—	—	—
97-98	Adirondack	AHL	43	1	4	5	313	3	0	0	0	41
98-99	Adirondack	AHL	63	5	7	12	345	3	0	0	0	14
	AHL	Totals	182	7	16	23	1186	9	0	0	0	55
	IHL	Totals	13	0	1	1	69	—	—	—	—	—
	CoHL	Totals	34	3	7	10	165	1	0	0	0	0

Born; 4/11/73, Cold Lake, Alberta. 6-1, 220. Last amateur club; Victoriaville (QMJHL).

Greg Lakovic — Left Wing

Regular Season / Playoffs

Season	Team	League	GP	G	A	PTS	PIM	GP	G	A	PTS	PIM
96-97	Las Vegas	IHL	4	0	0	0	20	—	—	—	—	—
96-97	Tallahassee	ECHL	16	1	1	2	70	—	—	—	—	—
96-97	Toledo	ECHL	32	2	7	9	76	4	0	0	0	16
97-98	Toledo	ECHL	22	3	5	8	52	—	—	—	—	—
97-98	Mississippi	ECHL	11	1	1	2	15	—	—	—	—	—
98-99	Huntsville	CHL	59	17	18	35	180	12	2	4	6	48
	ECHL	Totals	81	7	14	21	213	4	0	0	0	16

Born; 1/31/75, Vancouver, British Columbia. 6-2, 210. Sold to Mississippi by Toledo (1/98). Member of 1998-99 CHL Champion Hunstville Channel Cats.

Sasha Lakovic — Left Wing

Regular Season / Playoffs

Season	Team	League	GP	G	A	PTS	PIM	GP	G	A	PTS	PIM
92-93	Binghamton	AHL	3	0	0	0	0	—	—	—	—	—
92-93	Columbus	ECHL	27	7	9	16	162	—	—	—	—	—
92-93	Chatham	CoHL	28	7	5	12	235	5	2	1	3	62
93-94	Toledo	ECHL	24	5	10	15	198	—	—	—	—	—
93-94	Chatham	CoHL	13	11	7	18	61	—	—	—	—	—
94-95	Tulsa	CeHL	40	20	24	44	214	5	1	3	4	88
95-96	Las Vegas	IHL	49	1	2	3	416	13	1	1	2	57
96-97	Calgary	NHL	19	0	1	1	54	—	—	—	—	—
96-97	Saint John	AHL	18	1	8	9	182	—	—	—	—	—
96-97	Las Vegas	IHL	10	0	0	0	81	2	0	0	0	14
97-98	New Jersey	NHL	2	0	0	0	5	—	—	—	—	—
97-98	Albany	AHL	30	7	6	13	158	13	3	4	7	*84
98-99	New Jersey	NHL	16	0	3	3	59	—	—	—	—	—
98-99	Albany	AHL	10	1	1	2	93	—	—	—	—	—
	NHL	Totals	37	0	4	4	118	—	—	—	—	—
	AHL	Totals	61	9	15	24	433	13	3	4	7	84
	IHL	Totals	59	1	2	3	497	15	1	1	2	71
	ECHL	Totals	51	12	19	31	360	—	—	—	—	—
	CoHL	Totals	41	18	12	30	296	5	2	1	3	62

Born; 9/7/71, East Vancouver, British Columbia. 6-0, 198. Signed as a free agent by Calgary Flames (10/16/6). Signed as a free agent by New Jersey Devils

Patrick Lalime — Goaltender

Regular Season / Playoffs

Season	Team	League	GP	W	L	T	MIN	SO	AVG	GP	W	L	MIN	SO	AVG
94-95	Hampton Roads	ECHL	26	15	7	3	1470	2	3.35	—	—	—	—	—	—
94-95	Cleveland	IHL	23	7	10	4	1230	0	4.44	—	—	—	—	—	—
95-96	Cleveland	IHL	41	20	12	7	2314	0	3.86	—	—	—	—	—	—
96-97	Pittsburgh	NHL	39	21	12	2	2058	3	2.94	—	—	—	—	—	—
96-97	Cleveland	IHL	14	6	6	2	834	1	3.24	—	—	—	—	—	—
97-98	Grand Rapids	IHL	31	10	10	9	1749	2	2.61	1	0	1	77	0	3.11
98-99	Kansas City	IHL	*66	*39	20	4	*3789	2	3.01	3	1	2	179	1	2.01
	IHL	Totals	175	82	58	26	11140	5	2.97	4	1	3	256	1	2.34

Born; 7/7/74, St. Bonaventure, Quebec. 6-2, 170. Drafted by Pittsburgh Penguins (6th choice, 156th overall) in 1993 Entry Draft. Traded to Anaheim Mighty Ducks by Pittsburgh for Sean Pronger (3/24/98). Traded to Ottawa Senators by Anaheim for Ted Donato and the rights to Antti-Jussi Niemi (6/18/99). 1998-99 IHL First Team All-Star. Last amateur club; Shawinigan (QMJHL).

Martin Lamarche — Left Wing

Regular Season / Playoffs

Season	Team	League	GP	G	A	PTS	PIM	GP	G	A	PTS	PIM
95-96	Prince Edward Island	AHL	30	0	1	1	88	—	—	—	—	—
96-97	Saint John	AHL	33	4	5	9	114	4	0	0	0	21
97-98	Hershey	AHL	13	0	0	0	90	—	—	—	—	—
97-98	Binghamton	UHL	8	1	3	4	15	5	1	3	4	33
98-99	Fort Worth	WPHL	26	2	5	7	140	—	—	—	—	—
	AHL	Totals	76	4	6	10	292	4	0	0	0	21

Born; 10/2/75, Ste-Justine, Quebec. 6-1, 206. Signed as a free agent by Ottawa (3/3/95). Signed as a free agent by Colorado Avalanche (1/6/98). Last amateur club; Shawinigan (QMJHL).

Mark Lamb — Center

Regular Season / Playoffs

Season	Team	League	GP	G	A	PTS	PIM	GP	G	A	PTS	PIM
82-83	Nanaimo	WHL	30	14	37	51	16	—	—	—	—	—
82-83	Medicine Hat	WHL	46	22	43	65	33	5	3	2	5	4
82-83	Colorado	CHL	—	—	—	—	—	6	0	2	2	0
83-84	Medicine Hat	WHL	72	59	77	136	30	14	12	11	23	6
84-85	Moncton	AHL	80	23	49	72	53	—	—	—	—	—
85-86	Calgary	NHL	1	0	0	0	0	—	—	—	—	—
85-86	Moncton	AHL	79	26	50	76	51	10	2	6	8	17
86-87	Detroit	NHL	22	2	1	3	8	11	0	0	0	11
86-87	Adirondack	AHL	49	14	36	50	45	—	—	—	—	—
87-88	Edmonton	NHL	2	0	0	0	0	—	—	—	—	—
87-88	Nova Scotia	AHL	69	27	61	88	45	5	0	5	5	6
88-89	Edmonton	NHL	20	2	8	10	14	6	0	2	2	8
88-89	Cape Breton	AHL	54	33	49	82	29	—	—	—	—	—
89-90	Edmonton	NHL	58	12	26	28	42	22	6	11	17	2
90-91	Edmonton	NHL	37	4	8	12	25	15	0	5	5	20
91-92	Edmonton	NHL	59	6	22	28	46	16	1	1	2	10
92-93	Ottawa	NHL	71	7	19	26	64	—	—	—	—	—
93-94	Ottawa	NHL	66	11	18	29	56	—	—	—	—	—
93-94	Philadelphia	NHL	19	1	6	7	16	—	—	—	—	—
94-95	Philadelphia	NHL	8	0	2	2	2	—	—	—	—	—
94-95	Montreal	NHL	39	1	0	1	18	—	—	—	—	—
95-96	Houston	IHL	67	17	60	77	65	—	—	—	—	—
96-97	Houston	IHL	81	25	53	78	83	13	3	12	15	10
97-98	Landshut	Germany	46	7	21	28	36	6	3	1	4	8
98-99	Houston	IHL	79	21	49	70	72	19	1	10	11	12
	NHL	Totals	402	46	100	146	291	70	7	19	26	51
	AHL	Totals	331	123	245	368	223	15	2	11	13	23
	IHL	Totals	227	63	162	225	220	32	4	22	26	22

Born; 8/3/64, Swift Current, Saskatchewan. 5-9, 180. Drafted by Calgary Flames (5th choice, 72nd overall) in 1982 Entry Draft. Signed as a free agent by Detroit Red Wings (7/28/86). Claimed by Edmonton Oilers from Detroit in NHL Waiver Draft (10/5/87). Claimed by Ottawa from Edmonton in Expansion Draft (6/18/92). Traded to Philadelphia Flyers by Ottawa for Claude Boivin and Kirk Daubenspeck (3/5/94). Traded to Montreal Canadiens by Philadelphia for cash (2/10/95). Member of 1989-90 Stanley Cup champion Edmonton Oilers. Member of 1998-99 IHL Champion Houston Aeros. Last amateur club; Medicine Hat

Dale Lambert — Defenseman

Regular Season / Playoffs

Season	Team	League	GP	G	A	PTS	PIM	GP	G	A	PTS	PIM
91-92	Humberside	BHL	32	14	24	38	77	—	—	—	—	—
92-93	Humberside	BHL	34	11	27	38	42	—	—	—	—	—
93-94	Solihull	BHL	34	12	35	47	22	—	—	—	—	—
94-95	Milton-Keynes	BHL	43	5	15	19	51	—	—	—	—	—
95-96	Durham	BHL	49	10	18	28	160	—	—	—	—	—
96-97	Newcastle	BHL	41	2	2	4	42	9	0	0	0	25
97-98	Newcastle	BSL	31	1	3	4	10	4	1	0	1	0
98-99	Kingston	BNL										
98-99	Phoenix	WCHL	1	0	0	0	10	—	—	—	—	—

Born; 10/9/59, Saskatoon, Saskatchewan. 5-11, 185. Named coach of Kingston, BNL 10/99.

Dan Lambert — Defenseman

Regular Season / Playoffs

Season	Team	League	GP	G	A	PTS	PIM	GP	G	A	PTS	PIM
90-91	Quebec	NHL	1	0	0	0	0	—	—	—	—	—
90-91	Halifax	AHL	30	7	13	20	20	—	—	—	—	—
90-91	Fort Wayne	IHL	49	10	27	37	65	19	4	10	14	20
91-92	Quebec	NHL	28	6	9	15	22	—	—	—	—	—
91-92	Halifax	AHL	47	3	28	31	33	—	—	—	—	—
92-93	Moncton	AHL	73	11	30	41	100	5	1	2	3	2
93-94	Fort Wayne	IHL	62	10	27	37	138	18	3	12	15	20
94-95	San Diego	IHL	70	6	19	25	95	5	0	5	5	10
95-96	Los Angeles	IHL	81	22	65	87	121	—	—	—	—	—
96-97	Long Beach	IHL	71	15	50	65	70	18	2	8	10	8
97-98	Long Beach	IHL	81	19	59	78	112	17	3	14	17	16
98-99	Long Beach	IHL	50	17	36	53	91	8	0	6	6	12
	NHL	Totals	29	6	9	15	22	—	—	—	—	—
	IHL	Totals	464	99	283	382	692	85	12	55	67	86
	AHL	Totals	150	21	71	92	153	5	1	2	3	2

Born; 1/12/70, St. Boniface, Manitoba. 5-8, 177. Drafted by Quebec Nordiques (8th choice, 106th overall) in 1989 Entry Draft. Traded to Winnipeg Jets by Quebec for Shawn Cronin (8/25/92). 1997-98 IHL Governors Trophy (Best defenseman). 1997-98 IHL First Team All-Star. 1998-99 IHL Second Team All-Star. Last amateur club; Swift Current (WHL).

Judd Lambert — Goaltender

Regular Season / Playoffs

Season	Team	League	GP	W	L	T	MIN	SO	AVG	GP	W	L	MIN	SO	AVG
97-98	Fort Wayne	IHL	4	1	2	0	197	0	3.66	—	—	—	—	—	—
97-98	Albany	AHL	4	0	3	1	213	0	4.51	—	—	—	—	—	—
97-98	Dayton	ECHL	23	9	10	4	1373	0	3.28	3	1	2	177	0	3.39
98-99	Albany	AHL	2	1	0	0	102	0	1.76	—	—	—	—	—	—
98-99	Augusta	ECHL	51	24	20	5	2948	1	3.05	2	0	2	119	0	2.52
	AHL	Totals	6	1	3	1	315	0	3.62	—	—	—	—	—	—
	ECHL	Totals	74	33	30	9	4321	1	3.12	5	1	4	296	0	3.04

Born; 6/3/74, Richmond, British Columbia. 6-1, 175. Drafted by New Jersey Devils (9th choice, 221st overall) in 1993 Entry Draft. Last amateur club; Colorado (WCHA).

Lane Lambert — Right Wing

Regular Season / Playoffs

Season	Team	League	GP	G	A	PTS	PIM	GP	G	A	PTS	PIM
83-84	Detroit	NHL	73	20	15	35	115	4	0	0	0	10
84-85	Detroit	NHL	69	14	11	25	104	—	—	—	—	—
85-86	Adirondack	AHL	45	16	25	41	69	16	5	5	10	9
85-86	Detroit	NHL	34	2	3	5	130	—	—	—	—	—
86-87	New Haven	AHL	11	3	3	6	19	—	—	—	—	—
86-87	Rangers	NHL	18	2	2	4	33	—	—	—	—	—
86-87	Quebec	NHL	15	5	6	11	18	13	2	4	6	30
87-88	Quebec	NHL	61	13	28	41	98	—	—	—	—	—
88-89	Quebec	NHL	13	2	2	4	23	—	—	—	—	—
88-89	Halifax	AHL	59	25	35	60	162	4	0	2	2	2
89-90	Canada	National	54	28	36	64	48	—	—	—	—	—
90-91	Canada	National	4	1	0	1	0	—	—	—	—	—
91-92												
92-93												
93-94												
94-95												
95-96												
96-97	Cleveland	IHL	75	24	20	44	94	13	4	5	9	21
97-98	Cleveland	IHL	39	4	10	14	60	3	0	0	0	0
98-99	Cleveland	IHL	36	8	10	18	61	—	—	—	—	—
98-99	Houston	IHL	9	2	1	3	4	19	4	1	5	26
	NHL	Totals	283	58	66	124	521	17	2	4	6	40
	IHL	Totals	159	38	41	79	219	35	8	6	14	47
	AHL	Totals	115	44	63	107	250	20	5	7	12	11

Born; 11/18/64, Melfort, Saskatchewan. 6-0, 185. Drafted by Detroit Red Wings (2nd choice, 25th overall) in 1983 Entry Draft. Traded to New York Rangers with Kelly Kisio, Jim Leavins and a fifth round 1988 draft pick by Detroit for Glen Hanlon and third round 1987 (Dennis Holland) and 1988 draft picks and future considerations, (7/29/86). Traded to Quebec Nordiques by Rangers for Pat Price (3/5/87). Member of 1985-86 AHL Champion Adirondack Red Wings. Member of 1998-99 IHL Champion Houston Aeros. Last amateur club; Saskatoon (WHL).

David Lambeth — Defenseman

Regular Season / Playoffs

Season	Team	League	GP	G	A	PTS	PIM	GP	G	A	PTS	PIM
98-99	Kentucky	AHL	1	0	0	0	0	—	—	—	—	—
98-99	Richmond	ECHL	68	6	22	28	76	18	0	7	7	18

Born; 9/12/75, Clarkston, Michigan. 5-11, 195. Last amateur club; Lake Superior State (CCHA).

Jason Lammers — Defenseman

Regular Season / Playoffs

Season	Team	League	GP	G	A	PTS	PIM	GP	G	A	PTS	PIM
98-99	Idaho	WCHL	44	1	2	3	65	1	0	0	0	0

Born; 9/11/75, Pittsburgh, Pennsylvania. 6-4, 223. Last amateur club; SUNY-Genesco (NCAA 3).

Marc Lamothe — Goaltender

Regular Season / Playoffs

Season	Team	League	GP	W	L	T	MIN	SO	AVG	GP	W	L	MIN	SO	AVG
94-95	Fredericton	AHL	9	2	5	0	428	0	4.48	—	—	—	—	—	—
94-95	Wheeling	ECHL	12	9	2	1	736	0	3.10	—	—	—	—	—	—
95-96	Fredericton	AHL	23	5	9	3	1165	1	3.76	3	1	2	160	0	3.36
96-97	Indianapolis	IHL	38	20	14	4	2271	1	2.64	1	0	0	20	0	3.00
97-98	Indianapolis	IHL	31	18	10	2	1773	3	2.44	4	1	3	178	0	3.38
98-99	Indianapolis	IHL	32	9	16	6	1823	1	3.78	6	3	3	338	*2	1.78
98-99	Detroit	IHL	—	—	—	—	—	—	—	1	0	1	80	0	3.73
	IHL	Totals	101	47	40	12	5867	5	2.94	12	4	7	616	2	2.53
	AHL	Totals	32	7	14	3	1593	1	3.84	3	1	2	160	0	3.36

Born; 2/27/74, New Liskeard, Ontario. 6-1, 204. Drafted by Montreal Canadiens (6th choice, 92nd overall) in 1992 Entry Draft. Signed as a free agent by Chicago (9/26/96). Last amateur club; Kingston (OHL).

Denis Lamoureux — Forward

Regular Season / Playoffs

Season	Team	League	GP	G	A	PTS	PIM	GP	G	A	PTS	PIM
96-97	Hampton Roads	ECHL	18	4	6	10	4	—	—	—	—	—
96-97	Johnstown	ECHL	29	8	9	17	4	—	—	—	—	—
97-98	Johnstown	ECHL	5	0	0	0	0	—	—	—	—	—
97-98	Macon	CHL	36	20	22	42	30	—	—	—	—	—
97-98	Memphis	CHL	2	2	1	3	0	4	0	0	0	0
98-99	Memphis	CHL	69	67	54	121	20	4	3	2	5	10
	CHL	Totals	107	89	77	166	50	8	3	2	5	10
	ECHL	Totals	52	12	15	27	8	—	—	—	—	—

Born; 6/28/75, LaSalle, Quebec. 6-1, 195.

Mitch Lamoureux — Center

Regular Season / Playoffs

Season	Team	League	GP	G	A	PTS	PIM	GP	G	A	PTS	PIM
82-83	Baltimore	AHL	80	*57	50	107	107	—	—	—	—	—
83-84	Pittsburgh	NHL	8	1	1	2	6	—	—	—	—	—
83-84	Baltimore	AHL	68	30	38	68	136	9	1	3	4	2
84-85	Pittsburgh	NHL	62	11	8	19	53	—	—	—	—	—
84-85	Baltimore	AHL	18	10	14	24	34	—	—	—	—	—
85-86	Baltimore	AHL	75	22	31	53	129	—	—	—	—	—
86-87	Hershey	AHL	78	43	46	89	122	5	1	2	3	8
87-88	Philadelphia	NHL	3	0	0	0	0	—	—	—	—	—
87-88	Hershey	AHL	78	35	52	87	171	12	9	7	16	48
88-89	Hershey	AHL	9	9	7	16	14	9	1	4	5	14
89-90	Maine	AHL	10	4	7	11	10	—	—	—	—	—
89-90	Canada	National	4	1	2	3	6	—	—	—	—	—
90-91												
91-92												
92-93	San Diego	IHL	71	28	39	67	130	4	0	0	0	11
93-94	Hershey	AHL	80	45	60	105	92	11	3	4	7	26
94-95	Hershey	AHL	76	39	46	85	112	6	0	2	2	8
95-96	Providence	AHL	63	22	29	51	62	4	2	3	5	2
96-97	Providence	AHL	75	25	29	54	70	3	0	0	0	4
97-98	Hershey	AHL	22	4	9	13	22	7	2	4	6	12
97-98	Binghamton	UHL	16	18	15	33	10	—	—	—	—	—
98-99	Hershey	AHL	70	19	34	53	58	4	1	2	3	4
	NHL	Totals	73	12	9	21	59	—	—	—	—	—
	AHL	Totals	802	364	452	816	1139	70	20	31	51	128

Born; 8/22/62, Ottawa, Ontario. 5-6, 191. Drafted by Pittsburgh Penguins (6th choice, 154th overall) in 1981 Entry Draft. 1982-83 AHL Rookie of the Year. 1982-83 AHL Second Team All Star. 1998-99 AHL Fred T. Hunt Award (sportsmanship, determination and dedication). Last amateur club; Oshawa

Patrick Lampron — Defenseman

Regular Season / Playoffs

Season	Team	League	GP	G	A	PTS	PIM	GP	G	A	PTS	PIM
95-96	Brantford	CoHL	16	1	2	3	14	—	—	—	—	—
95-96	Quad City	CoHL	28	2	9	11	46	—	—	—	—	—
96-97	Central Texas	WPHL	33	7	11	18	61	—	—	—	—	—
96-97	Amarillo	WPHL	27	8	15	23	36	—	—	—	—	—
97-98	Odessa	WPHL	65	15	25	40	183	—	—	—	—	—
98-99	Bakersfield	WCHL	14	1	3	4	39	—	—	—	—	—
	WPHL	Totals	125	30	51	81	280	—	—	—	—	—
	CoHL	Totals	44	3	11	14	60	—	—	—	—	—

Born; 1/4/74, Cap De La Madeleine, Quebec. 6-1, 188.

Derek Landmesser — Defenseman

Regular Season / Playoffs

Season	Team	League	GP	G	A	PTS	PIM	GP	G	A	PTS	PIM
96-97	Thunder Bay	CoHL	17	0	3	3	11	—	—	—	—	—
97-98	Thunder Bay	UHL	73	2	19	21	80	5	1	1	2	2
98-99	Manitoba	IHL	1	0	0	0	0	—	—	—	—	—
98-99	Thunder Bay	UHL	72	7	36	43	180	13	3	3	6	26
	UHL	Totals	162	9	58	67	271	18	4	4	8	28

Born; 1/27/75, Cap-Rouge, Quebec. 6-1, 200.

Eric Landry — Center

Regular Season / Playoffs

Season	Team	League	GP	G	A	PTS	PIM	GP	G	A	PTS	PIM
95-96	Cape Breton	AHL	74	19	33	52	187	—	—	—	—	—
96-97	Hamilton	AHL	74	15	17	32	139	22	6	7	13	42
97-98	Calgary	NHL	12	1	0	1	4	—	—	—	—	—
97-98	Saint John	AHL	61	17	21	38	194	20	4	6	10	58
98-99	Calgary	NHL	3	0	1	1	0	—	—	—	—	—
98-99	Saint John	AHL	56	19	22	41	158	7	2	5	7	12
	NHL	Totals	15	1	1	2	4	—	—	—	—	—
	AHL	Totals	265	70	93	163	678	49	12	18	30	112

Born; 1/20/75, Hull, Quebec. 5-10, 180. Signed as a free agent by Calgary Flames (8/6/97). Traded to San Jose Sharks by Calgary for Frederik Oduya (7/21/99). Last amateur club; St. Hyacinthe (QMJHL).

Eric M. Landry — Center

Regular Season / Playoffs

Season	Team	League	GP	G	A	PTS	PIM	GP	G	A	PTS	PIM
96-97	Saint John	AHL	12	2	0	2	36	—	—	—	—	—
96-97	Roanoke	ECHL	1	0	0	0	0	4	2	2	4	17
97-98	Jacksonville	ECHL	49	6	4	10	122	—	—	—	—	—
97-98	Tallahassee	ECHL	16	4	1	5	82	—	—	—	—	—
98-99	Alexandria	WPHL	62	19	15	34	176	—	—	—	—	—
	ECHL	Totals	66	10	5	15	204	4	2	2	4	17

Born; 1/29/76, Cornwall, Ontario. 6-0, 200. Drafted by San Jose Sharks (8th choice, 193rd overall) in 1994 Entry Draft. Last amateur club; Peterborough

J.C. Lane — Forward

Regular Season / Playoffs

Season	Team	League	GP	G	A	PTS	PIM	GP	G	A	PTS	PIM
98-99	Amarillo	WPHL	5	0	1	1	0	—	—	—	—	—

Born; 9/30/77, Barrhead, Alberta. 5-10, 185.

Chad Lang — Goaltender

Regular Season / Playoffs

Season	Team	League	GP	W	L	T	MIN	SO	AVG	GP	W	L	MIN	SO	AVG
95-96	Raleigh	ECHL	8	2	6	0	461	0	3.64	—	—	—	—	—	—
95-96	Columbus	ECHL	4	3	1	0	237	1	2.27	3	0	2	147	0	2.85
96-97	Huntington	ECHL	15	5	5	2	738	0	4.55	—	—	—	—	—	—
97-98	Huntington	ECHL	40	18	16	4	2224	2	3.45	4	1	.3	238	0	3.03
98-99	Huntington	ECHL	16	4	9	2	798	0	4.06	—	—	—	—	—	—
98-99	Peoria	ECHL	20	12	6	1	1116	2	2.74	1	0	1	60	0	5.03
	ECHL	Totals	103	44	43	9	5574	5	3.51	8	1	6	445	0	3.23

Born; 2/11/75, Newmarket, Ontario. 5-11, 200. Drafted by Dallas Stars (3rd choice, 87th overall) in 1993 Entry Draft. Last amateur club; Peterborough

Daymond Langkow — Center

Regular Season / Playoffs

Season	Team	League	GP	G	A	PTS	PIM	GP	G	A	PTS	PIM
95-96	Tri-City	WHL	48	30	61	91	103	11	14	13	27	20
95-96	Tampa Bay	NHL	4	0	1	1	0	—	—	—	—	—
96-97	Tampa Bay	NHL	79	15	13	28	35	—	—	—	—	—
96-97	Adirondack	AHL	2	1	1	2	0	—	—	—	—	—
97-98	Tampa Bay	NHL	68	8	14	22	62	—	—	—	—	—
98-99	Tampa Bay	NHL	22	4	6	10	15	—	—	—	—	—
98-99	Philadelphia	NHL	56	10	13	23	24	6	0	2	2	2
98-99	Cleveland	IHL	4	1	1	2	18	—	—	—	—	—
	NHL	Totals	229	37	47	84	136	6	0	2	2	2

Born; 9/27/76, Edmonton, Alberta. 5-11, 175. Drafted by Tampa Bay Lightning (1st choice, 5th overall) in 1995 Entry Draft. Traded to Philadelphia Flyers by Tampa Bay with Mikael Renberg for Chris Gratton and Mike Sillinger (12/12/98). Last amateur club; Tri-City (WHL).

Scott Langkow — Goaltender

Regular Season / Playoffs

Season	Team	League	GP	W	L	T	MIN	SO	AVG	GP	W	L	MIN	SO	AVG
95-96	Winnipeg	NHL	1	0	0	0	6	0	0.00	—	—	—	—	—	—
95-96	Springfield	AHL	39	18	15	6	2329	3	2.99	7	4	2	392	0	3.51
96-97	Springfield	AHL	33	15	9	7	1929	0	2.64	—	—	—	—	—	—
97-98	Phoenix	NHL	3	0	1	1	137	0	4.38	—	—	—	—	—	—
97-98	Springfield	AHL	51	30	13	5	2875	3	2.67	4	1	3	216	0	3.88
98-99	Phoenix	NHL	1	0	0	0	35	0	5.14	—	—	—	—	—	—
98-99	Las Vegas	IHL	27	7	14	2	1402	1	4.15	—	—	—	—	—	—
98-99	Utah	IHL	21	10	9	2	1227	1	2.89	—	—	—	—	—	—
	NHL	Totals	5	0	1	1	178	0	4.38	—	—	—	—	—	—
	AHL	Totals	123	63	37	18	7133	6	2.77	11	5	5	608	0	3.65
	IHL	Totals	48	17	23	4	2628	2	3.56	—	—	—	—	—	—

Born; 4/21/75, Sherwood Park, Alberta. 5-11, 190. Drafted by Winnipeg Jets (2nd choice, 31st overall) in 1993 Entry Draft. Traded to Atlanta Thrashers for futuer considerations (6/25/99). 1995-96 AHL Harry "Hap" Holmes Trophy with Manny Legace (fewest goals against). 1997-98 AHL Baz Bastien Trophy (Top Goaltender). 1997-98 AHL First Team All-Star. Last amateur club; Portland (WHL).

Jocelyn Langlois — Left Wing

Regular Season / Playoffs

Season	Team	League	GP	G	A	PTS	PIM	GP	G	A	PTS	PIM
96-97	Jacksonville	ECHL	39	6	13	19	17	—	—	—	—	—
96-97	Macon	CeHL	5	1	5	6	15	5	4	2	6	8
97-98	Macon	CHL	70	34	50	84	55	3	0	0	0	6
98-99	Macon	CHL	70	38	65	103	34	3	0	2	2	0
	CHL	Totals	145	73	120	193	104	11	4	4	8	14

Born; 11/3/73, Montreal, Quebec. 6-0, 190.

Brian Langlot — Goaltender

Regular Season / Playoffs

Season	Team	League	GP	W	L	T	MIN	SO	AVG	GP	W	L	MIN	SO	AVG
93-94	Columbus	ECHL	3	1	1	0	159	0	3.76	—	—	—	—	—	—
93-94	Raleigh	ECHL	4	1	2	0	168	0	3.57	—	—	—	—	—	—
93-94	Albany	AHL	1	0	0	0	10	0	0.00	—	—	—	—	—	—
94-95															
95-96	Fresno	WCHL	1	0	0	0	12	0	0.00	—	—	—	—	—	—
96-97	Wichita	CeHL	25	7	5	3	1106	0	4.45	—	—	—	—	—	—
97-98	Wichita	CHL	1	0	0	0	23	0	7.77	—	—	—	—	—	—
98-99	Wichita	CHL	1	0	1	0	55	0	5.48	—	—	—	—	—	—
	CHL	Totals	27	7	6	3	1184	0	4.56	—	—	—	—	—	—
	ECHL	Totals	7	2	3	0	327	0	3.67	—	—	—	—	—	—

Born; 9/1/69, Seattle, Washington. 5-11, 190.

Marc Laniel — Defenseman

Regular Season / Playoffs

Season	Team	League	GP	G	A	PTS	PIM	GP	G	A	PTS	PIM
87-88	Oshawa	OHL	41	8	32	40	56	7	2	2	4	4
87-88	Utica	AHL	2	0	0	0	0	—	—	—	—	—
88-89	Utica	AHL	80	6	28	34	43	5	0	1	1	2
89-90	Utica	AHL	20	0	0	0	25	—	—	—	—	—
89-90	Phoenix	IHL	26	3	15	18	10	—	—	—	—	—
90-91	Utica	AHL	57	6	9	15	45	—	—	—	—	—
91-92	Winston-Salem	ECHL	57	15	36	51	90	5	2	5	7	4
91-92	San Diego	IHL	10	0	2	2	16	—	—	—	—	—
92-93	Birmingham	ECHL	21	5	9	14	26	—	—	—	—	—
92-93	Cincinnati	IHL	13	1	9	10	2	—	—	—	—	—
92-93	Fredericton	AHL	7	0	1	1	6	5	0	2	2	23
93-94	Fredericton	AHL	79	6	41	47	76	—	—	—	—	—
94-95	Cincinnati	IHL	70	5	29	34	34	—	—	—	—	—
94-95	Houston	IHL	2	0	0	0	0	4	0	2	2	6
95-96	Houston	IHL	65	5	25	30	40	—	—	—	—	—
95-96	Las Vegas	IHL	9	2	2	4	6	14	0	0	0	14
96-97	Cincinnati	IHL	61	4	14	18	30	—	—	—	—	—
96-97	Fort Wayne	IHL	21	2	5	7	19	—	—	—	—	—
97-98	Schwenningen	Germany	50	7	19	26	34	—	—	—	—	—
98-99	Schwenningen	Germany	52	8	10	18	53	—	—	—	—	—
	IHL	Totals	277	22	101	123	157	18	0	2	2	20
	AHL	Totals	245	18	79	97	195	10	0	3	3	25
	ECHL	Totals	78	20	45	65	116	5	2	5	7	4

Born; 1/16/68, Oshawa, Ontario. 6-1, 190. Drafted by New Jersey Devils (4th choice, 62nd overall) in 1986 Entry Draft. 1991-92 ECHL Second Team All-Star. Last amateur club; Oshawa (OHL).

Corey Laniuk — Defenseman

Regular Season / Playoffs

Season	Team	League	GP	G	A	PTS	PIM	GP	G	A	PTS	PIM
97-98	Phoenix	WCHL	6	0	0	0	0	5	0	0	0	10
98-99	Phoenix	WCHL	61	1	2	3	153	1	0	0	0	0
	WCHL	Totals	67	1	2	3	153	6	0	0	0	10

Born; 1/30/77, Vancouver, British Columbia. 6-2, 220. Last amateur club; Langley (BCJHL).

Jeff Lank — Defenseman

Regular Season / Playoffs

Season	Team	League	GP	G	A	PTS	PIM	GP	G	A	PTS	PIM
95-96	Hershey	AHL	72	7	13	20	70	5	0	0	0	8
96-97	Philadelphia	AHL	44	2	12	14	49	7	2	1	3	4
97-98	Philadelphia	AHL	69	7	9	16	59	20	1	4	5	22
98-99	Philadelphia	AHL	51	5	10	15	36	2	0	0	0	2
	AHL	Totals	185	16	34	50	178	32	3	5	8	34

Born; 3/1/75, Indian Head, Saskatchewan. 6-3, 185. Drafted by Montreal Canadiens (6th choice, 113th overall) in 1993 Entry Draft. Re-entered NHL Entry Draft. Drafted by Philadelphia Flyers (9th choice, 230th overall) in 1995 Entry Draft. Member of 1997-98 AHL Champion Philadelphia Phantoms. Last amateur club; Prince Albert (WHL).

Mike Lankshear — Defenseman

Regular Season / Playoffs

Season	Team	League	GP	G	A	PTS	PIM	GP	G	A	PTS	PIM
98-99	Owen Sound	OHL	26	2	5	7	44	16	3	13	16	23
98-99	Arkansas	WPHL	36	5	16	21	26	—	—	—	—	—

Born; 9/8/78, Calgary, Alberta. 6-2, 185. Drafted by Toronto Maple Leafs (3rd choice, 66th overall) in 1996 Entry Draft. Traded to Florida Panthers by Toronto for Per Gustafsson (6/12/97). Last amateur club; Owen Sound (OHL).

Daniel Laperriere — Defenseman

Regular Season / Playoffs

Season	Team	League	GP	G	A	PTS	PIM	GP	G	A	PTS	PIM
92-93	St. Louis	NHL	5	0	1	1	0	—	—	—	—	—
92-93	Peoria	IHL	54	4	20	24	28	—	—	—	—	—
93-94	St. Louis	NHL	20	1	3	4	8	—	—	—	—	—
93-94	Peoria	IHL	56	10	37	47	16	6	0	2	2	2
94-95	St. Louis	NHL	4	0	0	0	15	—	—	—	—	—
94-95	Ottawa	NHL	13	1	1	2	0	—	—	—	—	—
94-95	Peoria	IHL	65	19	33	52	42	—	—	—	—	—
95-96	Ottawa	NHL	6	0	0	0	4	—	—	—	—	—
95-96	Prince Edward Island	AHL	15	2	7	9	4	—	—	—	—	—
95-96	Atlanta	IHL	15	4	9	13	4	—	—	—	—	—
95-96	Kansas City	IHL	23	2	6	8	11	5	0	1	1	0
96-97	Portland	AHL	69	14	26	40	33	5	0	2	2	2
97-98	Schwenningen	Germany	50	14	27	41	18	—	—	—	—	—
98-99	Schwenningen	Germany	46	9	30	39	52	—	—	—	—	—
	NHL	Totals	48	2	5	7	27	—	—	—	—	—
	IHL	Totals	213	39	105	144	101	11	0	3	3	2
	AHL	Totals	84	16	33	49	37	5	0	2	2	2

Born; 3/28/69, Laval, Quebec. 6-1, 195. Drafted by St. Louis Blues (4th choice, 93rd overall) in 1989 Entry Draft. Traded to Ottawa Senators by St. Louis with St. Louis' ninth round choice (Erik Kasminski) in 1995 Entry Draft for Ottawa ninth round choice (Libor Zabransky) in 1995 Entry Draft (4/7/95). Signed as a free agent by Wasahington Capitals (7/12/96). Last amateur club; St. Lawrence

Darryl Laplante — Left Wing

Regular Season / Playoffs

Season	Team	League	GP	G	A	PTS	PIM	GP	G	A	PTS	PIM
97-98	Detroit	NHL	2	0	0	0	0	—	—	—	—	—
97-98	Adirondack	AHL	77	15	10	25	51	3	0	1	1	4
98-99	Detroit	NHL	3	0	0	0	0	—	—	—	—	—
98-99	Adirondack	AHL	71	17	15	32	96	3	0	1	1	0
	NHL	Totals	5	0	0	0	0	—	—	—	—	—
	AHL	Totals	148	32	25	57	147	6	0	2	2	4

Born; 3/28/77, Calgary, Alberta. 6-1, 185. Drafted by Detroit Red Wings (3rd choice, 58th overall) in 1995 Entry Draft. Last amateur club; Moose Jaw (WHL).

Martin Lapointe — Right Wing

Regular Season / Playoffs

Season	Team	League	GP	G	A	PTS	PIM	GP	G	A	PTS	PIM
98-99	South Carolina	ECHL	3	0	1	1	0	—	—	—	—	—

Born;

Alexandre LaPorte — Defenseman

Regular Season / Playoffs

Season	Team	League	GP	G	A	PTS	PIM	GP	G	A	PTS	PIM
95-96	Atlanta	IHL	14	0	1	1	5	—	—	—	—	—
95-96	Nashville	ECHL	38	2	9	11	60	5	0	0	0	8
96-97	Adirondack	AHL	38	0	3	3	39	1	0	0	0	0
97-98	Syracuse	AHL	4	1	0	1	2	—	—	—	—	—
97-98	Peoria	ECHL	3	0	0	0	2	—	—	—	—	—
97-98	Raleigh	ECHL	59	7	16	23	98	—	—	—	—	—
98-99	Augusta	ECHL	34	0	9	9	56	—	—	—	—	—
98-99	Tallahassee	ECHL	30	3	6	9	42	—	—	—	—	—
	AHL	Totals	42	1	3	4	41	1	0	0	0	0
	ECHL	Totals	164	12	40	52	258	5	0	0	0	8

Born; 5/1/75, Cowansville, Quebec. 6-3, 210. Drafted by Tampa Bay Lightning (9th choice, 211th overall) in 1993 Entry Draft. Traded to Raleigh by Peoria for future considerations (10/97). Traded to Tallahassee by Augusta with GarryGruber for Mark DeSantis (1/99). Last amateur club; Drummondville (QMJHL).

Georges Laraque — Right Wing

Regular Season / Playoffs

Season	Team	League	GP	G	A	PTS	PIM	GP	G	A	PTS	PIM
96-97	Hamilton	AHL	73	14	20	34	179	15	1	3	4	12
97-98	Edmonton	NHL	11	0	0	0	59	—	—	—	—	—
97-98	Hamilton	AHL	46	10	20	30	154	3	0	0	0	11
98-99	Edmonton	NHL	39	3	2	5	57	4	0	0	0	2
98-99	Hamilton	AHL	25	6	8	14	93	—	—	—	—	—
	NHL	Totals	50	3	2	5	116	4	0	0	0	2
	AHL	Totals	144	30	48	78	426	18	1	3	4	23

Born; 12/7/76, Montreal, Quebec. 6-3, 235. Drafted by Edmonton Oilers (2nd choice, 31st overall) in 1996 Entry Draft. Last amateur club; Granby (QMJHL).

Daniel Larin — Right Wing/Defenseman

Regular Season / Playoffs

Season	Team	League	GP	G	A	PTS	PIM	GP	G	A	PTS	PIM
90-91		France										
91-92		France										
92-93	Oklahoma City	CeHL	48	43	27	70	188	11	6	9	15	40
93-94												
94-95												
95-96	Kassel	Germany	8	0	6	6	0	—	—	—	—	—
96-97												
97-98	Central Texas	WPHL	9	6	10	16	15	4	3	1	4	4
98-99												
98-99												
98-99	Mohawk Valley	UHL	21	10	7	17	6	—	—	—	—	—
98-99	Oklahoma City	CHL	7	0	4	4	34	12	3	2	5	4
	CHL	Totals	55	43	31	74	222	23	9	11	20	44

Born; 11/20/67, Laval, Quebec. 5-11, 205. 1992-93 CeHL First Team All-Star. Last amateur club; Laval (QMJHL).

Francis Larivee — Goaltender

Regular Season / Playoffs

Season	Team	League	GP	W	L	T	MIN	SO	AVG	GP	W	L	MIN	SO	AVG
96-97	Granby	QMJHL	1	1	0	0	60	0	1.00	1	0	0	50	0	4.80
96-97	Laval	QMJHL	21	6	11	1	1068	1	4.33	—	—	—	—	—	—
96-97	St. John's	AHL	4	3	1	0	244	0	2.21	1	0	0	1	0	0.00
97-98	St. John's	AHL	30	6	12	5	1461	0	3.25	—	—	—	—	—	—
98-99	St. John's	AHL	17	4	7	2	851	0	4.16	—	—	—	—	—	—
98-99	Chicago	IHL	1	0	1	0	60	0	5.00	—	—	—	—	—	—
98-99	Huntington	ECHL	16	5	7	1	767	1	2.74	—	—	—	—	—	—
	AHL	Totals	51	13	20	7	2556	0	3.45	1	0	0	1	0	0.00

Born; 12/8/77, Montreal, Quebec. 6-2, 198. Drafted by Toronto Maple Leafs (2nd choice, 50th overall) in 1996 Entry Draft. Last amateur club; Granby (QMJHL).

Christian Lariviere — Defenseman
Regular Season / Playoffs

Season	Team	League	GP	G	A	PTS	PIM	GP	G	A	PTS	PIM
91-92	Johnstown	ECHL	62	3	16	19	142	6	1	3	4	24
92-93	Providence	AHL	9	0	1	1	6	—	—	—	—	—
92-93	Johnstown	ECHL	51	4	20	24	93	5	1	3	4	4
93-94	Fredericton	AHL	51	2	6	8	56	—	—	—	—	—
94-95	Fredericton	AHL	32	1	1	2	36	15	0	5	5	18
94-95	Wheeling	ECHL	17	0	8	8	40	—	—	—	—	—
95-96	Cornwall	AHL	43	1	4	5	49	2	0	0	0	0
96-97												
97-98	Las Vegas	IHL	13	1	1	2	17	—	—	—	—	—
97-98	Reno	WCHL	56	6	28	34	75	3	0	0	0	4
98-99	Shreveport	WPHL	68	5	27	32	83	12	0	5	5	12
	AHL	Totals	135	4	12	16	147	17	0	5	5	18
	AHL	Totals	130	7	44	51	275	11	2	6	8	28

Born; 4/25/70, Montreal, Quebec. 6-0, 195. Selected by Anchorage in 1998 WCHL Dispersal Draft. Member of 1998-99 WPHL Champion Shreveport Mudbugs. Last amateur club; St. Hyacinthe (QMJHL).

Mike Larkin — Defenseman
Regular Season / Playoffs

Season	Team	League	GP	G	A	PTS	PIM	GP	G	A	PTS	PIM
95-96	Hampton Roads	ECHL	9	2	10	12	8	—	—	—	—	—
95-96	Lakeland	SHL	33	5	29	34	47	4	1	0	1	8
96-97	Hampton Roads	ECHL	34	2	10	12	80	8	1	3	4	35
97-98	Hampton Roads	ECHL	24	2	8	10	85	—	—	—	—	—
97-98	Mobile	ECHL	34	10	15	25	53	—	—	—	—	—
98-99	Utah	IHL	2	0	1	1	0	—	—	—	—	—
98-99	Fresno	WCHL	55	10	30	40	109	7	0	6	6	27
	ECHL	Totals	101	16	43	59	226	8	1	3	4	35

Born; 3/15/73, South Weymouth, Massachusetts. 6-3, 210. Traded to Mobile by Hampton Roads for Mike Mayhew (1/98). Last amateur club; Vermont (H.E.).

Martin Laroche — Center
Regular Season / Playoffs

Season	Team	League	GP	G	A	PTS	PIM	GP	G	A	PTS	PIM
98-99	Baton Rouge	ECHL	25	9	4	13	2	—	—	—	—	—
98-99	Columbus	ECHL	37	8	18	26	10	4	0	4	4	4
	ECHL	Totals	62	17	22	39	12	4	0	4	4	4

Born; 6/3/75, Cornwall, Ontario. 5-11, 185. Selected by Greensboro in 1999 ECHL Dispersal Draft. Last amateur club; Merrimack (Hockey East).

Ian Larocque — Forward
Regular Season / Playoffs

Season	Team	League	GP	G	A	PTS	PIM	GP	G	A	PTS	PIM
98-99	Waco	WPHL	54	13	25	38	55	4	0	1	1	14

Born; 9/3/77, Kingston, Ontario. 6-0, 180. Last amateur club; Northern Michigan (CCHA).

J.C. Larocque — Center
Regular Season / Playoffs

Season	Team	League	GP	G	A	PTS	PIM	GP	G	A	PTS	PIM
97-98	Winston-Salem	UHL	15	2	2	4	6	—	—	—	—	—
98-99	Thunder Bay	UHL	4	0	0	0	0	—	—	—	—	—
	UHL	Totals	19	2	2	4	6	—	—	—	—	—

Born; 2/4/76, Toronto, Ontario. 5-9, 180.

Mario Larocque — Defenseman
Regular Season / Playoffs

Season	Team	League	GP	G	A	PTS	PIM	GP	G	A	PTS	PIM
98-99	Tampa Bay	NHL	5	0	0	0	16	—	—	—	—	—
98-99	Cleveland	IHL	59	5	7	12	202	—	—	—	—	—

Born; 4/24/76, Montreal, Quebec. 6-2, 182. Drafted by Tampa Bay Lightning (1st choice, 16th overall) in 1996 Entry Draft. Last amateur club; Sherbrooke

Stephane Larocque — Right Wing
Regular Season / Playoffs

Season	Team	League	GP	G	A	PTS	PIM	GP	G	A	PTS	PIM
95-96	South Carolina	ECHL	9	1	2	3	32	—	—	—	—	—
95-96	Thunder Bay	CoHL	44	22	35	57	110	18	4	7	11	24
96-97	Fort Worth	CeHL	59	41	39	80	354	17	*14	10	*24	66
97-98	Quebec	IHL	3	0	0	0	7	—	—	—	—	—
97-98	Fort Worth	WPHL	65	51	53	104	275	13	8	7	15	30
98-99	Fort Worth	WPHL	64	21	50	71	218	12	8	9	17	36
	WPHL	Totals	129	72	103	175	493	25	16	16	32	66

Born; 7/24/74, Hull, Quebec. 6-2, 205. Member of 1996-97 CeHL Champion Fort Worth Fire. Last amateur club; Halifax (QMJHL).

Guy Larose — Center
Regular Season / Playoffs

Season	Team	League	GP	G	A	PTS	PIM	GP	G	A	PTS	PIM
87-88	Moncton	AHL	77	22	31	53	127	—	—	—	—	—
88-89	Winnipeg	NHL	3	0	1	1	6	—	—	—	—	—
88-89	Moncton	AHL	72	32	27	59	176	10	4	4	8	37
89-90	Moncton	AHL	79	44	26	70	232	—	—	—	—	—
90-91	Winnipeg	NHL	7	0	0	0	8	—	—	—	—	—
90-91	Moncton	AHL	35	14	10	24	60	—	—	—	—	—
90-91	Binghamton	AHL	34	21	15	36	48	10	8	5	13	37
91-92	Toronto	NHL	34	9	5	14	27	—	—	—	—	—
91-92	Binghamton	AHL	30	10	11	21	36	—	—	—	—	—
91-92	St. John's	AHL	15	7	7	14	26	—	—	—	—	—
92-93	Toronto	NHL	9	0	0	0	8	—	—	—	—	—
92-93	St. John's	AHL	5	0	1	1	8	9	5	2	7	6
93-94	Toronto	NHL	10	1	2	3	10	—	—	—	—	—
93-94	Calgary	NHL	7	0	1	1	4	—	—	—	—	—
93-94	St. John's	AHL	23	13	16	29	41	—	—	—	—	—
93-94	Saint John	AHL	15	11	11	22	20	7	3	2	5	22
94-95	Boston	NHL	—	—	—	—	—	4	0	0	0	0
94-95	Providence	AHL	68	25	33	58	93	12	4	6	10	22
95-96	Detroit	IHL	50	28	15	43	53	—	—	—	—	—
95-96	Las Vegas	IHL	25	10	22	32	54	15	3	6	9	14
96-97	Houston	IHL	79	29	25	54	108	13	6	7	13	12
97-98	Revier Lowen	Germany	45	11	17	28	73	—	—	—	—	—
98-99	Chicago	IHL	80	19	22	41	117	10	1	3	4	14
	NHL	Totals	70	10	9	19	63	4	0	0	0	0
	AHL	Totals	453	186	188	374	867	48	24	19	43	124
	IHL	Totals	234	86	84	170	332	38	10	16	26	40

Born; 8/31/67, Hull, Quebec. 5-9, 175. Drafted by Buffalo Sabres (11th choice, 224th overall) in 1985 Entry Draft. Signed as a free agent by Winnipeg Jets 97/16/87). Traded to New York Rangers by Winnipeg for Rudy Poeschek (1/22/91). Traded to Toronto Maple Leafs by Rangers for Mike Stevens (12/26/91). Claimed on waivers by Calgary Flames from Toronto (1/1/94). Signed as a free agent by Boston Bruins (7/11/94). Last amateur club; Ottawa (OHL).

Steve Larouche
Regular Season — Center — Playoffs

Season	Team	League	GP	G	A	PTS	PIM	GP	G	A	PTS	PIM
91-92	Fredericton	AHL	74	21	35	56	41	7	1	0	1	0
92-93	Fredericton	AHL	77	27	65	92	52	5	2	5	7	6
93-94	Atlanta	IHL	80	43	53	96	73	14	*16	10	*26	16
94-95	Ottawa	NHL	18	8	7	15	6	—	—	—	—	—
94-95	Prince Edward Island	AHL	70	*53	48	101	54	2	1	0	1	0
95-96	Rangers	NHL	1	0	0	0	0	—	—	—	—	—
95-96	Los Angeles	NHL	7	1	2	3	4	—	—	—	—	—
95-96	Binghamton	AHL	39	20	46	66	47	—	—	—	—	—
95-96	Phoenix	IHL	33	19	17	36	14	4	0	1	1	8
96-97	Quebec	IHL	79	49	53	102	78	9	3	10	13	18
97-98	Quebec	IHL	68	23	44	67	40	—	—	—	—	—
97-98	Chicago	IHL	13	9	10	19	20	22	9	11	20	14
98-99	Chicago	IHL	33	13	25	38	18	—	—	—	—	—
	NHL	Totals	26	9	9	18	10	—	—	—	—	—
	IHL	Totals	306	156	202	358	243	49	28	32	60	56
	AHL	Totals	260	121	194	315	194	14	4	5	9	14

Born; 4/14/71, Rouyn, Quebec. 6-0, 180. Drafted by Montreal Canadiens (3rd choice, 41st overall) in 1989 Entry Draft. Signed as a free agent by Ottawa Senators (9/11/94). Traded to New York Rangers by Ottawa for Jean Yves-Roy (10/5/95). Traded to Los Angeles Kings by Rangers for Chris Snell (1/14/96). Traded to Chicago by Quebec with Marc Rodgers for Jack Williams and Dave Paradise (3/98). 1994-95 AHL First Team All-Star. 1994-95 AHL Fred Hunt Trophy winner (Sportmanship). 1994-95 AHL MVP. 1996-97 IHL First Team All-Star. Member of 1993-94 IHL Champion Atlanta Knights. Member of 1997-98 IHL Champion Chicago Wolves. Last amateur club; Chicoutimi (QMJHL).

Brad Larsen
Regular Season — Left Wing — Playoffs

Season	Team	League	GP	G	A	PTS	PIM	GP	G	A	PTS	PIM
97-98	Colorado	NHL	1	0	0	0	0	—	—	—	—	—
97-98	Hershey	AHL	65	12	10	22	80	7	3	2	5	2
98-99	Hershey	AHL	18	3	4	7	11	5	1	0	1	6
	AHL	Totals	83	15	14	29	91	12	4	2	6	8

Born; 1/28/77, Nakusp, British Columbia. 5-11, 212. Drafted by Ottawa Senators (3rd choice, 53rd overall) in 1995 Entry Draft. Traded to Colorado Avalanche by Ottawa for Janne Laukkanen (1/26/96). Re-entered NHL Entry Draft, Colorado's (5th choice, 87th overall) in 1997 Entry Draft. Last amateur club; Swift Current (WHL).

Brett Larson
Regular Season — Defenseman — Playoffs

Season	Team	League	GP	G	A	PTS	PIM	GP	G	A	PTS	PIM
95-96	Madison	CoHL	70	12	31	43	37	6	2	1	3	18
96-97	Louisville	ECHL	27	4	13	17	4	—	—	—	—	—
97-98	Utah	IHL	9	0	0	0	6	—	—	—	—	—
97-98	San Diego	WCHL	52	8	19	27	26	13	4	9	13	20
98-99	Long Beach	IHL	4	0	0	0	2	—	—	—	—	—
98-99	Utah	IHL	1	0	0	0	0	—	—	—	—	—
98-99	Las Vegas	IHL	2	0	0	0	0	—	—	—	—	—
98-99	San Diego	WCHL	60	10	36	46	42	12	7	7	14	6
	IHL	Totals	16	0	0	0	8	—	—	—	—	—
	WCHL	Totals	112	18	55	73	68	25	11	16	27	26

Born; 8/20/72, Duluth, Minnesota. 6-0, 175. Member of 1997-98 WCHL Champion San Diego Gulls. Last amateur club; Minnesota-Duluth (WCHA).

Dean Larson
Regular Season — Center — Playoffs

Season	Team	League	GP	G	A	PTS	PIM	GP	G	A	PTS	PIM
95-96	Anchorage	WCHL	54	31	61	92	71	—	—	—	—	—
96-97	Anchorage	WCHL	58	29	79	108	54	9	4	6	10	4
97-98	Anchorage	WCHL	60	36	67	103	47	8	1	4	5	22
98-99	Anchorage	WCHL	68	43	74	117	68	6	2	5	7	6
	WCHL	Totals	240	139	281	420	240	23	7	15	22	32

Born; 6/4/69, 5-8, 160. 1996-97 WCHL Second Team All-Star.

Frank LaScala
Regular Season — Left Wing — Playoffs

Season	Team	League	GP	G	A	PTS	PIM	GP	G	A	PTS	PIM
90-91	Richmond	ECHL	62	25	30	55	116	2	0	0	0	16
91-92	Columbus	ECHL	59	34	23	57	138	—	—	—	—	—
92-93	Dallas	CeHL	27	14	17	31	45	7	5	1	6	6
93-94	Dallas	CeHL	64	45	41	86	116	7	5	5	10	10
94-95	Dallas	CeHL	41	23	37	60	76	—	—	—	—	—
95-96	Knoxville	ECHL	69	45	50	95	112	8	5	4	9	30
96-97	Wedemark	Germany	47	9	16	25	122	4	0	1	1	6
97-98	Newcastle	BSL	56	19	18	37	71	6	2	4	6	4
97-98	Reno	WCHL	6	3	1	4	5	—	—	—	—	—
98-99	Bracknell	BSL	19	4	5	9	2	7	2	2	4	10
	ECHL	Totals	190	104	103	207	366	10	5	4	9	46
	CeHL	Totals	132	82	95	177	237	14	10	6	16	16

Born; 3/22/69, Thorold, Ontario. 6-3, 215. Selected by Colorado in 1998 WCHL Dispersal Draft.

Mike Latendresse
Regular Season — Right Wing — Playoffs

Season	Team	League	GP	G	A	PTS	PIM	GP	G	A	PTS	PIM
94-95	Adirondack	AHL	2	0	0	0	0	—	—	—	—	—
94-95	Toledo	ECHL	43	36	20	56	23	4	1	3	4	2
95-96	Detroit	IHL	1	0	0	0	0	—	—	—	—	—
95-96	Birmingham	ECHL	28	21	28	49	32	—	—	—	—	—
96-97	Birmingham	ECHL	61	20	28	48	82	2	0	1	1	0
97-98	Wheeling	ECHL	70	30	45	75	18	15	6	7	13	0
98-99	Wheeling	ECHL	63	15	17	32	34	—	—	—	—	—
	ECHL	Totals	265	122	138	260	189	21	7	11	18	2

Born; 2/11/71, Montreal, Quebec. 5-10, 160. Last amateur club; Maine (H.E).

Alain Latrielle
Regular Season — Forward — Playoffs

Season	Team	League	GP	G	A	PTS	PIM	GP	G	A	PTS	PIM
93-94	Solihull	BHL	44	78	69	147	52	—	—	—	—	—
94-95	Teeside	BHL	4	1	5	6	2	—	—	—	—	—
94-95	Medway	BHL	27	33	23	56	8	—	—	—	—	—
95-96												
96-97	Peterborough	BHL	13	8	8	16	4	—	—	—	—	—
97-98	Fayetteville	CHL	49	19	13	32	20	—	—	—	—	—
98-99												

Born; 12/15/65, Ottawa, Ontario. 6-1, 205.

Brad Lauer — Left Wing

Season	Team	League	GP	G	A	PTS	PIM	GP	G	A	PTS	PIM
			Regular Season					Playoffs				
86-87	Islanders	NHL	61	7	14	21	65	6	2	0	2	4
87-88	Islanders	NHL	69	17	18	35	67	5	3	1	4	4
88-89	Islanders	NHL	14	3	2	5	2	—	—	—	—	—
88-89	Springfield	AHL	8	1	5	6	0	—	—	—	—	—
89-90	Islanders	NHL	63	6	18	24	19	4	0	2	2	10
89-90	Springfield	AHL	7	4	2	6	0	—	—	—	—	—
90-91	Islanders	NHL	44	4	8	12	45	—	—	—	—	—
90-91	Capital District	AHL	11	5	11	16	14	—	—	—	—	—
91-92	Islanders	NHL	8	1	0	1	2	—	—	—	—	—
91-92	Chicago	NHL	6	0	0	0	4	7	1	1	2	2
91-92	Indianapolis	IHL	57	24	30	54	46	—	—	—	—	—
92-93	Chicago	NHL	7	0	1	1	2	—	—	—	—	—
92-93	Indianapolis	IHL	62	*50	41	91	80	5	3	1	4	6
93-94	Ottawa	NHL	30	2	5	7	6	—	—	—	—	—
93-94	Las Vegas	IHL	32	21	21	42	30	4	1	0	1	2
94-95	Cleveland	IHL	51	32	27	59	48	4	4	2	6	6
95-96	Pittsburgh	NHL	21	4	1	5	6	12	1	1	2	4
95-96	Cleveland	IHL	53	25	27	52	44	—	—	—	—	—
96-97	Cleveland	IHL	64	27	21	48	61	14	4	6	10	8
97-98	Cleveland	IHL	68	22	33	55	74	10	0	3	3	12
98-99	Utah	IHL	78	31	30	61	68	—	—	—	—	—
	NHL	Totals	323	44	67	111	218	34	7	5	12	24
	IHL	Totals	465	232	330	562	451	37	12	12	24	34
	AHL	Totals	26	10	18	28	14	—	—	—	—	—

Born; 10/27/66, Humboldt, Saskatchewan. 6-0, 195. Drafted by New York Islanders (3rd choice, 34th overall) in 1985 Entry Draft. Traded to Chicago Blackhawks by Islanders with Brent Sutter for Adam Creighton and Steve Thomas (10/25/91). Signed as a free agent by Ottawa Senators (1/3/94). Signed as a free agent by Pittsburgh Penguins (8/10/95). 1992-93 IHL First Team All-Star. Last amateur club; Regina (WHL).

Rob Laurie — Goaltender

Season	Team	League	GP	W	L	T	MIN	SO	AVG	GP	W	L	MIN	SO	AVG
			Regular Season							Playoffs					
92-93	Roanoke	ECHL	14	5	7	0	716	0	4.61	—	—	—	—	—	—
92-93	Dayton	ECHL	22	11	7	1	1197	0	4.51	1	0	1	68	0	3.53
93-94	Dayton	ECHL	2	1	1	0	120	0	4.50	—	—	—	—	—	—
93-94	Johnstown	ECHL	34	18	13	1	1942	0	3.96	3	1	2	153	0	4.31
94-95	Johnstown	ECHL	26	7	16	2	1456	0	4.66	—	—	—	—	—	—
94-95	Greensboro	ECHL	10	4	4	1	514	0	4.55	—	—	—	—	—	—
95-96	Adirondack	AHL	1	0	1	0	23	0	2.64	—	—	—	—	—	—
95-96	Toledo	ECHL	19	13	3	2	1125	0	3.73	—	—	—	—	—	—
95-96	Tallahassee	ECHL	17	8	5	0	774	0	3.49	3	1	2	196	0	2.76
96-97	Huntington	ECHL	56	27	25	2	3198	1	4.00	—	—	—	—	—	—
97-98	Fort Worth	WPHL	51	30	11	9	2992	*3	2.99	11	6	5	654	0	2.94
98-99	Flint	UHL	*66	*35	27	4	*3750	1	3.82	9	4	3	397	0	3.77
	ECHL	Totals	200	94	81	9	11042	1	4.14	7	2	5	417	0	3.45

Born; 5/19/70, East Lansing, Michigan. 5-10, 175. Selected by Fort Wayne in 1999 UHL Expansion Draft. Last amateur club; Western Michigan (CCHA).

Todd Laurin — Goaltender

Season	Team	League	GP	W	L	T	MIN	SO	AVG	GP	W	L	MIN	SO	AVG
			Regular Season							Playoffs					
96-97	Amarillo	WPHL	25	4	13	1	1200	0	5.40	—	—	—	—	—	—
97-98	Amarillo	WPHL	45	18	14	8	2378	0	3.58	—	—	—	—	—	—
97-98	San Diego	WCHL	—	—	—	—	—	—	—	1	0	0	0	0	0.00
98-99	Amarillo	WPHL	11	5	6	0	557	0	4.74	—	—	—	—	—	—
98-99	Fort Worth	WPHL	9	5	3	1	539	0	3.23	5	2	1	261	0	3.91
	WPHL	Totals	90	32	36	10	4674	0	4.15	5	2	1	261	0	3.91

Born; 3/10/75, Gloucester, Ontario. 5-6, 145. Member of 1997-98 WCHL Champion San Diego Gulls. Played 18 seconds in 1997-98 WCHL Playoffs, stopping the only shot on goal that he faced.

Dan Lavergne — Center

Season	Team	League	GP	G	A	PTS	PIM	GP	G	A	PTS	PIM
			Regular Season					Playoffs				
97-98	Odessa	WPHL	68	39	41	80	57	—	—	—	—	—
98-99	Odessa	WPHL	41	12	11	23	14	—	—	—	—	—
98-99	Abilene	WPHL	22	4	7	11	4	3	1	0	1	0
	WPHL	Totals	131	55	59	114	75	3	1	0	1	0

Born; 5/20/75, Woonsocket, Rhode Island. 5-9, 180. Traded to Abilene by Odessa for Mario Dumoulin (1/99). Last amateur club; Colby (NCAA 3).

Eric Lavigne — Defenseman

Season	Team	League	GP	G	A	PTS	PIM	GP	G	A	PTS	PIM
			Regular Season					Playoffs				
93-94	Phoenix	IHL	62	3	11	14	168	—	—	—	—	—
94-95	Los Angeles	NHL	2	0	0	0	0	—	—	—	—	—
94-95	Phoenix	IHL	69	4	10	14	233	—	—	—	—	—
94-95	Detroit	IHL	1	0	0	0	2	5	0	0	0	26
95-96	Prince Edward Island	AHL	72	5	13	18	154	2	0	0	0	6
96-97	Rochester	AHL	46	1	6	7	89	6	0	1	1	21
97-98	Rochester	AHL	28	0	1	1	118	—	—	—	—	—
97-98	Grand Rapids	IHL	4	0	1	1	13	—	—	—	—	—
97-98	Cleveland	IHL	16	0	0	0	34	10	1	1	2	44
98-99	Cleveland	IHL	66	11	7	18	259	—	—	—	—	—
	IHL	Totals	218	18	29	47	709	15	1	1	2	70
	AHL	Totals	146	6	20	26	361	8	0	1	1	27

Born; 10/14/72, Victoriaville, Quebec. 6-3, 194. Drafted by Washington Capitals (3rd choice, 25th overall) in 1991 Entry Draft. Signed as a free agent by Los Angeles Kings (10/13/93). Signed as a free agent by Ottawa Senators (8/10/95). Traded to Cleveland by Rochester for Darren Wetherill (3/98). Last amateur club; Hull (QMJHL).

Danny Laviolette — Goaltender

Season	Team	League	GP	W	L	T	MIN	SO	AVG	GP	W	L	MIN	SO	AVG
			Regular Season							Playoffs					
96-97	San Diego	WCHL	19	12	4	0	995	0	3.44	1	0	0	15	0	0.00
97-98	Tucson	WCHL	4	0	3	0	184	0	4.89	—	—	—	—	—	—
97-98	San Diego	WCHL	23	14	3	0	1039	2	2.89	4	0	1	106	0	3.95
98-99	Asheville	UHL	44	23	17	2	2434	0	4.19	2	0	2	119	0	4.54
	WCHL	Totals	46	26	10	0	2218	2	3.30	5	0	1	121	0	3.47

Born; 3/22/76, Sorel, Quebec. 6-0, 165. Traded to Tucson by San Diego for Bryan Masotta and Jason Shmyr (1/98). Member of 1996-97 WCHL Champion San Diego Gulls. Member of 1997-98 WCHL Champion San Diego Gulls. Last amateur club, Drummondville (QMJHL).

Ted Laviolette — Defenseman

Season	Team	League	GP	G	A	PTS	PIM	GP	G	A	PTS	PIM
			Regular Season					Playoffs				
98-99	Hamilton	AHL	1	0	0	0	0	—	—	—	—	—
98-99	New Orleans	ECHL	50	5	7	12	78	—	—	—	—	—

Born; 2/22/74, Montreal, Quebec. 6-1, 205. Last amateur club; Lake Superior (CCHA).

Darryl Lavoie — Defenseman

Season	Team	League	GP	G	A	PTS	PIM	GP	G	A	PTS	PIM
			Regular Season					Playoffs				
97-98	Columbus	ECHL	16	0	1	1	16	—	—	—	—	—
97-98	Dayton	ECHL	15	2	7	9	20	—	—	—	—	—
97-98	Richmond	ECHL	26	1	5	6	37	—	—	—	—	—
98-99	Austin	WPHL	40	8	18	26	69	—	—	—	—	—
98-99	New Mexico	WPHL	23	1	15	16	29	—	—	—	—	—
98-99	Flint	UHL	1	0	0	0	5	—	—	—	—	—
	WPHL	Totals	63	9	33	42	98	—	—	—	—	—
	ECHL	Totals	57	3	13	16	73	—	—	—	—	—

Born; 1/10/74, Chatham, New Brunswick. 5-11, 180. Traded to New Mexico by Austin for Aldo Iaquinta and future considerations (1/99). Last amateur club; University of Prince Edward Island (AUAA).

Kirby Law — Right Wing

Regular Season / Playoffs

Season	Team	League	GP	G	A	PTS	PIM	GP	G	A	PTS	PIM
98-99	Orlando	IHL	67	18	13	31	136	—	—	—	—	—
98-99	Adirondack	AHL	11	2	3	5	40	3	1	0	1	2

Born; 3/11/77, McCreary, Manitoba. 6-1, 180. Signed as a free agent by Atlanta Thrashers (7/6/99). Last amateur club; Brandon (WHL).

Paul Lawless — Left Wing

Regular Season / Playoffs

Season	Team	League	GP	G	A	PTS	PIM	GP	G	A	PTS	PIM
82-83	Hartford	NHL	47	6	9	15	4	—	—	—	—	—
83-84	Hartford	NHL	6	0	3	3	0	—	—	—	—	—
84-85	Binghamton	AHL	8	1	1	2	0	—	—	—	—	—
84-85	Salt Lake City	IHL	72	49	48	97	14	7	5	3	8	20
85-86	Hartford	NHL	64	17	21	38	20	1	0	0	0	0
86-87	Hartford	NHL	60	22	32	54	14	2	0	2	2	2
87-88	Hartford	NHL	27	4	5	9	16	—	—	—	—	—
87-88	Philadelphia	NHL	8	0	5	5	0	—	—	—	—	—
87-88	Vancouver	NHL	13	0	1	1	0	—	—	—	—	—
88-89	Toronto	NHL	7	0	0	0	0	—	—	—	—	—
88-89	Milwaukee	IHL	53	30	35	65	58	—	—	—	—	—
89-90	Toronto	NHL	6	0	1	1	0	—	—	—	—	—
89-90	Newmarket	AHL	3	1	0	1	0	—	—	—	—	—
92-93	New Haven	AHL	20	10	12	22	63	—	—	—	—	—
92-93	Cincinnati	IHL	29	29	25	54	64	—	—	—	—	—
93-94	Cincinnati	IHL	71	30	27	57	112	11	4	4	8	4
94-95	Cincinnati	IHL	64	44	52	96	119	10	9	9	18	8
95-96	Cincinnati	IHL	77	27	58	85	99	17	4	6	10	16
96-97	Cincinnati	IHL	14	2	10	12	14	—	—	—	—	—
96-97	Austin	WPHL	30	11	35	46	54	6	2	4	6	26
97-98	Austin	WPHL	1	1	0	1	14	—	—	—	—	—
98-99	Austin	WPHL	2	2	1	3	2	—	—	—	—	—
	NHL	Totals	238	49	77	126	54	3	0	2	2	2
	IHL	Totals	380	211	255	466	480	45	22	22	44	48
	AHL	Totals	31	12	13	25	63	—	—	—	—	—
	WPHL	Totals	33	14	36	50	70	6	2	4	6	26

Born; 7/2/64, Scarborough, Ontario. 5-11, 185. Drafted by Hartford Whalers (1st choice, 14th overall) in 1982 Entry Draft. Traded to Philadelphia Flyers by Hartford for Lindsay Carson (1/88). Traded to Vancouver Canucks by Philadelphia with Vancouver's fifth round choice (acquired 3/7/89) by Edmonton, who selected Peter White) in 1989 Entry Draft, acquired earlier by Philadelphia for Willie Huber (3/1/88). Traded to Toronto Maple Leafs by Vancouver for the rights to Peter Deboer (2/27/89). Last amateur club; Windsor (OHL). Assumed head coaching duties for Austin Ice Bats until the conclusion of 1997-98 season.

Doug Lawrence — Left Wing

Regular Season / Playoffs

Season	Team	League	GP	G	A	PTS	PIM	GP	G	A	PTS	PIM
89-90	Fort Wayne	IHL	3	0	0	0	0	—	—	—	—	—
89-90	Greensboro	ECHL	53	16	42	58	94	11	2	7	9	67
90-91	Greensboro	ECHL	47	17	44	61	89	—	—	—	—	—
90-91	Erie	ECHL	7	1	7	8	27	4	0	1	1	61
91-92	Erie	ECHL	60	19	74	93	120	4	1	1	2	35
92-93	Memphis	CeHL	19	8	*26	34	47	—	—	—	—	—
92-93	Tulsa	CeHL	38	14	*47	61	114	12	3	*15	18	43
93-94	Tulsa	CeHL	63	25	*93	118	199	11	3	11	14	52
94-95	Nashville	ECHL	33	7	37	44	129	—	—	—	—	—
94-95	Tulsa	CeHL	19	8	15	23	87	7	0	3	3	33
95-96	Oklahoma City	CeHL	54	6	53	59	346	10	2	5	7	61
96-97	Tulsa	CeHL	66	27	*100	127	250	3	1	1	2	43
97-98	Tulsa	CHL	67	23	*92	115	337	4	1	5	6	12
98-99	Shreveport	WPHL	40	24	45	69	145	—	—	—	—	—
98-99	Tulsa	CHL	23	6	39	45	159	—	—	—	—	—
	CeHL	Totals	349	117	465	582	1539	47	10	40	50	244
	ECHL	Totals	200	60	204	264	459	19	3	9	12	163

Born; 4/11/68, Richmond, British Columbia. 5-10, 180. 1992-93 CeHL Second Team All-Star. 1993-94 CeHL First Team All-Star. 1996-97 CeHL First Team All-Star. Member of 1989-90 ECHL champion Greensboro Monarchs. Member of 1992-93 CeHL champion Tulsa Oilers. Member of 1995-96 CeHL champion Oklahoma City Blazers.

Mark Lawrence — Right Wing

Regular Season / Playoffs

Season	Team	League	GP	G	A	PTS	PIM	GP	G	A	PTS	PIM
92-93	Dayton	ECHL	20	8	14	22	46	—	—	—	—	—
92-93	Kalamazoo	IHL	57	22	13	35	47	—	—	—	—	—
93-94	Kalamazoo	IHL	64	17	20	37	90	—	—	—	—	—
94-95	Dallas	NHL	2	0	0	0	0	—	—	—	—	—
94-95	Kalamazoo	IHL	77	21	29	50	92	16	3	7	10	28
95-96	Dallas	NHL	13	0	1	1	17	—	—	—	—	—
95-96	Michigan	IHL	55	15	14	29	92	10	3	4	7	30
96-97	Michigan	IHL	68	15	21	36	141	4	0	0	0	18
97-98	Islanders	NHL	2	0	0	0	2	—	—	—	—	—
97-98	Utah	IHL	80	36	28	64	102	4	1	1	2	4
98-99	Islanders	NHL	60	14	16	30	38	—	—	—	—	—
98-99	Lowell	AHL	21	10	6	16	28	—	—	—	—	—
	NHL	Totals	77	14	17	31	57	—	—	—	—	—
	IHL	Totals	401	126	125	251	564	34	7	12	19	80

Born; 1/27/72, Burlington, Ontario. 6-3, 210. Drafted by Minnesota North Stars (6th choice, 118th overall) in 1991 Entry Draft. Signed as a free agent by New York Islanders (7/29/97). Last amateur club; North Bay (OHL).

Charlie Lawson — Left Wing

Regular Season / Playoffs

Season	Team	League	GP	G	A	PTS	PIM	GP	G	A	PTS	PIM
98-99	Abilene	WPHL	14	1	2	3	12	—	—	—	—	—
98-99	Odessa	WPHL	18	3	2	5	20	—	—	—	—	—
98-99	Oklahoma City	CHL	1	0	0	0	0	—	—	—	—	—
98-99	Fort Worth	CHL	3	0	2	2	2	—	—	—	—	—
	CHL	Totals	32	4	4	8	32	—	—	—	—	—
	WPHL	Totals	4	0	2	2	2	—	—	—	—	—

Born; 7/5/75, Burlington, Ontario. 6-1, 225.

Cheyne Lazar — Forward

Regular Season / Playoffs

Season	Team	League	GP	G	A	PTS	PIM	GP	G	A	PTS	PIM
98-99	San Antonio	CHL	62	17	14	31	21	8	2	3	5	10

Born; 5/6/74, Montreal, Quebec. 5-10, 175. Selected by Indianapolis in 1999 CHL Expansion Draft. Last amateur club; Rochester Institute of Technology

Evgeny Lazarev — Left Wing

Regular Season / Playoffs

Season	Team	League	GP	G	A	PTS	PIM	GP	G	A	PTS	PIM
98-99	Hershey	AHL	53	6	15	21	18	—	—	—	—	—

Born; 4/25/80, Kharkov, USSR. 6-2, 215. Drafted by Colorado Avalanche (8th choice, 79th overall) in 1998 Entry Draft. Last amateur club; Kitchener (OJHL).

Jeff Lazaro — Left Wing

Regular Season / Playoffs

Season	Team	League	GP	G	A	PTS	PIM	GP	G	A	PTS	PIM
90-91	Maine	AHL	26	8	11	19	18	—	—	—	—	—
90-91	Boston	NHL	49	5	13	18	67	19	3	2	5	30
91-92	Boston	NHL	27	3	6	9	31	9	0	1	1	2
91-92	Maine	AHL	21	8	4	12	32	—	—	—	—	—
92-93	Ottawa	NHL	26	6	4	10	16	—	—	—	—	—
92-93	New Haven	AHL	27	12	13	25	49	—	—	—	—	—
93-94	United States	National	43	18	25	43	57	—	—	—	—	—
93-94	United States	Olympic	8	2	2	4	4	—	—	—	—	—
93-94	Providence	AHL	16	3	4	7	26	—	—	—	—	—
94-95												
95-96	Ratinger	Germany	49	29	42	71	85	—	—	—	—	—
96-97	Ratinger	Germany	44	13	23	36	69	7	5	3	8	8
97-98	Hamilton	AHL	2	2	0	2	0	8	2	3	5	2
97-98	New Orleans	ECHL	70	37	64	101	151	4	0	4	4	8
98-99	Adirondack	AHL	16	2	8	10	10	—	—	—	—	—
98-99	New Orleans	ECHL	52	26	44	70	81	11	9	7	16	14
	NHL	Totals	102	14	23	37	114	28	3	3	6	32
	AHL	Totals	108	35	40	75	135	8	2	3	5	2
	ECHL	Totals	122	63	108	171	232	15	9	11	20	22

Born; 3/21/68, Waltham, Massachusetts. 5-10, 180. Signed as a free agent by Boston Bruins (9/26/90). Selected by Ottawa Senators in NHL expansion draft (6/18/92). 1997-98 ECHL First All-Star Team. Last amateur club; New Hampshire (Hockey East).

Jamie Leach

Right Wing

Regular Season / Playoffs

Season	Team	League	GP	G	A	PTS	PIM	GP	G	A	PTS	PIM
89-90	Pittsburgh	NHL	10	0	3	3	0	—	—	—	—	—
89-90	Muskegon	IHL	72	22	36	58	39	15	9	4	13	14
90-91	Pittsburgh	NHL	7	2	0	2	0	—	—	—	—	—
90-91	Muskegon	IHL	43	33	22	55	26	—	—	—	—	—
91-92	Pittsburgh	NHL	38	5	4	9	8	—	—	—	—	—
91-92	Muskegon	IHL	3	1	1	2	2	—	—	—	—	—
92-93	Pittsburgh	NHL	5	0	0	0	2	—	—	—	—	—
92-93	Hartford	NHL	19	3	2	5	2	—	—	—	—	—
92-93	Cleveland	IHL	9	5	3	8	2	4	1	2	3	0
92-93	Springfield	AHL	29	13	15	28	33	—	—	—	—	—
93-94	Florida	NHL	2	1	0	1	0	—	—	—	—	—
93-94	Cincinnati	IHL	74	15	19	34	64	11	1	0	1	4
94-95	Cincinnati	IHL	11	0	2	2	9	—	—	—	—	—
94-95	San Diego	IHL	—	—	—	—	—	4	0	0	0	0
94-95	Canada	National	41	12	26	38	26	—	—	—	—	—
95-96	Rochester	AHL	47	12	14	26	52	2	0	0	0	0
95-96	South Carolina	ECHL	5	6	1	7	4	—	—	—	—	—
96-97	Sheffield	BHL	36	17	20	37	26	—	—	—	—	—
97-98	Nottingham	BSL	50	26	32	58	38	5	1	1	2	2
98-99	Nottingham	BSL	44	24	22	46	24	11	6	6	12	0
	NHL	Totals	81	11	9	20	12	—	—	—	—	—
	IHL	Totals	212	86	83	169	142	34	11	6	17	18
	AHL	Totals	76	25	29	54	85	2	0	0	0	0

Born; 8/25/69, Winnipeg, Manitoba. 6-1, 205. Drafted by Pittsburgh Penguins (3rd choice, 47th overall) in 1987 Entry Draft. Claimed on waivers by Hartford Whalers from Pittsburgh (11/21/92). Signed as a free agent by Florida Panthers (8/31/93). Signed as a free agent by Buffalo Sabres (7/21/95). Member of 1995-96 AHL champion Rochester Americans. Last amateur club; Niagara Falls

Steve Leach

Right Wing

Regular Season / Playoffs

Season	Team	League	GP	G	A	PTS	PIM	GP	G	A	PTS	PIM
85-86	New Hampshire	H.E.	25	22	6	28	30	—	—	—	—	—
85-86	Washington	NHL	11	1	1	2	2	6	0	1	1	0
86-87	Washington	NHL	15	1	0	1	6	—	—	—	—	—
86-87	Binghamton	AHL	54	18	21	39	39	13	3	1	4	6
87-88	United States	National	49	26	20	46	30	—	—	—	—	—
87-88	United States	Olympic	6	1	2	3	0	—	—	—	—	—
87-88	Washington	NHL	8	1	1	2	17	9	2	1	3	0
88-89	Washington	NHL	74	11	19	30	94	6	1	0	1	12
89-90	Washington	NHL	70	18	14	32	104	14	2	2	4	8
90-91	Washington	NHL	68	11	19	30	99	9	1	2	3	8
91-92	Boston	NHL	78	31	29	60	147	15	4	0	4	10
92-93	Boston	NHL	79	26	25	51	126	4	1	1	2	2
93-94	Boston	NHL	42	5	10	15	74	5	0	1	1	2
94-95	Boston	NHL	35	5	6	11	68	—	—	—	—	—
95-96	Boston	NHL	59	9	13	22	86	—	—	—	—	—
95-96	St. Louis	NHL	14	2	4	6	22	11	3	2	5	10
96-97	St. Louis	NHL	17	2	1	3	24	6	0	0	0	33
97-98	Carolina	NHL	45	4	5	9	42	—	—	—	—	—
98-99	Ottawa	NHL	9	0	2	2	6	—	—	—	—	—
98-99	Phoenix	NHL	22	1	1	2	37	7	1	1	2	2
98-99	Springfield	AHL	13	5	3	8	10	—	—	—	—	—
	NHL	Totals	646	128	150	278	954	92	15	11	26	87
	AHL	Totals	67	23	24	47	49	13	3	1	4	6

Born; 1/16/66, Cambridge, Massachusetts. 5-11, 197. Drafted by Washington Capitals (2nd choice, 34th overall) in 1984 Entry Draft. Traded to Boston Bruins by Washington for Randy Burridge (6/21/91). Traded to St. Louis Blues by Boston for Kevin Sawyer and Steve Staios (3/8/96). Traded to Carolina Hurricanes by St. Louis for Alexander Godynyuk and Carolina's sixth round choice (Brad Voth) in 1998 Entry Draft (6/27/97). Signed as a free agent by Ottawa Senators (9/16/98). Signed as a free agent by Phoenix Coyotes (12/3/98). Last amateur club; New Hampshire (Hockey East).

Carl LeBlanc

Defenseman

Regular Season / Playoffs

Season	Team	League	GP	G	A	PTS	PIM	GP	G	A	PTS	PIM
92-93	Knoxville	ECHL	59	6	16	22	110	—	—	—	—	—
93-94	Knoxville	ECHL	68	15	42	57	157	3	0	1	1	12
94-95	Houston	IHL	2	0	0	0	5	—	—	—	—	—
94-95	Knoxville	ECHL	62	6	47	53	192	4	0	2	2	19
95-96	Knoxville	ECHL	61	3	31	34	86	8	0	3	3	32
96-97	Quad City	CoHL	72	2	38	40	101	15	0	8	8	14
97-98	Portland	AHL	2	0	0	0	0	—	—	—	—	—
97-98	Quad City	UHL	70	8	39	47	180	20	2	7	9	14
98-99	Quad City	UHL	66	6	46	52	173	12	0	1	1	20
	ECHL	Totals	250	30	136	166	545	15	0	6	6	63
	UHL	Totals	208	16	123	139	454	47	2	16	18	48

Born; 9/6/71, Drummondville, Quebec. 6-0, 205. Drafted by Washington Capitals (11th choice, 212nd overall) in 1991 Entry Draft. Selected by Missouri in 1999 UHL Expansion Draft. 1997-98 UHL Second Team All-Star. Member of 1996-97 CoHL Champion Quad City Mallards. Member of 1997-98 UHL Champion Quad City Mallards. Last amateur club; Beauport (QMJHL).

Denis LeBlanc

Forward

Regular Season / Playoffs

Season	Team	League	GP	G	A	PTS	PIM	GP	G	A	PTS	PIM
93-94	Moncton	AHL	2	0	0	0	0	—	—	—	—	—
94-95												
95-96												
96-97												
97-98												
98-99	Port Huron	UHL	2	0	1	1	0	—	—	—	—	—

Born; 1/18/72, Montreal, Quebec. 6-0, 214.

Francois LeBlanc

Goaltender

Regular Season / Playoffs

Season	Team	League	GP	W	L	T	MIN	SO	AVG	GP	W	L	MIN	SO	AVG
98-99	Tupelo	WPHL	7	0	5	0	319	0	4.51	—	—	—	—	—	—

Born; 2/22/73, Fredericton, Quebec. 5-11, 180. Last amateur club; New Brunswick (AUAA).

Ray LeBlanc

Goaltender

Regular Season / Playoffs

Season	Team	League	GP	W	L	T	MIN	SO	AVG	GP	W	L	MIN	SO	AVG
84-85	Pinebridge	ACHL	40	-	-	-	2178	0	4.13	—	—	—	—	—	—
85-86	Carolina	ACHL	42	-	-	-	2505	3	3.19	—	—	—	—	—	—
86-87	Flint	IHL	64	33	23	1	3417	0	3.90	4	1	3	233	0	4.38
87-88	Flint	IHL	62	27	19	8	3269	1	4.39	16	10	6	925	1	3.57
88-89	Flint	IHL	15	5	9	0	852	0	4.72	—	—	—	—	—	—
88-89	Saginaw	IHL	29	19	7	2	1655	0	3.59	1	0	1	59	0	3.05
88-89	New Haven	AHL	1	0	0	0	20	0	9.00	—	—	—	—	—	—
89-90	Indianapolis	IHL	23	15	6	2	1334	2	3.19	—	—	—	—	—	—
89-90	Fort Wayne	IHL	15	3	3	3	680	0	3.88	3	0	2	139	0	4.75
90-91	Fort Wayne	IHL	21	10	8	0	1072	0	3.86	—	—	—	—	—	—
90-91	Indianapolis	IHL	3	2	0	0	145	0	2.90	1	0	0	19	0	3.20
91-92	United States	National	17	5	10	1	891	0	3.63	—	—	—	—	—	—
91-92	United States	Olympic	8	5	2	1	463	2	2.20	—	—	—	—	—	—
91-92	Chicago	NHL	1	1	0	0	60	0	1.00	—	—	—	—	—	—
91-92	Indianapolis	IHL	25	14	9	2	1468	2	3.43	—	—	—	—	—	—
92-93	Indianapolis	IHL	56	23	22	7	3201	0	3.86	5	1	4	276	0	5.00
93-94	Indianapolis	IHL	2	0	1	0	112	0	4.25	—	—	—	—	—	—
93-94	Cincinnati	IHL	34	17	9	3	1779	1	3.51	5	0	3	159	0	3.39
94-95	Chicago	IHL	44	19	14	6	2375	1	3.26	3	0	3	177	0	4.73
95-96	Chicago	IHL	31	10	14	2	1614	0	3.61	—	—	—	—	—	—
96-97	Chicago	IHL	38	15	14	2	1911	2	3.23	—	—	—	—	—	—
97-98	Chicago	IHL	14	9	3	0	728	0	2.80	—	—	—	—	—	—
97-98	Flint	UHL	29	12	4	5	1304	2	3.64	—	—	—	—	—	—
98-99	Jacksonville	ECHL	53	29	19	1	2982	1	3.28	2	0	2	118	0	4.06
	IHL	Totals	476	221	161	38	25612	9	3.71	38	12	22	1754	1	3.97
	ACHL	Totals	82	-	-	-	4683	3	3.63	—	—	—	—	—	—

Born; 10/24/64, Fitchburg, Massachusetts. 5-10, 170. Signed as a free agent by Chicago Blackhawks (7/5/89). Last amateur club; Kitchener (OHL).

Peter LeBoutillier — Right Wing

Regular Season / Playoffs

Season	Team	League	GP	G	A	PTS	PIM	GP	G	A	PTS	PIM
95-96	Baltimore	AHL	68	7	9	16	228	11	0	0	0	33
96-97	Anaheim	NHL	23	1	0	1	121	—	—	—	—	—
96-97	Baltimore	AHL	47	6	12	18	175	—	—	—	—	—
97-98	Anaheim	NHL	12	1	1	2	55	—	—	—	—	—
97-98	Cincinnati	AHL	51	9	11	20	143	—	—	—	—	—
98-99	Cincinnati	AHL	63	12	12	24	189	3	0	0	0	2
	NHL	Totals	35	2	1	3	176	—	—	—	—	—
	AHL	Totals	229	34	44	78	735	14	0	0	0	35

Born; 1/11/75, Neepawa, Manitoba. 6-1, 195. Drafted by New York Islanders (6th choice, 144th overall) in 1993 Entry Draft. Re-entered NHL Entry Draft, Anaheim Mighty Ducks (5th choice, 133rd overall) in 1995 Entry Draft. Last amateur club; Red Deer (WHL).

Shayne LeBreton — Left Wing

Regular Season / Playoffs

Season	Team	League	GP	G	A	PTS	PIM	GP	G	A	PTS	PIM
95-96	Winston-Salem	SHL	9	2	2	4	48	—	—	—	—	—
95-96	Jacksonville	SHL	2	0	0	0	6	—	—	—	—	—
96-97	Alaska	WCHL	21	2	2	4	57	—	—	—	—	—
97-98	Odessa	WPHL	38	2	10	12	146	—	—	—	—	—
98-99	Odessa	WPHL	22	6	3	9	42	—	—	—	—	—
	WPHL	Totals	60	8	13	21	188	—	—	—	—	—
	SHL	Totals	11	2	2	4	54	—	—	—	—	—

Born; 7/24/74, Manchester, New Hampshire. 6-2, 190.

Daniel Leckelt — Defenseman

Regular Season / Playoffs

Season	Team	League	GP	G	A	PTS	PIM	GP	G	A	PTS	PIM
98-99	Mohawk Valley	UHL	73	0	9	9	141	—	—	—	—	—

Born; 11/26/74, Sherwood Park, Alberta. 5-11, 195. Last amateur club; Stoney Plain (Sr. AAA).

Mike Leclerc — Left Wing

Regular Season / Playoffs

Season	Team	League	GP	G	A	PTS	PIM	GP	G	A	PTS	PIM
96-97	Anaheim	NHL	5	1	1	2	0	1	0	0	0	0
96-97	Baltimore	AHL	71	29	27	56	134	—	—	—	—	—
97-98	Anaheim	NHL	7	0	0	0	6	—	—	—	—	—
97-98	Cincinnati	AHL	48	18	22	40	83	—	—	—	—	—
98-99	Cincinnati	AHL	65	25	28	53	153	3	0	1	1	19
98-99	Anaheim	NHL	7	0	0	0	4	1	0	0	0	0
	NHL	Totals	19	1	1	2	10	2	0	0	0	0
	AHL	Totals	184	72	77	149	370	3	0	1	1	19

Born; 11/10/76, Winnipeg, Manitoba. 6-1, 205. Drafted by Anaheim Mighty Ducks (3rd choice, 55th overall) in 1995 Entry Draft. Member of AHL 1996-97 All Rookie Team. Last amateur club; Brandon (WHL).

Eric Lecompte — Left Wing

Regular Season / Playoffs

Season	Team	League	GP	G	A	PTS	PIM	GP	G	A	PTS	PIM
94-95	Hull	QMJHL	12	11	9	20	58	—	—	—	—	—
94-95	St-Jean	QMJHL	18	9	10	19	54	—	—	—	—	—
94-95	Sherbrooke	QMJHL	34	22	29	51	111	4	2	2	4	4
94-95	Indianapolis	IHL	3	2	0	2	2	—	—	—	—	—
95-96	Indianapolis	IHL	79	24	20	44	131	—	—	—	—	—
96-97	Indianapolis	IHL	35	2	3	5	74	—	—	—	—	—
96-97	Fort Wayne	IHL	14	1	2	3	62	—	—	—	—	—
96-97	Worcester	AHL	8	0	1	1	4	—	—	—	—	—
97-98	Cincinnati	AHL	26	11	8	19	68	—	—	—	—	—
97-98	Indianapolis	IHL	46	7	11	18	52	—	—	—	—	—
98-99	Cincinnati	AHL	67	11	22	33	183	3	1	2	3	0
	IHL	Totals	177	36	36	72	321	—	—	—	—	—
	AHL	Totals	34	11	9	20	72	—	—	—	—	—

Born; 4/4/75, Montreal, Quebec. 6-4, 190. Drafted by Chicago Blackhawks (1st choice, 24th overall) in 1993 Entry Draft. Signed as a free agent by Anaheim Mighty Ducks (8/18/98). Last amateur club; Sherbrooke (QMJHL).

Greg Leeb — Center

Regular Season / Playoffs

Season	Team	League	GP	G	A	PTS	PIM	GP	G	A	PTS	PIM
98-99	Michigan	IHL	77	16	27	43	18	5	0	3	3	4

Born; 5/31/77, Red Deer, Alberta. 5-9, 160. Signed as a free agent by Dallas Stars (7/24/98). Last amateur club; Spokane (WHL).

Patrice Lefebvre — Right Wing

Regular Season / Playoffs

Season	Team	League	GP	G	A	PTS	PIM	GP	G	A	PTS	PIM
90-91	Springfield	AHL	1	0	0	0	2	—	—	—	—	—
90-91	Louisville	ECHL	26	17	26	43	32	—	—	—	—	—
90-91	Milwaukee	IHL	16	6	4	10	13	—	—	—	—	—
91-92												
92-93	Billingham	BHL	36	56	109	165	NA	—	—	—	—	—
93-94	Las Vegas	IHL	76	31	67	98	71	5	3	4	7	4
94-95	Las Vegas	IHL	75	32	62	94	74	10	2	3	5	2
95-96	Las Vegas	IHL	77	36	78	114	85	15	9	11	20	12
96-97	Las Vegas	IHL	82	21	73	94	94	3	0	2	2	2
97-98	Las Vegas	IHL	77	27	*89	*116	113	4	2	0	2	2
98-99	Washington	NHL	3	0	0	0	2	—	—	—	—	—
98-99	Las Vegas	IHL	42	11	26	37	40	—	—	—	—	—
98-99	Long Beach	IHL	14	1	12	13	8	8	0	3	3	2
	IHL	Totals	459	165	411	576	498	45	16	23	39	24

Born; 6/28/67, Montreal, Quebec. 5-6, 160. Signed as a free agent by Las Vegas Thunder (1993) and (1996). Signed as a free agent by Washington Capitals (12/23/99). Traded to Long Beach by Las Vegas to complete an earlier trade (12/98). 1997-98 IHL MVP. 1997-98 IHL FIrst Team All-Star.

Steph Lefebvre — Left Wing

Regular Season / Playoffs

Season	Team	League	GP	G	A	PTS	PIM	GP	G	A	PTS	PIM
98-99	Tulsa	CHL	2	0	0	0	0	—	—	—	—	—

Born; 2/10/75, Timmins, Ontario. 6-1, 225.

Manny Legace — Goaltender

Regular Season / Playoffs

Season	Team	League	GP	W	L	T	MIN	SO	AVG	GP	W	L	MIN	SO	AVG
94-95	Springfield	AHL	39	12	17	6	2169	2	3.54	—	—	—	—	—	—
95-96	Springfield	AHL	37	20	12	4	2196	*5	*2.27	4	1	3	220	0	4.91
96-97	Springfield	AHL	36	17	14	5	2119	1	3.03	12	9	3	745	*2	2.01
96-97	Richmond	ECHL	3	2	1	0	158	0	3.05	—	—	—	—	—	—
97-98	Springfield	AHL	6	4	2	0	345	0	2.78	—	—	—	—	—	—
97-98	Las Vegas	IHL	41	18	16	4	2107	1	3.16	4	1	3	237	0	4.05
98-99	Los Ange-les	NHL	17	2	9	2	899	0	2.60	—	—	—	—	—	—
98-99	Long Beach	IHL	33	22	8	1	1796	2	2.24	6	4	2	338	0	1.60
	AHL	Totals	118	53	45	15	6829	8	2.93	16	10	6	965	2	2.67

Born; 2/4/73, Toronto, Ontario. 5-9, 162. Drafted by Hartford Whalers (5th choice, 188th overall) in 1993 Entry Draft. Traded to Los Angeles Kings by Carolina Hurricanes for a conditional 1999 Entry Draft choice (7/31/98). Signed as a free agent by Detroit Red Wings (7/15/99). 1995-96 AHL First Team All-Star. 1995-96 AHL Top Goaltender. 1995-96 AHL Shared Harry "Hap" Holmes Memorial Trophy (fewest goals against) with Scott Langkow. Last amateur club;

Martin Legault — Goaltender

Regular Season / Playoffs

Season	Team	League	GP	W	L	T	MIN	SO	AVG	GP	W	L	MIN	SO	AVG
97-98	Michigan	IHL	1	0	1	0	55	0	4.36	—	—	—	—	—	—
97-98	Dayton	ECHL	7	4	3	0	383	0	4.23	—	—	—	—	—	—
97-98	Chesapeake	ECHL	16	4	6	2	751	0	3.68	1	0	0	6	0	0.00
98-99	Tulsa	CHL	43	9	25	6	2369	1	4.56	—	—	—	—	—	—
	ECHL	Totals	23	8	9	2	1134	0	3.86	1	0	0	6	0	0.00

Born; 1/26/74, Gloucester, Ontario. 5-9, 184. Last amateur club; Merrimack (Hockey East).

Shawn Legault — Defenseman

Regular Season / Playoffs

Season	Team	League	GP	G	A	PTS	PIM	GP	G	A	PTS	PIM
98-99	Austin	WPHL	55	2	4	6	291	—	—	—	—	—

Born; 5/22/77, Lega, Alberta. 6-2, 205. Last amateur club; Lebret (SJHL).

Mike Legg — Left Wing
Regular Season — Playoffs

Season	Team	League	GP	G	A	PTS	PIM	GP	G	A	PTS	PIM
98-99	HIFK Helsinki	Finland	9	1	1	2	8	—	—	—	—	—
98-99	KalPa Kuopio	Finland	37	6	6	12	24	—	—	—	—	—
98-99	Fort Wayne	IHL	2	0	0	0	0	—	—	—	—	—
98-99	Columbus	ECHL	49	19	33	52	24	—	—	—	—	—
98-99	San Antonio	CHL	10	5	7	12	11	—	—	—	—	—

Born; 5/25/75, London, Ontario. 5-11, 165. Drafted by New Jersey Devils (11th choice, 273rd overall) in 1993 Entry Draft. Last amateur club; Michigan (CCHA).

Jason Lehman — Defenseman
Regular Season — Playoffs

Season	Team	League	GP	G	A	PTS	PIM	GP	G	A	PTS	PIM
98-99	Thunder Bay	UHL	59	5	12	17	43	—	—	—	—	—
98-99	Asheville	UHL	9	0	1	1	4	4	0	1	1	2
	UHL	Totals	68	5	13	18	47	4	0	1	1	2

Born; 8/13/72, Kingston, Ontario. 5-11, 185. Last amateur club; St. Thomas (AUAA).

Jody Lehman — Goaltender
Regular Season — Playoffs

Season	Team	League	GP	W	L	T	MIN	SO	AVG	GP	W	L	MIN	SO	AVG
97-98	Wichita	CHL	2	2	0	0	120	0	3.50	8	4	4	463	0	3.63
98-99	South Carolina	ECHL	33	18	7	4	1743	1	2.72	3	0	3	230	0	2.87

Born; 7/1/75, North Battleford, Saskatchewan. 5-10, 180. Last amateur club; Saskatchewan (CWUAA).

Tero Lehtera — Left Wing
Regular Season — Playoffs

Season	Team	League	GP	G	A	PTS	PIM	GP	G	A	PTS	PIM
98-99	Fort Wayne	IHL	69	15	24	39	8	2	0	1	1	0

Born; 4/21/72, Espoo, Finland. 6-0, 185. Drafted by Florida Panthers (9th choice, 235th overall) in 1994 Entry Draft.

Guy Lehoux — Defenseman
Regular Season — Playoffs

Season	Team	League	GP	G	A	PTS	PIM	GP	G	A	PTS	PIM
91-92	St. John's	AHL	67	1	7	8	134	—	—	—	—	—
92-93	St. John's	AHL	42	3	2	5	89	—	—	—	—	—
92-93	Brantford	CoHL	13	0	5	5	28	4	0	1	1	15
93-94	St. John's	AHL	71	2	8	10	217	9	1	1	2	8
94-95	St. John's	AHL	77	4	9	13	255	5	0	0	0	2
95-96	St. John's	AHL	66	1	5	6	211	4	0	0	0	2
96-97	St. John's	AHL	69	1	6	7	229	11	0	2	2	20
97-98	St. John's	AHL	4	0	2	2	13	4	0	0	0	20
97-98	Schwenninger	Germany	49	0	7	7	120	—	—	—	—	—
98-99	Schwenninger	Germany	43	1	6	7	127	—	—	—	—	—
	AHL	Totals	396	12	39	51	1148	33	1	3	4	52

Born; 10/19/71, Disraeli, Quebec. 5-11, 185. Drafted by Toronto Maple Leafs (10th choice, 179th overall) in 1991 Entry Draft. Last amateur club; Drummondville (QMJHL).

Jurgen Leitner — Defenseman
Regular Season — Playoffs

Season	Team	League	GP	G	A	PTS	PIM	GP	G	A	PTS	PIM
97-98	Chesapeake	ECHL	63	5	3	8	49	3	0	0	0	0
98-99	Vipiteno											

Born; 6/26/77, Feltweg, Austria. 6-1, 202.

Brian Leitza — Goaltender
Regular Season — Playoffs

Season	Team	League	GP	W	L	T	MIN	SO	AVG	GP	W	L	MIN	SO	AVG
98-99	Kansas City	IHL	3	0	2	0	131	0	4.58	—	—	—	—	—	—
98-99	Arkansas	WPHL	29	11	13	1	1584	1	3.64	3	1	2	201	0	3.58

Born; 3/16/74, Waukegon, Illinois. 6-2, 185. Drafted by Pittsburgh Penguins (14th choice, 284th overall) in 1994 Entry Draft. Last amateur club; St. Cloud

David Lemanowicz — Goaltender
Regular Season — Playoffs

Season	Team	League	GP	W	L	T	MIN	SO	AVG	GP	W	L	MIN	SO	AVG
96-97	Carolina	AHL	33	11	18	0	1796	2	3.91	—	—	—	—	—	—
96-97	Port Huron	CoHL	3	1	2	0	168	0	3.94	—	—	—	—	—	—
97-98	New Haven	AHL	16	5	9	0	880	0	3.34	—	—	—	—	—	—
97-98	Tallahassee	ECHL	25	6	16	0	1330	0	5.37	—	—	—	—	—	—
98-99	Austin	WPHL	47	16	*22	6	2576	3	4.05	—	—	—	—	—	—
	AHL	Totals	49	16	27	0	2676	2	3.72	—	—	—	—	—	—

Born; 3/8/76, Edmonton, Alberta. 6-2, 190. Drafted by Florida Panthers (9th choice, 218th overall) in 1996 Entry Draft. Last amateur club; Spokane (WHL).

Sandy Lemarre — Right Wing
Regular Season — Playoffs

Season	Team	League	GP	G	A	PTS	PIM	GP	G	A	PTS	PIM
97-98	El Paso	WPHL	69	26	32	58	76	12	0	1	1	19
98-99	El Paso	WPHL	59	23	20	43	146	—	—	—	—	—
	WPHL	Totals	128	49	52	101	222	12	0	1	1	19

Born; 6/3/76, Montreal, Quebec. 6-0, 185. Member of 1997-98 WPHL Champion El Paso Buzzards.

Eric LeMarque — Center
Regular Season — Playoffs

Season	Team	League	GP	G	A	PTS	PIM	GP	G	A	PTS	PIM
91-92	Greensboro	ECHL	55	29	37	66	110	3	0	0	0	8
92-93												
93-94												
94-95												
95-96												
96-97												
97-98												
98-99	Arkansas	WPHL	12	3	5	8	2	—	—	—	—	—

Born; 7/1/69, West Hills, California. 5-10, 185. Drafted by Boston Bruins (12th choice, 224th overall) in 1987 Entry Draft. Last amateur club; Northern Michigan (WCHA).

Jocelyn Lemieux — Left Wing

Regular Season / Playoffs

Season	Team	League	GP	G	A	PTS	PIM	GP	G	A	PTS	PIM
86-87	St. Louis	NHL	53	10	8	18	94	5	0	1	1	6
87-88	St. Louis	NHL	23	1	0	1	42	5	0	0	0	15
87-88	Peoria	IHL	8	0	5	5	35	—	—	—	—	—
88-89	Montreal	NHL	1	0	1	1	0	—	—	—	—	—
88-89	Sherbrooke	AHL	73	25	28	53	134	4	3	1	4	6
89-90	Montreal	NHL	34	4	2	6	61	—	—	—	—	—
89-90	Chicago	NHL	39	10	11	21	47	18	1	8	9	28
90-91	Chicago	NHL	67	6	7	13	119	4	0	0	0	0
91-92	Chicago	NHL	78	6	10	16	80	18	3	1	4	33
92-93	Chicago	NHL	81	10	21	31	111	4	1	0	1	2
93-94	Chicago	NHL	66	12	8	20	63	—	—	—	—	—
93-94	Hartford	NHL	16	6	1	7	19	—	—	—	—	—
94-95	Hartford	NHL	41	6	5	11	32	—	—	—	—	—
95-96	Hartford	NHL	29	1	2	3	31	—	—	—	—	—
95-96	New Jersey	NHL	18	0	1	1	4	—	—	—	—	—
95-96	Calgary	NHL	20	4	4	8	10	4	0	0	0	0
96-97	Long Beach	IHL	28	4	10	14	54	—	—	—	—	—
96-97	Phoenix	NHL	2	1	0	1	0	2	0	0	0	4
97-98	Phoenix	NHL	30	3	3	6	27	—	—	—	—	—
97-98	Long Beach	IHL	10	3	5	8	24	—	—	—	—	—
97-98	Springfield	AHL	6	3	1	4	0	4	2	2	4	2
98-99	Long Beach	IHL	17	4	4	8	16	8	0	2	2	15
	NHL	Totals	598	79	84	163	740	60	5	10	15	88
	AHL	Totals	79	28	29	57	134	8	5	3	8	8
	IHL	Totals	63	11	19	30	129	8	0	2	2	15

Born; 11/18/67, Mont-Laurier, Quebec. 5-10, 200. Drafted by St. Louis Blues (1st choice, 10th overall) in 1986 Entry Draft. Traded to Montreal Canadiens by St. Louis with Darrell May and St. Louis' second round choice (Patrice Brisebois) in 1989 Entry Draft for Sergio Momesso and Vincent Riendeau, (8/9/88). Traded to Chicago Blackhawks by Montreal for Chicago's third round choice (Charles Poulin) in 1990 Entry Draft, (1/5/90). Traded to Hartford Whalers by Chicago with Frantisek Kucera for Gary Suter, Randy Cunneyworth and Hartford's third round choice (later traded to Vancouver—Vancouver selected Larry Courville) in 1995 Entry Draft, (3/11/94). Traded to New Jersey Devils by Hartford with Hartford's second round choice in 1998 Entry Draft for Jim Dowd and New Jersey's choice in 1997 Entry Draft (later traded to Calgary—Calgary selected Dmitri Kokorev), (12/19/95). Traded to Calgary Flames by New Jersey with Tommy Albelin and Cal Hulse for Phil Housley and Dan Keczmer, (2/26/96). Signed as a free agent by Phoenix Coyotes (3/18/97). Last amateur club; Laval (QMJHL).

Mike Lenarduzzi — Goaltender

Regular Season / Playoffs

Season	Team	League	GP	W	L	T	MIN	SO	AVG	GP	W	L	MIN	SO	AVG
91-92	Sault Ste. Marie	OHL	9	5	3	0	486	0	4.07	—	—	—	—	—	—
91-92	Ottawa	OHL	18	5	12	1	986	1	3.65	—	—	—	—	—	—
91-92	Sudbury	OHL	22	11	5	4	1201	2	4.20	11	4	7	651	0	3.50
91-92	Springfield	AHL	—	—	—	—	—	—	—	1	0	0	39	0	3.08
92-93	Springfield	AHL	36	10	17	5	1945	0	4.38	2	1	0	100	0	3.00
92-93	Hartford	NHL	3	1	1	1	168	0	3.21	—	—	—	—	—	—
93-94	Hartford	NHL	1	0	0	0	21	0	2.86	—	—	—	—	—	—
93-94	Springfield	AHL	22	5	7	2	984	0	4.45	—	—	—	—	—	—
93-94	Salt Lake City	IHL	4	0	4	0	211	0	6.26	—	—	—	—	—	—
94-95	London	CoHL	43	19	16	0	2198	0	4.69	5	1	3	274	0	4.37
95-96	Saginaw	CoHL	43	14	15	3	2153	0	4.32	5	1	4	299	0	3.82
96-97	Hershey	AHL	2	0	0	0	13	0	0.00	—	—	—	—	—	—
96-97	Mobile	ECHL	37	15	10	8	1932	1	3.66	1	0	1	60	0	4.00
97-98	Mobile	ECHL	44	21	13	2	2202	2	3.32	3	0	2	133	0	4.96
98-99	Milan	Italy													
98-99	Amarillo	WPHL	9	2	3	2	344	0	4.19	—	—	—	—	—	—
	NHL	Totals	4	1	1	1	189	0	3.17	—	—	—	—	—	—
	AHL	Totals	60	15	24	7	2942	0	4.39	3	1	0	139	0	3.02
	ECHL	Totals	81	36	23	10	4134	3	3.48	4	0	3	193	0	4.66
	CoHL	Totals	86	33	31	3	4351	0	4.51	10	2	7	573	0	4.08

Born; 9/14/72, London, Ontario. 6-1, 165. Drafted by Hartford Whalers (3rd choice, 57th overall) in 1990 Entry Draft. Last amateur club; Sudbury (OHL).

Taras Lendzyk — Goaltender

Regular Season / Playoffs

Season	Team	League	GP	W	L	T	MIN	SO	AVG	GP	W	L	MIN	SO	AVG
96-97	South Carolina	ECHL	47	28	10	7	2590	0	3.20	1	0	0	20	0	0.00
97-98	Richmond	ECHL	39	13	17	5	2088	1	3.79	—	—	—	—	—	—
98-99	Charlotte	ECHL	36	14	14	6	2005	0	3.32	—	—	—	—	—	—
	ECHL	Totals	122	55	41	18	6683	1	3.42	1	0	0	20	0	0.00

Born; 3/7/72, Wynyard, Saskatchewan. 5-9, 180. Member of 1996-97 ECHL Champion South Carolina Stingrays. Last amateur club; Minnesota-Duluth

Dmitri Leonov — Left Wing

Regular Season / Playoffs

Season	Team	League	GP	G	A	PTS	PIM	GP	G	A	PTS	PIM
96-97	Worcester	AHL	9	0	1	1	6	—	—	—	—	—
96-97	Baton Rouge	ECHL	55	14	24	38	66	—	—	—	—	—
97-98	Idaho	WCHL	63	21	43	64	152	4	2	3	5	17
98-99	Long Beach	IHL	34	6	4	10	59	8	0	0	0	9
98-99	Idaho	WCHL	42	7	21	28	89	1	1	0	1	2
	WCHL	Totals	105	28	64	92	241	5	3	3	6	19

Born; 2/5/75, Chelyabinsk, Russia. 5-10, 185. Last amateur club; Spokane

Francois Leroux — Left Wing

Regular Season / Playoffs

Season	Team	League	GP	G	A	PTS	PIM	GP	G	A	PTS	PIM
94-95	Greensboro	ECHL	36	16	16	32	79	17	8	9	17	78
94-95	Cornwall	AHL	18	5	0	5	23	—	—	—	—	—
95-96	Saginaw	CoHL	15	3	8	11	21	—	—	—	—	—
95-96	Jacksonville	ECHL	21	6	14	20	57	—	—	—	—	—
96-97	Jacksonville	ECHL	41	5	14	19	60	—	—	—	—	—
96-97	Charlotte	ECHL	17	6	7	13	14	3	1	1	2	2
97-98	Macon	CHL	26	15	10	25	54	—	—	—	—	—
97-98	Tulsa	CHL	33	20	18	38	74	4	0	1	1	20
98-99	Tulsa	CHL	62	23	40	63	64	—	—	—	—	—
	CHL	Totals	121	58	68	126	192	4	0	1	1	20
	ECHL	Totals	115	33	51	84	210	20	9	10	19	80

Born; 3/1/73, La Praire, Quebec. 5-11, 190. Traded to Tulsa by Macon with Mike Anastasio for Craig Coxe and Dave Wilejto (12/97). Last amateur club; Verdun (QMJHL)

Francois Leroux — Left Wing

Regular Season / Playoffs

Season	Team	League	GP	G	A	PTS	PIM	GP	G	A	PTS	PIM
88-89	St-Jean	QMJHL	57	8	34	42	185	—	—	—	—	—
88-89	Edmonton	NHL	2	0	0	0	0	—	—	—	—	—
89-90	Victoriaville	QMJHL	54	4	33	37	169	—	—	—	—	—
89-90	Edmonton	NHL	3	0	1	1	0	—	—	—	—	—
90-91	Edmonton	NHL	1	0	2	2	0	—	—	—	—	—
90-91	Cape Breton	AHL	71	2	7	9	124	4	0	1	1	19
91-92	Edmonton	NHL	4	0	0	0	7	—	—	—	—	—
91-92	Cape Breton	AHL	61	7	22	29	114	5	0	0	0	8
92-93	Edmonton	NHL	1	0	0	0	4	—	—	—	—	—
92-93	Cape Breton	AHL	55	10	24	34	139	16	0	5	5	29
93-94	Ottawa	NHL	23	0	1	1	70	—	—	—	—	—
93-94	Prince Edward Island	AHL	25	4	6	10	52	—	—	—	—	—
94-95	Prince Edward Island	AHL	45	4	14	18	137	—	—	—	—	—
94-95	Pittsburgh	NHL	40	0	2	2	114	12	0	2	2	14
95-96	Pittsburgh	NHL	66	2	9	11	161	18	1	1	2	20
96-97	Pittsburgh	NHL	59	0	3	3	81	3	0	0	0	0
97-98	Colorado	NHL	50	1	2	3	140	—	—	—	—	—
98-99	Grand Rapids	IHL	13	1	1	2	22	—	—	—	—	—
	NHL	Totals	249	3	20	23	577	33	1	3	4	34
	AHL	Totals	257	27	73	100	566	25	0	6	6	56

Born; 4/18/70, Ste.-Adele, Quebec. 6-6, 235. Drafted by Edmonton Oiles (1st choice, 19th overall) in 1988 Entry Draft. Claimed on waivers by Ottawa Senators from Edmonton (10/6/93). Claimed by Pittsburgh Penguins on waivers from Ottawa in Waiver Draft (1/18/95). Traded to Colorado Avalanche by Pittsburgh for Colorado's 3rd round choice (David Cameron) in 1998 Entry Draft (9/28/97). Signed as a free agent by Phoenix Coyotes (7/16/99). Member of 1992-93 AHL Champion Cape Breton Oilers. Last amateur club; Victoriaville (QMJHL).

Jean-Yves Leroux — Left Wing

Regular Season / Playoffs

Season	Team	League	GP	G	A	PTS	PIM	GP	G	A	PTS	PIM
96-97	Chiacgo	NHL	1	0	1	1	5	—	—	—	—	—
96-97	Indianapolis	IHL	69	14	17	31	112	4	1	0	1	2
97-98	Chicago	NHL	66	6	7	13	55	—	—	—	—	—
98-99	Chicago	NHL	40	3	5	8	21	—	—	—	—	—
98-99	Chicago	IHL	—	—	—	—	—	10	1	1	2	18
	NHL	Totals	107	9	13	22	81	—	—	—	—	—
	IHL	Totals	69	14	17	31	112	14	2	1	3	20

Born; 6/24/76, Montreal, Quebec. 6-2, 211. Drafted by Chicago Blackhawks (2nd choice, 40th overall) in 1994 Entry Draft. Last amateur club; Beauport (QMJHL).

Kelly Leroux — Defenseman

Regular Season / Playoffs

Season	Team	League	GP	G	A	PTS	PIM	GP	G	A	PTS	PIM
96-97	Johnstown	ECHL	27	0	1	1	57	—	—	—	—	—
97-98	Johnstown	ECHL	62	5	5	10	160	—	—	—	—	—
98-99	Fort Worth	CHL	69	3	14	17	107	—	—	—	—	—
	ECHL	Totals	89	5	6	11	217	—	—	—	—	—

Born; 3/2/72, Abbotsford, Saskatchewan. 6-2, 215. Selected by Fayetteville in CHL Dispersal Draft. Played in goal in one game while with Ft. Worth for 17:09, facing 13 shots and stopping them all. Last amateur club; Canisius (NCAA 3).

Lance Leslie — Goaltender

Regular Season / Playoffs

Season	Team	League	GP	W	L	T	MIN	SO	AVG	GP	W	L	MIN	SO	AVG
94-95	PEI	AHL	1	0	0	1	65	0	1.85	—	—	—	—	—	—
94-95	Thunder Bay	CoHL	42	*29	10	3	2420	*2	3.22	10	*7	2	587	*1	3.58
95-96	PEI	AHL	28	12	12	3	1444	1	3.86	—	—	—	—	—	—
95-96	Thunder Bay	CoHL	11	5	3	2	588	0	3.57	—	—	—	—	—	—
95-96	Toledo	ECHL	4	3	0	0	212	0	2.83	—	—	—	—	—	—
96-97	Louisville	ECHL	22	10	8	3	1249	0	3.75	—	—	—	—	—	—
96-97	Kentucky	AHL	14	3	8	2	731	0	4.02	—	—	—	—	—	—
97-98	Louisville	ECHL	48	19	20	4	2691	2	3.50	—	—	—	—	—	—
98-99	Wichita	CHL	43	21	16	6	2484	1	3.45	—	—	—	—	—	—
	AHL	Totals	43	15	20	6	2240	1	3.86	—	—	—	—	—	—
	ECHL	Totals	74	32	28	7	4152	2	3.54	—	—	—	—	—	—
	CoHL	Totals	53	34	13	5	3008	2	3.29	10	7	2	587	1	3.58

Born; 6/21/74, Dawson Creek, British Columbia. 5-10, 190. Signed as a free agent by Ottawa Senators (10/4/93). 1994-95 CoHL First All-Star Team. 1994-95 CoHL Rookie of the Year. Member of 1994-95 CoHL champion Thunder Bay Senators. Last amateur club; Tri-City (WHL). Note: PEI=Prince Edward Island.

David Lessard — Forward

Regular Season / Playoffs

Season	Team	League	GP	G	A	PTS	PIM	GP	G	A	PTS	PIM
96-97	Bakersfield	WCHL	63	34	45	79	95	1	0	0	0	0
97-98	New Mexico	WPHL	62	50	37	87	96	9	5	6	11	28
98-99	Toledo	ECHL	66	30	31	61	130	7	1	3	4	6

Born; 6/18/75, Tring Junction, Quebec. 6-0, 205. Last amateur club; Drummondville (QMJHL).

Owen Lessard — Left Wing

Regular Season / Playoffs

Season	Team	League	GP	G	A	PTS	PIM	GP	G	A	PTS	PIM
90-91	Indianapolis	IHL	73	8	14	22	52	1	0	0	0	0
91-92	Indianapolis	IHL	41	3	2	5	53	—	—	—	—	—
92-93	Brantford	CoHL	5	1	3	4	2	—	—	—	—	—
92-93	Dayton	ECHL	8	2	2	4	4	—	—	—	—	—
92-93	Indianapolis	IHL	1	0	0	0	2	—	—	—	—	—
93-94												
94-95												
95-96	Brantford	CoHL	1	0	0	0	0	—	—	—	—	—
96-97	Huntington	ECHL	61	13	31	44	19	—	—	—	—	—
97-98	Huntington	ECHL	5	0	1	1	2	4	0	0	0	0
98-99	Huntington	ECHL	1	0	0	0	0	—	—	—	—	—
	IHL	Totals	115	11	16	27	107	1	0	0	0	0
	ECHL	Totals	75	15	34	49	25	—	—	—	—	—
	CoHL	Totals	6	1	3	4	2	—	—	—	—	—

Born; 1/11/70, Sudbury, Ontario. 6-1, 196. Last amateur club; Western Ontario (OUAA).

Don Lester — Defenseman

Regular Season / Playoffs

Season	Team	League	GP	G	A	PTS	PIM	GP	G	A	PTS	PIM
94-95	Richmond	ECHL	26	1	16	17	32	—	—	—	—	—
95-96	Alaska	WCHL	45	9	34	43	82	5	0	0	0	6
96-97	Alaska	WCHL	30	6	24	30	61	—	—	—	—	—
97-98	Idaho	WCHL	10	1	11	12	12	—	—	—	—	—
97-98	Bakersfield	WCHL	32	4	21	25	55	—	—	—	—	—
97-98	Phoenix	WCHL	21	1	5	6	38	9	1	4	5	6
98-99	Colorado	WCHL	52	4	23	27	75	3	0	0	0	4
	WCHL	Totals	148	20	86	106	256	17	1	4	5	16

Born; 4/29/70. Forest, Ontario. 5-11, 180. Selected by Idaho Steelheads in WCHL Dispersal Draft (1997). Traded to Bakersfield with Kelly Hrycun for Scott Davis (11/97). Traded to Tucson by Bakersfield for Aigars Mironovics (2/98). Traded to Phoenix by Tucson with Zdenek Sikl for Barry Cummins (2/98). Traded to Colorado by Phoenix with a player to be named later for Stu Kulak and Marc Salsman (9/98). Last amateur club; Alaska-Fairbanks (CCHA).

Alan Letang — Defenseman

Regular Season / Playoffs

Season	Team	League	GP	G	A	PTS	PIM	GP	G	A	PTS	PIM
95-96	Fredericton	AHL	71	0	26	26	40	10	0	3	3	4
96-97	Fredericton	AHL	60	2	9	11	8	—	—	—	—	—
97-98	Augsburg	Germany	17	0	1	1	4	—	—	—	—	—
98-99	Michigan	IHL	12	3	3	6	0	5	0	2	2	0
98-99	Canada	National	42	3	9	12	20	—	—	—	—	—
98-99	EV Zug	Switz.	—	—	—	—	—	9	0	4	4	4
	AHL	Totals	131	2	35	37	48	10	0	3	3	4

Born; 9/4/75, Renfrew, Ontario. 6-0, 185. Drafted by Montreal Canadiens (10th choice, 203rd overall) in 1993 Entry Draft. Last amateur club; Sarnia (OHL).

Trevor Letowski — Center

Regular Season / Playoffs

Season	Team	League	GP	G	A	PTS	PIM	GP	G	A	PTS	PIM
97-98	Springfield	AHL	75	11	20	31	26	4	1	0	1	2
98-99	Phoenix	NHL	14	2	2	4	2	—	—	—	—	—
98-99	Springfield	AHL	67	32	35	67	46	3	1	0	1	2
	AHL	Totals	142	43	55	98	72	7	2	0	2	4

Born; 4/5/77, Thunder Bay, Ontario. 5-10, 170. Drafted by Phoenix Coyotes (6th choice, 174th overall) in 1996 Entry Draft. Last amateur club; Sarnia (OHL).

Scott Levins — Right Wing

Regular Season / Playoffs

Season	Team	League	GP	G	A	PTS	PIM	GP	G	A	PTS	PIM
90-91	Moncton	AHL	74	12	26	38	133	4	0	0	0	4
91-92	Moncton	AHL	69	15	18	33	271	11	3	4	7	30
92-93	Winnipeg	NHL	9	0	1	1	18	—	—	—	—	—
92-93	Moncton	AHL	54	22	26	48	158	5	1	3	4	14
93-94	Florida	NHL	29	5	6	11	69	—	—	—	—	—
93-94	Ottawa	NHL	33	3	5	8	93	—	—	—	—	—
94-95	Ottawa	NHL	24	5	6	11	51	—	—	—	—	—
94-95	Prince Edward Island	AHL	6	0	4	4	14	—	—	—	—	—
95-96	Ottawa	NHL	27	0	2	2	80	—	—	—	—	—
95-96	Detroit	IHL	9	0	0	0	9	—	—	—	—	—
96-97	Springfield	AHL	68	24	23	47	267	11	5	4	9	37
97-98	Phoenix	NHL	2	0	0	0	5	—	—	—	—	—
97-98	Springfield	AHL	79	28	39	67	177	4	2	0	2	24
98-99	New Haven	AHL	80	32	26	58	189	—	—	—	—	—
	NHL	Totals	124	13	20	33	316	—	—	—	—	—
	AHL	Totals	430	133	162	295	1209	35	10	11	21	109

Born; 1/30/70, Apokane, Washington. 6-4, 210. Drafted by Winnipeg Jets (4th choice, 75th overall) in 1990 Entry Draft. Claimed by Florida Panthers in NHL Expansion Draft (6/24/93). Traded to Ottawa Senators by Florida with Evgeny Davydov, Florida's sixth round choice (Mike Gaffney) in 1994 Entry Draft and Dallas' fourth round choice (previously acquired by Florida—Ottawa selected Kevin Bolibruck) in 1995 Entry Draft for Bob Kudelski (1/6/94). Signed as a free agent by Phoenix Coyotes (10/3/96). Signed as a free agent by Carolina Hurricanes (8/18/98). Last amateur club; Tri-Cities (WHL).

Adam Lewis — Left Wing

Regular Season / Playoffs

Season	Team	League	GP	G	A	PTS	PIM	GP	G	A	PTS	PIM
98-99	Birmingham	ECHL	54	5	9	14	80	5	0	0	0	4

Born; 2/3/78, Woodstock, Ontario. 6-0, 198. Last amateur club; Kitchener (OHL).

Roger Lewis — Right Wing

Regular Season / Playoffs

Season	Team	League	GP	G	A	PTS	PIM	GP	G	A	PTS	PIM
97-98	Memphis	CHL	1	0	0	0	0	—	—	—	—	—
97-98	Muskegon	UHL	46	9	7	16	54	—	—	—	—	—
98-99	Corpus Christi	WPHL	66	4	17	21	65	4	0	1	1	9

Born; 4/30/72, Houghton, Michigan. 5-7, 172. Last amateur club; Northern Michigan (CCHA).

Jeff Libby — Defenseman

Regular Season / Playoffs

Season	Team	League	GP	G	A	PTS	PIM	GP	G	A	PTS	PIM
97-98	Utah	IHL	47	1	5	6	25	1	0	0	0	0
97-98	Kentucky	AHL	8	0	3	3	4	3	0	0	0	4
98-99	Lowell	AHL	5	0	0	0	2	—	—	—	—	—
	AHL	Totals	13	0	3	3	6	3	0	0	0	4

Born; 3/1/74, Waterville, Maine. 6-3, 215. Signed as a free agent by New York Islanders (5/12/97). Last amateur club; Maine (Hockey East).

Chris Libett — Defenseman

Regular Season / Playoffs

Season	Team	League	GP	G	A	PTS	PIM	GP	G	A	PTS	PIM
98-99	Richmond	ECHL	37	0	6	6	23	—	—	—	—	—
98-99	Pensacola	ECHL	28	1	4	5	36	—	—	—	—	—
	ECHL	Totals	65	1	10	11	59	—	—	—	—	—

Born; 1/29/75, West Bloomfield, Michigan. 6-2, 192. Last amateur club; Lowell (Hockey East).

Brett Lievers — Center

Regular Season / Playoffs

Season	Team	League	GP	G	A	PTS	PIM	GP	G	A	PTS	PIM
95-96	Utah	IHL	79	36	27	63	42	20	10	3	13	6
96-97	Utah	IHL	74	22	26	48	11	7	2	0	2	0
97-98	Revier Lowen	Germany	27	10	10	20	4	—	—	—	—	—
97-98	Fribiourg	Switz.	11	2	6	8	2	—	—	—	—	—
98-99	Kassel	Germany	29	5	14	19	8	—	—	—	—	—
	IHL	Totals	153	58	53	111	53	27	12	3	15	6

Born; 6/18/71, Syracuse, New York. 6-1, 190. Drafted by New York Rangers (13th choice, 223rd overall) in 1990 Entry Draft. Signed as a free agent by Ottawa Senators (7/29/96). 1995-96 IHL USA-born rookie of the year. Member of 1995-96 IHL champion Utah Grizzlies. Last amateur club; St. Cloud (WCHA).

John Lilley — Right Wing

Regular Season / Playoffs

Season	Team	League	GP	G	A	PTS	PIM	GP	G	A	PTS	PIM
93-94	United States	National	58	27	23	50	55	5	1	3	4	9
93-94	United States	Olympic	8	3	1	4	4	—	—	—	—	—
93-94	Anaheim	NHL	13	1	6	7	8	—	—	—	—	—
93-94	San Diego	IHL	2	2	1	3	0	—	—	—	—	—
94-95	San Diego	IHL	45	9	15	24	71	2	0	0	0	2
94-95	Anaheim	NHL	9	2	2	4	5	—	—	—	—	—
95-96	Baltimore	AHL	12	2	4	6	7	—	—	—	—	—
95-96	Anaheim	NHL	1	0	0	0	0	—	—	—	—	—
95-96	Los Angeles	IHL	64	12	20	32	112	—	—	—	—	—
96-97	Detroit	IHL	1	0	0	0	2	—	—	—	—	—
96-97	Rochester	AHL	1	0	2	2	15	—	—	—	—	—
96-97	Providence	AHL	63	12	25	37	130	10	3	0	3	24
97-98	Dusseldorf	Germany	44	9	14	23	120	3	0	0	0	4
98-99	Kassel	Germany	18	1	3	4	22	—	—	—	—	—
	NHL	Totals	23	3	8	11	13	—	—	—	—	—
	IHL	Totals	112	23	36	59	185	2	0	0	0	2
	AHL	Totals	76	14	31	45	152	10	3	0	3	24

Born; 8/3/72, Wakefield, Massachusetts. 5-9, 175. Drafted by Winnipeg Jets (8th choice, 140th overall) in 1990 Entry Draft. Signed as a free agent by Anaheim Mighty Ducks (3/9/94). Last amateur club; Seattle (WHL).

Billy Lincoln — Right Wing

Regular Season / Playoffs

Season	Team	League	GP	G	A	PTS	PIM	GP	G	A	PTS	PIM
97-98	Hampton Roads	ECHL	52	4	8	12	47	—	—	—	—	—
98-99	Fresno	WCHL	59	14	16	30	39	5	1	3	4	2

Born; 9/20/72, Norwell, Massachusetts. 6-1, 195. Last amateur club; Vermont (ECAC).

Juha Lind — Left Wing

Regular Season / Playoffs

Season	Team	League	GP	G	A	PTS	PIM	GP	G	A	PTS	PIM
97-98	Dallas	NHL	39	2	3	5	6	15	2	2	4	8
97-98	Michigan	IHL	8	2	2	4	2	—	—	—	—	—
98-99	Jokerit	Finland	50	20	19	39	22	3	3	1	4	2

Born; 2/2/74, Helsinki, Finland. 5-11, 178. Drafted by Dallas Stars (6th choice, 178th overall) in 1992 Entry Draft.

Pierre Lindahl — Defenseman

Regular Season / Playoffs

Season	Team	League	GP	G	A	PTS	PIM	GP	G	A	PTS	PIM
97-98	Wichita	CHL	18	0	2	2	81	—	—	—	—	—
97-98	Reno	WCHL	35	0	3	3	69	3	0	0	0	2
98-99	Paisley	BNL	38	3	4	7	66	—	—	—	—	—

Born; 9/22/76, Manmoe, Sweden. 6-0, 190.

Anders Lindberg — Defenseman

Regular Season / Playoffs

Season	Team	League	GP	G	A	PTS	PIM	GP	G	A	PTS	PIM
98-99	Odessa	WPHL	68	1	6	7	63	3	0	0	0	0

Born; 5/20/64. Vasby, Sweden. 6-1, 210.

Chris Lindberg — Right Wing

Regular Season / Playoffs

Season	Team	League	GP	G	A	PTS	PIM	GP	G	A	PTS	PIM
89-90	Binghamton	AHL	32	4	4	8	36	—	—	—	—	—
90-91	Canada	National	55	25	31	56	53	—	—	—	—	—
90-91	Springfield	AHL	1	0	0	0	2	1	0	0	0	0
91-92	Canada	National	56	33	35	68	63	—	—	—	—	—
91-92	Canada	Olympic	8	1	4	5	4	—	—	—	—	—
91-92	Calgary	NHL	17	2	5	7	17	—	—	—	—	—
92-93	Calgary	NHL	62	9	12	21	18	2	0	1	1	2
93-94	Quebec	NHL	37	6	8	14	12	—	—	—	—	—
93-94	Cornwall	AHL	23	14	13	27	28	13	11	3	14	10
94-95	Krefeld	Germany	42	25	41	66	103	15	4	10	14	20
95-96	Krefield	Germany	49	21	35	56	96	—	—	—	—	—
96-97	Krefeld	Germany	47	37	35	72	129	3	0	1	1	6
97-98	EV Zug	Switz.	2	1	1	2	0	17	6	15	21	22
97-98	Krefeld	Germany	15	2	7	9	33	—	—	—	—	—
97-98	Grand Rapids	IHL	18	8	14	22	25	—	—	—	—	—
98-99	Rapperswil-Jona	Switz.	43	22	28	50	114	5	1	2	3	4
	NHL	Totals	116	17	25	42	47	2	0	1	1	2
	AHL	Totals	56	18	17	35	66	14	11	3	14	10

Born; 4/16/67, Fort Francis, Ontario. 6-1, 185. Signed as a free agent by Hartford Whalers (3/17/89). Signed as a free agent by Calgary Flames (8/91). Selected by Ottawa Senators in NHL Expansion Draft (6/18/92). Traded to Calgary Flames by Ottawa for Mark Osiecki (6/23/92). Signed as a free agent by Quebec Nordiques (8/9/93). Last amateur club; Minnesota-Duluth (WCHA).

Terry Lindgren — Defenseman

Regular Season / Playoffs

Season	Team	League	GP	G	A	PTS	PIM	GP	G	A	PTS	PIM
96-97	Kentucky	AHL	35	4	3	7	58	1	0	0	0	0
96-97	Louisville	ECHL	29	1	9	10	66	—	—	—	—	—
97-98	Kentucky	AHL	16	0	3	3	33	2	0	0	0	0
97-98	Louisville	ECHL	56	6	16	22	142	—	—	—	—	—
98-99	Miami	ECHL	66	6	25	31	114	—	—	—	—	—
	AHL	Totals	51	4	6	10	91	3	0	0	0	0
	ECHL	Totals	85	7	25	32	208	—	—	—	—	—

Born; 10/11/75, Edmonton, Alberta. 6-1, 187. Last amateur club; Red Deer,

Craig Lindsay — Goaltender
Regular Season / Playoffs

Season	Team	League	GP	W	L	T	MIN	SO	AVG	GP	W	L	MIN	SO	AVG
97-98	Memphis	CHL	53	18	*29	4	2966	1	3.72	1	0	1	58	0	3.09
98-99	Paisley	BNL	40	—	—	—	2330	—	4.87	—	—	—	—	—	—
98-99	Sheffield	BSL	2	—	—	—	80	0	5.25	1	—	—	40	0	3.00

Born; 7/23/74, Toronto, Ontario. 6-3, 195. Last amateur club; Lowell (Hockey

Ryan Lindsay — Right Wing
Regular Season / Playoffs

Season	Team	League	GP	G	A	PTS	PIM	GP	G	A	PTS	PIM
98-99	Canada	National	48	11	19	30	42	—	—	—	—	—

Born; 4/13/76, Simcoe, Ontario. 5-11, 185. Last amateur club; New Brunswick (AUAA).

Scott Lindsay — Right Wing
Regular Season / Playoffs

Season	Team	League	GP	G	A	PTS	PIM	GP	G	A	PTS	PIM
93-94	Providence	AHL	2	0	1	1	0	—	—	—	—	—
93-94	Charlotte	ECHL	62	20	22	42	64	3	1	1	2	15
94-95	Charlotte	ECHL	9	2	0	2	13	—	—	—	—	—
94-95	Raleigh	ECHL	7	0	0	0	4	—	—	—	—	—
95-96												
96-97	Alberta	CWUAA	45	23	20	43	84	—	—	—	—	—
96-97	Alberta	CWUAA	35	7	13	20	97	—	—	—	—	—
98-99	Huntsville	CHL	14	6	1	7	36	15	5	6	11	16

Born; 8/29/72, Red Deer, Alberta. 6-2, 205. Member of 1998-99 CHL Champion Huntsville Channel Cats.

Fredrik Lindquist — Right Wing
Regular Season / Playoffs

Season	Team	League	GP	G	A	PTS	PIM	GP	G	A	PTS	PIM
98-99	Edmonton	NHL	8	0	0	0	2	—	—	—	—	—
98-99	Hamilton	AHL	57	18	36	54	20	11	2	2	4	2

Born; 6/21/73, Sodertalje, Sweden. 6-0, 190. Drafted by New Jersey Devils (4th choice, 55th overall) in 1991 Entry Draft. Traded to Edmonton Oilers by New Jersey with New Jersey's fourth (Kristian Antila) and fifth (Oleg Smirnov) round choices in 1998 Entry Draft for Pittsburgh's third round choice (previously acquired, New Jersey selected Brian Gionta) in 1998 Entry Draft (6/27/98). Previous European club; Djurgarden (Sweden).

David Ling — Right Wing
Regular Season / Playoffs

Season	Team	League	GP	G	A	PTS	PIM	GP	G	A	PTS	PIM
95-96	Saint John	AHL	75	24	32	56	179	9	0	5	5	12
96-97	Montreal	NHL	2	0	0	0	0	—	—	—	—	—
96-97	Saint John	AHL	5	0	2	2	19	—	—	—	—	—
96-97	Fredericton	AHL	48	22	36	58	229	—	—	—	—	—
97-98	Fredericton	AHL	67	25	41	66	148	—	—	—	—	—
97-98	Indianapolis	IHL	12	8	6	14	30	5	4	1	5	31
98-99	Kansas City	IHL	82	30	42	72	112	3	1	0	1	20
	AHL	Totals	195	71	111	182	575	9	0	5	5	12
	IHL	Totals	94	38	48	86	142	8	5	1	6	51

Born; 1/9/75, Halifax, Nova Scotia. 5-9, 185. Drafted by Quebec Nordiques (9th choice, 179th overall) in 1993 Entry Draft. Traded to Calgary Flames by Quebec with Quebec's 9th round choice (Steve Shirreffs) in 1995 Entry Draft for Calgary's 9th round choice (Chris George) in 1995 Entry Draft. Traded to Montreal Canadiens by Calgary with Calgary's 6th choice in 1998 Entry Draft (Gordie Dwyer) for Scott Fraser (10/24/96). Traded to Chicago Blackhawks by Montreal for Martin Gendron (3/14/98). Last amateur club; Kingston (OHL).

Jamie Ling — Center
Regular Season / Playoffs

Season	Team	League	GP	G	A	PTS	PIM	GP	G	A	PTS	PIM
96-97	Hershey	AHL	2	0	2	2	2	—	—	—	—	—
96-97	Milwaukee	IHL	3	0	0	0	0	—	—	—	—	—
96-97	Mobile	ECHL	66	19	61	80	51	3	0	0	0	2
97-98	Baton Rouge	ECHL	24	4	12	16	10	—	—	—	—	—
97-98	Chesapeake	ECHL	47	14	28	42	36	3	0	1	1	0
98-99	Cincinnati	IHL	2	1	2	3	0	—	—	—	—	—
98-99	Indianapolis	IHL	1	0	1	1	0	—	—	—	—	—
98-99	Dayton	ECHL	70	39	56	95	32	4	1	4	5	4
	IHL	Totals	6	1	3	4	0	—	—	—	—	—
	ECHL	Totals	207	76	157	233	129	10	1	5	6	6

Born; 2/22/73, Charlottetown, Prince Edward Island. 5-11, 190. Traded to Mobile by Baton Rouge for Anton Fedorov (12/97). Traded to Chesapeake by Mobile for Jon Larson (12/97). 1998-99 ECHL Sportsmanship Award. Last amateur club; Notre Dame (CCHA).

Steve Lingren — Defenseman
Regular Season / Playoffs

Season	Team	League	GP	G	A	PTS	PIM	GP	G	A	PTS	PIM
93-94	Victoria	WHL	56	14	21	35	118	—	—	—	—	—
93-94	Kalamazoo	IHL	2	0	0	0	0	—	—	—	—	—
94-95	Kalamazoo	IHL	4	0	0	0	0	—	—	—	—	—
94-95	Dayton	ECHL	64	11	23	34	128	9	2	8	10	16
95-96	Michigan	IHL	2	0	0	0	2	—	—	—	—	—
95-96	Cornwall	AHL	1	0	0	0	0	—	—	—	—	—
95-96	Dayton	ECHL	51	15	28	43	83	—	—	—	—	—
96-97	Hershey	AHL	40	3	10	13	67	12	1	2	3	8
96-97	Dayton	ECHL	9	2	5	7	15	—	—	—	—	—
97-98	Hershey	AHL	63	12	18	30	89	7	0	3	3	4
98-99	Kentucky	AHL	74	11	19	30	60	12	0	4	4	0
	AHL	Totals	178	26	47	73	216	31	1	9	10	12
	IHL	Totals	8	0	0	0	2	—	—	—	—	—
	ECHL	Totals	124	28	56	84	226	9	2	8	10	16

Born; 4/15/73, Lake Cowichan, British Columbia. 6-0, 185. 1995-96 ECHL First Team All-Star. Member of 1996-97 AHL Champion Hershey Bears. Signed as a free agent by San Jose Sharks (7/23/98). Last amateur club; Victoria (WHL).

Brad Link — Goaltender
Regular Season / Playoffs

Season	Team	League	GP	W	L	T	MIN	SO	AVG	GP	W	L	MIN	SO	AVG
98-99	Wichita	CHL	1	0	0	0	31	0	1.97	—	—	—	—	—	—

Born; 2/3/57, Buffalo, New York. 5-11, 190.

Tony Link — Defenseman
Regular Season / Playoffs

Season	Team	League	GP	G	A	PTS	PIM	GP	G	A	PTS	PIM
98-99	Anchorage	WCHL	16	1	2	3	12	2	0	0	0	0

Born; 6-2, 220.

Eric Linkowski — Defenseman
Regular Season / Playoffs

Season	Team	League	GP	G	A	PTS	PIM	GP	G	A	PTS	PIM
98-99	Chesapeake	ECHL	55	1	6	7	22	—	—	—	—	—

Born; 10/22/75, Mt. Vernon, New York. 5-10, 190. Last amateur club; Connecticut (NCAA 3).

Kaj Linna — Defenseman
Regular Season / Playoffs

Season	Team	League	GP	G	A	PTS	PIM	GP	G	A	PTS	PIM
95-96	Prince Edward Island	AHL	67	6	24	30	32	5	1	2	3	4
96-97	HIFK Helsinki	Finland	46	9	12	21	79	—	—	—	—	—
97-98	HIFK Helsinki	Finland	45	8	10	18	71	9	1	4	5	8
98-99	Milwaukee	IHL	11	0	1	1	25	—	—	—	—	—

Born; 1/24/71, Helsinki, Finland. 6-2, 209. Drafted by Ottawa Senators (7th choice, 183rd overall) in 1995 Entry Draft. Signed as a free agent by Nashville Predators (8/26/98). Last amateur club; Boston College (Hockey East).

Richard Lintner — Defenseman

Season	Team	League	GP	G	A	PTS	PIM	GP	G	A	PTS	PIM
			Regular Season					Playoffs				
97-98	Springfield	AHL	71	6	9	15	61	3	1	1	2	4
98-99	Springfield	AHL	8	0	1	1	16	—	—	—	—	—
98-99	Milwaukee	IHL	66	9	16	25	75	—	—	—	—	—
	AHL	Totals	79	6	10	16	77	3	1	1	2	4

Born; 11/15/77, Trencin, Czechoslovakia. 6-3, 194. Drafted by Phoenix Coyotes (4th choice, 119th overall) in 1996 Entry Draft. Traded to Nashville Predators by Phoenix with Cliff Ronning for future considerations (10/31/98). Last European club; Spisska (Slovakia).

Chris Lipsett — Forward

Season	Team	League	GP	G	A	PTS	PIM	GP	G	A	PTS	PIM
			Regular Season					Playoffs				
96-97	Roanoke	ECHL	70	19	27	46	40	3	1	2	3	0
97-98	Roanoke	ECHL	67	32	33	65	47	9	0	2	2	4
98-99	Lowell	AHL	2	1	0	1	0	—	—	—	—	—
98-99	Roanoke	ECHL	21	7	6	13	19	—	—	—	—	—
98-99	Pee Dee	ECHL	45	24	21	45	34	13	*13	4	17	20
	ECHL	Totals	203	82	87	169	140	25	14	8	22	24

Born; 9/24/74, Ottawa, Ontario. 6-0, 187. Last amateur club; Clarkson (ECAC).

Chris LiPuma — Defenseman

Season	Team	League	GP	G	A	PTS	PIM	GP	G	A	PTS	PIM
			Regular Season					Playoffs				
92-93	Tampa Bay	NHL	15	0	5	5	34	—	—	—	—	—
92-93	Atlanta	IHL	66	4	14	18	379	9	1	1	2	35
93-94	Tampa Bay	NHL	27	0	4	4	77	—	—	—	—	—
93-94	Atlanta	IHL	42	2	10	12	254	11	1	1	2	28
94-95	Tampa Bay	NHL	1	0	0	0	0	—	—	—	—	—
94-95	Atlanta	IHL	41	5	12	17	191	—	—	—	—	—
94-95	Nashville	ECHL	1	0	0	0	0	—	—	—	—	—
95-96	Tampa Bay	NHL	21	0	0	0	13	—	—	—	—	—
95-96	Atlanta	IHL	48	5	11	16	146	—	—	—	—	—
96-97	San Jose	NHL	8	0	0	0	22	—	—	—	—	—
96-97	Kentucky	AHL	48	6	17	23	93	4	0	3	3	6
97-98	Orlando	IHL	13	1	4	5	63	—	—	—	—	—
97-98	San Antonio	IHL	60	1	10	11	116	—	—	—	—	—
98-99	Chicago	IHL	34	0	10	10	186	—	—	—	—	—
	NHL	Totals	72	0	9	9	146	—	—	—	—	—
	IHL	Totals	304	18	71	89	1335	20	2	2	4	63

Born; 3/23/71, Bridgeview, Illinois. 6-1, 210. Signed as a free agent by Tampa Bay Lightning (6/29/92). Signed as a free agent by San Jose Sharks (8/26/96). Claimed on waivers by New Jersey Devils from San Jose (3/18/97). Traded to San Antonio by Orlando with Dave Smith and Dave Chyzowski for Scott Hollis, Grigori Pantaleyev and Dave MacIntyre (11/97). Member of 1993-94 IHL champion Atlanta Knights. Last amateur club; Kitchener (OHL).

Ron Lisczewski — Goaltender

Season	Team	League	GP	W	L	T	MIN	SO	AVG	GP	W	L	MIN	SO	AVG
			Regular Season							Playoffs					
98-99	Arkansas	WPHL	1	0	0	0	3	0	0.00	—	—	—	—	—	—

Born; 4/26/1960.

Dane Litke — Defenseman

Season	Team	League	GP	G	A	PTS	PIM	GP	G	A	PTS	PIM
			Regular Season					Playoffs				
97-98	Nashville	CHL	61	11	30	41	26	9	5	5	10	2
98-99	Florida	ECHL	67	10	25	35	21	5	0	1	1	0

Born; 8/11/72, Beausejour, Manitoba. 5-10, 180. Selected by Topeka in 1998 CHL Dispersal Draft. Last amateur club; North Dakota (WCHA).

Neil Little — Goaltender

Season	Team	League	GP	W	L	T	MIN	SO	AVG	GP	W	L	MIN	SO	AVG
			Regular Season							Playoffs					
93-94	RPI	ECAC	27	16	7	4	1570	0	3.36	—	—	—	—	—	—
93-94	Hershey	AHL	1	0	0	0	18	0	3.23	—	—	—	—	—	—
94-95	Hershey	AHL	19	5	7	3	919	0	3.91	—	—	—	—	—	—
94-95	Johnstown	ECHL	16	7	6	1	897	0	3.68	3	0	2	144	0	4.55
95-96	Hershey	AHL	48	21	18	6	2679	0	3.34	1	0	1	59	0	4.02
96-97	Philadelphia	AHL	54	31	12	7	3007	0	2.89	10	6	4	620	1	1.94
97-98	Philadelphia	AHL	51	*31	11	7	2961	0	2.94	*20	*15	*5	*1193	*3	*2.41
98-99	Grand Rapids	IHL	50	18	21	5	2740	3	3.15	—	—	—	—	—	—
	AHL	Totals	173	88	48	23	9584	0	3.13	31	21	10	1872	4	2.31

Born; 12/18/71, Medicine Hat, Alberta. 6-1, 175. Drafted by Philadelphia Flyers (11th choice, 226th overall) in 1991 Entry Draft. Member of 1997-98 AHL Champion Philadelphia Phantoms. Last amateur club; Rensselaer Polytechnic Institute (ECAC).

Frank Littlejohn — Right Wing

Season	Team	League	GP	G	A	PTS	PIM	GP	G	A	PTS	PIM
			Regular Season					Playoffs				
98-99	Arkansas	WPHL	43	3	4	7	71	—	—	—	—	—

Born; 2/3/77, Oshawa, Ontario. 5-11, 185. Last amateur club; Markham

David Littman — Goaltender

Season	Team	League	GP	W	L	T	MIN	SO	AVG	GP	W	L	MIN	SO	AVG
			Regular Season							Playoffs					
89-90	Rochester	AHL	14	5	6	1	681	0	3.26	—	—	—	—	—	—
89-90	Phoenix	IHL	18	8	7	2	1047	0	3.67	—	—	—	—	—	—
90-91	Buffalo	NHL	1	0	0	0	36	0	5.00	—	—	—	—	—	—
90-91	Rochester	AHL	*56	*33	13	5	*3155	3	3.04	8	4	2	378	0	2.54
91-92	Buffalo	NHL	1	0	1	0	60	0	4.00	—	—	—	—	—	—
91-92	Rochester	AHL	*61	*29	20	9	*3558	*3	2.93	15	8	7	879	*1	2.94
92-93	Tampa Bay	NHL	1	0	1	0	45	0	9.33	—	—	—	—	—	—
92-93	Atlanta	IHL	44	23	12	4	2390	0	3.36	3	1	2	178	0	2.70
93-94	Fredericton	AHL	16	8	7	0	872	0	4.33	—	—	—	—	—	—
93-94	Providence	AHL	25	10	11	3	1385	0	3.60	—	—	—	—	—	—
94-95	Richmond	ECHL	8	4	2	0	346	1	2.25	*17	*12	4	*952	*3	*2.33
95-96	Los Angeles	IHL	43	17	16	5	2244	1	3.88	—	—	—	—	—	—
96-97	San Antonio	IHL	45	20	16	5	2438	2	3.23	4	1	3	230	0	2.87
97-98	Orlando	IHL	44	21	13	6	2304	0	2.66	16	8	8	966	1	2.98
98-99	Orlando	IHL	55	32	17	1	2981	2	2.90	2	0	0	46	0	5.19
	NHL	Totals	3	0	2	0	141	0	5.96	—	—	—	—	—	—
	IHL	Totals	249	121	81	23	13404	5	3.25	25	10	13	1420	1	3.00
	AHL	Totals	172	85	57	18	9651	6	3.21	23	12	9	1257	1	2.82

Born; 6/13/67, Cranston, Rhode Island. 6-0, 175. Drafted by Buffalo Sabres (12th choice, 211th overall) in 1987 Entry Draft. Signed as a free agent by Tampa Bay Lightning (8/27/92). Signed as a free agent by Boston Bruins (8/6/93). 1990-91 Shared Harry "Hap" Holmes (fewest goals against-AHL) with Darcy Wakaluk. 1990-91 AHL First Team All-Star. 1991-92 AHL Second Team All-Star. Member of 1994-95 ECHL champion Richmond Renegades. Last amateur club; Boston College (Hockey East).

Kirk Llano — Defenseman

Season	Team	League	GP	G	A	PTS	PIM	GP	G	A	PTS	PIM
			Regular Season					Playoffs				
94-95		Belgium										
95-96	Winston-Salem	SHL	55	4	26	30	144	9	2	2	4	20
96-97		Germany										
97-98	Fort Wayne	IHL	2	0	0	0	0	—	—	—	—	—
97-98	Quad City	UHL	73	7	12	19	80	20	1	7	8	14
98-99	Colorado	WCHL	44	1	15	16	62	3	0	0	0	0

Born; 1/10/73, Calgary, Alberta. 5-11, 200. Member of 1997-98 UHL Champion Quad City Mallards.

Lonnie Loach — Left Wing

Season	Team	League	GP	G	A	PTS	PIM	GP	G	A	PTS	PIM
			Regular Season					Playoffs				
88-89	Flint	IHL	41	22	26	48	30	—	—	—	—	—
88-89	Saginaw	IHL	32	7	6	13	27	—	—	—	—	—
89-90	Indianapolis	IHL	3	0	0	0	0	—	—	—	—	—
89-90	Fort Wayne	IHL	54	15	33	48	40	5	4	2	6	15
90-91	Ft. Wayne	IHL	81	55	76	*131	45	19	5	11	16	13
91-92	Adirondack	AHL	67	37	49	86	69	19	*13	4	17	10
92-93	Ottawa	NHL	3	0	0	0	0	—	—	—	—	—
92-93	Los Angeles	NHL	50	10	13	23	27	1	0	0	0	0
92-93	Phoenix	IHL	4	2	3	5	10	—	—	—	—	—
93-94	Anaheim	NHL	3	0	0	0	2	—	—	—	—	—
93-94	San Diego	IHL	74	42	49	91	65	9	4	10	14	6
94-95	San Diego	IHL	13	3	10	13	21	—	—	—	—	—
94-95	Detroit	IHL	64	32	43	75	45	3	2	1	3	2
95-96	Detroit	IHL	79	35	51	86	75	11	1	5	6	8
96-97	San Antonio	IHL	70	24	37	61	45	9	1	3	4	10
97-98	San Antonio	IHL	52	7	29	36	22	—	—	—	—	—
97-98	Zuricher	Switz.	15	2	5	7	6	—	—	—	—	—
98-99	Laibach	Austria										
98-99	Long Beach	IHL	30	12	9	21	18	—	—	—	—	—
98-99	Kansas City	IHL	22	9	5	14	6	3	1	0	1	0
	NHL	Totals	56	10	13	23	29	1	0	0	0	0
	IHL	Totals	619	265	377	642	449	59	18	32	50	54

Born; 4/14/68, New Likseard, Ontario. 5-10, 185. Drafted by Chicago Blackhawks (4th choice, 98th overall) in 1986 Entry Draft. Signed as a free agent by Detroit Red Wings (6/7/91). Claimed by Ottawa Senators from Detroit in Expansion Draft (6/18/92). Claimed on waivers by Los Angeles Kings from Ottawa (10/21/92). Claimed by Anaheim Mighty Ducks from Los Angeles in Expansion Draft (6/24/93). 1990-91 IHL Second Team All-Star. Member of 1991-92 AHL champion Adirondack Red Wings. Last amateur club; Guelph (OHL).

Mike Loach — Right Wing

Season	Team	League	GP	G	A	PTS	PIM	GP	G	A	PTS	PIM
			Regular Season					Playoffs				
96-97	Belleville	OHL	67	22	27	49	144	6	4	1	5	6
96-97	Toledo	ECHL	3	0	1	1	0	4	0	0	0	6
97-98	Toledo	ECHL	60	15	14	29	71	7	0	1	1	25
98-99	Toledo	ECHL	3	0	0	0	12	—	—	—	—	—
98-99	Amarillo	WPHL	3	0	0	0	2	—	—	—	—	—
98-99	San Antonio	CHL	13	2	5	7	34	—	—	—	—	—
98-99	Tulsa	CHL	9	2	3	5	28	—	—	—	—	—
	ECHL	Totals	66	15	15	30	83	11	0	1	1	31
	CHL	Totals	22	4	8	12	62	—	—	—	—	—

Born; 9/6/76, New Likseard, Ontario. 6-1, 200. Drafted by New York Islanders (8th choice, 194th overall) in 1994 Entry Draft. Last amateur club; Belleville

Craig Lochead — Defenseman

Season	Team	League	GP	G	A	PTS	PIM	GP	G	A	PTS	PIM
			Regular Season					Playoffs				
97-98	Fort Worth	CHL	38	2	9	11	59	—	—	—	—	—
97-98	Wichita	CHL	2	0	0	0	0	—	—	—	—	—
98-99	Tulsa	CHL	2	0	0	0	4	—	—	—	—	—
98-99	Fort Worth	WPHL	1	0	0	0	0	—	—	—	—	—
	CHL	Totals	40	2	9	11	59	—	—	—	—	—

Born; 4/11/71, Brampton, Ontario. 6-1, 195.

Jeff Loder — Center

Season	Team	League	GP	G	A	PTS	PIM	GP	G	A	PTS	PIM
			Regular Season					Playoffs				
96-97	Manitoba	IHL	7	0	2	2	4	—	—	—	—	—
96-97	Roanoke	ECHL	54	23	22	45	53	4	2	4	6	0
97-98	Saint John	AHL	2	1	0	1	4	—	—	—	—	—
97-98	Roanoke	ECHL	67	16	26	42	73	9	0	2	2	10
98-99	Wheeling	ECHL	67	24	27	51	82	—	—	—	—	—
	ECHL	Totals	188	63	75	138	208	13	2	6	8	10

Born; 1/6/76, Cornerbrook, Newfoundland. 5-10, 195. Last amateur club; Beauport (QMJHL).

Matt Loen — Center

Season	Team	League	GP	G	A	PTS	PIM	GP	G	A	PTS	PIM
			Regular Season					Playoffs				
95-96	Madison	CoHL	68	36	39	75	26	6	4	3	7	2
96-97	Madison	CoHL	73	47	56	103	16	5	2	3	5	2
97-98	Milwaukee	IHL	9	0	3	3	0	2	0	0	0	0
97-98	Madison	UHL	50	34	53	87	20	5	5	2	7	4
98-99	Cincinnati	AHL	21	0	1	1	0	—	—	—	—	—
98-99	Madison	UHL	47	26	35	61	30	—	—	—	—	—
	UHL	Totals	238	143	183	326	92	16	11	8	19	8

Born; 11/9/92, Coon Rapids, Minnesota. 6-1, 190. 1995-96 CoHL Rookie of the Year. Last amateur club; Wisconsin Eau-Claire (NCHA).

Darcy Loewen — Left Wing

Season	Team	League	GP	G	A	PTS	PIM	GP	G	A	PTS	PIM
			Regular Season					Playoffs				
88-89	Spokane	WHL	60	31	27	58	194	—	—	—	—	—
88-89	Canada	National	2	0	0	0	0	—	—	—	—	—
89-90	Buffalo	NHL	4	0	0	0	4	—	—	—	—	—
89-90	Rochester	AHL	50	7	11	18	193	5	1	0	1	6
90-91	Buffalo	NHL	6	0	0	0	8	—	—	—	—	—
90-91	Rochester	AHL	71	13	15	28	130	15	1	5	6	14
91-92	Buffalo	NHL	2	0	0	0	2	—	—	—	—	—
91-92	Rochester	AHL	73	11	20	31	193	4	0	1	1	8
92-93	Ottawa	NHL	79	4	5	9	145	—	—	—	—	—
93-94	Ottawa	NHL	44	0	3	3	52	—	—	—	—	—
94-95	Las Vegas	IHL	64	9	21	30	183	7	1	1	2	16
95-96	Las Vegas	IHL	72	14	23	37	198	—	—	—	—	—
96-97	Las Vegas	IHL	76	14	19	33	177	3	0	0	0	0
97-98	Las Vegas	IHL	42	4	6	10	117	—	—	—	—	—
97-98	Utah	IHL	34	1	7	8	99	4	0	1	1	15
98-99	Idaho	WCHL	3	1	2	3	21	—	—	—	—	—
98-99	Nottingham	BSL	29	3	4	7	37	11	0	4	4	31
	NHL	Totals	135	4	8	12	211	—	—	—	—	—
	IHL	Totals	288	42	76	118	774	14	1	2	3	31

Born; 2/26/69, Calgary, Alberta. 5-10, 185. Drafted by Buffalo Sabres (2nd choice, 55th overall) in 1988 Entry Draft. Claimed by Ottawa Senators from Buffalo in Expansion Draft (6/18/92). Last amateur club; Spokane (WHL).

Jim Logan — Left Wing

Season	Team	League	GP	G	A	PTS	PIM	GP	G	A	PTS	PIM
			Regular Season					Playoffs				
98-99	Detroit	IHL	1	0	1	1	0	—	—	—	—	—
98-99	Michigan	IHL	20	2	1	3	54	—	—	—	—	—
98-99	Port Huron	UHL	8	1	2	3	9	7	2	0	2	8
98-99	Dayton	ECHL	23	7	9	16	27	—	—	—	—	—
	IHL	Totals	21	2	2	4	54	—	—	—	—	—

Born; 11/8/73, Nipigon, Ontario. 6-3, 210. Last amateur club; Bemidji State (NCHA).

Alexei Lojkin — Left Wing

Season	Team	League	GP	G	A	PTS	PIM	GP	G	A	PTS	PIM
			Regular Season					Playoffs				
94-95	Chicoutimi	QMJHL	57	43	58	101	26	11	6	5	11	2
94-95	Tallahassee	ECHL	1	3	1	4	0	—	—	—	—	—
95-96	Fredericton	AHL	74	24	33	57	16	7	1	3	4	0
96-97	Fredericton	AHL	79	33	56	89	41	—	—	—	—	—
97-98	Fredericton	AHL	61	13	22	35	18	2	0	1	1	0
98-99	Fredericton	AHL	71	20	20	40	16	—	—	—	—	—
98-99	Grand Rapids	IHL	10	1	2	3	4	—	—	—	—	—
	AHL	Totals	285	90	131	221	91	9	1	4	5	0

Born; 2/21/74, Minsk, Russia. 5-9, 170. Signed as a free agent by Montreal Canadiens (9/11/97). Last amateur club; Chicoutimi (QMJHL).

Clint Lomenda — Forward

Season	Team	League	GP	G	A	PTS	PIM	GP	G	A	PTS	PIM
			Regular Season					Playoffs				
98-99	Winston-Salem	UHL	2	0	0	0	0	—	—	—	—	—

Born; 11/4/78, Stockholm, Saskatchewan. 5-8, 170.

Brian Loney — Right Wing

Regular Season / Playoffs

Season	Team	League	GP	G	A	PTS	PIM	GP	G	A	PTS	PIM
92-93	Red Deer	WHL	66	39	36	75	147	4	1	1	2	19
92-93	Hamilton	AHL	3	0	2	2	0	—	—	—	—	—
92-93	Canadian	National	1	0	1	1	0	—	—	—	—	—
93-94	Hamilton	AHL	67	18	16	34	76	4	0	0	0	8
94-95	Syracuse	AHL	67	23	17	40	98	—	—	—	—	—
95-96	Vancouver	NHL	12	2	3	5	6	—	—	—	—	—
95-96	Syracuse	AHL	48	34	17	51	157	14	3	8	11	20
96-97	Syracuse	AHL	76	19	39	58	123	3	0	0	0	0
97-98	Lukko Rauma	Finland	12	5	2	7	45	—	—	—	—	—
97-98	Kassel	Germany	19	6	7	13	24	—	—	—	—	—
98-99	Balzano	Italy	18	11	9	20	NA	—	—	—	—	—
98-99	Central Texas	WPHL	25	18	33	51	43	—	—	—	—	—
	AHL	Totals	251	94	91	185	454	21	3	8	11	28

Born; 8/9/72, Winnipeg, Manitoba. 6-1, 195. Drafted by Vancouver Canucks (6th choice, 110th overall) in 1992 Entry Draft. Last amateur club; Red Deer (WHL).

Andrew Long — Center

Regular Season / Playoffs

Season	Team	League	GP	G	A	PTS	PIM	GP	G	A	PTS	PIM
98-99	New Haven	AHL	16	0	3	3	8	—	—	—	—	—
98-99	Miami	ECHL	25	7	8	15	16	—	—	—	—	—

Born; 8/10/78, Toronto, Ontario. 6-2, 181. Drafted by Florida Panthers (5th choice, 129th overall) in 1996 Entry Draft. Last amateur club; Guelph (OHL).

Eric Long — Defenseman

Regular Season / Playoffs

Season	Team	League	GP	G	A	PTS	PIM	GP	G	A	PTS	PIM
94-95	Raleigh	ECHL	53	4	15	19	55	—	—	—	—	—
95-96	Mobile	ECHL	54	6	25	31	87	—	—	—	—	—
96-97	Mobile	ECHL	65	11	15	26	69	3	0	3	3	6
97-98	San Antonio	IHL	6	0	1	1	2	—	—	—	—	—
97-98	Jacksonville	ECHL	38	2	17	19	53	—	—	—	—	—
98-99	Jacksonville	ECHL	68	13	35	48	78	2	1	0	1	2
	ECHL	Totals	278	36	107	143	342	5	1	3	4	8

Born; 7/26/72, Westfield, Massachusetts. 6-0, 190. Last amateur club; Saint Anselm (NCAA 2).

Chris Longo — Right Wing

Regular Season / Playoffs

Season	Team	League	GP	G	A	PTS	PIM	GP	G	A	PTS	PIM
92-93	Baltimore	AHL	74	7	18	25	52	7	0	1	1	0
93-94	Portland	AHL	69	6	19	25	69	17	2	4	6	11
94-95	Portland	AHL	57	8	13	21	33	2	0	0	0	0
95-96	Asiago	Italy	30	22	28	50	60	—	—	—	—	—
96-97	Springfield	AHL	71	9	22	31	24	17	1	4	5	4
97-98	Cleveland	IHL	81	9	12	21	80	10	0	0	0	12
98-99	Cleveland	IHL	69	13	23	36	109	—	—	—	—	—
	AHL	Totals	271	30	72	102	178	43	3	9	12	15
	IHL	Totals	150	22	35	57	189	10	0	0	0	12

Born; 1/5/72, Belleville, Ontario. 5-10, 180. Drafted by Washington Capitals (3rd choice, 51st overall) in 1990 Entry Draft. Signed as a free agent by Hartford Whalers (10/1/96). Last amateur club; Peterborough (OHL).

Jeff Longo — Goaltender

Regular Season / Playoffs

Season	Team	League	GP	W	L	T	MIN	SO	AVG	GP	W	L	MIN	SO	AVG
97-98	Anchorage	WCHL	1	0	0	0	1	0	0.00	—	—	—	—	—	—
98-99	San Diego	WCHL	1	0	0	0	0	0	0.00	—	—	—	—	—	—
	WCHL	Totals	2	0	0	0	1	0	0.00	—	—	—	—	—	—

Born; Last amateur club; Rutgers (ACHA). Played 22 seconds for San Diego during 1998-99 season.

Adam Lord — Goaltender

Regular Season / Playoffs

Season	Team	League	GP	W	L	T	MIN	SO	AVG	GP	W	L	MIN	SO	AVG
98-99	Amarillo	WPHL	52	22	18	6	2931	2	3.54	—	—	—	—	—	—

Born; 8/25/74, Vancouver, British Columbia. 6-1, 175. Last amateur club; Miami-Ohio (CCHA).

Danny Lorenz — Goaltender

Regular Season / Playoffs

Season	Team	League	GP	W	L	T	MIN	SO	AVG	GP	W	L	MIN	SO	AVG
88-89	Springfield	AHL	4	2	1	0	210	0	3.43	—	—	—	—	—	—
90-91	Islanders	NHL	2	0	1	0	80	0	3.75	—	—	—	—	—	—
90-91	Capital District	AHL	17	5	9	2	940	0	4.47	—	—	—	—	—	—
90-91	Richmond	ECHL	20	6	9	2	1020	0	4.41	—	—	—	—	—	—
91-92	Islanders	NHL	2	0	2	0	120	0	5.00	—	—	—	—	—	—
91-92	Capital District	AHL	53	22	22	7	3050	2	3.56	7	3	4	442	0	3.39
92-93	Islanders	NHL	4	1	2	0	157	0	3.82	—	—	—	—	—	—
92-93	Capital District	AHL	44	16	17	5	2412	1	3.63	4	0	3	219	0	3.29
93-94	Salt Lake City	IHL	20	4	12	0	982	0	5.56	—	—	—	—	—	—
93-94	Springfield	AHL	14	5	7	1	801	0	4.42	2	0	0	35	0	0.00
94-95	Cincinnati	IHL	41	24	10	2	2222	0	3.40	5	2	3	308	0	3.12
95-96	Cincinnati	IHL	46	28	12	5	2693	1	3.10	5	1	2	199	0	3.31
96-97	Milwaukee	IHL	67	33	27	6	3903	0	3.40	3	0	3	187	0	3.53
97-98	Milwaukee	IHL	54	28	18	4	2718	0	3.09	10	5	5	623	1	2.99
98-99	Mannheim	Germany	22	—	—	—	1051	2	3.08	—	—	—	—	—	—
98-99	Houston	IHL	7	3	2	2	418	0	1.86	1	0	0	38	0	3.19

Born; 12/12/69, Murrayville, British Columbia. 5-10, 185. Drafted by New York Islanders (4th choice, 58th overall) in 1988 Entry Draft. Signed as a free agent by Florida Panthers (6/14/94). Member of 1998-99 IHL Champion Houston Aeros. Last amateur club; Seattle (WHL).

John Lovell — Right Wing

Regular Season / Playoffs

Season	Team	League	GP	G	A	PTS	PIM	GP	G	A	PTS	PIM
96-97	Richmond	ECHL	29	7	7	14	10	—	—	—	—	—
98-99	Richmond	ECHL	12	2	1	3	12	—	—	—	—	—
	ECHL	Totals	41	9	8	17	22	—	—	—	—	—

Born; 11/20/65, Springfield, Massachusetts. 6-1, 205. Selected by Arkansas in 1999 ECHL Expansion Draft.

Tim Lovell — Center

Regular Season / Playoffs

Season	Team	League	GP	G	A	PTS	PIM	GP	G	A	PTS	PIM
97-98	Massachusetts	H.E.	26	8	14	22	58	—	—	—	—	—
97-98	Cincinnati	AHL	4	0	0	0	0	—	—	—	—	—
98-99	Tacoma	WCHL	54	33	43	76	68	5	2	6	8	0
98-99	Las Vegas	IHL	9	0	0	0	8	—	—	—	—	—

Born; 5/14/74, Norwood, Massachusetts. 5-9, 190. 1998-99 WCHL Rookie of the Year. Member of 1998-99 WCHL Champion Tacoma Sabrecats. Last amateur club; Massachusetts (Hockey East).

Chris Low — Forward

Regular Season / Playoffs

Season	Team	League	GP	G	A	PTS	PIM	GP	G	A	PTS	PIM
97-98	British Columbia	AUAA	35	13	20	33	38	—	—	—	—	—
97-98	Idaho	WCHL	11	3	4	7	4	2	0	0	0	6
98-99	Idaho	WCHL	13	2	1	3	10	—	—	—	—	—
98-99	Lake Charles	WPHL	30	7	5	12	8	—	—	—	—	—
98-99	Alexandria	WPHL	19	4	4	8	10	—	—	—	—	—
	WPHL	Totals	49	11	9	20	18	—	—	—	—	—
	WCHL	Totals	24	5	5	10	14	2	0	0	0	6

Born; 6/2/76, Foxwarren, Manitoba. 6-1, 190. Traded to Alexandria by Lake Charles for Mike Torkoff (2/99). Last amateur club; British Columbia (AUAA).

Reed Low — Right Wing

Regular Season / Playoffs

Season	Team	League	GP	G	A	PTS	PIM	GP	G	A	PTS	PIM
97-98	Worcester	AHL	17	1	1	2	75	3	0	0	0	0
97-98	Baton Rouge	ECHL	39	4	2	6	145	—	—	—	—	—
98-99	Worcester	AHL	77	5	6	11	239	4	0	0	0	2
	AHL	Totals	94	6	7	13	314	7	0	0	0	2

Born; 6/21/76, Moose Jaw, Saskatchewan. 6-4, 220. Drafted by St. Louis Blues (7th choice, 177th overall) in 1996 Entry Draft. Last amateur club; Moose Jaw

Steven Low — Defenseman

Regular Season / Playoffs

Season	Team	League	GP	G	A	PTS	PIM	GP	G	A	PTS	PIM
97-98	Quebec	IHL	25	0	4	4	56	—	—	—	—	—
97-98	Pensacola	ECHL	37	3	8	11	101	14	5	4	9	64
98-99	San Diego	WCHL	2	0	0	0	4	—	—	—	—	—
98-99	Long Beach	IHL	2	0	0	0	2	—	—	—	—	—
98-99	Kansas City	IHL	64	3	14	17	100	—	—	—	—	—
	IHL	Totals	91	3	18	21	158	—	—	—	—	—

Born; 5/21/76, Montreal, Quebec. 6-0, 170. Last amateur club; Hull (QMJHL).

Jason Lowe — Center

Regular Season / Playoffs

Season	Team	League	GP	G	A	PTS	PIM	GP	G	A	PTS	PIM
97-98	Fresno	WCHL	54	15	21	36	34	—	—	—	—	—
98-99	Fresno	WCHL	6	3	0	3	7	—	—	—	—	—
	WCHL	Totals	60	18	21	39	41	—	—	—	—	—

Born; 5-11, 175.

Tim Lozinik — Defenseman

Regular Season / Playoffs

Season	Team	League	GP	G	A	PTS	PIM	GP	G	A	PTS	PIM
98-99	Pensacola	ECHL	29	0	3	3	20	—	—	—	—	—

Born;

Andrew Luciuk — Left Wing

Regular Season / Playoffs

Season	Team	League	GP	G	A	PTS	PIM	GP	G	A	PTS	PIM
98-99	Florida	ECHL	11	2	0	2	4	—	—	—	—	—
98-99	Asheville	UHL	38	16	16	32	31	4	1	1	2	6

Born; 2/17/77, Barrhead, Alberta. 6-0, 200. Last amateur club; Prince George (WHL).

Warren Luhning — Right Wing

Regular Season / Playoffs

Season	Team	League	GP	G	A	PTS	PIM	GP	G	A	PTS	PIM
97-98	Islanders	NHL	8	0	0	0	0	—	—	—	—	—
97-98	Kentucky	AHL	51	6	7	13	82	—	—	—	—	—
98-99	Islanders	NHL	11	0	0	0	8	—	—	—	—	—
98-99	Lowell	AHL	56	20	20	40	67	3	0	3	3	16
	NHL	Totals	19	0	0	0	8	—	—	—	—	—
	AHL	Totals	107	26	27	53	149	3	0	3	3	16

Born; 7/3/75, Edmonton, Alberta. 6-2, 185. Drafted by New Yok Islanders (4th choice, 92nd overall) in 1993 Entry Draft. Last amateur club; Michigan (CCHA).

Rob Lukacs — Forward

Regular Season / Playoffs

Season	Team	League	GP	G	A	PTS	PIM	GP	G	A	PTS	PIM
98-99	Odessa	WPHL	66	4	14	18	198	3	0	1	1	2

Born; 11/24/77, Scarborough, Ontario. 6-1, 190.

Brad Lukowich — Defenseman

Regular Season / Playoffs

Season	Team	League	GP	G	A	PTS	PIM	GP	G	A	PTS	PIM
96-97	Michigan	IHL	69	2	6	8	77	4	0	1	1	2
97-98	Dallas	NHL	4	0	1	1	2	—	—	—	—	—
97-98	Michigan	IHL	60	6	27	33	104	4	0	4	4	14
98-99	Dallas	NHL	14	1	2	3	19	8	0	1	1	4
98-99	Michigan	IHL	67	8	21	29	95	—	—	—	—	—
	NHL	Totals	18	1	3	4	21	8	0	1	1	4
	IHL	Totals	196	16	54	70	276	8	0	5	5	16

Born; 8/12/76, Cranbrook, British Columbia. 6-1, 170. Drafted by New York Islanders (4th choice, 90th overall) in 1994 Entry Draft. Traded to Dallas Stars by Islanders for Dallas third round choice (Robert Schnabel) in 1997 Entry Draft (6/1/96). Member of 1998-99 Stanley Cup Champion Dallas Stars. Last amateur club; Kamloops (WHL).

Bill Lund — Center

Regular Season / Playoffs

Season	Team	League	GP	G	A	PTS	PIM	GP	G	A	PTS	PIM
97-98	Lake Charles	WPHL	69	18	40	58	34	4	2	2	4	8
98-99	Lake Charles	WPHL	68	36	49	85	100	11	3	8	11	18
	WPHL	Totals	137	54	89	143	134	15	5	10	15	26

Born; 12/16/71, Roseau, Minnesota. 5-9, 175. Drafted by Philadelphia Flyers (15th choice, 235th overall) in 1990 Entry Draft.

Justin Lund — Left Wing

Regular Season / Playoffs

Season	Team	League	GP	G	A	PTS	PIM	GP	G	A	PTS	PIM
96-97	Toledo	ECHL	1	0	0	0	2	—	—	—	—	—
96-97	Bakersfield	WCHL	3	0	0	0	2	—	—	—	—	—
96-97	Reno	WCHL	5	0	0	0	17	—	—	—	—	—
96-97	Memphis	CeHL	2	0	0	0	2	—	—	—	—	—
96-97	Nashville	CeHL	12	1	2	3	68	—	—	—	—	—
97-98	Fort Worth	CHL	4	0	1	1	44	—	—	—	—	—
98-99	Winston-Salem	UHL	2	0	0	0	0	—	—	—	—	—
	CHL	Totals	18	1	3	4	114	—	—	—	—	—
	WCHL	Totals	8	0	0	0	19	—	—	—	—	—

Born; 1/29/72, Toronto, Ontario. 5-11, 190.

Kevin Lune — Defenseman

Regular Season / Playoffs

Season	Team	League	GP	G	A	PTS	PIM	GP	G	A	PTS	PIM
95-96	Wheeling	ECHL	3	0	0	0	16	—	—	—	—	—
95-96	Oklahoma City	CeHL	48	24	20	44	186	9	2	3	5	17
96-97	Peoria	ECHL	43	9	14	23	111	—	—	—	—	—
97-98	Muskegon	UHL	67	5	14	19	126	11	1	0	1	9
98-99	Topeka	CHL	21	2	3	5	75	—	—	—	—	—
98-99	San Antonio	CHL	42	14	27	41	84	8	0	3	3	23
	CHL	Totals	111	40	50	90	345	17	2	6	8	40
	ECHL	Totals	46	9	14	23	127	—	—	—	—	—

Born; 6/8/71, Brantford, Ontario. 6-3, 214. Member of 1995-96 CeHL champion Oklahoma City Blazers. Last amateur club; Bowling Green (CCHA).

Chris Luongo — Defenseman

Regular Season / Playoffs

Season	Team	League	GP	G	A	PTS	PIM	GP	G	A	PTS	PIM
89-90	Adirondack	AHL	53	9	14	23	37	3	0	0	0	0
89-90	Phoenix	IHL	23	5	9	14	41	—	—	—	—	—
90-91	Detroit	NHL	4	0	1	1	4	—	—	—	—	—
90-91	Adirondack	AHL	76	14	25	39	71	2	0	0	0	7
91-92	Adirondack	AHL	80	6	20	26	60	19	3	5	8	10
92-93	Ottawa	NHL	76	3	9	12	68	—	—	—	—	—
92-93	New Haven	AHL	7	0	2	2	2	—	—	—	—	—
93-94	Islanders	NHL	17	1	3	4	13	—	—	—	—	—
93-94	Salt Lake City	IHL	51	9	31	40	54	—	—	—	—	—
94-95	Denver	IHL	41	1	14	15	26	—	—	—	—	—
94-95	Islanders	NHL	47	1	3	4	36	—	—	—	—	—
95-96	Islanders	NHL	74	3	7	10	55	—	—	—	—	—
96-97	Milwaukee	IHL	81	10	35	45	69	2	0	0	0	0
97-98	Landshut	Germany	48	5	13	18	54	6	0	2	2	18
98-99	Landshut	Germany	51	1	14	15	115	3	1	0	1	0
98-99	Detroit	IHL	11	0	1	1	4	11	0	4	4	16
	NHL	Totals	218	8	23	31	176	—	—	—	—	—
	AHL	Totals	216	29	61	90	170	24	3	5	8	10
	IHL	Totals	207	25	90	115	194	13	0	4	4	16

Born; 3/17/67, Detroit, Michigan. Drafted by Detroit Red Wings (5th choice, 92nd overall) in 1985 Entry Draft. Signed as a free agent by Ottawa Senators (9/9/92). Traded to New York Islanders by Ottawa for Jeff Finley, (6/30/93). Member of 1991-92 AHL Champion Adirondack Red Wings. Last amateur club; Michigan State (CCHA).

Andrei Lupandin — Defensman

Regular Season / Playoffs

Season	Team	League	GP	G	A	PTS	PIM	GP	G	A	PTS	PIM
98-99	Brandon	WHL	69	25	50	75	171	5	1	6	7	9
98-99	Utah	IHL	8	1	1	2	0	—	—	—	—	—

Born; 2/15/78, Kharkiv, Ukraine. 5-8, 186. Last amateur club; Brandon (WHL).

Dan Lupo — Right Wing

Regular Season / Playoffs

Season	Team	League	GP	G	A	PTS	PIM	GP	G	A	PTS	PIM
96-97	Utah	IHL	3	0	0	0	0	—	—	—	—	—
96-97	Tallahassee	ECHL	63	28	36	64	60	3	2	0	2	0
97-98	San Antonio	IHL	24	2	3	5	2	—	—	—	—	—
97-98	Quad City	UHL	5	2	0	2	2	—	—	—	—	—
97-98	Tallahassee	ECHL	29	20	13	33	26	—	—	—	—	—
98-99	Miami	ECHL	32	6	14	20	23	—	—	—	—	—
	IHL	Totals	27	2	3	5	2	—	—	—	—	—
	ECHL	Totals	124	54	63	117	109	3	2	0	2	0

Born; 11/1/72, Somerville, Massachusetts. 5-10, 190. Selected by Trenton in 1999 ECHL Dispersal Draft. Last amateur club; Northeastern (Hockey East).

Craig Lutes — Right Wing

Regular Season / Playoffs

Season	Team	League	GP	G	A	PTS	PIM	GP	G	A	PTS	PIM
94-95	Birmingham	ECHL	66	23	26	49	139	7	6	3	9	6
95-96	Birmingham	ECHL	24	9	10	19	50	—	—	—	—	—
95-96	Johnstown	ECHL	20	7	11	18	12	—	—	—	—	—
95-96	Jacksonville	ECHL	21	9	7	16	17	16	6	6	12	42
96-97	Jacksonville	ECHL	4	1	1	2	6	—	—	—	—	—
96-97	Birmingham	ECHL	63	35	29	64	36	8	4	6	10	2
97-98	Birmingham	ECHL	70	29	31	60	59	4	1	2	3	4
98-99	Birmingham	ECHL	68	23	25	48	64	5	1	2	3	10
	ECHL	Totals	336	136	140	276	383	40	18	19	37	64

Born; 2/18/73, Orillia, Ontario. 6-0, 195. Last amateur club; Windsor (OHL).

Yuri Lyaskovsky — Defensman

Regular Season / Playoffs

Season	Team	League	GP	G	A	PTS	PIM	GP	G	A	PTS	PIM
98-99	Corpus Christi	WPHL	10	0	4	4	6	—	—	—	—	—
98-99	New Mexico	WPHL	42	4	5	9	19	—	—	—	—	—
	WPHL	Totals	52	4	9	13	25	—	—	—	—	—

Born; 10/29/75.

Dave Lylyk — Left Wing

Regular Season / Playoffs

Season	Team	League	GP	G	A	PTS	PIM	GP	G	A	PTS	PIM
96-97	Charlotte	ECHL	4	0	0	0	0	—	—	—	—	—
96-97	San Antonio	CeHL	63	23	21	44	29	—	—	—	—	—
97-98	Memphis	CHL	43	5	8	13	20	—	—	—	—	—
97-98	Nashville	CHL	7	0	2	2	4	9	0	1	1	4
98-99	Abilene	WPHL	12	0	0	0	6	—	—	—	—	—
98-99	Memphis	CHL	15	5	3	8	24	—	—	—	—	—
98-99	Oklahoma City	CHL	8	0	2	2	8	—	—	—	—	—
98-99	Fort Worth	CHL	21	7	6	13	10	—	—	—	—	—
	CHL	Totals	157	40	42	82	95	9	0	1	1	4

Born; 12/22/75, Whitby, Ontario. 6-2, 190. Selected by Memphis in 1998 CHL Dispersal Draft. Selected by Oklahoma City in 1999 CHL Dispersal Draft. Last amateur club; Regina (WHL).

Corey Lyons — Right Wing

Regular Season / Playoffs

Season	Team	League	GP	G	A	PTS	PIM	GP	G	A	PTS	PIM
89-90	Lethbridge	WHL	72	63	79	142	26	19	11	15	26	4
89-90	Salt Lake City	IHL	—	—	—	—	—	1	0	0	0	0
90-91	Salt Lake City	IHL	51	15	12	27	22	3	0	2	2	0
91-92	Salt Lake City	IHL	26	3	3	6	4	—	—	—	—	—
91-92	Roanoke Valley	ECHL	22	10	13	23	13	7	4	3	7	4
92-93	Brantford	CoHL	4	0	1	1	0	—	—	—	—	—
93-94												
94-95												
95-96												
96-97	Fresno	WCHL	64	39	41	80	52	5	6	3	9	12
97-98	Fresno	WCHL	47	24	27	51	43	—	—	—	—	—
98-99	London	BSL	42	17	10	27	12	—	—	—	—	—
98-99	Ayr	BSL	15	5	3	8	0	6	1	1	2	0
	IHL	Totals	77	18	15	33	26	4	0	2	2	0
	WCHL	Totals	111	63	68	131	95	5	6	3	9	12

Born; 6/13/70, Calgary, Alberta. 5-11, 205. Drafted by Calgary Flames (4th choice, 63rd overall) in 1989 Entry Draft. Last amateur club; Lethbridge (WHL).

Craig Lyons — Right Wing

Regular Season / Playoffs

Season	Team	League	GP	G	A	PTS	PIM	GP	G	A	PTS	PIM
93-94	Springfield	AHL	46	7	14	21	16	2	0	0	0	0
94-95	South Carolina	ECHL	46	19	29	48	58	—	—	—	—	—
95-96	Dumfries	BHL	51	108	108	216	NA	—	—	—	—	—
96-97	Long Beach	IHL	1	0	0	0	0	—	—	—	—	—
96-97	Fresno	WCHL	61	51	60	111	108	5	3	2	5	6
97-98	Utah	IHL	5	0	2	2	0	—	—	—	—	—
97-98	Fresno	WCHL	50	33	59	92	78	5	5	4	9	19
98-99	Colorado	WCHL	68	42	73	115	106	3	1	5	6	4
	IHL	Totals	6	0	2	2	0	—	—	—	—	—
	WCHL	Totals	179	126	192	318	292	13	9	11	20	29

Born; 12/25/72, Calgary, Alberta. 6-2, 195. 1996-97 WCHL First Team All-Star. 1997-98 WCHL First Team All-Star. 1998-99 WCHL Second Team All-Star. Last amateur club; Kamloops (WHL).

Roddy MacCormick — Right Wing
Regular Season / Playoffs

Season	Team	League	GP	G	A	PTS	PIM	GP	G	A	PTS	PIM
96-97	South Carolina	ECHL	2	0	1	1	0	—	—	—	—	—
97-98	Fayetteville	CHL	70	19	33	52	175	—	—	—	—	—
98-99	Fayetteville	CHL	70	23	54	77	95	—	—	—	—	—
	CHL	Totals	140	42	87	129	270	—	—	—	—	—

Born; 1/25/73, Dartmouth, Nova Scotia. 6-1, 200. Last amateur club; Siant Mary's (AUAA).

Troy MacCormick — Left Wing
Regular Season / Playoffs

Season	Team	League	GP	G	A	PTS	PIM	GP	G	A	PTS	PIM
97-98	Tulsa	CHL	65	12	21	33	103	4	0	1	1	4
98-99	Tulsa	CHL	39	6	15	21	56	—	—	—	—	—
98-99	Oklahoma City	CHL	16	2	6	8	20	—	—	—	—	—
98-99	Fort Worth	CHL	10	2	5	7	4	—	—	—	—	—
	CHL	Totals	130	22	47	69	183	4	0	1	1	4

Born; 8/10/72, North Bay, Ontario. 6-2, 200. Selected by Memphis in 1999 CHL Dispersal Draft. Selected by Indianapolis in 1999 CHL Expansion Draft. Last amateur club; Canisius (MAAC).

Aaron MacDonald — Goaltender
Regular Season / Playoffs

Season	Team	League	GP	W	L	T	MIN	SO	AVG	GP	W	L	MIN	SO	AVG
97-98	Tallahassee	ECHL	37	11	19	2	1832	0	4.16	—	—	—	—	—	—
98-99	Miami	ECHL	29	7	8	5	1243	0	3.57	—	—	—	—	—	—
	ECHL	Totals	66	18	27	7	3075	0	3.92	—	—	—	—	—	—

Born; 8/29/77, Grand Prairie, Alberta. 6-1, 193. Drafted by Florida Panthers (2nd choice, 36th overall) in 1995 Entry Draft. Last amateur club; Kelowna (WHL).

Brett MacDonald — Defenseman
Regular Season / Playoffs

Season	Team	League	GP	G	A	PTS	PIM	GP	G	A	PTS	PIM
86-87	Fredericton	AHL	49	0	9	9	29	—	—	—	—	—
87-88	Vancouver	NHL	1	0	0	0	0	—	—	—	—	—
87-88	Fredericton	AHL	15	1	5	6	23	—	—	—	—	—
87-88	Flint	IHL	49	2	21	23	43	15	2	2	4	12
88-89	Flint	IHL	57	3	24	27	53	—	—	—	—	—
88-89	New Haven	AHL	15	2	4	6	6	—	—	—	—	—
90-91	Nashville	ECHL	64	19	62	81	56	—	—	—	—	—
90-91	San Diego	IHL	3	0	1	1	0	—	—	—	—	—
90-91	Moncton	AHL	2	0	0	0	0	7	1	3	4	4
91-92	Moncton	AHL	3	0	0	0	2	—	—	—	—	—
91-92	Flint	CoHL	46	12	33	45	23	—	—	—	—	—
92-93	Flint	CoHL	60	12	39	51	60	6	0	5	5	21
93-94	Chatham	CoHL	42	8	31	39	29	14	6	9	15	4
94-95	Saginaw	CoHL	62	17	42	59	42	—	—	—	—	—
94-95	Muskegon	CoHL	11	3	8	11	14	16	2	5	7	12
95-96	Flint	CoHL	62	16	39	55	55	15	1	8	9	2
96-97	Flint	CoHL	74	8	64	72	44	14	1	11	12	12
97-98	Flint	UHL	56	7	37	44	32	17	1	6	7	14
98-99	Flint	UHL	23	2	9	11	16	12	1	3	4	12
	IHL	Totals	109	5	46	51	96	15	2	2	4	12
	AHL	Totals	84	3	18	21	60	7	1	3	4	4
	UHL	Totals	441	85	302	387	317	101	13	50	63	81

Born; 1/5/66, Bothwell, Ontario. 6-1, 205. 1990-91 ECHL Defenseman of the Year. 1990-91 ECHL First Team All-Star. 1991-92 CoHL Second Team All-Star. 1992-93 CoHL First Team All-Star. 1995-96 CoHL First Team All-Star. 1996-97 CoHL First Team All-Star. Member of 1995-96 Colonial Cup Champion Flint Generals. Last amateur club; Kitchener (OHL).

Bruce MacDonald — Right Wing
Regular Season / Playoffs

Season	Team	League	GP	G	A	PTS	PIM	GP	G	A	PTS	PIM
91-92	Toledo	ECHL	42	29	26	55	32	5	0	4	4	22
92-93	Toledo	ECHL	55	20	27	47	80	14	5	3	8	16
93-94	Toledo	ECHL	17	3	6	9	4	—	—	—	—	—
93-94	Raleigh	ECHL	25	4	6	10	21	—	—	—	—	—
94-95	Tolede	ECHL	2	0	0	0	0	—	—	—	—	—
95-96	Toledo	ECHL	3	0	0	0	4	—	—	—	—	—
96-97	Toledo	ECHL	7	0	2	2	4	—	—	—	—	—
97-98	Toledo	ECHL	49	4	7	11	30	—	—	—	—	—
98-99	Toledo	ECHL	1	0	0	0	0	—	—	—	—	—
	ECHL	Totals	201	60	74	134	175	19	5	7	12	38

Born; 12/16/67, Reading, Massachusetts. 6-1, 192. Member of 1992-93 ECHL Champion Toledo Storm. Last amateur club; New Hampshire (Hockey East).

Craig MacDonald — Center
Regular Season / Playoffs

Season	Team	League	GP	G	A	PTS	PIM	GP	G	A	PTS	PIM
97-98	Canada	National	58	18	29	47	38	—	—	—	—	—
98-99	Carolina	NHL	11	0	0	0	0	1	0	0	0	0
98-99	New Haven	AHL	62	17	31	48	77	—	—	—	—	—

Born; 4/7/77, Antigonish, Nova Scotia. 6-2, 180. Drafted by Hartford Whalers (3rd choice, 88th overall) in 1996 Entry Draft. Last amateur club; Harvard

Doug Macdonald — Center
Regular Season / Playoffs

Season	Team	League	GP	G	A	PTS	PIM	GP	G	A	PTS	PIM
92-93	Buffalo	NHL	5	1	0	1	2	—	—	—	—	—
92-93	Rochester	AHL	64	25	33	58	58	7	0	2	2	4
93-94	Buffalo	NHL	4	0	0	0	0	—	—	—	—	—
93-94	Rochester	AHL	63	25	19	44	46	4	1	1	2	8
94-95	Buffalo	NHL	2	0	0	0	0	—	—	—	—	—
94-95	Rochester	AHL	58	21	25	46	73	5	0	1	1	0
95-96	Cincinnati	IHL	71	19	40	59	66	15	1	3	4	14
96-97	Cincinnati	IHL	65	20	34	54	36	3	0	0	0	0
97-98	Cincinnati	IHL	70	17	19	36	64	4	0	4	4	0
98-99	Cincinnati	IHL	33	7	11	18	22	—	—	—	—	—
	NHL	Totals	11	1	0	1	2	—	—	—	—	—
	IHL	Totals	239	63	104	167	188	22	1	7	8	14
	AHL	Totals	185	71	77	148	177	16	1	4	5	12

Born; 2/8/69, Assiniboia, British Columbia, 6-0, 198. Drafted by Buffalo Sabres (3rd choice, 77th overall) in 1989 Entry Draft. Last amateur club; Wisconsin

Ian MacDonald — Forward
Regular Season / Playoffs

Season	Team	League	GP	G	A	PTS	PIM	GP	G	A	PTS	PIM
98-99	Winston-Salem	UHL	2	0	0	0	5	—	—	—	—	—

Born;

Jason MacDonald — Right Wing
Regular Season / Playoffs

Season	Team	League	GP	G	A	PTS	PIM	GP	G	A	PTS	PIM
93-94	Owen Sound	OHL	66	55	61	116	177	9	7	11	18	36
93-94	Adirondack	AHL	—	—	—	—	—	1	0	0	0	0
94-95	Adirondack	AHL	68	14	21	35	238	4	0	0	0	2
95-96	Adirondack	AHL	43	9	13	22	99	—	—	—	—	—
95-96	Toledo	ECHL	9	5	5	10	26	9	3	1	4	39
96-97	Adirondack	AHL	1	0	0	0	2	—	—	—	—	—
96-97	Fredericton	AHL	63	22	25	47	189	—	—	—	—	—
97-98	Canadian	National	51	15	20	35	133	—	—	—	—	—
97-98	Saint John	AHL	6	2	0	2	27	11	1	3	4	17
98-99	Manitoba	IHL	82	25	27	52	283	5	2	2	4	13
	AHL	Totals	181	47	59	106	557	16	1	3	4	19

Born; 4/1/74, Charlottetown, Prince Edward Island. 6-0, 195. Drafted by Detroit Red Wings (5th choice, 142nd overall) in 1992 Entry Draft. Traded to Montreal Canadiens by Detroit for cash (11/8/96). Last amateur club; Owen Sound (OHL).

Rick MacDonald — Defenseman

Regular Season / Playoffs

Season	Team	League	GP	G	A	PTS	PIM	GP	G	A	PTS	PIM
98-99	Saginaw	UHL	9	0	1	1	4	—	—	—	—	—
98-99	Peoria	ECHL	15	0	1	1	8	—	—	—	—	—
98-99	Jacksonville	ECHL	8	0	0	0	6	—	—	—	—	—
	ECHL	Totals	23	0	1	1	14	—	—	—	—	—

Born; 1/24/76, Evergreen Park, Illinois. 5-11, 200.

Todd MacDonald — Goaltender

Regular Season / Playoffs

Season	Team	League	GP	W	L	T	MIN	SO	AVG	GP	W	L	MIN	SO	AVG
95-96	Detroit	CoHL	2	1	1	0	120	0	4.01	2	1	1	133	0	1.36
95-96	Carolina	AHL	18	3	12	2	979	0	4.78	—	—	—	—	—	—
96-97	Cincinnati	IHL	31	11	9	5	1617	2	2.71	1	0	0	20	0	3.00
96-97	Carolina	AHL	1	0	1	0	58	0	4.14	—	—	—	—	—	—
97-98	New Haven	AHL	13	8	3	2	790	1	2.28	3	0	3	177	0	5.07
97-98	Cincinnati	IHL	15	4	6	3	797	0	3.46	—	—	—	—	—	—
97-98	Birmingham	ECHL	3	1	1	1	180	0	2.67	—	—	—	—	—	—
98-99	New Haven	AHL	31	10	16	3	1775	0	3.08	—	—	—	—	—	—
	AHL	Totals	63	21	32	7	3602	1	3.38	3	0	3	177	0	5.07
	IHL	Totals	46	15	15	8	2414	2	2.96	1	0	0	20	0	3.00

Born; 7/5/75, Charlottetown, Prince Edward Island. 6-0, 167. Drafted by Florida Panthers (7th choice, 109th overall) in 1993 Entry Draft. Last amateur club, Tacoma (WHL).

Greg MacEachern — Defenseman

Regular Season / Playoffs

Season	Team	League	GP	G	A	PTS	PIM	GP	G	A	PTS	PIM
91-92	Laval	QMJHL	11	0	4	4	22	10	0	1	1	29
91-92	Fredericton	AHL	20	0	5	5	12	—	—	—	—	—
92-93	Lakeland	SUN	21	2	6	8	43	—	—	—	—	—
92-93	Tulsa	CeHL	56	4	3	7	107	12	1	1	2	32
93-94	Tulsa	CeHL	12	0	3	3	8	—	—	—	—	—
93-94	Dallas	CeHL	5	0	1	1	4	1	0	1	1	0
94-95	Dallas	CeHL	35	3	7	10	44	—	—	—	—	—
95-96	Reno	WCHL	57	7	17	24	108	3	2	2	4	2
96-97	New Mexico	WPHL	37	3	10	13	94	6	0	0	0	8
97-98	Reno	WCHL	46	6	11	17	86	—	—	—	—	—
98-99	New Mexico	WPHL	40	1	6	7	50	—	—	—	—	—
	CeHL	Totals	108	7	14	21	163	13	1	2	3	32
	WCHL	Totals	103	13	28	41	194	3	2	2	4	2
	WPHL	Totals	77	4	16	20	144	6	0	0	0	8

Born; 11/16/71, Port Hood, Nova Scotia. 6-3, 215. Drafted by the Montreal Canadiens (13th choice, 215th overall) in 1991 Entry Draft. Member of 1992-93 CeHL champion Tulsa Oilers. Last amateur club; Laval (QMJHL).

Mark Macera — Defenseman

Regular Season / Playoffs

Season	Team	League	GP	G	A	PTS	PIM	GP	G	A	PTS	PIM
96-97	Nashville	CeHL	4	1	0	1	23	—	—	—	—	—
96-97	Wichita	CeHL	31	4	11	15	75	—	—	—	—	—
96-97	San Antonio	CeHL	21	2	7	9	60	—	—	—	—	—
97-98	Nashville	CHL	6	1	0	1	25	—	—	—	—	—
97-98	Huntsville	CHL	55	6	28	34	143	3	1	1	2	4
98-99	Wichita	CHL	52	3	13	16	203	2	0	0	0	0
	CHL	Totals	169	17	59	76	529	5	1	1	2	4

Born; 12/20/71, London, Ontario. 5-11, 195. Last amateur club; Alabama-Huntsville (NCAA 2).

Eon MacFarlane — Defenseman

Regular Season / Playoffs

Season	Team	League	GP	G	A	PTS	PIM	GP	G	A	PTS	PIM
98-99	Pensacola	ECHL	36	3	4	7	26	—	—	—	—	—
98-99	Miami	ECHL	21	4	6	10	8	—	—	—	—	—
	ECHL	Totals	57	7	10	17	34	—	—	—	—	—

Born; 6/17/73, St. Andrews, New Brunswick. 5-10, 187. Selected by Trenton in 1999 ECHL Expansion Draft. Last amateur club; Alaska-Fairbanks (CCHA).

Martin Machacek — Center

Regular Season / Playoffs

Season	Team	League	GP	G	A	PTS	PIM	GP	G	A	PTS	PIM
96-97	Amarillo	WPHL	31	4	6	10	13	—	—	—	—	—
96-97	Raleigh	ECHL	1	0	0	0	0	—	—	—	—	—
97-98	Amarillo	WPHL	48	8	16	24	37	—	—	—	—	—
98-99	Fort Worth	WPHL	38	2	12	14	42	5	0	0	0	0
	WPHL	Totals	117	14	34	48	92	5	0	0	0	0

Born; 6/9/73, Scarborough, Ontario. 6-1, 200. Last amateur club; Michigan Tech (WCHA).

Andy MacIntyre — Left Wing

Regular Season / Playoffs

Season	Team	League	GP	G	A	PTS	PIM	GP	G	A	PTS	PIM
94-95	Indianapolis	IHL	51	9	8	17	17	—	—	—	—	—
94-95	Columbus	ECHL	22	7	8	15	5	—	—	—	—	—
95-96	Indianapolis	IHL	21	2	7	9	11	—	—	—	—	—
95-96	Columbus	ECHL	27	5	7	12	31	2	0	1	1	0
96-97	Indianapolis	IHL	22	2	4	6	26	—	—	—	—	—
96-97	Jacksonville	ECHL	37	13	13	26	17	—	—	—	—	—
97-98	Indianapolis	IHL	34	11	9	20	12	3	0	2	2	0
97-98	Jacksonville	ECHL	36	25	17	42	26	—	—	—	—	—
98-99	Kentucky	AHL	61	9	16	25	68	1	0	0	0	0
98-99	Richmond	ECHL	4	3	2	5	2	—	—	—	—	—
	IHL	Totals	128	24	28	52	66	3	0	2	2	0
	ECHL	Totals	136	53	47	100	81	2	0	1	1	0

Born; 4/16/74, Thunder Bay, Ontario. 6-1, 190. Drafted by Chicago Blackhawks (4th choice, 89th overall) in 1992 Entry Draft. Last amateur club; Saskatoon

Corey MacIntyre — Left Wing

Regular Season / Playoffs

Season	Team	League	GP	G	A	PTS	PIM	GP	G	A	PTS	PIM
95-96	Louisville	ECHL	4	0	0	0	4	—	—	—	—	—
96-97	Oklahoma City	CeHL	64	15	29	44	61	4	1	1	2	4
97-98	Oklahoma City	CHL	62	18	49	67	63	11	2	9	11	14
98-99	Oklahoma City	CHL	56	22	60	82	86	11	3	5	8	18
	CHL	Totals	182	55	138	193	210	26	6	15	21	36

Born; 8/10/70, Shawville, Quebec. 6-1, 190. Last amateur club; Dalhousie

Dave MacIntyre — Forward

Regular Season / Playoffs

Season	Team	League	GP	G	A	PTS	PIM	GP	G	A	PTS	PIM
97-98	Waco	WPHL	6	3	1	4	19	—	—	—	—	—
98-99	Long Beach	IHL	3	0	0	0	0	—	—	—	—	—
98-99	Waco	WPHL	60	28	18	46	138	4	0	0	0	10
	WPHL	Totals	66	31	19	50	157	4	0	0	0	10

Born; 3/12/73, Sydney, Nova Scotia. 6-0, 195. Last amateur club; St. Mary's (AUAA).

Jason MacIntyre — Defenseman

Regular Season / Playoffs

Season	Team	League	GP	G	A	PTS	PIM	GP	G	A	PTS	PIM
93-94	Hampton Roads	ECHL	55	10	8	18	195	5	0	0	0	13
94-95	Hampton Roads	ECHL	61	6	11	17	227	4	0	0	0	16
95-96	Hampton Roads	ECHL	15	1	1	2	49	—	—	—	—	—
96-97	Bakersfield	WCHL	41	3	18	21	270	4	0	0	0	32
97-98	San Antonio	IHL	1	0	0	0	0	—	—	—	—	—
97-98	Phoenix	WCHL	19	0	12	12	86	—	—	—	—	—
98-99	San Antonio	CHL	62	6	28	34	223	8	1	2	3	48
	ECHL	Totals	131	17	20	37	471	9	0	0	0	29
	WCHL	Totals	60	3	30	33	356	4	0	0	0	32

Born; 7/14/72, Halifax, Nova Scotia. 5-10, 190. Last amateur club; Antigonish (MJHL).

Dave MacIssac — Defenseman
Regular Season / Playoffs

Season	Team	League	GP	G	A	PTS	PIM	GP	G	A	PTS	PIM
94-95	Maine	H.E.	44	5	13	18	44	—	—	—	—	—
94-95	Milwaukee	IHL	2	0	0	0	5	9	0	2	2	2
95-96	Milwaukee	IHL	71	7	16	23	165	—	—	—	—	—
96-97	Philadelphia	AHL	61	3	15	18	187	10	0	1	1	31
97-98	Philadelphia	AHL	80	7	21	28	241	18	5	13	18	20
98-99	Philadelphia	AHL	47	6	15	21	98	16	2	5	7	50
	AHL	Totals	188	16	51	67	526	44	7	19	26	101
	IHL	Totals	73	7	16	23	170	9	0	2	2	2

Born; 4/23/72, Cambridge, Massachusetts. 6-2, 225. Signed as a free agent by Philadelphia Flyers (7/30/96). Member of 1997-98 AHL Champion Philadelphia Phantoms. Last amateur club; Maine (Hockey East).

Todd MacIssac — Center
Regular Season / Playoffs

Season	Team	League	GP	G	A	PTS	PIM	GP	G	A	PTS	PIM
95-96	Columbus	ECHL	38	11	13	24	95	—	—	—	—	—
95-96	Erie	ECHL	14	6	3	9	10	—	—	—	—	—
96-97	Baton Rouge	ECHL	48	8	19	27	44	—	—	—	—	—
96-97	Roanoke	ECHL	16	1	2	3	16	4	0	0	0	6
97-98	Macon	CHL	56	18	22	40	116	3	1	1	2	11
98-99	Macon	CHL	60	18	23	41	41	3	2	0	2	0
	ECHL	Totals	116	26	37	63	165	4	0	0	0	6
	CHL	Totals	116	36	45	81	157	6	3	1	4	11

Born; 5/25/74, Country Harbour, Nova Scotia. 5-10, 180. Last amateur club; Lethbridge (WHL).

Norm MacIver — Defenseman
Regular Season / Playoffs

Season	Team	League	GP	G	A	PTS	PIM	GP	G	A	PTS	PIM
86-87	Rangers	NHL	3	0	1	1	0	—	—	—	—	—
86-87	New Haven	AHL	71	6	30	36	73	7	0	0	0	9
87-88	Rangers	NHL	37	9	15	24	14	—	—	—	—	—
87-88	Colorado	IHL	27	6	20	26	22	—	—	—	—	—
88-89	Rangers	NHL	26	0	10	10	14	—	—	—	—	—
88-89	Hartford	NHL	37	1	22	23	24	1	0	0	0	2
89-90	Binghamton	AHL	2	0	0	0	0	—	—	—	—	—
89-90	Edmonton	NHL	1	0	0	0	0	—	—	—	—	—
89-90	Cape Breton	AHL	68	13	37	50	55	6	0	7	7	10
90-91	Edmonton	NHL	21	2	5	7	14	18	0	4	4	8
90-91	Cape Breton	AHL	56	13	46	59	60	—	—	—	—	—
91-92	Edmonton	NHL	57	6	34	40	38	13	1	2	3	10
92-93	Ottawa	NHL	80	17	46	63	84	—	—	—	—	—
93-94	Ottawa	NHL	53	3	20	23	26	—	—	—	—	—
94-95	Ottawa	NHL	28	4	7	11	10	—	—	—	—	—
94-95	Pittsburgh	NHL	13	0	9	9	6	12	1	4	5	8
95-96	Pittsburgh	NHL	32	2	21	23	32	—	—	—	—	—
95-96	Winnipeg	NHL	39	5	25	30	26	6	1	0	1	2
96-97	Phoenix	NHL	32	4	9	13	24	—	—	—	—	—
97-98	Phoenix	NHL	41	2	6	8	38	6	0	1	1	2
98-99	Houston	IHL	49	6	25	31	48	10	0	5	5	14
	NHL	Totals	500	55	230	285	350	56	3	11	14	32
	AHL	Totals	197	32	113	145	188	13	0	7	7	19
	IHL	Totals	76	12	45	57	70	10	0	5	5	14

Born; 9/8/64, Thunder Bay, Ontario. 5-11, 180. Signed as a free agent by New York Rangers (9/8/86). Traded to Hartford Whalers with Brian Lawton and Don Maloney for Carey Wilson and Hartford's fifth round choice (Lubos Rob) in 1990 Entry Draft (12/26/88). Traded to Edmonton Oilers by Hartford for Jim Ennis (10/10/89). Claimed by Ottawa Senators from Edmonton in NHL Waiver Draft (10/4/92). Traded to Pittsburgh Penguins by Ottawa with Troy Murray for Martin Straka (4/7/95). Traded to Winnipeg Jets by Pittsburgh for Neil Wilkinson (12/28/95). 1990-91 AHL Eddie Shore Award (Top Defenseman). 1990-91 AHL First All-Star Team. Member of 1998-99 IHL Champion Houston Aeros. Last amateur club; Minnesota (WCHA).

Mike MacKay — Left Wing
Regular Season / Playoffs

Season	Team	League	GP	G	A	PTS	PIM	GP	G	A	PTS	PIM
98-99	South Carolina	ECHL	23	3	2	5	2	—	—	—	—	—

Born; 9/10/78, New Glasgow, Nova Scotia. 5-10, 194.

Chris MacKenzie — Center
Regular Season / Playoffs

Season	Team	League	GP	G	A	PTS	PIM	GP	G	A	PTS	PIM
92-93	Hampton Roads	ECHL	3	0	1	1	0	—	—	—	—	—
92-93	Louisville	ECHL	2	0	0	0	0	—	—	—	—	—
92-93	Roanoke	ECHL	22	8	14	22	4	—	—	—	—	—
93-94	Daytona Beach	SHL	25	27	11	38	12	2	1	0	1	0
93-94	Detroit	CoHL	21	6	17	23	7	3	1	3	4	0
94-95	Detroit	CoHL	50	20	38	58	24	7	2	4	6	6
94-95	Durham	BHL	7	11	7	18	4	—	—	—	—	—
95-96												
96-97	El Paso	WPHL	55	29	55	84	50	11	*9	11	*20	10
97-98	Milwaukee	IHL	2	0	0	0	0	—	—	—	—	—
97-98	Brantford	UHL	3	2	0	2	2	—	—	—	—	—
97-98	El Paso	WPHL	46	33	46	79	39	15	10	14	24	26
98-99	Tacoma	WCHL	18	2	14	16	14	—	—	—	—	—
98-99	Shreveport	WPHL	24	7	18	25	13	12	8	11	19	10
	WPHL	Totals	101	62	101	163	89	26	19	25	44	36
	CoHL	Totals	74	28	55	83	33	10	3	7	10	6
	ECHL	Totals	27	8	15	23	4	—	—	—	—	—

Born; 9/16/71, Toronto, Ontario. 6-1, 210. Drafted by St. Louis Blues (10th choice, 219th overall) in 1991 Entry Draft.1996-97 WPHL Playoff MVP. Member of 1996-97 WPHL Champion El Paso Buzzards. Member of 1997-98 WPHL Champion El Paso Buzzards. Member of 1998-99 WPHL Champion Shreveport Mudbugs.Scored President's Cup-winning goal for Shreveport. Last amateur

Sandy MacKenzie — Right Wing
Regular Season / Playoffs

Season	Team	League	GP	G	A	PTS	PIM	GP	G	A	PTS	PIM
98-99	Mohawk Valley	UHL	49	15	8	23	46	—	—	—	—	—

Born; 7/21/73, Truro, Nova Scotia. 5-11, 171. Last amateur club; Truro (Sr.

Dave Mackey — Left Wing
Regular Season / Playoffs

Season	Team	League	GP	G	A	PTS	PIM	GP	G	A	PTS	PIM
86-87	Saginaw	IHL	81	26	49	75	173	10	3	7	10	44
87-88	Chicago	NHL	23	1	3	4	71	—	—	—	—	—
87-88	Saginaw	IHL	62	29	22	51	211	10	3	7	10	44
88-89	Chicago	NHL	23	1	2	3	78	—	—	—	—	—
88-89	Saginaw	IHL	57	22	23	45	223	—	—	—	—	—
89-90	Minnesota	NHL	16	2	0	2	28	—	—	—	—	—
90-91	Milwaukee	IHL	82	28	30	58	226	6	7	2	9	6
91-92	St. Louis	NHL	19	1	0	1	49	1	0	0	0	0
91-92	Peoria	IHL	35	20	17	37	90	—	—	—	—	—
92-93	St. Louis	NHL	15	1	4	5	23	—	—	—	—	—
92-93	Peoria	IHL	42	24	22	46	112	4	1	0	1	22
93-94	St. Louis	NHL	30	2	3	5	56	2	0	0	0	2
93-94	Peoria	IHL	49	14	21	35	132	—	—	—	—	—
94-95	Milwaukee	IHL	74	19	18	37	261	15	6	4	10	34
95-96	Milwaukee	IHL	77	15	16	31	235	4	2	1	3	10
96-97	Milwaukee	IHL	79	15	15	30	223	3	0	0	0	19
97-98	Milwaukee	IHL	36	3	6	9	134	—	—	—	—	—
97-98	Orlando	IHL	31	5	6	11	68	14	4	3	7	92
98-99	Orlando	IHL	78	21	20	41	192	17	3	0	3	38
	NHL	Totals	126	8	12	20	305	3	0	0	0	2
	IHL	Totals	783	241	265	506	2280	83	29	24	53	309

Born; 7/24/66, New Westminster, British Columbia. 6-3, 205. Drafted by Chicago Blackhawks (12th choice, 224th overall) in 1984 Entry Draft. Claimed by Minnesota North Stars from Chicago in Waiver Draft (10/2/89). Traded to Vancouver Canucks by Minnesota for future considerations (9/7/90). Signed as a free agent by St. Louis Blues (8/7/91). Traded to Orlando by Milwaukee with Sean McCann for Kelly Fairchild and Dave MacIntyre (1/98). Last amateur club;

Steve MacKinnan — Forward
Regular Season / Playoffs

Season	Team	League	GP	G	A	PTS	PIM	GP	G	A	PTS	PIM
98-99	Peoria	ECHL	34	7	6	13	21	—	—	—	—	—

Born; 8/20/76, Chelmsford, Massachusetts. 6-4, 215. Last amateur club; Massachusetts (Hockey East).

Dan MacKinnon — Left Wing
Regular Season / Playoffs

Season	Team	League	GP	G	A	PTS	PIM	GP	G	A	PTS	PIM
95-96	Wichita	CeHL	1	0	0	0	0	—	—	—	—	—
96-97	Waterloo	OUAA										
97-98	Waterloo	OUAA										
98-99	Columbus	ECHL	1	0	0	0	4	—	—	—	—	—

Born; 6/1/74, Vancouver, British Columbia. 5-11, 175. Last amateur club; Waterloo (OUAA).

Cail MacLean — Right Wing
Regular Season / Playoffs

Season	Team	League	GP	G	A	PTS	PIM	GP	G	A	PTS	PIM
97-98	Adirondack	AHL	7	0	1	1	4	—	—	—	—	—
97-98	Cleveland	IHL	1	0	0	0	0	—	—	—	—	—
97-98	Jacksonville	ECHL	66	30	35	65	44	—	—	—	—	—
98-99	Indianapolis	IHL	35	13	7	20	20	7	2	2	4	0
98-99	Jacksonville	ECHL	40	29	28	57	14	—	—	—	—	—
	IHL	Totals	43	13	8	21	24	7	2	2	4	0
	ECHL	Totals	106	59	63	122	58	—	—	—	—	—

Born; 9/30/76, Middletown, Nova Scotia. 5-11, 192. Last amateur club; Kingston (OHL).

Dave MacLean — Defenseman
Regular Season / Playoffs

Season	Team	League	GP	G	A	PTS	PIM	GP	G	A	PTS	PIM
98-99	Asheville	UHL	2	0	0	0	0	—	—	—	—	—
98-99	Fort Worth	CHL	1	0	0	0	0	—	—	—	—	—

Born; 4/8/75, Ancaster, Ontario. 6-1, 190.

Donald Maclean — Center
Regular Season / Playoffs

Season	Team	League	GP	G	A	PTS	PIM	GP	G	A	PTS	PIM
97-98	Los Angeles	NHL	22	5	2	7	4	—	—	—	—	—
97-98	Fredericton	AHL	39	9	5	14	32	4	1	3	4	2
98-99	Springfield	AHL	41	5	14	19	31	—	—	—	—	—
98-99	Grand Rapids	IHL	28	6	13	19	8	—	—	—	—	—
	AHL	Totals	80	14	19	33	63	4	1	3	4	2

Born; 1/14/77, Sydney, Nova Scotia. 6-2, 174. Drafted by Los Angeles Kings (2nd choice, 33rd overall) in 1995 Entry Draft. Last amateur club; Hull

Chad MacLeod — Goaltender
Regular Season / Playoffs

Season	Team	League	GP	W	L	T	MIN	SO	AVG	GP	W	L	MIN	SO	AVG
96-97	Flint	UHL	4	0	0	0	37	0	4.81	—	—	—	—	—	—
97-98															
98-99	Thunder Bay	UHL	3	1	1	0	111	0	7.55	—	—	—	—	—	—
	UHL	Totals	7	1	1	0	148	0	6.88	—	—	—	—	—	—

Born; 2/26/75, Toronto, Ontario.

Pat MacLeod — Defenseman
Regular Season / Playoffs

Season	Team	League	GP	G	A	PTS	PIM	GP	G	A	PTS	PIM
89-90	Kalamazoo	IHL	82	9	38	47	27	10	1	6	7	2
90-91	Minnesota	NHL	1	0	1	1	0	—	—	—	—	—
90-91	Kalamazoo	IHL	59	10	30	40	16	11	1	2	3	5
91-92	San Jose	NHL	37	5	11	16	4	—	—	—	—	—
91-92	Kansas City	IHL	45	9	21	30	19	11	1	4	5	4
92-93	San Jose	NHL	13	0	1	1	10	—	—	—	—	—
92-93	Kansas City	IHL	18	8	8	16	14	10	2	4	6	7
93-94	Milwaukee	IHL	73	21	52	73	18	3	1	2	3	0
94-95	Milwaukee	IHL	69	11	36	47	16	15	3	6	9	8
95-96	Dallas	NHL	2	0	0	0	0	—	—	—	—	—
95-96	Michigan	IHL	50	3	23	26	18	7	0	3	3	0
96-97	Kansas City	IHL	41	5	8	13	8	3	2	0	2	0
97-98	Cincinnati	IHL	78	16	39	55	51	9	0	6	6	8
98-99	Cincinnati	IHL	18	5	5	10	4	3	0	2	2	4
	NHL	Totals	53	5	13	18	14	—	—	—	—	—
	IHL	Totals	533	97	260	357	191	82	11	35	46	38

Born; 6/15/69, Melfort, Saskatchewan. 5-11, 190. Drafted by Minnesota North Stars (5th choice, 87th overall) in 1989 Entry Draft. Claimed by San Jose Sharks from Minnesota in Dispersal Draft (5/30/91). 1993-94 IHL First Team All-Star. Member of 1991-92 IHL champion Kansas City Blades. Last amateur club; Kamloops (WHL).

Tyler MacMillan — Forward
Regular Season / Playoffs

Season	Team	League	GP	G	A	PTS	PIM	GP	G	A	PTS	PIM
98-99	Dayton	ECHL	1	0	0	0	0	—	—	—	—	—
98-99	Columbus	ECHL	11	0	0	0	0	—	—	—	—	—
	ECHL	Totals	12	0	0	0	0	—	—	—	—	—

Born; Last amateur club; Wilfrid Laurier (OUAA)

Ian MacNeil — Center
Regular Season / Playoffs

Season	Team	League	GP	G	A	PTS	PIM	GP	G	A	PTS	PIM
97-98	New Haven	AHL	68	12	21	33	67	3	1	0	1	10
98-99	New Haven	AHL	47	6	4	10	62	—	—	—	—	—
	AHL	Totals	115	18	25	43	129	3	1	0	1	10

Born; 4/27/77, Halifax, Nova Scotia. 6-2, 171. Drafted by Hartford Whalers (3rd choice, 85th overall) in 1995 Entry Draft. Last amateur club; Oshawa (OHL).

B.J. MacPherson — Left Wing
Regular Season / Playoffs

Season	Team	League	GP	G	A	PTS	PIM	GP	G	A	PTS	PIM
94-95	Worcester	AHL	2	0	0	0	8	—	—	—	—	—
94-95	Greensboro	ECHL	15	4	7	11	34	—	—	—	—	—
94-95	Toledo	ECHL	54	16	30	46	117	3	1	3	4	18
95-96	Worcester	AHL	11	1	1	2	10	—	—	—	—	—
95-96	Toledo	ECHL	64	22	45	67	251	5	1	3	4	10
96-97	Long Beach	IHL	4	0	0	0	7	—	—	—	—	—
96-97	Las Vegas	IHL	1	0	0	0	0	—	—	—	—	—
96-97	San Diego	WCHL	60	29	47	76	157	8	4	8	12	30
97-98	Long Beach	IHL	1	1	0	1	2	—	—	—	—	—
97-98	San Diego	WCHL	63	25	50	75	181	13	3	6	9	45
98-99	Long Beach	IHL	4	1	2	3	2	—	—	—	—	—
98-99	San Diego	WCHL	61	37	43	80	160	12	5	4	9	14
	AHL	Totals	13	1	1	2	18	—	—	—	—	—
	IHL	Totals	10	2	2	4	11	—	—	—	—	—
	WCHL	Totals	184	91	140	231	498	33	12	18	30	89
	ECHL	Totals	133	42	82	124	402	8	2	6	8	28

Born; 9/23/73, Mississauga, Ontario. 6-2, 200. Drafted by Washington Capitals (10th choice, 263rd overall) in 1992 Entry Draft. Member of 1996-97 WCHL Champion San Diego Gulls. Member of 1997-98 WCHL Champion San Diego Gulls. Last amateur club; North Bay (OHL).

Don MacPherson — Left Wing

Regular Season / Playoffs

Season	Team	League	GP	G	A	PTS	PIM	GP	G	A	PTS	PIM
94-95	Daytona Beach	SUN	49	14	28	42	49	—	—	—	—	—
95-96	Daytona Beach	SHL	58	15	53	68	196	4	2	2	4	14
96-97	Huntsville	CeHL	54	14	47	61	64	9	3	5	8	12
97-98	Muskegon	UHL	10	0	3	3	10	—	—	—	—	—
97-98	Huntsville	CHL	47	22	28	50	72	3	1	0	1	2
98-99	Lake Charles	WPHL	17	1	5	6	27	—	—	—	—	—
98-99	Flint	UHL	35	10	13	23	57	12	2	3	5	11
	SHL	Totals	107	29	81	110	245	4	2	2	4	14
	CHL	Totals	101	36	75	111	136	12	4	5	9	14
	UHL	Totals	45	10	16	26	67	12	2	3	5	11

Born; 3/29/73, Fredericton, New Brunswick. 5-11, 189.

Forbes MacPherson — Center

Regular Season / Playoffs

Season	Team	League	GP	G	A	PTS	PIM	GP	G	A	PTS	PIM
96-97	Fort Wayne	IHL	2	0	1	1	4	—	—	—	—	—
96-97	Thunder Bay	CoHL	72	42	61	103	68	11	1	12	13	13
97-98	Mississippi	ECHL	55	16	27	43	65	—	—	—	—	—
97-98	Pee Dee	ECHL	12	4	3	7	8	8	1	2	3	0
98-99	Shreveport	WPHL	67	32	52	84	29	12	3	11	14	24
	ECHL	Totals	67	20	30	50	73	8	1	2	3	0

Born; 6/5/72, Charlottetown, Prince Edward Island. 5-10, 178. Traded to Pee Dee by Mississippi with Cody Bowtell for Vaclav Nedomansky (3/98). 1996-97 CoHL Rookie of the Year. 1996-97 CoHL All-Rookie Team. Member of 1998-99 WPHL Champion Shreveport Mudbugs. Last amateur club; Prince Edward Island

Michael MacPherson — Defenseman

Regular Season / Playoffs

Season	Team	League	GP	G	A	PTS	PIM	GP	G	A	PTS	PIM
98-99	Dayton	ECHL	1	0	0	0	0	—	—	—	—	—

Born;

Steve MacSwain — Right Wing

Regular Season / Playoffs

Season	Team	League	GP	G	A	PTS	PIM	GP	G	A	PTS	PIM
87-88	Salt Lake City	IHL	61	16	20	36	52	3	0	0	0	2
88-89	Konigsbrunn	Germany	24	41	31	72	58	—	—	—	—	—
89-90	Renon	Italy	32	42	54	96	26	—	—	—	—	—
90-91	Morrom	Sweden	30	26	17	43	22	—	—	—	—	—
91-92	Konigsbrunn	Germany	25	45	54	99	48	—	—	—	—	—
91-92	Zug	Switz.	3	1	0	1	0	—	—	—	—	—
92-93	Konigsbrunn	Germany	17	27	23	50	12	—	—	—	—	—
92-93	Sheffield	England	13	24	17	41	10	—	—	—	—	—
92-93	Fargo-Moorehead	AHA	3	3	3	6	0	—	—	—	—	—
92-93	Flint	CoHL	7	2	5	7	2	—	—	—	—	—
93-94	Vienna	Austria	19	21	17	38	22	—	—	—	—	—
94-95	Vienna	Austria	15	4	9	13	30	—	—	—	—	—
94-95	Konigsbrunn	Germany	16	17	24	41	41	—	—	—	—	—
95-96	Anchorage	WCHL	44	24	27	51	59	—	—	—	—	—
96-97	Anchorage	WCHL	41	13	17	30	33	—	—	—	—	—
97-98	Anchorage	WCHL	41	10	21	31	16	4	1	1	2	4
98-99	Anchorage	WCHL	8	2	2	4	17	2	0	0	0	0
	WCHL	Totals	224	49	67	116	125	6	1	1	2	4

Born; 8/8/65, Anchorage, Alaska. 5-8, 180. Selected in 1986 NHL Supplemental Draft by Calgary Flames. Member of 1987-88 IHL Champion Salt Lake City Golden Eagles. Last amateur club; Minnesota (WCHA).

Mike MacWilliam — Left Wing

Regular Season / Playoffs

Season	Team	League	GP	G	A	PTS	PIM	GP	G	A	PTS	PIM
88-89	Milwaukee	IHL	6	1	1	2	28	1	0	0	0	0
88-89	Flint	IHL	18	0	0	0	92	—	—	—	—	—
89-90	DNP	Injured										
90-91	Adirondack	AHL	8	0	0	0	32	—	—	—	—	—
90-91	Greensboro	ECHL	15	2	7	9	209	9	3	1	4	*118
91-92	St. John's	AHL	44	7	8	15	301	2	0	0	0	8
91-92	Greensboro	ECHL	8	2	5	7	94	—	—	—	—	—
92-93	Greensboro	ECHL	12	5	5	10	137	—	—	—	—	—
93-94	Tulsa	CeHL	39	16	12	28	326	8	4	0	4	88
94-95	Denver	IHL	30	5	6	11	218	12	2	2	4	56
95-96	Islanders	NHL	6	0	0	0	14	—	—	—	—	—
95-96	Utah	IHL	53	8	16	24	317	6	0	2	2	53
96-97	Phoenix	IHL	29	1	3	4	169	—	—	—	—	—
97-98	Cardiff	BSL	31	4	0	4	96	9	3	1	4	16
98-99	Cardiff	BSL	40	9	11	20	242	10	1	0	1	51
	IHL	Totals	136	15	26	41	791	19	6	4	10	109
	AHL	Totals	52	7	8	15	333	2	0	0	0	8
	BSL	Totals	71	13	11	24	338	19	4	1	5	67
	ECHL	Totals	35	9	17	26	440	9	3	1	4	118

Born; 2/14/67, Burnaby, British Columbia. 6-1, 195. Signed as a free agent by Philadelphia Flyers (10/7/86). Signed as a free agent by Toronto Maple Leafs (7/30/91). Signed as a free agent by New York Islanders (7/25/95). Signed as a free agent by Phoenix Roadrunners (1996). Member of 1994-95 IHL champion Denver Grizzlies. Member of 1995-96 IHL champion Utah Grizzlies.

John Madden — Center

Regular Season / Playoffs

Season	Team	League	GP	G	A	PTS	PIM	GP	G	A	PTS	PIM
97-98	Albany	AHL	74	20	36	56	40	13	3	13	16	14
98-99	New Jersey	NHL	4	0	1	1	0	—	—	—	—	—
98-99	Albany	AHL	75	38	60	98	44	5	2	2	4	6
	AHL	Totals	149	58	96	154	84	18	5	15	20	20

Born; 5/4/75, Barrie, Ontario. 5-11, 185. Signed as a free agent by New Jersey Devils (6/26/97). Last amateur club; Michigan (CCHA).

Darrin Madeley — Goaltender

Regular Season / Playoffs

Season	Team	League	GP	W	L	T	MIN	SO	AVG	GP	W	L	MIN	SO	AVG
92-93	Ottawa	NHL	2	0	2	0	90	0	6.67	—	—	—	—	—	—
92-93	New Haven	AHL	41	10	16	9	2295	0	3.32	—	—	—	—	—	—
93-94	Ottawa	NHL	32	3	18	5	1583	0	4.36	—	—	—	—	—	—
93-94	PEI	AHL	6	0	4	0	270	0	5.77	—	—	—	—	—	—
94-95	Ottawa	NHL	5	1	3	0	255	0	3.53	—	—	—	—	—	—
94-95	PEI	AHL	3	1	1	1	185	0	2.59	—	—	—	—	—	—
94-95	Detroit	IHL	9	7	2	0	498	1	2.41	—	—	—	—	—	—
95-96	PEI	AHL	1	1	0	0	60	0	4.00	—	—	—	—	—	—
95-96	Detroit	IHL	40	16	14	4	2047	0	3.17	7	3	3	354	0	3.89
96-97	Detroit	IHL	4	2	0	0	177	0	3.72	—	—	—	—	—	—
96-97	Saint John	AHL	46	11	18	11	2316	0	3.21	2	0	0	58	0	0.00
97-98	Richmond	ECHL	5	1	1	0	138	0	3.49	—	—	—	—	—	—
97-98	TPS Turku	Finland	2	1	0	0	85	0	1.41	—	—	—	—	—	—
98-99	Rosenheim	Germany	3	—	—	—	127	0	3.78	—	—	—	—	—	—
98-99	Pensacola	ECHL	32	12	16	3	1792	3	3.08	—	—	—	—	—	—
	NHL	Totals	39	4	23	5	1928	0	4.36	—	—	—	—	—	—
	AHL	Totals	97	23	39	21	5126	0	3.38	2	0	0	58	0	0.00
	IHL	Totals	53	25	16	4	2722	1	3.06	7	3	3	354	0	3.89
	ECHL	Totals	37	13	17	3	1930	3	3.11	—	—	—	—	—	—

Born; 2/25/68, Holland Landing, Ontario. 5-11, 165. Signed as a free agent by Ottawa Senators (6/20/92). 1992-93 AHL Second Team All-Star. Selected by Florida in 1998 ECHL Expansion Draft. Last amateur club; Lake Superior State (CCHA).

Mike Mader — Defenseman

Regular Season / Playoffs

Season	Team	League	GP	G	A	PTS	PIM	GP	G	A	PTS	PIM
97-98	Providence	H.E.	34	7	13	20	50	—	—	—	—	—
97-98	Springfield	AHL	2	0	0	0	0	—	—	—	—	—
98-99	Lowell	AHL	52	5	9	14	91	2	0	0	0	0
98-99	Roanoke	ECHL	14	3	2	5	38	—	—	—	—	—
	AHL	Totals	54	5	9	14	91	2	0	0	0	0

Born; 11/7/75, Manchester, Connecticut. 6-2, 180. Drafted by Winnipeg Jets (10th choice, 238th overall) in 1994 Entry Draft. Signed as a free agent by New York Islanders (9/5/98). Last amateur club; Providence (Hockey East).

Stephane Madore — Defenseman

Regular Season / Playoffs

Season	Team	League	GP	G	A	PTS	PIM	GP	G	A	PTS	PIM
95-96	Louisville	ECHL	59	1	7	8	179	2	1	0	1	6
96-97	Kentucky	AHL	7	0	1	1	32	—	—	—	—	—
96-97	Louisville	ECHL	56	5	14	19	200	—	—	—	—	—
97-98	Portland	AHL	4	0	2	2	12	—	—	—	—	—
97-98	Louisville	ECHL	54	8	27	35	175	—	—	—	—	—
98-99	Quad City	UHL	57	1	19	20	206	14	1	0	1	43
	AHL	Totals	11	0	3	3	44	—	—	—	—	—
	ECHL	Totals	169	14	48	62	554	2	1	0	1	6

Born; 3/13/74, Hull, Quebec. 6-2, 188. Selected by Knoxville in 1999 UHL Expansion Draft. Last amateur club; Beauport (QMJHL).

Marc Magliarditi — Goaltender

Regular Season / Playoffs

Season	Team	League	GP	W	L	T	MIN	SO	AVG	GP	W	L	MIN	SO	AVG
97-98	Indianapolis	IHL	3	1	2	0	179	0	3.35	—	—	—	—	—	—
97-98	Fort Wayne	IHL	2	0	1	1	120	0	3.01	—	—	—	—	—	—
97-98	Detroit	IHL	10	5	4	0	513	0	3.51	—	—	—	—	—	—
97-98	Columbus	ECHL	28	13	11	3	1644	2	3.14	—	—	—	—	—	—
98-99	Florida	ECHL	47	*32	10	3	2746	5	2.27	5	3	2	332	1	2.53
	IHL	Totals	15	6	7	1	812	0	3.40	—	—	—	—	—	—
	ECHL	Totals	75	45	21	6	4390	7	2.60	5	3	2	332	1	2.53

Born; 7/9/76, Niagara Falls, New York. 6-0, 180. Drafted by Chicago Blackhawks (6th choice, 146th overall) in 1995 Entry Draft. 1998-99 ECHL Second Team All-Star. Last amateur club; Red Deer (WHL).

Troy Maguire — Goaltender

Regular Season / Playoffs

Season	Team	League	GP	W	L	T	MIN	SO	AVG	GP	W	L	MIN	SO	AVG
98-99	Jacksonville	ECHL	2	0	1	1	119	0	4.52	—	—	—	—	—	—
98-99	Richmond	ECHL	1	1	0	0	40	0	1.50	—	—	—	—	—	—
	ECHL	Totals	3	1	1	1	159	0	3.76	—	—	—	—	—	—

Born;

Kim Maier — Left Wing

Regular Season / Playoffs

Season	Team	League	GP	G	A	PTS	PIM	GP	G	A	PTS	PIM
92-93	Wheeling	ECHL	5	1	0	1	2	—	—	—	—	—
92-93	Knoxville	ECHL	55	31	19	50	45	—	—	—	—	—
93-94	Knoxville	ECHL	66	35	32	67	54	3	4	0	4	0
94-95	Tilburg	Holland	34	45	27	72	38	—	—	—	—	—
95-96	Knoxville	ECHL	70	52	60	112	92	8	5	7	12	12
96-97	Asiago	Italy	32	31	35	66	32	—	—	—	—	—
97-98	Tacoma	WCHL	55	*56	47	103	57	12	6	11	17	10
98-99	Tacoma	WCHL	49	34	42	76	97	11	*10	5	15	18
	ECHL	Totals	196	119	111	230	193	11	9	7	16	12
	WCHL	Totals	104	90	89	179	154	23	16	16	32	28

Born; 3/25/71, Estevan, Saskatchewan. 5-10, 175. 1997-98 WCHL First Team All-Star. Member of 1998-99 WCHL Champion Tacoma Sabrecats.

Jacques Mailhot — Right Wing

Regular Season / Playoffs

Season	Team	League	GP	G	A	PTS	PIM	GP	G	A	PTS	PIM
87-88	Fredericton	AHL	28	2	6	8	137	8	0	0	0	18
87-88	Baltimore	AHL	15	2	0	2	167	—	—	—	—	—
88-89	Quebec	NHL	5	0	0	0	33	—	—	—	—	—
88-89	Halifax	AHL	35	4	1	5	259	1	0	0	0	5
89-90	Hampton Roads	ECHL	5	0	2	2	62	—	—	—	—	—
89-90	Phoenix	IHL	15	0	0	0	70	—	—	—	—	—
89-90	Cape Breton	AHL	6	0	1	1	12	—	—	—	—	—
89-90	Moncton	AHL	6	0	0	0	20	—	—	—	—	—
90-91	Moncton	AHL	13	0	0	0	43	—	—	—	—	—
90-91	San Diego	IHL	1	0	0	0	2	—	—	—	—	—
91-92	Flint	CoHL	29	15	12	27	237	—	—	—	—	—
91-92	Detroit	CoHL	5	2	2	4	44	4	0	1	1	27
92-93	Detroit	CoHL	48	14	21	35	273	4	2	4	6	12
93-94	Detroit	CoHL	21	1	9	10	122	3	0	1	1	49
94-95	Rochester	AHL	15	0	1	1	52	—	—	—	—	—
94-95	Utica	CoHL	59	11	17	28	302	—	—	—	—	—
95-96	Utica	CoHL	8	1	0	1	71	—	—	—	—	—
95-96	Quad City	CoHL	50	14	8	22	253	3	0	0	0	52
96-97	Utah	IHL	4	0	0	0	32	—	—	—	—	—
96-97	Central Texas	WPHL	34	5	8	13	247	8	0	3	3	24
97-98	Central Texas	WPHL	50	14	18	32	277	4	2	1	3	44
98-99	Fresno	WCHL	50	7	22	29	289	3	1	0	1	10
	AHL	Totals	118	8	9	17	690	9	0	0	0	23
	IHL	Totals	20	0	0	0	104	—	—	—	—	—
	CoHL	Totals	220	58	69	127	1302	14	2	6	8	140
	WPHL	Totals	84	19	26	45	524	12	2	4	6	68

Born; 12/5/61, Shawnigan, Quebec. 6-2, 208.

Chris Maillet — Defenseman

Regular Season / Playoffs

Season	Team	League	GP	G	A	PTS	PIM	GP	G	A	PTS	PIM
98-99	Muskegon	UHL	67	5	5	10	174	18	0	0	0	8

Born; 1/28/76, Moncton, New Brunswick. 6-5, 220. Drafted by Tampa Bay Lightning (7th choice, 164th overall) in 1994 Entry Draft. Selected by Madison in 1999 UHL Expansion Draft. Member of 1998-99 UHL Champion Muskegon Fury. Last amateur club; St. John (MHL).

Adam Mair — Center

Regular Season / Playoffs

Season	Team	League	GP	G	A	PTS	PIM	GP	G	A	PTS	PIM
98-99	Owen Sound	OHL	43	23	41	64	109	16	10	10	20	47
98-99	Toronto	NHL	—	—	—	—	—	5	1	0	1	14
98-99	St. John's	AHL	—	—	—	—	—	3	1	0	1	6

Born; 2/15/79, Hamilton, Ontario. 6-0, 189. Drafted by Toronto Maple Leafs (2nd choice, 84th overall) in 1997 Entry Draft. Last amateur club; Owen Sound

Ryan Mair — Forward

Regular Season / Playoffs

Season	Team	League	GP	G	A	PTS	PIM	GP	G	A	PTS	PIM
98-99	Amarillo	WPHL	9	1	2	3	2	—	—	—	—	—
98-99	Tulsa	CHL	8	1	2	3	6	—	—	—	—	—
98-99	Mohawk Valley	UHL	26	6	3	9	33	—	—	—	—	—

Born; 12/15/76, Timmins, Ontario. 5-11, 190.

Xavier Majic — Center

Regular Season / Playoffs

Season	Team	League	GP	G	A	PTS	PIM	GP	G	A	PTS	PIM
94-95	Fredericton	AHL	21	2	3	5	4	17	3	9	12	0
94-95	Wheeling	ECHL	49	20	31	51	41	—	—	—	—	—
95-96	Fredericton	AHL	70	13	25	38	38	10	1	5	6	2
96-97	Canada	National	57	14	27	41	58	—	—	—	—	—
97-98	Newcastle	BSL	26	10	15	25	14	2	1	0	1	2
98-99	Kentucky	AHL	1	0	1	1	0	—	—	—	—	—
98-99	Adirondack	AHL	33	2	15	17	12	2	0	0	0	0
98-99	Manitoba	IHL	1	0	0	0	0	—	—	—	—	—
98-99	Jacksonville	ECHL	33	16	28	44	30	—	—	—	—	—
	AHL	Totals	125	17	44	61	54	29	4	14	18	2
	ECHL	Totals	82	36	59	95	71	—	—	—	—	—

Born; 3/10/73, Fernie, British Columbia. 6-0, 190. Drafted by Vancouver Canucks (21th choice, 249th overall) in 1991 Entry Draft. Signed as a free agent by Montreal Canadiens (4/22/94). Last amateur club; RPI (ECAC).

Mark Major — Left Wing

Regular Season / Playoffs

Season	Team	League	GP	G	A	PTS	PIM	GP	G	A	PTS	PIM
90-91	Muskegon	IHL	60	8	10	18	160	5	0	0	0	0
91-92	Muskegon	IHL	80	13	18	31	302	12	1	3	4	29
92-93	Cleveland	IHL	82	13	15	28	155	3	0	0	0	0
93-94	Providence	AHL	61	17	9	26	176	—	—	—	—	—
94-95	Detroit	IHL	78	17	19	36	229	5	0	1	1	23
95-96	Adirondack	AHL	78	10	19	29	234	3	0	0	0	21
96-97	Detroit	NHL	2	0	0	0	5	—	—	—	—	—
96-97	Adirondack	AHL	78	17	18	35	213	4	0	0	0	13
97-98	Portland	AHL	79	13	2	15	343	10	2	1	3	52
98-99	Portland	AHL	66	5	4	9	250	—	—	—	—	—
	AHL	Totals	362	62	52	114	1216	17	2	1	3	86
	IHL	Totals	300	51	62	113	846	25	1	4	5	52

Born; 3/20/70, Toronto, Ontario. 6-4, 216. Drafted by Pittsburgh Penguins (2nd choice, 25th overall) in 1988 Entry Draft. Signed as a free agent by Boston Bruins (7/22/93). Signed as a free agent by Detroit Red Wings (6/26/95). Signed as a free agent by Washington Capitals (8/31/97). Last amateur club; Kingston (OHL).

Marko Makinen — Right Wing

Regular Season / Playoffs

Season	Team	League	GP	G	A	PTS	PIM	GP	G	A	PTS	PIM
97-98	Kentucky	AHL	26	2	2	4	15	—	—	—	—	—
97-98	Louisville	ECHL	38	10	6	16	19	—	—	—	—	—
98-99	Lukko Rauma	Finland	21	1	0	1	30	—	—	—	—	—
98-99	Indianapolis	IHL	5	0	0	0	0	—	—	—	—	—
98-99	Greenville	ECHL	20	3	5	8	14	—	—	—	—	—
	ECHL	Totals	58	13	11	24	33	—	—	—	—	—

Born; 3/31/77, Turku, Finland. 6-5, 200. Drafted by San Jose Sharks (3rd choice, 64th overall) in 1995 Entry Draft. Signed as a free agent by Chicago Blackhawks (9/2/98).

Thomas Makinen — Left Wing

Regular Season / Playoffs

Season	Team	League	GP	G	A	PTS	PIM	GP	G	A	PTS	PIM
98-99	Port Huron	UHL	4	0	1	1	0	—	—	—	—	—

Born; 4/21/75. 6-0, 190.

Eric Maksimenko — Center

Regular Season / Playoffs

Season	Team	League	GP	G	A	PTS	PIM	GP	G	A	PTS	PIM
98-99	Monroe	WPHL	1	0	0	0	0	—	—	—	—	—

Born; 1/2/78, Elk River, Minnesota. 5-10, 180.

Kevin Malgunas — Right Wing

Regular Season / Playoffs

Season	Team	League	GP	G	A	PTS	PIM	GP	G	A	PTS	PIM
92-93	Richmond	ECHL	29	7	5	12	106	—	—	—	—	—
92-93	Hampton Roads	ECHL	27	14	18	32	94	4	2	1	3	4
93-94	Hampton Roads	ECHL	37	12	28	40	132	—	—	—	—	—
93-94	Raleigh	ECHL	10	6	3	9	26	14	2	4	6	41
94-95	Detroit	CoHL	39	13	21	34	127	—	—	—	—	—
94-95	Detroit	IHL	17	0	1	1	52	—	—	—	—	—
94-95	Houston	IHL	20	2	5	7	58	2	1	0	1	12
95-96	Houston	IHL	31	1	4	5	60	—	—	—	—	—
96-97	Portland	AHL	3	0	0	0	4	—	—	—	—	—
96-97	Orlando	IHL	2	0	1	1	0	—	—	—	—	—
96-97	Tallahassee	ECHL	54	17	18	35	197	3	0	0	0	11
97-98	Lake Charles	WPHL	54	12	15	27	139	4	2	0	2	22
98-99	Lake Charles	WPHL	66	11	28	39	133	11	2	4	6	12
	IHL	Totals	70	3	11	14	170	2	1	0	1	12
	ECHL	Totals	157	56	72	128	555	21	4	5	9	56
	WPHL	Totals	120	23	43	66	272	15	4	4	8	34

Born; 7/12/71, Prince George, British Columbia. 5-11, 190. Last amateur club; Tacoma (WHL).

Stewart Malgunas — Defenseman

Regular Season / Playoffs

Season	Team	League	GP	G	A	PTS	PIM	GP	G	A	PTS	PIM
90-91	Adirondack	AHL	78	5	19	24	70	2	0	0	0	4
91-92	Adirondack	AHL	69	4	28	32	82	18	2	6	8	28
92-93	Adirondack	AHL	45	3	12	15	39	11	3	3	6	8
93-94	Philadelphia	NHL	67	1	3	4	86	—	—	—	—	—
94-95	Philadelphia	NHL	4	0	0	0	4	—	—	—	—	—
94-95	Hershey	AHL	32	3	5	8	28	6	2	1	3	31
95-96	Winnipeg	NHL	29	0	1	1	32	—	—	—	—	—
95-96	Washington	NHL	1	0	0	0	0	—	—	—	—	—
95-96	Portland	AHL	16	2	5	7	18	13	1	3	4	19
96-97	Washington	NHL	6	0	0	0	2	—	—	—	—	—
96-97	Portland	AHL	68	6	12	18	59	5	0	0	0	8
97-98	Washington	NHL	8	0	0	0	12	—	—	—	—	—
97-98	Portland	AHL	69	14	25	39	73	9	1	1	2	19
98-99	Washington	NHL	10	0	0	0	6	—	—	—	—	—
98-99	Portland	AHL	33	2	10	12	49	—	—	—	—	—
98-99	Detroit	IHL	9	0	2	2	10	11	0	1	1	21
	NHL	Totals	125	1	4	5	142	—	—	—	—	—
	AHL	Totals	410	39	116	155	418	64	9	14	23	117

Born; 4/21/70, Prince George, British Columbia. 5-11, 190. Drafted by Detroit Red Wings (3rd choice, 66th overall) in 1990 Entry Draft. Traded to Philadelphia Flyers by Detroit for Philadelphia's fifth round choice (David Arsenault) in 1995 Draft (9/9/93). Signed as a free agent by Winnipeg Jets (8/9/95). Traded to Washington Capitals by Winnipeg for Denis Chasse (2/15/96). Member of 1991-92 AHL champion Adirondack Red Wings. Last amateur club; Seattle (WHL).

Gregg Malicke — Goaltender

Regular Season / Playoffs

Season	Team	League	GP	W	L	T	MIN	SO	AVG	GP	W	L	MIN	SO	AVG
98-99	Alexandria	WPHL	22	4	9	4	925	0	4.60	—	—	—	—	—	—

Born; 4/20/75, Rochester Hills, Michigan. 6-0, 175. Last amateur club; Michigan (CCHA).

Marek Malik — Defenseman

Regular Season / Playoffs

Season	Team	League	GP	G	A	PTS	PIM	GP	G	A	PTS	PIM
94-95	Springfield	AHL	58	11	30	41	91	—	—	—	—	—
94-95	Hartford	NHL	1	0	1	1	0	—	—	—	—	—
95-96	Hartford	NHL	7	0	0	0	4	—	—	—	—	—
95-96	Springfield	AHL	68	8	14	22	135	8	1	3	4	20
96-97	Hartford	NHL	47	1	5	6	50	—	—	—	—	—
96-97	Springfield	AHL	3	0	3	3	4	—	—	—	—	—
97-98	Malmo IF	Sweden	37	1	5	6	21	—	—	—	—	—
98-99	Carolina	NHL	52	2	9	11	36	4	0	0	0	4
98-99	New Haven	AHL	21	2	8	10	28	—	—	—	—	—
	NHL	Totals	107	3	15	18	90	4	0	0	0	4
	AHL	Totals	150	21	55	76	258	8	1	3	4	20

Born; 6/24/75, Ostrava, Czechoslovakia. 6-5, 190. Drafted by Hartford Whalers (2nd choice, 72nd overall) in 1993 Entry Draft.

Dean Malkoc — Defenseman

Season	Team	League	GP	G	A	PTS	PIM	GP	G	A	PTS	PIM
			Regular Season					Playoffs				
90-91	Kamloops	WHL	8	1	4	5	47	—	—	—	—	—
90-91	Swift Current	WHL	56	10	23	33	248	3	0	2	2	5
90-91	Utica	AHL	1	0	0	0	0	—	—	—	—	—
91-92	Utica	AHL	66	1	11	12	274	4	0	2	2	6
92-93	Utica	AHL	73	5	19	24	255	5	0	1	1	8
93-94	Albany	AHL	79	0	9	9	296	5	0	0	0	21
94-95	Albany	AHL	9	0	1	1	52	—	—	—	—	—
94-95	Indianapolis	IHL	62	1	3	4	193	—	—	—	—	—
95-96	Vancouver	NHL	41	0	2	2	136	—	—	—	—	—
96-97	Boston	NHL	33	0	0	0	70	—	—	—	—	—
96-97	Providence	AHL	4	0	2	2	28	—	—	—	—	—
97-98	Boston	NHL	40	1	0	1	86	—	—	—	—	—
98-99	Islanders	NHL	2	0	1	1	7	—	—	—	—	—
98-99	Lowell	AHL	61	2	8	10	193	3	0	0	0	8
	NHL	Totals	116	2	2	4	299	—	—	—	—	—
	AHL	Totals	293	8	50	58	1098	17	0	3	3	43

Born; 1/26/70, Vancouver, British Columbia. 6-3, 215. Drafted by New Jersey Devils (7th choice, 95th overall) in 1990 Entry Draft. Traded to Chicago Blackhawks by New Jersey for Rob Conn (1/30/95). Signed as a free agent by Vancouver Canucks (9/8/95). Claimed by Boston Bruins from Vancouver in NHL Waiver Draft (9/30/96). Signed as a free agent by New York Islanders (8/19/98). Last amateur club; Swift Current (WHL).

Kurt Mallett — Right Wing

Season	Team	League	GP	G	A	PTS	PIM	GP	G	A	PTS	PIM
			Regular Season					Playoffs				
94-95	Richmond	ECHL	68	24	27	51	24	17	6	10	16	4
95-96	Richmond	ECHL	46	13	21	34	18	—	—	—	—	—
95-96	Jacksonville	ECHL	17	2	14	16	10	18	9	9	18	2
96-97	Jacksonville	ECHL	61	25	48	73	20	—	—	—	—	—
96-97	Phoenix	IHL	12	4	2	6	2	—	—	—	—	—
97-98	Fort Wayne	IHL	5	0	1	1	2	—	—	—	—	—
97-98	San Antonio	IHL	6	3	3	6	0	—	—	—	—	—
97-98	Jacksonville	ECHL	60	26	36	62	10	—	—	—	—	—
98-99	Pee Dee	ECHL	70	27	31	58	23	13	1	3	4	12
	IHL	Totals	23	7	6	13	4	—	—	—	—	—
	ECHL	Totals	322	117	177	294	105	48	16	22	38	18

Born; 3/27/71, Saugus, Massachusetts. 6-0, 185. Traded to Pee Dee by Jacksonville for Billy Pierce and Chad Wilson (7/98). Member of 1994-95 ECHL champion Richmond Renegades. Last amateur club: Salem State (NCAA 3).

Tony Malm — Right Wing

Season	Team	League	GP	G	A	PTS	PIM	GP	G	A	PTS	PIM
			Regular Season					Playoffs				
98-99	Edinburgh	BNL	17	8	13	21	12	—	—	—	—	—
98-99	Tucson	WCHL	20	2	3	5	6	—	—	—	—	—

Born; 5/9/74, Alfta, Sweden. 6-1, 210.

Darren Maloney — Defenseman

Season	Team	League	GP	G	A	PTS	PIM	GP	G	A	PTS	PIM
			Regular Season					Playoffs				
96-97	Chicago	IHL	8	0	0	0	6	—	—	—	—	—
96-97	San Antonio	IHL	3	0	0	0	2	—	—	—	—	—
96-97	Peoria	ECHL	49	5	22	27	56	10	0	3	3	8
97-98	Michigan	IHL	2	0	0	0	0	—	—	—	—	—
97-98	Peoria	ECHL	69	10	27	37	86	3	0	1	1	0
98-99	Worcester	AHL	6	1	0	1	6	—	—	—	—	—
98-99	Portland	AHL	4	0	0	0	6	—	—	—	—	—
98-99	Houston	IHL	2	0	0	0	4	—	—	—	—	—
98-99	Peoria	ECHL	61	9	30	39	120	4	2	1	3	21
	IHL	Totals	15	0	0	0	12	—	—	—	—	—
	AHL	Totals	10	1	0	1	12	—	—	—	—	—
	ECHL	Totals	179	24	79	103	262	17	2	5	7	29

Born; 3/10/72, Claresholm, Alberta. 6-2, 200. 1997-98 ECHL Second All-Star Team. Last amateur club; Western Michigan (CCHA).

Dominic Maltais — Center

Season	Team	League	GP	G	A	PTS	PIM	GP	G	A	PTS	PIM
			Regular Season					Playoffs				
93-94	Rochester	AHL	1	0	0	0	0	—	—	—	—	—
93-94	Fort Worth	CeHL	64	44	27	71	88	—	—	—	—	—
94-95	Fort Worth	CeHL	66	40	38	78	204	—	—	—	—	—
95-96	Hampton Roads	ECHL	54	31	32	63	163	—	—	—	—	—
96-97	Portland	AHL	3	0	0	0	4	—	—	—	—	—
96-97	Hampton Roads	ECHL	68	42	55	97	211	9	10	7	17	20
97-98	Manchester	BSL	43	21	23	44	79	—	—	—	—	—
97-98	Hampton Roads	ECHL	24	11	6	17	58	20	5	7	12	44
98-99	Hampton Roads	ECHL	70	22	37	59	217	4	4	1	5	15
	AHL	Totals	4	0	0	0	4	—	—	—	—	—
	ECHL	Totals	216	106	130	236	649	33	19	15	34	79
	CeHL	Totals	130	84	65	149	292	—	—	—	—	—

Born; 5/31/72, Longueil, Quebec. 5-11, 188. 1996-97 ECHL Second Team All-Star. Member of 1997-98 ECHL Champion Hampton Roads Admirals. Last amateur club; St. Jean (QMJHL).

Steve Maltais — Center

Season	Team	League	GP	G	A	PTS	PIM	GP	G	A	PTS	PIM
			Regular Season					Playoffs				
88-89	Cornwall	OHL	58	53	70	123	67	18	14	16	30	16
88-89	Fort Wayne	IHL	—	—	—	—	—	4	2	1	3	0
89-90	Washington	NHL	8	0	0	0	2	1	0	0	0	0
89-90	Baltimore	AHL	67	29	37	66	54	12	6	10	16	6
90-91	Washington	NHL	7	0	0	0	2	—	—	—	—	—
90-91	Baltimore	AHL	73	36	43	79	97	6	1	4	5	10
91-92	Minnesota	NHL	12	2	1	3	2	—	—	—	—	—
91-92	Kalamazoo	IHL	48	25	31	56	51	—	—	—	—	—
91-92	Halifax	AHL	10	3	3	6	0	—	—	—	—	—
92-93	Tampa Bay	NHL	63	7	13	20	35	—	—	—	—	—
92-93	Atlanta	IHL	16	14	10	24	22	—	—	—	—	—
93-94	Detroit	NHL	4	0	1	1	0	—	—	—	—	—
93-94	Adirondack	AHL	73	35	49	84	79	12	5	11	16	14
94-95	Chicago	IHL	79	*57	40	97	145	3	1	!	2	0
95-96	Chicago	IHL	81	56	66	122	161	9	7	7	14	20
96-97	Chicago	IHL	81	*60	54	114	62	4	2	0	2	4
97-98	Chicago	IHL	82	*46	57	103	120	22	8	11	19	28
98-99	Chicago	IHL	82	*56	44	100	164	10	4	6	10	2
	NHL	Totals	94	9	15	24	41	1	0	0	0	0
	IHL	Totals	469	314	302	616	725	52	24	26	50	54
	AHL	Totals	223	103	132	235	230	30	12	25	37	30

Born; 1/25/69, Arvida, Quebec. 6-2, 210. Drafted by Washington Capitals (2nd choice, 57th overall) in 1987 Entry Draft. Traded to Minnesota North Stars by Washington with Trent Klatt for Shawn Chambers (6/21/91). Traded to Quebec Nordiques by Minnesota for Kip Miller (3/8/92). Claimed by Tampa Bay Lightning from Quebec in Expansion Draft (6/18/92). Traded to Detroit Red Wings by Tampa Bay for Dennis Vial (6/8/93). 1994-95 IHL First Team All-Star. 1995-96 IHL Second Team All-Star. 1996-97 IHL Second team All-Star. Member of 1997-98 IHL Champion Chicago Wolves. 1998-99 IHL First Team All-Star. Last amateur club; Cornwall (OHL).

Shawn Maltby — Right Wing

Season	Team	League	GP	G	A	PTS	PIM	GP	G	A	PTS	PIM
			Regular Season					Playoffs				
97-98	Muskegon	UHL	11	2	1	3	18	—	—	—	—	—
97-98	Toledo	ECHL	14	3	3	6	12	—	—	—	—	—
97-98	Dayton	ECHL	8	2	1	3	21	—	—	—	—	—
97-98	Pee Dee	ECHL	20	0	2	2	14	—	—	—	—	—
98-99	Toledo	ECHL	64	15	15	30	94	7	2	6	8	6
	ECHL	Totals	106	20	21	41	141	7	2	6	8	6

Born; 7/22/76, Cambridge, Ontario. 5-10, 180.

Stephen Maltby — Right Wing

Season	Team	League	GP	G	A	PTS	PIM	GP	G	A	PTS	PIM
			Regular Season					Playoffs				
97-98	Hammer Eisbaren	Germany	39	53	48	101	54	—	—	—	—	—
98-99	Abilene	WPHL	58	15	18	33	26	3	0	0	0	2

Born; 1/10/71, Miramichi, New Brunswick. 6-0, 205.

Igor Malykhin — Defenseman

Season	Team	League	GP	G	A	PTS	PIM	GP	G	A	PTS	PIM
			Regular Season					Playoffs				
92-93	Adirondack	AHL	78	6	22	28	95	6	0	0	0	4
93-94	Adirondack	AHL	2	0	0	0	2	—	—	—	—	—
93-94	Fort Wayne	IHL	61	2	20	22	63	7	1	3	4	6
94-95	Fort Wayne	IHL	25	3	3	6	21	—	—	—	—	—
94-95	Detroit	IHL	13	1	8	9	8	2	0	1	1	0
95-96	Detroit	CoHL	12	1	2	3	24	—	—	—	—	—
95-96	Las Vegas	IHL	12	1	1	2	16	—	—	—	—	—
96-97												
97-98	Kassel	Germany	35	0	5	5	20	—	—	—	—	—
98-99	Muskegon	UHL	29	5	17	22	29	11	0	5	5	4
	IHL	Totals	111	7	32	39	108	9	1	4	5	6
	AHL	Totals	80	6	22	28	97	6	0	0	0	4
	UHL	Totals	41	6	19	25	53	11	0	5	5	4

Born; 6/6/69, Kharkov, USSR. 6-1, 189. Drafted by Detroit Red Wings (6th choice, 142nd overall) in 1991 Entry Draft. Selected by Knoxville in 1999 UHL Expansio Draft. Member of 1998-99 UHL Champion Muskegon Fury.

Jeff Mancini — Center

Season	Team	League	GP	G	A	PTS	PIM	GP	G	A	PTS	PIM
			Regular Season					Playoffs				
98-99	New Mexico	WPHL	69	30	28	58	70	—	—	—	—	—

Born; 4/14/75, Sudbury, Ontario. 6-2, 195.

Dean Mando — Left Wing

Season	Team	League	GP	G	A	PTS	PIM	GP	G	A	PTS	PIM
			Regular Season					Playoffs				
97-98	San Antonio	IHL	1	0	0	0	0	—	—	—	—	—
97-98	Austin	WPHL	35	8	7	15	52	1	0	0	0	0
98-99	Springfield	AHL	1	0	0	0	0	—	—	—	—	—
98-99	Mississippi	ECHL	68	13	17	30	156	8	1	1	2	25

Born; 4/29/77, West Bloomfield, Michigan. 6-4, 220. Member of 1998-99 ECHL Champion Mississippi SeaWolves. Last amateur club; Windsor (OHL).

Sal Manganaro — Right Wing

Season	Team	League	GP	G	A	PTS	PIM	GP	G	A	PTS	PIM
			Regular Season					Playoffs				
96-97	Fort Wayne	IHL	7	0	0	0	0	—	—	—	—	—
96-97	Dayton	ECHL	62	24	23	47	118	4	1	1	2	0
97-98	Michigan	IHL	3	0	0	0	2	—	—	—	—	—
97-98	Cleveland	IHL	3	0	0	0	0	—	—	—	—	—
97-98	Providence	AHL	1	0	0	0	5	—	—	—	—	—
97-98	Dayton	ECHL	39	16	28	44	76	—	—	—	—	—
97-98	Richmond	ECHL	26	13	15	28	70	—	—	—	—	—
98-99	Bracknell	BSL	34	16	15	31	56	—	—	—	—	—
98-99	Richmond	ECHL	26	10	14	24	33	18	3	5	8	37
	IHL	Totals	13	0	0	0	2	—	—	—	—	—
	ECHL	Totals	127	53	66	119	264	4	1	1	2	0

Born; 12/20/72, Boston, Massachusetts. 5-11, 183. Traded to Richmond by Dayton with Daryl Lavoie for Shayne Tomlinson and Mike Noble (1/98). Last amateur club; Massachusetts (Hockey East).

Eric Manlow — Center

Season	Team	League	GP	G	A	PTS	PIM	GP	G	A	PTS	PIM
			Regular Season					Playoffs				
95-96	Indianapolis	IHL	75	6	11	17	32	4	0	1	1	4
96-97	Baltimore	AHL	36	6	6	12	13	3	0	0	0	0
96-97	Columbus	ECHL	32	18	18	36	20	—	—	—	—	—
97-98	Indianapolis	IHL	60	8	11	19	25	3	1	0	1	0
98-99	Long Beach	IHL	51	9	19	28	30	8	0	0	0	8
98-99	Florida	ECHL	18	8	15	23	11	—	—	—	—	—
	IHL	Totals	186	23	41	64	87	15	1	1	2	12
	ECHL	Totals	50	26	33	59	31	—	—	—	—	—

Born; 4/7/75, Belleville, Ontario. 6-0, 190. Drafted by Chicago Blackhawks (2nd choice, 50th overall) in 1993 Entry Draft. Last amateur club; Detroit (OHL).

Cameron Mann — Right Wing

Season	Team	League	GP	G	A	PTS	PIM	GP	G	A	PTS	PIM
			Regular Season					Playoffs				
97-98	Boston	NHL	9	0	1	1	4	—	—	—	—	—
97-98	Providence	AHL	71	21	26	47	99	—	—	—	—	—
98-99	Boston	NHL	33	5	2	7	17	1	0	0	0	0
98-99	Providence	AHL	43	21	25	46	65	11	7	7	14	4
	NHL	Totals	40	5	3	8	21	1	0	0	0	0
	AHL	Totals	114	42	51	93	164	11	7	7	14	4

Born; 4/20/77, Thompson, Manitoba. 6-0, 194. Drafted by Boston Bruins (5th choice, 99th overall) in 1995 Entry Draft. Member of 1998-99 AHL Champion Providence Bruins. Last amateur club; Peterborough (OHL).

Dallas Mann — Left Wing

Season	Team	League	GP	G	A	PTS	PIM	GP	G	A	PTS	PIM
			Regular Season					Playoffs				
98-99	Binghamton	UHL	3	0	0	0	7	—	—	—	—	—

Born; 5/31/75, Thompson, Manitoba. 5-8, 189.

Doug Mann — Right Wing

Season	Team	League	GP	G	A	PTS	PIM	GP	G	A	PTS	PIM
			Regular Season					Playoffs				
94-95	Lakeland	SUN	15	2	3	5	109	—	—	—	—	—
95-96	Lakeland	SHL	46	6	6	12	141	5	1	1	2	17
96-97	Raleigh	ECHL	52	4	1	5	203	—	—	—	—	—
97-98	Columbus	CHL	40	3	5	8	199	9	0	1	1	76
98-99	Columbus	CHL	17	1	2	3	87	—	—	—	—	—
	SHL	Totals	61	8	9	17	250	5	1	1	2	17
	CHL	Totals	57	4	7	11	286	9	0	1	1	76

Born; 7/4/73, Etobicoke, Ontario. 6-0, 195. Member of 1997-98 CHL Champion Columbus Cottonmouths.

Troy Mann — Left Wing

Season	Team	League	GP	G	A	PTS	PIM	GP	G	A	PTS	PIM
			Regular Season					Playoffs				
95-96	Saginaw	CoHL	58	30	29	59	30	—	—	—	—	—
96-97	Mississippi	ECHL	63	33	33	66	38	3	1	0	1	6
97-98	Hampton Roads	ECHL	3	2	1	3	0	—	—	—	—	—
97-98	Tallahassee	ECHL	13	7	2	9	12	—	—	—	—	—
97-98	Mississippi	ECHL	48	20	15	35	30	—	—	—	—	—
98-99	Mississippi	ECHL	50	12	15	27	34	4	1	0	1	2
	ECHL	Totals	177	74	66	140	114	7	2	0	2	8

Born; 9/3/69, New Richmond, Quebec. 5-10, 185. Selected by Trenton in 1999 ECHL Expansion Draft. Traded to Hampton Roads by Mississippi for Mike Mayhew (1/98). Member of 1998-99 ECHL Champion Mississippi SeaWolves.

Blair Manning — Center

Season	Team	League	GP	G	A	PTS	PIM	GP	G	A	PTS	PIM
			Regular Season					Playoffs				
96-97	Grand Rapids	IHL	8	1	1	2	4	1	0	1	1	0
96-97	Saint John	AHL	2	0	0	0	0	—	—	—	—	—
96-97	Baton Rouge	ECHL	60	13	33	46	77	—	—	—	—	—
97-98	Cincinnati	AHL	2	0	0	0	0	—	—	—	—	—
97-98	Grand Rapids	IHL	2	0	0	0	0	—	—	—	—	—
97-98	Muskegon	UHL	68	22	57	79	57	11	1	0	1	8
98-99	Lowell	AHL	2	0	0	0	2	—	—	—	—	—
98-99	Louisiana	ECHL	65	9	19	28	57	5	0	1	1	6
	AHL	Totals	6	0	0	0	2	—	—	—	—	—
	IHL	Totals	10	1	1	2	4	1	0	1	1	0
	ECHL	Totals	125	22	52	74	134	5	0	1	1	6

Born; 5/27/75, Vancouver, British Columbia. 5-10, 185. Last amateur club; Medicine Hat (WHL).

Jason Mansoff — Defenseman

Regular Season / Playoffs

Season	Team	League	GP	G	A	PTS	PIM	GP	G	A	PTS	PIM
96-97	Maine	H.E.	33	11	18	29	40	—	—	—	—	—
96-97	Portland	AHL	7	0	0	0	0	—	—	—	—	—
97-98	Syracuse	AHL	3	0	1	1	0	—	—	—	—	—
97-98	Portland	AHL	3	0	0	0	0	—	—	—	—	—
97-98	Detroit	IHL	29	3	5	8	14	—	—	—	—	—
97-98	Las Vegas	IHL	13	0	1	1	4	4	0	1	1	0
97-98	Hampton Roads	ECHL	22	6	7	13	19	—	—	—	—	—
98-99	Rochester	AHL	26	0	3	3	14	—	—	—	—	—
	IHL	Totals	42	3	6	9	18	4	0	1	1	0
	AHL	Totals	39	0	4	4	14	—	—	—	—	—

Born; 12/11/72, Edmonton, Alberta. 5-11, 200. Last amateur club; Maine (Hockey East).

Grady Manson — Center

Regular Season / Playoffs

Season	Team	League	GP	G	A	PTS	PIM	GP	G	A	PTS	PIM
97-98	Columbus	CHL	29	11	16	27	30	13	3	3	6	8
98-99	Columbus	CHL	69	19	31	50	99	8	2	1	3	6
	CHL	Totals	98	30	47	77	129	21	5	4	9	14

Born; 5/26/75, Brandon, Manitoba. 5-8, 175. Member of 1997-98 CHL Champion Columbus Cottonmouths.

Norm Maracle — Goaltender

Regular Season / Playoffs

Season	Team	League	GP	W	L	T	MIN	SO	AVG	GP	W	L	MIN	SO	AVG
94-95	Adirondack	AHL	39	12	15	2	1997	0	3.57	—	—	—	—	—	—
95-96	Adirondack	AHL	54	24	18	6	2949	2	2.75	1	0	1	29	0	8.11
96-97	Adirondack	AHL	*68	*34	22	9	*3843	5	2.70	4	1	3	192	1	3.13
97-98	Detroit	NHL	4	2	0	1	178	0	2.02	—	—	—	—	—	—
97-98	Adirondack	AHL	*66	27	29	8	*3710	1	3.07	3	0	3	180	0	3.33
98-99	Detroit	NHL	16	6	5	2	821	0	2.27	2	0	0	58	0	3.10
98-99	Adirondack	AHL	6	3	3	0	359	0	3.01	—	—	—	—	—	—
	NHL	Totals	20	8	5	3	999	0	2.22	2	0	0	58	0	3.10
	AHL	Totals	233	100	87	25	12858	8	2.96	8	1	7	401	1	3.59

Born; 10/2/74, Belleville, Ontario. 5-9, 175. Drafted by Detroit Red Wings (6th choice, 126th overall) in 1993 Entry Draft. Selected by Atlanta Thrashers in NHL Expansion Draft (6/25/99). 1996-97 AHL Second Team All-Star. 1997-98 AHL Second Team All-Star. Last amateur club; Saskatoon (WHL).

Roman Marakhovski — Defenseman

Regular Season / Playoffs

Season	Team	League	GP	G	A	PTS	PIM	GP	G	A	PTS	PIM
98-99	Columbus	CHL	51	2	16	18	45	10	0	2	2	10

Born; 2/22/78, Kharkov, Ukraine. 6-2, 195. Last amateur club; Sherwood Park (AJHL).

Evan Marble — Defenseman

Regular Season / Playoffs

Season	Team	League	GP	G	A	PTS	PIM	GP	G	A	PTS	PIM
97-98	Canadian	National	56	6	17	23	50	—	—	—	—	—
97-98	Long Beach	IHL	—	—	—	—	—	1	0	0	0	0
98-99	Landshut	Germany	51	2	10	12	38	2	0	0	0	4

Born; Last amateur club; University of Calgary (CWUAA).

Todd Marcellus — Left Wing

Regular Season / Playoffs

Season	Team	League	GP	G	A	PTS	PIM	GP	G	A	PTS	PIM
97-98	New Mexico	WPHL	67	27	40	67	52	10	2	7	9	24
98-99	New Mexico	WPHL	63	30	45	75	69	—	—	—	—	—
	WPHL	Totals	130	57	85	142	121	10	2	7	9	24

Born; 2/14/73, Chesterville, Ontario. 5-10, 185. Last amateur club; McGill

Derek Marchand — Forward

Regular Season / Playoffs

Season	Team	League	GP	G	A	PTS	PIM	GP	G	A	PTS	PIM
95-96	Lakeland	SHL	59	27	29	56	36	5	0	3	3	0
96-97	Columbus	CeHL	60	16	16	32	57	3	0	0	0	22
97-98	Columbus	CHL	67	11	13	24	87	13	1	0	1	9
98-99	Columbus	CHL	8	0	1	1	8	—	—	—	—	—
	CHL	Totals	135	27	30	57	152	16	1	0	1	31

Born; 12/16/71, Mantunuck, Rhode Island. 6-2, 200. Member of 1997-98 CHL Champion Columbus Cottonmouths.

Terry Marchant — Center

Regular Season / Playoffs

Season	Team	League	GP	G	A	PTS	PIM	GP	G	A	PTS	PIM
98-99	Hamilton	AHL	47	12	8	20	10	2	1	0	1	0

Born; 2/24/76, Buffalo, New York. 6-2, 205. Drafted by Edmonton Oilers (9th choice, 136th overall) in 1994 Entry Draft. Last amateur club; Lake Superior (CCHA).

Sergei Marchkov — Forward

Regular Season / Playoffs

Season	Team	League	GP	G	A	PTS	PIM	GP	G	A	PTS	PIM
98-99	Tupelo	WPHL	10	3	3	6	6	—	—	—	—	—

Born; 12/3/73, Togliatti, Russia. 6-1, 200.

Frank Marciello — Left Wing

Regular Season / Playoffs

Season	Team	League	GP	G	A	PTS	PIM	GP	G	A	PTS	PIM
98-99	Memphis	CHL	3	0	0	0	0	—	—	—	—	—

Born;

Dave Marcinyshyn — Defenseman

Regular Season / Playoffs

Season	Team	League	GP	G	A	PTS	PIM	GP	G	A	PTS	PIM
87-88	Utica	AHL	73	2	7	9	179	—	—	—	—	—
87-88	Flint	UHL	3	0	0	0	4	16	0	2	2	31
88-89	Utica	AHL	74	4	14	18	101	5	0	0	0	13
89-90	Utica	AHL	74	6	18	24	164	5	0	2	2	21
90-91	New Jersey	NHL	9	0	1	1	21	—	—	—	—	—
90-91	Utica	AHL	52	4	9	13	81	—	—	—	—	—
91-92	Quebec	NHL	5	0	0	0	26	—	—	—	—	—
91-92	Halifax	AHL	74	10	42	52	138	—	—	—	—	—
92-93	Rangers	NHL	2	0	0	0	2	—	—	—	—	—
92-93	Binghamton	AHL	67	5	25	30	184	6	0	3	3	14
93-94	Milwaukee	IHL	1	0	0	0	0	—	—	—	—	—
94-95	Milwaukee	IHL	63	2	14	16	176	—	—	—	—	—
94-95	Kalamazoo	IHL	3	0	0	0	6	16	0	1	1	16
95-96	Cincinnati	IHL	65	6	13	19	160	17	0	2	2	10
96-97	Cincinnati	IHL	74	1	9	10	141	—	—	—	—	—
97-98	Dusseldorfer	Germany	47	6	16	22	99	3	0	0	0	4
98-99	Schwenninger	Germany	43	5	9	14	101	—	—	—	—	—
	NHL	Totals	16	0	1	1	49	—	—	—	—	—
	AHL	Totals	414	31	115	146	847	16	0	5	5	48
	IHL	Totals	209	9	36	45	487	49	0	5	5	57

Born; 6/2/76, Chavlickov, Czechoslovakia. 6-0, 170. Drafted by Quebec Nordiques (3rd choice, 35th overall) in 1994 Entry Draft. Member of 1996-97 AHL Champion Hershey Bears. Traded to Anaheim Mighty Ducks by Colorado for Warren Rychel and conditional 1999 Entry Draft Pick (3/24/98). Last amateur club; Kamloops (WHL).

Dan Marcotte — Left Wing

Regular Season / Playoffs

Season	Team	League	GP	G	A	PTS	PIM	GP	G	A	PTS	PIM
97-98	Pensacola	ECHL	24	4	3	7	46	—	—	—	—	—
97-98	Tucson	WCHL	19	5	1	6	59	—	—	—	—	—
98-99	Bakersfield	WCHL	25	5	5	10	51	—	—	—	—	—
98-99	Idaho	WCHL	12	1	3	4	16	2	0	0	0	0
	WCHL	Totals	80	15	12	27	172	2	0	0	0	0

Born; 8/10/76, Boxford, Massachusetts. 6-4, 225. Last amateur club; Laval (QMJHL).

Peter Marek — Center

Regular Season / Playoffs

Season	Team	League	GP	G	A	PTS	PIM	GP	G	A	PTS	PIM
93-94	Cape Breton	AHL	27	7	8	15	12	—	—	—	—	—
93-94	Wheeling	ECHL	14	7	13	20	27	7	1	3	4	12
94-95	Wheeling	ECHL	25	3	17	20	37	—	—	—	—	—
94-95	Birmingham	ECHL	23	8	16	24	26	7	3	5	8	2
95-96	Reno	WCHL	49	27	24	51	24	3	1	2	3	8
96-97	Reno	WCHL	56	28	35	63	80	—	—	—	—	—
97-98	Reno	WCHL	34	12	22	34	38	—	—	—	—	—
98-99	Long Beach	IHL	6	0	2	2	2	—	—	—	—	—
98-99	San Diego	WCHL	65	23	34	57	76	12	5	5	10	10
	WCHL	Totals	204	90	115	205	218	15	6	7	13	18
	ECHL	Totals	62	18	46	64	90	14	4	8	12	14

Born; 1/13/69, Slany, Czechoslovakia. 6-3, 205. Selected by San Diego in 1998 WCHL Dispersal Draft.

Don Margettie — Right Wing

Regular Season / Playoffs

Season	Team	League	GP	G	A	PTS	PIM	GP	G	A	PTS	PIM
96-97	Nashville	CeHL	24	13	14	27	89	—	—	—	—	—
96-97	San Antonio	CeHL	40	19	27	46	66	—	—	—	—	—
97-98	Odessa	WPHL	64	21	39	60	173	—	—	—	—	—
97-98	Central Texas	WPHL	6	2	2	4	9	2	0	0	0	2
98-99	Abilene	WPHL	53	15	21	36	142	—	—	—	—	—
	WPHL	Totals	123	38	62	100	324	2	.0	0	0	2
	CeHL	Totals	64	32	41	73	155	—	—	—	—	—

Born; 7/10/75, Niagara Falls, Ontario. 5-10, 186. Selected by Wichita Thunder in San Antonio Dispersal Draft (6/10/97). Traded to Central Texas by Odessa for Derek Prue (3/98). Selected by Abilene in 1998 WPHL Expansion Draft. Last amateur club; Niagara Falls (Jr. B).

Josef Marha — Center

Regular Season / Playoffs

Season	Team	League	GP	G	A	PTS	PIM	GP	G	A	PTS	PIM
95-96	Colorado	NHL	2	0	1	1	0	—	—	—	—	—
95-96	Cornwall	AHL	74	18	30	48	30	8	1	2	3	10
96-97	Colorado	NHL	6	0	1	1	0	—	—	—	—	—
96-97	Hershey	AHL	67	23	49	72	44	19	6	*16	*22	10
97-98	Colorado	NHL	11	2	5	7	4	—	—	—	—	—
97-98	Anaheim	NHL	12	7	4	11	0	—	—	—	—	—
97-98	Hershey	AHL	55	6	46	52	30	—	—	—	—	—
98-99	Anaheim	NHL	10	0	1	1	0	—	—	—	—	—
98-99	Chicago	NHL	22	2	5	7	4	—	—	—	—	—
98-99	Cincinnati	AHL	3	1	0	1	4	—	—	—	—	—
98-99	Portland	AHL	8	0	8	8	2	—	—	—	—	—
	NHL	Totals	63	11	17	28	8	—	—	—	—	—
	AHL	Totals	207	48	133	181	110	27	7	18	25	20

Born; 6/2/76, Chavlickov, Czechoslovakia. 6-0, 170. Drafted by Quebec Nordiques (3rd choice, 35th overall) in 1994 Entry Draft. Member of 1996-97 AHL Champion Hershey Bears. Traded to Anaheim Mighty Ducks by Colorado for Warren Rychel and future considerations (3/24/98). Traded to Chicago Blackhawks by Anaheim for a conditional draft pick (1/28/99). Last European Club;

Brett Marietti — Right Wing

Regular Season / Playoffs

Season	Team	League	GP	G	A	PTS	PIM	GP	G	A	PTS	PIM
93-94	Rochester	AHL	38	6	14	20	63	—	—	—	—	—
94-95	South Carolina	ECHL	67	23	33	56	103	9	2	0	2	16
95-96	South Carolina	ECHL	64	28	34	62	121	8	8	5	13	17
96-97	South Carolina	ECHL	61	25	41	66	103	18	*12	11	23	58
97-98	South Carolina	ECHL	65	26	28	54	107	5	0	3	3	8
98-99	South Carolina	ECHL	65	16	40	56	142	3	2	1	3	6
	ECHL	Totals	322	118	176	294	576	43	24	20	44	105

Born; 2/9/73, Haileybury, Ontario. 5-11, 183. Signed as a free agent by Buffalo Sabres (10/22/98). Member of 1996-97 ECHL Champion South Carolina Stingrays. Last amateur club; London (OHL).

Chris Marinucci — Center

Regular Season / Playoffs

Season	Team	League	GP	G	A	PTS	PIM	GP	G	A	PTS	PIM
94-95	Denver	IHL	74	29	40	69	42	14	3	4	7	12
94-95	Islanders	NHL	12	1	4	5	2	—	—	—	—	—
95-96	Utah	IHL	8	3	5	8	8	—	—	—	—	—
96-97	Los Angeles	NHL	1	0	0	0	0	—	—	—	—	—
96-97	Utah	IHL	21	3	13	16	6	—	—	—	—	—
96-97	Phoenix	IHL	62	23	29	52	26	—	—	—	—	—
97-98	Chicago	IHL	78	27	48	75	35	22	7	6	13	12
98-99	Chicago	IHL	82	41	40	81	24	10	3	5	8	10
	NHL	Totals	13	1	4	5	2	—	—	—	—	—
	IHL	Totals	325	126	175	301	141	46	13	15	238	34

Born; 12/29/71, Grand Rapids, Minnesota. 6-0, 188. Drafted by New York Islanders (4th choice, 90th overall) in 1990 Entry Draft. Traded to Los Angleles Kings by Islanders for Nicholas Vachon (1996). 1998-99 IHL Man of the Year. 1998-99 IHL Second Team All-Star. Member of 1994-95 IHL Champion Denver Grizzlies. Member of 1997-98 IHL Champion Chicago Wolves. Last amateur club; Minnesota-Duluth (WCHA).

Daniel Marois — Right Wing

Regular Season / Playoffs

Season	Team	League	GP	G	A	PTS	PIM	GP	G	A	PTS	PIM
87-88	Verdun	QMJHL	67	52	36	88	153	—	—	—	—	—
87-88	Newmarket	AHL	8	4	4	8	4	—	—	—	—	—
87-88	Toronto	NHL	—	—	—	—	—	3	1	0	1	0
88-89	Toronto	NHL	76	31	23	54	76	—	—	—	—	—
89-90	Toronto	NHL	68	39	37	76	82	5	2	2	4	12
90-91	Toronto	NHL	78	21	9	30	112	—	—	—	—	—
91-92	Toronto	NHL	63	15	11	26	76	—	—	—	—	—
91-92	Islanders	NHL	12	2	5	7	18	—	—	—	—	—
92-93	Islanders	NHL	28	2	5	7	35	—	—	—	—	—
92-93	Capital District	AHL	4	2	0	2	0	—	—	—	—	—
93-94	Boston	NHL	22	7	3	10	18	11	0	1	1	16
93-94	Providence	AHL	6	1	2	3	6	—	—	—	—	—
94-95	DNP	Injured										
95-96	Michigan	IHL	61	28	28	56	105	—	—	—	—	—
95-96	Minnesota	IHL	13	4	3	7	20	—	—	—	—	—
96-97	Quebec	IHL	7	1	1	2	12	—	—	—	—	—
96-97	Utah	IHL	29	7	9	16	58	—	—	—	—	—
97-98	Mannheim	Germany	19	3	6	9	38	—	—	—	—	—
97-98	SC Bern	Switz.	21	16	4	20	72	7	1	5	6	16
98-99	SC Bern	Switz.	45	27	31	58	93	6	3	2	5	18
	NHL	Totals	347	117	93	210	417	19	3	3	6	28
	IHL	Totals	110	40	41	81	195	—	—	—	—	—
	AHL	Totals	18	7	6	13	10	—	—	—	—	—

Born; 10/3/68, Montreal, Quebec. 6-0, 190. Drafted by Toronto Maple Leafs (2nd choice, 28th overall) in 1987 Entry Draft. Traded to New York Islanders by Toronto with Claude Loiselle for Ken Baumgartner and Dave McLlwain (3/10/92). Traded to Boston Bruins by Islanders for Boston's eighth round choice (Peter Hogradh) in 1994 Entry Draft (3/18/93). Signed as a free agent by Toronto (8/20/96). Last amateur club; Verdun (QMJHL).

Bobby Marshall — Defenseman

Regular Season / Playoffs

Season	Team	League	GP	G	A	PTS	PIM	GP	G	A	PTS	PIM
94-95	Saint John	AHL	77	7	24	31	62	5	0	0	0	4
95-96	Saint John	AHL	10	0	5	5	8	—	—	—	—	—
95-96	Baltimore	AHL	67	3	28	31	38	12	2	8	10	8
96-97	Baltimore	AHL	79	1	35	36	45	3	0	1	1	4
97-98	Hershey	AHL	6	0	4	4	4	—	—	—	—	—
97-98	Chicago	IHL	2	0	0	0	0	—	—	—	—	—
97-98	Columbus	CHL	55	11	63	74	79	13	2	12	14	28
98-99	Revier Lowen	Germany	52	4	16	20	50	—	—	—	—	—
98-99	San Angelo	WPHL	3	0	2	2	0	17	2	11	13	12
	AHL	Totals	239	11	96	107	157	20	2	9	11	16

Born; 4/11/72, North York, Ontario. 6-1, 190. Drafted by Calgary Flames (6th choice, 129th overall) in 1991 Entry Draft. Traded by Calgary to Anaheim Mighty Ducks for Jarrod Skalde (10/30/95). Member of 1997-98 CHL Champion Columbus Cottonmouths. Selected by Topeka in 1998 CHL Expansion Draft. Last amateur club; Miami of Ohio (CCHA).

Steve Martell — Right Wing

Regular Season — Playoffs

Season	Team	League	GP	G	A	PTS	PIM	GP	G	A	PTS	PIM
91-92	Baltimore	AHL	42	5	7	12	120	—	—	—	—	—
91-92	Hampton Roads	ECHL	20	9	25	34	34	11	4	5	9	47
92-93	Baltimore	AHL	5	3	2	5	0	—	—	—	—	—
92-93	Hampton Roads	ECHL	57	17	43	60	161	4	0	2	2	26
93-94	St. Francis	AUAA										
94-95	St. Francis	AUAA										
95-96	St. Francis	AUAA										
96-97	St. Francis	AUAA										
97-98	Port Huron	UHL	22	3	10	13	19	3	0	0	0	2
98-99	Port Huron	UHL	13	2	0	2	6	—	—	—	—	—
	AHL	Totals	47	8	9	17	120	—	—	—	—	—
	ECHL	Totals	77	26	68	94	195	15	4	7	11	73
	UHL	Totals	35	5	10	15	25	3	0	0	0	2

Born; 3/3/70, Sydney, Nova Scotia. 5-10, 185. Drafted by Washington Capitals (10th choice, 159th overall) in 1990 Entry Draft. Selected by Mohawk Valley in 1998 UHL Expansion Draft. Member of 1991-92 ECHL Champion Hampton Roads Admirals. Last amateur club; St. Francis Xavier (AUAA).

Mike Martens — Forward

Regular Season — Playoffs

Season	Team	League	GP	G	A	PTS	PIM	GP	G	A	PTS	PIM
92-93	Bismark	AHA	9	8	16	24	4	—	—	—	—	—
92-93	Thunder Bay	CoHL	27	12	21	33	31	—	—	—	—	—
92-93	Memphis	CeHL	19	10	18	28	10	6	1	2	3	8
93-94												
94-95												
95-96												
96-97	Regensberg	Germany										
97-98	Fayetteville	CHL	25	11	25	36	44	—	—	—	—	—
97-98	Columbus	CHL	11	13	9	22	4	13	*17	13	*30	16
98-99	Columbus	CHL	64	37	41	78	44	10	6	9	15	25
	CHL	Totals	119	71	93	164	102	29	24	24	48	49

Born; 3/5/68, Rosenort, Manitoba. 6-0, 205. 1997-98 CHL Playoff MVP. Member of 1997-98 CHL Champion Columbus Cottonmouths.

Craig Martin — Right Wing

Regular Season — Playoffs

Season	Team	League	GP	G	A	PTS	PIM	GP	G	A	PTS	PIM
91-92	Moncton	AHL	11	1	1	2	70	—	—	—	—	—
91-92	Fort Wayne	IHL	24	0	0	0	115	—	—	—	—	—
92-93	Moncton	AHL	64	5	13	18	198	5	0	1	1	22
93-94	Adirondack	AHL	76	15	24	39	297	12	2	2	4	63
94-95	Winnipeg	NHL	20	0	1	1	19	—	—	—	—	—
94-95	Springfield	AHL	6	0	1	1	21	—	—	—	—	—
95-96	Springfield	AHL	48	6	5	11	245	8	0	1	1	34
96-97	Carolina	AHL	44	1	2	3	239	—	—	—	—	—
96-97	San Antonio	IHL	15	3	3	6	99	6	0	1	1	25
97-98	San Antonio	IHL	6	1	1	2	21	—	—	—	—	—
97-98	Quebec	IHL	24	1	3	4	115	—	—	—	—	—
97-98	Manitoba	IHL	30	4	3	7	202	1	0	0	0	10
98-99	Berlin	Germany	45	0	1	1	183	—	—	—	—	—
	AHL	Totals	249	28	46	74	1060	25	2	4	6	119
	IHL	Totals	99	9	10	19	552	7	0	1	1	35

Born; 1/21/71, Amherst, Nova Scotia. 6-2, 215. Drafted by Winnipeg Jets (6th choice, 98th overall) in 1990 Entry Draft. Signed as a free agent by Detroit Red Wings (7/28/93). Traded to Manitoba by Quebec with Jeff Parrott and Michel Mongeau for Dale DeGray and Rick Girard (12/97). Last amateur club; St. Hyacinthe (QMJHL).

Don Martin — Defenseman

Regular Season — Playoffs

Season	Team	League	GP	G	A	PTS	PIM	GP	G	A	PTS	PIM
88-89	Fort Wayne	IHL	40	11	5	16	123	—	—	—	—	—
89-90	Phoenix	IHL	8	1	0	1	10	—	—	—	—	—
90-91	Richmond	ECHL	14	4	5	9	125	—	—	—	—	—
90-91	Winston-Salem	ECHL	14	7	6	13	24	—	—	—	—	—
91-92	Brantford	CoHL	40	13	19	32	62	4	0	0	0	39
92-93	Chatham	CoHL	28	7	10	17	75	—	—	—	—	—
92-93	Muskegon	CoHL	13	10	8	18	37	7	0	5	5	21
93-94	Muskegon	CoHL	7	4	3	7	4	3	1	0	1	4
93-94	St. Thomas	CoHL	50	24	28	52	199	—	—	—	—	—
94-95	Utica	CoHL	57	19	30	49	234	6	1	3	4	44
94-95	Milwaukee	IHL	1	0	0	0	0	—	—	—	—	—
94-95	Rochester	AHL	1	0	1	1	2	—	—	—	—	—
95-96	Utica	CoHL	3	0	0	0	4	—	—	—	—	—
97-98	Port Huron	UHL	60	20	17	37	114	4	1	2	3	8
98-99	Corpus Christi	WPHL	18	1	6	7	71	—	—	—	—	—
	IHL	Totals	49	12	5	17	133	—	—	—	—	—
	UHL	Totals	258	97	115	212	729	24	3	10	13	116
	ECHL	Totals	28	11	11	22	149	—	—	—	—	—

Born; 3/29/68, London, Ontario. 6-0, 210. Performed head coaching duties for the CoHL's Utica Blizzard during the 1995 and 1996 seasons. Last amateur club; London (OHL).

Justin Martin — Right Wing

Regular Season — Playoffs

Season	Team	League	GP	G	A	PTS	PIM	GP	G	A	PTS	PIM
98-99	Birmingham	ECHL	70	10	16	26	93	5	0	1	1	8

Born; 5/1/75, Syracuse, New York. 6-4, 210. Drafted by Los Angeles Kings (8th choice, 172nd overall) in 1993 Entry Draft. Last amateur club; Vermont (H.E.).

Matt Martin — Defenseman

Regular Season — Playoffs

Season	Team	League	GP	G	A	PTS	PIM	GP	G	A	PTS	PIM
92-93	St. John's	AHL	2	0	0	0	2	9	1	5	6	4
93-94	United States	National	39	7	8	15	127	—	—	—	—	—
93-94	United States	Olympic	8	0	2	2	8	—	—	—	—	—
93-94	Toronto	NHL	12	0	1	1	6	—	—	—	—	—
93-94	St. John's	AHL	12	1	5	6	9	11	1	5	6	33
94-95	St. John's	AHL	49	2	16	18	54	—	—	—	—	—
94-95	Toronto	NHL	15	0	0	0	13	—	—	—	—	—
95-96	Toronto	NHL	13	0	0	0	14	—	—	—	—	—
96-97	Toronto	NHL	36	0	4	4	38	—	—	—	—	—
96-97	St. John's	AHL	12	1	3	4	4	—	—	—	—	—
97-98	Chicago	IHL	78	7	22	29	95	19	0	5	5	24
98-99	Michigan	IHL	76	3	12	15	114	5	0	0	0	10
	NHL	Totals	76	0	5	5	71	—	—	—	—	—
	IHL	Totals	154	10	34	44	209	24	0	5	5	24
	AHL	Totals	75	4	24	28	69	20	2	10	12	37

Born; 4/30/71, Hamden, Connecticut. 6-3, 205. Drafted by Toronto Maple Leafs (4th choice, 66th overall) in 1989 Entry Draft. Signed as a free agent by Dallas Stars (7/28/98). Member of 1997-98 IHL Champion Chicago Wolves. Last amateur club; Maine (Hockey East).

Mike Martin — Defenseman

Regular Season — Playoffs

Season	Team	League	GP	G	A	PTS	PIM	GP	G	A	PTS	PIM
96-97	Binghamton	AHL	62	2	7	9	45	3	0	1	1	2
97-98	Hartford	AHL	60	4	11	15	70	4	0	0	0	2
98-99	Fort Wayne	IHL	75	6	20	26	89	2	0	0	0	4
	AHL	Totals	122	6	18	24	115	7	0	1	1	4

Born; 10/27/76, Stratford, Ontario. 6-2, 204. Drafted by New York Rangers (2nd choice, 65th overall) in 1995 Entry Draft. Last amateur club; Windsor (OHL).

Neil Martin
Regular Season — Defenseman — Playoffs

Season	Team	League	GP	G	A	PTS	PIM	GP	G	A	PTS	PIM
96-97	Portland	AHL	1	0	2	2	0	—	—	—	—	—
96-97	San Antonio	IHL	1	0	0	0	0	—	—	—	—	—
96-97	Hampton Roads	ECHL	54	3	19	22	89	9	0	2	2	4
97-98	Mississippi	ECHL	52	4	10	14	59	—	—	—	—	—
98-99	Long Beach	IHL	3	0	2	2	6	—	—	—	—	—
98-99	Chicago	IHL	8	0	1	1	2	—	—	—	—	—
98-99	Waco	WPHL	50	13	41	54	27	4	0	5	5	0
	IHL	Totals	12	0	3	3	8	—	—	—	—	—
	ECHL	Totals	106	7	29	36	148	9	0	2	2	4

Born; 9/8/75, Sudbury, Ontario. 5-10, 193. Last amateur club; Sudbury (OHL).

Tony Martino
Regular Season — Goaltender — Playoffs

Season	Team	League	GP	W	L	T	MIN	SO	AVG	GP	W	L	MIN	SO	AVG
88-89	Halmsted	Sweden	32	27	4	2	—	—	2.81	—	—	—	—	—	—
89-90	Gislaved	Sweden	28	16	10	3	—	—	3.88	—	—	—	—	—	—
90-91	Brunico	Italy	22	—	—	—	—	—	—	—	—	—	—	—	—
91-92	Clermont	France	20	13	6	1	—	—	3.77	—	—	—	—	—	—
92-93	Fassa	Italy	14	8	5	1	—	—	3.67	—	—	—	—	—	—
92-93	Tulsa	CeHL	39	23	13	2	2182	*2	*3.66	*11	*7	2	622	0	4.05
93-94	Tulsa	CeHL	48	30	12	4	2721	1	3.82	*11	4	7	*662	0	4.62
94-95	Tulsa	CeHL	42	25	14	3	2482	0	4.06	7	3	4	421	0	4.41
95-96	Tulsa	CeHL	*51	22	*25	4	*2952	0	4.47	6	2	4	386	0	2.64
96-97	Heilbronner	Germany	6	3	2	1	360	—	2.67	—	—	—	—	—	—
96-97	New Mexico	WPHL	51	*33	13	1	2846	1	3.50	5	2	3	312	0	*3.65
97-98	Aosta	Italy	8	3	4	1	—	—	3.93	—	—	—	—	—	—
97-98	New Mexico	WPHL	38	21	12	5	2219	2	3.57	10	5	4	560	0	4.18
98-99	Detroit	IHL	1	1	0	0	60	0	1.00	—	—	—	—	—	—
98-99	Abilene	WPHL	52	33	17	1	3065	0	3.11	3	0	3	189	0	3,18
	CeHL	Totals	180	100	64	13	10337	3	4.03	35	18	17	2091	0	4.05
	WPHL	Totals	141	87	42	7	8130	3	3.37	18	7	10	1061	0	3.85

Born; 8/13/64, Montreal, Quebec. 5-10, 185. 1992-93 CeHL Outstanding Goaltender. 1992-93 CeHL First Team All-Star. Member of 1992-93 CeHL Champion Tulsa Oilers. Named head coach of the New Mexico Scorpions beginning with the 1999-2000 season.

Patrick Martinovsky
Regular Season — Right Wing — Playoffs

Season	Team	League	GP	G	A	PTS	PIM	GP	G	A	PTS	PIM
98-99	Colorado	WCHL	21	5	3	8	0	—	—	—	—	—

Born; 9/11/74, Chomutov, Czech Republic. 5-11, 178.

Steve Martins
Regular Season — Center — Playoffs

Season	Team	League	GP	G	A	PTS	PIM	GP	G	A	PTS	PIM
95-96	Hartford	NHL	23	1	3	4	8	—	—	—	—	—
95-96	Springfield	AHL	30	9	20	29	10	—	—	—	—	—
96-97	Hartford	NHL	2	0	1	1	0	—	—	—	—	—
96-97	Springfield	AHL	63	12	31	43	78	17	1	3	4	26
97-98	Carolina	NHL	3	0	0	0	0	—	—	—	—	—
97-98	Chicago	IHL	78	20	41	61	122	21	6	14	20	28
98-99	Ottawa	NHL	36	4	3	7	10	—	—	—	—	—
98-99	Detroit	IHL	4	1	6	7	16	—	—	—	—	—
	NHL	Totals	64	5	7	12	18	—	—	—	—	—
	AHL	Totals	93	21	51	72	88	17	1	2	3	26
	IHL	Totals	82	21	47	68	138	21	6	14	20	28

Born; 4/13/72, Gatineau, Quebec. 5-9, 175. Drafted by Hartford Whalers (1st choice, 5th overall) in 1994 Supplemental Draft. Signed as a free agent by Ottawa Senators (7/22/98). Member of 1997-98 IHL Champion Chicago Wolves. Last amateur club; Harvard (ECAC).

Mike Martone
Regular Season — Defenseman — Playoffs

Season	Team	League	GP	G	A	PTS	PIM	GP	G	A	PTS	PIM
98-99	Springfield	AHL	2	0	0	0	2	—	—	—	—	—
98-99	Mississippi	ECHL	44	5	11	16	59	18	0	3	3	40

Born; 9/26/77, Sault Ste. Marie, Ontario. 6-2, 200. Drafted by Buffalo Sabres (6th choice, 106th overall) in 1996 Entry Draft. Signed as a free agent by Phoenix Coyotes (8/12/98). Member of 1998-99 ECHL Champion Mississippi SeaWolves. Last amateur club; Peterborough (OHL).

Dennis Maruk
Regular Season — Center — Playoffs

Season	Team	League	GP	G	A	PTS	PIM	GP	G	A	PTS	PIM
75-76	California	NHL	80	30	32	62	44	—	—	—	—	—
76-77	Cleveland	NHL	80	28	50	78	68	—	—	—	—	—
77-78	Cleveland	NHL	76	36	35	71	50	—	—	—	—	—
78-79	Minnesota	NHL	2	0	0	0	0	—	—	—	—	—
78-79	Washington	NHL	76	31	59	90	71	—	—	—	—	—
79-80	Washington	NHL	27	10	17	27	8	—	—	—	—	—
80-81	Washington	NHL	80	50	47	97	87	—	—	—	—	—
81-82	Washington	NHL	80	60	76	136	128	—	—	—	—	—
82-83	Washington	NHL	80	31	50	81	71	4	1	1	2	2
83-84	Minnesota	NHL	71	17	43	60	42	16	5	5	10	8
84-85	Minnesota	NHL	71	19	41	60	56	9	4	7	11	12
85-86	Minnesota	NHL	70	21	37	58	67	5	4	9	13	4
86-87	Minnesota	NHL	67	16	30	46	52	—	—	—	—	—
87-88	Minnesota	NHL	22	7	4	11	15	—	—	—	—	—
88-89	Minnesota	NHL	6	0	1	1	2	—	—	—	—	—
88-89	Kalamazoo	IHL	5	1	5	6	4	—	—	—	—	—
98-99	Lake Charles	WPHL	6	0	2	2	4	3	0	0	0	2
	NHL	Totals	888	356	522	878	761	34	14	22	36	26

Born; 11/17/55, Toronto, Ontario. 5-8, 175. Drafted by California Golden Seals (2nd choice, 21st overall) in 1975 Amateur Draft. Traded to Washington Capitals by Minnesota for Pittsburgh's first round choice (Tom McCarthy) in 1979 Entry Draft-Washington's property via earlier deal (10/18/78) Traded to Minnesota North Stars by Washington for Minnesota's second round choice (Stephen Leach) in 1984 Entry Draft (7/5/83). Last amateur club; London (OHA).

Tom Maryschak
Regular Season — Defenseman — Playoffs

Season	Team	League	GP	G	A	PTS	PIM	GP	G	A	PTS	PIM
98-99	New Mexico	WPHL	21	1	3	4	10	—	—	—	—	—

Born; 5/3/74, Penticton, British Columbia. 5-10, 180. Last amateur club; St. Norbert (NCAA 3).

Ralph Marziale
Regular Season — Center — Playoffs

Season	Team	League	GP	G	A	PTS	PIM	GP	G	A	PTS	PIM
95-96	West Palm Beach	SHL	39	10	13	23	59	—	—	—	—	—
95-96	Utica	CoHL	1	0	0	0	0	—	—	—	—	—
95-96	Tulsa	CHL	7	1	1	2	9	—	—	—	—	—
96-97	Utica	CoHL	2	0	0	0	0	—	—	—	—	—
97-98	Waco	WPHL	15	3	2	5	4	—	—	—	—	—
97-98	Reno	WCHL	6	1	4	5	2	—	—	—	—	—
98-99	Courmastra	Italy										
	CoHL	Totals	3	0	0	0	0	—	—	—	—	—

Born; 1/3/74, Providence, Rhode Island. 5-10, 195.

Martin Masa
Regular Season — Left Wing — Playoffs

Season	Team	League	GP	G	A	PTS	PIM	GP	G	A	PTS	PIM
94-95	Kansas City	IHL	3	0	0	0	0	—	—	—	—	—
94-95	Fort Worth	CeHL	61	31	35	66	104	—	—	—	—	—
95-96	Knoxville	ECHL	17	6	3	9	22	—	—	—	—	—
96-97	Johnstown	ECHL	59	36	32	68	114	—	—	—	—	—
97-98	Springfield	AHL	5	0	3	3	6	—	—	—	—	—
97-98	Saint John	AHL	10	0	2	2	4	—	—	—	—	—
97-98	Johnstown	ECHL	59	23	42	65	183	—	—	—	—	—
98-99	Orlando	IHL	2	0	0	0	2	—	—	—	—	—
98-99	Johnstown	ECHL	64	27	30	57	83	—	—	—	—	—
	AHL	Totals	15	0	5	5	10	—	—	—	—	—
	IHL	Totals	5	0	0	0	2	—	—	—	—	—
	ECHL	Totals	199	92	107	179	402	—	—	—	—	—

Born; 8/10/73, Sokolov, Czechoslovakia. 6-1, 205.

Mike Masini
Forward

			Regular Season					Playoffs				
Season	Team	League	GP	G	A	PTS	PIM	GP	G	A	PTS	PIM
97-98	San Angelo	WPHL	3	0	0	0	0	—	—	—	—	—
97-98	Saginaw	UHL	2	0	0	0	0	—	—	—	—	—
98-99	Amarillo	WPHL	5	1	1	2	0	—	—	—	—	—
98-99	Muskegon	UHL	4	0	0	0	0	—	—	—	—	—
	WPHL	Totals	7	0	0	0	0	—	—	—	—	—
	UHL	Totals	7	1	1	2	0	—	—	—	—	—

Born; 6/16/76, Everett, Massachusetts. 6-1, 185.

Chris Mason
Goaltender

			Regular Season							Playoffs					
Season	Team	League	GP	W	L	T	MIN	SO	AVG	GP	W	L	MIN	SO	AVG
97-98	Cincinnati	AHL	47	13	19	7	2368	0	3.45	—	—	—	—	—	—
98-99	Nashville	NHL	3	0	0	0	69	0	5.22	—	—	—	—	—	—
98-99	Milwaukee	IHL	34	15	12	6	1901	1	2.90	—	—	—	—	—	—

Born; 4/20/76, Red Deer, Alberta. 6-0, 200. Drafted by New Jersey Devils (7th choice, 122nd overall) in 1995 Entry Draft. Signed as a free agent by Anaheim Mighty Ducks (6/27/97). Traded to Nashville Predators by Anaheim with Marc Moro for Dominic Roussel (10/5/98). Last amateur club; Prince George (WHL).

Wes Mason
Left Wing

			Regular Season					Playoffs				
Season	Team	League	GP	G	A	PTS	PIM	GP	G	A	PTS	PIM
98-99	Albany	AHL	27	4	4	8	36	—	—	—	—	—
98-99	Augusta	ECHL	30	13	14	27	75	2	1	0	1	6

Born; 12/12/77, Windsor, Ontario. 6-2, 180. Drafted by New Jersey Devils (2nd choice, 38th overall) in 1996 Entry Draft. Last amateur club; Kingston (OHL).

Brian Masotta
Goaltender

			Regular Season							Playoffs					
Season	Team	League	GP	W	L	T	MIN	SO	AVG	GP	W	L	MIN	SO	AVG
97-98	San Diego	WCHL	1	0	0	0	40	0	3.00	—	—	—	—	—	—
97-98	Tucson	WCHL	6	1	3	1	261	0	4.37	—	—	—	—	—	—
98-99	Abilene	WPHL	8	5	2	0	459	0	3.92	—	—	—	—	—	—
98-99	Amarillo	WPHL	4	1	3	0	240	0	4.04	—	—	—	—	—	—
98-99	Central Texas	WPHL	6	2	1	2	335	0	3.23	—	—	—	—	—	—
	WPHL	Totals	18	8	6	2	1033	0	3,77	—	—	—	—	—	—
	WCHL	Totals	7	1	3	1	301	0	4.19	—	—	—	—	—	—

Born; 5/30/75, New Haven, Connecticut. 6-2, 195. Drafted by Ottawa Senators (3rd choice, 81st overall) in 1994 Entry Draft. Traded to San Diego by Tucson with Jason Shmyr for Danny Laviolette (1/98). Last amateur club; Maine (Hockey

Michel Massie
Left Wing

			Regular Season					Playoffs				
Season	Team	League	GP	G	A	PTS	PIM	GP	G	A	PTS	PIM
98-99	Baton Rouge	ECHL	20	2	4	6	9	—	—	—	—	—

Born; Last amateur club; Victoriaville (QMJHL).

Milt Mastad
Defenseman

			Regular Season					Playoffs				
Season	Team	League	GP	G	A	PTS	PIM	GP	G	A	PTS	PIM
95-96	Providence	AHL	18	0	2	2	52	—	—	—	—	—
96-97	Providence	AHL	33	0	2	2	106	—	—	—	—	—
96-97	Charlotte	ECHL	9	0	0	0	25	3	0	1	1	4
97-98	Charlotte	ECHL	50	6	12	18	54	7	0	2	2	10
98-99	Michigan	IHL	16	1	1	2	63	3	0	0	0	24
98-99	Hampton Roads	ECHL	44	2	6	8	142	—	—	—	—	—
	AHL	Totals	51	0	4	4	158	—	—	—	—	—
	ECHL	Totals	103	8	18	26	221	10	0	3	3	14

Born; 3/5/75, Regina, Saskatchewan. 6-4, 225. Drafted by Boston Bruins (6th choice, 155th overall) in 1993 Entry Draft. Last amateur club; Moose Jaw

Casson Masters
Right Wing

			Regular Season					Playoffs				
Season	Team	League	GP	G	A	PTS	PIM	GP	G	A	PTS	PIM
98-99	Canada	National	44	4	7	11	28	—	—	—	—	—

Born; 6/25/75, Bashaw, Alberta. 5-11, 180. Last amateur club; Princeton

Mike Mathers
Left Wing

			Regular Season					Playoffs				
Season	Team	League	GP	G	A	PTS	PIM	GP	G	A	PTS	PIM
96-97	Fresno	WCHL	51	24	37	61	31	5	0	0	0	7
97-98	Fresno	WCHL	60	24	26	50	78	5	1	5	6	0
98-99	Fresno	WCHL	49	9	24	33	35	5	2	2	4	0
	WCHL	Totals	160	57	87	144	144	15	3	7	10	7

Born; 6/20/72, Edmonton, Alberta. 6-0, 200. Drafted by Washington Capitals (7th choice, 191st overall) in 1992 Entry Draft.

Marquis Mathieu
Center

			Regular Season					Playoffs				
Season	Team	League	GP	G	A	PTS	PIM	GP	G	A	PTS	PIM
93-94	Fredericton	AHL	22	4	6	10	28	—	—	—	—	—
93-94	Wheeling	ECHL	42	12	11	23	75	9	1	3	4	23
94-95	Worcester	AHL	2	0	0	0	0	—	—	—	—	—
94-95	Toledo	ECHL	33	13	22	35	168	—	—	—	—	—
94-95	Raleigh	ECHL	33	15	17	32	181	—	—	—	—	—
95-96	Worcester	AHL	17	3	10	13	26	—	—	—	—	—
95-96	Houston	IHL	2	1	0	1	9	—	—	—	—	—
95-96	Johnstown	ECHL	25	4	17	21	89	—	—	—	—	—
95-96	Birmingham	ECHL	18	5	7	12	87	—	—	—	—	—
96-97	Worcester	AHL	30	8	16	24	88	1	0	0	0	0
97-98	Wheeling	ECHL	58	26	29	55	276	15	1	10	11	38
98-99	Boston	NHL	9	0	0	0	8	—	—	—	—	—
98-99	Providence	AHL	64	15	15	30	166	19	4	7	11	30
	AHL	Totals	135	30	47	77	308	20	4	7	11	30
	ECHL	Totals	209	75	103	178	876	24	2	13	15	61

Born; 5/31/73, Hartford, Connecticut. 5-11, 190. Signed as a free agent by Boston Bruins (10/29/98). Last amateur club; St. Jean (QMJHL).

Trevor Matschke
Defenseman

			Regular Season					Playoffs				
Season	Team	League	GP	G	A	PTS	PIM	GP	G	A	PTS	PIM
98-99	San Antonio	CHL	69	5	13	18	58	8	0	4	4	2

Born; 1/26/70, Saskatoon, Saskatchewan. 6-4, 195.

David Matsos
Left Wing

			Regular Season					Playoffs				
Season	Team	League	GP	G	A	PTS	PIM	GP	G	A	PTS	PIM
96-97	Adirondack	AHL	56	20	12	32	21	4	0	1	1	0
97-98	Adirondack	AHL	63	16	16	32	12	—	—	—	—	—
98-99	Hamilton	AHL	55	8	6	14	32	8	1	0	1	0
	AHL	Totals	174	44	34	78	65	12	1	1	2	0

Born; 11/12/73, Burlington, Ontario. 6-1, 201. Signed as a free agent by Tampa Bay Lightning (5/1/96). Last amateur club; Western Ontario (OUAA).

Christian Matte
Right Wing

			Regular Season					Playoffs				
Season	Team	League	GP	G	A	PTS	PIM	GP	G	A	PTS	PIM
93-94	Granby	QMJHL	59	50	47	97	103	7	5	5	10	12
93-94	Cornwall	AHL	1	0	0	0	0	—	—	—	—	—
94-95	Granby	QMJHL	66	50	66	116	86	13	11	7	18	12
94-95	Cornwall	AHL	—	—	—	—	—	3	0	1	1	2
95-96	Cornwall	AHL	64	20	32	52	51	7	1	1	2	6
96-97	Colorado	NHL	5	1	1	2	0	—	—	—	—	—
96-97	Hershey	AHL	49	18	18	36	78	22	8	3	11	25
97-98	Colorado	NHL	5	0	0	0	6	—	—	—	—	—
97-98	Hershey	AHL	71	33	40	73	109	7	3	2	5	4
98-99	Colorado	NHL	7	1	1	2	0	—	—	—	—	—
98-99	Hershey	AHL	60	31	47	78	48	5	2	1	3	8
	NHL	Totals	17	2	2	4	6	—	—	—	—	—
	AHL	Totals	245	102	137	239	286	44	14	8	22	45

Born; 1/20/75, Hull, Quebec. 5-11, 164. Drafted by Quebec Nordiques (8th choice, 153rd overall) in 1993 Entry Draft. Member of 1996-97 AHL Champion Hershey Bears. Last amateur club; Granby (QMJHL).

Trevor Matter — Goaltender
Regular Season — Playoffs

Season	Team	League	GP	W	L	T	MIN	SO	AVG	GP	W	L	MIN	SO	AVG
97-98	Tacoma	WCHL	25	9	8	2	1110	1	3.67	2	0	0	29	0	0.00
98-99	Tacoma	WCHL	20	8	8	2	1034	0	3.77	—	—	—	—	—	—
	WCHL	Totals	45	17	16	4	2144	1	3.72	2	0	0	29	0	0.00

Born; 9/3/76, Edmonton, Alberta. 6-2, 190. Member of 1998-99 WCHL Champion Tacoma Sabrecats.

Mike Matteucci — Defenseman
Regular Season — Playoffs

Season	Team	League	GP	G	A	PTS	PIM	GP	G	A	PTS	PIM
95-96	Lake Superior	CCHA	40	3	13	16	82	—	—	—	—	—
95-96	Los Angeles	IHL	4	0	0	0	7	—	—	—	—	—
96-97	Long Beach	IHL	81	4	4	8	254	18	0	1	1	42
97-98	Long Beach	IHL	79	1	7	8	258	17	0	2	2	57
98-99	Long Beach	IHL	79	3	9	12	253	8	0	1	1	12
	IHL	Totals	243	8	20	28	772	43	0	4	4	111

Born; 12/27/71, Trail, British Columbia. 6-2, 210. Signed as a free agent by Edmonton Oilers (9/10/98). Last amateur club; Lake Superior (CCHA).

Alex Matvichuk — Center
Regular Season — Playoffs

Season	Team	League	GP	G	A	PTS	PIM	GP	G	A	PTS	PIM
96-97	Toledo	ECHL	39	11	24	35	39	—	—	—	—	—
96-97	Wheeling	ECHL	26	8	23	31	23	3	0	3	3	2
97-98	Wheeling	ECHL	70	27	39	66	78	15	6	2	8	22
98-99	CSKA Moscow	Russia	10	4	2	6	12	—	—	—	—	—
	ECHL	Totals	135	46	86	132	140	18	6	5	11	24

Born; 5/13/75, Kiev, Ukraine. 5-8, 170. Traded to Peoria by Wheeling with J.F. Boutin for Rob Griffin (8/98). Last amateur club; North Bay (OHL).

Bob Maudie — Center
Regular Season — Playoffs

Season	Team	League	GP	G	A	PTS	PIM	GP	G	A	PTS	PIM
96-97	Binghamton	AHL	19	0	3	3	6	2	0	0	0	0
96-97	Charlotte	ECHL	6	1	1	2	4	—	—	—	—	—
97-98	Hartford	AHL	23	1	3	4	8	—	—	—	—	—
97-98	Canada	National	16	8	7	15	2	—	—	—	—	—
97-98	Charlotte	ECHL	13	3	10	13	6	—	—	—	—	—
98-99	Canada	National	41	14	15	29	22	—	—	—	—	—
	AHL	Totals	42	1	6	7	14	2	0	0	0	0
	ECHL	Totals	19	4	11	15	10	—	—	—	—	—

Born; 9/17/76, Cranbrook, British Columbia. 5-11, 180. Drafted by New York Rangers (9th choice, 221st overall) in 1995 Entry Draft. Last amateur club; Kamloops (WHL).

Mike Maurice — Center
Regular Season — Playoffs

Season	Team	League	GP	G	A	PTS	PIM	GP	G	A	PTS	PIM
91-92	Toledo	ECHL	62	39	72	111	51	5	1	2	3	6
92-93	Brantford	CoHL	11	11	6	17	14	—	—	—	—	—
92-93	Hamilton	AHL	13	3	7	10	6	—	—	—	—	—
92-93	Adirondack	AHL	25	4	7	11	4	2	0	0	0	2
93-94	Adirondack	AHL	70	25	30	55	53	12	7	6	13	4
94-95	Houston	IHL	71	20	26	46	64	4	1	2	3	6
95-96	Houston	IHL	68	17	19	36	32	—	—	—	—	—
96-97	St. John's	AHL	2	1	1	2	2	—	—	—	—	—
96-97	Grand Rapids	IHL	2	0	1	1	0	—	—	—	—	—
96-97	Mississippi	ECHL	6	2	5	7	2	—	—	—	—	—
96-97	Brantford	CoHL	60	48	76	124	48	10	6	14	20	16
97-98	Houston	IHL	36	9	11	20	14	—	—	—	—	—
97-98	Las Vegas	IHL	7	1	3	4	8	—	—	—	—	—
97-98	Springfield	AHL	12	2	3	5	10	3	0	2	2	0
98-99	Detroit	IHL	29	5	9	14	18	—	—	—	—	—
98-99	Madison	UHL	20	13	13	26	6	—	—	—	—	—
	IHL	Totals	213	52	69	121	136	4	1	2	3	6
	AHL	Totals	122	35	48	83	75	17	7	8	15	6
	UHL	Totals	91	72	95	167	68	10	6	14	20	16
	ECHL	Totals	68	41	77	118	53	5	1	2	3	6

Born; 4/22/66, Hamilton, Ontario. 6-1, 210. 1991-92 ECHL First Team All-Star. 1996-97 CoHL Second Team All-Star.

Jason Maurer — Goaltender
Regular Season — Playoffs

Season	Team	League	GP	W	L	T	MIN	SO	AVG	GP	W	L	MIN	SO	AVG
98-99	Austin	WPHL	1	0	0	0	5	0	0.00	—	—	—	—	—	—

Born; 7/19/73, 5-10, 180.

Dennis Maxwell — Left Wing
Regular Season — Playoffs

Season	Team	League	GP	G	A	PTS	PIM	GP	G	A	PTS	PIM
94-95	Sarnia	OHL	55	16	30	46	227	3	0	0	0	18
94-95	Muskegon	CoHL	—	—	—	—	—	10	0	1	1	36
95-96	Binghamton	AHL	8	0	1	1	7	—	—	—	—	—
95-96	Charlotte	ECHL	51	25	19	44	291	14	5	5	10	*78
96-97	Tallahassee	ECHL	30	13	22	35	175	—	—	—	—	—
96-97	Carolina	AHL	2	0	0	0	2	—	—	—	—	—
96-97	St. John's	AHL	20	2	2	4	97	—	—	—	—	—
96-97	San Antonio	IHL	14	1	4	5	32	4	1	0	1	41
97-98	San Antonio	IHL	6	0	0	0	49	—	—	—	—	—
97-98	Quebec	IHL	55	9	13	22	249	—	—	—	—	—
98-99	St. John's	AHL	41	9	16	25	212	5	0	3	3	8
	IHL	Totals	75	10	17	27	330	4	1	0	1	41
	AHL	Totals	71	11	19	30	318	5	0	3	3	8
	ECHL	Totals	81	38	41	79	466	14	5	5	10	78

Born; 6/4/74, Dauphin, Manitoba. 6-2, 210. Member of 1995-96 ECHL champion Charlotte Checkers. Last amateur club; Sarnia (OHL).

Roger Maxwell — Right Wing
Regular Season — Playoffs

Season	Team	League	GP	G	A	PTS	PIM	GP	G	A	PTS	PIM
96-97	Utah	IHL	1	0	0	0	5	—	—	—	—	—
96-97	Phoenix	IHL	2	0	0	0	12	—	—	—	—	—
96-97	Hershey	AHL	18	1	0	1	137	—	—	—	—	—
96-97	Mississippi	ECHL	38	2	4	6	276	—	—	—	—	—
97-98	Adirondack	AHL	23	1	1	2	88	—	—	—	—	—
97-98	Mississippi	ECHL	31	1	3	4	215	—	—	—	—	—
98-99	Louisiana	ECHL	36	1	2	3	285	—	—	—	—	—
98-99	Providence	AHL	29	2	3	5	153	7	0	0	0	6
	AHL	Totals	70	4	4	8	378	—	—	—	—	—
	IHL	Totals	3	0	0	0	17	—	—	—	—	—
	ECHL	Totals	105	4	9	13	776	—	—	—	—	—

Born; 11/21/75, Toronto, Ontario. 6-3, 237. Member of 1998-99 AHL Champion Providence Bruins.

Alan May
Right Wing

Regular Season / Playoffs

Season	Team	League	GP	G	A	PTS	PIM	GP	G	A	PTS	PIM
86-87	Springfield	AHL	4	0	2	2	11	—	—	—	—	—
86-87	Carolina	ACHL	42	23	14	37	310	5	2	2	4	57
87-88	Boston	NHL	3	0	0	0	15	—	—	—	—	—
87-88	Maine	AHL	61	14	11	25	*357	—	—	—	—	—
87-88	Nova Scotia	AHL	12	4	1	5	*54	4	0	0	0	51
88-89	Edmonton	NHL	3	1	0	1	7	—	—	—	—	—
88-89	Cape Breton	AHL	50	12	13	25	214	—	—	—	—	—
88-89	New Haven	AHL	12	2	8	10	99	16	6	3	9	*105
89-90	Washington	NHL	77	7	10	17	339	15	0	0	0	37
90-91	Washington	NHL	67	4	6	10	264	11	1	1	2	37
91-92	Washington	NHL	75	6	9	15	221	7	0	0	0	0
92-93	Washington	NHL	83	6	10	16	268	6	0	1	1	6
93-94	Washington	NHL	43	4	7	11	97	—	—	—	—	—
93-94	Dallas	NHL	8	1	0	1	18	1	0	0	0	0
94-95	Dallas	NHL	27	1	1	2	106	—	—	—	—	—
94-95	Calgary	NHL	7	1	2	3	13	—	—	—	—	—
95-96	Orlando	IHL	4	0	0	0	11	—	—	—	—	—
95-96	Detroit	IHL	17	2	5	7	49	—	—	—	—	—
95-96	Utah	IHL	53	13	12	25	108	14	1	2	3	14
96-97	Houston	IHL	82	7	11	18	270	13	1	2	3	28
97-98	DNP	Coaching										
98-99	Abilene	WPHL	22	6	10	16	48	3	1	0	1	9
	NHL	Totals	393	31	45	76	1348	40	1	2	3	80
	IHL	Totals	155	22	28	50	438	27	2	4	6	42
	AHL	Totals	140	32	35	67	735	20	6	3	9	156

Born; 1/14/65, Barrhead, Alberta. 6-1, 200. Signed as a free agent by Boston Bruins (10/30/87). Traded to Edmonton Oilers by Boston for Moe Lemay (3/8/88). Traded to Los Angeles Kings by Edmonton with Jim Wiemer for Brian Wilks and John English (3/7/89). Traded to Washington Capitals by Los Angeles for Washington's fifth round choice (Thomas Newman) in 1989 Entry Draft (6/17/89). Traded to Dallas Stars by Washington with Washington's seventh round choice (Jeff Dewar) in 1995 Entry Draft for Jim Johnson (3/21/94). Traded to Calgary Flames by Dallas for Calgary's eighth round choice (Sergei Luchinkin) in 1995 Entry Draft (4/7/95). Member of 1995-96 IHL Champion Utah Grizzlies. Last amateur club; New Westminster (WHL). Coached CHL's Fayetteville Force during 1997-98 season. Named Head Coach of WPHL's Lub-

Jamal Mayers
Right Wing

Regular Season / Playoffs

Season	Team	League	GP	G	A	PTS	PIM	GP	G	A	PTS	PIM
96-97	St. Louis	NHL	6	0	1	1	2	—	—	—	—	—
96-97	Worcester	AHL	62	12	14	26	104	5	4	5	9	4
97-98	Worcester	AHL	61	19	24	43	117	11	3	4	7	10
98-99	St. Louis	NHL	34	4	5	9	40	11	0	1	1	8
98-99	Worcester	AHL	20	9	7	16	34	—	—	—	—	—
	NHL	Totals	40	4	6	10	42	11	0	1	1	8
	AHL	Totals	143	40	45	85	255	16	7	9	16	14

Born; 10/24/74, Toronto, Ontario. 6-0, 190. Drafted by St. Louis Blues (3rd choice, 89th overall) in 1993 Entry Draft. Last amateur club; Western Michigan

David Mayes
Defenseman

Regular Season / Playoffs

Season	Team	League	GP	G	A	PTS	PIM	GP	G	A	PTS	PIM
96-97	St. John's	AHL	2	0	0	0	0	—	—	—	—	—
96-97	South Carolina	ECHL	66	10	22	32	61	11	3	3	6	28
97-98	South Carolina	ECHL	3	0	0	0	5	—	—	—	—	—
97-98	Thunder Bay	UHL	67	10	57	67	49	5	1	5	6	0
98-99	Thunder Bay	UHL	72	10	36	46	68	13	0	3	3	12
	UHL	Totals	139	20	93	113	117	18	1	8	9	12
	ECHL	Totals	69	10	22	32	66	11	3	3	6	28

Born; 7/26/74, Thunder Bay, Ontario. 6-0, 188. Member of 1996-97 ECHL Champion South Carolina Stingrays. Last amateur club; Lowell (Hockey East).

Mike Mayhew
Right Wing

Regular Season / Playoffs

Season	Team	League	GP	G	A	PTS	PIM	GP	G	A	PTS	PIM
96-97	Mobile	ECHL	55	16	22	38	215	1	0	0	0	0
96-97	Kansas City	IHL	1	0	0	0	0	—	—	—	—	—
97-98	Mobile	ECHL	23	10	6	16	93	—	—	—	—	—
97-98	Mississippi	ECHL	18	4	1	5	48	—	—	—	—	—
97-98	Pensacola	ECHL	11	1	1	2	26	8	1	0	1	24
98-99	Austin	WPHL	9	4	4	8	32	—	—	—	—	—
98-99	Tupelo	WPHL	28	14	5	19	79	—	—	—	—	—
	ECHL	Totals	107	31	30	61	382	9	1	0	1	24
	WPHL	Totals	37	18	9	27	111	—	—	—	—	—

Born; 3/10/74, Windsor, Ontario. 6-3, 220. Traded to Hampton Roads by Mobile for Mike Larkin (1/98). Traded to Mississippi by Hampton Roads for Troy Mann

Jay Mazur
Right Wing

Regular Season / Playoffs

Season	Team	League	GP	G	A	PTS	PIM	GP	G	A	PTS	PIM
87-88	Flint	IHL	39	17	11	28	28	—	—	—	—	—
87-88	Fredericton	AHL	31	14	6	20	28	15	4	2	6	38
88-89	Vancouver	NHL	1	0	0	0	0	—	—	—	—	—
88-89	Milwaukee	IHL	73	33	31	64	86	11	6	5	11	2
89-90	Vancouver	NHL	5	0	0	0	4	—	—	—	—	—
89-90	Milwaukee	IHL	70	20	27	47	63	6	3	0	3	6
90-91	Vancouver	NHL	36	11	7	18	14	6	0	1	1	8
90-91	Milwaukee	IHL	7	2	3	5	21	—	—	—	—	—
91-92	Vancouver	NHL	5	0	0	0	2	—	—	—	—	—
91-92	Milwaukee	IHL	56	17	20	37	49	5	2	3	5	0
92-93	Hamilton	AHL	59	21	17	38	30	—	—	—	—	—
93-94	Hamilton	AHL	78	40	55	95	40	4	2	2	4	4
94-95	Detroit	IHL	64	23	27	50	64	1	0	1	1	2
95-96	Rochester	AHL	16	5	2	7	16	—	—	—	—	—
95-96	Portland	AHL	54	16	9	25	55	19	3	7	10	19
95-96	Tallahassee	ECHL	10	7	8	15	6	—	—	—	—	—
96-97												
97-98	Pee Dee	ECHL	69	25	33	58	55	8	2	6	8	2
98-99	Alexandria	WPHL	61	22	53	75	12	—	—	—	—	—
	NHL	Totals	47	11	7	18	20	6	0	1	1	8
	IHL	Totals	309	112	119	231	311	23	11	9	20	10
	AHL	Totals	238	96	89	185	169	38	9	11	20	61
	ECHL	Totals	79	32	41	73	61	8	2	6	8	2

Born; 1/22/65, Hamilton, Ontario. 6-2, 205. Drafted by Vancouver Canucks (12th choice, 230th overall) in 1983 Entry Draft. Last amateur club; Maine (Hockey

Pat Mazzoli
Goaltender

Regular Season / Playoffs

Season	Team	League	GP	W	L	T	MIN	SO	AVG	GP	W	L	MIN	SO	AVG
96-97	Grand Rapids	IHL	5	2	0	0	169	0	3.56	—	—	—	—	—	—
96-97	Fort Wayne	IHL	15	1	6	0	673	0	3.75	—	—	—	—	—	—
96-97	Muskegon	CoHL	25	13	10	2	1429	1	3.02	—	—	—	—	—	—
97-98	Vipiteno	Italy	54	—	—	—	3221	0	3.05	—	—	—	—	—	—
98-99	Milan	Italy													
	IHL	Totals	20	3	6	0	841	0	3.71	—	—	—	—	—	—

Born; 3/16/70, Markham, Ontario. 5-10, 185. Drafted by Quebec Nordiques (8th choice, 169th overall) in 1990 Entry Draft.

Chris McAllister
Defenseman

Regular Season / Playoffs

Season	Team	League	GP	G	A	PTS	PIM	GP	G	A	PTS	PIM
95-96	Syracuse	AHL	68	0	2	2	142	16	0	0	0	34
96-97	Syracuse	AHL	43	3	1	4	108	3	0	0	0	6
97-98	Vancouver	NHL	36	1	2	3	106	—	—	—	—	—
97-98	Syracuse	AHL	23	0	1	1	71	5	0	0	0	21
98-99	Vancouver	NHL	28	1	1	2	63	—	—	—	—	—
98-99	Toronto	NHL	20	0	2	2	39	6	0	1	1	4
98-99	Syracuse	AHL	5	0	0	0	24	—	—	—	—	—
	NHL	Totals	84	2	3	5	208	6	0	1	1	4
	AHL	Totals	139	3	4	7	345	24	0	0	0	61

Born; 6/16/75, Saskatoon, Saskatchewan. 6-7, 238. Drafted by Vancouver Canucks (2nd choice, 40th overall) in 1995 Entry Draft. Traded to Toronto Maple Leafs by Vancouver for Darby Hendrickson (2/16/99). Last amateur club; Saska-

Dustin McArthur — Right Wing

Regular Season / Playoffs

Season	Team	League	GP	G	A	PTS	PIM	GP	G	A	PTS	PIM
95-96	Detroit	CoHL	7	1	0	1	5	—	—	—	—	—
96-97	Peoria	ECHL	46	11	15	26	106	—	—	—	—	—
97-98	Brantford	UHL	3	1	1	2	0	—	—	—	—	—
97-98	Monroe	WPHL	60	28	22	50	127	—	—	—	—	—
98-99	South Carolina	ECHL	19	2	2	4	48	—	—	—	—	—
98-99	Hampton Roads	ECHL	9	0	2	2	13	—	—	—	—	—
	ECHL	Totals	74	13	19	32	167	—	—	—	—	—
	UHL	Totals	10	2	1	3	5	—	—	—	—	—

Born; 2/21/75, Sarnia, Ontario. 6-0, 188. Last amateur club; Niagara Falls (OHL).

Mark McArthur — Goaltender

Regular Season / Playoffs

Season	Team	League	GP	W	L	T	MIN	SO	AVG	GP	W	L	MIN	SO	AVG
95-96	Utah	IHL	26	12	12	0	1482	0	3.12	—	—	—	—	—	—
96-97	Utah	IHL	56	28	20	6	3112	3	2.99	—	—	—	—	—	—
97-98	Utah	IHL	20	7	7	2	1060	0	3.40	1	0	1	63	0	3.78
98-99	Lowell	AHL	26	6	13	5	1457	3	3.09	—	—	—	—	—	—
98-99	Utah	IHL	1	0	1	0	60	0	5.00	—	—	—	—	—	—
	IHL	Totals	103	47	40	8	5714	3	3.12	1	0	1	63	0	3.78

Born; 11/16/75, Peterborough, Ontario. 5-11, 189. Drafted by New York Islanders (5th choice, 112th overall) in 1994 Entry Draft. 1995-96 Shared IHL Best Goaltender Award with Tommy Salo. Last amateur club; Guelph (OHL).

Darren McAusland — Defenseman

Regular Season / Playoffs

Season	Team	League	GP	G	A	PTS	PIM	GP	G	A	PTS	PIM
92-93	Baltimore	AHL	61	14	14	28	16	—	—	—	—	—
93-94	Portland	AHL	61	6	16	22	17	2	0	0	0	0
94-95	Portland	AHL	46	12	9	21	33	2	0	2	2	2
94-95	Wheeling	ECHL	11	6	1	7	8	—	—	—	—	—
95-96	Portland	AHL	69	7	24	31	39	21	6	5	11	6
96-97	Portland	AHL	65	9	20	29	32	1	0	0	0	4
97-98	Berlin	Germany	44	2	7	9	20	—	—	—	—	—
98-99	Newcastle	BSL	46	16	14	30	20	6	1	3	4	0
	AHL	Totals	302	48	83	131	137	26	6	7	13	12

Born; 3/3/72, Grovedale, Alberta. 5-11, 181. Signed as a free agent by Washington Capitals (7/92). Member of 1993-94 AHL Champion Portland Pirates. Last amateur club; Seattle (WHL).

Jason McBain — Defenseman

Regular Season / Playoffs

Season	Team	League	GP	G	A	PTS	PIM	GP	G	A	PTS	PIM
94-95	Springfield	AHL	77	16	28	44	92	—	—	—	—	—
95-96	Hartford	NHL	3	0	0	0	0	—	—	—	—	—
95-96	Springfield	AHL	73	11	33	44	43	8	1	1	2	2
96-97	Hartford	NHL	6	0	0	0	0	—	—	—	—	—
96-97	Springfield	AHL	58	8	26	34	40	16	0	8	8	12
97-98	Cleveland	IHL	65	8	22	30	62	3	0	2	2	2
98-99	Las Vegas	IHL	65	9	37	46	54	—	—	—	—	—
98-99	Providence	AHL	9	1	7	8	10	19	1	8	9	16
	NHL	Totals	9	0	0	0	0	—	—	—	—	—
	AHL	Totals	217	36	94	130	185	43	2	17	19	30
	IHL	Totals	130	17	59	76	116	3	0	2	2	2

Born; 4/12/74, Ilion, New York. 6-3, 210. Drafted by Hartford Whalers (5th choice, 81st overall) in 1992 Entry Draft.

Mike McBain — Defenseman

Regular Season / Playoffs

Season	Team	League	GP	G	A	PTS	PIM	GP	G	A	PTS	PIM
97-98	Tampa Bay	NHL	27	0	1	1	8	—	—	—	—	—
97-98	Adirondack	AHL	42	2	13	15	28	—	—	—	—	—
98-99	Tampa Bay	NHL	37	0	6	6	14	—	—	—	—	—
98-99	Cleveland	IHL	28	2	4	6	15	—	—	—	—	—
	NHL	Totals	64	0	7	7	22	—	—	—	—	—

Born; 1/12/77, Kimberley, British Columbia. 6-1, 191. Drafted by Tampa Bay Lightning (2nd choice, 30th overall) in 1995 Entry Draft. Last amateur club; Red Deer (WHL).

John McCabe — Left Wing

Regular Season / Playoffs

Season	Team	League	GP	G	A	PTS	PIM	GP	G	A	PTS	PIM
97-98	Alabama-Huntsville	NCAA2	30	16	32	48	—	—	—	—	—	—
97-98	Huntsville	CHL	5	1	2	3	2	2	0	0	0	0
98-99	Mobile	ECHL	7	0	0	0	5	—	—	—	—	—
98-99	El Paso	WPHL	50	8	6	14	76	3	0	0	0	0

Born; 5/30/74, Sudbury, Ontario. 6-4, 220. Last amateur club; Alabama-Huntsville (NCAA 2).

Rob McCaig — Defenseman

Regular Season / Playoffs

Season	Team	League	GP	G	A	PTS	PIM	GP	G	A	PTS	PIM
93-94	Lee Valley	BHL	24	12	14	26	162	—	—	—	—	—
94-95	Lee Valley	BHL	2	0	2	2	6	—	—	—	—	—
94-95	Dallas	CeHL	65	5	23	28	*380	—	—	—	—	—
95-96	Louisiana	ECHL	55	3	11	14	*512	5	0	1	1	10
96-97	Louisiana	ECHL	59	4	7	11	383	3	0	0	0	34
97-98	Newcastle	BSL	5	0	1	1	90	—	—	—	—	—
97-98	Baton Rouge	ECHL	6	0	1	1	28	—	—	—	—	—
97-98	Reno	WCHL	5	0	1	1	8	—	—	—	—	—
97-98	Lake Charles	WPHL	20	1	6	7	85	4	0	0	0	34
98-99	Courmastro	Italy										
98-99	Colorado	WCHL	41	2	7	9	157	3	0	1	1	31
	ECHL	Totals	120	7	19	26	923	8	0	1	1	44
	WCHL	Totals	46	2	8	10	165	3	0	1	1	31

Born; 1/5/72, Innisfall, Alberta. 6-3, 205. Traded to Baton Rouge by Louisiana with Dave Neilson for future considerations (10/97). Last amateur club; Prince Albert (WHL).

Keith McCambridge — Defenseman

Regular Season / Playoffs

Season	Team	League	GP	G	A	PTS	PIM	GP	G	A	PTS	PIM
95-96	Saint John	AHL	48	1	3	4	89	16	0	0	0	6
96-97	Saint John	AHL	56	2	1	3	109	—	—	—	—	—
97-98	Saint John	AHL	56	4	4	8	118	—	—	—	—	—
97-98	Las Vegas	IHL	10	0	1	1	16	4	0	0	0	9
98-99	Las Vegas	IHL	18	1	2	3	56	—	—	—	—	—
98-99	Long Beach	IHL	52	2	5	7	200	8	0	0	0	20
	AHL	Totals	160	7	8	15	316	16	0	0	0	6
	IHL	Totals	80	3	8	11	272	12	0	0	0	29

Born; 2/1/74, Thompson, Manitoba. 6-2, 205. Drafted by Calgary Flames (10th choice, 201st overall) in 1994 Entry Draft. Traded to Las Vegas by Saint John with Sami Helenius and Paxton Schulte for Steve Bancroft and Justin Kurtz (3/98). Traded to Long Beach by Las Vegas with a player to be named later (Patrice Lefebvre) for Shawn Wansborough and Scott Hollis (12/98). Last amateur club; Kamloops (WHL).

Sean McCann — Defenseman

Regular Season / Playoffs

Season	Team	League	GP	G	A	PTS	PIM	GP	G	A	PTS	PIM
94-95	Cincinnati	IHL	76	10	12	22	58	10	0	2	2	8
95-96	Carolina	AHL	80	14	33	47	61	—	—	—	—	—
96-97	Grand Rapids	IHL	76	8	26	34	46	5	0	0	0	2
97-98	Milwaukee	IHL	33	6	11	17	37	—	—	—	—	—
97-98	Orlando	IHL	26	5	3	8	30	—	—	—	—	—
98-99	Orlando	IHL	42	4	9	13	28	—	—	—	—	—
98-99	Springfield	AHL	31	8	15	23	31	3	0	1	1	4
	IHL	Totals	253	33	61	94	199	15	0	2	2	10
	AHL	Totals	111	22	48	70	92	3	0	1	1	4

Born; 9/18/71, North York, Ontario. 6-0, 195. Drafted by Florida Panthers (1st choice, 1st overall) in 1994 Supplemental Draft. Traded to Orlando by Milwaukee with Dave Mackey for Kelly Fairchild and Dave MacIntyre (1/98). Signed as a free agent by Phoenix Coyotes (2/11/99). Last amateur club; Harvard (ECAC).

Brian McCarthy — Center

Season	Team	League	GP	G	A	PTS	PIM	GP	G	A	PTS	PIM
		Regular Season						Playoffs				
94-95	Rochester	AHL	4	0	0	0	5	—	—	—	—	—
94-95	South Carolina	ECHL	21	3	5	8	25	—	—	—	—	—
94-95	Erie	ECHL	16	0	0	0	7	—	—	—	—	—
94-95	Johnstown	ECHL	12	4	4	8	2	5	4	1	5	2
95-96	Bakersfield	WCHL	39	19	17	36	24	—	—	—	—	—
96-97	Bakersfield	WCHL	62	25	46	71	34	4	0	3	3	17
97-98	Bakersfield	WCHL	62	14	18	32	52	4	0	1	1	2
98-99	Bakersfield	WCHL	69	12	21	33	30	2	0	0	0	0
	WCHL	Totals	232	70	102	172	140	10	0	4	4	19
	ECHL	Totals	49	7	9	16	34	5	4	1	5	2

Born; 12/6/71, Salem, Massachusetts. 6-2, 190. Drafted by Buffalo Sabres (2nd choice, 82nd overall) in 1990 Entry Draft. Last amateur club; St. Lawrence

Doug McCarthy — Center

Season	Team	League	GP	G	A	PTS	PIM	GP	G	A	PTS	PIM
		Regular Season						Playoffs				
85-86	Billings	CnHL	9	14	25	39	—	—	—	—	—	—
85-86	Carolina	ACHL	38	16	43	59	35	11	3	6	9	6
86-87	Carolina	ACHL	54	37	*73	*110	55	5	2	5	7	0
87-88	Alberta	CWUAA										
88-89	Alberta	CWUAA	47	35	70	105	24	—	—	—	—	—
89-90	Alberta	CWUAA	48	24	48	72	65	—	—	—	—	—
90-91	Alberta	CWUAA	48	38	36	74	78	—	—	—	—	—
91-92	Canada	National	1	0	0	0	0	—	—	—	—	—
91-92	Milano	Italy										
91-92	Milton-Keynes	BHL	12	20	21	41	22	—	—	—	—	—
92-93	Milton-Keynes	BHL	32	51	93	144	74	—	—	—	—	—
93-94	Milton-Keynes	BHL	43	87	156	243	139	—	—	—	—	—
94-95	Milton-Keynes	BHL	42	62	70	132	32	—	—	—	—	—
95-96	Milton-Keynes	BHL	36	34	46	80	40	—	—	—	—	—
96-97	Cardiff	BHL	42	28	26	54	16	—	—	—	—	—
97-98	Cardiff	BSL	47	16	15	31	16	9	4	7	11	4
98-99	Phoenix	WCHL	70	27	56	83	68	3	1	4	5	0
	ACHL	Totals	92	53	116	169	90	16	5	11	16	6

Born; 11/4/62, Edmonton, Alberta. 5-10, 180. 1986-87 ACHL First Team All-Star. Member of 1985-86 ACHL Champion Carolina Thunderbirds. Last amateur club; Alberta (CWUAA).

Jeremiah McCarthy — Defenseman

Season	Team	League	GP	G	A	PTS	PIM	GP	G	A	PTS	PIM
		Regular Season						Playoffs				
98-99	Worcester	AHL	59	5	10	15	37	4	0	2	2	0
98-99	Peoria	ECHL	6	1	2	3	6	—	—	—	—	—

Born; 3/1/76, Boston, Massachusetts. 6-0, 210. Last amateur club; Harvard

Bill McCauley — Center

Season	Team	League	GP	G	A	PTS	PIM	GP	G	A	PTS	PIM
		Regular Season						Playoffs				
95-96	Providence	AHL	62	11	17	28	71	—	—	—	—	—
96-97	Providence	AHL	19	2	3	5	10	—	—	—	—	—
96-97	Charlotte	ECHL	38	8	20	28	39	3	1	1	2	8
97-98	Providence	AHL	7	0	1	1	4	—	—	—	—	—
97-98	Charlotte	ECHL	58	10	34	44	58	6	1	5	6	6
98-99	Greenville	ECHL	61	11	29	40	74	—	—	—	—	—
	AHL	Totals	88	13	21	34	85	—	—	—	—	—
	ECHL	Totals	157	29	83	112	171	9	2	6	8	14

Born; 4/20/75, Detroit, Michigan. 6-1, 195. Drafted by Florida Panthers (6th choice, 83rd overall) in 1993 Entry Draft. Re-entered Entry Draft, selected by Boston Bruins (4th choice, 73rd overall) in 1995 Entry Draft. Last amateur club;

Tony McCauley — Defenseman

Season	Team	League	GP	G	A	PTS	PIM	GP	G	A	PTS	PIM
		Regular Season						Playoffs				
98-99	Chesapeake	ECHL	18	1	3	4	10	5	0	0	0	4

Born; Selected by Trenton in 1999 ECHL Expansion Draft.

Mike McCormick — Right Wing

Season	Team	League	GP	G	A	PTS	PIM	GP	G	A	PTS	PIM
		Regular Season						Playoffs				
89-90	North Dakota	WCHA	2	0	1	1	4	—	—	—	—	—
89-90	Greensboro	ECHL	29	16	3	19	13	11	7	4	11	19
90-91	Greensboro	ECHL	50	18	19	37	90	—	—	—	—	—
91-92	Greensboro	ECHL	31	6	4	10	110	—	—	—	—	—
91-92	Johnstown	ECHL	19	4	9	13	22	5	1	0	1	2
92-93	Fort Worth	CeHL	49	14	16	30	91	—	—	—	—	—
93-94	Fort Worth	CeHL	63	20	15	35	73	—	—	—	—	—
94-95	Fort Worth	CeHL	36	9	10	19	40	—	—	—	—	—
94-95	Wichita	CeHL	16	7	3	10	29	11	3	5	8	9
95-96												
96-97	Amarillo	WPHL	31	8	5	13	43	—	—	—	—	—
97-98	Amarillo	WPHL	11	7	4	11	6	—	—	—	—	—
97-98	Fort Worth	WPHL	53	17	6	23	82	13	0	2	2	55
98-99	Fort Worth	CHL	22	4	7	11	26	—	—	—	—	—
	CHL	Totals	186	54	51	105	259	11	3	5	8	9
	ECHL	Totals	129	44	35	79	235	16	8	4	12	21
	WPHL	Totals	95	32	15	47	131	13	0	2	2	55

Born; 5/14/68, Lynnwood, Washington. 6-3, 225. Drafted by Chicago Blackhawks (6th choice, 113rd overall) in 1987 Entry Draft. Traded to Fort Worth by Amarillo for Mike Reimann (11/97). Member of 1989-90 ECHL Champion Greensboro Monarchs. Member of 1994-95 CeHL Champion Wichita Thunder. Last amateur club; North Dakota (WCHA).

Shawn McCosh — Center

Season	Team	League	GP	G	A	PTS	PIM	GP	G	A	PTS	PIM
		Regular Season						Playoffs				
90-91	New Haven	AHL	66	16	21	37	104	—	—	—	—	—
91-92	Los Angeles	NHL	4	0	0	0	4	—	—	—	—	—
91-92	Phoenix	IHL	71	21	32	53	118	—	—	—	—	—
91-92	New Haven	AHL	—	—	—	—	—	5	0	1	1	0
92-93	New Haven	AHL	46	22	32	54	54	—	—	—	—	—
92-93	Phoenix	IHL	22	9	8	17	36	—	—	—	—	—
93-94	Binghamton	AHL	75	31	44	75	68	—	—	—	—	—
94-95	Rangers	NHL	5	1	0	1	2	—	—	—	—	—
94-95	Binghamton	AHL	67	23	60	83	73	8	3	9	12	6
95-96	Hershey	AHL	71	31	52	83	82	5	1	5	6	8
96-97	Philadelphia	AHL	79	30	51	81	110	10	3	9	12	23
97-98	Philadelphia	AHL	80	24	54	78	102	20	6	13	19	14
98-99	Philadelphia	AHL	38	12	25	37	43	—	—	—	—	—
98-99	Michigan	IHL	12	4	9	13	18	5	1	2	3	6
	NHL	Totals	9	1	0	1	6	—	—	—	—	—
	AHL	Totals	522	189	339	528	636	48	13	37	50	51
	IHL	Totals	105	34	49	83	172	5	1	2	3	6

Born; 6/5/69, Oshawa, Ontario. 6-0, 190. Drafted by Detroit Red Wings (5th choice, 95th overall) in 1989 Entry Draft. Traded to Los Angeles Kings by Detroit for Los Angeles' eighth round choice (Justin Krall) in 1992 Entry Draft (8/15/90). Traded to Ottawa Senators by Los Angeles with Bob Kudelski for Marc Fortier and Jim Thomson, (12/19/92). Signed as a free agent by New York Rangers (7/30/93). Signed as a free agent by Philadelphia Flyers (7/31/95). Member of 1997-98 AHL Champion Philadelphia Phantoms. Last amateur club;

Mike McCourt — Defenseman

Season	Team	League	GP	G	A	PTS	PIM	GP	G	A	PTS	PIM
		Regular Season						Playoffs				
94-95	Canada	National	2	0	1	1	0	—	—	—	—	—
94-95	Thunder Bay	CoHL	65	13	37	50	33	11	3	5	8	6
95-96	Thunder Bay	CoHL	13	1	8	9	14	19	1	5	6	18
96-97	Quebec	IHL	11	1	4	5	8	3	0	0	0	0
96-97	Carolina	AHL	7	0	0	0	7	—	—	—	—	—
96-97	Fort Worth	CeHL	50	15	52	67	73	—	—	—	—	—
97-98	Straubing	Germany	38	7	34	41	74	—	—	—	—	—
98-99	Fassa	Italy										
	CoHL	Totals	78	14	45	59	47	30	4	10	14	24

Born; 7/26/70, Brockville, Ontario. 6-1, 190. 1996-97 CeHL Second Team All-Star. Member of 1994-95 CoHL Champion Thunder Bay Senators. Last amateur club; St. Lawrence (ECAC).

Mark McCoy — Defenseman
Regular Season — Playoffs

Season	Team	League	GP	G	A	PTS	PIM	GP	G	A	PTS	PIM
93-94	Medicine Hat	WHL	1	0	0	0	0	—	—	—	—	—
93-94	Tulsa	CeHL	2	0	1	1	2	9	0	1	1	6
94-95												
95-96	Basingstoke	BHL	34	2	15	17	105	—	—	—	—	—
96-97												
97-98	Newcastle	BSL	18	1	2	3	8	6	1	0	1	4
97-98	Odessa	WPHL	17	0	2	2	24	—	—	—	—	—
97-98	Toledo	ECHL	13	0	3	3	33	—	—	—	—	—
98-99	Guildford	BNL	11	5	6	11	6	6	3	1	4	2

Born; 6/3/74, Prince Rupert, British Columbia. 6-0, 200. Last amateur club; Medicine Hat (WHL).

Scott McCrory — Center
Regular Season — Playoffs

Season	Team	League	GP	G	A	PTS	PIM	GP	G	A	PTS	PIM
87-88	Binghamton	AHL	72	18	33	51	29	4	0	1	1	2
88-89	Baltimore	AHL	80	38	51	89	25	—	—	—	—	—
89-90	Rochester	AHL	51	14	41	55	46	13	3	6	9	2
90-91	Rochester	AHL	58	27	25	52	39	2	0	0	0	0
94-95	Kalamazoo	IHL	22	3	12	15	12	—	—	—	—	—
94-95	Houston	IHL	3	1	4	5	0	4	2	2	4	2
95-96	Houston	IHL	25	5	6	11	12	—	—	—	—	—
95-96	San Francisco	IHL	51	13	39	52	24	4	3	1	4	2
96-97	Manitoba	IHL	82	24	47	71	30	—	—	—	—	—
97-98	Schwenninger	Germany	52	15	27	42	36	—	—	—	—	—
98-99	Schwenninger	Germany	52	18	27	45	52	—	—	—	—	—
	AHL	Totals	261	97	150	247	139	19	3	7	10	4
	IHL	Totals	183	46	108	154	78	8	5	3	8	6

Born; 2/27/67, Sudbury, Ontario. 5-10, 185. Drafted by Washington Capitals (13th choice, 250th overall) in 1986 Entry Draft. Traded to Buffalo Sabres by Washington for Mark Ferner (6/1/89). Last amateur club; Oshawa (OHL).

Kevin McDonald — Right Wing
Regular Season — Playoffs

Season	Team	League	GP	G	A	PTS	PIM	GP	G	A	PTS	PIM
98-99	New Haven	AHL	8	0	0	0	14	—	—	—	—	—
98-99	Florida	ECHL	41	17	24	41	153	6	3	2	5	10

Born; 4/29/77, Olds, Alberta. 5-11, 198. Last amateur club; Seattle (WHL).

Walker McDonald — Right Wing
Regular Season — Playoffs

Season	Team	League	GP	G	A	PTS	PIM	GP	G	A	PTS	PIM
98-99	Kansas City	IHL	3	0	0	0	7	—	—	—	—	—
98-99	Wichita	CHL	32	8	9	17	86	4	1	0	1	2

Born; 12/12/79, Thunder Bay, Ontario. 6-3, 215. Last amateur club; Barrie

Hubie McDonough — Center
Regular Season — Playoffs

Season	Team	League	GP	G	A	PTS	PIM	GP	G	A	PTS	PIM
86-87	Flint	IHL	82	27	52	79	59	6	3	2	5	0
87-88	New Haven	AHL	78	30	29	59	43	—	—	—	—	—
88-89	Los Angeles	NHL	4	0	1	1	0	—	—	—	—	—
88-89	New Haven	AHL	74	37	55	92	41	17	10	*21	*31	6
89-90	Los Angeles	NHL	22	3	4	7	10	—	—	—	—	—
89-90	Islanders	NHL	54	18	11	29	26	5	1	0	1	4
90-91	Islanders	NHL	52	6	6	12	10	—	—	—	—	—
90-91	Capital District	AHL	17	9	9	18	4	—	—	—	—	—
91-92	Islanders	NHL	33	7	2	9	15	—	—	—	—	—
91-92	Capital District	AHL	21	11	18	29	14	—	—	—	—	—
92-93	San Jose	NHL	30	6	2	8	6	—	—	—	—	—
92-93	San Diego	IHL	48	26	49	75	26	14	4	7	11	6
93-94	San Diego	IHL	69	31	48	79	61	8	0	7	7	6
94-95	San Diego	IHL	80	43	55	98	10	5	0	1	1	4
95-96	Los Angeles	IHL	11	11	9	20	10	—	—	—	—	—
95-96	Orlando	IHL	58	26	32	58	40	23	7	11	18	10
96-97	Orlando	IHL	68	30	25	55	60	10	5	8	13	6
97-98	Orlando	IHL	80	32	33	65	62	17	11	10	21	2
98-99	Orlando	IHL	74	20	33	53	52	17	2	12	14	14
	NHL	Totals	195	40	26	66	67	5	1	0	1	4
	IHL	Totals	570	246	336	582	380	100	32	58	90	54
	AHL	Totals	190	87	111	198	102	17	10	21	31	6

Born; 7/8/63, Manchester, New Hampshire. 5-9, 180. Signed as a free agent by Los Angeles Kings (4/18/88). Traded to New York Islanders by Los Angeles with Ken Baumgartner for Mikko Makela (11/29/89). Traded to San Jose Sharks for Islanders for cash (8/28/92). 1992-93 IHL Second All-Star Team. 1994-95 IHL Second Team All-Star. Last amateur club; Saint Anselm (NCAA 2).

John McEachern — Right Wing
Regular Season — Playoffs

Season	Team	League	GP	G	A	PTS	PIM	GP	G	A	PTS	PIM
98-99	Corpus Christi	WPHL	1	0	0	0	2	—	—	—	—	—

Born; 1/26/70.

Sean McEachern — Right Wing
Regular Season — Playoffs

Season	Team	League	GP	G	A	PTS	PIM	GP	G	A	PTS	PIM
97-98	Thunder Bay	UHL	51	3	1	4	74	—	—	—	—	—
98-99	Thunder Bay	UHL	66	10	3	13	186	8	0	0	0	7
	UHL	Totals	117	13	4	17	260	8	0	0	0	7

Born; 5/27/75, Winnipeg, Manitoba. 5-11, 200. Selected by Missouri in 1999 UHL Expansion Draft.

Dennis McEwen — Left Wing
Regular Season — Playoffs

Season	Team	League	GP	G	A	PTS	PIM	GP	G	A	PTS	PIM
89-90	Baltimore	AHL	1	0	0	0	0	—	—	—	—	—
89-90	Hampton Roads	ECHL	58	25	22	47	114	5	5	1	6	30
90-91	Hampton Roads	ECHL	44	16	28	44	66	14	4	10	14	37
91-92	Hampton Roads	ECHL	61	15	28	43	97	14	8	6	14	19
92-93												
93-94	Hampton Roads	ECHL	58	14	38	52	58	7	0	2	2	10
94-95	Hampton Roads	ECHL	25	6	8	14	32	—	—	—	—	—
95-96												
96-97												
97-98	Hampton Roads	ECHL	3	1	1	2	4	—	—	—	—	—
98-99	Hampton Roads	ECHL	13	0	1	1	8	—	—	—	—	—
	ECHL	Totals	262	77	126	203	379	40	17	19	36	96

Born; 1/30/68, Elliot Lake, Ontario. 5-11, 185. Member of 1990-91 ECHL Champion Hampton Roads Admirals. Member of 1991-92 ECHL Champion Hampton Roads Admirals. Last amateur club; London (OHL).

Harley McEwen — Center
Regular Season — Playoffs

Season	Team	League	GP	G	A	PTS	PIM	GP	G	A	PTS	PIM
98-99	Austin	WPHL	30	4	3	7	46	—	—	—	—	—

Born; 1/10/77, Lemberg, Saskatchewan. 5-9, 175. Last amateur club; Nipiwan (SJHL).

Mark McFarlane — Right Wing

Regular Season / Playoffs

Season	Team	League	GP	G	A	PTS	PIM	GP	G	A	PTS	PIM
95-96	Dayton	ECHL	7	1	0	1	34	—	—	—	—	—
95-96	Raleigh	ECHL	3	1	1	2	9	—	—	—	—	—
95-96	Hampton Roads	ECHL	12	1	2	3	89	—	—	—	—	—
95-96	Winston-Salem	SHL	24	14	6	20	131	8	5	5	10	53
96-97	Quad City	CoHL	70	19	28	47	201	6	1	2	3	22
97-98	Quad City	UHL	49	12	17	29	186	11	3	1	4	47
98-99	Quad City	UHL	72	31	25	56	274	13	2	5	7	43
	UHL	Totals	191	62	70	132	661	30	6	8	14	112
	ECHL	Totals	22	3	3	6	132	—	—	—	—	—

Born; 1/11/70, Amherst, Nova Scotia. 5-10, 185. Member of 1996-97 CoHL Champion Quad City Mallards. Member of 1997-98 UHL Champion Quad City Mallards. Selected by Mohawk Valley in 1998 UHL Expansion Draft.

Jay McGee — Defenseman

Regular Season / Playoffs

Season	Team	League	GP	G	A	PTS	PIM	GP	G	A	PTS	PIM
97-98	Huntington	ECHL	24	2	5	7	24	—	—	—	—	—
97-98	Birmingham	ECHL	41	0	7	7	16	4	0	1	1	4
98-99	Birmingham	ECHL	61	1	4	5	49	—	—	—	—	—
	ECHL	Totals	126	3	16	19	89	4	0	1	1	4

Born; 11/26/77, Edmonton, Alberta. 6-0, 205. Selected by Trenton in 1999 ECHL Expansion Draft. Last amateur club; North Battleford (SJHL).

Jim McGeough — Left Wing

Regular Season / Playoffs

Season	Team	League	GP	G	A	PTS	PIM	GP	G	A	PTS	PIM
81-82	Billings	WHL	71	*93	66	159	142	5	2	1	3	4
81-82	Washington	NHL	4	0	0	0	0	—	—	—	—	—
82-83	Hershey	AHL	5	1	1	2	10	5	0	2	2	25
83-84	Hershey	AHL	79	40	36	76	108	—	—	—	—	—
84-85	Washington	NHL	11	3	0	3	12	—	—	—	—	—
84-85	Pittsburgh	NHL	14	0	4	4	4	—	—	—	—	—
84-85	Binghamton	AHL	57	32	21	53	26	—	—	—	—	—
85-86	Pittsburgh	NHL	17	3	2	5	8	—	—	—	—	—
85-86	Baltimore	AHL	38	14	13	27	20	—	—	—	—	—
86-87	Pittsburgh	NHL	11	1	4	5	8	—	—	—	—	—
86-87	Baltimore	AHL	45	18	19	37	37	—	—	—	—	—
87-88	Springfield	AHL	30	11	13	24	28	—	—	—	—	—
88-89												
89-90	Phoenix	IHL	77	35	46	81	90	—	—	—	—	—
90-91	San Diego	IHL	10	2	4	6	4	—	—	—	—	—
90-91	Kalamazoo	IHL	7	0	0	0	2	—	—	—	—	—
90-91	Albany	IHL	12	9	3	12	4	—	—	—	—	—
90-91	Nashville	ECHL	4	2	1	3	0	—	—	—	—	—
91-92	Bracknell	BHL	12	15	9	24	20	—	—	—	—	—
91-92	Thunder Bay	CoHL	2	0	1	1	0	—	—	—	—	—
91-92	Richmond	ECHL	24	16	12	28	34	7	0	2	2	8
92-93	Richmond	ECHL	39	14	27	41	66	—	—	—	—	—
92-93	St. Petersburg	SUN	19	17	14	31	36	—	—	—	—	—
93-94	Richmond	ECHL	26	10	8	18	10	—	—	—	—	—
93-94	Dallas	CeHL	28	21	16	37	24	7	3	5	8	8
94-95	Dallas	CeHL	66	50	50	100	38	—	—	—	—	—
95-96	Reno	WCHL	15	4	10	14	4	—	—	—	—	—
95-96	Wichita	CeHL	31	11	20	31	16	—	—	—	—	—
96-97	Wichita	CEHL	21	6	20	26	4	9	9	2	11	8
97-98	Wichita	CHL	68	38	39	77	78	15	10	9	19	10
98-99	Wichita	CHL	27	18	22	40	24	4	1	3	4	6
	NHL	Totals	57	7	10	17	32	—	—	—	—	—
	AHL	Totals	254	116	103	219	237	5	0	2	2	25
	IHL	Totals	106	46	53	99	100	—	—	—	—	—
	CHL	Totals	241	144	167	311	184	35	23	19	42	32
	ECHL	Totals	89	40	47	87	110	7	0	2	2	8

Born; 4/13/63, Regina, Saskatchewan. 5-10, 180. Drafted by Washington Capitals (6th choice, 110th overall) in 1981 Entry Draft. Traded to Pittsburgh Penguins by Washington for Mark Taylor (3/12/85). Last amateur club; Billings (WHL).

Cal McGowan — Center

Regular Season / Playoffs

Season	Team	League	GP	G	A	PTS	PIM	GP	G	A	PTS	PIM
91-92	Kalamazoo	IHL	77	13	30	43	62	1	0	0	0	2
92-93	Kalamazoo	IHL	78	18	42	60	62	—	—	—	—	—
93-94	Kalamazoo	IHL	49	9	18	27	48	4	0	0	0	2
94-95	Worcester	AHL	64	22	21	43	28	—	—	—	—	—
94-95	Kalamazoo	IHL	1	0	0	0	0	—	—	—	—	—
95-96	Binghamton	AHL	77	14	21	35	42	4	0	1	1	2
96-97												
97-98												
98-99	Florida	ECHL	5	2	0	2	14	—	—	—	—	—
98-99	Amarillo	WPHL	58	8	28	36	20	—	—	—	—	—
	IHL	Totals	205	40	90	130	172	5	0	0	0	4
	AHL	Totals	141	36	42	78	70	4	0	1	1	2

Born; 6/19/70, Sidney, Nova Scotia. 6-1, 185. Drafted by Minnesota North Stars (3rd choice, 70th overall) in 1990 Entry Draft. Last amateur club; Kamloops

Don McGrath — Defenseman

Regular Season / Playoffs

Season	Team	League	GP	G	A	PTS	PIM	GP	G	A	PTS	PIM
87-88	Victoriaville	QMJHL	50	0	24	24	461	—	—	—	—	—
87-88	Baltimore	AHL	5	0	0	0	24	—	—	—	—	—
96-97	Central Texas	WPHL	46	2	9	11	141	6	0	1	1	25
97-98	Central Texas	WPHL	47	0	12	12	185	3	1	0	1	22
98-99	San Antonio	CHL	24	2	4	6	225	8	0	0	0	43
	WPHL	Totals	93	2	21	23	326	9	1	1	2	47

Born; 1/1/67, Tracadie-Shiela, Quebec. 6-3, 215. Last amateur club; Victoriaville (QMJHL).

Jim McGroarty — Defenseman

Regular Season / Playoffs

Season	Team	League	GP	G	A	PTS	PIM	GP	G	A	PTS	PIM
92-93	Erie	ECHL	3	1	1	2	2	—	—	—	—	—
93-94	Huntington	ECHL	13	5	8	13	4	—	—	—	—	—
93-94	Louisville	ECHL	30	4	11	15	6	6	1	4	5	4
93-94	Daytona Beach	SUN	5	2	4	6	2	—	—	—	—	—
94-95	Fresno	SUN	14	6	7	13	12	—	—	—	—	—
95-96	Bakersfield	WCHL	5	3	5	8	0	—	—	—	—	—
95-96	Alaska	WCHL	3	3	1	4	4	—	—	—	—	—
95-96	Fresno	WCHL	44	26	25	51	28	7	6	4	10	6
96-97	Fresno	WCHL	4	1	3	4	2	—	—	—	—	—
97-98	San Angelo	WPHL	17	6	3	9	4	—	—	—	—	—
97-98	Tacoma	WCHL	41	9	19	28	18	—	—	—	—	—
97-98	Bakersfield	WCHL	9	1	9	10	2	4	2	0	2	2
98-99	Asheville	UHL	61	13	34	47	36	4	0	0	0	2
	WCHL	Totals	106	43	62	105	54	11	8	4	12	8
	ECHL	Totals	46	10	20	30	12	6	1	4	5	4
	SUN	Totals	19	8	11	19	14	—	—	—	—	—

Born; 4/24/72, Toronto, Ontario. 5-8, 180.

Bill McGuigan — Right Wing

Regular Season / Playoffs

Season	Team	League	GP	G	A	PTS	PIM	GP	G	A	PTS	PIM
95-96	Detroit	CoHL	14	1	3	4	60	—	—	—	—	—
95-96	Saginaw	CoHL	41	5	6	11	69	—	—	—	—	—
96-97	Fort Worth	CeHL	8	3	3	6	25	—	—	—	—	—
96-97	Alaska	WCHL	47	12	18	30	201	—	—	—	—	—
97-98	Idaho	WCHL	58	6	16	22	222	4	1	0	1	8
98-99	Idaho	WCHL	20	0	8	8	43	—	—	—	—	—
	WCHL	Totals	125	18	42	60	466	4	1	0	1	8
	CoHL	Totals	55	6	9	15	129	—	—	—	—	—

Born; 5/30/75, Charlottetown, Prince Edward Island. 5-10, 190. Last amateur club; Kitchener (OHL).

Eoin McInerney — Goaltender

Regular Season / Playoffs

Season	Team	League	GP	W	L	T	MIN	SO	AVG	GP	W	L	MIN	SO	AVG
98-99	Monroe	WPHL	4	1	3	0	239	0	4.01	—	—	—	—	—	—
98-99	Macon	CHL	2	0	1	1	120	0	3.00	—	—	—	—	—	—
98-99	Port Huron	UHL	12	4	4	1	572	0	4.30	—	—	—	—	—	—

Born; 5/27/77, London, Ontario. 5-11, 185. Last amateur club; Owen Sound

Dan McIntyre — Goaltender

Regular Season / Playoffs

Season	Team	League	GP	W	L	T	MIN	SO	AVG	GP	W	L	MIN	SO	AVG
98-99	Flint	UHL	7	2	1	0	213	0	3.67	6	3	2	325	1	2.77

Born; 7/3/78, London, Ontario. 6-1, 190. Last amateur club; Trenton (Jr. A)

Ian McIntyre — Left Wing

Regular Season / Playoffs

Season	Team	League	GP	G	A	PTS	PIM	GP	G	A	PTS	PIM
95-96	Syracuse	AHL	57	6	7	13	108	2	0	0	0	0
96-97	Syracuse	AHL	40	3	12	15	57	—	—	—	—	—
96-97	Wheeling	ECHL	16	1	3	4	16	—	—	—	—	—
97-98	Cardiff	BSL	55	10	14	24	108	9	3	4	7	4
98-99	Cardiff	BSL	49	10	25	35	64	9	2	2	4	18
	AHL	Totals	97	9	19	28	165	2	0	0	0	0

Born; 2/12/74, Montreal, Quebec. 6-0, 192. Drafted by Quebec Nordiques (5th choice, 76th overall) in 1992 Entry Draft. Signed as a free agent by Vancouver Canucks (4/22/96). Last amateur club; Beauport (QMJHL).

Bill McKay — Forward

Regular Season / Playoffs

Season	Team	League	GP	G	A	PTS	PIM	GP	G	A	PTS	PIM
97-98	New Orleans	ECHL	65	6	10	16	117	4	0	1	1	12
98-99	New Orleans	ECHL	3	0	0	0	5	—	—	—	—	—
98-99	Jacksonville	ECHL	65	12	18	30	119	2	1	2	3	2
	ECHL	Totals	133	18	28	46	241	6	1	3	4	14

Born; 3/29/74, Ross River, Yukon Territory. 6-0, 200. Last amateur club; Brown (ECAC).

Sean McKegney — Right Wing

Regular Season / Playoffs

Season	Team	League	GP	G	A	PTS	PIM	GP	G	A	PTS	PIM
97-98	Saginaw	UHL	33	9	8	17	23	—	—	—	—	—
98-99	Oklahoma City	CHL	28	6	8	14	46	—	—	—	—	—

Born; 7/21/73, Waterloo, Ontario. 5-10, 180. Last amateur club; Waterloo

Rusty McKie — Right Wing

Regular Season / Playoffs

Season	Team	League	GP	G	A	PTS	PIM	GP	G	A	PTS	PIM
95-96	Huntsville	SHL	4	0	0	0	17	—	—	—	—	—
96-97	El Paso	WPHL	48	7	9	16	192	11	0	5	5	*74
97-98	El Paso	WPHL	58	6	12	18	274	15	2	0	2	49
98-99	Phoenix	WCHL	21	1	3	4	143	—	—	—	—	—
98-99	Colorado	WCHL	19	1	2	3	61	3	0	0	0	16
	WPHL	Totals	106	13	21	34	466	26	2	5	7	123
	WCHL	Totals	40	2	5	7	204	3	0	0	0	16

Born; 10/5/74, Toledo, Ohio. 6-1, 190. Member of 1996-97 WPHL Champion El Paso Buzzards. Member of 1997-98 WPHL Champion El Paso Buzzards. Selected by Arkansas in 1998 WPHL Expansion Draft.

Bobby McKillop — Right Wing

Regular Season / Playoffs

Season	Team	League	GP	G	A	PTS	PIM	GP	G	A	PTS	PIM
91-92	Michigan	CoHL	57	40	39	79	6	2	0	0	0	0
92-93	Detroit	CoHL	57	39	33	72	18	5	2	1	3	0
93-94	Huntsville	ECHL	31	15	23	38	24	—	—	—	—	—
93-94	Detroit	CoHL	15	9	7	16	4	3	4	1	5	12
94-95	Detroit	CoHL	63	32	45	77	37	9	6	2	8	4
95-96	San Diego	WCHL	27	26	17	43	32	—	—	—	—	—
95-96	Detroit	CoHL	37	21	20	41	24	10	5	9	14	6
96-97	Port Huron	CoHL	74	45	43	88	94	5	1	2	3	0
97-98	Port Huron	UHL	72	35	25	60	37	3	1	0	1	2
98-99	Port Huron	UHL	58	34	30	64	10	7	1	2	3	2
	UHL	Totals	433	255	242	497	230	44	20	17	37	26

Born; 3/19/70, Kitchener, Ontario. 5-11, 195. Last amateur club; Kingston

Barry McKinlay — Defenseman

Regular Season / Playoffs

Season	Team	League	GP	G	A	PTS	PIM	GP	G	A	PTS	PIM
91-92	Thunder Bay	CoHL	48	17	28	45	25	13	2	6	8	8
92-93	Thunder Bay	CoHL	55	17	39	56	47	11	2	3	5	11
93-94	Prince Edward Island	AHL	17	2	5	7	6	—	—	—	—	—
93-94	Thunder Bay	CoHL	40	14	43	57	53	9	3	6	9	11
94-95	Prince Edward Island	AHL	8	1	5	6	0	—	—	—	—	—
94-95	Thunder Bay	CoHL	65	26	54	80	100	11	4	13	17	4
95-96	Thunder Bay	CoHL	54	10	43	53	87	19	1	18	19	30
96-97	Thunder Bay	CoHL	65	32	58	90	82	11	6	10	16	16
97-98	Thunder Bay	UHL	74	36	90	126	40	5	3	4	7	2
98-99	Bracknell	BSL	19	6	11	17	6	—	—	—	—	—
98-99	Thunder Bay	UHL	34	15	27	42	24	13	5	4	9	8
	AHL	Totals	25	3	10	13	6	—	—	—	—	—
	UHL	Totals	435	167	382	549	458	92	26	64	90	90

Born; 8/8/67, Edmonton, Alberta. 6-3, 191. Drafted by Montreal Canadiens (12th choice, 206th overall) in 1987 Entry Draft. 1993-94 CoHL Top Defender. 1994-95 CoHL Top Defender. 1993-94 CoHL First Team All-Star. 1994-95 CoHL First Team All-Star. 1996-97 CoHL Defenseman of the Year. 1996-97 CoHL First Team All-Star. 1997-98 UHL First Team All-Star. Member of 1991-92 CoHL champion Thunder Bay Thunder Hawks. Member of 1993-94 CoHL champion Thunder Bay Senators. Member of 1994-95 CoHL champion Thunder Bay Sena-

Bryan McKinney — Defenseman

Regular Season / Playoffs

Season	Team	League	GP	G	A	PTS	PIM	GP	G	A	PTS	PIM
96-97	Detroit	OHL	50	11	30	41	62	5	1	0	1	10
96-97	Dayton	ECHL	3	0	0	0	2	3	0	0	0	2
97-98	Columbus	ECHL	4	0	0	0	0	—	—	—	—	—
97-98	Richmond	ECHL	60	4	15	19	97	—	—	—	—	—
98-99	Fort Wayne	IHL	1	0	0	0	0	—	—	—	—	—
98-99	Richmond	ECHL	7	1	1	2	7	—	—	—	—	—
98-99	Toledo	ECHL	24	1	4	5	25	—	—	—	—	—
98-99	Johnstown	ECHL	29	1	7	8	28	—	—	—	—	—
	ECHL	Totals	127	7	27	34	159	3	0	0	0	2

Born; 4/19/77, East Meadow, New York. 6-0, 190. Sold to Richmond by Columbus (10/97). Traded to Johnstown by Toledo for cash and future considerations (11/98). Last amateur club; Detroit (OHL).

Kevin C. McKinnon — Left Wing

Regular Season / Playoffs

Season	Team	League	GP	G	A	PTS	PIM	GP	G	A	PTS	PIM
94-95	Erie	ECHL	67	37	48	85	28	—	—	—	—	—
94-95	Minnesota	IHL	1	0	0	0	0	—	—	—	—	—
95-96	Canada	National	6	1	0	1	2	—	—	—	—	—
95-96	Lahti	Finland	44	18	13	31	61	—	—	—	—	—
96-97	Baton Rouge	ECHL	40	7	16	23	16	—	—	—	—	—
96-97	Mississippi	ECHL	13	3	5	8	6	2	0	1	1	9
97-98	Lahti	Finland	44	13	18	31	14	—	—	—	—	—
98-99	Colorado	WCHL	69	30	36	66	42	3	2	1	3	2
	ECHL	Totals	120	47	69	116	50	2	0	1	1	9

Born; 4/16/71, Fort Erie, Ontario. 5-9, 180. 1994-95 ECHL Rookie of the Year. Last amateur club; North Dakota (WCHA).

Kevin McKinnon — Left Wing

Regular Season / Playoffs

Season	Team	League	GP	G	A	PTS	PIM	GP	G	A	PTS	PIM
96-97	Pensacola	ECHL	2	0	0	0	2	—	—	—	—	—
96-97	Nashville	CeHL	52	30	33	63	73	—	—	—	—	—
96-97	Anchorage	WCHL	8	5	1	6	2	2	0	1	1	0
97-98	Nashville	CHL	69	29	45	74	44	9	6	3	9	4
98-99	San Angelo	WPHL	56	29	28	57	36	11	4	4	8	0
	CHL	Totals	121	59	78	137	117	9	6	3	9	4

Born; 6-0, 197. Selected by Topeka in 1998 CHL Expansion Draft. Last amateur club; Mercyhurst (NCAA 2).

Steve McLaren — Defenseman

Regular Season / Playoffs

Season	Team	League	GP	G	A	PTS	PIM	GP	G	A	PTS	PIM
95-96	Indianapolis	IHL	54	1	2	3	170	3	0	0	0	2
96-97	Indianapolis	IHL	63	2	5	7	309	4	0	0	0	10
97-98	Indianapolis	IHL	61	3	5	8	208	5	0	0	0	24
98-99	Philadelphia	AHL	52	4	3	7	216	7	0	0	0	2
	IHL	Totals	178	6	12	18	687	12	0	0	0	36

Born; 6-0, 194. Owen Sound, Ontario. 6-0, 194. Drafted by Chicago Blackhawks (3rd choice, 65th overall) in 1994 Entry Draft. Signed as a free agent by Philadelphia Flyers (8/24/98). Last amateur club; North Bay (OHL).

Brett McLean — Left Wing

Regular Season / Playoffs

Season	Team	League	GP	G	A	PTS	PIM	GP	G	A	PTS	PIM
98-99	Kelowna	WHL	44	32	38	70	46	—	—	—	—	—
98-99	Brandon	WHL	21	15	16	31	20	5	1	6	7	8
98-99	Cincinnati	AHL	7	0	3	3	6	—	—	—	—	—

Born; 8/14/78, Royston, British Columbia. 5-11, 186. Drafted by Dallas Stars (9th choice, 242nd overall) in 1997 Entry Draft. Last amateur club; Brandon (WHL).

Darren McLean — Defenseman

Regular Season / Playoffs

Season	Team	League	GP	G	A	PTS	PIM	GP	G	A	PTS	PIM
97-98	Fayetteville	CHL	50	1	3	4	248	—	—	—	—	—
98-99	Fayetteville	CHL	55	7	6	13	212	—	—	—	—	—
	CHL	Totals	105	8	9	17	460	—	—	—	—	—

Born; 10/30/74, Estevan, Saskatchewan. 6-2, 195.

Dave McLean — Left Wing

Regular Season / Playoffs

Season	Team	League	GP	G	A	PTS	PIM	GP	G	A	PTS	PIM
92-93	Minnesota	AHA	5	1	1	2	7	—	—	—	—	—
92-93	Dayton Beach	SUN	10	2	4	6	2	—	—	—	—	—
93-94												
94-95												
95-96												
96-97												
97-98												
98-99	Fort Worth	WPHL	1	0	0	0	15	—	—	—	—	—

Born; 6/14/68, Boston, Massachusetts. 5-11, 178.

Jeff McLean — Center

Regular Season / Playoffs

Season	Team	League	GP	G	A	PTS	PIM	GP	G	A	PTS	PIM
92-93	Kansas City	IHL	60	21	23	44	45	10	3	1	4	2
93-94	Kansas City	IHL	69	27	30	57	44	—	—	—	—	—
93-94	San Jose	NHL	6	1	0	1	0	—	—	—	—	—
94-95	Kansas City	IHL	41	16	18	34	22	4	1	4	5	0
95-96	Kansas City	IHL	71	17	27	44	34	3	0	3	3	2
96-97	Kansas City	IHL	39	8	15	23	14	—	—	—	—	—
96-97	Cincinnati	IHL	9	1	3	4	2	—	—	—	—	—
96-97	Fort Wayne	IHL	6	1	1	2	2	—	—	—	—	—
97-98	Kassel	Germany	12	3	5	8	12	—	—	—	—	—
98-99	South Carolina	ECHL	28	8	11	19	17	—	—	—	—	—
98-99	Tallahassee	ECHL	21	16	15	31	12	—	—	—	—	—
	IHL	Totals	295	91	117	208	163	17	4	8	12	4
	ECHL	Totals	49	24	26	50	29	—	—	—	—	—

Born; 10/6/69, Port Moody, British Columbia. 5-11, 190. Drafted by San Jose Sharks in Supplemental Draft (6/22/91). Traded to Tallahassee by South Carolina for Brendan Concannon (2/99). Last amateur club; North Dakota (WCHA).

Jim McLean — Defenseman

Regular Season / Playoffs

Season	Team	League	GP	G	A	PTS	PIM	GP	G	A	PTS	PIM
98-99	Monroe	WPHL	2	0	0	0	0	—	—	—	—	—
98-99	Amarillo	WPHL	45	0	7	7	14	—	—	—	—	—
	WPHL	Totals	47	0	7	7	14	—	—	—	—	—

Born; 10/28/73, Calgary, Alberta. 5-11, 185. Last amateur club; S.A.I.T (CIAU).

Dave McLlwain — Right Wing

Regular Season / Playoffs

Season	Team	League	GP	G	A	PTS	PIM	GP	G	A	PTS	PIM
87-88	Pittsburgh	NHL	66	11	8	19	40	—	—	—	—	—
87-88	Muskegon	IHL	9	4	6	10	23	6	2	3	5	8
88-89	Pittsburgh	NHL	24	1	2	3	4	3	0	1	1	0
88-89	Muskegon	IHL	46	37	35	72	51	7	8	2	10	6
89-90	Winnipeg	NHL	80	25	26	51	60	7	0	1	1	2
90-91	Winnipeg	NHL	60	14	11	25	46	—	—	—	—	—
91-92	Winnipeg	NHL	3	1	1	2	2	—	—	—	—	—
91-92	Buffalo	NHL	5	0	0	0	2	—	—	—	—	—
91-92	Islanders	NHL	54	8	15	23	28	—	—	—	—	—
91-92	Toronto	NHL	11	1	2	3	4	—	—	—	—	—
92-93	Toronto	NHL	66	14	4	18	30	4	0	0	0	0
93-94	Ottawa	NHL	66	17	26	43	48	—	—	—	—	—
94-95	Ottawa	NHL	43	5	6	11	22	—	—	—	—	—
95-96	Ottawa	NHL	1	0	1	1	2	—	—	—	—	—
95-96	Pittsburgh	NHL	18	2	4	6	4	—	—	—	—	—
95-96	Cleveland	IHL	60	30	45	75	80	—	—	—	—	—
96-97	Cleveland	IHL	63	29	46	75	85	14	8	15	23	6
97-98	Landshut	Germany	47	21	13	34	34	3	0	0	0	4
98-99	SC Bern	Switz.	39	20	34	54	30	6	2	2	4	6
	NHL	Totals	497	99	106	205	292	14	0	2	2	2
	IHL	Totals	178	100	132	232	239	27	18	20	38	20

Born; 1/9/67, Seaforth, Ontario. 6-0, 185. Drafted by Pittsburgh Penguins (9th choice, 172nd overall) in 1986 Entry Draft. Traded to Winnipeg Jets by Pittsburgh with Randy Cunneyworth and Rick Tabaracci for Jim Kyte, Andrew McBain and Randy Gilhen (6/17/89). Traded to Buffalo Sabres by Winnipeg with Gord Donnelly, Winnipeg's fifth round choice (Yuri Khmylev) in 1992 Entry Draft and future considerations for Darrin Shannon, Mike Hartman and Dean Kennedy (10/11/91). Traded to New York Islanders by Buffalo with Pierre Turgeon, Uwe Krupp and Benoit Hogue for Pat LaFontaine, Randy Hillier, Randy Wood and Islanders' fourth choice (Dean Melanson) in 1992 Entry Draft (10/25/91). Traded to Toronto Maple Leafs by Islanders with Ken Baumgartner for Daniel Marois and Claude Loiselle (3/10/92). Claimed by Ottawa Senators from Toronto in NHL Waiver Draft (10/3/93). Traded to Pittsburgh by Ottawa for Pittsburgh's eighth round draft choice (Erich Goldmann) in 1996 Entry Draft (3/1/96). Signed as a free agent by Islanders (7/29/96). Member of 1988-89 IHL Champion Muskegon Lumberjacks. Last amateur club; North Bay (OHL).

Mark McMahon — Defenseman

Regular Season / Playoffs

Season	Team	League	GP	G	A	PTS	PIM	GP	G	A	PTS	PIM
97-98	Kitchener	OHL	61	12	38	50	175	6	1	5	6	27
97-98	New Haven	AHL	4	0	1	1	6	2	0	0	0	16
98-99	Florida	ECHL	13	1	4	5	59	—	—	—	—	—
98-99	Plymouth	OHL	34	2	12	14	91	11	0	1	1	25

Born; 2/10/78, Geralton, Ontario. 6-1, 179. Drafted by Hartford Whalers (5th choice, 116th overall) in 1996 Entry Draft. Last amateur club; Kitchener (OHL).

Bryan McMullen — Goaltender

Regular Season / Playoffs

Season	Team	League	GP	W	L	T	MIN	SO	AVG	GP	W	L	MIN	SO	AVG
97-98	Detroit	IHL	1	0	0	0	0	0	0.00	—	—	—	—	—	—
97-98	Flint	UHL	32	12	13	1	1574	2	3.66	*13	4	5	649	0	3.05
98-99	Colorado	WCHL	43	16	16	5	2208	0	3.83	—	—	—	—	—	—

Born; 5/23/77, Buffalo, New York. 6-1, 193. Selected by Mohawk Valley in 1998 UHL Expansion Draft. Last amateur club; Guelph (OHL).

Jay McNeill — Right Wing

Regular Season / Playoffs

Season	Team	League	GP	G	A	PTS	PIM	GP	G	A	PTS	PIM
96-97	Richmond	ECHL	68	25	29	54	42	8	4	3	7	2
97-98	Richmond	ECHL	15	6	7	13	10	—	—	—	—	—
97-98	Columbus	ECHL	44	12	22	34	31	—	—	—	—	—
98-99	Adendorfer	Germany	51	32	36	68	34	—	—	—	—	—
	ECHL	Totals	127	43	58	101	83	8	4	3	7	2

Born; 8/28/72, Powell River, British Columbia. 5-9, 180. Traded to Columbus by Richmond for Pete Vandermeer (12/97). Last amateur club; Colorado College (WCHA).

Mike McNeill — Left Wing

Regular Season / Playoffs

Season	Team	League	GP	G	A	PTS	PIM	GP	G	A	PTS	PIM
88-89	Fort Wayne	IHL	75	27	35	62	12	11	1	5	6	2
88-89	Moncton	AHL	1	0	0	0	0	—	—	—	—	—
89-90	Indianapolis	IHL	74	17	24	41	15	14	6	4	10	21
90-91	Chicago	NHL	23	3	3	4	6	—	—	—	—	—
90-91	Quebec	NHL	14	2	5	7	4	—	—	—	—	—
90-91	Indianapolis	IHL	33	16	9	25	19	—	—	—	—	—
91-92	Quebec	NHL	26	1	4	5	8	—	—	—	—	—
91-92	Halifax	AHL	30	10	8	18	20	—	—	—	—	—
92-93	Milwaukee	IHL	75	17	17	34	34	6	2	0	2	0
93-94	Milwaukee	IHL	78	21	25	46	40	4	0	1	1	6
94-95	Milwaukee	IHL	80	23	15	38	30	15	2	2	4	14
95-96	Milwaukee	IHL	64	8	9	17	32	5	2	0	2	2
96-97	Milwaukee	IHL	74	18	26	44	24	3	0	1	1	0
97-98	Milwaukee	IHL	81	10	18	28	58	10	2	1	3	12
98-99	Revier Lowen	Germany	47	8	16	24	10	—	—	—	—	—
	NHL	Totals	63	5	11	16	18	—	—	—	—	—
	IHL	Totals	634	157	178	335	264	68	15	14	29	57
	AHL	Totals	31	10	8	18	20	—	—	—	—	—

Born; 7/22/66, Winona, Minnesota. 6-1, 185. Drafted by St. Louis Blues in supplemental draft (6/10/88). Signed as a free agent by Chicago Blackhawks (9/89). Traded to Quebec Nordiques by Chicago with Ryan McGill for Dan Vincelette and Paul Gillis (3/5/91). 1989-90 IHL Playoff MVP. Member of 1989-90 IHL champion Indianapolis Ice. Last amateur club; Notre Dame (CCHA).

Justin McPolin — Left Wing

Regular Season / Playoffs

Season	Team	League	GP	G	A	PTS	PIM	GP	G	A	PTS	PIM
96-97	London	OHL	20	1	6	7	97	—	—	—	—	—
96-97	Columbus	ECHL	20	1	0	1	45	3	0	0	0	11
97-98	Columbus	ECHL	43	1	5	6	281	—	—	—	—	—
98-99	Jacksonville	ECHL	7	0	0	0	55	—	—	—	—	—
	ECHL	Totals	70	2	5	7	381	3	0	0	0	11

Born; 7/13/76, Toronto, Ontario. 6-2, 220. Last amateur club; London (OHL).

Jason McQuat — Right Wing

Regular Season / Playoffs

Season	Team	League	GP	G	A	PTS	PIM	GP	G	A	PTS	PIM
94-95	Wichita	CeHL	7	0	0	0	45	—	—	—	—	—
95-96	Louisiana	ECHL	55	10	8	18	224	4	1	0	1	2
96-97	Manitoba	IHL	2	0	0	0	0	—	—	—	—	—
96-97	Louisiana	ECHL	51	7	5	12	268	12	2	0	2	38
97-98	Louisiana	ECHL	47	6	7	13	251	11	0	0	0	58
98-99	Louisiana	ECHL	26	3	1	4	112	5	0	0	0	13
	ECHL	Totals	179	26	21	47	855	32	3	0	3	111

Born; 3/24/74, Oshawa, Ontario. 6-1, 190. Last amateur club; Oshawa (OHL).

Rob McQuat — Defenseman

Regular Season / Playoffs

Season	Team	League	GP	G	A	PTS	PIM	GP	G	A	PTS	PIM
98-99	Louisiana	ECHL	14	1	2	3	36	—	—	—	—	—

Born; Last amateur club; Wilfrid Laurier (OUAA).

Don McSween — Defenseman

Regular Season / Playoffs

Season	Team	League	GP	G	A	PTS	PIM	GP	G	A	PTS	PIM
87-88	Buffalo	NHL	5	0	1	1	6	—	—	—	—	—
87-88	Rochester	AHL	63	9	29	38	18	6	0	1	1	15
88-89	Rochester	AHL	66	7	22	29	45	—	—	—	—	—
89-90	Buffalo	NHL	4	0	0	0	6	—	—	—	—	—
89-90	Rochester	AHL	70	16	43	59	43	17	3	10	13	12
90-91	Rochester	AHL	74	7	44	51	57	15	2	5	7	8
91-92	Rochester	AHL	75	6	32	38	60	16	5	6	11	18
92-93	San Diego	IHL	80	15	40	55	85	14	1	2	3	10
93-94	San Diego	IHL	38	5	13	18	36	—	—	—	—	—
93-94	Anaheim	NHL	32	3	9	12	39	—	—	—	—	—
94-95	Anaheim	NHL	2	0	0	0	0	—	—	—	—	—
95-96	Anaheim	NHL	4	0	0	0	4	—	—	—	—	—
95-96	Baltimore	AHL	12	1	9	10	2	—	—	—	—	—
96-97	Grand Rapids	IHL	75	7	20	27	66	3	0	1	1	8
97-98	Grand Rapids	IHL	2	0	0	0	4	—	—	—	—	—
97-98	Milwaukee	IHL	76	4	21	25	128	10	0	0	0	14
98-99	Muskegon	UHL	6	0	3	3	4	8	2	2	4	10
	NHL	Totals	47	3	10	13	55	—	—	—	—	—
	AHL	Totals	360	46	179	225	225	54	10	22	32	53
	IHL	Totals	271	31	94	125	319	27	1	3	4	32

Born; 6/9/64, Detroit, Michigan. 5-11, 197. Drafted by Buffalo Sabres (10th choice, 154th overall) in 1983 Entry Draft. Singed as a free agent by Anaheim Mighty Ducks (1/12/94). 1989-90 AHL First All-Star Team. Member of 1998-99 UHL Champion Muskegon Fury. Last amateur club; Michigan State (CCHA).

Dale McTavish — Center

Regular Season / Playoffs

Season	Team	League	GP	G	A	PTS	PIM	GP	G	A	PTS	PIM
95-96	Canada	National	53	24	32	56	91	—	—	—	—	—
95-96	Saint John	AHL	4	2	3	5	5	15	5	4	9	15
96-97	Calgary	NHL	9	1	2	3	2	—	—	—	—	—
96-97	Saint John	AHL	53	16	21	37	65	3	0	1	1	0
97-98	SaiPa	Finland	47	*25	18	43	73	3	0	3	3	4
98-99	SaiPa	Finland	44	22	17	39	117	7	4	5	9	2
	AHL	Totals	57	18	24	42	70	18	5	5	10	15

Born; 2/28/72, Eganville, Ontario. 6-1, 200. Signed as a free agent by Calgary Flames (8/1/96). Last amateur club; St. Francis (AUAA).

Jeff Mead — Right Wing

Regular Season / Playoffs

Season	Team	League	GP	G	A	PTS	PIM	GP	G	A	PTS	PIM
94-95	Jacksonville	SUN	36	5	10	15	10	—	—	—	—	—
94-95	West Palm Beach	SUN	19	9	10	19	10	5	1	3	4	0
95-96	Johnstown	ECHL	61	15	25	40	31	—	—	—	—	—
96-97	Pensacola	ECHL	37	6	15	21	2	—	—	—	—	—
96-97	Jacksonville	ECHL	27	5	14	19	4	—	—	—	—	—
97-98												
98-99	Alexandria	WPHL	2	0	1	1	0	—	—	—	—	—
98-99	Tupelo	WPHL	3	0	0	0	0	—	—	—	—	—
	ECHL	Totals	125	26	54	80	37	—	—	—	—	—
	SUN	Totals	55	14	20	34	20	5	1	3	4	0
	WPHL	Totals	5	0	1	1	0	—	—	—	—	—

Born; 2/10/71, Arlington, Massachusetts. 5-10, 165. Member of 1994-95 Sunshine League Champion West Palm Beach Blaze. Last amateur club; Massachusetts-Boston (NCAA 3).

Glen Mears — Defenseman
Regular Season / Playoffs

Season	Team	League	GP	G	A	PTS	PIM	GP	G	A	PTS	PIM
93-94	Greensboro	ECHL	25	1	3	4	29	—	—	—	—	—
94-95	Flint	CoHL	57	3	10	13	66	3	0	0	0	2
95-96	Toledo	ECHL	62	0	11	11	147	11	0	0	0	17
96-97	Utah	IHL	2	0	0	0	0	—	—	—	—	—
96-97	Port Huron	CoHL	7	0	1	1	11	—	—	—	—	—
96-97	Bakerfield	WCHL	57	8	41	49	190	4	2	5	7	18
97-98	Bakersfield	WCHL	32	3	20	23	115	—	—	—	—	—
98-99	Bakersfield	WCHL	69	10	37	47	189	2	0	2	2	6
	WCHL	Totals	158	21	98	119	494	6	2	7	9	24
	ECHL	Totals	87	1	14	15	176	11	0	0	0	17
	CoHL	Totals	64	3	11	14	77	3	0	0	0	0

Born; 7/14/72, Anchorage, Alaska. 6-3, 215. Drafted by Calgary Flames (5th choice, 62nd overall) in 1990 Entry Draft. 1996-97 WCHL First Team All-Star. Last amateur club; Bowling Green (CCHA).

Pat Meehan — Center
Regular Season / Playoffs

Season	Team	League	GP	G	A	PTS	PIM	GP	G	A	PTS	PIM
94-95	Dayton	ECHL	10	1	1	2	0	—	—	—	—	—
94-95	Columbus	ECHL	15	6	4	10	14	1	0	0	0	15
96-97	Central Texas	WPHL	39	10	9	19	26	—	—	—	—	—
96-97	Amarillo	WPHL	21	5	9	14	22	—	—	—	—	—
97-98	Amarillo	WPHL	57	15	17	32	49	—	—	—	—	—
98-99	New Mexico	WPHL	9	2	1	3	0	—	—	—	—	—
	WPHL	Totals	126	32	36	68	97	—	—	—	—	—
	ECHL	Totals	25	7	5	12	14	1	0	0	0	15

Born; 7/29/73, Prince George, British Columbia. 6-1, 190. Selected by Abilene in 1998 WPHL Expansion Draft.

Darren Meek — Defenseman
Regular Season / Playoffs

Season	Team	League	GP	G	A	PTS	PIM	GP	G	A	PTS	PIM
96-97	Richmond	ECHL	4	0	1	1	6	—	—	—	—	—
96-97	Huntington	ECHL	56	8	21	29	42	—	—	—	—	—
97-98	Amarillo	WPHL	68	3	25	28	50	—	—	—	—	—
98-99	Miami	ECHL	59	4	22	26	78	—	—	—	—	—
	ECHL	Totals	119	12	44	56	126	—	—	—	—	—

Born; 9/25/71, Williams Lake, British Columbia. 5-10, 190. Selected by Wheeling in 1999 ECHL Dispersal Draft. Last amateur club; Alaska-Anchorage

Brad Mehalko — Right Wing
Regular Season / Playoffs

Season	Team	League	GP	G	A	PTS	PIM	GP	G	A	PTS	PIM
98-99	Las Vegas	IHL	8	1	0	1	7	—	—	—	—	—
98-99	Tacoma	WCHL	49	14	22	36	75	—	—	—	—	—
98-99	Canada	National	7	1	0	1	4	—	—	—	—	—

Born; 1/4/77, Enchant, Alberta. 6-0, 190. Last amateur club; Calgary (WHL).

Tomas Meixner — Center
Regular Season / Playoffs

Season	Team	League	GP	G	A	PTS	PIM	GP	G	A	PTS	PIM
98-99	Macon	CHL	8	0	2	2	0	—	—	—	—	—

Born;

Dean Melanson — Defenseman
Regular Season / Playoffs

Season	Team	League	GP	G	A	PTS	PIM	GP	G	A	PTS	PIM
92-93	St-Hyacinthe	QMJHL	57	13	29	42	253	—	—	—	—	—
92-93	Rochester	AHL	8	0	12	1	6	14	1	6	7	18
93-94	Rochester	AHL	80	1	21	22	138	4	0	1	1	2
94-95	Buffalo	NHL	5	0	0	0	4	—	—	—	—	—
94-95	Rochester	AHL	43	4	7	11	84	—	—	—	—	—
95-96	Rochester	AHL	70	3	13	16	204	14	3	3	6	22
96-97	Quebec	IHL	72	3	21	24	95	7	0	2	2	12
97-98	Rochester	AHL	73	7	9	16	228	4	0	2	2	0
98-99	Rochester	AHL	79	7	27	34	192	17	3	2	5	32
	AHL	Totals	353	22	89	111	852	53	7	14	21	74

Born; 11/19/73, Antigonish, Nova Scotia. 5-11, 203. Drafted by Buffalo Sabres (4th choice, 80th overall) in 1992 Entry Draft. Signed as a free agent by Philadelphia Flyers (7/13/99). Member of 1995-96 AHL champion Rochester Americans. Last amateur club; St. Hyacinthe (QMJHL).

Rob Melanson — Defenseman
Regular Season / Playoffs

Season	Team	League	GP	G	A	PTS	PIM	GP	G	A	PTS	PIM
91-92	Knoxville	ECHL	49	0	11	11	186	—	—	—	—	—
91-92	Muskegon	IHL	7	0	2	2	2	1	0	0	0	0
92-93	Cleveland	IHL	27	0	5	5	123	1	0	0	0	0
92-93	Muskegon	CoHL	23	0	7	7	108	7	0	0	0	11
93-94	Rochester	AHL	13	0	1	1	24	—	—	—	—	—
93-94	Muskegon	CoHL	44	2	8	10	184	3	1	1	2	6
94-95	Worcester	AHL	59	0	3	3	210	—	—	—	—	—
95-96	Cornwall	AHL	10	0	0	0	67	—	—	—	—	—
95-96	Muskegon	CoHL	50	2	13	15	260	5	0	0	0	17
96-97	Muskegon	CoHL	63	3	13	16	217	3	0	1	1	16
97-98	Muskegon	UHL	55	3	10	13	178	11	0	0	0	21
98-99	Muskegon	UHL	69	0	13	13	251	18	0	1	1	46
	AHL	Totals	82	0	4	4	301	—	—	—	—	—
	IHL	Totals	34	0	7	7	125	2	0	0	0	0
	UHL	Totals	304	10	64	74	1198	47	1	3	4	117

Born; 3/5/71, Antigonish, Nova Scotia. 6-1, 202. Drafted by Pittsburgh Penguins (5th choice, 104th overall) in 1991 Entry Draft. Member of 1998-99 UHL Champion Muskegon Fury. Last amateur club; Hull (QMJHL).

Stan Melanson — Defenseman
Regular Season / Playoffs

Season	Team	League	GP	G	A	PTS	PIM	GP	G	A	PTS	PIM
92-93	St. Hyacinthe	QMJHL	48	4	16	20	107	—	—	—	—	—
92-93	New Haven	AHL	2	0	0	0	0	—	—	—	—	—
93-94												
94-95												
95-96	Peoria	IHL	4	0	0	0	17	—	—	—	—	—
95-96	Dayton	ECHL	8	1	1	2	35	—	—	—	—	—
95-96	Muskegon	CoHL	45	7	11	18	143	5	0	1	1	10
96-97	Louisiana	ECHL	56	3	8	11	201	17	0	1	1	36
97-98	Louisiana	ECHL	62	7	14	21	190	12	0	3	3	23
98-99	Louisiana	ECHL	49	2	2	4	191	5	0	0	0	4
	ECHL	Totals	175	13	25	38	617	34	0	4	4	63

Born; 6/15/72, Antigonish, Nova Scotia. 6-1, 198.

Mike Melas — Center
Regular Season / Playoffs

Season	Team	League	GP	G	A	PTS	PIM	GP	G	A	PTS	PIM
97-98	Western Michigan	CCHA	23	5	13	18	53	—	—	—	—	—
97-98	Wheeling	ECHL	17	9	11	20	8	15	7	5	12	16
98-99	Chicago	IHL	3	0	1	1	0	—	—	—	—	—
98-99	Quad City	UHL	67	40	52	92	111	5	1	1	2	2

Born; 3/10/75, Thornhill, Ontario. 5-10, 175. 1998-99 UHL All-Rookie Team. 1998-99 UHL Rookie of the Year. Last amateur club; Western Michigan

Jan Melichar — Defenseman
Regular Season / Playoffs

Season	Team	League	GP	G	A	PTS	PIM	GP	G	A	PTS	PIM
98-99	Bakersfield	WCHL	18	1	0	1	14	—	—	—	—	—
98-99	Topeka	CHL	43	2	14	16	28	3	0	0	0	2

Born; 2/24/78, Czech Republic. 6-1, 195. Last amateur club; Port Hope (Tier 2).

Marty Melnychuk — Defenseman

Regular Season / Playoffs

Season	Team	League	GP	G	A	PTS	PIM	GP	G	A	PTS	PIM
96-97	Wichita	CeHL	54	4	8	12	332	8	0	2	2	51
97-98	Huntington	ECHL	62	1	4	5	296	4	0	0	0	4
98-99	Kansas City	IHL	1	0	0	0	7	—	—	—	—	—
98-99	Arkansas	WPHL	28	1	3	4	268	3	0	0	0	7

Born; 2/13/75, New Westminster, British Columbia. 6-2, 210.

Taj Melson — Defenseman

Regular Season / Playoffs

Season	Team	League	GP	G	A	PTS	PIM	GP	G	A	PTS	PIM
96-97	San Diego	WCHL	36	8	16	24	47	8	1	5	6	23
97-98	Utah	IHL	1	0	0	0	0	—	—	—	—	—
97-98	San Diego	WCHL	51	17	26	43	59	13	2	6	8	26
98-99	Las Vegas	IHL	72	8	20	28	48	—	—	—	—	—
98-99	San Diego	WCHL	9	3	9	12	2	6	0	5	5	6
	IHL	Totals	73	8	20	28	48	—	—	—	—	—
	WCHL	Totals	96	28	51	79	208	27	3	16	19	55

Born; 4/10/74, Plymouth, Minnesota. 5-9, 170Member of 1996-97 WCHL Champion San Diego Gulls. Member of 1997-98 WCHL Champion San Diego Gulls. Last amateur club; St. Cloud State (WCHA).

Carl Menard — Right Wing

Regular Season / Playoffs

Season	Team	League	GP	G	A	PTS	PIM	GP	G	A	PTS	PIM
95-96	Memphis	CeHL	60	40	22	62	60	6	1	2	3	4
96-97	Memphis	CeHL	60	20	28	48	43	18	7	5	12	68
97-98	Idaho	WCHL	39	9	17	26	30	—	—	—	—	—
97-98	Macon	CHL	12	5	7	12	8	3	1	1	2	8
98-99	Macon	CHL	43	11	16	27	32	3	2	0	2	0
	CHL	Totals	175	76	73	149	143	30	11	8	19	80

Born; 1/19/72, Ottawa, Ontario. 6-0, 200.

Dan Menard — Right Wing

Regular Season / Playoffs

Season	Team	League	GP	G	A	PTS	PIM	GP	G	A	PTS	PIM
95-96	Brantford	CoHL	69	12	8	20	64	12	3	3	6	12
96-97	Brantford	CoHL	34	12	15	27	58	—	—	—	—	—
96-97	Utica	CoHL	33	8	13	21	6	3	0	0	0	4
97-98	Fort Worth	CHL	63	27	24	51	143	—	—	—	—	—
98-99	Fort Worth	CHL	58	19	23	42	104	—	—	—	—	—
	CoHL	Totals	136	32	36	68	128	15	3	3	6	16
	CHL	Totals	121	46	47	93	247	—	—	—	—	—

Born; 12/5/73, Ottawa, Ontario. 6-0, 188. Selected by Topeka in 1999 CHL Dispersal Draft.

Martin Menard — Center

Regular Season / Playoffs

Season	Team	League	GP	G	A	PTS	PIM	GP	G	A	PTS	PIM
97-98	Cincinnati	IHL	21	4	5	9	24	—	—	—	—	—
97-98	Rochester	AHL	47	18	13	31	30	—	—	—	—	—
97-98	Dayton	ECHL	7	4	3	7	6	5	2	2	4	4
98-99	Rosenheim	Germany	4	0	0	0	4	—	—	—	—	—
98-99	Essen	Germany	37	14	14	28	32	—	—	—	—	—

Born; 3/2/76, Hull, Quebec. 5-8, 165. Traded to Cincinnati by Rochester with Brent Fedyk for Steven King and Mike Casselman (2/98). Last amateur club; Hull (QMJHL).

Terry Menard — Center

Regular Season / Playoffs

Season	Team	League	GP	G	A	PTS	PIM	GP	G	A	PTS	PIM
89-90	Milwaukee	IHL	22	6	9	15	14	2	0	0	0	0
89-90	Virginia	ECHL	24	14	18	32	28	—	—	—	—	—
90-91												
91-92	Thunder Bay	CoHL	58	41	57	98	87	12	3	4	7	16
92-93	Thunder Bay	CoHL	36	10	27	37	38	11	4	6	10	36
93-94	Thunder Bay	CoHL	61	41	60	101	111	9	7	9	16	12
94-95	Thunder Bay	CoHL	71	39	60	99	152	11	6	7	13	16
95-96	Thunder Bay	CoHL	58	31	35	66	154	19	6	8	14	55
96-97	Fort Worth	CeHL	63	50	65	115	138	17	8	15	23	46
97-98	Fort Worth	WPHL	68	36	80	116	115	13	4	9	13	28
98-99	Fort Worth	WPHL	7	6	2	8	10	—	—	—	—	—
	CoHL	Totals	284	162	239	401	542	62	26	34	60	131
	WPHL	Totals	75	42	82	124	125	13	4	9	13	28

Born; 2/3/68, Timmins, Ontario. 5-10, 185. 1994-95 CoHL Top Defensive Forward. 1996-97 CeHL First Team All-Star. Member of 1991-92 CoHL champion Thunder Bay Thunder Hawks. Member of 1993-94 CoHL champion Thunder Bay Senators. Member of 1994-95 CoHL champion Thunder Bay Senators. Member of 1996-97 CeHL Champion Fort Worth Fire. Named coach of Fort Worth Brahmas beginning with 1998-99 season.

Tom Menicci — Defenseman

Regular Season / Playoffs

Season	Team	League	GP	G	A	PTS	PIM	GP	G	A	PTS	PIM
94-95	Hampton Roads	ECHL	50	11	12	23	47	4	1	0	1	0
95-96	Hampton Roads	ECHL	1	0	0	0	0	—	—	—	—	—
95-96	South Carolina	ECHL	20	1	2	3	14	—	—	—	—	—
95-96	Huntington	ECHL	42	5	7	12	18	—	—	—	—	—
96-97	Huntington	ECHL	70	15	29	44	52	—	—	—	—	—
97-98	Utah	IHL	1	0	0	0	0	—	—	—	—	—
97-98	Phoenix	WCHL	63	12	24	36	53	9	3	0	3	12
98-99	Phoenix	WCHL	62	14	35	49	55	3	1	0	1	6
	ECHL	Totals	183	32	50	82	131	4	1	0	1	0
	WCHL	Totals	125	26	59	85	108	12	4	0	4	18

Born; 7/23/71, Smithtown, New York. 5-10, 190. Last amateur club; St. Anselm (NCAA 2).

Jarno Mensonen — Left Wing

Regular Season / Playoffs

Season	Team	League	GP	G	A	PTS	PIM	GP	G	A	PTS	PIM
97-98	Waco	WPHL	21	7	6	13	0	—	—	—	—	—
98-99	Binghamton	UHL	49	3	8	11	8	—	—	—	—	—
98-99	Madison	UHL	18	3	6	9	4	—	—	—	—	—
	UHL	Totals	67	6	14	20	12	—	—	—	—	—

Born; 2/5/71, Imatra, Finland. 6-0, 182.

Jeff Mercer — Left Wing

Regular Season / Playoffs

Season	Team	League	GP	G	A	PTS	PIM	GP	G	A	PTS	PIM
98-99	Las Vegas	IHL	1	0	0	0	4	—	—	—	—	—
98-99	Tacoma	WCHL	1	0	0	0	2	10	2	1	3	12

Born; Cornerbrook, Newfoundland. 6-2, 215. Member of 1998-99 WCHL Champion Tacoma Sabrecats.

Rob Merrill — Left Wing

Regular Season / Playoffs

Season	Team	League	GP	G	A	PTS	PIM	GP	G	A	PTS	PIM
98-99	Toledo	ECHL	68	13	22	35	89	4	1	0	1	2

Born; 7/9/74, Glens Falls, New York. 6-2, 220. Last amateur club; Brown

Jan Mertzig — Defenseman

Regular Season / Playoffs

Season	Team	League	GP	G	A	PTS	PIM	GP	G	A	PTS	PIM
98-99	Rangers	NHL	23	0	2	2	8	—	—	—	—	—
98-99	Hartford	AHL	35	3	2	5	14	—	—	—	—	—
98-99	Utah	IHL	5	0	1	1	6	—	—	—	—	—

Born; 7/18/70, Huddinge, Sweden. 6-4, 218. Drafted by New York Rangers (9th choice, 235th overall) in 1998 Entry Draft. Last European club; Lulea (Sweden).

Eric Messier — Defenseman

Season	Team	League	GP	G	A	PTS	PIM	GP	G	A	PTS	PIM
			Regular Season					Playoffs				
95-96	Cornwall	AHL	72	5	9	14	111	8	1	1	2	20
96-97	Colorado	NHL	21	0	0	0	4	6	0	0	0	4
96-97	Hershey	AHL	55	16	26	42	69	5	2	4	6	12
97-98	Colorado	NHL	62	4	12	16	20	—	—	—	—	—
98-99	Colorado	NHL	31	4	2	6	14	3	0	0	0	0
98-99	Hershey	AHL	6	1	3	4	4	—	—	—	—	—
	NHL	Totals	114	8	14	22	38	9	0	0	0	4
	AHL	Totals	133	22	38	60	184	13	3	5	8	32

Born; 10/29/73, Drummondville, Quebec. 6-2, 200. Signed as a free agent by Colorado Avalanche (6/14/95). Last amateur club; Quebec (OUAA).

Scott Metcalfe — Center

Season	Team	League	GP	G	A	PTS	PIM	GP	G	A	PTS	PIM
			Regular Season					Playoffs				
87-88	Buffalo	NHL	1	0	1	1	0	—	—	—	—	—
87-88	Edmonton	NHL	2	0	0	0	0	—	—	—	—	—
87-88	Nova Scotia	AHL	43	9	19	28	87	—	—	—	—	—
87-88	Rochester	AHL	22	2	13	15	56	7	1	3	4	24
88-89	Buffalo	NHL	9	1	1	2	13	—	—	—	—	—
88-89	Rochester	AHL	60	20	31	51	241	—	—	—	—	—
89-90	Buffalo	NHL	7	0	0	0	5	—	—	—	—	—
89-90	Rochester	AHL	43	12	17	29	93	2	0	1	1	0
90-91	Rochester	AHL	69	17	22	39	177	14	4	1	5	27
91-92												
92-93												
93-94	Rochester	AHL	16	5	7	12	16	4	1	0	1	31
93-94	Knoxville	ECHL	56	25	56	81	136	3	0	1	1	20
94-95	Rochester	AHL	63	19	36	55	216	5	1	1	2	4
95-96	Rochester	AHL	71	21	24	45	228	19	6	8	14	23
96-97	Rochester	AHL	80	32	38	70	205	10	1	3	4	18
97-98	Rochester	AHL	75	9	24	33	192	4	0	0	0	11
98-99	Hannover	Germany	50	11	21	32	126	—	—	—	—	—
	NHL	Totals	19	1	2	3	18	—	—	—	—	—
	AHL	Totals	542	146	231	377	1511	65	14	17	31	138

Born; 1/6/67, Toronto, Ontario. 6-0, 200. Drafted by Edmonton Oilers (1st choice, 20th overall) in 1985 Entry Draft. Traded to Buffalo Sabres by Edmonton for Steve Dykstra (2/88). Member of 1995-96 AHL champion Rochester Americans. Last amateur club; Windsor (OHL).

Andy Meth — Center

Season	Team	League	GP	G	A	PTS	PIM	GP	G	A	PTS	PIM
			Regular Season					Playoffs				
95-96	Daytona Beach	SHL	3	0	0	0	5	—	—	—	—	—
96-97												
97-98												
98-99	San Antonio	CHL	3	0	0	0	2	—	—	—	—	—

Born; 9/2/69, Montreal, Quebec. 5-8, 175.

Francois Methot — Center

Season	Team	League	GP	G	A	PTS	PIM	GP	G	A	PTS	PIM
			Regular Season					Playoffs				
98-99	Rochester	AHL	58	5	8	13	8	9	0	1	1	0

Born; 4/26/78, Montreal, Quebec. 6-0, 175. Drafted by Buffalo Sabres (4th choice, 54th overall) in 1996 Entry Draft. Last amateur club; Shawinigan

Rich Metro — Forward

Season	Team	League	GP	G	A	PTS	PIM	GP	G	A	PTS	PIM
			Regular Season					Playoffs				
98-99	Northern Michigan	CCHA	40	9	13	22	42	—	—	—	—	—
98-99	Columbus	CHL	2	2	0	2	2	4	2	1	3	0

Born; 1/31/75, Sault Ste. Marie, Ontario. 5-11, 175. Last amateur club; Northern Michigan (CCHA).

Glen Metropolit — Center

Season	Team	League	GP	G	A	PTS	PIM	GP	G	A	PTS	PIM
			Regular Season					Playoffs				
95-96	Atlanta	IHL	1	0	0	0	0	—	—	—	—	—
95-96	Nashville	ECHL	58	30	31	61	62	5	3	8	11	2
96-97	Quebec	IHL	22	5	4	9	14	5	0	0	0	2
96-97	Pensacola	ECHL	54	35	47	82	45	12	9	16	25	28
97-98	Grand Rapids	IHL	79	20	35	55	90	3	1	1	2	0
98-99	Grand Rapids	IHL	77	28	53	81	92	—	—	—	—	—
	IHL	Totals	179	53	92	145	196	8	1	1	2	2
	ECHL	Totals	112	65	78	143	107	17	12	24	36	30

Born; 6/25/74, Toronto, Ontario. 6-0, 185. Signed as a free agent by Washington Capitals (7/20/99).

Bret Meyers — Right Wing

Season	Team	League	GP	G	A	PTS	PIM	GP	G	A	PTS	PIM
			Regular Season					Playoffs				
98-99	Lowell	AHL	11	5	2	7	2	—	—	—	—	—
98-99	Detroit	IHL	2	0	0	0	2	—	—	—	—	—
98-99	Indianapolis	IHL	4	0	0	0	4	—	—	—	—	—
98-99	Columbus	ECHL	53	33	30	63	104	4	2	1	3	2
	IHL	Totals	6	0	0	0	6	—	—	—	—	—

Born; 9/29/73, Uxbridge, Ontario. 6-0, 210. Last amateur club; Michigan Tech (WCHA).

Andrei Mezin — Goaltender

Season	Team	League	GP	W	L	T	MIN	SO	AVG	GP	W	L	MIN	SO	AVG
			Regular Season							Playoffs					
95-96	Fort Wayne	IHL	1	0	0	0	35	0	1.72	—	—	—	—	—	—
95-96	Flint	CoHL	40	27	9	2	2270	1	3.49	7	5	1	410	1	2.64
96-97	Las Vegas	IHL	10	4	5	0	490	0	4.04	—	—	—	—	—	—
96-97	Flint	CoHL	25	19	4	1	1417	2	*2.46	4	0	2	175	0	4.45
96-97	Rochester	AHL	7	3	3	1	386	0	4.82	—	—	—	—	—	—
97-98	Detroit	IHL	4	2	1	0	179	0	2.69	—	—	—	—	—	—
97-98	Flint	UHL	27	21	5	0	1489	1	3.47	8	*7	1	441	0	3.26
98-99	Nurnberg	Germany	49	—	—	—	2856	5	2.61	13	—	—	765	0	2.43
	IHL	Totals	15	6	6	0	704	0	3.58	—	—	—	—	—	—
	CoHL	Totals	92	67	18	3	5176	4	3.20	19	12	4	1026	1	3.22

Born; 7/8/74, Chelyabinsk, Russia. 6-0, 187. Member of 1995-96 CoHL Champion Flint Generals.

Phil Miaskowski — Center

Season	Team	League	GP	G	A	PTS	PIM	GP	G	A	PTS	PIM
			Regular Season					Playoffs				
95-96	Columbus	ECHL	2	0	0	0	6	—	—	—	—	—
95-96	Brantford	CoHL	71	31	25	56	104	12	9	6	15	14
96-97	Brantford	CoHL	61	34	33	67	77	10	8	3	11	8
97-98	Fort Worth	CHL	57	27	34	61	76	—	—	—	—	—
98-99	Fort Worth	WPHL	63	31	32	63	101	12	8	8	16	26
	CoHL	Totals	132	65	58	123	181	22	17	9	26	22

Born; 4/16/74, Toronto, Ontario. 6-3, 223.

Chad Michalchuk — Left Wing

Season	Team	League	GP	G	A	PTS	PIM	GP	G	A	PTS	PIM
			Regular Season					Playoffs				
96-97	Johnstown	ECHL	4	0	0	0	30	—	—	—	—	—
96-97	Madison	CoHL	36	5	9	14	98	—	—	—	—	—
96-97	Brantford	CoHL	7	1	0	1	23	10	0	2	2	16
97-98	Brantford	UHL	60	11	26	37	112	9	0	2	2	18
98-99	Waco	WPHL	64	32	29	61	224	4	1	0	1	15
	CoHL	Totals	103	17	35	52	233	19	0	4	4	34

Born; 7/10/73, Calgary, Alberta. 5-11, 185. Last amateur club; Brandon

Brad Michalski — Center

Regular Season / Playoffs

Season	Team	League	GP	G	A	PTS	PIM	GP	G	A	PTS	PIM
97-98	Tucson	WCHL	8	3	1	4	22	—	—	—	—	—
97-98	Port Huron	UHL	28	2	3	5	14	—	—	—	—	—
97-98	Brantford	UHL	3	0	1	1	2	—	—	—	—	—
98-99	Madison	UHL	9	0	0	0	11	—	—	—	—	—
98-99	Tupelo	WPHL	1	0	0	0	0	—	—	—	—	—
	UHL	Totals	40	2	4	6	27	—	—	—	—	—

Born; 3/24/76, Pittsburgh, Pennsylvania. 5-9, 160.

Thomas Migdel — Right Wing

Regular Season / Playoffs

Season	Team	League	GP	G	A	PTS	PIM	GP	G	A	PTS	PIM
98-99	Wichita	CHL	61	15	10	25	51	4	0	1	1	2

Born; 3/7/77, Lipton, Saskatchewan. 6-1, 190. Last amateur club; Calgary

Mike Migen — Defenseman

Regular Season / Playoffs

Season	Team	League	GP	G	A	PTS	PIM	GP	G	A	PTS	PIM
98-99	Topeka	CHL	2	0	0	0	0	—	—	—	—	—

Born; 6-0, 180.

Sonny Mignacca — Goaltender

Regular Season / Playoffs

Season	Team	League	GP	W	L	T	MIN	SO	AVG	GP	W	L	MIN	SO	AVG
94-95	Syracuse	AHL	19	4	11	2	1097	0	4.65	—	—	—	—	—	—
95-96	Syracuse	AHL	8	2	5	0	377	0	4.14	—	—	—	—	—	—
96-97	Tallahassee	ECHL	38	19	12	5	2027	4	3.23	3	0	2	132	0	3.64
97-98	Basingstoke	BSL	17	—	—	—	934	0	3.28	—	—	—	—	—	—
98-99	London	BSL	16	—	—	—	803	—	3.59	—	—	—	—	—	—
	AHL	Totals	27	6	16	2	1474	0	4.52	—	—	—	—	—	—

Born; 1/4/74, Winnipeg, Manitoba. 5-8, 178. Drafted by Vancouver Canucks (10th choice, 213th overall) in 1992 Entry Draft. Last amateur club; Moose Jaw

Jeff Mikesch — Center

Regular Season / Playoffs

Season	Team	League	GP	G	A	PTS	PIM	GP	G	A	PTS	PIM
97-98	Louisville	ECHL	45	10	12	22	68	—	—	—	—	—
98-99	Columbus	CHL	6	1	3	4	4	—	—	—	—	—

Born; 4/11/75, Hancock, Michigan. 6-0, 175. Drafted by Detroit Red Wings (8th choice, 231st overall) in 1994 Entry Draft. Last amateur club; Michigan Tech (WCHA).

Pat Mikesch — Center

Regular Season / Playoffs

Season	Team	League	GP	G	A	PTS	PIM	GP	G	A	PTS	PIM
95-96	Michigan Tech	WCHA	39	16	22	38	65	—	—	—	—	—
95-96	Louisville	ECHL	4	5	0	5	0	3	1	1	2	4
96-97	Kentucky	AHL	77	17	28	45	57	4	1	1	2	2
97-98	Orlando	IHL	64	6	23	29	46	6	1	0	1	0
98-99	New Haven	AHL	34	5	15	20	46	—	—	—	—	—
98-99	Florida	ECHL	45	23	37	60	67	4	1	5	6	4
	AHL	Totals	111	22	43	65	103	4	1	1	2	2
	ECHL	Totals	49	28	37	65	67	7	2	6	8	8

Born; 2/15/73, Hancock, Michigan. 5-10, 175. Last amateur club; Michigan Tech (WCHA).

Phil Milbourne — Defenseman

Regular Season / Playoffs

Season	Team	League	GP	G	A	PTS	PIM	GP	G	A	PTS	PIM
97-98	Chesapeake	ECHL	7	0	0	0	13	—	—	—	—	—
98-99	Chesapeake	ECHL	17	0	2	2	26	—	—	—	—	—
98-99	Augusta	ECHL	2	0	0	0	0	—	—	—	—	—
	ECHL	Totals	26	0	2	2	39	—	—	—	—	—

Born; 3/25/77, Annapolis, Maryland. 6-1, 200.

Ryan Miles — Goaltender

Regular Season / Playoffs

Season	Team	League	GP	W	L	T	MIN	SO	AVG	GP	W	L	MIN	SO	AVG
98-99	Flint	UHL	1	0	0	0	29	0	2.04	—	—	—	—	—	—

Born; 4/3/76, Barrie, Ontario.

Craig Millar — Defenseman

Regular Season / Playoffs

Season	Team	League	GP	G	A	PTS	PIM	GP	G	A	PTS	PIM
96-97	Edmonton	NHL	1	0	0	0	2	—	—	—	—	—
96-97	Rochester	AHL	64	7	18	25	65	—	—	—	—	—
96-97	Hamilton	AHL	10	1	3	4	10	22	4	4	8	21
97-98	Hamilton	AHL	60	10	22	32	113	9	3	1	4	22
98-99	Edmonton	NHL	24	0	2	2	19	—	—	—	—	—
98-99	Hamilton	AHL	43	3	17	20	38	11	1	5	6	18
	NHL	Totals	25	0	2	2	21	—	—	—	—	—
	AHL	Totals	177	21	60	81	226	42	8	10	18	61

Born; 7/12/76, Winnipeg, Manitoba. 6-2, 200. Drafted by Buffalo Sabres (10th choice, 225th overall) in 1994 Entry Draft. Member of 1996-97 AHL All-Rookie Team. Traded to Edmonton Oilers by Buffalo with Barrie Moore for Miroslav Satan (3/18/97). Traded to Nashville Predators by Edmonton for a third round choice (previously acquired from Detroit-Edmonton selected Mike Comrie) (6/25/99). Last amateur club; Swift Current (WHL).

Aren Miller — Goaltender

Regular Season / Playoffs

Season	Team	League	GP	W	L	T	MIN	SO	AVG	GP	W	L	MIN	SO	AVG
98-99	Adirondack	AHL	25	3	14	1	1155	1	3.53	2	0	2	123	0	3.92
98-99	Toledo	ECHL	7	1	4	1	374	0	5.30	—	—	—	—	—	—

Born; 1/13/78, Oxbow, Saskatchewan. 6-2, 208. Drafted by Detroit Red Wings (2nd choice, 52nd overall) in 1996 Entry Draft. Last amateur club; Spokane

Brad Miller — Defenseman

Regular Season / Playoffs

Season	Team	League	GP	G	A	PTS	PIM	GP	G	A	PTS	PIM
87-88	Rochester	AHL	3	0	0	0	4	2	0	0	0	2
88-89	Buffalo	NHL	7	0	0	0	6	—	—	—	—	—
88-89	Rochester	AHL	3	0	0	0	4	—	—	—	—	—
89-90	Rochester	NHL	1	0	0	0	0	—	—	—	—	—
89-90	Rochester	AHL	60	2	10	12	273	8	1	0	1	52
90-91	Buffalo	NHL	13	0	0	0	67	—	—	—	—	—
90-91	Rochester	AHL	49	0	9	9	248	12	0	4	4	67
91-92	Buffalo	NHL	42	1	4	5	192	—	—	—	—	—
91-92	Rochester	AHL	27	0	4	4	113	11	0	0	0	61
92-93	Ottawa	NHL	11	0	0	0	42	—	—	—	—	—
92-93	New Haven	AHL	41	1	9	10	138	—	—	—	—	—
92-93	St. John's	AHL	20	0	3	3	61	8	0	2	2	10
93-94	Calgary	NHL	8	0	1	1	14	—	—	—	—	—
93-94	Saint John	AHL	36	3	12	15	174	6	1	0	1	21
94-95	Minnesota	IHL	55	1	13	14	181	3	0	0	0	12
95-96	Utah	IHL	1	0	0	0	0	—	—	—	—	—
95-96	Minnesota	IHL	33	0	5	5	170	—	—	—	—	—
95-96	Atlanta	IHL	5	0	0	0	8	—	—	—	—	—
96-97	Quebec	IHL	57	1	7	8	132	4	0	0	0	2
97-98	San Antonio	IHL	58	3	6	9	228	—	—	—	—	—
97-98	Utah	IHL	9	0	1	1	46	4	0	0	0	8
98-99	Las Vegas	IHL	73	5	16	21	264	—	—	—	—	—
	NHL	Totals	82	1	5	6	321	—	—	—	—	—
	IHL	Totals	291	10	48	58	1029	11	0	0	0	22
	AHL	Totals	239	6	47	53	1015	45	2	6	8	211

Born; 7/23/69, Edmonton, Alberta. 6-4, 226. Drafted by Buffalo Sabres (2nd choice, 22nd overall) in 1987 Entry Draft. Selected by Ottawa Senators in NHL expansion draft (6/18/92). Traded to Toronto Maple Leafs by Ottawa for 9th round choice (Pavol Demitra) in 1993 Entry Draft (2/25/93). Traded to Calgary Flames by Toronto with Jeff Perry for Todd Gillingham and Paul Holden (9/3/93). Last amateur club; Regina (WHL).

Colin Miller — Center

Regular Season / Playoffs

Season	Team	League	GP	G	A	PTS	PIM	GP	G	A	PTS	PIM
92-93	Atlanta	IHL	76	20	39	59	52	9	2	4	6	22
93-94	Atlanta	IHL	80	13	32	45	48	3	2	3	5	0
94-95	Atlanta	IHL	36	5	14	19	29	—	—	—	—	—
94-95	Las Vegas	IHL	7	0	1	1	2	—	—	—	—	—
94-95	Indianapolis	IHL	13	5	6	11	10	—	—	—	—	—
94-95	Knoxville	ECHL	5	1	2	3	0	—	—	—	—	—
95-96	Dayton	ECHL	69	24	50	74	103	3	0	2	2	8
96-97	Michigan	IHL	1	0	0	0	0	—	—	—	—	—
96-97	Dayton	ECHL	68	20	58	78	60	4	2	2	4	18
97-98	Dayton	ECHL	66	19	48	67	144	5	0	2	2	12
98-99	Dayton	ECHL	68	20	36	56	126	4	0	1	1	16
	IHL	Totals	213	43	92	135	141	12	4	7	11	22
	ECHL	Totals	276	84	194	278	433	16	2	7	9	54

Born; 8/21/71, Grimsby, Ontario. 6-0, 200. Member of 1993-94 IHL champion Atlanta Knights. Last amateur club; Sault Ste. Marie (OHL).

Jason Miller — Center

Regular Season / Playoffs

Season	Team	League	GP	G	A	PTS	PIM	GP	G	A	PTS	PIM
90-91	Medicine Hat	WHL	66	60	76	136	31	12	9	10	19	8
90-91	New Jersey	NHL	1	0	0	0	0	—	—	—	—	—
91-92	New Jersey	NHL	3	0	0	0	0	—	—	—	—	—
91-92	Utica	AHL	71	23	32	55	31	4	1	3	4	0
92-93	New Jersey	NHL	2	0	0	0	0	—	—	—	—	—
92-93	Utica	AHL	72	28	42	70	43	5	4	4	8	2
93-94	Albany	AHL	77	22	53	75	65	5	1	1	2	4
94-95	Adirondack	AHL	77	32	33	65	39	4	1	0	1	0
95-96	Peoria	IHL	39	16	22	38	6	11	1	2	3	4
96-97	San Antonio	IHL	76	26	43	69	43	9	1	4	5	6
97-98	Dusseldorfer	Germany	46	15	19	34	26	3	1	2	3	0
98-99	Nurnberg	Germany	51	30	31	61	56	13	5	6	11	8
	NHL	Totals	6	0	0	0	0	—	—	—	—	—
	AHL	Totals	297	105	160	265	178	18	7	8	15	6
	IHL	Totals	115	42	65	107	49	20	2	6	8	10

Born; 3/1/71, Edmonton, Alberta. 6-1, 190. Drafted by New Jersey Devils (2nd choice, 18th overall) in 1989 Entry Draft. Signed as a free agent by Detroit Red Wings (7/28/94). Last amateur club; Medicine Hat (WHL).

Kevin Miller — Right Wing

Regular Season / Playoffs

Season	Team	League	GP	G	A	PTS	PIM	GP	G	A	PTS	PIM
88-89	Rangers	NHL	24	3	5	8	2	—	—	—	—	—
88-89	Denver	IHL	55	29	47	76	19	4	2	1	3	2
89-90	Rangers	NHL	16	0	5	5	2	1	0	0	0	0
89-90	Flint	IHL	48	19	23	42	41	—	—	—	—	—
90-91	Rangers	NHL	63	17	27	44	63	—	—	—	—	—
90-91	Detroit	NHL	11	5	2	7	4	7	3	2	5	20
91-92	Detroit	NHL	80	20	26	46	53	9	0	2	2	4
92-93	Washington	NHL	10	0	3	3	35	—	—	—	—	—
92-93	St. Louis	NHL	72	24	22	46	65	10	0	3	3	11
93-94	St. Louis	NHL	75	23	25	48	83	3	1	0	1	4
94-95	St. Louis	NHL	15	2	5	7	0	—	—	—	—	—
94-95	San Jose	NHL	21	6	7	13	13	6	0	0	0	2
95-96	San Jose	NHL	68	22	20	42	41	—	—	—	—	—
95-96	Pittsburgh	NHL	13	6	5	11	4	18	3	2	5	8
96-97	Chicago	NHL	69	14	17	31	41	6	0	1	1	0
97-98	Chicago	NHL	37	4	7	11	8	—	—	—	—	—
97-98	Indianapolis	IHL	26	11	11	22	41	2	1	1	2	0
98-99	Chicago	IHL	30	11	20	31	8	10	2	7	9	22
	NHL	Totals	574	146	176	322	414	60	7	10	17	49
	IHL	Totals	159	70	101	171	109	16	5	9	14	24

Born; 9/2/65, Lansing, Michigan. 5-11, 190. Drafted by New York Rangers (10th chocie, 202nd overall) in 1984 Entry Draft. Traded to Detroit Red Wings by Rangers with Jim Cummins and Dennis Vial for Joey Kocur and Per Djoos (3/5/91). Traded to Washington Capitals by Detroit for Dino Ciccarelli (6/20/92). Traded to St. Louis Blues by Washington for Paul Cavallini (11/2/92). Traded to San Jose Sharks by St. Louis for Todd Elik (3/23/95). Traded to Pittsburgh Penguins by San Jose for Pittsburgh's fifth round choice (later traded to Boston-Boston selected Elias Abrahamsson) in 1996 Entry Draft and future considerations (3/20/96). Signed as a free agent by Chicago Blackhawks (7/18/96). Last

Kris Miller — Defenseman

Regular Season / Playoffs

Season	Team	League	GP	G	A	PTS	PIM	GP	G	A	PTS	PIM
91-92	Raleigh	ECHL	42	12	27	39	78	4	2	3	5	8
91-92	Utica	AHL	1	0	0	0	0	—	—	—	—	—
91-92	Phoenix	IHL	16	1	2	3	17	—	—	—	—	—
92-93	Salt Lake City	IHL	45	4	21	25	45	—	—	—	—	—
92-93	Raleigh	ECHL	30	8	24	32	62	—	—	—	—	—
93-94	Saint John	AHL	58	2	17	19	38	—	—	—	—	—
94-95	Minnesota	IHL	71	4	16	20	61	3	1	0	1	0
95-96	Minnesota	IHL	70	5	10	15	84	—	—	—	—	—
96-97	Orlando	IHL	41	2	3	5	57	10	1	1	2	10
96-97	Raleigh	ECHL	30	3	23	26	61	—	—	—	—	—
97-98	Manchester	BSL	54	18	21	39	91	9	0	3	3	8
98-99	Manchester	BSL	41	8	18	26	42	9	1	0	1	10
	IHL	Totals	243	16	52	68	264	13	2	1	3	10
	AHL	Totals	59	2	17	19	38	—	—	—	—	—
	ECHL	Totals	102	23	74	97	201	4	2	3	5	8

Born; 3/30/69, Bemidji, Minnesota. 6-0, 200. Drafted by Montreal Canadiens (6th choice, 80th overall) in 1987 Entry Draft. Last amateur club; Minnesota

Rod Miller — Defenseman

Regular Season / Playoffs

Season	Team	League	GP	G	A	PTS	PIM	GP	G	A	PTS	PIM
94-95	Denver	IHL	47	2	5	7	65	12	1	3	4	11
95-96	Utah	IHL	49	2	1	3	61	—	—	—	—	—
95-96	Atlanta	IHL	21	1	1	2	28	3	0	0	0	2
96-97	Utah	IHL	79	0	12	12	111	6	0	1	1	4
97-98	Utah	IHL	41	1	1	2	55	—	—	—	—	—
98-99	Utah	IHL	72	2	8	10	95	—	—	—	—	—
	IHL	Totals	309	8	28	36	415	21	1	4	5	17

Born; 4/2/70, Prince Albert, Saskatchewan. 6-1, 205. 1997-98 IHL Man of the Year. Member of 1994-95 IHL champion Denver Grizzlies. Last amateur club; Minnesota-Duluth (WCHA).

Todd Miller — Center

Regular Season / Playoffs

Season	Team	League	GP	G	A	PTS	PIM	GP	G	A	PTS	PIM
98-99	Arkansas	WPHL	29	5	6	11	35	—	—	—	—	—
98-99	El Paso	WPHL	10	1	2	3	4	—	—	—	—	—
	WPHL	Totals	39	6	8	14	39	—	—	—	—	—

Born; 5/24/78, Elliot Lake, Ontario. 6-2, 200. Last amateur club; Sault Ste. Marie (OHL).

Rob Milliken — Defenseman

Regular Season / Playoffs

Season	Team	League	GP	G	A	PTS	PIM	GP	G	A	PTS	PIM
95-96	Bakersfield	WCHL	28	7	15	22	54	—	—	—	—	—
96-97	Bakersfield	WCHL	64	9	21	30	221	3	0	0	0	12
97-98	Bakersfield	WCHL	59	18	15	33	241	2	1	0	1	0
98-99	Asheville	UHL	61	15	38	53	119	3	0	2	2	4
	WCHL	Totals	151	34	51	85	516	5	1	0	1	12

Born; 10/27/74, Victoria, British Columbia. 6-1, 215. Last amateur club; Powell River (BCJHL).

Craig Mills — Right Wing

Regular Season / Playoffs

Season	Team	League	GP	G	A	PTS	PIM	GP	G	A	PTS	PIM
95-96	Belleville	OHL	48	10	19	29	113	14	4	5	9	32
95-96	Winnipeg	NHL	4	0	2	2	0	1	0	0	0	0
95-96	Springfield	AHL	—	—	—	—	—	2	0	0	0	0
96-97	Indianapolis	IHL	80	12	7	19	199	4	0	0	0	4
97-98	Chicago	NHL	20	0	3	3	34	—	—	—	—	—
97-98	Indianapolis	IHL	42	8	11	19	119	5	0	0	0	27
98-99	Chicago	NHL	7	0	0	0	2	—	—	—	—	—
98-99	Portland	AHL	48	7	11	18	59	—	—	—	—	—
98-99	Chicago	IHL	5	0	0	0	14	—	—	—	—	—
98-99	Indianapolis	IHL	12	2	3	5	14	6	1	0	1	5
	NHL	Totals	31	0	5	5	36	1	0	0	0	0
	IHL	Totals	139	22	21	43	346	15	1	0	1	36
	AHL	Totals	48	7	11	18	59	2	0	0	0	0

Born; 8/27/76, Toronto, Ontario. 5-11, 174. Drafted by Winnipeg Jets (5th choice, 108th overall) in 1994 Entry Draft. Traded to Chicago Blackhawks with Alexei Zhamnov, and Phoenix's first round choice (Ty Jones) for Jeremy Roenick (8/16/96). Last amateur club; Belleville (OHL).

Mike Minard — Goaltender

Regular Season / Playoffs

Season	Team	League	GP	W	L	T	MIN	SO	AVG	GP	W	L	MIN	SO	AVG
96-97	Hamilton	AHL	3	1	1	0	100	0	4.20	—	—	—	—	—	—
96-97	Wheeling	ECHL	23	3	7	1	899	0	4.60	3	0	2	148	0	6.47
97-98	Hamilton	AHL	2	1	0	0	80	0	1.50	—	—	—	—	—	—
97-98	Milwaukee	IHL	8	2	2	0	362	0	3.15	—	—	—	—	—	—
97-98	Brantford	UHL	2	1	1	0	75	0	5.63	—	—	—	—	—	—
97-98	New Orleans	ECHL	11	6	2	0	429	0	4.19	—	—	—	—	—	—
98-99	Hamilton	AHL	11	8	3	0	645	1	2.79	1	0	0	20	0	0.00
98-99	Milwaukee	IHL	10	3	5	0	531	0	3.05	—	—	—	—	—	—
98-99	Dayton	ECHL	15	8	5	2	788	1	3.20	—	—	—	—	—	—
	IHL	Totals	18	5	7	0	893	0	3.09	—	—	—	—	—	—
	AHL	Totals	16	10	4	0	825	1	2.84	1	0	0	20	0	0.00
	ECHL	Totals	49	17	14	3	2116	1	4.00	3	0	2	148	0	6.47

Born; 11/1/76, Owen Sound, Ontario. 6-3, 205. Drafted by Edmonton Oilers (4th choice, 83rd overall) in 1995 Entry Draft. Last amateur club; Detroit (OHL).

Chuck Mindel — Left Wing

Regular Season / Playoffs

Season	Team	League	GP	G	A	PTS	PIM	GP	G	A	PTS	PIM
98-99	Western Michigan	CCHA	34	14	9	23	44	—	—	—	—	—
98-99	Dayton	ECHL	4	1	1	2	2	2	1	0	1	0

Born; 8/28/77, Washington, Missouri. 5-10, 194. Last amateur club; Western Michigan (CCHA).

Aigars Mironovics — Defenseman

Regular Season / Playoffs

Season	Team	League	GP	G	A	PTS	PIM	GP	G	A	PTS	PIM
97-98	Tucson	WCHL	25	4	5	9	63	—	—	—	—	—
97-98	San Diego	WCHL	5	0	0	0	2	—	—	—	—	—
97-98	Bakersfield	WCHL	19	4	10	14	27	4	0	0	0	2
98-99	San Angelo	WPHL	36	3	5	8	47	—	—	—	—	—
98-99	Huntsville	CHL	15	3	4	7	19	15	1	6	7	8
	WCHL	Totals	49	8	15	23	92	4	0	0	0	2

Born; 1/3/76, Riga, Latvia. 5-11, 185. Traded to San Diego by Tucson for future considerations (1/98). Traded to Bakersfield by Tucson for Don Lester (2/98). Member of 1998-99 CHL Champion Huntsville Channel Cats.

Jeff Mitchell — Right Wing

Regular Season / Playoffs

Season	Team	League	GP	G	A	PTS	PIM	GP	G	A	PTS	PIM
95-96	Michigan	IHL	50	5	4	9	119	—	—	—	—	—
96-97	Michigan	IHL	24	0	3	3	40	—	—	—	—	—
96-97	Philadelphia	AHL	31	7	5	12	103	10	1	1	2	20
97-98	Dallas	NHL	7	0	0	0	7	—	—	—	—	—
97-98	Michigan	IHL	62	9	8	17	206	4	0	0	0	30
98-99	Michigan	IHL	50	4	4	8	122	2	0	0	0	0
	IHL	Totals	186	18	19	37	487	6	0	0	0	30

Born; 5/16/75, Wayne, Michigan. 6-1, 190. Drafted by Los Angeles Kings (2nd choice, 68th overall) in 1993 Entry Draft. Rights traded to Dallas Stars by Los Angeles for Vancouver's fifth round choice (previously acquired by Dallas-Los Angeles selected Jason Morgan) in 1995 Entry Draft (6/7/95). Last amateur club; Detroit (OHL).

Roy Mitchell — Defenseman

Regular Season / Playoffs

Season	Team	League	GP	G	A	PTS	PIM	GP	G	A	PTS	PIM
89-90	Sherbrooke	AHL	77	5	12	17	98	12	0	2	2	31
90-91	Fredericton	AHL	371	2	15	17	137	9	0	1	1	11
91-92	Kalamazoo	IHL	69	3	26	29	102	11	1	4	5	18
92-93	Minnesota	NHL	3	0	0	0	0	—	—	—	—	—
92-93	Kalamazoo	IHL	79	7	25	32	119	—	—	—	—	—
93-94	Binghamton	AHL	11	1	3	4	18	—	—	—	—	—
93-94	Albany	AHL	42	3	12	15	43	3	0	0	0	0
93-94	Kalamazoo	IHL	13	0	4	4	21	—	—	—	—	—
94-95	Worcester	AHL	80	5	25	30	97	—	—	—	—	—
95-96	Worcester	AHL	52	1	3	4	62	4	0	0	0	2
96-97	Central Texas	WPHL	20	1	8	9	12	11	2	7	9	10
97-98	Newcastle	BSL	55	5	19	24	46	6	0	0	0	0
98-99	Nottingham	BSL	55	6	9	15	46	11	0	2	2	12
	AHL	Totals	333	17	70	87	455	28	0	3	3	44
	IHL	Totals	161	10	55	65	242	11	1	4	5	18

Born; 3/14/69, Edmonton, Alberta. 6-2, 200. Drafted by Montreal Canadiens (9th choice, 188th overall) in 1989 Entry Draft. Signed as a free agent by Minnesota North Stars (7/25/91). Last amateur club; Portland (WHL).

Willie Mitchell — Defenseman

Regular Season / Playoffs

Season	Team	League	GP	G	A	PTS	PIM	GP	G	A	PTS	PIM
98-99	Clarkson	ECAC	34	10	19	29	40	—	—	—	—	—
98-99	Albany	AHL	6	1	3	4	29	—	—	—	—	—

Born; 4/23/77. Ft. McNeill, British Columbia. 6-3, 210. Drafted by New Jersey Devils (12th choice, 199th overall) in 1996 Entry Draft. Last amateur club; Clarkson (ECAC).

Savo Mitrovic — Center

Regular Season / Playoffs

Season	Team	League	GP	G	A	PTS	PIM	GP	G	A	PTS	PIM
92-93	Detroit	CoHL	46	13	36	49	37	6	3	2	5	24
93-94	Huntsville	ECHL	6	1	3	4	14	—	—	—	—	—
93-94	Greensboro	ECHL	29	3	14	17	12	—	—	—	—	—
93-94	Detroit	CoHL	12	8	10	18	8	3	1	2	3	4
94-95	Detroit	CoHL	68	23	45	68	38	12	5	5	10	21
95-96	Detroit	CoHL	29	5	16	21	20	8	3	8	11	19
96-97	Port Huron	CoHL	38	5	37	42	45	3	0	0	0	0
97-98	Phoenix	WCHL	54	20	35	55	83	9	5	5	10	10
98-99	Phoenix	WCHL	64	19	36	55	113	3	0	1	1	0
	CoHL	Totals	193	54	144	198	148	32	12	17	29	68
	WCHL	Totals	118	39	71	110	196	12	5	6	11	10

Born; 2/4/69, Etibicoke, Ontario. 5-11, 200. Last amateur club; New Hampshire (Hockey East).

Craig Mittleholt — Left Wing

Regular Season / Playoffs

Season	Team	League	GP	G	A	PTS	PIM	GP	G	A	PTS	PIM
94-95	Huntington	ECHL	10	1	1	2	2	—	—	—	—	—
94-95	Jacksonville	SUN	22	9	19	28	6	—	—	—	—	—
95-96	Jacksonville	ECHL	2	0	1	1	2	—	—	—	—	—
95-96	Birmingham	ECHL	2	0	0	0	2	—	—	—	—	—
95-96	Jacksonville	SHL	58	*60	44	104	26	—	—	—	—	—
96-97	Anchorage	WCHL	33	8	8	16	16	—	—	—	—	—
96-97	Thunder Bay	CoHL	14	5	11	16	4	11	4	5	9	4
97-98	Thunder Bay	UHL	74	16	29	45	30	5	1	2	3	0
98-99	Fort Worth	CHL	42	9	19	28	8	—	—	—	—	—
	UHL	Totals	88	21	40	61	34	16	5	7	12	4
	SHL	Totals	80	69	63	132	32	—	—	—	—	—
	ECHL	Totals	14	1	2	3	6	—	—	—	—	—

Born; 7/24/74, Ottawa, Ontario. 6-2, 190. Selected by Oklahoma City in 1999 CHL Dispersal Draft. Last amateur club; Seattle (WHL).

Joe Mittelsteadt — Defenseman

Regular Season / Playoffs

Season	Team	League	GP	G	A	PTS	PIM	GP	G	A	PTS	PIM
91-92	Columbus	ECHL	59	7	15	22	296	—	—	—	—	—
92-93	Dallas	CeHL	39	6	21	27	128	7	0	4	4	24
93-94	Dayton	ECHL	2	0	0	0	12	—	—	—	—	—
93-94	Dallas	CeHL	62	10	23	33	220	7	1	3	4	49
94-95	Cape Breton	AHL	37	2	3	5	74	—	—	—	—	—
94-95	Dallas	CeHL	8	1	1	2	29	—	—	—	—	—
95-96	Cape Breton	AHL	19	0	2	2	69	—	—	—	—	—
95-96	Reno	WCHL	31	2	15	17	88	3	0	0	0	9
96-97	Louisiana	ECHL	69	3	20	23	292	17	0	2	2	35
97-98	Ayr	BSL	60	1	8	9	66	9	0	0	0	12
98-99	Lake Charles	WPHL	69	4	22	26	122	11	0	3	3	8
	AHL	Totals	56	2	5	7	143	—	—	—	—	—
	ECHL	Totals	130	10	35	45	600	17	0	2	2	35
	CeHL	Totals	109	17	45	62	377	14	1	7	8	73

Born; 5/23/70, Scarborough, Ontario. 6-1, 220. Last amateur club; Kamloops (WHL).

Jason Modopoulos — Left Wing

Regular Season / Playoffs

Season	Team	League	GP	G	A	PTS	PIM	GP	G	A	PTS	PIM
97-98	Central Texas	WPHL	5	0	0	0	34	—	—	—	—	—
97-98	Amarillo	WPHL	13	0	1	1	37	—	—	—	—	—
98-99	Wichita	CHL	30	1	3	4	224	—	—	—	—	—
	WPHL	Totals	18	0	1	1	71	—	—	—	—	—

Born; 6/5/77, Toronto, Ontario. 6-1, 215. Last amateur club; Kitchener (OHL).

Jaroslav Modry — Defenseman

Regular Season / Playoffs

Season	Team	League	GP	G	A	PTS	PIM	GP	G	A	PTS	PIM
92-93	Utica	AHL	80	7	35	42	62	5	0	2	2	2
93-94	New Jersey	NHL	41	2	15	17	18	—	—	—	—	—
93-94	Albany	AHL	19	1	5	6	25	—	—	—	—	—
94-95	New Jersey	NHL	11	0	0	0	0	—	—	—	—	—
94-95	Albany	AHL	18	5	6	11	14	14	3	3	6	4
95-96	Ottawa	NHL	64	4	14	18	38	—	—	—	—	—
95-96	Los Angeles	NHL	9	0	3	3	6	—	—	—	—	—
96-97	Los Angeles	NHL	30	3	3	6	25	—	—	—	—	—
96-97	Phoenix	IHL	23	3	12	15	17	—	—	—	—	—
96-97	Utah	IHL	11	1	4	5	20	7	0	1	1	6
97-98	Utah	IHL	74	12	21	33	72	4	0	2	2	6
98-99	Los Angeles	NHL	5	0	1	1	0	—	—	—	—	—
98-99	Long Beach	IHL	64	6	29	35	44	8	4	2	6	4
	NHL	Totals	160	9	36	45	87	—	—	—	—	—
	IHL	Totals	172	22	66	88	153	19	4	5	9	16
	AHL	Totals	117	13	46	59	101	19	3	5	8	6

Born; 2/27/71, Ceske-Budejovice, Czechoslovakia. 6-2, 195. Drafted by New Jersey Devils (11th choice, 179th overall) in1990 Entry Draft. Traded to Ottawa Senators for Ottawa's fourth round choice (Alyn McCauley) in 1995 Entry Draft. Traded to Los Angeles by Ottawa with Ottawa's eighth round choice (Stephen Valiquette) in 1996 Entry Draft for Kevin Brown (3/20/96). Last European club; Budejovice (Czech Rep.)

Corri Moffat — Defenseman

Regular Season / Playoffs

Season	Team	League	GP	G	A	PTS	PIM	GP	G	A	PTS	PIM
97-98	El Paso	WPHL	64	9	29	38	43	15	2	6	8	10
98-99	El Paso	WPHL	57	2	27	29	20	3	0	2	2	2
	WPHL	Totals	121	11	56	67	63	18	2	8	10	12

Born; 8/7/72, Stoughton, Massachusetts. 5-11, 195. Member of 1997-98 WPHL Champion El Paso Buzzards. Last amateur club; Regina (CWUAA).

Steve Moffat — Right Wing

Regular Season / Playoffs

Season	Team	League	GP	G	A	PTS	PIM	GP	G	A	PTS	PIM
98-99	Columbus	ECHL	63	17	21	38	39	3	3	0	3	6

Born; Hatbord, Pennsylvania. Last amateur club; SUNY-Plattsburgh (NCAA 3).

Tony Mohagen — Center

Regular Season / Playoffs

Season	Team	League	GP	G	A	PTS	PIM	GP	G	A	PTS	PIM
98-99	Cincinnati	AHL	1	0	0	0	5	—	—	—	—	—

Born; 7/13/78, Regina, Saskatchewan. 6-4, 220. Drafted by Anaheim Mighty Ducks (5th choice, 178th overall) in 1997 Entry Draft. Last amateur club; Swift Current (WHL).

Sacha Molin — Left Wing

Regular Season / Playoffs

Season	Team	League	GP	G	A	PTS	PIM	GP	G	A	PTS	PIM
98-99	Long Beach	IHL	19	2	2	4	10	—	—	—	—	—
98-99	Fresno	WCHL	7	2	2	4	2	6	1	5	6	16

Born; 4/10/73, Stockholm, Sweden. 6-3, 200. Last amateur club; St. Cloud (WCHA).

Roland Monilaws — Defenseman

Regular Season / Playoffs

Season	Team	League	GP	G	A	PTS	PIM	GP	G	A	PTS	PIM
97-98	Fort Worth	CHL	32	3	6	9	57	—	—	—	—	—
97-98	San Angelo	WPHL	28	0	5	5	35	—	—	—	—	—
98-99	Amarillo	WPHL	6	0	0	0	17	—	—	—	—	—
98-99	Fort Worth	CHL	37	5	6	11	30	—	—	—	—	—
	CHL	Totals	69	8	12	20	87	—	—	—	—	—
	WPHL	Totals	34	0	5	5	52	—	—	—	—	—

Born; 4/5/76, Leduc, Alberta. 6-0, 205.

Russ Monteith — Left Wing

Regular Season / Playoffs

Season	Team	League	GP	G	A	PTS	PIM	GP	G	A	PTS	PIM
97-98	Mobile	ECHL	65	17	26	43	35	3	0	1	1	0
98-99	Mobile	ECHL	69	25	32	57	26	2	0	1	1	0
	ECHL	Totals	134	42	58	100	61	5	0	2	2	0

Born; 2/19/74, Toronto, Ontario. 6-1, 195. Traded to New Orleans by Mobile for Dalen Hrooshkin (7/99). Last amateur club; Union (ECAC).

Jim Montgomery — Center

Regular Season / Playoffs

Season	Team	League	GP	G	A	PTS	PIM	GP	G	A	PTS	PIM
93-94	St. Louis	NHL	67	6	14	20	44	—	—	—	—	—
93-94	Peoria	IHL	12	7	8	15	10	—	—	—	—	—
94-95	Montreal	NHL	5	0	0	0	2	—	—	—	—	—
94-95	Philadelphia	NHL	8	1	1	2	6	7	1	0	1	2
94-95	Hershey	AHL	16	8	6	14	14	6	3	2	5	25
95-96	Philadelphia	NHL	5	1	2	3	9	1	0	0	0	0
95-96	Hershey	AHL	78	34	*71	105	95	4	3	2	5	6
96-97	Koln	Germany	50	12	35	47	111	4	0	1	1	6
97-98	Philadelphia	AHL	68	19	43	62	75	20	13	16	29	55
98-99	Philadelphia	AHL	78	29	58	87	89	16	4	11	15	20
	NHL	Totals	85	8	17	25	61	8	1	0	1	2
	AHL	Totals	240	90	178	268	273	46	23	31	54	106

Born; 6/30/69, Montreal, Quebec. 5-10, 185. Signed as a free agent by St. Louis Blues (6/2/93). Traded to Montreal Canadiens by St. Louis for Guy Carbonneau (8/19/94). Claimed on waivers by Philadelphia Flyers from Montreal (2/10/95). 1995-96 AHL Second All-Star Team. Member of 1997-98 AHL Champion Philadelphia Phantoms. Last amateur club; Maine (Hockey East).

Eric Montreuil — Center

Regular Season / Playoffs

Season	Team	League	GP	G	A	PTS	PIM	GP	G	A	PTS	PIM
95-96	Carolina	AHL	66	7	8	15	81	—	—	—	—	—
96-97	Carolina	AHL	34	4	6	10	39	—	—	—	—	—
96-97	Port Huron	CoHL	3	0	2	2	4	—	—	—	—	—
96-97	Tallahassee	ECHL	3	0	1	1	25	—	—	—	—	—
97-98	New Orleans	ECHL	34	6	9	15	109	—	—	—	—	—
97-98	Baton Rouge	ECHL	27	2	5	7	32	—	—	—	—	—
98-99	Baton Rouge	ECHL	70	5	15	20	103	6	0	1	1	2
	AHL	Totals	100	11	14	25	120	—	—	—	—	—
	ECHL	Totals	134	13	30	43	269	6	0	1	1	2

Born; 5/18/75, Verdun, Quebec. 6-1, 177. Drafted by Florida Panthers (13th choice, 265th overall) in 1993 Entry Draft. Last amateur club; Beauport

Barrie Moore — Left Wing

Regular Season / Playoffs

Season	Team	League	GP	G	A	PTS	PIM	GP	G	A	PTS	PIM
95-96	Buffalo	NHL	3	0	0	0	0	—	—	—	—	—
95-96	Rochester	AHL	64	26	30	56	40	18	3	6	9	18
96-97	Buffalo	NHL	31	2	6	8	18	—	—	—	—	—
96-97	Edmonton	NHL	4	0	0	0	0	—	—	—	—	—
96-97	Rochester	AHL	32	14	15	29	14	—	—	—	—	—
96-97	Hamilton	AHL	9	5	2	7	0	22	2	6	8	15
97-98	Hamilton	AHL	70	22	29	51	64	8	0	1	1	4
98-99	Indianapolis	IHL	43	9	10	19	18	—	—	—	—	—
98-99	Portland	AHL	23	3	7	10	4	—	—	—	—	—
	NHL	Totals	38	2	6	8	18	—	—	—	—	—
	AHL	Totals	198	70	83	153	122	48	5	13	18	37

Born; 5/22/75, Barrie, Ontario. 5-11, 175. Drafted by Buffalo Sabres (7th choice, 220th overall) in 1993 Entry Draft. Traded to Edmonton Oilers by Buffalo with-Craig Millar for Miroslav Satan (3/18/97). Traded to Washington Capitals by Edmonton for Brad Church (2/3/99). Member of 1995-96 AHL champion Rochester Americans. Last amateur club; Barrie (OHL).

Blaine Moore — Center

Regular Season / Playoffs

Season	Team	League	GP	G	A	PTS	PIM	GP	G	A	PTS	PIM
94-95	Richmond	ECHL	60	30	33	63	181	17	17	17	34	34
95-96	Las Vegas	IHL	67	15	20	35	73	14	2	5	7	24
96-97	Las Vegas	IHL	18	1	3	4	14	—	—	—	—	—
96-97	Port Huron	CoHL	14	6	14	20	10	—	—	—	—	—
97-98	Fresno	WCHL	40	20	40	60	50	5	2	7	9	10
98-99	Fresno	WCHL	61	21	41	62	101	7	4	6	10	4
	IHL	Totals	85	16	23	39	87	14	2	5	7	24
	WCHL	Totals	101	41	81	122	151	12	6	13	19	14

Born; 10/8/69, Kitimat, British Columbia. 6-0, 185. 1994-95 ECHL Playoff MVP. Member of 1994-95 ECHL champion Richmond Renegades. Last amateur club; Wisconsin (WCHA). Named Head coach of the Fresno Falcons beginning with 1998-99 season.

David Moore — Defenseman

Regular Season / Playoffs

Season	Team	League	GP	G	A	PTS	PIM	GP	G	A	PTS	PIM
91-92	Cincinnati	ECHL	5	0	1	1	2	—	—	—	—	—
91-92	Louisville	ECHL	38	1	15	16	40	13	1	1	2	11
92-93	Louisville	ECHL	2	0	0	0	0	—	—	—	—	—
92-93	Memphis	CeHL	60	18	30	48	114	6	0	2	2	10
93-94	London	CoHL	3	0	0	0	5	—	—	—	—	—
93-94	Memphis	CeHL	53	16	38	54	71	—	—	—	—	—
93-94	Tulsa	CeHL	10	2	2	4	14	11	5	5	10	41
94-95	Tulsa	CeHL	66	20	41	61	127	5	4	3	7	24
95-96												
96-97	Austin	WPHL	61	10	22	32	84	6	0	1	1	8
97-98	Merano	Italy	16	16	18	34	18	—	—	—	—	—
97-98	New Mexico	WPHL	3	0	0	0	0	—	—	—	—	—
98-99	Odense	Denmark		8	10	18		—	—	—	—	—
98-99	Austin	WPHL	39	14	16	30	42	—	—	—	—	—
	CeHL	Totals	189	56	111	167	326	22	9	10	19	75
	WPHL	Totals	103	24	38	62	126	6	0	1	1	8

Born; 4/26/68, Hampstead, New Hampshire. 6-1, 200. 1993-94 Second Team CeHL All-Star.

Dean Moore — Right Wing

Regular Season / Playoffs

Season	Team	League	GP	G	A	PTS	PIM	GP	G	A	PTS	PIM
95-96	Knoxville	ECHL	34	3	6	9	154	6	0	1	1	13
96-97	Manitoba	IHL	3	0	0	0	7	—	—	—	—	—
96-97	Knoxville	ECHL	56	8	13	21	215	—	—	—	—	—
97-98	Charlotte	ECHL	31	7	2	9	91	—	—	—	—	—
97-98	New Orelans	ECHL	22	1	3	4	67	4	3	0	3	6
98-99	New Orleans	ECHL	67	10	9	19	248	10	0	1	1	25
	ECHL	Totals	208	29	33	62	775	20	3	2	5	44

Born; 7/6/73, Winnipeg, Manitoba. 6-2, 195. Traded to New Orleans by Charlotte with Stephane Soulliare for Mikhail Nemirovsky and Pierre Gendron (2/98).

Skeeter Moore — Center

Regular Season / Playoffs

Season	Team	League	GP	G	A	PTS	PIM	GP	G	A	PTS	PIM
96-97	Amarillo	WPHL	7	5	12	17	18	—	—	—	—	—
97-98	San Angelo	WPHL	59	17	32	49	93	3	3	2	5	2
98-99	San Angelo	WPHL	69	22	46	68	42	17	2	9	11	24
	WPHL	Totals	135	44	90	134	153	20	5	11	16	26

Born; 7/16/63, Duluth, Minnesota. 5-18, 175.

Steve Moore — Center

Regular Season / Playoffs

Season	Team	League	GP	G	A	PTS	PIM	GP	G	A	PTS	PIM
95-96	Charlotte	ECHL	6	2	2	4	6	—	—	—	—	—
95-96	Oklahoma City	CeHL	55	26	31	57	84	13	5	7	12	30
96-97	Oklahoma City	CeHL	66	37	28	65	138	4	3	4	7	17
97-98	Oklahoma City	CHL	67	38	59	97	142	11	10	3	13	28
98-99	Oklahoma City	CHL	53	30	41	71	136	10	3	6	9	31
	CHL	Totals	241	131	159	290	500	38	21	20	41	106

Born; 6/21/71, Gardiner, Maine. 6-0, 200. Member of 1995-96 CeHL champion Oklahoma City Blazers.

Kelly Morel — Defenseman

Regular Season / Playoffs

Season	Team	League	GP	G	A	PTS	PIM	GP	G	A	PTS	PIM
96-97	RIT	NCAA3	28	3	23	26	n/a	—	—	—	—	—
96-97	Jacksonville	ECHL	7	0	0	0	4	—	—	—	—	—
97-98	New Mexico	WPHL	47	3	9	12	17	10	1	3	4	13
98-99	New Mexico	WPHL	52	7	10	17	52	—	—	—	—	—
98-99	Amarillo	WPHL	7	2	3	5	4	—	—	—	—	—
	WPHL	Totals	106	12	22	34	73	10	1	3	4	13

Born; 8/30/73, Sudbury, Ontario. 5-11, 195. Selected by Abilene in 1998 WPHL Expansion Draft. Last amateur club; Rochester Institute of Technology (NCAA

Chris Morgan — Left Wing

Regular Season / Playoffs

Season	Team	League	GP	G	A	PTS	PIM	GP	G	A	PTS	PIM
98-99	Huntsville	CHL	15	1	2	3	32	—	—	—	—	—

Born; 1/11/75, Vernon, British Columbia. 5-10, 190.

Jason Morgan — Center

Regular Season / Playoffs

Season	Team	League	GP	G	A	PTS	PIM	GP	G	A	PTS	PIM
96-97	Los Angeles	NHL	3	0	0	0	0	—	—	—	—	—
96-97	Phoenix	IHL	57	3	6	9	29	—	—	—	—	—
96-97	Mississippi	ECHL	6	3	0	3	0	3	1	1	2	6
97-98	Los Angeles	NHL	11	1	0	1	4	—	—	—	—	—
97-98	Springfield	AHL	58	13	22	35	66	3	1	0	1	18
98-99	Springfield	AHL	46	6	16	22	51	3	0	0	0	6
98-99	Long Beach	IHL	13	4	6	10	18	—	—	—	—	—
	NHL	Totals	14	1	0	1	4	—	—	—	—	—
	AHL	Totals	104	19	38	57	117	6	1	0	1	24
	IHL	Totals	70	7	12	19	47	—	—	—	—	—

Born; 10/9/76, St. John's, Newfoundland. 6-1, 185. Drafted by Los Angeles Kings (fifth choice, 118th overall) in 1995 Entry Draft. Last amateur club; Kingston (OHL).

Gerald Moriarity — Defenseman

Regular Season / Playoffs

Season	Team	League	GP	G	A	PTS	PIM	GP	G	A	PTS	PIM
97-98	Louisiana	ECHL	2	0	0	0	30	—	—	—	—	—
97-98	Toronto	OHL	52	0	6	6	213	—	—	—	—	—
98-99	Toledo	ECHL	7	0	0	0	39	—	—	—	—	—
98-99	Toronto	OHL	53	0	1	1	199	—	—	—	—	—
	ECHL	Totals	9	0	0	0	69	—	—	—	—	—

Born; 3/29/78, Hamilton, Ontario. 6-2, 205. Last amateur club; Toronto (OHL).

Jesper Morin — Forward

Regular Season / Playoffs

Season	Team	League	GP	G	A	PTS	PIM	GP	G	A	PTS	PIM
97-98	Revier Lowen	Germany	13	1	2	3	0	—	—	—	—	—
98-99	Odessa	WPHL	8	1	1	2	6	—	—	—	—	—

Born; 5/27/75.

Olivier Morin — Left Wing

Regular Season / Playoffs

Season	Team	League	GP	G	A	PTS	PIM	GP	G	A	PTS	PIM
98-99	New Orleans	ECHL	54	9	8	17	61	9	0	0	0	2

Born; 4/2/78, Montreal, Quebec. 6-0, 176. Signed as a free agent by Montreal Canadiens (10/3/96). Last amateur club; Val d' Or (QMJHL).

Stephane Morin — Center

Regular Season / Playoffs

In Memoriam

Season	Team	League	GP	G	A	PTS	PIM	GP	G	A	PTS	PIM
89-90	Quebec	NHL	6	0	2	2	2	—	—	—	—	—
89-90	Halifax	AHL	65	28	32	60	60	6	3	4	7	6
90-91	Quebec	NHL	48	13	27	40	30	—	—	—	—	—
90-91	Halifax	AHL	17	8	14	22	18	—	—	—	—	—
91-92	Quebec	NHL	30	2	8	10	14	—	—	—	—	—
91-92	Halifax	AHL	30	17	13	30	29	—	—	—	—	—
92-93	Vancouver	NHL	1	0	1	1	0	—	—	—	—	—
92-93	Hamilton	AHL	70	31	54	85	49	—	—	—	—	—
93-94	Vancouver	NHL	5	1	1	2	6	—	—	—	—	—
93-94	Hamilton	AHL	69	38	71	109	48	4	3	2	5	4
94-95	Minnesota	IHL	81	33	*81	*114	53	2	0	1	1	0
95-96	Minnesota	IHL	80	27	51	78	75	—	—	—	—	—
96-97	Manitoba	IHL	12	3	6	9	4	—	—	—	—	—
96-97	Long Beach	IHL	65	25	57	82	73	18	6	13	19	14
97-98	Long Beach	IHL	27	10	17	27	30	13	1	10	11	18
98-99	Berlin	Germany	7	2	6	8	6	—	—	—	—	—
	NHL	Totals	90	16	39	55	52	—	—	—	—	—
	IHL	Totals	265	98	212	310	235	33	7	24	31	32
	AHL	Totals	251	122	184	306	204	10	6	6	12	10

Born; 3/27/69, Montreal, Quebec. 6-1, 175. Drafted by Quebec Nordiques (3rd choice, 43rd overall) in 1989 Entry Draft. Signed as a free agent by Vancouver Canucks (10/5/92). 1993-94 AHL Second Team All-Star. 1994-95 IHL First Team All-Star. Last amateur club; Chicoutimi (QMJHL).

Yvan Morin — Forward

Regular Season / Playoffs

Season	Team	League	GP	G	A	PTS	PIM	GP	G	A	PTS	PIM
98-99	Monroe	WPHL	1	0	0	0	0	—	—	—	—	—

Born;10/25/77.

Dave Morissette — Left Wing

Regular Season / Playoffs

Season	Team	League	GP	G	A	PTS	PIM	GP	G	A	PTS	PIM
91-92	Baltimore	AHL	2	0	0	0	6	—	—	—	—	—
91-92	Hampton Roads	ECHL	47	6	10	16	193	13	1	3	4	74
92-93	Hampton Roads	ECHL	54	9	13	22	226	2	0	0	0	2
93-94	Roanoke	ECHL	45	8	10	18	278	2	0	1	1	4
94-95	Minnesota	IHL	50	1	4	5	174	—	—	—	—	—
95-96	Minnesota	IHL	33	3	2	5	104	—	—	—	—	—
96-97	Houston	IHL	59	2	1	3	214	2	0	0	0	0
96-97	Austin	WPHL	5	2	3	5	10	—	—	—	—	—
97-98	Houston	IHL	67	4	4	8	254	2	0	0	0	2
98-99	Montreal	NHL	10	0	0	0	52	—	—	—	—	—
98-99	Fredericton	AHL	39	4	4	8	152	12	1	0	1	31
	IHL	Totals	209	10	11	21	746	4	0	0	0	2
	AHL	Totals	41	4	4	8	158	12	1	0	1	31
	ECHL	Totals	146	23	33	56	697	17	1	4	5	80

Born; 12/24/71, Quebec City, Quebec. 6-1, 210. Drafted by Washington Capitals (7th choice, 146th overall) in 1991 Entry Draft. Signed as a free agent by Montreal Canadiens (6/10/98). Member of 1991-92 ECHL champion Hampton Roads Admirals. Last amateur club; Shawinigan (QMJHL).

Marc Moro — Defenseman

Regular Season / Playoffs

Season	Team	League	GP	G	A	PTS	PIM	GP	G	A	PTS	PIM
95-96	Kingston	OHL	66	4	17	21	261	6	0	0	0	12
95-96	Prince Edward Island	AHL	2	0	0	0	7	2	0	0	0	4
96-97	Kingston	OHL	37	4	8	12	97	—	—	—	—	—
96-97	Sault Ste. Marie	OHL	26	0	5	5	74	11	1	6	7	38
97-98	Anaheim	NHL	1	0	0	0	0	—	—	—	—	—
97-98	Cincinnati	AHL	74	1	6	7	181	—	—	—	—	—
98-99	Milwaukee	IHL	80	0	5	5	264	2	0	0	0	4
	AHL	Totals	76	1	6	7	188	2	0	0	0	4

Born; 7/17/77, Toronto, Ontario. 6-1, 220. Drafted by Ottawa Senators (2nd choice, 27th overall) in 1995 Entry Draft. Rights traded to Anaheim Mighty Ducks by Ottawa with Ted Drury for Jason York and Shaun Van Allen (10/1/96). Traded to Nashville Predators by Anaheim with Chris Mason for Dominic Rousel (10/5/98). Last amateur club; Sault Ste. Marie (OHL).

Valentin Morozov — Center

Regular Season / Playoffs

Season	Team	League	GP	G	A	PTS	PIM	GP	G	A	PTS	PIM
98-99	Syracuse	AHL	63	17	23	40	10	—	—	—	—	—

Born; 6/1/75, Moscow, USSR. 5-11, 176. Drafted by Pittsburgh Penguins (8th choice, 154th overall) in 1994 Entry Draft. Last club; Soviet Wings (USSR).

Chris Morque — Defenseman

Regular Season / Playoffs

Season	Team	League	GP	G	A	PTS	PIM	GP	G	A	PTS	PIM
94-95	Erie	ECHL	26	3	8	11	83	—	—	—	—	—
94-95	Huntington	ECHL	36	1	9	10	126	—	—	—	—	—
95-96	Quad City	CoHL	2	0	0	0	4	—	—	—	—	—
95-96	Memphis	CeHL	60	9	33	42	235	6	1	2	3	45
96-97	Austin	WPHL	63	5	14	19	126	5	0	2	2	23
97-98	Austin	WPHL	48	4	13	17	131	—	—	—	—	—
97-98	El Paso	WPHL	22	2	9	11	65	15	0	4	4	*116
98-99	Odessa	WPHL	67	7	29	36	171	3	0	1	1	4
	WPHL	Totals	200	18	65	83	493	23	0	7	7	143
	ECHL	Totals	62	4	17	21	209	—	—	—	—	—

Born; 2/16/70, Grand Forks, South Dakota. 6-2, 200. Member of 1997-98 WPHL Champion El Paso Buzzards. Traded to El Paso by Austin with Corey Fletcher for Jason Rose and Derek Riley (1/98). Last amateur club; Bemidji State (NCAA 2).

Justin Morrison — Center
Regular Season — Playoffs

Season	Team	League	GP	G	A	PTS	PIM	GP	G	A	PTS	PIM
92-93	Toledo	ECHL	13	6	8	14	47	—	—	—	—	—
93-94	Muskegon	CoHL	64	27	33	60	86	3	1	1	2	12
94-95	Muskegon	CoHL	74	32	54	86	224	15	4	15	19	32
95-96	Madison	CoHL	61	21	30	51	179	4	1	6	7	2
96-97	Madison	CoHL	31	13	22	35	61	—	—	—	—	—
96-97	Muskegon	CoHL	41	19	23	42	50	3	0	1	1	17
97-98	Muskegon	UHL	73	28	42	70	132	11	0	3	3	12
98-99	Saginaw	UHL	59	24	27	51	109	—	—	—	—	—
98-99	Winston-Salem	UHL	11	3	9	12	27	5	1	3	4	29
	UHL	Totals	414	167	240	407	868	41	7	29	36	104

Born; 2/9/72, Newmarket, Ontario. 5-10, 174. Drafted by Washington Capitals (fourth round, 80th overall) 6/22/91. Last amateur club; Owen Sound (OHL).

Mike Morrone — Left Wing
Regular Season — Playoffs

Season	Team	League	GP	G	A	PTS	PIM	GP	G	A	PTS	PIM
96-97	Detroit	OHL	46	5	13	18	164	5	1	1	2	42
96-97	Richmond	ECHL	4	0	0	0	9	7	1	1	2	15
97-98	New Haven	AHL	1	0	0	0	4	—	—	—	—	—
97-98	Richmond	ECHL	65	4	4	8	281	—	—	—	—	—
98-99	New Orleans	ECHL	21	1	5	6	37	—	—	—	—	—
	ECHL	Totals	90	5	9	14	327	7	1	1	2	15

Born; 1/3/76, Windsor, Ontario. 5-11, 218. Signed as a free agent by Carolina Hurricanes (6/9/97). Last amateur club; Detroit (OHL).

Scott Morrow — Left Wing
Regular Season — Playoffs

Season	Team	League	GP	G	A	PTS	PIM	GP	G	A	PTS	PIM
91-92	Springfield	AHL	2	0	1	1	0	5	0	0	0	9
92-93	Springfield	AHL	70	22	29	51	80	15	6	9	15	21
93-94	Springfield	AHL	30	12	15	27	28	—	—	—	—	—
93-94	Saint John	AHL	8	2	2	4	0	7	2	1	3	10
94-95	Calgary	NHL	4	0	0	0	0	—	—	—	—	—
94-95	Saint John	AHL	64	18	21	39	105	5	2	0	2	4
95-96	Hershey	AHL	79	48	45	93	110	5	2	2	4	6
96-97	Cincinnati	IHL	67	14	23	37	50	—	—	—	—	—
96-97	Providence	AHL	11	3	4	7	15	7	2	1	3	0
97-98	Providence	AHL	5	1	4	5	7	—	—	—	—	—
97-98	Cincinnati	IHL	55	15	12	27	44	9	3	1	4	23
97-98	Binghamton	UHL	8	3	2	5	14	—	—	—	—	—
98-99	Cincinnati	IHL	80	29	22	51	116	3	0	2	2	2
	AHL	Totals	269	106	121	227	345	44	14	13	27	50
	IHL	Totals	202	58	57	115	210	12	3	3	6	25

Born; 6/18/69, Chicago, Illinois. 6-1, 185. Drafted by Hartford Whalers (4th choice, 95th overall) in 1988 Entry Draft. Traded to Calgary Flames by Hartford for Todd Harkins (1/24/94). Last amateur club; New Hampshire (H.E.).

Jay Moser — Right Wing
Regular Season — Playoffs

Season	Team	League	GP	G	A	PTS	PIM	GP	G	A	PTS	PIM
96-97	Providence	AHL	12	0	2	2	8	—	—	—	—	—
96-97	Rochester	AHL	22	4	9	13	4	9	1	1	2	4
96-97	South Carolina	ECHL	41	19	30	49	32	—	—	—	—	—
97-98	South Carolina	ECHL	16	7	4	11	14	—	—	—	—	—
97-98	Richmond	ECHL	14	8	5	13	13	—	—	—	—	—
98-99	South Carolina	ECHL	64	18	27	45	135	3	0	1	1	0
	AHL	Totals	34	4	11	15	12	9	1	1	2	4
	ECHL	Totals	135	52	66	118	194	3	0	1	1	0

Born; 12/26/72, Cottage Grove, Minnesota. 6-2, 170. Drafted by Boston Bruins (7th choice, 172nd overall) in 1991 Entry Draft. Traded to Richmond by South Carolina with Dan Fournel, Kevin Knopp and Mario Cormier for Mike Taylor and Jason Wright (12/97). Last amateur club; Minnesota (WCHA).

Tyler Moss — Goaltender
Regular Season — Playoffs

Season	Team	League	GP	W	L	T	MIN	SO	AVG	GP	W	L	MIN	SO	AVG
95-96	Atlanta	IHL	40	11	19	4	2029	1	4.08	3	0	3	213	0	3.10
96-97	Grand Rapids	IHL	15	5	6	1	715	0	2.94	—	—	—	—	—	—
96-97	Adirondack	AHL	11	1	5	2	507	1	4.97	—	—	—	—	—	—
96-97	Saint John	AHL	9	6	1	1	534	0	1.91	5	2	3	242	0	3.72
96-97	Muskegon	CoHL	2	1	1	0	119	0	2.51	—	—	—	—	—	—
97-98	Calgary	NHL	6	2	3	1	367	0	3.27	—	—	—	—	—	—
97-98	Saint John	AHL	39	19	10	7	2194	0	2.49	15	8	*5	762	0	2.91
98-99	Calgary	NHL	11	3	7	0	550	0	2.51	—	—	—	—	—	—
98-99	Saint John	AHL	9	2	5	1	475	0	3.16	—	—	—	—	—	—
98-99	Orlando	IHL	9	6	2	1	515	1	2.44	17	10	7	1017	0	3.13
	NHL	Totals	17	5	10	1	917	0	2.81	—	—	—	—	—	—
	AHL	Totals	68	28	21	13	3710	1	2.83	20	10	8	1004	0	3.11
	IHL	Totals	64	22	27	6	3259	2	3.57	20	10	10	1230	0	3.13

Born; 6/29/75, Ottawa, Ontario. 6-0, 168. Drafted by Tampa Bay Lightning (2nd choice, 29th overall) in 1993 Entry Draft. Traded to Calgary Flames by Tampa Bay for Jamie Huscroft (3/18/97). Traded to Orlando by Saint John with Eric Healey for Allan Egeland and Arthu Kayhko (3/99). 1997-98 AHL Hap Holmes Trophy with J-S Giguere (fewest goals against). Last amateur club; Kingston

Alex Motley — Center
Regular Season — Playoffs

Season	Team	League	GP	G	A	PTS	PIM	GP	G	A	PTS	PIM
98-99	Topeka	CHL	19	1	2	3	25	—	—	—	—	—

Born; 1/10/74, Pleasanton, California. 5-7, 175.

Ryan Mougenal — Right Wing
Regular Season — Playoffs

Season	Team	League	GP	G	A	PTS	PIM	GP	G	A	PTS	PIM
97-98	Quebec	IHL	13	2	3	5	2	—	—	—	—	—
97-98	Cleveland	IHL	37	2	6	8	58	—	—	—	—	—
97-98	Hampton Roads	ECHL	7	0	4	4	6	—	—	—	—	—
97-98	Chesapeake	ECHL	7	3	3	6	4	—	—	—	—	—
98-99	Cleveland	IHL	45	5	7	12	46	—	—	—	—	—
98-99	Chesapeake	ECHL	8	2	3	5	19	2	1	0	1	0
	IHL	Totals	95	9	16	25	106	—	—	—	—	—
	ECHL	Totals	22	5	10	15	29	2	1	0	1	0

Born; 3/2/76, Scarborough, Ontario. 6-1, 195. Traded to Cleveland by Quebec with Rick Hayward, John Craighead, Eric Perrin, Pat Jablonski and Burke Murphy for Rick Girard, Dale DeGray, Darcy Simon, Tom Draper and Jason Ruff (3/98). Last amateur club; Kitchener (OHL).

Tom Moulton — Defenseman
Regular Season — Playoffs

Season	Team	League	GP	G	A	PTS	PIM	GP	G	A	PTS	PIM
91-92	St. Thomas	CoHL	2	0	0	0	0	—	—	—	—	—
92-93	St. Thomas	CoHL	35	3	7	10	41	15	3	1	4	21
92-93	Green Bay	AHA	17	0	5	5	68	—	—	—	—	—
93-94	Brantford	CoHL	13	4	1	5	10	7	1	0	1	2
94-95												
95-96	Winston-Salem	SHL	59	5	26	31	200	9	1	1	2	51
96-97	Huntsville	CeHL	66	7	24	31	167	8	0	3	3	38
97-98	Huntsville	CHL	70	5	18	23	164	3	0	1	1	2
98-99	Amarillo	WPHL	13	1	4	5	18	—	—	—	—	—
98-99	Flint	UHL	30	0	6	6	31	—	—	—	—	—
98-99	Winston-Salem	UHL	28	1	1	2	51	5	0	0	0	10
	CHL	Totals	136	12	42	54	331	11	0	4	4	40
	UHL	Totals	108	8	15	23	132	27	4	1	5	33

Born; 3/28/70, London, Ontario. 6-1, 203. Traded to Winston-Salem by Flint for Jason Desloover (2/99).

Mark Mowers — Right Wing
Regular Season — Playoffs

Season	Team	League	GP	G	A	PTS	PIM	GP	G	A	PTS	PIM
98-99	Nashville	NHL	30	0	6	6	4	—	—	—	—	—
98-99	Milwaukee	IHL	51	14	22	36	24	1	0	0	0	0

Born; 1/6/74, Whitesboro, New York. 5-11, 188. Signed as a free agent by Nashville Predators (6/11/98). 1998-99 IHL U.S. Born Rookie of the Year. Last amateur club; New Hampshire (Hockey East).

Charlie Moxham — Left Wing
Regular Season / Playoffs

Season	Team	League	GP	G	A	PTS	PIM	GP	G	A	PTS	PIM
98-99	Greenville	ECHL	66	12	14	26	33	—	—	—	—	—

Born; 9/13/74, Calgary, Alberta. 6-1, 185. Last amateur club; Union (ECAC).

Jim Mroz — Center
Regular Season / Playoffs

Season	Team	League	GP	G	A	PTS	PIM	GP	G	A	PTS	PIM
98-99	Alexandria	WPHL	18	4	9	13	25	—	—	—	—	—

Born; 3/16/77, Durand, Michigan. 5-11, 195.

Rick Mrozik — Defenseman
Regular Season / Playoffs

Season	Team	League	GP	G	A	PTS	PIM	GP	G	A	PTS	PIM
97-98	Portland	AHL	75	2	15	17	52	10	1	3	4	2
98-99	Portland	AHL	70	4	8	12	63	—	—	—	—	—
	AHL	Totals	145	6	23	29	115	10	1	3	4	2

Born; 1/2/75, Duluth, Minnesota. 6-2, 185. Drafted by Dallas Stars (4th choice, 136th overall) in 1993 Entry Draft. Traded to Washington Capitals by Dallas with Mark Tinordi for Kevin Hatcher (1/18/95). Last amateur club; Minnesota-Duluth (WCHA).

John Mucciarone — Defenseman
Regular Season / Playoffs

Season	Team	League	GP	G	A	PTS	PIM	GP	G	A	PTS	PIM
98-99	Memphis	CHL	1	0	0	0	0	—	—	—	—	—
98-99	South Carolina	ECHL	8	0	0	0	4	—	—	—	—	—
98-99	Mohawk Valley	UHL	3	0	0	0	4	—	—	—	—	—

Born; 10/11/74, Milford, Massachusetts. 6-2, 220. Last amateur club; Alabama-Huntsville (NCAA 2).

Brian Mueller — Defenseman
Regular Season / Playoffs

Season	Team	League	GP	G	A	PTS	PIM	GP	G	A	PTS	PIM
95-96	Springfield	AHL	51	7	12	19	49	2	0	0	0	0
95-96	Richmond	ECHL	3	1	1	2	2	3	0	2	2	0
96-97	Springfield	AHL	42	7	20	27	28	7	0	2	2	0
96-97	Manitoba	IHL	6	1	1	2	2	—	—	—	—	—
96-97	Quebec	IHL	10	0	0	0	0	—	—	—	—	—
97-98	Hameenlinna	Finland	27	2	4	6	26	—	—	—	—	—
97-98	Hershey	AHL	2	0	0	0	0	—	—	—	—	—
98-99	Detroit	IHL	12	1	2	3	4	1	0	1	1	0
98-99	Saginaw	UHL	51	12	20	32	38	—	—	—	—	—
98-99	Port Huron	UHL	7	0	7	7	10	—	—	—	—	—
	AHL	Totals	95	14	32	46	77	9	0	2	2	0
	IHL	Totals	28	2	3	5	6	1	0	1	1	0
	UHL	Totals	58	12	27	39	48	—	—	—	—	—

Born; 6/2/72, Liverpool, New York. 5-11, 225. Drafted by Hartford Whalers (7th choice, 141st overall) in 1991 Entry Draft. Traded to Port Huron by Saginaw for Jeff Winter (3/99). Last amateur club; Clarkson (ECAC).

Bryan Muir — Defenseman
Regular Season / Playoffs

Season	Team	League	GP	G	A	PTS	PIM	GP	G	A	PTS	PIM
96-97	Hamilton	AHL	75	8	16	24	80	14	0	5	5	12
97-98	Edmonton	NHL	7	0	0	0	17	—	—	—	—	—
97-98	Hamilton	AHL	28	3	10	13	62	—	—	—	—	—
97-98	Albany	AHL	41	3	10	13	67	13	3	0	3	12
98-99	New Jersey	NHL	1	0	0	0	0	—	—	—	—	—
98-99	Chicago	NHL	53	1	4	5	50	—	—	—	—	—
98-99	Albany	AHL	10	0	0	0	29	—	—	—	—	—
98-99	Portland	AHL	2	1	1	2	2	—	—	—	—	—
	NHL	Totals	61	1	4	5	67	—	—	—	—	—
	AHL	Totals	156	15	37	52	240	27	3	5	8	24

Born; 6/8/73, Winnipeg, Manitoba. 6-4, 220. Signed as a free agent by Edmonton Oilers (4/30/96). Traded to New Jersey Devils by Edmonton with Jason Arnott for Valeri Zelepukin and Bill Guerin (1/4/98). Traded to Chicago Blackhawks by New Jersey for a conditional draft pick (11/13/98). Last amateur club; New Hampshire (Hockey East).

Wayne Muir — Left Wing
Regular Season / Playoffs

Season	Team	League	GP	G	A	PTS	PIM	GP	G	A	PTS	PIM
89-90	Sault Ste. Marie	OHL	62	40	21	61	210	—	—	—	—	—
89-90	Virginia	ECHL	1	1	2	3	0	1	0	0	0	0
90-91	Cape Breton	AHL	1	0	0	0	0	—	—	—	—	—
90-91	Roanoke	ECHL	61	31	24	55	239	—	—	—	—	—
91-92	Roanoke	ECHL	46	12	19	31	168	7	1	1	2	36
92-93	Greensboro	ECHL	50	28	24	52	200	—	—	—	—	—
92-93	Dayton	ECHL	6	4	2	6	38	3	1	0	1	16
93-94	Chatham	CoHL	62	29	41	70	269	15	5	4	9	54
94-95	Brantford	CoHL	71	38	46	84	232	—	—	—	—	—
95-96	Brantford	CoHL	74	40	47	87	261	12	8	6	14	31
96-97	Utah	IHL	1	0	0	0	0	—	—	—	—	—
96-97	Brantford	CoHL	73	52	65	117	212	10	5	10	15	27
97-98	Brantford	UHL	16	6	7	13	32	—	—	—	—	—
97-98	Quad City	UHL	51	23	25	48	161	19	4	1	5	51
98-99	Port Huron	UHL	47	16	22	38	83	—	—	—	—	—
	UHL	Totals	394	204	253	457	1250	56	22	21	43	163
	ECHL	Totals	164	76	71	147	645	11	2	1	3	52

Born; 1/9/69, Sydney, Nova Scotia. 5-11, 200. 1996-97 CoHL Second Team All-Star. Traded to Quad City by Brantford in a three-way deal with Winston-Salem. Muir went to Quad City while John Vecchiarelli went to Brantford and John Batten went to Winston-Salem (11/97). Traded to Port Huron by Mohawk Valley for Ryan Caley and Mike Hiebert (11/98). Member of 1997-98 UHL Champion Quad City Mallards. Last amateur club; Sault Ste. Marie (OHL).

Alex Mukhanov — Defenseman
Regular Season / Playoffs

Season	Team	League	GP	G	A	PTS	PIM	GP	G	A	PTS	PIM
98-99	Tacoma	WCHL	29	3	5	8	50	—	—	—	—	—

Born; 5/17/75, Moscow, Russia. 6-1, 190.

Colin Muldoon — Defenseman
Regular Season / Playoffs

Season	Team	League	GP	G	A	PTS	PIM	GP	G	A	PTS	PIM
97-98	Nashville	CHL	12	0	3	3	27	—	—	—	—	—
97-98	Columbus	ECHL	20	1	5	6	10	—	—	—	—	—
97-98	Dayton	ECHL	9	0	0	0	2	—	—	—	—	—
98-99	Fayetteville	CHL	70	2	10	12	53	—	—	—	—	—
	CHL	Totals	82	2	13	15	80	—	—	—	—	—
	ECHL	Totals	29	1	5	6	12	—	—	—	—	—

Born; 12/23/72, Red Lake Falls, Minnesota. 5-11, 195. Last amateur club; Ferris State (CCHA).

Ryan Mulhern — Left Wing
Regular Season / Playoffs

Season	Team	League	GP	G	A	PTS	PIM	GP	G	A	PTS	PIM
96-97	Portland	AHL	38	19	15	34	16	5	1	1	2	2
96-97	Hampton Roads	ECHL	40	22	16	38	52	—	—	—	—	—
97-98	Washington	NHL	3	0	0	0	0	—	—	—	—	—
97-98	Portland	AHL	71	25	40	65	85	6	1	0	1	12
98-99	Kansas City	IHL	59	7	11	18	82	—	—	—	—	—
98-99	Las Vegas	IHL	23	9	6	15	8	—	—	—	—	—
	AHL	Totals	109	44	55	99	101	11	2	1	3	14
	IHL	Totals	82	16	17	33	90	—	—	—	—	—

Born; 1/11/73, Philadelphia, Pennsylvania. 6-1, 180. Drafted by Calgary Flames (8th choice, 174th overall) in 1992 Entry Draft. Signed as a free agent by Washington Capitals (3/17/97). Traded to Las Vegas by Kansas City for Nick Naumenko (3/99). 1997-98 AHL First Team All-Star. Last amateur club; Brown

Dennis Mullen — Defenseman
Regular Season / Playoffs

Season	Team	League	GP	G	A	PTS	PIM	GP	G	A	PTS	PIM
98-99	Tucson	WCHL	13	0	10	10	93	—	—	—	—	—

Born; 8/14/77, Bonnyville, Alberta. 6-0, 185. Last amateur club; Calgary (WHL).

Matthias Muller — Goaltender
Regular Season / Playoffs

Season	Team	League	GP	W	L	T	MIN	SO	AVG	GP	W	L	MIN	SO	AVG
98-99	San Diego	WCHL	4	1	1	0	124	0	4.83	—	—	—	—	—	—

Born; 9/29/75, Uzwtl, Switzerland. 5-11, 195. Last European club; ZSC (Switz.)

Mike Muller — Defenseman

Regular Season — Playoffs

Season	Team	League	GP	G	A	PTS	PIM	GP	G	A	PTS	PIM
92-93	Dynamo Moscow	CIS	11	1	0	1	8	—	—	—	—	—
93-94	Moncton	AHL	61	2	14	16	88	—	—	—	—	—
94-95	Springfield	AHL	64	2	5	7	61	—	—	—	—	—
95-96	Minnesota	IHL	53	3	7	10	72	—	—	—	—	—
96-97	Grand Rapids	IHL	2	0	0	0	4	—	—	—	—	—
96-97	Mississippi	ECHL	54	15	24	39	36	—	—	—	—	—
96-97	Baton Rouge	ECHL	12	1	10	11	2	—	—	—	—	—
97-98												
98-99	Neuwied	Germany	48	5	22	27	30	—	—	—	—	—
	AHL	Totals	125	4	19	23	149	—	—	—	—	—
	IHL	Totals	55	3	7	10	76	—	—	—	—	—
	ECHL	Totasl	66	16	34	50	38	—	—	—	—	—

Born; 9/18/71, Edina, Minnesota. 6-2, 205. Drafted by Winnipeg Jets (2nd choice, 35th overall) in 1990 Entry Draft. Last amateur club; Minnesota

Jim Mullin — Goaltender

Regular Season — Playoffs

Season	Team	League	GP	W	L	T	MIN	SO	AVG	GP	W	L	MIN	SO	AVG
97-98	Jacksonville	ECHL	1	0	0	1	46	0	2.63	—	—	—	—	—	—
97-98	Austin	WPHL	8	3	4	1	412	0	3.35	—	—	—	—	—	—
97-98	Odessa	WPHL	5	0	1	1	191	0	4.08	—	—	—	—	—	—
98-99	Worcester	AHL	1	0	1	0	59	0	3.06	—	—	—	—	—	—
98-99	Peoria	ECHL	7	4	3	0	399	0	3.91	—	—	—	—	—	—
98-99	Huntington	ECHL	30	13	9	3	1446	0	3.57	—	—	—	—	—	—
	ECHL	Totals	38	17	12	4	1891	0	3.62	—	—	—	—	—	—
	WPHL	Totals	13	3	5	2	603	0	3.58	—	—	—	—	—	—

Born; 10/10/73, Chesterfield, Missouri. 5-11, 189. Last amateur club; Denver (WCHA).

Kory Mullin — Defenseman

Regular Season — Playoffs

Season	Team	League	GP	G	A	PTS	PIM	GP	G	A	PTS	PIM
95-96	St. John's	AHL	55	6	4	10	73	2	0	1	1	0
95-96	Brantford	CoHL	1	0	0	0	0	—	—	—	—	—
96-97	St. John's	AHL	29	3	2	5	62	—	—	—	—	—
96-97	Cincinnati	IHL	6	0	0	0	19	—	—	—	—	—
96-97	Birmingham	ECHL	21	5	13	18	102	5	4	1	5	10
97-98	Birmingham	ECHL	66	7	55	62	111	4	1	4	5	16
97-98	Cincinnati	IHL	5	0	0	0	21	5	0	0	0	2
98-99	Cardiff	BSL	15	3	5	8	74	—	—	—	—	—
98-99	Birmingham	ECHL	48	1	13	14	59	5	0	4	4	2
	AHL	Totals	84	9	6	15	135	2	0	1	1	0
	IHL	Totals	11	0	0	0	40	5	0	0	0	2
	ECHL	Totals	135	13	81	94	272	14	5	9	14	28

Born; 5/25/74, Lethbridge, Alberta. 6-2, 185. Signed as a free agent by Toronto Maple Leafs (9/23/93). Last amateur club; Lethbridge (WHL).

Matt Mullin — Goaltender

Regular Season — Playoffs

Season	Team	League	GP	W	L	T	MIN	SO	AVG	GP	W	L	MIN	SO	AVG
97-98	Jacksonville	ECHL	11	3	6	0	588	0	4.18	—	—	—	—	—	—
97-98	Flint	UHL	2	1	0	0	64	0	*5.59	—	—	—	—	—	—
97-98	Quad City	UHL	22	16	3	0	1171	2	*2.72	10	6	2	568	0	2.75
98-99	Toledo	ECHL	45	27	13	3	2480	0	2.93	7	3	4	419	0	3.73
	ECHL	Totals	56	30	19	3	3068	0	3.17	7	3	4	419	0	3.73
	UHL	Totals	24	17	3	0	1235	2	2.87	10	6	2	568	0	2.75

Born; 11/9/74, Guelph, Ontairo. 5-7, 165. Member of 1997-98 UHL Champion Quad City Mallards.

Glenn Mulvenna — Forward

Regular Season — Playoffs

Season	Team	League	GP	G	A	PTS	PIM	GP	G	A	PTS	PIM
88-89	Flint	IHL	32	9	14	23	12	—	—	—	—	—
88-89	Muskegon	IHL	11	3	2	5	0	—	—	—	—	—
88-89	Knoxville	ECHL	2	0	0	0	5	—	—	—	—	—
89-90	Muskegon	IHL	52	14	21	35	17	11	2	3	5	0
89-90	Fort Wayne	IHL	6	2	5	7	2	—	—	—	—	—
90-91	Muskegon	IHL	48	9	27	36	25	5	1	1	2	0
91-92	Pittsburgh	NHL	1	0	0	0	2	—	—	—	—	—
91-92	Muskegon	IHL	70	15	27	42	24	14	5	6	11	11
92-93	Philadelphia	NHL	1	0	0	0	2	—	—	—	—	—
92-93	Hershey	AHL	35	5	17	22	8	—	—	—	—	—
93-94	Kalamazoo	IHL	55	13	9	22	18	4	0	0	0	0
94-95	Peoria	IHL	48	7	9	16	20	7	3	0	3	2
95-96	Peoria	IHL	42	2	5	7	16	5	0	0	0	0
96-97	Sheffield	BHL	39	7	16	23	28	—	—	—	—	—
97-98	Feldkirch	Austria	3	0	0	0	8	—	—	—	—	—
97-98	Newcastle	BSL	23	4	8	12	2	5	0	1	1	0
97-98	Peoria	ECHL	4	0	1	1	14	—	—	—	—	—
98-99	Newcastle	BSL	40	8	13	21	18	5	1	2	3	0
	NHL	Totals	2	0	0	0	4	—	—	—	—	—
	IHL	Totals	364	74	119	193	134	46	11	10	21	13
	ECHL	Totals	6	0	1	1	19	—	—	—	—	—

Born; 2/18/67, Calgary, Alberta. 5-11, 187. Signed as a free agent by Pittsburgh Penguins (12/3/87). Signed as a free agent by Philadelphia Flyers (7/7/92). Last amateur club; Kamloops (WHL).

Dana Mulvihill — Forward

Regular Season — Playoffs

Season	Team	League	GP	G	A	PTS	PIM	GP	G	A	PTS	PIM
98-99	Providence	AHL	2	0	0	0	2	—	—	—	—	—
98-99	Greenville	ECHL	69	31	27	58	94	—	—	—	—	—

Born; 4/9/76, Nepean, Ontario. 5-11, 185. Last amateur club; Clarkson (ECAC).

Robert Murdoch — Goaltender

Regular Season — Playoffs

Season	Team	League	GP	W	L	T	MIN	SO	AVG	GP	W	L	MIN	SO	AVG
98-99	Roanoke	ECHL	1	0	1	0	59	0	1.02	—	—	—	—	—	—
98-99	Jacksonville	ECHL	16	2	7	0	591	0	4.97	—	—	—	—	—	—
	ECHL	Totals	17	2	8	0	650	0	4.62	—	—	—	—	—	—

Born; Last amateur club; Ottawa (OUAA).

John Murgatroyd — Center

Regular Season — Playoffs

Season	Team	League	GP	G	A	PTS	PIM	GP	G	A	PTS	PIM
98-99	Central Texas	WPHL	63	22	22	44	112	2	0	0	0	2

Born; 9/13/72, Port McNeil, British Columbia. 6-0, 200.

Alan Murphy — Defenseman

Regular Season — Playoffs

Season	Team	League	GP	G	A	PTS	PIM	GP	G	A	PTS	PIM
89-90	Greensboro	ECHL	3	0	0	0	0	—	—	—	—	—
89-90	Hampton Roads	ECHL	31	3	12	15	105	—	—	—	—	—
90-91	Kansas City	IHL	6	0	0	0	10	—	—	—	—	—
90-91	Hampton Roads	ECHL	33	11	16	27	123	10	3	4	7	34
91-92	Michigan	CoHL	43	10	14	24	85	4	2	0	2	16
92-93	Tulsa	CeHL	34	10	11	21	100	12	3	10	13	48
93-94	Tulsa	CeHL	6	1	3	4	47	—	—	—	—	—
94-95												
95-96	Reno	WCHL	56	9	25	34	227	3	0	0	0	6
96-97	Reno	WCHL	51	10	20	30	277	—	—	—	—	—
97-98	San Diego	WCHL	22	1	5	6	116	—	—	—	—	—
97-98	Idaho	WCHL	12	0	5	5	32	4	1	1	2	10
98-99	Idaho	WCHL	6	3	3	6	16	—	—	—	—	—
98-99	Bakersfield	WCHL	5	1	3	4	10	—	—	—	—	—
	WCHL	Totals	152	24	61	85	678	7	1	1	2	16
	ECHL	Totals	67	14	28	42	228	10	3	4	7	34
	CeHL	Totals	40	11	14	25	147	12	3	10	13	48

Born; 8/8/68, Toronto, Ontario. 6-3, 215. Traded to Bakersfield by Idaho for future considerations (11/98). Member of 1990-91 ECHL champion Hampton Roads Admirals. Member of 1992-93 CeHL champion Tulsa Oilers. Last amateur club; Cornwall (OHL).

Burke Murphy
Right Wing

Regular Season								Playoffs				
Season	Team	League	GP	G	A	PTS	PIM	GP	G	A	PTS	PIM
96-97	Saint John	AHL	54	8	18	26	20	—	—	—	—	—
97-98	Saint John	AHL	35	4	7	11	28	—	—	—	—	—
97-98	Cleveland	IHL	11	3	2	5	2	—	—	—	—	—
97-98	Quebec	IHL	13	10	6	16	4	—	—	—	—	—
98-99	Revier Lowen	Germany	52	22	15	37	30	—	—	—	—	—
	AHL	Totals	89	12	25	37	48	—	—	—	—	—
	IHL	Totals	24	13	8	21	6	—	—	—	—	—

Born; 6/5/73, Gloucester, Ontario. 6-0, 180. Drafted by Calgary Flames (11th choice, 278th overall) in 1993 Entry Draft. Traded to Quebec by Cleveland with Ryan Mougenel, Rick Hayward, John Craighead, Eric Perrin and Pat Jablonski for Rick Girard, Dale DeGray, Darcy Simon, Tom Draper and Jason Ruff (3/98). Last amateur club; St. Lawrence (ECAC).

Cory Murphy
Defenseman

Regular Season								Playoffs				
Season	Team	League	GP	G	A	PTS	PIM	GP	G	A	PTS	PIM
97-98	Mississippi	ECHL	5	0	1	1	6	—	—	—	—	—
97-98	Chesapeake	ECHL	64	1	4	5	106	3	0	0	0	2
98-99	Chesapeake	ECHL	62	2	12	14	87	8	0	1	1	8
	ECHL	Totals	131	3	17	20	199	11	0	1	1	10

Born; 10/22/76, Perth, Ontario. 6-2, 210.

Curtis Murphy
Defenseman

Regular Season								Playoffs				
Season	Team	League	GP	G	A	PTS	PIM	GP	G	A	PTS	PIM
98-99	Orlando	IHL	80	22	35	57	60	17	4	5	9	16

Born; 12/3/75, Kerrobert, Saskatchewan. 5-8, 185. Last amateur club; North Dakota (WCHA).

Dan Murphy
Goaltender

Regular Season										Playoffs					
Season	Team	League	GP	W	L	T	MIN	SO	AVG	GP	W	L	MIN	SO	AVG
98-99	Worcester	AHL	8	2	4	1	410	0	3.81	—	—	—	—	—	—
98-99	Peoria	ECHL	29	16	10	2	1672	0	3.30	3	1	2	180	0	3.67

Born; 6/13/70, New Haven, Connecticut. 6-1, 185. Last amateur club; Clarkson (ECAC).

Jay Murphy
Right Wing

Regular Season								Playoffs				
Season	Team	League	GP	G	A	PTS	PIM	GP	G	A	PTS	PIM
94-95	Richmond	ECHL	37	24	15	39	78	6	2	3	5	9
95-96	San Francisco	IHL	9	0	3	3	9	—	—	—	—	—
95-96	Richmond	ECHL	52	31	43	74	177	7	4	6	10	18
96-97	Louisiana	ECHL	15	5	5	10	42	17	7	5	12	91
96-97	Alaska	WCHL	28	15	22	37	65	—	—	—	—	—
97-98	Louisiana	ECHL	58	32	42	74	196	12	8	6	14	53
98-99	Louisiana	ECHL	47	29	29	58	189	5	1	1	2	23
	ECHL	Totals	209	121	134	255	682	47	22	21	43	194

Born; 1/10/72, Ypsilanti, Michigan. 6-2, 205. Member of 1994-95 ECHL champion Richmond Renegades. Last amateur club; Northeastern (H.E).

Jodi Murphy
Right Wing

Regular Season								Playoffs				
Season	Team	League	GP	G	A	PTS	PIM	GP	G	A	PTS	PIM
93-94	Hamilton	AHL	2	0	0	0	0	—	—	—	—	—
93-94	Richmond	ECHL	3	0	1	1	0	—	—	—	—	—
93-94	Muskegon	CoHL	36	4	1	5	150	1	0	0	0	2
94-95	Saginaw	CoHL	5	0	0	0	29	9	0	0	0	15
94-95	Muskegon	CoHL	39	1	0	1	178	—	—	—	—	—
95-96	Flint	CoHL	35	1	2	3	95	—	—	—	—	—
95-96	Madison	CoHL	17	0	1	1	5	5	0	0	0	7
96-97	Muskegon	CoHL	67	7	0	7	160	1	0	0	0	0
97-98	Bakersfield	WCHL	42	4	6	10	232	4	0	0	0	49
98-99	Tupelo	WPHL	63	5	6	11	207	—	—	—	—	—
	CoHL	Totals	132	6	4	10	457	15	0	0	0	24

Born; 8/1/73, Halifax, Nova Scotia. 6-5, 235. Last amateur club; Regina (WHL).

Joe Murphy
Right Wing

Regular Season								Playoffs				
Season	Team	League	GP	G	A	PTS	PIM	GP	G	A	PTS	PIM
98-99	Denver	WCHA	33	3	13	16	25	—	—	—	—	—
98-99	Huntsville	CHL	—	—	—	—	—	13	1	5	6	20

Born; 1/21/75, Didsbury, Alberta. 6-0, 190. Selected by Indianapolis in 1999 CHL Expansion Draft. Member of 1998-99 CHL Champion Huntsville Channel Cats. Last amateur club; Denver (WCHA).

John Murphy
Defenseman

Regular Season								Playoffs				
Season	Team	League	GP	G	A	PTS	PIM	GP	G	A	PTS	PIM
98-99	Waco	WPHL	39	3	3	6	243	4	0	1	1	32

Born; 10/7/76, Hunter Ridge, Prince Edward Island. 6-0, 185. Last amateur club; Summerside (MJHL).

Luke Murphy
Center

Regular Season								Playoffs				
Season	Team	League	GP	G	A	PTS	PIM	GP	G	A	PTS	PIM
98-99	Rochester Inst.	NCAA 3										
98-99	Augusta	ECHL	6	0	1	1	0	2	0	0	0	2

Born; Shawville, Quebec. 5-11, 180. Last amateur club; R.I. T. (NCAA 3).

Randy Murphy
Forward

Regular Season								Playoffs				
Season	Team	League	GP	G	A	PTS	PIM	GP	G	A	PTS	PIM
94-95	Elmira	NCAA 3	8	8	10	18	0	—	—	—	—	—
94-95	Raleigh	ECHL	2	0	0	0	0	—	—	—	—	—
95-96	Lakeland	SHL	60	40	69	109	35	5	1	2	3	4
96-97	Columbus	CeHL	65	36	69	105	42	3	0	3	3	2
97-98	Columbus	CHL	70	37	63	100	64	10	2	3	5	16
98-99	Odense	Denmark		21	26	47						
	CHL	Totals	135	73	132	205	106	13	2	6	8	18

Born; 7/25/72, Mississauga, Ontario. 5-7, 170. Last amateur club; Elmira (NCAA

Rob Murphy
Center

Regular Season								Playoffs				
Season	Team	League	GP	G	A	PTS	PIM	GP	G	A	PTS	PIM
87-88	Vancouver	NHL	5	0	0	0	2	—	—	—	—	—
87-88	Laval	QMJHL	26	11	25	36	82	—	—	—	—	—
87-88	Drummondville	QMJHL	33	16	28	44	41	17	4	15	19	45
88-89	Vancouver	NHL	8	0	1	1	2	—	—	—	—	—
88-89	Milwaukee	IHL	8	4	2	6	4	11	3	5	8	34
88-89	Drummondville	QMJHL	26	13	25	38	16	4	1	3	4	20
89-90	Vancouver	NHL	12	1	1	2	0	—	—	—	—	—
89-90	Milwaukee	IHL	64	24	47	71	87	6	2	6	8	12
90-91	Vancouver	NHL	42	5	1	6	90	4	0	0	0	2
90-91	Milwaukee	IHL	23	1	7	8	48	—	—	—	—	—
91-92	Vancouver	NHL	6	0	1	1	6	—	—	—	—	—
91-92	Milwaukee	IHL	73	26	38	64	141	5	0	3	3	2
92-93	Ottawa	NHL	44	3	7	10	30	—	—	—	—	—
92-93	New Haven	AHL	26	8	12	20	28	—	—	—	—	—
93-94	Los Angeles	NHL	8	0	1	1	22	—	—	—	—	—
93-94	Phoenix	IHL	72	23	34	57	101	—	—	—	—	—
94-95	Phoenix	IHL	2	0	0	0	10	2	0	1	1	0
94-95												
95-96	Fort Wayne	IHL	82	24	52	76	107	5	1	2	3	8
96-97	Fort Wayne	IHL	35	9	16	25	40	—	—	—	—	—
97-98	Rosenheim	Germany	44	9	24	33	68	—	—	—	—	—
98-99	Landshut	Germany	52	14	30	44	77	3	0	1	1	8
	NHL	Totals	125	9	12	21	152	4	0	0	0	2
	IHL	Totals	359	107	196	303	538	29	6	17	23	56

Born; 4/7/69, Hull, Quebec. 6-3, 205. Drafted by Vancouver Canucks (1st choice, 24th overall) in 1987 Entry Draft. Selected by Ottawa Senators in NHL Expansion Draft (6/18/92). Signed as a free agent by Los Angeles Kings (8/2/93). 1989-90 IHL Rookie of the Year. Last amateur club; Drummondville (QMJHL).

Marty Murray — Center

Regular Season / Playoffs

Season	Team	League	GP	G	A	PTS	PIM	GP	G	A	PTS	PIM
95-96	Calgary	NHL	15	3	3	6	0	—	—	—	—	—
95-96	Saint John	AHL	58	25	31	56	20	14	2	4	6	4
96-97	Calgary	NHL	2	0	0	0	4	—	—	—	—	—
96-97	Saint John	AHL	67	19	39	58	40	5	2	3	5	4
97-98	Calgary	NHL	2	0	0	0	2	—	—	—	—	—
97-98	Saint John	AHL	41	10	30	40	16	21	10	10	20	12
98-99	Heraklith	Austria	34	27	42	69	12	—	—	—	—	—
	NHL	Totals	19	3	3	6	6	—	—	—	—	—
	AHL	Totals	166	54	100	154	76	40	14	17	31	20

Born; 2/16/75, Deloraine, Manitoba. 5-9, 170. Drafted by Calgary Flames (5th choice, 96th overall) in 1993 Entry Draft. Last amateur club; Brandon (WHL).

Mike Murray — Right Wing

Regular Season / Playoffs

Season	Team	League	GP	G	A	PTS	PIM	GP	G	A	PTS	PIM
94-95	Saint John	AHL	65	8	27	35	53	4	0	0	0	6
95-96	Saint John	AHL	32	7	11	18	77	—	—	—	—	—
96-97	Saint John	AHL	17	2	5	7	8	4	1	1	2	12
97-98	Injured	DNP										
98-99	Louisiana	ECHL	66	31	40	71	97	5	2	3	5	6
	AHL	Totals	114	17	43	60	138	8	1	1	2	18

Born; 4/18/71, Cuberland, Rhode Island. 6-1, 200. Drafted by Calgary Flames (10th choice, 188th overall) in 1990 Entry Draft. Last amateur club; Lowell

Rob Murray — Center

Regular Season / Playoffs

Season	Team	League	GP	G	A	PTS	PIM	GP	G	A	PTS	PIM
87-88	Fort Wayne	IHL	80	12	21	33	139	6	0	2	2	16
88-89	Baltimore	AHL	80	11	23	34	235	—	—	—	—	—
89-90	Washington	NHL	41	2	7	9	58	9	0	0	0	18
89-90	Baltimore	AHL	23	5	4	9	63	—	—	—	—	—
90-91	Washington	NHL	17	0	3	3	19	—	—	—	—	—
90-91	Baltimore	AHL	48	6	20	26	177	4	0	0	0	12
91-92	Winnipeg	NHL	9	0	1	1	18	—	—	—	—	—
91-92	Moncton	AHL	60	16	15	31	247	8	0	1	1	56
92-93	Winnipeg	NHL	10	1	0	1	6	—	—	—	—	—
92-93	Moncton	AHL	56	16	21	37	147	3	0	0	0	6
93-94	Winnipeg	NHL	6	0	0	0	2	—	—	—	—	—
93-94	Moncton	AHL	69	25	32	57	280	21	2	3	5	60
94-95	Winnipeg	NHL	10	0	2	2	2	—	—	—	—	—
94-95	Springfield	AHL	78	16	38	54	373	—	—	—	—	—
95-96	Winnipeg	NHL	1	0	0	0	2	—	—	—	—	—
95-96	Springfield	AHL	74	10	28	38	263	10	1	6	7	32
96-97	Springfield	AHL	78	16	27	43	234	17	2	3	5	66
97-98	Springfield	AHL	80	7	30	37	255	4	0	2	2	2
98-99	Phoenix	NHL	13	1	2	3	4	—	—	—	—	—
98-99	Springfield	AHL	68	6	19	25	197	3	0	0	0	4
	NHL	Totals	107	4	15	19	109	9	0	0	0	18
	AHL	Totals	714	134	257	391	2471	70	5	15	20	238

Born; 4/4/67, Toronto, Ontario. 6-0, 180. Drafted by Washington Capitals (3rd choice, 61st overall) in 1985 Entry Draft. Claimed by Minnesota North Stars from Washington in Expansion Draft (5/30/91). Traded to Winnipeg Jets by Minnesota with future considerations for Winnipeg's seventh round draft choice (Geoff Finch) in 1991 Entry Draft and future considerations (5/31/91). AHL All-Time Leader in regular season penalty minutes. Last amateur club; Peterborough

Tim Murray — Defenseman

Regular Season / Playoffs

Season	Team	League	GP	G	A	PTS	PIM	GP	G	A	PTS	PIM
96-97	New Hampshire	H.E.	37	0	37	37	40	—	—	—	—	—
96-97	Detroit	IHL	5	0	4	4	2	—	—	—	—	—
97-98	Detroit	IHL	34	2	17	19	22	—	—	—	—	—
97-98	Rochester	AHL	26	3	13	16	18	—	—	—	—	—
97-98	Adirondack	AHL	7	1	6	7	6	3	0	1	1	0
98-99	Detroit	IHL	39	1	8	9	17	—	—	—	—	—
98-99	Portland	AHL	28	1	9	10	14	—	—	—	—	—
	IHL	Totals	78	3	29	32	41	—	—	—	—	—
	AHL	Totals	61	5	28	33	38	3	0	1	1	0

Born;11/11/74, Calgary, Alberta. 6-2, 195. Last amateur club; New Hampshire (Hockey East).

Dana Murzyn — Defenseman

Regular Season / Playoffs

Season	Team	League	GP	G	A	PTS	PIM	GP	G	A	PTS	PIM
85-86	Hartford	NHL	78	3	23	26	125	4	0	0	0	10
86-87	Hartford	NHL	74	9	19	28	95	6	2	1	3	29
87-88	Hartford	NHL	33	1	6	7	45	—	—	—	—	—
87-88	Calgary	NHL	41	6	5	11	94	5	2	0	2	13
88-89	Calgary	NHL	63	3	19	22	142	21	0	3	3	20
89-90	Calgary	NHL	78	7	13	20	140	6	2	2	4	2
90-91	Calgary	NHL	19	0	2	2	30	—	—	—	—	—
90-91	Vancouver	NHL	10	1	0	1	8	6	0	1	1	8
91-92	Vancouver	NHL	70	3	11	14	147	1	0	0	0	15
92-93	Vancouver	NHL	79	5	11	16	196	12	3	2	5	18
93-94	Vancouver	NHL	80	6	14	20	109	7	0	0	0	4
94-95	Vancouver	NHL	40	0	8	8	129	8	0	1	1	22
95-96	Vancouver	NHL	69	2	10	12	130	6	0	0	0	25
96-97	Vancouver	NHL	61	1	7	8	118	—	—	—	—	—
97-98	Vancouver	NHL	31	5	2	7	42	—	—	—	—	—
98-99	Vancouver	NHL	12	0	2	2	21	—	—	—	—	—
98-99	Syracuse	AHL	20	2	4	6	37	—	—	—	—	—
	NHL	Totals	838	52	152	204	1571	82	9	10	19	166

Born; 12/9/66, Calgary, Alberta. 6-2, 200. Drafted by Hartford Whalers (1st choice, 5th overall) in 1985 Entry Draft. Traded to Calgary Flames by Hartford with Shane Churla for Neil Sheehy, Carey Wilson and the rights to Lane MacDonald (1/3/88). Traded to Vancouver Canucks by Calgary for Ron Stern, Kevan Guy and future considerations (3/5/91). 1985-86 NHL All-Rookie Team. Member of 1988-89 Stanley Cup Champion Calgary Flames. Last amateur club; Calgary

Scott Muscutt — Left Wing

Regular Season / Playoffs

Season	Team	League	GP	G	A	PTS	PIM	GP	G	A	PTS	PIM
97-98	Shreveport	WPHL	43	5	15	20	89	8	1	2	3	16
98-99	Shreveport	WPHL	61	8	19	27	85	12	1	1	2	4
	WPHL	Totals	104	13	34	47	174	20	2	3	5	20

Born: 6/17/70, Appin, Ontario. 6-0, 185. Member of 1998-99 WPHL Champion Shreveport Mudbugs. Last amateur club; New Brunswick (AUAA).

Ivar Muzis — Defenseman

Regular Season / Playoffs

Season	Team	League	GP	G	A	PTS	PIM	GP	G	A	PTS	PIM
98-99	Colorado	WCHL	7	0	1	1	6	—	—	—	—	—
98-99	Tucson	WCHL	3	1	0	1	0	—	—	—	—	—
98-99	Tacoma	WCHL	7	0	0	0	0	—	—	—	—	—
	WCHL	Totals	17	1	1	2	6	—	—	—	—	—

Born; 7/22/73, Riga, Latvia. 5-10, 183.

Jason Muzzatti — Goaltender

Regular Season / Playoffs

Season	Team	League	GP	W	L	T	MIN	SO	AVG	GP	W	L	MIN	SO	AVG
91-92	Salt Lake City	IHL	52	24	22	5	3033	2	3.30	4	1	3	247	0	4.37
92-93	Canada	National	16	6	9	0	880	0	3.84	—	—	—	—	—	—
92-93	Indianapolis	IHL	12	5	6	1	707	0	4.07	—	—	—	—	—	—
92-93	Salt Lake City	IHL	13	5	6	1	747	0	4.18	—	—	—	—	—	—
93-94	Calgary	NHL	1	0	1	0	60	0	8.00	—	—	—	—	—	—
93-94	Saint John	AHL	51	26	21	3	2939	2	3.74	7	3	4	415	0	2.75
94-95	Saint John	AHL	31	10	14	4	1741	2	3.48	—	—	—	—	—	—
94-95	Calgary	NHL	1	0	0	0	10	0	0.00	—	—	—	—	—	—
95-96	Hartford	NHL	22	4	8	3	1013	1	2.90	—	—	—	—	—	—
95-96	Springfield	AHL	5	4	0	1	300	1	2.40	—	—	—	—	—	—
96-97	Hartford	NHL	31	9	13	5	1591	0	3.43	—	—	—	—	—	—
97-98	Rangers	NHL	6	0	3	2	313	0	3.26	—	—	—	—	—	—
97-98	San Jose	NHL	1	0	0	0	27	0	4.44	—	—	—	—	—	—
97-98	Hartford	AHL	17	11	5	1	999	0	3.42	—	—	—	—	—	—
97-98	Kentucky	AHL	7	2	3	2	430	0	3.49	3	0	3	154	0	5.07
98-99	Eisbaren Berlin	Germany	4	—	—	—	240	0	3.00	3	—	—	166	0	5.06
	NHL	Totals	62	13	25	10	3014	1	3.32	—	—	—	—	—	—
	AHL	Totals	111	53	43	11	6409	5	3.54	10	3	7	569	0	3.38

Born; 2/3/70, Toronto, Ontario. 6-2, 210. Drafted by Calgary Flames (1st choice, 21st overall) in 1988 Entry Draft. Claimed on waivers by Hartford Whalers from Calgary (10/6/95). Traded to New York Rangers by Carolina Hurricanes for Rangers' fourth round choice (Tommy Westlund) in 1998 entry Draft (8/8/97). Traded to San Jose Sharks by Rangers for Rich Brennan (3/24/98). Last amateur club; Michigan State (CCHA).

Brantt Myhres — Right Wing

Regular Season / Playoffs

Season	Team	League	GP	G	A	PTS	PIM	GP	G	A	PTS	PIM
93-94	Lethbridge	WHL	34	10	21	31	103	—	—	—	—	—
93-94	Spokane	WHL	27	10	22	32	139	3	1	4	5	7
93-94	Atlanta	IHL	2	0	0	0	17	—	—	—	—	—
94-95	Atlanta	IHL	40	5	5	10	213	—	—	—	—	—
94-95	Tampa Bay	NHL	15	2	0	2	81	—	—	—	—	—
95-96	Atlanta	IHL	12	0	2	2	58	—	—	—	—	—
96-97	Tampa Bay	NHL	47	3	1	4	136	—	—	—	—	—
96-97	San Antonio	IHL	12	0	0	0	98	—	—	—	—	—
97-98	Philadelphia	NHL	23	0	0	0	169	—	—	—	—	—
97-98	Philadelphia	AHL	18	4	4	8	67	—	—	—	—	—
98-99	San Jose	NHL	30	1	0	1	116	—	—	—	—	—
98-99	Kentucky	AHL	4	0	0	0	16	—	—	—	—	—
	NHL	Totals	85	5	1	6	386	—	—	—	—	—
	IHL	Totals	66	5	7	12	396	—	—	—	—	—
	AHL	Totals	22	4	4	8	83	—	—	—	—	—

Born; 3/18/74, Edmonton, Alberta. 6-4, 222. Drafted by Tampa Bay Lightning (6th choice, 97th overall) in 1992 Entry Draft. Traded to Edmonton Oilers by Tampa Bay with a conditional draft choice for Vladimir Vujtek and Edmonton's third round choice (Dimitry Afanasenkov) in 1998 Entry Draft (7/16/97). Traded to Philadelphia Flyers by Edmonton for Jason Bowen (10/15/97). Signed as a free agent by San Jose Sharks (9/11/98). Last amateur club; Spokane (WHL).

Jeremy Mylymok — Defenseman

Regular Season / Playoffs

Season	Team	League	GP	G	A	PTS	PIM	GP	G	A	PTS	PIM
95-96	Alaska-Anchorage	WCHA	35	3	10	13	79	—	—	—	—	—
95-96	Toledo	ECHL	9	1	0	1	24	8	0	0	0	10
96-97	Quebec	IHL	4	0	0	0	4	4	0	0	0	2
96-97	Toledo	ECHL	18	0	5	5	46	—	—	—	—	—
96-97	Pensacola	ECHL	43	2	13	15	113	11	0	1	1	46
97-98	Quebec	IHL	70	1	3	4	287	—	—	—	—	—
97-98	Chicago	IHL	8	0	2	2	2	22	0	1	1	49
98-99	Chicago	IHL	63	4	6	10	194	10	1	1	2	23
	IHL	Totals	145	5	11	16	487	36	1	2	3	74
	ECHL	Totals	70	3	18	21	183	19	0	1	1	56

Born; 1/12/72, London, Ontario. 6-0, 200. Traded to Chicago by Quebec for Craig Binns (3/98). Member of 1997-98 IHL Champion Chicago Wolves. Last amateur club; Alaska-Anchorage (WCHA).

Dan Myre — Center

Regular Season / Playoffs

Season	Team	League	GP	G	A	PTS	PIM	GP	G	A	PTS	PIM
98-99	Thunder Bay	UHL	59	11	19	30	36	—	—	—	—	—
98-99	Madison	UHL	9	0	4	4	2	—	—	—	—	—
	UHL	Totals	68	11	23	34	38	—	—	—	—	—

Born; 1/11/77, Ottawa, Ontario. 5-10, 180. Traded by Thunder Bay to Madison with Chris Torkoff for Jason Disher (3/99). Last amateur club; Gloucester

Anders Myrvold — Defenseman

Regular Season / Playoffs

Season	Team	League	GP	G	A	PTS	PIM	GP	G	A	PTS	PIM
94-95	Laval	QMJHL	64	14	50	64	173	20	4	10	14	68
94-95	Cornwall	AHL	—	—	—	—	—	3	0	1	1	2
95-96	Colorado	NHL	4	0	1	1	6	—	—	—	—	—
95-96	Cornwall	AHL	70	5	24	29	125	5	1	0	1	19
96-97	Hershey	AHL	20	0	3	3	16	—	—	—	—	—
96-97	Boston	NHL	9	0	2	2	4	—	—	—	—	—
96-97	Providence	AHL	53	6	15	21	107	10	0	1	1	6
97-98	Providence	AHL	75	4	21	25	91	—	—	—	—	—
98-99	AIK Solna	Sweden	19	1	3	4	24	—	—	—	—	—
	NHL	Totals	13	0	3	3	10	—	—	—	—	—
	AHL	Totals	218	15	63	78	349	18	1	2	3	27

Born; 8/12/75, Lorenskog, Norway. 6-2, 200. Drafted by Quebec Nordiques (6th choice, 127th overall) in 1993 Entry Draft. Traded to Boston Bruins with Landon Wilson for Boston's first round choice (Robyn Regehr) in 1998 Entry Draft (11/22/96).

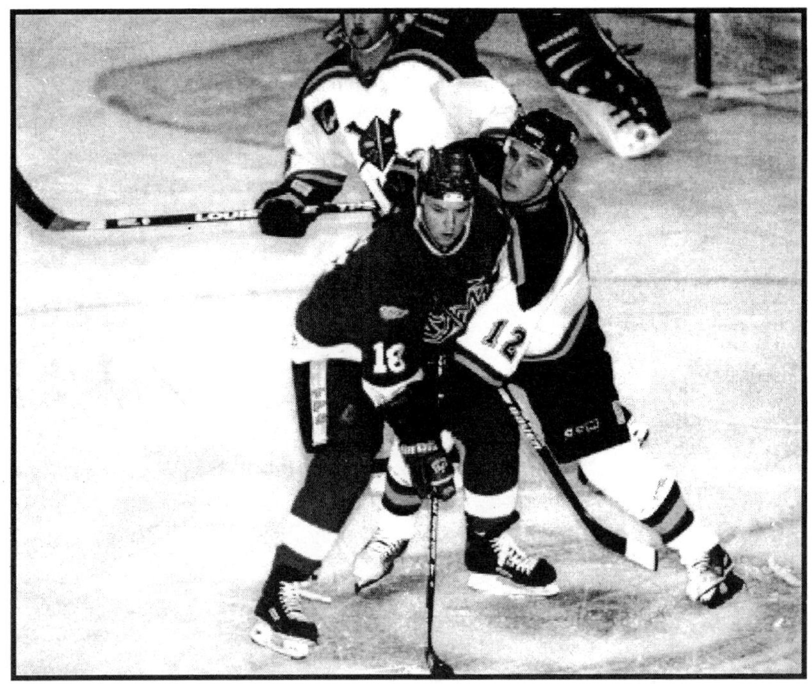

Toledo's Andrew Williamson and Wheeling's Keli Corpse battle for position after a face-off

Photo by John Gacioch

Dmitri Nabokov — Center

Season	Team	League	GP	G	A	PTS	PIM	GP	G	A	PTS	PIM
			Regular Season					Playoffs				
96-97	Soviet Wings	Russia	1	0	0	0	0	—	—	—	—	—
96-97	Regina	WHL	50	39	56	95	61	5	2	3	5	2
96-97	Indianapolis	IHL	2	0	0	0	0	—	—	—	—	—
97-98	Chicago	NHL	25	7	4	11	10	—	—	—	—	—
97-98	Indianapolis	IHL	46	6	15	21	16	5	2	1	3	0
98-99	Islanders	NHL	4	0	2	2	2	—	—	—	—	—
98-99	Lowell	AHL	73	17	25	42	46	3	0	1	1	0
	NHL	Totals	29	7	6	13	12	—	—	—	—	—
	IHL	Totals	48	6	15	21	16	5	2	1	3	0

Born; 1/4/77, Novosibirsk, USSR. 6-2, 209. Drafted by Chicago Blackhawks (1st choice, 19th overall) in 1995 Entry Draft. Traded to New York Islanders by Chicago for J.P. Dumont and Chicago's fifth round pick (later-traded to Philadelphia-Philadelphia selected Francis Belanger) (6/1/98). Last amateur club;

John Nabokov — Goaltender

Season	Team	League	GP	W	L	T	MIN	SO	AVG	GP	W	L	MIN	SO	AVG
			Regular Season							Playoffs					
97-98	Kentucky	AHL	33	10	21	2	1866	0	3.92	1	0	0	23	0	2.59
98-99	Kentucky	AHL	43	26	14	1	2429	5	2.62	11	6	5	599	*2	3.00
	AHL	Totals	76	36	35	3	4295	5	3.19	12	6	5	622	2	2.99

Born; 7/25/75, Ust-Kamenogorsk, USSR. 6-0, 180. Drafted by San Jose Sharks (9th choice, 219th overall) in 1994 Entry Draft. Last overseas club; Moscow

Chris Nadeau — Defenseman

Season	Team	League	GP	G	A	PTS	PIM	GP	G	A	PTS	PIM
			Regular Season					Playoffs				
96-97	Huntington	ECHL	66	2	10	12	42	—	—	—	—	—
97-98	Shreveport	WPHL	69	2	17	19	53	8	0	6	6	6
98-99	Shreveport	WPHL	68	6	23	29	37	12	2	2	4	4
	WPHL	Totals	137	8	40	48	90	20	2	8	10	10

Born; 4/10/72, Saint John, New Brunswick. 6-0, 200. Member of 1998-99 WPHL Champion Shreveport Mudbugs. Last amateur club; New Brunswick (AUAA).

Patrick Nadeau — Center

Season	Team	League	GP	G	A	PTS	PIM	GP	G	A	PTS	PIM
			Regular Season					Playoffs				
97-98	Quebec	QSPHL	33	23	37	60	47	—	—	—	—	—
98-99	Birmingham	ECHL	38	22	20	42	13	5	0	4	4	2

Born; 5-10, 180.

Ladislav Nagy — Center

Season	Team	League	GP	G	A	PTS	PIM	GP	G	A	PTS	PIM
			Regular Season					Playoffs				
98-99	Halifax	QMJHL	63	71	55	126	148	5	3	3	6	18
98-99	Worcester	AHL	—	—	—	—	—	3	2	2	4	0

Born; 6/1/79, Saca, Czechoslovakia. 5-11, 183. Drafted by St. Louis Blues (6th choice, 177th overall) in 1997 Entry Draft. Last amateur club; Halifax (QMJHL).

Yevgeny Namestnikov — Defenseman

Season	Team	League	GP	G	A	PTS	PIM	GP	G	A	PTS	PIM
			Regular Season					Playoffs				
93-94	Vancouver	NHL	17	0	5	5	10	—	—	—	—	—
93-94	Hamilton	AHL	59	7	27	34	97	4	0	2	2	19
94-95	Vancouver	NHL	16	0	3	3	4	1	0	0	0	2
94-95	Syracuse	AHL	59	11	22	33	59	—	—	—	—	—
95-96	Vancouver	NHL	—	—	—	—	—	1	0	0	0	0
95-96	Syracuse	AHL	59	13	34	47	85	15	1	8	9	16
96-97	Vancouver	NHL	2	0	0	0	4	—	—	—	—	—
96-97	Syracuse	AHL	55	9	37	46	73	3	2	0	2	0
97-98	Islanders	NHL	6	0	1	1	4	—	—	—	—	—
97-98	Utah	IHL	62	6	19	25	48	4	1	0	1	2
98-99	Lowell	AHL	42	12	14	26	42	—	—	—	—	—
	NHL	Totals	41	0	9	9	22	2	0	0	0	2
	AHL	Totals	336	58	153	211	404	26	4	10	14	37

Born; 10/9/71, Novgorod, Russia. 5-11, 190. Drafted by Vancouver Canucks (6th choice, 117th overall) in 1991 Entry Draft. Signed as a free agent by New York Islanders (7/21/97). Last overseas club; CKSA Moscow.

Bob Nardella — Defenseman

Season	Team	League	GP	G	A	PTS	PIM	GP	G	A	PTS	PIM
			Regular Season					Playoffs				
93-94	Alleghe HC	Italy	23	12	21	33	26	—	—	—	—	—
94-95	Chicago	IHL	74	9	40	49	36	3	1	2	3	0
95-96	Milan	Italy										
96-97	Mannheim	Germany	50	6	21	27	59	9	3	6	9	10
97-98	Chicago	IHL	65	13	35	48	40	22	5	13	18	24
98-99	Chicago	IHL	82	8	45	53	86	10	0	2	2	6
	IHL	Totals	221	30	120	150	162	35	6	17	23	30

Born; 2/2/68, Melrose Park, Illinois. 5-8, 169. Member of 1997-98 IHL Champion Chicago Wolves. Last amateur club; Ferris State (CCHA).

Luch Nasato — Defenseman

Season	Team	League	GP	G	A	PTS	PIM	GP	G	A	PTS	PIM
			Regular Season					Playoffs				
97-98	Barrie	OHL	61	12	57	69	254	6	1	2	3	23
97-98	Detroit	IHL	5	0	0	0	0	—	—	—	—	—
97-98	Flint	UHL	—	—	—	—	—	2	0	0	0	4
98-99	Detroit	IHL	26	2	4	6	111	—	—	—	—	—
98-99	Las Vegas	IHL	13	0	2	2	52	—	—	—	—	—
98-99	Flint	UHL	21	7	27	34	97	5	0	6	6	16
	IHL	Totals	44	2	6	8	163	—	—	—	—	—
	UHL	Totals	21	7	27	34	97	7	0	6	6	20

Born; 3/10/77, Mississauga, Ontario. 5-11, 205. Last amateur club; Barrie (OHL).

Tyson Nash — Left Wing

Season	Team	League	GP	G	A	PTS	PIM	GP	G	A	PTS	PIM
			Regular Season					Playoffs				
95-96	Syracuse	AHL	50	4	7	11	58	4	0	0	0	11
95-96	Raleigh	ECHL	6	1	1	2	8	—	—	—	—	—
96-97	Syracuse	AHL	77	17	17	34	105	3	0	2	2	0
97-98	Syracuse	AHL	74	20	20	40	184	5	0	2	2	28
98-99	St. Louis	NHL	2	0	0	0	5	1	0	0	0	2
98-99	Worcester	AHL	55	14	22	36	143	4	4	1	5	27
	AHL	Totals	256	55	66	121	490	16	4	5	9	66

Born; 3/11/75, Edmonton, Alberta. 6-0, 180. Drafted by Vancouver Canucks (10th choice, 247th overall) in 1994 Entry Draft. Signed as a free agent by St. Louis Blues (7/24/98). Last amateur club; Kamloops (WHL).

Alain Nasreddine — Defenseman

Season	Team	League	GP	G	A	PTS	PIM	GP	G	A	PTS	PIM
			Regular Season					Playoffs				
95-96	Carolina	AHL	63	0	5	5	245	—	—	—	—	—
96-97	Carolina	AHL	26	0	4	4	109	—	—	—	—	—
96-97	Indianapolis	IHL	49	0	2	2	248	4	1	1	2	27
97-98	Indianapolis	IHL	75	1	12	13	258	5	0	2	2	12
98-99	Montreal	NHL	15	0	0	0	52	—	—	—	—	—
98-99	Portland	AHL	7	0	1	1	36	—	—	—	—	—
98-99	Fredericton	AHL	38	0	10	10	108	15	0	3	3	39
	AHL	Totals	134	0	20	20	498	15	0	3	3	39
	IHL	Totals	124	1	14	15	506	9	1	3	4	39

Born; 7/10/75, Montreal, Quebec. 6-1, 201. Drafted by Florida Panthers (8th choice, 135th overall) in 1993 Entry Draft. Traded to Chicago Blackhawks with a conditional 1999 draft pick by Florida for Ivan Droppa (12/18/96). Traded to Montreal by Chicago with Jeff Hackett, Eric Weinrich and a conditional draft pick for Brad Brown, Jocelyn Thibault and Dave Manson (11/16/98). Last amateur club; Chicoutimi (QMJHL).

Samy Nasreddine — Defenseman

Season	Team	League	GP	G	A	PTS	PIM	GP	G	A	PTS	PIM
			Regular Season					Playoffs				
97-98	Quebec	IHL	1	0	0	0	0	—	—	—	—	—
97-98	Worcester	AHL	6	0	0	0	11	—	—	—	—	—
97-98	Peoria	ECHL	61	8	32	40	109	3	0	2	2	4
98-99	Fredericton	AHL	49	3	4	7	77	—	—	—	—	—
	AHL	Totals	55	3	4	7	88	—	—	—	—	—

Born; 8/28/76, Montreal, Quebec. 6-2, 198. Last amateur club; Granby (QMJHL).

Eric Naud
Left Wing

Season	Team	League	GP	G	A	PTS	PIM	GP	G	A	PTS	PIM
			Regular Season					Playoffs				
97-98	Providence	AHL	27	1	2	3	54	—	—	—	—	—
97-98	Charlotte	ECHL	16	0	0	0	42	—	—	—	—	—
98-99	Detroit	IHL	2	0	0	0	21	—	—	—	—	—
98-99	Abilene	WPHL	48	11	23	34	270	2	0	0	0	8

Born; 10/2/77, Lasarre, Quebec. 6-1, 187. Drafted by Boston Bruins (3rd choice, 53rd overall) in 1996 Entry Draft. Last amateur club; Hull (QMJHL).

Sylvain Naud
Right Wing

Season	Team	League	GP	G	A	PTS	PIM	GP	G	A	PTS	PIM
			Regular Season					Playoffs				
91-92	Trafford	BHL	18	38	29	67	58	—	—	—	—	—
91-92	Humberside	BHL	8	8	11	19	18	—	—	—	—	—
91-92	Murrayfield	BHL	7	4	1	5	12	—	—	—	—	—
92-93	Tulsa	CeHL	58	39	48	87	114	12	6	13	19	35
93-94	Saima	Italy	21	12	14	26	40	—	—	—	—	—
93-94	Tulsa	CeHL	24	19	22	41	71	—	—	—	—	—
94-95	Tulsa	CeHL	65	28	36	64	112	7	0	4	4	17
95-96	Tulsa	CeHL	64	32	44	76	107	6	3	1	4	14
96-97	Utah	IHL	8	1	0	1	4	—	—	—	—	—
96-97	New Mexico	WPHL	53	*47	44	91	131	6	1	1	2	12
97-98	New Mexico	WPHL	54	50	36	86	154	10	7	10	17	24
97-98	Utah	IHL	2	0	0	0	0	—	—	—	—	—
97-98	Quebec	IHL	15	5	4	9	8	—	—	—	—	—
97-98	Houston	IHL	3	0	0	0	4	3	0	0	0	6
98-99	New Mexico	WPHL	55	37	27	64	77	—	—	—	—	—
	IHL	Totals	28	6	4	10	16	3	0	0	0	6
	CeHL	Totals	211	118	150	268	404	25	9	18	27	66
	WPHL	Totals	162	134	107	241	362	16	8	11	19	36

Born; 3/29/70, LaSalle, Quebec. 5-11, 190. Drafted by Buffalo Sabres (9th choice, 208th overall) in 1990 Entry Draft. 1992-93 CeHL Second Team All-Star. Claimed on waivers by Fort Worth Fire (1993). Traded to Wichita Thunder by Fort Worth for Oleg Santurian and Kevin Stevens (1993). Traded to Tulsa Oilers by Wichita for Dave Doucette and Don Burke (1993). Member of 1992-93 CeHL champion Tulsa Oilers. Last amateur club; Laval (QMJHL).

Steve Naughton
Forward

Season	Team	League	GP	G	A	PTS	PIM	GP	G	A	PTS	PIM
			Regular Season					Playoffs				
98-99	Pensacola	ECHL	23	1	4	5	8	—	—	—	—	—

Born; Glendale, New York. 5-10, 180. Last amateur club; SUNY-Potsdam (NCAA 3).

Frankie Nault
Right Wing

Season	Team	League	GP	G	A	PTS	PIM	GP	G	A	PTS	PIM
			Regular Season					Playoffs				
98-99	Muskegon	UHL	73	11	16	27	62	18	0	7	7	24

Born; 2/10/78, Sherbrooke, Quebec. 5-11, 185. Member of 1998-99 UHL Champion Muskegon Fury. Last amateur club; Hull (QMJHL).

Nick Naumenko
Defenseman

Season	Team	League	GP	G	A	PTS	PIM	GP	G	A	PTS	PIM
			Regular Season					Playoffs				
96-97	Worcester	AHL	54	6	22	28	72	1	0	0	0	0
97-98	Worcester	AHL	72	12	34	46	63	11	1	7	8	8
98-99	Utah	IHL	20	4	3	7	20	—	—	—	—	—
98-99	Las Vegas	IHL	34	5	16	21	37	—	—	—	—	—
98-99	Kansas City	IHL	21	3	8	11	4	3	1	2	3	4
	AHL	Totals	126	18	56	74	135	12	1	7	8	8
	IHL	Totals	75	12	27	39	61	3	1	2	3	4

Born; 7/7/74, Chicago, Illinois. Drafted by St. Louis Blues (9th choice, 182nd overall) in 1992 Entry Draft. Traded to Kansas City by Las Vegas for Ryan Mulhern (3/99). Last amateur club; North Dakota (WCHA).

Sergei Naumov
Goaltender

Season	Team	League	GP	W	L	T	MIN	SO	AVG	GP	W	L	MIN	SO	AVG
			Regular Season							Playoffs					
94-95	Oklahoma City	CeHL	28	13	9	3	1467	0	4.29	1	0	1	60	0	8.00
95-96	San Diego	WCHL	*57	*48	7	2	*3380	*1	3.82	*9	*6	3	*537	0	*2.46
96-97	Las Vegas	IHL	1	1	0	0	60	0	4.00	—	—	—	—	—	—
96-97	San Diego	WCHL	49	*38	8	2	2832	1	*3.14	8	*7	1	465	0	*3.10
97-98	San Diego	WCHL	49	*39	7	1	2728	*4	*3.08	*12	*11	1	680	*1	2.47
98-99	Long Beach	IHL	15	10	4	0	808	0	3.49	—	—	—	—	—	—
98-99	San Diego	WCHL	42	27	11	3	2382	*3	3.15	10	5	*4	583	0	3.40
	IHL	Totals	16	11	4	0	868	0	3.52	—	—	—	—	—	—
	WCHL	Totals	197	152	33	8	11322	9	3.33	39	29	9	2265	1	2.83

Born; 4/4/69, Riga, Latvia. 5-9, 160. 1995-96 WCHL Goaltender of the Year. 1995-96 WCHL Playoff MVP. 1995-96 WCHL First Team All-Star. 1996-97 WCHL Goaltender of the Year. 1996-97 WCHL First Team All-Star. 1997-98 WCHL Playoff MVP. Member of 1995-96 WCHL champion San Diego Gulls. Member of 1996-97 WCHL Champion San Diego Gulls. Member of 1997-98 WCHL Champion San Diego Gulls.

Paval Navrat
Defenseman

Season	Team	League	GP	G	A	PTS	PIM	GP	G	A	PTS	PIM
			Regular Season					Playoffs				
98-99	Memphis	CHL	1	0	0	0	0	—	—	—	—	—

Born; 4/2/73, Prague, Czechoslovakia. 6-2, 198.

Rumun Ndur
Defenseman

Season	Team	League	GP	G	A	PTS	PIM	GP	G	A	PTS	PIM
			Regular Season					Playoffs				
95-96	Rochester	AHL	73	2	12	14	306	17	1	2	3	33
96-97	Buffalo	NHL	2	0	0	0	2	—	—	—	—	—
96-97	Rochester	AHL	68	5	11	16	282	10	3	1	4	21
97-98	Buffalo	NHL	1	0	0	0	2	—	—	—	—	—
97-98	Rochester	AHL	50	1	12	13	207	4	0	2	2	16
98-99	Buffalo	NHL	8	0	0	0	16	—	—	—	—	—
98-99	Rangers	NHL	31	1	3	4	46	—	—	—	—	—
98-99	Hartford	AHL	6	0	1	1	4	—	—	—	—	—
	NHL	Totals	42	1	3	4	66	—	—	—	—	—
	AHL	Totals	197	8	36	44	799	31	4	5	9	70

Born; 7/7/75, Zaria, Nigeria. 6-2, 200. Drafted by Buffalo Sabres Sabres (3rd choice, 69th overall) in 1994 Entry Draft. Claimed on waivers by New York Rangers from Buffalo (12/23/98). Member of 1995-96 AHL champion Rochester Americans. Last amateur club; Guelph (OHL).

Jay Neal
Right Wing

Season	Team	League	GP	G	A	PTS	PIM	GP	G	A	PTS	PIM
			Regular Season					Playoffs				
93-94	Huntington	ECHL	43	11	15	26	53	—	—	—	—	—
93-94	Toledo	ECHL	24	8	10	18	36	14	4	4	8	20
94-95	Toledo	ECHL	64	28	34	62	81	4	0	1	1	4
95-96	Raleigh	ECHL	46	11	23	34	33	4	2	1	3	0
96-97	Amarillo	WPHL	28	13	13	26	45	—	—	—	—	—
96-97	Central Texas	WPHL	25	10	10	20	20	11	4	9	13	6
97-98	Bakersfield	WCHL	55	25	31	56	72	4	1	2	3	2
98-99	Bakersfield	WCHL	44	17	18	35	61	2	1	0	1	7
	ECHL	Totals	177	58	82	140	203	22	6	6	12	24
	WCHL	Totals	99	42	49	91	133	6	2	2	4	9
	WPHL	Totals	53	23	23	46	65	11	4	9	13	6

Born; 6/3/70, Oshawa, Ontario. 6-0, 195. Member of 1993-94 ECHL champion Toledo Storm. Last amateur club; Kent (CCHA).

Jason Neath
Defenseman

Season	Team	League	GP	G	A	PTS	PIM	GP	G	A	PTS	PIM
			Regular Season					Playoffs				
98-99	Wichita	CHL	11	2	1	3	86	—	—	—	—	—

Born; 9/10/75, Ponoka, Alberta. 6-3, 220.

Patrick Neaton — Defenseman

Regular Season / Playoffs

Season	Team	League	GP	G	A	PTS	PIM	GP	G	A	PTS	PIM
93-94	Pittsburgh	NHL	9	1	1	2	12	—	—	—	—	—
93-94	Cleveland	IHL	71	8	24	32	78	—	—	—	—	—
94-95	Cleveland	IHL	2	0	0	0	4	—	—	—	—	—
94-95	San Diego	IHL	71	8	27	35	86	5	0	1	1	0
95-96	Orlando	IHL	77	8	27	35	148	21	3	5	8	34
96-97	Orlando	IHL	81	17	35	52	68	10	0	1	1	13
97-98	Orlando	IHL	78	11	24	35	114	17	3	11	14	12
98-99	Orlando	IHL	75	5	22	27	98	17	2	2	4	14
	IHL	Totals	455	57	159	216	596	70	8	20	28	73

Born; 5/21/71, Detroit, Michigan. 6-0, 180. Drafted by Pittsburgh Penguins (9th choice, 145th overall) in 1990 Entry Draft. Last amateur club; Michigan (CCHA).

Zybnek Neckar — Defenseman

Regular Season / Playoffs

Season	Team	League	GP	G	A	PTS	PIM	GP	G	A	PTS	PIM
98-99	Topeka	CHL	13	1	0	1	8	3	0	0	0	2
98-99	San Diego	WCHL	16	1	0	1	6	—	—	—	—	—
98-99	Bakersfield	WCHL	27	0	1	1	15	—	—	—	—	—
	WCHL	Totals	43	1	1	2	21	—	—	—	—	—

Born; 9/22/78, Pisek, Czech. Republic. 6-2, 210. Last overseas club; Jitex Pisek (Czech. Republic).

Vashi Nedomansky — Right Wing

Regular Season / Playoffs

Season	Team	League	GP	G	A	PTS	PIM	GP	G	A	PTS	PIM
92-93	Roanoke	ECHL	22	5	4	9	31	—	—	—	—	—
92-93	Knoxville	ECHL	27	8	11	19	117	—	—	—	—	—
93-94												
94-95	Phoenix	IHL	41	15	11	26	77	6	0	4	4	23
94-95	Knoxville	ECHL	26	14	9	23	107	—	—	—	—	—
95-96	Phoenix	IHL	3	0	0	0	4	—	—	—	—	—
95-96	Las Vegas	IHL	11	2	4	6	8	2	0	0	0	0
95-96	Knoxville	ECHL	37	32	17	49	160	8	4	4	8	28
96-97	Carolina	AHL	13	4	8	12	8	—	—	—	—	—
96-97	Knoxville	ECHL	45	26	30	56	194	—	—	—	—	—
97-98	Pee Dee	ECHL	56	24	31	55	126	—	—	—	—	—
97-98	Mississippi	ECHL	12	10	14	24	8	—	—	—	—	—
97-98	Grand Rapids	IHL	7	3	0	3	4	3	0	0	0	0
98-99	Lowell	AHL	11	4	1	5	4	—	—	—	—	—
98-99	Grand Rapids	IHL	12	3	4	7	6	—	—	—	—	—
98-99	Mississippi	ECHL	23	24	10	34	116	18	8	9	17	40
	IHL	Totals	74	23	19	42	99	11	0	4	4	23
	AHL	Totals	24	8	9	17	12	—	—	—	—	—
	ECHL	Totals	248	143	126	269	859	26	12	13	25	68

Born; 1/5/71, Bratislavia, Czechoslovakia. 6-1, 210. Traded to Mississippi from Pee Dee for Forbes MacPherson and Cody Bowtell (3/98). Last amateur club; Michigan (CCHA).

Petr Nedved — Center

Regular Season / Playoffs

Season	Team	League	GP	G	A	PTS	PIM	GP	G	A	PTS	PIM
90-91	Vancouver	NHL	61	10	6	16	20	6	0	1	1	0
91-92	Vancouver	NHL	77	15	22	37	36	10	1	4	5	16
92-93	Vancouver	NHL	84	38	33	71	96	12	2	3	5	2
93-94	Canadian	National	17	19	12	31	16	—	—	—	—	—
93-94	Canadian	Olympic	8	5	1	6	6	—	—	—	—	—
93-94	St. Louis	NHL	19	6	14	20	8	4	0	1	1	4
94-95	Rangers	NHL	46	11	12	23	26	10	3	2	5	6
95-96	Pittsburgh	NHL	80	45	54	99	68	18	10	10	20	16
96-97	Pittsburgh	NHL	74	33	38	71	66	5	1	2	3	12
97-98	Las Vegas	IHL	3	3	3	6	4	—	—	—	—	—
98-99	Rangers	NHL	56	20	27	47	50	—	—	—	—	—
98-99	Las Vegas	IHL	13	8	10	18	32	—	—	—	—	—
	NHL	Totaks	497	178	206	384	370	65	17	23	40	56
	IHL	Totals	16	11	13	24	36	—	—	—	—	—

Born; 12/9/71, Liberec, Czechoslovakia. 6-3, 195. Drafted by Vancouver Canucks (1st choice, 2nd overall) in 1990 Entry Draft. Signed as a free agent by St. Louis Blues (3/5/94). Traded to New York Rangers by St. Louis for Esa Tikkanen and Doug Lidster (7/24/94). Traded to Pittsburgh Penguins by Rangers with Sergei Zubov for Luc Robitaille and Ulf Samuelsson (8/31/95). Traded to Rangers by Pittsburgh with Sean Pronger and Chris Tamer for Harry York, Alexei Kovalev and cash (11/25/98). Last amateur club; Seattle (WHL).

Zdenek Nedved — Right Wing

Regular Season / Playoffs

Season	Team	League	GP	G	A	PTS	PIM	GP	G	A	PTS	PIM
94-95	Sudbury	OHL	59	47	51	98	36	18	12	16	28	16
94-95	Toronto	NHL	1	0	0	0	2	—	—	—	—	—
95-96	Toronto	NHL	7	1	1	2	6	—	—	—	—	—
95-96	St. John's	AHL	41	13	14	27	22	4	2	0	2	0
96-97	Toronto	NHL	23	3	5	8	6	—	—	—	—	—
96-97	St. John's	AHL	51	9	25	34	34	7	2	2	4	6
97-98	Long Beach	IHL	19	3	8	11	18	—	—	—	—	—
97-98	St. John's	AHL	45	7	8	15	24	3	1	0	1	2
98-99	Lukko Rauma	Finland	30	4	7	11	22	—	—	—	—	—
	NHL	Totals	31	4	6	10	14	—	—	—	—	—
	AHL	Totals	137	29	47	76	80	14	5	2	7	8

Born; 3/3/75, Lany, Czechoslovakia. 6-0, 180. Drafted by Toronto Maple Leafs (3rd choice, 123rd overall) in 1993 Entry Draft. Last amateur club; Sudbury

Chris Neil — Right Wing

Regular Season / Playoffs

Season	Team	League	GP	G	A	PTS	PIM	GP	G	A	PTS	PIM
98-99	North Bay	OHL	66	26	46	72	215	4	1	0	1	15
98-99	Muskegon	UHL	1	1	1	2	0	18	1	3	4	61

Born; 6/18/79, Flesherton, Ontario. 6-1, 203. Drafted by Ottawa Senators (7th choice, 161st overall) in 1999 Entry Draft. Traded to Muskegon by Flint with Kevin Boyd for Mike Bondy (3/99). Member of 1998-99 UHL Champion Muskegon Fury. Last amateur club; North Bay (OHL).

Wesley Neild — Left Wing/Defenseman

Regular Season / Playoffs

Season	Team	League	GP	G	A	PTS	PIM	GP	G	A	PTS	PIM
98-99	Memphis	CHL	4	0	1	1	2	—	—	—	—	—
98-99	Flint	UHL	7	0	0	0	2	—	—	—	—	—

Born; 2/25/77, Peterborough, Ontario. 6-0, 200.

Andrew Neilson — Goaltender

Regular Season / Playoffs

Season	Team	League	GP	W	L	T	MIN	SO	AVG	GP	W	L	MIN	SO	AVG
98-99	Amarillo	WPHL	1	1	0	0	60	0	3.00	—	—	—	—	—	—

Born; 12/3/68, Calgary, Alberta. 5-11, 175.

Dave Neilson — Left Wing

Regular Season / Playoffs

Season	Team	League	GP	G	A	PTS	PIM	GP	G	A	PTS	PIM
93-94	Las Vegas	IHL	12	1	3	4	14	—	—	—	—	—
94-95	Las Vegas	IHL	13	0	1	1	51	—	—	—	—	—
94-95	Knoxville	ECHL	33	11	14	25	129	—	—	—	—	—
95-96	Saint John	AHL	13	1	1	2	80	—	—	—	—	—
95-96	Cape Breton	AHL	47	7	10	17	121	—	—	—	—	—
96-97	Knoxville	ECHL	35	12	29	41	98	—	—	—	—	—
96-97	Louisiana	ECHL	30	5	12	17	102	13	1	2	3	38
97-98	Wheeling	ECHL	4	0	1	1	9	—	—	—	—	—
97-98	Baton Rouge	ECHL	6	0	3	3	19	—	—	—	—	—
98-99	Shreveport	WPHL	20	8	6	14	63	—	—	—	—	—
98-99	Columbus	CHL	50	22	26	48	122	10	5	1	6	13
	AHL	Totals	60	8	11	19	201	—	—	—	—	—
	IHL	Totals	25	1	4	5	65	—	—	—	—	—
	ECHL	Totals	108	28	59	87	357	13	1	2	3	38

Born; 1/25/71, Long Island, New York. 6-3, 215. Drafted by Vancouver Canucks (8th choice, 183rd overall) in 1991 Entry Draft. Traded to Baton Rouge by Wheeling with Rob McCaig for future considerations (10/97). Signed as a free agent by Las Vegas (3/19/94).

Chad Nelson — Defenseman
Regular Season / Playoffs

Season	Team	League	GP	G	A	PTS	PIM	GP	G	A	PTS	PIM
93-94	West Palm Beach	SUN	18	1	6	7	30	—	—	—	—	—
94-95												
95-96	Charlotte	ECHL	33	5	7	12	162	—	—	—	—	—
95-96	Louisiana	ECHL	19	0	3	3	89	3	0	0	0	27
96-97	Louisiana	ECHL	10	0	3	3	54	—	—	—	—	—
96-97	Wheeling	ECHL	25	1	3	4	79	—	—	—	—	—
96-97	Charlotte	ECHL	21	3	2	5	97	3	0	1	1	6
96-97	San Diego	WCHL	—	—	—	—	—	3	0	1	1	21
97-98	Charlotte	ECHL	2	1	0	1	7	—	—	—	—	—
97-98	Louisiana	ECHL	31	3	6	9	139	—	—	—	—	—
98-99	Louisiana	ECHL	15	2	0	2	73	—	—	—	—	—
98-99	Jacksonville	ECHL	12	2	0	2	57	—	—	—	—	—
	ECHL	Totals	168	17	24	41	757	6	0	1	1	33

Born; 6/3/74, Cranbrook, British Columbia. Member of 1996-97 WCHL Champion San Diego Gulls.

Chris Nelson — Defenseman
Regular Season / Playoffs

Season	Team	League	GP	G	A	PTS	PIM	GP	G	A	PTS	PIM
92-93	Utica	AHL	21	1	1	2	20	1	0	0	0	2
92-93	Cincinnati	IHL	58	4	26	30	69	—	—	—	—	—
93-94	Albany	AHL	7	0	2	2	4	—	—	—	—	—
93-94	Raleigh	ECHL	22	3	5	8	49	—	—	—	—	—
93-94	Erie	ECHL	26	2	13	15	53	—	—	—	—	—
94-95	Atlanta	IHL	49	0	9	9	46	—	—	—	—	—
94-95	Nashville	ECHL	21	3	11	14	46	—	—	—	—	—
95-96	Fresno	WCHL	24	4	7	11	36	7	0	3	3	37
97-98	Fresno	WCHL	33	3	9	12	63	—	—	—	—	—
98-99	Tacoma	WCHL	39	6	8	14	31	7	0	1	1	6
	IHL	Totals	107	4	35	39	115	—	—	—	—	—
	AHL	Totals	28	1	3	4	24	1	0	0	0	2
	WCHL	Totals	96	13	24	37	130	14	0	4	4	43
	ECHL	Totals	69	8	29	37	148	—	—	—	—	—

Born; 2/12/69, Philadelphia, Pennsylvania. 6-2, 190. Drafted by New Jersey Devils (6th choice, 96th overall) in 1988 Entry Draft. Member of 1998-99 WCHL Champion Tacoma Sabercats. Last amateur club; Wisconsin (WCHA).

Craig Nelson — Defenseman
Regular Season / Playoffs

Season	Team	League	GP	G	A	PTS	PIM	GP	G	A	PTS	PIM
97-98	Louisville	ECHL	64	3	18	21	62	—	—	—	—	—
98-99	Monroe	WPHL	58	6	13	19	48	6	0	0	0	2

Born; 7/8/76, Brampton, Ontario. 6-2, 200.

Jeff Nelson — Center
Regular Season / Playoffs

Season	Team	League	GP	G	A	PTS	PIM	GP	G	A	PTS	PIM
92-93	Baltimore	AHL	72	14	38	52	12	7	1	3	4	2
93-94	Portland	AHL	80	34	73	107	92	17	10	5	15	20
94-95	Washington	NHL	10	1	0	1	2	—	—	—	—	—
94-95	Portland	AHL	64	33	50	83	57	7	1	4	5	8
95-96	Washington	NHL	33	0	7	7	16	3	0	0	0	4
95-96	Portland	AHL	39	15	32	47	62	—	—	—	—	—
96-97	Grand Rapids	IHL	82	34	55	89	85	5	0	4	4	4
97-98	Milwaukee	IHL	52	20	34	54	30	10	2	7	9	15
98-99	Nashville	NHL	9	2	1	3	2	—	—	—	—	—
98-99	Milwaukee	IHL	70	20	31	51	66	2	0	0	0	0
	NHL	Totals	52	3	8	11	20	3	0	0	0	4
	AHL	Totals	255	96	193	289	223	31	12	12	24	30
	IHL	Totals	204	74	120	194	181	17	2	11	13	19

Born; 12/18/72, Prince Albert, Sakatchewan. 6-0, 180. Drafted by Washington Capitals (4th choice, 36th overall) in 1991 Entry Draft. Traded to Nashville Predators by Washington for future considerations (8/19/98). Traded to Washington by Nashville for future considerations (6/22/99). Member of 1993-94 AHL champion Portland Pirates. Last amateur club; Prince Albert (WHL).

John Nelson — Right Wing
Regular Season / Playoffs

Season	Team	League	GP	G	A	PTS	PIM	GP	G	A	PTS	PIM
95-96	St. John's	AHL	3	0	0	0	2	—	—	—	—	—
96-97	Port Huron	CoHL	58	30	39	69	166	5	2	0	2	16
97-98	Port Huron	UHL	20	5	16	21	36	—	—	—	—	—
97-98	Saginaw	UHL	16	4	13	17	69	—	—	—	—	—
98-99	Winston-Salem	UHL	12	2	3	5	67	—	—	—	—	—
98-99	Saginaw	UHL	34	7	18	25	93	—	—	—	—	—
	UHL	Totals	140	48	89	137	431	5	2	0	2	16

Born; 7/9/69, Scarborough, Ontario. Drafted by Buffalo Sabres (10th choice, 203rd overall) in 1989 Entry Draft. Traded to Saginaw by Winston-Salem with Kevin Tucker and Brian Kreft for Marc Delorme (1/99). Played in goal for seven minutes for Winston-Salem. Nelson faced two shots, saved one and posted a GAA of 8.57. Last amateur club; Prince Edward Island (AUAA).

Todd Nelson — Defenseman
Regular Season / Playoffs

Season	Team	League	GP	G	A	PTS	PIM	GP	G	A	PTS	PIM
90-91	Muskegon	IHL	79	4	20	24	32	3	0	0	0	4
91-92	Pittsburgh	NHL	1	0	0	0	0	—	—	—	—	—
91-92	Muskegon	IHL	80	6	35	41	46	14	1	11	12	4
92-93	Cleveland	IHL	76	7	35	42	115	4	0	2	2	4
93-94	Washington	NHL	2	1	0	1	2	4	0	0	0	0
93-94	Portland	AHL	80	11	34	45	69	11	0	6	6	6
94-95	Portland	AHL	75	10	35	45	76	7	0	4	4	6
95-96	Hershey	AHL	70	10	40	50	38	5	1	2	3	8
96-97	Grand Rapids	IHL	81	3	18	21	32	5	1	0	1	0
97-98	Grand Rapids	IHL	75	6	21	27	36	3	0	0	0	2
98-99	Berlin	Germany	44	5	10	15	26	—	—	—	—	—
	NHL	Totals	3	1	0	1	2	4	0	0	0	0
	IHL	Totals	310	26	129	155	261	29	2	13	15	14
	AHL	Totals	225	31	109	140	183	23	1	12	13	20

Born; 5/15/69, Prince Albert, Saskatchewan. 6-0, 200. Drafted by Pittsburgh Penguins (4th choice, 79th overall) in 1989 Entry Draft. Signed as a free agent by Washington Capitals (8/15/93). Member of 1993-94 AHL Champion Portland Pirates. Signed as a free agent by Grand Rapids Griffins (7/96). Last amateur club; Prince Albert (WHL).

Jan Nemecek — Defenseman
Regular Season / Playoffs

Season	Team	League	GP	G	A	PTS	PIM	GP	G	A	PTS	PIM
96-97	Phoenix	IHL	24	1	1	2	2	—	—	—	—	—
96-97	Mississippi	ECHL	20	3	9	12	16	3	0	0	0	4
97-98	Fredericton	AHL	65	7	24	31	43	2	0	0	0	0
98-99	Los Angeles	NHL	6	1	0	1	4	—	—	—	—	—
98-99	Long Beach	IHL	66	5	16	21	42	—	—	—	—	—
	IHL	Totals	90	6	17	23	44	—	—	—	—	—

Born; 2/14/76, Pisek, Czechoslovakia. 6-1, 194. Drafted by Los Angeles Kings (7th choice, 215th overall) in 1994 Entry Draft. Last amateur club; Hull

Tom Nemeth — Defenseman
Regular Season / Playoffs

Season	Team	League	GP	G	A	PTS	PIM	GP	G	A	PTS	PIM
92-93	Kalamazoo	IHL	48	6	13	19	24	—	—	—	—	—
92-93	Dayton	ECHL	26	9	28	37	14	—	—	—	—	—
93-94	Dayton	ECHL	66	16	82	98	91	3	1	1	2	16
94-95	Rochester	AHL	56	4	17	21	32	4	2	1	3	4
94-95	South Carolina	ECHL	5	3	3	6	2	—	—	—	—	—
95-96	DNP	Injured										
96-97	Dayton	ECHL	23	4	19	23	15	4	2	1	3	2
97-98	Fort Wayne	IHL	24	3	3	6	12	—	—	—	—	—
97-98	Rochester	AHL	11	0	3	3	6	—	—	—	—	—
97-98	Dayton	ECHL	31	8	24	32	19	—	—	—	—	—
98-99	Cincinnati	IHL	36	9	6	15	16	3	0	0	0	4
98-99	Dayton	ECHL	43	13	23	36	28	—	—	—	—	—
	IHL	Totals	108	18	22	40	52	3	0	0	0	4
	AHL	Totals	67	4	20	24	38	4	2	1	3	4
	ECHL	Totals	194	53	179	232	169	7	3	2	5	18

Born; 1/16/71, St. Catharines, Ontario. Drafted by Minnesota North Stars (8th choice, 206th overall) in 1991 Entry Draft. 1993-94 ECHL First All-Star Team. 1993-94 ECHL Outstanding Defenseman. Last amateur club; Cornwall (OHL).

David Nemirovsky — Right Wing

Regular Season / Playoffs

Season	Team	League	GP	G	A	PTS	PIM	GP	G	A	PTS	PIM
95-96	Sarnia	OHL	26	18	27	45	14	10	8	8	16	6
95-96	Florida	NHL	9	0	2	2	0	—	—	—	—	—
95-96	Carolina	AHL	5	1	2	3	0	—	—	—	—	—
96-97	Florida	NHL	39	7	7	14	32	3	1	0	1	0
96-97	Carolina	AHL	34	21	21	42	18	—	—	—	—	—
97-98	Florida	NHL	41	9	12	21	8	—	—	—	—	—
97-98	New Haven	AHL	29	10	15	25	10	1	1	0	1	0
98-99	Florida	NHL	2	0	1	1	0	—	—	—	—	—
98-99	Fort Wayne	IHL	44	22	13	35	24	—	—	—	—	—
98-99	St. John's	AHL	22	3	9	12	18	5	4	1	5	0
	NHL	Totals	91	16	22	38	40	3	1	0	1	0
	AHL	Totals	90	35	47	82	46	6	5	1	6	0

Born; 8/1/76, Toronto, Ontario. 6-1, 192. Drafted by Florida Panthers (5th choice, 84th overall) in 1994 Entry Draft. Traded to Toronto Maple Leafs by Florida for Jeff Ware (2/17/99). Last amateur club; Sarnia (OHL).

Mikhail Nemirovsky — Right Wing

Regular Season / Playoffs

Season	Team	League	GP	G	A	PTS	PIM	GP	G	A	PTS	PIM
94-95	Tallahassee	ECHL	6	0	2	2	0	—	—	—	—	—
94-95	Hampton Roads	ECHL	29	6	14	20	33	4	2	0	2	4
95-96	Flint	CoHL	65	29	52	81	121	14	5	10	15	10
96-97	Fredericton	AHL	7	1	0	1	0	—	—	—	—	—
96-97	Fort Wayne	IHL	16	2	4	6	18	—	—	—	—	—
96-97	Madison	CoHL	18	7	15	22	22	—	—	—	—	—
96-97	Flint	CoHL	3	0	5	5	2	9	4	5	9	24
97-98	New Orleans	ECHL	43	19	22	41	55	—	—	—	—	—
97-98	Charlotte	ECHL	25	7	17	24	40	—	—	—	—	—
98-99	Bracknell	BSL	12	1	3	4	8	7	1	4	5	0
98-99	Flint	UHL	40	17	16	33	28	—	—	—	—	—
	UHL	Totals	126	53	88	141	173	23	9	15	24	34
	ECHL	Totals	103	32	55	87	128	4	2	0	2	4

Born; 9/30/74, Moscow, Russia. 6-0, 190. Traded to Charlotte by New Orleans with Pierre Gendron for Dean Moore and Stephane Soulliere (2/98). Member of 1995-96 Colonial Cup Champion Flint Generals. Last amateur club; Newmarket

Pavel Nestak — Goaltender

Regular Season / Playoffs

Season	Team	League	GP	W	L	T	MIN	SO	AVG	GP	W	L	MIN	SO	AVG
98-99	Johnstown	ECHL	19	7	9	2	1061	2	3.68	—	—	—	—	—	—

Born; Last overseas club; Slezan Opava (Czech Republic).

Perry Neufeld — Right Wing

Regular Season / Playoffs

Season	Team	League	GP	G	A	PTS	PIM	GP	G	A	PTS	PIM
97-98	Shreveport	WPHL	58	23	37	60	55	8	0	5	5	8
98-99	Shreveport	WPHL	68	23	43	66	27	12	2	3	5	6
	WPHL	Totals	126	46	80	126	82	20	2	8	10	14

Born; 7/23/69, Lethbridge, Ontario. 6-2, 200. Member of 1998-99 WPHL Champion Shreveport Mudbugs.

Troy Neumeier — Defenseman

Regular Season / Playoffs

Season	Team	League	GP	G	A	PTS	PIM	GP	G	A	PTS	PIM
90-91	Prince Albert	WHL	72	6	27	33	56	3	0	0	0	0
90-91	Milwaukee	IHL	6	0	0	0	2	—	—	—	—	—
91-92	Milwaukee	IHL	72	1	9	10	55	3	0	0	0	0
92-93	Hamilton	AHL	79	3	11	14	73	—	—	—	—	—
93-94	Hamilton	AHL	44	1	7	8	21	—	—	—	—	—
93-94	Columbus	ECHL	2	0	2	2	2	—	—	—	—	—
94-95	Adirondack	AHL	60	4	17	21	26	4	0	0	0	2
94-95	Toledo	ECHL	10	0	5	5	18	—	—	—	—	—
95-96	Adirondack	AHL	16	0	3	3	10	—	—	—	—	—
95-96	Cape Breton	AHL	34	1	3	4	12	—	—	—	—	—
96-97	Hamilton	AHL	63	1	8	9	32	9	1	1	2	4
97-98	Manchester	BSL	53	3	15	18	48	9	0	2	2	4
98-99	Manchester	BSL	52	7	20	27	50	4	0	1	1	8
	AHL	Totals	296	10	49	59	174	13	1	1	2	6
	IHL	Totals	78	1	9	10	57	3	0	0	0	0
	ECHL	Totals	12	0	7	7	20	—	—	—	—	—
	BSL	Totals	105	10	35	45	98	13	0	3	3	12

Born; 9/3/70, Langenburg, Minnesota. 6-2, 195. Drafted by Vancouver Canucks (9th choice, 191st overall) in 1990 Entry Draft. Last amateur club; Prince Albert

Chris Newans — Defenseman

Regular Season / Playoffs

Season	Team	League	GP	G	A	PTS	PIM	GP	G	A	PTS	PIM
91-92	Raleigh	ECHL	13	5	4	9	26	—	—	—	—	—
91-92	Dayton	ECHL	23	4	8	12	42	—	—	—	—	—
91-92	Nashville	ECHL	9	6	5	11	16	—	—	—	—	—
91-92	Michigan	CoHL	8	2	6	8	8	—	—	—	—	—
92-93												
93-94	West Palm Beach	SUN	32	17	25	42	108	5	1	6	7	10
94-95	Saginaw	CoHL	6	4	1	5	27	—	—	—	—	—
94-95	West Palm Beach	SUN	11	4	6	10	33	5	4	4	8	16
95-96	Jacksonville	SHL	26	13	27	40	128	—	—	—	—	—
96-97	Anchorage	WCHL	60	26	57	83	331	9	2	7	9	46
97-98	Anchorage	WCHL	56	24	40	64	287	3	1	0	1	25
98-99	Fort Wayne	IHL	11	0	3	3	7	—	—	—	—	—
98-99	Asheville	UHL	21	6	19	25	81	—	—	—	—	—
98-99	Madison	UHL	18	2	7	9	27	—	—	—	—	—
98-99	Flint	UHL	7	0	3	3	22	4	1	4	5	12
	WCHL	Totals	116	50	97	147	618	12	3	7	10	71
	SHL	Totals	69	34	58	92	269	10	5	10	15	26
	UHL	Totals	52	12	30	42	157	4	1	4	5	12
	ECHL	Totals	45	15	17	32	84	—	—	—	—	—
	CoHL	Totals	14	6	7	13	35	—	—	—	—	—

Born; 10/6/69, Dauphin, Manitoba. 5-10, 175. 1996-97 WCHL Second Team All-Star. 1997-98 WCHL Second Team All-Star. Member of 1993-94 Sunshine Champion West Palm Beach Blaze. Member of 1994-95 Sunshine League Champion West Palm Beach Blaze. Traded to Madison by Asheville with Jeff Smith for Jason Dexter and Jeff Foster (1/99). Traded to Port Huron by Madison for Wayne Muir (3/99). Traded to Flint by Port Huron for Jeff Smith and Jamie

Ron Newhook — Center

Regular Season / Playoffs

Season	Team	League	GP	G	A	PTS	PIM	GP	G	A	PTS	PIM
96-97	London	OHL	67	28	33	61	41	—	—	—	—	—
96-97	Toledo	ECHL	9	1	9	10	2	5	2	0	2	0
97-98	Toledo	ECHL	59	10	11	21	42	—	—	—	—	—
98-99	Waco	WPHL	67	13	37	50	68	4	0	1	1	2
	ECHL	Totals	68	11	20	31	44	5	2	0	2	0

Born; 9/8/77, Worth Bay, Ontario. 5-5, 155. Last amateur club; London (OHL).

Todd Newton — Defenseman

Regular Season / Playoffs

Season	Team	League	GP	G	A	PTS	PIM	GP	G	A	PTS	PIM
96-97	Quad City	CoHL	69	4	16	20	131	—	—	—	—	—
97-98	Waco	WPHL	16	2	7	9	14	—	—	—	—	—
97-98	Fayetteville	CHL	11	0	3	3	24	—	—	—	—	—
97-98	Wichita	CHL	22	3	4	7	56	—	—	—	—	—
97-98	Binghamton	UHL	8	0	0	0	13	—	—	—	—	—
97-98	Madison	UHL	7	0	0	0	19	1	0	0	0	0
98-99	Waco	WPHL	5	0	0	0	17	—	—	—	—	—
98-99	Alexandria	WPHL	5	0	2	2	2	—	—	—	—	—
98-99	San Angelo	WPHL	45	3	11	14	66	9	0	0	0	11
	UHL	Totals	84	4	16	20	163	1	0	0	0	0
	WPHL	Totals	71	5	20	25	99	9	0	0	0	11
	CHL	Totals	33	3	7	10	80	—	—	—	—	—

Born; 12/9/75, St. Catharines, Ontario. 6-1, 220.

Rick Nichol — Goaltender

Regular Season / Playoffs

Season	Team	League	GP	W	L	T	MIN	SO	AVG	GP	W	L	MIN	SO	AVG
96-97	Oklahoma City	CeHL	23	15	3	1	1216	1	3.11	—	—	—	—	—	—
96-97	Columbus	CeHL	10	4	3	1	460	0	4.95	2	0	1	77	0	4.68
97-98	Waco	WPHL	7	2	5	0	371	0	5.33	—	—	—	—	—	—
97-98	Phoenix	WCHL	5	3	0	1	259	0	3.01	2	0	0	49	0	2.45
98-99	Tupelo	WPHL	2	0	2	0	100	0	4.82	—	—	—	—	—	—
98-99	Augusta	ECHL	1	0	0	0	11	0	0.00	—	—	—	—	—	—
98-99	Dayton	ECHL	3	0	1	1	164	0	4.46	—	—	—	—	—	—
98-99	Tallahassee	ECHL	5	0	1	0	144	0	4.17	—	—	—	—	—	—
	CeHL	Totals	33	19	6	1	1676	1	3.62	2	0	1	77	0	4.68
	WPHL	Totals	9	2	7	0	471	0	5.22	—	—	—	—	—	—
	ECHL	Totals	9	0	2	1	319	0	4.17	—	—	—	—	—	—

Born; 3/13/71, Calgary, Alberta. 5-10, 160. Last amateur club; Northern Alberta Institute (CIAU).

Scott Nichol — Center

Regular Season / Playoffs

Season	Team	League	GP	G	A	PTS	PIM	GP	G	A	PTS	PIM
94-95	Rochester	AHL	71	11	16	27	136	5	0	3	3	14
95-96	Buffalo	NHL	2	0	0	0	10	—	—	—	—	—
95-96	Rochester	AHL	62	14	18	32	170	19	7	6	13	36
96-97	Rochester	AHL	68	22	21	43	133	10	2	1	3	26
97-98	Buffalo	NHL	3	0	0	0	4	—	—	—	—	—
97-98	Rochester	AHL	35	13	7	20	113	—	—	—	—	—
98-99	Rochester	AHL	53	13	20	33	120	—	—	—	—	—
	NHL	Totlas	5	0	0	0	14	—	—	—	—	—
	AHL	Totals	289	73	82	155	672	34	9	10	19	76

Born; 12/31/74, Edmonton, Alberta. 5-8, 169. Drafted by Buffalo Sabres (9th choice, 272nd overall) in 1993 Entry Draft. Member of 1995-96 AHL champion Rochester Americans. Last amateur club; Portland (WHL).

Mike Nicholishen — Defenseman

Regular Season / Playoffs

Season	Team	League	GP	G	A	PTS	PIM	GP	G	A	PTS	PIM
98-99	Orlando	IHL	45	1	13	14	61	—	—	—	—	—
98-99	Utah	IHL	11	0	1	1	14	—	—	—	—	—
	IHL	Totals	56	1	14	15	75	—	—	—	—	—

Born; 2.28.75, Mississauga, Ontario. 6-1, 212. Last amateur club; Lowell (H.E.).

Brandon Nichols — Defenseman

Regular Season / Playoffs

Season	Team	League	GP	G	A	PTS	PIM	GP	G	A	PTS	PIM
98-99	Tupelo	WPHL	31	3	4	7	2	—	—	—	—	—
98-99	Odessa	WPHL	6	1	1	2	2	—	—	—	—	—
	WPHL	Totals	37	4	5	9	4	—	—	—	—	—

Born; 7/15/77, Edmonton, Alberta. 6-0, 180. Last amateur club; Bow Valley (AJHL).

Mike Nicholson — Left Wing

Regular Season / Playoffs

Season	Team	League	GP	G	A	PTS	PIM	GP	G	A	PTS	PIM
98-99	Wheeling	ECHL	4	0	2	2	0	—	—	—	—	—

Born;

Derek Nicolson — Defenseman

Regular Season / Playoffs

Season	Team	League	GP	G	A	PTS	PIM	GP	G	A	PTS	PIM
95-96	Thunder Bay	CoHL	56	0	5	5	69	—	—	—	—	—
95-96	Quad City	CoHL	14	2	0	2	11	3	0	0	0	5
97-98	Central Texas	WPHL	50	1	9	10	62	—	—	—	—	—
98-99	Central Texas	WPHL	58	2	17	19	58	2	0	0	0	0
	WPHL	Totals	108	3	26	29	120	2	0	0	0	0
	CoHL	Totals	70	2	5	7	80	3	0	0	0	5

Born; 1/1/73, Winnipeg, Manitoba. 6-0, 220. Last amateur club; Ohio State

Erik Nickulas — Right Wing

Regular Season / Playoffs

Season	Team	League	GP	G	A	PTS	PIM	GP	G	A	PTS	PIM
97-98	Orlando	IHL	76	22	9	31	77	6	0	0	0	10
98-99	Boston	NHL	2	0	0	0	0	1	0	0	0	2
98-99	Providence	AHL	75	31	27	58	83	18	8	12	20	33

Born; 3/25/75, Cape Cod, Massachusetts. 5-11, 190. Drafted by Boston Bruins (3rd choice, 99th overall) in 1994 Entry Draft. 1997-98 IHL US Rookie of the Year. Member of 1998-99 AHL Champion Providence Bruins. Last amateur club; New Hampshire (Hockey East).

Barry Nieckar — Left Wing

Regular Season / Playoffs

Season	Team	League	GP	G	A	PTS	PIM	GP	G	A	PTS	PIM
91-92	Phoenix	IHL	5	0	0	0	9	—	—	—	—	—
91-92	Raleigh	ECHL	46	10	18	28	229	4	4	0	4	22
92-93	Hartford	NHL	2	0	0	0	2	—	—	—	—	—
92-93	Springfield	AHL	21	2	4	6	65	6	1	0	1	14
93-94	Springfield	AHL	30	0	2	2	67	—	—	—	—	—
93-94	Raleigh	ECHL	18	4	6	10	126	15	5	7	12	51
94-95	Calgary	NHL	3	0	0	0	12	—	—	—	—	—
94-95	Saint John	AHL	65	8	7	15	*491	4	0	0	0	22
95-96	Utah	IHL	53	9	15	24	194	—	—	—	—	—
95-96	Peoria	IHL	10	3	3	6	72	12	4	6	10	48
96-97	Anaheim	NHL	2	0	0	0	5	—	—	—	—	—
96-97	Long Beach	IHL	63	3	10	13	386	5	0	0	0	22
97-98	Anaheim	NHL	1	0	0	0	2	—	—	—	—	—
97-98	Cincinnati	AHL	75	10	14	24	295	—	—	—	—	—
98-99	Springfield	AHL	67	11	6	17	270	1	0	0	0	2
	NHL	Totals	8	0	0	0	21	—	—	—	—	—
	AHL	Totals	238	31	33	64	1188	11	1	0	1	38
	IHL	Totals	131	15	28	43	661	17	4	6	10	70
	ECHL	Totals	64	14	24	38	355	19	9	7	16	73

Born; 12/16/67, Rama, Saskatchewan. 6-3, 205. Signed as a free agent by Hartford (9/25/92). Signed as a free agent by Calgary (2/11/95). Signed as a free agent by NY Islanders (8/8/95). Signed as a free agent by Anaheim Mighty Ducks (10/2/96). Signed as a free agent by Phoenix Coyotes (8/12/98).

Scott Niedermayer — Defenseman

Regular Season / Playoffs

Season	Team	League	GP	G	A	PTS	PIM	GP	G	A	PTS	PIM
91-92	Kamloops	WHL	35	7	32	39	61	17	9	14	23	28
91-92	New Jersey	NHL	4	0	1	1	2	—	—	—	—	—
92-93	New Jersey	NHL	80	11	29	40	47	5	0	3	3	2
93-94	New Jersey	NHL	81	10	36	46	42	20	2	2	4	8
94-95	New Jersey	NHL	48	4	15	19	18	20	4	7	11	10
95-96	New Jersey	NHL	79	8	25	33	46	—	—	—	—	—
96-97	New Jersey	NHL	81	5	30	35	64	10	2	4	6	6
97-98	New Jersey	NHL	81	14	43	57	27	6	0	2	2	4
98-99	New Jersey	NHL	72	11	35	46	26	7	1	3	4	18
98-99	Utah	IHL	5	0	2	2	0	—	—	—	—	—
	NHL	Totals	526	63	214	277	272	68	9	21	30	48

Born; 8/31/73, Edmonton, Alberta. 6-0, 205. Drafted by New Jersey Devils (1st choice, 3rd overall) in 1991 Entry Draft. 1992-93 NHL All-Rookie Team. 1997-98 NHL Second Team All-Star. Member of 1994-95 Stanley Cup Champion New Jersey Devils. Last amateur club; Kamloops (WHL).

Pasi Nielikainen — Forward

Regular Season — Playoffs

Season	Team	League	GP	G	A	PTS	PIM	GP	G	A	PTS	PIM
98-99	Miami	ECHL	39	5	6	11	40	—	—	—	—	—

Born; Selected by Tallahassee in 1999 ECHL Dispersal Draft.

Kirk Nielsen — Right Wing

Regular Season — Playoffs

Season	Team	League	GP	G	A	PTS	PIM	GP	G	A	PTS	PIM
96-97	Providence	AHL	68	12	23	35	30	9	2	1	3	2
97-98	Boston	NHL	6	0	0	0	0	—	—	—	—	—
97-98	Providence	AHL	72	19	29	48	40	—	—	—	—	—
98-99	Cincinnati	IHL	82	12	22	34	58	3	0	0	0	4
	AHL	Totals	140	31	52	83	70	9	2	1	3	2

Born; 10/19/73, Grand Rapids, Minnesota. 6-1, 190. Drafted by Philadelphia Flyers (1st choice, 10th overall) in 1994 Supplemental Draft. Signed as a free agent by Boston Bruins (6/7/96). Last amateur club; Harvard (ECAC).

Ville Nieminen — Left Wing

Regular Season — Playoffs

Season	Team	League	GP	G	A	PTS	PIM	GP	G	A	PTS	PIM
97-98	Hershey	AHL	74	14	22	36	85	—	—	—	—	—
98-99	Hershey	AHL	67	24	19	43	127	3	0	1	1	0
	AHL	Totals	141	38	41	79	212	3	0	1	1	0

Born; 4/6/77, Tampere, Finland. 5-11, 205. Drafted by Colorado Avalanche (4th choice, 78th overall) in 1997 Entry Draft. Last European club; Tappara (Finland)

Kraig Nienhuis — Left Wing

Regular Season — Playoffs

Season	Team	League	GP	G	A	PTS	PIM	GP	G	A	PTS	PIM
85-86	Boston	NHL	70	16	14	30	37	2	0	0	0	14
86-87	Boston	NHL	16	4	2	6	2	—	—	—	—	—
86-87	Moncton	AHL	54	10	17	27	44	—	—	—	—	—
87-88	Boston	NHL	1	0	0	0	0	—	—	—	—	—
87-88	Maine	AHL	36	16	17	33	57	—	—	—	—	—
88-89	Canada	National	4	0	0	0	12	—	—	—	—	—
88-89	Kaufbeuren	Germany	35	23	28	51	60	12	15	18	33	30
89-90												
90-91	Albany	IHL	3	3	1	4	0	—	—	—	—	—
91-92												
92-93												
93-94												
94-95												
95-96												
96-97	Berlin	Germany	48	12	22	34	79	8	0	0	0	10
97-98	Nottingham	BSL	54	25	28	53	45	6	0	5	5	8
98-99	Milan	Italy										
98-99	Port Huron	UHL	29	15	22	37	12	7	3	4	7	4
	NHL	Totals	87	20	16	36	39	2	0	0	0	14
	AHL	Totals	90	26	34	60	101	—	—	—	—	—

Born; 5/9/61, Sarnia, Ontario. 6-2, 205. Signed as a free agent by Boston Bruins (5/28/85). Last amateur club; RPI (ECAC).

Jiro Nihei — Goaltender

Regular Season — Playoffs

Season	Team	League	GP	W	L	T	MIN	SO	AVG	GP	W	L	MIN	SO	AVG
98-99	Tupelo	WPHL	12	3	7	0	565	0	4.99	—	—	—	—	—	—

Born; 3/9/71

Igor Nikulin — Right Wing

Regular Season — Playoffs

Season	Team	League	GP	G	A	PTS	PIM	GP	G	A	PTS	PIM
95-96	Cherepovets	CIS	47	20	13	33	28	4	1	0	1	0
95-96	Baltimore	AHL	4	2	2	4	2	—	—	—	—	—
96-97	Anaheim	NHL	—	—	—	—	—	1	0	0	0	0
96-97	Baltimore	AHL	61	27	25	52	14	3	2	1	3	2
96-97	Fort Wayne	IHL	10	1	2	3	4	—	—	—	—	—
97-98	Cincinnati	AHL	54	14	11	25	40	—	—	—	—	—
98-99	Cincinnati	AHL	74	18	26	44	26	3	0	1	1	4
	AHL	Totals	193	61	64	125	82	6	2	2	4	6

Born; 8/26/72, Cherepovets, USSR. 6-1, 190. Drafted by Anaheim Mighty Ducks (4th choice, 107th overall) in 1995 Entry Draft.

Marcus Nilson — Right Wing

Regular Season — Playoffs

Season	Team	League	GP	G	A	PTS	PIM	GP	G	A	PTS	PIM
98-99	Fresno	WCHL	2	0	0	0	2	—	—	—	—	—
98-99	Topeka	CHL	3	0	0	0	2	—	—	—	—	—

Born; 3/8/78, Balsta, Sweden. 6-2, 193.

Marcus Nilsson — Right Wing

Regular Season — Playoffs

Season	Team	League	GP	G	A	PTS	PIM	GP	G	A	PTS	PIM
98-99	Florida	NHL	8	1	1	2	5	—	—	—	—	—
98-99	New Haven	AHL	69	8	25	33	10	—	—	—	—	—

Born; 3/1/78, Stockholm, Sweden. 6-1, 183. Drafted by Florida Panthers (1st choice, 20th overall) in 1996 Entry Draft. Last European club; Djurgarden

Erik Noack — Defenseman

Regular Season — Playoffs

Season	Team	League	GP	G	A	PTS	PIM	GP	G	A	PTS	PIM
97-98	R.I.T.	NCAA 3	30	3	4	7	—	—	—	—	—	—
97-98	Roanoke	ECHL	3	0	0	0	0	—	—	—	—	—
98-99	Abilene	WPHL	49	0	5	5	25	2	0	0	0	0

Born; 4/23/73, Barrington, Rhode Island. 6-0, 210. Last amateur club; Rochester Institute of Technology. (NCAA 3).

Steve Noble — Forward

Regular Season — Playoffs

Season	Team	League	GP	G	A	PTS	PIM	GP	G	A	PTS	PIM
97-98	Fort Worth	CHL	9	0	0	0	6	—	—	—	—	—

Born; 8/17/76, Sault Ste. Marie, Ontario. 6-1, 185. Drafted by St. Louis Blues (5th choice, 198th overall) in 1994 Entry Draft. Last amateur club; Notre Dame

Tom Noble — Goaltender

Regular Season — Playoffs

Season	Team	League	GP	W	L	T	MIN	SO	AVG	GP	W	L	MIN	SO	AVG
98-99	Pensacola	ECHL	25	8	15	1	1380	1	4.26	—	—	—	—	—	—

Born; 3/21/75, Hanover, Massachusetts. 5-10, 165. Last amateur club; Boston University (Hockey East).

Tom Nolan — Center

Regular Season — Playoffs

Season	Team	League	GP	G	A	PTS	PIM	GP	G	A	PTS	PIM
97-98	New Hampshire	N.E.	37	18	41	59	73	—	—	—	—	—
97-98	Springfield	AHL	1	0	0	0	0	—	—	—	—	—
98-99	Grand Rapids	IHL	6	0	1	1	2	—	—	—	—	—
98-99	Houston	IHL	8	0	0	0	2	—	—	—	—	—
98-99	Austin	WPHL	4	2	6	8	2	—	—	—	—	—
98-99	Mobile	ECHL	42	18	17	35	44	2	0	0	0	10
	IHL	Totals	14	0	1	1	4	—	—	—	—	—

Born; 9/3/73, Springfield, Massachusetts. 5-01, 175. Last amateur club; New Hampshire (Hockey East).

Brian Noonan — Right Wing

Regular Season / Playoffs

Season	Team	League	GP	G	A	PTS	PIM	GP	G	A	PTS	PIM
85-86	Nova Scotia	AHL	2	0	0	0	0	—	—	—	—	—
85-86	Saginaw	IHL	76	39	39	78	69	11	6	3	9	6
86-87	Nova Scotia	AHL	70	25	26	51	30	5	3	1	4	4
87-88	Chicago	NHL	77	10	20	30	44	3	0	0	0	4
88-89	Chicago	NHL	45	4	12	16	28	1	0	0	0	0
88-89	Saginaw	IHL	19	18	13	31	36	1	0	0	0	0
89-90	Chicago	NHL	8	0	2	2	6	—	—	—	—	—
89-90	Indianapolis	IHL	56	40	36	76	85	14	6	9	15	20
90-91	Chicago	NHL	7	0	4	4	2	—	—	—	—	—
90-91	Indianapolis	IHL	59	38	53	91	67	7	6	4	10	18
91-92	Chicago	NHL	65	19	12	31	81	18	6	9	15	30
92-93	Chicago	NHL	63	16	14	30	82	4	3	0	3	4
93-94	Chicago	NHL	64	14	21	35	57	—	—	—	—	—
93-94	Rangers	NHL	12	4	2	6	12	22	4	7	11	17
94-95	Rangers	NHL	45	14	13	27	26	5	0	0	0	8
95-96	St. Louis	NHL	81	13	22	35	84	13	4	1	5	10
96-97	St. Louis	NHL	13	2	5	7	0	—	—	—	—	—
96-97	Rangers	NHL	44	6	9	15	28	—	—	—	—	—
96-97	Vancouver	NHL	16	4	8	12	6	—	—	—	—	—
97-98	Vancouver	NHL	82	10	15	25	62	—	—	—	—	—
98-99	Indianapolis	IHL	65	19	44	63	128	—	—	—	—	—
98-99	Phoenix	NHL	7	0	0	0	0	5	0	2	2	4
	NHL	Totals	629	116	159	275	518	71	17	19	36	77
	IHL	Totals	275	154	185	339	385	33	18	16	34	44
	AHL	Totals	72	25	26	51	30	5	3	1	4	4

Born; 5/29/65, Boston, Massachusetts. 6-1, 200. Drafted by Chicago Blackhawks (10th choice, 186th overall) in 1983 Entry Draft. Traded to New York Rangers by Chicago with Stephane Matteau for Tony Amonte and the rights to Matt Oates (3/21/94). Signed as a free agent by St. Louis Blues (7/24/95). Traded to Rangers by St. Louis for Sergio Momesso (11/13/96). Traded to Vancouver Canucks by Rangers with Sergei Nemchinov for Esa Tikkanen and Russ Courtnall (3/8/97). Signed as a free agent by Phoenix Coyotes (3/15/99). 1989-90 IHL First All-Star Team. 1990-91 IHL First Team All-Star. Member of 1989-90 IHL Champion Indianapolis Ice. Member of 1993-94 Stanley Cup Champion New York Rangers. Last amateur club; New Westminster (WHL).

Carlin Nordstrom — Right Wing

Regular Season / Playoffs

Season	Team	League	GP	G	A	PTS	PIM	GP	G	A	PTS	PIM
96-97	Western Michigan	CCHA	34	6	9	15	72	—	—	—	—	—
96-97	Fort Wayne	IHL	9	1	1	2	24	—	—	—	—	—
97-98	Fort Wayne	IHL	23	1	0	1	86	3	0	0	0	18
97-98	Baton Rouge	ECHL	5	0	2	2	21	—	—	—	—	—
98-99	Portland	AHL	10	0	1	1	36	—	—	—	—	—
98-99	Rochester	AHL	11	0	0	0	29	6	0	0	0	18
98-99	Detroit	IHL	3	0	0	0	6	—	—	—	—	—
98-99	Quad City	UHL	3	0	0	0	4	—	—	—	—	—
	IHL	Totals	35	2	1	3	116	3	0	0	0	18
	AHL	Totals	21	0	1	1	65	6	0	0	0	18

Born; 2/20/73, Saskatoon, Saskatchewan. 6-2, 213. Last amateur club; Western Michigan (CCHA).

Peter Nordstrom — Left Wing

Regular Season / Playoffs

Season	Team	League	GP	G	A	PTS	PIM	GP	G	A	PTS	PIM
98-99	Boston	NHL	2	0	0	0	0	—	—	—	—	—
98-99	Providence	AHL	13	2	1	3	2	—	—	—	—	—
98-99	Farjestads	Sweden	21	4	4	8	14	4	1	1	2	2

Born; 7/26/74, Munkfors, Sweden. 6-1, 200. Drafted by Boston Bruins (3rd choice, 78th overall) in 1998 Entry Draft.

Darryl Noren — Center

Regular Season / Playoffs

Season	Team	League	GP	G	A	PTS	PIM	GP	G	A	PTS	PIM
90-91	Albany	IHL	7	0	0	0	2	—	—	—	—	—
90-91	Greensboro	ECHL	43	27	23	50	29	13	2	5	7	18
91-92	New Haven	AHL	34	11	9	20	22	—	—	—	—	—
91-92	Halifax	AHL	3	0	0	0	0	—	—	—	—	—
91-92	Greensboro	ECHL	37	36	52	88	48	—	—	—	—	—
92-93	Halifax	AHL	1	0	0	0	0	—	—	—	—	—
92-93	Greensboro	ECHL	61	35	47	82	119	1	1	0	1	0
93-94	Detroit	CoHL	27	18	39	57	22	—	—	—	—	—
93-94	Greensboro	ECHL	26	16	23	39	41	8	1	3	4	20
94-95	Greensboro	ECHL	17	7	16	23	43	—	—	—	—	—
94-95	Charlotte	ECHL	45	39	25	64	63	3	5	1	6	2
95-96	Charlotte	ECHL	70	43	51	94	83	16	7	9	16	37
96-97	San Antonio	IHL	14	1	2	3	23	2	1	1	2	0
96-97	Charlotte	ECHL	57	25	33	58	57	—	—	—	—	—
97-98	Charlotte	ECHL	57	30	44	74	69	7	2	5	7	2
98-99	Charlotte	ECHL	70	26	50	76	89	—	—	—	—	—
	AHL	Totals	38	11	9	20	22	—	—	—	—	—
	IHL	Totals	21	1	2	3	25	2	1	1	2	0
	ECHL	Totals	483	284	364	648	641	48	18	23	41	79

Born; 8/7/68, Livonia, Michigan. 5-10, 180. ECHL's All-Time Scoring Leader. Member of 1995-96 ECHL champion Charlotte Checkers. Last amateur club; Illinois-Chicago (CCHA).

Todd Norman — Center

Regular Season / Playoffs

Season	Team	League	GP	G	A	PTS	PIM	GP	G	A	PTS	PIM
97-98	Saint John	AHL	1	0	0	0	0	—	—	—	—	—
97-98	Roanoke	ECHL	21	5	7	12	6	—	—	—	—	—
97-98	New Orleans	ECHL	34	13	9	22	18	4	1	0	1	4
98-99	New Orleans	ECHL	5	1	0	1	0	—	—	—	—	—
98-99	Columbus	ECHL	13	2	2	4	0	—	—	—	—	—
98-99	Pensacola	ECHL	45	7	7	14	12	—	—	—	—	—
	ECHL	Totals	118	28	25	53	36	4	1	0	1	4

Born; 1/29/77, Gloucester, Ontario. 5-11, 195. Traded to New Orleans by Roanoke for Wayne Strachan (1//98). Last amateur club; Guelph (OHL).

Eric Normandin — Right Wing

Regular Season / Playoffs

Season	Team	League	GP	G	A	PTS	PIM	GP	G	A	PTS	PIM
98-99	Johnstown	ECHL	31	9	11	20	30	—	—	—	—	—
98-99	Baton Rouge	ECHL	29	8	12	20	14	6	0	1	1	8
	ECHL	Totals	60	17	23	40	44	6	0	1	1	8

Born; 8/27/77, Laval, Quebec. 6-0, 195. Last amateur club; Sherbrooke

Jason Norrie — Right Wing

Regular Season / Playoffs

Season	Team	League	GP	G	A	PTS	PIM	GP	G	A	PTS	PIM
98-99	Charlotte	ECHL	11	1	0	1	30	—	—	—	—	—
98-99	Toledo	ECHL	55	9	18	27	164	7	1	1	2	15
	ECHL	Totals	66	10	18	28	194	7	1	1	2	15

Born; 10/8/77, Calgary, Alberta. 6-3, 205. Last amateur club; Kamloops (WHL).

Clayton Norris — Right Wing

Regular Season / Playoffs

Season	Team	League	GP	G	A	PTS	PIM	GP	G	A	PTS	PIM
92-93	Medicine Hat	WHL	41	21	16	37	128	10	3	2	5	14
92-93	Hershey	AHL	4	0	0	0	5	—	—	—	—	—
92-93	Roanoke	ECHL	4	0	0	0	0	—	—	—	—	—
93-94	Hershey	AHL	62	8	10	18	217	10	1	0	1	18
94-95	Hershey	AHL	76	12	21	33	287	4	0	0	0	8
95-96	Hershey	AHL	57	8	8	16	163	5	0	1	1	4
96-97	Philadelphia	AHL	1	0	0	0	17	—	—	—	—	—
96-97	Orlando	IHL	69	9	9	18	261	10	2	3	5	17
97-98	Orlando	IHL	13	0	3	3	51	—	—	—	—	—
97-98	St. John's	AHL	59	4	11	15	265	4	0	0	0	10
98-99	Orlando	IHL	67	6	5	11	327	7	0	0	0	25
	AHL	Totals	259	32	52	84	954	23	1	1	2	40
	IHL	Totals	149	15	17	32	639	17	2	3	5	42

Born; 3/8/72, Edmonton, Alberta. 6-2, 205. Drafted by Philadelphia Flyers (6th choice, 116th overall) in 1991 Entry Draft. Last amateur club; Medicine Hat

Warren Norris — Center

Regular Season / Playoffs

Season	Team	League	GP	G	A	PTS	PIM	GP	G	A	PTS	PIM
96-97	Massachusetts	H.E.	35	20	26	46	48	—	—	—	—	—
96-97	St. John's	AHL	9	1	0	1	4	—	—	—	—	—
97-98	St. John's	AHL	35	2	3	5	4	—	—	—	—	—
98-99	Canada	National	48	13	21	34	38	—	—	—	—	—
98-99	Grand Rapids	IHL	4	0	0	0	0	—	—	—	—	—
	AHL	Totals	44	3	3	6	8	—	—	—	—	—

Born; 9/19/74, St. John's Newfoundland. 6-1, 185. Last amateur club; Massachusetts (Hockey East).

Brad Norton — Defenseman

Regular Season / Playoffs

Season	Team	League	GP	G	A	PTS	PIM	GP	G	A	PTS	PIM
97-98	Massachusetts	H.E.	20	2	13	15	28	—	—	—	—	—
97-98	Detroit	IHL	33	1	4	5	56	22	0	2	2	87
98-99	Hamilton	AHL	58	1	8	9	134	11	0	1	1	6

Born; 2/13/75, Cambridge, Massachusetts. 6-4, 225. Drafted by Edmonton Oilers (9th choice, 215th overall) in 1993 Entry Draft. Last amateur club; Massachusetts (Hockey East).

Aaron Novak — Left Wing

Regular Season / Playoffs

Season	Team	League	GP	G	A	PTS	PIM	GP	G	A	PTS	PIM
98-99	Wichita	CHL	55	9	16	25	86	1	0	0	0	2

Born; 6/10/75, Cloquet, Minnesota. 6-0, 185. Last amateur club; Bemidji State (NCHA).

Stewart Nowasad — Forward

Regular Season / Playoffs

Season	Team	League	GP	G	A	PTS	PIM	GP	G	A	PTS	PIM
98-99	Bowling Green	CCHA	19	1	0	1	38	—	—	—	—	—
98-99	Toledo	ECHL	3	0	0	0	0	—	—	—	—	—
98-99	Columbus	CHL	1	0	0	0	2	—	—	—	—	—

Born; 11/9/77, LaSalle, Ontario. 6-1, 210. Last amateur club; Bowling Green State (CCHA).

Teemu Numminen — Forward

Regular Season / Playoffs

Season	Team	League	GP	G	A	PTS	PIM	GP	G	A	PTS	PIM
96-97	Fresno	WCHL	62	31	27	58	41	5	2	1	3	0
97-98	Mississippi	ECHL	56	4	12	16	18	—	—	—	—	—
98-99	Phoenix	WCHL	63	19	22	41	26	—	—	—	—	—
	WCHL	Totals	125	50	49	99	67	5	2	1	3	0

Born; 12/23/73, Tampero, Finland. 6-3, 205. Drafted by Winnipeg Jets (10th choice, 229th overall) in 1992 Entry Draft. Last overseas club; TPS Turku

Donovan Nunweiler — Goaltender

Regular Season / Playoffs

Season	Team	League	GP	W	L	T	MIN	SO	AVG	GP	W	L	MIN	SO	AVG
97-98	Moose Jaw	WHL	56	18	29	8	3098	2	3.49	4	0	4	264	0	3.86
97-98	Toledo	ECHL	3	1	1	0	99	0	4.24	—	—	—	—	—	—
98-99	Acadia	AUAA	26	—	—	—	846	—	2.76	—	—	—	—	—	—

Born; Redcliffe, Alberta. 5-9, 170. Last amateur club; Acadia (AUAA).

Hubie McDonough poses with the Frank Gallagher Trophy
Photo by Joe Costa

Mike Taylor picked up 105 points in his first WCHL season
Photo by Kelly Virtanen

Kevin Oakenfold — Left Wing

Season	Team	League	GP	G	A	PTS	PIM	GP	G	A	PTS	PIM
			Regular Season					Playoffs				
96-97	Alaska-Fairbanks	CCHA	29	3	5	8	65	—	—	—	—	—
96-97	Alaska	WCHL	6	0	0	0	0	—	—	—	—	—
97-98	Memphis	CHL	52	15	9	24	124	—	—	—	—	—
97-98	Huntsville	CHL	5	0	1	1	21	3	0	0	0	0
98-99	El Paso	WPHL	7	0	0	0	2	—	—	—	—	—
	CHL	Totals	57	15	10	25	145	3	0	0	0	0

Born; 6/7/73, Calgary, Alberta. 6-3, 205. Traded to Huntsville by Memphis for Tony Frenette (3/98). Last amateur club; Alaska-Fairbanks (CCHA).

Matt Oates — Left Wing

Season	Team	League	GP	G	A	PTS	PIM	GP	G	A	PTS	PIM
			Regular Season					Playoffs				
94-95	Indianapolis	IHL	59	3	6	9	18	—	—	—	—	—
94-95	Columbus	ECHL	11	4	5	9	11	—	—	—	—	—
95-96	Columbus	ECHL	46	12	28	40	63	3	1	0	1	4
96-97	Columbus	ECHL	70	22	43	65	59	8	2	3	5	16
97-98	Columbus	ECHL	60	18	34	52	68	—	—	—	—	—
97-98	Chicago	IHL	8	0	3	3	2	—	—	—	—	—
97-98	Kansas City	IHL	1	0	0	0	0	3	0	0	0	0
98-99	Columbus	ECHL	70	24	57	81	81	4	0	1	1	8
	IHL	Totals	68	3	9	12	20	3	0	0	0	0
	ECHL	Totals	257	80	167	247	282	15	3	4	7	28

Born; 12/20/72, Evanston, Illinois. 6-3, 208. Drafted by New York Rangers (7th choice, 168th overall) in 1992 Entry Draft. Traded to Chicago Blackhawks by Rangers with Tony Amonte for Stephane Matteau and Brian Noonan (3/21/94). Selected by Tallahassee in 1999 Dispersal Draft. Last amateur club; Miami of Ohio (CCHA).

Craig O'Brien — Left Wing

Season	Team	League	GP	G	A	PTS	PIM	GP	G	A	PTS	PIM
			Regular Season					Playoffs				
98-99	Flint	UHL	19	5	2	7	27	—	—	—	—	—

Born; 2/24/79, Peterborough, ONtario. 5-8, 175.

Keith O'Brien — Left Wing

Season	Team	League	GP	G	A	PTS	PIM	GP	G	A	PTS	PIM
			Regular Season					Playoffs				
97-98	Austin	WPHL	8	0	2	2	15	—	—	—	—	—
98-99	Austin	WPHL	8	2	1	3	11	—	—	—	—	—
	WPHL	Totals	16	2	3	5	26	—	—	—	—	—

Born; 1/12/74, Boston, Massachusetts 5-10, 175. Last amateur club; Princeton (ECAC).

Sean O'Brien — Left Wing/Defense

Season	Team	League	GP	G	A	PTS	PIM	GP	G	A	PTS	PIM
			Regular Season					Playoffs				
94-95	Houston	IHL	13	2	1	3	23	—	—	—	—	—
94-95	Richmond	ECHL	52	5	18	23	147	17	2	5	7	77
95-96	Utah	IHL	7	2	2	4	12	—	—	—	—	—
95-96	Las Vegas	IHL	1	0	0	0	2	—	—	—	—	—
95-96	Houston	IHL	4	0	1	1	12	—	—	—	—	—
95-96	Tallahassee	ECHL	54	9	19	28	179	8	0	2	2	23
96-97	Tallahassee	ECHL	10	7	3	10	29	—	—	—	—	—
96-97	Utah	IHL	50	21	10	31	135	—	—	—	—	—
96-97	Phoenix	IHL	10	3	3	6	20	—	—	—	—	—
97-98	Utah	IHL	36	3	8	11	77	—	—	—	—	—
97-98	Philadelphia	AHL	33	7	10	17	88	20	4	2	6	48
98-99	Syracuse	AHL	45	5	11	16	155	—	—	—	—	—
98-99	Philadelphia	AHL	18	1	2	3	60	16	3	4	7	24
	IHL	Totals	121	31	25	56	281	—	—	—	—	—
	AHL	Totals	96	13	23	36	303	36	7	6	13	72
	ECHL	Totals	116	21	40	61	355	25	2	7	9	100

Born; 2/9/72, Boston, Masachusetts. 6-1, 200. Signed as a free agent by Los Angeles Kings (6/26/97). Signed as a free agent by Pittsburgh Penguins (8/11/98). Traded to Philadelphia Flyers for future considerations (2/10/99). Member of 1994-95 ECHL champion Richmond Renegades. Member of 1997-98 AHL Champion Philadelphia Phantoms. Last amateur club; Princeton (ECAC).

Jaroslav Obsut — Defenseman

Season	Team	League	GP	G	A	PTS	PIM	GP	G	A	PTS	PIM
			Regular Season					Playoffs				
96-97	Edmonton	WHL	13	2	9	11	4	—	—	—	—	—
96-97	Medicine Hat	WHL	50	8	26	34	42	4	0	2	2	2
96-97	Toledo	ECHL	3	1	0	1	0	5	0	1	1	6
97-98	Syracuse	AHL	4	0	1	1	4	—	—	—	—	—
97-98	Raleigh	ECHL	60	6	26	32	46	—	—	—	—	—
98-99	Manitoba	IHL	2	0	0	0	0	—	—	—	—	—
98-99	Worcester	AHL	31	2	8	10	14	4	0	1	1	2
98-99	Augusta	ECHL	41	11	25	36	42	—	—	—	—	—
	AHL	Totals	35	2	9	11	18	4	0	1	1	2
	ECHL	Totals	104	18	51	69	88	5	0	1	1	6

Born; 9/3/76, Presov, Czechoslovakia. 6-1, 185. Drafted by Winnipeg Jets (9th choice, 188th overall) in 1995 Entry Draft. Signed as a free agent by St. Louis Blues (). Last amateur club; Medicine Hat (WHL).

Dan O'Connell — Center

Season	Team	League	GP	G	A	PTS	PIM	GP	G	A	PTS	PIM
			Regular Season					Playoffs				
94-95	Stavanger	Norway	32	37	21	58	NA	—	—	—	—	—
95-96	Assat Pori	Finland	20	0	6	6	34	—	—	—	—	—
96-97												
97-98	Morrum	Sweden	41	26	15	41	97	—	—	—	—	—
98-99	Roanoke	ECHL	37	9	14	23	85	11	0	2	2	22

Born; 12/16/70, Salisbury, Massachusetts. 5-9, 175. Last amateur club; Lowell (Hockey East).

Keith O'Connell — Defenseman

Season	Team	League	GP	G	A	PTS	PIM	GP	G	A	PTS	PIM
			Regular Season					Playoffs				
97-98	Pee Dee	ECHL	5	0	0	0	17	—	—	—	—	—
97-98	Raleigh	ECHL	2	0	0	0	0	—	—	—	—	—
97-98	Richmond	ECHL	42	2	10	12	107	—	—	—	—	—
97-98	Pensacola	ECHL	9	0	1	1	13	19	0	1	1	40
98-99	Pensacola	ECHL	22	1	2	3	60	—	—	—	—	—
98-99	Richmond	ECHL	35	0	6	6	72	—	—	—	—	—
	ECHL	Totals	115	3	19	22	269	19	0	1	1	40

Born; 8/9/72, South Boston, Massachusetts. 5-10, 180. Traded to Pensacola by Richmond with Etienne Beaudry and Brandon Gray (3/98). Last amateur club; Massachusetts (Hockey East).

J.P. O'Connor — Center

Season	Team	League	GP	G	A	PTS	PIM	GP	G	A	PTS	PIM
			Regular Season					Playoffs				
97-98	Hershey	AHL	2	0	0	0	2	—	—	—	—	—
97-98	Cleveland	IHL	1	0	0	0	2	—	—	—	—	—
97-98	Chesapeake	ECHL	62	13	17	30	28	3	0	0	0	4
98-99	Chesapeake	ECHL	70	11	20	31	86	8	2	0	2	2
	ECHL	Totals	132	24	37	61	114	11	2	0	2	6

Born; 5/31/74, Montreal, Quebec. 5-10, 185. Last amateur club; Princeton

Tom O'Connor — Defenseman

Season	Team	League	GP	G	A	PTS	PIM	GP	G	A	PTS	PIM
			Regular Season					Playoffs				
98-99	Syracuse	AHL	16	0	1	1	8	—	—	—	—	—
98-99	Wheeling	ECHL	54	5	20	25	58	—	—	—	—	—

Born; 1/9/76, Springfield, Massachusetts. 6-2, 190. Drafted by Pittsburgh Penguins (6th choice, 102nd overall) in 1994 Entry Draft. Last amateur club; Massachusetts (Hockey East).

Matt O'Dette — Defenseman

Season	Team	League	GP	G	A	PTS	PIM	GP	G	A	PTS	PIM
			Regular Season					Playoffs				
96-97	Roanoke	ECHL	69	6	16	22	139	4	0	0	0	10
97-98	Saint John	AHL	58	0	5	5	92	15	0	1	1	10
97-98	Roanoke	ECHL	5	0	0	0	29	—	—	—	—	—
98-99	Saint John	AHL	42	0	1	1	82	2	0	0	0	14
	AHL	Totals	100	0	6	6	174	17	0	1	1	24
	ECHL	Totals	74	6	16	22	168	4	0	0	0	10

Born; 11/9/75, Oshawa, Ontario. 6-5, 220. Drafted by Florida Panthers (7th choice, 157th overall) in 1994 Entry Draft. Last amateur club; Kitchener (OHL).

Mark O'Donnell — Left Wing

Regular Season / Playoffs

Season	Team	League	GP	G	A	PTS	PIM	GP	G	A	PTS	PIM
96-97	Fort Worth	CeHL	63	35	33	68	24	17	4	7	11	8
97-98	Jacksonville	ECHL	4	0	2	2	0	—	—	—	—	—
97-98	Fort Worth	WPHL	58	18	28	46	13	13	5	7	12	8
98-99	Fort Worth	WPHL	29	14	11	25	13	12	5	7	12	4
	WPHL	Totals	87	32	39	71	26	25	10	14	24	12

Born; 5/3/74, Kanata, Ontario. 6-3, 213. Member of 1996-97 CeHL Champion Fort Worth Fire. Last amateur club; Cape Breton (AUAA).

Fredrik Oduya — Left Wing

Regular Season / Playoffs

Season	Team	League	GP	G	A	PTS	PIM	GP	G	A	PTS	PIM
95-96	Kansas City	IHL	56	2	6	8	235	3	0	0	0	2
96-97	Kentucky	AHL	69	2	9	11	241	—	—	—	—	—
97-98	Kentucky	AHL	72	6	10	16	300	—	—	—	—	—
98-99	Orlando	IHL	64	2	14	16	259	—	—	—	—	—
98-99	Saint John	AHL	12	0	2	2	48	6	0	0	0	22
	AHL	Totals	153	8	21	29	589	6	0	0	0	22
	IHL	Totals	120	4	20	24	494	3	0	0	0	2

Born; 5/31/75, Stockholm, Sweden. 6-2, 185. Drafted by San Jose Sharks (8th choice, 154th overall) in 1993 Entry Draft. Traded to Calgary Flames by San Jose for Eric Landry (7/21/99). Last amateur club; Ottawa (OHL).

Michael O'Grady — Defenseman

Regular Season / Playoffs

Season	Team	League	GP	G	A	PTS	PIM	GP	G	A	PTS	PIM
97-98	New Haven	AHL	32	1	4	5	58	2	0	0	0	0
97-98	Tallahassee	ECHL	4	0	0	0	18	—	—	—	—	—
97-98	Port Huron	UHL	12	2	3	5	30	—	—	—	—	—
98-99	Port Huron	UHL	46	8	7	15	86	—	—	—	—	—
98-99	Binghamton	UHL	21	5	5	10	47	4	1	2	3	8
	UHL	Totals	79	15	15	30	163	4	1	2	3	8

Born; 3/22/77, Neilburg, Saskatchewan. 6-3, 227. Drafted by Florida Panthers (3rd choice, 62nd overall) in 1995 Entry Draft. Traded to Binghamton by Port Huron with Olie Sundstrom for Jon Hillebrandt (2/99). Last amateur club; Leth-

Colin O'Hara — Defenseman

Regular Season / Playoffs

Season	Team	League	GP	G	A	PTS	PIM	GP	G	A	PTS	PIM
98-99	Austin	WPHL	22	3	2	5	23	—	—	—	—	—

Born; 4/2/77, Vernon, British Columbia. 6-1, 210. Last amateur club; North Battleford (SJHL).

Martin Ohrstedt — Defenseman

Regular Season / Playoffs

Season	Team	League	GP	G	A	PTS	PIM	GP	G	A	PTS	PIM
98-99	Odessa	WPHL	69	15	16	31	38	3	2	0	2	0

Born; 2/19/75, Stockholm, Sweden. 6-3, 209. Last overseas club; Arlanda

Roman Oksiuta — Right Wing

Regular Season / Playoffs

Season	Team	League	GP	G	A	PTS	PIM	GP	G	A	PTS	PIM
92-93	Khimik	CIS	20	11	2	13	42	—	—	—	—	—
92-93	Cape Breton	AHL	43	26	25	51	22	16	9	19	28	12
93-94	Edmonton	NHL	10	1	2	3	4	—	—	—	—	—
93-94	Cape Breton	AHL	47	31	22	53	90	4	2	2	4	22
94-95	Cape Breton	AHL	25	9	7	16	20	—	—	—	—	—
94-95	Edmonton	NHL	26	11	2	13	8	—	—	—	—	—
94-95	Vancouver	NHL	12	5	2	7	2	10	2	3	5	0
95-96	Vancouver	NHL	56	16	23	39	42	—	—	—	—	—
95-96	Anaheim	NHL	14	7	5	12	18	—	—	—	—	—
96-97	Anaheim	NHL	28	6	7	13	22	—	—	—	—	—
96-97	Pittsburgh	NHL	7	0	0	0	4	—	—	—	—	—
97-98	Fort Wayne	IHL	19	5	8	13	50	3	0	0	0	12
98-99	Lukko Rauma	Finland	26	4	9	13	134	—	—	—	—	—
	NHL	Totals	153	46	41	87	100	10	2	3	5	0
	AHL	Totals	115	66	54	120	132	20	11	21	32	34

Born; 8/21/70, Murmanskk, USSR. 6-3, 230. Drafted by New York Rangers (11th chocie, 202nd overall) in 1989 Entry Draft. Traded to Edmonton Oilers by Rangers with Rangers' third round choice (Alexander Kerch) in 1993 Entry Draft for Kevin Lowe (12/11/92). Traded to Vancouver Canucks by Edmonton for Jiri Slegr (4/7/95). Traded to Anaheim Mighty Ducks by Vancouver for Mike Sillinger (3/15/96). Traded to Pittsburgh Penguins by Anaheim for Richard Park (3/18/97). Member of 1992-93 AHL Champion Cape Breton Oilers.

Mike Olaski — Right Wing

Regular Season / Playoffs

Season	Team	League	GP	G	A	PTS	PIM	GP	G	A	PTS	PIM
98-99	Wichita	CHL	3	3	0	3	2	—	—	—	—	—
98-99	Mobile	ECHL	52	2	6	8	25	2	0	0	0	2

Born; 4/25/74, Toronto, Ontario. 6-1, 195. Selected by Arkansas in 1999 ECHL Expansion Draft. Last amateur club; Ferris State (CCHA).

Ed Olczyk — Right Wing

Regular Season / Playoffs

Season	Team	League	GP	G	A	PTS	PIM	GP	G	A	PTS	PIM
83-84	United States	National	62	21	47	68	36	—	—	—	—	—
83-84	United States	Olympic	6	2	5	7	0	—	—	—	—	—
84-85	Chicago	NHL	70	20	30	50	67	15	6	5	11	11
85-86	Chicago	NHL	79	29	50	79	47	3	0	0	0	0
86-87	Chicago	NHL	79	16	35	51	119	4	1	1	2	4
87-88	Toronto	NHL	80	42	33	75	55	6	5	4	9	2
88-89	Toronto	NHL	80	38	52	90	75	—	—	—	—	—
89-90	Toronto	NHL	79	32	56	88	78	5	1	2	3	14
90-91	Toronto	NHL	18	4	10	14	13	—	—	—	—	—
90-91	Winnipeg	NHL	61	26	31	57	69	—	—	—	—	—
91-92	Winnipeg	NHL	64	32	33	65	67	6	2	1	3	4
92-93	Winnipeg	NHL	25	8	12	20	26	—	—	—	—	—
92-93	Rangers	NHL	46	13	16	29	26	—	—	—	—	—
93-94	Rangers	NHL	37	3	5	8	28	1	0	0	0	0
94-95	Rangers	NHL	20	2	1	3	4	—	—	—	—	—
94-95	Winnipeg	NHL	13	2	8	10	8	—	—	—	—	—
95-96	Winnipeg	NHL	51	27	22	49	65	6	1	2	3	6
96-97	Los Angeles	NHL	67	21	23	44	45	—	—	—	—	—
96-97	Pittsburgh	NHL	12	4	7	11	6	5	1	0	1	12
97-98	Pittsburgh	NHL	56	11	11	22	35	6	2	0	2	4
98-99	Chicago	NHL	61	10	15	25	29	—	—	—	—	—
98-99	Chicago	IHL	7	2	2	4	6	—	—	—	—	—
	NHL	Totals	998	340	450	790	862	57	19	15	34	57

Born; 8/16/66, Chicago, Illinois. 6-1, 205. Drafted by Chicago Blackhawks (1st choice, 3rd overall) in 1984 Entry Draft. Traded to Toronto Maple Leafs by Chicago with Al Secord for Steve Thomas, Rick Vaive, and Bob McGill (9/3/87). Traded to Winnipeg Jets by Toronto with Mark Osborne for Dave Ellett and Paul Fenton (11/10/90). Traded to New York Rangers by Winnipeg for Kris King and Tie Domi (12/28/92). Traded to Winnipeg by Rangers for Winnipeg's fifth round draft choice (Alexei Vasiliev) in 1995 Entry Draft (4/7/95). Signed as a free agent by Los Angeles Kings (7/8/96). Traded to Pittsburgh Penguins by Los Angeles Kings for Glen Murray (3/18/97). Signed as a free agent by Chicago (8/26/98). Member of 1993-94 Stanley Cup Champion New York Rangers.

Jamie O'Leary — Center
Regular Season / Playoffs

Season	Team	League	GP	G	A	PTS	PIM	GP	G	A	PTS	PIM
98-99	Chesapeake	ECHL	70	9	19	28	68	8	0	2	2	4

Born; 9/15/74, Needham, Massachusetts. 5-10, 175.

Mike Oliveira — Center
Regular Season / Playoffs

Season	Team	League	GP	G	A	PTS	PIM	GP	G	A	PTS	PIM
98-99	Kingston	OHL	68	37	52	89	26	5	0	4	4	2
98-99	Roanoke	ECHL	3	2	1	3	0	12	0	4	4	4

Born; 2/21/79, West Lorne, Ontario. 5-10, 195. Last amateur club; Kingston

David Oliver — Right Wing
Regular Season / Playoffs

Season	Team	League	GP	G	A	PTS	PIM	GP	G	A	PTS	PIM
94-95	Cape Breton	AHL	32	11	18	29	8	—	—	—	—	—
94-95	Edmonton	NHL	44	16	14	30	20	—	—	—	—	—
95-96	Edmonton	NHL	80	20	19	39	34	—	—	—	—	—
96-97	Edmonton	NHL	17	1	2	3	4	—	—	—	—	—
96-97	Rangers	NHL	14	2	1	3	4	3	0	0	0	0
97-98	Houston	IHL	78	38	27	65	60	4	3	0	3	4
98-99	Ottawa	NHL	17	2	5	7	4	—	—	—	—	—
98-99	Houston	IHL	37	18	17	35	30	19	10	6	16	22
	NHL	Totals	172	41	41	82	66	3	0	0	0	0
	IHL	Totals	115	56	44	100	90	23	13	6	19	26

Born; 4/17/71, Sechelt, British Columbia. 6-0, 190. Drafted by Edmonton Oilers (7th choice, 144th overall) in 1991 Entry Draft. Claimed on waivers by New York Rangers from Edmonton (2/21/97). Signed as a free agent by Ottawa Senators (7/2/98). Signed as a free agent by Phoenix Coyotes (7/16/99). Member of 1998-99 IHL Champion Houston Aeros. Last amateur club; Michigan (CCHA).

David Oliver — Forward
Regular Season / Playoffs

Season	Team	League	GP	G	A	PTS	PIM	GP	G	A	PTS	PIM
98-99	Hartford	AHL	4	0	0	0	29	—	—	—	—	—
98-99	Central Texas	WPHL	67	22	45	67	*357	2	0	1	1	4

Born; 5/4/76, Alberton, Prince Edward Island. 6-3, 215.

Matt Oliver — Left Wing
Regular Season / Playoffs

Season	Team	League	GP	G	A	PTS	PIM	GP	G	A	PTS	PIM
98-99	Phoenix	WCHL	60	5	6	11	28	—	—	—	—	—

Born; 3/16/74, Euclid, Ohio. 6-1, 210. Last amateur club; Maine (Hockey East).

Simon Olivier — Defenseman
Regular Season / Playoffs

Season	Team	League	GP	G	A	PTS	PIM	GP	G	A	PTS	PIM
95-96	Oklahoma City	CeHL	45	17	19	36	136	—	—	—	—	—
96-97	Mississippi	ECHL	67	8	13	21	230	3	1	1	2	12
97-98	Oklahoma City	CHL	64	12	31	43	302	11	1	6	7	58
98-99	Oklahoma City	CHL	51	14	34	48	153	—	—	—	—	—
	CHL	Totals	160	43	84	217	591	11	1	6	7	58

Born; 2/2/72, Quebec City, Quebec. 5-11, 190.

Jon Olofson — Forward
Regular Season / Playoffs

Season	Team	League	GP	G	A	PTS	PIM	GP	G	A	PTS	PIM
96-97	Waco	WPHL	51	1	12	13	34	—	—	—	—	—
97-98	Waco	WPHL	56	2	1	3	19	—	—	—	—	—
98-99	Fort Worth	WPHL	41	3	6	9	10	11	0	1	1	40
	WPHL	Totals	148	6	19	25	63	11	0	1	1	40

Born; Denver, Colorado. 6-1, 205. Last amateur club; Augsburg (NCAA 3).

Chris Olsen — Forward
Regular Season / Playoffs

Season	Team	League	GP	G	A	PTS	PIM	GP	G	A	PTS	PIM
98-99	Madison	UHL	4	0	0	0	0	—	—	—	—	—

Born; 6/14/71, Madison, Wisconsin. 6-0, 185.

Darryl Olsen — Defenseman
Regular Season / Playoffs

Season	Team	League	GP	G	A	PTS	PIM	GP	G	A	PTS	PIM
88-89	Canada	National	3	1	0	1	4	—	—	—	—	—
88-89	Northern Michigan	WCHA	45	16	26	42	88	—	—	—	—	—
89-90	Salt Lake City	IHL	72	16	50	66	90	11	3	6	9	2
90-91	Salt Lake City	IHL	76	15	40	55	89	4	1	5	6	2
91-92	Calgary	NHL	1	0	0	0	0	—	—	—	—	—
91-92	Salt Lake City	IHL	59	7	33	40	80	5	2	1	3	4
92-93	Providence	AHL	50	7	27	34	38	—	—	—	—	—
92-93	San Diego	IHL	21	2	8	10	26	10	1	3	4	30
93-94	Salt Lake City	IHL	73	17	32	49	97	—	—	—	—	—
94-95												
95-96												
96-97	Nottingham	BHL	39	7	21	28	24	—	—	—	—	—
97-98												
98-99	Phoenix	WCHL	11	0	3	3	12	3	0	0	0	6

Born; 10/7/66, Calgary, Alberta. 6-0, 180. Drafted by Calgary Flames (10th choice, 185th overall) in 1985 Entry Draft. Signed as a free agent by Boston Bruins (7/23/92). Last amateur club; Northern Michigan (WCHA).

Erik Olsen — Defenseman
Regular Season / Playoffs

Season	Team	League	GP	G	A	PTS	PIM	GP	G	A	PTS	PIM
97-98	Port Huron	UHL	52	2	17	19	53	—	—	—	—	—
97-98	Thunder Bay	UHL	8	1	3	4	11	5	0	0	0	4
98-99	Charlotte	ECHL	2	0	0	0	6	—	—	—	—	—
98-99	Jacksonville	ECHL	60	2	5	7	106	2	0	0	0	0
	ECHL	Totals	62	2	5	7	112	2	0	0	0	0
	UHL	Totals	60	3	20	23	64	5	0	0	0	4

Born; 12/16/77, Sarnia, Ontario. 6-0, 195. Last amateur club; Kingston (OHL).

Boyd Olson — Center
Regular Season / Playoffs

Season	Team	League	GP	G	A	PTS	PIM	GP	G	A	PTS	PIM
95-96	Tri-City	WHL	62	13	12	25	105	11	1	4	5	16
95-96	Fredericton	AHL	—	—	—	—	—	2	1	0	1	0
96-97	Fredericton	AHL	74	8	12	20	43	—	—	—	—	—
97-98	Fredericton	AHL	57	4	9	13	43	—	—	—	—	—
98-99	Fredericton	AHL	61	10	16	26	60	13	1	3	4	16
	AHL	Totals	192	22	37	59	146	15	2	3	5	16

Born; 4/4/76, Edmonton, Alberta. 6-1, 170. Drafted by Montreal Canadiens (6th choice, 138th overall) in 1995 Entry Draft. Last amateur club; Tri-City (WHL).

Christer Olsson — Defenseman
Regular Season / Playoffs

Season	Team	League	GP	G	A	PTS	PIM	GP	G	A	PTS	PIM
95-96	St. Louis	NHL	26	2	8	10	14	3	0	0	0	0
95-96	Worcester	AHL	39	7	7	14	22	—	—	—	—	—
96-97	St. Louis	NHL	5	0	1	1	0	—	—	—	—	—
96-97	Ottawa	NHL	25	2	3	5	10	—	—	—	—	—
96-97	Worcester	AHL	2	0	0	0	0	—	—	—	—	—
97-98	Vastra Frolunda	Sweden	45	13	8	21	54	7	0	1	1	18
98-99	Vastra Frolunda	Sweden	47	5	11	16	48	4	0	1	1	4
	NHL	Totals	56	4	12	16	24	3	0	0	0	0
	AHL	Totals	41	7	7	14	22	—	—	—	—	—

Born; 7/24/70, Arboga, Sweden. 5-11, 190. Drafted by St. Louis Blues (10th choice, 275th overall) in 1993 Entry Draft. Traded to Ottawa Senators by St. Louis for Pavol Demitra (11/27/96).

Sergei Olympiev — Left Wing
Regular Season / Playoffs

Season	Team	League	GP	G	A	PTS	PIM	GP	G	A	PTS	PIM
95-96	Johnstown	ECHL	3	0	1	1	0	—	—	—	—	—
96-97	Alaska	WCHL	56	16	16	32	53	—	—	—	—	—
97-98	Dayton	ECHL	4	0	0	0	2	—	—	—	—	—
97-98	Johnstown	ECHL	6	0	0	0	6	—	—	—	—	—
97-98	Muskegon	UHL	40	8	10	18	22	7	1	0	1	4
98-99	Topeka	CHL	43	10	9	19	45	3	0	1	1	7
	ECHL	Totals	13	0	1	1	8	—	—	—	—	—

Born; 1/12/75, lipetski, Russia. 6-4, 220. Drafted by New York Rangers (4th choice, 86th overall) in 1993 Entry Draft. Last amateur club; Kitchener (OHL).

Mike Omicioli — Center
Regular Season / Playoffs

Season	Team	League	GP	G	A	PTS	PIM	GP	G	A	PTS	PIM
98-99	Providence	H.E.	38	19	31	50	50	—	—	—	—	—
98-99	Portland	AHL	9	3	3	6	2	—	—	—	—	—

Born; 3/9/76, West Warwick, Rhode Island. 5-5, 160. Last amateur club; Providence College (Hockey East).

Mike O'Neill — Goaltender
Regular Season / Playoffs

Season	Team	League	GP	W	L	T	MIN	SO	AVG	GP	W	L	MIN	SO	AVG
89-90	Tappara	Finland	41	23	13	5	2369	2	3.22	—	—	—	—	—	—
90-91	Fort Wayne	IHL	8	5	2	1	490	0	3.80	—	—	—	—	—	—
90-91	Moncton	AHL	30	13	7	6	1613	0	3.12	8	3	4	435	0	4.00
91-92	Winnipeg	NHL	1	0	0	0	13	0	4.62	—	—	—	—	—	—
91-92	Moncton	AHL	32	14	16	2	1902	1	3.41	11	4	7	670	*1	3.85
91-92	Fort Wayne	IHL	33	22	6	3	1858	*4	3.13	—	—	—	—	—	—
92-93	Winnipeg	NHL	2	0	0	1	73	0	4.93	—	—	—	—	—	—
92-93	Moncton	AHL	30	13	10	1	1649	1	3.20	—	—	—	—	—	—
93-94	Winnipeg	NHL	17	0	9	1	738	0	4.15	—	—	—	—	—	—
93-94	Moncton	AHL	12	8	4	0	716	1	2.76	—	—	—	—	—	—
93-94	Fort Wayne	IHL	11	4	4	3	642	0	3.55	—	—	—	—	—	—
94-95	Fort Wayne	IHL	28	11	12	4	1603	0	4.08	—	—	—	—	—	—
94-95	Phoenix	IHL	21	13	4	4	1256	1	3.06	9	4	5	535	0	3.70
95-96	Baltimore	AHL	*74	31	31	7	*4250	2	3.53	12	6	6	689	0	3.75
96-97	Anaheim	NHL	1	0	0	0	31	0	5.81	—	—	—	—	—	—
96-97	Long Beach	IHL	45	26	12	6	2644	1	3.29	1	0	0	7	0	0.00
97-98	Portland	AHL	47	16	18	10	2640	1	3.07	6	2	3	305	0	3.15
98-99	Villach	Austria	42	35	5	1			2.49						
	NHL	Totals	21	0	9	2	855	0	4.28	—	—	—	—	—	—
	AHL	Totals	225	95	86	29	12770	6	3.28	37	15	20	2099	1	3.74
	IHL	Totals	146	81	40	21	8493	6	3.42	10	4	5	542	0	3.65

Born; 11/3/67, LaSalle, Quebec. 5-7, 160. Drafted by Winnipeg Jets (1st choice, 15th overall) in 1988 Supplemental Draft. Signed as a free agent by Anaheim Mighty Ducks (7/14/95). Signed as a free agent by Washington Capitals (8/3/97). Signed as a free agent by Los Angeles Kings (7/21/99). Last amateur club; Yale

Hayden O'Rear — Defenseman
Regular Season / Playoffs

Season	Team	League	GP	G	A	PTS	PIM	GP	G	A	PTS	PIM
92-93	Richmond	ECHL	1	0	0	0	2	—	—	—	—	—
92-93	Knoxville	ECHL	52	4	12	16	45	—	—	—	—	—
93-94	Knoxville	ECHL	61	7	20	27	83	3	0	0	0	0
94-95	Knoxville	ECHL	53	0	11	11	44	—	—	—	—	—
95-96	Winston-Salem	SHL	60	6	34	40	89	8	0	6	6	28
96-97	Anchorage	WCHL	64	8	37	45	70	9	2	4	6	2
97-98	Anchorage	WCHL	53	7	22	29	44	8	0	1	1	10
98-99	Anchorage	WCHL	71	3	19	22	58	6	0	3	3	2
	WCHL	Totals	188	18	78	96	172	23	2	8	10	14
	ECHL	Totals	167	11	43	54	174	3	0	0	0	0

Born; 10/8/70, Fairbanks, Alaska. 6-0, 190. Drafted by Vancouver Canucks (9th choice, 218th overall) in 1989 Entry Draft. 1996-97 WCHL Second Team All-

Sean O'Reilly — Defenseman
Regular Season / Playoffs

Season	Team	League	GP	G	A	PTS	PIM	GP	G	A	PTS	PIM
97-98	Wichita	CHL	53	3	21	24	195	15	2	5	7	60
98-99	Wichita	CHL	67	8	23	31	253	4	0	2	2	18
	CHL	Totals	120	11	44	55	448	19	2	7	9	78

Born; 10/1/71, London, Ontario. 5-11, 205. Last amateur club; Acadia (AUAA).

Chris O'Rourke — Defenseman
Regular Season / Playoffs

Season	Team	League	GP	G	A	PTS	PIM	GP	G	A	PTS	PIM
92-93	Detroit	CoHL	51	0	10	10	165	6	0	0	0	10
93-94	Flint	CoHL	47	1	13	14	168	10	0	2	2	56
94-95	Tallahassee	ECHL	15	0	1	1	79	—	—	—	—	—
94-95	Flint	CoHL	34	3	9	12	134	6	0	1	1	25
95-96	West Palm Beach	SHL	7	2	0	2	33	—	—	—	—	—
95-96	Winston-Salem	SHL	39	3	12	15	109	9	0	4	4	37
96-97	Waco	WPHL	29	1	5	6	70	—	—	—	—	—
96-97	Austin	WPHL	15	1	3	4	26	1	0	0	0	12
97-98	Waco	WPHL	35	1	10	11	112	—	—	—	—	—
97-98	Fort Worth	WPHL	11	0	1	1	48	—	—	—	—	—
98-99	Fort Worth	CHL	47	2	6	8	189	—	—	—	—	—
	CoHL	Totals	132	4	32	36	467	22	0	3	3	91
	WPHL	Totals	90	3	19	22	256	1	0	0	0	12
	SHL	Totals	46	5	12	17	142	9	0	4	4	37
	WPHL	Totals	44	2	8	10	96	1	0	0	0	12

Born; 1/6/71, Calgary, Alberta. 6-2, 195. Drafted by Toronto Maple Leafs (13th choice, 245th overall) in 1991 Entry Draft. Selected by Wichita in 1999 CHL Dispersal Draft. Last amateur club; Alaska-Fairbanks (CCHA).

Vladimir Orszagh — Right Wing
Regular Season / Playoffs

Season	Team	League	GP	G	A	PTS	PIM	GP	G	A	PTS	PIM
96-97	Utah	IHL	68	12	15	27	30	3	0	1	1	4
97-98	Islanders	NHL	11	0	1	1	2	—	—	—	—	—
97-98	Utah	IHL	62	13	10	23	60	4	2	0	2	0
98-99	Islanders	NHL	12	1	0	1	6	—	—	—	—	—
98-99	Lowell	AHL	68	18	23	41	57	3	2	2	4	2
	NHL	Totals	23	1	1	2	8	—	—	—	—	—
	IHL	Totals	130	25	25	50	90	7	2	1	3	4

Born; 5/24/77, Banska Bystrica, Czechoslovakia. 5-11, 173. Drafted by New York Islanders (4th choice, 106th overall) in 1995 Entry Draft. Last European club; Banska Bystrica (Slovakia).

Scott Orzoff — Defenseman
Regular Season / Playoffs

Season	Team	League	GP	G	A	PTS	PIM	GP	G	A	PTS	PIM
97-98	Amarillo	WPHL	54	1	4	5	63	—	—	—	—	—
98-99	Arkansas	WPHL	64	3	15	18	155	3	0	0	0	4
	WPHL	Totals	118	4	19	23	218	3	0	0	0	4

Born; 8/16/74, Riverwoods, Illinois. 6-0, 190. Last amateur club; Oswego (NCAA 3).

Keith Osborne — Right Wing
Regular Season / Playoffs

Season	Team	League	GP	G	A	PTS	PIM	GP	G	A	PTS	PIM
89-90	St. Louis	NHL	5	0	2	2	8	—	—	—	—	—
89-90	Peoria	IHL	56	23	24	47	58	—	—	—	—	—
90-91	Peoria	IHL	54	10	20	30	79	—	—	—	—	—
90-91	Newmarket	AHL	12	0	3	3	6	—	—	—	—	—
91-92	St. John's	AHL	53	11	16	27	21	4	0	1	1	2
92-93	Tampa Bay	NHL	11	1	1	2	8	—	—	—	—	—
92-93	Atlanta	IHL	72	40	49	89	91	8	1	5	6	2
93-94												
94-95												
95-96	Peoria	IHL	63	23	28	51	64	9	5	3	8	12
96-97	San Antonio	IHL	52	12	13	25	41	—	—	—	—	—
96-97	Utah	IHL	9	3	0	3	4	1	0	0	0	0
97-98	Winston-Salem	UHL	50	26	35	61	60	—	—	—	—	—
98-99	Saginaw	UHL	73	20	49	69	72	—	—	—	—	—
	NHL	Totals	16	1	3	4	8	—	—	—	—	—
	IHL	Totals	306	111	134	245	337	18	6	8	14	14
	AHL	Totals	65	11	19	30	27	4	0	1	1	2
	UHL	Totals	123	46	84	130	132	—	—	—	—	—

Born; 4/2/69, Toronto. 6-1, 180. Drafted by St. Louis Blues (1st choice, 12th overall) in 1987 Entry Draft. Traded to Toronto Maple Leafs by St. Louis for Darren Veitch (3/5/91). Selected by Tampa Bay Lightning in Expansion Draft (6/18/92). Last amateur club; Niagara Falls (OHL).

Matt Osiecki — Defenseman
Regular Season — Playoffs

Season	Team	League	GP	G	A	PTS	PIM	GP	G	A	PTS	PIM
94-95	Tallahassee	ECHL	68	6	27	33	28	13	0	0	0	18
95-96	Tallahassee	ECHL	68	6	24	30	108	12	0	4	4	6
96-97	Tallahassee	ECHL	67	5	21	26	61	3	0	1	1	2
97-98	Tallahassee	ECHL	70	3	12	15	49	—	—	—	—	—
98-99	Alexandria	WPHL	69	3	22	25	52	—	—	—	—	—
	ECHL	Totals	273	20	84	104	246	28	0	5	5	26

Born; 7/31/72, Burnsville, Minnesota. 6-2, 212. Last amateur club; Notre Dame (CCHA).

Chris O'Sullivan — Defenseman
Regular Season — Playoffs

Season	Team	League	GP	G	A	PTS	PIM	GP	G	A	PTS	PIM
96-97	Calgary	NHL	27	2	8	10	2	—	—	—	—	—
96-97	Saint John	AHL	29	3	8	11	17	5	0	4	4	0
97-98	Calgary	NHL	12	0	2	2	10	—	—	—	—	—
97-98	Saint John	AHL	32	4	10	14	2	21	2	17	19	18
98-99	Calgary	NHL	10	0	1	1	2	—	—	—	—	—
98-99	Saint John	AHL	41	7	29	36	24	—	—	—	—	—
98-99	Hartford	AHL	10	1	4	5	0	7	1	3	4	11
	NHL	Totals	49	2	11	13	14	—	—	—	—	—
	AHL	Totals	112	15	51	66	43	33	3	24	27	29

Born; 5/15/74, Dorchester, Massachusetts. 6-2, 185. Drafted by Calgary Flames (2nd choice, 30th overall) in 1992 Entry Draft. Traded to New York Rangers by Calgary for Lee Sorochan and conditional 2000 draft choice (3/23/99). Last amateur club; Boston University (Hockey East).

Francis Ouellette — Goaltender
Regular Season — Playoffs

Season	Team	League	GP	W	L	T	MIN	SO	AVG	GP	W	L	MIN	SO	AVG
91-92	Flint	CoHL	8	2	4	0	384	0	5.63	—	—	—	—	—	—
91-92	Dayton	ECHL	8	4	2	2	493	0	4.26	2	—	—	111	0	5.41
91-92	Peoria	IHL	12	—	—	—	700	0	3.17	—	—	—	—	—	—
92-93	Wheeling	ECHL	43	24	7	7	2376	2	3.48	9	4	4	560	0	3.54
93-94	South Carolina	ECHL	41	16	15	7	2336	0	4.26	—	—	—	—	—	—
94-95	Erie	ECHL	45	15	28	1	2559	1	4.74	—	—	—	—	—	—
95-96	Anchorage	WCHL	23	9	9	3	1296	1	3.75	—	—	—	—	—	—
96-97	Anchorage	WCHL	51	30	15	5	2959	0	3.85	*9	2	*7	*495	0	4.85
97-98	Columbus	CHL	35	26	5	2	2001	*2	2.97	9	*7	2	539	2	*2.00
98-99	Columbus	CHL	40	24	10	3	2262	0	2.76	10	4	4	503	0	3.34
	@ ECHL	Totals	137	59	52	17	7764	3	4.18	11	4	4	671	0	3.85
	CHL	Totals	75	50	15	5	4263	2	2.86	19	11	6	1042	2	2.65
	WCHL	Totals	74	39	24	8	4255	1	3.82	9	2	7	495	0	4.85

Born; 4/16/70, Victoriaville, Quebec. 5-10, 190. @ ECHL win/loss totals are not complete. 1992-93 ECHL First Team All-Star. 1995-96 WCHL Second Team All-Star. 1996-97 WCHL Second Team All-Star. Member of 1997-98 CHL Champion Columbus Cottonmouths. Last amateur club; Hull (QMJHL).

Marc Ouimet — Center
Regular Season — Playoffs

Season	Team	League	GP	G	A	PTS	PIM	GP	G	A	PTS	PIM
92-93	Michigan	CCHA	39	15	45	60	23	—	—	—	—	—
92-93	Baltimore	AHL	1	0	1	1	0	—	—	—	—	—
93-94												
94-95	Worcester	AHL	61	13	29	42	24	—	—	—	—	—
95-96	Adirondack	AHL	59	16	16	32	20	3	0	0	0	2
96-97	Worcester	AHL	2	0	1	1	0	—	—	—	—	—
96-97	Baton Rouge	ECHL	29	9	12	21	7	—	—	—	—	—
97-98												
98-99	Rapperswill	Switz.	37	5	10	15	12	5	1	0	1	0
	AHL	Totals	123	29	47	76	44	3	0	0	0	2

Born; 10/2/71, London, Ontario. 5-10, 183. Drafted by Washington Capitals (6th choice, 94th overall) in 1990 Entry Draft. Last amateur club; Michigan (CCHA).

Nicholas Ouimet — Center
Regular Season — Playoffs

Season	Team	League	GP	G	A	PTS	PIM	GP	G	A	PTS	PIM
98-99	Tulsa	CHL	2	0	0	0	0	—	—	—	—	—
98-99	San Antonio	CHL	15	3	1	4	29	8	1	1	2	6
	CHL	Totals	17	3	1	4	29	8	1	1	2	6

Born; 12/18/77, Elliott Lake, Ontario. 5-10, 190. Last amateur club; St. Cloud (WCHA).

Ronalds Ozolinsh — Defenseman
Regular Season — Playoffs

Season	Team	League	GP	G	A	PTS	PIM	GP	G	A	PTS	PIM
95-96	Jacksonville	ECHL	36	3	5	8	43	15	1	2	3	27
96-97	San Antonio	IHL	2	0	0	0	0	—	—	—	—	—
96-97	Jacksonville	ECHL	50	1	8	9	41	—	—	—	—	—
97-98	Jacksonville	ECHL	3	0	0	0	6	—	—	—	—	—
97-98	Pee Dee	ECHL	33	0	3	3	35	2	0	1	1	5
98-99	Fayetteville	CHL	31	1	4	5	22	—	—	—	—	—
	ECHL	Totals	122	4	16	20	125	17	1	3	4	32

Born; 2/7/73, Riga, Latvia. 6-0, 187. Selected by Florida in 1998 ECHL Expansion Draft.

Kevin Paden — Left Wing

Regular Season / Playoffs

Season	Team	League	GP	G	A	PTS	PIM	GP	G	A	PTS	PIM
95-96	Cape Breton	AHL	1	1	0	1	0	—	—	—	—	—
95-96	Tallahassee	ECHL	23	3	10	13	49	—	—	—	—	—
95-96	Huntington	ECHL	32	4	5	9	52	—	—	—	—	—
96-97	Huntington	ECHL	13	7	5	12	26	—	—	—	—	—
96-97	Nashville	CeHL	23	7	9	16	58	—	—	—	—	—
97-98	Huntington	ECHL	69	18	26	44	107	4	1	0	1	4
98-99	Huntington	ECHL	48	8	12	20	50	—	—	—	—	—
98-99	Peoria	ECHL	17	4	2	6	6	4	0	1	1	8
	ECHL	Totals	202	44	60	104	290	8	1	1	2	12

Born; 2/12/75, Woodhaven, Michigan. 6-4, 200. Drafted by Edmonton Oilers (4th choice, 59th overall) in 1993 Entry Draft. Traded to Peoria by Huntington for Joe Craigen (2/99). Last amateur club; Windsor (OHL).

Jim Paek — Defenseman

Regular Season / Playoffs

Season	Team	League	GP	G	A	PTS	PIM	GP	G	A	PTS	PIM
87-88	Muskegon	IHL	82	7	52	59	141	6	0	0	0	29
88-89	Muskegon	IHL	80	3	54	57	96	14	1	10	11	24
89-90	Muskegon	IHL	81	9	41	50	115	15	1	10	11	41
90-91	Canadian	National	48	2	12	14	24	—	—	—	—	—
90-91	Pittsburgh	NHL	3	0	0	0	9	8	1	0	1	2
91-92	Pittsburgh	NHL	49	1	7	8	36	19	0	4	4	6
92-93	Pittsburgh	NHL	77	3	15	18	64	—	—	—	—	—
93-94	Pittsburgh	NHL	41	0	4	4	8	—	—	—	—	—
93-94	Los Angeles	NHL	18	1	1	2	10	—	—	—	—	—
94-95	Ottawa	NHL	29	0	2	2	28	—	—	—	—	—
95-96	Houston	IHL	25	2	5	7	20	—	—	—	—	—
95-96	Minnesota	IHL	42	1	11	12	54	—	—	—	—	—
96-97	Manitoba	IHL	9	0	2	2	12	—	—	—	—	—
96-97	Cleveland	IHL	74	3	25	28	36	14	0	1	1	2
97-98	Cleveland	IHL	75	7	9	16	48	10	2	1	3	4
98-99	Cleveland	IHL	65	4	11	15	34	—	—	—	—	—
98-99	Houston	IHL	11	0	3	3	2	19	2	4	6	10
	NHL	Totals	217	5	29	34	155	27	1	4	5	8
	IHL	Totals	544	36	213	249	558	78	6	26	32	110

Born; 4/7/67, Weston, Ontario. 6-1, 195. Drafted by Pittsburgh Penguins (9th choice, 170th overall) in 1985 Entry Draft. Traded to Lcs Angeles Kings by Pittsburgh with Marty McSorley for Tomas Sandstrom and Shawn McEachern (2/16/94). Traded to Ottawa Senators by Los Angeles for Ottawa's seventh round choice (Benoit Larose) in 1995 Entry Draft (6/26/94). Member of 1988-89 IHL champion Muskegon Lumberjacks. Member of 1990-91 Stanley Cup Champion Pittsburgh Penguins. Member of 1991-92 Stanley Cup Champion Pittsburgh Penguins. Member of 1998-99 IHL Champion Houston Aeros. Last amateur club;

Francois Page — Right Wing

Regular Season / Playoffs

Season	Team	League	GP	G	A	PTS	PIM	GP	G	A	PTS	PIM
98-99	Rimouski	QMJHL	35	22	21	43	194	11	3	6	9	33
98-99	Mobile	ECHL	14	3	1	4	48	—	—	—	—	—

Born; Last amateur club; Rimouski (QMJHL).

Scott Page — Forward

Regular Season / Playoffs

Season	Team	League	GP	G	A	PTS	PIM	GP	G	A	PTS	PIM
98-99	Mississauga	OHL	66	20	30	50	251	—	—	—	—	—
98-99	Jacksonville	ECHL	3	0	0	0	4	2	0	0	0	0

Born; Selected by Arkansas in 1999 ECHL Expansion Draft. Last amateur club; Mississauga (OHL).

Matthew Pagnutti — Defenseman

Regular Season / Playoffs

Season	Team	League	GP	G	A	PTS	PIM	GP	G	A	PTS	PIM
96-97	Clarkson	ECAC	37	9	26	35	42	—	—	—	—	—
96-97	Carolina	AHL	1	0	0	0	0	—	—	—	—	—
97-98	Milwaukee	IHL	1	0	0	0	0	—	—	—	—	—
97-98	Louisiana	ECHL	68	5	15	20	63	12	1	6	7	12
98-99	Louisiana	ECHL	64	2	19	21	76	5	0	0	0	4
	ECHL	Totals	132	7	34	41	139	17	1	6	7	12

Born; 9/25/75, Springfield, Massachusetts. 6-0, 190. Last amateur club; Clarkson (ECAC).

Jason Pain — Center

Regular Season / Playoffs

Season	Team	League	GP	G	A	PTS	PIM	GP	G	A	PTS	PIM
97-98	Louisville	ECHL	52	14	17	31	24	—	—	—	—	—
98-99	Muskegon	UHL	18	3	1	4	6	—	—	—	—	—
98-99	Central Texas	WPHL	18	10	10	20	18	—	—	—	—	—

Born; 2/25/73, Toronto, Ontario. 5-11, 185. Last amateur club; York (OUAA).

Greg Pajor — Right Wing

Regular Season / Playoffs

Season	Team	League	GP	G	A	PTS	PIM	GP	G	A	PTS	PIM
96-97	Brantford	CoHL	55	8	17	25	16	10	1	2	3	4
97-98	Brantford	UHL	54	14	17	31	10	—	—	—	—	—
97-98	Binghamton	UHL	11	6	3	9	2	5	3	1	4	6
98-99	Binghamton	UHL	74	40	42	82	52	5	1	3	4	22
	UHL	Totals	194	68	79	147	80	20	5	6	11	32

Born; 9/6/71, Wilsonville, Ontario. 6-0, 180. Traded to Binghamton by Brantford with Cory Bricknell and Chris Grenville for Rob MacInnis (3/98). Last amateur club; Western Ontario University (OUAA).

Derek Pajot — Defenseman

Regular Season / Playoffs

Season	Team	League	GP	G	A	PTS	PIM	GP	G	A	PTS	PIM
97-98	Waco	WPHL	3	0	0	0	21	—	—	—	—	—
97-98	Odessa	WPHL	57	0	7	7	190	—	—	—	—	—
98-99	New Mexico	WPHL	4	0	0	0	10	—	—	—	—	—
98-99	Fort Worth	WPHL	3	0	1	1	6	—	—	—	—	—
	WPHL	Totals	67	0	8	8	227	—	—	—	—	—

Born; 11/16/76, LaSalle, Ontario. 6-4, 220. Traded to Odessa by Waco for Patrick Bergeron (10/97). Selected by Corpus Christi in 1998 WPHL Expansion Draft.

Ron Paleczny — Defenseman

Regular Season / Playoffs

Season	Team	League	GP	G	A	PTS	PIM	GP	G	A	PTS	PIM
96-97	Knoxville	ECHL	13	0	1	1	2	—	—	—	—	—
96-97	Columbus	ECHL	1	0	0	0	0	—	—	—	—	—
97-98	Fort Worth	WPHL	6	0	0	0	2	—	—	—	—	—
97-98	Fort Worth	CHL	3	0	0	0	4	—	—	—	—	—
98-99	Asheville	UHL	9	0	0	0	8	—	—	—	—	—
	ECHL	Totals	14	0	1	1	2	—	—	—	—	—

Born; 3/13/76, Kitchener, Ontario. 6-0, 205. Last amateur club; Waterloo

Rob Pallin — Defenseman

Regular Season / Playoffs

Season	Team	League	GP	G	A	PTS	PIM	GP	G	A	PTS	PIM
97-98	Reno	WCHL	2	0	1	1	4	—	—	—	—	—
98-99	Fresno	WCHL	2	1	0	1	0	—	—	—	—	—
	WCHL	Totals	4	1	1	2	4	—	—	—	—	—

Born;

Chris Palmer — Center

Regular Season / Playoffs

Season	Team	League	GP	G	A	PTS	PIM	GP	G	A	PTS	PIM
90-91	Utica	AHL	47	11	9	20	34	—	—	—	—	—
90-91	Johnstown	ECHL	25	3	20	23	13	1	0	0	0	7
91-92												
92-93	Murrayfield	BHL	36	96	86	182	97	—	—	—	—	—
93-94	Murrayfield	BHL	44	114	97	211	60	—	—	—	—	—
94-95	Canada	National	4	0	0	0	0	—	—	—	—	—
94-95	Edinburgh	BHL	37	77	85	162	55	—	—	—	—	—
95-96	Utica	CoHL	4	1	1	2	0	—	—	—	—	—
95-96	Fife	BHL	50	66	85	151	94	—	—	—	—	—
96-97												
97-98	HC Thurgen	Swiss	25	17	16	33	30	—	—	—	—	—
98-99	Winston-Salem	UHL	23	10	23	33	19	—	—	—	—	—
98-99	Saginaw	UHL	6	5	2	7	4	—	—	—	—	—
98-99	Mohawk Valley	UHL	13	11	7	18	18	—	—	—	—	—
	UHL	Totals	42	26	32	58	41	—	—	—	—	—

Born; 5/14/67, Midland, Ontario. 5-11, 175. Traded to Mohawk Valley by Saginaw for Mark Bultje (2/99).

Drew Palmer — Defenseman
Regular Season / Playoffs

Season	Team	League	GP	G	A	PTS	PIM	GP	G	A	PTS	PIM
96-97	Cleveland	IHL	13	0	0	0	21	—	—	—	—	—
96-97	Kansas City	IHL	26	0	2	2	55	—	—	—	—	—
96-97	Mobile	ECHL	5	0	2	2	25	—	—	—	—	—
97-98	Syracuse	AHL	5	0	0	0	11	—	—	—	—	—
97-98	Orlando	IHL	4	0	1	1	4	—	—	—	—	—
97-98	Tallahassee	ECHL	19	0	3	3	62	—	—	—	—	—
97-98	Hampton Roads	ECHL	19	0	1	1	53	6	0	2	2	2
98-99	Tallahassee	ECHL	41	0	4	4	86	—	—	—	—	—
	IHL	Totals	43	0	3	3	80	—	—	—	—	—
	ECHL	Totals	84	0	10	10	226	6	0	2	2	2

Born; 1/10/76, Wayzata, Minnesota. 6-3, 210. Member of 1997-98 ECHL Champion Hampton Roads Admirals. Last amateur club; Seattle (WHL).

Greg Pankewicz — Right Wing
Regular Season / Playoffs

Season	Team	League	GP	G	A	PTS	PIM	GP	G	A	PTS	PIM
91-92	Knoxville	ECHL	59	41	39	80	214	—	—	—	—	—
92-93	New Haven	AHL	62	23	20	43	163	—	—	—	—	—
93-94	Ottawa	NHL	3	0	0	0	2	—	—	—	—	—
93-94	Prince Edward Island	AHL	69	33	29	62	241	—	—	—	—	—
94-95	Prince Edward Island	AHL	75	37	30	67	161	6	1	1	2	24
95-96	Portland	AHL	28	9	12	21	99	—	—	—	—	—
95-96	Chicago	IHL	45	9	16	25	164	5	4	0	4	8
96-97	Chicago	IHL	79	32	34	66	222	—	—	—	—	—
97-98	Manitoba	IHL	76	42	34	76	246	3	0	0	0	6
98-99	Calgary	NHL	18	0	3	3	20	—	—	—	—	—
98-99	Saint John	AHL	30	10	14	24	84	—	—	—	—	—
98-99	Kentucky	AHL	10	2	3	5	7	11	4	1	5	10
	NHL	Totals	21	0	3	3	22	—	—	—	—	—
	AHL	Totals	274	114	108	222	755	22	9	2	11	42
	IHL	Totals	200	83	84	167	632	8	4	0	4	14

Born; 10/6/70, Drayton Valley, Alberta. 6-0, 180. Signed as a free agent by Ottawa Senators (5/27/93). Signed as a free agent by Washington Capitals (7/2/95). Signed as a free agent by Calgary Flames (9/1/98). Sold to San Jose Sharks by Calgary (3/23/99). Last amateur club; Regina (WHL).

Grigori Panteleyev — Right Wing
Regular Season / Playoffs

Season	Team	League	GP	G	A	PTS	PIM	GP	G	A	PTS	PIM
92-93	Boston	NHL	39	8	6	14	12	—	—	—	—	—
92-93	Providence	AHL	39	17	30	47	22	3	0	0	0	10
93-94	Boston	NHL	10	0	0	0	0	—	—	—	—	—
93-94	Providence	AHL	55	24	26	50	20	—	—	—	—	—
94-95	Boston	NHL	1	0	0	0	0	—	—	—	—	—
94-95	Providence	AHL	70	20	23	43	36	13	8	11	19	6
95-96	Utah	IHL	33	11	25	36	18	—	—	—	—	—
95-96	Las Vegas	IHL	29	15	21	36	14	15	4	7	11	2
95-96	Islanders	NHL	4	0	0	0	0	—	—	—	—	—
96-97	San Antonio	IHL	81	25	37	62	41	9	4	2	6	4
97-98	San Antonio	IHL	19	2	13	15	8	—	—	—	—	—
97-98	Orlando	IHL	63	27	29	56	44	17	6	9	15	2
98-99	Orlando	IHL	77	25	37	62	51	17	8	8	16	4
	NHL	Totals	54	8	6	14	12	—	—	—	—	—
	IHL	Totals	302	105	162	267	266	58	22	26	48	12
	AHL	Totals	164	61	79	160	78	16	8	11	19	16

Born; 11/13/72, Gastello, Russia. 5-9, 185. Drafted by Boston Bruins (5th choice, 136th overall) in 1992 Entry Draft. Signed as a free agent by New York Islanders (9/20/95). Traded to Orlando by San Antonio with Dave MacIntyre and Scott Hollis for Chirs Lipuma, Dave Smith and Dave Chyzowski (11/97).

Perry Pappas — Right Wing
Regular Season / Playoffs

Season	Team	League	GP	G	A	PTS	PIM	GP	G	A	PTS	PIM
96-97	Wheeling	ECHL	11	3	1	4	18	—	—	—	—	—
96-97	Baton Rouge	ECHL	39	17	6	23	89	—	—	—	—	—
97-98												
98-99	Slough	BNL										
	ECHL	Totals	50	20	7	27	107	—	—	—	—	—

Born; 11/3/73, Chatham, Ontario. 6-2, 210.

Normand Paquet — Center
Regular Season / Playoffs

Season	Team	League	GP	G	A	PTS	PIM	GP	G	A	PTS	PIM
96-97	Thunder Bay	CoHL	74	19	42	61	55	11	2	6	8	4
97-98	Thunder Bay	UHL	72	14	30	44	31	5	1	0	1	6
98-99	Thunder Bay	UHL	74	22	41	63	32	12	0	3	3	12
	UHL	Totals	220	55	113	168	118	28	3	9	12	22

Born; 7/5/73, Beauport, Quebec. 5-10, 195.

Charles Paquette — Defenseman
Regular Season / Playoffs

Season	Team	League	GP	G	A	PTS	PIM	GP	G	A	PTS	PIM
95-96	Providence	AHL	11	0	1	1	8	4	0	1	1	4
95-96	Charlotte	ECHL	45	4	5	9	114	3	0	1	1	6
96-97	Providence	AHL	18	0	3	3	25	6	0	0	0	8
97-98	Providence	AHL	23	0	0	0	85	—	—	—	—	—
97-98	Charlotte	ECHL	4	0	0	0	35	7	0	3	3	12
98-99	Greenville	ECHL	57	3	8	11	211	—	—	—	—	—
	AHL	Totals	52	0	4	4	118	10	0	1	1	12
	ECHL	Totals	106	7	13	20	360	10	0	4	4	18

Born; 6/17/75, Lachute, Quebec. 6-1, 193. Drafted by Boston Bruins (3rd choice, 88th overall) in 1993 Entry Draft. Member of 1995-96 ECHL champion Charlotte Checkers. Last amateur club; Sherbrooke (QMJHL).

Carl Paradis — Forward
Regular Season / Playoffs

Season	Team	League	GP	G	A	PTS	PIM	GP	G	A	PTS	PIM
97-98	New Mexico	WPHL	17	5	5	10	30	—	—	—	—	—
97-98	San Angelo	WPHL	31	8	3	11	30	3	0	0	0	4
98-99	San Angelo	WPHL	45	6	18	24	69	—	—	—	—	—
	WPHL	Totals	93	19	26	45	129	3	0	0	0	4

Born; 2/25/76, Beauport, Quebec. 6-1, 193. Last amateur club; Victoriaville (QMJHL).

Dave Paradise — Center
Regular Season / Playoffs

Season	Team	League	GP	G	A	PTS	PIM	GP	G	A	PTS	PIM
97-98	Saint John	AHL	18	4	1	5	12	—	—	—	—	—
97-98	Detroit	IHL	14	1	1	2	12	—	—	—	—	—
97-98	Chicago	IHL	11	3	2	5	12	—	—	—	—	—
97-98	Quebec	IHL	12	8	4	12	10	—	—	—	—	—
97-98	Peoria	ECHL	15	16	7	23	42	—	—	—	—	—
98-99	Adirondack	AHL	74	17	23	40	62	3	1	1	2	6
	AHL	Totals	92	21	24	45	74	3	1	1	2	6
	IHL	Totals	37	12	7	19	34	—	—	—	—	—

Born; 11/24/73, St. Paul, Minnesota. 6-0, 190. Traded to Quebec by Chicago with Jack Williams for Marc`Rodgers and Steve Larouche (3/98). Last amateur club; St. Cloud (WCHA).

Bob Pardy — Defenseman
Regular Season / Playoffs

Season	Team	League	GP	G	A	PTS	PIM	GP	G	A	PTS	PIM
97-98	Lake Charles	WPHL	42	5	9	14	42	—	—	—	—	—
98-99	Topeka	CHL	8	0	0	0	6	—	—	—	—	—

Born; 7/28/74, St. John's, Newfoundland. 6-0, 195.

Rich Parent — Goaltender

Regular Season / Playoffs

Season	Team	League	GP	W	L	T	MIN	SO	AVG	GP	W	L	MIN	SO	AVG
94-95	Muskegon	CoHL	35	17	11	3	1867	1	3.60	13	7	4	725	1	3.89
95-96	Rochester	AHL	2	0	1	0	90	0	4.02	—	—	—	—	—	—
95-96	Muskegon	CoHL	36	23	7	4	2087	2	2.44	—	—	—	—	—	—
95-96	Detroit	IHL	19	16	0	1	1040	2	2.77	7	3	3	362	0	3.64
96-97	Detroit	IHL	53	31	13	4	2815	4	2.22	15	8	3	786	1	*1.60
97-98	St. Louis	NHL	1	0	0	0	12	0	0.00	—	—	—	—	—	—
97-98	Manitoba	IHL	26	8	12	2	1334	3	3.10	—	—	—	—	—	—
97-98	Detroit	IHL	7	4	0	3	418	0	2.15	5	1	0	157	0	2.29
98-99	St. Louis	NHL	10	4	3	1	519	1	2.54	—	—	—	—	—	—
98-99	Worcester	AHL	20	8	8	2	1100	1	3.05	—	—	—	—	—	—
	NHL	Totals	11	4	3	1	531	1	2.49	—	—	—	—	—	—
	IHL	Totals	105	59	25	10	5607	9	2.53	27	12	6	1305	1	2.25
	AHL	Totals	22	8	9	2	1190	1	3.13	—	—	—	—	—	—
	CoHL	Totals	71	40	18	7	3954	3	2.99	13	7	4	725	1	3.89

Born; 3/29/73, Montreal, Quebec. 6-3, 215. Signed as a free agent by St. Louis Blues (7/31/97). Traded to Detroit by Manitoba for Steve Thomas (2/98). 1995-96 CoHL First Team All-Star. 1995-96 CoHL Best Goaltender. Shared 1996-97 IHL Norris Trophy (fewest goals against) with Jeff Reese. Member of 1996-97 IHL Champion Detroit Vipers.

Russ Parent — Defenseman

Regular Season / Playoffs

Season	Team	League	GP	G	A	PTS	PIM	GP	G	A	PTS	PIM
90-91	Ayr	BHL	15	6	21	27	22	—	—	—	—	—
91-92	Ayr	BHL	15	5	10	15	100	—	—	—	—	—
92-93	Basingstoke	BHL	32	19	55	74	42	—	—	—	—	—
93-94	Basingstoke	BHL	52	21	48	69	56	—	—	—	—	—
95-96	Basingstoke	BHL	31	3	9	12	26	—	—	—	—	—
96-97	Fife	BHL	26	24	40	64	57	—	—	—	—	—
97-98	Monroe	WPHL	69	12	29	41	72	—	—	—	—	—
98-99	Monroe	WPHL	69	10	27	37	54	6	0	1	1	0
	WPHL	Totals	138	22	56	78	126	6	0	1	1	0

Born; 5/6/68, Winnipeg, Manitoba. 5-10, 185. Selected by New York Rangers (11th choice, 219th overall) in 1986 Entry Draft. Last amateur club; North Dakota (WCHA).

Sebastien Parent — Forward

Regular Season / Playoffs

Season	Team	League	GP	G	A	PTS	PIM	GP	G	A	PTS	PIM
96-97	Memphis	CeHL	10	8	0	8	63	3	2	1	3	4
97-98	Macon	CHL	49	15	28	43	112	—	—	—	—	—
97-98	Memphis	CHL	11	10	7	17	23	4	1	1	2	10
98-99	Idaho	WCHL	58	24	33	57	157	2	0	0	0	8
	CHL	Totals	70	33	35	68	198	7	3	2	5	14

Born;7/8/71, Jonquiere, Quebec. 5-9, 172. Traded to Memphis by Macon with Matt McElwee and Marcel Chagnon for Dan Brown (3/98).

Richard Park — Center

Regular Season / Playoffs

Season	Team	League	GP	G	A	PTS	PIM	GP	G	A	PTS	PIM
94-95	Belleville	OHL	45	28	51	79	35	16	9	18	27	12
94-95	Pittsburgh	NHL	1	0	1	1	2	3	0	0	0	2
95-96	Pittsburgh	NHL	56	4	6	10	36	1	0	0	0	0
96-97	Pittsburgh	NHL	1	0	0	0	0	—	—	—	—	—
96-97	Anaheim	NHL	11	1	1	2	10	11	0	1	1	2
96-97	Cleveland	IHL	50	12	15	27	30	—	—	—	—	—
97-98	Anaheim	NHL	15	0	2	2	8	—	—	—	—	—
97-98	Cincinnati	AHL	56	17	26	43	36	—	—	—	—	—
98-99	Philadelphia	NHL	7	0	0	0	0	—	—	—	—	—
98-99	Philadelphia	AHL	75	41	42	83	33	16	9	6	15	4
	NHL	Totals	91	5	10	15	56	15	0	1	1	4
	AHL	Totals	131	58	68	126	69	16	9	6	15	4

Born; 5/27/76, Seoul, South Korea. 5-11, 190. Drafted by Pittsburgh Penguins (2nd choice, 50th overall) in 1994 Entry Draft. Traded to Anaheim Mighty Ducks by Pittsburgh for Roman Oksiuta, (3/18/97). Signed as a free agent by Philadelphia Flyers (8/24/98). 1998-99 ECHL Second Team All-Star. Last amateur club; Belleville (OHL).

Matt Parker — Forward

Regular Season / Playoffs

Season	Team	League	GP	G	A	PTS	PIM	GP	G	A	PTS	PIM
98-99	Tupelo	WPHL	2	0	1	1	4	—	—	—	—	—

Born; 7/28/75, Huntsville, Alabama. 5-11, 185. Last amateur club; Alabama-Huntsville (NCAA 2).

Scott Parker — Right Wing

Regular Season / Playoffs

Season	Team	League	GP	G	A	PTS	PIM	GP	G	A	PTS	PIM
98-99	Colorado	NHL	27	0	0	0	71	—	—	—	—	—
98-99	Hershey	AHL	32	4	3	7	143	4	0	0	0	6

Born; 1/29/78, Hanford, California. 6-4, 220. Drafted by New Jersey Devils (6th choice, 63rd overall) in 1996 Entry Draft. Re-entered Draft, selected by Colorado Avalanche (4th choice, 20th overall) in 1998 Entry Draft. Last amateur club; Kelowna (WHL).

Greg Parks — Right Wing

Regular Season / Playoffs

Season	Team	League	GP	G	A	PTS	PIM	GP	G	A	PTS	PIM
89-90	Springfield	AHL	49	22	32	54	30	18	9	*13	*22	22
89-90	Johnstown	ECHL	8	5	9	14	7	—	—	—	—	—
90-91	Capital District	AHL	48	32	43	75	67	—	—	—	—	—
90-91	Islanders	NHL	20	1	2	3	4	—	—	—	—	—
91-92	Islanders	NHL	1	0	0	0	2	—	—	—	—	—
91-92	Capital District	AHL	70	36	57	93	84	7	5	8	13	4
92-93	Leksand	Sweden	39	21	19	40	66	1	0	0	0	4
92-93	Canada	National	9	2	2	4	4	—	—	—	—	—
92-93	Islanders	NHL	2	0	0	0	0	2	0	0	0	0
93-94	Leksand	Sweden	39	21	18	39	44	4	3	1	4	—
93-94	Canada	National	21	2	3	5	122	—	—	—	—	—
93-94	Canada	Olympic	8	1	2	3	10	—	—	—	—	—
94-95	Krefeld	Germany	10	2	7	9	8	1	0	0	0	0
95-96	Canada	National	7	0	0	0	6	—	—	—	—	—
96-97	Langnau	Switz.	50	41	47	88	90	—	—	—	—	—
97-98	Langnau	Switz.	40	30	40	70	56	16	9	8	17	21
98-99	Langnau	Switz.	29	13	24	37	26	—	—	—	—	—
	NHL	Totals	23	1	2	3	6	2	0	0	0	0
	AHL	Totals	167	90	132	222	181	25	14	21	35	26

Born; 3/25/67, Edmonton, Alberta. 5-9, 180. Signed as a free agent by New York Islanders (8/13/90). Member of 1989-90 AHL Champion Springfield Indians. Last amateur club; Bowling Green (CCHA).

Scott Parmentier — Left Wing

Regular Season / Playoffs

Season	Team	League	GP	G	A	PTS	PIM	GP	G	A	PTS	PIM
98-99	Chesapeake	ECHL	1	0	0	0	2	—	—	—	—	—
98-99	Arkansas	WPHL	5	3	4	7	2	—	—	—	—	—
98-99	El Paso	WPHL	2	0	0	0	2	—	—	—	—	—
	WPHL	Totals	7	3	4	7	2	—	—	—	—	—

Born; 4/3/74, Blackstone, Massachusetts. 5-9, 180. Last amateur club; Maine

Dwight Parrish — Defenseman

Regular Season / Playoffs

Season	Team	League	GP	G	A	PTS	PIM	GP	G	A	PTS	PIM
96-97	Michigan	IHL	2	0	0	0	0	—	—	—	—	—
96-97	Fort Wayne	IHL	2	0	0	0	2	—	—	—	—	—
96-97	Dayton	ECHL	57	3	14	17	90	4	0	0	0	28
97-98	Syracuse	AHL	3	0	0	0	0	—	—	—	—	—
97-98	Providence	AHL	2	0	0	0	4	—	—	—	—	—
97-98	Michigan	IHL	2	0	0	0	0	—	—	—	—	—
97-98	Fort Wayne	IHL	3	0	1	1	4	—	—	—	—	—
97-98	Dayton	ECHL	62	9	18	27	139	5	0	1	1	12
98-99	Portland	AHL	54	2	4	6	138	—	—	—	—	—
	AHL	Totals	59	2	4	6	142	—	—	—	—	—
	IHL	Totals	9	0	1	1	6	—	—	—	—	—
	ECHL	Totals	119	12	32	44	229	9	0	1	1	40

Born; 4/6/72, Farmington, Michigan. 6-0, 195. Last amateur club; Ferris State (CCHA).

Mark Parrish — Right Wing

Regular Season — Playoffs

Season	Team	League	GP	G	A	PTS	PIM	GP	G	A	PTS	PIM
97-98	Seattle	WHL	54	54	38	92	29	5	2	3	5	2
97-98	New Haven	AHL	1	1	0	1	2	—	—	—	—	—
98-99	Florida	NHL	73	24	13	37	25	—	—	—	—	—
98-99	New Haven	AHL	2	1	0	1	0	—	—	—	—	—
	AHL	Totals	3	2	0	2	2	—	—	—	—	—

Born; 2/2/77, Edina, Minnesota. 6-0, 182. Drafted by Colorado Avalanche (3rd choice, 79th overall) in 1996 Entry Draft. Traded to Florida Panthers by Colorado with Anaheim's third round choice (previously acquired by Colorado-Florida selected Lance Ward) for Tom Fitzgerald (3/24/98). Last amateur club; Seattle (WHL).

Jeff Parrott — Defenseman

Regular Season — Playoffs

Season	Team	League	GP	G	A	PTS	PIM	GP	G	A	PTS	PIM
93-94	Cornwall	AHL	52	4	11	15	37	—	—	—	—	—
94-95	Cornwall	AHL	65	2	5	7	99	14	0	1	1	12
95-96	Cornwall	AHL	77	1	11	12	94	8	0	0	0	4
96-97	Detroit	IHL	78	2	8	10	63	18	0	2	2	12
97-98	Quebec	IHL	24	1	2	3	10	—	—	—	—	—
97-98	Manitoba	IHL	47	1	11	12	43	3	0	0	0	2
98-99	Manitoba	IHL	82	2	18	20	82	5	0	0	0	6
	IHL	Totals	231	6	39	45	198	26	0	2	2	20
	AHL	Totals	194	7	27	34	230	22	0	1	1	16

Born; 4/6/71, The Pas, Manitoba. Drafted by Quebec Nordiques (4th choice, 106th overall) in 1990 Entry Draft. Traded to Manitoba by Quebec with Craig Martin and Michel Mongeau for Dale DeGray and Rick Girard (12/97). Member of 1996-97 IHL Champion Detroit Vipers. Last amateur club; Minnesota-Duluth

Don Parsons — Left Wing

Regular Season — Playoffs

Season	Team	League	GP	G	A	PTS	PIM	GP	G	A	PTS	PIM
91-92	Lowell	H.E.	32	7	15	22	34					
91-92	Nashville	ECHL	3	0	3	3	0	—	—	—	—	—
92-93	Nashville	ECHL	60	27	34	61	62	9	3	2	5	12
93-94												
94-95	Tallahassee	ECHL	66	41	35	76	82	13	5	10	15	12
95-96	Johnstown	ECHL	66	50	39	89	104	—	—	—	—	—
96-97	Worcester	AHL	2	1	1	2	4	—	—	—	—	—
96-97	Baton Rouge	ECHL	19	13	14	27	8	—	—	—	—	—
96-97	Louisiana	ECHL	49	28	21	49	94	17	7	9	16	54
97-98	Louisiana	ECHL	70	*55	45	100	112	8	1	10	11	8
98-99	Manitoba	IHL	2	0	0	0	0	—	—	—	—	—
98-99	Louisiana	ECHL	44	34	29	63	44	4	0	1	1	4
	ECHL	Totals	379	248	217	465	506	51	16	32	48	90

Born; 1/17/69, Boston, Massachusetts. 5-10, 190. 1997-98 ECHL Second All-Star Team. Last amateur club; Lowell (Hockey East).

Jeremy Parsons — Center

Regular Season — Playoffs

Season	Team	League	GP	G	A	PTS	PIM	GP	G	A	PTS	PIM
97-98	Wheeling	ECHL	1	1	0	1	2	—	—	—	—	—
97-98	Binghamton	UHL	5	1	0	1	4	—	—	—	—	—
97-98	Central Texas	WPHL	2	0	0	0	2	—	—	—	—	—
98-99	Central Texas	WPHL	5	0	0	0	0	—	—	—	—	—
	WPHL	Totals	7	0	0	0	2	—	—	—	—	—

Born; 11/17/75, Binghamton, New York. 6-1, 200.

Jeff Parthenais — Defenseman

Regular Season — Playoffs

Season	Team	League	GP	G	A	PTS	PIM	GP	G	A	PTS	PIM
98-99	Brampton	OHL	46	0	8	8	55	—	—	—	—	—
98-99	Flint	UHL	6	0	0	0	4	3	0	0	0	0

Born; 7/17/79, Rochester, New York. 6-4, 210. Last amateur club; Brampton

Valentino Passarelli — Center

Regular Season — Playoffs

Season	Team	League	GP	G	A	PTS	PIM	GP	G	A	PTS	PIM
97-98	Quebec	IHL	13	4	4	8	6	—	—	—	—	—
97-98	Pensacola	ECHL	47	20	30	50	32	19	5	11	16	26
98-99	Richmond	ECHL	42	10	14	24	34	18	5	4	9	4
	ECHL	Totals	89	30	44	74	66	37	10	15	25	30

Born; 2/14/73, Montreal, Quebec. 5-11, 190.

Daniel Passero — Defenseman

Regular Season — Playoffs

Season	Team	League	GP	G	A	PTS	PIM	GP	G	A	PTS	PIM
98-99	Sault St. Marie	OHL	61	11	51	62	46	5	1	4	5	8
98-99	Birmingham	ECHL	2	0	0	0	0	4	0	2	2	6

Born; 6/4/79, Vaughan, Ontario. 6-2, 201. Last amateur club; Sault Ste. Marie (OHL).

Steve Passmore — Goaltender

Regular Season — Playoffs

Season	Team	League	GP	W	L	T	MIN	SO	AVG	GP	W	L	MIN	SO	AVG
94-95	Cape Breton	AHL	25	8	13	3	1455	0	3.83	—	—	—	—	—	—
95-96	Cape Breton	AHL	2	1	0	0	90	0	1.33	—	—	—	—	—	—
96-97	Hamilton	AHL	27	12	12	3	1568	1	2.68	22	12	*10	1325	*2	2.76
96-97	Raleigh	ECHL	2	1	1	0	119	0	6.56	—	—	—	—	—	—
97-98	Hamilton	AHL	27	11	10	6	1656	2	3.15	3	0	2	133	0	6.33
97-98	San Antonio	IHL	14	3	8	2	737	0	4.56	—	—	—	—	—	—
98-99	Edmonton	NHL	6	1	4	1	362	0	2.82	—	—	—	—	—	—
98-99	Hamilton	AHL	54	24	21	7	3148	4	2.23	11	5	6	680	0	2.74
	AHL	Totals	135	56	56	19	7917	7	2.80	36	17	18	2138	2	2.98

Born; 1/29/73, Thunder Bay, Ontario. 5-9, 165. Drafted by Quebec Nordiques (9th choice, 196th overall) in 1992 Entry Draft. Traded to Edmonton Oilers by Quebec for Brad Werenka (3/21/94). Signed as a free agent by Chicago Blackhawks (7/8/99). 1996-97 AHL Most Sportsmanlike Player. 1998-99 AHL Second Team All-Star. Last amateur club; Kamloops (WHL).

Craig Paterson — Defenseman

Regular Season — Playoffs

Season	Team	League	GP	G	A	PTS	PIM	GP	G	A	PTS	PIM
96-97	Richmond	ECHL	60	1	9	10	147	8	0	0	0	31
97-98	Syracuse	AHL	2	0	0	0	5	—	—	—	—	—
97-98	Richmond	ECHL	65	3	10	13	213	—	—	—	—	—
98-99	Kentucky	AHL	2	0	0	0	7	—	—	—	—	—
98-99	Richmond	ECHL	59	9	7	16	135	17	1	2	3	19
	AHL	Totals	4	0	0	0	12	—	—	—	—	—
	ECHL	Totals	184	13	26	39	495	25	1	2	3	50

Born; 11/6/72, Scarborough, Ontario. 6-2, 208. Last amateur club; Ohio State (CCHA).

Eric Patry — Goaltender

Regular Season — Playoffs

Season	Team	League	GP	W	L	T	MIN	SO	AVG	GP	W	L	MIN	SO	AVG
98-99	Macon	CHL	28	11	9	3	1342	1	3.13	—	—	—	—	—	—

Born; 3/5/77, Gatineau, Quebec. 6-3, 185.

Adam Patterson — Defenseman

Regular Season — Playoffs

Season	Team	League	GP	G	A	PTS	PIM	GP	G	A	PTS	PIM
98-99	Tulsa	CHL	7	0	1	1	38	—	—	—	—	—

Born; 8/16/74, Rochester, Minnesota. 6-2, 210.

Ed Patterson
Right Wing

Season	Team	League	GP	G	A	PTS	PIM	GP	G	A	PTS	PIM
		Regular Season						Playoffs				
92-93	Cleveland	IHL	63	4	16	20	131	3	1	1	2	2
93-94	Pittsburgh	NHL	27	3	1	4	10	—	—	—	—	—
93-94	Cleveland	IHL	55	21	32	53	73	—	—	—	—	—
94-95	Cleveland	IHL	58	13	17	30	93	4	1	2	3	6
95-96	Pittsburgh	NHL	35	0	2	2	38	—	—	—	—	—
96-97	Pittsburgh	NHL	6	0	0	0	8	—	—	—	—	—
96-97	Cleveland	IHL	40	6	12	18	75	13	2	4	6	61
97-98	Grand Rapids	IHL	81	12	31	43	226	3	2	1	3	8
98-99	Cincinnati	IHL	73	8	25	33	227	3	1	0	1	4
	NHL	Totals	68	3	3	6	56	—	—	—	—	—
	IHL	Totals	370	64	133	197	825	26	7	8	15	81

Born; 11/14/72, Delta, British Columbia. 6-2, 213. Drafted by Pittsburgh Penguins (7th choice, 148th overall) in 1991 Entry Draft. Last amateur club; Kamloops (WHL).

Rob Pattison
Left Wing

Season	Team	League	GP	G	A	PTS	PIM	GP	G	A	PTS	PIM
		Regular Season						Playoffs				
95-96	Albany	AHL	5	4	3	7	0	2	0	0	0	0
95-96	Raleigh	ECHL	67	14	23	37	122	4	1	2	3	0
96-97	Albany	AHL	61	24	16	40	31	16	5	1	6	20
96-97	Raleigh	ECHL	20	13	6	19	28	—	—	—	—	—
97-98	Adirondack	AHL	7	1	2	3	4	3	0	0	0	0
97-98	Las Vegas	IHL	61	13	13	26	68	—	—	—	—	—
98-99	Albany	AHL	40	9	6	15	17	5	0	1	1	0
98-99	Augusta	ECHL	30	11	13	24	63	—	—	—	—	—
	AHL	Totals	113	38	27	65	52	26	5	2	7	20
	ECHL	Totals	117	38	42	80	213	4	1	2	3	0

Born; 9/18/71, Sherborn, Massachusetts. 6-0, 195. Signed as a free agent by New Jersey Devils (10/1/95). Last amateur club; Vermont (ECAC).

Jeff Paul
Defenseman

Season	Team	League	GP	G	A	PTS	PIM	GP	G	A	PTS	PIM
		Regular Season						Playoffs				
98-99	Portland	AHL	6	0	0	0	4	—	—	—	—	—
98-99	Indianapolis	IHL	55	0	7	7	120	7	0	2	2	12

Born; 3/1/78, London, Ontario. 6-3, 196. Drafted by Chicago Blackhawks (2nd choice, 42nd overall) in 1996 Entry Draft. Last amateur club; Erie (OHL).

Rastislav Pavlikovsky
Left Wing

Season	Team	League	GP	G	A	PTS	PIM	GP	G	A	PTS	PIM
		Regular Season						Playoffs				
97-98	Las Vegas	IHL	1	0	0	0	0	—	—	—	—	—
97-98	Utah	IHL	74	17	29	46	54	2	0	0	0	6
98-99	Cincinnati	IHL	31	4	12	16	28	—	—	—	—	—
98-99	Cincinnati	AHL	36	12	23	35	59	2	0	1	1	4
	IHL	Totals	106	21	41	62	62	2	0	0	0	6

Born; 3/2/77, Dubnica, Slovakia. 5-10, 195. Drafted by Ottawa Senators (10th choice, 246th overall) in 1998 Entry Draft. Last European club; Dukla Trencin (Slovakia).

Jeff Pawluk
Defenseman

Season	Team	League	GP	G	A	PTS	PIM	GP	G	A	PTS	PIM
		Regular Season						Playoffs				
93-94	St. Thomas	CoHL	56	8	23	31	23	3	1	0	1	2
94-95	Lakeland	SUN	9	0	2	2	8	—	—	—	—	—
94-95	Huntington	ECHL	7	0	1	1	26	—	—	—	—	—
94-95	Brantford	CoHL	3	0	0	0	0	—	—	—	—	—
95-96	Detroit	CoHL	3	1	0	1	2	—	—	—	—	—
95-96	Wichita	CeHL	23	0	3	3	57	—	—	—	—	—
95-96	Jacksonville	ECHL	26	2	6	8	44	—	—	—	—	—
96-97	Wichita	CeHL	26	3	7	10	26	—	—	—	—	—
96-97	Nashville	CeHL	14	4	5	9	17	—	—	—	—	—
97-98	Nashville	CHL	70	6	19	25	62	9	0	4	4	8
98-99	Monroe	WPHL	68	5	26	31	34	6	1	2	3	12
	CeHL	Totals	133	13	34	47	162	9	0	4	4	8
	CoHL	Totals	59	9	23	32	25	3	1	0	1	2
	ECHL	Totals	33	2	7	9	70	—	—	—	—	—

Born; 7/23/73, Windsor, Ontario. 5-11, 212. Selected by Huntsville in 1998 CHL Dispersal Draft. Last amateur club; Belleville (OHL).

Ryan Pawluk
Left Wing

Season	Team	League	GP	G	A	PTS	PIM	GP	G	A	PTS	PIM
		Regular Season						Playoffs				
96-97	Windsor	OHL	64	38	47	85	34	5	1	4	5	4
96-97	Toledo	ECHL	4	2	0	2	2	5	2	2	4	0
97-98	Houston	IHL	5	0	1	1	2	—	—	—	—	—
97-98	Austin	WPHL	65	36	60	96	51	5	0	4	4	0
98-99	Arkansas	WPHL	69	43	58	101	20	3	2	1	3	6
	WPHL	Totals	134	79	118	197	71	8	2	5	7	6

Born; 3/28/76, Windsor, Ontario. 6-0, 190. Last amateur club; Windsor (OHL).

Andre Payette
Left Wing

Season	Team	League	GP	G	A	PTS	PIM	GP	G	A	PTS	PIM
		Regular Season						Playoffs				
97-98	Philadelphia	AHL	56	5	5	10	209	4	0	0	0	9
98-99	Philadelphia	AHL	12	0	1	1	34	—	—	—	—	—
98-99	Mohawk Valley	UHL	51	9	21	30	241	—	—	—	—	—
	AHL	Totals	68	5	6	11	243	4	0	0	0	9

Born; 7/29/76, Cornwall, Ontario. 6-2, 205. Drafted by Philadelphia Flyers (9th choice, 244th overall) in 1994 Entry Draft. Member of 1997-98 AHL Champion Philadelphia Phantoms. Last amateur club; Kingston (OHL).

Davis Payne
Right Wing

Season	Team	League	GP	G	A	PTS	PIM	GP	G	A	PTS	PIM
		Regular Season						Playoffs				
92-93	Greensboro	ECHL	57	15	20	35	178	1	0	0	0	4
93-94	Phoenix	IHL	22	6	3	9	51	—	—	—	—	—
93-94	Rochester	AHL	2	0	0	0	5	3	0	2	2	0
93-94	Greensboro	ECHL	36	17	17	34	139	8	2	1	3	27
94-95	Providence	AHL	2	1	0	1	0	—	—	—	—	—
94-95	Greensboro	ECHL	62	25	36	61	195	17	7	10	17	38
95-96	Boston	NHL	7	0	0	0	7	—	—	—	—	—
95-96	Providence	AHL	51	17	22	39	72	4	1	4	5	2
96-97	Boston	NHL	15	0	1	1	7	—	—	—	—	—
96-97	Providence	AHL	57	18	15	33	104	—	—	—	—	—
97-98	Providence	AHL	3	0	0	0	0	—	—	—	—	—
97-98	San Antonio	IHL	59	15	10	25	117	—	—	—	—	—
98-99	Greenville	ECHL	43	19	20	39	96	—	—	—	—	—
	NHL	Totals	22	0	1	1	14	—	—	—	—	—
	AHL	Totals	115	36	37	73	181	7	1	6	7	2
	IHL	Totals	81	21	13	34	168	—	—	—	—	—
	ECHL	Totals	198	76	93	169	608	26	9	11	20	69

Born; 9/24/70, Port Alberni, British Columbia. 6-2, 205. Drafted by Edmonton Oilers (6th choice, 140th overall) in 1989 Entry Draft. Signed as a free agent by Greensboro Monarchs (1992). Signed as a free agent by Boston Bruins (9/6/95). Signed as a free agent by San Antonio Dragons (8/97). Last amateur club; Michigan Tech (WCHA).

Jason Payne
Left Wing

Season	Team	League	GP	G	A	PTS	PIM	GP	G	A	PTS	PIM
		Regular Season						Playoffs				
95-96	Barrie	OHL	14	0	0	0	25	—	—	—	—	—
95-96	Utica	CoHL	14	0	1	1	85	—	—	—	—	—
96-97	Flint	CoHL	59	4	15	19	224	8	0	0	0	2
96-97	Carolina	AHL	4	1	0	1	5	—	—	—	—	—
96-97	Detroit	IHL	2	0	0	0	0	—	—	—	—	—
96-97	Michigan	IHL	1	0	0	0	5	—	—	—	—	—
97-98	Quad City	UHL	8	0	1	1	22	—	—	—	—	—
97-98	Binghamton	UHL	25	2	3	5	81	—	—	—	—	—
97-98	Thunder Bay	UHL	6	0	2	2	12	5	0	0	0	6
98-99	Thunder Bay	UHL	17	5	1	6	83	—	—	—	—	—
98-99	Flint	UHL	44	2	1	3	149	7	0	0	0	9
	IHL	Totals	3	0	0	0	5	—	—	—	—	—
	UHL	Totals	173	13	24	37	656	20	0	0	0	17

Born; 9/21/75, Toronto, Ontario. 6-1, 192. Last amateur club; Barrie (OHL).

Mike Payne
Left Wing

Season	Team	League	GP	G	A	PTS	PIM	GP	G	A	PTS	PIM
		Regular Season						Playoffs				
98-99	Pee Dee	ECHL	14	1	2	3	65	8	0	1	1	7

Born;

Rob Payne
Goaltender

Season	Team	League	GP	W	L	T	MIN	SO	AVG	GP	W	L	MIN	SO	AVG
		Regular Season								Playoffs					
98-99	Dayton	ECHL	1	0	0	0	27	0	8.74	—	—	—	—	—	—

Born; 1/19/72, Crofton, Maryland. 5-8, 200.

Chris Peach
Left Wing

Season	Team	League	GP	G	A	PTS	PIM	GP	G	A	PTS	PIM
		Regular Season						Playoffs				
96-97	Waco	WPHL	57	21	16	37	58	—	—	—	—	—
97-98	Waco	WPHL	49	6	15	21	56	—	—	—	—	—
98-99	Alexandria	WPHL	68	29	33	62	97	—	—	—	—	—
	WPHL	Totals	174	56	64	120	211	—	—	—	—	—

Born; 5/18/72, St. John's Newfoundland. 5-9, 175. Selected by Alexandria in 1998 WPHL Expansion Draft. Last amateur club; New Brunswick (AUAA).

Richard Peacock
Right Wing

Season	Team	League	GP	G	A	PTS	PIM	GP	G	A	PTS	PIM
		Regular Season						Playoffs				
98-99	Anchorage	WCHL	34	1	3	4	90	—	—	—	—	—

Born; 6/15/78, Salmon Arm, British Columbia. 5-10, 215. Last amateur club; Prince George (WHL).

Shayne Peacock
Defenseman

Season	Team	League	GP	G	A	PTS	PIM	GP	G	A	PTS	PIM
		Regular Season						Playoffs				
94-95	Kalamazoo	IHL	71	13	23	36	42	12	3	5	8	8
95-96	Michigan	IHL	79	24	43	67	26	10	0	4	4	6
96-97	Michigan	IHL	81	9	31	40	49	4	0	2	2	2
97-98	Dusseldorfer	Germany	38	11	18	29	73	3	2	1	3	2
98-99	Kassel	Germany	52	15	24	39	46	—	—	—	—	—
	IHL	Totals	231	46	97	143	117	26	3	11	14	16

Born; 7/7/73, Edmonton, Alberta. 5-10, 198. Drafted by Pittsburgh Penguins (3rd choice, 60th overall) in 1991 Entry Draft. Last amateur club; Lethbridge (WHL).

Andrew Pearsall
Defenseman

Season	Team	League	GP	G	A	PTS	PIM	GP	G	A	PTS	PIM
		Regular Season						Playoffs				
98-99	Charlotte	ECHL	6	0	0	0	4	—	—	—	—	—

Born; 9/30/74, Sandwich, Massachusetts. 6-2, 180.

Rob Pearson
Right Wing

Season	Team	League	GP	G	A	PTS	PIM	GP	G	A	PTS	PIM
		Regular Season						Playoffs				
90-91	Belleville	OHL	10	6	3	9	27	—	—	—	—	—
90-91	Oshawa	OHL	41	57	52	109	76	16	16	17	33	39
90-91	Newmarket	AHL	3	0	0	0	29	—	—	—	—	—
91-92	Toronto	NHL	47	14	10	24	58	—	—	—	—	—
91-92	St. John's	AHL	27	15	14	29	107	13	5	4	9	40
92-93	Toronto	NHL	78	23	14	37	211	14	2	2	4	31
93-94	Toronto	NHL	67	12	18	30	189	14	1	0	1	32
94-95	Washington	NHL	32	0	6	6	96	3	1	0	1	17
95-96	St. Louis	NHL	27	6	4	10	54	2	0	0	0	14
95-96	Portland	AHL	44	18	24	42	143	—	—	—	—	—
96-97	St. Louis	NHL	18	1	2	3	37	—	—	—	—	—
96-97	Worcester	AHL	46	11	16	27	199	5	3	0	3	16
97-98	Cleveland	IHL	46	17	14	31	118	10	6	4	10	43
98-99	Cleveland	IHL	20	3	10	13	27	—	—	—	—	—
98-99	Orlando	IHL	11	6	2	8	41	17	8	6	14	24
	NHL	Totals	269	56	54	110	645	33	4	2	6	94
	AHL	Totals	120	44	54	98	478	18	8	4	12	56
	IHL	Totals	77	26	26	52	186	27	14	10	24	67

Born; 3/8/71, Oshawa, Ontario. 6-1, 185. Drafted by Toronto Maple Leafs (2nd choice, 12th overall) in 1989 Entry Draft. Traded to Washington Capitals by Toronto with Philadelphia's first round pick (previously acquired by Toronto, Washington selected Nolan Baumgartner) in 1994 Entry Draft for Mike Ridley and St. Louis' first round pick, (previously acquired by Washington, Toronto selected Eric Fichaud) in 1994 Entry Draft (6/28/94). Last amateur club; Oshawa

Scott Pearson
Left Wing

Season	Team	League	GP	G	A	PTS	PIM	GP	G	A	PTS	PIM
		Regular Season						Playoffs				
88-89	Kingston	OHL	13	9	8	17	34	—	—	—	—	—
88-89	Niagara Falls	OHL	32	26	34	60	90	17	14	10	24	53
88-89	Toronto	NHL	9	0	1	1	2	—	—	—	—	—
89-90	Toronto	NHL	41	5	10	15	90	2	2	0	2	10
89-90	Newmarket	AHL	18	12	11	23	64	—	—	—	—	—
90-91	Toronto	NHL	12	0	0	0	20	—	—	—	—	—
90-91	Quebec	NHL	35	11	4	15	86	—	—	—	—	—
90-91	Halifax	AHL	24	12	15	27	44	—	—	—	—	—
91-92	Quebec	NHL	10	1	2	3	14	—	—	—	—	—
91-92	Halifax	AHL	5	2	1	3	4	—	—	—	—	—
92-93	Quebec	NHL	41	13	1	14	95	3	0	0	0	0
92-93	Halifax	AHL	5	3	1	4	25	—	—	—	—	—
93-94	Edmonton	NHL	72	19	18	37	165	—	—	—	—	—
94-95	Edmonton	NHL	28	1	4	5	54	—	—	—	—	—
94-95	Buffalo	NHL	14	2	1	3	20	5	0	0	0	4
95-96	Buffalo	NHL	27	4	0	4	67	—	—	—	—	—
95-96	Rochester	AHL	26	8	8	16	113	—	—	—	—	—
96-97	Toronto	NHL	1	0	0	0	2	—	—	—	—	—
96-97	St. John's	AHL	14	5	2	7	26	9	5	2	7	14
97-98	Chicago	IHL	78	34	17	51	225	22	12	6	18	50
98-99	Chicago	IHL	62	23	13	36	154	8	4	1	5	*50
	NHL	Totals	290	56	41	97	615	10	2	0	2	14
	AHL	Totals	92	42	38	80	276	9	5	2	7	14
	IHL	Totals	140	57	30	87	379	30	16	7	23	100

Born; 12/19/69, Cornwall, Ontario. 6-1, 205. Drafted by Toronto Maple Leafs (1st choice, 6th overall) in 1988 Entry Draft. Traded to Quebec Nordiques by Toronto with Toronto's second round choices in 1991 (later traded to Washington-Washington selected Eric Lavigne) and 1992 (Tuomas Gronman) Entry Drafts for Aaron Broten, Lucien DeBlois and Michel Petit. (11/17/90). Traded to Edmonton Oilers by Quebec for Martin Gelinas and Edmonton's sixth round choice (Nicholas Checco) in 1993 Entry Draft (6/20/93). Traded to Buffalo Sabres by Edmonton for Ken Sutton (4/7/95). Singed as a free agent by Toronto Maple Leafs (7/24/96). Member of 1997-98 IHL Champion Chicago Wolves. Last amateur club; Niagara Falls (OHL).

Jay Pecora
Defenseman

Season	Team	League	GP	G	A	PTS	PIM	GP	G	A	PTS	PIM
		Regular Season						Playoffs				
97-98	Kitzbuhel	Austria	35	32	42	74	—	—	—	—	—	—
98-99	Columbus	ECHL	50	12	15	27	45	4	0	2	2	4

Born; Stoneham, Massachusetts. 6-0, 205. Selected by Trenton in 1999 ECHL Dispersal Draft. Last amateur club; New England College (NCAA 3).

Tom Pederson
Defenseman

Season	Team	League	GP	G	A	PTS	PIM	GP	G	A	PTS	PIM
		Regular Season						Playoffs				
91-92	United States	National	44	3	11	14	41	—	—	—	—	—
91-92	Kansas City	IHL	20	6	9	15	16	13	1	6	7	14
92-93	San Jose	NHL	44	7	13	20	31	—	—	—	—	—
92-93	Kansas City	IHL	26	6	15	21	10	12	1	6	7	2
93-94	San Jose	NHL	74	6	19	25	31	14	1	6	7	2
93-94	Kansas City	IHL	7	3	1	4	0	—	—	—	—	—
94-95	San Jose	NHL	47	5	11	16	31	10	0	5	5	8
95-96	San Jose	NHL	60	1	4	5	40	—	—	—	—	—
96-97	Seibu Tetsudo	Japan	30	10	28	38	—	—	—	—	—	—
96-97	Toronto	NHL	15	1	2	3	9	—	—	—	—	—
96-97	St. John's	AHL	1	0	4	4	2	—	—	—	—	—
96-97	Utah	IHL	10	1	2	3	8	7	1	3	4	4
97-98	Fort Wayne	IHL	78	12	24	36	87	4	2	0	2	4
98-99	Hannover	Germany	50	10	22	32	53	—	—	—	—	—
	NHL	Totals	240	20	49	69	142	24	1	11	12	10
	IHL	Totals	141	28	51	79	121	36	5	15	20	24

Born; 1/14/70, Bloomington, Minnesota. 5-9, 175. Drafted by Minnesota North Stars (12th choice, 217th overall) in 1989 Entry Draft. Claimed by San Jose Sharks from Minnesota in NHL dispersal draft (5/30/91). Signed as a free agent by Toronto Maple Leafs (12/11/96). Member of 1991-92 IHL Champion Kansas City Blades. Last amateur club; Minnesota (WCHA).

Shaun Peet — Defenseman

Regular Season / Playoffs

Season	Team	League	GP	G	A	PTS	PIM	GP	G	A	PTS	PIM
98-99	Corpus Christi	WPHL	56	1	11	12	168	4	0	1	1	6

Born; 4/2/75, Nainamo, British Columbia. 6-2, 220. Last amateur club; Dartmouth (ECAC).

Jamie Pegg — Defenseman

Regular Season / Playoffs

Season	Team	League	GP	G	A	PTS	PIM	GP	G	A	PTS	PIM
97-98	Newcastle	BSL	56	2	19	21	75	6	1	2	3	4
98-99	Central Texas	WPHL	68	16	52	68	108	2	0	1	1	6

Born; 3/14/70, Flesherton, Ontario. 5-11, 185.

Pavol Pekarik — Defenseman

Regular Season / Playoffs

Season	Team	League	GP	G	A	PTS	PIM	GP	G	A	PTS	PIM
98-99	Mississippi	ECHL	48	4	1	5	54	—	—	—	—	—
98-99	Wheeling	ECHL	16	2	3	5	8	—	—	—	—	—
	ECHL	Totals	64	6	4	10	62	—	—	—	—	—

Born;

Brian Pellerin — Right Wing

Regular Season / Playoffs

Season	Team	League	GP	G	A	PTS	PIM	GP	G	A	PTS	PIM
91-92	Peoria	IHL	70	7	16	23	231	10	1	2	3	49
92-93	Peoria	IHL	78	15	25	40	204	4	1	1	2	8
93-94	Peoria	IHL	79	14	24	38	225	5	0	0	0	16
94-95	Houston	IHL	46	3	7	10	170	—	—	—	—	—
94-95	Chicago	IHL	24	4	1	5	80	3	0	2	2	13
95-96	Chicago	IHL	57	4	8	12	148	9	0	0	0	13
96-97												
97-98	Bracknell	BSL	56	17	20	37	127	6	2	3	5	10
98-99	Houston	IHL	6	1	0	1	16	—	—	—	—	—
98-99	Arkansas	WPHL	63	24	21	45	169	3	0	0	0	10
	IHL	Totals	360	48	81	129	1080	31	2	5	7	99

Born; 2/20/70, Hinton, Alberta. 5-10, 172. Signed as a free agent by St. Louis Blues (5/31/91). Signed as a free agent by Houston Aeros (7/14/94). Last amateur club; Prince Albert (WHL).

Jean-Marc Pelletier — Goaltender

Regular Season / Playoffs

Season	Team	League	GP	W	L	T	MIN	SO	AVG	GP	W	L	MIN	SO	AVG
98-99	Philadelphia	NHL	1	0	1	0	60	0	5.00	—	—	—	—	—	—
98-99	Philadelphia	AHL	47	25	16	4	2635	2	2.78	1	0	0	27	0	0.00

Born; 3/4/78, Atlanta, Georgia. 6-3, 200. Drafted by Philadelphia Flyers (1st choice, 30th overall) in 1997 Entry Draft. Last amateur club; Rimouski (QMJHL).

Mike Peluso — Right Wing

Regular Season / Playoffs

Season	Team	League	GP	G	A	PTS	PIM	GP	G	A	PTS	PIM
98-99	Portland	AHL	26	7	6	13	6	—	—	—	—	—

Born; 9/2/74, Denver, Colorado. 6-1, 200. Last amateur club; Minnesota

Darcy Pengelly — Left Wing

Regular Season / Playoffs

Season	Team	League	GP	G	A	PTS	PIM	GP	G	A	PTS	PIM
95-96	Oklahoma City	CeHL	46	17	13	30	161	11	1	1	2	32
96-97	Oklahoma City	CeHL	65	22	16	38	190	4	0	1	1	15
97-98	New Mexico	WPHL	69	17	26	43	183	5	3	3	6	4
98-99	New Mexico	WPHL	50	19	21	40	126	—	—	—	—	—
98-99	Flint	UHL	2	0	0	0	4	—	—	—	—	—
	WPHL	Totals	119	36	47	83	309	5	3	3	6	4
	CeHL	Totals	111	39	29	68	351	15	1	2	3	47

Born; 12/4/74, Reston, Manitoba. 5-11, 177. Member of 1995-96 CeHL champion Oklahoma City Blazers.

Shawn Penn — Left Wing

Regular Season / Playoffs

Season	Team	League	GP	G	A	PTS	PIM	GP	G	A	PTS	PIM
94-95	Toledo	ECHL	63	14	13	27	208	4	0	0	0	4
95-96	Toledo	ECHL	63	20	16	36	267	10	2	2	4	29
96-97	Chicago	IHL	62	3	7	10	208	4	0	0	0	6
97-98	Long Beach	IHL	66	5	9	14	261	8	0	0	0	40
98-99	Fort Wayne	IHL	78	3	13	16	308	2	0	0	0	2
	IHL	Totals	206	11	29	40	777	14	0	0	0	48
	ECHL	Totals	126	34	29	63	475	14	2	2	4	33

Born; 2/27/71, Madison Heights, Michigan. 6-2, 210. Last amateur club; Miami of Ohio (CCHA).

Chad Penney — Left Wing

Regular Season / Playoffs

Season	Team	League	GP	G	A	PTS	PIM	GP	G	A	PTS	PIM
93-94	Ottawa	NHL	3	0	0	0	2	—	—	—	—	—
93-94	Prince Edward Island	AHL	73	20	30	50	66	—	—	—	—	—
94-95	Prince Edward Island	AHL	66	16	16	32	19	11	2	2	4	2
95-96	Prince Edward Island	AHL	79	23	37	60	28	3	1	1	2	0
96-97	Manchester	BHL	39	9	16	25	48	—	—	—	—	—
97-98	Kentucky	AHL	78	16	21	37	43	2	0	0	0	0
98-99	Colorado	WCHL	67	31	46	77	58	3	0	2	2	4
	AHL	Totals	296	75	104	179	156	16	3	3	6	2

Born; 9/18/73, Labrador, Newfoundland. 6-0, 195. Drafted by Ottawa Senators (2nd choice, 25th overall) in 1992 Entry Draft. Last amateur club; Sault Ste. Marie (OHL).

Colin Pepperall — Left Wing

Regular Season / Playoffs

Season	Team	League	GP	G	A	PTS	PIM	GP	G	A	PTS	PIM
97-98	Erie	OHL	60	31	60	91	151	7	4	4	8	16
97-98	Hartford	AHL	3	1	0	1	2	—	—	—	—	—
98-99	Portland	AHL	4	0	0	0	6	—	—	—	—	—
98-99	Indianapolis	IHL	9	2	2	4	12	—	—	—	—	—
98-99	Greenville	ECHL	55	15	20	35	128	—	—	—	—	—
	AHL	Totals	7	1	0	1	8	—	—	—	—	—

Born; 4/28/78, Niagara Falls, Ontario. 5-10, 160. Drafted by New York Rangers (4th choice, 131st overall) in 1996 Entry Draft. Traded to Chicago Blackhawks by Rangers for future considerations (6/2/98). Last amateur club; Erie (OHL).

Ryan Pepperall — Right Wing

Regular Season / Playoffs

Season	Team	League	GP	G	A	PTS	PIM	GP	G	A	PTS	PIM
97-98	St. John's	AHL	63	3	4	7	50	1	0	0	0	0
98-99	St. John's	AHL	79	16	8	24	70	5	1	0	1	2
	AHL	Totals	142	19	12	31	120	6	1	0	1	2

Born; 1/26/77, Niagara Falls, Ontario. 6-1, 185. Drafted by Toronto Maple Leafs (2nd choice, 54th overall) in 1995 Entry Draft. Last amateur club; Kitchener

Darren Perkins — Defenseman

Regular Season / Playoffs

Season	Team	League	GP	G	A	PTS	PIM	GP	G	A	PTS	PIM
92-93	Columbus	ECHL	20	9	4	13	44	—	—	—	—	—
92-93	Erie	ECHL	28	7	17	24	40	—	—	—	—	—
93-94	Adirondack	AHL	2	0	2	2	2	—	—	—	—	—
93-94	Toledo	ECHL	64	23	31	54	160	14	4	8	12	46
94-95	Toledo	ECHL	59	7	29	36	138	4	1	2	3	4
95-96	San Diego	WCHL	54	19	46	65	168	9	5	7	12	25
96-97	Las Vegas	IHL	1	0	0	0	0	—	—	—	—	—
96-97	San Diego	WCHL	50	15	30	45	68	—	—	—	—	—
97-98	San Diego	WCHL	58	17	50	67	74	12	2	6	8	26
98-99	San Diego	WCHL	50	13	32	45	56	7	2	4	6	8
	WCHL	Totals	212	64	158	222	366	28	9	17	236	59
	ECHL	Totals	171	46	54	100	246	18	5	10	15	50

Born; 12/26/68, Fort Worth, Texas. 5-11, 190. 1995-96 WCHL Defenseman of the Year. 1995-96 WCHL First Team All Star. 1997-98 WCHL Defenseman of the Year. 1997-98 WCHL First Team All-Star. 1998-99 WCHL First Team All-Star. Member of 1993-94 ECHL champion Toledo Storm. Member of 1995-96 WCHL Champion San Diego Gulls. Member of 1997-98 WCHL Champion San Diego Gulls.

Mike Perna — Defenseman

Regular Season / Playoffs

Season	Team	League	GP	G	A	PTS	PIM	GP	G	A	PTS	PIM
96-97	Erie	OHL	35	2	13	15	90	5	1	0	1	14
96-97	Huntington	ECHL	16	1	0	1	59	—	—	—	—	—
97-98	Huntington	ECHL	46	1	13	14	160	4	0	0	0	10
98-99	Huntington	ECHL	49	1	7	8	200	—	—	—	—	—
	ECHL	Totals	111	3	20	23	419	4	0	0	0	10

Born; 1/24/76, Toronto, Ontario. 6-1, 200. Last amateur club; Erie (OHL).

Mike Peron — Center

Regular Season / Playoffs

Season	Team	League	GP	G	A	PTS	PIM	GP	G	A	PTS	PIM
97-98	Jacksonville	ECHL	6	1	0	1	0	—	—	—	—	—
97-98	Roanoke	ECHL	44	13	16	29	85	7	3	1	4	31
98-99	Lowell	AHL	5	1	1	2	2	—	—	—	—	—
98-99	Roanoke	ECHL	50	15	24	39	118	11	4	2	6	26
	ECHL	Totals	100	29	40	69	203	18	7	3	10	57

Born; 3/3/73, Newmarket, Ontario. 5-10, 195. Last amateur club; Lake Superior (CCHA).

Kelly Perreault — Defenseman

Regular Season / Playoffs

Season	Team	League	GP	G	A	PTS	PIM	GP	G	A	PTS	PIM
96-97	Bowling Green	CCHA	32	10	27	37	90	—	—	—	—	—
96-97	Chicago	IHL	8	0	3	3	6	4	0	1	1	6
97-98	Houston	IHL	53	3	4	7	58	1	0	0	0	0
97-98	Austin	WPHL	3	0	1	1	0	—	—	—	—	—
98-99	Manitoba	IHL	17	0	0	0	23	—	—	—	—	—
98-99	Birmingham	ECHL	50	7	32	39	59	—	—	—	—	—
	IHL	Totals	78	3	7	10	87	5	0	1	1	6

Born; 12/18/73, Fort Saskatchewan, Saskatchewan. 6-1, 195. Last amateur club; Bowling Green State (CCHA).

Nicolas Perreault — Defenseman

Regular Season / Playoffs

Season	Team	League	GP	G	A	PTS	PIM	GP	G	A	PTS	PIM
94-95	Saint John	AHL	36	3	2	5	46	—	—	—	—	—
95-96	Toledo	ECHL	46	12	16	28	103	—	—	—	—	—
96-97	St. Gabriel	QSPHL	27	2	8	10	67	—	—	—	—	—
97-98												
98-99	Toledo	ECHL	3	0	1	1	0	—	—	—	—	—
	ECHL	Totals	49	12	17	29	103	—	—	—	—	—

Born; 4/24/72, Loretteville, Quebec. 6-3, 200. Drafted by Calgary Flames (2nd choice, 26th overall) in 1990 Entry Draft. Last amateur club; Michigan State (CCHA).

Craig Perrett — Forward

Regular Season / Playoffs

Season	Team	League	GP	G	A	PTS	PIM	GP	G	A	PTS	PIM
98-99	Roanoke	ECHL	3	0	1	1	0	—	—	—	—	—
98-99	Mohawk Valley	UHL	6	0	0	0	5	—	—	—	—	—
98-99	Abilene	WPHL	51	9	12	21	23	3	0	0	0	0

Born; 7/10/73, Calgary, Alberta. 5-8, 175. Last amateur club; Michigan Tech (WCHA).

Eric Perrin — Center

Regular Season / Playoffs

Season	Team	League	GP	G	A	PTS	PIM	GP	G	A	PTS	PIM
97-98	Cleveland	IHL	69	12	31	43	34	—	—	—	—	—
97-98	Quebec	IHL	13	2	12	14	4	—	—	—	—	—
98-99	Kansas City	IHL	82	24	37	61	71	3	0	0	0	0
	IHL	Totals	164	38	80	118	109	3	0	0	0	0

Born; 11/1/75, Laval, Quebec. 5-9, 174. Traded to Quebec by Cleveland with Ryan Mougenel, Rick Hayward, John Craighead, Pat Jablonski and Burke Murphy for Rick Girard, Dale DeGray, Darcy Simon, Tom Draper and Jason Ruff (3/98). Last amateur club; Vermont (ECAC).

Nathan Perrott — Right Wing

Regular Season / Playoffs

Season	Team	League	GP	G	A	PTS	PIM	GP	G	A	PTS	PIM
97-98	Indianapolis	IHL	31	4	3	7	76	—	—	—	—	—
97-98	Jacksonville	ECHL	30	6	8	14	135	—	—	—	—	—
98-99	Indianapolis	IHL	72	14	11	25	307	7	3	1	4	45
	IHL	Totals	103	18	14	32	383	7	3	1	4	45

Born; 12/8/76, Owen Sound, Ontario. 6-0, 215. Last amateur club; Sault Ste. Marie (OHL).

Brad Perry — Right Wing

Regular Season / Playoffs

Season	Team	League	GP	G	A	PTS	PIM	GP	G	A	PTS	PIM
98-99	Toledo	ECHL	2	0	0	0	2	—	—	—	—	—

Born;

Tom Perry — Left Wing

Regular Season / Playoffs

Season	Team	League	GP	G	A	PTS	PIM	GP	G	A	PTS	PIM
97-98	Quad City	UHL	70	11	27	38	45	20	6	3	9	10
98-99	Colorado	WCHL	64	33	51	84	55	3	1	2	3	4

Born; 2/13/73, Humboldt, Saskatchewan. 6-0, 195. Member of 1997-98 UHL Champion Quad City Mallards. Last amateur club; Massachusetts (Hockey East).

Tyler Perry — Center

Regular Season / Playoffs

Season	Team	League	GP	G	A	PTS	PIM	GP	G	A	PTS	PIM
98-99	Austin	WPHL	26	8	11	19	6	—	—	—	—	—

Born; 8/31/77, 70 Mile House, British Columbia. 6-0, 192. Drafted by Detroit Red Wings (9th choice, 156th overall) in 1995 Entry Draft. Last amateur club; Kamloops (WHL).

Eduard Pershin — Center

Regular Season / Playoffs

Season	Team	League	GP	G	A	PTS	PIM	GP	G	A	PTS	PIM
97-98	Chesapeake	ECHL	38	12	21	33	38	3	0	0	0	4
98-99	Cleveland	IHL	68	9	12	21	71	—	—	—	—	—
98-99	Chesapeake	ECHL	2	0	1	1	2	—	—	—	—	—
	ECHL	Totals	40	12	22	34	40	3	0	0	0	4

Born; 9/1/77, Nizhnekamsk, USSR. 6-0, 191. Drafted by Tampa Bay Lightning (5th choice, 134th overall) in 1995 Entry Draft.

Pirre Persson — Defenseman

Regular Season / Playoffs

Season	Team	League	GP	G	A	PTS	PIM	GP	G	A	PTS	PIM
98-99	Tupelo	WPHL	66	1	11	12	71	—	—	—	—	—

Born; 2/21/76, Ostersund, Sweden. 6-1, 205. Traded to Monroe by Tupelo to complete an earlier trade for Steve Herniman (5/99).

Ricard Persson — Defenseman

Regular Season / Playoffs

Season	Team	League	GP	G	A	PTS	PIM	GP	G	A	PTS	PIM
94-95	Malmo IF	Sweden	31	3	13	16	38	9	0	2	2	8
94-95	Albany	AHL	3	0	0	0	0	9	3	5	8	7
95-96	New Jersey	NHL	12	2	1	3	8	—	—	—	—	—
95-96	Albany	AHL	67	15	31	46	59	4	0	0	0	7
96-97	New Jersey	NHL	1	0	0	0	0	—	—	—	—	—
96-97	Albany	AHL	13	1	4	5	8	—	—	—	—	—
96-97	St. Louis	NHL	53	4	8	12	45	6	0	0	0	27
97-98	St. Louis	NHL	1	0	0	0	0	—	—	—	—	—
97-98	Worcester	AHL	32	2	16	18	58	10	3	7	10	24
98-99	St. Louis	NHL	54	1	12	13	94	13	0	3	3	17
98-99	Worcester	AHL	19	6	4	10	42	—	—	—	—	—
	NHL	Totals	121	7	21	38	147	19	0	3	3	44
	AHL	Totals	134	24	55	79	167	23	6	12	18	38

Born; 8/24/69, Ostersund, Sweden. 6-2, 205. Drafted by New Jersey Devils (2nd choice, 23rd overall) in 1987 Entry Draft. Traded to St. Louis Blues with Mike Peluso for Ken Sutton and St. Louis' second round choice in 1999 Entry Draft (11/26/96).

Mark Petercak — Defenseman

Season	Team	League	GP	G	A	PTS	PIM	GP	G	A	PTS	PIM
			Regular Season					Playoffs				
98-99	Tulsa	CHL	3	0	0	0	6	—	—	—	—	—
98-99	Mohawk Valley	UHL	2	0	1	1	2	—	—	—	—	—
98-99	Toledo	ECHL	3	0	0	0	6	—	—	—	—	—
98-99	Huntington	ECHL	3	0	0	0	2	—	—	—	—	—
98-99	Peoria	ECHL	2	0	0	0	2	—	—	—	—	—
	ECHL	Totals	8	0	0	0	10	—	—	—	—	—

Born; 1/6/77, Edmonton, Alberta. 6-1, 205.

Geoff Peters — Center

Season	Team	League	GP	G	A	PTS	PIM	GP	G	A	PTS	PIM
			Regular Season					Playoffs				
97-98	Erie	OHL	31	15	11	26	36	—	—	—	—	—
97-98	North Bay	OHL	20	11	14	25	22	—	—	—	—	—
97-98	Indianapolis	IHL	2	0	0	0	10	—	—	—	—	—
98-99	Canada	National	38	9	4	13	50	—	—	—	—	—
98-99	Portland	AHL	4	1	1	2	9	—	—	—	—	—

Born; 4/30/78, Hamilton, Ontario. 6-0, 180. Drafted by Chicago Blackhawks (3rd choice, 46th overall) in 1996 Entry Draft. Last amateur club; North Bay (OHL).

Brent Peterson — Left Wing

Season	Team	League	GP	G	A	PTS	PIM	GP	G	A	PTS	PIM
			Regular Season					Playoffs				
95-96	Atlanta	IHL	69	9	19	28	33	3	0	0	0	0
96-97	Tampa Bay	NHL	17	2	0	2	4	—	—	—	—	—
96-97	Adirondack	AHL	52	22	23	45	56	4	3	1	4	2
97-98	Tampa Bay	NHL	19	5	0	5	2	—	—	—	—	—
97-98	Milwaukee	IHL	63	20	39	59	48	8	5	3	8	22
98-99	Tampa Bay	NHL	20	2	1	3	0	—	—	—	—	—
98-99	Cleveland	IHL	18	6	7	13	31	—	—	—	—	—
98-99	Grand Rapids	IHL	17	7	6	13	14	—	—	—	—	—
	NHL	Totals	56	9	1	10	6	—	—	—	—	—
	IHL	Totals	167	42	71	113	126	11	5	3	8	22

Born; 7/20/72, Calgary, Alberta. 6-3, 200. Drafted by Tampa Bay Lightning (1st choice, 3rd overall) in 1993 Supplemental Draft. Sold to Pittsburgh Penguins by Tampa Bay (3/18/99). Signed as a free agent by Nashville Predators (7/26/99). Last amateur club; Michigan Tech (WCHA).

Cory Peterson — Defenseman

Season	Team	League	GP	G	A	PTS	PIM	GP	G	A	PTS	PIM
			Regular Season					Playoffs				
95-96	Tulsa	CeHL	46	2	9	11	91	3	0	0	0	2
96-97	Raleigh	ECHL	12	0	2	2	4	—	—	—	—	—
96-97	Roanoke	ECHL	30	0	4	4	44	4	0	1	1	2
97-98	Roanoke	ECHL	67	2	15	17	93	9	1	2	3	2
98-99	Pee Dee	ECHL	49	1	7	8	50	—	—	—	—	—
	ECHL	Totals	158	3	28	31	191	13	1	3	4	4

Born; 6/10/75, Bloomington, Minnesota. 6-1, 205. Drafted by Dallas Stars (10th choice, 269th overall) in 1993 Entry Draft. Traded to Pee Dee by Roanoke for Doug Searle (9/98). Last amateur club; Peterborough (OHL).

Eric Peterson — Forward

Season	Team	League	GP	G	A	PTS	PIM	GP	G	A	PTS	PIM
			Regular Season					Playoffs				
96-97	Northeastern	H.E.	32	4	10	14	73	—	—	—	—	—
96-97	Jacksonville	ECHL	10	0	5	5	4	—	—	—	—	—
97-98		Holland	40	64	77	141	NA	—	—	—	—	—
98-99	El Paso	WPHL	65	14	26	40	89	—	—	—	—	—

Born; 10/27/73, Melrose, Massachusetts. 5-11, 185. Last amateur club; Northeastern (Hockey East).

Kyle Peterson — Left Wing

Season	Team	League	GP	G	A	PTS	PIM	GP	G	A	PTS	PIM
			Regular Season					Playoffs				
97-98	New Orleans	ECHL	25	5	9	14	37	—	—	—	—	—
98-99	New Orleans	ECHL	1	0	0	0	0	—	—	—	—	—
98-99	Memphis	CHL	61	18	30	48	48	4	0	2	2	8
	ECHL	Totals	26	5	9	14	37	—	—	—	—	—

Born; 4/17/74, Calgary, Alberta. 6-4, 220. Drafted by Minnesota North Stars (5th choice, 154th overall in 1992 Entry Draft. Signed as a free agent by Edmonton Oilers (6/5/97). Last amateur club; Michigan Tech (WCHA).

Matt Peterson — Defenseman

Season	Team	League	GP	G	A	PTS	PIM	GP	G	A	PTS	PIM
			Regular Season					Playoffs				
98-99	Columbus	CHL	70	3	9	12	44	4	0	0	0	6

Born; 2/15/75, Maple Grove, Minnesota. 6-1, 190. Drafted by Anaheim Mighty Ducks (7th choice, 160th overall) in 1993 Entry Draft. Selected by Johnstown in 1999 ECHL Dispersal Draft. Last amateur club; Wisconsin (WCHA).

Michel Petit — Defenseman

Season	Team	League	GP	G	A	PTS	PIM	GP	G	A	PTS	PIM
			Regular Season					Playoffs				
82-83	St. Jean	QMJHL	62	19	67	86	196	3	0	0	0	35
82-83	Vancouver	NHL	2	0	0	0	0	—	—	—	—	—
83-84	Canada	National	19	3	10	13	58	—	—	—	—	—
83-84	Vancouver	NHL	44	6	9	15	53	1	0	0	0	0
84-85	Vancouver	NHL	69	5	26	31	127	—	—	—	—	—
85-86	Vancouver	NHL	32	1	6	7	27	—	—	—	—	—
85-86	Fredericton	AHL	25	0	13	13	79	—	—	—	—	—
86-87	Vancouver	NHL	69	12	13	25	131	—	—	—	—	—
87-88	Vancouver	NHL	10	0	3	3	35	—	—	—	—	—
87-88	Rangers	NHL	64	9	24	33	223	—	—	—	—	—
88-89	Rangers	NHL	69	8	25	33	154	4	0	2	2	27
89-90	Quebec	NHL	63	12	24	36	215	—	—	—	—	—
90-91	Quebec	NHL	19	4	7	11	47	—	—	—	—	—
90-91	Toronto	NHL	54	9	19	28	132	—	—	—	—	—
91-92	Toronto	NHL	34	1	13	14	85	—	—	—	—	—
91-92	Calgary	NHL	36	3	10	13	79	—	—	—	—	—
92-93	Calgary	NHL	35	3	9	12	54	—	—	—	—	—
93-94	Calgary	NHL	63	2	21	23	110	—	—	—	—	—
94-95	Los Angeles	NHL	40	5	12	17	84	—	—	—	—	—
95-96	Los Angeles	NHL	9	0	1	1	27	—	—	—	—	—
95-96	Tampa Bay	NHL	45	4	7	11	108	6	0	0	0	20
96-97	Edmonton	NHL	18	2	4	6	20	—	—	—	—	—
96-97	Philadelphia	NHL	20	0	3	3	51	3	0	0	0	6
97-98	Detroit	IHL	9	2	3	5	24	—	—	—	—	—
97-98	Phoenix	NHL	32	4	2	6	77	5	0	0	0	8
98-99	Las Vegas	IHL	6	0	1	1	10	—	—	—	—	—
	NHL	Totals	827	90	238	328	1839	19	0	2	2	61
	IHL	Totals	15	2	4	6	34	—	—	—	—	—

Born; 2/12/64, St. Malo, Quebec. 6-1, 205. Drafted by Vancouver Canucks (1st choice, 11th overall) in 1982 Entry Draft. Traded to New York Rangers by Vancouver for Willie Huber and Larry Melnyk (11/4/87). Traded to Quebec Nordiques by Rangers for Randy Moller (10/5/89). Traded to Toronto Maple Leafs by Quebec with Aaron Broten and Lucien DeBlois for Scott Pearson and Toronto's second round choices in 1991 (later traded to Washington Capitals-Washington selected Eric Lavigne) and 1992 (Tuomas Gronman) Entry Draft (11/17/90). Traded to Calgary Flames by Toronto with Craig Berube, Alexander Godynyuk, Gary Leeman and Jeff Reese for Doug Gilmour, Jamie Macoun, Ric Nattress, Rick Wamsley and Kent Manderville (1/2/92). Signed as a free agent by Los Angeles Kings (6/16/94). Traded to Tampa Bay Lightning by Los Angeles for Steven Finn (11/13/95). Signed as a free agent by Edmonton Oilers (10/24/96). Claimed on waivers by Philadelphia Flyers from Edmonton (1/17/97). Signed as a free agent by Phoenix Coyotes (11/25/97). Last amateur club; St. Jean

Andrei Petrakov — Right Wing
Regular Season — Playoffs

Season	Team	League	GP	G	A	PTS	PIM	GP	G	A	PTS	PIM
98-99	Worcester	AHL	4	0	1	1	2	—	—	—	—	—
98-99	Fort Wayne	IHL	11	2	4	6	0	—	—	—	—	—
98-99	Muskegon	UHL	5	4	3	7	0	—	—	—	—	—
98-99	Magnotogorsk	Russia	10	4	4	8	8	15	4	8	12	4

Born; 4/26/76, Sverdlovsk, USSR. 6-0, 198. Drafted by St. Louis Blues (4th choice, 97th overall) in 1996 Entry Draft.

Sergei Petrov — Right Wing
Regular Season — Playoffs

Season	Team	League	GP	G	A	PTS	PIM	GP	G	A	PTS	PIM
97-98	Jacksonville	ECHL	63	14	26	40	81	—	—	—	—	—
98-99	Jacksonville	ECHL	4	0	0	0	0	—	—	—	—	—
98-99	Winston-Salem	UHL	66	30	39	69	121	5	2	2	4	14
	ECHL	Totals	67	14	26	40	81	—	—	—	—	—

Born; 1/22/75, Leningrad, USSR. 5-11, 185. Drafted by Chicago Blackhawks (9th choice, 206th overall) in 1993 Entry Draft. Last amateur club; Minnesota-Duluth (WCHA).

Robert Petrovicky — Center
Regular Season — Playoffs

Season	Team	League	GP	G	A	PTS	PIM	GP	G	A	PTS	PIM
92-93	Hartford	NHL	42	3	6	9	45	—	—	—	—	—
92-93	Springfield	AHL	16	5	3	8	39	15	5	6	11	14
93-94	Dukla Trencin	Czech.	1	0	0	0	0	—	—	—	—	—
93-94	Hartford	NHL	33	6	5	11	39	—	—	—	—	—
93-94	Springfield	AHL	30	16	8	24	39	4	0	2	2	4
94-95	Springfield	AHL	74	30	52	82	121	—	—	—	—	—
94-95	Hartford	NHL	2	0	0	0	0	—	—	—	—	—
95-96	Springfield	AHL	9	4	8	12	18	—	—	—	—	—
95-96	Detroit	IHL	12	5	3	8	16	—	—	—	—	—
95-96	Dallas	NHL	5	1	1	2	0	—	—	—	—	—
95-96	Michigan	IHL	50	23	23	46	63	7	3	1	4	16
96-97	St. Louis	NHL	44	7	12	19	10	2	0	0	0	0
96-97	Worcester	AHL	12	5	4	9	19	—	—	—	—	—
97-98	Worcester	AHL	65	27	34	61	97	10	3	4	7	12
98-99	Tampa Bay	NHL	28	3	4	7	6	—	—	—	—	—
98-99	Grand Rapids	IHL	49	26	32	58	87	—	—	—	—	—
	NHL	Totals	154	20	28	48	100	2	0	0	0	0
	AHL	Totals	206	87	109	196	333	29	8	12	20	30
	IHL	Totals	111	54	58	112	166	7	3	1	4	16

Born; 10/26/73, Kosice, Czechoslovakia. 5-11, 172. Drafted by Hartford Whalers (1st choice, 9th overall) in 1992 Entry Draft. Traded to Dallas Stars by Hartford for Dan Kesa and a conditional choice in the 1997 Entry Draft (11/29/95). Signed as a free agent by St. Louis Blues (9/6/96). Signed as a free agent by Tampa Bay Lightning (2/19/99).

Ronald Petrovicky — Right Wing
Regular Season — Playoffs

Season	Team	League	GP	G	A	PTS	PIM	GP	G	A	PTS	PIM
98-99	Saint John	AHL	78	21	21	33	114	7	1	2	3	19

Born; 2/15/77, Zilina, Czechoslovakia. 5-11, 185. Drafted by Calgary Flames (9th choice, 228th overall) in 1996 Entry Draft. Last amateur club; Regina (WHL).

Jeff Petruic — Left Wing
Regular Season — Playoffs

Season	Team	League	GP	G	A	PTS	PIM	GP	G	A	PTS	PIM
94-95	Regina	WHL	71	46	33	79	79	4	2	1	3	4
94-95	Peoria	IHL	3	0	1	1	0	—	—	—	—	—
95-96	Providence	AHL	3	1	0	1	2	—	—	—	—	—
95-96	Dayton	ECHL	38	13	9	22	26	3	0	1	1	17
96-97	Bakersfield	WCHL	62	36	37	73	50	4	2	1	3	2
97-98	Bakersfield	WCHL	7	2	0	2	4	—	—	—	—	—
97-98	Reno	WCHL	50	38	25	63	12	3	0	2	2	0
98-99	Alexandria	WPHL	68	46	44	90	8	—	—	—	—	—
	WCHL	Totals	119	76	62	138	16	3	0	2	2	0

Born; 5/19/74, Avonlea, Saskatchewan. 6-1, 202. Traded to Reno by Bakersfield for future considerations (11/97). Selected by Colorado Gold Kings in 1998 WCHL Dispersal Draft. Last amateur club; Regina (WHL).

Andrei Petrunin — Right Wing
Regular Season — Playoffs

Season	Team	League	GP	G	A	PTS	PIM	GP	G	A	PTS	PIM
98-99	Chicago	IHL	7	0	1	1	2	—	—	—	—	—
98-99	Muskegon	UHL	63	37	37	74	63	13	3	8	11	8

Born; 2/2/78, Moscow, USSR. 5-9, 169. Drafted by Hartford Whalers (2nd choice, 61st overall) in 1996 Entry Draft. 1998-99 UHL All-Rookie Team. Member of 1998-99 UHL Champion Muskegon Fury. Last overseas club; CKSA

Randy Petruk — Goaltender
Regular Season — Playoffs

Season	Team	League	GP	W	L	T	MIN	SO	AVG	GP	W	L	MIN	SO	AVG
98-99	New Haven	AHL	1	0	0	1	65	0	2.77	—	—	—	—	—	—
98-99	Florida	ECHL	25	13	10	2	1441	1	2.75	1	0	1	60	0	5.00

Born; 6/23/78, Cranbrook, Alberta. 5-9, 178. Drafted by Colorado Avalanche (5th choice, 107th overall) in 1996 Entry Draft. Traded to Carolina Hurricanes for Carolina's fifth round choice in 1999 Entry Draft. Last amateur club; Kamloops

Lars Petterson — Forward
Regular Season — Playoffs

Season	Team	League	GP	G	A	PTS	PIM	GP	G	A	PTS	PIM
97-98	Raleigh	ECHL	62	15	24	39	79	—	—	—	—	—
98-99	Augusta	ECHL	70	20	46	66	56	2	0	0	0	2
	ECHL	Totals	132	35	70	105	135	2	0	0	0	2

Born; 11/20/78, Okotoks, Alberta. 6-2, 210. Last amateur club; Regina (WHL).

Ryan Petz — Forward
Regular Season — Playoffs

Season	Team	League	GP	G	A	PTS	PIM	GP	G	A	PTS	PIM
95-96	Columbus	ECHL	28	7	10	17	39	—	—	—	—	—
95-96	Johnstown	ECHL	31	15	13	28	38	—	—	—	—	—
96-97	Johnstown	ECHL	69	25	27	52	90	—	—	—	—	—
97-98	Pee Dee	ECHL	69	22	24	46	113	8	2	2	4	12
98-99	Pee Dee	ECHL	70	28	34	62	71	13	7	6	13	14
	ECHL	Totals	267	97	108	205	351	21	9	8	17	26

Born; 9/9/74, Calgary, Alberta. 5-11, 185. Last amateur club; Moose Jaw (WHL).

Chris Phelps — Defenseman
Regular Season — Playoffs

Season	Team	League	GP	G	A	PTS	PIM	GP	G	A	PTS	PIM
94-95	Cornwall	AHL	3	0	0	0	0	1	1	0	1	0
94-95	Hampton Roads	ECHL	67	13	39	52	161	4	0	0	0	10
95-96	Utah	IHL	1	0	0	0	0	—	—	—	—	—
95-96	Portland	AHL	1	0	0	0	0	—	—	—	—	—
95-96	Baltimore	AHL	7	0	0	0	4	12	0	2	2	12
95-96	Hampton Roads	ECHL	40	2	22	24	117	3	0	0	0	0
96-97	Portland	AHL	11	0	4	4	10	—	—	—	—	—
96-97	Hampton Roads	ECHL	58	8	37	45	97	6	3	3	6	8
97-98	Hampton Roads	ECHL	66	4	39	43	88	20	1	10	11	26
98-99	Hampton Roads	ECHL	50	3	24	27	34	4	0	4	4	10
	AHL	Totals	22	0	4	4	14	13	1	2	3	12
	ECHL	Totals	281	30	161	191	502	37	4	17	21	54

Born; 2/21/73, Lapeer, Michigan. 6-0, 195. 1996-97 ECHL First All-Star Team. Member of 1997-98 ECHL Champion Hampton Roads Admirals. Last amateur club; Last amateur club; Ottawa (OHL).

Greg Phillips — Right Wing
Regular Season — Playoffs

Season	Team	League	GP	G	A	PTS	PIM	GP	G	A	PTS	PIM
98-99	Springfield	AHL	63	16	13	29	74	3	0	0	0	4

Born; 3/27/78, Winnipeg, Manitoba. 6-2, 205. Drafted by Los Angeles Kings (3rd choice, 57th overall) in 1996 Entry Draft. Last amateur club; Brandon (WHL).

Rob Phillips — Right Wing

Regular Season / Playoffs

Season	Team	League	GP	G	A	PTS	PIM	GP	G	A	PTS	PIM
97-98	Peoria	ECHL	48	7	10	17	25	—	—	—	—	—
98-99	Pensacola	ECHL	22	2	4	6	2	—	—	—	—	—
98-99	Macon	CHL	34	8	14	22	21	2	0	0	0	0
	ECHL	Totals	70	9	14	23	27	—	—	—	—	—

Born; 12/2/72, Merritt, British Columbia. 6-1, 190. Last amateur club; Alaska-Fairbanks (CCHA).

Ryan Phillips — Left Wing

Regular Season / Playoffs

Season	Team	League	GP	G	A	PTS	PIM	GP	G	A	PTS	PIM
95-96	Wichita	CeHL	18	7	4	11	8	—	—	—	—	—
96-97	Wichita	CeHL	19	3	8	11	49	—	—	—	—	—
96-97	Nashville	CeHL	27	9	14	23	21	—	—	—	—	—
97-98	Monroe	WPHL	26	11	10	21	40	—	—	—	—	—
97-98	Waco	WPHL	17	3	12	15	8	—	—	—	—	—
98-99	Wichita	CHL	4	2	1	3	0	—	—	—	—	—
98-99	Topeka	CHL	49	9	19	28	40	—	—	—	—	—
	CHL	Totals	117	30	46	76	118	—	—	—	—	—
	WPHL	Totals	43	14	22	36	48	—	—	—	—	—

Born; 7/8/75, North Vancouver, British Columbia. 6-0, 185. Traded to Waco by Monroe for Ryan MacDonald (1/98). Traded to San Antonio by Topeka for Roy Gray (2/99). Last amateur club; Regina (WHL).

Ethan Philpott — Right Wing

Regular Season / Playoffs

Season	Team	League	GP	G	A	PTS	PIM	GP	G	A	PTS	PIM
97-98	Richmond	ECHL	8	1	0	1	7	—	—	—	—	—
98-99	Central Texas	WPHL	10	2	2	4	12	2	0	0	0	0

Born; 2/11/75, Rochester, Minnesota. 6-4, 230. Drafted by Buffalo Sabres (2nd choice, 64th overall) in 1993 Entry Draft. Signed as a free agent by Carolina Hurricanes (8/28/97). Last amateur club; Harvard (ECAC).

Michel Picard — Left Wing

Regular Season / Playoffs

Season	Team	League	GP	G	A	PTS	PIM	GP	G	A	PTS	PIM
89-90	Binghamton	AHL	67	16	24	40	98	—	—	—	—	—
90-91	Hartford	NHL	5	1	0	1	2	—	—	—	—	—
90-91	Springfield	AHL	77	*56	40	96	61	18	8	13	21	18
91-92	Hartford	NHL	25	3	5	8	6	—	—	—	—	—
91-92	Springfield	AHL	40	21	17	38	44	11	2	0	2	34
92-93	San Jose	NHL	25	4	0	4	24	—	—	—	—	—
92-93	Kansas City	IHL	33	7	10	17	51	12	3	2	5	20
93-94	Portland	AHL	61	41	44	85	99	17	11	10	21	22
94-95	Ottawa	NHL	24	5	8	13	14	—	—	—	—	—
94-95	Prince Edward Island	AHL	57	32	57	89	58	8	4	4	8	6
95-96	Ottawa	NHL	17	2	6	8	10	—	—	—	—	—
95-96	Prince Edward Island	AHL	55	37	45	82	79	5	5	1	6	2
96-97	Grand Rapids	IHL	82	46	55	101	58	5	2	0	2	10
96-97	V. Frolunda	Sweden	3	0	1	1	0	—	—	—	—	—
97-98	St. Louis	NHL	16	1	8	9	29	—	—	—	—	—
97-98	Grand Rapids	IHL	58	28	41	69	42	—	—	—	—	—
98-99	St. Louis	NHL	45	11	11	22	16	5	0	0	0	2
98-99	Grand Rapids	IHL	6	2	2	4	2	—	—	—	—	—
	NHL	Totals	157	27	38	65	101	5	0	0	0	2
	AHL	Totals	357	203	227	430	439	59	30	28	58	82
	IHL	Totals	179	83	108	191	153	17	5	2	7	30

Born; 11/7/69, Beauport, Quebec. 5-11, 190. Drafted by Hartford Whalers (8th choice, 178th overall) in 1989 Entry Draft. Traded to San Jose Sharks by Hartford for future considerations (Yvon Corriveau, 1/21/93) 10/9/92. Signed as a free agent by Ottawa Senators (6/16/94). Traded to Washington Capitals for cash (5/21/96). Signed as a free agent by St. Louis Blues (1/3/98). Member of 1990-91 AHL champion Springfield Indians. Member of 1993-94 AHL champion Portland Pirates. 1990-91 AHL First Team All-Star. 1993-94 AHL Second Team All-Star. 1994-95 AHL First Team All-Star. 1996-97 IHL First All-Star Team. Last amateur club; Trois-Rivieres (QMJHL).

Billy Pierce — Forward

Regular Season / Playoffs

Season	Team	League	GP	G	A	PTS	PIM	GP	G	A	PTS	PIM
97-98	Chesapeake	ECHL	49	7	9	16	67	3	0	0	0	4
98-99	Jacksonville	ECHL	5	0	3	3	12	—	—	—	—	—
	ECHL	Totals	54	7	12	19	79	3	0	0	0	4

Born; 10/6/74, Burlington, Massachusetts. 6-1, 197. Drafted by Quebec Nordiques (4th choice, 75th overall) in 1993 Entry Draft. Traded to Pee Dee by Jacksonville with Chad Wilson for Kurt Mallett (7/98). Last amateur club; Boston University (Hockey East).

Jeff Pierce — Left Wing

Regular Season / Playoffs

Season	Team	League	GP	G	A	PTS	PIM	GP	G	A	PTS	PIM
97-98	Bakersfield	WCHL	18	2	1	3	40	1	0	0	0	17
98-99	Bakersfield	WCHL	5	2	0	2	11	—	—	—	—	—
	WCHL	Totals	23	4	1	5	51	1	0	0	0	17

Born; 10/13/70, Midland, Michigan. 6-0, 205.

Mike Pietrangelo — Right Wing

Regular Season / Playoffs

Season	Team	League	GP	G	A	PTS	PIM	GP	G	A	PTS	PIM
98-99	Wheeling	ECHL	4	2	0	2	0	—	—	—	—	—
98-99	Peoria	ECHL	31	0	1	1	17	—	—	—	—	—
98-99	Toledo	ECHL	6	0	0	0	2	—	—	—	—	—
	ECHL	Totals	41	2	1	3	19	—	—	—	—	—

Born;

Marco Pietroniro — Right Wing

Regular Season / Playoffs

Season	Team	League	GP	G	A	PTS	PIM	GP	G	A	PTS	PIM
92-93	Jacksonville	SUN	46	19	31	50	48	—	—	—	—	—
93-94		Italy										
94-95		Italy										
95-96		Italy										
96-97		Italy										
97-98	Idaho	WCHL	49	35	32	67	57	3	0	2	2	0
98-99	Idaho	WCHL	55	17	39	56	61	2	0	0	0	0
	WCHL	Totals	104	52	71	123	118	5	0	2	2	0

Born; 8/21/70, Montreal, Quebec. 5-8, 185.

Dave Piirto — Defenseman

Regular Season / Playoffs

Season	Team	League	GP	G	A	PTS	PIM	GP	G	A	PTS	PIM
92-93	Daytona Beach	SUN	2	0	2	2	0	—	—	—	—	—
92-93	Lakeland	SUN	1	1	0	1	0	—	—	—	—	—
94-95	Lakeland	SUN	7	0	5	5	2	—	—	—	—	—
94-95	Flint	CoHL	2	0	0	0	0	—	—	—	—	—
95-96	West Palm Beach	SHL	41	3	8	11	111	—	—	—	—	—
96-97	Waco	WPHL	15	0	0	0	36	—	—	—	—	—
97-98	Tucson	WCHL	40	1	6	7	141	—	—	—	—	—
98-99	Tucson	WCHL	9	0	1	1	29	—	—	—	—	—
98-99	Phoenix	WCHL	4	0	0	0	8	—	—	—	—	—
	WCHL	Totals	13	0	1	1	37	—	—	—	—	—
	SHL	Totals	51	4	15	19	113	—	—	—	—	—

Born; 8/26/71, Richmond Hill, Ontario. 6-3, 230.

Dennis Pinfold — Defenseman

Regular Season / Playoffs

Season	Team	League	GP	G	A	PTS	PIM	GP	G	A	PTS	PIM
95-96	Saginaw	CoHL	10	0	0	0	45	—	—	—	—	—
96-97	Birmingham	ECHL	57	0	7	7	316	—	—	—	—	—
97-98	Birmingham	ECHL	38	2	10	12	241	—	—	—	—	—
97-98	Syracuse	AHL	32	1	3	4	121	2	0	0	0	0
98-99	Birmingham	ECHL	43	4	5	9	323	1	1	0	1	2
	ECHL	Totals	138	6	22	28	880	1	1	0	1	2

Born; 2/28/74, Edmonton, Alberta. 6-0, 185. Last amateur club; Brandon (CWUAA).

Doug Pirnak — Left Wing

Regular Season / Playoffs

Season	Team	League	GP	G	A	PTS	PIM	GP	G	A	PTS	PIM
98-99	Tulsa	CHL	68	11	13	24	254	—	—	—	—	—

Born; 9/27/77, Glendon, Alberta. 6-0, 210.

John Pirrong — Defenseman

Regular Season / Playoffs

Season	Team	League	GP	G	A	PTS	PIM	GP	G	A	PTS	PIM
96-97	Johnstown	ECHL	1	0	0	0	0	—	—	—	—	—
96-97	Pensacola	ECHL	33	1	7	8	46	—	—	—	—	—
96-97	Columbus	ECHL	5	0	2	2	10	—	—	—	—	—
97-98	Odessa	WPHL	26	0	9	9	15	—	—	—	—	—
97-98	Fayetteville	CHL	30	2	5	7	53	—	—	—	—	—
98-99	Huntington	ECHL	1	0	0	0	0	—	—	—	—	—
98-99	Asheville	UHL	70	13	16	29	97	3	0	1	1	2
	ECHL	Totals	40	1	9	10	56	—	—	—	—	—

Born; 10/10/74, Norfolk, Massachusetts. 6-0, 190. Last amateur club; Rensselaer Polytechnic Institute (ECAC).

Ryan Pisiak — Right Wing

Regular Season / Playoffs

Season	Team	League	GP	G	A	PTS	PIM	GP	G	A	PTS	PIM
95-96	Wichita	CeHL	24	3	9	12	141	—	—	—	—	—
95-96	San Antonio	CeHL	11	3	0	3	70	13	0	1	1	66
96-97	San Antonio	CeHL	32	12	16	28	*327	—	—	—	—	—
96-97	Memphis	CeHL	13	5	4	9	*85	14	1	4	5	*126
97-98	Fort Wayne	IHL	11	0	0	0	24	—	—	—	—	—
97-98	Louisiana	ECHL	29	1	3	4	262	—	—	—	—	—
97-98	Wheeling	ECHL	—	—	—	—	—	9	0	0	0	*82
98-99	Pee Dee	ECHL	22	0	1	1	174	—	—	—	—	—
	CeHL	Totals	80	23	29	52	623	27	1	5	6	192
	ECHL	Totals	51	1	4	5	436	9	0	0	0	82

Born; 5/12/75, Swift Current, Saskatchewan. 6-3, 212. Drafted by Los Angeles Kings (7th choice, 231st overall) in 1992 Entry Draft.

Domenic Pittis — Center

Regular Season / Playoffs

Season	Team	League	GP	G	A	PTS	PIM	GP	G	A	PTS	PIM
94-95	Cleveland	IHL	62	18	32	50	66	3	0	2	2	2
95-96	Cleveland	IHL	74	10	28	38	100	3	0	0	0	2
96-97	Pittsburgh	NHL	1	0	0	0	0	—	—	—	—	—
96-97	Long Beach	IHL	65	23	43	66	91	18	5	9	14	26
97-98	Syracuse	AHL	75	23	41	64	90	5	1	3	4	4
98-99	Buffalo	NHL	3	0	0	0	2	—	—	—	—	—
98-99	Rochester	AHL	76	38	66	*104	110	20	7	*14	*21	40
	NHL	Totals	4	0	0	0	2	—	—	—	—	—
	IHL	Totals	201	51	103	154	257	24	5	11	16	30
	AHL	Totals	151	61	107	168	200	25	8	17	25	44

Born; 10/1/74, Calgary, Alberta. 5-11, 180. Drafted by Pittsburgh Penguins (2nd choice, 52nd overall) in 1993 Entry Draft. Signed as a free agent by Buffalo Sabres (7/30/98). Last amateur club; Lethbridge (WHL).

Mark Pivetz — Defenseman

Regular Season / Playoffs

Season	Team	League	GP	G	A	PTS	PIM	GP	G	A	PTS	PIM
96-97	North Dakota	WCHA	42	2	13	15	53	—	—	—	—	—
96-97	Hershey	AHL	5	0	0	0	4	—	—	—	—	—
97-98	Cincinnati	AHL	5	0	0	0	2	—	—	—	—	—
97-98	Columbus	ECHL	60	9	14	23	35	—	—	—	—	—
98-99	Chicago	IHL	1	0	0	0	0	—	—	—	—	—
98-99	Kentucky	AHL	3	0	0	0	0	—	—	—	—	—
98-99	Columbus	ECHL	59	4	10	14	57	4	1	0	1	2
	AHL	Totals	13	0	0	0	6	—	—	—	—	—

Born; 12/9/73, Edmonton, Alberta. 6-4, 215. Drafted by Quebec Nordiques (12th choice, 257th overall) in 1993 Entry Draft. Selected by Huntington in 1999 ECHL Dispersal Draft. Last amateur club; North Dakota (WCHA).

Kevin Plager — Right Wing

Regular Season / Playoffs

Season	Team	League	GP	G	A	PTS	PIM	GP	G	A	PTS	PIM
96-97	Baton Rouge	ECHL	46	10	6	16	54	—	—	—	—	—
97-98	Columbus	CHL	59	21	16	37	111	12	3	1	4	15
98-99	Columbus	CHL	45	10	16	26	137	3	0	0	0	0
	CHL	Total.s	104	31	32	63	248	15	3	1	4	15

Born; 4/27/71, St. Louis, Missouri. 6-1, 210. Drafted by St. Louis Blues (8th choice, 156th overall) in 1989 Entry Draft. Member of 1997-98 CHL Champion Columbus Cottonmouths. Last amateur club; Wisconsin-Stevens Point (NCHA).

Justin Plamondon — Left Wing

Regular Season / Playoffs

Season	Team	League	GP	G	A	PTS	PIM	GP	G	A	PTS	PIM
97-98	Binghamton	UHL	12	6	9	15	19	5	0	2	2	0
98-99	Binghamton	UHL	72	16	32	48	40	5	0	0	0	0
	UHL	Totals	84	22	41	63	59	10	0	2	2	0

Born; 1/28/77, Quebec City, Quebec. 6-0, 195.

Dan Plante — Right Wing

Regular Season / Playoffs

Season	Team	League	GP	G	A	PTS	PIM	GP	G	A	PTS	PIM
93-94	Islanders	NHL	12	0	1	1	4	1	1	0	1	2
93-94	Salt Lake City	IHL	66	7	17	24	148	—	—	—	—	—
94-95	Denver	IHL	2	0	0	0	4	—	—	—	—	—
95-96	Islanders	NHL	73	5	3	8	50	—	—	—	—	—
96-97	Islanders	NHL	67	4	9	13	75	—	—	—	—	—
97-98	Islanders	NHL	7	0	1	1	6	—	—	—	—	—
97-98	Utah	IHL	73	22	27	49	125	4	0	2	2	14
98-99	Chicago	IHL	81	21	12	33	119	10	1	5	6	10
	NHL	Totals	159	9	14	23	135	1	1	0	1	2
	IHL	Totals	222	50	56	106	396	14	1	7	8	24

Born; 10/5/71, Hayward, Wisconsin. 5-11, 202. Drafted by New York Islanders (3rd choice, 48th overall) in 1990 Entry Draft. Last amateur club; Wisconsin

Robert Plante — Defenseman

Regular Season / Playoffs

Season	Team	League	GP	G	A	PTS	PIM	GP	G	A	PTS	PIM
96-97	Wichita	CeHL	4	0	0	0	8	—	—	—	—	—
96-97	Alaska	WCHL	18	4	1	5	65	—	—	—	—	—
96-97	Reno	WCHL	8	0	1	1	15	—	—	—	—	—
96-97	El Paso	WPHL	14	0	0	0	75	—	—	—	—	—
96-97	New Mexico	WPHL	5	0	0	0	37	—	—	—	—	—
97-98	Fayetteville	CHL	50	0	2	2	171	—	—	—	—	—
98-99	Alexandria	WPHL	58	0	3	3	123	—	—	—	—	—
	WPHL	Totals	77	0	3	3	235	—	—	—	—	—
	CHL	Totals	54	0	2	2	179	—	—	—	—	—
	WCHL	Totals	26	4	2	6	80	—	—	—	—	—

Born; 12/24/70, Lake Isle, Alberta. 6-1, 225.

Ken Plaquin — Defenseman

Regular Season / Playoffs

Season	Team	League	GP	G	A	PTS	PIM	GP	G	A	PTS	PIM
93-94	Louisville	ECHL	65	9	35	44	72	6	2	4	6	52
94-95	San Antonio	CeHL	66	7	46	53	74	13	1	6	7	20
95-96	San Antonio	CeHL	26	3	8	11	37	—	—	—	—	—
95-96	Fort Worth	CeHL	36	3	12	15	28	—	—	—	—	—
96-97												
97-98	Reno	WCHL	45	4	13	17	22	—	—	—	—	—
98-99	Alexandria	WPHL	69	5	21	26	28	—	—	—	—	—
	CeHL	Totals	118	13	66	79	139	13	1	6	7	20

Born; 2/22/70, Calgary, Alberta. 6-2, 205. Selected by Colorado in 1998 WCHL Dispersal Draft. Last amateur club; Michigan Tech (WCHA).

Andrew Plumb
Defenseman

Season	Team	League	GP	G	A	PTS	PIM	GP	G	A	PTS	PIM
			Regular Season					Playoffs				
89-90	St. Louis	NHL	4	0	1	1	2	—	—	—	—	—
89-90	Vancouver	NHL	11	3	2	5	8	—	—	—	—	—
89-90	Peoria	IHL	51	7	14	21	87	—	—	—	—	—
89-90	Milwaukee	IHL	3	1	2	3	14	6	1	3	4	6
90-91	Vancouver	NHL	48	2	10	12	62	—	—	—	—	—
91-92	Canada	National	38	7	8	15	44	—	—	—	—	—
91-92	Vancouver	NHL	16	1	9	10	14	13	1	7	8	4
92-93	Vancouver	NHL	57	6	21	27	53	—	—	—	—	—
93-94	Vancouver	NHL	47	1	9	10	6	—	—	—	—	—
93-94	Hamilton	AHL	2	0	0	0	0	—	—	—	—	—
94-95	Vancouver	NHL	3	0	1	1	0	—	—	—	—	—
94-95	Tampa Bay	NHL	15	2	1	3	4	—	—	—	—	—
95-96	Tampa Bay	NHL	7	1	2	3	6	—	—	—	—	—
95-96	Atlanta	IHL	68	5	34	39	32	3	0	1	1	4
96-97	Anaheim	NHL	6	0	0	0	2	—	—	—	—	—
96-97	Long Beach	IHL	69	7	28	35	86	18	0	9	9	10
97-98	Revier Lowen	Germany	36	4	15	19	28	—	—	—	—	—
98-99	Zurich	Switz.	28	3	21	24	18	—	—	—	—	—
	NHL	Totals	214	16	56	72	161	13	1	7	8	4
	IHL	Totals	191	20	78	98	219	27	1	13	14	20

Born; 1/13/70, Montreal, Quebec. 6-1, 200. Drafted by St. Louis Blues (2nd choice, 30th overall) in 1988 Entry Draft. Traded to Vancouver Canucks by St. Louis with Montreal's first round choice (previously acquired by St. Louis-Vancouver selected Shawn Antoski) in 1990 Entry Draft and St. Louis' second round choice (later traded to Montreal-Montreal selected Craig Darby) in 1991 Entry Draft for Rich Sutter, Harold Snepts and St. Louis' second round choice (previously acquired by Vancouver-Vancouver selected Craig Johnson) in 1990 Entry Draft (3/6/90). Traded to Tampa Bay Lightning by Vancouver for Tampa Bay's fifth round choice (David Darguzas) in 1997 Entry Draft (3/23/95). Signed as a free agent by Anaheim Mighty Ducks (8/27/96). Last amateur club; New

Steve Plouffe
Goaltender

Season	Team	League	GP	W	L	T	MIN	SO	AVG	GP	W	L	MIN	SO	AVG
			Regular Season							Playoffs					
95-96	Fort Worth	CeHL	30	10	13	4	1582	0	4.17	—	—	—	—	—	—
96-97	Fort Worth	CeHL	52	*38	9	5	2983	*2	2.88	*17	*11	5	*1022	*1	3.11
97-98	Johnstown	ECHL	44	11	23	4	2229	1	3.90	—	—	—	—	—	—
98-99	Fort Worth	WPHL	52	27	17	6	2979	2	3.08	9	5	4	475	1	3.28
	CeHL	Totals	82	48	22	9	4565	2	3.33	17	11	5	1022	1	3.11

Born; 11/23/75, Montreal, Quebec. 6-0, 180. Drafted by Buffalo Sabres (6th choice, 168th overall) in 1994 Entry Draft. 1996-97 CeHL Playoff MVP. 1996-97 CeHL First Team All-Star. Last amateur club; Shawinigan (QMJHL).

Andrew Plumb
Defenseman

Season	Team	League	GP	G	A	PTS	PIM	GP	G	A	PTS	PIM
			Regular Season					Playoffs				
94-95	Utica	CoHL	8	0	1	1	9	—	—	—	—	—
94-95	London	CoHL	45	1	6	7	20	5	0	1	1	18
95-96	Huntsville	SHL	45	3	13	16	74	—	—	—	—	—
95-96	Jacksonville	SHL	8	0	3	3	25	—	—	—	—	—
96-97	Dayton	CoHL	71	2	14	16	71	—	—	—	—	—
97-98	Bakersfield	WCHL	36	1	11	12	67	—	—	—	—	—
97-98	Idaho	WCHL	17	0	4	4	33	4	0	0	0	2
98-99	Tupelo	WPHL	22	1	3	4	44	—	—	—	—	—
98-99	Abilene	WPHL	19	0	1	1	22	—	—	—	—	—
	CoHL	Totals	124	3	21	24	100	5	0	1	1	18
	WCHL	Totals	53	1	15	16	100	4	0	0	0	2
	SHL	Totals	53	3	16	19	99	—	—	—	—	—
	WPHL	Totals	41	1	4	5	66	—	—	—	—	—

Born; 2/6/72, Vancouver, British Columbia. 6-2, 205. Traded to Idaho by Bakersfield for future considerations (2/98).

Steve Poapst
Defenseman

Season	Team	League	GP	G	A	PTS	PIM	GP	G	A	PTS	PIM
			Regular Season					Playoffs				
91-92	Hampton Roads	ECHL	55	8	20	28	29	14	1	4	5	12
92-93	Baltimore	AHL	7	0	1	1	4	7	0	3	3	6
92-93	Hampton Roads	ECHL	63	10	35	45	57	4	0	1	1	4
93-94	Portland	AHL	78	14	21	35	47	12	0	3	3	8
94-95	Portland	AHL	71	8	22	30	60	7	0	1	1	16
95-96	Washington	NHL	3	1	0	1	0	6	0	0	0	0
95-96	Portland	AHL	70	10	24	34	79	20	2	6	8	16
96-97	Portland	AHL	47	1	20	21	34	5	0	1	1	6
97-98	Portland	AHL	76	8	29	37	46	10	2	3	5	8
98-99	Washington	NHL	22	0	0	0	8	—	—	—	—	—
98-99	Portland	AHL	54	3	21	24	36	—	—	—	—	—
	NHL	Totals	25	1	0	1	8	6	0	0	0	0
	AHL	Totals	403	44	138	182	306	61	4	17	21	60
	ECHL	Totals	118	18	55	73	86	18	1	5	6	16

Born; 1/3/69, Smith Falls, Ontario. 6-0, 195. Signed as a free agent by Washington Capitals (2/4/95). 1992-93 ECHL First Team All-Star. Member of 1991-92 ECHL Champion Hampton Roads Admirals. Member of 1993-94 AHL Champion Portland Pirates. Last amateur club; Colgate (ECAC).

Alexei Podalinski
Left Wing

Season	Team	League	GP	G	A	PTS	PIM	GP	G	A	PTS	PIM
			Regular Season					Playoffs				
96-97	Nashville	CeHL	7	2	3	5	4	—	—	—	—	—
97-98	Tacoma	WCHL	62	27	25	52	104	12	6	6	12	12
98-99	Las Vegas	IHL	4	0	0	0	0	—	—	—	—	—
98-99	Tacoma	WCHL	57	15	22	37	66	10	2	3	5	20
	WCHL	Totals	119	42	47	89	170	22	8	9	17	32

Born; 4/8/73, Moscow, Russia. 6-2, 205. Member of 1998-99 WCHL Champion Tacoma Sabrecats.

Andrej Podkonicky
Left Wing

Season	Team	League	GP	G	A	PTS	PIM	GP	G	A	PTS	PIM
			Regular Season					Playoffs				
98-99	Worcester	AHL	61	19	24	43	52	4	0	0	0	4

Born; 5/9/78, Zvolen, Czechoslovakia. 6-0, 174. Drafted by St. Louis Blues (8th choice, 196th overall) in 1996 Entry Draft. Last amateur club; Portland (WHL).

Michal Podolka
Goaltender

Season	Team	League	GP	W	L	T	MIN	SO	AVG	GP	W	L	MIN	SO	AVG
			Regular Season							Playoffs					
97-98	Windsor	OHL	23	5	13	1	1155	0	4.99	—	—	—	—	—	—
97-98	Muskegon	UHL	8	3	3	0	384	0	4.69	—	—	—	—	—	—
98-99	Topeka	CHL	22	7	10	3	1163	0	3.92	—	—	—	—	—	—

Born; 8/11/77, Most, Czechoslovakia. 5-11, 146. Drafted by Detroit Red Wings (4th choice, 135th overall) in 1996 Entry Draft. Last amateur club; Sault Ste. Marie (OHL).

Jason Podollan
Right Wing

Season	Team	League	GP	G	A	PTS	PIM	GP	G	A	PTS	PIM
			Regular Season					Playoffs				
94-95	Spokane	WHL	72	43	41	84	102	11	5	7	12	18
94-95	Cincinnati	IHL	—	—	—	—	—	3	0	0	0	2
95-96	Spokane	WHL	56	37	25	62	103	18	*21	12	33	28
96-97	Florida	NHL	19	1	1	2	4	—	—	—	—	—
96-97	Toronto	NHL	10	0	3	3	6	—	—	—	—	—
96-97	Carolina	AHL	39	21	25	46	36	—	—	—	—	—
96-97	St. John's	AHL	—	—	—	—	—	11	2	3	5	6
97-98	St. John's	AHL	70	30	31	61	116	4	1	0	1	10
98-99	Toronto	NHL	4	0	0	0	0	—	—	—	—	—
98-99	Los Angeles	NHL	6	0	0	0	5	—	—	—	—	—
98-99	St. John's	AHL	68	42	26	68	65	—	—	—	—	—
98-99	Long Beach	IHL	8	5	3	8	2	6	1	2	3	4
	NHL	Totals	39	1	4	5	15	—	—	—	—	—
	AHL	Totals	177	93	82	175	217	15	3	3	6	16
	IHL	Totals	8	5	3	8	2	9	1	2	3	6

Born; 2/18/76, Vernon, British Columbia. 6-1, 192. Drafted by Florida Panthers (3rd choice, 31st overall) in 1994 Entry Draft. Traded to Toronto Maple Leafs by Florida for Kirk Muller (3/18/97). Traded to Los Angeles Kings by Toronto with Toronto's third round choice (Cory Campbell) in 1999 Entry Draft for Yanic Perreault (3/23/99). Last amateur club; Spokane (WHL).

Vadim Podrezov — Defenseman

Regular Season / Playoffs

Season	Team	League	GP	G	A	PTS	PIM	GP	G	A	PTS	PIM
98-99	Michigan	IHL	2	0	0	0	2	—	—	—	—	—
98-99	Muskegon	UHL	69	8	53	61	78	18	3	9	12	14

Born; 9/23/65, Moscow, Russia. 6-0, 215. 1998-99 UHL All-Rookie Team. 1998-99 UHL Second Team All-Star. Member of 1998-99 UHL Champion Muskegon Fury. Last overseas club; Krylia (Russia).

Joel Poirier — Left Wing

Regular Season / Playoffs

Season	Team	League	GP	G	A	PTS	PIM	GP	G	A	PTS	PIM
95-96	Portland	AHL	30	5	3	8	34	1	0	0	0	0
95-96	Hampton Roads	ECHL	23	9	8	17	61	—	—	—	—	—
96-97	Hampton Roads	ECHL	70	20	21	41	85	9	1	4	5	4
97-98	Hampton Roads	ECHL	56	11	5	16	58	20	2	10	12	16
98-99	Hampton Roads	ECHL	67	11	32	43	93	4	1	3	4	2
	ECHL	Totals	216	51	66	117	297	33	4	17	21	22

Born; 1/15/75, Richmond Hill, Ontario. 6-1, 190. Drafted by Washington Capitals (7th choice, 199th overall) in 1993 Entry Draft. Member of 1997-98 ECHL Champion Hampton Roads Admirals. Last amateur club; Windsor (OHL).

Mark Polak — Center

Regular Season / Playoffs

Season	Team	League	GP	G	A	PTS	PIM	GP	G	A	PTS	PIM
97-98	Pensacola	ECHL	70	15	30	45	47	19	1	7	8	24
98-99	Florida	ECHL	5	0	2	2	8	—	—	—	—	—
98-99	Pensacola	ECHL	62	7	15	22	54	—	—	—	—	—
	ECHL	Totals	137	22	47	69	109	19	1	7	8	24

Born; 5/16/76, Spruce Grove, Alberta. 6-0, 175. Last amateur club; Medicine Hat (WHL).

Jason Polera — Right Wing

Regular Season / Playoffs

Season	Team	League	GP	G	A	PTS	PIM	GP	G	A	PTS	PIM
98-99	Windsor	OHL	65	33	22	55	64	5	0	4	4	0
98-99	Birmingham	ECHL	2	0	0	0	0	—	—	—	—	—

Born;3/21/79, Oshawa, Ontario. 6-0, 190. Last amateur club; Windsor (OHL).

Clark Polglase — Defenseman

Regular Season / Playoffs

Season	Team	League	GP	G	A	PTS	PIM	GP	G	A	PTS	PIM
92-93	Detroit	CoHL	38	4	11	15	113	6	0	0	0	15
93-94	Huntsville	ECHL	34	2	14	16	200	—	—	—	—	—
93-94	Detroit	CoHL	10	2	4	6	51	2	1	0	1	46
94-95	Adirondack	AHL	3	0	0	0	7	—	—	—	—	—
94-95	Detroit	IHL	5	1	0	1	7	—	—	—	—	—
94-95	Detroit	CoHL	34	11	13	24	116	12	1	6	7	4
95-96	San Diego	WCHL	49	9	16	25	138	9	3	3	6	8
96-97	San Diego	WCHL	54	8	33	41	123	8	0	1	1	21
97-98	San Diego	WCHL	48	1	14	15	109	12	0	4	4	14
98-99	San Diego	WCHL	16	2	2	4	56	—	—	—	—	—
98-99	Bakersfield	WCHL	23	4	10	14	58	2	0	2	2	0
	WCHL	Totals	190	24	75	99	484	31	3	10	13	43
	CoHL	Totals	82	17	28	45	429	20	2	6	8	65

Born; 4/7/69, Edmonton, Alberta. 6-2, 200. Member of 1995-96 WCHL Champion San Diego Gulls. Member of 1996-97 WCHL Champion San Diego Gulls. Member of 1997-98 WCHL Champion San Diego Gulls.

Paul Pollilo — Center

Regular Season / Playoffs

Season	Team	League	GP	G	A	PTS	PIM	GP	G	A	PTS	PIM
92-93	Brantford	CoHL	59	33	79	112	18	15	7	13	20	10
93-94	Brantford	CoHL	64	42	*99	*141	37	7	1	9	10	6
94-95	Brantford	CoHL	74	47	*99	*146	48	—	—	—	—	—
94-95	Denver	IHL	1	0	0	0	0	—	—	—	—	—
95-96	Brantford	CoHL	74	*64	*122	*186	62	12	9	16	25	2
96-97	Brantford	CoHL	73	61	*112	*173	49	10	5	19	24	14
97-98	Brantford	UHL	71	48	*117	*165	41	9	8	10	18	4
98-99	Port Huron	UHL	73	28	79	107	14	7	1	4	5	2
	UHL	Totals	488	323	707	1030	269	60	31	71	102	38

Born; 4/24/67, Brantford, Ontario. 5-11, 178. Traded to Port Huron by Asheville (Brantford) with Bernie John and Darryl Paquette for J.D. Eaton, Dale Greenwood, Gairin Smith and Chris Scourletis (7/98). 1992-93 CoHL Second Team All-Star. 1992-93 CoHL Sportsmanlike player. 1993-94 CoHL First All-Star team. 1993-94 CoHL sportsmanlike player. 1994-95 CoHL First Team All-Star. 1994-95 CoHL sportsmanlike player. 1994-95 Shared CoHL MVP award with Mark Green. 1995-96 CoHL 1st Team All-Star. 1995-96 CoHL MVP. 1996-97 CoHL MVP. 1996-97 CoHL First All-Star Team. 1997-98 UHL First Team All-Star. Member of 1992-93 CoHL champion Brantford Smoke.

Mike Pomichter — Left Wing

Regular Season / Playoffs

Season	Team	League	GP	G	A	PTS	PIM	GP	G	A	PTS	PIM
94-95	Indianapolis	IHL	76	13	9	22	47	—	—	—	—	—
95-96	Indianapolis	IHL	4	0	0	0	0	—	—	—	—	—
95-96	Portland	AHL	2	0	0	0	0	—	—	—	—	—
95-96	Cornwall	AHL	6	0	1	1	0	—	—	—	—	—
95-96	St. John's	AHL	19	2	4	6	4	—	—	—	—	—
96-97	Jacksonville	ECHL	61	37	40	77	26	—	—	—	—	—
96-97	Baltimore	AHL	4	2	1	3	4	3	0	0	0	0
96-97	Chicago	IHL	2	0	0	0	0	—	—	—	—	—
97-98	Springfield	AHL	20	7	6	13	14	—	—	—	—	—
97-98	Cincinnati	AHL	26	6	8	14	18	—	—	—	—	—
97-98	Jacksonville	ECHL	3	5	0	5	2	—	—	—	—	—
98-99	Cincinnati	AHL	25	2	2	4	14	—	—	—	—	—
98-99	Saginaw	UHL	10	8	2	10	0	—	—	—	—	—
98-99	Jacksonville	ECHL	33	10	18	28	31	2	1	2	3	0
	AHL	Totals	102	19	22	41	54	3	0	0	0	0
	IHL	Totals	82	13	9	22	47	—	—	—	—	—
	ECHL	Totals	97	52	58	110	59	—	—	—	—	—

Born; 9/10/73, New Haven, Connecticut. 6-2, 220. Drafted by Chicago Blackhawks (2nd choice, 39th overall) in 1991 Entry Draft. Traded to Toronto Maple Leafs by Chicago for cash (1/29/96). Signed as a free agent by Phoenix Coyotes (1997). Selected by Fort Wayne in 1999 UHL Expansion Draft. Last amateur club; Boston University (Hockey East).

Kevin Popp — Defenseman

Regular Season / Playoffs

Season	Team	League	GP	G	A	PTS	PIM	GP	G	A	PTS	PIM
97-98	Birmingham	ECHL	70	0	3	3	187	4	0	0	0	20
98-99	Birmingham	ECHL	59	3	4	7	300	—	—	—	—	—
	ECHL	Totals	129	3	7	10	487	4	0	0	0	20

Born; 2/26/76, Surrey, British Columbia. 6-1, 212. Last amateur club; Portland (WHL).

Kris Porter — Right Wing

Regular Season / Playoffs

Season	Team	League	GP	G	A	PTS	PIM	GP	G	A	PTS	PIM
98-99	Merrimack	H.E.	36	24	21	45	48	—	—	—	—	—
98-99	Worcester	AHL	3	0	0	0	2	—	—	—	—	—

Born; 9/13/78, Oxbow, Saskatchewan. 5-10, 175. Last amateur club; Merrimack (Hockey East).

Marek Posmyk — Defenseman

Regular Season / Playoffs

Season	Team	League	GP	G	A	PTS	PIM	GP	G	A	PTS	PIM
96-97	Dukla Jihlava	Czech. Rep.	24	1	7	8	44	—	—	—	—	—
96-97	St. John's	AHL	2	0	0	0	2	—	—	—	—	—
97-98	Sarnia	OHL	48	8	16	24	94	5	0	2	2	6
97-98	St. John's	AHL	3	0	0	0	4	—	—	—	—	—
98-99	St. John's	AHL	41	1	0	1	36	—	—	—	—	—
	AHL	Totals	46	1	0	1	42	—	—	—	—	—

Born; 9/15/78, Jihlava, Czechoslovakia. 6-5, 220. Drafted by Toronto Maple Leafs (1st choice, 36th overall) in 1996 Entry Draft.

Barry Potomski — Left Wing

Regular Season / Playoffs

Season	Team	League	GP	G	A	PTS	PIM	GP	G	A	PTS	PIM
92-93	Erie	ECHL	5	1	1	2	31	—	—	—	—	—
92-93	Toledo	ECHL	43	5	18	23	184	14	5	2	7	73
93-94	Toledo	ECHL	13	9	4	13	81	—	—	—	—	—
93-94	Adirondack	AHL	50	9	5	14	224	11	1	1	2	44
94-95	Phoenix	IHL	42	5	6	11	171	—	—	—	—	—
95-96	Los Angeles	NHL	33	3	2	5	104	—	—	—	—	—
95-96	Phoenix	IHL	24	5	2	7	74	3	1	0	1	8
96-97	Los Angeles	NHL	26	3	2	5	93	—	—	—	—	—
96-97	Phoenix	IHL	28	2	11	13	58	—	—	—	—	—
97-98	San Jose	NHL	9	0	1	1	30	—	—	—	—	—
97-98	Las Vegas	IHL	31	3	2	5	143	4	1	0	1	13
98-99	Adirondack	AHL	75	9	7	16	220	1	0	0	0	2
	NHL	Totals	68	6	5	11	227	—	—	—	—	—
	IHL	Totals	125	15	21	36	446	7	2	0	2	21
	AHL	Totals	125	18	12	30	444	12	1	1	2	46
	ECHL	Totals	61	15	23	38	296	14	5	2	7	73

Born; 11/24/72, Windsor, Ontario. 6-2, 210. Signed as a free agent by Los Angeles Kings (7/7/94). Signed as a free agent by San Jose Sharks (9/15/97). Signed as a free agent by Detroit Red Wings (7/21/98). Member of 1992-93 ECHL champion Toledo Storm. Last amateur club; London (OHL).

Steve Pottie — Goaltender

Regular Season / Playoffs

Season	Team	League	GP	W	L	T	MIN	SO	AVG	GP	W	L	MIN	SO	AVG
96-97	Nashville	CeHL	19	4	*7	1	806	0	4.84	—	—	—	—	—	—
96-97	San Antonio	CeHL	27	9	*13	1	1412	0	4.33	—	—	—	—	—	—
97-98	Huntsville	CHL	*54	*30	15	6	*3112	1	3.91	2	0	1	65	0	3.69
98-99	El Paso	WPHL	6	2	4	0	359	0	3.01	—	—	—	—	—	—
98-99	New Mexico	WPHL	24	10	10	1	1271	0	3.87	—	—	—	—	—	—
	CHL	Totals	100	43	35	8	5330	1	4.17	2	0	1	65	0	3.69
	WPHL	Totals	30	12	14	1	1630	0	3.68	—	—	—	—	—	—

Born; 9/28/73, Waverly, Nova Scotia. 6-0, 200. Last amateur club; Dalhousie (AUAA).

Steve Potvin — Right Wing

Regular Season / Playoffs

Season	Team	League	GP	G	A	PTS	PIM	GP	G	A	PTS	PIM
94-95	Niagara Falls	OHL	60	32	57	89	95	6	1	5	6	10
94-95	Peoria	IHL	2	1	0	1	0	2	0	0	0	0
95-96	Portland	AHL	1	0	0	0	0	—	—	—	—	—
95-96	Raleigh	ECHL	62	15	31	46	175	4	2	2	4	0
96-97	Albany	AHL	16	1	6	7	18	11	0	1	1	16
96-97	Raleigh	ECHL	49	27	39	66	62	—	—	—	—	—
97-98	Hamilton	AHL	66	20	14	34	84	9	1	4	5	8
98-99	Hamilton	AHL	71	9	21	30	79	7	0	1	1	6
	AHL	Totals	154	30	41	71	181	27	1	6	7	30
	ECHL	Totals	111	42	70	112	237	4	2	2	4	0

Born; 9/26/74, Montreal, Quebec. 5-11, 190. Last amateur club; Niagara Falls (OHL).

Charles Poulin — Center

Regular Season / Playoffs

Season	Team	League	GP	G	A	PTS	PIM	GP	G	A	PTS	PIM
92-93	Fredericton	AHL	58	12	19	31	99	1	0	0	0	0
93-94	Fredericton	AHL	35	9	15	24	70	—	—	—	—	—
94-95												
95-96	Canada	National	2	0	1	1	2	—	—	—	—	—
96-97												
97-98	Berlin	Germany	21	3	4	7	14	—	—	—	—	—
97-98	Quebec	IHL	18	1	2	3	33	—	—	—	—	—
97-98	Tallahassee	ECHL	5	2	2	4	2	—	—	—	—	—
98-99	Abilene	WPHL	58	41	55	96	136	2	0	1	1	2
	AHL	Totals	93	21	34	55	169	1	0	0	0	0

Born; 7/27/72, St. Jean d'Iberville, Quebec. 6-0, 172. Drafted by Montreal Canadiens (3rd choice, 58th overall) in 1990 Entry Draft. Last amateur club; St-Hyacinthe (QMJHL).

Kevin Powell — Left Wing

Regular Season / Playoffs

Season	Team	League	GP	G	A	PTS	PIM	GP	G	A	PTS	PIM
98-99	Miami	ECHL	4	0	0	0	2	—	—	—	—	—
98-99	Wichita	CHL	34	11	16	27	29	4	2	0	2	4

Born; 8/21/73, Regina, Saskatchewan. 5-9, 185. Last amateur club; Acadia

Andrew Power — Left Wing

Regular Season / Playoffs

Season	Team	League	GP	G	A	PTS	PIM	GP	G	A	PTS	PIM
97-98	Shreveport	WPHL	61	13	31	44	174	8	3	1	4	24
98-99	Shreveport	WPHL	43	16	28	44	179	12	4	6	10	58
	WPHL	Totals	104	29	59	88	353	20	7	7	14	82

Born; 1/19/76, London, Ontario. 6-2, 230. Member of 1998-99 WPHL Champion Shreveport Mudbugs.

Chad Power — Left Wing

Regular Season / Playoffs

Season	Team	League	GP	G	A	PTS	PIM	GP	G	A	PTS	PIM
96-97	Ohio State	CCHA	39	24	21	45	53	—	—	—	—	—
96-97	Detroit	IHL	7	0	1	1	11	—	—	—	—	—
97-98	Detroit	IHL	1	0	0	0	0	—	—	—	—	—
97-98	Baton Rouge	ECHL	67	29	19	48	46	—	—	—	—	—
98-99	New Orleans	ECHL	39	13	10	23	43	—	—	—	—	—
98-99	Birmingham	ECHL	30	22	10	32	8	5	2	1	3	4
	IHL	Totals	8	0	1	1	11	—	—	—	—	—
	ECHL	Totals	69	35	20	55	51	5	2	1	3	4

Born; 7/20/73, Corner Brook, Newfoundland. 6-0, 205. Last amateur club; Ohio State (CCHA).

Andy Powers — Left Wing

Regular Season / Playoffs

Season	Team	League	GP	G	A	PTS	PIM	GP	G	A	PTS	PIM
98-99	Boston College	H.E.	43	13	12	25	52	—	—	—	—	—
98-99	Syracuse	AHL	1	0	0	0	0	—	—	—	—	—
98-99	Long Beach	IHL	3	0	0	0	0	—	—	—	—	—

Born; Abington, Massachusetts. 5-11, 190. Last amateur club; Boston College

Mike Pozzo — Center

Regular Season / Playoffs

Season	Team	League	GP	G	A	PTS	PIM	GP	G	A	PTS	PIM
98-99	Oklahoma City	CHL	60	21	25	46	26	5	1	0	1	0

Born; 9/30/76, Calgary, Alberta. 5-11, 175. Last amateur club; Royal Military College (CIAU).

Kevin Pozzo — Defenseman

Season	Team	League	GP	G	A	PTS	PIM	GP	G	A	PTS	PIM
		Regular Season						Playoffs				
95-96	Chicago	IHL	51	3	6	9	97	9	2	3	5	6
96-97	Kansas City	IHL	1	0	0	0	2	—	—	—	—	—
96-97	Las Vegas	IHL	7	0	1	1	6	—	—	—	—	—
96-97	Tallahassee	ECHL	8	1	2	3	15	—	—	—	—	—
97-98	Hamilton	AHL	2	0	0	0	4	—	—	—	—	—
97-98	New Orleans	ECHL	54	5	22	27	114	4	0	2	2	2
98-99	Hamilton	AHL	3	0	0	0	4	—	—	—	—	—
98-99	New Orleans	ECHL	53	1	25	26	79	10	1	3	4	23
	IHL	Totals	59	3	7	10	105	9	2	3	5	6
	AHL	Totals	5	0	0	0	8	—	—	—	—	—
	ECHL	Totals	115	7	49	56	208	14	1	5	6	25

Born; 10/11/74, Calgary, Alberta. 6-2, 220. Drafted by Buffalo Sabres (4th choice, 142nd overall) in 1993 Entry Draft. Last amateur club; Brandon (WHL).

Harlan Pratt — Defenseman

Season	Team	League	GP	G	A	PTS	PIM	GP	G	A	PTS	PIM
		Regular Season						Playoffs				
98-99	Toledo	ECHL	61	4	35	39	32	3	0	0	0	0

Born; 12/10/78, Fort McMurray, Alberta. 6-2, 191. Drafted by Pittsburgh Penguins (5th choice, 124th overall) in 1997 Entry Draft. Last amateur club; Regina

Jon Pratt — Left Wing

Season	Team	League	GP	G	A	PTS	PIM	GP	G	A	PTS	PIM
		Regular Season						Playoffs				
94-95	Providence	AHL	44	12	6	18	31	9	1	1	2	8
95-96	Peoria	IHL	45	6	12	18	47	5	1	2	3	6
96-97	Long Beach	IHL	1	0	0	0	0	—	—	—	—	—
96-97	Peoria	ECHL	45	32	25	57	83	2	2	3	5	4
97-98	Peoria	ECHL	50	27	22	49	136	3	2	1	3	4
98-99	Wheeling	ECHL	25	11	11	22	49	—	—	—	—	—
98-99	Charlotte	ECHL	19	4	4	8	14	—	—	—	—	—
98-99	Greenville	ECHL	7	2	3	5	8	—	—	—	—	—
	IHL	Totals	46	6	12	18	47	5	1	2	3	6
	ECHL	Totals	146	76	65	141	290	5	4	4	8	8

Born; 9/25/70, Danvers, Massachusetts. 6-1, 195. Drafted by Minnesota North Stars (9th choice, 154th overall) in 1989 Entry Draft. Last amateur club; Boston University (Hockey East).

Jody Praznik — Defenseman

Season	Team	League	GP	G	A	PTS	PIM	GP	G	A	PTS	PIM
		Regular Season						Playoffs				
89-90	Hampton Roads	ECHL	55	7	35	42	40	5	0	4	4	0
90-91	Hampton Roads	ECHL	64	15	39	54	30	11	0	2	2	10
91-92	Toledo	ECHL	37	3	27	30	26	—	—	—	—	—
91-92	Knoxville	ECHL	19	4	12	16	17	—	—	—	—	—
92-93	Tulsa	CeHL	55	11	33	44	50	12	6	13	19	22
93-94	Tulsa	CeHL	59	5	25	30	52	10	2	2	4	12
94-95	Tulsa	CeHL	60	8	23	31	40	4	1	1	2	2
95-96	Reno	WCHL	57	12	40	52	39	3	0	0	0	0
96-97	New Mexico	WPHL	61	18	52	70	74	6	1	4	5	4
97-98	Esberg	Denmark	32	15	10	25	NA	—	—	—	—	—
98-99	Corpus Christi	WPHL	37	2	24	26	22	4	1	4	5	0
	ECHL	Totals	175	29	113	142	113	16	0	6	6	10
	CeHL	Totals	174	24	81	105	142	26	9	16	25	36
	WPHL	Totals	98	20	76	96	96	10	2	8	10	4

Born; 6/28/69, Winnipeg, Manitoba. 6-1, 200. Drafted by Detroit Red Wings (8th choice, 185th overall) in 1988 Entry Draft. 1996-97 WPHL Defenseman of the Year. Member of 1990-91 ECHL Champion Hampton Roads Admirals. Member of 1992-93 CeHL Champion Tulsa Oilers. Last amateur club; Saskatoon (WHL).

Brad Prefontaine — Defenseman

Season	Team	League	GP	G	A	PTS	PIM	GP	G	A	PTS	PIM
		Regular Season						Playoffs				
95-96	Birmingham	ECHL	60	1	7	8	279	—	—	—	—	—
96-97	Columbus	CeHL	63	6	11	17	197	3	0	0	0	30
97-98	Columbus	CHL	62	1	8	9	272	10	1	3	4	23
98-99	Columbus	CHL	65	0	10	10	177	8	0	1	1	6
	CHL	Totals	190	7	29	36	646	21	1	4	5	59

Born; 7/27/72, Camrose, Alberta. 6-2, 210. Member of 1997-98 CHL Champion Columbus Cottonmouths.

Jay Prentice — Right Wing

Season	Team	League	GP	G	A	PTS	PIM	GP	G	A	PTS	PIM
		Regular Season						Playoffs				
97-98	Baton Rouge	ECHL	59	10	23	33	66	—	—	—	—	—
98-99	Arkansas	WPHL	49	22	16	38	21	3	1	2	3	0

Born; 9/4/74, Coldwater, Ontario. 6-2, 200. Last amateur club; Union (ECAC).

Damian Prescott — Left Wing

Season	Team	League	GP	G	A	PTS	PIM	GP	G	A	PTS	PIM
		Regular Season						Playoffs				
98-99	South Carolina	ECHL	70	19	13	32	107	3	0	1	1	2

Born; 2/7/75, Danvers, Massachusetts. 5-11, 185. Last amateur club; Brown (ECAC).

Brad Preston — Center

Season	Team	League	GP	G	A	PTS	PIM	GP	G	A	PTS	PIM
		Regular Season						Playoffs				
97-98	New Orleans	ECHL	4	0	0	0	0	—	—	—	—	—
97-98	Oklahoma City	CHL	61	22	15	37	66	7	3	2	5	4
98-99	Oklahoma City	CHL	70	18	36	54	56	10	0	1	1	4
	CHL	Totals	131	40	51	91	122	17	3	3	6	8

Born; 9/6/74, Toronto, Ontario. 5-11, 185. Last amateur club; Fredonia-SUNY (NCAA 3).

Eric Preston — Right Wing

Season	Team	League	GP	G	A	PTS	PIM	GP	G	A	PTS	PIM
		Regular Season						Playoffs				
97-98	Oklahoma City	CHL	15	3	4	7	21	—	—	—	—	—
97-98	Memphis	CHL	36	6	23	29	18	4	0	1	1	0
98-99	Waco	WPHL	69	31	26	57	54	4	2	0	2	0
	CHL	Totals	51	9	27	36	39	4	0	1	1	0

Born; 6/18/73, Mission Viejo, California. 5-10, 185. Traded to Austin by San Angelo with future considerations for Marty Diamond (9/98). Traded to Waco by Austin for Jamie Hearn (9/98). Last amateur club; Fredonia-SUNY (NCAA 3).

Dan Price — Right Wing

Season	Team	League	GP	G	A	PTS	PIM	GP	G	A	PTS	PIM
		Regular Season						Playoffs				
98-99	Bowling Green	CCHA	38	21	32	53	56	—	—	—	—	—

Born; 9/23/74, Sarnia, Ontario. 6-1, 205. Last amateur cluh; Bowling Green (CCHA).

Jason Price — Defenseman

Season	Team	League	GP	G	A	PTS	PIM	GP	G	A	PTS	PIM
		Regular Season						Playoffs				
97-98	Maine	H.E.	23	1	6	7	28	—	—	—	—	—
97-98	Tucson	WCHL	9	0	2	2	26	—	—	—	—	—
98-99	Macon	CHL	49	6	13	19	64	3	0	0	0	2

Born; 3/22/78, Los Angeles, California. 6-3, 210. Last amateur club; Maine

Maxim Priyatel — Goaltender

Season	Team	League	GP	W	L	T	MIN	SO	AVG	GP	W	L	MIN	SO	AVG
		Regular Season								Playoffs					
98-99	Memphis	CHL	2	0	1	0	80	0	6.75	—	—	—	—	—	—

Born;

Mike Prokopec

Right Wing

Regular Season | Playoffs

Season	Team	League	GP	G	A	PTS	PIM	GP	G	A	PTS	PIM
94-95	Indianapolis	IHL	70	21	12	33	80	—	—	—	—	—
95-96	Chicago	NHL	9	0	0	0	5	—	—	—	—	—
95-96	Indianapolis	IHL	67	18	22	40	131	5	2	0	2	4
96-97	Chicago	NHL	6	0	0	0	6	—	—	—	—	—
96-97	Indianapolis	IHL	57	13	18	31	143	—	—	—	—	—
96-97	Detroit	IHL	3	2	0	2	4	8	2	1	3	14
97-98	Worcester	AHL	62	21	25	46	112	11	1	2	3	10
98-99	Detroit	IHL	75	25	28	53	125	10	3	6	9	26
	NHL	Totals	15	0	0	0	11	—	—	—	—	—
	IHL	Totals	272	79	80	159	483	23	7	7	14	34

Born; 5/17/74, Toronto, Ontario. 6-2, 190. Drafted by Chicago Blackhawks (7th choice, 161st overall) in 1992 Entry Draft. Traded to Ottawa Senators by Chicago for Denis Chasse, the rights to Kevin Bolibruck and future considerations (3/18/97). Last amateur club; Guelph (OHL).

Jason Prokopetz

Forward

Regular Season | Playoffs

Season	Team	League	GP	G	A	PTS	PIM	GP	G	A	PTS	PIM
98-99	Florida	ECHL	59	6	9	15	191	5	0	0	0	2

Born; 7/18/73, Esterhazy, Saskatchewan. 6-0, 185. Last amateur club; Michigan Tech (WCHA).

Andy Prokspec

Forward

Regular Season | Playoffs

Season	Team	League	GP	G	A	PTS	PIM	GP	G	A	PTS	PIM
98-99	Dayton	ECHL	1	0	0	0	0	—	—	—	—	—

Born;

Sean Pronger

Center

Regular Season | Playoffs

Season	Team	League	GP	G	A	PTS	PIM	GP	G	A	PTS	PIM
94-95	Knoxville	ECHL	34	18	23	41	55	—	—	—	—	—
94-95	Greensboro	ECHL	2	0	2	2	0	—	—	—	—	—
94-95	San Diego	IHL	8	0	0	0	2	—	—	—	—	—
95-96	Anaheim	NHL	7	0	1	1	6	—	—	—	—	—
95-96	Baltimore	AHL	72	16	17	33	61	12	3	7	10	16
96-97	Anaheim	NHL	39	7	7	14	20	9	0	2	2	4
96-97	Baltimore	AHL	41	26	17	43	17	—	—	—	—	—
97-98	Anaheim	NHL	62	5	15	20	30	—	—	—	—	—
97-98	Pittsburgh	NHL	5	1	0	1	2	5	0	0	0	4
98-99	Houston	IHL	16	11	7	18	32	—	—	—	—	—
98-99	Pittsburgh	NHL	2	0	0	0	0	—	—	—	—	—
98-99	Rangers	NHL	14	0	3	3	4	—	—	—	—	—
98-99	Los Angeles	NHL	13	0	1	1	4	—	—	—	—	—
	NHL	Totals	142	13	27	40	66	14	0	2	2	8
	AHL	Totals	113	42	34	76	78	12	3	7	10	16
	IHL	Totals	24	11	7	18	34	—	—	—	—	—
	ECHL	Totals	36	18	25	43	55	—	—	—	—	—

Born; 11/30/72, Dryden, Ontario. 6-2, 205. Drafted by Vancouver Canucks (3rd choice, 51st overall) in 1991 Entry Draft. Signed as a free agent by Anaheim Mighty Ducks (2/14/95). Traded to Pittsburgh Penguins by Anaheim for the rights to Patrick Lalime (3/24/98). Traded to New York Rangers by Pittsburgh with Petr Nedved and Chris Tamer for Alexei Kovalev, Harry York and cash (11/25/99). Traded to Los Angeles by Rangers for Eric Lacroix (2/12/99). Last amateur club; Bowling Green (CCHA).

Nikolai Pronin

Forward

Regular Season | Playoffs

Season	Team	League	GP	G	A	PTS	PIM	GP	G	A	PTS	PIM
98-99	Charlotte	ECHL	10	0	1	1	2	—	—	—	—	—
98-99	Toledo	ECHL	3	0	0	0	19	—	—	—	—	—
98-99	Thunder Bay	UHL	41	6	13	19	49	13	3	0	3	2
	ECHL	Totals	13	0	1	1	21	—	—	—	—	—

Born; 4/13/79, Moscow, Russia. 5-11, 200.

Andrew Proskurnicki

Left Wing

Regular Season | Playoffs

Season	Team	League	GP	G	A	PTS	PIM	GP	G	A	PTS	PIM
97-98	Sarnia	OHL	66	20	33	53	229	5	1	1	2	28
97-98	Hartford	AHL	4	0	1	1	7	—	—	—	—	—
98-99	Sarnia	OHL	36	4	14	18	136	—	—	—	—	—
98-99	Erie	OHL	15	6	5	11	39	5	2	2	4	16

Born; 7/24/78, Hamilton, Ontario. 6-3, 201. Drafted by New York Rangers (11th choice, 210th overall) in 1997 Entry Draft. Last amateur club; Sarnia (OHL).

Tyler Prosofsky

Right Wing

Regular Season | Playoffs

Season	Team	League	GP	G	A	PTS	PIM	GP	G	A	PTS	PIM
97-98	Providence	AHL	12	0	6	6	24	—	—	—	—	—
97-98	Utah	IHL	26	2	5	7	65	—	—	—	—	—
97-98	Las Vegas	IHL	17	2	3	5	21	—	—	—	—	—
97-98	Long Beach	IHL	1	0	0	0	2	—	—	—	—	—
97-98	Idaho	WCHL	4	4	4	8	25	—	—	—	—	—
98-99	Springfield	AHL	3	1	0	1	0	—	—	—	—	—
98-99	Birmingham	ECHL	27	15	14	29	115	—	—	—	—	—
	IHL	Totals	44	4	8	12	88	—	—	—	—	—
	AHL	Totals	15	1	6	7	24	—	—	—	—	—

Born; 2/19/76, Saskatoon, Saskatchewan. 5-11, 193. Drafted by Chicago Blackhawks (7th choice, 170th overall) in 1994 Entry Draft. Re-entered NHL Entry Draft, Vancouver's 4th choice, 121st overall in 1996 Entry Draft. Last amateur club; Kelowna (WHL).

Boris Protsenko

Right Wing

Regular Season | Playoffs

Season	Team	League	GP	G	A	PTS	PIM	GP	G	A	PTS	PIM
98-99	Syracuse	AHL	65	24	24	48	84	—	—	—	—	—

Born; 8/21/78, Kiev, USSR. 5-11, 194. Drafted by Pittsburgh Penguins (4th choice, 77th overall) in 1996 Entry Draft. Last amateur club; Calgary (WHL).

Christian Proulx

Defenseman

Regular Season | Playoffs

Season	Team	League	GP	G	A	PTS	PIM	GP	G	A	PTS	PIM
92-93	Fredericton	AHL	2	1	0	1	2	4	0	0	0	0
93-94	Montreal	NHL	7	1	2	3	20	—	—	—	—	—
93-94	Fredericton	AHL	70	2	12	14	183	—	—	—	—	—
94-95	Fredericton	AHL	75	1	9	10	184	9	0	1	1	8
95-96	San Francisco	IHL	80	1	15	16	154	4	0	0	0	6
96-97	Milwaukee	IHL	74	3	4	7	145	1	0	0	0	2
97-98	Hershey	AHL	32	2	2	4	76	—	—	—	—	—
97-98	Milwaukee	IHL	31	4	6	10	84	10	0	1	1	20
98-99	Asiago	Italy										
	IHL	Totals	185	8	25	33	383	15	0	1	1	28
	AHL	Totals	179	6	13	19	445	13	0	1	1	8

Born; 12/10/73, Coaticook, Quebec. 6-0, 190. Drafted by Montreal Canadiens (7th choice, 164th overall) in 1992 Entry Draft. Last amateur club; St. Jean

Hugo Proulx

Center

Regular Season | Playoffs

Season	Team	League	GP	G	A	PTS	PIM	GP	G	A	PTS	PIM
94-95	South Carolina	ECHL	10	0	1	1	12	—	—	—	—	—
94-95	Greensboro	ECHL	40	18	28	46	116	18	6	14	20	58
95-96	Saginaw	CoHL	4	2	3	5	14	—	—	—	—	—
95-96	Jacksonville	ECHL	24	11	8	19	43	18	9	9	18	46
96-97	Portland	AHL	2	0	0	0	2	—	—	—	—	—
96-97	Quad City	CoHL	69	48	58	106	82	15	8	11	19	12
97-98	San Antonio	IHL	3	0	0	0	2	—	—	—	—	—
97-98	Chicago	IHL	1	0	0	0	0	—	—	—	—	—
97-98	Quad City	UHL	54	33	48	81	95	12	3	2	5	6
98-99	Quad City	UHL	50	19	33	52	60	16	3	13	16	16
	IHL	Totals	4	0	0	0	2	—	—	—	—	—
	UHL	Totals	177	102	142	244	251	43	14	26	40	34
	ECHL	Totals	74	29	37	66	171	36	15	23	38	104

Born; 6/8/72, Drummondville, Quebec. 5-11, 185. Member of 1996-97 CoHL Champion Quad City Mallards. Member of 1997-98 UHL Champion Quad City Mallards. Last amateur club; Hull (QMJHL).

Joel Prpic — Center

Regular Season / Playoffs

Season	Team	League	GP	G	A	PTS	PIM	GP	G	A	PTS	PIM
97-98	Boston	NHL	1	0	0	0	2	—	—	—	—	—
97-98	Providence	AHL	73	17	18	35	53	—	—	—	—	—
98-99	Providence	AHL	75	14	16	30	163	18	4	6	10	48
	AHL	Totals	148	31	34	65	216	18	4	6	10	48

Born; 9/25/74, Sudbury, Ontario. 6-6, 200. Drafted by Boston Bruins (9th choice, 233rd overall) in 1993 Entry Draft. Member of 1998-99 AHL Champion Providence Bruins. Scored Calder Cup-winning goal for Providence (1999). Last amateur club; St. Lawrence (ECAC).

Tony Prpic — Right Wing

Regular Season / Playoffs

Season	Team	League	GP	G	A	PTS	PIM	GP	G	A	PTS	PIM
94-95	Tallahassee	ECHL	20	5	8	13	71	—	—	—	—	—
94-95	Wheeling	ECHL	30	11	16	27	64	3	1	1	2	2
95-96	Fredericton	AHL	26	3	3	6	60	9	2	2	4	18
95-96	Wheeling	ECHL	6	0	2	2	12	—	—	—	—	—
96-97	Fredericton	AHL	16	4	3	7	33	—	—	—	—	—
96-97	Quebec	IHL	3	0	0	0	2	—	—	—	—	—
96-97	Pensacola	ECHL	36	18	11	29	113	11	4	3	7	37
97-98	Toledo	ECHL	27	6	16	22	67	7	0	3	3	15
98-99	Idaho	WCHL	47	29	30	59	113	2	1	0	1	0
	AHL	Totals	42	7	6	13	93	9	2	2	4	18
	ECHL	Totals	119	40	53	93	327	21	5	7	12	54

Born; 6/16/73, Cleveland, Ohio. 6-4, 222. Last amateur club; Tri-City (WHL).

Derek Prue — Center

Regular Season / Playoffs

Season	Team	League	GP	G	A	PTS	PIM	GP	G	A	PTS	PIM
92-93	St. Petersburg	SUN	4	0	1	1	4	—	—	—	—	—
93-94	Chatham	CoHL	46	13	7	20	18	—	—	—	—	—
93-94	Utica	CoHL	2	0	0	0	0	—	—	—	—	—
93-94	St. Thomas	CoHL	11	2	4	6	2	3	0	0	0	0
94-95												
95-96												
96-97	Alaska	WCHL	10	2	2	4	10	—	—	—	—	—
96-97	Tulsa	CeHL	9	4	5	9	6	5	1	1	2	19
97-98	Tucson	WCHL	11	2	4	6	13	—	—	—	—	—
97-98	Central Texas	WPHL	19	5	6	11	18	—	—	—	—	—
97-98	Odessa	WPHL	4	2	0	2	20	—	—	—	—	—
98-99	Mohawk Valley	UHL	2	1	0	1	0	—	—	—	—	—
	UHL	Totals	61	15	11	26	20	3	0	0	0	0
	WPHL	Totals	23	7	6	13	38	—	—	—	—	—
	WCHL	Totals	21	4	6	10	23	—	—	—	—	—

Born; 3/24/72, Spruce Grove, Alberta. 6-0, 190. Signed as a free agent by Tucson Gila Monsters (1997). Traded to Odessa by Central Texas for Don Margettie

Brett Punchard — Center

Regular Season / Playoffs

Season	Team	League	GP	G	A	PTS	PIM	GP	G	A	PTS	PIM
97-98	Manitoba	IHL	41	8	14	22	31	—	—	—	—	—
97-98	Las Vegas	IHL	14	4	3	7	28	—	—	—	—	—
97-98	Tacoma	WCHL	12	4	8	12	34	11	3	12	15	18
98-99	Jacksonville	ECHL	20	6	9	15	38	—	—	—	—	—
98-99	Tallahassee	ECHL	49	20	29	49	40	—	—	—	—	—
	IHL	Totals	55	12	17	29	59	—	—	—	—	—
	ECHL	Totals	69	26	38	64	78	—	—	—	—	—

Born; 2/15/73, Toronto, Ontario. 6-0, 203. Last amateur club; Bowling Green (CCHA).

Derek Puppa — Goaltender

Regular Season / Playoffs

Season	Team	League	GP	W	L	T	MIN	SO	AVG	GP	W	L	MIN	SO	AVG
96-97	Pensacola	ECHL	1	0	1	0	60	0	5.00	—	—	—	—	—	—
96-97	Huntsville	CeHL	25	11	7	3	1219	1	4.87	—	—	—	—	—	—
97-98	Nashville	CHL	43	23	12	5	2391	1	3.16	6	3	2	308	0	3.89
98-99	Huntsville	CHL	55	*39	11	2	3104	1	3.13	*15	*11	4	*961	*1	*2.12
	CHL	Totals	123	73	30	10	6714	3	3.46	21	14	6	1269	1	2.55

Born; 2/18/72, Kirkland, Ontario. 5-9, 175. 1998-99 CHL MVP. 1998-99 CHL Playoff MVP. Member of 1998-99 CHL Champion Huntsville Channel Cats. Last amateur club; Alabama-Huntsville (NCAA 2).

Brad Purdie — Center

Regular Season / Playoffs

Season	Team	League	GP	G	A	PTS	PIM	GP	G	A	PTS	PIM
95-96	Maine	H.E.	39	17	20	37	36	—	—	—	—	—
95-96	Dayton	ECHL	3	1	1	2	0	—	—	—	—	—
95-96	Cornwall	AHL	1	0	0	0	0	—	—	—	—	—
96-97	Chicago	IHL	61	14	22	36	28	4	0	1	1	4
96-97	Peoria	ECHL	11	9	4	13	10	—	—	—	—	—
97-98	Manitoba	IHL	81	29	43	72	73	3	0	0	0	0
98-99	Fort Wayne	IHL	80	27	41	68	45	2	0	2	2	0
	IHL	Totals	222	70	106	176	146	9	0	3	3	4
	ECHL	Totals	14	10	5	15	10	—	—	—	—	—

Born; 9/11/72, Dollard-des-Or, Quebec. 6-0, 195. Last amateur club; Maine (Hockey East).

Dennis Purdie — Right Wing

Regular Season / Playoffs

Season	Team	League	GP	G	A	PTS	PIM	GP	G	A	PTS	PIM
92-93	Toledo	ECHL	6	0	0	0	17	—	—	—	—	—
92-93	Johnstown	ECHL	17	10	7	17	38	5	1	3	4	38
93-94	Johnstown	ECHL	57	36	46	82	171	3	3	2	5	8
94-95	Saint John	AHL	12	4	1	5	11	—	—	—	—	—
94-95	Johnstown	ECHL	36	27	33	60	125	5	5	3	8	12
95-96	Minnesota	IHL	2	0	0	0	0	—	—	—	—	—
95-96	Toledo	ECHL	48	23	36	59	187	11	9	4	13	24
96-97	Toledo	ECHL	58	37	43	80	169	5	1	3	4	25
97-98	Ayr	BSL	38	21	11	32	76	9	4	5	9	4
98-99	Ayr	BSL	47	17	13	30	156	5	1	0	1	2
	ECHL	Totals	222	133	165	298	707	29	19	14	33	107
	BSL	Totals	85	38	24	62	232	14	5	5	10	6

Born; 11/27/72, Amherstburg, Ontario. 5-10, 200. Last amateur club; London (OHL).

Dale Purinton — Defenseman

Regular Season / Playoffs

Season	Team	League	GP	G	A	PTS	PIM	GP	G	A	PTS	PIM
97-98	Hartford	AHL	17	0	0	0	95	—	—	—	—	—
97-98	Charlotte	ECHL	34	3	5	8	186	—	—	—	—	—
98-99	Hartford	AHL	45	1	3	4	306	7	0	2	2	24
	AHL	Totals	62	1	3	4	401	7	0	2	2	24

Born; 10/11/76, Fort Wayne, Indiana. 6-2, 190. Drafted by New York Rangers (5th choice, 117th overall) in 1995 Entry Draft. Signed as a free agent by Rangers (8/19/97). Last amateur club; Lethbridge (WHL).

Neal Purdon — Right Wing

Regular Season / Playoffs

Season	Team	League	GP	G	A	PTS	PIM	GP	G	A	PTS	PIM
94-95	Thunder Bay	CoHL	20	2	2	4	4	—	—	—	—	—
95-96	Thunder Bay	CoHL	56	13	9	22	16	13	0	1	1	4
96-97	Thunder Bay	CoHL	69	24	22	46	72	11	3	2	5	6
97-98	Thunder Bay	UHL	70	34	20	54	29	—	—	—	—	—
98-99	Thunder Bay	UHL	58	32	22	54	28	10	3	1	4	4
	CoHL	Totals	273	105	75	180	149	34	6	4	10	14

Born; 2/1/70, Thunder Bay, Ontario. 5-10, 175. Last amateur club; Kent State (CCHA).

John Purves
Right Wing

Regular Season / Playoffs

Season	Team	League	GP	G	A	PTS	PIM	GP	G	A	PTS	PIM
89-90	Baltimore	AHL	75	29	35	64	12	9	5	7	12	4
90-91	Washington	NHL	7	1	0	1	0	—	—	—	—	—
90-91	Baltimore	AHL	53	22	29	51	27	6	2	3	5	0
91-92	Baltimore	AHL	78	43	46	89	47	—	—	—	—	—
92-93	Kaufbeuren	Germany	43	15	17	32	34	—	—	—	—	—
93-94	Fort Wayne	IHL	69	38	48	86	29	18	10	14	24	12
94-95	Fort Wayne	IHL	60	30	33	63	16	4	4	1	5	6
95-96	San Francisco	IHL	75	56	49	105	32	4	0	3	3	0
96-97	Kansas City	IHL	66	25	47	72	17	3	0	0	0	0
97-98	Kansas City	IHL	21	6	10	16	9	—	—	—	—	—
97-98	San Antonio	IHL	59	22	21	43	12	—	—	—	—	—
98-99	Utah	IHL	80	24	39	63	24	—	—	—	—	—
	IHL	Totals	430	201	247	448	139	29	14	18	32	18
	AHL	Totals	206	94	110	204	86	15	7	10	17	4

Born; 2/12/68, Toronto, Ontario. 6-1, 201. Drafted by Washington Capitals (6th choice, 103rd overall) in 1986 Entry Draft. Signed as a free agent by Fort Wayne Komets (10/9/93). Traded to San Antonio by Kansas City with Darrin Kimble for Mike Craig and Reggie Savage (11/97). 1995-96 IHL Second Team All-Star. Last amateur club; North Bay (OHL).

Dennis Pybip
Forward

Regular Season / Playoffs

Season	Team	League	GP	G	A	PTS	PIM	GP	G	A	PTS	PIM
98-99	Jacksonville	ECHL	1	0	0	0	0	—	—	—	—	—

Born;

Bill Pye
Goaltender

Regular Season / Playoffs

Season	Team	League	GP	W	L	T	MIN	SO	AVG	GP	W	L	MIN	SO	AVG
91-92	Rochester	AHL	7	0	4	0	272	0	2.87	1	1	0	60	0	2.00
91-92	New Haven	AHL	4	0	3	1	200	0	5.70	—	—	—	—	—	—
91-92	Fort Wayne	IHL	8	5	2	1	451	0	3.86	—	—	—	—	—	—
91-92	Erie	ECHL	5	5	0	0	310	0	4.26	4	1	3	220	0	4.09
92-93	Rochester	AHL	26	9	14	2	1427	0	4.50	—	—	—	—	—	—
93-94	Rochester	AHL	19	7	7	2	980	0	4.29	—	—	—	—	—	—
93-94	South Carolina	ECHL	28	15	10	2	1578	1	3.61	3	1	2	179	0	4.03
94-95	Saginaw	CoHL	13	5	7	0	633	0	4.83	—	—	—	—	—	—
95-96	Columbus	ECHL	25	12	5	1	1227	0	4.50	—	—	—	—	—	—
96-97	Waco	WPHL	46	22	21	2	2620	0	3.64	—	—	—	—	—	—
97-98	Waco	WPHL	*15	2	*11	2	*861	0	4.81	—	—	—	—	—	—
97-98	Odessa	WPHL	*42	20	*18	3	*2349	1	4.47	—	—	—	—	—	—
98-99	Odessa	WPHL	45	20	22	2	2549	2	3.13	3	1	2	200	0	2.70
	AHL	Totals	56	16	28	5	2879	0	4.36	1	1	0	60	0	2.00
	WPHL	Totals	148	64	72	9	8379	3	3.84	3	1	2	200	0	2.70
	ECHL	Totals	58	32	15	3	3115	1	4.03	7	2	5	399	0	4.06

Born; 4/9/69, Canton, Michigan. Drafted by Buffalo Sabres (5th choice, 107th overall) in 1989 Entry Draft. Traded to Odessa from Waco for Petri Aaltonen (11/97). Last amateur club; Northern Michigan (WCHA).

Nico Pyka
Defenseman

Regular Season / Playoffs

Season	Team	League	GP	G	A	PTS	PIM	GP	G	A	PTS	PIM
98-99	Mobile	ECHL	1	0	0	0	0	—	—	—	—	—
98-99	Memphis	CHL	66	9	35	44	149	4	1	0	1	16

Born; 7/22/77, Berlin, Germany. 6-2, 190.

Jay Pylypuik
Defenseman

Regular Season / Playoffs

Season	Team	League	GP	G	A	PTS	PIM	GP	G	A	PTS	PIM
98-99	Toledo	ECHL	4	0	1	1	0	—	—	—	—	—
98-99	Wheeling	ECHL	6	0	1	1	15	—	—	—	—	—
98-99	Jacksonville	ECHL	3	0	0	0	0	—	—	—	—	—
98-99	San Antonio	CHL	17	1	4	5	4	—	—	—	—	—
98-99	Memphis	CHL	16	2	2	4	20	1	0	0	0	0
	CHL	Totals	10	0	2	2	15	—	—	—	—	—
	ECHL	Totals	33	3	6	9	24	1	0	0	0	0

Born; 1/2/74, Saskatoon, Saskatchewan. 6-0, 188. Traded to Jacksonville by Wheeling for future considerations (11/98). Last amateur club; Wisconsin-Eau Claire (NCAA 3).

Patrick Pysz
Right Wing

Regular Season / Playoffs

Season	Team	League	GP	G	A	PTS	PIM	GP	G	A	PTS	PIM
96-97	Columbus	ECHL	36	7	9	16	29	2	0	0	0	0
97-98												
98-99	Hamburg	Germany	46	17	27	44	65	—	—	—	—	—

Born; 1/15/75, Nowy Targ, Poland. 5-11, 187. Drafted by Chicago Blackhawks (6th choice, 102nd overall) in 1993 Entry Draft.

Chad Quenneville
Center

Regular Season / Playoffs

Season	Team	League	GP	G	A	PTS	PIM	GP	G	A	PTS	PIM
94-95	Providence	H.E.	36	25	29	54	51	—	—	—	—	—
94-95	Albany	AHL	8	1	5	6	0	—	—	—	—	—
95-96	Atlanta	IHL	6	1	1	2	2	—	—	—	—	—
95-96	Nashville	ECHL	54	16	25	41	24	4	1	2	3	6
96-97	Pensacola	ECHL	70	43	52	95	67	12	6	8	14	10
97-98	Pensacola	ECHL	70	26	44	70	38	19	4	6	10	4
98-99	Pensacola	ECHL	70	24	38	62	22	—	—	—	—	—
	ECHL	Totals	264	109	159	268	151	35	11	16	27	20

Born; 5/13/72, South Hadley, Massachusetts. 5-9, 175. Last amateur club; Providence (Hockey East).

Andre Quesnel
Forward

Regular Season / Playoffs

Season	Team	League	GP	G	A	PTS	PIM	GP	G	A	PTS	PIM
98-99	Fort Worth	CHL	51	18	24	42	37	—	—	—	—	—

Born; Selected by Topeka in 1999 CHL Dispersal Draft.

Bob Quinnell
Defenseman

Regular Season / Playoffs

Season	Team	League	GP	G	A	PTS	PIM	GP	G	A	PTS	PIM
98-99	Las Vegas	IHL	10	0	0	0	2	—	—	—	—	—
98-99	Corpus Christi	WPHL	62	10	31	41	73	3	0	0	0	14

Born; 1/12/73, Coquitlan, British Columbia. 6-1, 212. Last amateur club; Brown (ECAC).

Ken Quinney
Left Wing

Regular Season / Playoffs

Season	Team	League	GP	G	A	PTS	PIM	GP	G	A	PTS	PIM
85-86	Fredericton	AHL	61	11	26	37	34	6	2	2	4	9
86-87	Quebec	NHL	25	2	7	9	16	—	—	—	—	—
86-87	Fredericton	AHL	48	14	27	41	20	—	—	—	—	—
87-88	Quebec	NHL	15	2	2	4	5	—	—	—	—	—
87-88	Fredericton	AHL	58	37	39	76	39	13	3	5	8	35
88-89	Halifax	AHL	72	41	49	90	65	4	3	0	3	0
89-90	Halifax	AHL	44	9	16	25	63	2	0	0	0	2
90-91	Quebec	NHL	19	3	4	7	2	—	—	—	—	—
90-91	Halifax	AHL	44	20	20	40	76	—	—	—	—	—
91-92	Adirondack	AHL	63	31	29	60	33	19	7	12	19	9
92-93	Adirondack	AHL	63	32	34	66	15	10	2	9	11	9
93-94	Las Vegas	IHL	79	*55	53	108	52	5	3	3	6	2
94-95	Las Vegas	IHL	78	40	42	82	40	10	3	2	5	9
95-96	Las Vegas	IHL	66	33	36	69	59	9	2	5	7	15
96-97	Las Vegas	IHL	71	27	36	63	39	2	0	0	0	0
97-98	Las Vegas	IHL	82	34	57	91	19	4	1	2	3	2
98-99	Frankfurt	Germany	36	12	17	29	26	8	2	3	5	27
	NHL	Totals	59	7	13	20	23	—	—	—	—	—
	AHL	Totals	453	195	240	435	345	54	17	28	45	64
	IHL	Totals	376	189	224	413	209	30	9	12	21	28

Born; 5/23/65, New Westminster, British Columbia. 5-10, 190. Drafted by Quebec Nordiques (9th choice, 203rd overall) in 1984 Entry Draft. Signed as a free agent by DetroitRed Wings (8/12/91). 1993-94 IHL First Team All-Star. 1997-98 IHL Second Team All-Star. Member of 1991-92 AHL champion Adirondack Red Wings. Last amateur club; Calgary (WHL).

Tyler Quiring Left Wing
Regular Season Playoffs

Season	Team	League	GP	G	A	PTS	PIM	GP	G	A	PTS	PIM
96-97	El Paso	WPHL	26	11	7	18	12	—	—	—	—	—
98-99	Huntsville	CHL	61	17	42	59	78	12	5	5	10	15

Born; 1/1/75, Vernon, British Columbia. 5-8, 175. Member of 1998-99 CHL Champion Huntsville Channel Cats.

Richmond's Maxime Gingras dominated in his first professional season
Photo by Bill Vaughn

A blockbuster trade brought Paul Polillo to Port Huron
Photo by John Gacioch

Mathieu Raby

Regular Season — Defenseman — Playoffs

Season	Team	League	GP	G	A	PTS	PIM	GP	G	A	PTS	PIM
95-96	Atlanta	IHL	5	0	0	0	15	—	—	—	—	—
95-96	Nashville	ECHL	62	4	11	15	256	5	0	0	0	28
96-97	Adirondack	AHL	13	0	0	0	28	—	—	—	—	—
96-97	Wheeling	ECHL	39	5	3	8	130	3	0	1	1	6
97-98	Portland	AHL	3	0	0	0	6	—	—	—	—	—
97-98	Chesapeake	ECHL	66	10	25	35	230	3	1	2	3	6
98-99	Abilene	WPHL	28	2	9	11	173	—	—	—	—	—
98-99	Detroit	IHL	5	0	0	0	11	—	—	—	—	—
98-99	Kentucky	AHL	26	1	1	2	132	—	—	—	—	—
	AHL	Totals	42	1	1	2	166	—	—	—	—	—
	IHL	Totals	10	0	0	0	26	—	—	—	—	—
	ECHL	Totals	167	19	39	58	616	11	1	3	4	40

Born; 1/19/75, Hull, Quebec. 6-2, 204. Drafted by Tampa Bay Lightning (7th choice, 159th overall) in 1993 Entry Draft. Last amateur club; Sherbrooke

Andre Racicot

Regular Season — Goaltender — Playoffs

Season	Team	League	GP	W	L	T	MIN	SO	AVG	GP	W	L	MIN	SO	AVG
89-90	Montreal	NHL	1	0	0	0	13	0	13.85	—	—	—	—	—	—
89-90	Sherbrooke	AHL	33	19	11	2	1948	1	2.99	5	0	4	227	0	4.76
90-91	Montreal	NHL	21	7	9	2	975	1	3.20	2	0	1	12	0	10.00
90-91	Fredericton	AHL	22	13	8	1	1252	1	2.88	—	—	—	—	—	—
91-92	Montreal	NHL	9	0	3	3	436	0	3.17	1	0	0	1	0	0.00
91-92	Fredericton	AHL	28	14	8	5	1666	0	3.10	—	—	—	—	—	—
92-93	Montreal	NHL	26	17	5	1	1433	1	3.39	1	0	0	18	0	6.67
93-94	Montreal	NHL	11	2	6	2	500	0	4.44	—	—	—	—	—	—
93-94	Fredericton	AHL	6	1	4	0	292	0	3.28	—	—	—	—	—	—
94-95	Portland	AHL	19	10	7	0	1080	1	2.94	—	—	—	—	—	—
94-95	Phoenix	IHL	3	1	0	0	132	0	3.62	2	0	0	20	0	0.00
95-96	Columbus	ECHL	1	1	0	0	60	0	2.00	—	—	—	—	—	—
95-96	Albany	AHL	2	2	0	0	120	0	2.00	—	—	—	—	—	—
95-96	Indianapolis	IHL	11	3	6	0	547	0	4.71	—	—	—	—	—	—
95-96	Peoria	IHL	4	2	1	1	240	0	3.50	11	6	5	654	1	3.12
96-97	Indianapolis	IHL	2	1	0	1	120	1	1.50	—	—	—	—	—	—
96-97	Kansas City	IHL	6	1	4	0	274	0	4.60	—	—	—	—	—	—
96-97	Las Vegas	IHL	13	6	5	1	760	1	3.16	—	—	—	—	—	—
97-98	Monroe	WPHL	31	16	12	2	1789	1	2.68	—	—	—	—	—	—
97-98	Basingstoke	BSL	3	—	—	—	186	0	3.55	5	—	—	303	0	4.16
98-99	Monroe	WPHL	48	25	18	5	2806	1	3.16	6	2	4	380	*1	3.32
	NHL	Totals	68	26	23	8	3357	2	3.50	4	0	1	31	0	7.74
	AHL	Totals	110	59	38	8	6358	3	2.98	5	0	4	227	0	4.76
	IHL	Totals	38	14	16	3	2073	2	3.73	13	6	5	674	1	3.03
	WPHL	Totals	79	41	30	7	4595	2	2.98	6	2	4	380	1	3.32

Born; 6/9/69, Rouyn-Noranda, Quebec. 5-11, 165. Drafted by Montreal Canadiens (5th choice, 83rd overall) in 1989 Entry Draft. Signed as a free agent by Los Angeles (9/22/94). Signed as a free agent by Chicago Blackhawks (8/25/95). 1989-90 Shared Harry "Hap" Holmes (fewest goals against-AHL) with J.C. Bergeron. Last amateur club; Granby (QMJHL).

Bruce Racine

Regular Season — Goaltender — Playoffs

Season	Team	League	GP	W	L	T	MIN	SO	AVG	GP	W	L	MIN	SO	AVG
88-89	Muskegon	IHL	51	*37	11	0	*3039	*3	3.63	5	4	1	300	0	3.00
89-90	Muskegon	IHL	49	29	15	4	2911	1	3.75	9	5	4	566	1	3.34
90-91	Albany	IHL	29	7	18	1	1567	0	3.98	—	—	—	—	—	—
90-91	Muskegon	IHL	9	4	4	1	516	0	4.65	—	—	—	—	—	—
91-92	Muskegon	IHL	27	13	10	3	1559	1	3.50	1	0	1	60	0	6.00
92-93	Cleveland	IHL	35	13	16	6	1949	1	4.31	2	0	0	37	0	3.24
93-94	St. John's	AHL	37	20	9	2	1875	0	3.71	1	0	0	20	0	3.00
94-95	St. John's	AHL	27	11	10	4	1492	1	3.42	2	1	1	119	0	1.51
95-96	St. Louis	NHL	11	0	3	0	230	0	3.13	—	—	—	—	—	—
95-96	Peoria	IHL	22	11	10	1	1228	1	3.37	1	0	1	58	0	3.05
96-97	San Antonio	IHL	44	25	14	2	2426	6	3.02	6	3	2	326	0	3.13
97-98	San Antonio	IHL	*15	*4	9	1	*836	0	3.66	—	—	—	—	—	—
97-98	Fort Wayne	IHL	*45	*30	10	4	*2605	1	2.51	3	1	2	152	0	3.95
98-99	Fort Wayne	IHL	53	21	18	*11	3024	1	3.06	1	0	1	60	0	5.00
	IHL	Totals	379	194	135	34	21660	15	3.45	28	13	12	1559	1	3.46
	AHL	Totals	64	31	19	6	3367	1	3.58	3	1	1	139	0	1.72

Born; 8/9/66, Cornwall, Ontario. 6-0, 170. Drafted by Pittsburgh Penguins (3rd choice, 58th overall) in 1985 Entry Draft. Signed as a free agent by Toronto Maple Leafs (8/11/93). Signed as a free agent by St. Louis Blues (8/10/95). 1997-98 IHL First Team All-Star. Last amateur club; Northeastern (Hockey East).

Yves Racine

Regular Season — Defenseman — Playoffs

Season	Team	League	GP	G	A	PTS	PIM	GP	G	A	PTS	PIM
87-88	Victoriaville	QMJHL	69	10	84	94	150	5	0	0	0	13
87-88	Adirondack	AHL	—	—	—	—	—	9	4	2	6	2
88-89	Victoriaville	QMJHL	63	23	85	108	95	16	3	*30	*33	41
88-89	Adirondack	AHL	—	—	—	—	—	2	1	1	2	0
89-90	Detroit	NHL	28	4	9	13	23	—	—	—	—	—
89-90	Adirondack	AHL	46	8	27	35	31	—	—	—	—	—
90-91	Detroit	NHL	62	7	40	47	33	7	2	0	2	0
90-91	Adirondack	AHL	16	3	9	12	10	—	—	—	—	—
91-92	Detroit	NHL	61	2	22	24	94	11	2	1	3	10
92-93	Detroit	NHL	80	9	31	40	80	7	1	3	4	27
93-94	Philadelphia	NHL	67	9	43	52	48	—	—	—	—	—
94-95	Montreal	NHL	47	4	7	11	42	—	—	—	—	—
95-96	Montreal	NHL	25	0	3	3	26	—	—	—	—	—
95-96	San Jose	NHL	32	1	16	17	28	—	—	—	—	—
96-97	Kentucky	AHL	4	0	1	1	2	—	—	—	—	—
96-97	Quebec	IHL	6	0	4	4	4	—	—	—	—	—
96-97	Calgary	NHL	46	1	15	16	24	—	—	—	—	—
97-98	Tampa Bay	NHL	60	0	8	8	41	—	—	—	—	—
98-99	Jokerit	Finland	52	8	18	26	100	3	1	0	1	6
	NHL	Totals	508	37	194	231	439	25	5	4	9	37
	AHL	Totals	66	11	37	48	43	11	5	3	8	2

Born; 2/7/69, Matane, Quebec. 6-0, 205. Drafted by Detroit Red Wings (1st choice, 11th overall) in 1987 Entry Draft. Traded to Philadelphia Flyers by Detroit with Detroit's fourth round choice (Sebastien Vallee) in 1994 Entry Draft. for Terry Carkner (10/5/93). Traded to Montreal Canadiens by Philadelphia for Kevin Haller (6/29/94). Claimed on waivers by San Jose Sharks from Montreal (1/23/96). Traded to Calgary Flames by San Jose for cash (12/17/96). Signed as a free agent by Tampa Bay Lightning (7/16/97). Last amateur club; Victoriaville

Sergei Radchenko

Regular Season — Defenseman — Playoffs

Season	Team	League	GP	G	A	PTS	PIM	GP	G	A	PTS	PIM
97-98	Wheeling	ECHL	39	3	10	13	125	—	—	—	—	—
98-99	Wheeling	ECHL	28	2	3	5	98	—	—	—	—	—
98-99	Dayton	ECHL	7	0	0	0	24	2	1	0	1	0
98-99	Hamilton	AHL	3	0	0	0	7	—	—	—	—	—
	ECHL	Totals	74	5	13	18	247	2	1	0	1	0

Born; 2/22/78, Kiev, Ukraine. 6-1, 193. Last amateur club; Medicine Hat (WHL).

Brian Rafalski

Regular Season — Defenseman — Playoffs

Season	Team	League	GP	G	A	PTS	PIM	GP	G	A	PTS	PIM
96-97	Hameenlinna	Finland	49	11	24	35	26	10	6	5	11	4
97-98	HIFK Helsinki	Finland	40	13	10	23	24	9	5	6	11	0
98-99	HIFK Helsinki	Finland	53	19	34	53	18	11	5	9	14	4

Born; Signed as a free agent by New Jersey Devils (5/13/99). Last amateur club; Wisconsin (WCHA).

Ashkat Rakhmatulin

Regular Season — Forward — Playoffs

Season	Team	League	GP	G	A	PTS	PIM	GP	G	A	PTS	PIM
98-99	Florida	ECHL	6	0	1	1	2	—	—	—	—	—
98-99	Fayetteville	CHL	4	0	0	0	4	—	—	—	—	—
98-99	Asheville	UHL	31	6	10	16	23	4	1	0	1	0

Born; 5/31/78, Ufa, USSR. 5-11, 165. Drafted by Hartford Whalers (10th choice, 231st overall) in 1996 Entry Draft. Last overseas club; Ufa Salavat (Russia).

Jamie Ram — Goaltender

Regular Season / Playoffs

Season	Team	League	GP	W	L	T	MIN	SO	AVG	GP	W	L	MIN	SO	AVG
94-95	Binghamton	AHL	26	12	10	2	1472	1	3.30	11	6	5	663	1	2.62
95-96	Rangers	NHL	1	0	0	0	27	0	0.00	—	—	—	—	—	—
95-96	Binghamton	AHL	40	18	16	3	2262	1	4.01	1	0	0	34	0	1.75
96-97	Kentucky	AHL	50	25	19	5	2937	4	3.29	1	0	1	60	0	3.00
97-98	Kentucky	AHL	44	17	18	5	2554	3	2.91	—	—	—	—	—	—
97-98	Utah	IHL	7	3	4	0	399	0	3.61	1	0	1	59	0	3.04
98-99	Cincinnati	AHL	35	14	19	1	1916	2	3.41	—	—	—	—	—	—
	AHL	Totals	195	86	82	16	11141	11	3.37	13	6	6	757	1	2.61

Born; 1/18/71, Scarborough, Ontario. 5-11, 175. Drafted by New York Rangers (10th choice, 213th overall) in 1991 Entry Draft. Signed as a free agent by San Jose Sharks (8/13/97). Signed as a free agent by Anaheim Mighty Ducks (7/22/98). Last amateur club; Michigan Tech (WCHA).

Bruce Ramsay — Left Wing

Regular Season / Playoffs

Season	Team	League	GP	G	A	PTS	PIM	GP	G	A	PTS	PIM
91-92	Thunder Bay	CoHL	54	7	16	23	*313	12	1	2	3	55
92-93	Thunder Bay	CoHL	52	3	16	19	234	—	—	—	—	—
93-94	Thunder Bay	CoHL	63	9	22	31	313	8	1	2	3	45
94-95	Prince Edward Island	AHL	2	0	1	1	10	1	0	0	0	2
94-95	Thunder Bay	COHL	62	14	29	43	462	11	0	3	3	83
95-96	Milwaukee	IHL	3	0	0	0	5	—	—	—	—	—
95-96	Thunder Bay	CoHL	56	6	15	21	*400	18	2	3	5	*142
96-97	Grand Rapids	IHL	66	3	5	8	306	4	0	0	0	2
96-97	Thunder Bay	CoHL	9	6	4	10	71	—	—	—	—	—
97-98	Grand Rapids	IHL	62	5	6	11	310	—	—	—	—	—
98-99	Grand Rapids	IHL	47	1	3	4	165	—	—	—	—	—
	IHL	Totals	178	9	14	23	786	4	0	0	0	2
	CoHL	Totals	296	45	102	147	1793	50	4	10	14	325

Born; 5/13/69, Dryden, Ontario. 6-0, 178. Signed as a free agent by St. Louis Blues (7/31/97). Member of 1991-92 CoHL champion Thunder Bay Thunder Hawks. Member of 1993-94 CoHL champion Thunder Bay Senators. Member of 1994-95 CoHL champion Thunder Bay Senators.

Chad Ramsay — Forward

Regular Season / Playoffs

Season	Team	League	GP	G	A	PTS	PIM	GP	G	A	PTS	PIM
98-99	Tupelo	WPHL	20	1	1	2	16	—	—	—	—	—

Born; 7/31/76, Red Deer, Alberta. 5-10, 180. Last amateur club; Opaskwayak (MJHL).

Bryan Randall — Right Wing

Regular Season / Playoffs

Season	Team	League	GP	G	A	PTS	PIM	GP	G	A	PTS	PIM
98-99	Utah	IHL	9	0	2	2	8	—	—	—	—	—
98-99	Idaho	WCHL	55	12	16	28	108	2	0	1	1	2

Born; 8/8/78, Winnipeg, Manitoba. 6-3, 190. Drafted by Edmonton Oilers (6th choice, 141st overall) in 1996 Entry Draft. Last amateur club; Kelowna (WHL).

Shawn Randall — Right Wing

Regular Season / Playoffs

Season	Team	League	GP	G	A	PTS	PIM	GP	G	A	PTS	PIM
96-97	Huntsville	CeHL	48	3	12	15	135	5	0	1	1	4
97-98	Fort Worth	CHL	69	13	23	36	147	—	—	—	—	—
98-99	Topeka	CHL	47	5	7	12	136	3	0	0	0	17
	CHL	Totals	164	21	42	63	418	8	0	1	1	21

Born; 11/13/72, Montrose, Michigan. 5-9, 185. Selected by Indianapolis in 1999 CHL Expansion Draft. Last amateur club; R.I.T. (NCAA 3).

Trevor Rapchalk — Right Wing

Regular Season / Playoffs

Season	Team	League	GP	G	A	PTS	PIM	GP	G	A	PTS	PIM
98-99	Winston-Salem	UHL	32	4	3	7	58	5	0	1	1	6

Born; 5/19/74, Calder, Saskatchewan. 5-10, 190. Last amateur club; South Surrey (BCJHL).

Bob Rapoza — Defenseman

Regular Season / Playoffs

Season	Team	League	GP	G	A	PTS	PIM	GP	G	A	PTS	PIM
95-96	Daytona Beach	SHL	5	0	1	1	8	—	—	—	—	—
96-97	Dayton	CoHL	71	6	11	17	56	—	—	—	—	—
97-98	Tucson	WCHL	59	14	14	28	45	—	—	—	—	—
98-99	Phoenix	WCHL	62	14	20	34	73	3	1	1	2	2
	WCHL	Totals	121	28	34	62	118	3	1	1	2	2

Born; 9/29/74, Fall River, Massachusetts. 6-2, 225. Traded to Phoenix by Tucson to complete earlier trade (10/98).

Brian Rasmussen — Right Wing

Regular Season / Playoffs

Season	Team	League	GP	G	A	PTS	PIM	GP	G	A	PTS	PIM
97-98	Madison	UHL	2	0	0	0	0	—	—	—	—	—
98-99	Mohawk Valley	UHL	17	0	8	8	35	—	—	—	—	—
98-99	Tulsa	CHL	3	0	0	0	5	—	—	—	—	—
98-99	Tupelo	WPHL	21	0	3	3	48	—	—	—	—	—
	UHL	Totals	19	0	8	8	35	—	—	—	—	—

Born; 7/11/71, Thornhill, Ontario. 6-0, 200.

Erik Rasmussen — Center

Regular Season / Playoffs

Season	Team	League	GP	G	A	PTS	PIM	GP	G	A	PTS	PIM
97-98	Buffalo	NHL	21	2	3	5	14	—	—	—	—	—
97-98	Rochester	AHL	53	9	14	23	83	1	0	0	0	5
98-99	Buffalo	NHL	42	3	7	10	37	21	2	4	6	18
98-99	Rochester	AHL	37	12	14	26	47	—	—	—	—	—
	NHL	Totals	63	5	10	15	51	21	2	4	6	18
	AHL	Totals	90	21	28	49	130	1	0	0	0	5

Born; 3/28/77, Minneapolis, Minnesota. 6-2, 193. Drafted by Buffalo Sabres (1st choice, 7th overall) in 1996 Entry Draft. Last amateur club; Minnesota (WCHA).

Peter Ratchuk — Defenseman

Regular Season / Playoffs

Season	Team	League	GP	G	A	PTS	PIM	GP	G	A	PTS	PIM
98-99	Florida	NHL	24	1	1	2	10	—	—	—	—	—
98-99	New Haven	AHL	53	7	20	27	44	—	—	—	—	—

Born; 9/10/77, Buffalo, New York. 6-1, 180. Drafted by Colorado Avalanche (1st choice, 25th overall) in 1996 Entry Draft. Signed as a free agent by Florida Panthers (6/15/98). Last amateur club; Hull (QMJHL).

David Rattray — Forward

Regular Season / Playoffs

Season	Team	League	GP	G	A	PTS	PIM	GP	G	A	PTS	PIM
98-99	Amarillo	WPHL	61	15	16	31	271	—	—	—	—	—

Born; 1/17/73, Edmonton, Alberta. 5-11, 200.

Dan Ratushny — Defenseman

Regular Season / Playoffs

Season	Team	League	GP	G	A	PTS	PIM	GP	G	A	PTS	PIM
92-93	Vancouver	NHL	1	0	1	1	2	—	—	—	—	—
92-93	Fort Wayne	IHL	63	6	19	25	48	—	—	—	—	—
93-94	Hamilton	AHL	62	8	31	39	22	4	0	0	0	4
94-95	Fort Wayne	IHL	72	3	25	28	46	4	0	1	1	8
95-96	Carolina	AHL	23	5	10	15	28	—	—	—	—	—
95-96	Peoria	IHL	45	7	15	22	45	12	3	4	7	10
96-97	Quebec	IHL	50	14	23	37	34	—	—	—	—	—
97-98	Quebec	IHL	20	3	9	12	22	—	—	—	—	—
97-98	Albany	AHL	39	8	5	13	10	9	0	3	3	8
98-99	Kansas City	IHL	70	9	32	41	38	3	0	0	0	4
	IHL	Totals	320	42	123	165	233	19	3	5	8	22
	AHL	Totals	124	21	46	67	60	13	0	3	3	12

Born; 10/29/70, Nepean, Ontario. 6-1, 210. Drafted by Winnipeg Jets (2nd choice, 25th overall) in 1989 Entry Draft. Traded to Vancouver Canucks by Winnipeg for ninth round pick (Harjis Vitolinsh) in 1993 Entry Draft. Last amateur club; Cornell (ECAC).

Stacey Rayan — Forward

Regular Season / Playoffs

Season	Team	League	GP	G	A	PTS	PIM	GP	G	A	PTS	PIM
97-98	Raleigh	ECHL	64	24	24	48	34	—	—	—	—	—
98-99	Mobile	ECHL	44	10	26	36	16	—	—	—	—	—
	ECHL	Totals	108	34	50	84	50	—	—	—	—	—

Born; 3/12/72, Edmonton, Alberta. 5-9, 180.

Erik Raygor — Right Wing

Regular Season / Playoffs

Season	Team	League	GP	G	A	PTS	PIM	GP	G	A	PTS	PIM
98-99	Columbus	ECHL	2	0	0	0	10	—	—	—	—	—
98-99	Fayetteville	CHL	31	7	5	12	67	—	—	—	—	—

Born; 1/7/73, Superior, Wisconsin. 6-0, 210. Last amateur club; Wisconsin (WCHA).

Gennady Razin — Defenseman

Regular Season / Playoffs

Season	Team	League	GP	G	A	PTS	PIM	GP	G	A	PTS	PIM
98-99	Fredericton	AHL	48	0	3	3	16	4	0	0	0	2

Born; 2/3/78, Kharkov, USSR. 6-3, 175. Drafted by Montreal Canadiens (6th choice, 122nd overall) in 1997 Entry Draft. Last amateur club; Kamloops (WHL).

Clayton Read — Right Wing

Regular Season / Playoffs

Season	Team	League	GP	G	A	PTS	PIM	GP	G	A	PTS	PIM
98-99	Alaska-Anchorage	WCHA	36	6	7	13	20	—	—	—	—	—

Born; 5/13/76, Winnipeg, Manitoba. 6-2, 195. Last amateur club; Anchorage (WCHA).

Jake Ream — Defenseman

Regular Season / Playoffs

Season	Team	League	GP	G	A	PTS	PIM	GP	G	A	PTS	PIM
98-99	Colorado	WCHL	15	0	1	1	12	—	—	—	—	—
98-99	Tucson	WCHL	2	0	0	0	6	—	—	—	—	—
	WCHL	Totals	17	0	1	1	18	—	—	—	—	—

Born; 5/5/77, Tacoma, Washington. 6-1, 190. Last amateur club; Bozeman

Marty Reasoner — Center

Regular Season / Playoffs

Season	Team	League	GP	G	A	PTS	PIM	GP	G	A	PTS	PIM
98-99	St. Louis	NHL	22	3	7	10	8	—	—	—	—	—
98-99	Worcester	AHL	44	17	22	39	24	4	2	1	3	6

Born; 2/26/77, Rochester, New York. 6-1, 185. Drafted by St. Louis Blues (1st choice, 14th overall) in 1996 Entry Draft. Last amateur club; Boston College

Jeremy Rebek — Defenseman

Regular Season / Playoffs

Season	Team	League	GP	G	A	PTS	PIM	GP	G	A	PTS	PIM
97-98	Toledo	ECHL	70	9	22	31	69	7	0	2	2	2
98-99	Toledo	ECHL	70	10	39	49	90	7	1	3	4	6
	ECHL	Totals	140	19	61	80	159	14	1	5	6	8

Born; Sault Ste. Marie. 5-11, 185. Last amateur club; Laurentian (OUAA).

Pokey Reddick — Goaltender

Regular Season / Playoffs

Season	Team	League	GP	W	L	T	MIN	SO	AVG	GP	W	L	MIN	SO	AVG
85-86	Fort Wayne	IHL	29	15	11	0	1674	*3	3.00	—	—	—	—	—	—
86-87	Winnipeg	NHL	48	21	21	4	2762	0	3.24	3	0	2	166	0	3.61
87-88	Winnipeg	NHL	28	9	13	3	1487	0	4.12	—	—	—	—	—	—
87-88	Moncton	AHL	9	2	6	1	545	0	2.86	—	—	—	—	—	—
88-89	Winnipeg	NHL	41	11	17	7	2109	0	4.10	—	—	—	—	—	—
89-90	Edmonton	NHL	11	5	4	2	604	0	3.08	1	0	0	2	0	0.00
89-90	Cape Breton	AHL	15	9	4	1	821	0	3.95	—	—	—	—	—	—
89-90	Phoenix	IHL	3	2	1	0	185	0	2.27	—	—	—	—	—	—
90-91	Edmonton	NHL	2	0	2	0	120	0	4.50	—	—	—	—	—	—
90-91	Cape Breton	AHL	31	19	10	0	1673	2	3.48	2	0	2	124	0	4.84
91-92	Cape Breton	AHL	16	5	3	3	765	0	3.53	—	—	—	—	—	—
91-92	Fort Wayne	IHL	14	6	5	2	787	1	3.05	7	3	4	368	0	2.93
92-93	Fort Wayne	IHL	54	33	16	4	3043	3	3.08	12	*12	0	723	0	*1.49
93-94	Florida	NHL	2	0	1	0	80	0	6.00	—	—	—	—	—	—
93-94	Cincinnati	IHL	54	31	12	6	2894	*2	*3.05	10	6	2	498	*1	2.53
94-95	Las Vegas	IHL	40	23	13	1	2075	*3	3.01	10	4	6	592	0	3.14
95-96	Las Vegas	IHL	47	27	12	4	2636	1	2.94	15	8	6	770	0	3.35
96-97	Grand Rapids	IHL	61	30	14	10	3245	6	2.48	5	2	3	336	0	2.32
97-98	Grand Rapids	IHL	10	5	5	0	575	0	3.44	—	—	—	—	—	—
97-98	San Antonio	IHL	16	5	9	1	862	1	3.13	—	—	—	—	—	—
97-98	Kansas City	IHL	22	10	7	3	1255	1	2.63	4	2	1	203	0	4.14
98-99	Fort Wayne	IHL	33	12	15	5	1874	1	3.27	1	0	1	60	0	4.00
	NHL	Totals	132	46	58	16	7163	0	3.71	4	0	2	168	0	3.57
	IHL	Totals	383	199	120	36	21105	22	2.95	64	37	23	3551	1	2.74
	AHL	Totals	71	35	23	5	3804	2	3.50	2	0	2	124	0	4.84

Born; 10/6/64, Halifax, Nova Scotia. 5-8, 170. Signed as a free agent by Winnipeg Jets (9/27/85). Traded to Edmonton Oilers by Winnipeg for future considerations (9/28/89). Signed as a free agent by Florida Panthers (7/12/93). 1985-86 shared James Norris trophy (fewest goals allowed) with Rick St. Croix. 1992-93. 1992-93 IHL playoff MVP. Member of 1992-93 IHL champion Fort Wayne Komets. Last amateur club; Brandon (WHL).

Matt Redmond — Forward

Regular Season / Playoffs

Season	Team	League	GP	G	A	PTS	PIM	GP	G	A	PTS	PIM
98-99	Miami	ECHL	10	1	1	2	0	—	—	—	—	—
98-99	Monroe	WPHL	7	0	0	0	2	—	—	—	—	—

Born; 11/17/76. Selected by Greenville in 1999 ECHL Dispersal Draft.

Mike Rees — Defenseman

Regular Season / Playoffs

Season	Team	League	GP	G	A	PTS	PIM	GP	G	A	PTS	PIM
97-98	Fresno	WCHL	3	0	0	0	4	2	0	0	0	0
98-99	El Paso	WPHL	62	1	7	8	208	3	0	0	0	0

Born; 8/4/74, Calgary, Alberta. 5-11, 195. Last amateur club; S.A.I.T (ACAC).

Jeff Reese — Goaltender

Regular Season / Playoffs

Season	Team	League	GP	W	L	T	MIN	SO	AVG	GP	W	L	MIN	SO	AVG
86-87	Newmarket	AHL	50	11	29	0	2822	1	4.10	—	—	—	—	—	—
87-88	Toronto	NHL	5	1	2	1	249	0	4.10	—	—	—	—	—	—
87-88	Newmarket	AHL	28	10	14	3	1587	0	3.89	—	—	—	—	—	—
88-89	Toronto	NHL	10	2	6	1	486	0	4.94	—	—	—	—	—	—
88-89	Newmarket	AHL	37	17	14	3	2072	0	3.82	—	—	—	—	—	—
89-90	Toronto	NHL	21	9	6	3	1101	0	4.41	2	1	1	108	0	3.33
89-90	Newmarket	AHL	7	3	2	2	431	0	4.04	—	—	—	—	—	—
90-91	Toronto	NHL	30	6	13	3	1430	1	3.86	—	—	—	—	—	—
90-91	Newmarket	AHL	3	2	1	0	180	0	2.33	—	—	—	—	—	—
91-92	Toronto	NHL	8	1	5	1	413	1	2.91	—	—	—	—	—	—
91-92	Calgary	NHL	12	3	2	2	587	0	3.78	—	—	—	—	—	—
92-93	Calgary	NHL	26	14	4	1	1311	1	3.20	4	1	3	209	0	4.88
93-94	Calgary	NHL	1	0	0	0	13	0	4.62	—	—	—	—	—	—
93-94	Hartford	NHL	19	5	9	3	1086	1	3.09	—	—	—	—	—	—
94-95	Hartford	NHL	11	2	5	1	477	0	3.27	—	—	—	—	—	—
95-96	Hartford	NHL	7	2	3	0	275	1	3.05	—	—	—	—	—	—
95-96	Tampa Bay	NHL	19	7	7	1	994	0	3.26	5	1	1	198	0	3.64
96-97	New Jersey	NHL	3	0	2	0	139	0	5.61	—	—	—	—	—	—
96-97	Detroit	IHL	32	23	4	3	1763	4	*1.87	11	7	3	519	0	2.55
97-98	Detroit	IHL	46	27	9	8	2570	4	2.22	22	*13	*9	*1276	*2	2.44
98-99	Toronto	NHL	2	1	1	0	106	0	4.53	—	—	—	—	—	—
98-99	St. John's	AHL	27	17	7	3	1555	1	2.55	3	1	1	142	0	3.39
	NHL	Totals	174	53	65	17	8667	5	3.66	11	3	5	515	0	4.08
	AHL	Totals	152	60	67	11	8647	2	3.68	3	1	1	142	0	3.39
	IHL	Totals	78	50	13	11	4333	8	2.08	33	20	12	1795	2	2.47

Born; 3/24/66, Brantford, Ontario. 5-9, 180. Drafted by Toronto Maple Leafs (3rd choice, 67th overall) in 1984 Entry Draft. Traded to Calgary Flames with Craig Berube, Alexander Godynyuk, Gary Leeman and Michel Petit for Doug Gilmour, Jamie Macoun, Ric Nattress, Rick Wamsley and Kent Manderville, (1/2/92). Traded to Hartford Whalers by Calgary for Dan Keczmer, (11/19/93). Traded to Tampa Bay Lightning by Hartford for Tampa Bay's ninth round choice (Askhat Rakhmatullin) in 1996 Entry Draft (12/1/95). Traded to New Jersey Devils by Tampa Bay with Chicago's second round choice (previously acquired by Tampa Bay—New Jersey selected Pierre Dagenais) in 1996 Entry Draft and Tampa Bay's eighth round choice (Jay Bertsch) in 1996 Entry Draft for Corey Schwab, (6/22/96). Traded to Tampa Bay by Toronto with a ninth round draft choice in 2000 for a ninth round choice in the 2000 Entry Draft. 1996-97 IHL Second Team All-Star. 1997-98 IHl Second Team All-Star. Member of 1996-97 IHL Champion Detroit Vipers. Last amateur club; London (OHL).

Kyle Reeves — Right Wing

Regular Season / Playoffs

Season	Team	League	GP	G	A	PTS	PIM	GP	G	A	PTS	PIM
91-92	Peoria	IHL	60	12	7	19	92	—	—	—	—	—
92-93	Peoria	IHL	50	17	14	31	83	3	0	2	2	2
93-94	Peoria	IHL	3	0	1	1	2	—	—	—	—	—
93-94	Toledo	ECHL	33	12	13	25	75	—	—	—	—	—
94-95	Fort Wayne	IHL	7	0	0	0	17	—	—	—	—	—
94-95	South Carolina	ECHL	2	0	1	1	4	—	—	—	—	—
94-95	Flint	CoHL	36	38	16	54	133	—	—	—	—	—
94-95	Utica	CoHL	13	12	5	17	28	6	2	2	4	12
95-96	Utah	IHL	2	0	0	0	2	—	—	—	—	—
95-96	Fort Worth	CeHL	63	*68	47	115	179	—	—	—	—	—
96-97	Knoxville	ECHL	31	29	22	51	90	—	—	—	—	—
96-97	Baton Rouge	ECHL	24	6	8	14	30	—	—	—	—	—
97-98	San Diego	WCHL	54	36	35	71	167	13	10	5	15	78
98-99	San Diego	WCHL	69	59	31	90	228	12	9	8	17	22
	IHL	Totals	122	29	22	51	196	3	0	2	2	2
	WCHL	Totals	123	95	66	161	395	25	19	13	32	100
	ECHL	Totals	90	47	44	91	199	—	—	—	—	—
	CoHL	Totals	49	50	21	71	161	6	2	2	4	12

Born; 5/12/71, Swan River, Manitoba. 6-0, 200. Drafted by St. Louis Blues (2nd choice, 64th overall) in 1989 Entry Draft. Traded to Anchorage by San Diego for Wade Brookbank and Kevin Epp (6/99). 1995-96 CeHL First Team All-Star. 1998-99 WCHL First Team All-Star. Member of 1997-98 WCHL Champion San Diego Gulls. Last amateur club; Tri-City (WHL).

Brian Regan — Goaltender

Regular Season / Playoffs

Season	Team	League	GP	W	L	T	MIN	SO	AVG	GP	W	L	MIN	SO	AVG
98-99	Cleveland	IHL	1	0	1	0	60	0	3.02	—	—	—	—	—	—
98-99	Cincinnati	IHL	4	2	1	0	197	0	2.73	1	0	0	43	0	1.41
98-99	Peoria	ECHL	10	4	2	2	500	1	2.76	—	—	—	—	—	—
98-99	Dayton	ECHL	32	14	12	5	1831	3	3.01	1	0	1	36	0	6.68
	IHL	Totals	5	2	2	0	257	0	2.80	1	0	0	43	0	1.41
	ECHL	Totals	42	18	14	7	2331	4	2.96	1	0	1	36	0	6.68

Born; New Milford, Connecticut, 6-0, 195. Last amateur club; Massachusetts

Curt Regnier — Left Wing

Regular Season / Playoffs

Season	Team	League	GP	G	A	PTS	PIM	GP	G	A	PTS	PIM
92-93	Utica	AHL	37	6	4	10	21	2	0	1	1	0
93-94	Albany	AHL	34	12	20	32	4	—	—	—	—	—
93-94	Raleigh	ECHL	7	6	5	11	10	16	6	9	15	6
94-95	Albany	AHL	73	20	26	46	34	6	1	1	2	2
95-96	Albany	AHL	7	0	1	1	0	—	—	—	—	—
95-96	Raleigh	ECHL	57	19	21	40	26	—	—	—	—	—
96-97												
97-98												
97-98	New Mexico	WPHL	9	7	2	9	4	10	4	4	8	6
98-99	Odense	Denmark		28	26	54		—	—	—	—	—
	AHL	Totals	151	38	51	89	59	8	1	2	3	2
	ECHL	Totals	64	25	26	51	36	16	6	9	15	6

Born; 1/24/72, Prince Albert, Saskatchewan. 6-1, 210. Drafted by New Jersey Devils (6th choice, 121st overall) in 1991 Entry Draft. Member of 1994-95 AHL Champion Albany RiverRats. Last amateur club; Prince Albert (WHL).

Henrik Rehnberg — Defenseman

Regular Season / Playoffs

Season	Team	League	GP	G	A	PTS	PIM	GP	G	A	PTS	PIM
98-99	Albany	AHL	55	1	4	5	49	2	0	0	0	0

Born; 6/20/77, Grava, Sweden. 6-2, 195. Drafted by New Jersey Devils (6th choice, 96th overall) in 1995 Entry Draft. Last European club; Farjestad

Craig Reichert — Right Wing

Regular Season / Playoffs

Season	Team	League	GP	G	A	PTS	PIM	GP	G	A	PTS	PIM
94-95	San Diego	IHL	49	4	12	16	28	—	—	—	—	—
95-96	Baltimore	AHL	68	10	17	27	50	1	0	0	0	0
96-97	Baltimore	AHL	77	22	53	75	54	3	0	2	2	0
96-97	Anaheim	NHL	3	0	0	0	0	—	—	—	—	—
97-98	Cincinnati	AHL	78	28	59	87	28	—	—	—	—	—
98-99	Cincinnati	AHL	72	28	41	69	56	3	2	0	2	0
	AHL	Totals	295	88	170	258	188	7	2	2	4	0

Born; 5/11/74, Calgary, Alberta. 6-1, 196. Drafted by Anaheim Mighty Ducks (3rd choice, 67th overall) in 1994 Entry Draft. Signed as a free agent by Florida Panthers (7/8/99). Last amateur club; Red Deer (WHL).

Ryan Reid — Defenseman

Regular Season / Playoffs

Season	Team	League	GP	G	A	PTS	PIM	GP	G	A	PTS	PIM
95-96	Jacksonville	ECHL	1	0	0	0	19	—	—	—	—	—
95-96	Utica	CoHL	10	0	0	0	29	—	—	—	—	—
95-96	Jacksonville	SHL	21	1	8	9	103	—	—	—	—	—
96-97	Columbus	CeHL	47	1	5	6	142	1	0	0	0	0
97-98	Fayetteville	CHL	49	5	7	12	362	—	—	—	—	—
98-99	San Angelo	WPHL	43	0	3	3	185	11	0	0	0	13
	CHL	Totals	96	6	12	18	504	1	0	0	0	0

Born; 5/2/71, Fort Saskatchewan, Saskatchewan. 6-2, 190. Last amateur club; Plattsburgh (NCAA 3).

Dan Reimann — Defenseman

Regular Season / Playoffs

Season	Team	League	GP	G	A	PTS	PIM	GP	G	A	PTS	PIM
96-97	Johnstown	ECHL	33	1	3	4	34	—	—	—	—	—
96-97	Louisville	ECHL	28	0	3	3	19	—	—	—	—	—
97-98	Louisville	ECHL	67	0	5	5	54	—	—	—	—	—
98-99	Florida	ECHL	59	0	3	3	53	5	0	0	0	0
	ECHL	Totals	187	1	14	15	160	5	0	0	0	0

Born; 12/17/72, Ramsey, Minnesota. 6-1, 205. Drafted by New Jersey Devils (9th choice, 187th overall) in 1991 Entry Draft. Traded to Florida by Miami (Louisville) for Jim Paradise (9/98). Selected by Greensboro in 1999 ECHL Expansion Draft. Last amateur club; St. Cloud (WCHA).

Mike Reimann — Left Wing

Regular Season / Playoffs

Season	Team	League	GP	G	A	PTS	PIM	GP	G	A	PTS	PIM
97-98	Amarillo	WPHL	20	3	2	5	35	—	—	—	—	—
97-98	Fort Worth	WPHL	26	5	5	10	61	3	1	1	2	17
98-99	Fort Worth	WPHL	33	1	4	5	161	—	—	—	—	—
	WPHL	Totals	79	9	11	20	257	3	1	1	2	17

Born; 3/19/75, Anoka, Minnesota. 6-1, 207. Traded to Fort Worth by Amarillo for Mike McCormick (11/97).

Todd Reirden — Defenseman

Regular Season / Playoffs

Season	Team	League	GP	G	A	PTS	PIM	GP	G	A	PTS	PIM
94-95	Raleigh	ECHL	26	2	13	15	33	—	—	—	—	—
94-95	Tallahassee	ECHL	43	5	25	30	61	13	2	5	7	10
95-96	Chicago	IHL	31	0	2	2	39	9	0	2	2	16
95-96	Tallahassee	ECHL	7	1	3	4	10	—	—	—	—	—
95-96	Jacksonville	ECHL	15	1	10	11	41	1	0	2	2	4
96-97	Chicago	IHL	57	3	10	13	108	—	—	—	—	—
96-97	San Antonio	IHL	23	2	5	7	51	9	0	1	1	17
97-98	San Antonio	IHL	70	5	14	19	132	—	—	—	—	—
97-98	Fort Wayne	IHL	11	2	2	4	16	4	0	2	2	4
98-99	Edmonton	NHL	17	2	3	5	20	—	—	—	—	—
98-99	Hamilton	AHL	58	9	25	34	84	11	0	5	5	6
	IHL	Totals	192	12	33	45	346	22	0	5	5	37
	ECHL	Totals	91	9	51	60	145	14	2	7	9	14

Born; 6/25/71, Arlington Heights, Illinois. 6-4, 205. Drafted by New Jersey Devils (14th choice, 242nd overall) in 1990 Entry Draft. Last amateur club; Bowling Green (CCHA).

Danny Reja — Left Wing

Regular Season / Playoffs

Season	Team	League	GP	G	A	PTS	PIM	GP	G	A	PTS	PIM
96-97	Hampton Roads	ECHL	7	1	0	1	16	—	—	—	—	—
96-97	Louisville	ECHL	38	11	17	28	43	—	—	—	—	—
97-98	Louisville	ECHL	58	16	24	40	73	—	—	—	—	—
98-99	Tucson	WCHL	14	12	7	19	22	—	—	—	—	—
98-99	Phoenix	WCHL	4	1	2	3	0	—	—	—	—	—
98-99	Bakersfield	WCHL	44	18	19	37	83	2	0	0	0	4
	ECHL	Totals	103	28	41	69	132	—	—	—	—	—
	WCHL	Totals	62	31	28	59	105	2	0	0	0	4

Born; 5/16/76, Toronto, Ontario. 6-1, 193. Drafted by Washington Capitals (7th choice, 171st overall) in 1994 Entry Draft. Selected by Bakersfield in 1998 WCHL Dispersal Draft. Last amateur club; Belleville (OHL).

Chad Remackel — Left Wing

Regular Season / Playoffs

Season	Team	League	GP	G	A	PTS	PIM	GP	G	A	PTS	PIM
96-97	Portland	AHL	1	0	0	0	0	—	—	—	—	—
96-97	Grand Rapids	IHL	70	9	18	27	36	1	0	0	0	0
97-98	Chicago	IHL	3	0	1	1	0	—	—	—	—	—
97-98	Rochester	AHL	4	0	0	0	0	—	—	—	—	—
97-98	Mobile	ECHL	53	19	36	55	51	3	2	1	3	2
98-99	Fayetteville	UHL	70	36	67	103	68	—	—	—	—	—
	IHL	Totals	73	9	19	28	36	1	0	0	0	0
	AHL	Totals	5	0	0	0	0	—	—	—	—	—

Born; 11/9/71, St. Paul, Minnesota. 6-1, 198. Last amateur club; Colorado College (WCHA).

Jon Rempel — Defenseman

Regular Season / Playoffs

Season	Team	League	GP	G	A	PTS	PIM	GP	G	A	PTS	PIM
96-97	Baton Rouge	ECHL	26	1	4	5	63	—	—	—	—	—
97-98	Portland	AHL	2	0	1	1	5	—	—	—	—	—
97-98	Baton Rouge	ECHL	55	0	8	8	144	—	—	—	—	—
98-99	Slough	BNL										
98-99	Baton Rouge	ECHL	12	1	1	2	39	—	—	—	—	—
	ECHL	Totals	81	1	12	13	205	—	—	—	—	—

Born; 9/11/71, Steinbach, Manitoba. 6-3, 225. Last amateur club; Manitoba (CWUAA).

Iannique Renaud — Right Wing

Regular Season / Playoffs

Season	Team	League	GP	G	A	PTS	PIM	GP	G	A	PTS	PIM
96-97	Pensacola	ECHL	3	0	0	0	10	—	—	—	—	—
96-97	Anchorage	WCHL	9	0	0	0	52	—	—	—	—	—
96-97	Alaska	WCHL	20	5	5	10	147	—	—	—	—	—
96-97	Bakersfield	WCHL	3	0	3	3	8	3	0	1	1	50
97-98	Bakersfield	WCHL	6	0	0	0	95	—	—	—	—	—
98-99	El Paso	WPHL	23	3	5	8	180	—	—	—	—	—
98-99	Phoenix	WCHL	36	5	5	10	254	3	0	0	0	20
	WCHL	Totals	74	10	13	23	556	6	0	1	1	70

Born; 9/19/75, Winnipeg, Manitoba. 6-3, 215.

Jason Renard — Right Wing

Regular Season / Playoffs

Season	Team	League	GP	G	A	PTS	PIM	GP	G	A	PTS	PIM
93-94	Richmond	ECHL	35	12	12	24	262	—	—	—	—	—
94-95	Fort Wayne	IHL	27	4	2	6	129	3	0	1	1	16
94-95	Saginaw	CoHL	27	6	11	17	117	—	—	—	—	—
95-96	Johnstown	ECHL	10	2	1	3	43	—	—	—	—	—
95-96	South Carolina	ECHL	8	2	2	4	89	—	—	—	—	—
95-96	Saginaw	CoHL	35	7	7	14	187	5	0	2	2	33
96-97	Utica	CoHL	30	9	7	16	152	—	—	—	—	—
96-97	Port Huron	CoHL	35	7	21	28	85	5	4	2	6	30
97-98	Port Huron	UHL	25	5	7	12	132	—	—	—	—	—
97-98	Saginaw	UHL	19	5	12	17	90	—	—	—	—	—
97-98	Brantford	UHL	13	11	4	15	32	7	3	5	8	55
98-99	Macon	CHL	41	15	20	35	376	3	1	0	1	21
	UHL	Totals	184	50	69	119	795	17	7	9	16	118
	ECHL	Totals	53	14	15	29	394	—	—	—	—	—

Born; 4/22/73, Brooks, Alberta. 6-1, 190. Traded to Port Huron by Saginaw with Dale Greenwood and Bobby Ferraris for J.D. Eaton, Joel Gardner and David Geris (12/97). Last amateur club; Tri-City (WHL).

Bruce Rendall — Left Wing

Regular Season / Playoffs

Season	Team	League	GP	G	A	PTS	PIM	GP	G	A	PTS	PIM
88-89	Indianapolis	IHL	15	2	2	4	9	—	—	—	—	—
88-89	Hershey	AHL	37	7	8	15	12	—	—	—	—	—
89-90	Fort Wayne	IHL	2	1	0	1	0	—	—	—	—	—
89-90	Hershey	AHL	9	2	1	3	4	—	—	—	—	—
90-91												
91-92												
92-93	Thunder Bay	CoHL	17	6	5	11	12	—	—	—	—	—
93-94												
94-95												
95-96												
96-97												
97-98												
98-99	Port Huron	UHL	3	1	1	2	5	—	—	—	—	—
	AHL	Totals	46	9	9	18	16	—	—	—	—	—
	IHL	Totals	17	3	2	5	9	—	—	—	—	—
	UHL	Totals	20	7	6	13	17	—	—	—	—	—

Born; 4/18/67, Thunder Bay, Ontario. 6-1, 190. Drafted by Philadelphia Flyers (2nd choice, 42nd overall) in 1985 Entry Draft. Last amateur club; Michigan State (CCHA).

Brian Renfrew — Goaltender

Regular Season / Playoffs

Season	Team	League	GP	W	L	T	MIN	SO	AVG	GP	W	L	MIN	SO	AVG
95-96	Oklahoma City	CeHL	5	2	3	0	269	0	5.13	—	—	—	—	—	—
95-96	Dayton	ECHL	21	6	5	3	912	0	3.09	—	—	—	—	—	—
95-96	Jacksonville	ECHL	8	4	4	0	440	0	4.37	16	9	7	901	0	3.93
96-97	Jacksonville	ECHL	10	0	8	0	517	0	6.15	—	—	—	—	—	—
96-97	Dayton	CoHL	37	7	23	4	2051	0	5.09	—	—	—	—	—	—
97-98	Anchorage	WCHL	33	16	13	4	1971	1	4.02	3	0	3	180	0	7.00
98-99	Alexandria	WPHL	25	8	12	3	1389	0	4.97	—	—	—	—	—	—
98-99	Memphis	CHL	20	12	3	3	1140	0	3.37	4	1	3	243	0	4.45
	ECHL	Totals	39	10	17	3	1869	0	4.24	16	9	7	901	0	3.93
	CHL	Totals	25	14	6	6	1409	0	3.71	4	1	3	243	0	4.45

Born; 5/1/72, Fairbanks, Alaska. 5-9, 165. Last amateur club; Western Michigan (CCHA).

Charlie Retter — Center

Regular Season / Playoffs

Season	Team	League	GP	G	A	PTS	PIM	GP	G	A	PTS	PIM
98-99	Hampton Roads	ECHL	10	0	0	0	7	—	—	—	—	—
98-99	Mobile	ECHL	47	8	11	19	26	2	1	0	1	2
	ECHL	Totals	57	8	11	19	33	2	1	0	1	2

Born; 2/11/76, Toronto, Ontario. 6-1, 190. Last amateur club; Dartmouth

Bob Revermann — Goaltender

Regular Season / Playoffs

Season	Team	League	GP	W	L	T	MIN	SO	AVG	GP	W	L	MIN	SO	AVG
98-99	Colorado	WCHL	24	8	9	1	1168	1	4.31	—	—	—	—	—	—

Born; 4/5/77, Fairbanks, Alaska. 6-2, 195.

Bobby Reynolds — Left Wing

Regular Season / Playoffs

Season	Team	League	GP	G	A	PTS	PIM	GP	G	A	PTS	PIM
89-90	Newmarket	AHL	66	22	28	50	55	—	—	—	—	—
89-90	Toronto	NHL	7	1	1	2	0	—	—	—	—	—
90-91	Newmarket	AHL	65	24	22	46	59	—	—	—	—	—
90-91	Baltimore	AHL	14	4	9	13	8	6	2	2	4	10
91-92	Baltimore	AHL	53	12	18	30	39	—	—	—	—	—
91-92	Kalamazoo	IHL	13	8	10	18	19	12	5	4	9	4
92-93												
93-94												
94-95												
95-96	Ratinger	Germany	50	44	36	80	40	—	—	—	—	—
96-97	Ratinger	Germany	48	21	16	37	28	6	1	1	2	52
97-98	Revier Lowen	Germany	27	9	13	22	12	—	—	—	—	—
98-99	Flint	UHL	4	4	2	6	0	—	—	—	—	—
98-99	Detroit	IHL	67	21	20	41	60	10	2	4	6	6
	AHL	Totals	198	62	77	139	161	6	2	2	4	10
	IHL	Totals	80	29	30	59	79	22	7	8	15	10

Born; 7/14/67, Flint, Michigan. 5-11, 175. Drafted by Toronto Maple Leafs (10th choice, 190th overall) in 1985 Entry Draft. Traded to Washington Capitals by Toronto for Robert Mendel (4/5/91). Traded to Minnesota North Stars by Washington for future considerations (3/10/92). Last amateur club; Michigan State

Doug Reynolds — Center

Regular Season / Playoffs

Season	Team	League	GP	G	A	PTS	PIM	GP	G	A	PTS	PIM
98-99	Winston-Salem	UHL	44	7	13	20	12	—	—	—	—	—
98-99	Mohawk Valley	UHL	12	0	1	1	2	—	—	—	—	—
98-99	Saginaw	UHL	7	2	5	7	2	—	—	—	—	—
	UHL	Totals	63	9	19	28	16	—	—	—	—	—

Born; 6/14/73, St. John's Newfoundland. 6-1, 195. Traded to Mohawk Valley by Winston-Salem with Josh Tymchak for Ryan Caley (2/99). Last amateur club; Acadia (AUAA).

Jesse Rezansoff — Right Wing

Regular Season / Playoffs

Season	Team	League	GP	G	A	PTS	PIM	GP	G	A	PTS	PIM
96-97	Fredericton	AHL	68	0	8	8	208	—	—	—	—	—
97-98	Raleigh	ECHL	63	6	15	21	234	—	—	—	—	—
98-99	Augusta	ECHL	67	8	17	25	283	2	0	1	1	2
	ECHL	Totals	130	14	32	46	517	2	0	1	1	2

Born; 1/31/76, Regina, Saskatchewan. 6-4, 201. Last amateur club; Calgary

Alex Riadinsky — Defenseman

Regular Season / Playoffs

Season	Team	League	GP	G	A	PTS	PIM	GP	G	A	PTS	PIM
98-99	Anchorage	WCHL	4	0	0	0	4	—	—	—	—	—

Born; 4/1/78, Minsk, Belarus. 6-2, 190.

Mike Ribeiro — Center

Regular Season / Playoffs

Season	Team	League	GP	G	A	PTS	PIM	GP	G	A	PTS	PIM
98-99	Rouyn-Noranda	QMJHL	69	67	100	167	137	11	5	11	16	12
98-99	Fredericton	AHL	—	—	—	—	—	5	0	1	1	2

Born; 2/10/80, Montreal, Quebec. 5-11, 150. Drafted by Montreal Canadiens (2nd choice, 45th overall) in 1998 Entry Draft. Last amateur club; Rouyn-Noranda (QMJHL).

Eric Ricard — Defenseman

Regular Season / Playoffs

Season	Team	League	GP	G	A	PTS	PIM	GP	G	A	PTS	PIM
89-90	New Haven	AHL	28	1	1	2	55	—	—	—	—	—
90-91	New Haven	AHL	35	1	4	5	65	—	—	—	—	—
90-91	Phoenix	IHL	16	1	3	4	24	—	—	—	—	—
91-92	New Haven	AHL	38	2	9	11	85	2	1	0	1	2
91-92	Louisville	ECHL	23	4	13	17	8	—	—	—	—	—
92-93	Fredericton	AHL	14	0	5	5	18	—	—	—	—	—
93-94	Fort Worth	CeHL	12	0	6	6	14	—	—	—	—	—
94-95	Denver	IHL	1	0	0	0	0	—	—	—	—	—
94-95	Fort Worth	CeHL	60	11	45	56	141	—	—	—	—	—
95-96	Tulsa	CeHL	6	2	3	5	2	6	0	4	4	8
96-97	New Mexico	WPHL	58	13	36	49	131	6	1	1	2	6
97-98	Las Vegas	IHL	—	—	—	—	—	4	0	0	0	2
97-98	New Mexico	WPHL	69	16	62	78	120	10	0	8	8	20
98-99	Florida	ECHL	47	1	12	13	100	6	0	5	5	12
	AHL	Totals	115	4	19	23	223	2	1	0	1	2
	IHL	Totals	17	1	3	4	24	4	0	0	0	2
	WPHL	Totals	127	29	98	127	251	16	1	9	10	26
	ECHL	Totals	70	5	25	30	108	6	0	5	5	12
	CeHL	Totals	78	13	54	67	157	6	0	4	4	8

Born; 2/29/69, St. Cesaire, Quebec. 6-4, 235. Drafted by Los Angeles Kings (3rd choice, 102nd overall) in 1989 Entry Draft. 1994-95 CeHL Defenseman of the Year. 1994-95 CeHL First Team All-Star. 1997-98 WPHL Defenseman of the Year. Last amateur club; Granby (WHL).

Jason Ricci — Defenseman

Regular Season / Playoffs

Season	Team	League	GP	G	A	PTS	PIM	GP	G	A	PTS	PIM
97-98	Tucson	WCHL	42	7	26	33	22	—	—	—	—	—
98-99	Fort Worth	CHL	7	0	1	1	0	—	—	—	—	—
98-99	Port Huron	UHL	6	0	0	0	0	—	—	—	—	—
98-99	Saginaw	UHL	14	0	7	7	10	—	—	—	—	—
	UHL	Totals	20	0	7	7	10	—	—	—	—	—

Born; 9/4/72, Toronto, Ontario. 5-10, 180.

Scott Ricci — Defenseman

Regular Season / Playoffs

Season	Team	League	GP	G	A	PTS	PIM	GP	G	A	PTS	PIM
98-99	Springfield	AHL	9	0	1	1	4	—	—	—	—	—
98-99	Hershey	AHL	4	0	0	0	2	—	—	—	—	—
98-99	Binghamton	UHL	57	6	20	26	70	5	0	2	2	2
	AHL	Totals	13	0	1	1	6	—	—	—	—	—

Born; 4/3/74, St. Catherines, Ontario. 6-3, 212. 1998-99 UHL All-Rookie Team. Last amateur club; Colgate (ECAC).

Jeff Ricciardi — Defenseman

Regular Season / Playoffs

Season	Team	League	GP	G	A	PTS	PIM	GP	G	A	PTS	PIM
92-93	Providence	AHL	3	0	0	0	0	—	—	—	—	—
92-93	Johnstown	ECHL	61	7	29	36	248	5	2	2	4	6
93-94	Indianapolis	IHL	75	3	20	23	307	—	—	—	—	—
94-95	Indianapolis	IHL	60	2	11	13	187	—	—	—	—	—
95-96	Las Vegas	IHL	75	4	13	17	303	15	2	0	2	42
96-97	Manitoba	IHL	81	3	22	25	271	—	—	—	—	—
97-98	Revier Lowen	Germany	28	0	6	6	110	—	—	—	—	—
97-98	Kassell	Germany	18	0	2	2	20	—	—	—	—	—
98-99	Kolner Haie	Germany	50	4	8	12	122	4	0	1	1	33
	IHL	Totals	291	12	66	78	1068	15	2	0	2	42

Born; 6/21/71, Thunder Bay, Ontario. 5-11, 203. Drafted by Winnipeg Jets (8th choice, 159th overall) in 1991 Entry Draft. Traded to Boston Bruins by Winnipeg for future considerations (9/8/92). Signed as a free agent by Chicago Blackhawks (7/28/93). Last amateur club; Ottawa (OHL).

Eric Rice — Right Wing

Regular Season / Playoffs

Season	Team	League	GP	G	A	PTS	PIM	GP	G	A	PTS	PIM
98-99	Tacoma	WCHL	2	0	0	0	0	—	—	—	—	—

Born;

Tyler Rice — Right Wing

Regular Season / Playoffs

Season	Team	League	GP	G	A	PTS	PIM	GP	G	A	PTS	PIM
97-98	Wichita	CHL	61	35	27	62	176	15	4	3	7	26
98-99	Fort Worth	WPHL	19	12	12	24	22	—	—	—	—	—
98-99	Waco	WPHL	1	0	0	0	2	—	—	—	—	—
	WPHL	Totals	20	12	12	24	24	—	—	—	—	—

Born; 6/4/73, Winnipeg, Manitoba. 6-1, 200. Selected by San Antonio in CHL 1998 Expansion Draft. Traded to Waco by Fort Worth for Tim Green (12/98). Last amateur club; North Dakota (WCHA).

Chad Richard — Left Wing

Regular Season / Playoffs

Season	Team	League	GP	G	A	PTS	PIM	GP	G	A	PTS	PIM
95-96	Anchorage	WCHL	37	3	3	6	*356	—	—	—	—	—
96-97	Anchorage	WCHL	25	7	9	16	313	—	—	—	—	—
96-97	Port Huron	CoHL	15	4	2	6	53	—	—	—	—	—
97-98	Anchorage	WCHL	14	2	3	5	144	—	—	—	—	—
97-98	Louisiana	ECHL	17	1	1	2	77	—	—	—	—	—
97-98	Louisville	ECHL	4	0	0	0	0	—	—	—	—	—
97-98	Johnstown	ECHL	10	0	7	7	77	—	—	—	—	—
98-99	Tacoma	WCHL	42	4	6	10	347	6	0	1	1	10
	WCHL	Totals	118	16	21	37	1160	6	0	1	1	10
	ECHL	Totals	31	1	8	9	154	—	—	—	—	—

Born; 6/23/74, Anchorage, Alaska. 6-6, 235. Sold to Louisville by Louisiana (2/98). Member of 1998-99 WCHL Champion Tacoma Sabrecats.

Jean-Marc Richard — Defenseman

Regular Season / Playoffs

Season	Team	League	GP	G	A	PTS	PIM	GP	G	A	PTS	PIM
87-88	Fredericton	AHL	68	14	42	56	52	7	2	1	3	4
87-88	Quebec	NHL	4	2	1	3	2	—	—	—	—	—
88-89	Halifax	AHL	57	8	25	33	38	4	1	0	1	4
89-90	Quebec	NHL	1	0	0	0	0	—	—	—	—	—
89-90	Halifax	AHL	40	1	24	25	38	—	—	—	—	—
90-91	Halifax	AHL	80	7	41	48	78	—	—	—	—	—
90-91	Fort Wayne	IHL	1	0	0	0	0	19	3	9	12	8
91-92	Fort Wayne	IHL	82	18	68	86	109	7	0	5	5	20
92-93	San Diego	IHL	6	1	0	1	4	—	—	—	—	—
92-93	Fort Wayne	IHL	52	10	33	43	48	12	6	11	17	6
93-94	Las Vegas	IHL	59	15	33	48	44	5	0	3	3	0
94-95	Las Vegas	IHL	81	16	41	57	76	10	0	3	3	4
95-96	Las Vegas	IHL	82	12	40	52	92	15	1	7	8	23
96-97	Quebec	IHL	56	8	26	34	31	9	1	1	2	10
97-98	Frankfurt	Germany	48	4	17	21	40	7	1	2	3	2
98-99	Frankfurt	Germany	49	8	18	26	74	8	1	0	1	12
	NHL	Totals	5	2	1	3	2	—	—	—	—	—
	IHL	Totals	419	80	241	321	404	77	11	39	50	71
	AHL	Totals	245	30	132	162	206	11	3	1	4	8

Born; 10/8/66, St. Raymond, Quebec. 5-11, 178. Signed as a free agent by Quebec Nordiques (4/87). Loaned to Fort Wayne Komets (3/91). Signed as a free agent by Fort Wayne (9/91). Signed as a free agent by Las Vegas Thunder (7/8/93). 1991-92 IHL First Team All-Star. 1993-94 IHL First Team All-Star. 1991-92 IHL Best Defenseman (Governor's Trophy). Member of 1992-93 IHL Champion Fort Wayne Komets. Last amateur club; Chicoutimi (QMJHL).

Marcel Richard — Right Wing

Regular Season / Playoffs

Season	Team	League	GP	G	A	PTS	PIM	GP	G	A	PTS	PIM
93-94	Erie	ECHL	1	0	1	1	0	—	—	—	—	—
94-95	Bracknell	BHL	1	0	0	0	0	—	—	—	—	—
94-95	Lakeland	SUN	2	0	0	0	0	—	—	—	—	—
94-95	London	CoHL	22	7	8	15	2	5	4	2	6	0
95-96	Madison	CoHL	70	24	31	55	48	6	1	2	3	4
96-97	Columbus	CeHL	63	51	58	109	74	3	1	1	2	0
97-98	Columbus	CHL	61	39	57	96	45	13	9	13	22	19
98-99	Tucson	WCHL	21	15	17	32	34	—	—	—	—	—
98-99	Columbus	CHL	43	19	24	43	35	10	4	6	10	26
	CHL	Totals	167	109	139	248	154	26	14	20	34	45
	CoHL	Totals	92	31	39	70	50	11	5	4	9	4

Born; 5/21/69, Kingston, Ontario. 6-0, 200. Selected by San Antonio in 1998 CHL Expansion Draft. Member of 1997-98 CHL Champion Columbus Cottonmouths. Last amateur club; Colgate (ECAC).

Mark Richards — Goaltender

Regular Season / Playoffs

Season	Team	League	GP	W	L	T	MIN	SO	AVG	GP	W	L	MIN	SO	AVG
92-93	Moncton	AHL	13	6	6	1	736	0	3.99	4	1	3	231	0	4.94
92-93	Fort Wayne	IHL	3	1	0	0	139	0	4.75	—	—	—	—	—	—
92-93	Toledo	ECHL	11	5	4	1	612	1	2.75	—	—	—	—	—	—
93-94	Moncton	AHL	29	8	16	0	1419	0	4.35	—	—	—	—	—	—
94-95	Tallahassee	ECHL	*59	31	16	7	*3369	0	2.90	13	8	5	760	1	3.16
95-96	Tallahassee	ECHL	50	28	11	5	2627	*2	3.49	9	6	3	537	*2	*2.12
96-97	Carolina	AHL	1	0	1	0	40	0	4.50	—	—	—	—	—	—
96-97	Tallahassee	ECHL	38	20	11	3	2086	2	3.28	1	0	1	52	0	4.64
97-98	Saint John	AHL	6	3	2	0	240	1	2.25	—	—	—	—	—	—
97-98	Chicago	IHL	7	5	1	0	350	0	2.75	—	—	—	—	—	—
97-98	Winston-Salem	UHL	33	16	14	2	1909	1	3.52	—	—	—	—	—	—
98-99	Pee Dee	ECHL	40	29	4	3	2234	3	2.82	5	0	2	226	0	2.38
	AHL	Totals	49	17	25	1	2435	1	4.04	4	1	3	231	0	4.94
	IHL	Totals	10	6	1	0	489	0	3.31	—	—	—	—	—	—

Born; 7/24/69, Abington, Pennsylvania. 5-8, 185. Drafted by Winnipeg Jets (1st choice, 19th overall) in 1990 Supplemental Draft. Last amateur club; Lowell (Hockey East).

Todd Richards — Defenseman

Regular Season / Playoffs

Season	Team	League	GP	G	A	PTS	PIM	GP	G	A	PTS	PIM
89-90	Sherbrooke	AHL	71	6	18	24	73	5	1	2	3	6
90-91	Hartford	NHL	2	0	4	4	2	6	0	0	0	2
90-91	Fredericton	AHL	3	0	1	1	2	—	—	—	—	—
90-91	Springfield	AHL	71	10	41	51	62	14	2	8	10	2
91-92	Hartford	NHL	6	0	0	0	2	5	0	3	3	4
91-92	Springfield	AHL	43	6	23	29	33	8	0	3	3	2
92-93	Springfield	AHL	78	13	42	55	53	9	1	5	6	2
93-94	Las Vegas	IHL	80	11	35	46	122	5	1	4	5	18
94-95	Las Vegas	IHL	80	12	49	61	130	9	1	2	3	6
95-96	Orlando	IHL	81	19	54	73	59	23	4	9	13	8
96-97	Orlando	IHL	82	9	36	45	134	10	0	1	1	4
97-98	Orlando	IHL	75	6	37	43	68	17	3	8	11	13
98-99	Orlando	IHL	67	11	26	37	61	16	3	7	10	14
	NHL	Totals	8	0	4	4	4	11	0	3	3	6
	IHL	Totals	465	68	237	305	574	80	12	31	43	63
	AHL	Totals	266	35	125	160	223	36	4	18	22	12

Born; 10/20/66, Crystal, Minnesota. 6-0, 194. Drafted by Montreal Canadiens (3rd choice, 33rd overall) in 1985 Entry Draft. Traded to Hartford Whalers by Montreal for future considerations (10/90). Signed as a free agent by Las Vegas Thunder (7/14/93). Signed as a free agent by Orlando Solar Bears (7/10/95). 1993-94 IHL Second Team All-Star. 1994-95 IHL First Team All-Star. 1994-95 IHL Governors Trophy (Best Defenseman). 1995-96 IHL First Team All-Star. Member of 1990-91 AHL champion Springfield Indians. Last amateur club;

Travis Richards — Defenseman

Regular Season / Playoffs

Season	Team	League	GP	G	A	PTS	PIM	GP	G	A	PTS	PIM
93-94	United States	National	51	1	11	12	12	—	—	—	—	—
93-94	United States	Olympic	8	0	0	0	2	—	—	—	—	—
93-94	Kalamazoo	IHL	19	2	10	12	20	4	1	1	2	0
94-95	Dallas	NHL	2	0	0	0	0	—	—	—	—	—
94-95	Kalamazoo	IHL	63	4	16	20	53	15	1	5	6	12
95-96	Dallas	NHL	1	0	0	0	2	—	—	—	—	—
95-96	Michigan	IHL	65	8	15	23	55	9	2	2	4	4
96-97	Grand Rapids	IHL	77	10	13	23	83	5	1	3	4	2
97-98	Grand Rapids	IHL	81	12	20	32	70	3	1	1	2	4
98-99	Grand Rapids	IHL	82	9	23	32	84	—	—	—	—	—
	NHL	Totals	3	0	0	0	2	—	—	—	—	—
	IHL	Totals	387	45	97	142	365	36	6	12	18	22

Born; 3/22/70, Crystal, Minnesota. 6-1, 195. Drafted by Minnesota North Stars (6th choice, 169th overall) in 1988 Entry Draft. Last amateur club; Minnesota

Bruce Richardson — Center

Regular Season / Playoffs

Season	Team	League	GP	G	A	PTS	PIM	GP	G	A	PTS	PIM
97-98	Chicoutimi	QMJHL	43	7	20	27	264	6	2	4	6	11
97-98	Hershey	AHL	10	0	0	0	87	—	—	—	—	—
97-98	Chesapeake	ECHL	2	0	0	0	26	—	—	—	—	—
98-99	Hershey	AHL	44	4	7	11	132	3	0	0	0	15
98-99	Quad City	UHL	16	4	7	11	75	—	—	—	—	—
	AHL	Totals	54	4	7	11	219	3	0	0	0	15

Born; 6/8/77, Ville St. Pierre, Quebec. 5-9, 175. Selected by Missouri River Otters in 1999 UHL Expansion Draft. Last amateur club; Chicoutimi (QMJHL).

Bryan Richardson — Center

Regular Season / Playoffs

Season	Team	League	GP	G	A	PTS	PIM	GP	G	A	PTS	PIM
96-97	Dayton	ECHL	25	5	16	21	28	1	0	0	0	4
97-98	Baton Rouge	ECHL	27	12	10	22	18	—	—	—	—	—
98-99	Baton Rouge	ECHL	69	32	47	79	56	6	2	4	6	4
	ECHL	Totals	121	49	73	122	102	7	2	4	6	8

Born; 7/28/73, Montreal, Quebec. 5-9, 188. Last amateur club; Rensselaer Polytechnic Institute (ECAC).

Ken Richardson — Defenseman

Regular Season / Playoffs

Season	Team	League	GP	G	A	PTS	PIM	GP	G	A	PTS	PIM
97-98	Fresno	WCHL	45	20	22	42	84	5	0	1	1	28
98-99	Huntsville	CHL	53	17	21	38	240	15	6	9	15	44

Born; 1/11/73, Red Deer, Alberta. 6-0, 210. Member of 1998-99 CHL Champion Huntsville Channel Cats. Scored Levins Cup-winning goal for Channel Cats.

Grant Richison — Defenseman

Regular Season / Playoffs

Season	Team	League	GP	G	A	PTS	PIM	GP	G	A	PTS	PIM
89-90	Moncton	AHL	50	2	10	12	28	—	—	—	—	—
90-91	Moncton	AHL	49	4	10	14	57	—	—	—	—	—
91-92	Fort Wayne	IHL	48	6	10	16	84	5	0	2	2	9
92-93	Muskegon	CoHL	2	0	1	1	0	—	—	—	—	—
92-93	Fort Wayne	IHL	52	5	18	23	73	12	1	7	8	20
93-94	Fort Wayne	IHL	59	3	17	20	50	17	0	3	3	28
94-95	Fort Wayne	IHL	72	3	16	19	62	4	0	3	3	2
95-96	Fort Wayne	IHL	3	0	1	1	6	—	—	—	—	—
96-97	Fort Wayne	IHL	51	1	7	8	57	—	—	—	—	—
96-97	Quad City	CoHL	6	0	3	3	2	—	—	—	—	—
97-98	Fort Wayne	IHL	23	0	1	1	20	—	—	—	—	—
97-98	Orlando	IHL	24	1	4	5	31	17	2	3	5	16
97-98	Muskegon	UHL	3	0	1	1	0	—	—	—	—	—
98-99	Kansas City	IHL	65	0	8	8	58	3	0	0	0	4
98-99	Muskegon	UHL	2	1	0	1	2	—	—	—	—	—
	IHL	Totals	397	19	82	101	441	58	3	18	21	79
	AHL	Totals	99	6	20	26	85	—	—	—	—	—
	UHL	Totals	13	1	5	6	4	—	—	—	—	—

Born; 5/5/67, Detroit, Michigan. 6-2, 205. Member of 1992-93 IHL Champion Fort Wayne Komets.

Chris Riddell — Defenseman

Regular Season / Playoffs

Season	Team	League	GP	G	A	PTS	PIM	GP	G	A	PTS	PIM
98-99	Austin	WPHL	7	0	0	0	26	—	—	—	—	—

Born; 1/9/77, Naicam, Saskatchewan. 6-1, 220.

Brian Ridolfi — Left Wing

Regular Season / Playoffs

Season	Team	League	GP	G	A	PTS	PIM	GP	G	A	PTS	PIM
96-97	Dayton	ECHL	67	21	28	49	62	4	0	1	1	8
97-98	Michigan	IHL	2	0	0	0	0	—	—	—	—	—
97-98	Dayton	ECHL	67	34	36	70	62	5	1	1	2	11
98-99	Dayton	ECHL	70	17	35	52	73	4	1	0	1	4
	ECHL	Totals	204	72	99	171	197	13	2	2	4	23

Born; 10/3/71, Cumberland, Rhode Island. 5-8, 180. Last amateur club; Providence (Hockey East).

Don Riendeau — Forward

Regular Season / Playoffs

Season	Team	League	GP	G	A	PTS	PIM	GP	G	A	PTS	PIM
98-99	Lake Charles	WPHL	13	3	1	4	4	—	—	—	—	—
98-99	Odessa	WPHL	13	1	5	6	2	—	—	—	—	—
	WPHL	Totals	26	4	6	10	6	—	—	—	—	—

Born; 10/30/70, E. Grand Forks, Minnesota. 5-10, 180. Traded to Odessa by Lake Charles for a player to be named later (Jamie Dunn) (2/99).

Vincent Riendeau — Goaltender

Regular Season / Playoffs

Season	Team	League	GP	W	L	T	MIN	SO	AVG	GP	W	L	MIN	SO	AVG
86-87	Sherbrooke	AHL	41	25	14	0	2363	2	2.89	13	8	5	742	0	3.80
87-88	Montreal	NHL	1	0	0	0	36	0	8.33	—	—	—	—	—	—
87-88	Sherbrooke	AHL	44	27	13	3	2521	*4	*2.67	2	0	2	127	0	3.31
88-89	St. Louis	NHL	32	11	15	5	1842	0	3.52	—	—	—	—	—	—
89-90	St. Louis	NHL	43	17	19	5	2551	1	3.50	8	3	4	397	0	3.63
90-91	St. Louis	NHL	44	29	9	6	2671	3	3.01	13	6	7	687	*1	3.06
91-92	St. Louis	NHL	3	1	2	0	157	0	4.20	—	—	—	—	—	—
91-92	Detroit	NHL	2	2	0	0	87	0	1.38	2	1	0	73	0	3.29
91-92	Adirondack	AHL	3	2	1	0	179	0	2.68	—	—	—	—	—	—
92-93	Detroit	NHL	22	13	4	2	1193	0	3.22	—	—	—	—	—	—
93-94	Detroit	NHL	8	2	4	0	345	0	4.00	—	—	—	—	—	—
93-94	Adirondack	AHL	10	6	3	0	582	0	3.09	—	—	—	—	—	—
93-94	Boston	NHL	18	7	6	1	976	1	3.07	2	1	1	120	0	4.00
94-95	Boston	NHL	11	3	6	1	565	0	2.87	—	—	—	—	—	—
94-95	Providence	AHL	—	—	—	—	—	—	—	1	1	0	60	0	3.00
95-96															
96-97	Manitoba	IHL	41	10	18	5	1941	0	3.49	—	—	—	—	—	—
97-98	Lugano	Italy													
97-98	Revier Lowen	Germany	14	—	—	—	750	0	3.04	—	—	—	—	—	—
98-99	Lada Toglietti	USSR	5	—	—	—	235	0	1.53	7	—	—	407	1	2.06
98-99	Ayr	BSL	27	—	—	—	1651	—	2.94	—	—	—	—	—	—
	NHL	Totals	184	85	65	20	10423	5	3.30	25	11	12	1277	1	3.34
	AHL	Totals	98	60	31	3	5645	6	2.81	16	9	7	929	0	3.68

Born; 4/20/66, St. Hyancinthe, Quebec. 5-10, 185. Signed as a free agent by Montreal Canadiens (10/9/85). Traded to St. Louis Blues by Montreal with Sergio Momesso for Jocelyn Lemiuex, Darrell May and St. Louis' second round choice (Patrice Brisebois) in 1989 Entry Draft (8/9/88). Traded to Detroit Red Wings by St. Louis for Rick Zombo (10/18/91). Traded to Boston Bruins by Detroit for Boston's fifth round choice (Chad Wilchynski) in 1995 Entry Draft (1/17/94). 1987-88 AHL Harry "Hap" Holmes Trophy (fewest goals against) with Jocelyn Perreault. 1987-88 AHL Second Team All-Star. Last amateur club; Drum-

Michel Riesen — Right Wing

Regular Season / Playoffs

Season	Team	League	GP	G	A	PTS	PIM	GP	G	A	PTS	PIM
98-99	Hamilton	AHL	60	6	17	23	6	3	0	0	0	0

Born; 4/11/79, Oberbalm, Switzerland. 6-2, 190. Drafted by Edmonton Oilers (1st choice, 14th overall) in 1997 Entry Draft. Last European club; HC Davos (Switzerland).

Travis Riggin — Forward

Regular Season / Playoffs

Season	Team	League	GP	G	A	PTS	PIM	GP	G	A	PTS	PIM
97-98	Oklahoma City	CHL	66	16	14	30	65	2	0	1	1	6
98-99	Oklahoma City	CHL	8	0	1	1	30	—	—	—	—	—
98-99	Columbus	CHL	14	5	0	5	8	—	—	—	—	—
98-99	Topeka	CHL	32	9	6	15	17	—	—	—	—	—
	CHL	Totals	120	30	21	51	120	2	0	1	1	6

Born; 4/26/77, Kincardine, Ontario. 6-0, 200. Traded to Topeka by Columbus with Oleg Tsirkounov for Thomas Stewart (12/98).

Jasen Rintala — Center

Regular Season / Playoffs

Season	Team	League	GP	G	A	PTS	PIM	GP	G	A	PTS	PIM
97-98	Mankato State	NCAA	38	6	6	12	24	—	—	—	—	—
97-98	Nashville	CHL	6	2	0	2	6	9	0	0	0	18
98-99	Oklahoma City	CHL	45	13	14	27	78	—	—	—	—	—
98-99	Fayetteville	CHL	25	5	6	11	26	—	—	—	—	—
	CHL	Totals	76	20	20	40	110	9	0	0	0	18

Born; 4/20/74, Calumet, Michigan. 6-0, 190. Selected by Oklahoma City in 1998 CHL Dispersal Draft. Traded to Fayetteville by Oklahoma City for Rod Butler (1/99). Last amateur club; Mankato State (NCAA 1).

Ken Riplinger — Left Wing

Regular Season / Playoffs

Season	Team	League	GP	G	A	PTS	PIM	GP	G	A	PTS	PIM
98-99	Fresno	WCHL	1	0	0	0	2	—	—	—	—	—

Born;

Ryan Risidore — Defenseman

Regular Season / Playoffs

Season	Team	League	GP	G	A	PTS	PIM	GP	G	A	PTS	PIM
96-97	Springfield	AHL	63	1	9	10	90	15	0	1	1	12
97-98	Indianapolis	IHL	75	3	8	11	123	4	0	1	1	6
98-99	Hartford	AHL	49	1	4	5	81	1	0	0	0	0
	AHL	Totals	112	2	13	15	171	16	0	1	1	12

Born; 4/4/76, Hamilton, Ontario. 6-4, 195. Drafted by Hartford Whalers (3rd choice, 109th overall) in 1994 Entry Draft. Traded to Chicago Blackhawks by Carolina Hurricanes with Carolina's fifth round choice in 1998 Entry Draft (later traded to Toronto-Toronto selected Morgan Warren) for Enrico Ciccone (7/25/97). Traded to New York Rangers by Chicago for Ryan Vandenbussche (3/24/98). Last amateur club; Guelph (OHL).

Dave Risk — Defenseman

Regular Season / Playoffs

Season	Team	League	GP	G	A	PTS	PIM	GP	G	A	PTS	PIM
98-99	Dartmouth	ECAC	29	2	12	14	6	—	—	—	—	—
98-99	Charlotte	ECHL	7	0	0	0	2	—	—	—	—	—

Born; 9/6/76, Morristown, New Jersey. 6-0, 220. Last amateur club; Dartmouth (ECAC).

Jaynen Rissling — Defenseman

Regular Season / Playoffs

Season	Team	League	GP	G	A	PTS	PIM	GP	G	A	PTS	PIM
96-97	Johnstown	ECHL	20	2	7	9	23	—	—	—	—	—
97-98	Richmond	ECHL	14	0	0	0	26	—	—	—	—	—
97-98	Toledo	ECHL	10	1	2	3	8	—	—	—	—	—
98-99	Amarillo	WPHL	69	7	13	20	114	—	—	—	—	—
	ECHL	Totals	44	3	9	12	57	—	—	—	—	—

Born; 8/4/72, Edmnonton, Alberta. 6-1, 200. Last amateur club; Massachusetts (Hockey East).

Andy Ristau — Defenseman

Regular Season / Playoffs

Season	Team	League	GP	G	A	PTS	PIM	GP	G	A	PTS	PIM
80-81	Tulsa	CHL	5	1	0	1	0	—	—	—	—	—
85-86	Carolina	ACHL	15	10	4	14	148	—	—	—	—	—
85-86	Rochester	AHL	46	1	2	3	170	—	—	—	—	—
86-87	Flint	IHL	31	5	7	12	267	—	—	—	—	—
86-87	Rochester	AHL	23	1	1	2	113	5	0	0	0	31
98-99	Winston-Salem	UHL	2	0	0	0	0	—	—	—	—	—
	AHL	Totals	69	2	3	5	283	5	0	0	0	31

Born; 1/28/61, Winnipeg, Manitoba. 6-5, 240. Signed as a free agent by Buffalo Sabres (3/7/86). Member of 1986-87 AHL Champion Rochester Amerks.

Byron Ritchie — Center

Regular Season / Playoffs

Season	Team	League	GP	G	A	PTS	PIM	GP	G	A	PTS	PIM
95-96	Springfield	AHL	6	2	1	3	4	8	0	3	3	0
95-96	Lethbridge	WHL	66	55	51	106	163	4	0	2	2	4
96-97	Lethbridge	WHL	63	50	76	126	115	18	*16	12	*28	28
97-98	New Haven	AHL	65	13	18	31	97	—	—	—	—	—
98-99	Carolina	NHL	3	0	0	0	0	—	—	—	—	—
98-99	New Haven	AHL	66	24	33	57	139	—	—	—	—	—
	AHL	Totals	137	39	52	91	240	8	0	3	3	0

Born; 4/24/97, Burnaby, British Columbia. 5-10, 180. Drafted by Hartford Whalers (6th choice, 165th overall) in 1995 Entry Draft. Last amateur club; Lethbridge (WHL).

Darren Ritchie — Right Wing

Regular Season / Playoffs

Season	Team	League	GP	G	A	PTS	PIM	GP	G	A	PTS	PIM
95-96	St. John's	AHL	32	9	5	14	12	—	—	—	—	—
95-96	South Carolina	ECHL	25	6	16	22	4	6	1	2	3	4
96-97	Central Texas	WPHL	14	20	3	23	8	—	—	—	—	—
96-97	Baton Rouge	ECHL	15	8	3	11	4	—	—	—	—	—
97-98	Merano	Italy	26	14	16	30	6	—	—	—	—	—
98-99	Bietigheim	Germany	59	44	48	92	28	—	—	—	—	—
	ECHL	Totals	40	14	19	33	8	6	1	2	3	4

Born; 3/10/74, Minnesdosa, Manitoba. 5-10, 185. Last amateur club; Brandon (WHL).

Dan Riva — Forward

Regular Season / Playoffs

Season	Team	League	GP	G	A	PTS	PIM	GP	G	A	PTS	PIM
98-99	RPI	ECAC	36	22	35	57	35	—	—	—	—	—
98-99	Milwaukee	IHL	8	0	2	2	4	1	0	1	1	0

Born; 9/17/75, Framingham, Massachusetts. 6-0, 195. Signed as a free agent by Nashville Predators (5/7/99). Last amateur club; RPI (ECAC).

J.F. Rivard — Goaltender

Regular Season / Playoffs

Season	Team	League	GP	W	L	T	MIN	SO	AVG	GP	W	L	MIN	SO	AVG
96-97	Thunder Bay	CoHL	37	21	12	4	2094	0	3.29	11	5	4	602	0	3.39
97-98	Thunder Bay	UHL	*69	*39	21	6	*3856	3	3.69	5	1	4	288	0	4.16
98-99	Thunder Bay	UHL	55	34	14	6	3159	2	3.10	13	6	*7	849	1	*2.12
	UHL	Totals	161	94	47	16	9109	5	3.39	29	12	15	1739	1	2.90

Born; 2/10/72, Lorettaville, Quebec. 5-9, 155. 1997-98 UHL Second All-Star Team. Last amateur club; Ottawa (OUAA).

Stefan Rivard — Center

Regular Season / Playoffs

Season	Team	League	GP	G	A	PTS	PIM	GP	G	A	PTS	PIM
95-96	Columbus	ECHL	50	11	14	25	158	—	—	—	—	—
97-98	Birmingham	ECHL	65	14	20	34	182	4	0	0	0	10
98-99	Birmingham	ECHL	70	21	26	47	149	5	2	1	3	10
	ECHL	Totals	185	46	60	106	489	9	2	1	3	20

Born; 3/14/74, New Likseard, Ontario. 5-11, 183. Last amateur club; North Bay (OHL).

Andy Roach — Defenseman

Regular Season / Playoffs

Season	Team	League	GP	G	A	PTS	PIM	GP	G	A	PTS	PIM
97-98	San Antonio	IHL	67	8	16	24	30	—	—	—	—	—
98-99	Long Beach	IHL	41	5	21	26	34	—	—	—	—	—
98-99	Utah	IHL	44	7	10	17	18	—	—	—	—	—
	IHL	Totals	152	20	47	67	82	—	—	—	—	—

Born; 8/22/73, Mattawan, Michigan. 5-11, 181. Last amateur club; Ferris State (CCHA).

Dean Roach — Center

Regular Season / Playoffs

Season	Team	League	GP	G	A	PTS	PIM	GP	G	A	PTS	PIM
98-99	Winston-Salem	UHL	64	7	19	26	93	5	3	0	3	2

Born; 2/1/74, Moose Factory, Ontario. 5-9, 178. Last amateur club; Lebret

Gary Roach — Defenseman

Regular Season / Playoffs

Season	Team	League	GP	G	A	PTS	PIM	GP	G	A	PTS	PIM
95-96	Detroit	CoHL	5	0	2	2	6	—	—	—	—	—
95-96	Carolina	AHL	44	1	14	15	20	—	—	—	—	—
96-97	Laurentian	AUAA	14	3	13	16	20	—	—	—	—	—
97-98	Louisville	ECHL	11	1	4	5	17	—	—	—	—	—
97-98	Louisiana	ECHL	51	8	32	40	32	10	1	6	7	19
98-99	Louisiana	ECHL	65	9	37	46	45	5	0	2	2	6
	ECHL	Totals	127	18	73	91	94	15	1	8	9	25

Born; 2/4/75, Sault Ste. Marie, Ontario. 6-1, 195. Traded to Louisiana by Louisville for Tobias Ablad (12/97). Last amateur club; Laurentian (OUAA).

Adam Robbins — Left Wing

Regular Season / Playoffs

Season	Team	League	GP	G	A	PTS	PIM	GP	G	A	PTS	PIM
96-97	Fort Worth	CeHL	58	8	16	24	139	17	5	5	10	25
97-98	Fort Worth	WPHL	65	11	10	21	154	13	1	2	3	18
98-99	Port Huron	UHL	70	16	25	41	85	4	0	0	0	12

Born; 10/17/77, Bancroft, Ontario. 5-11, 195. Member of 1996-97 CeHL Champion Fort Worth Fire. Last amateur club; Belleville, (OHL).

Serge Roberge — Right Wing

Regular Season / Playoffs

Season	Team	League	GP	G	A	PTS	PIM	GP	G	A	PTS	PIM
86-87	Virginia	ACHL	49	9	16	25	*353	12	4	2	6	*104
87-88	Sherbrooke	AHL	30	0	1	1	130	5	0	0	0	21
88-89	Sherbrooke	AHL	65	5	7	12	353	6	0	1	1	10
89-90	Sherbrooke	AHL	66	8	5	13	343	12	2	0	2	44
90-91	Quebec	NHL	9	0	0	0	24	—	—	—	—	—
90-91	Halifax	AHL	52	0	5	5	152	—	—	—	—	—
91-92	Halifax	AHL	66	2	8	10	319	—	—	—	—	—
92-93	Halifax	AHL	16	2	2	4	34	—	—	—	—	—
92-93	Utica	AHL	28	0	3	3	85	1	0	0	0	0
93-94	Cape Breton	AHL	51	3	5	8	130	1	0	0	0	0
94-95	Cornwall	AHL	73	0	3	3	342	11	0	0	0	29
95-96	Rochester	AHL	32	0	1	1	42	—	—	—	—	—
95-96	Fredericton	AHL	14	1	1	2	45	7	0	0	0	10
96-97	Quebec	IHL	61	2	4	6	273	—	—	—	—	—
97-98	Quebec	IHL	35	2	0	2	115	—	—	—	—	—
98-99	Mohawk Valley	UHL	61	7	4	11	268	—	—	—	—	—
	AHL	Totals	493	21	41	62	1975	43	2	1	3	114
	IHL	Totals	96	4	4	8	388	—	—	—	—	—

Born; 3/31/65, Quebec City, Quebec. 6-1, 195. Signed as a free agent by Montreal Canadiens (1/25/88). Signed as a free agent by Quebec Nordiques (12/28/90). Member of 1986-87 ACHL champion Virginia Lancers. Last amateur club; Drummondville (QMJHL).

Dave Roberts — Left Wing

Regular Season / Playoffs

Season	Team	League	GP	G	A	PTS	PIM	GP	G	A	PTS	PIM
93-94	United States	National	49	17	28	45	68	—	—	—	—	—
93-94	United States	Olympic	8	1	5	6	4	—	—	—	—	—
93-94	St. Louis	NHL	1	0	0	0	2	3	0	0	0	12
93-94	Peoria	IHL	10	4	6	10	4	—	—	—	—	—
94-95	Peoria	IHL	65	30	38	68	65	—	—	—	—	—
94-95	St. Louis	NHL	19	6	5	11	10	6	0	0	0	4
95-96	St. Louis	NHL	28	1	6	7	12	—	—	—	—	—
95-96	Worcester	AHL	22	8	17	25	46	—	—	—	—	—
95-96	Edmonton	NHL	6	2	4	6	6	—	—	—	—	—
96-97	Vancouver	NHL	58	10	17	27	51	—	—	—	—	—
97-98	Vancouver	NHL	13	1	1	2	4	—	—	—	—	—
97-98	Syracuse	AHL	37	17	22	39	44	5	2	1	3	2
98-99	Michigan	IHL	75	32	38	70	77	4	1	2	3	2
	NHL	Totals	125	20	33	53	85	9	0	0	0	16
	IHL	Totals	150	66	82	148	146	4	1	2	3	2
	AHL	Totals	59	25	39	64	90	5	2	1	3	2

Born; 5/28/70, Alameda, California. 6-0, 185. Drafted by St. Louis Blues (5th choice, 114th overall) in 1989 Entry Draft. Traded to Edmonton Oilers by St. Louis for future considerations (3/12/96). Signed as a free agent by Vancouver Canucks (7/31/96). Signed as a free agent by Dallas Stars (7/30/98). Last amateur club; Michigan (CCHA).

Kurt Roberts — Defenseman

Regular Season / Playoffs

Season	Team	League	GP	G	A	PTS	PIM	GP	G	A	PTS	PIM
98-99	Asheville	UHL	3	0	1	1	0	—	—	—	—	—
98-99	Mohawk Valley	UHL	2	0	0	0	0	—	—	—	—	—
	UHL	Totals	5	0	1	1	0	—	—	—	—	—

Born; 7/5/76, Woodstock, Ontario. 6-1, 180.

Steve Roberts — Right Wing

Season	Team	League	GP	G	A	PTS	PIM	GP	G	A	PTS	PIM
			Regular Season					Playoffs				
95-96	Dayton	ECHL	41	20	16	36	39	—	—	—	—	—
96-97	Michigan	IHL	2	0	0	0	0	—	—	—	—	—
96-97	Baltimore	AHL	2	0	0	0	0	—	—	—	—	—
96-97	Dayton	ECHL	62	46	26	72	38	4	2	4	6	2
97-98	Providence	AHL	1	0	0	0	0	—	—	—	—	—
97-98	Cincinnati	IHL	15	3	3	6	4	5	1	0	1	0
97-98	Detroit	IHL	1	0	0	0	0	—	—	—	—	—
97-98	Dayton	ECHL	50	37	17	54	61	5	1	1	2	4
98-99	Nottingham	BSL	13	11	5	16	4	—	—	—	—	—
	IHL	Totals	18	3	3	6	4	5	1	0	1	0
	AHL	Totals	3	0	0	0	0	—	—	—	—	—
	ECHL	Totals	153	103	59	162	138	9	3	5	8	6

Born; 2/17/74, Saskatoon, Saskatchewan. 5-11, 190. Last amateur club; Lethbridge (WHL).

Chris Robertson — Center

Season	Team	League	GP	G	A	PTS	PIM	GP	G	A	PTS	PIM
			Regular Season					Playoffs				
89-90	Greensboro	ECHL	59	32	43	75	51	11	5	8	13	7
90-91	Greensboro	ECHL	3	0	1	1	2	—	—	—	—	—
90-91	Richmond	ECHL	21	8	12	20	27	—	—	—	—	—
93-94	Tulsa	CeHL	26	23	14	37	24	11	7	4	11	16
94-95	Tulsa	CeHL	17	6	10	16	24	7	5	4	9	6
95-96	Tulsa	CeHL	54	31	55	86	96	3	1	0	1	4
96-97	New Mexico	WPHL	40	29	39	68	60	6	5	5	10	14
97-98	Esberg	Denmark	47	26	30	56	88	—	—	—	—	—
98-99	Corpus Christi	WPHL	64	42	67	109	69	4	2	4	6	4
	WPHL	Totals	104	71	106	177	129	10	7	9	16	18
	CeHL	Totals	97	60	79	139	144	21	13	8	21	26
	ECHL	Totals	83	40	56	96	80	11	5	8	13	7

Born; 3/28/68, Calgary, Alberta. 6-0, 185. Member of 1989-90 ECHL champion Greensboro Monarchs. 1998-99 WPHL Most Valuable Player. Last amateur club; Brandon (WHL).

Bert Robertsson — Defenseman

Season	Team	League	GP	G	A	PTS	PIM	GP	G	A	PTS	PIM
			Regular Season					Playoffs				
95-96	Syracuse	AHL	65	1	7	8	109	16	0	1	1	26
96-97	Syracuse	AHL	80	4	9	13	132	3	1	0	1	4
97-98	Vancouver	NHL	30	2	4	6	24	—	—	—	—	—
97-98	Syracuse	AHL	42	5	9	14	87	3	0	0	0	6
98-99	Vancouver	NHL	39	2	2	4	13	—	—	—	—	—
98-99	Syracuse	AHL	8	1	0	1	21	—	—	—	—	—
	NHL	Totals	69	4	6	10	37	—	—	—	—	—
	AHL	Totals	195	11	25	36	349	22	1	1	2	36

Born; 6/30/74, Sodertalje, Sweden. 6-2, 198. Drafted by Vancouver Canucks (8th choice, 254th overall) in 1993 Entry Draft. Last European club; Sodertalje-2 (Sweden).

Stephane Robidas — Defenseman

Season	Team	League	GP	G	A	PTS	PIM	GP	G	A	PTS	PIM
			Regular Season					Playoffs				
97-98	Fredericton	AHL	79	10	21	31	50	4	0	2	2	0
98-99	Fredericton	AHL	79	8	33	41	59	15	1	5	6	10
	AHL	Totals	158	18	54	72	109	19	1	7	8	10

Born; 3/3/77, Sherbrooke, Quebec. 5-11, 192. Drafted by Montreal Canadiens (7th choice, 164th overall) in 1995 Entry Draft. Last amateur club; Shawinigan (QMJHL).

Jason Robinson — Defenseman

Season	Team	League	GP	G	A	PTS	PIM	GP	G	A	PTS	PIM
			Regular Season					Playoffs				
98-99	Cleveland	IHL	29	2	3	5	26	—	—	—	—	—
98-99	Chesapeake	ECHL	37	1	5	6	57	—	—	—	—	—

Born; 8/22/78, Goderich, Ontario. 6-2, 190. Drafted by Tampa Bay Lightning (3rd choice, 125th overall) in 1996 Entry Draft. Last amateur club; Erie (OHL).

Mark Robinson — Defenseman

Season	Team	League	GP	G	A	PTS	PIM	GP	G	A	PTS	PIM
			Regular Season					Playoffs				
98-99	Flint	UHL	3	0	0	0	9	—	—	—	—	—

Born; 4/3/78, Parry Sound, Ontario. 6-0, 210. Last amateur club; Huntsville

Nick Robinson — Defenseman

Season	Team	League	GP	G	A	PTS	PIM	GP	G	A	PTS	PIM
			Regular Season					Playoffs				
98-99	Kitchener	OHL	66	11	22	33	80	1	0	0	0	0
98-99	Dayton	ECHL	3	0	0	0	0	3	0	0	0	4

Born; Last amateur club; Kitchener (OHL).

Marc Robitaille — Goaltender

Season	Team	League	GP	W	L	T	MIN	SO	AVG	GP	W	L	MIN	SO	AVG
			Regular Season							Playoffs					
98-99	St. John's	AHL	42	13	22	1	2269	1	3.28	3	1	2	158	0	3.04

Born; 6/7/76, Gloucester, Ontario. 5-10, 185. Signed as a free agent by Toronto Maple Leafs (6/4/98). Last amateur club; Northeastern (Hockey East).

Patrice Robitaille — Right Wing

Season	Team	League	GP	G	A	PTS	PIM	GP	G	A	PTS	PIM
			Regular Season					Playoffs				
95-96	Peoria	IHL	69	27	28	55	49	—	—	—	—	—
95-96	Indianapolis	IHL	10	1	1	2	8	—	—	—	—	—
96-97	Milwaukee	IHL	12	1	2	3	4	—	—	—	—	—
96-97	Cincinnati	IHL	20	3	8	11	4	—	—	—	—	—
97-98	Phoenix	WCHL	30	16	19	35	12	9	6	7	13	6
98-99	Binghamton	UHL	71	18	57	75	38	5	2	1	3	0
	IHL	Totals	111	32	39	71	65	—	—	—	—	—

Born; 12/4/70, St. Catharine, Quebec. 6-0, 190. Last amateur club; Clarkson (ECAC).

Randy Robitaille — Center

Season	Team	League	GP	G	A	PTS	PIM	GP	G	A	PTS	PIM
			Regular Season					Playoffs				
96-97	Miami-Ohio	CCHA	39	27	34	61	44	—	—	—	—	—
96-97	Boston	NHL	1	0	0	0	0	—	—	—	—	—
97-98	Boston	NHL	4	0	0	0	0	—	—	—	—	—
97-98	Providence	AHL	48	15	29	44	16	—	—	—	—	—
98-99	Boston	NHL	4	0	2	2	0	1	0	0	0	0
98-99	Providence	AHL	74	28	*74	102	34	19	6	*14	20	20
	NHL	Totals	9	0	2	2	0	1	0	0	0	0
	AHL	Totals	122	43	103	146	50	19	6	14	20	20

Born; 10/12/75, Ottawa, Ontario. 5-11, 195. Signed as a free agent by Boston Bruins (3/27/97). Traded to Atlanta Thrashers by Boston for Peter Ferraro (6/25/99). 1998-99 AHL MVP. 1998-99 AHL First All-Star Team. Member of 1998-99 AHL Champion Providence Bruins. Last amateur club; Miami of Ohio

Derrick Robson — Defenseman

Season	Team	League	GP	G	A	PTS	PIM	GP	G	A	PTS	PIM
			Regular Season					Playoffs				
98-99	Winston-Salem	UHL	4	1	0	1	0	—	—	—	—	—

Born; 12/10/74, Acton, Ontario. 5-10, 190.

Lance Robson — Forward

Season	Team	League	GP	G	A	PTS	PIM	GP	G	A	PTS	PIM
			Regular Season					Playoffs				
97-98	Fayetteville	CHL	1	0	0	0	0	—	—	—	—	—
98-99	Fayetteville	CHL	10	0	2	2	0	—	—	—	—	—
	CHL	Totals	11	0	2	2	0	—	—	—	—	—

Born; Detroit, Michigan. 5-9, 190.

Dave Roche — Center
Regular Season — Playoffs

Season	Team	League	GP	G	A	PTS	PIM	GP	G	A	PTS	PIM
95-96	Pittsburgh	NHL	71	7	7	14	130	16	2	7	9	26
96-97	Pittsburgh	NHL	61	5	5	10	155	—	—	—	—	—
96-97	Cleveland	IHL	18	5	5	10	25	13	6	3	9	*87
97-98	Syracuse	AHL	73	12	20	32	307	5	2	0	2	10
98-99	Calgary	NHL	36	3	3	6	44	—	—	—	—	—
98-99	Saint John	AHL	7	0	3	3	6	—	—	—	—	—
	NHL	Totals	168	15	15	30	329	16	2	7	9	26
	AHL	Totals	80	12	23	35	313	5	2	0	2	10

Born; 6/13/75, Lindsay, Ontario. 6-4, 224. Drafted by Pittsburgh Penguins (3rd choice, 62nd overall) in 1993 Entry Draft. Traded to Calgary Flames with Ken Wregget for German Titov and Todd Hlushko (6/17/98). Last amateur club; Windsor (OHL).

Scott Roche — Goaltender
Regular Season — Playoffs

Season	Team	League	GP	W	L	T	MIN	SO	AVG	GP	W	L	MIN	SO	AVG
97-98	Detroit	IHL	4	0	1	0	147	0	3.27	—	—	—	—	—	—
97-98	Peoria	ECHL	38	23	11	3	2229	1	2.93	2	0	2	122	0	2.95
98-99	Worcester	AHL	9	2	3	1	339	0	3.19	—	—	—	—	—	—
98-99	Peoria	ECHL	7	3	3	1	418	0	2.72	—	—	—	—	—	—
	ECHL	Totals	45	26	14	4	2647	1	2.90	2	0	2	122	0	2.95

Born; 3/19/77, Lindsay, Ontario. 6-4, 220. Drafted by St. Louis Blues (2nd choice, 75th overall) in 1995 Entry Draft. Last amateur club; Windsor (OHL).

Richard Rochefort — Center
Regular Season — Playoffs

Season	Team	League	GP	G	A	PTS	PIM	GP	G	A	PTS	PIM
97-98	Albany	AHL	59	7	14	21	16	13	1	0	1	4
98-99	Albany	AHL	70	16	10	26	26	5	1	0	1	0
	AHL	Totals	129	23	24	47	42	18	2	0	2	4

Born; 1/7/77, North Bay, Ontario. 5-9, 180. Drafted by New Jersey Devils (9th choice, 174th overall) in 1995 Entry Draft. Last amateur club; Sarnia (OHL).

Patrick Rochon — Defenseman
Regular Season — Playoffs

Season	Team	League	GP	G	A	PTS	PIM	GP	G	A	PTS	PIM
96-97	Hershey	AHL	16	1	2	3	8	—	—	—	—	—
96-97	Mississippi	ECHL	54	5	23	28	88	3	0	2	2	26
97-98	Springfield	AHL	2	1	1	2	0	—	—	—	—	—
97-98	Mississippi	ECHL	68	10	30	40	74	—	—	—	—	—
98-99	Chicago	IHL	1	0	0	0	2	—	—	—	—	—
98-99	Mississippi	ECHL	70	3	35	38	113	17	2	7	9	28
	AHL	Totals	18	2	3	5	38	—	—	—	—	—
	ECHL	Totals	192	18	88	106	275	20	2	9	11	54

Born; 4/8/75, Ste. Martins, Quebec. 5-9, 182. Member of 1998-99 ECHL Champion Mississippi SeaWolves. Last amateur club; RIP (ECAC).

John Rockbrune — Defenseman
Regular Season — Playoffs

Season	Team	League	GP	G	A	PTS	PIM	GP	G	A	PTS	PIM
97-98	Shreveport	WPHL	2	0	0	0	15	—	—	—	—	—
98-99	Tulsa	CHL	18	1	0	1	56	—	—	—	—	—
98-99	Tucson	WCHL	6	0	0	0	50	—	—	—	—	—

Born; 7/24/74, Barrie, Ontario. 6-1, 215.

Andrew Rodgers — Left Wing
Regular Season — Playoffs

Season	Team	League	GP	G	A	PTS	PIM	GP	G	A	PTS	PIM
97-98	Odessa	WPHL	19	1	1	2	106	—	—	—	—	—
97-98	Fort Worth	CHL	2	0	0	0	4	—	—	—	—	—
97-98	Pensacola	ECHL	6	0	0	0	15	—	—	—	—	—
98-99	Odessa	WPHL	7	0	0	0	46	2	0	0	0	4
98-99	Pensacola	ECHL	41	2	1	3	105	—	—	—	—	—
	ECHL	Totals	47	2	1	3	120	—	—	—	—	—
	WPHL	Totals	26	1	1	2	152	—	—	—	—	—

Born; 12/21/75, Sterling, Ontario. 6-2, 200.

Marc Rodgers — Right Wing
Regular Season — Playoffs

Season	Team	League	GP	G	A	PTS	PIM	GP	G	A	PTS	PIM
92-93	Wheeling	ECHL	64	23	40	63	91	6	1	1	2	8
93-94	Las Vegas	IHL	40	7	7	14	110	4	0	2	2	17
93-94	Knoxville	ECHL	27	12	18	30	83	—	—	—	—	—
94-95	Las Vegas	IHL	58	17	19	36	131	10	2	6	8	16
95-96	Las Vegas	IHL	51	13	16	29	65	—	—	—	—	—
95-96	Utah	IHL	31	6	14	20	51	21	4	4	8	16
96-97	Utah	IHL	5	2	2	4	10	—	—	—	—	—
96-97	Quebec	IHL	70	25	42	67	115	9	1	9	10	14
97-98	Quebec	IHL	61	20	22	42	61	—	—	—	—	—
97-98	Chicago	IHL	11	5	5	10	22	22	9	9	18	10
98-99	Adirondack	AHL	80	19	38	57	66	3	0	0	0	10
	IHL	Totals	327	95	127	222	555	66	16	30	46	73
	ECHL	Totals	91	35	58	93	174	6	1	1	2	8

Born; 3/16/72, Bryson, Quebec. 5-10, 185. Traded to Chicago by Quebec with Steve Larouche for Dave Paradise and Jack Williams (3/98)Signed as a free agent by Detroit Red Wings (8/3/98). Member of 1995-96 IHL Champion Utah Grizzlies. Member of 1997-98 IHL Champion Chicago Wolves. Last amateur club; Longueuil (QMJHL).

Dmitri Rodine — Defenseman
Regular Season — Playoffs

Season	Team	League	GP	G	A	PTS	PIM	GP	G	A	PTS	PIM
96-97	Utah	IHL	3	0	0	0	4	—	—	—	—	—
96-97	Detroit	IHL	10	0	0	0	4	—	—	—	—	—
96-97	Flint	CoHL	58	7	25	32	35	11	0	0	0	6
97-98	Long Beach	IHL	2	0	1	1	0	—	—	—	—	—
97-98	Detroit	IHL	6	0	0	0	2	—	—	—	—	—
97-98	Michigan	IHL	5	1	0	1	4	—	—	—	—	—
97-98	Rochester	AHL	1	0	1	1	0	—	—	—	—	—
97-98	Flint	UHL	32	3	21	24	16	—	—	—	—	—
97-98	Winston-Salem	UHL	28	6	10	16	10	—	—	—	—	—
98-99	Winston-Salem	UHL	73	11	44	55	57	5	1	4	5	4
	IHL	Totals	26	1	1	2	14	—	—	—	—	—
	UHL	Totals	191	27	100	127	118	16	1	4	5	10

Born; 2/25/75, Tallinn, Estonia. 6-1, 205. Traded to Winston-Salem by Flint for John Batten, Brent Daugherty and Paul Vincent (1/98). Member of 1996-97 CoHL All-Rookie Team.

Jacque Rodrique — Defenseman
Regular Season — Playoffs

Season	Team	League	GP	G	A	PTS	PIM	GP	G	A	PTS	PIM
94-95	Maine	H.E.	43	11	26	37	44	—	—	—	—	—
94-95	Syracuse	AHL	2	0	1	1	0	—	—	—	—	—
95-96	Dayton	ECHL	30	1	10	11	31	—	—	—	—	—
95-96	Richmond	ECHL	5	2	2	4	10	—	—	—	—	—
95-96	Columbus	ECHL	13	4	9	13	12	3	0	1	1	12
96-97	Fort Wayne	IHL	1	0	0	0	0	—	—	—	—	—
96-97	Utica	CoHL	37	9	20	29	28	—	—	—	—	—
96-97	Dayton	CoHL	35	6	24	30	36	—	—	—	—	—
97-98	Phoenix	WCHL	32	3	12	15	52	—	—	—	—	—
97-98	Odessa	WPHL	18	4	15	19	45	—	—	—	—	—
98-99	Odessa	WPHL	68	11	40	51	124	3	0	2	2	6
	WPHL	Totals	86	15	55	70	169	3	0	2	2	6
	CoHL	Totals	72	15	44	59	64	—	—	—	—	—
	ECHL	Totals	48	7	21	28	53	3	0	1	1	12

Born; 5/7/71, Nashua, New Hampshire. 6-0, 195. Last amateur club; Maine (Hockey East).

Peter Roed — Center
Regular Season — Playoffs

Season	Team	League	GP	G	A	PTS	PIM	GP	G	A	PTS	PIM
96-97	Prince George	WHL	51	21	16	37	8	14	5	2	7	9
96-97	Louisville	ECHL	7	1	0	1	4	—	—	—	—	—
97-98	Kentucky	AHL	67	6	7	13	44	—	—	—	—	—
97-98	Louisville	ECHL	4	0	2	2	10	—	—	—	—	—
98-99	Richmond	ECHL	60	26	24	50	68	18	6	10	16	14

Born; 11/15/76, St. Paul, Minnesota. 5-10, 210. Drafted by San Jose Sharks (2nd choice, 38th overall) in 1995 Entry Draft. Last amateur club; Prince George

Trevor Roenick — Right Wing
Regular Season — Playoffs

Season	Team	League	GP	G	A	PTS	PIM	GP	G	A	PTS	PIM
96-97	Maine	H.E.	35	16	14	30	54	—	—	—	—	—
96-97	Springfield	AHL	7	1	1	2	8	—	—	—	—	—
96-97	Phoenix	IHL	8	2	2	4	22	—	—	—	—	—
97-98	Las Vegas	IHL	69	14	12	26	105	4	0	3	3	14
97-98	Tacoma	WCHL	11	7	7	14	17	—	—	—	—	—
98-99	Las Vegas	IHL	32	3	4	7	43	—	—	—	—	—
98-99	Utah	IHL	21	0	2	2	17	—	—	—	—	—
98-99	Tacoma	WCHL	12	3	12	15	15	11	6	8	14	44
	IHL	Totals	130	19	20	39	187	4	0	3	3	14
	WCHL	Totals	23	10	19	29	32	11	6	8	14	44

Born; 10/7/74, Derby, Connecticut. 6-1, 200. Drafted by Hartford Whalers (3rd choice, 84th overall) in 1993 Entry Draft. Last amateur club; Maine (H.E.)

Stacy Roest — Center
Regular Season — Playoffs

Season	Team	League	GP	G	A	PTS	PIM	GP	G	A	PTS	PIM
94-95	Medicine Hat	WHL	69	37	78	115	32	5	2	7	9	2
94-95	Adirondack	AHL	3	0	0	0	0	—	—	—	—	—
95-96	Adirondack	AHL	76	16	39	55	40	3	0	0	0	2
96-97	Adirondack	AHL	78	25	41	66	30	4	1	1	2	0
97-98	Adirondack	AHL	80	34	58	92	30	3	2	1	3	6
98-99	Detroit	NHL	59	4	8	12	14	—	—	—	—	—
98-99	Adirondack	AHL	2	0	1	1	0	—	—	—	—	—
	AHL	Totals	239	75	139	214	100	10	3	2	5	8

Born; 3/15/74, Lethbridge, Alberta. 5-9, 191. Signed as a free agent by Detroit Red Wings (6/9/97). 1997-98 In The Crease Minor-Pro Player of the Year. Last amateur club; Medicine Hat (WHL).

John Rohloff — Defenseman
Regular Season — Playoffs

Season	Team	League	GP	G	A	PTS	PIM	GP	G	A	PTS	PIM
93-94	Providence	AHL	55	12	23	35	59	—	—	—	—	—
94-95	Boston	NHL	34	3	8	11	39	5	0	0	0	6
94-95	Providence	AHL	4	2	1	3	6	—	—	—	—	—
95-96	Boston	NHL	79	1	12	13	59	5	1	2	3	2
96-97	Boston	NHL	37	3	5	8	31	—	—	—	—	—
96-97	Providence	AHL	3	1	1	2	0	—	—	—	—	—
97-98	Providence	AHL	58	6	17	23	46	—	—	—	—	—
98-99	Kentucky	AHL	12	0	1	1	8	—	—	—	—	—
98-99	Kansas City	IHL	41	5	13	18	42	3	0	0	0	18
	NHL	Totals	150	7	25	32	129	10	1	2	3	8
	AHL	Totals	132	21	43	64	119	—	—	—	—	—

Born; 10/3/69, Mankato, Minnesota. 6-0, 221. Drafted by Boston Bruins (7th chocie, 186th overall) in 1988 Entry Draft. Signed as a free agent by San Jose Sharks (7/22/98). Last amateur club; Minnesota-Duluth (WCHA).

Todd Rohloff — Defenseman
Regular Season — Playoffs

Season	Team	League	GP	G	A	PTS	PIM	GP	G	A	PTS	PIM
97-98	Miami-Ohio	CCHA	17	2	5	7	38	—	—	—	—	—
97-98	Indianapolis	IHL	5	0	1	1	6	1	0	0	0	0
98-99	Portland	AHL	58	1	6	7	59	—	—	—	—	—
98-99	Indianapolis	IHL	12	2	0	2	8	5	1	1	2	6
	IHL	Totals	17	2	1	3	14	6	1	1	2	6

Born; 1/16/74, Grand Rapids, Minnesota. 6-3, 213. Signed as a free agent by Chicago Blackhawks (7/8/98). Last amateur club; Miami of Ohio (CCHA).

Layne Roland — Right Wing
Regular Season — Playoffs

Season	Team	League	GP	G	A	PTS	PIM	GP	G	A	PTS	PIM
95-96	Dayton	ECHL	3	0	2	2	2	—	—	—	—	—
95-96	Erie	ECHL	64	27	33	60	40	—	—	—	—	—
96-97	Amarillo	WPHL	28	16	12	28	23	—	—	—	—	—
96-97	Central Texas	WPHL	22	8	7	15	6	11	7	10	17	14
97-98	Central Texas	WPHL	69	53	42	95	44	4	0	1	1	8
98-99	Amberg	Germany	35	37	30	67	100	—	—	—	—	—
	WPHL	Totals	119	77	61	138	73	15	7	11	18	22
	ECHL	Totals	67	27	35	62	42	—	—	—	—	—

Born; 2/6/74, Vernon, British Columbia. 6-2, 205. Drafted by Chicago Blackhawks (8th choice, 185th overall) in 1992 Entry Draft. Last amateur club; Port-

Dwayne Roloson — Goaltender
Regular Season — Playoffs

Season	Team	League	GP	W	L	T	MIN	SO	AVG	GP	W	L	MIN	SO	AVG
94-95	Saint John	AHL	46	16	21	8	2734	1	3.42	5	1	4	298	0	2.61
95-96	Saint John	AHL	67	*33	22	11	4026	1	2.83	16	10	6	1027	1	2.86
96-97	Calgary	NHL	31	9	14	3	1618	1	2.89	—	—	—	—	—	—
96-97	Saint John	AHL	8	6	2	0	480	1	2.75	—	—	—	—	—	—
97-98	Calgary	NHL	39	11	16	8	2205	0	2.99	—	—	—	—	—	—
97-98	Saint John	AHL	4	3	0	1	245	0	1.96	—	—	—	—	—	—
98-99	Buffalo	NHL	18	6	8	2	911	1	2.77	4	1	1	139	0	4.32
98-99	Rochester	AHL	2	2	0	0	120	0	2.00	—	—	—	—	—	—
	NHL	Totals	88	26	38	13	4734	2	2.92	4	1	1	139	0	4.32
	AHL	Totals	127	60	45	20	7605	3	3.00	21	11	10	1325	1	2.81

Born; 10/12/69, Simcoe, Ontario. 6-1, 180. Signed as afree agent by Calgary Flames (7/4/94). Signed as a free agent by Buffalo Sabres (7/9/98). Last amateur club; Lowell (Hockey East).

Russ Romaniuk — Left Wing
Regular Season — Playoffs

Season	Team	League	GP	G	A	PTS	PIM	GP	G	A	PTS	PIM
91-92	Winnipeg	NHL	27	3	5	8	18	—	—	—	—	—
91-92	Moncton	AHL	45	16	15	31	25	10	5	4	9	19
92-93	Winnipeg	NHL	28	3	1	4	22	1	0	0	0	0
92-93	Moncton	AHL	28	18	8	26	40	5	0	4	4	2
92-93	Fort Wayne	IHL	4	2	0	2	7	—	—	—	—	—
93-94	Canadian	National	34	8	9	17	17	—	—	—	—	—
93-94	Winnipeg	NHL	24	4	8	12	6	—	—	—	—	—
93-94	Moncton	AHL	18	16	8	24	24	17	2	6	8	30
94-95	Winnipeg	NHL	6	0	0	0	0	—	—	—	—	—
94-95	Springfield	AHL	17	5	7	12	29	—	—	—	—	—
95-96	Philadelphia	NHL	17	3	0	3	17	1	0	0	0	0
95-96	Hershey	AHL	27	19	10	29	43	—	—	—	—	—
96-97	Manitoba	IHL	46	14	13	27	43	—	—	—	—	—
97-98	Manitoba	IHL	5	0	1	1	8	—	—	—	—	—
97-98	Long Beach	IHL	49	16	11	27	37	—	—	—	—	—
97-98	Las Vegas	IHL	22	6	4	10	10	4	2	2	4	4
98-99	Las Vegas	IHL	82	43	20	63	91	—	—	—	—	—
	NHL	Totals	102	13	14	27	63	2	0	0	0	0
	IHL	Totals	208	81	49	130	196	4	2	2	4	4
	AHL	Totals	135	74	48	122	161	32	7	14	21	51

Born; 5/9/70, Winnipeg, Manitoba. 6-0, 185. Drafted by Winnipeg Jets (2nd choice, 31st overall) in 1988 Entry Draft. Traded to Philadelphia Flyers by Winnipeg for Jeff Finley (6/27/95). Traded to Long Beach by Manitoba for Brian Chapman (10/97). Last amateur club; North Dakota (WCHA).

Peter Romeo — Right Wing
Regular Season — Playoffs

Season	Team	League	GP	G	A	PTS	PIM	GP	G	A	PTS	PIM
94-95	Thunder Bay	CoHL	25	2	6	8	19	—	—	—	—	—
94-95	Brantford	CoHL	1	0	0	0	5	—	—	—	—	—
94-95	Johnstown	ECHL	11	0	4	4	16	—	—	—	—	—
95-96												
96-97	Bracknell	BHL	36	14	9	23	42	—	—	—	—	—
97-98	Columbus	CHL	7	1	1	2	12	—	—	—	—	—
97-98	Tucson	WCHL	42	13	34	47	97	—	—	—	—	—
98-99	Saginaw	UHL	30	3	9	12	41	—	—	—	—	—
98-99	Mohawk Valley	UHL	4	0	1	1	2	—	—	—	—	—
	UHL	Totals	60	5	16	21	67	—	—	—	—	—

Born; 6/25/71, Ancaster, Ontario. 6-1, 205. Last amateur club; Elmira (NCAA 3).

Jeff Romfo — Right Wing
Regular Season — Playoffs

Season	Team	League	GP	G	A	PTS	PIM	GP	G	A	PTS	PIM
96-97	South Carolina	ECHL	51	15	33	48	36	15	4	4	8	10
97-98	South Carolina	ECHL	70	14	26	40	82	5	1	1	2	8
98-99	Lowell	AHL	3	0	0	0	2	—	—	—	—	—
98-99	South Carolina	ECHL	69	25	44	69	124	3	1	0	1	0
	ECHL	Totals	190	54	103	157	242	23	6	5	11	18

Born; 2/9/74, Blaine, Minnesota. 5-11, 195. Drafted by Minnesota North Stars (8th choice, 226th overall) in 1992 Entry Draft. Member of 1996-97 ECHL Champion South Carolina Stingrays. Last amateur club; Minnesota-Duluth

Allan Rooney — Goaltender

Regular Season / Playoffs

Season	Team	League	GP	W	L	T	MIN	SO	AVG	GP	W	L	MIN	SO	AVG
96-97	Nashville	CeHL	17	3	13	0	918	0	4.44	—	—	—	—	—	—
96-97	Port Huron	CoHL	9	3	3	0	394	0	4.27	—	—	—	—	—	—
97-98	San Angelo	WPHL	24	12	8	0	1267	0	4.26	3	0	3	159	0	5.28
98-99	San Angelo	WPHL	22	7	10	2	1165	1	4.12	3	0	1	31	0	9.81
	WPHL	Totals	46	19	18	2	2432	1	4.19	6	0	4	190	0	5.99

Born; 12/28/72, North Babylon, New York. 5-10, 175. Last amateur club; Buffalo State (SUNY).

Ryan Root — Defenseman

Regular Season / Playoffs

Season	Team	League	GP	G	A	PTS	PIM	GP	G	A	PTS	PIM
98-99	Columbus	ECHL	8	0	2	2	4	—	—	—	—	—
98-99	El Paso	WPHL	6	0	1	1	4	—	—	—	—	—
98-99	Central Texas	WPHL	10	1	0	1	8	—	—	—	—	—
98-99	Austin	WPHL	1	0	0	0	0	—	—	—	—	—
	WPHL	Totals	17	1	1	2	12	—	—	—	—	—

Born; 1/18/75, Pueblo, Colorado. 5-11, 215. Last amateur club; Ohio State

Pavel Rosa — Right Wing

Regular Season / Playoffs

Season	Team	League	GP	G	A	PTS	PIM	GP	G	A	PTS	PIM
97-98	Fredericton	AHL	1	0	0	0	0	—	—	—	—	—
97-98	Long Beach	IHL	2	0	1	1	0	1	1	1	2	0
98-99	Los Angeles	NHL	29	4	12	16	6	—	—	—	—	—
98-99	Long Beach	IHL	31	17	13	30	28	6	1	2	3	0
	IHL	Totals	33	17	14	31	28	7	2	3	5	0

Born; 6/7/77, Most, Czechoslovakia. 5-11, 180. Drafted by Los Angeles Kings (3rd choice, 50th overall) in 1995 Entry Draft. Last amateur club; Hull (QJMHL).

Mike Rosati — Goaltender

Regular Season / Playoffs

Season	Team	League	GP	W	L	T	MIN	SO	AVG	GP	W	L	MIN	SO	AVG
89-90	Erie	ECHL	18	12	5	0	1056	0	4.14	—	—	—	—	—	—
90-91	Bolzano	Italy	46	—	—	—	2700	0	4.71	—	—	—	—	—	—
91-92	Bolzano	Italy	18	11	6	1	1022	2	3.22	7	5	2	409	0	4.28
92-93	Bolzano	Italy	NA												
93-94	Bolzano	Italy	NA												
94-95	Bolzano	Italy	47	—	—	—	2705	1	3.30	—	—	—	—	—	—
95-96	Bolzano	Italy	42	—	—	—	2465	3	3.33	—	—	—	—	—	—
96-97	Mannheim	Germany	44	—	—	—	2625	6	2.38	9	—	—	514	0	2.80
97-98	Mannheim	Germany	43	—	—	—	2567	2	2.71	*10	*9	1	569	*1	*2.00
98-99	Washington	NHL	1	1	0	0	28	0	0.00	—	—	—	—	—	—
98-99	Portland	AHL	32	9	23	0	1783	1	3.74	—	—	—	—	—	—
98-99	Manitoba	IHL	8	5	1	2	479	1	2.00	5	2	3	314	0	3.44

Born; 1/7/68, Toronto, Ontario. 5-10, 170. Drafted by New York Rangers (6th choice, 131st overall) in 1988 Entry Draft. Signed as a free agent by Washington Capitals (7/15/88). Last amateur club; Niagara Falls (OHL).

Jason Rose — Defenseman

Regular Season / Playoffs

Season	Team	League	GP	G	A	PTS	PIM	GP	G	A	PTS	PIM
96-97	El Paso	WPHL	60	6	14	20	103	9	1	4	5	15
97-98	El Paso	WPHL	39	2	11	13	104	—	—	—	—	—
97-98	Austin	WPHL	10	0	1	1	11	—	—	—	—	—
97-98	Waco	WPHL	7	1	2	3	2	—	—	—	—	—
98-99	Phoenix	WCHL	42	3	7	10	102	—	—	—	—	—
98-99	Idaho	WCHL	9	1	4	5	13	1	0	0	0	2
	WPHL	Totals	116	9	28	37	220	9	1	4	5	15
	WCHL	Totals	51	4	11	15	115	1	0	0	0	2

Born; 1/12/75, Martensville, Saskatchewan. 6-0, 180. Traded to Austin by El Paso with Derek Riley for Corey Fletcher and Chris Morque (1/98). Traded to Waco by Austin with Derek Riley and Chris Haskett for Rob Schriner (3/98). Traded to Idaho by Phoenix with Stu Kulak for Mario Therrien and Alex Alepin (2/99). Member of 1996-97 WPHL Champion El Paso Buzzards.

Paul Rosebush — Left Wing

Regular Season / Playoffs

Season	Team	League	GP	G	A	PTS	PIM	GP	G	A	PTS	PIM
98-99	Guelph	OUAA										
98-99	Port Huron	UHL	7	4	4	8	0	5	0	2	2	0

Born; 7/5/75, Wellington, Ontario. 5-11, 185. Last amateur club; Guelph

Howie Rosenblatt — Right Wing

Regular Season / Playoffs

Season	Team	League	GP	G	A	PTS	PIM	GP	G	A	PTS	PIM
91-92	Maine	AHL	2	0	0	0	9	—	—	—	—	—
91-92	Cincinnati	ECHL	50	26	16	42	235	9	3	8	11	55
92-93	Cincinnati	IHL	45	10	7	17	201	—	—	—	—	—
92-93	Birmingham	ECHL	6	4	3	7	23	—	—	—	—	—
93-94	Providence	AHL	19	6	4	10	59	—	—	—	—	—
93-94	Charlotte	ECHL	44	21	17	38	173	3	3	3	6	2
94-95	Providence	AHL	3	0	0	0	7	1	0	0	0	0
94-95	Charlotte	ECHL	5	1	1	2	38	—	—	—	—	—
94-95	Greensboro	ECHL	41	12	34	46	245	14	5	1	6	76
95-96	Raleigh	ECHL	25	4	13	17	109	—	—	—	—	—
95-96	Dayton	ECHL	7	2	2	4	27	—	—	—	—	—
96-97	San Antonio	IHL	15	2	4	6	26	—	—	—	—	—
96-97	Quad City	CoHL	40	13	32	45	123	14	3	9	12	*58
97-98	Portland	AHL	1	0	0	0	0	—	—	—	—	—
97-98	Quad City	UHL	24	8	14	22	71	—	—	—	—	—
98-99	Quad City	UHL	29	6	7	13	119	10	3	7	10	14
	IHL	Totals	60	12	11	23	227	—	—	—	—	—
	AHL	Totals	25	6	4	10	75	1	0	0	0	0
	ECHL	Totals	178	70	86	156	850	26	11	12	23	133
	UHL	Totals	93	27	53	80	313	24	6	16	22	72

Born; 1/3/69, Philadelphia, Pennsylvania. 6-0, 205. Member of 1996-97 CoHL Champion Quad City Mallards. Last amateur club; Merrimack (Hockey East).

Andy Ross — Left Wing

Regular Season / Playoffs

Season	Team	League	GP	G	A	PTS	PIM	GP	G	A	PTS	PIM
90-91	Erie	ECHL	54	10	19	29	96	1	0	0	0	0
91-92	Knoxville	ECHL	9	2	3	5	2	—	—	—	—	—
91-92	Erie	ECHL	36	13	16	29	53	—	—	—	—	—
92-93	Memphis	CeHL	50	23	24	47	130	6	1	1	2	11
93-94	Memphis	CeHL	55	18	21	39	56	—	—	—	—	—
94-95	Memphis	CeHL	47	18	17	35	55	—	—	—	—	—
94-95	Tulsa	CeHL	17	4	6	10	12	—	—	—	—	—
95-96	Memphis	CeHL	62	12	20	32	118	5	1	0	1	0
96-97	Austin	WPHL	61	35	34	69	34	6	3	0	3	10
97-98	Austin	WPHL	69	27	37	64	60	5	0	1	1	0
98-99	Austin	WPHL	69	12	26	38	76	—	—	—	—	—
	CeHL	Totals	231	75	88	163	371	11	2	1	3	11
	WPHL	Totals	199	74	97	171	170	11	3	1	4	10
	ECHL	Totals	99	25	38	63	151	1	0	0	0	0

Born; 5/24/70, Philadelphia, Pennsylvania. 6-3, 215.

Mike Ross — Defense

Regular Season / Playoffs

Season	Team	League	GP	G	A	PTS	PIM	GP	G	A	PTS	PIM
92-93	Fargo-Moorhead	AHA	30	10	27	37	28	—	—	—	—	—
92-93	Louisville	ECHL	5	0	0	0	2	—	—	—	—	—
93-94												
94-95												
95-96												
96-97												
97-98	Lake Charles	WPHL	22	1	8	9	29	4	0	1	1	13
98-99	Odessa	WPHL	61	4	11	15	38	3	0	0	0	0
	WPHL	Totals	83	5	19	24	67	7	0	1	1	13

Born; 6/7/67, Roseau, Minnesota. 5-10, 175. Last amateur club; Western Michigan University (CCHA).

Nick Ross — Defense

Regular Season / Playoffs

Season	Team	League	GP	G	A	PTS	PIM	GP	G	A	PTS	PIM
98-99	Flint	UHL	5	0	0	0	0	—	—	—	—	—

Born;

Scott Ross — Forward
Regular Season / Playoffs

Season	Team	League	GP	G	A	PTS	PIM	GP	G	A	PTS	PIM
98-99	Fort Worth	WPHL	5	1	0	1	26	—	—	—	—	—

Born; 11/4/77, Bonnyville, Alberta. 6-1, 210.

Steve Ross — Defense
Regular Season / Playoffs

Season	Team	League	GP	G	A	PTS	PIM	GP	G	A	PTS	PIM
94-95	Fresno	SUN	5	0	1	1	6	—	—	—	—	—
95-96												
96-97												
97-98	Lake Charles	WPHL	22	2	11	13	8	4	0	2	2	0
98-99	Arkansas	WPHL	56	5	18	23	18	—	—	—	—	—
	WPHL	Totals	78	7	29	36	36	4	0	2	2	0

Born; 11/19/68, Roseau, Minnesota. 5-11, 190. Selected in 1998 WPHL Expansion Draft by Arkansas (5/30/98).

Blair Rota — Left Wing
Regular Season / Playoffs

Season	Team	League	GP	G	A	PTS	PIM	GP	G	A	PTS	PIM
98-99	San Antonio	CHL	70	16	16	32	82	7	3	1	4	12

Born; 11/6/77, Kamloops, British Columbia. 5-10, 185.

Guy Rouleau — Center
Regular Season / Playoffs

Season	Team	League	GP	G	A	PTS	PIM	GP	G	A	PTS	PIM
86-87	Sherbrooke	AHL	10	4	3	7	2	2	0	0	0	0
87-88	Sherbrooke	AHL	76	26	47	73	42	4	0	1	1	2
88-89												
89-90	Erie	ECHL	13	9	10	19	9	—	—	—	—	—
89-90	Springfield	AHL	52	18	26	44	14	18	9	9	18	20
90-91												
91-92												
92-93												
93-94	Peoria	IHL	6	0	2	2	0	—	—	—	—	—
94-95												
95-96												
96-97												
97-98	Reno	WCHL	12	5	7	12	4	—	—	—	—	—
98-99	Erford											
	AHL	Totals	138	48	76	124	58	24	9	10	19	22

Born; 2/16/65, Beloeil, Quebec. 5-9, 175. Signed as a free agent by Montreal Canadiens (4/30/86). Member of 1989-90 AHL Champion Springfield Indians. Last amateur club; Hull (QMJHL).

Alan Roulette — Defenseman
Regular Season / Playoffs

Season	Team	League	GP	G	A	PTS	PIM	GP	G	A	PTS	PIM
97-98	Thunder Bay	UHL	14	1	1	2	26	—	—	—	—	—
98-99	Thunder Bay	UHL	63	11	16	27	53	13	1	1	2	4
	UHL	Totals	77	12	17	29	79	13	1	1	2	4

Born; 1/25/75, Portage la Prairie, Quebec. 6-0, 185. Selected by Missouri River Otters in 1999 UHL Expansion Draft.

Ivan Roulette — Forward
Regular Season / Playoffs

Season	Team	League	GP	G	A	PTS	PIM	GP	G	A	PTS	PIM
94-95	Dallas	CeHL	9	1	2	3	0	—	—	—	—	—
95-96												
96-97												
97-98	Thunder Bay	UHL	4	0	0	0	5	—	—	—	—	—
98-99	Fort Worth	WPHL	14	2	0	2	6	—	—	—	—	—

Born; 7/31/72, Portage la Prairie, Quebec. 6-2, 210.

Sean Rowe — Right Wing
Regular Season / Playoffs

Season	Team	League	GP	G	A	PTS	PIM	GP	G	A	PTS	PIM
93-94	Fort Worth	CeHL	61	22	35	57	43	—	—	—	—	—
94-95	Fort Worth	CeHL	56	22	40	62	19	—	—	—	—	—
95-96	Louisiana	ECHL	47	24	22	46	28	—	—	—	—	—
95-96	Columbus	ECHL	13	14	10	24	8	3	0	2	2	0
96-97	Anchorage	WCHL	58	43	53	96	40	9	5	6	11	6
97-98	Anchorage	WCHL	56	35	42	77	24	8	5	3	8	12
98-99	Anchorage	WCHL	66	32	64	96	39	6	2	2	4	6
	WCHL	Totals	180	110	159	269	103	23	12	11	23	24
	CeHL	Totals	117	44	75	119	62	—	—	—	—	—
	ECHL	Totals	60	38	32	70	36	3	0	2	2	0

Born; 12/17/70, Montreal, Quebec. 6-1, 200. 1996-97 ECHL Second Team All-

Chris Rowland — Right Wing
Regular Season / Playoffs

Season	Team	League	GP	G	A	PTS	PIM	GP	G	A	PTS	PIM
92-93	Prince Edward Island	AHL	34	4	4	8	65	—	—	—	—	—
92-93	Thunder Bay	CoHL	22	5	3	8	65	11	3	4	7	44
93-94	Prince Edward Island	AHL	40	6	2	8	122	—	—	—	—	—
93-94	Thunder Bay	CoHL	14	4	6	10	13	9	3	2	5	31
94-95	Fort Wayne	IHL	5	0	1	1	14	—	—	—	—	—
94-95	Prince Edward Island	AHL	8	1	0	1	5	—	—	—	—	—
94-95	Thunder Bay	CoHL	64	30	44	74	255	11	7	7	14	34
95-96	Fort Wayne	IHL	1	0	0	0	2	—	—	—	—	—
95-96	Louisville	ECHL	65	28	23	51	373	1	0	0	0	10
96-97	Baltimore	AHL	5	0	1	1	15	—	—	—	—	—
96-97	Louisville	ECHL	46	9	25	34	256	—	—	—	—	—
96-97	South Carolina	ECHL	14	4	6	10	69	18	5	5	10	39
97-98	South Carolina	ECHL	13	0	0	0	61	—	—	—	—	—
97-98	New Orleans	ECHL	13	3	4	7	73	—	—	—	—	—
97-98	Fresno	WCHL	9	5	7	12	50	5	2	2	4	8
98-99	Miami	ECHL	70	14	12	26	264	—	—	—	—	—
	AHL	Totals	87	11	7	18	197	—	—	—	—	—
	IHL	Totals	6	0	1	1	16	—	—	—	—	—
	ECHL	Totals	221	58	70	128	1096	19	5	5	10	49
	CoHL	Totals	100	39	53	92	333	31	13	13	26	109

Born; 3/30/71, Sylvan Lake, Manitoba. 6-1, 195. Sold to New Orleans by South Carolina (11/97). Selected by Wheeling in 1999 ECHL Dispersal Draft. Member of 1993-94 CoHL champion Thunder Bay Senators. Member of 1994-95 CoHL champion Thunder Bay Senators. Member of 1996-97 ECHL Champion South Carolina Stingrays. Last amateur club; Portland (WHL).

Andre Roy — Left Wing
Regular Season / Playoffs

Season	Team	League	GP	G	A	PTS	PIM	GP	G	A	PTS	PIM
95-96	Boston	NHL	3	0	0	0	0	—	—	—	—	—
95-96	Providence	AHL	58	7	8	15	167	1	0	0	0	10
96-97	Boston	NHL	10	0	2	2	12	—	—	—	—	—
96-97	Providence	AHL	50	17	11	28	234	—	—	—	—	—
97-98	Providence	AHL	36	3	11	14	154	—	—	—	—	—
97-98	Charlotte	ECHL	27	10	8	18	132	7	2	3	5	34
98-99	Fort Wayne	IHL	65	15	6	21	395	2	0	0	0	11
	NHL	Totals	13	0	2	2	12	—	—	—	—	—
	AHL	Totals	144	27	30	57	555	1	0	0	0	10

Born; 2/8/75, Port Chester, New York. 6-3, 178. Drafted by Boston Bruins (5th choice, 151st overall) in 1994 Entry Draft. Signed as a free agent by Ottawa Senators (3/19/99). Last amateur club; Drummondville (QMJHL).

Jean-Yves Roy — Right Wing

Regular Season / Playoffs

Season	Team	League	GP	G	A	PTS	PIM	GP	G	A	PTS	PIM
92-93	Binghamton	AHL	49	13	15	28	21	14	5	2	7	4
92-93	Canada	National	23	9	6	15	35	—	—	—	—	—
93-94	Binghamton	AHL	65	41	24	65	33	—	—	—	—	—
93-94	Canada	National	6	3	2	5	2	—	—	—	—	—
93-94	Canada	Olympic	8	1	0	1	0	—	—	—	—	—
94-95	Rangers	NHL	3	1	0	1	2	—	—	—	—	—
94-95	Binghamton	AHL	67	41	36	77	28	11	4	6	10	12
95-96	Ottawa	NHL	4	1	1	2	2	—	—	—	—	—
95-96	Prince Edward Island	AHL	67	40	55	95	64	5	4	8	12	6
96-97	Boston	NHL	52	10	15	25	22	—	—	—	—	—
96-97	Providence	AHL	27	9	16	25	30	10	2	7	9	2
97-98	Boston	NHL	2	0	0	0	0	—	—	—	—	—
97-98	Providence	AHL	65	28	34	62	60	—	—	—	—	—
98-99	Heraklith	Austria	30	26	32	58	26	—	—	—	—	—
	NHL	Totals	59	12	16	28	26	—	—	—	—	—
	AHL	Totals	340	172	180	352	236	40	15	23	38	24

Born; 2/17/69, Rosemere, Quebec. 5-10, 180. Signed as a free agent by the New York Rangers (7/20/92). Traded to Ottawa Senators by Rangers for Steve Larouche (10/5/92). Signed as a free agent by Boston Bruins (7/15/96). Last amateur club; Maine (Hockey East).

Jimmy Roy — Right Wing

Regular Season / Playoffs

Season	Team	League	GP	G	A	PTS	PIM	GP	G	A	PTS	PIM
96-97	Canada	National	55	10	17	27	82	—	—	—	—	—
97-98	Manitoba	IHL	61	8	10	18	133	3	0	0	0	6
98-99	Manitoba	IHL	78	10	16	26	185	5	0	1	1	6
	IHL	Totals	139	18	26	44	318	8	0	1	1	12

Born; 9/22/75, Sioux Lookout, Ontario. 5-11, 170. Drafted by Dallas Stars (7th choice, 254th overall) in 1994 Entry Draft. Last amateur club; Michigan Tech (WCHA).

Serge Roy — Defenseman

Regular Season / Playoffs

Season	Team	League	GP	G	A	PTS	PIM	GP	G	A	PTS	PIM
83-84	Nova Scotia	AHL	5	0	2	2	0	—	—	—	—	—
84-85												
85-86	Canada	National	67	8	34	42	53	—	—	—	—	—
86-87	National	National	16	1	2	3	14	—	—	—	—	—
87-88	Adirondack	AHL	9	0	1	1	0	5	1	2	3	9
88-89												
89-90	Fort Wayne	IHL	19	1	4	5	13	—	—	—	—	—
90-91	Canada	National	5	0	2	2	4	—	—	—	—	—
90-91	Phoenix	IHL	7	1	4	5	25	—	—	—	—	—
90-91	New Haven	AHL	46	3	12	15	25	—	—	—	—	—
91-92	Brantford	CoHL	11	2	9	11	16	—	—	—	—	—
92-93												
93-94												
94-95												
95-96	San Diego	WCHL	53	9	46	55	61	8	0	2	2	14
96-97	San Diego	WCHL	45	8	22	30	48	6	1	1	2	4
97-98	San Diego	WCHL	56	7	27	34	76	3	0	0	0	6
98-99	San Diego	WCHL	15	4	10	14	11	—	—	—	—	—
98-99	Fresno	WCHL	12	1	6	7	8	7	0	4	4	6
	IHL	Totals	26	2	8	10	38	—	—	—	—	—
	AHL	Totals	14	0	3	3	0	5	1	2	3	9
	WCHL	Totals	181	29	111	140	204	24	1	7	8	30

Born; 6/25/62, Sept-Iles, Quebec. 5-9, 190. Traded to Fresno by San Diego by Hakan Jansson (1/99). 1995-96 WCHL First Team All-Star. Member of 1995-96 WCHL champion San Diego Gulls. Member of 1996-97 WCHL Champion San Diego Gulls. Member of 1997-98 WCHL Champion San Diego Gulls.

Stephane Roy — Center

Regular Season / Playoffs

Season	Team	League	GP	G	A	PTS	PIM	GP	G	A	PTS	PIM
87-88	Minnesota	NHL	12	1	0	1	0	—	—	—	—	—
87-88	Kalamazoo	IHL	58	21	12	33	52	5	1	2	3	11
88-89	Kalamazoo	IHL	20	5	4	9	27	—	—	—	—	—
88-89	Halifax	AHL	42	8	16	24	28	1	0	0	0	0
89-90												
90-91	Canada	National	52	22	22	44	6	—	—	—	—	—
91-92	Canada	National	49	10	24	34	15	—	—	—	—	—
92-93	Canada	National	55	12	31	43	38	—	—	—	—	—
93-94												
94-95												
95-96	Memphis	CeHL	60	18	44	62	33	6	1	2	3	8
96-97	Memphis	CeHL	38	16	28	44	25	—	—	—	—	—
96-97	Anchorage	WCHL	22	3	12	15	27	2	1	2	3	0
97-98	Macon	CHL	4	1	6	7	8	3	1	0	1	10
97-98	Quebec	QSPHL	8	2	5	7	6	—	—	—	—	—
98-99	Abilene	WPHL	29	9	18	27	13	—	—	—	—	—
	IHL	Totals	78	26	16	42	79	5	1	2	3	11
	CeHL	Totals	102	35	78	113	66	9	2	2	4	18

Born; 6/29/67, Quebec City, Quebec. 6-0, 195. Drafted by Minnesota North Stars (1st choice, 51st overall) in 1985 Draft. Traded to Quebec Nordiques by Minnesota for future considerations (12/15/88). Last amateur club; Granby (QMJHL).

Stephane Roy — Center

Regular Season / Playoffs

Season	Team	League	GP	G	A	PTS	PIM	GP	G	A	PTS	PIM
95-96	Val d' Or	QMJHL	62	43	72	115	89	13	9	15	24	10
95-96	Worcester	AHL	1	0	0	0	2	—	—	—	—	—
96-97	Worcester	AHL	66	24	23	47	57	5	2	0	2	4
97-98	Worcester	AHL	77	21	27	48	95	10	4	4	8	10
98-99	Worcester	AHL	64	16	28	44	41	4	0	2	2	2
	AHL	Totals	208	61	78	139	195	19	6	6	12	16

Born; 1/26/76, Ste-Martine, Quebec. 5-10, 173. Drafted by St. Louis Blues (1st choice, 68th overall) in 1994 Entry Draft. Last amateur club; Val d'Or (QMJHL).

Eric Royal — Center

Regular Season / Playoffs

Season	Team	League	GP	G	A	PTS	PIM	GP	G	A	PTS	PIM
95-96	Wheeling	ECHL	30	5	9	14	34	—	—	—	—	—
96-97	Wheeling	ECHL	70	31	61	92	68	3	0	0	0	0
97-98	Pee Dee	ECHL	66	12	39	51	8	8	0	8	8	2
98-99	Newcastle	BSL	50	9	26	35	14	6	0	5	5	0
	ECHL	Totals	166	48	109	157	110	11	0	8	8	2

Born; 2/16/72, Rochester, New Hampshire. 6-0, 185. Traded to Pee Dee by Wheeling for Joe Harney and Matt Garzone (10/97). Last amateur club; New Hampshire (Hockey East).

Gaetan Royer — Right Wing

Regular Season / Playoffs

Season	Team	League	GP	G	A	PTS	PIM	GP	G	A	PTS	PIM
96-97	Indianapolis	IHL	29	2	4	6	60	—	—	—	—	—
96-97	Jacksonville	ECHL	28	7	8	15	149	—	—	—	—	—
97-98	Canada	National	55	10	17	27	101	—	—	—	—	—
98-99	Grand Rapids	IHL	52	12	6	18	177	—	—	—	—	—
98-99	Saint John	AHL	15	1	0	1	36	7	0	1	1	8
	IHL	Totals	81	14	10	24	237	—	—	—	—	—

Born; 3/13/76, Donnacona, Quebec. 6-3, 193. Signed as a free agent by Chicago Blackhawks (9/9/94). Traded to Saint John by Grand Rapids for Mickey Elick (3/99). Last amateur club; Beauport (QMJHL).

Remi Royer — Defenseman

Regular Season / Playoffs

Season	Team	League	GP	G	A	PTS	PIM	GP	G	A	PTS	PIM
96-97	Rouyn-Noranda	QMJHL	29	3	12	15	85	—	—	—	—	—
96-97	Indianapolis	IHL	10	0	1	1	17	—	—	—	—	—
97-98	Indianapolis	IHL	5	0	2	2	4	5	1	2	3	12
98-99	Chicago	NHL	18	0	0	0	67	—	—	—	—	—
98-99	Indianapolis	IHL	54	4	15	19	164	7	0	0	0	44
98-99	Portland	AHL	2	0	1	1	2	—	—	—	—	—
	IHL	Totals	69	4	18	22	185	12	1	2	3	56

Born; 2/12/78, Donnacona, Quebec. 6-2, 185. Drafted by Chicago Blackhawks (1st choice, 31st overall) in 1996 Entry Draft. Last amateur club; Rouyn-Noranda (QMJHL).

Michal Rozsival — Defense

Regular Season / Playoffs

Season	Team	League	GP	G	A	PTS	PIM	GP	G	A	PTS	PIM
98-99	Syracuse	AHL	49	3	22	25	72	—	—	—	—	—

Born; 9/3/78, Vlasim, Czechoslovakia. 6-1, 194. Drafted by Pittsburgh Penguins (5th choice, 105th overall) in 1996 Entry Draft. Last amateur club; Swift Current

Mike Ruark — Defenseman

Regular Season / Playoffs

Season	Team	League	GP	G	A	PTS	PIM	GP	G	A	PTS	PIM
91-92	Phoenix	IHL	16	1	2	3	91	—	—	—	—	—
92-93	Phoenix	IHL	57	3	3	6	168	—	—	—	—	—
92-93	Muskegon	CoHL	1	0	0	0	0	—	—	—	—	—
93-94												
94-95	Canada	National	1	0	0	0	2	—	—	—	—	—
94-95	Calgary	CWUAA	24	2	2	4	82	—	—	—	—	—
95-96	Calgary	CWUAA	25	5	8	13	73	—	—	—	—	—
96-97	Calgary	CWUAA	25	9	8	17	85	—	—	—	—	—
97-98	Manitoba	IHL	71	1	7	8	204	3	0	0	0	4
98-99	Manitoba	IHL	53	5	6	11	179	—	—	—	—	—
	IHL	Totals	197	10	18	28	642	3	0	0	0	4

Born; 4/18/71, Calgary, Alberta. 6-2, 190. Last amateur club; Calgary (CWUAA).

Vladimir Rubes — Center

Regular Season / Playoffs

Season	Team	League	GP	G	A	PTS	PIM	GP	G	A	PTS	PIM
93-94	West Palm Beach	SHL	6	2	1	3	0	—	—	—	—	—
93-94	Daytona Beach	SHL	41	14	19	33	54	—	—	—	—	—
94-95												
95-96												
96-97												
97-98												
98-99	Memphis	CHL	56	24	20	44	34	4	0	1	1	2
	SHL	Totals	47	16	20	36	54	—	—	—	—	—

Born; 8/9/70, Prague, Czechoslovakia. 6-0, 193.

Matt Ruchty — Left Wing

Regular Season / Playoffs

Season	Team	League	GP	G	A	PTS	PIM	GP	G	A	PTS	PIM
91-92	Utica	AHL	73	9	14	23	250	4	0	0	0	25
92-93	Utica	AHL	74	4	14	18	253	4	0	2	2	15
93-94	Albany	AHL	68	11	11	22	303	5	0	1	1	18
94-95	Albany	AHL	78	26	23	49	348	12	5	10	15	43
95-96	Syracuse	AHL	68	12	16	28	321	—	—	—	—	—
95-96	Atlanta	IHL	12	3	4	7	38	3	1	1	2	36
96-97	Grand Rapids	IHL	63	14	20	34	364	5	0	1	1	23
96-97	Utica	CoHL	10	2	3	5	45	—	—	—	—	—
97-98	Rochester	AHL	6	2	3	5	21	—	—	—	—	—
97-98	Grand Rapids	IHL	64	8	14	22	259	3	1	2	3	20
98-99	Anchorage	WCHL	7	3	3	6	20	—	—	—	—	—
98-99	Providence	AHL	17	1	3	4	54	—	—	—	—	—
98-99	Adirondack	AHL	29	6	6	12	134	5	1	0	1	16
98-99	Grand Rapids	IHL	13	1	0	1	59	—	—	—	—	—
	AHL	Totals	413	71	90	161	1336	30	6	13	19	117
	IHL	Totals	152	26	38	64	720	11	2	4	6	79

Born; 11/27/69, Kitchener, Ontario. 6-1, 225. Drafted by New Jersey Devils (4th choice, 65th overall) in 1988 Entry Draft. Member of 1994-95 AHL champion Albany RiverRats. Last amateur club; Bowling Green (CCHA).

Jeff Rucinski — Defenseman

Regular Season / Playoffs

Season	Team	League	GP	G	A	PTS	PIM	GP	G	A	PTS	PIM
97-98	Western Michigan	CCHA	35	6	7	13	60	—	—	—	—	—
97-98	Wheeling	ECHL	3	0	0	0	0	—	—	—	—	—
97-98	Orlando	IHL	5	0	0	0	10	2	0	0	0	14
98-99	Chesapeake	ECHL	17	1	3	4	27	2	0	1	1	0
98-99	Cleveland	IHL	63	4	5	9	72	—	—	—	—	—
	IHL	Totals	68	4	5	9	82	2	0	0	0	14
	ECHL	Totals	20	1	3	4	27	2	0	1	1	0

Born; 9/29/74, Independence, Ohio. 5-10, 195. Selected by Memphis in CHL 1998 Disperal Draft. Last amateur club; Western Michigan (CCHA).

Mike Rucinski — Defenseman

Regular Season / Playoffs

Season	Team	League	GP	G	A	PTS	PIM	GP	G	A	PTS	PIM
96-97	Springfield	AHL	6	0	1	1	0	—	—	—	—	—
96-97	Raleigh	ECHL	61	20	23	43	85	—	—	—	—	—
97-98	Carolina	NHL	9	0	1	1	2	—	—	—	—	—
97-98	New Haven	AHL	65	5	17	22	50	1	0	0	0	0
97-98	Cleveland	IHL	2	0	0	0	4	—	—	—	—	—
98-99	New Haven	AHL	23	2	6	8	27	—	—	—	—	—
98-99	Florida	ECHL	16	2	5	7	13	—	—	—	—	—
98-99	Charlotte	ECHL	16	6	10	16	4	—	—	—	—	—
	AHL	Totals	94	7	24	31	77	1	0	0	0	0
	ECHL	Totals	93	28	38	66	102	—	—	—	—	—

Born; 3/30/75, Trenton, Michigan. 5-11, 179. Drafted by Hartford Whalers (8th choice, 217th overall) in 1995 Entry Draft. Last amateur club; Detroit (OHL).

Eric Rud — Defenseman

Regular Season / Playoffs

Season	Team	League	GP	G	A	PTS	PIM	GP	G	A	PTS	PIM
97-98	San Antonio	IHL	6	0	1	1	4	—	—	—	—	—
97-98	Quebec	IHL	63	8	19	27	57	—	—	—	—	—
98-99	Kansas City	IHL	11	0	1	1	6	—	—	—	—	—
98-99	Florida	ECHL	50	11	18	29	36	6	3	2	5	2
	IHL	Totals	80	8	21	29	67	—	—	—	—	—

Born; 11/20/72, Inver Grove, Minnesota. 6-0, 196. Last amateur club; Colorado College (WCHA).

Ken Ruddick — Defenseman

Regular Season / Playoffs

Season	Team	League	GP	G	A	PTS	PIM	GP	G	A	PTS	PIM
96-97	Louisiana	ECHL	56	7	4	11	93	—	—	—	—	—
97-98	Austin	WPHL	32	5	21	26	28	—	—	—	—	—
97-98	Phoenix	WCHL	5	0	5	5	4	—	—	—	—	—
97-98	Louisiana	ECHL	7	0	0	0	2	11	0	1	1	12
98-99	Louisiana	ECHL	25	2	5	7	23	—	—	—	—	—
98-99	Augusta	ECHL	15	2	4	6	26	2	0	0	0	4
	ECHL	Totals	103	11	13	24	144	13	0	1	1	16

Born; 8/15/72, Hamilton, Ontario. 6-1, 205. Traded to Mobile by Tallahassee with Mitch Vig for Greg Callahan (2/99). Traded to Augusta by Mobile for Russ Guzior (2/99). Last amateur club; Wilfrid Laurier (OUAA).

Bogdan Rudenko — Right Wing

Regular Season / Playoffs

Season	Team	League	GP	G	A	PTS	PIM	GP	G	A	PTS	PIM
97-98	Quad City	UHL	69	22	27	49	174	13	2	3	5	16
98-99	Colorado	WCHL	51	12	12	24	174	3	0	2	2	6

Born; 9/13/77, Drummondville, Quebec. 6-0, 200. Last amateur club; Sarnia

Jason Ruff — Left Wing

Regular Season / Playoffs

Season	Team	League	GP	G	A	PTS	PIM	GP	G	A	PTS	PIM
90-91	Lethbridge	WHL	66	61	75	136	154	16	12	17	29	18
90-91	Peoria	IHL	—	—	—	—	—	5	0	0	0	2
91-92	Peoria	IHL	67	27	45	72	148	10	7	7	14	19
92-93	St. Louis	NHL	7	2	1	3	8	—	—	—	—	—
92-93	Tampa Bay	NHL	1	0	0	0	0	—	—	—	—	—
92-93	Peoria	IHL	40	22	21	43	81	—	—	—	—	—
92-93	Atlanta	IHL	26	11	14	25	90	7	2	1	3	26
93-94	Tampa Bay	NHL	6	1	2	3	2	—	—	—	—	—
93-94	Atlanta	IHL	71	24	25	49	122	14	6	*17	23	41
94-95	Atlanta	IHL	64	42	34	76	161	3	3	1	4	10
95-96	Atlanta	IHL	59	39	33	72	135	2	0	0	0	16
96-97	Quebec	IHL	80	35	50	85	93	9	8	5	13	10
97-98	Quebec	IHL	54	21	24	45	77	—	—	—	—	—
97-98	Cleveland	IHL	6	2	3	5	9	10	6	6	12	4
98-99	Cleveland	IHL	44	13	27	40	57	—	—	—	—	—
98-99	Houston	IHL	1	0	0	0	0	19	5	5	10	12
	NHL	Totals	14	3	3	6	10	—	—	—	—	—
	IHL	Totals	512	236	276	512	953	79	37	42	79	140

Born; 1/27/70, Kelowna, British Columbia. 6-2, 205. Drafted by St. Louis Blues (3rd choice, 96th overall) in 1990 Entry Draft. Traded to Tampa Bay Lightning by St. Louis with future considerations for Doug Crossman, Basil McRae and fourth round choice (Andrei Petrakov) in 1996 Entry Draft (1/28/93). Traded to Cleveland by Quebec with Rick Girard, Dale DeGray, Darcy Simon and Tom Draper for Ryan Mougenal, Rick Hayward, John Craighead, Eric Perrin, Burke Murphy and Pat Jablonski (3/98). Member of 1990-91 IHL champion Peoria Rivermen. Member of 1993-94 IHL champion Atlanta Knights. Member of 1998-99 IHL Champion Houston Aeros. Last amateur club; Lethbridge (WHL).

J.C. Ruid — Left Wing

Regular Season / Playoffs

Season	Team	League	GP	G	A	PTS	PIM	GP	G	A	PTS	PIM
97-98	Baton Rouge	ECHL	36	8	17	25	20	—	—	—	—	—
97-98	Roanoke	ECHL	24	4	8	12	14	9	2	1	3	2
98-99	Roanoke	ECHL	39	6	18	24	38	—	—	—	—	—
	ECHL	Totals	99	18	43	61	72	9	2	1	3	2

Born; 12/31/74, Ballston Spa, New York. 6-4, 215. Traded to Roanoke by Baton Rouge for Kelly Hollingshead (1/98). Last amateur club; Vermont (ECAC).

Darren Rumble — Defenseman

Regular Season / Playoffs

Season	Team	League	GP	G	A	PTS	PIM	GP	G	A	PTS	PIM
89-90	Hershey	AHL	57	2	13	15	31	—	—	—	—	—
90-91	Philadelphia	NHL	3	1	0	1	0	—	—	—	—	—
90-91	Hershey	AHL	73	6	35	41	48	3	0	5	5	2
91-92	Hershey	AHL	79	12	54	66	118	6	0	3	3	2
92-93	Ottawa	NHL	69	3	13	16	61	—	—	—	—	—
92-93	New Haven	AHL	2	1	0	1	0	—	—	—	—	—
93-94	Ottawa	NHL	70	6	9	15	116	—	—	—	—	—
93-94	Prince Edward Island	AHL	3	2	0	2	0	—	—	—	—	—
94-95	Prince Edward Island	AHL	70	7	46	53	77	11	0	6	6	4
95-96	Philadelphia	NHL	5	0	0	0	4	—	—	—	—	—
95-96	Hershey	AHL	58	13	37	50	83	5	0	0	0	6
96-97	Philadelphia	NHL	10	0	0	0	0	—	—	—	—	—
96-97	Philadelphia	AHL	72	18	44	62	83	7	0	3	3	19
97-98	San Antonio	IHL	46	7	22	29	47	—	—	—	—	—
98-99	Grand Rapids	IHL	53	6	22	28	44	—	—	—	—	—
98-99	Utah	IHL	10	1	4	5	10	—	—	—	—	—
	NHL	Totals	157	10	22	32	181	—	—	—	—	—
	AHL	Totals	414	60	229	289	440	32	0	17	17	33
	IHL	Totals	109	14	48	62	101	—	—	—	—	—

Born; 1/23/69, Barrie, Ontario. 6-1, 200. Drafted by Philadelphia Flyers (1st choice, 20th overall) in 1987 Entry Draft. Claimed by Ottawa Senators from Philadelphia in Expansion Draft (6/18/92). Signed as a free agent by Philadelphia (7/31/95). Acquired from San Antonio to complete earlier trade (7/98). Traded to Utah by Grand Rapids for Yan Kaminsky (3/99). 1994-95 AHL Second Team All-Star. 1996-97 AHL First Team All-Star. 1996-97 AHL Outstanding Defenseman. Last amateur club; Kitchener (OHL).

John Rumeo — Forward

Regular Season / Playoffs

Season	Team	League	GP	G	A	PTS	PIM	GP	G	A	PTS	PIM
98-99	Pensacola	ECHL	6	0	1	1	0	—	—	—	—	—

Born; Toronto, Ontario. 6-0, 165. Selected by Arkansas in 1999 ECHL Expansion Draft.

Daniel Ruoho — Left Wing

Regular Season / Playoffs

Season	Team	League	GP	G	A	PTS	PIM	GP	G	A	PTS	PIM
93-94	South Carolina	ECHL	56	7	22	29	106	3	0	2	2	2
94-95	South Carolina	ECHL	22	7	6	13	25	—	—	—	—	—
94-95	Charlotte	ECHL	28	8	6	14	41	3	0	1	1	2
95-96	Madison	CoHL	72	9	30	39	46	6	3	1	4	9
96-97	Madison	CoHL	62	14	33	47	61	5	0	1	1	6
97-98	Madison	UHL	73	13	21	34	90	7	0	2	2	6
98-99	Madison	UHL	25	3	5	8	30	—	—	—	—	—
	UHL	Totals	232	39	89	128	227	18	3	4	7	21
	ECHL	Totals	106	22	34	56	172	6	0	3	3	4

Born; 6/22/70, Madison, Wisconsin. 6-4, 215. Drafted by Buffalo Sabres (9th choice 160th overall) in 1988 Entry Draft. Last amateur club; Northern Michigan

Mark Rupnow — Left Wing

Regular Season / Playoffs

Season	Team	League	GP	G	A	PTS	PIM	GP	G	A	PTS	PIM
95-96	South Carolina	ECHL	59	12	14	26	35	—	—	—	—	—
96-97	Mississippi	ECHL	30	11	7	18	17	—	—	—	—	—
97-98	Mississippi	ECHL	66	23	21	44	59	—	—	—	—	—
98-99	Springfield	AHL	3	0	1	1	0	—	—	—	—	—
98-99	Mississippi	ECHL	67	13	39	52	36	18	6	9	15	10
	ECHL	Totals	222	59	81	140	147	18	6	9	15	10

Born; 2/21/70, Belleville, Ontario. 5-11, 200. Member of 1998-99 ECHL Champion Mississippi SeaWolves. Last amateur club; St. Thomas (AUAA).

Paul Rushforth — Center

Regular Season / Playoffs

Season	Team	League	GP	G	A	PTS	PIM	GP	G	A	PTS	PIM
94-95	Rochester	AHL	25	8	6	14	10	2	0	0	0	0
94-95	South Carolina	ECHL	41	6	8	14	130	—	—	—	—	—
95-96	South Carolina	ECHL	56	20	26	46	141	7	1	0	1	8
96-97	Rochester	AHL	7	0	2	2	4	1	0	0	0	0
96-97	Birmingham	ECHL	17	7	8	15	52	8	3	9	12	34
97-98	Louisiana	ECHL	50	14	36	50	136	12	4	4	8	40
98-99	Fresno	WCHL	52	25	37	62	148	7	1	5	6	16
	AHL	Totals	32	8	8	16	14	3	0	0	0	0
	ECHL	Totals	164	47	78	125	459	27	8	13	21	82

Born; 4/22/74, Prince George, British Columbia. 6-0, 189. Drafted by Buffalo Sabres (8th choice, 131st overall) in 1992 Entry Draft. Last amateur club;

Jason Rushton — Right Wing

Regular Season / Playoffs

Season	Team	League	GP	G	A	PTS	PIM	GP	G	A	PTS	PIM
94-95	Chicago	IHL	2	0	0	0	10	—	—	—	—	—
95-96	Jacksonville	SHL	8	3	6	9	24	—	—	—	—	—
95-96	Wichita	CeHL	44	17	13	30	263	—	—	—	—	—
96-97	Tulsa	CeHL	64	37	29	66	341	5	5	4	9	22
96-97	Syracuse	AHL	3	3	0	3	7	2	0	0	0	5
97-98	Tulsa	CHL	45	20	31	51	142	—	—	—	—	—
97-98	Fayetteville	CHL	4	2	6	8	9	—	—	—	—	—
98-99	El Paso	WPHL	25	11	13	24	103	—	—	—	—	—
98-99	Arkansas	WPHL	34	6	17	23	128	3	0	0	0	2
	CHL	Totals	157	76	79	155	755	5	5	4	9	22
	WPHL	Totals	59	17	30	47	231	3	0	0	0	2

Born; 12/12/74, Victoria, British Columbia. 5-11, 205.

Mike Rusk — Defenseman

Regular Season / Playoffs

Season	Team	League	GP	G	A	PTS	PIM	GP	G	A	PTS	PIM
95-96	Columbus	ECHL	47	3	13	16	63	3	1	0	1	2
96-97	Columbus	ECHL	59	4	26	30	80	4	0	0	0	2
97-98	St. John's	AHL	2	0	0	0	2	—	—	—	—	—
97-98	New Orleans	ECHL	8	0	3	3	6	—	—	—	—	—
97-98	Johnstown	ECHL	28	2	5	7	31	—	—	—	—	—
98-99	Columbus	CHL	2	0	0	0	0	—	—	—	—	—
98-99	Topeka	CHL	62	4	23	27	87	3	0	0	0	8
	ECHL	Totals	142	9	47	56	180	7	1	0	1	4
	CHL	Totals	64	4	23	27	87	3	0	0	0	8

Born; 4/26/75, Milton, Ontario. 6-1, 175. Drafted by Chicago Blackhawks (10th choice, 232nd overall) in 1993 Entry Draft. Traded to Johnstown by New Orleans with Chris Bowen for Martin Woods (11/97). Last amateur club; Guelph (OHL).

Blaine Russell — Goaltender

Regular Season / Playoffs

Season	Team	League	GP	W	L	T	MIN	SO	AVG	GP	W	L	MIN	SO	AVG
97-98	Cincinnati	AHL	20	0	9	2	748	0	4.65	—	—	—	—	—	—
97-98	Columbus	ECHL	4	1	2	0	200	0	5.71	—	—	—	—	—	—
97-98	Huntington	ECHL	1	0	1	0	60	0	6.00	—	—	—	—	—	—
97-98	New Orleans	ECHL	4	0	0	2	184	0	3.59	—	—	—	—	—	—
98-99	Huntington	ECHL	12	6	1	0	516	1	2.90	—	—	—	—	—	—
	ECHL	Totals	21	7	4	2	960	1	43.81	—	—	—	—	—	—

Born; 1/11/77, Wetaskawin, Saskatchewan. 5-11, 180. Drafted by Anaheim Mighty Ducks (4th choice, 149th overall) in 1996 Entry Draft. Last amateur club; Prince Albert (WHL).

Bobby Russell — Right Wing

Regular Season / Playoffs

Season	Team	League	GP	G	A	PTS	PIM	GP	G	A	PTS	PIM
98-99	Milwaukee	IHL	31	3	3	6	8	—	—	—	—	—
98-99	Hampton Roads	ECHL	44	15	8	23	25	—	—	—	—	—

Born; 3/9/78, Surrey, British Columbia. 6-1, 185. Signed as a free agent by Nashville Predators (10/22/99). Last amateur club; Portland (WHL).

Ted Russell — Defenseman

Regular Season / Playoffs

Season	Team	League	GP	G	A	PTS	PIM	GP	G	A	PTS	PIM
95-96	Dayton	ECHL	43	4	14	18	40	—	—	—	—	—
95-96	Johnstown	ECHL	18	2	6	8	4	—	—	—	—	—
96-97	Johnstown	ECHL	64	9	41	50	92	—	—	—	—	—
97-98	Peterborough	BNL	54	41	60	101	82	8	9	9	18	24
98-99	Peterborough	BNL										
	ECHL	Totals	215	15	61	76	136	—	—	—	—	—

Born; 5/7/71, Saint John, Newfoundland. 5-10, 190.

Virgil Rutili — Defenseman

Regular Season / Playoffs

Season	Team	League	GP	G	A	PTS	PIM	GP	G	A	PTS	PIM
97-98	Fort Worth	CHL	69	9	20	29	43	—	—	—	—	—
98-99	Topeka	CHL	2	0	0	0	0	—	—	—	—	—
98-99	Tulsa	CHL	8	1	1	2	6	—	—	—	—	—
	CHL	Totals	79	10	21	31	49	—	—	—	—	—

Born; 2/17/73, Addison, Illinois. 5-11, 180. Last amateur club; Lake Forest (NCAA 3).

Yevgeny Ryabchikov — Goaltender

Regular Season / Playoffs

Season	Team	League	GP	W	L	T	MIN	SO	AVG	GP	W	L	MIN	SO	AVG
94-95	Providence	AHL	14	6	3	1	721	0	3.49	—	—	—	—	—	—
95-96	Providence	AHL	1	0	0	0	40	0	3.00	—	—	—	—	—	—
95-96	Charlotte	ECHL	1	0	1	0	29	0	8.24	—	—	—	—	—	—
95-96	Huntington	ECHL	8	3	3	0	360	0	4.17	—	—	—	—	—	—
95-96	Erie	ECHL	16	2	7	1	858	0	3.50	—	—	—	—	—	—
96-97	Providence	AHL	1	0	0	0	20	0	6.00	—	—	—	—	—	—
96-97	Charlotte	ECHL	14	5	6	2	734	1	3.84	—	—	—	—	—	—
96-97	Dayton	ECHL	15	6	4	3	842	0	4.28	—	—	—	—	—	—
97-98	Odessa	WPHL	7	2	4	0	345	0	7.83	—	—	—	—	—	—
97-98	Waco	WPHL	10	2	8	0	591	0	4.77	—	—	—	—	—	—
98-99	Molot-Prikamje	Russia	12	—	—	—	694	1	2.59	5	—	—	272	1	2.43
	AHL	Totals	16	6	3	1	781	0	3.53	—	—	—	—	—	—
	ECHL	Totals	54	16	21	6	2823	1	3.95	—	—	—	—	—	—
	WPHL	Totals	17	4	12	0	936	0	5.90	—	—	—	—	—	—

Born; 1/16/74, Yaroslavl, Soviet Union. 5-11, 167. Drafted by Boston Bruins (1st choice, 21st overall) in 1994 Entry Draft.

Terry Ryan — Left Wing

Regular Season / Playoffs

Season	Team	League	GP	G	A	PTS	PIM	GP	G	A	PTS	PIM
95-96	Tri-City	WHL	59	32	37	69	133	5	0	0	0	4
95-96	Fredericton	AHL	—	—	—	—	—	3	0	0	0	2
96-97	Red Deer	WHL	16	13	22	35	10	16	18	6	24	32
96-97	Montreal	NHL	3	0	0	0	0	—	—	—	—	—
97-98	Montreal	NHL	4	0	0	0	31	—	—	—	—	—
97-98	Fredericton	AHL	71	21	18	39	256	3	1	1	2	0
98-99	Montreal	NHL	1	0	0	0	5	—	—	—	—	—
98-99	Fredericton	AHL	55	16	27	43	189	11	1	3	4	10
	NHL	Totals	8	0	0	0	36	—	—	—	—	—
	AHL	Totals	126	37	45	82	445	17	2	4	6	12

Born; 1/14/77, St. John's Newfoundland. 6-2, 198. Drafted by Montreal Canadiens (1st choice, 8th overall) in 1995 Entry Draft. Last amateur club; Red Deer

Alexandre Ryazantsev — Defenseman

Regular Season / Playoffs

Season	Team	League	GP	G	A	PTS	PIM	GP	G	A	PTS	PIM
98-99	Victoriaville	QMJHL	64	17	40	57	57	6	0	3	3	10
98-99	Hershey	AHL	2	0	0	0	0	—	—	—	—	—

Born; 3/15/80, Moscow, USSR. 5-11, 200. Drafted by Colorado Avalanche (10th choice, 167th overall) in 1998 Entry Draft. Last amateur club; Victoriaville (QMJHL).

Joe Rybar — Center

Regular Season / Playoffs

Season	Team	League	GP	G	A	PTS	PIM	GP	G	A	PTS	PIM
98-99	Peoria	ECHL	70	32	41	73	30	4	1	4	5	0

Born; 3/10/74, Fernie, British Columbia. 5-11, 170. Last amateur club; Minnesota-Duluth (WCHA).

Thierry Ryckman — Left Wing

Regular Season / Playoffs

Season	Team	League	GP	G	A	PTS	PIM	GP	G	A	PTS	PIM
98-99	Mobile	ECHL	1	0	0	0	0	—	—	—	—	—
98-99	Memphis	CHL	12	5	4	9	31	—	—	—	—	—
98-99	Mohawk Valley	UHL	12	1	0	1	22	—	—	—	—	—

Born; 4/21/75, Rimouski, Quebec. 6-0, 190.

Jason Saal
Goaltender

Season	Team	League	Regular Season GP	W	L	T	MIN	SO	AVG	Playoffs GP	W	L	MIN	SO	AVG
95-96	St. John's	AHL	24	9	8	1	1083	0	3.76	1	0	0	13	0	0.00
95-96	South Carolina	ECHL	8	5	3	0	428	0	3.51	—	—	—	—	—	—
96-97	St. John's	AHL	12	2	5	2	569	0	4.11	—	—	—	—	—	—
96-97	Peoria	ECHL	17	8	6	1	924	1	2.79	—	—	—	—	—	—
97-98	Portland	AHL	1	0	0	1	65	0	2.77	—	—	—	—	—	—
97-98	Hampton Roads	ECHL	31	12	12	4	1753	0	3.01	2	0	2	120	0	3.00
98-99	Hampton Roads	ECHL	44	20	17	5	2478	4	2.76	4	1	2	179	0	4.02
	AHL	Totals	37	11	13	4	1717	0	3.84	1	0	0	13	0	0.00
	ECHL	Totals	100	45	38	10	5583	5	2.90	6	1	4	299	0	3.61

Born; 2/1/75, Sterling Heights, Michigan. 5-11, 175. Drafted by Los Angeles Kings (5th choice, 117th overall) in 1993 Entry Draft. Signed as a free agent by Toronto Maple Leafs (8/3/95). Member of 1997-98 ECHL Champion Hampton Roads Admirals. Last amateur club; Detroit (OHL).

Steve Sabo
Defenseman

Season	Team	League	Regular Season GP	G	A	PTS	PIM	Playoffs GP	G	A	PTS	PIM
98-99	Dayton	ECHL	18	1	0	1	12	—	—	—	—	—
98-99	Roanoke	ECHL	47	2	5	7	75	11	0	0	0	16
	ECHL	Totals	65	3	5	8	87	11	0	0	0	16

Born; 1/7/73, Madison, Wisconsin. 6-1, 195. Last amateur club; Wisconsin (WCHA).

Dany Sabourin
Goaltender

Season	Team	League	Regular Season GP	W	L	T	MIN	SO	AVG	Playoffs GP	W	L	MIN	SO	AVG
98-99	Sherbrooke	QMJHL	30	8	13	2	1477	1	4.14	1	0	1	49	0	2.45
98-99	Saint John	AHL	—	—	—	—	—	—	—	1	0	1	57	0	4.19

Born; 9/2/80, Val D'Or, Quebec. 6-2, 165. Drafted by Calgary Flames (5th choice, 108th overall) in 1998 Entry Draft. Last amateur club; Sherbrooke

Ken Sabourin
Defenseman

Season	Team	League	Regular Season GP	G	A	PTS	PIM	Playoffs GP	G	A	PTS	PIM
85-86	Sault Ste. Marie	OHL	25	1	5	6	77	—	—	—	—	—
85-86	Cornwall	OHL	37	3	12	15	94	6	1	2	3	6
85-86	Moncton	AHL	3	0	0	0	0	6	0	1	1	2
86-87	Moncton	AHL	75	1	10	11	166	6	0	1	1	27
87-88	Salt Lake City	IHL	71	2	8	10	186	16	1	6	7	57
88-89	Calgary	NHL	6	0	1	1	26	1	0	0	0	0
88-89	Salt Lake City	IHL	74	2	18	20	197	11	0	1	1	26
89-90	Calgary	NHL	5	0	0	0	10	—	—	—	—	—
89-90	Salt Lake City	IHL	76	5	19	24	336	11	0	2	2	40
90-91	Calgary	NHL	16	1	3	4	36	—	—	—	—	—
90-91	Washington	NHL	28	1	4	5	81	11	0	0	0	34
90-91	Salt Lake City	IHL	28	2	15	17	77	—	—	—	—	—
91-92	Washington	NHL	19	0	0	0	48	—	—	—	—	—
91-92	Baltimore	AHL	30	3	8	11	106	—	—	—	—	—
92-93	Baltimore	AHL	30	5	14	19	68	—	—	—	—	—
92-93	Salt Lake City	IHL	52	2	11	13	140	—	—	—	—	—
93-94	Milwaukee	IHL	81	6	13	19	279	4	0	0	0	10
94-95	Milwaukee	IHL	75	3	16	19	297	15	1	1	2	69
95-96	Milwaukee	IHL	82	2	8	10	252	5	0	1	1	24
96-97	Milwaukee	IHL	81	2	9	11	233	3	0	0	0	2
97-98	Milwaukee	IHL	71	1	5	6	172	10	0	1	1	55
98-99	Orlando	IHL	72	3	4	7	248	14	0	0	0	49
	NHL	Totals	74	2	8	10	201	12	0	0	0	34
	IHL	Totals	763	30	126	156	2417	89	2	12	14	332

Born; 4/28/66, Scarbrough, Ontario. 6-3, 205. Drafted by Calgary Flames (2nd choice, 33rd overall) in 1984 Entry Draft. Traded to Washington Capitals for Paul Fenton (1/24/91). Traded to Calgary by Washington for future considerations (12/16/92). Member of 1987-88 IHL Champion Salt Lake City Golden Eagles. Last amateur club; Cornwall (OHL).

Warren Sachs
Right Wing

Season	Team	League	Regular Season GP	G	A	PTS	PIM	Playoffs GP	G	A	PTS	PIM
98-99	Space Coast	SEHL	18	30	28	58	69	8	13	11	24	18
98-99	San Antonio	CHL	14	3	5	8	14	—	—	—	—	—
98-99	Fort Worth	CHL	12	3	4	7	0	—	—	—	—	—
	CHL	Totals	26	6	9	15	14	—	—	—	—	—

Born; 2/18/77, Saskatoon, Saskatchewan. 5-8, 165. Last amateur club; Space Coast (SEHL).

Rostislav Saglo
Left Wing

Season	Team	League	Regular Season GP	G	A	PTS	PIM	Playoffs GP	G	A	PTS	PIM
96-97	Pensacola	ECHL	11	0	1	1	4	—	—	—	—	—
97-98	Macon	CHL	7	1	2	3	4	—	—	—	—	—
97-98	Saginaw	UHL	14	0	3	3	2	—	—	—	—	—
97-98	Idaho	WCHL	14	2	2	4	8	4	1	0	1	0
98-99	Phoenix	WCHL	11	0	1	1	9	—	—	—	—	—
98-99	El Paso	WPHL	10	0	0	0	2	—	—	—	—	—
	WCHL	Totals	25	2	3	5	17	4	1	0	1	0

Born; 5/8/78, Kiev, Russia. 6-1, 190. Last amateur club; Laval (QMJHL).

Brian Sakic
Center

Season	Team	League	Regular Season GP	G	A	PTS	PIM	Playoffs GP	G	A	PTS	PIM
92-93	Erie	ECHL	51	18	33	51	22	—	—	—	—	—
93-94	Flint	CoHL	64	39	86	125	30	10	6	7	13	2
94-95	Flint	CoHL	62	38	85	113	22	6	1	5	6	0
95-96	Flint	CoHL	74	30	66	96	30	15	8	12	20	0
96-97	Austin	WPHL	16	2	8	10	23	—	—	—	—	—
96-97	Flint	CoHL	53	19	47	66	4	13	5	15	20	4
97-98	Flint	UHL	72	21	99	120	10	3	0	2	2	0
98-99	Flint	UHL	71	36	72	108	10	12	4	15	19	2
	UHL	Totals	396	173	455	628	106	59	24	56	80	8

Born; 9/4/71, Burnaby, British Columbia. 5-10, 179. Drafted by Washington Capitals (5th round, 93rd overall) 6/16/90. Signed by New York Rangers as a free agent 8/13/92. 1997-98 UHL Most Sportsmanlike Player. 1998-99 UHL Second Team All-Star. 1998-99 UHL Most Sportsmanlike Player. Member of 1995-96 CoHL Champion Flint Generals. Last amateur club; Tri-City, WHL.

Jeff Salajko
Goaltender

Season	Team	League	Regular Season GP	W	L	T	MIN	SO	AVG	Playoffs GP	W	L	MIN	SO	AVG
96-97	Indianapolis	IHL	1	1	0	0	60	0	1.00	—	—	—	—	—	—
96-97	Columbus	ECHL	54	35	14	3	3085	1	3.35	8	3	5	516	0	2.79
97-98	Kansas City	IHL	26	12	6	6	1449	2	3.15	—	—	—	—	—	—
97-98	Columbus	ECHL	18	9	7	2	1042	2	2.30	—	—	—	—	—	—
97-98	Wichita	CHL	—	—	—	—	—	—	—	8	3	4	445	0	4.05
98-99	Portland	AHL	2	0	1	0	80	0	5.25	—	—	—	—	—	—
98-99	Indianapolis	IHL	2	0	0	1	80	0	3.75	—	—	—	—	—	—
98-99	Columbus	ECHL	*54	30	16	6	*3077	2	3.16	3	1	2	139	0	4.32
	IHL	Totals	29	13	6	7	1589	2	3.10	—	—	—	—	—	—

Born; 4/18/75, Toronto, Ontario. 6-1, 190. Drafted by San Jose Sharks (12th choice, 236th overall) in 1993 Entry Draft. Selected by Topeka in CHL 1998 Expansion Draft. Last amateur club; Sarnia (OHL).

Sami Salo
Defenseman

Season	Team	League	Regular Season GP	G	A	PTS	PIM	Playoffs GP	G	A	PTS	PIM
98-99	Ottawa	NHL	61	7	12	19	24	4	0	0	0	0
98-99	Detroit	IHL	5	0	2	2	0	—	—	—	—	—

Born; 9/2/74, Turku, Finland. 6-3, 190. Drafted by Ottawa Senators (7th choice, 239th overall) in 1996 Entry Draft. Last European club; Jokerit (Finland).

Marc Salsman — Right Wing
Regular Season — Playoffs

Season	Team	League	GP	G	A	PTS	PIM	GP	G	A	PTS	PIM
96-97	Lowell	H.E.	37	13	16	29	38	—	—	—	—	—
96-97	Jacksonville	ECHL	7	1	1	2	9	—	—	—	—	—
97-98	Tacoma	WCHL	29	6	9	15	60	—	—	—	—	—
97-98	Reno	WCHL	—	—	—	—	—	3	1	1	2	4
98-99	Asheville	UHL	14	0	2	2	41	—	—	—	—	—
98-99	Tupelo	WPHL	36	14	10	24	80	—	—	—	—	—
	WCHL	Totals	29	6	9	15	60	3	1	1	2	4

Born; 2/27/74, Malden, Massachusetts. 5-11, 202. Selected by Colorado in 1998 WCHL Disperal Draft. Last amateur club; Lowell (Hockey East).

Bryce Salvador — Defenseman
Regular Season — Playoffs

Season	Team	League	GP	G	A	PTS	PIM	GP	G	A	PTS	PIM
97-98	Worcester	AHL	46	2	8	10	74	11	0	1	1	45
98-99	Worcester	AHL	69	5	13	18	129	4	0	1	1	2
	AHL	Totals	115	7	21	28	203	15	0	2	2	47

Born; 2/11/76, Brandon, Manitoba. 6-3, 205. Drafted by Tampa Bay Lightning (6th choice, 138th overall) in 1994 Entry Draft. Signed as a free agent by St. Louis Blues (12/16/96). Last amateur club; Lethbridge (WHL).

Erasmo Saltarelli — Goaltender
Regular Season — Playoffs

Season	Team	League	GP	W	L	T	MIN	SO	AVG	GP	W	L	MIN	SO	AVG
98-99	Chesapeake	ECHL	27	8	11	5	1421	1	3.12	—	—	—	—	—	—
98-99	Tallahassee	ECHL	6	1	1	1	216	1	3.61	—	—	—	—	—	—
	ECHL	Totals	33	9	12	6	1637	2	3.19	—	—	—	—	—	—

Born; 2/20/74, Montreal, Quebec. 5-10, 185. Last amateur club; Princeton

Mike Sancimino — Center
Regular Season — Playoffs

Season	Team	League	GP	G	A	PTS	PIM	GP	G	A	PTS	PIM
96-97	Louisville	ECHL	70	28	33	61	58	—	—	—	—	—
97-98	Louisville	ECHL	70	14	37	51	84	—	—	—	—	—
98-99	Miami	ECHL	11	4	3	7	12	—	—	—	—	—
98-99	Tallahassee	ECHL	45	6	9	15	51	—	—	—	—	—
	ECHL	Totals	196	52	82	134	205	—	—	—	—	—

Born; 2/15/74, Warren, Michigan. 6-2, 205. Last amateur club; Cornell (ECAC).

Mike Sanderson — Center
Regular Season — Playoffs

Season	Team	League	GP	G	A	PTS	PIM	GP	G	A	PTS	PIM
91-92	Nashville	ECHL	4	2	1	3	2	—	—	—	—	—
91-92	Johnstown	ECHL	6	1	2	3	4	—	—	—	—	—
92-93	Fort Worth	CeHL	60	37	31	68	33	—	—	—	—	—
93-94	Fort Worth	CeHL	63	27	34	61	37	—	—	—	—	—
94-95	Bracknell	BHL	18	11	14	25	14	—	—	—	—	—
94-95	Dallas	CeHL	3	0	0	0	2	—	—	—	—	—
94-95	Tulsa	CeHL	25	18	14	32	10	7	2	3	5	2
95-96	Bakersfield	WCHL	57	19	27	46	22	—	—	—	—	—
96-97	Guildford	BHL	8	7	3	10	4	—	—	—	—	—
96-97	Fort Worth	CeHL	56	16	32	48	16	15	6	3	9	8
97-98	New Mexico	WPHL	61	34	34	68	104	10	7	3	10	4
98-99	New Mexico	WPHL	56	15	28	43	25	—	—	—	—	—
	CeHL	Totals	207	98	111	209	98	22	8	6	14	10
	WPHL	Totals	117	49	62	111	129	10	7	3	10	4
	ECHL	Totals	10	3	3	6	6	—	—	—	—	—

Born; 5/31/70, Moose Jaw, Saskatchewan. 5-11, 185. Member of 1996-97 CeHL Champion Fort Worth Fire.

Terran Sandwith — Defenseman
Regular Season — Playoffs

Season	Team	League	GP	G	A	PTS	PIM	GP	G	A	PTS	PIM
92-93	Hershey	AHL	61	1	12	13	140	—	—	—	—	—
93-94	Hershey	AHL	62	3	5	8	169	2	0	1	1	4
94-95	Hershey	AHL	11	1	1	2	32	—	—	—	—	—
94-95	Kansas City	IHL	25	0	3	3	73	—	—	—	—	—
95-96	Canada	National	47	3	12	15	63	—	—	—	—	—
95-96	Hamilton	AHL	5	0	2	2	4	—	—	—	—	—
96-97	Hamilton	AHL	78	3	6	9	213	22	0	2	2	27
97-98	Edmonton	NHL	8	0	0	0	6	—	—	—	—	—
97-98	Hamilton	AHL	54	4	8	12	131	9	0	0	0	10
98-99	Cincinnati	AHL	40	0	6	6	77	—	—	—	—	—
	AHL	Totals	311	12	40	52	766	33	0	3	3	41

Born; 4/17/72, Stoney Plain, Alberta. 6-4, 210. Drafted by Philadelphia Flyers (4th choice, 42nd overall) in 1990 Entry Draft. Signed as a free agent by Edmonton Oilers (4/10/96). Signed as a free agent by Anaheim Mighty Ducks (7/14/98). Signed as a free agent by Toronto Maple Leafs (7/9/99). Last amateur club; Saskatoon (WHL).

Steve Sangermano — Center
Regular Season — Playoffs

Season	Team	League	GP	G	A	PTS	PIM	GP	G	A	PTS	PIM
93-94	Johnstown	ECHL	2	1	0	1	0	—	—	—	—	—
93-94	South Carolina	ECHL	2	0	0	0	0	—	—	—	—	—
94-95	Dallas	CeHL	3	0	0	0	0	—	—	—	—	—
94-95	Jacksonville	SUN	6	0	3	3	2	—	—	—	—	—
95-96	Jacksonville	ECHL	1	0	1	1	0	—	—	—	—	—
95-96	Daytona Beach	SHL	53	34	*60	94	148	4	1	1	2	23
96-97	Adirondack	AHL	11	5	0	5	4	—	—	—	—	—
96-97	Quad City	CoHL	54	25	57	82	82	15	10	10	20	16
97-98	Quad City	UHL	26	11	15	26	60	—	—	—	—	—
97-98	Port Huron	UHL	8	4	5	9	8	4	3	4	7	2
98-99	Fayetteville	CHL	47	35	41	76	174	—	—	—	—	—
	UHL	Totals	88	40	77	117	150	19	13	14	27	18
	CHL	Totals	50	35	41	76	174	—	—	—	—	—
	ECHL	Totals	5	1	1	2	0	—	—	—	—	—
	SHL	Totals	59	34	63	97	150	4	1	1	2	23

Born; 10/11/72, Burrillville, Rhode Island. 5-11, 170. Traded to Port Huron by Quad City for Ryan Black (3/98). Member of 1996-97 CoHL Champion Quad City Mallards.

Jason Sangiuliano — Forward
Regular Season — Playoffs

Season	Team	League	GP	G	A	PTS	PIM	GP	G	A	PTS	PIM
98-99	Memphis	CHL	69	17	28	45	71	4	0	0	0	2

Born; 7/11/76, South Porcupine, Ontario. 5-9, 170.

Gino Santerre — Defenseman
Regular Season — Playoffs

Season	Team	League	GP	G	A	PTS	PIM	GP	G	A	PTS	PIM
95-96	Louisville	ECHL	59	10	37	47	49	3	0	0	0	0
96-97	Louisville	ECHL	42	8	30	38	18	—	—	—	—	—
96-97	Kingston	BHL	27	12	25	37	16	—	—	—	—	—
97-98												
98-99	Lake Charles	WPHL	62	12	25	37	30	11	1	2	3	6
	ECHL	Totals	101	18	67	85	67	3	0	0	0	0

Born; 7/22/70. Ste. Foy, Quebec. 5-10, 180. Last amateur club; St. Cloud

Yves Sarault — Left Wing
Regular Season — Playoffs

Season	Team	League	GP	G	A	PTS	PIM	GP	G	A	PTS	PIM
92-93	Fredericton	AHL	59	14	17	31	41	3	0	1	1	2
92-93	Wheeling	ECHL	2	1	3	4	0	—	—	—	—	—
93-94	Fredericton	AHL	60	13	14	27	72	—	—	—	—	—
94-95	Fredericton	AHL	69	24	21	45	96	13	2	1	3	33
94-95	Montreal	NHL	8	0	1	1	0	—	—	—	—	—
95-96	Montreal	NHL	14	0	0	0	4	—	—	—	—	—
95-96	Calgary	NHL	11	2	1	3	4	—	—	—	—	—
95-96	Saint John	AHL	26	10	12	22	34	16	6	2	8	33
96-97	Colorado	NHL	28	2	1	3	6	5	0	0	0	2
96-97	Hershey	AHL	6	2	3	5	8	—	—	—	—	—
97-98	Colorado	NHL	2	1	0	1	0	—	—	—	—	—
97-98	Hershey	AHL	63	23	36	59	43	7	1	2	3	14
98-99	Ottawa	NHL	11	0	1	1	4	—	—	—	—	—
98-99	Detroit	IHL	36	11	12	23	52	11	7	2	9	40
	NHL	Totals	74	5	4	9	18	5	0	0	0	2
	AHL	Totals	283	86	103	189	294	39	9	6	15	82

Born; 12/23/72, Valleyfield, Quebec. 6-1, 170. Drafted by Montreal Canadiens (3rd choice, 61st overall) in 1991 Entry Draft. Traded to Calgary Flames by Montreal with Craig Ferguson for Calgary's eighth round choice (Peter Kubos) in 1997 Entry Draft (11/26/95). Signed as a free agent by Colorado Avalanche (9/13/96). Signed as a free agent by Ottawa Senators (7/28/98). Last amateur club; Trois-Rivieres (QMJHL).

Cory Sarich — Defenseman
Regular Season — Playoffs

Season	Team	League	GP	G	A	PTS	PIM	GP	G	A	PTS	PIM
98-99	Buffalo	NHL	4	0	0	0	0	—	—	—	—	—
98-99	Rochester	AHL	77	3	26	29	82	20	2	4	6	14

Born; 8/16/78, Saskatoon, Saskatchewan. 6-3, 175. Drafted by Buffalo Sabres (2nd choice, 27th overall) in 1996 Entry Draft. 1998-99 AHL All-Rookie Team. Last amateur club; Seattle (WHL).

Geoff Sarjeant — Goaltender
Regular Season — Playoffs

Season	Team	League	GP	W	L	T	MIN	SO	AVG	GP	W	L	MIN	SO	AVG
92-93	Peoria	IHL	41	22	14	3	2356	0	3.31	3	0	3	179	0	4.36
93-94	Peoria	IHL	41	25	9	2	2275	*2	*2.45	4	2	2	211	0	3.69
94-95	St. Louis	NHL	4	1	0	0	120	0	3.00	—	—	—	—	—	—
94-95	Peoria	IHL	55	32	12	8	3146	0	3.01	4	0	3	206	0	5.81
95-96	San Jose	NHL	4	0	2	1	171	0	4.91	—	—	—	—	—	—
95-96	Kansas City	IHL	41	18	18	1	2166	1	3.88	2	0	1	99	0	1.82
96-97	Cincinnati	IHL	59	32	20	5	3287	1	2.87	3	0	3	158	0	4.55
97-98	Cincinnati	IHL	54	25	19	9	3118	5	2.73	5	4	1	353	0	2.38
98-99	Cincinnati	IHL	14	6	5	1	733	1	3.44	—	—	—	—	—	—
98-99	Detroit	IHL	8	1	5	1	421	0	3.70	—	—	—	—	—	—
98-99	Long Beach	IHL	1	1	0	0	60	0	1.00	—	—	—	—	—	—
98-99	Indianapolis	IHL	23	13	7	2	1354	2	2.53	3	0	1	115	0	5.21
98-99	Flint	UHL	3	0	2	1	179	0	3.69	—	—	—	—	—	—
	NHL	Totals	8	1	2	1	291	0	4.12	—	—	—	—	—	—
	IHL	Totals	337	175	109	32	18917	12	3.00	24	6	14	1321	0	3.86

Born; 11/30/69, Newmarket, Ontario. 5-9, 180. Drafted by St. Louis Blues (1st choice, 17th overall) in 1990 Supplemental Draft. Signed as a free agent by San Jose Sharks (9/23/95). Traded to Detroit by Cincinnati for future considerations (12/98). 1993-94 IHL First Team All-Star. Last amateur club; Michigan Tech

Peter Sarno — Center
Regular Season — Playoffs

Season	Team	League	GP	G	A	PTS	PIM	GP	G	A	PTS	PIM
97-98	Hamilton	AHL	8	1	1	2	2	—	—	—	—	—
97-98	Windsor	OHL	64	33	88	121	18	—	—	—	—	—
98-99	Sarnia	OHL	68	37	93	*130	49	6	1	7	8	2

Born; 7/26/79, Toronto, Ontario. 5-11, 185. Drafted by Edmonton Oilers (6th choice, 141st overall) in 1997 Entry Draft. Last amateur club; Windsor (OHL).

Francois Sasseville — Right Wing
Regular Season — Playoffs

Season	Team	League	GP	G	A	PTS	PIM	GP	G	A	PTS	PIM
97-98	Quebec	IHL	52	6	5	11	34	—	—	—	—	—
97-98	Pensacola	ECHL	21	5	4	9	4	—	—	—	—	—
98-99	Grand Rapids	IHL	3	0	0	0	2	—	—	—	—	—
98-99	Saginaw	UHL	70	23	30	53	49	—	—	—	—	—
	IHL	Totals	55	6	5	11	36	—	—	—	—	—

Born; 2/7/77, St. Bruno, Quebec. 5-11, 195. Last amateur club; Halifax

Corwin Saurdiff — Goaltender
Regular Season — Playoffs

Season	Team	League	GP	W	L	T	MIN	SO	AVG	GP	W	L	MIN	SO	AVG
93-94	Kansas City	IHL	17	6	9	1	946	0	4.69	—	—	—	—	—	—
93-94	Fort Worth	CeHL	5	1	4	0	292	0	4.51	—	—	—	—	—	—
94-95	Kansas City	IHL	6	1	5	0	299	0	5.42	—	—	—	—	—	—
94-95	Hampton Roads	ECHL	22	13	6	2	1261	1	3.14	4	1	3	241	0	2.99
95-96	Hampton Roads	ECHL	5	2	2	0	272	0	4.63	—	—	—	—	—	—
97-98	Hampton Roads	ECHL	1	0	0	0	23	0	0.00	—	—	—	—	—	—
97-98	Nashville	CHL	32	17	6	4	1577	*2	3.35	5	2	2	230	0	4.69
98-99	Columbus	CHL	34	17	11	5	1939	1	2.91	2	1	1	105	0	5.14
	IHL	Totals	23	7	14	1	1245	0	4.87	—	—	—	—	—	—
	CHL	Totals	71	35	21	7	3808	3	3.21	7	3	3	335	0	4.84
	ECHL	Totals	28	15	8	2	1556	1	3.36	4	1	3	241	0	2.99

Born; 10/17/72, Warroad, Minnesota. 6-1, 195. Scored a goal for the Hampton Roads Admirals during the 1994-95 season. Selected by Columbus Cottonmouths in 1998 CHL Dispersal Draft. Traded to San Antonio by Columbus for future considerations (7/99). Last amateur club; Northern Michigan (WCHA).

Hardy Sauter — Defenseman
Regular Season — Playoffs

Season	Team	League	GP	G	A	PTS	PIM	GP	G	A	PTS	PIM
95-96	Tallahassee	ECHL	63	16	32	48	44	12	1	6	7	8
96-97	Houston	IHL	1	0	0	0	0	—	—	—	—	—
96-97	Oklahoma City	CeHL	66	32	69	101	54	4	3	2	5	12
97-98	Oklahoma City	CHL	69	22	87	109	87	11	3	8	11	8
98-99	Oklahoma City	CHL	70	20	80	100	56	13	5	9	14	37
	CHL	Totals	205	74	236	310	197	28	11	19	30	57

Born; 2/25/71, Dayton, Ohio. 5-10, 180. Played goal for 3:47 during the 1998-99 season for Blazers allowing one goal on four shots and finished with a 15.86 GAA. 1996-97 CeHL First Team All-Star. 1996-97 CeHL Defenseman of the Year. 1997-98 CHL Defenseman of the Year. Last amateur club; Regina

Alain Savage — Left Wing
Regular Season — Playoffs

Season	Team	League	GP	G	A	PTS	PIM	GP	G	A	PTS	PIM
96-97	Cleveland	IHL	3	0	0	0	0	—	—	—	—	—
96-97	Hampton Roads	ECHL	64	26	25	51	147	9	5	4	9	2
97-98	Utah	IHL	4	0	1	1	0	—	—	—	—	—
97-98	Idaho	WCHL	59	48	47	95	175	3	0	3	3	25
98-99	Mobile	ECHL	19	3	12	15	27	—	—	—	—	—
98-99	Idaho	WCHL	41	19	19	38	122	2	0	0	0	2
	WCHL	Totals	100	67	66	133	297	5	0	3	3	27
	ECHL	Totals	83	29	37	66	174	9	5	4	9	2
	IHL	Totals	7	0	1	1	0	—	—	—	—	—

Born; 11/13/74, Montreal, Quebec. 5-7, 190.

Andre Savage — Center
Regular Season — Playoffs

Season	Team	League	GP	G	A	PTS	PIM	GP	G	A	PTS	PIM
98-99	Boston	NHL	6	1	0	1	0	—	—	—	—	—
98-99	Providence	AHL	63	27	42	69	54	5	0	1	1	0

Born; 5/27/75, Ottawa, Ontario. 6-0, 195. Signed as a free agent by Boston Bruins (6/18/98). 1998-99 AHL All-Rookie Team. Member of 1998-99 AHL Champion Providence Bruins. Last amateur club; Michigan Tech (WCHA).

Reggie Savage — Right Wing

Regular Season / Playoffs

Season	Team	League	GP	G	A	PTS	PIM	GP	G	A	PTS	PIM
90-91	Washington	NHL	1	0	0	0	0	—	—	—	—	—
90-91	Baltimore	AHL	62	32	29	61	10	6	1	1	2	6
91-92	Baltimore	AHL	77	42	28	70	51	—	—	—	—	—
92-93	Washington	NHL	16	2	3	5	12	—	—	—	—	—
92-93	Baltimore	AHL	40	37	18	55	28	—	—	—	—	—
93-94	Quebec	NHL	17	3	4	7	16	—	—	—	—	—
93-94	Cornwall	AHL	33	21	13	34	56	—	—	—	—	—
94-95	Cornwall	AHL	34	13	7	20	56	14	5	6	11	40
95-96	Atlanta	IHL	66	22	14	36	118	—	—	—	—	—
95-96	Syracuse	AHL	10	9	5	14	28	16	9	6	15	54
96-97	Springfield	AHL	68	32	25	57	103	17	6	7	13	24
97-98	San Antonio	IHL	22	6	12	18	24	—	—	—	—	—
97-98	Kansas City	IHL	51	6	10	16	60	—	—	—	—	—
97-98	Orlando	IHL	10	5	5	10	18	17	2	9	11	60
98-99	Asiago	Italy	27	25	27	52	NA	—	—	—	—	—
	NHL	Totals	34	5	7	12	28	—	—	—	—	—
	AHL	Totals	324	186	125	311	332	53	21	20	41	124
	IHL	Totals	149	39	41	80	220	17	2	9	11	60

Born; 5/1/70, Montreal, Quebec. 5-10, 187. Drafted by Washington Capitals (1st choice, 15th overall) in 1988 Entry Draft. Traded to Quebec Nordiques by Washington with Paul MacDermid for Mike Hough (6/20/93). Signed as a free agent by Phoenix Coyotes (8/28/96). Traded to Kansas City by San Antonio with Mike Craig for John Purves and Darin Kimble (11/97). Traded to Orlando by Kansas City with Jason Herter for Bill H. Armstrong and Jeff Buchanan (3/98). Last amateur club; Victoriaville (QMJHL).

Marc Savard — Center

Regular Season / Playoffs

Season	Team	League	GP	G	A	PTS	PIM	GP	G	A	PTS	PIM
97-98	Rangers	NHL	28	1	5	6	4	—	—	—	—	—
97-98	Hartford	AHL	58	21	53	74	66	15	8	19	27	24
98-99	Rangers	NHL	70	9	36	45	38	—	—	—	—	—
98-99	Hartford	AHL	9	3	10	13	16	7	1	12	13	16
	NHL	Totals	98	10	41	51	42	—	—	—	—	—
	AHL	Totals	67	24	63	87	82	22	9	31	40	40

Born; 7/17/77, Ottawa, Ontario. 5-10, 174. Drafted by New York Rangers (3rd choice, 91st overall) in 1995 Entry Draft. Traded to Calgary Flames by Rangers with Rangers' first round choice (Oleg Saprykin) in 1999 Entry Draft for the rights to Jan Hlavac and Calgary's first round choice (Jamie Lundmark) in 1999 Entry Draft (6/26/99). 1997-98 AHL All-Rookie Team. Last amateur club; Os-

Ryan Savoia — Center

Regular Season / Playoffs

Season	Team	League	GP	G	A	PTS	PIM	GP	G	A	PTS	PIM
94-95	Brock	OUAA	38	35	48	83	24	—	—	—	—	—
94-95	Cleveland	IHL	1	0	0	0	0	—	—	—	—	—
95-96	Cleveland	IHL	49	6	7	13	31	—	—	—	—	—
96-97	Cleveland	IHL	4	1	0	1	2	—	—	—	—	—
96-97	Fort Wayne	IHL	8	0	2	2	2	—	—	—	—	—
96-97	Johnstown	ECHL	60	35	44	79	100	—	—	—	—	—
97-98	Syracuse	AHL	7	0	4	4	2	—	—	—	—	—
97-98	Johnstown	ECHL	6	1	5	6	0	—	—	—	—	—
98-99	Pittsburgh	NHL	3	0	0	0	0	—	—	—	—	—
98-99	Syracuse	AHL	54	9	22	31	40	—	—	—	—	—
	IHL	Totals	62	7	9	16	31	—	—	—	—	—
	AHL	Totals	61	9	26	35	42	—	—	—	—	—
	ECHL	Totals	66	36	49	85	100	—	—	—	—	—

Born; 5/6/73, Thorold, Ontario. 6-1, 205. Signed as a free agent by Pittsburgh Penguins (4/7/95). Last amateur club; Brock (OUAA).

Kevin Sawyer — Right Wing

Regular Season / Playoffs

Season	Team	League	GP	G	A	PTS	PIM	GP	G	A	PTS	PIM
94-95	Spokane	WHL	54	7	9	16	365	11	2	0	2	58
94-95	Peoria	IHL	—	—	—	—	—	2	0	0	0	12
95-96	Boston	NHL	2	0	0	0	5	—	—	—	—	—
95-96	St. Louis	NHL	6	0	0	0	23	—	—	—	—	—
95-96	Providence	AHL	4	0	0	0	29	4	0	1	1	9
95-96	Worcester	AHL	41	3	4	7	268	—	—	—	—	—
96-97	Boston	NHL	2	0	0	0	0	—	—	—	—	—
96-97	Providence	AHL	60	8	9	17	367	6	0	0	0	32
97-98	Kalamazoo	IHL	60	2	5	7	*398	3	0	0	0	23
98-99	Worcester	AHL	70	8	14	22	299	4	0	1	1	4
	NHL	Totals	10	0	0	0	28	—	—	—	—	—
	AHL	Totals	175	19	27	46	963	10	0	1	1	36
	IHL	Totals	60	2	5	7	398	5	0	0	0	35

Born; 2/21/74, Christina Lake, British Columbia. 6-2, 205. Signed as a free agent by St. Louis Blues (2/28/95). Traded to Boston Bruins by St. Louis with Steve Staois for Steve Leach (3/8/96). Signed as a free agent by Dallas Stars (8/19/97). Signed as a free agent by St. Louis (9/4/98). Last amateur club; Spokane (WHL).

Curtis Sayler — Right Wing

Regular Season / Playoffs

Season	Team	League	GP	G	A	PTS	PIM	GP	G	A	PTS	PIM
96-97	Central Texas	WPHL	1	0	0	0	0	—	—	—	—	—
96-97	San Antonio	CeHL	25	2	4	6	120	—	—	—	—	—
96-97	Port Huron	CoHL	38	4	3	7	176	5	0	0	0	10
97-98	Port Huron	UHL	69	6	13	19	217	2	0	0	0	2
98-99	Port Huron	UHL	66	4	4	8	201	5	0	0	0	5
	UHL	Totals	173	14	20	34	594	12	0	0	0	17

Born; 3/30/75, Beauvallon, Alberta. 5-11, 200. Selected by Missouri River Otters in 1999 UHL Expansion Draft. Last amateur club; Bow Valley (AJHL).

Chris Sbrocca — Center

Regular Season / Playoffs

Season	Team	League	GP	G	A	PTS	PIM	GP	G	A	PTS	PIM
96-97	Quebec	IHL	6	1	2	3	8	—	—	—	—	—
96-97	Pensacola	ECHL	65	25	46	71	201	12	4	5	9	26
97-98	Verosta	Italy	26	22	9	31	16	—	—	—	—	—
98-99	Laval	QSPHL	18	9	20	29	NA	—	—	—	—	—
98-99	Pensacola	ECHL	3	1	4	5	6	—	—	—	—	—
	ECHL	Totals	68	26	50	76	207	12	4	5	9	26

Born; 1/22/74, Montreal, Quebec. 5-10, 185. Last amateur club; Lowell (Hockey East).

Trent Schachle — Defenseman

Regular Season / Playoffs

Season	Team	League	GP	G	A	PTS	PIM	GP	G	A	PTS	PIM
96-97	Dayton	ECHL	61	10	25	35	109	4	0	3	3	8
97-98	Oklahoma City	CHL	64	10	20	30	137	11	3	3	6	8
98-99	Winston-Salem	UHL	74	14	35	49	145	5	0	2	2	0

Born; 8/31/72, Wasilla, Alaska. 6-4, 208. Selected by San Antonio in CHL 1998 Expansion Draft. Last amateur club; Alaska-Fairbanks (CCHA).

Jeff Schachterle — Center

Regular Season / Playoffs

Season	Team	League	GP	G	A	PTS	PIM	GP	G	A	PTS	PIM
97-98	Brandon	CWUAA	41	15	18	33	54	—	—	—	—	—
97-98	Huntsville	CHL	6	2	1	3	4	—	—	—	—	—
98-99	Tupelo	WPHL	59	15	14	29	84	—	—	—	—	—

Born; 5/3/73, Red Deer, Alberta. 6-2, 210. Last amateur club; Brandon

Jeremy Schaefer — Forward

Regular Season / Playoffs

Season	Team	League	GP	G	A	PTS	PIM	GP	G	A	PTS	PIM
97-98	Roanoke	ECHL	62	9	9	18	253	9	1	0	1	22
98-99	Roanoke	ECHL	39	4	2	6	182	—	—	—	—	—
	ECHL	Totals	101	13	11	24	435	9	1	0	1	22

Born; 2/27/76, Spruce Grove, Alberta. 6-3, 210. Last amateur club; Calgary

Peter Schaefer — Left Wing

Season	Team	League	GP	G	A	PTS	PIM	GP	G	A	PTS	PIM
			Regular Season					Playoffs				
96-97	Brandon	WHL	61	49	74	123	85	6	1	4	5	4
96-97	Syracuse	AHL	5	0	3	3	0	3	1	3	4	14
97-98	Syracuse	AHL	73	19	44	63	41	5	2	1	3	2
98-99	Vancouver	NHL	25	4	4	8	8	—	—	—	—	—
98-99	Syracuse	AHL	41	10	19	29	66	—	—	—	—	—
	AHL	Totals	119	29	66	95	107	8	3	4	7	16

Born; 7/12/77, Yellow Grass, Saskatchewan. 5-11, 187. Drafted by Vancouver Canucks (3rd choice, 66th overall) in 1995 Entry Draft. Last amateur club; Brandon (WHL).

Paxton Schafer — Goaltender

Season	Team	League	GP	W	L	T	MIN	SO	AVG	GP	W	L	MIN	SO	AVG
			Regular Season							Playoffs					
96-97	Boston	NHL	3	0	0	0	77	0	4.68	—	—	—	—	—	—
96-97	Providence	AHL	22	9	10	0	1206	1	3.73	—	—	—	—	—	—
96-97	Charlotte	ECHL	4	3	1	0	239	0	1.75	—	—	—	—	—	—
97-98	Providence	AHL	3	1	1	0	159	0	4.16	—	—	—	—	—	—
97-98	Charlotte	ECHL	44	21	17	5	2539	1	3.10	7	3	4	429	0	2.94
98-99	Providence	AHL	1	1	0	0	61	0	2.94	—	—	—	—	—	—
98-99	Greenville	ECHL	40	17	16	7	2326	2	2.97	—	—	—	—	—	—
	AHL	Totals	26	11	11	0	1426	1	3.74	—	—	—	—	—	—
	ECHL	Totals	88	41	34	12	5104	3	2.97	7	3	4	429	0	2.94

Born; 2/26/76, Medicine Hat, Alberta. 5-9, 152. Drafted by Boston Bruins (3rd choice, 47th overall) in 1995 Entry Draft. Last amateur club; Medicine Hat

Taj Schaffnit — Defenseman

Season	Team	League	GP	G	A	PTS	PIM	GP	G	A	PTS	PIM
			Regular Season					Playoffs				
98-99	Tallahassee	ECHL	23	1	4	5	37	—	—	—	—	—
98-99	Pensacola	ECHL	30	1	3	4	35	—	—	—	—	—
	ECHL	Totals	53	2	7	9	72	—	—	—	—	—

Born; 5/15/74, Gloucester, Ontario. 6-3, 210. Last amateur club; Ohio State (CCHA).

Jeff Scharf — Center

Season	Team	League	GP	G	A	PTS	PIM	GP	G	A	PTS	PIM
			Regular Season					Playoffs				
96-97	North Bay	OHL	66	23	36	59	57	—	—	—	—	—
96-97	Charlotte	ECHL	6	0	1	1	23	2	0	0	0	0
97-98	Belleville	OHL	63	34	51	85	60	10	3	7	10	12
98-99	Greenville	ECHL	6	1	3	4	2	—	—	—	—	—
98-99	Toledo	ECHL	12	1	5	6	12	—	—	—	—	—
98-99	Birmingham	ECHL	41	5	21	26	29	5	0	1	1	2
	ECHL	Totals	65	7	30	37	66	7	0	1	1	2

Born; 3/6/77, Sudbury, Ontario. 6-1, 190. Last amateur club; Belleville (OHL).

Lee Schill — Goaltender

Season	Team	League	GP	W	L	T	MIN	SO	AVG	GP	W	L	MIN	SO	AVG
			Regular Season							Playoffs					
95-96	Bakersfield	WCHL	26	12	11	0	1360	0	4.85	—	—	—	—	—	—
96-97	Bakersfield	WCHL	*55	27	*22	3	*3034	*2	4.81	4	1	3	224	0	4.28
97-98	Utah	IHL	4	2	1	0	656	1	3.67	—	—	—	—	—	—
97-98	Reno	WCHL	45	14	*26	2	2521	0	4.05	3	0	3	162	0	5.19
98-99	Asheville	UHL	34	13	16	1	1919	0	4.38	2	0	2	119	0	4.04
	WCHL	Totals	126	53	59	5	6915	2	4.54	7	1	6	386	0	4.67

Born; 5/12/71, Vancouver, British Columbia. 5-10, 190. Last amateur club; Alaska-Anchorage (WCHA).

Per Schlyter — Defenseman

Season	Team	League	GP	G	A	PTS	PIM	GP	G	A	PTS	PIM
			Regular Season					Playoffs				
98-99	Amarillo	WPHL	32	2	9	11	10	—	—	—	—	—
98-99	Asheville	UHL	9	0	2	2	6	—	—	—	—	—
98-99	Macon	CHL	15	2	4	6	12	3	0	2	2	0

Born; 9/3/71, Kristiansand, Sweden. 6-5, 205.

Chris Schmidt — Left Wing

Season	Team	League	GP	G	A	PTS	PIM	GP	G	A	PTS	PIM
			Regular Season					Playoffs				
96-97	Phoenix	IHL	37	3	6	9	60	—	—	—	—	—
96-97	Mississippi	ECHL	18	7	7	14	35	—	—	—	—	—
97-98	Fredericton	AHL	69	8	5	13	67	4	0	0	0	2
98-99	Springfield	AHL	17	3	2	5	19	1	0	0	0	0
98-99	Mississippi	ECHL	6	1	0	1	2	18	5	8	13	10
	AHL	Totals	86	11	7	18	86	5	0	0	0	2
	ECHL	Totals	24	8	7	15	37	18	5	8	13	10

Born; 3/1/76, Beaverlodge, Alberta. 6-3, 200. Drafted by Los Angeles Kings (4th choice, 111th overall) in 1994 Entry Draft. Member of 1998-99 ECHL Champion Mississippi SeaWolves. Last amateur club; Seattle (WHL).

Colin Schmidt — Center

Season	Team	League	GP	G	A	PTS	PIM	GP	G	A	PTS	PIM
			Regular Season					Playoffs				
96-97	Hamilton	AHL	15	2	2	4	2	—	—	—	—	—
96-97	Wheeling	ECHL	37	9	19	28	25	—	—	—	—	—
97-98												
98-99	Dayton	ECHL	10	1	2	3	7	—	—	—	—	—
	ECHL	Totals	47	10	21	31	32	—	—	—	—	—

Born; 2/3/74, Regina, Saskatchewan. 5-11, 185. Drafted by Edmonton Oilers (9th choice, 190th overall) in 1992 Entry Draft. Selected by Greensboro in 1999 ECHL Expansion Draft. Last amateur club; Colorado (WCHA).

Greg Schmidt — Center

Season	Team	League	GP	G	A	PTS	PIM	GP	G	A	PTS	PIM
			Regular Season					Playoffs				
97-98	Quebec	IHL	23	3	3	6	14	—	—	—	—	—
97-98	Pensacola	ECHL	2	0	1	1	4	—	—	—	—	—
98-99	South Carolina	ECHL	62	13	18	31	99	3	0	0	0	0
	ECHL	Totals	64	13	19	32	103	3	0	0	0	0

Born; 4/19/76, North Battleford, Saskatchewan. 5-10, 180. Last amateur club; Red Deer (WHL).

Ryan Schmidt — Defenseman

Season	Team	League	GP	G	A	PTS	PIM	GP	G	A	PTS	PIM
			Regular Season					Playoffs				
93-94	Dallas	CeHL	6	0	0	0	9	—	—	—	—	—
94-95	Roanoke	ECHL	4	0	0	0	0	—	—	—	—	—
94-95	Utica	CoHL	11	1	0	1	6	—	—	—	—	—
94-95	Detroit	CoHL	19	2	3	5	50	—	—	—	—	—
95-96	West Palm Beach	SHL	8	0	0	0	28	—	—	—	—	—
95-96	Wichita	CeHL	26	2	5	7	66	—	—	—	—	—
96-97	Dayton	CeHL	3	0	1	1	0	—	—	—	—	—
96-97	Amarillo	WPHL	39	0	4	4	81	—	—	—	—	—
97-98	Fayetteville	CHL	62	2	9	11	108	—	—	—	—	—
98-99	Mobile	ECHL	8	0	0	0	8	—	—	—	—	—
98-99	Macon	CHL	27	0	6	6	60	—	—	—	—	—
98-99	Fort Worth	CHL	7	0	1	1	24	—	—	—	—	—
	CHL	Totals	128	4	21	25	267	—	—	—	—	—
	CoHL	Totals	33	3	4	7	56	—	—	—	—	—
	ECHL	Totals	12	0	0	0	8	—	—	—	—	—

Born; 5/23/73, Grosse Ile, Michigan. 6-1, 215. Selected by Fayetteville in 1999 CHL Dispersal Draft.

Robert Schnabel — Defenseman

Season	Team	League	GP	G	A	PTS	PIM	GP	G	A	PTS	PIM
			Regular Season					Playoffs				
98-99	Springfield	AHL	77	1	7	8	155	3	1	0	1	4

Born; 11/10/78, Prague, Czechoslovakia. 6-6, 216. Drafted by New York Islanders (5th choice, 79th overall) in 1997 Entry Draft. Re-entered draft; selected by Phoenix Coyotes (7th choice, 129th overall) in 1998 Entry Draft. Last amateur club; Red Deer (WHL).

Andy Schneider — Left Wing

Regular Season / Playoffs

Season	Team	League	GP	G	A	PTS	PIM	GP	G	A	PTS	PIM
92-93	Swift Current	WHL	38	19	66	85	78	17	13	26	39	40
92-93	New Haven	AHL	19	2	2	4	13	—	—	—	—	—
93-94	Ottawa	NHL	10	0	0	0	15	—	—	—	—	—
93-94	Prince Edward Island	AHL	61	15	46	61	119	—	—	—	—	—
94-95	Leksand	Sweden	39	6	8	14	71	4	1	1	2	31
94-95	Canada	National	3	1	0	1	0	—	—	—	—	—
94-95	Prince Edward Island	AHL	10	1	5	6	25	11	5	5	10	11
95-96	Minnesota	IHL	81	12	28	40	85	—	—	—	—	—
96-97	Manitoba	IHL	79	14	37	51	142	—	—	—	—	—
97-98	Revier Lowen	Germany	26	3	12	15	46	—	—	—	—	—
97-98	Schwenningen	Germany	22	7	13	20	91	—	—	—	—	—
98-99	Schwenningen	Germany	52	17	29	46	90	—	—	—	—	—
	IHL	Totals	160	26	65	91	227	—	—	—	—	—
	AHL	Totals	90	18	53	71	157	11	5	5	10	11

Born; 3/29/72, Edmonton, Alberta. 5-9, 170. Signed as a free agent by Ottawa Senators (10/9/92). Last amateur club; Swift Current (WHL).

J.A. Schneider — Forward

Regular Season / Playoffs

Season	Team	League	GP	G	A	PTS	PIM	GP	G	A	PTS	PIM
92-93	Birmingham	ECHL	45	2	10	12	104	—	—	—	—	—
93-94	Birmingham	ECHL	63	3	16	19	202	10	0	2	2	40
94-95												
95-96	McGill	OUAA	16	4	6	10	63	—	—	—	—	—
96-97	McGill	OUAA	32	3	12	15	87	—	—	—	—	—
97-98	McGill	OUAA	27	2	8	10	90	—	—	—	—	—
98-99	Columbus	CHL	36	2	3	5	31	—	—	—	—	—
98-99	Tulsa	CHL	16	1	2	3	20	—	—	—	—	—
	ECHL	Totals	108	5	26	31	306	10	0	2	2	40
	CHL	Totals	52	3	5	8	51	—	—	—	—	—

Born; 2/16/72, Colchester, Vermont. 5-11, 185. Last amateur club; McGill

Bryan Schoen — Goaltender

Regular Season / Playoffs

Season	Team	League	GP	W	L	T	MIN	SO	AVG	GP	W	L	MIN	SO	AVG
93-94	Roanoke	ECHL	6	1	4	0	279	0	4.94	—	—	—	—	—	—
93-94	Louisville	ECHL	11	3	7	0	576	0	4.48	6	2	4	351	*1	4.62
93-94	Fort Worth	CeHL	4	2	1	0	211	0	3.98	—	—	—	—	—	—
94-95	Fort Worth	CeHL	32	11	10	2	1503	0	4.43	—	—	—	—	—	—
95-96	Los Angeles	IHL	2	0	1	1	110	0	4.36	—	—	—	—	—	—
95-96	Louisiana	ECHL	11	5	3	2	605	1	3.07	—	—	—	—	—	—
95-96	Louisville	ECHL	26	18	4	2	1418	0	3.34	—	—	—	—	—	—
96-97	Louisiana	ECHL	13	6	2	0	552	0	3.91	7	3	1	307	0	3.52
97-98	Louisiana	ECHL	19	7	6	4	1030	1	3.49	2	0	0	14	0	4.15
98-99	Lake Charles	WPHL	*61	*37	19	3	*3382	3	3.16	1	0	0	4	0	0.00
	ECHL	Totals	86	40	26	8	4460	2	3.66	15	5	5	672	1	4.11
	CeHL	Totals	36	13	11	2	1714	0	4.38	—	—	—	—	—	—

Born; 9/9/71, Minneapolis, Minnesota. 6-2, 195. Drafted by Minnesota North Stars (6th choice, 91st overall) in 1989 Entry Draft. Last amateur club; Denver

Drew Schoneck — Defenseman

Regular Season / Playoffs

Season	Team	League	GP	G	A	PTS	PIM	GP	G	A	PTS	PIM
97-98	Canada	National	50	4	14	18	63	—	—	—	—	—
98-99	Oklahoma City	CHL	—	—	—	—	—	7	0	0	0	7

Born;

Robert Schrader — Goaltender

Regular Season / Playoffs

Season	Team	League	GP	W	L	T	MIN	SO	AVG	GP	W	L	MIN	SO	AVG
98-99	Austin	WPHL	5	0	2	1	191	0	4.40	—	—	—	—	—	—

Born; 1/14/77, Prince Albert, Saskatchewan. 6-3, 200.

Rob Schriner — Center

Regular Season / Playoffs

Season	Team	League	GP	G	A	PTS	PIM	GP	G	A	PTS	PIM
92-93	Columbus	ECHL	64	26	24	50	64	—	—	—	—	—
93-94	Columbus	ECHL	65	29	31	60	45	6	2	2	4	4
94-95	Columbus	ECHL	42	14	8	22	29	—	—	—	—	—
95-96	Columbus	ECHL	63	20	19	39	54	3	0	0	0	3
96-97	Waco	WPHL	15	10	7	17	6	—	—	—	—	—
97-98	Waco	WPHL	30	24	10	34	14	—	—	—	—	—
97-98	Austin	WPHL	4	1	3	4	0	5	3	1	4	0
98-99	Columbus	ECHL	5	2	1	3	0	—	—	—	—	—
	ECHL	Totals	239	91	83	174	192	9	2	2	4	6
	WPHL	Totals	49	35	20	55	20	5	3	1	4	0

Born; 1/24/69, Colonsay, Saskatchewan. 5-11, 185. Traded to Austin by Waco for Derek Riley, Jason Rose and Chris Haskett (3/98). Last amateur club; Ohio State (CCHA). Has served as head coach of the Waco Wizards (WPHL).

Paxton Schulte — Left Wing

Regular Season / Playoffs

Season	Team	League	GP	G	A	PTS	PIM	GP	G	A	PTS	PIM
93-94	Quebec	NHL	1	0	0	0	2	—	—	—	—	—
93-94	Cornwall	AHL	56	15	15	30	102	—	—	—	—	—
94-95	Cornwall	AHL	74	14	22	36	217	14	3	3	6	29
95-96	Cornwall	AHL	*69	25	31	56	171	—	—	—	—	—
95-96	Saint John	AHL	*14	4	5	9	25	14	4	7	11	40
96-97	Calgary	NHL	1	0	0	0	2	—	—	—	—	—
96-97	Saint John	AHL	71	14	23	37	274	4	2	0	2	35
97-98	Saint John	AHL	59	8	17	25	133	—	—	—	—	—
97-98	Las Vegas	IHL	10	0	1	1	32	4	0	0	0	4
98-99	Bracknell	BSL	44	10	14	24	203	3	0	0	0	14
	NHL	Totals	2	0	0	0	4	—	—	—	—	—
	AHL	Totals	333	80	113	193	922	32	9	10	19	104

Born; 7/16/72, Ionaway, Alberta. 6-2, 210. Drafted by Quebec Nordiques (7th choice, 124th ovwerall) in 1992 Entry Draft. Traded to Calgary Flames by Quebec for Vesa Viitakoski (3/19/96). Traded to Las Vegas by Saint John with Sami Helenius and Keith McCambridge for Steve Bancroft and Justin Kurtz (3/98). Last amateur club; Spokane (WHL).

Kris Schultz — Left Wing

Regular Season / Playoffs

Season	Team	League	GP	G	A	PTS	PIM	GP	G	A	PTS	PIM
98-99	Asheville	UHL	70	5	5	10	281	4	0	1	1	9

Born; 10/20/78, Strasbourg, Saskatchewan. 6-2, 200. Last amateur club; Estevan (SJHL).

Mike Schultz — Right Wing

Regular Season / Playoffs

Season	Team	League	GP	G	A	PTS	PIM	GP	G	A	PTS	PIM
98-99	Toledo	ECHL	7	0	1	1	0	—	—	—	—	—
98-99	Huntington	ECHL	11	2	0	2	4	—	—	—	—	—
98-99	Peoria	ECHL	39	8	6	14	11	—	—	—	—	—
	ECHL	Totals	57	10	7	17	15	—	—	—	—	—

Born; 1/27/75, Hartford, Connecticut. 5-10, 210. Last amateur club; Connecticut (NCAA 3).

Ray Schultz — Defenseman

Regular Season / Playoffs

Season	Team	League	GP	G	A	PTS	PIM	GP	G	A	PTS	PIM
97-98	Islanders	NHL	13	0	1	1	45	—	—	—	—	—
97-98	Kentucky	AHL	51	2	4	6	179	1	0	0	0	25
98-99	Islanders	NHL	4	0	0	0	7	—	—	—	—	—
98-99	Lowell	AHL	54	0	3	3	184	1	0	0	0	4
	NHL	Totals	17	0	1	1	52	—	—	—	—	—
	AHL	Totals	105	2	7	9	363	2	0	0	0	29

Born; 11/14/76, Red Deer, Alberta. 6-2, 199. Drafted by Ottawa Senators (8th choice, 184th overall) in 1995 Entry Draft. Signed as a free agent by New York Islanders (6/9/97). Last amateur club; Kelowna (WHL).

Ben Schust — Center

Regular Season / Playoffs

Season	Team	League	GP	G	A	PTS	PIM	GP	G	A	PTS	PIM
98-99	Roanoke	ECHL	67	10	22	32	34	12	2	0	2	8

Born; 4/16/77, 5-11, 175. Last amateur club; Kitchener (OHL).

Corey Schwab — Goaltender

Regular Season / Playoffs

Season	Team	League	GP	W	L	T	MIN	SO	AVG	GP	W	L	MIN	SO	AVG
91-92	Utica	AHL	24	9	12	1	1322	0	4.31	—	—	—	—	—	—
91-92	Cincinnati	ECHL	8	6	0	1	450	0	4.13	9	6	3	540	0	3.22
92-93	Utica	AHL	40	18	16	5	2387	*2	4.25	1	0	1	59	0	6.10
92-93	Cincinnati	IHL	3	1	2	0	185	0	5.51	—	—	—	—	—	—
93-94	Albany	AHL	51	27	21	3	3058	0	3.61	5	1	4	298	0	4.02
94-95	Albany	AHL	45	25	10	9	2711	3	*2.59	7	6	1	425	0	2.68
95-96	New Jersey	NHL	10	0	3	0	331	0	2.18	—	—	—	—	—	—
95-96	Albany	AHL	5	3	2	0	299	0	2.61	—	—	—	—	—	—
96-97	Tampa Bay	NHL	31	11	12	1	1462	2	3.04	—	—	—	—	—	—
97-98	Tampa Bay	NHL	16	2	9	1	821	1	2.92	—	—	—	—	—	—
98-99	Tampa Bay	NHL	40	8	25	3	2146	0	3.52	—	—	—	—	—	—
98-99	Cleveland	IHL	8	1	6	1	477	0	3.90	—	—	—	—	—	—
	NHL	Totals	97	21	49	5	4760	3	3.18	—	—	—	—	—	—
	AHL	Totals	165	82	51	18	9777	5	3.55	13	7	6	782	0	3.45
	IHL	Totals	11	2	8	1	662	0	4.35	—	—	—	—	—	—

Born; 11/4/70, North Battleford, Saskatchewan. 6-0, 180. Drafted by New Jersey Devils (12th choice, 200th overall) in 1990 Entry Draft. Traded to Tampa Bay Lightning by New Jersey for Jeff Reese, Chicago's second round choice (previously acquired, New Jersey selected Pierre Dagenais) in 1996 Entry Draft and Tampa Bay's eighth round choice (Jay Bertsch) in 1996 Entry Draft (6/22/96). Selected by Atlanta Thrashers in 1999 NHL Expansion Draft (6/25/99). 1994-95 AHL Second Team All-Star. 1994-95 AHL shared Harry "Hap" Holmes Trophy (fewest goals against) with Mike Dunham. 1994-95 AHL shared Playoff MVP with Mike Dunham. Shared shutout with Kevin Hodson Vs Boston (4/8/99). Member of 1994-95 AHL Champion Albany RiverRats. Last amateur

Darren Schwartz — Left Wing

Regular Season / Playoffs

Season	Team	League	GP	G	A	PTS	PIM	GP	G	A	PTS	PIM
89-90	Johnstown	ECHL	50	26	27	53	270	—	—	—	—	—
90-91	Johnstown	ECHL	62	33	34	67	254	10	2	0	2	74
91-92	Winston-Salem	ECHL	55	25	21	46	345	5	1	4	5	61
92-93	Baltimore	AHL	2	0	0	0	4	—	—	—	—	—
92-93	Wheeling	ECHL	62	62	52	114	212	16	*13	18	*31	43
93-94	Wheeling	ECHL	67	54	38	92	201	9	8	3	11	35
94-95	Nottingham	BHL	1	1	0	1	8	—	—	—	—	—
94-95	Denver	IHL	1	0	0	0	0	—	—	—	—	—
94-95	Tallahassee	ECHL	66	47	35	82	150	15	5	9	14	18
95-96	Tallahassee	ECHL	60	39	22	61	159	11	3	4	7	10
96-97												
97-98	Winston-Salem	UHL	73	42	35	77	187	—	—	—	—	—
98-99	Wheeling	ECHL	68	27	29	56	148	—	—	—	—	—
	ECHL	Totals	490	313	258	571	1739	66	32	38	70	235

Born; 3/28/68, Kamsack, Saskatchewan. 5-11, 205. 1992-93 ECHL First Team All-Star. 1993-94 ECHL First Team All-Star. 1994-95 ECHL First Team All-Star.

Aaron Schweitzer — Goaltender

Regular Season / Playoffs

Season	Team	League	GP	W	L	T	MIN	SO	AVG	GP	W	L	MIN	SO	AVG
98-99	Canada	Na-	48	11	6	6	1284	—	3.13	—	—	—	—	—	—

Born; 12/1/78, Regina, Saskatchewan. 5-10, 175. Last amateur club; North Dakota (WCHA).

Blair Scott — Defenseman

Regular Season / Playoffs

Season	Team	League	GP	G	A	PTS	PIM	GP	G	A	PTS	PIM
93-94	Cornwall	AHL	19	1	2	3	13	—	—	—	—	—
94-95	Cornwall	AHL	56	8	16	24	108	14	3	5	8	12
95-96	Chicago	IHL	14	0	2	2	32	—	—	—	—	—
95-96	Atlanta	IHL	19	1	1	2	38	—	—	—	—	—
95-96	Cape Breton	AHL	30	4	4	8	42	—	—	—	—	—
96-97	Hershey	AHL	47	2	12	14	100	—	—	—	—	—
97-98	Basingstoke	BSL	47	7	12	19	148	6	2	1	3	4
98-99	Manchester	BSL	53	5	21	26	66	9	3	1	4	32
	AHL	Totals	152	15	34	49	273	14	3	5	8	12
	IHL	Totals	33	1	3	4	70	—	—	—	—	—

Born; 2/25/72, Winnipeg, Manitoba. 6-0, 194. Signed as a free agent by Quebec Nordiques (7/6/93). Last amateur club; Detroit (OHL).

Brent Scott — Right Wing

Regular Season / Playoffs

Season	Team	League	GP	G	A	PTS	PIM	GP	G	A	PTS	PIM
95-96	Bakersfield	WCHL	54	29	42	71	251	—	—	—	—	—
96-97	El Paso	WPHL	60	19	31	50	235	9	4	2	6	44
97-98	El Paso	WPHL	61	22	31	53	98	15	1	4	5	33
98-99	Alexandria	WPHL	49	20	47	67	147	—	—	—	—	—
98-99	Amarillo	WPHL	14	4	4	8	44	—	—	—	—	—
	WPHL	Totals	184	65	113	178	524	24	5	6	11	77

Born; 9/9/66, Calgary, Alberta. 5-10, 200. Selected by Alexandria in 1998 WPHL Expansion Draft. Traded to Amarillo by ALexandria for Trevor Jobe (2/99). Member of 1996-97 WPHL Champion El Paso Buzzards. Member of 1997-98 WPHL Champion El Paso Buzzards.

Brian Scott — Forward

Regular Season / Playoffs

Season	Team	League	GP	G	A	PTS	PIM	GP	G	A	PTS	PIM
96-97	Johnstown	ECHL	7	2	1	3	4	—	—	—	—	—
97-98	Johnstown	ECHL	12	1	1	2	2	—	—	—	—	—
98-99	Saginaw	UHL	12	0	1	1	5	—	—	—	—	—
	ECHL	Totals	19	3	2	5	6	—	—	—	—	—

Born; 5/22/77, Brampton, Ontario. 6-2, 200. Last amateur club; Sudbury (OHL).

Travis Scott — Goaltender

Regular Season / Playoffs

Season	Team	League	GP	W	L	T	MIN	SO	AVG	GP	W	L	MIN	SO	AVG
96-97	Worcester	AHL	29	14	10	1	1482	1	3.04	—	—	—	—	—	—
96-97	Baton Rouge	ECHL	10	5	2	1	501	0	2.63	—	—	—	—	—	—
97-98	Baton Rouge	ECHL	36	14	11	6	1949	1	2.96	—	—	—	—	—	—
98-99	Mississippi	ECHL	44	22	12	5	2337	1	2.88	*18	*14	4	*1252	3	2.01
	ECHL	Totals	90	31	25	12	4787	2	2.88	18	14	4	1252	3	2.01

Born; 9/14/75, Kanata, Ontario. 6-2, 185. Signed as a free agent by St. Louis Blues (12/30/96). 1998-99 ECHL Playoff MVP. Member of 1998-99 ECHL Champion Mississippi SeaWolves. Last amateur club; Ottawa (OHL).

Darrel Scoville — Defenseman

Regular Season / Playoffs

Season	Team	League	GP	G	A	PTS	PIM	GP	G	A	PTS	PIM
98-99	Saint John	AHL	61	1	7	8	66	7	1	2	3	13

Born; 10/13/75, Regina, Saskatchewan. 6-3, 215. Signed as a free agent by Calgary Flames (6/12/98). Last amateur club; Merrimack (Hockey East).

Claudio Scremin

Regular Season — Defenseman — Playoffs

Season	Team	League	GP	G	A	PTS	PIM	GP	G	A	PTS	PIM
90-91	Kansas City	IHL	77	7	14	21	60	—	—	—	—	—
91-92	Kansas City	IHL	70	5	23	28	44	15	1	6	7	14
91-92	San Jose	NHL	13	0	0	0	25	—	—	—	—	—
92-93	San Jose	NHL	4	0	1	1	4	—	—	—	—	—
92-93	Kansas City	IHL	75	10	22	32	93	12	0	5	5	18
93-94	Kansas City	IHL	38	7	17	24	39	—	—	—	—	—
94-95	Kansas City	IHL	61	8	30	38	29	20	8	12	20	14
95-96	Kansas City	IHL	79	6	47	53	83	5	0	1	1	6
96-97	Kansas City	IHL	69	7	25	32	71	3	1	1	2	2
97-98	Kansas City	IHL	81	12	46	58	66	11	2	12	14	4
98-99	Hannover	Germany	52	7	17	24	40	—	—	—	—	—
	NHL	Totals	17	0	1	1	29	—	—	—	—	—
	IHL	Totals	550	62	224	286	485	66	12	37	49	58

Born; 5/28/68, Burnaby, British Columbia. 6-2, 205. Drafted by Washington Capitals (12th choice, 204th overall) in 1988 Entry Draft. Traded to Minnesota North Stars by Washington for Don Beaupre (11/1/88). Signed as a free agent by San Jose Sharks (9/3/91). Member of 1991-92 IHL champion Kansas City Blades. Last amateur club; Maine (Hockey East).

Doug Searle

Regular Season — Defenseman — Playoffs

Season	Team	League	GP	G	A	PTS	PIM	GP	G	A	PTS	PIM
93-94	Las Vegas	IHL	1	0	0	0	0	—	—	—	—	—
93-94	Knoxville	ECHL	65	6	12	18	154	3	0	1	1	4
94-95	Las Vegas	IHL	7	0	1	1	18	—	—	—	—	—
94-95	Knoxville	ECHL	56	7	11	18	205	4	0	0	0	15
95-96	Phoenix	IHL	4	0	0	0	17	—	—	—	—	—
95-96	Knoxville	ECHL	58	4	30	34	261	7	1	1	2	31
96-97	Roanoke	ECHL	70	4	8	12	102	4	0	1	1	0
97-98	Pee Dee	ECHL	70	4	12	16	99	8	0	2	2	6
98-99	Roanoke	ECHL	68	1	10	11	70	12	0	0	0	8
	IHL	Totals	12	0	1	1	35	—	—	—	—	—
	ECHL	Totals	387	26	83	109	891	38	1	6	7	64

Born; 3/21/72, Toronto, Ontario. 6-4, 220. Traded to Roanoke by Pee Dee for Cory Peterson (9/98). Last amateur club; Peterborough (OHL).

Jeff Sebastien

Regular Season — Defenseman — Playoffs

Season	Team	League	GP	G	A	PTS	PIM	GP	G	A	PTS	PIM
92-93	Canada	National	2	0	2	2	0	—	—	—	—	—
92-93	Louisville	ECHL	63	14	28	42	52	—	—	—	—	—
93-94	Louisville	ECHL	66	11	19	30	51	6	0	0	0	8
94-95	Canada	National	50	10	12	22	14	—	—	—	—	—
94-95	Saint John	AHL	11	1	1	2	0	5	0	1	1	0
95-96	Daytona Beach	SHL	1	0	0	0	0	—	—	—	—	—
96-97	Manchester	BHL	39	4	15	19	14	—	—	—	—	—
97-98	Nottingham	BSL	56	12	25	37	103	6	0	5	5	2
98-99	Revier Lowen	Germany	52	9	18	27	57	—	—	—	—	—
98-99	San Angelo	WPHL	3	0	1	1	0	17	4	7	11	8
	ECHL	Totals	129	25	47	72	103	6	0	0	0	8

Born; 11/21/71, Regina, Saskatchewan. 6-2, 195. Last amateur club; Seattle

Brian Secord

Regular Season — Center — Playoffs

Season	Team	League	GP	G	A	PTS	PIM	GP	G	A	PTS	PIM
95-96	Sault Ste. Marie	OHL	59	28	45	73	100	4	0	0	0	4
95-96	Springfield	AHL	1	0	0	0	0	—	—	—	—	—
96-97	Springfield	AHL	6	1	2	3	2	—	—	—	—	—
96-97	Hamilton	AHL	3	1	1	2	0	—	—	—	—	—
96-97	Quebec	IHL	3	1	0	1	4	—	—	—	—	—
96-97	Richmond	ECHL	31	14	8	22	58	—	—	—	—	—
96-97	Pensacola	ECHL	19	5	9	14	20	12	2	3	5	14
97-98	Michigan	IHL	1	0	0	0	2	—	—	—	—	—
97-98	Manitoba	IHL	26	2	6	8	54	1	0	0	0	0
97-98	Raleigh	ECHL	16	6	5	11	26	—	—	—	—	—
97-98	Dayton	ECHL	26	7	14	21	54	—	—	—	—	—
98-99	Cincinnati	IHL	31	1	6	7	26	—	—	—	—	—
98-99	Dayton	ECHL	37	11	20	31	66	4	0	1	1	24
	IHL	Totals	61	4	12	16	86	1	0	0	0	0
	AHL	Totals	10	2	3	5	2	—	—	—	—	—
	ECHL	Totals	129	43	56	99	224	16	2	4	6	38

Born; 1/19/75, Ridgetown, Ontario. 5-11, 180. Signed as a free agent by Hartford Whalers (9/27/95). Last amateur club; Sault Ste. Marie (OHL).

Boris Sedivy

Regular Season — Left Wing — Playoffs

Season	Team	League	GP	G	A	PTS	PIM	GP	G	A	PTS	PIM
98-99	Austin	WPHL	8	0	1	1	0	—	—	—	—	—

Born; 11/21/77, Tabor, Czech. Republic. 6-1, 195.

Anthony Segala

Regular Season — Defenseman — Playoffs

Season	Team	League	GP	G	A	PTS	PIM	GP	G	A	PTS	PIM
97-98	Binghamton	UHL	50	0	6	6	27	1	0	0	0	0
98-99	Saginaw	UHL	28	0	3	3	16	—	—	—	—	—
98-99	Memphis	CHL	3	0	0	0	0	—	—	—	—	—
	UHL	Totals	78	0	9	9	43	1	0	0	0	0

Born; 6/10/74, Pittsfield, Massachusetts. 6-1, 185.

Brett Seguin

Regular Season — Center — Playoffs

Season	Team	League	GP	G	A	PTS	PIM	GP	G	A	PTS	PIM
92-93	Muskegon	CoHL	49	24	40	64	48	7	6	8	14	20
92-93	Phoenix	IHL	16	2	7	9	8	—	—	—	—	—
93-94	Fort Wayne	IHL	6	0	0	0	4	—	—	—	—	—
93-94	Muskegon	CoHL	46	24	50	74	105	3	1	3	4	8
94-95	Phoenix	IHL	2	0	2	2	0	—	—	—	—	—
94-95	Muskegon	CoHL	74	55	67	122	74	17	13	20	33	10
95-96	Detroit	IHL	3	0	0	0	0	—	—	—	—	—
95-96	Muskegon	CoHL	62	31	75	106	70	5	4	3	7	28
96-97	Austin	WPHL	53	35	54	89	26	6	1	5	6	2
97-98	Austin	WPHL	53	22	46	68	24	5	1	3	4	12
98-99	Topeka	CHL	70	24	56	80	34	3	0	1	1	8
	IHL	Totals	27	2	9	11	12	—	—	—	—	—
	CoHL	Totals	231	134	232	366	297	32	24	34	58	66
	WPHL	Totals	106	57	100	157	50	11	2	8	10	14

Born; 2/20/72, Rochester, New York. 5-9, 185. Drafted by Los Angeles Kings (6th round, 130th overall) 6/6/22/91. 1994-95 CoHL Second Team All-Star. Last amateur club; Ottawa (OHL).

Kurt Seher — Defenseman

Regular Season / Playoffs

Season	Team	League	GP	G	A	PTS	PIM	GP	G	A	PTS	PIM
92-93	Seattle	WHL	69	9	20	29	125	5	0	3	3	10
92-93	Providence	AHL	2	0	0	0	2	3	0	0	0	2
93-94	Providence	AHL	8	0	0	0	8	—	—	—	—	—
93-94	Charlotte	ECHL	51	6	21	27	54	3	0	0	0	2
94-95	Providence	AHL	15	0	3	3	4	6	0	0	0	2
94-95	Charlotte	ECHL	49	8	13	21	51	1	1	0	1	0
95-96	Charlotte	ECHL	68	10	37	47	71	16	3	10	13	14
96-97	Utah	IHL	16	0	5	5	4	—	—	—	—	—
96-97	Manitoba	IHL	3	0	1	1	2	—	—	—	—	—
96-97	Charlotte	ECHL	28	4	10	14	24	3	0	1	1	18
97-98	Charlotte	ECHL	62	3	19	22	62	—	—	—	—	—
98-99	Charlotte	ECHL	68	7	17	24	65	—	—	—	—	—
	AHL	Totals	25	0	3	3	14	9	0	0	0	4
	IHL	Totals	19	0	6	6	6	—	—	—	—	—
	ECHL	Totals	326	38	117	155	327	23	4	11	15	34

Born; 4/15/73, Lethbridge, Alberta. 6-2, 200. Drafted by Boston Bruins (6th choice, 184th overall) in 1993 Entry Draft. Member of 1995-96 ECHL champion Charlotte Checkers. Last amateur club; Seattle (WHL).

Troy Seibel — Goaltender

Regular Season / Playoffs

Season	Team	League	GP	W	L	T	MIN	SO	AVG	GP	W	L	MIN	SO	AVG
95-96	Huntsville	SHL	30	15	14	0	1719	1	4.40	10	7	2	584	0	3.91
96-97	Huntsville	CeHL	49	28	17	0	2710	0	4.12	9	5	4	545	0	3.75
97-98	Fayetteville	CHL	27	5	16	0	1291	0	4.97	—	—	—	—	—	—
97-98	Amarillo	WPHL	5	0	1	0	151	0	5.96	—	—	—	—	—	—
98-99	Huntsville	CHL	7	4	2	1	379	0	5.06	—	—	—	—	—	—
	CHL	Totals	83	37	35	1	4380	0	4.45	9	5	4	545	0	3.75

Born; 6/16/70, Drumheller, Alberta. 6-2, 198. Member of 1995-96 SHL champion Huntsville Channel Cats.

Dave Seitz — Center

Regular Season / Playoffs

Season	Team	League	GP	G	A	PTS	PIM	GP	G	A	PTS	PIM
96-97	Rochester	AHL	13	0	2	2	4	—	—	—	—	—
96-97	South Carolina	ECHL	58	43	54	97	48	17	9	15	24	30
97-98	Rochester	AHL	4	1	0	1	2	—	—	—	—	—
97-98	South Carolina	ECHL	66	33	50	83	56	5	1	3	4	2
98-99	Chicago	IHL	7	1	2	3	2	—	—	—	—	—
98-99	South Carolina	ECHL	53	30	37	67	69	3	0	1	1	4
	AHL	Totals	17	1	2	3	6	—	—	—	—	—
	ECHL	Totals	177	106	141	247	173	25	10	19	29	36

Born; 2/2/74, Buffalo, New York. 5-10, 180. Last amateur club; Clarkson

Marc Seliger — Goaltender

Regular Season / Playoffs

Season	Team	League	GP	W	L	T	MIN	SO	AVG	GP	W	L	MIN	SO	AVG
96-97	Portland	AHL	6	0	3	1	253	0	4.98	—	—	—	—	—	—
96-97	Hampton Roads	ECHL	16	10	3	1	723	0	3.40	2	0	1	90	0	4.68
97-98	Revier Lowen	Germany	28	—	—	—	1645	0	3.90	—	—	—	—	—	—
98-99	Revier Lowen	Germany	32	—	—	—	1743	0	4.72	—	—	—	—	—	—

Born; 5/1/74, Rosenheim, Germany. 5-11, 165. Drafted by Washington Capitals (9th choice, 251st overall) in 1993 Entry Draft.

Alexander Selivanov — Right Wing

Regular Season / Playoffs

Season	Team	League	GP	G	A	PTS	PIM	GP	G	A	PTS	PIM
94-95	Atlanta	IHL	4	0	3	3	2	—	—	—	—	—
94-95	Chicago	IHL	14	4	1	5	8	—	—	—	—	—
94-95	Tampa Bay	NHL	43	10	6	16	14	—	—	—	—	—
95-96	Tampa Bay	NHL	79	31	21	52	93	6	2	2	4	6
96-97	Tampa Bay	NHL	69	15	18	33	61	—	—	—	—	—
97-98	Tampa Bay	NHL	70	16	19	35	85	—	—	—	—	—
98-99	Tampa Bay	NHL	43	6	13	19	18	—	—	—	—	—
98-99	Edmonton	NHL	29	8	6	14	24	2	0	1	1	2
98-99	Cleveland	IHL	2	0	1	1	4	—	—	—	—	—
	NHL	Totals	332	86	83	169	295	8	2	3	5	8
	IHL	Totals	20	4	5	9	14	—	—	—	—	—

Born; 3/23/71, Moscow, USSR. 6-0, 206. Drafted by Philadelphia Flyers (4th choice, 140th overall) in 1994 Entry Draft. Traded to Tampa Bay Lightning by Philadelphia for Philadelphia's fourth round choice (previously acquired, Philadelphia selected Radovan Somik) in 1995 Entry Draft (9/6/94). Traded to Edmonton Oilers by Tampa Bay for Alexandre Daigle (1/29/99).

Sean Selmser — Left Wing

Regular Season / Playoffs

Season	Team	League	GP	G	A	PTS	PIM	GP	G	A	PTS	PIM
95-96	Portland	AHL	6	4	1	5	28	5	2	3	5	11
95-96	Hampton Roads	ECHL	70	23	31	54	211	3	2	0	2	8
96-97	Canada	National	59	20	18	38	150	—	—	—	—	—
96-97	Manitoba	IHL	4	0	2	2	12	—	—	—	—	—
97-98	Canada	National	52	8	22	30	122	—	—	—	—	—
97-98	Portland	AHL	—	—	—	—	—	1	0	1	1	0
98-99	Fort Wayne	IHL	80	9	15	24	200	2	0	0	0	2
	IHL	Totals	84	9	17	26	212	2	0	0	0	2
	AHL	Totals	6	4	1	5	28	6	2	4	6	11

Born; 11/10/74, Calgary, Alberta. 6-1, 190. Last amateur club; Red Deer (WHL).

Alexander Semak — Center

Regular Season / Playoffs

Season	Team	League	GP	G	A	PTS	PIM	GP	G	A	PTS	PIM
91-92	New Jersey	AHL	25	5	6	11	0	1	0	0	0	0
91-92	Utica	AHL	7	3	2	5	0	—	—	—	—	—
92-93	New Jersey	NHL	82	37	42	79	70	5	1	1	2	0
93-94	New Jersey	NHL	54	12	17	29	22	2	0	0	0	0
94-95	New Jersey	NHL	19	2	6	8	13	—	—	—	—	—
94-95	Tampa Bay	NHL	22	5	5	10	12	—	—	—	—	—
95-96	Islanders	NHL	69	20	14	34	68	—	—	—	—	—
96-97	Vancouver	NHL	18	2	1	3	2	—	—	—	—	—
96-97	Syracuse	AHL	23	10	14	24	12	—	—	—	—	—
96-97	Las Vegas	IHL	13	11	13	24	10	3	0	4	4	4
97-98	Chicago	IHL	67	26	35	61	90	22	10	*17	*27	35
98-99	Albany	AHL	70	20	42	62	62	5	0	2	2	4
	NHL	Totals	289	83	91	174	187	8	1	1	2	0
	AHL	Totals	125	38	64	102	74	6	0	2	2	4
	IHL	Totals	80	37	48	85	100	25	10	21	31	39

Born; 2/11/66, Ufa, Russia. 5-10, 185. Drafted by New Jersey Devils (12th choice, 207th overall) in 1988 Entry Draft. Traded to Tampa Bay Lightning by New Jersey with Ben Hankinson for Shawn Chambers and Danton Cole, (3/14/95). Traded to New York Islanders by Tampa Bay for Islanders fifth round choice (Karel Betik) in 1997 Entry Draft (9/14/95). 1997-98 IHL Playoff MVP. Member of 1997-98 IHL Champion Chicago Wolves.

Kurt Semandel — Right Wing

Regular Season / Playoffs

Season	Team	League	GP	G	A	PTS	PIM	GP	G	A	PTS	PIM
90-91	Kansas City	IHL	11	0	1	1	4	—	—	—	—	—
90-91	Nashville	ECHL	49	21	29	50	66	—	—	—	—	—
91-92	Columbus	ECHL	61	26	36	62	72	—	—	—	—	—
92-93	Columbus	ECHL	62	27	28	55	86	—	—	—	—	—
93-94	Toledo	ECHL	5	1	0	1	6	—	—	—	—	—
94-95												
95-96												
96-97												
97-98	Madison	UHL	18	4	8	12	20	6	0	1	1	2
98-99	Madison	UHL	3	0	0	0	0	—	—	—	—	—
	ECHL	Totals	177	75	93	168	230	—	—	—	—	—
	UHL	Totals	21	4	8	12	20	6	0	1	1	2

Born; 5/21/67, West Allis, Wisconsin. 6-0, 192.

Brandy Semchuk — Left Wing

Regular Season / Playoffs

Season	Team	League	GP	G	A	PTS	PIM	GP	G	A	PTS	PIM
90-91	Lethbridge	WHL	14	9	8	17	10	15	8	5	13	18
90-91	New Haven	AHL	21	1	4	5	6	—	—	—	—	—
91-92	Phoenix	IHL	15	1	5	6	6	—	—	—	—	—
91-92	Raleigh	ECHL	5	1	2	3	16	2	1	0	!	4
92-93	Phoenix	IHL	56	13	12	25	58	—	—	—	—	—
92-93	Los Angeles	NHL	1	0	0	0	2	—	—	—	—	—
93-94	Phoenix	IHL	2	0	0	0	6	—	—	—	—	—
93-94	Erie	ECHL	44	17	15	32	37	—	—	—	—	—
94-95	Nashville	ECHL	9	3	2	5	2	—	—	—	—	—
94-95	San Antonio	CeHL	29	17	16	33	34	13	1	5	6	33
95-96	San Antonio	CeHL	12	5	2	7	43	—	—	—	—	—
96-97	San Antonio	CeHL	10	4	6	10	2	—	—	—	—	—
96-97	Columbus	CeHL	13	5	5	10	8	3	0	1	1	12
97-98	Shreveport	WPHL	34	20	11	31	33	—	—	—	—	—
97-98	Fresno	WCHL	25	20	18	38	21	5	2	3	5	0
98-99	Fresno	WCHL	39	10	11	21	40	—	—	—	—	—
	IHL	Totals	73	14	17	31	70	—	—	—	—	—
	WCHL	Totals	64	30	29	59	61	5	2	3	5	0
	CeHL	Totals	64	31	29	60	87	16	1	6	7	45
	ECHL	Totals	58	21	19	40	55	2	1	0	1	4

Born; 9/22/71, Calgary, Alberta. 6-1, 215. Drafted by Los Angeles Kings (2nd choice, 28th overall) in 1990 Entry Draft. Last amateur club; Lethbridge (WHL).

Mike Senior — Right Wing

Regular Season / Playoffs

Season	Team	League	GP	G	A	PTS	PIM	GP	G	A	PTS	PIM
96-97	Nashville	CHL	9	1	5	6	9	—	—	—	—	—
97-98												
98-99	Saginaw	UHL	64	11	5	16	30	—	—	—	—	—

Born; 9/10/75, Trenton, Ontario. 5-11, 176.

Trevor Senn — Right Wing

Regular Season / Playoffs

Season	Team	League	GP	G	A	PTS	PIM	GP	G	A	PTS	PIM
91-92	Winston-Salem	ECHL	41	16	25	41	196	4	0	0	0	60
92-93	Wheeling	ECHL	53	14	21	35	301	14	3	2	5	89
93-94	Greensboro	ECHL	4	2	3	5	50	8	0	2	2	37
94-95	Greensboro	ECHL	15	5	3	8	141	—	—	—	—	—
94-95	South Carolina	ECHL	15	2	1	3	139	—	—	—	—	—
94-95	Richmond	ECHL	9	1	0	1	98	16	5	8	13	*138
95-96	Houston	IHL	2	0	0	0	22	—	—	—	—	—
95-96	Richmond	ECHL	57	18	31	49	507	7	3	3	6	21
96-97	Baltimore	AHL	27	4	5	9	167	—	—	—	—	—
96-97	Richmond	ECHL	28	8	14	22	211	8	2	5	7	58
97-98	Winston-Salem	UHL	43	8	28	36	280	—	—	—	—	—
98-99	Richmond	ECHL	42	7	11	18	271	18	4	4	8	*89
	ECHL	Totals	264	73	109	182	1914	75	17	24	41	492

Born; 4/7/70, Saskatoon, Saskatchewan. 5-9, 185. Member of 1994-95 ECHL Champion Richmond Renegades.

Dmitri Sergeev — Center

Regular Season / Playoffs

Season	Team	League	GP	G	A	PTS	PIM	GP	G	A	PTS	PIM
98-99	Tacoma	WCHL	13	0	1	1	2	—	—	—	—	—
98-99	Wheeling	ECHL	31	8	9	17	12	—	—	—	—	—

Born; 3/15/73, Moscow, Russia. 6-1, 190.

Joe Seroski — Right Wing

Regular Season / Playoffs

Season	Team	League	GP	G	A	PTS	PIM	GP	G	A	PTS	PIM
97-98	Hamilton	AHL	2	1	0	1	0	—	—	—	—	—
97-98	New Orleans	ECHL	68	43	36	79	12	4	6	1	7	6
98-99	Hamilton	AHL	2	0	0	0	0	—	—	—	—	—
98-99	New Orleans	ECHL	36	9	10	19	8	—	—	—	—	—
98-99	Birmingham	ECHL	29	12	18	30	8	5	0	1	1	0
	AHL	Totals	4	1	0	1	0	—	—	—	—	—
	ECHL	Totals	133	64	64	128	28	9	6	2	8	6

Born; 1/3/77, Hamilton, Ontario. 5-10, 175. Last amateur club; Sault Ste. Marie (OHL).

Jason Sessa — Right Wing

Regular Season / Playoffs

Season	Team	League	GP	G	A	PTS	PIM	GP	G	A	PTS	PIM
97-98	Lake Superior	CCHA	32	16	13	29	55	—	—	—	—	—
97-98	St. John's	AHL	5	0	0	0	6	—	—	—	—	—
98-99	St. John's	AHL	56	9	4	13	25	—	—	—	—	—
	AHL	Totals	61	9	4	13	31	—	—	—	—	—

Born; 7/17/77, Long Island, New York. 6-1, 173. Drafted by Toronto Maple Leafs (5th choice, 86th overall) in 1996 Entry Draft. Last amateur club; Lake Superior (CCHA).

Tom Severance — Forward

Regular Season / Playoffs

Season	Team	League	GP	G	A	PTS	PIM	GP	G	A	PTS	PIM
98-99	Colorado	WCHL	1	0	0	0	0	—	—	—	—	—

Born;

Cam Severson — Left Wing

Regular Season / Playoffs

Season	Team	League	GP	G	A	PTS	PIM	GP	G	A	PTS	PIM
98-99	Spokane	WHL	47	16	17	33	190	—	—	—	—	—
98-99	Oklahoma City	CHL	5	6	3	9	4	10	4	0	4	26

Born; 1/15/78, Canora, Saskatchewan. 6-1, 215. Drafted by San Jose Sharks (6th choice, 192nd overall) in 1997 Entry Draft. Last amateur club; Spokane (WHL).

Brent Severyn — Left Wing

Season	Team	League	GP	G	A	PTS	PIM	GP	G	A	PTS	PIM
			Regular Season					Playoffs				
88-89	Halifax	AHL	47	2	12	14	141	—	—	—	—	—
89-90	Quebec	NHL	35	0	2	2	42	—	—	—	—	—
89-90	Halifax	AHL	43	6	9	15	105	6	1	2	3	49
90-91	Halifax	AHL	50	7	26	33	202	—	—	—	—	—
91-92	Utica	AHL	80	11	33	44	211	4	0	1	1	4
92-93	Utica	AHL	77	20	32	52	240	5	0	0	0	35
93-94	Florida	NHL	67	4	7	11	156	—	—	—	—	—
94-95	Florida	NHL	9	1	1	2	37	—	—	—	—	—
94-95	Islanders	NHL	19	1	3	4	34	—	—	—	—	—
95-96	Islanders	NHL	65	1	8	9	180	—	—	—	—	—
96-97	Colorado	NHL	66	1	4	5	193	8	0	0	0	12
97-98	Anaheim	NHL	37	1	3	4	133	—	—	—	—	—
98-99	Michigan	IHL	3	0	0	0	0	—	—	—	—	—
98-99	Dallas	NHL	30	1	2	3	50	—	—	—	—	—
	NHL	Totals	328	10	30	40	825	8	0	0	0	12
	AHL	Totals	297	46	122	168	899	15	1	3	4	88

Born; 2/22/66, Vegreville, Alberta. 6-2, 211. Drafted by Winnipeg Jets (5th choice, 99th overall) in 1984 Entry Draft. Signed as a free agent by Quebec Nordiques (7/15/88). Traded to New Jersey Devils by Quebec for Dave Marcinyshyn (6/3/91). Traded to Winnipeg by New Jersey for New Jersey's sixth round choice (Ryan Smart) in 1994 Entry Draft (9/30/93). Traded to Florida Panthers by Winnipeg for Milan Tichy (10/3/93). Traded to New York Islanders by Florida for Islanders fourth round choice (Dave Duerden) in 1995 Entry Draft (3/3/95). Traded to Colorado Avalanche by Islanders for Colorado's third round choice (later traded to Calgary-later traded to Carolina Hurricanes-Carolina selected Francis Lessard) in 1997 Entry Draft (9/4/96). Claimed by Anaheim Mighty Ducks from Colorado in NHL Waiver Draft (9/28/97). Signed as a free agent by Dallas Stars (8/26/98). Last amateur club; Alberta (CWUAA).

Pierre Sevigny — Left Wing

Season	Team	League	GP	G	A	PTS	PIM	GP	G	A	PTS	PIM
			Regular Season					Playoffs				
91-92	Fredericton	AHL	74	22	37	59	145	7	1	1	2	26
92-93	Fredericton	AHL	80	36	40	76	113	5	1	1	2	2
93-94	Montreal	NHL	43	4	5	9	42	3	0	1	1	0
94-95	Montreal	NHL	19	0	0	0	15	—	—	—	—	—
95-96	Fredericton	AHL	76	39	42	81	188	10	5	9	14	20
96-97	Montreal	NHL	13	0	0	0	5	—	—	—	—	—
96-97	Fredericton	AHL	32	9	17	26	58	—	—	—	—	—
97-98	Rangers	NHL	3	0	0	0	2	—	—	—	—	—
97-98	Hartford	AHL	40	18	13	31	94	12	3	5	8	14
98-99	Long Beach	IHL	6	1	3	4	7	—	—	—	—	—
98-99	Orlando	IHL	43	11	21	32	44	15	4	5	9	32
	NHL	Totals	78	4	5	9	74	3	0	1	1	0
	AHL	Totals	302	124	149	275	598	34	10	16	26	62
	IHL	Totals	49	12	24	36	51	15	4	5	9	32

Born; 8/9/71, Trois-Rivieries, Quebec. 6-0, 189. Drafted by Montreal Canadiens (4th choice, 51st overall) in 1989 Entry Draft. Signed as a free agent by New York Rangers (8/27/97). Last amateur club; Ste. Hyacinthe (QMJHL).

Konstantin Shafranov — Defenseman

Season	Team	League	GP	G	A	PTS	PIM	GP	G	A	PTS	PIM
			Regular Season					Playoffs				
93-94	Detroit	CoHL	4	3	2	5	0	—	—	—	—	—
93-94	Kamenogorsk	CIS	27	18	21	39	6	—	—	—	—	—
94-95	Magnitogorsk	CIS	47	21	30	51	24	7	5	4	9	12
95-96	Magnitogorsk	CIS	6	3	3	6	0	—	—	—	—	—
95-96	Fort Wayne	IHL	74	46	28	74	26	5	1	2	3	4
96-97	St. Louis	NHL	5	2	1	4	0	—	—	—	—	—
96-97	Worcester	AHL	62	23	25	48	16	5	0	2	2	0
97-98	Fort Wayne	IHL	67	28	52	80	50	4	2	4	6	2
97-98	Kazakhstan	Olympics	7	4	3	7	6	—	—	—	—	—
98-99												
98-99	Fort Wayne	IHL	—	—	—	—	—	2	0	1	1	0
	IHL	Totals	141	74	80	154	76	9	3	4	7	6

Born; 9/11/68, Usf-Kamenogorak, Russia. 5-11, 176. Drafted by St. Louis Blues (10th choice, 229th overall) in 1996 Entry Draft. 1995-96 IHL Rookie of the Year. 1997-98 IHL Second Team All-Star.

Yevgeny Shaldybin — Defenseman

Season	Team	League	GP	G	A	PTS	PIM	GP	G	A	PTS	PIM
			Regular Season					Playoffs				
96-97	Boston	NHL	3	1	0	1	0	—	—	—	—	—
96-97	Providence	AHL	65	4	13	17	28	3	0	0	0	0
97-98	Providence	AHL	63	5	7	12	54	—	—	—	—	—
98-99	Providence	AHL	1	0	0	0	0	—	—	—	—	—
98-99	Las Vegas	IHL	13	1	3	4	6	—	—	—	—	—
98-99	Binghamton	UHL	61	14	38	52	38	—	—	—	—	—
	AHL	Totals	129	9	20	29	82	3	0	0	0	0

Born; 7/29/75, Novosibirsk, Russia. 6-1, 198. Drafted by Boston Bruins (6th choice, 151st overall) in 1995 Entry Draft.

Ryan Shanahan — Right Wing

Season	Team	League	GP	G	A	PTS	PIM	GP	G	A	PTS	PIM
			Regular Season					Playoffs				
95-96	Louisiana	ECHL	4	3	2	5	2	5	2	0	2	20
96-97	Louisiana	ECHL	11	4	3	7	66	—	—	—	—	—
96-97	Wheeling	ECHL	39	6	21	27	101	3	0	0	0	0
97-98	Louisiana	ECHL	35	3	8	11	87	5	0	0	0	29
98-99	Louisiana	ECHL	27	3	3	6	91	5	0	0	0	8
	ECHL	Totals	116	19	37	56	347	18	2	0	2	57

Born; 4/3/75, Buffalo, New York. 6-1, 195. Drafted by Detroit Red Wings (10th choice, 230th overall) in 1993 Entry Draft. Traded to Louisiana by Birmingham with Mario Dumoulin and cash for Marc Delorme (1/98). Last amateur club; SUNY-Genesco (NCAA 3).

Daniel Shank — Right Wing

Season	Team	League	GP	G	A	PTS	PIM	GP	G	A	PTS	PIM
			Regular Season					Playoffs				
88-89	Adirondack	AHL	42	5	20	25	113	17	11	8	19	102
89-90	Detroit	NHL	57	11	13	24	143	—	—	—	—	—
89-90	Adirondack	AHL	14	8	8	16	36	—	—	—	—	—
90-91	Detroit	NHL	7	0	1	1	14	—	—	—	—	—
90-91	Adirondack	AHL	60	26	49	75	278	—	—	—	—	—
91-92	Hartford	NHL	13	2	0	2	18	5	0	0	0	22
91-92	Adirondack	AHL	27	13	21	34	112	—	—	—	—	—
91-92	Springfield	AHL	31	9	19	28	83	8	8	0	8	48
92-93	San Diego	IHL	77	39	53	92	*495	14	5	10	15	*131
93-94	San Diego	IHL	63	27	36	63	273	—	—	—	—	—
93-94	Phoenix	IHL	7	4	6	10	26	—	—	—	—	—
94-95	Minnesota	IHL	19	4	11	15	30	—	—	—	—	—
94-95	Detroit	IHL	54	44	27	71	142	5	2	2	4	6
95-96	Las Vegas	IHL	49	36	29	65	191	—	—	—	—	—
95-96	Detroit	IHL	29	14	19	33	96	12	4	5	9	38
96-97	San Antonio	IHL	81	33	58	91	293	9	3	3	6	32
97-98	San Antonio	IHL	80	39	43	82	141	—	—	—	—	—
98-99	Frankfurt	Germany	9	2	5	7	12	8	3	2	5	33
98-99	Phoenix	WCHL	17	13	16	29	26	—	—	—	—	—
	NHL	Totals	77	13	14	27	175	5	0	0	0	22
	IHL	Totals	459	240	282	522	1687	40	14	20	34	207
	AHL	Totals	174	61	117	168	622	25	19	8	27	150

Born; 5/12/67, Montreal, Quebec. 5-11, 200. Signed as a free agent by Detroit Red Wings (5/26/89). Traded to Hartford Whalers by Detroit for Chris Tancill (12/18/91). 1992-93 IHL First Team All-Star. Member of 1988-89 AHL champion Adirondack Red Wings. Last amateur club; Hull (QMJHL).

Darrin Shannon — Left Wing
Regular Season — Playoffs

Season	Team	League	GP	G	A	PTS	PIM	GP	G	A	PTS	PIM
88-89	Windsor	OHL	54	33	48	81	47	4	1	6	7	2
88-89	Buffalo	NHL	3	0	0	0	0	2	0	0	0	0
89-90	Buffalo	NHL	17	2	7	9	4	6	0	1	1	4
89-90	Rochester	AHL	50	20	23	43	25	9	4	1	5	2
90-91	Buffalo	NHL	34	8	6	14	12	6	1	2	3	4
90-91	Rochester	AHL	49	26	34	60	56	10	3	5	8	22
91-92	Buffalo	NHL	1	0	1	1	0	—	—	—	—	—
91-92	Winnipeg	NHL	68	13	26	39	41	7	0	1	1	10
92-93	Winnipeg	NHL	84	20	40	60	91	6	2	4	6	6
93-94	Winnipeg	NHL	77	21	37	58	87	—	—	—	—	—
94-95	Winnipeg	NHL	19	5	3	8	14	—	—	—	—	—
95-96	Winnipeg	NHL	63	5	18	23	28	6	1	0	1	6
96-97	Phoenix	NHL	82	11	13	24	41	7	3	1	4	4
97-98	Phoenix	NHL	58	2	12	14	26	5	0	1	1	4
98-99	Grand Rapids	IHL	10	1	5	6	12	—	—	—	—	—
	NHL	Totals	506	87	163	250	344	45	7	10	17	38
	AHL	Totals	99	46	57	103	81	19	7	6	13	26

Born; 12/8/69, Barrie, Ontario. 6-2, 210. Drafted by Pittsburgh Penguins (1st choie, 4th overall) in 1988 Entry Draft. Traded to Buffalo Sabres by Pittsburgh with Doug Bodger for Tom Barrasso and Buffalo's third round choice (Joe Dziedzic) in 1990 Entry Draft (11/12/88). Traded to Winnipeg Jets by Buffalo with Mike Hartman and Dean Kennedy for Dave McLlwain, Gord Donnelly, Winnipeg's fifth round choice (Yuri Khmylev) in 1992 Entry Draft and future considerations (10/11/91). Last amateur club; Windsor (OHL).

Brian Shantz — Center
Regular Season — Playoffs

Season	Team	League	GP	G	A	PTS	PIM	GP	G	A	PTS	PIM
92-93	Erie	ECHL	38	14	26	40	44	5	2	3	4	23
93-94	Tulsa	CeHL	4	0	1	1	0	—	—	—	—	—
93-94	Erie	ECHL	54	25	43	68	58	—	—	—	—	—
94-95	San Antonio	CeHL	66	39	*80	*119	125	13	10	17	27	27
95-96	San Antonio	CeHL	64	54	*85	*139	90	12	3	11	14	22
96-97	San Antonio	IHL	26	2	9	11	21	—	—	—	—	—
96-97	Fort Wayne	IHL	18	2	5	7	4	—	—	—	—	—
96-97	Quad City	CoHL	9	1	13	14	2	—	—	—	—	—
97-98	Shreveport	WPHL	69	30	82	112	64	8	5	7	12	6
98-99	San Antonio	CHL	69	26	63	89	48	8	3	9	12	16
	IHL	Totals	44	4	14	18	25	—	—	—	—	—
	CHL	Totals	203	119	229	348	263	33	16	37	53	65
	ECHL	Totals	92	39	69	108	102	5	2	3	5	23

Born; 5/15/70, Edmonton, Alberta. 5-9, 180. 1995-96 CeHL MVP. 1995-96 CeHL First Team All-Star.

Paul Shantz — Center
Regular Season — Playoffs

Season	Team	League	GP	G	A	PTS	PIM	GP	G	A	PTS	PIM
97-98	Tucson	WCHL	9	0	0	0	48	—	—	—	—	—
97-98	Mississippi	ECHL	16	0	1	1	58	—	—	—	—	—
98-99	Memphis	CHL	2	0	0	0	4	—	—	—	—	—

Born; 7/21/76, Joliette, Quebec. 5-11, 206. Last amateur club; Laval (QMJHL).

Larry Shapley — Right Wing
Regular Season — Playoffs

Season	Team	League	GP	G	A	PTS	PIM	GP	G	A	PTS	PIM
98-99	Syracuse	AHL	50	1	1	2	254	—	—	—	—	—

Born; 2/6/78, 6-6, 215. Drafted by Vancouver Canucks (9th choice, 148th overall) in 1997 Entry Draft. Last amateur club; Peterborough (OHL).

Vadim Sharapov — Left Wing
Regular Season — Playoffs

Season	Team	League	GP	G	A	PTS	PIM	GP	G	A	PTS	PIM
98-99	Las Vegas	IHL	2	0	2	2	0	—	—	—	—	—
98-99	Corpus Christi	WPHL	47	20	27	47	48	—	—	—	—	—
98-99	Odessa	WPHL	8	1	3	4	24	2	0	0	0	0
	WPHL	Totals	55	21	30	51	72	2	0	0	0	0

Born; 1/13/78, Moscow, Russia. 5-10, 179. Traded to Odessa by Corpus Christi to complete earlier trade for Dave Shute (2/99). Last amateur club; Erie (OHL).

Oleg Shargorodsky — Defenseman
Regular Season — Playoffs

Season	Team	League	GP	G	A	PTS	PIM	GP	G	A	PTS	PIM
94-95	Houston	IHL	62	7	26	33	52	—	—	—	—	—
94-95	Detroit	IHL	10	3	4	7	10	5	0	2	2	11
95-96	Detroit	IHL	11	2	5	7	22	—	—	—	—	—
95-96	Phoenix	IHL	67	9	21	30	89	3	0	2	2	9
96-97	Detroit	IHL	3	0	3	3	4	—	—	—	—	—
96-97												
97-98	Hameenlinna	Finland	47	7	14	21	134	—	—	—	—	—
98-99	Fort Wayne	IHL	79	18	30	48	100	2	0	0	0	0
	IHL	Totals	232	39	89	128	277	10	0	4	4	20

Born; 11/16/69, Kharkovj, Ukraine. 6-1, 195.

Vadim Sharifijanov — Left Wing
Regular Season — Playoffs

Season	Team	League	GP	G	A	PTS	PIM	GP	G	A	PTS	PIM
94-95	CKSA Moscow	CIS	34	7	3	10	26	2	0	0	0	0
94-95	Albany	AHL	1	1	1	2	0	9	3	3	6	10
95-96	Albany	AHL	69	14	28	42	28	—	—	—	—	—
96-97	New Jersey	NHL	2	0	0	0	0	—	—	—	—	—
96-97	Albany	AHL	70	14	27	41	89	10	3	3	6	6
97-98	Albany	AHL	72	23	27	50	69	12	4	9	13	6
98-99	Albany	AHL	2	1	1	2	0	—	—	—	—	—
98-99	New Jersey	NHL	53	11	16	27	28	4	0	0	0	0
	NHL	Totals	55	11	16	27	28	4	0	0	0	0
	AHL	Totals	214	53	84	137	186	31	10	15	25	22

Born; 12/23/75, Ufa, Russia. 5-11, 210. Drafted by New Jersey Devils (1st choice, 25th overall) in 1994 Entry Draft. Member of 1994-95 Calder Cup Champion Albany RiverRats.

Chris Sharland — Goaltender
Regular Season — Playoffs

Season	Team	League	GP	W	L	T	MIN	SO	AVG	GP	W	L	MIN	SO	AVG
98-99	New Mexico	WPHL	31	8	13	6	1627	0	4.13	—	—	—	—	—	—

Born; 10/25/74, Orilla, Ontario. 5-10, 170. Traded to San Angelo by New Mexico for future considerations (7/99).

Jeff Sharples — Defenseman
Regular Season — Playoffs

Season	Team	League	GP	G	A	PTS	PIM	GP	G	A	PTS	PIM
86-87	Detroit	NHL	3	0	1	1	2	2	0	0	0	2
87-88	Detroit	NHL	56	10	25	35	42	4	0	3	3	4
87-88	Adirondack	AHL	4	2	1	3	4	—	—	—	—	—
88-89	Detroit	NHL	46	4	9	13	26	1	0	0	0	0
88-89	Adirondack	AHL	10	0	4	4	8	—	—	—	—	—
89-90	Adirondack	AHL	9	2	5	7	6	—	—	—	—	—
89-90	Cape Breton	AHL	38	4	13	17	28	—	—	—	—	—
89-90	Utica	AHL	13	2	5	7	19	5	1	2	3	15
90-91	Utica	AHL	64	16	29	45	42	—	—	—	—	—
91-92	Capital District	AHL	31	3	12	15	18	7	6	5	11	4
92-93	Kansas City	IHL	39	5	21	26	43	8	0	0	0	6
93-94	Las Vegas	IHL	68	18	32	50	68	5	2	1	3	6
94-95	Las Vegas	IHL	72	20	33	53	63	10	4	4	8	16
95-96	Las Vegas	IHL	41	6	14	20	56	—	—	—	—	—
95-96	Utah	IHL	31	2	15	17	18	21	3	10	13	16
96-97	Utah	IHL	49	9	26	35	54	7	0	2	2	10
97-98	Utah	IHL	76	10	28	38	82	4	1	1	2	6
98-99	Utah	IHL	78	8	29	37	93	—	—	—	—	—
	NHL	Totals	105	14	35	49	70	7	0	3	3	6
	IHL	Totals	378	68	170	238	395	51	9	17	26	56
	AHL	Totals	245	39	97	136	207	16	8	8	16	25

Born; 7/28/67, Terrace, British Columbia. 6-1, 195. Drafted by Detroit Red Wings (2nd choice, 29th overall) in 1985 Entry Draft. Traded to Edmonton Oilers by Detroit with Petr Klima, Joe Murphy and Adam Graves for Jimmy Carson, Kevin McClelland and Edmonton's fifth round choice (later traded to Montreal-Montreal selected Brad Layzell) in 1991 Entry Draft (11/2/89). Traded to New Jersey Devils by Edmonton for Reijo Ruotsalainen (3/6/90). Member of 1995-96 IHL champion Utah Grizzlies. Last amateur club; Portland (WHL).

Scott Shaunessy — Defenseman

Season	Team	League	GP	G	A	PTS	PIM	GP	G	A	PTS	PIM
			Regular Season					Playoffs				
86-87	Boston University	H.E.	32	2	13	15	71	—	—	—	—	—
86-87	Quebec	NHL	3	0	0	0	7	—	—	—	—	—
87-88	Fredericton	AHL	60	0	9	9	257	1	0	0	0	2
88-89	Quebec	NHL	4	0	0	0	16	—	—	—	—	—
88-89	Halifax	AHL	41	3	10	13	106	—	—	—	—	—
89-90	Halifax	AHL	27	3	5	8	105	—	—	—	—	—
89-90	Fort Wayne	IHL	45	3	9	12	267	5	0	1	1	31
90-91	Albany	IHL	34	3	9	12	126	—	—	—	—	—
90-91	Muskegon	IHL	23	1	4	5	104	5	0	0	0	21
91-92	Fort Wayne	IHL	53	3	8	11	243	7	0	1	1	27
92-93	Cincinnati	IHL	71	2	7	9	222	—	—	—	—	—
93-94												
94-95												
95-96												
96-97	Austin	WPHL	32	3	4	7	138	6	3	0	3	22
97-98												
98-99	Fort Worth	WPHL	55	9	13	22	190	12	0	3	3	26
	NHL	Totals	7	0	0	0	23	—	—	—	—	—
	IHL	Totals	226	12	37	49	962	17	0	2	2	79
	AHL	Totals	128	6	24	30	468	1	0	0	0	2
	WPHL	Totals	87	12	17	29	328	18	3	3	6	48

Born; 1/22/64, Newport, Rhode Island. 6-4, 220. Drafted by Quebec Nordiques (9th choice, 192nd overall) in 1983 Entry Draft. Last amateur club; Boston University (Hockey East).

Steve Shaunessy — Defenseman

Season	Team	League	GP	G	A	PTS	PIM	GP	G	A	PTS	PIM
			Regular Season					Playoffs				
88-89	Muskegon	IHL	11	0	2	2	40	—	—	—	—	—
88-89	Flint	IHL	21	1	2	3	81	—	—	—	—	—
89-90	Winston-Salem	ECHL	51	2	12	14	247	10	0	1	1	68
90-91	Cincinnati	ECHL	55	6	21	27	264	4	0	0	0	39
91-92	Cincinnati	ECHL	40	0	12	12	241	—	—	—	—	—
91-92	San Diego	IHL	27	1	5	6	183	1	0	0	0	2
92-93	Louisville	ECHL	38	2	5	7	200	—	—	—	—	—
92-93	Memphis	CHL	13	1	3	4	79	6	0	0	0	14
93-94	Memphis	CHL	46	5	6	11	221	—	—	—	—	—
93-94	Wichita	CHL	11	1	5	6	42	11	0	5	5	44
94-95												
95-96												
96-97												
97-98												
98-99	Fort Worth	WPHL	3	0	0	0	4	—	—	—	—	—
	IHL	Totals	59	2	9	11	304	1	0	0	0	2
	ECHL	Totals	184	10	50	60	732	14	0	1	1	107
	CHL	Totals	70	7	14	21	342	17	0	5	5	58

Born; 5/7/67, Reading, Massachusetts. 6-4, 220. Member of 1993-94 CHL Champion Wichita Thunder. Last amateur club; Boston University (Hockey East).

Brad Shaw — Defenseman

Season	Team	League	GP	G	A	PTS	PIM	GP	G	A	PTS	PIM
			Regular Season					Playoffs				
84-85	Binghamton	AHL	24	1	10	11	4	8	1	8	9	6
84-85	Salt Lake City	IHL	44	3	29	32	25	—	—	—	—	—
85-86	Hartford	NHL	8	0	2	2	4	—	—	—	—	—
85-86	Binghamton	AHL	64	10	44	54	33	5	0	2	2	6
86-87	Hartford	NHL	2	0	0	0	0	—	—	—	—	—
86-87	Binghamton	AHL	77	9	30	39	43	12	1	8	9	2
87-88	Hartford	NHL	1	0	0	0	0	—	—	—	—	—
87-88	Binghamton	AHL	73	12	50	62	50	4	0	5	5	4
88-89	Hartford	NHL	3	1	0	1	0	3	1	0	1	0
88-89	Canada	National	4	1	0	1	2	—	—	—	—	—
89-90	Hartford	NHL	64	3	32	35	30	7	2	5	7	0
90-91	Hartford	NHL	72	4	28	32	29	6	1	2	3	2
91-92	Hartford	NHL	62	3	22	25	44	3	0	1	1	4
92-93	Ottawa	NHL	81	7	34	41	34	—	—	—	—	—
93-94	Ottawa	NHL	66	4	19	23	59	—	—	—	—	—
94-95	Ottawa	NHL	2	0	0	0	0	—	—	—	—	—
94-95	Atlanta	IHL	26	1	18	19	17	5	3	4	7	9
95-96	Detroit	IHL	79	7	54	61	46	8	2	3	5	8
96-97	Detroit	IHL	59	6	32	38	30	21	2	9	11	10
97-98	Detroit	IHL	64	2	33	35	47	23	1	11	12	30
98-99	Detroit	IHL	61	10	35	45	44	—	—	—	—	—
98-99	Washington	NHL	4	0	0	0	4	—	—	—	—	—
98-99	St. Louis	NHL	12	0	0	0	4	4	0	0	0	0
	NHL	Totals	377	22	137	159	208	23	4	8	12	6
	IHL	Totals	333	29	201	230	209	57	8	27	35	57
	AHL	Totals	238	32	134	166	130	29	2	23	25	18

Born; 4/28/64, Mississauga, Ontario. 6-0, 190. Drafted by Detroit Red Wings (5th choice, 86th overall) in 1982 Entry Draft. Rigths traded to Hartford Whalers by Detroit for Hartford's eighth round choice (Urban Nordin) in 1984 Entry Draft (5/29/84). Traded to New Jersey Devils by Hartford for cash (6/13/92). Claimed by Ottawa Senators from New Jersey in Expansion Draft (6/18/92). Signed as a free agent by Ottawa (3/11/99). Claimed on waivers by Washington Capitals (3/11/99). Traded to St. Louis Blues by Washington with Washington's eighth round selection (Colin Hemingway) in 1999 Entry Draft for St. Louis' sixth round choice (Kyle Clark) in 1999 Entry Draft (3/18/99). 1986-87 AHL First Team All-Star. 1987-88 AHL First Team All-Star. 1986-87 AHL Best Defenseman. 1996-97 IHL First Team All-Star. Member of 1996-97 IHL Champion Detroit Vipers. Last amateur club; Ottawa (OHL).

David Shaw — Defenseman

Regular Season / Playoffs

Season	Team	League	GP	G	A	PTS	PIM	GP	G	A	PTS	PIM
82-83	Kitchener	OHL	57	18	56	74	78	12	2	10	12	18
82-83	Quebec	NHL	2	0	0	0	0	—	—	—	—	—
83-84	Kitchener	OHL	58	14	34	48	73	16	4	9	13	12
83-84	Quebec	NHL	3	0	0	0	0	—	—	—	—	—
84-85	Quebec	NHL	14	0	0	0	11	—	—	—	—	—
84-85	Fredericton	AHL	48	7	6	13	73	2	0	0	0	7
85-86	Quebec	NHL	73	7	19	26	78	—	—	—	—	—
86-87	Quebec	NHL	75	0	19	19	69	—	—	—	—	—
87-88	Rangers	NHL	68	7	25	32	100	—	—	—	—	—
88-89	Rangers	NHL	63	6	11	17	88	4	0	2	2	30
89-90	Rangers	NHL	22	2	10	12	22	—	—	—	—	—
90-91	Rangers	NHL	77	2	10	12	89	6	0	0	0	11
91-92	Rangers	NHL	10	0	1	1	15	—	—	—	—	—
91-92	Edmonton	NHL	12	1	1	2	8	—	—	—	—	—
91-92	Minnesota	NHL	37	0	7	7	49	7	2	2	4	10
92-93	Boston	NHL	77	10	14	24	108	4	0	1	1	6
93-94	Boston	NHL	55	1	9	10	85	13	1	2	3	16
94-95	Boston	NHL	44	3	4	7	36	5	0	1	1	4
95-96	Tampa Bay	NHL	66	1	11	12	64	6	0	1	1	4
96-97	Tampa Bay	NHL	57	1	10	11	72	—	—	—	—	—
97-98	Tampa Bay	NHL	14	0	2	2	12	—	—	—	—	—
97-98	Las Vegas	IHL	26	6	13	19	28	—	—	—	—	—
98-99	Las Vegas	IHL	24	3	10	13	22	—	—	—	—	—
	NHL	Totals	769	41	153	194	906	45	3	9	12	81
	IHL	Totals	50	9	23	32	50	—	—	—	—	—

Born; 5/25/64, St. Thomas, Ontario. 6-2, 205. Drafted by Quebec Nordiques (1st choice, 13th overall) in 1982 Entry Draft. Traded to New York Rangers by Quebec with John Ogrodnick for Jeff Jackson and Terry Carkner (9/30/87). Traded to Edmonton Oilers by Rangers for Jeff Beukeboom (11/12/91). Traded to Minnesota North Stars by Edmonton for Brian Glynn (1/21/92). Traded to Boston Bruins by Minnesota for future considerations (9/2/92). Traded to Tampa Bay Lightning by Boston for Detroit's third round draft choice (previously acquired by Tampa Bay-Boston selected Jason Doyle) in 1996 Entry Draft (8/17/96). Traded to San Jose Sharks with Bryan Marchment and Tampa Bay's first round choice (later traded to Nashville-Nashville selected David Legwand) in 1998 Entry Draft for Andrei Nazarov and Florida's first round draft choice (previously acquired, Tampa Bay selected Vincent Lecavalier) in 1998 Entry Draft (3/24/98). Last amateur club; Kitchener (OHL).

Lloyd Shaw — Right Wing

Regular Season / Playoffs

Season	Team	League	GP	G	A	PTS	PIM	GP	G	A	PTS	PIM
97-98	Cincinnati	AHL	60	1	2	3	138	—	—	—	—	—
97-98	Columbus	ECHL	4	0	0	0	7	—	—	—	—	—
98-99	Cincinnati	AHL	50	2	0	2	170	—	—	—	—	—
98-99	Huntington	ECHL	2	0	0	0	4	—	—	—	—	—
	AHL	Totals	110	3	2	5	308	—	—	—	—	—
	ECHL	Totals	6	0	0	0	11	—	—	—	—	—

Born; 9/26/76, Regina, Saskatchewan. 6-3, 220. Drafted by Vancouver Cancucks (4th choice, 92nd overall) in 1995 Entry Draft. Signed as a free agent by Anaheim Mighty Ducks (7/7/97). Last amateur club; Red Deer (WHL).

Mitch Shawara — Left Wing

Regular Season / Playoffs

Season	Team	League	GP	G	A	PTS	PIM	GP	G	A	PTS	PIM
97-98	Fresno	WCHL	50	10	12	22	189	5	2	0	2	11
98-99	New Mexico	WPHL	26	1	3	4	112	—	—	—	—	—

Born; 2/18/76, McBride, British Columbia. 6-1, 205. Traded to Amarillo by New Mexico for Brendan Kenny (6/99). Last amateur club; Calgary (WHL).

Blake Sheane — Right Wing

Regular Season / Playoffs

Season	Team	League	GP	G	A	PTS	PIM	GP	G	A	PTS	PIM
97-98	N. Battleford	SJHL	49	40	42	82	NA	—	—	—	—	—
97-98	Wichita	CHL	4	1	0	1	10	—	—	—	—	—
98-99	El Paso	WPHL	69	37	23	60	117	3	2	3	5	2

Born; 5/5/77, Virden, Manitoba. 5-11, 190. Last amateur club; North Battleford (SJHL).

Rob Shearer — Right Wing

Regular Season / Playoffs

Season	Team	League	GP	G	A	PTS	PIM	GP	G	A	PTS	PIM
96-97	Hershey	AHL	78	12	16	28	88	23	0	4	4	9
97-98	Hershey	AHL	79	30	30	60	44	7	0	5	5	6
98-99	Hershey	AHL	77	24	42	66	43	3	0	0	0	6
	AHL	Totals	234	66	88	154	175	33	0	9	9	21

Born; 10/19/76, Kitchener, Ontario. 5-10, 190. Signed as a free agent by Colorado Avalanche (10/5/95). Member of 1996-97 AHL Champion Hershey Bears. Last amateur club; Windsor (OHL).

Bobby Sheehan — Defenseman

Regular Season / Playoffs

Season	Team	League	GP	G	A	PTS	PIM	GP	G	A	PTS	PIM
98-99	Charlotte	ECHL	24	2	7	9	26	—	—	—	—	—

Born; 1/1/75, Medford, Massachusetts. 6-3, 198. Last amateur club; Northeastern (Hockey East).

Murray Sheehan — Forward

Regular Season / Playoffs

Season	Team	League	GP	G	A	PTS	PIM	GP	G	A	PTS	PIM
98-99	Odessa	WPHL	5	0	0	0	0	—	—	—	—	—

Born; 6/17/77, Toronto, Ontario. 6-2, 180.

Jody Shelley — Left Wing

Regular Season / Playoffs

Season	Team	League	GP	G	A	PTS	PIM	GP	G	A	PTS	PIM
97-98	Dalhousie	OUAA	19	6	11	17	145	—	—	—	—	—
97-98	Saint John	AHL	18	1	1	2	50	—	—	—	—	—
98-99	Saint John	AHL	8	0	0	0	46	—	—	—	—	—
98-99	Johnstown	ECHL	52	12	17	29	325	—	—	—	—	—
	AHL	Totals	26	1	1	2	96	—	—	—	—	—

Born; 2/6/76, Yarmouth, Nova Scotia. 6-3, 230. Signed as a free agent by Calgary Flames (9/1/98). Last amateur club; Dallhousie (OUAA).

Ken Shepard — Goaltender

Regular Season / Playoffs

Season	Team	League	GP	W	L	T	MIN	SO	AVG	GP	W	L	MIN	SO	AVG
95-96	Binghamton	AHL	14	6	4	2	726	1	3.14	1	0	0	38	0	3.13
95-96	Charlotte	ECHL	17	10	4	1	952	0	3.15	8	6	1	374	0	2.89
96-97	Binghamton	AHL	14	3	7	2	747	0	3.78	—	—	—	—	—	—
96-97	Charlotte	ECHL	21	7	11	1	1185	0	4.45	—	—	—	—	—	—
97-98	Charlotte	ECHL	2	0	0	0	29	0	4.21	—	—	—	—	—	—
98-99	San Antonio	CHL	31	16	11	2	1778	1	3.64	—	—	—	—	—	—
98-99	Fayetteville	CHL	16	11	3	1	894	0	2.88	—	—	—	—	—	—
	AHL	Totals	28	9	11	4	1473	1	3.46	1	0	0	38	0	3.13
	CHL	Totals	47	27	14	3	2673	1	3.39	—	—	—	—	—	—
	ECHL	Totals	40	17	15	2	2166	0	3.88	8	6	1	374	0	2.89

Born; 1/20/74, Toronto, Ontario. 5-10, 192. Drafted by New York Rangers (10th choice, 216th overall) in 1993 Entry Draft. Member of 1995-96 ECHL champion Charlotte Checkers. Last amateur club; Oshawa (OHL).

Jim Shepherd — Center

Regular Season / Playoffs

Season	Team	League	GP	G	A	PTS	PIM	GP	G	A	PTS	PIM
98-99	Houston	IHL	5	2	2	4	0	—	—	—	—	—
98-99	Mobile	ECHL	68	21	40	61	161	2	1	2	3	6

Born; 5/13/77, Calgary, Alberta. 6-0, 205. Last amateur club; Laval (QMJHL).

Curtis Sheptak — Left Wing

Regular Season / Playoffs

Season	Team	League	GP	G	A	PTS	PIM	GP	G	A	PTS	PIM
98-99	Portland	AHL	13	0	3	3	32	—	—	—	—	—
98-99	Utah	IHL	60	7	8	15	99	—	—	—	—	—

Born; 11/19/74, Leduc, Alberta. 6-3, 196. Last amateur club; Northern Michigan (CCHA).

Trevor Sherban
Defenseman

Regular Season / Playoffs

Season	Team	League	GP	G	A	PTS	PIM	GP	G	A	PTS	PIM
97-98	Alberta	CWUAA	45	9	35	44	66	—	—	—	—	—
97-98	Kansas City	IHL	3	0	0	0	9	—	—	—	—	—
98-99	Kansas City	IHL	35	1	1	2	40	—	—	—	—	—
98-99	Wichita	CHL	4	0	2	2	0	—	—	—	—	—
	IHL	Totals	38	1	1	2	49	—	—	—	—	—

Born; 12/11/72, Edmonton, Alberta. 6-2, 200. Last amateur club; Alberta (CWUAA).

Dan Shermerhorn
Center

Regular Season / Playoffs

Season	Team	League	GP	G	A	PTS	PIM	GP	G	A	PTS	PIM
96-97	Maine	H.E.	35	16	13	29	46	—	—	—	—	—
96-97	Hampton Roads	ECHL	12	2	5	7	6	9	2	2	4	6
97-98	Las Vegas	IHL	17	0	4	4	10	—	—	—	—	—
97-98	Tacoma	WCHL	54	45	69	114	56	11	*11	7	18	12
98-99	Tallahassee	ECHL	10	2	2	4	8	—	—	—	—	—
98-99	Baton Rouge	ECHL	61	25	34	59	63	6	0	2	2	4
	ECHL	Totals	83	29	41	70	77	15	2	4	6	10

Born; 7/15/73, Calgary, Alberta. 5-11, 200. 1997-98 WCHL MVP. 1997-98 WCHL First All-Star Team. Last amateur club; Maine (Hockey East).

Todd Shestok
Goaltender

Regular Season / Playoffs

Season	Team	League	GP	W	L	T	MIN	SO	AVG	GP	W	L	MIN	SO	AVG
96-97	Fresno	WCHL	18	12	2	0	935	1	3.59	2	0	0	12	0	5.16
97-98	Fresno	WCHL	12	5	5	0	637	0	4.90	—	—	—	—	—	—
98-99	Fresno	WCHL	18	4	7	1	850	0	4.38	—	—	—	—	—	—
	WCHL	Totals	48	21	14	1	2422	1	4.21	2	0	0	12	0	5.16

Born; 8/28/74, Westford, Massachusetts. 5-10, 165. Last amateur club; Connecticut College (NCAA 3).

Jeff Shevalier
Left Wing

Regular Season / Playoffs

Season	Team	League	GP	G	A	PTS	PIM	GP	G	A	PTS	PIM
94-95	Los Angeles	NHL	1	1	0	1	0	—	—	—	—	—
94-95	Phoenix	IHL	68	31	39	70	44	9	5	4	9	0
95-96	Phoenix	IHL	79	29	38	67	72	4	2	2	4	2
96-97	Los Angeles	NHL	26	4	9	13	6	—	—	—	—	—
96-97	Phoenix	IHL	46	16	21	37	26	—	—	—	—	—
97-98	Springfield	AHL	66	23	30	53	38	4	1	1	2	0
98-99	Cincinnati	IHL	76	29	34	63	57	3	1	1	2	0
	NHL	Totals	27	5	9	14	6	—	—	—	—	—
	IHL	Totals	223	89	111	200	173	16	8	7	15	2

Born; 3/14/74, Mississauga, Ontario. 5-11, 185. Drafted by Los Angeles Kings (4th choice, 111th overall) in 1992 Entry Draft. Signed as a free agent by Tampa Bay Lightning (7/12/99). Last amateur club; North Bay (OHL).

Jordon Shields
Left Wing

Regular Season / Playoffs

Season	Team	League	GP	G	A	PTS	PIM	GP	G	A	PTS	PIM
96-97	Dayton	ECHL	45	18	21	39	8	—	—	—	—	—
97-98	New Mexico	WPHL	8	2	3	5	4	—	—	—	—	—
97-98	Amarillo	WPHL	20	6	4	10	16	—	—	—	—	—
97-98	Waco	WPHL	7	2	2	4	6	—	—	—	—	—
98-99	Bakersfield	WCHL	9	0	1	1	10	—	—	—	—	—
98-99	Topeka	CHL	44	14	11	25	16	2	0	0	0	2
	WPHL	Totals	35	10	9	19	26	—	—	—	—	—

Born; 4/27/72, Gloucester, Ontario. 5-10, 180. Last amateur club; Northeastern (Hockey East).

Andrew Shier
Right Wing

Regular Season / Playoffs

Season	Team	League	GP	G	A	PTS	PIM	GP	G	A	PTS	PIM
94-95	Richmond	ECHL	64	28	37	65	126	17	8	19	27	33
95-96	Milwaukee	IHL	39	2	1	3	8	—	—	—	—	—
95-96	Madison	CoHL	2	2	2	4	0	—	—	—	—	—
95-96	Richmond	ECHL	4	3	1	4	6	7	7	7	14	2
96-97	Baltimore	AHL	3	1	0	1	0	—	—	—	—	—
96-97	Richmond	ECHL	52	29	39	68	127	8	7	6	13	28
97-98	Richmond	ECHL	69	35	42	77	100	—	—	—	—	—
98-99	Richmond	ECHL	70	27	37	64	76	18	2	*14	16	22
	ECHL	Totals	259	122	156	278	435	50	24	46	70	85

Born; 8/15/71, Lansing, Michigan. 5-11, 165. Member of 1994-95 ECHL champion Richmond Renegades. Last amateur club; Wisconsin (WCHA).

Dean Shmyr
Right Wing

Regular Season / Playoffs

Season	Team	League	GP	G	A	PTS	PIM	GP	G	A	PTS	PIM
92-93	Dallas	CeHL	57	5	18	23	163	7	0	1	1	12
93-94	Dallas	CeHL	50	2	12	14	96	7	0	3	3	35
94-95	San Antonio	CeHL	60	3	29	32	225	12	0	1	1	30
95-96	Quad City	CoHL	72	3	20	23	195	4	0	3	3	6
96-97	Utah	IHL	9	0	0	0	31	—	—	—	—	—
96-97	New Mexico	WPHL	44	7	6	13	240	1	0	0	0	0
97-98	Reno	WCHL	50	0	10	10	172	3	0	1	1	14
98-99	Cleveland	IHL	3	0	0	0	8	—	—	—	—	—
98-99	New Mexico	WPHL	41	4	8	12	309	—	—	—	—	—
	IHL	Totals	23	0	0	0	39	—	—	—	—	—
	CeHL	Totals	167	10	59	69	484	26	0	5	5	77
	WPHL	Totals	85	11	14	25	549	1	0	0	0	0

Born; 4/29/71, Vancouver, British Columbia. 6-0, 170. Traded to Odessa by New Mexico for future considerations (5/99).

Jason Shmyr
Left Wing

Regular Season / Playoffs

Season	Team	League	GP	G	A	PTS	PIM	GP	G	A	PTS	PIM
96-97	Pensacola	ECHL	1	0	0	0	2	—	—	—	—	—
96-97	Anchorage	WCHL	51	8	12	20	388	9	1	1	2	50
97-98	Utah	IHL	3	0	0	0	7	—	—	—	—	—
97-98	Anchorage	WCHL	31	4	6	10	172	—	—	—	—	—
97-98	San Diego	WCHL	14	0	3	3	50	11	3	3	6	78
98-99	Long Beach	IHL	8	0	0	0	35	—	—	—	—	—
98-99	Manitoba	IHL	57	1	1	2	227	3	0	0	0	0
98-99	San Diego	WCHL	2	0	0	0	7	—	—	—	—	—
	IHL	Totals	68	1	1	2	269	3	0	0	0	0
	WCHL	Totals	98	12	21	33	617	20	4	4	8	128

Born; 7/27/75, Fairview, Alberta. 6-4, 215. Traded to San Diego by Tucson with Bryan Masotta for Danny Laviolette (1/98). Signed as a free agent by Washington Capitals (5/8/99). Member of 1997-98 WCHL Champion San Diego Gulls. Last amateur club; Bonnyville (AJHL).

Ryan Shmyr
Left Wing

Regular Season / Playoffs

Season	Team	League	GP	G	A	PTS	PIM	GP	G	A	PTS	PIM
97-98	Bonnyville	AJHL	57	10	12	22	443	—	—	—	—	—
97-98	San Diego	WCHL	7	3	2	5	37	—	—	—	—	—
98-99	San Diego	WCHL	27	0	0	0	176	—	—	—	—	—
	WCHL	Totals	34	3	2	5	213	—	—	—	—	—

Born; 4/29/77, Fairview, Alberta. 6-6, 230. Last amateur club; Bonnyville

Johnathon Shockey
Defenseman

Regular Season / Playoffs

Season	Team	League	GP	G	A	PTS	PIM	GP	G	A	PTS	PIM
98-99	Idaho	WCHL	62	4	10	14	244	1	0	0	0	15

Born; 6/8/76, Lethbridge, Alberta. 6-3, 195. Last amateur club; Spokane (WHL).

Kayle Short — Defenseman
Regular Season / Playoffs

Season	Team	League	GP	G	A	PTS	PIM	GP	G	A	PTS	PIM
96-97	Canada	National	59	7	6	13	91	—	—	—	—	—
96-97	Portland	AHL	1	0	1	1	0	—	—	—	—	—
97-98	Portland	AHL	25	1	2	3	27	—	—	—	—	—
97-98	Hampton Roads	ECHL	40	1	10	11	86	13	1	0	1	18
98-99	Sheffield	BSL	47	5	9	14	50	9	0	2	2	34
	AHL	Totals	26	1	3	4	27	—	—	—	—	—

Born; 5/16/73, Barrie, Ontario. 6-1, 198. Member of 1997-98 ECHL Champion Hampton Roads Admirals. Last amateur club; New Brunswick (AUAA)

Gary Shuchuk — Right Wing
Regular Season / Playoffs

Season	Team	League	GP	G	A	PTS	PIM	GP	G	A	PTS	PIM
90-91	Detroit	NHL	6	1	2	3	6	3	0	0	0	0
90-91	Adirondack	AHL	59	23	24	47	32	—	—	—	—	—
91-92	Adirondack	AHL	79	32	48	80	48	19	4	9	13	18
92-93	Adirondack	AHL	47	24	53	77	66	—	—	—	—	—
92-93	Los Angeles	NHL	25	2	4	6	16	17	2	2	4	12
93-94	Los Angeles	NHL	56	3	4	7	30	—	—	—	—	—
94-95	Los Angeles	NHL	22	3	6	9	6	—	—	—	—	—
94-95	Phoenix	IHL	13	8	7	15	12	—	—	—	—	—
95-96	Los Angeles	NHL	33	4	10	14	12	—	—	—	—	—
96-97	Houston	IHL	55	18	23	41	48	13	5	2	7	18
97-98	Herisau	Switz.	40	15	33	48	60	—	—	—	—	—
98-99	Klagenfurter	Austria										
	NHL	Totals	142	13	26	39	70	20	2	2	4	12
	AHL	Totals	185	79	125	204	146	19	4	9	13	18
	IHL	Totals	68	26	30	56	60	13	5	2	7	18

Born; 2/17/67, Edmonton, Alberta. 5-11, 190. Drafted by Detroit Red Wings (1st choice, 22nd overall) in 1998 Supplemental Draft. Traded to Los Angeles Kings by Detroit with Jimmy Carson and Marc Potvin for Paul Coffey, Sylvain Couturier and Jim Hiller (1/29/93). Member of 1991-92 AHL Champion Adirondack Red Wings. Last amateur club; Wisconsin (WCHA).

Richard Shulmistra — Goaltender
Regular Season / Playoffs

Season	Team	League	GP	W	L	T	MIN	SO	AVG	GP	W	L	MIN	SO	AVG
94-95	Cornwall	AHL	20	4	9	2	937	0	3.71	8	4	3	446	0	2.95
95-96	Cornwall	AHL	36	9	18	2	1844	0	3.25	1	0	0	8	0	6.75
96-97	Albany	AHL	23	5	9	2	1062	2	2.43	2	1	0	77	0	1.56
97-98	New Jersey	NHL	1	0	1	0	92	0	1.94	—	—	—	—	—	—
97-98	Fort Wayne	IHL	11	3	8	0	656	1	3.11	—	—	—	—	—	—
97-98	Albany	AHL	35	20	8	4	2022	2	2.31	13	8	3	696	1	2.76
98-99	Albany	AHL	12	6	4	0	596	0	3.42	2	0	2	64	0	2.82
98-99	Manitoba	IHL	44	25	11	7	2469	2	2.84	—	—	—	—	—	—
	AHL	Totals	126	44	48	10	6461	4	2.91	26	13	8	1291	1	2.79
	IHL	Totals	55	28	19	7	3125	3	2.90	—	—	—	—	—	—

Born; 4/1/71, Sudbury, Ontario. 6-2, 186. Drafted by Quebec Nordiques (1st choice, 4th overall) in 1992 Supplemental Draft. Signed as a free agent by New Jersey Devils (10/11/96). Signed as a free agent by Florida Panthers (7/21/99). 1997-98 AHL Second Team All-Star. Last amateur club; Miami-Ohio (CCHA).

Andrei Shurupov — Center
Regular Season / Playoffs

Season	Team	League	GP	G	A	PTS	PIM	GP	G	A	PTS	PIM
98-99	Toledo	ECHL	30	7	12	19	50	—	—	—	—	—

Born; 2/27/78, Moscow, Russia. 6-1, 185. Last amateur club; Belleville (OHL).

David Shute — Left Wing
Regular Season / Playoffs

Season	Team	League	GP	G	A	PTS	PIM	GP	G	A	PTS	PIM
91-92	Muskegon	IHL	7	1	2	3	6	—	—	—	—	—
91-92	Knoxville	ECHL	57	18	35	53	91	—	—	—	—	—
92-93	Chatham	CoHL	15	4	9	13	10	—	—	—	—	—
93-94	Raleigh	ECHL	27	10	13	23	21	—	—	—	—	—
93-94	Hampton Roads	ECHL	8	2	4	6	6	5	0	2	2	2
94-95	San Antonio	CeHL	53	22	31	53	68	13	11	5	16	12
95-96	San Antonio	CeHL	17	7	6	13	41	—	—	—	—	—
95-96	Wichita	CeHL	46	42	27	69	42	—	—	—	—	—
96-97	Waco	WPHL	5	3	0	3	2	—	—	—	—	—
96-97	Wichita	CeHL	16	8	2	10	29	—	—	—	—	—
96-97	Oklahoma City	CeHL	32	15	15	30	51	—	—	—	—	—
97-98	Lake Charles	WPHL	39	12	14	26	34	—	—	—	—	—
97-98	Odessa	WPHL	1	1	1	2	0	—	—	—	—	—
98-99	Corpus Christi	WPHL	69	22	26	48	79	4	1	2	3	8
	CeHL	Totals	164	94	81	175	251	13	11	5	16	12
	WPHL	Totals	114	38	41	79	115	4	1	2	3	8
	ECHL	Totals	92	30	52	82	118	5	0	2	2	2

Born; 2/10/71, Carlyle, Pennsylvania. 6-0. 190. Drafted by Pittsburgh Penguins (9th choice, 163rd overall) in 1989 Entry Draft. Traded to Wichita Thunder by San Antonio Iguanas for Rob Weingartner. 1995-96 Traded to Odessa by Lake Charles with Ryan Connolly for Greg Bailey (1/98). CeHL First Team All-Star. Last amateur club; Medicine Hat (WHL).

Konstantin Sidulov — Defenseman
Regular Season / Playoffs

Season	Team	League	GP	G	A	PTS	PIM	GP	G	A	PTS	PIM
98-99	Fredericton	AHL	5	0	0	0	6	—	—	—	—	—
98-99	Miami	ECHL	45	1	4	5	60	—	—	—	—	—

Born; 1/1/77, Ufa, USSR. 6-1, 176. Drafted by Montreal Canadiens (5th choice, 118th overall) in 1997 Entry Draft. Last overseas club; Chelyabinsk (Russia).

Marc Siegel — Goaltender
Regular Season / Playoffs

Season	Team	League	GP	W	L	T	MIN	SO	AVG	GP	W	L	MIN	SO	AVG
96-97	Johnstown	ECHL	10	0	6	0	440	0	5.31	—	—	—	—	—	—
96-97	Toledo	ECHL	8	4	3	1	462	0	4.16	—	—	—	—	—	—
97-98	Johnstown	ECHL	1	0	1	0	60	0	7.00	—	—	—	—	—	—
97-98	New Mexico	WPHL	7	4	1	1	387	0	3.72	2	1	0	45	0	*1.32
98-99	New Mexico	WPHL	7	2	2	1	243	0	5.19	—	—	—	—	—	—
	ECHL	Totals	19	4	10	1	962	0	4.87	—	—	—	—	—	—
	WPHL	Totals	14	6	3	2	630	0	4.29	2	1	0	45	0	1.32

Born; 12/23/73, Pompano Beach, Florida. 6-2, 185. Last amateur club; Williams College (NCAA 3).

Jon Sikkema — Goaltender
Regular Season / Playoffs

Season	Team	League	GP	W	L	T	MIN	SO	AVG	GP	W	L	MIN	SO	AVG
98-99	Huntsville	CHL	12	2	6	1	589	0	4.48	—	—	—	—	—	—

Born; Last amateur club; University of British Columbia (CWUAA).

Andy Silverman — Defenseman
Regular Season / Playoffs

Season	Team	League	GP	G	A	PTS	PIM	GP	G	A	PTS	PIM
94-95	Binghamton	AHL	5	0	1	1	2	—	—	—	—	—
94-95	Charlotte	ECHL	64	3	11	14	57	3	0	0	0	2
95-96	Binghamton	AHL	75	5	15	20	92	4	0	0	0	6
96-97	Binghamton	AHL	20	0	1	1	28	—	—	—	—	—
96-97	Baltimore	AHL	42	2	1	3	24	1	0	0	0	0
97-98	Berlin	Germany	39	0	3	3	57	—	—	—	—	—
98-99	Tallahassee	ECHL	26	1	4	5	14	—	—	—	—	—
	AHL	Totals	142	7	18	25	146	5	0	0	0	6
	ECHL	Totals	90	4	15	19	71	3	0	0	0	2

Born; 8/23/72, Beverly, Massachusetts. 6-3, 210. Drafted by New York Rangers (11th choice, 181st overall) in 1990 Entry Draft. Last amateur club; Maine (H.E.).

John Sim — Center

Regular Season / Playoffs

Season	Team	League	GP	G	A	PTS	PIM	GP	G	A	PTS	PIM
98-99	Dallas	NHL	7	1	0	1	12	4	0	0	0	0
98-99	Michigan	IHL	68	24	27	51	91	5	3	1	4	18

Born; 9/29/77, New Glasgow, Nova Scotia. 5-9, 175. Drafted by Dallas Stars (2nd choice, 70th overall) in 1996 Entry Draft. Member of 1998-99 Stanley Cup Champion Dallas Stars. Last amateur club; Sarnia (OHL).

Trevor Sim — Right Wing

Regular Season / Playoffs

Season	Team	League	GP	G	A	PTS	PIM	GP	G	A	PTS	PIM
89-90	Swift Current	WHL	6	3	2	5	21	—	—	—	—	—
89-90	Kamloops	WHL	43	27	35	62	53	17	3	13	16	28
89-90	Edmonton	NHL	3	0	1	1	2	—	—	—	—	—
90-91	Cape Breton	AHL	62	20	9	29	39	2	0	0	0	0
91-92	Cape Breton	AHL	2	0	1	1	0	—	—	—	—	—
91-92	Wheeling	ECHL	53	25	29	54	110	5	7	2	9	4
92-93	Canada	National	53	24	19	43	49	—	—	—	—	—
92-94	Canada	National	49	16	20	36	18	—	—	—	—	—
93-94	Milwaukee	IHL	32	7	13	20	10	4	1	0	1	0
94-95	Milwaukee	IHL	37	9	10	19	26	7	1	2	3	4
94-95	Syracuse	AHL	3	2	0	2	0	—	—	—	—	—
95-96	Canada	National	3	0	0	0	0	—	—	—	—	—
95-96	Milwaukee	IHL	7	0	0	0	0	—	—	—	—	—
95-96	Raleigh	ECHL	28	11	17	28	26	4	0	0	0	0
96-97	Orlando	IHL	58	9	21	30	32	2	0	1	1	0
97-98	Orlando	IHL	36	8	3	11	17	—	—	—	—	—
97-98	New Orleans	ECHL	13	4	11	15	23	4	0	3	3	2
98-99	Charlotte	ECHL	9	3	5	8	12	—	—	—	—	—
	IHL	Totals	170	33	47	80	85	13	2	3	5	4
	AHL	Totals	67	22	10	32	39	2	0	0	0	0
	ECHL	Totals	103	43	62	105	171	13	7	5	12	6

Born; 6/9/70, Calgary, Alberta. 6-2, 192. Drafted by Edmonton Oilers (3rd choice, 53rd overall) in 1988 Entry Draft. Last amateur club; Kamloops (WHL).

Konstantin Simchuk — Goaltender

Regular Season / Playoffs

Season	Team	League	GP	W	L	T	MIN	SO	AVG	GP	W	L	MIN	SO	AVG
97-98	Las Vegas	IHL	16	6	6	1	846	2	3.19	—	—	—	—	—	—
97-98	Tacoma	WCHL	46	33	11	1	2632	3	3.08	*12	8	4	*700	0	3.25
98-99	Las Vegas	IHL	30	10	10	3	1471	0	3.06	—	—	—	—	—	—
98-99	Bakersfield	WCHL	4	1	2	1	240	0	3.50	—	—	—	—	—	—
98-99	Port Huron	UHL	8	5	1	1	405	0	2.22	—	—	—	—	—	—
	IHL	Totals	46	16	16	4	2317	2	3.11	—	—	—	—	—	—
	WCHL	Totals	50	34	13	2	2872	3	3.11	12	8	4	700	0	3.25

Born; Kiev, Ukraine. 6-0, 175. 1997-98 WCHL Goaltender of the Year. 1997-98 WCHL First Team All-Star. Selected by Knoxville in 1999 UHL Expansion

Chris Simms — Center

Regular Season / Playoffs

Season	Team	League	GP	G	A	PTS	PIM	GP	G	A	PTS	PIM
96-97	Alaska	WCHL	18	3	7	10	8	—	—	—	—	—
97-98	Tulsa	CHL	6	1	2	3	0	—	—	—	—	—
98-99	Asheville	UHL	1	0	0	0	0	—	—	—	—	—

Born; 5/5/75, Toronto, Ontario. 5-10, 170.

Jason Simon — Defenseman

Regular Season / Playoffs

Season	Team	League	GP	G	A	PTS	PIM	GP	G	A	PTS	PIM
89-90	Utica	AHL	16	3	4	7	28	2	0	0	0	12
89-90	Nashville	ECHL	13	4	3	7	81	5	1	3	4	17
90-91	Utica	AHL	50	2	12	14	189	—	—	—	—	—
90-91	Johnstown	ECHL	22	11	9	20	55	—	—	—	—	—
91-92	Utica	AHL	1	0	0	0	12	—	—	—	—	—
91-92	San Diego	IHL	13	1	4	5	45	3	0	1	1	9
91-92	Flint	CoHL	33	9	33	42	261	—	—	—	—	—
92-93	Detroit	CoHL	11	7	13	20	38	—	—	—	—	—
92-93	Flint	CoHL	44	17	32	49	202	—	—	—	—	—
93-94	Islanders	NHL	4	0	0	0	34	—	—	—	—	—
93-94	Salt Lake City	IHL	50	7	7	14	*323	—	—	—	—	—
93-94	Detroit	CoHL	13	9	16	25	87	—	—	—	—	—
94-95	Denver	IHL	61	3	6	9	300	1	0	0	0	12
95-96	Springfield	AHL	18	2	2	4	90	7	1	0	1	26
96-97	Phoenix	NHL	1	0	0	0	0	—	—	—	—	—
96-97	Las Vegas	IHL	64	4	3	7	402	3	0	0	0	0
97-98	Hershey	AHL	26	0	1	1	170	—	—	—	—	—
97-98	Quebec	IHL	30	6	3	9	127	—	—	—	—	—
98-99	Colorado	WCHL	60	16	23	39	419	3	1	1	2	17
	NHL	Totals	5	0	0	0	34	—	—	—	—	—
	IHL	Totals	218	21	23	44	1197	7	0	1	1	21
	AHL	Totals	111	7	19	26	489	9	1	0	1	38
	CoHL	Totals	101	42	94	136	588	—	—	—	—	—
	ECHL	Totals	35	15	12	27	136	5	1	3	4	17

Born; 3/21/69, Sarnia Reserve, Ontario. 6-1, 210. Drafted by New Jersey Devils (9th choice, 215th overall) in 1989 Entry Draft. Signed as a free agent by New York Islanders (1/6/94). Signed as a free agent by Winnipeg Jets (8/9/95). Signed as a free agent by Colorado Avalanche (8/20/97). Member of 1994-95 IHL champion Denver Grizzlies. Last amateur club; Windsor (OHL).

Todd Simon — Center

Regular Season / Playoffs

Season	Team	League	GP	G	A	PTS	PIM	GP	G	A	PTS	PIM
92-93	Rochester	AHL	67	27	66	93	54	12	3	14	17	15
93-94	Buffalo	NHL	15	0	1	1	0	5	1	0	1	0
93-94	Rochester	AHL	55	33	52	85	79	—	—	—	—	—
94-95	Rochester	AHL	69	25	65	90	78	5	0	2	2	21
95-96	Las Vegas	IHL	52	26	48	74	48	—	—	—	—	—
95-96	Detroit	IHL	29	19	16	35	20	12	2	12	14	6
96-97	Detroit	IHL	80	21	51	72	46	18	4	6	10	12
97-98	Cincinnati	IHL	81	33	72	105	115	9	2	4	6	12
98-99	Cincinnati	IHL	81	26	61	87	72	3	1	1	2	12
	IHL	Totals	323	125	248	373	301	42	9	23	32	42
	AHL	Totals	191	85	183	268	211	17	3	16	19	36

Born; 4/21/72, Toronto, Ontario. 5-10, 187. Drafted by Buffalo Sabres (9th choice, 203rd overall) in 1992 Entry Draft. 1995-96 IHL First Team All-Star. Member of 1996-97 IHL Champion Detroit Vipers. Last amateur club; Niagara

Kent Simpson — Left Wing

Regular Season / Playoffs

Season	Team	League	GP	G	A	PTS	PIM	GP	G	A	PTS	PIM
98-99	Johnstown	ECHL	55	6	21	27	56	—	—	—	—	—

Born; 7/20/75, North Vancouver, British Columbia. 5-10, 175. Last amateur club; Alberta (CWUAA).

Wade Simpson — Defenseman

Regular Season / Playoffs

Season	Team	League	GP	G	A	PTS	PIM	GP	G	A	PTS	PIM
97-98	Chesapeake	ECHL	13	0	0	0	21	—	—	—	—	—
97-98	Raleigh	ECHL	52	2	9	11	53	—	—	—	—	—
98-99	Shreveport	WPHL	69	14	20	34	103	12	0	5	5	16
	ECHL	Totals	65	2	9	11	74	—	—	—	—	—

Born; 3/19/73, Ottawa, Ontario. 6-3, 225. Member of 1998-99 WPHL Champion Shreveport Mudbugs. Last amateur club; New Brunswick (AUAA).

Darren Sinclair — Left Wing
Regular Season — Playoffs

Season	Team	League	GP	G	A	PTS	PIM	GP	G	A	PTS	PIM
96-97	Syracuse	AHL	68	12	16	28	32	3	0	2	2	0
97-98	Syracuse	AHL	57	5	15	20	23	4	0	0	0	2
97-98	Raleigh	ECHL	6	2	0	2	0	—	—	—	—	—
98-99	Syracuse	AHL	68	7	6	13	38	—	—	—	—	—
	AHL	Totals	193	24	37	61	93	7	0	2	2	2

Born; 11/24/76, Brooks, Alberta. 6-0, 200. Signed as a free agent by Vancouver Canucks (10/5/95). Last amateur club; Spokane (WHL).

Darryl Sinclair — Center
Regular Season — Playoffs

Season	Team	League	GP	G	A	PTS	PIM	GP	G	A	PTS	PIM
98-99	Saginaw	UHL	6	3	0	3	4	—	—	—	—	—
98-99	Fort Worth	CHL	1	0	0	0	0	—	—	—	—	—
98-99	Arkansas	WPHL	6	0	1	1	4	—	—	—	—	—

Born; 5/27/74, Hamilton, Ohio. 6-0, 187.

Rob Sinclair — Forward
Regular Season — Playoffs

Season	Team	League	GP	G	A	PTS	PIM	GP	G	A	PTS	PIM
98-99	Columbus	CHL	70	40	34	74	8	9	0	3	3	5

Born; 10/27/76, Glace Bay, Nova Scotia. 5-11, 192. Last amateur club; Princeton (ECAC).

Travis Sinden — Goaltender
Regular Season — Playoffs

Season	Team	League	GP	W	L	T	MIN	SO	AVG	GP	W	L	MIN	SO	AVG
98-99	Topeka	CHL	1	0	1	0	40	0	7.50	—	—	—	—	—	—

Born; 3/31/76, Phoenix, Arizona. 6-1, 165.

Harkie Singh — Defenseman
Regular Season — Playoffs

Season	Team	League	GP	G	A	PTS	PIM	GP	G	A	PTS	PIM
98-99	Thunder Bay	UHL	6	0	2	2	32	—	—	—	—	—

Born; 9/15/78, Toronto, Ontario. 6-3, 218. Last amateur club; Windsor (OHL).

Nick Sinerate — Left Wing
Regular Season — Playoffs

Season	Team	League	GP	G	A	PTS	PIM	GP	G	A	PTS	PIM
97-98	Providence	H.E.	33	4	4	8	18	—	—	—	—	—
97-98	Columbus	CHL	7	1	0	1	19	—	—	—	—	—
98-99	Columbus	CHL	1	0	0	0	0	—	—	—	—	—
98-99	Amarillo	WPHL	63	16	16	32	89	—	—	—	—	—
	CHL	Totals	8	1	0	1	19	—	—	—	—	—

Born; 1/18/75, Northboro, Massachusetts. 6-3, 210. Last amateur club; Providence (Hockey East).

Jeff Sirrka — Defenseman
Regular Season — Playoffs

Season	Team	League	GP	G	A	PTS	PIM	GP	G	A	PTS	PIM
89-90	Maine	AHL	56	0	9	9	110	—	—	—	—	—
89-90	Binghamton	AHL	16	0	1	1	38	—	—	—	—	—
90-91	Indianapolis	IHL	69	6	12	18	203	6	0	0	0	6
91-92	Indianapolis	IHL	71	3	17	20	146	—	—	—	—	—
92-93	Rochester	AHL	59	6	11	17	132	3	0	0	0	7
93-94	Portland	AHL	76	6	18	24	113	15	2	6	8	47
94-95	Denver	IHL	58	4	18	22	86	5	0	1	1	19
95-96	Orlando	IHL	47	2	15	17	122	—	—	—	—	—
95-96	Kansas City	IHL	25	1	2	3	41	4	0	0	0	10
96-97	Kansas City	IHL	5	0	0	0	9	—	—	—	—	—
96-97	Long Beach	IHL	45	3	3	6	44	—	—	—	—	—
96-97	Utah	IHL	6	0	0	0	12	1	0	1	1	0
97-98	Cincinnati	IHL	64	3	2	5	97	—	—	—	—	—
97-98	Hershey	AHL	7	1	1	2	4	5	0	0	0	10
98-99	Colorado	WCHL	46	3	13	16	80	3	0	0	0	8
	IHL	Totals	390	22	69	91	760	16	0	2	2	35
	AHL	Totals	214	13	40	53	397	23	2	6	8	64

Born; 6/17/68, Sudbury, Ontario. 6-0, 193. Signed as a free agent by Boston Bruins (9/89). Traded to Hartford Whalers by Boston for Steve Dykstra (3/3/90). Signed as a free agent by Chicago Blackhawks (9/20/90). 1998-99 WCHL Second Team All-Star. Member of 1993-94 AHL champion Portland Pirates. Member of 1994-95 IHL champion Denver Grizzlies. Last amateur club; Toronto

Allan Sirois — Center
Regular Season — Playoffs

Season	Team	League	GP	G	A	PTS	PIM	GP	G	A	PTS	PIM
95-96	Rimouski	QMJHL	69	59	68	127	172	10	4	10	14	15
95-96	Worcester	AHL	2	1	0	1	0	—	—	—	—	—
96-97	Worcester	AHL	2	0	0	0	0	—	—	—	—	—
96-97	Baton Rouge	ECHL	62	29	29	58	64	—	—	—	—	—
97-98	Worcester	AHL	3	0	0	0	2	—	—	—	—	—
97-98	Baton Rouge	ECHL	37	7	17	24	80	—	—	—	—	—
97-98	Jacksonville	ECHL	28	16	13	29	40	—	—	—	—	—
98-99	Pee Dee	ECHL	70	35	49	84	105	13	4	13	17	14
	AHL	Totals	4	1	0	1	0	—	—	—	—	—
	ECHL	Totals	197	87	108	195	289	13	4	13	17	14

Born; 2/19/75, Riviere du Loup, Quebec. 6-0, 195. 1998-99 ECHL First All-Star Team. Last amateur club; Rimouski (QMJHL).

Ryan Sittler — Left Wing
Regular Season — Playoffs

Season	Team	League	GP	G	A	PTS	PIM	GP	G	A	PTS	PIM
94-95	Hershey	AHL	42	2	7	9	48	—	—	—	—	—
94-95	Johnstown	ECHL	1	1	1	2	0	—	—	—	—	—
95-96	Hershey	AHL	7	0	1	1	6	—	—	—	—	—
95-96	St. John's	AHL	6	1	2	3	18	4	0	0	0	4
95-96	Raleigh	ECHL	12	2	8	10	8	—	—	—	—	—
95-96	Mobile	ECHL	21	3	11	14	30	—	—	—	—	—
96-97	Baltimore	AHL	66	4	22	26	167	3	1	0	1	0
97-98	South Carolina	ECHL	44	12	15	27	66	4	0	0	0	8
98-99	Charlotte	ECHL	33	3	9	12	112	—	—	—	—	—
	AHL	Totals	121	7	32	39	239	7	1	0	1	4
	ECHL	Totals	111	21	44	65	216	4	0	0	0	8

Born; 1/28/74, London, Ontario. 6-2, 195. Drafted by Philadelphia Flyers (1st choice, 7th overall) in 1992 Entry Draft. Last amateur club; Michigan (CCHA).

Grant Sjerven — Goaltender
Regular Season — Playoffs

Season	Team	League	GP	W	L	T	MIN	SO	AVG	GP	W	L	MIN	SO	AVG
94-95	Chicago	IHL	7	0	3	1	252	0	4.29	—	—	—	—	—	—
94-95	Richmond	ECHL	26	17	6	2	1438	1	3.01	—	—	—	—	—	—
95-96	Houston	IHL	12	4	6	1	628	0	3.63	—	—	—	—	—	—
95-96	Richmond	ECHL	22	15	2	4	1292	0	*2.65	5	2	3	328	0	4.40
96-97	Richmond	ECHL	33	19	9	3	1854	0	3.40	7	3	4	419	0	3.87
97-98	Manchester	BSL	24	—	—	—	1471	1	3.08	9	—	—	553	0	3.91
98-99	Sheffield	BSL	37	—	—	—	2078	—	2.77	9	—	—	503	—	2.51
	IHL	Totals	19	4	9	2	880	0	3.82	—	—	—	—	—	—
	ECHL	Totals	81	51	17	9	4584	1	3.06	12	5	7	747	0	4.10

Born; 3/13/70, Brandon, Manitoba. 6-0, 195. Last amateur club; St. Cloud

Andreas Sjolund
Regular Season — Left Wing — Playoffs

Season	Team	League	GP	G	A	PTS	PIM	GP	G	A	PTS	PIM
97-98	Odessa	WPHL	13	1	1	2	23	—	—	—	—	—
97-98	Idaho	WCHL	46	7	14	21	77	3	0	0	0	2
98-99	Idaho	WCHL	67	5	8	13	151	2	0	0	0	27
	WCHL	Totals	113	12	22	34	228	5	0	0	0	29

Born; 1/7/77, Knivsta, Sweden. 6-1, 190. Last European club; Arlanda (Sweden).

Jarrod Skalde
Regular Season — Center — Playoffs

Season	Team	League	GP	G	A	PTS	PIM	GP	G	A	PTS	PIM
90-91	Oshawa	OHL	15	8	14	22	14	—	—	—	—	—
90-91	Belleville	OHL	40	30	52	82	21	6	9	6	15	10
90-91	New Jersey	NHL	1	0	1	1	0	—	—	—	—	—
90-91	Utica	AHL	3	3	2	5	0	—	—	—	—	—
91-92	New Jersey	NHL	15	2	4	6	4	—	—	—	—	—
91-92	Utica	AHL	62	20	20	40	56	4	3	1	4	8
92-93	New Jersey	NHL	11	0	2	2	4	—	—	—	—	—
92-93	Utica	AHL	59	21	39	60	76	5	0	2	2	19
92-93	Cincinnati	IHL	4	1	2	3	4	—	—	—	—	—
93-94	Anaheim	NHL	20	5	4	9	10	—	—	—	—	—
93-94	San Diego	IHL	57	25	38	63	73	9	3	12	15	10
94-95	Las Vegas	IHL	74	34	41	75	103	9	2	4	6	8
95-96	Calgary	NHL	1	0	0	0	0	—	—	—	—	—
95-96	Baltimore	AHL	11	2	6	8	55	—	—	—	—	—
95-96	Saint John	AHL	68	27	40	67	98	16	4	9	13	6
96-97	Saint John	AHL	65	32	36	68	94	3	0	0	0	14
97-98	San Jose	NHL	22	4	6	10	14	—	—	—	—	—
97-98	Chicago	NHL	7	0	1	1	0	—	—	—	—	—
97-98	Dallas	NHL	1	0	0	0	0	—	—	—	—	—
97-98	Indianapolis	IHL	2	0	2	2	0	—	—	—	—	—
97-98	Kentucky	AHL	23	5	15	20	48	3	3	0	3	6
98-99	San Jose	NHL	17	1	1	2	4	—	—	—	—	—
98-99	Kentucky	AHL	54	17	40	57	75	12	4	5	9	16
	NHL	Totals	95	12	19	31	36	—	—	—	—	—
	AHL	Totals	345	127	198	325	502	43	14	17	31	69
	IHL	Totals	137	60	83	143	180	18	5	16	21	18

Born; 2/26/71, Niagara Falls, Ontario. 6-0, 180. Drafted by New Jersey Devils (3rd choice, 26th overall) in 1989 Entry Draft. Claimed by Anaheim Mighty Ducks from New Jersey in Expansion Draft (6/24/93). Signed as a free agent by Anaheim (5/31/95). Traded to Calgary Flames by Anaheim for Bobby Marshall (10/30/95). Signed as a free agent by San Jose Sharks (8/13/97). Claimed on waivers by Chicago Blackhawks from San Jose (1/8/98). Claimed on waivers by San Jose from Chicago (1/23/98). Claimed on waivers by Dallas Stars from San Jose (1/27/98). Claimed on waivers by Chicago from Dallas (2/10/98). Claimed on waivers by San Jose from Chicago (3/6/98). Last amateur club; Belleville

Eddy Skazyk
Regular Season — Goaltender — Playoffs

Season	Team	League	GP	W	L	T	MIN	SO	AVG	GP	W	L	MIN	SO	AVG
97-98	Bakersfield	WCHL	32	5	16	4	1678	0	5.69	2	0	0	28	0	8.58
98-99	Bakersfield	WCHL	5	2	1	0	202	0	2.96	—	—	—	—	—	—
98-99	San Diego	WCHL	4	1	0	0	118	0	3.05	—	—	—	—	—	—
98-99	Phoenix	WCHL	4	2	2	0	239	0	4.51	—	—	—	—	—	—
	WCHL	Totals	45	10	19	4	2237	0	5.18	2	0	0	28	0	8.58

Born; 9/4/74, Lockport, Manitoba. 5-11, 170.

Andrei Skopintsev
Regular Season — Defenseman — Playoffs

Season	Team	League	GP	G	A	PTS	PIM	GP	G	A	PTS	PIM
98-99	Tampa Bay	NHL	19	1	1	2	10	—	—	—	—	—
98-99	Cleveland	IHL	19	3	2	5	8	—	—	—	—	—

Born; 9/28/71, Elekrostal, USSR. 6-0, 185. Drafted by Tampa Bay Lightning (7th choice, 153rd overall) in 1997 Entry Draft. Last European club; TPS Turko (Finland).

Christian Skoryna
Regular Season — Center — Playoffs

Season	Team	League	GP	G	A	PTS	PIM	GP	G	A	PTS	PIM
97-98	South Carolina	ECHL	23	6	10	16	0	—	—	—	—	—
98-99	Fresno	WCHL	51	27	39	66	89	7	3	2	5	14

Born; 9/4/74, Elgin, Ontario. 5-10, 192. Last amateur club; Acadia (AUAA).

Martin Skoula
Regular Season — Defenseman — Playoffs

Season	Team	League	GP	G	A	PTS	PIM	GP	G	A	PTS	PIM
98-99	Barrie	OHL	67	13	46	59	46	12	3	10	13	13
98-99	Hershey	AHL	—	—	—	—	—	1	0	0	0	0

Born; 10/28/79, Litvinov, Czechoslovakia. 6-2, 195. Drafted by Colorado Avalanche (2nd choice, 17th overall) in 1998 Entry Draft. Last amateur club;

Karlis Skrastins
Regular Season — Defenseman — Playoffs

Season	Team	League	GP	G	A	PTS	PIM	GP	G	A	PTS	PIM
98-99	Nashville	NHL	2	0	1	1	0	—	—	—	—	—
98-99	Milwaukee	IHL	75	8	36	44	47	2	0	1	1	2

Born; 8/9/74, Riga, Latvia. 6-1, 196. Drafted by Nashville Predators (8th choice, 230th overall) in 1998 Entry Draft. Last European club; TPS Turku (Finland).

Pavel Skrbek
Regular Season — Defenseman — Playoffs

Season	Team	League	GP	G	A	PTS	PIM	GP	G	A	PTS	PIM
98-99	Syracuse	AHL	64	6	16	22	38	—	—	—	—	—

Born; 8/9/78, Kladno, Czechoslovakia. 6-3, 191. Drafted by Pittsburgh Penguins (2nd choice, 28th overall) in 1996 Entry Draft. Last European club; Poldi Kladno (Czech Republic).

Rob Skrlac
Regular Season — Left Wing — Playoffs

Season	Team	League	GP	G	A	PTS	PIM	GP	G	A	PTS	PIM
97-98	Albany	AHL	53	0	2	2	256	—	—	—	—	—
98-99	Albany	AHL	61	1	1	2	203	1	0	0	0	0
	AHL	Totals	114	1	3	4	459	1	0	0	0	0

Born; 6/10/76, Campbell, British Columbia. 6-4, 230. Drafted by Buffalo Sabres (11th choice, 224th overall) in 1995 Entry Draft. Signed as a free agent by New Jersey Devils (6/17/97). Last amateur club; Kamloops (WHL).

Jeremy Sladovnik
Regular Season — Defenseman — Playoffs

Season	Team	League	GP	G	A	PTS	PIM	GP	G	A	PTS	PIM
97-98	Flint	UHL	55	2	7	9	*301	11	0	0	0	34
98-99	Flint	UHL	6	0	1	1	34	—	—	—	—	—
	UHL	Totals	61	2	8	10	335	11	0	0	0	34

Born; 5/14/76, Trenton, Michigan. 6-1, 205.

John Slaney — Defenseman
Regular Season / Playoffs

Season	Team	League	GP	G	A	PTS	PIM	GP	G	A	PTS	PIM
91-92	Cornwall	OHL	34	19	41	60	43	6	3	8	11	0
91-92	Baltimore	AHL	6	2	4	6	0	—	—	—	—	—
92-93	Baltimore	AHL	79	20	46	66	60	7	0	7	7	8
93-94	Washington	NHL	47	7	9	16	27	11	1	1	2	2
93-94	Portland	AHL	29	14	13	27	17	—	—	—	—	—
94-95	Washington	NHL	16	0	3	3	6	—	—	—	—	—
94-95	Portland	AHL	8	3	10	13	4	7	1	3	4	4
95-96	Colorado	NHL	7	0	3	3	4	—	—	—	—	—
95-96	Cornwall	AHL	5	0	4	4	2	—	—	—	—	—
95-96	Los Angeles	NHL	31	6	11	17	10	—	—	—	—	—
96-97	Los Angeles	NHL	32	3	11	14	4	—	—	—	—	—
96-97	Phoenix	IHL	35	9	25	34	8	—	—	—	—	—
97-98	Phoenix	NHL	55	3	14	17	24	—	—	—	—	—
97-98	Las Vegas	IHL	5	2	2	4	10	—	—	—	—	—
98-99	Nashville	NHL	46	2	12	14	14	—	—	—	—	—
98-99	Milwaukee	IHL	7	0	1	1	0	—	—	—	—	—
	NHL	Totals	188	19	51	70	75	11	1	1	2	2
	AHL	Totals	127	39	77	116	83	14	1	10	11	12
	IHL	Totals	40	11	27	38	18	—	—	—	—	—

Born; 2/7/72, St. John's Newfoundland. 6-0, 185. Drafted by Washington Capitals (1st choice, 9th overall) in 1990 Entry Draft. Traded to Colorado Avalanche by Washington for Philadelphia's third round choice (previously acquired by Colorado—Washington selected Shawn McNeil) in 1996 Entry Draft, (7/12/95). Traded to Los Angeles Kings by Colorado for Winnipeg's sixth round choice (previously acquired by Los Angeles—Colorado selected Brian Willsie) in 1996 Entry Draft, (12/28/95). Signed as a free agent by Phoenix Coyotes (8/18/97). Selected by Nashville Predators in 1998 NHL Expansion Draft (6/26/98). Last amateur club; Cornwall (OHL).

Chris Slater — Forward
Regular Season / Playoffs

Season	Team	League	GP	G	A	PTS	PIM	GP	G	A	PTS	PIM
98-99	Alexandria	WPHL	43	10	12	22	69	—	—	—	—	—
98-99	New Orleans	ECHL	9	0	2	2	10	11	0	1	1	16

Born; 12/25/74, Mattawan, Michigan. 5-10, 200. Last amateur club; Western Michigan (CCHA).

Jan Slavik — Defenseman
Regular Season / Playoffs

Season	Team	League	GP	G	A	PTS	PIM	GP	G	A	PTS	PIM
96-97	Peoria	ECHL	29	1	3	4	25	1	0	0	0	4
97-98	Huntington	ECHL	70	15	43	58	62	4	0	0	0	4
98-99	Kentucky	AHL	3	0	2	2	2	—	—	—	—	—
98-99	Huntington	ECHL	68	12	37	49	75	—	—	—	—	—
	ECHL	Totals	167	28	83	111	162	5	0	0	0	8

Born; 5/18/75, Vlasmin, Czechoslovakia. 6-1, 205.

Blake Sloan — Right Wing
Regular Season / Playoffs

Season	Team	League	GP	G	A	PTS	PIM	GP	G	A	PTS	PIM
97-98	Houston	IHL	70	2	13	15	86	2	0	0	0	0
98-99	Houston	IHL	62	8	10	18	76	—	—	—	—	—
98-99	Dallas	NHL	14	0	0	0	10	19	0	2	2	8
	IHL	Totals	132	10	23	33	162	2	0	0	0	0

Born; 7/27/75, Park Ridge, Illinois. 5-10, 193. Signed as a free agent by Dallas Stars (3/11/99). Member of 1998-99 Stanley Cup Champion Dallas Stars. Last amateur club; Michigan (CCHA).

Kevin Slota — Forward
Regular Season / Playoffs

Season	Team	League	GP	G	A	PTS	PIM	GP	G	A	PTS	PIM
98-99	Arkansas	WPHL	54	3	7	10	121	2	0	0	0	0

Born; 4/1/76, London, Ontario. 5-9, 175.

Henrik Smangs — Goaltender
Regular Season / Playoffs

Season	Team	League	GP	W	L	T	MIN	SO	AVG	GP	W	L	MIN	SO	AVG
98-99	Tupelo	WPHL	31	7	15	1	1497	0	4.33	—	—	—	—	—	—

Born; 1/19/76, Leksand, Sweden. 5-11, 174. Drafted by Winnipeg Jets (9th choice, 212th overall) in 1994 Entry Draft. Last European club; Mora (Sweden-

Kelly Smart — Center
Regular Season / Playoffs

Season	Team	League	GP	G	A	PTS	PIM	GP	G	A	PTS	PIM
98-99	Houston	IHL	1	0	0	0	0	—	—	—	—	—
98-99	Austin	WPHL	38	13	24	37	4	—	—	—	—	—

Born; 9/9/77, McAuly, Manitoba. 6-0, 186. Last amateur club; Brandon (WHL).

Joe Smaza — Defenseman
Regular Season / Playoffs

Season	Team	League	GP	G	A	PTS	PIM	GP	G	A	PTS	PIM
97-98	Wisc. River-Falls	NCAA 3	11	0	5	5	na	—	—	—	—	—
97-98	Dayton	ECHL	10	1	2	3	8	—	—	—	—	—
97-98	Wheeling	ECHL	2	0	0	0	2	—	—	—	—	—
98-99	Saginaw	UHL	7	0	1	1	2	—	—	—	—	—
	ECHL	Totals	12	1	2	3	10	—	—	—	—	—

Born; 12/4/73, Farmington, Michigan. 6-1, 200. Last amateur club; Wisconsin-River Falls (NCAA 3).

Rob Smillie — Left Wing
Regular Season / Playoffs

Season	Team	League	GP	G	A	PTS	PIM	GP	G	A	PTS	PIM
98-99	St. Norbert	NCAA 3	32	21	29	50	NA	—	—	—	—	—
98-99	Charlotte	ECHL	9	0	2	2	0	—	—	—	—	—

Born; Richmond, British Columbia. 5-11, 190. Last amateur club; St. Norbert (NCAA 3).

Pavel Smirnov — Forward
Regular Season / Playoffs

Season	Team	League	GP	G	A	PTS	PIM	GP	G	A	PTS	PIM
98-99	Lowell	AHL	1	0	0	0	2	—	—	—	—	—
98-99	Tallahassee	ECHL	64	26	21	47	125	—	—	—	—	—

Born; 5/12/77, Moscow, Russia. 6-2, 206. Last amateur club; Shawinigan

Lukas Smital — Right Wing
Regular Season / Playoffs

Season	Team	League	GP	G	A	PTS	PIM	GP	G	A	PTS	PIM
96-97	Johnstown	ECHL	68	19	29	48	62	—	—	—	—	—
97-98	Saint John	AHL	9	2	0	2	4	—	—	—	—	—
97-98	Johnstown	ECHL	62	39	26	65	95	—	—	—	—	—
98-99	Johnstown	ECHL	34	12	21	33	38	—	—	—	—	—
98-99	Jacksonville	ECHL	23	12	9	21	19	2	0	0	0	0
	ECHL	Totals	187	82	85	167	214	2	0	0	0	0

Born; 8/15/74, Brno, Czech Republic. 6-1, 200. Traded to Jacksonville by Johnstown for Matt Eldred (2/99).

Adam Smith — Defenseman
Regular Season / Playoffs

Season	Team	League	GP	G	A	PTS	PIM	GP	G	A	PTS	PIM
96-97	Binghamton	AHL	56	0	8	8	59	2	0	0	0	0
97-98	Hartford	AHL	64	7	5	12	120	4	0	0	0	12
98-99	Hartford	AHL	29	1	4	5	54	—	—	—	—	—
98-99	Grand Rapids	IHL	5	0	0	0	12	—	—	—	—	—
98-99	Fort Wayne	IHL	27	3	1	4	44	2	1	0	1	0
	AHL	Totals	149	8	17	25	233	6	0	0	0	12
	IHL	Totals	32	3	1	4	56	2	1	0	1	0

Born; 5/24/76, Digby, Nova Scotia. 6-0, 190. Drafted by New York Rangers (3rd choice, 78th overall) in 1994 Entry Draft. Last amateur club; Kelowna (WHL).

Brad Smith
Defenseman

Regular Season / Playoffs

Season	Team	League	GP	G	A	PTS	PIM	GP	G	A	PTS	PIM
97-98	Saginaw	UHL	1	0	0	0	0	—	—	—	—	—
97-98	Lake Charles	WPHL	39	8	15	23	4	4	0	1	1	2
98-99	Lake Charles	WPHL	64	4	11	15	20	11	1	7	8	0
	WPHL	Totals	103	12	26	38	24	15	1	8	9	2

Born; 11/9/70, Prince George, British Columbia. 5-11, 205.

Brandon Smith
Defenseman

Regular Season / Playoffs

Season	Team	League	GP	G	A	PTS	PIM	GP	G	A	PTS	PIM
94-95	Adirondack	AHL	14	1	2	3	7	3	0	0	0	2
94-95	Minnesota	IHL	1	0	0	0	0	—	—	—	—	—
94-95	Dayton	ECHL	60	16	49	65	57	4	2	3	5	0
95-96	Adirondack	AHL	48	4	13	17	22	3	0	1	1	2
96-97	Adirondack	AHL	80	8	26	34	30	4	0	0	0	0
97-98	Adirondack	AHL	64	9	27	36	26	1	0	1	1	0
98-99	Boston	NHL	5	0	0	0	0	—	—	—	—	—
98-99	Providence	AHL	72	16	46	62	32	19	1	9	10	12
	AHL	Totals	278	38	114	152	117	30	1	11	12	16

Born; 2/25/73, Prince George, British Columbia. 6-0, 195. Signed as a free agent by Detroit Red Wings (7/28/97). Signed as a free agent by Boston Bruins (7/22/98). 1994-95 ECHL Defenseman of the Year. 1994-95 ECHL First Team All-Star. 1998-99 AHL First Team All-Star. Member of 1998-99 AHL Champion Providence Bruins. Last amateur club; Portland (WHL).

Buddy Smith
Center

Regular Season / Playoffs

Season	Team	League	GP	G	A	PTS	PIM	GP	G	A	PTS	PIM
98-99	Northern Michigan	CCHA	42	9	35	44	40	—	—	—	—	—
98-99	Columbus	CHL	2	1	1	2	4	9	2	6	8	0

Born; 2/1/75, Rochfort Bridge, Alberta. 5-8, 155. Last amateur club; Northern Michigan (CCHA).

Chris Smith
Defenseman

Regular Season / Playoffs

Season	Team	League	GP	G	A	PTS	PIM	GP	G	A	PTS	PIM
96-97	Tulsa	CeHL	66	13	29	42	117	5	0	1	1	4
97-98	Roanoke	ECHL	2	0	1	1	2	—	—	—	—	—
97-98	Tulsa	CHL	62	26	31	57	131	4	0	4	4	8
98-99	Tulsa	CHL	66	18	56	74	136	—	—	—	—	—
	CHL	Totals	194	57	116	173	384	9	0	5	5	12

Born; 1/19/73, Hamburg, Michigan. 5-10, 190. Last amateur club; Michigan State (CCHA).

Dan Smith
Defenseman

Regular Season / Playoffs

Season	Team	League	GP	G	A	PTS	PIM	GP	G	A	PTS	PIM
96-97	Tri-City	WHL	72	5	19	24	174	—	—	—	—	—
96-97	Hershey	AHL	8	0	1	1	6	15	0	1	1	25
97-98	Hershey	AHL	50	1	2	3	71	6	0	0	0	4
98-99	Colorado	NHL	12	0	0	0	9	—	—	—	—	—
98-99	Hershey	AHL	54	5	7	12	72	5	0	1	1	0
	AHL	Totals	112	6	10	16	149	26	0	2	2	29

Born; 5/2/76, Vernon, British Columbia. 5-11, 180. Drafted by Colorado Avalanche (7th choice, 181st overall) in 1995 Entry Draft. Member of 1996-97 AHL Champion Hershey Bears. Last amateur club; Tri-City (WHL).

Darcy Smith
Defenseman

Regular Season / Playoffs

Season	Team	League	GP	G	A	PTS	PIM	GP	G	A	PTS	PIM
97-98	Detroit	IHL	1	0	0	0	2	—	—	—	—	—
97-98	Peoria	ECHL	52	2	7	9	207	3	0	0	0	4
98-99	Peoria	ECHL	42	1	3	4	175	—	—	—	—	—
	ECHL	Totals	94	3	10	13	382	3	0	0	0	4

Born; 4/1/76, Sherwood Park, Alberta. 6-3, 210. Last amateur club; Kamloops (WHL).

Dave Smith
Center

Regular Season / Playoffs

Season	Team	League	GP	G	A	PTS	PIM	GP	G	A	PTS	PIM
92-93	Dayton	ECHL	49	22	29	51	183	3	0	0	0	26
92-93	Fort Wayne	IHL	25	7	6	13	77	10	4	5	9	46
93-94	Fort Wayne	IHL	65	22	22	44	196	18	2	6	8	68
94-95	Binghamton	AHL	77	20	40	60	225	8	2	4	6	38
95-96	Detroit	IHL	24	6	9	15	81	—	—	—	—	—
95-96	Los Angeles	IHL	53	21	37	58	150	—	—	—	—	—
96-97	Long Beach	IHL	61	17	17	34	175	—	—	—	—	—
96-97	Orlando	IHL	15	4	3	7	54	10	2	3	5	53
97-98	Orlando	IHL	16	2	2	4	34	—	—	—	—	—
97-98	San Antonio	IHL	63	19	19	38	195	—	—	—	—	—
98-99	Dayton	ECHL	1	0	0	0	0	—	—	—	—	—
	IHL	Totals	322	98	115	213	962	38	8	14	22	167
	ECHL	Totals	50	22	29	51	183	3	0	0	0	26

Born; 11/21/68, Arthur, Ontario. 6-0, 191. Traded to San Antonio by Orlando with Chris Lipuma and Dave Chyzowski for Scott Hollis, Grigori Panteleyev and Dave MacIntyre (11/97). Last amateur club; Ohio State (CCHA).

D.J. (Denis) Smith
Defenseman

Regular Season / Playoffs

Season	Team	League	GP	G	A	PTS	PIM	GP	G	A	PTS	PIM
95-96	Windsor	OHL	64	14	45	59	260	7	1	7	8	23
95-96	St. John's	AHL	1	0	0	0	0	—	—	—	—	—
96-97	Windsor	OHL	63	15	52	67	190	5	1	7	8	11
96-97	Toronto	NHL	8	0	1	1	7	—	—	—	—	—
96-97	St. John's	AHL	—	—	—	—	—	1	0	0	0	0
97-98	St. John's	AHL	65	4	11	15	237	4	0	0	0	4
98-99	St. John's	AHL	79	7	28	35	216	5	0	1	1	0
	AHL	Totals	145	11	39	50	453	10	0	1	1	4

Born; 5/13/77, Windsor, Ontario. 6-1, 200. Drafted by New York Islanders (3rd choice, 41st overall) in 1995 Entry Draft. Traded to Toronto Maple Leafs by Islanders with Wendel Clark and Mathieu Schneider for Darby Hendrickson, Kenny Jonsson, Sean Haggerty and Toronto's first round choice (Roberto Luongo) in the 1997 Entry Draft (3/13/96). Last amateur club; Windsor (OHL).

Derek Smith
Center

Regular Season / Playoffs

Season	Team	League	GP	G	A	PTS	PIM	GP	G	A	PTS	PIM
97-98	Huntington	ECHL	70	14	17	31	35	4	0	2	2	2
98-99	Huntington	ECHL	70	8	15	23	95	—	—	—	—	—
	ECHL	Totals	140	22	32	54	130					

Born; 4/22/75, Edmonton, Alberta. 5-9, 185.

Derrick Smith
Left Wing

Regular Season / Playoffs

Season	Team	League	GP	G	A	PTS	PIM	GP	G	A	PTS	PIM
84-85	Philadelphia	NHL	77	17	22	39	31	19	2	5	7	16
85-86	Philadelphia	NHL	69	6	6	12	57	4	0	0	0	10
86-87	Philadelphia	NHL	71	11	21	32	34	26	6	4	10	26
87-88	Philadelphia	NHL	76	16	8	24	104	7	0	0	0	6
88-89	Philadelphia	NHL	74	16	14	30	43	19	5	2	7	12
89-90	Philadelphia	NHL	55	3	6	9	32	—	—	—	—	—
90-91	Philadelphia	NHL	72	11	10	21	37	—	—	—	—	—
91-92	Minnesota	NHL	33	2	4	6	33	7	1	0	1	9
91-92	Kalamazoo	IHL	6	1	5	6	4	—	—	—	—	—
92-93	Minnesota	NHL	9	0	1	1	2	—	—	—	—	—
92-93	Kalamazoo	IHL	52	22	13	35	43	—	—	—	—	—
93-94	Dallas	NHL	1	0	0	0	0	—	—	—	—	—
93-94	Kalamazoo	IHL	77	44	37	81	90	5	0	0	0	18
94-95	Kalamazoo	IHL	68	30	21	51	103	16	3	8	11	8
95-96	Michigan	IHL	69	15	26	41	79	10	4	3	7	16
96-97	Michigan	IHL	68	8	21	29	55	4	1	0	1	16
97-98	Michigan	IHL	64	15	26	41	39	4	1	1	2	2
98-99	Baton Rouge	ECHL	6	3	7	10	9	6	0	0	0	0
	NHL	Totals	537	82	92	175	373	82	14	11	25	79
	IHL	Totals	404	135	149	284	413	39	9	12	21	60

Born; 1/22/65, Scarborough, Ontario. 6-2, 215. Drafted by Philadelphia Flyers (2nd choice, 44th overall) in 1983 Entry Draft. Claimed on waivers by Minnesota North Stars from Philadelphia (10/26/91). Selected by Greensboro in 1999 ECHL Expansion Draft. Last amateur club; Peterborough (OHL).

Gairin Smith

Regular Season — Defenseman — Playoffs

Season	Team	League	GP	G	A	PTS	PIM	GP	G	A	PTS	PIM
93-94	Charlotte	ECHL	17	5	2	7	77	—	—	—	—	—
93-94	Roanoke	ECHL	38	6	11	17	137	2	1	1	2	0
94-95	Cape Breton	AHL	6	0	1	1	16	—	—	—	—	—
94-95	Saginaw	CoHL	1	0	0	0	0	—	—	—	—	—
94-95	Wheeling	ECHL	48	8	11	19	195	—	—	—	—	—
95-96	Wheeling	ECHL	67	13	23	36	239	7	3	1	4	10
96-97	Carolina	AHL	6	0	0	0	30	—	—	—	—	—
96-97	Port Huron	CoHL	19	16	9	25	101	—	—	—	—	—
97-98	Port Huron	UHL	49	18	16	34	135	3	0	0	0	4
98-99	Fayetteville	CHL	3	3	1	4	25	—	—	—	—	—
98-99	Asheville	UHL	4	1	2	3	9	—	—	—	—	—
	AHL	Totals	12	0	1	1	46	—	—	—	—	—
	ECHL	Totals	170	32	47	79	648	9	4	2	6	10
	UHL	Totals	73	35	27	62	245	3	0	0	0	4

Born; 4/15/72, Tillsonburg, Ontario. 6-0, 195. Selected by Missouri in 1999 UHL Expansion Draft. Traded to Asheville by Port Huron with J.D. Eaton, Dale Greenwood and Chris Scourletis for Paul Polillo, Bernie John and Daryl Paquette (7/98). Last amateur club; Kitchener (OHL).

Geoff Smith

Regular Season — Defenseman — Playoffs

Season	Team	League	GP	G	A	PTS	PIM	GP	G	A	PTS	PIM
89-90	Edmonton	NHL	74	4	11	15	52	3	0	0	0	0
90-91	Edmonton	NHL	59	1	12	13	55	4	0	0	0	0
91-92	Edmonton	NHL	74	2	16	18	43	5	0	1	1	6
92-93	Edmonton	NHL	78	4	14	18	30	—	—	—	—	—
93-94	Edmonton	NHL	21	0	3	3	12	—	—	—	—	—
93-94	Florida	NHL	56	1	5	6	38	—	—	—	—	—
94-95	Florida	NHL	47	2	4	6	22	—	—	—	—	—
95-96	Florida	NHL	31	3	7	10	20	1	0	0	0	2
96-97	Florida	NHL	3	0	0	0	2	—	—	—	—	—
96-97	Carolina	AHL	27	3	4	7	20	—	—	—	—	—
97-98	Rangers	NHL	15	1	1	2	6	—	—	—	—	—
97-98	Hartford	AHL	59	1	12	13	34	—	—	—	—	—
98-99	Rangers	NHL	4	0	0	0	2	—	—	—	—	—
98-99	Hartford	AHL	9	1	4	5	10	—	—	—	—	—
98-99	Worcester	AHL	25	1	3	4	16	4	0	0	0	4
98-99	Cincinnati	IHL	31	3	3	6	20	—	—	—	—	—
	NHL	Totals	462	18	73	91	282	13	0	1	1	8
	AHL	Totals	120	6	23	29	80	4	0	0	0	4

Born; 3/7/69, Edmonton, Alberta. 6-3, 194. Drafted by Edmonton Oilers (3rd choice, 67th overall) in 1987 Entry Draft. Traded to Florida Panthers by Edmonton with Edmonton's fourth round choice (David Nemirovsky) in 1994 Entry Draft for Florida's third round choice (Corey Neilson) in 1994 Entry Draft and St. Louis' sixth round choice (previosuly acquired by Florida—later traded to Winnipeg—Winnipeg selected Chris Kibermanis) in 1994 Entry Draft, (12/6/93). Signed as a free agent by New York Rangers (9/29/97). Traded to St. Louis Blues with Jeff Finley and cash for Chris Kenady (2/13/99). Member of 1989-90 Stanley Cup Champion Edmonton Oilers. Last amateur club; North Dakota

Greg Smith

Regular Season — Goaltender — Playoffs

Season	Team	League	GP	W	L	T	MIN	SO	AVG	GP	W	L	MIN	SO	AVG
92-93	Dallas	CeHL	21	7	11	2	1243	0	4.15	1	0	0	8	0	15.00
93-94	Dallas	CeHL	33	12	13	6	1860	0	5.06	—	—	—	—	—	—
93-94	Wichita	CeHL	5	1	2	0	210	0	6.01	2	0	1	67	0	3.58
94-95	Wichita	CeHL	29	17	8	2	1515	1	4.08	5	2	0	183	0	*2.30
95-96	Wichita	CeHL	12	2	9	0	608	0	5.82	—	—	—	—	—	—
95-96	Bakersfield	WCHL	19	5	8	4	1037	0	5.56	—	—	—	—	—	—
96-97	Knoxville	ECHL	6	4	2	0	331	0	4.53	—	—	—	—	—	—
96-97	Nashville	CeHL	26	4	18	0	1365	0	5.32	—	—	—	—	—	—
97-98	Central Texas	WPHL	26	11	7	2	1312	0	4.02	—	—	—	—	—	—
98-99	Kansas City	IHL	3	0	0	1	98	0	1.83	—	—	—	—	—	—
98-99	Wichita	CHL	17	9	4	2	932	3	3.41	3	1	2	165	0	4.71
	CeHL	Totals	143	52	65	12	7733	4	4.66	11	3	3	423	0	3.69

Born; 8/11/71, Southgate, Michigan. 6-0, 190. Member of 1993-94 CeHL champion Wichita Thunder. Member of 1994-95 CeHL champion Wichita Thunder.

Ian Smith

Regular Season — Defenseman — Playoffs

Season	Team	League	GP	G	A	PTS	PIM	GP	G	A	PTS	PIM
97-98	Mobile	ECHL	4	2	0	2	2	—	—	—	—	—
97-98	Jacksonville	ECHL	4	0	0	0	2	—	—	—	—	—
97-98	Johnstown	ECHL	51	10	33	43	47	—	—	—	—	—
98-99	Johnstown	ECHL	60	4	28	32	72	—	—	—	—	—
	ECHL	Totals	119	16	61	77	123	—	—	—	—	—

Born; 2/13/73, Montreal, Quebec. 5-10, 195. Selected by Greensboro in 1999 Expansion Draft.

Jason Smith

Regular Season — Defenseman — Playoffs

Season	Team	League	GP	G	A	PTS	PIM	GP	G	A	PTS	PIM
92-93	Erie	ECHL	22	3	8	11	2	5	1	1	2	2
93-94	Erie	ECHL	68	22	37	59	44	—	—	—	—	—
94-95	Erie	ECHL	56	7	34	41	38	—	—	—	—	—
94-95	Utica	CoHL	1	0	1	1	2	—	—	—	—	—
95-96	Utica	CoHL	74	23	64	87	38	—	—	—	—	—
96-97	Mobile	ECHL	19	4	5	9	7	—	—	—	—	—
96-97	Austin	WPHL	31	3	16	19	10	6	0	2	2	2
97-98	Madison	UHL	31	6	20	26	4	—	—	—	—	—
97-98	Saginaw	UHL	34	7	19	26	0	—	—	—	—	—
98-99	Monroe	WPHL	69	15	39	54	22	6	3	0	3	0
	ECHL	Totals	165	36	84	120	91	5	1	1	2	2
	UHL	Totals	140	36	104	140	44	—	—	—	—	—
	WPHL	Totals	100	18	55	73	32	12	3	2	5	2

Born; 5/21/72, Winnipeg, Manitoba. 5-10, 200. Traded to Saginaw by Madison for Dave Ivaska and Ken Blum (1/98). 1995-96 CoHL Second Team All-Star. Last amateur club; Tri-City (WHL).

Jeff Smith

Regular Season — Defenseman — Playoffs

Season	Team	League	GP	G	A	PTS	PIM	GP	G	A	PTS	PIM
96-97	Amarillo	WPHL	30	7	9	16	74	—	—	—	—	—
96-97	Mobile	ECHL	18	0	5	5	12	—	—	—	—	—
97-98	Odessa	WPHL	13	2	6	8	54	—	—	—	—	—
97-98	Lake Charles	WPHL	25	1	8	9	29	—	—	—	—	—
97-98	Bakersfield	WCHL	21	1	3	4	28	4	1	0	1	6
98-99	Thunder Bay	UHL	17	3	3	6	34	—	—	—	—	—
98-99	Asheville	UHL	21	2	2	4	46	—	—	—	—	—
98-99	Madison	UHL	4	0	0	0	4	—	—	—	—	—
98-99	Flint	UHL	15	1	2	3	4	—	—	—	—	—
	WPHL	Totals	68	10	23	33	157	—	—	—	—	—
	UHL	Totals	57	6	7	13	88	—	—	—	—	—

Born; 5/3/74, Belleville, Ontario. 6-0, 200. Traded to Lake Charles by Odessa with Mike Henderson for Paul Fiorini (11/97). Traded to Madison by Asheville with Chris Newans for Jason Dexter and Jeff Foster (1/99). Traded to Port Huron by Flint with Jamie Weatherspoon for Chris Newans (3/99).

Mark Smith

Regular Season — Center — Playoffs

Season	Team	League	GP	G	A	PTS	PIM	GP	G	A	PTS	PIM
97-98	Lethbridge	WHL	70	42	67	109	206	3	0	2	2	18
97-98	Kentucky	AHL	—	—	—	—	—	2	0	0	0	0
98-99	Kentucky	AHL	78	18	21	39	101	12	2	7	9	16
	AHL	Totals	78	18	21	39	101	14	2	7	9	16

Born; 10/24/77, Edmonton, Alberta. 5-10, 190. Drafted by San Jose Sharks (9th choice, 219th overall) in 1997 Entry Draft. Last amateur club; Lethbridge (WHL).

Matt Smith

Regular Season — Defenseman — Playoffs

Season	Team	League	GP	G	A	PTS	PIM	GP	G	A	PTS	PIM
97-98	Massachusetts	H.E.	33	5	8	13	48	—	—	—	—	—
97-98	Worcester	AHL	4	1	0	1	4	3	0	0	0	10
98-99	Worcester	AHL	44	3	8	11	81	—	—	—	—	—
98-99	Peoria	ECHL	6	0	3	3	6	4	1	1	2	6
	AHL	Totals	48	4	8	12	85	3	0	0	0	10

Born; 12/23/76, Kent, England. 6-6, 215. Signed as a free agent by St. Louis Blues (3/27/98). Last amateur club; Massaachusetts (Hockey East).

Rick Smith — Defenseman

Regular Season / Playoffs

Season	Team	League	GP	G	A	PTS	PIM	GP	G	A	PTS	PIM
98-99	Plymouth	OHL	30	13	12	25	44	—	—	—	—	—
98-99	Kitchener	OHL	30	9	9	18	37	1	0	0	0	4
98-99	Birmingham	ECHL	4	1	1	2	0	5	0	1	1	0

Born; 7/29/78, Brighton, Michigan. 6-0, 187. Last amateur club; Kitchener

Shawn Smith — Defenseman

Regular Season / Playoffs

Season	Team	League	GP	G	A	PTS	PIM	GP	G	A	PTS	PIM
97-98	Binghamton	UHL	12	0	0	0	20	—	—	—	—	—
97-98	Thunder Bay	UHL	26	1	3	4	48	5	0	0	0	8
98-99	Thunder Bay	UHL	46	1	12	13	66	10	0	0	0	10
	UHL	Totals	84	2	15	17	134	15	0	0	0	18

Born; 1/5/73, Winnipeg, Manitoba. 6-0, 195. Selected by Fort Wayne in 1999 UHL Expansion Draft.

Travis Smith — Defenseman

Regular Season / Playoffs

Season	Team	League	GP	G	A	PTS	PIM	GP	G	A	PTS	PIM
97-98	Roanoke	ECHL	46	2	8	10	38	9	2	1	3	8
98-99	Lowell	AHL	7	0	0	0	0	—	—	—	—	—
98-99	Roanoke	ECHL	59	7	11	18	83	12	0	0	0	44
	ECHL	Totals	105	9	19	28	121	21	2	1	3	52

Born; 8/27/73, Moose Jaw, Saskatchewan. 6-0, 195. Last amateur club; Denver (WCHA).

Brad Smyth — Right Wing

Regular Season / Playoffs

Season	Team	League	GP	G	A	PTS	PIM	GP	G	A	PTS	PIM
93-94	Cincinnati	IHL	30	7	3	10	54	—	—	—	—	—
93-94	Birmingham	ECHL	29	26	30	56	38	10	8	8	16	19
94-95	Springfield	AHL	3	0	0	0	7	—	—	—	—	—
94-95	Birmingham	ECHL	36	33	35	68	52	3	5	2	7	0
94-95	Cincinnati	IHL	26	2	11	13	34	1	0	0	0	2
95-96	Florida	NHL	7	1	1	2	4	—	—	—	—	—
95-96	Carolina	AHL	68	*68	58	*126	80	—	—	—	—	—
96-97	Florida	NHL	8	1	0	1	2	—	—	—	—	—
96-97	Los Angeles	NHL	44	8	8	16	74	—	—	—	—	—
96-97	Phoenix	IHL	3	5	2	7	0	—	—	—	—	—
97-98	Los Angeles	NHL	9	1	3	4	4	—	—	—	—	—
97-98	Rangers	NHL	1	0	0	0	0	—	—	—	—	—
97-98	Hartford	AHL	57	29	33	62	79	15	12	8	20	11
98-99	Nashville	NHL	3	0	0	0	6	—	—	—	—	—
98-99	Milwaukee	IHL	34	11	16	27	21	—	—	—	—	—
98-99	Hartford	AHL	36	25	19	44	48	7	6	0	6	14
	NHL	Totals	72	11	12	23	90	—	—	—	—	—
	AHL	Totals	164	122	110	232	214	22	18	8	26	25
	IHL	Totals	93	25	32	57	109	1	0	0	0	2
	ECHL	Totals	65	59	65	124	90	13	13	10	23	19

Born; 3/13/73, Ottawa, Ontario. 6-0, 200. Signed as a free agent by Florida Panthers (10/4/93). Traded to Los Angeles Kings by Florida for Los Angeles' third round choice (Vratislav Czech) in 1997 Entry Draft (11/28/96). Traded to New York Rangers by Los Angeles for a conditional draft pick (11/14/97). Signed as a a free agent by Nashville Predators (7/16/98). Sold to Rangers by Nashville (4/30/99). Last amateur club; London (OHL).

Greg Smyth — Defenseman

Regular Season / Playoffs

Season	Team	League	GP	G	A	PTS	PIM	GP	G	A	PTS	PIM
85-86	London	OHL	46	12	42	54	199	4	1	2	3	28
85-86	Hershey	AHL	2	0	1	1	5	8	0	0	0	60
86-87	Philadelphia	NHL	1	0	0	0	0	1	0	0	0	2
86-87	Hershey	AHL	35	0	2	2	158	2	0	0	0	19
87-88	Philadelphia	NHL	48	1	6	7	192	5	0	0	0	38
87-88	Hershey	AHL	21	0	10	10	102	—	—	—	—	—
88-89	Quebec	NHL	10	0	1	1	70	—	—	—	—	—
88-89	Halifax	AHL	43	3	9	12	310	4	0	1	1	35
89-90	Quebec	NHL	13	0	0	0	57	—	—	—	—	—
89-90	Halifax	AHL	49	5	14	19	235	6	1	0	1	52
90-91	Quebec	NHL	1	0	0	0	0	—	—	—	—	—
90-91	Halifax	AHL	56	6	23	29	340	—	—	—	—	—
91-92	Quebec	NHL	29	0	2	2	138	—	—	—	—	—
91-92	Calgary	NHL	7	1	1	2	15	—	—	—	—	—
91-92	Halifax	AHL	9	1	3	4	35	—	—	—	—	—
92-93	Calgary	NHL	35	1	2	3	95	—	—	—	—	—
92-93	Salt Lake City	IHL	5	0	1	1	31	—	—	—	—	—
93-94	Florida	NHL	12	1	0	1	37	—	—	—	—	—
93-94	Toronto	NHL	11	0	1	1	38	—	—	—	—	—
93-94	Chicago	NHL	38	0	0	0	108	6	0	0	0	0
94-95	Chicago	NHL	22	0	3	3	33	—	—	—	—	—
94-95	Indianapolis	IHL	2	0	0	0	0	—	—	—	—	—
95-96	Chicago	IHL	15	1	3	4	53	—	—	—	—	—
95-96	Los Angeles	IHL	41	2	7	9	231	—	—	—	—	—
96-97	St. John's	AHL	43	2	4	6	273	5	0	1	1	14
97-98	St. John's	AHL	63	5	6	11	353	4	0	1	1	6
98-99	St. John's	AHL	40	0	7	7	159	5	0	1	1	19
	NHL	Totals	227	4	16	20	783	12	0	0	0	40
	AHL	Totals	361	22	78	100	1965	26	1	4	5	145
	IHL	Totals	63	3	11	14	315	—	—	—	—	—

Born; 4/23/66, Oakville, Ontario. 6-3, 212. Drafted by Philadelphia Flyers (1st choice, 22nd overall) in 1984 Entry Draft. Traded to Quebec Nordiques by Philadelphia with Philadelphia's third round choice (John Tanner) in the 1989 Entry Draft for Terry Carkner (7/25/88). Traded to Calgary Flames by Quebec for Martin Simard (3/10/92). Signed as a free agent by Florida Panthers (8/10/93). Traded to Toronto Maple Leafs by Florida for cash (12/7/93). Claimed on waivers by Chicago Blackhawks from Toronto (1/8/94). Signed as a free agent by Toronto (8/22/96). Last amateur club; London (OHL).

Kevin Smyth — Left Wing

Regular Season / Playoffs

Season	Team	League	GP	G	A	PTS	PIM	GP	G	A	PTS	PIM
93-94	Hartford	NHL	21	3	2	5	10	—	—	—	—	—
93-94	Springfield	AHL	42	22	27	49	72	6	4	5	9	0
94-95	Hartford	NHL	16	1	5	6	13	—	—	—	—	—
94-95	Springfield	AHL	57	17	22	39	72	—	—	—	—	—
95-96	Hartford	NHL	21	2	1	3	8	—	—	—	—	—
95-96	Springfield	AHL	47	15	33	48	87	10	5	5	10	8
96-97	Orlando	IHL	38	14	17	31	49	10	1	2	3	6
97-98	Orlando	IHL	43	10	5	15	59	1	0	0	0	2
98-99	Las Vegas	IHL	1	0	0	0	0	—	—	—	—	—
98-99	Tacoma	WCHL	42	25	21	46	83	11	7	*13	*20	10
	NHL	Totals	58	6	8	14	31	—	—	—	—	—
	AHL	Totals	146	54	82	136	231	16	9	10	19	8
	IHL	Totals	82	24	22	46	108	11	1	2	3	6

Born; 11/22/73, Banff, Alberta. 6-2, 220. Drafted by Hartford Whalers (4th choice, 79th overall) in 1992 Entry Draft. Member of 1998-99 WCHL Champion Tacoma Sabrecats. Last amatuer club; Moose Jaw (WHL).

Chris Snell — Defenseman

Regular Season / Playoffs

Season	Team	League	GP	G	A	PTS	PIM	GP	G	A	PTS	PIM
97-98	Monroe	WPHL	69	4	11	15	66	—	—	—	—	—
98-99	South Carolina	ECHL	1	0	0	0	0	—	—	—	—	—

Born; 12/15/73, Grand Rapids, Minnesota. 6-1, 200. Selected by Tupelo in 1998 WPHL Expansion Draft. Last amateur club; Minnesota-Duluth (WCHA).

Chris Snell — Defenseman

Regular Season / Playoffs

Season	Team	League	GP	G	A	PTS	PIM	GP	G	A	PTS	PIM
91-92	Rochester	AHL	65	5	27	32	66	10	2	1	3	6
92-93	Rochester	AHL	76	14	57	71	83	17	5	8	13	39
93-94	Toronto	NHL	2	0	0	0	2	—	—	—	—	—
93-94	St. John's	AHL	75	22	74	96	92	11	1	15	16	10
94-95	Los Angeles	NHL	32	2	7	9	22	—	—	—	—	—
94-95	Phoenix	IHL	57	15	49	64	122	—	—	—	—	—
95-96	Phoenix	IHL	40	9	22	31	113	—	—	—	—	—
95-96	Binghamton	AHL	32	7	25	32	48	4	2	2	4	6
96-97	Indianapolis	IHL	73	22	45	67	130	2	0	0	0	2
97-98	Frankfurt	Germany	44	13	23	36	161	7	3	2	5	22
98-99	Frankfurt	Germany	49	22	29	51	157	8	2	4	6	6
	NHL	Totals	34	2	7	9	24	—	—	—	—	—
	AHL	Totals	248	48	183	231	289	42	10	26	36	61
	IHL	Totals	170	46	116	162	365	2	0	0	0	2

Born; 7/12/71, Regina, Saskatchewan. 5-11, 184. Drafted by Buffalo Sabres (8th choice, 145th overall) in 1991 Entry Draft. Signed as a free agent by Toronto Maple Leafs (8/3/93). Traded to Los Angeles Kings by Toronto with Eric Lacroix and Toronto's fourth round choice (Eric Belanger) in 1996 Entry Draft for Dixon Ward, Guy Leveque and Kelly Fairchild (10/3/94). Traded to New York Rangers by Los Angeles for Steve Larouche (1/14/96). Signed as a free agent by Chicago Blackhawks (7/96). 1993-94 AHL First Team All-Star. 1993-94 AHL Top Defenseman. 1994-95 IHL First Team All-Star. 1996-97 IHL Second Team All-Star. Last amateur club; Ottawa (OHL).

Shawn Snesar — Defenseman

Regular Season / Playoffs

Season	Team	League	GP	G	A	PTS	PIM	GP	G	A	PTS	PIM
91-92	Hampton Roads	ECHL	57	5	17	22	272	14	0	2	2	21
92-93	Hampton Roads	ECHL	53	7	24	31	251	4	2	1	3	6
93-94	Hampton Roads	ECHL	67	12	44	56	151	7	0	2	2	34
94-95	Richmond	ECHL	63	8	23	31	259	14	1	1	2	39
95-96	Bracknell	BHL	22	3	9	12	100	—	—	—	—	—
96-97	Bracknell	BHL	19	2	3	5	79	—	—	—	—	—
97-98	Fresno	WCHL	41	5	14	19	106	5	0	4	4	8
98-99	Corpus Christi	WPHL	28	0	3	3	34	4	0	0	0	10
	ECHL	Totals	240	32	108	140	933	39	3	6	9	100

Born; 3/23/69, Ottawa, Ontario. 5-11, 210. Member of 1991-92 ECHL Champion Hampton Roads Admirals. Member of 1994-95 ECHL Champion Richmond Renegades.

Jamie Sokolsky — Defenseman

Regular Season / Playoffs

Season	Team	League	GP	G	A	PTS	PIM	GP	G	A	PTS	PIM
97-98	New Orleans	ECHL	23	0	3	3	24	—	—	—	—	—
97-98	Huntington	ECHL	22	4	6	10	26	4	3	1	4	6
98-99	Huntington	ECHL	65	12	30	42	79	—	—	—	—	—
	ECHL	Totals	110	16	39	55	129	4	3	1	4	6

Born; 3/11/77, Toronto, Ontario. 6-2, 205. Drafted by Philadelphia Flyers (5th choice, 135th overall) in 1995 Entry Draft. Last amateur club; Owen Sound

Kevin Solari — Left Wing

Regular Season / Playoffs

Season	Team	League	GP	G	A	PTS	PIM	GP	G	A	PTS	PIM
94-95	Columbus	ECHL	11	1	1	2	25	—	—	—	—	—
95-96												
96-97	Grand Rapids	IHL	1	0	0	0	2	—	—	—	—	—
96-97	Muskegon	CoHL	48	14	12	26	65	—	—	—	—	—
96-97	Utica	CoHL	21	6	5	11	39	3	0	1	1	0
97-98	Winston-Salem	UHL	54	13	24	37	107	—	—	—	—	—
98-99	Monroe	WPHL	65	13	17	30	188	5	1	1	2	9
	UHL	Totals	123	33	41	74	211	3	0	1	1	0

Born; 3/7/74, Hamilton, Ontario. 6-0, 203. Last amateur club; Peterborough

Jonas Soling — Right Wing

Regular Season / Playoffs

Season	Team	League	GP	G	A	PTS	PIM	GP	G	A	PTS	PIM
98-99	Augusta	ECHL	50	27	20	47	71	—	—	—	—	—
98-99	Syracuse	AHL	29	2	2	4	4	—	—	—	—	—

Born; 9/7/78, Stockholm, Sweden. 6-4, 192. Drafted by Vancouver Canucks (3rd choice, 93rd overall) in 1996 Entry Draft. Last amateur club; Sudbury (OHL).

Martin Sonnenberg — Left Wing

Regular Season / Playoffs

Season	Team	League	GP	G	A	PTS	PIM	GP	G	A	PTS	PIM
98-99	Pittsburgh	NHL	44	1	1	2	19	7	0	0	0	0
98-99	Syracuse	AHL	37	16	9	25	31	—	—	—	—	—

Born; 1/23/78, Wetaskiwin, Alberta. Signed as a free agent by Pittsburgh Penguins (1998). Last amateur club; Saskatoon (WHL).

Brent Sopel — Defenseman

Regular Season / Playoffs

Season	Team	League	GP	G	A	PTS	PIM	GP	G	A	PTS	PIM
95-96	Swift Current	WHL	71	13	48	61	87	6	1	2	3	4
95-96	Syracuse	AHL	1	0	0	0	0	—	—	—	—	—
96-97	Swift Current	WHL	62	15	41	56	109	10	5	11	16	32
96-97	Syracuse	AHL	2	0	0	0	0	3	0	0	0	0
97-98	Syracuse	AHL	76	10	33	43	70	5	0	7	7	12
98-99	Vancouver	NHL	5	1	0	1	4	—	—	—	—	—
98-99	Syracuse	AHL	53	10	21	31	59	—	—	—	—	—
	AHL	Totals	132	20	54	74	129	8	0	7	7	12

Born; 1/7/77, Calgary, Alberta. 6-1, 185. Drafted by Vancouver Canucks (6th choice, 144th overall) in 1995 Entry Draft. Last amateur club; Swift Current

Anders Sorenson — Defenseman

Regular Season / Playoffs

Season	Team	League	GP	G	A	PTS	PIM	GP	G	A	PTS	PIM
98-99	Fort Worth	CHL	17	3	6	9	4	—	—	—	—	—
98-99	Tupelo	WPHL	8	0	1	1	8	—	—	—	—	—

Born; 5/11/75, Sodertalje, Sweden. 5-9, 180. Selected by Huntsville in 1999 CHL Dispersal Draft.

Jonathan Sorg — Defenseman

Regular Season / Playoffs

Season	Team	League	GP	G	A	PTS	PIM	GP	G	A	PTS	PIM
97-98	Hershey	AHL	2	0	0	0	2	—	—	—	—	—
97-98	Johnstown	ECHL	70	6	10	16	119	—	—	—	—	—
98-99	Lowell	AHL	3	0	2	2	2	—	—	—	—	—
98-99	Johnstown	ECHL	38	4	13	17	99	—	—	—	—	—
98-99	Wheeling	ECHL	27	1	6	7	42	—	—	—	—	—
	AHL	Totals	5	0	2	2	4	—	—	—	—	—
	ECHL	Totals	135	11	29	40	260	—	—	—	—	—

Born; 5/21/74, Branchville, New Jersey. 6-2, 205. Last amateur club; Vermont (ECAC).

Lee Sorochan — Defenseman

Regular Season / Playoffs

Season	Team	League	GP	G	A	PTS	PIM	GP	G	A	PTS	PIM
94-95	Lethbridge	WHL	29	4	15	19	93	—	—	—	—	—
94-95	Saskatoon	WHL	24	5	13	18	63	10	3	6	9	34
94-95	Binghamton	AHL	—	—	—	—	—	8	0	0	0	11
95-96	Binghamton	AHL	45	2	8	10	26	1	0	0	0	0
96-97	Binghamton	AHL	77	4	27	31	160	4	0	2	2	18
97-98	Hartford	AHL	73	7	11	18	197	13	0	2	2	51
98-99	Calgary	NHL	2	0	0	0	0	—	—	—	—	—
98-99	Hartford	AHL	16	0	2	2	33	—	—	—	—	—
98-99	Saint John	AHL	3	1	3	4	4	7	3	3	6	29
98-99	Fort Wayne	IHL	45	0	10	10	204	—	—	—	—	—
	AHL	Totals	214	14	51	65	420	33	3	7	10	109

Born; 9/9/75, Edmonton, Alberta. 6-1, 210. Drafted by New York Rangers (2nd choice, 34th overall) in 1993 Entry Draft. Traded to Calgary Flames with a conditional draft choice in 2000 by Rangers for Chris O'Sullivan (3/23/99). Last amateur club; Saskatoon (WHL).

Christian Soucy — Goaltender

Regular Season / Playoffs

Season	Team	League	GP	W	L	T	MIN	SO	AVG	GP	W	L	MIN	SO	AVG
93-94	Chicago	NHL	1	0	0	0	3	0	0.00	—	—	—	—	—	—
93-94	Indianapolis	IHL	46	14	25	1	2302	1	4.14	—	—	—	—	—	—
94-95	Indianapolis	IHL	42	15	17	5	2216	0	4.01	—	—	—	—	—	—
95-96	Indianapolis	IHL	22	12	9	0	1197	0	3.11	—	—	—	—	—	—
96-97	Kentucky	AHL	3	0	2	0	138	0	4.77	—	—	—	—	—	—
96-97	Baton Rouge	ECHL	46	18	20	1	2421	3	3.17	—	—	—	—	—	—
97-98	Houston	IHL	5	4	1	0	288	0	1.87	—	—	—	—	—	—
97-98	Austin	WPHL	11	6	5	0	659	0	3.46	5	2	3	322	0	2.61
98-99	Tucson	WCHL	16	6	7	2	903	0	3.72	—	—	—	—	—	—
98-99	Baton Rouge	ECHL	25	9	9	4	1386	2	2.99	—	—	—	—	—	—
	IHL	Totals	115	45	52	6	6003	1	3.78	—	—	—	—	—	—
	ECHL	Totals	71	27	29	5	3807	5	3.10	—	—	—	—	—	—

Born; 9/14/70, Gatineau, Quebec. 5-11, 160. Signed as a free agent by Chicago Blackhawks (6/21/93). Last amateur club; Vermont (ECAC).

Jean-Phillipe Soucy — Defenseman

Regular Season / Playoffs

Season	Team	League	GP	G	A	PTS	PIM	GP	G	A	PTS	PIM
98-99	Bathurst	QMJHL	36	1	17	18	108	—	—	—	—	—
98-99	Chicoutimi	QMJHL	5	0	4	4	9	—	—	—	—	—
98-99	Drummondville	QMJHL	24	2	13	15	53	—	—	—	—	—
98-99	Jacksonville	ECHL	6	0	0	0	5	2	0	0	0	0

Born; Last amateur club; Drummondville (QMJHL).

Scott Souffel — Forward

Regular Season / Playoffs

Season	Team	League	GP	G	A	PTS	PIM	GP	G	A	PTS	PIM
98-99	Binghamton	UHL	2	0	0	0	0	—	—	—	—	—

Born; 7/25/75, Oradell, New Jersey. 5-10, 190.

Stephane Soulliere — Left Wing

Regular Season / Playoffs

Season	Team	League	GP	G	A	PTS	PIM	GP	G	A	PTS	PIM
95-96	Phoenix	IHL	5	0	0	0	2	—	—	—	—	—
95-96	Knoxville	ECHL	59	26	26	52	124	5	0	2	2	16
96-97	Phoenix	IHL	6	0	1	1	2	—	—	—	—	—
96-97	Knoxcville	ECHL	58	25	42	67	63	—	—	—	—	—
97-98	Charlotte	ECHL	42	11	24	35	21	—	—	—	—	—
97-98	New Orleans	ECHL	14	3	4	7	32	—	—	—	—	—
98-99	Hamilton	AHL	2	1	0	1	0	—	—	—	—	—
98-99	New Orleans	ECHL	59	20	22	42	94	10	0	3	3	8
	IHL	Totals	11	0	1	1	4	—	—	—	—	—
	ECHL	Totals	232	85	118	203	334	15	0	5	5	24

Born; 5/30/75, Greenfield Park, Quebec. 5-11, 180. Signed as a free agent by Los Angeles Kings (7/1/94). Traded to New Orleans by Charlotte with Dean Moore for Mikhail Nemirovsky and Pierre Gendron (2/98). Last amateur club; Guelph

Jaroslav Spacek — Defenseman

Regular Season / Playoffs

Season	Team	League	GP	G	A	PTS	PIM	GP	G	A	PTS	PIM
98-99	Florida	NHL	63	3	12	15	28	—	—	—	—	—
98-99	New Haven	AHL	14	4	8	12	15	—	—	—	—	—

Born; 2/11/74, Rokycany, Czechoslovakia. 5-11, 198. Drafted by Florida Panthers (5th choice, 117th overall) in 1998 Entry Draft. Last European club; Farjestad (Sweden).

Todd Sparks — Left Wing

Regular Season / Playoffs

Season	Team	League	GP	G	A	PTS	PIM	GP	G	A	PTS	PIM
95-96	Springfield	AHL	3	0	0	0	2	—	—	—	—	—
95-96	Richmond	ECHL	49	17	26	43	100	6	1	5	6	6
96-97	Fredericton	AHL	67	17	23	40	83	—	—	—	—	—
97-98												
98-99	Vojers	Belgium	33	21	37	58	154	—	—	—	—	—
	AHL	Totals	70	17	23	40	85	—	—	—	—	—

Born; 6/9/71, Edmunston, New Brunswick. 6-0, 190. Drafted by New York Islanders (8th choice, 158th overall) in 1991 Entry Draft. Last amateur club; New Brunswick (AUAA).

Mark Spence — Left Wing

Regular Season / Playoffs

Season	Team	League	GP	G	A	PTS	PIM	GP	G	A	PTS	PIM
98-99	Tucson	WCHL	21	7	11	18	23	—	—	—	—	—
98-99	Phoenix	WCHL	43	13	15	28	40	—	—	—	—	—
98-99	Fresno	WCHL	12	6	5	11	12	5	0	2	2	2
	WCHL	Totals	76	26	31	57	75	5	0	2	2	2

Born; 4/21/75, Montreal, Quebec. 6-1, 190. Last amateur club; Middlebury (NCAA 3).

Joe Spencer — Center

Regular Season / Playoffs

Season	Team	League	GP	G	A	PTS	PIM	GP	G	A	PTS	PIM
98-99	Birmingham	ECHL	1	0	0	0	0	—	—	—	—	—

Born;

Greg Spenrath — Left Wing

Regular Season / Playoffs

Season	Team	League	GP	G	A	PTS	PIM	GP	G	A	PTS	PIM
90-91	Binghamton	AHL	2	0	0	0	14	—	—	—	—	—
90-91	Erie	ECHL	61	29	36	65	*407	4	1	2	3	46
91-92	Kalamazoo	IHL	69	4	7	11	237	—	—	—	—	—
92-93	Indianapolis	IHL	9	0	1	1	68	1	0	0	0	5
92-93	Binghamton	AHL	1	0	0	0	2	—	—	—	—	—
92-93	Erie	ECHL	55	17	28	45	344	3	1	0	1	77
93-94	Las Vegas	IHL	43	2	0	2	222	—	—	—	—	—
94-95	Prince Edward Island	AHL	58	3	5	8	216	9	0	2	2	28
95-96	Fresno	WCHL	57	20	35	55	206	7	4	5	9	16
96-97	Utah	IHL	2	0	1	1	8	—	—	—	—	—
96-97	Fresno	WCHL	61	14	32	46	375	5	0	4	4	53
97-98	Utah	IHL	46	13	11	24	101	4	1	1	2	9
97-98	Fresno	WCHL	7	1	4	5	59	—	—	—	—	—
98-99	Fresno	WCHL	49	10	20	30	223	7	2	4	6	25
	IHL	Totals	168	19	20	39	636	5	1	1	2	14
	AHL	Totals	61	3	5	8	232	9	0	2	2	28
	WCHL	Totals	174	45	91	136	863	19	6	13	19	94
	ECHL	Totals	116	46	64	110	751	7	2	2	4	123

Born; 9/27/69, Edmonton, Alberta. 6-3, 225. Drafted by New York Rangers (9th choice, 160th overall) in 1989 Entry Draft. Signed as a free agent by Minnesota North Stars (7/25/91). Last amateur club; Tri-City (WHL).

Maxim Spirodonov — Right Wing

Regular Season / Playoffs

Season	Team	League	GP	G	A	PTS	PIM	GP	G	A	PTS	PIM
97-98	London	OHL	66	54	44	98	52	16	3	4	7	4
97-98	Grand Rapids	IHL	—	—	—	—	—	3	0	0	0	0
98-99	Grand Rapids	IHL	41	11	17	28	12	—	—	—	—	—
98-99	Springfield	AHL	23	8	8	16	2	2	0	0	0	2
	IHL	Totals	41	11	17	28	12	3	0	0	0	0

Born; 5-11, 182. Drafted by Edmonton Oilers (10th choice, 241st overall) in 1998 Entry Draft. Last amateur club; London (OHL).

John Spoltore — Center

Regular Season / Playoffs

Season	Team	League	GP	G	A	PTS	PIM	GP	G	A	PTS	PIM
95-96	Louisiana	ECHL	70	33	68	101	99	5	4	4	8	2
96-97	Louisiana	ECHL	9	0	8	8	8	17	10	13	23	20
97-98	Michigan	IHL	2	0	1	1	0	—	—	—	—	—
97-98	Louisiana	ECHL	68	32	*79	111	51	12	4	15	19	15
98-99	Providence	AHL	—	—	—	—	—	11	6	6	12	4
98-99	Louisiana	ECHL	69	36	73	*109	96	5	2	3	5	0
	ECHL	Totals	216	101	228	329	254	39	20	35	55	37

Born; 8/25/71, Bridgeton, New Jersey. 5-10, 195. 1997-98 ECHL Second Team All-Star. 1998-99 ECHL First Team All-Star. Member of 1998-99 AHL Champion Providence Bruins. Last amateur club; Wilfrid Laurier (OUAA).

Doug Spooner — Left Wing

Regular Season / Playoffs

Season	Team	League	GP	G	A	PTS	PIM	GP	G	A	PTS	PIM
98-99	Anchorage	WCHL	1	0	0	0	0	—	—	—	—	—

Born; Cache Creek, British Columbia. 6-0, 185.

Corey Spring — Right Wing

Regular Season / Playoffs

Season	Team	League	GP	G	A	PTS	PIM	GP	G	A	PTS	PIM
95-96	Atlanta	IHL	73	14	14	28	104	2	0	0	0	0
96-97	Adirondack	AHL	69	20	26	46	118	4	0	0	0	14
97-98	Tampa Bay	NHL	8	1	0	1	10	—	—	—	—	—
97-98	Adirondack	AHL	57	19	25	44	120	3	0	0	0	6
98-99	Tampa Bay	NHL	8	0	1	1	2	—	—	—	—	—
98-99	Cleveland	IHL	48	18	10	28	98	—	—	—	—	—
	NHL	Totals	16	1	1	2	12	—	—	—	—	—
	AHL	Totals	126	39	51	90	238	7	0	0	0	20
	IHL	Totals	121	32	24	56	202	2	0	0	0	0

Born; 5/31/71, Cranbrook, British Columbia. 6-4, 214. Signed as a free agent by Tampa Bay Lightning (7/24/95). Last amateur club; Alaska-Anchorage (CCHA).

Jim Sprott — Defenseman

Regular Season / Playoffs

Season	Team	League	GP	G	A	PTS	PIM	GP	G	A	PTS	PIM
89-90	Halifax	AHL	22	2	1	3	103	—	—	—	—	—
90-91	Halifax	AHL	9	0	2	2	17	—	—	—	—	—
90-91	Fort Wayne	IHL	19	0	1	1	67	—	—	—	—	—
90-91	Peoria	IHL	31	2	5	7	92	—	—	—	—	—
90-91	Greensboro	ECHL	3	0	0	0	31	—	—	—	—	—
91-92	New Haven	AHL	54	4	11	15	140	3	0	0	0	17
92-93	Halifax	AHL	77	6	21	27	180	—	—	—	—	—
93-94	St. John's	AHL	9	1	0	1	35	—	—	—	—	—
93-94	South Carolina	ECHL	46	8	25	33	221	3	0	0	0	5
93-94	Brantford	CoHL	12	1	3	4	55	—	—	—	—	—
94-95	South Carolina	ECHL	21	1	6	7	100	—	—	—	—	—
95-96	South Carolina	ECHL	2	0	0	0	24	—	—	—	—	—
95-96	San Antonio	CeHL	51	11	33	44	220	13	2	8	10	51
96-97	San Antonio	CeHL	64	15	42	57	209	—	—	—	—	—
97-98	Shreveport	WPHL	66	8	21	29	241	8	1	4	5	31
98-99	Shreveport	WPHL	59	13	34	47	228	12	2	6	8	41
	AHL	Totals	171	13	35	48	475	3	0	0	0	17
	IHL	Totals	50	2	6	8	159	—	—	—	—	—
	WPHL	Totals	125	21	55	76	469	20	3	10	13	72
	CeHL	Totals	115	26	75	101	429	13	2	8	10	51
	ECHL	Totals	72	9	31	40	376	3	0	0	0	5

Born; 4/11/69, Hanover, Ontario. 6-2, 220. Drafted by Quebec Nordiques (3rd choice, 51st overall) in 1987 Entry Draft. Member of 1998-99 WPHL Champion Shreveport Mudbugs. Last amateur club; London (OHL).

Chad Spurr — Right Wing

Regular Season / Playoffs

Season	Team	League	GP	G	A	PTS	PIM	GP	G	A	PTS	PIM
98-99	Sault Ste. Marie	OHL	65	27	45	72	73	5	4	3	7	4
98-99	Roanoke	ECHL	3	2	0	2	2	12	4	2	6	12

Born; 5/13/79, Hamilton, Ontario. 6-0, 190. Last amateur club; S.S. Marie (OHL).

Darren Srochenski — Defenseman

Regular Season / Playoffs

Season	Team	League	GP	G	A	PTS	PIM	GP	G	A	PTS	PIM
88-89	Carolina	ECHL	3	0	0	0	2	—	—	—	—	—
89-90	Knoxville	ECHL	5	0	1	1	13	—	—	—	—	—
90-91	Winston-Salem	ECHL	2	0	0	0	0	—	—	—	—	—
90-91	Louisville	ECHL	29	3	4	7	84	—	—	—	—	—
91-92	Thunder Bay	CoHL	6	0	0	0	2	—	—	—	—	—
92-93	Wichita	CeHL	43	2	7	9	196	—	—	—	—	—
93-94	Wichita	CeHL	50	4	9	13	140	—	—	—	—	—
93-94	Fort Worth	CeHL	16	1	3	4	55	—	—	—	—	—
94-95	Fort Worth	CeHL	14	0	0	0	47	—	—	—	—	—
94-95	Wichita	CeHL	14	0	2	2	40	3	0	0	0	26
95-96	Birmingham	ECHL	31	1	4	5	108	—	—	—	—	—
96-97	Reno	WCHL	7	0	1	1	24	—	—	—	—	—
97-98												
98-99	Winston-Salem	UHL	5	0	0	0	13	—	—	—	—	—
	CeHL	Totals	137	7	21	28	478	3	0	0	0	26
	ECHL	Totals	70	1	9	10	207	—	—	—	—	—
	UHL	Totals	11	0	0	0	15	—	—	—	—	—

Born; 2/20/69, Regina, Saskatchewan. 6-2, 220. Member of 1994-95 CeHL Champion Wichita Thunder.

Andrei Sryubko — Defenseman

Regular Season / Playoffs

Season	Team	League	GP	G	A	PTS	PIM	GP	G	A	PTS	PIM
96-97	Toledo	ECHL	62	0	8	8	238	5	0	0	0	4
97-98	Las Vegas	IHL	13	0	0	0	57	—	—	—	—	—
97-98	Toledo	ECHL	50	1	12	13	165	7	0	0	0	8
98-99	Fort Wayne	IHL	1	0	0	0	0	—	—	—	—	—
98-99	Las Vegas	IHL	51	0	8	8	164	—	—	—	—	—
98-99	Port Huron	UHL	22	2	2	4	78	2	0	0	0	4
	IHL	Totals	65	0	8	8	221	—	—	—	—	—
	ECHL	Totals	112	1	20	21	403	12	0	0	0	12

Born; 10/21/75, Liev, Ukraine. 6-2, 205. Kiev, Ukraine. 6-2, 205.

Martin St. Amour — Left Wing

Regular Season / Playoffs

Season	Team	League	GP	G	A	PTS	PIM	GP	G	A	PTS	PIM
90-91	Fredericton	AHL	45	13	16	29	51	1	0	0	0	0
91-92	Cincinnati	ECHL	60	44	44	88	183	9	4	9	13	18
92-93	New Haven	AHL	71	21	39	60	78	—	—	—	—	—
93-94	Prince Edward Island	AHL	37	13	12	25	65	—	—	—	—	—
93-94	Providence	AHL	12	0	3	3	22	—	—	—	—	—
94-95	Whitley	BHL	2	1	1	2	16	—	—	—	—	—
95-96	San Francisco	IHL	4	0	2	2	6	—	—	—	—	—
95-96	Los Angeles	IHL	1	0	0	0	0	—	—	—	—	—
95-96	San Diego	WCHL	53	*61	48	*109	182	9	6	7	13	10
96-97	San Diego	WCHL	59	*60	67	*127	170	8	*8	4	12	23
97-98	San Diego	WCHL	61	35	44	79	203	12	*11	7	18	28
98-99	San Diego	WCHL	59	15	31	46	176	12	2	7	9	18
	AHL	Totals	165	47	70	117	226	1	0	0	0	0
	IHL	Totals	5	0	2	2	6	—	—	—	—	—
	WCHL	Totals	232	171	190	361	731	41	27	25	52	79

Born; 1/30/70, Montreal, Quebec. 6-3, 195. Drafted by Montreal Canadiens (2nd choice, 34th overall) in 1988 Entry Draft. 1995-96 WCHL First Team All-Star. 1996-97 WCHL MVP. 1996-97 WCHL First Team All-Star. Member of 1995-96 WCHL champion San Diego Gulls. Member of 1996-97 WCHL Champion San Diego Gulls. Member of 1997-98 WCHL Champion San Diego Gulls. Last amateur club; Trois-Rivieres (QMJHL).

Stephane St. Amour — Center

Regular Season / Playoffs

Season	Team	League	GP	G	A	PTS	PIM	GP	G	A	PTS	PIM
95-96	Raleigh	ECHL	3	0	0	0	0	—	—	—	—	--
95-96	Jacksonville	ECHL	32	14	11	25	43	—	—	—	—	—
95-96	San Diego	WCHL	17	12	7	19	32	9	2	2	4	8
96-97	San Diego	WCHL	61	56	51	107	167	4	0	2	2	6
97-98	Long Beach	IHL	2	0	0	0	0	—	—	—	—	—
97-98	San Diego	WCHL	49	28	27	55	79	12	3	6	9	12
98-99	San Diego	WCHL	32	14	16	30	88	12	2	3	5	12
98-99	Bakersfield	WCHL	23	5	10	15	26	—	—	—	—	—
	WCHL	Totals	182	115	111	226	392	37	7	13	20	38
	ECHL	Totals	35	14	11	25	43	—	—	—	—	—

Born; 1/20/74, St. Hippolyte, Quebec. 5-11, 190. Traded to San Diego by Bakersfield for Sandy Gasseau (2/99). Member of 1995-96 WCHL champion San Diego Gulls. 1996-97 WCHL Second Team All-Star. Member of 1996-97 WCHL Champion San Diego Gulls. Member of 1997-98 WCHL Champion San Diego Gulls. Last amateur club; Drummondville (QMJHL).

Alain St.Hilaire — Center

Regular Season / Playoffs

Season	Team	League	GP	G	A	PTS	PIM	GP	G	A	PTS	PIM
98-99	R.P.I.	ECAC	33	16	32	48	34	—	—	—	—	—
98-99	Portland	AHL	9	1	1	2	0	—	—	—	—	—

Born; 3/28/75, Montreal, Quebec. 6-0, 190. Last amateur club; R.P.I. (ECAC).

Kevin St. Jacques — Left Wing

Regular Season / Playoffs

Season	Team	League	GP	G	A	PTS	PIM	GP	G	A	PTS	PIM
92-93	Indianapolis	IHL	71	10	21	31	93	4	0	0	0	0
93-94	Indianapolis	IHL	49	5	23	28	91	—	—	—	—	—
93-94	Flint	CoHL	10	5	13	18	2	10	4	14	18	19
94-95	Indianapolis	IHL	12	4	5	9	10	—	—	—	—	—
94-95	Columbus	ECHL	46	14	38	52	88	—	—	—	—	—
95-96	Fife	BHL	20	25	14	39	53	—	—	—	—	—
95-96	Detroit	CoHL	21	11	10	21	32	—	—	—	—	—
95-96	Saginaw	CoHL	—	—	—	—	—	5	1	2	3	4
96-97	Las Vegas	IHL	7	2	2	4	4	—	—	—	—	—
96-97	San Diego	WCHL	57	41	62	103	148	8	4	8	12	31
97-98	Long Beach	IHL	2	0	0	0	0	—	—	—	—	—
97-98	San Diego	WCHL	56	38	47	85	123	13	7	10	17	20
98-99	Las Vegas	IHL	2	1	1	2	2	—	—	—	—	—
98-99	San Diego	WCHL	56	32	45	77	146	12	6	5	11	12
	IHL	Totals	143	22	52	74	200	4	0	0	0	0
	WCHL	Totals	169	111	154	265	417	33	17	23	40	63
	CoHL	Totals	31	16	23	39	34	15	5	16	21	23

Born; 2/25/71, Edmonton, Alberta. 5-11, 190. Selected by Chicago Blackhawks (8th choice, 112th overall) 1991 Entry Draft. Member of 1996-97 WCHL Champion San Diego Gulls. Member of 1997-98 WCHL Champion San Diego Gulls. Last amateur club; Lethbridge (WHL).

Martin St. Louis — Right Wing

Regular Season / Playoffs

Season	Team	League	GP	G	A	PTS	PIM	GP	G	A	PTS	PIM
97-98	Cleveland	IHL	56	16	34	50	24	—	—	—	—	—
97-98	Saint John	AHL	25	15	11	26	20	20	5	15	20	16
98-99	Calgary	NHL	13	1	1	2	10	—	—	—	—	—
98-99	Saint John	AHL	53	28	34	62	30	7	4	4	8	2
	AHL	Totals	78	43	45	88	50	27	9	19	28	18

Born; 6/18/75, Laval, Quebec. 5-9, 180. Signed as a free agent by Calgary Flames (2/18/98). Last amateur club; Vermont (ECAC).

Todd St. Louis — Defenseman

Regular Season / Playoffs

Season	Team	League	GP	G	A	PTS	PIM	GP	G	A	PTS	PIM
97-98	Lake Charles	WPHL	2	0	0	0	0	—	—	—	—	—
97-98	Fort Worth	WPHL	41	2	2	4	150	10	0	1	1	32
98-99	Arkansas	WPHL	67	3	10	13	331	2	0	0	0	0
	WPHL	Totals	110	5	12	17	481	12	0	1	1	32

Born; 5/1/76, Windsor, Ontario. 6-1, 200. Selected by Arkansas in 1998 WPHL Expansion Draft.

Kevin St. Pierre — Goaltender

Regular Season / Playoffs

Season	Team	League	GP	W	L	T	MIN	SO	AVG	GP	W	L	MIN	SO	AVG
95-96	Wichita	CeHL	14	6	5	1	661	0	4.54	—	—	—	—	—	—
96-97	Wichita	CeHL	16	7	8	1	899	0	4.14	—	—	—	—	—	—
96-97	Nashville	CeHL	3	0	2	0	91	0	5.95	—	—	—	—	—	—
96-97	San Antonio	CeHL	12	9	3	0	664	0	3.34	—	—	—	—	—	—
97-98	Shreveport	WPHL	55	*36	16	2	3141	*3	3.00	5	2	2	297	0	3.44
98-99	Shreveport	WPHL	35	21	8	2	1946	2	3.21	8	7	1	478	*1	2.01
	WPHL	Totals	90	57	24	4	5087	5	3.08	13	9	3	775	1	2.55
	CeHL	Totals	45	22	18	2	2315	0	4.10	—	—	—	—	—	—

Born; 4/7/75, Sherbrooke, Quebec. 6-3, 205. Selected by Wichita Thunder in San Antonio CHL Dispersal Draft (6/10/97). Selected by Lubbock in 1999 WPHL Expansion Draft. 1997-98 WPHL Goaltender of the Year. Member of 1998-99 WPHL Champion Shreveport Mudbugs. Last amateur club; Drummondville

Samuel St. Pierre — Right Wing

Regular Season / Playoffs

Season	Team	League	GP	G	A	PTS	PIM	GP	G	A	PTS	PIM
98-99	Drummondville	QMJHL	68	47	28	75	65	—	—	—	—	—
98-99	Cleveland	IHL	13	2	5	7	4	—	—	—	—	—

Born; 6/28/79, Laurierville, Quebec. 6-1, 170. Drafted by Tampa Bay Lightning (10th choice, 185th overall) in 1997 Entry Draft. Last amateur club; Drummondville (QMJHL).

Brian Stacey — Defenseman

Regular Season / Playoffs

Season	Team	League	GP	G	A	PTS	PIM	GP	G	A	PTS	PIM
96-97	Kansas City	IHL	53	2	8	10	43	1	0	0	0	2
96-97	Mobile	ECHL	5	2	2	4	6	—	—	—	—	—
97-98	Kansas City	IHL	21	0	0	0	10	—	—	—	—	—
97-98	Orlando	IHL	4	0	1	1	0	17	1	9	10	14
97-98	Wichita	CHL	37	18	20	38	63	—	—	—	—	—
98-99	Arkansas	WPHL	42	10	24	34	72	3	1	1	2	2
	IHL	Totals	78	2	9	11	53	18	1	9	10	16

Born; 6/28/75, East York, Ontario. 6-3, 200. Last amateur club; Sault Ste. Marie (OHL).

Nick Stajduhar — Defenseman

Regular Season / Playoffs

Season	Team	League	GP	G	A	PTS	PIM	GP	G	A	PTS	PIM
94-95	Cape Breton	AHL	54	12	26	38	55	—	—	—	—	—
95-96	Edmonton	NHL	2	0	0	0	4	—	—	—	—	—
95-96	Cape Breton	AHL	8	2	0	2	11	—	—	—	—	—
95-96	Canadian	National	46	7	21	28	60	—	—	—	—	—
96-97	Hamilton	AHL	11	1	2	3	2	—	—	—	—	—
96-97	Quebec	IHL	7	1	3	4	2	—	—	—	—	—
96-97	Pensacola	ECHL	30	9	15	24	32	12	1	6	7	34
97-98	Cincinnati	AHL	13	0	0	0	16	—	—	—	—	—
97-98	Fort Wayne	IHL	15	2	0	2	27	—	—	—	—	—
97-98	Pensacola	ECHL	19	4	8	12	36	19	5	*21	*26	10
98-99	Pensacola	ECHL	33	7	18	25	66	—	—	—	—	—
98-99	Louisiana	ECHL	30	5	18	23	26	5	1	1	2	10
	AHL	Totals	86	15	28	43	84	—	—	—	—	—
	IHL	Totals	22	3	3	6	29	—	—	—	—	—
	ECHL	Totals	112	25	59	84	160	36	7	28	35	54

Born; 12/6/74, Kitchener, Ontario. 6-3, 206. Drafted by Edmonton Oilers (2nd choice, 16th overall) in 1993 Entry Draft. Last amateur club; London (OHL).

Craig Stahl — Right Wing

Regular Season / Playoffs

Season	Team	League	GP	G	A	PTS	PIM	GP	G	A	PTS	PIM
96-97	Tri-City	WHL	61	21	15	36	177	—	—	—	—	—
96-97	Charlotte	ECHL	5	0	1	1	12	—	—	—	—	—
97-98	Tri-City	WHL	51	8	8	16	105	—	—	—	—	—
98-99	Austin	WPHL	45	13	29	42	52	—	—	—	—	—

Born; 3/19/77, Cranbrook, British Columbia. 6-0, 198. Last amateur club; Tri-City (WHL).

Sergei Stakhovich — Center

Regular Season / Playoffs

Season	Team	League	GP	G	A	PTS	PIM	GP	G	A	PTS	PIM
97-98	Port Huron	UHL	20	2	3	5	4	—	—	—	—	—
98-99	Mohawk Valley	UHL	2	0	0	0	2	—	—	—	—	—
	UHL	Totals	22	2	3	5	6	—	—	—	—	—

Born; 3/4/78, Minsk, Belarus. 6-0, 192.

Rob Stanfield — Defenseman

Regular Season / Playoffs

Season	Team	League	GP	G	A	PTS	PIM	GP	G	A	PTS	PIM
98-99	Huntington	ECHL	54	3	9	12	108	—	—	—	—	—

Born; Last amateur club; North Bay (OHL).

Jeff Staples — Defenseman

Regular Season / Playoffs

Season	Team	League	GP	G	A	PTS	PIM	GP	G	A	PTS	PIM
95-96	Hershey	AHL	61	7	3	10	100	5	0	1	1	0
96-97	Philadelphia	AHL	74	4	11	15	157	8	0	2	2	10
97-98	Philadelphia	AHL	63	4	16	20	187	19	0	0	0	23
98-99	Milwaukee	IHL	69	2	10	12	155	2	0	0	0	2
	AHL	Totals	198	15	30	45	444	32	0	3	3	33

Born; 3/4/75, Kitimat, British Columbia. 6-2, 207. Drafted by Philadelphia Flyers (10th choice, 244th overall) in 1993 Entry Draft. Traded to Nashville Predators with Dominic Roussel for Nashville's seventh round choice (Cam Ondrik) in 1998 Entry Draft (6/25/98). Member of 1997-98 AHL Champion Philadelphia Phantoms. Last amateur club; Brandon (WHL).

Aaron Starnyski — Defenseman
Regular Season — Playoffs

Season	Team	League	GP	G	A	PTS	PIM	GP	G	A	PTS	PIM
98-99	Fort Worth	CHL	1	0	0	0	0	—	—	—	—	—

Born; 7/7/77, Elliott Lake, Ontario. 6-2, 205. Selected by Memphis in 1999 CHL Dispersal Draft.

Sergei Stas — Defenseman
Regular Season — Playoffs

Season	Team	League	GP	G	A	PTS	PIM	GP	G	A	PTS	PIM
93-94	Erie	ECHL	2	1	2	3	4	—	—	—	—	—
94-95	Erie	ECHL	35	1	15	16	108	—	—	—	—	—
95-96	Fort Wayne	IHL	38	1	2	3	90	—	—	—	—	—
95-96	Phoenix	IHL	3	0	0	0	6	—	—	—	—	—
95-96	Quad City	CoHL	15	2	7	9	30	4	0	1	1	4
96-97	Las Vegas	IHL	12	0	1	1	39	—	—	—	—	—
96-97	San Antonio	IHL	9	1	1	2	40	—	—	—	—	—
96-97	Fort Wayne	IHL	14	1	3	4	23	—	—	—	—	—
96-97	Saginaw	CoHL	29	5	17	22	63	—	—	—	—	—
97-98	Nurnberg	Germany	43	12	15	27	76	—	—	—	—	—
98-99	Nurnburg	Germany	51	2	18	20	163	6	1	0	1	35
	IHL	Totals	76	3	7	10	198	—	—	—	—	—
	CoHL	Totals	44	7	24	31	93	4	0	1	1	4
	ECHL	Totals	37	2	17	19	112	—	—	—	—	—

Born; 4/28/74, Rlinsk, Russia. 6-0, 190.

Robb Stauber — Goaltender
Regular Season — Playoffs

Season	Team	League	GP	W	L	T	MIN	SO	AVG	GP	W	L	MIN	SO	AVG
89-90	Los Angeles	NHL	2	0	1	0	83	0	7.95	—	—	—	—	—	—
89-90	New Haven	AHL	14	6	6	2	851	0	3.03	5	2	3	302	0	4.77
90-91	New Haven	AHL	33	13	16	4	1882	1	3.67	—	—	—	—	—	—
90-91	Phoenix	IHL	4	1	2	0	160	0	4.13	—	—	—	—	—	—
91-92	Phoenix	IHL	22	8	12	1	1242	0	3.86	—	—	—	—	—	—
92-93	Los Angeles	NHL	31	15	8	4	1735	0	3.84	4	3	1	240	0	4.00
93-94	Los Angeles	NHL	22	4	11	5	1144	1	3.41	—	—	—	—	—	—
93-94	Phoenix	IHL	3	1	1	0	121	0	6.42	—	—	—	—	—	—
94-95	Los Angeles	NHL	1	0	0	0	16	0	7.50	—	—	—	—	—	—
94-95	Buffalo	NHL	6	2	3	0	317	0	3.79	—	—	—	—	—	—
95-96	Rochester	AHL	16	6	7	1	833	0	3.53	—	—	—	—	—	—
96-97	Portland	AHL	30	13	13	2	1606	0	3.06	—	—	—	—	—	—
97-98	Hartford	AHL	39	20	10	6	2221	2	2.40	7	3	4	420	0	4.29
98-99	Manitoba	IHL	5	2	1	1	213	0	4.78	—	—	—	—	—	—
	NHL	Totals	62	21	23	9	3295	1	3.81	4	3	1	240	0	4.00
	AHL	Totals	93	38	42	9	5172	1	3.35	5	2	3	302	0	4.77
	IHL	Totals	34	12	16	2	1736	0	4.18	—	—	—	—	—	—

Born; 11/25/67, Duluth, Minnesota. 5-11, 180. Drafted by Los Angeles Kings (5th choice, 107th overall) in 1986 Entry Draft. Traded to Buffalo Sabres by Los Angeles with Alexei Zhitnik, Charlie Huddy and Los Angeles' fifth round choice (Marian Menhart) in 1996 Entry Draft for Philippe Boucher, Denis Tsygurov and Grant Fuhr (2/14/95). Signed as a free agent by Washington Capitals (8/20/96). Signed as a free agent by New York Rangers (9/2/97). Last amateur club; Min-

Patrik Stefan — Center
Regular Season — Playoffs

Season	Team	League	GP	G	A	PTS	PIM	GP	G	A	PTS	PIM
97-98	Long Beach	IHL	25	5	10	15	10	10	1	1	2	2
98-99	Long Beach	IHL	33	11	24	35	26	—	—	—	—	—
	IHL	Totals	58	16	34	50	36	10	1	1	2	2

Born; 9/16/80, Pribram, Czech. Republic. 6-2, 195. Drafted by Atlanta Thrashers (1st choice, 1st overall) in 1999 Entry Draft.

Brian Steiner — Center
Regular Season — Playoffs

Season	Team	League	GP	G	A	PTS	PIM	GP	G	A	PTS	PIM
98-99	Amarillo	WPHL	6	0	0	0	15	—	—	—	—	—
98-99	Saginaw	UHL	9	0	1	1	12	—	—	—	—	—

Born; 4/18/77, Huntington Beach, California. 6-3, 198.

Kelly Stephens — Right Wing
Regular Season — Playoffs

Season	Team	League	GP	G	A	PTS	PIM	GP	G	A	PTS	PIM
98-99	Madison	UHL	67	6	4	10	92	—	—	—	—	—

Born; 8/28/73, Grand Rapids, Michigan. 5-11, 190. Last amateur club; Wisconsin-Eau Claire (NCAA 3).

Scott Stephens — Right Wing
Regular Season — Playoffs

Season	Team	League	GP	G	A	PTS	PIM	GP	G	A	PTS	PIM
97-98	Johnstown	ECHL	66	13	18	31	150	—	—	—	—	—
98-99	Abilene	WPHL	5	0	0	0	2	—	—	—	—	—

Born; 10/20/76, Barrier, Ontario. 5-9, 160.

Troy Stephens — Center
Regular Season — Playoffs

Season	Team	League	GP	G	A	PTS	PIM	GP	G	A	PTS	PIM
94-95	Saginaw	CoHL	37	15	18	33	24	11	4	8	12	12
95-96	Fort Worth	CeHL	63	20	40	60	129	—	—	—	—	—
96-97	Utica	CoHL	69	41	48	89	78	3	0	1	1	2
97-98	Phoenix	WCHL	63	33	36	69	81	9	1	3	4	20
98-99	Adendorfer	Germany	42	32	44	76	112	—	—	—	—	—
	CoHL	Totals	106	56	66	122	102	14	4	9	13	14

Born; 2/28/71, Mississauga, Ontario. 5-8, 170.

John Stevens — Defenseman
Regular Season — Playoffs

Season	Team	League	GP	G	A	PTS	PIM	GP	G	A	PTS	PIM
84-85	Oshawa	OHL	44	2	10	12	61	5	0	2	2	4
84-85	Hershey	AHL	3	0	0	0	0	—	—	—	—	—
85-86	Oshawa	OHL	65	1	7	8	146	6	0	2	2	14
85-86	Kalamazoo	IHL	6	0	1	1	8	6	0	3	3	9
86-87	Philadelphia	NHL	6	0	2	2	14	—	—	—	—	—
86-87	Hershey	AHL	63	1	15	16	131	3	0	0	0	7
87-88	Philadelphia	NHL	3	0	0	0	0	—	—	—	—	—
87-88	Hershey	AHL	59	1	15	16	108	—	—	—	—	—
88-89	Hershey	AHL	78	3	13	16	129	12	1	1	2	29
89-90	Hershey	AHL	79	3	10	13	193	—	—	—	—	—
90-91	Hartford	NHL	14	0	1	1	11	—	—	—	—	—
90-91	Springfield	AHL	65	0	12	12	139	18	0	6	6	35
91-92	Hartford	NHL	21	0	4	4	19	—	—	—	—	—
91-92	Springfield	AHL	45	1	12	13	73	11	1	3	4	27
92-93	Springfield	AHL	74	1	19	20	111	15	0	1	1	18
93-94	Hartford	NHL	9	0	3	3	4	—	—	—	—	—
93-94	Springfield	AHL	71	3	9	12	85	3	0	0	0	0
94-95	Springfield	AHL	79	5	15	20	122	—	—	—	—	—
95-96	Springfield	AHL	69	0	19	19	95	10	0	1	1	31
96-97	Philadelphia	AHL	74	2	18	20	116	10	0	2	2	8
97-98	Philadelphia	AHL	50	1	9	10	76	20	0	6	6	44
98-99	Philadelphia	AHL	25	0	1	1	19	—	—	—	—	—
	NHL	Totals	53	0	10	10	48	—	—	—	—	—
	AHL	Totals	837	21	167	188	1397	102	2	20	22	199

Born; 5/4/66, Campbellton, New Brunswick. 6-1, 195. Drafted by Philadelphia Flyers (5th choice, 47th overall) in 1984 Entry Draft. Signed as a free agent by Hartford (7/30/90). Signed as a free agent by Philadelphia (8/6/96). Member of 1990-91 AHL champion Springfield Indians. Member of 1997-98 AHL Champion Philadelphia Phantoms. Last amateur club; Oshawa (OHL).

Mike Stevens — Left Wing

Regular Season / Playoffs

Season	Team	League	GP	G	A	PTS	PIM	GP	G	A	PTS	PIM
84-85	Kitchener	OHL	37	17	18	35	121	4	1	1	2	8
84-85	Vancouver	NHL	6	0	3	3	6	—	—	—	—	—
85-86	Vancouver	NHL	79	12	19	31	208	6	1	1	2	35
86-87	Ferdericton	AHL	71	7	18	25	258	—	—	—	—	—
87-88	Boston	NHL	7	0	1	1	9	—	—	—	—	—
87-88	Maine	AHL	63	30	25	55	265	7	1	2	3	37
88-89	Islanders	NHL	9	1	0	1	14	—	—	—	—	—
88-89	Springfield	AHL	42	17	13	30	120	—	—	—	—	—
89-90	Toronto	NHL	1	0	0	0	0	—	—	—	—	—
89-90	Springfield	AHL	28	12	10	22	75	—	—	—	—	—
89-90	Newmarket	AHL	46	16	28	44	86	—	—	—	—	—
90-91	Newmarket	AHL	68	24	23	47	229	—	—	—	—	—
91-92	St. John's	AHL	30	13	11	24	65	—	—	—	—	—
91-92	Binghamton	AHL	44	15	15	30	87	11	7	6	13	45
92-93	Binghamton	AHL	68	31	61	92	230	14	5	5	10	63
93-94	Saint John	AHL	79	20	37	57	293	6	1	3	4	34
94-95	Cincinnati	IHL	80	34	43	77	274	10	6	3	9	16
95-96	Cleveland	IHL	81	31	43	74	252	3	1	0	1	8
96-97	Cleveland	IHL	6	1	4	5	32	—	—	—	—	—
96-97	Manitoba	IHL	22	8	4	12	54	—	—	—	—	—
96-97	Cincinnati	IHL	46	16	18	34	140	3	0	2	2	8
97-98	Schwenningen	Germany	50	18	32	50	197	—	—	—	—	—
98-99	Adler Mannheim	Germany	44	8	18	26	233	11	4	4	8	49
	NHL	Totals	23	1	4	5	29	—	—	—	—	—
	AHL	Totals	618	197	260	457	1916	44	15	17	32	214
	IHL	Totals	235	90	112	202	752	16	7	5	12	32

Born; 12/30/65, Kitchener, Ontario. 5-11, 195. Drafted by Vancouver Canucks (5th choice, 58th overall) in 1984 Entry Draft. Traded to Boston Bruins by Vancouver for cash (10/6/87). Signed as a free agent by New York Islanders (8/20/88). Traded to Toronto Maple Leafs by Islanders with Gilles Thibaudeau for Jack Capuano, Paul Gagne and Derek Laxdal (12/20/89). Traded to New York Rangers by Toronto for Guy Larose (12/26/91). Signed as a free agent by Calgary Flames (8/10/93). Last amateur club; Kitchener (OHL).

Randy Stevens — Right Wing

Regular Season / Playoffs

Season	Team	League	GP	G	A	PTS	PIM	GP	G	A	PTS	PIM
95-96	Las Vegas	IHL	2	0	0	0	2	—	—	—	—	—
95-96	Knoxville	ECHL	47	5	17	22	28	4	0	0	0	6
96-97	Kentucky	AHL	26	3	2	5	25	—	—	—	—	—
96-97	Louisville	ECHL	38	7	14	21	35	—	—	—	—	—
97-98	Memphis	CHL	60	33	29	62	55	4	1	1	2	7
98-99	Memphis	CHL	62	30	34	64	90	4	2	2	4	0
	CHL	Totals	122	63	63	126	145	8	3	3	6	7
	ECHL	Totals	85	12	31	43	63	4	0	0	0	6

Born; 8/9/73, Sault Ste. Marie, Michigan. 6-0, 195. Last amateur club; Michigan Tech (WCHA).

Rod Stevens — Center

Regular Season / Playoffs

Season	Team	League	GP	G	A	PTS	PIM	GP	G	A	PTS	PIM
94-95	Syracuse	AHL	78	21	21	42	63	—	—	—	—	—
95-96	Syracuse	AHL	60	13	17	30	30	16	3	4	7	14
96-97	Syracuse	AHL	74	20	9	29	26	—	—	—	—	—
97-98	Canada	National	62	10	16	26	69	—	—	—	—	—
98-99	Milan	Italy										
	AHL	Totals	212	54	47	101	119	16	3	4	7	14

Born; 4/5/74, Fort St. John. British Columbia. 5-10, 175. Signed as a free agent by Vancouver Canucks (10/4/93). Last amateur club; Kamloops (WHL).

Scott Stevens — Right Wing

Regular Season / Playoffs

Season	Team	League	GP	G	A	PTS	PIM	GP	G	A	PTS	PIM
97-98	Amarillo	WPHL	65	39	23	62	16	—	—	—	—	—
98-99	Amarillo	WPHL	66	28	32	60	25	—	—	—	—	—
	WPHL	Totals	131	67	55	122	41	—	—	—	—	—

Born; 11/14/73, Waterloo, Ontario. 5-10, 190. Last amateur club; St. Lawrence (ECAC).

Troy Stevens — Center

Regular Season / Playoffs

Season	Team	League	GP	G	A	PTS	PIM	GP	G	A	PTS	PIM
94-95	Union	ECAC	18	4	13	17	8	—	—	—	—	—
94-95	Nashville	ECHL	25	5	16	21	23	12	4	1	5	8
95-96	Nashville	ECHL	4	0	0	0	5	—	—	—	—	—
95-96	South Carolina	ECHL	6	0	1	1	4	—	—	—	—	—
95-96	Raleigh	ECHL	13	2	6	8	16	—	—	—	—	—
95-96	Muskegon	CoHL	29	3	2	5	15	4	0	1	1	0
96-97	Utica	CoHL	47	9	31	40	25	—	—	—	—	—
97-98	Binghamton	UHL	63	14	26	40	30	2	0	0	0	0
98-99	Tupelo	WPHL	66	10	32	42	60	—	—	—	—	—
	UHL	Totals	139	26	59	85	70	6	0	1	1	0
	ECHL	Totals	48	7	23	30	48	12	4	1	5	8

Born; 9/3/72, Phoenix, Arizona. 5-10, 180. Last amateur club; Union (ECAC).

Jeremy Stevenson — Left Wing

Regular Season / Playoffs

Season	Team	League	GP	G	A	PTS	PIM	GP	G	A	PTS	PIM
94-95	Greensboro	ECHL	43	14	13	27	231	17	6	11	17	64
95-96	Anaheim	NHL	3	0	1	1	12	—	—	—	—	—
95-96	Baltimore	AHL	60	11	10	21	295	12	4	2	6	23
96-97	Anaheim	NHL	5	0	0	0	14	—	—	—	—	—
96-97	Baltimore	AHL	25	8	8	16	125	3	0	0	0	8
97-98	Anaheim	NHL	45	3	5	8	101	—	—	—	—	—
97-98	Cincinnati	AHL	10	5	0	5	34	—	—	—	—	—
98-99	Cincinnati	AHL	22	4	4	8	83	3	1	0	1	2
	NHL	Totals	53	3	6	9	127	—	—	—	—	—
	AHL	Totals	117	28	22	50	537	18	5	2	7	33

Born; 7/28/74, Elliot Lake, Ontario. 6-2, 215. Drafted by Winnipeg Jets (3rd choice, 60th overall) in 1992 Entry Draft. Re-entered Entry Draft, Anaheim's 10th choice, 262nd overall in 1994 Entry Draft. Last amateur club; Sault Ste.

Shayne Stevenson — Center

Regular Season / Playoffs

Season	Team	League	GP	G	A	PTS	PIM	GP	G	A	PTS	PIM
90-91	Boston	NHL	14	0	0	0	26	—	—	—	—	—
90-91	Maine	AHL	58	22	28	50	112	—	—	—	—	—
91-92	Boston	NHL	5	0	1	1	2	—	—	—	—	—
91-92	Maine	AHL	54	10	23	33	150	—	—	—	—	—
92-93	Tampa Bay	NHL	8	0	1	1	7	—	—	—	—	—
92-93	Atlanta	IHL	53	17	17	34	160	6	0	2	2	2
93-94	Fort Wayne	IHL	22	3	5	8	116	—	—	—	—	—
93-94	Muskegon	CoHL	1	2	0	2	0	—	—	—	—	—
93-94	St. Thomas	CoHL	6	3	3	6	15	2	0	2	2	9
94-95	Utica	CoHL	43	17	40	57	37	6	0	3	3	14
95-96	Utica	CoHL	27	11	21	32	72	—	—	—	—	—
96-97	Utica	CoHL	10	2	6	8	18	—	—	—	—	—
96-97	Saginaw	CoHL	17	2	23	25	30	—	—	—	—	—
96-97	Brantford	CoHL	10	3	9	12	25	6	5	3	8	24
97-98	Port Huron	UHL	18	8	9	17	27	3	2	0	2	4
98-99	San Angelo	WPHL	48	28	28	56	41	13	7	8	15	51
	NHL	Totals	27	0	2	2	35	—	—	—	—	—
	AHL	Totals	112	32	51	83	262	—	—	—	—	—
	IHL	Totals	75	20	22	42	276	6	0	2	2	2
	UHL	Totals	132	48	111	159	224	17	7	8	15	51

Born; 10/26/70, Aurora, Ontario. 6-1, 190. Drafted by Boston Bruins (1st choice, 17th overall) in 1989 Entry Draft. Selected by Tampa Bay Lightning in NHL Expansion Draft (6/18/92). Last amateur club; Kitchener (OHL).

Andy Stewart — Defenseman
Regular Season — Playoffs

Season	Team	League	GP	G	A	PTS	PIM	GP	G	A	PTS	PIM
89-90	Knoxville	ECHL	3	0	0	0	0	—	—	—	—	—
90-91												
91-92												
92-93												
93-94	Utica	CoHL	50	6	13	19	84	—	—	—	—	—
94-95	Fort Worth	CeHL	35	2	10	12	73	—	—	—	—	—
94-95	Dallas	CeHL	23	0	6	6	79	—	—	—	—	—
95-96	Wichita	CeHL	10	0	3	3	23	—	—	—	—	—
95-96	Tulsa	CeHL	40	5	4	9	52	6	0	2	2	15
96-97	Waldkraiburg	Germany	40	10	20	30	126	—	—	—	—	—
97-98	Hammer	Germany										
98-99	Alexandria	WPHL	64	5	11	16	84	—	—	—	—	—
	CeHL	Totals	108	7	23	30	227	6	0	2	2	15

Born; 1/28/69, Montreal, Quebec. 6-0, 195

Bobby Stewart — Left Wing
Regular Season — Playoffs

Season	Team	League	GP	G	A	PTS	PIM	GP	G	A	PTS	PIM
98-99	Maine	H.E.	31	8	5	13	28	—	—	—	—	—
98-99	Syracuse	AHL	3	0	0	0	0	—	—	—	—	—

Born; 6/3/74, Fort McMurray, Alberta. 5-9, 174. Last amateur club; Maine

Cam Stewart — Left Wing
Regular Season — Playoffs

Season	Team	League	GP	G	A	PTS	PIM	GP	G	A	PTS	PIM
93-94	Boston	NHL	57	3	6	9	66	8	0	3	3	7
93-94	Providence	AHL	14	3	2	5	5	—	—	—	—	—
94-95	Boston	NHL	5	0	0	0	2	—	—	—	—	—
94-95	Providence	AHL	31	13	11	24	38	9	2	5	7	0
95-96	Boston	NHL	6	0	0	0	0	5	1	0	1	2
95-96	Providence	AHL	54	17	25	42	39	—	—	—	—	—
96-97	Boston	NHL	15	0	1	1	4	—	—	—	—	—
96-97	Providence	AHL	18	4	3	7	37	—	—	—	—	—
96-97	Cincinnati	IHL	7	3	2	5	8	1	0	0	0	0
97-98	Houston	IHL	63	18	27	45	51	4	0	1	1	18
98-99	Houston	IHL	61	36	26	62	75	19	10	5	15	26
	NHL	Totals	83	3	7	10	72	13	1	3	4	9
	IHL	Totals	131	57	55	112	134	24	10	6	16	44
	AHL	Totals	117	37	41	78	119	9	2	5	7	0

Born; 9/18/71, Kitchener, Ontario. 5-11, 196. Drafted by Boston Bruins (2nd choice, 63rd overall) in 1990 Entry Draft. Signed as a free agent by Florida Panthers (7/9/99). Member of 1998-99 IHL Champion Houston Aeros. Last amateur club; Michigan (CCHA).

Dave Stewart — Defenseman
Regular Season — Playoffs

Season	Team	League	GP	G	A	PTS	PIM	GP	G	A	PTS	PIM
91-92	Kingston	OHL	65	14	45	60	143	—	—	—	—	—
91-92	Toledo	ECHL	3	0	2	2	2	—	—	—	—	—
92-93	Muskegon	CoHL	17	3	11	14	35	2	0	0	0	0
93-94	Flint	CoHL	8	1	14	15	8	—	—	—	—	—
94-95	Roanoke	ECHL	68	14	46	60	200	8	2	1	3	20
95-96	Roanoke	ECHL	65	13	28	41	239	3	0	1	1	4
96-97	Roanoke	ECHL	57	9	30	39	168	4	0	1	1	4
97-98	Roanoke	ECHL	67	10	20	30	119	9	4	4	8	23
98-99	Thunder Bay	UHL	6	0	2	2	12	12	0	1	1	37
	ECHL	Totals	260	46	126	172	728	24	6	7	13	51
	CoHL	Totals	25	4	25	29	43	2	0	0	0	0

Born; 1/11/72, Norwood, Ontario. 6-1, 205. Selected by Madison in 1999 UHL Expansion Draft. Last amateur club; Kingston (OHL).

Glenn Stewart — Left Wing
Regular Season — Playoffs

Season	Team	League	GP	G	A	PTS	PIM	GP	G	A	PTS	PIM
94-95	Greensboro	ECHL	57	33	45	78	51	6	2	5	7	27
95-96	Erie	ECHL	69	41	51	92	145	—	—	—	—	—
96-97	Utah	IHL	1	0	0	0	0	—	—	—	—	—
96-97	Fort Wayne	IHL	8	0	0	0	2	—	—	—	—	—
96-97	Quad City	CoHL	65	66	69	135	30	14	6	12	16	10
97-98	Portland	AHL	10	2	2	4	0	—	—	—	—	—
97-98	Quad City	UHL	59	46	38	84	45	20	7	*18	25	10
98-99	Chicago	IHL	16	7	6	13	4	—	—	—	—	—
98-99	Quad City	UHL	56	50	49	99	38	16	10	7	17	8
	IHL	Totals	25	7	6	13	6	—	—	—	—	—
	UHL	Totals	180	162	156	318	113	50	23	37	60	28
	ECHL	Totals	126	74	96	170	196	6	2	5	7	27

Born; 7/30/70, Scarborough, Ontario. 6-0, 185. 1995-96 ECHL First Team All-Star. 1996-97 CoHL First Team All-Star. 1998-99 UHL First Team All-Star. Member of 1996-97 CoHL Champion Quad City Mallards. Member of 1997-98 UHL Champion Quad City Mallards. Last amateur club; New Hampshire

Jason Stewart — Center
Regular Season — Playoffs

Season	Team	League	GP	G	A	PTS	PIM	GP	G	A	PTS	PIM
98-99	Lowell	AHL	31	0	2	2	7	—	—	—	—	—
98-99	Roanoke	ECHL	31	7	13	20	39	12	0	0	0	2

Born; 4/30/76, St. Paul, Minnesota. 5-11, 185. Drafted by New York Islanders (7th choice, 142nd overall) in 1994 Entry Draft. Last amateur club; St. Cloud State (WCHA).

Michael Stewart — Defenseman
Regular Season — Playoffs

Season	Team	League	GP	G	A	PTS	PIM	GP	G	A	PTS	PIM
92-93	Binghamton	AHL	68	2	10	12	71	1	0	0	0	0
93-94	Binghamton	AHL	79	8	42	50	75	—	—	—	—	—
94-95	Binghamton	AHL	68	6	21	27	83	—	—	—	—	—
94-95	Springfield	AHL	7	0	3	3	21	—	—	—	—	—
95-96	Detroit	IHL	41	6	6	12	95	—	—	—	—	—
95-96	Springfield	AHL	29	2	6	8	44	10	1	3	4	22
96-97	Rochester	AHL	4	0	0	0	0	9	1	3	4	23
97-98	Canada	National	60	12	20	32	87	—	—	—	—	—
97-98	Manitoba	IHL	69	5	19	24	133	3	0	1	1	8
98-99	Manitoba	IHL	77	5	10	15	136	5	0	1	1	11
	AHL	Totals	255	18	82	100	294	20	2	6	8	45
	IHL	Totals	187	16	35	51	364	8	0	2	2	19

Born; 5/30/72, Calgary, Alberta. 6-2, 210. Drafted by New York Rangers (1st choice, 13th overall) in 1990 Entry Draft. Traded to Hartford Whalers by Rangers with Glen Featherstone, NY Rangers' first round choice (Jean-Sebastien Giguere) in 1995 Entry Draft and fourth round choice (Steve Wasylko) in 1996 Entry Draft for Pat Verbeek (3/23/95). Last amateur club; Michigan State (CCHA).

Ryan Stewart — Right Wing
Regular Season — Playoffs

Season	Team	League	GP	G	A	PTS	PIM	GP	G	A	PTS	PIM
97-98	Tulsa	CHL	10	4	7	11	6	4	2	2	4	11
98-99	Greenville	ECHL	39	8	13	21	43	—	—	—	—	—

Born; 4/27/74, Niagara Falls, Ontario. 6-0, 202. Last amateur club; Canisius (MAAC).

Thomas Stewart — Right Wing
Regular Season — Playoffs

Season	Team	League	GP	G	A	PTS	PIM	GP	G	A	PTS	PIM
96-97	Macon	CeHL	64	24	27	51	164	5	0	1	1	17
97-98	Brantford	UHL	73	31	40	71	74	9	3	1	4	7
98-99	Topeka	CHL	26	12	6	18	50	—	—	—	—	—
98-99	Columbus	CHL	45	22	30	52	48	8	2	2	4	12
	CHL	Totals	135	58	63	121	262	13	2	3	5	29

Born; 5/19/75, Brantford, Ontario. 6-2, 202. Traded to Columbus by Topeka for Oleg Tsirkounov and Travis Riggin (12/98). Selected by Indianapolis in 1999 CHL Expansion Draft.

Mark Stitt — Center
Regular Season / Playoffs

Season	Team	League	GP	G	A	PTS	PIM	GP	G	A	PTS	PIM
95-96	Toledo	ECHL	67	15	36	51	86	11	1	6	7	12
96-97	San Diego	WCHL	63	31	75	106	99	8	2	6	8	8
97-98	San Diego	WCHL	58	20	33	53	42	13	4	9	13	16
98-99	San Diego	WCHL	71	29	42	71	73	12	4	10	14	15
	WCHL	Totals	192	80	150	230	214	33	10	25	35	39

Born; 2/14/71, Hamilton, Ontario. 6-0, 190. Member of 1996-97 WCHL Champion San Diego Gulls. Member of 1997-98 WCHL Champion San Diego Gulls. Last amateur club; Alaska-Anchorage (WCHA).

Regan Stocco — Defenseman
Regular Season / Playoffs

Season	Team	League	GP	G	A	PTS	PIM	GP	G	A	PTS	PIM
97-98	Roanoke	ECHL	15	1	2	3	15	—	—	—	—	—
98-99	London	BSL	38	1	5	6	40	—	—	—	—	—

Born; 8/16/75, Guelph, Ontario. 6-1, 190. Last amateur club; Guelph (OHL).

P.J. Stock — Left Wing
Regular Season / Playoffs

Season	Team	League	GP	G	A	PTS	PIM	GP	G	A	PTS	PIM
97-98	Rangers	NHL	38	2	3	5	114	—	—	—	—	—
97-98	Hartford	AHL	41	8	8	16	202	11	1	3	4	79
98-99	Rangers	NHL	5	0	0	0	6	—	—	—	—	—
98-99	Hartford	AHL	55	4	14	18	250	6	0	1	1	35
	NHL	Totals	43	2	3	5	120	—	—	—	—	—
	AHL	Totals	96	12	22	34	452	17	1	4	5	114

Born; 5/26/75, Victoriaville, Quebec. 5-11, 183. Signed as a free agent by New York Rangers (9/2/97). Last amateur club; St. Francis Xavier (AUAA).

Alek Stojanov — Right Wing
Regular Season / Playoffs

Season	Team	League	GP	G	A	PTS	PIM	GP	G	A	PTS	PIM
92-93	Guelph	OHL	36	27	28	55	62	—	—	—	—	—
92-93	Newmarket	OHL	14	9	7	16	26	7	1	3	4	26
92-93	Hamilton	AHL	4	4	0	4	0	—	—	—	—	—
93-94	Hamilton	AHL	4	0	1	1	5	—	—	—	—	—
94-95	Syracuse	AHL	73	18	12	30	270	—	—	—	—	—
94-95	Vancouver	NHL	4	0	0	0	13	5	0	0	0	3
95-96	Vancouver	NHL	58	0	1	1	123	—	—	—	—	—
95-96	Pittsburgh	NHL	10	1	0	1	7	9	0	0	0	19
96-97	Pittsburgh	NHL	35	1	4	5	79	—	—	—	—	—
97-98	Syracuse	AHL	41	5	4	9	215	3	1	0	1	4
98-99	Hamilton	AHL	12	0	1	1	35	—	—	—	—	—
98-99	Milwaukee	IHL	13	0	1	1	58	—	—	—	—	
98-99	Detroit	IHL	27	1	3	4	91	—	—	—	—	—
	NHL	Totals	107	2	5	7	222	14	0	0	0	21
	AHL	Totals	134	27	18	45	525	3	1	0	1	4
	IHL	Totals	40	1	4	5	149	—	—	—	—	—

Born; 4/25/73, Windsor, Ontario. 6-4, 225. Drafted by Vancouver Canucks (1st choice,7th overall) in 1991 Entry Draft. Traded to Pittsburgh Penguins by Vancouver for Markus Naslund (3/20/96). Last amateur club; Newmarket (OHL).

Darren Stolk — Defenseman
Regular Season / Playoffs

Season	Team	League	GP	G	A	PTS	PIM	GP	G	A	PTS	PIM
89-90	Muskegon	IHL	65	3	3	6	59	6	1	0	1	2
90-91	Muskegon	IHL	47	2	8	10	40	—	—	—	—	—
90-91	Kansas City	IHL	23	2	10	12	36	—	—	—	—	—
91-92	Salt Lake City	IHL	65	2	8	10	68	5	0	0	0	2
92-93	Salt Lake City	IHL	64	4	5	9	65	—	—	—	—	—
93-94	Providence	AHL	57	4	10	14	56	—	—	—	—	—
94-95	Providence	AHL	23	3	6	9	13	4	0	1	1	4
95-96	Fresno	WCHL	29	4	14	18	58	2	0	0	0	0
96-97	Fresno	WCHL	32	3	16	19	50	5	2	2	4	31
97-98	Jokerit	Finland	34	0	1	1	2	8	0	0	0	0
98-99	London	BSL	21	0	7	7	22	—	—	—	—	—
	IHL	Totals	264	13	34	47	268	11	1	0	1	4
	AHL	Totals	80	7	16	23	121	4	0	1	1	4
	WCHL	Totals	61	7	30	37	108	7	2	2	4	31

Born; 7/22/68, Taber, Alberta. 6-4, 225. Drafted by Pittsburgh Penguins (11th choice, 235th overall) in 1988 Entry Draft. Last amateur club; Medicine Hat

Matt Stone — Right Wing
Regular Season / Playoffs

Season	Team	League	GP	G	A	PTS	PIM	GP	G	A	PTS	PIM
97-98	Huntsville	CHL	53	6	12	18	237	—	—	—	—	—
98-99	Central Texas	WPHL	3	0	0	0	17	—	—	—	—	—
98-99	Huntsville	CHL	2	0	0	0	4	—	—	—	—	—
	CHL	Totals	55	6	12	18	241	—	—	—	—	—

Born; 2/11/72, Sarnia, Ontario. 6-0,215.

Troy Stonier — Center
Regular Season / Playoffs

Season	Team	League	GP	G	A	PTS	PIM	GP	G	A	PTS	PIM
98-99	Canada	National	38	6	15	21	18	—	—	—	—	—

Born; 6/5/77, Ottawa, Ontario. 6-0, 185. Last amateur club; Spokane (WHL).

Ben Storey — Defenseman
Regular Season / Playoffs

Season	Team	League	GP	G	A	PTS	PIM	GP	G	A	PTS	PIM
98-99	Harvard	ECAC	23	4	11	15	30	—	—	—	—	—
98-99	Hershey	AHL	5	0	0	0	0	—	—	—	—	—

Born; 6/22/77, Ottawa, Ontario. 6-2, 180. Drafted by Colorado Avalanche (4th choice, 98th overall) in 1996 Entry Draft. Last amateur club; Harvard (ECAC).

Dean Stork — Defenseman
Regular Season / Playoffs

Season	Team	League	GP	G	A	PTS	PIM	GP	G	A	PTS	PIM
98-99	Massachusetts	H.E.	34	9	7	16	44	—	—	—	—	—
98-99	Portland	AHL	10	0	2	2	13	—	—	—	—	—

Born; 2/10/75, Edmonton, Alberta. 6-3, 215. Signed as a free agent by Washington Capitals (3/24/99). Last amateur club; Massachusetts (Hockey East).

Wayne Strachan — Center
Regular Season / Playoffs

Season	Team	League	GP	G	A	PTS	PIM	GP	G	A	PTS	PIM
95-96	Los Angeles	IHL	75	19	30	49	55	—	—	—	—	—
96-97	Long Beach	IHL	6	3	0	3	2	—	—	—	—	—
96-97	Manitoba	IHL	25	3	10	13	24	—	—	—	—	—
96-97	Roanoke	ECHL	25	19	13	32	23	—	—	—	—	—
96-97	Thunder Bay	CoHL	8	4	6	10	2	4	3	3	6	10
97-98	South Carolina	ECHL	10	4	3	7	2	—	—	—	—	—
97-98	Roanoke	ECHL	33	11	20	31	20	9	4	7	11	2
97-98	Thunder Bay	UHL	2	2	0	2	0	—	—	—	—	—
98-99	Thunder Bay	UHL	72	*57	71	128	91	13	6	6	12	14
	IHL	Totals	106	25	40	65	81	—	—	—	—	—
	UHL	Totals	82	63	77	140	93	17	39	9	18	24
	ECHL	Totals	68	34	36	70	45	9	4	7	11	2

Born; 12/12/72, Fort Francis, Ontario. 5-9, 185. Selected by New York Rangers in 1993 Supplemental Draft. Traded to New Orleans by South Carolina for John Blessman (11/97). Traded to Roanoke by New Orleans for Todd Norman (1/98). 1998-99 UHL First Team All-Star. Last amateur club; Lake Superior (CCHA).

Luke Strand — Right Wing
Regular Season / Playoffs

Season	Team	League	GP	G	A	PTS	PIM	GP	G	A	PTS	PIM
97-98	Madison	UHL	72	8	19	27	86	7	0	1	1	2
98-99	Madison	UHL	74	4	17	21	130	—	—	—	—	—
	UHL	Totals	146	12	36	48	216	7	0	1	1	2

Born; 2/12/73, Eau Claire, Wisconsin. 5-8, 175. Last amateur club; Wisconsin-Eau Claire (NCAA 3).

Paul Strand — Center
Regular Season / Playoffs

Season	Team	League	GP	G	A	PTS	PIM	GP	G	A	PTS	PIM
97-98	Baton Rouge	ECHL	10	2	1	3	8	—	—	—	—	—
97-98	Raliegh	ECHL	54	25	26	51	119	—	—	—	—	—
98-99	Hamburg	Germany	41	15	20	35	134	—	—	—	—	—
	ECHL	Totals	64	27	27	54	127	—	—	—	—	—

Born; 1/12/72, Edmonton, Alberta. 5-11, 190. Last amateur club; Alberta (CWUAA).

Keith Street — Center

Regular Season / Playoffs

Season	Team	League	GP	G	A	PTS	PIM	GP	G	A	PTS	PIM
88-89	Milwaukee	IHL	40	10	11	21	22	—	—	—	—	—
89-90	Milwaukee	IHL	55	5	13	18	25	—	—	—	—	—
90-91												
91-92												
92-93												
93-94												
94-95												
95-96	Anchorage	WCHL	54	44	40	84	68	—	—	—	—	—
96-97	Anchorage	WCHL	64	44	70	114	61	6	4	2	6	4
97-98	Anchorage	WCHL	64	30	*90	*120	64	7	4	2	6	11
98-99	Anchorage	WCHL	71	47	*88	*135	71	6	1	6	7	2
	IHL	Totals	95	15	24	39	47	—	—	—	—	—
	WCHL	Totals	253	165	288	453	264	19	9	10	19	17

Born; 3/18/65, Moose Jaw, Saskatchewan. 6-0, 175. Signed as a free agent by Vancouver Canucks (7/22/88). 1997-98 WCHL Second Team All-Star. 1998-99 WCHL First Team All-Star.

Mikhail Strelkov — Defenseman

Regular Season / Playoffs

Season	Team	League	GP	G	A	PTS	PIM	GP	G	A	PTS	PIM
98-99	Johnstown	ECHL	8	0	1	1	67	—	—	—	—	—
98-99	Pensacola	ECHL	4	0	0	0	35	—	—	—	—	—
98-99	Alexandria	WPHL	34	1	6	7	175	—	—	—	—	—
	ECHL	Totals	12	0	1	1	102	—	—	—	—	—

Born; 3/17/75, Sankt-Peterbyrg, Russia. 6-3, 245.

Rob Striar — Defenseman

Regular Season / Playoffs

Season	Team	League	GP	G	A	PTS	PIM	GP	G	A	PTS	PIM
93-94	Jacksonville	SUN	28	2	5	7	30	—	—	—	—	—
93-94	Daytona Beach	SUN	4	0	0	0	2	—	—	—	—	—
93-94	Fort Worth	CeHL	8	0	4	4	34	—	—	—	—	—
94-95												
95-96	Utica	CoHL	1	0	0	0	0	—	—	—	—	—
95-96	Erie	ECHL	10	0	0	0	26	—	—	—	—	—
95-96	Hampton Roads	ECHL	2	0	0	0	2	—	—	—	—	—
96-97	Saginaw	CoHL	71	3	8	11	115	—	—	—	—	—
97-98	Binghamton	UHL	55	5	5	10	61	—	—	—	—	—
98-99	Tupelo	WPHL	43	1	12	13	133	—	—	—	—	—
	UHL	Totals	127	8	13	21	176	—	—	—	—	—
	SUN	Totals	32	2	5	7	32	—	—	—	—	—
	ECHL	Totals	12	0	0	0	28	—	—	—	—	—

Born; 8/24/72, New York, New York. 6-0, 200.

Mark Strohack — Defenseman

Regular Season / Playoffs

Season	Team	League	GP	G	A	PTS	PIM	GP	G	A	PTS	PIM
96-97	Utica	CoHL	1	0	0	0	0	—	—	—	—	—
96-97	Fort Worth	CeHL	66	13	38	51	79	17	2	13	15	14
97-98	Fort Worth	WPHL	69	13	38	51	67	13	1	4	5	10
98-99	Fort Worth	WPHL	68	6	30	36	69	12	1	8	9	14
	WPHL	Totals	137	19	68	87	136	25	2	12	14	24

Born; 2/12/71, Waterloo, Ontario. 6-1, 215. Member of 1996-97 CeHL Champion Fort Worth Fire. Last amateur club; Wilfrid Laurier (OUAA).

John Sturgis — Forward

Regular Season / Playoffs

Season	Team	League	GP	G	A	PTS	PIM	GP	G	A	PTS	PIM
98-99	Florida	ECHL	11	2	2	4	4	—	—	—	—	—
98-99	Charlotte	ECHL	53	18	16	34	14	—	—	—	—	—
	ECHL	Totals	64	20	18	38	18	—	—	—	—	—

Born; Sold to Charlotte by Florida (11/98). Last amateur club; Dartmouth

Radoslav Suchy — Defenseman

Regular Season / Playoffs

Season	Team	League	GP	G	A	PTS	PIM	GP	G	A	PTS	PIM
97-98	Las Vegas	IHL	26	1	4	5	10	—	—	—	—	—
97-98	Springfield	AHL	41	6	15	21	16	4	0	1	1	2
98-99	Springfield	AHL	69	4	32	36	10	3	0	1	1	0
	AHL	Totals	110	10	47	57	26	7	0	2	2	2

Born; 7/4/76, Poprad, Slovakia. 6-2, 185. Signed as a free agent by Phoenix Coyotes (9/26/97). Last amateur club; Chicoutimi (QMJHL).

Brandon Sugden — Right Wing

Regular Season / Playoffs

Season	Team	League	GP	G	A	PTS	PIM	GP	G	A	PTS	PIM
98-99	Cincinnati	IHL	6	0	2	2	51	—	—	—	—	—
98-99	Dayton	ECHL	44	0	1	1	233	1	0	0	0	17

Born; 6/23/78, Toronto, Ontario. 6-2, 178. Drafted by Toronto Maple Leafs (8th choice, 111th overall) in 1996 Entry Draft. Last amateur club; Barrie (OHL).

Jeff Suggitt — Center

Regular Season / Playoffs

Season	Team	League	GP	G	A	PTS	PIM	GP	G	A	PTS	PIM
98-99	Bakersfield	WCHL	6	1	0	1	18	—	—	—	—	—

Born;

Joe Suk — Center

Regular Season / Playoffs

Season	Team	League	GP	G	A	PTS	PIM	GP	G	A	PTS	PIM
95-96	Louisville	ECHL	67	19	37	56	63	3	0	1	1	2
96-97	Macon	CeHL	65	21	37	58	71	5	2	0	2	2
97-98	Macon	CHL	38	12	29	41	16	3	0	0	0	0
98-99	Macon	CHL	68	15	26	41	63	3	0	1	1	4
	CHL	Totals	171	48	92	140	150	11	2	1	3	6

Born; 2/26/70, Chicago, Illinois. 5-11, 200.

Steve Suk — Center

Regular Season / Playoffs

Season	Team	League	GP	G	A	PTS	PIM	GP	G	A	PTS	PIM
95-96	Louisville	ECHL	31	10	19	29	22	—	—	—	—	—
95-96	Mobile	ECHL	39	11	28	39	22	—	—	—	—	—
96-97	Mobile	ECHL	59	19	44	63	60	3	0	4	4	0
97-98	Mobile	ECHL	47	12	23	35	37	3	1	3	4	4
98-99	Macon	CHL	63	18	44	62	40	3	0	2	2	0
	ECHL	Totals	239	70	158	228	181	9	1	9	10	4

Born; 3/21/73, Highland Park, Illinois. 5-11, 185. Selected by Greenville in ECHL 1998 Expansion Draft. Last amateur club; Michigan State (CCHA).

Brian Sullivan — Right Wing

Regular Season / Playoffs

Season	Team	League	GP	G	A	PTS	PIM	GP	G	A	PTS	PIM
91-92	Utica	AHL	70	23	24	47	58	4	0	4	4	6
92-93	Utica	AHL	75	30	27	57	88	5	0	0	0	12
92-93	New Jersey	NHL	2	0	1	1	0	—	—	—	—	—
93-94	Albany	AHL	77	31	30	61	140	5	1	1	2	18
94-95	San Diego	IHL	74	24	23	47	97	5	0	1	1	7
95-96												
96-97	San Antonio	IHL	77	22	24	46	115	9	1	2	3	11
97-98	Grand Rapids	IHL	54	12	7	19	49	—	—	—	—	—
97-98	Springfield	AHL	11	2	4	6	29	1	0	0	0	0
98-99	Houston	IHL	53	9	7	16	32	—	—	—	—	—
98-99	Kansas City	IHL	2	0	0	0	0	—	—	—	—	—
	IHL	Totals	260	67	61	128	293	14	1	3	4	18
	AHL	Totals	233	86	85	171	315	15	1	5	6	36

Born; 4/23/69, South Windsor, Connecticut. 6-4, 215. Drafted by New Jersey Devils (3rd choice, 65th overall) in 1987 Entry Draft. Signed as a free agent by Anaheim Mighty Ducks (9/2/74). Last amateur club; Northeastern (Hockey East).

Mike Sullivan — Center

Regular Season / Playoffs

Season	Team	League	GP	G	A	PTS	PIM	GP	G	A	PTS	PIM
96-97	Adirondack	AHL	17	1	3	4	2	—	—	—	—	—
96-97	Toledo	ECHL	36	9	23	32	18	5	0	3	3	4
97-98	Quebec	IHL	6	0	1	1	6	—	—	—	—	—
97-98	Pensacola	ECHL	64	30	49	79	30	19	9	13	22	6
98-99	Pensacola	ECHL	56	27	34	61	22	—	—	—	—	—
	ECHL	Totals	156	66	106	172	70	24	9	16	25	10

Born; 10/16/73, Woburn, Massachusetts. 6-0, 190. Drafted by Detroit Red Wings (4th choice, 118th overall) in 1992 Entry Draft. Last amateur club; North Hampshire (Hockey East).

Ronnie Sundin — Defenseman

Regular Season / Playoffs

Season	Team	League	GP	G	A	PTS	PIM	GP	G	A	PTS	PIM
97-98	Rangers	NHL	1	0	0	0	0	—	—	—	—	—
97-98	Hartford	AHL	67	3	19	22	59	14	2	5	7	15
98-99	Vastra Frolunda	Sweden	50	5	3	8	26	4	0	1	1	2

Born; 10/3/70, Ludvika, Sweden. 6-1, 220. Drafted by New York Rangers (8th choice, 237th overall) in 1996 Entry Draft.

Olie Sundstrom — Goaltender

Regular Season / Playoffs

Season	Team	League	GP	W	L	T	MIN	SO	AVG	GP	W	L	MIN	SO	AVG
92-93	Columbus	ECHL	8	4	3	0	416	0	4.04	—	—	—	—	—	—
92-93	Nashville	ECHL	21	8	7	0	1087	0	5.46	—	—	—	—	—	—
93-94	Cleveland	IHL	46	20	19	4	2521	0	4.09	—	—	—	—	—	—
94-95	Cleveland	IHL	23	3	17	1	1235	0	5.05	—	—	—	—	—	—
95-96	Erie	ECHL	47	20	22	3	2430	0	4.07	—	—	—	—	—	—
96-97	Johnstown	ECHL	*24	8	*15	1	1349	0	4.89	—	—	—	—	—	—
96-97	Wheeling	ECHL	*37	23	*11	2	2011	0	3.82	1	0	1	31	0	13.43
97-98	Providence	AHL	11	0	7	1	427	0	4.08	—	—	—	—	—	—
97-98	Wheeling	ECHL	27	14	9	2	1428	0	3.95	—	—	—	—	—	—
97-98	New Orleans	ECHL	3	1	1	0	172	0	3.49	—	—	—	—	—	—
98-99	Port Huron	UHL	33	17	10	3	1712	2	2.98	—	—	—	—	—	—
98-99	Binghamton	UHL	19	13	6	0	1133	0	2.97	2	0	2	95	0	5.06
	IHL	Totals	69	23	36	5	3756	0	4.41	—	—	—	—	—	—
	ECHL	Totals	167	78	68	8	8893	0	4.28	1	0	1	31	0	13.43
	UHL	Totals	52	30	16	3	2845	2	2.97	2	0	2	95	0	5.06

Born; 4/2/68, Ange, Sweden. 6-0, 180. Traded to Binghamton by Port Huron with Mike O'Grady for Jon Hillebrandt (2/99). Selected by Missouri in 1999 UHL Expansion Draft.

Jari Suorsa — Left Wing

Regular Season / Playoffs

Season	Team	League	GP	G	A	PTS	PIM	GP	G	A	PTS	PIM
98-99	Fresno	WCHL	44	13	16	29	149	3	2	0	2	6

Born; 1/27/76, Kuusankoski, Finland. 6-2, 206. Last overseas club; Hermes (Finland).

Andy Sutton — Defenseman

Regular Season / Playoffs

Season	Team	League	GP	G	A	PTS	PIM	GP	G	A	PTS	PIM
97-98	Michigan Tech	WCHA	38	16	24	40	97	—	—	—	—	—
97-98	Kentucky	AHL	7	0	0	0	33	—	—	—	—	—
98-99	San Jose	NHL	31	0	3	3	65	—	—	—	—	—
98-99	Kentucky	AHL	21	5	10	15	53	5	0	0	0	23
	AHL	Totals	28	5	10	15	86	5	0	0	0	23

Born; 10/24/77, Edmonton, Alberta. 5-10, 192. Signed as a free agent by San Jose Sharks (3/20/98). Last amateur club; Michigan Tech (WCHA).

Ken Sutton — Defenseman

Regular Season / Playoffs

Season	Team	League	GP	G	A	PTS	PIM	GP	G	A	PTS	PIM
89-90	Rochester	AHL	57	5	14	19	83	11	1	6	7	15
90-91	Buffalo	NHL	15	3	6	9	13	6	0	1	1	2
90-91	Rochester	AHL	62	7	24	31	65	3	1	1	2	14
91-92	Buffalo	NHL	64	2	18	20	71	7	0	2	2	4
92-93	Buffalo	NHL	63	8	14	22	30	8	3	1	4	8
93-94	Buffalo	NHL	78	4	20	24	71	4	0	0	0	2
94-95	Buffalo	NHL	12	1	2	3	30	—	—	—	—	—
94-95	Edmonton	NHL	12	3	1	4	12	—	—	—	—	—
95-96	Edmonton	NHL	32	0	8	8	43	—	—	—	—	—
95-96	St. Louis	NHL	6	0	0	0	4	1	0	0	0	0
95-96	Worcester	AHL	32	4	16	20	60	4	0	2	2	21
96-97	Manitoba	IHL	20	3	10	13	48	—	—	—	—	—
96-97	Albany	AHL	61	6	13	19	79	16	4	8	12	55
97-98	New Jersey	NHL	13	0	0	0	6	—	—	—	—	—
97-98	San Jose	NHL	8	0	0	0	15	—	—	—	—	—
97-98	Albany	AHL	10	0	7	7	15	—	—	—	—	—
98-99	New Jersey	NHL	5	1	0	1	0	—	—	—	—	—
98-99	Albany	AHL	75	13	42	55	118	5	0	2	2	12
	NHL	Totals	308	22	69	91	295	26	3	4	7	16
	AHL	Totals	297	35	116	151	420	39	6	19	25	117

Born; 5/11/69, Edmonton, Alberta. 6-0, 198. Drafted by Buffalo Sabres (4th choice, 98th overall) in 1989 Entry Draft. Traded to Edmonton Oilers by Buffalo for Scott Pearson (4/7/95). Traded to St. Louis Blues by Edmonton with Igor Kravchuk for Jeff Norton and Donald Dufresne (1/4/96). Traded to New Jersey Devils with St. Louis' second round choice in the 1999 Entry Draft for Ricard Persson and Mike Peluso, (11/26/96). Traded to San Jose Sharks by New Jersey with John MacLean for Doug Bodger and Dody Wood (12/7/97). Traded to New Jersey by San Jose for future considerations (8/26/98). 1998-99 AHL First All-Star Team. 1998-99 AHL Top Defenseman. Last amateur club; Saskatoon

Toivo Suursoo — Left Wing

Regular Season / Playoffs

Season	Team	League	GP	G	A	PTS	PIM	GP	G	A	PTS	PIM
98-99	Malmo	Sweden	29	8	6	14	57	8	4	3	7	12
98-99	Adirondack	AHL	2	0	0	0	0	—	—	—	—	—

Born; 11/23/75, Tallinn, USSR. 6-0, 175. Drafted by Detroit Red Wings (10th choice, 283rd overall) in 1994 Entry Draft.

Lee Svangstu — Left Wing

Regular Season / Playoffs

Season	Team	League	GP	G	A	PTS	PIM	GP	G	A	PTS	PIM
97-98	Utah	IHL	1	0	0	0	0	—	—	—	—	—
97-98	Idaho	WCHL	51	21	19	40	312	4	0	0	0	22
98-99	DNP	Injured										

Born; Crosby, North Dakota. 6-5, 230. Last amateur club; Medicine Hat (WHL).

Per Sveder — Defenseman

Regular Season / Playoffs

Season	Team	League	GP	G	A	PTS	PIM	GP	G	A	PTS	PIM
98-99	Waco	WPHL	30	1	4	5	10	—	—	—	—	—

Born; 3/11/75, Sweden. 6-1, 193.

Fredrik Svensson — Left Wing

Regular Season / Playoffs

Season	Team	League	GP	G	A	PTS	PIM	GP	G	A	PTS	PIM
97-98	Wheeling	ECHL	49	5	10	15	38	—	—	—	—	—
97-98	Johnstown	ECHL	15	0	1	1	2	—	—	—	—	—
98-99	Asheville	UHL	68	19	19	38	69	4	2	0	2	0
	ECHL	Totals	64	5	11	16	40	—	—	—	—	—

Born; 6/29/73, Stockholm, Sweden. 6-1, 190. Selected by Florida in ECHL 1998 Expansion Draft. Last European club; Keikko-Espoo (Finland).

Libor Svindle — Defenseman

Regular Season / Playoffs

Season	Team	League	GP	G	A	PTS	PIM	GP	G	A	PTS	PIM
94-95	Brantford	CoHL	1	0	0	0	0	—	—	—	—	—
95-96												
96-97	El Paso	WPHL	11	0	2	2	8	—	—	—	—	—
97-98												
98-99	Flint	UHL	4	0	0	0	2	—	—	—	—	—
98-99	Mohawk Valley	UHL	43	3	10	13	31	—	—	—	—	—
	UHL	Totals	48	3	10	13	33	—	—	—	—	—

Born; 6/14/73, Stany, Czechoslovakia. 6-4, 225. Last European club; EHC Waldkriburg (Germany).

Brian Swanson — Center

Regular Season / Playoffs

Season	Team	League	GP	G	A	PTS	PIM	GP	G	A	PTS	PIM
98-99	Colorado	WCHA	42	25	41	66	28	—	—	—	—	—
98-99	Hartford	AHL	4	0	0	0	4	—	—	—	—	—

Born; 3/24/76, Anchorage, Alaska. 5-10, 180. Drafted by San Jose Sharks (5th choice, 115th overall) in 1994 Entry Draft. Traded to New York Rangers by San Jose with Jayson More and future considerations for Marty McSorley (8/20/96). Last amateur club; Colorado (WCHA).

Brent Swarbrick — Center

Regular Season / Playoffs

Season	Team	League	GP	G	A	PTS	PIM	GP	G	A	PTS	PIM
97-98	Fort Worth	CHL	3	0	0	0	0	—	—	—	—	—
98-99	Fort Worth	CHL	2	0	0	0	0	—	—	—	—	—
	CHL	Totals	5	0	0	0	0	—	—	—	—	—

Born;

Bob Sweeney — Center

Regular Season / Playoffs

Season	Team	League	GP	G	A	PTS	PIM	GP	G	A	PTS	PIM
86-87	Boston	NHL	14	2	4	6	21	3	0	0	0	0
86-87	Moncton	AHL	58	29	26	55	81	4	0	2	2	13
87-88	Boston	NHL	80	22	23	45	73	23	6	8	14	66
88-89	Boston	NHL	75	14	14	28	99	10	2	4	6	19
89-90	Boston	NHL	70	22	24	46	93	20	0	2	2	30
90-91	Boston	NHL	80	15	33	48	115	17	4	2	6	45
91-92	Boston	NHL	63	6	14	20	103	14	1	0	1	25
91-92	Maine	AHL	1	1	0	1	0	—	—	—	—	—
92-93	Buffalo	NHL	80	21	26	47	118	8	2	2	4	8
93-94	Buffalo	NHL	60	11	14	25	94	1	0	0	0	0
94-95	Buffalo	NHL	45	5	4	9	18	5	0	0	0	4
95-96	Islanders	NHL	66	6	6	12	59	—	—	—	—	—
95-96	Calgary	NHL	6	1	1	2	6	2	0	0	0	0
96-97	Quebec	IHL	69	10	21	31	120	9	2	0	2	8
97-98	Frankfurt	Germany	20	7	8	15	32	7	1	3	4	6
97-98	Revior Lowen	Germany	29	9	4	13	77	—	—	—	—	—
98-99	Frankfurt	Germany	46	6	21	27	30	1	0	1	1	8
	NHL	Totals	639	125	163	288	799	103	15	18	33	197
	AHL	Totals	59	30	26	56	81	4	0	2	2	13

Born; 1/25/64, Concord, Massachusetts. 6-3, 200. Drafted by Boston Bruins (6th choice, 123rd overall) in 1982 Entry Draft. Claimed on waivers by Buffalo Sabres from Boston (10/9/92). Claimed on waivers by New York Islanders from Buffalo in NHL Waiver Draft (10/2/95). Traded to Calgary Flames by Islanders for Pat Conacher and Calgary's sixth round choice (Ilja Demidov) in 1997 Entry Draft (3/20/96). Last amateur club; Boston College (Hockey East).

Tim Sweeney — Right Wing

Regular Season / Playoffs

Season	Team	League	GP	G	A	PTS	PIM	GP	G	A	PTS	PIM
89-90	Salt Lake City	IHL	81	46	51	97	32	11	5	4	9	4
90-91	Calgary	NHL	42	7	9	16	8	—	—	—	—	—
90-91	Salt Lake City	IHL	31	19	16	35	8	4	3	3	6	0
91-92	United States	National	21	9	11	20	10	—	—	—	—	—
91-92	United States	Olympic	8	3	4	7	6	—	—	—	—	—
91-92	Calgary	NHL	11	1	2	3	4	—	—	—	—	—
92-93	Boston	NHL	14	1	7	8	6	3	0	0	0	0
92-93	Providence	AHL	60	41	55	96	32	3	2	2	4	0
93-94	Anaheim	NHL	78	16	27	43	49	—	—	—	—	—
94-95	Anaheim	NHL	13	1	1	2	2	—	—	—	—	—
94-95	Providence	AHL	2	2	2	4	0	13	8	*17	*25	6
95-96	Boston	NHL	41	8	8	16	14	1	0	0	0	2
95-96	Providence	AHL	34	17	22	39	12	—	—	—	—	—
96-97	Boston	NHL	36	10	11	21	14	—	—	—	—	—
96-97	Providence	AHL	23	11	22	33	6	—	—	—	—	—
97-98	Rangers	NHL	56	11	18	29	26	—	—	—	—	—
97-98	Hartford	AHL	7	2	6	8	8	—	—	—	—	—
98-99	Providence	AHL	2	0	0	0	0	—	—	—	—	—
	NHL	Totals	291	55	83	138	123	4	0	0	0	2
	AHL	Totals	128	73	107	180	58	16	10	19	29	6
	IHL	Totals	112	65	67	132	40	15	8	7	15	4

Born; 4/12/67, Boston, Massachusetts. 5-11, 185. Drafted by Calgary Flames (7th choice, 122nd overall) in 1985 Entry Draft. Signed as a free agent by Boston Bruins (9/16/92). Claimed by Anaheim Mighty Ducks from Boston in Expansion Draft (6/24/93). Signed as a free agent by Boston (8/9/95). Signed as a free agent by New York Rangers (9/11/97). 1989-90 IHL Second Team All-Star. 1992-93 AHL Second Team All-Star. Last amateur club; Boston College (Hockey East).

Wes Swinson — Defenseman

Regular Season / Playoffs

Season	Team	League	GP	G	A	PTS	PIM	GP	G	A	PTS	PIM
96-97	Carolina	AHL	10	0	0	0	10	—	—	—	—	—
96-97	Tallahassee	ECHL	17	3	9	12	28	3	0	1	1	4
97-98	New Haven	AHL	22	0	2	2	26	—	—	—	—	—
97-98	Fort Wayne	IHL	18	1	2	3	21	—	—	—	—	—
98-99	Miami	ECHL	17	1	11	12	37	—	—	—	—	—
98-99	Tallahassee	ECHL	26	3	18	21	67	—	—	—	—	—
	AHL	Totals	32	0	2	2	36	—	—	—	—	—
	ECHL	Totals	60	7	38	45	132	3	0	1	1	4

Born; 5/26/75, Peterborough, Ontario. Drafted by Hartford Whalers (7th choice, 240th overall) in 1993 Entry Draft. Signed as a free agent by Florida Panthers (3/19/96). Last amateur club; Kingston (OHL).

Martin Sychra — Right Wing

Regular Season / Playoffs

Season	Team	League	GP	G	A	PTS	PIM	GP	G	A	PTS	PIM
94-95	Fredericton	AHL	39	4	10	14	4	—	—	—	—	—
95-96	Fredericton	AHL	9	1	1	2	0	—	—	—	—	—
95-96	Wheeling	ECHL	23	9	8	17	4	—	—	—	—	—
96-97												
97-98												
98-99	Charlotte	ECHL	64	20	25	45	41	—	—	—	—	—
	AHL	Totals	48	5	11	16	4	—	—	—	—	—
	ECHL	Totals	87	29	33	62	45	—	—	—	—	—

Born; 6/19/74, Brno, Czech Republic. 6-1, 180. Last amateur club; Kingston

Petr Sykora — Center

Regular Season / Playoffs

Season	Team	League	GP	G	A	PTS	PIM	GP	G	A	PTS	PIM
98-99	Nashville	NHL	2	0	0	0	0	—	—	—	—	—
98-99	Milwaukee	IHL	73	14	15	29	50	2	1	1	2	0

Born; 12/21/78, Pardubice, Czechoslovakia. 6-2, 180. Drafted by Detroit Red Wings (2nd choice, 76th overall) in 1997 Entry Draft. Traded to Nashville Predators by Detroit with Detroit's third round choice in 1999 Entry Draft for Doug Brown (7/14/98). Last European club; Pardobice (Czech-Republic).

Dean Sylvester — Right Wing

Regular Season / Playoffs

Season	Team	League	GP	G	A	PTS	PIM	GP	G	A	PTS	PIM
95-96	Kansas City	IHL	36	11	10	21	15	4	0	0	0	2
95-96	Mobile	ECHL	44	24	27	51	35	—	—	—	—	—
96-97	Kansas City	IHL	77	23	22	45	47	3	1	1	2	0
97-98	Kansas City	IHL	77	33	20	53	63	11	5	2	7	4
98-99	Buffalo	NHL	1	0	0	0	0	4	0	0	0	2
98-99	Rochester	AHL	76	35	30	65	46	18	*12	5	17	8
	IHL	Totals	190	67	52	119	125	18	6	3	9	6

Born; 12/30/72, Weymouth, Massachusetts. 6-2, 200. Signed as a free agent by Buffalo Sabres (9/10/98). Traded to Atlanta Thrashers by Buffalo for future considerations (6/25/99). Last amateur club; Michigan State (CCHA).

Yanic Sylvester — Defenseman

Regular Season / Playoffs

Season	Team	League	GP	G	A	PTS	PIM	GP	G	A	PTS	PIM
98-99	Memphis	CHL	5	0	3	3	0	—	—	—	—	—

Born;

Mike Sylvia — Right Wing

Regular Season / Playoffs

Season	Team	League	GP	G	A	PTS	PIM	GP	G	A	PTS	PIM
98-99	Hartford	AHL	3	0	0	0	0	—	—	—	—	—
98-99	Cincinnati	IHL	1	0	0	0	0	—	—	—	—	—
98-99	Dayton	ECHL	9	0	3	3	4	—	—	—	—	—
98-99	Charlotte	ECHL	56	9	26	35	56	—	—	—	—	—
	ECHL	Totals	65	9	29	38	60	—	—	—	—	—

Born; 2/5/76, Newton, Massachusetts. 5-11, 180. Traded to Charlotte by Dayton for future considerations (11/98). Last amateur club; Boston University (Hockey

Brad Symes — Defenseman

Regular Season / Playoffs

Season	Team	League	GP	G	A	PTS	PIM	GP	G	A	PTS	PIM
96-97	Hamilton	AHL	5	0	0	0	7	—	—	—	—	—
96-97	Wheeling	ECHL	51	6	17	23	63	1	0	0	0	0
97-98	New Orleans	ECHL	18	1	4	5	28	—	—	—	—	—
98-99	New Orleans	ECHL	67	3	6	9	76	11	0	0	0	21
	ECHL	Totals	136	10	27	37	167	12	0	0	0	21

Born; 4/26/76, Edmonton, Alberta. 6-2, 210. Drafted by Edmonton Oilers (5th choice, 60th overall) in 1994 Entry Draft. Last amateur club; Portland (WHL).

Nikolai Syrston — Defenseman

Regular Season / Playoffs

Season	Team	League	GP	G	A	PTS	PIM	GP	G	A	PTS	PIM
98-99	Las Vegas	IHL	12	0	0	0	4	—	—	—	—	—
98-99	Port Huron	UHL	58	7	18	25	69	7	0	0	0	8

Born; 6/24/71, Russia. 6-1. 205. Selected by Fort Wayne in 1999 UHL Expansion Draft. Last overseas club; Novgorod (Russia).

Dave Szabo — Forward

Regular Season / Playoffs

Season	Team	League	GP	G	A	PTS	PIM	GP	G	A	PTS	PIM
98-99	Tupelo	WPHL	66	33	27	60	25	—	—	—	—	—

Born; 6/18/74, Courtice, Ontario. 6-0, 200. Last amateur club; Concordia

Darren Szczygiel — Center

Regular Season / Playoffs

Season	Team	League	GP	G	A	PTS	PIM	GP	G	A	PTS	PIM
97-98	Thunder Bay	UHL	13	3	7	10	12	5	1	4	5	4
98-99	Thunder Bay	UHL	53	8	22	30	63	6	0	2	2	4
	UHL	Totals	66	11	29	40	75	11	1	6	7	8

Born; 12/2/74, Bancroft, Ontario. 5-10, 190

Chris Szysky — Forward

Regular Season / Playoffs

Season	Team	League	GP	G	A	PTS	PIM	GP	G	A	PTS	PIM
97-98	Canada	National	50	9	20	29	111	—	—	—	—	—
98-99	Canada	National	41	9	13	22	58	—	—	—	—	—
98-99	Grand Rapids	IHL	6	1	1	2	10	—	—	—	—	—

Born; 6/8/76, White City, Saskatchewan. 5-11, 205. Signed as a free agent by Ottawa Senators (6/11/99) Last amateur club; Swift Current (WHL).

Greg Hawgood won his third professional top defenseman trophy last season

Photo by John Gacioch

John Taggart — Left Wing
Regular Season — Playoffs

Season	Team	League	GP	G	A	PTS	PIM	GP	G	A	PTS	PIM
98-99	Winston-Salem	UHL	8	0	0	0	0	4	0	0	0	0

Born; 9/20/78, Whitecourt, Alberta. 6-0, 190.

Gerald Tallaire — Forward
Regular Season — Playoffs

Season	Team	League	GP	G	A	PTS	PIM	GP	G	A	PTS	PIM
97-98	Karhut	Finland	23	5	13	18	12	—	—	—	—	—
98-99	Central Texas	WPHL	66	43	57	100	61	2	1	0	1	0

Born; 3/10/72, Winnipeg, Manitoba. 5-11, 185.

Sean Tallaire — Right Wing
Regular Season — Playoffs

Season	Team	League	GP	G	A	PTS	PIM	GP	G	A	PTS	PIM
96-97	Manitoba	IHL	74	21	29	50	67	—	—	—	—	—
97-98	Manitoba	IHL	73	13	17	30	65	—	—	—	—	—
97-98	Cleveland	IHL	7	1	1	2	4	10	2	2	4	4
98-99	Springfield	AHL	6	2	1	3	0	—	—	—	—	—
98-99	Grand Rapids	IHL	4	0	0	0	0	—	—	—	—	—
98-99	Long Beach	IHL	56	24	19	43	68	8	4	1	5	8
98-99	Central Texas	WPHL	2	1	3	4	0	—	—	—	—	—
	IHL	Totals	211	59	66	125	204	18	6	3	9	12

Born; 10/3/73, Steinbach, Minnesota. 5-10, 185. Drafted by Vancouver Canucks (7th choice, 202nd overall) in 1993 Entry Draft. Last amateur club; Lake Superior (CCHA).

Mike Tamburro — Goaltender
Regular Season — Playoffs

Season	Team	League	GP	W	L	T	MIN	SO	AVG	GP	W	L	MIN	SO	AVG
96-97	Cleveland	IHL	26	13	8	2	1326	1	2.99	1	0	0	12	0	0.00
96-97	Louisville	ECHL	1	0	1	0	60	0	6.00	—	—	—	—	—	—
97-98	Cleveland	IHL	19	9	9	0	1059	1	3.29	—	—	—	—	—	—
97-98	Chesapeake	ECHL	25	16	6	1	1411	2	2.68	3	0	3	189	0	3.17
98-99	Cleveland	IHL	17	5	11	0	835	0	4.17	—	—	—	—	—	—
98-99	Chesapeake	ECHL	35	19	11	2	1935	2	2.45	1	1	0	60	0	2.00
	IHL	Totals	62	27	28	2	3220	2	3.39	1	0	0	12	0	0.00
	ECHL	Totals	61	35	18	3	3406	4	2.61	4	1	3	249	0	2.89

Born; 3/26/73, Toronto, Ontario. 5-8, 170. Last amateur club; Rennsalaer Polytechnic Institute (ECAC).

T.J. Tanberg — Forward
Regular Season — Playoffs

Season	Team	League	GP	G	A	PTS	PIM	GP	G	A	PTS	PIM
98-99	Tallahassee	ECHL	42	2	7	9	22	—	—	—	—	—

Born; 3/4/74, Littleton, Colorado. 6-1, 180. Last amateur club; Colorado

Chris Tancill — Right Wing
Regular Season — Playoffs

Season	Team	League	GP	G	A	PTS	PIM	GP	G	A	PTS	PIM
90-91	Hartford	NHL	9	1	1	2	4	—	—	—	—	—
90-91	Springfield	AHL	72	37	35	72	46	17	8	4	12	32
91-92	Hartford	NHL	10	0	0	0	2	—	—	—	—	—
91-92	Detroit	NHL	1	0	0	0	0	—	—	—	—	—
91-92	Springfield	AHL	17	12	7	19	20	—	—	—	—	—
91-92	Adirondack	AHL	50	36	34	70	42	19	7	9	16	31
92-93	Detroit	NHL	4	1	0	1	2	—	—	—	—	—
92-93	Adirondack	AHL	68	*59	43	102	62	10	7	7	14	10
93-94	Dallas	NHL	12	1	3	4	8	—	—	—	—	—
93-94	Kalamazoo	IHL	60	41	54	95	55	5	0	2	2	8
94-95	San Jose	NHL	26	3	11	14	10	11	1	1	2	8
94-95	Kansas City	IHL	64	31	28	59	40	—	—	—	—	—
95-96	San Jose	NHL	45	7	16	23	20	—	—	—	—	—
95-96	Kansas City	IHL	27	12	16	28	18	—	—	—	—	—
96-97	San Jose	NHL	25	4	0	4	8	—	—	—	—	—
96-97	Kentucky	AHL	42	19	26	45	31	4	2	0	2	2
97-98	Dallas	NHL	2	0	1	1	0	—	—	—	—	—
97-98	Michigan	IHL	70	30	39	69	86	4	3	0	3	14
98-99	Kloten	Switz.	42	19	30	49	46	12	4	2	6	16
	NHL	Totals	116	22	32	54	54	11	1	1	2	8
	AHL	Totals	249	163	145	308	201	50	24	20	44	75
	IHL	Totals	221	114	137	251	199	9	3	2	5	22

Born; 2/7/68, Livonia, Michigan. 5-10, 185. Drafted by Hartford Whalers (1st choice, 15th overall) in 1989 Supplemental Draft. Traded to Detroit Red Wings to Hartford for daniel Shank (12/18/91). Signed as a free agent by Dallas Stars (8/28/93). Signed as a free agent by San Jose Sharks (8/24/94). Signed as a free agent by Dallas (7/25/97). Member of 1990-91 AHL champion Springfield Indians. Member of 1991-92 AHL champion Adirondack Red Wings. Last amateur club; Wisconsin (WCHA).

Alex Tanguay — Center
Regular Season — Playoffs

Season	Team	League	GP	G	A	PTS	PIM	GP	G	A	PTS	PIM
98-99	Halifax	QMJHL	31	27	34	61	30	5	1	2	3	2
98-99	Hershey	AHL	5	1	2	3	2	5	0	2	2	0

Born; 11/21/79, Ste.-Justine, Quebec. 6-0, 180. Drafted by Colorado Avalanche (1st choice, 12th overall) in 1998 Entry Draft. Last amateur club; Halifax

Bryan Tapper — Defenseman
Regular Season — Playoffs

Season	Team	League	GP	G	A	PTS	PIM	GP	G	A	PTS	PIM
98-99	Pee Dee	ECHL	70	5	15	20	58	13	0	0	0	10

Born; 3/13/75, Scarborough, Ontario. 6-2, 195. Last amateur club; R.P.I (ECAC).

Dmitri Tarabrin — Right Wing
Regular Season — Playoffs

Season	Team	League	GP	G	A	PTS	PIM	GP	G	A	PTS	PIM
97-98	Wheeling	ECHL	60	12	16	28	77	15	2	1	3	16
98-99	Wheeling	ECHL	41	12	22	34	30	—	—	—	—	—
98-99	Johnstown	ECHL	31	7	6	13	6	—	—	—	—	—
	ECHL	Totals	132	31	44	75	113	15	2	1	3	16

Born; 9/17/76, Moscow, Russia. 5-8, 180.

Marc Tardif — Left Wing
Regular Season — Playoffs

Season	Team	League	GP	G	A	PTS	PIM	GP	G	A	PTS	PIM
93-94	Atlanta	IHL	65	9	13	22	154	—	—	—	—	—
94-95	Atlanta	IHL	5	0	0	0	2	—	—	—	—	—
94-95	Nashville	ECHL	54	16	26	42	263	8	1	0	1	30
95-96	Worcester	AHL	3	0	0	0	0	—	—	—	—	—
95-96	South Carolina	ECHL	52	25	18	43	206	8	3	4	7	41
96-97	Rochester	AHL	1	0	0	0	0	—	—	—	—	—
96-97	South Carolina	ECHL	56	15	22	37	187	18	4	12	16	*114
97-98	South Carolina	ECHL	26	4	12	16	82	5	1	2	3	22
98-99	South Carolina	ECHL	36	9	15	24	149	3	0	0	0	18
	IHL	Totals	70	9	13	22	156	—	—	—	—	—
	AHL	Totals	4	0	0	0	0	—	—	—	—	—
	ECHL	Totals	224	69	93	162	887	42	9	18	27	225

Born; 1/6/73, Montreal, Quebec. 6-1, 190. Drafted by Tampa Bay Lightning (10th choice, 218th overall) in 1992 Entry Draft. Member of 1996-97 ECHL Champion South Carolina Stingrays. Last amateur club; Sherbrooke (QMJHL).

Patrice Tardif — Center

Regular Season / Playoffs

Season	Team	League	GP	G	A	PTS	PIM	GP	G	A	PTS	PIM
93-94	Peoria	IHL	11	4	4	8	21	4	2	0	2	4
94-95	St. Louis	NHL	27	3	10	13	29	—	—	—	—	—
94-95	Peoria	IHL	53	27	18	45	83	—	—	—	—	—
95-96	Los Angeles	NHL	15	1	1	2	37	—	—	—	—	—
95-96	St. Louis	NHL	23	3	0	3	12	—	—	—	—	—
95-96	Worcester	AHL	30	13	13	26	69	—	—	—	—	—
96-97	Phoenix	IHL	9	0	3	3	13	—	—	—	—	—
96-97	Detroit	IHL	66	24	23	47	70	11	0	1	1	8
97-98	Detroit	IHL	28	10	9	19	24	15	3	7	10	14
97-98	Rochester	AHL	41	13	13	26	68	—	—	—	—	—
98-99	Manitoba	IHL	63	21	35	56	88	5	1	2	3	0
	NHL	Totals	65	7	11	18	78	—	—	—	—	—
	IHL	Totals	230	86	92	178	299	35	6	10	16	26
	AHL	Totals	71	26	26	52	137	—	—	—	—	—

Born; 10/30/70, Thetford Mines, Quebec. Drafted by St. Louis Blues (2nd choice, 54th overall) in 1990 Entry Draft. Traded to Los Angeles Kings with Craig Johnson, Roman Vopat, St. Louis first round pick (Matt Zultek) in 1997 Entry Draft and fifth round pick (Peter Hogan) in 1996 Entry Draft for Wayne Gretzky (2/27/96). Signed as a free agent by Buffalo Sabres (8/11/97). Member of 1996-97 IHL Champion Detroit Vipers. Last amateur club; Maine (Hockey East).

Steve Tardif — Center

Regular Season / Playoffs

Season	Team	League	GP	G	A	PTS	PIM	GP	G	A	PTS	PIM
97-98	Jacksonville	ECHL	15	4	3	7	48	—	—	—	—	—
97-98	Indianapolis	IHL	42	3	4	7	113	—	—	—	—	—
98-99	Portland	AHL	33	2	9	11	48	—	—	—	—	—
98-99	Indianapolis	IHL	6	0	0	0	40	—	—	—	—	—
98-99	Florida	ECHL	25	13	12	25	75	6	4	3	7	18
	IHL	Totals	48	3	4	7	153	—	—	—	—	—
	ECHL	Totals	40	17	15	32	123	6	4	3	7	18

Born; 3/29/77, St. Agnes, Quebec. 6-1, 180. Drafted by Chicago Blackhawks (8th chocie, 175th overall) in 1995 Entry Draft. Last amateur club; Drummondville (QMJHL).

Ken Tasker — Right Wing

Regular Season / Playoffs

Season	Team	League	GP	G	A	PTS	PIM	GP	G	A	PTS	PIM
97-98	Thunder Bay	UHL	55	3	5	8	281	2	0	0	0	9
98-99	Birmingham	ECHL	18	0	0	0	131	—	—	—	—	—
98-99	Toledo	ECHL	29	1	2	3	188	—	—	—	—	—
	ECHL	Totals	47	1	2	3	319	—	—	—	—	—

Born; 1/21/76, Ottawa, Ontario. 6-0, 205.

Andrew Taylor — Left Wing

Regular Season / Playoffs

Season	Team	League	GP	G	A	PTS	PIM	GP	G	A	PTS	PIM
98-99	Florida	ECHL	70	12	33	45	77	6	1	3	4	0

Born; 1/17/77, Stratford, Ontario. 6-1, 182. Drafted by New York Islanders (5th choice, 158th overall) in 1995 Entry Draft. Last amateur club; Plymouth (OHL).

Chris Taylor — Center

Regular Season / Playoffs

Season	Team	League	GP	G	A	PTS	PIM	GP	G	A	PTS	PIM
92-93	Capital District	AHL	77	19	43	62	32	4	0	1	1	2
93-94	Salt Lake City	IHL	79	21	20	41	38	—	—	—	—	—
94-95	Islanders	NHL	10	0	3	3	2	—	—	—	—	—
94-95	Denver	IHL	78	38	48	86	47	14	7	6	13	10
95-96	Islanders	NHL	11	0	1	1	2	—	—	—	—	—
95-96	Utah	IHL	50	18	23	41	60	22	5	11	16	26
96-97	Islanders	NHL	1	0	0	0	0	—	—	—	—	—
96-97	Utah	IHL	71	27	40	67	24	7	1	2	3	0
97-98	Utah	IHL	79	28	56	84	66	4	0	2	2	6
98-99	Boston	NHL	37	3	5	8	12	—	—	—	—	—
98-99	Providence	AHL	21	6	11	17	6	—	—	—	—	—
98-99	Las Vegas	IHL	14	3	12	15	2	—	—	—	—	—
	NHL	Totals	59	3	9	12	16	—	—	—	—	—
	IHL	Totals	371	135	199	334	237	47	13	21	34	42
	AHL	Totals	98	25	54	79	38	4	0	1	1	2

Born; 3/6/72, Stratford, Ontario. 6-1, 196. Drafted by New York Islanders (2nd choice, 27th overall) in 1990 Entry Draft. Signed as a free agent by Los Angeles Kings (7/25/97). Signed as a free agent by Boston Bruins (7/22/98). Member of 1994-95 IHL champion Denver Grizzlies. Member of 1995-96 IHL champion Utah Grizzlies. Last amateur club; London (OHL).

Greg Taylor — Goaltender

Regular Season / Playoffs

Season	Team	League	GP	W	L	T	MIN	SO	AVG	GP	W	L	MIN	SO	AVG
97-98	Columbus	CHL	38	25	8	4	2173	*2	3.04	4	4	0	240	0	2.75
98-99	Tallahassee	ECHL	35	11	14	4	1664	1	3.39	—	—	—	—	—	—
98-99	Columbus	CHL	—	—	—	—	—	—	—	1	0	0	20	0	0.00
	CHL	Totals	38	25	8	4	2173	2	3.04	5	4	0	260	0	2.54

Born; 11/5/73, Alberta. 6-0, 190. Member of 1997-98 CHL Champion Columbus Cottonmouths. Last amateur club; Boston College (Hockey East).

Jason Taylor — Center

Regular Season / Playoffs

Season	Team	League	GP	G	A	PTS	PIM	GP	G	A	PTS	PIM
91-92	Columbus	ECHL	21	7	9	16	147	—	—	—	—	—
92-93	Dallas	CeHL	60	38	32	70	210	7	1	2	3	23
93-94	Brantford	CoHL	43	4	6	10	176	5	0	0	0	22
94-95	Dallas	CeHL	26	6	12	18	118	—	—	—	—	—
94-95	London	CoHL	18	1	3	4	165	—	—	—	—	—
94-95	Brantford	CoHL	13	1	3	4	36	—	—	—	—	—
95-96	Detroit	CoHL	30	10	18	28	66	8	0	2	2	35
96-97	Central Texas	WPHL	44	10	31	41	250	11	4	7	11	12
97-98	Central Texas	WPHL	57	22	22	44	160	4	0	4	4	10
98-99	Mohawk Valley	UHL	36	5	15	20	24	—	—	—	—	—
98-99	Shreveport	WPHL	14	2	12	14	12	12	3	2	5	35
	UHL	Totals	140	21	45	66	467	13	0	2	2	57
	WPHL	Totals	115	34	65	99	422	27	7	13	20	57
	CeHL	Totals	86	44	44	88	328	7	1	2	3	23

Born; 7/19/67, Oak Lake, Manitoba. 5-10, 188. Member of 1998-99 WPHL Champion Shreveport Mudbugs.

Mike Taylor — Center
Regular Season / Playoffs

Season	Team	League	GP	G	A	PTS	PIM	GP	G	A	PTS	PIM
94-95	St. John's	AHL	4	0	1	1	0	—	—	—	—	—
94-95	Cornwall	AHL	3	0	0	0	2	—	—	—	—	—
94-95	Richmond	ECHL	42	7	21	28	90	17	3	14	17	23
95-96	Springfield	AHL	2	1	1	2	2	—	—	—	—	—
95-96	Portland	AHL	1	0	0	0	2	—	—	—	—	—
95-96	Richmond	ECHL	65	27	48	75	261	7	1	6	7	21
96-97	Orlando	IHL	2	0	0	0	2	—	—	—	—	—
96-97	Chicago	IHL	43	8	16	24	60	4	0	2	2	0
96-97	Baltimore	AHL	5	0	1	1	4	—	—	—	—	—
96-97	Richmond	ECHL	28	16	19	35	43	—	—	—	—	—
97-98	Fort Wayne	IHL	21	3	5	8	20	—	—	—	—	—
97-98	South Carolina	ECHL	47	12	34	46	78	5	2	1	3	18
98-99	Utah	IHL	1	0	1	1	4	—	—	—	—	—
98-99	Tucson	WCHL	21	18	21	39	67	—	—	—	—	—
98-99	San Diego	WCHL	54	24	42	66	48	12	4	8	12	*49
	IHL	Totals	67	11	22	33	86	4	0	2	2	0
	AHL	Totals	10	1	2	3	6	—	—	—	—	—
	ECHL	Totals	182	62	122	184	472	29	6	21	27	62
	WCHL	Totals	75	42	63	105	115	12	4	8	12	49

Born; 8/18/71, Kingston, Ontario. 5-9, 180. Traded to South Carolina by Richmond with Jason Wright for Dan Fournel, Kevin Knopp, Mario Cormier and Jay Moser (12/97). Member of 1994-95 ECHL champion Richmond Renegades. Last amateur club; Northeastern (Hockey East).

Paul Taylor — Goaltender
Regular Season / Playoffs

Season	Team	League	GP	W	L	T	MIN	SO	AVG	GP	W	L	MIN	SO	AVG
94-95	Dayton	ECHL	32	18	11	2	1685	3	3.45	2	0	1	108	0	1.67
94-95	Peoria	IHL	2	2	0	0	120	0	2.50	—	—	—	—	—	—
95-96	Kaufbeurer	Germany	5	—	—	—	300	0	5.60	—	—	—	—	—	—
95-96	Peoria	IHL	16	5	8	1	913	0	4.34	1	0	0	20	0	3.00
95-96	Dayton	ECHL	5	3	1	0	260	0	4.62	—	—	—	—	—	—
96-97	Saint John	AHL	4	0	4	0	238	0	5.04	—	—	—	—	—	—
96-97	Fort Wayne	IHL	1	1	0	0	60	0	3.00	—	—	—	—	—	—
96-97	Roanoke	ECHL	2	1	1	0	120	0	2.50	—	—	—	—	—	—
97-98	Fayetteville	CHL	25	12	10	2	1443	0	4.45	—	—	—	—	—	—
97-98	Pee Dee	ECHL	5	2	2	1	248	0	3.39	—	—	—	—	—	—
98-99	Las Vegas	IHL	1	0	0	1	9	0	7.02	—	—	—	—	—	—
98-99	Tacoma	WCHL	11	3	5	1	557	0	4.63	—	—	—	—	—	—
98-99	San Antonio	CHL	19	9	5	2	1019	0	3.89	8	3	5	488	0	3.69
	IHL	Totals	20	8	8	2	1102	0	4.08	1	0	0	20	0	3.00
	ECHL	Totals	44	24	15	1	2313	3	3.53	2	0	1	108	0	1.67
	CHL	Totals	44	21	15	4	2462	0	4.22	8	3	5	488	0	3.69

Born; 8/20/71, Vancouver, British Columbia. 6-1, 190. Last amateur club; Northern Michigan (WCHA).

Rod Taylor — Left Wing
Regular Season / Playoffs

Season	Team	League	GP	G	A	PTS	PIM	GP	G	A	PTS	PIM
91-92	Hampton Roads	ECHL	40	26	24	50	29	14	*16	10	*26	26
92-93	Baltimore	AHL	18	3	4	7	2	4	0	0	0	10
92-93	Hampton Roads	ECHL	37	30	22	52	63	2	3	0	3	10
93-94	Hampton Roads	ECHL	65	54	34	88	133	7	1	5	6	24
94-95	Hampton Roads	ECHL	68	38	40	78	118	4	2	1	3	6
95-96	Hampton Roads	ECHL	62	40	17	57	102	3	2	1	3	8
96-97	Hampton Roads	ECHL	68	33	33	66	137	9	3	1	4	6
97-98	Hampton Roads	ECHL	58	32	23	55	88	20	9	4	13	48
98-99	Hampton Roads	ECHL	70	23	27	50	97	4	0	0	0	30
	ECHL	Totals	468	276	220	496	767	63	36	22	58	158

Born; 12/1/66, Lake Orion, Michigan. 5-10, 185. Member of 1991-92 ECHL Champion Hampton Roads Admirals. Member of 1997-98 ECHL Champion Hampton Roads Admirals. Last amateur club; Ferris State (CCHA).

Marc Terris — Left Wing
Regular Season / Playoffs

Season	Team	League	GP	G	A	PTS	PIM	GP	G	A	PTS	PIM
94-95	Canada	National	53	4	13	17	14	—	—	—	—	—
95-96	Mobile	ECHL	30	6	13	19	18	—	—	—	—	—
95-96	Louisville	ECHL	2	0	1	1	0	—	—	—	—	—
95-96	Huntington	ECHL	31	7	10	17	4	—	—	—	—	—
96-97	Peoria	ECHL	68	20	31	51	19	10	3	7	10	2
97-98	Peoria	ECHL	50	20	19	39	20	3	0	1	1	0
98-99	Peoria	ECHL	1	0	0	0	0	—	—	—	—	—
	ECHL	Totals	182	53	74	127	61	13	3	8	11	2

Born; 9/2/72, Edmonton, Alberta. 6-1, 190. Last amateur club; Concordia

Anthony Terzo — Center
Regular Season / Playoffs

Season	Team	League	GP	G	A	PTS	PIM	GP	G	A	PTS	PIM
97-98	Toronto	OHL	66	20	20	40	57	—	—	—	—	—
97-98	Toledo	ECHL	7	1	0	1	0	2	0	0	0	0
98-99	Toledo	ECHL	70	32	36	68	37	4	1	1	2	4
	ECHL	Totals	77	33	36	69	37	6	1	1	2	4

Born; 1/18/78, Scarborough, Ontario. 6-0, 180. Traded to Charlotte by Toledo to complete earlier deal (7/99). Last amateur club; Toronto (OHL).

Doug Teskey — Goaltender
Regular Season / Playoffs

Season	Team	League	GP	W	L	T	MIN	SO	AVG	GP	W	L	MIN	SO	AVG
98-99	Alaska-Anchorage	WCHA	8	2	5	0	461	1	2.99	—	—	—	—	—	—
98-99	Anchorage	WCHL	9	6	1	0	439	0	3.41	4	2	1	187	0	3.86

Born; 4/13/75, Dryden, Ontario. 6-1, 185. Last amateur club; Alaska-Anchorage (WCHA).

Jean Paul Tessier — Defenseman
Regular Season / Playoffs

Season	Team	League	GP	G	A	PTS	PIM	GP	G	A	PTS	PIM
98-99	Ferris State	CCHA	36	0	7	7	56	—	—	—	—	—
98-99	Richmond	ECHL	9	0	0	0	4	14	0	1	1	15

Born; 8/19/74, Salol, Minnesota. 6-0, 200. Last amateur club; Ferris State

Joey Tetarenko — Defenseman
Regular Season / Playoffs

Season	Team	League	GP	G	A	PTS	PIM	GP	G	A	PTS	PIM
98-99	New Haven	AHL	65	4	10	14	154	—	—	—	—	—

Born; 3/3/78, Prince Albert, Saskatchewan. 6-1, 215. Drafted by Florida Panthers (4th choice, 82nd overall) in 1996 Entry Draft. Last amateur club; Portland

Alexei Tezikov — Defenseman
Regular Season / Playoffs

Season	Team	League	GP	G	A	PTS	PIM	GP	G	A	PTS	PIM
98-99	Washington	NHL	5	0	0	0	0	—	—	—	—	—
98-99	Rochester	AHL	31	3	7	10	41	—	—	—	—	—
98-99	Cincinnati	IHL	5	0	0	0	2	3	0	0	0	10

Born; 6/22/78, Togliatti, USSR. 6-1, 198. Drafted by Buffalo Sabres (7th choice, 115th overall) in 1996 Entry Draft. Traded to Washington Capitals with future considerations by Buffalo for Joe Juneau and 1999 third round pick (Tim Preston), 3/22/99. Last amateur club; Moncton (QMJHL).

Jose Theodore — Goaltender

Regular Season / Playoffs

Season	Team	League	GP	W	L	T	MIN	SO	AVG	GP	W	L	MIN	SO	AVG
94-95	Hull	QMJHL	*58	*32	22	2	*3348	5	3.46	*21	*15	6	*1263	*1	2.80
94-95	Fredericton	AHL	—	—	—	—	—	—	—	1	0	1	60	0	3.00
95-96	Hull	QMJHL	48	33	11	2	2807	0	3.38	5	2	3	299	0	4.01
95-96	Montreal	NHL	1	0	0	0	9	0	6.67	—	—	—	—	—	—
96-97	Montreal	NHL	16	5	6	2	821	0	3.87	2	1	1	168	0	2.50
96-97	Fredericton	AHL	26	12	12	0	1469	0	3.55	—	—	—	—	—	—
97-98	Montreal	NHL	—	—	—	—	—	—	—	3	0	1	120	0	0.50
97-98	Fredericton	AHL	53	20	23	8	3053	2	2.85	4	1	3	237	0	3.28
98-99	Montreal	NHL	18	4	12	0	913	1	3.29	—	—	—	—	—	—
98-99	Fredericton	AHL	27	12	13	2	1609	2	2.87	13	8	5	694	1	3.03
	NHL	Totals	35	9	18	2	1743	1	3.58	5	1	2	288	0	1.67

Born; 9/13/76, Laval, Quebec. 5-11, 180. Drafted by Montreal Canadiens (2nd choice, 44th overall) in 1994 Entry Draft. Last amateur club; Hull (QMJHL).

Joel Theriault — Defenseman

Regular Season / Playoffs

Season	Team	League	GP	G	A	PTS	PIM	GP	G	A	PTS	PIM
96-97	Hampton Roads	ECHL	50	2	4	6	206	6	0	0	0	10
97-98	Portland	AHL	15	0	2	2	89	—	—	—	—	—
97-98	Hampton Roads	ECHL	32	2	4	6	161	—	—	—	—	—
97-98	Mobile	ECHL	10	1	1	2	43	2	2	1	3	18
98-99	Mobile	ECHL	19	2	0	2	95	—	—	—	—	—
98-99	Jacksonville	ECHL	43	4	5	9	164	2	0	0	0	19
	ECHL	Totals	154	11	14	25	669	10	2	1	3	47

Born; 10/30/76, Montreal, Quebec. 6-3, 201. Drafted by Washington Capitals (5th choice, 95th overall) in 1995 Entry Draft. Last amateur club; Drummondville (QMJHL).

Mario Therrien — Left Wing

Regular Season / Playoffs

Season	Team	League	GP	G	A	PTS	PIM	GP	G	A	PTS	PIM
96-97	Macon	CeHL	66	30	22	52	96	5	0	3	3	32
97-98	Idaho	WCHL	48	24	21	45	85	4	1	2	3	2
98-99	Idaho	WCHL	35	15	21	36	100	—	—	—	—	—
98-99	Phoenix	WCHL	14	14	7	21	40	3	1	0	1	2
	WCHL	Totals	97	53	49	102	140	7	2	2	4	4

Born; 5/18/72, Ste. Anne Des Plaines, Quebec. 6-3, 225. Traded to Phoenix by Idaho with Alex Alepin for Stu Kulak and Jason Rose (2/99).

Benoit Thibert — Goaltender

Regular Season / Playoffs

Season	Team	League	GP	W	L	T	MIN	SO	AVG	GP	W	L	MIN	SO	AVG
98-99	Memphis	CHL	2	0	2	0	91	0	9.21	—	—	—	—	—	—
98-99	Alexandria	WPHL	32	13	9	7	1813	0	3.61	—	—	—	—	—	—

Born; 7/22/77, Chateauguay, Quebec. 5-11, 180.

Travis Thiessen — Defenseman

Regular Season / Playoffs

Season	Team	League	GP	G	A	PTS	PIM	GP	G	A	PTS	PIM
92-93	Cleveland	IHL	64	3	7	10	69	4	0	0	0	16
93-94	Cleveland	IHL	74	2	13	15	75	—	—	—	—	—
94-95	Indianapolis	IHL	41	2	3	5	36	—	—	—	—	—
94-95	Saint John	AHL	9	1	2	3	12	5	0	1	1	0
94-95	Flint	CoHL	5	0	1	1	2	—	—	—	—	—
95-96	Indianapolis	IHL	4	0	1	1	8	—	—	—	—	—
95-96	Peoria	IHL	63	3	12	15	102	12	1	4	5	8
96-97	Indianapolis	IHL	8	0	3	3	8	—	—	—	—	—
96-97	Manitoba	IHL	25	0	8	8	28	—	—	—	—	—
96-97	Peoria	ECHL	14	1	6	7	12	10	0	6	6	12
97-98	Rosenheim	Germany	39	2	12	14	56	—	—	—	—	—
98-99	London	BSL	29	2	11	13	28	5	0	1	1	4
	IHL	Totals	279	10	47	57	326	16	1	4	5	24

Born; 7/11/72, North Battleford, Saskatchewan. 6-3, 202. Drafted by Pittsburgh Penguins (3rd choice, 67th overall) in 1992 Entry Draft. Signed as a free agent by Chicago Blackhawks (6/9/94). Last amateur club; Moose Jaw (WHL).

Darren Thomas — Goaltender

Regular Season / Playoffs

Season	Team	League	GP	W	L	T	MIN	SO	AVG	GP	W	L	MIN	SO	AVG
97-98	Winston-Salem	UHL	12	3	7	0	649	0	5.82	—	—	—	—	—	—
98-99	Memphis	CHL	3	1	1	0	93	1	3.89	—	—	—	—	—	—

Born; 12/2/75, Concord, Massachusetts. 5-10, 180. Last amateur club; Salem State (NCAA 3).

Kahlil Thomas — Center

Regular Season / Playoffs

Season	Team	League	GP	G	A	PTS	PIM	GP	G	A	PTS	PIM
96-97	Columbus	CeHL	1	0	0	0	0	—	—	—	—	—
96-97	Detroit	IHL	1	1	0	1	0	—	—	—	—	—
96-97	Pensacola	ECHL	5	0	1	1	0	—	—	—	—	—
96-97	Flint	CoHL	50	26	26	52	51	14	4	4	8	6
97-98	Flint	UHL	61	24	58	82	34	17	12	9	21	8
98-99	Flint	UHL	35	19	20	39	26	12	5	0	5	6
	UHL	Totals	146	69	104	173	111	43	21	13	34	20

Born; 12/22/75, Toronto, Ontario. 5-9, 190.

Scott Thomas — Right Wing

Regular Season / Playoffs

Season	Team	League	GP	G	A	PTS	PIM	GP	G	A	PTS	PIM
91-92	Clarkson	ECAC	30	*25	21	46	62	—	—	—	—	—
91-92	Rochester	AHL	—	—	—	—	—	9	0	1	1	17
92-93	Buffalo	NHL	7	1	1	2	15	—	—	—	—	—
92-93	Rochester	AHL	65	32	27	59	38	17	8	5	13	6
93-94	Buffalo	NHL	32	2	2	4	8	—	—	—	—	—
93-94	Rochester	AHL	11	4	5	9	0	—	—	—	—	—
94-95	Rochester	AHL	55	21	25	46	115	5	4	0	4	4
95-96	Cincinnati	IHL	78	32	28	60	54	17	13	2	15	4
96-97	Cincinnati	IHL	71	32	29	61	46	3	0	0	0	0
97-98	Detroit	IHL	44	11	16	27	18	—	—	—	—	—
97-98	Manitoba	IHL	26	12	4	16	8	3	0	1	1	2
98-99	Manitoba	IHL	78	45	25	70	32	5	3	4	7	4
	NHL	Totals	39	3	3	6	23	—	—	—	—	—
	IHL	Totals	297	132	102	234	158	28	16	7	23	10
	AHL	Totals	131	57	57	114	153	31	12	6	18	27

Born; 1/18/70, Buffalo, New York. 6-2, 202. Drafted by Buffalo Sabres (2nd choice, 56th overall) in 1989 Entry Draft. Traded to Manitoba by Detroit for Rich Parent (2/98). 1998-99 IHL First Team All-Star. Last amateur club; Clarkson

Tim Thomas — Goaltender

Regular Season / Playoffs

Season	Team	League	GP	W	L	T	MIN	SO	AVG	GP	W	L	MIN	SO	AVG
97-98	Houston	IHL	1	0	1	0	60	0	4.01	—	—	—	—	—	—
97-98	Birmingham	ECHL	6	4	1	1	360	1	2.17	—	—	—	—	—	—
97-98	Helsinki	Finland	22	13	4	1	1035	2	1.62	9	9	0	551	3	1.52
98-99	Hamilton	AHL	15	6	8	0	837	0	3.23	—	—	—	—	—	—
98-99	Helsinki	Finland	14	8	3	3	833	2	2.23	11	7	4	658	0	2.28

Born; 4/15/74, Flint, Michigan. 5-11, 180. Drafted by Quebec Nordiques (11th choice, 217th overall) in 1994 Entry Draft. Signed as a free agent by Edmonton Oilers (6/4/98). Last amateur club; Vermont (ECAC).

Brent Thompson
Defenseman

Regular Season / Playoffs

Season	Team	League	GP	G	A	PTS	PIM	GP	G	A	PTS	PIM
90-91	Medicine Hat	WHL	51	5	40	45	87	12	1	7	8	16
90-91	Phoenix	IHL	—	—	—	—	—	4	0	1	1	6
91-92	Los Angeles	NHL	27	0	5	5	89	4	0	0	0	4
91-92	Phoenix	IHL	42	4	13	17	139	—	—	—	—	—
92-93	Los Angeles	NHL	30	0	4	4	76	—	—	—	—	—
92-93	Phoenix	IHL	22	0	5	5	112	—	—	—	—	—
93-94	Los Angeles	NHL	24	1	0	1	81	—	—	—	—	—
93-94	Phoenix	IHL	26	1	11	12	118	—	—	—	—	—
94-95	Winnipeg	NHL	29	0	0	0	78	—	—	—	—	—
95-96	Winnipeg	NHL	10	0	1	1	21	—	—	—	—	—
95-96	Springfield	AHL	58	2	10	12	203	10	1	4	5	*55
96-97	Phoenix	NHL	1	0	0	0	7	—	—	—	—	—
96-97	Phoenix	IHL	12	0	1	1	67	—	—	—	—	—
96-97	Springfield	AHL	64	2	15	17	215	17	0	2	2	31
97-98	Hartford	AHL	77	4	15	19	308	15	0	4	4	25
98-99	Hartford	AHL	76	3	15	18	265	7	0	0	0	23
	NHL	Totals	121	1	10	11	352	4	0	0	0	4
	AHL	Totals	275	11	55	66	991	49	1	10	11	134
	IHL	Totals	102	5	30	35	436	4	0	1	1	6

Born; 1/9/71, Calgary, Alberta. 6-2, 190. Drafted by Los Angeles Kings (1st choice, 39th overall) in 1989 Entry Draft. Traded to Winnipeg Jets by Los Angeles with future considerations for the rights to Ruslan Batyrshin and Phoenix Coyotes' second round choice (Marian Cisar) in 1986 Entry Draft (8/8/94). Signed as a free agent by New York Rangers (8/26/97). Signed as a free agent by Florida Panthers (7/21/99). 1998-99 AHL Man of the Year. Last amateur club;

Briane Thompson
Defenseman

Regular Season / Playoffs

Season	Team	League	GP	G	A	PTS	PIM	GP	G	A	PTS	PIM
98-99	Bakersfield	WCHL	44	7	17	24	142	2	0	0	0	4

Born; 4/17/74, Millbrooke, Ontario. 6-4, 220. Last amateur club; Guelph

Chris Thompson
Defenseman/Left Wing

Regular Season / Playoffs

Season	Team	League	GP	G	A	PTS	PIM	GP	G	A	PTS	PIM
98-99	Albany	AHL	9	0	0	0	14	—	—	—	—	—
98-99	Augusta	ECHL	57	16	14	30	221	2	0	0	0	4

Born; 4/10/78, Prince Albert, Saskatchewan. 6-0, 180. Signed as a free agent by New Jersey Devils (7/23/98). Last amateur club; Seattle (WHL).

Jamie Thompson
Left Wing

Regular Season / Playoffs

Season	Team	League	GP	G	A	PTS	PIM	GP	G	A	PTS	PIM
96-97	El Paso	WPHL	50	34	28	62	65	9	4	8	12	12
97-98	Utah	IHL	6	2	1	3	2	—	—	—	—	—
97-98	El Paso	WPHL	58	*71	51	122	34	15	*15	11	*26	8
98-99	Worcester	AHL	25	7	3	10	12	1	0	0	0	0
98-99	Peoria	ECHL	43	21	22	43	37	2	3	0	3	2
	WPHL	Totals	108	105	79	184	99	24	19	19	38	20

Born; 3/24/74, Framingham, Massachusetts. 6-0, 200. Signed as a free agent by St. Louis Blues (7/15/98). 1997-98 WPHL MVP. 1997-98 WPHL Man Of the Year. Member of 1996-97 WPHL Champion El Paso Buzzards. Member of 1997-98 WPHL Champion El Paso Buzzards. Last amateur club; Maine (Hockey East).

Jeremy Thompson
Right Wing

Regular Season / Playoffs

Season	Team	League	GP	G	A	PTS	PIM	GP	G	A	PTS	PIM
95-96	Tri-City	WHL	42	4	3	7	102	—	—	—	—	—
95-96	Moose Jaw	WHL	23	4	3	7	52	—	—	—	—	—
95-96	Nashville	CeHL	3	2	0	2	6	5	2	0	2	5
96-97	Austin	WPHL	8	4	3	7	20	6	3	1	4	31
96-97	Reno	WCHL	48	11	18	29	150	—	—	—	—	—
97-98	Austin	WPHL	36	1	6	7	222	5	1	0	1	22
98-99	Hershey	AHL	1	0	0	0	2	—	—	—	—	—
98-99	Johnstown	ECHL	54	3	6	9	224	—	—	—	—	—
	WPHL	Totals	44	5	9	14	242	11	4	1	5	53

Born; 4/8/75, Whitecourt, Alberta. 5-11, 190. Last amateur club; Moose Jaw

Rocky Thompson
Defenseman

Regular Season / Playoffs

Season	Team	League	GP	G	A	PTS	PIM	GP	G	A	PTS	PIM
95-96	Medicine Hat	WHL	71	9	20	29	260	5	2	3	5	26
95-96	Saint John	AHL	4	0	0	0	33	—	—	—	—	—
96-97	Medicine Hat	WHL	47	6	9	15	170	—	—	—	—	—
96-97	Swift Current	WHL	22	3	5	8	90	10	1	2	3	22
97-98	Calgary	NHL	12	0	0	0	61	—	—	—	—	—
97-98	Saint John	AHL	51	3	0	3	187	18	1	1	2	47
98-99	Calgary	NHL	3	0	0	0	25	—	—	—	—	—
98-99	Saint John	AHL	27	2	2	4	108	—	—	—	—	—
	NHL	Totals	15	0	0	0	86	—	—	—	—	—
	AHL	Totals	82	5	2	7	328	18	1	1	2	47

Born; 8/8/77, Calgary, Alberta. 6-2, 192. Drafted by Calgary Flames (3rd choice, 72nd overall) in 1995 Entry Draft. Last amateur club; Swift Current (WHL).

Scott Thompson
Defenseman

Regular Season / Playoffs

Season	Team	League	GP	G	A	PTS	PIM	GP	G	A	PTS	PIM
97-98	London	OHL	5	0	0	0	2	—	—	—	—	—
97-98	Manitoba	IHL	1	0	0	0	0	—	—	—	—	—
97-98	Jacksonville	ECHL	22	0	1	1	27	—	—	—	—	—
97-98	Dayton	ECHL	41	2	5	7	67	5	0	0	0	4
98-99	Dayton	ECHL	1	0	0	0	0	—	—	—	—	—
98-99	Quad City	UHL	49	1	8	9	120	—	—	—	—	—
	ECHL	Totals	64	2	6	8	94	5	0	0	0	4

Born; 1/27/76, Kingston, Ontario. 6-2, 220. Traded to Dayton by Jacksonville for Jean-ian Filiatrault (12/97). Selected by Madison in 1999 UHL Expansion Draft. Last amateur club; London (OHL).

Tim Thompson
Defenseman

Regular Season / Playoffs

Season	Team	League	GP	G	A	PTS	PIM	GP	G	A	PTS	PIM
98-99	New Mexico	WPHL	41	2	9	11	10	—	—	—	—	—

Born; 2/19/74, Toronto, Ontario. 6-2, 205. Last amateur club; Guelph (OUAA).

Bobby Thornton
Center

Regular Season / Playoffs

Season	Team	League	GP	G	A	PTS	PIM	GP	G	A	PTS	PIM
96-97	San Diego	WCHL	7	0	0	0	0	—	—	—	—	—
96-97	Alaska	WCHL	23	5	13	18	8	—	—	—	—	—
97-98	Tacoma	WCHL	20	3	2	5	10	—	—	—	—	—
97-98	Tucson	WCHL	18	1	4	5	10	—	—	—	—	—
97-98	Bakersfield	WCHL	7	2	1	3	2	4	0	0	0	4
98-99	Bakersfield	WCHL	5	0	0	0	2	—	—	—	—	—
98-99	Dayton	ECHL	13	2	0	2	10	—	—	—	—	—
98-99	Chesapeake	ECHL	27	7	7	14	19	8	0	1	1	12
	WCHL	Totals	80	11	20	31	32	4	0	0	0	4
	ECHL	Totals	40	9	7	16	29	8	0	1	1	12

Born; 2/18/75, Manhasset, New York. 6-1, 195. Last amateur club; Seattle

Shawn Thornton
Right Wing

Regular Season / Playoffs

Season	Team	League	GP	G	A	PTS	PIM	GP	G	A	PTS	PIM
97-98	St. John's	AHL	59	0	3	3	225	—	—	—	—	—
98-99	St. John's	AHL	78	8	11	19	354	5	0	0	0	9
	AHL	Totals	137	8	14	22	579	5	0	0	0	9

Born; 7/23/79, Oshawa, Ontario. 6-1, 202. Drafted by Toronto Maple Leafs (6th choice, 190th overall) in 1997 Entry Draft. Last amateur club; Peterborough

Rob Thorpe
Right Wing

Regular Season / Playoffs

Season	Team	League	GP	G	A	PTS	PIM	GP	G	A	PTS	PIM
96-97	Michigan	IHL	1	0	0	0	0	—	—	—	—	—
96-97	Toledo	ECHL	68	47	28	75	64	2	1	1	2	0
97-98	Toledo	ECHL	69	39	26	65	80	7	5	3	8	12
98-99	Toledo	ECHL	40	20	13	33	63	7	3	0	3	12
	ECHL	Totals	177	106	67	173	207	16	9	4	13	24

Born; 7/22/73, Hamilton, Ontario. 6-0, 200. Last amateur club; Guelph (OUAA).

Chuck Thuss — Goaltender

Regular Season / Playoffs

Season	Team	League	GP	W	L	T	MIN	SO	AVG	GP	W	L	MIN	SO	AVG
95-96	Los Angeles	IHL	22	5	10	1	976	0	3.93	—	—	—	—	—	—
95-96	Louisiana	ECHL	15	6	4	1	686	0	3.67	3	2	1	143	0	4.62
96-97	Birmingham	ECHL	27	10	8	5	1435	1	4.31	—	—	—	—	—	—
96-97	Mobile	ECHL	9	4	3	1	442	0	3.12	2	0	2	119	0	4.04
97-98	Houston	IHL	1	1	0	0	60	0	4.00	—	—	—	—	—	—
97-98	Mobile	ECHL	38	14	14	6	1983	2	3.06	2	0	1	72	0	5.02
98-99	Mississippi	ECHL	37	19	10	2	1850	3	3.02	—	—	—	—	—	—
	IHL	Totals	23	6	10	1	1036	0	3.94	—	—	—	—	—	—
	ECHL	Totals	126	53	39	15	6396	6	3.40	7	2	4	334	0	4.49

Born; 2/15/72, Arkona, Ontario. 6-1, 193. Member of 1998-99 ECHL Champion Mississippi SeaWolves. Last amateur club; Miami of Ohio (CCHA).

Dan Tice — Right Wing

Regular Season / Playoffs

Season	Team	League	GP	G	A	PTS	PIM	GP	G	A	PTS	PIM
98-99	Winston-Salem	UHL	5	0	0	0	45	—	—	—	—	—

Born; 3/9/72, London, Ontario. 5-11, 205.

Brad Tiley — Defenseman

Regular Season / Playoffs

Season	Team	League	GP	G	A	PTS	PIM	GP	G	A	PTS	PIM
91-92	Maine	AHL	62	7	22	29	36	—	—	—	—	—
92-93	Binghamton	AHL	26	6	10	16	19	8	0	1	1	2
92-93	Phoenix	IHL	46	11	27	38	35	—	—	—	—	—
93-94	Binghamton	AHL	29	6	10	16	6	—	—	—	—	—
93-94	Phoenix	IHL	35	8	15	23	21	—	—	—	—	—
94-95	Detroit	IHL	56	7	19	26	32	—	—	—	—	—
94-95	Fort Wayne	IHL	14	1	6	7	2	3	1	2	3	0
95-96	Orlando	IHL	69	11	23	34	82	23	2	4	6	16
96-97	Long Beach	IHL	3	1	0	1	2	—	—	—	—	—
96-97	Phoenix	IHL	66	8	28	36	34	—	—	—	—	—
97-98	Phoenix	NHL	1	0	0	0	0	—	—	—	—	—
97-98	Springfield	AHL	60	10	31	41	36	4	0	4	4	2
98-99	Phoenix	NHL	8	0	0	0	0	1	0	0	0	0
98-99	Springfield	AHL	69	9	35	44	14	1	0	0	0	0
	NHL	Totals	9	0	0	0	0	1	0	0	0	0
	IHL	Totals	289	47	118	165	208	26	3	6	9	16
	AHL	Totals	246	38	108	146	111	13	0	5	5	4

Born; 7/5/71, Markdale, Ontario. 6-1, 190. Drafted by Boston Bruins (fourth choice, 84th overall) in 1991 Entry Draft. Signed as a free agent by New York Rangers (9/4/92). Signed as a free agent by Phoenix Coyotes (8/28/97). Last amateur club; Sault Ste. Marie (OHL).

Tom Tilley — Defenseman

Regular Season / Playoffs

Season	Team	League	GP	G	A	PTS	PIM	GP	G	A	PTS	PIM
88-89	St. Louis	NHL	70	1	22	23	47	10	1	2	3	17
89-90	St. Louis	NHL	34	0	5	5	6	—	—	—	—	—
89-90	Peoria	IHL	22	1	8	9	13	—	—	—	—	—
90-91	St. Louis	NHL	22	2	4	6	4	—	—	—	—	—
90-91	Peoria	IHL	48	7	38	45	53	13	2	9	11	25
91-92	Milan	Italy	18	7	13	20	12	12	5	12	17	10
92-93	Milan	Alpenliga	32	5	17	22	21	—	—	—	—	—
92-93	Milan	Italy	14	8	3	11	2	8	1	5	6	4
93-94	St. Louis	NHL	48	1	7	8	32	4	0	1	1	2
94-95	Atlanta	IHL	10	2	6	8	14	—	—	—	—	—
94-95	Indianapolis	IHL	25	2	13	15	19	—	—	—	—	—
95-96	Milwaukee	IHL	80	11	68	79	58	4	2	2	4	4
96-97	Milwaukee	IHL	25	1	10	11	8	3	0	1	1	0
97-98	Chicago	IHL	73	9	49	58	49	22	2	*17	19	14
98-99	Chicago	IHL	73	5	55	60	32	10	1	1	2	2
	NHL	Totals	174	4	38	42	89	14	1	3	4	19
	IHL	Totals	356	38	247	285	246	52	7	30	37	45

Born; 3/28/65, Trenton, Ontario. 6-0, 190. Drafted by St. Louis Blues (13th choice, 196th overall) in 1984 Entry Draft. Traded to Tampa Bay Lightning by St. Louis for Adam Creighton (10/6/94). Traded to Chicago Blackhawks by Tampa Bay with Jim Cummins and Jeff Buchanan for Paul Ysebaert and Rich Sutter(2/22/95). 1990-91 IHL Second Team All-Star. 1995-96 IHL Second Team All-Star. 1998-99 IHL Second Team All-Star. Member of 1990-91 IHL champion Peoria Rivermen. Member of 1997-98 IHL Champion Chicago Wolves. Last amateur club; Michigan State (CCHA).

Mike Tilson — Defenseman

Regular Season / Playoffs

Season	Team	League	GP	G	A	PTS	PIM	GP	G	A	PTS	PIM
98-99	Topeka	CHL	—	—	—	—	—	1	0	0	0	0

Born;

Dean Tiltgen — Center

Regular Season / Playoffs

Season	Team	League	GP	G	A	PTS	PIM	GP	G	A	PTS	PIM
97-98	Baton Rouge	ECHL	61	14	15	29	41	—	—	—	—	—
98-99	Arkansas	WPHL	69	30	39	69	79	3	1	1	2	0

Born; 2/3/74, Edmonton, Alberta. 6-0, 188. Last amateur club; Alberta

Mattias Timander — Defenseman

Regular Season / Playoffs

Season	Team	League	GP	G	A	PTS	PIM	GP	G	A	PTS	PIM
96-97	Boston	NHL	41	1	8	9	14	—	—	—	—	—
96-97	Providence	AHL	32	3	11	14	20	10	1	1	2	12
97-98	Boston	NHL	23	1	1	2	6	—	—	—	—	—
97-98	Providence	AHL	31	3	7	10	25	—	—	—	—	—
98-99	Boston	NHL	22	0	6	6	10	4	1	1	2	2
98-99	Providence	AHL	43	2	22	24	24	—	—	—	—	—
	NHL	Totals	86	2	15	17	30	4	1	1	2	2
	AHL	Totals	106	8	40	48	69	10	1	1	2	12

Born; 4/16/74, Solleftea, Sweden. 6-1, 194. Drafted by Boston Bruins (7th choice, 208th overall) in 1992 Entry Draft.

Kimmo Timonen — Defenseman

Regular Season / Playoffs

Season	Team	League	GP	G	A	PTS	PIM	GP	G	A	PTS	PIM
98-99	Nashville	NHL	50	4	8	12	30	—	—	—	—	—
98-99	Milwaukee	IHL	29	2	13	15	22	—	—	—	—	—

Born; 3/18/75, Kuopio, Finland. 5-9, 180. Drafted by Los Angeles Kings (11th choice, 250th overall) in 1993 Entry Draft. Traded to Nashville Predators by Los Angeles with Jan Vopat for future considerations (6/26/98). Last European club; Helsinki (Finland).

Travis Tipler — Left Wing

Regular Season / Playoffs

Season	Team	League	GP	G	A	PTS	PIM	GP	G	A	PTS	PIM
98-99	Wichita	CHL	10	4	3	7	14	4	1	0	1	7

Born; 1/10/78, Wainwright, Manitoba. 6-1, 210. Last amateur club; Weyburn (SJHL).

Mikael Tjallden — Defenseman

Regular Season / Playoffs

Season	Team	League	GP	G	A	PTS	PIM	GP	G	A	PTS	PIM
97-98	Syracuse	AHL	3	0	1	1	0	—	—	—	—	—
97-98	Tallahassee	ECHL	37	3	13	16	60	—	—	—	—	—
98-99	Asiago	Italy										

Born; 2/16/75, Ornskoldsvik, Sweden. 6-2, 194. Drafted by Florida Panthers (4th choice, 67th overall) in 1993 Entry Draft.

Sergei Tkachenko — Goaltender

Regular Season / Playoffs

Season	Team	League	GP	W	L	T	MIN	SO	AVG	GP	W	L	MIN	SO	AVG
92-93	Hamilton	AHL	1	1	0	0	60	0	3.00	—	—	—	—	—	—
92-93	Brantford	CoHL	4	0	1	0	96	0	6.88	—	—	—	—	—	—
93-94	Hamilton	AHL	2	0	1	1	125	0	4.32	—	—	—	—	—	—
93-94	Columbus	ECHL	34	18	7	4	1884	0	4.11	4	1	2	182	0	5.27
94-95	Syracuse	AHL	2	0	2	0	118	0	4.57	—	—	—	—	—	—
94-95	South Carolina	ECHL	16	7	7	1	868	0	3.25	—	—	—	—	—	—
94-95	Birmingham	ECHL	6	2	4	0	359	0	4.17	—	—	—	—	—	—
95-96	Syracuse	AHL	14	2	8	1	733	2	4.26	1	0	1	60	0	5.00
95-96	Oklahoma City	CeHL	16	12	3	1	944	1	2.35	1	0	1	63	0	4.73
95-96	Raleigh	ECHL	3	0	2	1	179	0	4.69	—	—	—	—	—	—
96-97	Louisiana	ECHL	10	5	3	1	524	0	4.46	—	—	—	—	—	—
96-97	Knoxville	ECHL	22	6	14	0	1234	0	3.79	—	—	—	—	—	—
96-97	Utica	CoHL	—	—	—	—	—	—	—	3	0	3	178	0	4.73
97-98	Anchorage	WCHL	32	20	7	4	1861	1	3.80	5	3	2	300	*1	2.40
98-99	Anchorage	WCHL	56	*35	15	2	3106	2	3.36	4	0	3	175	0	5.84
	AHL	Totals	19	3	11	2	1036	2	4.23	1	0	1	60	0	5.00
	ECHL	Totals	91	38	37	7	5049	0	3.95	4	1	2	182	0	5.27
	WCHL	Totals	88	55	22	6	4967	3	3.53	9	3	5	475	1	3.67
	CoHL	Totals	4	0	1	0	96	0	6.88	3	0	3	178	0	4.73

Born; 6/6/71, Kiev, USSR. 6-2, 198. Drafted by Vancouver Canucks (9th choice, 280th overall) in 1993 Entry Draft. Member of 1995-96 CeHL champion Oklahoma City Blazers.

Stas Tkatch — Left Wing

Regular Season / Playoffs

Season	Team	League	GP	G	A	PTS	PIM	GP	G	A	PTS	PIM
92-93	Nashville	ECHL	52	13	18	31	96	8	2	1	3	15
93-94	Nashville	ECHL	67	36	35	71	143	2	0	0	0	5
94-95	Detroit	CoHL	74	39	45	84	72	12	0	2	2	6
95-96	Madison	CoHL	68	39	23	62	117	6	0	2	2	4
96-97	Madison	CoHL	46	23	33	56	53	—	—	—	—	—
96-97	Quad City	CoHL	23	13	18	31	36	15	3	7	10	24
97-98	Portland	AHL	1	0	0	0	0	—	—	—	—	—
97-98	Quad City	UHL	72	43	58	101	113	20	6	12	18	26
98-99	Chicago	IHL	1	0	0	0	0	—	—	—	—	—
98-99	Memphis	CHL	30	12	19	31	24	2	1	2	3	4
	UHL	Totals	214	121	126	247	302	53	9	23	32	60
	ECHL	Totals	119	49	53	102	239	10	2	1	3	20

Born; 7/12/71, Moscow, Russia. 6-1, 183. 1997-98 UHL Second Team All-Star. Member of 1996-97 CoHL Champion Quad City Mallards. Member of 1997-98 UHL Champion Quad City Mallards.

Mike Tobin — Defenseman

Regular Season / Playoffs

Season	Team	League	GP	G	A	PTS	PIM	GP	G	A	PTS	PIM
96-97	Brantford	CoHL	1	0	0	0	0	—	—	—	—	—
96-97	El Paso	WPHL	24	1	3	4	66	10	0	0	0	12
97-98	Phoenix	WCHL	61	4	2	6	211	9	0	2	2	70
98-99	San Antonio	CHL	51	5	16	21	186	—	—	—	—	—
98-99	Oklahoma City	CHL	10	1	2	3	53	13	0	6	6	34
	CHL	Totals	61	6	18	24	239	13	0	6	6	34

Born; 4/25/71, Toronto, Ontario. 5-11, 217. Traded to Fort Worth by San Antonio for Gatis Tseplis (2/99). Member of 1996-97 WPHL Champion El Paso Buzzards.

Ryan Tobler — Left Wing

Regular Season / Playoffs

Season	Team	League	GP	G	A	PTS	PIM	GP	G	A	PTS	PIM
97-98	Utah	IHL	3	1	0	1	2	—	—	—	—	—
97-98	Lake Charles	WPHL	66	22	34	56	204	4	2	3	5	18
98-99	Adirondack	AHL	64	9	18	27	157	3	0	0	0	2

Born; 5/13/76, Calgary, Alberta. 6-3, 215. Last amateur club; Moose Jaw (WHL).

Kevin Todd — Center

Regular Season / Playoffs

Season	Team	League	GP	G	A	PTS	PIM	GP	G	A	PTS	PIM
88-89	New Jersey	NHL	1	0	0	0	0	—	—	—	—	—
88-89	Utica	AHL	78	26	45	61	62	4	2	0	2	6
89-90	Utica	AHL	71	18	36	54	72	5	2	4	6	2
90-91	New Jersey	NHL	1	0	0	0	0	1	0	0	0	6
90-91	Utica	AHL	75	37	*81	*118	75	—	—	—	—	—
91-92	New Jersey	NHL	80	21	42	63	69	7	3	2	5	8
92-93	New Jersey	NHL	30	5	5	10	16	—	—	—	—	—
92-93	Utica	AHL	2	2	1	3	0	—	—	—	—	—
92-93	Edmonton	NHL	25	4	9	13	10	—	—	—	—	—
93-94	Chicago	NHL	35	5	6	11	16	—	—	—	—	—
93-94	Los Angeles	NHL	12	3	8	11	8	—	—	—	—	—
94-95	Utica	CoHL	2	1	3	4	0	—	—	—	—	—
94-95	Los Angeles	NHL	33	3	8	11	12	—	—	—	—	—
95-96	Los Angeles	NHL	74	16	27	43	38	—	—	—	—	—
96-97	Anaheim	NHL	65	9	21	30	44	4	0	0	0	2
97-98	Anaheim	NHL	27	4	7	11	12	—	—	—	—	—
97-98	Long Beach	IHL	30	18	28	46	54	13	1	10	11	38
98-99	EV Zug	Switz.	40	9	41	50	81	5	0	2	2	2
	NHL	Totals	383	70	133	203	225	12	3	2	5	16
	AHL	Totals	226	83	163	246	209	9	2	6	8	8

Born; 5/4/68, Winnipeg, Manitoba. 5-10, 180. Drafted by New Jersey Devils (7th choice, 129th overall) in 1986 Entry Draft. Traded to Edmonton Oilers by New Jersey with Zdeno Ciger for Bernie Nicholls (1/13/93). Traded to Chicago Blackhawks by Edmonton for Adam Bennett (10/7/93). Traded to Los Angeles Kings by Chicago for Los Angeles' fourth round choice (Steve McLaren) in 1994 Entry Draft (3/21/94). Signed as a free agent by Pittsburgh Penguins (7/10/96). Claimed on waivers by Anaheim Mighty Ducks from Pittsburgh (10/4/96). 1990-91 AHL MVP. 1990-91 AHL First Team All-Star. 1991-92 NHL All-Rookie Team. Last amateur club; Prince Albert (WHL).

Lorne Toews — Left Wing

Regular Season / Playoffs

Season	Team	League	GP	G	A	PTS	PIM	GP	G	A	PTS	PIM
94-95	Wheeling	ECHL	54	8	11	19	71	3	0	1	1	2
95-96	Wheeling	ECHL	35	3	7	10	88	—	—	—	—	—
95-96	Columbus	ECHL	16	3	6	9	65	3	2	1	3	4
96-97	Baltimore	AHL	1	0	0	0	0	—	—	—	—	—
96-97	Columbus	ECHL	70	25	25	50	198	8	1	5	6	14
97-98	Las Vegas	IHL	3	0	0	0	0	—	—	—	—	—
97-98	Portland	AHL	6	1	1	2	0	2	0	1	1	0
97-98	Columbus	ECHL	67	29	23	52	248	—	—	—	—	—
98-99	Las Vegas	IHL	13	1	0	1	15	—	—	—	—	—
98-99	Corpus Christi	WPHL	64	34	32	66	252	4	3	3	6	10
	AHL	Totals	7	1	1	2	0	2	0	1	1	0
	IHL	Totals	16	1	0	1	15	—	—	—	—	—
	ECHL	Totals	172	43	47	90	472	6	2	2	4	6

Born; 6/17/73, Winnipeg, Manitoba. 6-0, 195. Last amateur club; Medicine Hat (WHL).

Chris Tok — Defenseman

Regular Season / Playoffs

Season	Team	League	GP	G	A	PTS	PIM	GP	G	A	PTS	PIM
95-96	Jacksonville	ECHL	8	1	3	4	21	—	—	—	—	—
95-96	Fort Wayne	IHL	60	2	4	6	120	4	0	0	0	19
96-97	Fort Wayne	IHL	19	1	3	4	35	—	—	—	—	—
96-97	Manitoba	IHL	48	0	4	4	74	—	—	—	—	—
97-98	Cincinnati	AHL	48	3	9	12	58	—	—	—	—	—
98-99	Ljubljana	Austria										
	IHL	Totals	127	3	11	14	229	4	0	0	0	19

Born; 3/19/73, Grand Rapids, Michigan. 6-1, 185. Drafted by Pittsburgh Penguins (10th choice, 214th overall) in 1991 Entry Draft. Last amateur club; Wisconsin (WCHA).

Steven Toll — Right Wing
Regular Season / Playoffs

Season	Team	League	GP	G	A	PTS	PIM	GP	G	A	PTS	PIM
96-97	R.I.T.	Div. 3	30	39	45	84	NA	—	—	—	—	—
96-97	Raleigh	ECHL	7	1	3	4	2	—	—	—	—	—
97-98	Columbus	CHL	12	2	3	5	4	—	—	—	—	—
97-98	Fayetteville	CHL	50	23	38	61	41	—	—	—	—	—
98-99	Fayetteville	CHL	59	19	26	45	21	—	—	—	—	—
	CHL	Totals	121	44	67	111	66	—	—	—	—	—

Born; 6/16/74, Thurold, Ontario. 6-0, 186. Traded by Columbus to Fayetteville for Kevin Hastings (12/97). Selected by Indianapolis in 1999 CHL Expansion Draft. Last amateur club; Rochester Institute of Technology (NCAA 3).

Scott Tollestrup — Goaltender
Regular Season / Playoffs

Season	Team	League	GP	W	L	T	MIN	SO	AVG	GP	W	L	MIN	SO	AVG
98-99	Toledo	ECHL	4	1	1	0	141	0	3.83	—	—	—	—	—	—

Born; Last amateur club; Lethbridge (CWUAA).

Janis Tomans — Left Wing
Regular Season / Playoffs

Season	Team	League	GP	G	A	PTS	PIM	GP	G	A	PTS	PIM
95-96	Jacksonville	ECHL	32	17	18	35	35	18	6	7	13	21
96-97	San Antonio	IHL	8	1	2	3	6	—	—	—	—	—
96-97	Madison	CoHL	37	24	33	57	44	5	4	1	5	6
97-98	Orlando	IHL	2	0	0	0	0	—	—	—	—	—
97-98	Detroit	IHL	6	0	1	1	4	—	—	—	—	—
97-98	Baton Rouge	ECHL	44	18	20	38	42	—	—	—	—	—
97-98	Madison	UHL	8	4	7	11	4	—	—	—	—	—
97-98	Flint	UHL	1	0	0	0	0	15	3	4	7	6
98-99	Tallahassee	ECHL	14	1	3	4	12	—	—	—	—	—
98-99	Fayetteville	CHL	37	12	16	28	48	—	—	—	—	—
	IHL	Totals	16	1	3	4	10	—	—	—	—	—
	ECHL	Totals	90	36	41	77	89	18	6	7	13	21
	UHL	Totals	46	28	40	68	48	20	7	5	12	12

Born; 2/5/75, Riga, Latvia. 6-1, 200.

Justin Tomberlin — Forward
Regular Season / Playoffs

Season	Team	League	GP	G	A	PTS	PIM	GP	G	A	PTS	PIM
94-95	Raleigh	ECHL	53	11	18	29	17	—	—	—	—	—
95-96	Quad City	CoHL	8	1	1	2	2	—	—	—	—	—
95-96	Lakeland	SHL	46	46	48	94	42	5	4	5	9	0
96-97	Columbus	CeHL	51	24	27	51	61	3	1	2	3	0
97-98	Nashville	CHL	67	27	29	56	61	9	1	1	2	4
98-99	Fayetteville	CHL	70	29	37	66	42	—	—	—	—	—
	CHL	Totals	188	80	93	173	164	12	2	3	5	4

Born; 11/15/70, Grand Rapids, Michigan. 6-1, 195. Drafted by Toronto Maple Leafs (11th choice, 192nd overall) in 1989 Entry Draft. Selected by Fayetteville in 1998 CHL Dispersal Draft.

Mike Tomlak — Center
Regular Season / Playoffs

Season	Team	League	GP	G	A	PTS	PIM	GP	G	A	PTS	PIM
89-90	Hartford	NHL	70	7	14	21	48	7	0	1	1	2
90-91	Hartford	NHL	64	8	8	16	55	3	0	0	0	2
90-91	Springfield	AHL	15	4	9	13	15	—	—	—	—	—
91-92	Hartford	NHL	6	0	0	0	0	—	—	—	—	—
91-92	Springfield	AHL	39	16	21	37	24	—	—	—	—	—
92-93	Springfield	AHL	38	16	21	37	56	5	1	1	2	2
93-94	Hartford	NHL	1	0	0	0	0	—	—	—	—	—
93-94	Springfield	AHL	79	44	56	100	53	4	2	5	7	4
94-95	Milwaukee	IHL	63	27	41	68	54	15	4	5	9	8
95-96	Milwaukee	IHL	82	11	32	43	68	5	0	2	2	6
96-97	Milwaukee	IHL	47	8	23	31	44	—	—	—	—	—
97-98	Milwaukee	IHL	82	19	32	51	62	10	1	3	4	10
98-99	Ljubljana	Austria										
	NHL	Totals	141	15	22	37	103	10	0	1	1	4
	IHL	Totals	274	65	128	193	228	30	5	10	15	24
	AHL	Totals	171	80	107	187	148	9	3	6	9	6

Born; 10/17/65, Thunder Bay, Ontario. 6-3, 205. Drafted by Toronto Maple Leafs (10th choice, 208th overall) in 1983 Entry Draft. Signed as a free agent by Hartford Whalers (11/14/88). Last amateur club; Western Ontario (OUAA).

Mike Tomlinson — Center
Regular Season / Playoffs

Season	Team	League	GP	G	A	PTS	PIM	GP	G	A	PTS	PIM
92-93	Chatham	CoHL	48	14	27	41	58	—	—	—	—	—
92-93	Brantford	CoHL	3	0	0	0	2	—	—	—	—	—
93-94	Utica	CoHL	63	24	31	55	148	—	—	—	—	—
94-95	Utica	CoHL	52	16	20	36	128	6	0	2	2	16
95-96	Utica	CoHL	74	21	41	62	203	—	—	—	—	—
96-97	New Mexico	WPHL	58	32	45	77	143	6	1	3	4	2
97-98	Saginaw	UHL	52	17	20	37	72	—	—	—	—	—
97-98	Madison	UHL	15	6	7	13	18	6	2	1	3	16
98-99	Corpus Christi	WPHL	68	17	28	45	104	4	1	0	1	21
	UHL	Totals	307	98	146	244	629	12	2	3	5	32
	WPHL	Totals	126	49	73	122	247	10	2	3	5	23

Born; 3/23/71, Peterborough, Ontario. 6-0, 183. Last amateur club; Peterborough (OHL).

Shayne Tomlinson — Defenseman
Regular Season / Playoffs

Season	Team	League	GP	G	A	PTS	PIM	GP	G	A	PTS	PIM
96-97	Northern Michigan	WCHA	35	3	13	16	52	—	—	—	—	—
96-97	Richmond	ECHL	6	1	1	2	2	3	0	2	2	0
97-98	Richmond	ECHL	44	7	23	30	80	—	—	—	—	—
97-98	Dayton	ECHL	24	0	6	6	32	4	1	0	1	2
98-99	Dayton	ECHL	34	0	2	2	30	—	—	—	—	—
98-99	Tacoma	WCHL	13	1	5	6	10	8	0	3	3	25
	ECHL	Totals	74	8	30	38	114	7	1	2	3	2

Born; 6/13/73, Toronto, Ontario. 6-0, 195. Traded to Dayton by Richmond with Mike Noble for Sal Manganaro and Darryl Lavoie (1/98). Member of 1998-99 WCHL Champion Tacoma Sabrecats. Last amateur club; Northern Michigan (WCHA).

Jeff Toms — Left Wing
Regular Season / Playoffs

Season	Team	League	GP	G	A	PTS	PIM	GP	G	A	PTS	PIM
94-95	Atlanta	IHL	40	7	8	15	10	4	0	0	0	4
95-96	Tampa Bay	NHL	1	0	0	0	0	—	—	—	—	—
95-96	Atlanta	IHL	68	16	18	34	18	1	0	0	0	0
96-97	Tampa Bay	NHL	34	2	8	10	10	—	—	—	—	—
96-97	Adirondack	AHL	37	11	16	27	8	4	1	2	3	0
97-98	Tampa Bay	NHL	13	1	2	3	7	—	—	—	—	—
97-98	Washington	NHL	33	3	4	7	8	1	0	0	0	0
98-99	Washington	NHL	21	1	5	6	2	—	—	—	—	—
98-99	Portland	AHL	20	3	7	10	8	—	—	—	—	—
	NHL	Totals	102	7	19	26	27	1	0	0	0	0
	IHL	Totals	108	23	26	49	28	5	0	0	0	4
	AHL	Totals	57	14	23	37	16	4	1	2	3	0

Born; 6/4/74, Swift Current, Saskatchewan. 6-5, 200. Drafted by New Jersey Devils (10th choice, 210th overall) in 1992 Entry Draft. Traded to Tampa Bay Lightning by New Jersey for Vancouver's fourth round choice (previously acquired by Tampa Bay-later traded to Calgary-Calgary selected Ryan Duthie) in 1994 Entry Draft (5/31/94). Claimed on waivers by Washington Capitals from Tampa Bay (11/19/97). Last amateur club; Sault Ste. Marie (OHL).

Brad Toporowski — Defenseman
Regular Season / Playoffs

Season	Team	League	GP	G	A	PTS	PIM	GP	G	A	PTS	PIM
95-96	Erie	ECHL	65	5	12	17	154	—	—	—	—	—
96-97	Thunder Bay	CoHL	71	6	32	38	117	11	0	0	0	22
97-98	Louisiana	ECHL	6	0	0	0	6	—	—	—	—	—
97-98	Central Texas	WPHL	34	2	5	7	42	4	0	1	1	20
98-99	Colorado	WCHL	35	3	11	14	97	—	—	—	—	—
98-99	Bakersfield	WCHL	14	0	3	3	32	2	0	0	0	0
	ECHL	Totals	71	5	12	17	160	—	—	—	—	—
	WCHL	Totals	49	3	14	17	129	2	0	0	0	0

Born; 6/30/73, Paddockwood, Saskatchewan. 6-1,180. Last amateur club; Saskatchewan (CWUAA).

Shayne Toporowski — Right Wing
Regular Season — Playoffs

Season	Team	League	GP	G	A	PTS	PIM	GP	G	A	PTS	PIM
95-96	St. John's	AHL	72	11	26	37	216	4	1	1	2	4
96-97	Toronto	NHL	3	0	0	0	7	—	—	—	—	—
96-97	St. John's	AHL	72	20	17	37	210	11	3	2	5	16
97-98	Worcester	AHL	73	9	21	30	128	11	5	3	8	44
98-99	Worcester	AHL	75	18	29	47	124	4	1	0	1	6
	AHL	Totals	292	58	93	151	678	30	10	6	16	70

Born; 8/6/75, Paddockwood, Saskatchewan. 6-2, 216. Drafted by Los Angeles Kings (1st choice, 42nd overall) in 1993 Entry Draft. Traded to Toronto Maple Leafs by Los Angeles with Dixon Ward, Guy Leveque and Kelly Fairchild for Eric Lacroix, Chris Snell and Toronto's fourth round choice (Eric Belanger) in the 1996 Entry Draft. Signed as a free agent by St. Louis Blues (8/29/97). Last amateur club; Prince Albert (WHL).

Mike Torchia — Goaltender
Regular Season — Playoffs

Season	Team	League	GP	W	L	T	MIN	SO	AVG	GP	W	L	MIN	SO	AVG
92-93	Canada	Nation.	5	5	0	0	300	1	2.20	—	—	—	—	—	—
92-93	Kalamazoo	IHL	48	19	17	9	2729	0	3.80	—	—	—	—	—	—
93-94	Kalamazoo	IHL	43	23	12	2	2168	0	3.68	4	1	3	221	*1	3.80
94-95	Dallas	NHL	6	3	2	1	327	0	3.30	—	—	—	—	—	—
94-95	Kalamazoo	IHL	41	19	14	5	2140	*3	2.97	6	0	4	257	0	3.97
95-96	Michigan	IHL	1	1	0	0	60	0	1.00	—	—	—	—	—	—
95-96	Orlando	IHL	7	3	1	1	341	0	2.99	—	—	—	—	—	—
95-96	Portland	AHL	12	2	6	2	577	0	4.79	—	—	—	—	—	—
95-96	Baltimore	AHL	5	2	1	1	257	0	4.61	1	0	0	40	0	0.00
95-96	Hampton Roads	ECHL	5	2	2	0	260	0	3.92	—	—	—	—	—	—
96-97	Fort Wayne	IHL	57	20	*31	3	2971	1	3.47	—	—	—	—	—	—
96-97	Baltimore	AHL	—	—	—	—	—	—	—	1	0	0	40	0	6.00
97-98	Milwaukee	IHL	34	13	14	1	1828	1	3.09	—	—	—	—	—	—
97-98	San Antonio	IHL	2	0	2	0	119	0	6.07	—	—	—	—	—	—
97-98	Peoria	ECHL	5	4	1	0	299	0	3.21	1	0	1	60	0	7.00
98-99	Asiago	Italy													
	IHL	Totals	233	98	91	21	12356	5	3.44	10	1	7	478	1	3.89
	AHL	Totals	17	4	7	3	833	0	4.61	2	0	0	80	0	3.01
	ECHL	Totals	10	6	3	0	559	0	3.54	—	—	—	—	—	—

Born; 2/23/72, Toronto, Ontario. 5-11, 215. Drafted by Minnesota North Stars (2nd choice, 74th overall) in 1991 Entry Draft. Traded to Washington Capitals by Dallas for future considerations (7/14/95). Traded to Anaheim Mighty Ducks by Washington for Todd Krygier (3/8/96). Last amateur club; Kitchener (OHL).

Chris Torkoff — Right Wing
Regular Season — Playoffs

Season	Team	League	GP	G	A	PTS	PIM	GP	G	A	PTS	PIM
98-99	Quad City	UHL	4	0	0	0	28	—	—	—	—	—
98-99	Winston-Salem	UHL	27	6	6	12	61	—	—	—	—	—
98-99	Asheville	UHL	24	1	4	5	59	—	—	—	—	—
98-99	Madison	UHL	9	2	3	5	18	—	—	—	—	—
	UHL	Totals	64	9	13	22	166	—	—	—	—	—

Born; 12/7/74, Richmond Hills, Ontario. 6-0, 190. Traded to Winston-Salem by Quad City for Steve Richards (10/98). Traded to Asheville by Winston-Salem for Bob Brandon (1/99). Traded to Madison by Thunder Bay with Dan Myre for Jason Disher (3/99). Last amateur club; Senaca College.

Mike Torkoff — Defenseman
Regular Season — Playoffs

Season	Team	League	GP	G	A	PTS	PIM	GP	G	A	PTS	PIM
92-93	Chatham	CoHL	1	0	0	0	0	—	—	—	—	—
93-94												
94-95												
95-96												
96-97												
97-98	Tucson	WCHL	20	3	7	10	44	—	—	—	—	—
97-98	Fayetteville	CHL	18	5	9	14	15	—	—	—	—	—
98-99	Alexandria	WPHL	41	11	20	31	33	—	—	—	—	—
98-99	Lake Charles	WPHL	13	2	3	5	2	2	1	0	1	2
	WPHL	Totals	54	13	23	36	35	2	1	0	1	2

Born; 11/27/71, Richmond Hill, Ontario. 5-11, 195. Traded to Lake Charles by Alexandria for Chris Low (2/99). Last amateur club; York (OUAA).

Michael Tornquist — Goaltender
Regular Season — Playoffs

Season	Team	League	GP	W	L	T	MIN	SO	AVG	GP	W	L	MIN	SO	AVG
97-98	Odessa	WPHL	22	2	8	1	753	0	5.66	—	—	—	—	—	—
98-99	Odessa	WPHL	27	15	7	3	1572	1	3.05	—	—	—	—	—	—
	WPHL	Totals	49	17	15	4	2325	1	3.90	—	—	—	—	—	—

Born; 4/18/76, Stockholm, Sweden. 6-1, 185.

Andrew Tortorella — Center
Regular Season — Playoffs

Season	Team	League	GP	G	A	PTS	PIM	GP	G	A	PTS	PIM
98-99	Roanoke	ECHL	5	0	1	1	4	—	—	—	—	—

Born; 5/17/77, Glen Head, New York. 5-5, 150.

Kaleb Toth — Right Wing
Regular Season — Playoffs

Season	Team	League	GP	G	A	PTS	PIM	GP	G	A	PTS	PIM
98-99	Baton Rouge	ECHL	7	0	1	1	2	—	—	—	—	—
98-99	Chesapeake	ECHL	57	26	15	41	37	8	2	1	3	4
	ECHL	Totals	64	26	16	42	39	8	2	1	3	4

Born; 8/8/77, Calgary, Alberta. 6-1, 195. Traded to Chesapeake by Baton Rouge for future considerations (11/98). Last amateur club; Lethbridge (WHL).

Jeff Tory — Defenseman
Regular Season — Playoffs

Season	Team	League	GP	G	A	PTS	PIM	GP	G	A	PTS	PIM
96-97	Kentucky	AHL	3	0	2	2	0	4	0	0	0	2
96-97	Canada	National	54	8	37	45	30	—	—	—	—	—
97-98	Houston	IHL	74	11	27	38	35	4	0	1	1	2
98-99	Houston	IHL	79	19	36	55	46	18	2	6	8	8
	IHL	Totals	153	30	63	93	81	22	2	7	9	10

Born; 5/9/73, Burnaby, British Columbia. 5-11, 195. Signed as a free agent by Philadelphia Flyers (7/13/99). Member of 1998-99 IHL Champion Houston Aeros. Last amateur club; Maine (Hockey East).

Graeme Townshend — Right Wing
Regular Season — Playoffs

Season	Team	League	GP	G	A	PTS	PIM	GP	G	A	PTS	PIM
88-89	R.P.I.	ECAC	31	6	16	22	50	—	—	—	—	—
88-89	Maine	AHL	5	2	1	3	11	—	—	—	—	—
89-90	Boston	NHL	4	0	0	0	7	—	—	—	—	—
89-90	Maine	AHL	64	15	13	28	162	—	—	—	—	—
90-91	Boston	NHL	18	2	5	7	12	—	—	—	—	—
90-91	Maine	AHL	46	16	10	26	119	2	2	0	2	4
91-92	Islanders	NHL	7	1	2	3	0	—	—	—	—	—
91-92	Capital District	AHL	61	14	23	37	94	4	0	2	2	0
92-93	Islanders	NHL	2	0	0	0	0	—	—	—	—	—
92-93	Capital District	AHL	67	29	21	50	45	2	0	0	0	0
93-94	Ottawa	NHL	14	0	0	0	9	—	—	—	—	—
93-94	Prince Edward Island	AHL	56	16	13	29	107	—	—	—	—	—
94-95	Houston	IHL	71	19	21	40	204	4	0	2	2	22
95-96	Minnesota	IHL	3	0	0	0	0	—	—	—	—	—
95-96	Houston	IHL	63	21	11	32	97	—	—	—	—	—
96-97	Houston	IHL	74	21	15	36	68	3	0	0	0	2
97-98	Utah	IHL	1	0	0	0	0	—	—	—	—	—
97-98	Houston	IHL	1	0	0	0	0	—	—	—	—	—
97-98	Lake Charles	WPHL	68	43	44	87	67	4	0	4	4	14
98-99	Lake Charles	WPHL	60	28	29	57	113	11	7	3	10	12
	NHL	Totals	45	3	7	10	28	—	—	—	—	—
	AHL	Totals	299	92	81	173	538	8	2	2	4	4
	IHL	Totals	213	61	47	108	369	7	0	2	2	24
	WPHL	Totals	128	71	73	144	180	15	7	7	14	26

Born; 10/23/65, Kingston, Jamaica. 6-2, 215. Signed as a free agent by Boston Bruins (5/12/89). Signed as a free agent by New York Islanders (9/3/91). Signed as a free agent by Ottawa Senators (8/24/93). 1998-99 WPHL Man of the Year. Named head coach of Macon Whoopee (CHL) beginning with 1999-2000 season. Last amateur club; Rensselaer Polytechnic Institute (ECAC).

Paul Traynor — Defenseman

Regular Season / Playoffs

Season	Team	League	GP	G	A	PTS	PIM	GP	G	A	PTS	PIM
97-98	Albany	AHL	25	0	3	3	2	—	—	—	—	—
97-98	Raleigh	ECHL	20	1	1	2	31	—	—	—	—	—
98-99	Michigan	IHL	39	3	9	12	12	5	0	0	0	2
98-99	South Carolina	ECHL	27	0	9	9	31	—	—	—	—	—
	ECHL	Totals	47	1	10	11	62	—	—	—	—	—

Born; 9/14/77, Thunder Bay, Ontario. 6-1, 190. Drafted by Winnipeg Jets (8th choice, 162nd overall) in 1995 Entry Draft. Last amateur club; Kitchener (OHL).

Dean Trboyovich — Defenseman

Regular Season / Playoffs

Season	Team	League	GP	G	A	PTS	PIM	GP	G	A	PTS	PIM
91-92	Capital District	AHL	22	0	3	3	65	—	—	—	—	—
91-92	Richmond	ECHL	23	1	6	7	100	—	—	—	—	—
91-92	Salt Lake City	IHL	5	0	1	1	7	—	—	—	—	—
92-93												
93-94												
94-95												
95-96	Detroit	IHL	—	—	—	—	—	1	0	0	0	2
95-96	Anchorage	WCHL	31	5	12	17	121	—	—	—	—	—
95-96	Detroit	CoHL	25	2	6	8	136	10	3	3	6	53
96-97	Grand Rapids	IHL	30	1	1	2	73	5	0	1	1	14
96-97	Anchorage	WCHL	38	6	18	24	118	—	—	—	—	—
97-98	Grand Rapids	IHL	66	2	5	7	94	—	—	—	—	—
97-98	Milwaukee	IHL	11	1	2	3	27	10	1	0	1	14
98-99	Anchorage	WCHL	43	2	10	12	133	6	0	2	2	4
	IHL	Totals	112	4	9	13	201	16	1	1	2	30
	WCHL	Totals	69	11	30	41	239	—	—	—	—	—

Born; 6/6/68, Bovey, Minnesota. 6-1, 200. Traded to Milwaukee by Grand Rapids for Mike Harder (3/98). Last amateur club; Alaska-Anchorage (WCHA).

Dan Trebil — Defenseman

Regular Season / Playoffs

Season	Team	League	GP	G	A	PTS	PIM	GP	G	A	PTS	PIM
96-97	Anaheim	NHL	29	3	3	6	23	9	0	1	1	6
96-97	Baltimore	AHL	49	4	20	24	38	—	—	—	—	—
97-98	Anaheim	NHL	21	0	1	1	2	—	—	—	—	—
97-98	Cincinnati	AHL	32	5	15	20	21	—	—	—	—	—
98-99	Anaheim	NHL	6	0	0	0	0	1	0	0	0	2
98-99	Cincinnati	AHL	52	6	15	21	31	—	—	—	—	—
	NHL	Totals	56	3	4	7	25	10	0	1	1	8
	AHL	Totals	133	15	50	65	90	—	—	—	—	—

Born; 4/10/74, Edina, Minnesota. 6-3, 185. Drafted by New Jersey Devils (7th choice, 138th overall) in 1992 Entry Draft. Signed as a free agent by Anaheim Mighty Ducks (5/30/96). Last amateur club; Minnesota (WCHA).

Andrei Trefilov — Goaltender

Regular Season / Playoffs

Season	Team	League	GP	W	L	T	MIN	SO	AVG	GP	W	L	MIN	SO	AVG
92-93	Calgary	NHL	1	0	0	1	65	0	4.62	—	—	—	—	—	—
92-93	Salt Lake City	IHL	44	23	17	3	2536	0	3.19	—	—	—	—	—	—
93-94	Calgary	NHL	11	3	4	2	623	2	2.50	—	—	—	—	—	—
93-94	Saint John	AHL	28	10	10	7	1629	0	3.42	—	—	—	—	—	—
94-95	Calgary	NHL	6	0	3	0	236	0	4.07	—	—	—	—	—	—
94-95	Saint John	AHL	7	1	5	1	383	0	3.13	—	—	—	—	—	—
95-96	Buffalo	NHL	22	8	8	1	1094	0	3.51	—	—	—	—	—	—
95-96	Rochester	AHL	5	4	1	0	299	0	2.61	—	—	—	—	—	—
96-97	Buffalo	NHL	3	0	2	0	159	0	3.77	1	0	0	5	0	0.00
97-98	Russia	Olympics	2	1	0	0	69	0	3.45	—	—	—	—	—	—
97-98	Chicago	NHL	6	1	4	0	299	0	3.41	—	—	—	—	—	—
97-98	Rochester	AHL	3	1	0	1	139	0	2.60	—	—	—	—	—	—
97-98	Indianapolis	IHL	1	0	1	0	59	0	3.03	—	—	—	—	—	—
98-99	Ak Bars Kazan	Russia	3	—	—	—	160	1	2.63	—	—	—	—	—	—
98-99	Chicago	NHL	1	0	1	0	25	0	9.60	—	—	—	—	—	—
98-99	Calgary	NHL	4	0	3	0	162	0	4.07	—	—	—	—	—	—
98-99	Indianapolis	IHL	18	9	6	2	986	0	2.37	—	—	—	—	—	—
98-99	Detroit	IHL	27	17	8	2	1613	3	1.97	10	6	4	647	0	2.04
	NHL	Totals	54	12	25	4	2663	2	3.45	1	0	0	5	0	0.00
	IHL	Totals	90	49	32	7	5195	3	2.66	10	6	4	647	0	2.04
	AHL	Totals	43	16	16	9	2450	0	3.23	—	—	—	—	—	—

Born; 8/31/69, Kirovo-Chepetsk, USSR. 6-0, 190. Drafted by Calgary Flames (14th choice, 261st overall) in 1991 Entry Draft. Signed as a free agent by Buffalo Sabres (7/11/95). Traded to Chicago Blackhawks by Buffalo for future considerations (11/12/97). Traded to Calgary Flames by Chicago for Calgary's seventh round choice (Yorick Treille) in 1999 Entry Draft (12/28/98). 1998-99 IHL Shared lowest goals against average award with Kevin Weekes. 1998-99 IHL

Jeff Trembecky — Center

Regular Season / Playoffs

Season	Team	League	GP	G	A	PTS	PIM	GP	G	A	PTS	PIM
98-99	Peoria	ECHL	68	21	26	47	40	4	1	1	2	4

Born; 10/19/74, Drumheller, Alberta. 5-10, 184. Last amateur club; Alaska-Fairbanks (CCHA).

Frederic Tremblay — Defenseman

Regular Season / Playoffs

Season	Team	League	GP	G	A	PTS	PIM	GP	G	A	PTS	PIM
98-99	Augusta	ECHL	3	0	0	0	0	—	—	—	—	—
98-99	Mobile	ECHL	10	0	1	1	4	—	—	—	—	—
	ECHL	Totals	13	0	1	1	4	—	—	—	—	—

Born; Last amateur club; Laval (QMJHL).

J.F. Tremblay — Forward

Regular Season / Playoffs

Season	Team	League	GP	G	A	PTS	PIM	GP	G	A	PTS	PIM
96-97	Roanoke	ECHL	36	6	7	13	140	4	0	1	1	4
97-98	Roanoke	ECHL	61	20	10	30	183	7	2	4	6	26
98-99	Roanoke	ECHL	54	17	14	31	153	6	0	2	2	12
	ECHL	Totals	151	43	31	74	476	17	2	7	9	42

Born; 4/3/75, Montreal, Quebec. 5-11, 185. Last amateur club; Beauport

Philippe Tremblay — Center

Regular Season / Playoffs

Season	Team	League	GP	G	A	PTS	PIM	GP	G	A	PTS	PIM
98-99	Cape Breton	QMJHL	64	30	55	85	101	3	2	2	4	4
98-99	Mohawk Valley	UHL	4	1	2	3	0	—	—	—	—	—

Born; 7/16/78, Beauport, Quebec. 5-9, 170. Selected by Fort Wayne in 1999 UHL Expansion Draft. Last amateur club; Cape Breton (QMJHL).

Bill Trew — Center

Regular Season / Playoffs

Season	Team	League	GP	G	A	PTS	PIM	GP	G	A	PTS	PIM
96-97	El Paso	WPHL	62	33	29	62	18	11	6	7	13	0
97-98	El Paso	WPHL	69	39	42	81	29	15	10	*16	*26	27
98-99	El Paso	WPHL	69	44	47	91	46	3	0	2	2	0
	WPHL	Totals	200	116	118	234	93	29	16	25	41	27

Born; 1/1/74, Garden Hill, Ontario. 5-11, 175. 1997-98 WPHL Playoff MVP. Member of 1996-97 WPHL Champion El Paso Buzzards. Member of 1997-98 WPHL Champion El Paso Buzzards. Last amateur club; North Dakota (WCHA).

Jeff Trigg — Goaltender

Regular Season / Playoffs

Season	Team	League	GP	W	L	T	MIN	SO	AVG	GP	W	L	MIN	SO	AVG
96-97	Anchorage	WCHL	17	11	3	0	871	1	4.14	3	0	0	42	0	9.96
97-98	Detroit	IHL	1	0	1	0	59	0	4.07	—	—	—	—	—	—
97-98	Richmond	ECHL	1	0	0	0	20	0	9.00	—	—	—	—	—	—
97-98	Idaho	WCHL	3	2	1	0	180	0	4.33	—	—	—	—	—	—
98-99	Idaho	WCHL	12	4	5	2	619	0	4.17	—	—	—	—	—	—
	WCHL	Totals	32	17	9	2	1670	1	4.17	3	0	0	42	0	9.96

Born; 10/3/69, Vancouver, British Columbia. 6-0, 177.

John Tripp — Right Wing

Regular Season / Playoffs

Season	Team	League	GP	G	A	PTS	PIM	GP	G	A	PTS	PIM
97-98	Saint John	AHL	61	1	11	12	66	2	0	1	1	0
97-98	Roanoke	ECHL	9	0	2	2	22	—	—	—	—	—
98-99	Saint John	AHL	2	0	0	0	10	—	—	—	—	—
98-99	Johnstown	ECHL	7	2	0	2	12	—	—	—	—	—
	AHL	Totals	63	1	11	12	76	2	0	1	1	0
	ECHL	Totals	16	2	2	4	34	—	—	—	—	—

Born; 5/4/77, Kingston, Ontario. 6-2, 207. Drafted by Colorado Avalanche (3rd choice, 77th overall) in 1995 Entry Draft. Re-entered NHL Entry Draft, Drafted by Calgary Flames (3rd choice, 42nd overall). Last amateur club; Oshawa (OHL).

Anders Troberg — Defenseman

Regular Season / Playoffs

Season	Team	League	GP	G	A	PTS	PIM	GP	G	A	PTS	PIM
98-99	Tupelo	WPHL	9	0	0	0	14	—	—	—	—	—

Born; 2/27/76, Linkoping, Sweden. 6-3, 210.

Rhett Trombley — Right Wing

Regular Season / Playoffs

Season	Team	League	GP	G	A	PTS	PIM	GP	G	A	PTS	PIM
94-95	Las Vegas	IHL	30	4	0	4	141	3	0	0	0	10
94-95	Toledo	ECHL	13	0	2	2	80	—	—	—	—	—
95-96	Las Vegas	IHL	15	0	2	2	56	—	—	—	—	—
95-96	Carolina	AHL	34	2	2	4	163	—	—	—	—	—
96-97	Syracuse	AHL	10	0	0	0	30	1	0	0	0	2
96-97	Las Vegas	IHL	44	4	3	7	199	1	0	0	0	2
96-97	Toledo	ECHL	4	0	1	1	25	—	—	—	—	—
97-98	Las Vegas	IHL	20	1	0	1	95	—	—	—	—	—
97-98	Utah	IHL	47	1	5	6	205	2	0	0	0	2
98-99	San Antonio	CHL	4	0	5	5	44	—	—	—	—	—
98-99	Utah	IHL	36	0	0	0	86	—	—	—	—	—
	IHL	Totals	192	10	8	18	782	6	0	0	0	14
	AHL	Totals	44	2	2	4	193	1	0	0	0	2

Born; 12/9/74, New Westminster, British Columbia. 6-3, 225. Signed as a free agent by Florida (4/5/95). Last amateur club; Victoria (WHL).

Marc Tropper — Right Wing

Regular Season / Playoffs

Season	Team	League	GP	G	A	PTS	PIM	GP	G	A	PTS	PIM
98-99	Chesapeake	ECHL	63	26	24	50	83	6	1	1	2	4

Born; 4/14/76, Toronto, Ontario. 5-10, 195. Last amateur club; Miami-Ohio (CCHA).

Joel Trottier — Right Wing

Regular Season / Playoffs

Season	Team	League	GP	G	A	PTS	PIM	GP	G	A	PTS	PIM
98-99	Providence	AHL	7	3	0	3	17	—	—	—	—	—
98-99	Greenville	ECHL	53	15	15	30	49	—	—	—	—	—

Born; 2/11/77, Alexandria, Ontario. 6-0, 190. Drafted by Boston Bruins (8th choice, 162nd overall) in 1997 Entry Draft. Last amateur club; Belleville (OHL).

Jean-Guy Trudel — Center

Regular Season / Playoffs

Season	Team	League	GP	G	A	PTS	PIM	GP	G	A	PTS	PIM
96-97	Peoria	ECHL	37	25	29	54	47	9	9	10	19	22
96-97	Quad City	CoHL	5	8	7	15	4	—	—	—	—	—
96-97	San Antonio	IHL	12	1	5	6	4	—	—	—	—	—
96-97	Chicago	IHL	6	1	2	3	2	—	—	—	—	—
97-98	Peoria	ECHL	62	39	74	113	147	3	0	0	0	2
98-99	Kansas City	IHL	76	24	25	49	66	3	1	0	1	0
	IHL	Totals	94	26	32	58	72	3	1	0	1	2
	ECHL	Totals	99	64	103	167	194	12	9	10	19	24

Born; 10/18/75, Sudbury, Ontario. 6-0, 194. Signed as a free agent by Phoenix Coyotes (7/16/99). 1997-98 ECHL First Team All-Star. Last amateur club; Hull (QMJHL).

Rob Trumbley — Right Wing

Regular Season / Playoffs

Season	Team	League	GP	G	A	PTS	PIM	GP	G	A	PTS	PIM
95-96	Cape Breton	AHL	11	1	2	3	31	—	—	—	—	—
95-96	Wheeling	ECHL	51	8	10	18	321	7	0	2	2	44
96-97	Hamilton	AHL	25	2	3	5	97	—	—	—	—	—
96-97	Wheeling	ECHL	34	15	22	37	164	2	1	0	1	14
97-98	Newcastle	BSL	50	4	11	15	258	4	0	1	1	36
98-99	Newcastle	BSL	48	10	12	22	107	6	1	0	1	16
	AHL	Totals	36	3	5	8	128	—	—	—	—	—
	ECHL	Totals	85	23	32	55	485	9	1	2	3	58

Born; 8/9/74, Regina, Saskatchewan. 5-10, 180. Drafted by Vancouver Canucks (8th choice, 195th overall) in 1994 Entry Draft. Last amateur club; Moose Jaw

Gatis Tseplis — Defenseman

Regular Season / Playoffs

Season	Team	League	GP	G	A	PTS	PIM	GP	G	A	PTS	PIM
96-97	Huntsville	CeHL	10	1	0	1	4	—	—	—	—	—
96-97	San Antonio	CeHL	21	5	12	17	10	—	—	—	—	—
96-97	Nashville	CeHL	12	2	4	6	6	—	—	—	—	—
97-98	Detroit	IHL	2	0	0	0	4	—	—	—	—	—
97-98	Fort Worth	WPHL	56	19	45	64	24	13	2	8	10	14
98-99	Fort Worth	CHL	52	16	37	53	26	—	—	—	—	—
98-99	San Antonio	CHL	18	5	14	19	18	8	4	5	9	4
	CHL	Totals	113	29	67	96	64	8	4	5	9	4

Born; 5/1/71, Riga, Latvia. 6-1, 195. Traded to San Antonio by Fort Worth for Mike Tobin (2/99).

Oleg Tsirkounov — Forward

Regular Season / Playoffs

Season	Team	League	GP	G	A	PTS	PIM	GP	G	A	PTS	PIM
98-99	Columbus	CHL	20	4	8	12	15	—	—	—	—	—
98-99	Topeka	CHL	44	19	17	36	61	3	1	0	1	9
	CHL	Totals	64	23	25	48	76	3	1	0	1	9

Born; 3/15/77, Kiev, Ukraine. 6-0, 195. Traded to Topeka by Columbus with Travis Riggin for Thomas Stewart (12/98).

Nikolai Tsulygin — Defenseman

Regular Season / Playoffs

Season	Team	League	GP	G	A	PTS	PIM	GP	G	A	PTS	PIM
95-96	Baltimore	AHL	78	3	18	21	109	12	0	5	5	18
96-97	Anaheim	NHL	22	0	1	1	8	—	—	—	—	—
96-97	Fort Wayne	IHL	5	2	1	3	8	—	—	—	—	—
96-97	Baltimore	AHL	17	4	13	17	8	3	0	0	0	0
97-98	Cincinnati	AHL	77	5	31	36	63	—	—	—	—	—
98-99	Fort Wayne	IHL	17	1	4	5	8	—	—	—	—	—
	AHL	Totals	172	12	62	74	180	15	0	5	5	18
	IHL	Totals	22	3	5	8	16	—	—	—	—	—

Born; 6/29/75, Ufa, USSR. 6-4, 205. Drafted by Anaheim Mighty Ducks (2nd choice, 30th overall) in 1993 Entry Draft.

Yevgeny Tsybuk — Defenseman

Regular Season / Playoffs

Season	Team	League	GP	G	A	PTS	PIM	GP	G	A	PTS	PIM
98-99	Michigan	IHL	42	1	3	4	69	2	0	0	0	2

Born; 2/2/78, Chebarkul, USSR. 6-0, 183. Drafted by Dallas Stars (5th choice, 113th overall) in 1996 Entry Draft. Last amateur club; Lethbridge (WHL).

Kevin Tucker — Right Wing

Regular Season / Playoffs

Season	Team	League	GP	G	A	PTS	PIM	GP	G	A	PTS	PIM
98-99	Winston-Salem	UHL	35	11	11	22	24	—	—	—	—	—
98-99	Saginaw	UHL	35	7	14	21	0	—	—	—	—	—
	UHL	Totals	70	18	25	43	24	—	—	—	—	—

Born; 5/27/74, Cambridge, Ontario. 5-10, 190. Traded to Saginaw with John Nelson and Brian Kreft for Marc Delorme (1/99). Last amateur club; Acadia

Travis Tucker — Defenseman

Regular Season / Playoffs

Season	Team	League	GP	G	A	PTS	PIM	GP	G	A	PTS	PIM
94-95	Syracuse	AHL	2	0	0	0	2	—	—	—	—	—
94-95	Charlotte	ECHL	62	5	11	16	250	3	1	0	1	6
95-96	Louisville	ECHL	62	17	23	40	211	3	0	0	0	14
96-97	Portland	AHL	2	0	0	0	4	—	—	—	—	—
96-97	Kansas City	IHL	2	0	0	0	5	—	—	—	—	—
96-97	Quad City	CoHL	68	15	27	42	163	15	0	1	1	22
97-98	Portland	AHL	17	1	0	1	24	—	—	—	—	—
97-98	Grand Rapids	IHL	2	0	0	0	7	—	—	—	—	—
97-98	Quad City	UHL	51	7	20	27	97	18	1	6	7	34
98-99	Mississippi	ECHL	3	0	2	2	20	—	—	—	—	—
98-99	Quad City	UHL	27	2	8	10	71	10	0	1	1	44
98-99	Grand Rapids	IHL	10	0	0	0	31	—	—	—	—	—
98-99	Portland	AHL	2	0	0	0	0	—	—	—	—	—
98-99	Hershey	AHL	5	0	0	0	0	—	—	—	—	—
	AHL	Totals	28	1	0	1	30	—	—	—	—	—
	IHL	Totals	14	0	0	0	43	—	—	—	—	—
	UHL	Totals	146	24	55	79	331	43	1	8	9	100
	ECHL	Totals	127	22	36	58	481	6	1	0	1	20

Born; 3/15/71, Hartford, Connecticut. 6-3, 220. Drafted by Detroit Red Wings (9th choice, 192nd overall) in 1990 Entry Draft. Member of 1996-97 CoHL Champion Quad City Mallards. Member of 1997-98 UHL Champion Quad City Mallards. Selected by Missouri in 1999 UHL Expansion Draft. Last amateur club; Lowell (Hockey East).

Brent Tully — Defenseman

Regular Season / Playoffs

Season	Team	League	GP	G	A	PTS	PIM	GP	G	A	PTS	PIM
93-94	Peterborough	OHL	37	17	26	43	81	7	5	3	8	12
93-94	Canada	National	1	0	1	1	0	—	—	—	—	—
93-94	Hamilton	AHL	1	0	0	0	0	1	1	0	1	0
94-95	Syracuse	AHL	63	6	3	9	106	—	—	—	—	—
95-96	Syracuse	AHL	52	3	13	16	114	—	—	—	—	—
96-97	Syracuse	AHL	26	4	2	6	19	—	—	—	—	—
97-98	Augsburg	Germany	17	1	1	2	43	—	—	—	—	—
98-99	Dusseldorfer	Germany	29	2	2	4	49	3	0	0	0	14
98-99	Hannover	Germany	48	7	16	23	87	—	—	—	—	—
	AHL	Totals	142	13	18	31	239	1	1	0	1	0

Born; 3/26/74, Peterborough, Ontario. 6-3, 190. Drafted by Vancouver Canucks (5th choice, 93rd overall) in 1992 Entry Draft. Last amateur club; Peterborough

Marty Turco — Goaltender

Regular Season / Playoffs

Season	Team	League	GP	W	L	T	MIN	SO	AVG	GP	W	L	MIN	SO	AVG
98-99	Michigan	IHL	54	24	17	10	3127	1	2.61	5	2	3	300	0	2.80

Born; 8/13/75, Sault Ste. Marie, Ontario. 5-11, 175. Drafted by Dallas Stars (4th choice, 124th overall) in 1994 Entry Draft. 1998-99 IHL Rookie of the Year. Last amateur club; Michigan (CCHA).

Alfie Turcotte — Center

Regular Season / Playoffs

Season	Team	League	GP	G	A	PTS	PIM	GP	G	A	PTS	PIM
83-84	Montreal	NHL	30	7	7	14	10	—	—	—	—	—
84-85	Montreal	NHL	53	8	16	24	35	5	0	0	0	0
85-86	Montreal	NHL	2	0	0	0	2	—	—	—	—	—
85-86	Sherbrooke	AHL	75	29	36	65	60	—	—	—	—	—
86-87	Nova Scotia	AHL	70	27	41	68	37	5	2	4	6	2
87-88	Winnipeg	NHL	3	0	0	0	0	—	—	—	—	—
87-88	Baltimore	AHL	33	21	33	54	42	—	—	—	—	—
87-88	Moncton	AHL	25	12	25	37	18	—	—	—	—	—
87-88	Sherbrooke	AHL	8	3	8	11	4	—	—	—	—	—
88-89	Winnipeg	NHL	14	1	3	4	2	—	—	—	—	—
88-89	Moncton	AHL	54	27	39	66	74	10	3	9	12	17
89-90	Washington	NHL	4	0	2	2	0	—	—	—	—	—
89-90	Baltimore	AHL	65	26	40	66	42	12	7	9	16	14
90-91	Washington	NHL	6	1	1	2	0	—	—	—	—	—
90-91	Baltimore	AHL	65	33	52	85	20	6	3	3	6	4
91-92												
92-93												
93-94												
94-95	Schwenninger	Germany	33	7	40	47	30	11	7	5	12	12
95-96	Orlando	IHL	73	22	47	69	44	23	3	10	13	8
96-97	Schwenninger	Germany	1	0	0	0	0	—	—	—	—	—
97-98	Frankfurt	Germany	26	2	6	8	12	7	0	0	0	0
97-98	Indianapolis	IHL	17	5	6	11	8	—	—	—	—	—
98-99	Arkansas	WPHL	2	0	0	0	0	—	—	—	—	—
	NHL	Totals	112	17	29	46	49	5	0	0	0	0
	AHL	Totals	395	178	274	452	297	33	15	25	40	37
	IHL	Totals	90	27	53	80	52	23	3	10	13	8

Born; 6/5/65, Gary, Indiana. 5-9, 170. Drafted by Montreal Canadians (1st choice, 17th overall) in 1983 Entry Draft. Traded to Edmonton Oilers by Montreal for future considerations (7/86). Sold to Montreal by Edmonton (5/87). Traded to Winnipeg Jets by Montreal for future considerations (1/88). 1987-88 AHL Second Team All-Star. Last amateur club; Portland (WHL).

Matt Turek — Center

Regular Season / Playoffs

Season	Team	League	GP	G	A	PTS	PIM	GP	G	A	PTS	PIM
96-97	Knoxville	ECHL	62	11	20	31	62	—	—	—	—	—
97-98	Pee Dee	ECHL	70	16	23	39	62	8	3	1	4	8
98-99	Hamburg	Germany	45	16	24	40	75	—	—	—	—	—
	ECHL	Totals	132	27	43	70	124	8	3	1	4	8

Born; 2/14/73, Toronto, Ontario. 5-11, 190. Last amateur club; Wilfrid Laurier (OUAA).

Mark Turner — Center

Regular Season / Playoffs

Season	Team	League	GP	G	A	PTS	PIM	GP	G	A	PTS	PIM
90-91	Cincinnati	ECHL	54	25	27	52	89	4	0	1	1	13
90-91	Fort Wayne	IHL	20	6	6	12	21	4	0	0	0	2
91-92	Fort Wayne	IHL	49	8	10	18	68	5	2	0	2	6
92-93	Muskegon	CoHL	37	25	33	58	33	2	2	1	3	4
92-93	Chatham	CoHL	15	9	10	19	30	—	—	—	—	—
93-94	Muskegon	CoHL	61	46	58	104	57	2	0	0	0	0
94-95	Muskegon	CoHL	20	7	13	20	48	—	—	—	—	—
94-95	Utica	CoHL	18	6	10	16	28	—	—	—	—	—
94-95	Flint	CoHL	10	1	11	12	16	6	2	2	4	33
95-96	Muskegon	CoHL	67	32	69	101	99	1	1	1	2	0
96-97	Columbus	ECHL	55	20	48	68	81	8	3	5	8	6
97-98	Fort Wayne	IHL	8	0	1	1	4	—	—	—	—	—
97-98	Columbus	ECHL	65	25	35	60	109	—	—	—	—	—
98-99	New Orleans	ECHL	63	14	38	52	47	11	2	5	7	22
	IHL	Totals	77	14	17	31	93	9	2	0	2	8
	ECHL	Totals	237	84	148	232	326	23	5	11	16	41
	CoHL	Totals	228	126	204	330	311	11	5	4	9	37

Born; 5/9/68, Windsor, Ontario. 5-10, 185. Traded to Mobile by New Orleans for Yannick Jean (6/99).

Tony Tuzzolino — Right Wing

Regular Season / Playoffs

Season	Team	League	GP	G	A	PTS	PIM	GP	G	A	PTS	PIM
97-98	Anaheim	NHL	1	0	0	0	2	—	—	—	—	—
97-98	Kentucky	AHL	35	9	14	23	83	—	—	—	—	—
97-98	Cincinnati	AHL	13	3	3	6	6	—	—	—	—	—
98-99	Cincinnati	AHL	50	4	10	14	55	—	—	—	—	—
98-99	Cleveland	IHL	15	2	4	6	22	—	—	—	—	—
	AHL	Totals	98	16	27	43	144	—	—	—	—	—

Born; 10/9/75, Buffalo, New York. 6-2, 180. Drafted by Quebec Nordiques (7th choice, 113th overall) in 1994 Entry Draft. Signed as a free agent by New York Islanders (4/26/97). Traded to Anaheim Mighty Ducks by Islanders with Travis Green and Doug Houda for Joe Sacco, J.J. Daigneault and Mark Janssens (2/6/98). Last amateur club; Michigan State (CCHA).

Josh Tymchak — Center

Regular Season / Playoffs

Season	Team	League	GP	G	A	PTS	PIM	GP	G	A	PTS	PIM
97-98	Binghamton	UHL	1	0	0	0	7	—	—	—	—	—
97-98	Winston-Salem	UHL	8	1	0	1	15	—	—	—	—	—
98-99	Winston-Salem	UHL	46	4	3	7	135	—	—	—	—	—
98-99	Mohawk Valley	UHL	12	1	0	1	36	—	—	—	—	—
98-99	Asheville	UHL	11	0	1	1	35	4	0	1	1	0
	UHL	Totals	78	6	4	10	228	4	0	1	1	0

Born; 2/4/74, Winnipeg, Manitoba. 6-1, 170. Traded to Mohawk Valley by Winston-Salem with Doug Reynolds for Ryan Caley (2/99).

Paul Tzountzouris — Defenseman

Regular Season / Playoffs

Season	Team	League	GP	G	A	PTS	PIM	GP	G	A	PTS	PIM
95-96	Quad City	CoHL	1	0	0	0	0	—	—	—	—	—
95-96	Winston-Salem	SHL	9	0	2	2	17	—	—	—	—	—
95-96	Daytona Beach	SHL	17	2	3	5	52	—	—	—	—	—
96-97	Flint	CoHL	21	2	5	7	29	—	—	—	—	—
96-97	Madison	CoHL	7	2	1	3	2	3	0	0	0	2
97-98	Madison	UHL	50	11	13	24	24	—	—	—	—	—
97-98	Brantford	UHL	14	5	8	13	10	9	2	2	4	2
98-99	Waco	WPHL	54	7	13	20	48	4	0	1	1	4
	UHL	Totals	93	20	27	47	65	12	2	2	4	4
	SHL	Totals	26	2	5	7	69	—	—	—	—	—

Born; 8/25/74, Toronto, Ontario. 6-2, 201.

Shawn Ulrich — Center

Regular Season / Playoffs

Season	Team	League	GP	G	A	PTS	PIM	GP	G	A	PTS	PIM
95-96	Alaska	WCHL	58	34	64	98	62	5	3	6	9	2
96-97	Alaska	WCHL	53	30	36	66	30	—	—	—	—	—
96-97	Anchorage	WCHL	16	5	7	12	32	9	3	2	5	10
97-98	Waco	WPHL	16	7	7	14	11	—	—	—	—	—
97-98	Reno	WCHL	50	18	33	51	48	3	1	3	4	12
98-99	Asheville	UHL	67	39	57	96	71	3	0	0	0	0
	WCHL	Totals	177	87	140	227	172	17	7	11	18	24

Born; 10/31/69, Saskatoon, Saskatchewan. 5-8, 190.

Richard Uniacke — Center

Regular Season / Playoffs

Season	Team	League	GP	G	A	PTS	PIM	GP	G	A	PTS	PIM
97-98	Providence	AHL	6	1	0	1	0	—	—	—	—	—
97-98	San Antonio	IHL	1	0	1	1	0	—	—	—	—	—
97-98	Houston	IHL	1	0	0	0	0	—	—	—	—	—
97-98	Charlotte	ECHL	2	0	2	2	0	—	—	—	—	—
97-98	Austin	WPHL	32	14	20	34	13	—	—	—	—	—
98-99	Sheffield	BSL	33	11	5	16	6	—	—	—	—	—
98-99	Manchester	BSL	14	2	2	4	2	7	0	0	0	0
	IHL	Totals	2	0	1	1	0	—	—	—	—	—

Born; 11/2/76, Toronto, Ontario. 6-0, 190. Selected by Arkansas in 1998 WPHL Expansion Draft. Last amateur club; Sault Ste. Marie (OHL).

Scott Usmail — Defenseman

Regular Season / Playoffs

Season	Team	League	GP	G	A	PTS	PIM	GP	G	A	PTS	PIM
98-99	Mohawk Valley	UHL	9	0	0	0	17	—	—	—	—	—
98-99	Tulsa	CHL	19	1	2	3	25	—	—	—	—	—
98-99	San Antonio	CHL	5	0	0	0	0	—	—	—	—	—
98-99	Fort Worth	CHL	7	2	3	5	6	—	—	—	—	—
	CHL	Totals	31	3	5	8	31	—	—	—	—	—

Born; 11/8/73, New Hartford, New York. 5-11, 198. Selected by San Antonio in 1999 CHL Dispersal Draft.

Stefan Ustorf — Center

Regular Season / Playoffs

Season	Team	League	GP	G	A	PTS	PIM	GP	G	A	PTS	PIM
94-95	Portland	AHL	63	21	38	59	51	7	1	6	7	7
95-96	Washington	NHL	48	7	10	17	14	5	0	0	0	0
95-96	Portland	AHL	8	1	4	5	6	—	—	—	—	—
96-97	Washington	NHL	6	0	0	0	2	—	—	—	—	—
96-97	Portland	AHL	36	7	17	24	27	—	—	—	—	—
97-98	Berlin	Germany	45	17	23	40	54	—	—	—	—	—
97-98	Germany	Olympics	4	0	0	0	0	—	—	—	—	—
98-99	Las Vegas	IHL	40	11	17	28	40	—	—	—	—	—
98-99	Detroit	IHL	14	3	7	10	11	11	4	7	11	2
	NHL	Totals	54	7	10	17	16	5	0	0	0	0
	AHL	Totals	107	29	59	88	84	7	1	6	7	7
	IHL	Totals	54	14	24	38	51	11	4	7	11	2

Born; 1/3/74, Kaufbeuren, Germany. 6-0, 185. Drafted by Washington Capitals (3rd choice, 53rd overall) in 1992 Entry Draft. Signed as a free agent by Las Vegas Thunder (7/29/98).

Dmitri Ustyuzhanin — Forward

Regular Season / Playoffs

Season	Team	League	GP	G	A	PTS	PIM	GP	G	A	PTS	PIM
98-99	Tupelo	WPHL	21	1	6	7	12	—	—	—	—	—

Born; 2/2/76, Ekaterinaburg, Russia. 5-10, 190.

Joe Vandermeer Defenseman
Regular Season Playoffs

Season	Team	League	GP	G	A	PTS	PIM	GP	G	A	PTS	PIM
98-99	Richmond	ECHL	70	1	35	36	80	18	4	7	11	8

Born; 1/8/77, Red Deer, Alberta. 5-10, 170. Last amateur club; South Surrey (BCJHL).

Peter Vandermeer Left Wing
Regular Season Playoffs

Season	Team	League	GP	G	A	PTS	PIM	GP	G	A	PTS	PIM
96-97	Columbus	ECHL	30	6	11	17	195	7	2	1	3	26
97-98	Rochester	AHL	30	4	2	6	140	4	1	0	1	13
97-98	Columbus	ECHL	20	4	7	11	78	—	—	—	—	—
97-98	Richmond	ECHL	18	2	5	7	165	—	—	—	—	—
98-99	Rochester	AHL	2	1	0	1	16	16	1	0	1	38
98-99	Binghamton	UHL	62	15	21	36	*390	5	2	2	4	0
	AHL	Totals	32	5	2	7	156	20	2	0	2	51
	ECHL	Totals	68	12	23	35	500	7	2	1	3	26

Born; 10/14/74, Caroline, Alberta. 6-0, 195. Traded to Richmond by Columbus for Jay McNeill (12/97). Last amateur club; Red Deer (WHL).

Jeremy Vanin Forward
Regular Season Playoffs

Season	Team	League	GP	G	A	PTS	PIM	GP	G	A	PTS	PIM
98-99	El Paso	WPHL	52	10	19	29	49	3	3	1	4	0

Born; 5/4/77, Vancouver, British Columbia. 5-10, 175. Last amateur club; South Surrey (BCJHL).

John Varga Left Wing
Regular Season Playoffs

Season	Team	League	GP	G	A	PTS	PIM	GP	G	A	PTS	PIM
94-95	Portland	AHL	2	0	1	1	0	—	—	—	—	—
94-95	Milwaukee	IHL	1	0	0	0	0	—	—	—	—	—
95-96	Cornwall	AHL	10	1	0	1	6	—	—	—	—	—
95-96	Columbus	ECHL	33	19	17	36	38	—	—	—	—	—
95-96	Wheeling	ECHL	17	10	6	16	13	7	1	3	4	16
96-97	Wheeling	ECHL	66	*56	45	101	84	3	0	1	1	6
97-98	Providence	AHL	41	7	13	20	22	—	—	—	—	—
97-98	Louisiana	ECHL	8	3	4	7	6	12	9	8	17	20
98-99	Louisiana	ECHL	65	39	44	83	77	5	1	2	3	10
	AHL	Totals	53	8	14	22	28	—	—	—	—	—
	ECHL	Totals	189	127	116	243	218	27	11	14	25	52

Born; 1/31/74, Chicago, Illinois. 5-10, 180. Drafted by Washington Capitals (5th choice, 119th overall) in 1992 Entry Draft. Last amateur club; Tacoma (WHL).

Mike Varhaug Right Wing
Regular Season Playoffs

Season	Team	League	GP	G	A	PTS	PIM	GP	G	A	PTS	PIM
98-99	Lethbridge	WHL	15	0	1	1	60	—	—	—	—	—
98-99	Austin	WPHL	11	0	2	2	20	—	—	—	—	—

Born; 8/23/78, Brooks, Alberta. 6-7, 245. Last amateur club; Lethbridge (WHL).

Petri Varis Left Wing
Regular Season Playoffs

Season	Team	League	GP	G	A	PTS	PIM	GP	G	A	PTS	PIM
97-98	Chicago	NHL	1	0	0	0	0	—	—	—	—	—
97-98	Indianapolis	IHL	77	18	54	72	32	5	3	4	7	4
98-99	Kolner Haie	Germany	52	10	25	35	22	5	3	0	3	4

Born; 5/13/69, Varkaus, Finland. 6-1, 200. Drafted by San Jose Sharks (7th choice, 132nd overall) in 1993 Entry Draft. Rights traded to Chicago Blackhawks by San Jose with San Jose's sixth round choice (Jair Viuhkola) for Murray Craven (7/25/97).

Sergei Varlamov Left Wing
Regular Season Playoffs

Season	Team	League	GP	G	A	PTS	PIM	GP	G	A	PTS	PIM
96-97	Swift Current	WHL	72	46	39	85	94	10	3	8	11	10
96-97	Saint John	AHL	1	0	0	0	2	—	—	—	—	—
97-98	Swift Current	WHL	72	*66	53	*119	132	12	10	5	15	28
97-98	Calgary	NHL	1	0	0	0	0	—	—	—	—	—76
97-98	Saint John	AHL	—	—	—	—	—	3	0	0	0	0
98-99	Saint John	AHL	76	24	33	57	66	7	0	4	4	8
	AHL	Totals	77	24	33	57	68	10	0	4	4	8

Born; 7/21/78, Kiev, USSR. 5-11, 190. Signed as a free agent by Calgary Flames (9/18/96). Last amateur club; Swift Current (WHL).

John Vary Defenseman
Regular Season Playoffs

Season	Team	League	GP	G	A	PTS	PIM	GP	G	A	PTS	PIM
91-92	Kingston	OHL	54	11	38	49	102	—	—	—	—	—
91-92	Binghamton	AHL	1	0	0	0	0	—	—	—	—	—
92-93	Binghamton	AHL	12	0	2	2	8	—	—	—	—	—
92-93	Phoenix	IHL	9	0	6	6	10	—	—	—	—	—
92-93	Erie	ECHL	46	15	31	46	158	5	1	2	3	20
93-94	Erie	ECHL	55	10	29	39	129	—	—	—	—	—
94-95	Wichita	CeHL	63	12	38	50	163	11	3	5	8	16
95-96	Louisiana	ECHL	70	2	27	29	174	5	1	3	4	10
96-97	Muskegon	CoHL	74	14	54	68	106	3	1	2	3	2
97-98	Muskegon	UHL	74	13	48	61	71	11	2	8	10	10
98-99	Muskegon	UHL	62	14	47	61	75	17	6	12	18	16
	AHL	Totals	13	0	2	2	8	—	—	—	—	—
	UHL	Totals	210	41	149	190	252	31	9	22	31	28
	ECHL	Totals	171	27	87	114	461	10	2	5	7	30

Born; 2/1/72, Owen Sound, Ontario. 6-1, 207. Drafted by New York Rangers (3rd choice, 55th overall) in 1990 Entry Draft. 1997-98 UHL Best Defenseman. 1997-98 UHL First All-Star Team. 1998-99 UHL Second Team All-Star. Member of 1994-95 CeHL champion Wichita Thunder. Member of 1998-99 UHL Champion Muskegon Fury. Scored Colonial Cup-winning goal for Muskegon. Last amateur club; Kingston (OHL).

Alexei Vasiliev Defenseman
Regular Season Playoffs

Season	Team	League	GP	G	A	PTS	PIM	GP	G	A	PTS	PIM
97-98	Injured	DNP										
98-99	Hartford	AHL	75	8	19	27	24	6	0	1	1	2

Born; 9/1/77, Yaroslavl, USSR. 6-1, 190. Drafted by New York Rangers (4th choice, 110th overall) in 1995 Entry Draft. Last overseas club; Yaroslavl

Herbert Vasiljevs Center
Regular Season Playoffs

Season	Team	League	GP	G	A	PTS	PIM	GP	G	A	PTS	PIM
96-97	Carolina	AHL	54	13	18	31	30	—	—	—	—	—
96-97	Port Huron	CoHL	3	3	2	5	4	—	—	—	—	—
96-97	Knoxville	ECHL	3	1	1	2	0	—	—	—	—	—
97-98	New Haven	AHL	76	36	30	66	60	3	1	0	1	2
98-99	Florida	NHL	5	0	0	0	2	—	—	—	—	—
98-99	Kentucky	AHL	76	28	48	76	66	12	2	1	3	4
	AHL	Totals	206	77	96	173	156	15	3	1	4	6

Born; 5/27/76, Riga, Latvia. 5-11, 170. Signed as a free agent by Florida Panthers (10/3/96). Traded to Atlanta Thrashers with Gord Murphy, Daniel Tjarnqvist and Ottawa's sixth round draft choice (previously acquired-later traded to Dallas-Dallas selected Justin Cox) in 1999 Entry Draft for Trevor Kidd (6/25/99). Last amateur club; Guelph (OHL).

Andrei Vasilyev — Left Wing

Regular Season / Playoffs

Season	Team	League	GP	G	A	PTS	PIM	GP	G	A	PTS	PIM
94-95	Denver	IHL	74	28	37	65	48	13	9	4	13	22
94-95	Islanders	NHL	2	0	0	0	2	—	—	—	—	—
95-96	Islanders	NHL	10	2	5	7	2	—	—	—	—	—
95-96	Utah	IHL	43	26	20	46	34	22	12	4	16	18
96-97	Islanders	NHL	3	0	0	0	2	—	—	—	—	—
96-97	Utah	IHL	56	16	18	34	42	7	4	1	5	0
97-98	Long Beach	IHL	62	33	34	67	60	17	9	4	13	14
98-99	Phoenix	NHL	1	0	0	0	0	—	—	—	—	—
98-99	Las Vegas	IHL	15	3	6	9	6	—	—	—	—	—
98-99	Grand Rapids	IHL	59	21	27	48	24	—	—	—	—	—
	NHL	Totals	16	2	5	7	6	—	—	—	—	—
	IHL	Totals	309	127	142	269	214	59	34	13	47	54

Born; 3/30/72, Voskresensk, Russia. 5-8, 176. Drafted by New York Islanders (11th choice, 248th overall) in 1992 Entry Draft. Signed as a free agent by Phoenix Coyotes (8/5/98). Member of 1994-95 IHL champion Denver Grizzlies. Member of 1995-96 IHL champion Utah Grizzlies. Last overseas club; Moscow

Dennis Vaske — Defenseman

Regular Season / Playoffs

Season	Team	League	GP	G	A	PTS	PIM	GP	G	A	PTS	PIM
90-91	Islanders	NHL	5	0	0	0	2	—	—	—	—	—
90-91	Capital District	AHL	67	10	10	20	65	—	—	—	—	—
91-92	Islanders	NHL	39	0	1	1	39	—	—	—	—	—
91-92	Capital District	AHL	31	1	11	12	59	—	—	—	—	—
92-93	Islanders	NHL	27	1	5	6	32	18	0	6	6	14
92-93	Capital District	AHL	42	4	15	19	70	—	—	—	—	—
93-94	Islanders	NHL	65	2	11	13	76	4	0	1	1	2
94-95	Islanders	NHL	41	1	11	12	53	—	—	—	—	—
95-96	Islanders	NHL	19	1	6	7	21	—	—	—	—	—
96-97	Islanders	NHL	17	0	4	4	12	—	—	—	—	—
97-98	Islanders	NHL	19	0	3	3	12	—	—	—	—	—
98-99	Boston	NHL	3	0	0	0	6	—	—	—	—	—
98-99	Providence	AHL	43	2	13	15	56	19	1	5	6	26
	NHL	Totals	235	5	41	46	253	22	0	7	7	16
	AHL	Totals	183	17	49	66	250	19	1	5	6	26

Born; 10/11/67, Rockford, Illinois. 6-2, 210. Drafted by New York Islanders (2nd choice, 38th overall) in 1986 Entry Draft. Signed as a free agent by Boston Bruins (9/10/99). Member of 1998-99 AHL Champion Providence Bruins. Last amateur club; Minnesota (WCHA).

John Vecchiarelli — Center

Regular Season / Playoffs

Season	Team	League	GP	G	A	PTS	PIM	GP	G	A	PTS	PIM
85-86	Flint	IHL	81	40	52	92	89	—	—	—	—	—
86-87	Flint	IHL	12	4	3	7	23	—	—	—	—	—
86-87	Peoria	IHL	65	18	34	52	91	—	—	—	—	—
87-88												
88-89												
89-90												
90-91	Milan	Italy										
91-92	Milan	Italy										
92-93												
93-94	Dallas	CeHL	6	4	3	7	14	—	—	—	—	—
93-94	Chatham	CoHL	48	45	64	109	105	15	10	*18	*28	41
94-95	Saginaw	CoHL	40	33	46	79	155	11	8	13	21	22
95-96	Las Vegas	IHL	2	0	1	1	4	—	—	—	—	—
95-96	Utica	CoHL	58	32	50	82	165	—	—	—	—	—
96-97	Utica	CoHL	73	56	50	106	153	3	3	1	4	8
97-98	Schwennigen	Germany	7	1	0	1	60	—	—	—	—	—
97-98	Brantford	UHL	51	33	43	76	60	9	6	10	16	22
98-99	Shreveport	WPHL	55	43	46	89	128	12	10	11	21	18
	IHL	Totals	158	62	89	151	203	—	—	—	—	—
	UHL	Totals	270	199	253	452	635	38	27	42	69	93

Born; 7/24/64, Toronto, Ontario. 6-0, 190. Traded to Brantford by Winston-Salem in a three-way trade. John Batten went to Winston-Salem while Wayne Muir went to Quad City (11/97). 1993-94 CoHL First All-Star Team. 1998-99 WPHL Playoff MVP. Member of 1998-99 WPHL Champion Shreveport Mudbugs. Last amateur club; Peterborough (OHL).

Eric Vellieux — Center

Regular Season / Playoffs

Season	Team	League	GP	G	A	PTS	PIM	GP	G	A	PTS	PIM
93-94	Cornwall	AHL	77	8	19	27	69	13	1	7	8	20
94-95	Cornwall	AHL	70	13	23	36	93	13	1	1	2	20
95-96	Cornwall	AHL	71	25	35	60	119	8	2	6	8	2
96-97	Hershey	AHL	68	28	33	61	118	23	*11	10	21	14
97-98	Hershey	AHL	78	24	38	62	127	7	4	2	6	8
98-99	Sai Pa Lappeenranta	Finland	9	1	2	3	14	—	—	—	—	—
98-99	Kentucky	AHL	68	8	25	33	114	6	0	2	2	6
	AHL	Totals	432	106	173	279	640	70	19	28	47	70

Born; 2/20/72, Quebec City, Quebec. 5-7, 148. Signed as a free agent by Quebec Nordiques (10/6/93). Member of 1996-97 AHL Champion Hersey Bears. Last amateur club; Laval (QMJHL).

Darren Veitch — Defenseman

Regular Season / Playoffs

Season	Team	League	GP	G	A	PTS	PIM	GP	G	A	PTS	PIM
80-81	Washington	NHL	59	4	21	25	46	—	—	—	—	—
80-81	Hershey	AHL	26	6	22	28	12	10	6	3	9	15
81-82	Washington	NHL	67	9	44	53	54	—	—	—	—	—
81-82	Hershey	AHL	10	5	10	15	16	—	—	—	—	—
82-83	Washington	NHL	10	0	8	8	0	—	—	—	—	—
82-83	Hershey	AHL	5	0	1	1	2	—	—	—	—	—
83-84	Washington	NHL	46	6	18	24	17	5	0	1	1	15
83-84	Hershey	AHL	11	1	6	7	4	—	—	—	—	—
84-85	Washington	NHL	75	3	18	21	37	5	0	1	1	4
85-86	Washington	NHL	62	3	9	12	27	—	—	—	—	—
85-86	Detroit	NHL	13	0	5	5	2	—	—	—	—	—
86-87	Detroit	NHL	77	13	45	58	52	12	3	4	7	8
87-88	Detroit	NHL	63	7	33	40	45	11	1	5	6	6
88-89	Toronto	NHL	37	3	7	10	16	—	—	—	—	—
88-89	Newmarket	AHL	33	5	19	24	29	5	0	4	4	4
89-90	Newmarket	AHL	78	13	54	67	30	—	—	—	—	—
90-91	Toronto	NHL	2	0	1	1	0	—	—	—	—	—
90-91	Newmarket	AHL	56	7	28	35	26	—	—	—	—	—
90-91	Peoria	IHL	18	2	14	16	10	19	4	12	16	10
91-92	Moncton	AHL	61	6	23	29	47	11	0	6	6	2
92-93	Peoria	IHL	79	12	37	49	16	4	2	0	2	4
93-94	Peoria	IHL	76	21	54	75	16	6	1	1	2	0
94-95	Peoria	IHL	75	8	42	50	42	9	0	2	2	8
95-96	Peoria	IHL	15	1	9	10	8	—	—	—	—	—
95-96	Phoenix	IHL	43	1	15	16	12	1	0	0	0	0
96-97	DNP											
97-98	Phoenix	WCHL	59	6	31	37	40	9	3	6	9	12
98-99	Phoenix	WCHL	52	3	29	32	46	3	0	1	1	2
	NHL	Totals	511	48	209	257	296	33	4	11	15	33
	IHL	Totals	306	45	171	216	104	39	7	15	22	22
	AHL	Totals	280	43	163	206	140	36	6	13	19	21
	WCHL	Totals	111	9	60	69	86	12	3	7	10	14

Born; 4/24/60, Saskatoon, Saskatchewan. 6-0, 200. Drafted by Washington Capitals (1st choice, 5th overall) in 1980 Entry Draft. Traded to Detroit Red Wings by Washington for Greg Smith and John Barrett (3/86). Traded to Toronto Maple Leafs by Detroit for Miroslav Frycer (6/88). Traded to St. Louis Blues by Toronto for Keith Osborne (3/5/91). Signed as a free agent by Moncton Hawks (11/8/91). Signed as a free agent by Peoria Rivermen (7/27/92). Traded to Phoenix Roadrunners by Peoria for Steve Wilson. 1989-90 AHL Second Team All-Star. 1993-94 IHL Governor's Trophy (outstanding defenseman). Member of 1990-91 IHL Champion Peoria Rivermen. Last amateur club; Regina (WHL).

Mike Vellinga — Defenseman

Regular Season / Playoffs

Season	Team	League	GP	G	A	PTS	PIM	GP	G	A	PTS	PIM
98-99	Saint John	AHL	15	0	1	1	6	—	—	—	—	—
98-99	Orlando	IHL	1	0	0	0	4	—	—	—	—	—
98-99	Johnstown	ECHL	45	1	14	15	22	—	—	—	—	—

Born; 8/19/78, Chatham, Ontario. 6-1, 218. Drafted by Chicago Blackhawks (5th choice, 184th overall) in 1996 Entry Draft. Signed as a free agent by Calgary Flames (7/21/98). Last amateur club; Guelph (OHL).

Sean Venedam — Center

Regular Season / Playoffs

Season	Team	League	GP	G	A	PTS	PIM	GP	G	A	PTS	PIM
96-97	Sudbury	OHL	66	36	55	91	54	—	—	—	—	—
96-97	Adirondack	AHL	13	0	1	1	4	—	—	—	—	—
97-98	Toledo	ECHL	70	29	43	72	91	7	0	1	1	12
98-99	Greenville	ECHL	70	29	24	53	42	—	—	—	—	—
	ECHL	Totals	140	58	67	125	133	7	0	1	1	12

Born; 7/31/76, Sudbury, Ontario. 5-10, 185. 1997-98 ECHL Rookie of the Year. Last amateur club; Sudbury (OHL).

Jim Verdule — Defenseman

Regular Season / Playoffs

Season	Team	League	GP	G	A	PTS	PIM	GP	G	A	PTS	PIM
98-99	Rouyn-Noranda	QMJHL	42	5	33	38	172	—	—	—	—	—
98-99	New Mexico	WPHL	17	2	2	4	98	—	—	—	—	—

Born; 5/3/78, Montreal, Quebec. 6-1, 190. Last amateur club; Rouyn-Noranda (QMJHL).

Ben Verhaagh — Defenseman

Regular Season / Playoffs

Season	Team	League	GP	G	A	PTS	PIM	GP	G	A	PTS	PIM
98-99	Madison	UHL	39	0	2	2	19	—	—	—	—	—
98-99	Monroe	WPHL	20	0	0	0	10	—	—	—	—	—

Born; 4/17/74, Green Bay, Wisconsin. 6-0, 200.

Darcy Verot — Center

Regular Season / Playoffs

Season	Team	League	GP	G	A	PTS	PIM	GP	G	A	PTS	PIM
97-98	Lake Charles	WPHL	68	11	26	37	269	4	0	1	1	25
98-99	Lake Charles	WPHL	68	17	23	40	236	9	2	4	6	53
	WPHL	Totals	136	28	49	77	505	13	2	5	7	78

Born; 7/13/76, Radville, Saskatchewan. 6-0, 190.

Steve Vezina — Goaltender

Regular Season / Playoffs

Season	Team	League	GP	W	L	T	MIN	SO	AVG	GP	W	L	MIN	SO	AVG
95-96	Saginaw	CoHL	43	17	19	4	2158	0	4.67	—	—	—	—	—	—
96-97	Binghamton	AHL	1	0	0	0	20	0	6.00	—	—	—	—	—	—
96-97	Jacksonville	ECHL	44	14	19	8	2440	0	3.54	—	—	—	—	—	—
97-98	Lake Charles	WPHL	2	0	2	0	119	0	5.54	—	—	—	—	—	—
97-98	Macon	CHL	48	20	18	4	2532	*2	3.10	2	0	2	119	0	5.02
98-99	Long Beach	IHL	2	0	1	0	52	0	3.48	—	—	—	—	—	—
98-99	Utah	IHL	20	12	4	1	1066	0	2.76	—	—	—	—	—	—
98-99	San Diego	WCHL	13	5	4	3	710	1	3.30	—	—	—	—	—	—
98-99	Bakersfield	WCHL	5	2	2	1	297	0	3.69	—	—	—	—	—	—
98-99	Colorado	WCHL	9	4	5	0	538	0	3.01	3	1	2	183	0	3.61
	IHL	Totals	22	12	5	1	1117	0	2.79	—	—	—	—	—	—
	WCHL	Totals	27	11	11	4	1545	1	3.46	3	1	2	183	0	3.61

Born; 10/25/75, Montreal, Quebec. 5-11, 175. Drafted by Winnipeg Jets (6th choice, 143rd overall) in 1994 Entry Draft. Last amateur club; Drummondville

Dennis Vial — Defenseman

Regular Season / Playoffs

Season	Team	League	GP	G	A	PTS	PIM	GP	G	A	PTS	PIM
89-90	Flint	IHL	79	6	29	35	351	4	0	0	0	10
90-91	Rangers	NHL	21	0	0	0	61	—	—	—	—	—
90-91	Binghamton	AHL	40	2	7	9	250	—	—	—	—	—
90-91	Detroit	NHL	9	0	0	0	16	—	—	—	—	—
91-92	Detroit	NHL	27	1	0	1	72	—	—	—	—	—
91-92	Adirondack	AHL	20	2	4	6	107	17	1	3	4	43
92-93	Detroit	NHL	9	0	1	1	20	—	—	—	—	—
92-93	Adirondack	AHL	30	2	11	13	177	11	1	1	2	14
93-94	Ottawa	NHL	55	2	5	7	214	—	—	—	—	—
94-95	Ottawa	NHL	27	0	4	4	65	—	—	—	—	—
95-96	Ottawa	NHL	64	1	4	5	276	—	—	—	—	—
96-97	Ottawa	NHL	11	0	1	1	25	—	—	—	—	—
97-98	Ottawa	NHL	19	0	0	0	45	—	—	—	—	—
97-98	Chicago	IHL	24	1	3	4	86	1	0	0	0	2
98-99	Chicago	IHL	55	1	4	5	213	—	—	—	—	—
	NHL	Totals	242	4	15	19	794	—	—	—	—	—
	IHL	Totals	158	8	36	44	650	5	0	0	0	12
	AHL	Totals	90	6	22	28	534	28	2	4	6	57

Born; 4/10/69, Sault Ste. Marie, Ontario. 6-1, 220. Drafted by New York Rangers (5th choice, 110th overall) in 1988 Entry Draft. Traded to Detroit Red Wings by Rangers with Kevin Miller and Jim Cummins for Joey Kocur and Per Djoos (3/5/91). Traded to Quebec Nordiques by Detroit with Doug Crossman for cash (6/15/92). Traded to Detroit by Quebec for cash (9/9/92). Traded to Tampa Bay Lightning by Detroit for Steve Maltais (6/8/93). Claimed by Anaheim Mighty Ducks from Tampa Bay in Expansion Draft (6/24/93). Claimed by Ottawa Senators from Anaheim in Phase II of Expansion Draft (6/25/93). Member of 1991-92 AHL Champion Adirondack Red Wings. Member of 1997-98 IHL Champion Chicago Wolves. Last amateur club; Niagara Falls (OHL).

Mitch Vig — Defenseman

Regular Season / Playoffs

Season	Team	League	GP	G	A	PTS	PIM	GP	G	A	PTS	PIM
98-99	Tallahassee	ECHL	45	2	5	7	87	—	—	—	—	—
98-99	Mobile	ECHL	20	1	6	7	14	2	0	0	0	14
	ECHL	Totals	65	3	11	14	101	2	0	0	0	14

Born; 5/18/74, Bismark, North Dakota. 6-3, 200. Traded to Mobile by Tallahassee with Ken Ruddick for Greg Callahan (2/99). Last amateur club; North Dakota (WCHA).

Bruno Villeneuve — Right Wing

Regular Season / Playoffs

Season	Team	League	GP	G	A	PTS	PIM	GP	G	A	PTS	PIM
91-92	Knoxville	ECHL	48	38	35	72	12	—	—	—	—	—
91-92	Raleigh	ECHL	8	5	2	7	9	4	0	2	2	2
92-93	Raleigh	ECHL	54	30	19	49	47	10	3	5	8	2
93-94	Knoxville	ECHL	48	27	29	56	65	3	2	0	2	2
94-95	Brantford	CoHL	10	3	2	5	0	—	—	—	—	—
94-95	Utica	CoHL	49	22	25	47	30	6	2	0	2	2
95-96	Winston-Salem	SHL	60	23	33	56	82	9	3	2	5	0
96-97	Macon	CeHL	66	49	46	95	14	5	1	4	5	0
97-98	Winston-Salem	UHL	9	3	5	8	4	—	—	—	—	—
98-99	Macon	CHL	31	11	6	17	4	—	—	—	—	—
98-99	Winston-Salem	UHL	24	7	6	13	2	3	0	1	1	0
	ECHL	Totals	158	100	85	185	133	17	5	7	12	6
	CHL	Totals	97	60	52	112	18	5	1	4	5	0
	UHL	Totals	92	35	38	73	36	9	2	1	3	2

Born; 7/4/70, Hull, Quebec. 5-11, 187. Last amateur club; Hull (QMJHL).

Daniel Villeneuve — Defenseman

Regular Season / Playoffs

Season	Team	League	GP	G	A	PTS	PIM	GP	G	A	PTS	PIM
95-96	Val D' Or	QMJHL										
95-96	Saginaw	CoHL	8	0	0	0	43	—	—	—	—	—
96-97	San Antonio	CeHL	60	3	8	11	334	—	—	—	—	—
97-98	Tulsa	CHL	55	4	9	13	321	4	0	0	0	30
98-99	Tulsa	CHL	56	3	16	19	266	—	—	—	—	—
	CHL	Totals	171	10	33	43	921	4	0	0	0	30

Born; 3/21/75, Buckingham, Quebec. 6-2, 200. Last amateur club; Val D'Or (QMJHL).

Martin Villeneuve — Goaltender

Regular Season / Playoffs

Season	Team	League	GP	W	L	T	MIN	SO	AVG	GP	W	L	MIN	SO	AVG
96-97	Rouyn-Noranda	QMJHL	56	15	33	5	3200	1	4.05	—	—	—	—	—	—
96-97	Fredericton	AHL	3	1	1	0	114	0	2.11	—	—	—	—	—	—
97-98	Fredericton	AHL	1	0	1	0	60	0	2.01	—	—	—	—	—	—
97-98	New Orleans	ECHL	54	26	17	7	2960	0	3.32	4	1	3	270	0	3.56
98-99	Fredericton	AHL	2	1	0	0	75	0	3.22	—	—	—	—	—	—
98-99	New Orleans	ECHL	43	17	14	8	2334	0	3.42	8	5	3	479	2	2.25
	AHL	Totals	6	2	2	0	249	0	2.41	—	—	—	—	—	—
	ECHL	Totals	97	43	31	15	5294	0	3.37	12	6	6	749	2	2.72

Born; 1/1/76, Montreal, Quebec. 5-10, 178. Signed as a free agent by Montreal Canadiens (8/29/97). Last amateur club; Rouyn-Noranda (QMJHL).

Mark Vilneff — Defenseman

Regular Season / Playoffs

Season	Team	League	GP	G	A	PTS	PIM	GP	G	A	PTS	PIM
94-95	Muskegon	CoHL	71	1	10	11	60	14	1	3	4	6
95-96	Muskegon	CoHL	69	3	3	6	27	5	0	1	1	0
96-97	Muskegon	CoHL	66	1	10	11	38	3	0	0	0	4
97-98	Grand Rapids	IHL	5	0	0	0	0	—	—	—	—	—
97-98	Michigan	IHL	1	0	0	0	0	—	—	—	—	—
97-98	Muskegon	UHL	71	3	19	22	57	11	0	1	1	4
98-99	Utah	IHL	3	0	0	0	0	—	—	—	—	—
98-99	Detroit	IHL	7	0	0	0	2	—	—	—	—	—
98-99	Muskegon	UHL	37	0	11	11	45	—	—	—	—	—
98-99	Flint	UHL	13	1	2	3	25	11	0	2	2	12
	IHL	Totals	16	0	0	0	2	—	—	—	—	—
	UHL	Totals	327	9	55	64	252	44	1	7	8	26

Born; 11/28/73, Cobourg, Ontario. 6-2, 195. Traded to Flint by Muskegon with Jan Klimes and David Beauregard for Mike Bondy and Chad Grills (2/99). Last amateur club; Peterborough (OHL).

Paul Vincent — Center

Regular Season / Playoffs

Season	Team	League	GP	G	A	PTS	PIM	GP	G	A	PTS	PIM
94-95	St. John's	AHL	2	0	2	2	0	—	—	—	—	—
95-96	St. John's	AHL	16	2	3	5	2	1	0	0	0	2
95-96	Raleigh	ECHL	30	12	9	21	29	—	—	—	—	—
96-97	St. John's	AHL	3	0	2	2	12	—	—	—	—	—
96-97	Peoria	ECHL	45	31	29	60	72	10	7	8	15	8
97-98	Winston-Salem	UHL	22	16	15	31	29	—	—	—	—	—
97-98	Flint	UHL	16	7	8	15	10	—	—	—	—	—
97-98	Saginaw	UHL	13	6	8	14	4	—	—	—	—	—
98-99	Michigan	IHL	2	2	1	3	0	—	—	—	—	—
98-99	Lake Charles	WPHL	17	9	8	17	13	—	—	—	—	—
98-99	Odessa	WPHL	15	18	11	29	6	3	1	2	3	2
	AHL	Totals	21	2	7	9	14	1	0	0	0	2
	ECHL	Totals	75	43	38	81	101	10	7	8	15	8
	UHL	Totals	51	29	31	60	43	—	—	—	—	—
	WPHL	Totals	32	27	19	46	19	3	1	2	3	2

Born; 1/4/75, Utica, New York. 6-4, 200. Drafted by Toronto Maple Leafs (4th choice, 149th overall) in 1993 Entry Draft. Traded to Flint by Winston-Salem with John Batten and Brent Daugherty for Dmitri Rodine (1/98). Traded to Saginaw by Flint for David Grant (3/98). Traded to Odessa by Lake Charles for Ryan Equale (2/99). Last amateur club; Swift Current (WHL).

Kelly Vipond — Right Wing

Regular Season / Playoffs

Season	Team	League	GP	G	A	PTS	PIM	GP	G	A	PTS	PIM
95-96	San Diego	WCHL	54	13	17	30	97	9	2	0	2	17
96-97	San Diego	WCHL	8	1	5	6	41	—	—	—	—	—
97-98	San Diego	WCHL	3	0	0	0	15	—	—	—	—	—
97-98	Reno	WCHL	8	0	1	1	12	—	—	—	—	—
98-99	Monroe	WPHL	32	4	2	6	53	3	0	0	0	10
	WCHL	Totals	73	14	23	37	165	9	2	0	2	17

Born; 1/26/74, Brooklin, Ontario. 6-1, 190. Member of 1995-96 WCHL Champion San Diego Gulls.

Terry Virtue — Defenseman

Regular Season / Playoffs

Season	Team	League	GP	G	A	PTS	PIM	GP	G	A	PTS	PIM
91-92	Roanoke	ECHL	38	4	22	26	165	—	—	—	—	—
91-92	Louisville	ECHL	23	1	15	16	58	13	0	8	8	49
92-93	Louisville	ECHL	28	0	17	17	84	—	—	—	—	—
92-93	Wheeling	ECHL	31	3	15	18	86	16	3	5	8	18
93-94	Cape Breton	AHL	26	4	6	10	10	—	—	—	—	—
93-94	Wheeling	ECHL	34	5	28	33	61	6	2	2	4	4
94-95	Atlanta	IHL	1	0	0	0	2	—	—	—	—	—
94-95	Worcester	AHL	73	14	25	39	186	—	—	—	—	—
95-96	Worcester	AHL	76	7	31	38	234	4	0	0	0	4
96-97	Worcester	AHL	80	16	26	42	220	5	0	4	4	8
97-98	Worcester	AHL	74	8	26	34	233	11	1	4	5	41
98-99	Boston	NHL	4	0	0	0	0	—	—	—	—	—
98-99	Providence	AHL	76	8	48	56	117	17	2	12	14	29
	AHL	Totals	329	49	114	163	883	20	1	8	9	53
	ECHL	Totals	154	13	97	110	454	35	5	15	20	71

Born; 8/12/70, Scarborough, Ontario. 6-0, 200. Signed as a free agent by St. Louis Blues (1/29/96). Signed as a free agent by Boston Bruins (9/10/98). Signed as a free agent by New York Rangers (7/29/99). 1998-99 AHL Second Team All-Star. Member of 1998-99 AHL Champion Providence Bruins. Last amateur club; Portland (WHL).

Sergejs Visegorodcevs — Defenseman

Regular Season / Playoffs

Season	Team	League	GP	G	A	PTS	PIM	GP	G	A	PTS	PIM
98-99	San Diego	WCHL	51	3	24	27	28	11	1	1	2	4

Born; 5/22/76, Riga, Latvia. 6-3, 190. Last European club; CSKA Moscow.

Nick Vitucci — Goaltender

Regular Season / Playoffs

Season	Team	League	GP	W	L	T	MIN	SO	AVG	GP	W	L	MIN	SO	AVG
88-89	Carolina	ECHL	22	11	9	0	1238	1	4.65	10	*8	2	592	0	3.55
89-90	Winston-Salem	ECHL	6	4	2	0	360	0	4.67	—	—	—	—	—	—
89-90	Greensboro	ECHL	28	10	9	5	1496	0	4.57	3	1	1	153	0	2.75
90-91	Greensboro	ECHL	41	22	16	2	2225	1	3.82	*13	8	5	*813	0	3.17
91-92	Hershey	AHL	4	2	1	0	191	0	4.71	—	—	—	—	—	—
91-92	Maine	AHL	1	0	0	1	65	0	2.77	—	—	—	—	—	—
91-92	Greensboro	ECHL	42	28	8	2	2358	1	3.46	11	5	6	673	0	2.67
92-93	Peoria	IHL	8	3	4	1	479	0	3.38	—	—	—	—	—	—
92-93	Hampton Roads	ECHL	29	17	7	3	1669	1	*3.06	3	1	2	206	0	2.33
93-94	Peoria	IHL	11	3	4	1	422	0	4.98	—	—	—	—	—	—
93-94	Toledo	ECHL	27	15	6	4	1532	0	3.64	—	—	—	—	—	—
94-95	Toledo	ECHL	56	*35	16	3	3273	*3	3.23	4	1	3	239	0	3.01
95-96	Charlotte	ECHL	48	*32	13	3	2794	0	3.52	11	7	2	585	1	2.46
96-97	Binghamton	AHL	2	0	0	2	129	0	4.17	—	—	—	—	—	—
96-97	Charlotte	ECHL	36	20	10	4	2029	0	3.46	3	0	3	178	0	3.37
97-98	Toledo	ECHL	49	27	16	5	2827	2	2.76	7	4	3	440	0	2.59
98-99	Greenville	ECHL	32	9	17	4	1855	0	3.33	—	—	—	—	—	—
	IHL	Totals	19	6	8	2	901	0	4.13	—	—	—	—	—	—
	AHL	Totals	7	2	1	3	385	0	4.21	—	—	—	—	—	—
	[illegible]	[illegible]	[illegible]	[illegible]	[illegible]	[illegible]	[illegible]	[illegible]	[illegible]	[illegible]	[illegible]	[illegible]	[illegible]	[illegible]	[illegible]

Born; 6/16/67, Welland, Ontario. 5-9, 175, 1989-90 ECHL playoff MVP. 1995-96 ECHL playoff MVP. 1991-92 ECHL First All-Star Team. 1992-93 ECHL Top Goaltender. 1997-98 ECHL Top Goaltender. 1997-98 ECHL First All-Star Team. Member of 1988-89 ECHL champion Carolina Thunderbirds. Member of 1989-90 ECHL champion Greensboro Monarchs. Back-up goaltender for 1993-94 ECHL champion Toledo Storm. Member of 1995-96 ECHL champion Charlotte

Jan Vodrazka — Defenseman

Regular Season / Playoffs

Season	Team	League	GP	G	A	PTS	PIM	GP	G	A	PTS	PIM
96-97	Detroit	OHL	61	7	21	28	238	5	0	1	1	17
96-97	Richmond	ECHL	4	0	0	0	12	7	0	1	1	36
97-98	Milwaukee	IHL	10	0	0	0	32	—	—	—	—	—
97-98	Madison	UHL	55	3	15	18	224	6	1	1	2	36
98-99	Pee Dee	ECHL	64	8	12	20	262	13	0	0	0	56
	ECHL	Totals	68	8	12	20	274	20	0	1	1	92

Born; 11/10/76, Pizen, Czechoslovakia. 6-1, 200. Last amateur club; Detroit

Thomas Vokoun — Goaltender
Regular Season / Playoffs

Season	Team	League	GP	W	L	T	MIN	SO	AVG	GP	W	L	MIN	SO	AVG
95-96	Fredericton	AHL	—	—	—	—	—	—	—	1	0	1	59	0	4.09
95-96	Wheeling	ECHL	35	20	10	2	1912	0	3.67	7	4	3	436	0	2.61
96-97	Montreal	NHL	1	0	0	0	20	0	12.00	—	—	—	—	—	—
96-97	Fredericton	AHL	47	12	26	7	2645	2	3.49	—	—	—	—	—	—
97-98	Fredericton	AHL	31	13	13	2	1735	0	3.11	—	—	—	—	—	—
98-99	Nashville	NHL	37	12	18	4	1954	1	2.95	—	—	—	—	—	—
98-99	Milwaukee	IHL	9	3	2	4	539	1	2.45	2	0	2	149	0	3.22
	NHL	Totals	38	12	18	4	1974	1	3.04	—	—	—	—	—	—
	AHL	Totals	78	25	39	9	4380	2	3.34	1	0	1	59	0	4.09

Born; 7/2/76, Karlovy Vary, Czechoslovakia. 5-11, 180. Drafted by Montreal Canadiens (11th choice, 226th overall) in 1994 Entry Draft. Selected by Nashville Predators in NHL Expansion Draft (6/26/98).

Alexandre Volchkov — Right Wing
Regular Season / Playoffs

Season	Team	League	GP	G	A	PTS	PIM	GP	G	A	PTS	PIM
96-97	Barrie	OHL	56	29	53	82	76	9	6	9	15	12
96-97	Portland	AHL	—	—	—	—	—	4	0	0	0	0
97-98	Portland	AHL	34	2	5	7	20	1	0	0	0	0
98-99	Portland	AHL	27	3	8	11	24	—	—	—	—	—
98-99	Cincinnati	IHL	25	1	3	4	8	—	—	—	—	—
	AHL	Totals	61	5	13	18	44	5	0	0	0	0

Born; 9/25/77, Moscow, Russia. 6-1, 194. Drafted by Washington Capitals (1st choice, 4th overall) in 1996 Entry Draft. Last amateur club; Barrie (OHL).

Kelly Von Hiltgen — Defenseman
Regular Season / Playoffs

Season	Team	League	GP	G	A	PTS	PIM	GP	G	A	PTS	PIM
97-98	Fort Worth	CHL	5	0	1	1	8	—	—	—	—	—
97-98	Thunder Bay	UHL	22	0	4	4	27	—	—	—	—	—
98-99	Tupelo	WPHL	30	3	7	10	148	—	—	—	—	—

Born; 12/6/73, Vancouver, British Columbia. 6-4, 220.

Phil von Stefenelli — Defenseman
Regular Season / Playoffs

Season	Team	League	GP	G	A	PTS	PIM	GP	G	A	PTS	PIM
91-92	Milwaukee	IHL	80	2	34	36	40	5	1	2	3	2
92-93	Hamilton	AHL	78	11	20	31	75	—	—	—	—	—
93-94	Hamilton	AHL	80	10	31	41	89	4	1	0	1	2
94-95	Providence	AHL	75	6	13	19	93	11	2	4	6	6
95-96	Boston	NHL	27	0	4	4	16	—	—	—	—	—
95-96	Providence	AHL	42	9	21	30	52	—	—	—	—	—
96-97	Ottawa	NHL	6	0	1	1	7	—	—	—	—	—
96-97	Detroit	IHL	67	14	26	40	86	21	2	4	6	20
97-98												
98-99	Frankfurt	Germany	51	4	12	16	75	8	0	0	0	6
	NHL	Totals	33	0	5	5	23	—	—	—	—	—
	AHL	Totals	275	36	85	121	309	15	3	4	7	8
	IHL	Totals	147	16	60	76	126	26	3	6	9	22

Born; 4/10/69, Vancouver, British Columbia. 6-1, 200. Drafted by Vancouver Canucks (5th choice, 122nd overall) in 1988 Entry Draft. Signed as a free agent by Boston Bruins (9/10/94). Signed as a free agent by Ottawa Seantors (7/17/96). Signed as a free agent by Tampa Bay Lightning (7/22/99). Last amateur club; Boston University (Hockey East).

Vladimir Vorobiev — Right Wing
Regular Season / Playoffs

Season	Team	League	GP	G	A	PTS	PIM	GP	G	A	PTS	PIM
96-97	Rangers	NHL	16	5	5	10	6	—	—	—	—	—
96-97	Binghamton	AHL	61	22	27	49	6	4	1	1	2	2
97-98	Rangers	NHL	15	2	2	4	6	—	—	—	—	—
97-98	Hartford	AHL	56	20	28	48	18	15	11	8	19	4
98-99	Edmonton	NHL	2	2	0	2	2	1	0	0	0	0
98-99	Hartford	AHL	65	24	41	65	22	—	—	—	—	—
98-99	Hamilton	AHL	8	3	6	9	2	6	0	1	1	2
	NHL	Totals	33	9	7	16	14	1	0	0	0	0
	AHL	Totals	190	69	102	171	48	25	12	10	22	8

Born; 10/2/72, Cherepovets, Russia. 5-11, 185. Drafted by New York Rangers (10th choice, 240th overall) in 1992 Entry Draft. Traded to Edmonton Oilers by Rangers for Kevin Brown (3/23/99). Last overseas club; Moscow Dynamo (CIS).

Curtis Voth — Right Wing
Regular Season / Playoffs

Season	Team	League	GP	G	A	PTS	PIM	GP	G	A	PTS	PIM
96-97	Amarillo	WPHL	11	2	1	3	40	—	—	—	—	—
97-98	Fort Worth	WPHL	4	0	0	0	17	—	—	—	—	—
97-98	Wichita	CHL	60	8	12	20	267	11	0	1	1	*98
98-99	Tulsa	CHL	56	7	4	11	*426	—	—	—	—	—
	CHL	Totals	116	15	16	31	693	11	0	1	1	98
	WPHL	Totals	15	2	1	3	57	—	—	—	—	—

Born; 4/4/75, Riverhurst, Saskatchewan. 6-0, 180.

Vladomir Vujtek — Left Wing
Regular Season / Playoffs

Season	Team	League	GP	G	A	PTS	PIM	GP	G	A	PTS	PIM
91-92	Tri-City	WHL	53	41	61	102	114	—	—	—	—	—
91-92	Montreal	NHL	2	0	0	0	0	—	—	—	—	—
92-93	Edmonton	NHL	30	1	10	11	8	—	—	—	—	—
92-93	Cape Breton	AHL	20	10	9	19	14	1	0	0	0	0
93-94	Edmonton	NHL	40	4	15	19	14	—	—	—	—	—
94-95	Vitkovice	Czech.	18	5	7	12	51	—	—	—	—	—
94-95	Cape Breton	AHL	30	10	11	21	30	—	—	—	—	—
94-95	Las Vegas	IHL	1	0	0	0	0	—	—	—	—	—
95-96	Vitkovice	Czech.	26	6	7	13	—	4	1	1	2	—
96-97	Assat Pori	Finland	50	27	31	58	48	4	1	2	3	2
97-98	Tampa Bay	NHL	30	2	4	6	16	—	—	—	—	—
97-98	Adirondack	AHL	2	1	2	3	0	—	—	—	—	—
98-99	Vitkovice	Czech.	47	20	35	55	75	—	—	—	—	—
	NHL	Totals	102	7	29	36	38	—	—	—	—	—
	AHL	Totals	52	21	22	43	44	1	0	0	0	0

Born; 2/17/72, Ostrava, Czech Republic. 6-1, 190. Drafted by Montreal Canadiens (5th choice, 73rd overall) in 1991 Entry Draft. Traded to Edmonton Oilers by Montreal with Shayne Corson and Brent Gilchrist for Vincent Damphousse and Edmonton's fourth round choice (Adam Wiesel) in 1993 Entry Draft (8/27/92). Traded to Tampa Bay Lightning by Edmonton with Edmonton's third round choice (Dmitri Afanasenkov) in 1998 Entry Draft for Brant Myhres and Toronto's third round choice (previously acquired-Edmonton selected Alex Henry) in 1998 Entry Draft (7/16/97). Signed as a free agent by Atlanta Thrashers (7/19/99).

Mike Vukonich — Center
Regular Season / Playoffs

Season	Team	League	GP	G	A	PTS	PIM	GP	G	A	PTS	PIM
91-92	Phoenix	IHL	68	17	11	28	21	—	—	—	—	—
92-93	Phoenix	IHL	70	25	15	40	27	—	—	—	—	—
93-94	Phoenix	IHL	22	4	6	10	8	—	—	—	—	—
93-94	Binghamton	AHL	3	1	0	1	0	—	—	—	—	—
93-94	Flint	CoHL	8	7	8	15	12	10	7	7	14	12
94-95	Albany	AHL	61	16	14	30	16	4	0	0	0	0
95-96	Albany	AHL	1	0	0	0	0	—	—	—	—	—
95-96	Raleigh	ECHL	7	0	4	4	8	—	—	—	—	—
95-96	Indianapolis	IHL	53	11	15	26	40	5	1	1	2	2
96-97												
97-98	Rosenheim	Germany	42	14	14	28	40	—	—	—	—	—
98-99	Indianapolis	IHL	70	9	17	26	20	4	0	0	0	0
	IHL	Totals	283	66	64	130	116	9	1	1	2	2
	AHL	Totals	65	17	14	31	16	4	0	0	0	0

Born; 11/5/68, Duluth, Minnesota. 6-2, 220. Drafted by Los Angeles Kings (4th choice, 90th overall) in 1987 Entry Draft. Signed as a free agent by New Jersey Devils (9/28/94). Traded to Chicago Blackhawks by New Jersey with Bill Armstrong for Darin Kimble (11/1/95). Member of 1994-95 AHL Champion Albany RiverRats. Last amateur club; Harvard (ECAC).

Mick Vukota — Right Wing

Regular Season / Playoffs

Season	Team	League	GP	G	A	PTS	PIM	GP	G	A	PTS	PIM
87-88	Islanders	NHL	17	1	0	1	82	2	0	0	0	23
87-88	Springfield	AHL	52	7	9	16	375	—	—	—	—	—
88-89	Islanders	NHL	48	2	2	4	237	—	—	—	—	—
88-89	Springfield	AHL	3	1	0	1	33	—	—	—	—	—
89-90	Islanders	NHL	76	4	8	12	290	1	0	0	0	17
90-91	Islanders	NHL	60	2	4	6	238	—	—	—	—	—
90-91	Capital District	AHL	2	0	0	0	9	—	—	—	—	—
91-92	Islanders	NHL	74	0	6	6	293	—	—	—	—	—
92-93	Islanders	NHL	74	2	5	7	216	15	0	0	0	16
93-94	Islanders	NHL	72	3	1	4	237	4	0	0	0	17
94-95	Islanders	NHL	40	0	2	2	109	—	—	—	—	—
95-96	Islanders	NHL	32	1	1	2	106	—	—	—	—	—
96-97	Islanders	NHL	17	1	0	1	71	—	—	—	—	—
96-97	Utah	IHL	43	11	11	22	185	7	1	2	3	20
97-98	Tampa Bay	NHL	42	1	0	1	116	—	—	—	—	—
97-98	Montreal	NHL	22	0	0	0	76	1	0	0	0	0
98-99	Utah	IHL	48	8	7	15	226	—	—	—	—	—
	NHL	Totals	574	17	29	46	2071	23	0	0	0	73
	IHL	Totals	91	19	18	37	411	7	1	2	3	20
	AHL	Totals	57	8	9	17	417	—	—	—	—	—

Born; 9/14/66, Saskatoon, Saskatchewan. 6-1, 225. Signed as a free agent by New York Islanders (3/2/87). Claimed by Tampa Bay Lightning from Islanders in NHL Waiver Draft (9/28/97). Traded to Montreal Canadiens by Tampa Bay with Patrick Poulin and Igor Ulanov for Stephane Richer, Darcy Tucker and David Wilkie (1/15/98). Last amateur club; Spokane (WHL).

Sergei Vyshedkevich — Defenseman

Regular Season / Playoffs

Season	Team	League	GP	G	A	PTS	PIM	GP	G	A	PTS	PIM
96-97	Albany	AHL	65	8	27	35	16	12	0	6	6	0
97-98	Albany	AHL	54	12	16	28	12	13	0	10	10	4
98-99	Albany	AHL	79	11	38	49	28	5	0	3	3	0
	AHL	Totals	198	31	81	112	56	30	0	19	19	4

Born; 1/3/75, Dedovsk, Russia. 6-0, 185. Drafted by New Jersey Devils (3rd choice, 70th overall) in 1995 Entry Draft. Traded to Atlanta Thrashers by New Jersey Devils for future considerations (6/25/99).

Fedor Fedorov was selected by the Tampa Bay Lightning in the NHL Draft
Photo by Joe Costa

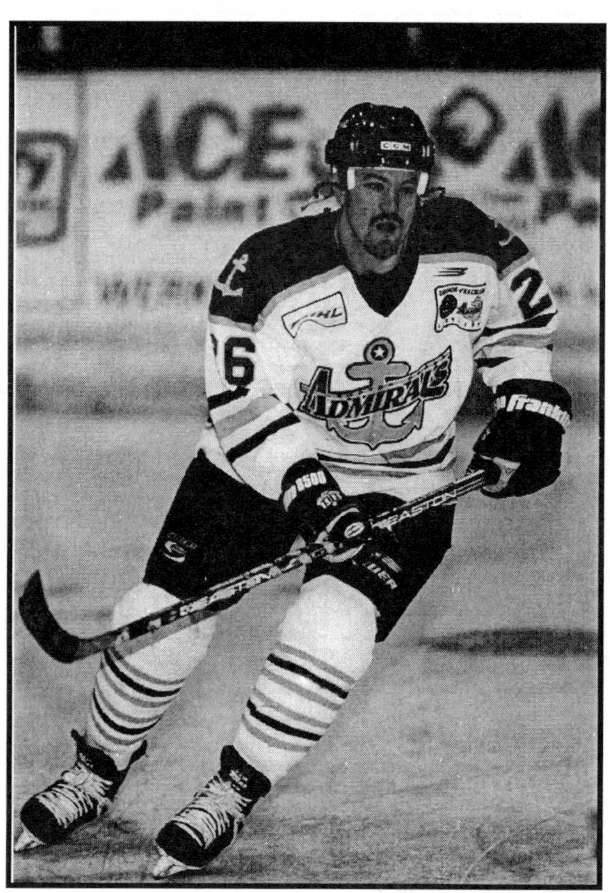

Dan Ceman should see plenty of action in the IHL or AHL next year
Photo by John Gacioch

Steve Wachter — Goaltender

Regular Season / Playoffs

Season	Team	League	GP	W	L	T	MIN	SO	AVG	GP	W	L	MIN	SO	AVG
91-92	Columbus	ECHL	3	—	—	—	84	0	7.86	—	—	—	—	—	—
91-92	Erie	ECHL	1	—	—	—	9	0	13.33	—	—	—	—	—	—
92-93	Wichita	CHL	2	0	0	0	24	0	12.50	—	—	—	—	—	—
93-94															
94-95	Muskegon	CoHL	1	0	0	0	15	0	0.00	—	—	—	—	—	—
95-96	Anchorage	WCHL	10	7	2	0	566	0	5.19						
96-97	Mississippi	ECHL	1	0	0	1	19	0	0.00	—	—	—	—	—	—
97-98															
98-99	Fort Worth	CHL	1	0	1	0	58	0	4.15	—	—	—	—	—	—
	ECHL	Totals	5	0	0	1	112	0	6.95	—	—	—	—	—	—
	CHL	Totals	3	0	1	0	82	0	6.57	—	—	—	—	—	—

Born; 1/3/66, Pittsburgh, Pennsylvania. 6-1, 180.

Steve Wagg — Center

Regular Season / Playoffs

Season	Team	League	GP	G	A	PTS	PIM	GP	G	A	PTS	PIM
97-98	Fort Worth	CHL	56	13	11	24	52	—	—	—	—	—
98-99	San Antonio	CHL	26	4	3	7	10	—	—	—	—	—
98-99	Austin	WPHL	18	2	6	8	2	—	—	—	—	—
98-99	Fort Worth	WPHL	13	1	4	5	2	10	2	0	2	4
	CHL	Totals	82	17	14	31	62	—	—	—	—	—
	WPHL	Totals	31	3	10	13	4	10	2	0	2	4

Born; 8/13/73, Bridgewater, Saskatchewan. 5-11, 198. Selected by San Antonio in 1998 CHL Expansion Draft. Last amateur club; St. Francis Xavier (AUAA).

Chad Wagner — Right Wing

Regular Season / Playoffs

Season	Team	League	GP	G	A	PTS	PIM	GP	G	A	PTS	PIM
95-96	San Diego	WCHL	45	5	12	17	289	2	0	0	0	29
96-97	San Diego	WCHL	45	6	10	16	*503	5	2	1	3	*80
97-98	Las Vegas	IHL	22	0	1	1	210	—	—	—	—	—
97-98	San Diego	WCHL	34	5	4	9	*439	5	0	0	0	63
98-99	Las Vegas	IHL	4	0	0	0	29	—	—	—	—	—
98-99	San Diego	WCHL	43	3	6	9	*521	3	0	0	0	26
	IHL	Totals	26	0	1	1	239	—	—	—	—	—
	WCHL	Totals	167	19	32	51	1752	15	2	1	3	198

Born; 11/12/74, Calgary, Alberta. 6-5, 225. Member of 1995-96 WCHL Champion San Diego Gulls. Member of 1996-97 WCHL Champion San Diego Gulls. Member of 1997-98 WCHL Champion San Diego Gulls.

Jimmy Waite — Goaltender

Regular Season / Playoffs

Season	Team	League	GP	W	L	T	MIN	SO	AVG	GP	W	L	MIN	SO	AVG
88-89	Chicago	NHL	11	0	7	1	494	0	5.22	—	—	—	—	—	—
88-89	Saginaw	IHL	5	3	1	0	304	0	1.97	—	—	—	—	—	—
89-90	Chicago	NHL	4	2	0	0	183	0	4.59	—	—	—	—	—	—
89-90	Indianapolis	IHL	54	*34	14	5	*3207	*5	*2.53	*10	*9	1	*602	*1	*1.89
90-91	Chicago	NHL	1	1	0	0	60	0	2.00	—	—	—	—	—	—
90-91	Indianapolis	IHL	49	*26	18	4	2888	3	3.47	6	2	4	369	0	3.25
91-92	Chicago	NHL	17	4	7	4	877	0	3.69	—	—	—	—	—	—
91-92	Indianapolis	IHL	13	4	7	1	702	0	4.53	—	—	—	—	—	—
91-92	Hershey	AHL	11	6	4	1	631	0	4.18	6	2	4	360	0	3.17
92-93	Chicago	NHL	20	6	7	1	996	2	2.95	—	—	—	—	—	—
93-94	San Jose	NHL	15	3	7	0	697	0	4.30	2	0	0	40	0	4.50
94-95	Chicago	NHL	2	1	1	0	119	0	2.52	—	—	—	—	—	—
94-95	Indianapolis	IHL	4	2	1	1	239	0	3.25	—	—	—	—	—	—
95-96	Chicago	NHL	1	0	0	0	31	0	0.00	—	—	—	—	—	—
95-96	Indianapolis	IHL	56	28	18	6	3157	0	3.40	5	2	3	298	1	3.02
96-97	Chicago	NHL	2	0	1	1	105	0	4.00	—	—	—	—	—	—
96-97	Indianapolis	IHL	41	22	15	4	2450	4	2.74	4	1	3	222	0	3.51
97-98	Phoenix	NHL	17	5	6	1	793	1	2.12	4	0	3	171	0	3.86
98-99	Phoenix	NHL	16	6	5	4	898	1	2.74	—	—	—	—	—	—
98-99	Utah	IHL	11	6	3	2	622	0	2.89	—	—	—	—	—	—
98-99	Springfield	AHL	8	3	4	1	483	0	2.36	2	0	2	118	0	3.05
	NHL	Totals	106	28	41	12	5253	4	3.35	6	0	3	211	0	3.98
	IHL	Totals	233	125	77	23	13569	12	3.09	25	14	11	1491	2	2.70
	AHL	Totals	19	9	8	2	1114	0	3.39	8	2	6	478	0	3.14

Born; 4/15/69, Sherbrooke, Quebec. 6-1, 180. Drafted by Chicago Blackhawks (1st choice, 8th overall) in 1987 Entry Draft. Traded to San Jose Sharks by Chicago for future considerations (Neil Wilkinson, 7/9/93) (6/19/93). Traded to Chicago by San Jose for Chicago's fourth round choice-later traded to New York Rangers-Rangers selected Tomi Kallarsson) in 1997 Entry Draft. (2/5/95). Claimed by Phoenix Coyotes in NHL Waiver Draft (9/28/97). 1989-90 IHL First All-Star Team. 1989-90 James Norris Trophy (IHL-fewest goals against). Member of 1989-90 IHL Champion Indianapolis Ice. Last amateur club; Chicoutimi

Steffon Walby — Right Wing

Regular Season / Playoffs

Season	Team	League	GP	G	A	PTS	PIM	GP	G	A	PTS	PIM
93-94	St. John's	AHL	63	15	22	37	79	2	0	0	0	2
94-95	St. John's	AHL	70	23	23	46	30	5	1	1	2	4
95-96	St. John's	AHL	57	23	31	54	61	4	2	2	4	17
96-97	Hershey	AHL	74	24	23	47	61	23	9	5	14	38
97-98	Fort Wayne	IHL	77	28	26	54	53	4	1	1	2	6
98-99	Rochester	AHL	48	15	13	28	52	—	—	—	—	—
98-99	Kentucky	AHL	11	8	4	12	6	12	3	2	5	14
	AHL	Totals	323	108	116	224	289	46	15	10	25	75

Born; 11/22/72, Madison, Wisconsin. 6-1, 198. Signed as a free agent by Toronto Maple Leafs (8/20/93). Signed as a free agent by Buffalo Sabres (8/31/98). Member of 1996-97 AHL Champion Hershey Bears. Last amateur club; Kelowna

Richie Walcott — Right Wing

Regular Season / Playoffs

Season	Team	League	GP	G	A	PTS	PIM	GP	G	A	PTS	PIM
91-92	Baltimore	AHL	51	1	1	2	277	—	—	—	—	—
91-92	Hampton Roads	ECHL	7	1	0	1	23	—	—	—	—	—
92-93	Hampton Roads	ECHL	14	1	1	2	116	—	—	—	—	—
92-93	Wheeling	ECHL	8	0	0	0	46	—	—	—	—	—
93-94	Rochester	AHL	17	1	0	1	66	—	—	—	—	—
93-94	Hampton Roads	ECHL	41	2	1	3	143	—	—	—	—	—
94-95	Utica	CoHL	61	6	9	15	309	6	0	0	0	16
95-96	Dayton	ECHL	3	1	1	2	40	—	—	—	—	—
95-96	Birmingham	ECHL	17	2	1	3	78	—	—	—	—	—
95-96	Utica	CoHL	23	1	0	1	99	—	—	—	—	—
96-97	Brantford	CoHL	41	4	5	9	86	—	—	—	—	—
96-97	Madison	CoHL	5	0	2	2	21	5	0	1	1	11
97-98	Fort Worth	CHL	36	8	10	18	89	—	—	—	—	—
97-98	Macon	CHL	28	9	7	16	86	2	0	0	0	26
98-99	Macon	CHL	16	3	0	3	54	—	—	—	—	—
98-99	Fort Worth	WPHL	22	4	5	9	113	12	1	2	3	20
	AHL	Totals	68	1	1	2	323	—	—	—	—	—
	CoHL	Totals	130	11	16	27	515	11	0	1	1	27
	ECHL	Totals	90	7	4	11	446	—	—	—	—	—
	CHL	Totals	80	20	17	37	229	2	0	0	0	26

Born; 5/17/70, Grand Cache, Alberta. 6-2, 225. Traded to Macon by Fort Worth for Jason Carriere and Claude Fillion (1/98).

Troy Walczak — Center

Regular Season / Playoffs

Season	Team	League	GP	G	A	PTS	PIM	GP	G	A	PTS	PIM
98-99	Madison	UHL	2	0	0	0	0	—	—	—	—	—

Born; 6/7/77, Toronto, Ontario.

Brian Walker — Defenseman

Regular Season / Playoffs

Season	Team	League	GP	G	A	PTS	PIM	GP	G	A	PTS	PIM
98-99	Thunder Bay	UHL	2	0	0	0	20	—	—	—	—	—

Born; 1/21/69, Red Deer, Alberta.

Darby Walker — Forward

Regular Season / Playoffs

Season	Team	League	GP	G	A	PTS	PIM	GP	G	A	PTS	PIM
97-98	Fayetteville	CHL	12	0	2	2	77	—	—	—	—	—
98-99	Newcastle	BSL	16	0	3	3	10	6	0	0	0	6

Born; 8/5/74, Beaver Lodge, Alberta. 6-4, 225.

Steve Walker — Left Wing

Regular Season / Playoffs

Season	Team	League	GP	G	A	PTS	PIM	GP	G	A	PTS	PIM
93-94	Wheeling	ECHL	9	1	0	1	2	—	—	—	—	—
94-95	Muskegon	CoHL	56	18	28	46	35	17	4	1	5	19
95-96	Muskegon	CoHL	69	43	57	100	121	5	2	3	6	0
96-97	Detroit	IHL	54	12	12	24	27	20	10	9	19	8
96-97	Rochester	AHL	3	0	0	0	17	—	—	—	—	—
96-97	Flint	CoHL	16	13	16	29	34	—	—	—	—	—
97-98	Detroit	IHL	78	27	49	76	53	23	7	9	16	13
98-99	Detroit	IHL	80	25	32	57	72	11	1	4	5	4
	IHL	Totals	212	64	93	157	152	54	18	22	40	25
	CoHL	Totals	141	74	101	175	190	22	6	4	10	19

Born; 1/12/73, Collingwood, Ontario. 6-0, 190. 1995-96 CoHL Second Team All-Star. Member of 1996-97 IHL Champion Detroit Vipers. Last amateur club; Owen Sound (OHL).

Buddy Wallace — Center

Regular Season / Playoffs

Season	Team	League	GP	G	A	PTS	PIM	GP	G	A	PTS	PIM
98-99	Lowell	AHL	70	11	11	22	57	3	1	1	2	2

Born; 12/18/75, Palatine, Illinois. 6-1, 195. Last amateur club; Clarkson (ECAC).

Jesse Wallin — Defenseman

Regular Season / Playoffs

Season	Team	League	GP	G	A	PTS	PIM	GP	G	A	PTS	PIM
98-99	Adirondack	AHL	76	4	12	16	34	3	0	2	2	2

Born; 3/10/78, Saskatoon, Saskatchewan. 6-2, 190. Drafted by Detroit Red Wings (1st choice, 26th overall) in 1996 Entry Draft. Last amateur club; Red Deer

Sinuhe Wallinheimo — Goaltender

Regular Season / Playoffs

Season	Team	League	GP	W	L	T	MIN	SO	AVG	GP	W	L	MIN	SO	AVG
96-97	Hershey	AHL	13	5	4	1	581	0	3.30	2	0	0	4	0	16.14
96-97	Mobile	ECHL	26	14	9	1	1453	0	3.26	—	—	—	—	—	—
97-98	Springfield	AHL	10	4	4	0	516	0	3.49	—	—	—	—	—	—
97-98	Mississippi	ECHL	37	19	12	3	1902	1	2.81	—	—	—	—	—	—
98-99	Lukko Rauma	Finland	33	9	21	2	1853	0	3.53	—	—	—	—	—	—
	AHL	Totals	23	9	8	1	1097	0	3.39	2	0	0	4	0	16.14
	ECHL	Totals	63	33	21	4	3355	1	3.00	—	—	—	—	—	—

Born; 3/9/72, Jyvasklya, Finland. 6-2, 200. Member of 1996-97 AHL Champion Hershey Bears. Last amateur club; Denver (WCHA).

Bobby Wallwork — Right Wing

Regular Season / Playoffs

Season	Team	League	GP	G	A	PTS	PIM	GP	G	A	PTS	PIM
90-91	Cincinnati	ECHL	18	7	11	18	18	2	0	0	0	0
91-92	Cincinnati	ECHL	63	22	46	68	48	9	5	7	12	6
92-93		Italy										
93-94	Memphis	CeHL	64	43	40	83	83	—	—	—	—	—
94-95	Memphis	CeHL	64	42	50	92	66	—	—	—	—	—
95-96	Muskegon	CoHL	71	40	39	79	61	5	3	5	8	2
96-97	Austin	WPHL	61	42	53	95	80	6	2	2	4	12
97-98	Lake Charles	WPHL	69	28	51	79	26	4	4	1	5	8
98-99	Lake Charles	WPHL	68	27	34	61	48	11	1	8	9	6
	WPHL	Totals	198	97	138	235	154	21	7	11	18	26
	CeHL	Totals	128	85	90	175	149	—	—	—	—	—
	ECHL	Totals	81	29	57	86	66	11	5	7	12	6

Born; 3/15/68, Boston, Massachusetts. 5-9, 185. Drafted by Buffalo Sabres (12th round, 244th overall) 6/11/88. 1993-94 CeHL First Team All-Star. 1994-95 CeHL Second Team All-Star. Last amateur club; Miami of Ohio (CCHA).

Derrick Walser — Defenseman

Regular Season / Playoffs

Season	Team	League	GP	G	A	PTS	PIM	GP	G	A	PTS	PIM
98-99	Saint John	AHL	40	3	7	10	24	—	—	—	—	—
98-99	Johnstown	ECHL	24	8	12	20	29	—	—	—	—	—

Born; 5/12/78. New Glasgow, Nova Scotia. 5-10, 200. Signed as a free agent by Calgary Flames (10/22/98). Last amateur club; Rimouski (QMJHL).

Kurt Walston — Defenseman

Regular Season / Playoffs

Season	Team	League	GP	G	A	PTS	PIM	GP	G	A	PTS	PIM
93-94	Huntsville	ECHL	13	1	2	3	107	—	—	—	—	—
94-95	Dallas	CeHL	2	0	1	1	2	—	—	—	—	—
95-96												
96-97	Fresno	WCHL	23	0	1	1	112	—	—	—	—	—
96-97	Anchorage	WCHL	32	6	10	16	60	—	—	—	—	—
97-98	Fort Worth	CHL	2	0	0	0	10	—	—	—	—	—
98-99	Fort Worth	CHL	3	1	1	2	4	—	—	—	—	—
	WCHL	Totals	55	6	11	17	172	—	—	—	—	—
	CHL	Totals	7	1	2	3	16	—	—	—	—	—

Born; 5/5/68, Kenora, Ontario. 6-0, 215.

Greg Walters — Left Wing

Regular Season — Playoffs

Season	Team	League	GP	G	A	PTS	PIM	GP	G	A	PTS	PIM
90-91	Newmarket	AHL	54	7	14	21	58	—	—	—	—	—
91-92	St. John's	AHL	10	0	2	2	20	—	—	—	—	—
91-92	Raleigh	ECHL	18	9	13	22	30	4	1	2	3	8
92-93	St. John's	AHL	27	4	5	9	82	1	0	1	1	4
92-93	Brantford	CoHL	26	14	19	33	44	10	11	8	19	20
93-94	St. John's	AHL	13	0	2	2	67	—	—	—	—	—
93-94	Brantford	CoHL	42	42	62	104	88	7	5	3	8	8
94-95	Fort Wayne	IHL	44	4	9	13	142	—	—	—	—	—
94-95	Chicago	IHL	18	1	4	5	110	2	0	0	0	0
95-96	Chicago	IHL	50	4	7	11	254	5	0	0	0	12
96-97	Rochester	AHL	55	5	10	15	247	10	3	6	9	20
97-98	Rochester	AHL	33	4	3	7	81	—	—	—	—	—
98-99	Rochester	AHL	56	6	8	14	200	15	1	3	4	14
	AHL	Totals	248	26	44	70	755	26	4	10	14	38
	IHL	Totals	112	9	22	31	506	7	0	0	0	12
	CoHL	Totals	68	56	81	137	132	17	16	11	27	28

Born; 8/12/70, Calgary, Alberta. 6-1, 195. Drafted by Toronto Maple Leafs (3rd pick, 80th overall) in 1990 Entry Draft. 1993-94 CoHL Second Team All-Star. Member of 1992-93 CoHL champion Brantford Smoke. Last amateur club; Ottawa (OHL).

Kris Waltze — Left Wing

Regular Season — Playoffs

Season	Team	League	GP	G	A	PTS	PIM	GP	G	A	PTS	PIM
98-99	San Angelo	WPHL	62	6	10	16	285	15	2	3	5	28

Born; 5/30/78, Two Hills, Alberta. 6-0, 210. Last amateur club; Spokane (WHL).

Dion Wandler — Left Wing

Regular Season — Playoffs

Season	Team	League	GP	G	A	PTS	PIM	GP	G	A	PTS	PIM
97-98	Reno	WCHL	8	1	0	1	2	—	—	—	—	—
98-99	Milan	Italy										

Born; Calgary, Alberta. 6-1, 210.

Shawn Wansborough — Right Wing

Regular Season — Playoffs

Season	Team	League	GP	G	A	PTS	PIM	GP	G	A	PTS	PIM
97-98	Maine	H.E.	32	15	19	34	77	—	—	—	—	—
97-98	Cincinnati	AHL	1	0	0	0	0	—	—	—	—	—
97-98	Orlando	IHL	3	3	3	6	4	17	8	8	16	14
98-99	Orlando	IHL	3	0	0	0	6	—	—	—	—	—
98-99	Long Beach	IHL	8	1	5	6	16	—	—	—	—	—
98-99	Las Vegas	IHL	62	7	20	27	144	—	—	—	—	—
	IHL	Totals	76	11	28	39	170	17	8	8	16	14

Born; 6/3/74, Etobicoke, Ontario. 5-11, 195. Traded to Las Vegas by Long Beach with Scott Hollis for Keith McCambridge and a player to be named later (Patrice Lefebvre) (12/98). Signed as a free agent by Phoenix Coyotes (7/6/99). Last amateur club; Maine (H.E.)

Duane Ward — Center

Regular Season — Playoffs

Season	Team	League	GP	G	A	PTS	PIM	GP	G	A	PTS	PIM
97-98	Revier Lowen	Germany	5	0	0	0	0	—	—	—	—	—
98-99	Flint	UHL	6	0	1	1	15	—	—	—	—	—
98-99	Tulsa	CHL	15	2	4	6	2	—	—	—	—	—

Born; 2/20/76, Shawville, Ontario. 6-2, 215.

Jason Ward — Right Wing

Regular Season — Playoffs

Season	Team	League	GP	G	A	PTS	PIM	GP	G	A	PTS	PIM
97-98	Erie	OHL	21	7	9	16	42	—	—	—	—	—
97-98	Windsor	OHL	26	19	27	46	34	—	—	—	—	—
97-98	Fredericton	AHL	7	1	0	1	2	1	0	0	0	2
98-99	Windsor	OHL	12	8	11	19	25	—	—	—	—	—
98-99	Plymouth	OHL	23	14	13	27	28	11	6	8	14	12
98-99	Fredericton	AHL	—	—	—	—	—	10	4	2	6	22
	AHL	Totals	7	1	0	1	2	11	4	2	6	24

Born; 1/16/79, Chapleau, Ontario. 6-2, 184. Drafted by Montreal Canadiens (1st choice, 11th overall) in 1997 Entry Draft. Last amateur club; Plymouth (OHL).

Lance Ward — Defenseman

Regular Season — Playoffs

Season	Team	League	GP	G	A	PTS	PIM	GP	G	A	PTS	PIM
98-99	New Haven	AHL	43	2	5	7	51	—	—	—	—	—
98-99	Fort Wayne	IHL	13	0	2	2	28	—	—	—	—	—
98-99	Miami	ECHL	6	1	0	1	12	—	—	—	—	—

Born; 6/2/78, Lloydminster, Alberta. 6-3, 195. Drafted by New Jersey Devils (1st choice, 10th overall) in 1996 Entry Draft. Re-entered Draft, selected by Florida Panthers (3rd choice, 63rd overall) in 1998 Entry Draft. Last amateur club; Red Deer (WHL).

Jeff Ware — Defenseman

Regular Season — Playoffs

Season	Team	League	GP	G	A	PTS	PIM	GP	G	A	PTS	PIM
95-96	Oshawa	OHL	62	4	19	23	128	5	0	1	1	8
95-96	St. John's	AHL	4	0	0	0	4	4	0	0	0	2
96-97	Oshawa	OHL	24	1	10	11	38	13	0	3	3	34
96-97	Toronto	NHL	13	0	0	0	6	—	—	—	—	—
97-98	Toronto	NHL	2	0	0	0	0	—	—	—	—	—
97-98	St. John's	AHL	67	0	3	3	182	4	0	0	0	4
98-99	Florida	NHL	6	0	1	1	6	—	—	—	—	—
98-99	St. John's	AHL	55	1	4	5	130	—	—	—	—	—
98-99	New Haven	AHL	20	0	1	1	26	—	—	—	—	—
	NHL	Totals	21	0	1	1	12	—	—	—	—	—
	AHL	Totals	146	1	8	9	342	8	0	0	0	6

Born; 5/19/77, Toronto, Ontario. 6-4, 220. Drafted by Toronto Maple Leafs (1st choice, 15th overall) in 1995 Entry Draft. Traded to Florida Panthers by Toronto for David Nemirovsky (2/17/99). Last amateur club; Oshawa (OHL).

Steve Washburn — Center

Regular Season — Playoffs

Season	Team	League	GP	G	A	PTS	PIM	GP	G	A	PTS	PIM
94-95	Ottawa	OHL	63	43	63	106	72	—	—	—	—	—
94-95	Cincinnati	IHL	6	3	1	4	0	9	1	3	4	4
95-96	Florida	NHL	1	0	1	1	0	1	0	1	1	0
95-96	Carolina	AHL	78	29	54	83	45	—	—	—	—	—
96-97	Florida	NHL	18	3	6	9	4	—	—	—	—	—
96-97	Carolina	AHL	60	23	40	63	66	—	—	—	—	—
97-98	Florida	NHL	58	11	8	19	32	—	—	—	—	—
97-98	New Haven	AHL	6	3	5	8	4	3	2	0	2	15
98-99	Florida	NHL	4	0	0	0	4	—	—	—	—	—
98-99	Vancouver	NHL	8	0	0	0	2	—	—	—	—	—
98-99	New Haven	AHL	10	4	3	7	6	—	—	—	—	—
98-99	Syracuse	AHL	13	1	6	7	6	—	—	—	—	—
	NHL	Totals	89	14	15	29	42	1	0	1	1	0
	AHL	Totals	167	60	108	168	127	—	—	—	—	—

Born; 4/10/75, Ottawa, Ontario. 6-2, 191. Drafted by Florida Panthers (5th choice, 78th overall) in 1993 Entry Draft. Claimed on waivers by Vancouver Canucks from Florida (2/18/99). Last amateur club; Ottawa (OHL).

Joakim Wassberger — Center

Regular Season — Playoffs

Season	Team	League	GP	G	A	PTS	PIM	GP	G	A	PTS	PIM
94-95	Oklahoma City	CHL	4	1	1	2	2	—	—	—	—	—
94-95	Daytona Beach	SUN	2	0	0	0	0	—	—	—	—	—
95-96	Quad City	CoHL	73	24	48	72	34	4	2	0	2	0
96-97	Mississippi	ECHL	26	6	9	15	6	—	—	—	—	—
96-97	Raleigh	ECHL	35	9	17	26	17	—	—	—	—	—
97-98												
98-99	Asheville	UHL	9	1	5	6	2	—	—	—	—	—
98-99	Muskegon	UHL	50	8	18	26	18	13	3	4	7	0
	UHL	Totals	132	33	71	104	54	17	5	4	9	0
	ECHL	Totals	61	15	26	41	23	—	—	—	—	—

Born; 3/12/70, Stockholm, Sweden. 5-10, 183. Traded to Muskegon by Asheville for Bob Brandon and Lubos Krajkovic (12/98). Member of 1998-99 UHL Champion Muskegon Fury.

Bruce Watson — Left Wing

Regular Season — Playoffs

Season	Team	League	GP	G	A	PTS	PIM	GP	G	A	PTS	PIM
98-99	Port Huron	UHL	66	12	15	27	136	7	0	0	0	31

Born; 12/22/76, Pembroke, Ontario. 6-2, 227. Last amateur club; Acadia

Mike Watt — Left Wing
Regular Season — Playoffs

Season	Team	League	GP	G	A	PTS	PIM	GP	G	A	PTS	PIM
97-98	Edmonton	NHL	14	1	2	3	4	—	—	—	—	—
97-98	Hamilton	AHL	63	24	25	49	65	9	2	2	4	8
98-99	Islanders	NHL	75	8	17	25	12	—	—	—	—	—
98-99	Lowell	AHL	—	—	—	—	—	2	1	0	1	2
	NHL	Totals	89	9	19	28	16	—	—	—	—	—
	AHL	Totals	63	24	25	49	65	11	3	2	5	10

Born; 3/31/76, Seaforth, Ontario. 6-2, 212. Drafted by Edmonton Oilers (3rd choice, 32nd overall) in 1994 Entry Draft. Traded to New York Islanders by Edmonton for Eric Fichaud (6/18/98). Last amateur club; Michigan State

Jamie Weatherston — Defenseman
Regular Season — Playoffs

Season	Team	League	GP	G	A	PTS	PIM	GP	G	A	PTS	PIM
98-99												
98-99	Flint	UHL	3	0	0	0	0	—	—	—	—	—

Born; 2/7/78, Barrie, Ontario. 6-3, 205. Traded by Port Huron to Flint with Jeff Smith for Chris Newans (3/99).

Jason Weaver — Left Wing
Regular Season — Playoffs

Season	Team	League	GP	G	A	PTS	PIM	GP	G	A	PTS	PIM
97-98	Grand Rapids	IHL	44	4	5	9	56	2	0	1	1	0
97-98	Muskegon	UHL	29	19	21	40	44	4	1	1	2	6
98-99	Nottingham	BSL	24	7	13	20	79	10	5	5	10	8
98-99	Grand Rapids	IHL	10	0	1	1	28	—	—	—	—	—
	IHL	Totals	54	4	6	10	84	2	0	1	1	0

Born; 9/22/72, Mississauga, Ontario. 6-3, 215. 1997-98 UHL Rookie of the Year. Last amateur club; Acadia (AUAA).

Steve Webb — Right Wing
Regular Season — Playoffs

Season	Team	League	GP	G	A	PTS	PIM	GP	G	A	PTS	PIM
95-96	Detroit	IHL	4	0	0	0	24	—	—	—	—	—
95-96	Muskegon	CoHL	58	18	24	42	263	5	1	2	3	22
96-97	Islanders	NHL	41	1	4	5	144	—	—	—	—	—
96-97	Kentucky	AHL	25	6	6	12	103	2	0	0	0	19
97-98	Islanders	NHL	20	0	0	0	35	—	—	—	—	—
97-98	Kentucky	AHL	37	5	13	18	139	3	0	1	1	10
98-99	Islanders	NHL	45	0	0	0	32	—	—	—	—	—
98-99	Lowell	AHL	23	2	4	6	80	—	—	—	—	—
	NHL	Totals	106	1	4	5	211	—	—	—	—	—
	AHL	Totals	85	13	23	36	322	5	0	1	1	29

Born; 4/30/75, Peterborough, Ontario. 4/30/75. Drafted by Buffalo Sabres (8th choice, 176th overall) in 1994 Entry Draft. Signed as a free agent by New York Islanders (10/10/96). Last amateur club; Peterborough (OHL).

Kevin Weekes — Goaltender
Regular Season — Playoffs

Season	Team	League	GP	W	L	T	MIN	SO	AVG	GP	W	L	MIN	SO	AVG
95-96	Carolina	AHL	60	24	25	8	3403	2	4.04	—	—	—	—	—	—
96-97	Carolina	AHL	51	17	*28	4	2899	1	3.56	—	—	—	—	—	—
97-98	Florida	NHL	11	0	5	1	485	0	3.96	—	—	—	—	—	—
97-98	Fort Wayne	IHL	12	9	2	1	719	1	2.84	—	—	—	—	—	—
98-99	Vancouver	NHL	11	0	8	1	532	0	3.83	—	—	—	—	—	—
98-99	Detroit	IHL	33	19	5	7	1857	*4	2.07	—	—	—	—	—	—
	NHL	Totals	22	0	13	2	1017	0	3.89	—	—	—	—	—	—
	AHL	Totals	111	41	53	12	6302	3	3.82	—	—	—	—	—	—
	IHL	Totals	45	19	7	8	2576	5	2.28	—	—	—	—	—	—

Born; 4/4/75, Toronto, Ontario. 6-0, 158. Drafted by Florida Panthers (2nd choice, 41st overall) in 1993 Entry Draft. Traded to Vancouver Canucks with Ed Jovanovski, Dave Gagner, Mike Brown and an optional pick in 1999 or 2000 for Pavel Bure, Bret Hedican, Brad Ference and an optional pick in 1999 or 2000 (1/17/99). 1998-99 IHL Shared lowest goals against with Andrei Trefilov. 1998-99 IHL Second Team All-Star. Last amateur club; Ottawa (OHL).

Eric Weichselbaumer — Center
Regular Season — Playoffs

Season	Team	League	GP	G	A	PTS	PIM	GP	G	A	PTS	PIM
97-98	Huntington	ECHL	27	5	7	12	20	—	—	—	—	—
97-98	Tucson	WCHL	2	0	0	0	2	—	—	—	—	—
97-98	Bakersfield	WCHL	24	9	12	21	33	4	2	2	4	4
98-99	Alexandria	WPHL	69	45	39	84	34	—	—	—	—	—
	ECHL	Totals	26	9	12	21	35	4	2	2	4	4

Born; 5/17/74, Valley Stream, New York. 6-2, 205. Last amateur club; Merrimack (Hockey East).

Rob Weingartner — Right Wing
Regular Season — Playoffs

Season	Team	League	GP	G	A	PTS	PIM	GP	G	A	PTS	PIM
92-93	Wichita	CeHL	35	10	4	14	71	—	—	—	—	—
93-94	Wichita	CeHL	50	16	17	33	150	11	1	4	5	49
94-95	Wichita	CeHL	49	20	11	31	274	11	4	6	10	30
95-96	Wichita	CeHL	15	1	6	7	69	—	—	—	—	—
95-96	San Antonio	CeHL	45	20	30	50	184	13	5	10	15	45
96-97	Manitoba	IHL	4	0	1	1	11	—	—	—	—	—
96-97	Louisiana	ECHL	59	20	15	35	334	17	5	10	15	46
97-98	Fort Wayne	IHL	14	1	1	2	26	—	—	—	—	—
97-98	Louisiana	ECHL	50	26	27	53	198	12	*12	3	15	30
98-99	Louisiana	ECHL	59	20	22	42	203	2	1	0	1	19
	IHL	Totals	18	1	2	3	37	—	—	—	—	—
	CeHL	Totals	194	67	68	135	748	35	10	20	30	124
	ECHL	Totals	168	66	64	130	735	31	18	13	31	95

Born; 10/22/71, Lake Ronkonkoma, New York. 5-10, 190. Member of 1993-94 CeHL champion Wichita Thunder. Member of 1994-95 CeHL champion Wichita Thunder. Selected by Arkansas in 1999 ECHL Expansion Draft.

Alex Weinrich — Defenseman
Regular Season — Playoffs

Season	Team	League	GP	G	A	PTS	PIM	GP	G	A	PTS	PIM
94-95	London	CoHL	8	0	0	0	0	—	—	—	—	—
95-96												
96-97												
97-98												
98-99	Odense	Austria		4	6	10	NA	—	—	—	—	—
98-99	Tucson	WCHL	9	1	7	8	10	—	—	—	—	—

Born; 3/12/69, Gardiner, Maine. 6-0, 190.

Jason Weinrich — Defenseman
Regular Season — Playoffs

Season	Team	League	GP	G	A	PTS	PIM	GP	G	A	PTS	PIM
94-95	Huntington	ECHL	21	1	9	10	42	—	—	—	—	—
95-96	Johnstown	ECHL	68	3	22	25	115	—	—	—	—	—
96-97	Basingstoke	BHL	39	5	5	10	46	—	—	—	—	—
97-98	Tallahassee	ECHL	46	5	11	16	50	—	—	—	—	—
98-99	Milan	Italy										
	ECHL	Totals	135	9	42	51	207	—	—	—	—	—

Born; 2/13/72, Lewiston, Maine. 6-3, 220. Last amateur club; Maine (H.E.).

Bill Weir — Center
Regular Season — Playoffs

Season	Team	League	GP	G	A	PTS	PIM	GP	G	A	PTS	PIM
97-98	Louisville	ECHL	9	2	6	8	2	—	—	—	—	—
98-99	Quad City	UHL	63	10	19	29	68	10	0	1	1	2

Born; 5/21/73, London, Ontario. 5-10, 185. Last amateur club; St. Thomas

Nolan Weir — Left Wing
Regular Season — Playoffs

Season	Team	League	GP	G	A	PTS	PIM	GP	G	A	PTS	PIM
98-99	Wichita	CHL	51	10	12	22	101	—	—	—	—	—
98-99	Tulsa	CHL	12	2	3	5	15	—	—	—	—	—
	CHL	Totals	63	12	15	27	116	—	—	—	—	—

Born; 5/3/72, Toronto, Ontario. 6-1, 205.

Jason Welch — Center

Regular Season / Playoffs

Season	Team	League	GP	G	A	PTS	PIM	GP	G	A	PTS	PIM
96-97	El Paso	WPHL	51	27	31	58	30	11	5	9	14	12
97-98	Utah	IHL	2	0	0	0	0	—	—	—	—	—
97-98	El Paso	WPHL	60	31	65	96	70	14	12	12	24	28
98-99	El Paso	WPHL	52	22	34	56	57	3	0	2	2	4
	WPHL	Totals	163	80	130	210	157	28	17	23	40	44

Born; 8/2/73, Sault Ste. Marie, Ontario. 5-11, 200. Member of 1996-97 WPHL Champion El Paso Buzzards. Member of 1997-98 WPHL Champion El Paso Buzzards. Last amateur club; Northern Michigan (WCHA).

Chris Wells — Center

Regular Season / Playoffs

Season	Team	League	GP	G	A	PTS	PIM	GP	G	A	PTS	PIM
94-95	Seattle	WHL	69	45	63	108	148	3	0	1	1	4
94-95	Cleveland	IHL	3	0	1	1	2	—	—	—	—	—
95-96	Pittsburgh	NHL	54	2	2	4	59	—	—	—	—	—
96-97	Cleveland	IHL	15	4	6	10	9	—	—	—	—	—
96-97	Florida	NHL	47	2	6	8	42	3	0	0	0	0
97-98	Florida	NHL	61	5	10	15	47	—	—	—	—	—
98-99	New Haven	AHL	9	3	1	4	28	—	—	—	—	—
98-99	Florida	NHL	20	0	2	2	31	—	—	—	—	—
	NHL	Totals	182	9	20	29	179	3	0	0	0	0
	IHL	Totals	18	4	7	11	11	—	—	—	—	—

Born; 11/12/75, Calgary, Alberta. 6-6, 223. Drafted by Pittsburgh Penguins (1st choice, 24th overall) in 1994 Entry Draft. Traded to Florida Panthers by Pittsburgh for Stu Barnes and Jason Woolley (11/19/96). Last amateur club; Seattle

Jeff Wells — Defenseman

Regular Season / Playoffs

Season	Team	League	GP	G	A	PTS	PIM	GP	G	A	PTS	PIM
94-95	Providence	AHL	51	3	11	14	23	9	2	1	3	0
95-96	Cincinnati	IHL	62	10	19	29	46	17	2	4	6	8
95-96	Birmingham	ECHL	3	1	2	3	4	—	—	—	—	—
96-97	Cincinnati	IHL	79	10	11	21	41	3	0	0	0	4
97-98	Cincinnati	IHL	82	10	30	40	50	9	1	2	3	16
98-99	Cincinnati	IHL	82	9	29	38	41	3	0	1	1	0
	IHL	Totals	325	39	89	128	178	32	3	7	10	28

Born; 3/19/70, Brockville, Ontario. 6-0, 195. Last amateur club; Bowling Green State (CCHA).

Marty Wells — Left Wing

Regular Season / Playoffs

Season	Team	League	GP	G	A	PTS	PIM	GP	G	A	PTS	PIM
93-94	Chatham	CoHL	49	21	24	45	28	15	9	8	17	11
94-95	Thunder Bay	CoHL	11	0	3	3	4	—	—	—	—	—
95-96	Alaska	WCHL	10	4	7	11	2	—	—	—	—	—
95-96	Bakersfield	WCHL	17	8	5	13	24	—	—	—	—	—
95-96	Anchorage	WCHL	7	1	2	3	13	—	—	—	—	—
96-97	Quad City	CoHL	2	1	0	1	6	—	—	—	—	—
96-97	Saginaw	CoHL	27	8	6	14	30	—	—	—	—	—
96-97	Dayton	CoHL	27	9	6	15	6	—	—	—	—	—
97-98	Binghamton	UHL	66	43	26	69	39	5	4	5	9	2
98-99	Macon	CHL	2	0	0	0	2	—	—	—	—	—
98-99	Fort Worth	CHL	10	1	2	3	19	—	—	—	—	—
98-99	Tupelo	WPHL	5	0	2	2	0	—	—	—	—	—
98-99	Mohawk Valley	UHL	5	2	1	3	2	—	—	—	—	—
98-99	Saginaw	UHL	11	1	3	4	4	—	—	—	—	—
	UHL	Totals	198	85	69	154	119	20	13	13	26	13
	WCHL	Totals	34	13	14	27	39	—	—	—	—	—
	CHL	Totals	12	1	2	3	21	—	—	—	—	—

Born; 11/3/72, Toronto, Ontario. 5-8, 200.

Jorin Welsh — Defenseman

Regular Season / Playoffs

Season	Team	League	GP	G	A	PTS	PIM	GP	G	A	PTS	PIM
98-99	New Mexico	WPHL	68	5	16	21	42	—	—	—	—	—

Born; 11/21/73, Arthur, Ontario. 6-1, 200. Last amateur club; Windsor (OUAA).

Rocky Welsing — Defenseman

Regular Season / Playoffs

Season	Team	League	GP	G	A	PTS	PIM	GP	G	A	PTS	PIM
98-99	Charlotte	ECHL	7	0	0	0	8	—	—	—	—	—
98-99	Kansas City	IHL	45	3	2	5	79	—	—	—	—	—

Born; 2/8/76, Beloit, Wisconsin. 6-3, 196. Drafted by Anaheim Mighty Ducks (7th choice, 158th overall) in 1994 Entry Draft. Last amateur club; Northern Michigan (CCHA).

Wade Welte — Left Wing

Regular Season / Playoffs

Season	Team	League	GP	G	A	PTS	PIM	GP	G	A	PTS	PIM
94-95	West Palm Beach	SUN	52	25	18	43	163	5	1	1	2	20
95-96	Jacksonville	SHL	8	0	0	0	26	—	—	—	—	—
95-96	Fresno	WCHL	12	5	2	7	35	—	—	—	—	—
95-96	Bakersfield	WCHL	32	16	16	32	84	—	—	—	—	—
96-97	Bakersfield	WCHL	61	28	21	49	280	4	0	2	2	58
97-98	Bakersfield	WCHL	57	9	17	26	346	1	0	0	0	45
98-99	Asheville	UHL	67	18	20	38	258	4	0	2	2	13
	WCHL	Totals	162	58	56	114	745	5	0	2	2	103
	SHL	Totals	60	25	18	43	189	5	1	1	2	20

Born; 5/24/73, Richmond, Saskatoon. 5-8, 190.

Darcy Werenka — Defenseman

Regular Season / Playoffs

Season	Team	League	GP	G	A	PTS	PIM	GP	G	A	PTS	PIM
92-93	Lethbridge	WHL	19	4	17	21	12	—	—	—	—	—
92-93	Brandon	WHL	36	4	25	29	19	3	0	0	0	2
92-93	Binghamton	AHL	3	0	1	1	2	3	0	0	0	0
93-94	Binghamton	AHL	53	5	22	27	10	—	—	—	—	—
94-95	Binghamton	AHL	73	17	29	46	12	11	4	3	7	2
95-96	Chicago	IHL	12	2	5	7	10	—	—	—	—	—
95-96	Atlanta	IHL	58	6	20	26	22	—	—	—	—	—
96-97	Quebec	IHL	5	1	1	2	2	—	—	—	—	—
96-97	Houston	IHL	74	12	20	32	31	13	2	1	3	2
97-98	Vienna	Austria	42	5	15	20	18	—	—	—	—	—
98-99	Vienna	Austria										
	IHL	Totals	149	21	46	67	89	13	2	1	3	2
	AHL	Totals	129	22	52	74	24	14	4	3	7	4

Born; 5/13/73, Edmonton, Alberta. 6-1, 210. Drafted by New York Rangers (2nd choice, 37th overall) in 1991 Entry Draft. Last amateur club; Brandon (WHL).

Brian Wesenberg — Right Wing

Regular Season / Playoffs

Season	Team	League	GP	G	A	PTS	PIM	GP	G	A	PTS	PIM
96-97	Guelph	OHL	64	37	43	80	186	18	4	9	13	59
96-97	Philadelphia	AHL	—	—	—	—	—	3	0	0	0	7
97-98	Philadelphia	AHL	74	17	22	39	93	19	1	4	5	34
98-99	Philadelphia	NHL	1	0	0	0	5	—	—	—	—	—
98-99	Philadelphia	AHL	71	23	20	43	169	16	5	3	8	28
	AHL	Totals	145	40	42	82	262	38	6	7	13	69

Born; 5/9/77, Peterborough, Ontario. 6-3, 187. Drafted by Anaheim Mighty Ducks (2nd choice, 29th overall) in 1995 Entry Draft. Traded to Philadelphia Flyers by Anaheim for Anatoli Semenov and Mike Crowley (3/19/96). Member of 1997-98 AHL Champion Philadelphia Phantoms. Last amateur club; Guelph

Bob Westerby — Left Wing

Regular Season / Playoffs

Season	Team	League	GP	G	A	PTS	PIM	GP	G	A	PTS	PIM
95-96	Rochester	AHL	40	2	6	8	155	—	—	—	—	—
96-97	Baton Rouge	ECHL	54	6	14	20	310	—	—	—	—	—
97-98	Baton Rouge	ECHL	3	0	0	0	22	—	—	—	—	—
97-98	Memphis	CHL	28	9	8	17	212	4	1	2	3	31
98-99	Baton Rouge	ECHL	59	5	10	15	211	6	0	0	0	28
	ECHL	Totals	116	11	24	35	543	6	0	0	0	28

Born; 10/29/75, Kelowna, British Columbia. 6-1, 195. Drafted by Buffalo Sabres (9th choice, 199th overall) in 1994 Entry Draft. Last amateur club; Kamloops (WHL).

Tom Westfall
Forward

Regular Season / Playoffs

Season	Team	League	GP	G	A	PTS	PIM	GP	G	A	PTS	PIM
98-99	El Paso	WPHL	2	0	0	0	0					

Born; 12/26/74

Kevin Westlake
Center

Regular Season / Playoffs

Season	Team	League	GP	G	A	PTS	PIM	GP	G	A	PTS	PIM
98-99	Mohawk Valley	UHL	2	1	0	1	0	—	—	—	—	—
98-99	Saginaw	UHL	4	1	1	2	0	—	—	—	—	—
	UHL	Totals	6	2	1	3	0	—	—	—	—	—

Born; 5/15/75, Oshawa, Ontario. 5-11, 218.

Tommy Westland
Right Wing

Regular Season / Playoffs

Season	Team	League	GP	G	A	PTS	PIM	GP	G	A	PTS	PIM
98-99	New Haven	AHL	50	8	18	26	31	—	—	—	—	—

Born; 12/29/74, Fors, Sweden. 6-0, 210. Drafted by Carolina Hurricanes (5th choice, 93rd overall) in 1998 Entry Draft. Last European club; Brynas Gavle

Darren Wetherill
Defenseman

Regular Season / Playoffs

Season	Team	League	GP	G	A	PTS	PIM	GP	G	A	PTS	PIM
94-95	Richmond	ECHL	56	6	12	18	114	17	1	2	3	41
94-95	Cornwall	AHL	3	0	0	0	12	—	—	—	—	—
95-96	Orlando	IHL	14	1	1	2	15	10	0	0	0	11
95-96	Baltimore	AHL	2	0	0	0	2	—	—	—	—	—
95-96	Richmond	ECHL	63	6	19	25	166	—	—	—	—	—
96-97	Orlando	IHL	32	0	0	0	43	8	0	1	1	25
97-98	Rochester	AHL	8	0	0	0	10	—	—	—	—	—
97-98	Cleveland	IHL	51	1	2	3	89	—	—	—	—	—
97-98	Chesapeake	ECHL	4	1	0	1	2	—	—	—	—	—
98-99	Portland	AHL	5	0	0	0	2	—	—	—	—	—
98-99	Kentucky	AHL	4	0	0	0	4	—	—	—	—	—
98-99	Richmond	ECHL	68	1	14	15	146	18	1	1	2	26
	IHL	Totals	97	2	3	5	147	18	0	1	1	36
	AHL	Totals	22	0	0	0	30	—	—	—	—	—
	ECHL	Totals	191	14	45	59	428	35	2	3	5	67

Born; 1/28/70, Regina, Saskatchewan. 6-0, 185. Drafted by Boston Bruins (8th choice, 189th overall) in 1990 Entry Draft. Signed as a free agent by Orlando Solar Bears (8/96). Traded to Rochester by Cleveland for Eric Lavigne (3/98). Member of 1994-95 ECHL champion Richmond Renegades. Last amateur club; Lake Superior State (CCHA).

Chris Wheaton
Left Wing

Regular Season / Playoffs

Season	Team	League	GP	G	A	PTS	PIM	GP	G	A	PTS	PIM
97-98	Fayetteville	CHL	2	0	0	0	5	—	—	—	—	—
97-98	Odessa	WPHL	2	0	0	0	0	—	—	—	—	—
98-99	South Carolina	ECHL	70	7	4	11	112	1	0	0	0	17

Born; 8/20/76, Fredericton, New Brunswick. 6-2, 215.

Jarrett Whidden
Center

Regular Season / Playoffs

Season	Team	League	GP	G	A	PTS	PIM	GP	G	A	PTS	PIM
97-98	Winston-Salem	UHL	70	24	34	58	40	—	—	—	—	—
98-99	Cleveland	IHL	3	0	1	1	2	—	—	—	—	—
98-99	Arkansas	WPHL	69	41	55	96	23	3	1	2	3	2

Born; 4/15/73. 5-10, 190. Last amateur club; Ohio State (CCHA).

Ben White
Defenseman

Regular Season / Playoffs

Season	Team	League	GP	G	A	PTS	PIM	GP	G	A	PTS	PIM
96-97	Utica	CoHL	17	0	5	5	11	3	0	0	0	4
97-98	Winston-Salem	UHL	32	1	3	4	40	—	—	—	—	—
97-98	Fort Worth	WPHL	4	0	0	0	7	—	—	—	—	—
97-98	Waco	WPHL	38	2	11	13	46	—	—	—	—	—
98-99	Fort Worth	CHL	39	3	14	17	110	—	—	—	—	—
98-99	Tulsa	CHL	12	1	2	3	18	—	—	—	—	—
98-99	Binghamton	UHL	12	1	2	3	11	5	0	1	1	2
	UHL	Totals	61	2	10	12	62	8	0	1	1	6
	CHL	Totals	51	4	16	20	128	—	—	—	—	—
	WPHL	Totals	42	2	11	13	53	—	—	—	—	—

Born; 6/1/74, Sudbury, Ontario. 6-3, 215. Traded to Waco by Fort Worth for Darren McClellan (10/97). Last amateur club; Rochester Institute of Technology

Brian White
Defenseman

Regular Season / Playoffs

Season	Team	League	GP	G	A	PTS	PIM	GP	G	A	PTS	PIM
97-98	Maine	H.E.	33	0	12	12	45	—	—	—	—	—
97-98	Long Beach	IHL	1	0	0	0	0	—	—	—	—	—
98-99	Colorado	NHL	2	0	0	0	0	—	—	—	—	—
98-99	Hershey	AHL	71	4	8	12	41	4	0	1	1	2

Born; 2/7/76, Winchester, Massachusetts. 6-1, 180. Drafted by Tampa Bay Lightning (11th choice, 268th overall) in 1994 Entry Draft. Signed as a free agent by Colorado Avalanche (7/7/98). Last amateur club; Maine (Hockey East).

Colin White
Defenseman

Regular Season / Playoffs

Season	Team	League	GP	G	A	PTS	PIM	GP	G	A	PTS	PIM
97-98	Albany	AHL	76	3	13	16	235	13	0	0	0	55
98-99	Albany	AHL	77	2	12	14	265	5	0	1	1	8
	AHL	Totals	153	5	25	30	500	18	0	1	1	63

Born; 12/12/77, New Glasgow, Nova Scotia. 6-3, 215. Drafted by New Jersey Devils (5th choice, 49th overall) in 1996 Entry Draft. Last amateur club; Hull

Jason White
Goaltender

Regular Season / Playoffs

Season	Team	League	GP	W	L	T	MIN	SO	AVG	GP	W	L	MIN	SO	AVG
98-99	Winston-Salem	UHL	3	1	2	0	164	0	5.48	—	—	—	—	—	—

Born; 4/27/73, Dartmouth, Nova Scotia. 6-0, 210.

Kam White
Defenseman

Regular Season / Playoffs

Season	Team	League	GP	G	A	PTS	PIM	GP	G	A	PTS	PIM
95-96	North Bay	OHL	54	2	15	17	141	—	—	—	—	—
95-96	South Carolina	ECHL	6	0	1	1	10	—	—	—	—	—
96-97	Mississippi	ECHL	3	0	0	0	4	—	—	—	—	—
96-97	Johnstown	ECHL	47	0	5	5	261	—	—	—	—	—
97-98	Jacksonville	ECHL	36	0	5	5	83	—	—	—	—	—
98-99	New Orleans	ECHL	1	0	0	0	6	—	—	—	—	—
98-99	Greenville	ECHL	34	1	4	5	127	—	—	—	—	—
98-99	Chesapeake	ECHL	13	1	1	2	59	8	0	0	0	24
98-99	Saint John	AHL	6	0	0	0	17	—	—	—	—	—
	ECHL	Totals	140	2	16	18	550	8	0	0	0	24

Born; 2/13/76, Toronto, Ontario. 6-3, 217. Drafted by Toronto Maple Leafs (5th choice, 152nd overall) in 1994 Entry Draft. Last amateur club; North Bay (OHL).

Peter White — Center

Regular Season / Playoffs

Season	Team	League	GP	G	A	PTS	PIM	GP	G	A	PTS	PIM
92-93	Cape Breton	AHL	64	12	28	40	10	16	3	3	6	12
93-94	Edmonton	NHL	26	3	5	8	2	—	—	—	—	—
93-94	Cape Breton	AHL	45	21	49	70	12	5	2	3	5	2
94-95	Edmonton	NHL	9	2	4	6	0	—	—	—	—	—
94-95	Cape Breton	AHL	65	36	*69	*105	30	—	—	—	—	—
95-96	Edmonton	NHL	26	5	3	8	0	—	—	—	—	—
95-96	Toronto	NHL	1	0	0	0	0	—	—	—	—	—
95-96	St. John's	AHL	17	6	7	13	6	—	—	—	—	—
95-96	Atlanta	IHL	36	21	20	41	4	3	0	3	3	2
96-97	Philadelphia	AHL	80	*44	61	*105	28	10	6	8	14	6
97-98	Philadelphia	AHL	80	27	*78	*105	28	20	9	9	18	6
98-99	Philadelphia	NHL	3	0	0	0	0	—	—	—	—	—
98-99	Philadelphia	AHL	77	31	59	90	20	16	4	13	17	12
	NHL	Totals	65	10	12	22	2	—	—	—	—	—
	AHL	Totals	428	177	351	528	134	67	24	39	63	50

Born; 3/15/69, Montreal, Quebec. 5-11, 195. Drafted by Edmonton Oilers' (4rth choice, 92 overall) in 1989 Entry Draft. Traded to Toronto Maple Leafs by Edmonton with Edmonton's fourth round choice (Jason Sessa) in 1996 Entry Draft for Kent Manderville (12/4/95). Signed as a free agent by Philadelphia Flyers (8/19/96). 1994-95 AHL Second Team All-Star. 1996-97 AHL Second Team All-Star. Member of 1997-98 AHL Champion Philadelphia Phantoms. Last amateur club; Michigan State (CCHA).

Rob White — Forward

Regular Season / Playoffs

Season	Team	League	GP	G	A	PTS	PIM	GP	G	A	PTS	PIM
98-99	Columbus	ECHL	8	1	2	3	21	4	0	1	1	7

Born; Selected by Pensacola in 1999 ECHL Dispersal Draft.

Scott White — Defenseman

Regular Season / Playoffs

Season	Team	League	GP	G	A	PTS	PIM	GP	G	A	PTS	PIM
89-90	Greensboro	ECHL	30	9	13	22	67	11	4	10	14	24
90-91	Kalamazoo	IHL	6	0	1	1	21	—	—	—	—	—
90-91	Kansas City	IHL	18	3	2	5	33	—	—	—	—	—
90-91	Greensboro	ECHL	42	8	29	37	93	13	2	11	13	10
91-92	Greensboro	ECHL	57	21	63	84	204	8	1	6	7	12
92-93	New Haven	AHL	80	10	44	54	72	—	—	—	—	—
93-94	Prince Edward Island	AHL	15	1	4	5	6	—	—	—	—	—
93-94	Salt Lake City	IHL	15	0	3	3	8	—	—	—	—	—
93-94	Greensboro	ECHL	27	3	21	24	65	8	1	5	6	8
	AHL	Totals	95	11	48	59	78	—	—	—	—	—
	IHL	Totals	39	3	6	9	62	—	—	—	—	—
	ECHL	Totals	156	41	126	167	429	40	8	32	40	54

Born; 4/21/68, Ormstown, Quebec. 6-1, 195. Last amateur club; Michigan Tech (WCHA). 1991-92 ECHL First Team All-Star. 1991-92 ECHL Defenseman of the Year. Member of 1989-90 ECHL Champion Greensboro Monarchs.

Todd White — Center

Regular Season / Playoffs

Season	Team	League	GP	G	A	PTS	PIM	GP	G	A	PTS	PIM
97-98	Chicago	NHL	7	1	0	1	2	—	—	—	—	—
97-98	Indianapolis	IHL	65	46	36	82	28	5	2	3	5	4
98-99	Chicago	NHL	35	5	8	13	20	—	—	—	—	—
98-99	Chicago	IHL	25	11	13	24	8	10	1	4	5	8
	NHL	Totals	42	6	8	14	22	—	—	—	—	—
	IHL	Totals	90	57	49	106	36	15	3	7	10	12

Born; 5/21/75. Kanata, Ontario. 5-10, 180. Signed as a free agent by Chicago Blackhawks (8/6/97). 1997-98 IHL Rookie of the Year. Last amateur club; Clarkson (ECAC).

Trent Whitfield — Center

Regular Season / Playoffs

Season	Team	League	GP	G	A	PTS	PIM	GP	G	A	PTS	PIM
98-99	Portland	AHL	50	10	8	18	20	—	—	—	—	—
98-99	Hampton Roads	ECHL	19	13	12	25	12	4	2	0	2	14

Born; 6/17/77, Estevan, Saskatchewan. 5-11, 176. Drafted by Boston Bruins (5th choice, 100th overall) in 1996 Entry Draft. Signed as a free agent by Washington Capitals (9/3/98). Last amateur club; Spokane (WHL).

Kay Whitmore — Goaltender

Regular Season / Playoffs

Season	Team	League	GP	W	L	T	MIN	SO	AVG	GP	W	L	MIN	SO	AVG
87-88	Binghamton	AHL	38	17	15	4	2137	*3	3.40	2	0	2	118	0	5.08
88-89	Hartford	NHL	3	2	1	0	180	0	3.33	2	0	2	135	0	4.44
88-89	Binghamton	AHL	*56	21	29	4	*3200	1	4.52	—	—	—	—	—	—
89-90	Hartford	NHL	9	4	2	1	442	0	3.53	—	—	—	—	—	—
89-90	Binghamton	AHL	24	3	19	2	1386	0	4.72	—	—	—	—	—	—
90-91	Hartford	NHL	18	3	9	3	850	0	3.67	—	—	—	—	—	—
90-91	Springfield	AHL	33	22	9	1	1916	1	3.07	*15	*11	4	*926	0	*2.40
91-92	Hartford	NHL	45	14	21	6	2567	3	3.62	1	0	0	19	0	3.16
92-93	Vancouver	NHL	31	18	8	4	1817	1	3.10	—	—	—	—	—	—
93-94	Vancouver	NHL	32	18	14	0	1921	0	3.53	—	—	—	—	—	—
94-95	Vancouver	NHL	11	0	6	2	558	0	3.98	1	0	0	20	0	6.00
95-96	Detroit	IHL	10	3	5	0	501	0	3.95	—	—	—	—	—	—
95-96	Los Angeles	IHL	30	10	9	7	1563	1	3.80	—	—	—	—	—	—
95-96	Binghamton	AHL	11	6	4	1	663	0	3.35	2	0	2	127	0	4.27
96-97	Sodertalje	Sweden	25	—	—	—	1320	0	3.86	—	—	—	—	—	—
97-98	Long Beach	IHL	46	28	12	3	2516	3	2.60	14	9	5	839	0	3.08
98-99	Hartford	AHL	18	8	8	2	1080	0	2.61	—	—	—	—	—	—
98-99	Milwaukee	IHL	23	10	6	4	1304	0	2.95	—	—	—	—	—	—
	NHL	Totals	149	59	61	16	8335	4	3.51	4	0	2	174	0	4.48
	AHL	Totals	180	77	84	14	10382	6	3.77	19	11	8	1170	0	2.87
	IHL	Totals	109	51	32	14	5884	4	3.11	14	9	5	839	0	3.08

Born; 4/10/67, Sudbury, Ontario. 5-11, 175. Drafted by Hartford Whalers (2nd choice, 26th overall) in 1985 Entry Draft. Traded to Vancouver Canucks by Hartford for Corrie D'Alessio and future considerations (10/1/92). Traded to New York Rangers by Vancouver for Joe Kocur (3/20/96). Signed as a free agent by San Jose Sharks (9/2/97). Traded to Buffalo Sabres by San Jose with Colorado's second round choice in 1998 Entry Draft (previously acquired by San Jose-Buffalo selected Jaroslav Kristek) and San Jose's fifth round pick in the 2000 Entry Draft for Steve Shields and Buffalo's fourth round choice (Miroslav Zalesak) in 1998 Entry Draft (6/18/98). Signed as a free agent by Rangers (8/17/98). 1990-91 AHL Playoff MVP. 1997-98 Shared IHL Norris Trophy (fewest goals against) with Mike Buzak. Member of 1990-91 AHL Champion Springfield Indians. Last amateur club; Peterborough (OHL).

Jeff Whittle — Right Wing

Regular Season / Playoffs

Season	Team	League	GP	G	A	PTS	PIM	GP	G	A	PTS	PIM
92-93	Hampton Roads	ECHL	5	1	0	1	19	—	—	—	—	—
92-93	Erie	ECHL	45	9	16	25	133	—	—	—	—	—
93-94	Erie	ECHL	67	47	42	89	126	—	—	—	—	—
94-95	Fort Wayne	IHL	2	2	0	2	0	—	—	—	—	—
94-95	Flint	CoHL	58	31	44	75	133	6	2	2	4	15
95-96	Detroit	IHL	1	0	0	0	0	—	—	—	—	—
95-96	Flint	CoHL	54	24	31	55	98	—	—	—	—	—
95-96	Utica	CoHL	15	6	6	12	26	—	—	—	—	—
96-97	Detroit	IHL	1	0	0	0	0	—	—	—	—	—
96-97	Flint	CoHL	74	28	55	83	111	14	*12	12	24	14
97-98	Detroit	IHL	15	1	2	3	0	—	—	—	—	—
97-98	Flint	UHL	38	21	32	53	37	13	6	12	18	22
98-99	Detroit	IHL	8	0	3	3	2	—	—	—	—	—
98-99	Flint	UHL	5	1	4	5	54	—	—	—	—	—
	IHL	Totals	27	3	5	8	2	—	—	—	—	—
	UHL	Totals	244	111	172	283	459	33	20	26	46	51
	ECHL	Totals	117	57	58	115	278	—	—	—	—	—

Born; 3/22/71, Toronto, Ontario. 5-9, 187. Last amateur club; Tacoma (WHL).

John Whitwell — Defenseman

Regular Season / Playoffs

Season	Team	League	GP	G	A	PTS	PIM	GP	G	A	PTS	PIM
98-99	Augusta	ECHL	70	3	13	16	92	2	0	0	0	2

Born; 12/2/75, Niagara Falls, Ontario. 6-1, 210. Last amateur club; Hamilton College (NCAA 3).

Sean Whyte — Right Wing

Regular Season / Playoffs

Season	Team	League	GP	G	A	PTS	PIM	GP	G	A	PTS	PIM
90-91	Phoenix	IHL	60	18	17	35	61	4	1	0	1	2
91-92	Los Angeles	NHL	3	0	0	0	0	—	—	—	—	—
91-92	Phoenix	IHL	72	24	30	54	113	—	—	—	—	—
92-93	Los Angeles	NHL	18	0	2	2	12	—	—	—	—	—
92-93	Phoenix	IHL	51	11	35	46	65	—	—	—	—	—
93-94	Cornwall	AHL	18	6	9	15	16	9	1	2	3	2
93-94	Tulsa	CeHL	50	42	29	71	93	—	—	—	—	—
94-95	Worcester	AHL	59	13	8	21	76	—	—	—	—	—
95-96	Phoenix	IHL	11	0	2	2	4	—	—	—	—	—
95-96	Fort Worth	CeHL	51	15	37	52	94	—	—	—	—	—
96-97	El Paso	WPHL	60	21	39	60	105	11	2	*14	16	36
97-98	Phoenix	WCHL	53	19	23	42	93	9	4	10	14	10
98-99	Phoenix	WCHL	65	16	34	50	80	3	2	0	2	4
	IHL	Totals	194	53	84	137	243	4	1	0	1	2
	AHL	Totals	77	19	17	36	92	9	1	2	3	2
	WCHL	Totals	118	35	57	92	173	12	6	10	16	14
	CeHL	Totals	101	57	66	123	187	—	—	—	—	—

Born; 5/4/70, Sudbury, Ontario. Drafted by Los Angeles Kings (7th choice, 165th overall) in 1989 Entry Draft. Member of 1996-97 WPHL Champion El Paso Buzzards. Last amateur club; Owen Sound (OHL).

Christian Wibner — Forward

Regular Season / Playoffs

Season	Team	League	GP	G	A	PTS	PIM	GP	G	A	PTS	PIM
98-99	Odessa	WPHL	23	8	6	14	25	—	—	—	—	—

Born; 1/2/70, Norrkoping, Sweden. 6-1, 189.

Chris Wickenheiser — Goaltender

Regular Season / Playoffs

Season	Team	League	GP	W	L	T	MIN	SO	AVG	GP	W	L	MIN	SO	AVG
97-98	Hamilton	AHL	2	0	0	0	20	0	2.96	—	—	—	—	—	—
97-98	Huntington	ECHL	32	16	10	3	1758	2	3.38	—	—	—	—	—	—
98-99	Hamilton	AHL	2	1	0	0	80	0	2.25	—	—	—	—	—	—
98-99	New Orleans	ECHL	35	13	13	5	1848	0	3.60	3	1	2	180	0	4.01
	AHL	Totals	4	1	0	0	100	0	2.40	—	—	—	—	—	—
	ECHL	Totals	67	29	23	8	3606	2	3.49	3	1	2	180	0	4.01

Born; 1/20/76, Lethbridge, Alberta. 6-1, 185. Drafted by Edmonton Oilers (12th choice, 179th overall) in 1994 Entry Draft. Last amateur club; Portland (WHL).

Kurt Wickenheiser — Right Wing

Regular Season / Playoffs

Season	Team	League	GP	G	A	PTS	PIM	GP	G	A	PTS	PIM
85-86	Troy	ACHL	2	0	1	1	18	—	—	—	—	—
85-86	Flint	IHL	13	2	1	3	0	—	—	—	—	—
85-86	Muskegon	IHL	6	0	0	0	0	—	—	—	—	—
86-87	Stratham	BHL										
87-88												
88-89												
89-90	EHC Unna		45	65	42	117	NA	—	—	—	—	—
90-91	EHC Unna		40	45	42	87	NA	—	—	—	—	—
91-92												
92-93	Westfaler		62	115	80	195	NA	—	—	—	—	—
93-94	Westfaler											
94-95	Westfaler		18	22	18	40	NA	—	—	—	—	—
95-96	Westfaler		40	22	33	55	44	—	—	—	—	—
96-97	New Mexico	WPHL	55	46	28	74	62	6	6	3	9	4
97-98	Riessersee	Germany	42	22	33	55	65	—	—	—	—	—
98-99	Heilbronner	Germany	42	13	23	36	70	—	—	—	—	—
	IHL	Totals	19	2	1	3	0	—	—	—	—	—

Born; 8/24/64, Regina, Saskatchewan. 5-11, 183. Last amateur club; Regina

Jason Widmer — Defenseman

Regular Season / Playoffs

Season	Team	League	GP	G	A	PTS	PIM	GP	G	A	PTS	PIM
92-93	Lethbridge	WHL	55	3	15	18	140	4	0	3	3	2
92-93	Capital District	AHL	4	0	0	0	2	—	—	—	—	—
93-94	Lethbridge	WHL	64	11	31	42	191	9	3	5	8	34
94-95	Islanders	NHL	1	0	0	0	0	—	—	—	—	—
94-95	Worcester	AHL	73	8	26	34	136	—	—	—	—	—
94-95	Canada	National	6	1	4	5	4	—	—	—	—	—
95-96	Islanders	NHL	4	0	0	0	7	—	—	—	—	—
95-96	Worcester	AHL	76	6	21	27	129	4	2	0	2	9
96-97	Kentucky	AHL	76	4	24	28	105	4	0	0	0	8
97-98	Kentucky	AHL	71	5	13	18	176	3	0	0	0	6
98-99	Worcester	AHL	25	2	3	5	42	—	—	—	—	—
	NHL	Totals	5	0	0	0	7	—	—	—	—	—
	AHL	Totals	325	25	87	112	590	11	2	0	2	23

Born; 8/1/73, Calgary, Alberta. 6-0, 205. Drafted by New York Islanders (8th choice, 176th overall) in 1992 Entry Draft. Signed as a free agent by San Jose Sharks (9/11/96). Signed as a free agent by St. Louis Blues (7/24/98). Last amateur club; Lethbridge (WHL).

Nando Wieser — Goaltender

Regular Season / Playoffs

Season	Team	League	GP	W	L	T	MIN	SO	AVG	GP	W	L	MIN	SO	AVG
98-99	Central Texas	WPHL	26	9	11	2	1370	0	4.47	—	—	—	—	—	—
98-99	Davos	Switz.	—	—	—	—	—	—	—	1	—	—			

Born; 9/22/72, Davos, Switzerland. 5-11, 185.

Chad Wilchynski — Defenseman

Regular Season / Playoffs

Season	Team	League	GP	G	A	PTS	PIM	GP	G	A	PTS	PIM
97-98	Kelowna	WHL	39	9	24	33	53	—	—	—	—	—
97-98	Birmingham	ECHL	19	0	2	2	15	—	—	—	—	—
98-99	Birmingham	ECHL	5	0	0	0	2	—	—	—	—	—
98-99	Mobile	ECHL	4	1	0	1	2	2	0	0	0	2
98-99	Alexandria	WPHL	40	3	14	17	71	—	—	—	—	—
	ECHL	Totals	28	1	2	3	19	2	0	0	0	2

Born; 4/4/77, Regina, Saskatchewan. 6-3, 179. Drafted by Detroit Red Wings (5th choice, 125th overall) in 1995 Entry Draft. Last amateur club; Kelowna (WHL).

George Wilcox — Center

Regular Season / Playoffs

Season	Team	League	GP	G	A	PTS	PIM	GP	G	A	PTS	PIM
95-96	Louisville	ECHL	62	25	29	54	151	1	0	0	0	12
96-97	Anchorage	WCHL	52	18	30	48	165	9	3	4	7	42
97-98	Anchorage	WCHL	59	17	29	46	192	8	3	2	5	58
98-99	Anchorage	WCHL	68	26	47	73	217	6	1	2	3	41
	WCHL	Totals	179	61	106	167	574	23	7	8	15	141

Born; 2/16/70, Sept Isles, Quebec. 6-1, 190.

Dan Wildfong — Left Wing

Regular Season / Playoffs

Season	Team	League	GP	G	A	PTS	PIM	GP	G	A	PTS	PIM
98-99	Colgate	ECAC	35	9	16	25	54	—	—	—	—	—
98-99	Mohawk Valley	UHL	4	0	3	3	2	—	—	—	—	—

Born; 12/29/75, Stratford, Ontario. 5-10, 190. Last amateur club; Colgate

Dave Wilejto — Defenseman

Regular Season / Playoffs

Season	Team	League	GP	G	A	PTS	PIM	GP	G	A	PTS	PIM
97-98	Raleigh	ECHL	14	0	0	0	30	—	—	—	—	—
97-98	Tulsa	CHL	13	2	2	4	9	—	—	—	—	—
97-98	Macon	CHL	38	3	8	11	76	3	0	0	0	2
98-99	Macon	CHL	70	8	14	22	117	3	0	0	0	2
	CHL	Totals	121	13	24	37	202	6	0	0	0	4

Born; 1/17/76, Burns Lake, Alberta. 6-4, 230. Traded to Macon by Tulsa with Craig Coxe for Francois Leroux and Mike Anastasio (12/97).

Marty Wilford — Defenseman

Regular Season / Playoffs

Season	Team	League	GP	G	A	PTS	PIM	GP	G	A	PTS	PIM
97-98	Indianapolis	IHL	26	0	4	4	16	—	—	—	—	—
97-98	Columbus	ECHL	46	8	27	35	123	—	—	—	—	—
98-99	Indianapolis	IHL	80	3	13	16	116	7	0	1	1	16
	IHL	Totals	106	3	17	20	132	7	0	1	1	16

Born; 4/17/77, Cobourg, Ontario. 6-0, 216. Drafted by Chicago Blackhawks (7th choice, 149th overall) in 1995 Entry Draft. Last amateur club; Oshawa (OHL).

Bob Wilkie — Defenseman

Regular Season / Playoffs

Season	Team	League	GP	G	A	PTS	PIM	GP	G	A	PTS	PIM
89-90	Adirondack	AHL	58	5	33	38	64	6	1	4	5	2
90-91	Detroit	NHL	8	1	2	3	2	—	—	—	—	—
90-91	Adirondack	AHL	43	6	18	24	71	2	1	0	1	2
91-92	Adirondack	AHL	7	1	4	5	6	16	2	5	7	12
92-93	Fort Wayne	IHL	32	7	14	21	82	12	4	6	10	10
92-93	Hershey	AHL	28	7	25	32	18	—	—	—	—	—
93-94	Philadelphia	NHL	10	1	3	4	8	—	—	—	—	—
93-94	Hershey	AHL	69	8	53	61	100	9	1	4	5	8
94-95	Hershey	AHL	50	9	30	39	46	—	—	—	—	—
94-95	Indianapolis	IHL	29	5	22	27	30	—	—	—	—	—
95-96	Cincinnati	IHL	22	4	6	10	32	—	—	—	—	—
95-96	Augsburg	Germany	6	0	1	1	43	—	—	—	—	—
96-97												
97-98	Las Vegas	IHL	3	0	1	1	0	—	—	—	—	—
97-98	Fresno	WCHL	54	13	50	63	60	5	1	7	8	38
98-99	Pensacola	ECHL	16	2	11	13	18	—	—	—	—	—
98-99	Fresno	WCHL	10	3	4	7	21	7	1	2	3	18
	NHL	Totals	18	2	5	7	10	—	—	—	—	—
	AHL	Totals	269	36	168	204	325	33	5	13	18	24
	IHL	Totals	86	16	43	59	144	12	4	6	10	10
	WCHL	Totals	64	16	54	70	81	12	2	9	11	56

Born; 2/11/69, Calgary. Alberta. 6-2, 215. Drafted by Detroit Red Wings (3rd choice, 41st overall) in 1987 Entry Draft. Traded to Philadelphia Flyers by Detroit for future considerations (2/2/93). Traded to Chicago Blackhawks by Philadelphia with a possible conditional draft choice in 1997 Entry Draft for Karl Dykhuis (2/16/95). 1993-94 AHL Second All-Star Team. 1997-98 WCHL First All-Star Team. Member of 1991-92 AHL Champion Adirondack Red Wings. Member of 1992-93 IHL Champion Fort Wayne Komets. Last amateur club; Swift Current (WHL). Named coach of Anchorage Aces (WCHL) beginning with 1999-2000

David Wilkie — Defenseman

Regular Season / Playoffs

Season	Team	League	GP	G	A	PTS	PIM	GP	G	A	PTS	PIM
94-95	Fredericton	AHL	70	10	43	53	34	1	0	0	0	0
94-95	Montreal	NHL	1	0	0	0	0	—	—	—	—	—
95-96	Montreal	NHL	24	1	5	6	10	6	1	2	3	12
95-96	Fredericton	AHL	23	5	12	17	20	—	—	—	—	—
96-97	Montreal	NHL	61	6	9	15	63	2	0	0	0	2
97-98	Montreal	NHL	5	1	0	1	4	—	—	—	—	—
97-98	Tampa Bay	NHL	29	1	5	6	17	—	—	—	—	—
98-99	Tampa Bay	NHL	46	1	7	8	69	—	—	—	—	—
98-99	Clevelamd	IHL	2	0	2	2	0	—	—	—	—	—
	NHL	Totals	166	10	26	36	163	8	1	2	3	14
	AHL	Totals	93	15	55	70	54	1	0	0	0	0

Born; 5/30/74, Ellensburgh, Washington. 6-2, 210. Drafted by Montreal Canadiens (1st choice, 20th overall) in 1992 Entry Draft. Traded to Tampa Bay Lightning by Montreal with Stephane Richer and Darcy Tucker for Patrick Poulin, Mick Vukota and Igor Ulanov (1/15/98). Last amateur club; Regina (WHL).

Derek Wilkinson — Goaltender

Regular Season / Playoffs

Season	Team	League	GP	W	L	T	MIN	SO	AVG	GP	W	L	MIN	SO	AVG
94-95	Atlanta	IHL	46	22	17	2	2414	1	3.01	4	2	1	197	0	2.43
95-96	Tampa Bay	NHL	4	0	3	0	200	0	4.50	—	—	—	—	—	—
95-96	Atlanta	IHL	28	11	11	2	1432	1	4.10	—	—	—	—	—	—
96-97	Tampa Bay	NHL	5	0	2	1	169	0	4.26	—	—	—	—	—	—
96-97	Cleveland	IHL	46	20	17	6	2595	1	3.19	14	8	*6	893	0	2.95
97-98	Tampa Bay	NHL	8	2	4	1	311	0	3.28	—	—	—	—	—	—
97-98	Cleveland	IHL	25	9	12	2	1295	1	2.92	1	0	0	27	0	2.19
98-99	Tampa Bay	NHL	5	1	3	1	253	0	3.08	—	—	—	—	—	—
98-99	Cleveland	IHL	34	10	15	2	1760	1	3.68	—	—	—	—	—	—
	NHL	Totals	22	3	12	3	933	0	3.67	—	—	—	—	—	—
	IHL	Totals	179	72	72	14	9496	5	3.34	19	10	7	1117	0	2.85

Born; 7/29/74, Lasalle, Quebec. 6-0, 170. Drafted by Tampa Bay Lightning (7th choice, 145th overall) in 1992 Entry Draft. Last amateur club; Belleville (OHL).

Andrew Will — Defenseman

Regular Season / Playoffs

Season	Team	League	GP	G	A	PTS	PIM	GP	G	A	PTS	PIM
97-98	Mobile	ECHL	68	3	9	12	30	3	0	0	0	0
98-99	Mobile	ECHL	70	9	23	32	34	2	0	1	1	0
	ECHL	Totals	138	12	32	44	64	5	0	1	1	0

Born; 3/27/74, Willowdale, Ontario. 5-11, 200. Last amateur club; Union

Craig Willard — Defenseman

Regular Season / Playoffs

Season	Team	League	GP	G	A	PTS	PIM	GP	G	A	PTS	PIM
96-97	Macon	CeHL	55	4	5	9	116	—	—	—	—	—
97-98	Macon	CHL	52	2	4	6	85	—	—	—	—	—
98-99	Columbus	CHL	1	0	0	0	2	—	—	—	—	—
98-99	Oklahoma City	CHL	14	1	2	3	48	—	—	—	—	—
	CHL	Totals	122	7	11	18	251	—	—	—	—	—

Born; 8/22/71, St. Charles, Illinois. 6-1, 190.

Paul Willett — Center

Regular Season / Playoffs

Season	Team	League	GP	G	A	PTS	PIM	GP	G	A	PTS	PIM
89-90	Longueuil	QMJHL	68	57	75	132	68	7	3	7	10	12
89-90	Sherbrooke	AHL	2	0	1	1	2	—	—	—	—	—
90-91	Roanoke	ECHL	29	21	29	50	26	—	—	—	—	—
90-91	New Haven	AHL	42	11	19	30	18	—	—	—	—	—
91-92	New Haven	AHL	69	29	51	80	68	5	3	1	4	2
92-93	Fort Wayne	IHL	74	33	52	85	109	10	7	6	13	22
93-94	Greensboro	ECHL	2	1	0	1	4	—	—	—	—	—
93-94	Cornwall	AHL	56	24	34	58	60	13	2	10	12	0
94-95	Fort Wayne	IHL	80	26	47	73	74	1	0	1	1	0
95-96	Fort Wayne	IHL	81	24	37	61	118	5	2	1	3	4
96-97	Fort Wayne	IHL	36	7	10	17	50	—	—	—	—	—
97-98	Fort Wayne	IHL	1	1	0	1	2	—	—	—	—	—
97-98	Muskegon	UHL	60	47	64	111	83	11	8	10	18	22
98-99	Chicago	IHL	3	0	0	0	0	—	—	—	—	—
98-99	Fort Wayne	IHL	1	0	0	0	2	—	—	—	—	—
98-99	Muskegon	UHL	62	24	68	92	37	18	11	15	*26	22
	IHL	Totals	276	91	146	237	355	16	9	8	17	26
	AHL	Totals	169	64	105	169	148	18	5	11	16	2
	UHL	Totals	122	71	132	203	120	29	19	25	44	44
	ECHL	Totals	31	22	29	51	30	—	—	—	—	—

Born; 10/15/69, New Richmond, Quebec. 5-10, 180. 1997-98 UHL Second Team All-Star. 1998-99 UHL Best Defensive Forward. Member of 1992-93 IHL champion Fort Wayne Komets. Member of 1998-99 UHL Champion Muskegon Fury. Last amateur club; Longueuil (QMJHL).

Darryl Williams — Left Wing

Regular Season / Playoffs

Season	Team	League	GP	G	A	PTS	PIM	GP	G	A	PTS	PIM
88-89	Belleville	OHL	45	24	21	45	137	—	—	—	—	—
88-89	New Haven	AHL	15	5	5	10	24	—	—	—	—	—
89-90	New Haven	AHL	51	9	13	22	124	—	—	—	—	—
90-91	New Haven	AHL	57	14	11	25	278	—	—	—	—	—
90-91	Phoenix	IHL	12	2	1	3	53	7	1	0	1	12
91-92	New Haven	AHL	13	0	2	2	69	—	—	—	—	—
91-92	Phoenix	IHL	48	8	19	27	219	—	—	—	—	—
92-93	Los Angeles	NHL	2	0	0	0	10	—	—	—	—	—
92-93	Phoenix	IHL	61	18	7	25	314	—	—	—	—	—
93-94	Phoenix	IHL	52	11	18	29	237	—	—	—	—	—
94-95	Detroit	IHL	66	10	12	22	268	4	0	0	0	14
95-96	Detroit	IHL	72	8	19	27	294	12	0	3	3	30
96-97	Long Beach	IHL	82	13	17	30	285	14	2	2	4	26
97-98	Long Beach	IHL	82	16	17	33	184	17	6	6	12	52
98-99	Long Beach	IHL	65	13	15	28	122	—	—	—	—	—
	IHL	Totals	540	99	125	224	1976	54	9	11	20	134
	AHL	Totals	136	28	31	59	495	—	—	—	—	—

Born; 2/29/68, Mt. Pearl, Newfoundland. 5-11, 190. Signed as a free agent by Los Angeles Kings (5/19/89). Last amateur club; Belleville (OHL).

Jeff Williams — Left Wing

Regular Season / Playoffs

Season	Team	League	GP	G	A	PTS	PIM	GP	G	A	PTS	PIM
96-97	Albany	AHL	46	13	21	34	12	15	1	2	3	15
96-97	Raleigh	ECHL	20	4	8	12	8	—	—	—	—	—
97-98	Albany	AHL	58	13	12	25	20	12	5	6	11	2
98-99	Albany	AHL	74	*46	27	73	39	5	1	2	3	0
	AHL	Totals	178	72	60	132	71	32	7	10	17	17

Born; 2/11/76, Pinte-Claire, Quebec. 6-0, 175. Drafted by New Jersey Devils (8th choice, 181st overall) in 1994 Entry Draft. 1998-99 AHL Second Team All-Star. Last amateur club; Guelph (OHL).

Mike Williams — Goaltender

Regular Season / Playoffs

Season	Team	League	GP	W	L	T	MIN	SO	AVG	GP	W	L	MIN	SO	AVG
90-91	Cincinnati	ECHL	12	6	6	0	671	0	5.18	—	—	—	—	—	—
90-91	Nashville	ECHL	3	1	1	0	121	0	5.95	—	—	—	—	—	—
91-92	Toledo	ECHL	44	32	8	2	2490	0	3.81	1	0	1	59	0	6.10
92-93	Toledo	ECHL	8	2	1	2	376	0	4.47	—	—	—	—	—	—
92-93	Knoxville	ECHL	21	3	13	2	1145	0	4.98	—	—	—	—	—	—
93-94	Oklahoma City	CeHL	41	20	12	4	2350	1	3.75	7	3	3	422	0	3.69
94-95	San Antonio	CeHL	38	15	12	4	2000	0	4.17	4	1	1	144	0	2.91
95-96	San Antonio	CeHL	48	27	10	5	2481	*3	3.60	13	7	6	749	0	3.45
96-97	Oklahoma City	CeHL	11	7	0	1	552	1	2.94	4	1	3	241	0	3.49
97-98	Oklahoma City	CHL	34	20	11	2	1933	0	3.94	1	0	0	20	0	6.00
98-99	Oklahoma City	CHL	23	14	7	1	1335	1	3.24	—	—	—	—	—	—
	CHL	Totals	195	103	52	17	10651	6	3.72	29	12	13	1576	0	3.50

Born; 4/16/67, Brownstown, Michigan. 6-0, 200. Drafted by Quebec Nordiques (12th choice, 219th overall) in 1987 Entry Draft. Last amateur club; Ferris State (CCHA).

Paul Williams — Right Wing

Regular Season / Playoffs

Season	Team	League	GP	G	A	PTS	PIM	GP	G	A	PTS	PIM
95-96	Anchorage	WCHL	48	27	23	50	10	—	—	—	—	—
96-97	Anchorage	WCHL	62	41	35	76	8	9	3	1	4	12
97-98	Anchorage	WCHL	61	46	39	85	22	8	2	5	7	2
98-99	Anchorage	WCHL	66	31	55	86	34	5	2	4	6	2
	WCHL	Totals	237	145	152	297	74	22	7	10	17	16

Born; 11/16/70, Anchorage, Alaska. 6-0, 205. 1997-98 WCHL Second Team All-Star. Last amateur club; Alaska-Anchorage (WCHA).

Vince Williams — Defenseman

Regular Season / Playoffs

Season	Team	League	GP	G	A	PTS	PIM	GP	G	A	PTS	PIM
98-99	Indianapolis	IHL	33	2	3	5	30	7	0	0	0	10
98-99	Columbus	ECHL	43	5	8	13	57	—	—	—	—	—

Born; Selected by Pensacola in 1999 ECHL Dispersal Draft. Last amateur club; Concordia (OUAA).

Andrew Williamson — Left Wing

Regular Season / Playoffs

Season	Team	League	GP	G	A	PTS	PIM	GP	G	A	PTS	PIM
97-98	Columbus	ECHL	5	1	0	1	4	—	—	—	—	—
97-98	Toledo	ECHL	49	32	23	55	56	7	0	1	1	6
98-99	Cleveland	IHL	3	2	0	2	0	—	—	—	—	—
98-99	Toledo	ECHL	55	34	20	54	65	7	2	3	5	10
	ECHL	Totals	109	67	43	110	125	14	2	4	6	16

Born; 1/21/76, Thorold, Ontario. 5-10, 195. Traded to Toledo by Columbus for future considerations (10/97). Last amateur club; Owen Sound (OHL).

Jordan Willis — Goaltender

Regular Season / Playoffs

Season	Team	League	GP	W	L	T	MIN	SO	AVG	GP	W	L	MIN	SO	AVG
95-96	Dallas	NHL	1	0	1	0	19	0	3.16	—	—	—	—	—	—
95-96	Michigan	IHL	38	17	9	9	2184	1	3.24	4	1	3	238	0	4.29
96-97	Canada	National	15	7	4	2	804	—	3.13	—	—	—	—	—	—
96-97	Dayton	ECHL	8	4	4	0	429	0	3.50	—	—	—	—	—	—
96-97	Michigan	IHL	2	0	2	0	102	0	4.70	—	—	—	—	—	—
97-98	Michigan	IHL	31	8	18	2	1584	1	3.52	—	—	—	—	—	—
98-99	Baton Rouge	ECHL	47	19	20	5	2521	4	3.12	6	3	3	374	1	2.89
	IHL	Totals	71	25	29	11	3870	2	3.40	4	1	3	238	0	4.29
	ECHL	Totals	55	23	24	5	2950	4	3.17	6	3	3	374	1	2.89

Born; 2/28/75, Kincardine, Ontario. 5-9, 155. Drafted by Dallas Stars (8th choice, 243rd overall) in 1993 Entry Draft. Last amateur club; London (OHL).

Shane Willis — Right Wing

Regular Season / Playoffs

Season	Team	League	GP	G	A	PTS	PIM	GP	G	A	PTS	PIM
97-98	Lethbridge	WHL	64	58	54	112	73	4	2	3	5	6
97-98	New Haven	AHL	1	0	1	1	2	—	—	—	—	—
98-99	Carolina	NHL	7	0	0	0	0	—	—	—	—	—
98-99	New Haven	AHL	73	31	50	81	49	—	—	—	—	—
	AHL	Totals	74	31	51	82	51	—	—	—	—	—

Born; 6/13/77, Edmonton, Alberta. 6-0, 176. Drafted by Tampa Bay Lightning (3rd choice, 56th overall) in 1995 Entry Draft. Re-entered NHL Entry Draft, drafted by Carolina Hurricanes (fourth choice, 88th overall) in 1997 Entry Draft. 1998-99 AHL Rookie of the Year. 1998-99 AHL First All-Star Team. 1998-99 AHL All-Rookie Team. Last amateur club; Lethbridge (WHL).

Tyler Willis — Right Wing

Regular Season / Playoffs

Season	Team	League	GP	G	A	PTS	PIM	GP	G	A	PTS	PIM
97-98	Worcester	AHL	24	2	1	3	140	—	—	—	—	—
97-98	Baton Rouge	ECHL	21	4	10	14	112	—	—	—	—	—
98-99	Worcester	AHL	55	8	10	18	227	—	—	—	—	—
	AHL	Totals	79	10	11	21	367	—	—	—	—	—

Born; 4/8/77, Princeton, British Columbia. 5-9, 173. Last amateur club; Seattle (WHL).

Brian Willsie — Right Wing

Regular Season / Playoffs

Season	Team	League	GP	G	A	PTS	PIM	GP	G	A	PTS	PIM
98-99	Hershey	AHL	72	19	10	29	28	3	1	0	1	0

Born; 3/16/78, London, Ontario. 6-0, 190. Drafted by Colorado Avalanche (7th choice, 146th overall) in 1996 Entry Draft. Last amateur club; Guelph (OHL).

Sean Wilmert — Defenseman

Regular Season / Playoffs

Season	Team	League	GP	G	A	PTS	PIM	GP	G	A	PTS	PIM
95-96	Madison	CoHL	47	1	5	6	89	3	0	1	1	7
96-97	Reno	WCHL	11	2	0	2	39	—	—	—	—	—
96-97	Amarillo	WPHL	1	0	0	0	0	—	—	—	—	—
96-97	Columbus	CeHL	3	0	0	0	2	—	—	—	—	—
96-97	Nashville	CeHL	2	0	0	0	7	—	—	—	—	—
97-98	Nashville	CHL	34	2	1	3	164	—	—	—	—	—
98-99	Tucson	WCHL	3	0	0	0	11	—	—	—	—	—
	CHL	Totals	39	2	1	3	173	—	—	—	—	—

Born; 5/26/69, Atlanta, Georgia. 6-0, 200.

Brian Wilson — Center

Regular Season / Playoffs

Season	Team	League	GP	G	A	PTS	PIM	GP	G	A	PTS	PIM
97-98	Madison	UHL	74	14	17	31	30	7	0	1	1	2
98-99	Madison	UHL	2	3	0	3	0	—	—	—	—	—
	UHL	Totals	76	17	17	34	30	7	0	1	1	2

Born; 4/4/73, Sun Prairie, Wisconsin. 5-11, 185. Last amateur club; Wisconsin-River Falls (NCAA 3).

Chad Wilson — Defenseman

Regular Season / Playoffs

Season	Team	League	GP	G	A	PTS	PIM	GP	G	A	PTS	PIM
97-98	Pee Dee	ECHL	70	7	15	22	69	8	0	0	0	10
98-99	Jacksonville	ECHL	5	3	0	3	6	—	—	—	—	—
98-99	Augusta	ECHL	46	3	7	10	35	—	—	—	—	—
	ECHL	Totals	121	13	22	35	110	8	0	0	0	10

Born; 1/16/74, Terrace, British Columbia. 6-0, 205. Traded to Jacksonville by Pee Dee with Billy Pierce for Kurt Mallett (7/98). Last amateur club; Cornell

Dean Wilson — Left Wing

Regular Season / Playoffs

Season	Team	League	GP	G	A	PTS	PIM	GP	G	A	PTS	PIM
95-96	Bakersfield	WCHL	3	0	0	0	4	—	—	—	—	—
95-96	San Diego	WCHL	7	0	1	1	19	—	—	—	—	—
97-98	Tucson	WCHL	4	0	1	1	12	—	—	—	—	—
98-99	Fresno	WCHL	6	1	0	1	7	—	—	—	—	—
98-99	Bakersfield	WCHL	1	0	0	0	4	—	—	—	—	—
	WCHL	Totals	21	1	2	3	46	—	—	—	—	—

Born; 8/20/71, San Diego, California. 5-10, 180.

Landon Wilson — Right Wing

Regular Season / Playoffs

Season	Team	League	GP	G	A	PTS	PIM	GP	G	A	PTS	PIM
94-95	North Dakota	WCHA	31	7	16	23	141	—	—	—	—	—
94-95	Cornwall	AHL	8	4	4	8	25	13	3	4	7	68
95-96	Colorado	NHL	7	1	0	1	6	—	—	—	—	—
95-96	Cornwall	AHL	53	21	13	34	154	8	1	3	4	22
96-97	Colorado	NHL	9	1	2	3	23	—	—	—	—	—
96-97	Boston	NHL	40	7	10	17	49	—	—	—	—	—
96-97	Providence	AHL	2	2	1	3	2	10	3	4	7	16
97-98	Boston	NHL	28	1	5	6	7	1	0	0	0	0
97-98	Providence	AHL	42	18	10	28	146	—	—	—	—	—
98-99	Boston	NHL	22	3	3	6	17	8	1	1	2	8
98-99	Providence	AHL	48	31	22	53	89	11	7	1	8	19
	NHL	Totals	106	13	20	33	102	9	1	1	2	8
	AHL	Totals	153	76	50	126	416	42	14	12	26	125

Born; 3/3/75, St. Louis, Missouri. 6-2, 216. Drafted by Toronto Maple Leafs (2nd choice, 19th overall) in 1993 Entry Draft. Traded to Quebec Nordiques by Toronto with Wendel Clark, Sylvain Lefebvre and Toronto's first round choice (Jeff Kealty) in 1994 Entry Draft for Garth Butcher, Todd Warriner, Mats Sundin and Philadelphia's first round choice-later traded to Washington (Capitals selected Nolan Baumgartner) in 1994 Entry Draft (6/28/94). Traded to Boston Bruins with Anders Myrvold by Colorado for Boston's first round choice (Robin Regehr) in the 1998 Entry Draft, (11/22/96). 1998-99 AHL First Team All-Star. Member of 1998-99 AHL Champion Providence Bruins. Last amateur club;

Mike Wilson — Defenseman

Regular Season / Playoffs

Season	Team	League	GP	G	A	PTS	PIM	GP	G	A	PTS	PIM
95-96	Buffalo	NHL	58	4	8	12	41	—	—	—	—	—
95-96	Rochester	AHL	15	0	5	5	38	—	—	—	—	—
96-97	Buffalo	NHL	77	2	9	11	51	10	0	1	1	2
97-98	Buffalo	NHL	66	4	4	8	48	15	0	1	1	13
98-99	Buffalo	NHL	30	1	2	3	47	—	—	—	—	—
98-99	Florida	NHL	4	0	0	0	0	—	—	—	—	—
98-99	Las Vegas	IHL	6	3	1	4	6	—	—	—	—	—
	NHL	Totals	235	11	23	34	187	25	0	2	2	15

Born; 2/26/75, Brampton, Ontario. 6-6, 212. Drafted by Vancouver Canucks (1st choice, 20th overall) in 1993 Entry Draft. Traded to Buffalo Sabres with Mike Peca and Vancouver's first round choie (Jay McKee) in 1995 Entry Draft for Alexander Mogilny and Buffalo's fifth round choice (Todd Norman) in 1995 Entry Draft (7/8/95). Traded to Florida Panthers by Buffalo for Rhett Warrener and Florida's fifth round pick (Ryan Miller) in 1999 Entry Draft (3/23/99). Last amateur club; Sudbury (OHL).

Ross Wilson — Right Wing

Regular Season / Playoffs

Season	Team	League	GP	G	A	PTS	PIM	GP	G	A	PTS	PIM
89-90	New Haven	AHL	61	19	14	33	39	—	—	—	—	—
90-91	New Haven	AHL	68	29	17	46	28	—	—	—	—	—
91-92	Phoenix	IHL	28	9	9	18	81	—	—	—	—	—
91-92	Kalamazoo	IHL	31	18	6	24	38	11	9	1	10	6
92-93	Kalamazoo	IHL	58	15	14	29	49	—	—	—	—	—
93-94	Moncton	AHL	75	29	38	67	49	21	10	9	19	18
94-95	Minnesota	IHL	2	0	1	1	0	—	—	—	—	—
94-95	Worcester	AHL	70	17	24	41	82	—	—	—	—	—
95-96	Saginaw	CoHL	42	38	30	68	68	—	—	—	—	—
95-96	Portland	AHL	14	5	2	7	14	—	—	—	—	—
95-96	Fort Wayne	IHL	21	3	8	11	10	5	1	1	2	0
96-97	Detroit	IHL	2	0	0	0	0	—	—	—	—	—
96-97	Fort Wayne	IHL	5	0	1	1	4	—	—	—	—	—
96-97	Flint	CoHL	68	53	56	109	47	14	9	11	20	10
97-98	Flint	UHL	57	50	31	81	46	12	8	4	12	4
98-99	Flint	UHL	74	43	66	109	36	12	11	2	13	14
	AHL	Totals	288	99	95	194	212	21	10	9	19	18
	IHL	Totals	140	45	38	83	178	16	10	2	12	6
	UHL	Totals	241	184	183	367	207	38	28	17	45	28

Born; 6/26/69, The Pas, Manitoba. 6-3, 210. Drafted by Los Angeles Kings (3rd choice, 43rd overall) in 1987 Entry Draft. 1998-99 UHL Second Team All-Star. Last amateur club; Peterborough (OHL).

Steve Wilson — Defenseman

Regular Season / Playoffs

Season	Team	League	GP	G	A	PTS	PIM	GP	G	A	PTS	PIM
92-93	Dayton	ECHL	63	11	18	29	49	3	0	0	0	7
93-94	Dayton	ECHL	60	13	26	39	134	3	1	0	1	2
93-94	Kalamazoo	IHL	3	0	0	0	2	—	—	—	—	—
93-94	Peoria	IHL	1	0	0	0	0	—	—	—	—	—
93-94	Salt Lake City	IHL	2	0	0	0	0	—	—	—	—	—
94-95	Dayton	ECHL	16	12	9	21	30	—	—	—	—	—
94-95	Phoenix	IHL	54	3	6	9	61	9	0	6	6	0
95-96	Phoenix	IHL	22	1	0	1	18	—	—	—	—	—
95-96	Peoria	IHL	54	5	15	20	44	12	0	2	2	8
96-97	Manitoba	IHL	81	4	10	14	75	—	—	—	—	—
97-98	Manitoba	IHL	2	1	1	2	8	—	—	—	—	—
97-98	Cleveland	IHL	17	0	4	4	16	8	0	1	1	0
97-98	Chesapeake	ECHL	51	6	23	29	26	—	—	—	—	—
98-99	Cleveland	IHL	18	1	5	6	21	—	—	—	—	—
98-99	Chesapeake	ECHL	47	5	18	23	128	8	0	2	2	10
	IHL	Totals	254	15	41	56	245	29	0	9	9	8
	ECHL	Totals	237	47	94	141	367	14	1	2	3	19

Born; 9/3/68, Kingston, Ontario. 6-2, 205. Last amateur club; Miami of Ohio (CCHA).

Tom Wilson — Defenseman

Season	Team	League	GP	G	A	PTS	PIM	GP	G	A	PTS	PIM
			Regular Season					Playoffs				
94-95	Lakeland	SUN	44	2	8	10	156	—	—	—	—	—
95-96	Mobile	ECHL	2	0	0	0	11	—	—	—	—	—
95-96	Lakeland	SHL	51	2	10	12	160	5	0	3	3	15
96-97	Columbus	CeHL	55	7	8	15	218	2	0	0	0	2
97-98	Columbus	CHL	62	1	3	4	252	10	1	0	1	40
98-99	Columbus	CHL	51	1	4	5	243	10	0	0	0	20
	CHL	Totals	168	9	15	24	713	22	1	0	1	62
	SHL	Totals	95	4	18	22	316	5	0	3	3	15

Born; 1/14/73, Toronto, Ontario. 6-1, 205. Member of 1997-98 CHL Champion Columbus Cottonmouths.

Nicholas Windsor — Defenseman

Season	Team	League	GP	G	A	PTS	PIM	GP	G	A	PTS	PIM
			Regular Season					Playoffs				
98-99	Lowell	AHL	8	0	1	1	0	—	—	—	—	—
98-99	Roanoke	ECHL	59	14	22	36	48	12	1	1	2	8

Born; 1/24/76, Waterloo, Ontario. 6-1, 190. Last amateur club; Clarkson (ECAC).

Brad Wingfield — Left Wing

Season	Team	League	GP	G	A	PTS	PIM	GP	G	A	PTS	PIM
			Regular Season					Playoffs				
96-97	Central Texas	WPHL	35	4	4	8	176	2	0	0	0	0
97-98	Utah	IHL	3	0	0	0	5	—	—	—	—	—
97-98	Bakersfield	WCHL	11	1	3	4	46	—	—	—	—	—
97-98	Central Texas	WPHL	10	1	2	3	43	—	—	—	—	—
97-98	New Mexico	WPHL	17	1	1	2	95	7	0	1	1	22
98-99	Corpus Christi	WPHL	54	12	11	23	233	—	—	—	—	—
	WPHL	Totals	116	18	18	36	547	9	0	1	1	22

Born; 6/24/75, Vancouver, British Columbia. 6-0, 212. Traded to New Mexico by Central Texas for Francois Chaput (1/98). Selected by Corpus Christi in 1998 WPHL Expansion Draft.

Tim Winkleman — Defenseman

Season	Team	League	GP	G	A	PTS	PIM	GP	G	A	PTS	PIM
			Regular Season					Playoffs				
98-99	Winston-Salem	UHL	8	0	1	1	48	—	—	—	—	—
98-99	Jacksonville	ECHL	3	0	0	0	7	—	—	—	—	—

Born; 8/24/77, Roblin, Manitoba. 5-9, 190.

Chris Winnes — Left Wing

Season	Team	League	GP	G	A	PTS	PIM	GP	G	A	PTS	PIM
			Regular Season					Playoffs				
90-91	New Hampshire	H.E.	33	15	16	31	24	—	—	—	—	—
90-91	Boston	NHL	—	—	—	—	—	1	0	0	0	0
90-91	Maine	AHL	7	3	1	4	0	1	0	2	2	0
91-92	Boston	NHL	24	1	3	4	6	—	—	—	—	—
91-92	Maine	AHL	45	12	35	47	30	—	—	—	—	—
92-93	Boston	NHL	5	0	1	1	0	—	—	—	—	—
92-93	Providence	AHL	64	23	36	59	34	4	0	2	2	5
93-94	Philadelphia	NHL	4	0	2	2	0	—	—	—	—	—
93-94	Hershey	AHL	70	29	21	50	20	7	1	3	4	0
94-95	Hershey	AHL	78	26	40	66	39	6	2	2	4	17
95-96	Michigan	IHL	27	6	13	19	14	—	—	—	—	—
95-96	Fort Wayne	IHL	39	6	7	13	12	2	0	0	0	0
96-97	Murano	Italy	12	11	5	16	10	—	—	—	—	—
96-97	Utah	IHL	5	0	0	0	0	—	—	—	—	—
97-98	San Antonio	IHL	3	0	0	0	0	—	—	—	—	—
97-98	Hartford	AHL	64	17	23	40	16	13	1	4	5	2
98-99	Manitoba	IHL	11	2	0	2	0	—	—	—	—	—
98-99	Hartford	AHL	33	7	6	13	25	1	0	0	0	0
	NHL	Totals	33	1	6	7	6	1	0	0	0	0
	AHL	Totals	361	117	162	279	164	32	4	13	17	24
	IHL	Totals	85	14	20	34	26	2	0	0	0	0

Born; 2/12/68, Columbus, Ohio. 6-0, 170. Drafted by Boston Bruins (9th choice, 161st overall) in 1987 Entry Draft. Signed as a free agent by Philadelphia Flyers (8/4/93). Signed as a free agent by New York Rangers (7/21/98). Last amateur club; New Hampshire (Hockey East).

Jeff Winter — Defenseman

Season	Team	League	GP	G	A	PTS	PIM	GP	G	A	PTS	PIM
			Regular Season					Playoffs				
96-97	Madison	CoHL	73	7	19	26	73	5	2	2	4	2
97-98	Cincinnati	AHL	26	0	4	4	21	—	—	—	—	—
97-98	Madison	UHL	38	3	16	19	49	—	—	—	—	—
98-99	Cincinnati	AHL	55	1	0	1	42	—	—	—	—	—
98-99	Port Huron	UHL	13	0	6	6	2	—	—	—	—	—
	AHL	Totals	81	1	4	5	63	—	—	—	—	—
	UHL	Totals	124	10	41	51	124	5	2	2	4	2

Born; 2/26/72, New Milford, Connecticut. 6-4, 210. Traded to Saginaw by Port Huron for Brian Mueller (3/99). Member of 1996-97 CoHL All-Rookie Team. Last amateur club; Ohio State (CCHA).

Brian Wiseman — Center

Season	Team	League	GP	G	A	PTS	PIM	GP	G	A	PTS	PIM
			Regular Season					Playoffs				
94-95	Chicago	IHL	75	17	55	72	52	3	1	1	2	4
95-96	Chicago	IHL	73	33	55	88	117	—	—	—	—	—
96-97	Toronto	NHL	3	0	0	0	0	—	—	—	—	—
96-97	St. John's	AHL	71	33	62	95	83	7	5	4	9	8
97-98	Houston	IHL	78	26	72	98	86	4	0	3	3	8
98-99	Houston	IHL	71	21	*88	*109	106	19	3	*13	16	26
	IHL	Totals	297	97	270	367	361	26	4	17	21	38

Born; 7/13/71, Chatham, Ontario. 5-7, 185. Drafted by New York Rangers (11th choice, 257th overall) in 1991 Entry Draft. Signed as a free agent by Toronto Maple Leafs (8/14/96). Signed as a free agent by Toronto (7/9/99). 1997-98 IHL First All-Star Team. 1998-99 IHL MVP. 1998-99 IHL First Team All-Star. Member of 1998-99 IHL Champion Houston Aeros. Last amateur club; Michigan

Chris Wismer — Defenseman

Season	Team	League	GP	G	A	PTS	PIM	GP	G	A	PTS	PIM
			Regular Season					Playoffs				
96-97	Owen Sound	OHL	62	4	26	30	100	4	0	1	1	6
96-97	Roanoke	ECHL	3	0	0	0	2	—	—	—	—	—
97-98	Owen Sound	OHL	42	3	18	21	126	10	1	4	5	16
98-99	Roanoke	ECHL	20	0	2	2	33	—	—	—	—	—
98-99	Dayton	ECHL	40	2	8	10	107	4	0	0	0	16
98-99	Detroit	IHL	4	0	0	0	21	—	—	—	—	—
98-99	Cincinnati	IHL	4	0	0	0	6	—	—	—	—	—
	IHL	Totals	8	0	0	0	27	—	—	—	—	—
	ECHL	Totals	63	2	10	12	142	4	0	0	0	16

Born; 9/23/77, Cambridge, Ontario. 6-2, 190. Last amateur club; Owen Sound (OHL).

Johan Witehall — Left Wing

Season	Team	League	GP	G	A	PTS	PIM	GP	G	A	PTS	PIM
			Regular Season					Playoffs				
98-99	Rangers	NHL	4	0	0	0	0	—	—	—	—	—
98-99	Hartford	AHL	62	14	15	29	56	7	1	2	3	6

Born; 1/7/72, Kungsbacka, Sweden. 6-1, 198. Drafted by New York Rangers (8th choice, 207th overall) in 1998 Entry Draft. Last European club; Leksand

Casey Wolak — Forward

Season	Team	League	GP	G	A	PTS	PIM	GP	G	A	PTS	PIM
			Regular Season					Playoffs				
98-99	Mississauga	OHL	1	0	0	0	0	—	—	—	—	—
98-99	Sarnia	OHL	15	1	1	2	31	—	—	—	—	—
98-99	Kitchener	OHL	14	10	14	24	117	1	0	0	0	4
98-99	Baton Rouge	ECHL	3	0	0	0	17	6	0	0	0	18

Born; 3/26/78, Point Claire, Quebec. 5-11, 182. Last amateur club; Kitchener (OHL).

Craig Wolanin — Defenseman

Regular Season / Playoffs

Season	Team	League	GP	G	A	PTS	PIM	GP	G	A	PTS	PIM
85-86	New Jersey	NHL	44	2	16	18	74	—	—	—	—	—
86-87	New Jersey	NHL	68	4	6	10	109	—	—	—	—	—
87-88	New Jersey	NHL	78	6	25	31	170	18	2	5	7	51
88-89	New Jersey	NHL	56	3	8	11	69	—	—	—	—	—
89-90	New Jersey	NHL	37	1	7	8	47	—	—	—	—	—
89-90	Utica	AHL	6	2	4	6	2	—	—	—	—	—
89-90	Quebec	NHL	13	0	3	3	10	—	—	—	—	—
90-91	Quebec	NHL	80	5	13	18	89	—	—	—	—	—
91-92	Quebec	NHL	69	2	11	13	80	—	—	—	—	—
92-93	Quebec	NHL	24	1	4	5	49	4	0	0	0	4
93-94	Quebec	NHL	63	6	10	16	80	—	—	—	—	—
94-95	Quebec	NHL	40	3	6	9	40	6	1	1	2	4
95-96	Colorado	NHL	75	7	20	27	50	7	1	0	1	8
96-97	Tampa Bay	NHL	15	0	0	0	8	—	—	—	—	—
96-97	Toronto	NHL	23	0	4	4	13	—	—	—	—	—
97-98	Toronto	NHL	10	0	0	0	6	—	—	—	—	—
98-99	Detroit	IHL	16	0	5	5	21	11	0	0	0	12
	NHL	Totals	695	40	133	173	894	35	4	6	10	67

Born; 7/27/67, Grosse Pointe, Michigan. 6-4, 215. Drafted by New Jersey Devils (1st choice, 3rd overall) in 1985 Entry Draft. Traded to Quebec Nordiques by New Jersey with future considerations (Randy Velischek, 8/13/90) for Peter Stastny (3/6/90). Traded to Tampa Bay Lightning by Colorado Avalanche for Tampa Bay's second round choice (Ramzi Abid) in 1998 Entry Draft (7/29/96). Traded to Toronto Maple Leafs for Toronto's third round selection (later traded to Edmonton-Edmonton selected Alex Henry) in 1998 Entry Draft (1/31/97). Member of 1995-96 Stanley Cup Champion Colorado Avalanche. Last amateur club;

Derek Wood — Center

Regular Season / Playoffs

Season	Team	League	GP	G	A	PTS	PIM	GP	G	A	PTS	PIM
96-97	Columbus	ECHL	66	27	30	57	181	8	1	2	3	35
97-98	Rochester	AHL	31	3	7	10	75	4	0	0	0	21
97-98	Columbus	ECHL	23	5	7	12	107	—	—	—	—	—
98-99	Rochester	AHL	3	0	0	0	0	20	2	4	6	24
98-99	Fort Wayne	IHL	25	0	8	8	36	—	—	—	—	—
98-99	Binghamton	UHL	18	12	10	22	29	5	0	3	3	2
	AHL	Totals	34	3	7	10	75	24	2	4	6	45
	ECHL	Totals	89	32	37	69	288	8	1	2	3	35

Born; 7/8/75, Prince George, British Columbia. 5-10, 190. Last amateur club; Medicine Hat (WHL).

Dody Wood — Left Wing

Regular Season / Playoffs

Season	Team	League	GP	G	A	PTS	PIM	GP	G	A	PTS	PIM
92-93	San Jose	NHL	13	1	1	2	71	—	—	—	—	—
92-93	Kansas City	IHL	36	3	2	5	216	6	0	1	1	15
93-94	Kansas City	IHL	48	5	15	20	320	—	—	—	—	—
94-95	Kansas City	IHL	44	5	13	18	255	21	7	10	17	87
94-95	San Jose	NHL	9	1	1	2	29	—	—	—	—	—
95-96	San Jose	NHL	32	3	6	9	138	—	—	—	—	—
96-97	San Jose	NHL	44	3	2	5	193	—	—	—	—	—
96-97	Kansas City	IHL	6	3	6	9	35	—	—	—	—	—
97-98	San Jose	NHL	8	0	0	0	40	—	—	—	—	—
97-98	Kansas City	IHL	2	0	1	1	31	—	—	—	—	—
97-98	Albany	AHL	34	4	13	17	185	13	2	0	2	55
98-99	Kansas City	IHL	60	11	16	27	286	3	0	1	1	25
	NHL	Totals	106	8	10	18	471	—	—	—	—	—
	IHL	Totals	196	27	53	80	1143	30	7	12	19	127

Born; 3/18/72, Chetwynd, British Columbia. 6-0, 200. Drafted by San Jose Sharks (4th choice, 45th overall) in 1991 Entry Draft. Traded to New Jersey Devils by San Jose with Doug Bodger for John MacLean and Ken Sutton (12/7/97). Last amateur club; Swift Current (WHL).

Doug Wood — Defenseman

Regular Season / Playoffs

Season	Team	League	GP	G	A	PTS	PIM	GP	G	A	PTS	PIM
96-97	Syracuse	AHL	19	1	3	4	16	1	0	0	0	0
96-97	South Carolina	ECHL	43	1	14	15	65	—	—	—	—	—
96-97	Raleigh	ECHL	6	0	1	1	14	—	—	—	—	—
97-98	Kassel	Germany	34	2	5	7	28	—	—	—	—	—
98-99	Degendorf	Germany	52	7	22	29	132	—	—	—	—	—
	ECHL	Totals	49	1	15	16	79	—	—	—	—	—

Born; 1/7/74, Waltham, Massachusetts. 6-2, 215. Last amateur club; Boston University (Hockey East).

Ryan Wood — Left Wing

Regular Season / Playoffs

Season	Team	League	GP	G	A	PTS	PIM	GP	G	A	PTS	PIM
97-98	Huntsville	CHL	64	35	35	70	51	3	2	4	6	2
98-99	San Angelo	WPHL	2	0	0	0	0	—	—	—	—	—
98-99	Huntsville	CHL	64	14	27	41	61	15	4	1	5	6
	CHL	Totals	128	49	62	111	112	18	6	5	11	8

Born; Mordin, Manitoba. 5-11, 190. Member of 1998-99 CHL Champion Huntsville Channel Cats.

Bob Woods — Defenseman

Regular Season / Playoffs

Season	Team	League	GP	G	A	PTS	PIM	GP	G	A	PTS	PIM
88-89	Utica	AHL	11	0	1	1	2	4	0	0	0	2
89-90	Utica	AHL	58	2	12	14	30	5	0	0	0	6
90-91	Utica	AHL	33	4	6	10	21	—	—	—	—	—
90-91	Johnstown	ECHL	23	12	25	37	32	—	—	—	—	—
91-92	Johnstown	ECHL	63	18	43	61	44	6	4	1	5	14
92-93	Johnstown	ECHL	61	11	36	47	72	5	1	1	2	8
93-94	Hershey	AHL	28	2	9	11	21	11	2	4	6	8
93-94	Johnstown	ECHL	43	18	37	55	57	3	1	3	4	4
94-95	Utica	CoHL	1	0	0	0	0	—	—	—	—	—
95-96	Portland	AHL	5	0	1	1	2	2	0	0	0	9
95-96	Hampton Roads	ECHL	66	3	26	29	106	3	1	2	3	17
96-97	Hershey	AHL	6	1	0	1	2	16	0	1	1	4
96-97	Mobile	ECHL	69	19	50	69	68	3	1	0	1	2
97-98	Fort Wayne	IHL	10	0	0	0	2	3	0	1	1	0
97-98	Tallahassee	ECHL	65	18	31	49	62	—	—	—	—	—
98-99	Fort Wayue	IHL	1	2	0	2	0	—	—	—	—	—
98-99	Mississippi	ECHL	70	24	38	62	41	18	2	6	8	12
	AHL	Totals	141	9	29	38	78	38	2	5	7	29
	IHL	Totals	11	2	0	2	2	3	0	1	1	0
	ECHL	Totals	460	123	286	409	482	38	10	13	23	57

Born; 1/24/68, LeRoy, Saskatchewan. 6-1, 192. Drafted by New Jersey Devils (11th choice, 201st overall) in 1988 Entry Draft. 1996-97 ECHL Second Team All-Star. 1998-99 ECHL Second Team All-Star. Member of 1996-97 AHL Champion Hershey Bears. Member of 1998-99 ECHL Champion Mississippi Sea-Wolves. Last amateur club; Brandon (WHL).

Martin Woods — Defenseman

Regular Season / Playoffs

Season	Team	League	GP	G	A	PTS	PIM	GP	G	A	PTS	PIM
95-96	Hampton Roads	ECHL	7	0	1	1	14	—	—	—	—	—
95-96	Jacksonville	ECHL	33	6	12	18	80	—	—	—	—	—
95-96	Johnstown	ECHL	22	4	8	12	95	—	—	—	—	—
96-97	Philadelphia	AHL	1	0	0	0	0	—	—	—	—	—
96-97	Johnstown	ECHL	67	16	34	50	233	—	—	—	—	—
97-98	Hamilton	AHL	2	0	0	0	2	—	—	—	—	—
97-98	Johnstown	ECHL	15	1	3	4	54	—	—	—	—	—
97-98	New Orleans	ECHL	52	8	19	27	177	4	0	1	1	14
98-99	New Orleans	ECHL	67	9	27	36	170	11	1	6	7	12
	AHL	Totals	3	0	0	0	2	—	—	—	—	—
	ECHL	Totals	263	44	104	148	823	15	1	7	8	26

Born; 5/14/75, Hull, Quebec. 6-1, 200. Drafted by Winnipeg Jets (8th choice, 171st overall) in 1993 Entry Draft. Traded to New Orleans by Johnstown for Mike Rusk and Chris Bowen (11/97). Last amateur club; Drummondville

Rob Woodward — Left Wing

Regular Season / Playoffs

Season	Team	League	GP	G	A	PTS	PIM	GP	G	A	PTS	PIM
93-94	Hamilton	AHL	60	11	14	25	45	2	0	0	0	0
94-95												
95-96												
96-97												
97-98												
98-99	Columbus	ECHL	50	11	16	27	48	4	0	0	0	0
98-99	Indianapolis	IHL	1	0	0	0	0	—	—	—	—	—

Born; 1/15/71, Evanston, Illinois. 6-4, 225. Drafted by Vancouver Canucks (2nd choice, 29th overall) in 1989 Entry Draft. Last amateur club; Michigan State (CCHA).

Mark Woolf

Regular Season / Playoffs

Season	Team	League	GP	G	A	PTS	PIM	GP	G	A	PTS	PIM
91-92	Roanoke Valley	ECHL	63	50	51	101	93	7	6	2	8	4
91-92	Salt Lake City	IHL	1	0	0	0	0	—	—	—	—	—
92-93	Thunder Bay	CoHL	33	16	20	36	18	—	—	—	—	—
92-93	Columbus	ECHL	26	8	10	18	45	—	—	—	—	—
92-93	Adirondack	AHL	1	0	0	0	0	—	—	—	—	—
93-94	Springfield	AHL	15	2	3	5	4	2	0	0	0	0
93-94	Columbus	ECHL	51	42	29	71	103	6	1	2	3	8
94-95	Worcester	AHL	7	1	0	1	0	—	—	—	—	—
94-95	Huntington	ECHL	59	38	36	74	96	4	0	2	2	8
95-96	Kapfenberg	Austria	26	13	10	23	78	—	—	—	—	—
96-97	Ayr	BSL	53	22	23	45	76	7	4	1	5	2
97-98	Ayr	BSL	60	26	36	62	44	9	1	5	6	8
98-99	Ayr	BSL	50	27	27	54	22	4	0	2	2	2
	AHL	Totals	23	3	3	6	4	2	0	0	0	0
	ECHL	Totals	199	138	126	264	337	17	7	6	13	20
	BSL	Totals	163	75	86	161	142	20	5	8	13	12

Born; 9/30/70, Brandon, Manitoba. 6-0, 210. Last amateur club; Spokane (WHL).

Peter Worrell — Left Wing

Regular Season / Playoffs

Season	Team	League	GP	G	A	PTS	PIM	GP	G	A	PTS	PIM
97-98	Florida	NHL	19	0	0	0	153	—	—	—	—	—
97-98	New Haven	AHL	50	15	12	27	309	1	0	1	1	6
98-99	Florida	NHL	62	4	5	9	258	—	—	—	—	—
98-99	New Haven	AHL	10	3	1	4	65	—	—	—	—	—
	NHL	Totals	81	4	5	9	411	—	—	—	—	—
	AHL	Totals	60	18	13	31	374	1	0	1	1	6

Born; 8/18/77, Pierre Fonds, Quebec. 6-6, 249. Drafted by Florida Panthers (7th choice, 166th overall) in 1995 Entry Draft. Last amateur club; Hull (QMJHL).

Mark Wotton — Defenseman

Regular Season / Playoffs

Season	Team	League	GP	G	A	PTS	PIM	GP	G	A	PTS	PIM
94-95	Vancouver	NHL	1	0	0	0	0	5	0	0	0	4
94-95	Syracuse	AHL	75	12	29	41	50	—	—	—	—	—
95-96	Syracuse	AHL	80	10	35	45	96	15	1	12	13	20
96-97	Vancouver	NHL	36	3	6	9	19	—	—	—	—	—
96-97	Syracuse	AHL	27	2	8	10	25	2	0	0	0	4
97-98	Vancouver	NHL	5	0	0	0	6	—	—	—	—	—
97-98	Syracuse	AHL	56	12	21	33	80	5	0	0	0	12
98-99	Syracuse	AHL	72	4	31	35	74	—	—	—	—	—
	NHL	Totals	42	3	6	9	25	5	0	0	0	4
	AHL	Totals	310	40	124	164	325	22	1	12	13	36

Born; 1/16/73, Foxwarren, Manitoba. 5-11, 187. Drafted by Vancouver Canucks (11th choice, 237th overall) in 1992 Entry Draft. Signed as a free agent by Dallas Stars (7/9/99). Last amateur club; Saskatoon (WHL).

Scott Wray — Left Wing

Regular Season / Playoffs

Season	Team	League	GP	G	A	PTS	PIM	GP	G	A	PTS	PIM
98-99	North Bay	OHL	61	23	18	41	61	4	0	0	0	6
98-99	San Antonio	CHL	—	—	—	—	—	8	1	3	4	2

Born; 12/19/79. 5-11, 183. Last amateur club; North Bay (OHL).

Bob Wren — Center

Regular Season / Playoffs

Season	Team	League	GP	G	A	PTS	PIM	GP	G	A	PTS	PIM
94-95	Springfield	AHL	61	16	15	31	118	—	—	—	—	—
94-95	Richmond	ECHL	2	0	1	1	0	—	—	—	—	—
95-96	Detroit	IHL	1	0	0	0	0	—	—	—	—	—
95-96	Knoxville	ECHL	50	21	35	56	257	8	4	11	15	32
96-97	Baltimore	AHL	73	23	36	59	97	3	1	1	2	0
97-98	Anaheim	NHL	3	0	0	0	0	—	—	—	—	—
97-98	Cincinnati	AHL	77	42	58	100	151	—	—	—	—	—
98-99	Cincinnati	AHL	73	27	43	70	102	3	1	2	3	8
	AHL	Totals	284	108	152	260	468	6	2	3	5	8
	ECHL	Totals	52	21	36	57	257	8	4	11	15	32

Born; 9/16/74, Preston, Ontario. 5-10, 185. Drafted by Los Angeles Kings (3rd choice, 94th overall) in 1993 Entry Draft. Signed as a free agent by Hartford Whalers (9/6/94). Signed as a free agent by Anaheim Mighty Ducks (8/1/97). Last amateur club; Detroit (OHL).

Billy Wright — Left Wing

Regular Season / Playoffs

Season	Team	League	GP	G	A	PTS	PIM	GP	G	A	PTS	PIM
97-98	Shreveport	WPHL	29	5	13	18	51	—	—	—	—	—
97-98	Waco	WPHL	24	9	15	24	28	—	—	—	—	—
97-98	Amarillo	WPHL	7	2	1	3	4	—	—	—	—	—
98-99	Waco	WPHL	63	25	29	54	52	4	0	0	0	4
	WPHL	Totals	123	41	58	99	135	4	0	0	0	4

Born; 10/23/72, North Bay, Ontario. 5-10, 180. Last amateur club; New Brunswick (AUAA).

Darren Wright — Defenseman

Regular Season / Playoffs

Season	Team	League	GP	G	A	PTS	PIM	GP	G	A	PTS	PIM
97-98	New Mexico	WPHL	62	1	11	12	178	10	0	1	1	40
98-99	Toledo	ECHL	32	1	3	4	93	—	—	—	—	—

Born; 5/22/76, Duncan, British Columbia. 6-2, 196. Drafted by Boston Bruins (4th choice, 125th overall) in 1994 Entry Draft. Last amateur club; Kamloops

Jamie Wright — Left Wing

Regular Season / Playoffs

Season	Team	League	GP	G	A	PTS	PIM	GP	G	A	PTS	PIM
96-97	Michigan	IHL	60	6	8	14	34	1	0	0	0	0
97-98	Dallas	NHL	21	4	2	6	2	5	0	0	0	0
97-98	Michigan	IHL	53	15	11	26	31	—	—	—	—	—
98-99	Dallas	NHL	11	0	0	0	0	—	—	—	—	—
98-99	Michigan	IHL	64	16	15	31	92	2	0	0	0	2
	NHL	Totals	32	4	2	6	2	5	0	0	0	0
	IHL	Totals	177	37	34	71	157	3	0	0	0	2

Born; 5/13/76, Kitchener, Ontario. 6-0, 172. Drafted by Dallas Stars (3rd choice, 98th overall) in 1994 Entry Draft. Last amateur club; Guelph (OHL).

Jason Wright — Defenseman

Regular Season / Playoffs

Season	Team	League	GP	G	A	PTS	PIM	GP	G	A	PTS	PIM
95-96	Michigan Tech	WCHA	42	9	22	31	36	—	—	—	—	—
95-96	Richmond	ECHL	3	0	1	1	2	—	—	—	—	—
96-97	Richmond	ECHL	67	6	14	20	84	4	0	1	1	2
97-98	Richmond	ECHL	23	2	12	14	31	—	—	—	—	—
97-98	South Carolina	ECHL	47	3	14	17	41	5	0	1	1	6
98-99	Fayetteville	CHL	70	8	40	48	68	—	—	—	—	—
	ECHL	Totals	140	11	41	52	158	9	0	2	2	8

Born; 7/6/72, Thunder Bay, Ontario. 6-0, 195. Traded to South Carolina by Richmond with Mike Taylor for Dan Fournel, Kevin Knopp, Mario Cormier and Jay Moser (12/97). Last amateur club; Michigan Tech (WCHA).

Shayne Wright — Defenseman

Regular Season / Playoffs

Season	Team	League	GP	G	A	PTS	PIM	GP	G	A	PTS	PIM
94-95	Owen Sound	OHL	63	11	50	61	114	10	1	9	10	34
94-95	Rochester	AHL	2	0	0	0	0	4	0	1	1	0
95-96	Rochester	AHL	48	0	7	7	99	5	0	1	1	8
96-97	Rochester	AHL	80	7	30	37	124	10	2	3	5	6
97-98	Rochester	AHL	70	2	18	20	122	4	0	2	2	0
98-99	Canada	National	48	7	9	16	52	—	—	—	—	—
98-99	Zurich	Switz.	7	1	2	3	20	6	0	2	2	10
	AHL	Totals	200	9	55	64	345	23	2	7	9	14

Born; 6/30/75, Welland, Ontario. 6-0, 189. Drafted by Buffalo Sabres (12th choice, 277th overall) in 1994 Entry Draft. Member of 1995-96 AHL champion Rochester Americans. Last amateur club; Owen Sound (OHL).

Bartek Wrobel — Left Wing

Regular Season / Playoffs

Season	Team	League	GP	G	A	PTS	PIM	GP	G	A	PTS	PIM
98-99	Mohawk Valley	UHL	3	0	0	0	4	—	—	—	—	—

Born; 8/12/77, Gdansk, Poland. 6-4, 205.

Wally Wuttunee — Defenseman

Regular Season / Playoffs

Season	Team	League	GP	G	A	PTS	PIM	GP	G	A	PTS	PIM
98-99	Wheeling	ECHL	25	0	3	3	44	—	—	—	—	—
98-99	Birmingham	ECHL	11	0	0	0	2	—	—	—	—	—
98-99	Port Huron	UHL	19	0	0	0	8	—	—	—	—	—

Born; 8/17/77, North Battleford, Saskatchewan. 6-1, 220. Traded to Birmingham by Wheeling to complete an earlier trade (3/99).

Deuce Wynes — Defenseman

Regular Season / Playoffs

Season	Team	League	GP	G	A	PTS	PIM	GP	G	A	PTS	PIM
98-99	El Paso	WPHL	64	2	7	9	41	3	0	0	0	0

Born; 11/2/74, Apple Valley, Minnesota. 5-10, 190. Last amateur club; Lake Superior (CCHA).

Caleb Wyse — Forward

Regular Season / Playoffs

Season	Team	League	GP	G	A	PTS	PIM	GP	G	A	PTS	PIM
98-99	Tupelo	WPHL	58	7	10	17	44	—	—	—	—	—

Born; 4/18/72, Cleveland Heights, Ohio. 5-8, 190. Last amateur club; Curry College (NCAA 3).

Derek Puppa won the CHL's Regular and Playoff MVP Awards
Photo by Lindy Frank

David Lessard's goal-scoring abilities make him an attractive AA player
Photo by Bill Vaughn

Vitali Yachmenev — Right Wing

Regular Season / Playoffs

Season	Team	League	GP	G	A	PTS	PIM	GP	G	A	PTS	PIM
94-95	North Bay	OHL	59	53	52	105	8	6	1	8	9	2
94-95	Phoenix	IHL	—	—	—	—	—	4	1	0	1	0
95-96	Los Angeles	NHL	80	19	34	53	16	—	—	—	—	—
96-97	Los Angeles	NHL	65	10	22	32	10	—	—	—	—	—
97-98	Los Angeles	NHL	4	0	1	1	4	—	—	—	—	—
97-98	Long Beach	IHL	59	23	28	51	14	17	8	9	17	4
98-99	Nashville	NHL	55	7	10	17	10	—	—	—	—	—
98-99	Milwaukee	IHL	16	7	6	13	0	—	—	—	—	—
	NHL	Totals	204	36	67	103	40	—	—	—	—	—
	IHL	Totals	59	23	28	51	14	21	9	9	18	4

Born; 1/8/75, Chelyabinsk, USSR. 5-9, 180. Drafted by Los Angeles Kings (3rd choice, 59th overall) in 1994 Entry Draft. Traded to Nashville Predators by Los Angeles for future considerations (7/7/98). Last amateur club: North Bay (OHL).

Terry Yake — Center

Regular Season / Playoffs

Season	Team	League	GP	G	A	PTS	PIM	GP	G	A	PTS	PIM
88-89	Hartford	NHL	2	0	0	0	0	—	—	—	—	—
88-89	Binghamton	AHL	75	39	56	95	57	—	—	—	—	—
89-90	Hartford	NHL	2	0	1	1	0	—	—	—	—	—
89-90	Binghamton	AHL	77	13	42	55	37	—	—	—	—	—
90-91	Hartford	NHL	19	1	4	5	10	6	1	1	2	16
90-91	Springfield	AHL	60	35	42	77	56	15	9	9	18	10
91-92	Hartford	NHL	15	1	1	2	4	—	—	—	—	—
91-92	Springfield	AHL	53	21	34	55	63	8	3	4	7	2
92-93	Hartford	NHL	66	22	31	53	46	—	—	—	—	—
92-93	Springfield	AHL	16	8	14	22	27	—	—	—	—	—
93-94	Anaheim	NHL	82	21	31	52	44	—	—	—	—	—
94-95	Toronto	NHL	19	3	2	5	2	—	—	—	—	—
94-95	Denver	IHL	2	0	3	3	2	17	4	11	15	16
95-96	Milwaukee	IHL	70	32	56	88	70	5	3	6	9	4
96-97	Rochester	AHL	78	34	*67	101	77	10	8	8	16	2
97-98	St. Louis	NHL	65	10	15	25	38	10	2	1	3	6
98-99	St. Louis	NHL	60	9	18	27	34	13	1	2	3	14
98-99	Worcester	AHL	24	8	11	19	26	—	—	—	—	—
	NHL	Totals	330	67	103	170	178	29	4	4	8	36
	AHL	Totals	383	158	266	424	343	33	20	21	41	14
	IHL	Totals	72	32	59	91	72	22	7	17	24	20

Born; 10/22/68, New Westminster, British Columbia. 5-11, 185. Drafted by Harftord Whalers (3rd choice, 81st overall) in 1987 Entry Draft. Claimed by Anaheim Mighty Ducks from Hartford in NHL Expansion Draft (6/24/93). Traded to Toronto Maple Leafs by Anaheim for David Sacco (9/28/94). Signed as a free agent by St. Louis Blues (8/24/97). Selected by Atlanta Thrashers in NHL Expansion Draft (6/25/99). Member of 1990-91 AHL Champion Springfield Indians. Member of 1994-95 IHL Champion Denver Grizzlies. Last amateur club;

Shawn Yakimishyn — Center

Regular Season / Playoffs

Season	Team	League	GP	G	A	PTS	PIM	GP	G	A	PTS	PIM
93-94	Columbus	ECHL	7	1	4	5	25	6	0	1	1	18
94-95	Columbus	ECHL	6	0	1	1	24	—	—	—	—	—
94-95	Tallahassee	ECHL	1	0	0	0	0	—	—	—	—	—
94-95	Saginaw	CoHL	33	3	8	11	16	11	5	3	8	55
95-96	Saginaw	CoHL	69	13	23	36	184	3	1	0	1	2
96-97	Utica	CoHL	72	21	26	47	144	3	0	1	1	6
97-98	Winston-Salem	UHL	55	12	20	32	129	—	—	—	—	—
98-99	Winston-Salem	UHL	65	24	26	50	172	—	—	—	—	—
	UHL	Totals	294	73	103	176	645	17	6	4	10	63
	ECHL	Totals	14	1	5	6	49	6	0	1	1	18

Born; 2/15/72, Roblin, Manitoba. 5-9, 180. Last amateur club; Saskatoon (WHL).

Dmitri Yakushin — Defenseman

Regular Season / Playoffs

Season	Team	League	GP	G	A	PTS	PIM	GP	G	A	PTS	PIM
98-99	St. John's	AHL	71	2	6	8	65	4	0	0	0	0

Born; 1/21/78, Kharkov, USSR. 6-0, 200. Drafted by Toronto Maple Leafs (9th choice, 140th overall) in 1996 Entry Draft. Last amateur club; Regina (WHL).

Igor Yankovitch — Defenseman

Regular Season / Playoffs

Season	Team	League	GP	G	A	PTS	PIM	GP	G	A	PTS	PIM
95-96	Flint	CoHL	6	0	0	0	6	—	—	—	—	—
95-96	Saginaw	CoHL	51	2	11	13	101	—	—	—	—	—
95-96	Utica	CoHL	6	0	1	1	12	—	—	—	—	—
96-97	Muskegon	CoHL	52	5	15	20	65	—	—	—	—	—
96-97	Port Huron	CoHL	22	0	7	7	20	5	1	2	3	6
97-98	Pensacola	ECHL	2	0	0	0	18	—	—	—	—	—
97-98	Birmingham	ECHL	4	0	0	0	2	—	—	—	—	—
98-99	Augusta	ECHL	1	0	0	0	2	—	—	—	—	—
98-99	Flint	UHL	7	0	1	1	40	—	—	—	—	—
	UHL	Totals	137	7	34	41	204	5	1	2	3	6
	ECHL	Totals	6	0	0	0	20	—	—	—	—	—

Born; 2/26/75, Kiev, Russia. 6-4, 205.

Mark Yannetti — Defenseman

Regular Season / Playoffs

Season	Team	League	GP	G	A	PTS	PIM	GP	G	A	PTS	PIM
94-95	San Antonio	CeHL	48	2	11	13	47	13	0	2	2	14
95-96	San Antonio	CeHL	64	2	16	18	68	13	1	1	2	11
96-97	San Antonio	CeHL	66	8	16	24	51	—	—	—	—	—
97-98	Johnstown	ECHL	21	1	5	6	20	—	—	—	—	—
97-98	Columbus	ECHL	46	4	2	6	23	—	—	—	—	—
98-99	Syracuse	AHL	1	0	0	0	0	—	—	—	—	—
98-99	Mohawk Valley	UHL	66	7	39	46	15	—	—	—	—	—
	CeHL	Totals	178	12	43	55	166	26	1	3	4	25
	ECHL	Totals	67	5	7	12	43	—	—	—	—	—

Born; 6/7/71, Bayford, Massachusetts. 5-11, 195. Last amateur club; Williams College (NCAA 3).

Brendan Yarema — Center

Regular Season / Playoffs

Season	Team	League	GP	G	A	PTS	PIM	GP	G	A	PTS	PIM
96-97	St. John's	AHL	9	1	4	5	8	—	—	—	—	—
96-97	South Carolina	ECHL	12	3	6	9	28	9	1	0	1	38
97-98	Kentucky	AHL	64	8	14	22	172	3	0	0	0	0
98-99	Kansas City	IHL	69	11	21	32	163	3	0	0	0	12
	AHL	Totals	73	9	18	27	180	3	0	0	0	0

Born; 7/16/76, Sault Ste. Marie, Ontario. 6-0, 195. Member of 1996-97 ECHL Champion South Carolina Stingrays. Last amateur club; Sarnia (OHL).

Troy Yarosh — Defenseman

Regular Season / Playoffs

Season	Team	League	GP	G	A	PTS	PIM	GP	G	A	PTS	PIM
98-99	Phoenix	WCHL	4	0	0	0	19	—	—	—	—	—
98-99	Tulsa	CHL	26	1	3	4	53	—	—	—	—	—
98-99	Wichita	CHL	9	0	0	0	23	—	—	—	—	—
	CHL	Totals	35	1	3	4	76	—	—	—	—	—

Born; 5/26/76, Slave Lake, Alberta. 6-1, 195. Last amateur club; Bernon

Mike Yates — Forward

Regular Season / Playoffs

Season	Team	League	GP	G	A	PTS	PIM	GP	G	A	PTS	PIM
98-99	Central Texas	WPHL	48	7	6	13	92	1	0	0	0	0

Born; 4/9/77, Sechelt, British Columbia. 6-0, 195.

Igor Yefimov — Center

Regular Season / Playoffs

Season	Team	League	GP	G	A	PTS	PIM	GP	G	A	PTS	PIM
98-99	Binghamton	UHL	25	5	3	8	21	—	—	—	—	—

Born; 1/22/74, Moscow, Russia. 6-0, 180.

Alexei Yegorov — Right Wing

Regular Season / Playoffs

Season	Team	League	GP	G	A	PTS	PIM	GP	G	A	PTS	PIM
94-95	Fort Worth	CeHL	18	4	10	14	15	—	—	—	—	—
95-96	San Jose	NHL	9	3	2	5	2	—	—	—	—	—
95-96	Kansas City	IHL	65	31	25	56	84	5	2	0	2	8
96-97	San Jose	NHL	2	0	1	1	0	—	—	—	—	—
96-97	Kentucky	AHL	75	26	32	58	59	4	0	1	1	2
97-98	Kentucky	AHL	79	32	52	84	56	3	2	0	2	0
98-99	St. Petersburg	Russia	25	8	8	16	30	—	—	—	—	—
	NHL	Totals	11	3	3	6	2	—	—	—	—	—
	AHL	Totals	154	58	84	142	115	7	2	1	3	2

Born; 5/21/75, St. Petersburg, Russia. 5-11, 185. Drafted by San Jose Sharks (3rd choice, 66th overall) in 1994 Entry Draft. Selected by Atlanta Thrashers in 1999 NHL Expansion Draft (6/25/99).

Mike Yeo — Left Wing

Regular Season / Playoffs

Season	Team	League	GP	G	A	PTS	PIM	GP	G	A	PTS	PIM
94-95	Houston	IHL	63	5	12	17	100	—	—	—	—	—
95-96	Houston	IHL	69	14	16	30	113	—	—	—	—	—
96-97	Houston	IHL	56	10	11	21	105	13	2	3	5	2
97-98	Houston	IHL	72	20	21	41	128	3	0	1	1	2
98-99	Houston	IHL	57	6	12	18	65	9	0	4	4	11
	IHL	Totals	260	49	60	109	446	16	2	4	6	4

Born; 7/31/73, Thunder Bay, Ontario. 6-1, 190. Member of 1998-99 IHL Champion Houston Aeros. Last amateur club; Sudbury (OHL).

Sergei Yerkovich — Defenseman

Regular Season / Playoffs

Season	Team	League	GP	G	A	PTS	PIM	GP	G	A	PTS	PIM
96-97	Las Vegas	IHL	76	6	19	25	167	—	—	—	—	—
97-98	Las Vegas	IHL	69	7	15	22	130	4	0	0	0	6
98-99	Hamilton	AHL	69	7	11	18	103	8	0	2	2	2
	IHL	Totals	145	13	34	47	297	4	0	0	0	6

Born; 3/9/74, Minsk, Russia. 6-3, 210. Drafted by Edmonton Oilers (3rd choice, 68th overall) in 1997 Entry Draft. Last European club; Minsk (CIS).

C.J. Yoder — Center

Regular Season / Playoffs

Season	Team	League	GP	G	A	PTS	PIM	GP	G	A	PTS	PIM
98-99	Phoenix	WCHL	24	4	7	11	4	3	0	0	0	4

Born; 7/17/75, Hershey, Pennsylvania. 6-2, 190.

Jami Yoder — Defenseman

Regular Season / Playoffs

Season	Team	League	GP	G	A	PTS	PIM	GP	G	A	PTS	PIM
97-98	Richmond	ECHL	69	6	12	18	70	—	—	—	—	—
98-99	Hampton Roads	ECHL	17	0	3	3	29	—	—	—	—	—
98-99	Jacksonville	ECHL	47	2	9	11	30	2	0	0	0	0
	ECHL	Totals	133	8	24	32	129	2	0	0	0	0

Born; 9/15/77, Harrisburg, Pennsylvania. 6-0, 190. Last amateur club; Omaha (USHL).

Michael York — Center

Regular Season / Playoffs

Season	Team	League	GP	G	A	PTS	PIM	GP	G	A	PTS	PIM
98-99	Michigan State	CCHA	42	22	32	54	41	—	—	—	—	—
98-99	Hartford	AHL	3	2	2	4	0	6	3	1	4	0

Born; 1/3/78, Pontiac, Michigan. 5-9, 179. Drafted by New York Rangers (7th choice, 136th overall) in 1997 Entry Draft. Last amateur club; Michigan State (CCHA).

B.J. Young — Right Wing

Regular Season / Playoffs

Season	Team	League	GP	G	A	PTS	PIM	GP	G	A	PTS	PIM
97-98	Adirondack	AHL	65	15	22	37	191	3	0	2	2	6
98-99	Adirondack	AHL	58	13	17	30	150	3	1	0	1	6
	AHL	Totals	123	28	39	67	341	6	1	2	3	12

Born; 7/23/77, Anchorage, Alaska. 5-10, 178. Drafted by Detroit Red Wings (5th choice, 157th overall) in 1997 Entry Draft. Last amateur club; Red Deer (WHL).

Wendell Young — Goaltender

Regular Season / Playoffs

Season	Team	League	GP	W	L	T	MIN	SO	AVG	GP	W	L	MIN	SO	AVG
83-84	Fredericton	AHL	11	7	3	0	569	1	4.11	—	—	—	—	—	—
83-84	Milwaukee	IHL	6	4	1	1	339	0	3.01	—	—	—	—	—	—
83-84	Salt Lake City	CHL	20	11	6	0	1094	0	4.39	4	0	2	122	0	5.42
84-85	Fredericton	AHL	22	7	11	3	1242	0	4.01	—	—	—	—	—	—
85-86	Vancouver	NHL	22	4	9	3	1023	0	3.58	1	0	1	60	0	5.00
85-86	Fredericton	AHL	24	12	8	4	1457	0	3.21	—	—	—	—	—	—
86-87	Vancouver	NHL	8	1	6	1	420	0	5.00	—	—	—	—	—	—
86-87	Fredericton	AHL	30	11	16	0	1676	0	4.22	—	—	—	—	—	—
87-88	Philadelphia	NHL	6	3	2	0	320	0	3.75	—	—	—	—	—	—
87-88	Hershey	AHL	51	*33	15	1	2922	1	2.77	12	*12	0	*767	*1	*2.19
88-89	Pittsburgh	NHL	22	12	9	0	1150	0	4.80	1	0	0	39	0	1.54
88-89	Muskegon	IHL	2	1	0	1	125	0	3.36	—	—	—	—	—	—
89-90	Pittsburgh	NHL	43	16	20	3	2318	1	4.17	—	—	—	—	—	—
90-91	Pittsburgh	NHL	18	4	6	2	773	0	4.04	—	—	—	—	—	—
91-92	Pittsburgh	NHL	18	7	6	0	838	0	3.79	—	—	—	—	—	—
92-93	Tampa Bay	NHL	31	7	19	2	1591	0	3.66	—	—	—	—	—	—
92-93	Atlanta	IHL	3	3	0	0	183	0	2.62	—	—	—	—	—	—
93-94	Tampa Bay	NHL	9	2	3	1	480	1	2.50	—	—	—	—	—	—
93-94	Atlanta	IHL	2	2	0	0	120	0	3.00	—	—	—	—	—	—
94-95	Pittsburgh	NHL	10	3	6	0	497	0	3.26	—	—	—	—	—	—
94-95	Chicago	IHL	37	14	11	7	1882	0	3.57	—	—	—	—	—	—
95-96	Chicago	IHL	61	30	20	6	3285	1	3.63	9	4	5	540	0	3.33
96-97	Chicago	IHL	52	25	21	4	2931	1	3.48	4	1	3	257	0	3.04
97-98	Chicago	IHL	51	31	14	3	2912	2	3.07	9	5	3	515	1	2.79
98-99	Chicago	IHL	35	20	10	4	2047	3	2.46	7	4	3	421	1	2.70
	NHL	Totals	187	59	86	12	9410	2	3.94	2	0	1	99	0	3.64
	IHL	Totals	249	130	77	26	13824	27	3.26	29	14	14	1733	2	2.98
	AHL	Totals	138	70	50	8	7866	1	3.16	12	12	0	767	1	2.19

Born; 8/1/63, Haifax, Nova Scotia. 5-9, 181. Drafted by Vancouver Canucks (3rd choice, 73rd overall) in 1981 Entry Draft. Traded to Philadelphia Flyers by Vancouver with Vancouver's third round choice (Kimbi Daniels) in 1990 Entry Draft for Darren Jensen and Darryl Stanley (8/28/87). Traded to Pittsburgh Penguins by Philadelphia with Philadelphia's seventh round choice (Mika Valila) in 1990 Entry Draft for Pittsburgh's third round choice (Chris Therien) in 1990 Entry Draft (9/1/88). Claimed by Tampa Bay Lightning from Pittsburgh in Expansion Draft (6/18/92). Traded to Pittsburgh by Tampa Bay for future considerations (2/16/95). 1987-88 AHL First Team All-Star. 1987-88 AHL Top Goaltender. 1987-88 AHL Playoff MVP. Member of 1987-88 AHL champion Hershey Bears. Member of 1997-98 IHL Champion Chicago Wolves. Last amateur club; Kitch-

Paul Ysebart — Left Wing

Regular Season / Playoffs

Season	Team	League	GP	G	A	PTS	PIM	GP	G	A	PTS	PIM
87-88	Utica	AHL	78	30	49	79	60	—	—	—	—	—
88-89	New Jersey	NHL	5	0	4	4	0	—	—	—	—	—
88-89	Utica	AHL	56	36	44	80	22	5	0	1	1	4
89-90	New Jersey	NHL	5	1	2	3	0	—	—	—	—	—
89-90	Utica	AHL	74	53	52	*105	61	5	2	4	6	0
90-91	New Jersey	NHL	11	4	3	7	6	—	—	—	—	—
90-91	Detroit	NHL	51	15	18	33	16	2	0	2	2	0
91-92	Detroit	NHL	79	35	40	75	55	10	1	0	1	10
92-93	Detroit	NHL	80	34	28	62	42	7	3	1	4	2
93-94	Winnipeg	NHL	60	9	18	27	18	—	—	—	—	—
93-94	Chicago	NHL	11	5	3	8	8	6	0	0	0	8
94-95	Chicago	NHL	15	4	5	9	6	—	—	—	—	—
94-95	Tampa Bay	NHL	29	8	11	19	12	—	—	—	—	—
95-96	Tampa Bay	NHL	55	16	15	31	16	5	0	0	0	0
96-97	Tampa Bay	NHL	39	5	12	17	4	—	—	—	—	—
97-98	Tampa Bay	NHL	82	13	27	40	32	—	—	—	—	—
98-99	Tampa Bay	NHL	10	0	1	1	2	—	—	—	—	—
98-99	Cleveland	IHL	27	6	11	17	14	—	—	—	—	—
	NHL	Totals	532	149	187	336	217	30	4	3	7	20
	AHL	Totals	208	119	145	264	143	10	2	5	7	4

Born; 5/15/66, Sarnia, Ontario. 6-1, 194. Drafted by New Jersey Devils (4th choice, 74th overall) in 1984 Entry Draft. Traded to Detroit Red Wings by New Jersey for Lee Norwood and Detroit's fourth round draft choice (Scott McCabe) in 1992 Entry Draft (11/27/90). Traded to Winnipeg Jets by Detroit with future considerations (Alan Kerr, 6/18/93) for Aaron Ward and Toronto's fourth round choice (previously acquired by Winnipeg-Detroit selected John Jakopin) in 1993 Entry Draft (6/11/93). Traded to Chicago Blackhawks by Winnipeg for Chicago's third round draft choice (later traded back to Chicago-Chicago selected Kevin MacKay) in 1995 Entry Draft (3/21/94). Traded to Tampa Bay Lightning by Chicago with Rich Sutter for Jim Cummins, Tom Tilley and Jeff Buchanan (2/22/95). 1989-90 AHL MVP. 1989-90 AHL First All-Star Team. Last amateur

Libor Zabransky
Defenseman
Regular Season / Playoffs

Season	Team	League	GP	G	A	PTS	PIM	GP	G	A	PTS	PIM
96-97	St. Louis	NHL	34	1	5	6	44	—	—	—	—	—
96-97	Worcester	AHL	23	3	6	9	24	5	2	5	7	6
97-98	St. Louis	NHL	6	0	1	1	6	—	—	—	—	—
97-98	Worcester	AHL	54	2	17	19	61	6	1	1	2	8
98-99	Slovnaft Vsetin	Czech.	31	3	9	12	57	12	1	2	3	—
98-99	Worcester	AHL	6	0	0	0	18	—	—	—	—	—
	NHL	Totals	40	1	6	7	50	—	—	—	—	—
	AHL	Totals	777	5	23	28	85	11	3	6	9	14

Born; 11/25/73, Brno, Czechoslovakia. 6-3, 196. Drafted by St. Louis Blues (7th choice, 209th overall) in 1995 Entry Draft.

Mark Zacharias
Center
Regular Season / Playoffs

Season	Team	League	GP	G	A	PTS	PIM	GP	G	A	PTS	PIM
98-99	Austin	WPHL	51	14	14	28	54	—	—	—	—	—

Born; 7/13/73, Miami, Manitoba. 5-11, 185. Last amateur club; Mankato State (NCAA).

Erik Zachrisson
Forward
Regular Season / Playoffs

Season	Team	League	GP	G	A	PTS	PIM	GP	G	A	PTS	PIM
98-99	Quad City	UHL	9	2	0	2	6	—	—	—	—	—
98-99	Madison	UHL	4	0	0	0	0	—	—	—	—	—
	UHL	Totals	13	2	0	2	6	—	—	—	—	—

Born; 10/11/77, Stockholm, Sweden. 6-6, 220.

Edgars Zaltkovskis
Left Wing
Regular Season / Playoffs

Season	Team	League	GP	G	A	PTS	PIM	GP	G	A	PTS	PIM
97-98	Tacoma	WCHL	61	18	21	39	50	12	6	2	8	10
98-99	Las Vegas	IHL	1	0	0	0	0	—	—	—	—	—
98-99	Tacoma	WCHL	70	32	26	58	48	11	3	2	5	4
	WCHL	Totals	131	50	47	97	98	23	9	4	13	14

Born; 4/25/74, Riga, Latvia. 6-0, 180. Member of 1998-99 WCHL Champion Tacoma Sabrecats.

Mike Zanutto
Center
Regular Season / Playoffs

Season	Team	League	GP	G	A	PTS	PIM	GP	G	A	PTS	PIM
97-98	Rochester	AHL	9	0	0	0	0	—	—	—	—	—
97-98	South Carolina	ECHL	49	18	17	35	6	5	0	0	0	0
98-99	Canada	National	10	2	1	3	0	—	—	—	—	—

Born; 1/1/77, Burlington, Ontario. 6-0, 190. Drafted by Buffalo Sabres (10th choice, 198th overall) in 1995 Entry Draft. Last amateur club; Oshawa (OHL).

Dean Zayonce
Defenseman
Regular Season / Playoffs

Season	Team	League	GP	G	A	PTS	PIM	GP	G	A	PTS	PIM
91-92	Greensboro	ECHL	26	2	7	9	151	—	—	—	—	—
91-92	Halifax	AHL	24	0	3	3	26	—	—	—	—	—
92-93	Greensboro	ECHL	26	1	9	10	73	1	0	0	0	0
92-93	Halifax	AHL	22	0	1	1	6	—	—	—	—	—
93-94	Greensboro	ECHL	56	11	16	27	260	8	0	0	0	14
94-95	Greensboro	ECHL	60	2	14	16	245	17	0	2	2	54
95-96	Atlanta	IHL	24	0	5	5	58	—	—	—	—	—
95-96	San Antonio	CeHL	49	7	14	21	140	—	—	—	—	—
96-97	Carolina	AHL	32	0	0	0	49	—	—	—	—	—
96-97	Tallahassee	ECHL	6	2	5	7	2	—	—	—	—	—
97-98	Winston-Salem	UHL	69	6	13	19	109	—	—	—	—	—
98-99	Charlotte	ECHL	62	2	14	16	118	—	—	—	—	—
	AHL	Totals	78	0	4	4	81	—	—	—	—	—
	ECHL	Totals	236	20	65	85	851	26	0	2	2	68

Born; 10/28/70, Kelowna, British Columbia. 6-0, 192. Last amateur club; Tri-City (WHL).

Boris Zelenko
Forward
Regular Season / Playoffs

Season	Team	League	GP	G	A	PTS	PIM	GP	G	A	PTS	PIM
97-98	CSKA Moscow	Russia	25	5	5	10	14	—	—	—	—	—
97-98	Hampton Roads	ECHL	37	9	17	26	18	20	7	8	15	6
98-99	Hampton Roads	ECHL	29	11	10	21	20	—	—	—	—	—
	ECHL	Totals	66	20	27	47	38	20	7	8	15	6

Born; 9/12/75, Moscow, USSR. 6-1, 172. Drafted by Pittsburgh Penguins (11th choice, 206th overall) in 1994 Entry Draft. Member of 1997-98 ECHL Champion Hampton Roads Admirals.

Jason Zent
Left Wing
Regular Season / Playoffs

Season	Team	League	GP	G	A	PTS	PIM	GP	G	A	PTS	PIM
94-95	Prince Edward Island	AHL	55	15	11	26	46	9	6	1	7	6
95-96	Prince Edward Island	AHL	68	14	5	19	61	5	2	1	3	4
96-97	Ottawa	NHL	22	3	3	6	9	—	—	—	—	—
96-97	Worcester	AHL	45	14	10	24	45	5	3	4	7	4
97-98	Ottawa	NHL	3	0	0	0	4	—	—	—	—	—
97-98	Worcester	AHL	66	25	17	42	67	11	2	0	2	6
97-98	Detroit	IHL	4	1	0	1	0	—	—	—	—	—
98-99	Philadelphia	NHL	2	0	0	0	0	—	—	—	—	—
98-99	Philadelphia	AHL	64	13	13	26	82	16	2	4	6	22
	NHL	Totals	27	3	3	6	13	—	—	—	—	—
	AHL	Totals	298	81	56	137	301	46	15	10	25	42

Born; 4/15/71, Buffalo, New York. 5-11, 180. Drafted by New York Islanders (3rd choice, 44th overall) in 1989 Entry Draft. Traded to Ottawa Senators by Islanders for fith round choice in 1996 (Andrew Berenzweig) (10/15/94). Signed as a free agent by Philadelphia Flyers (8/4/98). Last amateur club; Wisconsin

Rob Zettler
Defenseman
Regular Season / Playoffs

Season	Team	League	GP	G	A	PTS	PIM	GP	G	A	PTS	PIM
87-88	Sault Ste. Marie	OHL	64	7	41	48	77	6	2	2	4	9
87-88	Kalamazoo	IHL	2	0	1	1	0	7	0	2	2	2
88-89	Minnesota	NHL	2	0	0	0	0	—	—	—	—	—
88-89	Kalamazoo	IHL	80	5	21	26	79	6	0	1	1	26
89-90	Minnesota	NHL	31	0	8	8	45	—	—	—	—	—
89-90	Kalamazoo	IHL	41	6	10	16	64	7	0	0	0	6
90-91	Minnesota	NHL	47	1	4	5	119	—	—	—	—	—
90-91	Kalamazoo	IHL	1	0	0	0	2	—	—	—	—	—
91-92	San Jose	NHL	74	1	8	9	99	—	—	—	—	—
92-93	San Jose	NHL	80	0	7	7	150	—	—	—	—	—
93-94	San Jose	NHL	42	0	3	3	65	—	—	—	—	—
93-94	Philadelphia	NHL	33	0	4	4	69	—	—	—	—	—
94-95	Philadelphia	NHL	32	0	1	1	34	1	0	0	0	2
95-96	Toronto	NHL	29	0	1	1	48	2	0	0	0	0
96-97	Toronto	NHL	48	2	12	14	51	—	—	—	—	—
96-97	Utah	IHL	30	0	10	10	60	—	—	—	—	—
97-98	Toronto	NHL	59	0	7	7	108	—	—	—	—	—
98-99	Nashville	NHL	2	0	0	0	2	—	—	—	—	—
98-99	Utah	IHL	77	2	16	18	136	—	—	—	—	—
	NHL	Totals	479	4	55	59	790	3	0	0	0	2
	IHL	Totals	231	13	58	71	341	20	0	3	3	34

Born; 3/8/68, Sept Isles, Quebec. 6-3, 200. Drafted by Minnesota North Stars (5th choice, 55th overall) in 1986 Entry Draft. Claimed by San Jose Sharks from Minnesota in Dispersal Draft (5/30/91). Traded to Philadelphia Flyers by San Jose for Viacheslav Butsayev (2/1/94). Traded to Toronto Maple Leafs by Philadelphia for Toronto's fifth round choice (Per-Ragna Bergqvist) in 1996 Entry Draft (7/8/95). Claimed by Nashville Predators from Toronto in Expansion Draft (6/26/98). Last amateur club; Sault Ste. Marie (OHL).

Sergei Zholtok — Center
Regular Season / Playoffs

Season	Team	League	GP	G	A	PTS	PIM	GP	G	A	PTS	PIM
92-93	Boston	NHL	1	0	1	1	0	—	—	—	—	—
92-93	Providence	AHL	64	31	35	66	57	6	3	5	8	4
93-94	Boston	NHL	24	2	1	3	2	—	—	—	—	—
93-94	Providence	AHL	54	29	33	62	16	—	—	—	—	—
94-95	Providence	AHL	78	23	35	58	42	13	8	5	13	6
95-96	Las Vegas	IHL	82	51	50	101	30	15	7	13	20	6
96-97	Ottawa	NHL	57	12	16	28	19	7	1	1	2	0
96-97	Las Vegas	IHL	19	13	14	27	20	—	—	—	—	—
97-98	Ottawa	NHL	78	10	13	23	16	11	0	2	2	0
98-99	Montreal	NHL	70	7	15	22	6	—	—	—	—	—
98-99	Fredericton	AHL	7	3	4	7	0	—	—	—	—	—
	NHL	Totals	230	31	46	77	43	18	1	3	4	0
	AHL	Totals	203	86	107	193	115	19	11	10	21	10
	IHL	Totals	101	64	64	128	50	15	7	13	20	6

Born; 12/2/72, Riga, Latvia. 6-0, 190. Drafted by Boston Bruins (2nd choice, 55th overall) in 1992 Entry Draft. Signed as a free agent by Ottawa Senators (7/10/96). Signed as a free agent by Montreal Canadiens (9/9/98). Last overseas club; Riga (CIS).

Alexander Zhurik — Defenseman
Regular Season / Playoffs

Season	Team	League	GP	G	A	PTS	PIM	GP	G	A	PTS	PIM
95-96	Cape Breton	AHL	80	5	36	41	85	—	—	—	—	—
96-97	Hamilton	AHL	72	5	16	21	49	22	2	11	13	14
97-98	Belarus	Olympics	4	0	0	0	10	—	—	—	—	—
97-98	Hamilton	AHL	63	1	23	24	84	9	0	4	4	8
98-99	Dynamo Moscow	Russia	42	1	7	8	88	15	0	0	0	12
	AHL	Totals	215	11	75	86	218	31	2	15	17	22

Born; 5/29/75, Minsk, Russia. 6-3, 195. Drafted by Edmonton Oilers (7th choice, 163rd overall) in 1993 Entry Draft. Last amateur club; Kingston (OHL).

Shane Zimmer — Right Wing
Regular Season / Playoffs

Season	Team	League	GP	G	A	PTS	PIM	GP	G	A	PTS	PIM
97-98	Anchorage	WCHL	7	4	1	5	30	—	—	—	—	—
98-99	Anchorage	WCHL	11	3	0	3	62	—	—	—	—	—
	WCHL	Totals	18	7	1	8	92	—	—	—	—	—

Born; 7/23/79, Tisdale, Saskatchewan. 6-2, 215.

Myles Zomok — Right Wing
Regular Season / Playoffs

Season	Team	League	GP	G	A	PTS	PIM	GP	G	A	PTS	PIM
98-99	Madison	UHL	3	0	1	1	5	—	—	—	—	—
98-99	Asheville	UHL	62	2	2	4	53	—	—	—	—	—
	UHL	Totals	65	2	3	5	58	—	—	—	—	—

Born; 4/8/73, Welland, Ontario. 6-0, 220.

Steve Zoryk — Left Wing
Regular Season / Playoffs

Season	Team	League	GP	G	A	PTS	PIM	GP	G	A	PTS	PIM
97-98	Toronto	OHL	66	34	27	61	36	—	—	—	—	—
97-98	South Carolina	ECHL	5	1	1	2	2	5	0	0	0	2
98-99	South Carolina	ECHL	9	2	0	2	0	—	—	—	—	—
	ECHL	Totals	14	3	1	4	2	5	0	0	0	2

Born; 3/22/77. 6-1, 210. Last amateur club; Toronto (OHL).

Pavel Zubov — Defenseman
Regular Season / Playoffs

Season	Team	League	GP	G	A	PTS	PIM	GP	G	A	PTS	PIM
98-99	Tupelo	WPHL	10	0	2	2	2	—	—	—	—	—

Born; 6/8/73, Togliatti, Russia. 6-3, 200.

Jarrett Zukiwsky — Right Wing
Regular Season / Playoffs

Season	Team	League	GP	G	A	PTS	PIM	GP	G	A	PTS	PIM
96-97	Lethbridge	CWUA	26	24	14	38	NA	—	—	—	—	—
96-97	Mobile	ECHL	5	2	1	3	14	2	1	0	1	2
97-98	Brunico	Italy	25	16	21	37	12	—	—	—	—	—
98-99	Nottingham	BSL	47	11	23	34	151	11	1	2	3	18

Born; 12/7/72, Pincher Creek, Alberta. 5-11, 200. Last amateur club; Lethbridge (CWUHA).

Shane Zulyniak
Regular Season / Playoffs

Season	Team	League	GP	G	A	PTS	PIM	GP	G	A	PTS	PIM
98-99	Abilene	WPHL	3	0	0	0	2	1	0	0	0	0

Born; 6/21/74.

Peter Zurba — Left Wing
Regular Season / Playoffs

Season	Team	League	GP	G	A	PTS	PIM	GP	G	A	PTS	PIM
95-96	Huntsville	SHL	27	2	18	20	168	10	1	1	2	23
96-97	Utah	IHL	4	0	0	0	37	—	—	—	—	—
96-97	Central Texas	WPHL	44	10	7	17	*291	11	3	3	6	52
97-98	Utah	IHL	1	0	0	0	0	—	—	—	—	—
97-98	Central Texas	WPHL	62	18	23	41	311	4	0	4	4	33
98-99	Las Vegas	IHL	24	2	3	5	89	—	—	—	—	—
98-99	Louisiana	ECHL	14	0	1	1	103	—	—	—	—	—
98-99	Bakersfield	WCHL	28	7	7	14	133	—	—	—	—	—
	IHL	Totals	29	2	3	5	126	—	—	—	—	—
	WPHL	Totals	106	28	30	58	602	15	3	7	10	85

Born; 11/15/74, Thompson, Manitoba. 5-11, 174. Member of 1995-96 SHL champion Huntsville Channel Cats.

Anthony Zurfluh — Defenseman
Regular Season / Playoffs

Season	Team	League	GP	G	A	PTS	PIM	GP	G	A	PTS	PIM
98-99	Fresno	WCHL	51	0	7	7	91	—	—	—	—	—

Born; 1/24/77, Soldotna, Alaska. 6-1, 205. Last amateur club; Bozeman (AFHL).

Sergei Zvyagin — Goaltender
Regular Season / Playoffs

Season	Team	League	GP	W	L	T	MIN	SO	AVG	GP	W	L	MIN	SO	AVG
94-95	Detroit	CoHL	32	12	15	2	1705	0	4.36	8	4	3	407	0	3.24
95-96	Detroit	CoHL	40	14	13	6	1873	1	3.62	—	—	—	—	—	—
95-96	Quad City	CoHL	9	6	3	0	538	0	2.90	3	0	3	179	0	6.69
96-97	Michigan	IHL	2	1	1	0	79	0	3.03	—	—	—	—	—	—
96-97	Quad City	CoHL	*60	*42	15	2	*3475	1	2.99	*15	*11	3	*912	0	3.22
97-98	San Antonio	IHL	8	2	4	1	445	0	4.72	—	—	—	—	—	—
97-98	Quad City	UHL	33	25	7	0	1841	2	3.45	12	6	*6	*721	0	2.91
98-99	Quad City	UHL	20	11	5	1	1084	2	3.15	14	9	*5	847	*2	2.27
	IHL	Totals	10	3	5	1	524	0	4.47	—	—	—	—	—	—
	UHL	Totals	194	110	58	11	10516	6	3.42	52	30	20	3066	2	3.09

Born; 2/17/71, Moscow, Russia. 5-8, 167. 1996-97 CoHL Outstanding Netminder. 1996-97 Playoff MVP. 1996-97 CoHL First Team All-Star. Member of 1996-97 CoHL Champion Quad City Mallards. Member of 1997-98 UHL Champion Quad City Mallards.

Andrei Zyuzin — Defenseman
Regular Season / Playoffs

Season	Team	League	GP	G	A	PTS	PIM	GP	G	A	PTS	PIM
97-98	San Jose	NHL	56	6	7	13	66	6	1	0	1	14
97-98	Kentucky	AHL	17	4	5	9	28	—	—	—	—	—
98-99	San Jose	NHL	25	3	1	4	38	—	—	—	—	—
98-99	Kentucky	AHL	23	2	12	14	42	—	—	—	—	—
	NHL	Totals	81	9	8	17	104	6	1	0	1	14
	AHL	Totals	40	6	17	23	70	—	—	—	—	—

Born; 1/21/78, Ufa, USSR. 6-1, 187. Drafted by San Jose Sharks (1st choice, 2nd overall) in 1996 Entry Draft. Traded to Tampa Bay Lightning by San Jose with Bill Houlder, Shawn Burr and Steve Guolla for Niklas Sundstrom and a third round choice in 2000 (8/4/99). Last overseas club; Ufa Salavat (Russia).

The Leagues
The Teams

The following section contains final regular season and playoff results from the seven minor-pro leagues functioning during the 1998-99 hockey season.

Included are final standings, playoff results, league directories and statistical leaders from the 1998-99 season. The statistics were compiled from team and league sources and Howe Sports Data.

Muskegon captain Scott Feasby leads his club in a victory lap

Photo by Chuck Barton

American Hockey League

1998-99 Final Standings

EASTERN CONFERENCE

ATLANTIC	GP	W	L	OTL	T	PTS	PCT	GF	GA	PIM
Lowell	80	33	32	2	13	81	.506	219	237	1750
St. John's	80	34	35	4	7	79	.494	246	270	2116
Fredericton	80	33	36	5	6	77	.481	246	246	2086
Saint John	80	31	40	1	8	71	.444	238	296	2217
Portland	80	23	48	2	7	55	.344	214	273	1970
NEW ENGLAND										
Providence	80	56	16	4	4	120	.750	321	223	2332
Hartford	80	38	31	6	5	87	.544	256	256	1938
Springfield	80	35	35	1	9	80	.500	245	232	1973
Worcester	80	34	36	2	8	78	.488	237	260	2108
New Haven	80	33	35	5	7	78	.488	240	250	1854

WESTERN CONFERENCE

EMPIRE	GP	W	L	OTL	T	PTS	PCT	GF	GA	PIM
Rochester	80	52	21	1	6	111	.694	287	176	1663
Albany	80	46	26	2	6	100	.625	275	230	2070
Hamilton	80	40	29	4	7	91	.569	229	206	1661
Adirondack	80	21	48	3	8	53	.331	184	280	2043
Syracuse	80	18	50	3	9	48	.300	220	327	2018
MID-ATLANTIC										
Philadelphia	80	47	22	2	9	105	.656	272	221	2223
Kentucky	80	44	26	3	7	98	.613	272	214	2153
Hershey	80	37	32	1	10	85	.531	242	224	1795
Cincinnati	80	35	39	2	4	76	.475	227	249	1911

Teams awarded one point for an overtime loss

	GP	W	L	OTL	T	PTS	PCT	GF	GA	PIM
TOTAL	760	690	690	53	140	1573		4670		37881

ATTENDANCE REPORT

TEAM	TOTAL	GAMES	AVERAGE
Philadelphia	480,106	40	12,002
Rochester	336,284	40	8,407
Hartford	288,859	40	7,221
Providence	287,648	40	7,191
Hershey	251,510	40	6,287
Worcester	246,176	40	6,154
Kentucky	245,779	40	6,144
Springfield	205,127	40	5,128
Syracuse	204,373	40	5,109
Hamilton	193,781	40	4,844
Albany	183,639	40	4,590
Saint John	174,591	40	4,364
Cincinnati	174,239	40	4,355
New Haven	172,040	40	4,301
Portland	171,414	40	4,285
Fredericton	137,834	40	3,445
Adirondack	137,646	40	3,441
Lowell	131,870	40	3,296
St. John's	126,834	40	3,170

LEADING SCORERS

POINTS	TEAM	GP	G	A	PTS
Pittis, Domenic	ROC	76	38	66	104
Robitaille, Randy	PRO	74	28	74	102
Madden, John	ALB	75	38	60	98
White, Peter	PHL	77	31	59	90
Montgomery, Jim	PHL	78	29	58	87
Brule, Steve	ALB	78	32	52	84
Park, Richard	PHL	75	41	42	83
Bohonos, Lonny	SJS	70	34	48	82
Willis, Shane	NHV	73	31	50	81
Fisher, Craig	ROC	70	29	52	81
Armstrong, Derek	HRT	59	29	51	80
Harder, Mike	ROC	79	31	48	79
Matte, Christian	HER	60	31	47	78
Ferraro, Chris	HAM	72	35	41	76
Guolla, Steve	KEN	53	29	47	76
Vasiljevs, Herbert	KEN	76	28	48	76
Vorobiev, Vladimir	HAM	73	27	47	74
Williams, Jeff	ALB	74	46	27	73
Wren, Bob	CIN	73	27	43	70
Several Players Tied at					69

GOALS	TEAM	GP	G
Williams, Jeff	ALB	74	46
Podollan, Jason	SJS	68	42
Park, Richard	PHL	75	41
Madden, John	ALB	75	38
Pittis, Domenic	ROC	76	38

ASSISTS	TEAM	GP	A
Robitaille, Randy	PRO	74	74
Pittis, Domenic	ROC	76	66
Madden, John	ALB	75	60
White, Peter	PHL	77	59
Montgomery, Jim	PHL	78	58

PENALTY MINUTES	TEAM	GP	PIM
Downey, Aaron	PRO	75	401
Thornton, Shawn	SJS	78	354
Laitre, Martin	ADK	63	345
Blouin, Sylvain	FRE	67	333
Gagnon, Sean	SPR	68	331

POWER PLAY GOALS	TEAM	PPG
Levins, Scott	NHV	21
Fisher, Craig	ROC	19
Several Players Tied at		15

SHORT HANDED GOALS	TEAM	SHG
Park, Richard	PHL	8
Madden, John	ALB	6
Bates, Shawn	PRO	5
Several Players Tied at		4

SHOTS	TEAM	SHOTS
Madden, John	ALB	334
Park, Richard	PHL	312
Brule, Steve	ALB	302
Bohonos, Lonny	SJS	289
Banham, Frank	CIN	265

SHOOTING PERCENTAGE	TEAM	GOALS	SHOTS	PCT
Deyell, Mark	SJS	20	89	0.225
Pittis, Domenic	ROC	38	190	0.200
Davidson, Matt	ROC	26	131	0.198
Savage, Andre	PRO	27	137	0.197
Walby, Steffon	KEN	23	117	0.197

PLUS-MINUS	TEAM	+/-
Laaksonen, Antti	PRO	40
Smith, Brandon	PRO	36
Virtue, Terry	PRO	34
Several Players Tied at		33

LEADING GOALTENDERS
(Based on 1590 or more minutes)

	TEAM	GPI	MIN	AVG	W	L	T	EN	SO	GA	SAVES	SPCT
Biron, Martin	ROC	52	3129:20	2.07	36	13	3	1	6	108	1424	0.930
Passmore, Steve	HAM	54	3148:08	2.23	24	21	7	4	4	117	1539	0.929
Carey, Jim	PRO	30	1749:34	2.33	17	8	3	1	3	68	770	0.919
Aebischer, David	HER	38	1932:24	2.45	17	10	5	2	2	79	912	0.920
Gauthier, Sean	KEN	40	2376:02	2.50	18	15	6	6	1	99	1074	0.916
Buzak, Mike	ALB	48	2382:23	2.57	22	13	3	2	0	102	1091	0.915
Boucher, Brian	PHL	36	2060:44	2.59	20	8	5	0	2	89	906	0.911
Nabokov, John	KEN	43	2429:05	2.62	26	14	1	1	5	106	1063	0.909
Askey, Tom	CIN	53	2892:44	2.72	21	22	3	7	3	131	1473	0.918
Cousineau, Marcel	LOW	53	3034:21	2.75	26	17	7	2	3	139	1398	0.910
Pelletier, John	PHL	47	2635:30	2.78	25	16	4	3	2	122	1212	0.909
Esche, Robert	SPR	55	2956:39	2.80	24	20	6	4	1	138	1318	0.905
Denis, Marc	HER	52	2907:44	2.83	20	23	5	6	4	137	1447	0.914
Theodore, Jose	FRE	27	1609:00	2.87	12	13	2	2	2	77	852	0.917
Grahame, John	PRO	48	2771:09	2.90	37	9	1	1	3	134	1149	0.896
Henry, Frederic	ALB	35	1689:35	2.98	17	10	3	1	1	84	803	0.905
Johnson, Brent	WOR	49	2924:59	2.99	22	22	4	7	2	146	1256	0.896
Fountain, Mike	NHV	51	2988:54	3.01	23	24	3	4	2	150	1595	0.914
Garon, Mathieu	FRE	40	2222:19	3.08	14	22	2	3	3	114	1076	0.904
MacDonald, Todd	NHV	31	1775:19	3.08	10	16	3	2	0	91	871	0.905

WINS	TEAM	WINS
Grahame, John	PRO	37
Biron, Martin	ROC	36
Labbe, Jean-Francois	HRT	28
Cousineau, Marcel	LOW	26
Nabokov, John	KEN	26

LOSSES	TEAM	LOSSES
Elliott, Jason	ADK	27
Labbe, Jean-Francois	HRT	26
Fountain, Mike	NHV	24
Rosati, Mike	POR	23
Denis, Marc	HER	23

MINUTES	TEAM	MIN
Labbe, Jean-Francois	HRT	3392
Passmore, Steve	HAM	3148
Biron, Martin	ROC	3129
Cousineau, Marcel	LOW	3034
Fountain, Mike	NHV	2988

SHUTOUTS	TEAM	SHUTOUTS
Biron, Martin	ROC	6
Nabokov, John	KEN	5
Passmore, Steve	HAM	4
Denis, Marc	HER	4
Several Players Tied at		3

SAVES	TEAM	SAVES
Labbe, Jean-Francois	HRT	1606
Fountain, Mike	NHV	1595
Passmore, Steve	HAM	1539
Askey, Tom	CIN	1473
Denis, Marc	HER	1447

SAVE PERCENTAGE	TEAM	GOALS	SAVES	PCT
Biron, Martin	ROC	108	1424	0.930
Passmore, Steve	HAM	117	1539	0.929
Draper, Tom	ROC	60	728	0.924
Reese, Jeff	SJS	66	765	0.921
Aebischer, David	HER	79	912	0.920

Division Quarterfinals

Saint John vs. Lowell
Saint John wins series 3 games to 0

Providence vs. Worcester
Providence wins series 3 games to 1

Rochester vs. Adirondack
Rochester wins series 3 games to 0

Philadelphia vs. Cincinnati
Philadelphia wins series 3 games to 0

Fredericton vs. St. John's
Fredericton wins series 3 games to 2

Hartford vs. Springfield
Hartford wins series 3 games to 0

Hamilton vs. Albany
Hamilton wins series 3 games to 2

Hershey vs. Kentucky
Kentucky wins series 3 games to 2

Division Finals

Saint John vs. Fredericton
Fredericton wins series 4 games to 0

Rochester vs. Hamilton
Rochester wins series 4 games to 2

Hartford vs. Providence
Providence wins series 4 games to 0

Philadelphia vs. Kentucky
Philadelphia wins series 4 games to 3

Conference Finals

Fredericton vs. Providence
Providence wins series 4 games to 2

Philadelphia vs. Rochester
Rochester wins series 4 games to 2

Calder Cup Finals

Providence vs. Rochester
Providence wins series 4 games to 1

LEADING SCORERS

POINTS	TEAM	GP	G	A	PTS
Ferraro, Peter	PRO	19	9	12	21
Pittis, Domenic	ROC	20	7	14	21
Fisher, Craig	ROC	20	9	11	20
Nickulas, Eric	PRO	18	8	12	20
Robitaille, Randy	PRO	19	6	14	20
Gendron, Martin	FRE	15	12	5	17
Sylvester, Dean	ROC	18	12	5	17
White, Peter	PHL	16	4	13	17
Cunneyworth, Randy	ROC	20	3	14	17
Jomphe, J.F.	FRE	15	5	11	16
Park, Richard	PHL	16	9	6	15
Montgomery, Jim	PHL	16	4	11	15
Asham, Aaron	FRE	13	8	6	14
Mann, Cameron	PRO	11	7	7	14
Virtue, Terry	PRO	17	2	12	14
Several Players Tied at					13

GOALS	TEAM	GP	G
Gendron, Martin	FRE	15	12
Sylvester, Dean	ROC	18	12
Park, Richard	PHL	16	9
Fisher, Craig	ROC	20	9
Ferraro, Peter	PRO	19	9

ASSISTS	TEAM	GP	A
Cunneyworth, Randy	ROC	20	14
Pittis, Domenic	ROC	20	14
Robitaille, Randy	PRO	19	14
White, Peter	PHL	16	13
Several Players Tied at			12

PENALTY MINUTES	TEAM	GP	PIM
Blouin, Sylvain	FRE	15	87
Lacroix, Daniel	HAM	11	65
Cunneyworth, Randy	ROC	20	58
MacIsaac, Dave	PHL	16	50
Jomphe, J.F.	FRE	15	49

POWER PLAY GOALS	TEAM	PPG
Gendron, Martin	FRE	6
Wilson, Landon	PRO	6
Sylvester, Dean	ROC	4
Several Players Tied at		3

SHORT HANDED GOALS	TEAM	SHG
Sylvester, Dean	ROC	3
Domenichelli, Hnat	SJN	2
O'Brien, Sean	PHL	2
Several Players Tied at		1

LEADING GOALTENDERS

(Based on 90 or more minutes)

	TEAM	GPI	MIN	AVG	W	L	EN	SO	GA	SAVES	SPCT
Biron, Martin	ROC	20	1166:43	2.16	12	8	2	1	42	590	0.934
Aebischer, David	HER	3	152:07	2.37	1	2	0	0	6	74	0.925
Grahame, John	PRO	19	1208:36	2.38	15	4	1	1	48	498	0.912
Buzak, Mike	ALB	5	272:10	2.65	2	1	0	0	12	117	0.907
Passmore, Steve	HAM	11	679:44	2.74	5	6	1	0	31	354	0.919
Boucher, Brian	PHL	16	947:14	2.85	9	7	2	0	45	435	0.906
Denis, Marc	HER	3	143:26	2.93	1	1	0	0	7	70	0.909
Labbe, Jean-Francois	HRT	7	447:26	2.95	3	4	0	0	22	226	0.911
Nabokov, John	KEN	11	599:28	3.00	6	5	1	2	30	294	0.907
Johnson, Brent	WOR	4	238:03	3.02	1	3	4	0	12	131	0.916
Theodore, Jose	FRE	13	693:41	3.03	8	5	0	1	35	437	0.926
Robitaille, Marc	SJS	3	157:49	3.04	1	2	0	0	8	64	0.889
Waite, Jimmy	SPR	2	117:59	3.05	0	2	2	0	6	62	0.912
Reese, Jeff	SJS	3	141:40	3.39	1	1	1	0	8	61	0.884
Garon, Mathieu	FRE	6	207:47	3.47	1	1	1	0	12	123	0.911
Gauthier, Sean	KEN	4	130:21	3.68	0	1	0	0	8	58	0.879
Miller, Aren	ADK	2	122:34	3.92	0	2	0	0	8	60	0.882
Giguere, J-Sebastien	SJN	7	304:12	4.14	3	2	1	0	21	128	0.859
Cousineau, Marcel	LOW	3	185:48	4.20	0	3	1	0	13	85	0.867
Askey, Tom	CIN	3	177:42	4.39	0	3	1	0	13	85	0.867

SAVES	TEAM	SAVES
Biron, Martin	ROC	590
Grahame, John	PRO	498
Theodore, Jose	FRE	437
Boucher, Brian	PHL	435
Passmore, Steve	HAM	354

SAVE PERCENTAGE	TEAM	GOALS	SAVES	PCT
Biron, Martin	ROC	42	590	0.934
Theodore, Jose	FRE	35	437	0.926
Passmore, Steve	HAM	31	354	0.919
Johnson, Brent	WOR	12	131	0.916
Grahame, John	PRO	48	498	0.912

American Hockey League Directory

American Hockey League
1 Monarch Place, Suite 2400
Springfield, MA 01144
Phone: (413) 781-2030
Fax: (413) 747-5061

Albany RiverRats
51 South Pearl Street
Albany, New York 12207
Phone: (518) 487-2244
Fax: (518) 487-2248
Coach: John Cunniff

Cincinnati Mighty Ducks
2250 Seymour Avenue
Cincinnati, Ohio 45212
Phone: (513) 351-3999
Fax: (513) 351-5898
Coach: Moe Mantha

Hamilton Bulldogs
85 York Blvd.
Hamilton, Ontario L8R 3L4
Phone: (905) 529-8500
Fax: (905) 529-1188
Coach: Walt Kyle

Hartford Wolf Pack
196 Trumbull Street, 3rd Floor
Hartford, Connecticut 06103
Phone: (860) 246-7825
Fax: (860) 240-7618
Coach: John Paddock

Hershey Bears
P.O. Box 866
Hershey, Pennsylvania 17033
Phone: (717) 534-3380
Fax: (717) 534-3383
Coach: Mike Foligno

Kentucky Thoroughblades
410 West Vine Street
Lexington, Kentucky 40507
Phone: (606) 259-1996
Fax: (606) 252-3684
Coach: Roy Sommer

Louisville Panthers
P.O. Box 9227
Louisville, Kentucky 40209
Phone: (502) 992-7825
Fax: (502) 992-7834
Coach: Joe Paterson

Lowell Lock Monsters
300 Arcand Drive
Lowell, Massachusetts 01852
Phone: (978) 458-7825
Fax: (978) 453-8452
Coach: Bruce Boudreau

Philadelphia Phantoms
First Union Spectrum
3601 S. Broad Street
Philadelphia, Pennsylvania 19148
Phone: (215) 465-4522
Fax: (215) 952-5245
Coach: Bill Barber

Portland Pirates
85 Free Street
Portland, Maine 04101
Phone: (207) 828-4665
Fax: (207) 773-3278
Coach: Glen Hanlon

Providence Bruins
1 LaSalle Square
Providence, Rhode Island 02903
Phone: (401) 273-5000
Fax: (401) 273-5004
Coach: Peter Laviolette

Quebec Citadelles
250 Hamel Boulevard
Quebec City, Quebec G1L 5A7
Phone: (418) 525-5333
Fax: (418) 525-2242
Coach: Michel Therrien

Rochester Americans
1 War Memorial Square
Rochester, New York 14614
Phone: (716) 454-5335
Fax: (716) 454-3954
Coach: Brian McCutcheon

Saint John Flames
P.O. Box 4040, Station B
Saint John, New Brunswick E2M 5E6
Phone: (506) 635-2637
Phone: (506) 633-4625
Coach: Rick Vaive

Springfield Falcons
P.O. Box 3190
Springfield, Massachusetts 01101
Phone: (413) 739-3344
Fax: (413) 739-3389
Coach: Dave Farrish

St. John's Maple Leafs
6 Logy Bay Road
St. John's, Newfoundland A1A 1J3
Phone: (709) 726-1010
Fax: (709) 726-1511
Coach: Al MacAdam

Syracuse Crunch
800 South State Street
Syracuse, New York 13202
Phone: (315) 473-4444
Fax: (315) 473-4449
Coach: Stan Smyl

Wilkes-Barre/Scranton Penguins
60 Public Square, Suite 150
Wilkes-Barre, Pennsylvania 18701
Phone: (570) 208-7367
Fax: (570) 208-5432
Coach: Glenn Patrick

Worcester IceCats
303 Main Street
Worcester, Massachusetts 01608
Phone: (508) 798-5400
Fax: (508) 799-5267
Coach: Greg Gilbert

Syracuse Crunch
800 South State Street
Syracuse, New York 13202
Phone: (315) 473-4444
Fax: (315) 473-4449
GM: Vance Lederman
Coach: Jack McIlhargey

Worcester IceCats
303 Main Street
Worcester, Massachusetts 01608
Phone: (508) 798-5400
Fax: (508) 799-5267
Vice President: Peter Ricciardi
Coach: Greg Gilbert

AHL Awards

All-Star Teams

First Team	Position	Second Team
Martin Biron, Rochester	Goaltender	Steve Passmore, Hamilton
Ken Sutton, Albany	Defenseman	Terry Virtue, Providence
Brandon Smith, Providence	Defenseman	Dan Boyle, Kentucky
Randy Robitaille, Providence	Center	Steve Guolla, Kentucky
Shane Willis, New Haven	Right Wing	Richard Park, Philadelphia
Landon Wilson, Providence	Left Wing	Jeff Williams, Albany

Les Cunningham (MVP)	Randy Robitaille, Providence
Eddie Shore (Defenseman)	Ken Sutton, Albany
Fred T. Hunt (sportmanship, determination, dedication)	Mitch Lamoureux, Hershey
"Red" Garrett (rookie)	Shane Willis, New Haven
"Baz" Bastien (Goalie)	Martin Biron, Rochester
Louis Pieri (Coach)	Peter Laviolette, Providence
Calder Cup (AHL Champions)	Providence Bruins
Jack Butterfield (Playoff MVP)	Peter Ferraro, Providence
Yanick Dupre Memorial Award (AHL Man of the Year)	Brent Thompson, Hartford WolfPack

The Providence Bruins went from worst to first to claim the Calder Cup

Photo by David Silverman

International Hockey League

1998-99 Final Standings

EASTERN CONFERENCE

NORTHEAST	GP	W	L	SOL	PTS	PCT	GF	GA	PIM
Detroit	82	50	21	11	111	.677	259	195	2216
Orlando	82	45	33	4	94	.573	264	253	2324
Cincinnati	82	44	32	6	94	.573	269	270	1835
Grand Rapids	82	34	40	8	76	.463	256	281	1842
CENTRAL									
Michigan	82	35	34	13	83	.506	232	253	2275
Fort Wayne	82	33	33	16	82	.500	250	280	2615
Indianapolis	82	33	37	12	78	.476	243	277	1946
Cleveland	82	28	47	7	63	.384	248	310	1847

WESTERN CONFERENCE

MIDWEST	GP	W	L	SOL	PTS	PCT	GF	GA	PIM
Chicago	82	49	21	12	110	.671	285	246	2044
Manitoba	82	47	21	14	108	.659	269	236	1922
Kansas City	82	44	31	7	95	.579	256	270	1776
Milwaukee	82	38	28	16	92	.561	254	265	1810
SOUTHWEST									
Houston	82	54	15	13	121	.738	307	209	1955
Long Beach	82	48	28	6	102	.622	260	237	2274
Utah	82	39	34	9	87	.530	244	254	1482
Las Vegas	82	35	39	8	78	.476	247	307	2597

ATTENDANCE REPORT

TEAM	TOTAL	OPENINGS	AVERAGE
Detroit	474,217	41	11,566
Grand Rapids	410,498	41	10,012
Chicago	381,008	41	9,292
Cleveland	342,620	41	8,356
Utah	333,325	41	8,129
Milwaukee	312,525	41	7,622
Manitoba	300,873	41	7,338
Houston	300,332	41	7,325
Orlando	270,178	41	6,589
Cincinnati	257,413	41	6,278
Fort Wayne	256,669	41	6,260
Kansas City	246,427	41	6,010
Las Vegas	205,065	41	5,001
Indianapolis	189,689	41	4,626
Long Beach	170,713	41	4,163
Michigan	152,686	41	3,724
LEAGUE (98-99)	4,604,238	656	7,019
LEAGUE (97-98)	5,343,490	738	7,241

LEADING SCORERS

POINTS	TEAM	GP	G	A	PTS
Wiseman, Brian	HOU	77	21	88	109
Maltais, Steve	CHI	82	56	44	100
Bowler, Bill	MAN	82	26	67	93
Dionne, Gilbert	CIN	76	35	53	88
Simon, Todd	CIN	81	26	61	87
Harkins, Brett	CLV	74	20	67	87
Christian, Jeff	HOU	80	45	41	86
Marinucci, Chris	CHI	82	41	40	81
Metropolit, Glen	GR	77	28	53	81
Hymovitz, Dave	IND	78	46	30	76
Drulia, Stan	DET	82	23	52	75
Biggs, Don	UTA	83	22	53	75
Hawgood, Greg	HOU	76	17	57	74
Ling, David	KCT	82	30	42	72
Butsayev, Viacheslav	FTW	71	28	44	72
Beaufait, Mark	ORL	71	28	43	71
Hauer, Brett	MAN	81	15	56	71
Thomas, Scott	MAN	78	45	25	70
Roberts, Dave	MCH	75	32	38	70
Lamb, Mark	HOU	79	21	49	70

GOALS	TEAM	GP	G
Maltais, Steve	CHI	82	56
Hymovitz, Dave	IND	78	46
Thomas, Scott	MAN	78	45
Christian, Jeff	HOU	80	45
Romaniuk, Russ	LVG	82	43

ASSISTS	TEAM	GP	A
Wiseman, Brian	HOU	77	88
Bowler, Bill	MAN	82	67
Harkins, Brett	CLV	74	67
Simon, Todd	CIN	81	61
Hawgood, Greg	HOU	76	57

PENALTY MINUTES	TEAM	GP	PIM
Angelstad, Mel	MCH	78	421
Jutras, Claude	LB	74	408
Roy, Andre	FTW	65	395
Norris, Clayton	ORL	66	327
Several Players Tied	at		308

SHOTS	TEAM	SHOTS
Maltais, Steve	CHI	376
Ling, David	KCT	297
Fairchild, Kelly	MCH	283
Hawgood, Greg	HOU	278
Christian, Jeff	HOU	263

SHOOTING PERCENTAGE	TEAM	GOALS	SHOTS	PCT
Romaniuk, Russ	LVG	43	180	0.239
Ciavaglia, Peter	DET	27	117	0.231
Stewart, Cam	HOU	36	171	0.211
Boguniecki, Eric	FTW	32	156	0.205
Hymovitz, Dave	IND	46	227	0.203

GAME WINNING GOALS	TEAM	GWG
Marinucci, Chris	CHI	10
Thomas, Scott	MAN	8
Several Players Tied	at	7

PLUS-MINUS	TEAM	+/-
Dyck, Paul	HOU	38
Drulia, Stan	DET	33
Aldridge, Keith	DET	30
Wiseman, Brian	HOU	28
Ferschweiler, Pat	KCT	27

(Based on 1620 or more minutes)

	TEAM	GPI	MIN	AVG	W	L	SOL	SOW	EN	SHO	SOG	SOA	GA	SAVES	SPCT
Weekes, Kevin	DET	33	1857:11	2.07	19	5	7	5	1	4	17	52	64	726	0.919
Trefilov, Andrei	DET	45	2599:48	2.12	26	14	4	6	3	3	15	67	92	1210	0.929
Legace, Manny	LB	33	1795:36	2.24	22	8	1	5	3	2	4	29	67	691	0.912
Fernandez, Manny	HOU	50	2948:32	2.36	34	6	9	7	2	2	24	88	116	1263	0.916
Bronsard, Christian	MAN	33	1746:15	2.44	15	8	4	0	1	1	12	26	71	800	0.918
Young, Wendell	CHI	35	2047:14	2.46	20	10	4	3	2	3	10	32	84	894	0.914
Turco, Marty	MCH	54	3127:23	2.61	24	17	10	5	4	1	31	94	136	1565	0.920
Shulmistra, Richard	MAN	44	2468:40	2.84	25	11	7	7	0	2	19	68	117	1153	0.908
Littman, David	ORL	55	2980:53	2.90	32	17	1	7	5	2	6	38	144	1298	0.900
Mason, Chris	MIL	34	1900:54	2.90	15	12	6	1	4	1	14	31	92	887	0.906
Sarjeant, Geoff	IND	46	2568:55	2.94	21	17	4	10	2	3	17	68	126	1292	0.911
Bach, Ryan	LB	31	1688:30	2.95	12	10	5	3	3	1	14	42	83	711	0.895
Jablonski, Pat	CHI	36	2118:37	3.00	22	7	7	5	0	1	19	57	106	949	0.900
Lalime, Patrick	KCT	66	3789:17	3.01	39	20	4	10	7	2	19	70	190	1708	0.900
Cassivi, Frederic	CIN	44	2417:58	3.05	21	17	2	4	4	1	7	32	123	1149	0.903
Racine, Bruce	FTW	53	3023:55	3.06	21	18	11	4	5	1	25	76	154	1534	0.909
Hurme, Jani	CIN	38	2070:22	3.10	21	12	3	6	2	1	10	55	107	919	0.896
Little, Neil	GR	50	2739:56	3.15	18	21	5	3	3	3	13	37	144	1218	0.894
Bales, Mike	MCH	32	1773:12	3.25	11	17	3	5	4	1	8	34	96	859	0.899
Reddick, Pokey	FTW	33	1873:34	3.27	12	15	5	3	3	1	12	39	102	973	0.905

WINS	TEAM	WINS
Lalime, Patrick	KCT	39
Fernandez, Manny	HOU	34
Littman, David	ORL	32
Trefilov, Andrei	DET	26
Shulmistra, Richard	MAN	25

LOSSES	TEAM	LOSSES
Langkow, Scott	UTA	23
Little, Neil	GR	21
Lalime, Patrick	KCT	20
Gordon, Ian	GR	19
Franek, Petr	LVG	19

MINUTES	TEAM	MIN
Lalime, Patrick	KCT	3789
Turco, Marty	MCH	3127
Racine, Bruce	FTW	3023
Littman, David	ORL	2980
Fernandez, Manny	HOU	2948

SHUTOUTS	TEAM	SHUTOUTS
Weekes, Kevin	DET	4
Several Players Tied	at	3

SAVES	TEAM	SAVES
Lalime, Patrick	KCT	1708
Turco, Marty	MCH	1565
Racine, Bruce	FTW	1534
Littman, David	ORL	1298
Sarjeant, Geoff	IND	1292

SAVE PERCENTAGE	TEAM	GOALS	SAVES	PCT
Trefilov, Andrei	DET	92	1210	0.929
Turco, Marty	MCH	136	1565	0.920
Weekes, Kevin	DET	64	726	0.919
Bronsard, Christian	MAN	71	800	0.918
Fernandez, Manny	HOU	116	1263	0.916

Conference Quarterfinals

Fort Wayne vs. Michigan
Michigan wins series 2 games to 0

Fort Wayne vs. Cleveland
Cleveland wins series 3 games to 1

Milwaukee vs. Manitoba
Manitoba wins series 2 games to 0

Cincinnati vs. Indianapolis
Indianapolis wins series 2 games to 1

Orlando vs. Indianapolis
Orlando wins series 3 games to 2

Long Beach vs. Kansas City
Long Beach wins series 2 games to 1

Conference Semifinals

Detroit vs. Indianapolis
Detroit wins series 3 games to 1

Long Beach vs. Houston
Houston wins series 3 games to 2

Orlando vs. Michigan
Orlando wins series 3 games to 0

Chicago vs. Manitoba
Chicago wins series 3 games to 0

Conference Finals

Detroit vs. Orlando
Orlando wins series 4 games to 3

Chicago vs. Houston
Houston wins series 4 games to 3

Turner Cup Finals

Houston vs. Orlando
Houston wins series 4 games to 3

LEADING SCORERS

POINTS	TEAM	GP	G	A	PTS
Freer, Mark	HOU	19	11	11	22
Krygier, Todd	ORL	17	9	10	19
Valicevic, Rob	HOU	19	7	10	17
Oliver, David	HOU	19	10	6	16
Panteleyev, Grigori	ORL	17	8	8	16
Christian, Jeff	HOU	18	4	12	16
Wiseman, Brian	HOU	19	3	13	16
Stewart, Cam	HOU	19	10	5	15
Pearson, Rob	ORL	17	8	6	14
McDonough, Hubie	ORL	17	2	12	14
Beaufait, Mark	ORL	15	2	12	14
Hawgood, Greg	HOU	19	4	8	12
Bowler, Bill	MAN	5	6	5	11
Ustorf, Stefan	DET	11	4	7	11
Lamb, Mark	HOU	19	1	10	11
Ruff, Jason	HOU	19	5	5	10
Augusta, Patrik	LB	8	4	6	10
Maltais, Steve	CHI	10	4	6	10
Felsner, Brian	DET	11	4	6	10
Richards, Todd	ORL	16	3	7	10

GOALS	TEAM	GP	G
Freer, Mark	HOU	19	11
Stewart, Cam	HOU	19	10
Oliver, David	HOU	19	10
Krygier, Todd	ORL	17	9
Several Players Tied	at		8

ASSISTS	TEAM	GP	A
Wiseman, Brian	HOU	19	13
McDonough, Hubie	ORL	17	12
Beaufait, Mark	ORL	15	12
Christian, Jeff	HOU	18	12
Freer, Mark	HOU	19	11

PENALTY MINUTES	TEAM	GP	PIM
Pearson, Scott	CHI	8	50
Aldridge, Keith	DET	11	49
Sabourin, Ken	ORL	14	49
Perrott, Nathan	IND	7	45
Royer, Remi	IND	7	44

GAME WINNING GOALS	TEAM	GWG
Pearson, Rob	ORL	3
Several Players Tied	at	2

PLUS-MINUS	TEAM	+/-
Panteleyev, Grigori	ORL	9
Ustorf, Stefan	DET	8
Paek, Jim	HOU	8
Felsner, Brian	DET	7
Dyck, Paul	HOU	7

LEADING GOALTENDERS
(Based on 90 or more minutes)

	TEAM	GPI	MIN	AVG	W	L	EN	SO	SOG	SOA	GA	SAVES	SPCT
Legace, Manny	LB	6	337:34	1.60	4	2	2	0	0	0	9	153	0.944
Lalime, Patrick	KCT	3	179:12	2.01	1	2	0	1	0	0	6	98	0.942
Trefilov, Andrei	DET	10	647:21	2.04	6	4	0	0	0	0	22	256	0.921
Lamothe, Marc	DET	7	418:09	2.15	3	4	0	2	0	0	15	212	0.934
Cassivi, Frederic	CIN	3	138:47	2.59	1	2	0	0	0	0	6	66	0.917
Fernandez, Manny	HOU	19	1126:26	2.61	11	8	1	1	0	0	49	463	0.904
Young, Wendell	CHI	7	421:29	2.70	4	3	0	1	0	0	19	182	0.905
Bach, Ryan	LB	3	151:43	2.77	0	2	0	0	0	0	7	80	0.920
Turco, Marty	MCH	5	300:25	2.80	2	3	0	0	0	0	14	156	0.918
Moss, Tyler	ORL	17	1016:45	3.13	10	7	1	0	0	0	53	455	0.896
Vokoun, Tomas	MIL	2	149:18	3.22	0	2	0	0	0	0	8	80	0.909
Rosati, Mike	MAN	5	314:14	3.44	2	3	0	0	0	0	18	145	0.890
Jablonski, Pat	CHI	3	185:05	3.57	2	1	2	0	0	0	11	73	0.869
Sarjeant, Geoff	IND	3	115:07	5.21	0	1	0	0	0	0	10	48	0.828

WINS	TEAM	WINS
Fernandez, Manny	HOU	11
Moss, Tyler	ORL	10
Trefilov, Andrei	DET	6
Legace, Manny	LB	4
Young, Wendell	CHI	4

LOSSES	TEAM	LOSSES
Fernandez, Manny	HOU	6
Moss, Tyler	ORL	5
Trefilov, Andrei	DET	3
Young, Wendell	CHI	3
Several Players Tied	at	2

SAVES	TEAM	SAVES
Fernandez, Manny	HOU	463
Moss, Tyler	ORL	455
Trefilov, Andrei	DET	256
Lamothe, Marc	DET	212
Several Players Tied	at	182

SAVE PERCENTAGE	TEAM	GOALS	SAVES	PCT
Legace, Manny	LB	9	153	0.944
Lalime, Patrick	KCT	6	98	0.942
Lamothe, Marc	DET	15	212	0.934
Trefilov, Andrei	DET	22	256	0.921
Bach, Ryan	LB	7	80	0.920

IHL Awards

First Team	Position	Second Team
Patrick Lalime, Kansas City	Goaltender	Andrei Trefilov, Detroit
Brett Hauer, Manitoba	Defenseman	Dan Lambert, Long Beach
Greg Hawgood, Houston	Defenseman	Tom Tilley, Milwaukee
Brian Wiseman, Houston	Center	Bill Bowler, Manitoba
Scott Thomas, Manitoba	Left Wing	Chris Marinucci, Chicago
Steve Maltais, Chicago	Right Wing	Dave Hymovitz, Indianapolis

James Gatschene Memorial (MVP)	Brian Wiseman, Houston
Governors' Trophy (Defenseman)	Greg Hawgood, Houston
Ironman Award (offense, defense and all games played)	Stan Drulia, Detroit
U.S. Born Rookie of the Year	Mark Mowers, Milwaukee
James Norris (Lowest goals against per team)	Kevin Weekes and Andrei Trefilov, Detroit
Rookie-of-the-Year	Marty Turco, Michigan
Coach of the Year	Dave Tippett, Houston
Man of the Year	Chris Marinucci, Chicago
Turner Cup (IHL Champions)	Houston Aeros
Bud Poile (Playoff MVP)	Mark Freer, Houston

Detroit's Andrei Trefilov shows Kansas City's Dody Wood the door

Photo by John Gacioch

International Hockey League

International Hockey League
1395 East Twelve Mile Road
Madison Heights, Michigan 48701
Phone: (248) 546-3200
Fax: (248) 546-1811

Chicago Wolves
2301 Ravine Way
Glenview, Illinois 60025
Phone: (847) 724-4625
Fax: (847) 724-1652
Coach: John Anderson

Cincinnati Cyclones
100 Broadway
Cincinnati, Ohio 45202
Phone: (513) 421-7825
Fax: (513) 421-1210
Coach: Ron Smith

Cleveland Lumberjacks
One Center Ice, 200 Huron Road
Cleveland, Ohio 44115
Phone: (216) 420-0000
Fax: (216) 420-2500
Coaches: Perry Ganchar,
Blair MacDonald, Phil Russell

Detroit Vipers
2 Championship Drive
Auburn Hills, Michigan 48326
Phone: (810) 377-8613
Fax: (810) 377-2695
Coach: Paulin Bordeleau

Grand Rapids Griffins
130 West Fulton
Grand Rapids, MI 49503
Phone: (616) 774-4585
Fax: (616) 336-5464
Coach: Guy Charron

Houston Aeros
Wilcrest Drive, Suite 260
Houston, Texas 77042
Phone: (713) 974-7825
Fax: (713) 361-7900
Coach: Ron Low

Kansas City Blades
1800 Genesee
Kansas City, Missouri 64102
Phone: (816) 842-5233
Fax: (816) 842-5610
Coach: Paul MacLean

Long Beach Ice Dogs
300 E. Ocean Blvd.
Long Beach, CA 90802
Phone: (562) 423-3647
Fax: (562) 437-5116
Coach: John Van Boxmeer

Manitoba Moose
1430 Maroons Road
Winnipeg, Manitoba R3G 0L5
Phone: (204) 987-7825
Fax: (204) 896-6673
Coach: Randy Carlyle

Michigan K-Wings
3620 Van Rick Drive
Kalamazoo, Michigan 49001
Phone: (616) 349-9772
Fax: (616) 345-6584
Coach: Bill McDonald

Milwaukee Admirals
1001 N 4th Street
Milwaukee, Wisconsin 53203
Phone: (414) 227-0550
Fax: (414) 227-0568
Coach: Al Sims

Orlando Solar Bears
Two Magic Place
8701 Maitland Summit Blvd.
Orlando, Florida 32810
Phone: (407) 916-2400
Fax: (407) 916-2830
Coach: TBD

Utah Grizzlies
The "E" Center
3200 S. Decker Lake Drive
West Valley City, Utah 84119
Phone: (801) 988-8000
Fax: (801) 988-8001
Coach: Bob Bourne

Central Hockey League

1998-99 Final Standings

EASTERN	GP	W	L	SOL	PTS	PCT	GF	GA	PIM
Huntsville	70	47	19	4	98	.700	310	251	2313
Columbus	70	41	21	8	90	.643	276	210	2008
Macon	70	36	25	9	81	.579	241	233	1468
Memphis	70	36	27	7	79	.564	313	307	1747
Fayetteville	70	35	27	8	78	.557	267	285	1529
WESTERN									
Oklahoma City	70	49	19	2	100	.714	322	203	2194
San Antonio	70	37	26	7	81	.579	286	283	2128
Wichita	70	34	26	10	78	.557	257	262	2158
Topeka	70	28	38	4	60	.429	189	251	1584
Fort Worth	70	22	43	5	49	.350	245	322	1694
Tulsa	70	20	41	9	49	.350	261	360	2276

ATTENDANCE REPORT

TEAM	TOTAL	OPENINGS	AVERAGE
Oklahoma City	318,511	35	9,100
Wichita	173,089	35	4,945
Tulsa	171,604	35	4,902
Topeka	167,788	35	4,793
Columbus	148,723	35	4,249
Memphis	136,310	35	3,894
Fayetteville	134,122	35	3,832
San Antonio	127,619	35	3,646
Macon	126,002	35	3,600
Huntsville	95,088	35	2,716
Fort Worth	77,565	35	2,216
LEAGUE (98-99)	1,676,421	385	4,354
LEAGUE (97-98)	1,520,218	350	4,343

CENTRAL HOCKEY LEAGUE REGULAR SEASON STATISTICS 1998-1999
LEADING SCORERS

POINTS	TEAM	GP	G	A	PTS
Grant, Derek	MEM	65	45	78	123
Lamoureux, Denis	MEM	69	67	54	121
Brdarovic, Johnny	SAN	68	56	59	115
Burton, Joe	OKC	69	73	37	110
George, Chris	HVL	70	59	48	107
Bondarev, Igor	HVL	64	26	78	104
Jackson, Paul	SAN	62	41	62	103
Langlois, Jocelyn	MAC	70	38	65	103
Remackel, Chad	FAY	70	36	67	103
Antonovich, Jeff	TUL	70	40	60	100
Sauter, Hardy	OKC	70	20	80	100
DuBois, Jonathan	HVL	58	28	71	99
Shantz, Brian	SAN	69	26	63	89
Clayton, Travis	WCH	69	25	57	82
MacIntyre, Corey	OKC	56	22	60	82
Karpen, Mark	WCH	69	35	46	81
Seguin, Brett	TOP	70	24	56	80
Bonanno, Leonard	MEM	67	26	53	79
Martens, Mike	COL	64	37	41	78
Several Players Tied at					77

GOALS	TEAM	GP	G
Burton, Joe	OKC	69	73
Lamoureux, Denis	MEM	69	67
George, Chris	HVL	70	59
Brdarovic, Johnny	SAN	68	56
Grant, Derek	MEM	65	45

ASSISTS	TEAM	GP	A
Sauter, Hardy	OKC	70	80
Bondarev, Igor	HVL	64	78
Grant, Derek	MEM	65	78
DuBois, Jonathan	HVL	58	71
Remackel, Chad	FAY	70	67

PENALTY MINUTES	TEAM	GP	PIM
Voth, Curtis	TUL	56	426
Renard, Jason	MAC	41	376
LaForge, Marc	SAN	58	302
Bechard, Jerome	COL	70	298
Arvanitis, Peter	OKC	58	280

POWER PLAY GOALS	TEAM	PPG
George, Chris	HVL	24
Lamoureux, Denis	MEM	24
Burton, Joe	OKC	22
Brdarovic, Johnny	SAN	20
Martens, Mike	COL	19

SHORT HANDED GOALS	TEAM	SHG
Chunchukov, Alexsand	FAY	5
George, Chris	HVL	5
Shantz, Brian	SAN	5
Langlois, Jocelyn	MAC	5
Several Players Tied at		4

GAME WINNING GOALS	TEAM	GWG
Burton, Joe	OKC	14
Langlois, Jocelyn	MAC	10
Sinclair, Rob	COL	8
Brdarovic, Johnny	SAN	7

PLUS-MINUS	TEAM	+/-
Bondarev, Igor	HVL	64
Sauter, Hardy	OKC	62
Burton, Joe	OKC	49
MacIntyre, Corey	OKC	40

CENTRAL HOCKEY LEAGUE REGULAR SEASON STATISTICS 1998-1999

LEADING GOALTENDERS

(Based on 1380 or more minutes)

	TEAM	GPI	MIN	AVG	W	L	SOL	SOW	EN	SHO	SOG	SOA	GA	SAVES	SPCT
Filiatrault, Jean-Ia	OKC	43	2532:09	2.54	30	12	1	1	3	6	2	8	107	1057	0.908
Ouellette, Francis	COL	40	2261:46	2.76	24	10	3	7	1	0	12	59	104	1025	0.908
Saurdiff, Corwin	COL	34	1939:17	2.91	17	11	5	4	3	1	8	41	94	854	0.901
Puppa, Derek	HVL	55	3103:57	3.13	39	11	2	8	2	1	15	72	162	1461	0.900
Branch, Rod	TOP	48	2816:24	3.17	22	21	2	8	5	3	13	47	149	1407	0.904
Gagnon, Pierre	MAC	50	2734:59	3.27	25	16	4	7	0	0	11	52	149	1393	0.903
Shepard, Ken	FAY	47	2672:37	3.39	27	14	3	0	2	1	6	13	151	1277	0.894
Leslie, Lance	WCH	43	2484:16	3.45	21	16	6	6	2	1	19	63	143	1002	0.875
Friesen, Rob	MEM	48	2691:55	4.26	23	18	4	5	4	0	13	34	191	1226	0.865
Grobins, Nathan	FTW	60	3503:40	4.38	18	37	4	6	3	1	15	58	256	2111	0.892
Legault, Martin	TUL	43	2368:32	4.56	9	25	6	1	7	1	12	31	180	1478	0.891

WINS	TEAM	WINS
Puppa, Derek	HVL	39
Filiatrault, Jean-Ia	OKC	30
Shepard, Ken	FAY	27
Gagnon, Pierre	MAC	25
Ouellette, Francis	COL	24

LOSSES	TEAM	LOSSES
Grobins, Nathan	FTW	37
Legault, Martin	TUL	25
Branch, Rod	TOP	21
Friesen, Rob	MEM	18
Several Players Tied	at	16

MINUTES	TEAM	MIN
Grobins, Nathan	FTW	3503
Puppa, Derek	HVL	3103
Branch, Rod	TOP	2816
Gagnon, Pierre	MAC	2734
Friesen, Rob	MEM	2691

SHUTOUTS	TEAM	SHUTOUTS
Filiatrault, Jean-Ia	OKC	6
Branch, Rod	TOP	3
Smith, Greg	WCH	3
Several Players Tied	at	1

SAVES	TEAM	SAVES
Grobins, Nathan	FTW	2111
Legault, Martin	TUL	1478
Puppa, Derek	HVL	1461
Branch, Rod	TOP	1407
Gagnon, Pierre	MAC	1393

SAVE PERCENTAGE	TEAM	GOALS	SAVES	PCT
Patry, Eric	MAC	70	716	0.911
Filiatrault, Jean-Ia	OKC	107	1057	0.908
Ouellette, Francis	COL	104	1025	0.908
Branch, Rod	TOP	149	1407	0.904
Gagnon, Pierre	MAC	149	1393	0.903

SHOOTOUT WINS	TEAM	SOW
Puppa, Derek	HVL	8
Branch, Rod	TOP	8
Ouellette, Francis	COL	7
Gagnon, Pierre	MAC	7
Several Players Tied	at	6

SHOOTOUT PERCENTAGE	TEAM	SAVES	SOA	PCT
Saurdiff, Corwin	COL	33	41	0.805
Ouellette, Francis	COL	47	59	0.797
Williams, Mike	OKC	19	24	0.792
Puppa, Derek	HVL	57	72	0.792
Gagnon, Pierre	MAC	41	52	0.788

Division Semifinals

Oklahoma City vs. Topeka
Oklahoma City wins series 3 games to o

Huntsville vs. Macon
Huntsville wins series 3 games to 0

San Antonio vs. Wichita
San Antonio wins series 3 games to 1

Columbus vs. Memphis
Columbus wins series 3 games to 1

Division Finals

Columbus vs. Huntsville
Huntsville wins series 4 games to 2

Oklahoma City vs. San Antonio
Oklahoma City wins series 4 games to 0

Levins Cup Finals

Huntsville vs. Oklahoma City
Huntsville wins series 4 games to 2

CENTRAL HOCKEY LEAGUE PLAYOFF STATISTICS -- 1998-1999

LEADING SCORERS

POINTS	TEAM	GP	G	A	PTS
DuBois, Jonathan	HVL	15	3	16	19
Bondarev, Igor	HVL	15	5	11	16
Kempffer, Mick	COL	10	3	13	16
Martens, Mike	COL	10	6	9	15
Richardson, Ken	HVL	15	6	9	15
Sauter, Hardy	OKC	13	5	9	14
Burton, Joe	OKC	11	6	7	13
Jensen, Jim	OKC	13	5	8	13
Green, Scott	SAN	8	8	4	12
George, Chris	HVL	15	6	6	12
Brdarovic, Johnny	SAN	8	4	8	12
Shantz, Brian	SAN	8	3	9	12
Johnston, Chris	OKC	13	6	5	11
Lindsay, Scott	HVL	15	5	6	11
Jackson, Paul	SAN	8	1	10	11
Kholomeyev, Alex	HVL	15	6	4	10
Quiring, Tyler	HVL	12	5	5	10
Richard, Marcel	COL	10	4	6	10
Tseplis, Gatis	SAN	8	4	5	9
Moore, Steve	OKC	10	3	6	9

GOALS	TEAM	GP	G
Green, Scott	SAN	8	8
DeGurse, Mike	HVL	14	8
Several Players Tied	at		6

ASSISTS	TEAM	GP	A
DuBois, Jonathan	HVL	15	16
Kempffer, Mick	COL	10	13
Bondarev, Igor	HVL	15	11
Jackson, Paul	SAN	8	10
Several Players Tied	at		9

PENALTY MINUTES	TEAM	GP	PIM
Johnson, Craig	OKC	10	73
Jackson, Paul	SAN	8	67
Johnston, Chris	OKC	13	49
MacIntyre, Jason	SAN	8	48
Lakovic, Greg	HVL	12	48

GAME WINNING GOALS	TEAM	GWG
Richardson, Ken	HVL	3
Crimin, Derek	COL	2
Kjenstad, Olaf	COL	2
Quiring, Tyler	HVL	2
Sauter, Hardy	OKC	2

PLUS-MINUS	TEAM	+/-
Sauter, Hardy	OKC	13
MacIntyre, Corey	OKC	12
Burton, Joe	OKC	12
DuBois, Jonathan	HVL	11
Jensen, Jim	OKC	10

LEADING GOALTENDERS
(Based on 90 or more minutes)

	TEAM	GPI	MIN	AVG	W	L	EN	SO	SOG	SOA	GA	SAVES	SPCT
Puppa, Derek	HVL	15	961:14	2.12	11	4	0	1	0	0	34	389	0.920
Filiatrault, Jean-Ia	OKC	12	733:23	2.45	9	3	0	1	0	0	30	331	0.917
Ouellette, Francis	COL	10	502:49	3.34	4	4	2	0	0	0	28	233	0.893
Gagnon, Pierre	MAC	3	205:10	3.51	0	3	2	0	0	0	12	115	0.906
Taylor, Paul	SAN	8	487:33	3.69	3	5	2	0	0	0	30	294	0.907
Renfrew, Brian	MEM	4	242:41	4.45	1	3	1	0	0	0	18	118	0.868
Branch, Rod	TOP	3	178:50	4.70	0	3	0	0	0	0	14	109	0.886
Smith, Greg	WCH	3	165:29	4.71	1	2	0	0	0	0	13	64	0.831
Saurdiff, Corwin	COL	2	105:04	5.14	1	1	0	0	0	0	9	47	0.839

WINS	TEAM	WINS
Puppa, Derek	HVL	11
Filiatrault, Jean-Ia	OKC	9
Ouellette, Francis	COL	4
Taylor, Paul	SAN	3
Several Players Tied	at	1

LOSSES	TEAM	LOSSES
Taylor, Paul	SAN	4
Branch, Rod	TOP	3
Renfrew, Brian	MEM	3
Ouellette, Francis	COL	3
Several Players Tied	at	2

SAVES	TEAM	SAVES
Puppa, Derek	HVL	389
Filiatrault, Jean-Ia	OKC	331
Taylor, Paul	SAN	294
Ouellette, Francis	COL	233
Renfrew, Brian	MEM	118

SAVE PERCENTAGE	TEAM	GOALS	SAVES	PCT
Puppa, Derek	HVL	34	389	0.920
Filiatrault, Jean-Ia	OKC	30	331	0.917
Taylor, Paul	SAN	30	294	0.907
Gagnon, Pierre	MAC	12	115	0.906
Ouellette, Francis	COL	28	233	0.893

CeHL Regular Season Award Winners

Most Valuable Player	Derek Puppa, Huntsville
Defenseman of the Year	Igor Bondarev, Huntsville
Rookie of the Year	Johnny Brdarovic, San Antonio
Goaltender of the Year	Jean-ian Filiatrault, Oklahoma City
Coach of the Year	Chris Stewart, Huntsville
Community Service	Mike Berger, Tulsa
Levins Trophy (CeHL Champions)	Huntsville Channel Cats
President's Trophy (Playoff MVP)	Derek Puppa, Huntsville
Public Relations Director of the Year	Josh Evans, Oklahoma City
CHL Employee of the Year	Chris Presson, Topeka

Central Hockey League

1202 East 38th Street
Indianapolis, Indiana 46205
Phone: (317) 931-4245
Fax: (317) 931-4244

Columbus Cottonmouths
P.O. Box 1886
Columbus Civic Center, 400 Fourth Street
Columbus, Georgia. 31902-1886
Phone: (706) 571-0086
Fax: (706) 571-0080
Coach: Bruce Garber

Huntsville Channel Cats
700 Monroe Street
Huntsville, Alabama 35801
Phone: (256) 551-2383
Fax: (256) 551-2382
Coach: Pat Bingham

Macon Whoopee
Macon Centroplex
200 Coliseum Drive
Macon, Georgia 31217
Phone (912) 741-1000
Fax: (912) 464-0655
Coach: Graeme Townshend

Oklahoma City Blazers
119 N. Robinson, Suite 230
Oklahoma City, OK 73102
Phone: (405) 235-7825
Fax: (405) 272-9875
Coach: Doug Sauter

Topeka Scarecrows
P.O. Box 57
Topeka, Kansas 66612-1442
Phone (785) 232-7697
Fax: (785) 232-7423
Coach: Paul Kelly

Wichita Thunder
505 W. Maple, Suite 100
Wichita, Kansas 67213
Phone (316) 264-4625
Fax: (316) 264-3037
Coach: Bryan Wells

Fayetteville Force
1960 Coliseum Drive
Fayetteville, North Carolina 28306
Phone: (910) 438-9000
Fax: (910) 438-9004
Coach: Dave Lohrei

Indianapolis Ice
1202 East 38th Street
Indianapolis, Indiana 46205
Phone: (317) 925-4423
Fax: (317) 931-4511
Coach: TBA

Memphis RiverKings
315 S. Hollywood
Building E
Memphis, Tennessee 38104
Phone (901) 278-9009
Fax (901) 323-3262
Coach: Kevin Evans

San Antonio Iguanas
5757 Hwy. 90 W.
San Antonio, Texas 78227
Phone: (210) 227-4449
Fax: (210) 670-0001
Coach: Chris Stewart

Tulsa Oilers
6413 S. Mingo, Suite 200
Tulsa, Oklahoma 74133
Phone: (918) 252-7825
Fax: (918) 249-0310
Coach: Shaun Clouston

East Coast Hockey League

1998-99 Final Standings

NORTHERN CONFERENCE

NORTHEAST	GP	W	L	T	PTS	PCT	GF	GA	PIM
Roanoke	70	38	22	10	86	.614	224	201	1499
Hampton Roads	70	38	24	8	84	.600	215	213	2147
Richmond	70	40	27	3	83	.593	239	196	1796
Chesapeake	70	34	25	11	79	.564	229	206	1713
Johnstown	70	27	34	9	63	.450	218	265	1734
NORTHWEST									
Columbus	70	39	24	7	85	.607	257	242	1614
Peoria	70	39	25	6	84	.600	243	230	1839
Toledo	70	39	26	5	83	.593	256	246	1915
Dayton	70	34	27	9	77	.550	239	241	1984
Huntington	70	31	33	6	68	.486	221	253	1420
Wheeling	70	27	37	6	60	.429	206	249	2220

SOUTHERN CONFERENCE

SOUTHEAST									
Pee Dee	70	51	15	4	106	.757	289	191	1674
Florida	70	45	20	5	95	.679	253	180	1517
South Carolina	70	40	20	10	90	.643	235	216	1839
Augusta	70	38	27	5	81	.579	235	233	1984
Jacksonville	70	35	33	2	72	.514	235	255	1533
Charlotte	70	29	30	11	69	.493	221	262	1264
Miami	70	28	32	10	66	.471	208	266	1618
Greenville	70	26	33	11	63	.450	208	241	1589
SOUTHWEST									
Louisiana	70	46	18	6	98	.700	297	205	2425
Mississippi	70	41	22	7	89	.636	251	215	1357
Birmingham	70	37	29	4	78	.557	251	267	2020
New Orleans	70	30	27	13	73	.521	244	261	1903
Mobile	70	31	31	8	70	.500	231	259	1431
Baton Rouge	70	30	30	10	70	.500	222	228	1566
Tallahassee	70	27	34	9	63	.450	212	250	1838
Pensacola	70	25	41	4	54	.386	199	267	1267

ATTENDANCE REPORT

TEAM	TOTAL	OPENINGS	AVERAGE
Louisiana	345,003	35	9,857
Greenville	324,417	35	9,269
South Carolina	230,743	35	6,592
Florida	222,978	35	6,370
Hampton Roads	215,225	35	6,149
Pensacola	213,690	35	6,105
Pee Dee	200,174	35	5,719
Richmond	193,360	35	5,524
Augusta	190,525	35	5,443
Charlotte	178,446	35	5,098
Mississippi	175,030	35	5,000
Toledo	173,601	35	4,960
Roanoke	165,929	35	4,740
Peoria	160,567	35	4,587
Dayton	158,492	35	4,528
Birmingham	156,015	35	4,457
Baton Rouge	155,150	35	4,432
Columbus	154,264	35	4,407
Jacksonville	143,062	35	4,087
New Orleans	136,430	35	3,898
Tallahassee	136,455	35	3,898
Mobile	135,609	35	3,874
Wheeling	121,155	35	3,461
Johnstown	84,159	35	2,404
Chesapeake	82,152	35	2,347
Huntington	78,860	35	2,253
Miami	52,191	35	1,491
LEAGUE (98-99)	4,583,682	945	4,850
LEAGUE (97-98)	4,386,194	875	5,013

EAST COAST HOCKEY LEAGUE REGULAR SEASON STATISTICS -- 1998-1999

LEADING SCORERS

POINTS	TEAM	GP	G	A	PTS
Spoltore, John	LA	69	36	73	109
Ling, Jamie	DAY	70	39	56	95
Valicevic, Chris	LA	70	20	72	92
Hicks, Jamey	BIR	65	16	75	91
Bousquet, Dany	PD	62	36	54	90
DeCiantis, Rob	NO	70	47	41	88
Sirois, Allan	PD	70	35	49	84
Varga, John	LA	65	39	44	83
Aube, J.F.	CHR	70	32	50	82
Oates, Matt	COL	70	24	57	81
Richardson, Bryan	BR	69	32	47	79
Clancey, Derek	CHS	70	21	58	79
Bermingham, Jim	HGN	64	16	63	79
LaFrance, Darryl	NO	55	39	39	78
Ceman, Dan	HRD	70	38	39	77
Gendron, Pierre	PEN	68	34	42	76
Noren, Darryl	CHR	70	26	50	76
Elders, Jason	MOB	68	29	46	75
Several Players Tied at					74

GOALS	TEAM	GP	G
DeCiantis, Rob	NO	70	47
LaFrance, Darryl	NO	55	39
Varga, John	LA	65	39
Ling, Jamie	DAY	70	39
Several Players Tied at			38

ASSISTS	TEAM	GP	A
Hicks, Jamey	BIR	65	75
Spoltore, John	LA	69	73
Valicevic, Chris	LA	70	72
Bermingham, Jim	HGN	64	63
Clancey, Derek	CHS	70	58

PENALTY MINUTES	TEAM	GP	PIM
Charbonneau, L.P.	GRE	65	366
Bedard, Louis	HRD	64	325
Shelley, Jody	JHN	52	325
Pinfold, Dennis	BIR	43	323
Tasker, Ken	TOL	47	319

GAME WINNING GOALS	TEAM	GWG
Seitz, Dave	SC	11
Dumont, Louis	LA	9
Ceman, Dan	HRD	9
Curtin, Luke	BR	9
Several Players Tied at		8

PLUS-MINUS	TEAM	+/-
Vodrazka, Jan	PD	44
Valicevic, Chris	LA	40
Sirois, Allan	PD	33
Pagnutti, Matthew	LA	32
Petz, Ryan	PD	32

LEADING GOALTENDERS
(Based on 1380 or more minutes)

	TEAM	GPI	MIN	AVG	W	L	SOL	SOW	EN	SHO	SOG	SOA	GA	SAVES	SPCT
Gingras, Maxime	RMD	50	2808:10	2.26	30	13	3	7	3	7	14	48	106	1291	0.924
Magliarditi, Marc	FLA	47	2745:31	2.27	32	10	3	5	1	5	9	41	104	1102	0.914
Amidovski, Bujar	LA	27	1524:59	2.32	17	5	3	0	1	3	7	12	59	706	0.923
Tamburro, Mike	CHS	35	1934:45	2.45	19	11	2	3	3	2	7	22	79	926	0.921
Allan, Sandy	PD	35	1958:03	2.48	21	11	2	2	2	1	7	19	81	899	0.917
Gagnon, Dave	RNK	34	2032:37	2.57	20	9	5	6	2	2	21	58	87	973	0.918
Lehman, Jody	SC	33	1743:03	2.72	18	7	4	5	0	1	10	42	79	862	0.916
Petruk, Randy	FLA	25	1441:25	2.75	13	10	2	3	4	1	6	23	66	569	0.896
Saal, Jason	HRD	44	2477:53	2.76	20	17	5	7	4	4	17	61	114	1253	0.917
Berthiaume, Daniel	RNK	35	2104:48	2.77	18	12	5	3	4	2	15	42	97	959	0.908
Richards, Mark	PD	40	2233:59	2.82	29	4	3	4	0	3	13	40	105	956	0.901
Scott, Travis	MIS	44	2336:37	2.88	22	12	5	5	2	1	15	48	112	1111	0.908
Mullin, Matt	TOL	45	2480:08	2.93	27	13	3	4	2	0	10	30	121	1241	0.911
Valiquette, Steve	HRD	31	1713:02	2.94	18	7	3	2	3	1	10	36	84	913	0.916
Regan, Brian	DAY	42	2331:00	2.96	18	14	7	3	4	4	18	46	115	1074	0.903
Schafer, Paxton	GRE	40	2325:49	2.97	17	16	7	4	3	2	22	54	115	1133	0.908
Soucy, Christian	BR	25	1385:50	2.99	9	9	4	2	2	2	11	32	69	730	0.914
Thuss, Chuck	MIS	37	1849:53	3.02	19	10	2	6	1	3	12	43	93	858	0.902
Bonner, Doug	LA	45	2592:43	3.03	28	13	3	6	3	1	12	44	131	1224	0.903
Lambert, Judd	AUG	51	2948:30	3.05	24	20	5	8	7	1	17	67	150	1497	0.909

WINS	TEAM	WINS
Magliarditi, Marc	FLA	32
Salajko, Jeff	COL	30
Gingras, Maxime	RMD	30
LeBlanc, Ray	JAX	29
Richards, Mark	PD	29

LOSSES	TEAM	LOSSES
Belecki, Brent	MIA	24
Caravaggio, Luciano	WHL	22
Lambert, Judd	AUG	20
Willis, Jordan	BR	20
Eisler, Matt	JHN	20

MINUTES	TEAM	MIN
Salajko, Jeff	COL	3076
LeBlanc, Ray	JAX	2982
Lambert, Judd	AUG	2948
Belecki, Brent	MIA	2937
Gingras, Maxime	RMD	2808

SHUTOUTS	TEAM	SHUTOUTS
Gingras, Maxime	RMD	7
Magliarditi, Marc	FLA	5
Regan, Brian	DAY	4
Willis, Jordan	BR	4
Saal, Jason	HRD	4

SAVES	TEAM	SAVES
Belecki, Brent	MIA	1577
Lambert, Judd	AUG	1497
LeBlanc, Ray	JAX	1461
Salajko, Jeff	COL	1435
Gingras, Maxime	RMD	1291

SAVE PERCENTAGE	TEAM	GOALS	SAVES	PCT
Gingras, Maxime	RMD	106	1291	0.924
Amidovski, Bujar	LA	59	706	0.923
Tamburro, Mike	CHS	79	926	0.921
Gagnon, Dave	RNK	87	973	0.918
Allan, Sandy	PD	81	899	0.917

Preliminary Round

Augusta vs. Baton Rouge
Baton Rouge wins series 2 games to 0

Birmingham vs. Mobile
Birmingham wins series 2 games to 0

New Orleans vs. Jacksonville
New Orleans wins series 2 games to 0

Conference Quarterfinals

Louisiana vs. New Orleans
New Orleans wins series 3 games to 2

Birmingham vs. Florida
Florida wins series 3 games to 0

Richmond vs Hampton Roads
Richmond wins series 3 games to 1

Toledo vs Peoria
Toledo wins series 3 games to 1

Baton Rouge vs. Pee Dee
Pee Dee wins series 3 games to 1

South Carolina vs. Mississippi
Mississippi wins series 3 games to 0

Roanoke vs. Dayton
Roanoke wins series 3 games to 1

Chesapeake vs Columbus
Chesapeake wins series 3 games to 1

Conference Semifinals

New Orleans vs. Pee Dee
Pee Dee wins series 3 games to 1

Roanoke vs. Chesapeake
Roanoke wins series 3 games to 1

Florida vs. Mississippi
Mississippi wins series 3 games to 0

Richmond vs. Toledo
Richmond wins series 3 games to 0

Conference Finals

Pee Dee vs. Mississippi
Mississippi wins series 4 games to 1

Roanoke vs. Richmond
Richmond wins series 4 games to 0

Riley Cup Finals

Mississippi vs Richmond
Mississippi wins series 4 games to 3

LEADING SCORERS

POINTS	TEAM	GP	G	A	PTS
DeCiantis, Rob	NO	11	11	11	22
Kraft, Ryan	RMD	18	10	10	20
Hurd, Kelly	MIS	18	9	11	20
Bousquet, Dany	PD	13	7	12	19
Lipsett, Chris	PD	13	13	4	17
Nedomansky, Vaclav	MIS	18	8	9	17
LaFrance, Darryl	NO	11	6	11	17
Sirois, Allan	PD	13	4	13	17
Lazaro, Jeff	NO	11	9	7	16
Roed, Peter	RMD	18	6	10	16
Shier, Andrew	RMD	18	2	14	16
Blaznek, Joe	RMD	18	10	5	15
Hilton, Kevin	MIS	18	7	8	15
Rupnow, Mark	MIS	18	6	9	15
Petz, Ryan	PD	13	7	6	13
Schmidt, Chris	MIS	18	5	8	13
Kravets, Mikhail	MIS	18	5	8	13
Fair, Quinn	MIS	18	3	10	13
Bianchi, Joe	RMD	18	7	5	12
Knopp, Kevin	RMD	15	2	10	12

GOALS	TEAM	GP	G
Lipsett, Chris	PD	13	13
DeCiantis, Rob	NO	11	11
Blaznek, Joe	RMD	18	10
Kraft, Ryan	RMD	18	10
Several Players Tied at			9

ASSISTS	TEAM	GP	A
Shier, Andrew	RMD	18	14
Sirois, Allan	PD	13	13
Bousquet, Dany	PD	13	12
Several Players Tied at			11

PENALTY MINUTES	TEAM	GP	PIM
Senn, Trevor	RMD	18	89
Goudie, Brian	PD	13	66
Vodrazka, Jan	PD	13	56
Smith, Travis	RNK	12	44
Several Players Tied at			42

EAST COAST HOCKEY LEAGUE PLAYOFF STATISTICS -- 1998-1999
(Based on 90 or more minutes)

	TEAM	GPI	MIN	AVG	W	L	EN	SO	SOG	SOA	GA	SAVES	SPCT
Hayes, Harlin	COL	2	106:45	1.12	0	1	1	0	0	0	2	41	0.953
Daubenspeck, Kirk	CHS	7	424:08	1.70	3	4	1	1	0	0	12	196	0.942
Koenig, Trevor	DAY	4	202:46	1.78	1	2	2	1	0	0	6	84	0.933
Berthiaume, Daniel	RNK	10	608:08	1.87	6	4	0	1	0	0	19	317	0.943
Scott, Travis	MIS	18	1252:28	2.01	14	4	0	3	0	0	42	599	0.934
Villeneuve, Martin	NO	8	479:12	2.25	5	3	0	2	0	0	18	336	0.949
Gingras, Maxime	RMD	18	1117:03	2.31	12	5	0	5	0	0	43	531	0.925
Richards, Mark	PD	5	226:29	2.38	0	2	1	0	0	0	9	96	0.914
Lambert, Judd	AUG	2	119:13	2.52	0	2	1	0	0	0	5	72	0.935
Magliarditi, Marc	FLA	5	332:18	2.53	3	2	0	1	0	0	14	139	0.908
Gagnon, Dave	RNK	3	138:45	2.59	0	2	2	0	0	0	6	72	0.923
Bonner, Doug	LA	5	298:58	2.61	2	3	0	0	0	0	13	134	0.912
Allan, Sandy	PD	11	626:38	2.68	7	4	0	0	0	0	28	233	0.893

WINS	TEAM	WINS
Scott, Travis	MIS	14
Gingras, Maxime	RMD	12
Allan, Sandy	PD	7
Berthiaume, Daniel	RNK	6
Villeneuve, Martin	NO	5

LOSSES	TEAM	LOSSES
Mullin, Matt	TOL	4
Daubenspeck, Kirk	CHS	4
Gingras, Maxime	RMD	4
Several Players Tied at		3

ECHL Regular Season Awards

First Team	Position	Second Team
Maxime Gingras, Richmond	Goaltender	Marc Magliarditi, Florida
Chris Valicevic, Louisiana	Defenseman	Bob Woods, Mississippi
Arturs Kupaks, Chesapeake	Defenseman	Brad Dexter, South Carolina
John Spoltore, Louisiana	Center	Jamey Hicks, Mobile
Denny Felsner, Chesapeake	Right Wing	Rob DeCiantis, Baton Rouge
Allan Sirois, Pee Dee	Left Wing	Jason Elders, Mobile

Most Valuable Player	Chris Valicevic, Louisiana
Best Defenseman	Chris Valicevic, Louisiana
Rookie of the Year	Maxime Gingras, Richmond
Best Goalie	Maxime Gingras, Richmond
Best Coach	Bob Ferguson, Florida
Riley Cup (ECHL Champions)	Mississippi SeaWolves
Playoff MVP	Travis Scott, Mississippi
Sportsmanship	Jamie Ling, Dayton

East Coast Hockey League
125 Village Boulevard, Suite 210
Princeton, New Jersey 08540
Phone (609) 452-0770
Fax: (609) 452-7147

Arkansas RiverBlades
425 W. Broadway, Suite B
North Little Rock, Arkansas 72114
Phone: (501) 975-2327
Fax: (501) 907-2327
Coach: Geoff Ward

Augusta Lynx
712 Telfair Street
Augusta, Georgia 30901
Phone: (706) 724-4423
Fax: (706) 724-2423
Coach: Dan Wiebe

Baton Rouge Kingfish
PO Box 2142
Baton Rouge, Louisiana 70821
Phone: (504) 336-4625
Fax: (504) 336-4011
Coach: Bob McGill

Birmingham Bulls
P.O. Box 1506
Birmingham, Alabama 35201
Phone: (205) 458-8833
Fax: (205) 458-8489
Coach: Dennis Desrosiers

Charlotte Checkers
2700 E. Independance Boulevard
Charlotte, NC 28205
Phone: (704) 342-4423
Fax: (704) 377-4595
Coach: Shawn Wheeler

Dayton Bombers
3640 Colonel Glenn Hwy. #417
Dayton, Ohio 43435
Phone: (937) 775-4747
Fax: (937) 775-4749
Coach: Greg Ireland

Florida Everblades
11000 Everblades Parkway
Estero, Florida 33928
Phone: (941) 948-7825
Fax: (941) 948-9299
Coach: Bob Ferguson

Greensboro
P.O. Box 3387
Greensboro, North Carolina 27402
Phone: (336) 218-5428
Fax: (336) 218-5498
Coach: Jeff Brubaker

Greenville Grrrowl
P.O. Box 10348
Greenville, South Carolina 29603
Phone: (864) 467-4777
Fax: (864) 241-3872
Coach: John Marks

Hampton Roads Admirals
PO Box 58230
Virginia Beach, Virginia 23501
Phone: (757) 430-8873
Fax: (757) 430-8803
Coach: John Brophy

Huntington Blizzard
763 Third Avenue
Huntington, West Virginia 25701
Phone: (304) 697-7825
Fax: (304) 697-7832
Coach: Ray Edwards

Jackson Bandits

Jackson, Mississippi
Phone: (601)
Fax: (601)
Coach: Derek Clancey

Jacksonville Lizard Kings
1000 W. Bay Street
Jacksonville, Florida. 32204
Phone: (904) 358-7825
Fax: (904) 358-9999
Coach: Alain Lemieux

Johnstown Chiefs
326 Napoleon Street
Johnstown, Pennsylvania 15901
Phone: (814) 539-1799
Fax: (814) 536-1316
Coach: Scott Allen

Louisiana IceGators
444 Cajundome Boulevard
Lafayette, Louisiana 70506
Phone: (318) 234-4423
Fax: (318) 232-1254
Coach: Don Murdoch

Mississippi Sea Wolves
2350 Beach Blvd.
Biloxi, Mississippi 39531
Phone: (228) 388-6151
Fax: (228) 388-5848
Coach: Marc Potvin

Mobile Mysticks
P.O. Box 263
Mobile, Alabama 36601-0263
Phone: (334) 208-7825
Fax: (334) 434-7931
Coach: Jeff Pyle

New Orleans Brass
Municipal Auditorum
1201 St. Peter Street, Suite 200
New Orleans, Louisiana 70116
Phone: (504) 522-7825
Fax: (504) 523-7295
Coach: Ted Sator

Pee Dee Pride
One Civic Center Plaza
3300 West Radio Drive
Florence, South Carolina 29501
Phone (843) 669-7825
Fax: (843) 669-7149
Coach: Frank Anzalone

Pensacola Ice Pilots
East Gregory Street-Rear
Pensacola, Florida 32501-4956
Phone: (850) 432-7825
Fax: (850) 432-1929
Coach: Al Pederson

Peoria Rivermen
201 SW Jefferson
Peoria, Illinois 61602
Phone: (309) 676-1040
Fax: (309) 676-2488
Coach: Don Granato

Richmond Renegades
601 East Leigh Street
Richmond, Virgina 23219
Phone: (804) 643-7865
Fax: (804) 649-0651
Coach: Mark Kaufman

Roanoke Express
4502 Starkey Rd. SW Suite 208
Roanoke, Virginia 24014
Phone: (540) 989-4625
Fax: (540) 989-8681
Coach: Scott Gordon

South Carolina Stingrays
3107 Firestone Road
North Charleston, SC 29418
Phone: (843) 744-2248
Fax: (843) 744-2898
Coach: Rick Adduono

Tallahassee Tiger Sharks
505 W. Pensacola St. Suite B
Tallahassee, Florida 32301
Phone (850) 224-4625
Phone: (850) 224-6300
Coach: Terry Christensen

Toledo Storm
One Main Street
Toledo, Ohio 43605
Phone: (419) 691-0200
Fax: (419) 698-8998
Coach: Todd Gordon

Trenton Titans
P.O. Box 4570
Trenton, New Jersey 08811
Phone: (609) 599-9500
Fax: (609) 599-3600
Coach: Bruce Cassidy

Wheeling Nailers
1144 Market Street, Suite 202
Wheeling, WV 26003
Phone: (304) 234-4625
Fax: (304) 233-4846
Coach: Murray Eaves

United Hockey League

1998-99 Final Standings

CENTRAL	GP	W	L	SOL	PTS	PCT	GF	GA	PIM
Muskegon	74	50	18	6	106	.716	304	208	1670
Port Huron	74	41	26	7	89	.601	261	239	1441
Flint	74	37	32	5	79	.534	318	299	1872
Saginaw	74	20	46	8	48	.324	212	332	1325
EASTERN									
Binghamton	74	39	30	5	83	.561	280	238	1499
Asheville	74	36	35	3	75	.507	292	331	1761
Winston-Salem	74	31	40	3	65	.439	245	311	1837
Mohawk Valley	74	27	39	8	62	.419	214	300	1811
WESTERN									
Quad City	74	50	19	5	105	.709	364	253	2514
Thunder Bay	74	47	20	7	101	.682	325	247	1922
Madison	74	29	40	5	63	.426	237	294	1496

ATTENDANCE REPORT

TEAM	TOTAL	OPENINGS	AVERAGE
Quad City	311,468	37	8,418
Muskegon	134,619	37	3,638
Asheville	124,429	37	3,362
Binghamton	113,717	37	3,073
Flint	112,393	37	3,037
Port Huron	97,386	37	2,632
Saginaw	87,118	37	2,354
Mohawk Valley	82,269	37	2,223
Thunder Bay	80,538	37	2,176
Winston-Salem	72,136	37	1,949
Madison	70,159	37	1,896
LEAGUE (98-99)	1,286,232	407	3,160
LEAGUE (97-98)	1,129,921	370	3,054

LEADING SCORERS

POINTS	TEAM	GP	G	A	PTS
Firth, Jason	TBY	73	50	91	141
Strachan, Wayne	TBY	72	57	71	128
Wilson, Ross	FLT	74	43	66	109
Sakic, Brian	FLT	71	36	72	108
Polillo, Paul	PH	73	28	79	107
Kharin, Sergei	MUS	70	37	63	100
Vallis, Lindsay	ASH	66	27	73	100
Stewart, Glenn	QCY	56	50	49	99
Glover, Jason	FLT	66	48	48	96
Blackned, Brant	TBY	70	41	55	96
Ulrich, Shawn	ASH	67	39	57	96
Delmonte, Dion	MAD	72	40	53	93
Melas, Mike	QCY	67	40	52	92
Willett, Paul	MUS	62	24	68	92
Deev, Alexei	W-S	74	35	49	84
Azar, Jeff	W-S	71	38	45	83
Bouchard, Robin	MUS	70	48	34	82
Pajor, Greg	BNG	74	40	42	82
Beauregard, David	FLT	69	52	29	81
Burfoot, Scott	QCY	58	18	61	79

GOALS	TEAM	GP	G
Strachan, Wayne	TBY	72	57
Beauregard, David	FLT	69	52
Stewart, Glenn	QCY	56	50
Firth, Jason	TBY	73	50
Several Players Tied at			48

ASSISTS	TEAM	GP	A
Firth, Jason	TBY	73	91
Polillo, Paul	PH	73	79
Vallis, Lindsay	ASH	66	73
Sakic, Brian	FLT	71	72
Strachan, Wayne	TBY	72	71

PENALTY MINUTES	TEAM	GP	PIM
Vandermeer, Pete	BNG	62	390
Holliday, Kevin	TBY	41	352
Gulash, Garry	QCY	56	342
Henderson, Michael	TBY	57	287
Schultz, Kris	ASH	70	281

SHOTS	TEAM	SHOTS
Wilson, Ross	FLT	334
Bouchard, Robin	MUS	329
Grenville, Chris	BNG	322
Strachan, Wayne	TBY	308
Glover, Jason	FLT	297

SHOOTING PERCENTAGE	TEAM	GOALS	SHOTS	PCT
Kharin, Sergei	MUS	37	142	0.261
Sakic, Brian	FLT	36	139	0.259
Firth, Jason	TBY	50	226	0.221
Purdon, Neal	TBY	32	152	0.211
Beauregard, David	FLT	52	251	0.207

GAME WINNING GOALS	TEAM	GWG
Bouchard, Robin	MUS	11
Grenville, Chris	BNG	10
Polillo, Paul	PH	7
Vallis, Lindsay	ASH	7
Several Players Tied at		6

PLUS-MINUS	TEAM	+/-
LaFleur, Brian	QCY	63
Mayes, David	TBY	60
Strachan, Wayne	TBY	56
Firth, Jason	TBY	54
Gulash, Garry	QCY	51

LEADING GOALTENDERS
(Based on 1470 or more minutes)

	TEAM	GPI	MIN	AVG	W	L	SOL	SOW	EN	SHO	SOG	SOA	GA	SAVES	SPCT
Dimaline, Joe	MUS	44	2412:20	2.36	29	9	4	4	5	4	11	40	95	1075	0.919
Hillebrandt, Jon	PH	34	1868:28	2.89	18	12	1	3	4	4	3	16	90	945	0.913
Sundstrom, Olie	BNG	52	2845:21	2.97	30	16	3	6	3	2	12	53	141	1254	0.899
Kochan, Dieter	BNG	40	2321:30	2.97	18	16	5	2	1	2	10	43	115	1125	0.907
Khlopotnov, Denis	MUS	37	1950:09	3.02	21	8	2	6	0	1	11	43	98	803	0.891
Rivard, J.F.	TBY	55	3159:00	3.10	34	14	6	3	2	2	13	43	163	1588	0.907
Fillion, Martin	QCY	38	2027:45	3.37	21	8	3	3	1	1	11	27	114	1031	0.900
Caley, Ryan	W-S	37	1973:09	3.41	14	14	4	3	2	0	6	28	112	1018	0.901
Ford, Chad	MV	29	1483:46	3.52	19	8	1	3	1	1	5	30	87	725	0.893
Fletcher, David	MAD	36	2000:33	3.54	13	16	3	4	4	2	11	35	118	938	0.888
Charbonneau, Patrick	MV	54	2881:28	3.60	19	26	5	4	7	2	16	45	173	1678	0.907
Laurie, Rob	FLT	66	3749:54	3.82	35	27	4	2	3	1	6	20	239	1895	0.888
Delorme, Marc	W-S	60	3411:24	3.94	22	32	5	8	1	2	24	75	224	1726	0.885
Gilmour, Darryl	MAD	43	2423:56	4.06	16	24	2	2	3	1	6	19	164	1194	0.879
Laviolette, Danny	ASH	44	2433:38	4.19	23	17	2	3	5	0	9	26	170	1310	0.885
Kreft, Brian	SAG	36	1978:27	4.22	11	20	1	2	4	1	4	11	139	971	0.875
Schill, Lee	ASH	34	1919:24	4.38	13	16	1	1	4	0	2	8	140	1103	0.887
Karunakar, Avi	SAG	28	1516:18	4.59	7	17	3	1	2	1	8	17	116	874	0.883

WINS	TEAM	WINS
Laurie, Rob	FLT	35
Rivard, J.F.	TBY	34
Sundstrom, Olie	BNG	30
Dimaline, Joe	MUS	29
Laviolette, Danny	ASH	23

LOSSES	TEAM	LOSSES
Delorme, Marc	W-S	32
Laurie, Rob	FLT	27
Charbonneau, Patrick	MV	26
Gilmour, Darryl	MAD	24
Kreft, Brian	SAG	20

MINUTES	TEAM	MIN
Laurie, Rob	FLT	3749
Delorme, Marc	W-S	3411
Rivard, J.F.	TBY	3159
Charbonneau, Patrick	MV	2881
Sundstrom, Olie	BNG	2845

SHUTOUTS	TEAM	SHUTOUTS
Hillebrandt, Jon	PH	4
Dimaline, Joe	MUS	4
Several Players Tied at		2

Division Semifinals

Flint vs. Binghamton
Flint wins series 4 games to 1

Quad City vs. Asheville
Quad City wins series 4 games to 0

Port Huron vs. Thunder Bay
Thunder Bay wins series 4 games to 3

Muskegon vs. Winston-Salem
Muskegon wins series 4 games to 1

Division Finals

Flint vs. Muskegon
Muskegon wins series 4 games to 3

Quad City vs. Thunder Bay
Quad City wins series 4 games to 2

Colonial Cup Finals

Quad City vs Muskegon
Muskegon wins series 4 games to 2

LEADING SCORERS

POINTS	TEAM	GP	G	A	PTS
Willett, Paul	MUS	18	11	15	26
Kharin, Sergei	MUS	18	7	17	24
Bouchard, Robin	MUS	18	13	9	22
Firth, Jason	TBY	13	6	13	19
Sakic, Brian	FLT	12	4	15	19
Vary, John	MUS	17	6	12	18
Stewart, Glenn	QCY	16	10	7	17
Grills, Chad	MUS	18	5	11	16
Proulx, Hugo	QCY	16	3	13	16
Burfoot, Scott	QCY	16	4	11	15
Gibson, Steve	QCY	14	8	6	14
Wilson, Ross	FLT	12	11	2	13
Afinogenov, Denis	MUS	17	7	6	13
Blackned, Brant	TBY	13	5	8	13
Strachan, Wayne	TBY	13	6	6	12
Podrezov, Vadim	MUS	18	3	9	12
Gaffney, Mike	QCY	10	2	10	12
Kerr, Kevin	QCY	16	5	6	11
Petrunin, Andrei	MUS	13	3	8	11
Rosenblatt, Howie	QCY	10	3	7	10

GOALS	TEAM	GP	G
Bouchard, Robin	MUS	18	13
Wilson, Ross	FLT	12	11
Willett, Paul	MUS	18	11
Stewart, Glenn	QCY	16	10
Gibson, Steve	QCY	14	8

ASSISTS	TEAM	GP	A
Kharin, Sergei	MUS	18	17
Sakic, Brian	FLT	12	15
Willett, Paul	MUS	18	15
Firth, Jason	TBY	13	13
Proulx, Hugo	QCY	16	13

PENALTY MINUTES	TEAM	GP	PIM
Henderson, Michael	TBY	12	65
Neil, Chris	MUS	18	61
Banika, Cory	MUS	15	58
Gulash, Garry	QCY	16	53
Knauft, Lorne	FLT	10	50

GAME WINNING GOALS	TEAM	GWG
Wilson, Ross	FLT	3
Stewart, Glenn	QCY	3
Several Players Tied at		2

PLUS-MINUS	TEAM	+/-
Sakic, Brian	FLT	10
Firth, Jason	TBY	8
Strachan, Wayne	TBY	8
Afinogenov, Denis	MUS	8
Several Players Tied at		7

LEADING GOALTENDERS

(Based on 120 or more minutes)

	TEAM	GPI	MIN	AVG	W	L	EN	SO	SOG	SOA	GA	SAVES	SPCT
Rivard, J.F.	TBY	13	849:17	2.12	6	7	0	1	0	0	30	437	0.936
Hillebrandt, Jon	PH	7	437:51	2.19	3	4	0	1	0	0	16	187	0.921
Zvyagin, Sergei	QCY	14	847:03	2.27	9	5	0	2	0	0	32	374	0.921
Fillion, Martin	QCY	3	163:35	2.57	1	1	1	0	0	0	7	79	0.919
Kochan, Dieter	BNG	4	207:35	2.60	1	2	2	0	0	0	9	94	0.913
Dimaline, Joe	MUS	16	920:58	2.74	11	5	0	2	0	0	42	407	0.906
McIntyre, Dan	FLT	6	325:09	2.77	3	2	0	1	0	0	15	143	0.905
Khlopotnov, Denis	MUS	4	165:34	3.26	1	1	1	0	0	0	9	45	0.833
Laurie, Rob	FLT	9	397:28	3.77	4	3	0	0	0	0	25	220	0.898
Delorme, Marc	W-S	4	246:43	4.86	1	3	0	0	0	0	20	161	0.890

WINS	TEAM	WINS
Dimaline, Joe	MUS	11
Zvyagin, Sergei	QCY	9
Rivard, J.F.	TBY	6
Laurie, Rob	FLT	4
Several Players Tied at		3

LOSSES	TEAM	LOSSES
Dimaline, Joe	MUS	5
Rivard, J.F.	TBY	4
Zvyagin, Sergei	QCY	4
Hillebrandt, Jon	PH	3
Laurie, Rob	FLT	3

MINUTES	TEAM	MIN
Dimaline, Joe	MUS	920
Rivard, J.F.	TBY	849
Zvyagin, Sergei	QCY	847
Hillebrandt, Jon	PH	437
Laurie, Rob	FLT	397

SHUTOUTS	TEAM	SHUTOUTS
Dimaline, Joe	MUS	2
Zvyagin, Sergei	QCY	2
Hillebrandt, Jon	PH	1
Rivard, J.F.	TBY	1
McIntyre, Dan	FLT	1

UHL Regular Season Awards

First Team	Position	Second Team
Joe Dimaline, Muskegon	Goaltender	J.F. Rivard, Thunder Bay
Stephan Brochu, Flint	Defenseman	John Vary, Muskegon
Brian LaFleur, Quad City	Defenseman	Vadim Podrezov, Muskegon
Jason Firth, Thunder Bay	Center	Brian Sakic, Flint
Wayne Strachan, Thunder Bay	Right Wing	Ross Wilson, Flint
Glenn Stewart, Quad City	Left Wing	Sergei Kharin, Muskegon

MVP	Jason Firth, Thunder Bay
Defenseman	Stephan Brochu, Flint
Sportmanship	Brian Sakic, Flint
Rookie	Mike Melas, Quad City
Goalie	Joe Dimaline, Muskegon
Best Defensive Forward	Paul Willett, Muskegon
Coach	Rich Kromm, Muskegon
Colonial Cup (CoHL Champions)	Muskegon Fury
Playoff MVP	Sergei Kharin, Muskegon

United Hockey League
1301 Edgewater Point Suite 301
Lake St. Louis, Missouri 63367
Phone: (314) 625-6011
Fax: (314) 625-2009

Adirondack IceHawks
1 Civic Center Plaza
Glens Falls, New York 12801
Phone: (518) 926-7825
Fax: (518) 761-9112
Coach: Robbie Nichols

Asheville Smoke
87 Haywood Street
Asheville, North Carolina 28801
Phone (828) 252-7825
Fax: (828) 252-8756
Coach: Keith Gretzky

B.C. Icemen
One Stuart Street
Binghamton, New York 13901
Phone: (607) 772-9300
Fax: (607) 772-0707
Coach: Brad Jones

Flint Generals
3501 Lapeer Road
Flint, Michigan 48503
Phone: (810) 742-9422
Fax: (810) 742-5892
Coach: Doug Shedden

Fort Wayne Komets
1010 Memorial Way, Suite 100
Fort Wayne, Indiana 46805
Phone: (219) 483-0011
Phone: (219) 483-3899
Coach: Dave Allison

Knoxville Speed
500 East Church Street
Knoxville, Tennessee 37915
Phone: (423) 521-9991
Fax: (423) 524-2639
Coach: Terry Ruskowski

Madison Kodiaks
1881 Expo Mall East
Madison, Wisconsin 53713
Phone: (608) 251-2884
Fax: (608) 251-2923
Coach: Kent Hawley

Missouri River Otters
324 Main Street
St. Charles, Missouri 63301
Phone: (314) 946-0003
Fax: (314) 946-3844
Coach: Mark Reeds

Mohawk Valley Prowlers
400 West Oriskany Street
Utica, New York 13502
Phone: (315) 733-0100
Fax: (315) 733-8154
Coach: Shawn Evans

Muskegon Fury
470 West Michigan Avenue
Muskegon, Michigan 49440
Phone: (616) 726-3879
Fax: (616) 728-0428
Coach: Rich Kromm

Port Huron Border Cats
215 Huron Avenue
Port Huron, Michigan 48060
Phone: (810) 982-2287
Fax: (810) 982-9838
Coach: Greg Puhalski

Quad City Mallards
1509 3rd Avenue A
Moline, Illinois 61265
Phone: (309) 764-7825
Fax: (309) 764-7858
Coach: Matt Shaw

Rockford IceHogs
P.O. Box 5984
Rockford, Illinois 61125-0984
Phone: (815) 986-6465
Fax: (815) 963-0974
Coach:TBA

Saginaw Gears
310 Johnson Street, Suite 105
Saginaw, Michigan 48607
Phone: (517) 753-4801
Fax: (517) 753-4907
Coach: Robert Dirk

West Coast Hockey League

1998-99 Final Standings

NORTHERN	GP	W	L	OTL	PTS	PCT	GF	GA	PIM
Tacoma	70	44	18	8	96	.686	278	234	1627
Anchorage	71	46	22	3	95	.669	332	260	1759
Colorado	71	32	33	6	70	.493	270	288	2233
Idaho	71	31	34	6	68	.479	265	298	2027
SOUTHERN									
San Diego	71	45	19	7	97	.683	342	242	2746
Fresno	70	35	31	4	74	.529	257	296	2172
Phoenix	71	32	33	6	70	.493	260	284	1932
Bakersfield	70	21	40	9	51	.364	213	308	2010
*Tucson	21	7	11	3	17	.405	83	90	650

* Disbanded after 21 games

ATTENDANCE REPORT

TEAM	TOTAL	OPENINGS	AVERAGE
San Diego	228,135	35	6,518
Anchorage	180,350	35	5,152
Idaho	171,734	35	4,906
Tacoma	170,745	35	4,878
Bakersfield	161,785	35	4,622
Colorado	106,598	35	3,045
Fresno	89,893	35	2,568
Phoenix	83,986	35	2,399
Tucson	17,916	13	1,378
LEAGUE (98-99)	1,211,142	293	4,134
LEAGUE (97-98)	1,051,234	287	3,663

LEADING SCORERS

POINTS	TEAM	GP	G	A	PTS
Street, Keith	ANC	71	47	88	135
Corbin, Yvan	ANC	71	60	63	123
Larson, Dean	ANC	68	43	74	117
Lyons, Craig	COL	68	42	73	115
Belanger, Hugo	PHX	61	51	61	112
Ingraham, Cal	IDH	71	50	60	110
Taylor, Mike	SD	75	42	63	105
Enga, Richard (R.J.)	COL	71	38	64	102
Rowe, Sean	ANC	66	32	64	96
Reeves, Kyle	SD	69	59	31	90
Dowhy, Steve	BAK	67	33	55	88
Hachborn, Len	SD	49	23	64	87
Williams, Paul	ANC	66	31	55	86
Perry, Tom	COL	64	33	51	84
McCarthy, Doug	PHX	70	27	56	83
MacPherson, B.J.	SD	61	37	43	80
St. Jacques, Kevin	SD	56	32	45	77
Penney, Chad	COL	67	31	46	77
Maier, Kim	TAC	49	34	42	76
Lovell, Tim	TAC	54	33	43	76

GOALS	TEAM	GP	G
Corbin, Yvan	ANC	71	60
Reeves, Kyle	SD	69	59
Belanger, Hugo	PHX	61	51
Ingraham, Cal	IDH	71	50
Street, Keith	ANC	71	47

ASSISTS	TEAM	GP	A
Street, Keith	ANC	71	88
Larson, Dean	ANC	68	74
Lyons, Craig	COL	68	73
Several Players Tied at			64

PENALTY MINUTES	TEAM	GP	PIM
Wagner, Chad	SD	43	521
Simon, Jason	COL	60	419
Richard, Chad	TAC	42	347
Brookbank, Wade	ANC	56	337
Mailhot, Jacques	FRE	50	289

SHOTS	TEAM	SHOTS
Street, Keith	ANC	356
Lyons, Craig	COL	352
Reeves, Kyle	SD	314
Corbin, Yvan	ANC	310
Taylor, Mike	SD	296

SHOOTING PERCENTAGE	TEAM	GOALS	SHOTS	PCT
Gulutzan, Glen	FRE	32	116	0.276
Brar, Dampy	TAC	33	151	0.219
Ingraham, Cal	IDH	50	234	0.214
Belanger, Hugo	PHX	51	244	0.209
Cunningham, Bob	ANC	29	140	0.207

GAME WINNING GOALS	TEAM	GWG
Street, Keith	ANC	8
Corbin, Yvan	ANC	8
Belanger, Hugo	PHX	8
MacPherson, B.J.	SD	7
Stitt, Mark	SD	7

PLUS-MINUS	TEAM	+/-
Perkins, Darren	SD	39
Corbin, Yvan	ANC	37
MacPherson, B.J.	SD	37
Rowe, Sean	ANC	34
Stitt, Mark	SD	31

LEADING GOALTENDERS
(Based on 1290 or more minutes)

	TEAM	GPI	MIN	AVG	W	L	OTL	EN	SO	GA	SAVES	SPCT
Allison, Blair	TAC	48	2592:18	2.66	33	5	5	1	2	115	1053	0.902
Naumov, Sergei	SD	42	2382:13	3.15	27	11	3	2	3	125	1073	0.896
Tkachenko, Sergei	ANC	56	3106:23	3.36	35	15	2	1	2	174	1510	0.897
Vezina, Steve	COL	27	1545:11	3.46	11	11	4	3	1	89	781	0.898
Beaubien, Frederick	IDH	45	2531:56	3.72	22	18	3	6	0	157	1246	0.888
Goverde, David	PHX	58	3378:24	3.75	26	25	6	2	2	211	1690	0.889
McMullen, Bryan	COL	43	2207:34	3.83	16	16	5	2	0	141	1033	0.880
Ferguson, Jeff	FRE	59	3336:44	4.06	31	24	3	2	1	226	1716	0.884
Guzda, Brad	BAK	45	2496:48	4.49	11	28	4	5	1	187	1423	0.884

WINS	TEAM	WINS
Tkachenko, Sergei	ANC	35
Allison, Blair	TAC	33
Ferguson, Jeff	FRE	31
Naumov, Sergei	SD	27
Goverde, David	PHX	26

LOSSES	TEAM	LOSSES
Guzda, Brad	BAK	28
Goverde, David	PHX	25
Ferguson, Jeff	FRE	24
Beaubien, Frederick	IDH	18
McMullen, Bryan	COL	16

MINUTES	TEAM	MIN
Goverde, David	PHX	3378
Ferguson, Jeff	FRE	3336
Tkachenko, Sergei	ANC	3106
Allison, Blair	TAC	2592
Beaubien, Frederick	IDH	2531

SHUTOUTS	TEAM	SHUTOUTS
Naumov, Sergei	SD	3
Allison, Blair	TAC	2
Tkachenko, Sergei	ANC	2
Goverde, David	PHX	2
Several Players Tied at		1

Division Semifinals

San Diego vs. Bakersfield
San Diego wins series 2 games to 0

Tacoma vs. Idaho
Tacoma wins series 2 games to 0

Phoenix vs. Fresno
Fresno wins series 2 games to 1

Anchorage vs. Colorado
Anchorage wins series 2 games to 1

Division Finals

San Diego vs. Fresno
San Diego wins series 3 games to 1

Anchorage vs. Tacoma
Tacoma wins series 3 games to 0

Taylor Cup Finals

Tacoma vs San Diego
Tacoma wins series 4 games to 2

LEADING SCORERS

POINTS	TEAM	GP	G	A	PTS
Smyth, Kevin	TAC	11	7	13	20
Reeves, Kyle	SD	12	9	8	17
Hachborn, Len	SD	12	4	12	16
Maier, Kim	TAC	11	10	5	15
Boston, Scott	TAC	11	5	10	15
Drevitch, Scott	TAC	11	4	11	15
Larson, Brett	SD	12	7	7	14
Roenick, Trevor	TAC	11	6	8	14
Stitt, Mark	SD	12	4	10	14
Alexeev, Alex	TAC	10	1	12	13
Taylor, Mike	SD	12	4	8	12
St. Jacques, Kevin	SD	12	6	5	11
Marek, Petr	SD	12	5	5	10
Moore, Blaine	FRE	7	4	6	10
MacPherson, B.J.	SD	12	5	4	9
Brar, Dampy	TAC	11	5	4	9
St. Amour, Martin	SD	12	2	7	9
Enga, Richard (R.J.)	COL	3	5	3	8
Lovell, Tim	TAC	5	2	6	8
Jobin, Frederick	SD	11	1	7	8

GOALS	TEAM	GP	G
Maier, Kim	TAC	11	10
Reeves, Kyle	SD	12	9
Larson, Brett	SD	12	7
Smyth, Kevin	TAC	11	7
Several Players Tied at			6

ASSISTS	TEAM	GP	A
Smyth, Kevin	TAC	11	13
Hachborn, Len	SD	12	12
Alexeev, Alex	TAC	10	12
Drevitch, Scott	TAC	11	11
Several Players Tied at			10

PENALTY MINUTES	TEAM	GP	PIM
Taylor, Mike	SD	12	49
Brookbank, Wade	ANC	5	47
Jobin, Frederick	SD	11	47
Roenick, Trevor	TAC	11	44
Wilcox, George	ANC	6	41

SHOTS	TEAM	SHOTS
Maier, Kim	TAC	64
Reeves, Kyle	SD	53
Smyth, Kevin	TAC	45
Wilkie, Bob	FRE	38
Drevitch, Scott	TAC	37

SHOOTING PERCENTAGE	TEAM	GOALS	SHOTS	PCT
Enga, Richard (R.J.)	COL	5	17	0.294
St. Jacques, Kevin	SD	6	21	0.286
Gulutzan, Glen	FRE	4	15	0.267
Whyte, Sean	PHX	2	8	0.250
Mathers, Mike	FRE	2	8	0.250

GAME WINNING GOALS	TEAM	GWG
Boston, Scott	TAC	2
Smyth, Kevin	TAC	2
Several Players Tied at		1

PLUS-MINUS	TEAM	+/-
Boston, Scott	TAC	11
Alexeev, Alex	TAC	9
Marek, Petr	SD	8
Stitt, Mark	SD	8
Maier, Kim	TAC	7

LEADING GOALTENDERS
(Based on 90 or more minutes)

	TEAM	GPI	MIN	AVG	W	L	EN	SO	GA	SAVES	SPCT
Allison, Blair	TAC	11	671:36	2.05	9	2	1	2	23	298	0.928
Couture, Patrick	SD	4	148:47	2.82	2	1	0	0	7	81	0.920
Naumov, Sergei	SD	10	582:40	3.40	5	4	1	0	33	245	0.881
Vezina, Steve	COL	3	182:40	3.61	1	2	1	0	11	82	0.882
Goverde, David	PHX	3	178:57	3.69	1	2	0	0	11	124	0.919
Teskey, Doug	ANC	4	186:46	3.86	2	1	0	0	12	106	0.898
Ferguson, Jeff	FRE	7	417:35	3.88	3	4	2	0	27	212	0.887
Tkachenko, Sergei	ANC	4	174:43	5.84	0	3	1	0	17	60	0.779
Guzda, Brad	BAK	2	120:00	7.00	0	2	0	0	14	62	0.816

WINS	TEAM	WINS
Allison, Blair	TAC	9
Naumov, Sergei	SD	5
Ferguson, Jeff	FRE	3
Teskey, Doug	ANC	2
Couture, Patrick	SD	2

LOSSES	TEAM	LOSSES
Ferguson, Jeff	FRE	4
Tkachenko, Sergei	ANC	3
Naumov, Sergei	SD	3
Several Players Tied at		2

MINUTES	TEAM	MIN
Allison, Blair	TAC	671
Naumov, Sergei	SD	582
Ferguson, Jeff	FRE	417
Teskey, Doug	ANC	186
Vezina, Steve	COL	182

SHUTOUTS	TEAM	SHUTOUTS
Allison, Blair	TAC	2
Several Players Tied at		0

WCHL Awards

First Team	Position	Second Team
Blair Allison, Tacoma	Goaltender	David Goverde, Phoenix
Darren Perkins, San Diego	Defenseman	Jeff Sirkka, Colorado
Scott Drevitch, Tacoma	Defenseman	Scott Boston, Tacoma
Keith Street, Anchorage	Center	Len Hachborn, Phoenix
Hugo Belanger, Phoenix	Left Wing	Yvan Corbin, Anchorage
Kyle Reeves, San Diego	Right Wing	Craig Lyons, Colorado

MVP	Hugo Belanger, Phoenix
Defenseman	Scott Drevitch, Tacoma
Goalie	Blair Allison, Tacoma
Rookie	Tim Lovell, Tacoma
Coach	John Olver, Tacoma
Taylor Cup (WCHL Champions)	Tacoma Sabercats
Playoff MVP	Blair Allison, Tacoma

West Coast Hockey League
805 West Idaho Street, Suite 304
Boise, Idaho 83702
Phone: (208) 367-1400
Fax: (208) 367-1500

Anchorage Aces
245 West 5th Avenue, Suite 128
Anchorage, Alaska 99501
Phone: (907) 258-2237
Fax: (907) 278-4297
Coach: Bob Wilkie

Bakersfield Condors
P.O. Box 1806
Bakersfield, California 93303
Phone: (805) 324-7825
Fax: (805) 324-6929
Coach: Kevin MacDonald

Colorado Gold Kings
Colorado Springs World Arena
3185 Venelucci Boulevard
Colorado Springs, Colorado 80906
Phone (719) 579-9000
Fax: (719) 579-7609
Coach: Kirk Tomlinson

Fresno Falcons
P.O. Box 232, Suite 150
Fresno, California 93704
Phone: (559) 650-4000
Fax: (559) 497-6077
Coach: Blaine Moore

Idaho Steelheads
251 South Capitol Boulevard
Boise, Idaho 837202
Phone: (208) 383-0080
Fax: (208) 383-0194
Coach: Clint Malarchuk

Phoenix Mustangs
1826 West McDowell Road
Phoenix, Arizona 85007
Phone: (602) 340-0001
Fax: (602) 251-0528
Coach: Brad McCaughey

San Diego Gulls
3500 Sports Arena Blvd.
San Diego, California 92110
Phone: (619) 224-4625
Fax: (619) 224-3010
Coach: Steve Martinson

Tacoma Sabrecats
1111 Fawcett Avenue Suite 204
Tacoma, WA 98402
Phone: (253) 627-2673
Fax: (253) 573-1009
Coach: John Olver

Cal Ingraham scored 110 points in his first WCHL season

Photo by Kelly Virtanen

Western Professional Hockey League

1998-99 Final Standings

CENTRAL	GP	W	L	OTL	PTS	PCT	GF	GA	PIM
Waco	69	40	22	7	87	.630	275	232	1898
Corpus Christi	69	40	23	6	86	.623	253	210	2242
Central Texas	69	33	24	12	78	.565	286	266	2282
Fort Worth	69	34	26	9	77	.558	227	235	1862
Austin*	69	26	33	10	54	.391	211	287	2062
EASTERN									
Shreveport	69	47	17	5	99	.717	315	234	1751
Lake Charles	69	40	25	4	84	.609	275	232	1697
Monroe	69	37	26	6	80	.580	252	248	1218
Arkansas	69	37	27	5	79	.572	272	247	2131
Alexandria	69	25	30	14	64	.464	264	310	1750
Tupelo	69	20	45	4	44	.319	195	316	1549
WESTERN									
Abilene	69	43	23	3	89	.645	261	230	1739
San Angelo	69	39	25	5	83	.601	284	253	1661
El Paso	69	36	27	6	78	.565	246	231	1775
Odessa	69	35	29	5	75	.543	233	221	1351
Amarillo	69	31	30	8	70	.507	246	271	1588
New Mexico	69	27	34	8	62	.449	245	293	1811
Kristall Elek.	8	3	4	1	7	.438	23	35	116
Traktor Chelyab.	9	2	6	1	5	.278	26	38	88

*-Penalized 8 points by WPHL

ATTENDANCE REPORT

TEAM	YESTERDAY	TOTAL	OPENINGS	AVERAGE
Shreveport		171,878	35	4,910
Austin		176,748	36	4,909
New Mexico		152,503	35	4,357
Arkansas		148,283	35	4,236
El Paso		145,750	35	4,164
San Angelo		143,960	35	4,113
Lake Charles		142,612	35	4,074
Odessa		137,250	35	3,921
Abilene		115,777	35	3,307
Corpus Christi		115,560	35	3,301
Amarillo		112,503	35	3,214
Alexandria		100,814	35	2,880
Tupelo		97,128	35	2,775
Central Texas		90,133	35	2,575
Monroe		88,744	35	2,535
Fort Worth		85,895	35	2,454
Waco		74,825	35	2,137
LEAGUE (98-99)		2,100,363	596	3,524
LEAGUE (97-98)		1,651,990	420	3,933

WESTERN PROFESSIONAL HOCKEY LEAGUE LEADING SCORERS

Through Games of 07/01/1999

POINTS	TEAM	GP	G	A	PTS
Boudreau, Carl	SAN	68	33	85	118
Findlay, Tim	ARK	69	45	64	109
Robertson, Chris	CRP	64	42	67	109
Boni, Josh	MON	65	38	68	106
Brooks, Chris	AMA	61	48	57	105
Pawluk, Ryan	ARK	69	43	58	101
Tallaire, Gerald	CTX	66	43	57	100
Harris, Ross	SAN	69	41	56	97
Poulin, Charles	ABL	58	41	55	96
Whidden, Jarret	ARK	69	41	55	96
Dougan, Darren	CTX	69	28	66	94
Blouin, Jean	SAN	57	47	44	91
Trew, Bill	ELP	69	44	47	91
Petruic, Jeff	ALX	68	46	44	90
Vecchiarelli, John	SHR	55	43	46	89
Anneck, Dorian	MON	69	44	41	85
Lund, Bill	LKC	68	36	49	85
Weichselbaumer, Eric	ALX	69	45	39	84
MacPherson, Forbes	SHR	67	32	52	84
Holmes, Randy	WAC	69	33	50	83

GAME WINNING GOALS	TEAM	GWG
Cimellaro, Tony	WAC	10
Trew, Bill	ELP	10
Anneck, Dorian	MON	10
Several Players Tied at		9

GOALS	TEAM	GP	G
Brooks, Chris	AMA	61	48
Blouin, Jean	SAN	57	47
Petruic, Jeff	ALX	68	46
Findlay, Tim	ARK	69	45
Weichselbaumer, Eric	ALX	69	45

ASSISTS	TEAM	GP	A
Boudreau, Carl	SAN	68	85
Boni, Josh	MON	65	68
Robertson, Chris	CRP	64	67
Dougan, Darren	CTX	69	66
Findlay, Tim	ARK	69	64

PENALTY MINUTES	TEAM	GP	PIM
Oliver, David	CTX	67	357
Bland, Keith	CTX	57	333
St. Louis, Todd	ARK	67	331
Jesiolowski, Dave	ALX	59	329
Domonsky, Brad	WAC	56	314

PLUS-MINUS	TEAM	+/-
Whidden, Jarret	ARK	50
Findlay, Tim	ARK	50
Pawluk, Ryan	ARK	48
Sprott, Jim	SHR	42
Haddock, Robert	ELP	37

LEADING GOALTENDERS
(Based on 1230 or more minutes)

	TEAM	GPI	MIN	AVG	W	L	OTL	EN	SO	GA	SAVES	SPCT
Genik, Jason	CRP	29	1682:52	2.10	21	5	2	2	4	59	750	0.927
Cooper, Kory	WAC	59	3231:46	2.77	36	14	4	7	4	149	1512	0.910
Tornquist, Michael	ODE	27	1572:00	3.05	15	7	3	1	1	80	891	0.918
Gordon, Chris	ELP	45	2561:08	3.07	23	18	3	4	4	131	1059	0.890
Plouffe, Steve	FTW	52	2978:41	3.08	27	17	6	3	2	153	1529	0.909
Martino, Tony	ABL	52	3064:39	3.11	33	17	1	2	0	159	1489	0.904
Pye, Billy	ODE	45	2548:35	3.13	20	22	2	2	2	133	1172	0.898
Schoen, Bryan	LKC	61	3382:07	3.16	37	19	3	2	3	178	1652	0.903
Racicot, Andre	MON	48	2806:01	3.16	25	18	5	4	1	148	1510	0.911
Carey, Jason	CTX	45	2420:56	3.20	22	12	8	2	4	129	1257	0.907
St. Pierre, Kevin	SHR	35	1945:45	3.21	21	8	2	2	2	104	850	0.891
Barber, Scott	CRP	25	1391:54	3.23	9	11	2	6	1	75	656	0.897
Hoople, Ryan	ARK	44	2536:32	3.24	26	14	4	3	3	137	1256	0.902
Erickson, Chad	SAN	49	2841:00	3.29	31	14	3	4	0	156	1733	0.917
Hamelin, Hugo	SHR	39	2183:40	3.30	26	9	3	3	2	120	958	0.889
Lord, Adam	AMA	52	2931:19	3.54	22	18	6	2	2	173	1535	0.899
Thibert, Benoit	ALX	32	1813:15	3.61	13	9	7	0	0	109	1049	0.906
Leitza, Brian	ARK	29	1584:09	3.64	11	13	1	6	1	96	843	0.898
Pottie, Steve	NMX	30	1629:34	3.68	12	14	1	2	0	100	765	0.884
Lemanowicz, David	AUS	47	2576:23	4.05	16	22	6	0	3	174	1454	0.893

WINS	TEAM	WINS
Schoen, Bryan	LKC	37
Cooper, Kory	WAC	36
Martino, Tony	ABL	33
Erickson, Chad	SAN	31
Plouffe, Steve	FTW	27

MINUTES	TEAM	MIN
Schoen, Bryan	LKC	3382
Cooper, Kory	WAC	3231
Martino, Tony	ABL	3064
Plouffe, Steve	FTW	2978
Lord, Adam	AMA	2931

LOSSES	TEAM	LOSSES
Pye, Billy	ODE	22
Lemanowicz, David	AUS	22
Schoen, Bryan	LKC	19
Several Players Tied at		18

SHUTOUTS	TEAM	SHUTOUTS
Genik, Jason	CRP	4
Cooper, Kory	WAC	4
Gordon, Chris	ELP	4
Carey, Jason	CTX	4
Several Players Tied at		3

Preliminary

San Angelo vs. Odessa
San Angelo wins series 2-1

Lake Charles vs Central Texas
Lake Charles wins series 2-0

El Paso vs Fort Worth
Fort Worth wins series 2-1

Arkansas vs Monroe
Monroe wins series 2-1

Quarterfinals

Waco vs. San Angelo
San Angelo wins series 3 games to 1

Fort Worth vs. Abilene
Fort Worth wins series 3 games to 0

Corpus Christi vs. Lake Charles
Lake Charles wins series 3 games to 1

Shreveport vs. Monroe
Shreveport wins series 3 games to 0

Semifinals

Shreveport vs. Lake Charles
Shreveport wins series 4 games to 1

Fort Worth vs. San Angelo
San Angelo wins series 4 games to 2

President's Cup Finals

Shreveport vs San Angelo
Shreveport wins series 4 games to 0

Through Games of 07/01/1999

POINTS	TEAM	GP	G	A	PTS
Boudreau, Carl	SAN	17	7	18	25
Blouin, Jean	SAN	17	13	9	22
Vecchiarelli, John	SHR	12	10	11	21
MacKenzie, Chris	SHR	12	8	11	19
DuPaul, Cosmo	FTW	12	7	11	18
Larocque, Stephane	FTW	12	8	9	17
Harris, Ross	SAN	17	6	11	17
Miaskowski, Phil	FTW	12	8	8	16
Buchanan, Trevor	SHR	12	5	11	16
Clark, Jason	SAN	17	4	12	16
Stevenson, Shayne	SAN	13	7	8	15
Burkitt, Toby	SHR	12	4	11	15
Henry, Dale	SHR	12	7	7	14
MacPherson, Forbes	SHR	12	3	11	14
Marshall, Bobby	SAN	17	2	11	13
Black, Ryan	FTW	12	7	5	12
O'Donnell, Mark	FTW	12	5	7	12
Several Players Tied at					11

GOALS	TEAM	GP	G
Blouin, Jean	SAN	17	13
Vecchiarelli, John	SHR	12	10
Miaskowski, Phil	FTW	12	8
Larocque, Stephane	FTW	12	8
MacKenzie, Chris	SHR	12	8

ASSISTS	TEAM	GP	A
Boudreau, Carl	SAN	17	18
Clark, Jason	SAN	17	12
Several Players Tied at			11

PENALTY MINUTES	TEAM	GP	PIM
Diamond, Marty	SAN	12	63
Power, Andrew	SHR	12	58
Verot, Darcy	LKC	9	53
Stevenson, Shayne	SAN	13	51
Sprott, Jim	SHR	12	41

LEADING GOALTENDERS

(Based on 60 or more minutes)

	TEAM	GPI	MIN	AVG	W	L	EN	SO	GA	SAVES	SPCT
Galt, Scott	LKC	2	115:38	0.52	2	0	0	1	1	61	0.984
Hamelin, Hugo	SHR	4	239:53	1.75	4	0	0	0	7	135	0.951
St. Pierre, Kevin	SHR	8	478:14	2.01	7	1	0	1	16	236	0.937
Pye, Billy	ODE	3	200:08	2.70	1	2	0	0	9	110	0.924
Martino, Tony	ABL	3	188:51	3.18	0	3	0	0	10	68	0.872
Dopson, Rob	LKC	9	541:29	3.21	4	5	1	1	29	285	0.908
Plouffe, Steve	FTW	9	475:29	3.28	5	4	1	1	26	248	0.905
Racicot, Andre	MON	6	379:39	3.32	2	4	0	1	21	212	0.910
Erickson, Chad	SAN	17	1032:34	3.37	9	7	2	0	58	565	0.907
Cooper, Kory	WAC	4	251:27	3.58	1	3	0	0	15	103	0.873
Leitza, Brian	ARK	3	200:52	3.58	1	2	1	0	12	115	0.906
Laurin, Todd	FTW	5	261:03	3.91	2	1	0	0	17	135	0.888
Gordon, Chris	ELP	3	178:58	4.02	1	2	1	0	12	65	0.844
Carey, Jason	CTX	2	120:00	4.50	0	2	0	0	9	82	0.901
Genik, Jason	CRP	4	239:25	5.26	1	3	0	0	21	124	0.855

WPHL Awards

MVP	Chris Robertson, Corpus Christi
Top Defenseman	Eric Brule, Abilene
Top Goaltender	Kory Cooper, Waco
Rookie of the Year	Kory Cooper, Waco
Coach of the Year	Todd Lalonde, Waco
Man of the Year	Graeme Townshend, Lake Charles
President's Cup (WPHL Champions)	Shreveport Mudbugs
Playoff MVP	John Vecchiarelli, Shreveport

Western Professional Hockey League
14040 North Cave Creek Road, Suite #100
Phoenix, Arizona
Phone (602) 485-9399
Fax: (602) 485-9449

Abilene Aviators
1215 East South 11th Street Suite A
Abilene, Texas 79602
Phone: (915) 695-4625
Fax: (915) 695-2110
Coach: Marty Dallman

Alexandria Warthogs
5503-B, John Eskew Drive
Alexandria, Louisiana 71303
Phone: (318) 445-3927
Fax: (318) 445-3817
Coach: Mike Zruna

Amarillo Rattlers
P.O. Box 9087
Amarillo, Texas 79106
Phone: (806) 374-7825
Fax: (806) 374-7835
Coach: Ken Karpuk

Arkansas Glaciercats
2600 Howard Street
Little Rock, Arkansas 72206
Phone: (501) 374-7825
Fax: (501) 374-1225
Coach: Jim Burton

Austin Ice Bats
7311 Decker Lane
Austin, Texas 78724
Phone: (512) 927-7825
Fax: (512) 927-7828
Coach: Brent Hughes

Central Texas Stampede
600 Forest Drive
Belton, Texas 76513
Phone: (254) 933-3500
Fax: (254) 933-9490
Coach: Todd Lalonde

Corpus Christi IceRays
500 North Water Street #412
Corpus Christi, Texas 78471
Phone (512) 814-7825
Fax: (512) 980-0003
Coach: Taylor Hall

El Paso Buzzards
1035 Belvedere, Suite 200
El Paso, Texas 79912
Phone: (915) 581-6666
Fax (915) 581-6650
Coach: Todd Brost

Fort Worth Brahmas
1314 Lake Street, Suite #200
Fort Worth, Texas 76102
Phone: (817) 336-4423
Fax: (817) 336-3334
Coach: Terry Menard

Lake Charles Ice Pirates
900 Lakeshore Drive, 2nd Floor
Lake Charles, Louisiana 70602
Phone: (318) 436-0055
Fax: (318) 436-0054
Coach: Bob Loucks

Lubbock Cotton Kings
4405 Brownfield Highway
Lubbock, Texas 79407
Phone: (806) 747-7825
Fax: (806) 792-8396
Coach: Alan May

Monroe Moccasins
P.O. Box 14110
Monroe, Louisiana 71207
Phone: (318) 398-9434
Fax: (318) 398-0000
Coach: Brian Curran

New Mexico Scorpions
5111 San Mateo NE
Albuquerque, New Mexico 87109
Phone: (505) 881-7825
Fax: (505) 883-7829
Coach: Tony Martino

Odessa Jackalopes
PO Box 51187
Midland, Texas 79710
Phone: (915) 552-7825
Fax: (915) 550-6670
Coach: Joe Clark

San Angelo Outlaws
3260 Sherwood Way
San Angelo, Texas 76901
Phone: (915) 949-7825
Fax: (915) 223-0999
Coach: Mike Collins

Shreveport Mudbugs
3701 Hudson Street, 2nd Floor
Shreveport, Louisiana 71109
Phone: (318) 636-2847
Fax: (318) 636-2280
Coach: Jean Laforest

Tupelo T-Rex
375 East Main Street
Tupelo, Mississippi 38801
Phone: (601) 620-7543
Fax: (601) 620-7540
Coach: George Dupont

Waco Wizards
4601 Bosque, Blvd.
Waco, Texas 76710
Phone: (254) 741-9226
Fax: (254) 741-6208
Coach: Kevin Abrams

1999-2000 Season

The following section will contain the current divisional alignments of all the minor-pro clubs for the upcoming section. Also included will be some player transactions and incoming rookies. This list is by no means comprehensive. Information up to August 10th is included in this section.

American Hockey League

Atlantic Division
Lowell Lock Monsters
Quebec Citadelles
Saint John Flames
St. John's Maple Leafs

New England Division
Hartford Wolf Pack
Portland Pirates
Providence Bruins
Springfield Falcons
Worcester IceCats

Empire Division
Albany RiverRats
Hamilton Bulldogs
Rochester Americans
Syracuse Crunch
Wilkes-Barre/Scranton Penguins

Mid-Atlantic
Cincinnati Mighty Ducks
Hershey Bears
Kentucky Thoroughblades
Louisville Panthers
Philadelphia Phantoms

International Hockey League

Eastern Conference
Cincinnati Cyclones
Cleveland Lumberjacks
Detroit Vipers
Grand Rapids Griffins
Michigan K-Wings
Milwaukee Admirals
Orlando Solar Bears

Western Conference
Chicago Wolves
Houston Aeros
Kansas City Blades
Long Beach Ice Dogs
Manitoba Moose
Utah Grizzlies

East Coast Hockey League

Northeast Division
Charlotte Checkers
Greensboro
Hampton Roads Admirals
Richmond Renegades
Roanoke Express
Trenton Titans

Northwest Division
Dayton Bombers
Huntington Blizzard
Johnstown Chiefs
Peoria Rivermen
Toledo Storm
Wheeling Nailers

Southeast
Augusta Lynx
Florida Everblades
Greenville Grrrowl
Jacksonville Lizard Kings
Pee Dee Pride
South Carolina Stingrays
Tallahassee Tiger Sharks

Southwest Division
Arkansas RiverBlades
Baton Rouge Kingfish
Birmingham Bulls
Jackson Bandits
Louisiana IceGators
Mississippi Sea Wolves
Mobile Mysticks
New Orleans Brass
Pensacola Ice Pilots

Central Hockey League

Eastern Division
Columbus Cottonmouths
Huntsville Channel Cats
Macon Whoopee
Fayetteville Force
Memphis RiverKings

Western Division
Indianapolis Ice
Oklahoma City Blazers
San Antonio Iguanas
Topeka ScareCrows
Tulsa Oilers
Wichita Thunder

United Hockey League

Eastern Division
Adirondack IceHawks
Asheville Smoke
B.C. Icemen
Knoxville Speed
Mohawk Valley Prowlers

Central Division
Flint Generals
Fort Wayne Komets
Muskegon Fury
Port Huron Border Cats
Saginaw Gears

Western Division
Madison Kodiaks
Missouri River Otters
Rockford IceHogs
Quad City Mallards

West Coast Hockey League

Northern
Anchorage Aces
Colorado Gold Kings
Idaho Steelheads
Tacoma Sabercats

Southern
Bakersfield Condors
Fresno Falcons
Phoenix Mustangs
San Diego Gulls

Western Professional Hockey League

Eastern
Alexandria Warthogs
Arkansas GlacierCats
Lake Charles Ice Pirates
Monroe Moccasins
Shreveport Mudbugs
Tupelo T-Rex

Central
Abilene Aviators
Austin IceBats
Central Texas Stampede
Corpus Christi IceRays
Fort Worth Brahmas
Waco Wizards

Western
Amarillo Rattlers
El Paso Buzzards
Lubbock Cotton Kings
New Mexico Scorpions
Odessa Jackalopes
San Angelo Outlaws

All-Star Games

This season's All-Star slate became even more interesting that usual when the CHL and WCHL announced that they would play each other in a two-season series. The first game will take place on CHL turf this January while the rematch will take place in a WCHL venue in 2001. You can check www.inthecrease.com throughout the season for all of the latest on each of the events

League	Location	Date
American	Rochester, New York	1/17/2000
International	Chicago, Illinois	*
East Coast	Greenville, South Carolina	1/19/2000
United	Muskegon, Michigan	2/2/2000
Western Professional	Amarillo, Texas	1/15/2000
Central League vs West Coast Hockey League	Fayetteville, North Carolina	1/25/2000

* Date not set at time of publication

New Faces

Every season a new flux of talent heads into the world of minor-professional hockey. The players come from Canadian Junior Hockey, both major and "A" classes, United States colleges (Divisions 1-3), overseas and from Canadian colleges.

The following list contains players who may find their way into the minor-pros next season. Due to the many options available to each player they may or may not choose to go that route in their personal development. For example, players coming out of Canadian Major Junior could stay in their leagues for another season as an "overage" player. They could also attend a Canadian college (a popular option) or head overseas. This season players who were drafted in the 1997 NHL Entry Draft are eligible to turn pro as are players from the 1997 Entry Draft who were born in 1978. An asterik next to the player's name means that he has already seen pro action.

First Name	Last Name	Position	Last Season	League	G	A	PTS	PIM
Hugo	Boisvert	Forward	Ohio State	CCHA	24	27	51	54
Yuri	Butsayev	Forward	Togliatti	Russia	10	7	17	55
Roman	Lyashenko	Forward	Yaroslavl	Russia	10	9	19	51
Brendan	Morrow	Foward	Portland	WHL	41	44	85	248
*Brian	Campbell	Defense	Ottawa	OHL	12	75	87	27
Alex	Andreyev	Defense	Moose Jaw	WHL	11	11	22	80
Jason	Krog	Forward	New Hampshire	ECAC	34	51	85	38
*Mike	Ribeiro	Forward	Rouyn-Noranda	QMJHL	67	100	167	137
Daniel	Tkachuk	Forward	Barrie	OHL	43	62	105	58
Gavin	Morgan	Forward	Denver	WCHA	13	16	29	85
*Andrew	Ference	Defense	Portland	WHL	11	21	32	104
Syl	Apps	Forward	Princeton	ECAC	13	21	34	45
Ben	Clymer	Defense	Seattle	WHL	12	44	56	93
David	Cullen	Defense	Maine	H. East	11	33	44	24
*Danny	Riva	Forward	R.P. I.	ECAC	22	35	57	35
*Mike	York	Forward	Michigan State	CCHA	20	25	45	33
*Brian	Swanson	Forward	Colorado College	WCHA	25	41	66	28
Francis	Lessard	Defense	Drummondville	QMJHL	12	36	48	295
*Mike	Omicioli	Forward	Providence College	H. East	19	31	50	50
Mike	Brown	Forward	Kamloops	WHL	28	26	44	285
Wes	Jarvis	Defense	Kitchener	OHL	5	18	23	80
Randy	Ready	Forward	Belleville	OHL	33	59	92	73
*Samuel	St. Pierre	Forward	Drummondville	QMJHL	47	28	75	65
*Jason	Blake	Forward	North Dakota	WCHA	28	41	69	49
Scott	Swanson	Defense	Colorado College	WCHA	11	41	52	16
Jason	Reid	Defense	Vermont	ECAC	7	12	19	54
Jarrett	Smith	Forward	Prince George	WHL	20	37	57	54

Goaltenders

First Name	Last Name	Last Season	League	G	W	L	T	SO	GAVG
Mika	Noronen	Tappara Tampere	Sweden	43	18	20	5	2	3.25
Danny	Lavoie	Rouyn-Nornanda	QMJHL	28	11	13	3	0	3.36
Curtis	Cruickshank	Kingston-Sarnia	OHL	44	23	14	1	3	3.24
Evan	Lindsay	Prince Albert	WHL	56	34	16	5	1	2.84
Scott	Fankhouser	Lowell	Lowell	32	16	14	0	1	2.78
Milan	Hnilicka	Sparta Praha	Czech.	50	—	—	—	—	2.27
*Tyrone	Garner	Oshawa	OHL	44	24	15	3	4	2.98
Roberto	Luongo	Val d' Or-Bathurst	QMJHL	43	20	27	3	1	3.60
Patrick	DesRochers	Sarnia-Kingston	OHL	52	17	27	3	1	4.33
Alfie	Michaud	Maine	H. East	37	28	6	3	3	2.32

Feature Articles

That season we introduced feature articles to the Ice Pages. We have continued to do so with the Ice Pages IV. I hope that you enjoy these columns this season as we tried to find a different an interesting way to look at the sport of hockey.

Included in this season's features are a column on Patrik Stefan. Stefan was selected first overall by the NHL's Atlanta Thrashers after deciding to play in the IHL for two seasons before his draft eligibility kicked in. We also have an article on how hockey took ahold of the North Carolina city of Asheville. Rounding out our coverage is a British Hockey Primer, a Year in the Life of a minor-pro broadcaster/media relations director and and we report on a summer of change for the IHL and a look at the changes in the WPHL coaching ranks.

The Las Vegas Thunder will not return for the 1999-2000 season

Photo by John Gacioch

I-OPENER

Stefan Proved Worth In IHL

by Sean Broderick

Patrik Stefan's initial exposure to North America -- and the International Hockey League was supposed to be for two or so week during the 1998 Winter Olympics. With his Czech Extraleague team, Sparta Praque, on break for the Negano games, Stefan— who at 17 was already considered a top prospect for the 1999 draft— had a perfect chance to get a quick education on life on and off the ice in North America.

But what started as a sojourn turned into a full-season contract and a follow-on deal for 1998-99. And while Stefan did his fair share of learning, his skills were advanced enough to allow him to do some teaching, too.

In 68 IHL regular-season games, Stefan racked up 17 goals and 40 assists -- not bad for a kid that turned 18 during his only IHL training camp, and who wasn't planning to spend a year in pro hockey before he was eligible for the NHL draft.

"I didn't know I was going to stay," Stefan admits. "I was just coming and thinking about trying the hockey. I didn't know I'd like it like that. I loved it, and I decided to stay."

His on-ice performance surely figured into the equation. The IHL is no garage league, and it was clear early on that Stefan could hang with the big boys. After just 10 games, he had three goals, five points, and the desire to stick with the Ice Dogs and further his NHL development. So he did.

"Everything was hard," Stefan recalls. "I couldn't speak English. I didn't know what to do on the ice. It was small ice. Everything was different ...but after a couple months I was very comfortable in the league and this season [1998-99] was just great."

Stefan gives credit for his rapid adjustment to several people, including countryman and fellow Ice Dog Patrik Augusta. In his sixth North American season when Stefan arrived, Augusta took in the young centerman, letting him move in to an apartment shared with fellow Czech Zdenek Nedved and showing him around both in Long Beach and on the road.

"He was like my father," Stefan says of Augusta. "He told me what I had to do, what I had to say, what to do on the ice. He explained everything to me."

Stefan obviously got the message. He followed up his stellar stint as a 17-year old with an even better 1998-99. He captured the IHL Player of the Week award by scoring five goals and six points from Nov. 2-8.

He was named to the IHL's Western Conference All-Star Team and also had a four-game assist streak, the longest of the season by any IHL player. He finished the season with 35 points (11-24-35) in 33 games, eliminating any lingering doubt about whether he had the skills to compete in North America.

Based on skill alone, there's no argument: Stefan is considered by players and interested observers alike to be the most promising prospect to come out of his country since Pittsburgh Penguin Jaromir Jagr.

The IHL is no garage league, and it was clear early on that Stefan could hang with the big boys.

"He's got all the tools to be a star in the National Hockey League," says Petr Nedved, who knows his young countryman from the rinks in and around Prague and played against him in 1997-98 in the IHL. "I think it's just more like you've got to wait and see if he does become a star or not."

Adds Augusta: "Patrik is going to be a good hockey player. He is still young but you can see that he has a great desire and work ethic. ... He is just unbelievable with the puck. He is a great puck-handler and a great skater."

The one question mark with Stefan is well known to anyone that followed the Ice Dogs or the NHL draft this past year: concussions. Stefan suffered two pretty good ones in 1998-99, leaving some to question whether he really can handle himself against bigger, faster opponents on smaller North American ice.

The Atlanta Thrashers, whose future rests a great deal on the 6-1, 205-pound Stefan's broad shoulders, did their homework. A clean bill of health for Stefan just before the draft eased their minds regarding lingering damage, and their own scouting allowed them to eliminate the theory that Stefan isn't cut out for the rugged North American game.

"We had scouts at both games he got hurt," says Atlanta GM Don Waddell. "The first was a mild one and included a neck injury. The second" -- which ended Stefan's season -- "he hit a player's knee and the player tore an MCL. I don't think you can say he's prone to concussions, it was just the situations."

For Stefan, getting picked No. 1 by the Thrashers provided some satisfaction in light of the doubters that insist the IHL did more damage to him than vise-versa. But he's looking forward to proving his worth once and for all -- on the ice.

"I will be same like I played before," Stefan says. "After [the] second one, I was coming back, I play same game I play before. I'm not scared about going into corner. Lots of persons have concussions, they come back. They are still great players. That's what I want do."

Sean Broderick is managing editor of The Pro Hockey EuroReport (www.euroreport.com)

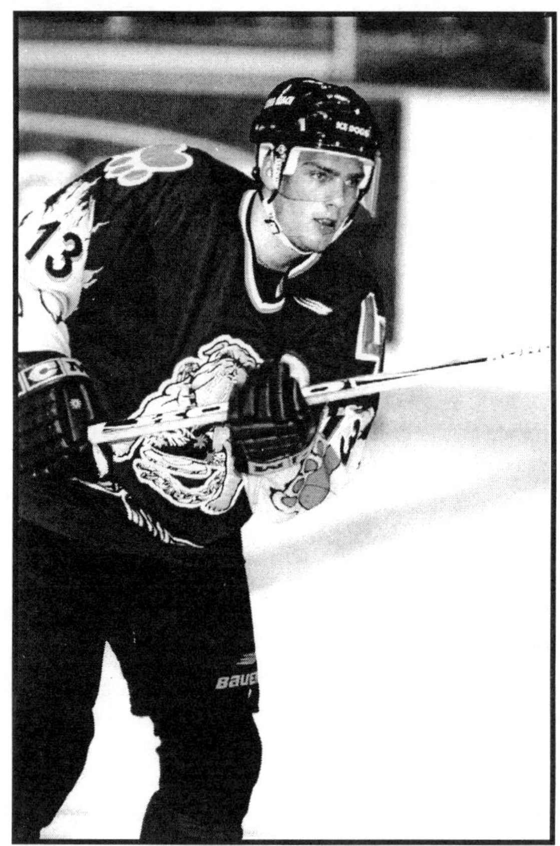

Atlanta is hoping that #13 will be lucky for them
Photo by John Gacioch

Smokin'! Hockey a Hit in Asheville

by Joseph H. Bloom

"It'll never work," said the pessimists when the Brantford (Ontario) Smoke announced it was moving its franchise to Asheville, North Carolina for the 1998-99 UHL season. "It's too far south," said some. "No one here will understand ice hockey," said others.

Wrong. In their first year in the mountains of western North Carolina, the Smoke drew close to 125,000 paying customers for 37 home dates at the aging Asheville Civic Center. (The Smoke's best year in Canada was 1993-1994 when it drew 64,174.) The team averaged 3,362 fans per game, compared to 1,464 the previous year in Brantford. The first two hockey games ever played in this part of the world each attracted more than 5,000 fans, and a meaningless late season game against intrastate rival Winston-Salem drew 5,481.

"I love it," said Smoke winger Shawn Ulrich, who played his previous professional hockey in Alaska, Waco, and Reno. "The crowds here definitely get me pumped up to play better."

At first, the loudest cheers were for the fights and board-rattling checks ... or even missed checks. By mid-season, the crowd was booing linesmen for what it saw as questionable off-sides calls. Quick learners.

"I was really impressed how the people of the area took to us," said Smoke president and general manager, Dan Wilhelm. "To get support like we got for a new sport and a first-year franchise was more than I ever expected."

None of the Asheville players played the previous year in Brantford. The team was put together via free-agent signings, trades, and invitees who impressed during training camp, among them, Brent Gretzky, younger brother of the NHL's Wayne Gretzky and Smoke coach, Keith Gretzky. Although Brent played only half a season in North Carolina before being called up to the Chicago Wolves of the IHL, his and Keith's name recognition undoubtedly helped sell the team in the early going.

One explanation for the success may lie in the make-up of the area itself. Asheville, a city of some 65,000, in the midst of a rapidly growing county of more than 200,000, is not your typical 'sleepy' southern city. Many of the inhabitants are transplants from places like the midwest and the northeast. And the city prides itself on its eclectic quality. The number of bookstores rivals the number of NASCAR-souvenir shops.

On any given night, the seats at the Civic Center were populated by everyone from college presidents to hard-working blue-collar types. Families came in droves ~ Mom, Dad, youngsters who got a handshake from the team's dragon mascot, even infants in car seats.

As much as the community reached out to the team, the team reached out to the community, visiting area hospitals, appearing at blood drives, and helping beginners at public skating sessions.

Promotions helped, too. Games began with the players skating out in a spotlight between the open jaws of a large inflatable dragon as the lights were dimmed throughout the arena. Intermissions featured contests with selected fans shooting pucks for a free car or tossing numbered pucks toward a target on the ice in the hopes of earning a free team jersey. Area organizations sponsored give-aways. Friday nights offered reduced prices on selected beverages. And the team made its players available for post-game autograph and "skate-with-the-team" sessions.

Box-office success contributed to merchandising success, with a usually crowded booth between periods offering T-shirts, sweatshirts, golfing shirts, game jerseys, souvenir pucks, and more. As one news service writer noted, "Almost anything with the smoking dragon logo is a hot item in Asheville these days."

Things have come a long way since early last year when forward Kris Schultz, the team's long-haired, teen-popular 'enforcer' was asked, "How do you stand up on the ice? It's so slippery."

Brent Gretzky helped brother Keith's efforts to coach the Smoke by providing 70 points in just 32 games

Photo by Joe Costa

ONE STEP BACKWARD, TWO STEPS AHEAD
GLOOMY FRANCHISE NEWS CAN'T ECLIPSE NHL AFFILIATIONS

BY LARRY NADER

It was an offseason of good news/bad news for the International Hockey League as new NHL affiliations were announced amid the departure of three IHL franchises. Overall, five teams have left the once growing league over the last two seasons, for a total of 7 in the last four years.

Following last season, the Las Vegas Thunder suspended operations, hopefully only short term, as their lease on the Thomas & Mack Center expired and the team was unable to secure a new venue for the upcoming year. In the meantime the West Coast Hockey League muddied the waters further when they announced they would field a team in Vegas beginning with the 2000-01 season. Then, in June, both the Fort Wayne Komets and the Indianapolis Ice left for other leagues citing financial difficulties.

"The situation in Vegas, is that we don't have a building in which to play," remarked IHL President and CEO Douglas Moss. "We are looking at a longer term solution to that. With Indianapolis and Fort Wayne, we have two franchises that have had some difficulty for the last couple of years, so we are not surprised by their announcements."

At the time of this article, the Expansion and Transfer Committee was still considering the teams' request to suspend operations. The Committee would make their recommendation to the Board of Governors in mid-July for the Board's decision.

Prior to this past offseason, the Quebec Rafales and San Antonio Dragons ceased operations following the 97-98 season, while the Phoenix Roadrunners and San Francisco Spiders were mothballed following the 96-97 and 95-96 seasons, respectively.

Attempts to revive the Spiders franchise have been unsuccessful, as the ownership's attempts to relocate the team to Victoria, British Columbia have thusfar been futile.

The Phoenix franchise, however, is gaining momentum in their attempt to relocate to the Toronto area in time for the 2000-01 season, as talks continue with local officials there. The proposed plan would put Edmonton businessman Lyle Abraham's team playing in the Exhibition Place Coliseum which would be converted from 6,200-seats to hold a capacity of 11,000.

"I think most of this was inevitable," stated Moss. "The league has made some decisions in the past that didn't pan out. That's why we had problems in San Francisco and Quebec. I think we went into markets and situations that we didn't entirely study or understand."

The IHL will begin the 1999-2000 season with only 13 teams - their lowest level since the 1992-93 season when they scheduled 12 franchises. While this downward trend is cause for concern, there is also reason to be optimistic as several new National Hockey League affiliations have sprouted.

"I think there were some perceived negatives," related Moss. "The first Board of Governors meeting I ever attended in this league, people didn't talk; however there were a lot of conversations behind the scenes. I thought the meeting we had in Cabo San Lucas, in the winter, was good, but after the meeting we just came out of in Chicago (this past summer), I don't think this board has ever been more unified in the history of the league.

"I like the position that this league is headed. Yes we have problems - every professional league does - but we know what they are, we have a plan on how to address them and we are going to move forward. I am very excited about the future."

All seven Eastern Conference teams this season will have full NHL affiliations - Cincinnati (Carolina Huricanes), Cleveland (Chicago Blackhawks), Detroit (Tampa Bay Lightning), Grand Rapids (Ottawa Senators), Michigan (Dallas Stars), Milwaukee (Nashville Predators) and Orlando (Atlanta Thrashers).

"That's up from 2 teams, just two years ago," Moss remarked of the seven NHL affiliations. "We have made significant progress there and we are not finished. It's up to each individual team if they want to do this, but I think an affiliation, with the right number of young players mixed in with the right number of veterans, gives the best product on the ice."

During the summer Board of Governors and General Managers Meeting in late June, several changes were

Each IHL team will be required to have a minimum of five players 25-years-old or younger on their roster. Two of those 5 players are required to be 22-years-old or younger, and have less than 50 games of professional hockey experience.

"The National Hockey League drafts 17-year-cld kids," Moss remarked. "You really don't know what they are going to be like at 21 or 22. If you put them in a situation where they can flourish, get a little more travel and play against kids their own age, as well as learn from having some really solid veterans in the dressing room, you are going to find out who can play and who can't play very quickly.

"We've seen our league get old, average-age wise, and I think you need more of a blend. The Youth Rule helps us to get there. We can't unilaterally implement that rule, it has to be ratified by the players union before it becomes a reality. I don't know if it will be done this year, but it's something that this league thinks it needs."

In addition the league will begin to use a Video Replay Rule in arenas that have the video capability. Usage of the video replay is at the sole discretion of the referee and will not be utilized to determine if a player was in the crease or not. It will be for the sole purpose of determining if the puck crossed the goal line or not.

All in all, Doug Moss remains bullish on the league and feels that they are heading into the rebuilding of a new, stronger IHL. Sometimes you have to take a few steps back to move forward.

"We're looking at areas of the country where we have some teams, and we are trying to find some rivals to take up with them," outlined Moss. "We're looking at the Southeast and the West. There are even some opportunities in the Northeast. We are going to take our time and strategize this. We have an expansion and transfer plan, now we are just going to execute it.

"We have terrific markets, buildings and ownership, which is probably the strongest key to this league. I wouldn't be surprised if we have some expansion announcements towards the end of the summer, or the beginning of the fall."

Michigan's Marty Flichel tries to go backhand on Detroit's Kevin Weekes

Photo by John Gacioch

HOW DO YOU STOP THIS CRAZY THING?! WPHL COACHING STAFF CHANGES BY 50%

By Thomas Schettino

When you read about it's invariably called the "coaching carousel". But this season's WPHL carousel has been more like George Jetson's whacked-out treadmill as coaches have been flung about in all different directions before, during and after the league's 1998-99 campaign. Out of the eighteen available leadership positions in the loop, nine will be helmed by a new captains this season.

Typically, most of the changes were brought about by teams trying to become more competitive within the league. No one can blame Tupelo (George Dupont), Alexandria (Mike Zruna), Austin (Brent Hughes) and/or New Mexico (Tony Martino) for making a move; after all, those squads missed the playoffs last season. We can let Lubbock (Alan May) off the hook too, because, well, they've never had a coach before.

Natural attrition cost San Angelo (Mike Collins) and Waco (Kevin Abrams) their coaches, but what happened in Monroe (Brian Curran) and Abilene (Marty Dallman), are a little tougher to explain.

The Moccasins made the playoffs last season for the first time in franchise history, but when a chance to bring in a former NHL'er in Brian Curran came about, the Mocs made their move. Abilene's change can be traced to new ownership. However one needs to wonder if they used a microscope when examining Jeff Triano's All-Star, first-place rookie season behind the bench. Triano's regular season accomplishments will be hard to duplicate, but Dallman was brought in to improve the bottom line in the playoffs.

Two of the coaching changes around the loop really stood out. In Central Texas GM Deborah Lackey looked to Waco and registered a coup when Todd Lalonde decided to move south. After taking the Wizards from out of the playoffs in 1997-98 into a first place finish and a Coach-of-the-Year season in his first WPHL season, Lalonde became available when the Wizards changed ownership.

While some have attributed Lalonde's departure to problems with then-Wizards owner Joe Milano, the coach disputes those claims. "In this profession, specifically at this level, comfort is pretty important," related Lalonde. "Contrary to public belief Joe Milano treated me extremely well. With the change in ownership, and the uncertainty as to the direction they were going, I just felt at League Meeting time it was important for me to establish a different entity in a different market."

Off the ice he might be able to do that, but on the ice his club will sort of be like the Central Texas Wizards. On the day we completed this article Waco and the Stampede finalize a nine-player deal that brought many of Lalonde's former players to Waco.

In addition to Lalonde in Central Texas, many eyes are on rookie head coach Tony Martino in New Mexico. No one doubts his ability to recruit after he helped put together strong teams in Abilene and New Mexico when he was still playing, but behind the bench he is an x-factor. The question remaining is whether or not he will be a good X's and O's guy.

"I know that I am going to have a good team" admitted Martino. "But when it comes to systems, I've been working with that with the help of John Torchetti (Tampa Bay Lightning assistant coach). We're trying to mirror pretty much what they (Torchetti and Steve Ludzik, Tampa Bay Lightning head coach) did in Detroit with the Vipers...With the help of Peter Ambroziak (Scorpions player/ assistant coach), especially since he played for the Vipers and knows the system, he will be able to help me with any obstacles I might have knowing the system inside out."

On the other side of the coaching coin is El Paso's Todd Brost. Brost is the only coach who has remained with his club since the WPHL began play three seasons ago.

The University of Michigan Hall-of-Famer claimed the first two WPHL Championships before being waylaid by the Fort Worth Brahmas last season while trying to three-peat.

But it hasn't all been wine and roses for Brost, "it didn't start out smoothly, that's for sure," said Brost about the start of his head coaching career. "We were 2-8 to start the season and I made a ton of changes. Some of those changes turned out incredibly well."

Indeed they did. Brost was able to pick up two pretty fair players by the names of Jamie Thompson and Chris MacKenzie, who were idle because no coach was willing to give them a chance at the time. The last piece of the puzzle was defenseman Mark Hilton who was acquired in a trade with Waco late in the season.

Thanks to the two championships, organizations in higher leagues have contacted Brost about assistant coaching positions with them. It is an offer the Buzzards boss has turned down several times.

"I've been treated very well here (El Paso) and the league is run very well here," said Brost about his decision to stay on. "I like having the control over the players as a coach, where for sure I wouldn't have that at the next level. It's been a great experience. At this level the coaches wear a lot of hats. We do everything from booking the flights, the hotels and the busses to running practice. I've been treated very well."

Now if the WPHL could just get a few more coaches to have the same tenure as Brost they could give that carousel a rest!

Todd Lalonde and Deborah Lackey at the press conference announcing his arrival in Belton
Photo by Larry Furnace

A Year by Air
A Play-by-Play Announcer's Rookie Season

By Ron Matejko

After spending four years as a sportswriter, I found myself on the other side of the fence during the 1998-99 season as the director of media relations and broadcasting for the Phoenix Mustangs.

The most appealing aspect of the job for me was serving as the radio play-by-play voice for both the home and road games. The only city in the West Coast Hockey League that I had previously visited was San Diego, so the prospect of visiting new places and traveling with the team was very interesting.

Working in the minor leagues offers plenty of room for growth and creativity during the radio broadcasts. In addition to the play-by-play, I was responsible for filling the 17 minutes of intermission time with interviews, news reports and other interesting league related items.

Most afternoons are spent either at my desk gathering information for the game notes or on my hotel room bed digging up ditties to regurgitate during the broadcast. Add on some research on the web about the other teams in the league along with a daily check that all is well on the Mustangs official web page and I usually log in two to three hours on the Internet per game day. Luckily I'm part hockey information junkie, part stats geek.

Being the lone one-man media relations and broadcaster operation in the league, there are many other duties to perform at home or on the road during the season. The main duty for a P.R. person is to serve as the mouthpiece between the franchise and the public while utilizing the different media avenues to get the word out.

Road games offer more free time following the games because the home team is responsible for disseminating the game sheets to the list of media outlets who are required to receive them. It allows for more time to enjoy a soda after the game instead of at home where I am usually married to the fax machine and phone for close to an hour.

Of course, there is something to be said for sleeping in your own bed. Ask any WCHLer about the small, hard beds in Anchorage. The larger ice sheet and crazy fans are only part of the reason why the Aces have been so difficult to beat at home the last few years.

One of the major perks of working in the WCHL is that approximately 80 percent of the travel is done by plane. The Mustangs only bus trips last season were the six-hour treks to Bakersfield and the eight-hour jaunts to Fresno. Return bus trips to Phoenix usually begin about an hour and a half after the game to load the equipment and grab a bite to eat before the red-eye highway haul begins. Sleeping is the best way to kill time although watching movies are a close second.

Overall this job is very enjoyable with just a few aspects that are less desirable. Mustangs game days meant my fighting the constant losing battles with the copying machine. Dealing with the copier was a necessary evil in assembling the game notes but often resulted in a profanity-laced tirade as the refurbished piece of crap would invariably jam up on every other copy. By the end of the season, the machine owned more dimples than a box of golf balls from the frequent collisions with the front of my foot.

Seven months of my being "on the inside" generated a better understanding and appreciation for the inner workings of a sports franchise and the fragile makeup of team chemistry. Last season also provided many memories and spawned many stories.

The wildest tale from last season occurred on the first night of the season. With just one pre-season game of radio experience under my belt, my color analyst, and Ice Pages author, Tom Schettino, and I were in San Diego to provide the call on the season opener between the Phoenix Mustangs and the rival San Diego Gulls.

The surroundings where less than friendly as we were led to a table positioned just in front of the upper level, very much within reach of the restless natives. With nearly 9,000 boisterous Gulls supporters at the Sports Arena, General Custer crossed my mind more than once.

The game was close until the Gulls scored twice in the third period to open a three-goal lead. We spoke on air of the heated playoff matchup between the clubs the previous year and the chippy play that dominated the final games of the series. The tension was evident throughout the contest with the threat of retaliation from that series seemingly waning as the third period was drawing to a close.

That was until a fan exercised bad judgment with under two minutes to play by throwing a partially filled glass beer bottle onto the ice, shattering just a few feet from two Mustangs players. All that action did was fan what was a flickering flame.

With 11 seconds remaining in the game and the outcome already decided, Mustangs left wing Rusty McKie hit San Diego's Martin St. Amour along the side of the head with his stick, touching off a melee. A five-on-five brawl ensued, with one battle floating toward the Mustangs net.

Phoenix goaltender David Goverde found himself in heavy traffic, and although he didn't interject himself into the action, San Diego goaltender Mattias Muller (pronounced mule-er) took exception. Like a scene out of the movie Slap Shot, Muller skated from his crease and challenged Goverde near center ice. The two netminders squared off, exchanging swings as the fans went wild.

Remember, this is my first regular season game on the radio. At this point, I'm wondering what the hell I got myself involved in, but my adrenaline was pumping. All 12 players on the ice are either in a fight or wrestling match. The fans are going nuts. Some are throwing gumballs at us in the booth. It was a hectic scene, but incredibly electric and the passion for this level of hockey, albeit the uglier side, was evident.

In hockey, the constant travel for close to seven months pulls fathers and husbands away from their families for long stretches which proved to be the toughest part of the job for me to adjust to. Quite often players are seen at pay phones (players phones in their rooms have the long distance shut off) calling loved ones back home.

The Mustangs begin every season on the road while the state fair occupies the building resulting in a 12-game, 18-day introductory road trip last year. It's one thing to be in the NHL and pulling down seven figures while being away from home, because the financial security provides the ability to walk away from the game at any time.

I gained an added respect for the many players and coaches who are able to maintain a stable home life despite the hectic schedule. It is strange how as the end of the season nears, you can't wait for it. But after a few weeks, the beginning of the new season can't come soon enough.

Two of the new leagues we included in this season's book were the British Superleague and the British National League. In order for us to get up to speed on those leagues I asked Dave Qua, who runs a Bracknell Bees (ISL) website, to give us a primer.

UK Hockey

By Dave Qua

(Bracknell Bees Web Page - http://www.bees.nu/)

There are two main leagues at the moment in the UK Hockey scene. They are the Ice Hockey Superleague (ISL) and the British National League (BNL). Of the two the ISL is by far the senior league and is composed primarily of imported (non-British national) players. The BNL also contains a fair number of imports but has a significantly greater number of Brits playing.

ISL

The ISL came into existence 3 years ago and consists of 8 teams (Ayr Scottish Raiders, Bracknell Bees, Cardiff Devils, London Knights, Manchester Storm, Newcastle Riverkings, Nottingham Panthers and Sheffield Steelers). The emergence of the ISL raised hockey to new levels of skill not seen previously in the UK

Besides the league there are a couple of cup competitions during the season (The Benson & Hedges Cup and the Challenge Cup) and the league finishes off with a series of playoffs culminating in the play-off finals.

The hockey season runs from September through to end March although the league proper does not start until October. During September the opening rounds of the B&H Cup are played.

The Teams

This season the governing body has imposed a wage cap of =A3500,000 ($750,000) so teams have had to adjust their playing staff accordingly. Teams go with a playing squad of 18-21 players (21 is the maximum allowed) There are very few home grown players on any of the teams and most of the squad comes from North America with a few Europeans thrown in for good measure. Most of the players come from the AHL, ECHL,etc with several having had NHL experience.

Ayr Scottish Eagles (coach: Jim Lynch): Ayr won everything two seasons ago and went with a virtually unchanged team last season. It didn't work and the season was a disaster for them. They have changed their squad a lot for this season with Rob Trumblay and Jamie Steer being two of their prominent players

Bracknell Bees (coach: Dave Whistle): Bracknell (with Whistle in his rookie year as coach) had their most successful season ever in senior hockey last year. They finished fourth in the league and got to the semis in the play-offs. Whistle has kept a core of players from last season (Bruno Campese - net-minder, Denis Chasse and PC Drouin being the stars) and has also brought in several apparently strong additions so they could be the team to watch this season

Cardiff Devils (coach: Paul Heavey): Heavey is the only UK born coach in the ISL and guided Cardiff to second place in the league and victory in the Play-off finals. Notable players are Ivan Matulik and Steve Thornton. One of their best D-men (Kip Noble) has moved to Sheffield this season.

London Knights (coach: Chris McSorley): London are the new boys of the ISL and only came into existence last season when they had a disaster finishing bottom of the league and being knocked out early in all the cup competitions. They haven't yet put together a full squad of players so it's difficult to say how they will do this year. They are owned by the same organisation that owns the LA Kings and with McSorley in charge they could be the surprise package.

Manchester Storm (coach: Kurt Kleinendorst): Traditionally viewed as the 'money-bags' team they play out of a new 19,000 capacity stadium but only really fulfilled their potential last season when they won the league. They have one of the best netminders (Frank Pietrangelo) in the ISL and will do well this season.

Newcastle Riverkings (coach: Alex Dampier): Newcastle came into existence three seasons ago as the Newcastle Cobras (they changed their name last season). They have permanent financial problems which shows in terms of the quality of players they are able to sign. They are expected to be the whipping boys of the league this season.

Nottingham Panthers (coach: Mike Blaisdell): Nottingham are one of the oldest teams in UK hockey and are always there or thereabouts when it comes to deciding the honours. They are in t process of building a new ice stadium (ready next year) and it is rumoured they are on a tight budget this season. They won the Benson & Hedges Cup last season and can't be ruled out for more honours this season.

Sheffield Steelers (coach: Don McKee): They were all conquering up to a couple of seasons ago but have slipped since then. However they showed signs of regaining some of their former glory when they won the Challenge Cup last season. In Ed Courteney they have one of the best goal scorers in the league and the addition of Shayne McCosh (from Bracknell) will boost the attacking side of their defence.he

The League

In the league each team plays the other six times (three home and three away) with one pair of games also counting towards the Challenge Cup. It get sort of complicated around here so I'll describe the Challenge Cup in more detail later. The scoring system is such that a team gets 2 points for a win in normal time. If the teams are tied after normal time then there is a sudden death overtime with the winner (if there is one) getting another point.

At the end of the season all the teams progress into the playoffs. They are split into two groups of four, according to final league position, for the initial round of the playoffs. In the initial round teams in each group play each other home and away with the top two teams in each group progressing to the Play-off semi-finals. The semis are a single game knockout with the winners going through to the single game final.

Benson & Hedges (B&H) Cup

This gets fairly complicated so you may want to read the following paragraph twice (or even three or four times!) All the teams in the ISL plus teams from the BNL compete in the B&H Cup. The ISL teams are split into two groups of four and the BNL teams into 3 groups. The top 3 teams in the ISL groups automatically qualify for the quarter finals of the B&H Cup. The teams which finish fourth in the ISL groups enter into a challenge round with two teams from the BNL groups decided after a playoff. This challenge round will be played as a home tie for the BNL team and the winning teams will qualify for the quarter finals. The Quarter-finals are played on a home and away basis as will be the Semifinals. The final takes place in December and is a single game.

The Challenge Cup

Results of two of the league games between ISL sides (defined before the season starts) also count towards the Challenge Cup. These results are used to calculate a mini-league table with the top four in this 'mini-league' progressing to the semi-finals of the Cup. The semis are two leg games (home and away) with the winners progressing to the single game final.

The British National League

This season it has been agreed that the BNL teams will all work to a playing roster of 18 players to ensure financial stability by reducing costs. The BNL consists of nine teams (Slough Jets, Basingstoke Bison, Guildford Flames, Peterborough Pirates, Fife Flyers, Kingstone Hawks, Telford Tigers, Edinburgh Capitals, Paisley Pirates) who play each other 4 times during the season (twice home and away) for the league title. In addition to the league competition there is a Benson & Hedges Plate competition to play for. The end of season league finals format has been changed this year to a North American series style play-off finals.

The top 8 teams in the league will be divided into 2 groups and the top two teams in each group will play cross-over semi-finals using a best of 3 series. The two winning teams will then go into a best of five series to decide the champions.

Benson & Hedges Plate competition: The BNL teams which are not successful in the B&H Cup (described above) will take part in the B&H Plate competition which is a similar format to the B&H Cup.

Late Signings

At some point I had to quit adding transactions into each player's respective page. The transactions that took place this season after the player templates were set will be added into their respective records in Volume 5 of the Ice Pages (2000-2001). Below are some of the transactions that took place just before we went to press.

8/9/99
New York Rangers -- Signed goaltender Jean-Francois Labbe.
Montreal Canadiens -- Agreed to terms with unrestricted free agent defenseman Barry Richter, who had been with the New York Islanders, on a two-year contract.
Vancouver Canucks -- Re-signed defenseman Jason Strudwick.
Charlotte Checkers (ECHL) -- Signed right wing Tracy Egeland
Abilene Aviators (WPHL) -- Re-signed forward Francois Archambault; signed goaltender Patrick Mazzoli.
Odessa Jackalopes (WPHL) -- Re-signed forward Andrew Rodgers.

8/10/99
Nashville Predators -- Signed unrestricted free agent goaltender Corey Hirsch and center Steve Washburn, both of whom had been with the Vancouver Canucks.
Houston Aeros (IHL) -- Re-signed center Mark Freer to a two-year contract.
Utah Grizzlies (IHL) -- Signed right wings Joe Frederick and Sean Tallaire and defenseman Pat Neaton.
Flint Generals (UHL) -- Named Ross Wilson player assistant coach; re-signed defenseman Lorne Knauft.

8/11/99
New York Rangers -- Agreed to terms with right wing Ken Gernander.
Vancouver Canucks -- Signed free agent defenseman Chris O'Sullivan, who had been with the New York Rangers.
Mobile Mysticks (ECHL) -- Signed defenseman Anders Sorensen.
Portland Pirates (AHL) -- Re-signed defenseman Dwight Parrish to a one-year contract.
Madison Kodiaks (UHL) -- Signed forward Brian Wilson.
Alexandria Warthogs (WPHL) -- Re-signed defenseman Chad Wilchynski; signed golatender Jeff Blair.
El Paso Buzzards (WPHL) -- Signed forward Martin Menard and goaltender Patrick Couture.
Monroe Moccasins (WPHL) -- Signed defenseman Bill McKay.
New Mexico Scorpions (WPHL) -- Signed forward Nick Forbes.
Odessa Jackalopes (WPHL) -- Signed forward Mark Smith and defenseman Brandon Nichols.
San Angelo Outlaws (WPHL) -- Traded the rights to defenseman Mike Vandenberghe to the Odessa Jackalopes for the rights to forward Rob Lukacs.
Tupelo T-Rex (WPHL) -- Signed defenseman Mark Collicutt.
Waco Wizards (WPHL) -- Traded the rights to forwards Luc Gagne and Ron Newhook and defensemen Paul Tzountzouris, Jens Andersson and John Murphy to the Central Texas Stampede for the rights to defensemen Jamie Pegg and Keith Bland and forwards Darren Dougan and Mike Dairon.

8/12/99
Atlanta Thrashers -- Signed Geordie Kinnear and Sean Ritchlin
Dayton Bombers (ECHL) -- Signed defenseman Julian Dal Cin.
New Mexico Scorpions (WPHL)— Traded Mike Sanderson to Fort Worth for future considerations

Proud To Be Loud!

For More Information Contact:
Western Professional Hockey League
14040 N. Cave Creek Road, Suite 100
Phoenix, Arizona 85022
1-602-485-9399
website: www.wphlhockey.com
e-mail: info@wphlhockey.com

Bugs Rule!
Shreveport Claims First WPHL Championship

THE

Steve Martinson has won three Taylor Cup Championships with the San Diego Gulls

Photo by Kelly Virtanen

Coaches

John Brophy's legendary coaching career includes three championships and a NHL gig

Photo by Bill Vaughn

THE

The Stanley Cup Champion Dallas Stars hope that IHL Rookie of the Year Marty Turco can someday play in the NHL

Photo by John Gacioch—Just Hockey

Rookies

Johhny Brdarovic enjoyed a tremendous CHL rookie season and went up to the IHL twice. He was voted CHL Rookie of the Year

Photo by Angie Riemersman

League Enforcers

Michigan's Mel Angelstad (L) led the IHL in penalty minutes last season

Photo by John Gacioch—Just Hockey

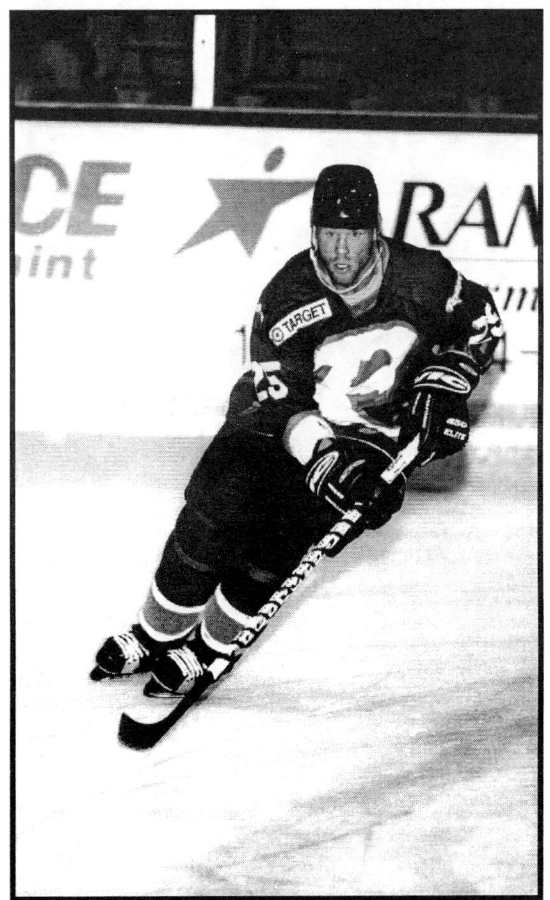

Trevor Senn is the ECHL's All-Time PIM leader spending much of his time with Richmond

Photo by Bill Vaughn

Second

Bakersfield's Briane Thompson shows off the Condors "Lucky" shamrock jersey

Photo courtesy of Bakersfield Condors

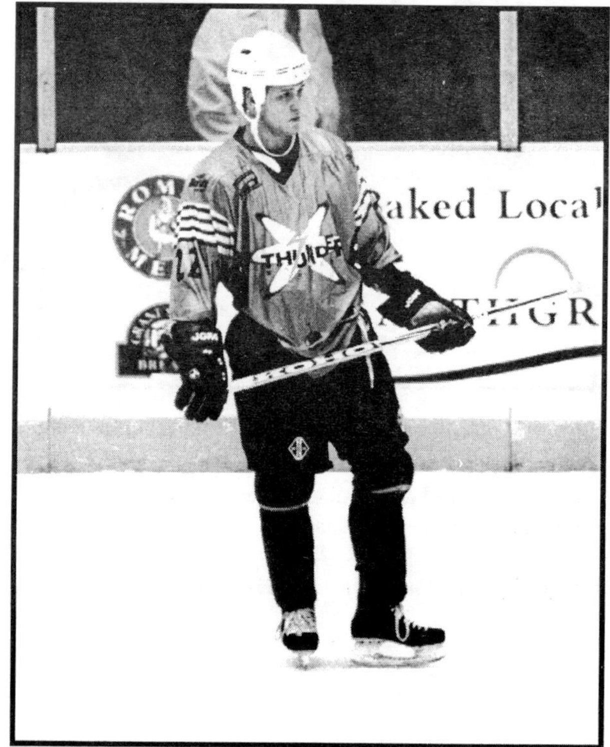

Uniforms

Rhett Dudley shows off his Back-to-the-Future Wichita Thunder uniform

Photo by Jorge Martinez

Multiple

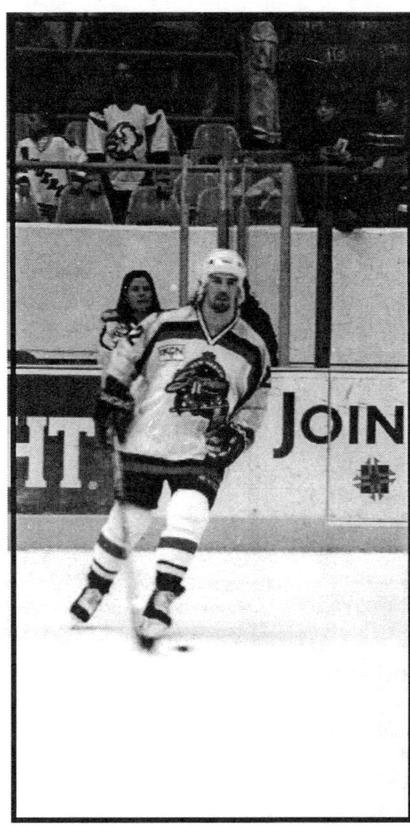

Dean Shmyr shows off the New Mexico Scorpions New Year's Eve Jersey

Photo by Lou Lafrado

Uniforms

This jersey was worn by Shmyr on Halloween. Like many clubs, the Scorpions auction off their special jerseys for charity.

Photo by Lou Lafrado